MW00914465

CONTRACT LAW

Aspen Casebook Series

CONTRACT LAW

A Case & Problem-Based Approach

MARCO J. JIMENEZ
Professor of Law
Stetson University College of Law

Published by Wolters Kluwer in New York.

Wolters Kluwer Legal & Regulatory US customers worldwide with CCH, Aspen Publishers, and Kluwer Law International products. (www.WKLegaledu.com)

To contact Customer Service, e-mail customer.service@wolterskluwer.com, call 1-800-234-1660, fax 1-800-901-9075, or mail correspondence to:

Wolters Kluwer
Attn: Order Department
PO Box 990
Frederick, MD 21705

Printed in the United States of America.

1 2 3 4 5 6 7 8 9 0

ISBN 978-1-4548-6330-4

Library of Congress Cataloging-in-Publication Data

Names: Jimenez, Marco J., author.
Title: Contract law : a case & problem-based approach / Marco J. Jimenez, Professor of Law, Stetson University College of Law.
Description: New York : Wolters Kluwer, 2017.
Identifiers: LCCN 2016028169 | ISBN 9781454863304
Subjects: LCSH: Contracts—United States. | LCGFT: Casebooks.
Classification: LCC KF801.A7 J56 2017 | DDC 346.7302/2—dc23
LC record available at https://lccn.loc.gov/2016028169

Certified Chain of Custody
Promoting Sustainable Forestry
www.sfiprogram.org
SFI-01042

SFI label applies to the text stock

About Wolters Kluwer Legal & Regulatory US

Wolters Kluwer Legal & Regulatory US delivers expert content and solutions in the areas of law, corporate compliance, health compliance, reimbursement, and legal education. Its practical solutions help customers successfully navigate the demands of a changing environment to drive their daily activities, enhance decision quality and inspire confident outcomes.

Serving customers worldwide, its legal and regulatory portfolio includes products under the Aspen Publishers, CCH Incorporated, Kluwer Law International, ftwilliam.com and MediRegs names. They are regarded as exceptional and trusted resources for general legal and practice-specific knowledge, compliance and risk management, dynamic workflow solutions, and expert commentary.

To my family, for their love, support, and encouragement

SUMMARY OF CONTENTS

Contents

PART II
A GENERAL OVERVIEW OF CONTRACT LAW 27

CHAPTER 2
A General Overview of the Major Doctrines of Contract Law 29

PREFACE

IMPETUS FOR A NEW CASEBOOK—A NOTE TO PROFESSORS

Does the world really need another contracts casebook? As it currently stands, there are already numerous casebooks on the market from a variety of publishers, many of whose authors offer strong and frequently divergent views of what material should be included and how it should be organized, presented, and taught. Yet, given the traditional presentation of these materials—both from the perspective of a student, and, more frequently, from the perspective of a law professor choosing a casebook—the choice sometimes appears to be between six of one and half a dozen of the other.

For instance, in its December 2013 symposium issue on contracts education, the *Washington Law Review* published the results of a survey of 136 law professors on the current state of contracts casebooks.* Based on the survey, the most common complaints about the current contracts casebooks on the market concerned an insufficient inclusion of problems and drafting exercises, the need for more recent cases, improving the extent and quality of UCC and CISG coverage, including "comparative elements from other legal systems," and the need to "reorganize or expand interpretation materials." Additional concerns addressed the inclusion of "excessive ideology" and "idiosyncratic theory" in current casebooks, in addition to "insufficient cross-referenc[ing] to other 1L subjects." Finally, there were several comments reflecting the need for current casebooks to supplement the traditional case method with "other methods for conveying doctrine," including the need for a "hybrid" textbook that, like more traditional graduate level textbooks, would include "(1) full explanations of the law, (2) case summaries illustrating the law, (3) the full opinion of a select group of cases[, and] (4) problems to work through." This more modern casebook would "optimize readability" by "using pictures, graphics, sidebars, etc."

Although it was disconcerting, on the one hand, to see the current dissatisfaction with the current state of contracts casebooks, on the other hand I was delighted because I had been thinking about many of these issues for a long time, and had taken steps in my own course to organize the materials in a way

* Jennifer Taub, *Unpopular Contracts and Why They Matter: Burying Langdell and Enlivening Students*, 88 Wash. L. Rev. 1227, 1427 (2013).

that addressed many of the above-related concerns, in addition to other concerns (discussed below) not discussed in the survey. In writing this contracts casebook, it was my goal to offer a new and pedagogically sound approach to the study of contract law that takes into account many of these considerations while drawing on what has (and has not) worked for me in the classroom.

To begin, a glance at the casebooks currently on the market reveals that many authors approach their subject with the belief that contract law, as a whole, cannot be properly grasped until one specific part of contract law (e.g., enforceability, or mutual assent, or remedies) is *first* grasped by the student. Consequently, casebooks are inevitably organized with this general approach in mind: The student will dive, headfirst, into (for example) the topic of enforceability, covering consideration, promissory estoppel, and unjust enrichment, before marching to the next area of contract law (e.g., mutual assent), covering offer, acceptance, and the mirror image rule, all the while never quite understanding how the material they have just read fits together, and never quite understanding how one part of contract law (e.g., enforceability) relates to other parts of contract law (e.g., mutual assent). Other casebook authors, seeing the error of beginning with, say, enforceability before the student is even able to grasp what, exactly, judges are enforcing in the first place, will attempt to remedy this perceived defect by diving headfirst into contract formation, i.e., offer, acceptance, and mutual assent. Or, perceiving the weakness of *this* approach, another author might insist instead that no part of contract law can be understood until the student first understands what the parties want, in the case of the plaintiff, or wants to avoid, in the case of the defendant, and therefore begin with remedies. And so it goes.

Personally, I have taught contracts over the years by beginning with remedies, with mutual assent, and with enforceability, and I even strongly considered beginning with defenses. In so doing, I have come to realize that all of these approaches are "correct" in the sense that no one part of contract law can be understood until all other parts of contract law to which that part is related are understood. But, for the same reason, I have also come to realize that all of these approaches are "incorrect" in that whatever part the student begins with will usually not be well understood (if it is understood at all) until the student begins preparing their outline at the end of the course, during which time they may find themselves thinking, "If only I'd known *that* earlier, contract law would have made so much more sense!" The unique organization of this casebook, which provides the student with an overview of all areas of contract law before delving into any one area in great depth, is designed to address this problem. By providing the student with the framework to understand contract law holistically early on, not only will the student have the tools to see how each part of contract law relates other parts of contract law as the material is presented, but it should also lead to greater appreciation of the material, richer class discussion, and more enjoyment! The specific organization of this casebook is outlined in greater depth in "Casebook Description—A Note to Students and Professors" below.

The second major innovation of this casebook requires some explanation. In his recent book called *The Legal Analyst: A Toolkit for Thinking about the Law*, Professor Ward Farnsworth points out that "[t]here are, in general, two sorts of things one learns at a law school. First, there are lots of legal rules—principles that tell you whether a contract is valid, for example, or when people have to pay for accidents they cause, or what the difference is between murder and manslaughter. Second, there are tools for thinking about legal problems—ideas such as the prisoner's dilemma, or the differences between rules and standards, or the notion of a baseline problem, or the problem of hindsight bias."* Needless to say, the traditional contracts casebook typically focuses on the first category—the rules—while failing to provide the student with the mental tools necessary for thinking about these rules. Yet, when we call on our students in class, it is often this sort of thoughtful discussion we hope to have, although we have not equipped them to do so, expecting, perhaps, that their analysis should flow fully formed like Athena from Zeus's brow. This is not only unfair to our students, but a shame to boot. As Professor Farnsworth points out, the

> tools for thought are by far the more interesting, useful, and fun part of a legal education. They enable you to see more deeply into all sorts of questions, old and new, and say better, more penetrating things about them. The problem is that law schools generally don't teach those tools carefully or systematically.... Law tends to be taught, in other words, as if legal rules were the most important things one could learn, and as if the tools for thinking about them were valuable but secondary—nice to know if someone happens to explain them, but nothing urgent.†

This casebook attempts to address this shortcoming by providing our students with a series of "thinking tools" throughout the book. These "thinking tools" are set off from the main text in color-coded text boxes, and discussion questions throughout the book will refer back to them where applicable.

In sum, the approach of the casebook is to provide an organizational structure that allows the student to gain a basic introduction of all aspects of contract law, covering not only the black-letter law itself, but teaching them how to think about that law as well. In addition, the casebook will emphasize the manner in which the various parts of contract law fit together with one another, showing how contract law is but one part of the larger fabric of our common law system, and revealing how the practice of that body of law is informed by history, governed by philosophy, and shaped by practice. It is my hope that students who grasp these relationships will not only have more fun in the course, but will also become better lawyers, as they will have a solid foundation in contract law and be equipped with the analytic tools necessary to look for and appreciate the connections between and among various legal subjects throughout the rest of their legal career.

* WARD FARNSWORTH, THE LEGAL ANALYST: A TOOLKIT FOR THINKING ABOUT THE LAW vii (2007).
† *Id.*

CASEBOOK DESCRIPTION—A NOTE TO STUDENTS AND PROFESSORS

To bring about the approach discussed above, this casebook is organized in the following manner. First, in Part I, which consists of the opening chapter, the student is oriented to the world of contract law with a "30,000-foot view" in which they are introduced to each of the major substantive areas that will be studied during the remainder of the course. Specifically, this section of the book is designed to familiarize the student with a basic understanding of contract law, the sorts of problems with which it attempts to deal, and some of the basic rules and theories underlying its structure. It has been my experience that by broadly introducing the types of issues that come up in a typical contracts course before studying them in more depth, students are better positioned to not only draw connections between each of the various areas in contract law, but to focus more on each aspect of contract law when the material is presented later in the course.

Second, once students grasp the general lay of the land at the 30,000-foot level, Part II of this book will fly a little closer to the surface (to about the 5,000-foot level) and expose students to each major substantive area of contract law in a bit more depth. To do this, one classic case from each substantive area of contract law will be presented (e.g., *Hamer v. Sidway* for enforceability, *Embry v. Hargadine* for mutual assent, *Hawkins v. McGee* for remedies), which will enable the student to delve deeper than he was able to in the first part of the book, while drawing connections between and among the various areas of contract law to which he has been exposed (to see, for example, how the issue of enforceability is related to the issue of mutual assent, which is in turn related to interpretation, which is itself related to performance, breach, remedies, and defenses). Before each case there will be a clear statement of the black-letter rule "governing" the case, so that students can focus less on trying to figure out what the rule is, and more on synthesizing the material and understanding how law is really made when these black-letter rules are applied by judges—operating within an historical context and influenced by theory—to the facts of the dispute.

Finally, after completing Part II of the course, the student should have a pretty good sense of the way the pieces of the contracts puzzle fit together, and will know something about why certain promises and agreements should be enforced, what tests for enforceability are used by courts, how judges determine whether the parties have made a contract, etc. At this point, students will be well prepared to delve into each substantive area in much more depth, and will be provided with the material to do so in Part III, which includes a healthy mix of classic and modern cases, background and contextual materials, explanatory excerpts, and problems. Because students will have already gained a basic understanding of the way the different parts of contract law fit together, along with the general black-letter rules governing each major substantive area, the focus in Part III will be, to the extent possible, on mastery—on ensuring that the student is not only familiar with the black-letter law, but that she appreciates the manner in which one substantive area is related to another. For instance, the student will come to appreciate how, in a case like *Jacob & Youngs v. Kent,* a court's decision about the type of *performance* rendered by one party (e.g., substantial performance versus material breach) can have a significant impact on the *remedy* available to another party (e.g., diminution in value versus cost of performance), but that in figuring out what type of performance was *promised,* a court must first *interpret* the contract, which in turn requires them to consider what the parties *intended* when they *bargained* with one another. Each italicized term in the previous sentence corresponds to a different area of contract law (each of which is typically presented in its own separate chapter), which reveals at a glance why a student taught in the traditional manner (chapter by chapter, and concept by concept) has little hope of understanding such a case until the end of the course!

The second unique feature of the casebook (unlike some casebooks that have a particular historical, philosophical, or practice-oriented focus) is that my own experience has shown that students learn best when they are exposed to the history of their field, the philosophy undergirding it, *and* the practical lessons that can be drawn from their study. Therefore, throughout the casebook, there is sprinkled in what I hope is just enough history, philosophy, judicial biography, comparative material, background material, black-letter doctrine, and practice-oriented tips to salt the dish, but not so much as to spoil the meal. These materials are frequently set off from the main text in sidebar boxes (allowing communication with the student in real time as they are reading the cases), in slightly longer excerpts before and after the cases, and in the notes and questions. This format is designed to help to keep the material interesting for the student without overwhelming them.

Where relevant, this casebook also draws upon connections between contract law and other areas of law. For instance, the connection between contract law and tort law will be highlighted in the context of tortuous interference with contract (e.g., *Lumley v. Gye*), the connection between contracts law and criminal law will be illustrated in discussing the defense of incompetence (e.g., *Ortelere v. Teachers' Retirement Board of New York*), and other such connections will be made, as appropriate.

Finally, I believe the student can better understand the settled and flexible points in their own law by embracing a comparative approach. Therefore, this casebook draws upon, as appropriate, the CISG when teaching the UCC, civil law systems when teaching the common law, and the UNIDROIT Principles when discussing the *Restatements (First) and (Second) of Contract Law.* The professor may make as much (or as little) use of these additional resources as he or she likes, which are presented in the appendix to spare the student the expense of purchasing an additional supplement. Each of these bodies of law will be explained for the student in the first chapter.

M.J.
August 2016

ACKNOWLEDGMENTS

First of all, I would like to thank my amazing wife and wonderful son who have patiently encouraged and put up with me during the long process it has taken to write this book. I could not have done it without you—thank you!

Second, I would like to thank the Stetson University College of Law for its generous research support, in addition to all of the students and colleagues I have had over the years who have helped me think deeply about many of the materials that appear in this casebook. In particular, I would like to thank Professor Jamie Fox at Stetson (and a few anonymous reviewers provided by Aspen/Wolters Kluwer), who read an earlier draft of a few chapters of this casebook and provided critical feedback and positive encouragement that, despite the errors of mine that inevitably remain, has made this casebook better than it otherwise would have been. Also, this book could not have been written without the wonderful research assistance provided by the following students over the years: David Brunell, Rebecca Csikos, Kimberly Dukes, Martin Musichi, Kira Ramirez, Amy Ray, Carolina Saavedra, Aisha Sanchez, Catherine Selm, and Adam Saunders. Thank you!

Third, I would like to thank my former Dean, Darby Dickerson, who learned that I was writing and organizing my own contracts materials for use in my class and generously put me in touch with Rick Mixter at Aspen/Wolters Kluwer. Rick and I had a number of amazing and enjoyable conversations over the years, during which time I have benefited tremendously from his insight and experience publishing textbooks at the undergraduate and graduate levels. He has helped me think carefully about what a casebook should do, what it should look like, and how it should be organized to have a strong pedagogical impact on students. Many of his ideas, such as the sidebars and text boxes accompanying many of the cases, have made their way into this casebook, and the final product would have been much poorer without his help. Thank you!

Fourth, I would like to thank everyone at Aspen/Wolters Kluwer for the opportunity, guidance, and assistance you have provided to me in writing this casebook. I would like to give special thanks to Darren Kelly at Bullpen Publishing Solutions, who has been very helpful in walking a first-time book author through the publishing process, working with me on the design for the casebook, helping to obtain copyright permissions, and patiently putting up with me throughout the entire process. Thank you! I would also like to thank The Froebe Group, in particular Andrew Blevins for managing production of the book, Susan Junkin for compiling the table of cases and index, and Cambridge Ridley Lynch for her incredibly helpful copyediting. She caught a number of errors that would have remained in the final text, although responsibility for any errors that do remain, of course, is my own.

Finally, I would like to thank the following copyright holders for their generous permission to reprint the article excerpts and images throughout this casebook:

Books and Articles

Atiyah, P.S., THE RISE AND FALL OF FREEDOM OF CONTRACT (1979). Republished with permission of Oxford University Press; permission conveyed through Copyright Clearance Center, Inc.

Chirelstein, Marvin, CONCEPTS AND CASE ANALYSIS IN THE LAW OF CONTRACTS. Copyright © 2013 by Marvin Chirelstein. Reprinted with permission of West Academic.

Christie, George C. and Martin, Patrick H., JURISPRUDENCE: TEXT AND READINGS ON THE PHILOSOPHY OF LAW, Third Edition (2008). Copyright © 2008 by West Academic Publishing. Reprinted with permission of West Academic.

Cohen, Morris, *The Basis of Contract*, 46 HARV. L. REV. 571-85 (1933). Republished with permission of Harvard Law Review; permission conveyed through Copyright Clearance Center, Inc.

Corbin, Arthur Linton, *The Parol Evidence Rule*, 53 YALE L.J. 622-624 (1944). Republished with permission of Yale Law Journal; permission conveyed through Copyright Clearance Center, Inc.

Cunningham, Lawrence A., CONTRACTS IN THE REAL WORLD: STORIES OF POPULAR CONTRACTS AND WHY THEY MATTER. Copyright © 2012 Lawrence A. Cunningham. Reprinted with the permission of Cambridge University Press.

Danzig, Richard, THE CAPABILITY PROBLEM IN CONTRACT LAW. Copyright © 1978 by Richard Danzig. Reprinted with permission of West Academic.

Danzig, Richard, *Hadley v. Baxendale: A Study in the Industrialization of the Law*, 4 J. LEG. STUD. 249-51, 254-55, 259-60, 267-68, 271-76, 284 (1975). Copyright © 1975 The University of Chicago. Reprinted with permission of the publisher, The University of Chicago Press.

Delson, Jennifer, *Landing in an O.C. Court, This IOU Was Red All Over*, Los Angeles Times, May 31, 2006. Copyright © 2006 Los Angeles Times. Reprinted by permission.

Dodge, William S., *Teaching the CISG in Contracts*, 50 J. LEGAL EDUC. 74-75, 80-83, 86-87, 90-91 (2000). Journal of Legal Education © 2000 AALS; article copyright © 2000 William S. Dodge. Reprinted with the permission of AALS and the author.

Dubroff, Harold, *The Implied Covenant of Good Faith in Contract Interpretation and Gap-Filling: Reviling a Revered Relic*, St. John's Law Review, Vol. 80:

No. 2, Article 3 (2006). Available at: http://scholarship.law.stjohns.edu/lawreview/vol80/iss2/3. Reprinted with the permission of St. John's Law Review.

Eisenberg, Melvin Aron, *The Principles of Consideration*, 67 CORNELL L. REV. 659-61 (1982). Reprinted with permission of Cornell Law Review.

Fajans, Elizabeth and Falk, Mary R., *Against the Tyranny of Paraphrase: Talking Back to Texts*, 78 CORNELL L. REV. 163-65 (1995). Reprinted with permission of Cornell Law Review.

Farnsworth, E. Allan, CONTRACTS, Copyright © 2004 E. Allan Farnsworth. Used by permission of Wolters Kluwer Legal & Regulatory US.

Farnsworth, E. Allan, *The Past of Promise: An Historical Introduction to Contract*, 69 COLUM. L. REV. 591-96, 598-99 (1969). Republished with permission of Columbia Law Review; permission conveyed through Copyright Clearance Center, Inc.

Farnsworth, Ward, THE LEGAL ANALYST: A TOOLKIT FOR THINKING ABOUT THE LAW (2007). Republished with permission of University of Chicago Press; permission conveyed through Copyright Clearance Center, Inc.

Fried, Charles, CONTRACT AS PROMISE, Second Edition (2015). Copyright © 2015 by Oxford University Press. Reprinted with permission.

Fuller, Lon L., *Consideration and Form*, 41 COLUM. L. REV. 800-06 (1941). Republished with permission of Columbia Law Review; permission conveyed through Copyright Clearance Center, Inc.

Gilmore, Grant, THE DEATH OF CONTRACT (1974). Reprinted by permission of Ohio State University Press.

Gordon, Robert W., *Britton v. Turner: A Signpost on the Crooked Road to "Freedom" in the Employment Contract*, from Baird, Douglas G. (Ed.), CONTRACTS STORIES. Copyright © 2007 by Foundation Press. Reprinted with permission of West Academic.

Hyde, Alan, BODIES OF LAW (1997). Republished with permission of Princeton University Press; permission conveyed through Copyright Clearance Center, Inc.

Jimenez, Marco, *Finding the Good in Holmes's Bad Man*, 79 FORDHAM L. REV. 2080-87 (2011). Copyright © 2011 Marco Jimenez.

Jimenez, Marco, *Remedial Consilience*, 62 EMORY L.J. 1328-34 (2013). Copyright © 2013 Marco Jimenez.

Jimenez, Marco J., *The Many Faces of Promissory Estoppel: An Empirical Analysis Under the Restatement (Second) of Contracts*, 57 UCLA L. REV. 673-79 (2010). Copyright © 2010 Marco J. Jimenez.

Jimenez, Marco J., *The Value Of A Promise: A Utilitarian Approach To Contract Law Remedies*, 56 UCLA L. REV. 63-72 (2008). Copyright © 2008 Marco J. Jimenez.

Kelly, Kevin M., *Drafting Enforceable Covenants Not to Compete in Author-Publisher Agreements Under New York Law*, 36 UCLA L. REV. 119-20 (1988). Reprinted by permission of UCLA Law Review.

Kessler, Friedrich, Kronman, Anthony T., and Gilmore, Grant, CONTRACTS: CASES AND MATERIALS, Third Edition. Copyright © 1986 Aspen Publishers. Used by permission of Wolters Kluwer Legal & Regulatory US.

Konefsky, Alfred S., *How To Read, Or at Least Not Misread, Cardozo in the Allegheny College Case*, 36 BUFF. L. REV. 686-87 (1987). Republished with permission of Buffalo Law Review; permission conveyed through Copyright Clearance Center, Inc.

Kronman, Anthony T., *Mistake, Disclosure, Information, and the Law of Contracts*, 7 J. LEGAL STUDIES 2-5, 9, 13-18 (1978). Copyright © 1978 The University of Chicago. Reprinted with permission of the publisher, The University of Chicago Press.

Kull, Andrew, *Mistake, Frustration, and the Windfall Principle of Contract Remedies*, 43 HASTINGS L.J. 5-6 (1991). Reprinted with the permission of Hastings Law Journal and the author.

Linzer, Peter, *On the Amorality of Contract Remedies—Efficiency, Equity, and the Second Restatement*, 81 COLUM. L. REV. 134-39 (1981). Republished with permission of Columbia Law Review; permission conveyed through Copyright Clearance Center, Inc.

Llewellyn, Karl N., *A Lecture on Appellate Advocacy*, 29 U. CHI. L. REV. 637-38 (1962). Republished with permission of The University of Chicago Press; permission conveyed through Copyright Clearance Center, Inc.

Macaulay, Stewart, *Justice Traynor and the Law of Contracts*, 13 STAN. L. REV. 812-18 (1961). Republished with permission of Stanford Law Review; permission conveyed through Copyright Clearance Center, Inc.

Mehta, Prakash, *An Essay on Hamlet: Emblems of Truth in Law and Literature*, 83 GEO. L.J. 181-82 (1994). Copyright © 1994. Reprinted with the permission of the publisher, Georgetown Law Journal.

Nyquist, Curtis, *Teaching Wesley Hohfeld's Theory of Legal Relations*, 52 J. LEGAL EDUC. 239-43, 246-47, 249-50, 253-55 (2002). Journal of Legal Education © 2002 AALS; article copyright © 2002 Curtis Nyquist. Reprinted with the permission of AALS and the author.

Patterson, Edwin W., *The Interpretation and Construction of Contracts*, 64 COLUM. L. REV. 853-55 (1964). Republished with permission of Columbia Law Review; permission conveyed through Copyright Clearance Center, Inc.

Posner, Eric A., *ProCD v Zeidenberg and Cognitive Overload in Contractual Bargaining*, 77 U. CHI. L. REV. 1181-83 (2010). Republished with permission of The University of Chicago Press; permission conveyed through Copyright Clearance Center, Inc.

Posner, Richard A. and Rosenfield, Andrew M., *Impossibility and Related Doctrines In Contract Law: An Economic Analysis*, 6 J. LEGAL STUD. 85-86, 88-95, 106, 108-11 (1977). Copyright © 1977 The University of Chicago. Reprinted with permission of the publisher, The University of Chicago Press.

Roberts, Jorie, *Hawkins Case: A Hair-Raising Experience*, 66 HARV. L. REC. 1 (March 17, 1978). Reprinted with permission of The Harvard Law Record.

Sandel, Michael J., "Surrogacy Contracts" from *Markets and Morals* from JUSTICE: WHAT'S THE RIGHT THING TO DO? Copyright © 2009 by Michael J. Sandel. Reprinted by permission of Farrar, Straus and Giroux, LLC.

Simpson, A.W.B., *Quackery and Contract Law: The Case of the Carbolic Smoke Ball*, 14 J. LEG. STUD. 345, 348, 350-52, 354-56, 358-60, 363-67, 370-71, 375-79, 388-89 (1985). Copyright © 1985 The University of Chicago. Reprinted with permission of the publisher, The University of Chicago Press.

Tiersma, Peter Meijes, *Reassessing Unilateral Contracts: The Role of Offer, Acceptance and Promise*, 26 U.C. DAVIS L. REV. 29, 32-33 (1992). Republished with permission of UC Davis Law Review; permission conveyed through Copyright Clearance Center, Inc.

Wade, John W., *Restitution for Benefits Conferred Without Request*, 19 VAND. L. REV. 1183-84, 1211-12 (1966). Reprinted with the permission of Vanderbilt Law Review.

Watson, Geoffrey R., *In the Tribunal of Conscience: Mills v. Wyman Reconsidered*, 71 TUL. L. REV. 1749 (1997). Reprinted by permission of Tulane Law Review.

Whitford, William C. and Macaulay, Stewart, *Hoffman v. Red Owl Stores: The Rest of the Story*, 61 HASTINGS L.J. 855-56 (2010). Reprinted with the permission of Hastings Law Journal and the authors.

Illustrations

Brooklyn Bridge, photograph. Permission granted by Postdlf at the English language Wikipedia, the copyright holder of this work.

Cardozo, Justice Benjamin N., photograph. From the Library of Congress, Prints & Photographs Division. Photograph by Harris & Ewing.

The City Flour Mills in the 1920s, photograph. Copyright © 2003-04 Hugh Conway-Jones, from http://www.gloucesterdocks.me.uk. Used with permission.

Darlington North Road Station, photograph. From http://www.railwayarchitecture.org.uk/.

Traynor, Honorable Roger J., photograph. Copyright © 2016 UC Hastings College of the Law. Used by permission.

Author's Note

I have edited the materials in this casebook by using ellipses where text has been removed and brackets where text has been summarized. I have also removed, without indication, footnotes and citations that had, in my judgment, little pedagogical value, but have retained citations and footnotes that were needed to make sense of, or shed light on, material retained within the text. Where I have kept footnotes, I have retained their original numbers. Finally, to facilitate readability, I have inserted paragraph breaks where appropriate, standardized a number of spellings, and fixed small grammatical errors, all without indication.

PART I

AN INTRODUCTION TO CONTRACT LAW

Part I is designed to provide you, the student, with an introduction to contract law from the 30,000-foot level, introducing you to (1) the study of contract law, including the sources of contract law and how to brief cases for this class, (2) some of the historical and theoretical forces that have shaped contract law, and (3) a quick overview of each of the major doctrines of contract law that will be studied in this casebook. After reading this part, you will have some familiarity with each of the major components of contract law that we will be examining throughout the casebook (e.g., forming agreements, interpreting contracts, remedying breaches), in addition to having a rough sense of how each of these issues fit together to form a cohesive picture of contract law as a whole.

CHAPTER 1

AN INTRODUCTION TO THE SOURCES, BACKGROUND, AND DOCTRINES OF CONTRACT LAW

At its heart, contract law is about the law governing enforceable promises. As such, it focuses on questions such as what promises and agreements are, why we need and make them, and how courts interpret and enforce them. To be sure, we will spend much time exploring these issues in the pages that follow. But, before we do so, it makes sense to first become familiar with (a) some of the main sources of contract law and (b) how you, the student, should consider learning and studying contract law, including how you should read and brief cases for this class. So, without further ado, let's get started.

A. SOURCES OF LAW

American contract law comes from a variety of sources, but the majority of it comes from judge-made case law. Specifically, whenever a judge decides a case in a common law system (which, influenced by English common law, prevails in all federal and state courts in the United States with the exception of Louisiana, which was influenced by continental Europe's civil law tradition), the rule of law announced by the judge becomes *stare decisis*, or binding precedent on lower courts in the same jurisdiction deciding similar cases. It is largely because much of contract law is made up of legal rules and principles invented by judges that much of the material in this casebook consists of judicial opinions, where one can see first-hand how these rules and principles are often generated in response to the particular facts of the case. Learning contract law by studying cases allows us to critically examine these laws, testing the extent to which the black-letter rules announced by judges are capable of enduring—or must be altered—when confronted with a different or only somewhat related set of facts.

As judges decide thousands of cases every year, and have been doing so for centuries, one can easily imagine the large number of rules that have been built up over time. One can also easily imagine the chaos that resulted for judges, practitioners, and those wishing to know what the law was at any particular time from a process in which courts in fifty different states each announced their own particular rules—rules that, in turn, sometimes sat uneasily alongside other rules announced by federal courts and those inherited from the English common-law tradition. In fact, in large part because of this chaos, the problem was addressed in the early twentieth century by the newly-formed American Law Institute ("ALI"), consisting of a group of prominent scholars, judges, and practitioners from around the country tasked with unifying these principles into a grand restatement of contract law.

Under the guidance of the Reporter Samuel Williston, a Harvard Law professor and leading contracts scholar, the *Restatement (First) of Contracts* was published in 1932 to great acclaim. Although the provisions that make up the *Restatement* are not "law" in that they are now binding on courts, they constitute highly persuasive authority due to the fact that they were carefully drafted after receiving extensive input from leading judges, academicians, and practitioners. Indeed, with a few important exceptions that will be addressed in later chapters, the principles of contract law announced in the *Restatement* are based on commonly-accepted legal principles that have been gathered together after combing through thousands of judicial decisions across multiple jurisdictions. The result is a work that stands as "something less than a code" but "more than a treatise," a work that persuades rather than commands by "embody[ing] a composite thought and speak[ing with] a composite voice."* And persuade it has. The *Restatement (First) of Contracts*, along with the *Restatement (Second) of Contracts* (which was published in 1981 and written under the guidance of both Professor Robert Braucher, the initial Reporter, and Professor Allan Farnsworth, who succeeded him as Reporter when the former was appointed to the Massachusetts Supreme Judicial Court in 1971), have influenced countless courts and been cited thousands of times in judicial opinions across the country. Of course, once a provision from a *Restatement* is used by a court to decide a case, it becomes binding as part of that jurisdiction's case law. Throughout this casebook, we will come across a number of instances in which courts rely on a legal principle taken from the *Restatement of Contracts* (usually from the more recent *Restatement [Second] of Contracts*) to resolve a legal dispute. In addition, whenever a legal principle is discussed in the casebook, the relevant section of the *Restatement* will be referenced in the text and excerpted in the appendix, often along with accompanying comments and illustrations.

In addition to case law and the *Restatement*, another important source of contract law is the Uniform Commercial Code ("UCC"). The UCC is a uniform

* Benjamin Cardozo, The Growth of the Law 9 (1924).

act that was developed jointly by the ALI and the National Conference of Commissioners on Uniform State Laws ("NCCUSL") to unify the law of sales and important commercial transactions across the United States. The project was completed in 1952, and the uniform act has since been enacted as statutory law in every state except Louisiana, which means that, unlike the *Restatement*, the content found in the UCC is binding law. In this course, we will primarily be concerned with Article 2 of the UCC, which is concerned with the sales of goods. Specifically, whenever this casebook addresses a legal principle covered by the UCC, the relevant provision of the UCC will be referenced in the text and excerpted in the appendix, frequently along with the UCC's official comments, which provide guidance to courts charged with interpreting and applying these provisions to the facts before them.

As the *Restatement* is to U.S. domestic contract law, the UNIDROIT Principles of International Commercial Contracts ("UNIDROIT Principles") are to international contract law. Specifically, like the *Restatement*, the UNIDROIT Principles were published by an influential body (the International Institute for the Unification of Private Law, or "UNIDROIT") with the aim of compiling in a single place the principles of international contract law. Again, like the *Restatement*, the provisions contained in the UNIDROIT Principles are nonbinding but highly influential to courts resolving disputes requiring the application of international contract law. The UNIDROIT Principles were first published in 1994, updated in 2004, and updated again in a third edition published in 2010, primarily to include new articles dealing with topics like restitution, illegality, and conditions. As with the *Restatement* and UCC, articles of the UNIDROIT Principles are referenced throughout the casebook where relevant, and can be found in a separate appendix.

Similarly, as the UCC is to U.S. domestic sales law, so too is the United Nations Convention on Contracts for the International Sale of Goods (the "CISG" or "Vienna Convention") to international sales law. Specifically, the CISG is an international treaty that was put forward by the United Nations Commission on International Trade Law ("UNCITRAL") in 1980 to make international sales law more uniform across various nations. As of December 2015, it has been ratified by 84 states, including most of the nations responsible for the vast majority of the world's international commerce. The CISG applies whenever a contract for the sale of goods is entered into between parties whose places of business are in one of the contracting states. Because the CISG is a treaty that was ratified by the United States, whenever a place of business anywhere in the U.S. (including Louisiana!) does business with a party in another signatory state, the CISG will apply unless the parties have opted out of the CISG in their contract. As with the other bodies of law discussed above, the articles of the CISG are referenced throughout the casebook whenever relevant, and are included in a separate appendix.

In addition to the sources named above, courts will sometimes rely on contract treatises and scholarly books and articles when deciding cases. This casebook will include excerpts from both of these sources. Specifically, this casebook will often introduce new material by providing excerpts from Professor E. Allan Farnsworth's treatise *Contracts* (4th ed. 2004), in large part to provide the student with legal context for the cases and materials that follow. Similarly, this casebook will use excerpts from scholarly books and articles, usually after (but sometimes before) cases to provide the student with materials for thinking critically about less well-settled areas of law.

B. HOW TO BRIEF LEGAL CASES

Reading a legal case for the first time can be daunting. There is so much going on—from who the parties are to what they did to one another to how the legal dispute between them arose—that it can be difficult for a student to process all this information and to know what he or she should be taking away from a case. Therefore, although there is no single "correct" way to read or brief a case, one way to successfully brief your cases (for this and other classes) is offered below. You should feel free to depart from it as you develop your own style, but by following the suggestions below, you should feel confident that you are getting most of the important information from a legal case.

1. *Parties.* First, find out what court you are in (a trial court, an intermediate appellate court, or a state's highest appellate court), and identify the plaintiff and defendant. Most of the decisions you will read in law school are appellate decisions, which means that, in addition to identifying the plaintiff and defendant, you will also need to identify the appellant (the party appealing the decision below) and the appellee (the party against whom the decision is being appealed). Finally, if this is the second round of appeals (i.e., if the case is now before the state's highest appellate court), keep in mind that the party referred to by the court as the "appellant below" may actually be the appellee here, and vice versa. Unless you clearly identify the parties early on, it can often be difficult to figure out who the court is talking about, so take the extra time to carefully note who the parties are, and how the court is referring to them.

2. *Procedural History.* Closely related to identifying the parties is figuring out the procedural history of the case. This means clearly identifying who won at trial, who won on appeal, and what is being disputed before the instant court. So, for instance, combining steps one and two above, your case brief (so far) might look something like this:

> Plaintiff "X" brought a breach of contract action against Defendant "Y" for non-payment of delivery of 10,000 pounds of oranges in the United States District Court for the Southern District of Florida. The judge granted Defendant Y's motion for summary judgment, and Plaintiff X appealed. The issue is now before the Circuit Court of Appeals.

3. *Facts.* Next, you should identify and summarize the facts that were important to the court's disposition of the case. You will often not be able to tell

the difference between important and unimportant facts from a single reading, especially early on in law school. Therefore, it is highly recommended that you read each case several times until you feel comfortable distilling the important facts into a paragraph or so. An example of an effective summary of facts might look something like this:

> Plaintiff "X" is a Florida farmer engaged in the retail sale of oranges. Defendant "Y" is a Georgia company that makes and distributes orange juice to grocery stores. In 2015, X's president met representatives of Y at a trade fair in Tampa, Florida, where Y agreed to purchase 10,000 pounds of oranges from X. Specifically, the parties arrived at an oral agreement on the terms of price, quality, quantity, delivery, and payment, and recorded these agreements on one of Y's standard, pre-printed order forms and X's president signed it. The preprinted order forms contained terms and conditions on both the front and back, which X's president claims to have never read. Indeed, according to X, Y's representatives told X "not to worry about those other terms, as the only terms between us are the ones we're agreeing to here." One of the terms that X's president claimed to have not read stated that "Any late delivery shall constitute a material breach of this contract, allowing Y to cancel the contract." Due to bad weather, the first 1,000 pounds of oranges arrived one day later than scheduled, and Y's president called X's president to cancel the contract, claiming that X's late shipment constituted a material breach of the contract pursuant to the clause on the back of the contract. X's president ignored Y's president, told her that she was told by Y's representatives that those terms were not part of the agreement, and proceeded to deliver 9,000 additional pounds of oranges to Y over the next 10 days. When Y refused to pay, X sued Y for breach of contract, but Y claimed it under no obligation to accept or pay for the oranges on account of X's first delivery being late.

4. *Arguments.* Here, you should identify each argument that was (or should have been) raised by each of the parties. So, for instance, your case brief might include something like the following:

> *Plaintiff.* X argued that the parties never intended the terms and conditions printed on the reverse of the order form to apply to their agreements, submitting a number of affidavits from Y's own representatives, all of which demonstrated that X had no subjective intention of being bound by those terms and that Y was aware of this intent.
>
> *Defendant.* Y argued that the clause on the reverseside of the order form clearly allowed Y to cancel the contract for any late deliveries whatsoever. Because X's first delivery was late, and because the contract terms are clear, no oral evidence should be admitted to prove the veracity of X's assertion.

5. *Issues.* Next, identify any legal issues being asserted by the parties, including, where applicable, any relevant defenses. So, to continue our sample brief, you might write something like the following under the heading "issue":

> The issue before the court is whether oral evidence should be admitted to interpret the written contract between X and Y.

6. *Rules.* After you've identified the relevant issues before the court, identify any legal rules, principles, theories, or policies that were used by the court to resolve the dispute. So, for instance, one of the rules that might have been used by a court to resolve the fact pattern above might have been something like:

> Statements made by, or conduct of, a party are to be interpreted according to that party's intent only where the other party knew or could not have been unaware what that intent was.

7. *Analysis.* Next, you will want to pay careful attention to the court's *reasoning*, i.e., the way in which the court applied the relevant rules, principles, theories, or policies identified above to the facts to resolve the dispute between the parties. Do you agree with the court's analysis? Why or why not? Do you agree with the way in which the court applied the law? Should the court have used a different rule or principle to decide the case? Do you think the case will create good precedent for future cases? Were there any arguments or policy implications the court failed to consider? If so, write them down. It is only by engaging critically with the court's analysis of the case that you will begin to understand how legal rules and principles get applied to the facts of the case to "resolve" disputes, including the extent to which law and policy determine legal outcomes.

8. *Conclusion and Disposition.* Here, you should indicate how the court ruled (e.g., "the lower court erred in refusing to admit the affidavits discussing the subjective intent of Y's representatives") and disposed of the case (e.g., "reversed and remanded").

9. *Impressions.* Finally, you might include a place in your case brief to note your general impression of the case. So, for instance, if the court's decision seems unjust to you, or is brilliantly written but shallow on legal authority, or puts forth a rule inconsistent with another concept you learned earlier, make a note of it here. Sometimes, the casebook will provide materials before and/or after the cases that provide additional insight into the cases themselves. If so, this is a good place to capture such information. Finally, if you have any other thoughts about the case that do not easily fit into one of the previously-mentioned categories but which seem important, this is a good place to include such information.

C. AN INTRODUCTION TO THE FORCES SHAPING CONTRACT LAW

As stated above, contract law is concerned with the law governing enforceable promises. But the law we shall study—the oracles pronounced by our jurisprudential high priests—often constitute the practical working out of our market economy's dominant religion: capitalism. Indeed, if we wish to demystify and understand (rather than simply memorize) what is often called the "black-letter" law, it behooves one to not only become familiar with the orthodox religion of contract law—or the "classical view" of contracts, as it is sometimes called, centered around ideas like freedom of contract, party autonomy, and laissez-faire capitalism—but also with the historical context in which it arose. Indeed, doing so not only allows one to see past contract law's seemingly static exterior and appreciate it for the dynamic, exciting, and evolving force that it is, but also to gain access to the Sibylline leaves on which these legal oracles (or, if you prefer, the "black-letter rules") are written, thereby allowing one to foretell the law's prophesies for oneself (and, of course, for one's clients).*

As suggested above, a good introduction to contract law should familiarize the student with the main tenets of the classical view of contract law, from which much of our modern case law developed, in addition to exploring some of the critiques leveled against that view. The best introduction I know of was provided in a wonderful essay appearing in the beginning of Kessler, Gilmore, and Kronman's magisterial casebook on contract law. A significantly edited version of that essay appears below, and is provided to introduce the student to some of the forces that continue to shape contract law to this day.

CONTRACT AS A PRINCIPLE OF ORDER†

A profitable approach to the law of contract, and perhaps to law in general, is to view legal doctrine, rules, principles, and standards as reflecting the value system of the culture in which the legal system is embedded. In our modern society, a tension exists between those values favoring individual freedom and those favoring social control.[4] Whatever the merits of the claim that a society without tension is conceivable (and desirable), in our society we encounter every day the tension between individual freedom and social control in debates over government regulation of the economy, abortion, use of marijuana and laetrile, sexual practices between consenting adults, gun control, the rights of criminal defendants, busing, affirmative action, and the teaching of evolution. The list is virtually endless. Small wonder, then, that modern contract law reproduces this same tension within itself, drawing much of its drama and vitality from our divided commitment to individual freedom and social control.

The law of contracts comprises many different doctrinal elements and encompasses exchange relationships of limitless variety. If these relationships were arranged along a continuum, we would find at one end transactions based on free

* For the classic expression of this view, see Oliver Wendell Holmes, *The Path of the Law*, 10 HARV. L. 468 (1897).

† Excerpted from KESSLER, GILMORE, AND KRONMAN, CONTRACTS: CASES AND MATERIALS 1-6, 7-8, 11-12, 13-14, 15, 16-17 (3d ed. 1986).

4. This conflict is reflected in the two main theories of contractual liability. One, the will theory, emphasizes the autonomy of the individual. The other, the objective theory, bases contractual liability on the social consequences of promise-making, or, as Hume put it, on the fact that "[p]romises are human inventions founded on the necessity and interests of society." [DAVID HUME, A TREATISE ON HUMAN NATURE, Book III: of Morals, ch. 6, at 287 (T. H. Greene & T. H. Grose eds. 1890).] . . .

bargain and genuine agreement, or at least on promises voluntarily given. Here, the dominant theme is respect for the autonomy of the parties and noninterference in the arrangements they have made for themselves, provided all the ground rules laid down to insure the smooth working of the system have been observed. Social control is at a minimum. As we proceed along the continuum, the freedom of the parties increasingly is limited by a system of judicial and legislative control designed to protect the community interest. And finally, at the opposite end of the scale, we find the so-called compulsory and adhesive contracts, the first type entered into under an enforceable duty to serve the public and the second unilaterally dictated by the stronger to the weaker party in need of goods or services. In recent years, there has undoubtedly been a shift all along this vast continuum in the direction of greater social control, a phenomenon reflecting the socialization of modern law in general. But the idea of private autonomy remains influential in wide areas of contract law and even where it is no longer dominant, its appeal can still be heard, albeit often only as a distant echo.

To better understand the main tenets of modern contract law, and its distinctive tendencies, it will be helpful to [understand] the "classical" theory of contractual obligation. Classical contract theory starts from the belief that the individual is the best judge of his own welfare and of the means of securing it, and is inspired by the hope that given a "suitable system of general rules and institutions there will arise spontaneous relationships also deserving the term 'order' but which are self-sustaining and within the limits prescribed by the rules need no detailed and specific regulation."[8] To achieve such order, according to the proponents of the classical theory, all that is required besides a system of general rules is "a free market guaranteeing and guiding the division of labor through a system of incentives it provides to the interest of the individual producers."[9] Within this framework, contract provides the legal machinery required by an economic system that relies on free exchange rather than tradition, custom, or command.

The triumph of capitalism during the eighteenth and nineteenth centuries, with its spectacular increase in the productivity of labor, was possible only because of a constant refinement of the division of labor. This development in turn presupposed that enterprisers could depend on a continuous flow of goods and services exchanged in a free market. And to be able to exploit the factors of production in the most efficient way, enterprisers had (and still have) to be able to bargain for goods and services to be delivered in the future and to rely on promises for future delivery. Thus, it became one of the main functions of our law of contracts to keep this flow running smoothly, making certain that bargains would be kept and that legitimate expectations created by contractual promises would be honored.

---

8. LORD ROBBINS, POLITICAL ECONOMY PAST AND PRESENT 5-9 (1976).

9. T. SOWELL, CLASSICAL ECONOMICS RECONSIDERED, ch. 1 (1974). ADAM SMITH, WEALTH OF NATIONS 13 (Cannan ed. 1937):

> This division of labor, from which so many advantages are derived, is not originally the effect of any human wisdom which foresees and intends the general opulence to which it gives occasion. It is the necessary, though very slow and gradual, consequence of a certain propensity in human nature which has in view no such extensive utility: the propensity to truck, barter and exchange one thing for another.

"The foundation of contract," in the language of Adam Smith, "is the reasonable expectation, which the person who promises raises in the person to whom he binds himself; of which the satisfaction may be extorted by force."[11] In this sense, contract liability is promissory liability. In an industrial and commercial society, whose wealth, as Pound said, is largely made up of promises, the interest of society as a whole demands protection of the interest of the individual promisee. . . .

Within the framework of a free-enterprise system the essential prerequisite of contractual liability is volition, that is, consent freely given, and not coercion or status.[13] Contract, in this view, is the "meeting place of the ideas of agreement and obligation."[14] As a matter of historical fact the rise of free and informal contract within western civilization reflected the erosion of a status-organized society; contract became, at an ever-increasing rate, a tool of change and of growing self-determination and self-assertion. Self-determination during the nineteenth century was regarded as the goal towards which society progressed; the movement of progressive societies, in the words of Sir Henry Maine, is a movement from status to contract, *Ancient Law* [163-65 (1864)]. "It is through contract that man attains freedom. Although it appears to be the subordination of one man's will to another, the former gains more than he loses."[15] Contract, in this view, is the principle of order par excellence and the only legitimate means of social integration in a free society. Translated into legal language this means that in a progressive society all law is ultimately based on contract. And since contract as a social phenomenon is the result of a "coincidence of free choices" on the part of the members of the community, merging their egoistical and altruistic tendencies, a contractual society safeguards its own stability. Contract is an instrument of peace in society. It reconciles freedom with order. . . .

The high hopes with regard to the potentialities inherent in the contractual mechanism found admirable expression in Henry Sidgwick's *Elements of Politics* 82 (1879):

> In a summary view of the civil order of society, as constituted in accordance with the individualistic ideal, performance of contract presents itself as the chief *positive* element, protection of life and property being the chief *negative* element. Withdraw contract—suppose that no one can count upon the fulfillment of any engagement—and the members of a human community are atoms that cannot effectively combine; the complex cooperation and division of employments that are the essential characteristics of modern industry cannot be introduced among such beings. Suppose contracts freely made and effectively sanctioned, and the most elaborate social organization becomes possible, at least in a society of such human beings as the

11. LECTURES ON JUSTICE, POLICE, REVENUE AND ARMS 7 (Cannan ed. 1896).

13. Freedom of contract thus means that, subject to narrow limits, the law, in the field of contracts, has delegated legislation to the contracting parties. As far as the parties are concerned, the law of contracts is of their own making; society merely lends its machinery of enforcement to the party injured by the breach. . . .

14. W. WATT, THE THEORY OF CONTRACT IN ITS SOCIAL LIGHT 2 (1897).

15. W. G. MILLER, LECTURES IN THE PHILOSOPHY OF LAW 216 (1884).

individualistic theory contemplates—gifted with mature reason, and governed by enlightened self-interest. . . .

Thus, a system of free contract did not recommend itself solely for reasons of sheer expediency and utilitarianism; it was deeply rooted in the moral sentiments of the period in which it found strongest expression. The dominant current of belief inspiring nineteenth-century industrial society . . . was the deep-felt conviction that individual and cooperative action should be left unrestrained in family, church, and market, and that such a system of laissez-faire would protect the freedom and dignity of the individual and secure the greatest possible measure of social justice. The representatives of this school of thought were firmly convinced, to state it somewhat roughly, of the existence of a natural law according to which, at least in the long run, the individual serving his own interest was also serving the interest of the community.[18] Profits, under this system, could be earned only by supplying desired commodities and freedom of competition would prevent profits from rising unduly. The play of the market, if left to itself, would therefore maximize net satisfactions and establish the ideal conditions for the distribution of wealth. Justice within this context has a very definite meaning. It means freedom of property and of contract, of profit making and of trade. A social system based on freedom of enterprise and competition sees to it that the private autonomy of contracting parties is kept within bounds and works for the benefit of society as a whole. . . .

It was taken for granted that oppressive bargains could be avoided by careful shopping around. Contracting parties were expected to look out for their own interest and their own protection. "Let the bargainer beware" was (and to some extent still is) the ordinary rule of contract. It is not the function of courts to strike down improvident bargains. Courts have only to interpret contracts made by the parties. They do not make them. Within this framework contract justice is commutative and not distributive justice. This attitude is in keeping with liberal social and moral philosophy according to which it pertains to the dignity of man to lead his own life as a reasonable person and to accept responsibility for his own mistakes. If the diligent is not to be deprived of the fruits of his own superior skill and knowledge acquired by legitimate means, the law cannot afford to go to the "romantic length of giving indemnity against the consequences of indolence and folly, or a careless indifference to the ordinary and accessible means of information."[29] Sir George Jessel, one of the great defenders of freedom of contract remarked,

---

18. Adam Smith, Wealth of Nations 423 (Cannan ed. 1937): "By pursuing his own interest the individual member of society promotes that of the society more effectively than when he really intends to promote it." . . .

29. 2 J. Kent, Commentaries 485 (O. W. Holmes 12th ed. 1873); Bolden, *Voluntary Assumption of Risk*, 20 Harv. L. Rev. 14, 22 (1906):

> While the common law makes no pretense of being a social reformer and does not profess to reduce all persons to an absolutely equal position by eliminating all natural advantages, but rather, recognizing society as it is, considers social inequalities as the natural inevitable tactical advantages of those lucky enough to possess them, it does prohibit their misuse while permitting their use within fair limits.

> [I]f there is one thing more than another which public policy requires, it is that men of full age and competent understanding shall have the utmost liberty of contracting, and that their contracts entered into freely and voluntarily shall be held sacred and shall be enforced by Courts of Justice. . . .[30]

Only slowly did American courts recognize the dangers inherent in the inequality of bargaining power. . . . State statutes attempting to protect the weaker contracting party against abuses of freedom of contract by fixing minimum wages and maximum hours in employment and by attempting to outlaw discrimination against union members by means of yellow dog contracts* did not fare any better at the hands of American courts. The climate of opinion prevailing at the end of the last century and well into this one is strikingly illustrated by the celebrated cases of *Lochner v. New York*, 198 U.S. 45 (1904), *Adair v. United States*, 208 U.S. 161 (1907), and *Coppage v. Kansas*, 236 U.S. 1 (1914). Declaring such statutes unconstitutional under the due process clause of the fourteenth amendment, these decisions elevated liberty of contract to the status of a fundamental property right. Pitney, J., speaking for the majority of the court in *Coppage v. Kansas*, which declared an anti-yellow dog statute unconstitutional, formulated the then-prevailing philosophy of Social Darwinism.

> . . . No doubt, wherever the right of private property exists, there must and will be inequalities of fortune; and thus it naturally happens that parties negotiating about a contract are not equally unhampered by circumstances. This applies to all contracts, and not merely to that between employer and employee. Indeed a little reflection will show that wherever the right of private property and the right of free contract co-exist, each party when contracting is inevitably more or less influenced by the question whether he has much property, or little, or none; for the contract is made to the very end that each may gain something that he needs or desires more urgently than that which he proposes to give in exchange. And, since it is self-evident that, unless all things are held in common, some persons must have more property than others, it is from the nature of things impossible to uphold freedom of contract and the right of private property without at the same time recognizing as legitimate those inequalities of fortune that are the necessary result of the exercise of those rights. But the Fourteenth Amendment, in declaring that a State shall not "deprive any person of life, liberty or property without due process of law," gives to each of these an equal sanction; it recognizes "liberty" and "property" as co-existent human rights, and debars the States from any unwarranted interference with either. . . .[44]

---

30. *Printing and Numerical Registering Co. v. Sampson*, 19 L.R.-Eq. 462, 465 (1875).

* [Yellow-dog contracts are contracts in which employees agree, as a condition of their employment, not to be a member of a union.—Ed.]

44. 236 U.S. 1, 17 (1914).

Very gradually the conviction took hold that political democracy is not sufficient by itself to secure the meaningful liberty men rightly desire. To overcome the deep sense of frustration felt by many, and to establish the material conditions needed to give existing legal freedoms something more than paper worth, political democracy (many argued) had to be supplemented by economic and social democracy. In the course of this debate, the rhetoric of freedom of contract was drowned out by the rhetoric of freedom from contract, and equality of opportunity.

Social control of contractual association, which began as a countercurrent in the early days of laissez-faire libertarianism, has finally swelled into a main current of thought. . . .

Today, . . . the individual member of the community continuously finds himself involved in contractual relations, the contents of which are predetermined for him by statute, public authority, or group action. The terms and conditions under which he obtains his supply of electricity and gas will in all likelihood be regulated by a public utility commission. So will his fare, should he use a public conveyance going to work. The rent he will have to pay may be fixed by governmental authority. The price of his food will depend partly on the government's farm support program and not solely on the interplay of supply and demand in a free market. Many of the goods he uses in daily consumption will have prices that reflect suggested list prices. The wages he earns, or must pay, may also have been fixed for him beforehand. And if he is a businessman, he must take care not to violate the antitrust laws which, during the last half century, have grown steadily in importance, transforming the business environment.

This picture of our world has led many to the conclusion that the idea of contract has undergone a dramatic change. Some view contract as an anachronistic concept, anticipating its merger with the general law of obligations, or argue that Maine's famous formula has to be qualified if not reversed. Closely connected with this criticism is the idea that more attention should be given to the difference between discrete (transactional) exchanges and continuing relations, since many of the terms of the latter type of transaction must be left open for further negotiation. It has also been suggested that the modern law of contracts can be more meaningfully explained in terms of a tripartite distinction between benefit-based, detriment-based, and promise-based obligations. . . .

These observations doubtless have some validity. Today, few judges (and fewer legislatures) feel enthusiasm, or even respect, for the elegant simplicities of the classical law of contracts. On the contrary, the carefully delimited classical defenses of mistake, fraud, and duress—the only defenses allowable in a strict libertarian regime—seem continually on the verge of further expansion and have recently been supplemented by a revitalized, and potentially far-reaching concept of unconscionabilty. Social policy arguments are frequently advanced to strike down obnoxious clauses. Caveat emptor is a mere shadow of its former self. The rules of the contracting game have been softened, and bargainers are expected to act in good faith toward one another. The old model of arm's length dealing is in retreat, along with the notion that a contractual relation is one of "limited commitment." In their place, the confidential relation—the relation of fiduciary

> trust—has emerged or is emerging as the new model for both bargaining and contract performance in a large number of cases.
>
> Despite all this, however, the classical theory of contract reflects a set of values that continue to enjoy wide acceptance in our society. Most special legislation leaves considerable freedom to the parties to arrange their affairs as they wish. . . . Faith in market forces, or perhaps a lack of faith in governmental controls, is widespread and growing. Despite paternalistic arguments for directly regulating the consuming habits of the poor, consumer legislation has not gone so far. Self-reliance, it would seem, is still a valued concept in late twentieth-century America, and even those who argue that we are turning back to status after a brief flirtation with contract recognize that the roles that define a person's rights and responsibilities are not ascribed to one at birth, but are assumed more or less freely, and just as freely given up. Finally, the planning element of contract, so important in the field of business, has in recent years become increasingly important in the domain of interpersonal relations, such as marriage and cohabitation, where traditionally the contractual freedom of the individual was restricted or nonexistent. As freedom of contract wanes in one area, it waxes in another, and the overall result is a world that may well be more free than its nineteenth-century counterpart (though it is certainly free in different ways). . . .

D. AN INTRODUCTION TO CONTRACT LAW DOCTRINE

Finally, before we get to the cases themselves, the materials in this casebook will be organized around seven broad issues, and can be understood as contract law's attempt to provide answers to the following seven questions: (1) Have the parties promised or agreed to do something? (2) If so, should a court enforce their promises? (3) If so, then we have a contract, and the question becomes *how* should a court enforce this contract (i.e., what remedy should it enforce)? (4) How should a court interpret the parties' contract? (5) How should a court determine whether a party has breached its contract? (6) Where a party has breached, what defenses (if any) may a party allege to avoid performance of its contractual duties? Finally, (7) how, if at all, does the contract affect third parties? That's it! Although courts have slowly developed answers to these questions over hundreds of years, which means that we have plenty of cases, doctrines, principles, theories, and history to look at over the course of our study, all of the big questions one can ask about contract law will fit into one of these seven broad categories. It's nice to remember this fact if you ever find yourself feeling lost amidst the vast number of doctrinal trees making up the contractual forest. So, to orient you with the lay of the land and give you some familiarity with the major doctrines of contract law, the rest of this chapter is designed to give you a 30,000-foot overview of the contracts landscape, providing you with an overview of the types of situations and cases that will arise under each of these seven categories before we delve into them in greater depth in the chapters to follow.

1. Promises and Agreements: Have the parties promised or agreed to do something?

The first question a court can ask is whether the parties promised or agreed to do something. To answer this question, of course, we must first know something about the nature of promises and agreements. In fact, this is all the more important because the *Restatement (Second) of Contracts* itself defines a contract as an enforceable *promise*;* so unless we know what a promise is, we're sure to not get very far in our study of contract law. So, what's a promise? According to the *Restatement*, "[a] promise is a manifestation of intention to act or refrain from acting in a specified way, so made as to justify a promisee in understanding that a commitment has been made."† A rather unwieldy definition, to be sure, but if we read over it a few times, what we will notice is that a party who makes a promise to another party is doing something much more than merely expressing its present intention to do or refrain from doing something in the future—it is actually *committing* itself to a certain course of action that it was previously at liberty to avoid. So, if I tell you that I plan on giving you my car when you graduate from law school, it is true that I have expressed my intention about how I plan on behaving in the future, but because I have not actually made a *commitment* to you, I would still be at liberty to change my mind when you graduated, notwithstanding your displeasure at my having done so. On the other hand, if I *promise* to give you my car when you graduate, I have not merely indicated to you my present intention regarding my future conduct, I have actually *committed* myself to behave in a certain way in the future. This commitment, in turn, cuts off a course of conduct previously available to me (i.e., the ability to change my mind and keep my car), compelling me to keep my promise even though I may no longer feel like doing so when the time for performance arrives.

As you may have noticed, promises have somewhat of a unilateral dimension to them: Although it is true that they join two parties, they do so in a rather one-dimensional way in that they are given *by* one party (the "promisor") *to* another party (the "promisee"). *Agreements*, on the other hand, have much more of a bilateral dimension to them, in that they are formed where two (or more) parties exchange their promises so that each of the parties receives something back for the promise it has given. If, for instance, I promise to give you my car in exchange for your promise to graduate from law school, then each of us has not merely made a promise, we have actually formed an *agreement* (or, more colloquially, we've made a deal) with each other. As we shall soon see, this distinction between promises and agreements is important because the law is much more inclined to enforce agreements than stand-alone

* *See* RESTATEMENT (SECOND) OF CONTRACTS § 1 ("A contract is a promise or a set of promises for the breach of which the law gives a remedy, or the performance of which the law in some way recognizes as a duty").

† RESTATEMENT (SECOND) OF CONTRACTS § 2(1).

promises because the former are often supported by "consideration" (we will see what this means soon) whereas the latter are not.

But before discussing consideration (and a few other doctrines capable of turning non-enforceable promises into enforceable ones), we should pause first to consider how courts go about determining whether parties have made a promise, or formed an agreement, in the first place. How, in other words, do courts go about determining whether the parties have merely expressed their intention to behave in a certain way in the future, or have actually made a *commitment* obligating themselves to behave in a certain way in the future? For instance, if I say something like "My car is yours when you graduate" and you say something like "Well then, I will graduate," have we actually exchanged promises with one another, thereby forming an agreement, or have we merely expressed our future plans without obligating us to follow through with them, preserving our freedom to change our minds when the future arrives? And, more complicatedly, how should courts deal with a situation in which one party understands another party's words or conduct to constitute a promise, but that other party had no such understanding, and never in fact intended to make a commitment?

Consider, for instance, the well-known case of *Embry v. Hargadine, McKittrick Dry Goods Co.* (1907). In that case, Embry, who selected samples for traveling salesmen of a dry goods company, worked under a contract that expired on December 15. After his contract expired, on December 23, Embry approached his boss McKittrick and told him that he would quit unless he was given a new contract. According to Embry, McKittrick responded by telling him "Go ahead, you're all right; get your men out and don't let that worry you." According to McKittrick, however, he told Embry that he was too busy to take up the matter just then, and told him to "Go back upstairs and get your men out on the road." Embry, in any event, believed that his contract had been renewed, and continued to work for McKittrick until one day, on February 15 of the following year, he was notified that his services were no longer needed after March 1. Embry sued McKittrick for breach of contract, and the question before the court was whether Embry and McKittrick had formed an agreement.

How do you think the court should decide this case? How, in short, do you think the court should go about determining whether Embry and McKittrick formed an agreement? This is one of the cases we will look at in the materials below.

2. Enforceability: Should the court enforce the promise or agreement between the parties?

Just because a party has made a promise to, or formed an agreement with, another party, does not necessarily mean that that promise or agreement should be enforced. And, if the promise or agreement is not enforceable, then, according to the *Restatement (Second) of Contracts*, it is not a contract, which the *Restatement* defines as an *enforceable* promise.* But what, exactly, makes a promise or agreement enforceable? In fact, to even define a contract as an enforceable promise presumes that we have already worked out answers to at least two questions that lay at the heart of contract law itself. First, it assumes that we have thought about *why* courts should enforce promises at all. After all, most promises concern private commitments made between private parties operating in the private sphere. How, then, can we justify using a taxpayer-subsidized court system to force a private party to do something it no longer wants to do? Second, assuming we have satisfactorily answered our first question, the *Restatement's* definition of a contract assumes that our courts have some way of distinguishing between enforceable and unenforceable promises. If your uncle promises to meet you for dinner but doesn't show up, I suspect that many of us would view his actions as morally blameworthy, but most of us probably wouldn't want our courts to *force* him to keep his promise. On the other hand, if you entered into a contract to buy someone's car—even your uncle's car—for $5,000, but the seller refused to deliver the car to you when the time for performance came due, I suspect that most of us *would* want the courts to get involved in some way, either to force the seller to deliver the car, or to compensate you. And if you relied on your uncle's promise in some way (say, by purchasing a new set of tires for the car you expected to receive), I suspect that we would feel even *more* justified inenforcing your uncle's promise. And, finally, if you already paid the $5,000 to your uncle, we would feel even more justified still. But why? What, exactly, is responsible for these intuitions? Why do many of us feel that some promises, like your uncle's promise to meet you for dinner, should probably not be enforced at all, but other promises, like the one where you paid $5,000 for your uncle's car, should almost certainly be enforced? How, in short, should courts go about distinguishing between enforceable and unenforceable promises?

Consider, for instance, *Hamer v. Sidway* (1891), in which an uncle, during a wedding celebration, promised to give his nephew $5,000 "if he would refrain from drinking, using tobacco, swearing and playing cards or billiards for money until he became twenty-one years of age." Assume, further, that the nephew performs his promise and, having never been paid, seeks to collect $5,000 from his uncle. Do you think this is the kind of promise a court should enforce? Why or why not? Would it matter to you that the uncle may have derived no benefit from making his promise, except perhaps a psychological one, and that the nephew may have suffered no detriment by foregoing liquor and tobacco, except the liberty he had to give up by not engaging in a few activities he was legally privileged to enjoy? How, in short, do you think a court should decide

* *See Restatement (Second) of Contracts* § 1 ("A contract is a promise or a set of promises for the breach of which the law gives a remedy, or the performance of which the law in some way recognizes as a duty").

such a case, and what test or tests should it use to distinguish between enforceable and non-enforceable promises? This, too, we will study in the materials below.

3. Remedies: How should the court enforce the parties' contract?

Once a court decides that a promise or agreement should be enforced, it next needs to decide *how* it should be enforced. In other words, what should the court do where a party refuses to perform its contractual obligations? Suppose, for instance, that you already paid your uncle $5,000 for his car, and also purchased a new set of tires (say, for $500) in expectation of receiving his car. Suppose, further, that you can buy an equivalent car on the open market for $6,000. What should the court do if your uncle refuses to deliver the car to you as promised?

One option is that the court could force your uncle to give you the car. This remedy, called specific performance, is sometimes awarded by common law courts, but, for historical reasons that we will discuss in greater detail in the cases and materials below, it is typically not awarded unless the contracted-for item is unique, i.e., where an adequate substitute is not readily available on the open market. Here, because a substitute car is available on the open market (although for $1,000 more than you paid for your uncle's car), most courts will enforce the contract between you and your uncle by requiring your uncle to pay money damages.

So now the question becomes: How much in money damages should your uncle be required to pay? Courts can measure the harm done to you by your uncle's breach in at least three different ways. First, courts can require your uncle to pay *restitution damages,* which attempts to measure the benefit you conferred on your uncle. Here, because you gave your uncle $5,000, a court could simply require your uncle to return your money, thereby returning him to the position he occupied before the contract was made. Alternatively, the court could require your uncle to pay *reliance damages,* which attempts to measure the harm you suffered in reliance on your uncle's promise. Here, you not only paid your uncle $5,000, but you also purchased a new set of tires for $500. Suppose that, after learning of your uncle's breach, you're only able to resell these tires for $250. In this case, a court measuring your recovery by the reliance measure damages would require your uncle to pay you $5,250, which would restore you to the position you occupied before you contracted with your uncle. Finally, a court could require your uncle to pay *expectation damages,* which attempts to measure the value of the unperformed contract. Here, had your uncle performed his promise, you would have obtained a $6,000 car for $5,000. The value of this bargain was therefore worth $1,000 to you. Therefore, by awarding this amount, plus the $5,000 you already paid to your uncle (for a total of $6,000), the court would (in theory, anyway) put you in the position you would have occupied had your uncle performed his promise, because you could use this money, if you so desired, to buy a substitute car on the open market.

Unfortunately for you, notice that all three of these damages measures fail to compensate you for your frustration, your lost time, or your court costs. Further, if you attached some sentimental value to owning your uncle's car, it would not compensate you for that either. Finally, all three of these damages measures would fail to compensate you for any additional damages you might have suffered where such damages were (1) unforeseeable to your uncle at the time of entering into the contract, (2) difficult to prove with certainty, or (3) avoidable by you. We will discuss all of these remedies, in addition to the three limitations courts typically place on these remedies, in the cases and materials below.

For now, you should ask yourself, of all of the possible remedies we have discussed—specific performance, restitution damages, reliance damages, and expectation damages—which damages do you prefer and think that courts should typically award, and why? Why do you suppose common-law courts have typically favored money damages over specific performance, and why do you suppose they have traditionally limited money damages with the three limitations discussed above? And what about punishment? Do you think that, in addition to requiring your uncle to perform his promise or pay damages, the court should also impose punitive damages to punish you uncle for his behavior and/or deter other parties from behaving like your uncle in the future? Why or why not?

4. Interpretation: How should the court interpret the parties' contract?

Another issue that courts must frequently deal with is how to interpret the parties' contract. For instance, what if your uncle agreed to sell you his "car" for $5,000, but he actually had two cars, a Buick and a Honda, and you thought he meant "Honda," but he thought you meant "Buick." Is there a contract and, if so, for which car? (One of the cases we will look at, *Raffles v. Wichelhaus* (1864), deals with precisely this issue.) Or, suppose, to draw upon the facts of another famous case we will study, *Frigaliment Importing Co. v. B.N.S. International Sales Corp.* (1960), two parties make a contract for the sale and delivery of chickens, but one party thinks chicken means "young chicken, suitable for broiling and frying," whereas the other party thinks chicken means "any bird of that genus." Where the parties have not defined the term "chicken" in their contract, how should a court go about determining whose meaning should prevail? There is, of course, no easy answer to this question, but courts will generally start by looking carefully at (1) the *express terms* used by the parties in their contract to try to figure out what they intended to bargain for. They may also consider things like (2) the *course of performance* between the parties, or how they have performed with respect to previous shipments of chicken, if applicable; (3) the course of dealing between the parties, or how they have behaved towards one another in any previous transactions, if applicable; and (4) usage of trade, which focuses on the types of practices other parties in the industry tend to observe.

But not only are courts called upon to interpret terms (like "car" or "chicken") used by the parties in their contract, they are also called upon to decide if they will supply terms for the parties where a dispute arises over a situation that the parties did not anticipate when they formed their contract, and therefore provided no terms to govern in that scenario. Consider, for instance, *Wood v. Lucy, Lady Duff-Gordon* (1917), which we will study when we get to Chapter 6. In that case, Lucy, Lady Duff-Gordon, who was a famous fashion designer (and survivor of the sinking of the *Titanic*), contracted with Wood, an advertising agent, giving him the "exclusive right" to market her brand in exchange for "one-half of 'all profits and revenues' derived from any contracts he [Wood] might make." Lucy later changed her mind about the deal and wanted to go a different direction with respect to the marketing of her clothes line, and repudiated her agreement with Wood. Wood, of course, sued for breach of contract, and Lucy defended on the ground that no valid contract existed between them because Wood never actually promised to do anything concrete—he merely promised to give her half of the profits and revenues from his efforts *if* he attempted to, and succeeded in, marketing her clothes line. In resolving this dispute, the court had a choice before it: Should it interpret the contract as written, which said nothing about the efforts that Wood promised to use, or should it try to figure out what the parties probably intended for Wood to do when they first formed their agreement? What would you do? What do you think a reasonable person in Lucy's or Wood's shoes would have intended when they first formed their agreement?

In this particular case, the court found that unless it implied a promise on Wood's behalf "to use reasonable efforts to bring profits and revenues into existence," the agreement would have been without "such business 'efficacy as both parties must have intended'" when they formed their agreement. It could, of course, have refused to imply such a promise, holding that Wood should have foreseen this contingency and provided for this eventuality in the contract itself. Either way, courts need a way for determining when, and under what conditions, it will imply terms into a parties' contract when an event arises that the parties did not anticipate when they first formed their contract. We will take a look at some of these techniques in the cases and materials below.

5. Performance: How should the court determine whether a party has breached its contract?

Another issue we will explore in the cases and materials below is how courts go about determining whether a party has substantially performed its contractual obligations, on the one hand, or materially breached them, on the other. There are, of course, the easy cases, such as where you pay $5,000 to your uncle for a car you never receive. There, it should be clear not only that you've substantially performed your end of the bargain, but that your uncle has materially breached his. Such cases, because they don't trouble the courts, need not detain us here.

But let's consider a more difficult case. Suppose someone hires a construction company to build a mansion for him, and insists in his contract that only "Reading Pipe" be used throughout the house. Suppose further that, through the oversight a subcontractor, less than half of the pipe installed is actually manufactured by the Reading Pipe Company, although the other pipe was identical in price and quality (and, it might be added, hidden behind the walls). Do you think the construction company has substantially performed its obligations to the homeowner, or have they materially breached their contract? Should the homeowner be required to pay for the house built by the construction company, or should he instead be allowed to force the construction company to rip out the non-conforming pipe from behind the walls and replace it with Reading Pipe before he is required to pay? More importantly, how should a court make this determination?

As you might have guessed, the "hypothetical" discussed above is taken from an actual case, *Jacob & Youngs, Inc. v. Kent* (1921). There, the homeowner, Kent, believed that the general contractor, Jacob & Youngs, Inc. ("J&Y"), should be required to strictly perform every condition of the contract to the letter before its own obligation to pay the construction company arose. On the one hand, doing so would result in economic waste by requiring the construction company to incur a significant expense that would have no effect on the final value of the mansion. On the other hand, not doing so would fail to respect Kent's personal autonomy by forcing upon Kent a contract he never made, thereby violating the principle of freedom of contract.

So, how do you think a court should decide this case? Should it find that J&Y has substantially performed its contract (it did, after all, build an entire mansion for Kent that conformed to the contract in every respect except for installation of the non-conforming pipe), or should it instead find that J&Y has materially breached (it didn't, after all, do everything it promised to do under the contract)? And you should probably know that the court's determination as to whether J&Y substantially performed or materially breached will have significant consequences for the remedy it owes to Kent. If, for instance, the court finds that J&Y has substantially performed its contract, then Kent will only be entitled to the difference in value between a mansion with and without Reading Pipe. Here, because the non-conforming pipe was equivalent in quality and price to Reading Pipe, the mansion as built without Reading Pipe would be worth the same amount as if it were built exclusively with Reading Pipe. Therefore, the remedy J&Y would owe to Kent would be $0. If, on the other hand, the court finds that J&Y has materially breached, then it will owe Kent the cost of completing the contracted-for performance (i.e., Kent would be able to deduct from the amount he owed J&Y the cost of ripping out the non-conforming pipe and installing Reading Pipe in its place).

All of what has been said above, of course, assumes that J&Y doesn't have a defense it can allege that would excuse them from performing their contractual obligations. It is therefore to defenses that we next turn.

6. Defenses: Can the breaching party assert any defenses to excuse its nonperformance?

A breaching party that has not performed its promise may still be able to avoid its contractual obligations if it can assert a defense excusing its nonperformance. For instance, contract law presumes that minors and the mentally incompetent lack the necessary capacity to enter into meaningful contracts, and any obligations undertaken by such individuals are voidable—i.e., they can be avoided at the election of the incompetent party. These defenses can be justified on the ground that contract law is based, at least in part, on the principle of freedom of contract, which allows autonomous individuals to meaningfully exercise their will in making promises and agreements that tend to improve their welfare. Without the court's protection, a party lacking the capacity to make meaningful choices would often find themselves entering into bargains that were contrary to their own interests.

But what should a court do where one or both parties make assumptions about presently-existing facts that turn out to be wrong? For instance, what should a court do if a buyer and seller enter into a contract for the sale of a cow for $80, believing it to be barren, if it later turns out that the cow is not only not barren, but actually pregnant and worth ten times as much? Should the buyer or the seller bear this risk (or, to ask the same question differently, should the buyer or the seller get the windfall)? Or, similarly, what should a court do where one party sells a gem to a jeweler for $1 if both of them believe it to be a topaz but it turns out to be an uncut diamond worth a thousand times that amount? These facts are taken from *Sherwood v. Walker* (1887) and *Wood v. Boynton* (1885), respectively, and the issue in both cases is on which party the court should place the risk of loss where the parties themselves did not foresee this risk when they made their contract. We will deal with these and other similar cases in Chapter 8, but for now, how do you think such cases should be resolved, and why? Do you think it should matter whether the mistake was made by both parties as opposed to only one of the parties? Why? As it turns out, courts do tend to treat mutual mistake cases differently from unilateral cases. Can you think of any good reasons as to why this might be so?

On a related issue, do you think courts should treat mistakes made by parties about the future in the same way they treat mistakes made by parties about presently-existing facts? There are a group of related defenses known as impossibility, impracticability, and frustration of purpose that are designed to deal with such cases. Consider, for instance, *Taylor v. Caldwell* (1863), where a party rented a music hall to hold a series of concerts and spent money advertising these events. Unfortunately, before the concerts could take place, the music hall burned down. Should a court excuse the music hall owner's performance on account that it was impossible for it to perform? What if performance was not impossible but merely impractical—i.e., the music hall was severely damaged by the fire and could be repaired before the performance, but only at great cost? Or, consider *Krell v. Henry* (1903), in which a party advertised to rent out its apartment for the purpose of viewing the coronation of Edward VII. If the coronation was postponed due to the King's appendicitis, should the lessee still have to pay for the use of the room, or should a court let him off on account that his purpose for renting the room had been frustrated? In each of these cases, note that the question before the court is which of the two parties should bear the risk of loss where neither party anticipated the risk when they made their contract.

Finally, what should a court do where a party withholds critical facts from another party, or where it uses its superior bargaining power to obtain an advantage vis-a-vis the other party, or where the resulting terms of the contract appear to be unfair—or where a little bit of all three happens in the same case? Consider, for instance, a case in which a relatively uninformed welfare recipient bargains with a furniture store to buy furniture on an installment plan in which a difficult-to-understand clause is included in their contract that operates with particularly harsh effects.* Should the welfare recipient be allowed to get out of her bargain? The court in *Williams v. Walker-Thomas Furniture Co.* (1965) was called upon to answer such a question, and we will see how the court answered this question in the next chapter. For now, it is enough to realize that it would undermine the very idea of freedom of contract itself if courts either (1) never enforced contracts where there was a disparity of bargaining power or seemingly unfair terms, on the one hand, or (2) always enforced such contracts regardless of what unsavory bargaining tactics were used (think of a gun put to a parties head, forcing them to sign a contract), or regardless of how unfair the resulting terms turned out to be (think fraud). In short, courts must develop tools to walk a fine line between these two extremes, but it isn't always easy.

7. Third Parties: How, if at all, does the parties' agreement affect third parties?

The final issue we will explore in this casebook is the extent to which an agreement may affect the rights and duties of third parties. Consider, for instance, a situation in which Party A (Holly), who already owes $300 to Party B (Lawrence), makes a loan for the same amount to Party C (Fox), and gets Party C (Fox) to promise to repay the $300 to Party B (Lawrence). If Party C

* Specifically, the clause read as follows: "The amount of each periodical installment payment to be made by purchaser to the Company under this present lease shall be inclusive of and not in addition to the amount of each installment payment to be made by purchaser under such prior leases, bills or accounts; and all payments now and hereafter made by purchaser shall be credited pro rata on all outstanding leases, bills and accounts due the Company by purchaser at the time each such payment is made." Can you make any sense of this?

(Fox) fails to pay $300 to Party B (Lawrence) as promised, it is clear that Party A can bring suit against C for breach of contract, but can B? After all, C never had a contract with B, although C did expect to benefit from the contract that B had with A. This was the issue in the famous case of *Lawrence v. Fox* (1859), and the issue before the court was whether B, a non-party to the A/C contract, nevertheless had rights under the A/C contract. Is, in other words, B a third-party beneficiary of the contract between A and C? How do you think such a court should rule, and why?

Or, to consider a slightly different scenario, suppose the city you live in reaches an agreement to bring a new major league baseball team into town, promising to build them a brand-new stadium in the downtown area. Based on this knowledge, you purchase a building next to where the stadium will be built and open up a restaurant, which you expect to do extremely well once the stadium is completed. Meanwhile, after your restaurant is up and running, the major league baseball team welches on its agreement, and moves to a different city instead. Do you have any rights under the contract between the baseball team and your city? Why or why not? We will look at these and similar issues when we discuss third parties in Chapter 9.

By now, I'm sure that you can't wait to dive in and see how the issues discussed in this brief overview have actually been approached and decided by courts—so, without further ado, let's get started!

PART II

A GENERAL OVERVIEW OF CONTRACT LAW

CHAPTER 2

A General Overview of the Major Doctrines of Contract Law

Part II of this casebook has been designed to introduce you to contract law from the 5,000-foot level, and has several major goals. The first goal is to familiarize you, at the beginning of the course, with each of the major substantive areas of contract law. This will generally be done by using a classic (and fun) case from the contracts law canon, and then by accompanying that case with explanatory materials, notes, and questions. By introducing you to these substantive areas early in the course, it is hoped that you will be in a better position to engage with the materials more deeply in Part III, where a separate chapter is set aside for each substantive area.

In addition to introducing you to the major areas of contract law, the second goal of Part II is to familiarize you with the lay of the contracts land, where it is hoped that you will learn to view the contractual forest as a whole rather than viewing each of the concepts and doctrines as separate contractual trees. Unfortunately, this "holistic" perspective, if it is attained at all, is often only attained at the end of the course, when the student puts together his or her outline for the final exam. This is both a wonderful and frustrating moment: wonderful, because you finally have that "aha" moment and feel like you now "get" contract law, frustrating because it did not happen earlier. *If only I'd known X,* you will think to yourself, *Y would have made so much more sense!* But there are so many X's and Y's in contract law! Indeed, many casebook authors, aware of the fact that some "X" is needed to understand some "Y," will often begin their casebooks with the substantive area they deem most important (e.g., remedies, enforceability, mutual assent), accompanied by an explanation as to why the particular X they selected helps the reader make sense of the rest of the course.

The problem with the belief that contract law must be started with remedies, or enforceability, or mutual assent, or . . . , is not that it is wrong, but that it is right. You really do need to understand the substantive area identified by the author—whichever area that is—to make sense of the rest of the course. But *something* must come first, of course, and whatever does come first, although it will help the student grasp materials to come, will itself not be fully understood until these later materials are grasped. And so, the vicious cycle. This book takes the approach, therefore, that what is needed from the beginning of the course is familiarity with *all* of the major concepts of contract law. Previous students, in addition to finding the overview fun, have found that their exposure to these doctrines early on has helped them better grasp—and see connections between—the materials that followed.

The third and final goal of Part II is to provide you not simply with an understanding of black-letter legal doctrines, but also with tools for thinking *about* these doctrines. The need for such "thinking tools," as they are called throughout this casebook, was beautifully captured in a recent (and wonderful) book by Ward Farnsworth called *The Legal Analyst: A Toolkit for Thinking about the Law*. In it, Professor Farnsworth points out that

> There are, in general, two sorts of things one learns at a law school. First, there are lots of legal rules—principles that tell you whether a contract is valid, for example, or when people have to pay for accidents they cause, or what the difference is between murder and manslaughter. Second, there are tools for thinking about legal problems—ideas such as the prisoner's dilemma, or the differences between rules and standards, or the notion of a baseline problem, or the problem of hindsight bias.*

Some contracts casebooks only focus on the first category—the rules—but fail to provide the student with the tools necessary for thinking about the legal problems these rules were designed to address. This is unfortunate, however, because any meaningful discussion of a rule should include a discussion about the rule's purpose, about the legal problems the rule was designed to solve, and about whether the rule is doing a good or poor job of solving those problems. Can we convince the judge that there is a better rule? If so, how? Can we help move the law in a new direction favorable to our client? If so, how? Ironically, when professors call on their students in class, it is often *this* type of thoughtful discussion that we wish to have—discussions about whether the rules are just, or efficient, or useful; about whether they should be kept or changed, about whether they are achieving or interfering with important public policy goals—although we have too often failed to equip them with the tools to have these conversations. This is not only unfair, but a shame to boot. As Professor Farnsworth points out, these

> tools for thought are by far the more interesting, useful, and fun part of a legal education. They enable you to see more deeply into all sorts of questions, old and new, and say better, more penetrating things about them. The problem is that law schools generally don't teach those tools carefully or systematically. . . . Law tends to be taught, in other words, as if legal rules were the most important things one could learn, and as if the tools for thinking about them were valuable

* Ward Farnsworth, The Legal Analyst: A Toolkit for Thinking about the Law vii (2007).

but secondary—nice to know if someone happens to explain them, but nothing urgent.*

This casebook was influenced by these comments, and proposes to address the shortcoming identified by Professor Farnsworth by providing "thinking tools" throughout the book, tools that are designed to help you "think like a lawyer" directly by not only learning, but also evaluating, the black-letter doctrine. These "thinking tools" will be set off from the main text in color-coded text boxes, and discussion questions throughout the book will refer back to them where applicable.

In fact, as it happens, we turn to one now:

THINKING TOOL: READING CRITICALLY†

In reading we produce text within text*; in* interpreting *we produce* text upon text*; in criticizing we produce* text against text.

- *Robert Scholes,* Textual Power

If imagination is "the prime agent of all human perception," then most law students (and the lawyers they become) perceive very dimly indeed the text-world they inhabit.[2] Even the best and brightest students too often scan judicial opinions for issue, holding, and reasoning and call that "reading," produce a paraphrase of the text and call that "writing." Yet surely, the callings of advocate, counselor, judge, and scholar all require more. . . .

To be effective counselors and advocates, lawyers cannot take legal documents at their word. They ought to be able to read between the lines and to link texts to larger contexts. Yet our students are all too often simply seduced by the text; their gullibility as readers has become a source of perplexity and frustration. . . . Although we spend hours focusing students on the invisible workings of a text . . . when our students revert to being readers, they forget the lessons they learned as writers. In a shocking suspension of disbelief, they fail to see how another author "worked" the text on them. . . .

We began to feel that we should address some of our time and energy to the activity of reading. We speculated that close, critical reading—reading which attends to the implicit text as well as the explicit text and which puts more of it in question[3]—might inspire our students to go past conventional notions of reading and writing to meaningful analysis.

Helping law students to get beyond purely denotative, case-briefing notions of reading is, however, no easy thing. In an age of reading comprehension tests,

---

* *Id.*

† Excerpted from Elizabeth Fajans & Mary R. Falk, *Against the Tyranny of Paraphrase: Talking Back to Texts,* 78 CORNELL L. REV. 163, 163-65 (1995) (some internal citations omitted).

2. All humans, Berthoff says, "read the world; we all make sense of our experience, construing and constructing and representing it by means of language." But, she adds, our students are much less successful at "reading the word" than at "reading the world." *Id.* at 124, 126.

3. Critical consciousness, Berthoff says, requires "initiating and sustaining the dialectic of *what is said* and *what is meant* as we read what others and what we ourselves have written." *Id.* at 127.

students are trained to read only for facts, for information. . . . Indeed, mainstream legal education too often creates the conviction that class rank and future earnings are dependent on consuming facts-holding-reasoning (reading) and producing a paraphrase of them (writing). . . . These habits of mind are all the more difficult to change because they are in a conventional sense efficient, enabling students to get through large masses of course material in relatively small amounts of time. And few full-time law students have the leisure to devote themselves full-time to the intellectual project of reading law; they have tuition to earn and families to care for. Close and critical reading and the strong writing it promotes take more time than case-briefing and paraphrase. Indeed, they take even more than the actual reading and writing time, requiring solitary moments of percolation and germination.

The central challenge is to help students learn techniques of patient intellectual inquiry, even though this lesson goes against the grain of a society that wants results in a hurry. Further, although those few students with a background in the close reading of texts are better equipped to dig below the surface of judicial opinions, almost all students will come up against an inhibition present in no other secular discipline. **Judicial opinions are not just interpretation—they are adjudication, and adjudication is power, coercion, even violence.[7] To read judicial opinions closely and critically is to talk back to power.**

Yet, there are at least three good reasons to talk back to power, to resist the tyranny of paraphrase. First, ours is explicitly a "text-oriented"[7] democracy—from the Declaration of Independence to the Constitution to the written opinions of courts—and unexamined authority is incompatible with democracy. Second, the close examination of legal rhetoric is fun of a particularly edifying sort; there is a healthy zaniness to searching for *all* of a text's texts, intended and hidden. Third, cognitive psychology teaches that *all* readers of legal texts, judges as well as law students, subconsciously supply multiple contexts when they read, whether they believe they do or not. When judges interpret precedent, they respond "personally" to the text, and bring their subjective readings into their decisions, even while claiming in good faith that they merely "find" the law in the first case and "apply" it to the second. Thus, close reading not only helps readers to understand and make use of their own reading response, but also illuminates the judicial decision-making process. . . .

The violence of interpretation

This is an important point, and one that must never be lost sight of in this or any other course. Unlike, say, literary interpretation, legal interpretation has *consequences* for the parties involved. Especially in criminal law, but even in contract law, the lives of the parties will often change as a result of the way a judge interprets a legal text, and the judge's decision, if necessary, will be enforced by the power of the state. Because legal texts frequently lend themselves to numerous legitimate (and not so legitimate) interpretations, it is our obligation, both as citizens and lawyers, to pay careful attention to, and examine the legitimacy of, any given interpretation of a legal text.

7. *See, e.g.*, Robert Cover, *The Bonds of Constitutional Interpretation: Of the Word, the Deed and the Role*, 20 GA. L. REV. 815, 817-20 (1986); Robin L. West, *Adjudication Is Not Interpretation: Some Reservations About the Law-As-Literature Movement*, 54 TENN. L. REV. 203, 244 (1987).

8. Robert A. Ferguson, *'We Do Ordain and Establish': The Constitution as Literary Text*, 29 WM. & MARY L. REV. 3, 24-25 (1987). Ferguson argues that our "text-oriented culture requires [of us] the knowledge of the scholar, the craft of the writer, the sympathy of the accomplished reader. . . ." *Id.* at 25.

NOTES AND QUESTIONS

1. ***More on interpretation.*** In the last paragraph, the authors note that judges do not—indeed, cannot—simply "find" and "apply" the law to resolve legal disputes, but must make a number of interpretive decisions along the way. This point was powerfully illustrated in a famous debate between H.L.A. Hart and Lon L. Fuller on the interpretation of legal texts. Given the tremendous importance that these interpretive decisions will play in resolving most of the legal disputes you will read about in this* and other courses, a few paragraphs of that debate is reproduced below. Reading it should help prepare you to think critically (i.e., like a lawyer) about the cases and materials you will encounter in this and other courses, and will also illustrate how indeterminate even seemingly crystalline black-letter law can sometimes be. Let us begin, then, with this famous passage from H.L.A. Hart:

> A legal rule forbids you to take a vehicle into the public park. Plainly this forbids an automobile, but what about bicycles, roller skates, toy automobiles? What about airplanes? Are these, as we say, to be called "vehicles" for the purpose of the rule or not? If we are to communicate with each other at all, and if, as in the most elementary form of law, we are to express our intentions that a certain type of behavior be regulated by rules, then the general words we use—like "vehicle" in the case I consider—must have some standard instance in which no doubts are felt about its application. There must be a core of settled meaning, but there will be, as well, a penumbra of debatable cases in which words are neither obviously applicable nor obviously ruled out.†

For Hart, then, interpretation seems more appropriate in the "penumbra" (e.g., when resolving questions like "is a tricycle a vehicle for the purpose of the statute?") than in the "core," where the meaning is more settled. But Fuller, in response, denies even this:

> What would Professor Hart say if some local patriots wanted to mount on a pedestal in the park a truck used in World War II, while other citizens, regarding the proposed memorial as an eyesore, support their stand by the "no vehicle" rule? Does this truck, in perfect working order, fall within the core or the penumbra?
>
> Professor Hart seems to assert that unless words have "standard instances" that remain constant regardless of context, effective communication would break down and it would become impossible to construct a system of "rules which have authority." If in every context words took on a unique meaning, peculiar to that

* For instance, all of the major questions of contract law (questions like: did the parties manifest their mutual assent to one another, or did the promisee reasonably rely on the promisor's promise, or did the parties intend for their language to operate as a promise or condition) can only be answered through interpretation. And, as the numerous conflicting opinions sprinkled throughout this casebook reveal, similar disputes can and have been resolved in different ways by different judges employing different but equally legitimate interpretative techniques.

† H.L.A. Hart, *Positivism and the Separation of Law and Morals*, 71 HARV. J. REV. 593, 607 (1958).

> context, the whole process of interpretation would become so uncertain and subjective that the ideal of a rule of law would lose its meaning. In other words, Professor Hart seems to be saying that unless we are prepared to accept his analysis of interpretation, we must surrender all hope of giving an effective meaning to the ideal of fidelity to law. This presents a very dark prospect indeed, if one believes, as I do, that we cannot accept his theory of interpretation. I do not take so gloomy a view of the future of the ideal of fidelity to law.
>
> An illustration will help to test, not only Professor Hart's theory of the core and the penumbra, but its relevance to the ideal of fidelity to law as well. Let us suppose that in leafing through the statutes, we come upon the following enactment: "It shall be a misdemeanor, punishable by a fine of five dollars, to sleep in any railway station." We have no trouble in perceiving the general nature of the target toward which this statute is aimed. Indeed, we are likely at once to call to mind the picture of a disheveled tramp, spread out in an ungainly fashion on one of the benches of the station, keeping weary passengers on their feet and filling their ears with raucous and alcoholic snores. This vision may fairly be said to represent the "obvious instance" contemplated by the statute, though certainly it is far from being the "standard instance" of the physiological state called "sleep."
>
> Now let us see how this example bears on the ideal of fidelity to law. Suppose I am a judge, and that two men are brought before me for violating this statute. The first is a passenger who was waiting at 3 A.M. for a delayed train. When he was arrested he was sitting upright in an orderly fashion, but was heard by the arresting officer to be gently snoring. The second is a man who had brought a blanket and pillow to the station and had obviously settled himself down for the night. He was arrested, however, before he had a chance to go to sleep. Which of these cases presents the "standard instance" of the word "sleep"? If I disregard that question, and decide to fine the second man and set free the first, have I violated a duty of fidelity to law? Have I violated that duty if I interpret the word "sleep" as used in this statute to mean something like "to spread oneself out on a bench or floor to spend the night, or as if to spend the night"?*

We are not going to resolve the debate between Hart and Fuller here, of course. The point is to get you thinking about the various ways that even seemingly clear laws (e.g., no vehicles in the park, no sleep in a railway station) can be legitimately interpreted in different ways, even where the facts are not in dispute.†

* Lon L. Fuller, *Positivism and Fidelity to Law—A Reply to Professor Hart*, 71 HARV. L. REV. 630, 663-64 (1958).

† The facts, however, are almost always in dispute. When judges write "the facts" of a case, they are not only selecting a particular subset of facts from among a much larger set, but they are treating some facts as more important than others, and are focusing on some facts in a *different* way than they are focusing on others. This will be pointed out in various places throughout the casebook, but for an immediate illustration of this principle, pay attention, in this and other classes, to the various ways in which majority and dissenting opinions often focus on different facts, and even focus on the same facts in different ways.

A. PUBLIC POLICY, FREEDOM OF CONTRACT, AND THE LIMITS OF CONTRACT LAW

Public policy is a very unruly horse, and when once you get astride it you never know where it will carry you. It may lead you from the sound law. It is never argued at all but when other points fail.

Richardson v. Mellish, 130 Eng. Rep. 294, 303 (1824) (Burrough, J.)

It must not be forgotten that you are not to extend arbitrarily those rules which say that a given contract is void as being against public policy, because if there is one thing which more than another public policy requires it is that men of full age and competent understanding shall have the utmost liberty of contracting, and that their contracts when entered into freely and voluntarily shall be held sacred and shall be enforced by Courts of justice. Therefore, you have this paramount public policy to consider—that you are not lightly to interfere with this freedom of contract.

Printing and Numerical Registering Co v Sampson,
L.R. 19 Eq. 462 (1875) (Jessel, M.R.)

The power to contract is not unlimited. While as a general rule there is the utmost freedom of action in this regard, some restrictions are placed upon the right by legislation, by public policy, and by the nature of things. Parties cannot make a binding contract in violation of law or of public policy.

Sternamen v. Metropolitan Life Ins. Co., 62 N.E. 763 (N.Y. 1902)

Before we delve into our overview of each of the substantive areas that make up this course (forming agreements, remedies, interpretation, etc.), these introductory materials will explore, from both a legal and public policy perspective, the limits of contract law itself, and what restrictions—if any—the law should place on the types of bargains that parties are allowed to make with one another. Relatedly, these materials ask you to think about *who* should decide which bargains should be allowed and which should be forbidden, and how such determinations should be made.

It is important to realize, at the outset, that all contract law doctrines are, at their core, based on public policy considerations. These public policy considerations, however, are often implicit, masked by the ostensible "objectiveness" of black-letter "rules." In the next case, however, which caused quite a stir in its time and is still a gripping read, we confront these public policy considerations head on. Here, one party (Mr. Stern) contracted with another party (Mrs. Whitehead) to have Mrs. Whitehead artificially inseminated with Mr. Stern's sperm, carry the baby to term, and then hand it over to Mr. Stern and his wife, all in exchange for $10,000. Once the baby was born, however, Mrs. Whitehead changed her mind and wanted to keep it, and the Sterns sued her for breach of contract, asking the court to force her to turn over the baby.

In deciding this issue, the court had to confront squarely the issue of whether the parties should be permitted the freedom to make such contracts in the first place, or whether such contracts should be forbidden on public policy grounds. But the "Baby M" case is about much more than surrogacy contracts: It is about the limits of markets themselves. It is about, in short, whether some things—from drugs to prostitution to the sale of body organs—should be beyond the reach of money and markets.

In the Matter of Baby "M" (A Pseudonym for an Actual Person)

Supreme Court of New Jersey
537 A.2d 1227 (1988)

> **A Media Frenzy**
>
> "[*Baby M*] can easily be called the custody trial of the twentieth century. Every aspect of the six-week trial — from Tuesday's tears to Betsy's (real) hair color to expert testimony on the best way to play patty cake — was covered in depth and worldwide, as was the trial court's decision ordering specific performance of the contract and awarding the Sterns custody of the baby. The case remained in the news during Mary Beth's appeal to the New Jersey Supreme Court as paparazzi snapped away at Mary Beth arriving for her weekly supervised visitation and as partisans on both sides prepared amici briefs and battled it out on op-ed pages." Carol Sanger, *Developing Markets in Baby-Making:* In the Matter of Baby M, 30 HARV. J. L. & GENDER 67, 69 (2007).

WILENTZ, C.J. In this matter the Court is asked to determine the validity of a contract that purports to provide a new way of bringing children into a family. For a fee of $10,000, a woman agrees to be artificially inseminated with the semen of another woman's husband; she is to conceive a child, carry it to term, and after its birth surrender it to the natural father and his wife. The intent of the contract is that the child's natural mother will thereafter be forever separated from her child. The wife is to adopt the child, and she and the natural father are to be regarded as its parents for all purposes. The contract providing for this is called a "surrogacy contract," the natural mother inappropriately called the "surrogate mother."

We invalidate the surrogacy contract because it conflicts with the law and public policy of this State. While we recognize the depth of the yearning of infertile couples to have their own children, we find the payment of money to a "surrogate" mother illegal, perhaps criminal, and potentially degrading to women. Although in this case we grant custody to the natural father, the evidence having clearly proved such custody to be in the best interests of the infant, we void both the termination of the surrogate mother's parental rights and the adoption of the child by the wife/stepparent. We thus restore the "surrogate" as the mother of the child. We remand the issue of the natural mother's visitation rights to the trial court, since that issue was not reached below and the record before us is not sufficient to permit us to decide it de novo.

We find no offense to our present laws where a woman voluntarily and without payment agrees to act as a "surrogate" mother, provided that she is not subject to a binding agreement to surrender her child. Moreover, our holding today does not preclude the Legislature from altering the current statutory scheme, within constitutional limits, so as to permit surrogacy contracts. Under current law, however, the surrogacy agreement before us is illegal and invalid.

I. FACTS

In February 1985, William Stern and Mary Beth Whitehead entered into a surrogacy contract. It recited that Stern's wife, Elizabeth, was infertile, that they wanted a child, and that Mrs. Whitehead was willing to provide that child as the mother with Mr. Stern as the father.

The contract provided that through artificial insemination using Mr. Stern's sperm, Mrs. Whitehead would become pregnant, carry the child to term, bear it, deliver it to the Sterns, and thereafter do whatever was necessary to terminate her maternal rights so that Mrs. Stern could thereafter adopt the child. Mrs. Whitehead's husband, Richard, was also a party to the contract; Mrs. Stern was not. Mr. Whitehead promised to do all acts necessary to rebut the presumption of paternity under the Parentage Act. Although Mrs. Stern was not a party to the surrogacy agreement, the contract gave her sole custody of the child in the event of Mr. Stern's death. Mrs. Stern's status as a nonparty to the surrogate parenting agreement presumably was to avoid the application of the baby-selling statute to this arrangement.

Mr. Stern, on his part, agreed to attempt the artificial insemination and to pay Mrs. Whitehead $10,000 after the child's birth, on its delivery to him. In a separate contract, Mr. Stern agreed to pay $7,500 to the Infertility Center of New York ("ICNY"). The Center's advertising campaigns solicit surrogate mothers and encourage infertile couples to consider surrogacy. ICNY arranged for the surrogacy contract by bringing the parties together, explaining the process to them, furnishing the contractual form, and providing legal counsel.

The history of the parties' involvement in this arrangement suggests their good faith. William and Elizabeth Stern were married in July 1974, having met at the University of Michigan, where both were Ph.D. candidates. Due to financial considerations and Mrs. Stern's pursuit of a medical degree and residency, they decided to defer starting a family until 1981. Before then, however, Mrs. Stern learned that she might have multiple sclerosis and that the disease in some cases renders pregnancy a serious health risk. Her anxiety appears to have exceeded the actual risk, which current medical authorities assess as minimal. Nonetheless that anxiety was evidently quite real, Mrs. Stern fearing that pregnancy might precipitate blindness, paraplegia, or other forms of debilitation. Based on the perceived risk, the Sterns decided to forego having their own children. The decision had special significance for Mr. Stern. Most of his family had been destroyed in the Holocaust. As the family's only survivor, he very much wanted to continue his bloodline.

Initially the Sterns considered adoption, but were discouraged by the substantial delay apparently involved and by the potential problem they saw arising from their age and their differing religious backgrounds. They were most eager for some other means to start a family.

The paths of Mrs. Whitehead and the Sterns to surrogacy were similar. Both responded to advertising by ICNY. The Sterns' response, following their inquiries into adoption, was the result of their long-standing decision to have a child. Mrs. Whitehead's response apparently resulted from her sympathy with family members and others who could have no children (she stated that she wanted to give another couple the "gift of life"); she also wanted the $10,000 to help her family.

> *"Implications of the transaction"?*
>
> What, exactly, is Chief Justice Wilentz's argument here? Do you agree with it? Is it generalizable beyond this case? If so, what are its implications for contract law?

Both parties, undoubtedly because of their own self-interest, were less sensitive to the implications of the transaction than they might otherwise have been. Mrs. Whitehead, for instance, appears not to have been concerned about whether the Sterns would make good parents for her child; the Sterns, on their part, while conscious of the obvious possibility that surrendering the child might cause grief to Mrs. Whitehead, overcame their qualms because of their desire for a child. At any rate, both the Sterns and Mrs. Whitehead were committed to the arrangement; both thought it right and constructive.

Mrs. Whitehead had reached her decision concerning surrogacy before the Sterns, and had actually been involved as a potential surrogate mother with another couple. After numerous unsuccessful artificial inseminations, that effort was abandoned. Thereafter, the Sterns learned of the Infertility Center, the possibilities of surrogacy, and of Mary Beth Whitehead. The two couples met to discuss the surrogacy arrangement and decided to go forward. On February 6, 1985, Mr. Stern and Mr. and Mrs. Whitehead executed the surrogate parenting agreement. After several artificial inseminations over a period of months, Mrs. Whitehead became pregnant. The pregnancy was uneventful and on March 27, 1986, Baby M was born.

Not wishing anyone at the hospital to be aware of the surrogacy arrangement, Mr. and Mrs. Whitehead appeared to all as the proud parents of a healthy female child. Her birth certificate indicated her name to be Sara Elizabeth Whitehead and her father to be Richard Whitehead. In accordance with Mrs. Whitehead's request, the Sterns visited the hospital unobtrusively to see the newborn child.

Mrs. Whitehead realized, almost from the moment of birth, that she could not part with this child. She had felt a bond with it even during pregnancy. Some indication of the attachment was conveyed to the Sterns at the hospital when they told Mrs. Whitehead what they were going to name the baby. She apparently broke into tears and indicated that she did not know if she could give up the child. She talked about how the baby looked like her other daughter, and made it clear that she was experiencing great difficulty with the decision.

Nonetheless, Mrs. Whitehead was, for the moment, true to her word. Despite powerful inclinations to the contrary, she turned her child over to the Sterns on March 30 at the Whiteheads' home.

The Sterns were thrilled with their new child. They had planned extensively for its arrival, far beyond the practical furnishing of a room for her. It was a time of joyful celebration—not just for them but for their friends as well. The Sterns looked forward to raising their daughter, whom they named Melissa.

While aware by then that Mrs. Whitehead was undergoing an emotional crisis, they were as yet not cognizant of the depth of that crisis and its implications for their newly-enlarged family.

Later in the evening of March 30, Mrs. Whitehead became deeply disturbed, disconsolate, stricken with unbearable sadness. She had to have her child. She could not eat, sleep, or concentrate on anything other than her need for her baby. The next day she went to the Sterns' home and told them how much she was suffering.

The depth of Mrs. Whitehead's despair surprised and frightened the Sterns. She told them that she could not live without her baby, that she must have her, even if only for one week, that thereafter she would surrender her child. The Sterns, concerned that Mrs. Whitehead might indeed commit suicide, not wanting under any circumstances to risk that, and in any event believing that Mrs. Whitehead would keep her word, turned the child over to her. It was not until four months later, after a series of attempts to regain possession of the child, that Melissa was returned to the Sterns, having been forcibly removed from the home where she was then living with Mr. and Mrs. Whitehead, the home in Florida owned by Mary Beth Whitehead's parents.

The struggle over Baby M began when it became apparent that Mrs. Whitehead could not return the child to Mr. Stern. Due to Mrs. Whitehead's refusal to relinquish the baby, Mr. Stern filed a complaint seeking enforcement of the surrogacy contract. He alleged, accurately, that Mrs. Whitehead had not only refused to comply with the surrogacy contract but had threatened to flee from New Jersey with the child in order to avoid even the possibility of his obtaining custody. The court papers asserted that if Mrs. Whitehead were to be given notice of the application for an order requiring her to relinquish custody, she would, prior to the hearing, leave the state with the baby. And that is precisely what she did. After the order was entered, **ex parte**, the process server, aided by the police, in the presence of the Sterns, entered Mrs. Whitehead's home to execute the order. Mr. Whitehead fled with the child, who had been handed to him through a window while those who came to enforce the order were thrown off balance by a dispute over the child's current name.

> ***Ex parte motion***
>
> "A motion made to the court without notice to the adverse party; a motion that a court considers and rules on without hearing from all sides." BLACK'S LAW DICTIONARY (10th ed. 2014).

The Whiteheads immediately fled to Florida with Baby M. They stayed initially with Mrs. Whitehead's parents, where one of Mrs. Whitehead's children had been living. For the next three months, the Whiteheads and Melissa lived at roughly twenty different hotels, motels, and homes in order to avoid apprehension. From time to time Mrs. Whitehead would call Mr. Stern to discuss the matter; the conversations, recorded by Mr. Stern on advice of counsel, show an escalating dispute about rights, morality, and power, accompanied by threats of Mrs. Whitehead to kill herself, to kill the child, and falsely to accuse Mr. Stern of sexually molesting Mrs. Whitehead's other daughter.

Eventually the Sterns discovered where the Whiteheads were staying, commenced supplementary proceedings in Florida, and obtained an order requiring the Whiteheads to turn over the child. Police in Florida enforced the order, forcibly removing the child from her grandparents' home. She was soon thereafter brought to New Jersey and turned over to the Sterns. . . .

The Sterns' complaint, in addition to seeking possession and ultimately custody of the child, sought enforcement of the surrogacy contract. Pursuant to the contract, it asked that the child be permanently placed in their custody, that Mrs. Whitehead's parental rights be terminated, and that Mrs. Stern be allowed to adopt the child, i.e., that, for all purposes, Melissa become the Sterns' child.

The trial took thirty-two days over a period of more than two months. It included numerous interlocutory appeals and attempted interlocutory appeals. There were twenty-three witnesses to the facts recited above and fifteen expert witnesses. . . . Soon after the conclusion of the trial, the trial court announced its opinion from the bench. It held that the surrogacy contract was valid; ordered that Mrs. Whitehead's parental rights be terminated and that sole custody of the child be granted to Mr. Stern; and, after hearing brief testimony from Mrs. Stern, immediately entered an order allowing the adoption of Melissa by Mrs. Stern, all in accordance with the surrogacy contract. Pending the outcome of the appeal, we granted a continuation of visitation to Mrs. Whitehead, although slightly more limited than the visitation allowed during the trial.

Although clearly expressing its view that the surrogacy contract was valid, the trial court devoted the major portion of its opinion to the question of the baby's best interests. The inconsistency is apparent. The surrogacy contract calls for the surrender of the child to the Sterns, permanent and sole custody in the Sterns, and termination of Mrs. Whitehead's parental rights, all without qualification, all regardless of any evaluation of the best interests of the child. As a matter of fact the contract recites (even before the child was conceived) that it is in the best interests of the child to be placed with Mr. Stern. In effect, the trial court awarded custody to Mr. Stern, the natural father, based on the same kind of evidence and analysis as might be expected had no surrogacy contract existed. Its rationalization, however, was that while the surrogacy contract was valid, specific performance would not be granted unless that remedy was in the best interests of the child. The factual issues confronted and decided by the trial court were the same as if Mr. Stern and Mrs. Whitehead had had the child out of wedlock, intended or unintended, and then disagreed about custody. The trial court's awareness of the irrelevance of the contract in the court's determination of custody is suggested by its remark that beyond the question of the child's best interests, "[a]ll other concerns raised by counsel constitute commentary."

On the question of best interests—and we agree, but for different reasons, that custody was the critical issue—the court's analysis of the testimony was perceptive, demonstrating both its understanding of the case and its considerable experience in these matters. We agree substantially with both its analysis and conclusions on the matter of custody.

The court's review and analysis of the surrogacy contract, however, is not at all in accord with ours. The trial court concluded that the various statutes governing this matter, including those concerning adoption, termination of parental rights, and payment of money in connection with adoptions, do not apply to surrogacy contracts. It reasoned that because the Legislature did not have surrogacy contracts in mind when it passed those laws, those laws were therefore irrelevant. Thus, assuming it was writing on a clean slate, the trial court analyzed the interests involved and the power of the court to accommodate them. It then held that surrogacy contracts are valid and should be enforced, and furthermore that Mr. Stern's rights under the surrogacy contract were constitutionally protected.

Mrs. Whitehead appealed. This Court granted direct certification. The briefs of the parties on appeal were joined by numerous briefs filed by amici expressing various interests and views on surrogacy and on this case. We have found many of them helpful in resolving the issues before us.

Mrs. Whitehead contends that the surrogacy contract, for a variety of reasons, is invalid. She contends that it conflicts with public policy since it guarantees that the child will not have the nurturing of both natural parents—presumably New Jersey's goal for families. She further argues that it deprives the mother of her constitutional right to the companionship of her child, and that it conflicts with statutes concerning termination of parental rights and adoption. With the contract thus void, Mrs. Whitehead claims primary custody (with visitation rights in Mr. Stern) both on a best interests basis (stressing the "tender years" doctrine) as well as on the policy basis of discouraging surrogacy contracts. She maintains that even if custody would ordinarily go to Mr. Stern, here it should be awarded to Mrs. Whitehead to deter future surrogacy arrangements. . . .

The Sterns claim that the surrogacy contract is valid and should be enforced, largely for the reasons given by the trial court. . . .

II. INVALIDITY AND UNENFORCEABILITY OF SURROGACY CONTRACT

We have concluded that this surrogacy contract is invalid. Our conclusion has two bases: direct conflict with existing statutes and conflict with the public policies of this State, as expressed in its statutory and decisional law.

One of the surrogacy contract's basic purposes, to achieve the adoption of a child through private placement, though permitted in New Jersey "is very much disfavored." *Sees v. Baber*, 377 A.2d 628, 636 (1977). **Its use of money for this purpose—and we have no doubt whatsoever that the money is being paid to obtain an adoption and not, as the Sterns argue, for the personal services of Mary Beth Whitehead—is illegal and perhaps criminal.** In addition to the inducement of money, there is the coercion of contract: the natural mother's irrevocable agreement, prior to birth, even prior to conception, to surrender

> ***"No doubt whatsoever"?***
>
> Do you agree with Wilentz that the Sterns were contracting for an adoption, or were they contracting for Mrs. Whitehead's services? As you read the rest of the opinion, pay careful attention to the facts that bear on this point either way. Do you think this distinction should make a legal difference? Why or why not?

the child to the adoptive couple. Such an agreement is totally unenforceable in private placement adoption. Even where the adoption is through an approved agency, the formal agreement to surrender occurs only after birth, and then, by regulation, only after the birth mother has been offered counseling. Integral to these invalid provisions of the surrogacy contract is the related agreement, equally invalid, on the part of the natural mother to cooperate with, and not to contest, proceedings to terminate her parental rights, as well as her contractual concession, in aid of the adoption, that the child's best interests would be served by awarding custody to the natural father and his wife—all of this before she has even conceived, and, in some cases, before she has the slightest idea of what the natural father and adoptive mother are like.

The foregoing provisions not only directly conflict with New Jersey statutes, but also offend long-established State policies. These critical terms, which are at the heart of the contract, are invalid and unenforceable; the conclusion therefore follows, without more, that the entire contract is unenforceable.

A. Conflict with Statutory Provisions

The surrogacy contract conflicts with: (1) laws prohibiting the use of money in connection with adoptions; (2) laws requiring proof of parental unfitness or abandonment before termination of parental rights is ordered or an adoption is granted; and (3) laws that make surrender of custody and consent to adoption revocable in private placement adoptions.

(1) Our law prohibits paying or accepting money in connection with any placement of a child for adoption. Violation is a high misdemeanor. Excepted are fees of an approved agency (which must be a non-profit entity) and certain expenses in connection with childbirth. . . .

Considerable care was taken in this case to structure the surrogacy arrangement so as not to violate this prohibition. The arrangement was structured as follows: the adopting parent, Mrs. Stern, was not a party to the surrogacy contract; the money paid to Mrs. Whitehead was stated to be for her services—not for the adoption; the sole purpose of the contract was stated as being that "of giving a child to William Stern, its natural and biological father," the money was purported to be "compensation for services and expenses and in no way . . . a fee for termination of parental rights or a payment in exchange for consent to surrender a child for adoption," the fee to the Infertility Center ($7,500) was stated to be for legal representation, advice, administrative work, and other "services." Nevertheless, it seems clear that the money was paid and accepted in connection with an adoption.

The Infertility Center's major role was first as a "finder" of the surrogate mother whose child was to be adopted, and second as the arranger of all proceedings that led to the adoption. Its role as adoption finder is demonstrated by the provision requiring Mr. Stern to pay another $7,500 if he uses Mary Beth Whitehead again as a surrogate, and by ICNY's agreement to "coordinate arrangements for the adoption of the child by the wife." The surrogacy agreement requires Mrs. Whitehead to surrender Baby M for the purposes of adoption. The agreement notes that Mr. and Mrs. Stern wanted to have a child, and provides that the child be "placed" with Mrs. Stern in the event Mr. Stern dies before the child is born. The payment of the $10,000 occurs only on surrender of custody of the child and "completion of the duties and obligations" of Mrs. Whitehead, including termination of her parental rights to facilitate adoption by Mrs. Stern. As for the contention that the Sterns are paying only for services and not for an adoption, we need note only that they would pay nothing in the event the child died before the fourth month of pregnancy, and only $1,000 if the child were stillborn, even though the "services" had been fully rendered. Additionally, one of Mrs. Whitehead's estimated costs, to be assumed by Mr. Stern, was an "Adoption Fee," presumably for Mrs. Whitehead's incidental costs in connection with the adoption.

Mr. Stern knew he was paying for the adoption of a child; Mrs. Whitehead knew she was accepting money so that a child might be adopted; the Infertility Center knew that it was being paid for assisting in the adoption of a child. The actions of all three worked to frustrate the goals of the statute. It strains credulity to claim that these arrangements, touted by those in the surrogacy business as an attractive alternative to the usual route leading to an adoption, really amount to something other than a private placement adoption for money.

The prohibition of our statute is strong. Violation constitutes a high misdemeanor, a third-degree crime, carrying a penalty of three to five years imprisonment. The evils inherent in baby-bartering are loathsome for a myriad of reasons. The child is sold without regard for whether the purchasers will be suitable parents. The natural mother does not receive the benefit of counseling and guidance to assist her in making a decision that may affect her for a lifetime. In fact, the monetary incentive to sell her child may, depending on her financial circumstances, make her decision less voluntary. Furthermore, the adoptive parents may not be fully informed of the natural parents' medical history.

Baby-selling potentially results in the exploitation of all parties involved. Conversely, adoption statutes seek to further humanitarian goals, foremost among them the best interests of the child. The negative consequences of baby-buying are potentially present in the surrogacy context, especially the potential for placing and adopting a child without regard to the interest of the child or the natural mother. . . .

B. Public Policy Considerations

The surrogacy contract's invalidity, resulting from its direct conflict with the above statutory provisions, is further underlined when its goals and means are measured against New Jersey's public policy. The contract's basic premise, that the natural parents can decide in advance of birth which one is to have custody of the child, bears no relationship to the settled law that the child's best interests shall determine custody. The fact that the trial court remedied that aspect of the contract through the "best interests" phase does not make the contractual provision any less offensive to the public policy of this State.

The surrogacy contract guarantees permanent separation of the child from one of its natural parents. Our policy, however, has long been that to the extent possible, children should remain with and be brought up by both of their natural parents. . . . While not so stated in the present adoption law, this purpose remains part of the public policy of this State. This is not simply some theoretical ideal that in practice has no meaning. The impact of failure to follow that policy is nowhere better shown than in the results of this surrogacy contract. A child, instead of starting off its life with as much peace and security as possible, finds itself immediately in a tug-of-war between contending mother and father.[9]

The surrogacy contract violates the policy of this State that the rights of natural parents are equal concerning their child, the father's right no greater than the mother's. . . . The whole purpose and effect of the surrogacy contract was to give the father the exclusive right to the child by destroying the rights of the mother.

The policies expressed in our comprehensive laws governing consent to the surrender of a child, stand in stark contrast to the surrogacy contract and what it implies. Here there is no counseling, independent or otherwise, of the natural mother, no evaluation, no warning.

The only legal advice Mary Beth Whitehead received regarding the surrogacy contract was provided in connection with the contract that she previously entered into with another couple. Mrs. Whitehead's lawyer was referred to her by the Infertility Center, with which he had an agreement to act as counsel for surrogate candidates. His services consisted of spending one hour going through the contract with the Whiteheads, section by section, and answering their questions. Mrs. Whitehead received no further legal advice prior to signing the contract with the Sterns.

Mrs. Whitehead was examined and psychologically evaluated, but if it was for her benefit, the record does not disclose that fact. The Sterns regarded the evaluation as important, particularly in connection with the question of whether she would change her mind. Yet they never asked to see it, and were content with the assumption that the Infertility Center had made an evaluation and had concluded that there was no danger that the surrogate mother would change her mind. From Mrs. Whitehead's point of view, all that she learned from the evaluation was that "she had passed." It is apparent that the profit

9. And the impact on the natural parents, Mr. Stern and Mrs. Whitehead, is severe and dramatic. The depth of their conflict about Baby M, about custody, visitation, about the goodness or badness of each of them, comes through in their telephone conversations, in which each tried to persuade the other to give up the child. The potential adverse consequences of surrogacy are poignantly captured here—Mrs. Whitehead threatening to kill herself and the baby, Mr. Stern begging her not to, each blaming the other. The dashed hopes of the Sterns, the agony of Mrs. Whitehead, their suffering, their hatred—all were caused by the unraveling of this arrangement.

motive got the better of the Infertility Center. Although the evaluation was made, it was not put to any use, and understandably so, for the psychologist warned that Mrs. Whitehead demonstrated certain traits that might make surrender of the child difficult and that there should be further inquiry into this issue in connection with her surrogacy. To inquire further, however, might have jeopardized the Infertility Center's fee. The record indicates that neither Mrs. Whitehead nor the Sterns were ever told of this fact, a fact that might have ended their surrogacy arrangement.

Under the contract, the natural mother is irrevocably committed before she knows the strength of her bond with her child. She never makes a totally voluntary, informed decision, for quite clearly any decision prior to the baby's birth is, in the most important sense, uninformed, and any decision after that, compelled by a pre-existing contractual commitment, the threat of a lawsuit, and the inducement of a $10,000 payment, is less than totally voluntary. Her interests are of little concern to those who controlled this transaction.

> ***Involuntary and uninformed***
>
> Do you agree that Mrs. Whitehead's consent was involuntary? Was it uninformed? Couldn't Justice Wilentz's logic be applied to *all* contracts? If so, should *this* contract be treated differently? Why or why not?

Although the interest of the natural father and adoptive mother is certainly the predominant interest, realistically the only interest served, even they are left with less than what public policy requires. They know little about the natural mother, her genetic makeup, and her psychological and medical history. Moreover, not even a superficial attempt is made to determine their awareness of their responsibilities as parents.

Worst of all, however, is the contract's total disregard of the best interests of the child. There is not the slightest suggestion that any inquiry will be made at any time to determine the fitness of the Sterns as custodial parents, of Mrs. Stern as an adoptive parent, their superiority to Mrs. Whitehead, or the effect on the child of not living with her natural mother.

This is the sale of a child, or, at the very least, the sale of a mother's right to her child, the only mitigating factor being that one of the purchasers is the father. Almost every evil that prompted the prohibition on the payment of money in connection with adoptions exists here.

> ***Baby selling?***
>
> Do you agree that this is this baby selling? Judge Sorkow, the trial court judge, didn't think so. He thought the Sterns were paying Mrs. Whitehead for her services, and that a purchase wasn't even possible: "At birth, the father does not purchase the child. It is his own biological genetically related child. He cannot purchase what is already his." Who has the better argument, and why?

The differences between an adoption and a surrogacy contract should be noted, since it is asserted that the use of money in connection with surrogacy does not pose the risks found where money buys an adoption.

First, and perhaps most important, all parties concede that it is unlikely that surrogacy will survive without money. Despite the alleged selfless motivation of surrogate mothers, if there is no payment, there will be no surrogates, or very few. That conclusion contrasts with adoption; for obvious reasons, there remains a steady supply, albeit insufficient, despite the prohibitions against payment. The adoption itself, relieving the natural mother of the financial burden of supporting an infant, is in some sense the equivalent of payment.

Second, the use of money in adoptions does not produce the problem—conception occurs, and usually the birth itself, before illicit funds are offered. With surrogacy, the "problem," if one views it as such, consisting of the purchase of a woman's procreative capacity, at the risk of her life, is caused by and originates with the offer of money.

Third, with the law prohibiting the use of money in connection with adoptions, the built-in financial pressure of the unwanted pregnancy and the consequent support obligation do not lead the mother to the highest paying, ill-suited, adoptive parents. She is just as well-off surrendering the child to an approved agency. In surrogacy, the highest bidders will presumably become the adoptive parents regardless of suitability, so long as payment of money is permitted.

Fourth, the mother's consent to surrender her child in adoptions is revocable, even after surrender of the child, unless it be to an approved agency, where by regulation there are protections against an ill-advised surrender. In surrogacy, consent occurs so early that no amount of advice would satisfy the potential mother's need, yet the consent is irrevocable.

The main difference, that the unwanted pregnancy is unintended while the situation of the surrogate mother is voluntary and intended, is really not significant. Initially, it produces stronger reactions of sympathy for the mother whose pregnancy was unwanted than for the surrogate mother, who "went into this with her eyes wide open." On reflection, however, it appears that the essential evil is the same, taking advantage of a woman's circumstances (the unwanted pregnancy or the need for money) in order to take away her child, the difference being one of degree.

In the scheme contemplated by the surrogacy contract in this case, a middle man, propelled by profit, promotes the sale. Whatever idealism may have motivated any of the participants, the profit motive predominates, permeates, and ultimately governs the transaction. The demand for children is great and the supply small. The availability of contraception, abortion, and the greater willingness of single mothers to bring up their children has led to a shortage of babies offered for adoption. The situation is ripe for the entry of the middleman who will bring some equilibrium into the market by increasing the supply through the use of money.

> ***The profit motive***
>
> Do you agree? Is it really "the profit motive" that "predominates, permeates, and ultimately governs the transaction"? Even if so, should this be relevant? Is there something wrong with "a middle man, propelled by profit, promot[ing] the sale"? Why or why not?

Intimated, but disputed, is the assertion that surrogacy will be used for the benefit of the rich at the expense of the poor. In response it is noted that the Sterns are not rich and the Whiteheads not poor. Nevertheless, it is clear to us that it is unlikely that surrogate mothers will be as proportionately numerous among those women in the top twenty percent income bracket as among those in the bottom twenty percent. Put differently, **we doubt that infertile couples**

in the low-income bracket will find upper income surrogates.

In any event, even in this case one should not pretend that disparate wealth does not play a part simply because the contrast is not the dramatic "rich versus poor." At the time of trial, the Whiteheads' net assets were probably negative—Mrs. Whitehead's own sister was foreclosing on a second mortgage. Their income derived from Mr. Whitehead's labors. Mrs. Whitehead is a homemaker, having previously held part-time jobs. The Sterns are both professionals, she a medical doctor, he a biochemist. Their combined income when both were working was about $89,500 a year and their assets sufficient to pay for the surrogacy contract arrangements.

The point is made that Mrs. Whitehead agreed to the surrogacy arrangement, supposedly fully understanding the consequences. Putting aside the issue of how compelling her need for money may have been, and how significant her understanding of the consequences, we suggest that her consent is irrelevant. **There are, in a civilized society, some things that money cannot buy.** In America, we decided long ago that merely because conduct purchased by money was "voluntary" did not mean that it was good or beyond regulation and prohibition. *West Coast Hotel Co. v. Parrish*, 300 U.S. 379 (1937). Employers can no longer buy labor at the lowest price they can bargain for, even though that labor is "voluntary," 29 U.S.C. § 206 (1982), or buy women's labor for less money than paid to men for the same job, 29 U.S.C. § 206(d), or purchase the agreement of children to perform oppressive labor, 29 U.S.C. § 212, or purchase the agreement of workers to subject themselves to unsafe or unhealthful working conditions, 29 U.S.C. §§ 651 to 678. (Occupational Safety and Health Act of 1970). There are, in short, values that society deems more important than granting to wealth whatever it can buy, be it labor, love, or life. Whether this principle recommends prohibition of surrogacy, which presumably sometimes results in great satisfaction to all of the parties, is not for us to say. We note here only that, under existing law, the fact that Mrs. Whitehead "agreed" to the arrangement is not dispositive.

The long-term effects of surrogacy contracts are not known, but feared—the impact on the child who learns her life was bought, that she is the offspring of someone who gave birth to her only to obtain money; the impact on the natural mother as the full weight of her isolation is felt along with the full reality of the sale of her body and her child; the impact on the natural father and adoptive mother once they realize the consequences of their conduct. Literature in related areas suggests these are substantial considerations, although, given the newness of surrogacy, there is little information.

Rich v. poor?

As a general rule, should courts consider the relative economic prosperity of the parties? Should they, as a general rule, consider the *types* of parties that tend to enter into certain *types* of contracts? Why or why not? What about here — do you think the relative economic positions of the parties should be relevant? Why or why not? Was Wilentz worried about the relative bargaining power of the parties? If so, consider what trial court judge Sorkow said on this point: "Neither party has a superior bargaining position. Each had what the other wanted. A price for the service each was to perform was struck and a bargain reached. One did not force the other. Neither had expertise that left the other at a disadvantage. Neither had disproportionate bargaining power." Who has the better argument here, and why?

The limits of markets

Do you agree that Mrs. Whitehead's consent was irrelevant because there are "some things that money cannot buy"? Or do you instead think that everything should be for sale? Why? If you think markets should have limits, who should determine these limits, and how?

The surrogacy contract is based on principles that are directly contrary to the objectives of our laws. It guarantees the separation of a child from its mother; it looks to adoption regardless of suitability; it totally ignores the child; it takes the child from the mother regardless of her wishes and her maternal fitness; and it does all of this, it accomplishes all of its goals, through the use of money.

Beyond that is the potential degradation of some women that may result from this arrangement. In many cases, of course, surrogacy may bring satisfaction, not only to the infertile couple, but to the surrogate mother herself. The fact, however, that many women may not perceive surrogacy negatively but rather see it as an opportunity does not diminish its potential for devastation to other women.

In sum, the harmful consequences of this surrogacy arrangement appear to us all too palpable. In New Jersey the surrogate mother's agreement to sell her child is void. Its irrevocability infects the entire contract, as does the money that purports to buy it. . . .

CONCLUSION

This case affords some insight into a new reproductive arrangement: the artificial insemination of a surrogate mother. The unfortunate events that have unfolded illustrate that its unregulated use can bring suffering to all involved. Potential victims include the surrogate mother and her family, the natural father and his wife, and most importantly, the child. Although surrogacy has apparently provided positive results for some infertile couples, it can also, as this case demonstrates, cause suffering to participants, here essentially innocent and well-intended.

We have found that our present laws do not permit the surrogacy contract used in this case. Nowhere, however, do we find any legal prohibition against surrogacy when the surrogate mother volunteers, without any payment, to act as a surrogate and is given the right to change her mind and to assert her parental rights. Moreover, the Legislature remains free to deal with this most sensitive issue as it sees fit, subject only to constitutional constraints.

If the Legislature decides to address surrogacy, consideration of this case will highlight many of its potential harms. We do not underestimate the difficulties of legislating on this subject. In addition to the inevitable confrontation with the ethical and moral issues involved, there is the question of the wisdom and effectiveness of regulating a matter so private, yet of such public interest. Legislative consideration of surrogacy may also provide the opportunity to begin to focus on the overall implications of the new reproductive biotechnology—in vitro fertilization, preservation of sperm and eggs, embryo implantation and the like. The problem is how to enjoy the benefits of the technology—especially for infertile couples—while minimizing the risk of abuse. The problem can be addressed only when society decides what its values and objectives are in this troubling, yet promising, area.

The judgment is affirmed in part, reversed in part, and remanded for further proceedings consistent with this opinion.

RELEVANT PROVISIONS

For the *Restatement (Second) of Contracts*, consult §§ 178, 179, and 191.

NOTES AND QUESTIONS

1. ***Was this case correctly decided?*** Do you agree with the result reached by Chief Justice Wilentz? Do you agree with his reasoning? Why or why not? Should parties be allowed to make such contracts? Why or why not? How, if at all, would you have written the opinion differently?

2. ***Let me count the ways.*** This case raises so many interesting issues, it is difficult to know where to begin. But, since we have to start somewhere, consider this: Before a court could even think about simply following the public's admonition to simply "apply the law" (preferably "like an umpire," in the language of U.S. Supreme Court Chief Justice John Roberts) to resolve the dispute before it, the judge first had to select what area of law should govern the transaction in the first place (contract law, adoption law, or even criminal law, as hinted at by Chief Justice Wilentz). The trial court judge, who was the first to take a crack at this, thought that a contract-based approach was appropriate, but the Supreme Court of New Jersey disagreed. Once this question was decided, the judge next had to weigh the relevance of various relevant competing principles *within* contract law. Here, those principles included party autonomy and freedom of contract, on the one hand, and the extent to which a party's consent must be voluntary and fully informed, on the other. Finally, once these principles were settled, it was then necessary for the judge to examine various *doctrines* within contract law (e.g., capacity, mutual assent, consideration, the absence of defenses like fraud, duress, or unconscionability) to see whether an enforceable bargain was struck (putting aside the issue of whether a bargain *should* have been allowed in the first place). Many of these choices are often unseen and unnoticed, but far from irrelevant to the final outcome. This point was beautifully captured in the following brief excerpt, which, interestingly enough, referred to *Baby M* as a "relatively simple surrogacy case." Imagine a complex one! As you read the excerpt below, pay attention to the number of different ways this case *could* have been resolved. How would *you* have resolved the dispute, and why?

> [T]he advent of "reproductive technologies" such as in vitro fertilization, artificial insemination, and embryo transfer have transformed radically the landscape of family law. The assumptions that lay behind existing systems of sexual and reproductive morality have been fundamentally altered. Who is a father or a mother? Who has rights and duties with respect to a child? Consider for example a relatively simple surrogacy case in which A and B (husband and wife) contract with C (who is married to D) to receive A's sperm and bear a child E for which A and B will be parents. At birth of E, C decides to breach the contract and keep "her" child. What are to be the legal relations among A, B, C, D & E for the rest of their respective lives?
>
> A judge (or legal system) could try to answer such questions by looking to a contract approach, a natural rights approach, a common law approach or if

there is one, a statutory approach, each with a very different resolution. Under a contract approach A and B would be the parents and C and D would have no relationship to E. Under a natural rights approach (and there could be various natural rights approaches), a judge might decide that genes are destiny and that A and C are the source of E's genes and therefore they are exclusively the parents of E. A common law approach might start with the presumption that the husband of the mother is the father of the child, so the judge could decide that C and D are the parents of E and that A and B have no rights or duties with respect to E. . . . A statute might sort things out in a variety of ways but a judge might decide that Liberty trumps statute. . . . Has the science of DNA identification made the old presumptions of the common law invalid? Can a principle or standard like "best interests of the child" sort out the problems raised here? Note that "best interests" is another example in law that requires recourse to a range of contentious facts and values in order to make a judgment.*

3. *Regret.* We are told that, even during her pregnancy, Mrs. Whitehead began to regret her decision to enter into a contract obligating her to give up Baby M. Should this matter? Generally speaking, a party enters into a contract because it believes, at the time it is making the contract, that what it will receive is worth more than what it must give up to obtain it. Part of the risk inherent in every contract is that, before the time for performance comes due, these expected values may change. As a general rule, courts are not usually sympathetic to the argument that a contract should not be enforced because a party no longer values the thing it contracted for (e.g., $10,000) more than the consideration given up to obtain it (e.g., a baby). Should this case be treated differently? Why or why not?

4. *Drafting.* As mentioned in the margin note above, Justice Wilentz thought the Sterns were contracting for an adoption rather than for Mrs. Whitehead's services. How would you redraft the contract to structure the transaction as one for services rather than for an adoption?

5. *A case of lasting importance.* Not only did the case cause a media frenzy in its time, but it brought up a number of extremely important issues of lasting importance, among them the limits of contract law. As explained by Professor Sanger:

> The case provoked philosophical debate, political organizing, and legislative action as ethicists, feminists, theologians, lawmakers, and local men and women weighed in on surrogacy's moral, legal, and practical significance. *Baby M* set the stage for debates about the commoditization of children, women's reproductive autonomy, and the meaning of family in an era of technological possibilities, concerns now directed at the ever more sophisticated forms of assisted reproduction that have come into being since 1985. . . .†

---

* George C. Christie and Patrick H. Martin, Jurisprudence: Text and Readings on the Philosophy of Law 1, 11-12 (3d ed. 2008).

† Carol Sanger, *Developing Markets in Baby-Making:* In the Matter of Baby M, 30 Harv. J. L. & Gender 67, 69-70 (2007).

6. ***Paternalism and the limits of contract law.*** Should courts enforce surrogacy contracts? Why or why not? More broadly, under what circumstances (if any) is legislative or judicial paternalism justified?* Are there certain things money shouldn't be able to buy, or should everything (or just about everything) be for sale? If the former, how should courts determine the limits of markets? Is the *Restatement (Second) of Contracts* § 178 of any help? In the next thinking tool, noted philosopher Michael Sandel attempts to shed light on some of these issues, both in the context of the *Baby M* case and in the context of contract law in general, by looking at them through the broader lens of social justice.

Professor Sandel believes that contracts derive their moral force from two independent sources: the principle of autonomy and the principle of reciprocity. In the excerpt below, the principle of autonomy is reflected in the libertarian view of contract law, and the principle of reciprocity is reflected in the utilitarian view. These principles are important because they suggest that, where the parties' choices are free (according to the libertarians) or welfare-maximizing (according to the utilitarians), contracts should be upheld—but not otherwise. Although judges obviously don't decide cases by saying "I'm a libertarian, and this contract should be enforced because it upholds party autonomy," if you look carefully, you will often see arguments based on these principles lurking beneath the surface of many judicial decisions. But sometimes, it is argued, even these principles are not enough. Some contracts—regardless of whether they are formed by autonomous individuals exercising their freedom or by fully-informed parties entering into welfare-maximizing bargains—should simply not be enforced. Or so the argument goes. As you read the following excerpt, ask yourself the extent to which you think courts should take into account broader concerns about justice when resolving contracts disputes, and whether you agree that some areas of life are simply beyond contract law.

THINKING TOOL: CONTRACTS AND JUSTICE†

Surrogacy Contracts and Justice

So who was right in the Baby M case—the trial court that enforced the contract, or the higher court that invalidated it? To answer this question, we need to assess the moral force of contracts, and the two objections that were raised against the surrogacy contract.

[At least two different theories of justice can be used to uphold contracts, including surrogacy contracts]—libertarianism and utilitarianism. The libertarian case for contracts is that they reflect freedom of choice; to uphold a contract between two consenting adults is to respect their liberty. The utilitarian case for contracts is that they promote the general welfare; if both parties agree to a deal,

* For a thoughtful discussion on the role of paternalism in contract law, see the appropriately titled Anthony T. Kronman, *Paternalism and the Law of Contracts*, 92 YALE. L.J. 763 (1983).

† Excerpted from MICHAEL J. SANDEL, JUSTICE: WHAT'S THE RIGHT THING TO DO? 95-98 (2009).

both must derive some benefit or happiness from the agreement—otherwise, they wouldn't have made it. So, unless it can be shown that the deal reduces someone else's utility (and by more than it benefits the parties), mutually advantageous exchanges—including surrogacy contracts—should be upheld.

What about the objections? How convincing are they?

Objection 1: Tainted consent

The first objection, about whether Mary Beth Whitehead's agreement was truly voluntary, raises a question about the conditions under which people make choices. It argues that we can exercise free choice only if we're not unduly pressured (by the need for money, say), and if we're reasonably well informed about the alternatives. Exactly what counts as undue pressure or the lack of informed consent is open to argument. But the point of such arguments is to determine when a supposedly voluntary agreement is really voluntary—and when it's not. This question loomed large in the Baby M case. . . .

As we've already seen, libertarianism . . . holds that justice requires respect for whatever choices people make, provided the choices don't violate anyone's rights. Other theories that view justice as respecting freedom impose some restrictions on the conditions of choice. They say—as did Justice Wilentz in the Baby M case—that choices made under pressure, or in the absence of informed consent, are not truly voluntary. . . .

Objection 2: Degradation and higher goods

What about the second objection to surrogacy contracts—the one that says there are some things money shouldn't buy, including babies and women's reproductive capacities? What exactly is wrong with buying and selling these things? The most compelling answer is that treating babies and pregnancy as commodities degrades them, or fails to value them appropriately.

Underlying this answer is a far-reaching idea: The right way of valuing goods and social practices is not simply up to us. Certain modes of valuation are appropriate to certain goods and practices. In the case of commodities, such as cars and toasters, the proper way of valuing them is to use them, or to make them and sell them for profit. But it's a mistake to treat all things as if they were commodities. It would be wrong, for example, to treat human beings as commodities, mere things to be bought and sold. That's because human beings are persons worthy of respect, not objects to be used. Respect and use are two different modes of valuation.

Elizabeth Anderson, a contemporary moral philosopher, has applied a version of this argument to the surrogacy debate. She argues that surrogacy contracts degrade children and women's labor by treating them as if they were commodities.[43] By degradation, she means treating something "in accordance with a lower mode of valuation than is proper to it. We value things not just 'more' or 'less,' but in qualitatively higher and lower ways. To love or respect someone is to value her in a higher way than one would if one merely used her. . . . Commercial

43. Elizabeth S. Anderson, *Is Women's Labor a Commodity?*, 19 PHIL. & PUB. AFF. 71 (1990).

surrogacy degrades children insofar as it treats them as commodities."[44] It uses them as instruments of profit rather than cherishes them as persons worthy of love and care.

Commercial surrogacy also degrades women, Anderson argues, by treating their bodies as factories and by paying them not to bond with the children they bear. It replaces "the parental norms which usually govern the practice of gestating children with the economic norms which govern ordinary production." By requiring the surrogate mother "to repress whatever parental love she feels for the child," Anderson writes surrogacy contracts "convert women's labor into a form of alienated labor."[45]

> In the surrogate contract, [the mother] agrees not to form or to attempt to form a parent-child relationship with her offspring. Her labor is alienated, because she must divert it from the end which the social practices of pregnancy rightly promote—an emotional bond with her child.

Central to Anderson's argument is the idea that goods differ in kind; it's therefore a mistake to value all goods in the same way, as instruments of profit or objects of use. If this idea is right, it explains why there are some things money shouldn't buy.

It also poses a challenge to utilitarianism. If justice is simply a matter of maximizing the balance of pleasure over pain, we need a single, uniform way of weighing and valuing all goods and the pleasure or pain they give us. Bentham invented the concept of utility for precisely this purpose. But Anderson argues that valuing everything according to utility (or money) degrades those goods and social practices—including children, pregnancy, and parenting—that are properly valued according to higher norms.

But what are those higher norms, and how can we know what modes of valuation are appropriate to what goods and social practices? One approach to this question begins with the idea of freedom. Since human beings are capable of freedom, we shouldn't be used as if we were mere objects, but should be treated instead with dignity and respect. This approach emphasizes the distinction between persons (worthy of respect) and mere objects or things (open to use) as the fundamental distinction in morality. . . .

Another approach to higher norms begins with the idea that the right way of valuing goods and social practices depends on the purposes and ends those practices serve. Recall that, in opposing surrogacy, Anderson argues that "the social practices of pregnancy rightly promote" a certain end, namely an emotional bond of a mother with her child. A contract that requires the mother not to form such a bond is degrading because it diverts her from this end. It replaces a "norm of parenthood" with a "norm of commercial production." . . .

Until we examine these theories of morality and justice, we can't really determine what goods and social practices should be governed by markets. But the debate over surrogacy . . . gives us a glimpse of what's at stake.

44. *Id.* at 77.
45. *Id.* at 80-81.

7. *Thinking tools applied.* So, what do you think? Should concerns for justice play a role (and, if so, how) in determining which contracts should be enforced? What about efficiency? Should it play a role in influencing which bargains (if any) should be off limits? If you answered yes to either of these questions, then how should lawmakers balance the concern for promoting the formation of just or efficient contracts (or at least preventing unjust and inefficient contracts) with other public policy objectives?

8. *Economic pressure.* To what extent (if any) do you think that the disparity between the bargaining power of the parties should make a *legal* difference? Recall that, in the "Rich v. poor" margin note on p. 47 above, Justice Wilentz made much of this point; Judge Sorkow, the trial court judge, not so much. In another highly publicized opinion on surrogacy contracts, here is what a California court had to say:

> Anna and some commentators have expressed concern that surrogacy contracts tend to exploit or dehumanize women, especially women of lower economic status. Anna's objections center around the psychological harm she asserts may result from the gestator's relinquishing the child to whom she has given birth. Some have also cautioned that the practice of surrogacy may encourage society to view children as commodities, subject to trade at their parents' will. . . .
>
> We are unpersuaded that gestational surrogacy arrangements are so likely to cause the untoward results Anna cites as to demand their invalidation on public policy grounds. Although common sense suggests that women of lesser means serve as surrogate mothers more often than do wealthy women, there has been no proof that surrogacy contracts exploit poor women to any greater degree than economic necessity in general exploits them by inducing them to accept lower-paid or otherwise undesirable employment. We are likewise unpersuaded by the claim that surrogacy will foster the attitude that children are mere commodities; no evidence is offered to support it. The limited data available seem to reflect an absence of significant adverse effects of surrogacy on all participants.
>
> The argument that a woman cannot knowingly and intelligently agree to gestate and deliver a baby for intending parents carries overtones of the reasoning that for centuries prevented women from attaining equal economic rights and professional status under the law. To resurrect this view is both to foreclose a personal and economic choice on the part of the surrogate mother, and to deny intending parents what may be their only means of procreating a child of their own genetic stock.*

Are you persuaded? In the second paragraph above, the court seems to suggest that because the poor are already somewhat exploited anyway, we shouldn't be troubled that they're also somewhat exploited in surrogacy contracts. If so, is this the court's way of saying that courts shouldn't fix problems that

---

* *Johnson v. Calvert*, 851 P.2d 776, 784-85 (1993).

society (presumably, through its legislative bodies) doesn't take the trouble to fix itself? If this *is* what the court is saying, do you agree?

9. ***Baby M as a remedy?*** Mr. Stern originally sued for breach of contract, asking the court to specifically enforce his contract (i.e., protecting his contractual right with a property rule). Had the court done so, it would have meant awarding Baby M as a remedy. Does this seem proper? Is this the *kind* of remedy contract law should award? If not, what other remedies would be possible? How would damages, measured by a liability rule, be determined? Would such a remedy even make sense here?

10. *Avoiding a rule of inalienability?* Unlike most of the rules of contract law, which are default rules that can be contracted around, the rule established by Justice Wilentz is not such a rule. It is, in the parlance of Calabresi and Melamed (who we will meet in the excerpt "Thinking Tool: Property Rules and Liability Rules," p. 109), a "rule of inalienability," meaning that it cannot be altered by the parties. They're stuck with it. But we humans, being the clever little creatures we are, still find creative ways to get what we want. What (if anything) should courts and legislatures do about the fact that individuals prevented from obtaining something in one place can simply go somewhere else to get it? Again, Professor Sanger:

> In removing surrogacy from the realm of permissible commercial activity in New Jersey, Justice Wilentz focused on what he saw as the pernicious role of the middleman. By taking money out of the equation, entrepreneurs would have to go elsewhere to extract surplus from trades like this, and that is certainly what happened. Surrogacy brokers decamped to jurisdictions where surrogacy was permitted or to those still in legal limbo, as New Jersey had been. But *Baby M* had revealed surrogacy's potential for heartbreak—or as many contended, heartbreak's inevitability—and many state legislatures took note. Some banned commercial surrogacy outright; others were content to make surrogacy contracts legal but unenforceable.
>
> In many jurisdictions, brokers have come in for special mention. Some states, such as Colorado, ban payment to the mothers but permit it to the broker. Some countries, such as the United Kingdom, permit payment to the mother but completely ban it to the broker. It is an offense in the U.K. not only to broker a commercial deal but even to arrange without compensation for a volunteer surrogate. And where surrogacy is legal, as in California, it appears to thrive. In sum, couples can now choose from an array of surrogacy options. They can stay close to home if the local market satisfies, or they can forum shop in the global market of reproductive tourism. . . .*

* Carol Sanger, *Developing Markets in Baby-Making:* In the Matter of Baby M, 30 HARV. J. L. & GENDER 67, 95-96 (2007).

B. PROMISES AND AGREEMENTS

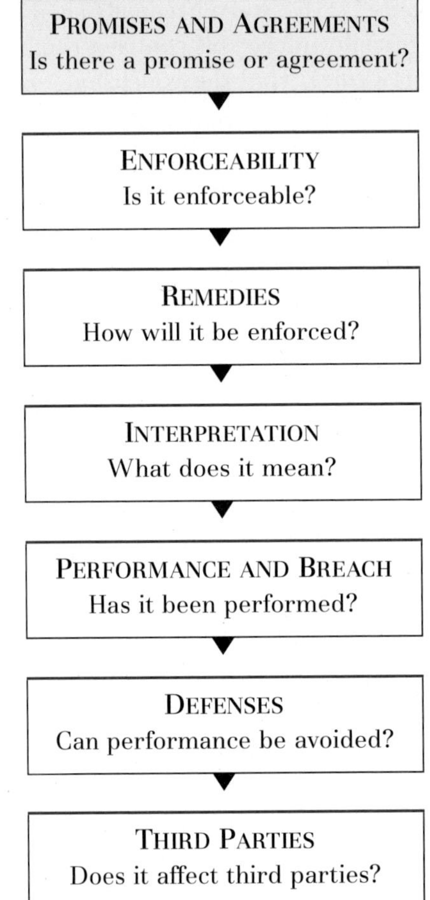
PROMISES AND AGREEMENTS
Is there a promise or agreement?
ENFORCEABILITY
Is it enforceable?
REMEDIES
How will it be enforced?
INTERPRETATION
What does it mean?
PERFORMANCE AND BREACH
Has it been performed?
DEFENSES
Can performance be avoided?
THIRD PARTIES
Does it affect third parties?

> *We do not have promises because we have a law of contracts; we have a law of contracts because we have promises.*
>
> H. Havighurst, THE NATURE OF PRIVATE CONTRACT 10 (1961)

We have all made promises. Some have been important, others, trivial. Some we have remembered, others we have forgotten. And some have brought us unforgettable happiness, while others have caused us unspeakable woe. But what, exactly, *are* these promises, these spirit-like forces capable of animating our waking life while dissolving in our dreams? And how, if at all, do they relate to contracts?

"Promises," to paraphrase Shakespeare's Prospero, "are such stuff as contracts are made on." They are the internal spirit animating contract's external form. While the contract, like the body, provides shape, it is the promise, like the soul, that provides direction. And so it is appropriate for a course in contract law to begin by attempting to understand what it can about the nature of promise.

In this section, we will take a brief look at *what*, exactly, promises are, *why* people make them, and *how* they can create obligations binding those who make them to a future course of action. After all, but for this strange tendency of our species to make promises, there would be no need for contract law at all. After finishing this section on promises and agreements, we will be armed with important insights that will help us tackle some related questions raised in the next section on enforceability, questions central to contract law itself, such as which promises people expect to be kept, and—perhaps more importantly for contract law—which promises people expect courts to enforce.

Before reading the material below, take a moment and try to answer the following questions, which you should be prepared to discuss in class. How would *you* define a promise? When you promise, *why* do you do so? And *which* promises do you expect to be kept? Do you believe that all, some, or none of the promises we make should be *morally* binding—committing us to some future act—and what is it that potentially makes them morally binding in the first place? What promises do you think should be *legally* binding, and why? Do you think your answer to the previous (moral) question should have any bearing on your answer to this (legal) question?

1. Making Promises: The Manifestation of Intention

So, what, exactly, is a promise, and what is its relation to contract? Beginning with the second question first, the *Restatement (Second) of Contracts* § 1 defines "contract" as "a promise or a set of promises for the breach of which the law gives a remedy, or the performance of which the law in some way recognizes as a duty." Condensing this definition further, we could say that contracts are enforceable promises. Given this definition, of course, one cannot hope to understand contracts until one first understand promises. So what's a promise? Below, we look at two answers to that question, the first from Professor Gardner's article *An Inquiry into the Principles of the Law of Contracts*, and the second taken, once again, from the *Restatement (Second) of Contracts*.

ON THE NATURE OF PROMISE*

The reader can doubtless recognize a promise without the aid of definition; but since we are to study its consequences a brief survey of its characteristics is required. In the first place, a promise does not differ from other predictions either in the fact that it arouses expectations or in the strength and precision of the expectations that are aroused. Citizen *A* opens his morning paper and

* Excerpted from George K. Gardner, *An Inquiry into the Principles of the Law of Contracts*, 46 HARV. L. REV. 1, 4-5 (1932).

learns that astronomer *X* says that there will be an eclipse of the sun visible in a neighboring city on August 31, 1932, beginning at 3:29:17 p.m. He also learns that candidate *Y* says that he will, if elected, reduce the municipal payroll and pay no regard to party services or affiliations in appointments to municipal posts. Citizen *A* probably has complete confidence in the fulfillment of astronomer *X's* prediction, and he may or may not have confidence in the assurance of candidate *Y*. But, whether his faith in candidate *Y* is large or little, he would probably speak of his assurance as a promise, a name which he would never think of applying to the prediction of astronomer *X*. What, then, is the essential difference between these two predictions? It seems to lie in the character of the causal relationship asserted between the fact predicted and the prediction itself. Astronomer *X* says that he makes his statement because he is compelled to make it by the facts. Candidate *Y* says that certain events will happen because they are compelled to happen by his word. Either statement may be true; events may prove either to be false. The essence of a promise is that it asserts the power of the speaker's mind over the future; a prediction asserts the power of the future over the speaker's mind.

Either kind of assertion may, of course, be conditional, that is, limited by one or more contingencies which are neither promised nor foretold. Candidate *Y's* promise is conditional on his election, and the prediction that an eclipse will be visible in a certain city is conditional on the absence of clouds. And it is to be observed that every promise is always conditional on one contingency which is neither promised nor predicted, namely, on an act of will by someone other than the promisor. A man may vow himself to lifelong celibacy, to the pursuit of medicine, or to the discovery of the North Pole, and thereby affirm the power of his present will over all his future conduct in the most emphatic terms. But such assertions are not promises, at least not in any sense which concerns the common law. To be of interest to lawyers a promise must concern at least two persons; it must assert not only that the speaker has a power over the future but that he confers a part of this power on someone else. We may, therefore, propose the following tentative definition:

A promise is an assertion that someone other than the speaker possesses, by force of the assertion, some power over the future which he did not previously possess. . . .

Let's now take a look at how the *Restatement (Second) of Contracts* defines promise before we compare these definitions in the "Notes and Questions" section below. According to the *Restatement*, "[a] promise is a manifestation of intention to act or refrain from acting in a specified way, so made as to justify a promisee in understanding that a commitment has been made."* Read that sentence over a few times. Memorize it if you can. We will come back to it again and again throughout this course. The *Restatement* goes on to provide that the party "manifesting the intention" is called the promisor, and the party "to whom the manifestation is

* RESTATEMENT (SECOND) OF CONTRACTS § 2(1).

addressed" is called the promisee.* Because courts will use the terms "promisor" and "promisee," along with the terms "offeror" (the person making the offer) and "offeree" (the person to whom the offer is made) throughout the materials in this casebook, the sooner you become familiar with these terms, the better.

Now that we've established some basic terminology, we're ready to move on to a few more interesting questions raised by the definition above. Specifically, (1) what, exactly, does it mean to manifest one's intention, (2) how should the parties go about manifesting their intention to one another, and (3) how should a court determine whether the parties have actually manifested their intention? These questions, of course, are related, and will consume a tremendous amount of judicial energy both in this introductory part, and in the next chapter, where we examine promises and agreements in greater depth.

RELEVANT PROVISIONS

For the *Restatement (Second) of Contracts,* consult §§ 1 and 2.

NOTES AND QUESTIONS

1. *Defining promise.* How do the definitions of "promise" offered by Professor Gardner and the *Restatement (Second) of Contracts* differ from one another? How do they differ, if at all, from your own understanding of promise?

2. *Distinguishing between the internal and external aspects of promise.* Although many of us probably think of promises as something quite personal, which can only be understood from within the promisor's own mind, the *Restatement (Second) of Contracts* takes a different approach, focusing not on what the promisor *intended* when he or she promised, but on how his or her intention was *manifested* to the external world.† Why might this be so? Is this a sound approach? The tension between the internal and external realms will run throughout our study of contract law, and will be taken up in greater detail later in this section, as well as in the next chapter.

3. *Intention versus promise.* How would you distinguish between a party's mere expression of intention, on the one hand, and a promise, on the other? It is a subtle distinction, to be sure, and there is always a risk, even where the promisor is careful, of the promisee misinterpreting an intended expression of intention as a promise. The following case provides a nice introduction to this distinction. As you read it, ask yourself whether you believe the promisor to

* *Id.* at § 2(2) and § 2(3).

† See *Restatement (Second) of Contracts* § 2, Comment b ("The phrase "manifestation of intention" adopts an external or objective standard for interpreting conduct; it means the external expression of intention as distinguished from undisclosed intention.")

have made (and the promisee to have understood the promisor to have made) a mere expression of intention, on the one hand, or a promise, on the other.

Pappas v. Bever

Supreme Court of Iowa
219 N.W.2d 720 (1974)

> ***Receiver***
>
> "A disinterested person appointed by a court, or by a corporation or other person, for the protection or collection of property that is the subject of diverse claims (for example, because it belongs to a bankrupt or is otherwise being litigated)." BLACK'S LAW DICTIONARY (10th ed. 2014).

> ***Executor***
>
> "A person named by a testator to carry out the provisions in the testator's will." BLACK'S LAW DICTIONARY (10th ed. 2014).

MCCORMICK, JUSTICE. Plaintiff William Pappas, **receiver** for Charles City College, appeals trial court's judgment denying enforcement of a fundraising pledge against defendant Sondra Bever, **executor** of the estate of Philip Bissonnette, Jr. No evidence was offered bearing on the meaning of the pledge instrument. The court held the instrument alone was insufficient to show the pledge was obligatory. We affirm.

In relevant part the executed form read as follows:

> I/we intend to subscribe to the College Founder's Fund the sum of Five Thousand—no/100 Dollars.
>
> I intend to pay ( ) Monthly ( ) Quarterly ( ) Semi-Annually ( ) Annually over ( ) 60 ( ) 36 months beginning 1967.
>
> Philip Bissonette (signature). . . .

The form was printed except for the blanks designating the amount of the pledge, terms of payment, signature and address of the pledgor. Bissonnette paid $1,000 on the pledge in 1967 and $1,000 in 1968. The college closed in May 1968, and he made no further payments prior to his death May 15, 1969.

[The question before the court is] whether the pledge form standing alone is obligatory or not.

Without extrinsic evidence bearing upon the intention of the participants, we must attempt to ascertain the meaning and legal effect of the pledge form by giving the language used in the instrument its common and ordinary meaning. No useful purpose would be served by repetition of the authorities treating the meaning of the word "intend" in various contexts. These authorities demonstrate that when words expressing an intention to do something in the future stand alone, they are not a promise and hence do not create an obligation. A mere expression of intention is not a promise.

The distinction between a statement of intention and a promise is explained in 1 *Corbin on Contracts* § 15 at 35 (1963):

> A statement of intention is the mere expression of a state of mind, put in such a form as neither to invite nor to justify action in reliance by another person. A promise is also the expression of a state of mind, but put in such a form as to invite reliance by another person. . . .

The language of the pledge form in this case, standing alone, shows nothing more than a statement of intention. There is no evidence the pledge was intended to be obligatory.

Even if the language were viewed as uncertain, the conclusion is the same. We are dealing with language printed on the pledge form by the fund-raiser in this case, and doubtful language in a written instrument is construed against the party who selected it.

Plaintiff contends the fact two payments were made proves the pledge was obligatory. This is a bootstrap argument. The mere fact a person carries out in part what he said he intended to do does not convert his statement of intention into a promise.

It was plaintiff's burden to prove the pledge was intended to be obligatory. We agree with trial court he failed to do so.

Affirmed.

NOTES AND QUESTIONS

1. ***Was this case correctly decided?*** Do you agree with the result reached by Justice McCormick? Why? What about his reasoning? What are the strengths and weaknesses of his approach? How, if at all, would you have written the opinion differently?

2. ***Intention or promise?*** The court believed that the pledge form filled out by Mr. Bissonnette merely indicated his intention—but not his promise—to contribute to Charles City College. Do you agree? If you filled out a pledge form to your alma mater, would you believe yourself to have made a commitment, or merely expressed an intention to giveor not to give as fit your fancy? If the latter, what do you suppose is the purpose of obtaining pledge forms from potential subscribers in the first place? Would these subscriptions merely constitute "illusory" promises?* Keep your answers to these questions in mind, for we will come across a strikingly similar fact pattern in which the court reached a very different result when we come to *Allegheny College v. National Chautauqua County Bank of Jamestown* in Chapter 4, one of the most famous cases in contract law, and a case that Justice McCormick was almost certainly aware of.

3. Contra proferentem. The court wrote that "doubtful language in a written instrument is construed against the party who selected it." This well-known maxim of contract interpretation, known as *contra proferentem,* is designed to put the onus for clear contractual language on the party in the best position to supply it—the drafting party. Additionally, by requiring the drafting party to invest additional resources on the front end to draft clearer contracts, not only

* *See Restatement (Second) of Contracts* § 2, Comment e.

will each party have a better sense of its rights and duties under the contract during performance, but both parties (and the courts) can save resources on the back end by minimizing needless litigation costs.

4. *Significance of previous payments.* The court did not place much emphasis on the two previous payments made by Mr. Bissonnette. Do you agree with the court? Can you think of any good policy arguments for or against the court's rule? The court accused the plaintiff of making a "bootstrap argument," and noted that "[t]he mere fact a person carries out in part what he said he intended to do does not convert his statement of intention into a promise." Do you agree? Do you think a person doing what they said they would do should have *any* bearing on whether their statement should be construed as an intention or promise?

5. *Burden of proof.* In a criminal proceeding, the state must prove "beyond a reasonable doubt" that the defendant committed the crime(s) brought against him or her. But in most civil proceedings, the plaintiff need only satisfy its burden "beyond a preponderance of the evidence." This means that the plaintiff need only show that its allegations are more likely (i.e., greater than 50% probability) true than not. Do you agree that the plaintiff failed to meet his burden here?

PROBLEM: PROMISING DIGITAL LOVE?

Yahoo! Inc. ("Yahoo!") offers two online dating services: Yahoo! Personals and Yahoo! Premier. The former is "for dates and fun," while the latter caters to people looking for "loving, lasting relationships." Yahoo! represents that both services "will help the subscriber find better first dates and more second dates." Yahoo! advises users to be truthful and reserves the right to remove deceptive profiles, thus "giving all subscribers and potential subscribers a sense of confidence in the authenticity of the images displayed on its website."

Plaintiff Perry claims that Yahoo! has "deliberately and intentionally originated, created, and perpetuated false and/or non-existent profiles on its site" to trick people like him into joining the service and renewing their memberships. In addition, Perry claims that, when a subscription nears its end date, Yahoo! sends the subscriber a fake profile, heralding it as a "potential 'new match.'" Perry has twenty-three examples of these "false and/or non-existent profiles," which include (1) "using recurrent phrases for multiple images with such unique dictation and vernacular that such a random occurrence would not be possible" and (2) "identical images with multiple 'identities.'" Perry also claims that Yahoo! continues to circulate profiles of "actual, legitimate former subscribers whose subscriptions had expired," thus giving the misleading impression that these individuals are still available for dates.

Perry alleges that subscribers must agree to Yahoo!'s Terms of Service, Personals' Additional Terms of Service, and Personals' Guidelines. He asserts that (1) "Yahoo! entered into a valid, fully integrated contract representing its online dating services as genuine," (2) "all parties to the contract understood the nature of the contract was intended to provide each paying subscriber with access to a legitimate and genuine online dating service," and (3) Yahoo! "breached the aforementioned contract by creating and forwarding false and/or nonexistent profiles."

Perry wants to sue Yahoo! for breach of contract. To do so, he must first be able to identify a promise that Yahoo! made and broke. *See Restatement (Second) of Contracts* §§ 1 and 2. Can he do so? More specifically, do you think Perry will be successful in identifying for the court any contractual term that requires Yahoo! not to create or forward false profiles?

2. Why Do We Make Promises?

Now that we have a sense of what a promise *is*, the next question we must address is *why* do we make promises at all? One way of approaching this question is to ask: What problems would exist in a world without promise for which the institution of promising would be a solution? To answer this, imagine the following scenario arising in a world without promise.

You and I are strangers. I have an avocado tree, and you have a lemon tree. I like avocados, but life for me would be even better if I could add some lemons to my diet. You feel the same way about your lemons and my avocados. So, naturally, I want some of your lemons, and you want some of my avocados. What to do? Well, one answer, unlikely to be very successful, is that I could approach you when I thought you were in a particularly generous mood and ask you to give me some of your lemons. And who knows? Maybe I get lucky. But I probably have a much better chance of getting what I want if I propose a bargain, offering to trade what I have for what I desire. As Adam Smith explained:

> [M]an has almost constant occasion for the help of his brethren, and it is vain for him to expect it from their benevolences only. He will be more likely to prevail if he can interest their self-love in his favour, and shew them that it is for their own advantage to do for him what he requires of them. Whoever offers to another a bargain of any kind, proposes to do this. Give me that which I want, and you shall have this which you want, is the meaning of every such offer; and it is in this manner that we obtain from one another the far greater part of those good offices which we stand in need of. We address ourselves, not to their humanity but to their self-love, and never talk to them of our own necessities but of their advantages. Nobody but a beggar chooses to depend chiefly upon the benevolence of his fellow citizens.*

So, following Adam Smith's insight, the logical thing for me to do is to offer to trade some of my avocados for some of your lemons. Because each of

* A. SMITH, AN INQUIRY INTO THE NATURE AND CAUSES OF THE WEALTH OF NATIONS 19 (1811 ed., bk. 1, ch. II).

us wants what the other has, we should be able to make a deal. Assuming I have avocados on hand right now, and you have lemons right now, the solution is simple: we should both enter into an *immediate* exchange of avocados for lemons.

THINKING TOOL: MARGINAL ANALYSIS AND EFFICIENCY

How many avocados will I trade, and for how many of your lemons? Parties looking to maximize their welfare will make these decisions using **marginal analysis**, trading up to the point where the marginal (or additional) benefit of obtaining one more unit equals the marginal cost needed to obtain that unit. According to marginal analysis, I can maximize my welfare by trading avocados for lemons up to the point where I no longer valued the next lemon I would get from you more than I valued the avocados I would need to give you to obtain it. Before this point is reached, I can always do better trading avocados for lemons, but once this point is reached, any additional trade would require me to give up some of my remaining avocados (which I value more) for lemons (which I value less).

We can also understand the transaction above in terms of "efficiency," of which there are two varieties. First, a trade is "Pareto efficient" if, as a result of the trade, at least one party is made better off without another party being made worse off. If trading avocados for lemons increases my welfare without decreasing yours, this trade is "Pareto efficient." Where no additional Pareto efficient trades are possible, the resource allocation is "Pareto optimal." Most voluntary trades will be Pareto efficient, because if either party feels that it will be worse off after the exchange (i.e., if marginal costs exceed marginal benefits for either party), it will refuse to trade.

But might there be some cases in which society as a whole might benefit by violating Pareto efficiency? Yes, according to the Kaldor-Hicks test of efficiency, which states that an allocation of resources is efficient where the sum of the gains resulting from the new allocation exceeds the sum of the losses. So long as the winners could theoretically compensate the losers (even if they don't), the wealth of society as a whole would still be maximized by such transactions.*

Marginal Analysis

Marginal analysis, or thinking at the margin, is a simple but powerful tool that can help us make better decisions about larger problems (e.g., what is the best combination of avocados and lemons to maximize my welfare?) by viewing these problems incrementally (e.g., will trading one more avocado for one more lemon make me better or worse off?). In contract law, marginal analysis can be used to analyze a wide variety of problems, ranging from (1) whether courts should enforce more or fewer promises, to (2) how courts should determine the optimal remedy in case of breach, to (3) whether courts should admit oral testimony altering the terms of a written agreement, and so on. So, for instance, rather than asking whether courts should enforce more or fewer promises, as a general matter, marginal analysis would focus our attention on how enforcing more or fewer promises would, by altering incentives, likely change human behavior. We could then look at whether these new patterns of behavior are likely to be better or worse than before. Whenever courts can resolve a legal dispute in more than one way, you should, in this and other classes, consider how each approach is likely to affect human behavior at the margin, which in turn can help you decide which approach is best—again, at the margin.

* *See, e.g.*, Nicholas Kaldor, *Welfare Propositions of Economics and Interpersonal Comparisons of Utility*, 49 ECON. J. 549 (1939) (allocation A is preferable to allocation B if the

These three concepts, (1) thinking at the margin, (2) Pareto efficiency, and (3) Kaldor-Hicks efficiency, are important thinking tools that we will come back to again and again throughout this casebook. They are important not only for understanding whether (and on what terms) you and I will enter into a bargain, but for thinking about the law in general. Marginal analysis, for instance, suggests that we can think about legal problems and legal rules incrementally by paying attention to how small changes in the law are likely to affect individual behavior. Meanwhile, thinking about the law in terms of efficiency provides an important framework for structuring our legal rules to allow parties and/or society to achieve important objectives, such as minimizing waste and maximizing welfare. We will return to these concepts again in future chapters, but for now, just let these ideas simmer, and be on the lookout—in this and other classes—for ways in which changing the legal rules is likely to affect incentives, whether these incentives will bring about generally efficient or inefficient patterns of behavior, and how these considerations interact with other important policy goals, such as freedom of contract or ensuring that the exchange does not violate principles of fairness and justice.

But what if an immediate exchange is not possible? Suppose you grow a variety of lemons that are best picked from late winter to early summer, and I grow a variety of avocados that are best picked from late summer to early winter. In that case, if we are to trade at all, it will have to take the form of a *deferred* exchange in which our performance is sequential rather than simultaneous—one of us will have to perform first.

And now we come to our first major problem with deferred exchanges: each of us will want the other one to go first! Why? Because the party who goes first takes on more risk, and this is for at least two reasons. First, things may change in the external world in the time that elapses between the first and second party's performances. For instance, after I perform, your lemon tree might catch some disease and produce far fewer lemons than expected, or—even worse—no lemons at all. If this happens, I will be the one to suffer. And second, things may change in your internal world. Once you have my avocados, you may realize that you can do even better if you keep your lemons when they ripen, and may find yourself with little incentive to perform when performance comes due.

But the problem is even worse than this, because everything just said will be obvious to both of us *while* we are considering whether to enter into the deferred exchange in the first place, locking us into a prisoners' dilemma of sorts. At the time of *negotiations,* each of us realizes that we will benefit from trade, and therefore each of us has a strong incentive to come to an agreement.

---

gainers from A could theoretically compensate the losers from B while still remaining better off); J.R. Hicks, *The Foundations of Welfare Economics*, 49 ECON. J. 696 (1939) (allocation A is preferable to allocation B if those who would lose from allocation A could not profitably bribe the gainers into not switching from B to A).

But we also realize that, when *performance* comes due, whichever party gets to perform second will have a strong incentive to *not* perform.

These incentives can be modeled as follows:

		You	
Me		Perform	Not Perform
	Perform	5, 5	-10, 10
	Not Perform	10, -10	0, 0

Assuming the payoffs above, a few things become obvious. We both realize that if we each perform our end of the bargain when performance comes due, we will both increase our satisfaction by five units (upper left cell). But each of us also realizes that whoever agrees to perform second can always do better by not performing: if I can get you to perform first, then I can obtain your lemons *and* keep my avocados, giving me a gain, and you a loss, of ten (bottom left cell). You, of course, realize the same thing (upper right cell). And because our incentives are obvious to both of us while are negotiating, we are unlikely to trade at all (lower right cell), which is a bad result for both of us. It is now that the true irony of the prisoners' dilemma can be seen: Although each of us would be better off if we both performed (upper left cell), each of us acting in our own self-interest when performance comes due will cause us to breach (upper right and lower left cells). And each of us anticipating this result will mean that no trade takes place at all (lower right cell).*

So what we really need is a way of moving us from the lower-right to the upper-left cell, allowing us to take advantage of the mutually beneficial trades prevented by the prisoners' dilemma. What we need, in short, is some method to ensure that we cooperate when performance comes due. How to achieve this? Well, where we are repeat players (i.e., where we have dealt with each other in the past and are likely to do so in the future), then (1) our *previous* interactions will have built up trust between us, establishing our reputations as cooperative (i.e., not breaching) trading partners, and (2) the prospect of engaging in mutually beneficial *future* transactions will ensure that we cooperate in *this* transaction, if only to avoid being retaliated against in the future.

But what do we do where we are one-shot players (i.e., if we have not dealt with each other in the past, and are unlikely to do so in the future)? Well, we don't know each other, so we can't trust each other, and because there is little prospect of dealing with each other in the future, we can't even count on our behaving well now for the sake of some future benefit. Even the threat of retaliation in this context is a nonsequitur. What each of us would really like,

* The dilemma lies in the fact that each individual's dominant strategy (do not perform) is inferior to the collective gain that can be gotten when each party *does* perform. *See, e.g.*, Richard H. McAdams, *Beyond the Prisoners' Dilemma: Coordination, Game Theory, and Law*, 82 S. CAL. L. REV. 209, 215-16 (2009) ("The game is termed a 'dilemma' because this theoretically inevitable outcome is worse *for each* [*party*] than another possible outcome," Perform/Perform.)

therefore, is to obtain some assurance that the person we are dealing with is trustworthy, i.e., that they are the kind of person that has performed in the past, and is likely to perform in the future. And, though far from perfect, what better mechanism for communicating this trustworthiness, especially among strangers, than the institution of promise! Promises give parties, especially strangers, the ability to make commitments to each other, allowing room for many efficient and mutually beneficial exchanges to take place that otherwise would not.*

But to *really* be effective, these promises must be credible, which brings us to our next question: how do parties make *credible* commitments to one another? Well, where we know one another, as previously stated, then *trust* can fulfill this role. Or, I might know someone who knows you, in which case I can obtain information about your *reputation* for keeping your promises, allowing me to place faith in the credibility of your commitment, and threatening to damage your reputation if you do not. But again, where individuals are complete strangers, as many individuals are in a modern, post-industrial society, there is perhaps no better way to make promises credible than by converting them into contracts and backing them up with the power of the state, which can make trouble for a party that does not keep its promises.†

But should all promises be treated this way, as enforceable commitments? The issue of *which* promises the law should enforce, and why, will be taken up in greater detail in the next section, "Introduction to Enforceability." However, before we broach that question, we must take one small detour.

3. Forming Agreements: The Manifestation of Mutual Assent

We now turn to mutual assent, a fundamental idea in contract law concerned with the process by which parties, through their promises, form agreements with one another. Here, we will focus on how courts expect parties to manifest their assent to one another, reserving for the next section the question of whether these agreements are enforceable. So long as a dispute does not arise, of course, the manner in which the parties manifest their assent, or whether they are enforceable, makes little difference—as the parties will, by definition, go about their business without interference from the courts.

The real problem, of course, occurs where a dispute arises, causing one party to believe that the parties have formed an agreement that should govern their dispute, whereas the other party believes that no such agreement has

---

* The institution of promise-keeping, of course, can also be justified on other grounds. *See, e.g.*, CHARLES FRIED, CONTRACT AS PROMISE 13 (1981) (arguing that the institution of promise-keeping allows parties to expand the range of their wills by making nonoptional a future course of conduct that would otherwise be optional).

† See KARL N. LLEWELLYN, THE BRAMBLE BUSH 85 (New York, 1960). We will study the way in which courts "make trouble" for breaching parties in much greater detail when we take up remedies in Chapter 5, *infra*.

been formed. Where the matter is unclear, the courts must address the issue of how they should go about determining whether the parties have, or have not, formed an agreement in the first place. It is this issue that we turn to in our next case.

Embry v. Hargadine, McKittrick Dry Goods Co.

St. Louis Court of Appeals
105 S.W. 777 (1907)

GOODE, J. . . . The appellant was an employee of the respondent company under a written contract to expire December 15, 1903, at a salary of $2,000 per annum. His duties were to attend to the sample department of respondent, of which he was given complete charge. It was his business to select samples for the traveling salesmen of the company, which is a wholesale dry goods concern, to use in selling goods to retail merchants. Appellant contends that on December 23, 1903, he was re-engaged by respondent, through its president, Thos. H. McKittrick, for another year at the same compensation and for the same duties stipulated in his previous written contract. On March 1, 1904, he was discharged, having been notified in February, that on account of the necessity of retrenching expenses, his services and that of some other employees, would no longer be required. The respondent company contends that its president never re-employed appellant after the termination of his written contract and hence that it had a right to discharge him when it chose. The point with which we are concerned requires an epitome of the testimony of appellant and the counter-testimony of McKittrick, the president of the company, in reference to the alleged re-employment. Appellant testified that several times prior to the termination of his written contract on December 15, 1903, he had endeavored to get an understanding with McKittrick for another year, but had been put off from time to time; that on December 23d, eight days after the expiration of said contract, he called on McKittrick, in the latter's office, and said to him that as appellant's written employment had lapsed eight days before, and as there were only a few days between then and the first of January in which to seek employment with other firms, if respondent wished to retain his services longer he must have a contract for another year or he would quit respondent's service then and there; that he had been put off twice before and wanted an understanding or contract at once so that he could go ahead without worry; that McKittrick asked him how he was getting along in his department, and appellant said he was very busy as they were in the height of the season getting men out—had about 110 salesmen on the line and others in preparation; that McKittrick then said: "Go ahead, you're all right; get your men out and don't let that worry you;" that appellant took McKittrick at his word and worked until February 15th without any question in his mind. It was on February 15th that he was notified his services would be discontinued on March 1st. McKittrick denied this conversation as related by appellant and said that when accosted by the latter on December 23d, he (McKittrick) was working on his books in order to get out a report for a stockholders' meeting and when appellant said if he did not get a contract he would leave, that he (McKittrick) said: "Mr. Embry, I am just getting ready for the stockholders' meeting to-morrow, I have no time to take it up now; I have told you before I would not take it up until I had these matters out of the way; you will have to see me at a later time. I said: 'Go back upstairs and get your men out on the road.' I may have asked him one or two other questions relative to the department; I don't remember. The whole conversation did not take more than a minute."

Embry also swore that when he was notified he would be discharged, he complained to McKittrick about it, as being a violation of their contract, and McKittrick said it was due to the action of the board of directors and not to any personal action of his and that others would suffer by what the board had done as well as Embry. Appellant requested an instruction to the jury setting out in substance the conversation between him and McKittrick according to his version and declaring that those facts, if found to be true, constituted a contract between the parties that defendant would pay plaintiff the sum of $2,000 for another year, provided the jury believed from the evidence that plaintiff commenced said work believing he was to have $2,000 for the year's work. This instruction was refused but the court gave another embodying in substance appellant's version of the conversation, and declaring it made a contract "if you (the jury) find both parties thereby intended and did contract with each other for plaintiff's employment for one year from and including December 23, 1903, at a salary of $2,000 per annum." Embry swore that on several occasions when he spoke to McKittrick about employment for the ensuing year, he asked for a renewal of his former contract and that on December 23d, the date of the alleged renewal, he went into Mr. McKittrick's office and told him his contract had expired and he wanted to renew it for a year, having always worked under year contracts. Neither the refused instruction nor the one given by the court embodied facts quite as strong as appellant's testimony, because neither referred to appellant's alleged statement to McKittrick, that unless he was re-employed he would stop work for respondent then and there.

It is assigned for error that the court required the jury, in order to return a verdict for appellant, not only to find (1) the conversation occurred as appellant swore, but (2) that both parties intended by such conversation to contract with each other for plaintiff's employment for the year from December, 1903, at a salary of $2,000.

(1) If it appeared from the record that there was a dispute between the parties as to the terms on which appellant wanted re-employment, there might have been sound reason for inserting this clause in the instruction; but no issue was made that they split on terms; the testimony of McKittrick tending to prove only that he refused to enter into a contract with appellant regarding another year's employment until the annual meeting of stockholders was out of the way. Indeed, as to the proposed terms McKittrick agrees with Embry; for the former swore as follows: "Mr. Embry said he wanted to know about the renewal of his contract; said if he did not have the contract made he would leave." As the two witnesses coincided as to the terms of the proposed re-employment, there was

no reason for inserting the above mentioned clause in the instruction in order that it might be settled by the jury whether or not plaintiff, if employed for one year from December 23, 1903, was to be paid $2,000 a year.

(2) Therefore it remains to determine whether or not this part of the instruction was a correct statement of the law in regard to what was necessary to constitute a contract between the parties; that is to say, whether the formation of a contract by what, according to Embry was said, depended on the intention of both Embry and McKittrick. Or, to put the question more precisely, did what was said constitute a contract of re-employment on the previous terms irrespective of the intention or purpose of McKittrick?

Judicial opinion and elementary treatises abound in statements of the rule that to constitute a contract there must be a meeting of the minds of the parties and both must agree to the same thing in the same sense. Generally speaking this may be true; but it is not literally or universally true. That is to say, the inner intention of parties to a conversation subsequently alleged to create a contract, cannot either make a contract of what transpired or prevent one from arising, if the words used were sufficient to constitute a contract. In so far as their intention is an influential element, it is only such intention as the words or acts of the parties indicate; not one secretly cherished which is inconsistent with those words or acts. The rule is thus stated by a text-writer and many decisions are cited in support of his text:

> The primary object of construction in contract law is to discover the intention of the parties. This intention in express contracts is, in the first instance, embodied in the words which the parties have used and is to be deduced therefrom. . . .

2 Paige, *Contracts* § 1104. . . .

In *Brewington v. Mesker*, 51 Mo. App. 348, 356, it is said that the meeting of minds which is essential to the formation of a contract, is not determined by the secret intention of the parties, but by their expressed intention, which may be wholly at variance with the former. . . . In view of those authorities we hold that though McKittrick may not have intended to employ Embry by what transpired between them according to the latter's testimony, yet if what McKittrick said would have been taken by **a reasonable man** to be an employment, and Embry so understood it, it constituted a valid contract of employment for the ensuing year.

The next question is whether or not the language used was of that character; namely, was such that Embry, as a reasonable man, might consider he was re-employed for the ensuing year on the previous terms, and act accordingly. . . . The general rule is that it is for the court to construe the effect of writing relied on to make a contract and also the effect of unambiguous oral words. However, if the words are in dispute, the question of whether they were

A Brief History of the Reasonable Person

"The rise of the reasonable person standard and the objective theory of contract during the twentieth century was not without ancestral roots. The use of formality to provide objective guidance for assessing contractual liability can be traced back to Roman times. Roman contract law was structured upon objective formality, not subjective agreement. . . . Our Anglo-American tradition is filled with similar formality. Examples include the sealed instrument . . . and the Statute of Frauds. The seeds

used or not is for the jury. With those rules of law in mind, let us recur to the conversation of December 23d between Embry and McKittrick as related by the former. Embry was demanding a renewal of his contract, saying he had been put off from time to time and that he had only a few days before the end of the year in which to seek employment from other houses, and that he would quit then and there unless he was re-employed. McKittrick inquired how he was getting along with the department and Embry said they (i.e., the employees of the department) were very busy getting out salesmen; whereupon McKittrick said: "Go ahead, you are all right; get your men out and do not let that worry you." We think no reasonable man would construe that answer to Embry's demand that he be employed for another year, otherwise than as an assent to the demand, and that Embry had the right to rely on it as an assent. . . . The answer was unambiguous, and we rule that if the conversation was according to appellant's version and he understood he was employed, it constituted in law a valid contract of re-employment, and the court erred in making the formation of a contract depend on a finding that both parties intended to make one. It was only necessary that Embry, as a reasonable man, had a right to and did so understand. . . .

The judgment is reversed and the cause remanded. All concur.

of the reasonable person as applied to manifestations of intent are found in these historical formalities. . . . Durkheim has written that it was 'these ceremonies that gave an objective character to the word and to the resolve of the promisor.' The notion of manifestation of intent can be seen as a modern substitute for these ancient rituals. Implicit in the notion of manifestation of intent is the need to measure and judge that manifestation. In order to fairly attribute legal consequences to a person's manifestations, a neutral, third party arbiter was needed. This fair-minded, all-knowing figure had to be available to judge a potentially infinite number of factual situations. This desideratum was the impetus for the development of the reasonable person standard." Larry A. DiMatteo, *The Counterpoise of Contracts: The Reasonable Person Standard and the Subjectivity of Judgment*, 48 S.C. L. REV. 293, 295-96 (1997).

RELEVANT PROVISIONS

For the *Restatement (Second) of Contracts*, consult § 3.

NOTES AND QUESTIONS

1. ***What happened?*** Who sued whom for what and why? Procedurally, how did the case get before this court? What arguments were made by plaintiff and defendant?

2. ***Was this case correctly decided?*** Do you agree with the result reached by Judge Goode? Why? What about his reasoning? What are the strengths and weaknesses of his approach? How, if at all, would you have written the opinion differently?

3. *Actual versus legal assent.* In *Embry*, the court struggled to determine whether Embry and McKittrick intended to form, and actually did form, an agreement with one another. If you look carefully, you will notice that there are two separate questions here. On the one hand, there is the philosophical question of whether Embry and McKittrick *really* intended to form an agreement with each other. Of course, it would be nice if we could answer this question, but knowing whether anything *really* is or is not the case is tricky business.* On the other hand, therefore, courts focus on the much more manageable question of whether Embry and McKittrick satisfied the legal test for forming such an agreement. This is by no means an easy question, but, as demonstrated by courts like *Embry*, it is at least answerable. But to acknowledge this is to raise yet another question: What legal test *do* courts use for ascertaining legal assent?

4. *Three tests for ascertaining assent.* Courts, in fact, have used at least three different approaches to ascertain whether parties have formed an agreement with one another: the subjective, objective, and mixed approaches to mutual assent. Each approach is examined in greater detail in the excerpt below.

THREE VIEWS OF ASSENT

How does a court determine whether the parties have come to an agreement? Historically, courts have approached this problem from a variety of perspectives. We will look at a few of these below.

The Subjective Approach: According to the subjective approach to mutual assent, which, according to some, held sway over contract law until the nineteenth century,† courts ascertained assent by determining whether there was a "meeting of the minds"‡ between the parties, which was understood as a process whereby the parties willed themselves, at a particular moment in time, to form an

* Indeed, there is an entire sub-branch of philosophy called "ontology" that is dedicated to figuring out what things *really* exist in our universe. If we approached the issue of assent ontologically, we would be asking ourselves such questions as "what is assent," "what is existence," "what does it mean for assent to exist," etc. Interesting questions, to be sure, but well beyond the scope of this casebook. For those interested in pursuing this line of questioning, a fun place to start is with the movie *The Matrix* (1999), preferably after a long weekend of studying contract law.

† *See, e.g.*, Clare Dalton, *An Essay in the Deconstruction of Contract Doctrine*, 94 YALE L.J. 997, 1042 (1985) ("A standard history of contract doctrine represents that, from the sixteenth to the early nineteenth century, contract formation depended upon a subjective 'meeting of the minds'"). Professor Perillo, however, believes this view is mistaken, and that "objective approaches have predominated in the common law of contracts since time immemorial." For a fascinating account of the battle between the subjective and objective schools, *see* Joseph M. Perillo, *The Origins of the Objective Theory of Contract Formation and Interpretation*, 69 FORDHAM L. REV. 427 (2000).

‡ *See, e.g.*, E. ALLAN FARNSWORTH, CONTRACTS § 3.6 (4th ed. 2004) ("The subjectivists looked to the actual or subjective intentions of the parties. The subjectivists did not go so far as to advocate that subjective assent alone was *sufficient* to make a contract. Even under the subjective theory there had to be some manifestation of assent. But actual assent to the agreement on the part of both parties was *necessary*, and without it there could be no contract. In the much-abused metaphor, there had to be a 'meeting of the minds'").

agreement with one another.* This approach was given expression by the court in *Dickinson v. Dodds* (*see* p. 287, *infra*), which wrote:

> It must, to constitute a contract, appear that the two minds were at one, at the same moment of time, that is, that there was an offer continuing up to the time of the acceptance. If there was not such a continuing offer, then the acceptance comes to nothing.

Although it is sometimes the case that courts can obtain evidence about the parties' mental states, this is more often than not a fool's errand, for "the intent inward in the heart, man's law cannot judge."† Therefore, although some courts still employ the subjective test where it is feasible to do so,‡ most courts reject it in favor of . . .

The Objective Approach: According to the objective approach to mutual assent, the internal mental states of the parties are irrelevant: All that matters is the external manifestation of their internal states. The most forceful expression of the objective view from the bench was by Judge Learned Hand, who wrote in *Hotchkiss v. National City Bank*, 200 F. 287, 293 (S.D.N.Y. 1911):

> A contract has, strictly speaking, nothing to do with the personal, or individual, intent of the parties. A contract is an obligation attached by the mere force of law to certain acts of the parties, usually words, which ordinarily accompany and represent a known intent. If, however, it were proved by twenty bishops that either party when he used the words intended something else than the usual meaning which the law imposes on them, he would still be held,unless there were mutual mistake or something else of the sort.§

Although the objective approach plays a dominant role in contract law today,¶ it, like the subjective approach, arguably went too far,** which may account for

---

* *See* CHRISTOPHER COLUMBUS LANGDELL, LAW OF CONTRACTS § 78 (2d ed. 1880) ("[I]t is indispensable to the making of a contract that the wills of the contracting parties do, in legal contemplation, concur at the moment of making it").

† CHRISTOPHER SAINT GERMAIN, DOCTOR AND STUDENT; OR, DIALOGUES BETWEEN A DOCTOR OF DIVINITY AND A STUDENT IN THE LAWS OF ENGLAND 179 (Legal Classics Library 1988) (1530-41).

‡ *See, e.g.*, CISG Article 8(1) ("For the purposes of this Convention statements made by and other conduct of a party are to be interpreted according to his intent where the other party knew or could not have been unaware what that intent was.")

§ *See also* Oliver Wendell Holmes, Jr., *The Path of the Law*, 10 HARV. L. REV. 457, 464 (1897) ("In my opinion no one will understand the true theory of contract or be able even to discuss some fundamental questions intelligently until he has understood that all contracts are formal, that the making of a contract depends not on the agreement of two minds in one intention, but on the agreement of two sets of external signs—not on the parties' having meant the same thing but on their having said the same thing").

¶ *See, e.g.*, E. ALLAN FARNSWORTH, CONTRACTS § 3.6 (4th ed. 2004) ("By the end of the nineteenth century, the objective theory had become ascendant and courts universally accept it today").

** *See, e.g.*, *Ricketts v. Pennsylvania R.R.*, 153 F.2d 757, 760-62 (2d Cir. 1946) (Frank, J., concurring). ("In the early days of this century a struggle went on between the respective proponents of two theories of contracts, [a] the . . . 'meeting of the minds' or 'will' theory—and [b] the so-called 'objective theory. Without doubt, the first theory had been carried too far: Once a contract

the more nuanced approach adopted by the *Embry* court. For lack of a better term, we may call this . . .

The Mixed Approach: According to the mixed approach, both the objective and subjective theories of mutual assent are relevant in determining whether the parties have formed an agreement with each other. More specifically, the mixed approach requires courts to determine not only how a reasonable person *would have understood* the external manifestation of another party's intention, but it further requires courts to determine how a party's external manifestation of intention was *actually understood* by the party to whom it was directed. So, for instance, in *Embry*, the court tells us that "if what McKittrick said would have been taken by a reasonable man to be an employment, and Embry so understood it, it constituted a valid contract of employment for the ensuing year." Another example is provided in *Kabil Development Corp. v. Mignot*, 566 P.2d 505 (1977). There, the defendant-appellant thought it was error for the trial court to permit the jury to hear testimony on plaintiff-appellee's subjective intention as to whether it formed a contract. The Supreme Court of Oregon rejected appellant's argument, noting that even a theory focusing on manifested assent need not prevent "a party from testifying whether he thought at the time of the events that he was in fact entering into an agreement. Here the witness was permitted to testify that he did, indeed, act in the belief that he was making a contract." *Id.* at 508.

5. *Formulating the tests.* In the excerpt above, we saw how the *Embry* court actually adopted a mixed approach to ascertaining the parties' intent. Pretend you are the judge deciding *Embry*, and try formulating the test from both a subjective and objective perspective.

6. *The reasonable man?* Note that the court asks us to consider how a "reasonable man" would have interpreted McKittrick's words. But who, exactly, is this reasonable person, and how should he behave?* Is he a hypothetical reasonable person, divorced from the realities of the case, or a reasonable person in the promisee's (here, Embry's) position? According to Farnsworth, "it seems preferable to state the test in terms of what [a promisee such as Embry] had reason to know or to believe, rather than in terms of a hypothetical 'reasonable

---

has been validly made, the courts attach legal consequences to the relation created by the contract, consequences of which the parties usually never dreamed. . . . But the objectivists also went too far. They tried [1] to treat virtually all the varieties of contractual arrangements in the same way, and [2], as to all contracts in all their phases, to exclude, as legally irrelevant, consideration of the actual intention of the parties or either of them, as distinguished from the outward manifestation of that intention. The objectivists transferred from the field of torts that stubborn anti-subjectivist, the 'reasonable man'; so that, in part at least, advocacy of the 'objective' standard in contracts appears to have represented a desire for legal symmetry [and] legal uniformity.")

* For an insightful discussion of this question, see Larry A. DiMatteo, *The Counterpoise of Contracts: The Reasonable Person Standard and the Subjectivity of Judgment*, 48 S.C. L. REV. 293, 294 (1997). ("Who is this all-knowing arbiter of reasonableness known as the reasonable person? From what organic and metaphysical antecedents has this person evolved? Is the reasonable person one and the same with Kant's rational being or tort's reasonably prudent man or Lord Denning's officious bystander? How do courts go about creating this contractual mystic?")

person.' A court should be able to take account of the other party's [Embry's] particular circumstances, at least to the extent that the first party [McKittrick] was or should have been aware of them."* Do you agree?

7. *Evaluating the tests.* What do you think are the strengths and weaknesses of the (a) subjective, (b) objective, and (c) mixed approaches we have discussed thus far? Which approach do you favor? Why?

THINKING TOOL: ADMINISTRATIVE COSTS AND STANDARDS V. RULES†

In *Embry*, the court struggled to come up with a standard for determining whether Embry and McKittrick intended to form a contract. In doing so, the court, like all courts called upon to settle disputes, imposed at least two different costs on the parties. First, it imposed the cost of administering the legal proceedings themselves, which was borne not only by the parties, who had to invest time and resources to litigate their dispute, but by the taxpayers, who had to subsidize the operation of the legal system by paying for its judges, bailiffs, law clerks, etc. Second, though perhaps less obviously, it imposed on the parties the cost of error, or the cost that the court might get it wrong.[36] For instance, a court might find that the parties intended to form a contract where they actually didn't, or it might find that the parties didn't intend to form a contract where they actually did.[37] Together, these costs will, at the margin,[38] prevent at least some efficient trades from being made, resulting in waste.

This suggests that courts, when deciding whether to adopt a particular standard (i.e., subjective, objective, or mixed view of assent), should consider not only the effects that adopting that standard might have on future parties, but also how accurately and inexpensively such a standard can be administered. In some cases, these considerations will clash, and courts will be forced to make difficult decisions between competing policy goals. For instance, returning to *Embry*, a standard that focused exclusively on ascertaining the parties' subjective intent might prove to be relatively difficult to administer (imagine all the evidence and testimony that courts would have to collect and sift through), thereby increasing the courts' administrative costs, but could improve accuracy by ensuring that courts only enforced agreements they could be pretty sure the parties intended to make. Conversely, a standard that focused exclusively on ascertaining the parties' objective intent would be easier to administer, thereby reducing administrative costs, but would probably sacrifice accuracy in the process by (a) failing to enforce

* E. ALLAN FARNSWORTH, CONTRACTS § 3.6, n.10 (4th ed. 2004).

† The excerpt below is indebted to the excellent discussion of these concepts in WARD FARNSWORTH, THE LEGAL ANALYST: A TOOLKIT FOR THINKING ABOUT THE LAW 57-65, 163-171 (2007).

36. Theoretically, this cost would be equal to the probability of error multiplied by its magnitude.

37. The first type of error is sometimes referred to as a false positive, or "type I error," because there, the court wrongly finds assent where none existed. The second type of error is sometimes referred to as a false negative, or "type II error," because there the court failed to find assent where, in fact, it existed.

38. *See* "Thinking Tool: Marginal Analysis and Efficiency," p. 64, *supra*.

some agreements that the parties intended to be enforced, (b) enforcing some agreements that the parties intended to remain unenforced, and even (c) enforcing some agreements that the parties intended to be enforced, but on terms they never intended. This last (and seemingly strange) result was expressed by Oliver Wendell Holmes, Jr., who we will encounter many times throughout this course:

> We talk about a contract as a meeting of the minds of the parties, and thence it is inferred in various cases that there is no contract because their minds have not met; that is, because they have intended different things or because one party has not known of the assent of the other. Yet nothing is more certain than that parties may be bound by a contract to things which neither of them intended, and when one does not know of the other's assent. Suppose a contract is executed in due form and in writing to deliver a lecture, mentioning no time. One of the parties thinks that the promise will be construed to mean at once, within a week. The other thinks that it means when he is ready. The court says that it means within a reasonable time. The parties are bound by the contract as it is interpreted by the court, yet neither of them meant what the court declares that they have said.[39]

Up until now we have been discussing which standard a court should adopt, but a court doesn't have to adopt a standard at all. Instead, it could adopt a rule stating, for example, that no promises shall be enforced unless an exact verbal formula is adhered to (as required by the ancient Roman form of contract known as *stipulation*) or unless the promise was memorialized in a sealed instrument (as required by the form of contract known as *covenant* in early English common law).

So what's the difference between a standard and a rule? Painting with a broad brush, standards give courts more discretion than rules.[40] Whereas a standard might look to see whether the parties intended to form an agreement, a rule might instead look to see whether the parties performed a certain action (presumably one related to intent), such as affixing a wax seal to a written instrument. As such, a rule can often be interpreted and administered more cheaply by a court, but probably only by increasing the cost of error, whereas a standard may be more expensive to administer, but might do a better job of reducing the cost of error.

So, how should lawmakers decide whether to adopt a standard or a rule? This question is at the heart of many of the cases you will read in this and other courses,[41] and we shall consider it at greater length throughout this casebook. For the time being, however, take a moment to brainstorm some of the factors you think are important in making this determination. How, for instance, would the choice between a standard and a rule impact efficiency and administrative costs at the margin?

---

39. Oliver Wendell Holmes, Jr., *The Path of the Law*, 10 HARV. L. REV. 457, 463-64 (1897).

40. *See, e.g.*, WARD FARNSWORTH, THE LEGAL ANALYST: A TOOLKIT FOR THINKING ABOUT THE LAW 164 (2007) ("the consequences of a rule are triggered once we settle the facts; a standard requires a judgment about the facts before it kicks in").

41. *See, e.g.*, Pierre J. Schlag, *Rules and Standards*, 33 UCLA L. REV. 379, 380 (1985). (". . . [D]isputes that pit a rule against a standard are extremely common in legal discourse. Indeed, the battles of legal adversaries (whether they be judges, lawyers, or legal academics) are often joined so that one side is arguing for a rule while the other is promoting a standard.")

NOTES AND QUESTIONS

1. *Evaluating the tests, redux.* If we take into account administrative costs, which of the three standards for ascertaining mutual assent do you believe is best, and why? More specifically, which test do you think best takes into account the combination of (a) the effect such a rule might have on future parties, (b) the accuracy of such a rule, (c) the costs of administering such a rule, and (d) any other factors you deem relevant?

2. *The stuff that rules and standards are made of.* Which of the following factors do you think are most important for courts to consider when developing a rule or standard: (a) the effect the rule/standard might have on future parties, (b) the accuracy of the rule/standard, or (c) the costs of administering the rule/standard? Are there any other factors that you think are important for courts to consider in making and applying the rules and standards of contract law? Which ones, and why?

4. Why Do We Keep Our Promises and Agreements?

Now that we have explored some of the reasons why parties might make promises and agreements with each other, we now briefly explore some of the reasons why parties might feel inclined to keep these promises and agreements. Some of these reasons overlap, of course. For instance, if someone does not keep her promises, then others will lose trust in that individual, not only damaging her reputation, but harming her ability to enter into mutually beneficial exchanges in the future. Yet another reason for keeping one's promises is to avoid the legal remedies that courts might impose for breaking one's promise.* But this, of course, assumes that the promise is legally enforceable in the first place, which is a *contractual* question taken up in the next section. But for many, keeping one's promises is simply the right thing to do. Indeed, taking this argument one step further, many individuals keep—and believe that they should be *legally* obligated to keep—their promises, in no small part, because they are *morally* obligated to do so. Although it is beyond the scope of a contracts casebook to explore this issue in depth,† we would be remiss if we left

---

* The various remedies that courts can award to protect the contractual entitlements of the parties will be taken up in Section D, "Remedies," p. 104, *infra*, and then again in Chapter 5.

† There are a number of excellent works that explore the nature of the moral and legal obligations created by promise. *See, e.g.*, P.S. ATIYAH, PROMISES, MORALS AND THE LAW (1981), Brian Bix, *Theories of Contract Law and Enforcing Promissory Morality: Comments on Charles Fried*, 45 SUFFOLK U. L. REV. 719 (2012), CHARLES FRIED, CONTRACT AS PROMISE (1981), JAMES GORDLEY, THE PHILOSOPHICAL ORIGINS OF MODERN CONTRACT DOCTRINE (1991), DORI KIMEL, FROM PROMISE TO CONTRACT: TOWARD A LIBERAL THEORY OF CONTRACT (2003), Ann De Moor, *Are Contracts Promises?*, in OXFORD ESSAYS IN JURISPRUDENCE 103 (1987), Michael G. Pratt, *Promise, Contracts and Voluntary Obligations*, 26 LAW AND PHILOSOPHY 531 (2007), Joseph Raz, *Promises in Morality and Law*, 95 HARV. L. REV. 916 (1982), Seana Shiffrin, *The Divergence of Contract and Promise*, 120 HARV. L. REV 709 (2007), Seana Shiffrin, *Are Contracts Promises?*, in THE

this section without at least touching upon one of the most important and enduring issues surrounding promise, which is how promises can create moral and legal obligations in the first place. One of the most popular answers to this question was provided by Charles Fried, who attempted to rest contractual liability on promissory obligation. We end this section with that account.

In the excerpt below, Fried attempts to answer the question of why it is wrong to break one's promise. As you read it, ask yourself whether you agree with Fried, and whether you think that contract law should rest mostly, partly, or not at all on the moral obligation to keep one's promise.

THE MORAL OBLIGATION OF PROMISE*

Considerations of self-interest cannot supply the moral basis of my obligation to keep a promise. By an analogous argument neither can considerations of utility. For however sincerely and impartially I may apply the utilitarian injunction to consider at each step how I might increase the sum of happiness or utility in the world, it will allow me to break my promise whenever the balance of advantage (including, of course, my own advantages) tips in that direction. . . .

The obligation to keep a promise is grounded not in arguments of utility but in respect for individual autonomy and in trust. . . . An individual is morally bound to keep his promises because he has intentionally invoked a convention whose function it is to give grounds—moral grounds—for another to expect the promised performance. To renege is to abuse a confidence he was free to invite or not, and which he intentionally did invite. To abuse that confidence now is like (but only *like*) lying: the abuse of a shared social institution that is intended to invoke the bonds of trust. A liar and a promise-breaker each *use* another person. In both speech and promising there is an invitation to the other to trust, to make himself vulnerable; the liar and the promise-breaker then abuse that trust. The obligation to keep a promise is thus similar to but more constraining than the obligation to tell the truth. To avoid lying you need only believe in the truth of what you say when you say it, but a promise binds into the future, well past the moment when the promise is made. . . .

The utilitarian counting the advantages affirms the general importance of enforcing *contracts*. The moralist of duty, however, sees *promising* as a device that free, moral individuals have fashioned on the premise of mutual trust, and which gathers its moral force from that premise. The moralist of duty thus posits a general obligation to keep promises, of which the obligation of contract will be only a special case—that special case in which certain promises have attained legal as well as moral force. But since a contract is first of all a promise, the contract must be kept because a promise must be kept.

ROUTLEDGE COMPANION TO THE PHILOSOPHY OF LAW (2012), STEPHEN SMITH, CONTRACT THEORY (2004), and Warren Swain, *Contract as Promise: The Role of Promising in the Contract Law. An Historical Account*, 17 EDINBURGH L. REV. 1 (2013).

* Excerpted from CHARLES FRIED, CONTRACT AS PROMISE 15-17 (1981).

To summarize: There exists a convention that defines the practice of promising and its entailments. This convention provides a way that a person may create expectations in others. By virtue of the basic Kantian principles of trust and respect, it is wrong to invoke that convention in order to make a promise, and then to break it.

C. ENFORCEABILITY

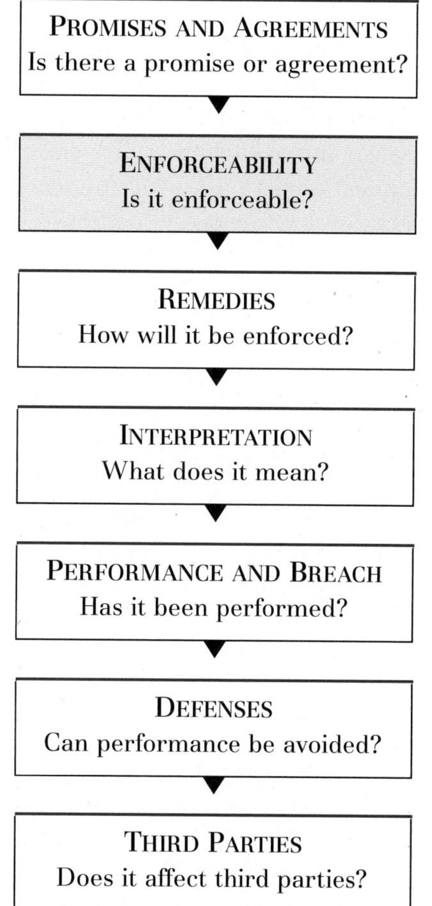
PROMISES AND AGREEMENTS
Is there a promise or agreement?
ENFORCEABILITY
Is it enforceable?
REMEDIES
How will it be enforced?
INTERPRETATION
What does it mean?
PERFORMANCE AND BREACH
Has it been performed?
DEFENSES
Can performance be avoided?
THIRD PARTIES
Does it affect third parties?

No legal system has even been reckless enough to make all promises enforceable. As a legal philosopher expressed it, some freedom to change one's mind is essential "for free intercourse between those who lack omniscience," and most of us "would shudder at the idea of being bound by every promise, no matter how foolish, without any chance of letting increased wisdom undo past foolishness." In framing a basis for enforcing promises, however, one can approach the goal from two opposite extremes. One can begin with the assumption that

promises are generally enforceable, and then create exceptions for promises considered undesirable to enforce. Or one can begin with the assumption that promises are generally unenforceable, and then create exceptions for promises thought desirable to enforce.

Farnsworth, CONTRACTS § 1.5 (4th ed. 2004)

This section is designed to familiarize you with the main issues governing the enforceability of promises (i.e., contracts) from about the 5,000-foot level. In it, you will become familiar with some of the main justifications for enforcing promises,* learn a little about the history of promissory enforcement,† and become familiar with the doctrine of consideration,‡ the main approach used by courts to distinguish between enforceable and non-enforceable promises. After reading this section, you should feel comfortable with the main issues governing the enforceability of promises, and be prepared to engage in a more in-depth exploration of these issues, which we take up in Chapter 4. But first, now is a great time to pause and ask why we have contract law at all. Another way of approaching this question is to ask what the world would look like without contract law. The short excerpt below, in addition to providing an amusing footnote to one of the greatest movies ever made (especially while studying for finals), provides one answer to that question, and leads nicely into the materials that follow.

THE PHILOSOPHICAL FOUNDATIONS OF CONTRACT LAW§

Before the state, there was the family and the clan. Before courts, there was the feud—private vengeance wreaked by members of the aggrieved party's extended family or the aggrieved party personally. It is well-recognized that the law of crimes and torts owe their origin to the state's desire to eliminate private vengeance and to minimize other forms of self-help. It is not as well known that contract law has the same genesis. Among the earliest executory contracts were compositions—agreements settling claims of personal injury or property damages. To the extent they were executory, performance was secured by the delivery of hostages to the promisee. In the event of breach, the hostage could be executed or enslaved.

In modern law, where contract law refuses to enter, vengeance and self-help fill the vacuum. On nearly a daily basis, residents of our major cities are informed by the media of a "drug-related" murder or kidnapping. The relationship between the victim and the enforcer is usually that of debtor and creditor. Because the legal system will not aid in the collection of the debt formed by a criminal sale, vengeance or hostage-taking substitutes for law. It is not only drug-related

* *See, e.g.*, "Justifying Contract Law," at p. 81, *infra*.

† *See, e.g.*, "The Rise of Contracts," at p. 87, *infra*.

‡ *See, e.g.*, *Hamer v. Sidway* and accompanying materials, beginning at p. 93, *infra*.

§ Excerpted from JOSEPH M. PERILLO, CALAMARI AND PERILLO ON CONTRACTS § 1.4 (5th ed. 2003).

transactions that give rise to extra-legal punishment or enforcement. Take the example of a builder who went to a prospective lender for a loan. Not realizing the nature of the business of the person he was applying to, he inquired about the collateral the lender might want. He was told: "Your body is your collateral."[4]

Anthropology and history prove that a basis of contract law is the desire to keep the public peace. Nonetheless, contract law serves other functions and other rationales are given for its existence. For centuries, philosophers of the law have attempted to explain why, in addition to the keeping of the public peace, the legal system recognizes and enforces private agreements. Asis so frequently the case in philosophical discourse no consensus has been reached, but the range of disagreement, although significant, is surprisingly small. . . .

1. Which Promises Should Courts Enforce?

So, what do *you* think? Do you think courts should enforce all, some, or none of our promises? Why? If you believe that courts should enforce at least *some* promises, then the next question practically asks (but does not answer) itself: *Which* promises should they enforce, and why? In this subsection, we will read a short excerpt from a classic article written by Professor Cohen, who attempts to answer these questions by taking a closer look at some of the most important justifications for enforcing promises. You will get a lot more out of the reading if you pause before reading the next excerpt and take a moment to make a list of all of the reasons you can think of as to (a) why you think courts should enforce promises, and (b) what tests you think courts should use to distinguish between enforceable and non-enforceable promises. In doing so, you may find it helpful to consider some of the promises you've made in the past, or promises that others have made to you. Which of these promises (if any) did you expect courts to enforce, and why? Once you've made your list, read the following excerpt, and consider how your justifications differ, if at all, from those offered below.

JUSTIFYING CONTRACT LAW*

A. The Sanctity of Promises

Contract law is commonly supposed to enforce promises. Why should promises be enforced?

The simplest answer is that of the intuitionists, namely, that promises are sacred *per se*, that there is something inherently despicable about not keeping a

4. N.Y. State Comm. of Investigation, The Loan Shark Racket 11 (1965). See also the film "Rocky."

* Excerpted from Morris Cohen, *The Basis of Contract*, 46 HARV. L. REV. 553, 571-85 (1933).

promise, and that a properly organized society should not tolerate this. This may also be said to be the common man's theory. . . .

Now there can be no doubt that common sense does generally find something revolting about the breaking of a promise, and this, if a fact, must be taken into account by the law, though it may be balanced by other factors or considerations. . . .

If, then, we find ourselves in a state of society in which men are, as a matter of fact, repelled by the breaking of promises and feel that such practice should be discouraged or minimized, that is a primary fact which the law must not ignore.

But while this intuitionist theory contains an element of truth, it is clearly inadequate. No legal system does or can attempt to enforce all promises. . . . And when we come to draw a distinction between those promises which should be and those which should not be enforced, the intuitionist theory, that all promises should be kept, gives us no light or guiding principle.

Similar to the intuitionist theory is the view of Kantians . . . that the duty to keep one's promise is one without which rational society would be impossible. There can be no doubt that . . . the ability to rely on the promises of others adds to the confidence necessary for social intercourse and enterprise. But as an absolute proposition this is untenable. The actual world . . . is not one in which all promises are kept, and there are many people . . . who prefer a world in which they and others occasionally depart from the truth and go back on some promise. It is indeed very doubtful whether there are many who would prefer to live in an entirely rigid world in which one would be obliged to keep *all* one's promises instead of the present more viable system, in which a vaguely fair proportion is sufficient. Many of us indeed would shudder at the idea of being bound by every promise, no matter how foolish, without any chance of letting increased wisdom undo past foolishness. Certainly, some freedom to change one's mind is necessary for free intercourse between those who lack omniscience. . . .

B. The Will Theory of Contract

According to the classical view, the law of contract gives expression to and protects the will of the parties, for the will is something inherently worthy of respect. Hence [numerous] authorities . . . hold that the first essential of a contract is the agreement of wills, or the meeting of minds.

The metaphysical difficulties of this view have often been pointed out. Minds or wills are not in themselves existing things that we can look at and recognize. We are restricted in our earthly experience to the observation of the changes or actions of more or less animated bodies in time and space; and disembodied minds or wills are beyond the scope and reach of earthly law. . . .

A more important objection to the theory that every contract expresses the consensus or agreed wills of the two parties is the fact that most litigation in this field arises precisely because of the advent of conditions that the two parties did not foresee when they entered into the transaction. Litigation usually reveals the absence of genuine agreement between the parties *ab initio*. If both parties had foreseen the difficulty, provision would have been made for it in the beginning when the contract was drawn up. When courts thus proceed to interpret the terms of the contract they are generally not merely seeking to discover the actual past meanings (though these may sometimes be investigated), but more generally they decide the "equities," the rights and obligations of the parties, in such circumstances; and these legal relations are determined by the courts and the jural system and not by the agreed will of the contesting parties.

[Some scholars] have argued that while certain effects of a contract may not have been foreseen by the parties, nevertheless these are effects following from the original objective and are therefore the will of the two contractors. But to argue that, because the law fixes certain obligations, you did foresee something that in fact you did not see is a confusion which would be too ridiculous to criticize were it not so prevalent in juristic discussions. . . . So in contracts men are liable for things that they did not actually foresee; and to say that they intended or willed these results is a fiction designed to save the will theory. . . .

C. The Injurious-Reliance Theory

[According to the injurious-reliance theory, c]ontractual liability arises (or should arise) only where (1) someone makes a promise explicitly in words or implicitly by some act, (2) someone else relies on it, and (3) suffers some loss thereby.

This theory appeals to the general moral feeling that not only ought promises to be kept, but that anyone innocently injured by relying on them is entitled to have his loss "made good" by the one who thus caused it. If, as Schopenhauer has maintained, the sense of wrong is the ultimate human source of the law, then to base the obligation of the promise on the injury of the one who has relied on it, is to appeal to something really fundamental.

This theory also appeals powerfully to modern legal theorists because it seems to be entirely objective and social. It does not ask the court to examine the intention of the promisor. Instead, the court is asked to consider whether what the defendant has said or done is such that reasonable people generally do rely on it under the circumstances. The resulting loss can be directly proved and, to some extent, even measured. . . .

Nevertheless, this theory is not entirely consistent with existing law, nor does it give an altogether satisfactory account of what the law should do.

Contractual obligation is not coextensive with injurious reliance because (1) there are instances of both injury and reliance for which there is no contractual obligation, and (2) there are cases of such obligation where there is no reliance or injury.

(1) Clearly, not all cases of injury resulting from reliance on the word or act of another are actionable, and the theory before us offers no clue as to what distinguishes those which are. There is, first, the whole class of instances of definite financial injury caused by reliance on an explicit promise made in social relations, such as dinner parties and the like. Suppose I say to *A*, "If you agree to meet my friends and talk to them about your travels in Africa, I will hire an appropriate room in a hotel and give a dinner in your honor." *A* agrees but fails to come, or notifies me too late to prevent my financial loss. Here the law gives me no redress. Cases like these are often said to be properly ruled out on the ground that those who make them do not intend to be legally bound. . . . But this argument is rather circular, since liability does not generally depend on knowledge or ignorance of the law. Men are held liable in many cases where they do not intend to be bound legally. There are doubtless good reasons why there should be no legal liability for "social" promises; but our theory does not account for them.

Even clearer are those cases where someone advertises goods for sale or a position to be filled, and, when I come, tells me that he has changed his mind. The fact that I have suffered actual loss from relying on this public statement does not in this case give me a cause of action. The law does not help everyone who has relied on the word or act of another.

(2) In formal contracts, such as promises under seal, stipulation in court, and the like, it is clearly not necessary for the promisee to prove reliance and injury. Certain formalities are binding *per se*. . . . Actual reliance, it seems, is not always a necessary element in the case. . . .

(3) Finally, the recovery that the law allows to the injured promisee is not determined by what he lost in relying on the promise, but rather by what he would have gained if the promise had been kept. There are obviously many cases where the injured party is substantially no worse after the breach than if the contract had never been made. He has thus not been in fact injured. And yet he may recover heavy damages if he would have gained heavily by the performance of the contract. The policy of the law, then, is not merely to redress injuries but also to protect certain kinds of expectation by making men live up to certain promises.

There can be no question about the soundness of the injurious reliance theory in accounting for a dominant phase of the law of contract, and the foregoing difficulties may thus seem petty. But they do call attention to fundamental obscurities in the very idea of "reliance" as well as in the criteria of "injury." The injurious-reliance theory, like others, calls attention to a necessary element but does not give an adequate account of the whole of the law of contract. . . .

D. The Equivalent Theory

Popular sentiment generally favors the enforcement of those promises which involve some *quid pro quo*. It is generally considered unfair that after *A* has given something of value or rendered *B* some service, *B* should fail to render anything in return. Even if what *A* did was by way of gift, *B* owes him gratitude and should express it in some appropriate way. And if, in addition, *B* has promised to pay *A* for the value or services received, the moral sense of the community condemns *B's* failure to do so as even more unfair. The demand for justice behind the law is but an elaboration of such feelings of what is fair and unfair.

The equivalent theory of contract has the advantage of being supported by this popular sentiment. This sentiment also explains the primacy of *real* contracts.

While a legal theory must not ignore common sense, it must also go beyond it. For common sense, while generally sound at its core, is almost always vague and inadequate. Common sentiment, for instance, demands an equivalent. But what things are equivalent? It is easy to answer this in regard to goods or services that have a standard market value. But how shall we measure things that are dissimilar in nature, or in a market where monopolistic or other factors prevent a fair or just price? Modern law therefore professes to abandon the effort of more primitive systems to enforce material fairness within the contract. The parties to the contract must themselves determine what is fair. Thereby, however, the law loses a good deal of support in the moral sense of the community. . . .

E. Formalism in Contract

. . . [R]eflection shows that our modern practices of shaking hands to close a bargain, signing papers, and protesting a note are, like the taking of an oath on assuming office, not only designed to make evidence secure, but are in large part also expressions of the fundamental human need for formality and ceremony, to make sharp distinctions where otherwise lines of demarcation would not be so clearly apprehended.

Ceremonies are the channels that the stream of social life creates by its ceaseless flow through the sands of human circumstance. Psychologically, they are habits; socially, they are customary ways of doing things; and ethically, they have what Jellinek has called the normative power of the actual, that is, they control what we do by creating a standard of respectability or a pattern to which we feel bound to conform. The daily obedience to the act of the government, which is the basis of all political and legal institutions, is thus largely a matter of conformity to established ritual or form of behavior. For the most part, we obey the law or the policeman as a matter of course, without deliberation. The customs of other people seem to us strange and we try to explain them as ceremonies symbolic of things that are familiar or seem useful to us. But many of our own customs can appear to an outsider as equally non-rational rituals that we follow from habit. We may justify them as the sacred vessels through which we obtain the substance of life's goods. But the maintenance of old forms may also be an end in itself to all those to whom change from the familiar is abhorrent.

F. Contract and the Distribution of Risks

Mr. Justice Holmes has suggested that a legal promise may be viewed as a wager: I assure you of a certain event (which may or may not be within my control) and I pay in case of failure.

This view has not found much favor. The first objection that has been urged against it is that when men make a contract, they contemplate its performance rather than its breach. This is hardly fatal. Men can and do sometimes deliberately plan to pay damages in certain contingencies rather than carry out their legal promises. It might even be said that the law sometimes encourages that attitude. . . .

Nevertheless, when taken in a wider sense in connection with Mr. Justice Holmes's general philosophy concerning the risk in all human affairs, his theory is illuminating and important.

All human transactions are directed to a future that is never free from elements of uncertainty. Every one of our ventures, therefore, involves the taking of a risk. . . . Now a contract or agreement may be viewed as an agreement for the distribution of anticipated gains or losses. . . . [But] the human power to foresee all the consequences of an agreement is limited, even if we suppose that the two parties understand each other's meaning to begin with. Disputes or disagreements are therefore bound to come up; and the law of contract may thus be viewed as an attempt to determine the rights and duties of the two parties under circumstances that were not anticipated exactly in the same way by the two contracting parties, or at any rate were not expressly provided for in an unambiguous way. One can therefore say that the court's adjudication supplements the original contract as a method of distributing gains and losses.

From this point of view, we may look upon the law of contract as a number of rules according to which courts distribute gains and losses according to the equities of such cases; and the pretense that the result follows exclusively from the agreement of the two parties is fictional. Just as the process of interpreting a statute is really a process of subsidiary legislation, so is the interpretation of a contract really a method of supplementing the original agreement by such provisions as are necessary to determine the point at issue.

If we view the law of contract as directed to strengthening the security of transactions by enabling men to rely more fully on promises, we see only one phase of its actual workings. The other phase is the determination of the rights of the contracting parties as to contingencies that they have not foreseen, and for which they have not provided. In this latter respect the law of contract is a way of enforcing some kind of distributive justice within the legal system. And technical doctrines of contract may thus be viewed as a set of rules that will systematize decisions in this field and thus give lawyers and their clients some guidance in the problem of anticipating future decisions. Thus, for instance, if the question arises as to who should suffer a loss caused by the destruction of goods in transit, the technical doctrine of when title passes enables us to deal with the problem more definitely. In any case, the essential problem of the law of contract is the problem of distribution of risks. The other phase, namely, the assurance that what the parties have actually agreed on will be fulfilled, is a limiting principle.

NOTES AND QUESTIONS

1. *Why enforce promises?* In what ways did the justifications offered by Cohen in the excerpt above differ from the justifications you came up with before you began reading it? Did you think of any justifications not mentioned by Cohen?

2. *Weighing competing claims.* Of the various justifications offered by Cohen, which ones did you find most persuasive, and why?

3. *From theory to practice.* Many of the justifications discussed by Cohen have found expression in numerous black-letter doctrines scattered throughout our common law, many of which we will study in the upcoming chapters. For instance, the "will theory of contract" discussed by Cohen has found expression in the "subjective test" of mutual assent courts have sometimes relied on to determine whether parties intended to form an agreement,* the "injurious-reliance theory" has found expression in the doctrines of equitable† and promissory estoppel‡ sometimes used by courts to protect parties harmed by their reliance on another party's statement or promise, and "formalism in contract law" has found expression in a number of contract doctrines, such as the statute

* *See, e.g., Dickinson v. Dodds* and CISG Article 8(1), in Chapter 3, *infra.*

† *See, e.g., Ricketts v. Scothorn,* in Chapter 4, *infra.*

‡ *See, e.g., Hoffman v. Red Owl Stores, Inc.* and Restatement (Second) of Contracts § 90 in Chapter 4, *infra.*

of frauds,* requiring that certain promises be put in writing to be enforceable. You might consider revisiting this excerpt throughout this course, perhaps at the end of each chapter, to see how many of the theories discussed by Cohen you can find given concrete expression in our common law's black-letter doctrines.

2. Which Promises Have Courts Enforced?

In the previous subsection, we learned to approach the problem of distinguishing between enforceable and non-enforceable promises *theoretically*, by examining the various justifications undergirding the institution of promise-keeping. In this subsection, we will approach the institution of promise-keeping *historically*, by briefly examining our law's fascinating history of promissory enforcement. Specifically, we will watch as our common law courts struggle to develop a general theory of promissory enforcement that was broad enough to include a widerange of important promises in its ambit, but nimble enough to allow courts to distinguish between enforceable and non-enforceable promises. As we shall see in the next subsection, the fruits of their struggle, and the doctrines they have developed, are still with us today.

THE RISE OF CONTRACTS†

No legal system devised by man has even been reckless enough to make all promises enforceable. In Morris Cohen's words:

> It is indeed very doubtful whether there are many who would prefer to live in an entirely rigid world in which one would be obliged to keep *all* one's promises instead of the present more viable system, in which a vaguely fair proportion is sufficient. Many of us indeed would shudder at the idea of being bound by every promise, no matter how foolish, without any chance of letting increased wisdom undo past foolishness. Certainly, some freedom to change one's mind is necessary for free intercourse between those who lack omniscience.[66]

But in framing a general theory for the enforcement of promises, this goal can be approached from two extremes. One can begin with the premise that promises are generally enforceable and then create exceptions for promises which it is thought undesirable to enforce. Or one can begin with the premise that promises are generally unenforceable and then create exceptions for promises which it is thought desirable to enforce. In the centuries following the Conquest in England, both views had substantial support.

---

* *See* Chapter 8, *infra*.

† Excerpted from E. Allan Farnsworth, *The Past of Promise: An Historical Introduction to Contract*, 69 COLUM. L. REV. 576, 591-96, 598-99 (1969).

66. Cohen, *The Basis of Contract*, 46 HARV. L. REV. 553, 573 (1932).

Canon law

"The laws of the Christian Church; esp., a body of western ecclesiastical law that was first compiled from the 12th to 14th centuries. It has grown steadily since that time and is now codified in the *Codex Juris Canonici* of 1983, replacing that of 1918." BLACK'S LAW DICTIONARY (10th ed. 2014).

Law merchant

"A system of customary law that developed in Europe during the Middle Ages and regulated the dealings of mariners and merchants in the commercial countries of the world until the 17th century. Many of the law merchant's principles came to be incorporated into the common law, which in turn formed the basis of the Uniform Commercial Code. Also termed *commercial law; lexmercatoria.*" BLACK'S LAW DICTIONARY (10th ed. 2014).

Equity

Equity refers to the body of rules traditionally administered by Courts of Equity, which grew up alongside, and competed with, Courts of Law in medieval England. *See* F.W. MAITLAND, EQUITY 1 (2d rev. ed., Cambridge Univ. Press 1969). Today, federal law and all but three states—Delaware, Mississippi, and Tennessee—have merged their courts of law and equity. For a fascinating history of these mergers in the United States, *see* Thomas O. Main, *Traditional Equity and Contemporary Procedure*, 78 WASH. L. REV. 429 (2003).

Chancellor

A judge who presides over the proceedings in a court of equity or chancery is called a "Chancellor."

The former view, which laid emphasis on the force of the promise itself, was held by the **canon law**, the **law merchant**, and **equity**. As for the canon law, [it] regarded a promise made with a pledge of faith as enforceable and its breach as a mortal sin, and was moving toward the view that even a simple promise, without a pledge of faith, was sacred and therefore enforceable. As for the law merchant, the fair and market courts entertained numerous actions, as commerce required, upon simple promises made by merchants. And as for equity, the **Chancellor** held the view that the law of man must accord with the law of God and, in his own words in the fifteenth century, because a man was "damaged by the non-performance of the promise, he shall have a remedy."[67]

The view that promises are not generally enforceable, which started from the premise of Roman law that a mere agreement did not beget an action, was held by the common law. Its choice was scarcely surprising. It accorded well with the procedural niceties of common law courts, where recovery was not to be had unless the claim could be fitted within one of the established **forms of action**; and it suited the status-oriented society of the Middle Ages, which was anything but conducive to the flowering of promise. Furthermore, there was no great pressure for enforceability as contracts were not a significant part of the business of the common law courts. At the end of the twelfth century **Ranulf de Glanville** apologized for the scant treatment of the subject in his treatise on English common law with the remark that "it is not the custom of the court of the lord King to protect private agreements, nor does it even concern itself with such contracts as can be considered to be like private agreements."[68]

Nonetheless, it was the common law view that was ultimately to prevail. It achieved its success less on its intrinsic merits than as a by-product of the victories of the common law courts in their jurisdictional struggles with their competitors. As for the canon law, through the Constitutions of Clarendon of 1164, born of the quarrel between Henry II and Thomas á Becket, the common law courts were able to deprive the Church of its jurisdiction over breach of faith in temporal matters

67. Anon. (1468) Y. B. Pasch. 8 Edw. 4 at f. 4, pl. 11, C. H. S. FIFOOT, [HISTORY AND SOURCES OF THE COMMON LAW: TORT AND CONTRACT pt. 2], at 304 [1949].

68. R. DE GLANVILLE, THE TREATISE ON THE LAWS AND CUSTOMS OF THE REALM OF ENGLAND bk. 10, ch. 18 (G. D. G. Hall ed. 1965). *See also* bk. 10, ch. 8.

and to snuff out the attempts of the ecclesiastical courts to implement their view that promises were in themselves sacred. As for the law merchant, by the sixteenth century the common law courts had begun their successful attempt to wrest jurisdiction from the commercial courts and to stifle the view that simple promises made in commerce should be enforced. And as for equity, although it alone among the three competing jurisdictions was to survive the jurisdictional ambitions of the common law courts, the Chancellor hesitated to intervene unless the common law was wanting. It is a tribute to the ingenuity and flexibility of the common law judges that they succeeded in moving fast enough to stay the Chancellor's hand so that credit for the development of the general basis for the enforcement of promises that we know today was theirs and theirs alone. The challenge that faced them was to work within the framework of the forms of action, first to develop exceptions as the Romans had done, and then to so fashion these exceptions as ultimately to achieve what the Romans had never achieved—a general theory of contract. This challenge was met by the common law courts in the course of the fifteenth and sixteenth centuries. . . . The achievement was all the more remarkable in view of the fact that when this development began, the English law of contracts was little more advanced than that of many primitive societies. How was it brought about? . . .

The common law courts found the answer in the law of torts. They had already recognized that liability in tort arose when a person undertook (***assumpsit***) to perform a duty and then performed it in such a way as to cause harm. Suit could be brought on the special variety of trespass on the case that came to be known as assumpsit. At the beginning of the fifteenth century it was available only where there had been misfeasance in performance of the undertaking. This example was given in 1436: "If a carpenter makes a covenant with me to make me a house good and strong and of a certain form, and he makes me a house which is weak and bad and of another form, I shall have an action of trespass on my case."[74] In such cases of misfeasance it was not hard to justify liability in tort. But might not the same remedy lie when there had merely been nonfeasance, a failure to perform the undertaking? At first the answer was no. In 1410 it was said: "Certainly [an action] would lie [if the carpenter had built the house badly], because he would then answer for the wrong which he had done, but when a man makes a covenant and does nothing under

Forms of action

Under the old medieval writ system, a party could bring a legal action against another only if it could couch its grievance in terms of a previously existing form of action, each of which had its own procedural method for resolving the dispute, some allowing trial by jury, others allowing trial by battle, oath, ordeal, etc. Choosing the appropriate form of action from a court was likened to choosing the appropriate weapon from an armory: "[t]he choice is large; but he must remember that he will not be able to change weapons in the middle of the combat and also that every weapon has its proper use and may be put to none other. If he selects a sword, he must observe the rules of sword-play; he must not try to use his cross-bow as a mace." 2 FREDERICK POLLOCK & FREDERIC W. MAITLAND, THE HISTORY OF ENGLISH LAW BEFORE THE TIME OF EDWARD I 561-62 (2d ed. 1898). Although we have long abandoned this antiquated procedure, the names of many forms of action developed during this time, such as "covenant," "debt," "detinue," "replevin," "assumpsit," and "action on the case" will pop up in various places throughout this casebook. As F.W. Maitland once colorfully put it, "[t]he forms of action we have buried, but they still rule us from their graves." F.W. MAITLAND, THE FORMS OF ACTION AT COMMON LAW (1909).

74. Y.B. 14 Hy. VI, at 18.

that covenant, how can you have an action against him without a deed?"[75]

Nevertheless, by the second half of the fifteenth century there was a growing tendency among the common law judges to make the first major extension in the action of assumpsit by enforcing such promises even where there had been only nonfeasance. This inclination was encouraged by the fear that if they did not do so the Chancellor would. But some limits had to be placed on what promises would be enforced, for the judges were not about to allow "that one shall have trespass for any breach of covenant in the world."[76] The courts were therefore forced to find a test to distinguish instances where nonfeasance was actionable from those where it was not. Since the misfeasance cases that had originally given rise to the action in assumpsit were characterized by a detriment incurred by the promisee in reliance on the promise, it was natural to formulate an analogous test and to allow enforcement where the promisee had changed his position on the faith of the promise, and had been consequently damaged by its nonperformance.

Illustration 7. Builder promises to do specified work on Owner's house in return for which Owner promises to pay $10,000 on its completion. In reliance on Builder's promise, Owner rents another house and moves into it to permit Builder to do the work. Builder fails to do the work.

Here the law's justification in protecting Owner is based on the detriment sustained by him through his reliance on the promise, not on any benefit received by Builder. . . . To the extent that the promisee has incurred expenditures in preparing for performance, or has suffered loss by foregoing other opportunities, without conferring any benefit upon the promisor, the broken promise has resulted in a waste that cannot be undone by a simple reversal as in the case of recognition of the restitution interest. Nevertheless, in a society that depends upon promises for cooperation, there is justification in protecting those who rely on promises by placing the cost of the waste occasioned by broken promises on those that break them through requiring the party in breach to compensate the injured party in an amount sufficient to put him in as good a position as he would have been in had the promise never been made. This interest is called the "reliance interest" by Fuller and Perdue.[77] But since some action in reliance on the

Ranulf de Glanville

Glanville was a major figure in English law. During the reign of Henry II, he held the post of Chief Justiciar (1180-89), the highest judicial official in the land, and an office that, at times, rivaled the power of the Crown itself. It was during this time, probably at Henry II's insistence, that Glanvill wrote the first treatise on English law, *Treatise on the laws and customs of the Kingdom of England*, earning him the title of "the father of English jurisprudence." Glanville died fighting at the siege of Acre during the Third Crusade in 1190. For a fascinating account of his life, see JOHN LORD CAMPBELL, THE LIVES OF THE CHIEF JUSTICES OF ENGLAND: FROM THE NORMAN CONQUEST TILL THE DEATH OF LORD TENTERDEN 22-40 (1894).

Assumpsit

From the Latin *assumere*, to "take on" or "assume." A common-law form of action (see margin note "Forms of action," *supra*) to recover damages for the breach of contract not under seal.

75. Y.B. 14 Hy. VI, at 18.
76. Y.B. Hil. 3 Hy. VI, pl. 33,
77. Fuller and Perdue, [*The Reliance Interest in Contract Damages*: 1, 46 YALE L.J. 52, 5[4] (1936).]. "[I]n the early stages of its growth the action of assumpsit was clearly dominated by the

promise was required, this first major extension of the action of assumpsit did not make a mere exchange of promises, without more, enforceable.

As the sixteenth century drew to a close, however, the common law courts, conscious of the expanding jurisdiction of Chancery and anxious to preserve their own powers, made a second major extension of the action of assumpsit. Thus it was held that a party who had given only a promise in exchange for the other's promise had, nonetheless, suffered a detriment by having his freedom of action fettered, since he was in turn bound by his own promise.

> *Illustration 8.* Builder promises to do specified work on Owner's house in return for which Owner promises to pay $10,000 on completion. Before Owner has done anything in reliance on Builder's promise, Builder repudiates the bargain.

The reasoning was, of course, circular, since the detriment to the promisee, in this case the Owner, assumed that he was bound by his own promise, for which only a promise had in turn been given. Nevertheless, by the end of the sixteenth century the common law courts were enforcing exchanges of promise, as in Illustration 8, where nothing had been done on either side. . . .

Over the course of the fifteenth and sixteenth centuries the common law courts had succeeded in evolving a general basis for the enforceability of promises through the action of assumpsit. During the sixteenth century the word "consideration," which had earlier been used without technical significance, came to be used as a word of art to express the sum of the conditions necessary for an action in assumpsit to lie. It was therefore a tautology that a promise, if not under seal, was enforceable only where there was "consideration," for this was to say no more than that it was enforceable only under those circumstances in which the action of assumpsit was allowed. In this fashion, however, the word "consideration" came to be applied to the test of enforceability of a simple promise and to be used to distinguish those promises that in the eyes of the common law were of sufficient significance to society to justify the legal sanctions of assumpsit for their enforcement.

It was, to be sure, neither a simple nor a logical test. Bound up in it were several elements. Most important, from the *quid pro quo* of debt . . . had come the idea that there must have been an exchange arrived at by way of bargain. This precept has remained at the core of the concept of consideration down to today.[85] From the same source had come the notion that there must be a benefit to the promisor, while from the reliance of special assumpsit came the notion that there must be a detriment to the promisee—both notions that have proved less durable than those of exchange and bargain. The requirement of an exchange

---

reliance interest, so much so that Ames assumed, even in the absence of cases in point, that recovery in assumpsit must originally have been limited to compensation for change of position." *Id.* at 68. *But see* Washington, *Damages in Contract at Common Law*, 47 L.Q. Rev. 345, 371-79 (1959).

85. According to the *Restatement Second*, "To constitute consideration, a performance or a return promise must be bargained for," which means that "it is sought by the promisor in exchange for his promise and is given by the promisee in exchange for that promise." *Restatement (Second) of Contracts* § [71]. . . .

accorded well with what has been called the "theory of equivalents," under which an abstract promise is enforceable only when supported by an equivalent. And in a society based on free enterprise it is scarcely surprising that courts declined to meddle in the determination of equivalence, leaving that to the parties themselves. The focus of the law was on the process by which the parties determined equivalence, with bargain as the touchstone. The doctrine of consideration provided no ground for the enforceability of gratuitous promises, for which nothing is given in exchange, but it took good care of the bulk of economically vital commercial agreements. . . .

As a cornerstone for the law of contract, the doctrine of consideration has been widely criticized, and it would be foolhardy to attempt to defend it through an exercise in logic. It can be understood only in the light of its history and of the society that produced it. Yet in view of the difficulty that mankind the world over has had in developing any general basis at all for enforcing promises, it is perhaps less remarkable that the common law developed a theory that is logically flawed than that it succeeded in developing any theory at all.

NOTES AND QUESTIONS

1. *From theory to history.* As Farnsworth pointed out in the excerpt above, historically, "consideration" embraced several different tests, ranging from a promisor-based "benefit" to a promisee-based "detriment" to an exchange-based "bargain." Each of these doctrinal tests, in turn, map on to one of the theoretical justifications offered by Cohen in *The Basis of Contracts*. Can you see how?

2. *What's missing?* Cohen provided several justifications for enforcing promises that do not appear in Farnsworth's brief account of the history of consideration. But this does not mean that these justifications have not played a role, or do not continue to play a role, in the development of contract law today. As you read the cases and materials in this section and in Chapter 4 on "Enforceability," keep your eyes open for instances in which courts seem concerned with some of the other justifications for enforcing promises discussed by Cohen.

3. *From history to practice.* All three of the concepts discussed by Farnsworth (benefit, detriment, and bargain) will reappear when we examine the doctrine of consideration in action in our next case, *Hamer v. Sidway*, and in the *Restatement (Second) of Contracts* provisions following that case. As you read, pay careful attention to which test is being adopted by the *Hamer* court, and which test is adopted by the *Restatement*. Does one test seem better than the other? If so, which one, and why?

3. Which Promises Do Courts Enforce?

From the excerpt above, we learned that the doctrine of consideration often requires "an exchange arrived at by way of bargain," and that this exchange is often accompanied by "a benefit to the promisor" and/or "a detriment to the promisee," although, it should be pointed out, the requirement that there be a benefit or detriment, which was common in the nineteenth century, has not been adopted by the *Restatement (Second) of Contracts*. Finally, we learned that although consideration has its strengths, in that it was capable of taking "good care of the bulk of economically vital commercial agreements," it also has its weaknesses, and has "been widely criticized" in part because it "provided no ground for the enforceability of gratuitous promises, for which nothing is given in exchange."

As you read the next case, ask yourself whether you think consideration provides a good test for determining whether the uncle's promise to his nephew should be enforceable, and whether the concepts of "benefit" and "detriment," which play a role in Judge Parker's analysis, are useful in answering this question.

Hamer v. Sidway

Court of Appeals of New York
27 N.E. 256 (1891)

Appeal from order of the General Term of the Supreme Court in the fourth judicial department, made July 1, 1890, which reversed a judgment in favor of plaintiff entered upon a decision of the court on trial at Special Term and granted a new trial.

This action was brought upon an alleged contract.

The plaintiff presented a claim to the **executor** of William E. Story, Sr., for $5,000 and interest from the 6th day of February, 1875. She acquired it through **several mesne assignments** from William E. Story, 2d. The claim being rejected by the executor, this action was brought. It appears that William E. Story, Sr., was the uncle of William E. Story, 2d; that at the celebration of the golden wedding of Samuel Story and wife, father and mother of William E. Story, Sr., on the 20th day of March, 1869, in the presence of the family and invited guests he promised his nephew that if he would refrain from drinking, using tobacco, swearing and playing cards or billiards for money until he became twenty-one years of age he would pay him a sum of $5,000. The nephew assented thereto and fully performed the conditions inducing the promise. When the nephew arrived at the age of twenty-one years and on the 31st day of January, 1875, he wrote to his uncle informing him that he had performed his part of the agreement and had thereby become entitled to the sum of $5,000. The uncle received the letter and a few days later and on the sixth of February, he wrote and mailed to his nephew the following letter:

Executor

"A person [here, Sidway] named by a testator to carry out the provisions in the testator's will." BLACK'S LAW DICTIONARY (10th ed. 2014).

Several mesne assignments?

Although the facts are less than clear, it appears that the nephew, William E. Story, 2d, assigned his uncle's promise to his wife, who in turn assigned it to his mother-in-law, Louise Hamer, on the day of his uncle's funeral. *See* DOUGLAS G. BAIRD, CONTRACT STORIES 175-77 (2007). This explains why the case is captioned "*Hamer v. Sidway*," rather than "*Story v. Story*."

BUFFALO, *Feb.* 6, 1875.

W. E. STORY, Jr.:

DEAR NEPHEW—Your letter of the 31st ult. came to hand all right, saying that you had lived up to the promise made to me several years ago. I have no doubt but you have, for which you shall have five thousand dollars as I promised you. I had the money in the bank the day you was 21 years old that I intend for you, and you shall have the money certain. Now, Willie I do not intend to interfere with this money in any way till I think you are capable of taking care of it and the sooner that time comes the better it will please me. I would hate very much to have you start out in some adventure that you thought all right and lose this money in one year. The first five thousand dollars that I got together cost me a heap of hard work. . . . All the money I have saved I know just how I got it. It did not come to me in any mysterious way, and the reason I speak of this is that money got in this way stops longer with a fellow that gets it with hard knocks than it does when he finds it. Willie, you are 21 and you have many a thing to learn yet. This money you have earned much easier than I did besides acquiring good habits at the same time and you are quite welcome to the money; hope you will make good use of it. I was ten long years getting this together after I was your age. Now, hoping this will be satisfactory, I stop. . . .

Truly Yours,

W. E. STORY.

P. S.—You can consider this money on interest.

The nephew received the letter and thereafter consented that the money should remain with his uncle in accordance with the terms and conditions of the letters. The uncle died on the 29th day of January, 1887, without having paid over to his nephew any portion of the said $5,000 and interest. . . .

Alton Brooks Parker

Judge Parker (1852-1926) practiced law in Kingston, New York, before being appointed to the New York Supreme Court. He was later elected to the New York Court of Appeals, where he served as Chief Judge from 1898 to 1904, when he resigned to run for president against the popular incumbent Theodore Roosevelt. In the election, he was defeated in a landslide (336 electoral votes to 140), and thereafter returned to the practice of law.

Testator

"Someone who has made a will; esp., a person who dies leaving a will." BLACK'S LAW DICTIONARY (10th ed. 2014).

Parker, J. The question which provoked the most discussion by counsel on this appeal, and which lies at the foundation of plaintiff's asserted right of recovery, is whether by virtue of a contract defendant's **testator** William E. Story became indebted to his nephew William E. Story, 2d, on his twenty-first birthday in the sum of five thousand dollars. The trial court found as a fact that "on the 20th day of March, 1869, William E. Story agreed to and with William E. Story, 2d, that if he would refrain from drinking liquor, using tobacco, swearing, and playing cards or billiards for money until he should become 21 years of age then he, the said William E. Story, would at that time pay him, the said William E. Story, 2d, the sum of $5,000 for such refraining, to which the said William E. Story, 2d, agreed," and that he "in all things fully performed his part of said agreement."

The defendant contends that the contract was without consideration to support it, and, therefore, invalid. He asserts that the promisee by refraining from the use of liquor and tobacco was not harmed but benefited; that that which he did was best for him to do independently of his uncle's promise, and insists that it follows that unless the promisor was benefited, the contract was without consideration. A contention, which if well founded, would seem to leave open for controversy in many cases whether that which the promisee did or omitted to do was, in fact, of such benefit to him as to leave no consideration to support the enforcement of the promisor's agreement. Such a rule could not be tolerated, and is without foundation in the law. The Exchequer Chamber, in 1875, defined consideration as follows: "A valuable consideration in the sense of the law may consist either in some right, interest, profit or benefit accruing to the one party, or some forbearance, detriment, loss or responsibility given, suffered or undertaken by the other." Courts "will not ask whether the thing which forms the consideration does in fact benefit the promisee or a third party, or is of any substantial value to anyone. It is enough that something is promised, done, forborne or suffered by the party to whom the promise is made as consideration for the promise made to him." (Anson's Prin. of Con. 63.)

"In general a waiver of any legal right at the request of another party is a sufficient consideration for a promise." (Parsons on Contracts, 444.)

"Any damage, or suspension, or forbearance of a right will be sufficient to sustain a promise." (Kent, vol. 2, 465, 12th ed.)

Pollock, in his work on contracts, page 166, after citing the definition given by the Exchequer Chamber already quoted, says: "The second branch of this judicial description is really the most important one. Consideration means not so much that one party is profiting as that the other abandons some legal right in the present or limits his legal freedom of action in the future as an inducement for the promise of the first."

Now, applying this rule to the facts before us, the promisee used tobacco, occasionally drank liquor, and he had a legal right to do so. That right he abandoned for a period of years upon the strength of the promise of the testator that for such forbearance he would give him $5,000. We need not speculate on the effort which may have been required to give up the use of those stimulants. It is sufficient that he restricted his lawful freedom of action within certain prescribed limits upon the faith of his uncle's agreement, and now having fully performed the conditions imposed, it is of no moment whether such performance actually proved a benefit to the promisor, and the court will not inquire into it, but were it a proper subject of inquiry, we see nothing in this record that would permit a determination that the uncle was not benefited in a legal sense. Few cases have been found which may be said to be precisely in point, but such as have been support the position we have taken. . . .

The order appealed from should be reversed and the judgment of the Special Term affirmed, with costs payable out of the estate.

All concur.

RELEVANT PROVISIONS

For the *Restatement (Second) of Contracts,* consult §§ 17 and 71.

NOTES AND QUESTIONS

1. *A note on legal terminology.* You probably noticed that the word "right" appeared no fewer than seven times in *Hamer v. Sidway* (the word was underlined each time it appeared), but were you also aware that this term was not consistently used to refer to the same legal concept? This is unfortunate, because "rights," along with other legal concepts like "duties," "powers," "privileges," and "immunities," not only appear frequently throughout the law (a perusal of the U.S. Constitution should convince you of this), but constitute the building blocks upon which our entire legal edifice is erected. In fact, the only difference between contract law, tort law, property law—or any other area of law, for that matter—is the way these building blocks are arranged, just as it is the arrangement of atoms that accounts for the difference between, say, your contracts casebook and a platypus.* Without a clear understanding of these fundamental building blocks, therefore, it is easy to slip back and forth between two or more possible legal meanings (imagine asking a friend to borrow her casebook and getting a platypus instead), often without even realizing it, thereby making legal analysis difficult at best, and impossible at worst. A firm grasp of these concepts, on the other hand, will not only allow you to view legal problems with greater clarity, but will also help you make sense of, and thereby sharpen your analysis of, even the most difficult legal problems. So, now is the time, early in your law school career, to learn how to understand and use these concepts with some precision. Otherwise, next time you ask to borrow a contracts casebook . . .

THINKING TOOL: THINKING CLEARLY ABOUT LEGAL RELATIONSHIPS†

Hohfeld's* central insight is that certain words of critical importance in law have no agreed meaning and that muddled language leads to muddled thought. As Llewellyn put it, "This invites confusion, it makes bad logic almost inevitable,

* The fact that casebooks don't at all resemble platypuses, or that tort law bears little resemblance to property law, should alert you to the importance of these arrangements.

† Excerpted from Curtis Nyquist, *Teaching Wesley Hohfeld's Theory of Legal Relations,* 52 J. LEGAL EDUC. 238, 239-41 (2002).

* [Editors' note: Wesley Newcomb Hohfeld (1879-1918) was a professor of law during the early twentieth century, first at Stanford Law School (1905-1913), and then at Yale Law School (1914-1918). He was the first legal thinker to clearly identify and distinguish between the eight fundamental legal concepts that constituted the fundamental building blocks or "elements" of the law, in addition to working out the logical relationships between each of these concepts. Ironically, by precisely revealing and laying bare the logical structure of the law, Professor Hohfeld's work made it clear what legal conclusions could *not* be deduced as a matter of logic, thus increasing the role and importance of policy in legal analysis and decision making.]

it makes clear statement of clear thought difficult, it makes clear thought itself improbable."[7] In particular, the word *right* is used in four different senses. Consider the following statements.

1. A party to a binding contract has a right to the other party's performance.
2. Since flag burning is protected speech, a person has a right to burn a flag.
3. The state of Massachusetts has a right to call me to jury duty (since Massachusetts is my domicile).
4. I have a right not to be called to jury duty in Rhode Island (since Rhode Island is not my domicile).

These sentences are typical of the way the legal community discusses legal relations. For example, a first-year law student might attend a Contracts class discussing issues related to statement 1 and a Constitutional Law class discussing issues related to statement 2, without anyone pointing out that the word right is being used in two different ways.[8]

Hohfeld provides a vocabulary that captures the four different uses of the word *right:* right (in a Hohfeldian sense), privilege, power, and immunity. He argues that a legal relation is always between two persons and that a right, privilege, power, or immunity is always linked to a correlative (duty, no-right, liability, and disability). In other words, if someone has a Hohfeldian right, another person has a duty. Privilege is linked to no-right, power to liability, and immunity to disability. A legal relation is similar to two persons holding opposite ends of the same stick.[9] Hohfeld displays the four relations in a table of correlatives.[10]

Jural Correlatives

right	privilege	power	immunity
duty	no-right	liability	disability

A person with a Hohfeldian *right* against another person (who is under a *duty*) has a claim if the other does not act in accordance with the duty. A person with a *privilege* may act without liability to another (who has a *no-right*). A person with

7. KARL N. LLEWELLYN, THE BRAMBLE BUSH 85 (New York, 1960).

8. In fact, the meanings are opposite. In sentence 1 the word right means a person has a claim against another person, while in sentence 2 it means a person is not subject to a claim from another.

9. Llewellyn provides the following explanation of correlatives: "There is a person on *each* end, always. A has a right that B shall do something, I repeat, when should B fail to do it, A can get the court to make trouble for B. But the right has B on the other end. The right *is indeed a duty,* a duty seen [from the] other end. . . . The relation is identical; the only difference is in the point of observation." Llewellyn, *supra* note 7, at 85.

10. Wesley Newcomb Hohfeld, *Some Fundamental Legal Conceptions as Applied in Judicial Reasoning,* 23 YALE L.J. 16, 30 (1913). The eight concepts can also be sorted into a table of opposites. For example, if a person has a privilege of performing an act vis-à-vis another person, it also means that she does not have a duty to that person with respect to the act.

Jural Opposites

right	privilege	power	immunity
no-right	duty	disability	liability

a *power* is able to change a legal relation of another (who is under a *liability*). A person with an *immunity* cannot have a particular legal relation changed by another (who is under a *disability*). Using Hohfeld's vocabulary, the four statements would read:

1. A party to a binding contract has a right to the other party's performance.
2. Since flag burning is protected speech, a person has a privilege to burn a flag.
3. The state of Massachusetts has a power to call me to jury duty.
4. I have an immunity from being called to jury duty in Rhode Island.

The two legal relations on the left side of Hohfeld's table of correlatives (right/duty and privilege/no-right) form a grid that is focused on a current state of affairs. A person who burns a flag, for example, either is privileged to do so or has a duty to refrain. The relations on the table's right side (power/liability and immunity/disability) form a second grid that is focused both on a current state of affairs and on a potential future state. My relationship with Massachusetts on the jury issue, for example, is that I am under a liability to be called if Massachusetts follows the proper procedure for summoning me. My liability is a statement both about a current situation and about the future. Defining legal issues under Hohfeld's system demands clarity about which grid is being addressed. The question *Does Curt Nyquist have to report for jury duty in Massachusetts today?* is a question focused on the right/duty or privilege/no-right grid and the answer is no, I have a privilege of not reporting since I have not been summoned. The question *Might Curt Nyquist have to report for jury duty in Massachusetts in the future?* is a question focused on the power/liability or immunity/disability grid and the answer is yes, I have a liability of being summoned.

2. *Hohfeld and critical reading.* Having now read the excerpt above (preferably a couple of times), go back to Parker's opinion and try to identify where his use of "right" was being used in a manner inconsistent with Hohfeld's understanding of that concept. In each instance, replace the term "right" with the Hohfeldian term that should have been used instead. This exercise underscores an important point, and one that should help you read and think more critically about the law: Whenever you come across a Hohfeldian term such as "right" or "duty," ask yourself whether the author is using this terms consistently, or whether they are carelessly moving back and forth between two or more senses of the word. Doing so may help you identify previously hidden logical errors, and think critically about whether you should reject the reasoning upon which a legal principle rests, or place it on a steadier foundation.

3. *Should this promise be enforced?* Do you think the promise made by the uncle in *Hamer v. Sidway* is the type of promise courts should enforce? Why or why not?

4. *Some additional facts.* Do any of the facts brought out in the excerpt below shed light on the difficulties of determining whether to enforce such promises?

CONTEXTUAL PERSPECTIVE: MORE ON *HAMER V. SIDWAY**

One way to look at the story of *Hamer v. Sidway* is from the point of view of Franklin Sidway. William Story dies twelve years after Willie turned twenty-one without, by Willie's account, making good on a promise made many years before. Franklin Sidway is William's executor, and he is the person in the first instance who has to decide whether there was a legally enforceable promise. Sidway is vice president of the Farmers and Mechanics National Bank, a man who is "prudent, conservative, quick of decision, and not afraid of large undertakings." As a banker whose job it was to handle such matters, Sidway is used to such controversies. Precisely because he is neither a family member nor a friend who cares about sorting out the equities after the fact, his focus is narrowly on the legal technicalities. Moreover, the legal fees the case generates do not trouble him greatly.

The lawyers who have represented Willie and his family for years approach Franklin Sidway and ask him to honor a promise William made to Willie long before. Formally, they are representing not Willie himself, but rather Louise Hamer. She is Willie's mother-in-law, and, Sidway is told, she is entitled to enforce this odd promise because Willie assigned it to her on the day of his uncle's funeral.

Franklin Sidway is skeptical. The evidence that the promise had even been made is not ironclad. There is only a copy, in Willie's hand, of the uncle's letter.[33] Even if Sidway believes that the letter was a faithful copy, he has to ask whether he was bound by the uncle's statement in the letter that he believed Willie kept the promise, for Sidway can reasonably doubt that Willie lived up to his part of the bargain. Willie freely admits that he smoked, drank, and gambled both before he was fifteen and again after he was twenty-one. He spent a good part of the intervening time at college in Ann Arbor, Michigan, hundreds of miles away from the eyes of anyone in his hometown. When asked about his college experiences, Willie has trouble remembering the names of his classmates or where they might be found. The only one Willie can remember and locate is, it appears, a relative of his lawyer.

5. *From theory to history to doctrine.* Compare the reasons offered by Judge Parker for enforcing promises to the reasons we explored for enforcing promises in the excerpts "Justifying Contract Law" (p. 81, *supra*) and "The Rise of Contracts" (p. 87, *supra*). Do any of the reasons offered by Judge Parker link up with the historical or theoretical justifications we previously studied? If so, which ones?

6. *Was this case correctly decided?* Do you agree with the result reached by Judge Parker? Why? What about his reasoning? What are the strengths and weaknesses of his approach? How, if at all, would you have written the opinion differently?

---

* Excerpted from DOUGLAS G. BAIRD, CONTRACT STORIES 174-75 (2007).

33. Willie returned the original to his uncle at his uncle's request many years before, but it was not found among the uncle's effects until later.

7. *Williston's Tramp.* What light, if any, does the following excerpt shed on the case above?

> If a benevolent man says to a tramp: "If you go around the corner to the clothing shop there, you may purchase an overcoat on my credit," no reasonable person would understand that the short walk was requested as the consideration for the promise, but that in the event of the tramp going to the shop the promisor would make him a gift. Yet the walk to the shop is in its nature capable of being consideration. It is a legal detriment to the tramp to make the walk, and the only reason why the walk is not consideration is because on a reasonable construction it must be held that the walk was not requested as the price of the promise, but was merely a condition of a gratuitous promise. It is often difficult to determine whether words of condition in a promise indicate a request for consideration or state a mere condition in a gratuitous promise. An aid, though not a conclusive test, in determining which construction of the promise is more reasonable is an inquiry whether the happening of the condition will be a benefit to the promisor. If so, it is a fair inference that the happening was requested as a consideration. On the other hand, if, as in the case of the tramp stated above, the happening of the condition will be not only of no benefit to the promisor but is obviously merely for the purpose of enabling the promisee to receive a gift, the happening of the event on which the promise is conditional, though brought about by the promisee in reliance on the promise, will not properly be construed as consideration. In case of doubt where the promisee has incurred a detriment on the faith of the promise, courts will naturally be loath to regard the promise as a mere gratuity and the detriment incurred as merely a condition. But in some cases it is so clear that a conditional gift was intended that even though the promisee has incurred detriment, the promise has been held unenforceable.*

8. *Why all the hostility towards gratuitous promises?* By now you are probably getting the sense that the doctrine of consideration makes it difficult for courts to enforce gratuitous promises. Well, you're right. The question, however, is whether this is simply a result of the doctrine we are stuck with, or whether it can be justified on other grounds. We will return to this question again in Chapter 4, when we will examine the enforceability of gratuitous promises in greater depth. For now, here is one justification (which, as it happens, relies in part on administrative costs, which we've examined in an earlier thinking tool).† Do you agree with the author's explanation?

THE NONENFORCEABILITY OF GRATUITOUS PROMISES‡

The general rule is that gratuitous promises are not enforceable. A good example of the rule and its economic logic would be a case where a man promised to

* WILLISTON ON CONTRACTS § 112, p. 445 (3d ed. 1957).

† *See* "Thinking Tool: Administrative Costs and Standards v. Rules", p. 75, *supra*.

‡ Excerpted from Richard A. Posner, *Gratuitous Promises in Economics and Law*, 6 J. LEGAL STUD. 411, 416-17 (1977).

take a woman to dinner but later reneged. The man presumably derived some utility from making the promise, and his utility might be greater if the promise were legally binding on him. But the increment in utility, if any, is probably small, both compared to that of the dinner itself and absolutely given the small size of the promised transfer. Moreover, the legal-error costs of enforcing such promises would be high because of the difficulty of distinguishing in casual social relations between a mere present intention, subject to change at will, and a promise intended to be binding on the promisor.

An additional factor reinforces the conclusion that it would be uneconomical to enforce such promises. The administrative costs of enforcement in such a case, while not high in absolute terms, are so high relative to the stakes that legal enforcement would be attempted only rarely. The man in our example would derive only a negligible increment in utility from being able to make a legally binding promise because the woman would know that he knew that in the event he reneged she would not sue. The binding character of the promise would be illusory, and the benefits from its formal status as a binding promise therefore few. But the costs of enforcement would not be negligible.

A moment's reflection will suggest, however, that the analysis would not be materially altered if the dinner promise had been bilateral—if, that is, in return for the man's promise to take her out the woman had promised to accompany him. Where the utility of the promises being exchanged is small, the gains from legal enforcement are likely to be swamped by the costs of enforcement. The law recognizes this and refuses to enforce trivial social promises, especially within the family—where an additional factor, pointing in the same direction, is the existence of an inexpensive alternative to legal enforcement: refusal to engage in promissory transactions in the future. If the husband reneges on his promise, the wife will refuse in the future to perform services in exchange for his promises. Perhaps, then, the real reason for the law's generally not enforcing gratuitous promises is not a belief, which would be economically unsound, that there is a difference in kind between the gratuitous and the bargained-for promise, but an empirical hunch that gratuitous promises tend both to involve small stakes and to be made in family settings where there are economically superior alternatives to legal enforcement.

9. ***How Would* Hamer v. Sidway *Be Decided Today?*** Recall that the uncle's executor in *Hamer v. Sidway* asserted not only that the nephew was not harmed (but actually benefited) by refraining from the use of liquor and tobacco, but also argued that unless the promisor (the uncle) benefited in some way, there could be no consideration. Towards the end of the nineteenth century, however, "the traditional requirement that the consideration be either a benefit to the promisor or a detriment to the promisee had begun to be replaced by a requirement that the consideration be 'bargained for.'"* This "bargain-based" theory of promissory liability was memorably asserted by Oliver Wendell Holmes, Jr. in 1881 in the following terms:

* E. ALLAN FARNSWORTH, CONTRACTS § 2.2 (4th ed. 2004).

> [I]t is the essence of a consideration, that by the terms of the agreement, it is given and accepted as the motive or inducement for furnishing the consideration. The root of the whole matter is the relation of reciprocal conventional inducement, each for the other, between consideration and promise.*

10. *Consideration as Bargain.* The bargain-based theory of consideration was formally adopted by the *Restatement (First) of Contracts* in 1932, and has been retained in the *Restatement (Second) of Contracts* in 1981. *See* "Relevant Provisions," *supra*. This does not mean, however, that the benefit/detriment test is dead. Indeed, as explained by Professor Farnsworth, the Reporter for the *Restatement (Second)*:

> Despite its age, *Hamer* is still very much alive, along with the notion that either a benefit or a detriment will suffice. See Weiner v. McGraw-Hill, 443 N.E.2d 441 (N.Y. 1982) ("any basic contemporary definition would include the idea that it consists of either a benefit to the promisor or a detriment to the promisee" as "elaborated in Hamer v. Sidway, the seminal case on the subject").†

Professor Farnsworth went on to note that

> [g]iven a sufficiently expansive definition of *benefit* and *detriment*, judges might have avoided inquiry into the substance of the exchange even without adoption of the bargain test. After all, if a promisor chooses to bargain for something it must be a benefit to the promisor, and if the promisor needs to bargain for something in order to extract it from the promisee, it must be a detriment to the promisee.‡

11. *Why bargain?* Although the bargain-based doctrine of consideration would require the nephew to argue for the enforceability of his uncle's promises in terms of whether there was a bargain, isn't it foreseeable that anyone in the nephew's position might detrimentally rely on such a promise, thereby suffering a loss? In response to such concerns, today's contract law is more flexible than would be indicated by too narrow a focus on the bargain-based doctrine of consideration, and other competing doctrines (e.g., the doctrine of promissory estoppel) now exist that might allow recovery in such a case. We will discuss this and other bases for promissory liability in Chapter 4 on "Enforceability." But for now, let's get a little practice applying the bargain-based theory of consideration as set forth in the *Restatement (Second) of Contracts*. Consult the "Relevant Provisions" above, and see if you can answer the following questions.

---

* OLIVER WENDELL HOLMES, JR., THE COMMON LAW 230 (1881).
† E. ALLAN FARNSWORTH, CONTRACTS § 2.4, n.9 (4th ED. 2004).
‡ E. ALLAN FARNSWORTH, CONTRACTS § 2.4 (4th ED. 2004).

APPLYING THE RESTATEMENT 

1. *Applying the* Restatement, *Part I.* According to the bargain test of consideration outlined in the *Restatement (Second) of Contracts,* do you think that the uncle's promise to his nephew was supported by consideration? Why or why not?

2. *Applying the* Restatement, *Part II.* According to the bargain test of consideration, would it have mattered if the uncle's executor could prove that the nephew's forbearance did not harm him, but actually benefited him, as he argued in the original case?

3. *Varying the facts, Part I.* Would the uncle's promise be enforceable if he bargained not for the nephew's refraining from drinking, smoking, swearing, and gambling, as in the actual case, but merely for the nephew's promise to refrain from such activities (assuming the nephew promised to do so)? Why?

4. *Varying the facts, Part II.* Suppose that the nephew stopped drinking, smoking, swearing, and gambling all on his own and the uncle, overcome with joy, promised him $5,000. Is the promise enforceable?

5. *Varying the facts, Part III.* The nephew approaches the uncle and promises to stop drinking, smoking, swearing, and gambling. The uncle, overcome with joy, promises to pay the nephew $5,000. Is the promise enforceable?

6. *Varying the facts, Part IV.* The nephew is addicted to cocaine. The uncle, wishing his nephew to stop, approaches him and says: "Nephew, if you stop your cocaine habit until you're 21, I'll give you $5,000." The nephew does so. When he turns 21, Nephew walks up to Uncle, puts out his hand, and says "Pay up. I need $5,000 to buy some cocaine." The uncle refuses, and the nephew sues. Result?

HAMER HYPOS

How would you apply the *Restatement (Second) of Contracts* to the hypotheticals below?

Hypo 1: During the celebration of the golden wedding of Samuel Story and his wife, Uncle shouts to Nephew from across the room: "*Come* over here, lad, and I'll give you $5,000." Nephew walks over. Uncle refuses to pay, stating that he intended to make a gift, but Nephew took too long, and Uncle changed his mind. Nephew sues Uncle. Who will prevail, and why?

Hypo 2: Same facts as above, but this time Uncle shouts across the room: "*Skip* over here, lad, and I'll give you $5,000." Nephew walks over and demands the money. Uncle refuses to pay, saying: "I asked you to *skip* over here, not *walk* over here." Nephew goes back and *skips* to Uncle, then demands the $5,000. Uncle refuses to pay, and Nephew sues. Result?

Hypo 3: Same facts as above, but now assume that Nephew never learned how to skip properly, and can only do so with great awkwardness. Uncle, knowing this fact, and wanting to embarrass Nephew in front of everyone at the wedding, shouts across the room "*Skip* over here, lad, and I'll give you $5,000." Nephew tries his best to do so, gets his feet entangled, and falls down several times along the way, knocking over several drinks and dinner plates. By the time Nephew makes it to Uncle, everyone at the wedding is doubled over in laughter, some with tears streaming from their eyes. Nephew demands payment, and Uncle refuses. Result?

Hypo 4: Same facts as Hypo 1, above, but this time Uncle shouts across the room: "*Walk* over here, lad, and I'll give you $5,000." Nephew walks over and demands $5,000, but Uncle refuses to pay. Result?

D. REMEDIES

PROMISES AND AGREEMENTS
Is there a promise or agreement?

▼

ENFORCEABILITY
Is it enforceable?

▼

REMEDIES
How will it be enforced?

▼

INTERPRETATION
What does it mean?

▼

PERFORMANCE AND BREACH
Has it been performed?

▼

DEFENSES
Can performance be avoided?

▼

THIRD PARTIES
Does it affect third parties?

We will now take a look at remedies from the 5,000-foot level, but before we proceed, let us pause and consider our journey so far. To reach the issue of remedies, a court must have already determined that the parties, through their promises (*Pappas*), formed an enforceable (*Hamer*) agreement (*Embry*). The question now is how the court will protect this agreement, i.e., what remedy the court will award in the event of breach. This section addresses that question.

Before you read the next case, one of the most famous in the contract law canon, brainstorm for a few moments and try to answer the following question: What do you think should be the main purpose of contract remedies? In other words, once a party has breached its contract, what do you think the court should *do* about it? Then, as you read the following case, (1) make a list of all the possible remedies that you think *could* have been requested by the plaintiff, and (2) indicate whether you agree with the remedy that was ultimately awarded by the court. Did the court's remedy reflect the purpose that you thought should be served by contract remedies?

Hawkins v. McGee

Supreme Court of New Hampshire
146 A. 641 (1929)

Assumpsit, against a surgeon for breach of an alleged warranty of the success of an operation. Trial by jury, and verdict for the plaintiff. The **writ** also contained a count in negligence upon which a **nonsuit** was ordered, without **exception**. The defendant seasonably moved to set aside the verdict because the damages awarded by the jury were excessive. The court found that the damages were excessive and made an order that the verdict be set aside unless the plaintiff elected to **remit**, the verdict was set aside as "excessive and against the weight of the evidence," and the plaintiff excepted.

> ***Assumpsit***
>
> From the Latin *assumere*, to "take on" or "assume." A common-law form of action (see "Forms of action" at p. 89, *supra*) to recover damages for the breach of contract not under seal.

> ***Writ***
>
> Here, the court is referring to the writ of assumpsit. For more on the writ system, see "Forms of action" at p. 89, *supra*.

> ***Nonsuit***
>
> "A court's dismissal of a case . . . because the plaintiff has failed to make out a legal case or to bring forward sufficient evidence." BLACK'S LAW DICTIONARY (10th ed. 2014).

> ***Exception***
>
> "A formal objection to a court's ruling by a party who wants to preserve an overruled objection or rejected proffer for appeal." BLACK'S LAW DICTIONARY (10th ed. 2014).

BRANCH, J.

1. The operation in question consisted in the removal of a considerable quantity of scar tissue from the palm of the plaintiff's right hand and the grafting of skin taken from the plaintiff's chest in place thereof. The scar tissue was the result of a severe burn caused by contact with an electric wire, which the plaintiff received about nine years before the time of the transactions here involved. There was evidence to the effect that before the operation was performed the plaintiff and his father went to the defendant's office, and that the defendant, in answer to the question, "How long will the boy be in the hospital?" replied, "Three or four days, not over four; then the boy can go home and it will be just a few days when he will go back to

Remit

A **remittitur** refers to either (a) "[a]n order awarding a new trial, or a damages amount lower than that awarded by the jury, and requiring the plaintiff to choose between those alternatives" or (b) "[t]he process by which a court requires either that the case be retried, or that the damages awarded by the jury be reduced." BLACK'S LAW DICTIONARY (10th ed. 2014).

work with a good hand." Clearly this and other testimony to the same effect would not justify a finding that the doctor contracted to complete the hospital treatment in three or four days or that the plaintiff would be able to go back to work within a few days thereafter. The above statements could only be construed as expressions of opinion or predictions as to the probable duration of the treatment and plaintiff's resulting disability, and the fact that these estimates were exceeded would impose no contractual liability upon the defendant. The only substantial basis for the plaintiff's claim is the testimony that the defendant also said before the operation was decided upon, "I will guarantee to make the hand a hundred per cent perfect hand or a hundred per cent good hand." The plaintiff was present when these words were alleged to have been spoken, and, if they are to be taken at their face value, it seems obvious that proof of their utterance would establish the giving of a warranty in accordance with his contention.

The defendant argues, however, that, even if these words were uttered by him, no reasonable man would understand that they were used with the intention of entering "into any contractual relation whatever," and that they could reasonably be understood only "as his expression in strong language that he believed and expected that as a result of the operation he would give the plaintiff a very good hand." It may be conceded, as the defendant contends, that, before the question of the making of a contract should be submitted to a jury, there is a preliminary question of law for the trial court to pass upon, i.e. "whether the words could possibly have the meaning imputed to them by the party who founds his case upon a certain interpretation," but it cannot be held that the trial court decided this question erroneously in the present case. It is unnecessary to determine at this time whether the argument of the defendant, based upon "common knowledge of the uncertainty which attends all surgical operations," and the improbability that a surgeon would ever contract to make a damaged part of the human body "one hundred per cent perfect," would, in the absence of countervailing considerations, be regarded as conclusive, for there were other factors in the present case which tended to support the contention of the plaintiff. There was evidence that the defendant repeatedly solicited from the plaintiff's father the opportunity to perform this operation, and the theory was advanced by plaintiff's counsel in cross-examination of defendant that he sought an opportunity to "experiment on skin grafting," in which he had had little previous experience. If the jury accepted this part of plaintiff's contention, there would be a reasonable basis for the further conclusion that, if defendant spoke the words attributed to him, he did so with the intention that they should be accepted at their face value, as an inducement for the granting of consent to the operation by the plaintiff and his father, and there was ample evidence that they were so accepted by them. The question of the making of the alleged contract was properly submitted to the jury.

2. The substance of the charge to the jury on the question of damages appears in the following quotation: "If you find the plaintiff entitled to anything, he is entitled to recover for what pain and suffering he has been made to endure and for what injury he has sustained over and above what injury he had before." To this instruction the defendant seasonably excepted. By it, the jury was permitted to consider two elements of damage: (1) Pain and suffering due to the operation; and (2) positive ill effects of the operation upon the plaintiff's hand. Authority for any specific rule of damages in cases of this kind seems to be lacking, but, when tested by general principle and by analogy, it appears that the foregoing instruction was erroneous.

"By 'damages,' as that term is used in the law of contracts, is intended compensation for a breach, measured in the terms of the contract." The purpose of the law is "to put the plaintiff in as good a position as he would have been in had the defendant kept his contract." 3 Williston, *Contracts* § 1338. The measure of recovery "is based upon what the defendant should have given the plaintiff, not what the plaintiff has given the defendant or otherwise expended." 3 Williston, *Contracts* § 1341. "The only losses that can be said fairly to come within the terms of a contract are such as the parties must have had in mind when the contract was made, or such as they either knew or ought to have known would probably result from a failure to comply with its terms." *Davis v. New England Cotton Yarn Co.*, 77 N.H. 403, 404 (1914).

The present case is closely analogous to one in which a machine is built for a certain purpose and warranted to do certain work. In such cases, the usual rule of damages for breach of warranty in the sale of chattels is applied, and it is held that the measure of damages is the difference between the value of the machine, if it had corresponded with the warranty and its actual value, together with such incidental losses as the parties knew, or ought to have known, would probably result from a failure to comply with its terms.

The rule thus applied is well settled in this state. "As a general rule, the measure of the vendee's damages is the difference between the value of the goods as they would have been if the warranty as to quality had been true, and the actual value at the time of the sale, including gains prevented and losses sustained, and such other damages as could be reasonably anticipated by the parties as likely to be caused by the vendor's failure to keep his agreement, and could not by reasonable care on the part of the vendee have been avoided." We therefore conclude that the true measure of the plaintiff's damage in the present case is the difference between the value to him of a perfect hand or a good hand, such as the jury found the defendant promised him, and the value of his hand in its present condition, including any incidental consequences fairly within the contemplation of the parties when they made their contract. Damages not thus limited, although naturally resulting, are not to be given.

The extent of the plaintiff's suffering does not measure this difference in value. The pain necessarily incident to a serious surgical operation was a part of the contribution which the plaintiff was willing to make to his joint undertaking with the defendant to produce a good hand. It was a legal detriment suffered by him which constituted a part of the consideration given by him for the contract. It represented a part of the price which he was willing to pay for a good hand, but it furnished no test of the value of a good hand or the difference between the value of the hand which the defendant promised and the one which resulted from the operation.

It was also erroneous and misleading to submit to the jury as a separate element of damage any change for the worse in the condition of the plaintiff's hand resulting from the operation, although this error was probably more prejudicial to the plaintiff than to the defendant. Any such ill effect of the operation would be included under the true rule of damages set forth above, but damages might properly be assessed for the defendant's failure to improve the condition of the hand, even if there were no evidence that its condition was made worse as a result of the operation.

It must be assumed that the trial court, in setting aside the verdict, undertook to apply the same rule of damages which he had previously given to the jury, and, since this rule was erroneous, it is unnecessary for us to consider whether there was any evidence to justify his finding that all damages awarded by the jury above $500 were excessive.

3. Defendant's requests for instructions were loosely drawn, and were properly denied. A considerable number of issues of fact were raised by the evidence, and it would have been extremely misleading to instruct the jury in accordance with defendant's request No. 2, that "the only issue on which you have to pass is whether or not there was a special contract between the plaintiff and the defendant to produce a perfect hand." Equally inaccurate was defendant's request No. 5, which reads as follows: "You would have to find, in order to hold the defendant liable in this case, that Dr. McGee and the plaintiff both understood that the doctor was guaranteeing a perfect result from this operation." If the defendant said that he would guarantee a perfect result, and the plaintiff relied upon that promise, any mental reservations which he may have had are immaterial. The standard by which his conduct is to be judged is not internal, but external.

Defendant's request No. 7 was as follows: "If you should get so far as to find that there was a special contract guaranteeing a perfect result, you would still have to find for the defendant unless you also found that a further operation would not correct the disability claimed by the plaintiff." In view of the testimony that the defendant had refused to perform a further operation, it would clearly have been erroneous to give this instruction. The evidence would have justified a verdict for an amount sufficient to cover the cost of such an operation, even if the theory underlying this request were correct.

4. It is unlikely that the questions now presented in regard to the argument of plaintiff's counsel will arise at another trial, and therefore they have not been considered.

New trial.

Before you read Hawkins v. McGee, *you were asked to brainstorm what you believed to be the main purpose of contract remedies. Then, as you read the case, you were asked to make a list of all the possible remedies the plaintiff could have requested, and which the court could have awarded. What many of you probably ended up with was an unordered and chaotic morass of remedial confusion: You wrote down a lot of different individual remedies but perhaps had no way of organizing them into categories that made sense. Fortunately, however, there is a way of doing so.*

The excerpt below argues that, generally speaking, a remedy may protect an injured promisee in two different ways. First, an injured promisee can be protected with (1) a "property rule," which protects its right to the promisor's performance by forcing the promisor to give it the very thing it bargained for. As applied to Hawkins v. McGee, *protecting the promisee with a property rule would have meant requiring Dr. McGee to give Mr. Hawkins the very thing he bargained for, i.e., a perfect hand. For obvious reasons, the court didn't even consider this option, but where the breached contract is, say, for the sale of land or a rare painting, protecting the promisee's right with a property rule makes more sense. Alternatively, an injured promisee can be protected with (2) a "liability rule," which would award the injured promisee money damages approximating the value of the promised performance. This is a bit closer to what happened in the actual case, although we can (and should) discuss whether the remedy actually approximated the value of the promised performance.*

In general, we can think of property rules as constituting "specific relief," because the injured promisee gets the very thing he or she contracted for, whereas liability rules generally constitute "substitutionary relief," because the injured party is getting a monetary substitute designed to represent the value of the promised performance. As you read the excerpt below, ask yourself how you think a court should decide between these two broad remedial categories. We will revisit this issue in greater depth in Chapter 5, where we discuss contract remedies in much greater detail.

THINKING TOOL: PROPERTY RULES AND LIABILITY RULES*

A primitive way to think about law is that for the most part it simply creates *rights*. You have the right not to be mugged, the right not to be run over by a driver who isn't paying attention to the road, the right not to be disappointed by someone with whom you make a contract, and so forth. A first step toward sophistication is realizing that rights are only as good as their protections, and that rights like those just listed can be protected in different ways; the penalties for people who violate them vary not only in degree but in kind. A mugger is put

* Excerpted from WARD FARNSWORTH, THE LEGAL ANALYST: A TOOLKIT FOR THINKING ABOUT THE LAW 188-89 (2007).

in prison, but an inattentive driver just pays for the damage he causes. Someone who breaks a contract probably just pays damages, too, but occasionally a court might order him to perform his promise or else be held in contempt of court, with heavy monetary penalties or even jail time then a possibility. We will talk about these examples and some others in a moment, but the important initial idea is just the perspective: you can understand law better by looking not so much at the rights it creates per se as at the remedies it gives when rights are invaded. Experiment with the idea that remedies *define* rights.

Perhaps the most famous law review article ever written is *Property Rules, Liability Rules, and Inalienability: One View of the Cathedral* by Guido Calabresi and Douglas Melamed.[52] The article suggested that we might think about remedies in ways that go beyond the usual boundaries between legal subjects; instead of thinking about remedies in property cases versus tort cases, for example, we might carve up the remedies used in both of those areas, and others, into two major categories: property rules and liability rules. A right is protected by a property rule if it can't be invaded without its owner's consent. A right is protected by a liability rule if someone can get away with destroying it so long as he pays the cost. The rules don't apply to things; they apply to situations. Thus your car is protected against outright taking by a property rule: a miscreant who steals it will be arrested. The same car is protected against accidental damage by a liability rule: a careless driver who demolishes it will have to pay damages. In effect the careless driver can force a transaction on you that you might have declined. He damages your car and writes you a check—and the legal system is satisfied. But the system isn't satisfied if the thief gets caught and writes you a check. He goes to prison.

So property rules and liability rules differ in the extent to which they require permission from their owners before they are invaded. But we also just saw another way of looking at the difference: the consequences one suffers for infringing them. If a right is protected by a property rule, invasions of it are punished, whether with jail, fines, or punitive damages. A liability rule requires only that the violator of a right pay for whatever damage he has caused. Nobody likes to do that, but it isn't considered *punishment*. Punishments try to force people to behave in a certain way, whereas holding people liable doesn't necessarily do that; it just puts them to a choice: respect the right or pay for the costs created by invading it. Of course one *could* look at punishments the same way. Someone might choose to break a law and accept jail time as the price of the disobedience. But punishments generally aren't designed to encourage that sort of thought. We don't set the punishment for theft at, say, ten years in prison because we want people to steal from others if they think the benefits of the theft will offset the penalty. Rather, we don't want people to steal at all, and the punishment is set to make it unattractive (the fact that it is only ten years, and not more, is the result of other considerations: the cost of imprisoning people, the need to have marginal deterrence, perhaps a sense of mercy, and so on). Now compare the law's instruction not to break a contract, which is enforced just by a liability rule. Some would say this means there really *isn't* an instruction from the law not to break

52. 85 Harv. L. Rev. 1089 (1972).

contracts. There merely is a choice: perform your promise or pay for the damage caused when you don't. On an economic view, the rule invites you to compare the cost of keeping a promise with the cost of breaking it, and to do whichever is cheaper. (Breaking a contract because that's cheaper than performing it is what economists sometimes call *efficient breach*.)

RELEVANT PROVISIONS

For the *Restatement (Second) of Contracts*, consult § 344.

NOTES AND QUESTIONS

1. *Was this case correctly decided?* Do you agree with the result reached by Justice Branch? Do you think he adopted the right measure of damages? Why or why not? Were you convinced by Justice Branch's reasoning? Why or why not? How, if at all, would you have written the opinion differently?

2. *Punishment?* In the introduction to the excerpt above, you were told that the court protected Mr. Hawkins with a liability rule rather than with a property rule. Yet another possibility was mentioned: punishment. Do you think it would be appropriate to punish Dr. McGee for what he did to Mr. Hawkins? Why or why not?

3. *The famous "Hairy Hand" case.* *Hawkins v. McGee*, also called the "Hairy Hand" case, was featured prominently in John Jay Osborn, Jr.'s legal novel *The Paper Chase*, which was adapted into a popular film and TV series. John Houseman won an Oscar for Best Supporting Actor for his portrayal of Professor Kingsfield, a role he reprised in the TV series. So where did the case get its ominous name? Keep reading.

4. *Some additional facts.* According to Hawkins's original complaint, "[T]he defendant so unskillfully and negligently operated and treated the [hand] that by his unskillfulness and negligence, the new tissue grafted upon said hand became matted, unsightly, and so healed and attached to said hand as to practically fill the hand with an unsightly growth, restricting the motion of the plaintiff's hand so that said hand has become useless to the plaintiff wherein, previous to said operation by the said defendant, it was a practical, useful hand." McGee v. U.S. Fidelity & Guaranty, 53 F.2d 953 (1st Cir. 1931).

5. *Even more facts.* How did Hawkins go from having "a practical, useful hand" to one that "has become useless"? Some fascinating background information shedding light on this tragic story was discovered by Jorie Roberts, reproduced in the excerpt below.

CONTEXTUAL PERSPECTIVE: MORE ON *HAWKINS V. MCGEE**

Perhaps nothing is more hair-raising for 1L's than the famed "case of the hairy hand."

Many first-year law students initially encounter the different contract and tort damage principles in the tragic case of *Hawkins v. McGee*. The case originated in 1922 in Berlin, New Hampshire, a small mill town near the Canadian border, when Dr. Edward McGee, a general practitioner, promised to restore George Hawkins' slightly scarred hand to "perfect condition" through surgery. Instead, Hawkins' hand was permanently disfigured and crippled. . . .

One morning in 1915, 11-year-old George burned his right hand while preparing breakfast for his father on the family's wood-burning stove. At the time, George was trying to turn on the kitchen light to illuminate the stove, but an electrical storm the night before had damaged the wiring so that George received a severe shock.

One of George's younger brothers, Howard Hawkins, now an insurance agent in Berlin, described George's initial scar as a "small pencil-size scar" which was between his thumb and index finger and did not substantially affect his use of the hand. Nevertheless, Charles Hawkins took his son George to skin specialists in Montreal after the accident; but there the doctors advised the Hawkinses against doing anything to restore the hand.

During this period, the family physician, Edward McGee, while treating one of George's younger brothers for pneumonia, also became aware of George's scarred hand. Later, in 1919, after returning from several years of medical service in Europe during World War I, McGee requested George and his parents to let him operate on the hand in order to restore it to "perfect condition."

According to Dorothy St. Hilaire, George's younger sister, McGee claimed to have done a number of similar skin grafts on soldiers in Germany during the war, although he later admitted that he had really only observed such operations.

St. Hilaire recollects that McGee, in persuading George to undergo the surgery, emphasized the social problems which his scarred hand might create. McGee encouraged the Hawkinses to allow him to operate on the hand for three years, until finally George agreed shortly after his 18th birthday. St. Hilaire remembers that, while her parents had strong doubts about the operation, they trusted McGee's judgment and were hesitant to oppose George's decision and the physician's advice.

McGee operated on George's hand in the St. Louis Hospital in Berlin in March of 1922. The skin graft operation was supposed to be quick, simple, and effective, and to require only a few days of hospitalization. Instead, St. Hilaire recalls that her brother bled very badly for several days; the sight of the saturated surgical dressings caused her mother to faint when they first visited George at the hospital after what they thought to be minor surgery.

Moreover, while McGee had earlier stated that the skin for the graft was to come from George's thigh, Mrs. Hawkins and Dorothy, then age 13, saw that George's hand was bandaged to his chest. George was, in the words of his brother

* Jorie Roberts, *Hawkins Case: A Hair-Raising Experience*, 66 HARV. L. REC. 1 (March 17, 1978).

Howard, "in the throes of death" for quite a while after the operation because of his extensive bleeding and the ensuing infection. Moreover, the post-operation scar covered this thumb and two fingers and was densely covered with hair.

Howard Hawkins remembered that George's hand was partially curled up and continued to bleed periodically throughout his life. St. Hilaire, in describing the skin on George's chest from where McGee had taken the graft, compared it to thin onion skin.

After the operation failed so completely to give George the "100 percent perfect hand" which McGee had promised, Ovide Coulombe, a lawyer friend of the Hawkinses and mayor of Berlin, encouraged the Hawkinses to take the case to court. He represented the Hawkinses, while McGee engaged three lawyers from Concord.

The jury only awarded the Hawkinses $3,000 for damages, and the final settlement was for $1,400 and lawyer's fees. St. Hilaire believes the jurors, while at heart solidly behind the Hawkinses' cause, were afraid to return heavier damages against McGee because he was one of the more prominent physicians in the area. Charles Hawkins took the $1,400 and his injured son to Montreal to see if any subsequent operations would alleviate George's deformity, but the doctors there said that the grafted skin was so tough that nothing more could be done. . . .

Hawkins' crippled hand affected his employment and outlook throughout his lifetime. After the operation, George Hawkins never returned to high school, even though, in Howard's opinion, "George was very bright, learned quickly, and had a pleasing personality." He was encouraged by his parents to finish school, but would not because, in his siblings' view, he was embarrassed by his hand.

George also gave up tennis and riflery after the operation, although previously he had won several medals as a marksman for the State Home Guard. Because of his hand, George was unable to perform any heavy manual labor or learn to type. He worked for many years in the printing division of the Brown Company, a pulp and paper manufacturer in Berlin, and later in a tire store. He then entered the military service for a short time in 1943, where he was stationed at Fort Devens in eastern Massachusetts.

George married late in life and never had any children. He and his wife worked as a chauffeur-maid team for a wealthy couple in Massachusetts for several years, then returned to Berlin in 1952. After George died of a heart attack in 1958, his widow went to work in North Conway, New Hampshire. According to his family members, George was always very sensitive about his hand and suffered lifelong emotional distress. His parents also grieved until their deaths because of the tragic and unnecessary crippling of their son's hand. . . .

6. ***Revisiting the remedy.*** In light of the excerpt above, do you think that the method proposed by Justice Branch for calculating damages accurately reflected the harm suffered by Hawkins? How might the court have improved its analysis to better capture the harm suffered by Hawkins? What would you have awarded?

7. ***The hand as a machine.*** In an attempt to make the problem of ascertaining damages more tractable, the court analogized Hawkins's hand to a machine. Is this analogy appropriate, or is the machine metaphor more harmful than

useful? In what ways are hands (or body parts, generally) like, and unlike, machines? Keep these questions in mind as you read the following excerpt, which contains a thoughtful discussion of the court's use (or misuse) of the machine analogy. Do you agree with the author's take on the case? Why or why not?

THE HAND AS A MACHINE?*

Something is wrong with law's language of the body. . . .

Quite literally the first analogy taught to many American law students concerns the proper measure of damages in an action in which a surgeon promised to a boy, George Hawkins, with scars from an earlier burn "a hundred per cent perfect hand." The operation resulted in a hand less attractive and functional than it had been in the preoperative state. In the court's opinion, we read, "The present case is closely analogous to one in which a machine is built for a certain purpose and warranted to do certain work." Closely analogous?

Law's language of the body is typically just this cold, this clinical, and this self-consciously metaphorical. . . .

The court's manifest purpose in introducing this far-fetched analogy is to explain its theory of damages: Hawkins recovers (1) his anticipated gain from the operation, that is, the value of the hand as promised less its present value, (2) but no damages for pain and suffering. . . .

If the court introduces the machine metaphor to limit a damage award, the metaphor becomes functional. Presumably if the case is retried, the defendant can get a jury instruction based on the machine metaphor, something like: "Gentlemen . . . of the jury, in determining the value to George Hawkins of a perfect hand, you should regard that hand as if it were a machine that George Hawkins bought." If the metaphor is used in this jury instruction, it is functional, but also clearly a bad analogy; indeed it is functional just because it is a bad analogy. A machine ordered from the Sears catalog is priced to reflect a competitive market in which buyers will demand machines on the basis of their marginal contribution to productivity, and manufacturers will produce them if they can make a profit on the marginal sale. Obviously Hawkins cannot order a hand from Sears or anyone else, and we have no assurance that the price he agreed to pay Dr. McGee reflected only, or primarily, the enhanced economic value of a perfect hand.

In any case, if the court's purpose in introducing the machine metaphor is to provide an economic analogy to limit the jury's award of damages, it does not follow through on this intention. The jury still has discretion to determine the "value of the hand, if perfect"; it is not expressly limited to its economic value and is not told that the price of the operation equals the anticipated value of the hand. Moreover, the court permits the jury to award "incidental damages," without defining these or limiting them to economic losses.

Perhaps all this is wrong, and the machine metaphor is a pro-plaintiff metaphor, and not pro-defendant. Perhaps the *Hawkins* court is not haunted by the specter of a runaway jury award, but rather by the specter of a jury that fails even

---

* Alan Hyde, Bodies of Law 4-5, 22, 23, 25-26, 28, 30-31 (1997).

to see an injury here. Perhaps in an isolated farming community in northern New Hampshire, scarred hands are common, as common as other body scars, missing digits and limbs, the myriad injuries that farming inflicts on the body. Perhaps the court fears that the jury, unless properly guided, might not regard George Hawkins's scarred hand as a legal injury at all. Ah, but if the hand is not a hand but a machine, a machine that failed to perform as warranted, any farmer should be able to see the legal and economic injury, if a scarred hand is not just a scarred hand. Perhaps in the consumer society of today, it is easier to get any jury to imagine that people have a sort of right to a perfect body, but if the New Hampshire jury did not start from this point, both Dr. McGee's promise, and the machine metaphor, might be necessary to get the jury to see that George Hawkins, at least, had a right to a perfect hand. . . .

The notion that George Hawkins's arrangement for an operation on his hand was "closely analogous" to the purchase of a machine was, perhaps, cold and legalistic. The internal evidence from the opinion sustaining this interpretation is mainly silence. The opinion is silent about physical description of Hawkins's hand, details of his life, his feelings about his body, indeed, any detail about the "person" George Hawkins other than the fact that his doctor promised him a perfect hand. I said above that this coldness is not necessarily functional for analysis of the legal issues presented by the case, and I think we can see it as chronically legal. Legal thought absorbed, without much difficulty, the invitation of Adam Smith to imagine economic life as the workings of an invisible hand. *Hawkins v. McGee* makes this metaphor embarrassingly literal. Insofar as it assumes economic meaning, George Hawkins's is the invisible hand; it is made "visible" in the opinion only through the machine metaphor. . . .

[A]ny reader in our culture can, at this point, imagine a counter-opinion that would seek to arouse identification, pity, sympathy, or desire for George Hawkins's body. Such an opinion would include, at a minimum, physical description of Hawkins and personal details about his life. . . .

By imagining this counter-opinion, we may readily see that the actual opinion is careful to efface any erotic aspects of the body of George Hawkins. Its very abstention from physical description creates a legal voice from which desire is absent, so the reader is prevented any emotional engagement with George Hawkins as a person. . . .

Instead, Hawkins's hand is a machine that is bought, constructed, warranted, but not performing. This hand is thus inscribed into the normal regulatory mechanisms of consumer capitalism, mechanisms that include lawsuits and expectation damages.

George Hawkins's hand is constructed as a machine, then, for no particular purpose internal to the opinion, but rather as a typical example of a legal culture oriented away from erotic desire and toward economic self-understandings. . . .

The machine metaphor performs another function in Hawkins that characterizes all constructions of the body in law: it mediates between the "public" and "private" aspects of George Hawkins's body. . . .

Because the injured hand is a machine that George Hawkins ordered, it is private to him; he "owned" it; and the injury to his hand, or the failure to deliver the "perfect" hand he was promised, calls for compensation to him. But because the hand is public, we can analogize it to other objects in our experience, we can evaluate it, we can put a dollar figure on it—and we do so "objectively," by reference

> to "public" or social valuations of a "perfect hand," and not to "subjective" or emotional valuations internal to George Hawkins—or to us. A marvelous metaphor, property, that is always and everywhere public and private! . . .
>
> For many years, when I have taught contracts, I have tried to . . . mak[e] the students conscious of the weirdness of the machine metaphor. I refer to some selected, recent, well-publicized injury, usually of a wellknown sports figure. I ask the students to imagine a lunch table conversation in which people are commiserating with the victim, speculating about the impact of the injury on the victim and on his team, whatever people have actually been saying about the injury in question. I then ask them to imagine a law student saying what the *Hawkins* court said: "You have to think about this as if Bo Jackson's hip were a machine, and now his machine is damaged." Wouldn't people feel that a psychopath was sitting at the table with them?
>
> I pulled this stunt in my contracts class for many years before I understood its structure. When I ask the students to imagine lunch table conversation about Bo Jackson's hip, I am not sending them into their own experience of their own bodies (however problematic the idea of "experience" of your body). The contrast works equally well for students who have had hip injuries and students who have not. Rather, I was playing on . . . the contrast between the "nice" sentimental body and the estranged legal body, that is, between two competing discursive constructions. . . .
>
> Because each of my students can call up the image of the "nice" sentimental body, the felt, sensed, empathized-with body, they can readily grasp the function of the machine analogy as used in *Hawkins* or elsewhere in legal analysis. The very purpose of the analogy may be to estrange the reader or hearer, specifically, the juror who hears the jury instruction based on it, from those feelings of human empathy and commiseration that dominate "normal," "lunch table" conversations about someone else's injury and thus come to seem "natural." I raised above the possibility that this is not how the analogy worked in 1929, when it may rather have created such empathy when it was lacking. However, a contemporary audience almost surely will value a perfect body more highly than a perfect machine.

8. ***What does Hawkins* really *want?*** Why, a perfect hand, of course! But, unfortunately, this remedy is unavailable for both practical and legal reasons. Practically, it's probably a bad idea to *force* Dr. McGee to operate on Hawkins's hand under these circumstances, even if such an operation had the possibility of being successful (can you see why?). And legally, for reasons that will be explored in greater depth in Chapter 8, the court would run afoul of both public policy and the 13th Amendment by *requiring* Dr. McGee to perform an operation. So what *can* the court do? Well, Hawkins was promised "a hundred per cent perfect hand or a hundred per cent good hand." If the court cannot give Hawkins the very thing he bargained for (specific relief), it can try to give him what might amount to the next best thing, an amount of money reflecting the *value* of a perfect hand (substitutionary relief).* But how should such *value* be measured? Keep reading.

* We will explore in greater depth the issue of how courts determine whether to protect an injured party's contractual entitlement with specific or substitutionary relief in Chapter 5.

9. ***Three damage interests.*** In one the most influential law review articles ever written, Fuller and Perdue suggested that courts can protect one of three distinct damage interests when they award money damages: the expectation, reliance, and restitution interests. (Pop quiz: Are Fuller and Perdue discussing property rules or liability rules here?) As you read the following excerpt, which defines and offers justifications for each of these interests, ask yourself (1) which of these interests you think contract law should generally seek to protect and why, (2) which interest was protected by the court in *Hawkins v. McGee*, and (3) what damages would the court have awarded if it had protected one of the other damage interests not identified in your answer to (2) above?

THREE DAMAGE INTERESTS*

It is convenient to distinguish three principal purposes which may be pursued in awarding contract damages. These purposes, and the situations in which they become appropriate, may be stated briefly as follows:

First, the plaintiff has in reliance on the promise of the defendant conferred some value on the defendant. The defendant fails to perform his promise. The court may force the defendant to disgorge the value he received from the plaintiff. The object here may be termed the prevention of gain by the defaulting promisor at the expense of the promisee; more briefly, the prevention of unjust enrichment. The interest protected may be called the *restitution interest.* For our present purposes it is quite immaterial how the suit in such a case be classified, whether as contractual or quasi-contractual, whether as a suit to enforce the contract or as a suit based upon a rescission of the contract. These questions relate to the superstructure of the law, not to the basic policies with which we are concerned.

Secondly, the plaintiff has in reliance on the promise of the defendant changed his position. For example, the buyer under a contract for the sale of land has incurred expense in the investigation of the seller's title, or has neglected the opportunity to enter other contracts. We may award damages to the plaintiff for the purpose of undoing the harm which his reliance on the defendant's promise has caused him. Our object is to put him in as good a position as he was in before the promise was made. The interest protected in this case may be called the *reliance interest.*

Thirdly, without insisting on reliance by the promisee or enrichment of the promisor, we may seek to give the promisee the value of the expectancy which the promise created. We may in a suit for specific performance actually compel the defendant to render the promised performance to the plaintiff, or, in a suit for damages, we may make the defendant pay the money value of this performance. Here our object is to put the plaintiff in as good a position as he would have occupied had the defendant performed his promise. The interest protected in this case we may call the *expectation interest.* . . .

* Excerpted from Lon L. Fuller and William R. Perdue, Jr., *The Reliance Interest in Contract Damages: I,* 46 YALE L.J. 52, 53-54, 56-57 (1936).

It is obvious that the three "interests" we have distinguished do not present equal claims to judicial intervention. It may be assumed that ordinary standards of justice would regard the need for judicial intervention as decreasing in the order in which we have listed the three interests. The "restitution interest," involving a combination of unjust impoverishment with unjust gain, presents the strongest case for relief. If, following Aristotle, we regard the purpose of justice as the maintenance of an equilibrium of goods among members of society, the restitution interest presents twice as strong a claim to judicial intervention as the reliance interest, since if A not only causes B to lose one unit but appropriates that unit to himself, the resulting discrepancy between A and B is not one unit but two.[6]

On the other hand, the promisee who has actually relied on the promise, even though he may not thereby have enriched the promisor, certainly presents a more pressing case for relief than the promisee who merely demands satisfaction for his disappointment in not getting what was promised him. In passing from compensation for change of position to compensation for loss of expectancy we pass, to use Aristotle's terms again, from the realm of corrective justice to that of distributive justice. The law no longer seeks merely to heal a disturbed status quo, but to bring into being a new situation. It ceases to act defensively or restoratively, and assumes a more active role. With the transition, the justification for legal relief loses its self-evident quality. It is as a matter of fact no easy thing to explain why the normal rule of contract recovery should be that which measures damages by the value of the promised performance.

Although Fuller and Perdue, in the excerpt above, express some skepticism with respect to justifying expectation damages, Fried, in the excerpt below, is much more confident that expectation damages are appropriate in the event of breach. Which of the two accounts do you find more persuasive? Why?

WHAT A PROMISE IS WORTH*

If I make a promise to you, I should do as I promise; and if I fail to keep my promise, it is fair that I should be made to hand over the equivalent of the promised performance. In contract doctrine this proposition appears as the expectation measure of damages for breach. The expectation standard gives the victim of a breach no more or less than he would have had had there been no breach—in other words, he gets the benefit of his bargain. . . .

Put simply, I am bound to do what I promised you I would do—or I am bound to put you in as good a position as if I had done so. To bind me to do no more than to reimburse your reliance is to excuse me to that extent from the obligation I undertook. If your reliance is less than your expectation . . . , then to that extent a reliance standard excuses me from the very obligation I undertook and so weakens the force of an obligation I chose to assume. Since by hypothesis I chose

6. ARISTOTLE, NICOMACHEAN ETHICS, 1132a-1132b.

* Excerpted from CHARLES FRIED, CONTRACT AS PROMISE 17, 19-21 (1981).

to assume the obligation in its stronger form (that is, to render the performance promised), the reliance rule indeed precludes me from incurring the very obligation I chose to undertake at the time of promising. . . .

[H]olding people to their obligations is a way of taking them seriously and thus of giving the concept of sincerity itself serious content. Taking this intuition to a more abstract level, I would say that respect for others as free and rational requires taking seriously their capacity to determine their own values. . . . Others must respect our capacity as free and rational persons to choose our own good, and that respect means allowing persons to take responsibility for the good they choose. . . . If we decline to take seriously the assumption of an obligation because we do not take seriously the promisor's prior conception of the good that led him to assume it, to that extent we do not take him seriously as a person. We infantilize him, as we do quite properly when we release the very young from the consequences of their choices.

E. INTERPRETATION

PROMISES AND AGREEMENTS
Is there a promise or agreement?

▼

ENFORCEABILITY
Is it enforceable?

▼

REMEDIES
How will it be enforced?

▼

INTERPRETATION
What does it mean?

▼

PERFORMANCE AND BREACH
Has it been performed?

▼

DEFENSES
Can performance be avoided?

▼

THIRD PARTIES
Does it affect third parties?

> *"I don't know what you mean by 'glory,'" Alice said.*
> *Humpty Dumpty smiled contemptuously. "Of course you don't—till I tell you. I meant 'there's a nice knock-down argument for you!'"*
> *"But 'glory' doesn't mean 'a nice knock-down argument'," Alice objected.*
> *"When I use a word," Humpty Dumpty said, in rather a scornful tone, "it means just what I choose it to mean—neither more nor less."*
> *"The question is," said Alice, "whether you can make words mean so many different things."*
> *"The question is," said Humpty Dumpty, "which is to be master—that's all."*
>
> Lewis Carroll, THROUGH THE LOOKING-GLASS 72 (1872)

Having now explored the nature of promises and assent, the main issues governing the enforceability of promises (i.e., contracts), and how these contracts are enforced by courts (i.e., remedies), we now turn to the problem of interpretation from the 5,000-foot level. When it comes to interpretation, there are three broad categories of problems with which courts are generally concerned: (1) identifying any terms in need of interpretation, (2) interpreting those terms, resolving any potential vagueness or ambiguity in the process, and, where necessary, (3) filling contractual gaps by providing terms for the parties where they have failed to do so themselves. The next case, an old chestnut of contract law, touches on all three issues as the court struggles to ascertain the meaning of the word "chicken." The case is famous, among other reasons, for employing multiple interpretive devices in a well-thought-out opinion to get at "meaning" in contract law.

Frigaliment Importing Co. v. B.N.S. International Sales Corp.

United States District Court, Southern District of New York
190 F. Supp. 116 (1960)

Henry Jacob Friendly (1903-86)

Judge Friendly was a great legal mind and one of our nation's greatest judges. He was the first student to graduate from Harvard Law School *summa cum laude*, and would go on to practice law in New York for over 30 years (1928-59), serving as a founding partner (in 1946) of one the nation's most prestigious law firms, Cleary Gottlieb Steen & Hamilton LLP. In 1959 he was appointed to the United States Court of Appeals for the Second Circuit, where he remained until 1986, when he took his own life. His former clerks include the likes of current Chief Justice John Roberts, and his decisions, which are still cited today, are models of clear, insightful, and penetrating legal prose. According to Judge Richard Posner, Judge Friendly "was the greatest

FRIENDLY, C.J. The issue is, what is chicken? Plaintiff says "chicken" means a young chicken, suitable for broiling and frying. Defendant says "chicken" means any bird of that genus that meets contract specifications on weight and quality, including what it calls "stewing chicken" and plaintiff pejoratively terms "fowl". Dictionaries give both meanings, as well as some others not relevant here. To support its [interpretation], plaintiff sends a number of volleys over the net; defendant essays to return them and adds a few serves of its own. Assuming that both parties were acting in good faith, the case nicely illustrates Holmes' remark "that the making of a contract depends not on the agreement of two minds in one intention, but on the agreement of two sets of external signs—not on the parties' having meant the same thing but on their having said the same thing." *The Path of the Law,* in *Collected Legal Papers,* p. 178. I have concluded that plaintiff has not sustained its burden of persuasion that the contract used "chicken" in the narrower sense.

The action is for breach of the warranty that goods sold shall correspond to the description. Two contracts are in suit. In the first, dated May 2, 1957, defendant, a New York sales corporation, confirmed the sale to plaintiff, a Swiss corporation, of

> US Fresh Frozen Chicken, Grade A, Government Inspected, Eviscerated 2½-3 lbs. and 1½-2 lbs. each all chicken individually wrapped in cryovac, packed in secured fiber cartons or wooden boxes, suitable for export
>
> 75,000 lbs. 2½-3 lbs. . . . . @$33.00
> 25,000 lbs. 1½-2 lbs. . . . . @$36.50
> Per 100 lbs. FAS New York
> scheduled May 10, 1957 pursuant to instructions from Penson& Co., New York.[24]

federal appellate judge of his time—in analytic power, memory, and application perhaps of any time. His opinions have exhibited greater staying power than that of any of his contemporaries on the federal courts of appeals. In addition, his extrajudicial scholarship has been extraordinarily influential, more so, perhaps, than any judge's since Cardozo." Richard Posner, *In Memoriam: Henry J. Friendly*, 99 HARV. L. REV. 1724, 1724 (1986). For a wonderful recent biography, *see* DAVID M. DORSEN, HENRY FRIENDLY, GREATEST JUDGE OF HIS ERA (2012).

The second contract, also dated May 2, 1957, was identical save that only 50,000 lbs. of the heavier "chicken" were called for, the price of the smaller birds was $37 per 100 lbs., and shipment was scheduled for May 30. The initial shipment under the first contract was short but the balance was shipped on May 17. When the initial shipment arrived in Switzerland, plaintiff found, on May 28, that the 2½-3 lbs. birds were not young chicken suitable for broiling and frying but stewing chicken or "fowl"; indeed, many of the cartons and bags plainly so indicated. Protests ensued. Nevertheless, shipment under the second contract was made on May 29, the 2½-3 lbs. birds again being stewing chicken. Defendant stopped the transportation of these at Rotterdam.

This action followed. Plaintiff says that, notwithstanding that its acceptance was in Switzerland, New York law controls under the principle of *Rubin v. Irving Trust Co.*, 113 N.E.2d 424, 431 (1953); defendant does not dispute this, and relies on New York decisions. I shall follow the apparent agreement of the parties as to the applicable law.

Since the word "chicken" standing alone is ambiguous, I turn first to see whether the contract itself offers any aid to its interpretation. Plaintiff says the 1½-2 lbs. birds necessarily had to be young chicken since the older birds do not come in that size, hence the 2½-3 lbs. birds must likewise be young. This is unpersuasive—a contract for "apples" of two different sizes could be filled with different kinds of apples even though only one species came in both sizes. Defendant notes that the contract called not simply for chicken but for "US Fresh Frozen Chicken,

24. The Court notes the contract provision whereby any disputes are to be settled by arbitration by the New York Produce Exchange; it treats the parties' failure to avail themselves of this remedy as an agreement eliminating that clause of the contract.

Grade A, Government Inspected." It says the contract thereby incorporated by reference the Department of Agriculture's regulations, which favor its interpretation; I shall return to this after reviewing plaintiff's other contentions.

The first hinges on an exchange of cablegrams which preceded execution of the formal contracts. The negotiations leading up to the contracts were conducted in New York between defendant's secretary, Ernest R. Bauer, and a Mr. Stovicek, who was in New York for the Czechoslovak government at the World Trade Fair. A few days after meeting Bauer at the fair, Stovicek telephoned and inquired whether defendant would be interested in exporting poultry to Switzerland. Bauer then met with Stovicek, who showed him a cable from plaintiff dated April 26, 1957, announcing that they "are buyer" of 25,000 lbs. of chicken 2½-3 lbs. weight, Cryovac packed, grade A Government inspected, at a price up to 33 cents per pound, for shipment on May 10, to be confirmed by the following morning, and were interested in further offerings. After testing the market for price, Bauer accepted, and Stovicek sent a confirmation that evening. Plaintiff stresses that, although these and subsequent cables between plaintiff and defendant, which laid the basis for the additional quantities under the first and for all of the second contract, were predominantly in German, they used the English word "chicken"; it claims this was done because it understood "chicken" meant young chicken whereas the German word, "Huhn," included both "Brathuhn" (broilers) and "Suppenhuhn" (stewing chicken), and that defendant, whose officers were thoroughly conversant with German, should have realized this. Whatever force this argument might otherwise have is largely drained away by Bauer's testimony that he asked Stovicek what kind of chickens were wanted, received the answer "any kind of chickens," and then, in German, asked whether the cable meant "Huhn" and received an affirmative response. . . .

Plaintiff's next contention is that there was a definite trade usage that "chicken" meant "young chicken." Defendant showed that it was only beginning in the poultry trade in 1957, thereby bringing itself within the principle that "when one of the parties is not a member of the trade or other circle, his acceptance of the standard must be made to appear" by proving either that he had actual knowledge of the usage or that the usage is "so generally known in the community that his actual individual knowledge of it may be inferred." 9 Wigmore, *Evidence* (3d ed. § 1940). Here there was no proof of actual knowledge of the alleged usage; indeed, it is quite plain that defendant's belief was to the contrary. In order to meet the alternative requirement, the law of New York demands a showing that "the usage is of so long continuance, so well established, so notorious, so universal and so reasonable in itself, as that the presumption is violent that the parties contracted with reference to it, and made it a part of their agreement." *Walls v. Bailey*, 49 N.Y. 464, 472-73 (1872).

Plaintiff endeavored to establish such a usage by the testimony of three witnesses and certain other evidence. Strasser, resident buyer in New York for a large chain of Swiss cooperatives, testified that "on chicken I would definitely understand a broiler." However, the force of this testimony was considerably weakened by the fact that in his own transactions the witness, a careful businessman, protected himself by using "broiler" when that was what he wanted and "fowl" when he wished older birds. . . . Niesielowski, an officer of one of the companies that had furnished the stewing chicken to defendant, testified that "chicken" meant "the male species of the poultry industry. That could be a broiler, a fryer or a roaster", but not a stewing chicken; however, he also testified that upon receiving defendant's inquiry for "chickens", he asked whether the desire was for "fowl or frying chickens" and, in fact, supplied fowl, although taking the precaution of asking defendant, a day or two after plaintiff's acceptance of the contracts in suit, to change its confirmation of its order from "chickens," as defendant had originally prepared it, to "stewing chickens." Dates, an employee of Urner-Barry Company, which publishes a daily market report on the poultry trade, gave it as his view that the trade meaning of "chicken" was "broilers and fryers." In addition to this opinion testimony, plaintiff relied on the fact that the Urner-Barry service, the Journal of Commerce, and Weinberg Bros. & Co. of Chicago, a large supplier of poultry, published quotations in a manner which, in one way or another, distinguish between "chicken," comprising broilers, fryers and certain other categories, and "fowl," which, Bauer acknowledged, included stewing chickens. This material would be impressive if there were nothing to the contrary. However, there was, as will now be seen.

Defendant's witness Weininger, who operates a chicken eviscerating plant in New Jersey, testified "Chicken is everything except a goose, a duck, and a turkey. Everything is a chicken, but then you have to say, you have to specify which category you want or that you are talking about." Its witness Fox said that in the trade "chicken" would encompass all the various classifications. Sadina, who conducts a food inspection service, testified that he would consider any bird coming within the classes of "chicken" in the Department of Agriculture's regulations to be a chicken. The specifications approved by the General Services Administration include fowl as well as broilers and fryers under the classification "chickens." Statistics of the Institute of American Poultry Industries use the phrases "Young chickens" and "Mature chickens," under the general heading "Total chickens," and the Department of Agriculture's daily and weekly price reports avoid use of the word "chicken" without specification.

Defendant advances several other points which it claims affirmatively support its construction. Primary among these is the regulation of the Department of Agriculture, 7 C.F.R. § 70.300-70.370, entitled, "Grading and Inspection of Poultry and Edible Products Thereof," and in particular 70.301 which recited:

> *Chickens.* The following are the various classes of chickens:
>
> (a) Broiler or fryer . . .
> (b) Roaster . . .
> (c) Capon . . .
> (d) Stag . . .
> (e) Hen or stewing chicken or fowl . . .
> (f) Cock or old rooster . . .

Defendant argues, as previously noted, that the contract incorporated these regulations by reference. Plaintiff answers that the contract provision related simply to grade and Government inspection and did not incorporate the Government definition of "chicken," and also that the definition in the Regulations is ignored in the trade. However, the latter contention was contradicted by Weininger and Sadina; and there is force in defendant's argument that the contract made the regulations a dictionary, particularly since the reference to Government grading was already in plaintiff's initial cable to Stovicek.

Defendant makes a further argument based on the impossibility of its obtaining broilers and fryers at the 33 cents price offered by plaintiff for the 2½-3 lbs. birds. There is no substantial dispute that, in late April, 1957, the price for 2½-3 lbs. broilers was between 35 and 37 cents per pound, and that when defendant entered into the contracts, it was well aware of this and intended to fill them by supplying fowl in these weights. It claims that plaintiff must likewise have known the market since plaintiff had reserved shipping space on April 23, three days before plaintiff's cable to Stovicek, or, at least, that Stovicek was chargeable with such knowledge. It is scarcely an answer to say, as plaintiff does in its brief, that the 33 cents price offered by the 2½-3 lbs. "chickens" was closer to the prevailing 35 cents price for broilers than to the 30 cents at which defendant procured fowl. Plaintiff must have expected defendant to make some profit—certainly it could not have expected defendant deliberately to incur a loss.

Finally, defendant relies on conduct by the plaintiff after the first shipment had been received. On May 28 plaintiff sent two cables complaining that the larger birds in the first shipment constituted "fowl." Defendant answered with a cable refusing to recognize plaintiff's objection and announcing "We have today ready for shipment 50,000 lbs. chicken 2½-3 lbs. 25,000 lbs. broilers 1½-2 lbs.," these being the goods procured for shipment under the second contract, and asked immediate answer "whether we are to ship this merchandise to you and whether you will accept the merchandise." After several other cable exchanges, plaintiff replied on May 29 "Confirm again that merchandise is to be shipped since resold by us if not enough pursuant to contract chickens are shipped the missing quantity is to be shipped within ten days stop we resold to our customers pursuant to your contract chickens grade A you have to deliver us said merchandise we again state that we shall make you fully responsible for all resulting costs."[25] Defendant argues that if plaintiff was sincere in thinking it was entitled to young chickens, plaintiff would not have allowed the shipment under the second contract to go forward, since the distinction between broilers and chickens drawn in defendant's cablegram must have made it clear that the larger birds would not be broilers. However, plaintiff answers that the cables show plaintiff was insisting on delivery of young chickens and that defendant shipped old ones at its peril. Defendant's point would be highly relevant on another disputed

25. These cables were in German; "chicken," "broilers" and, on some occasions, "fowl," were in English.

issue—whether if liability were established, the measure of damages should be the difference in market value of broilers and stewing chicken in New York or the larger difference in Europe, but I cannot give it weight on the issue of interpretation. Defendant points out also that plaintiff proceeded to deliver some of the larger birds in Europe, describing them as "poulets"; defendant argues that it was only when plaintiff's customers complained about this that plaintiff developed the idea that "chicken" meant "young chicken." There is little force in this in view of plaintiff's immediate and consistent protests.

When all the evidence is reviewed, it is clear that defendant believed it could comply with the contracts by delivering stewing chicken in the 2½-3 lbs. size. Defendant's subjective intent would not be significant if this did not coincide with an objective meaning of "chicken." Here it did coincide with one of the dictionary meanings, with the definition in the Department of Agriculture Regulations to which the contract made at least oblique reference, with at least some usage in the trade, with the realities of the market, and with what plaintiff's spokesman had said. Plaintiff asserts it to be equally plain that plaintiff's own subjective intent was to obtain broilers and fryers; the only evidence against this is the material as to market prices and this may not have been sufficiently brought home. In any event it is unnecessary to determine that issue. For plaintiff has the burden of showing that "chicken" was used in the narrower rather than in the broader sense, and this it has not sustained.

This opinion constitutes the Court's findings of fact and conclusions of law. Judgment shall be entered dismissing the complaint with costs.

RELEVANT PROVISIONS

For the *Restatement (Second) of Contracts*, consult §§ 201 and 202. For the UCC, consult §§ 1-205 and 2-208. For the CISG, consult Articles 8 and 9.

NOTES AND QUESTIONS

1. ***Why did the chicken cross the road?*** Who knows, but if this opinion is any indication, perhaps it suffered from an identity crisis. On the other hand, maybe it was just depressed because a seemingly friendly judge kept referring to it as fowl.

2. ***Was this case correctly decided?*** Do you agree with the result reached by Judge Friendly? Why? What about his reasoning? What are the strengths and weaknesses of his approach? How, if at all, would you have written the opinion differently?

3. ***Burden of proof.*** In the first paragraph of the opinion, Judge Friendly concluded "that plaintiff has not sustained its burden of persuasion that the contract used 'chicken' in the narrower sense." Suppose defendant, rather than

plaintiff, initially brought suit, arguing for a broader interpretation of "chicken." Would the case have been decided differently? Why or why not?

4. *The meaning of "chicken."* Where the parties are in disagreement over the meaning of a contract term, such as "chicken," how should a court determine what the term *really* means for purposes of resolving a dispute? Indeed, how should courts ascertain meaning *generally,* whenever the meaning of a term or phrase is in dispute? We will tackle this question in greater depth in Chapter 6, "Interpretation."

5. *Default rules.* By not defining "chicken" during their negotiations, the parties left a gap in their contract, a gap that can only be filled—if it is to be filled at all—by the courts. Courts traditionally do this by applying default rules or, where none are available, by relying on policy to fill these gaps. We will look at the role of policy in filling such gaps in greater detail in Chapter 6, "Interpretation," but for now, let's focus on default rules. What, exactly, are default rules, and how do they work? As it turns out, most of the rules of contract law, such as the rules that make up the *Restatement (Second) of Contracts,* the UCC, the UNIDROIT principles and the CISG, are made up of default rules, rules that will govern the contract between the parties unless the parties specifically "contract around" them by providing their own rules in their place.* But if the default rules can simply be contracted around by the parties, why have them at all? Quite simply, because most parties do not have the time, resources, or foresight to negotiate around any more than a small fraction of these rules. Therefore, because it is frequently the case that most of the rules that govern a particular contract are not the rules chosen by the parties, but the default rules chosen by the law, their importance cannot be overstated. The following brief excerpt provides a nice introduction to one of the main purposes of default rules—to fill gaps in contracts that the parties themselves did not fill. We will return to the concept of default rules, and how such rules should be chosen by courts, throughout this course.

THINKING TOOL: GAP FILLING AND DEFAULT RULES†

One further . . . set of observations should be made concerning the purpose and function of legal rules in the Contracts field. . . . [C]ontracts are voluntary arrangements created by the parties themselves to carry out their own particular aims. People exchange things with one another because they want to not because they have to, and in fashioning the terms of exchange—who is obliged to do what for whom—they are likewise free, within broad limits, to invent their own rules of conduct and to structure their relationship in the way that best suits their

* While most of the rules of contract law are made up of default rules, some rules—such as the rule prohibiting the enforcement of contracts violating public policy—are "mandatory" or "immutable" rules, i.e., rules that cannot be altered or contracted around by the parties.

† Excerpted from MARVIN CHIRELSTEIN, CONCEPTS AND CASE ANALYSIS IN THE LAW OF CONTRACTS 9-11 (2013).

personal interests. As usual, the structure finally adopted will be the product of negotiation—sometimes protracted, sometimes instantaneous—with each party seeking his own advantage but with both parties, presumably, feeling better off as a result of the exchange.

The role of legal rules in this setting—whether we speak of statutory rules, as in the case of Uniform Commercial Code, or of common law rules—is important but, in a sense, subordinate. If the parties to a contract had the time and the vision to negotiate and articulate every element that could conceivably bear upon their relationship, weighing every contingency and imagining all possible future states of the world, there would be little need for contract rules as such. The resulting agreement, under these idealized circumstances, would be complete and self-contained; there would be no gaps of meaning and no ambiguity of language or expression, and hence nothing would be left for judicial interpolation of surmise. The courts, then, would function solely as an enforcement mechanism, automatically converting known obligations and entitlements into legal judgments.

The difficulty, of course, is that no contract, however detailed, can or will be wholly comprehensive. Apart from limitations on human foresight, the cost in time and money of sorting out all possible contingencies and then drafting the relevant contract provisions would be prohibitive even for large transactions, and the resulting contract would be as thick as the proverbial phone-book (actually, some are). For the smaller, routine transactions of daily business or personal life, anything more complex and time-consuming than a one- or two-page purchase order is obviously impractical.

Having this circumstance in mind, the primary function of legal rules becomes apparent. Thus, the presence of standing rules on which the parties can rely in the absence of a fully articulated agreement makes it unnecessary to burden every contractual undertaking with the costly process just referred to. By saying nothing in their agreement to the contrary, the contracting parties will be deemed to have adopted the legal rules supplied by statue or common law just as if those rules had been agreed to and written into the contract itself. In effect, the parties can go forward on the assumption that they have completed contract *without* the need to reach express agreement on each and every question that might have bearing on their relationship. The legal rules serve to fill in the gaps.

This, in turn, means that the legal rules themselves—if they are to play their gap-filling role in a useful fashion—should reflect the arrangements that the contracting parties, in the generality of cases, would have wanted and chosen had they actually gone to the trouble and expense of reaching an agreed position on the particular point at issue. If it were otherwise, that is, if the standing rules of contract law ran contrary to the arrangements likely, then in order to escape those rules the parties would have to incur additional negotiation and drafting costs, which they would obviously prefer to avoid. Over time, presumably, such ill-fitting rules would come to be viewed as obstacles to agreement and would be changed or discarded.

But how do we know just what arrangements the parties *would* have chosen and agreed to? How can the law, long afterwards, go back and, putting itself in the parties' place, reconstruct a hypothetical bargain between them? The answer is: it can't. All that can really be done by courts and legislatures is to make the very general assumption that the parties to a contract, acting in their own interest, would normally seek to maximize their *combined* benefits under the contracts by allocating risks and responsibilities in the least costly manner. If, for example, it appears that Party A would usually be in a position to deal with a particular risk or responsibility more cheaply and efficiently than Party B, then it is reasonable to assume that the parties would have allocated that risk or responsibility to Party A had they actually taken time to reach agreement on the matter. Minimizing the *joint* costs of performance means that the net value of the contractual pie will be larger. With more to divide up, each of the parties would be likely to get a bigger slice than otherwise. It follows that the "default" rule—the rule supplied by contract law in default of express agreement—should be fashioned with that objective in view.

Once again, however, we should be aware that the legal rules in this field are not obligatory elements of every contract. The parties are by no means bound to adopt those rules, and if their particular interests dictate otherwise, then, in general, they are free to create their own "rules" by explicit contractual provision. Their freedom in this regard is not unlimited—in a very few instances the legal rules are mandatory—but for the most part the parties can either accept or "contract around" the standing rules at will.

6. ***Default rules, party intent, and other considerations.*** In the excerpt above, the author points out that courts traditionally plug contract gaps by selecting default rules that reflect the types of terms the parties would have agreed to had they taken the time and trouble to do so. While this is generally true, this is not the only way of thinking about default rules. Sometimes, it might make sense for a court to pick a default rule having little (or nothing) to do with the parties' intentions if doing so would advance important public policy goals, such as promoting efficiency, fairness, or justice. And, even more radically, the court might even pick default rules that are the opposite of what one or both of the parties would have intended if doing so would incentivize one or both of the parties to contract around this default rule, which would likely have an information-revealing effect while leading to more efficient contracts (can you see how?). Therefore, whenever a court is interpreting a contract, it is important to pause and ask whether it is (1) interpreting the express terms supplied by the parties themselves, (2) implying terms that the parties failed to express but probably intended to govern their contract, or (3) selecting default terms where the parties never intended any terms to govern at all, perhaps because they never considered the dispute that arose before the court. Where (3) is the case, you should next ask whether the court should fill this gap in the contract by choosing default terms (a) that the parties would have selected themselves had they foreseen the contingency before the court, or (b) that advance other important public policy goals, such as efficiency, fairness, or justice.

7. *Speaking of filling gaps.* Notice how Judge Friendly relied on trade usage to fill the gap regarding the meaning of chicken. Do you think the intention of the parties was consistent with such usage? Ought it to have been? Should it matter whether one or both parties were aware of such usage? Why or why not?

8. *"Chicken" and the objective approach.* In the last full paragraph of the opinion, the *Frigaliment* court found that the defendant's understanding "coincide[d] with an objective meaning of 'chicken.'" Read that paragraph again carefully. Is the court saying that the word "chicken" has an objective meaning?

9. *"Chicken" and the subjective approach.* If "chicken" does not have an objective meaning, does the subjective approach offer a better solution? Or is such an approach destined to be plagued by Humpty Dumptyism, where each party insists, as was arguably the case here, that a word means exactly what each party chooses it to mean, neither more nor less?

10. *"Chicken" and the mixed approach.* How do you think the *Embry* court, adopting the mixed approach to mutual assent, would have resolved the dispute in *Frigaliment*?

11. *Resolving* Frigaliment *today.* Judge Friendly applied the common law to resolve the dispute before him, and his approach is, by and large, reflected in the *Restatement (Second) of Contracts* (see "Relevant Provisions" above). If this dispute arose today, however, it would likely be resolved in one of the following three ways:

a. *Arbitration.* First, as the court pointed out in Footnote 24, the parties themselves originally agreed to settle their dispute by arbitration, but never availed themselves of this procedure. Had they done so, the parties would have likely found themselves presenting their case to one or three individuals (depending on the terms of their arbitration agreement) who, though not necessarily legally trained, would probably possess some expertise in this particular area. Do you think this case would have been resolved differently before a panel of experts? Why or why not?

b. *UCC.* New York adopted the UCC in 1962, meaning that if the parties brought their dispute just a few years later, Judge Friendly would have applied the UCC rather than common law. Applying the UCC provisions listed under "Relevant Provisions" above, how do you think this case would have been resolved?

c. *CISG.* According to CISG Article 1, any dispute relating "to contracts of sale of goods between parties whose places of business are in different States" are subject to the CISG where "the States are Contracting States." Because the United States (since January 1, 1988) and Switzerland (since March 1, 1991) are Contracting States, this dispute would be governed by the CISG if it arose today. Applying the CISG provisions listed in "Relevant Provisions" above, how do you think this case would have been resolved?

12. *Maxims of interpretation.* In addition to the techniques discussed above, judges sometimes rely on well-settled "legal maxims" for guidance in interpreting promises and agreements. We have already seen an example of this in our first case, *Pappas v. Bever,* where the court invoked the principle of "contra proferentem" (see Maxim 5 in excerpt below) when it stated that "doubtful language in a written instrument is construed against the party who selected it." Other well-known maxims are discussed below, and will pop up, from time to time, in this and other courses.

SOME MAXIMS OF INTERPRETATION AND CONSTRUCTION*

In this brief treatment we can only quote a list of standard maxims, which may not be complete. The ones most often phrased in Latin are given first:

1. *Noscitur a sociis.* The meaning of a word in a series is affected by others in the same series; or, a word may be affected by its immediate context. The example for the next maxim may be taken to illustrate this one.

2. *Ejusdem generis.* A general term joined with a specific one will be deemed to include only things that are like (of the same genus as) the specific one. This one if applied usually leads to a restrictive interpretation. *E.g., S* contracts to sell *B* his farm together with the "cattle, hogs, and other animals." This would probably not include S's favorite house-dog, but might include a few sheep that *S* was raising for the market.

3. *Expressio unius exclusio alterius.* If one or more specific items are listed, without any more general or inclusive terms, other items although similar in kind are excluded. *E.g., S* contracts to sell *B* his farm together with "the cattle and hogs on the farm." This language would be interpreted to exclude the sheep and *S's* favorite house-dog.

4. *Ut magis valeat quam pereat.* By this maxim an interpretation that makes the contract valid is preferred to one that makes it invalid.

5. *Omnia praesumuntur contra proferentem.* This maxim states that if a written contract contains a word or phrase which is capable of two reasonable meanings, one of which favors one party and the other of which favors the other, that interpretation will be preferred which is less favorable to the one by whom the contract was drafted. This maxim favors the party of lesser bargaining power, who has little or no opportunity to choose the terms of the contract, and perforce accepts one drawn by the stronger party. [These are called] "contracts of adhesion." . . . However, the maxim is commonly invoked in cases that do not reveal any disparity of bargaining power between the parties.

* Excerpted from Edwin W. Patterson, *The Interpretation and Construction of Contracts,* 64 COLUM. L. REV. 833, 853-55 (1964).

6. *Interpret contract as a whole.* A writing or writings that form part of the same transaction should be interpreted together as a whole, that is, every term should be interpreted as a part of the whole and not as if isolated from it. This maxim expresses the contextual theory of meaning, which is, perhaps, a truism.

7. *"Purpose of the parties."* "The principal apparent purpose of the parties is given great weight in determining the meaning to be given to manifestations of intention or to any part thereof."[86] This maxim must be used with caution. In fact, the two parties to a (bargain) contract necessarily have different purposes, and if these are apparent, then the court can construe a principal or common purpose from the two as a guide to the interpretation of language or the filling of gaps. . . . However, if the purposes of the parties are obscure the court may well fall back upon "plain meaning."*

8. *Specific provision is exception to a general one.* If two provisions of a contract are inconsistent with each other and if one is "general" enough to include the specific situation to which the other is confined, the specific provision will be deemed to qualify the more general one, that is, to state an exception to it. . . .

9. *Handwritten or typed provisions control printed provisions.* Where a written contract contains both printed provisions and handwritten or typed provisions, and the two are inconsistent, the handwritten or typed provisions are preferred. This maxim is based on the inference that the language inserted by handwriting or by typewriter for this particular contract is a more recent and more reliable expression of their intentions than is the language of a printed form. . . .

10. *Public interest preferred.* If a public interest is affected by a contract, that interpretation or construction is preferred which favors the public interest. The proper scope of application of this rule seems doubtful. It may have some appropriate uses in construing contracts between private parties. However, as applied to government contracts it would, if applied, be used to save the taxpayers' money as against those contracting with the government. But this is not, it is believed, a standard of interpretation or construction uniformly applied to government contracts.

This battery of maxims is never fired all together. The judge or other interpreter-construer of a contract may, by making prudent choices, possibly obtain some useful guides for his reasoning and justifications for his conclusion.

86. *Restatement (First) of Contracts* § 236(b) (1932).

* [The author here references an earlier part of his article, where he wrote: "The 'plain meaning' rule serves as a last resort, to guide a court that has found no aids to interpretation nor signs of intention in the transactional context and no basis for an 'equitable construction,' and thus falls back upon the literal wording of the contract for which the court does not see any rational basis. Either poor drafting of the contract or supervening unforeseen circumstances have made the contract scarcely intelligible, and the court refuses, under the guise of 'equitable interpretation,' to make a new contract for the parties."—ED.]

F. PERFORMANCE AND BREACH

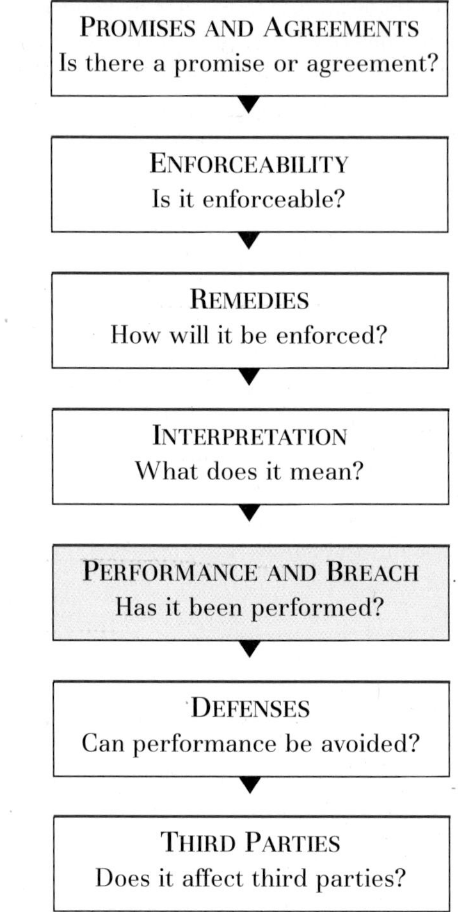
PROMISES AND AGREEMENTS
Is there a promise or agreement?
ENFORCEABILITY
Is it enforceable?
REMEDIES
How will it be enforced?
INTERPRETATION
What does it mean?
PERFORMANCE AND BREACH
Has it been performed?
DEFENSES
Can performance be avoided?
THIRD PARTIES
Does it affect third parties?

How does a court determine whether a party performed or breached its contractual obligations to another party? Let us begin with an easy case. Where a seller has contracted to deliver 100 widgets to a buyer, but fails to do so without any justification or excuse whatsoever, then it is pretty clear that the seller is in breach. Similarly, if, having made this contract, a buyer receives from the seller widgets that conform perfectly to the contract, but refuses to pay, it is pretty clear that the buyer is in breach.

Now let's consider some slightly more complicated variations on the previous case. Suppose the seller delivered 50 of 100 contracted-for widgets, and then promised to deliver the other 50 widgets upon full payment by the buyer. Would this be a breach? Or, suppose that the buyer, having received 50 widgets, refused to pay anything until all 100 widgets were delivered. Would this be a breach? Of course, if the contract had something to say about any of these situations, we would begin our analysis there, but what if the contract was silent on these issues?

In this section, we will examine some of the tools courts use to determine whether a party has performed or breached its obligations, and we will begin our journey by examining one of the most famous (and, for some, frustrating) contract cases of all time: *Jacob & Youngs v. Kent*. After reading this case, you should have a good sense of some of the factors that courts take into account in determining whether parties have performed or breached their contractual obligations.

Jacob & Youngs, Inc. v. Kent

Court of Appeals of New York
129 N.E. 889 (1921)

CARDOZO, J. The plaintiff built a country residence for the defendant at a cost of upwards of $77,000, and now sues to recover a balance of $3,483.46, remaining unpaid. The work of construction ceased in June, 1914, and the defendant then began to occupy the dwelling. There was no complaint of defective performance until March, 1915. One of the specifications for the plumbing work provides that "all wrought iron pipe must be well galvanized, lap welded pipe of the grade known as 'standard pipe' of Reading manufacture." The defendant learned in March, 1915, that some of the pipe, instead of being made in Reading, was the product of other factories. The plaintiff was accordingly directed by the architect to do the work anew. The plumbing was then encased within the walls except in a few places where it had to be exposed. Obedience to the order meant more than the substitution of other pipe. It meant the demolition at great expense of substantial parts of the completed structure. The plaintiff left the work untouched, and asked for a certificate that the final payment was due. Refusal of the certificate was followed by this suit.

The evidence sustains a finding that the omission of the prescribed brand of pipe was neither fraudulent nor willful. It was the result of the oversight and inattention of the plaintiff's subcontractor. Reading pipe is distinguished from Cohoes pipe and other brands only by the name of the manufacturer stamped upon it at intervals of between six and seven feet. Even the defendant's architect, though he inspected the pipe upon arrival, failed to notice the discrepancy. The plaintiff tried to show that the brands installed, though made by other manufacturers, were the same

Benjamin Nathan Cardozo (1870-1938)

Justice Cardozo was one of America's greatest judges, sitting on both the New York Court of Appeals (1914-32) and the United States Supreme Court (1932-1938), occupying the seat left vacant by the retirement of Oliver Wendell Holmes, Jr. Cardozo's influence on American law was profound, not only as a judge who issued many canonical opinions (particularly in tort and contract law) still studied today, but as an author, legal philosopher, and founding member of the American Law Institute, which was responsible for publishing two of the most influential texts in the history of American contract law: the *Restatements (First)* and *(Second) of Contracts*. Cardozo not only possessed a great legal mind, but a penetrating, lucid, and flowery literary style, much to the delight (or chagrin) of law students everywhere. Several excellent biographies on Cardozo have been written. *See, e.g.*, Richard A. Posner, *Cardozo: A Study in*

Reputation (1993), Richard Polenberg, *The World of Benjamin Cardozo: Personal Values and the Judicial Process* (1999), and Andrew L. Kaufman, *Cardozo* (2000).

in quality, in appearance, in market value and in cost as the brand stated in the contract—that they were, indeed, the same thing, though manufactured in another place. The evidence was excluded, and a verdict directed for the defendant. The Appellate Division reversed, and granted a new trial.

We think the evidence, if admitted, would have supplied some basis for the inference that the defect was insignificant in its relation to the project. The courts never say that one who makes a contract fills the measure of his duty by less than full performance. They do say, however, that an omission, both trivial and innocent, will sometimes be atoned for by allowance of the resulting damage, and will not always be the breach of a condition to be followed by a forfeiture. The distinction is akin to that between dependent and independent promises, or between promises and conditions. Some promises are so plainly independent that they can never by fair construction be conditions of one another. Others are so plainly dependent that they must always be conditions. Others, though dependent and thus conditions when there is departure in point of substance, will be viewed as independent and collateral when the departure is insignificant. Considerations partly of justice and partly of presumable intention are to tell us whether this or that promise shall be placed in one class or in another. The simple and the uniform will call for different remedies from the multifarious and the intricate. The margin of departure within the range of normal expectation upon a sale of common chattels will vary from the margin to be expected upon a contract for the construction of a mansion or a "skyscraper." There will be harshness sometimes and oppression in the implication of a condition when the thing upon which labor has been expended is incapable of surrender because united to the land, and equity and reason in the implication of a like condition when the subject-matter, if defective, is in shape to be returned. From the conclusion that promises may not be treated as dependent to the extent of their uttermost minutiae without a sacrifice of justice, the progress is a short one to the conclusion that they may not be so treated without a perversion of intention. Intention not otherwise revealed may be presumed to hold in contemplation the reasonable and probable. If something else is in view, it must not be left to implication. There will be no assumption of a purpose to visit venial faults with oppressive retribution.

Those who think more of symmetry and logic in the development of legal rules than of practical adaptation to the attainment of a just result will be troubled by a classification where the lines of division are so wavering and blurred. Something, doubtless, may be said on the score of consistency and certainty in favor of a stricter standard. The courts have balanced such considerations against those of equity and fairness, and found the latter to be the weightier. The decisions in this state commit us to the liberal view, which is making its way, nowadays, in jurisdictions slow to welcome it. Where the line is to be drawn between the important and the trivial cannot be settled by a formula. "In the nature of the case precise boundaries are impossible" (2 *Williston on Contracts* § 841). The same omission may take on one aspect or another according to its setting. Substitution of equivalents may not have the same significance in fields of art on the one side and in those of mere utility on the other. Nowhere will change be tolerated, however, if it is so dominant or pervasive as in any real or substantial measure to frustrate the purpose of the contract. There is no general license to install whatever, in the builder's judgment, may be regarded as "just as good". The question is one of degree, to be answered, if there is doubt, by the triers of the facts, and, if the inferences are certain, by the judges of the law. We must weigh the purpose to be served, the desire to be gratified, the excuse for deviation from the letter, the cruelty of enforced adherence. Then only can we tell whether literal fulfilment is to be implied by law as a condition. **This is not to say that the parties are not free by apt and certain words to effectuate a purpose that performance of every term shall be a condition of recovery**. That question is not here. This is merely to say that the law will be slow to impute the purpose, in the silence of the parties, where the significance of the default is grievously out of proportion to the oppression of the forfeiture. The willful transgressor must accept the penalty of his transgression. For him there is no occasion to mitigate the rigor of implied conditions. The transgressor whose default is unintentional and trivial may hope for mercy if he will offer atonement for his wrong.

> ***"This is not to say that the parties are not free by apt and certain words . . ."***
>
> With this language, the court is informing future parties that they can contract around the court's announced default rule by providing specific terms to the contrary. *See* "Thinking Tool: Gap Filling and Default Rules" on p. 126, *supra*.

In the circumstances of this case, we think the measure of the allowance is not the cost of replacement, which would be great, but the difference in value, which would be either nominal or nothing. Some of the exposed sections might perhaps have been replaced at moderate expense. The defendant did not limit his demand to them, but treated the plumbing as a unit to be corrected from cellar to roof. In point of fact, the plaintiff never reached the stage at which evidence of the extent of the allowance became necessary. The trial court had excluded evidence that the defect was unsubstantial, and in view of that ruling there was no occasion for the plaintiff to go farther with an offer of proof. We think, however, that the offer, if it had been made, would not of necessity have been defective because directed to difference in value. It is true that in most cases the cost of replacement is the measure. The owner is entitled to the money which will permit him to complete, unless the cost of completion is grossly and unfairly out of proportion to the good to be attained. When that is true, the measure is the difference in value. Specifications call, let us say, for a foundation built of granite quarried in Vermont. On the completion of the building, the owner learns that through the blunder of a subcontractor part of the foundation has been built of granite of the same quality quarried in New Hampshire. The measure of allowance is not the cost of reconstruction. "There may be omissions of that which could not afterwards be supplied exactly as called for by the contract without taking down the building to its foundations, and at the same time the omission may not affect the value of the building for use or otherwise, except so slightly as to be hardly appreciable" (*Handy v. Bliss*, 204 Mass. 513, 519). The rule that gives a remedy in cases of substantial performance with compensation for defects of trivial or inappreciable importance, has been developed by the courts as an instrument of justice. The measure of the allowance must be shaped to the same end.

The order should be affirmed, and judgment absolute directed in favor of the plaintiff upon the stipulation, with costs in all courts.

MCLAUGHLIN, J. **(dissenting).** I dissent. The plaintiff did not perform its contract. Its failure to do so was either intentional or due to gross neglect which, under the uncontradicted facts, amounted to the same thing, nor did it make any proof of the cost of compliance, where compliance was possible.

Under its contract it obligated itself to use in the plumbing only pipe (between 2,000 and 2,500 feet) made by the Reading Manufacturing Company. The first pipe delivered was about 1,000 feet and the plaintiff's superintendent then called the attention of the foreman of the subcontractor, who was doing the plumbing, to the fact that the specifications annexed to the contract required all pipe used in the plumbing to be of the Reading Manufacturing Company. They then examined it for the purpose of ascertaining whether this delivery was of that manufacture and found it was. Thereafter, as pipe was required in the progress of the work, the foreman of the subcontractor would leave word at its shop that he wanted a specified number of feet of pipe, without in any way indicating of what manufacture. Pipe would thereafter be delivered and installed in the building, without any examination whatever. Indeed, no examination, so far as appears, was made by the plaintiff, the subcontractor, defendant's architect, or any one else, of any of the pipe except the first delivery, until after the building had been completed. [Defendant's] architect then refused to give the certificate of completion, upon which the final payment depended, because all of the pipe used in the plumbing was not of the kind called for by the contract. After such refusal, the subcontractor removed the covering or insulation from about 900 feet of pipe which was exposed in the basement, cellar and attic, and all but 70 feet was found to have been manufactured, not by the Reading Company, but by other manufacturers, some by the Cohoes Rolling Mill Company, some by the National Steel Works, some by the South Chester Tubing Company, and some which bore no manufacturer's mark at all. The balance of the pipe had been so installed in the building that an inspection of it could not be had without demolishing, in part at least, the building itself.

I am of the opinion the trial court was right in directing a verdict for the defendant. The plaintiff agreed that all the pipe used should be of the Reading Manufacturing Company. Only about two-fifths of it, so far as appears, was of that kind. If more were used, then the burden of proving that fact was upon the plaintiff, which it could easily have done, since it knew where the pipe was obtained. The question of substantial performance of a contract of the character of the one under consideration depends in no small degree upon the good faith of the contractor. If the plaintiff had intended to, and had complied with the terms of the contract except as to minor omissions, due to inadvertence, then he might be allowed to recover the contract price, less the amount necessary to fully compensate the defendant for damages caused by such omissions. But that is not this case. It installed between 2,000 and 2,500 feet of pipe, of which only 1,000 feet at most complied with the contract. No explanation was given why pipe called for by the contract was not used, nor was any effort made to show what it would cost to remove the pipe of other manufacturers and install that of the Reading Manufacturing Company. The defendant had a right to contract for what he wanted. He had a right before making payment to get what the contract called for. It is no answer to this suggestion to say that the pipe put in was just as good as that made by the Reading Manufacturing Company, or that the difference in value between such pipe and the pipe made by the Reading Manufacturing Company would be either "nominal or nothing." Defendant contracted for pipe made by the Reading Manufacturing Company. What his reason was for requiring this kind of pipe is of no importance. He wanted that and was entitled to it. It may have been a mere whim on his part, but even so, he had a right to this kind of pipe, regardless of whether some other kind, according to the opinion of the contractor or experts, would have been "just as good, better, or done just as well." He agreed to pay only upon condition that the pipe installed were made by that company and he ought not to be compelled to pay unless that condition be performed. The rule, therefore, of substantial performance, with damages for unsubstantial omissions, has no application.

What was said by this court in *Smith v. Brady*[, 17 N.Y. 173, 186 (1858),] is quite applicable here:

> I suppose it will be conceded that everyone has a right to build his house, his cottage or his store after such a model and in such style as shall best accord with his notions of utility or be most agreeable to his fancy. The specifications of the contract become the law between the parties until voluntarily changed. If the owner prefers a plain and simple Doric column, and has so provided in the agreement, the contractor has no right to put in its place the more costly and elegant Corinthian. If the owner, having regard to strength and durability, has contracted for walls of specified materials to be laid in a particular manner, or for a given number of joists and beams, the builder has no right to substitute his own judgment or that of others. Having departed from the agreement, if performance has not been waived by the other party, the law will not allow him to allege that he has made as good a building as the one he engaged to erect. He can demand payment only upon and according to the terms of his contract, and if the conditions on which payment is due have not been performed, then the right to demand it does not exist. To hold a different doctrine would be simply to make another contract, and would be giving to parties an encouragement to violate their engagements, which the just policy of the law does not permit.

I am of the opinion the trial court did not err in ruling on the admission of evidence or in directing a verdict for the defendant.

For the foregoing reasons I think the judgment of the Appellate Division should be reversed and the judgment of the Trial Term affirmed.

HISCOCK, C.J., HOGAN and CRANE, J.J., concur with CARDOZO, J., POUND and ANDREWS, J.J., concur with MCLAUGHLIN, J.

Order affirmed, etc.

RELEVANT PROVISIONS

For the *Restatement (Second) of Contracts,* consult § 241.

NOTES AND QUESTIONS

1. *Was this case correctly decided?* Do you agree with the result reached by Judge Cardozo, and believe that a little leniency was called for, or do you agree with Judge McLaughlin, and believe that the court should have enforced the contract as written? Why? What about their reasoning? What are the strengths and weaknesses of Cardozo's and McLaughlin's approaches? How, if at all, would you have written either of the opinions differently?

2. *Varying the facts.* Suppose that Jacob & Youngs, Inc. ("J&Y") had, at great expense, finished installing Cohoes pipe throughout the entire home and covered up all of the walls. Suppose further that Kent had not yet made a single payment to J&Y. When J&Y sought payment, Kent, learning of the nonconformity, refused to pay until (1) all of the walls were torn down, (2) all of the nonconforming pipe was torn out, (3) all of the pipe was replaced with Reading pipe, and (4) all of the walls were repaired. What result? Suppose it would cost $100,000 for J&Y to complete steps 1-4, but the amount due was only $50,000, and it would not have any effect on the value of Kent's home?

3. *Additional facts.* Does the following excerpt shed any light on the case, or affect how you think the case should have been decided?

CONTEXTUAL PERSPECTIVE: MORE ON *JACOB & YOUNGS v. KENT**

The Reading Company was by its account the largest manufacturer of wrought iron pipe in the country, having provided it for such famous New York buildings as the Metropolitan Life Insurance Building and the Chrysler Building. Indeed, its 1911 brochure asserted that "the majority of the modern and most prominent buildings in New York City are equipped with READING wrought iron pipe" and that "many leading architects and engineers have drawn their specifications in favor of wrought iron pipe, in instances prohibiting steel pipe entirely."

Interestingly, as this last comment suggests, these trade publications made their comparative claims not so much with reference to their competitors who

* Excerpted from RICHARD DANZIG, THE CAPABILITY PROBLEM IN CONTRACT LAW 121-23 (1978).

made wrought iron pipe, as to those who made steel pipe. According to a pipe wholesaler interviewed in New York City in 1975, genuine wrought iron pipe was manufactured in the pre-war period by four largely non-competing companies: Reading, Cohoes, Byers and Southchester. According to this informant, all of these brands "were of the same quality and price. The manufacturer's name would make absolutely no difference in pipe or in price."

The testimony prepared for the Kent trial was to the same effect. If one reads between and around objections and exclusions of evidence it is apparent that Jacob and Youngs were prepared to show equality of price, weight, size, appearance, composition, and durability for all four major brands of wrought iron pipe. Indeed, in addition to other witnesses, an employee of the Reading Company was prepared to testify to this effect. Probably because of this evidence, Kent's briefs on appeal conceded that "experts could have testified that the substitute pipe was the same in quality in all respects. . . ." It appears that this concession crystallized into a "stipulation" before argument in the Court of Appeals, and that Cardozo's reference was to this when he directed a judgment for Jacob and Youngs.

Why then was Reading Pipe specified? Apparently because it was the normal trade practice to assure wrought iron pipe quality by naming a manufacturer. In contemporary trade bulletins put out by Byers and Reading, prospective buyers were cautioned that some steel pipe manufacturers used iron pipe and often sold under misleading names like "wrought pipe." To avoid such inferior products, Byers warned: "When wrought iron pipe is desired, the specifications often read 'genuine wrought iron pipe' but as this does not always exclude wrought iron containing steel scrap, it is safer to mention the name of a manufacturer known not to use scrap." Reading's brochure said: "If you want the best pipe, specify 'Genuine wrought iron pipe made from Puddled Pig Iron' and have the Pipe-Fitter furnish you with the name of the manufacturer."

The contract makes it especially clear that the use of Reading was primarily as a standard. Specification twenty-two says: "Where any particular brand of manufactured article is specified, it is to be considered as a standard. Contractors desiring to use another shall first make application in writing to the Architect stating the difference in cost and obtain their written approval of change." (Jacob and Youngs stressed the implications of this first sentence in their court of appeals brief.)

Why, given a realistic indifference to the maker of the pipe, did Kent refuse to pay for anything but Reading Pipe through three levels of litigation? Mr. Kent, according to some who knew him, carried cost consciousness "to an extreme point." As one put it: "The old man would go all over town to save a buck." Perhaps having paid the extra cost of wrought iron pipe, he felt cheated when not indisputably assured of the highest quality and purity with which Reading's name was associated. However, a Reading representative's willingness to testify for the plaintiff, and the apparent ability of Jacob and Youngs to show the equality of Byers, Cohoes, Southchester and Reading pipes (an equality probably realized by Kent's architect) suggest that Kent may have seized upon the pipe substitution as an expression of other dissatisfactions in his relationship with Jacob and Youngs. A summary of the construction process as revealed during the suit suggests anything but a harmonious relationship between builder and owner. . . .

4. *Apt and certain words?* Cardozo noted that "the parties [were] free by apt and certain words to effectuate a purpose that performance of every term shall be a condition of recovery." What, exactly, does Cardozo mean by this statement? What words should Kent have used?

5. *What words* were *used in the contract?* Here are the words the parties actually included in their contract:

> Any work furnished by the Contractor, the material or workmanship of which is defective or which is not fully in accordance with the drawings and specifications, in every respect, will be rejected and is to be immediately torn down, removed and remade or replaced in accordance with the drawings and specifications, whenever discovered.

Why weren't these words enough? Part of the answer, which cannot be fully appreciated at this time, lies in understanding the law of conditions, which we will explore in greater detail in Chapter 7, *infra*. For now, suffice it to say that Cardozo believed the words used by Kent in the actual contract, though strong, fell short of the "apt and certain words" necessary to create an express condition, which would have required Jacob & Youngs, Inc. to perform every term of their contract before obtaining recovery. But another part of the answer might lie in understanding a little-known but powerful concept called "acoustic separation," bringing us to our next thinking tool.

THINKING TOOL: ACOUSTIC SEPARATION*

[Many of the thinking tools that appear in this casebook are based on the idea of incentives]: people know how the courts will react to various things they might do, and they take this into account when they decide how to act. . . . If courts won't allow the attorney-client privilege to protect conversations lawyers have with clients in crowded elevators, lawyers will know this and will do their talking elsewhere. But sometimes the situation may be more complicated. Jeremy Bentham suggested that laws might be split into two types of commands—the ones that tell people how to act, called *conduct rules*, and the ones that tell judges how to decide cases, called *decision rules*. On the surface these two sorts of rules usually look the same. [A rule, for instance, stating that promises will not be enforced unless certain formal requirements are met (e.g., there is "bargained for" consideration) has two different functions: first, it announces a *conduct rule* that tells the parties what to do to make their promises enforceable, and second, it announces a *decision rule* that tells judges which promises to enforce.]

The interesting question is whether there sometimes *can* be differences between the rules told to people in the world and the rules that courts actually enforce—and whether any such differences are a good thing. Meir Dan-Cohen proposed a thought experiment to illustrate the idea: imagine that the law gave

* Excerpted from Ward Farnsworth, The Legal Analyst: A Toolkit for Thinking about the Law 182-85 (2007).

completely different instructions to the public and the courts, and that neither could hear what was said to the other; imagine, in his phrase, acoustic separation between those audiences. Might this not be useful—and sometimes possible? His leading example is the necessity defense in criminal law. Sometimes committing a crime is the lesser of two evils, and in that case letting the defendant off seems attractive; by hypothesis he did the right thing. But it's worrisome to announce this rule in advance, because then people might be too eager to take advantage of it when deciding whether to commit a tempting crime. . . .

You see the problem, and presumably you see that it would go away if there were acoustic separation—in other words, if we were able to tell people that we never admit the "lesser of two evils" defense but then secretly allow it after all. Dan-Cohen's suggestion is that in fact we do (and should) allow defenses of this kind precisely in those situations where there is some acoustic separation—where the law can permit the defense without worrying much that it will be known and relied upon in the future by people planning their affairs. . . .

The idea of acoustic separation has been applied outside the criminal law as well. In contract law, for example, it has been argued that the legal system has conflicting goals. From the standpoint of efficiency we want to enforce rather strictly the terms of the agreements people make, so they will think hard about their contracts before entering into them. But in some cases there may be an interest as well in giving relief from agreements that have a whiff of unfairness about them. It is hard to have it both ways, but a degree of acoustic separation might relieve the tension between those wishes. The general message sent by the law is that contracts almost always get enforced without reference to the sense of fairness in the particular case; there are standard defenses you might raise, but you won't get very far by claiming that you didn't understand the contract before signing it or that enforcement will be hard on you. At the same time, though, those last considerations may be treated as relevant to a court's choice of *remedy*—whether to limit the winner to an award of money, or to make an order of specific performance requiring that the defendant actually carry out the contract.* The second option is known as an *equitable* remedy. As a historical matter, specific performance was available only from a court of equity; now that there are no separate equity courts in most places, the greatest significance of the "equity" label is that courts can take into account a wide range of considerations in deciding whether to order the remedy. The practical point is that contracts very commonly aren't strictly enforced, at least not in the sense that one *must* perform them. The disappointed party usually just wins money, and often will find in this something less that the full benefit of the contract. But these details of remedy are beyond the understanding of many parties operating outside the sophisticated commercial settings, and perhaps that bit of acoustic separation is for the best. Let people enter into contracts with the thought that

* [We may have seen an example of this in *Jacob & Youngs v. Kent*, where one type of monetary remedy, "cost of completion" damages, was available and would presumably have been awarded had the breach been particularly wrongful or egregious, but where another type of monetary remedy, "difference in value" damages, was actually awarded because the breach was thought by Cardozo to be presumably minor or innocuous.—ED.]

enforcement is strict, and let any lenity come as a surprise. Hide the role of fairness in a maze of obscure doctrines of equity that most parties won't learn about in advance. The conduct rule is clear: honor your contracts. The decision rule is mumbled.

6. *Should courts provide relief from unfair agreements?* Should courts sometimes "giv[e] relief from agreements that have a whiff of unfairness about them"? Why or why not? Do you think that the agreement in *Jacob & Youngs, Inc. v. Kent* constituted such a case?

7. *Or, should courts enforce contracts as written?* Do you think it is wrong to let people "enter into contracts with the thought that enforcement is strict," while intentionally hiding "the role of fairness in a maze of obscure doctrines of equity that most parties won't learn about in advance"? What about the fairness of enforcing contracts as written?

8. *Cardozo, Shakespeare, and acoustic separation.* Might Shakespeare have had the concept of acoustic separation in mind when he wrote *The Merchant of Venice*? In *The Merchant of Venice*, Shylock agreed to lend 3,000 ducats to his rival, Antonio, provided that if Antonio did not repay him by the agreed-upon date, Shylock would be entitled to take a pound of Antonio's flesh. Venice led its citizens to believe that if they detailed the terms of their agreements in a recognized legal instrument (e.g., a bond), then the Venetian courts would strictly enforce these instruments. This is Venice's "conduct rule." However, when Antonio did not repay Shylock in time, and Shylock brought a lawsuit to enforce his bond, the court was (understandably) reluctant to do so. Be that as it may, the court could not simply refuse to enforce the bond, because doing so would reveal that Venice's "decision rules" differed from its "conduct rules," which would weaken its laws in the process. Therefore, a court wishing to avoid the harsh results of enforcing Shylock's bond would have to be quite clever if it were to preserve the ostensible integrity of its laws. Shakespeare, of course, was up to the task.

Shakespeare had Portia disguise herself as Balthazar, a "doctor of the law," to serve as judge in the case. As Balthazar, Portia attempts to craft a decision rule that achieves an equitable result while preserving the conduct rule that keeps Venice's laws strong. In a famous scene, Portia strictly construed the terms of Shylock's bond to allow him to take the pound of flesh from Antonio, but nothing more. If, warned Portia, Shylock took too much or too little flesh, or spilled a single drop of blood, all of his wealth would be confiscated by the state, and he would be condemned to death. In doing so, Portia's hyper-strict interpretation achieved acoustic separation because, functionally, the conduct rule *really did* differ from the decision rule, but formalistically, the two rules *appeared* to be in harmony.

9. *Acoustic separation in contract law.* Maintaining such acoustic separation, which has a long tradition in contract law, also has its dangers, as explained

by Meir Dan-Cohen, *Decision Rules and Conduct Rules: On Acoustic Separation in Criminal Law*, 97 HARV. L. REV. 625, 665, n. 109 (1984):

> Professor P.S. Atiyah suggests an essentially similar account of the role played by equity in contract law: "[H]istorically [equity] may have been especially useful when its existence and extent was not widely known among the mass of the people. If equitable rules are applied on a regular and uniform basis so that they come to supplant the legal rules altogether, then the deterrent effect of the legal rules may be greatly weakened. Who will pay his debts punctually if everybody knows that the legal sanction for failing to do so is, as a matter of course, disregarded by Courts of Equity?" Atiyah, *Judges and Policy*, 15 ISR. L. REV. 346, 361 (1980). "It is, therefore, not surprising that attempts were made to conceal the likelihood of equitable relief or mercy being available, and rather to emphasize the threat itself." P. ATIYAH, THE RISE AND FALL OF FREEDOM OF CONTRACT 193 (1979).

G. DEFENSES

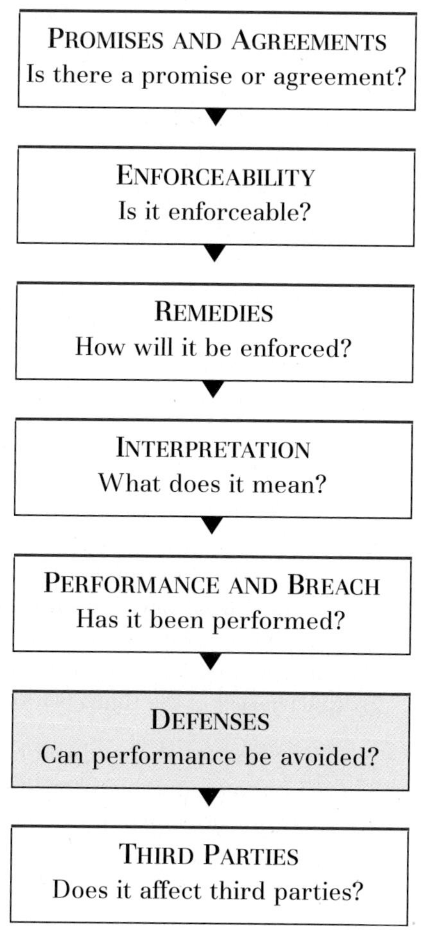
PROMISES AND AGREEMENTS
Is there a promise or agreement?
ENFORCEABILITY
Is it enforceable?
REMEDIES
How will it be enforced?
INTERPRETATION
What does it mean?
PERFORMANCE AND BREACH
Has it been performed?
DEFENSES
Can performance be avoided?
THIRD PARTIES
Does it affect third parties?

Under what circumstances, if any, should courts let parties out of bargains they have made? We will study defenses in greater detail in Chapter 8, *infra*, but it is important to recognize that contract defenses, perhaps more so than any other area of contract law, reflect public policy considerations about the types of bargains that should and should not be allowed. In the next case, we will read about a welfare recipient who defaulted on payments pursuant to a contract containing difficult-to-understand terms. The question confronting the court is whether the terms of the contract ought to be enforceable, and whether factors like the welfare recipient's bargaining power, her legal and economic sophistication, and the fairness of the terms ultimately agreed upon ought to be taken into account in answering this question. As you read the next case, think broadly about the types of promises, if any, that you think courts should refuse to enforce, and whether you believe the promise below should fit into this category.

Williams v. Walker-Thomas Furniture Co.

United States Court of Appeals, D.C. Circuit
350 F.2d 445 (1965)

J. SKELLY WRIGHT, CIRCUIT JUDGE. Appellee, Walker-Thomas Furniture Company, operates a retail furniture store in the District of Columbia. During the period from 1957 to 1962 each appellant in these cases purchased a number of household items from Walker-Thomas, for which payment was to be made in installments. The terms of each purchase were contained in a printed form contract which set forth the value of the purchased item and purported to lease the item to appellant for a stipulated monthly rent payment. The contract then provided, in substance, that title would remain in Walker-Thomas until the total of all the monthly payments made equaled the stated value of the item, at which time appellants could take title. In the event of a default in the payment of any monthly installment, Walker-Thomas could repossess the item.

The contract further provided that

> **the amount of each periodical installment payment to be made by (purchaser) to the Company under this present lease shall be inclusive of and not in addition to the amount of each installment payment to be made by (purchaser) under such prior leases, bills or accounts; and all payments now and hereafter made by (purchaser) shall be credited pro rata on all outstanding leases, bills and accounts due the Company by (purchaser) at the time each such payment is made.**

> ***The "anaconda" clause***
>
> This type of clause is called a "cross-collateral," "dragnet," "wrap around," or "anaconda" clause. What do you think this clause means? Read over it several times to see if you can understand how it operates, as it will be crucial to the resolution of this case. If you can understand it on the first (or second, or third) reading, congratulations! If not, consider whether courts should expect those who are not legally trained to understand it. Keep your answer in mind as you read the rest of the court's opinion.

The effect of this rather obscure provision was to keep a balance due on every item purchased until the balance due on all items, whenever purchased, was liquidated. As a result, the debt incurred at the time of purchase of each item was secured by the right to repossess all the items previously purchased by the same purchaser, and each new item purchased automatically became subject to a security interest arising out of the previous dealings.

On May 12, 1962, appellant Thorne purchased an item described as a Daveno, three tables, and two lamps, having total stated value of $391.10. Shortly thereafter, he defaulted on his monthly payments and appellee sought to replevy all the items purchased since the first transaction in 1958. Similarly, on April 17, 1962, appellant Williams bought a stereo set of stated value of $514.95.[1] She too defaulted shortly thereafter, and appellee sought to replevy all the items purchased since December, 1957. The Court of General Sessions granted judgment for appellee. The District of Columbia Court of Appeals affirmed, and we granted appellants' motion for leave to appeal to this court.

Appellants' principal contention, rejected by both the trial and the appellate courts below, is that these contracts, or at least some of them, are unconscionable and, hence, not enforceable. In its opinion in *Williams v. Walker-Thomas Furniture Company*, 198 A.2d 914, 916 (1964), the District of Columbia Court of Appeals explained its rejection of this contention as follows:

> Appellant's second argument presents a more serious question. The record reveals that prior to the last purchase appellant had reduced the balance in her account to $164. The last purchase, a stereo set, raised the balance due to $678. Significantly, at the time of this and the preceding purchases, appellee was aware of appellant's financial position. The reverse side of the stereo contract listed the name of appellant's social worker and her $218 monthly stipend from the government. Nevertheless, with full knowledge that appellant had to feed, clothe and support both herself and seven children on this amount, appellee sold her a $514 stereo set.
>
> We cannot condemn too strongly appellee's conduct. It raises serious questions of sharp practice and irresponsible business dealings. A review of the legislation in the District of Columbia affecting retail sales and the pertinent decisions of the highest court in this jurisdiction disclose, however, no ground upon which this court can declare the contracts in question contrary to public policy. We note that were the Maryland Retail Installment Sales Act, Art. 83 §§ 128-153, or its equivalent, in force in the District of Columbia, we could grant appellant appropriate relief. We think Congress should consider corrective legislation to protect the public from such exploitive contracts as were utilized in the case at bar.

We do not agree that the court lacked the power to refuse enforcement to contracts found to be unconscionable. In other jurisdictions, it has been held as a matter of common law that unconscionable contracts are not enforceable.[2] While no decision of this court so holding has been found, the notion that an unconscionable

---

1. At the time of this purchase her account showed a balance of $164 still owing from her prior purchases. The total of all the purchases made over the years in question came to $1,800. The total payments amounted to $1,400.

2. *Campbell Soup Co. v. Wentz*, 3 Cir., 172 F.2d 80 (1948); *Indianapolis Morris Plan Corporation v. Sparks*, 172 N.E.2d 899 (1961); *Henningsen v. Bloomfield Motors, Inc.*, 161 A.2d 69, 84-96 (1960). *Cf.* 1 Corbin, *Contracts* § 128 (1963).

bargain should not be given full enforcement is by no means novel. In *Scott v. United States*, 79 U.S. 443, 445 (1870), the Supreme Court stated:

> If a contract be unreasonable and unconscionable, but not void for fraud, a court of law will give to the party who sues for its breach damages, not according to its letter, but only such as he is equitably entitled to.

Since we have never adopted or rejected such a rule, the question here presented is actually one of first impression.

Congress has recently enacted the Uniform Commercial Code, which specifically provides that the court may refuse to enforce a contract which it finds to be unconscionable at the time it was made. [UCC] § 2-302. The enactment of this section, which occurred subsequent to the contracts here in suit, does not mean that the common law of the District of Columbia was otherwise at the time of enactment, nor does it preclude the court from adopting a similar rule in the exercise of its powers to develop the common law for the District of Columbia. In fact, in view of the absence of prior authority on the point, we consider the congressional adoption of § 2-302 persuasive authority for following the rationale of the cases from which the section is explicitly derived. Accordingly, we hold that where the element of unconscionability is present at the time a contract is made, the contract should not be enforced.

Unconscionability has generally been recognized to include an absence of meaningful choice on the part of one of the parties together with contract terms which are unreasonably favorable to the other party.[6] Whether a meaningful choice is present in a particular case can only be determined by consideration of all the circumstances surrounding the transaction. In many cases the meaningfulness of the choice is negated by a gross inequality of bargaining power.[7] The manner in which the contract was entered is also relevant to this consideration. Did each party to the contract, considering his obvious education or lack of it, have a reasonable opportunity to understand the terms of the contract, or were the important terms hidden in a maze of fine print and minimized by deceptive sales practices? Ordinarily, one who signs an agreement without full knowledge of its terms might be held to assume the risk that he has entered a one-sided bargain. But when a party of little bargaining power, and hence

The elements of unconscionability

Note carefully the two separate elements that make up the defense of unconscionability. According to Professor Leff, in a colorful article, the first element ("an absence of meaningful choice") can be thought of as "procedural unconscionability" and refers to "bargaining naughtiness," whereas the second element ("terms which are unreasonably favorable to the other party") can be thought of as "substantive unconscionability" and refers to the "evils in the resulting contract." Arthur Allen Leff, *Unconscionability and the Code — The Emperor's New Clause*, 115 U. PA. L. REV. 485, 487-88 (1967).

6. See *Henningsen v. Bloomfield Motors, Inc.*, supra Note 2; *Campbell Soup Co. v. Wentz*, supra Note 2.

7. See *Henningsen v. Bloomfield Motors, Inc.*, supra Note 2, 161 A.2d at 86, and authorities there cited. Inquiry into the relative bargaining power of the two parties is not an inquiry wholly divorced from the general question of unconscionability, since a one-sided bargain is itself evidence of the inequality of the bargaining parties. . . .

little real choice, signs a commercially unreasonable contract with little or no knowledge of its terms, it is hardly likely that his consent, or even an objective manifestation of his consent, was ever given to all the terms. In such a case the usual rule that the terms of the agreement are not to be questioned should be abandoned and the court should consider whether the terms of the contract are so unfair that enforcement should be withheld.

In determining reasonableness or fairness, the primary concern must be with the terms of the contract considered in light of the circumstances existing when the contract was made. The test is not simple, nor can it be mechanically applied. The terms are to be considered "in the light of the general commercial background and the commercial needs of the particular trade or case."[11] Corbin suggests the test as being whether the terms are "so extreme as to appear unconscionable according to the mores and business practices of the time and place." 1 Corbin, *Contracts* § 128 (1963).[12] We think this formulation correctly states the test to be applied in those cases where no meaningful choice was exercised upon entering the contract.

Because the trial court and the appellate court did not feel that enforcement could be refused, no findings were made on the possible unconscionability of the contracts in these cases. Since the record is not sufficient for our deciding the issue as a matter of law, the cases must be remanded to the trial court for further proceedings.

So ordered.

DANAHER, CIRCUIT JUDGE **(dissenting)**. The District of Columbia Court of Appeals obviously was as unhappy about the situation here presented as any of us can possibly be. Its opinion in the *Williams* case, quoted in the majority text, concludes: "We think Congress should consider corrective legislation to protect the public from such exploitive contracts as were utilized in the case at bar."

My view is thus summed up by an able court which made no finding that there had actually been sharp practice. Rather the appellant seems to have known precisely where she stood.

There are many aspects of public policy here involved. What is a luxury to some may seem an outright necessity to others. Is public oversight to be required of the expenditures of relief funds? A washing machine, e.g., in the hands of a relief client might become a fruitful source of income. Many relief clients may well need credit, and certain business establishments will take long chances on the sale of items, expecting their pricing policies will afford a degree of protection commensurate with the risk. Perhaps a remedy when

11. Comment, UCC § 2-307.

12. See *Henningsen v. Bloomfield Motors, Inc.*, supra Note 2. The traditional test as stated in *Greer v. Tweed*, N.Y.C.P., 13 Abb. Pr., N.S., 427, 429 (1872), is "such as no man in his senses and not under delusion would make on the one hand, and as no honest or fair man would accept, on the other."

necessary will be found within the provisions of the "Loan Shark" law, D.C.Code §§ 26-601 et seq. (1961).

I mention such matters only to emphasize the desirability of a cautious approach to any such problem, particularly since the law for so long has allowed parties such great latitude in making their own contracts. I dare say there must annually be thousands upon thousands of installment credit transactions in this jurisdiction, and one can only speculate as to the effect the decision in these cases will have.

I join the District of Columbia Court of Appeals in its disposition of the issues.

RELEVANT PROVISIONS

For the *Restatement (Second) of Contracts,* consult § 208. For the UCC, consult § 2-302. For the UNIDROIT Principles, consult Article 3.2.7.

NOTES AND QUESTIONS

1. ***Was this case correctly decided?*** Do you agree with the result reached in this case? Why or why not? Do you agree with the court's reasoning? Why or why not? How, if at all, would you have written the opinion differently?

2. ***Some additional facts.*** The following additional facts appear in Kessler, Gilmore, and Kronman's casebook on contract law. How, if at all, do they change your view of the case?

> Mrs. Williams was represented by the Legal Assistance Office of the Bar Association. Her lawyers were willing to allow repossession of the stereo, but plaintiff insisted on repossessing all the items. . . .
>
> Some of the items were bought in door-to-door sales. Frequently the defendants signed the documents "in blank" (the [lower] court's phrase, apparently meaning that blank spaces were left for plaintiffs to fill in later), and the add-on clauses were in extremely fine print, not to mention "obscure" language. Mrs. Williams had made payments of $1,400 on a total debt of $1,800 over the years. Under the add-on [or "anaconda"] clause, each payment was applied proportionately to the outstanding balance of each item so that Mrs. Williams still owed $.25 out of $54.67 on the first item and $.03 out of $13.21 on another item. There were no finance charges. . . .
>
> One major objection to the type of add-on clause used in the *Williams* case is that it gives the secured party, the seller, a continuous security interest in property which, under most if not all state statutes, would be exempt from execution by creditors otherwise unsecured. On the other hand, Professor Epstein defends this type of add-on clause as commercially sound. He argues that since consumer goods rapidly depreciate in value, the merchant selling on credit needs the added measure of protection of additional security to guard against the risk that the buyer will not be able to pay and the items most recently sold will not be

of sufficient value to cover the remaining payments and the costs of collection. Richard Epstein, *Unconscionability, a Critical Reappraisal*, 18 J.L. & ECON. 293, 307 (1975).*

3. ***Was the contract unconscionable?*** The court thought it was, but do you? Specifically, can you find both procedural and substantive unconscionability? According to Professor Leff in the excerpt below, although the contract may have been procedurally unconscionable, it may not have been substantively unconscionable. Do you agree?

> [I]t is not clear . . . about *what* in the contract is bad. It seems, however, that there are two possibilities. First, it may be that the provisions by which each item purchased became security for all items purchased was the objectionable feature of the contract. Or it might be that the furniture company sold this expensive stereo set to this particular party which forms the unconscionability of the contract. If the vice is the add-on clause, then one encounters the now-familiar problem: such a clause is hardly such a moral outrage as by itself meets Judge Wright's standard of being "so extreme as to appear unconscionable according to the mores and business practices of the time and place."
>
> The lower court in the *Williams* case called attention, for instance, to a Maryland statute regulating retail installment sales under which Mrs. Williams might have been relieved, noting with regret that the statute was not in effect in the District. What was not pointed out by the lower court (and *certainly* not by the upper court) was that the State of Maryland had found nothing illegal per se about add-on provisions, in fact specifically permitting them and setting out to regulate them in some detail. Of the thirty-seven jurisdictions which have statutes regulating retail installment sales, only one has a provision making add-on clauses impermissible. In such circumstances it does seem a bit much to find "so extreme as to appear unconscionable according to the mores and business practices of the time and place" an add-on clause in the District of Columbia which is used and statutorily permitted almost every place else, including contiguous Maryland. One's gorge can hardly be expected to rise with such nice geographic selectivity.
>
> If one is not convinced that the unconscionability inheres in the add-on provision, it may be argued that it inheres in the contract as a whole, in the act of having sold this expensive item to a poor person knowing of her poverty. This is quite clearly the primary significance of the case to some of the commentators. That is the kind of action which the Maryland statute does not deal with, nor do any of the statutes like it: the unconscionability of aiding or encouraging a person to live beyond his means (without much hope of eventual success).†

4. ***Paternalism?*** This decision strikes some as overly paternalistic (see excerpts below). Do you agree? If so, do you think it was *justifiably* paternalistic? Why or why not? In answering this question, do you think the fact that

---

* KESSLER, GILMORE, AND KRONMAN, CONTRACTS: CASES AND MATERIALS 600-01 (1986)

† Arthur Allen Leff, *Unconscionability and the Code—The Emperor's New Clause*, 115 U. PA. L. REV. 485, 554-55 (1967).

Williams was financially strapped, on welfare, or had seven children was (or should have been) relevant in deciding this dispute? If so, why? If not, why not? Regardless of your answer to the previous questions, do you think that laws or policies designed to prohibit the type of clause at issue in *Walker-Thomas* are more beneficial or detrimental to the parties they are designed to protect (e.g., the poor, the unsophisticated)? If the former, does this mean that entire markets (e.g., the rent-to-own market) should be unavailable to parties below a certain socio-economic threshold, or perhaps that their contracts should be policed differently by courts to protect them from unsavory business practices? Can such a practice even be justified? If so, how? If not, what does your answer suggest (if anything) about the merits of the unconscionability doctrine? Would you agree or disagree with the following view, expressed by Judge Posner in *Amoco Oil Company v. Ashcraft*, 791 F.2d 519, 522 (7th Cir. 1986):

> The problem with unconscionability as a legal doctrine comes in making sense out of lack of "meaningful choice" in a situation where the promisor was not deceived or compelled and really did agree to the provision that he contends was unconscionable. Suppose that for reasons unrelated to any conduct by the promisee the promisor has very restricted opportunities. Maybe he is so poor that he can be induced to sell the clothes off his back for a pittance, or is such a poor credit risk that he can be made (in the absence of usury laws) to pay an extraordinarily high interest rate to borrow money that he wants desperately. Does he have a "meaningful choice" in such circumstances? If not he may actually be made worse off by a rule of nonenforcement of hard bargains; for, knowing that a contract with him will not be enforced, merchants may be unwilling to buy his clothes or lend him money. Since the law of contracts cannot compel the making of contracts on terms favorable to one party, but can only refuse to enforce contracts with unfavorable terms, it is not an institution well designed to rectify inequalities in wealth.

5. ***Judicial activism?*** Did Judge Wright overstep his judicial role, or was his activism not only appropriate, but necessary? One take on this question is provided in the excerpt below. Do you agree?

> It is of course true that some of his most notable decisions were greeted with harsh and bitter invective. The charge was that he was an "activist judge," exceeding his proper role. This, of course, is not an unfamiliar charge. But since our beginnings, lively, even acrimonious, debate about the proper role of judges in a democratic society has been with us. The judge who believes that the judicial power should be made creative and vigorously effective is labeled "activist." The judge inclined to question the propriety of judicial intervention to redress even the most egregious failures of democracy is labeled "neutralist" or "passivist." The labels are not synonymous with "conservative" or "liberal"; where yesterday "activist" was pinned on liberals, today it's on conservatives. As often as not, however, such labels are used merely to express disapproval of a particular judge's decisions. If useful at all, the labels may be more serviceable to distinguish the judge who sees his role as guided by the principle that "justice or righteousness is the source, the substance and the ultimate end of the

law," from the judge for whom the guiding principle is that "courts do not sit to administer justice, but to administer the law." Such legendary names as Justice Holmes and Judge Learned Hand have been associated with the latter view. Holmes' imaginary society of Jobbists is limited to judges who hold a tight rein on humanitarian impulse and compassionate action, stoically doing their best to discover and apply already existing rules. But judges acting on the former view, and Skelly Wright was one, believe that the judicial process demands a good deal more than that. Because constitutions, statutes, and precedents rarely speak unambiguously, a just choice between competing alternatives has to be made to decide concrete cases. Skelly Wright would argue that in such cases "the judge's role necessarily is a creative one - he must legislate; there is no help for it; when the critical moment comes and he must say yea or nay, he is on his own; he has nothing to rely on but his own intellect, experience and conscience."*

6. *Thinking tools.* Can you think of any thinking tools that we previously examined that either support or militate against the ruling here?

What influence (if any) should the wealth of the contracting parties have on the judge? One approach, offered by Professor Schwartz, is excerpted below. Do you agree with his take? Why or why not? Might defenses like unconscionability actually hurt poor people, or are they more beneficial than harmful? Please explain.

A REEXAMINATION OF NONSUBSTANTIVE UNCONSCIONABILITY†

The doctrine of unconscionability, which a court may invoke to invalidate a contract, has a nonsubstantive and a substantive branch. Nonsubstantive unconscionability arises when certain factors, such as a lack of commercial sophistication, apparently prevent a contracting party from exercising his freedom to choose the terms of an agreement. Substantive unconscionability arises when a contract yields a result that affects a contracting party too harshly or that affects a non-contracting party adversely. Such contracts may include an agreement containing a disclaimer of warranties or an assignment of wages. These two branches of unconscionability hereinafter are labeled "nonsubstantive" factors or objections and "substantive" factors or objections, respectively.[4]

This article explores the nonsubstantive objections to the enforcement of a contract. These objections fall into four categories. The first category, poverty, involves those situations where a poor consumer, although he would prefer not to bear certain risks under a contract, can afford only with great difficulty an agreement that allocates these risks to the seller. . . .

---

* William J. Brennan, Jr., *In Memoriam: J. Skelly Wright*, 102 HARV. L. REV. 361, 361-62 (1988).

† Excerpted from Alan Schwartz, *A Reexamination of Nonsubstantive Unconscionability*, 63 VA. L. REV. 1053, 1053-54, 1054-55, 1056-59 (1977).

4. The nonsubstantive factors are more commonly labeled "procedural" factors. . . .

This article seeks to demonstrate that the first three categories of nonsubstantive objections described above do not support a decision to invalidate a contract. To the contrary, the factor relating to poverty actually weighs in favor of enforcing an agreement. . . .

A contracting party's poverty is commonly thought to militate in four ways against enforcing an agreement. First, poverty may impede the buyer's efforts to purchase a "fair" contract. The cost of a contract reflects, among other things, the agreement's allocation of risk between buyer and seller. For example, a contract disclaiming product warranties usually is cheaper than a contract providing such warranties. Although an affluent buyer often can pay the premium necessary to induce a seller to assume significant risks under a contract, a poor buyer may experience great difficulty in trying to buy away disfavored terms.

Second, poverty is thought to correlate strongly with a buyer's lack of commercial sophistication. A poor consumer, therefore, is often said to be at a disadvantage relative to more affluent parties in understanding and negotiating contracts. Third, poverty may restrict the flow of commercial information to poor consumers. If sellers provide less information in ghetto markets than in other markets, even a poor consumer skilled in bargaining may be unable to evaluate the terms of a proposed agreement. Fourth, poverty may exacerbate the consequences of certain contract clauses. An acceleration clause, for example, may bear more harshly upon a poor consumer than upon an affluent consumer. . . .

Prohibiting a contract clause because a poor buyer finds it difficult to purchase more favorable terms yields a nonoptimal result. Assume, for example, that a retailer is offering two contracts that are identical except for one clause: the first contract, which costs $100, includes a warranty against product defects, while the second contract, which costs $90, includes a disclaimer of the warranty. The hypothetical retailer has customers for both contracts, but the state, by statute or judicial opinion, later bans the warranty disclaimer. Under these circumstances, the prohibition against warranty disclaimers neither helps nor hurts those customers who would have purchased warranty coverage. The prohibition, however, harms the customers who would have purchased a contract disclaiming all warranties. These consumers apparently value the insurance against product defects provided by a warranty less than they value other uses for their $10. Therefore, the prohibition against disclaimers yields a nonoptimal result: some buyers regard themselves as worse off than before the ban, and no buyers regard themselves as better off.

This result is particularly undesirable because banning warranty disclaimers is likely to affect the poor more adversely than the affluent. A poor person spends a large percentage of his income on goods for which his demand is income-inelastic, *e.g.*, food, shelter, and clothing. As his income rises, he will begin to purchase goods for which his demand is more income-elastic. Analysis indicates that a poor person's demand for warranty protection is probably more income-elastic than that for "necessities." Many of the contract clauses that are now of concern, such as warranty disclaimers, shift purchase risks to buyers. Poor people generally are more risk averse than rich people because they cannot withstand large losses. The poor, however, may lose relatively less than the middle class when purchase risks materialize because, in the circumstances discussed here, the poor have less at stake. For example, middle class buyers who default may lose valuable property, while poor buyers have much less property to lose. Also, accidents may cause middle class buyers to lose wages, while poor buyers on welfare may lose no income at all. Because a poor person, thus, is probably more anxious than a rich person to forego the insurance a warranty affords, prohibiting warranty disclaimers or other contract clauses will bear more harshly upon the poor than upon the affluent. Therefore, a contracting party's poverty, other things being equal, should militate in favor of, rather than against, enforcing a contract clause.

Does the Walker-Thomas *decision strike you as paternalistic? If so, is this a bad thing? Should the law sometimes be paternalistic? Why or why not? We dealt with this argument once before, when we discussed* Baby M, *and revisit it again in the excerpt below. Do you agree with the author? Why or why not?*

LEGISLATURES AND PATERNALISM*

In the sphere of contract, the judicial decisions most likely to be paternalist in their motivation, at least in substantial part, are those in which a contract term is imposed or invalidated despite the contrary intention of the parties. Even these outcomes may be substantially induced by a desire to achieve a greater measure of efficiency or a fairer distribution of resources. But I agree with those who find the notions of unfair overreaching and unequal bargaining power in these cases (and to a lesser extent, some uses of the notions of coercion and duress) proxies for the idea that one of the contracting parties simply did not know what was in his own best interest.

For present purposes, the important point is that in a wide range of human activity—even those touching sensitive moral nerves—the courts are reluctant to invoke common law principles to invalidate private choice. And despite the charter granted to the courts by the Uniform Commercial Code's unconscionability provision,[66] such decisions remain especially rare in the realm of commercial and consumer sales. The landmark decisions declining enforcement of written provisions—decisions like *Henningsen v. Bloomfield Motors, Inc.*, and *Williams v. Walker-Thomas Furniture Co.*—are beginning to stand out in the casebooks as curiosities.

Indeed, the *Williams* case, which cast doubt on the validity of a particularly troublesome credit arrangement in an installment sale of consumer goods to a person on welfare, was far from clear about the basis of the holding: was it the procedural irregularities suggested by the record, the unfairness of the arrangement, or some combination of both? To the extent that procedural irregularities (such as lack of adequate notice of the nature and impact of the arrangement) lay at the root of the holding, it can hardly be classified as paternalist. To the extent that the court's true goal was substantive but was dressed in procedural

---

* Excerpted from David L. Shapiro, *Courts, Legislatures and Paternalism*, 74 VA. L. REV. 519, 534-36 (1988).

66. U.C.C. § 2-302 (1978).

clothing, the decision may underscore even reformist judges' unwillingness to take an openly paternalist stance. Finally, to the extent that the opinion reveals a paternalist readiness to invalidate a credit arrangement that a consumer was willing to enter in order to get the goods she wanted, that readiness has not met with universal approval. One critic, for example, has suggested that such an approach smacks of condescension toward a class: "[T]he benevolent have a tendency to colonize, whether geographically or legally."[70]

For the most part, then, courts are still reluctant—at least when acting without legislative guidance or mandate—to interfere with sales agreements that people apparently regard as in their interests, even though if the world were a better and fairer place, they might not have to enter such bargains.

As you read the excerpt below, try to see how the theory of second best, which is related to the concepts of marginal analysis and efficiency that we discussed earlier, applies to Williams v. Walker-Thomas *and other similar cases. Should the considerations discussed below be taken into account by courts like* Walker-Thomas *when deciding whether to apply a given defense to a contract dispute? Why or why not?*

THINKING TOOL: THE THEORY OF SECOND BEST*

One view of the danger we are discussing is known as the theory of second best. It's complicated to demonstrate formally, but the thrust of it is this: suppose there is some set of conditions that you would like to create; they are "optimal," or first best. Unfortunately you can't fulfill all the conditions, but perhaps you can fulfill three out of four. Is it clear that you should? Not necessarily; satisfying some of the conditions (but not all) might be worse than doing nothing. To say it in slightly less abstract terms . . . : ideally—or at least ideally from an economic standpoint—we might like to see the whole world running efficiently. But if we can't get to that result, we should at least make as much of it go efficiently as we can, right? Again, not necessarily. Settling for a "second best" change might actually do more harm than good because it might cause substitutions elsewhere that are inefficient (i.e., that cause waste) and offset whatever good the first change did. That wouldn't be a problem in a first-best world, because in that world there is efficiency at every margin. But in a world where we can only control some margins, changes that improve the ones we can control might make things worse along the others we can't control. And sometimes the bad effects can outweigh the good.

Here is an example of how this line of thinking works, suggested by Thomas Ulen.[30] A man named Tunkl showed up at a public hospital in California. The

70. Leff, *Unconscionability and the Code—The Emperor's New Clause*, 115 U. PA. L. REV. 485, 557 (1967).

* Excerpted from WARD FARNSWORTH, THE LEGAL ANALYST: A TOOLKIT FOR THINKING ABOUT THE LAW 30-32 (2007).

30. The following discussion is condensed from Thomas S. Ulen, *Courts, Legislatures, and the General Theory of Second Best in Law and Economics*, 73 CHI.-KENT L. REV. 189 (1998).

hospital wouldn't treat him unless he signed a waiver of his right to site (or his estate's right to sue) if anything went wrong. Tunkl signed the waiver and died in the hospital soon after. His wife sued. The waiver Tunkl signed was held to be unenforceable; the California Supreme Court said, among other things, that the imbalance of bargaining power between the parties was too great to treat the contract as valid. It was a "contract of adhesion," meaning that Tunkl had to take it or leave it; there was no chance to negotiate over the terms, and under the circumstances he might have been likely to sign it no matter what it said.

Was the decision in Tunkl's case efficient? Normally it would seem inefficient to stop two parties from making any sort of contract that suits them, including a waiver of the right of one to sue the other. Presumably they wouldn't sign it unless they both thought it would make them better off, and the loss of that amount by which they would be made better off seems like a waste. To put it concretely, maybe some hospitals won't treat people like Tunkl because they are too afraid of being sued—and that would be a shame if the patients in Tunkl's position would have been willing to waive their right to sue in order to get treated. In that case there would be an outcome—treatment, but with a waiver—that both sides would have liked, yet instead the patient gets no help. But maybe all this is wrong. Perhaps this particular contract might not have been efficient after all because there was no chance to negotiate over it. Maybe if there were time to bargain (imagine that the patient isn't in such a hurry to pick a hospital), no such waiver would ever be signed. In that case it's more efficient not to allow these waivers because that is the result the parties would reach for themselves if they were making their decisions in a well-functioning market rather than at the front door of an emergency room.

If this last idea is right, it might seem like a strong argument against enforcing the waiver. And maybe it is. But a possible problem with this analysis is suggested by the theory of the second best. We can control one margin of this situation, but not all the margins. If research hospitals can't get patients to sign waivers that stand up in court, maybe they react to the financial consequences by making other changes: they stop paying their doctors quite as much, and those doctors leave and work at other hospitals with different priorities. Now less research is conducted and fewer discoveries are made. This overall result might be inefficient; the lost value of those discoveries might be greater than the losses you would get if you simply enforced those nasty waivers despite the imbalance of bargaining power. We got rid of a small source of waste but created a bigger one. Maybe to get real efficiency the courts should forbid the waivers and then the legislature should give larger subsidies to research hospitals. But if it turns out that we can do the former but not the latter, it's not clear that the former is worth doing at all; that is the point of second-best theory. Just forbidding the waiver might appear to be the second-best solution (getting rid of one market failure is better than nothing), but sometimes the second-best solution actually makes things worse because of its side effects (or "external costs"). . . . When you correct one failure of the market, you might just shift more pressure onto some other failure you didn't correct, perhaps because you couldn't.

How would you complete the following opinion? Would you follow Walker-Thomas *above, or do the facts here dictate a different outcome?*

PROBLEM: COMPLETE THE OPINION

On August 31, 1965, the plaintiffs, who are welfare recipients, agreed to purchase a home freezer unit for $900 as the result of a visit from a salesman representing Your Shop At Home Service, Inc. With the addition of the time credit charges, credit life insurance, credit property insurance, and sales tax, the purchase price totaled $1,234.80. Thus far the plaintiffs have paid $619.88 toward their purchase. The defendant claims that with various added credit charges paid for an extension of time there is a balance of $819.81 still due from the plaintiffs. The uncontroverted proof at the trial established that the freezer unit, when purchased, had a maximum retail value of approximately $300. The question is whether this transaction and the resulting contract could be considered unconscionable within the meaning of UCC § 2-302. . . .

H. THIRD PARTIES

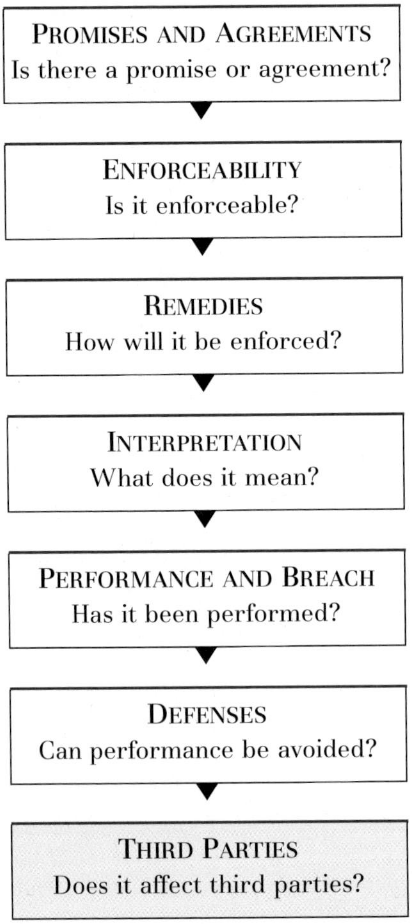

PROMISES AND AGREEMENTS
Is there a promise or agreement?

▼

ENFORCEABILITY
Is it enforceable?

▼

REMEDIES
How will it be enforced?

▼

INTERPRETATION
What does it mean?

▼

PERFORMANCE AND BREACH
Has it been performed?

▼

DEFENSES
Can performance be avoided?

▼

THIRD PARTIES
Does it affect third parties?

We conclude our 5,000-foot overview of contract law by taking a look at the leading case on the rights and duties of third parties. To set it up, imagine the following scenario: You were kind enough to loan me $300 last week (thank you!), and I'm heading to your house, cash in hand, to pay you back. On my way, I'm stopped by an old friend, Mr. Deadbeat, who asks me if he can borrow some money. Deadbeat's a mischievous fellow, and there's no telling what he will do with the money, but that's a story for later.* Anyway, I tell Mr. Deadbeat I only have $300, but that I owe it to a student in my contracts class. "Look here," he says, "I get paid tomorrow, and you know I'm good for it. Lend me the money for a day, and I promise I'll pay your student $300 tomorrow." "Okeydokey," I say, partly because one of your classmates, who was standing nearby, heard the entire conversation, and I didn't want her to think that her professor was too cheap (or unwilling) to help an old friend. So, I loan my friend the money, and we all know what happens next (this is, after all, a hypothetical scenario ominously appearing before a contracts case that features a party named "Mr. Deadbeat"). One day passes, then two, then three . . . but my friend, of course, never pays you. What should you do?

Well, because I'm the one who borrowed $300 from you, you could always sue me, and that would certainly be a logical thing to do. On the other hand, Mr. Deadbeat *did* promise me that he would pay the money to you, and one of your friends *did* hear him make that promise. After giving the matter some thought, you think it's probably not a great idea, as a general rule, to go around suing professors while you're still taking classes from them, and you are downright convinced that it's a bad idea to sue a contracts professor in a contract dispute—who knows what kind of wily arguments they'll cook up. So, naturally, you do the next best thing: you sue my friend. Your argument, of course, is that you were a third-party beneficiary of Mr. Deadbeat's promise. Mr. Deadbeat's defense, on the other hand, is that because his contract was with me, not you, he should owe you nothing. Pretty interesting case so far, right? What should a court hearing this dispute do? Funny you should ask. Roughly the same thing happened about a century and a half ago, and the court, in its decision, established a rule that still governs the case between you and my friend today. So, let's jump in our legal time machine and go back to the year 1859 to see what happened!

Lawrence v. Fox

Court of Appeals of New York
20 N.Y. 268 (1859)

Appeal from the Superior Court of the City of Buffalo. On the trial before Mr. Justice Masten, it appeared by the evidence of a by-stander that one Holly, in November, 1857, at the request of the defendant [Fox], loaned and advanced to him $300, stating at the time that he owed that sum to the plaintiff [Lawrence]

* *See* "Contextual Perspective: More on *Lawrence v. Fox*," following the case.

for money borrowed of him, and had agreed to pay it to him the then next day; that the defendant in consideration thereof, at the time of receiving the money, promised to pay it to the plaintiff the then next day. Upon this state of facts the defendant moved for a nonsuit, upon three several grounds, viz.: That there was no proof tending to show that Holly was indebted to the plaintiff; that the agreement by the defendant with Holly to pay the plaintiff was void for want of consideration, and that there was no privity between the plaintiff and defendant. The court overruled the motion, and the counsel for the defendant excepted. The cause was then submitted to the jury, and they found a verdict for the plaintiff for the amount of the loan and interest, $344.66, upon which judgment was entered; from which the defendant appealed to the Superior Court, at general term, where the judgment was affirmed, and the defendant appealed to this court. . . .

H. GRAY, J. . . . [On appeal, defendant argues that his promise to pay plaintiff $300] was void for the want of consideration. It is now more than a quarter of a century since it was settled by the Supreme Court of this State . . . that a promise . . . like the one under consideration was valid. . . . *Farley v. Cleaveland,* 4 *Cow.* 432. In that case one Moon owed Farley and sold to Cleaveland a quantity of hay, in consideration of which Cleaveland promised to pay Moon's debt to Farley; and the decision in favor of Farley's right to recover was placed upon the ground that the hay received by Cleaveland from Moon was a valid consideration for Cleaveland's promise to pay Farley. . . . The report of that case shows that the promise was not only made to Moon but to the plaintiff Farley. **In this case the promise was made to Holly and not expressly to the plaintiff**; and this difference between the two cases presents the question, raised by the defendant's objection, as to the want of privity between the plaintiff and defendant. . . .

But it is urged that because the defendant was not in any sense a trustee of the property of Holly for the benefit of the plaintiff, the law will not imply a promise. I agree that many of the cases where a promise was implied were cases of trusts, created for the benefit of the promiser . . . , [but] it proves nothing against the application of the rule to this case. . . . In this case the defendant, upon ample consideration received from Holly, promised Holly to pay his debt to the plaintiff; the consideration received and the promise to Holly made it as plainly his duty to pay the plaintiff as if the money had been remitted to him for that purpose, and as well implied a promise to do so as if he had been made a trustee of property. . . . **The principle illustrated by the example so frequently quoted (which concisely states the case in hand) "that a promise made to one for the benefit of another, he for whose benefit it is made may bring an action for its breach," has been applied to trust cases, not because it was exclusively applicable to**

Should the court imply a promise?

Because the defendant never expressly made a promise to the plaintiff to pay him $300, the court struggles (see paragraph below) with whether such a promise should be implied. Do you think the court should imply such a promise? Why or why not?

A principle of law?

The theory animating trust law is that a trustee has a fiduciary duty to act for the benefit of the named beneficiaries. The traditional theory animating contract law, on the other hand, is that each party bargains with one another at arm's

those cases, but because it was a principle of law, and as such applicable to those cases. . . .

No one can doubt that he owes the sum of money demanded of him, or that in accordance with his promise it was his duty to have paid it to the plaintiff; nor can it be doubted that whatever may be the diversity of opinion elsewhere, the adjudications in this State, from a very early period, approved by experience, have established the defendant's liability; if, therefore, it could be shown that a more strict and technically accurate application of the rules applied, would lead to a different result (which I by no means concede), the effort should not be made in the face of manifest justice.

The judgment should be affirmed. . . .

length to advance its own interests. Despite the court's rhetoric, therefore, the principle referred to here is far from being a general "principle of law," otherwise the case would have never made its way to the state's highest court. Rather, what the court is being asked to decide is *whether* this principle should become operative either (a) in this case, or (b) in contract law in general. What do you think? *See* "Thinking Tool: Ex Ante v. Ex Post, and a Note on Formalism v. Realism" following this case (p. 163).

COMSTOCK, J. **(dissenting.)** The plaintiff had nothing to do with the promise on which he brought this action. It was not made to him, nor did the consideration proceed from him. If he can maintain the suit, it is because an anomaly has found its way into the law on this subject. In general, there must be privity of contract. The party who sues upon a promise must be the promisee, or he must have some legal interest in the undertaking. In this case, it is plain that Holly, who loaned the money to the defendant, and to whom the promise in question was made, could at any time have claimed that it should be performed to himself personally. He had lent the money to the defendant, and at the same time directed the latter to pay the sum to the plaintiff. This direction he could countermand, and if he had done so, manifestly the defendant's promise to pay according to the direction would have ceased to exist. The plaintiff would receive a benefit by a complete execution of the arrangement, but the arrangement itself was between other parties, and was under their exclusive control. If the defendant had paid the money to Holly, his debt would have been discharged thereby. So Holly might have released the demand or assigned it to another person, or the parties might have annulled the promise now in question, and designated some other creditor of Holly as the party to whom the money should be paid. It has never been claimed, that in a case thus situated, the right of a third person to sue upon the promise rested on any sound principle of law. We are to inquire whether the rule has been so established by positive authority. . . .

In the case before us there was nothing in the nature of a trust or agency. The defendant borrowed the money of Holly and received it as his own. The plaintiff had no right in the fund, legal or equitable. The promise to repay the money created an obligation in favor of the lender to whom it was made and not in favor of any one else. . . .

The judgment of the court below should therefore be reversed, and a new trial granted. . . .

Judgment affirmed.

RELEVANT PROVISIONS

For the *Restatement (Second) of Contracts*, consult §§ 302 and 304.

NOTES AND QUESTIONS

1. *Who sued whom for what and why?* Before you consider the questions below, make sure you understand exactly who is suing whom for what, and why. The introduction before the case should help, but whenever there are multiple parties, you may find it helpful to grab a sheet of paper and map things out. Here, start by identifying the promisor, promisee, and third-party beneficiary (reread *Restatement (Second) of Contracts* § 2 if any of these terms are unclear). Next, using arrows, diagram who promised what to whom, who is suing whom, and what arguments are being made. You might also find it helpful to do this for *Farley v. Cleaveland*, the case on which the *Lawrence* court relied.

2. *Was there consideration?* Defendant argues "that the agreement by the defendant with Holly to pay the plaintiff was void for want of consideration." Applying what you learned from *Hamer* and the materials in that section, do you think there was consideration in this case? Why or why not? Further, do you think the answer to this question should determine whether plaintiff should be allowed to bring suit against defendant? Why or why not?

3. *Was this case correctly decided?* Do you agree with the result reached, and the approach used, by the majority, or do you instead favor the result/approach of the dissent? Why? After considering both views, do you think third-party beneficiary contracts should generally be enforceable by the beneficiaries? Why or why not? (Keep your answer in mind as you read the "Thinking Tool" following the "Contextual Perspective" below.) How, if at all, would you have written either of the opinions differently? Finally, how would you state the rule in *Lawrence v. Fox*?

4. *To be continued . . .* In this introductory section, you were introduced to third-party beneficiaries, and learned one way a third party may acquire rights under another party's contract. In Chapter 9 ("Third Parties"), we will discuss two additional methods—the "assignment of rights" and "delegation of duties"—by which a third party may acquire rights and/or duties under another party's contract. Stay tuned.

CONTEXTUAL PERSPECTIVE: MORE ON LAWRENCE V. FOX*

The facts of *Lawrence v. Fox*, as recounted by the New York Court of Appeals, are these: One Holly, declaring that he owed Lawrence three hundred dollars, lent that

* Excerpted from Anthony Jon Waters, *The Property in the Promise: A Study of the Third Party Beneficiary Rule*, 98 HARV. L. REV. 1109, 1122-27 (1985).

amount to Fox, who promised Holly that he would repay it to Lawrence the next day. Fox did not pay, and Lawrence sued him. Lawrence prevailed at trial, on appeal, and, finally, in the New York Court of Appeals. What the Court of Appeals called the "principle of law" of the case is "that [when] a promise [is] made to one for the benefit of another, he for whose benefit it is made may bring an action for its breach." The mystery of *Lawrence v. Fox* is why Lawrence chose the tortuous route of suing Fox, with whom he had not dealt, rather than sue Holly, who was, it appears, his debtor.

1. Suing the Debtor's Debtor.—From the records of the case, we learn that "Holly" was in fact one Hawley, referred to in the complaint as Samuel Hawley. The Buffalo census of 1855 lists no Samuel Hawley, but of the eighteen Hawleys who are listed, only one appears to have had sufficient means to have been involved in a three hundred dollar cash transaction. He was Merwin Spencer Hawley, a prominent merchant. In 1856, Hawley was President of the Buffalo Board of Trade, an organization with which Fox, at some point, was also connected. It is admittedly possible that the Hawley who dealt with Fox, and who was allegedly indebted to Lawrence, was another Hawley from out of town, or out of state. That would explain his absence from the census and from the courtroom. But there are indications of other reasons why Lawrence may have avoided suing Hawley, even if he was affluent and available. Those reasons—which I shall deal with shortly—taken together with the fact that Merwin Hawley was a wealthy Buffalonian who moved in the same social circles as Arthur Fox, make it more likely that he is the Hawley of *Lawrence v. Fox*. The assumption that Hawley was affluent and available in Buffalo when Lawrence sued Fox does nothing, however, to solve the mystery of why Lawrence chose not to sue him. The solution to that mystery lies in the nature of Lawrence's transaction with Hawley, of which Hawley's dealings with Fox on the next day are highly suggestive.

In 1854, when the transaction took place, three hundred dollars was a very large amount of money. Even among successful entrepreneurs, a loan the size of Hawley's to Fox, to be repaid a day later, must have been out of the ordinary. At trial in the Superior Court in Buffalo, Fox's attorney, Jared Torrance, shed some light on the nature of that transaction. The only witness in the case was William Riley, by whom Lawrence's attorney, Edward Chapin, had proved that Hawley paid three hundred dollars to Fox; that Hawley told Fox that he, Hawley, owed that amount to Lawrence; and that Fox promised Hawley that he would repay that amount to Lawrence. On cross-examination, Torrance elicited four facts: that Lawrence was not present when Hawley made the loan to Fox; that the deal took place at Mr. Purdy Merritt's on Washington Street; that there were "two or three persons present . . . doing nothing but standing near them"; and that Hawley counted out the money as he handed it to Fox.

The first fact, that Lawrence was not present, formed the basis of Fox's privity defense. This defense makes sense only in an action based on contract, a point to which we shall return. For now, it is the other three facts—the location, the bystanders, and the cash being counted out—that are noteworthy, for they suggest the milieu in which the transaction took place, and help to explain its character.

William Riley, the witness, was a horse dealer. He did his business near the canal, the life line of Buffalo's then-thriving commerce. Not many steps away was Mr. Purdy Merritt's establishment, where the transaction took place; Merritt was also a horse dealer. Torrance's cross-examination presented a more complete picture: two well-to-do merchants in a horse dealer's establishment down by the canal; a large amount of cash changing hands; and several other people present, loitering. Of these facts, not the least significant was the location:

> Canal Street was more than a street. It was the name of a district, a small and sinful neighborhood. . . . As late as the 1800's, there were ninety-three saloons there, among which were sprinkled fifteen other dives known as concert halls plus sundry establishments designed to separate the sucker from his money as swiftly as possible, painlessly by preference, but painfully if necessary. . . . It must have been an eternal mystery to the clergy and the good people of the town why the Lord never wiped out this nineteenth century example of Sodom and Gomorrah with a storm or a great wave from Lake Erie.[53]

In his cross-examination of Riley, Attorney Torrance had gone as far as he could go to set the scene for what he then sought to prove directly, also by William Riley: that Hawley lent the money to Fox for Fox to gamble with it, and that this unlawful purpose was known to Hawley.

Trial Judge Joseph Masten did not, however, permit Riley to testify to the alleged link with gambling. Attorney Chapin, for Lawrence, successfully objected on two grounds, neither of which bears upon the probable truth or untruth of the evidence that Riley was prepared to give. As to that question, the facts that Torrance had already elicited do suggest a setting in which gambling could have been taking place. But there is one more fact, this one uncontroverted, that is entirely consistent with the allegation of a connection with gambling and is difficult to explain otherwise. That fact—the central mystery of this case—is that Lawrence chose to sue not his debtor, Hawley, but his debtor's debtor, Fox. If, as seems to be the fact, Hawley was a person of considerable wealth in Buffalo, and if, as alleged, he owed three hundred dollars to Lawrence, then Lawrence must have had compelling reason to neglect the obvious action—suing Hawley—in favor of the much more difficult task of seeking recovery from Fox. A gambling debt would have presented just such a reason. If Hawley's debt to Lawrence from the day before, in the round sum of three hundred dollars, was itself the outcome of gambling and thus unenforceable at law, Lawrence was well advised to look for someone other than Hawley to sue. Furthermore, if we look to the law of gamblers rather than the law of commerce, it is clear that Fox, and not Hawley, was both the villain and the obvious person to pursue.

Commercial transactions were not then and are not now structured in such a way as to leave a creditor with no better means of recovery than to sue his debtor's debtor. The series of events described in *Lawrence v. Fox* makes no commercial sense. Had Hawley's dealings with Fox conformed to the norms of commercial behavior, Hawley would have requested a negotiable instrument either made out to Lawrence, or to be endorsed in his favor, in return for his loan to Fox. And had Lawrence's dealings with Hawley been of a kind condoned and upheld by the law of the land, then Lawrence would surely have sued Hawley, and not Fox. It is not surprising, therefore, that there was no theory of recovery in the law of contract by which Lawrence could collect from Fox.

53. L. Graham, Niagara Country 205-06 (1949).

THINKING TOOL: EX ANTE V. EX POST, AND A NOTE ON FORMALISM V. REALISM

The life of the law has not been logic; it has been experience. . . . The law embodies the story of a nation's development through many centuries, and it cannot be dealt with as if it contained only the axioms and corollaries of a book of mathematics.

Oliver Wendell Holmes, Common Law *1 (1881)*

There are two ways courts can think about legal disputes, and both methods were on display in *Lawrence v. Fox*. First, a court can view a dispute from an *ex post* (or after-the-fact) perspective, looking to the past and asking questions like: (1) Who did what to whom?; (2) What rule (or standard)* governs their dispute?; and (3) Applying this rule or standard, did one party violate the rights of another?† Where a right has been violated, a court must further determine (4) how that right should be protected,‡ but once this is done, it is possible for a court to simply issue its decision and move on, not worrying too much about whether the rule or standard it applied was a good one, and even without regard for the broader social or legal consequences of its decision. This is not quite the "mechanical jurisprudence"§ it appears to be on its surface, because courts can and must still exercise a tremendous amount of (mostly hidden) discretion at every point along steps 1-4, but there is a lot less discretion involved in this way of deciding a case than in the next approach, to which we now turn.

The second way a court can think about a legal dispute is from an *ex ante* (or before-the-fact) perspective. This approach, which recognizes that a court's resolution of *this* dispute will act as precedent in *future* cases, requires a court to make its decision with an eye to the future, and ask questions like: (1) How will our decision affect the behavior of similarly situated parties in the future?; (2) How should the rule or standard governing these types of disputes be crafted to provide future parties with better incentives to achieve important public policy goals?; and (3) What decision will most likely have the best consequences, not only for these parties, but for future parties?

The first approach, reflected in the dissent in *Lawrence v. Fox*, is often associated with legal formalism and classical contract law, whereas the second approach, reflected in the majority's opinion, is often associated with legal realism and reflects a more instrumentalist approach to contracts. Speaking generally, legal formalism promotes "the use of deductive logic to derive the outcome of a case from premises accepted as authoritative."¶ Because, at the time

---

* *See* "Thinking Tool: Administrative Costs and Standards v. Rules", p. 75, *infra*.

† *See* "Thinking Tool: Thinking Clearly About Legal Relationships", p. 96, *infra*.

‡ *See* "Thinking Tool: Property Rules and Liability Rules", p. 109, *infra*.

§ The term "mechanical jurisprudence" was first used and discussed in Roscoe Pound, *Mechanical Jurisprudence*, 8 COLUM. L. REV. 605 (1908).

¶ Richard A. Posner, *Legal Formalism, Legal Realism, and the Interpretation of Statutes and the Constitution*, 37 CASE W. RES. L. REV. 179, 181 (1986). Judge Posner further provides that

Lawrence was decided, there was no black-letter rule allowing a third-party beneficiary in the plaintiff's position to recover, there was, according to the dissent, no major premise from which a court could reason: "[t]he plaintiff had no right in the fund, legal or equitable." Legal realism, on the other hand, focuses on "deciding a case so that its outcome best promotes public welfare in nonlegalistic terms."* We see evidence that Judge Gray was thinking along these lines in the last paragraph of the opinion, where he acknowledged that although "a more strict and technically accurate application of the [existing] rules" *may* have "lead to a different result," such a result should nevertheless be shunned here in favor of a result that achieves "manifest justice."

The "formalist" ex post and "realist" ex ante perspectives both have their merits, and you should be equally comfortable in both worlds, as there is no one "correct" way of thinking about legal disputes. Indeed, it should come as no surprise that common law courts themselves often move back and forth between the two perspectives, as their decisions necessarily must do two things at the same time: (1) resolve an existing dispute about a past conflict between the parties before it *and* (2) establish a rule to guide the conduct of similarly situated parties in the future. You will have to decide for yourself, after careful consideration of many cases, whether you generally favor one approach or the other, or perhaps one approach in some situations but another approach in other situations. For the time being, however, understanding these various approaches will make you a better and more critical reader of legal texts, and will allow you to understand and critically examine arguments and judicial reasoning in a more revealing light.

Therefore, in both this and in other classes, try to be on the lookout for how judges approach the legal disputes before them, and ask yourself questions like: Does the court seem more concerned with resolving the dispute before it, or with how their decision will impact future parties? Does the court seem more concerned with issuing a decision that is logically consistent with past decisions, or with issuing a decision that advances some greater public policy goal? Does the court seem to assume (or want the reader to believe) that there is only one way of construing the facts, only one rule or principle that applies to the facts, or only one correct way of applying the rule or principle, or does it instead suggest (or perhaps even openly acknowledge) the discretion available to them? Finally, and most importantly, whenever you read a case, don't forget to ask yourself which approach, based on the facts of the case and on the totality of the surrounding circumstances, seems best to you, and why.

"[f]ormalism enables a commentator to pronounce the outcome of the case as being correct or incorrect, in approximately the same way that the solution to a mathematical problem can be pronounced correct or incorrect." *Id.*

* *Id.* Judge Posner goes on to note that "[a] 'realist' decision is more likely to be judged sound or unsound than correct or incorrect—the latter pair suggests a more demonstrable, verifiable mode of analysis than will usually be possible in weighing considerations of policy."

PART III

AN IN-DEPTH EXAMINATION OF CONTRACT LAW

In Part III of this casebook, we will delve more deeply into each of the major areas of contract law we explored in Parts I and II. As Part I was designed to provide you with a 30,000-foot view of contract law, and Part II was designed to provide you with a 5,000-foot view, Part III of the casebook, consisting of seven chapters, is designed to provide you with a ground-level view of contract law, fleshing out and exploring in greater detail many of the concepts and doctrines you were introduced to in the previous two parts. For this reason, the material below will often refer back to earlier materials. As you read it, you, too, should try to draw on the knowledge, and build on the framework, you were introduced to in Parts I and II, which should help you understand and organize the material below into a coherent framework.

CHAPTER 3

PROMISES AND AGREEMENTS

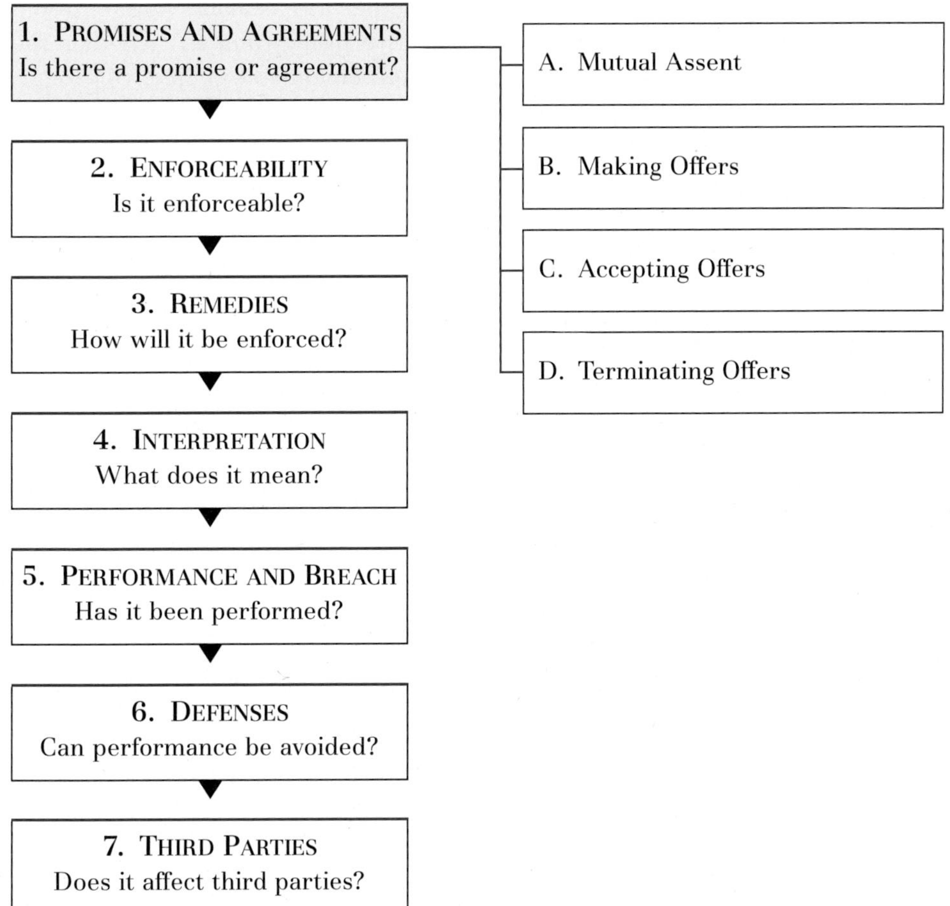

1. Promises And Agreements
Is there a promise or agreement?
2. Enforceability
Is it enforceable?
3. Remedies
How will it be enforced?
4. Interpretation
What does it mean?
5. Performance and Breach
Has it been performed?
6. Defenses
Can performance be avoided?
7. Third Parties
Does it affect third parties?
A. Mutual Assent
B. Making Offers
C. Accepting Offers
D. Terminating Offers

> *A contract has, strictly speaking, nothing to do with the personal, or individual, intent of the parties. A contract is an obligation attached by the mere force of law to certain acts of the parties, usually words, which ordinarily accompany and represent a known intent. If, however, it were proved by twenty bishops that either party when he used the words intended something else than the usual meaning which the law imposes on them, he would still be held, unless there were mutual mistake or something else of the sort.*
>
> *Judge Learned Hand, Hotchkiss v. National City Bank, 200 F. 287, 293 (S.D.N.Y. 1911)*

Recall that, in Part II.2.B, *supra*, you were introduced to the subjective, objective, and mixed theories of assent. To briefly summarize those materials, in determining whether the parties have formed an agreement, the subjective test looked to see whether there was a subjective meeting of the minds between the parties, the objective test looked to see whether a reasonable person viewing the parties' conduct would believe there to be an agreement, and the mixed test combined both approaches to see (1) whether a reasonable person would believe there to be an agreement (the objective prong) *and* (2) whether the promisee actually understood there to be an agreement (the subjective prong).

In this chapter, we will now undertake an in-depth exploration of mutual assent, looking at the concept in general terms (as expressed, for instance, in cases like *Embry*) and through some of its more specific manifestations in the making, accepting, and terminating of offers. In doing so, we will be examining some of the most common tools parties use to make promises to one another that have the potential to ripen into contracts.*

Specifically, in Section A, we pick up right where we left off in Part II.2.B ("Introduction to Promises and Agreements"), taking a closer look at the various approaches courts use to ascertain mutual assent. After reviewing *Embry*, we will read the classic "joke" case *Lucy v. Zehmer*, where a seller finds to his chagrin that, in life as well as in the eyes of the law, there is such a thing as taking a good joke too far. We then explore how the principles of mutual assent operate in the international context (*MCC-Marble*) and with respect to internet commerce (*Nguyen v. Barnes & Noble Inc.*).

Having wrapped up Section A, we next turn to the traditional tools parties use to manifest their willingness (or unwillingness) to form agreements with one another. Specifically, we will look at how parties make (Section B), accept (Section C), and terminate (Section D) offers. In the process, we will explore a number of other important concepts, ranging from the legal status of advertisements and rewards to the formation of contracts in the mail to whether promises to leave offers open for a period of time may be revoked before that

---

* From Part II, you should recall that, to ripen into a contract, the promise will also have to be enforceable, and to be enforceable, the promise will have to satisfy one of the law's tests for enforceability. In the next chapter, we will look at three of the most common tests by which the enforceability of promises is determined: the bargain-based test of consideration (which you were introduced to in *Hamer v. Sidway* and the *Restatement (Second) of Contracts*), the reliance-based test of promissory estoppel, and the benefit-based test of unjust enrichment.

time has elapsed. Even better, we will do so by studying a number of interesting, quirky, and (sometimes) downright entertaining cases, many of which are likely to stay with you long after you graduate from law school.*

The chapter concludes with Section E, consisting of a single case that brings together many of the above-mentioned concepts with one of the wildest fact patterns you've ever read. So, without further ado, let's get started!

A. MUTUAL ASSENT

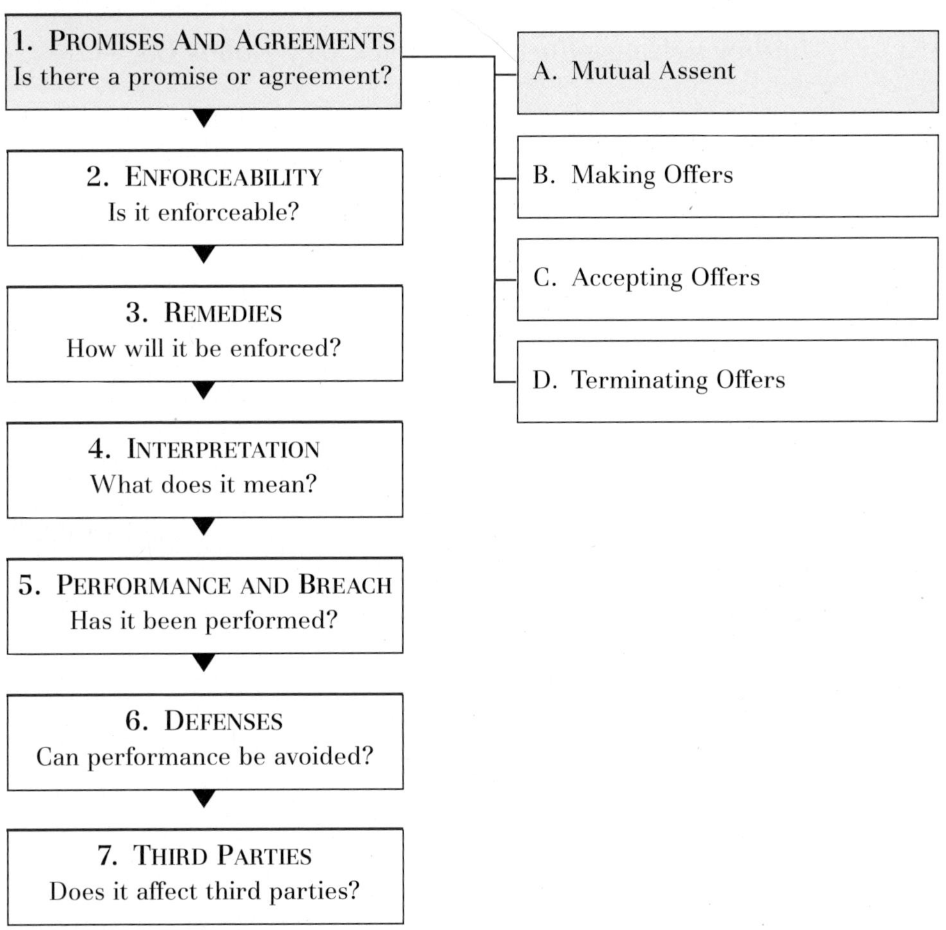
1. PROMISES AND AGREEMENTS
Is there a promise or agreement?
2. ENFORCEABILITY
Is it enforceable?
3. REMEDIES
How will it be enforced?
4. INTERPRETATION
What does it mean?
5. PERFORMANCE AND BREACH
Has it been performed?
6. DEFENSES
Can performance be avoided?
7. THIRD PARTIES
Does it affect third parties?
A. Mutual Assent
B. Making Offers
C. Accepting Offers
D. Terminating Offers

1. Mutual Assent in General

In this section, we explore in greater depth the various methods courts use to ascertain whether the parties have formed an agreement: the subjective,

* *Lucy v. Zehmer*, *Leonard v. Pepsico*, *Carlill v. Carbolic Smoke Ball Co.*, *Petterson v. Pattberg*, *Dickinson v. Dodds*, *Baird v. Gimble Bros.*, and *Drennan v. Star Paving* are a few that immediately jump to mind.

objective, and mixed approaches to mutual assent.* As you read the cases below, ask yourself which (if any) of the three approaches the court seems to have adopted, and how the case might have been decided differently had the court adopted a different approach. This exercise should also get you thinking about the various advantages and disadvantages of each approach. For instance, which of the three approaches do you think best captured the true intentions of the parties? Which approach seems easiest or least expensive for the courts to apply? Which approach seems most just? Can you think of any ways to improve on any of the traditional tests?

Embry v. Hargadine, McKittrick Dry Goods Co.

St. Louis Court of Appeals
105 S.W. 777 (1907)

For a report of the case and accompanying materials, see p. 68, *supra*.

RELEVANT PROVISIONS

For the *Restatement (Second) of Contracts*, consult § 3.

Lucy v. Zehmer

Supreme Court of Virginia
84 S.E.2d 516 (1954)

BUCHANAN, J. This suit was instituted by W. O. Lucy and J. C. Lucy, complainants, against A. H. Zehmer and Ida S. Zehmer, his wife, defendants, to have specific performance of a contract by which it was alleged the Zehmers had sold to W. O. Lucy a tract of land owned by A. H. Zehmer in Dinwiddie county containing 471.6 acres, more or less, known as the Ferguson farm, for $50,000. J. C. Lucy, the other complainant, is a brother of W. O. Lucy, to whom W. O. Lucy transferred a half interest in his alleged purchase.

The instrument sought to be enforced was written by A. H. Zehmer on December 20, 1952, in these words: "We hereby agree to sell to W. O. Lucy the Ferguson Farm complete for $50,000.00, title satisfactory to buyer," and signed by the defendants, A. H. Zehmer and Ida S. Zehmer.

The answer of A. H. Zehmer admitted that at the time mentioned W. O. Lucy offered him $50,000 cash for the farm, but that he, Zehmer, considered that the offer was made in jest; that so thinking, and both he and Lucy having had several drinks, he wrote out "the memorandum" quoted above and induced his wife to sign it; that he did not deliver the memorandum to Lucy, but that Lucy picked it up, read it, put it in his pocket, attempted to offer Zehmer $5 to bind the bargain, which Zehmer refused to accept, and realizing for the first

* *See* Section II.2.B, "Introduction to Promises and Agreements."

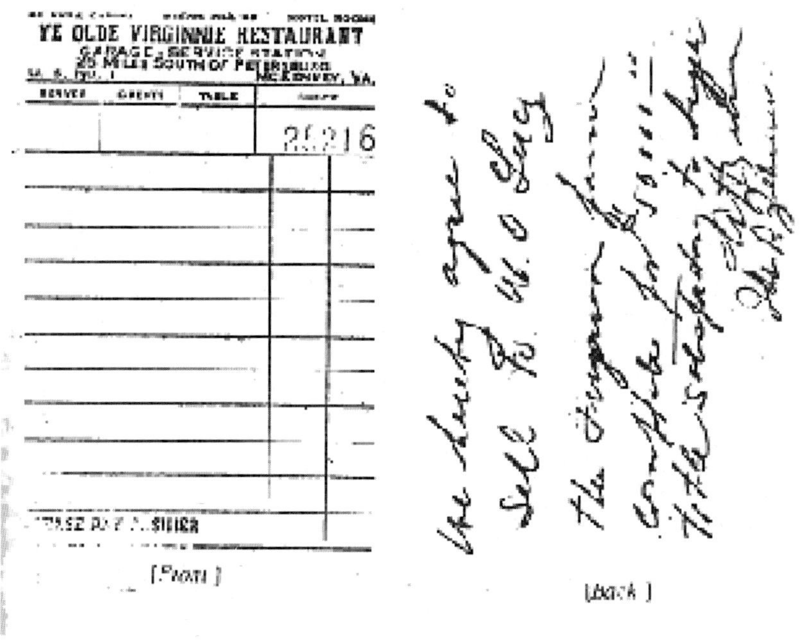

time that Lucy was serious, Zehmer assured him that he had no intention of selling the farm and that the whole matter was a joke. Lucy left the premises insisting that he had purchased the farm.

Depositions were taken and the decree appealed from was entered holding that the complainants had failed to establish their right to specific performance, and dismissing their bill. The assignment of error is to this action of the court.

W. O. Lucy, a lumberman and farmer, thus testified in substance: He had known Zehmer for fifteen or twenty years and had been familiar with the Ferguson farm for ten years. Seven or eight years ago he had offered Zehmer $20,000 for the farm which Zehmer had accepted, but the agreement was verbal and Zehmer backed out. On the night of December 20, 1952, around eight o'clock, he took an employee to McKenney, where Zehmer lived and operated a restaurant, filling station and motor court. While there he decided to see Zehmer and again try to buy the Ferguson farm. He entered the restaurant and talked to Mrs. Zehmer until Zehmer came in. He asked Zehmer if he had sold the Ferguson farm. Zehmer replied that he had not. Lucy said, "I bet you wouldn't take $50,000.00 for that place." Zehmer replied, "Yes, I would too; you wouldn't give fifty." Lucy said he would and told Zehmer to write up an agreement to that effect. Zehmer took a restaurant check and wrote on the back of it, "I do hereby agree to sell to W. O. Lucy the Ferguson Farm for $50,000 complete." Lucy told him he had better change it to "We" because Mrs. Zehmer would have to sign it too. Zehmer then tore up what he had written, wrote the agreement quoted above and asked Mrs. Zehmer, who was at the other end of the counter ten or twelve feet away, to sign it. Mrs. Zehmer said she would for

$50,000 and signed it. Zehmer brought it back and gave it to Lucy, who offered him $5 which Zehmer refused, saying, "You don't need to give me any money, you got the agreement there signed by both of us."

The discussion leading to the signing of the agreement, said Lucy, lasted thirty or forty minutes, during which Zehmer seemed to doubt that Lucy could raise $50,000. Lucy suggested the provision for having the title examined and Zehmer made the suggestion that he would sell it "complete, everything there," and stated that all he had on the farm was three heifers.

Lucy took a partly filled bottle of whiskey into the restaurant with him for the purpose of giving Zehmer a drink if he wanted it. Zehmer did, and he and Lucy had one or two drinks together. Lucy said that while he felt the drinks he took he was not intoxicated, and from the way Zehmer handled the transaction he did not think he was either.

December 20 was on Saturday. Next day Lucy telephoned to J. C. Lucy and arranged with the latter to take a half interest in the purchase and pay half of the consideration. On Monday he engaged an attorney to examine the title. The attorney reported favorably on December 31 and on January 2 Lucy wrote Zehmer stating that the title was satisfactory, that he was ready to pay the purchase price in cash and asking when Zehmer would be ready to close the deal. Zehmer replied by letter, mailed on January 13, asserting that he had never agreed or intended to sell.

Mr. and Mrs. Zehmer were called by the complainants as adverse witnesses. Zehmer testified in substance as follows: He bought this farm more than ten years ago for $11,000. He had had twenty-five offers, more or less, to buy it, including several from Lucy, who had never offered any specific sum of money. He had given them all the same answer, that he was not interested in selling it. On this Saturday night before Christmas it looked like everybody and his brother came by there to have a drink. He took a good many drinks during the afternoon and had a pint of his own. When he entered the restaurant around eight-thirty Lucy was there and he could see that he was "pretty high." He said to Lucy, "Boy, you got some good liquor, drinking, ain't you?" Lucy then offered him a drink. "I was already high as a Georgia pine, and didn't have any more better sense than to pour another great big slug out and gulp it down, and he took one too."

After they had talked a while Lucy asked whether he still had the Ferguson farm. He replied that he had not sold it and Lucy said, "I bet you wouldn't take $50,000.00 for it." Zehmer asked him if he would give $50,000 and Lucy said yes. Zehmer replied, "You haven't got $50,000 in cash." Lucy said he did and Zehmer replied that he did not believe it. They argued "pro and con for a long time," mainly about "whether he had $50,000 in cash that he could put up right then and buy that farm."

Finally, said Zehmer, Lucy told him if he didn't believe he had $50,000, "you sign that piece of paper here and say you will take $50,000.00 for the farm." He, Zehmer, "just grabbed the back off of a guest check there" and wrote on the back of it. At that point in his testimony Zehmer asked to see what he had written to "see if I recognize my own handwriting." He examined the paper and exclaimed, "Great balls of fire, I got 'Firgerson' for Ferguson. I have got satisfactory spelled wrong. I don't recognize that writing if I would see it, wouldn't know it was mine."

After Zehmer had, as he described it, "scribbled this thing off," Lucy said, "Get your wife to sign it." Zehmer walked over to where she was and she at first refused to sign but did so after he told her that he "was just needling him [Lucy], and didn't mean a thing in the world, that I was not selling the farm." Zehmer then "took it back over there . . . and I was still looking at the dern thing. I had the drink right there by my hand, and I reached over to get a drink, and he said, 'Let me see it.' He reached and picked it up, and when I looked back again he had it in his pocket and he dropped a five dollar bill over there, and he said, 'Here is five dollars payment on it.' . . . I said, 'Hell no, that is beer and liquor talking. I am not going to sell you the farm. I have told you that too many times before.'"

Mrs. Zehmer testified that when Lucy came into the restaurant he looked as if he had had a drink. When Zehmer came in he took a drink out of a bottle that Lucy handed him. She went back to help the waitress who was getting things ready for next day. Lucy and Zehmer were talking but she did not pay too much attention to what they were saying. She heard Lucy ask Zehmer if he had sold the Ferguson farm, and Zehmer replied that he had not and did not want to sell it. Lucy said, "I bet you wouldn't take $50,000 cash for that farm," and Zehmer replied, "You haven't got $50,000 cash." Lucy said, "I can get it." Zehmer said he might form a company and get it, "but you haven't got $50,000.00 cash to pay me tonight." Lucy asked him if he would put it in writing that he would sell him this farm. Zehmer then wrote on the back of a pad, "I agree to sell the Ferguson Place to W. O. Lucy for $50,000.00 cash." Lucy said, "All right, get your wife to sign it." Zehmer came back to where she was standing and said, "You want to put your name to this?" She said "No," but he said in an undertone, "It is nothing but a joke," and she signed it.

She said that only one paper was written and it said: "I hereby agree to sell," but the "I" had been changed to "We." However, she said she read what she signed and was then asked, "When you read 'We hereby agree to sell to W. O. Lucy,' what did you interpret that to mean, that particular phrase?" She said she thought that was a cash sale that night; but she also said that when she read that part about "title satisfactory to buyer" she understood that if the title was good Lucy would pay $50,000 but if the title was bad he would have a right to reject it, and that that was her understanding at the time she signed her name.

On examination by her own counsel she said that her husband laid this piece of paper down after it was signed; that Lucy said to let him see it, took it, folded it and put it in his wallet, then said to Zehmer, "Let me give you $5.00," but Zehmer said, "No, this is liquor talking. I don't want to sell the farm, I have told you that I want my son to have it. This is all a joke." Lucy then said at least twice, "Zehmer, you have sold your farm," wheeled around and started for the door. He paused at the door and said, "I will bring you $50,000.00

tomorrow. . . . No, tomorrow is Sunday. I will bring it to you Monday." She said you could tell definitely that he was drinking and she said to her husband, "You should have taken him home," but he said, "Well, I am just about as bad off as he is."

The waitress referred to by Mrs. Zehmer testified that when Lucy first came in "he was mouthy." When Zehmer came in they were laughing and joking and she thought they took a drink or two. She was sweeping and cleaning up for next day. She said she heard Lucy tell Zehmer, "I will give you so much for the farm," and Zehmer said, "You haven't got that much." Lucy answered, "Oh, yes, I will give you that much." Then "they jotted down something on paper . . . and Mr. Lucy reached over and took it, said let me see it." He looked at it, put it in his pocket and in about a minute he left. She was asked whether she saw Lucy offer Zehmer any money and replied, "He had five dollars laying up there, they didn't take it." She said Zehmer told Lucy he didn't want his money "because he didn't have enough money to pay for his property, and wasn't going to sell his farm." Both of them appeared to be drinking right much, she said.

She repeated on cross-examination that she was busy and paying no attention to what was going on. She was some distance away and did not see either of them sign the paper. She was asked whether she saw Zehmer put the agreement down on the table in front of Lucy, and her answer was this: "Time he got through writing whatever it was on the paper, Mr. Lucy reached over and said, 'Let's see it.' He took it and put it in his pocket," before showing it to Mrs. Zehmer. Her version was that Lucy kept raising his offer until it got to $50,000.

The defendants insist that the evidence was ample to support their contention that the writing sought to be enforced was prepared as a bluff or dare to force Lucy to admit that he did not have $50,000; that the whole matter was a joke; that the writing was not delivered to Lucy and no binding contract was ever made between the parties.

It is an unusual, if not bizarre, defense. When made to the writing admittedly prepared by one of the defendants and signed by both, clear evidence is required to sustain it.

In his testimony Zehmer claimed that he "was high as a Georgia pine," and that the transaction "was just a bunch of two doggoned drunks bluffing to see who could talk the biggest and say the most." That claim is inconsistent with his attempt to testify in great detail as to what was said and what was done. It is contradicted by other evidence as to the condition of both parties, and rendered of no weight by the testimony of his wife that when Lucy left the restaurant she suggested that Zehmer drive him home. The record is convincing that Zehmer was not intoxicated to the extent of being unable to comprehend the nature and consequences of the instrument he executed, and hence that instrument is not to be invalidated on that ground. It was in fact conceded by defendants' counsel in oral argument that under the evidence Zehmer was not too drunk to make a valid contract.

The evidence is convincing also that Zehmer wrote two agreements, the first one beginning "I hereby agree to sell." Zehmer first said he could not remember about that, then that "I don't think I wrote but one out." Mrs. Zehmer said that what he wrote was "I hereby agree," but that the "I" was changed to "We" after that night. The agreement that was written and signed is in the record and indicates no such change. Neither are the mistakes in spelling that Zehmer sought to point out readily apparent.

The appearance of the contract, the fact that it was under discussion for forty minutes or more before it was signed; Lucy's objection to the first draft because it was written in the singular, and he wanted Mrs. Zehmer to sign it also; the rewriting to meet that objection and the signing by Mrs. Zehmer; the discussion of what was to be included in the sale, the provision for the examination of the title, the completeness of the instrument that was executed, the taking possession of it by Lucy with no request or suggestion by either of the defendants that he give it back, are facts which furnish persuasive evidence that the execution of the contract was a serious business transaction rather than a casual, jesting matter as defendants now contend.

On Sunday, the day after the instrument was signed on Saturday night, there was a social gathering in a home in the town of McKenney at which there were general comments that the sale had been made. Mrs. Zehmer testified that on that occasion as she passed by a group of people, including Lucy, who were talking about the transaction, $50,000 was mentioned, whereupon she stepped up and said, "Well, with the high-price whiskey you were drinking last night you should have paid more. That was cheap." Lucy testified that at that time Zehmer told him that he did not want to "stick" him or hold him to the agreement because he, Lucy, was too tight and didn't know what he was doing, to which Lucy replied that he was not too tight; that he had been stuck before and was going through with it. Zehmer's version was that he said to Lucy: "I am not trying to claim it wasn't a deal on account of the fact the price was too low. If I had wanted to sell $50,000.00 would be a good price, in fact I think you would get stuck at $50,000.00." A disinterested witness testified that what Zehmer said to Lucy was that "he was going to let him up off the deal, because he thought he was too tight, didn't know what he was doing. Lucy said something to the effect that 'I have been stuck before and I will go through with it.'"

If it be assumed, contrary to what we think the evidence shows, that Zehmer was jesting about selling his farm to Lucy and that the transaction was intended by him to be a joke, nevertheless the evidence shows that Lucy did not so understand it but considered it to be a serious business transaction and the contract to be binding on the Zehmers as well as on himself. The very next day he arranged with his brother to put up half the money and take a half interest in the land. The day after that he employed an attorney to examine the title. The next night, Tuesday, he was back at Zehmer's place and there Zehmer told him for the first time, Lucy said,

> ***"If it be assumed . . ."***
>
> What is the legal consequence of this language? For one approach, see *Restatement (Second) of Contracts* § 201. Does this approach to mutual assent reflect the objective, subjective, or mixed approach? How would the case have been decided if the court would have adopted a different approach? As you will recall, both *Embry* and *Frigaliment* also involved cases where different parties attached different meanings to the same set of facts.

that he wasn't going to sell and he told Zehmer, "You know you sold that place fair and square." After receiving the report from his attorney that the title was good he wrote to Zehmer that he was ready to close the deal.

> ***"Not only did Lucy . . ."***
>
> Do you see how this language reflects *Embry's* mixed approach to mutual assent?

Not only did Lucy actually believe, but the evidence shows he was warranted in believing, that the contract represented a serious business transaction and a good faith sale and purchase of the farm.

In the field of contracts, as generally elsewhere, "We must look to the outward expression of a person as manifesting his intention rather than to his secret and unexpressed intention. 'The law imputes to a person an intention corresponding to the reasonable meaning of his words and acts.'" *First Nat. Bank v. Roanoke Oil Co.*, 192 S.E. 764, 770 (1937).

At no time prior to the execution of the contract had Zehmer indicated to Lucy by word or act that he was not in earnest about selling the farm. They had argued about it and discussed its terms, as Zehmer admitted, for a long time. Lucy testified that if there was any jesting it was about paying $50,000 that night. The contract and the evidence show that he was not expected to pay the money that night. Zehmer said that after the writing was signed he laid it down on the counter in front of Lucy. Lucy said Zehmer handed it to him. In any event there had been what appeared to be a good faith offer and a good faith acceptance, followed by the execution and apparent delivery of a written contract. Both said that Lucy put the writing in his pocket and then offered Zehmer $5 to seal the bargain. Not until then, even under the defendants' evidence, was anything said or done to indicate that the matter was a joke. Both of the Zehmers testified that when Zehmer asked his wife to sign he whispered that it was a joke so Lucy wouldn't hear and that it was not intended that he should hear.

The mental assent of the parties is not requisite for the formation of a contract. If the words or other acts of one of the parties have but one reasonable meaning, his undisclosed intention is immaterial except when an unreasonable meaning which he attaches to his manifestations is known to the other party. *Restatement (First) of Contracts* § 71.

". . . The law, therefore, judges of an agreement between two persons exclusively from those expressions of their intentions which are communicated between them. . . ." *Clark on Contracts*, 4 ed., § 3, p. 4.

An agreement or mutual assent is of course essential to a valid contract but the law imputes to a person an intention corresponding to the reasonable meaning of his words and acts. If his words and acts, judged by a reasonable standard, manifest an intention to agree, it is immaterial what may be the real but unexpressed state of his mind.

So a person cannot set up that he was merely jesting when his conduct and words would warrant a reasonable person in believing that he intended a real agreement.

Whether the writing signed by the defendants and now sought to be enforced by the complainants was the result of a serious offer by Lucy and a serious acceptance by the defendants, or was a serious offer by Lucy and an acceptance in secret jest by the defendants, in either event it constituted a binding contract of sale between the parties.

Defendants contend further, however, that even though a contract was made, equity should decline to enforce it under the circumstances. These circumstances have been set forth in detail above. They disclose some drinking by the two parties but not to an extent that they were unable to understand fully what they were doing. There was no fraud, no misrepresentation, no sharp practice and no dealing between unequal parties. The farm had been bought for $11,000 and was assessed for taxation at $6,300. The purchase price was $50,000. Zehmer admitted that it was a good price. There is in fact present in this case none of the grounds usually urged against specific performance.

Specific performance, it is true, is not a matter of absolute or arbitrary right, but is addressed to the reasonable and sound discretion of the court. But it is likewise true that the discretion which may be exercised is not an arbitrary or capricious one, but one which is controlled by the established doctrines and settled principles of equity; and, generally, where a contract is in its nature and circumstances unobjectionable, it is as much a matter of course for courts of equity to decree a specific performance of it as it is for a court of law to give damages for a breach of it.

"Specific performance, it is true . . ."

We will study the circumstances in which a party is entitled to the remedy of specific performance in greater detail in Chapter 5. For the time being, however, suffice it to say that specific performance is generally available for contracts involving land, but it is ultimately a matter of the judge's discretion. Here, Zehmer is calling on the court to exercise its discretion to *refuse* to award specific performance. Assume that the judge found Zehmer to have both made and breached his contract with Lucy, but that specific performance should not be awarded. What remedy should the court have awarded instead, and how should it be measured?

The complainants are entitled to have specific performance of the contracts sued on. The decree appealed from is therefore reversed and the cause is remanded for the entry of a proper decree requiring the defendants to perform the contract in accordance with the prayer of the bill.

Reversed and remanded.

RELEVANT PROVISIONS

For the *Restatement (Second) of Contracts*, consult §§ 3, 17(1), and 201(2). For the UCC, consult § 2-204.

NOTES AND QUESTIONS

1. ***What happened?*** Who sued whom for what? Procedurally, how did the case get before this court? Factually, what happened between the parties?

What arguments did the plaintiff and defendant make? What rule or rules did the court apply? How did the court analyze the dispute between the parties? How did the court decide the case?

2. *Was this case correctly decided?* Do you agree with the result reached by Buchanan? Do you think Zehmer was serious, or was he joking? Do you believe that Lucy thought Zehmer was serious? Before reading this case, did you think a court would have enforced a contract for the sale of land scrawled by hand, over drinks, on the back of a piece of paper?

3. *Objective, subjective, or mixed?* Did the court adopt an objective, subjective, or mixed approach to ascertaining the intent of the parties? Do you agree with the approach adopted by the court, and its application of the law to the facts? How would the case have turned out if the court had adopted a different approach?

4. *Intoxication?* Was Zehmer drunk? Keep in mind that, despite Zehmer's testimony that he was "already high as a Georgia pine" when he agreed to sell the land to Lucy, the court must not have found him to be so drunk as to be mentally incapacitated. In other words, it did not find his intoxication to be "so extreme as to prevent any manifestation of assent." *See Restatement (Second) of Contracts* § 16, Comment b. If Zehmer was *that* drunk, then he would be off the hook by asserting the defense of incapacity (specifically, through intoxication), which we will cover in greater depth in Chapter 8.

5. *The writing.* The fact that this particular promise *was* written down, however, was important. Although all promises do not have to be in writing to be enforceable, the statute of frauds requires that certain promises—usually important promises, such as promises for the sale of land, goods priced at $500 or more, or services that cannot be performed within a year—must be in writing to be enforceable. We will cover the statute of frauds in greater detail in Chapter 8.

6. *A joke gone too far?* Well, it's not that the joke went too far, but that the court thought there was no joke at all, at least from a legal perspective. Although Zehmer may have intended to sell his farm in "jest," Lucy did not understand it this way, and a reasonable person in Lucy's position would also not have understood it this way. $50,000 seemed, after all, to be a fair price. In any event, we can draw an important lesson from this case: When you tell a joke, make sure the person you tell it to gets the punchline. If you can do this, then a world full of contractual fun will open up to you. For instance, you can jokingly offer to buy a product (say, a watch) for more than its worth, and, if you later get sued by the disappointed seller, you can just quote this language, which uncannily tracks this hypo: "[Because] 'the whole transaction between the parties was a frolic and a banter, the plaintiff not expecting to sell, nor the defendant intending to buy the watch at the sum for which the check was drawn,' the conclusion should have been that no contract was ever made by the parties." *Keller v. Holderman*, 11 Mich. 248 (1863).

7. *Joking and the Restatement.* Here is what the *Restatement (Second) of Contracts* § 18, Comment c, has to say about shams and jests:

> *c. Sham or jest.* Where all the parties to what would otherwise be a bargain manifest an intention that the transaction is not to be taken seriously, there is no such manifestation of assent to the exchange as is required by this Section. In some cases the setting makes it clear that there is no contract, as where a business transaction is simulated on a stage during a dramatic performance. In other cases, there may be doubt as to whether there is a joke, or one of the parties may take the joke seriously. If one party is deceived and has no reason to know of the joke the law takes the joker at his word. Even if the deceived party had reason to know of the joke, there may be a claim for fraud or unjust enrichment by virtue of the promise made. Where the parties to a sham transaction intend to deceive third parties, considerations of public policy may sometimes preclude a defense of sham.

PROBLEM: SOMEONE OWES YOU MONEY, JUST NOT ME

Owner was the owner of a shopping plaza. In January, Owner entered into a written contract with General Contractor, who agreed to build a section of the plaza. At about the same time, General Contractor, in turn, subcontracted in writing with Subcontractor for electrical work. Starting as early as March, General Contractor, running into some financial difficulties, went into arrears in paying Subcontractor for work performed. As a result, Subcontractor began to entertain serious doubts about whether General Contractor would carry out its end of their agreement and threatened to bring suit against the General Contractor unless the payments were brought up to date. Just as the Subcontractor feared, before the end of July, General Contractor found himself in such financial distress that it abandoned the job entirely. After General Contractor departed the project, Subcontractor, with the knowledge, consent, and co-operation of Owner, nevertheless continued to perform the electrical work, completing everything by the end of August. In early September, in response to an invoice from Subcontractor to Owner for the amount still due for its work on the project, Owner wrote back that it would send its check for "payment of the balance" upon receiving the underwriters' inspection certificates from Subcontractor. Nevertheless, when Subcontractor sent the certificates, Owner failed to make the promised payment, and Subcontractor sued for breach of contract. Owner's position is that there was no mutual assent between Owner and Subcontractor, and that no contract was ever entered into between Owner and Subcontractor. Further, Owner alleged that Subcontractor, in completing the electrical work, did no more than fulfill its obligation to General Contractor.

Drawing on the materials in this section, how do you think the court should resolve this dispute? Would your answer vary based on whether the court applied an objective, subjective, or mixed test to ascertain mutual assent?

PROBLEM: DEVELOPING COLD FEET

Patty, a realtor, published an ad in the newspaper looking for developers, offering for sale several hundred acres of land. Dennis contacted Patty and offered to purchase the land through his company, Dennis Construction Corporation. Shortly after entering this sales agreement, on July 18, 2015, Patty and Dennis met in Patty's office, where Patty alleges that Dennis and she entered into an oral contract for Patty to advertise for a new development on the tract of land Dennis's company had purchased. Patty and Dennis allegedly agreed that Patty would be in charge of sales and would have exclusive rights to the first 1200 homes built by Dennis's company at a commission of between $300 and $400 per house sold. A week after this meeting, Patty wrote Dennis a letter setting forth the commission agreed upon and stating: "This will confirm our discussion in my office on July 18, 2015 regarding sale commissions payable under an exclusive agreement for all houses constructed in your development project." Nowhere in the letter did it mention any promise on Dennis's part to build the houses. Dennis did not respond to the letter.

Shortly after sending the letter, Patty employed salespeople to promote sales of the houses to be constructed. Patty spent $5,600 promoting the development. Four months after the meeting between Patty and Dennis, construction had yet to begin on the development and only three model homes had been built. After Patty complained to Dennis about the lack of progress, Dennis discharged Patty claiming that she had not performed her advertising services adequately. Dennis also claimed that there was no firm guarantee he would be building 1200 homes within any deadline, but that it was his intention, if conditions were favorable to sell and build at a rapid rate. Patty filed a motion for judgment against Dennis for $400,000 as damages resulting from an alleged breach of oral contract entered into by the parties on the July 18th meeting.

Drawing on the materials in this section, how do you think the court should resolve this dispute? Would your answer vary based on whether the court applied an objective, subjective, or mixed test to ascertain mutual assent?

PROBLEM: FOOL'S GOLD

Mary is the proprietor of a well-known antique shop. To supply inventory for her shop, Mary attends estate auctions and bids on interesting and unique items to resell. On August 13, 2013, Mary attended the auction of the estate of the late Peter Locke and won the auction for a used vintage safe for $75. After submitting the winning bid, the auctioneer gave Mary the combination to the safe, told her that there was a small inside compartment that was corroded shut, and that all sales were final. When Mary opened the safe to examine the corroded inside compartment, she determined that it would require a welder to break it open. Several days after the auction, Mary took the safe to a welder to have the compartment forcibly opened. Upon opening the compartment, the welder found 33 troy ounces of gold, which was worth approximately $45,000. The Pinellas County Police Department, notified by the welder, impounded the gold. The beneficiaries of Locke's estate claim that the gold belongs to them because they did not intend to sell it. Mary argues that the gold belongs to her because the estate knowingly sold an object with unknown contents.

Drawing on the materials in this section, how do you think the court should resolve this dispute? Would your answer vary based on whether the court applied an objective, subjective, or mixed test to ascertain mutual assent?

2. International Perspective: Mutual Assent and the CISG

How do the various approaches to mutual assent that we have previously examined differ from the approach adopted by the CISG and applied by the court below? After reading the following case, which of the various approaches to mutual assent that we have studied thus far do you think is best, and why?

MCC-Marble Ceramic Center v. Ceramica Nuova D'Agostino

United States Circuit Court of Appeals, Eleventh Circuit
144 F.3d 1384 (1998)

BIRCH, J. This case requires us to determine whether a court must consider **parol evidence** in a contract dispute governed by the United Nations Convention on Contracts for the International Sale of Goods ("CISG").[1] The district court granted **summary judgment** on behalf of the defendant-appellee, relying on certain terms and provisions that appeared on the reverse of a pre-printed form contract for the sale of ceramic tiles. The plaintiff-appellant sought to rely on a number of affidavits that tended to show both that the parties had arrived at an oral contract before memorializing their agreement in writing and that they subjectively intended not to apply the terms on the reverse of the contract to their agreements. The magistrate judge held that the affidavits did not raise an issue of material fact and recommended that the district court grant summary judgment based on the terms of the contract. The district court agreed with the magistrate judge's reasoning and entered summary judgment in the defendant-appellee's favor. We reverse.

Parol evidence

Parol evidence refers to extrinsic evidence found outside of the four corners of a written contract. Often, one party will seek to introduce (and the other party will seek to prevent the introduction of) parol evidence for the purposes of adding to, subtracting from, varying, or interpreting the text of a written contract. We will discuss the parol evidence rule, which governs the admissibility of extrinsic evidence, in greater detail in Chapter 6.

Summary judgment

To avoid a potentially lengthy and expensive trial, a court will, upon motion, grant summary judgment where there is no genuine dispute of material facts between the parties and the moving party is entitled to judgment as a matter of law. If you haven't already done so, you will soon be covering summary judgment in your civil procedure class. *See* Fed. R. Civ. P. 56.

1. United Nations Convention on Contracts for the International Sale of Goods, opened for signature April 11, 1980, S. Treaty Doc. No. 9, 98th Cong., 1st Sess. 22 (1983), 19 I.L.M. 671, reprinted at 15 U.S.C. app. 52 (1997).

BACKGROUND

The plaintiff-appellant, MCC-Marble Ceramic, Inc. ("MCC"), is a Florida corporation engaged in the retail sale of tiles, and the defendant-appellee, Ceramica Nuova d'Agostino S.p.A. ("D'Agostino") is an Italian corporation engaged in the manufacture of ceramic tiles. In October 1990, MCC's president, Juan Carlos Monzon, met representatives of D'Agostino at a trade fair in Bologna, Italy and negotiated an agreement to purchase ceramic tiles from D'Agostino based on samples he examined at the trade fair. Monzon, who spoke no Italian, communicated with Gianni Silingardi, then D'Agostino's commercial director, through a translator, Gianfranco Copelli, who was himself an agent of D'Agostino.[2] The parties apparently arrived at an oral agreement on the crucial terms of price, quality, quantity, delivery and payment. The parties then recorded these terms on one of D'Agostino's standard, pre-printed order forms and Monzon signed the contract on MCC's behalf. According to MCC, the parties also entered into a **requirements contract** in February 1991, subject to which D'Agostino agreed to supply MCC with high grade ceramic tile at specific discounts as long as MCC purchased sufficient quantities of tile. MCC completed a number of additional order forms requesting tile deliveries pursuant to that agreement.

> ***Requirements contract***
>
> "A contract in which a buyer promises to buy, and a seller to supply, all the goods or services that a buyer needs during a specified period. The quantity term is measured by the buyer's requirements. A requirements contract assures the buyer of a source for the term of the contract." BLACK'S LAW DICTIONARY (10th ed. 2014). We will discuss requirements contracts in greater detail in *Eastern Air Lines, Inc. v. Gulf Oil Corporation*, p. 818, *infra*.

MCC brought suit against D'Agostino claiming a breach of the February 1991 requirements contract when D'Agostino failed to satisfy orders in April, May, and August of 1991. In addition to other defenses, **D'Agostino responded that it was under no obligation to fill MCC's orders because MCC had defaulted on payment for previous shipments.** In support of its position, D'Agostino relied on the pre-printed terms of the contracts that MCC had executed. The executed forms were printed in Italian and contained terms and conditions on both the front and reverse. According to an English translation of the October 1990 contract,[3] the front of the order form contained the following language directly beneath Monzon's signature:

> ***"D'Agostino responded . . ."***
>
> It often happens that one party refuses to perform its obligations under a contract in response to its belief that the other party has breached its obligations under that same contract. Where the first party is correct, it is usually justified in withholding its own performance. However, where the first party is mistaken, it will (often painfully and expensively) learn that it, by withholding performance, is now the party in breach. We will examine these issues, and some of the circumstances in which a party is entitled to withhold its own performance, in much greater detail in Chapter 7.

> [T]he buyer hereby states that he is aware of the sales conditions stated on the reverse and that he expressly approves of them with special reference to those numbered 1-2-3-4-5-6-7-8.

2. Since this case is before us on summary judgment, we consider the facts in the light most favorable to MCC, the non-moving party, and grant MCC the benefit of every factual inference. See *Welch v. Celotex Corp.*, 951 F.2d 1235, 1237 (11th Cir.1992).

3. D'Agostino provided the translation of the contract. MCC has never contested its accuracy.

Clause 6(b), printed on the back of the form states:

> [D]efault or delay in payment within the time agreed upon gives D'Agostino the right to . . . suspend or cancel the contract itself and to cancel possible other pending contracts and the buyer does not have the right to indemnification or damages.

D'Agostino also brought a number of counterclaims against MCC, seeking damages for MCC's alleged nonpayment for deliveries of tile that D'Agostino had made between February 28, 1991 and July 4, 1991. MCC responded that the tile it had received was of a lower quality than contracted for, and that, pursuant to the CISG, MCC was entitled to reduce payment in proportion to the defects.[4] D'Agostino, however, noted that clause 4 on the reverse of the contract states, in pertinent part:

> Possible complaints for defects of the merchandise must be made in writing by means of a certified letter within and not later than 10 days after receipt of the merchandise.

Although there is evidence to support MCC's claims that it complained about the quality of the deliveries it received, MCC never submitted any written complaints.

MCC did not dispute these underlying facts before the district court, but argued that the parties never intended the terms and conditions printed on the reverse of the order form to apply to their agreements. As evidence for this assertion, MCC submitted Monzon's affidavit, which claims that MCC had no subjective intent to be bound by those terms and that D'Agostino was aware of this intent. MCC also filed affidavits from Silingardi and Copelli, D'Agostino's representatives at the trade fair, which support Monzon's claim that the parties subjectively intended not to be bound by the terms on the reverse of the order form. The magistrate judge held that the affidavits, even if true, did not raise an issue of material fact regarding the interpretation or applicability of the terms of the written contracts and the district court accepted his recommendation to award summary judgment in D'Agostino's favor. MCC then filed this timely appeal.

> ***"MCC did not dispute . . ."***
>
> Before you read the rest of the court's opinion, pause and ask yourself what you think of this argument. As a general rule, it is a bad idea to sign a document containing terms that you don't want to be part of your contract, and an even worse idea to argue that such terms should not apply because you did not intend them to apply. That being said, might there be something to MCC's argument? As a judge, what kind of proof would you need before finding such an argument to be valid? Do you think MCC's intent should be tested according to the objective, subjective, or mixed approach to mutual assent? And finally, if, at the time of entering into the contract, MCC really did not intend these terms and conditions to apply, what should it have done?

DISCUSSION

. . . The parties to this case agree that the CISG governs their dispute because the United States, where MCC has its place of business, and Italy,

4. Article 50 of the CISG permits a buyer to reduce payment for nonconforming goods in proportion to the nonconformity under certain conditions. *See* CISG, art. 50.

where D'Agostino has its place of business, are both States Party to the Convention.[5] *See* CISG, art. 1.[6] Article 8 of the CISG governs the interpretation of international contracts for the sale of goods and forms the basis of MCC's appeal from the district court's grant of summary judgment in D'Agostino's favor.[7] MCC argues that the magistrate judge and the district court improperly ignored evidence that MCC submitted regarding the parties' subjective intent when they memorialized the terms of their agreement on D'Agostino's pre-printed form contract, and that the magistrate judge erred by applying the parol evidence rule in derogation of the CISG.

> ***"Contrary to what is familiar practice..."***
>
> Do you agree with the court's statement here? To what extent does the CISG's approach to mutual assent actually differ from "familiar practice in United States courts"? Look carefully at CISG Article 8. Does it adopt the objective, subjective, or mixed view of assent? In what ways does it differ from the common law, as reflected, say, in *Restatement (Second) of Contracts* § 201?

I. Subjective Intent Under the CISG

Contrary to what is familiar practice in United States courts, the CISG appears to permit a substantial inquiry into the parties' subjective intent, even if the parties did not engage in any objectively ascertainable means of registering this intent.[8] Article 8(1) of the CISG instructs courts to interpret the "statements . . . and other conduct of a party . . . according to his intent" as long as the other party

5. The United States Senate ratified the CISG in 1986, and the United States deposited its instrument of ratification at the United Nations Headquarters in New York on December 11, 1986. *See Preface to Convention*, reprinted at 15 U.S.C. app. 52 (1997). The Convention entered into force between the United States and the other States Parties, including Italy, on January 1, 1988. *See id.*; *Filanto S.p.A. v. Chilewich Int'l Corp.*, 789 F. Supp. 1229, 1237 (S.D.N.Y. 1992).

6. Article 1 of the CISG states in relevant part:

> (1) This Convention applies to contracts of sale of goods between parties whose places of business are in different States:
>
> (a) When the States are Contracting States. . . .

CISG, art. 1.

7. Article 8 provides:

> (1) For the purposes of this Convention statements made by and other conduct of a party are to be interpreted according to his intent where the other party knew or could not have been unaware what that intent was.
>
> (2) If the preceding paragraph is not applicable, statements made by and conduct of a party are to be interpreted according to the understanding a reasonable person of the same kind as the other party would have had in the same circumstances.
>
> (3) In determining the intent of a party or the understanding a reasonable person would have had, due consideration is to be given to all relevant circumstances of the case including the negotiations, any practices which the parties have established between themselves, usages and any subsequent conduct of the parties.

CISG, art. 8.

8. In the United States, the legislatures, courts, and the legal academy have voiced a preference for relying on objective manifestations of the parties' intentions. For example, Article Two of the *Uniform Commercial Code*, which most states have enacted in some form or another to govern contracts for the sale of goods, is replete with references to standards of commercial reasonableness. *See e.g.*, U.C.C. § 2-206 (referring to reasonable means of accepting an offer); *see also Lucy v. Zehmer*, 84 S.E.2d 516, 522 (1954) ("Whether the writing signed . . . as the result of a serious

"knew or could not have been unaware" of that intent. The plain language of the Convention, therefore, requires an inquiry into a party's subjective intent as long as the other party to the contract was aware of that intent.

In this case, MCC has submitted three affidavits that discuss the purported subjective intent of the parties to the initial agreement concluded between MCC and D'Agostino in October 1990. All three affidavits discuss the preliminary negotiations and report that the parties arrived at an oral agreement for D'Agostino to supply quantities of a specific grade of ceramic tile to MCC at an agreed upon price. The affidavits state that the "oral agreement established the essential terms of quality, quantity, description of goods, delivery, price and payment." . . . **The affidavits also note that the parties memorialized the terms of their oral agreement on a standard D'Agostino order form, but all three affiants contend that the parties subjectively intended not to be bound by the terms on the reverse of that form despite a provision directly below the signature line that expressly and specifically incorporated those terms.**[9]

> ***"The affidavits also note . . ."***
>
> Read Footnote 9 carefully. Are you more or less sympathetic to MCC's argument after learning that (a) the written order form was entirely in Italian and (b) Monzon neither spoke nor read Italian?

The terms on the reverse of the contract give D'Agostino the right to suspend or cancel all contracts in the event of a buyer's non-payment and require a buyer to make a written report of all defects within ten days. As the magistrate judge's report and recommendation makes clear, if these terms applied to the agreements between MCC and D'Agostino, summary judgment would be appropriate because MCC failed to make any written complaints about the quality of tile it received and D'Agostino has established MCC's non-payment of a number of invoices amounting to $108,389.40 and 102,053,846.00 Italian lira.

---

offer . . . and a serious acceptance . . . , or was a serious offer . . . and an acceptance in secret jest . . . , in either event it constituted a binding contract of sale between the parties."). Justice Holmes expressed the philosophy behind this focus on the objective in forceful terms: "The law has nothing to do with the actual state of the parties' minds. In contract, as elsewhere, it must go by externals, and judge parties by their conduct." OLIVER W. HOLMES, THE COMMON LAW 242 (Howe ed. 1963) *quoted in* JOHN O. HONNOLD, UNIFORM LAW FOR INTERNATIONAL SALES UNDER THE 1980 UNITED NATIONS CONVENTION § 107 at 164 (2d ed. 1991) (hereinafter HONNOLD, UNIFORM LAW).

9. MCC makes much of the fact that the written order form is entirely in Italian and that Monzon, who signed the contract on MCC's behalf directly below this provision incorporating the terms on the reverse of the form, neither spoke nor read Italian. This fact is of no assistance to MCC's position. We find it nothing short of astounding that an individual, purportedly experienced in commercial matters, would sign a contract in a foreign language and expect not to be bound simply because he could not comprehend its terms. We find nothing in the CISG that might counsel this type of reckless behavior and nothing that signals any retreat from the proposition that parties who sign contracts will be bound by them regardless of whether they have read them or understood them. *See, e.g., Samson Plastic Conduit and Pipe Corp. v. Battenfeld Extrusionstechnik GMBH*, 718 F. Supp. 886, 890 (M.D. Ala. 1989) ("A good and recurring illustration of the problem . . . involves a person who is . . . unfamiliar with the language in which a contract is written and who has signed a document which was not read to him. There is all but unanimous agreement that he is bound. . . .")

Article 8(1) of the CISG requires a court to consider this evidence of the parties' subjective intent. Contrary to the magistrate judge's report, which the district court endorsed and adopted, article 8(1) does not focus on interpreting the parties' statements alone. Although we agree with the magistrate judge's conclusion that no "interpretation" of the contract's terms could support MCC's position,[10] article 8(1) also requires a court to consider subjective intent while interpreting the conduct of the parties. The CISG's language, therefore, requires courts to consider evidence of a party's subjective intent when signing a contract if the other party to the contract was aware of that intent at the time. This is precisely the type of evidence that MCC has provided through the . . . affidavits, which discuss not only Monzon's intent as MCC's representative but also discuss the intent of D'Agostino's representatives and their knowledge that Monzon did not intend to agree to the terms on the reverse of the form contract. This acknowledgment that D'Agostino's representatives were aware of Monzon's subjective intent puts this case squarely within article 8(1) of the CISG, and therefore requires the court to consider MCC's evidence as it interprets the parties' conduct.[11] . . .

CONCLUSION

MCC asks us to reverse the district court's grant of summary judgment in favor of D'Agostino. The district court's decision rests on pre-printed contractual terms and conditions incorporated on the reverse of a standard order form that MCC's president signed on the company's behalf. Nevertheless, we conclude that the CISG, which governs international contracts for the sale of goods, precludes summary judgment in this case because MCC has raised an issue of material fact concerning the parties' subjective intent to be bound by the terms on the reverse of the pre-printed contract. [The court also held that summary judgment was precluded because there is no parol evidence rule under the CISG, as discussed on p. 785, *infra*.] Accordingly, we reverse the district court's grant of summary judgment and remand this case for further proceedings consistent with this opinion.

10. The magistrate judge's report correctly notes that MCC has not sought an interpretation of those terms, but rather to exclude them altogether. We agree that such an approach "would render terms of written contracts virtually meaningless and severely diminish the reliability of commercial contracts."

11. Without this crucial acknowledgment, we would interpret the contract and the parties' actions according to article 8(2), which directs courts to rely on objective evidence of the parties' intent. On the facts of this case it seems readily apparent that MCC's affidavits provide *no evidence* that Monzon's actions would have made his alleged subjective intent not to be bound by the terms of the contract known to "the understanding that a reasonable person . . . would have had in the same circumstances." CISG, art 8(2).

RELEVANT PROVISIONS

For the CISG, consult Articles 1 and 8. For the UNIDROIT Principles, consult Articles 4.1-4.3.

NOTES AND QUESTIONS

1. *What happened?* Who sued whom for what? Procedurally, how did the case get before this court? Factually, what happened between the parties? What arguments did the plaintiff and defendant make? What rule or rules did the court apply? How did the court analyze the dispute between the parties? How did the court decide the case?

2. *Was this case correctly decided?* Do you agree with the result reached in this case? Why or why not? Do you agree with the court's reasoning? Why or why not? How, if at all, would you have written the opinion differently?

3. *Is the CISG International Law?* Well, yes and no. It is international law insofar as it applies to the sale of goods between parties whose places of business are in countries that have ratified the CISG. *See* CISG Article 1. But it also constitutes the domestic "law of the land" insofar as the CISG is a treatise ratified by Congress (see the court's Footnote 5). For this reason, *both* the UCC (which has been enacted by all state legislatures except Louisiana's) *and* the CISG govern the sale of goods in the United States. This means that if you have a business in California that buys or sells widgets to a company in Massachusetts, your contract is governed by the UCC. But if your company in California buys or sells widgets to your business partner in, say, Amsterdam, the capital of the Netherlands, which has ratified the CISG (as have most of world's economic powerhouses),* then your contract is likely governed by the CISG. See *Filanto, S.p.A. v. Chilewich Intern. Corp.*, 789 F. Supp. 1229, 1237 (S.D.N.Y. 1992) (absent a clear choice of law, "the Convention governs *all* contracts between parties with places of business in different nations, so long as both nations are signatories to the Convention"). We will discuss *Filanto* in greater depth on p. 719, *infra*.

4. *Drafting exercise. What if you don't want the CISG to govern your contract?* Good question. Try to draft a clause between you and your business partner in Amsterdam (you do remember your business partner, don't you?) ensuring that, if a dispute arises, the governing law will be the law of California. Such a clause, called a choice of law provision, is often the cornerstone of any successful international contract. But be careful: simply writing something

---

* For a list of countries that have ratified the CISG, see *http://www.cisg.law.pace.edu/cisg/countries/cntries.html*.

like "In the event of a dispute, the law of California will apply" would probably not work (do you see why?), and the law that ended up governing your contract would probably turn out to be as different from what you expected as the quantity of goods measured by the metric system (in kilograms) would be different from the quantity of goods measured by the imperial system (in pounds).

5. *Applying the CISG.* Revisiting the facts of *Lucy v. Zehmer,* and putting to the side for the moment the fact that the case did not involve the sale of goods, do you think a court would have found mutual assent under CISG Article 8?

3. Internet Commerce: Contracts in the Digital Age

Before we conclude this general unit on mutual assent, it is worth pausing to ask whether the general principles of contract law we have learned so far—many of which were developed in the horse and buggy age—are still relevant to the types of contract disputes that arise in the digital age. The answer, of course, is yes (otherwise, we'd need to seriously rethink the way we teach contract law). Anthropologists are in wide agreement that human nature (to be distinguished from human culture) has remained unchanged for at least the past 50,000 years, and contract law, broadly conceived, is about regulating those aspects of human behavior responsible for delayed exchanges, often with promises involved. As long as we humans continue to desire to maximize our welfare (broadly conceived) by giving and taking, buying and selling, trading, bartering, and promising, there will be a place for contract law. And, as long as we care about ascertaining intent before enforcing any old promise, then the various approaches to mutual assent that we examined will continue to be relevant. So, onwards we go! We say goodbye to our cavemen ancestors of 50,000 years ago, jump in our DeLorean time machines, set the year to 2014, and find ourselves smack in the thick of the modern world.* Here, we find ourselves surrounded by Barnes & Noble stores, computers, the internet, arbitration clauses, clickwrap agreements, and browsewrap agreements. But don't let any of that confuse you. The question before the court is the same as it's always been: Is there evidence that the parties have manifested their assent to one another?

* Of course, everyone knows that time travel isn't *that* easy. We must first bring the DeLorean up to 88 miles per hour to activate the flux capacitor, and we must make sure it is powered by a source capable of generating 1.21 gigawatts of electricity. Plutonium works well here, but a bolt of lightning will also do in a pinch.

Nguyen v. Barnes & Noble, Inc.

United States Court of Appeals, Ninth Circuit
763 F.3d 1171 (2014)

NOONAN, CIRCUIT JUDGE. Barnes & Noble, Inc. ("Barnes & Noble") appeals the district court's denial of its motion to compel arbitration against Kevin Khoa Nguyen ("Nguyen") pursuant to the arbitration agreement contained in its website's Terms of Use. In order to resolve the issue of arbitrability, we must address whether Nguyen, by merely using Barnes & Noble's website, agreed to be bound by the Terms of Use, even though Nguyen was never prompted to assent to the Terms of Use and never in fact read them. We agree with the district court that Barnes & Noble did not provide reasonable notice of its Terms of Use, and that Nguyen therefore did not unambiguously manifest assent to the arbitration provision contained therein. . . .

We therefore affirm the district court's denial of Barnes & Noble's motion to compel arbitration and to stay court proceedings.

I. BACKGROUND

The underlying facts are not in dispute. Barnes & Noble is a national bookseller that owns and operates hundreds of bookstores as well as the website <www.barnesandnoble.com>. In August 2011, Barnes & Noble, along with other retailers across the country, liquidated its inventory of discontinued Hewlett-Packard Touchpads ("Touchpads"), an unsuccessful competitor to Apple's iPad, by advertising a "fire sale" of Touchpads at a heavily discounted price. Acting quickly on the nationwide liquidation of Touchpads, Nguyen purchased two units on Barnes & Noble's website on August 21, 2011, and received an email confirming the transaction. The following day, Nguyen received another email informing him that his order had been cancelled due to unexpectedly high demand. Nguyen alleges that, as a result of "Barnes & Noble's representations, as well as the delay in informing him it would not honor the sale," he was "unable to obtain an HP Tablet during the liquidation period for the discounted price," and was "forced to rely on substitute tablet technology, which he subsequently purchased . . . [at] considerable expense."

In April 2012, Nguyen filed this lawsuit in California Superior Court on behalf of himself and a putative class of consumers whose Touchpad orders had been cancelled, alleging that Barnes & Noble had engaged in deceptive business practices and false advertising in violation of both California and New York law. Barnes & Noble removed the action to federal court and moved to compel arbitration under the Federal Arbitration Act ("FAA"), arguing that Nguyen was bound by the arbitration agreement in the website's Terms of Use.

The website's Terms of Use are available via a "Terms of Use" hyperlink located in the bottom left-hand corner of every page on the Barnes & Noble website, which appears alongside other hyperlinks labeled "NOOK Store

Terms," "Copyright," and "Privacy Policy." These hyperlinks also appear underlined and set in green typeface in the lower left-hand corner of every page in the online checkout process.

Nguyen neither clicked on the "Terms of Use" hyperlink nor actually read the Terms of Use. Had he clicked on the hyperlink, he would have been taken to a page containing the full text of Barnes & Noble's Terms of Use, which state, in relevant part: "By visiting any area in the Barnes & Noble.com Site, creating an account, [or] making a purchase via the Barnes & Noble.com Site . . . a User is deemed to have accepted the Terms of Use." Nguyen also would have come across an arbitration provision, which states:

XVIII. DISPUTE RESOLUTION

> Any claim or controversy at law or equity that arises out of the Terms of Use, the Barnes & Noble.com Site or any Barnes & Noble.com Service (each a "Claim"), shall be resolved through binding arbitration conducted by telephone, online or based solely upon written submissions where no in-person appearance is required. In such cases, arbitration shall be administered by the American Arbitration Association under its Commercial Arbitration Rules (including without limitation the Supplementary Procedures for Consumer-Related Disputes, if applicable), and judgment on the award rendered by the arbitrator(s) may be entered in any court having jurisdiction thereof. . . .
>
> Any claim shall be arbitrated or litigated, as the case may be, on an individual basis and shall not be consolidated with any Claim of any other party whether through class action proceedings, class arbitration proceedings or otherwise. . . .
>
> Each of the parties hereby knowingly, voluntarily and intentionally waives any right it may have to a trial by jury in respect of any litigation (including but not limited to any claims, counterclaims, cross-claims, or third party claims) arising out of, under or in connection with these Terms of Use. Further, each party hereto certifies that no representative or agent of either party has represented, expressly or otherwise, that such a party would not in the event of such litigation, seek to enforce this waiver of right to jury trial provision. Each of the parties acknowledges that this section is a material inducement for the other party entering into these Terms of Use.

Nguyen contends that he cannot be bound to the arbitration provision because he neither had notice of nor assented to the website's Terms of Use. Barnes & Noble, for its part, asserts that the placement of the "Terms of Use" hyperlink on its website put Nguyen on constructive notice of the arbitration agreement. Barnes & Noble contends that this notice, combined with Nguyen's subsequent use of the website, was enough to bind him to the Terms of Use. The district court disagreed, and Barnes & Noble now appeals. . . .

III. DISCUSSION

The FAA requires federal district courts to stay judicial proceedings and compel arbitration of claims covered by a written and enforceable arbitration agreement. The FAA limits the district court's role to determining whether a valid arbitration agreement exists, and whether the agreement encompasses the disputes at issue. The parties do not quarrel that Barnes & Noble's arbitration agreement, should it be found enforceable, encompasses Nguyen's claims. The only issue is whether a valid arbitration agreement exists. . . .

For the reasons that follow, we hold that Nguyen did not enter into Barnes & Noble's agreement to arbitrate.

"While new commerce on the Internet has exposed courts to many new situations, it has not fundamentally changed the principles of contract." *Register.com, Inc. v. Verio, Inc.*, 356 F.3d 393, 403 (2d Cir. 2004). One such principle is the requirement that "[m]utual manifestation of assent, whether by written or spoken word or by conduct, is the touchstone of contract." *Specht v. Netscape Commc'ns Corp.*, 306 F.3d 17, 29 (2d Cir. 2002).

Contracts formed on the Internet come primarily in two flavors: "clickwrap" (or "click-through") agreements, in which website users are required to click on an "I agree" box after being presented with a list of terms and conditions of use; and "browsewrap" agreements, where a website's terms and conditions of use are generally posted on the website via a hyperlink at the bottom of the screen. *See Register.com*, 356 F.3d at 428-30. Barnes & Noble's Terms of Use fall in the latter category.

"Unlike a clickwrap agreement, a browsewrap agreement does not require the user to manifest assent to the terms and conditions expressly . . . [a] party instead gives his assent simply by using the website." *Hines v. Overstock.com, Inc.*, 668 F. Supp. 2d 362, 366-67 (E.D.N.Y. 2009). Indeed, "in a pure-form browsewrap agreement, 'the website will contain a notice that—by merely using the services of, obtaining information from, or initiating applications within the website—the user is agreeing to and is bound by the site's terms of service.'" *Fteja v. Facebook, Inc.*, 841 F. Supp. 2d 829, 837 (S.D.N.Y. 2012). Thus, "by visiting the website—something that the user has already done—the user agrees to the Terms of Use not listed on the site itself but available only by clicking a hyperlink." *Id.* "The defining feature of browsewrap agreements is that the user can continue to use the website or its services without visiting the page hosting the browsewrap agreement or even knowing that such a webpage exists." *Be In, Inc. v. Google Inc.*, No. 12-CV-03373-LHK, 2013 WL 5568706, at *6 (N.D. Cal. Oct. 9, 2013). "Because no affirmative action is required by the website user to agree to the terms of a contract other than his or her use of the website, the determination of the validity of the browsewrap contract depends on whether the user has actual or constructive knowledge of a website's terms and conditions." *Van Tassell v. United Mktg. Grp., LLC*, 795 F. Supp. 2d 770, 790 (N.D. Ill. 2011); *see also* Mark A. Lemley, *Terms of Use*, 91 MINN. L. REV. 459, 477 (2006) ("Courts may be willing to overlook the utter absence of assent only when there are reasons to believe that the [website user] is aware of the [website owner's] terms.").

Were there any evidence in the record that Nguyen had actual notice of the Terms of Use or was required to affirmatively acknowledge the Terms of Use before completing his online purchase, the outcome of this case might be different. Indeed, courts have consistently enforced browsewrap agreements where the user had actual notice of the agreement. *See, e.g., Register.com*, 356 F.3d at 401-04 (finding likelihood of success on the merits in a breach of browsewrap claim where the defendant "admitted that . . . it was fully aware of the terms" of the offer); *Sw. Airlines Co.*, 2007 WL 4823761, at *4-6 (finding proper contract formation where defendant continued its breach after being notified of the terms in a cease and desist letter); *Ticketmaster Corp. v. Tickets. Com, Inc.*, No. CV-997654, 2003 WL 21406289, at *2C (C.D. Cal. Mar. 7, 2003) (denying defendants' summary judgment motion on browsewrap contract claim where defendants continued breaching contract after receiving letter quoting the browsewrap contract terms). Courts have also been more willing to find the requisite notice for constructive assent where the browsewrap agreement resembles a clickwrap agreement—that is, where the user is required to affirmatively acknowledge the agreement before proceeding with use of the website. *See, e.g., Zaltz v. JDATE*, 952 F. Supp. 2d 439, 451-52 (E.D.N.Y. 2013) (enforcing forum selection clause where prospective members had to check box confirming that they both read and agreed to the website's Terms and Conditions of Service to obtain account); *Fteja*, 841 F. Supp. 2d at 838-40 (enforcing forum selection clause in website's terms of service where a notice below the "Sign Up" button stated, "By clicking Sign Up, you are indicating that you have read and agree to the Terms of Service," and user had clicked "Sign Up").

But where, as here, there is no evidence that the website user had actual knowledge of the agreement, the validity of the browsewrap agreement turns on whether the website puts a reasonably prudent user on inquiry notice of the terms of the contract. Whether a user has inquiry notice of a browsewrap agreement, in turn, depends on the design and content of the website and the agreement's webpage. Where the link to a website's terms of use is buried at the bottom of the page or tucked away in obscure corners of the website where users are unlikely to see it, courts have refused to enforce the browsewrap agreement. *See, e.g., Specht*, 306 F.3d at 23 (refusing to enforce terms of use that "would have become visible to plaintiffs only if they had scrolled down to the next screen"); *In re Zappos.com*, 893 F. Supp. 2d at 1064 ("The Terms of Use is inconspicuous, buried in the middle to bottom of every Zappos.com webpage among many other links, and the website never directs a user to the Terms of Use."); *Van Tassell*, 795 F. Supp. 2d at 792-93 (refusing to enforce arbitration clause in browsewrap agreement that was only noticeable after a "multistep process" of clicking through non-obvious links); *Hines*, 668 F. Supp. 2d at 367 (plaintiff "could not even see the link to [the terms and conditions] without scrolling down to the bottom of the screen—an action that was not required to effectuate her purchase").

On the other hand, where the website contains an explicit textual notice that continued use will act as a manifestation of the user's intent to be bound, courts have been more amenable to enforcing browsewrap agreements. *See, e.g., Cairo, Inc. v. Crossmedia Servs., Inc.*, No. 04-04825, 2005 WL 756610, at *2, *4-5 (N.D. Cal. Apr. 1, 2005) (enforcing forum selection clause in website's terms of use where every page on the website had a textual notice that read: "By continuing past this page and/or using this site, you agree to abide by the Terms of Use for this site, which prohibit commercial use of any information on this site"). *But see Pollstar v. Gigmania, Ltd.*, 170 F. Supp. 2d 974, 981 (E.D. Cal. 2000) (refusing to enforce browsewrap agreement where textual notice appeared in small gray print against a gray background). In short, the conspicuousness and placement of the "Terms of Use" hyperlink, other notices given to users of the terms of use, and the website's general design all contribute to whether a reasonably prudent user would have inquiry notice of a browsewrap agreement.

Barnes & Noble argues that the placement of the "Terms of Use" hyperlink in the bottom left-hand corner of every page on the Barnes & Noble website, and its close proximity to the buttons a user must click on to complete an online purchase, is enough to place a reasonably prudent user on constructive notice. It is true that the location of the hyperlink on Barnes & Noble's website distinguishes this case from *Specht,* the leading authority on the enforceability of browsewrap terms under New York law. There, the Second Circuit refused to enforce an arbitration provision in a website's licensing terms where the hyperlink to the terms was located at the bottom of the page, hidden below the "Download" button that users had to click to initiate the software download. Then-Second Circuit Judge Sotomayor, writing for the panel, held that "a reference to the existence of license terms on a submerged screen is not sufficient to place consumers on inquiry or constructive notice of those terms." *Specht,* 306 F.3d at 32. By contrast, here the "Terms of Use" link appears either directly below the relevant button a user must click on to proceed in the checkout process or just a few inches away. On some pages, the content of the webpage is compact enough that a user can view the link without scrolling. On the remaining pages, the hyperlink is close enough to the "Proceed with Checkout" button that a user would have to bring the link within his field of vision in order to complete his order.

But the proximity or conspicuousness of the hyperlink alone is not enough to give rise to constructive notice, and Barnes & Noble directs us to no case law that supports this proposition.[1] The most analogous case the court was able to

1. Indeed, in cases where courts have relied on the proximity of the hyperlink to enforce a browsewrap agreement, the websites at issue have also included something more to capture the user's attention and secure her assent. *See, e.g., 5381 Partners LLC v. Sharesale.com, Inc.*, No. 12-CV-4263 JFB AKT, 2013 WL 5328324, at *7 (E.D.N.Y. Sept. 23, 2013) (in addition to hyperlink that appeared adjacent to the activation button users had to click on, website also contained a text warning near the button that stated "By clicking and making a request to Activate, you agree to the terms and conditions in the [agreement]"); *Zaltz,* 952 F. Supp. 2d at 451-52 (users required to check box confirming that they had reviewed and agreed to website's Terms and Conditions, even though hyperlink to Terms and Conditions was located on the same screen as the button users had to click on to complete registration).

locate is *PDC Labs., Inc. v. Hach Co.,* an unpublished district court order cited by neither party. No. 09-1110, 2009 WL 2605270 (C.D. Ill. Aug. 25, 2009). There, the "Terms [and Conditions of Sale] were hyperlinked on three separate pages of the online . . . order process in underlined, blue, contrasting text." *Id.* at *3. The court held that "[t]his contrasting text is sufficient to be considered conspicuous," thereby placing a reasonable user on notice that the terms applied. *Id.* It also observed, however, that the terms' conspicuousness was reinforced by the language of the final checkout screen, which read, "'STEP 4 of 4: *Review terms,* add any comments, and submit order,'" and was followed by a hyperlink to the Terms. *Id.* (emphasis added).

As in *PDC,* the checkout screens here contained "Terms of Use" hyperlinks in underlined, color-contrasting text. But *PDC* is dissimilar in that the final screen on that website contained the phrase "Review terms." *PDC Labs.,* 2009 WL 2605270, at *3. This admonition makes *PDC* distinguishable, despite the court's explanation that the blue contrasting hyperlinks were sufficiently conspicuous on their own. That the *PDC* decision couched its holding in terms of procedural unconscionability rather than contract formation further distinguishes it from our case. *See id.*

In light of the lack of controlling authority on point, and in keeping with courts' traditional reluctance to enforce browsewrap agreements against individual consumers,[2] we therefore hold that where a website makes its terms of use available via a conspicuous hyperlink on every page of the website but otherwise provides no notice to users nor prompts them to take any affirmative action to demonstrate assent, even close proximity of the hyperlink to relevant buttons users must click on—without more—is insufficient to give rise to constructive notice. While failure to read a contract before agreeing to its terms does not relieve a party of its obligations under the contract, the onus must be on website owners to put users on notice of the terms to which they wish to bind consumers. Given the breadth of the range of technological savvy of online purchasers, consumers cannot be expected to ferret out hyperlinks to terms and conditions to which they have no reason to suspect they will be bound.

Barnes & Noble's argument that Nguyen's familiarity with other websites governed by similar browsewrap terms, including his personal website

2. *See* Woodrow Hartzog, *Website Design as Contract,* 60 AM. U. L. REV. 1635, 1644 (2011) (observing that courts "tend to shy away from enforcing browsewrap agreements that require no outward manifestation of assent"); Lemley, 91 MINN. L. REV. at 472-77 ("An examination of the cases that have considered browsewraps in the last five years demonstrates that the courts have been willing to enforce terms of use against corporations, but have not been willing to do so against individuals.").

<www.kevinkhoa.com>, gives rise to an inference of constructive notice is also of no moment. Whether Nguyen has experience with the browsewrap agreements found on other websites such as Facebook, LinkedIn, MySpace, or Twitter, has no bearing on whether he had constructive notice of Barnes & Noble's Terms of Use. There is nothing in the record to suggest that those browsewrap terms are enforceable by or against Nguyen, much less why they should give rise to constructive notice of Barnes & Noble's browsewrap terms. . . .

We hold that Nguyen had insufficient notice of Barnes & Noble's Terms of Use, and thus did not enter into an agreement with Barnes & Noble to arbitrate his claims.

Affirmed.

NOTES AND QUESTIONS

1. *What happened?* Who sued whom for what? Procedurally, how did the case get before this court? Factually, what happened between the parties? What arguments did the plaintiff and defendant make? What rule or rules did the court apply? How did the court analyze the dispute between the parties? How did the court decide the case?

2. *Was this case correctly decided?* Do you agree with the result reached here? How about the reasoning? How, if at all, would you have written the opinion differently?

3. *What approach was used?* Did the court use the objective, subjective, or mixed approach to ascertain intent? Would the case have come out differently if the court used a different approach? How?

4. *A note on terminology.* The terms "clickwrap" and "browsewrap" agreements are adapted from the older term "shrink wrap" agreements, which refer to the boilerplate inserts one often finds packaged, along with one's product, in a cellophane shrink-wrapped box.

5. *Clickwrap versus browsewrap.* The court distinguished between clickwrap and browsewrap agreements. What's the difference? And what should we call an agreement that requires you to check an "I agree" box indicating you've clicked on (and presumably read) the information contained in the "Terms and Conditions" and "Privacy Policy" links next to it? You could (and probably do) check the box (making it look like clickwrap) without ever having to read the information contained in the either of the two links (making it look like browsewrap).

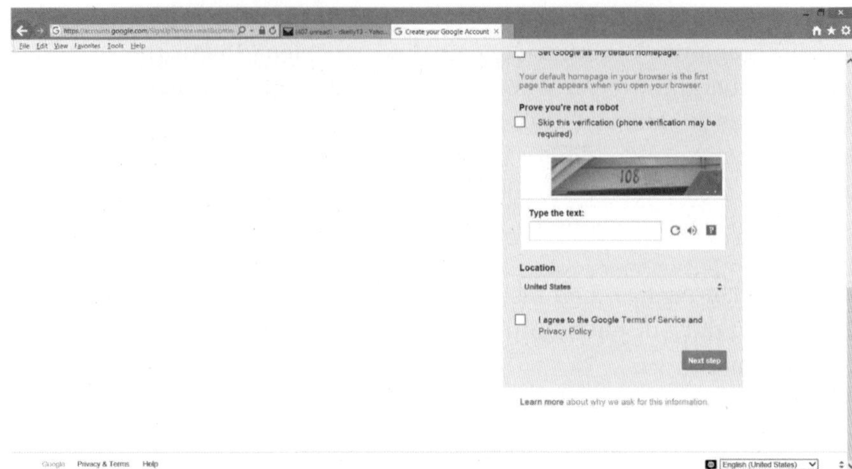

6. ***Clickthrough agreements?*** For some of the reasons mentioned in the note above, some commentators think we should ditch the "clickwrap" and "browsewrap" language, and focus instead on whether the user must mandatorily "click through" an agreement, ticking boxes along the way, indicating that they have read the agreements referenced next to the boxes. Is this helpful?

7. ***Back to assent.*** More important than terminology, do courts have a basis for treating any of these agreements (e.g., clickwrap) differently from any of the others (e.g., browsewrap)? Why? We all know that most customers don't read the terms of their license agreements, whether they're accessible via a "clickwrap," "browsewrap," or "mandatory clickthrough" link. So does it make sense for the court to find assent in one case, but not the other? Can you think of a better approach?

8. ***So what happens now?*** Now that the court has ruled for Nguyen, is the case over? What will happen next?

PROBLEM: SUBSTANDARD SERVICE SORROWS

InTech, a Delaware corporation with its principal place of business in Virginia, offered fiber Internet service at speeds it claims are ten times greater than DSL Internet. InTech has signed up hundreds of thousands of subscribers, including Danielle, a resident of Florida. After Danielle purchased the best service package available, it took InTech over a month and a half to send a technician to install her Internet modem. Danielle noticed immediately after the installation that the service experienced frequent disruptions where no Internet was available and operated at speeds much lower than those advertised. After enduring poor service for five months, Danielle cancelled her service.

Shortly afterwards, Danielle filed a class action lawsuit against InTech in Florida. InTech responded to the lawsuit by filing a motion to dismiss based on a forum selection clause in its Services Access Agreement. To become an InTech subscriber, each customer must agree to all the terms in the Services Access Agreement, including the forum selection clause. When a customer agrees to the

Services Access Agreement, the customer reads the agreement in a scroll box on their computer monitor, where only a small portion of the document is visible at any one time. The contract is entered when the subscriber clicks the "Accept" button below the scroll box. The forum selection clause reads:

> 30.2 You and INTECH agree that this Agreement shall be interpreted in accordance with the substantive laws of the Commonwealth of Virginia, without reference to its principles of conflicts of laws. You and INTECH consent to the exclusive personal jurisdiction of and venue in a court of competent jurisdiction located in Richmond, Virginia. Any cause of action or claim you may have with respect to the Service must be commenced within one (1) year after the claim or cause of action arises or such claim or cause of action is barred.

The contract does not mention that Virginia is one of only two states that does not allow class action lawsuits.

Is Danielle able to pursue her class-action lawsuit in Florida? In Virginia? Is the forum selection clause in this agreement enforceable?

PROBLEM: WHERE SHOULD I SUE?

Giovanni, an attorney residing in New Jersey, purchased a subscription to Metware, a cloud-computing storage service located in Washington State. After using the service for three months, Giovanni noticed that Metware had, without notice or permission, unilaterally charged him an increased subscription fee attributed to an "upgrade" in service plans. Giovanni reviewed Metware's service agreement and did not find any provision that gave notice that Metware would upgrade his plan after a certain amount of time. Giovanni filed a class action lawsuit in his home state of New Jersey due to its strong consumer protection laws. The class purported to represent 800,000 similarly aggrieved Metware subscribers from around the country. Metware immediately moved to dismiss the complaint for lack of jurisdiction and improper venue by reason of its forum selection clause which, Metware argues, is in every service agreement and bound Giovanni and all the members of the class. The service agreement's forum selection clause reads:

> This Agreement is governed by the laws of the State of Washington and you consent to the exclusive jurisdiction and venue in Pierce County, Washington in any dispute arising out of or relating to your use of Metware Cloud-Computing Storage Service or Metware Membership.

During the sign-up process on Metware's website, a prospective subscriber is prompted to view multiple pages of information, including the service agreement containing the forum selection clause. The service agreement is eighteen pages long and appears on the computer screen in a small scrollable window, below which there is an "I Agree" and an "I Don't Agree" button. Registration can only be completed if a prospective subscriber clicks the "I Agree" button. Metware does not begin charging subscribers until they have fully completed the registration process.

Can Metware enforce its forum selection clause? What is Giovanni's best argument against enforcement of the forum selection clause?

B. MAKING OFFERS

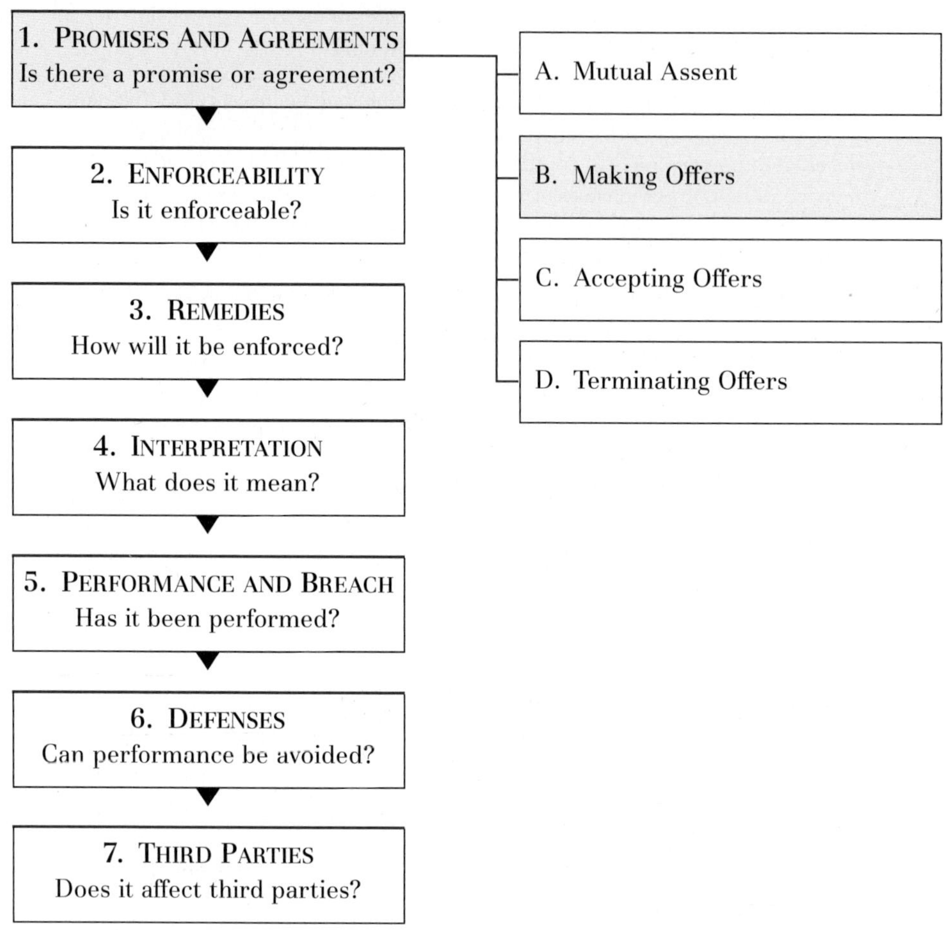
1. Promises And Agreements
Is there a promise or agreement?
2. Enforceability
Is it enforceable?
3. Remedies
How will it be enforced?
4. Interpretation
What does it mean?
5. Performance and Breach
Has it been performed?
6. Defenses
Can performance be avoided?
7. Third Parties
Does it affect third parties?
A. Mutual Assent
B. Making Offers
C. Accepting Offers
D. Terminating Offers

1. Offers in General

Now that we have examined mutual assent in some detail, and have considered the three main perspectives used by courts to ascertain the intent of the parties (the objective, subjective, and mixed approaches), we are now ready to turn to the mechanics of assent—to its nuts and bolts, as it were—to learn how courts test whether parties have formed enforceable agreements with one another. As it turns out, although there are a variety of ways in which parties can manifest their assent to one another, contract law favors analyzing these manifestations through the lens of offer and acceptance.

We begin this part of the chapter with three short excerpts. In the first, you will be introduced to the relationship between mutual assent and the doctrines of offer and acceptance. In the second, you will be provided with a doctrinal overview to offers themselves. Finally, in the last excerpt, we will draw on an earlier thinking tool to examine the various legal relationships that offers may create between parties.

ON THE RELATIONSHIP BETWEEN MUTUAL ASSENT AND OFFER AND ACCEPTANCE*

The rule generally laid down is that the acts of offer and acceptance must be expressions of assent. This has long been the theory upon which contractual obligations have been enforced. The test question usually put is, what was the intention of the parties? It must not be supposed from this, however, that no contractual relation can exist unless the parties both foresaw and intended it. If two parties have gone through the form of offering and accepting, the law determines the legal relations that follow. Frequently these come with surprise and shock to the parties themselves. It may be said here, as in the law of torts, that the parties are presumed to intend the consequences of their acts, but this is often a violent presumption contrary to fact. To indulge such a presumption is merely to hold that the actual intention of the parties is not the determinative fact, or even that it is wholly immaterial.

Parties are bound by the reasonable meaning of what they said and not by what they thought. If A makes an offer to B which B reasonably understands to have a particular meaning, and so accepts, A is bound in accordance with B's understanding. So also, if A's offer has only one reasonable meaning, B is bound in accordance therewith, even though he accepted supposing the meaning to be otherwise. The operative act creating an obligation is the expression of intention and not the thought process. It may be said that the purpose of the rule is to carry out the intentions of the parties in the great majority of cases; but it seems better to say that its purpose is to secure the fulfilment of the promisee's reasonable expectations as induced by the promisor's act. In the law of contract as in the law of tort, men are expected to live up to the standard of the reasonably prudent man. If there is a misunderstanding and neither party was negligent, there is no contract. The same is true if both are equally negligent.

The legal relations consequent upon offer and acceptance are not wholly dependent, even upon the reasonable meaning of the words and acts of the parties. The law determines these relations in the light of subsequent circumstances, these often being totally unforeseen by the parties. In such cases it is sometimes said that the law will create that relation which the parties would have intended had they foreseen.[85] The fact is, however, that the decision will depend upon the

* Excerpted from Arthur L. Corbin, *Offer and Acceptance, and Some of the Resulting Legal Relations*, 26 YALE L.J. 169, 204-06 (1917).

85. "Supposing a contract to have been duly formed, what is its result? An obligation has been created between the contracting parties, by which rights are conferred upon the one and duties are imposed upon the other, partly stipulated for in the agreement, but partly also implied by law, which, as Bentham observes (Works III, 190) 'has thus in every country supplied the short-sightedness of individuals, by doing for them what they would have done for themselves, if their imagination had anticipated the march of nature.'" Holland, *Juris.* (10th ed.) p. 278. In *Leonard v. Dyer*, 26 Conn. 172, 178 (1857), the court said: "And if we were to add stipulations to the contract which the parties themselves did not make, it appears to us that such only should be inferred as

notions of the court as to policy, welfare, justice, right and wrong, such notions often being inarticulate and subconscious.[86]

DOCTRINAL OVERVIEW: THE OFFER*

The outward appearance of the agreement process . . . varies widely according to the circumstances. It may, for example, involve face-to-face negotiations, an exchange of letters or facsimiles, a transaction between computers, or merely the perfunctory signing of a printed form supplied by the other party. Whatever the outward appearance, it is common to analyze the process in terms of two distinct steps: first, a manifestation of assent that is called an *offer*, made by one party (the *offeror*) to another (the *offeree*); and second, a manifestation of assent in response that is called an *acceptance*, made by the offeree to the offeror. Although courts apply this analysis on a case-by-case basis, depending on the circumstances, it gives a reassuring appearance of consistency.

What is an "offer"? It can be defined as a manifestation to another of assent to enter into a contract if the other manifests assent in return by some action, often a promise but sometimes a performance. By making an offer, the offeror thus confers upon the offeree the power to create a contract. An offer is nearly always a promise and, in a sense, the action (promise or performance) on which the offeror conditions the promise is the "price" of its becoming enforceable. *Offer*, then, is the name given to a promise that is conditional on some action by the promisee *if* the legal effect of the promisee's taking that action is to make the promise enforceable. Empowerment of the offeree to make the offeror's promise enforceable is thus the essence of an offer. . . .

No formalities are generally required for an offer. It may be made by spoken or written words or by other conduct. Sometimes a contract that results from words is described as "express," while one that results from conduct is described as "implied in fact," but the distinction as such has no legal consequences. Conduct that would lead a reasonable person in the other party's position to infer a promise in return for performance or promise may amount to an offer. . . .

An offer is not effective until it reaches the offeree. . . . The offer, however, need not be communicated directly by the offeror to the offeree. For example, it may be enough in the case of an offer of a reward that the offeree hears from a third person that a reward has been offered. But until the offer reaches the offeree, it is not effective and the offeror can withdraw it.

---

the parties themselves would have made, had they foreseen the circumstances that rendered such stipulations important." *See also* Bankes, L. J., *in Grove v. Webb* 114 L. T. 1082, 1089 (1916).

86. "You can always imply a condition in a contract. But why do you imply it? It is because of some belief as to the practice of the community or of a class, or because of some opinion as to policy, or, in short, because of some attitude of yours upon a matter not capable of exact quantitative measurement, and therefore not capable of founding exact logical conclusions." Justice Holmes, *The Path of the Law*, 10 HARV. L. REV. 466 (1897).

* Excerpted from E. ALLAN FARNSWORTH, CONTRACTS §§ 3.3, 3.10 (4th ed. 2004).

Whether a particular proposal amounts to an offer is a question of intention. The question most commonly arises when the maker of the proposal denies having had any intention to make an offer, while the one to whom the proposal was made claims to have believed that it was intended as an offer. Under the objective theory the issue then becomes whether the one to whom the proposal was made had reason to believe that it was intended as an offer. . . .

Before reading the next excerpt, you may find it helpful to review "Thinking Tool: Thinking Clearly About Legal Relationships" at p. 96, supra.

THINKING TOOL APPLIED: UNDERSTANDING OFFERS

Before we dive into the cases, let's pause and make sure that we understand exactly how an offer operates by couching it in Hohfeldian terms. I walk up to you—a complete stranger—in a parking lot and say "I agree to buy your car for $10,000." Do we have a contract? Of course not, and you don't even need to go to law school to figure that out. But why, exactly, is there no contract? If we pop open the hood on our contracts vehicle (I always imagine mine as a Ferrari, but you are free to imagine yours as you like), we will see some cool analytical stuff happening underneath, stuff that is responsible for powering not only the vehicle of contract law, but the very law itself. So, let's pop that hood open and see what kind of engine we've got.

As I walk up to you in that parking lot, only one of two possible legal relationships can currently exist between us with respect to your car. We can either have (a) a right/duty relationship or (b) a privilege/no-right relationship. Which one do you think we have? If you guessed (b), correctamundo! But why? Because you currently have the *privilege* of not selling your car to me, which means that I currently have *no right* to purchase it from you. So far, so good. But we've only discussed the relationship *currently* existing between us. Can this legal relationship be altered in the *future*? Why yes, through an offer! An offer allows us to change our privilege/no-right relationship into a right/duty relationship. But how does it work? Read on.

Recall that, with respect to our ability (at some point in the future) to change our *current* legal relationship, Hohfeld tells us that we either have (c) a power/liability relationship or (d) an immunity/disability relationship. Which one is it? If you said (d), then, once again, right you are! The answer is (d) because, as we have seen, my lack of *power* to change our current privilege/no-right relationship (by uttering "I agree to buy your car for $10,000") constitutes a *disability*, which is another way of saying that you are *immune* from having our current legal relationship changed. So far, so good? Then let's press on, introducing the offer.

For clarity's sake, let's erase the previous hypothetical from our minds and say that, as I am approaching you in the parking lot, you beat me to the punch and say "I'll hereby offer to sell you my car for $10,000." If we could pause time, the first thing I'd do is ask you why you talk like that. But the second thing I'd do is pop open the hood (not on your car, but on that contracts Ferrari we talked about earlier) to see what sort of crazy Hohfeldianism is going on underneath. Quite a bit, as it turns out. By making what the law calls "an offer," you have converted the immunity/disability relationship that once existed between us into a power/liability relationship. And what does *this* mean? It means that, unlike before, I now have a *power* to convert our privilege/no-right relationship into a right/duty relationship by saying "I accept." If I do so, then I now have the *right* to buy your car for $10,000, and you will now have a corresponding *duty* to sell it to me. And, for the sake of completeness, as we are talking about reciprocal promises here, you will also have a *right* to receive $10,000 from me, and I will have a corresponding *duty* to pay $10,000 to you.

So, whenever you see an offer in this course, or out there in the real world, you will now know what's happening analytically under the hood: An immunity/disability relationship is being changed to a power/liability relationship, thereby allowing the party on whom the power is conferred to convert the presently-existing privilege/no-right relationship into a right/duty relationship. Whew, that was a mouthful! When you start thinking about legal relationships in this way, you will soon find that many complicated legal problems can be broken down into much simpler components, making legal analysis more precise and—once the initial analytical work is done—easier to resolve. And, as an added benefit, you will understand the issues before you much more clearly. (Just don't try to explain it to any of your friends this way.)

As you read the following case, try to characterize each item of correspondence (there are four) passing between the parties. Which document (if any) constitutes the offer? Which document (if any) constitutes the acceptance? How would you characterize the other two items? Then, as you read the case, see if the court's analysis reflects your own.

Fairmount Glass Works v. Crunden-Martin Woodenware Co.

Court of Appeals of Kentucky
51 S.W. 196 (1899)

HOBSON, J. On April 20, 1895, appellee wrote appellant the following letter:

St. Louis, Mo., April 20, 1895. Gentlemen: Please advise us the lowest price you can make us on our order for ten car loads of Mason green jars, complete, with caps, packed one dozen in a case, either delivered here, or **f.o.b.** cars your place, as you prefer. State terms and cash discount. Very truly, Crunden-Martin W. W. Co.

> ***f.o.b.***
>
> "In an F.O.B. ('free on board') contract, the goods must be delivered on board by the seller, free of expense to the purchaser, and they are not at the latter's risk until actually delivered on board, when the property in them passes to him." 2 E.W. CHANCE, PRINCIPLES OF MERCANTILE LAW 86-87 (P.W. French ed., 10th ed. 1951).

To this letter appellant answered as follows:

Fairmount, Ind., April 23, 1895. Crunden-Martin Wooden Ware Co., St. Louis, Mo.—Gentlemen: Replying to your favor of April 20, **we quote you** Mason fruit jars, complete, in one-dozen boxes, delivered in East St. Louis, Ill.: Pints $4.50, quarts $5.00, half

> gallons $6.50, per gross, for immediate acceptance, and shipment not later than May 15, 1895; sixty days' acceptance, or 2 off, cash in ten days. Yours, truly, Fairmount Glass Works.
>
> Please note that we make all quotations and contracts subject to the contingencies of agencies or transportation, delays or accidents beyond our control.

For reply thereto, appellee sent the following telegram on April 24, 1895:

> Fairmount Glass Works, Fairmount, Ind.: Your letter twenty-third received. Enter order ten car loads as per your quotation. Specifications mailed. Crunden-Martin W. W. Co.

In response to this telegram, appellant sent the following:

> Fairmount, Ind., April 24, 1895. Crunden-Martin W. W. Co., St. Louis, Mo.: **Impossible to book your order.** Output all sold. See letter. Fairmount Glass Works.

Appellee insists that, by its telegram sent in answer to the letter of April 23d, the contract was closed for the purchase of 10 car loads of Mason fruit jars. Appellant insists that the contract was not closed by this telegram, and that it had the right to decline to fill the order at the time it sent its telegram of April 24. This is the chief question in the case. The court below gave judgment in favor of appellee, and appellant has appealed, earnestly insisting that the judgment is erroneous.

We are referred to a number of authorities holding that a quotation of prices is not an offer to sell, in the sense that a completed contract will arise out of the giving of an order for merchandise in accordance with the proposed terms. There are a number of cases holding that the transaction is not completed until the order so made is accepted. **But each case must turn largely upon the language there used.**

In this case we think there was more than a quotation of prices, although appellant's letter uses the word "quote" in stating the prices given. The true meaning of the correspondence must be determined by reading it as a whole. Appellee's letter of April 20th, which began the transaction, did not ask for a quotation of prices. It reads:

"[W]e quote you . . ."

Standing alone, what legal effect do you attribute to the words "we quote you"? Does your answer change when you read those words in the context of the correspondence between the parties? Why or why not?

"Impossible to book your order . . ."

Courts sometimes excuse a party's contractual obligations when performance becomes impossible. We will study this defense in greater detail in Chapter 8, but there is nothing to prevent you from thinking about the problem now. Do you think performance is impossible here? Do you think the seller's obligations should be excused?

"[E]ach case must turn largely upon the language there used."

In law school, as in the practice of law, the response "it depends," despite its frequent use, should not be mistaken for some trite and unimaginative way of answering a legal question, but as the inspired beginning of good legal analysis. Why? Because, as the court points out, the resolution of each case really does depend upon the facts and circumstances peculiar to that case. This is why, both in law school and in the practice of law, it is never enough to simply know the "black letter" law: You must also know how to apply the law to the facts before you, and you must do so in light of all relevant circumstances. The court recognizes this fact when it notes that "[t]he true meaning of the correspondence must be determined by reading it as a whole." As you can imagine, there is a great deal of choice involved in ascertaining which circumstances are relevant, and the extent to which these circumstances should be taken into account when deciding legal issues, such as reading the contract "as a whole." We will take up many of these issues when we examine interpretation in Chapter 6, but they will appear periodically throughout this casebook, and in your other courses as well.

> Please advise us the lowest price you can make us on our order for ten car loads of Mason green jars. . . . State terms and cash discount.

From this appellant could not fail to understand that appellee wanted to know at what price it would sell it ten car loads of these jars; so when, in answer, it wrote:

> We quote you Mason fruit jars . . . pints $4.50, quarts $5.00, half gallons $6.50, per gross, for immediate acceptance; . . . 2 off, cash in ten days,

—it must be deemed as intending to give appellee the information it had asked for. We can hardly understand what was meant by the words "for immediate acceptance," unless the latter was intended as a proposition to sell at these prices if accepted immediately. **In construing every contract, the aim of the court is to arrive at the intention of the parties. . . .** The expression in appellant's letter, "for immediate acceptance," taken in connection with appellee's letter, in effect, at what price it would sell it the goods, is, it seems to us, much stronger evidence of a present offer, which, when accepted immediately, closed the contract. Appellee's letter was plainly an inquiry for the price and terms on which appellant would sell it the goods, and appellant's answer to it was not a quotation of prices, but a definite offer to sell on the terms indicated, and could not be withdrawn after the terms had been accepted. . . .

Judgment affirmed.

> ***"In construing every contract . . ."***
>
> This is true, but don't forget that the intention of the parties can be ascertained in at least three different ways: by using the objective, subjective, and mixed approaches to mutual assent.

RELEVANT PROVISIONS

For the *Restatement (Second) of Contracts*, consult §§ 22, 24, and 30. For the UCC, consult §§ 2-204(1) and 2-206(1). For the CISG, consult Articles 8 and 14(1). For the UNIDROIT Principles, consult Articles 2.1.1 and 2.1.2.

NOTES AND QUESTIONS

1. *What happened?* Who sued whom for what? Procedurally, how did the case get before this court? Factually, what happened between the parties? What arguments did the plaintiff and defendant make? What rule or rules did the court apply? How did the court analyze the dispute between the parties? How did the court decide the case?

2. *Was this case correctly decided?* Do you agree with the result reached in this case? Why or why not? What about the court's reasoning? Do you think the result would have changed if the purchaser attempted to buy 100 car loads rather than 10? How about 1,000? How about a million? If so, what explains the difference in result?

3. ***Remedy?*** Recall that the seller refused to fill the buyer's order because it was "[i]mpossible to book" on account of its inventory being sold out. If the buyer can't get the product it ordered, what remedy should the court award?

4. *Modernizing* Fairmount. If you replace the words "telegraph" and "letter" with "internet" and "email," respectively, you have before you a case that could have been decided a year ago rather than a century ago. In resolving this dispute, however, the court would apply the UCC because the case involves the sale of goods between parties in states (Indiana and Missouri) that have adopted the UCC. (Recall that every state except Louisiana has done so). Note that we could modify the case even further by having the CISG apply if we put one of the parties in a country that ratified the CISG. Would the case come out any differently under the UCC or CISG? For the UCC, consult UCC § 2-204, and for the CISG, consult Articles 8 and 14.

Lonergan v. Scolnick

Court of Appeals of California
276 P.2d 8 (1954)

BARNARD, PRESIDING JUSTICE. This is an action for specific performance or for damages in the event specific performance was impossible.

The complaint alleged that on April 15, 1952, the parties entered into a contract whereby the defendant agreed to sell, and plaintiff agreed to buy a 40-acre tract of land for $2,500; that this was a fair, just and reasonable value of the property; that on April 28, 1952, the defendant repudiated the contract and refused to deliver a deed; that on April 28, 1952, the property was worth $6,081; and that plaintiff has been damaged in the amount of $3,581. The answer denied that any contract had been entered into, or that anything was due to the plaintiff.

By stipulation, the issue of whether or not a contract was entered into between the parties was first tried, reserving the other issues for a further trial if that became necessary. The issue as to the existence of a contract was submitted upon an agreed statement, including certain letters between the parties, without the introduction of other evidence.

The stipulated facts are as follows: During March, 1952, the defendant placed an ad in a Los Angeles paper reading, so far as material here, "Joshua Tree vic. 40 acres, need cash, will sacrifice." In response to an inquiry resulting from this ad the defendant, who lived in New York, wrote a letter to the plaintiff dated March 26, briefly describing the property, giving directions as to how to get there, stating that his rock-bottom price was $2,500 cash, and further stating that "This is a form letter." On April 7, the plaintiff wrote a letter to the defendant saying that he was not sure he had found the property, asking for its legal description, asking whether the land was all level or whether it included certain jutting rock hills, and suggesting a certain bank as escrow agent "should I desire to purchase the land." **On April 8, the defendant wrote to the plaintiff saying**

The April 8 Letter

Read over this letter several times, as it will play an important role in the outcome of the case. How, exactly, would you characterize it? Is it an offer, or something else?

"From your description you have found the property"; that this bank "is O.K. for escrow agent"; that the land was fairly level; giving the legal description; and then saying, "If you are really interested, you will have to decide fast, as I expect to have a buyer in the next week or so." On April 12, the defendant sold the property to a third party for $2,500. The plaintiff received defendant's letter of April 8 on April 14. On April 15 he wrote to the defendant thanking him for his letter "confirming that I was on the right land", stating that he would immediately proceed to have the escrow opened and would deposit $2,500 therein "in conformity with your offer", and asking the defendant to forward a deed with his instructions to the escrow agent. On April 17, 1952, the plaintiff started an escrow and placed in the hands of the escrow agent $100, agreeing to furnish an additional $2,400 at an unspecified time, with the provision that if the escrow was not closed by May 15, 1952, it should be completed as soon thereafter as possible unless a written demand for a return of the money or instruments was made by either party after that date. It was further stipulated that the plaintiff was ready and willing at all times to deposit the $2,400.

The matter was submitted on June 11, 1953. On July 10, 1953, the judge filed a memorandum opinion stating that it was his opinion that the letter of April 8, 1952, when considered with the previous correspondence, constituted an offer of sale which offer was, however, qualified and conditioned upon prompt acceptance by the plaintiff; that in spite of the condition thus imposed, the plaintiff delayed more than a week before notifying the defendant of his acceptance; and that since the plaintiff was aware of the necessity of promptly communicating his acceptance to the defendant his delay was not the prompt action required by the terms of the offer. Findings of fact were filed on October 2, 1953, finding that each and all of the statements in the agreed statement are true, and that all allegations to the contrary in the complaint are untrue. As conclusions of law, it was found that the plaintiff and defendant did not enter into a contract as alleged in the complaint or otherwise, and that the defendant is entitled to judgment against the plaintiff. Judgment was entered accordingly, from which the plaintiff has appealed.

The appellant contends that the judgment is contrary to the evidence and to the law since the facts, as found, do not support the conclusions of law upon which the judgment is based. It is argued that there is no conflict in the evidence, and this court is not bound by the trial court's construction of the written instruments involved; that the evidence conclusively shows that an offer was made to the plaintiff by the defendant, which offer was accepted by the mailing of plaintiff's letter of April 15; that upon receipt of defendant's letter of April 8 the plaintiff had a reasonable time within which to accept the offer that had been made; that by his letter of April 15 and his starting of an escrow the plaintiff accepted said offer; and that the agreed statement of facts establishes that a valid contract was entered into between the parties. In his briefs the appellant assumes that an offer was made by the defendant, and confined his argument to contending that the evidence shows that he accepted that offer within a reasonable time.

There can be no contract unless the minds of the parties have met and mutually agreed upon some specific thing. This is usually evidenced by one party making an offer which is accepted by the other party. **The *Restatement (First) of Contracts* § 25 reads:**

> If from a promise, or manifestation of intention, or from the circumstances existing at the time, the person to whom the promise or manifestation is addressed knows or has reason to know that the person making it does not intend it as an expression of his fixed purpose until he has given a further expression of assent, he has not made an offer.

The Restatement (First) of Contracts §25

The provision corresponds with the *Restatement (Second) of Contracts* § 26 (see "Relevant Provisions" after the case).

The language used in *Niles v. Hancock*, 73 P. 840, 842 (1903), "It is also clear from the correspondence that it was the intention of the defendant that the negotiations between him and the plaintiff were to be purely preliminary," is applicable here. **The correspondence here indicates an intention on the part of the defendant to find out whether the plaintiff was interested, rather than an intention to make a definite offer to the plaintiff.** The language used by the defendant in his letters of March 26 and April 8 rather clearly discloses that they were not intended as an expression of fixed purpose to make a definite offer, and was sufficient to advise the plaintiff that some further expression of assent on the part of the defendant was necessary.

"An intention to find out whether the plaintiff was interested"

First, what does this mean? Second, do you agree? If the court is right, then, legally speaking, what should we call such a correspondence?

The advertisement in the paper was a mere request for an offer. The letter of March 26 contains no definite offer, and clearly states that it is a form letter. It merely gives further particulars, in clarification of the advertisement, and tells the plaintiff how to locate the property if he was interested in looking into the matter. The letter of April 8 added nothing in the way of a definite offer. It merely answered some questions asked by the plaintiff, and stated that if the plaintiff was really interested he would have to act fast. The statement that he expected to have a buyer in the next week or so indicated that the defendant intended to sell to the first-comer, and was reserving the right to do so. From this statement, alone, the plaintiff knew or should have known that he was not being given time in which to accept an offer that was being made, but that some further assent on the part of the defendant was required. Under the language used the plaintiff was not being given a right to act within a reasonable time after receiving the letter; he was plainly told that the defendant intended to sell to another, if possible, and warned that he would have to act fast if he was interested in buying the land.

Regardless of any opinion previously expressed, the court found that no contract had been entered into between these parties, and we are in accord with the court's conclusion on that controlling issue. The court's construction of the letters involved was a reasonable one, and we think the most reasonable one, even if it be assumed that another construction was possible.

The judgment is affirmed.

RELEVANT PROVISIONS

For the *Restatement (Second) of Contracts*, consult § 26.

NOTES AND QUESTIONS

1. ***What happened?*** Who sued whom for what? Procedurally, how did the case get before this court? Factually, what happened between the parties? What arguments did the plaintiff and defendant make? What rule or rules did the court apply? How did the court analyze the dispute between the parties? How did the court decide the case?

2. ***Was this case correctly decided?*** Do you agree with the result reached in this case? Why or why not? Were you convinced by the court's reasoning? Note the last line in the court's opinion, which admits that other constructions were possible.

3. ***Trial versus appellate court.*** The appellate court reached the same conclusion as the trial court, but on different grounds. How did their opinions differ?

4. ***Was there an offer?*** In your judgment, was there an offer? In short, did the defendant ever confer on the plaintiff a *power* to create a right/duty relationship (i.e., a contract) through the act of acceptance? What is the plaintiff's best argument that there was an offer?

5. ***What was the legal significance of the April 15 letter?*** According to the plaintiff's theory of the case, the April 8 letter constituted the offer, and his April 15 letter constituted an acceptance. As the court rejected this argument, what is the legal significance of his April 15 letter?

6. ***Previewing acceptance and termination.*** Assuming that the April 8 letter constituted an offer, would the plaintiff's April 15 letter have constituted an acceptance, especially in light of the seller's request for him "to decide fast"? The offeror, as master of the offer, seems to indicate that, even if the April 8 letter *was* an offer, it would self-terminate after a period of time. How long should this period be?

PROBLEM: MINERAL SELLER'S REMORSE

Stanley is a dealer of lithium metal, used in batteries, located in Cheyenne, Wyoming. Francine is a purchasing agent for EnerGlow, Inc., a major supplier of industrial batteries located in Milwaukee, Wisconsin. On September 23, 2007, Stanley sent an email to Francine, stating:

> DEAR MADAM: In consequence of an oversupply in lithium due to a large deposit found in Wyoming, we are authorized to offer lithium metal, in lots of 0.5 to 1 metric ton, delivered to your company, at $95,000 per metric ton, to be shipped per Union Pacific R.R. only. At this price it is a bargain, as the price of lithium metal on the open market remains unchanged. Shall be pleased to receive your order.
>
> Yours truly,
>
> Stanley

The very same day, Francine responded to Stanley's email asking for the immediate shipment of 500 metric tons of lithium metal in accordance with the offer in Stanley's letter. Stanley received Francine's response the next day. Although lithium purchasers typically order large quantities and Stanley knew that EnerGlow was a major supplier of batteries, Stanley was not prepared for such a large order and did not have nearly enough supply to fill the order. Stanley knows that 500 metric tons is typically a year supply of lithium for most battery manufacturers. On September 25, 2007, Stanley sent Francine an email to withdraw the offer in his original email. Shortly after, Francine sent a reply email demanding that Stanley deliver to EnerGlow the 500 metric tons of lithium metal, in accordance with the terms of the offer. Stanley replied back, categorically refusing to deliver that amount at that price. In December 2007, EnerGlow filed suit against Stanley, claiming damages of $28 million, the price difference between what EnerGlow paid for the equivalent lithium metal from an alternative supplier and the offer in Stanley's email.

Drawing on any assigned cases or materials, how do you think this dispute should be resolved, and why? What could Stanley have written instead to make it clear that his email was not an offer? Do you think that the damages remedy that EnerGlow sought is appropriate?

2. Advertisements, Rewards, and Auctions as Offers

DOCTRINAL OVERVIEW: ADVERTISEMENTS, REWARDS, AND AUCTIONS AS OFFERS*

Whether a particular proposal amounts to an offer is a question of intention. The question most commonly arises when the maker of the proposal denies having

* Excerpted from E. ALLAN FARNSWORTH, CONTRACTS § 3.10 (4th ed. 2004).

had any intention to make an offer, while the one to whom the proposal was made claims to have believed that it was intended as an offer. Under the objective theory the issue then becomes whether the one to whom the proposal was made had reason to believe that it was intended as an offer. . . .

The fact that the proposal itself uses the word *offer* or is sent in response to a request for an *offer* is deserving of weight, but it is not controlling, and a court may decide that what is called an *offer* is merely an invitation to the recipient to make an offer. More important is whether the proposal contains language suggesting that it is within the power of the recipient to close the deal by acceptance. . . .

A proposal will not usually be interpreted as an offer if such an interpretation would expose its maker to the risk of liability for performance far beyond the maker's means. . . .

The same rationale extends to proposals made to the public through advertisements, posters, circulars, and the like, and these are generally held not to be offers. . . . A customer would not usually have reason to believe that the shopkeeper intended exposure to the risk of a multitude of acceptances resulting in a number of contracts exceeding the shopkeeper's inventory. . . . Of course, if the very nature of a proposal restricts its maker's potential liability to a reasonable number of people, there is no reason why it cannot be an offer. The nature of the proposal may be such that only a limited number of people can accept. An example is the offer of a reward for the return of lost property. Or, although an unlimited number of people can accept, it may be that only a limited number can meet the conditions that the proposal imposes for the offeror's liability. An example is the offer of a reward for the furnishing of information that leads to the apprehension of a criminal.

The reasoning behind these reward cases is not, however, applied to proposals to sell to the highest bidder. When an auctioneer puts property up for sale to the highest bidder, the auctioneer is taken, in the absence of a contrary understanding or usage, to be interested in entertaining offers in the form of bids, not in making an offer. Although only one of the many possible bidders could claim the property as the highest bidder, even the highest bid might be too low, and it would not be reasonable to assume an intention to sell in that case. The auctioneer's proposal is therefore not an offer, but each bid is an offer that the auctioneer may accept or reject. Under the Uniform Commercial Code [§ 2-328(2)], there is no contract until the auctioneer accepts by "the fall of the hammer or in other customary manner." Such a typical auction is often described as being "with reserve" to distinguish it from an auction "without reserve," in which putting up an item for bids amounts to a commitment, irrevocable for a reasonable time, to sell the item to the highest bidder. . . . The rule for auctions "with reserve" is applied by analogy to construction contracts that are to be awarded on the basis of public bidding. Generally the owner merely "invites" offers, and it is the contractor's bid that is the offer.

Suppose you see a commercial on television, hear about a "two-for-one" deal at the grocery store, or click on an advertisement to buy a product over the internet. You are excited by the deal, and rush to buy the item advertised, only to find out that it was a hoax, that they are out of stock, or that they are no longer willing to honor the terms in their ad. What can you do? Are advertisements offers, capable of being accepted? We take up this question in the following two cases, which are likely to forever change how you look at advertisements.

Lefkowitz v. Great Minneapolis Surplus Store, Inc.

Supreme Court of Minnesota
86 N.W. 2d 689 (1957)

MURPHY, JUSTICE. This is an appeal from an order of the Municipal Court of Minneapolis denying the motion of the defendant for amended findings of fact, or, in the alternative, for a new trial. The order for judgment awarded the plaintiff the sum of $138.50 as damages for breach of contract.

This case grows out of the alleged refusal of the defendant to sell to the plaintiff a certain fur piece which it had offered for sale in a newspaper advertisement. It appears from the record that on April 6, 1956, the defendant published the following advertisement in a Minneapolis newspaper:

Saturday 9 A.M. Sharp
3 Brand New
Fur Coats
Worth to $100.00
First Come
First Served
$1
Each

On April 13, the defendant again published an advertisement in the same newspaper as follows:

Saturday 9 A.M.
2 Brand New Pastel
Mink 3-Skin Scarfs
Selling for $89.50
Out they go
Saturday. Each . . . $1.00
1 Black Lapin Stole
Beautiful,
worth $139.50 . . . $1.00
First Come
First Served

The record supports the findings of the court that on each of the Saturdays following the publication of the above-described ads the plaintiff was the first to present himself at the appropriate counter in the defendant's store and on each occasion demanded the coat and the stole so advertised and indicated his readiness to pay the sale price of $1. On both occasions, the defendant refused to sell the merchandise to the plaintiff, stating on the first occasion that by a "house rule" the offer was intended for women only and sales would not be made to men, and on the second visit that plaintiff knew defendant's house rules.

The trial court properly disallowed plaintiff's claim for the value of the fur coats since the value of these articles was speculative and uncertain. The only evidence of value was the advertisement itself to the effect that the coats were "Worth to $100.00," how much less being speculative especially in view of the price for which they were offered for sale. With reference to the offer of the defendant on April 13, 1956, to sell the "1 Black Lapin Stole . . . worth $139.50 . . ." the trial court held that the value of this article was established and granted judgment in favor of the plaintiff for that amount less the $1 quoted purchase price.

1. The defendant contends that a newspaper advertisement offering items of merchandise for sale at a named price is a "unilateral offer" which may be withdrawn without notice. He relies upon authorities which hold that, where an advertiser publishes in a newspaper that he has a certain quantity or quality of goods which he wants to dispose of at certain prices and on certain terms, such advertisements are not offers which become contracts as soon as any person to whose notice they may come signifies his acceptance by notifying the other that he will take a certain quantity of them. Such advertisements have been construed as an invitation for an offer of sale on the terms stated, which offer, when received, may be accepted or rejected and which therefore does not become a contract of sale until accepted by the seller; and until a contract has been so made, the seller may modify or revoke such prices or terms.

The defendant relies principally on *Craft v. Elder & Johnston Co.*, 38 N.E.2d 416 (1941). In that case, the court discussed the legal effect of an advertisement offering for sale, as a one-day special, an electric sewing machine at a named price. The view was expressed that the advertisement was "not an offer made to any specific person but was made to the public generally. Thereby it would be properly designated as a unilateral offer and not being supported by any consideration could be withdrawn at will and without notice." It is true that such an offer may be withdrawn before acceptance. Since all offers are by their nature unilateral because they are necessarily made by one party or on one side in the negotiation of a contract, the distinction made in that decision between a unilateral offer and a **unilateral contract** is not clear. On the facts before us we are concerned with whether the advertisement constituted an offer, and, if so, whether the plaintiff's conduct constituted an acceptance.

There are numerous authorities which hold that a particular advertisement in a newspaper or circular letter relating to a sale of articles may be construed by the court as constituting an offer, acceptance of which would complete a contract.

> ***Unilateral contract***
>
> Whereas, in a bilateral contract, parties typically exchange promises with each other (i.e., the promise contained in A's offer is exchanged for the promise contained in B's acceptance), in a unilateral contract, one party exchanges its promise (as contained in the offer) for the other party's performance (the completion of which constitutes the acceptance of that offer). We will cover unilateral contracts in greater depth in Section C. 4.

The test of whether a binding obligation may originate in advertisements addressed to the general public is "whether the facts show that some performance was promised in positive terms in return for something requested." 1 WILLISTON, CONTRACTS (Rev. ed.) § 27.

The authorities above cited emphasize that, where the offer is clear, definite, and explicit, and leaves nothing open for negotiation, it constitutes an offer, acceptance of which will complete the contract. The most recent case on the subject is *Johnson v. Capital City Ford Co.*, 85 So. 2d 75 (1955), in which the court pointed out that a newspaper advertisement relating to the purchase and sale of automobiles may constitute an offer, acceptance of which will consummate a contract and create an obligation in the offeror to perform according to the terms of the published offer.

Whether in any individual instance a newspaper advertisement is an offer rather than an invitation to make an offer depends on the legal intention of the parties and the surrounding circumstances. We are of the view on the facts before us that the offer by the defendant of the sale of the Lapin fur was clear, definite, and explicit, and left nothing open for negotiation. The plaintiff having successful [sic] managed to be the first one to appear at the seller's place of business to be served, as requested by the advertisement, and having offered the stated purchase price of the article, he was entitled to performance on the part of the defendant. We think the trial court was correct in holding that there was in the conduct of the parties a sufficient mutuality of obligation to constitute a contract of sale.

Intention again!

By this point, these words should start to look very familiar to you. As mentioned previously, most of the rules of contract law—as with law in general—are not to be applied mechanistically, but in regard to achieving some underlying purpose. In contract law, more often than not, that purpose is to take into account, for the sake of realizing, the intent of the parties.

2. The defendant contends that the offer was modified by a "house rule" to the effect that only women were qualified to receive the bargains advertised. The advertisement contained no such restriction. This objection may be disposed of briefly by stating that, while an advertiser has the right at any time before acceptance to modify his offer, he does not have the right, after acceptance, to impose new or arbitrary conditions not contained in the published offer.

Affirmed.

RELEVANT PROVISIONS

For the *Restatement (Second) of Contracts*, consult §§ 24 and 26. For the UCC, consult § 2-204. For the CISG, consult Article 14. For the UNIDROIT Principles, consult Article 2.1.2.

NOTES AND QUESTIONS

1. *What happened?* Who sued whom for what? Procedurally, how did the case get before this court? Factually, what happened between the parties? What arguments did the plaintiff and defendant make? What rule or rules did the court apply? How did the court analyze the dispute between the parties? How did the court decide the case?

2. *Was this case correctly decided?* Do you agree with the result reached by the court in *Lefkowitz*? Did the court find that the Great Minneapolis Surplus Store only *offered* to sell the black lapin stole but not the fur coat? Do you think the store *intended* to offer the former but merely advertise the latter? As a customer, how would you have read the ads? What, if anything, explains the court's different treatment of the two items?

3. *Counseling.* In light of the court's decision, how would you advise the Great Minneapolis Surplus Store to advertise its products in the future?

4. *First come, first served?* What significance did the court attribute to these words? Would most customers have given these words the same significance?

5. *House rule.* What significance did the court attribute to the house rules? What significance, if any, do you think the house rules should have had?

6. *Clear, definite, and explicit?* Although it is not always easy to distinguish between advertisements that constitute offers and advertisements that constitute invitations to bargain, the court in *Lefkowitz* provides some guidance by focusing our attention on the advertisement itself, and requiring us to ask whether it is clear, definite, and explicit, and leaves nothing open for negotiation. Do you think this test is helpful? Do most customers expect advertised products to be offers? If so, should the law follow these expectations? Keep your answers to these questions in mind, and see if they help you sort through the following notes and problems.

7. *The eager home seller.* The *Restatement (Second) of Contracts* § 26, Illustration 4, provides the following example illustrating the principle in *Lefkowitz*:

> A writes B, "I am eager to sell my house. I would consider $20,000 for it." B promptly answers, "I will buy your house for $20,000 cash." There is no contract. A's letter is a request or suggestion that an offer be made to him. B has made an offer.

8. *The reluctant shopkeeper.* Because advertisements are a ubiquitous part of the commercial world we inhabit, a little practice in distinguishing ads from offers is very useful. Try to apply the *Lefkowitz* test to the problem struggled with by the author of the short excerpt below. As you read it, ask

yourself whether you agree with the judge's, the treatise writer's, or the author's analysis of the problem, and why. How does the author's analysis differ from the analysis employed by the judge in *Lefkowitz*? And, speaking of judges, do you agree with the reasons articulated by the judge below (in the second paragraph) for not construing the advertisement as an offer? Why or why not?

DISTINGUISHING BETWEEN OFFERS AND INVITATIONS TO BARGAIN*

A familiar rule is that one who accepts an invitation to do business is not thereby accepting any offer of the invitor so as to constitute a contract between them. On the contrary, it is the invitee who makes the offer, if any. It must always be a question of interpreting facts in order to ascertain whether they amount to an offer or to a mere invitation to do business.

One illustration is worth discussion here. What is the effect of display in a shop window of goods with a price marked upon them? . . . [In] *Crawley v. R.*, . . . [a] tradesman advertised goods at a specified price. X entered the shop and persisted in demanding the goods at that price. The tradesman refused to deliver them and at last told X to leave the shop. X would not do so. He was prosecuted for, and convicted of, unlawfully remaining on premises after being requested to leave them. . . . [The judge] said that the advertisement was not an offer and that extraordinary consequences would follow if it were, for thousands of people might crowd into the shop at once and demand to be served, and each would have a right of action against the shopkeeper.

Sir J. Wessels, in his learned treatise on the *Law of Contract in South Africa*, disagreed with this opinion, at least in so far as it related to goods with a price affixed to them. He was unable to see what interpretation could be put upon the shopkeeper's act except to regard it as an offer, and he cited French law to the effect that such an advertisement is an offer, though the shopkeeper need sell only so long as he has the goods in his possession. He admitted, however, that if circumstances negatived an intent to make an unqualified offer, it would not be construed as such.

We would respectfully suggest a rather different line of reasoning which would support the decision in *Crawley v. R.*, but which would also carry it farther. . . . [A] more natural interpretation of the display of goods in a shop with a marked price upon them would be that the shopkeeper impliedly reserves to himself a right of selecting his customer. A shop is a place for bargaining, not for compulsory sales. Presumptively, the importance of the personality of the customer cannot be eliminated. If the display of such goods were an offer, then the shopkeeper might be forced to contract with his worst enemy, his greatest trade rival, a reeling drunkard, or a ragged and verminous tramp. That would be a result scarcely likely to be countenanced by the law.

* Excerpted from P.H. Winfield, *Some Aspects of Offer and Acceptance*, 55 L.Q. Rev. 499, 516-18 (1939).

Even in a business like that of the innkeeper or the common carrier, where there is by law a duty to render services to such persons as may apply for them, the personal element is never entirely excluded. An innkeeper is not bound to accommodate a common prostitute, a railway company is not bound to find transport for one who is not in a fit condition to travel. Of course, a tradesman may frame his proposal in such a way as to abrogate any choice in his selection of a customer. But it is not easy to imagine a case in which he would be likely to do so, and some instances, which might at first sight appear to amount to such abrogation, are more likely to be construed as retaining it. Thus, even if the ticket on a clock in a jeweler's window were "For sale for £1, cash down, to first comer," we still think that it is only an invitation to do business and that the first comer must be one of whom the jeweler approves.

Before you read the next case, see if you can apply what you have learned so far to the following problem. Then, test your answer against the court's answer in the next case.

PROBLEM: COLLECTOR'S EDITION

In February 2002, Congress passed the Twin Towers Commemorative Coin Act directing the U.S. Mint to create one-dollar and five-dollar gold coins to be released for public purchase to help fund the redevelopment of downtown New York City. The Act specified that the initial release would be in September 2002, but the Mint could take pre-orders and bulk orders, which would provide a substantial discount to purchasers. Acting at the direction of the Secretary of the Treasury, the Mint sent advertising materials to individuals that had made previous coin purchases from the Mint. The advertising materials included an order form and stated that the Mint would accept payment by check, money order, or credit card.

Lauren, a collector of rare coins, received this advertisement and forwarded to the Mint an order for 24 commemorative five-dollar gold coins. Along with the details of her order, she also sent her credit card information. A month after Lauren placed her order, she received a letter from the Mint that "they had tried but were unable to process" her credit card order. Along with the letter was a new order form that did not include the five-dollar gold coins that Lauren had previously ordered. Shortly after receiving this rejection letter, Lauren began to hear talk amongst other coin collectors that they had received similar rejection letters from the Mint when placing credit card orders for the commemorative five-dollar gold coins. Lauren, deciding to investigate why her order was rejected, called the U.S. Mint. The Mint told her that credit card orders had to be approved by the Bank of Mellon in New York before being certified as valid and returned to the Mint to be filled. Because the credit card certification was such a slow process, before most of the credit card orders were certified, the Mint had sold all of the five-dollar gold coins to those who placed cash orders. The Mint revealed that the credit card orders that were received after the Mint had sold out received the rejection letters. In March 2003, Lauren filed suit against the Mint in New York seeking damages on a breach of contract theory. Lauren argued that the order form sent by the Mint constituted an offer that, upon acceptance, created a binding contract whereby the government was bound and obligated to deliver the coins ordered.

What is the Mint's best argument against the existence of a contract? How might Lauren respond? Drawing on any assigned cases or materials, how do you think this dispute should be resolved, and why?

The following case is fun both for its facts and for the style in which it was written, and does a wonderful job of bringing together many of the concepts we have previously covered in this chapter,* in addition to previewing a few concepts we will soon cover.† Not only did this case garner much media attention when it was decided, but it continues to live a strong afterlife as a staple in most contracts casebooks. As you read it, try to apply what you have learned about mutual assent, offers, and advertisements, and ask yourself how you would have resolved this dispute if you were the judge assigned to the case. In general, do you agree with this judge's approach? Why or why not? What test does the court use to ascertain the intent of the parties? Is this the test you would have applied? Would the court's analysis have changed if it adopted a different approach?

Leonard v. Pepsico

United States District Court, Southern District of New York
88 F. Supp. 2d 116 (1999)

WOOD, J. Plaintiff brought this action seeking, among other things, specific performance of an alleged offer of a Harrier Jet, featured in a television advertisement for defendant's "Pepsi Stuff" promotion. Defendant has moved for summary judgment pursuant to *Federal Rule of Civil Procedure 56*. For the reasons stated below, defendant's motion is granted.

I. BACKGROUND

This case arises out of a promotional campaign conducted by defendant, the producer and distributor of the soft drinks Pepsi and Diet Pepsi. The promotion, entitled "Pepsi Stuff," encouraged consumers to collect "Pepsi Points" from specially marked packages of Pepsi or Diet Pepsi and redeem these points for merchandise featuring the Pepsi logo. Before introducing the promotion nationally, defendant conducted a test of the promotion in the Pacific Northwest from October 1995 to March 1996. A Pepsi Stuff catalog was distributed to consumers in the test market, including Washington State. Plaintiff is a resident of

* *See, e.g.*, the court's discussion of *Lefkowitz v. Great Minneapolis Surplus Store, Inc.*, and its wink to *Lucy v. Zehmer*.

† *See, e.g.*, the court's discussion of *Carlill v. Carbolic Smoke Ball Co.*, which we will discuss in the next section on "Accepting Offers."

Seattle, Washington. While living in Seattle, plaintiff saw the Pepsi Stuff commercial that he contends constituted an offer of a Harrier Jet.

A. The Alleged Offer

Because whether the television commercial constituted an offer is the central question in this case, the Court will describe the commercial in detail. The commercial opens upon an idyllic, suburban morning, where the chirping of birds in sun-dappled trees welcomes a paperboy on his morning route. As the newspaper hits the stoop of a conventional two-story house, the tattoo of a military drum introduces the subtitle, "MONDAY 7:58 AM." The stirring strains of a martial air mark the appearance of a well-coiffed teenager preparing to leave for school, dressed in a shirt emblazoned with the Pepsi logo, a red-white-and-blue ball. While the teenager confidently preens, the military drumroll again sounds as the subtitle "T-SHIRT 75 PEPSI POINTS" scrolls across the screen. Bursting from his room, the teenager strides down the hallway wearing a leather jacket. The drumroll sounds again, as the subtitle "LEATHER JACKET 1450 PEPSI POINTS" appears. The teenager opens the door of his house and, unfazed by the glare of the early morning sunshine, puts on a pair of sunglasses. The drumroll then accompanies the subtitle "SHADES 175 PEPSI POINTS." A voiceover then intones, "Introducing the new Pepsi Stuff catalog," as the camera focuses on the cover of the catalog.

The scene then shifts to three young boys sitting in front of a high school building. The boy in the middle is intent on his Pepsi Stuff Catalog, while the boys on either side are each drinking Pepsi. The three boys gaze in awe at an object rushing overhead, as the military march builds to a crescendo. The Harrier Jet is not yet visible, but the observer senses the presence of a mighty plane as the extreme winds generated by its flight create a paper maelstrom in a classroom devoted to an otherwise dull physics lesson. Finally, the Harrier Jet swings into view and lands by the side of the school building, next to a bicycle rack. Several students run for cover, and the velocity of the wind strips one hapless faculty member down to his underwear. While the faculty member is being deprived of his dignity, the voiceover announces: "Now the more Pepsi you drink, the more great stuff you're gonna get."

The teenager opens the cockpit of the fighter and can be seen, helmetless, holding a Pepsi. "Looking very pleased with himself," the teenager exclaims, "Sure beats the bus," and chortles. The military drumroll sounds a final time, as the following words appear: "HARRIER FIGHTER 7,000,000 PEPSI POINTS." A few seconds later, the following appears in more stylized script: "Drink Pepsi—Get Stuff." With that message, the music and the commercial end with a triumphant flourish.

Inspired by this commercial, plaintiff set out to obtain a Harrier Jet. Plaintiff explains that he is "typical of the 'Pepsi Generation' . . . he is young, has an adventurous spirit, and the notion of obtaining a Harrier Jet appealed to him enormously." Plaintiff consulted the Pepsi Stuff Catalog. The Catalog features youths dressed in Pepsi Stuff regalia or enjoying Pepsi Stuff accessories, such as

"Blue Shades" ("As if you need another reason to look forward to sunny days."), "Pepsi Tees" ("Live in 'em. Laugh in 'em. Get in 'em."), "Bag of Balls" ("Three balls. One bag. No rules."), and "Pepsi Phone Card" ("Call your mom!"). The Catalog specifies the number of Pepsi Points required to obtain promotional merchandise. The Catalog includes an Order Form which lists, on one side, fifty-three items of Pepsi Stuff merchandise redeemable for Pepsi Points. Conspicuously absent from the Order Form is any entry or description of a Harrier Jet. The amount of Pepsi Points required to obtain the listed merchandise ranges from 15 (for a "Jacket Tattoo" ("Sew 'em on your jacket, not your arm.")) to 3300 (for a "Fila Mountain Bike" ("Rugged. All-terrain. Exclusively for Pepsi.")). It should be noted that plaintiff objects to the implication that because an item was not shown in the Catalog, it was unavailable.

The rear foldout pages of the Catalog contain directions for redeeming Pepsi Points for merchandise. These directions note that merchandise may be ordered "only" with the original Order Form. The Catalog notes that in the event that a consumer lacks enough Pepsi Points to obtain a desired item, additional Pepsi Points may be purchased for ten cents each; however, at least fifteen original Pepsi Points must accompany each order.

Although plaintiff initially set out to collect 7,000,000 Pepsi Points by consuming Pepsi products, it soon became clear to him that he "would not be able to buy (let alone drink) enough Pepsi to collect the necessary Pepsi Points fast enough." Reevaluating his strategy, plaintiff "focused for the first time on the packaging materials in the Pepsi Stuff promotion," and realized that buying Pepsi Points would be a more promising option. Through acquaintances, plaintiff ultimately raised about $700,000.

B. PLAINTIFF'S EFFORTS TO REDEEM THE ALLEGED OFFER

On or about March 27, 1996, plaintiff submitted an Order Form, fifteen original Pepsi Points, and a check for $700,008.50. Plaintiff appears to have been represented by counsel at the time he mailed his check; the check is drawn on an account of plaintiff's first set of attorneys. At the bottom of the Order Form, plaintiff wrote in "1 Harrier Jet" in the "Item" column and "7,000,000" in the "Total Points" column. In a letter accompanying his submission, plaintiff stated that the check was to purchase additional Pepsi Points "expressly for obtaining a new Harrier jet as advertised in your Pepsi Stuff commercial."

On or about May 7, 1996, defendant's fulfillment house rejected plaintiff's submission and returned the check, explaining that:

> The item that you have requested is not part of the Pepsi Stuff collection. It is not included in the catalogue or on the order form, and only catalogue merchandise can be redeemed under this program.
>
> The Harrier jet in the Pepsi commercial is fanciful and is simply included to create a humorous and entertaining ad. We apologize for any misunderstanding or confusion that you may have experienced and are enclosing some free product coupons for your use.

Plaintiff's previous counsel responded on or about May 14, 1996, as follows:

> Your letter of May 7, 1996 is totally unacceptable. We have reviewed the video tape of the Pepsi Stuff commercial . . . and it clearly offers the new Harrier jet for 7,000,000 Pepsi Points. Our client followed your rules explicitly. . . .
>
> This is a formal demand that you honor your commitment and make immediate arrangements to transfer the new Harrier jet to our client. If we do not receive transfer instructions within ten (10) business days of the date of this letter you will leave us no choice but to file an appropriate action against Pepsi. . . .

This letter was apparently sent onward to the advertising company responsible for the actual commercial, BBDO New York ("BBDO"). In a letter dated May 30, 1996, BBDO Vice President Raymond E. McGovern, Jr., explained to plaintiff that:

> I find it hard to believe that you are of the opinion that the Pepsi Stuff commercial ("Commercial") really offers a new Harrier Jet. The use of the Jet was clearly a joke that was meant to make the Commercial more humorous and entertaining. In my opinion, no reasonable person would agree with your analysis of the Commercial.

On or about June 17, 1996, plaintiff mailed a similar demand letter to defendant. [On the following day, PepsiCo sought] a **declaratory judgment** stating that it had no obligation to furnish plaintiff with a Harrier Jet. . . .

Declaratory judgment

Declaratory judgments are an important form of preventive relief seeking to clarify the legal relationship existing between the parties. As with other forms of preventive relief, declaratory injunctions, by reducing legal uncertainty, attempt to avoid future harm rather than seeking damages to remedy past harm. *See* Samuel Bray, *Preventive Adjudication,* 77 U. CHI. L. REV. 1275, 1276 (2010).

II. DISCUSSION

B. DEFENDANT'S ADVERTISEMENT WAS NOT AN OFFER

1. *Advertisements as Offers*

The general rule is that an advertisement does not constitute an offer. The *Restatement (Second) of Contracts* explains that:

> Advertisements of goods by display, sign, handbill, newspaper, radio or television are not ordinarily intended or understood as offers to sell. The same is true of catalogues, price lists and circulars, even though the terms of suggested bargains may be stated in some detail. It is of course possible to make an offer by an advertisement directed to the general public (see § 29), but there must ordinarily be some language of commitment or some invitation to take action without further communication.

Restatement (Second) of Contracts § 26 cmt. b (1979). Similarly, a leading treatise notes that:

> It is quite possible to make a definite and operative offer to buy or sell goods by advertisement, in a newspaper, by a handbill, a catalog or circular or on a placard in a store window. *It is not customary to do this, however; and the*

> *presumption is the other way*. . . . Such advertisements are understood to be mere requests to consider and examine and negotiate; and no one can reasonably regard them as otherwise unless the circumstances are exceptional and the words used are very plain and clear.

1 Arthur Linton Corbin & Joseph M. Perillo, *Corbin on Contracts* § 2.4, at 116-17 (rev. ed. 1993) (emphasis added). New York courts adhere to this general principle. *See Lovett v. Frederick Loeser & Co.*, 207 N.Y.S. 753, 755 (Mun. Ct. N.Y. City 1924) (noting that an "advertisement is nothing but an invitation to enter into negotiations, and is not an offer which may be turned into a contract by a person who signifies his intention to purchase some of the articles mentioned in the advertisement"); *see also People v. Gimbel Bros. Inc.*, 115 N.Y.S.2d 857, 858 (Ct. Spec. Sess. 1952) (because an "advertisement does not constitute an offer of sale but is solely an invitation to customers to make an offer to purchase," defendant not guilty of selling property on Sunday).

An advertisement is not transformed into an enforceable offer merely by a potential offeree's expression of willingness to accept the offer through, among other means, completion of an order form. In *Mesaros v. United States*, 845 F.2d 1576 (Fed. Cir. 1988), for example, the plaintiffs sued the United States Mint for failure to deliver a number of Statue of Liberty commemorative coins that they had ordered. When demand for the coins proved unexpectedly robust, a number of individuals who had sent in their orders in a timely fashion were left empty-handed. The court began by noting the "well-established" rule that advertisements and order forms are "mere notices and solicitations for offers which create no power of acceptance in the recipient." *Id.* at 1580; *see also Foremost Pro Color, Inc. v. Eastman Kodak Co.*, 703 F.2d 534, 538-39 (9th Cir. 1983) ("The weight of authority is that purchase orders such as those at issue here are not enforceable contracts until they are accepted by the seller."); *Restatement (Second) of Contracts* § 26 ("A manifestation of willingness to enter a bargain is not an offer if the person to whom it is addressed knows or has reason to know that the person making it does not intend to conclude a bargain until he has made a further manifestation of assent."). The spurned coin collectors could not maintain a breach of contract action because no contract would be formed until the advertiser accepted the order form and processed payment. Under these principles, plaintiff's letter of March 27, 1996, with the Order Form and the appropriate number of Pepsi Points, constituted the offer. There would be no enforceable contract until defendant accepted the Order Form and cashed the check.

The exception to the rule that advertisements do not create any power of acceptance in potential offerees is where the advertisement is "clear, definite, and explicit, and leaves nothing open for negotiation," in that circumstance, "it constitutes an offer, acceptance of which will complete the contract." *Lefkowitz v. Great Minneapolis Surplus Store*, 86 N.W.2d 689, 691 (Minn. 1957). In *Lefkowitz*, defendant had published a newspaper announcement stating: "Saturday 9 AM Sharp, 3 Brand New Fur Coats, Worth to $100.00, First Come First Served $1 Each." Mr. Morris Lefkowitz arrived at the store, dollar in hand, but was informed that under defendant's "house rules," the offer was open to ladies, but not gentlemen. The court ruled that because plaintiff had fulfilled all of the terms of the advertisement and the advertisement was specific and left nothing open for negotiation, a contract had been formed.

The present case is distinguishable from *Lefkowitz*. First, the commercial cannot be regarded in itself as sufficiently definite, because it specifically reserved the details of the offer to a separate writing, the Catalog. The commercial itself made no mention of the steps a potential offeree would be required to take to accept the alleged offer of a Harrier Jet. The advertisement in *Lefkowitz*, in contrast, "identified the person who could accept." Corbin, *supra*, § 2.4, at 119. *See generally* 1 E. Allan Farnsworth, *Farnsworth on Contracts* § 3.10, at 239 (2d ed. 1998) ("The fact that a proposal is very detailed suggests that it is an offer, while omission of many terms suggests that it is not."). **Second, even if the Catalog had included a Harrier Jet among the items that could be obtained by redemption of Pepsi Points, the advertisement of a Harrier Jet by both television commercial and catalog would still not constitute an offer. As the *Mesaros* court explained, the absence of any words of limitation such as "first come, first served," renders the alleged offer sufficiently indefinite that no contract could be formed.** "A customer would not usually have reason to believe that the shopkeeper intended exposure to the risk of a multitude of acceptances resulting in a number of contracts exceeding the shopkeeper's inventory." Farnsworth, *supra*, at 242. There was no such danger in *Lefkowitz*, owing to the limitation "first come, first served."

No Harrier Jet, no matter what?

Do you agree? Under these facts, wouldn't it be reasonable for a customer to believe that Pepsi had at least one Harrier Jet available to be redeemed? Why or why not? If so, should Pepsi be bound to fill at least the first order it gets?

The Court finds, in sum, that the Harrier Jet commercial was merely an advertisement. The Court now turns to the line of cases upon which plaintiff rests much of his argument.

2. *Rewards as Offers*

In opposing the present motion, plaintiff largely relies on a different species of unilateral offer, involving public offers of a reward for performance of a specified act. . . . The most venerable of these precedents is the case of *Carlill v. Carbolic Smoke Ball Co.*, 1 Q.B. 256 (Court of Appeal, 1892), a quote from which heads plaintiff's memorandum of law: "If a person chooses to make extravagant promises . . . he probably does so because it pays him to make them, and, if he has made them, the extravagance of the promises is no reason in law why he should not be bound by them."

Long a staple of law school curricula,* *Carbolic Smoke Ball* owes its fame not merely to "the comic and slightly mysterious object involved," A.W. Brian Simpson, *Quackery and Contract Law: Carlill v. Carbolic Smoke Ball Company (1893)*, in *Leading Cases in the Common Law* 259, 281 (1995), but also to

* [This case is, indeed, "a staple of law school curricula," and appears at p. 243, *infra*.—ED.]

its role in developing the law of unilateral offers. The case arose during the London influenza epidemic of the 1890s. Among other advertisements of the time, for Clarke's World Famous Blood Mixture, Towle's Pennyroyal and Steel Pills for Females, Sequah's Prairie Flower, and Epp's Glycerine Jube-Jubes, *see* Simpson, *supra*, at 267, appeared solicitations for the Carbolic Smoke Ball. The specific advertisement that Mrs. Carlill saw, and relied upon, read as follows:

> £100 reward will be paid by the Carbolic Smoke Ball Company to any person who contracts the increasing epidemic influenza, colds, or any diseases caused by taking cold, after having used the ball three times daily for two weeks according to the printed directions supplied with each ball. £1000 is deposited with the Alliance Bank, Regent Street, shewing our sincerity in the matter.
>
> During the last epidemic of influenza many thousand carbolic smoke balls were sold as preventives against this disease, and in no ascertained case was the disease contracted by those using the carbolic smoke ball.

Carbolic Smoke Ball, 1 Q.B. at 256-57. "On the faith of this advertisement," Mrs. Carlill purchased the smoke ball and used it as directed, but contracted influenza nevertheless.[8] The lower court held that she was entitled to recover the promised reward.

Affirming the lower court's decision, Lord Justice Lindley began by noting that the advertisement was an express promise to pay £100 in the event that a consumer of the Carbolic Smoke Ball was stricken with influenza. The advertisement was construed as offering a reward because it sought to induce performance, unlike an invitation to negotiate, which seeks a reciprocal promise. As Lord Justice Lindley explained, "advertisements offering rewards . . . are offers to anybody who performs the conditions named in the advertisement, and anybody who does perform the condition accepts the offer." *Id.* at 262; *see also id.* at 268 (Bowen, L.J.).[9] Because Mrs. Carlill had complied with the terms of the offer, yet contracted influenza, she was entitled to £100.

Like *Carbolic Smoke Ball*, the decisions relied upon by plaintiff involve offers of reward. In *Barnes v. Treece*, 549 P.2d 1152 (Wash. Ct. App. 1976), for example, the vice-president of a punchboard distributor, in the course of hearings before the Washington State Gambling Commission, asserted that, "'I'll put a hundred thousand dollars to anyone to find a crooked board. If they find it, I'll pay it.'" 549 P.2d at 1154. Plaintiff, a former bartender, heard of the offer and located two crooked punchboards. Defendant, after reiterating

8. Although the Court of Appeals' opinion is silent as to exactly what a carbolic smoke ball was, the historical record reveals it to have been a compressible hollow ball, about the size of an apple or orange, with a small opening covered by some porous material such as silk or gauze. The ball was partially filled with carbolic acid in powder form. When the ball was squeezed, the powder would be forced through the opening as a small cloud of smoke. *See* Simpson, *supra*, at 262-63. At the time, carbolic acid was considered fatal if consumed in more than small amounts.

9. *Carbolic Smoke Ball* includes a classic formulation of this principle: "If I advertise to the world that my dog is lost, and that anybody who brings the dog to a particular place will be paid some money, are all the police or other persons whose business it is to find lost dogs to be expected to sit down and write a note saying that they have accepted my proposal?"

that the offer was serious, providing plaintiff with a receipt for the punchboard on company stationery, and assuring plaintiff that the reward was being held in escrow, nevertheless repudiated the offer. *See id.* at 1154. The court ruled that the offer was valid and that plaintiff was entitled to his reward. *See id.* at 1155. The plaintiff in this case also cites cases involving prizes for skill (or luck) in the game of golf. *See Las Vegas Hacienda v. Gibson*, 359 P.2d 85 (Nev. 1961) (awarding $5,000 to plaintiff, who successfully shot a hole-in-one); *see also Grove v. Charbonneau Buick-Pontiac, Inc.*, 240 N.W.2d 853 (N.D. 1976) (awarding automobile to plaintiff, who successfully shot a hole-in-one).

Other "reward" cases underscore the distinction between typical advertisements, in which the alleged offer is merely an invitation to negotiate for purchase of commercial goods, and promises of reward, in which the alleged offer is intended to induce a potential offeree to perform a specific action, often for noncommercial reasons. In *Newman v. Schiff*, 778 F.2d 460 (5th Cir. 1985), for example, the Fifth Circuit held that a tax protestor's assertion that, "If anybody calls this show . . . and cites any section of the code that says an individual is required to file a tax return, I'll pay them $100,000," would have been an enforceable offer had the plaintiff called the television show to claim the reward while the tax protestor was appearing. The court noted that, like *Carbolic Smoke Ball*, the case "concerns a special type of offer: an offer for a reward." *James v. Turilli*, 473 S.W.2d 757 (Mo. Ct. App. 1971), arose from a boast by defendant that the "notorious Missouri desperado" Jesse James had not been killed in 1882, as portrayed in song and legend, but had lived under the alias "J. Frank Dalton" at the "Jesse James Museum" operated by none other than defendant. Defendant offered $10,000 "to anyone who could prove me wrong." The widow of the outlaw's son demonstrated, at trial, that the outlaw had in fact been killed in 1882. On appeal, the court held that defendant should be liable to pay the amount offered.

In the present case, the Harrier Jet commercial did not direct that anyone who appeared at Pepsi headquarters with 7,000,000 Pepsi Points on the Fourth of July would receive a Harrier Jet. Instead, the commercial urged consumers to accumulate Pepsi Points and to refer to the Catalog to determine how they could redeem their Pepsi Points. The commercial sought a reciprocal promise, expressed through acceptance of, and compliance with, the terms of the Order Form. As noted previously, the Catalog contains no mention of the Harrier Jet. Plaintiff states that he "noted that the Harrier Jet was not among the items described in the catalog, but this did not affect [his] understanding of the offer."

Carbolic Smoke Ball itself draws a distinction between the offer of reward in that case, and typical advertisements, which are merely offers to negotiate. As Lord Justice Bowen explains:

> It is an offer to become liable to any one who, before it is retracted, performs the condition. . . . It is not like cases in which you offer to negotiate, or you issue advertisements that you have got a stock of books to sell, or houses to let, in which case there is no offer to be bound by any contract. Such advertisements are offers to negotiate—offers to receive offers—offers to chaffer, as, I think, some learned judge in one of the cases has said.

Carbolic Smoke Ball, 1 Q.B. at 268. Because the alleged offer in this case was, at most, an advertisement to receive offers rather than an offer of reward, plaintiff cannot show that there was an offer made in the circumstances of this case.

C. An Objective, Reasonable Person Would Not Have Considered the Commercial an Offer

Plaintiff's understanding of the commercial as an offer must also be rejected because the Court finds that no objective person could reasonably have concluded that the commercial actually offered consumers a Harrier Jet.

1. Objective Reasonable Person Standard

In evaluating the commercial, the Court must not consider defendant's subjective intent in making the commercial, or plaintiff's subjective view of what the commercial offered, but what an objective, reasonable person would have understood the commercial to convey. *See Kay-R Elec. Corp. v. Stone & Weber Constr. Co.*, 23 F.3d 55, 57 (2d Cir. 1994) ("We are not concerned with what was going through the heads of the parties at the time [of the alleged contract]. Rather, we are talking about the objective principles of contract law."); *Mesaros*, 845 F.2d at 1581 ("A basic rule of contracts holds that whether an offer has been made depends on the objective reasonableness of the alleged offeree's belief that the advertisement or solicitation was intended as an offer.").

If it is clear that an offer was not serious, then no offer has been made:

> What kind of act creates a power of acceptance and is therefore an offer? It must be an expression of will or intention. It must be an act that leads the offeree reasonably to conclude that a power to create a contract is conferred. This applies to the content of the power as well as to the fact of its existence. *It is on this ground that we must exclude* invitations to deal or acts of mere preliminary negotiation, and *acts evidently done in jest* or without intent to create legal relations.

Corbin on Contracts, § 1.11 at 30 (emphasis added). An obvious joke, of course, would not give rise to a contract. On the other hand, if there is no indication that the offer is "evidently in jest," and that an objective, reasonable person would find that the offer was serious, then there may be a valid offer. *See Barnes*, 549 P.2d at 1155 ("If the jest is not apparent and a reasonable hearer would believe that an offer was being made, then the speaker risks the formation of a contract which was not intended."); *see also Lucy v. Zehmer*, 84 S.E.2d 516, 518, 520 (Va. 1954) (ordering specific performance of a contract to purchase a farm despite defendant's protestation that the transaction was done in jest as "'just a bunch of two doggoned drunks bluffing'"). . . .

3. Whether the Commercial Was "Evidently Done In Jest"

Plaintiff's insistence that the commercial appears to be a serious offer requires the Court to explain why the commercial is funny. Explaining why a joke is funny is a daunting task; as the essayist E.B. White has remarked,

"Humor can be dissected, as a frog can, but the thing dies in the process. . . ."[11] [Tempted by the prospect, the Court proceeded to perform vivisection on the commercial's humor over the next five paragraphs, killing the joke in the process. We rejoin the court in its post mortem.]

Plaintiff argues that a reasonable, objective person would have understood the commercial to make a serious offer of a Harrier Jet because there was "absolutely no distinction in the manner" in which the items in the commercial were presented. Plaintiff also relies upon a press release highlighting the promotional campaign, issued by defendant, in which "no mention is made by [defendant] of humor, or anything of the sort." These arguments suggest merely that the humor of the promotional campaign was tongue in cheek. Humor is not limited to what Justice Cardozo called "the rough and boisterous joke . . . [that] evokes its own guffaws." *Murphy v. Steeplechase Amusement Co.*, 166 N.E. 173, 174 (1929). In light of the obvious absurdity of the commercial, the Court rejects plaintiff's argument that the commercial was not clearly in jest. . . .

D. The Alleged Contract Does Not Satisfy the Statute of Frauds

[The court also found that the absence of any writing failed to satisfy the Statute of Frauds. We will take up this part of the court's opinion when we discuss the Statute of Frauds in Chapter 8, *infra*.]

III. CONCLUSION

In sum, there are three reasons why plaintiff's demand cannot prevail as a matter of law. First, the commercial was merely an advertisement, not a unilateral offer. Second, the tongue-in-cheek attitude of the commercial would not cause a reasonable person to conclude that a soft drink company would be giving away fighter planes as part of a promotion. Third, there is no writing between the parties sufficient to satisfy the Statute of Frauds.

For the reasons stated above, the Court grants defendant's motion for summary judgment. The Clerk of Court is instructed to close these cases. Any pending motions are moot.

So ordered.

RELEVANT PROVISIONS

For the *Restatement (Second) of Contracts,* consult §§ 24 and 26. For the UCC, consult § 2-204(1). For the CISG, consult Article 14. For the UNIDROIT Principles, consult Article 2.1.2.

11. *Quoted in* Gerald R. Ford, *Humor and the Presidency* 23 (1987).

NOTES AND QUESTIONS

1. *YouTube*. You can watch the commercial discussed in the court's opinion on YouTube. *See http://www.youtube.com/watch?v=U_n5SNrMaL8.*

2. *What happened?* Who sued whom for what? Procedurally, how did the case get before this court? Factually, what happened between the parties? What arguments did the plaintiff and defendant make? What rule or rules did the court apply? How did the court analyze the dispute between the parties? How did the court decide the case?

3. *Was this case correctly decided?* Do you agree with the result reached by Judge Wood in this case? Why or why not? Do you agree with her reasoning? Why or why not? How, if at all, would you have written the opinion differently?

4. *What did Leonard really think*? Even if PepsiCo intended the commercial as a joke, did Leonard understand it that way? How do we know? Does it even matter? How would we have to change the facts so that it would be reasonable for Leonard to believe that the commercial constituted an offer?

5. *Mutual assent, reprised.* How would the case come out under the various approaches to mutual assent that we have discussed (the objective, subjective, and mixed)?

6. *Speaking of jokes.* This is our second joke case. In the first case, *Lucy v. Zehmer*, the court found that there was no joke and enforced the contract. Here, the court found that there was a joke, and thus, no contract to enforce. Can the cases be reconciled, or was one of them wrongly decided?

7. *What information should the court consider?* In determining whether Pepsi's ad was an offer, should the court consult only the information available in the commercial, only the Pepsi Stuff Catalog, or a combination of both? Why? Would your answer change if Leonard only saw the commercial but did not read the catalog, or vice versa? Why?

8. *The importance of facts.* The court mentioned that the plaintiff realized that he would never be able to drink 7,000,000 Pepsi Points worth of Pepsi products, and had to resort to purchasing additional Pepsi Points at ten cents each. What relevance (if any) should the court attribute to these facts in determining whether the commercial should be construed as an offer? Would your answer change if additional Pepsi Points could not be purchased?

9. *Varying the facts.* Suppose the court found that the commercial, standing alone, constituted an offer, but the information in the Pepsi Stuff Catalog, when read in conjunction with the commercial, indicated the commercial was only an ad, and not an offer. Should Leonard, who both watched the commercial and read the catalog, win? Why or why not? Finally, how would your answer change if the plaintiff was someone who only had the commercial described to her by her friend, but never saw it?

10. *Counseling.* In light of the court's decision, how would you advise PepsiCo to advertise its products in the future?

C. ACCEPTING OFFERS

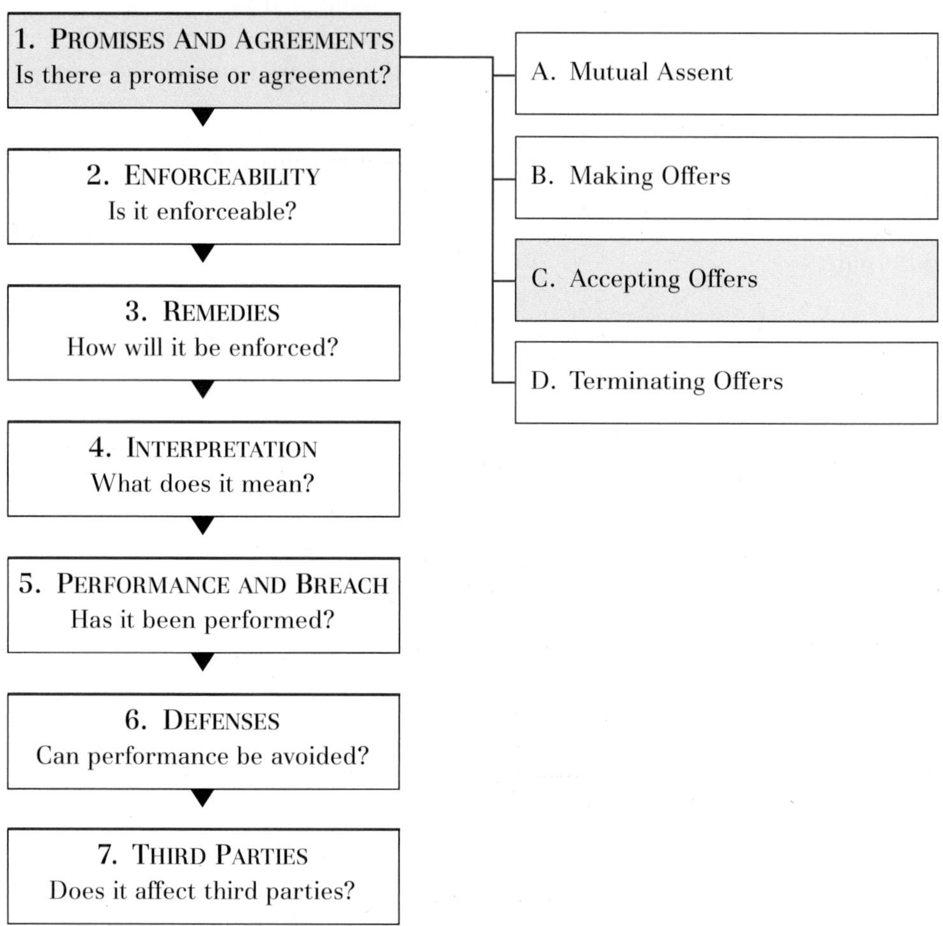
1. Promises And Agreements
Is there a promise or agreement?
2. Enforceability
Is it enforceable?
3. Remedies
How will it be enforced?
4. Interpretation
What does it mean?
5. Performance and Breach
Has it been performed?
6. Defenses
Can performance be avoided?
7. Third Parties
Does it affect third parties?
A. Mutual Assent
B. Making Offers
C. Accepting Offers
D. Terminating Offers

1. Acceptance in General

Now that we have looked at mutual assent in general, and the making of offices in particular, it is time to turn to acceptance. The moment the offer is made, of course, the offeror is inwardly wishing for the offeree to accept.* And, if the acceptance is immediate, we can feel pretty comfortable that the parties have made a welfare-enhancing contract. This is because the offeror is only likely to make an offer if it values what it is offering (say, a car) less than it values what it

* Unless, of course the "offer" was a joke à la *Lucy v. Zehmer* or *Leonard v. Pepsico*.

will receive in return (say, $10,000). And, as with the offeror, so too with the offeree: the offeree will only accept the offer if it values what it is accepting (the car) more than it values what it is promising to give up to obtain it ($10,000).

But offers and acceptances are rarely simultaneous, and a lot can change during the period of time in which an offeror makes an offer and the offeree attempts to accept it. For instance, an offeree may dispatch an acceptance only to learn that the value of the offeror's promise has decreased, and may wish to retract its acceptance before it is received. Can it do so? The opposite may also happen: The value of the offeror's promise may increase before it is accepted, and the offeror may no longer wish to form a contract on the previously offered terms. May it retract its offer?* The principles and rules you will learn in this section will help you deal with such problems, and others besides. As before, we will begin this section with a doctrinal overview to get you familiar with the lay of the land.

DOCTRINAL OVERVIEW: THE ACCEPTANCE†

We have seen that an offer is a manifestation of assent that empowers another to enter into a contract by manifesting assent in return. If the offeree exercises this power by manifesting assent, the offeree is said to "accept" the offer. This acceptance is the final step in the making of a contract. Upon acceptance, the offeror is bound by the contract proposed by the offer. Whether the offer invites acceptance by a promise or by performance, the offeror is "the master of the offer" and acceptance must be on the terms of the offer. There are, however, limits to what the offeror can turn into an acceptance, and the offeror cannot, for example, turn an offeree's silence into acceptance.*

If the offer invites acceptance by performance, the offeree cannot accept by promising the performance. Nor can the offeree accept by rendering a performance that does not conform to all of the terms of the offer. An offer of a reward, for example, cannot be accepted by one who does not do all that the terms of the reward require. . . .

Most offers invite acceptance by a promise rather than by performance, and most of the law of offer and acceptance has developed in connection with such offers. Under the objective theory, the offeree's undisclosed intention is irrelevant, as long as the offeree's conduct gives the offeror reason to believe that the offeree intends to accept by making a promise. . . . As Judge Easterbrook put it, "You can't escape contractual obligation by signing with your fingers crossed behind your back, even if that clearly shows your intent not to be bound."[9]

---

* We deal with the problem of retracting an offer in the next section, "Terminating Offers," p. 285, *infra*.

† Excerpted from E. ALLAN FARNSWORTH, CONTRACTS § 3.13 (4th ed. 2004).

* [We will discuss acceptance by silence in greater detail in subsection C.5., p. 281, *infra*.—ED.]

9. *Robbins v. Lynch*, 836 F.2d 330, 332 (7th Cir. 1988).

The fact that an offer invites acceptance by a promise does not mean the promise must be in words. A promise may be implied from other conduct, such as a nod of the head, and in some circumstances beginning performance or even preparing for performance may as effectively indicate a commitment to finish as a promise in words. . . .

According to UCC 2-206(1)(a):

> Unless otherwise unambiguously indicated by the language or circumstances . . . an offer to make a contract shall be construed as inviting acceptance in any manner and by any medium reasonable in the circumstances . . . .

The language or other conduct that will suffice as acceptance by a promise depends on the circumstances, and cases tend to turn on their special facts. . . . Three general requirements for an acceptance by a promise can be identified.

First, there must be an expression of commitment. A mere acknowledgment of receipt of the offer or an expression of interest in it is not enough. . . .

Second, the commitment must not be conditional on any further act by either party. . . .

Third, at least according to traditional contract doctrine, the commitment must be one on the terms proposed by the offer without the slightest variation. The offeree's promise, embodied in the acceptance, must be identical with the offeror's promise, embodied in the offer. Under traditional doctrine, the offeror as the master of the offer enjoys freedom from contract except on the terms of the offer. . . .

In addition to these three requirements, which courts have deduced from the nature of an acceptance, the offeror as the master of the offer may impose further requirements. . . .

Before reading the excerpt below, you may wish to review both "Thinking Tool: Thinking Clearly About Legal Relationships" at p. 96, supra, *and "Thinking Tool Applied: Understanding Offers" at p. 201,* supra. *Note how Corbin, who was influenced by Hohfeld, is very careful to use Hohfeldian concepts like "power" and "disability" precisely.*

THINKING TOOL APPLIED: UNDERSTANDING ACCEPTANCES*

An acceptance is a voluntary act of the offeree whereby he exercises the power conferred upon him by the offer, and thereby creates the set of legal relations called a contract. What acts are sufficient to serve this purpose? We must look first to the terms in which the offer was expressed, either by words or by other conduct. The offeror is the creator of the power and at the time of its creation he has full control over both the fact of its existence and its terms. The offeror has,

* Excerpted from Arthur L. Corbin, *Offer and Acceptance, and Some of the Resulting Legal Relations*, 26 YALE L.J. 169, 199-200 (1917).

in the beginning, full power to determine the acts that are to constitute acceptance. After he has once created the power, he may lose his control over it, and may become disabled to change or to revoke it; but the fact that, in the beginning, the offeror has full control of the immediately succeeding relation called a power, is the characteristic that distinguishes contractual relations from non-contractual ones. After the offeror has created the power, the legal consequences thereof are out of his hands, and he may be brought into numerous consequential relations of which he did not dream, and to which he might not have consented. These later relations are nevertheless called contractual.

RELEVANT PROVISIONS

For the *Restatement (Second) of Contracts,* consult §§ 30, 32, 35(1), 50, 52, and 58. For the UCC, consult § 2-206(1)(a). For the CISG, consult Articles 18 and 23. For the UNIDROIT Principles, consult Articles 2.1.1, 2.1.6, and 2.1.7.

2. The Mirror Image Rule

DOCTRINAL OVERVIEW: THE MIRROR IMAGE RULE

In the Farnsworth excerpt "On Acceptance" above, you read that, "according to traditional contract doctrine, the commitment must be one on the terms proposed by the offer without the slightest variation. The offeree's promise, embodied in the acceptance, must be identical with the offeror's promise, embodied in the offer." This is known as the "mirror image" rule, and means that, to be effective, the terms of the acceptance must mirror the terms of the offer. Any attempted acceptance that deviates from this rule is treated as a rejection of the original offer, which destroys the offeree's power of acceptance. Where, however, the attempted acceptance "relate[s] to the same matter as the original offer and propos[es] a substituted bargain different from that proposed by the original offer,"* the court will usually treat it as a counteroffer on the new terms proposed therein. Where this is the case, the old offeree becomes the new offeror, and vice versa. In the next case, *Ardente v. Horan*, we will see the mirror image rule in action. As you read *Ardente*, ask yourself whether this rule makes sense. Does it seem to comport with the reasonable expectations of most people who make contracts? What are its pros and cons? Do you think contract law would be better off with a different rule? If so, what would such a rule look like? We will take up these questions again in the notes following this case.

* Restatement (Second) of Contracts § 39(1).

Ardente v. Horan

Supreme Court of Rhode Island
366 A.2d 162 (1976)

DORIS, JUSTICE. Ernest P. Ardente, the plaintiff, brought this civil action in Superior Court to specifically enforce an agreement between himself and William A. and Katherine L. Horan, the defendants, to sell certain real property. The defendants filed an **answer** together with a motion for summary judgment. Following the submission of affidavits by both the plaintiff and the defendants and a hearing on the motion, judgment was entered by a Superior Court justice for the defendants. The plaintiff now appeals.

> ***Answer***
>
> "A defendant's first pleading that addresses the merits of the case, usually by denying the plaintiff's allegations. An answer usually sets forth the defendant's defenses and counterclaims." BLACK'S LAW DICTIONARY (10th ed. 2014).

In August 1975, certain residential property in the city of Newport was offered for sale by defendants. The plaintiff made a bid of $250,000 for the property which was communicated to defendants by their attorney. After defendants' attorney advised plaintiff that the bid was acceptable to defendants, he prepared a purchase and sale agreement at the direction of defendants and forwarded it to plaintiff's attorney for plaintiff's signature. After investigating certain title conditions, plaintiff executed the agreement. Thereafter plaintiff's attorney returned the document to defendants along with a check in the amount of $20,000 and a letter dated September 8, 1975, which read in relevant part as follows:

> My clients are concerned that the following items remain with the real estate: a) dining room set and tapestry wall covering in dining room; b) fireplace fixtures throughout; c) the sun parlor furniture. I would appreciate your confirming that these items are a part of the transaction, as they would be difficult to replace.

The defendants refused to agree to sell the enumerated items and did not sign the purchase and sale agreement. They directed their attorney to return the agreement and the deposit check to plaintiff and subsequently refused to sell the property to plaintiff. This action for specific performance followed.

In Superior Court, defendants moved for summary judgment on the ground that the facts were not in dispute and no contract had been formed as a matter of law.[1] The trial justice ruled that the letter quoted above constituted a conditional acceptance of defendants' offer to sell the property and consequently must be construed as a counteroffer. Since defendants never accepted the counteroffer, it followed that no contract was formed, and summary judgment was granted.

1. Although the contract would appear to be within the statute of frauds, defendants did not raise this defense in the trial court, nor do they raise it here. Where a party makes no claim to the benefit of the statute, the court *sua sponte* will not interpose it for him. [We will discuss the statute of frauds in Chapter 8, *infra*.—ED.]

Summary judgment is a drastic remedy and should be cautiously applied; nevertheless, where there is no genuine issue as to any material fact and the moving party is entitled to judgment as a matter of law, summary judgment properly issues. . . .

The plaintiff's . . . contention is that the trial justice incorrectly applied the principles of contract law in deciding that the facts did not disclose a valid acceptance of defendants' offer. . . . [W]e cannot agree.

The trial justice proceeded on the theory that the delivery of the purchase and sale agreement to plaintiff constituted an offer by defendants to sell the property. Because we must view the evidence in the light most favorable to the party against whom summary judgment was entered, in this case plaintiff, we assume as the trial justice did that the delivery of the agreement was in fact an offer.[3]

The question we must answer next is whether there was an acceptance of that offer. The general rule is that where, as here, there is an offer to form a bilateral contract, the offeree must communicate his acceptance to the offeror before any contractual obligation can come into being. **A mere mental intent to accept the offer, no matter how carefully formed, is not sufficient. The acceptance must be transmitted to the offeror in some overt manner.** A review of the record shows that the only expression of acceptance which was communicated to defendants was the delivery of the executed purchase and sale agreement accompanied by the letter of September 8. Therefore it is solely on the basis of the language used in these two documents that we must determine whether there was a valid acceptance. **Whatever plaintiff's unexpressed intention may have been in sending the documents is irrelevant. We must be concerned only with the language actually used, not the language plaintiff thought he was using or intended to use.**

> ***Subjective intent, revisited***
>
> Here, the court seems to allude to the subjective, "meeting of the minds" approach to mutual assent. Note, however, that all but the most ardent plaintiffs (near pun intended) would agree that a party's intent, to be effective, must be manifested, or "transmitted . . . in some overt manner," to be effective. *See, e.g., Household Fire and Carriage Accident Insurance Co. Ltd. v. Grant*, 4 Ex. D. 21 (1879) (accepting the meeting of the minds approach but noting that "[a]n acceptance, which only remains in the breast of the acceptor without being actually and by legal implication communicated to the offeror, is no binding acceptance").

> ***Hidden intentions, again***
>
> This language should immediately remind you of both *Embry* and *Lucy*. If not, you probably know what you should do as soon as you finish this case.

There is no doubt that the execution and delivery of the purchase and sale agreement by plaintiff, without more, would have operated as an acceptance. The terms of the accompanying letter, however, apparently conditioned the acceptance upon the inclusion of various items of personalty. In assessing the effect of the terms of that letter we must keep in mind certain generally

3. The conclusion that the delivery of the agreement was an offer is not unassailable in view of the fact that defendants did not sign the agreement before sending it to plaintiff, and the fact that plaintiff told defendants' attorney *after* the agreement was received that he would have to investigate certain conditions of title before signing the agreement. If it was not an offer, plaintiff's execution of the agreement could itself be no more than an offer, which defendants never accepted.

accepted rules. To be effective, an acceptance must be definite and unequivocal. "An offeror is entitled to know in clear terms whether the offeree accepts his proposal. It is not enough that the words of a reply justify a probable inference of assent." 1 *Restatement Contracts* § 58, comment a (1932). The acceptance may not impose additional conditions on the offer, nor may it add limitations. "An acceptance which is equivocal or upon condition or with a limitation is a counteroffer and requires acceptance by the original offeror before a contractual relationship can exist." *John Hancock Mut. Life Ins. Co. v. Dietlin*, 199 A.2d 311, 313 (1964).

However, an acceptance may be valid despite conditional language if the acceptance is clearly independent of the condition. Many cases have so held. Williston states the rule as follows:

> Frequently an offeree, while making a positive acceptance of the offer, also makes a request or suggestion that some addition or modification be made. So long as it is clear that the meaning of the acceptance is positively and unequivocally to accept the offer whether such request is granted or not, a contract is formed. 1 Williston, *Contracts* § 79 at 261-62 (3d ed. 1957).

Thus our task is to decide whether plaintiff's letter is more reasonably interpreted as a qualified acceptance or as an absolute acceptance together with a mere inquiry concerning a collateral matter.

In making our decision we recognize that, as one text states, "The question whether a communication by an offeree is a conditional acceptance or counteroffer is not always easy to answer. It must be determined by the same commonsense process of interpretation that must be applied in so many other cases." 1 Corbin, [*Contracts*] § 82 at 353. In our opinion, the language used in plaintiff's letter of September 8 is not consistent with an absolute acceptance accompanied by a request for a gratuitous benefit. We interpret the letter to impose a condition on plaintiff's acceptance of defendants' offer. The letter does not unequivocally state that even without the enumerated items plaintiff is willing to complete the contract. In fact, the letter seeks "confirmation" that the listed items "are a part of the transaction." Thus, far from being an independent, collateral request, the sale of the items in question is explicitly referred to as a part of the real estate transaction. Moreover, the letter goes on to stress the difficulty of finding replacements for these items. This is a further indication that plaintiff did not view the inclusion of the listed items as merely collateral or incidental to the real estate transaction. . . .

Accordingly, we hold that since the plaintiff's letter of acceptance dated September 8 was conditional, it operated as a rejection of the defendants' offer and no contractual obligation was created.

The plaintiff's appeal is denied and dismissed, the judgment appealed from is affirmed and the case is remanded to the Superior Court.

RELEVANT PROVISIONS

For the *Restatement (Second) of Contracts*, consult §§ 38, 39, 59, and 61. For the UCC, consult § 2-207. For the CISG, consult Articles 17 and 19. For the UNIDROIT Principles, consult Articles 2.1.5 and 2.1.11.

NOTES AND QUESTIONS

1. *What happened?* Who sued whom for what? Procedurally, how did the case get before this court? Factually, what happened between the parties? What arguments did the plaintiff and defendant make? What rule or rules did the court apply? How did the court analyze the dispute between the parties? How did the court decide the case?

2. *Was this case correctly decided?* Do you agree with the result reached in this case? Why or why not? Do you agree with the court's reasoning? Why or why not? How, if at all, would you have written the opinion differently?

3. *Cause for concern?* The court rightly focused on the language in the September 8 letter from the plaintiff's attorney, but do you agree with the conclusions it drew? For instance, the court focused on the fact that the clients were "concerned" that certain items came with the real estate, but these concerns were expressed *along with* a check for $20,000 and plaintiff's execution of the purchase and sale agreement. Why not just treat the concern as a concern, rather than as a rejection and counteroffer? What other facts allowed the court to rule as it did? Do you agree with the court?

4. *Absolute or conditional?* Do you think the plaintiff's language in the September 8 letter constitutes (1) an absolute or unqualified acceptance, along with "a mere inquiry concerning a collateral matter," or (2) a "conditional acceptance," which is to say, no acceptance at all, but a rejection of the original offer and counteroffer? We know what the court thought, but what do you think? Did the court get it right? How can you tell?

5. *Drafting exercise.* The court, citing Williston, acknowledges that a party can accept an offer while also "mak[ing] a request or suggestion that some addition or modification be made." Isn't that what happened here? In any event, pretend you are the plaintiff's lawyer, and try to redraft the September 8 letter so as to (1) accept the offer while (2) giving your client the best chance of obtaining the three additional items referred to in that letter.

6. *How does the mirror image rule fare outside of the common law?* Take a look at the UCC, CISG, and UNIDROIT Principles referenced above. To what extent do they appear to accept or reject the mirror image rule? Regarding UCC § 2-207, don't focus too much on the details, as we will cover it in greater depth in Chapter 6, *infra*. Instead, just peruse it once or twice to get a sense of how (if at all) it differs from the mirror image rule.

7. *Thinking tools applied.* Now that you have considered some alternatives to the mirror image rule, do you think the common law is better off with or without it? If the latter, what rule would you replace it with? In thinking about your answer, here are some things to consider: What rule would be best from the perspective of reducing administrative costs? What rule would best reflect the intention of the parties and comport with notions of justice and fair play? What rule would reduce the transaction costs between the parties? Do you think the principle of acoustic separation should play a role here? For instance, might it be a good idea to announce a rather strict conduct rule to the parties (e.g., such as the mirror image rule), even though such a rule might sometimes lead to unjust results or results that don't comport with the parties' intent, because courts could always apply a decision rule that is more just or fair under the circumstances?

3. The Mailbox Rule

DOCTRINAL OVERVIEW: CONTRACTS BY CORRESPONDENCE*

It is more difficult to work out the mechanics of assent if the parties are at a distance and communicate by mail or some other means that takes time. Suppose that the offeree has dispatched an acceptance that has not yet been received by the offeror. Is it too late for the offeror to reconsider and revoke the offer? Is it too late for the offeree to reconsider and reject the offer? Is there a contract even if the acceptance is lost in transit and never received by the offeror? These questions are further complicated if either party has relied on what it assumes to be the state of affairs. The common law has tended, however, to answer such questions without regard to reliance, on the simple assumption that there must be a single moment that is decisive in all cases—a moment after which the offeror's power to revoke is terminated, after which the offerees power to reject is at an end, and after which any further risks of transmission are on the offeror.[1]

The question that has been most often presented is that of the offeror's power to revoke. Suppose that a seller mails an offer to an offeree, and the offeree accepts by return mail. But while the acceptance is in transit, the offeror telephones the offeree to revoke the offer. Is the acceptance effective on dispatch, so that the revocation comes too late, and there is then a contract? Or is the acceptance effective only on receipt, so that the revocation comes in time, and there is then no contract? The Court of King's Bench addressed that question in 1818 in *Adams v. Lindsell,* once one of the most celebrated cases in the field of contracts. . . .

---

* Excerpted from E. Allan Farnsworth, Contracts § 3.22 (4th ed. 2004).

1. In this context, "dispatch" occurs when the communication is put out of the sender's possession. Giving a letter to one's employee to be mailed will not suffice. "Receipt" occurs when the communication comes into the possession of the addressee or is delivered to a person or place authorized by the addressee for such communications. The addressee need not have read it or even seen it. . . .

Adams v. Lindsell

King's Bench

106 Eng. Rep. 250 (1818)

Action for non-delivery of wool according to agreement. At the trial . . . before BURROUGH J. it appeared that the defendants, who were dealers in wool, at St. Ives, in the county of Huntingdon, had, on Tuesday the 2d of September 1817, written the following letter to the plaintiffs, who were woolen manufacturers residing in Bromsgrove, Worcestershire.

> We now offer you eight hundred tons of weather fleeces, of a good fair quality of our country wool, at 35s. 6d. per ton, to be delivered at Leicester, and to be paid for by two months' bill in two months, and to be weighed up by your agent within fourteen days, receiving your answer in course of post.

This letter was misdirected by the defendants, to Bromsgrove, Leicestershire, in consequence of which it was not received by the plaintiffs in Worcestershire till 7 P.M. on Friday, September 5th. On that evening the plaintiffs wrote an answer, agreeing to accept the wool on the terms proposed. The course of the post between St. Ives and Bromsgrove is through London, and consequently this answer was not received by the defendants till Tuesday, September 9th. On the Monday September 8th, the defendants not having, as they expected, received an answer on Sunday September 7th, (which in case their letter had not been misdirected, would have been in the usual course of the post,) sold the wool in question to another person. Under these circumstances, the learned Judge held, that the delay having been occasioned by the neglect of the defendants, the jury must take it, that the answer did come back in due course of post; and that then the defendants were liable for the loss that had been sustained; and the plaintiffs accordingly recovered a verdict.

Jervis having in Easter term obtained a **rule nisi** for a new trial, on the ground that there was no binding contract between the parties.

Dauncey, Puller, and Richardson, shewed cause. They contended, that at the moment of the acceptance of the offer of the defendants by the plaintiffs, the former became bound. And that was on the Friday evening, when there had been no change of circumstances. **They were then stopped by the Court, who called upon Jervis and Campbell in support of the**

> ***Rule nisi***
>
> A rule nisi is like a temporary ruling that will become permanent (or "absolute") *unless* the party adversely affected by the rule can show cause as to why the rule should be set aside. Here, the trial judge (Burrough) found that there *was* a contract. The rule nisi, however, threatens to grant a new trial, which would adversely affect the plaintiff/offeree, who prevailed below. Therefore, the plaintiff must show cause as to why the rule nisi (granting a new trial) should be set aside.

> ***Dauncey, Puller, and Richardson***
>
> Here, the attorneys for the plaintiff/offeree present their argument as to why the rule nisi granting a new trial should be set aside.

> ***The court did what?***
>
> Apparently convinced by their argument, the court stopped plaintiff's attorneys, mid-argument, and called upon defendant's attorneys to argue in support of the rule.

rule. They relied on *Payne v Cave* (3 T.R. 148), and more particularly on *Cooke v Oxley* (Ibid. 653). In that case, Oxley, who had proposed to sell goods to Cooke, and given him a certain time at his request, to determine whether he would buy them or not, was held not liable to the performance of the contract, even though Cooke, within the specified time, had determined to buy them, and given Oxley notice to that effect. So here the defendants who have proposed by letter to sell this wool, are not to be held liable, even though it be now admitted that the answer did come back in due course of post. Till the plaintiffs answer was actually received, there could be no binding contract between the parties; and before then, the defendants had retracted their offer, by selling the wool to other persons. But—

The Court said, that if that were so, no contract could ever be completed by the post. For if the defendants were not bound by their offer when accepted by the plaintiffs till the answer was received, then the plaintiffs ought not to be bound till after they had received the notification that the defendants had received their answer and assented to it. And so it might go on ad infinitum. The defendants must be considered in law as making, during every instant of the time their letter was travelling, the same identical offer to the plaintiffs; and then the contract is completed by the acceptance of it by the latter. Then as to the delay in notifying the acceptance, that arises entirely from the mistake of the defendants, and it therefore must be taken as against them, that the plaintiffs answer was received in course of post.

Rule discharged.

> ***Judgment day***
>
> The arguments have ended, and we finally get to hear what the court thinks about all this. If convinced by the plaintiff's arguments, the court will discharge the rule nisi, there will be no new trial, and the original judgment for plaintiff will stand. If the court is convinced by the plaintiff, however, it will convert the rule nisi into a "rule absolute," and there will be a new trial.

> ***Rule discharged***
>
> The court sides with plaintiff! There will not be a new trial, and the original verdict for the plaintiff will stand.

RELEVANT PROVISIONS

For the *Restatement (Second) of Contracts*, consult §§ 40, 42, 43, 63, and 68. For the CISG, consult Articles 15, 16(1), 18(2), and 22-24. For the UNIDROIT Principles, consult Articles 2.1.3-2.1.5, 2.1.6(2), and 2.1.10.

NOTES AND QUESTIONS

1. *What happened?* Who sued whom for what? Procedurally, how did the case get before this court? Factually, what happened between the parties? What arguments did the plaintiff and defendant make? What rule or rules did the court apply? How did the court analyze the dispute between the parties? How did the court decide the case?

2. *Was this case correctly decided?* Do you agree with the result reached in this case? Why or why not? Do you agree with the court's reasoning? Why or why not? How, if at all, would you have written the opinion differently?

3. *The mailbox rule.* This case established the "mailbox rule," which states that although offers are effective upon receipt, acceptances are effective upon dispatch, rather than upon receipt. The rule is now codified in *Restatement (Second) of Contracts* § 63. Recall that revocations are effective upon receipt (§§ 42, 43), as are rejections (§ 40). The interaction of these rules produces a number of interesting implications . . .

4. *Implications of the mailbox rule.* For instance, in response to an offer, an offeree may dispatch an acceptance that subsequently gets delayed or, even worse, lost, but the offeror will still find itself bound to a contract it knows nothing about. And, even more tragic, as we saw in *Adams v. Lindsell*, an offeror in such a position may, thinking there to be no contract, sell its goods elsewhere, with the result that it may find itself in no position to perform upon ultimately learning of the offeree's acceptance. Is this fair?

5. *Allocating risk.* The mailbox rule puts the risk of a lost acceptance on the offeror, but the opposite rule (i.e., one in which acceptances are only effective upon receipt) would place that risk on the offeree. Between the two, is it generally better to place this risk on the offeror or offeree? Why?

6. *Mutual assent and the mailbox rule.* Do you think the mailbox rule can be reconciled with any of the approaches to mutual assent that we have examined? Before answering, consider the following: Suppose that, on Day 1, Offeror mails an offer to Offeree. On Day 2, Offeror changes her mind and mails a revocation. On Day 3, Offeree receives the offer and posts an acceptance. On Day 4, Offeree receives the revocation. On Day 5, Offeror receives Offeree's acceptance. According to the mailbox rule, a contract is formed on Day 3, despite the fact that Offeror has not wanted to contract since Day 2.

7. *Holmes's response.* Here's how Holmes would respond to the question above: "The existence of a written contract depends on the fact that the offeror and offeree have interchanged their written expressions, not on the continued existence of those expressions."* How would you reply?

8. *Drafting exercise.* Keep in mind that, like most contract rules, the mailbox rule is a default rule (*see Restatement (Second) Contracts* § 30(2) ["unless otherwise indicated . . ."]), meaning that the offeror, as master of the offer, can contract around it. You are the offeror in *Adams v. Lindsell*. Redraft the September 2 letter to avoid the mailbox rule.

* Oliver Wendell Holmes, *The Path of the Law*, 10 Harv. L. Rev. 457, 473 (1897).

9. ***Justifying the mailbox rule.*** Some commentators think that the mailbox rule is arbitrary. According to these folks, it is less important what the rule *is* than that we have a rule at all—a clear way for courts to determine whether the parties have, or have not, established a contract through their correspondence. Other folks, however, think the issue is far from arbitrary, and have offered strong justifications both for and against the mailbox rule. For instance, according to Professor Fried, in support of the rule:

> In the context of a postal system that in the nineteenth century was remarkably swift and reliable, the mailbox rule had the virtue of creating maximum certainty at the earliest point. The promisee knew he had a deal as soon as he posted his acceptance, and he could proceed on that basis without awaiting a confirmation. True, the promisor had to consider the risk that he might be bound to a contract without knowing it, but that is both a lesser and a controllable hardship: The promisor initiates the transaction by making the offer, so he can make enquiries if no answer is forthcoming. And if he does not wish to assume even this burden, he can reverse the law's presumption and require actual receipt of the acceptance as a term of his offer. The contrary presumption—that the contract is complete only on receipt of the acceptance—would leave the promisee in exactly the same doubt about his situation as the mailbox rule leaves the promisor. And the effective date of the obligation would be delayed by that one step without any gain in certainty.*

According to critics like Langdell, however, the mailbox rule violates the well-established notion that bilateral contracts should only be formed upon receipt of the bargained-for return promise:

> The consideration for the offer was the offeree's return promise. But a promise by its nature is not complete until communicated; a "promise" into the air is no promise at all. Since there was no promise, there was no consideration and there could be no contract, until the letter of acceptance was received and read. The mailbox rule could not be good law.†

Which of the above views do you find most convincing? How did the court in *Adams v. Lindsell* justify the mailbox rule? How would you justify it?

10. ***Thinking tools applied.*** Using the thinking tools we previously examined, do you think the mailbox rule is the best way of governing contracts created by correspondence, or is there a better approach? In answering this question, here are some questions you may wish to consider: Do you think the mailbox rule, or a different approach, would be most consistent with the ex ante expectations of the parties? Does one approach seem more just than another? Should contracts by correspondence be governed by a standard or a rule? What approach would reduce administrative costs by allowing courts to administer it most accurately and inexpensively? What approach would minimize the transaction costs between the parties?

---

* CHARLES FRIED, CONTRACT AS PROMISE 51 (1981).

† Thomas C. Grey, *Langdell's Orthodoxy*, 45 U. PITT. L. REV. 1, 4 (1983).

11. *Comparative analysis.* Do the rules set forth in the CISG or UNIDROIT Principles, listed above under "Relevant Provisions," accept or reject the mailbox rule? Consult the following excerpt, and especially CISG Articles 16(1) and 18(2).

INTERNATIONAL PERSPECTIVE: THE MAILBOX RULE AND THE CISG*

Under the common law, acceptances are effective upon dispatch, even if they never reach the offeror. This rule performs two functions: it protects the offeree against the possibility of revocation once the acceptance is dispatched, and it places the risk of a lost communication on the offeror. In contrast to the common law mailbox rule, Article 18(2) of the CISG adopts a receipt rule: "An acceptance of an offer becomes effective at the moment the indication of assent reaches the offeror." But this provision must be read in conjunction with Article 16(1), which says that "an offer may be revoked if the revocation reaches the offeree *before he has dispatched an acceptance*" (emphasis added). In other words, once the offeree has dispatched an acceptance, the offeror may no longer revoke, but if the acceptance is lost in the mail there is no contract. So the CISG and the common law both protect the offeree against the possibility of revocation once the acceptance is dispatched, but the CISG places the risk of a lost communication on the offeree rather than the offeror.

PROBLEM: *LONERGAN* REVISITED

Go back and review the facts in *Lonergan v. Scolnick* (p. 205, *infra*). Assume that the seller's April 8 letter constituted an offer, but that the seller sold his land to another person on April 14. Would the April 15 letter posted by the buyer have constituted an acceptance? Why or why not?

PROBLEM: MAILBOX HYPOS

How would you apply the mailbox rule to the hypotheticals below? ("R" is the offeror, and "E" is the offeree.)

Hypo 1: Day 1: R dispatches offer to sell 100 widgets to E. Day 2: E dispatches acceptance. Day 3 passes. Day 4 passes. Day 5 passes. Not hearing from E, R sells widgets to another buyer and dispatches his revocation to E. Day 6: E receives revocation, and calls R, explaining that he dispatched his acceptance days ago. Day 7, R finally receives acceptance. Result?

---

* Excerpted from William S. Dodge, *Teaching the CISG in Contracts*, 50 J. LEGAL EDUC. 72, 81 (2000).

Hypo 2: Day 1: R dispatches offer to sell 100 widgets to E. Day 2: E dispatches acceptance. Day 3: E changes mind, dispatches rejection, which overtakes E's acceptance in the mail. Day 4, R receives rejection, and sells widgets elsewhere. Day 5, R receives acceptance. Result?

Hypo 3: Day 1: R dispatches offer to sell 100 widgets to E. Day 2: E dispatches rejection. Day 3, R dispatches revocation. Day 4, R receives E's rejection. Day 5, E receives R's revocation. Result?

Hypo 4: Day 1: R dispatches offer to sell 100 widgets to E. Day 2: E dispatches rejection. Day 3, E changes mind, and dispatches acceptance. Day 4, R receives E's rejection. Day 5, R receives E's acceptance. Result?

Hypo 5: Day 1: R dispatches offer to sell 100 widgets to E. Day 2: E dispatches rejection. Day 3, E changes mind, and dispatches acceptance, which overtakes E's rejection in the mail. Day 4, R receives E's acceptance. Day 5, R receives E's rejection. Result?

4. Acceptance by Performance: Unilateral Contracts

DOCTRINAL OVERVIEW: BILATERAL AND UNILATERAL CONTRACTS*

Traditional analysis of the bargaining process developed a dichotomy between "bilateral" and "unilateral" contracts. In forming a bilateral contract each party makes a promise: the offeror makes the promise contained in the offer, and the offeree makes a promise in return as acceptance. For example, a buyer offers to pay the price 30 days after delivery in return for a seller's *promise* to deliver apples. In forming a unilateral contract only one party makes a promise: the offeror makes the promise contained in the offer, and the offeree renders some performance as acceptance. For example, a buyer offers to pay the price 30 days after delivery in return for a seller's delivery of apples. Traditional analysis has it that in a bilateral contract there are promises on both sides (the buyer's promise to pay and the seller's promise to deliver); there are *duties* on both sides (the buyer's duty to pay and the seller's duty to deliver) and *rights* on both sides (the seller's right to payment and the buyer's right to delivery).[3] In a unilateral contract, however, there is a promise on only one side (the buyer's promise to pay);

---

* Excerpted from E. ALLAN FARNSWORTH, CONTRACTS §§ 3.4 and 3.15 (4th ed. 2004).

3. For the precise use of terms such as *right* and *duty*, the legal profession is indebted to Professor Wesley Newcomb Hohfeld, whose elaborate system of "Hohfeldian terminology" is set out in HOHFELD, FUNDAMENTAL LEGAL CONCEPTIONS (1919). A is said to have a *right* that B shall do an act when, if B does not do the act, A can initiate legal proceedings that will result in coercing B. B in such a situation is said to have a *duty* to do the act. *Right* and *duty* are therefore correlatives, since in this sense there can never be a *duty* without a *right*. A *power* is the capacity to change a legal relationship. In this terminology the offeree has, before the contract is made, a *power* to create a contract by means of acceptance.

there is a *duty* on only one side (the buyer's duty to pay) and a *right* on the other side (the seller's right to payment). . . .

If an offer invites acceptance by performance rather than a promise, the offeree must ordinarily notify the offeror that the offer has been accepted if the offeree has reason to believe that the offeror will not learn of the acceptance without notice.[1] [An offeree failing to give required notice will result in the offeror not be bound] . . .

[However, s]ometimes an offer that invites performance expressly dispenses with notice, or it is apparent from the circumstances that acceptance of the offer does not require notice. [We will see an example of this in our next case, *Carlill v. Carbolic Smoke Ball Co. . . .*]

Carlill v. Carbolic Smoke Ball Co.

In the Court of Appeal
1 Q.B. 256 (1893)

Appeal from a decision of **Hawkins, J.** The defendants, who were the proprietors and vendors of a medical preparation called "The Carbolic Smoke Ball," inserted in the Pall Mall Gazette of November 13, 1891, and in other newspapers, the following advertisement:

> **£100 reward will be paid by the Carbolic Smoke Ball Company to any person who contracts the increasing epidemic influenza, colds, or any disease caused by taking cold, after having used the ball three times daily for two weeks according to the printed directions supplied with each ball. £1000. is deposited with the Alliance Bank, Regent Street, shewing our sincerity in the matter.**
>
> **During the last epidemic of influenza many thousand carbolic smoke balls were sold as preventives against this disease, and in no ascertained case was the disease contracted by those using the carbolic smoke ball.**
>
> **One carbolic smoke ball will last a family several months, making it the cheapest remedy in the world at the price, 10s., post free.**

1. *Restatement Second* § 54.

The ball can be refilled at a cost of 5s. Address, Carbolic Smoke Ball Company, 27, Princes Street, Hanover Square, London.

The plaintiff, a lady, on the faith of this advertisement, bought one of the balls at a chemist's, and used it as directed, three times a day, from November 20, 1891, to January 17, 1892, when she was attacked by influenza. Hawkins, J., held that she was entitled to recover the £100. The defendants appealed. . . .

LINDLEY, L.J: . . . We must first consider whether this was intended to be a promise at all, or whether it was a mere puff which meant nothing. Was it a mere puff? My answer to that question is No, and I base my answer upon this passage: "£1000 is deposited with the Alliance Bank, shewing our sincerity in the matter." Now, for what was that money deposited or that statement made except to negative the suggestion that this was a mere puff and meant nothing at all? The deposit is called in aid by the advertiser as proof of his sincerity in the matter—that is, the sincerity of his promise to pay this £100 in the event which he has specified. I say this for the purpose of giving point to the observation that we are not inferring a promise; there is the promise, as plain as words can make it.

Then it is contended that it is not binding. In the first place, it is said that it is not made with anybody in particular. Now that point is common to the words of this advertisement and to the words of all other advertisements offering rewards. They are offers to anybody who performs the conditions named in the advertisement, and anybody who does perform the condition accepts the offer. In point of law this advertisement is an offer to pay £100 to anybody who will perform these conditions, and the performance of the conditions is the acceptance of the offer. . . .

We, therefore, find here all the elements which are necessary to form a binding contract enforceable in point of law. . . .

It appears to me, therefore, that the defendants must perform their promise, and, if they have been so unwary as to expose themselves to a great many actions, so much the worse for them.

BOWEN, L.J: I am of the same opinion. . . .

Was it intended that the £100 should, if the conditions were fulfilled, be paid? The advertisement says that £1000 is lodged at the bank for the purpose. Therefore, it cannot be said that the statement that £100 would be paid was intended to be a mere puff. I **think it was intended to be understood by the public as an offer which was to be acted upon.**

But it was said there was no check on the part of the persons who issued the advertisement, and that it would be an insensate thing to promise £100 to a person who used the smoke ball unless you could check or superintend his manner of using it. The answer to

Is this an offer?

In *Lefkowitz*, we learned that an advertisement is an offer only where it is "clear, definite, and explicit, and leaves nothing open for negotiation" (see p. 211, *supra*). Based on those criteria, is this ad an offer?

that argument seems to me to be that if a person chooses to make extravagant promises of this kind he probably does so because it pays him to make them, and, if he has made them, **the extravagance of the promises is no reason in law why he should not be bound by them.**

No matter how extravagant?

Do you agree that a promisor should be bound to their promises no matter how extravagant? Are there no limits to this principle?

It was also said that the contract is made with all the world—that is, with everybody; and that you cannot contract with everybody. It is not a contract made with all the world. There is the fallacy of the argument. It is an offer made to all the world; and why should not an offer be made to all the world which is to ripen into a contract with anybody who comes forward and performs the condition? It is an offer to become liable to anyone who, before it is retracted, performs the condition, and, although the offer is made to the world, the contract is made with that limited portion of the public who come forward and perform the condition on the faith of the advertisement. . . .

Then it was said that there was no notification of the acceptance of the contract. **One cannot doubt that, as an ordinary rule of law, an acceptance of an offer made ought to be notified to the person who makes the offer, in order that the two minds may come together. Unless this is done the two minds may be apart, and there is not that consensus which is necessary according to the English law . . . to make a contract.** But there is this clear gloss to be made upon that doctrine, that as notification of acceptance is required for the benefit of the person who makes the offer, the person who makes the offer may dispense with notice to himself if he thinks it desirable to do so, and I suppose there can be no doubt that where a person in an offer made by him to another person, expressly or impliedly intimates a particular mode of acceptance as sufficient to make the bargain binding, it is only necessary for the other person to whom such offer is made to follow the indicated method of acceptance; and if the person making the offer, expressly or impliedly intimates in his offer that it will be sufficient to act on the proposal without communicating acceptance of it to himself, performance of the condition is a sufficient acceptance without notification. . . .

The "subjective" approach in action

Here is a rather clear expression, in context, of the "subjective" or "meeting of the minds" approach to mutual assent. But note how the thoughtful judges who adhere to this view do not do so dogmatically, but allow contracts to be formed even where it is clear that the minds have not met. You can see this in the very next sentence, where Lord Bowen qualifies the meeting of the minds approach ("there is this clear gloss to be made upon that doctrine . . .") by allowing the offeror to contract around the traditional default rule requiring the offeree to notify the offeror of acceptance. The result of this is that, as with the mailbox rule (see *Adams v. Lindsell*, p. 237, *supra*), a contract can be formed without the offeror even knowing about it.

Now, if that is the law, how are we to find out whether the person who makes the offer does intimate that notification of acceptance will not be necessary in order to constitute a binding bargain? In many cases you look to the offer itself. In many

Mutual assent applied

How would you answer this question through the lens of each of the three approaches to mutual assent that we have examined in this casebook?

cases you extract from the character of the transaction that notification is not required, and in the advertisement cases it seems to me to follow as an inference to be drawn from the transaction itself that a person is not to notify his acceptance of the offer before he performs the condition, but that if he performs the condition notification is dispensed with. It seems to me that from the point of view of common sense no other idea could be entertained. **If I advertise to the world that my dog is lost, and that anybody who brings the dog to a particular place will be paid some money, are all the police or other persons whose business it is to find lost dogs to be expected to sit down and write me a note saying that they have accepted my proposal? Why, of course, they at once look after the dog, and as soon as they find the dog they have performed the condition.** The essence of the transaction is that the dog should be found, and it is not necessary under such circumstances, as it seems to me, that in order to make the contract binding there should be any notification of acceptance. It follows from the nature of the thing that the performance of the condition is sufficient acceptance without the notification of it, and a person who makes an offer in an advertisement of that kind makes an offer which must be read by the light of that common sense reflection. He does, therefore, in his offer impliedly indicate that he does not require notification of the acceptance of the offer.

> ***Transaction costs***
>
> In an earlier thinking tool, we explored how it may be beneficial to establish default rules that minimize transaction costs (see p. 126, *infra*). The rule established in *Carlill*, which dispenses with the notice requirement where a large number of potential acceptances are possible, seems to be justified on these grounds. Would another rule even be possible? Here, Professors Kronman and Posner explain: "Because the potential finders of lost property will often be numerous and unidentified, there is no feasible way in which the owner could negotiate with each of them for the return of his property. The unilateral-contract approach enables voluntary transacting without actual negotiations with potential transactors." ANTHONY KRONMAN AND RICHARD POSNER, THE ECONOMICS OF CONTRACT LAW 58 (1979).

A further argument for the defendants was that this was a *nudum pactum*—that there was no consideration for the promise—that taking the influenza was only a condition, and that the using the smoke ball was only a condition, and that there was no consideration at all; in fact, that there was no request, express or implied, to use the smoke ball. . . . **The definition of "consideration" . . . is this: "Any act of the plaintiff from which the defendant derives a benefit or advantage, or any labour, detriment, or inconvenience sustained by the plaintiff, provided such act is performed or such inconvenience suffered by the plaintiff, with the consent, either express or implied, of the defendant."** Can it be said here that if the person who reads this advertisement applies thrice daily, for such time as may seem to him tolerable, the carbolic smoke ball to his nostrils for a whole fortnight, he is doing nothing at all—that it is a mere act which is not to count towards consideration to support a promise (for the law does not require us to measure the adequacy of the consideration). Inconvenience sustained by one party at the request of the other is enough to create a consideration. I think, therefore, that it is consideration

> ***Consideration as benefit or detriment***
>
> Note the similarity between this view of consideration, and the view expressed by the court in *Hamer v. Sidway* (see p. 93, *supra*). How does it differ from the view embraced by the *Restatement (Second) of Contracts* §71?

enough that the plaintiff took the trouble of using the smoke ball. But I think also that the defendants received a benefit from this user, for the use of the smoke ball was contemplated by the defendants as being indirectly a benefit to them, because the use of the smoke balls would promote their sale. . . .

Appeal dismissed.

RELEVANT PROVISIONS

For the *Restatement (Second) of Contracts,* consult §§ 29(2), 30, 32, 50(2), 53(1), and (especially) 54. For the UCC, consult §§ 2-204(1) and 2-206. For the CISG, consult Article 18(3).

NOTES AND QUESTIONS

1. *What happened?* Who sued whom for what? Procedurally, how did the case get before this court? Factually, what happened between the parties? What arguments did the plaintiff and defendant make? What rule or rules did the court apply? How did the court analyze the dispute between the parties? How did the court decide the case?

2. *Was this case correctly decided?* Do you agree with the result reached in this case? Why or why not? Do you agree with the reasoning used by each of the judges? Why or why not? How, if at all, would you have written the opinion differently?

3. *Look familiar?* It should. Recall that there was a substantial discussion of this case, along with several "reward" cases, in *Leonard v. Pepsico.* You may want to review the portion of the court's opinion dealing with "Rewards as Offers" at this time. See p. 222, *supra*.

4. *Was there an offer?* Do you agree that the Carbolic Smoke Ball Co. made an offer? Why or why not?

5. *Did Carlill accept this offer? If so, when?* Do you think Carlill accepted the offer? If so, when, exactly, did the acceptance take place? Here are some possibilities: (1) When she purchased the smoke ball, (2) when she first used it, (3) when she completed her course of treatment according to the printed directions (i.e., three times daily for two weeks), or (4) when she contracted influenza. If you answered anything other than (1), does this mean that Carlill could buy the smoke ball, *then* learn about the offer, and *then* accept at (2)-(4)? Conversely, does it mean that the Carbolic Smoke Ball Co. could simply retract their offer after (1), but prior to Carlill's attempted acceptance at point (2), (3), or (4)? If so, does this seem fair? Can it be justified? (Here, you may wish to consult some of the thinking tools we have previously examined.) Might

there be a better rule available, perhaps one that protects Carlill's reliance on the promise between points (1) and (2)-(4)? Does this mean there is . . .

6. ***A potential problem with unilateral contracts?*** Because unilateral contracts can only be accepted by performance, there will usually be a period of time (and, sometimes, a long period of time) between the point at which a promisee begins to perform the invited performance and the point at which the promisee completes such performance. Therefore, the promisee will assume a disproportionate share of risk in performing such contracts, for at least two reasons. First, because the promisee is agreeing to perform 100% of his contractual obligations before getting anything in return, he is taking on the entire risk of the promisor's nonperformance, which is only due *after* the promisee's performance (e.g., the promisor may go bankrupt or refuse to perform its promise *after* obtaining the full benefit of the promisee's performance). And second, because "acceptance" in the context of unilateral contracts means complete performance, the promisee will also be vulnerable *while* they are performing *so long as* we allow the promisor to revoke her offer prior to acceptance (which is the traditional rule). However, this traditional rule creates special problems as applied to unilateral contracts. In theory, it means that a promisor can obtain 99% of the promisee's performance and then revoke the offer before the last 1% is completed. In practice, of course, courts have and will continue to find ways to prevent such an unjust outcome (e.g., allowing the promisee to recover under a theory of unjust enrichment immediately comes to mind), but is there any way the general doctrine can be justified? And, relatedly, can you think of any way the general doctrine should be modified? Keep these questions in mind, as we will return to them again at the end of this section, after having considered several more cases involving unilateral contracts. At that time, we will be in a better position to appreciate more fully some of the intricacies involved.

7. *Counseling.* In light of the court's decision, how would you advise the Carbolic Smoke Ball Co. to advertise its smoke ball in the future? As you read the following excerpt, note that a portion of it discusses the new advertising campaign launched by the Carbolic Smoke Ball Co. in response to this case.

8. *Digging deeper.* The following excerpt is wonderful in so many ways. Not only does it explore more deeply the richness of the facts of the case, many of which never made it into the court's final decision, but it also sets these facts against the medical and social background of the time and delves into the patterns of legal thought prevailing during that time concerning such important issues as the will theory of assent and the acceptance of unilateral contracts. As you read it, ask yourself which of these facts, if any, should have influenced (or perhaps *did* influence) the court's decision. Are these the kinds of facts that courts *ought* to take into account? Why or why not? Are these the kinds of facts that courts have the *expertise* to take into account? Why or why not? Those of you who answered "yes" to the first question but "no" to

the second should feel mildly uncomfortable with your answer, especially when you consider that such information could theoretically be provided for *all* of the cases in *all* of your courses. Because courts can't focus on everything, do any of the thinking tools we previously discussed help us sort out which facts courts should consider, which they should ignore, and, more generally, how they should make legal decisions against such a rich tapestry of "background" material? "Background" is put in quotations because it is important to keep in mind that what ultimately gets considered as background material, as opposed to material necessary to decide a case, does not exist as some kind of *a priori* fact, but is a product of the legal system itself, and is determined, in part, by the sorts of answers judges provide to the types of questions raised in this note when they are deciding cases.

CONTEXTUAL PERSPECTIVE: MORE ON *CARLILL V. CARBOLIC SMOKE BALL CO.**

All lawyers, and indeed many nonlawyers, are familiar with the case of *Carlill v. Carbolic Smoke Ball Company.* Continuously studied though it has been by lawyers and law students for close to a century, it has never been investigated historically. . . .

The Patenting of the Smoke Ball

On October 30, 1889, one Frederick Augustus Roe . . . submitted an application to patent what he described as "An Improved Device for Facilitating the Distribution, Inhalation and Application of Medicated and Other Powder." . . .

By a fortunate chance the directions for use of the ball as marketed survive in the *Inventor.*

> Hold the ball by the loose end below the silk floss, with the thumb and forefinger in front of the mouth. Snap or flip rapidly on the side of the ball, on the place marked "S" and a fine powder resembling smoke will arise. Inhale this smoke or powder as it arises, as shown in the above illustration. This will cause sneezing, and for a few moments you will feel as if you were taking cold. This feeling will soon pass away and the cure has commenced. If you do not feel the effects at the first inhalation by it making you sneeze, take a second in the same manner.

The Marketing of the Ball

Whether the ball was in fact marketed in America, perhaps as "the Pulverator," is unknown, but late in 1889 or early in 1890 Roe began to market his Carbolic Smoke Ball in England. . . . The influenza epidemic which had begun . . . in December of 1889, must have come as a godsend to his new enterprise, but the

* Excerpted from A.W.B. Simpson, *Quackery and Contract Law: The Case of the Carbolic Smoke Ball*, 14 J. Legal Stud. 345, 345, 348, 350, 351-52, 354-55, 356, 358-60, 363, 364-66, 367, 370-71, 375-76, 377-79, 388-89 (1985).

utility of the ball was by no means restricted to this single ailment. The earliest of his advertisements that I have located appeared in the *Illustrated London News* on January 11, 1890. He claimed that the ball . . . "Will positively cure Influenza, Catarrh, Asthma, Bronchitis, Hay Fever, Neuralgia, Throat Deafness, Hoarseness, Loss of Voice, Whooping Cough, Croup, Coughs, Colds, and all other ailments caused by Taking Cold." Behind this optimism lay a theory . . . that all these ailments arose from a single cause, taking cold, and were therefore all amenable to the same single remedy, the Carbolic Smoke Ball. His advertisements exhibited a note of caution in insisting that the ball was to be used for inhalation only. Carbolic acid, though not at the time a scheduled poison, could be fatal if taken internally in more than small amounts. . . .

Frederick Roe was only one of many advertisers who made claims to cure or ward off influenza. It was the practice of the patent medicine vendors to adapt their claims, rather than their products, to the current needs of the market, and Roe was merely doing what was normal in the trade. The product remained the same; its function changed. . . .

The Recurrence of Influenza, 1891-92

Influenza again became established in London during 1891. . . . According to Dr. Parson's meticulous report, the winter epidemic started in November and reached its peak in the week ending January 23, 1892, when 506 deaths were attributed to it, as a primary cause, in London alone and a further eighty-six as a secondary cause. . . . The epidemic died out in February of 1892. At this time Frederick Roe was, as we have seen, advertising heavily. . . .

The advertisement that gave rise to the litigation first appeared . . . in the *Pall Mall Gazette* on November 13, 1891, and again on November 24 and December 8; apparently it also appeared in substantially the same form in other newspapers. . . .

The Carlill Family

Her full name was Louisa Elizabeth Carlill . . . She . . . was born . . . on October 22, 1845. . . . On December 17, 1873, . . . she married James Briggs Carlill. . . . [A]ccording to family tradition he was an actuary. . . . Whatever he eventually became, he was originally a solicitor. He was admitted to the roll in 1870, and practiced in Hull until 1882. . . . James Briggs moved to London in about 1882 and established a legal practice . . . with William Crook, under the style of Crook and Carlill. This appears to have come to an end by 1885, when he is back in Hull in partnership with one Simon Crawshaw. This practice does not seem to have continued long, as he is not in later law lists, and at the time of the action the Carlills were living in West Dulwich; what occupation James Briggs then followed is uncertain. . . . As for Mrs. Carlill herself, she was described by counsel in the legal proceedings as "a literary lady." This was a slightly mocking expression at the time, but it is clear that she had, as a writer, an income of her own. . . .

Mrs. Carlill saw the advertisement, and on November 20 she purchased a smoke ball from Messrs. Wilcox and Company, who operated a druggist's shop. . . . She paid for the ball out of her literary earnings. The vendors, as we have seen, were actively promoting the ball at the time. According to her account of the matter, which was given in evidence at the trial and not disputed, she assiduously used the ball three times daily for two weeks, in accordance with the already quoted printed instructions supplied with it: "In the morning before breakfast, at about 2 o'clock, and again when I went to bed." Whether she continued to use the ball thereafter does not appear. On January 17, that is, at the height of the epidemic, she contracted influenza. She remained ill under the care of a Dr. Robertson for some two weeks.

On January 20 her husband, James Briggs Carlill, wrote to the Carbolic Smoke Ball Company informing them of what had occurred; possibly her letter was only one of many received at this time:

> Dear Sir,
>
> Seeing your offer of a reward, dated July 20, in the "Pall Mall Gazette" of November 13, my wife purchased one of your smoke balls, and has used it three times a day since the beginning of December. She was, however, attacked by influenza. Dr. Robertson, of West Dulwich, attended, and will no doubt be able to certify in the matter. I think it right to give you notice of this, and shall be prepared to answer any inquiry or furnish any evidence you require. I am, yours obediently,
>
> J. B. Carlill.

This was ignored. He wrote again, threatening to place the matter in the hands of his solicitors, and received in reply a post card saying the matter would receive attention. He wrote a third time, and received in reply a printed circular, undated, endorsed "In answer to your letter of January 20." This remarkable document read:

> Re reward of £100—The Carbolic Smoke Ball Company, seeing that claims for the above reward have been made by persons who have either not purchased the smoke ball at all, or else have failed to use it as directed, consider it necessary that they should state the conditions in which alone such reward would be paid. They have such confidence in the efficacy of the carbolic smoke ball, if used according to the printed directions supplied to each person, that they made the aforesaid offer in entire good faith, believing it impossible for the influenza to be taken during the daily inhalation of the smoke ball as prescribed. In order to protect themselves against all fraudulent claims, the Carbolic Smoke Ball Company require that the smoke ball be administered, free of charge, at their office, to those who have already purchased it. Intending claimants must attend three times daily for three weeks, and inhale the smoke ball under the directions of the Smoke Ball Company. These visits will be specially recorded by the secretary in a book. 27 Princes St. Hanover Square, London.

[This letter] certainly irritated James Briggs Carlill, who replied, insisting his claim was perfectly honest. To this Roe replied that "the company considered his letter impertinent and gave him the names of his solicitors." And so it was that on February 15 an action was commenced to claim the £100 promised. . . .

[The trial began on June 16, 1892]. [T[he facts of the case were not in any real dispute, and a full trial before the special jury would have further inflated the costs. Mrs. Carlill did indeed go into the witness box, and the judge inspected the letters and the document setting out the instructions for use, and showing a lady using the ball—the picture appears in many of Roe's advertisements and in the *Inventor*. **Asquith** asked her when she used the ball, but did not cross examine as the facts were undisputed. Counsel agreed to leave the decision to the judge, giving him power to enter whatever verdict the jurymen, in his view, ought to have found; the jury was discharged. The case was then adjourned until Saturday June 18, when the judge heard counsels' argument on the points of law involved. He then reserved judgment to consider their arguments, eventually, on July 4, entering a verdict in favor of Mrs. Carlill for the £100 claimed, together with costs, and refusing an application for a stay of execution of the judgment. The form of procedure adopted, which bypassed the jury, was a significant factor in the conversion of the dispute into a leading case, for the judge gave reasons for his decision in a complex written opinion. Had the matter gone to a jury the case would have terminated in a laconic jury verdict, and although there could have been an appeal based on the judge's directions to the jury, it is unlikely that the legal elaboration of the case would have proceeded so far as it did. . . .

Herbert Henry Asquith

Herbert Henry Asquith (12 September 1852-15 February 1928), 1st Earl of Oxford and Asquith, was counsel for the Carbolic Smoke Ball Co. during the initial trial before Hawkins. He would later become the Prime Minister of the United Kingdom (5 April 1908-5 December 1916), leading that nation into the First World War.

Comical though the facts appear to us today, the decision in favor of Mrs. Carlill excited only limited comment in the press of the time. The *Pall Mall Gazette*, however, published a deeply hypocritical leader on December 8:

> As Mr. Justice Lindley pointed out, for once advertisers have counted too much on the gullibility of the public . . . . The plaintiff bought the ball and carried out the instructions. Three times a day for two weeks she did it, with faith and with industry and yet the foul fiend gripped her. In vain the ball was smoked in the sight of any germ. Carbolic smoke positively braced the bacilli. But convalescence came, and the plaintiff rose in wrath and smote the company. Mr. Justice Hawkins backed her case, and the Court of Appeal has backed Mr. Justice Hawkins. Smoke is good, but the carbolic smoke, we fear, will have lost its savour.

The *Spectator's* lead writer, in a piece entitled "A Novel Breach of Contract," revealed that he had personally sampled the ball: "To judge from our own experiences, twenty-five violent sneezes is the least result that can be expected from a single application. Therefore, we may suppose that in the course of these two weeks, this heroic lady suffered forty-two applications of the ball, and sneezed violently more than a thousand times." He argued that no *man* would have pressed the claim to its conclusion; Mrs. Carlill showed "all that patient determination and persistent importunity of which only a woman is capable."

The *Chemist and Druggist* welcomed the decision and took the opportunity to voice disgust on the cynicism of lawyers, in particular Asquith, quoting him as saying: "We are not discussing the honourable obligation to pay." In the medical press too the case was noticed, and Sir Henry Hawkins's decision was welcomed in a leader in the *Lancet*, then (and now) one of the leading organs of the legitimate medical profession. This was published on July 9, and the journal did not trouble to repeat its grudging approval when the decision was upheld in December:

> To those amongst our readers who are familiar with the way of the quack medicine vendor the facts proved the other day by Mrs. Carlill in the action she has brought against the Carbolic Smoke Ball Company will occasion no surprise. . . . We are glad to learn that in spite of the ingenuity of their legal advisers the defendants have been held liable to make good their promise. People who are silly enough to adopt a medicine simply because a tradesman is reckless enough to make extravagant promises and wild representations as to its efficiency may thank themselves chiefly for any disappointment that ensues. Still for this folly, which is only foolish and nothing worse, it is possible to feel sympathy when the disappointment comes. It is a pleasant alternative to learn that the dupe has been able, in the present instance, to enforce a sharp penalty. . . .

The doctors at this time were fighting a continuous and not very successful battle against various forms of quack medicine; in particular they took strong exception to the extravagant claims made by advertisers. No doubt there were at the time genuinely satisfied users of the Carbolic Smoke Ball; indeed, initially Mrs. Carlill was one, for in the witness box she explained how she had recommended the ball to her friends. Although the claims made for its efficacy were ludicrously optimistic, the puffing of carbolic powder up the nostrils as a mode of treatment was not in itself any odder than many of the procedures employed at the time by orthodox medicine.

For in the Victorian world the distinction between quackery and legitimate scientific medicine was by no means as clear as it now seems. It depended, at least in part, purely on who was prescribing the treatment. Much of what the doctors did was either useless or positively harmful, except insofar as it may have improved the morale of the patient. Quack medicine was not obviously any worse as a morale booster and could, especially if available on mail order, be considerably cheaper. Considered merely as an appliance the ball was not in itself in any way unorthodox. It was what was and indeed still is known in the business as an insufflator, close cousin to an inhaler. . . .

The smoke ball's active ingredient, carbolic acid, is a poison, and from 1882 onward the Pharmaceutical Society had waged a campaign to persuade the Privy Council to add it to the list of scheduled poisons, a campaign which was eventually partially successful in 1900. . . . [B]ut we must not judge Frederick Roe too harshly for his optimism. And, so far as influenza is concerned the use of the ball compares favorably with the heroic measures adopted for the same condition by Dr. J. C. Voight, a product of the medical school at Edinburgh: rectal injections of eucalyptus oil. . . .

Roe Goes Public

A flood of claims ought surely to have arrived to drive Roe into the bankruptcy court, for his personal liability for the payment of the £100 rewards. . . . Counsel in the argument before Hawkins indicated that there had been other claims, and the *Chemist and Druggist* noted one such, from the Chester area. In the Court of Appeal much was made of this by Finlay [representing Carbolic Smoke Ball Co.]:

"At the present there might be 10,000 people watching for the result of this appeal. There might be a swarm of imposters in the industry of smelling smoke-balls who might continue to march in as long as there was anything to be squeezed out of this unfortunate company." But in fact no flood of claims seems to have occurred. On February 25 we find [Roe] boldly publishing in the *Illustrated London News* a new advertisement, cunningly framed in order to turn the whole affair to his advantage.* In it he pointed out that a reward of £100 pounds had recently been promised to anyone who contracted influenza, or eleven other diseases "caused by taking cold," after using the ball according to the instructions. The text continues: "Many thousand Carbolic Smoke Balls were sold on these advertisements, but only three persons claimed the reward of £100, thus proving conclusively that this invaluable remedy will prevent and cure the above mentioned diseases. THE CARBOLIC SMOKE BALL COMPANY LTD. now offer £200 REWARD to the person who purchases a Carbolic Smoke Ball and afterwards contracts any of the following diseases. . . ." There followed a list of nineteen ailments: influenza, coughs, cold in the head, cold in the chest, catarrh, asthma, bronchitis, sore throat, hoarseness, throat deafness, loss of voice, laryngitis, snoring, sore eyes, diphtheria, croup, whooping cough, neuralgia, headache. It will be noted that this offer appears to envisage only a single prize, and the small print went on to restrict the scope of the offer still further in a way which suggests legal advice: "This offer is made to those who have purchased a Carbolic Smoke Ball since Jan. 1, 1893, and is subject to conditions to be obtained on application, a duplicate of which must be signed and deposited with the Company in London by the applicant before commencing the treatment specified in the conditions. This offer will remain open only till March 31, 1893."

FEB. 25, 1893 THE ILLUSTRATED LONDON NEWS 253

FREE TRIALS AT OUR CONSULTING ROOMS.

FOR INHALATION ONLY.

£100 REWARD

WAS RECENTLY OFFERED BY THE

CARBOLIC SMOKE BALL CO.

To any person who contracted Influenza, Coughs, Colds, Catarrh, Asthma, Bronchitis, Sore Throat, Hoarseness, Loss of Voice, Throat Deafness, Croup, Whooping Cough, or any Disease caused by taking Cold, after having used the Carbolic Smoke Ball according to the printed directions.

Many thousand Carbolic Smoke Balls were sold on these advertisements, but only three persons claimed the reward of £100, thus proving conclusively that this invaluable remedy will prevent and cure the above-mentioned diseases.

THE CARBOLIC SMOKE BALL CO., Ltd.,

NOW OFFER

£200 REWARD

to the person who purchases a Carbolic Smoke Ball and afterwards contracts any of the following diseases, viz.—

INFLUENZA	CATARRH	THROAT DEAFNESS	DIPHTHERIA
COUGHS	ASTHMA	LOSS OF VOICE	CROUP
COLD IN THE HEAD	BRONCHITIS	LARYNGITIS	WHOOPING COUGH
COLD ON THE CHEST,	SORE THROAT	SNORING	NEURALGIA
	HOARSENESS	SORE EYES	HEADACHE

or any disease caused by taking cold while using the Carbolic Smoke Ball. This offer is made to those who have purchased a Carbolic Smoke Ball since Jan. 1, 1893, and is subject to conditions to be obtained on application, a duplicate of which must be signed and deposited with the Company in London by the applicant before commencing the treatment specified in the conditions. This offer will remain open only till March 31, 1893.

As all the diseases mentioned above arise from one cause, they can therefore be cured by the remedy which stops the cause, viz.—

THE CARBOLIC SMOKE BALL.

One CARBOLIC SMOKE BALL will last a family for several months, making it the cheapest remedy in the world at the price—10s. post free.

The CARBOLIC SMOKE BALL will be refilled and returned, post free, the same day, on receipt of Money or Postal Order for 5s.

ADDRESS—

CARBOLIC SMOKE BALL CO., LTD.,

27, PRINCES STREET, HANOVER SQUARE, LONDON, W.

PARIS DEPOT—14, Rue de la Paix. AMERICAN DEPOT—196, Broadway, New York. CANADIAN DEPOT—71 & 73, Front Street, Toronto, Ontario.

* [This advertisement is reproduced above.—ED.]

What these conditions were, or whether anyone succeeded in claiming the reward, does not appear. But no similar offer appears to have been made in later advertisements, so perhaps the experiment proved costly. The ball continued to be advertised enthusiastically in the early part of 1893, and the summer number of the *Illustrated London News* for that year carried one principally directed toward hay fever.

The Smoke Ball and Contractual Theory

For lawyers, and particularly for law students, *Carlill v. Carbolic Smoke Ball Co.* rapidly achieved the status of a leading case, a status which it has retained perhaps more securely in England than in the United States. Part of its success derived from the comic and slightly mysterious object involved, but there were two reasons of a legal character that suggest that it deserves its place in the firmament. The first, which is not always fully appreciated, is historical; it was the vehicle whereby a new legal doctrine was introduced into the law of contract.[96] The second is that the decision could be used by expositors of the law of contract to illustrate the arcane mysteries surrounding the conception of a unilateral or one-sided contract.

So far as the first point is concerned, the so-called will theory of contract supposed that all contractual obligations were the product of the joint wills of the contracting parties, embodied in their agreement. The function of law courts, according to this theory, was merely that of faithfully carrying into effect the wishes of the parties to the contract. Further reflection on the implications of this theory, which had powerful support in nineteenth-century thought, suggested that it must necessarily follow that a court should not enforce an agreement unless it was the will of the parties that it should be legally enforced. . . . But until Mrs. Carlill brought her action there was no case which had clearly recognized the requirement of an intention to create legal relations; her case did. It was indeed explicitly argued in this trial by Asquith that "the advertisement was a mere representation of what the advertisers intended to do in a certain event. The defendants did not by issuing it mean to impose upon themselves any obligations enforceable by law." . . . This argument was firmly rejected by the trial judge, who relied in particular on the fact that the advertisement had stated that £1,000 had been deposited in the Alliance Bank "showing our sincerity in the matter." This, he argued, "could only have been inserted with the object of leading those who read it to believe that the defendants were serious in their proposal." In the Court of Appeal the same view was taken. Thus Lord Justice Lindley, early in his opinion said: "We must first consider whether this was intended to be a promise at all, or whether it was a mere puff which meant nothing. Was it a mere puff? My answer to that question is No, and I base my answer on this passage: '£1000 is deposited with the Alliance Bank, shewing our sincerity in the matter.'" . . .

As for the second point, most contracts that concern the courts involve two-sided agreements, two-sided in the sense that the parties enter into reciprocal obligations to each other. A typical example is a sale of goods, where the seller

96. *See generally* A. W. B. Simpson, *Innovation in Nineteenth Century Contract Law*, 91 LAW Q. REV. 247 (1975).

has to deliver the goods and the buyer to pay for them. The doctrines of nineteenth-century contract law were adapted to such bilateral contracts, but the law also somewhat uneasily recognized that there could be contracts in which only one party was ever under any obligation to the other. The standard example was a published promise to pay a reward for information on the recovery of lost property: £10 to anyone who finds and returns my dog. In such a case obviously nobody is obligated to search for the dog, but if they do so successfully, they are entitled to the reward. Such contracts seem odd in another way; there is a promise, but no agreement, for the parties never even meet until the reward is claimed. Promises of rewards, made to the world at large, will not involve an indefinite number of claims—there is only one reward offered—and the courts will uphold the claimant's right to the reward although he has never communicated any acceptance of the promise. Classified as "unilateral" contracts, such arrangements presented special problems of analysis to contract theorists, whose standard doctrines had not been evolved to fit them. Thus it was by 1892 orthodox to say that all contracts were formed by the exchange of an offer and an acceptance, but it was by no means easy to see how this could be true of unilateral contracts, where there was, to the eyes of common sense, no acceptance needed.

The analytical problems arose in a particularly acute form in the smoke ball case. Thus it seemed very peculiar to say there had been any sort of agreement between Mrs. Carlill and the company, which did not even know of her existence until January 20, when her husband wrote to them to complain. There were indeed earlier cases permitting the recovery of advertised rewards; the leading case here was *Williams v. Cawardine*, where a reward of £20 had been promised by handbill for information leading to the conviction of the murderer of Walter Cawardine, and Williams, who gave such information, successfully sued to recover the reward. But this was long before the more modern doctrines had become so firmly embodied in legal thinking, and in any event the case was quite distinguishable. It concerned a reward, whereas Mrs. Carlill was seeking compensation. There could be at most only a few claimants for this, but there is no limit on the number of those who may catch influenza. Furthermore, the Carbolic Smoke Ball Company had had no chance to check the validity of claims, of which there could be an indefinite number; much was made of this point in the argument. But the judges were not impressed with these difficulties, and their attitude was no doubt influenced by the view that the defendants were rogues. They fit their decision into the structure of the law by boldly declaring that the performance of the conditions was the acceptance, thus fictitiously extending the concept of acceptance to cover the facts. And, since 1893, law students have been introduced to the mysteries of the unilateral contract through the vehicle of *Carlill v. Carbolic Smoke Ball Co.* and taught to repeat, as a sort of magical incantation of contract law, that in the case of unilateral contracts performance of the act specified in the offer constitutes acceptance, and need not be communicated to the offeror.

Lord Justice Bowen's analysis of the facts places the moment of acceptance as the moment when Mrs. Carlill completed the three-week period of use stipulated by the directions for use. This was not the only possible view. In argument Finlay attributed the one-sniff theory to his opponents: "According to the plaintiff, having taken one sniff at the ball, the defendant would not be at liberty to withdraw from the contract—(laughter)—because she had altered her position by sniffing." But Dickens did not agree that this was his view, though he is reported as saying that "Here the contract arose when the plaintiff began to sniff the ball," he thought that the contract only became binding on the defendants on completion of the course. A difficulty with Bowen and Dickens's view is that it leads to the conclusion that the offer could be withdrawn up to the moment of the last sniff, although the act of reliance by Mrs. Carlill took place earlier than this—either when she bought the ball or when she started to use it. This apparently unjust result has encouraged the further complexity of supposing there to be two contracts involved—a contract to pay the £100 if the complete course fails, and a second promise not to revoke the promise to pay the £100 once the purchaser of the ball starts the course of treatment. Other complexities somewhat inadequately dealt with in the case centered on the scope of the promise. Did it cover influenza contracted at any date in the future, or within the period of the epidemic, or while the ball was being used, or within a reasonable time thereafter? The court settled for the last possibility. And did the offer apply to any user—even one who had stolen the ball? But the judges were clearly not impressed with these problems—the defendants had not behaved as gentlemen, and that was essentially that.

Epilogue

And as for Louisa Elizabeth Carlill herself, . . . she long survived her adventure with the law. After her husband died on October 6, 1930, she lived in a flat in Blackheath, but by 1939 she was established in a hotel on the south coast, probably in Hastings, where she was renowned for her punctuality and her settled practice of drinking one glass of claret with her lunch. She then went to live with her daughter Dorothy Brousson at Swan House, in the village of Sellindge, near Folkestone, a lively spot to choose at the time of the Battle of Britain. There she died on March 10, 1942, at the age of ninety-six years, principally, as her death certificate records, of old age.

The other cause noted by her medical man, Dr. Joseph M. Yarman, was influenza.

Petterson v. Pattberg

Court of Appeals of New York
161 N.E. 428 (1928)

KELLOGG, J. The evidence given upon the trial sanctions the following statement of facts: John Petterson, of whose last will and testament the plaintiff is the **executrix**, was the owner of a parcel of real estate in Brooklyn, known as 5301 Sixth Avenue. The defendant was the owner of a bond executed by Petterson, which was secured by a third mortgage upon the parcel. On April 4th, 1924, there remained unpaid upon the principal the sum of $5,450. This amount was payable in installments of $250 on April 25th, 1924, and

> **Executrix**
>
> An **executrix** is a female executor. Recall that an **executor** is "[a] person named by a testator to carry out the provisions in the testator's will." BLACK'S LAW DICTIONARY (10th ed. 2014).

upon a like monthly date every three months thereafter. Thus the bond and mortgage had more than five years to run before the entire sum became due. Under date of the 4th of April, 1924, the defendant wrote Petterson as follows:

> **I hereby agree to accept** cash for the mortgage which I hold against premises 5301 6th Ave., Brooklyn, N.Y. It is understood and agreed as a consideration I will allow you $780 providing said mortgage is paid on or before May 31, 1924, and the regular quarterly payment due April 25, 1924, is paid when due.

I hereby agree to accept?

What does this mean? Is defendant making an offer, or encouraging plaintiff to make an offer, which he "agrees" to accept? Here, you may find the context more helpful than the text.

On April 25, 1924, Petterson paid the defendant the installment of principal due on that date. Subsequently, on a day in the latter part of May, 1924, Petterson presented himself at the defendant's home, and knocked at the door. The defendant demanded the name of his caller. Petterson replied:

> **It is Mr. Petterson. I have come to pay off the mortgage.**

Knock, knock

These facts have the trappings of a bad "knock knock" joke. But to tell that joke well (any takers?), we need to know the legal significance of Mr. Petterson's actions. What is he doing here? Is he making an offer? Accepting an offer? Announcing his intention to accept an offer? Recall from earlier* that an offer creates in the offeree a power to change the legal relationship between the parties, through the act of acceptance. However, as master of the offer, it is the offeror who gets to decide how the offeree must exercise this power. Here, what is it that the offeror bargained for?

The defendant answered that he had sold the mortgage. Petterson stated that he would like to talk with the defendant, so the defendant partly opened the door. Thereupon Petterson exhibited the cash and said he was ready to pay off the mortgage according to the agreement. The defendant refused to take the money. Prior to this conversation Petterson had made a contract to sell the land to a third person free and clear of the mortgage to the defendant. Meanwhile, also, the defendant had sold the bond and mortgage to a third party. It, therefore, became necessary for Petterson to pay to such person the full amount of the bond and mortgage. It is claimed that he thereby sustained a loss of $780, the sum which the defendant agreed to allow upon the bond and mortgage if payment in full of principal, less that sum, was made on or before May 31st, 1924. The plaintiff has had a recovery for the sum thus claimed, with interest.

Clearly the defendant's letter proposed to Petterson the making of a unilateral contract, the gift of a promise in exchange for the performance of an act. The thing conditionally promised by the defendant was the reduction of the mortgage debt. The act requested to be done, in consideration of the offered promise, was payment in full of the reduced principal of the debt prior to the due date thereof. "If an act is requested, that very act and no other must be given." *Williston on Contracts* § 73. "In case of offers for a consideration, the performance of the consideration is always deemed a condition." *Langdell's Summary of the Law of Contracts* § 4. **It is elementary that any offer to enter**

* *See* "Thinking Tool Applied: Understanding Offers", at p. 201, *infra*.

into a unilateral contract may be withdrawn before the act requested to be done has been performed. *Williston on Contracts* § 60; *Langdell's Summary* § 4. . . . An interesting question arises when, as here, the offeree approaches the offeror with the intention of proffering performance and, before actual tender is made, the offer is withdrawn. Of such a case Williston says:

> The offeror may see the approach of the offeree and know that an acceptance is contemplated. If the offeror can say "I revoke" before the offeree accepts, however brief the interval of time between the two acts, there is no escape from the conclusion that the offer is terminated.

Williston on Contracts § 60-b. In this instance Petterson, standing at the door of the defendant's house, stated to the defendant that he had come to pay off the mortgage. Before a tender of the necessary moneys had been made the defendant informed Petterson that he had sold the mortgage. That was a definite notice to Petterson that the defendant could not perform his offered promise and that a tender to the defendant, who was no longer the creditor, would be ineffective to satisfy the debt.

> An offer to sell property may be withdrawn before acceptance without any formal notice to the person to whom the offer is made. It is sufficient if that person has actual knowledge that the person who made the offer has done some act inconsistent with the continuance of the offer, such as selling the property to a third person.

Dickinson v. Dodds, 2 Ch. Div. 463, headnote. . . . **Thus, it clearly appears that the defendant's offer was withdrawn before its acceptance had been tendered. It is unnecessary to determine, therefore, what the legal situation might have been had tender been made before withdrawal. It is the individual view of the writer that the same result would follow. This would be so, for the act requested to be performed was the completed act of payment, a**

Performance and unilateral contracts.

To make this point even more vividly, one of the leading contracts treatises describes the rule this way: "If A says to B, 'If you walk across the Brooklyn Bridge I will pay you $100,' A has made a promise but has not asked B for a return promise. A has asked B to perform, not a commitment to perform. A has thus made an offer looking to a unilateral contract. B cannot accept this offer by promising to walk the bridge. B must accept, if at all, by performing the act. Because no return promise is requested, at no point is B bound to perform. If B does perform, a contract involving two parties is created, but the contract is classified as unilateral because only one party is ever under an obligation."* We shall return to the famous "Brooklyn Bridge" hypothetical after this case.

Critical reading

Earlier, we talked about the importance of critical reading,† and this passage calls for it in spades. There are a few things to notice. First: Whenever a court tells you that something is "obvious" or "clearly appears" to be a certain way, your skeptical antennae should stand on end. In fact, Lehman, who wrote the dissent, did not find this point so "obvious." Second: Don't mistake the rest of Kellogg's passage, beginning with "It is unnecessary to determine" and ending with "the supposed case is not before us for decision," as part of the court's holding. Because, as Kellogg states, the hypothetical case he manufactures was *not* before the court, the court cannot rule on how it should be resolved. It is, in short, pure rhetoric, with another "clearly" squeezed in the middle for good measure. But if it was just rhetoric, then why do you think he wrote it?

* John D. Calamari & Joseph M. Perillo, The Law of Contracts § 2-10(a), at 64-65 (4th ed. 1998).

† *See* "Thinking Tool Applied: Reading Critically," at p. 610, *infra*.

thing incapable of performance unless assented to by the person to be paid. *Williston on Contracts* § 60-b. Clearly an offering party has the right to name the precise act performance of which would convert his offer into a binding promise. Whatever the act may be until it is performed the offer must be revocable. However, the supposed case is not before us for decision. We think that in this particular instance the offer of the defendant was withdrawn before it became a binding promise, and, therefore, that no contract was ever made for the breach of which the plaintiff may claim damages.

The judgment of the Appellate Division and that of the Trial Term should be reversed and the complaint dismissed, with costs in all courts.

> ***Does this matter?***
>
> Did the defendant have to accept payment? On the one hand, recall from earlier that Petterson did say that he "hereby agree[d] to accept cash," and this sounds like a promise (though perhaps an unenforceable one). On the other hand, Petterson seems to have bargained for Pattberg's payment, not for Pattberg's announcement of his intention to pay. At the end of the day, the fact remains that payment was never made. Should it matter that this might have been Petterson's fault? How do you think this issue should be resolved?

LEHMAN, J. **(dissenting)**. The defendant's letter to Petterson constituted a promise on his part to accept payment at a discount of the mortgage he held, provided the mortgage is paid on or before May 31st, 1924. Doubtless by the terms of the promise itself, the defendant made payment of the mortgage by the plaintiff, before the stipulated time, a condition precedent to performance by the defendant of his promise to accept payment at a discount. **If the condition precedent has not been performed, it is because the defendant made performance impossible by refusing to accept payment, when the plaintiff came with an offer of immediate performance.**

> It is a principle of fundamental justice that if a promisor is himself the cause of the failure of performance either of an obligation due him or of a condition upon which his own liability depends, he cannot take advantage of the failure.

Williston on Contracts § 677. The question in this case is not whether payment of the mortgage is a condition precedent to the performance of a promise made by the defendant, but, rather, whether at the time the defendant refused the offer of payment, he had assumed any binding obligation, even though subject to condition.

The promise made by the defendant lacked consideration at the time it was made. Nevertheless the promise was not made as a gift or mere gratuity to the plaintiff. It was made for the purpose of obtaining from the defendant something which the plaintiff desired. It constituted an offer which was to become binding whenever the plaintiff should give, in return for the defendant's promise, exactly the consideration which the defendant requested.

Here the defendant requested no counter promise from the plaintiff. The consideration requested by the defendant for his promise to accept payment was, I agree, some act to be performed by the plaintiff. Until the act requested was performed, the defendant might undoubtedly revoke his offer. Our problem is to determine from the words of the letter read in the light of surrounding circumstances what act the defendant requested as consideration for his promise.

The defendant undoubtedly made his offer as an inducement to the plaintiff to "pay" the mortgage before it was due. Therefore, it is said, that "the act requested to be performed was the completed act of payment, a thing incapable of performance unless assented to by the person to be paid." In unmistakable terms the defendant agreed to accept payment, yet we are told that the defendant intended, and the plaintiff should have understood, that the act requested by the defendant, as consideration for his promise to accept payment, included performance by the defendant himself of the very promise for which the act was to be consideration. The defendant's promise was to become binding only when fully performed; and part of the consideration to be furnished by the plaintiff for the defendant's promise was to be the performance of that promise by the defendant. So construed, the defendant's promise or offer, though intended to induce action by the plaintiff, is but a snare and delusion. The plaintiff could not reasonably suppose that the defendant was asking him to procure the performance by the defendant of the very act which the defendant promised to do, yet we are told that even after the plaintiff had done all else which the defendant requested, the defendant's promise was still not binding because the defendant chose not to perform.

I cannot believe that a result so extraordinary could have been intended when the defendant wrote the letter. **"The thought behind the phrase proclaims itself misread when the outcome of the reading is injustice or absurdity." (See opinion of Cardozo, Ch. J., in *Surace v. Danna*, 248 N.Y. 18.)** If the defendant intended to induce payment by the plaintiff and yet reserve the right to refuse payment when offered he should have used a phrase better calculated to express his meaning than the words: "I agree to accept." A promise to accept payment, by its very terms, must necessarily become binding, if at all, not later than when a present offer to pay is made.

> ***Judicial drama***
>
> Here we see an oh-so-subtle jab at Cardozo, who concurred with Kellogg's majority opinion. Lehman could have easily made his point without citing Cardozo (actually, he *did* make his point before he cited Cardozo!), so this gratuitous citation is his way of asking Cardozo, "What happened here? I thought we had an understanding about these things."

I recognize that in this case only an offer of payment, and not a formal tender of payment, was made before the defendant withdrew his offer to accept payment. Even the plaintiff's part in the act of payment was then not technically complete. Even so, under a fair construction of the words of the letter I think the plaintiff had done the act which the defendant requested as consideration for his promise. The plaintiff offered to pay with present intention and ability to make that payment. A formal tender is seldom made in business transactions, except to lay the foundation for subsequent assertion in a court of justice of rights which spring from refusal of the tender. If the defendant acted in good faith in making his offer to accept payment, he could not well have intended to draw a distinction

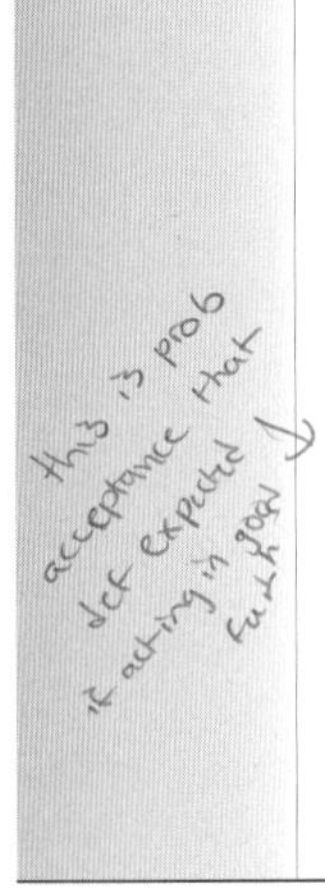

in the act requested of the plaintiff in return, between an offer which unless refused would ripen into completed payment, and a formal tender. Certainly the defendant could not have expected or intended that the plaintiff would make a formal tender of payment without first stating that he had come to make payment. We should not read into the language of the defendant's offer a meaning which would prevent enforcement of the defendant's promise after it had been accepted by the plaintiff in the very way which the defendant must have intended it should be accepted, if he acted in good faith.

The judgment should be affirmed.

CARDOZO, Ch. J., POUND, CRANE and O'BRIEN, JJ., concur with KELLOGG, J.; LEHMAN, J., dissents in opinion, in which ANDREWS, J., concurs.

Judgments reversed, etc.

RELEVANT PROVISIONS

For the *Restatement (Second) of Contracts,* consult §§ 50, 54, and 58.

NOTES AND QUESTIONS

1. *What happened?* Who sued whom for what? Procedurally, how did the case get before this court? Factually, what happened between the parties? What arguments did the plaintiff and defendant make? What rule or rules did the court apply? How did the court analyze the dispute between the parties? How did the court decide the case?

2. *Was this case correctly decided?* Do you agree with Kellogg (majority) or Lehman (dissent)? Why? What are the strengths and weaknesses of each approach? How, if at all, would you have written the opinion differently?

3. *Additional facts.* Here are some additional facts that did not find their way into the court's opinion. Do they change how you look at the case? Keep in mind, in this course and in other courses you are taking, that there are *always* more facts—and sometimes very important facts—that can be, but are not, included in a court's final written decision. Why do you think that is? We will sometimes explore these additional facts in the various "Contextual Perspectives" that are included throughout this casebook.

> Other facts in the case, not appearing in the opinion, may have influenced the court. The record of the trial . . . reveals that the defendant was prevented from testifying as to a letter, sent to the plaintiff's testator, revoking the offer because such testimony was inadmissible under § 347 of the Civil Practice Act, which excludes the testimony of one of the interested parties, to a transaction, where the other is dead and so unable to contradict the evidence. The record . . . also

> seems to suggest that the mortgagor knew of the previous sale of the mortgage, since he brought $4,000 in cash with him, and was accompanied by his wife and a notary public as witnesses; anticipation of the defendant's refusal by seeking to get evidence on which to base this action seems to be a plausible explanation. There was no actual proof of knowledge of the defendant's inability to carry out his offer but the situation was suspicious.*

4. *Acceptance?* Do you think Petterson accepted Pattberg's offer? Why or why not? According to Kellogg, at what moment of time would there be acceptance? When Petterson announces himself at Pattberg's door, along with his intention to pay? When Petterson tenders the money? When Pattberg accepts Petterson's tender? What about according to Lehman? Which view is better? Why?

5. *Revocation.* Do you think Pattberg should be allowed to revoke the moment before Petterson was about to perform? Does it matter that he said in his April 4, 1924 letter that "I hereby agree to accept cash for the mortgage which I hold"? In general, should offerors be allowed to bargain for performance, and then revoke the moment before the bargained-for performance is completed? What if the offeree has completed nearly all of the required performance?

6. *Justifying unilateral contracts.* What arguments can you think of in favor of the traditional rule governing unilateral contracts, that the offer may be withdrawn any time prior to the completion of the bargained-for act? What arguments can you think of in favor of a more lenient rule? What might such a rule look like? For instance, consulting some of the earlier thinking tools we've examined, what type of rule do you think would be easiest to enforce, thereby reducing administrative costs? What type of rule would be most consistent with the ex ante expectations of the parties? What type of rule would be most consistent with principles of justice? Keep these answers in mind, as we will now turn to a few arguments in favor and against the traditional rule governing unilateral contracts, and a few modern attempts to deal with these problems.

THE TRUE CONCEPTION OF UNILATERAL CONTRACTS†

Suppose A says to B, "I will give you $100 if you walk across the Brooklyn Bridge," and B walks—is there a contract? It is clear that A is not asking B for B's *promise* to walk across the Brooklyn Bridge. What A wants from B is the act of walking across the bridge. When B has walked across the bridge there is a contract, and A is then bound to pay to B $100. At that moment there arises a unilateral contract.

* Note, 14 CORNELL L.Q. 81, 84-85 n. 18 (1928).

† Excerpted from I. Maurice Wormser, *The True Conception of Unilateral Contracts*, 26 YALE L.J. 136, 136-39, 142 (1916).

A has bartered away his volition for B's act of walking across the Brooklyn Bridge.

When an act is thus wanted in return for a promise, a unilateral contract is created when the act is done. It is clear that only one party is bound. B is not bound to walk across the Brooklyn Bridge, but A is bound to pay B $100 if B does so. Thus, in unilateral contracts, on one side we find merely an act, on the other side a promise. On the other hand, in bilateral contracts, . . . there is an exchange of promises or assurances. In the case of the bilateral contract both parties, A and B, are bound from the moment that their promises are exchanged. Thus, if A says to B, "I will give you $100 if you will promise to walk across the Brooklyn Bridge," and B then promises to walk across the bridge, a bilateral contract is created at the moment when B promises, and both parties are thereafter bound. . . .

It is plain that in the Brooklyn Bridge case as first put, what A wants from B is the act of walking across the Brooklyn Bridge. A does not ask for B's promise to walk across the bridge and B has never given it. B has never bound himself to walk across the bridge. A, however, has bound himself to pay $100 to B, if B does so. Let us suppose that B starts to walk across the Brooklyn Bridge and has gone about one-half of the way across. At that moment A overtakes B and says to him, "I withdraw my offer." Has B then any rights against A? Again, let us suppose that after A has said "I withdraw my offer," B continues to walk across the Brooklyn Bridge and completes the act of crossing. Under these circumstances, has B any rights against A?

In the first of the cases just suggested, A withdrew his offer before B had walked across the bridge. What A wanted from B, what A asked for, was the act of walking across the bridge. Until that was done, B had not given to A what A had requested. The acceptance by B of A's offer could be nothing but the act on B's part of crossing the bridge. It is elementary that an offeror may withdraw his offer until it has been accepted. **It follows logically that A is perfectly within his rights in withdrawing his offer before B has accepted it by walking across the bridge—the act contemplated by the offeror and the offeree as the acceptance of the offer. A did not want B to walk half-way across or three-quarters of the way across the bridge. What A wanted from B, and what A asked for from B, was a certain and entire act. B understood this.** It was for that act that A was willing to barter his volition with regard to $100. B understood this also. Until this act is done, therefore, A is not

Is Wormser right?

Do you agree with Wormser that the "act contemplated" by A *and* B was that that A could withdraw his offer at *any* moment, up to and including the last moment before B crossed the bridge? What view of mutual assent (if any) would support such a notion? Or is his argument that the default rule governing unilateral offers does (or should) *create* this understanding between the parties? If you agree with Wormser, how would you strengthen his argument? If you disagree, how would you respond?

bound, since no contract arises until the completion of the act called for. Then, and not before, would a unilateral contract arise. Then, and not before, would A be bound.

The objection is made, however, that it is very "hard" upon B that he should have walked half-way across the Brooklyn Bridge and should get no compensation. This suggestion, **invariably advanced, might be dismissed with the remark that "hard" cases should not make bad law.** But going a step further, by way of reply, the pertinent inquiry at once suggests itself, "Was B bound to walk across the Brooklyn Bridge?" The answer to this is obvious. By hypothesis, B was not bound to walk across the Brooklyn Bridge [because] B had never promised A that he would walk across the bridge. . . . A was bound to pay B $100 in the event that B should walk across the bridge, but B had not bound himself to walk. It follows that at the moment when A overtook B, after B had walked half-way across the bridge, that B was not then bound to complete the crossing of the bridge. B, on his side, could have refused at that time, or at any other time, to continue to cross the bridge without making himself in any way legally liable to A. If B is not bound to continue to cross the bridge, if B is will-free, why should not A also be will-free? Suppose that after B has crossed half the bridge he gets tired and tells A that he refuses to continue crossing. B, concededly, would be perfectly within his rights in so speaking and acting. A would have no cause of action against B for damages. If B has a ***locus poenitentiae,*** so has A. They each have, and should have, the opportunity to reconsider and withdraw. Not until B has crossed the bridge, thereby doing the act called for, and accepting the offer, is a contract born. At that moment, and not one instant before, A is bound, and there is a unilateral contract. **Critics of the doctrine of unilateral contract on the ground that the rule is "hard" on B, forget the primary need for mutuality of withdrawal and in lamenting the alleged hardships of B, they completely lose sight of the fact that B has the same right of withdrawal that A has.** To the writer's mind, the doctrine of unilateral contract is thus as just

"Hard cases make bad law."

This famous legal maxim means that law should be made to cover the ordinary cases expected to fall within its purview, and should not seek to accommodate the extraordinary cases, which, though they may make a claim on our emotional heartstrings, will be far and few between, and will skew the law for the rest of us. Can you think of a solution to this problem? (Hint: look over your thinking tools.) Do you think courts should enforce the law as it is written, regardless of its consequences, or should they adjust it or its application to accommodate circumstances not taken into account when the law was made? Here is one view, expressed a long, long time ago in an ancient land far, far away, but perhaps with some relevance for us today: "[W]here the lawgiver has passed over some consideration and made an error through having spoken in the abstract, we should in practice correct this aberration—an aberration which even the lawgiver himself would prescribe if he were present, and for which he would have legislated if he had foreseen. . . . [T]his is the nature of what is equitable—a rectification of law on points where law is at fault owing to its universality."* Do you agree?

opp. to reconsider and withdraw

Locus poenitentiae

A ***locus poenitentiae*** is "[a] point at which it is not too late for one to change one's legal position," and expresses "the possibility of withdrawing from a contemplated course of action." BLACK'S LAW DICTIONARY (10th ed. 2014).

Should there be mutuality?

This is an important point, and one that (arguably) is not taken into account very well by some of the newer solutions to the problem of unilateral contracts. Keep this argument in mind, for example, as you read *Restatement (Second) of Contracts* § 45, following this excerpt.

* ARISTOTLE, NICOMACHEAN ETHICS V, 14 (Walter M. Hatch trans., 1879).

and equitable as it is logical. So long as there is freedom of contract and parties see fit to integrate their understanding in the form of a unilateral contract, the courts should not interfere with their evident understanding and intention simply because of alleged fanciful hardship.

Suppose, reverting to the second case, that B completes the act of crossing the bridge after A has told him that the offer it withdrawn. Here too, B has no rights against A, since B had not accepted the offer until after A had duly communicated to B its revocation. An offer cannot be accepted after it has been revoked. B is laboring under an unrelievable error of law in proceeding to accept an offer which, as far as he was concerned, had ceased to exist. . . .

The writer can see no injustice whatever in the operation of the doctrine of unilateral contract. *It is logical in theory, simple in application, and just in result.*

REASSESSING UNILATERAL CONTRACTS*

[N]o reasonable person would intentionally create the sort of agreement that the traditional theory of unilateral contracts assumes. Suppose that a person, asserting his freedom to contract and his mastery over his offer, specifically intends to make a promise that will bind him not at the time he makes it, but only after the other party has completed a particular act in exchange. In other words, this promisor wishes to create the traditional unilateral contract. For example, he might tell the offeree that if she paints his house, he will—once she is finished—commit himself to paying her $1000. He makes it clear that he does not wish to be bound until she is completely finished, explaining to her that before she is finished he may revoke with impunity. What rational person would even buy the paint if she believed the speaker had not committed himself? No one would realistically begin to perform such an agreement. Nor should the law give damages to an offeree injured by acting so rashly; expending money and effort on the basis of such a non-promise is hardly justifiable reliance, and the law is loath to protect fools.[94]

The primary purpose of unilateral contracts, such as reward offers or promises to pay a commission to a real estate broker, is to motivate the offeree to do the requested act. In other words, their goal is precisely to induce reliance. Obviously, an "offer" to pay someone to paint a fence or find a lost dog provides precious little inducement if it remains freely revocable until full performance. . . .

The fact of the matter, as the *Restatement* implicitly recognizes, is that very reasonable people spend substantial time and money doing the sorts of things that

* Peter Meijes Tiersma, *Reassessing Unilateral Contracts: The Role of Offer, Acceptance and Promise*, 26 U.C. DAVIS L. REV. 1, 29, 32-33 (1992).

94. A similar point is made by Samuel J. Stoljar, *The False Distinction Between Bilateral and Unilateral Contracts*, 64 YALE L.J. 515, 522-23 (1955): Suppose X tells Y "I'll give you $50 if you go to Rome, but remember that I'm at liberty to revoke this promise at any time before you reach the Holy City." A promise of this type would be as unusual as it is absurd. Because it is merely a statement of intention that X might give Y the money, but X is free to change his mind, the promise is illusory.

unilateral contracts attempt to induce them to do. The only rational explanation for such behavior is that . . . people believe the speaker is in fact committed *then and there* to paying the price if the conditions of the offer are met.

RELEVANT PROVISIONS

For the *Restatement (Second) of Contracts,* consult §§ 25 and 45.

NOTES AND QUESTIONS

1. *The verdict?* So, who do you think has the better argument, Wormser in "The True Conception of Unilateral Contracts," or Tiersma in "Reassessing Unilateral Contracts"?

2. *Retraction.* Some of you will be disappointed to learn that Wormser changed his mind about unilateral contracts in a book review he wrote some thirty-four years later: "Since that time I have repented, so that now, clad in sackcloth, I state frankly, that my point of view has changed. I agree, at this time, with the rule set forth in the *Restatement of the Law of Contracts* . . . § 45."*

3. *A new default rule.* If you haven't already done so, now is a good time to read § 45 carefully. How does it change the default rule we learned about in *Petterson v. Pattberg* and argued for by (the old) Wormser? Do you think the new rule adequately responded to Wormser's concern that *both* the offeror *and* the offeree were vulnerable under the old rule because *both* had the privilege of withdrawing any time prior to the offeree's acceptance? Stated another way, if the old default rule was overly harsh on offerees, do you think the new default rule is overly harsh on offerors? Why or why not?

4. *Thinking tool applied.* You should find the next excerpt helpful, not only in helping you to understand the black-letter rule as it now exists, but in helping you to critically examine whether, and how, it might be improved.

The following excerpt does an excellent job of helping us think clearly about the legal relationships that are created under both the old and new default rules governing option contracts. Before reading it, you may wish to review "Thinking Tool: Thinking Clearly About Legal Relationships" at p. 96, supra.

* I. Maurice Wormser, *Book Review*, 3 J. LEGAL EDUC. 145, 146 (1950).

THINKING TOOL APPLIED: OPTION CONTRACTS*

Option contracts (irrevocable offers) create a thicket of issues for students, but a Hohfeldian analysis helps to sort out the issues and clarify them. In the classroom I begin the discussion with Maurice Wormser's Brooklyn Bridge hypothetical: "Suppose A says to B, 'I will give you $100 if you walk across the Brooklyn Bridge.'" The offer does not invite acceptance by promise; it can be accepted only if B completes the walk. If B starts walking and A revokes the offer before B has completed the walk, is there a contract? Wormser argued that no contract has been formed: "It is elementary that an offeror may withdraw his offer until it has been accepted. . . . Until this act is done, therefore, A is not bound, since no contract arises until the completion of the act called for."[16] This result is problematic because it fails to protect B's reliance, and current law changes the outcome by making the offer irrevocable.[17] A Hohfeldian analysis of Wormser's position (the offer is revocable) both clarifies the issue and points to the difficulty with his answer.

First, consider the legal relations between A and B before A issues the offer. . . . Hohfeld demands a precise issue statement and absolute clarity about which grid is being addressed. *"Does A have an obligation to pay B $100?"* is a duty-or-privilege question and the answer is no, A is privileged not to pay and B has no-right to recover $100. *"Does B have an obligation to walk across the bridge?"* is focused on the same grid and the answer again is no, B is privileged not to walk and A has no-right against him. The question *"Is there anything B can do (without A's participation) to change A's privilege of not paying $100?"* is focused on the second grid (power/liability or immunity/disability) and the answer is no, there is nothing B can do. In Hohfeldian terms, B is disabled from changing A's privilege of not paying $100 and A has an immunity. In other words, as A is standing at the bridge (before issuing the offer), she can say to herself, "I have a privilege of not paying B $100, and there is nothing B can do to change that state of affairs."[18] Similarly B has an immunity of having his privilege of not walking changed by A.

---

* Excerpted from Curtis Nyquist, *Teaching Wesley Hohfeld's Theory of Legal Relations*, 52 J. LEGAL EDUC. 238, 242-43 (2002).

16. I. Maurice Wormser, *The True Conception of Unilateral Contracts*, 26 YALE L.J. 136, 136-37 (1916).

17. Section 45 of *Restatement (Second)* provides:

> (1) Where an offer invites an offeree to accept by rendering a performance and does not invite a promissory acceptance, an option contract is created when the offeree tenders or begins the invited performance or tenders a beginning of it.
>
> (2) The offeror's duty of performance under any option contract so created is conditional on completion or tender of the invited performance in accordance with the terms of the offer.

18. A's situation is similar to my legal relationship with Rhode Island on the jury issue. I am privileged not to report for jury duty, and there is nothing Rhode Island can do (without my participation) to change that state of affairs. Of course, if I changed my domicile to Rhode Island, it would then have the power to summon me.

When A issues an offer, the legal relationship changes since B now has a power of acceptance by completing the walk.[19] From A's perspective, she is now under a liability of having her privilege of not paying $100 changed to a duty to pay if B completes the walk. If the offer is revocable, however, A also has a power of changing her liability/power relationship with B to immunity/disability by saying, "I revoke." Revocation of an offer terminates the offeree's power of acceptance. From B's perspective, if the offer is revocable, he is subject throughout the walk to a liability of having his power of acceptance changed to a disability.

The *Restatement (Second) of Contracts* § 45 provides that where an offer can be accepted only by performance, "an option contract is created when the offeree tenders or begins the invited performance or tenders a beginning of it." As applied to the Brooklyn Bridge hypothetical, the offer becomes irrevocable when B starts walking. In Hohfeldian terms, when B starts walking, he has an immunity from having his power of acceptance changed by A. From A's perspective, she is disabled from changing B's power of acceptance. Furthermore, under Section 45, B has no duty to complete the walk; he is privileged to abandon it at any point.[20] If B completes the walk, he has accepted the offer, and A then has a duty to pay him $100. During the walk B is both protected from a revocation of the offer and privileged to abandon the walk at any time.

A Hohfeldian analysis helps students distinguish legal relations during the offer-and-acceptance phase from legal relations under the contract. The critical issue related to option contracts is found on the power/liability or immunity/disability grid. An offeree of a revocable offer is subject to a liability of having the offer revoked. An offeree of an irrevocable offer has an immunity.

As we just learned, the drafters of the *Restatement* responded to the perceived harshness of traditional unilateral contracts by advocating replacement of the old default rule with a new one (§ 45). Courts had their techniques as well. One solution they used was to sever, where possible, a single unilateral contract into a series of smaller units, thereby allowing the offeree to recover for the portions performed. Professor Farnsworth offers this example:

---

19. It is common to speak of the offeree's "power" of acceptance, but issuance of an offer is also a power since it changes a legal relationship of another (the offeree).

20. *See Restatement (Second) of Contracts* § 45(2) (1981). If an offer can be accepted either by performance or by promising to perform, the analysis is fundamentally different. Section 62 of *Restatement (Second)* provides:

> (1) Where an offer invites an offeree to choose between acceptance by promise and acceptance by performance, the tender or beginning of the invited performance or a tender of a beginning of it is an acceptance by performance.
>
> (2) Such an acceptance operates as a promise to render complete performance.

Hohfeld's system clarifies the differences between the sections. If the Brooklyn Bridge hypothetical is changed so that B can accept either by performing or by promising, then as soon as B takes the first step he has accepted the offer. He then has a duty to complete the walk, and A has rights against him if he does not. A also has a duty to perform. Under Section 62 the revocability of the offer is never an issue since a contract is formed immediately when the offeree begins performance. The entire discussion of the power/liability or immunity/disability grid, essential to an understanding of Section 45, does not apply to Section 62.

If, for example, A had said to B, "I will give you $100 for each time that you walk across the Brooklyn Bridge up to a maximum of $1,000," and had revoked during B's seventh crossing, a court could award B $600 on the ground that the offer proposed a series of ten unilateral contracts, of which six had been made at the time of revocation.

Another solution is presented in the case below. In it, we learn that, where there is any doubt regarding the offeror's intentions, courts are more likely to construe an offer as proposing a bilateral—rather than a unilateral—contract. Doing so will tend to result in the contract being formed much sooner (can you see why?), with the result that the offeree will be exposed to much less risk. This is also the position adopted by the *Restatement (Second) of Contracts* § 32.

Davis v. Jacoby

Supreme Court of California
34 P.2d 1026 (1934)

Per Curiam. Plaintiffs appeal from a judgment refusing to grant specific performance of an alleged contract to make a will. The facts are not in dispute and are as follows:

The plaintiff Caro M. Davis was the niece of Blanche Whitehead, who was married to Rupert Whitehead. Prior to her marriage in 1913 to her coplaintiff Frank M. Davis, Caro lived for a considerable time at the home of the Whiteheads, in Piedmont, Cal. The Whiteheads were childless and extremely fond of Caro. The record is replete with uncontradicted testimony of the close and loving relationship that existed between Caro and her aunt and uncle. During the period that Caro lived with the Whiteheads, she was treated as and often referred to by the Whiteheads as their daughter. In 1913, when Caro was married to Frank Davis, the marriage was arranged at the Whitehead home and a reception held there. After the marriage Mr. and Mrs. Davis went to Mr. Davis' home in Canada, where they have resided ever since. During the period 1913 to 1931 Caro made many visits to the Whiteheads, several of them being of long duration. The Whiteheads visited Mr. and Mrs. Davis in Canada on several occasions. After the marriage and continuing down to 1931 the closest and most friendly relationship at all times existed between these two families. They corresponded frequently, the record being replete with letters showing the loving relationship.

By the year 1930 Mrs. Whitehead had become seriously ill. She had suffered several strokes and her mind was failing. Early in 1931 Mr. Whitehead had her removed to a private hospital. The doctors in attendance had informed him that she might die at any time or she might linger for many months. Mr. Whitehead had suffered severe financial reverses. He had had several sieges of sickness and was in poor health. The record shows that during the early part of

1931 he was desperately in need of assistance with his wife, and in his business affairs, and that he did not trust his friends in Piedmont. On March 18, 1931, he wrote to Mrs. Davis telling her of Mrs. Whitehead's condition and added that Mrs. Whitehead was very wistful.

> Today I endeavored to find out what she wanted. I finally asked her if she wanted to see you. She burst out crying and we had great difficulty in getting her to stop. Evidently, that is what is on her mind. It is a very difficult matter to decide. If you come it will mean that you will have to leave again, and then things may be serious. I am going to see the doctor, and get his candid opinion and will then write you again. . . . Since writing the above, I have seen the doctor, and he thinks it will help considerably if you come.

Shortly thereafter, Mr. Whitehead wrote to Caro Davis further explaining the physical condition of Mrs. Whitehead and himself. On March 24, 1931, Mr. Davis, at the request of his wife, telegraphed to Mr. Whitehead as follows:

> Your letter received. Sorry to hear Blanche not so well. Hope you are feeling better yourself. If you wish Caro to go to you can arrange for her to leave in about two weeks. Please wire me if you think it advisable for her to go.

On March 30, 1931, Mr. Whitehead wrote a long letter to Mr. Davis, in which he explained in detail the condition of Mrs. Whitehead's health and also referred to his own health. He pointed out that he had lost a considerable portion of his cash assets but still owned considerable realty, that he needed some one to help him with his wife and some friend he could trust to help him with his business affairs and suggested that perhaps Mr. Davis might come to California. He then pointed out that all his property was community property; that under his will all the property was to go to Mrs. Whitehead; that he believed that under Mrs. Whitehead's will practically everything was to go to Caro.

Mr. Whitehead again wrote to Mr. Davis under date of April 9, 1931, pointing out how badly he needed some one he could trust to assist him, and giving it as his belief that if properly handled he could still save about $150,000. He then stated: "Having you [Mr. Davis] here to depend on and to help me regain my mind and courage would be a big thing."

Three days later, on April 12, 1931, Mr. Whitehead again wrote, addressing his letter to "Dear Frank and Caro," and in this letter made the definite offer, which offer it is claimed was accepted and is the basis of this action. In this letter he first pointed out that Blanche, his wife, was in a private hospital and that "she cannot last much longer . . . my affairs are not as bad as I supposed at first. Cutting everything down I figure $150,000 can be saved from the wreck." He then enumerated the values placed upon his various properties and then continued:

> ***Critical reading***
>
> The court has signaled to us that the April 12 letter will be of critical importance. Therefore, read it over carefully several times, and, as you do so, ask yourself (1) whether you think it constitutes an offer, and (2) if so, whether it constitutes an offer to enter into a (a) bilateral or (b) unilateral contract.

> My trouble was caused by my friends taking advantage of my illness and my position to skin me.

> Now if Frank could come out here and be with me, and look after my affairs, we could easily save the balance I mention, provided I dont get into another panic and do some more foolish things.
>
> The next attack will be my end, I am 65 and my health had been bad for years, so, the Drs. dont give me much longer to live. So if you can come, Caro will inherit everything and you will make our lives happier and see Blanche is provided for to the end.
>
> My eyesight had gone back on me, I cant read only for a few lines at a time. I am at the house alone with Stanley [the chauffeur] who does everything for me and is a fine fellow. Now, what I want is some one who will take charge of my affairs and see I dont lose any more. Frank can do it, if he will and cut out the booze.
>
> Will you let me hear from you as soon as possible, I know it will be a sacrifice but times are still bad and likely to be, so by settling down you can help me and Blanche and gain in the end. If I had you here my mind would get better and my courage return, and we could work things out.

This letter was received by Mr. Davis at his office in Windsor, Canada, about 9:30 a.m. April 14, 1931. After reading the letter to Mrs. Davis over the telephone, and after getting her belief that they must go to California, Mr. Davis immediately wrote Mr. Whitehead a letter, which, after reading it to his wife, he sent by air mail. This letter was lost, but there is no doubt that it was sent by Davis and received by Whitehead; in fact, the trial court expressly so found. Mr. Davis testified in substance as to the contents of this letter. After acknowledging receipt of the letter of April 12, 1931, Mr. Davis unequivocally stated that he and Mrs. Davis accepted the proposition of Mr. Whitehead and both would leave Windsor to go to him on April 25. This letter of acceptance also contained the information that the reason they could not leave prior to April 25 was that Mr. Davis had to appear in court on April 22 as one of the executors of his mother's estate. The testimony is uncontradicted and ample to support the trial court's finding that this letter was sent by Davis and received by Whitehead. In fact, under date of April 15, 1931, Mr. Whitehead again wrote to Mr. Davis and stated:

> Your letter by air mail received this a.m. Now, I am wondering if I have put you to unnecessary trouble and expense, if you are making any money dont leave it, as things are bad here. . . . You know your business and I dont and I am half crazy in the bargain, but I dont want to hurt you or Caro.
>
> Then on the other hand if I could get some one to trust and keep me straight I can save a good deal, about what I told you in my former letter.

This letter was received by Mr. Davis on April 17, 1931, and the same day Mr. Davis telegraphed to Mr. Whitehead: "Cheer up—we will soon be there, we will wire you from the train."

Between April 14, 1931, the date the letter of acceptance was sent by Mr. Davis, and April 22, Mr. Davis was engaged in closing out his business affairs, and Mrs. Davis in closing up their home and in making other arrangements to leave. On April 22, 1931, Mr. Whitehead committed suicide. Mr. and Mrs. Davis were immediately notified and they at once came to California. From almost the moment of her arrival Mrs. Davis devoted herself to the care and comfort of her aunt, and gave her aunt constant attention and care until Mrs. Whitehead's death on May 30, 1931. On this point the trial court found:

> From the time of their arrival in Piedmont, Caro M. Davis administered in every way to the comforts of Blanche Whitehead and saw that she was cared for and provided for down to the time of the death of Blanche Whitehead on May 30, 1931; during said time Caro M. Davis nursed Blanche Whitehead, cared for her and administered to her wants as a natural daughter would have done toward and for her mother.

This finding is supported by uncontradicted evidence and in fact is conceded by respondents to be correct. In fact, the record shows that after their arrival in California Mr. and Mrs. Davis fully performed their side of the agreement.

After the death of Mrs. Whitehead, for the first time it was discovered that the information contained in Mr. Whitehead's letter of March 30, 1931, in reference to the contents of his and Mrs. Whitehead's wills was incorrect. By a duly witnessed will dated February 28, 1931, Mr. Whitehead, after making several specific bequests, had bequeathed all of the balance of his estate to his wife for life, and upon her death to respondents Geoff Doubble and Rupert Ross Whitehead, his nephews. Neither appellant was mentioned in his will. It was also discovered that Mrs. Whitehead by a will dated December 17, 1927, had devised all of her estate to her husband. The evidence is clear and uncontradicted that the relationship existing between Whitehead and his two nephews, respondents herein, was not nearly as close and confidential as that existing between Whitehead and appellants.

After the discovery of the manner in which the property had been devised was made, this action was commenced upon the theory that Rupert Whitehead had assumed a contractual obligation to make a will whereby "Caro Davis would inherit everything"; that he had failed to do so; that plaintiffs had fully performed their part of the contract; that damages being insufficient, quasi specific performance should be granted in order to remedy the alleged wrong, upon the equitable principle that equity regards that done which ought to have been done. The requested relief is that the beneficiaries under the will of Rupert Whitehead, respondents herein, be declared to be involuntary trustees for plaintiffs of Whitehead's estate.

It should also be added that the evidence shows that as a result of Frank Davis leaving his business in Canada he forfeited not only all insurance business he might have written if he had remained, but also

> ### *Dynamic contract law*
>
> This is a really neat paragraph, as it reveals that contract law does not exist in a vacuum, but interacts dynamically with other areas of law. Here, plaintiffs argue that Mr. Whitehead had a contract-based duty to structure his will in a certain manner, and that plaintiffs, by performing their obligations under the contract, have a right to Mr. Whitehead's estate. Mr. Whitehead, however, has breached his duty, but now that he is dead, it is too late for the law to require him to perform. But what the law *can* do is to use other areas of the law (here, trust and estates law) to craft a solution that mimics the state of affairs Mr. Whitehead promised to bring about. Specifically, the court is asked to require those who inherited under the will (the beneficiaries) to be treated *as* trustees, who will in turn be required to turn the estate's assets over to the equitable beneficiaries, i.e., the plaintiffs. The result of all this is that, if the plaintiffs prevail, the court will have used tools from another area of the law (here, trusts and estates) to virtually create the contract that *should* have existed had Mr. Whitehead performed his duty.

forfeited all renewal commissions earned on past business. According to his testimony this loss was over $8,000.

The trial court found that the relationship between Mr. and Mrs. Davis and the Whiteheads was substantially as above recounted and that the other facts above stated were true; that prior to April 12, 1931, Rupert Whitehead had suffered business reverses and was depressed in mind and ill in body; that his wife was very ill; that because of his mental condition he "was unable to properly care for or look after his property or affairs"; that on April 12, 1931, Rupert Whitehead in writing made an offer to plaintiffs that, if within a reasonable time thereafter plaintiffs would leave and abandon their said home in Windsor, and if Frank M. Davis would abandon or dispose of his said business, and if both of the plaintiffs would come to Piedmont in the said county of Alameda where Rupert Whitehead then resided and thereafter reside at said place and be with or near him, and if Frank M. Davis would thereupon and thereafter look after the business and affairs of said Rupert Whitehead until his condition improved to such an extent as to permit him so to do, and if the plaintiffs would look after and administer to the comforts of Blanche Whitehead and see that she was properly cared for until the time of her death, that, in consideration thereof, Caro M. Davis would inherit everything that Rupert Whitehead possessed at the time of his death and that by last will and testament Rupert Whitehead would devise and bequeath to Caro M. Davis all property and estate owned by him at the time of his death, other than the property constituting the community interest of Blanche Whitehead; that shortly prior to April 12, 1931, Rupert Whitehead informed plaintiffs of the supposed terms of his will and the will of Mrs. Whitehead. The court then finds that the offer of April 12 was not accepted. As already stated, the court found that plaintiffs sent a letter to Rupert Whitehead on April 14 purporting to accept the offer of April 12, and also found that this letter was received by the Whiteheads, but finds that in fact such letter was not a legal acceptance. The court also found that the offer of April 12 was

> fair and just and reasonable, and the consideration therefor, namely, the performance by plaintiffs of the terms and conditions thereof, if the same had been performed, would have been an adequate consideration for said offer and for the agreement that would have resulted from such performance; said offer was not, and said agreement would not have been, either harsh or oppressive or unjust to the heirs at law, or devisees, or legatees, of Rupert Whitehead, or to each or any of them, or otherwise.

The court also found that plaintiffs did not know that the statements made by Whitehead in reference to the wills were not correct until after Mrs. Whitehead's death, that after plaintiffs arrived in Piedmont they cared for Mrs. Whitehead until her death and "Blanche Whitehead was greatly comforted by the presence, companionship and association of Caro M. Davis, and by her administering to her wants."

The theory of the trial court and of respondents on this appeal is that the letter of April 12 was an offer to contract, but that such offer could

only be accepted by performance and could not be accepted by a promise to perform, and that said offer was revoked by the death of Mr. Whitehead before performance. In other words, it is contended that the offer was an offer to enter into a unilateral contract, and that the purported acceptance of April 14 was of no legal effect.

The distinction between unilateral and bilateral contracts is well settled in the law. It is well stated in *Restatement (First) of the Law of Contracts* § 12 as follows: "A unilateral contract is one in which no promisor receives a promise as consideration for his promise. A bilateral contract is one in which there are mutual promises between two parties to the contract; each party being both a promisor and a promisee." This definition is in accord with the law of California.

In the case of unilateral contracts no notice of acceptance by performance is required. Section 1584 of the Civil Code provides: "Performance of the conditions of a proposal . . . is an acceptance of the proposal."

Although the legal distinction between unilateral and bilateral contracts is thus well settled, the difficulty in any particular case is to determine whether the particular offer is one to enter into a bilateral or unilateral contract. Some cases are quite clear cut. Thus an offer to sell which is accepted is clearly a bilateral contract, while an offer of a reward is a clear-cut offer of a unilateral contract which cannot be accepted by a promise to perform, but only by performance. Between these two extremes is a vague field where the particular contract may be unilateral or bilateral depending upon the intent of the offer and the facts and circumstances of each case. The offer to contract involved in this case falls within this category. By the provisions of the *Restatement of the Law of Contracts* it is expressly provided that there is a *presumption* that the offer is to enter into a bilateral contract. **§ 31 provides:**

> In case of doubt it is presumed that an offer invites the formation of a bilateral contract by an acceptance amounting in effect to a promise by the offeree to perform what the offer requests, rather than the formation of one or more unilateral contracts by actual performance on the part of the offeree.

Professor Williston, in his *Treatise on Contracts*, volume 1, § 60, also takes the position that a presumption in favor of bilateral contracts exists.

How did you do?

Did the trial court agree or disagree with your earlier assessment of the April 12 letter? Do you now see why the construction of the offer as unilateral or bilateral is so important?

More critical reading

"Uh oh." If you're the defendant, and you're reading these lines, this is what you're thinking, because you probably know that this will not end well. As you read cases in this and other classes, always be on the lookout for these subtle clues in the court's language. A careful reader will realize that a court is often setting you up to accept a particular outcome as inevitable by crafting its opinion to make a non-obvious solution seem obvious. Indeed, very few of the cases you will read about in law school will have obvious solutions, and with good reason. First, remember that the parties went to court in the first place because both sides believed in the merits of their case. If you think your side will lose, settling is often a much better option. Second, if you are reading about a dispute in an appellate decision, this means that even after a trial court told one of the parties "you lose," that party *still* kept fighting, because they *still* believed in the merits of their case. Finally, note that, even when these cases do get resolved, there is often a dissenting opinion reminding us that the outcome was anything but certain.

Restatement change

§ 31 under the *Restatement (First) of Contracts* has changed residence, and now lives its life under *Restatement (Second) of Contracts* § 32.

In the comment following § 31 of the *Restatement* the reason for such presumption is stated as follows:

> It is not always easy to determine whether an offeror requests an act or a promise to do the act. As a bilateral contract immediately and fully protects both parties, the interpretation is favored that a bilateral contract is proposed.

While the California cases have never expressly held that a presumption in favor of bilateral contracts exists, the cases clearly indicate a tendency to treat offers as offers of bilateral rather than of unilateral contracts. ***See also Wood v. Lucy, Lady Duff-Gordon***, 118 N.E. 214 (1917).

> ***A rhetorical masterpiece***
>
> We will study this famous case in chapter 6, *infra*. Justice Cardozo, whom you met previously in *Jacob & Youngs v. Kent* (see p. 133, *supra*), was a master of making non-obvious outcomes seem inevitable. And, as we were just discussing making non-obvious outcomes seem inevitable, read the court's next sentence. It has come far since ominously warning us, a few paragraphs back, that "the difficulty in any particular case is to determine whether the particular offer is one to enter into a bilateral or unilateral contract." Didn't seem that difficult at all, did it?

Keeping these principles in mind, we are of the opinion that the offer of April 12 was an offer to enter into a bilateral as distinguished from a unilateral contract. Respondents argue that Mr. Whitehead had the right as offeror to designate his offer as either unilateral or bilateral. That is undoubtedly the law. It is then argued that from all the facts and circumstances it must be implied that what Whitehead wanted was performance and not a mere promise to perform. We think this is a non sequitur, in fact the surrounding circumstances lead to just the opposite conclusion. These parties were not dealing at arm's length. Not only were they related, but a very close and intimate friendship existed between them. The record indisputably demonstrates that Mr. Whitehead had confidence in Mr. and Mrs. Davis, in fact that he had lost all confidence in every one else. The record amply shows that by an accumulation of occurrences Mr. Whitehead had become desperate, and that what he wanted was the promise of appellants that he could look to them for assistance. He knew from his past relationship with appellants that if they gave their promise to perform he could rely upon them. The correspondence between them indicates how desperately he desired this assurance. Under these circumstances he wrote his offer of April 12, above quoted, in which he stated, after disclosing his desperate mental and physical condition, and after setting forth the terms of his offer:

> *Will you let me hear from you as soon as possible*—I know it will be a sacrifice but times are still bad and likely to be, so by settling down you can help me and Blanche and gain in the end.

By thus specifically requesting an immediate reply Whitehead expressly indicated the nature of the acceptance desired by him, namely, appellants' promise that they would come to California and do the things requested by him. This promise was immediately sent by appellants upon receipt of the offer, and was received by Whitehead. It is elementary that when an offer has indicated the mode and means of acceptance, an acceptance in accordance with that mode or means is binding on the offeror.

Another factor which indicates that Whitehead must have contemplated a bilateral rather than an unilateral contract, is that the contract required Mr. and Mrs. Davis to perform services until the death of both Mr. and Mrs. Whitehead. It is obvious that if Mr. Whitehead died first some of these services were to be performed after his death, so that he would have to rely on the promise of appellants to perform these services. It is also of some evidentiary force that Whitehead received the letter of acceptance and acquiesced in that means of acceptance.

Shaw v. King, 218 P. 50 (1923), relied on by respondents, is clearly not in point. In that case there was no written acceptance, nor was there an acceptance by partial or total performance.

For the foregoing reasons we are of the opinion that the offer of April 12, 1931, was an offer to enter into a bilateral contract which was accepted by the letter of April 14, 1931. Subsequently appellants fully performed their part of the contract. Under such circumstances it is well settled that damages are insufficient and specific performance will be granted. Since the consideration has been fully rendered by appellants the question as to mutuality of remedy becomes of no importance.

Respondents also contend the complaint definitely binds appellants to the theory of a unilateral contract. This contention is without merit. The complaint expressly alleges the parties entered into a contract. It is true that the complaint also alleged that the contract became effective by performance. However, this is an action in equity. Respondents were not misled. No objection was made to the testimony offered to show the acceptance of April 14. A fair reading of the record clearly indicates the case was tried by the parties on the theory that the sole question was whether there was a contract—unilateral or bilateral.

For the foregoing reasons the judgment appealed from is reversed.

RELEVANT PROVISIONS

For the *Restatement (Second) of Contracts*, consult § 32. For the UCC, consult § 2-206(1)(a).

NOTES AND QUESTIONS

1. ***What happened?*** Who sued whom for what? Procedurally, how did the case get before this court? Factually, what happened between the parties? What arguments did the plaintiff and defendant make? What rule or rules did the court apply? How did the court analyze the dispute between the parties? How did the court decide the case?

2. ***Was this case correctly decided?*** Do you agree with the result reached in this case? Why or why not? Do you agree with the reasoning? Why or why not? How, if at all, would you have written the opinion differently?

3. *Unilateral or bilateral?* What kind of offer did Mr. Whitehead propose? Was he bargaining for performance or for a return promise? How can you tell? What would a reasonable person in the offeree's position think? Finally, was the offer accepted?

4. *Justifying the decision.* Do you think the result here can be justified on doctrinal grounds, or is this a case where Mr. Whitehead was bargaining for performance, but the court found otherwise to prevent an injustice (i.e., the non-enforcement of the promise)?

5. *Legal consequences of court's decision.* If the court is right and the offer was one to enter into a bilateral contract, does that mean that the offeree could have formed a contract by simply writing back and saying "I accept"? If so, does this also mean that (1) if Mr. Whitehead died the next day after receiving this letter, the offeree could have recovered?, and (2) if the offeree never showed up, Mr. Whitehead could have prevailed against plaintiffs in a breach of action suit?

6. *Justifying the rule.* Do the issues raised in this case explain why, where there is doubt, courts are more likely to interpret an offer as one proposing to enter a bilateral (rather than a unilateral) contract?

PROBLEM: EXPANDING A SUBWAY

On November 23, 2006, the City of Seattle prepared a written instrument to serve as payment to STBM, Inc. for the expansion the Seattle subway network. The written instrument in part read:

> 5. Thirty days after the completion of the Subway Track of STBM, Inc. from Westlake Station to Boren Avenue Station, for value received, the City of Seattle promises to pay to the order of STBM, Inc., the sum of five million six hundred thousand dollars ($5,600,000), negotiable and payable at Key Bank, with interest at the rate of five percent per annum, payable after maturity.

The written instrument, along with an escrow agreement was placed in the control of Key Bank. On the faith of the written instrument, four months later, STBM bid and paid to the city $15,000 for a permit to begin construction on the subway expansion. Once started, STBM worked on the project only intermittently over the course of three years and the project remained incomplete. At the end of the third year of construction, the city served STBM with a written notice that they no longer recognized any liability to pay because the subway had not been completed within the time agreed upon. Shortly after receiving this notice, STBM diverted its construction assets to finish the project and completed the expansion before the expiration of the fourth year. When STBM went to the city to demand payment, the city referenced the written notice to deny compensation. STBM commenced an action against the city for breach of contract. The City claimed that their liability to STBM was conditional upon STBM's completion of the subway expansion at a much earlier date than at which it was actually finished.

Is this a unilateral or bilateral contract? Why? When was the contract formed? May the city withdraw from the contract?

PROBLEM: MUNICIPAL BONDS

A representative of the City of New York's City Council and a New York developer agree on a contract that reads in part:

> Stephanie Pringle agrees to sell two hundred fifty (250) municipal bonds on behalf of the City of New York, New York to aid in the expansion of the Brooklyn-Battery Tunnel by Paul Jones III, unless prevented by some means, which he cannot control. The bonds shall be under the control of Pringle within sixty days (60), properly issued and dated with the certificate of the City Council upon the bonds so as to allow the bonds to be lawfully registered. Out of the proceeds of the sale of the bonds Pringle shall pay Jones sixteen million. If the bonds sell for less than sixteen million, Pringle will pay Jones the deficit; and if they sell for more than sixteen million, Jones may retain the excess for his fees for selling.

What kind of contract is this? What is Stephanie Pringle's obligation under the contract? What is Paul Jones III's obligation?

PROBLEM: ENCYCLOPEDIAS, ANYONE?

On September 1, 2015, Alex Jones mailed a proposal to sell a 164-volume collection of the *Corpus Juris Secundum* encyclopedia to Lawrence Hoven at a fixed price. On September 8, Jones received an offer to buy his encyclopedia collection for double the price that he had offered to sell it to Hoven. After receiving this new offer, the same day, Jones mailed a revocation of his original offer to Hoven, although Hoven did not receive the revocation until September 20. In the interim, on September 10, Hoven received the original offer and sent an overnight mail reply accepting the offer. Before hearing back from Jones or receiving the books, Hoven turned around and resold the books to a prominent Tampa lawyer on September 15.

Was Jones's revocation of the offer effective? If not, when was a contract formed?

PROBLEM: CONTRACTING FOR BERYLLIUM

Debra Rothford is a beryllium merchant who purchases beryllium to sell to third party computer chip manufacturers. Carlos Miguel owns a beryllium processing plant in Utah and had a 40-ton surplus of unsold refined beryllium from a particularly successful mining operation. By email on Saturday, April 27, Miguel offered to sell the refined beryllium to Rothford for "40 tons, net cash, open till Monday." On Monday, Rothford sent Miguel an email asking whether he would accept the forty tons for delivery over three months, or if not, what would be the longest time he would allow the delivery to be spaced out. Miguel did not respond to the email and later that day sold the 40 tons of refined beryllium to another party. At 1:30 P.M. the same Monday, Miguel then sent Rothford an email saying that the refined beryllium had been sold. Two minutes prior, at 1:28 P.M., Rothford sent Miguel another email advising acceptance of the offer in Miguel's first email. When Miguel failed to deliver the refined beryllium, Rothford sued for breach of contract.

Did Rothford's original reply to Miguel constitute a counteroffer? Did the email that was sent by Rothford, which stated that the refined beryllium had been sold, constitute an effective revocation of the original offer?

PROBLEM: AN ARGUMENT AT THE COURT

During oral arguments in *Offord v. Dazies,* 12 C.B.N.S. 748 (1862), the following exchange took place:

> JUSTICE WILLIAMS: "Suppose I guarantee the price of a carriage to be built for a third party who, before the carriage is finished and consequently before I am bound to pay for it, becomes insolvent, may I recall my guaranty?"
>
> MR. JAMES (lawyer): "Not after the coach-builder has commenced the carriage."
>
> CHIEF JUSTICE ERLE: "Before it ripens into a contract either party may withdraw and so put an end to the matter. But the moment the coach-builder has prepared the materials he would probably be found by the jury to have contracted."

Who's right here? How do you think this case should be resolved?

PROBLEM: THE NIFFI ESTATE

Katrina Agneau, a retired attorney, lived in Dallas, Texas her entire life along with her two brothers, until her eldest brother, Peter Niffi, moved to California at the height of the oil boom. Peter made a small fortune investing in oil companies. As the siblings got on later in life, Katrina became ill more frequently and when Peter found out, in concern for her health, he sent her a letter reading:

> Dear Katrina,
>
> I am soon to cash out my stockholdings in Standard CalOil and I anticipate receiving a substantial sum of money. As we have talked about in past correspondence, I would greatly like to bring you out to California at my expense, with the hopes that the more moderate climate may improve your health. I can make arrangements to provide for you here in California. It would bring my great joy to have you close by in our remaining days.
>
> Peter

Enclosed in the letter was a personal check for $8,000 and a request to stop and see her younger brother before making her way to California. After receiving the letter, Katrina arranged to have her things moved and set out via train to visit her younger brother on the way to California. One day before Katrina left Dallas, unbeknownst to her, Peter died. Katrina did not find out that Peter had died until she arrived in California. When Peter's estate entered probate his wife was the estate administrator and refused to honor Peter's letter to Katrina. Katrina then made a claim for specific performance against the estate, submitting Peter's letter to her as proof he promised to take care of her in California.

Is Peter's letter to Katrina an offer? Did Katrina accept the offer? Do you think Katrina has any additional remedies she may be able to pursue? What additional facts, if proved, would help Katrina's case?

5. Acceptance by Silence

DOCTRINAL OVERVIEW: ACCEPTANCE BY SILENCE*

As a general rule, a promise will not be inferred from the offeree's mere inaction. Thus an offeree's silence in the face of an offer to sell goods is not ordinarily an acceptance, because the offeror has no reason to believe from the offeree's silence that the offeree promises to buy. The same is true if the offeror delivers the goods to the offeree, which retains them in silence. If there are additional circumstances, however, a promise may be inferred, resulting in a contract that is sometimes described as "implied-in-fact" as distinguished from "express."

If, for example, the offeree exercises dominion over the goods by acting inconsistently with the offeror's ownership, as by carrying them from the railroad station to the offeree's place of business, the offeree is taken to have accepted the offer and is bound to pay the price. The same principle applies if dominion is exercised over real property. . . .

Analogous principles are applied to services. . . . In contrast to [goods and real property], the offeree is expected not only to refrain from affirmative action that would appropriate the services . . . , but also to speak up in protest. Services, unlike property, cannot be returned, and the recipient of a nonreturnable benefit that silently watches another confer the benefit in apparent expectation of compensation is liable. . . .

So fundamental is the tenet that mere silence is not acceptance that, even as the master of the offer, the offeror is powerless to alter the rule. The seller cannot turn the buyer's silence into acceptance by adding to the offer, "If I do not hear from you in a week, I will take it that you have accepted my offer" [or by making] some usual and routine action or inaction of the buyer amount to acceptance. It will not avail the seller to add to the offer, for example: "If you go to work on Monday, I will take it that you have accepted my offer"; or, "If you do not go to

* Excerpted from E. ALLAN FARNSWORTH, CONTRACTS § 3.14 (4th ed. 2004).

work on Sunday, I will take it that you have accepted my offer." By neither of these phrases can the offeror impose liability on the offeree that remains silent or continues in established ways. . . .

There are, however, exceptional situations in which silence has been held to be acceptance. . . . [I]n these situations the offeror has reason to believe from the offeree's silence that the offeree assents. Each case turns on its own facts. . . .

And speaking of a case turning on its facts, we now turn to a leading case, decided by America's preeminent jurist of the age, in which the seller argued that silence *should* constitute acceptance. As you read it, pay close attention to the specific facts seller focused on to support its argument that the traditional default rule governing silence should not apply here.

Hobbs v. Massasoit Whip Co.

Supreme Judicial Court of Massachusetts
33 N.E. 495 (1893)

HOLMES, J. This is an action for the price of eelskins sent by the plaintiff to the defendant, and kept by the defendant some months, until they were destroyed. It must be taken that the plaintiff received no notice that the defendants declined to accept the skins. The **case comes before us on exceptions to an instruction to the jury, that, whether there was any prior contract or not, if skins are sent to the defendant, and it sees fit, whether it has agreed to take them or not, to lie back, and to say nothing, having reason to suppose that the man who has sent them believes that it is taking them, since it says nothing about it, then, if it fails to notify, the jury would be warranted in finding for the plaintiff.**

Standing alone, and unexplained, this proposition might seem to imply that one stranger may impose a duty upon another, and make him a purchaser, in spite of himself, by sending goods to him, unless he will take the trouble, and be at the expense, of notifying the sender that he will not buy. The case was argued for the defendant on that interpretation. But, in view of the evidence, we do not understand that to have been the meaning of the judge, and we do not think that the jury can have understood that to have been his meaning. The plaintiff was not a stranger to the defendant, even if there was no

Critical reading

Read this sentence carefully, as it is masterfully crafted. Note not only the light in which Holmes paints the defendant, but how this personality sketch gets incorporated into the issue to be decided. From this point on, there can be little question how the case will be decided. This is even more remarkable when you consider that this seemingly inevitable outcome cuts against the traditional default rule we learned about above, that silence generally cannot constitute acceptance.

Oliver Wendell Holmes, Jr.

Justice Holmes (1841-1935), Civil War veteran and son of the famous poet Oliver

contract between them. He had sent eelskins in the same way four or five times before, and they had been accepted and paid for. On the defendant's testimony, it is fair to assume that, if it had admitted the eelskins to be over twenty-two inches in length, and fit for its business, as the plaintiff testified, and the jury found that they were, it would have accepted them; that this was understood by the plaintiff; and, indeed, that there was a standing offer to him for such skins. In such a condition of things, the plaintiff was warranted in sending the defendant skins conforming to the requirements, and even if the offer was not such that the contract was made as soon as skins corresponding to its terms were sent, sending them did impose on the defendant a duty to act about them; and silence on its part, coupled with a retention of the skins for an unreasonable time, might be found by the jury to warrant the plaintiff in assuming that they were accepted, and thus to amount to an acceptance. **The proposition stands on the general principle that conduct which imports acceptance or assent is acceptance or assent in the view of the law, whatever may have been the actual state of mind of the party.**

Exceptions overruled.

Wendell Holmes, Sr., was one of the greatest legal scholars and judges in American history. As a legal scholar, he wrote one of the most influential books (*The Common Law,* in 1881) and law review articles ("The Path of the Law," in 1897) of all time. Both of these works continue to influence American law in general, and contract law in particular. The latter, especially, is short, accessible, and cannot be recommended highly enough. As a judge, Holmes sat as a justice on the Massachusetts Supreme Judicial Court from 1882-1902, and then as a justice on the United States Supreme Court from 1902-1932, retiring at the age of 90. For a sampling of Holmes's work, with an excellent introduction to the man himself, highly recommended is Oliver Wendell Holmes, Jr., *The Essential Holmes: Selections from the Letters, Speeches, Judicial Opinions, and Other Writings of Oliver Wendell Holmes, Jr.* (Richard A. Posner ed., 1992). Several excellent biographies on Holmes have also been written. *See, e.g.,* G. Edward White, *Oliver Wendell Holmes, Jr.* (2006), and Sheldon M. Novick, *Honorable Justice: The Life of Oliver Wendell Holmes* (2013).

Mutual assent

In this sentence, does Holmes adopt the subjective, objective, or mixed approach to mutual assent? Would adopting an alternative view change the result in this case?

RELEVANT PROVISIONS

For the *Restatement (Second) of Contracts,* consult §§ 41 and 69. For the UCC, consult § 2-204(1). For the CISG, consult Article 18(1) and (3). For the UNIDROIT Principles, consult Article 2.1.6(1) and (3).

NOTES AND QUESTIONS

1. ***What happened?*** Who sued whom for what? Procedurally, how did the case get before this court? Factually, what happened between the parties?

What arguments did the plaintiff and defendant make? What rule or rules did the court apply? How did the court analyze the dispute between the parties? How did the court decide the case?

2. ***Was this case correctly decided?*** Do you agree with the result reached in this case? Why or why not? Do you agree with Holmes's reasoning? Why or why not? How, if at all, would you have written the opinion differently?

3. ***The importance of facts.*** What specific facts allow Holmes to find that the traditional default rule governing silence should not apply here? What facts would you need to change to support the alternative conclusion, i.e., that the traditional default rule does apply?

4. ***An unwilling buyer?*** How does Holmes respond to the defendant's argument that the principle urged by plaintiff would allow a stranger to impose a duty on an unwilling buyer by sending the buyer unwanted goods? Imagine finding yourself in such a position (it's easy if you try), where a book or music club sends you unwanted merchandise, and then bills you for it.

5. ***Speculating at the seller's expense?*** Does Holmes's solution allow a buyer to speculate at the seller's expense? For instance, if silence constitutes acceptance, does this mean that the buyer can simply hold onto goods sent by the seller while it shops around for a better price? If the market price rises, the buyer can argue that its silence constituted acceptance of the previously sent goods at the old market price, and if the market price drops, the buyer can send the goods back to the seller, and buy on the open market. First, do you think this is a problem, and second, how do you think Holmes would respond to this argument?

PROBLEM: DOUGHY DILEMMA

Amy's Dough Company is a Delaware corporation engaged in producing and shipping dough to local bakeries. Amy, the owner of the company, has an ongoing business relationship with Steven's Bakery. Amy had made numerous deliveries to Steven's Bakery over the course of two years and had always responded to each order within one week and delivered the product shortly thereafter. In February 2015, Steven's Bakery booked Amy's Dough Company to deliver 20,000 pounds of raw dough on a 10 cents per pound basis. The booking was a service provided by Amy's Dough Company that allowed bakeries to send in orders, subject to Amy's acceptance, up to the amount they have booked. A bakery is not obligated to order all or any part of the requested amount and Amy's Dough Company is not obligated to accept any order. On February 23, Steven's Bakery ordered 5,248 pounds of dough from Amy's Dough Company. Steven's Bakery did not hear any response from Amy until March 4 when the company was advised that their order had been declined. At the time the price of dough was 12 cents per pound instead of the 10 cents per pound that Steven's Bakery had booked. Steven's Bakery had to find an alternative supplier and paid 15 cents per pound. Steven's Bakery sued Amy's Dough Company on the theory that Amy's silence in response to the bakery's order operated as an acceptance due to their ongoing business relationship. Steven's Bakery claimed that they relied upon Amy to their detriment.

Drawing on any assigned cases or materials, how do you think this dispute should be resolved, and why? Specifically, do you think plaintiff can maintain a promissory estoppel cause of action against defendant? What additional facts, if proved, would help plaintiff's case? Defendant's? Assuming plaintiff prevails, what should the court award as a remedy?

D. TERMINATING OFFERS

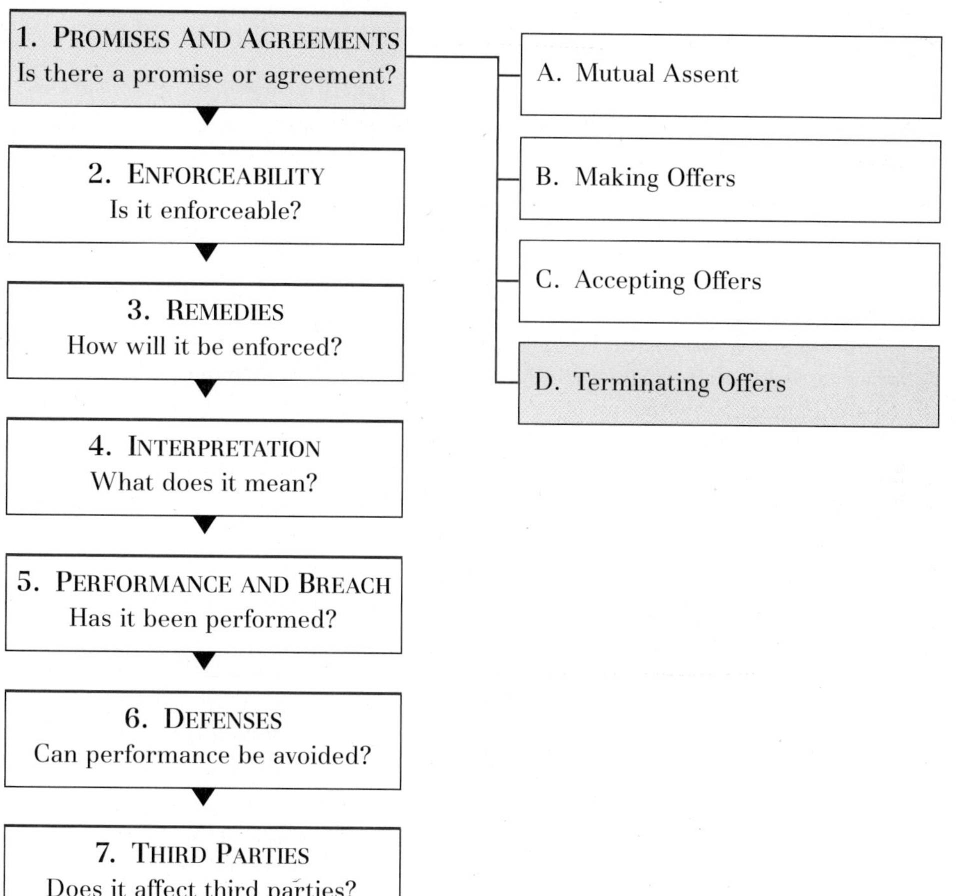
1. Promises And Agreements
Is there a promise or agreement?
2. Enforceability
Is it enforceable?
3. Remedies
How will it be enforced?
4. Interpretation
What does it mean?
5. Performance and Breach
Has it been performed?
6. Defenses
Can performance be avoided?
7. Third Parties
Does it affect third parties?
A. Mutual Assent
B. Making Offers
C. Accepting Offers
D. Terminating Offers

1. Termination in General

According to Restatement (Second) of Contracts *§ 36, an offeree's power of acceptance may be terminated by: (1) the offeree's rejection or counteroffer, (2) lapse of time, (3) the offeror's revocation, or (4) the offeror's or offeree's subsequent death or incapacity. You will recall that we already touched on (1) and (2) when we discussed the mirror image rule, the mailbox rule, acceptance by performance, and acceptance by silence. In fact, we even touched on (3) indirectly in many of the cases we discussed above, and a bit more directly when we covered* Petterson v. Pattberg *and the Brooklyn Bridge hypothetical. As for (4), while interesting in that it constitutes "a glaring exception to the objective theory of assent,"* it rather speaks for itself and need not detain us here. Therefore, this section will primarily focus on (3), revocation by the offeror.†*

DOCTRINAL OVERVIEW: REVOCATION‡

Revocation of an offer must be distinguished from withdrawal. An offer can be withdrawn if notice of withdrawal reaches the offeree no later than the offer does. This is a corollary of the principle that an offer is not effective until it has been communicated to the offeree. But revocation of an offer after it has become effective is a different matter.

It is a fundamental tenet of the common law that an offer is generally freely revocable and can be countermanded by the offeror at any time before it has been accepted by the offeree. . . . That the rule is not inevitable can be seen from the law of some civil law countries, including Germany, where an offer is irrevocable for a reasonable time, unless the offeror expresses a different intention. However, the common law view that an offer is freely revocable is accepted throughout the United States, with rare exceptions.[4] . . .

What sort of manifestation of the offeror's intention suffices as a revocation of the offer? Just as the offeror need not say "offer" to offer, so too the offeror need not say "revoke" to revoke. It is enough that the offeror indicate an intention not to make the proposed contract. A subsequent offer, inconsistent with the original offer, may suffice to revoke the original offer. Action without words may suffice if the action is inconsistent with an intention to contract. . . .

The revocation is not effective, however, until it is received by the offeree. In keeping with the objective theory, an uncommunicated change of mind does not suffice.[16] According to Holmes, "It would be monstrous to allow an inconsistent

---

* *See* E. ALLAN FARNSWORTH, CONTRACTS § 3.18 (4th ed. 2004). *See also Restatement (Second) of Contracts* § 48 cmt. *a* (noting that the rule "seems to be a relic of the obsolete view that a contract requires a 'meeting of the minds,' and it is out of harmony with the modern doctrine that a manifestation of assent is effective without regard to actual mental assent.")

† It should also be noted that, per *Restatement (Second) of Contracts* § 36(2), "an offeree's power of acceptance" may also be "terminated by the non-occurrence of any condition of acceptance under the terms of the offer." We will discuss conditions in greater detail in Chapter 7.

‡ Excerpted from E. ALLAN FARNSWORTH, CONTRACTS § 3.18 (4th ed. 2004).

4. Restatement Second § 42.

16. No discussion of revocation would be complete without a reference to *Cooke v. Oxley*, 100 Eng. Rep. 785 (K.B. 1790), a confusing relic of the subjective era. It became the *bête noire*

act of the offeror, not known or brought to the notice of the offeree, to affect the making of the contract."[17] . . . The difficulties that arise out of attempts at revocation when the negotiations are by correspondence [have been discussed in Section 2, *infra*]. Two other problems, however, remain. . . .

[One problem] involves the revocation of a general offer, such as one made by a newspaper advertisement, a poster, or other general notification to the public. If the offeror can reasonably notify everyone who might accept the offer, revocation is not effective as to a particular offeree unless it has been communicated to that offeree. Ordinarily, however, the maker of a general offer cannot do this. Even if the revocation receives publicity equal to that of the offer, it may not reach everyone. If that is so, giving equal publicity has been held to be enough, even as to an offeree that read the offer and missed the revocation. Giving equal publicity ordinarily takes time, but even before the revocation has received equal notoriety, it is too late for an offeree that has seen the revocation to accept. . . .

[The other problem is] that of the indirect communication of revocation, a problem associated with *Dickinson v. Dodds*. . . .

Dickinson v. Dodds

Court of Appeal, Chancery Division

2 Ch. D. 463 (1876)

On Wednesday, the 10th of June, 1874, the Defendant John Dodds signed and delivered to the Plaintiff, George Dickinson, a memorandum, of which the material part was as follows:

> I hereby agree to sell to Mr. George Dickinson the whole of the dwelling-houses, garden ground, stabling, and outbuildings thereto belonging, situate at Croft, belonging to me, for the sum of £800. As witness my hand this tenth day of June, 1874.
>
> £800 (Signed) John Dodds.
>
> P.S.—This offer to be left over until Friday, 9 o'clock, A.M. J. D. (the twelfth), 12th June, 1874.
>
> (Signed) J. Dodds.

The **bill** alleged that Dodds understood and intended that the Plaintiff should have until Friday 9 A.M. within which to determine whether he would or would not

Bill

"An equitable pleading by which a claimant brings a claim in a court of equity.

of the objectivists, who regarded it as standing for the proposition that an offeror of goods could prevent acceptance by the offeree by a mere change of mind, as by an uncommunicated sale of the goods to another.

17. *Brauer v. Shaw*, 46 N.E. 617, 618 (Mass. 1897).

Before the merger of law and equity, the bill in equity was analogous to a declaration in law." BLACK'S LAW DICTIONARY (10th ed. 2014).

purchase, and that he should absolutely have until that time the refusal of the property at the price of £800, and that the Plaintiff in fact determined to accept the offer on the morning of Thursday, the 11th of June, but did not at once signify his acceptance to Dodds, believing that he had the power to accept it until 9 A.M. on the Friday.

Critical reading I

Read this sentence carefully, slowly, several times. What, exactly, did plaintiff know, and when did he know it?

In the afternoon of the Thursday the Plaintiff was informed by a Mr. Berry that Dodds had been offering or agreeing to sell the property to Thomas Allan, the other Defendant. Thereupon the Plaintiff, at about half-past seven in the evening, went to the house of Mrs. Burgess, the mother-in-law of Dodds, where he was then staying, and left with her a formal acceptance in writing of the offer to sell the property. According to the evidence of Mrs. Burgess this document never in fact reached Dodds, she having forgotten to give it to him.

On the following (Friday) morning, at about seven o'clock, Berry, who was acting as agent for Dickinson, found Dodds at the Darlington railway station, and handed to him a duplicate of the acceptance by Dickinson, and explained to Dodds its purport. He replied that it was too late, as he had sold the property. A few minutes later Dickinson himself found Dodds entering a railway carriage, and handed him another duplicate of the notice of acceptance, but Dodds declined to receive it, saying, "You are too late. I have sold the property."

It appeared that on the day before, Thursday, the 11th of June, Dodds had signed a formal contract for the sale of the property to the Defendant Allan for £800, and had received from him a deposit of £40.

Look familiar?

Do you see how the remedies requested here are strikingly similar to the remedies requested in *Davis v. Jacoby*? If not, now is a good time to review the margin note "Dynamic contract law" on p. 273, *supra*.

The bill in this suit prayed that the Defendant Dodds might be decreed specifically to perform the contract of the 10th of June, 1874; that he might be restrained from conveying the property to Allan; that Allan might be restrained from taking any such conveyance; that, if any such conveyance had been or should be made, Allan might be declared a trustee of the property for, and might be directed to convey the property to, the Plaintiff; and for damages.

The cause came on for hearing before Vice-Chancellor Bacon on the 25th of January, 1876. . . .

JAMES, L.J., after referring to the document of the 10th of June, 1874, continued: The document, though beginning "I hereby agree to sell," was nothing but an offer, and was only intended to be an offer, for the Plaintiff himself tells us that he required time to consider whether he would enter into an agreement or not. Unless both parties had then agreed there was no concluded agreement then made; it was in effect and substance only an offer to sell. The Plaintiff, being minded not to complete the bargain at that time, added this memorandum—"This offer to be left over until Friday, 9 o'clock A.M., 12th June, 1874." That shews it was only an offer. There was no consideration given for the undertaking or promise, to whatever extent it may be considered binding, to keep the property unsold until 9 o'clock on Friday morning; but **apparently Dickinson was of opinion, and probably Dodds was of the same opinion, that he (Dodds) was bound by that promise, and could not in any way withdraw from it, or retract it, until 9 o'clock on Friday morning, and this probably explains a good deal of what afterwards took place.** But it is clear settled law, on one of the clearest principles of law, that this promise, being a mere *nudum pactum*, was not binding, and that at any moment before a complete acceptance by Dickinson of the offer, Dodds was as free as Dickinson himself.

> ***Meeting of the minds?***
>
> If James is right about this, that each party believed the promise in the June 10 postscript to be enforceable, then it reveals that contract law is about more than giving legal effect to the parties' intent. Indeed, this passage makes clear that, even for a court that adopts the subjective approach hook, line, and sinker (see next paragraph), a meetings of the minds is merely a necessary—though not sufficient—condition for forming a contract. Is this the right approach? Where the parties' intent is clear, shouldn't a court enforce their agreements? Why or why not?

Well, that being the state of things, it is said that the only mode in which Dodds could assert that freedom was by actually and distinctly saying to Dickinson, "Now I withdraw my offer." It appears to me that there is neither principle nor authority for the proposition that there must be an express and actual withdrawal of the offer, or what is called a retractation. It must, to constitute a contract, appear that the two minds were at one, at the same moment of time, that is, that there was an offer continuing up to the time of the acceptance. If there was not such a continuing offer, then the acceptance comes to nothing. Of course it may well be that the one man is bound in some way or other to let the other man know that his mind with regard to the offer has been changed; but **in this case, beyond all question, the Plaintiff knew that Dodds was no longer minded to sell the property to him as plainly and clearly as if Dodds had told him in so many words, "I withdraw the offer."** This is evident from the Plaintiff's own statements in the bill.

> ***Critical reading II***
>
> Recall the sentence associated with "Critical reading I" above. Now read this sentence. Do you agree with it? What is Dickinson's best response? What is Dodds's best response to Dickinson?

The Plaintiff says in effect that, having heard and knowing that Dodds was no longer minded to sell to him, and that he was selling or had sold to someone else, thinking that he could not in point of law withdraw his offer, meaning to fix him to it, and endeavouring to bind him, "I went to the house where he was lodging, and saw his mother-in-law, and left with her an acceptance of the offer, knowing all the while that he had entirely changed his mind. I got an agent to watch for him at 7 o'clock the next morning, and I went to the train just before 9 o'clock, in order that I might catch him and give him my notice of acceptance just before 9 o'clock, and when that occurred he told my agent, and he told me, you are too late, and he then threw back the paper." It is to my mind quite clear that before there was any attempt at acceptance by the Plaintiff, he was perfectly well aware that Dodds had changed his mind, and that he had in fact agreed to sell the property to Allan. It is impossible, therefore, to say there was ever that existence of the same mind between the two parties which is essential in point of law to the making of an agreement. I am of opinion, therefore, that the Plaintiff has failed to prove that there was any binding contract between Dodds and himself.

Critical reading III

Reread the sentences associated with the previous "critical reading" boxes. How does Mellish's understanding of the facts differ from these previous accounts, and what difference does this make? Are you beginning to see how it is not simply the black-letter rule that decides disputes, but (in part) what rule or standard is chosen, how the facts are interpreted, and only then how the rule or standard is applied to the facts?

MELLISH, L.J.: I am of the same opinion. . . . **[T]he question which arises is this—If an offer has been made for the sale of property, and before that offer is accepted, the person who has made the offer enters into a binding agreement to sell the property to somebody else, and the person to whom the offer was first made receives notice in some way that the property has been sold to another person, can he after that make a binding contract by the acceptance of the offer?** I am of opinion that he cannot. The law may be right or wrong in saying that a person who has given to another a certain time within which to accept an offer is not bound by his promise to give that time; but, if he is not bound by that promise, and may still sell the property to someone else, and if it be the law that, in order to make a contract, the two minds must be in agreement at some one time, that is, at the time of the acceptance, how is it possible that when the person to whom the offer has been made knows that the person who has made the offer has sold the property to someone else, and that, in fact, he has not remained in the same mind to sell it to him, he can be at liberty to accept the offer and thereby make a binding contract? It seems to me that would be simply absurd.

If a man makes an offer to sell a particular horse in his stable, and says, "I will give you until the day after to-morrow to accept the offer," and the next day goes and sells the horse to somebody else, and receives the purchase-money from him, can the person to whom the offer was originally made then come and say, "I accept," so as to make a binding contract, and so as to be entitled to recover damages for the non-delivery of the horse? If the rule of law is that a mere offer to sell property, which can be withdrawn at any time, and which is made dependent on the acceptance of the person to whom it is made, is a mere *nudum pactum*, how is it possible that the person to whom the offer has been made can by acceptance make a binding contract after he knows that the person who has made the offer has sold the property to someone else?

It is admitted law that, if a man who makes an offer dies, the offer cannot be accepted after he is dead, and parting with the property has very much the same effect as the death of the owner, for it makes the performance of the offer impossible. I am clearly of opinion that, just as when a man who has made an offer dies before it is accepted it is impossible that it can then be accepted, so when once the person to whom the offer was made knows that the property has been sold to someone else, it is too late for him to accept the offer, and on that ground I am clearly of opinion that there was no binding contract for the sale of this property by Dodds to Dickinson, and even if there had been, it seems to me that the sale of the property to Allan was first in point of time. However, it is not necessary to consider, if there had been two binding contracts, which of them would be entitled to priority in equity, because there is no binding contract between Dodds and Dickinson.

RELEVANT PROVISIONS

For the *Restatement (Second) of Contracts,* consult §§ 25, 35(2), 36, 42, and 43. For the UCC, consult §§ 2-104(a) and 2-205. For the CISG, consult Articles 15(2), 16, and 17. For the UNIDROIT Principles, consult Articles 2.1.3(2), 2.1.4(1), and 2.1.5.

NOTES AND QUESTIONS

1. *What happened?* Who sued whom for what? Procedurally, how did the case get before this court? Factually, what happened between the parties? What arguments did the plaintiff and defendant make? What rule or rules did the court apply? How did the court analyze the dispute between the parties? How did the court decide the case?

2. *Was this case correctly decided?* Do you agree with the result reached in this case? Why or why not? Do you agree with the reasoning used by each of the judges? Why or why not? How, if at all, would you have written the opinion differently? By the way, we will meet Mellish again (he wrote the second opinion in *Dickinson*) in the famous case of *Raffles v. Wichelhaus* (p. 747, *infra*), where we shall find him, 12 years earlier, making the winning argument as the attorney for the defendant-buyer.

3. *Plain meaning and a preview of the parol evidence rule.* In the June 10 letter, what do the words "I hereby agree to sell" mean? At first glance, they may seem to indicate that the seller is making a contract. Indeed, if this is all the text we had to work with, that conclusion seems nearly inescapable. But then we come to the postscript and immediately realize that this seemingly obvious interpretation is wrong, and what we just read was really an offer. Oops. Now imagine that the postscript was never included in the June 10 letter, but that the exact words contained in the postscript were spoken by the seller to the buyer when he handed over the June 10 letter. On these facts, do you think a court should consider this evidence, or should it interpret the document according to its "plain meaning"? Good arguments can be made both for admitting and for excluding such evidence, but one argument—that the written

words carry a plain meaning that indicates party intent—seems dead in the water. Keep these points in mind when we come to the parol evidence rule in Chapter 6, which explores the circumstances in which evidence outside the four corners of a written contract may be admitted to interpret the agreement.

4. *Acceptance?* If Dickinson did accept Dodds's offer, there are at least three possible points at which this acceptance might have taken place. Let's go through each of them here. First, Dickinson might have accepted Dodds's offer when he left a written acceptance with Dodds's mother-in-law on Thursday evening. Second, Dickinson might have accepted when Berry (his agent) handed an acceptance to Dodds around 7:00 A.M. Friday morning. Finally, Dickinson might have accepted when he himself handed Dodds a notice of acceptance a few minutes later. If there was an acceptance, which of these three possibilities seems most likely?

5. ***Consideration and option contracts.*** As you will recall from our discussion of *Hamer v. Sidway* (see p. 93, *supra*), and as we shall discuss in greater detail in the next chapter, contracts, to be enforceable, must generally be supported by consideration. Subject to a few exceptions, which we turn explore in the next subsection, our common law courts have taken the position that option contracts—by which one party promises to leave an offer open for a period of time—are still contracts, and therefore must also be supported by consideration to be valid. It is for this reason that Dodds's promise to leave his offer open until 9:00 A.M. on Friday is treated as a *nudum pactum*, or a naked promise not properly clothed in consideration's illustrious raiment.

6. ***Déjà vu all over again.*** A strikingly similar case arose in North Carolina over a hundred years later. Not surprisingly, it had a strikingly similar outcome:

> [T]he record is devoid of any evidence that any consideration was given which would have made the offer irrevocable as an option. Since the promise to hold the offer open until 5:00 P.M., 5 August 1980, was not supported by consideration, it could be revoked at any time. "An offeree's power of acceptance is terminated when the offeror takes definite action inconsistent with an intention to enter into the proposed contract and the offeree acquires reliable information to that effect." *Restatement (Second) of Contracts* § 43 (1981). By accepting Segal's offer to convey the property, Miller revoked her offer to Normile and Kurniawan. Once they received notice from Byer that the property had been sold, the revocation became effective and their power to accept Miller's counteroffer was terminated. Thus, their subsequent signing of the counteroffer and its delivery to the realtor's office was an insufficient attempt to bind Miller to the contract.*

Perhaps more surprisingly, however, the venerable *Dickinson v. Dodds* was never cited by the court.

* *Normile v. Miller*, 306 S.E.2d 147, 150 (N.C. Ct. App. 1983).

PROBLEM: DOUBLE DEALING IN REAL ESTATE

On June 9, 1999, Larry Lenard entered into a 365-day exclusive listing agreement with Century 21, a real estate brokerage firm, to sell a piece of riverfront property for $750,000. Gary Gilmore is the accounting agent for Century 21.

On August 16, 1999, FREP, through its president, Brett Butler, a sophisticated real estate broker and developer, submitted an offer to purchase the property for $300,000. The offer was submitted contingent upon several open-ended conditions and was accompanied by an earnest money deposit of $1,000 payable to Century 21. The deposit was fully refundable if transfer to FREP was not completed for any reason except FREP's failure to perform. If the offer were accepted the $1,000 would go into the purchase price. The offer to purchase was to expire on September 16, 1999 at 6:00 p.m.

Both the offer to purchase and the contingent conditions were totally unacceptable to Lenard so he allowed the offer to expire without response. Immediately at the expiration of FREP's offer to purchase, Butler convinced Gilmore to seek a counteroffer from Lenard.

In an effort to accommodate Butler, Gilmore persuaded Lenard to propose a counteroffer. Lenard sent a counteroffer on September 29 proposing a $550,000 purchase price in cash with $20,000 earnest money and an option to close the sale within a two-month window. Lenard stipulated that the counteroffer was to remain open for thirty days until October 28.

Upon receipt of the counteroffer Gilmore immediately communicated the contents to Butler. Butler received the counteroffer but took no action on it until October 20, when Gilmore advised him that negotiations for the sale of the property to Harrison Property were about to be concluded.

Harrison Property had initiated negotiations with Lenard to purchase the property within days after FREP's initial offer expired. After hearing of the Harrison Property negotiation, on October 20, Butler decided to accept the September 29 offer by Lenard. Butler prepared the $20,000 earnest payment and the letter of acceptance and mailed it to Gilmore. When Butler learned that Lenard had executed the option to sell the property to Harrison Property, he filed an action to enjoin Lenard from selling the property to Harrison Property and ordering Lenard to convey the property to FREP.

Was Butler's acceptance of the September 29 offer effective? Did the $1,000 earnest money from Butler's original offer create a 30-day irrevocable option for Butler to accept Lenard's September 29 offer?

PROBLEM: WATCH YOUR TIME

Chronovex, Inc. wanted to purchase watch components from a parts manufacturer, Goheim, LLC. On May 14, Goheim offered to sell Chronovex watch components. The offer was firm until June 31. On September 18, more than three months after the original offer was made, Chronovex, unhappy with the terms in Goheim's offer, forwarded to Goheim a counteroffer stating different price terms for the watch components. On December 4, Goheim attempted to accept the offer made on May 14.

Was Goheim, LLC's acceptance effective?

PROBLEM: A CABIN FOR SALE

Bexley Madison owned a cabin in Maggie Valley, North Carolina. On January 4, the property was listed for sale with a local realtor. The same day it was listed, the realtor showed the cabin to a prospective purchaser, Joseph Taylor. After viewing the cabin, Taylor prepared a written offer to purchase the property. The offer contained standard provisions and listed the time and date for acceptance as: "OFFER & CLOSING DATE. Time is of the essence, therefore this offer must be accepted before 6:00 P.M. on January 6, 2003. A signed copy shall be promptly returned to the purchaser." Madison took Taylor's offer and made several changes including increasing the earnest money deposit. For each change, Madison initialed next to the provision. The evening of January 5, Taylor received Madison's counteroffer but was not sure if he had the additional earnest money requested by Madison. Taylor sat on the offer thinking that Madison's counteroffer gave him the first option on the property. The morning of January 6, Madison's realtor showed the property to Elizabeth Cromworth, a wealthy property investor, who immediately after a tour of the property signed an offer to purchase with terms very similar to the counteroffer presented to Taylor. Madison accepted this offer without change. At 2:00 P.M. the same day, Madison informed Taylor that the property had been sold and that her counteroffer was revoked. Shortly thereafter, Taylor signed the counteroffer he had received from Madison and delivered it with the earnest money to Madison's realtor. When Madison refused to sell the cabin to him, Taylor sued for specific performance.

What is Taylor's best argument in favor of specific performance? What would Madison's best defense to Taylor's claim be? If Taylor had delivered his acceptance before 2:00 p.m., would that have made a difference?

PROBLEM: I'D LIKE TO RETIRE, PLEASE

In 2007, the Arizona legislature passed a modification to teachers' retirement incentive packages to ease the growing burden on school districts in Arizona. The Marion School District sought to take advantage of this proposed legislation. The school board of the district directed their district manager, Andrew Martin, to determine how the district could alter their retirement incentives based on the legislature's proposal. The district manager proposed that the school board could save money by offering teachers an additional retirement payment that would pay off a portion of the teacher's indebtedness to the district's collective retirement fund. Taking the district manager's advice, on August 2 the school board voted on the following motion, which read in part:

> MOTION . . . to offer an additional retirement incentive payment equal to the employee's indebtedness for two years to all certified and classified employees who are eligible to retire at the end of the school year and/or meet the requirements established for a retirement incentive package. The employee must notify the District by August 30, 2007 if they plan to participate.

Within days of the motion passing, Martin realized he had erred and that the district's new retirement payment would cost the district more than it would save.

In early August, several teachers heard of the school board's new retirement incentive. One of the teachers, Shelly Winsley, decided to approach Martin about the new program established by the school board. Martin advised Winsley that "the school board intended to rescind the new retirement incentive program at the next school board meeting on September 5." Winsley and several teachers decided to accept the offer before this meeting. On August 28, Winsley and several teachers delivered a letter communicating their acceptance of the terms of the August 2 program. On September 5 when the school board met, they rescinded the August 2 motion and passed a new motion modifying the retirement incentive program. Winsley and the teachers that had accepted the August 2 retirement incentives demanded that those benefits be honored and when the school district refused, they sued for breach of contract.

Was the school board's motion to create the new incentive program an offer that the teachers could accept? If there was an offer, was it revoked when Andrew Martin told Shelly Winsley that the school board intended to rescind the August 2 motion? What additional facts would be necessary for a court to make a determination on this breach of contract claim?

2. Revocation and Option Contracts

As you may recall, we briefly touched upon option contracts when we read *Dickinson v. Dodds*. There, Dodds promised to leave his offer open until Friday at 9:00 A.M., but because his promise wasn't supported by consideration (you'll recall that the court amusingly* referred to this promise as a "mere *nudum pactum*"), it was unenforceable. In this unit, we consider option contracts more directly, including some of the circumstances in which courts and legislatures have expressed a willingness to imply them, even absent consideration. But before we get to that, let's start with an overview of option contracts in general.

* Well, amusing to a 21st century reader, anyway. For the Victorian judges who wrote it, probably not so much. Random fact: the expression "we are not amused" is attributed to Queen Victoria. Even more amusingly, some think she never said it. But as anyone who watched *The Man Who Shot Liberty Valance* knows, "when the legend becomes fact, print the legend." So I did. Okay, back to contracts.

DOCTRINAL OVERVIEW: OPTION CONTRACTS*

An offeree may need time to decide whether to accept the offer and, during that time, may need to spend money and effort. Even if the offeror is willing to assure the offeree that the offer will be held open for that time, the traditional common law rules make it difficult to protect the offeree against the offeror's power of revocation. Not only does the common law posit that offers are generally revocable, but the offeror's mere promise not to revoke the offer—or its mere statement that the offer is not revocable—has traditionally been regarded as unenforceable unless under seal or supported by consideration. The doctrine of consideration, combined with the rule of free revocability, makes it impossible for the offeror to give the offeree the desired protection merely by saying so. The result has been increasingly subjected to criticism, especially where irrevocability does not expose the offeror to a substantial risk of speculation by the offeree. . . . The conventional way for the offeree to overcome the obstacles imposed by the common law and get the desired protection is by means of an option.

An irrevocable offer is commonly called an *option.* Like any other offer, an option imposes no duty on the offeree. The offeree has unfettered discretion to either accept the offer or not. An offeree that accepts the offer is said to "exercise" the option. An option is itself a contract, sometimes called an *option contract* to distinguish it from the main contract to be formed on acceptance of the offer.

Before the abolition of the seal, the offeror could make an option by promising under seal not to revoke the offer.[5] Now that the seal has been generally abolished, the offeror can still make an option if the promise not to revoke is supported by consideration. The consideration may consist of either a promise or a performance. . . .

The *Restatement Second* favors the enforceability of what it calls *option contracts.*[16] . . .

If an offer is irrevocable, a purported revocation by the offeror has no effect on the offeree's power of acceptance. The offeree can accept despite the purported revocation and can sue for breach of the contract if the offeror fails to perform. The same is true of the offeror's death or incapacity. . . .

RELEVANT PROVISIONS

For the *Restatement (Second) of Contracts,* consult §§ 25 and 37.

---

* Excerpted from E. ALLAN FARNSWORTH, CONTRACTS § 3.23 (4th ed. 2004).

5. . . . The offeror may put the promise in this form: "If you pay me $100, I promise not to revoke my offer to sell you apples for $10,000 for a period of 30 days." Or the offeror may put it in this form: "If you pay me $100, I will sell you apples for $10.000 on condition that you accept my offer within 30 days." The effect is the same.

16. *Restatement Second* § 25 ("option contract is a promise which meets the requirements for the formation of a contract and limits the promisor's power to revoke an offer").

So, here's the situation. A general contractor ("general") is preparing its bid to build a shopping center for the city. As part of the process, it invites a number of subcontractors ("subs") to submit bids on a wide variety of projects needed to complete the shopping center (e.g., roads, drywall, plumbing). Hundreds of bids come in, and the general takes the lowest bid for each of these projects, adds them up, adds in a profit margin, and submits its bid to the city. The next day, a sub calls to inform the general that it made a mistake—say, it forgot to carry a "1"—and explains that it cannot possibly do the work for less than twice the amount of their previous bid. The general says no way, informs the sub that the bid has already been submitted to the city, and tells the sub that it expects them to perform if the city awards them the contract. The sub says it won't, explains to the general that its bid was just an offer, and further explains that because the general never accepted their offer—in fact, couldn't accept their offer because the city hasn't even awarded them the contract yet—they're privileged to withdraw it. The general, not surprisingly, sees things differently.

"Although it is true," the general explains to the sub, "that we didn't formally accept your offer, we did rely on it, and you knew when you submitted it to us that we'd rely on it. Now that we've submitted our bid to the city, it's too late for us to withdraw it, which means that it's too late for you to withdraw your bid from us. As for your price, if we pay you twice as much, where do you suppose that money will come from? I'll tell you—from us! You're basically asking us to grab money from our own pocket and put it in yours. But why should we do that? Had you done your math correctly, we probably wouldn't have used your bid at all. Other subs submitted bids lower than the price you're now quoting us." The sub was about to respond (you'll have to imagine what it would have said or, better yet, why not grab a pen and paper or laptop and continue the dialogue yourself?), but the general had to take another call. It was from the city, who informed the general that its bid had been accepted. The general and sub spoke again, but never could work out their issues, as each party adamantly stuck to its guns. Unfortunately for them, but great for law students everywhere, who can now read about their conflict, the general and the sub found no way of resolving their dispute except through the courts.

As the judge assigned to the case, what would you do, and why? In fact, why don't you stop reading and take a moment and write down how you'd resolve this dispute, and the reasons you'd use to support your conclusion. Then, go ahead and read the next two cases, which are basically variations on the story just told. Although the problems are the same, the legal solution presented in each case is very different, as you'll soon see. As you read these cases, do you find yourself drawn more to one legal solution than the other? Do you find yourself more drawn to one style of legal reasoning than the other? Did you, by any chance, change your mind?

Because these cases go together, the notes and questions for both of them will appear at the end of the second case.

James Baird Co. v. Gimbel Bros., Inc.

United States Court of Appeals, Second Circuit
64 F.2d 344 (1933)

L. Hand, Circuit Judge. The plaintiff sued the defendant for breach of a contract to deliver linoleum under a contract of sale; the defendant denied the making of the contract; the parties tried the case to the judge under a written stipulation and he directed judgment for the defendant. The facts as found, bearing on the making of the contract, the only issue necessary to discuss, were as follows: The defendant, a New York merchant, knew that the Department of Highways in Pennsylvania had asked for bids for the construction of a public building. It sent an employee to the office of a contractor in Philadelphia, who had possession of the specifications, and the employee there computed the amount of the linoleum which would be required on the job, underestimating the total yardage by about one-half the proper amount. In ignorance of this mistake, on December twenty-fourth the defendant sent to some twenty or thirty contractors, likely to bid on the job, an offer to supply all the linoleum required by the specifications at two different lump sums, depending upon the quality used. These offers concluded as follows: "If successful in being awarded this contract, it will be absolutely guaranteed, . . . and . . . we are offering these prices for reasonable" (sic), "prompt acceptance after the general contract has been awarded." The plaintiff, a contractor in Washington, got one of these on the twenty-eighth, and on the same day the defendant learned its mistake and telegraphed all the contractors to whom it had sent the offer, that it withdrew it and would substitute a new one at about double the amount of the old. This withdrawal reached the plaintiff at Washington on the afternoon of the same day, but not until after it had put in a bid at Harrisburg at a lump sum, based as to linoleum upon the prices quoted by the defendant. The public authorities accepted the plaintiff's bid on December thirtieth, the defendant having meanwhile written a letter of confirmation of its withdrawal, received on the thirty-first. The plaintiff formally accepted the offer on January second, and, as the defendant persisted in declining to recognize the existence of a contract, sued it for damages on a breach.

Billings Learned Hand

Judge Jearned Hand (1872-1961) (yup, that's his real name) was one of the most influential judges and judicial philosophers in American history. He was appointed to the U.S. District Court for the Southern District of New York in 1909 and to the Second Circuit in 1924, where he sat until his death in 1961. During his long tenure, he penned a number of influential decisions that continue to shape today's legal landscape. Not only was he called "the greatest living American jurist" by no less a figure than Cardozo, but his opinions have been cited by the U.S. Supreme Court more frequently than any other lower-court judge, earning him the nickname "the tenth Justice of the Supreme Court." Hand was also a founding member of the American Law Institute and wrote several successful books, including *The Spirit of Liberty* (1952) and *Bill of Rights* (1958), which became a national bestseller.

Mistake

A party's contractual obligations are generally excused where the mistake is mutual. *Restatement (Second) of Contracts* §152(1). We will cover this defense in greater detail in Chapter 8.

Unless there are circumstances to take it out of the ordinary doctrine, since the offer was withdrawn before it was accepted, the acceptance was too late. *Restatement of Contracts* § 35. To meet this the plaintiff argues as follows: It was a reasonable implication from the defendant's offer that it should be irrevocable in case the plaintiff acted upon it, that is to say, used the prices quoted in making its bid, thus putting itself in a position from which it could not withdraw without great loss. While it might have withdrawn its bid after receiving the revocation, the time had passed to submit another, and as the item of linoleum was a very trifling part of the cost of the whole building, it would have been an unreasonable hardship to expect it to lose the contract on that account, and probably forfeit its deposit. While it is true that the plaintiff might in advance have secured a contract conditional upon the success of its bid, this was not what the defendant suggested. It understood that the contractors would use its offer in their bids, and would thus in fact commit themselves to supplying the linoleum at the proposed prices. The inevitable implication from all this was that when the contractors acted upon it, they accepted the offer and promised to pay for the linoleum, in case their bid were accepted.

It was of course possible for the parties to make such a contract, and the question is merely as to what they meant; that is, what is to be imputed to the words they used. Whatever plausibility there is in the argument, is in the fact that the defendant must have known the predicament in which the contractors would be put if it withdrew its offer after the bids went in. **However, it seems entirely clear that the contractors did not suppose that they accepted the offer merely by putting in their bids. If, for example, the successful one had repudiated the contract with the public authorities after it had been awarded to him, certainly the defendant could not have sued him for a breach. If he had become bankrupt, the defendant could not prove against his estate. It seems plain therefore that there was no contract between them. And if there be any doubt as to this, the language of the offer sets it at rest.** The phrase, "if successful in being awarded this contract," is scarcely met by the mere use of the prices in the bids. Surely such a use was not an "award" of the contract to the defendant. Again, the phrase, "we are offering these prices for . . . prompt acceptance after the general contract has been awarded," looks to the usual communication of an acceptance, and precludes the idea that the use of the offer in the bidding shall be the equivalent. It may indeed be argued that this last language contemplated no more than an early notice that the offer had been accepted, the actual acceptance being the bid, but that would wrench its natural meaning too far, especially in the light of the preceding phrase. The contractors had a ready escape from their difficulty by insisting upon a contract before they used the figures; and in commercial transactions it does not in the end promote justice to seek strained interpretations in aid of those who do not protect themselves.

> ***Stay alert!***
>
> What is the general contractor's argument as to why the subcontractor should not be allowed to withdraw its bid? Does Hand's response meet that argument? Be on the lookout: Hand will soon offer a much more direct (and forceful) response to plaintiff's argument. What is it?

But the plaintiff says that even though no bilateral contract was made, the defendant should be held under the doctrine of "promissory estoppel." This is to be chiefly found in those cases where persons subscribe to a venture, usually charitable, and are held to their promises after it has been completed. It has been applied much more broadly, however, and has now been generalized in the *Restatement of Contracts* § 90. We may arguendo accept it as it there reads, for it does not apply to the case at bar. Offers are ordinarily made in exchange for a consideration, either a counter-promise or some other act which the promisor wishes to secure. In such cases they propose bargains; they presuppose that each promise or performance is an inducement to the other. But a man may make a promise without expecting an equivalent; a donative promise, conditional or absolute. The common law provided for such by sealed instruments, and it is unfortunate that these are no longer generally available. The doctrine of "promissory estoppel" is to avoid the harsh results of allowing the promisor in such a case to repudiate, when the promisee has acted in reliance upon the promise. *Cf. Allegheny College v. National Bank*, 159 N. E. 173. But an offer for an exchange is not meant to become a promise until a consideration has been received, either a counter-promise or whatever else is stipulated. To extend it would be to hold the offeror regardless of the stipulated condition of his offer. **In the case at bar the defendant offered to deliver the linoleum in exchange for the plaintiff's acceptance, not for its bid, which was a matter of indifference to it.** That offer could become a promise to deliver only when the equivalent was received; that is, when the plaintiff promised to take and pay for it. There is no room in such a situation for the doctrine of "promissory estoppel."

Comparative reading, part one

Mark this sentence well. In the next opinion, Justice Traynor will respond to it directly.

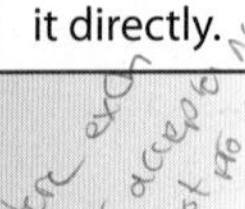

Nor can the offer be regarded as of an option, giving the plaintiff the right seasonably to accept the linoleum at the quoted prices if its bid was accepted, but not binding it to take and pay, if it could get a better bargain elsewhere. There is not the least reason to suppose that the defendant meant to subject itself to such one-sided obligation. True, if so construed, the doctrine of "promissory estoppel" might apply, the plaintiff having acted in reliance upon it, though, so far as we have found, the decisions are otherwise. As to that, however, we need not declare ourselves.

Judgment affirmed.

Drennan v. Star Paving Co.

Supreme Court of California
333 P.2d 757 (1958)

TRAYNOR, JUSTICE. Defendant appeals from a judgment for plaintiff in an action to recover damages caused by defendant's refusal to perform certain paving work according to a bid it submitted to plaintiff.

On July 28, 1955, plaintiff, a licensed general contractor, was preparing a bid on the "Monte Vista School Job" in the Lancaster school district. Bids had to be submitted before 8:00 P.M. Plaintiff testified that it was customary in that area for general contractors to receive the bids of subcontractors by telephone on the day set for bidding and to rely on them in computing their own bids. Thus on that day plaintiff's secretary, Mrs. Johnson, received by telephone between fifty and seventy-five subcontractors' bids for various parts of the school job. As each bid came in, she wrote it on a special form, which she brought into plaintiff's office. He then posted it on a master cost sheet setting forth the names and bids of all subcontractors. His own bid had to include the names of subcontractors who were to perform one-half of one per cent or more of the construction work, and he had also to provide a bidder's bond of ten per cent of his total bid of $317,385 as a guarantee that he would enter the contract if awarded the work.

Roger Traynor

Justice Traynor (1900-1983) (whose name isn't nearly as spiffy as "Learned Hand") was a professor at U.C. Berkeley before beginning his 30-year tenure on the Supreme Court of California. He first sat as an Associate Justice from 1940-1964, and then as Chief Justice from 1964-1970. During his long and distinguished career, he penned over 900 decisions that had an influence far beyond the borders of California, and established himself as "one of the greatest judicial talents never to sit on the United States Supreme Court" according to the *New York Times*. We will meet Judge Traynor again in Chapter 6, where we will have occasion to consider his judicial philosophy and its impact on contract law in greater detail. See "Justice Traynor and the Law of Contracts" on p. 771, *infra*.

Late in the afternoon, Mrs. Johnson had a telephone conversation with Kenneth R. Hoon, an estimator for defendant. He gave his name and telephone number and stated that he was bidding for defendant for the paving work at the Monte Vista School according to plans and specifications and that his bid was $7,131.60. At Mrs. Johnson's request he repeated his bid. Plaintiff listened to the bid over an extension telephone in his office and posted it on the master sheet after receiving the bid form from Mrs. Johnson. Defendant's was the lowest bid for the paving. Plaintiff computed his own bid accordingly and submitted it with the name of defendant as the subcontractor for the paving. When the bids were opened on July 28th, plaintiff's proved to be the lowest, and he was awarded the contract.

On his way to Los Angeles the next morning plaintiff stopped at defendant's office. The first person he met was defendant's construction engineer, Mr. Oppenheimer. Plaintiff testified:

> I introduced myself and he immediately told me that they had made a mistake in their bid to me the night before, they couldn't do it for the price they had bid, and I told him I would expect him to carry through with their original bid because I had used it in compiling my bid and the job was being awarded them. And I would have to go and do the job according to my bid and I would expect them to do the same.

Defendant refused to do the paving work for less than $15,000. Plaintiff testified that he "got figures from other people" and after trying for several months to get as low a bid as possible engaged L & H Paving Company, a firm in Lancaster, to do the work for $10,948.60.

The trial court found on substantial evidence that defendant made a definite offer to do the paving on the Monte Vista job according to the plans and specifications for $7,131.60, and that plaintiff relied on defendant's bid in computing his own bid for the school job and naming defendant therein as the subcontractor for the paving work. Accordingly, it entered judgment for plaintiff in the amount of $3,817.00 (the difference between defendant's bid and the cost of the paving to plaintiff) plus costs.

Defendant contends that there was no enforceable contract between the parties on the ground that it made a revocable offer and revoked it before plaintiff communicated his acceptance to defendant.

There is no evidence that defendant offered to make its bid irrevocable in exchange for plaintiff's use of its figures in computing his bid. Nor is there evidence that would warrant interpreting plaintiff's use of defendant's bid as the acceptance thereof, binding plaintiff, on condition he received the main contract, to award the subcontract to defendant. In sum, there was neither an option supported by consideration nor a bilateral contract binding on both parties.

> **Look familiar?**
>
> Up to this point, not only are the facts in *Baird* and *Drennan* similar, but the parties' arguments are identical! Must have taken a lot of work to write those briefs.

Plaintiff contends, however, that he relied to his detriment on defendant's offer and that defendant must therefore answer in damages for its refusal to perform. Thus the question is squarely presented: Did plaintiff's reliance make defendant's offer irrevocable?

Restatement of Contracts § 90 states:

> A promise which the promisor should reasonably expect to induce action or forbearance of a definite and substantial character on the part of the promisee and which does induce such action or forbearance is binding if injustice can be avoided only by enforcement of the promise.

This rule applies in this state.

Defendant's offer constituted a promise to perform on such conditions as were stated expressly or by implication therein or annexed thereto by operation of law. Defendant had reason to expect that if its bid proved the lowest it would be used by plaintiff. It induced "action . . . of a definite and substantial character on the part of the promisee."

Had defendant's bid expressly stated or clearly implied that it was revocable at any time before acceptance we would treat it accordingly. It was silent on revocation, however, and we must therefore determine whether there are conditions to the right of revocation imposed by law or reasonably inferable in fact. In the analogous problem of an offer for a unilateral contract, the theory is now obsolete that the offer is revocable at any time before

> **Interpreting silence**
>
> In each case, *both* parties were silent regarding whether the bid was revocable, and in each case, *neither* party said anything about how this silence was to be treated. According to Hand, where an offer is silent, it is incumbent upon the *general contractors* to "protect themselves" by "insisting upon a

complete performance. Thus the *Restatement of Contracts* § 45 provides:

> If an offer for a unilateral contract is made, and part of the consideration requested in the offer is given or tendered by the offeree in response thereto, the offeror is bound by a contract, the duty of immediate performance of which is conditional on the full consideration being given or tendered within the time stated in the offer, or, if no time is stated therein, within a reasonable time.

In explanation, comment b states that the

> main offer includes as a subsidiary promise, necessarily implied, that if part of the requested performance is given, the offeror will not revoke his offer, and that if tender is made it will be accepted. Part performance or tender may thus furnish consideration for the subsidiary promise. Moreover, merely acting in justifiable reliance on an offer may in some cases serve as sufficient reason for making a promise binding (see § 90).

contract" that makes the offer irrevocable. According to Traynor, however, where a bid is "silent on revocation," it is up to the *subcontractor* to "expressly state[] or clearly impl[y] that [its bid] was revocable at any time prior to acceptance." Who's right? In the absence of an express provision by either party, how should courts determine (1) which default rule should govern the offer, and, relatedly, (2) which party should have the obligation to contract around it? Now is a great opportunity to apply many of the thinking tools you have learned about earlier! For more on this issue, see Note 8 entitled "Default Rules" following this case.

Whether implied in fact or law, the subsidiary promise serves to preclude the injustice that would result if the offer could be revoked after the offeree had acted in detrimental reliance thereon. Reasonable reliance resulting in a foreseeable prejudicial change in position affords a compelling basis also for implying a subsidiary promise not to revoke an offer for a bilateral contract.

The absence of consideration is not fatal to the enforcement of such a promise. It is true that in the case of unilateral contracts the *Restatement* finds consideration for the implied subsidiary promise in the part performance of the bargained-for exchange, but its reference to § 90 makes clear that consideration for such a promise is not always necessary. The very purpose of § 90 is to make a promise binding even though there was no consideration "in the sense of something that is bargained for and given in exchange." (*See* 1 Corbin, *Contracts* 634 et seq.) Reasonable reliance serves to hold the offeror in lieu of the consideration ordinarily required to make the offer binding. In a case involving similar facts the Supreme Court of South Dakota stated that

> we believe that reason and justice demand that the doctrine (of § 90) be applied to the present facts. We cannot believe that by accepting this doctrine as controlling in the state of facts before us we will abolish the requirement of a consideration in contract cases, in any different sense than an ordinary estoppel abolishes some legal requirement in its application. We are of the opinion, therefore, that the defendants in executing the agreement (which was not supported by consideration) made a promise which they should have reasonably expected would induce the plaintiff to submit a bid based thereon to the Government, that such promise did induce this action, and that injustice can be avoided only by enforcement of the promise.

> **Wink wink, nudge nudge**
>
> About the slyest "cf." you'll ever see. Don't forget that Hand was still on the bench when Traynor wrote this.

> **Comparative reading, part two**
>
> This sentence was written in direct response to Hand's sentence referred to in "Comparative reading, part one" on p. 300, *supra*. The short excerpt following the cases will have something to say about this, but for now, who's right: Hand or Traynor?

Northwestern Engineering Co. v. Ellerman, 10 N.W.2d 879, 884; ***cf. James Baird Co. v. Gimbel Bros.*, 2 Cir., 64 F.2d 344.**

When plaintiff used defendant's offer in computing his own bid, he bound himself to perform in reliance on defendant's terms. **Though defendant did not bargain for this use of its bid neither did defendant make it idly, indifferent to whether it would be used or not.** On the contrary it is reasonable to suppose that defendant submitted its bid to obtain the subcontract. It was bound to realize the substantial possibility that its bid would be the lowest, and that it would be included by plaintiff in his bid. It was to its own interest that the contractor be awarded the general contract; the lower the subcontract bid, the lower the general contractor's bid was likely to be and the greater its chance of acceptance and hence the greater defendant's chance of getting the paving subcontract. Defendant had reason not only to expect plaintiff to rely on its bid but to want him to. Clearly defendant had a stake in plaintiff's reliance on its bid. Given this interest and the fact that plaintiff is bound by his own bid, it is only fair that plaintiff should have at least an opportunity to accept defendant's bid after the general contract has been awarded to him.

It bears noting that a general contractor is not free to delay acceptance after he has been awarded the general contract in the hope of getting a better price. Nor can he reopen bargaining with the subcontractor and at the same time claim a continuing right to accept the original offer. In the present case plaintiff promptly informed defendant that plaintiff was being awarded the job and that the subcontract was being awarded to defendant.

Defendant contends, however, that its bid was the result of mistake and that it was therefore entitled to revoke it. It relies on [several] rescission cases . . . In those cases, however, the bidder's mistake was known or should have been known to the offeree, and the offeree could be placed in status quo. Of course, if plaintiff had reason to believe that defendant's bid was in error, he could not justifiably rely on it, and § 90 would afford no basis for enforcing it. Plaintiff, however, had no reason to know that defendant had made a mistake in submitting its bid, since there was usually a variance of 160 per cent between the highest and lowest bids for paving in the desert around Lancaster. He committed himself to performing the main contract in reliance on defendant's figures. Under these circumstances defendant's mistake, far from relieving it of its obligation, constitutes an additional reason for enforcing it, for it misled plaintiff as to the cost of doing the paving. Even had it been clearly understood that defendant's offer was revocable until accepted, it would not necessarily follow that defendant had no duty to exercise reasonable care in preparing its bid. It presented its bid with knowledge of the substantial possibility that it would be used by plaintiff; it could foresee the harm that would ensue from an erroneous underestimate of the cost. Moreover, it was motivated by its own business interest. Whether or not these considerations alone would justify recovery for negligence had the case been tried on that theory, they are persuasive that defendant's mistake should not defeat recovery under the rule of § 90.

As between the subcontractor who made the bid and the general contractor who reasonably relied on it, the loss resulting from the mistake should fall on the party who caused it. . . .

The judgment is affirmed.

Who should bear the risk of loss?

Do you agree with Traynor? How would Judge Hand respond?

Mistake should fall on party who caused it.

FREEDOM AND INTERDEPENDENCE IN TWENTIETH-CENTURY CONTRACT LAW*

In 1958, Judge Roger Traynor, writing for a unanimous California Supreme Court in *Drennan v. Star Paving*, rejected a form of analysis offered exactly twenty-five years before by Judge Learned Hand in the Second Circuit Court of Appeals decision of *Baird v. Gimbel*. Both cases addressed a contractual problem in the bidding process in the construction industry: What are the legal consequences of a general contractor's use of a subcontractor's low bid that is subsequently discovered to have contained a mistake? Although the decisions have often invited comparison, I believe those comparisons have overlooked the evidence that Traynor deliberately targeted and rejected the *Baird* decision and Hand's reasoning.

Applying traditional common-law rules of consideration and offer and acceptance, Hand determined that no liability for breach of contract flowed from subcontractor to general contractor because the subcontractor had exercised the right to revoke the offer before the general contractor had accepted. Therefore, according to Hand, no bilateral contract had been formed. He also went on to say that no liability could be assessed against the subcontractor as a result of reliance-based notions of promissory estoppel, strongly suggesting that promissory estoppel had no place in the rough and tumble world of commercial practice.

A generation later, Traynor also concluded that no legal liability arose in the situation if the conventional rules of offer and acceptance applied. Unlike Hand, however, Traynor believed that liability should be imposed in this factual context by application of the doctrine of promissory estoppel, which, from his point of view, accurately reflected the true vulnerability of general contractors in the marketplace caused by their reliance on bids prepared and submitted to them by subcontractors.

Baird and *Drennan* are frequently juxtaposed in contracts casebooks as a "textbook" example of contrasting doctrinal approaches to a legal problem. Students are often asked in notes following the cases to evaluate the relative strengths and weaknesses of the analyses developed by the judges.[4] Treatise and textbook

---

* Excerpted from Alfred S. Konefsky, *Freedom and Interdependence in Twentieth-Century Contract Law: Traynor and Hand and Promissory Estoppel*, 65 U. CIN. L. REV. 1169, 1169-75 (1997) (internal citations omitted).

4. *See, e.g.*, . . . JOHN E. MURRAY, JR., CASES AND MATERIALS ON CONTRACTS 290 (3d ed. 1983) ("In a jurisdiction taking the position urged by Judge Hand, can you draft a provision that would protect the general contractor? In a jurisdiction following the Traynor position, can you draft a provision protecting the subcontractor?"); ROBERT E. SCOTT & DOUGLAS L. LESLIE,

writers, concerned with a higher level of generality and theory, have likewise noted the relationship between the two opinions—commenting that *Drennan* "is inevitably to be contrasted with" *Baird*, or that *Drennan* "made a dramatic departure from the traditional analysis" in *Baird*. . . .

The historical change from Hand's approach to Traynor's analysis focuses on the introduction of the modern innovation of promissory estoppel into the realm of commercial litigation. The conventional interpretation of the rise of promissory estoppel positions it as a primary example of the shift from the "highly individualistic" contract doctrine of the late nineteenth century to a twentieth century contract environment emphasizing an "interventionist, protectionist spirit" leading "to the welfare state and beyond." Under this view, "promissory estoppel is probably best seen as an outgrowth of a more interdependent, community-oriented moral climate. . . ." The norm of "discrete transactions among autonomous actors" is replaced by "integrated exchanges" in which people rely on one another. Therefore, in order to encourage reliance, modern doctrinal devices in contract law have been created stressing the value of "fostering trust between economic actors. Trust is viewed as a moral good, as well as an economic asset. It allows coordination and planning between economic actors and fosters the formation of valuable economic institutions." Historically, "perhaps . . . traditional contract law was adequate to foster the degree of trust society needed in economic activities. Today, an increasingly interdependent society needs to foster trust in a variety of relationships not readily organized through the device of the formal contract."

The presumption, then, is that the triggering mechanism for doctrinal change in twentieth century contract law is the recognition of the concept of "interdependence" in modern capitalist relations. In the aftermath of the Depression, Lon Fuller observed that "with an increasing interdependence among members of society, we may expect to see reliance . . . become increasingly important as a basis of liability."[16] In *Baird*, Learned Hand viewed the commercial transaction at issue through the lens of individualism and formalism. Traynor, however, impatient with the traditional application of individualism to contract law, sought to transform that law by sanctioning the increasingly interdependent activities of marketplace actors. Hand apparently feared that sanctioning such inroads into conventional contract doctrine would inhibit the individual exercise of freedom in a democratic society. Traynor, on the contrary, believed that individual autonomy would be encouraged by freeing economic actors to arrange their transactions in light of an "increasingly" interrelated world. Therefore, Traynor thought that the reliance principle recognized and enhanced individual freedom in an interdependent universe.

Traynor offered a modern doctrinal revision of the ideology of contract law, forged in the late nineteenth and early twentieth centuries, that Hand had

CONTRACT LAW AND THEORY 244 (2d ed. 1993) ("Questions on *Baird* and *Drennan*. Compare the two opinions carefully. Exactly what point of disagreement separates Justice Traynor and Judge Hand?"); EDWARD J. MURPHY & RICHARD E. SPEIDEL, STUDIES IN CONTRACT LAW 409 (4th ed. 1991) ("How does [Justice Traynor] avoid Judge Hand's reasoning in *Baird* ?"); KNAPP & CRYSTAL, supra note 3, at 239 ("Does Justice Traynor in his *Drennan* opinion effectively counter [Judge Hand's] arguments?").

16. Lon Fuller, *Consideration and Form*, 41 COLUM. L REV. 799, 823 (1941).

embraced. Traynor did not entirely reject the individualistic rationale of contract law. Rather, by altering the relationship between freedom and individualism, Traynor sought to insure the survival of individualism and to contribute to its growth by refurbishing the ideology with a current, modern version. Freedom and individualism became compatible with trust, reliance, and interdependence because, in a modern economy, it would be in one's self-interest to behave in this rational, related way rather than in an atomistic manner that pitted everyone against each other. Traynor seems to be treating promissory estoppel not as an idealistic concept derived from altruism and community, nor as an alternative to an individualistic ethic—as some historical accounts would have it—but instead as a modern adaptation or strain of individualism. Although it would be easy to portray Hand as the "formalist" and Traynor as the "progressive," this characterization would miscast the complexities of their ideas. Both believed in the efficacy of legal rules and in the primacy of individual freedom and its attendant responsibilities and opportunities. . . .

I propose to study *Baird* and *Drennan* by addressing the extent to which Traynor specifically focused on reforming Hand's solution to the legal problem in *Baird*. There is internal and external evidence for this claim. Within the cases, for example, Traynor's *Drennan* opinion in 1958 directly uses Hand's language from 1933 in reaching an opposite conclusion. In other words, Traynor carefully selected words that Hand employed and turned the phraseology on its head. I do not think that Traynor's use of Hand's words was accidental. In addition, some of Traynor's opinion is parallel in structure to Hand's organization. Traynor also provides an ideological justification for the result in 1958 that directly repudiates Hand's rationale in defense of the result in *Baird*.

The external evidence that Traynor discarded Hand's mode of analysis stems from Traynor's general attitudes about the relationship between precedent, social change, and legal change. In his extrajudicial writings, as well as in his opinions, Traynor evinced a certain impatience with what he perceived to be roadblocks to effective legal change. Traynor, in fact, indicated not just that the doctrinal result in *Baird* ought to be different, but that a fundamental rethinking of contract law was in order. To Traynor, Hand represented a remnant of the past—the iron rule of formalism. Traynor suggested a new model of contract analysis, and he forthrightly proposed to jettison both the outcome and the reasoning reached by Hand's generation of judges. What better way to accomplish this purpose than to demonstrate that Hand's own language could be used to justify a directly opposite approach and conclusion? More importantly, Traynor wrote about the *Drennan* case on more than one occasion, revealing what he thought the case signified as he detailed its doctrinal contribution and consequences. He was engaged in and defended self-conscious change.

RELEVANT PROVISIONS

For the *Restatement (Second) of Contracts,* consult § 87. For the UCC, consult § 2-205. For the CISG, consult Article 16(2). For the UNIDROIT Principles, consult 2.1.4(2).

NOTES AND QUESTIONS

1. *The Restatement.* The approach of the *Drennan* court has been adopted by the *Restatement (Second) of Contracts* § 87(2).

2. *What happened?* In each of these cases, who sued whom for what? Procedurally, how did the cases get before their respective court? Factually, what happened between the parties? What arguments did the plaintiffs and defendants make? What rule or rules did the court apply? How did each court analyze the dispute between the parties? How did each court decide its respective case?

3. *Which case (if any) was correctly decided?* How would you have resolved the dispute if you were the judge? Were there any arguments not brought up in either of the opinions that you would have made?

4. *Footnote 4.* In the excerpt following *Drennan,* you read that "[s]tudents are often asked in notes following the cases to evaluate the relative strengths and weaknesses of the analyses developed by the judges." Great idea! Rather than rehash those questions here, go back and re-read Footnote 4 and see if you can answer the questions that appear there.

5. *Overcoming the default rule?* In *Baird,* Judge Hand wrote that "[u]nless there are circumstances to take it out of the ordinary doctrine, since the offer was withdrawn before it was accepted, the acceptance was too late." How does plaintiff try to meet this challenge? Are you convinced?

6. *Option contracts.* Why didn't the general contractors in *Baird* and *Drennan* simply protect themselves with an option contract?

7. *Revocability and option contracts.* Because neither party spoke out against the background of silence (see margin note "Interpreting silence," p. 302), do you think the offer in *Baird* should have been revocable, or should the offer in *Drennan* have been irrevocable? Why? Isn't this just an argument about . . .

8. *Default rules.* Which default rule is better: to refuse to imply an option contract, even where there is reliance, as in *Baird,* or to imply an option contract where there is reliance, as in *Drennan*? In answering this, you may find it helpful to consult some of the thinking tools we examined earlier. Which rule, for instance, seems most consistent with the ex ante expectations of the parties? Which seems most consistent with commonly accepted principles of justice? Which would best reduce administrative and transaction costs? Between the contractor and the subcontractor, which party seemed best situated to avoid the risk of the mistake that materialized? How, if at all, should this be taken into account by the courts in setting the default rule?

9. ***Bid shopping.*** Suppose that the general contractor in *Drennan* was awarded the contract, but then decided to shop around for a lower bid. Would the subcontractor have a cause of action for breach of contract against the general? Should it? If not, does that change your intuition about which of the two cases was correctly decided? Does it change your intuition about how the default rule should be structured?

10. ***Counseling.*** After reading *Baird* and *Drennan,* how would you advise a client concerning the submitting and/or accepting of bids? What would you warn them about, and what language would you advise them to use in their communications with one another?

11. ***Drafting exercise.*** In *Baird,* Hand wrote that "[t]he contractors had a ready escape from their difficulty by insisting upon a contract before they used the figures; and in commercial transactions it does not in the end promote justice to seek strained interpretations in aid of those who do not protect themselves." Suppose that, after this decision was handed down, the general contractor asked you, its attorney, to draft a clause that it could include in its future contracts to ensure this didn't happen to them again. What would you write?

12. ***Promissory estoppel.*** We will discuss promissory estoppel in greater depth in the next chapter. For the time being, however, it is enough to know that the general doctrine allows promises to sometimes be enforced without consideration where there is (1) a promise that (2) induces reliance upon which (3) a promisee actually relies if (4) injustice can be prevented only by enforcing the promise. Do you think promissory estoppel was appropriate in *Drennan*? Why or why not? If so, should it have been available in *Baird*?

13. ***Other solutions.*** The introduction to this unit noted that courts and legislatures are sometimes willing to imply an option contract even where there is no consideration. We saw an example of this in *Drennan,* which is also reflected in *Restatement (Second) of Contracts* § 87(2). Another approach is offered by the UCC. According to § 2-205, also called the "firm offer" rule, a merchant who makes an offer to buy or sell goods and promises to leave its offer open in a signed writing will find that its offer is irrevocable "during the stated time or if no time is stated for a reasonable time, but in no event may such period of irrevocability exceed three months." (Pop quiz: if the dispute in *Dickinson v. Dodds* came up today in a state that adopted UCC § 2-205—i.e., anywhere but Louisiana—how, if at all, would the outcome change?) Yet another solution is presented by the CISG and the UNIDROIT Principles (whose language tracks the CISG), as discussed in the excerpt below. As you read it, ask yourself what you think is the best approach to the problem of revocability (e.g., the common law approach, the UCC approach, or the CISG approach).

INTERNATIONAL PERSPECTIVE: FIRM OFFERS AND THE CISG*

Under the common law, an offer is freely revocable, even if the offeror has promised to hold it open, unless that promise is supported by consideration or reliance. The UCC, of course, changes this rule, allowing a merchant to make an irrevocable offer—a "firm offer"—without the need for consideration. But the UCC's firm-offer rule contains a number of restrictions: the offeror must be a merchant; the offer must be in a signed writing; the offer must contain an "assurance that it will be held open"; and the period of irrevocability may not exceed three months.[40]

CISG Article 16 allows an offeror to make a firm offer without these limitations:

> (1) Until a contract is concluded an offer may be revoked if the revocation reaches the offeree before he has dispatched an acceptance.
>
> (2) However, an offer cannot be revoked:
>
> (a) if it indicates, whether by stating a fixed time for acceptance or otherwise, that it is irrevocable; or
>
> (b) if it was reasonable for the offeree to rely on the offer as being irrevocable and the offeree has acted in reliance on the offer.

As one can see, Article 16 does not require that the offeror be a merchant[41] or that the offer be in a signed writing, and there is no limit on the period of irrevocability. Article 16 does not even require an express assurance that the offer will be held open. It requires only that the offer "indicate that it is irrevocable" and it makes clear that an offer may do this "by stating a fixed time for acceptance." If an offer simply stated that it would expire after thirty days, the UCC would not treat the offer as "firm" and would allow the offeror to revoke before the thirty days were up. The CISG, on the other hand, would treat the offer as being irrevocable during the thirty-day period. Article 16(2)(b), like *Restatement (Second)* § 87(2), provides for an offer to become irrevocable because of the offeree's reliance.[41]

Article 16 reflects a compromise between the civil law tradition, which presumes that offers are irrevocable, and the common law tradition, which presumes the opposite. Article 16(1) provides that offers are revocable, as under the common law, but Article 16(2) creates broad exceptions that will lead many offers to be irrevocable in practice.

---

* Excerpted from William S. Dodge, *Teaching the CISG in Contracts,* 50 J. LEGAL EDUC. 72, 80-81 (2000).

40. UCC § 2-205.

41. But one should recall that Article 2's exclusion of consumer goods from the scope of the CISG means that most contracts to which the CISG applies will be between merchants.

43. Article 16(2)(b), unlike *Restatement (Second) of Contracts.* § 87(2) (1981), does not require that the offeree's reliance be "substantial," and the commentary suggests that investigation of an offer may be sufficient to make it irrevocable under the CISG but not under the *Restatement (Second)*.

PROBLEM: BIDDING FOR PERLITE

Brownstein Construction, a general contractor firm, sought bids for a construction project in Pasco County involving large quantities of perlite, a mineral used in roofing insulation. Stewart Linkton, a local subcontracting firm, asked the Pasco County Environmental Lands Division if perlite could be sourced from within Pasco County. The Environmental Lands Division recommended a local source of the mineral located in Seven Springs Quarry. On March 12, 2011, without waiting to hear the price of the perlite, Stewart Linkton began drawing up a bid. On March 16, an agent from Stewart Linkton met a representative from Seven Springs Quarry who quoted the perlite at $3.50 per cubic yard. Stewart Linkton used this figure to complete a bid for Brownstein Construction's project. Accompanying the bid was a bid bond of $24,468. On April 20, the bids on the project closed with Stewart Linkton as the low bid by more than $103,000. The same day the winning bid was announced; Stewart Linkton heard from Seven Springs Quarry that its perlite was no longer available for purchase. Immediately after receiving this news, an agent from Stewart Linkton hand delivered a written withdrawal of the company's bid to Brownstein Construction. On April 25, Brownstein Construction awarded the bid to Stewart Linkton. Stewart Linkton sued to relieve itself of any obligation under the bid and for the return of its bid bond claiming it had withdrawn its bid. Brownstein Construction counter-claimed seeking forfeiture of the bid bond.

Did Stewart Linkton effectively withdraw its bid? If you were the presiding judge in this case, what remedy would you give to Stewart Linkton? To Brownstein Construction?

PROBLEM: DISCOUNTING WAVE RUNNERS

On May 16, 2014, Carlos Monique, a West Palm Beach jet-ski vendor, sent a mailer out to local residents in the West Palm Beach area that had previously purchased from him that he was offering a 10 percent discount on 2013 wave runners. The ad specifically mentioned that the offer was redeemable until June 1, 2014. As a part of the advertisement, the jet-ski vendor included his stylized digital signature at the bottom of the ad. Marissa Delaney, a local resident and jet-skiing enthusiast, received this mailer and was interested in purchasing a discounted jet ski. On May 26, Delaney drove to the jet-ski vendor's store with the mailer with the intent of using the discount to purchase a wave runner. When Delaney arrived at Monique's store, she saw a sign in the window that read, "All discounts on 2013 wave runners have been discontinued." Concerned, Delaney walks into the shop to find Monique. She showed the mailer to Monique and asked about the 10 percent discount. Monique told her that the promotion had been cancelled after too many people had attempted to redeem the discount and it had become unprofitable.

What recourse would Delaney have against the jet-ski vendor under the UCC? If this were an international sale of goods, what recourse would Delaney have under the CISG?

E. CHAPTER CAPSTONE: PUTTING IN ALL TOGETHER

We end this chapter with an incredibly fun (and recent) case that brings together many of the issues and themes we've covered so far. There are no notes at the end; just read it and enjoy. Whenever the court is faced with a new problem, put down your book and ask yourself how you think it should be resolved. Then, when you have your answer, pick up your book and compare your answer with the court's solution.* And finally, don't ignore the footnotes or gloss over the citations within the case. In them, you'll find a treasure trove of interesting and familiar cases, many of which should start to feel like old friends by now.

Kolodziej v. Mason

United States Court of Appeals, Eleventh Circuit
774 F.3d 736 (2014)

WILSON, CIRCUIT JUDGE. This case involves a law student's efforts to form a contract by accepting a "million-dollar challenge" that a lawyer extended on national television while representing a client accused of murder. Since we find that the challenge did not give rise to an enforceable unilateral contract, we hold that the district court properly entered summary judgment for the lawyer and his law firm, Defendants-Appellees James Cheney Mason (Mason) and J. Cheney Mason, P.A., with regard to the breach-of-contract claim brought by the law student, Plaintiff-Appellant Dustin S. Kolodziej.

I.

The current dispute—whether Mason formed a unilateral contract with Kolodziej—arose from comments Mason made while representing criminal defendant Nelson Serrano, who stood accused of murdering his former business partner as well as the son, daughter, and son-in-law of a third business partner. During Serrano's highly publicized capital murder trial, Mason participated in an interview with NBC News in which he focused on the seeming implausibility of the prosecution's theory of the case. Indeed, his client ostensibly had an alibi—on the day of the murders, Serrano claimed to be on a business trip in an entirely different state, several hundred miles away from the scene of the crimes in central Florida. Hotel surveillance video confirmed that Serrano was at a La Quinta Inn (La Quinta) in Atlanta, Georgia, several hours before and after the murders occurred in Bartow, Florida.

However, the prosecution maintained that Serrano committed the murders in an approximately ten-hour span between the times that he was seen on the security camera. According to the prosecution, after being recorded by the

* Incidentally, this is a great way to practice answering the sorts of questions that you may encounter on your final exams.

hotel security camera in the early afternoon, Serrano slipped out of the hotel and, traveling under several aliases, flew from Atlanta to Orlando, where he rented a car, drove to Bartow, Florida, and committed the murders. From there, Serrano allegedly drove to the Tampa International Airport, flew back to Atlanta, and drove from the Atlanta International Airport to the La Quinta, to make an appearance on the hotel's security footage once again that evening.

Mason argued that it was impossible for his client to have committed the murders in accordance with this timeline; for instance, for the last leg of the journey, Serrano would have had to get off a flight in Atlanta's busy airport, travel to the La Quinta several miles away, and arrive in that hotel lobby in only twenty-eight minutes. After extensively describing the delays that would take place to render that twenty-eight-minute timeline even more unlikely,[1] Mason stated, "I challenge anybody to show me, and guess what? Did they bring in any evidence to say that somebody made that route, did so? State's burden of proof. If they can do it, I'll challenge 'em. I'll pay them a million dollars if they can do it."

NBC did not broadcast Mason's original interview during Serrano's trial. At the conclusion of the trial, the jury returned a guilty verdict in Serrano's case. Thereafter, in December 2006, NBC featured an edited version of Mason's interview in a national broadcast of its "Dateline" television program. The edited version removed much of the surrounding commentary, including Mason's references to the State's burden of proof, and Mason's statement aired as, "I challenge anybody to show me—I'll pay them a million dollars if they can do it."

Enter Kolodziej, then a law student at the South Texas College of Law, who had been following the Serrano case. Kolodziej saw the edited version of Mason's interview and understood the statement as a serious challenge, open to anyone, to "make it off the plane and back to the hotel within [twenty-eight] minutes"—that is, in the prosecution's timeline—in return for one million dollars.

Kolodziej subsequently ordered and studied the transcript of the edited interview, interpreting it as an offer to form a unilateral contract—an offer he decided to accept by performing the challenge. In December 2007, Kolodziej recorded himself retracing Serrano's alleged route, traveling from a flight at the Atlanta airport to what he believed was the former location of the now-defunct La Quinta within twenty-eight minutes. Kolodziej then sent Mason a copy of the recording of his journey and a letter stating that Kolodziej had performed

1. For example, Mason noted that, "in Atlanta, depending on which concourse you're landing in, you're going to have to wait to get off the airplane. . . . You got people boxed in—the lady with the kids in the carriage. Or people getting down their bags. Or the fat one can't get down the aisle. I mean, whatever the story is, you've got delays in getting off the airplane. . . . Then you have to go from whatever gate you are, . . . to catch the subway train to the terminal. Wait for that. Wait while it stops in the meantime. People getting on and off. Get to that. Go up again, the escalators. Get to where you're in the terminal, out the terminal to ground transportation. And from there to be on the videotape in 28 minutes."

the challenge and requested payment. Mason responded with a letter in which he refused payment and denied that he made a serious offer in the interview. Kolodziej again demanded payment, and Mason again refused.

Considering Mason's refusal to pay a breach of contract, Kolodziej sued Mason and Mason's law firm, J. Cheney Mason, P.A., in the United States District Court for the Southern District of Texas. Although the court dismissed the case for lack of personal jurisdiction, it was then that Kolodziej discovered the existence of Mason's unedited interview with NBC and learned that Dateline had independently edited the interview before it aired.[2] Kolodziej subsequently filed suit in . . . the Middle District of Florida, where Mason moved for summary judgment.

The district court granted summary judgment on two grounds: first, Kolodziej was unaware of the unedited Mason interview at the time he attempted to perform the challenge, and thus he could not accept an offer he did not know existed; second, the challenge in the unedited interview was unambiguously directed to the prosecution only, and thus Kolodziej could not accept an offer not open to him. The district court declined to address the arguments that Mason's challenge was not a serious offer and that, in any event, Kolodziej did not adequately perform the challenge. This appeal ensued. . . .

III.

The case before us involves the potential creation of an oral, unilateral contract.[3] Under Florida law, the question of whether a valid contract exists is a threshold question of law that may be properly decided by the court.

"To prove the existence of a contract, a plaintiff must plead: (1) offer; (2) acceptance; (3) consideration; and (4) sufficient specification of the essential terms." *Vega v. T-Mobile USA, Inc.*, 564 F.3d 1256, 1272 (11th Cir. 2009). An oral contract is subject to all basic requirements of contract law, and mutual assent is a prerequisite for the formation of any contract.

Mutual assent is not necessarily an independent "element" unto itself; rather, we evaluate the existence of assent by analyzing the parties' agreement process in terms of offer and acceptance.[4] A valid contract—premised on the

---

2. The parties do not dispute that Mason was not involved in any of the editing or broadcast decisions made by the network; that he did not see the program when it aired; and that he was not even aware that Dateline edited his interview until Kolodziej contacted him to demand payment.

3. While most contracts are bilateral, with promises exchanged between two parties, a unilateral contract is, as the name implies, one-sided—one party promises to do something (for example, pay money) in exchange for performance (an act, forbearance, or conduct producing a certain result). . . .

4. The scholarly definitions of an offer reflect this concept by including the integral component of assent. *See, e.g., Corbin on Contracts* § 1.11 (revised ed. 1993) (defining an offer as "an expression by one party of assent to certain definite terms, provided that the other party involved in the bargaining transaction will likewise express assent to the same terms"); *Restatement (Second) of Contracts* § 24 (1981) ("An offer is the manifestation of willingness to enter into a bargain, so made as to justify another person in understanding that his assent to that bargain is invited and will conclude it.").

parties' requisite willingness to contract—may be "manifested through written or spoken words, or inferred in whole or in part from the parties' conduct." *L & H Constr. Co. v. Circle Redmont, Inc.*, 55 So. 3d 630, 634 (Fla. Dist. Ct. App. 2011). We use "an objective test . . . to determine whether a contract is enforceable." *See Robbie v. City of Miami*, 469 So. 2d 1384, 1385 (Fla. 1985); see also *Leonard v. Pepsico, Inc.*, 88 F. Supp. 2d 116, 128 (S.D.N.Y. 1999) (noting that the determination of whether a party made an offer to enter into a contract requires "the [c]ourt to determine how a reasonable, objective person would have understood" the potential offeror's communication).

IV.

We do not find that Mason's statements were such that a reasonable, objective person would have understood them to be an invitation to contract, regardless of whether we look to the unedited interview or the edited television broadcast seen by Kolodziej. Neither the content of Mason's statements, nor the circumstances in which he made them, nor the conduct of the parties reflects the assent necessary to establish an actionable offer—which is, of course, essential to the creation of a contract.

As a threshold matter, the "spoken words" of Mason's purported challenge do not indicate a willingness to enter into a contract. Even removed from its surrounding context, the edited sentence that Kolodziej claims creates Mason's obligation to pay (that is, "I challenge anybody to show me—I'll pay them a million dollars if they can do it") appears colloquial. The exaggerated amount of "a million dollars"—the common choice of movie villains and schoolyard wagerers alike—indicates that this was hyperbole. As the district court noted, "courts have viewed such indicia of jest or hyperbole as providing a reason for an individual to doubt that an 'offer' was serious." *See Kolodziej v. Mason*, 996 F. Supp. 2d 1237, 1252 (M.D. Fla. 2014) (discussing, in dicta, a laughter-eliciting joke made by Mason's co-counsel during the interview). Thus, the very content of Mason's spoken words "would have given any reasonable person pause, considering all of the attendant circumstances in this case." *See id.*

Those attendant circumstances are further notable when we place Mason's statements in context. As Judge Learned Hand once noted, "the circumstances in which the words are used is always relevant and usually indispensable." *N.Y. Trust Co. v. Island Oil & Transp. Corp.*, 34 F.2d 655, 656 (2d Cir. 1929); *see Lefkowitz v. Great Minneapolis Surplus Store, Inc.*, 251 Minn. 188, 86 N.W.2d 689, 691 (1957) (noting that the existence of an offer "depends on the legal intention of the parties and the surrounding circumstances"). Here, Mason made the comments in the course of representing a criminal defendant accused of quadruple homicide and did so during an interview solely related to that representation. Such circumstances would lead a reasonable person to question whether the requisite assent and actionable offer giving rise to contractual liability existed. Certainly, Mason's statements—made as a defense attorney in response to the prosecution's theory against his client—were far more likely to be a descriptive illustration of what that attorney saw as serious holes in the prosecution's theory instead of a serious offer to enter into a contract.

Nor can a valid contract be "inferred in whole or in part from the parties' conduct" in this case. *See L & H Constr. Co.*, 55 So. 3d at 634; *see also Commerce P'ship 8098 LP v. Equity Contracting Co.*, 695 So. 2d 383, 385 (Fla. Dist. Ct. App. 1997) (noting that contracts that have not been "put into promissory words with sufficient clarity" may still be enforceable, but they "rest upon the assent of the parties"). By way of comparison, consider *Lucy v. Zehmer*, 84 S.E.2d 516 (1954), the classic case describing and applying what we now know as the objective standard of assent.[5] That court held that statements allegedly made "in jest" *could* result in an offer binding the parties to a contract, since "the law imputes to a person an intention corresponding to the reasonable meaning of his words and acts." *Id.* at 522. Therefore, "a person cannot set up that he was merely jesting when his conduct and words would warrant a reasonable person in believing that he intended a real agreement." *Id.*

In so holding, the *Lucy* court considered that the offeror wrote, prepared, and executed a writing for sale; the parties engaged in extensive, serious discussion prior to preparing the writing; the offeror prepared a second written agreement, having changed the content of the writing in response to the offeree's request; the offeror had his wife separately sign the writing; and the offeror allowed the offeree to leave with the signed writing without ever indicating that it was in jest. *Id.* at 519-22. Given that these "words and acts, judged by a reasonable standard, manifest[ed] an intention to agree," the offeror's "unexpressed state of . . . mind" was immaterial. *Id.* at 522. Under the objective standard of assent, the *Lucy* court found that the parties had formed a contract. *See id.*

Applying the objective standard here leads us to the real million-dollar question: "What did the party say and do?" *See Newman v. Schiff*, 778 F.2d 460, 464 (8th Cir. 1985). Here, it is what both parties did not say and did not do that clearly distinguishes this case from those cases where an enforceable contract was formed. Mason did not engage in any discussion regarding his statements to NBC with Kolodziej, and, prior to Kolodziej demanding payment, there was no contact or communication between the parties.[6] Mason neither confirmed that he made an offer nor asserted that the offer was serious.[7] Mason did not

---

5. *See, e.g.*, Keith A. Rowley, *You Asked for It, You Got It . . . Toy Yoda: Practical Jokes, Prizes, and Contract Law*, 3 NEV. L.J. 526, 527 & n.7 (2003) (characterizing Lucy v. Zehmer as "[t]he case best known to contemporary American attorneys, judges, and law professors" for the objective assent standard and collecting the plethora of contracts casebooks in which Lucy appears as a principal case).

6. *Cf. Lucy*, 84 S.E.2d at 520-21 (describing the parties' extensive discussion prior to and during the creation of the contract).

7. Compare with *Barnes v. Treece*, where, after seeing news reports that Treece stated he would "put a hundred thousand dollars to anyone to find a crooked board," Barnes telephoned Treece and asked if his earlier statement had been made seriously. 549 P.2d 1152, 1154 (1976). Treece "assured Barnes that the statement had been made seriously [and] advised Barnes that the statement was firm." *Id.* Thus, the trial court found that "Treece's statements before the gambling commission and reiterated to Barnes personally on the telephone constituted a valid offer for a unilateral contract." *Id.*; *see also Newman*, 778 F.2d at 463, 466 (finding that the confirmative statement, "I did make an offer," was pertinent to the question of whether a rebroadcast of an offer also constituted an offer).

have the payment set aside in escrow;[8] nor had he ever declared that he had money set aside in case someone proved him wrong.[9] Mason had not made his career out of the contention that the prosecution's case was implausible;[10] nor did he make the statements in a commercial context for the "obvious purpose of advertising or promoting [his] goods or business."[11] He did not create or promote the video that included his statement, nor did he increase the amount at issue.[12] He did not, nor did the show include, any information to contact Mason about the challenge.[13] Simply put, Mason's conduct lacks any indicia of assent to contract.[14]

In fact, none of Mason's surrounding commentary—either in the unedited original interview or in the edited television broadcast—gave the slightest

---

8. In the seminal case of *Carlill v. Carbolic Smoke Ball Co.*, which found that an advertisement can constitute an offer to form a unilateral contract, the same advertisement promising the reward included the statement: "£1000 is deposited with the Alliance Bank, Regent Street, shewing our sincerity in the matter." (1892) 2 Q.B. 484, 484-85, *aff'd*, (1893) 1 Q.B. 256 (Eng.); see also *Barnes*, 549 P.2d at 1154 ("[Treece] informed Barnes that the $100,000 was safely being held in escrow.").

9. *Cf. James v. Turilli*, 473 S.W.2d 757, 761 (Mo. Ct. App. 1971). In *James*, Turilli stated before a nationwide television audience that Jesse James didn't die in 1882 and that Turilli "would pay Ten Thousand Dollars ($10,000.00) to anyone . . . who could prove [him] wrong." *Id.* at 759 (internal quotation marks omitted). In finding that this constituted an offer, the court noted that, in addition to other evidence, Turilli had previously said that he had a "certified check of ten thousand dollars" to be collected upon proof that Jesse James had actually died in 1882. *Id.* at 761.

10. In *Newman*, a "self-styled 'tax rebel,'" who "made a career and substantial profits out of his tax protest activities" and "promoted his books by appearing on over five hundred radio and television programs," 778 F.2d at 461-62, made a valid, time-limited offer when, in a live television appearance, he stated, "If anybody calls this show . . . and cites any section of this Code that says an individual is required to file a tax return, I will pay them $100,000," *id.* at 462 (internal quotation marks omitted); *see also James*, 473 S.W.2d at 761 (noting that "[Turilli] had virtually made a career out of his contention Jesse W. James was not killed in 1882").

11. *Rosenthal v. Al Packer Ford, Inc.*, 374 A.2d 377, 379 (1977). Here, any promotional benefit that Mason might have received by appearing in the interview was incidental, not the "obvious purpose." Rather, his televised appearance and his statements were on behalf of his client and went to the implausibility of the prosecution's case against his client. Further, even a commercial advertisement will generally constitute an offer only when it is "clear, definite, and explicit, and leaves nothing open for negotiation." *See Lefkowitz*, 86 N.W.2d at 691.

12. Compare with *Augstein v. Leslie*, where, in YouTube videos, news articles, and online postings on social media, Leslie stated he would pay a reward to anyone who returned his stolen laptop, gradually increasing the sum to one million dollars. No. 11 Civ. 7512, 2012 WL 4928914, *2-3 (S.D.N.Y. Oct. 17, 2012). Given the increase in the offer amount, the value of the property lost, and Leslie's postings, the court found that "Leslie's videos and other activities together [were] best characterized as an offer for a reward." *Id.* at *2.

13. *Cf. Newman*, 778 F.2d at 462. During Schiff's live interview on national television program, wherein Schiff made statements constituting an offer, "[t]he words 'Nightwatch Phone-In' and the telephone number [for the show] were flashed on the screen periodically during Schiff's appearance. In addition, [the interviewer] repeated the telephone number and encouraged viewers to call and speak directly with Schiff on the air." *Id.*

14. Correspondingly, in *Leonard v. Pepsico, Inc.*, Pepsi's advertisement of a Harrier Fighter jet for 7,000,000 "Pepsi Points" did not result in a valid offer or enforceable contract because "no reasonable, objective person would have understood the commercial to make a serious offer." 88 F. Supp. 2d at 130-31.

indication that his statement was anything other than a figure of speech. In the course of representing his client, Mason merely used a rhetorical expression to raise questions as to the prosecution's case. We could just as easily substitute a comparable idiom such as "I'll eat my hat" or "I'll be a monkey's uncle" into Mason's interview in the place of "I'll pay them a million dollars," and the outcome would be the same. We would not be inclined to make him either consume his headwear or assume a simian relationship were he to be proven wrong; nor will we make him pay one million dollars here.[15]

Additionally, an enforceable contract requires mutual assent as to sufficiently definite essential terms. *See Tiara Condo. Ass'n v. Marsh & McLennan Cos.*, 607 F.3d 742, 746 (11th Cir. 2010), *certified question answered,* 110 So. 3d 399 (Fla. 2013) ("Under Florida law, a claim for breach of an oral contract arises only when the parties mutually assented to a certain and definite proposition and left no essential terms open."); *Holloway v. Gutman*, 707 So. 2d 356, 357 (Fla. Dist. Ct. App. 1998) ("Whether a contract is oral or written, it is essential that the parties mutually agree upon the material terms."). Here, even the proper starting and ending points for Mason's purported challenge were unspecified and indefinite; Kolodziej had to speculate and decide for himself what constituted the essential terms of the challenge. For instance, in the prosecution's theory of the case, Serrano, using an alias, was seated in the coach section of an aircraft loaded with over one hundred other passengers. Kolodziej, however, purchased a front row aisle seat in first class and started the twenty-eight-minute countdown from that prime location. Comparably, Kolodziej did not finish his performance in the La Quinta lobby; rather, Kolodziej ended the challenge at an EconoLodge, which, based on anecdotal information, he believed was the former location of the La Quinta in which Serrano stayed.

We highlight these differences not to comment as to whether Kolodziej adequately performed the challenge—which the parties dispute for a multitude of additional reasons—but instead to illustrate the lack of definiteness and specificity in any purported offer (and absence of mutual assent thereto). It is challenging to point to anything Mason said or did that evinces a "display of willingness to enter into a contract on specified terms, made in a way that would lead a reasonable person to understand that an acceptance, having been sought, will result in a binding contract." *See Black's Law Dictionary* 1189 (9th ed. 2009) (defining "offer" in contract law); *see also Tiara Condo. Ass'n*, 607

15. However, unenforceable is not quite the same as "unlitigable," since some people might still take such a challenge literally. For example, Donald Trump recently sued Bill Maher for breach of contract after Maher stated on national television that he would offer five million dollars to Trump, donatable to the charity of Trump's choice, if Trump proved that he was not the spawn of an orangutan. *See* Compl., *Trump v. Maher*, No. BC499537 (Cal. Sup. Ct. filed Feb. 4, 2013), available at http://pmcdeadline2.files.wordpress.com/2013/02/trump-maher_130205003242.pdf. Trump claimed to accept this offer by providing a copy of his birth certificate as proof of his non-orangutan origin, filing suit when Maher did not respond to his demand for payment. Trump later voluntarily dismissed the suit.

F.3d at 746. Therefore, we conclude that Mason did not manifest the requisite willingness to contract through his words or conduct, and no amount of subsequent effort by Kolodziej could turn Mason's statements into an actionable offer.

In further illustration of the lack of assent to contract in this case, we question whether even Kolodziej's conduct—his "acceptance"—manifested assent to any perceived offer. Under the objective standard of assent, we do not look into the subjective minds of the parties; the law imputes an intention that corresponds with the reasonable meaning of a party's words and acts. *See Lucy*, 84 S.E.2d at 522. We thus find it troublesome that, in all this time—ordering the transcript, studying it, purchasing tickets, recording himself making the trip—Kolodziej never made any effort to contact Mason to confirm the existence of an offer, to ensure any such offer was still valid after Serrano's conviction, or to address the details and terms of the challenge.[16] However, we will not attribute bad intent when inexperience may suffice. Kolodziej may have learned in his contracts class that acceptance by performance results in an immediate, binding contract and that notice may not be necessary, but he apparently did not consider the absolute necessity of first having a specific, definite offer and the basic requirement of mutual assent. We simply are driven to ask, as Mason did in his response letter: "Why did you not just call?" Perhaps a jurist's interpretation of an old aphorism provides the answer: "If, as Alexander Pope wrote, 'a little learning is a dangerous thing,' then a little learning in law is particularly perilous."[17]

V.

Finally, summary judgment was procedurally appropriate in this case. Mason's spoken words, the circumstances in which those words were said, and the parties' conduct are all undisputed, and we find "no genuine issue as to whether the parties' conduct implied a contractual understanding." *See Bourque v. F.D.I.C.*, 42 F.3d 704, 708 (1st Cir. 1994) (affirming district court's grant of summary judgment when the "words and actions that allegedly formed a contract" are "so clear themselves that reasonable people could not differ over their meaning").

---

16. This is additionally problematic considering the timeline of events. The murders took place in 1997; the interview, trial, conviction, sentencing, and broadcast of the edited interview all occurred in 2006. Yet Kolodziej claims to have accepted Mason's "offer" by attempting the challenge in 2007, a year after the trial had concluded and the sentence had been returned. These factors raise serious doubts as to whether Kolodziej could even accept the purported offer, given that offers must be accepted within a reasonable time and Mason's client had already been convicted. *See* 1 *Williston on Contracts* § 5:7 (4th ed.) (observing that, although offers of reward generally do not lapse for a substantial length of time, the reasonable-time analysis requires "taking into account the circumstances surrounding any particular offer"). A reasonable person would have had, at a minimum, hesitations as to whether any actionable offer had lapsed.

17. Chief Judge Gilbert in *Ginn v. Farley*, 43 Md. App. 229, 403 A.2d 858, 859 (1979) (quoting Alexander Pope, *An Essay on Criticism*, Part II, line 15 (n.p. 1711)).

As the district court noted, "'It is basic contract law that one cannot suppose, believe, suspect, imagine or hope that an offer has been made.'" *Kolodziej,* 996 F. Supp. 2d at 1251 [internal citations omitted]; *see Lucy,* 84 S.E.2d at 522 ("[T]he law imputes to a person an intention corresponding to the reasonable meaning of his words and acts."). No reasonable person and no reasonable juror would think, absent any other indicia of seriousness, that Mason manifested willingness to enter into a contract in either the unedited interview or the edited broadcast relied upon by Kolodziej. Accordingly, Kolodziej cannot establish the basic requirements for contract formation. With no assent, there is no actionable offer; with no offer, there is no enforceable contract. *See Gibson v. Courtois,* 539 So. 2d 459, 460 (Fla. 1989) ("Absent mutual assent, neither the contract nor any of its provisions come into existence."). Thus, Kolodziej's breach-of-contract claim was appropriately dismissed on summary judgment.[18]

VI.

Just as people are free to contract, they are also free *from* contract, and we find it neither prudent nor permissible to impose contractual liability for offhand remarks or grandstanding. Nor would it be advisable to scrutinize a defense attorney's hyperbolic commentary for a hidden contractual agenda, particularly when that commentary concerns the substantial protections in place for criminal defendants. Having considered the content of Mason's statements, the context in which they were made, and the conduct of the parties, we do not find it reasonable to conclude that Mason assented to enter into a contract with anyone for one million dollars. We affirm the district court's judgment in favor of Mason and J. Cheney Mason, P.A.

---

18. Because we find that Mason's statements in these circumstances do not constitute an enforceable contractual offer, regardless of which version of the statements is considered, we need not address Kolodziej's additional arguments with regard to the district court's reasoning. . . .

CHAPTER 4

ENFORCEABILITY

PROMISES AND AGREEMENTS
Is there a promise or agreement?

ENFORCEABILITY
Is it enforceable?

- A. Bargain-Based Contracts: The Doctrine of Consideration
- B. Reliance-Based Contracts: The Doctrine of Promissory Estoppel
- C. Benefit-Based Contracts: The Doctrine of Unjust Enrichment

REMEDIES
How will it be enforced?

INTERPRETATION
What does it mean?

PERFORMANCE AND BREACH
Has it been performed?

DEFENSES
Can performance be avoided?

THIRD PARTIES
Does it affect third parties?

In "Introduction to Enforceability" (Part II.2.C, *supra*), we examined some of the most important justifications for enforcing promises, looked at how common law courts came to enforce promises historically, and learned how judges apply the doctrine of consideration to decide whether to enforce promises. In this chapter, which is divided into three main parts, we will examine the principles of enforceability in greater detail.

In Section A, we will pick up where we left off, taking a closer look at the bargain-based theory of promissory liability as enshrined in the doctrine of consideration. Additionally, we will examine some of the doctrine's potential shortcomings, such as its attempt to (1) distinguish between bargains and gifts, (2) identify valid and invalid forms of consideration, and (3) provide a sensible set of rules to govern contract modification.

Then, in Section B, we will consider the reliance-based theory of promissory liability as enshrined in the doctrine of promissory estoppel. This doctrine has probably made the most significant contribution to contract law in the twentieth century. In the materials below, we will see why, witnessing the evolution of the doctrine of promissory estoppel in new and interesting ways—primarily to meet many of the shortcomings associated with the doctrine of consideration, but creating some new problems along the way.

Finally, in Section C, we will turn our attention to the benefit-based theory of promissory liability exemplified by the doctrine of unjust enrichment. Unlike promissory estoppel, the doctrine of unjust enrichment is not a new development, and has ancient roots planted deeply in the sands of time. However, even here, there are some exciting new developments that have come out of the recent publication of the *Restatement (Third) of Restitution and Unjust Enrichment*, many of which we will explore in greater detail below, and some of which promise (or threaten, depending on one's view) to change some fundamental aspects of contract law in the years to come. Time will tell.

It is important to note that each of these three major theories that we will discuss is designed to provide courts with a distinctive method for determining whether a particular promise or set of promises ought to be enforced. The important question of *how* these promises are to be enforced, however, with respect to the types of remedies that may be available to an aggrieved party, will be taken up in the next chapter.

The excerpt below outlines (in rough form) each of the three major theories of promissory liability that will be discussed in this chapter. As you read it (and the other materials in this chapter), ask yourself whether you find the justifications for enforcing or refusing to enforce particular types of promises to be compelling. Are there other (perhaps better) justifications the courts may be overlooking? Which ones, and why?

THREE THEORIES OF PROMISSORY LIABILITY*

[T]o understand [the theory of contractual and promissory liability] it is necessary at the outset to distinguish three situations in which contracts may be held legally binding, or promises may be found morally binding:

(1) In the first situation a contract or promise may be found binding after a price has been paid for it. For example, a person may borrow £100 from a friend and may simultaneously promise to repay it. In this situation there would, both legally and morally, be a liability to repay even if there were no promise. The promise may, indeed, be said to be "implied" but my contention is that in this situation the primary justification for imposing a legal or moral obligation on the party borrowing the money is that he has received a benefit at the expense of the other party, and that is, in a property-owning society, usually sufficient to establish a liability. I express this conclusion by saying that the liability is benefit-based in this type of case; it could also be said to arise from broad notions of unjust enrichment. If it should be asked what is the function of the promise in such circumstances, one answer might be that the promise has evidentiary value. It is evidence that the promisor has received a benefit (for if it was not a benefit would he have promised to pay for it?) and it may be evidence of many ancillary matters such as the precise terms of the arrangement, the date of repayment and so on.

(2) In the second situation, a contract or promise may be enforced where the promisee has acted in reliance on the promise, or on the promisor's conduct, and would in consequence be in a worse situation than if no promise had ever been made. The case of a simple loan discussed above may, of course, also be a case of such action in reliance, for the lender may only have lent his money in reliance on the borrower's promise to repay. But cases of action in reliance may arise without any element of benefit or unjust enrichment. In the law, a common example is to be found in the typical contract of guarantee, as where A promises to guarantee repayment of a loan to be made by B to C. In this situation if B acts in reliance on the guarantee, he will lend money to C and may (if C is himself not good for the money) thus make his position worse than it would be if there had been no promise. In my terminology I would refer to liability in such a case as reliance-based. As in the previous case, I suggest that many forms of reliance-based liability arise, or would arise even in the absence of a promise. The party relying may be relying, not on a promise, but on other words, or mere conduct. Such reliance is commonplace in modern societies and often gives rise to liabilities even in the absence of a promise. For instance, a person who buys a new house, in reliance on the proper performance by the local authority of its duties of ensuring compliance with the Building Regulations, may have remedy against the authority for malperformance even though they give no promise. Here again, as with benefit-based liability, the result may be justified or explained by saying that there is an "implied" promise. But it will be observed that in such circumstances the liability comes first, and the implication is made subsequently to justify the decision already arrived at. Once the liability itself is well established (whether in law or in social custom) it is easy to make the implication. But in the first instance, it is the conduct of one party,

* Excerpted from P.S. ATIYAH, THE RISE AND FALL OF FREEDOM OF CONTRACT 1-4 (1979).

followed by the action in reliance of the other, which creates the liability. As with the case of benefit-based liability, it is likely that an actual, express promise, will serve a useful evidentiary role in reliance-based liability. Whether the party acting did in fact rely on the other (or, for example, on his own judgment) and if so, whether in so acting, he acted reasonably by the standards of the society in question, are questions whose answer may be greatly assisted by the presence of an express promise. But again, it does not follow that it is the promise which creates the liability.

(3) The third situation concerns a promise or a contract which has not been paid for, and which has not yet been relied upon. In the law such a contract or promise would be called "wholly executory." If such a promise or contract generates any liability, the liability must be promise-based, since it cannot be benefit-based or reliance-based. In the first two cases, distinct grounds exist for imposing the liability, apart altogether from the promise. In this case, no such distinct grounds exist. If the promise is held to be "binding" or to create some liability, it must be for some reason which is inherent in the promise itself. The principal grounds which (it is suggested) can be found for imposing such liability in this case are these. First, it may be said that a promise, even while executory, creates expectations, and that these expectations will be disappointed if the promise is not performed. In this sense, there is a similarity between a promise-based and a reliance-based liability. The promise whose expectations are disappointed may feel he is worse off that he would have been if no promise had been made at all. Psychologically this may be true; but in a pecuniary sense, it is not. The party who acts in reliance may spend money which he would lose if he could not claim recompense from the party on whose conduct he relied. But the promisee who has not yet acted in reliance on a promise, and not yet paid any price for it, will not be worse off in a pecuniary sense merely because his expectations are disappointed.

Secondly, it may be said that contracts and promises are essentially risk-allocation devices, like simple bets. The nature of this device is such that the transaction must generally remain executory prior to the occurrence of the risk, and the whole point of the transaction would be lose if the arrangement could not be made binding for the future.

The third possible ground for the enforcement of executory promises or contracts is that it may be desirable to uphold the *principle* of promissory liability, even in cases where the non-performance of the promise has little practical effect. The argument here comes to this, that if executory promises are held binding (whether in law or in social custom and morality) then people are more likely to perform promises which have been paid for, or relied upon.

Now it will be seen that many promises and contracts are likely to be wholly executory at the outset, but may quickly pass into one or other of the first two situations discussed above. A promise may be given which is at first executory, and only subsequently is it acted upon by the promisee, or paid for by the promisee. . . . I suggest that once this happens, the ground for imposing a liability shifts. The liability becomes benefit-based or reliance-based, where it was previously promise-based. . . . If benefit-based and reliance-based liabilities are taken as the paradigm cases of obligation, whether legal or moral, it may be suggested that promise-based liabilities are neither paradigmatic nor of central importance. Far from being the typical case of obligation, a promise-based liability may be a projection of liabilities normally based on benefit or reliance. Because these are normally found such powerful grounds for imposing obligations, it has been thought that the element of promise (express or implied) which is often combined with benefit-based and reliance-based liability, is itself the ground for the obligation. And from this, it has been an easy move to the inference that promise-based liability, even without any element of benefit or reliance, carries its own justification.

A. BARGAIN-BASED CONTRACTS: THE DOCTRINE OF CONSIDERATION

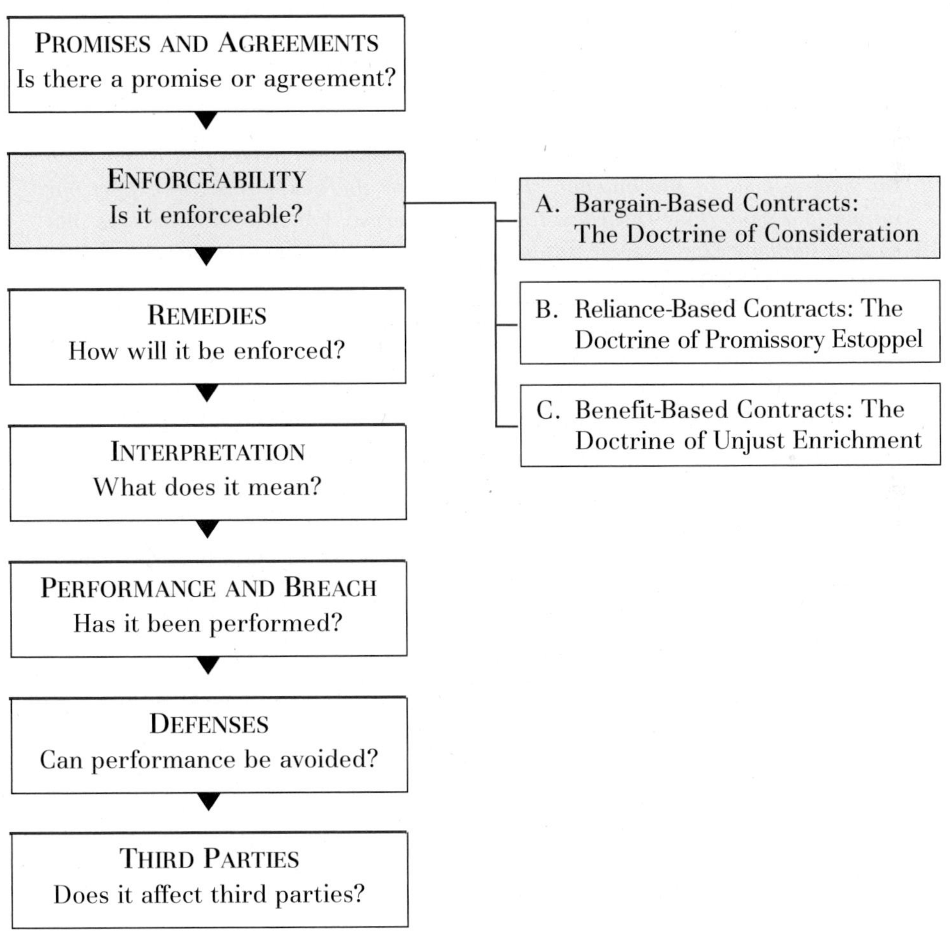
PROMISES AND AGREEMENTS
Is there a promise or agreement?
ENFORCEABILITY
Is it enforceable?
REMEDIES
How will it be enforced?
INTERPRETATION
What does it mean?
PERFORMANCE AND BREACH
Has it been performed?
DEFENSES
Can performance be avoided?
THIRD PARTIES
Does it affect third parties?
A. Bargain-Based Contracts: The Doctrine of Consideration
B. Reliance-Based Contracts: The Doctrine of Promissory Estoppel
C. Benefit-Based Contracts: The Doctrine of Unjust Enrichment

> *Learned Americans are still engaged from time to time in valiant efforts to reduce the common-law rules of contract, and the doctrine of consideration in particular, to strict logical consistency. That quest is, in my humble judgment, misconceived. Legal rules exist not for their own sake, but to further justice and convenience in the business of human life; dialectic is the servant of their purpose, not their master. Reasonableness, no doubt, is the ideal of the common law; and the words "reason" and "logic" go back to Latin and Greek words of like or nearly like original import; nevertheless the field of reason, as we understand it in English, includes many things outside strict logical deduction. One could say more of this, but it would be superfluous for the greater part of English readers.*
>
> Pollock, PRINCIPLES OF CONTRACT x-xi (9th ed. 1921)

1. Consideration and the Bargain Principle: Distinguishing Bargains from Gifts

> *Whoever offers to another a bargain of any kind, proposes to do this. Give me that which I want, and you shall have this which you want, is the meaning of every such offer; and it is in this manner that we obtain from one another the far greater part of those good offices which we stand in need of. It is not from the benevolence of the butcher, the brewer, or the baker that we expect our dinner, but from their regard to their own interest. We address ourselves, not to their humanity but to their self-love, and never talk to them of our own necessities but of their advantages.*
>
> Adam Smith, WEALTH OF NATIONS, Book I, Chapter 2 (1776)

In this subsection you will be introduced to some of the justifications for enforcing promises, learn about the history of promissory enforcement, and become familiar with the doctrine of consideration, which is the doctrine most frequently used by common law courts to determine whether a particular promise should or should not be enforced. In addition, you will learn how to distinguish bargains from gifts, analyze the adequacy of consideration, become familiar with the concepts of past and moral consideration, and learn the rules governing contract modification. As you read the materials below, ask yourself whether you think the purpose of contract law should be to facilitate bargains that move resources to higher valued uses, consistent with Adam Smith's understanding of bargain, or whether it should more broadly encompass other types of promises as well.

Hamer v. Sidway

Court of Appeals of New York
27 N.E. 256 (1891)

For a report of the case and accompanying materials, see p. 93, *supra*.

RELEVANT PROVISIONS

For the *Restatement (Second) of Contracts*, consult §§ 17, 71, 79(a), and 81.

DOCTRINAL OVERVIEW: THE BARGAIN TEST OF CONSIDERATION*

Among the limitations on the enforcement of promises, the most fundamental is the requirement of consideration. For a time during the nineteenth century a "will theory," under which a promise was enforceable because the promisor had "willed" to be bound by the promise, was prevalent. But that notion was to give way to one based on bargain. We have already seen how, out of the common law action of assumpsit [and reflected in cases like *Hamer v. Sidway*], it came to be required that the promisee give something in exchange for the promise that is either a detriment to the promisee or a benefit to the promisor. By the end of the nineteenth century, at least in the United States, the traditional requirement that the consideration be either a benefit to the promisor or a detriment to the promisee had begun to be replaced by a requirement that the consideration be "bargained for." At first it was said that the benefit or detriment had to be bargained for. But when the first *Restatement of Contracts* was promulgated in 1933, it defined *consideration* with no mention of benefit or detriment, exclusively in terms of bargain.[5] The *Restatement Second* does the same and adds a definition. Something is said to be bargained for "if it is sought by the promisor in exchange for his promise and is given by the promisee in exchange for that promise."[6]

It should be noted that testing a promise's enforceability on the basis of bargain might put pressure on transactions occurring outside of the marketplace, and especially on those that take place in a family setting. An example of such a transaction can be seen in our next principal case, *Kirksey v. Kirksey*. As you read it, ask yourself whether you think the promise should be enforceable, and, if so, on what basis. If you haven't already done so, you may find it helpful to review the materials in the "Introduction to Enforceability" unit (p. 67, *supra*) at this time.

Kirksey v. Kirksey

Supreme Court of Alabama
8 Ala. 131 (1845)

The plaintiff was the wife of defendant's brother, but had for some time been a widow, and had several children. In 1840, the plaintiff resided on public land, under a contract of lease, she had held over, and was comfortably settled, and

* Excerpted from E. ALLAN FARNSWORTH, CONTRACTS § 2.2 (4th ed. 2004).

5. RESTATEMENT FIRST § 75.

6. RESTATEMENT SECOND § 71. *See* § 3 (defining "bargain"), § 79 (stating that if the requirement of consideration is met, there is no further requirement of "benefit to the promisor" or "detriment to the promisee"). The Uniform Commercial Code has no comparable provision.

would have attempted to secure the land she lived on. The defendant resided in Talladega County, some sixty, or seventy miles off. On the 10th October, 1840, he wrote to her the following letter:

> Dear sister Antillico—Much to my mortification, I heard, that brother Henry was dead, and one of his children. I know that your situation is one of grief, and difficulty. You had a bad chance before, but a great deal worse now. I should like to come and see you, but cannot with convenience at present. . . . I do not know whether you have a preference on the place you live on, or not. If you had, I would advise you to obtain your preference, and sell the land and quit the country, as I understand it is very unhealthy, and I know society is very bad. If you will come down and see me, I will let you have a place to raise your family, and I have more open land than I can tend; and on the account of your situation, and that of your family, I feel like I want you and the children to do well.

Within a month or two after the receipt of this letter, the plaintiff abandoned her possession, without disposing of it, and removed with her family, to the residence of the defendant, who put her in comfortable houses, and gave her land to cultivate for two years, at the end of which time he notified her to remove, and put her in a house, not comfortable, in the woods, which he afterwards required her to leave.

A verdict being found for the plaintiff, for two hundred dollars, the above facts were agreed, and if they will sustain the action, the judgment is to be affirmed, otherwise it is to be reversed. . . .

Sufficient consideration?

Based on our discussion of the benefit-detriment test of consideration in *Hamer v. Sidway*, or the bargain-based test of *Restatement (Second) of Contracts* § 71, do you agree with Judge Ormond, the dissenting judge (see Note 1 below), that there is sufficient consideration to support the defendant's promise? Why or why not? Would it matter which test you used?

ORMOND, J. The inclination of my mind, is, that **the loss and inconvenience, which the plaintiff sustained in breaking up, and moving to the defendant's, a distance of sixty miles, is a sufficient consideration to support the promise**, to furnish her with a house, and land to cultivate, until she could raise her family. My brothers, however think, that the promise on the part of the defendant, was a mere gratuity, and that an action will not lie for its breach.

The judgment of the Court below must therefore be reversed, pursuant to the agreement of the parties.

NOTES AND QUESTIONS

1. *A note on reading* Kirksey. Note that Judge Ormond, who believes that there is sufficient consideration to support defendant's promise, is actually dissenting from the majority, who believes that defendant's promise was "a mere gratuity." Who has the better argument, Judge Ormond or the majority? Why?

2. *What happened?* Who sued whom for what? Procedurally, how did the case get before this court? Factually, what happened between the parties?

What arguments did the plaintiff and defendant make? What rule or rules did the court apply? How did the court analyze the dispute between the parties? How did the court decide the case?

3. *Was this case correctly decided?* Do you agree with the result reached in this case? Why or why not? Do you agree with the court's reasoning? Why or why not? How, if at all, would you have written the opinion differently?

4. *Do you agree with the court?* Suppose it is true that defendant's promise was "a mere gratuity." Should it follow that a court should refuse to enforce it? Should courts only enforce promises that are "bargained for," or promises leading to a promisor-based benefit or a promisee-based detriment? Why or why not?

5. *Why the hostility to gratuitous promises?* Why do you think common law courts have traditionally been reluctant to enforce gratuitous promises? Perhaps, as Kessler, Gilmore, and Kronman have argued, courts are concerned that these "promises are often made impulsively and with little reflection." Or perhaps, reflecting an idea we explored earlier,* courts are worried about the fact that "[t]he administrative cost of determining the existence of an informal gift promise may be great, and the possibilities of error substantial." "Finally," conclude the authors, "it has been argued that legal enforcement either would decrease the quantity of donative promises, or would have little effect on the accuracy and reliability of such promises."† Are you convinced?

6. *Distinguishing bargain from gift.* Because courts traditionally drew such a hard line between bargains and gifts, it is important not only to look at *what* the promisor did, but *why* the promisor did it. Recall, for instance, the uncle's promise in *Hamer v. Sidway*. Because the uncle promised his nephew money to induce his nephew to change his behavior, even modern courts could find a bargain. Had the uncle instead promised his nephew the same amount of money "to be nice," however, the promise would have been unenforceable as "a mere gratuity." See, for instance, Illustration 2 of the *Restatement (Second) of Contracts* § 24, which provides the following example: "A promises B $100 if B goes to college. If the circumstances give B reason to know that A is not undertaking to pay B to go to college but is promising a gratuity, there is no offer."

The first few paragraphs of the next opinion are a little rough going, but it's a short case, and once you get to defendant's counterclaim, you'll know why it was included. This brings us to the following: Do you think the promise below was not enforced because it was not bargained for, or perhaps because there are certain bargains that courts won't enforce? How can you tell?

* *See* "Thinking Tool: Administrative Costs and Standards v. Rules" in Part II.2.B, *supra*.

† Kessler, Gilmore, and Kronman, Contracts: Cases and Materials (3d ed. 1986).

Whitten v. Greeley-Shaw

Supreme Judicial Court of Maine
520 A.2d 1307 (1987)

NICHOLS, JUSTICE. On appeal the Defendant, Shirley C. Greeley-Shaw, contends that the Superior Court (Cumberland County) committed error when it entered judgment against her upon a **promissory note** in favor of the Plaintiff, George D. Whitten, in a foreclosure action, and when the court refused to recognize a certain writing entered into by the parties as a valid contract, that writing being the basis of the Defendant's counterclaim.

> **Promissory note**
>
> "An unconditional written promise, signed by the maker, to pay absolutely and in any event a certain sum of money either to, or to the order of, the bearer or a designated person." BLACK'S LAW DICTIONARY (10th ed. 2014).

We reject both of the Defendant's claims of error and deny the appeal.

The Defendant's first claim of error originates from the foreclosure action brought by the Plaintiff. . . . As assignee of a promissory note secured by a mortgage deed of a home in Harpswell, he sought to foreclose due to the Defendant's failure to pay any portion of the $64,000.00 long since overdue him on the promissory note. The Defendant alleged that she was the owner of the home, that it was given to her by the Plaintiff as an incident of their four-year romantic relationship, and as assistance toward her efforts to start life anew with her fiancee. While the Defendant admits to having executed both the promissory note and the mortgage deed in favor of the Plaintiff's assignor, she argues that neither the Plaintiff, nor his attorney (who was the assignor), had informed her of what the documents were that she was signing, their legal significance, or that she would be responsible for annual payments on the note. She claims that it was not until a week later, when photocopying the documents, that she thoroughly examined them and realized their legal significance. Not until the foreclosure action was commenced, however, did she make known to the Plaintiff her misunderstanding.

The Plaintiff asserts that at all times the funds he advanced to the Defendant to purchase the home was in the form of a loan, and that both he and his attorney made this clear to the Defendant. He testified that he had encouraged her to purchase a home in Maine and that he originally had his attorney's name on the deed and note to save himself possible embarrassment.

While she alleges facts that might possibly give rise to claims of misrepresentation or breach of fiduciary duty, the Defendant does not expressly claim either ground for relief. Based upon evidence adduced at trial, that included the deposition of a second attorney who actually conducted the closing, there was ample evidence to support the finding of the Superior Court that the Defendant was aware of the nature of the documents and her legal responsibilities, and entered into the contract voluntarily. It is to no avail that the Defendant objects to the contents of a contract, that she admits she "barely looked at," despite having been given the opportunity, and indeed encouragement, to read.

Emerging as a counterclaim to the Plaintiff's foreclosure action is the Defendant's request that the court enforce the terms of a written "agreement" entered into by the parties. The parties had engaged in an intermittent extramarital affair from 1972 until March, 1980. At the time of this writing the Plaintiff, a Massachusetts contractor, had travelled to his Bermuda home to vacation with friends, and expected to soon be joined there by his wife. The precise facts surrounding the creation of the agreement are in dispute. However, it is the testimony of the Defendant that she wanted to have "something in writing" because of all the past promises to her that she said the Plaintiff had broken. She testified that the Plaintiff told her, "You figure out what you want and I will sign it." She added that she unilaterally drew up the "agreement" while in Bermuda, and the Plaintiff signed it without objection. There was an original and a copy, and only he signed the original.

On his part the Plaintiff testified that he had agreed to visit with the Defendant, who had come to his Bermuda home uninvited, because "[S]he demanded I see her or she would come up and raise hell with my friends" and embarrass him in front of his wife.

Basically, the "agreement" is a one-page typewritten document, prepared by the Defendant, that begins "I, George D. Whitten . . . agree to the following conditions made by Mrs. Shirley C. Shaw . . ." and then goes on to list four "conditions" required of the Plaintiff. The "conditions" require the Plaintiff to make payments to the Defendant of $500.00 per month for an indeterminate period, make any "major repairs" to the Harpswell home, pay for any medical needs, take one trip with the Defendant and supply her with one piece of jewelry per year, and visit and phone the Defendant at various stated intervals. The only "condition" that approaches the recital of a promise or duty of the Defendant is the statement "[U]nder no circumstances will there be any calls made to my homes or offices without prior permission from me."

The Plaintiff contends that, *inter alia*, this writing is unenforceable because of a lack of consideration. The Defendant argues that the writing is enforceable because there is the necessary objective manifestation of assent on each side, supported by the "stated" consideration of the Defendant not to call the Plaintiff without his prior permission, that, she asserts, constituted her "promise."

The Superior Court found that no legally enforceable contract had been created. We agree. Every contract requires "consideration" to support it, and any promise not supported by consideration is unenforceable. The Defendant asks this Court to recognize the "agreement" as an enforceable bilateral contract, where the necessary consideration is the parties' promise of performance. 1 S. Williston, *A Treatise on the Law of Contracts* § 13 (3d ed. 1957). Generally, the Defendant's promise to forbear from engaging in an activity that she had the legal right to engage in, can provide her necessary consideration for the Plaintiff's return promises. 1 Williston § 135. However, the Plaintiff's allegation of lack of consideration draws attention to the bargaining process; although the Defendant's promise to forbear could constitute consideration, it cannot if it was not sought after by the Plaintiff, and motivated by his request that the Defendant not disturb him. *Id.* Of this there was no evidence whatsoever. This clause, the only one that operates in the Plaintiff's favor, was only included in the contract by the Defendant, because, she asserts, she felt the Plaintiff should get something in exchange for his promises. Clearly, this clause was not "bargained for" by the Plaintiff, and not given in exchange for his promises, and as such cannot constitute the consideration necessary to support a contract. *Restatement (Second) of Contracts* §§ 75, 71(1)(2).

Judgment affirmed.

NOTES AND QUESTIONS

1. *What happened?* Who sued whom for what? Procedurally, how did the case get before this court? Factually, what happened between the parties? What arguments did the plaintiff and defendant make? What rule or rules did the court apply? How did the court analyze the dispute between the parties? How did the court decide the case?

2. *Was this case correctly decided?* Do you agree with the result reached in this case? Why or why not? Do you agree with the court's reasoning? Why or why not? How, if at all, would you have written the opinion differently?

3. *The promises.* What, exactly, were the promises that each party made to the other? There are actually two potential contracts here. Make sure you can identify both of them, and are familiar with defendant's arguments with respect to each of the potential contracts.

4. *The bargain.* Why, exactly, did the court say that there was no consideration to support the contract that is the subject of defendant's counterclaim? Was it because there was no bargain, or for some other reason? Do you agree with the court's reasoning? Do you agree with its result?

5. *Problem.* Let's pause for a moment and see if you can apply the principles you've learned so far to the problem below.

PROBLEM: HOW MUCH IS A 50 CENT PROMISE WORTH?*

The rap artist 50 Cent, whose real name is Curtis Jackson, secured his first recording contract in October 2003. It came with a $300,000 advance. To boost his professional image as a rapper, he bought a Hummer and a Connecticut mansion once owned by boxer Mike Tyson. The mansion boasted a state-of-the-art recording studio, and the rapper hired a full-time caretaker and professional cleaning crew to maintain it. In 2004, Jackson bought another house in Valley Stream, the small village in New York's Nassau County where his grandmother

* Excerpted from LAWRENCE A. CUNNINGHAM, CONTRACTS IN THE REAL WORLD: STORIES OF POPULAR CONTRACTS AND WHY THEY MATTER 44-48 (2012).

and other relatives lived; in December 2006, he added to his real estate holdings a $2 million house at 2 Sandra Lane, Dix Hills, on Long Island, New York. By then, he had sold tens of millions of recordings, toured the world, and amassed hundreds of millions of dollars in net worth, as chronicled in his 2005 autobiographical film, "Get Rich, or Die Tryin."

This success came after hard knocks. Jackson had dealt crack cocaine as a teenager. In 1995, at age twenty, he was released from jail and became involved with Shaniqua Tompkins in his hometown of Jamaica in Queens, New York. The two had a son, Marquise, out of wedlock in 1996. Jackson and Tompkins had no money and no real home, living with his grandmother or hers. In May 2000, Jackson nearly died when he was shot nine times during a gangland ambush. He was in the hospital for weeks, followed by months of rehab spent at his mother's house, near the Pocono Mountains in Pennsylvania. Before the shooting, Jackson had been negotiating with Columbia Records; following it, the record company stopped returning his calls.

Jackson, however, persevered. In November 2001, he launched a recording company, Rotten Apple Records. The rising rap star Eminem brought Jackson's 2002 self-produced record to the industry's attention. As a result, Interscope Records offered Jackson the 2003 deal that propelled him to fame and fortune. With money flowing in and Jackson leading the high life, Tompkins asserted her right to a share. But Jackson's relationship with Tompkins was tumultuous. They did not always live together and fought often, sometimes physically.

When Jackson bought the Dix Hills house in 2006, both agreed it was the best place to raise Marquise, then almost ten years old, and Tompkins pled with Jackson to put it in her name. Although Jackson promised to do so, he never did. After the relationship soured, Jackson tried to evict Tompkins from the Dix Hills house. During that battle, the house burned to the ground under circumstances that authorities considered suspicious. The house had been insured against fire, but the policy lapsed for nonpayment of the premium a few weeks before. In response to Jackson's eviction lawsuit, Tompkins asserted a claim of her own: that the two had a contract entitling her to $50 million.

Tompkins claimed that in September 1996, one month before Marquise was born, she and Jackson made a deal. She claimed that Jackson promised her, in exchange for putting up with him and helping him through tough times, that when he "makes it big," he would take care of her for the "rest of her life," sharing everything he ever owns equally. They were "down for life," Tompkins recalls Jackson saying. In exchange, Tompkins said, she agreed to support him until he "got it together." Tompkins alleged that formed a binding contract. She elaborated this claim:

> I agreed to continue to live with him, maintain his home, perform homemaking and domestic services for him as well as support him mentally, emotionally and financially to the best of my abilities. I also agreed to accompany him to social and other events. . . . Jackson agreed that he would vigorously pursue a professional recording career with the understanding that our combined efforts could result in the accumulation of substantial wealth and assets that we would divide and share equally.

Tompkins said they were in love at that time. She explained:

> He was a corner crack dealer parolee. He did not have anything. . . . So I was going to be with him whether he was 50 Cent, with a hundred million dollars, or Curtis Jackson, working for sanitation, making $50,000 a year. I would have been with him, because I loved him. It was not about him saying that he would give me everything he had. It is when you love a person, you don't—it is not about the monetary. If you're a prostitute, then it is a monetary thing. We were two people in love with each other.

Jackson denied making any lifetime promise and argued that, even if he had, it was unenforceable. Instead, Jackson argued, these were merely expressions of support by two unmarried lovers. Their commitments sprung from mutual regard and affection—not money—and even if done for money, they resembled arrangements law historically frowned on.

Jackson could cite many precedents, from decades earlier, that refused to enforce as contracts agreements between paramours (unmarried cohabitants). Tompkins countered that the deal went beyond ordinary domestic management and could cite other, more modern cases recognizing the enforceability of contracts between unmarried cohabitants. The Jackson-Tompkins dispute was thus wedged between these lines of authority.

Before the 1960s, courts were disinclined to enforce contracts like this, for the two reasons Jackson urged. Well into the twentieth century, a social stigma attached to unmarried cohabitation and law reflected that distaste by refusing to recognize bargains made in those settings as valid contracts. The law's main discomfort around these types of bargains stemmed from concerns about whether the deal was a type of disguised prostitution. Early cases called this type of consideration—money for sex—meretricious, referring to a harlot's traits. Because prostitution was and remains illegal by statute throughout the United States, courts refuse to enforce these contracts; this repugnance extended to include deals made among unmarried cohabitants. . . .

Social norms have, of course, evolved. . . . [Some states], like New York, where Jackson and Tompkins disputed, have reversed the historical hostility toward unmarried cohabitation so that such contracts are not automatically invalid. Most states now regard express contracts in these settings as they do others, enforcing those supported by consideration and manifest mutual assent to be bound. But relics of the past persist. Courts struggle in paramour cases to determine whether the evidence shows a bargain. They must discern whether promises were made with or without expectation of payment and whether primarily out of love and affection or with an intention to make a deal.

Jackson argued that the arrangement Tompkins asserted was all about love and personal affection and not any sort of exchange transaction intended as an enforceable bargain. The promises Tompkins made addressed daily attention, support, companionship, and household chores; in exchange, Jackson promised to take care of her for life. Those are the things couples do for each other in day-to-day living without intending, expecting, or manifesting a bargain.

Tompkins contended the deal was not only about love, but also amounted to a bargain, noting that Jackson's promise did not depend on whether the two were living together or involved romantically. Although originating in love, the promises were a bargained-for exchange, she argued.

Drawing on the assigned cases and materials, how do you think this dispute should be resolved, and why? In your answer, be sure to address any relevant arguments that were (or could have been) raised in the excerpt above.

RELEVANT PROVISIONS

For the *Restatement (Second) of Contracts,* consult the provisions included after *Hamer v. Sidway* (i.e., §§ 17, 71, 79(a), and 81). For the UCC, consult § 2-204(1). For the CISG, consult Article 29(1). For the UNIDROIT Principles, consult Article 3.2.

In the United States, employment is typically "at will": you can quit your job whenever you want, and your boss can fire you whenever she wants. But suppose you have a job, and along comes a better offer to work elsewhere. Being a nice person—even though you're not required to by the "at will" doctrine—you decide to give your boss a two-week notice. Your boss, however, really likes you (for now) and wants you to stay. So she promises to give you a little something to keep you (more money, let's say; that's always nice). So you stay, and your boss is happy. And you're happy too. But, this being a contracts hypothetical, things have to go wrong sooner or later, and so they do. After a few months, your boss changes her mind about this whole employment thing and decides to fire you. Which gets you to thinking: Was that bargain you made a few months back enforceable? Did your boss bargain away her privilege of terminating your employment? As luck would have it, the next case is a variation on this sad little story. So let's keep reading and see what happens.

McInerney v. Charter Golf, Inc.

Supreme Court of Illinois
680 N.E.2d 1347 (1997)

JUSTICE HEIPLE. Is an employee's promise to forgo another job opportunity in exchange for a guarantee of lifetime employment sufficient consideration to modify an existing employment-at-will relationship? If "yes," must such an agreement be in writing to satisfy the requirements of the statute of frauds? These questions, among others, must be answered in plaintiff Dennis McInerney's appeal from an order of the appellate court affirming a grant of summary judgment in favor of the defendant, Charter Golf, Inc. Although we conclude that a promise for a promise is sufficient consideration to modify a contract—even an employment contract—we further conclude that the statute of frauds requires that a contract for lifetime employment be in writing.

The facts are uncomplicated. . . . From 1988 through 1992, Dennis McInerney worked as a sales representative for Charter Golf, Inc., a company which manufactures and sells golf apparel and supplies. Initially, McInerney's territory included Illinois but was later expanded to include Indiana and Wisconsin. In 1989, McInerney allegedly was offered a position as an exclusive sales representative for Hickey-Freeman, an elite clothier which manufactured a competing line of golf apparel. Hickey-Freeman purportedly offered McInerney an 8% commission.

Intending to inform Charter Golf of his decision to accept the Hickey-Freeman offer of employment, McInerney called Jerry Montiel, Charter Golf's president. Montiel wanted McInerney to continue to work for Charter Golf and urged McInerney to turn down the Hickey-Freeman offer. Montiel promised to guarantee McInerney a 10% commission on sales in Illinois and Wisconsin "for the remainder of his life," in a position where he would be subject to discharge only for dishonesty or disability. McInerney allegedly accepted Charter Golf's offer and, in exchange for the guarantee of lifetime employment, gave up the Hickey-Freeman offer. McInerney then continued to work for Charter Golf.

In 1992, the relationship between Charter Golf and McInerney soured: Charter Golf fired McInerney. McInerney then filed a complaint in the circuit court of Cook County, alleging breach of contract. The trial court granted Charter Golf's motion for summary judgment after concluding that the alleged oral contract was unenforceable under the statute of frauds because the contract amounted to an agreement which could not be performed within a year from its making. The appellate court affirmed, but on a wholly different ground. The appellate court held that the putative contract between McInerney and Charter Golf suffered from a more fundamental flaw, namely, that no contract for lifetime employment even existed because a promise to forbear another job opportunity was insufficient consideration to convert an existing employment-at-will relationship into a contract for lifetime employment.

This court accepted McInerney's petition for leave to appeal, and for the reasons set forth below, we affirm on other grounds.

ANALYSIS

Employment contracts in Illinois are presumed to be at-will and are terminable by either party; this rule, of course, is one of construction which may be overcome by showing that the parties agreed otherwise. As with any contract, the terms of an employment contract must be clear and definite and the contract must be supported by consideration.

A. Consideration

Although the rules of contract law are well-established and straightforward, a conflict has emerged in the appellate court decisions on the subject of consideration in the context of a lifetime employment contract. Several decisions have held that a promise of lifetime employment, which by its terms purports to alter an employment-at-will contract, must be supported by "additional" consideration beyond the standard employment duties. These cases have held that an employee's rejecting an outside job offer in exchange for a promised guarantee of lifetime employment is not sufficient consideration to alter an employment-at-will relationship. The premise underlying these cases is that the employee simply weighs the benefits of the two positions, and by accepting one offer the employee necessarily rejects the other. As such, these cases have reasoned that the employee has not given up anything of value, and thus there is no consideration to support the promise of lifetime employment.

One case, however, has taken issue with this analysis. In *Martin v. Federal Life Insurance Co.*, the appellate court held that an enforceable contract for lifetime employment was formed when an employee relinquished a job offer in exchange for a promise of permanent employment from his current employer. *Martin v. Federal Life Insurance Co.*, 109 Ill. App. 3d 596, 601 (1982). **The *Martin* court recognized that there was consideration in an exchange of promises: the employer promised to give up his right to terminate the employee at-will, and in exchange the employee agreed to continue working for his current employer and to forgo a lucrative opportunity with a competitor.**

What is consideration? Under the prevailing view, embodied in the *Restatement (Second) of Contracts*, consideration is the bargained-for exchange of promises or performances, and may consist of a promise, an act or a forbearance. *Restatement (Second) of Contracts* § 71. Thus, a promise for a promise is, without more, enforceable. *Restatement (Second) of Contracts* § 79, Comment a. In past cases, this court has recognized this basic precept, i.e., mutual assent and an exchange of promises provides consideration to support the formation of a contract. *See, e.g., Steinberg v. Chicago Medical School*, 371 N.E.2d 634 (1977) (holding that any act or promise which is of benefit to one party or disadvantage to the other is sufficient "consideration" to support a contract).

While this court has never directly addressed the specific requirements to establish a permanent employment contract, it has held more generally that the employment relationship is governed by the law of contract. Existence of an employment contract, express or implied, is essential to the employer-employee relationship. As with any contract, it is not possible for a contract of employment to exist without consent of the parties. Indeed, this court held in

> ***An option contract in disguise!***
>
> In this sentence, the court incorrectly refers to the employer's promise to give up his "right" to terminate the employee at will. Referring to Hohfeld's juridical concepts, which we examined in "Thinking Tool: Thinking Clearly About Legal Relationships" (p. 96, *supra*), the court should have used the term "power" instead of "right." Why is this important? Because it allows us to see an important legal relationship that might otherwise escape our notice. Before their agreement, the employer had the *power* to change its legal relationship with the employee by firing him, and the employee, in turn, was *liable* to having his legal relationship changed. Once the new contract is made, however, the employer's power is replaced with its jural opposite, i.e., a *disability*, which means that the employee is now *immune* from having his legal relationship changed by the employer. In other words, what we have here is an option contract, a nifty little insight provided by applying Hohfeld's jural concepts! And once we know what we're dealing with, i.e., an option contract, it becomes much easier to follow this idea to its logical conclusion: It is only the employee, and not the employer, who retains the power of changing (by quitting) the relationship between them. That's how option contracts work, by giving one party a power, and the other a disability, to change the currently existing legal relationship! Had the court recognized this fact, it could have dealt with the issues involved in this case in a much less confusing manner.

Duldulao v. Saint Mary of Nazareth Hosp. Center, 505 N.E.2d 314 (1987), that an employee handbook or other policy statement creates enforceable contractual rights governed by the traditional requirements for contract formation.

In the instant case, Charter Golf argues that an employee's promise to forgo another employment offer in exchange for an employer's promise of lifetime employment is not sufficient consideration. But why not? The defendant has failed to articulate any principled reason why this court should depart from traditional notions of contract law in deciding this case. While we recognize that some cases have indeed held that such an exchange is "inadequate" or "insufficient" consideration to modify an employment-at-will relationship, we believe that those cases have confused the conceptual element of consideration with more practical problems of proof. As we discussed above, this court has held that a promise for a promise constitutes consideration to support the existence of a contract. To hold otherwise in the instant case would ignore the economic realities underlying the case. Here McInerney gave up a lucrative job offer in exchange for a guarantee of lifetime employment; and in exchange for giving up its right to terminate McInerney at will, Charter Golf retained a valued employee. Clearly both parties exchanged bargained-for benefits in what appears to be a near textbook illustration of consideration.

Of course, not every relinquishment of a job offer will necessarily constitute consideration to support a contract. On the related issue of mutuality of obligation, Charter Golf complains that McInerney's promise to continue working was somehow illusory, because it alleges that McInerney had the power to terminate the employment relationship at his discretion while it lacked any corresponding right. The court's decision in *Armstrong Paint & Varnish Works v. Continental Can Co.,* 301 Ill. 102, 108 (1922), teaches that "where there is any other consideration for the contract mutuality of obligation is not essential." Charter Golf's argument on this point fails because McInerney continued working for Charter Golf *and* relinquished his right to accept another job opportunity. When, as here, the employee relinquishes something of value in a bargained-for exchange for the employer's guarantee of permanent employment, a contract is formed.

B. Statute of Frauds

[The majority, over a scathing dissent, ultimately refused to enforce the oral contract because it was not in writing as required by the Statute of Frauds. We will take up this part of the court's opinion when we discuss the Statute of Frauds in Chapter 8, *infra*.]

NOTES AND QUESTIONS

1. ***The statute of frauds.*** We briefly touched on the statute of frauds in the "Notes and Questions" after *Lucy v. Zehmer* (p. 170), and will cover it in greater detail in Chapter 8.

2. ***What happened?*** Who sued whom for what? Procedurally, how did the case get before this court? Factually, what happened between the parties? What arguments did the plaintiff and defendant make? What rule or rules did the court apply? How did the court analyze the dispute between the parties? How did the court decide the case?

3. ***Was this case correctly decided?*** Was there consideration? If so—and forgetting about the statute of frauds for the moment—do you think the promise should have been enforced? What arguments can you think of in favor and against enforcement? Do you think the fact that the employee, by relying on the employer's promise, lost out on an opportunity elsewhere should count for anything? Keep your answer in mind, as a good deal of the theory of promissory estoppel (which we turn to in Section B of this chapter) is concerned with deciding whether to enforce promises that a party relied upon to its detriment.

As we have seen, doctrines like consideration and the statute of frauds, even with their flaws, continue to survive. Why? Take consideration, for instance. Most legal systems have long made do without it,[*] the UCC[†] and UNIDROIT Principles[‡] don't require it, and the CISG, although it does not directly address the enforceability of the agreement itself, allows contracts to be "modified or terminated by the mere agreement of the parties."[§] So why does our legal system continue to insist on "consideration" as the touchstone of enforceability? Part of the answer lies in the fact that consideration, like the statute of frauds and other contract doctrines, serves an important role as a legal formality, a sort of ritual used by the parties to signal to courts (and to each other) that they are serious about keeping their promises. Indeed, the more one thinks about the role of ritual in promise keeping, or in any area of law for that matter, the more one is struck by the strangeness of the enterprise. Consider, for instance, why it is that, over the centuries, parties have engaged in such strange behaviors as signing one's mark on a sheet of parchment, or impressing one's seal into hot melted wax, or grasping another's hand firmly and shaking it up and down in a vigorous fashion. Is all this *really* needed to "seal" a deal? Many humans certainly behave as though this

[*] This point is not new. For instance, in a 1936 article, Lord Wright noted that "consideration has no place" in a number of jurisdictions, including "civilised countries with a highly developed system of law" such as "France, Italy, Spain, Germany, Switzerland and Japan." Wright went on to question how it was "possible to regard the common law rule of consideration as axiomatic or as an inevitable element in any code of law?" Wright, *Ought the Doctrine of Consideration to Be Abolished from the Common Law?*, 49 HARV. L. REV. 1225, 1226 (1936).

[†] *See* UCC § 2-204(1) ("A contract for sale of goods may be made in any manner sufficient to show agreement, including offer and acceptance, conduct by both parties which recognizes the existence of a contract, the interaction of electronic agents, and the interaction of an electronic agent and an individual.")

[‡] See UNIDROIT Principles Article 3.2 ("A contract is concluded, modified or terminated by the mere agreement of the parties, without any further requirement.")

[§] CISG Article 29(1).

were so, as if the need for complying with certain forms were in our legal DNA. Watch young children make promises to one another on the playground, crossing their fingers behind their backs when they don't intend to keep their promises, or raising their hand to the sky as if taking a solemn oath or crossing their hearts with their fingers when they do, sometimes even ominously calling down curses on themselves in a sing-song manner should they break their promises (e.g., "cross my heart, swear to die, stick a needle in my eye"). Ouch!

And if these promises—the kinds *we* make—look strange, consider some of the formalities the ancients used when promising. The Romans, for instance, once made binding promises through an elaborate form of question and answer called the *stipulatio*. To invoke this form, the parties had to be Roman citizens standing in one another's presence. The promisee would then ask the promisor, according to the precise verbal formula, "Spondesne 'X'" (*Do you promise me "X"*). The promisor, in turn, would respond by using the precise word "Spondeo" (*I agree*).* Any slip of the tongue, or any hesitation or delay between the question and the answer, rendered the promise unenforceable. In an earlier form of this type of contract, the *sponsio*, the promisor would go one step further and "seal" the deal by pouring a libation before an altar, signaling to the promisee that "if he broke his word, he wished his blood to be shed like that wine."† In so doing, the promisor thereby indicated that his promise was being made not only to the other party, but to the gods as well.‡ Not unlike the promises made by those young school children we met earlier, when you come to think about it.§ Which brings us back full circle to the question we started with, why do we have these strange things called "formalities" at all? Lon Fuller, in his classic article *Consideration and Form*, was one of the first commentators to give systematic treatment to this question. In so doing, he identified several

* This reflects, even more strictly, the mirror image rule we discussed in the previous chapter. But note that, with the Roman *stipulatio*, it is the *promisee* who couches the promise in terms of an offer, and the *promisor* who accepts!

† William Henry Hastings Kelke, An Epitome of Roman Law 150 (1901).

‡ *Id.*

§ Another interesting use of a rather bizarre-looking formality to "seal a deal" in the ancient world comes from the Bible, where God makes a promise to give land to Abram (later to become Abraham) and his descendants in the following manner:

> Then He said to him, "I am the Lord who brought you out from Ur of the Chaldeans to assign this land to you as a possession." And he [Abram] said, "O Lord God, how shall I know that I am to possess it?" He answered, "Bring Me a three-year-old heifer, a three-year-old she-goat, a three-year-old ram, a turtledove, and a young bird." He brought Him all these and cut them in two, placing each half opposite the other; but he did not cut up the bird. . . . When the sun set and it was very dark, there appeared a smoking oven, and a flaming torch which passed between those pieces. On that day the Lord made a covenant with Abram, saying, "To your offspring I assign this land, from the river of Egypt to the great river, the river Euphrates. . . ."

Genesis 15:7-18, *in* The Jewish Study Bible. (Tanakh Translation, Adele Berlin & Marc Zvi Brettler eds. 2004).

important functions served by legal formalities, and showed that the doctrine of consideration can be thought of as a formality useful to contract law, like memorializing an agreement in writing or shaking another party's hand to seal a deal. After reading the excerpt below, you should come away with more insight into why the doctrine of consideration, despite its flaws, has persisted, and continues to persist, well into the twenty-first century.

THE ROLE OF LEGAL FORMALITIES*

§ 2. *The Evidentiary Function.*—The most obvious function of a legal formality is, to use Austin's words, that of providing "evidence of the existence and purport of the contract, in case of controversy." The need for evidentiary security may be satisfied in a variety of ways: by requiring a writing, or attestation, or the certification of a notary. It may even be satisfied, to some extent, by such a device as the Roman stipulatio, which compelled an oral spelling out of the promise in a manner sufficiently ceremonious to impress its terms on participants and possible bystanders.

§ 3. *The Cautionary Function.*—A formality may also perform a cautionary or deterrent function by acting as a check against inconsiderate action. The seal in its original form fulfilled this purpose remarkably well. The affixing and impressing of a wax wafer—symbol in the popular mind of legalism and weightiness—was an excellent device for inducing the circumspective frame of mind appropriate in one pledging his future. To a less extent any requirement of a writing, of course, serves the same purpose, as do requirements of attestation, notarization, etc.

§ 4. *The Channeling Function.*—Though most discussions of the purposes served by formalities go no further than the analysis just presented, this analysis stops short of recognizing one of the most important functions of form. That a legal formality may perform a function not yet described can be shown by the seal. The seal not only insures a satisfactory memorial of the promise and induces deliberation in the making of it. It serves also to mark or signalize the enforceable promise; it furnishes a simple and external test of enforceability. This function of form Ihering described as "the facilitation of judicial diagnosis," and he employed the analogy of coinage in explaining it.

> Form is for a legal transaction what the stamp is for a coin. Just as the stamp of the coin relieves us from the necessity of testing the metallic content and weight—in short, the value of the coin (a test which we could not avoid if uncoined metal were offered to us in payment), in the same way legal formalities relieve the judge of an inquiry whether a legal transaction was intended, and—in case different forms are fixed for different legal transactions—which was intended.

In this passage it is apparent that Ihering has placed an undue emphasis on the utility of form for the judge, to the neglect of its significance for those transacting

* Excerpted from Lon L. Fuller, *Consideration and Form*, 41 COLUM. L. REV. 799, 800-06 (1941).

business out of court. If we look at the matter purely from the standpoint of the convenience of the judge, there is nothing to distinguish the forms used in legal transactions from the "formal" element which to some degree permeates all legal thinking. Even in the field of criminal law "judicial diagnosis" is "facilitated" by formal definitions, presumptions, and artificial constructions of fact. The thing which characterizes the law of contracts and conveyances is that in this field forms are deliberately used, and are intended to be so used, by the parties whose acts are to be judged by the law. To the business man who wishes to make his own or another's promise binding, the seal was at common law available as a device for the accomplishment of his objective. In this aspect form offers a legal framework into which the party may fit his actions, or, to change the figure, it offers channels for the legally effective expression of intention. It is with this aspect of form in mind that I have described the third function of legal formalities as "the channeling function." . . .

§ 5. *Interrelations of the Three Functions.*—Though I have stated the three functions of legal form separately, it is obvious that there is an intimate connection between them. Generally speaking, whatever tends to accomplish one of these purposes will also tend to accomplish the other two. He who is compelled to do something which will furnish a satisfactory memorial of his intention will be induced to deliberate. Conversely, devices which induce deliberation will usually have an evidentiary value. Devices which insure evidence or prevent inconsiderateness will normally advance the desideratum of channeling, in two different ways. In the first place, he who is compelled to formulate his intention carefully will tend to fit it into legal and business categories. In this way the party is induced to canalize his own intention. In the second place, wherever the requirement of a formality is backed by the sanction of the invalidity of the informal transaction (and this is the means by which requirements of form are normally made effective), a degree of channeling results automatically. Whatever may be its legislative motive, the formality in such a case tends to effect a categorization of transactions into legal and non-legal.

Just as channeling may result unintentionally from formalities directed toward other ends, so these other ends tend to be satisfied by any device which accomplishes a channeling of expression. There is an evidentiary value in the clarity and definiteness of contour which such a device accomplishes. Anything which effects a neat division between the legal and the non-legal, or between different kinds of legal transactions, will tend also to make apparent to the party the consequences of his action and will suggest deliberation where deliberation is needed. . . .

Despite the close interrelationship of the three functions of form, it is necessary to keep the distinctions between them in mind since the disposition of borderline cases of compliance may turn on our assumptions as to the end primarily sought by a particular formality. . . .

§ 6. *When are Formalities Needed? The Effect of an Informal Satisfaction of the Desiderata Underlying the Use of Formalities.*—The analysis of the functions of legal form which has just been presented is useful in answering a question which will assume importance in the later portion of this discussion when a detailed treatment of consideration is undertaken. That question is: In what situations does good legislative policy demand the use of a legal formality? One part of the answer to the question is clear at the outset. Forms must be reserved for relatively important transactions. We must preserve a proportion between means and end; it will scarcely do to require a sealed and witnessed document for the effective sale of a loaf of bread.

But assuming that the transaction in question is of sufficient importance to support the use of a form if a form is needed, how is the existence of this need to be determined? A general answer would run somewhat as follows: The need for investing a particular transaction with some legal formality will depend upon the extent to which the guaranties that the formality would afford are rendered superfluous by forces native to the situation out of which the transaction arises—including in these "forces" the habits and conceptions of the transacting parties.

Whether there is any need, for example, to set up a formality designed to induce deliberation will depend upon the degree to which the factual situation, innocent of any legal remolding, tends to bring about the desired circumspective frame of mind. An example from the law of gifts will make this point clear. To accomplish an effective gift of a chattel without resort to the use of documents, delivery of the chattel is ordinarily required and mere donative words are ineffective. It is thought, among other things, that mere words do not sufficiently impress on the donor the significance and seriousness of his act. In an Oregon case however, the donor declared his intention to give a sum of money to the donee and at the same time disclosed to the donee the secret hiding place where he had placed the money. Though the whole donative act consisted merely of words, the court held the gift to be effective. The words which gave access to the money which the donor had so carefully concealed would presumably be accompanied by the same sense of present deprivation which the act of handing over the money would have produced. The situation contained its own guaranty against inconsiderateness.

So far as the channeling function of a formality is concerned it has no place where men's activities are already divided into definite, clear-cut business categories. Where life has already organized itself effectively, there is no need for the law to intervene. It is for this reason that important transactions on the stock and produce markets can safely be carried on in the most "informal" manner. At the other extreme we may cite the negotiations between a house-to-house book salesman and the housewife. Here the situation may be such that the housewife is not certain whether she is being presented with a set of books as a gift, whether she is being asked to trade her letter of recommendation for the books, whether the books are being offered to her on approval, or whether—what is, alas, the fact—a simple sale of the books is being proposed. The ambiguity of the situation is, of course, carefully cultivated and exploited by the canvasser. Some "channeling" here would be highly desirable, though whether a legal form is the most practicable means of bringing it about is, of course, another question.

What has been said in this section demonstrates, I believe, that the problem of "form," when reduced to its underlying policies, extends not merely to "formal" transactions in the usual sense, but to the whole law of contracts and conveyances. Demogue has suggested that even the requirement, imposed in certain cases, that the intention of the parties be express, rather than implied or tacit, is in essence a requirement of form. If our object is to avoid giving sanction to inconsiderate engagements, surely the case for legal redress is stronger against the man who has spelled out his promise than it is against the man who has merely drifted into a situation where he appears to hold out an assurance for the future.

2. Determining the Validity of Consideration

a. Adequacy of Consideration

DOCTRINAL OVERVIEW: THE PEPPERCORN THEORY OF CONSIDERATION

Contract law can police bargains in one of two ways: it can police them substantively, requiring that the promises exchanged between parties be of roughly equal value, or it can police them procedurally, ensuring that the bargaining process itself, rather than the result achieved, is a fair one.

The former view, which can be supported under an ancient "theory of just price," operates on the assumption that things (e.g., land, goods, services) have an "intrinsic" value, and that the prices charged for these things should reflect these values. Where the price charged does not reflect an item's true value, then, so holds the theory, courts should provide a remedy to the aggrieved party.* For instance, under the ancient principle of *laesio enormis* (abnormal harm), a seller of goods is entitled to rescind an agreement where the price it receives from the buyer is less than a certain percentage (say, one-half) of the value of the goods sold.† The logic underlying the theory of just price, however, has been attacked by critics as unsound. These critics maintain that things don't have objective or intrinsic values. Rather, the very notion of "value" is a product of the forces of supply and demand: "[I]t is precisely the disparity in the value attached to the objects exchanged that results in their being exchanged. People buy and sell only because they appraise the things given up less than those received."‡ Although the theory of "just price" has been embraced by a number of legal systems around the world, contract law in the United States, with the notable exception of Louisiana,§ has rejected it in favor of "market price."¶ Indeed, it has often been said that, in American contract law, a mere "peppercorn" is sufficient consideration to support a promise, with a few important exceptions. First, the bargain itself must be genuine and not a "sham" transaction. This means that a party cannot, for instance, try to "trick" the courts and convert an otherwise unenforceable promise (e.g., a promise to make a gift) into an enforceable bargain by simply requiring the other party to promise a peppercorn in return. Second, one party may not take inappropriate advantage of the other party during the bargaining process itself by, for example, forcing the other party to sign under duress. In this subsection, we will focus on how courts handle cases where one party alleges that their

---

* *See generally* James Gordley, *Equality in Exchange*, 69 CAL. L. REV. 1587 (1981).

† *See, e.g.*, Arthur Taylor Voh Mehren, *The French Doctrine of Lesion in the Sale of Immovable Property*, 49 TUL. L. REV. 321, 324 (1975) ("The *laesio* doctrine rested on ethical views which required a fair exchange of values and on the proposition that values, including economic values, were not inherently individualistic and subjective").

‡ LUDWIG VON MISES, HUMAN ACTION, THE SCHOLAR'S EDITION 205 (2008). This view is also reflected in *Restatement (Second) of Contracts* § 79, Comment c, reproduced in the appendix.

§ *See, e.g.*, Louisiana Civil Code Art. 2589 ("The sale of an immovable may be rescinded . . . when the price is less than one half of the fair market value of the immovable.")

¶ *See Restatement (Second) of Contracts* § 79, reproduced in the appendix.

promise is unenforceable because the other party's consideration was inadequate. Then, when we come to chapter 8, we will take a closer look at some of the factors that may suggest that the bargaining process itself was defective, and some of the defenses that may be available to an aggrieved party.

Schnell v. Nell

Supreme Court of Indiana

17 Ind. 29 (1861)

PERKINS, J. Action by *J. B. Nell* against *Zacharias Schnell,* upon the following instrument:

> This agreement, entered into this 13th day of *February,* 1856, between *Zach. Schnell,* of *Indianapolis, Marion* county, State of *Indiana,* as party of the first part, and *J. B. Nell,* of the same place, *Wendelin Lorenz,* of *Stilesville, Hendricks* county, State of *Indiana,* and *Donata Lorenz,* of *Frickinger, Grand Duchy of Baden, Germany,* as parties of the second part, witnesseth: The said *Zacharias Schnell* agrees as follows: whereas his wife, *Theresa Schnell,* now deceased, has made a last will and testament, in which, among other provisions, it was ordained that every one of the above named second parties, should receive the sum of $200; and whereas the said provisions of the will must remain a nullity, for the reason that no property, real or personal, was in the possession of the said *Theresa Schnell,* deceased, in her own name, at the time of her death, and all property held by *Zacharias* and *Theresa Schnell* jointly, therefore reverts to her husband; and whereas the said *Theresa Schnell* has also been a dutiful and loving wife to the said *Zach. Schnell,* and has materially aided him in the acquisition of all property, real and personal, now possessed by him; for, and in consideration of all this, and the love and respect he bears to his wife; and, furthermore, in consideration of one cent, received by him of the second parties, he, the said *Zach, Schnell,* agrees to pay the above named sums of money to the parties of the second part, to wit: $200 to the said *J. B. Nell;* $200 to the said *Wendelin Lorenz;* and $200 to the said *Donata Lorenz,* in the following installments, viz., $200 in one year from the date of these presents; $200 in two years, and $200 in three years; to be divided between the parties in equal portions of $66 2/3 each year, or as they may agree, till each one has received his full sum of $200.
>
> And the said parties of the second part, for, and in consideration of this, agree to pay the above named sum of money [one cent], and to deliver up to said *Schnell,* and abstain from collecting any real or supposed claims upon him or his estate, arising from the said last will and testament of the said *Theresa Schnell,* deceased.
>
> In witness whereof, the said parties have, on this 13th day of *February,* 1856, set hereunto their hands and seals.
>
> ZACHARIAS SCHNELL, [SEAL.]
> J. B. NELL, [SEAL.]
> WEN. LORENZ. [SEAL.]

The complaint contained no averment of a consideration for the instrument, outside of those expressed in it; and did not aver that the one cent agreed to be paid, had been paid or tendered.

A **demurrer** to the complaint was overruled.

The defendant answered, that the instrument sued on was given for no consideration whatever.

He further answered, that it was given for no consideration, because his said wife, *Theresa,* at the time she made the will mentioned, and at the time of her death, owned, neither separately, nor jointly with her husband, or any one else (except so far as the law gave her an interest in her husband's property), any property, real or personal, etc.

The will is copied into the record, but need not be into this opinion.

> **Demurrer**
>
> More commonly known as a "**motion to dismiss**" today, a demurrer is "[a] pleading stating that although the facts alleged in a complaint may be true, they are insufficient for the plaintiff to state a claim for relief and for the defendant to frame an answer." BLACK'S LAW DICTIONARY (10th ed. 2014).

The Court sustained a demurrer to these answers, evidently on the ground that they were regarded as contradicting the instrument sued on, which particularly set out the considerations upon which it was executed. But the instrument is latently ambiguous on this point.

The case turned below, and must turn here, upon the question whether the instrument sued on does express a consideration sufficient to give it legal obligation, as against *Zacharias Schnell.* It specifies three distinct considerations for his promise to pay $600:

1. A promise, on the part of the plaintiffs, to pay him one cent.
2. The love and affection he bore his deceased wife, and the fact that she had done her part, as his wife, in the acquisition of property.
3. The fact that she had expressed her desire, in the form of an inoperative will, that the persons named therein should have the sums of money specified.

The consideration of one cent will not support the promise of *Schnell.* **It is true, that as a general proposition, inadequacy of consideration will not vitiate an agreement. But this doctrine does not apply to a mere exchange of sums of money, of coin, whose value is exactly fixed, but to the exchange of something of, in itself, indeterminate value, for money, or, perhaps, for some other thing of indeterminate value.** In this case, had the one cent mentioned, been some particular one cent, a family piece, or ancient, remarkable coin, possessing an indeterminate value, extrinsic from its simple money value, a different view might be taken. As it is, the mere promise to pay six hundred dollars for one cent, even had the portion of that cent due from the plaintiff been tendered, is an unconscionable contract, void, at first blush, upon its face, if it be regarded as an earnest one. The consideration of one cent is, plainly, in this case, merely nominal, and intended to be so.

> **Why the exception?**
>
> Why do you think this exception to the general rule (that inadequacy of consideration will ordinarily not vitiate an agreement) exists? Or, to approach the question from a slightly different angle, why are courts generally hesitant to inquire into the adequacy of consideration in most cases, and what's different about cases where there is "a mere exchange of sums of money"?

As the will and testament of *Schnell's* wife imposed no legal obligation upon him to discharge her bequests out of his property, and as she had none of her own, his promise to discharge them was not legally binding upon him, on that ground. A moral consideration, only, will not support a promise. And for the same reason, a valid consideration for his promise can not be found in the fact of a compromise of a disputed claim; for where such claim is legally groundless, a promise upon a compromise of it, or of a suit upon it, is not legally binding. There was no mistake of law or fact in this case, as the agreement admits the will inoperative and void. The promise was simply one to make a gift.

The past services of his wife, and the love and affection he had borne her, are objectionable as legal considerations for *Schnell's* promise, on two grounds: (1) They are past considerations. (2) The fact that *Schnell* loved his wife, and that she had been industrious, constituted no consideration for his promise to pay *J. B. Nell,* and the *Lorenzes,* a sum of money. Whether, if his wife, in her lifetime, had made a bargain with *Schnell,* that, in consideration of his promising to pay, after her death, to the persons named, a sum of money, she would be industrious, and worthy of his affection, such a promise would have been valid and consistent with public policy, we need not decide. Nor is the fact that *Schnell* now venerates the memory of his deceased wife, a legal consideration for a promise to pay any third person money.

The instrument sued on, interpreted in the light of the facts alleged in the second paragraph of the answer, will not support an action. The demurrer to the answer should have been overruled.

PER CURIAM.

The judgment is reversed, with costs. Cause remanded, etc.

RELEVANT PROVISIONS

For the *Restatement (Second) of Contracts,* consult §§ 71, 74(1), 79(b), and 95(1)(a).

NOTES AND QUESTIONS

1. ***What happened?*** Who sued whom for what? Procedurally, how did the case get before this court? Factually, what happened between the parties? What arguments did the plaintiff and defendant make? What rule or rules did the court apply? How did the court analyze the dispute between the parties? How did the court decide the case?

2. ***Was this case correctly decided?*** Do you agree with the result reached in this case? Why or why not? Do you agree with the court's reasoning? Why or why not? How, if at all, would you have written the opinion differently?

3. ***Should the promise have been enforced?*** There were a number of grounds upon which the court *could* have enforced Schnell's promise. Make a

list of these reasons, and next to each, indicate why the court rejected it. Do you agree with the court's decision? Are you convinced by the court's reasons? Why or why not?

4. ***What was the role of Schnell's stated considerations?*** The instrument that was signed and sealed by the parties indicates that Schnell's promise was supported by consideration (the phrase "in consideration of" appears three times). Why did the court reject Schnell's stated considerations? Should it have? Why or why not?

5. ***Moral and past consideration.*** The court said that moral consideration and past consideration were insufficient to render a promise enforceable. Why do you think this might be? We will explore these concepts later in this chapter in a pair of fascinating cases, *Mills v. Wyman* and *Webb v. McGowin*.

6. ***Applying the* Restatement.** Was Schnell's promise enforceable based on any of the *Restatement* provisions listed under "Relevant Provisions" above? Why or why not?

7. ***The role of the seal.*** Should the fact that Schnell's promise was in writing and "signed, sealed, delivered" have made it enforceable? Stevie Wonder might have thought so, but do you? In thinking about this question, you might want to consider the excerpt "The Role of Legal Formalities" in the previous section (p. 341). One wonders why the plaintiff did not even make this argument. Was it an oversight, or did he simply think the court would not have given it the consideration it deserved? Historically, the seal predated the doctrine of consideration, and once upon a time, common law courts wouldn't even enforce a written promise under the writ of covenant unless a seal was affixed thereto. Indeed, the seal once served an important function by signaling to courts and promisees alike that the promisor was serious about its promise and intended it to be enforced.* Should contract law begin enforcing such promises once again? Why or why not? If not, should there be some other device by which parties can make their promises binding without a bargain? See if you can answer these questions as you read the two short excerpts below. Also, focus on the way the two authors disagree with each other about the merits of the seal. Who seems to have the better argument, and why?

THE SEAL (I)†

Promises under seal are a traditional and, again, an economically appropriate exception to the requirement that an enforceable promise must be supported by consideration. The requirement of the seal eliminates the major administrative

---

* *See* "The Role of Legal Formalities," Section A.1, *supra*.

† Excerpted from Richard A. Posner, *Gratuitous Promises in Economics and Law*, 6 J. LEGAL STUD. 411, 419-20 (1977).

costs associated with the enforcement of unilateral promises. The formalities and written character of the promise reduce both the costs of determining the content of the promise and the probability that the promise was not made or was not intended to be binding.

The abolition by statute of the seal in many states is therefore a mysterious development from the standpoint of efficiency. The decline of this simple but reliable method of making a gratuitous promise binding has been deplored, and various proposals for a substitute method suggested. The legislative character of the abolition movement may reflect simply the difference between the courts and legislatures in the emphasis placed on efficiency. Or, less probably, it may reflect the rise of alternative methods of imparting enforceability to gratuitous promises, such as [doctrines like promissory estoppel]. One way of making a unilateral promise enforceable is for the promisor to exact a merely nominal consideration from the promisee, since courts normally inquire only into the existence and not into the adequacy of the consideration. But not only is this a cumbersome alternative to the promise under seal; increasingly, there is the danger that such a "contract" may be deemed unconscionably one-sided and so not enforced.

THE SEAL (II)*

At early common law the seal [allowed a party to legally obligate itself to make a gift]. In modern times, most state legislatures have either abolished the distinction between sealed and unsealed promises, abolished the use of a seal in contracts, or otherwise limited the seal's effect. The axiomatic school, however, never rejected the rule that a seal makes a promise enforceable, and that rule is now embodied in section 95(1)(a) of the Restatement Second, which provides that "[i]n the absence of statute a promise is binding without consideration if . . . it is in writing and sealed. . . ."

The *Restatement Second* makes no attempt to justify this rule. That is not surprising, because justification would be hard to find. Originally, the seal was a natural formality—that is, a promissory form popularly understood to carry legal significance—which ensured both deliberation and proof by involving a writing, a ritual of hot wax, and a physical object that personified its owner. Later, however, the elements of ritual and personification eroded away, so that in most states by statute or decision a seal may now take the form of a printed device, word, or scrawl, the printed initials "L.S.," or a printed recital of sealing. Few promisors today have even the vaguest idea of the significance of such words, letters, or signs, if they notice them at all. The *Restatement Second* itself admits that "the seal has come to seem archaic." Considering this drastic change in circumstances, the rule that a seal renders a promise enforceable has ceased to be tenable under modern conditions. The rule has been changed by statute in about two-thirds of

* Excerpted from Melvin Aron Eisenberg, *The Principles of Consideration*, 67 CORNELL L. REV. 640, 659-61 (1982).

the states, and at least one modern case held even without the benefit of statute that the rule should no longer be strictly applied.[62] Other courts can and should follow suit. Should the law then recognize some new formality to play the role once played by the seal? An obvious candidate is nominal consideration—that is, the form of a bargain—because it can be safely assumed that parties who falsely cast a nonbargain promise as a bargain do so for the express purpose of making the promise legally enforceable. A rule that promises in this form were enforceable would have obvious substantive advantages, but would also involve serious difficulties of administration. As a practical matter, such a form would be primarily employed to render donative promises enforceable. Both morally and legally, however, an obligation created by a donative promise should normally be excused either by acts of the promisee amounting to ingratitude, or by personal circumstances of the promisor that render it improvident to keep the promise. If Uncle promises to give Nephew $20,000 in two years, and Nephew later wrecks Uncle's living room in an angry rage, Uncle should not remain obliged. The same result should ordinarily follow if Uncle suffers a serious financial setback and is barely able to take care of the needs of his immediate family, or if Uncle's wealth remains constant but his personal obligations significantly increase in an unexpected manner, as through illness or the birth of children.

8. *A penny for your thoughts.* The court noted, in the first paragraph after the parties' agreement, that the plaintiffs never alleged that the one cent that was agreed to be paid was ever actually paid or tendered to Mr. Schnell. Should this matter?

9. *Speaking of pennies, what happened to the peppercorn theory of consideration?* Was the court's ruling consistent with the common law's general prohibition against inquiring into the adequacy of consideration? Why or why not? Can this decision be squared with *Whitney v. Stearns*, 16 Me. 394 (1939)? In that case, the court wrote "[a] cent or a peppercorn, in legal estimation, would constitute consideration." *Id.* at 397.

10. *Illustrations.* To say that a mere peppercorn is sufficient to constitute consideration is not to say that parties can make otherwise unenforceable promises binding by providing sham consideration. The consideration exchanged must actually form part of the parties' bargain. The *Restatement (Second) of Contracts* § 71 offers the following Illustrations:

> 4. A desires to make a binding promise to give $1000 to his son B. Being advised that a gratuitous promise is not binding, A writes out and signs a false

62. *Hartford-Connecticut Trust Co. v. Devine*, 116 A. 239 (1922); *cf. Ortez v. Bargas*, 29 Hawaii 548 (1927) (instrument is sealed only if it bears actual wax seal, and even if sealed, it may be attacked for lack of consideration).

recital that B has sold him a car for $1000 and a promise to pay that amount. There is no consideration for A's promise.

5. A desires to make a binding promise to give $1000 to his son B. Being advised that a gratuitous promise is not binding, A offers to buy from B for $1000 a book worth less than $1. B accepts the offer knowing that the purchase of the book is a mere pretense. There is no consideration for A's promise to pay $1000.

Can the result in *Schnell* can be reconciled with the result in the next case?

Batsakis v. Demotsis

Court of Civil Appeals of Texas, El Paso
226 S.W.2d 673 (1949)

MCGILL, JUSTICE. This is an appeal from a judgment of the 57th judicial District Court of Bexar County. Appellant was plaintiff and appellee was defendant in the trial court. The parties will be so designated.

Plaintiff sued defendant to recover $2,000 with interest at the rate of 8% per annum from April 2, 1942, alleged to be due on the following instrument, being a translation from the original, which is written in the Greek language:

Peiraeus

April 2, 1942

Mr. George Batsakis
Konstantinou Diadohou #7
Peiraeus

Mr. Batsakis:

I state by my present (letter) that I received today from you the amount of two thousand dollars ($2,000.00) of United States of America money, which I borrowed from you for the support of my family during these difficult days and because it is impossible for me to transfer dollars of my own from America.

The above amount I accept with the expressed promise that I will return to you again in American dollars either at the end of the present war or even before in the event that you might be able to find a way to collect them (dollars) from my representative in America to whom I shall write and give him an order relative to this. You understand until the final execution (payment) to the above amount an eight per cent interest will be added and paid together with the principal.

I thank you and I remain yours with respects.

The recipient,

(Signed) Eugenia The. Demotsis.

Trial to the court without the intervention of a jury resulted in a judgment in favor of plaintiff for $750.00 principal, and interest at the rate of 8% per annum from April 2, 1942 to the date of judgment, totaling $1163.83, with interest thereon at the rate of 8% per annum until paid. Plaintiff has perfected his appeal.

The court sustained certain special exceptions of plaintiff to defendant's first amended original answer on which the case was tried, and struck therefrom paragraphs II, III and V. Defendant excepted to such action of the court, but has not cross-assigned error here. The answer, stripped of such paragraphs, consisted of a general denial contained in paragraph I thereof, and of paragraph IV, which is as follows:

> IV. That under the circumstances alleged in Paragraph II of this answer, the consideration upon which said written instrument sued upon by plaintiff herein is founded, is wanting and has failed to the extent of $1975.00, and defendant pleads specially under the verification hereinafter made the want and failure of consideration stated, and now tenders, as defendant has heretofore tendered to plaintiff, $25.00 as the value of the loan of money received by defendant from plaintiff, together with interest thereon.
>
> Further, in connection with this plea of want and failure of consideration defendant alleges that she at no time received from plaintiff himself or from anyone for plaintiff any money or thing of value other than, as hereinbefore alleged, the original loan of 500,000 drachmae. That at the time of the loan by plaintiff to defendant of said 500,000 drachmae the value of 500,000 drachmae in the Kingdom of Greece in dollars of money of the United States of America, was $25.00, and also at said time the value of 500,000 drachmae of Greek money in the United States of America in dollars was $25.00 of money of the United States of America. The plea of want and failure of consideration is verified by defendant as follows.

The allegations in paragraph II which were stricken, referred to in paragraph IV, were that the instrument sued on was signed and delivered in the Kingdom of Greece on or about April 2, 1942, at which time both plaintiff and defendant were residents of and residing in the Kingdom of Greece, and

> Plaintiff . . . avers that on or about April 2, 1942 she owned money and property and had credit in the United States of America, but was then and there in the Kingdom of Greece in straitened financial circumstances due to the conditions produced by World War II and could not make use of her money and property and credit existing in the United States of America. That in the circumstances the plaintiff agreed to and did lend to defendant the sum of 500,000 drachmae, which at that time, on or about April 2, 1942, had the value of $25.00 in money of the United States of America. That the said plaintiff, knowing defendant's financial distress and desire to return to the United States of America, exacted of her the written instrument plaintiff sues upon, which was a promise by her to pay to him the sum of $2,000.00 of United States of America money.

Plaintiff specially excepted to paragraph IV because the allegations thereof were insufficient to allege **either want of consideration or failure of**

consideration, in that it affirmatively appears therefrom that defendant received what was agreed to be delivered to her, and that plaintiff breached no agreement. The court overruled this exception, and such action is assigned as error. Error is also assigned because of the court's failure to enter judgment for the whole unpaid balance of the principal of the instrument with interest as therein provided.

> ***Want versus failure of consideration***
>
> Make sure you understand the difference between the plaintiff's arguments that defendant's allegations were insufficient *both* for "want of consideration" and "failure of consideration." How did the court address each of these claims? Do you agree?

Defendant testified that she did receive 500,000 drachmas from plaintiff. It is not clear whether she received all the 500,000 drachmas or only a portion of them before she signed the instrument in question. Her testimony clearly shows that the understanding of the parties was that plaintiff would give her the 500,000 drachmas if she would sign the instrument. She testified:

> Q. . . . who suggested the figure of $2,000.00?
>
> A. That was how he asked me from the beginning. He said he will give me five hundred thousand drachmas provided I signed that I would pay him $2,000.00 American money.

The transaction amounted to a sale by plaintiff of the 500,000 drachmas in consideration of the execution of the instrument sued on, by defendant. It is not contended that the drachmas had no value. Indeed, the judgment indicates that the trial court placed a value of $750.00 on them or on the other consideration which plaintiff gave defendant for the instrument if he believed plaintiff's testimony. Therefore the plea of want of consideration was unavailing. A plea of want of consideration amounts to a contention that the instrument never became a valid obligation in the first place.

Mere inadequacy of consideration will not void a contract.

> ***Mere inadequacy will not void a contract***
>
> How, if at all, would you square the result here with *Schnell*?

Nor was the plea of failure of consideration availing. Defendant got exactly what she contracted for according to her own testimony. The court should have rendered judgment in favor of plaintiff against defendant for the principal sum of $2,000.00 evidenced by the instrument sued on, with interest as therein provided. We construe the provision relating to interest as providing for interest at the rate of 8% per annum. The judgment is reformed so as to award appellant a recovery against appellee of $2,000.00 with interest thereon at the rate of 8% per annum from April 2, 1942. Such judgment will bear interest at the rate of 8% per annum until paid on $2,000.00 thereof and on the balance interest at the rate of 6% per annum. As so reformed, the judgment is affirmed.

Reformed and affirmed.

RELEVANT PROVISIONS

For the *Restatement (Second) of Contracts*, consult §§ 71 and 79(b).

NOTES AND QUESTIONS

1. *What happened?* Who sued whom for what? Procedurally, how did the case get before this court? Factually, what happened between the parties? What arguments did the plaintiff and defendant make? What rule or rules did the court apply? How did the court analyze the dispute between the parties? How did the court decide the case?

2. *Was this case correctly decided?* Do you agree with the result reached in this case? Why or why not? Do you agree with the court's reasoning? Why or why not? How, if at all, would you have written the opinion differently?

3. *Can these cases be reconciled?* Can *Schnell* and *Batsakis* be reconciled? Why did the court find no consideration in *Schnell*, but consideration here? Do you agree or disagree with the different outcomes reached in these cases?

4. *Should the promise have been enforced?* Regardless of whether or not there was consideration, do you think the promise here should have been enforced? Why or why not?

5. *Currency.* Is the fact that this transaction involved two different currencies relevant? Why or why not? Should it matter that the market value of the drachma vis-à-vis the dollar was so low? What if the 500,000 drachmae had a market value of one cent? Same result?

6. *Adequacy of consideration reconsidered.* The introduction to this unit indicated that most U.S. courts do not inquire into the adequacy of consideration, and *Batsakis* is about as strong a case in support of that principle as one could ask for. But is this a good policy? If taken to extremes, wouldn't it allow nominal consideration to be used as a mere form? If so, is there a problem with this? In answering this, you may want to reread the two excerpts that appear immediately before this case.

7. *Should the circumstances under which the contract was made matter?* Consider the following:

> It has been said that Greece suffered more heavily during the war than any other Allied country except Soviet Russia. From 1941 to 1944 the country was visited by famine, destruction, and inflation. Greece normally requires to import some 600,000 tons of grain a year. Most of this comes by sea. As soon as the Axis occupied Greece the usual sea routes ceased to be available—except those from the Black Sea and the Adriatic. And in any case there were few ships on which the Axis could lay their hands for feeding the country. Moreover, the only

> other main line of communication, the railway to Belgrade and Sofia, was fully occupied in supplying the Axis armies of occupation. Even if the Axis had been determined to maintain the existing standard of nutrition in Greece, it would have been a difficult task. As things were, the standard fell disastrously. It is estimated that the average daily diet in 1941, the worst of the three war winters, fell to 900 calories per person, and that it never exceeded 1,400 calories during the occupation. As the daily diet of a healthy man should be in the region of 3,000 calories, it is hardly surprising that Greece fell a prey to famine, especially in the towns. At one period in the winter of 1941-2 people were dying daily in the streets of Athens by the score. It will probably never be known how many perished of malnutrition and the diseases occasioned thereby, but the figure may well run into hundreds of thousands.*

8. *Unconscionability.* Might this agreement have been unconscionable? We will postpone this question for now, taking it up again when we discuss the defense of unconscionability in greater detail in Chapter 8. For those wishing to peek ahead, however, the relevant *Restatement (Second) of Contracts* provision is § 208.

9. *Application.* Can you apply the principles we have learned above to the problems below?

PROBLEM: A MOTHER'S GOOD DEED?

On September 18, 2013, Shannon Fischer conveyed a warranty deed for Jefferson and Calvin Street properties to her daughter, Laura Fischer. The Jefferson Street property was encumbered by a $15,000 mortgage. Laura took the deed and read it. The deed mentioned that it was encumbered by the mortgage but said that "the grantor agrees to pay the mortgage" when it came due. A year and a half after the conveyance, Shannon Fischer died. Her will made no provision for the payment of the mortgage on the Jefferson Street property. Within two months of her death, the bank that held the mortgage on the Jefferson Street property threatened to foreclose for failure to make payments.

What remedy, if any, would Laura have against the bank? Against her mother's estate? What course of action would you recommend the bank take in this situation?

PROBLEM: TAKING ADVANTAGE

At age sixteen Bridgett Watts was awarded $1.5 million as a settlement for a botched medical procedure that left her with large visible scars. When she was nineteen she became romantically involved with Peter Kilman, an ex-convict,

* BICKHAM SWEET-ESCOTT, GREECE—A POLITICAL AND ECONOMIC SURVEY 93-96 (1954).

who introduced her to crack cocaine. Peter suggested to Bridgett that she should sell her annuity contract for an immediate payout. Peter approached Lancaster Insurance Company to have them draft the contract documents to purchase the annuity. Peter brought the contract back to Bridgett and she signed part of it on the hood of an automobile in a parking lot and the rest in a restaurant. The contract stipulated that Lancaster Insurance Company would pay Bridgett $350,000 for the annuity policy which would return to the company almost $1.85 million over its guaranteed term of twenty-five years, and which had a cash value at the time the contract was executed of $1.25 million. As part of a deposit on the annuity contract, Peter negotiated debt forgiveness on a $2,500 debt he owed to Lancaster Insurance Company. Shortly afterwards, Bridgett brought suit against Lancaster Insurance Company to rescind the contract. Lancaster Insurance counterclaimed for specific performance.

What grounds does Bridgett have to argue for rescission of the contract? What grounds does Lancaster Insurance Company have to argue for specific performance?

PROBLEM: A GOLDEN OPPORTUNITY

About ten years ago, Drew bought some property in Nevada and began prospecting for gold. After prospecting for several years, Drew was adjudged insane and committed to an asylum in Las Vegas, Nevada. After being confined for about four years, Drew was finally released. Upon his release, Drew learned that his guardian, Gary, sold his property during his confinement, and that gold was subsequently found on his property. Drew, destitute and without work, met with his old friend, Perry, to ask for a loan to recover his property. Although the chance of Drew recovering his property was slim, Drew promised Perry a very significant sum if his mining property—now worth around $5 million—were recovered. Specifically, Drew told Perry:

> You have already let me have $1,000 in the past. If you will give me $1,000 more so I can get my property back, I will pay you a hundred thousand dollars if and when I win back my property.
>
> Perry accepted this offer, and advanced Drew the sum of $1,000. A few years later, after some litigation, Drew recovered his property. Drew, remembering his agreement with Perry, instructed that Gary, as his trustee, pay the full amount due to Perry. Gary refused to do so, and Perry brought an action for breach of contract to recover the $100,000.

As Drew's guardian and trustee, Gary argued that no contract was made between Perry and Drew because any promise was not supported by adequate consideration. Specifically, Gary alleged that the sum of $1,000 was not an adequate consideration to support a promise to repay $100,000.

Assume that Drew was of sound mind when he first voluntarily offered to pay $100,000 to Perry if he successfully recovered his property. Drawing on the cases and *Restatement* provisions above, how should a court rule, and why?

Specifically, do you think a court should enforce the contract between Perry and Drew, or should it refuse to do so on account of the $1,000 consideration being inadequate to support a $100,000 return promise?

One of the neat things about knowing a little contract law is that it will enable you to make sense of a wide range of social phenomena you encounter every day, phenomena that were always there—in pop culture, on television, in novels, newspapers, and the movies—but that somehow flew beneath your radar. No more! In the excerpt below, we take a new look—a contractual look—at an old story that many of you may already be familiar with: Esau's selling of his birthright to his brother Jacob under somewhat dubious circumstances. Are there any similarities between the bargain below and the bargain that took place between Batsakis and Demotsis in the previous case?

COMPARATIVE PERSPECTIVE: THE SALE OF A BIRTHRIGHT*

Consider . . . the famous story of Esau's sale of his birthright in Genesis 25:27-34. Jacob and Esau are twins, but Esau has the birthright as firstborn. Esau becomes a hunter and Jacob a farmer. Esau comes in from the field famished and finds Jacob with some pottage of lentils. Jacob refuses to give him any until Esau agrees to sell him his birthright; and, even when Esau indicates a willingness to sell because "I am at death's door,"[19] Jacob insists that he swear an oath. Esau swears the oath, and Jacob gives him the food. In modern terms, this story describes a contract for sale in which Esau and Jacob exchange Esau's birthright for a mess of pottage owned by Jacob. . . . The fact that Jacob insists that Esau swear an oath, I believe, is immediate evidence that the text fulfilled a legal function. An oath is a specifically legal act. It formalizes and bonds a promise by invoking the deity as witness or even as cobeneficiary of the promise. . . . Delivery in the form of a handing over would not be possible for a birthright as it was for tangible personal property. The oath takes the place of delivery and establishes with the requisite formality that the property in fact has been transferred. The likelihood of future disputes over whether ownership of intangible property in fact has been conveyed is greatly mitigated if the party transferring the property swears an oath, particularly if he does so in the presence of witnesses. . . .

The other remarkable feature of the story . . . is the gross inequality of bargaining power between the parties. . . . The text . . . sets out to establish the sharpest possible contrast between the value in market terms of the thing Jacob has—pottage, which was among the meanest of foods—and that which Esau provides in

* Excerpted from Geoffrey P. Miller, *Contracts of Genesis*, 22 J. LEGAL STUD. 15, 23 (1993) (internal citations omitted).

19. GEN. 25:32.

exchange—his birthright, his most valuable asset. . . . Esau was fully aware of the value of the thing he was giving up and did so only because he had no choice in the matter; if he died for want of food his birthright would pass to Jacob in any event. . . . [I]t is evident that the parties are shown as being in grossly unequal bargaining positions, and Jacob is portrayed as extracting compensation that far exceeds in objective value the value of the item he gives up.

Part of the fascination of this story is the lesson it teaches about economics. The Jacob-Esau saga illustrates that the utility of a good to an individual can far exceed its market value and that a monopolistic seller is in the position to extract all of the consumer surplus in a transaction with such an individual. The story emphasizes this proposition by specifically recounting the fact that Esau discloses his condition to Jacob before the parties engage in their negotiations. Jacob would not have been likely to seek such an above-market price had he not known of Esau's weak bargaining position. By implication, Esau was very unwise to give Jacob this information before seeking to strike a deal. . . .

Turning to the actual contract itself, the story seems to carry the rule that a contract is legally binding even if made under conditions of grossly unequal bargaining power. It is noteworthy that Esau, after having sworn an oath and sold the birthright, never denies that the sale was valid and binding as a matter of contract. The legal validity of the contract is never an issue.

The rule that a contract is valid and binding despite grossly unfair terms and extreme inequality of bargaining power seems dubious from today's perspective. Today, at least, this contract would not be enforceable, either under an expansive notion of duress or under principles of unconscionability. . . .

[However,] [t]he rule of the Jacob-Esau story is simply that duress or inequality of bargaining power is no defense: if the contract is made—here, the oath is sworn and the birthright transferred—that is the end of it. . . .

One other point is worth mentioning. Why is it that the oral tradition should have remembered this particular story? I think the answer is that this story is quite recognizable as what we would today call a "hard case." In fact, it is about as hard a case as one can imagine. Why would the hard case be transmitted in oral tradition and the easy cases not? Because the hard case conveys information in the most economical fashion. Given the Jacob-Esau story, other fact patterns that might arise seem a fortiori. In an oral tradition where economy of meaning is at a premium because of the costs of memorization, it is exactly the hard case that we would expect to see passed through the culture. The easy cases will be forgotten for the same reason that we forget the easy cases today: they simply do not convey as much information.

NOTES AND QUESTIONS

1. *Legal formalities.* As should be clear from the excerpt above, the problems we have confronted in this chapter are not new, and have been with us for as long as humans have been exchanging things with one another, which is to say, for a long, long time. Indeed, whenever a society—like our own, or like

that of ancient Canaan where the Jacob-Esau story is set—is willing to enforce unwritten promises, it seems inevitable that the society will soon establish a set of formalities to test whether any particular unwritten promise should be enforced. In our society, this role is largely performed by the doctrine of consideration. In many ancient societies, such as Canaan, that role was often performed by taking an oath. Can you see how the oath satisfied all three functions of legal formalities identified by Fuller in the excerpt "The Role of Legal Formalities"? (See p. 341, *supra*.)

2. ***Consideration.*** Do you think the Jacob-Esau bargain would satisfy the test of consideration used by our courts today? Does the doctrine of consideration care whether the bargain was fair? Should it? If not, do you think Esau should be able to assert a defense to get out of the contract? (We will discuss several defenses that Esau could have argued, such as duress and unconscionability, in chapter 8, *infra*.)

3. ***Hard cases.*** Finally, note that the author describes the Jacob-Esau story as a "hard case," but seems to view such cases in a much kinder light than Wormser in *The True Conception of Unilateral Contracts* (see p. 263, *supra*).

b. Forbearing to Sue as Consideration

This overview provides a brief introduction to the problem of enforcing promises to settle invalid claims. As you read, pay attention not only to the split among courts in dealing with this problem, but, in the last paragraph, how the benefit/detriment theory of consideration we learned about in Hamer *has been used to hold such promises unenforceable, whereas the bargain-based theory of consideration we learned about in the* Restatement *has often been used to uphold them.*

DOCTRINAL OVERVIEW: SETTLEMENT OF INVALID CLAIMS AS CONSIDERATION*

Suppose that a claimant asserts a claim against another—perhaps in contract, in tort, or under a will—and the other promises to pay $1,000 if the claimant releases the claim or forbears or promises to forbear from pursuing it. If the claim is a valid one, and the promisor bargains for its settlement in return for his promise to pay $1,000, there is clearly consideration for the promise. But what if it later turns out that the claim is invalid? Is settlement of an invalid claim enough of a peppercorn to support a promise?

It may make sense to enforce the promise even if the claim is invalid. The law favors settlement by the parties of disputed claims in the interests of alleviating discord and promoting certainty. . . . The policy favoring such compromises of

* Excerpted from E. Allan Farnsworth, Contracts § 2.12 (4th ed. 2004).

disputed claims suggests that the claimant be allowed to enforce the promise, even if the settled claim later proves to be invalid.

Most courts have taken a position favorable to compromise and have upheld promises made in settlement of invalid claims as long as the claim was disputed. A few courts have rejected this view, however, on the ground that there is no consideration for the promise if the claim that is settled turns out to be invalid. . . .

Courts following the prevailing view invariably require that the claim be asserted in good faith, that is, with an honest belief that it may fairly be determined to be valid. . . . A claim that is neither valid nor asserted in good faith will not suffice as a peppercorn.

In addition to the requirement of the claimant's good faith, many courts have imposed a requirement that the claim itself have enough substance to be "doubtful," as opposed to unfounded, though there is little agreement on what is meant by "doubtful." One court gave the following graphic summary of the problem:

> It is difficult to reconcile the antinomous rules and statements which are applied to the "doubtful claims" and to find the words which will exactly draw the line between the compromise (on the one hand) of an honestly disputed claim which has some fair element of doubt and is therefore to he regarded as consideration and (on the other hand) a claim, though honestly made, which is so lacking in substance and virility as to be entirely baseless. . . . But . . . we would say that if the claimant *in good faith,* makes a mountain out of a mole hill the claim is "doubtful." But if there is no discernable mole hill in the beginning, then the claim has no substance.[7]

. . . These cases on the settlement of claims show the interplay of the several theories of consideration. If a court chooses not to enforce the promise made in settlement of an invalid claim, it can find support in the argument that the relinquishment of such a claim is no detriment—no "legal" detriment, it is sometimes said—to the promisee, the claimant. Somewhat less convincing is the argument that its settlement is no benefit to the promisor, which has at least managed to "buy its peace." If, however, the court chooses to enforce the promise, it can find support in the bargain test for, as one court pointed out, the promisor "can hardly be heard to say that the claim . . . was obviously invalid and frivolous when it attached enough importance to it to make the contract in question."[9]

Fiege v. Boehm

Court of Appeals of Maryland
123 A.2d 316 (1956)

DELAPLAINE, J. This suit was brought in the Superior Court of Baltimore City by Hilda Louise Boehm against Louis Gail Fiege to recover for breach of a contract to pay the expenses incident to the birth of his bastard child and to provide

7. *Duncan v. Black,* 324 S.W.2d 483, 486-87 (Mo. App. 1959).

9. *Ralston v. Mathew,* 250 P.2d 841 (Kan. 1952) (tort claim against church "was not obviously invalid or frivolous" although churches were not liable for their torts).

for its support upon condition that she would refrain from prosecuting him for bastardy.

Plaintiff alleged in her declaration substantially as follows: (1) that early in 1951 defendant had sexual intercourse with her although she was unmarried, and as a result thereof she became pregnant, and defendant acknowledged that he was responsible for her pregnancy; (2) that on September 29, 1951, she gave birth to a female child; that defendant is the father of the child; and that he acknowledged on many occasions that he is its father; (3) that before the child was born, defendant agreed to pay all her medical and miscellaneous expenses and to compensate her for the loss of her salary caused by the child's birth, and also to pay her ten dollars per week for its support until it reached the age of 21, upon condition that she would not institute bastardy proceedings against him as long as he made the payments in accordance with the agreement; (4) that she placed the child for adoption on July 13, 1954, and she claimed the following sums: Union Memorial Hospital, \$110; Florence Crittenton Home, \$100; Dr. George Merrill, her physician, \$50; medicines \$70.35; miscellaneous expenses, \$20.45; loss of earnings for 26 weeks, \$1,105; support of the child, \$1,440; total, \$2,895.80; and (5) that defendant paid her only \$480, and she demanded that he pay her the further sum of \$2,415.80, the balance due under the agreement, but he failed and refused to pay the same. . . .

Plaintiff, a typist, now over 35 years old, who has been employed by the Government in Washington and Baltimore for over thirteen years, testified in the Court below that she had never been married, but that at about midnight on January 21, 1951, defendant, after taking her to a moving picture theater on York Road and then to a restaurant, had sexual intercourse with her in his automobile. She further testified that he agreed to pay all her medical and hospital expenses, to compensate her for loss of salary caused by the pregnancy and birth, and to pay her ten dollars per week for the support of the child upon condition that she would refrain from instituting bastardy proceedings against him. She further testified that between September 17, 1951, and May, 1953, defendant paid her a total of \$480.

Defendant admitted that he had taken plaintiff to restaurants, had danced with her several times, had taken her to Washington, and had brought her home in the country; but he asserted that he had never had sexual intercourse with her. He also claimed that he did not enter into any agreement with her. He admitted, however, that he had paid her a total of \$480. His father also testified that he stated "that he did not want his mother to know, and if it were just kept quiet, kept principally away from his mother and the public and the courts, that he would take care of it."

Defendant further testified that in May, 1953, he went to see plaintiff's physician to make inquiry about blood tests to show the paternity of the child; and that those tests were made and they indicated that it was not possible that he could have been the child's father. He then stopped making payments. Plaintiff thereupon filed a charge of bastardy with the State's Attorney.

The testimony which was given in the Criminal Court by Dr. Milton Sachs, hematologist at the University Hospital, was read to the jury in the Superior Court. . . . Dr. Sachs reported that Fiege's blood group was Type O, Miss Boehm's was Type B, and the infant's was Type A. He further testified that on the basis of these tests, Fiege could not have been the father of the child, as it is impossible for a mating of Type O and Type B to result in a child of Type A.

Although defendant was acquitted by the Criminal Court, the Superior Court overruled his **motion for a directed verdict**. In the charge to the jury the Court instructed them that defendant's acquittal in the Criminal Court was not binding upon them. The jury found a verdict in favor of plaintiff for $2,415.80, the full amount of her claim.

> ***Motion for directed verdict***
>
> "A party's request that the court enter judgment in its favor before submitting the case to the jury because there is no legally sufficient evidentiary foundation on which a reasonable jury could find for the other party." BLACK'S LAW DICTIONARY (10th ed. 2014).

Defendant filed a **motion for judgment n.o.v.** or a new trial. The Court overruled that motion also, and entered judgment on the verdict of the jury. Defendant appealed from that judgment.

> ***Motion for judgment notwithstanding the verdict (or j.n.o.v.)***
>
> "A party's request that the court enter a judgment in its favor despite the jury's contrary verdict because there is no legally sufficient evidentiary basis for a jury to find for the other party." BLACK'S LAW DICTIONARY (10th ed. 2014).

Defendant contends that, even if he did enter into the contract as alleged, it was not enforceable, because plaintiff's forbearance to prosecute was not based on a valid claim, and hence the contract was without consideration. He, therefore, asserts that the Court erred in overruling . . . his motion for a directed verdict, and . . . his motion for judgment n.o.v. or a new trial.

> ***Filius nullius***
>
> "[Latin 'son of nobody'] Hist. (17c) An illegitimate child." BLACK'S LAW DICTIONARY (10th ed. 2014).

It was originally held at common law that a child born out of wedlock is ***filius nullius***, and a putative father is not under any legal liability to contribute to the support of his illegitimate child, and his promise to do so is unenforceable because it is based on purely a moral obligation. Some of the courts in this country have held that, in the absence of any statutory obligation on the father to aid in the support of his bastard child, his promise to the child's mother to pay her for its maintenance, resting solely on his natural affection for it and his moral obligation to provide for it, is a promise which the law cannot enforce because of lack of sufficient consideration. On the contrary, a few courts have stated that the natural affection of a father for his child and the moral obligation upon him to support it and to aid the woman he has wronged furnish sufficient consideration for his promise to the mother to pay for the support of the child to make the agreement enforceable at law.

However, where statutes are in force to compel the father of a bastard to contribute to its support, the courts have invariably held that a contract by the putative father with the mother of his bastard child to provide for the support of the child upon the agreement of the mother to refrain from invoking the bastardy statute against the father, or to abandon proceedings already commenced, is supported by sufficient consideration.

In Maryland it is now provided by statute that whenever a person is found guilty of bastardy, the court shall issue an order directing such person (1) to pay for the maintenance and support of the child until it reaches the age of eighteen years, such sum as may be agreed upon, if consent proceedings be had, or in the absence of agreement, such sum as the court may fix, with due regard to the circumstances of the accused person; and (2) to give bond to the State of Maryland in such penalty as the court may fix, with good and sufficient securities, conditioned on making the payments required by the court's order, or any amendments thereof. Failure to give such bond shall be punished by commitment to the jail or the House of Correction until bond is given but not exceeding two years.

Prosecutions for bastardy are treated in Maryland as criminal proceedings, but they are actually civil in purpose. While the prime object of the Maryland Bastardy Act is to protect the public from the burden of maintaining illegitimate children, it is so distinctly in the interest of the mother that she becomes the beneficiary of it. Accordingly a contract by the putative father of an illegitimate child to provide for its support upon condition that bastardy proceedings will not be instituted is a compromise of civil injuries resulting from a criminal act, and not a contract to compound a criminal prosecution, and if it is fair and reasonable, it is in accord with the Bastardy Act and the public policy of the State.

Of course, a contract of a putative father to provide for the support of his illegitimate child must be based, like any other contract, upon sufficient consideration. The early English law made no distinction in regard to the sufficiency of a claim which the claimant promised to forbear to prosecute, as the consideration of a promise, other than the broad distinction between good claims and bad claims. No promise to forbear to prosecute an unfounded claim was sufficient consideration. In the early part of the Nineteenth Century, an advance was made from the criterion of the early authorities when it was held that forbearance to prosecute a suit which had already been instituted was sufficient consideration, without inquiring whether the suit would have been successful or not.

In 1867 the Maryland Court of Appeals, in the opinion delivered by Judge Bartol in *Hartle v. Stahl*, 27 Md. 157, 172, held: (1) that forbearance to assert a claim before institution of suit, if not in fact a legal claim, is not of itself sufficient consideration to support a promise; but (2) that a compromise of a doubtful claim or a relinquishment of a pending suit is good consideration for a promise; and (3) that in order to support a compromise, it is sufficient that the parties entering into it thought at the time that there was a *bona fide* question between them, although it may eventually be found that there was in fact no such question.

We have thus adopted the rule that the surrender of, or forbearance to assert, an invalid claim by one who has not an honest and reasonable belief in its possible validity is not sufficient consideration for a contract. ***Restatement (First) of Contracts* § 76(b)**. We combine the subjective requisite that the claim be *bona fide* with the objective requisite that it must have a reasonable basis of support. Accordingly a promise not to prosecute a claim which is not founded in good faith does

Restatement (First) of Contracts § 76(b)

This provision provides that "[t]he surrender of, or forbearance to assert an invalid claim or defense by one who has not an honest and reasonable belief in its possible validity" cannot constitute sufficient consideration.

not of itself give a right of action on an agreement to pay for refraining from so acting, because a release from mere annoyance and unfounded litigation does not furnish valuable consideration.

Professor Williston was not entirely certain whether the test of reasonableness is based upon the intelligence of the claimant himself, who may be an ignorant person with no knowledge of law and little sense as to facts; but he seemed inclined to favor the view that "the claim forborne must be neither absurd in fact from the standpoint of a reasonable man in the position of the claimant, nor, obviously unfounded in law to one who has an elementary knowledge of legal principles." 1 *Williston on Contracts*, Rev. Ed. § 135. We agree that while stress is placed upon the honesty and good faith of the claimant, forbearance to prosecute a claim is insufficient consideration if the claim forborne is so lacking in foundation as to make its assertion incompatible with honesty and a reasonable degree of intelligence. Thus, if the mother of a bastard knows that there is no foundation, either in law or fact, for a charge against a certain man that he is the father of the child, but that man promises to pay her in order to prevent bastardy proceedings against him, the forbearance to institute proceedings is not sufficient consideration.

On the other hand, forbearance to sue for a lawful claim or demand is sufficient consideration for a promise to pay for the forbearance if the party forbearing had an honest intention to prosecute litigation which is not frivolous, vexatious, or unlawful, and which he believed to be well founded. Thus the promise of a woman who is expecting an illegitimate child that she will not institute bastardy proceedings against a certain man is sufficient consideration for his promise to pay for the child's support, even though it may not be certain whether the man is the father or whether the prosecution would be successful, if she makes the charge in good faith. The fact that a man accused of bastardy is forced to enter into a contract to pay for the support of his bastard child from fear of exposure and the shame that might be case [sic] upon him as a result, as well as a sense of justice to render some compensation for the injury he inflicted upon the mother, does not lessen the merit of the contract, but greatly increases it. . . .

In the case at bar there was no proof of fraud or unfairness. Assuming that the hematologists were accurate in their laboratory tests and findings, nevertheless plaintiff gave testimony which indicated that she made the charge of bastardy against defendant in good faith. For these reasons the Court acted properly in overruling . . . the motion for a directed verdict. . . .

It is immaterial whether defendant was the father of the child or not. In the light of what we have said, we need not make any specific determination on this subject. . . .

As we have found no reversible error in the rulings and instructions of the trial Court, we will affirm the judgment entered on the verdict of the jury.

Judgment affirmed, with costs.

RELEVANT PROVISIONS

For the *Restatement (Second) of Contracts*, consult § 74.

NOTES AND QUESTIONS

1. *What happened?* Who sued whom for what? Procedurally, how did the case get before this court? Factually, what happened between the parties? What arguments did the plaintiff and defendant make? What rule or rules did the court apply? How did the court analyze the dispute between the parties? How did the court decide the case?

2. *Was this case correctly decided?* Do you agree with the result reached in this case? Why or why not? Do you agree with the court's reasoning? Why or why not? How, if at all, would you have written the opinion differently?

3. *Promises.* What promises did each party make to the other?

4. *Consideration.* Were these promises supported by consideration? Why or why not?

5. *Good faith.* This court cited an earlier Maryland Court of Appeals decision holding that "a compromise of a doubtful claim or a relinquishment of a pending suit is good consideration for a promise." But it was also made clear by the court (and later, in Comment b to the *Restatement (Second) of Contracts* § 74) that the dispute between the parties must be in good faith to constitute consideration. This brings up two questions: First, should the good faith of the claim be the deciding factor in determining whether the promise is enforceable? In other words, would you agree with the court that, so long as the claim here was made in good faith, "[i]t is immaterial whether defendant was the father of the child or not"? Second, do you think the dispute here was made in good faith? Why or why not?

6. *Is this the right test?* Is consideration really the appropriate doctrine to govern such cases? Why or why not?

7. *Application.* Try to apply the principles you have learned in this unit to the problem below.

PROBLEM: ONE NIGHT COST

Daniel Forrest is a professional golfer who had an extramarital affair with Shawna Kent in 2000. At the time, Daniel was the favorite to win the PGA Championship and had secured numerous endorsement deals worth more than $12 million. Shortly before the start of the tournament, Shawna approached Daniel and told him that she was pregnant and would not be aborting the baby due to her personal beliefs. Daniel, worried that his reputation would be ruined if this extramarital affair were exposed to the public, proposed to Shawna a settlement agreement that would resolve their problem. Daniel offered to pay her "$5 million when he retired from professional golf in return for her agreement not to file a paternity suit against him and for her agreement to keep their romantic involvement confidential." Shawna accepted Daniel's offer. In 2008, when rumors began to spread that Daniel was retiring from golf, Shawna's counsel contacted Daniel's counsel to remind him of the obligation to pay the $5 million. Daniel denied that he promised to pay Shawna $5 million and filed a complaint for declaratory judgment and an injunction claiming the contract was extortion. Shawna counterclaimed for $5 million for breach of contract.

Does Shawna have a valid contract upon which to base her lawsuit? As the judge in this case, how would you rule on Daniel's counterclaim? What additional facts, if proved, would help Daniel's case? Shawna's?

c. Past and Moral Consideration

DOCTRINAL OVERVIEW: PAST CONSIDERATION AND MORAL OBLIGATIONS*

Imagine an exchange consisting of a promise on one side and some action, either promise or performance, on the other. Only if that action has not yet been taken when the promise is made can the promisor be bargaining for it when making the promise. If the action has already been taken, the promisor cannot be seeking to induce it. Such "past consideration"—action already taken before a promise is made—cannot be consideration for the promise. Suppose that an employer promises an employee a gold watch "in return for your good work during the year just ended," but then reconsiders. The employee's "good work" in the past is no consideration for the employer's promise, and the promise is not enforceable. Although the employer may have made a promise, and the employee may have done work, the exchange was not the result of bargain. This principle has had its main impact in cases that have refused to enforce promises to pay pensions for past services.† It is often possible for the parties to restructure the transaction to make the promise enforceable. The requirement of consideration will be met if the employer bargains for some future performance by the employee—remaining on the job for a stated time, retiring within a stated time, refraining from competing with the employer after retirement—or for a return promise by the employee to do any of these things.The conclusion that past consideration cannot be consideration is inevitable under the bargain test. . . . Other situations were to arise later, however, in which it would be argued that a promise was enforceable though supported only by past consideration. . . .

---

* Excerpted from E. ALLAN FARNSWORTH, CONTRACTS §§ 2.7 and 2.8 (4th ed. 2004).

† [We will deal with such a case, *Feinberg v. Pfeiffer Co.*, in the next section on promissory estoppel.—ED.]

> There was, [for instance], pressure to allow exceptions for promises to perform what could be regarded as a "moral obligation."

The "pressure" referred to in the excerpt above is on display in the next case, one of the most famous "moral obligation" cases in contract law. In it, you will learn how courts deal with cases of moral obligation as a general matter, and some of the exceptions they have carved out from the general rule. As you read it, ask yourself whether you think the promise below should be enforced.

Mills v. Wyman

Supreme Judicial Court of Massachusetts
20 Mass. 207 (1825)

This was an action of ***assumpsit*** brought to recover a compensation for the board, nursing, &c., of Levi Wyman, son of the defendant, from the 5th to the 20th of February, 1821. The plaintiff then lived at Hartford, in Connecticut; the defendant, at Shrewsbury, in this county. Levi Wyman, at the time when the services were rendered, was about 25 years of age, and had long ceased to be a member of his father's family. He was on his return from a voyage at sea, and being suddenly taken sick at Hartford, and being poor and in distress, was relieved by the plaintiff in the manner and to the extent above stated. On the 24th of February, after all the expenses had been incurred, the defendant wrote a letter to the plaintiff, promising to pay him such expenses. There was no consideration for this promise, except what grew out of the relation which subsisted between Levi Wyman and the defendant, and Howe J., before whom the cause was tried in the Court of Common Pleas, thinking this not sufficient to support the action, directed a nonsuit. To this direction the plaintiff filed exceptions.

> ***Assumpsit***
>
> From the Latin *assumere*, to "take on" or "assume." A common-law form of action (see "Forms of action" at 89, *supra*) to recover damages for the breach of contract not under seal.

PARKER, C.J. General rules of law established for the protection and security of honest and fair-minded men, who may inconsiderately make promises without any equivalent, will sometimes screen men of a different character from engagements which they are bound ***in foro conscientiae*** to perform. This is a defect inherent in all human systems of legislation. The rule that a mere verbal promise, without any consideration, cannot be enforced by action, is universal in its application, and cannot be departed from to suit particular cases in which a refusal to perform such a promise may be disgraceful.

> ***In foro conscientiae***
>
> "[Latin 'in the forum of conscience'] Privately or morally rather than legally." BLACK'S LAW DICTIONARY (10th ed. 2014).

The promise declared on in this case appears to have been made without any legal consideration. The kindness and services towards the sick son of the defendant were not bestowed at his request. The son was in no respect under the care of the defendant. He was twenty-five years old, and had long left his father's family. On his return from a foreign country, he fell sick among strangers, and the plaintiff acted the part of the **good Samaritan**, giving him shelter and comfort until he died. The defendant, his father, on being informed of this event, influenced by a transient feeling of gratitude, promises in writing to pay the plaintiff for the expenses he had incurred. But he has determined to break this promise, and is willing to have his case appear on record as a strong example of particular injustice sometimes necessarily resulting from the operation of general rules.

It is said a moral obligation is a sufficient consideration to support an express promise; and some authorities lay down the rule thus broadly; but upon examination of the cases we are satisfied that the universality of the rule cannot be supported, and that there must have been some preexisting obligation, which has become inoperative by positive law, to form a basis for an effective promise. **The cases of debts barred by the statute of limitations, of debts incurred by infants, of debts of bankrupts, are generally put for illustration of the rule.** Express promises founded on such preexisting equitable obligations may be enforced; there is a good consideration for them; they merely remove an impediment created by law to the recovery of debts honestly due, but which public policy protects the debtors from being compelled to pay. In all these cases there was originally a *quid pro quo;* and according to the principles of natural justice the party receiving ought to pay; but the legislature has said he shall not be coerced; then comes the promise to pay the debt that is barred, the promise of the man to pay the debt of the infant, of the discharged bankrupt to restore to his creditor what by the law he had lost. In all these cases there is a moral obligation founded upon an antecedent valuable consideration. These promises therefore have a sound legal basis. They are not promises to pay something for nothing; not naked pacts; but the voluntary revival or creation of obligation which before existed in natural law, but which had been dispensed

The good Samaritan

The story of the good Samaritan comes from Luke 10:30-35, in which Jesus related the following parable to an expert in the law: "A certain man went down from Jerusalem to Jericho, and fell among thieves, which stripped him of his raiment, and wounded him, and departed, leaving him half dead. And by chance there came down a certain priest that way: and when he saw him, he passed by on the other side. And likewise a Levite, when he was at the place, came and looked on him, and passed by on the other side. But a certain Samaritan, as he journeyed, came where he was: and when he saw him, he had compassion on him, And went to him, and bound up his wounds, pouring in oil and wine, and set him on his own beast, and brought him to an inn, and took care of him. And on the morrow when he departed, he took out two pence, and gave them to the host, and said unto him, Take care of him; and whatsoever thou spendest more, when I come again, I will repay thee." KING JAMES BIBLE (1611).

*Why these promises?**

Why do you suppose that, for these types of promises, "a moral obligation is a sufficient consideration to support an express promise"? Compare your answer to the one given in the excerpt "Why Past Consideration is Sometimes Enforceable," found in Note 9 following this case. Do you agree with the author's analysis? Why or why not?

* The "bankruptcy" exception has been altered by the Bankruptcy Code. *See* 11 U.S.C. § 524(c), (d).

with, not for the benefit of the party obliged solely, but principally for the public convenience. If moral obligation, in its fullest sense, is a good substratum for an express promise, it is not easy to perceive why it is not equally good to support an implied promise. **What a man ought to do, generally he ought to be made to do, whether he promise or refuse. But the law of society has left most of such obligations to the *interior* forum, as the tribunal of conscience has been aptly called.** Is there not a moral obligation upon every son who has become affluent by means of the education and advantages bestowed upon him by his father, to relieve that father from pecuniary embarrassment, to promote his comfort and happiness, and even to share with him his riches, if thereby he will be made happy? And yet such a son may, with impunity, leave such a father in any degree of penury above that which will expose the community in which he dwells, to the danger of being obliged to preserve him from absolute want. Is not a wealthy father under strong moral obligation to advance the interest of an obedient, well-disposed son, to furnish him with the means of acquiring and maintaining a becoming rank in life, to rescue him from the horrors of debt incurred by misfortune? Yet the law will uphold him in any degree of parsimony, short of that which would reduce his son to the necessity of seeking public charity.

Law v. Morality?

Justice Parker suggests that we should be forced to keep our obligations, bringing law and morality closer together, but that "the law of society" has done otherwise, drawing a somewhat sharper distinction between moral and legal commitments.* Which of these views seems better, and why? Should courts enforce (at least some) moral commitments (and if so, which ones), or is it better that we draw a clear line between law and morality?

Without doubt there are great interests of society which justify withholding the coercive arm of the law from these duties of imperfect obligation, as they are called; imperfect, not because they are less binding upon the conscience than those which are called perfect, but because the wisdom of the social law does not impose sanctions upon them.

A deliberate promise, in writing, made freely and without any mistake, one which may lead the party to whom it is made into contracts and expenses, cannot be broken without a violation of moral duty. But if there was nothing paid or promised for it, the law, perhaps wisely, leaves the execution of it to the conscience of him who makes it. It is only when the party making the promise gains something, or he to whom it is made loses something, that the law gives the promise validity. And in the case of the promise of the adult to pay the debt of the infant, of the debtor discharged by the statute of limitations or bankruptcy, the principle is preserved by looking back to the origin of the transaction, where an equivalent is to be found. An exact equivalent is not required by the law; for there being a consideration, the parties are left to estimate its value:

* The tension between moral and legal commitments was memorably explored, but with a different result, in the classic case of *Lumley v. Wagner*, 42 Eng. Rep. 687 (1852) ("Wherever this Court has not proper jurisdiction to enforce specific performance, it operates to bind men's consciences, as far as they can be bound, to a true and literal performance of their agreements.") We will explore this case in the next chapter on contract remedies.

though here the courts of equity will step in to relieve from gross inadequacy between the consideration and the promise.

These principles are deduced from the general current of decided cases upon the subject, as well as from the known maxims of the common law. The general position, that moral obligation is a sufficient consideration for an express promise, is to be limited in its application, to cases where at some time or other a good or valuable consideration has existed.

A legal obligation is always a sufficient consideration to support either an express or an implied promise; such as an infant's debt for necessaries, or a father's promise to pay for the support and education of his minor children. But when the child shall have attained to manhood, and shall have become his own agent in the world's business, the debts he incurs, whatever may be their nature, create no obligation upon the father; and it seems to follow, that his promise founded upon such a debt has no legally binding force. . . .

For the foregoing reasons we are all of opinion that the nonsuit directed by the Court of Common Pleas was right, and that judgment be entered thereon for costs for the defendant.

RELEVANT PROVISIONS

For the *Restatement (Second) of Contracts,* consult §§ 82, 83, and 86.

NOTES AND QUESTIONS

1. *What happened?* Who sued whom for what? Procedurally, how did the case get before this court? Factually, what happened between the parties? What arguments did the plaintiff and defendant make? What rule or rules did the court apply? How did the court analyze the dispute between the parties? How did the court decide the case?

2. *Was this case correctly decided?* Do you agree with the result reached in this case? Why or why not? Do you agree with the court's reasoning? Why or why not? How, if at all, would you have written the opinion differently?

3. *Consideration?* Do you think there was consideration here under the test articulated in *Hamer*? Under the *Restatement (Second) of Contracts* § 71? Regardless of your answer, would you have enforced this promise if you were the judge? Why or why not?

4. *Moral consideration as legal consideration?* Do you think these types of promises should generally be enforced? Why or why not? You may find it helpful to go back and review some of the justifications offered for enforcing promises in the "Introduction to Enforceability" unit in Part II.2.C, *supra* (p.

79). Would you agree with Professor Williston, who offered the following argument in favor of not enforcing agreements supported only with "moral consideration"?

> However much one may wish to extend the number of promises which are enforceable by law, it is essential that the classes of promises which are so enforceable shall be clearly defined. The test of moral consideration must vary with the opinion of every individual. Indeed, . . . since there is a moral obligation to perform every promise, it would seem that if morality was to be the guide, every promise would be enforced and if the existence of a past moral obligation is to be the test, every promise which repeats or restates a prior gratuitous promise would be binding.*

5. *A lesser recovery?* If the court was unwilling to enforce the promise, should Mills at least have been able to recover the reasonable value of the services he rendered? Why or why not? If so, from whom?

6. *A new approach?* Would the promise have been enforceable under the *Restatement (Second) of Contracts* § 86? Why or why not? We will explore this provision in greater depth when we come to the similar case of *Webb v. McGowin*, and p. 479, *infra*, which also involves past and moral consideration.

7. *Lawyering.* As the plaintiff's attorney, what's the best argument you can think of as to why this particular promise should be enforced? As the defendant's attorney, how would you meet this argument?

8. *Counseling.* Based on the holding in *Mills v. Wyman*, how would you advise future clients in the plaintiff's position?

9. *Why past consideration is sometimes enforceable.* In *Mills v. Wyman*, Parker noted that, in some cases, a "preexisting obligation, which has become inoperative by positive law, [may] form a basis for an effective promise" and cited as examples "cases of debts barred by the statute of limitations, of debts incurred by infants, [and] of debts of bankrupts." This can be understood as an exception to the general rule that gratuitous promises are unenforceable. But why does such an exception exist? One explanation is provided by Professor (now Judge) Posner in the excerpt below, which builds on several of the thinking tools we have previously examined.† Do you agree with his analysis?

> Among the exceptions to the general principle that gratuitous promises will not be enforced are several which are grouped under the rubric of "past consideration." A subsequent promise to pay a debt barred by the statute of limitations, or to pay a debt discharged in bankruptcy, or to pay a debt that is uncollectable because the debtor was a minor at the time the debt was contracted, is legally

* SAMUEL WILLISTON, CONTRACTS § 148 (1st ed. 1920).

† *See, e.g.*, "Thinking Tool: Marginal Analysis and Efficiency," Part II.2.B.2, *supra*, and "Thinking Tool: Administrative Costs and Standards v. Rules," Part II.2.B.3, *supra*.

> enforceable even though there is no fresh consideration for the promise. These are classes of promise in which the utility of the promise to the promisor is often great and the costs of enforcement low. First, as regards utility, it should be noted not only that the stakes are often substantial (these are formal debts after all) but that the *incremental* gain in utility from the enforceable character of the promise may be great. The legal promise conveys information (which a mere stated intention to pay would not) about the promisor's attitude toward the payment of debts barred by a technicality. The information conveyed enhances the promisor's reputation for credit-worthiness and may induce people—not necessarily the promisee himself, which is why the promise itself may not be bilateral—to extend credit to him in the future. And enforcement costs are likely to be low or at least no higher than in conventional bilateral-contract cases because the underlying obligation—the original debt—is fully bilateral. The original debt is not directly enforceable only because of a condition which in the case of the statute of limitations slightly, and in the case of discharge in bankruptcy or voidability by reason of minority not at all, increases the likelihood of error compared to what it would have been in a suit on the original bilateral contract that gave rise to the debt.*

10. *Additional facts and critical reading.* As it turns out, *Mills v. Wyman* has a fascinating history that may help explain some of the strange goings-on represented in Justice Parker's opinion. As the excerpt below (and all such excerpts throughout this book) should make clear, the set of facts you read about in a judicial opinion is merely one of an infinite number of possible stories that could have (and would have) been told by another judge writing the same opinion. Therefore, as you approach such materials (or, more generally, whenever you read a case), you should always ask yourself (1) why a judge focused on *this* particular subset of available facts, and (2) why the court *interpreted* these facts as it did. Forming such a habit early in your law school career will not only reveal to you an entire world of hidden judicial possibilities, but will help you critically examine some of the deeper, perhaps hidden, reasons responsible for the court deciding the case as it did.

CONTEXTUAL PERSPECTIVE: MORE ON MILLS V. WYMAN†

It is not clear why the Supreme Judicial Court thought Levi was dead. No surviving court records suggest that he had died. Perhaps a stray suggestion of counsel at oral argument influenced the court; only the plaintiff's attorneys appeared in person. But it would hardly have been in Mills's interest to suggest that Levi had died while under his care.

---

* Richard A. Posner, *Gratuitous Promises in Economics and Law*, 6 J. LEGAL STUD. 411, 418 (1977).

† Excerpted from Geoffrey R. Watson, *In the Tribunal of Conscience: Mills v. Wyman Reconsidered*, 71 TUL. L. REV. 1749, 1757-62, 1767-68 (1997).

Whatever his physical health in 1821—sick or well, dead or alive—Levi's financial health was indisputably wretched. He was a "stranger" in Hartford, "totally unable to pay" for his room, board, and medical expenses. Those expenses amounted to about twenty-two dollars—a considerable sum in those days—and included six dollars for fourteen days' board and lodging, three dollars for "Room pine & Candles," one dollar for a gallon of "Spirits," six dollars in expenses for the two men hired to restrain Levi, and six dollars for Dr. Comstock's fee. Levi apparently did, however, volunteer that his father Seth Wyman would reimburse Mills. He was "confident that his father, Col. Seth Wyman, would readily pay" the bill. This confidence was either misplaced or feigned.

Levi Wyman left Hartford without paying Daniel Mills a penny. As Mills's acquaintances put it: "We never have known of any property of Levi Wyman since his sickness nor have we ever seen him since." The date of Levi's departure is uncertain. That date is of interest because it roughly corresponds with the date on which Seth Wyman supposedly promised to pay for Levi's expenses. Mills billed Seth for fourteen days lodging, but Mills didn't clearly indicate which fourteen days were involved. One bill carries the date February 20; another carries the date February 27. But on March 3, Mills reported to Seth Wyman that Levi Wyman had "left this place a day or two since," suggesting that Levi had left Mills's house at the very end of February or even early March.

Daniel Mills was not willing to let this bill go unpaid. He does not appear to have been wealthy. Court papers identify Mills as an "innkeeper" and a "yeoman," a term that usually meant a farmer. Unlike Seth Wyman, Mills is never referred to as a "gentleman" in the papers. . . .

Anxious to be paid, Mills did not wait to contact Levi's father until Levi had departed. In early or middle February, Mills contacted Seth Wyman and advised him of Levi's condition. We don't have the text of Mills's first communication to Wyman, but Mills apparently suggested that Seth Wyman come see his son. On February 24, while Levi was probably still at Mills's house, Seth Wyman responded. This was the ostensible promise to pay Mills for services already rendered and the writing on which the litigation in Mills v. Wyman turned. It is worth quoting in full:

> Dear Sir
>
> I received a line from you relating to my Son Levi's sickness and requesting me to come up and see him, but as the going is very bad I cannot come up at the present, but I wish you to take all possible care of him and if you cannot have him at your house I wish you to remove him to some convenient place and if he cannot satisfy you for it I will.
>
> I want that you should write me again immediately how he does and greatly oblige your most obedient servant
>
> Seth Wyman
Feb 24th 1821
Mr. Daniel Mills

By this letter, Seth Wyman supposedly promised to pay Mills for services already rendered, for so-called "past consideration." But the letter does not clearly promise to pay for the services already rendered. It seems more directed at procuring future services from Daniel Mills—i.e., that he either "have him at your house" or "remove him to some convenient place." Wyman can be more fairly said to have been bargaining for future conduct and for real consideration than to have been making a sterile promise to pay for past services. The letter is understandably preoccupied with ensuring his son's safety hereafter, not in settling his debts heretofore. Not surprisingly, when the case came to trial, Wyman's first defense was that he never promised to pay Mills for past expenses.

Mills, however, interpreted Wyman's letter as a promise to pay Levi's existing debt, not just an offer to pay for future services. Mills was not concerned with arranging future accommodations for Levi. Mills wanted Levi's bill paid. By the time Mills received Seth Wyman's letter, i.e., in late February or even early March, Levi Wyman was leaving or perhaps already gone. Anxious to collect on his debt, Mills interpreted Wyman's letter as a guarantee of Levi's existing obligations. After advising Seth of Levi's departure, Mills wrote:

> [Levi] did not nor was not in any situation for to compensate me or the Phisitian in the Senst [?] For my trouble and expense I shall therefore agreeable to your Letter of guarantee make out any bill against you which you will find annexed to this—amounting to—$16.00—Which I can assure you is more reasonable than it otherwise would have been—had it not been so unfortunate on your part—you will have the goodness to enclose said amount and forward it to me by mail as soon as convenient and oblige yours etc.
>
> Daniel Mills
> City of Hartford 3d March 1821

The letter included Mills's itemized expenses and Dr. Comstock's bill for six dollars. There is no record of any response from Seth Wyman. Mills repeated his demand, to no avail, one month later.

[The author then raised a number of intriguing questions, ranging from why Seth or his wife Mary Wyman never visited their son Levi to why they refused "to pay the man who nursed Levi back to health?" But most intriguing of all, perhaps, is the following:]

Why did these two men take a twenty-five dollar dispute all the way to the Supreme Judicial Court of Massachusetts? Granted, twenty-five dollars was a significant sum of money, the equivalent of a month's pay or more, but it was not that large a sum when compared to court costs and attorney's fees. Moreover, not only did the Massachusetts court award costs to the victor, as is the practice today; it also still followed the English rule on attorney's fees, thereby magnifying the risks of litigation for both parties. At the trial level, for example, Daniel Mills was ordered to pay Wyman's costs and fees, which totaled $10.74, $1.50 of which represented the attorney's fee. When Mills lost again on appeal, he was saddled with Wyman's costs in the Supreme Judicial Court as well; these totaled an additional $9.94, $2.50 of which represented defense counsel's fee on appeal, for a total of $20.68. In addition to all this, Mills presumably had to pay his own attorneys; he was represented by respected counsel at trial and by fairly prominent attorneys on appeal, and they presumably charged similarly for fees and costs. Thus he paid out more than he expected to win. In retrospect, it seems remarkable that either Mills or Wyman took the risk of being saddled with costs and fees that exceeded the actual amount in controversy. But they did. . . .

As with *Mills v. Wyman*, the next case, *Webb v. McGowin*, is treated in many contracts casebooks as illustrating the principle that past or moral "consideration" is no consideration at all. As such, *Webb* can profitably be read at this time and juxtaposed with *Mills*. However, whereas the *Mills* court denied recovery because there was no bargain-based promise (i.e., consideration), the *Webb* court allowed it, not because there was consideration (there still wasn't), but because there was a benefit-based promise (i.e., a promise to pay for a benefit already received). The theory of promissory recovery in *Webb*, in other words, wasn't the bargain-based theory of consideration, but the benefit-based theory of unjust enrichment. For this reason, *Webb* is also included in Part C of this chapter, under "Benefit-Based Contracts." Whether your professor covers it now or in Part C, you should include it in both places when you prepare your outline for the course.

Webb v. McGowin

Court of Appeals of Alabama
168 So. 196 (1935)

For a report of the case and accompanying materials, see p. 479, *infra*.

3. Consideration and Contract Modification

DOCTRINAL OVERVIEW: THE PRE-EXISTING DUTY RULE

Suppose that Luke and Han have entered into a valid, consideration-based contract with each other, whereby Luke promises to do "X" for Han, and Han promises to do "Z" for Luke. A few weeks later, the parties agree that Luke should also do "Y" for Han. If the parties subsequently get into a dispute, should the court enforce the contract on the first or second set of terms? To answer this, a court will first need to determine whether the parties' modification was valid. But how should a court make *this* determination?

One response is to say that this is the parties' contract, not the court's, so if the parties mutually agree to modify their terms, a court should simply enforce the agreement on the modified terms. But another response is to say that because the law generally requires agreements to be supported by consideration, and because the modification is technically a new agreement, the modification must also be supported by consideration. Why? Otherwise, one of the parties (Han) would be getting something ("Y") for nothing. How so? Because although Luke has to now do "X" and "Y," Han only has to do "Z," which he already had a pre-existing duty to do anyway. According to this rule, called (logically enough) the "pre-existing duty rule," unless each party gives fresh consideration, a court should refuse to enforce the contract on the modified terms. This rule is enshrined in *Restatement (Second) of Contracts* § 73.

But is this right? Is modifying a contract, where the parties already have a relationship with each other, really like forming an entirely new agreement? All things equal, the answer is probably no. Except on a hyper-technical reading, Luke and Han are not forming an entirely new agreement, but modifying an existing one. This brings us to our next question: If modifying and creating agreements are different activities, should the legal system apply the same test (e.g., consideration) to govern the enforceability both of the creation *and* modification of agreements? Well, that depends on what the legal system is aiming for.

If our legal system is aiming for doctrinal consistency, and wants a rule that can decide particular disputes with some degree of certainty, then there are good arguments for applying a single doctrine to both types of problems. If, however, the legal system is more interested in solving the types of problems for which the individual doctrines were created, then we would probably first want to (a) determine the purpose (or purposes) behind a particular doctrine like consideration, and (b) ask ourselves whether that purpose (or those purposes) will be served in this particular case before deciding on whether contract modification should be governed by a different doctrine than contract formation.* And this, in turn, brings us to our final two questions: First, what purposes *are* served by the doctrine of consideration, and second, are these purposes being satisfied by applying the doctrine of consideration equally to issues of contract formation and contract modification? What previous thinking tools that we have discussed might help us navigate these questions? Keep your answers in mind as you consider the cases and materials below.

Stilk v. Myrick

In the High Court of Justice, King's Bench Division
170 Eng. Rep. 1168 (1809)

This was an action for seaman's wages, on a voyage from London to the Baltic and back.

By the ship's articles, executed before the commencement of the voyage, the plaintiff was to be paid at the rate of £5 a month; and the principal question in the cause was, whether he was entitled to a higher rate of wages? In the course of the voyage two of the men deserted and the captain having in vain attempted to supply their places at **Cronstadt**, there entered into an agreement with the rest of the crew, that they should have the wages of the two who

> ***Cronstadt***
>
> **Cronstadt**, or Kronstadt, is the main seaport of St. Petersburg, Russia.

* Roughly speaking, but only roughly, the first view is more doctrine-based and likely to find supporters among the legal formalists, whereas the second view is more policy-based and likely to find supporters among the legal realists. For a review of these different ways of viewing the law, *see* "Thinking Tool: Ex Ante v. Ex Post, and a Note on Formalism v. Realism," p. 163, *supra*.

had deserted equally divided among them, if he could not procure two other hands at **Gottenburgh**. This was found impossible; and the ship was worked back to London by the plaintiff and eight more of the original crew, with whom the agreement had been made at Cronstadt.

> ### *Gottenburgh*
>
> **Gottenburgh**, or **Gothenburg**, is Sweden's second-largest city, and boasts the largest seaport of all the Nordic countries.

Garrow for the defendant insisted, that this agreement was contrary to public policy, and utterly void. In West India voyages, crews are often thinned greatly by death and desertion; and if a promise of advanced wages were valid, exorbitant claims would be set up on all such occasions. This ground was strongly taken by Lord Kenyon in *Harris v. Watson*, Peak. Cas. 72, where that learned Judge held, that no action would lie at the suit of a sailor on a promise of a captain to pay him extra wages, in consideration of his doing more than the ordinary share of duty in navigating the ship; and his Lordship said, that if such a promise could be enforced, sailors would in many cases suffer a ship to sink unless the captain would accede to any extravagant demand they might think proper to make.

The Attorney-General, contra, distinguished this case from *Harris v. Watson*, as the agreement here was made on shore, when there was no danger or pressing emergency, and when the captain could not be supposed to be under any constraint or apprehension. The mariners were not to be permitted on any sudden danger to force concessions from the captain; but why should they be deprived of the compensation he voluntarily offers them in perfect security for their extra labour during the remainder of the voyage?

LORD ELLENBOROUGH. I think *Harris v. Watson* was rightly decided; but I doubt whether the ground of public policy, upon which Lord Kenyon is stated to have proceeded, be the true principle on which the decision is to be supported. Here, I say, the agreement is void for want of consideration. There was no consideration for the ulterior pay promised to the mariners who remained with the ship. Before they sailed from London they had undertaken to do all that they could under all the emergencies of the voyage. They had sold all their services till the voyage should be completed. If they had been at liberty to quit the vessel at Cronstadt, the case would have been quite different; or if the captain had capriciously discharged the two men who were wanting, the others might not have been compellable to take the whole duty upon themselves, and their agreeing to do so might have been a sufficient consideration for the promise of an advance of wages. But the desertion of a part of the crew is to be considered an emergency of the voyage as much as their death; and those who remain are bound by the terms of their original contract to exert themselves to the utmost to bring the ship in safety to her destined port. Therefore, without looking to the policy of this agreement, I think it is void for want of consideration, and that the plaintiff can only recover at the rate of £5 a month.

Verdict accordingly.

NOTES AND QUESTIONS

1. ***What happened?*** Who sued whom for what? Procedurally, how did the case get before this court? Factually, what happened between the parties? What arguments did the plaintiff and defendant make? What rule or rules did the court apply? How did the court analyze the dispute between the parties? How did the court decide the case?

2. ***Was this case correctly decided?*** Do you agree with the result reached in this case? Why or why not? Do you agree with the court's reasoning? Why or why not? How, if at all, would you have written the opinion differently?

3. ***Comparing* Stilk *and* Harris.** The courts in *Stilk v. Myrick* and *Harris v. Watson* (cited in *Stilk*) reached similar results (both refused to allow the contract modification, enforcing the contracts on their original terms), but by employing different methods. Whereas Lord Ellenborough, deciding *Stilk*, based his decision on the doctrine of consideration, Lord Kenyon seems to have decided *Harris* on grounds of public policy (Lord Ellenborough's characterization of the case notwithstanding). Which method seems better, and why?

4. ***A creative argument.*** Suppose the plaintiffs presented their argument in the following terms: "Originally, there were 11 of us, so each of us only bargained to do 1/11 (or 9%) of the work. When the two seamen deserted, however, only 9 of us remained, requiring each of us to do 1/9 (or 11%) of the work, or 2% more work than we bargained for. Therefore, the modification is valid." Would this have changed the result? What if the number of seamen who abandoned ship was 3, or 4, or 5, or more? What is the captain's best response to these arguments, and how would you, as the judge, have handled such a dispute?

5. ***A variation.*** Would your answer to the above questions change if the seamen presented their argument not in terms of the extra work they would have to do, but in terms of the extra danger that would be involved in sailing back to London with a reduced crew? Once again, what arguments do you think the captain would present in response, and how would you, as judge, handle this dispute?

Alaska Packers' Assn. v. Domenico

United States Circuit Court of Appeals, Ninth Circuit
117 F. 99 (1902)

> ***Libel***
>
> "The complaint or initial pleading in an admiralty or ecclesiastical case." BLACK'S LAW DICTIONARY (10th ed. 2014).

ROSS, CIRCUIT JUDGE. The **libel** in this case was based upon a contract alleged to have been entered into between the **libelants** and the appellant corporation on the 22d day of May, 1900, at Pyramid Harbor, Alaska, by which it is claimed the appellant promised to pay each of the libelants, among other things, the sum of $100 for services rendered and to be rendered. In its answer the respondent denied the execution, on its part, of the contract sued upon, averred that it was without consideration, and for a third defense alleged that the work performed by the libelants for it was performed under other and different contracts than that sued on, and that, prior to the filing of the libel, each of the libelants was paid by the respondent the full amount due him thereunder, in consideration of which each of them executed a full release of all his claims and demands against the respondent.

> ***Libelant***
>
> "The party who institutes a suit in admiralty or ecclesiastical court by filing a libel." BLACK'S LAW DICTIONARY (10th ed. 2014).

The evidence shows without conflict that on March 26, 1900, at the city and county of San Francisco, the libelants entered into a written contract with the appellant, whereby they agreed to go from San Francisco to Pyramid Harbor, Alaska, and return, on board such vessel as might be designated by the appellant, and to work for the appellant during the fishing season of 1900, at Pyramid Harbor, as sailors and fishermen, agreeing to do "regular ship's duty, both up and down, discharging and loading; and to do any other work whatsover when requested to do so by the captain or agent of the Alaska Packers' Association." By the terms of this agreement, the appellant was to pay each of the libelants $50 for the season, and two cents for each red salmon in the catching of which he took part.

On the 15th day of April, 1900, 21 of the libelants signed shipping articles by which they shipped as seamen on the Two Brothers, a vessel chartered by the appellant for the voyage between San Francisco and Pyramid Harbor, and also bound themselves to perform the same work for the appellant provided for by the previous contract of March 26th; the appellant agreeing to pay them therefor the sum of $60 for the season, and two cents each for each red salmon in the catching of which they should respectively take part. Under these contracts, the libelants sailed on board the Two Brothers for Pyramid Harbor, where the appellant had about $150,000 invested in a salmon cannery. The libelants arrived there early in April of the year mentioned, and began to unload the vessel and fit up the cannery. A few days thereafter, to wit, May 19th, they stopped work in a body, and demanded of the company's superintendent there in charge $100 for services in operating the vessel to and from Pyramid Harbor, instead of the sums stipulated for in and by the contracts; stating that unless they were paid this additional wage they would stop work entirely, and return to San Francisco. The evidence showed, and the court below found, that it was impossible for the appellant to get other men to take the places of the libelants, the place being remote, the season short and just opening; so that, after endeavoring for several days without success to induce the libelants to proceed with their work in accordance with their contracts, the company's superintendent, on the 22d day of May, so far yielded to their demands as to instruct his clerk to copy the contracts executed in San Francisco, including the words "Alaska Packers' Association" at the end, substituting, for the $50 and $60 payments, respectively, of those contracts, the sum of $100, which document, so prepared, was signed by the libelants before a shipping commissioner whom they had requested to be brought from Northeast Point; the superintendent, however, testifying that he at the time told the libelants that he was without authority to enter into any such contract, or to in any way alter the contracts made between them and the company in San Francisco. Upon the return of the libelants to San Francisco at the close of the fishing season, they demanded pay in accordance with the terms of the alleged contract of May 22d, when the company denied its validity, and refused to pay other than as provided for by the contracts of March 26th and April 5th, respectively. Some of the libelants, at least, consulted counsel, and, after receiving his advice, those of them who had signed the shipping articles before the shipping commissioner at San Francisco went before that officer, and received the amount due them thereunder, executing in consideration thereof a release in full, and the others being paid at the office of the company, also receipting in full for their demands.

On the trial in the court below, the libelants undertook to show that the fishing nets provided by the respondent were defective, and that it was on that account that they demanded increased wages. On that point, the evidence was substantially conflicting, and the finding of the court was against the libelants, the court saying:

> The contention of libelants that the nets provided them were rotten and unserviceable is not sustained by the evidence. The defendant's interest required that libelants should be provided with every facility necessary to their success as fishermen, for on such success depended the profits defendant would be able to realize that season from its packing plant, and the large capital invested therein. In view of this self-evident fact, it is highly improbable that the defendant gave libelants rotten and unserviceable nets with which to fish. It follows from this finding that libelants were not justified in refusing performance of their original contract.

112 Fed. 554.

The evidence being sharply conflicting in respect to these facts, the conclusions of the court, who heard and saw the witnesses, will not be disturbed.

The real questions in the case as brought here are questions of law, and, in the view that we take of the case, it will be necessary to consider but one of those. Assuming that the appellant's superintendent at Pyramid Harbor was authorized to make the alleged contract of May 22d, and that he executed it on behalf of the appellant, was it supported by a sufficient consideration? From the foregoing statement of the case, it will have been seen that **the libelants agreed in writing, for certain stated compensation, to render their services to the appellant in remote waters where the season for conducting fishing operations is extremely short, and in which enterprise the appellant had a large amount of money invested; and, after having entered upon the discharge of their contract, and at a time when it was**

> ***Critical reading***
>
> Why do you think Judge Ross is highlighting these particular facts surrounding the circumstances in which the promise was made? Do these facts have anything to do with whether the modification is supported by consideration, or might the court be getting at something else?

impossible for the appellant to secure other men in their places, the libelants, without any valid cause, absolutely refused to continue the services they were under contract to perform unless the appellant would consent to pay them more money. Consent to such a demand, under such circumstances, if given, was, in our opinion, without consideration, for the reason that it was based solely upon the libelants' agreement to render the exact services, and none other, that they were already under contract to render. The case shows that they willfully and arbitrarily broke that obligation. As a matter of course, they were liable to the appellant in damages, and it is quite probable, as suggested by the court below in its opinion, that they may have been unable to respond in damages. But we are unable to agree with the conclusions there drawn, from these facts, in these words:

> Under such circumstances, it would be strange, indeed, if the law would not permit the defendant to waive the damages caused by the libelants' breach, and enter into the contract sued upon,—a contract mutually beneficial to all the parties thereto, in that it gave to the libelants reasonable compensation for their labor, and enabled the defendant to employ to advantage the large capital it had invested in its canning and fishing plant.

Certainly, it cannot be justly held, upon the record in this case, that there was any voluntary **waiver** on the part of the appellant of the breach of the original contract. The company itself knew nothing of such breach until the expedition returned to San Francisco, and the testimony is uncontradicted that its superintendent at Pyramid Harbor, who, it is claimed, made on its behalf the contract sued on, distinctly informed the libelants that he had no power to alter the original or to make a new contract; and it would, of course, follow that, if he had no power to change the original, he would have no authority to waive any rights thereunder. The circumstances of the present case bring it, we think, directly within the sound and just observations of the supreme court of Minnesota in the case of *King v. Railway Co.*, 63 N.W. 1105:

> **Waiver**
>
> "The voluntary relinquishment or abandonment—express or implied—of a legal right or advantage." BLACK'S LAW DICTIONARY (10th ed. 2014). We will explore waiver in greater detail when we come to *Clark v. West* in Chapter 8.

> No astute reasoning can change the plain fact that the party who refuses to perform, and thereby coerces a promise from the other party to the contract to pay him an increased compensation for doing that which he is legally bound to do, takes an unjustifiable advantage of the necessities of the other party. Surely it would be a travesty on justice to hold that the party so making the promise for extra pay was **estopped** from asserting that the promise was without consideration. . . .

It results from the views above expressed that the judgment must be reversed, and the cause remanded, with directions to the court below to enter judgment for the respondent, with costs. It is so ordered.

> **Estoppel**
>
> A party is "estopped" when it is prevented "from asserting a claim or right that contradicts what one has said or done before." BLACK'S LAW DICTIONARY (10th ed. 2014). We will be introduced to estoppel in our next principal case, *Ricketts v. Scothorn*.

CONTEXTUAL PERSPECTIVE: MORE ON *ALASKA PACKERS**

In a fascinating article, Professor Threedy argued that, upon arriving in Alaska, the fishermen learned that the fishing nets provided by the company were of a much lower quality than they were used to, testifying that "they could tear the meshes by pulling on them with two fingers" and that "fish broke right through the bottom of the nets where the mesh was old." While the fishermen expected to get most of their money from the amount of fish they caught, the nets provided by the company prevented them from doing so. Interestingly, it may have been in the company's best interest to provide these lower-quality nets. According to Professor Threedy, although "the canneries needed the fishermen to catch sufficient fish," they didn't want the fishermen to catch "too many." This is because "[t]here were no facilities in 1900 for preserving the fish until they could be canned," and "[i]f the salmon harvest was too bountiful, the cannery workers would not be able to keep up and fish would rot before they could be canned."

NOTES AND QUESTIONS

1. *What happened?* Who sued whom for what? Procedurally, how did the case get before this court? Factually, what happened between the parties? What arguments did the plaintiff and defendant make? What rule or rules did the court apply? How did the court analyze the dispute between the parties? How did the court decide the case?

2. *Was this case correctly decided?* Given the facts as presented by Judge Ross, do you think the case was correctly decided? Why or why not? How, if at all, do the facts presented by Professor Threedy, discussed in the excerpt above, change your view?

3. *Thinking tools applied.* The courts in *Stilk v. Myrick* and *Alaska Packers' Assn. v. Domenico* were presented with the same basic question (i.e., whether the contract modification is valid, or whether the contract should be enforced on its original terms), but each court approached the problem in a slightly different way. In *Stilk*, Lord Ellenborough seemed to take a primary interest in approaching the problem from a doctrinal perspective, making consideration the touchstone for determining the enforceability of contract modifications. Recall, for instance, Lord Ellenborough's "doubt" that Lord Kenyon decided *Harris v. Watson* on grounds of public policy, as defense counsel claimed, and his preference of the view that Lord Kenyon decided *Harris* by applying the doctrine of consideration, which he then applied himself to resolve *Stilk*.

---

* The following account is based on Debora L. Threedy, *A Fish Story: Alaska Packers' Association v. Domenico*, 2000 UTAH L. REV. 185 (2000).

In deciding *Alaska Packers*, on the other hand, Judge Ross seemed to lean, ever so slightly, back in the direction of Lord Kenyon's policy-based jurisprudence. For instance, although he ultimately refused to enforce the modification on the ground that it lacked consideration, he seemed quite interested in the policies buttressing the doctrine. For instance, note his concern with the fact that the waters were remote, the season was short, the amount of money already invested was large, that it was impossible to hire other men, et cetera.

Drawing on any of the thinking tools we have previously discussed, which of these approaches do you think is best, and why?

Angel v. Murray

Rhode Island Supreme Court
322 A.2d 630 (1974)

ROBERTS, CHIEF JUSTICE. This is a civil action brought by Alfred L. Angel and others against John E. Murray, Jr., Director of Finance of the City of Newport, the city of Newport, and James L. Maher, alleging that Maher had illegally been paid the sum of $20,000 by the Director of Finance and praying that the defendant Maher be ordered to repay the city such sum. The case was heard by a justice of the Superior Court, sitting without a jury, who entered a judgment ordering Maher to repay the sum of $20,000 to the city of Newport. Maher is now before this court prosecuting an appeal.

The record discloses that Maher has provided the city of Newport with a refuse-collection service under a series of five-year contracts beginning in 1946. On March 12, 1964, Maher and the city entered into another such contract for a period of five years commencing on July 1, 1964, and terminating on June 30, 1969. The contract provided, among other things, that Maher would receive $137,000 per year in return for collecting and removing all combustible and noncombustible waste materials generated within the city.

In June of 1967 Maher requested an additional $10,000 per year from the city council because there had been a substantial increase in the cost of collection due to an unexpected and unanticipated increase of 400 new dwelling units. Maher's testimony, which is uncontradicted, indicates the 1964 contract had been predicated on the fact that since 1946 there had been an average increase of 20 to 25 new dwelling units per year. After a public meeting of the city council where Maher explained in detail the reasons for his request and was questioned by members of the city council, the city council agreed to pay him an additional $10,000 for the year ending on June 30, 1968. Maher made a similar request again in June of 1968 for the same reasons, and the city council again agreed to pay an additional $10,000 for the year ending on June 30, 1969.

The trial justice found that each such $10,000 payment was made in violation of law. His decision . . . is premised on [the] ground[] [that] Maher was not entitled to extra compensation because the original contract already required him to collect all refuse generated within the city and, therefore, included the 400 additional units. The trial justice further found that these 400 additional units were within the contemplation of the parties when they entered into the contract. It appears that he based this portion of the decision upon the rule that Maher had a preexisting duty to collect the refuse generated by the 400 additional units, and thus there was no consideration for the two additional payments. . . .

[W]e are . . . confronted with the question of whether the additional payments were illegal because they were not supported by consideration.

A

As previously stated, the city council made two $10,000 payments. The first was made in June of 1967 for the year beginning on July 1, 1967, and ending on June 30, 1968. Thus, by the time this action was commenced in October of 1968, the modification was completely executed. That is, the money had been paid by the city council, and Maher had collected all of the refuse. Since consideration is only a test of the enforceability of executory promises, the presence or absence of consideration for the first payment is unimportant because the city council's agreement to make the first payment was fully executed at the time of the commencement of this action. However, since both payments were made under similar circumstances, our decision regarding the second payment (Part B, infra) is fully applicable to the first payment.

B

It is generally held that a modification of a contract is itself a contract, which is unenforceable unless supported by consideration. In *Rose v. Daniels*, 8 R.I. 381 (1866), this court held that an agreement by a debtor with a creditor to discharge a debt for a sum of money less than the amount due is unenforceable because it was not supported by consideration.

Rose is a perfect example of the preexisting duty rule. Under this rule an agreement modifying a contract is not supported by consideration if one of the parties to the agreement does or promises to do something that he is legally obligated to do or refrains or promises to refrain from doing something he is not legally privileged to do. In *Rose* there was no consideration for the new agreement because the debtor was already legally obligated to repay the full amount of the debt.

Although the preexisting duty rule is followed by most jurisdictions, a small minority of jurisdictions, Massachusetts, for example, find that there is consideration for a promise to perform what one is already legally obligated to do because the new promise is given in place of an action for damages to secure performance. *See Swartz v. Lieberman*, 80 N.E.2d 5 (1948). *Swartz* is premised on the theory that a promisor's forbearance of the power to breach his original agreement and be sued in an action for damages is consideration for a subsequent agreement by the promisee to pay extra compensation. This rule, however, has been widely criticized as an anomaly.

The primary purpose of the preexisting duty rule is to prevent what has been referred to as the "hold-up game." *See* 1A *Corbin*, Contracts § 171 (1963). A classic example of the "hold-up game" is found in *Alaska Packers' Ass'n v. Domenico*, 117 F. 99 (9th Cir. 1902). There 21 seamen entered into a written contract with Domenico to sail from San Francisco to Pyramid Harbor, Alaska. They were to work as sailors and fishermen out of Pyramid Harbor during the fishing season of 1900. The contract specified that each man would be paid $50 plus two cents for each red salmon he caught. Subsequent to their arrival at Pyramid Harbor, the men stopped work and demanded an additional $50. They threatened to return to San Francisco if Domenico did not agree to their demand. Since it was impossible for Domenico to find other men, he agreed to pay the men an additional $50. After they returned to San Francisco, Domenico refused to pay the men an additional $50. The court found that the subsequent agreement to pay the men an additional $50 was not supported by consideration because the men had a preexisting duty to work on the ship under the original contract, and thus the subsequent agreement was unenforceable.

Another example of the "hold-up game" is found in the area of construction contracts. Frequently, a contractor will refuse to complete work under an unprofitable contract unless he is awarded additional compensation. The courts have generally held that a subsequent agreement to award additional compensation is unenforceable if the contractor is only performing work which would have been required of him under the original contract.

These examples clearly illustrate that the courts will not enforce an agreement that has been procured by **coercion or duress** and will hold the parties to their original contract regardless of whether it is profitable or unprofitable. However, the courts have been reluctant to apply the preexisting duty rule when a party to a contract encounters unanticipated difficulties and the other party, not influenced by coercion or duress, voluntarily agrees to pay additional compensation for work already required to be performed under the contract. For example, the courts have found that the original contract was rescinded, abandoned, or waived.

> ***Coercion and Duress***
>
> The defenses of coercion and duress will be explored in greater detail in Chapter 8, Section D.

Although the preexisting duty rule has served a useful purpose insofar as it deters parties from using coercion and duress to obtain additional compensation, it has been widely criticized as a general rule of law. With regard to the preexisting duty rule, one legal scholar has stated:

> There has been a growing doubt as to the soundness of this doctrine as a matter of social policy. . . . In certain classes of cases, this doubt has influenced courts to refuse to apply the rule, or to ignore it, in their actual decisions. Like other legal rules, this rule is in process of growth and change, the process being more active here than in most instances. The result of this is that a court should no longer accept this rule as fully established. It should never use it as the major premise of a decision, at least without giving careful thought to the circumstances of the particular case, to the moral deserts of the parties, and to the

> social feelings and interests that are involved. It is certain that the rule, stated in general and all-inclusive terms, is no longer so well-settled that a court must apply it though the heavens fall.

1A Corbin, *supra*, § 171.

The modern trend appears to recognize the necessity that courts should enforce agreements modifying contracts when unexpected or unanticipated difficulties arise during the course of the performance of a contract, even though there is no consideration for the modification, as long as the parties agree voluntarily.

Under the UCC § 2-209(1), which has been adopted by 49 states, "(a)n agreement modifying a contract (for the sale of goods) needs no consideration to be binding." Although at first blush this section appears to validate modifications obtained by coercion and duress, the comments to this section indicate that a modification under this section must meet the test of good faith imposed by the Code, and a modification obtained by extortion without a legitimate commercial reason is unenforceable.

The modern trend away from a rigid application of the preexisting duty rule is reflected by *Restatement Second of the Law of Contracts* § 89(a), which provides: "A promise modifying a duty under a contract not fully performed on either side is binding (a) if the modification is fair and equitable in view of circumstances not anticipated by the parties when the contract was made. . . ."

We believe that § 89(a) is the proper rule of law and find it applicable to the facts of this case. It not only prohibits modifications obtained by coercion, duress, or extortion but also fulfills society's expectation that agreements entered into voluntarily will be enforced by the courts.[3] § 89(a), of course,

---

3. The drafters of § 89(a) of the *Restatement Second of the Law of Contracts* use the following illustrations in comment (b) as examples of how this rule is applied to certain transactions: 1. By a written contract A agrees to excavate a cellar for B for a stated price. Solid rock is unexpectedly encountered and A so notifies B. A and B then orally agree that A will remove the rock at a unit price which is reasonable but nine times that used in computing the original price, and A completes the job. B is bound to pay the increased amount. 2. A contracts with B to supply for $300 a laundry chute for a building B has contracted to build for the Government for $150,000. Later A discovers that he made an error as to the type of material to be used and should have bid $1,200. A offers to supply the chute for $1,000, eliminating overhead and profit. After ascertaining that other suppliers would charge more, B agrees. The new agreement is binding. 3. A is employed by B as a designer of coats at $90 a week for a year beginning November 1 under a written contract executed September 1. A is offered $115 a week by another employer and so informs B. A and B then agree that A will be paid $100 a week and in October execute a new written contract to that effect, simultaneously tearing up the prior contract. The new contract is binding.

4. A contracts to manufacture and sell to B 2,000 steel roofs for corn cribs at $60. Before A begins manufacture a threat of a nationwide steel strike raises the cost of steel about $10 per roof, and A and B agree orally to increase the price to $70 per roof. A thereafter manufactures and delivers 1,700 of the roofs, and B pays for 1,500 of them at the increased price without protest, increasing the selling price of the corn cribs by $10. The new agreement is binding.

5. A contracts to manufacture and sell to B 100,000 castings for lawn mowers at 50 cents each. After partial delivery and after B has contracted to sell a substantial number of lawn mowers at a fixed price, A notifies B that increased metal costs require that the price be increased to 75 cents. Substitute castings are available at 55 cents, but only after several months' delay. B protests but is forced to agree to the new price to keep its plant in operation. The modification is not binding.

does not compel a modification of an unprofitable or unfair contract; it only enforces a modification if the parties voluntarily agree and if (1) the promise modifying the original contract was made before the contract was fully performed on either side, (2) the underlying circumstances which prompted the modification were unanticipated by the parties, and (3) the modification is fair and equitable.

The evidence, which is uncontradicted, reveals that in June of 1968 Maher requested the city council to pay him an additional $10,000 for the year beginning on July 1, 1968, and ending on June 30, 1969. This request was made at a public meeting of the city council, where Maher explained in detail his reasons for making the request. Thereafter, the city council voted to authorize the Mayor to sign an amendment to the 1964 contract which provided that Maher would receive an additional $10,000 per year for the duration of the contract. Under such circumstances we have no doubt that the city voluntarily agreed to modify the 1964 contract.

Having determined the voluntariness of this agreement, we turn our attention to the three criteria delineated above. First, the modification was made in June of 1968 at a time when the five-year contract which was made in 1964 had not been fully performed by either party. Second, although the 1964 contract provided that Maher collect all refuse generated within the city, it appears this contract was premised on Maher's past experience that the number of refuse-generating units would increase at a rate of 20 to 25 per year. Furthermore, the evidence is uncontradicted that the 1967-1968 increase of 400 units "went beyond any previous expectation." Clearly, the circumstances which prompted the city council to modify the 1964 contract were unanticipated. Third, although the evidence does not indicate what proportion of the total this increase comprised, the evidence does indicate that it was a "substantial" increase. In light of this, we cannot say that the council's agreement to pay Maher the $10,000 increase was not fair and equitable in the circumstances.

The judgment appealed from is reversed, and the cause is remanded to the Superior Court for entry of judgment for the defendants.

RELEVANT PROVISIONS

For the *Restatement (Second) of Contracts,* consult §§ 73 and 89. For the UCC, consult § 2-209. For the CISG, consult Article 29.

NOTES AND QUESTIONS

1. ***What happened?*** Who sued whom for what? Procedurally, how did the case get before this court? Factually, what happened between the parties? What arguments did the plaintiff and defendant make? What rule or rules did the court apply? How did the court analyze the dispute between the parties? How did the court decide the case?

2. *Was this case correctly decided?* Do you agree with the result reached in this case? Why or why not? Do you agree with the court's reasoning? Why or why not? How, if at all, would you have written the opinion differently?

3. *Consideration?* Was there consideration to support the modification here? If not, why was the modification enforced?

4. *Thinking tools applied.* Modifications often occur due to some unforeseen event that arises after the parties have made their contract. Here, Maher claims that he requested additional money "because there had been a substantial increase in the cost of collection due to an unexpected and unanticipated increase of 400 new dwelling units." Did Maher assume this risk? How do we know? If neither party assumed this risk, on which party should the court place it? Which of the parties was in the best position to either foresee or avoid this risk? Can any of the thinking tools we've previously discussed help us here?

5. *Critical reading.* Did you catch that the court cited UCC § 2-209(1) on contract modifications, and even bolstered its authority by telling us that it "has been adopted by 49 states," but said nothing about *Restatement (Second) of Contracts* § 73, which enshrines the pre-existing duty rule? Is there anything strange about that?

6. *A better approach?* Read the relevant provisions above. To what extent do they alter the pre-existing duty rule? Do you think that they provide a better approach to the underlying problem that the pre-existing duty rule is designed to address?

7. *How* should *modifications be policed?* You probably realized that the question above requires you to think about what basic problem the pre-existing duty rule is designed to address. One view, expressed in the opinion above, is to prevent the "hold-up game." What's the hold-up game, why is it so bad, and do you think the doctrine of consideration is the best way of dealing with it? A similar view was expressed in an opinion by Judge Posner, which offers a concise distillation of some of the critical issues governing how contract modifications should be policed:

> The black-letter rule is indeed that a contract may not be modified without consideration. (The UCC abrogates the rule for sales of goods, UCC § 2-209(1). . . .) And yet the cautionary, evidential, and other policies behind the requirement of consideration do not apply, or apply only with much attenuated strength, in the context of written modification. By hypothesis the parties already have a contract, so that the danger of mistaking casual promissory language for an intention to be legally bound is slight. . . .
>
> The requirement of consideration has, however, a distinct function in the modification setting—although one it does not perform well—and that is to prevent coercive modifications. Since one of the main purposes of contracts and of contract law is to facilitate long-term commitments, there is often an interval in the life of a contract during which one party is at the mercy of the other. A

> may have ordered a machine from B that A wants to place in operation on a given date, specified in their contract; and in expectation of B's complying with the contract, A may have made commitments to his customers that it would be costly to renege on. As the date of scheduled delivery approaches, B may be tempted to demand that A agree to renegotiate the contract price, knowing that A will incur heavy expenses if B fails to deliver on time. A can always refuse to renegotiate, relying instead on his right to sue B for breach of contract if B fails to make delivery by the agreed date. But legal remedies are costly and uncertain, thereby opening the way to duress. Considerations of commercial reputation will deter taking advantage of an opportunity to exert duress on a contract partner in many cases, but not in all: For examples of duress in the contract-modification setting, see *Austin Instrument, Inc. v. Loral Corp.* and *Alaska Packers' Ass'n v. Domenico.*
>
> The rule that modifications are unenforceable unless supported by consideration strengthens A's position by reducing B's incentive to seek a modification. But it strengthens it feebly. . . . The law does not require that consideration be adequate—that it be commensurate with what the party accepting it is giving up. Slight consideration, therefore, will suffice to make a contract or a contract modification enforceable. And slight consideration is consistent with coercion. To surrender one's contractual rights in exchange for a peppercorn is not functionally different from surrendering them for nothing.
>
> The sensible course would be to enforce contract modifications (at least if written) regardless of consideration and rely on the defense of duress to prevent abuse. All coercive modifications would then be unenforceable, and there would be no need to worry about consideration, an inadequate safeguard against duress. . . .*

According to Judge Posner, how should contract modifications be policed? Do you agree? Why or why not?

8. ***Reevaluating the doctrine of consideration to police contract modifications.*** Having now considered *Stilk, Alaska Packers,* and *Angel,* let us return to some of the questions we considered at the beginning of this section: Do you think that the doctrine of consideration should be applied to govern both (a) the enforceability of new contracts and (b) the enforceability of modifications to existing contracts? Why or why not?

PROBLEM: SUPPLY AND DEMAND

Bakerfield Inc. is a large producer of ethanol and has a contract with Leon's Farm, Inc. to supply them with corn in 2004 at $5.25 per ton, or $8.50 if the harvest was small. The contract was made in 2003. The 2004 rainy season delivered so little water that the corn crop suitable for harvest was greatly diminished from previous years. In October 2004, Leon's Farm notified Bakerfield that no more

* Excerpted from *United States v. Stump Home Specialties Manufacturing*, 905 F.2d 1117 (7th Cir. 1990) (Posner, J.).

corn would be furnished to them that year under the contract. Bakerfield had a considerable amount of unfulfilled orders of ethanol, all of which it was contractually bound to fulfill, and under the stress of the circumstances it made a new arrangement with Leon's Farm, and agreed to pay $12 per ton for more corn. At this rate, Leon's Farm delivered additional corn to Bakerfield. In February 2005, Bakerfield sued Leon's Farm, claiming that the $12 rate that it paid for the corn was obtained without consideration and under duress.

Does Bakerfield have a valid claim for duress? What defense can Leon's Farm raise to Bakerfield's assertion of duress? What, if anything, can Leon's Farm point to as the consideration for this contract modification?

B. RELIANCE-BASED CONTRACTS: THE DOCTRINE OF PROMISSORY ESTOPPEL

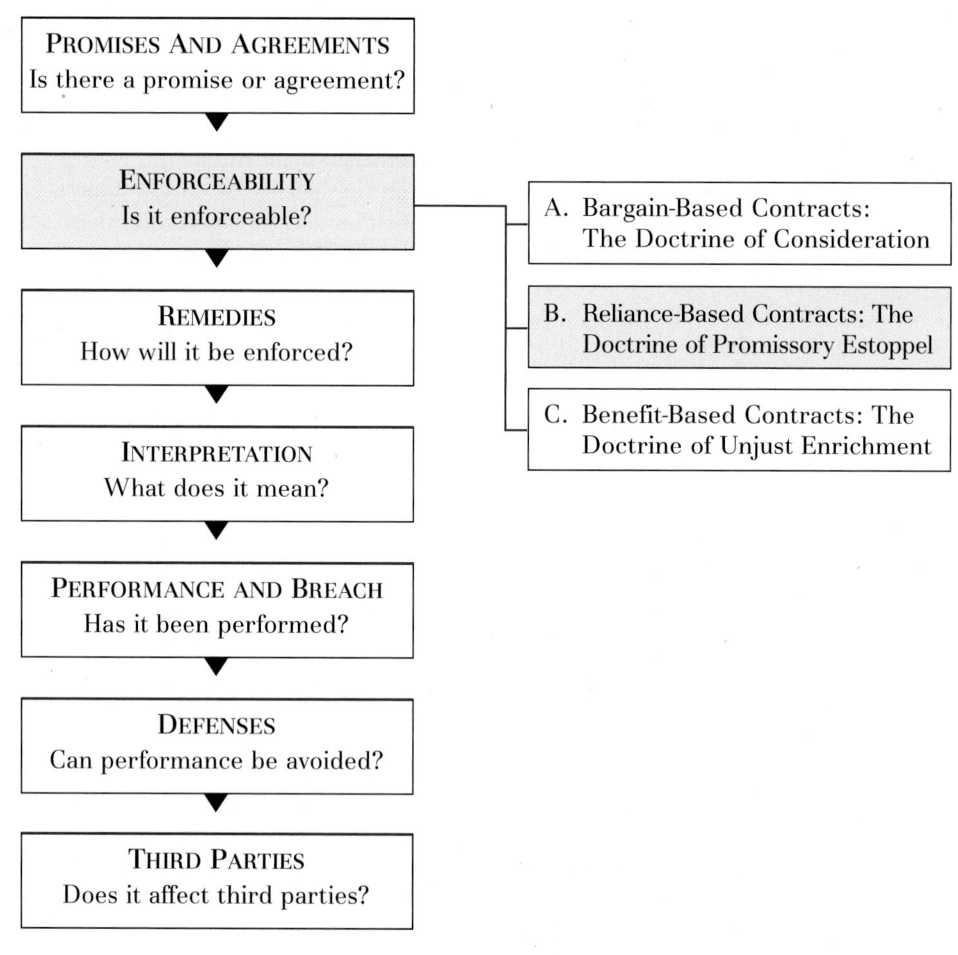
PROMISES AND AGREEMENTS
Is there a promise or agreement?
ENFORCEABILITY
Is it enforceable?
A. Bargain-Based Contracts: The Doctrine of Consideration
B. Reliance-Based Contracts: The Doctrine of Promissory Estoppel
C. Benefit-Based Contracts: The Doctrine of Unjust Enrichment
REMEDIES
How will it be enforced?
INTERPRETATION
What does it mean?
PERFORMANCE AND BREACH
Has it been performed?
DEFENSES
Can performance be avoided?
THIRD PARTIES
Does it affect third parties?

In this section you will be introduced to the reliance-based theory of promissory liability known as promissory estoppel, the second main theory of promissory liability we will consider. As we have seen, the growth of the doctrine of consideration, particularly in the nineteenth century, crowded out other bases of promissory liability, with the result that some promises that perhaps ought to have been enforced were no longer enforced (recall, for instance, *Kirksey v. Kirksey*), or could only be enforced by putting a great deal of strain on the doctrine itself (as we will see, for instance, in *Allegheny College*). Promissory estoppel evolved, in large part, to patch up many of consideration's holes, making enforceable a broad range of reliance-based promises that would have otherwise been unenforceable. But in doing so, promissory estoppel has evolved to become much more than a mere "substitute" for consideration, and it now stands as an independent ground of promissory liability in its own right. The cases in this section have been organized chronologically, in part to give you a sense of the types of problems promissory estoppel was designed to respond to, and in part to give you a sense of the way the doctrine has evolved (and continues to evolve), becoming more and more progressive over time.

1. Cracks in the Foundation: Consideration and its Limitations

We have seen how the rise of the bargain-based theory of consideration, particularly as embodied in the *Restatement (First)* and *(Second) of Contracts*, came to supplant the older benefit- and detriment-based notions of consideration enshrined in such memorable decisions as *Hamer v. Sidway* and *Kirksey v. Kirksey*. The rise of this doctrine, however, had several important consequences on the law of contracts, as described in the excerpt below:

DOCTRINAL OVERVIEW: THE LIMITATIONS OF THE BARGAIN PRINCIPLE*

The rise of th[e] bargain test of consideration had two consequences. First, to the extent that it imposed a new requirement, that of bargain, the test made some promises unenforceable that might previously have been enforceable. The requirement of bargain had little impact on transactions that took place in the marketplace, where bargain was an almost inevitable ingredient. But bargain might well be lacking in transactions taking place outside or on the periphery of the marketplace. Exchanges in a family setting, for example, are often not arrived at by bargain, and promises made in such settings often turned out to be unenforceable under the bargain test. This consequence is scarcely startling, given nineteenth-century America's preeminent concern with the marketplace. New doctrines would have to be devised if such promises were to result in liability.

effects — some family enf. etc.

* Excerpted from E. ALLAN FARNSWORTH, CONTRACTS § 2.3 (4th ed. 2004).

Second, to the extent that the test eliminated any requirement of benefit or detriment, it made some promises enforceable that might previously have been unenforceable. It did so by shifting the concern of judges away from the substance of the exchange. Their sole inquiry now was into the process by which the parties had arrived at that exchange—was it the product of "bargain"? this development accorded well with the prevailing mood of nineteenth-century America, which placed its trust in free enterprise and in the dignity and creativity of the individual. Had not Adam Smith written that it was through the competitive process of "bargaining" that society could best take advantage of what he called man's "self-love"? Under the bargain test a promise that had been exchanged as a result of that process satisfied the fundamental test of enforceability without anything more. Of course, if neither the benefit to one party nor the detriment to the other was relevant, that doctrine could scarcely serve as a safeguard against unfairness in the exchange. New doctrines would have to be developed if judges were to inquire into fairness.

As pointed out in excerpt above, the doctrine of consideration sometimes interfered with the courts' ability to enforce promises that took place outside of a commercial setting (recall, for example, the family-based background of *Kirksey v. Kirksey*), and this, in turn, put pressure on courts to develop new doctrines of promissory liability to circumvent these perceived injustices. In this subsection, we will consider some of the cases evidencing the strain put on the doctrine of consideration, and examine some of the (often messy) solutions developed by courts to circumvent the doctrine's formal requirements. Then, in the next subsection, we will focus on the development of a new and important theory of promissory liability: the doctrine of promissory estoppel, which not only helped tidy up this doctrinal messiness, but expanded the reach of contract law itself to areas beyond consideration's grasp.

Ricketts v. Scothorn

Supreme Court of Nebraska
77 N.W. 365 (1898)

SULLIVAN, J. In the district court of Lancaster county the plaintiff Katie Scothorn recovered judgment against the defendant Andrew D. Ricketts, as executor of the last will and testament of John C. Ricketts, deceased. The action was based upon a promissory note, of which the following is a copy:

> May the first, 1891. I promise to pay to Katie Scothorn on demand, $2,000, to be at 6 per cent per annum.
>
> J. C. Ricketts.

Petition

A "petition" is another term for "complaint," the first pleading filed by plaintiff to initiate a lawsuit.

In the **petition** the plaintiff alleges that the consideration for the execution of the note was that she should surrender her employment as bookkeeper for Mayer Bros. and cease to work for a living. She also alleges that the note was given to induce her to abandon her occupation, and that, relying on it, and on the annual interest, as a means of support, she gave up the employment in which she was then engaged. These allegations of the petition are denied by the executor.

The material facts are undisputed. They are as follows: John C. Ricketts, the maker of the note, was the grandfather of the plaintiff. Early in May,—presumably on the day the note bears date,—he called on her at the store where she was working. What transpired between them is thus described by Mr. Flodene, one of the plaintiff's witnesses:

> A. Well the old gentleman came in there one morning about 9 o'clock,—probably a little before or a little after, but early in the morning,—and he unbuttoned his vest and took out a piece of paper in the shape of a note; that is the way it looked to me; and he says to Miss Scothorn, "I have fixed out something that you have not got to work any more." He says, "None of my grandchildren work and you don't have to."
>
> Q. Where was she?
>
> A. She took the piece of paper and kissed him; and kissed the old gentleman and commenced to cry.

It seems Miss Scothorn immediately notified her employer of her intention to quit work and that she did soon after abandon her occupation. The mother of the plaintiff was a witness and testified that she had a conversation with her father, Mr. Ricketts, shortly after the note was executed in which he informed her that he had given the note to the plaintiff to enable her to quit work; that none of his grandchildren worked and he did not think she ought to. For something more than a year the plaintiff was without an occupation; but in September, 1892, with the consent of her grandfather, and by his assistance, she secured a position as bookkeeper with Messrs. Funke & Ogden. On June 8, 1894, Mr. Ricketts died. He had paid one year's interest on the note, and a short time before his death expressed regret that he had not been able to pay the balance. In the summer or fall of 1892 he stated to his daughter, Mrs. Scothorn, that if he could sell his farm in Ohio he would pay the note out of the proceeds. He at no time repudiated the obligation.

We quite agree with counsel for the defendant that upon this evidence there was nothing to submit to the jury, and that a verdict should have been directed peremptorily for one of the parties. The testimony of Flodene and Mrs. Scothorn, taken together, conclusively establishes the fact that the note was not given in consideration of the plaintiff pursuing, or agreeing to pursue, any particular line of conduct. There was no promise on the part of the plaintiff to do or refrain from doing anything. Her right to the money promised in the note was not made to depend upon an abandonment of her employment with Mayer Bros. and future abstention from like service. Mr. Ricketts made no condition, requirement, or request. He exacted no *quid pro quo*. He gave the note as a gratuity and looked for nothing in return. So far as the evidence discloses, it was his purpose to place the plaintiff in a position of independence where she could work or remain idle as she might choose. The abandonment by Miss Scothorn of her position as bookkeeper was altogether voluntary. It was not an act done in fulfillment of any contract obligation assumed when she accepted the note. The instrument in suit being given without any valuable consideration, was nothing more than a promise to make a gift in the future of the sum of money therein named. Ordinarily, such promises are not enforceable even when put in the form of a promissory note.

But it has often been held that an action on a note given to a church, college, or other like institution, upon the faith of which money has been expended or obligations incurred, could not be successfully defended on the ground of a want of consideration. In this class of cases the note in suit is nearly always spoken of as a gift or donation, but the decision is generally put on the ground that the expenditure of money or assumption of liability by the **donee**, on the faith of the promise, constitutes a valuable and sufficient consideration. It seems to us that the true reason is the preclusion of the defendant, under the doctrine of estoppel, to deny the consideration. . . . It has been held that a note given in expectation of the payee performing certain services, but without any contract binding him to serve, will not support an action. But when the payee changes his position to his disadvantage, in reliance on the promise, a right of action does arise.

Donee

"One to whom a gift is made; the recipient of a gift." To be contrasted with **donor**: "Someone who gives something without receiving consideration for the transfer." BLACK'S LAW DICTIONARY (10th ed. 2014).

Under the circumstances of this case is there an **equitable estoppel** which ought to preclude the defendant from alleging that the note in controversy is lacking in one of the essential elements of a valid contract? We think there is. An estoppel *in pais* is defined to be "a right arising from acts, admissions, or conduct which have induced a change of position in accordance with the real or apparent intention of the party against whom they are alleged." Mr. Pomeroy has formulated the following definition:

> Equitable estoppel is the effect of the voluntary conduct of a party whereby he is absolutely precluded, both at law and in equity, from asserting rights which might perhaps have otherwise existed, either of property, or contract, or of remedy, as against another person who in good faith relied upon such conduct, and has been led thereby to change his position for the worse, and who on his part acquires some corresponding right either of property, of contract, or of remedy

(2 Pomeroy, *Equity Jurisprudence* 804.)

According to the undisputed proof, as shown by the record before us, the plaintiff was a working girl, holding a position in which she earned a salary of $10

The elements of equitable estoppel

Although there is no perfect definition of equitable estoppel, and each court tends to define it according to their own needs based on the facts of the case before it, one definition that has stood the test of time comes from Professor Pomeroy, who stated that equitable estoppel contains the following six elements: "(1) There must be conduct—acts, language, or silence-amounting to a representation or concealment of material facts; (2) These facts must be known to the party estopped at the time of this said conduct or at least the circumstances must be such that knowledge of them is necessarily imputed to him; (3) The truth concerning these facts must not be known to the other party; (4) The conduct must be done with the intention, or at least the expectation, that it will be acted upon by the other party . . . ; (5) The conduct must be relied upon by the other party, and thus relying, he must be led to act upon it; [and]

per week. Her grandfather, desiring to put her in a position of independence, gave her the note, accompanying it with the remark that his other grandchildren did not work, and that she would not be obliged to work any longer. In effect he suggested that she might abandon her employment and rely in the future upon the bounty which he promised. He, doubtless, desired that she should give up her occupation, but whether he did or not, it is entirely certain that he contemplated such action on her part as a reasonable and probable consequence of his gift. Having intentionally influenced the plaintiff to alter her position for the worse on the faith of the note being paid when due, it would be grossly inequitable to permit the maker, or his executor, to resist payment on the ground that the promise was given without consideration. The petition charges the elements of an equitable estoppel, and the evidence conclusively establishes them. If errors intervened at the trial they could not have been prejudicial. A verdict for the defendant would be unwarranted. The judgment is right and is

Affirmed.

(6) He must in fact act upon it in such a manner as to change his position for the worse." Based on this definition, do you think there is equitable estoppel in this case? Why or why not?

NOTES AND QUESTIONS

1. *What happened?* Who sued whom for what? Procedurally, how did the case get before this court? Factually, what happened between the parties? What arguments did the plaintiff and defendant make? What rule or rules did the court apply? How did the court analyze the dispute between the parties? How did the court decide the case?

2. *Was this case correctly decided?* Do you agree with the result reached in this case? Why or why not? Do you agree with the court's reasoning? Why or why not? How, if at all, would you have written the opinion differently?

3. *Explaining* Ricketts. We learned earlier that courts were traditionally uncomfortable enforcing (1) gratuitous promises and (2) promises made within the family setting, yet here, both factors were present and the court enforced the grandfather's promise anyway. Why?

4. *The relevance of intent.* The facts seem to indicate that Mr. Ricketts, who memorialized his promise in the form of a promissory note, intended to be bound to his promise. What significance do (and should) courts attribute to a party's intent for the purposes of determining whether to enforce promises?

5. *Was the promise's form important?* Even though Mr. Ricketts's promise took the form of a promissory note, and even though he had already paid one year's interest on the note, the court tells us that, "[o]rdinarily, such promises are not enforceable." Nevertheless, the court went on to point out that

"an action on a note given to a church, college, or other like institution, upon the faith of which money has been expended or obligations incurred, could not be successfully defended on the ground of a want of consideration." Why not? What significance should we attribute to the fact that the grandfather's promise was put into a particular legal form (i.e., a promissory note)? Does Fuller's article *Consideration and Form* (p. 341) shed any light on the court's actions, or on the broader question of whether this promise ought to have been enforced?

6. *Equitable estoppel.* Note that this case relied on a theory of equitable estoppel (rather than promissory estoppel, which was not yet in existence) to enforce Mr. Ricketts's promise. What, exactly, is equitable estoppel, and how was it used by the court to enforce Mr. Ricketts's promise?

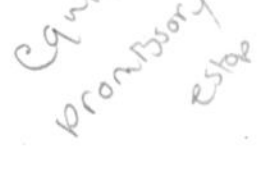

7. *The emergence of promissory estoppel.* By relying on the doctrine of equitable estoppel to enforce a promise, *Ricketts* proved to be an important case in demonstrating the need for a reliance-based theory of promissory liability, a need that would eventually be met by the doctrine of promissory estoppel. This development, however, was still several decades away. Meanwhile, cases continued to come before judges in which the application of the traditional doctrine of consideration would arguably result in unjust outcomes. Therefore, even before the doctrine of promissory estoppel was developed, the doctrine of consideration adapted to some of these changes as well. We see an example of this in the next case, a famous opinion written by Judge Cardozo (whom you met earlier in *Jacob & Youngs v. Kent*). As you read it, try to keep in mind the main problem facing Cardozo in deciding the case: How should one enforce (if at all) a reliance-based promise where there is not yet in existence a widely accepted reliance-based theory of promissory liability?

Allegheny College v. National Chautauqua County Bank of Jamestown

Court of Appeals of New York

159 N.E. 173 (1927)

CARDOZO, C.J. The plaintiff, Allegheny College, is an institution of liberal learning at Meadville, Pennsylvania. In June 1921, a "drive" was in progress to secure for it an additional endowment of $1,250,000. An appeal to contribute to this fund was made to Mary Yates Johnston of Jamestown, New York. In response thereto, she signed and delivered on June 15, 1921, the following writing:

Estate Pledge,

Allegheny College Second Century Endowment

Jamestown, N. Y., June 15, 1921

In consideration of my interest in Christian Education, and in consideration of others subscribing, I hereby subscribe and will pay to the order of

> the Treasurer of Allegheny College, Meadville, Pennsylvania, the sum of Five Thousand Dollars; $5,000.
>
> This obligation shall become due thirty days after my death, and I hereby instruct my Executor, or Administrator, to pay the same out of my estate. This pledge shall bear interest at the rate of __ per cent per annum, payable annually, from __ till paid. The proceeds of this obligation shall be added to the Endowment of said Institution, or expended in accordance with instructions on reverse side of this pledge.
>
> Name MARY YATES JOHNSTON . . .

On the reverse side of the writing is the following indorsement:

> In loving memory this gift shall be known as the Mary Yates Johnston Memorial Fund, the proceeds from which shall be used to educate students preparing for the Ministry, either in the United States or in the Foreign Field.
>
> This pledge shall be valid only on the condition that the provisions of my Will, now extant, shall be first met.
>
> MARY YATES JOHNSTON.

The subscription was not payable by its terms until thirty days after the death of the promisor. The sum of $1,000 was paid, however, upon account in December, 1923, while the promisor was alive. The college set the money aside to be held as a scholarship fund for the benefit of students preparing for the ministry. Later, in July, 1924, the promisor gave notice to the college that she repudiated the promise. Upon the expiration of thirty days following her death, this action was brought against the executor of her will to recover the unpaid balance.

The law of charitable subscriptions has been a prolific source of controversy in this State and elsewhere. We have held that a promise of that order is unenforceable like any other if made without consideration. On the other hand, though professing to apply to such subscriptions the general law of contract, we have found consideration present where the general law of contract, at least as then declared, would have said that it was absent.

A classic form of statement identifies consideration with detriment to the promisee sustained by virtue of the promise (*Hamer v. Sidway*, 124 N.Y. 538). So compendious a formula is little more than a half truth. There is need of many a supplementary gloss before the outline can be so filled in as to depict the classic doctrine. "The promise and the consideration must purport to be the motive each for the other, in whole or at least in part. It is not enough that the promise induces the detriment or that the detriment induces the promise if the other half is wanting" (*Wisc. & Mich. Ry. Co. v. Powers*, 191 U.S. 379, 386). If A promises B to make him a gift, consideration may be lacking, though B has

Reconsidering consideration

Recall that the court in *Hamer* understood consideration as "either . . . some right, interest, profit or benefit accruing to the one party, or some forbearance, detriment, loss or responsibility given, suffered or undertaken by the other." According to Cardozo, however, this benefit-detriment test constituted but a "half truth," to be *supplemented with*, rather than *replaced by*, the bargain theory of consideration (see next sentence, quoting Holmes). Putting these "half truths" together, Cardozo suggests that consideration can be understood in two different ways: as (1) a bargain-based benefit to the promisor, *or* (2) a bargain-based detriment to the promisee.

renounced other opportunities for betterment in the faith that the promise will be kept.

The half truths of one generation tend at times to perpetuate themselves in the law as the whole truths of another, when constant repetition brings it about that qualifications, taken once for granted, are disregarded or forgotten. The doctrine of consideration has not escaped the common lot. As far back as 1881, Judge Holmes in his lectures on the Common Law, separated the detriment which is merely a consequence of the promise from the detriment which is in truth the motive or inducement, and yet added that the courts "have gone far in obliterating this distinction." The tendency toward effacement has not lessened with the years. On the contrary, there has grown up of recent days a doctrine that a substitute for consideration or an exception to its ordinary requirements can be found in what is styled "a promissory estoppel" (Williston, *Contracts*, §§ 139, 116). Whether the exception has made its way in this State to such an extent as to permit us to say that the general law of consideration has been modified accordingly, we do not now attempt to say. . . . Certain, at least, it is that we have adopted the doctrine of promissory estoppel as the equivalent of consideration in connection with our law of charitable subscriptions. So long as those decisions stand, the question is not merely whether the enforcement of a charitable subscription can be squared with the doctrine of consideration in all its ancient rigor. The question may also be whether it can be squared with the doctrine of consideration as qualified by the doctrine of promissory estoppel.

We have said that the cases in this State have recognized this exception, if exception it is thought to be. . . . Very likely, conceptions of public policy have shaped, more or less subconsciously, the rulings thus made. Judges have been affected by the thought that "defenses of that character" are "breaches of faith toward the public, and especially toward those engaged in the same enterprise, and an unwarrantable disappointment of the reasonable expectations of those interested." . . .

It is in this background of precedent that we are to view the problem now before us. The background helps to an understanding of the implications inherent in subscription and acceptance. This is so though we may find in the end that without recourse to the innovation of promissory estoppel the transaction can be fitted within the mold of consideration as established by tradition.

The evolution of law

Cardozo's warning about blindly imitating legal traditions without understanding their origins, or reasons for being, packs quite a punch, and reminds one of an old joke: A young bride makes her first Thanksgiving turkey and, following her mom's old recipe, cuts the bird in half before putting it in the pan. The husband asks, "Why do you cut the turkey in half before cooking it?" "I don't know," she replies, "My mom's been doing it that way since I was a little girl, and I'm following her recipe. I'll call her and ask." So she calls and asks her mom, who explains: "Well, my mom made it that way when I was a little girl, so when I started making the turkey, I just followed her recipe." Not satisfied, the bride calls her grandmother, who says, "Oh, well I just cut the turkey that way because the pan we had back then was too small!"

Traditions are to laws what pans are to turkeys. As Holmes once remarked, when it comes to understanding the law, "[a] page of history is worth a volume of logic." *New York Trust Co. v. Eisner*, 256 U.S. 345, 349 (1921). But to *understand* the law, of course, is not to *justify* it, but to prepare us to accept or reject it on its own terms. Again, Holmes: "It is revolting to have no better reason for a rule of law than that so it was laid down in the time of Henry IV. It is still more revolting if the grounds upon which it was laid down have vanished long since, and the rule simply persists from blind imitation of the past." Oliver Wendell Holmes, *The Path of the Law*, 10 HARV. L. REV. 457, 468 (1897).

The promisor wished to have a memorial to perpetuate her name. She imposed a condition that the "gift" should "be known as the Mary Yates Johnston Memorial Fund." The **moment that the college accepted $1,000 as a payment on account, there was an assumption of a duty to do whatever acts were customary or reasonably necessary to maintain the memorial fairly and justly in the spirit of its creation.** The college could not accept the money, and hold itself free thereafter from personal responsibility to give effect to the condition. More is involved in the receipt of such a fund than a mere acceptance of money to be held to a corporate use. The purpose of the founder would be unfairly thwarted or at least inadequately served if the college failed to communicate to the world, or in any event to applicants for the scholarship, the title of the memorial. By implication it undertook, when it accepted a portion of the "gift," that in its circulars of information and in other customary ways, when making announcement of this scholarship, it would couple with the announcement the name of the donor. The donor was not at liberty to gain the benefit of such an undertaking upon the payment of a part and disappoint the expectation that there would be payment of the residue. If the college had stated after receiving $1,000 upon account of the subscription that it would apply the money to the prescribed use, but that in its circulars of information and when responding to prospective applicants it would deal with the fund as an anonymous donation, there is little doubt that the subscriber would have been at liberty to treat this statement as the repudiation of a duty impliedly assumed, a repudiation justifying a refusal to make payments in the future. Obligation in such circumstances is correlative and mutual.

> **Thinking tool applied**
>
> Do you agree? Doesn't the obligation Cardozo speaks of depend in the first place on whether the court deems the $1,000 to be part of a gift, or part of a bargained-for promise? If the college has a duty, does Ms. Johnston have a corresponding right? If so, what is it? Consult "Thinking Tool: Thinking Clearly About Legal Relationships" (p. 96).

A case much in point is *N.J. Hospital v. Wright* (95 N.J.L. 462, 464), where a subscription for the maintenance of a bed in a hospital was held to be enforceable by virtue of an implied promise by the hospital that the bed should be maintained in the name of the subscriber. A parallel situation might arise upon the endowment of a chair or a fellowship in a university by the aid of annual payments with the condition that it should commemorate the name of the founder or that of a member of his family. The university would fail to live up to the fair meaning of its promise if it were to publish in its circulars of information and elsewhere the existence of a chair or a fellowship in the prescribed subject, and omit the benefactor's name. A duty to act in ways beneficial to the promisor and beyond the application of the fund to the mere uses of the trust would be cast upon the promisee by the acceptance of the money.

We do not need to measure the extent either of benefit to the promisor or of detriment to the promisee implicit in this duty. "If a person chooses to make an extravagant promise for an inadequate consideration it is his own affair." It was long ago said that "when a thing is to be done by the plaintiff, be it never so small, this is a sufficient consideration to ground an action." The longing for posthumous remembrance is an emotion not so weak as to justify us in saying that its gratification is a negligible good.

We think the duty assumed by the plaintiff to perpetuate the name of the founder of the memorial is sufficient in itself to give validity to the subscription within the rules that define consideration for a promise of that order. When the promisee subjected itself to such a duty at the implied request of the promisor, the result was the creation of a bilateral agreement. There was a promise on the one side and on the other a return promise, made, it is true, by implication, but expressing an obligation that had been exacted as a condition of the payment. A bilateral agreement may exist though one of the mutual promises be a promise "implied in fact," an inference from conduct as opposed to an inference from words. We think the fair inference to be drawn from the acceptance of a payment on account of the subscription is a promise by the college to do what may be necessary on its part to make the scholarship effective. . . .

The conclusion thus reached makes it needless to consider whether, aside from the feature of a memorial, a promissory estoppel may result from the assumption of a duty to apply the fund. . . .

The judgment of the Appellate Division and that of the Trial Term should be reversed, and judgment ordered for the plaintiff as prayed for in the complaint, with costs in all courts.

KELLOGG, J. **(dissenting).** The Chief Judge finds in the expression "In loving memory this gift shall be known as the Mary Yates Johnston Memorial Fund" an offer on the part of Mary Yates Johnston to contract with Allegheny College. The expression makes no such appeal to me. Allegheny College was not requested to perform any act through which the sum offered might bear the title by which the offeror states that it shall be known. The sum offered was termed a "gift" by the offeror. Consequently, I can see no reason why we should strain ourselves to make it, not a gift, but a trade. Moreover, since the donor specified that the gift was made "In consideration of my interest in Christian education, and in consideration of others subscribing," considerations not adequate in law, I can see no excuse for asserting that it was otherwise made in consideration of an act or promise on the part of the donee, constituting a sufficient *quid quo pro* to convert the gift into a contract obligation. To me the words used merely expressed an expectation or wish on the part of the donor and failed to exact the return of an adequate consideration.

But if an offer indeed was present, then clearly it was an offer to enter into a unilateral contract. The offeror was to be bound provided the offeree performed such acts as might be necessary to make the gift offered become known under the proposed name. This is evidently the thought of the Chief Judge, for he says: "She imposed a condition that the 'gift' should be known as the Mary Yates Johnston Memorial Fund." In other words, she proposed to exchange her offer of a donation in return for acts to be performed. Even so there was never any acceptance of the offer and, therefore, no contract, for the acts requested have never been performed. The gift has never been made known as demanded. Indeed, the requested acts, under the very terms of the assumed offer, could never have been performed at a time to convert the offer into a promise. This is so for the reason that the donation was not to take effect until after the death of the donor, and by her death her offer was withdrawn. Clearly, although a promise of the college to make the gift known, as requested, may be implied, that promise was not the acceptance of an offer which gave rise to a contract. The donor stipulated for acts, not promises.

> In order to make a bargain it is necessary that the acceptor shall give in return for the offer or the promise exactly the consideration which the offeror requests. If an act is requested, that very act and no other must be given. If a promise is requested, that promise must be made absolutely and unqualifiedly.

Williston on Contracts § 73.

> It does not follow that an offer becomes a promise because it is accepted; it may be, and frequently is, conditional, and then it does not become a promise until the conditions are satisfied; and in case of offers for a consideration, the performance of the consideration is always deemed a condition.

Langdell, *Summary of the Law of Contracts* § 4.

It seems clear to me that there was here no offer, no acceptance of an offer, and no contract. . . . I do not understand that the holding about to be made in this case is other than a holding that consideration was given to convert the offer into a promise. With that result I cannot agree and, accordingly, must dissent.

POUND, CRANE, LEHMAN and O'BRIEN, JJ., concur with CARDOZO, C. J.; KELLOGG, J. dissents in opinion, in which ANDREWS, J., concurs.

Judgment accordingly.

NOTES AND QUESTIONS

1. ***What happened?*** Who sued whom for what? Procedurally, how did the case get before this court? Factually, what happened between the parties? What arguments did the plaintiff and defendant make? What rule or rules did the court apply? How did the court analyze the dispute between the parties? How did the court decide the case?

2. ***Was this case correctly decided?*** Should this promise have been enforced? Why or why not? Do you agree with the result reached, and reasoning used, by the majority or by the dissent? How, if at all, would you have written the opinion or dissent differently?

3. ***Consideration or promissory estoppel?*** Did the court find that there was sufficient consideration to support the enforcement of the promise? If yes, why all this talk about promissory estoppel? If no, why all this talk about consideration? In short, why do you suppose Judge Cardozo oscillated back and forth between promissory estoppel and consideration?

4. *The Thaumatrope.* Professor Leon Lipson provided one answer to this question in a fascinating article that analyzed the rhetorical features of Cardozo's opinion:

> When we look at the oscillation of argument in the opinion, we are reminded rather of another image, one that was suggested a hundred years before the Allegheny College Case by that odd and engaging logician, Richard Whately, sometime later to be Archbishop of Dublin. Judge Cardozo goes from consideration to promissory estoppel to consideration to duty-&-obligation to promise to consideration to promissory estoppel to victory for Allegheny College. Whenever his argument emphasizing consideration runs thin, he moves on to promissory estoppel; whenever his hints in favor of promissory estoppel approach the edge of becoming a committed ground of decision, he veers off in the direction of the doctrine of consideration. Arguments that oscillate in this way, repeatedly promoting each other by the alternation, call to mind Whately's simile of "the optical illusion effected by that ingenious and philosophical toy call the Thaumatrope: in which two objects are painted on opposite sides of a card,—for instance, a man and a horse, [or]—a bird and a cage"; the card is fitted into a frame with a handle, and the two objects are, "by a sort of rapid whirl [of the handle], presented to the mind as combined in one picture—the man *on* the horse's back, the bird *in* the cage."
>
> Now what were the objects painted on the opposite sides of Judge Cardozo's Thaumatrope? His trouble was that on the consideration side he had a solid rule but shaky facts; on the promissory-estoppel side he had a shaky rule but (potentially) solid facts. He twirled the Thaumatrope in order to give the impression that he had solid facts fitting a solid rule. Some lawyers think that what emerges instead is a picture of a bird on the horse's back.*

5. *Breaking away from formalism?* Another explanation is that Cardozo was trying to break away from the classical school's formalistic grip on contract law—as exemplified by the doctrine of consideration—in favor of a more flexible, instrumentalist approach to enforceability, paving the way for such doctrines as promissory estoppel. As Professor Konefsky explains:

> At the same time, one should notice that as a judge with a mission—loosening up, maybe even disjointing, the classical law of contracts, torts, etc.—Cardozo faced difficult conceptual problems and made substantial advances. *Hamer* was hardly a secure precedent around which a great edifice had been erected. Indeed, it was more of a lighthouse than a castle. And promissory estoppel was hardly developed beyond the most classic of charitable subscription cases. With facts as weak as in *Allegheny College*, it would have been difficult for most judges to move the doctrine along in the direction that Cardozo wished. Normally, strong facts drag the doctrine with them. Yet, here again Cardozo's craft shows how much can be done with just a few raw materials, for he manages to push forward simultaneously on both doctrinal fronts. Simply by using *Hamer*, drawing a few inferences about the nature of reasonable conduct, and

* Leon S. Lipson, *The Allegheny College Case*, YALE L. REP. 8, 11 (Spring 1977).

> turning a piece of Holmes's objective theory on its head to create liability rather than limit it, Cardozo was able both to reinforce Hamer as a precedent and suggest a new and at the same time familiar way of thinking about what might be consideration. In so doing, Cardozo demonstrated that a formal exchange requirement might be "implied" or met in the most attenuated way.
>
> By positioning, if only in dictum, promissory estoppel not as an exception to consideration doctrine, but squarely within it, Cardozo opened the possibility (though never realized by him or his court) that in the next case promissory estoppel could be found in a commercial circumstance. Bargain theory was used to make all doctrinal moves appear as mainstream as possible. To make such gains, in a two-front war with such poor troops on such unpromising terrain, bordered on the inspired.
>
> What are we left with at the end of this opinion? The free-standing structure of the analysis looks something like this: After the statement of "facts," there is an opening foray of several paragraphs into the problem area of consideration doctrine in charitable subscription cases in New York, focusing on a definition of consideration. The conclusion is that whatever consideration is, it is, at the least, an expansive, flexible, and adaptable doctrine. Then, as evidence of that insight, the concept of promissory estoppel is introduced, not as an exception to consideration doctrine, but as a continuation of the process of enlarging it. In other words, promissory estoppel is used informatively, as an historical lesson, and instrumentally, as a means to expand consideration. The "background of precedent" allows Cardozo to fit charitable subscription cases into "the mould of consideration as established by tradition," but more particularly, by his understanding and reshaping of that tradition. . . .*

6. *More on formalism.* Professor Townsend also believes that Cardozo used *Allegheny* to move contract law away from formalism: "*Allegheny College* often is cited as an example of 'Cardozo's commitment to the elevation of a realistic approach' to judging that goes beyond 'the technicalities of precedent and doctrine.'"† Assuming this is correct, do you think this is a good or bad way of judging? Why?

7. *The indeterminacy of legal doctrine.* In addition to helping establish the doctrine of promissory estoppel, Cardozo's opinion is significant for another reason, as explained by Prakash Mehta:

> Cardozo's opinion . . . openly conveys the indeterminacy of legal doctrine in order to establish the result more persuasively. Cardozo makes sweeping statements about how "the half truths of one generation" become "the whole truths of another." He then uses this refrain to introduce the complexities of consideration, including the "innovation of promissory estoppel." As quickly as

* Alfred S. Konefsky, *How To Read, Or at Least Not Misread, Cardozo in the* Allegheny College *Case*, 36 BUFF. L. REV. 645, 686-87 (1987).

† Mike Townsend, *Cardozo's* Allegheny College *Opinion: A Case Study in Law as an Art*, 33 HOUS. L. REV. 1103, 1113 (1996), *citing* Andrew L. Kaufman, *Judging New York Style: A Brief Retrospective of Two New York Judges*, in 1988 YEARBOOK OF THE SUPREME COURT HISTORICAL SOCIETY 60, 65 (1988).

he canvasses this innovation, Cardozo puts it aside, molding Johnston's contract into more traditional notions of consideration.

In light of his ultimate reliance on traditional doctrine, Cardozo's references to promissory estoppel and the other "public policy" driven modifications of consideration are interesting. To my mind, these references to doctrinal indeterminacy are acknowledgements of legal doubt. At first blush, this type of "concession" appears unnecessary or, even worse, it appears to undermine the decision. However, in this case, the acknowledgements work to persuade, to reinforce the validity of the "implied promise" that Cardozo ultimately finds. . . .

[H]e is persuasive because he acknowledges what is true: that law is at times indeterminate, particularly in cases in which the policies reflected in law are in flux.

Just as *Hamlet* remains focused on the role of doubt in moral life, *Allegheny College* reflects a judge consumed by the realities of doubt in legal life. Whereas Hamlet's is a case of first impression that calls forth no clear "rule," Cardozo's dilemma in *Allegheny College* is one in which he must deal with the circumstances of a consideration doctrine in flux. In both cases, the acknowledgement of doubt is unnecessary to the substantive outcome or decision. But without those acknowledgements I do not think we would tap these works for their beauty. Hamlet's musings do not change the stakes of the decision he has to make, nor do Cardozo's gymnastics alter the facts of the case. The musings in Hamlet's case are simply the charm that draws us to him, and Cardozo's intricately patterned rationale the sign of legal beauty, or persuasiveness.*

8. *On the early history of promissory estoppel.* In 1926, one year before this case was decided, Judge Cardozo was in attendance at a meeting of the American Law Institute, in which the Reporter for the *Restatement (First) of Contracts*, Professor Williston, was defending the inclusion of what would become § 90, which established promissory estoppel as a new fixture in American contract law.† Although Cardozo was silent during these hearings, according to Professor Townsend, he would later use *Allegheny College* to "purposely inject[] himself into the debate over the Restatement's position that reliance could provide a nonbargain basis for promissory liability."‡ (Can you see how?) But it is not clear whether Williston, Cardozo, or anyone else originally associated with the *Restatement (First) of Contracts* knew just how revolutionary the doctrine of promissory estoppel would turn out to be. In the excerpt below, the author attempts to put into perspective the significance of this new doctrine, the extent to which it differed from the traditional, consideration-based theory of contract, and a word or two about promissory estoppel remedies.

---

* Prakash Mehta, Note, *An Essay on Hamlet: Emblems of Truth in Law and Literature*, 83 GEO. L.J. 165, 181-82 (1994).

† The fascinating debate, which is well worth the read, is excerpted in PETER LINZER, A CONTRACTS ANTHOLOGY 339-49 (2d ed. 1995).

‡ Mike Townsend, *Cardozo's* Allegheny College *Opinion: A Case Study in Law as an Art*, 33 HOUS. L. REV. 1103, 1118 (1996).

HISTORICAL PERSPECTIVE: THE BIRTH OF PROMISSORY ESTOPPEL*

In 1932, the American Law Institute published the much-anticipated *Restatement (First) of Contracts,* which contained within its pages two completely different and, some would say, irreconcilable theories of contract law. On the one hand, the relatively innocuous § 75 endorsed the centuries-old, bargain-based theory of contracts in which a promise, to be enforceable, must be supported by "consideration," which was defined as "an act," "forbearance," or "return promise bargained for and given in exchange for the promise." On the other hand, tucked away several pages later, the drafters of the *Restatement* enshrined in § 90 a completely different and contradictory theory of contractual obligation based on the normative principle of reliance, as opposed to the more settled principle of bargain. This provision, which established what is today commonly referred to as "promissory estoppel," provided:

> A promise which the promisor should reasonably expect to induce action or forbearance of a definite and substantial character on the part of the promisee and which does induce such action or forbearance is binding if injustice can be avoided only by enforcement of the promise.[9]

Several generations later, it is difficult to appreciate how innovative these forty-six words were when they were first penned over seventy-five years ago, but one commentator neatly captured their revolutionary spirit when he wrote that the inclusion of § 90 in the *Restatement (First) of Contracts* was "the most important event in twentieth century American contract law."[10] These are strong words, to be sure. But despite the seemingly hyperbolic nature of these remarks, few commentators would disagree with this characterization. Similarly, it is no easy task to describe how different § 90 was from the prevailing bargain-based theory of consideration, or the challenge that it would, in time, pose to the dominant theory of contractual obligation. Professor Gilmore came close when he colorfully described the differences between § 75 and § 90 as analogous to "matter and anti-matter," "Restatement and anti-Restatement," and, most poignantly, "Contract and anti-Contract."[12] It was the more traditional, consideration-based view that played the starring role of "Contract" opposite the newer, tort-like theory of promissory estoppel, which was left to play the villainous role of "anti-Contract." Professor Gilmore went on to predict that "these two contradictory propositions cannot live comfortably together: in the end one must swallow the other up." Surprisingly, Professor Gilmore predicted that the promissory estoppel underdog would prove victorious by "swallow[ing] up" contract, thereby merging these two fields of law into the single, unified subject of "Contorts," which would soon be taught to first year law students in place of the traditional (and soon to be obsolete) courses in Contracts and Torts. Given Professor Gilmore's belief that promissory estoppel was originally intended to apply to noncommercial transactions that lay just beyond consideration's grasp, his

* Excerpted from Marco Jimenez, *The Many Faces of Promissory Estoppel: An Empirical Analysis Under the Restatement (Second) of Contracts,* 57 UCLA L. Rev. 669, 673-79 (2010).

9. Restatement (First) of Contracts § 90 (1932).

10. Peter Linzer, A Contracts Anthology 221 (1989).

12. Grant Gilmore, The Death of Contract 61 (1974).

claim that promissory estoppel would soon operate as a general theory of obligation must have come as quite a shock to his contemporaries. And, although Professor Gilmore's prophecy has not yet come to pass, the tension that he described has grown, and these doctrines continue to battle each other to this day.But what exactly makes these two theories of promissory recovery so different from one another? Here is one explanation: Under the traditional, bargain-based theory of contract, a party who wishes to form a binding contract with another must offer something by way of performance or return promise in exchange for the desired promise. Under this view, because each promisee has given something in exchange for the other's promised performance, when the other party breaches, the promisee may "feel that he has been 'deprived' of something" that belonged to him, and can therefore justifiably demand as a remedy the very thing that was promised to him by way of specific performance or, where that remedy is unavailable, expectation damages. The justification behind promissory estoppel, however, is entirely different. As one commentator explained, the wrong complained of in a promissory estoppel claim "is not primarily in depriving the plaintiff of the promised reward but in causing the plaintiff to change position to his detriment."[22] Therefore, because the right that the law seeks to protect in a bargain-based contract (the promised performance) is distinct from the right involved in a reliance-based contract (detrimental reliance), the remedies invoked to protect these rights should also be distinct. Thus, rather than protecting the promisee's expectation interest, as would be customary in a bargain-based contract, some commentators and judges have suggested that promissory estoppel damages "should not exceed the loss caused by the change of position, which would never be more in amount, but might be less, than the promised reward."[23] Stated differently, the remedy for promissory estoppel should never exceed what are frequently referred to as "reliance damages." Although many commentators think about the difference between consideration-based contracts and promissory estoppel in these terms today, as an historical matter, this was simply not true. Instead, "the original Restatement was conceived and drafted primarily in terms of promise," rather than reliance.[25] Therefore, because promissory estoppel was originally conceived of as a promise-based theory of recovery (that also required reliance), rather than a reliance-based theory of recovery (that just so happened to require a promise), it should come as no surprise that Professor Samuel Williston, the Reporter and primary drafter of the *Restatement (First) of Contracts,* thought that the remedy awarded in promissory estoppel cases should be the same as the remedy awarded for an ordinary breach of contract action. In other words, they should both be protected with the (usually) more generous expectation remedy. This point can be seen most clearly in a famous debate over promissory estoppel that took place in 1926 on the floor of the American Law Institute (ALI) between Professor Williston and Frederick Coudert, a New York attorney. In this debate, which took place six years before promissory estoppel was officially adopted by the ALI, Williston was asked about an Uncle's liability if Uncle

22. Warren A. Seavey, *Reliance Upon Gratuitous Promises or Other Conduct*, 64 HARV. L. REV. 913, 926 (1951).

23. *Id.*

25. Edward Yorio & Stev Thel, *The Promissory Basis of Section 90*, 101 YALE L.J. 111, 112 (1991).

promised his nephew Johnny $1000 to buy a car, Johnny went out and purchased a car for $500, and Uncle refused to pay. Professor Williston stated that he thought Uncle should be liable for $1000, the amount he promised to pay, rather than the $500 that Johnny had spent in reliance on his Uncle's promise. Professor Williston's response provoked a strong reaction from several members of the ALI, including Mr. Coudert. Their exchange, part of which has been excerpted below, has been immortalized in the contract law canon:

> MR. COUDERT: Please let me see if I understand it rightly. Would you say, Mr. Reporter, in your case of Johnny and the uncle, the uncle promising the $1000 and Johnny buying the car—say, he goes out and buys the car for $500—that uncle would be liable for $1000 or would he be liable for $500?
>
> MR. WILLISTON: If Johnny had done what he was expected to do, or is acting within the limits of his uncle's expectation, I think the uncle would be liable for $1000; but not otherwise.
>
> MR. COUDERT: In other words, substantial justice would require that uncle should be penalized in the sum of $500.
>
> MR. WILLISTON: Why do you say "penalized"?
>
> . . .
>
> MR. COUDERT: Because substantial justice there would require, it seems to me, that Johnny get [sic] his money for his car, but should he get his car and $500 more? I don't see. . . .
>
> . . .
>
> MR. WILLISTON: Either the promise is binding or it is not. If the promise is binding it has to be enforced as it is made.[26]

As the Reporter and primary drafter of the *Restatement*, it is not surprising that Professor Williston's view, even if controversial, initially won out. In spite of this, forty-two years later Professor Grant Gilmore predicted that promissory estoppel would eventually swallow up the traditional, consideration-based theory of contract to form a single theory of promissory enforcement based on reliance. Professor Gilmore's claim seemed to suggest that, at its core, the normative basis of promissory estoppel law had shifted over the years from one initially based on promise to one based on reliance. Indeed, so powerful was Professor Gilmore's belief that the reliance principle now undergirded cases in this area that he would argue, as early as 1974, that even "the 'probability of reliance' may be a sufficient reason for enforcement" of a promise.

The disparity between Professor Williston's original intent and Professor Gilmore's descriptive claims begged the obvious normative question: How should promises be enforced under a theory of promissory estoppel? If one were inclined to look to history as a guide, then one might conclude that, because promissory estoppel was initially conceived of as a distinctly contractual theory of recovery, plaintiffs who prevailed under this theory of promissory recovery ought to be awarded full contractual damages (that is, expectation damages), as the drafters of the *Restatement* originally intended. If, on the other hand, one looked to

26. *Discussion of the Tentative Draft, Contracts Restatement No. 2*, 4 A.L.I. PROC. 61, 98-103 (1926).

contemporary evidence as a guide, one might be tempted to follow Professor Gilmore and view promissory estoppel as a tort-like theory of recovery, which would suggest that the damages that ought to be awarded should reflect tort-like reliance damages, rather than contract-like expectation damages.

To summarize, Professor Gilmore made three important but controversial claims regarding promissory estoppel that continue to impact the case law and influence scholars, lawyers, and judges to this day. First, Professor Gilmore believed that promissory estoppel was an increasingly significant cause of action that would eventually swallow up the entire field of contract law. Second, he thought that the normative principle underlying promissory estoppel was, and ought to be, reliance, not promise. And third, because he viewed promissory estoppel as more akin to tort than contract law, he thought that the remedy that ought to be awarded to successful litigants ought to reflect reliance damages rather than expectation damages.

You will recall that *James Baird Co. v. Gimbel Bros, Inc.* discussed (but rejected) the applicability of promissory estoppel in the context of offer and acceptance. For this reason, it is sometimes included in contracts casebooks alongside cases dealing with promissory estoppel, and sometimes (as in this book) included alongside cases dealing with offer and acceptance. Wherever it is placed, it is almost always juxtaposed with *Drennan v. Star Paving Co.*, which, as you will recall, had a similar fact pattern but reached a completely different result: Whereas the court in *Baird* held that there was no place for promissory estoppel where a traditional, consideration-based contract was contemplated, *Drennan* disagreed, and expanded the role of promissory estoppel in the process. Because both cases considered the doctrine of promissory estoppel as a possible solution to traditional offer and acceptance problems, a decision has been made to include the full report of both cases in the section of the casebook dealing with offer and acceptance. The opposite decision, of course, could also have been justified, as all such arrangements are somewhat artificial. Indeed, it is because so many aspects of contract law are interrelated that we began this course with an overview and introduction to each major area. Therefore, whether your professor covered *Baird* and *Drennan* earlier, or chooses to cover it here, you should include them in both places when you prepare your outline for this course.

James Baird Co. v. Gimbel Bros., Inc.

United States Court of Appeals, Second Circuit
64 F.2d 344 (1933)

For a report of the case and accompanying materials, see p. 298, *supra*.

2. The Rise of Promissory Estoppel

In the previous subsection, we looked at a few of the classic cases that arguably demonstrated the limitations of the doctrine of consideration and the need for a reliance-based form of promissory liability. We also saw how judges struggled to deal with promises that invited reliance in the absence of such a theory. In this subsection, we turn to the doctrine of promissory estoppel itself, which provides a much cleaner doctrinal solution to the types of problems explored in the previous subsection.

DOCTRINAL OVERVIEW: PROMISSORY ESTOPPEL*

We have seen that the promisee's unsolicited reliance is not consideration because it is not bargained for. Promises made outside or on the periphery of the marketplace are particularly likely to lack this element of bargain. The failure of the doctrine of consideration to provide a more satisfactory basis for enforcing such promises might have brought greater pressure to reform the doctrine had it not been for the increasing recognition of reliance as an alternative ground for recovery.

[I]t was not until the twentieth century that a generalized theory of recovery based on reliance developed. . . . Late in the nineteenth century, Holmes expressed the common law's traditional view of reliance: "It would cut up the doctrine of consideration by the roots, if a promisee could make a gratuitous promise binding by subsequently acting in reliance on it."[5] Nevertheless, even during the nineteenth century, reliance on a gratuitous promise came to be recognized as a basis for recovery in a few categories of cases.One category was made up of gratuitous promises to convey land. Courts enforced such promises if the promisee had relied by moving onto the land and making improvements (e.g., by putting up a building). A second category consisted of gratuitous promises made by bailees in connection with gratuitous bailments. If, when the bailor delivered goods to the bailee, the bailee promised to obtain insurance on them but then failed to do so, the bailor's reliance by not obtaining insurance made the bailee's promise enforceable when the goods were later destroyed. . . .

A third category was made up of promises to make gifts to charitable institutions ("charitable subscriptions"). Such a promise seems the archetype of the unenforceable gratuitous promise. . . . [The desire of American courts] to support private philanthropy . . . spawned a variety of tenuous arguments designed to show that such promises were supported by consideration. . . . [*Allegheny College* provides a striking example of such a case.] Now, however, it has come to be recognized that such promises are enforceable when relied on by the charitable institution, without resort to the doctrine of consideration.

The fourth category consisted of gratuitous promises made within the family. Because the pattern of the bargained-for exchange, so common in the marketplace, seems out of place within the family, promisors within a family may not actually bargain for something in return, even though they desire and expect it. . . . [*Ricketts v. Scothorn* provides a striking example of such a case. Although the *Ricketts* court ultimately had to resort to "equitable estoppel" to enforce the

* Excerpted from E. ALLAN FARNSWORTH, CONTRACTS § 2.19 (4th ed. 2004).

5. *Commonwealth v. Scituate Sav. Bank*, 137 Mass. 301, 302 (1884).

promise,] [s]uch decisions took much of the sting out of the requirement of consideration in family transactions. Courts no longer needed to search for a bargain in cases such as *Hamer v. Sidway*, in which one was found, and in *Kirksey*, in which one was not.

These decisions based on reliance, however, involved far more than a routine application of "equitable estoppel." That concept applied to a representation *of fact* made by one party and relied on by the other. The estopped party was precluded from alleging or proving facts that contradicted its representation. But cases like *Ricketts* involved a *promise*, not a representation of a fact. The promisor was "estopped" to raise the defense of lack of consideration in his promise. This type of estoppel came to be known as "promissory estoppel."

In 1933, on the authority of such cases as these, the American Law Institute promulgated § 90 of the *Restatement of Contracts*, which was destined to become its most notable and influential rule. It states, in terms generally applicable to all promises, the principle that courts had applied to the four narrow categories of promise just described:

> A promise which the promisor should reasonably expect to induce action or forbearance of a definite and substantial character on the part of the promisee and which does induce such action or forbearance is binding if injustice can be avoided only by enforcement of the promise.

The following version appears as § 90 in the *Restatement Second*:

> (1) A promise which the promisor should reasonably expect to induce action or forbearance on the part of the promisee or a third person and which does induce such action or forbearance is binding if injustice can be avoided only by enforcement of the promise. The remedy granted for breach may be limited as justice requires.
>
> (2) A charitable subscription or a marriage settlement is binding under Subsection (1) without proof that the promise induced action or forbearance.

Section 90 is the *Restatement*'s most significant departure from its stated policy of following precedents and has been the fountainhead of recovery based on reliance in a broad range of situations. Most of these situations involve commercial transactions and are far removed from the original settings, such as that in *Ricketts*, in which the doctrine originated. Although the rule that it states does not lend itself to precision, four requirements are of special interest. First, there must have been a promise. Second, the promisor must have had reason to expect reliance on the promise. Third, the promise must have induced such reliance.[28] Fourth, the circumstances must have been such that injustice can be avoided only by enforcement of the promise.It is to this doctrine, enshrined in the *Restatement (First) and (Second) of Contracts* § 90, that we now turn.

---

28. The requirement of the first *Restatement* that the reliance be "of a definite and substantial character" has been dropped in the *Restatement Second*. . . .

Drennan v. Star Paving Co.

Supreme Court of California
333 P.2d 757 (1958)

For a report of the case and accompanying materials, see p. 300, *supra*.

PROMISSORY ESTOPPEL AND TRADITIONAL CONTRACT DOCTRINE*

While the general problems relating to the revocability of offers, particularly those presented in the construction bidding cases, have been the subject of much study and discussion, the application of § 90 to offers raises a number of questions which have not yet been answered.

It should be recalled that contract doctrine generally classifies offers under the same consideration rules as promises. Thus, unless an offer is supported by consideration, the offeror retains the power to revoke until the moment of acceptance. If the offer is expressly or impliedly "firm," the potential injustice of the operation of the revocation rule is obvious. One avenue of escape is made available by consideration doctrine in the part performance rule of § 45 of the *Restatement*. The principle of that section, however, does not provide a foundation sufficiently broad to include many cases of justifiable reliance arising today.[118] It is expressly limited to offers for unilateral contracts and precludes revocation prior to acceptance only where the action in reliance constitutes a part of the actual performance made the price of the offer. If justifiable reliance in the form of *preparations* to perform is to have the effect of preventing revocation, the most readily available theory is that of promissory estoppel. Yet, aside from the construction bidding cases, there is little evidence that nonperformance reliance upon unaccepted offers prompts explicit use of § 90 as a ground of irrevocability. And even in those cases in which the section is applied, the mode of application is vulnerable to objections of inconsistency, invalid analogy, and circuitous reasoning. The outcome of current construction bidding litigation usually depends upon the extent to which a particular court accepts the *Drennan* rout around the obstacles of *Baird*.[123] In view of the frequent applications of § 90 to bargains, it is surprising that *Baird* has retained as much vitality as it has. Aside from

* Excerpted from Stanley D. Henderson, *Promissory Estoppel and Traditional Contract Doctrine*, 78 YALE L.J. 343, 365-67 (1969).

118. Even a casual examination of the reports should make it clear that Section 45 is invoked in contract litigation much less often than is Section 90. This may suggest that a greater number of reliance claims arise from the bilateral than the unilateral setting. It may also suggest that Section 90 is operating as a substitute for Section 45.

123. . . . Though *Baird* and *Drennan* produce widely divergent results, it is interesting that they both purport to observe traditional offer-acceptance rules. In *Baird* it is the offer which authorizes revocation until acceptance, thereby precluding the application of promissory estoppel. On the other hand, the offer in *Drennan* provides assurance against revocation and makes the general's reliance reasonable. At the same time, even *Drennan* concedes the common law effect of a deviant response to an offer. Thus, again in contrast to other factual settings, the continuation of negotiations past the point of the general's use of the sub's bid operates to remove the conditions which justify the use of promissory estoppel. . . .

the technicalities of theory, the blunt thrust of the case is that § 90 has no relevance to a promise which offers a bargain. A number of courts have, in effect, adopted this philosophy, depriving themselves of a flexible tool for conforming law to common commercial expectations and practices. The liberalizing effect of Justice Traynor's opinion in *Drennan* is therefore a valuable contribution to legal doctrine. However, because the opinion may well be relied upon to justify continued expansion of § 90, the difficulties with the *Drennan* application of promissory estoppel to offers ought to be kept in mind.

Recall how, when we studied past and moral consideration, we noticed a reluctance among courts to enforce promises for services already rendered. But what if the promise, although technically unenforceable under a bargain-based theory of consideration, induced the promisee's reliance? And what if this reliance resulted in the promisee being in a *worse* position than she would have been in had the promise never been made? Should a court, in such a case, enforce the promise? If so, to what extent (e.g., should a court protect the promisee's reliance or expectation interest)?* These issues are both dealt with in the following case.

Feinberg v. Pfeiffer Co.

St. Louis Court of Appeal, Missouri
322 S.W.2d 163 (1959)

DOERNER, COMMISSIONER. This is a suit brought in the Circuit Court of the City of St. Louis by plaintiff, a former employee of the defendant corporation, on an alleged contract whereby defendant agreed to pay plaintiff the sum of $200 per month for life upon her retirement. A jury being waived, the case was tried by the court alone. Judgment below was for plaintiff for $5100, the amount of the pension claimed to be due as of the date of the trial, together with interest thereon, and defendant duly appealed.

The parties are in substantial agreement on the essential facts. Plaintiff began working for the defendant, a manufacturer of pharmaceuticals, in 1910, when she was but 17 years of age. By 1947 she had attained the position of bookkeeper, office manager, and assistant treasurer of the defendant, and owned 70 shares of its stock out of a total of 6503 shares issued and outstanding. . . .

On December 27, 1947, the annual meeting of the defendant's Board of Directors was held. . . . At that meeting the Board of Directors adopted the following resolution, which, because it is the crux of the case, we quote in full:

> The Chairman thereupon pointed out that the Assistant Treasurer, Mrs. Anna Sacks Feinberg, has given the corporation many years of long and faithful

* For a review, see "Three Damage Interests" on p. 117, *supra*.

> service. Not only has she served the corporation devotedly, but with exceptional ability and skill. The President pointed out that although all of the officers and directors sincerely hoped and desired that Mrs. Feinberg would continue in her present position for as long as she felt able, nevertheless, in view of the length of service which she has contributed provision should be made to afford her retirement privileges and benefits which should become a firm obligation of the corporation to be available to her whenever she should see fit to retire from active duty, however many years in the future such retirement may become effective. It was, accordingly, proposed that Mrs. Feinberg's salary which is presently $350.00 per month, be increased to $400.00 per month, and that Mrs. Feinberg would be given the privilege of retiring from active duty at any time she may elect to see fit so to do upon a retirement pay of $200.00 per month for life, with the distinct understanding that the retirement plan is merely being adopted at the present time in order to afford Mrs. Feinberg security for the future and in the hope that her active services will continue with the corporation for many years to come. After due discussion and consideration, and upon motion duly made and seconded, it was—
>
> RESOLVED, that the salary of Anna Sacks Feinberg be increased from $350.00 to $400.00 per month and that she be afforded the privilege of retiring from active duty in the corporation at any time she may elect to see fit so to do upon retirement pay of $200.00 per month, for the remainder of her life.

At the request of Mr. Lippman, his sons-in-law, Messrs. Harris and Flammer, called upon the plaintiff at her apartment on the same day to advise her of the passage of the resolution. Plaintiff testified on cross-examination that she had no prior information that such a pension plan was contemplated, that it came as a surprise to her, and that she would have continued in her employment whether or not such a resolution had been adopted. It is clear from the evidence that there was no contract, oral or written, as to plaintiff's length of employment, and that she was free to quit, and the defendant to discharge her, at any time.

Plaintiff did continue to work for the defendant through June 30, 1949, on which date she retired. In accordance with the foregoing resolution, the defendant began paying her the sum of $200 on the first of each month. Mr. Lippman died on November 18, 1949, and was succeeded as president of the company by his widow. Because of an illness, she retired from that office and was succeeded in October, 1953, by her son-in-law, Sidney M. Harris. Mr. Harris testified that while Mrs. Lippman had been president she signed the monthly pension check paid plaintiff, but fussed about doing so, and considered the payments as gifts. After his election, he stated, a new accounting firm employed by the defendant questioned the validity of the payments to plaintiff on several occasions, and in the Spring of 1956, upon its recommendation, he consulted the Company's then attorney, Mr. Ralph Kalish. Harris testified that both Ernst and Ernst, the accounting firm, and Kalish told him there was no need of giving plaintiff the money. He also stated that he had concurred in the view that the payments to plaintiff were mere gratuities rather than amounts due under a contractual obligation, and that following his discussion with the Company's attorney plaintiff was sent a check for $100 on April 1, 1956. Plaintiff declined to accept the reduced amount, and this action followed. Additional facts will be referred to later in this opinion. . . .

[Appellant argues] that there was insufficient evidence to support the court's findings that plaintiff would not have quit defendant's employ had she not known and relied upon the promise of defendant to pay her $200 a month for life, and the finding that, from her voluntary retirement until April 1, 1956, plaintiff relied upon the continued receipt of the pension installments. The trial court so found, and, in our opinion, justifiably so. Plaintiff testified, and was corroborated by Harris, defendant's witness, that knowledge of the passage of the resolution was communicated to her on December 27, 1947, the very day it was adopted. She was told at that time by Harris and Flammer, she stated, that she could take the pension as of that day, if she wished. She testified further that she continued to work for another year and a half, through June 30, 1949; that at that time her health was good and she could have continued to work, but that after working for almost forty years she thought she would take a rest. Her testimony continued:

Q. What was the reason that you left?
A. Well, I thought almost forty years, it was a long time and I thought I would take a little rest.
Q. Yes.
A. And with the pension and what earnings my husband had, we figured we could get along.
Q. Did you rely upon this pension?
A. We certainly did.
Q. Being paid?
A. Very much so. We relied upon it because I was positive that I was going to get it as long as I lived.
Q. Would you have left the employment of the company at that time had it not been for this pension?
A. No.
Mr. Allen: Just a minute, I object to that as calling for a conclusion and conjecture on the part of this witness.
The Court: It will be overruled.
Q. (Mr. Agatstein continuing): Go ahead, now. The question is whether you would have quit the employment of the company at that time had you not relied upon this pension plan?
A. No, I wouldn't.
Q. You would not have. Did you ever seek employment while this pension was being paid to you—
A. (interrupting): No.
Q. Wait a minute, at any time prior—at any other place?
A. No, sir.
Q. Were you able to hold any other employment during that time?
A. Yes, I think so.
Q. Was your health good?
A. My health was good.

It is obvious from the foregoing that there was ample evidence to support the findings of fact made by the court below.

We come, then, to the basic issue in the case. While otherwise defined in defendant's third and fourth assignments of error, it is thus succinctly stated in the argument in its brief: ". . . whether plaintiff has proved that she has a right to recover from defendant based upon a legally binding contractual obligation to pay her $200 per month for life."

It is defendant's contention, in essence, that the resolution adopted by its Board of Directors was a mere promise to make a gift, and that no contract resulted either thereby, or when plaintiff retired, because there was no consideration given or paid by the plaintiff. It urges that a promise to make a gift is not binding unless supported by a legal consideration; that the only apparent consideration for the adoption of the foregoing resolution was the "many years of long and faithful service" expressed therein; and that **past services are not a valid consideration for a promise.** Defendant argues further that there is nothing in the resolution which made its effectiveness conditional upon plaintiff's continued employment, that she was not under contract to work for any length of time but was free to quit whenever she wished, and that she had no contractual right to her position and could have been discharged at any time.

> ***Past consideration***
>
> Recall from cases like *Mills v. Wyman* (p. 367) and *Webb v. McGowin* (p. 479) that "past consideration" is generally not treated as legally sufficient consideration because, by definition, it cannot be bargained for.

Plaintiff concedes that a promise based upon past services would be without consideration, but contends that there were two other elements which supplied the required element: First, the continuation by plaintiff in the employ of the defendant for the period from December 27, 1947, the date when the resolution was adopted, until the date of her retirement on June 30, 1949. And, second, her change of position, i.e., her retirement, and the abandonment by her of her opportunity to continue in gainful employment, made in reliance on defendant's promise to pay her $200 per month for life.

> ***Why fight it?***
>
> Like you, counsel for plaintiff read *Mills v. Wyman*, and knew that the whole "past consideration is sufficient consideration" argument was a losing one, conceded the point, and let it die. Good lawyers do this: concede weak points to focus on stronger ones. Counsel also seems to have been familiar with the hydra of Greek mythology, and offered two stronger arguments in its place. What were these arguments, and how did the court deal with them? Do you agree with the court's approach?

We must agree with the defendant that the evidence does not support the first of these contentions. There is no language in the resolution predicating plaintiff's right to a pension upon her continued employment. She was not required to work for the defendant for any period of time as a condition to gaining such retirement benefits. She was told that she could quit the day upon which the resolution was adopted, as she herself testified, and it is clear from her own testimony that she made no promise or agreement to continue in the employ of the defendant in return for its promise to pay her a pension. Hence there was lacking that mutuality of obligation which is essential to the validity of a contract.

But as to the second of these contentions we must agree with plaintiff. By the terms of the resolution defendant promised to pay plaintiff the sum of $200 a month upon her retirement. Consideration for a promise has been defined in the ***Restatement of the Law of Contracts*** § 75, as:

> **Look familiar?**
>
> *Restatement (First) of Contracts* § 75 has undergone a few minor (and mostly cosmetic) changes and now appears as *Restatement (Second) of Contracts* § 71.

(1) Consideration for a promise is
(a) an act other than a promise, or
(b) a forbearance, or
(c) the creation, modification or destruction of a legal relation, or
(d) a return promise, bargained for and given in exchange for the promise.

As the parties agree, the consideration sufficient to support a contract may be either a benefit to the promisor or a loss or detriment to the promisee. § 90 of the ***Restatement of the Law of Contracts*** states that:

> **Comparing the Restatements.**
>
> Unlike § 75, which has remained relatively unchanged, § 90 has undergone several important changes between the first and second *Restatements of Contracts*. The student should undertake a side-by-side comparison of the two provisions,* which will provide important insight into some of the important doctrinal shifts that have occurred in contract law in general—and promissory estoppel in particular—during the middle of the twentieth century.

> A promise which the promisor should reasonably expect to induce action or forbearance of a definite and substantial character on the part of the promisee and which does induce such action or forbearance is binding if injustice can be avoided only by enforcement of the promise.

This doctrine has been described as that of "promissory estoppel," as distinguished from that of equitable estoppel or estoppel in pais, the reason for the differentiation being stated as follows:

> It is generally true that one who has led another to act in reasonable reliance on his representations of fact cannot afterwards in litigation between the two deny the truth of the representations, and some courts have sought to apply this principle to the formation of contracts, where, relying on a gratuitous promise, the promisee has suffered detriment. It is to be noticed, however, that such a case does not come within the ordinary definition of estoppel. If there is any representation of an existing fact, it is only that the promisor at the time of making the promise intends to fulfill it. As to such intention there is usually no misrepresentation and if there is, it is not that which has injured the promisee. In other words, he relies on a promise and not on a misstatement of fact; and the term "promissory" estoppel or something equivalent should be used to make the distinction.

Williston on Contracts, Rev. Ed., § 139, Vol. 1.

---

* The two provisions are placed next to each other in "Doctrinal Overview: Promissory Estoppel," at the beginning of this unit (p. 409).

In speaking of this doctrine, **Judge Learned Hand said in *Porter v. Commissioner of Internal Revenue*, 60 F.2d 673, 675, that " . . . 'promissory estoppel' is now a recognized species of consideration."** . . .

He said this, but was he right?

Is promissory estoppel a "species" of consideration? Or is it something different? And, for that matter, is promissory estoppel even a contractual form of liability, or is it something else? As it turns out, this seemingly banal question has important consequences for contract law, and courts are currently split. If promissory estoppel is contractual, then the default remedy should be specific performance or expectation damages, and all of the contract-based defenses (which we cover in Chapter 8) should ostensibly apply. If, however, promissory estoppel is non-contractual, then the remedial question is an open one, as is the applicability of traditional contract-based defenses. You are not expected to be able to resolve this issue here, of course. It is simply raised so that you know that there *is* an issue, one to which we will return several times throughout these materials.

Was there such an act on the part of plaintiff, in reliance upon the promise contained in the resolution, as will estop the defendant, and therefore create an enforceable contract under the doctrine of promissory estoppel? We think there was. One of the illustrations cited under § 90 of the *Restatement* is:

> 2. A promises B to pay him an annuity during B's life. B thereupon resigns a profitable employment, as A expected that he might. B receives the annuity for some years, in the meantime becoming disqualified from again obtaining good employment. A's promise is binding. . . .

The fact of the matter is that plaintiff's subsequent illness was not the "action or forbearance" which was induced by the promise contained in the resolution. As the trial court correctly decided, such action on plaintiff's part was her retirement from a lucrative position in reliance upon defendant's promise to pay her an annuity or pension. In a very similar case, *Ricketts v. Scothorn,* the Supreme Court of Nebraska said:

> . . . According to the undisputed proof, as shown by the record before us, the plaintiff was a working girl, holding a position in which she earned a salary of $10 per week. Her grandfather, desiring to put her in a position of independence, gave her the note, accompanying it with the remark that his other grandchildren did not work, and that she would not be obliged to work any longer. In effect, he suggested that she might abandon her employment, and rely in the future upon the bounty which he promised. He doubtless desired that she should give up her occupation, but, whether he did or not, it is entirely certain that he contemplated such action on her part as a reasonable and probable consequence of his gift. Having intentionally influenced the plaintiff to alter her position for the worse on the faith of the note being paid when due, it would be grossly inequitable to permit the maker, or his executor, to resist payment on the ground that the promise was given without consideration.

The Commissioner therefore recommends, for the reasons stated, that the judgment be affirmed.

PER CURIAM.

The foregoing opinion by DOERNER, C., is adopted as the opinion of the court. The judgment is, accordingly, affirmed.

RELEVANT PROVISIONS

For the *Restatement (Second) of Contracts*, consult § 90.

NOTES AND QUESTIONS

1. ***What happened?*** Who sued whom for what? Procedurally, how did the case get before this court? Factually, what happened between the parties? What arguments did the plaintiff and defendant make? What rule or rules did the court apply? How did the court analyze the dispute between the parties? How did the court decide the case?

2. ***Was this case correctly decided?*** Do you agree with the result reached in this case? Why or why not? Do you agree with the court's reasoning? Why or why not? How, if at all, would you have written the opinion differently?

3. ***Should the promise be enforced?*** Do you think the promise to pay Ms. Feinberg a pension should be enforceable? Why or why not? If so, on what grounds? Here are some possibilities:

a. Would equitable estoppel have worked, à la *Ricketts*?

b. What about consideration, perhaps in the hands of someone like Cardozo, à la *Allegheny College*? Can *you* find a bargain here? Or would doing so simply be stretching the doctrine of consideration beyond its breaking point?

c. What about promissory estoppel? Are you sure all four elements are satisfied? How?

d. Can you think of any other grounds for enforcing the promise?

4. ***What remedy should be awarded?*** Assuming that the company's promise is found to be enforceable, as in this case, to what extent should it be enforced (i.e., what remedy should the court award: expectation, reliance, or something else)? Why?*

5. ***Counseling.*** This case was a close call for Ms. Feinberg. Looking forward, how would you advise future clients in Ms. Feinberg's position who receive such promises before they retire?

6. ***Comparing the Restatements.*** Did you compare *Restatements (First)* and *(Second)* § 90 yet? If not, you should stop reading and do so at this time. Done? Good, keep reading. What differences did you notice, and what difference do you think these differences make? For instance, do you think a promise is more or less likely to be enforced under the *Restatement (Second)*? Do you

* See "Empirical Perspective: Promissory Estoppel and the Remedial Landscape," p. 443, *infra*.

think the remedy is likely to be more or less generous under the *Restatement (Second)*? Did you notice that the charitable subscription at issue in *Allegheny* could now be enforced, without a showing of consideration *or reliance*, under *Restatement (Second) of Contracts* § 90(2)? For an example of one court using this approach, *see Salsbury v. Northwestern Bell Telephone Co.*, 221 N.W.2d 609, 613 (Iowa 1974) ("We believe public policy supports [the] view [expressed in § 90(2)]. It is more logical to bind charitable subscriptions without requiring a showing of consideration or detrimental reliance.") The court justified its approach by noting that

> Charitable subscriptions often serve the public interest by making possible projects which otherwise could never come about. It is true some fund raising campaigns are not conducted on a plan which calls for subscriptions to be binding. In such cases we do not hesitate to hold them not binding. However where a subscription is unequivocal the pledgor should be made to keep his word.

Of course, this does not mean that the court *must* apply the *Restatement* to afford relief whenever a promise is made to a charitable institution. Because the *Restatement* states that the promise is only "binding if injustice can be avoided only by enforcement of the promise," a judge who believes it is not unjust to enforce a promise need not do so. Consider, for example, *Congregation Kadimah Toras-Moshe v. DeLeo*, 405 Mass. 365 (1989), a case remarkably similar to *Allegheny College*. In this case, a decedent made an oral promise to give her Orthodox Jewish synagogue ("Congregation") $25,000, which they planned on using to transform a storage room in the synagogue into a library and name it after the decedent. After the decedent passed away, the administrator of the decedent's estate refused to fulfill the oral promise, and Congregation brought suit, alleging that the promise was enforceable both (1) because it was supported by consideration, and (2) on a theory of promissory estoppel because the synagogue relied on receiving the $25,000. In its decision, the court rejected both claims. With respect to the consideration claim, the court pithily noted that "[t]here was no legal benefit to the promisor nor detriment to the promisee, and thus no consideration." With respect to the synagogue's promissory estoppel claim, the court noted that the mere fact that the Congregation allocated $25,000 in its budget merely reduced to writing its "expectation that it would have additional funds," but that "[a] hope or expectation, even though well founded, is not equivalent to either legal detriment or reliance." True, notes the court, reliance is not required under *Restatement (Second) of Contracts* § 90(2), which *allows* a charitable subscription to be enforced "without proof that the promise induced action or forbearance." But to "allow" is not to "require." Therefore, the court refused to apply this section because it thought that, in this particular case, "there is no injustice in declining to enforce the decedent's promise." A different judge, of course, could have ruled otherwise.

Hoffman v. Red Owl Stores, Inc.

Supreme Court of Wisconsin
133 N.W.2d 267 (1965)

Action by Joseph Hoffman (hereinafter "Hoffman") and wife, plaintiffs, against defendants Red Owl Stores, Inc. (hereinafter "Red Owl") and Edward Lukowitz.

The complaint alleged that Lukowitz, as agent for Red Owl, represented to and agreed with plaintiffs that Red Owl would build a store building in Chilton and stock it with merchandise for Hoffman to operate in return for which plaintiffs were to put up and invest a total sum of $18,000; that in reliance upon the above mentioned agreement and representations plaintiffs sold their bakery building and business and their grocery store and business; also in reliance on the agreement and representations Hoffman purchased the building site in Chilton and rented a residence for himself and his family in Chilton; plaintiffs' actions in reliance on the representations and agreement disrupted their personal and business life; plaintiffs lost substantial amounts of income and expended large sums of money as expenses. Plaintiffs demanded recovery of damages for the breach of defendants' representations and agreements.

The action was tried to a court and jury. The facts hereafter stated are taken from the evidence adduced at the trial. Where there was a conflict in the evidence the version favorable to plaintiffs has been accepted since the verdict rendered was in favor of plaintiffs.

Hoffman assisted by his wife operated a bakery at Wautoma from 1956 until sale of the building late in 1961. The building was owned in joint tenancy by him and his wife. Red Owl is a Minnesota corporation having its home office at Hopkins, Minnesota. It owns and operates a number of grocery supermarket stores and also extends franchises to agency stores which are owned by individuals, partnerships and corporations. Lukowitz resides at Green Bay and since September, 1960, has been divisional manager for Red Owl in a territory comprising Upper Michigan and most of Wisconsin in charge of 84 stores. Prior to September, 1960, he was district manager having charge of approximately 20 stores.

In November, 1959, Hoffman was desirous of expanding his operations by establishing a grocery store and contacted a Red Owl representative by the name of Jansen, now deceased. Numerous conversations were had in 1960 with the idea of establishing a Red Owl franchise store in Wautoma. In September, 1960, Lukowitz succeeded Jansen as Red Owl's representative in the negotiations. Hoffman mentioned that $18,000 was all the capital he had available to invest and he was repeatedly assured that this would be sufficient to set him up in business as a Red Owl store. About Christmastime, 1960, Hoffman thought it would be a good idea if he bought a small grocery store in Wautoma and operated it in order that he gain experience in the grocery business prior to operating a Red Owl store in some larger community. On February 6, 1961, on the advice of Lukowitz and Sykes, who had succeeded Lukowitz as Red Owl's district manager, Hoffman bought the inventory and fixtures of a small grocery store in Wautoma and leased the building in which it was operated.

After three months of operating this Wautoma store, the Red Owl representatives came in and took inventory and checked the operations and found the store was operating at a profit. Lukowitz advised Hoffman to sell the store to his manager, and assured him that Red Owl would find a larger store from him elsewhere. Acting on this advice and assurance, Hoffman sold the fixtures and inventory to his manager on June 6, 1961. Hoffman was reluctant to sell at that time because it meant losing the summer tourist business, but he sold on the assurance that he would be operating in a new location by fall and that he must sell this store if he wanted a bigger one. Before selling, Hoffman told the Red Owl representatives that he had $18,000 for "getting set up in business" and they assured him that there would be no problems in establishing him in a bigger operation. The makeup of the $18,000 was not discussed; it was understood plaintiff's father-in-law would furnish part of it. By June, 1961, the towns for the new grocery store had been narrowed down to two, Kewaunee and Chilton. In Kewaunee, Red Owl had an option on a building site. In Chilton, Red Owl had nothing under option, but it did select a site to which plaintiff obtained an option at Red Owl's suggestion. The option stipulated a purchase price of $6,000 with $1,000 to be paid on election to purchase and the balance to be paid within 30 days. On Lukowitz's assurance that everything was all set plaintiff paid $1,000 down on the lot on September 15th.

On September 27, 1961, plaintiff met at Chilton with Lukowitz and Mr. Reymund and Mr. Carlson from the home office who prepared a projected financial statement. Part of the funds plaintiffs were to supply as their investment in the venture were to be obtained by sale of their Wautoma bakery building.

On the basis of this meeting Lukowitz assured Hoffman: ". . . [E]verything is ready to go. Get your money together and we are set." Shortly after this meeting Lukowitz told plaintiffs that they would have to sell their bakery business and bakery building, and that their retaining this property was the only "hitch" in the entire plan. On November 6, 1961, plaintiffs sold their bakery building for $10,000. Hoffman was to retain the bakery equipment as he contemplated using it to operate a bakery in connection with his Red Owl store. After sale of the bakery Hoffman obtained employment on the night shift at an Appleton bakery.

The record contains different exhibits which were prepared in September and October, some of which were projections of the fiscal operation of the business and others were proposed building and floor plans. Red Owl was to procure some third party to buy the Chilton lot from Hoffman, construct the building, and then lease it to Hoffman. No final plans were ever made, nor were bids let or a construction contract entered. Some time prior to November 20, 1961, certain of the terms of the lease under which the building was to be rented by Hoffman were understood between him and Lukowitz. The lease was to be for 10 years with a rental approximating $550 a month calculated on the basis of 1 percent per month on the building cost, plus 6 percent of the land cost divided on a monthly basis. At the end of the 10-year term he was to have an option to renew the lease for an additional 10-year period or to buy the property at cost on an instalment basis. There was no discussion as to what the instalments would be or with respect to repairs and maintenance.

On November 22nd or 23rd, Lukowitz and plaintiffs met in Minneapolis with Red Owl's credit manager to confer on Hoffman's financial standing and on financing the agency. Another projected financial statement was there drawn up entitled, "Proposed Financing For An Agency Store." This showed Hoffman contributing $24,100 of cash capital of which only $4,600 was to be cash possessed by plaintiffs. Eight thousand was to be procured as a loan from a Chilton bank secured by a mortgage on the bakery fixtures, $7,500 was to be obtained on a 5 percent loan from the father-in-law, and $4,000 was to be obtained by sale of the lot to the lessor at a profit.

A week or two after the Minneapolis meeting Lukowitz showed Hoffman a telegram from the home office to the effect that if plaintiff could get another $2,000 for promotional purposes the deal could go through for $26,000. Hoffman stated he would have to find out if he could get another $2,000. He met with his father-in-law, who agreed to put $13,000 into the business provided he could come into the business as a partner. Lukowitz told Hoffman the partnership arrangement "sounds fine" and that Hoffman should not go into the partnership arrangement with the "front office." On January 16, 1962, the Red Owl credit manager teletyped Lukowitz that the father-in-law would have to sign an agreement that the $13,000 was either a gift or a loan subordinate to all general creditors and that he would prepare the agreement. On January 31, 1962, Lukowitz teletyped the home office that the father-in-law would sign one or other of the agreements. However, Hoffman testified that it was not until the final meeting some time between January 26th and February 2nd, 1962, that he was told that his father-in-law was expected to sign an agreement that the $13,000 he was advancing was to be an outright gift. No mention was then made by the Red Owl representatives of the alternative of the father-in-law signing a subordination agreement. At this meeting the Red Owl agents presented Hoffman with [a] financial statement [that] Hoffman interpreted . . . [as requiring him to come up with] $34,000 cash made up of $13,000 gift from his father-in-law, $2,000 on mortgage, $8,000 on Chilton bank loan, $5,000 in cash from plaintiff, and $6,000 on the resale of the Chilton lot. Red Owl claims $18,000 is the total of the unborrowed or unencumbered cash, that is, $13,000 from the father-in-law and $5,000 cash from Hoffman himself. Hoffman informed Red Owl he could not go along with this proposal, and particularly objected to the requirement that his father-in-law sign an agreement that his $13,000 advancement was an absolute gift. This terminated the negotiations between the parties.

The case was submitted to the jury on a **special verdict** with the first two questions answered by the court. This verdict, as returned by the jury, was as follows:

Special verdict

"A verdict in which the jury makes findings only on factual issues submitted to them by the judge, who then decides the legal effect of the verdict. *See* Fed. R. Civ. P. 49." BLACK'S LAW DICTIONARY (10th ed. 2014).

Question No. 1: Did the Red Owl Stores, Inc. and Joseph Hoffman on or about mid-May of 1961 initiate negotiations looking to the establishment of Joseph Hoffman as a franchise operator of a Red Owl Store in Chilton? *Answer*: Yes. (Answered by the Court.)

Question No. 2: Did the parties mutually agree on all of the details of the proposal so as to reach a final agreement thereon? *Answer*: No. (Answered by the Court.)

Question No. 3: Did the Red Owl Stores, Inc., in the course of said negotiations, make representations to Joseph Hoffman that if he fulfilled certain conditions that they would establish him as franchise operator of a Red Owl Store in Chilton? *Answer*: Yes.

Question No. 4: If you have answered Question No. 3 "Yes," then answer this question: Did Joseph Hoffman rely on said representations and was he induced to act thereon? *Answer*: Yes.

Question No. 5: If you have answered Question No. 4 "Yes," then answer this question: Ought Joseph Hoffman, in the exercise of ordinary care, to have relied on said representations? *Answer*: Yes.

Question No. 6: If you have answered Question No. 3 "Yes," then answer this question: Did Joseph Hoffman fulfill all the conditions he was required to fulfill by the terms of the negotiations between the parties up to January 26, 1962? *Answer*: Yes.

Question No. 7: What sum of money will reasonably compensate the plaintiffs for such damages as they sustained by reason of:

(a) The sale of the Wautoma store fixtures and inventory?
Answer: $16,735.00.
(b) The sale of the bakery building?
Answer: $2,000.00.
(c) Taking up the option on the Chilton lot?
Answer: $1,000.00.
(d) Expenses of moving his family to Neenah?
Answer: $140.00.
(e) House rental in Chilton?
Answer: $125.00.

Plaintiffs moved for judgment on the verdict while defendants moved to change the answers to Questions 3, 4, 5, and 6 from "Yes" to "No," and in the alternative for relief from the answers to the subdivisions of Question 7 or new trial. On March 31, 1964, the circuit court entered the following order:

IT IS ORDERED in accordance with said decision on motions after verdict hereby incorporated herein by reference:

1. That the answer of the jury to Question No. 7(a) be and the same is hereby vacated and set aside and that a new trial be had on the sole issue of the damages for loss, if any, on the sale of the Wautoma store, fixtures and inventory.

2. That all other portions of the verdict of the jury be and hereby are approved and confirmed and all afterverdict motions of the parties inconsistent with this order are hereby denied.

Defendants have appealed from this order and plaintiffs have cross-appealed from paragraph 1. thereof. . . .

CURRIE, C.J. The instant appeal and cross-appeal present these questions:

(1) Whether this court should recognize causes of action grounded on promissory estoppel as exemplified by § 90 of *Restatement, 1 Contracts*?

(2) Do the facts in this case make out a cause of action for promissory estoppel?

(3) Are the jury's findings with respect to damages sustained by the evidence?

RECOGNITION OF A CAUSE OF ACTION GROUNDED ON PROMISSORY ESTOPPEL.

§ 90 of *Restatement, 1 Contracts,* provides (at p. 110):

> A promise which the promisor should reasonably expect to induce action or forbearance of a definite and substantial character on the part of the promisee and which does induce such action of forbearance is binding if injustice can be avoided only by enforcement of the promise.

The Wisconsin Annotations to *Restatement, Contracts,* prepared under the direction of the late Professor William H. Page and issued in 1933, stated (at p. 53, sec. 90):

> The Wisconsin cases do not seem to be in accord with this section of the *Restatement.* It is certain that no such proposition has ever been announced by the Wisconsin court and it is at least doubtful if it would be approved by the court.

Since 1933, the closest approach this court has made to adopting the rule of the Restatement occurred in the recent case of *Lazarus v. American Motors Corp.,* 123 N.W.2d 548, 553 (1963), wherein the court stated:

> We recognize that upon different facts it would be possible for a seller of steel to have altered his position so as to effectuate the equitable considerations inherent in § 90 of the *Restatement.*

While it was not necessary to the disposition of the Lazarus Case to adopt the promissory estoppel rule of the *Restatement,* we are squarely faced in the instant case with that issue. Not only did the trial court frame the special verdict on the theory of § 90 of *Restatement, 1 Contracts,* but no other possible theory has been presented to or discovered by this court which would permit plaintiffs to recover. Of other remedies considered that of an action for fraud and deceit seemed to be the most comparable. An action at law for fraud, however, cannot be predicated on unfulfilled promises unless the promisor possessed the present intent not to perform. Here, there is no evidence that would support a finding that Lukowitz made any of the promises, upon which plaintiffs' complaint is predicated, in bad faith with any present intent that they would not be fulfilled by Red Owl.

Many courts of other jurisdictions have seen fit over the years to adopt the principle of promissory estoppel, and the tendency in that direction continues. As Mr. Justice McFaddin, speaking in behalf of the Arkansas court, well stated, that the development of the law of promissory estoppel "is an attempt by the courts to keep remedies abreast of increased moral consciousness of honesty and fair representations in all business dealings."

The *Restatement* avoids use of the term "promissory estoppel," and there has been criticism of it as an inaccurate term. On the other hand, Williston advocated the use of this term or something equivalent. Use of the word "estoppel" to describe a doctrine upon which a party to a lawsuit may obtain affirmative relief offends the traditional concept that estoppel merely serves as a shield and cannot serve as a sword to create a cause of action. . . . However, . . . [w]e have employed [the term "promissory estoppel"] in this opinion not only because of its extensive use by other courts but also since a more accurate equivalent has not been devised.

Because we deem the doctrine of promissory estoppel, as stated in § 90 of *Restatement, 1 Contracts,* is one which supplies a needed tool which courts may employ in a proper case to prevent injustice, we endorse and adopt it.

APPLICABILITY OF DOCTRINE TO FACTS OF THIS CASE.

The record here discloses a number of promises and assurances given to Hoffman by Lukowitz in behalf of Red Owl upon which plaintiffs relied and acted upon to their detriment.

Foremost were the promises that for the sum of $18,000 Red Owl would establish Hoffman in a store. After Hoffman had sold his grocery store and paid the $1,000 on the Chilton lot, the $18,000 figure was changed to $24,100. Then in November, 1961, Hoffman was assured that if the $24,100 figure were increased by $2,000 the deal would go through. Hoffman was induced to sell his grocery store fixtures and inventory in June, 1961, on the promise that he would be in his new store by fall. In November, plaintiffs sold their bakery building on the urging of defendants and on the assurance that this was the last step necessary to have the deal with Red Owl go through.

We determine that there was ample evidence to sustain the answers of the jury to the questions of the verdict with respect to the promissory representations made by Red Owl, Hoffman's reliance thereon in the exercise of ordinary care, and his fulfillment of the conditions required of him by the terms of the negotiations had with Red Owl.

There remains for consideration the question of law raised by defendants that agreement was never reached on essential factors necessary to establish a contract between Hoffman and Red Owl. Among these were the size, cost, design, and layout of the store building; and the terms of the lease with respect to rent, maintenance, renewal, and purchase options. This poses the question of whether the promise necessary to sustain a cause of action for promissory estoppel must embrace all essential details of a proposed transaction between promisor and promisee so as to be the equivalent of an offer that would result in a binding contract between the parties if the promisee were to accept the same.

Originally the doctrine of promissory estoppel was invoked as a substitute for consideration rendering a gratuitous promise enforceable as a contract. In other words, the acts of reliance by the promisee to his detriment provided a substitute for consideration. If promissory estoppel were to be limited to only those situations where the promise giving rise to the cause of action must be so definite with respect to all details that a contract would result were the promise supported by consideration, then the defendants' instant promises to Hoffman would not meet this test. However, § 90 of *Restatement, 1 Contracts,* does not impose the requirement that the promise giving rise to the cause of action must be so comprehensive in scope as to meet the requirements of an offer that would ripen into a contract if accepted by the promisee. Rather the conditions imposed are:

> (1) Was the promise one which the promisor should reasonably expect to induce action or forbearance of a definite and substantial character on the part of the promisee?
> (2) Did the promise induce such action or forbearance?
> (3) Can injustice be avoided only by enforcement of the promise?

To be or not to be . . . a contract?

With apologies to the Bard, this really *is* the question when it comes to promissory estoppel. When we discussed *Feinberg*, it was brought to your attention in a margin note that Judge Hand's understanding of promissory estoppel as a contractual cause of action ("'promissory estoppel' is now a recognized species of consideration") was up for debate, and it took a grand total of one case before you were exposed to a different view. Although you need not weigh in (at this time, anyway) on whether you think promissory estoppel is or is not a contract, you *should* ask yourself whether the judge's understanding of promissory estoppel as a non-contractual cause of action affected the court's understanding of what remedy Hoffman should get.

We deem it would be a mistake to regard an action grounded on promissory estoppel as the equivalent of a breach of contract action. As Dean Boyer points out, it is desirable that fluidity in the application of the concept be maintained. While the first two of the above listed three requirements of promissory estoppel present issues of fact which ordinarily will be resolved by a jury, the third requirement, that the remedy can only be invoked where necessary to avoid injustice, is one that involves a policy decision by the court. Such a policy decision necessarily embraces an element of discretion.

We conclude that injustice would result here if plaintiffs were not granted some relief because of the failure of defendants to keep their promises which induced plaintiffs to act to their detriment.

DAMAGES

Defendants attack all the items of damages awarded by the jury.

The bakery building at Wautoma was sold at defendants' instigation in order that Hoffman might have the net proceeds available as part of the cash capital he was to invest in the Chilton store venture. The evidence clearly establishes that it was sold at a loss of $2,000. Defendants contend that half of this loss was sustained by Mrs. Hoffman because title stood in joint tenancy. They point out that no dealings took place between her and defendants as all negotiations were had with her husband. Ordinarily only the promisee and not third persons are entitled to enforce the remedy of promissory estoppel against the promisor. However, if the promisor actually foresees, or has reason to foresee, action by

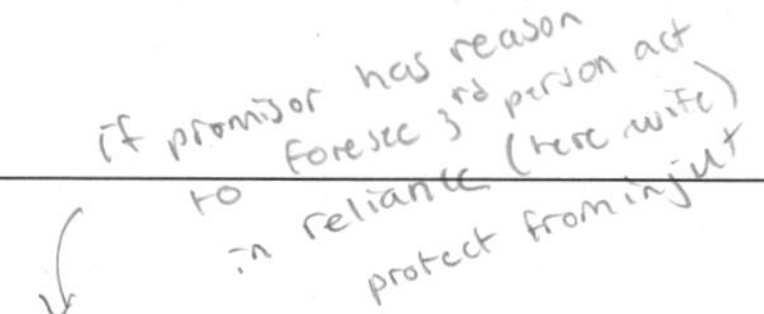

a third person in reliance on the promise, it may be quite unjust to refuse to perform the promise. Here not only did defendants foresee that it would be necessary for Mrs. Hoffman to sell her joint interest in the bakery building, but defendants actually requested that this be done. We approve the jury's award of $2,000 damages for the loss incurred by both plaintiffs in this sale.

Defendants attack on two grounds the $1,000 awarded because of Hoffman's payment of that amount on the purchase price of the Chilton lot. The first is that this $1,000 had already been lost at the time the final negotiations with Red Owl fell through in January, 1962, because the remaining $5,000 of purchase price had been due on October 15, 1961. The record does not disclose that the lot owner had foreclosed Hoffman's interest in the lot for failure to pay this $5,000. The $1,000 was not paid for the option, but had been paid as part of the purchase price at the time Hoffman elected to exercise the option. This gave him an equity in the lot which could not be legally foreclosed without affording Hoffman an opportunity to pay the balance. The second ground of attack is that the lot may have had a fair market value of $6,000, and Hoffman should have paid the remaining $5,000 of purchase price. We determine that it would be unreasonable to require Hoffman to have invested an additional $5,000 in order to protect the $1,000 he had paid. Therefore, we find no merit to defendants' attack upon this item of damages.

We also determine it was reasonable for Hoffman to have paid $125 for one month's rent of a home in Chilton after defendants assured him everything would be set when plaintiff sold the bakery building. This was a proper item of damage.

Plaintiffs never moved to Chilton because defendants suggested that Hoffman get some experience by working in a Red Owl store in the Fox River Valley. Plaintiffs, therefore, moved to Neenah instead of Chilton. After moving, Hoffman worked at night in an Appleton bakery but held himself available for work in a Red Owl store. The $140 moving expense would not have been incurred if plaintiffs had not sold their bakery building in Wautoma in reliance upon defendants' promises. We consider the $140 moving expense to be a proper item of damage.

We turn now to the damage item with respect to which the trial court granted a new trial, i.e., that arising from the sale of the Wautoma grocery store fixtures and inventory for which the jury awarded $16,735. The trial court ruled that Hoffman could not recover for any loss of future profits for the summer months following the sale on June 6, 1961, but that damages would be limited to the difference between the sales price received and fair market value of the assets sold, giving consideration to any goodwill attaching thereto by reason of the transfer of a going business. There was no direct evidence presented as to what this fair market value was on June 6, 1961. The evidence did disclose that Hoffman paid $9,000 for the inventory, added $1,500 to it and sold it for $10,000 or a loss of $500. His 1961 federal income tax return showed that the grocery equipment had been purchased for $7,000 and sold for $7,955.96. Plaintiffs introduced evidence of the buyer that during the first eleven weeks of operation of the grocery store his gross sales were $44,000 and his profit was $6,000 or roughly 15 percent. On cross-examination he admitted that this was gross and not net profit. Plaintiffs contend that in a breach of contract action damages may include loss of profits. **However, this is not a breach of contract action.**

Once more unto the breach, dear friends, once more

With more apologies to Shakespeare, the court is leaving future parties with no doubt as to where it stands on the issue of whether promissory estoppel is or isn't contractual.

The only relevancy of evidence relating to profits would be with respect to proving the element of goodwill in establishing the fair market value of the grocery inventory and fixtures sold. Therefore, evidence of profits would be admissible to afford a foundation for expert opinion as to fair market value.

Where damages are awarded in promissory estoppel instead of specifically enforcing the promisor's promise, they should be only such as in the opinion of the court are necessary to prevent injustice. Mechanical or rule of thumb approaches to the damage problem should be avoided. . . .

At the time Hoffman bought the equipment and inventory of the small grocery store at Wautoma he did so in order to gain experience in the grocery store business. At that time discussion had already been had with Red Owl representatives that Wautoma might be too small for a Red Owl operation and that a larger city might be more desirable. Thus Hoffman made this purchase more or less as a temporary experiment. Justice does not require that the damages awarded him, because of selling these assets at the behest of defendants, should exceed any actual loss sustained measured by the difference between the sales price and the fair market value.

Since the evidence does not sustain the large award of damages arising from the sale of the Wautoma grocery business, the trial court properly ordered a new trial on this issue.

Order affirmed. . . .

NOTES AND QUESTIONS

1. ***Pop quiz.*** According to this court, is promissory estoppel a contractual cause of action?

2. ***What happened?*** Who sued whom for what? Procedurally, how did the case get before this court? Factually, what happened between the parties? What arguments did the plaintiff and defendant make? What rule or rules did the court apply? How did the court analyze the dispute between the parties? How did the court decide the case?

3. ***Was this case correctly decided?*** Do you agree with the result reached in this case? Why or why not? Do you agree with the court's reasoning? Why or why not? How, if at all, would you have written the opinion differently?

4. ***Enforceability?*** If you were the judge, would you have enforced Lukowitz's promise? Why or why not? Did Red Owl take advantage of Joseph Hoffmann's* vulnerability, or ought he to have known better?

5. ***Promissory estoppel.*** Do you think Hoffmann satisfied all four prongs of the promissory estoppel test? Specifically, do you think Lukowitz made a "promise"? If so, should Lukowitz have "reasonably expect[ed] it to induce [Hoffmann to take] action or forbearance of a definite and substantial character? If so, was Hoffmann so induced? If so, could injustice "be avoided only by enforcement of the promise"?

6. ***Remedy.*** What remedy did the court award: expectation, reliance, or something else? Was this the appropriate remedy? Did the court's conceptualization of promissory estoppel as a contractual or non-contractual cause of action affect its remedial decision?

7. ***Pre-contract negotiations.*** As the following excerpts suggest, *Hoffman* was an important case in regulating how parties are expected to deal with one another during pre-contract negotiations. Did the court go too far? Or not far enough? How might such a decision affect the way future parties will negotiate with one another? How would you advise future clients in Hoffmann's or Red Owl's position? Keep in mind that although the court did not go so far as to impose a duty requiring parties to bargain with each other in good faith, it did help nudge the law in that direction.

HOFFMAN, THE DUTY TO BARGAIN IN GOOD FAITH, AND THE FIRM OFFER RULE†

The importance of the Hoffman case . . . lies as much in the way the decision is explained as in the decision itself. With commendable candor, the court makes no attempt to obscure the fact that the parties had not reached final agreement on all material terms when the deal fell through. The defendant thus could not be said to have made an offer so definite that plaintiff, simply by accepting, could cause a contract to come into being. The court compensated plaintiff for his reliance on defendant's assurance not that agreement had been reached, but only that it would be reached—and on terms satisfactory to the plaintiff.

It is thus reasonable to interpret *Hoffman* as furnishing authority for the proposition that one may in some circumstances come under a duty to bargain in good

---

* *See, e.g.*, William C. Whitford and Stewart Macaulay, Hoffman v. Red Owl Stores*: The Rest of the Story*, 61 HASTINGS L.J. 801, 804 n.9 (2010) ("Mr. Hoffmann has always spelled his name with two n's, as is made clear in the trial record. Transcript of Trial at 2, Hoffmann v. Red Owl Stores, Inc., No. 14954 (Wis. Cir. Ct. Oct. 21, 1963), microformed on File No. 14,900-14,954 C1985/026, Roll CC-159 POS (State Historical Soc'y of Wis.). For unknown reasons, the Wisconsin Supreme Court used only one n, and the case name has been spelled that way ever since. . . .")

† Excerpted from Charles L. Knapp, *Enforcing the Contract to Bargain*, 44 N.Y.U. L. REV. 673, 688, 690 (1969).

faith, breach of which duty may result in liability for damages, at least to the extent of compensating the detrimental reliance of the injured party. . . .

Whatever its consequences in terms of legal recognition of rights and granting of remedies, the contract to bargain is basically a bilateral arrangement; its claim for legal recognition is principally based upon the contention that there are cases where a level of agreement has been reached, and manifested, which is sufficient in the eyes of the parties themselves to bind them, absent good faith justification for withdrawal. A fundamental characteristic of promissory estoppel is its one-sidedness—only one party having enforceable rights against the other. In that respect, *Hoffman*, if it is truly a promissory estoppel situation, is closer to the "firm offer" cases than to the contract to bargain situation.

To what extent does the problem of precontractual reliance discussed in the first paragraph below remind you of the problem of the "hold-up game" discussed in Angel v. Murray *in the context of the pre-existing duty rule? If, in fact, the two problems are related, might some of the solutions discussed in that unit work here? In the second paragraph, the authors discuss two different approaches to filling the "gap" that existed in the Hoffman-Red Owl contract. Which of these approaches do you favor, and why? Do any of the previous thinking tools that we've discussed shed light on this question?*

HOFFMAN V. RED OWL STORES: THE REST OF THE STORY*

[T]he Hoffman case is best known as the leading early American case to allow recovery for precontractual reliance, in a situation where the parties clearly contemplated at all relevant times later negotiations and agreement. Though still controversial, a considerable majority of commentators now support a legal remedy for precontractual reliance in some circumstances. It is now widely recognized that when, in precontractual bargaining, only one party detrimentally relies, the other party is immediately in a stronger bargaining position. The relying party now has an investment it wants to protect, while the other party can walk away from the deal without loss. For reasons of both efficiency and fairness, scholars who advocate various positions are now willing to accept, at least in some circumstances, recovery of reliance loss caused by a failed negotiation. Most are comfortable with such a recovery where the reliance was at the defendant's urging or was a foreseeable and desired response to a strong assurance that a deal would be reached. The efficiency concern is that without some legal protection, the relying party will be reluctant to make a precontractual investment that will likely benefit the parties' prospective project. The fairness concern is that because of

* Excerpted from William C. Whitford and Stewart Macaulay, Hoffman v. Red Owl Stores: *The Rest of the Story*, 61 HASTINGS L.J. 801, 855-56 (2010).

its stronger bargaining position, the nonrelying party may be able in later negotiations to secure an undue share of the joint benefits from the deal.

It also is possible to justify recovery of precontractual reliance on freedom of contract or autonomy principles. If parties agree explicitly, before any precontractual reliance occurs, that such losses will or will not be reimbursed or shared, few would object to respecting their explicit agreement. However, we think that this is a rare situation. In *Hoffman* there was no such explicit agreement, and so we have a "gap" situation that is so common in the law of contract interpretation. Some scholars prefer very predictable and determinative default rules in such situations—rules that allow courts little discretion in their application and require parties to enter explicit agreements if they want something else.[297] We would allow courts, and where appropriate juries, to consider all the facts in context to fashion a rule for the case that approximates the parties' "tacit" agreement or probable assumptions. And from that perspective, at least a sharing of Hoffmann's losses with respect to his bakery business seems to us consistent with the parties' reasonable assumptions. Notice, too, that the very uncertainty of the situation when the Supreme Court of Wisconsin remanded the case helped provoke a settlement. As is true in most precontractual reliance situations, the amount Red Owl paid to Hoffmann was not a huge sum. Nonetheless, it helped the Hoffmanns cope with the way their lives had been upset by the failed pursuit of a Red Owl franchise.

Cohen v. Cowles Media Co.

Supreme Court of Minnesota
479 N.W.2d 387 (1992)

SIMONETT, JUSTICE. This case comes to us on remand from the United States Supreme Court. We previously held that plaintiff's verdict of $200,000 could not be sustained on a theory of breach of contract. On remand, we now conclude the verdict is sustainable on the theory of promissory estoppel and affirm the jury's award of damages.

The facts are set out in *Cohen v. Cowles Media Co.*, 457 N.W.2d 199, 200-02 (Minn. 1990), and will be only briefly restated here. On October 28, 1982, the Minneapolis Star and Tribune (now the Star Tribune) and the St. Paul Pioneer Press each published a story on the gubernatorial election campaign, reporting that Marlene Johnson, the DFL nominee for lieutenant governor, had been charged in 1969 for three counts of unlawful assembly and in 1970 had been convicted of shoplifting. Both newspapers revealed that Dan Cohen had supplied this information to them. The Star Tribune identified Cohen as a

297. *See, e.g.*, Allan Schwartz & Robert E. Scott, *Contract Theory and the Limits of Contract Law*, 113 YALE L.J. 541, 618 (2003) ("An efficient default rule . . . is simple in form, conditioned on few states of the world, [and maximizes joint gains in a wide variety of contexts].")

political associate of the Independent-Republican gubernatorial candidate and named the advertising firm where Cohen was employed.

Cohen then commenced this lawsuit against defendants Cowles Media Company, publisher of the Minneapolis Star Tribune, and Northwest Publications, Inc., publisher of the St. Paul Pioneer Press Dispatch. **It was undisputed that Cohen had given the information about Marlene Johnson's arrests and conviction to a reporter for each of the newspapers in return for the reporters' promises that Cohen's identity be kept confidential.** The newspapers' editors overruled these promises. The disparaging information about the candidate leaked in the closing days of the election campaign was such, decided the editors, that the identity of the source of the information was as important, as newsworthy, as the information itself. Put another way, the real news story was one of political intrigue, and the information about the particular candidate was only a part, an incomplete part, of that story. Moreover, not to reveal the source, felt the editors, would be misleading, as it would cast suspicion on others; and, in any event, it was likely only a matter of time before competing news media would uncover Cohen's identity. Finally, the Star Tribune had endorsed the Perpich-Johnson ticket in its opinion section, and thus to withhold Cohen's identity might be construed as an effort by the newspaper to protect its favored candidates. On the same day as the newspaper stories were published, Cohen was fired.

> ***Consideration?***
>
> Does Cohen's act seem to be supported by consideration? Why or why not?

The case was submitted to the jury on theories of breach of contract and fraudulent misrepresentation. The jury found liability on both theories and awarded $200,000 compensatory damages against the two defendants, jointly and severally. The jury also awarded $250,000 punitive damages against each newspaper on the misrepresentation claim. The court of appeals set aside recovery on the basis of fraudulent misrepresentation (and with it the punitive damages award), but affirmed recovery of the compensatory damages on the basis of a breach of contract. *Cohen v. Cowles Media Co.*, 445 N.W.2d 248, 262 (Minn. App. 1989).

We affirmed denial of recovery for fraudulent misrepresentation but also held that there could be no recovery for breach of contract. **While the newspapers may have had a moral and ethical commitment to keep their source anonymous, we said this was not a situation where the parties were thinking in terms of a legally binding contract.** *Cohen I*, 457 N.W.2d at 203. "To impose a contract theory on this arrangement," we said, "puts an unwarranted legal rigidity on a special ethical relationship, precluding necessary consideration of factors underlying that ethical relationship." *Id.*

> ***Moral consideration only?***
>
> Is it relevant whether the parties *thought* they were making a contract? Should it be? We have seen a number of cases in which courts have found contracts contrary to the parties' intent, and have also seen cases in which courts have failed to find contracts where the parties intended to form a contractual relationship. Why, then, do you think the court ruled as it did in the previous case?

The evidence at trial might be characterized as the pot calling the kettle black, with each side insinuating that the other's behavior was unethical or underhanded. We observed that when applying a contract analysis in this context "the focus was more on whether a binding promise was intended and breached, not so much on the contents of that promise or the nature of the information exchanged for the promise." *Id.* at 204. We concluded that a contract theory, which looks only to whether there was a promise and an acceptance, does not fit a situation where the essential concern is with the intrinsic nature of the overall transaction.

We went on in *Cohen I* to consider enforcement of a confidentiality promise under the doctrine of promissory estoppel. Under this theory, the court would consider all aspects of the transaction's substance in determining whether enforcement was necessary to prevent an injustice. We found this approach, which differed from the neutral approach of the classic contract analysis, best fit the kind of confidential commitments that news media in newsgathering made. There was, however, a problem. To shed the neutrality of a contract analysis for an inquiry into the editorial process of deciding whether the identity of the news source was needed for a proper reporting of a news story constituted, we concluded, an impermissible intrusion into the newspaper's First Amendment free press rights. Consequently, we held plaintiff Cohen's verdict was not sustainable. 457 N.W.2d at 205.

The United States Supreme Court granted certiorari and held that the doctrine of promissory estoppel does not implicate the First Amendment. The doctrine is one of general application, said the Court, and its employment to enforce confidentiality promises has only "incidental effects" on news gathering and reporting, so that the First Amendment is not offended. *Cohen v. Cowles Media Co.*, 501 U.S. 663 (1991). The Court refused to reinstate the jury verdict for $200,000 in compensatory damages, stating this was a matter for our consideration, and remanded the case.

On remand, we must address four issues: (1) Does Cohen's failure to plead promissory estoppel bar him from pursuing that theory now; (2) does our state constitutional guarantee of a free press bar use of promissory estoppel to enforce promises of confidentiality; (3) does public policy bar Cohen from enforcing the newspapers' promises of confidentiality; and (4) if Cohen may proceed under promissory estoppel, should the case be remanded for retrial or should the jury's award of compensatory damages be reinstated?

I.

Generally, litigants are bound on appeal by the theory or theories upon which the case was tried. Here, promissory estoppel was neither pled nor presented at the trial, and this court first raised the applicability of that theory during oral argument in *Cohen I. See* 457 N.W.2d at 204 n.5. Nevertheless, this court considered promissory estoppel and held that the First Amendment barred recovery under that theory.

The defendant newspapers argue it is too late for Cohen to proceed now under promissory estoppel, and this case should be at an end. We have, however, on rare occasions exercised our discretion to allow a party to proceed on a theory not raised at trial. . . .

We conclude it would be unfair not to allow Cohen to proceed under promissory estoppel. Throughout the litigation, the issue has been the legal enforceability of a promise of anonymity. **Promissory estoppel is essentially a variation of contract theory**, a theory on which plaintiff prevailed through the court of appeals. The evidence received at trial was as relevant to promissory estoppel as it was to contract, and the parties now have briefed the issue thoroughly.

> ***Yet another court weighs in . . .***
>
> This is just one more example of a court weighing in on the debate of whether promissory estoppel is or is not contractual.

What we have here is a novel legal issue of first impression where this court has adopted an approach closely akin to the theory on which the case was originally pled and tried; under these unique circumstances we conclude it is not unfair to the defendants to allow the case to be decided under principles of promissory estoppel.

II.

[In this section of its opinion, the court held that Minnesota's constitutional guarantee of a free press did not bar the use of promissory estoppel to enforce promises of confidentiality.]

III.

What, then, should be the appropriate disposition of this case? We conclude a retrial is unnecessary.

Under promissory estoppel, a promise which is expected to induce definite action by the promisee, and does induce the action, is binding if injustice can be avoided only by enforcing the promise. *Cohen I,* 457 N.W.2d at 204; *Restatement (Second) of Contracts* § 90(1) (1981). First of all, the promise must be clear and definite. As a matter of law, such a promise was given here. *Cohen I,* 457 N.W.2d at 204 ("[W]e have, without dispute, the reporters' unambiguous promise to treat Cohen as an anonymous source."). Secondly, the promisor must have intended to induce reliance on the part of the promisee, and such reliance must have occurred to the promisee's detriment. Here again, these facts appear as a matter of law. In reliance on the promise of anonymity, Cohen turned over the court records and, when the promises to keep his name confidential were broken, he lost his job. *Id.*

This leads to the third step in a promissory estoppel analysis: Must the promise be enforced to prevent an injustice? As the Wisconsin Supreme Court has held, this is a legal question for the court, as it involves a policy decision. *Hoffman v. Red Owl Stores, Inc.,* 133 N.W.2d 267, 275 (1965).

It is perhaps worth noting that the test is not whether the promise should be enforced to do justice, but whether enforcement is required to prevent an injustice. As has been observed elsewhere, it is easier to recognize an unjust result than a just one, particularly in a morally ambiguous situation. *Cf.* Edmond Cahn, *The Sense of Injustice* (1964).

> ***Justice versus injustice***
>
> This is an important point that is sometimes overlooked. A court enforcing a promise under the theory of promissory estoppel is not (ostensibly, anyway) attempting to "do justice," but to

"prevent an injustice." However, once a court decides to enforce a promise, it is still an open question as to whether the remedy should do the former (perhaps by awarding expectation damages) or the latter (perhaps by awarding reliance expenditures). See the bolded sentence three paragraphs down. Some of these issues are discussed in "Empirical Perspective: Promissory Estoppel and the Remedial Landscape," at p. 443, *supra*.

The newspapers argue it is unjust to be penalized for publishing the whole truth, but it is not clear this would result in an injustice in this case. For example, it would seem veiling Cohen's identity by publishing the source as someone close to the opposing gubernatorial ticket would have sufficed as a sufficient reporting of the "whole truth."

Cohen, on the other hand, argues that it would be unjust for the law to countenance, at least in this instance, the breaking of a promise. We agree that denying Cohen any recourse would be unjust. What is significant in this case is that the record shows the defendant newspapers themselves believed that they generally must keep promises of confidentiality given a news source. The reporters who actually gave the promises adamantly testified that their promises should have been honored. The editors who countermanded the promises conceded that never before or since have they reneged on a promise of confidentiality. A former Minneapolis Star managing editor testified that the newspapers had "hung Mr. Cohen out to dry because they didn't regard him very highly as a source." The Pioneer Press Dispatch editor stated nothing like this had happened in her 27 years in journalism. The Star Tribune's editor testified that protection of sources was "extremely important." Other experts, too, stressed the ethical importance, except on rare occasions, of keeping promises of confidentiality. It was this long-standing journalistic tradition that Cohen, who has worked in journalism, relied upon in asking for and receiving a promise of anonymity.

Neither side in this case clearly holds the higher moral ground, but in view of the defendants' concurrence in the importance of honoring promises of confidentiality, and absent the showing of any compelling need in this case to break that promise, we conclude that the resultant harm to Cohen requires a remedy here to avoid an injustice. In short, defendants are liable in damages to plaintiff for their broken promise.

This leaves, then, the issue of damages. **For promissory estoppel, "[t]he remedy granted for breach may be limited as justice requires."** *Restatement (Second) of Contracts* § 90(1) (1981). In this case the jury was instructed:

> A party is entitled to recover for a breach of contract only those damages which: (a) arise directly and naturally in the usual course of things from the breach itself; or (b) are the consequences of special circumstances known to or reasonably supposed to have been contemplated by the parties when the contract was made.

This instruction, we think, provided an appropriate damages remedy for the defendants' broken promise, whether considered under a breach of contract or a promissory estoppel theory. There was evidence to support the jury's award of $200,000, and we see no reason to remand this case for a new trial on damages alone.

Our prior reversal of the verdict having been vacated, we now affirm the court of appeals' decision, but on promissory estoppel grounds. We affirm, therefore, plaintiff's verdict and judgment for $200,000 compensatory damages.

Affirmed on remand on different grounds.

NOTES AND QUESTIONS

1. ***Pop quiz.*** According to this court, does promissory estoppel seem to operate as a contractual or non-contractual cause of action?

2. ***What happened?*** Who sued whom for what? Procedurally, how did the case get before this court? Factually, what happened between the parties? What arguments did the plaintiff and defendant make? What rule or rules did the court apply? How did the court analyze the dispute between the parties? How did the court decide the case?

3. ***Was this case correctly decided?*** Do you agree with the result reached in this case? Why or why not? Do you agree with the court's reasoning? Why or why not? How, if at all, would you have written the opinion differently?

4. ***Was there a consideration-based contract?*** Do you think there was a consideration-based contract here? Did the parties think they were making a contract? If so, should the court have enforced it? Why or why not?

5. ***Promissory estoppel.*** Do you think promissory estoppel was appropriate here? Why or why not? Do you agree that all four prongs were met? Go through each one to make sure.

6. ***Remedy.*** What remedy did the court award? How can you tell? Do you think this remedy was appropriate? Why or why not?

The next case looks at whether promissory estoppel can operate to enforce a promise for continued employment in a context where the principle of at-will employment is the traditional rule. It further examines whether the remedy to an aggrieved party should be limited to reliance damages, as per *Hoffman*, or whether an award of "contract damages" (i.e., specific performance or expectation damages) is more appropriate. Finally, the case explores the connection between the final prong of the promissory estoppel test (i.e., that a promise is "binding if injustice can be avoided only by enforcement of the promise") and the remedy necessary to avoid that injustice. This final point is an important one, as it links together two of the biggest issues in contract law: (1) the enforceability of a promise, which we have explored in this chapter, and (2) the remedy needed to protect that promise, which we will take up in the next chapter.

Skebba v. Kasch

Court of Appeals of Wisconsin
297 Wis. 2d 401 (2006)

KESSLER, J. We conclude that the trial court misinterpreted *Hoffman v. Red Owl Stores*, 26 Wis. 2d 683, 133 N.W.2d 267 (1965), when it determined that under the holding of that case, it could not specifically enforce the promise which the jury found that Jeffrey Kasch had made, and on which the jury found that William Skebba had relied. On the facts in this case, specific performance of the promise is the only remedy that will compensate Skebba for his loss because, as the jury found, the amount Kasch promised to pay is the exact measure of what Skebba lost when Kasch refused to honor the promise. Consequently, we reverse and remand for further proceedings consistent with this opinion.

BACKGROUND

Skebba, a salesman, worked for many years for a company that eventually experienced serious financial difficulties. Kasch, with his brother, owned M.W. Kasch Co. Kasch hired Skebba as a sales representative, and over the years promoted him first to account manager, then to customer service manager, field sales manager, vice president of sales, senior vice president of sales and purchasing and finally to vice president of sales. Kasch's father was the original owner of the business, and had hired Skebba's father. Skebba's father mentored Kasch.

When M.W. Kasch Co. experienced serious financial problems in 1993, Skebba was solicited by another company to leave Kasch and work for them. When Skebba told Kasch he was accepting the new opportunity, Kasch asked what it would take to get him to stay, and noted that Skebba's leaving at this time would be viewed very negatively within the industry. Shortly thereafter, Skebba told Kasch that he needed security for his retirement and family and would stay if Kasch agreed to pay Skebba $250,000 if one of these three conditions occurred: (1) the company was sold; (2) Skebba was lawfully terminated; or (3) Skebba retired. Skebba reports, and the jury apparently found, that Kasch agreed to this proposal and Kasch promised to have the agreement drawn up. Skebba turned down the job opportunity and stayed with Kasch from December 1993 (when this discussion occurred) through 1999 when the company assets were sold.

Over the years, Skebba repeatedly asked Kasch for a written summary of this agreement; however, none was forthcoming. Eventually, Kasch sold the business. Kasch received $5.1 million dollars for his fifty-one percent share of the business when it was sold. Upon the sale of the business, Skebba asked Kasch for the $250,000 Kasch had previously promised to him, but Kasch refused, and denied ever having made such an agreement. Instead, Kasch gave Skebba a severance agreement which had been drafted by Kasch's lawyers in 1993. This agreement promised two years of salary continuation on the sale of the company, but only if Skebba was not hired by the successor company and the severance agreement required a set-off against the salary continuation of any sums Skebba earned from any activity during the two years of the severance agreement. Skebba sued, alleging breach of contract and promissory estoppel.

The jury found there was no contract, but that Kasch had made a promise upon which Skebba relied to his detriment, that the reliance was foreseeable, and that Skebba was damaged in the amount of $250,000. The trial court concluded that, based on its reading of applicable case law, it could not specifically enforce the promise the jury found Kasch made to Skebba because there were other ways to measure damages. In motions after verdict, the trial court struck the jury's answer on damages, concluding that under *Hoffman,* because Skebba did not prove what he would have earned had he taken the job with the other company, he could not establish what he had lost by relying on Kasch's promise and, therefore, had not proved his damages. We conclude that the trial court misread *Hoffman*. . . .

DISCUSSION

Kasch did *not* promise to pay Skebba more than Skebba would have earned at the job Skebba turned down. Kasch did *not* promise that total income to Skebba would be greater than in the turned-down job, no matter how long he remained with Kasch. Kasch *only* promised that if Skebba stayed, Kasch would pay Skebba $250,000 (the sum Skebba wanted for his retirement), at the earliest of (1) Kasch selling the business, (2) Skebba retiring, or (3) Skebba being lawfully terminated. Skebba stayed. Kasch sold the business while Skebba was still employed by Kasch. Kasch refused to pay as promised.

PROMISSORY ESTOPPEL

The purpose of promissory estoppel is to enforce promises where the failure to do so is unjust. In this case, the trial court specifically relied on parts of *Hoffman* in determining that specific performance of the promise could not be awarded and in concluding that Skebba had not properly established damages. *Hoffman* was the first case in Wisconsin to adopt promissory estoppel. The facts in *Hoffman* present a long and complex history of Red Owl Food Stores inducing Mr. Hoffman to do a number of things (sell his bakery; sell his grocery store; move to another city to get larger grocery store management experience; commit to investing ever increasing sums of money in order to get a Red Owl store; buy a lot on which the store would be built, then sell the same lot; and other activities) in order to own a Red Owl grocery store to be built in the future. Mr. Hoffman did all of the things required, but finally balked at the last demand for increased capital. Although there was never a specific contract between Mr. Hoffman and Red Owl, yet Mr. Hoffman had obviously changed position in a number of ways in reliance on Red Owl's promise of a store, the court was faced with the need to provide a remedy to Mr. Hoffman and the impracticality of enforcing the promise of a store against Red Owl. In that context, the *Hoffman* court explained its adoption of a cause of action based on promissory estoppel as grounded in § 90 of the *Restatement of Contracts* which:

> does not impose the requirement that the promise giving rise to the cause of action must be so comprehensive in scope as to meet the requirements of an offer that would ripen into a contract if accepted by the promisee. Rather the conditions imposed are:
>
> (1) Was the promise one which the promisor should reasonably expect to induce action or forbearance of a definite and substantial character on the part of the promisee?
> (2) Did the promise induce such action or forbearance?
> (3) Can injustice be avoided only by enforcement of the promise?

The *Hoffman* court explains that the first two of these requirements are facts to be found by a jury or other factfinder, while the third is a policy decision to be made by the court. In making this policy decision, a court must consider a number of factors in determining whether injustice can only be avoided by enforcement of the promise. The court in *U.S. Oil Company, Inc. v. Midwest Auto Care Services, Inc.*, 150 Wis. 2d 80, 92 (1989) adopted those considerations set forth in the *Restatement (Second) of Contracts* § 139(2):

> (a) the availability and adequacy of other remedies, particularly cancellation and restitution;
>
> (b) the definite and substantial character of the action or forbearance in relation to the remedy sought;
>
> (c) the extent to which the action or forbearance corroborates evidence of the making and terms of the promise, or the making and terms are otherwise established by clear and convincing evidence;
>
> (d) the reasonableness of the action or forbearance; [and]
>
> (e) the extent to which the action or forbearance was foreseeable by the promisor.

The record does not indicate that the trial court here applied the considerations our supreme court announced in *U.S. Oil.* Instead, the trial court apparently relied on the *Hoffman* court's discussion of various damage theories that the court explained might be appropriate once the determination had been made to enforce the promise by application of promissory estoppel. The *Hoffman* court, discussing alternatives to specific performance of the promise to be enforced, quoted alternative damage theories from one treatise and two law review articles. These academics suggested, as measures of damages, the value to the plaintiff of the promised performance or the loss to the plaintiff caused by his change in position, and opined that there was no requirement that contract damages be awarded in promissory estoppel. The *Hoffman* court, in determining how to measure the part of Mr. Hoffman's loss caused specifically by his sale of the grocery store, concluded that only the actual loss Mr. Hoffman sustained was proper and that this loss was to be measured as the difference between the sales price and the fair market value, rather than by awarding the entire sales price as the jury had determined. *Ibid.*

Here, the trial court referred to *Hoffman*'s reference to a 1951 Harvard Law Review article written by Seavy, which argued that "damages should not exceed the loss caused by the change of position, which would never be more in amount, but might be less, than the promised reward." *Ibid.* The trial court then concluded that the only way it could measure Skebba's change in position was by calculating the difference in what he would have earned had he taken the job he turned down, minus what he actually earned during the time he remained with Kasch. In coming to that conclusion, the trial court misunderstood the holding of *Hoffman*.

A court, in fashioning a remedy, can consider any equitable *or* legal remedy which will "prevent injustice." [Quoting *Corbin, Contracts* § 200, the court went on to note that]:

> Enforcement of a promise does not necessarily mean Specific Performance. It does not necessarily mean Damages for breach. Moreover, the amount allowed as Damages may be determined by the plaintiff's expenditures or change of position in reliance as well as by the value to him of the promised performance. . . . *In determining what justice requires, the court must remember all of its powers, derived from equity, law merchant, and other sources, as well as the common law.* Its decree should be molded accordingly (emphasis added).

As later commentators have noted, Wisconsin, with its landmark *Hoffman* decision, is one of a small group of states which recognizes that to fulfill the purpose of promissory estoppel—*i.e.,* prevent injustice—a court must be able to fashion a remedy that restores the promisee to where he or she would be if the promisor had fulfilled the promise. In this case, Skebba performed—he remained at M.W. Kasch—in reliance on Kasch's promise to pay $250,000 to him if one of three conditions occurred. Kasch enjoyed the fruits of Skebba's reliance—he kept on a top salesperson to help the company through tough financial times and he avoided the damage that he believed Skebba's leaving could have had on M.W. Kasch's reputation in the industry. Accordingly, to prevent injustice, the equitable remedy for Skebba to receive is Kasch's specific performance promised—payment of the $250,000.

The record in this case, considered in light of the *U.S. Oil* tests and the jury's findings, compels specific performance of the promise because otherwise Kasch will enjoy all of the benefits of induced reliance while Skebba will be deprived of that which he was promised, with no other available remedy to substitute fairly for the promised reward. "[T]he availability and adequacy of other remedies, particularly cancellation and restitution" supports enforcement of the promise because, unlike Mr. Hoffman, Skebba did not spend money in reliance on the promise, so neither restitution

Remedial flexibility

Remedial flexibility is a hallmark of promissory estoppel cases, although many judges have their own views as to what remedy (e.g., reliance or expectation) is generally appropriate. Are you in favor of such remedial flexibility, or do you think that courts should have less discretion, perhaps being required to enforce all promises the same way? You should note that, by making a promise easier to enforce on the front end (e.g., with promissory estoppel) and then fully enforcing that promise on the back end (e.g., with expectation damages), the promisee gets the best of both worlds. Do you think this is being too harsh on promisors? Or should promisors simply be more careful about the types of promises they make? Break out your thinking tools, and consider how such remedial flexibility might affect the way parties interact with one other in the future.

nor cancellation of an obligation Skebba incurred would be relevant to these facts. "[T]he definite and substantial character of the action or forbearance in relation to the remedy sought" supports enforcing the promise. **Skebba's forbearance of other employment for six years from the 1993 promise the jury found occurred was both definite and substantial.** "[T]he extent to which the action or forbearance corroborates evidence of the making and terms of the promise, or the making and terms are otherwise established by clear and convincing evidence," is established by the jury finding that Kasch made the promise, by no evidence that the promise was made any time other than December 1993 or early in 1994, and it is undisputed that Skebba not only turned down other employment at that time but also remained with Kasch through financially difficult times for the company until the sale of the business in 1999. "[T]he reasonableness of the action or forbearance" and "the extent to which the action or forbearance was foreseeable by the promisor" is supported by the undisputed fact that Kasch knew Skebba had another job opportunity in 1993, that Kasch believed Skebba's leaving would damage the company in the industry, and that Kasch wanted Skebba to stay. Kasch's promise achieved Kasch's objectives: Skebba stayed even though the company was in severe financial difficulties. In short, every factor this court requires to be considered supports enforcement of the promise through promissory estoppel. The trial court submitted the promissory estoppel cause of action to the jury. The jury concluded that the promise had been made, that Skebba relied on the promise to his detriment, and that such reliance was foreseeable by Kasch. The jury also found that Skebba's damages were the amount Skebba testified Kasch promised to pay Skebba if he was still employed when the company was sold, that is, $250,000. The jury heard no evidence of any other damages.

> ***Definite and substantial***
>
> Recall from your comparison of the *Restatements (First)* and *(Second) of Contracts* § 90 (you *did* compare these provisions, didn't you?) that the *Restatement (Second)* no longer requires that the promisee's action or forbearance be of a "definite and substantial character." This means that promissory estoppel actions are more available than ever before for parties in jurisdictions following the approach of the *Restatement (Second)*.

Skebba's loss has nothing to do with what he might have earned on another job. Income from the rejected job was never a part of the calculus of the promise made and relied upon. Kasch never proposed to better the salary or bonus offered. Neither Kasch nor Skebba mention any discussion about a way for Kasch to retain Skebba other than the now disputed payment. Rather, Kasch's promise was to pay Skebba $250,000 if one of three conditions occurred. One triggering condition occurred—the business was sold while Skebba was still employed by Kasch. Hence, the damage calculation required by the trial court, which might be appropriate in other cases, has no reasonable application to the facts here. Rather, as noted by the *Hoffman* court, while "[e]nforcement of a promise does not necessarily mean Specific Performance," specific performance is neither precluded nor disfavored as a remedy for promissory estoppel; preventing injustice is the objective. **In this case, specific performance *is* the**

> ***Was specific performance necessary?***
>
> Notice the court's view concerning the link between the fourth prong of the promissory estoppel test (the "injustice" prong, which must be satisfied for there to be promissory liability at all) and the

"specific performance" remedy the court ultimately awarded to Skebba. Generally, the remedial issue is thought to be distinct from the liability issue (and to be determined after liability is settled), but here, the court sees the two as inextricably linked. In other words, in the court's view, the scope of the remedy (which we will cover in the next chapter) is an integral part of the enforceability of right itself (which we have concerned ourselves with in this chapter). This integrated way of viewing contract law is consistent with the approach adopted throughout this casebook, but it doesn't mean, of course, that the court is right about specific performance being "necessary . . . to prevent injustice." What do you think?

***necessary* enforcement mechanism to prevent injustice for Skebba's reliance on the promise the jury found Kasch had made to him.**

Accordingly, we conclude that the trial court erred in holding that specific performance was not available on this promissory estoppel claim. We further conclude that the trial court erred in its application of *Hoffman* to the facts of this case. We reverse and remand for further proceedings consistent with this opinion.

NOTES AND QUESTIONS

1. *What happened?* Who sued whom for what? Procedurally, how did the case get before this court? Factually, what happened between the parties? What arguments did the plaintiff and defendant make? What rule or rules did the court apply? How did the court analyze the dispute between the parties? How did the court decide the case?

2. *Was this case correctly decided?* Do you agree with the result reached in this case? Why or why not? Do you agree with the court's reasoning? Why or why not? How, if at all, would you have written the opinion differently?

3. *Was there a consideration-based contract?* Was promissory estoppel necessary here? Didn't Skebba bargain with Kasch to remain on the job for a conditional payment of $250,000? The jury, we are told, found that there was no contract. Do you agree?

4. *Promissory estoppel.* Do you think promissory estoppel was appropriate here? Why or why not? Once again, go through and make sure that each of the four prongs was satisfied. Is it relevant that Kasch never drew up the paperwork, despite Skebba's repeated requests for him to do so?

5. *Remedy.* Note that the court ultimately awarded specific performance of the money promised, which, in the context of this case, is identical to expectation damages. Do you think this remedy was appropriate? Why or why not?

We conclude this section with a brief excerpt discussing how the constantly evolving promissory estoppel cause of action, including the remedies available to an injured party, is most commonly viewed today by scholars and judges alike.

EMPIRICAL PERSPECTIVE: PROMISSORY ESTOPPEL AND THE REMEDIAL LANDSCAPE*

1985 can be said to be the year when the reliance-based edifice of the promissory estoppel cathedral began to crumble, or at least show numerous cracks in its foundation. In their extremely influential (and still controversial) article, Professors Daniel A. Farber and John H. Matheson examined more than two hundred promissory estoppel cases decided between 1975 and 1985 and concluded that many of the claims reached by Professor Gilmore were simply wrong.

Unlike Professor Gilmore, who believed that the normative basis underlying promissory estoppel rested on the principle of reliance, Professors Farber and Matheson found no support for this view in the case law. Rather, they argued that, based on their reading of the cases, promissory estoppel rested four-square on the normative principle of promise, and that even those decisions in which judges "purportedly" denied recovery to promissory estoppel claimants on the principle of reliance could "be readily explained on other grounds." They went on to claim that:

> Based on our survey of recent promissory estoppel cases, we believe that promissory estoppel is losing its link with reliance. In key cases promises have been enforced with only the weakest showing of any detriment to the promisee. Reliance-based damages are the exception, not the rule. With the decline of reliance, promissory estoppel is moving away from tort law.

Professors Farber and Matheson's argument amounted to the claim that the traditional elements making up the promissory estoppel cause of action were a mere subterfuge concealing the manner in which judges really decided promissory estoppel cases. Instead, Farber and Matheson postulated that judges actually enforce "any promise made in furtherance of an economic activity."

As astonishing as this claim was, Farber and Matheson were just getting warmed up. In what bordered on promissory estoppel heresy at the time, they claimed that, among plaintiffs who tend to prevail in their promissory estoppel actions, "reliance plays little role in the determination of remedies." According to their study, judges tended to award full expectation damages in five-sixths, or 83 percent, of the cases, relegating reliance damages (which were thought, at that time, to be de rigueur in promissory estoppel actions) to plug the remedial gap in the remaining one-sixth of cases.

They did, however, agree with Professor Gilmore in one respect: they too thought that promissory estoppel was "no longer merely a fall-back theory of recovery" left to play second fiddle to traditional, consideration-based contracts, but was now being used by courts "as a primary basis of enforcement."

Professors Farber and Matheson's work was followed up by another article by Professors Edward Yorio and Steve Thel that echoed many of the same findings. For instance, Professors Yorio and Thel wrote that "the prominence of reliance in

* Excerpted from Marco Jimenez, *The Many Faces of Promissory Estoppel: An Empirical Analysis Under the Restatement (Second) of Contracts*, 57 UCLA L. Rev. 669, 680-81 (2010) (internal citations omitted).

the text of Section 90 and in the commentary on the section does not correspond to what courts do in fact," and further claimed that, "[r]ather than using Section 90 to compensate promisees for losses suffered in reliance, judges use it to hold people to their promises by granting specific performance or by awarding expectation damages."

PROBLEM: THE BATTLE FOR MLK'S PAPERS*

Dr. Martin Luther King, Jr. is among the most consequential figures in America's civil rights movement. As an activist and leader, he corresponded with luminaries of his time and wrote passionately. His voluminous papers have historical significance, so valuable that many have bid hefty prices to buy them. Most spectacularly, in June 2006, King family members planned to auction the bulk of his papers to the highest bidder at Sotheby's in New York City. Civic leaders in Atlanta, where King was born and raised, worried about the papers landing in private hands, never to be available for public reviewing or scholarly research. To avert that fate, distinguished civic-minded citizens, led by Atlanta Mayor Shirley Franklin, engineered a $32 million loan to a new foundation to buy the papers. The foundation deposited the papers for permanent public access with Atlanta's Morehouse College, where King studied as an undergraduate.

The Morehouse College episode was not the first drama surrounding where King's papers would reside, nor was it the most controversial. That distinction goes to an earlier batch of his papers that King deposited in the 1960s with Boston University, where he earned the PhD that made him "Dr. King." A July 16, 1964 letter that King wrote and signed, and on which he followed up by delivering many papers, read, in part:

> I name the Boston University Library the Repository of my correspondence, manuscripts and other papers. . . . It is my intention that after the end of each calendar year, [additional] files of materials . . . should be sent to Boston University. All papers and other objects which thus pass into the custody of Boston University remain my legal property until otherwise indicated. . . .
>
> I intend each year to indicate a portion of the materials deposited with Boston University to become the absolute property of Boston University as an outright gift from me, until all shall have been thus given to the University. In the event of my death, all such materials deposited with the University shall become from that date the absolute property of Boston University.

Dr. King was assassinated on April 4, 1968. He left no will. Decades later, after years of BU's custodianship, Dr. King's widow, Coretta Scott King, challenged the archive arrangement in Massachusetts court. Mrs. King argued that

* Excerpted from LAWRENCE A. CUNNINGHAM, CONTRACTS IN THE REAL WORLD: STORIES OF POPULAR CONTRACTS AND WHY THEY MATTER 11-14 (2012).

the letter and Dr. King's delivery of the materials showed he had merely loaned them to BU. She said he made no promise to do more, and that any promise he did make was merely to make a gift, as opposed to a legally valid commitment. BU contended just the opposite, saying the promise was clear and binding.

The King case raised profound issues in a struggle dating as far back as the Middle Ages: how to distinguish enforceable statements from those that are not. A long-standing social and moral norm treats promises as sacred. An important strand of philosophy considers promise keeping a social or civic duty. If these principles were followed, law would be obliged to enforce all promises as contracts, which, of course, it cannot. It would simply be impracticable for any court system to handle, and undesirable for judges to resolve, every fight over a breached promise. Courts are therefore more circumspect about what makes for a legally binding contract.

Mrs. King stressed the lack of formality in Dr. King's statements. His letter, though signed, was merely a gesture of kindness. For example, he did not take the trouble of having any witnesses attest to it, getting it notarized, or affixing a waxed seal on it to evidence an intention that it be legally binding.

BU urged more substantive tests than this emphasis on formalities. True, such formal tests can be probative of intent, and the law for centuries, in America and Europe, looked to such formalities. But modern law appreciates that such formal tests become diluted or supplanted over time. The seal can become a mere habit, meaning nothing, and people gradually adopt other norms of bargaining, from shaking hands to writing letters. Fixating on such formalities could enable legitimate claims to be defeated.

BU stressed two more useful tests to determine the enforceability of a promise. The first is based on an intuitive sense of a bargain: whether parties agreed to an exchange that one side disappointed. Called "consideration," this has been our law's most important test to determine the enforceability of a contract since the eighteenth century. Unlike a seal or notary, consideration offers both a formal and a substantive test. The presence of an exchange—a quid pro quo—establishes an intention and cautions against impulsively made promises.

The second ground BU urged was reliance, an alternative reason to enforce a promise, which gained increasing recognition throughout the twentieth century. Reliance refers to a change of position made on the basis of a promise someone else made. This doctrine, often called "promissory estoppel," means that unsealed, unwritten, and unbargained-for promises can be enforced when the person making them should expect another to rely on them and did so. Today, this is an available alternative to consideration to justify enforcing a promise, so long as the reliance is reasonable.

The fight in the King case, then, was whether BU gave consideration for Dr. King's commitment of his papers to it or, alternatively, Dr. King made a promise on which BU foreseeably and reasonably relied. Mrs. King argued that Dr. King's statement was not binding because it lacked consideration. In his letter, Dr. King indicated that, in the future, a portion of the deposited materials were "to become" BU's property "as an outright gift" until all papers had been given. To Mrs. King, that language amounted to a mere gratuitous promise to make a gift—not a binding deal. Mrs. King emphasized the letter's qualifying language, when Dr. King wrote that all papers BU takes into custody "remain my legal property" until further steps occurred.

In opposition, BU argued that Dr. King's promise was supported by consideration and by the University's reliance. The statement that deposited property would become BU's by gift must be read alongside the statement that, upon Dr. King's death, all the property would "become from that date the absolute property of" BU. Dr. King delivered property upon signing the letter and another installment the following year. BU took possession of the materials and cared for them. The delivery signaled BU's reciprocal obligation and amounted to consideration, a trade: the papers in exchange for appropriate curating. Alternatively, that same language and context justified the interpretation that Dr. King made a promise that he should have foreseen BU would rely on. By archiving the material in its special collection for many years, the University did reasonably rely on that promise.

Drawing on any assigned cases or materials, how do you think this dispute should be resolved, and why? In your answer, be sure to address any relevant arguments that were (or could have been) raised in the excerpt above.

PROBLEM: TERMINATION OF A SALESMAN

Willy Salesman ("Willy") worked as a traveling representative for the Great Northeastern Insurance Company ("Company") for several years, when, one day, he was arrested for the crimes of rape, kidnapping, and gross sexual imposition. He was suspended from his job without pay because of the accusations, until such time as the criminal charges would be favorably resolved. The trial resulted in a hung jury, and the charges were subsequently dismissed because the alleged victim no longer desired to prosecute the case.

Company subsequently notified Willy that he would not be reinstated and terminated his employment. Willy filed suit against Company alleging that under the terms of his oral employment agreement he was improperly fired. Specifically, Willy argued that his good employment record, oral promises made to him by Company at the time of hiring and suspension, dismissal of the criminal charges, provisions in Company's handbook, and the Company's failure to follow its own published internal grievance procedures all combined to provide grounds for this action. Willy claims he is entitled to relief either on a breach of contract or promissory estoppel basis.

Company denied any breach of the employment agreement and alleged Willy was an employee-at-will, subject to discharge for any reason. Willy argues that promissory estoppel may constitute an exception to the doctrine of employment-at-will.

Drawing on any assigned cases or materials, how do you think this dispute should be resolved, and why? Specifically, do you think Willy can maintain a promissory estoppel cause of action against defendant? What additional facts, if proved, would help Willy's case? Defendant's? Assuming Willy prevails, what should the court award as a remedy?

PROBLEM: HOTEL CALIFORNIA

Vulcan Developers ("Vulcan") wanted to build a hotel near San Francisco International Airport, and sought financing for the project. After some negotiations, on January 9, 2013, Goldrush Bank ("Bank") sent to Vulcan a letter of conditional commitment which read as follows:

> Dear Vulcan Developers:
>
> Re: Hotel at San Francisco International Airport.
>
> Goldrush Bank is pleased to move from our letter of intent to commit, dated December 11, 2012, to this conditional commitment, as follows:
>
> Loan Amount and Interest Rate: $70,000,000 at 5%; which must be supported by appraised value with resulting loan to value ratio not in excess of 75%.
>
> Ownership of proposed project between Vulcan Developers to be clarified; Dun & Bradstreet reports required on both. Final Limited Partnership Agreement subject to Goldrush Bank review and approval.
>
> Property Management: Management of subject property subject to review and approval by Goldrush Bank. Resume of owners management history plus copies of Management Contract, if applicable, to be forwarded for review. Plans, specifications and detailed cost breakdown requested on proposed project.
>
> Cordially,
>
> (s) Goldrush Bank
> Date: 1-15-2013

Bank subsequently refused to make the loan, and Vulcan brought suit for breach of contract. Vulcan claims that the conditional commitment letter is binding because (1) all of the conditions to Bank's commitment set forth in the letter were either met or waived by Bank, and (2) Vulcan relied on it to their detriment in that they proceeded with the development of the project including forbearance from seeking other financing. Vulcan also argues that, at the time Bank repudiated the conditional commitment, Vulcan only had 45 days within which to break ground on the project in order to maintain their permit. The alternative financing was substantially more expensive than that which was conditionally committed by Bank. Vulcan did, however, succeed in building the hotel, which is now in operation.

For their part, Bank argues that Vulcan failed to allege facts sufficient to constitute a cause of action, and that the letter is not an enforceable contract because it is missing the following essential terms: (1) The letter lists no schedule of payment for the loan as required by applicable regulations; (2) the security for the loan is not identified; (3) the identity of the borrower is not clear; and (4) miscellaneous items are missing; namely, prepayment conditions, terms for interest calculations, method for loan disbursements, and rights and remedies of the lender in the case of default.

Drawing on any assigned cases or materials, how do you think this dispute should be resolved, and why? Specifically, do you think Vulcan can maintain a promissory estoppel cause of action against Bank? What additional facts, if proved, would help Vulcan's case? Bank's case? Assuming Vulcan prevails, what remedy should the court award?

PROBLEM: CHILD SUPPORT AND PROMISSORY ESTOPPEL

Seeking to recover child support for her daughter and her son, Kim Newman filed suit against Bruce Wright. Wright's answer admitted his paternity only as to Newman's daughter and DNA testing subsequently showed that he is not the father of her son. The trial court nevertheless ordered Wright to pay child support for both children. As to Newman's son, the trial court based its order upon Wright's "actions in having himself listed on the child's birth certificate, giving the child his surname and establishing a parent-child relationship. . . ." According to the trial court, Wright had thereby

> allow[ed] the child to consider him his father and in so doing deterr[ed Newman] from seeking to establish the paternity of the child's natural father[,] thus denying the child an opportunity to establish a parent-child relationship with the natural father.

The Court of Appeals granted Wright's application for a discretionary appeal so as to review the trial court's order requiring that he pay child support for Newman's son.

Wright does not contest the trial court's factual findings. He asserts only that the trial court erred in its legal conclusion that the facts authorized the imposition of an obligation to provide support for Newman's son. If Wright were the natural father of Newman's son, he would be legally obligated to provide support. Likewise, if Wright had formally adopted Newman's son, he would be legally obligated to provide support. However, Wright is neither the natural nor the formally adoptive father of the child.

Does Wright have a contractual obligation to support the child under a theory of promissory estoppel? Drawing on any assigned cases or materials, how do you think the Court of Appeals should resolve this dispute, and why? Are there any additional facts you would like to know that would change your answer? Assuming plaintiff prevails, what remedy should the Court award?

PROBLEM: A CAREFUL PROMISE

The Al-Farooq Masjid Mosque brought an action against the estate of Aaban Reza to compel the administrator of the estate to fulfil an oral promise Mr. Reza made to give the mosque $35,000. Mr. Reza had suffered through a prolonged illness and throughout his last days he visited with the mosque's Imam, Abdul Khalid. During five or six of those visits, and in the presence of other witnesses, Mr. Reza made an oral promise to give to the mosque $35,000. The mosque had planned in its yearly budget to use the money that Mr. Reza would be donating to pay for restorative work on the mosque's iconic minaret and to place a plaque on the outside of the mosque noting Mr. Reza contribution. The oral promise was never reduced to writing. Mr. Reza died intestate with no children, but was survived by his wife. The mosque asserts that Mr. Reza's oral promise is an enforceable contract because it was supported by consideration, or alternatively, because the mosque relied on Mr. Reza's promise to donate in compiling its yearly budget.

Drawing on any assigned cases or materials, how do you think this dispute should be resolved, and why? Specifically, do you think the mosque can either (a) show that there was consideration to support Mr. Reza's promise or (b) maintain a promissory estoppel cause of action against Mr. Reza? What additional facts, if proved, would help the mosque's case? What facts would help Mr. Reza's case? Assuming the mosque prevails, what remedy should the court award, and why?

PROBLEM: TO GIVE AND TAKE

Diana McClaren, a 2010 graduate of Yale Law School, was employed as a document reviewer at Tannan Law Offices in Chicago, Illinois. She worked approximately 60 hours per week earning about $18 per hour. Diana desired employment as a law firm associate. In the summer of 2012 she advised the Yale Law School Career Development Office that she was seeking an associate position. The Career Development Office connected her with Johnson, LLP who told Diana to come in for an interview. Approximately two weeks after the interview, Diana phoned the office of Johnson, LLP and was told to be patient as it was necessary to interview recent graduates before making an offer. A month after phoning the office, Diana received a call from Johnson, LLP offering her a position as a junior associate at the firm. Diana accepted the offer but mentioned that she had to give two weeks notice of her resignation to Tannan Law Offices. That afternoon, Diana also received another offer for an associate position at a small firm in the Chicago area, which she declined. Shortly before Diana's two week notice period at Tannan Law Offices was over, a representative from Johnson, LLP contacted Diana to confirm that she had resigned. A week later, the representative from Johnson, LLP contacted Diana and mentioned that before becoming an associate she must provide a favorable written reference. After her former employer refused to provide a reference, Diana communicated with Johnson, LLP that she couldn't provide a reference at this time. Because Diana was unable to produce a favorable reference, Johnson, LLP hired another person to fill their junior associate position. When Diana phoned to inform Johnson, LLP that she had obtained a favorable written reference from a former law school professor, they informed her that someone else had been hired. Diana experienced difficulty regaining full employment and suffered wage loss as a result. Diana sued Johnson, LLP for damages resulting from repudiation of an employment offer.

Drawing on any assigned cases or materials, how do you think this dispute should be resolved, and why? Specifically, do you think Diana can maintain a promissory estoppel cause of action against Johnson, LLP? What additional facts, if proved, would help Diana's case? What facts would help Johnson, LLP's case? Assuming Diana prevails, what remedy should the court award?

C. BENEFIT-BASED CONTRACTS: THE DOCTRINE OF UNJUST ENRICHMENT

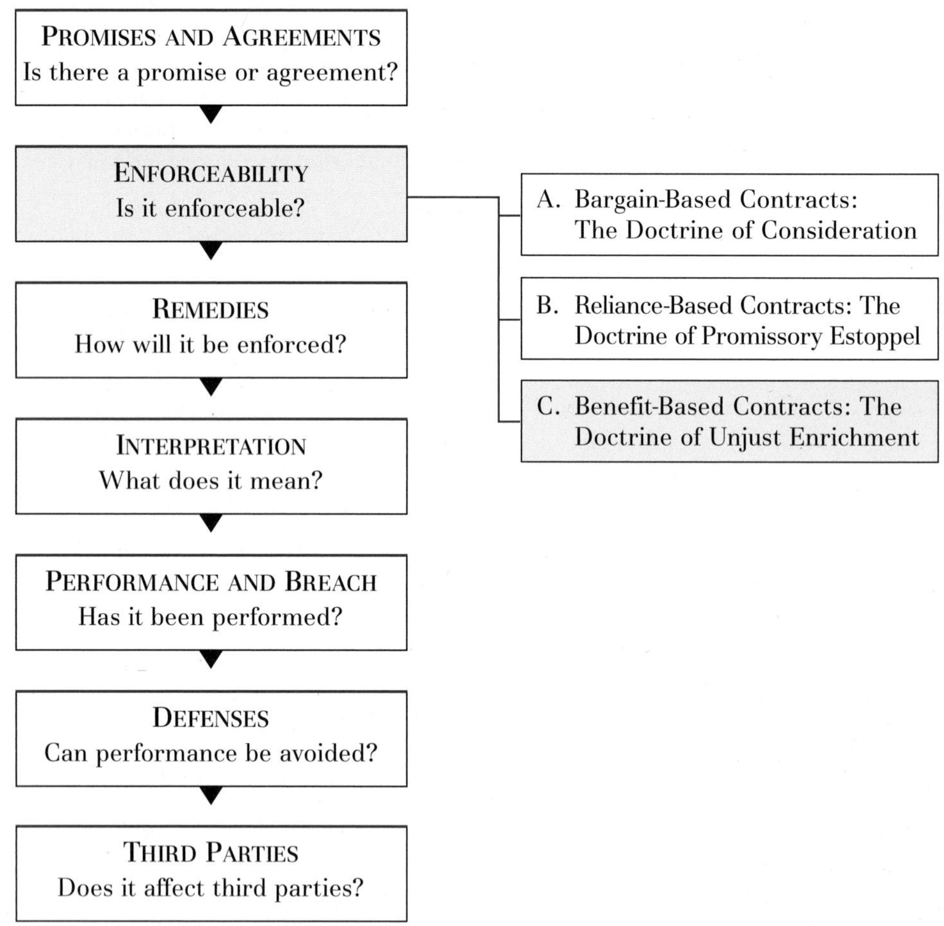
PROMISES AND AGREEMENTS
Is there a promise or agreement?
ENFORCEABILITY
Is it enforceable?
REMEDIES
How will it be enforced?
INTERPRETATION
What does it mean?
PERFORMANCE AND BREACH
Has it been performed?
DEFENSES
Can performance be avoided?
THIRD PARTIES
Does it affect third parties?
A. Bargain-Based Contracts: The Doctrine of Consideration
B. Reliance-Based Contracts: The Doctrine of Promissory Estoppel
C. Benefit-Based Contracts: The Doctrine of Unjust Enrichment

In this section, you will be introduced to the doctrine of unjust enrichment as a third, independent ground of promissory liability. Unjust enrichment represents one of the three great pillars of civil liability: Whereas contract liability is based on promise, and tort liability is based on wrongdoing, unjust enrichment liability is based on the simple but powerful notion that a party must not unjustly retain a benefit to which it is not entitled.* Indeed, whenever a party ("A") confers a benefit on another party ("B"), and a court finds that it would be unjust for B to retain that benefit, A may bring a cause of action against B for unjust enrichment.† As an independent basis of civil liability, unjust enrichment is broad, and covers a number of situations having little or nothing to do with contract law. Therefore, we will only concern ourselves with those situations in which promise and unjust enrichment overlap (sometimes called promissory restitution). This situation usually arises where one party promises to pay for a benefit received, but the promise turns out to be unenforceable (e.g., because it is unsupported by consideration). So, for instance, some of the cases we will look at in this section include: (1) a case in which a party conferred a benefit on another party pursuant to a promise that could no longer be enforced (*Britton v. Turner*), (2) a case where two doctors conferred a benefit on an a patient without first making a contract because the patient, being unconscious, did not have the opportunity to make one (*Cotnam v. Wisdom*), (3) a case in which a party thought it had a contract (or, in the alternative, thought that the court should impose a constructive contract) to recover for caring for another party's horse (*Bailey v. West*), and (4) a case where a party subsequently promised to pay for a benefit it received but didn't bargain for, but probably would have had there been time to do so (*Webb v. McGowin*). One final note before we get to the cases. Nowadays, the term "unjust enrichment" is often used to refer to any situation in which one party seeks to recover against another for the other party's unjust retention of a benefit. However, over the course of its long and complicated history,‡ the concept we today know as "unjust enrichment" has been cobbled together in piecemeal fashion from a number of individual causes of action, such as "quantum meruit," "quasi contract," and "restitution."§ For our purposes, you should try to think of these individual causes of action as a

* See *Restatement (Third) of Restitution and Unjust Enrichment* § 1 ("A person who is unjustly enriched at the expense of another is subject to liability in restitution.")

† See *Restatement (Third) of Restitution and Unjust Enrichment* § 1 Comment b (2011) (As you might imagine, most of the law in this area is "concerned with identifying those forms of enrichment that the law treats as 'unjust' for purposes of imposing liability.")

‡ *See, e.g.*, Andrew Kull, *James Barr Ames and the Early Modern History of Unjust Enrichment*, 25 OXFORD J. LEGAL STUD. 297 (2005) *and* Douglas Laycock, *How Remedies Became a Field: A History*, 27 REV. LITIG. 161 (2008).

§ Commentators sometimes use the term "restitution" as a synonym for "unjust enrichment," and although this is not historically inaccurate, doing so can lead to confusion. *See, e.g.*, *Restatement (Third) of Restitution and Unjust Enrichment* § 1 Comment e (2011) ("The fact that the word 'restitution' is used to designate both liabilities and remedies in unjust enrichment leads to a series of common misunderstandings.") This is especially so in contract law, where the term "restitution" is frequently used to refer not to liability at all, but to the remedy that requires one party (e.g., the promisor) to return any unjustly retained gains to another party (e.g., the promisee). Therefore, for the sake of clarity, this casebook will use the term "unjust enrichment" only when referring to a cause of action giving rise to liability for the unjust retention of a benefit, and the term "restitution" when referring to the remedy that returns the promisor to its status quo ante, by taking from it any unjustly retained benefits.

species of "unjust enrichment," and focus on the more important question of whether recovery should be allowed.

1. Quantum Meruit

Before reading the next case, it is worth pointing out that the court below is not trying to determine whether the plaintiff should be allowed to recover *on* the contract, because the plaintiff, having breached the contract, has no contract to enforce. Rather, the court is trying to determine whether the plaintiff should be allowed to recover *off* the contract, as it were, under a theory of unjust enrichment. As is the case with many unjust enrichment claims, the particular cause of action being alleged here, *quantum meruit*, is often used to refer to both (1) the cause of action allowing recovery, and (2) the "quantum" or amount of recovery due. The *Britton v. Turner* court helpfully uses the term only in first sense.

Britton v. Turner

Superior Court of Judicature of New Hampshire
6 N.H. 481 (1834)

Assumpsit for work and labor, performed by the plaintiff, in the service of the defendant, from March 9th, 1831, to December 27, 1831.

The declaration contained the common counts, and among them a count in **quantum meruit**, for the labor, averring it to be worth one hundred dollars.

At the trial in the C. C. Pleas, the plaintiff proved the performance of the labor as set forth in the declaration.

The defense was that it was performed under a special contract—that the plaintiff agreed to work one year, from some time in March, 1831, to March 1832, and that the defendant was to pay him for said year's labor the sum of one hundred and twenty dollars; and the defendant offered evidence tending to show that such was the contract under which the work was done.

Evidence was also offered to show that the plaintiff left the defendant's service without his consent, and it was contended by the defendant that the plaintiff had no good cause for not continuing in his employment.

There was no evidence offered of any damage arising from the plaintiffs departure, farther than was to be inferred from his non fulfilment of the entire contract.

The court instructed the jury, that if they were satisfied from the evidence that the labor was performed, under a contract to labor a year, for the sum of one hundred and twenty dollars, and if they were satisfied that the plaintiff

> ***Assumpsit***
>
> From the Latin *assumere*, to "take on" or "assume." A common-law form of action (see "Forms of action" at 89, *supra*) to recover damages for the breach of contract not under seal.

> ***Quantum meruit***
>
> "[Latin 'as much as he has deserved.'] *Quantum meruit* has several meanings, but as used in *Britton v. Turner*, is closest to the following: "A claim for the value of benefits provided without a contract, as when the plaintiff brings a claim for restitution and that value provides the measure of recovery." BLACK'S LAW DICTIONARY (10th ed. 2014).

labored only the time specified in the declaration, and then left the defendant's service, against his consent, and without any good cause, yet the plaintiff was entitled to recover, under his quantum meruit count, as much as the labor he performed was reasonably worth, and under this direction the jury gave a verdict for the plaintiff for the sum of $95.

The defendant excepted to the instructions thus given to the jury. . . .

PARKER, **J. delivered the opinion of the court.** It may be assumed, that the labor performed by the plaintiff, and for which he seeks to recover a compensation in this action, was commenced under a special contract to labor for the defendant the term of one year, for the sum of one hundred and twenty dollars, and that the plaintiff has labored but a portion of that time, and has voluntarily failed to complete the entire contract.

It is clear, then, that he is not entitled to recover upon the contract itself, because the service, which was to entitle him to the sum agreed upon, has never been performed.

But the question arises, can the plaintiff, under these circumstances, recover a reasonable sum for the service he has actually performed, under the count in quantum meruit. . . .

It has been held, upon contracts of this kind for labor to be performed at a specified price, that the party who voluntarily fails to fulfil the contract by performing the whole labor contracted for, is not entitled to recover any thing for the labor actually performed, however much he may have done towards the performance, and this has been considered the settled rule of law upon this subject.

That such rule in its operation may be very unequal, not to say unjust, is apparent.

A party who contracts to perform certain specified labor, and who breaks his contract in the first instance, without any attempt to perform it, can only be made liable to pay the damages which the other party has sustained by reason of such nonperformance, which in many instances may be trifling—whereas a party who in good faith has entered upon the performance of his contract, and nearly completed it, and then abandoned the further performance—although the other party has had the full benefit of all that has been done, and has perhaps sustained no actual damage—is in fact subjected to a loss of all which has been performed, in the nature of damages for the non fulfilment of the remainder, upon the technical rule, that the contract must be fully performed in order to a recovery of any part of the compensation.

By the operation of this rule, then, the party who attempts performance may be placed in a much worse situation than he who wholly disregards his contract, and the other party may receive much more, by the breach of the contract, than the injury which he has sustained by such breach, and more than he could be entitled to were he seeking to recover damages by an action.

The case before us presents an illustration. Had the plaintiff in this case never entered upon the performance of his contract, the damage could not probably have been greater than some small expense and trouble incurred in procuring another to do the labor which he had contracted to perform. But having entered upon the performance, and labored nine and a half months, the value of which labor to the defendant as found by the jury is $95, if the defendant can succeed in this defense, he in fact receives nearly five sixths of the value of a whole year's labor, by reason of the breach of contract by the plaintiff a sum not only utterly disproportionate to any probable, not to say possible damage which could have resulted from the neglect of the plaintiff to continue the remaining two and an half months, but altogether beyond any damage which could have been recovered by the defendant, had the plaintiff done nothing towards the fulfilment of his contract. . . .

It is said, that where a party contracts to perform certain work, and to furnish materials, as, for instance, to build a house, and the work is done, but with some variations from the mode prescribed by the contract, yet if the other party has the benefit of the labor and materials he should be bound to pay so much as they are reasonably worth. . . .

The party who contracts for labor merely, for a certain period, does so with full knowledge that he must, from the nature of the case, be accepting part performance from day to day, if the other party commences the performance, and with knowledge also that the other may eventually fail of completing the entire term.

If under such circumstances he actually receives a benefit from the labor performed, over and above the damage occasioned by the failure to complete, there is as much reason why he should pay the reasonable worth of what has thus been done for his benefit, as there is when he enters and occupies the house which has been built for him, but not according to the stipulations of the contract, and which he perhaps enters, not because he is satisfied with what has been done, but because circumstances compel him to accept it such as it is, that he should pay for the value of the house. . . .

[W]here the contract is to labor from day to day, for a certain period, the party for whom the labor is done in truth stipulates to receive it from day to day, as it is performed, and although the other may not eventually do all he has contracted to do, there has been, necessarily, an acceptance of what has been done in pursuance of the contract, and the party must have understood when he made the contract that there was to be such acceptance.

If then the party stipulates in the outset to receive part performance from time to time, with a knowledge that the whole may not be completed, we see no reason why he should not equally be holden to pay for the amount of value received, as where he afterwards takes the benefit of what has been done, with a knowledge that the whole which was contracted for has not been performed. . . .

[W]here the party receives value—takes and uses the materials, or has advantage from the labor, he is liable to pay the reasonable worth of what he has received. . . .

In fact we think the technical reasoning, that the performance of the whole labor is a condition precedent, and the right to recover any thing dependent upon it . . . is not properly applicable to this species of contract, where a beneficial service has been actually performed; for we have abundant reason to believe, that the general understanding of the community is, that the hired laborer shall be entitled to compensation for the service actually performed, though he do not continue the entire term contracted for, and such contracts must be presumed to be made with reference to that understanding, unless an express stipulation shows the contrary. . . .

It is easy, if parties so choose, to provide by an express agreement that nothing shall be earned, if the laborer leaves his employer without having performed the whole service contemplated, and then there can be no pretense for a recovery if he voluntarily deserts the service before the expiration of the time.

> **Contracting around the rule**
>
> With this language, the court is informing future parties that they can contract around the court's announced default rule by providing specific terms to the contrary. The concept of default rules was explored in much greater depth in "Thinking Tool: Gap Filling and Default Rules" in Part II.2.E, supra (p. 126).

The amount, however, for which the employer ought to be charged, where the laborer abandons his contract, is only the reasonable worth, or the amount of advantage he receives upon the whole transaction, and, in estimating the value of the labor, the contract price for the service cannot be exceeded.

If a person makes a contract fairly he is entitled to have it fully performed, and if this is not done he is entitled to damages. He may maintain a suit to recover the amount of damage sustained by the non-performance.

The benefit and advantage which the party takes by the labor, therefore, is the amount of value which he receives, if any, after deducting the amount of damage; and if he elects to put this in defense he is entitled so to do, and the implied promise which the law will raise, in such case, is to pay such amount of the stipulated price for the whole labor, as remains after deducting what it would cost to procure a completion of the residue of the service, and also any damage which has been sustained by reason of the non fulfilment of the contract.

If in such case it be found that the damages are equal to, or greater than the amount of the labor performed, so that the employer, having a right to the full performance of the contract, has not upon the whole case received a beneficial service, the plaintiff cannot recover.

This rule, by binding the employer to pay the value of the service he actually receives, and the laborer to answer in damages where he does not complete the entire contract, will leave no temptation to the former to drive the laborer from his service, near the close of his term, by ill treatment, in order to escape from payment; nor to the latter to desert his service before the stipulated time, without a sufficient reason; and it will in most instances settle the whole controversy in one action, and prevent a multiplicity of suits and cross actions.

There may be instances, however, where the damage occasioned is much greater than the value of the labor performed, and if the party elects to permit himself to be charged for the value of the labor, without interposing the damages in defense, he is entitled to do so, and may have an action to recover his damages for the non-performance, whatever, they may be. . . .

Applying the principles thus laid down, to this case, the plaintiff is entitled to judgment on the verdict.

The defendant sets up a mere breach of the contract in defense of the action, but this cannot avail him. He does not appear to have offered evidence to show that he was damnified by such breach, or to have asked that a deduction should be made upon that account. The direction to the jury was therefore correct, that the plaintiff was entitled to recover as much as the labor performed was reasonably worth, and the jury appear to have allowed a *pro rata* compensation, for the time which the plaintiff labored in the defendant's service.

As the defendant has not claimed or had any adjustment of damages, for the breach of the contract, in this action, if he has actually sustained damage he is still entitled to a suit to recover the amount. . . .

Judgment on the verdict.

The short excerpt below reveals that much more is going on in Britton v. Turner *than first meets the eye. Specifically, the case raises important questions regarding (1) how a court should deal with precedent where its application may lead to an unjust result, (2) whether the aim of contract law should be to encourage parties to perform their promises by deterring and/or punishing breaching parties, or whether it should merely ensure that the injured party is compensated for damages resulting from the promisor's breach, and (3) how the default rules of contract law should be selected, a concept we explored in several earlier thinking tools.*

CONTEXTUAL PERSPECTIVE: MORE ON BRITTON V. TURNER*

Britton v. Turner—as some but not all the casebooks point out—was an outlier when it was decided. The standard rule that emerged and persisted in most American jurisdictions in the nineteenth century was the "entire contract" or "entirety" rule. A contract of hiring that did not specify its duration was presumed to be for a year and to be "entire," that is, not divisible into increments of time. Thus the worker who quits without cause before the year is out has not performed his side of the bargain and therefore forfeits all claims to unpaid wages. The leading American case is from Massachusetts, Stark v. Parker (1824).[8] This case also involved a farm laborer who had contracted for a year's labor at $120 for the year, who walked off the job partway through his term and asked for payment for the work done so far. The Supreme Judicial Court held . . . that serving out the year is the condition precedent for his right to recover payment for the work,

* Excerpted from Robert W. Gordon, Britton v. Turner*: A Signpost on the Crooked Road to "Freedom" in the Employment Contract*, in DOUGLAS G. BAIRD (ed.), CONTRACT STORIES 189-93 (2007).

8. Mass. (2 Pick.) 267 (1824).

and that this is a good rule because it discourages contract breach and rewards faithful service. . . . Ten years later, Judge Parker in Britton starts out by noting the Stark rule, but immediately points out that such a "technical rule . . . in its operation may be very unequal, not to say unjust," because the employer will realize a windfall by being allowed to appropriate the benefit of all the employee's work even if the damage is "trifling," while the employee who serves nearly to the end will lose everything. . . . Parker concludes with a policy argument of his own about incentives: His rule will "leave no temptation to the [employer] to drive the laborer from his service, near the end of his term, by ill treatment, in order to escape from payment; nor to the latter to desert his service before the stipulated time, without a sufficient reason. . . ."

So we have two cases on nearly identical facts in adjoining New England states, decided ten years apart, looking at the world through two subtly different conceptual lenses. The opinions differ on customary expectations of the parties; on the likely incentive effects of different rules; and most basically on the grand eternal contest of principle within contract law: Is it to be a mechanism for forcing people to perform their promises, and to deter or punish immoral breachers? Or is it to be indifferent as between performance and breach so long as the breacher pays damages?[21] Note that in this contest the *Stark* rule straddles both sides. The employer who breaches must only pay compensatory damages, the contract wage reduced by whatever the employee earned or could have earned at another job. The breaching employee forfeits his entire wage.On many basic matters the cases are in accord. Both cases supply implied (default) terms to the contractual relationship: Yearlong contracts are entire; payment on the contract is not due until the year's end; the worker breaches by quitting early. The parties *could* expressly spell out their own times and terms of payment in exchange for performance. The *Britton* court itself points out that the parties could if they wished contract around its holding and specify the result of the majority *Stark* doctrine—no payment until and unless a full year's work had been performed. Since these are default rules, the party whom the rules favor can reap their benefits without having to say anything at the onset of the contract about the term in question. Under the majority *Stark* rule, unless a worker is prepared to lose a year's wages, he is effectively indentured to his employer for the entire term, even if he gets a better offer elsewhere, even if he wants to quit because the boss is abusive. If he is not deterred from quitting because he doesn't know about the secret term, he may be in for a nasty surprise when he actually quits. If the boss were abusive enough, of course, the boss would himself be in material breach of contract, which would entitle the worker both to quit work and to damages. But this is not much comfort to the worker: It leaves a farm laborer who has not yet been paid for his work with the burden of having to bring and finance a lawsuit. Besides . . . , because employment law gave masters so much authority over their servants, it was much easier for the master to put his servant in breach than the other way around: All he had to do was to give orders that the servant disobeyed, or just provoke him to

21. And it touches on another grand contest: Is the role of contract law to enforce even harsh bargains to the limit? Or is it to enforce only within a range of results securing fair and equitable returns to both sides?

insolent or defiant behavior. Anyway, the default rule allows even the manifestly abusive employer the self-help remedy of holding on to the money, to withhold back wages without going to court. Even *Britton's* more generous rule requires the worker to incur the costs and risks of a lawsuit to recover his wage. And even if he got past those barriers, as Robert Steinfeld has pointed out, "it was always possible for an unsympathetic judge . . . to find that the damage to the employer from the worker's breach fully equaled the value of any labor performed, leaving the worker to recover nothing."[23] A builder or contractor supplying materials and labor on a building contract, likely to be a business-savvy repeat-playing party, will, of course, usually insist on structuring the contract to get around the rule that he must finish the entire job before being entitled to any payment, and provide for periodic payments to finance the work as it proceeds. (He will also get a mechanic's lien on the realty.) A farm laborer or factory worker, we may speculate, is more likely to accept work on the terms offered, less likely to be aware of the invisible terms of the contract, and even if aware of them to be much less likely, unless labor is scarce and his skills unusual, to be able to contract around them. . . .

RELEVANT PROVISIONS

For the *Restatement (Second) of Contracts,* consult § 374. For the *Restatement (Third) of Restitution and Unjust Enrichment,* consult § 36.

NOTES AND QUESTIONS

1. *Significance of original contract.* Is it significant that there was originally a contract between Britton and Turner? Suppose Britton just showed up on Turner's farm one day and started working. Same result? Why or why not? Does Cohen's article, excerpted as "Justifying Contract Law" in Part II.2.C, *supra* (p. 81), or Fuller's article, excerpted as "The Role of Legal Formalities" in Section 4.A.1, *supra* (p. 341), shed any light on this question?

2. *What happened?* Who sued whom for what? Procedurally, how did the case get before this court? Factually, what happened between the parties? What arguments did the plaintiff and defendant make? What rule or rules did the court apply? How did the court analyze the dispute between the parties? How did the court decide the case?

3. *Was this case correctly decided?* Do you agree with the result reached by Judge Parker? Why? What about his reasoning? What are the strengths and

---

23. Robert J. Steinfeld, Coercion, Contract and Free Labor in the Nineteenth Century 300 (2001).

weaknesses of his approach? How, if at all, would you have written the opinion differently? In answering these questions, you may find it helpful to first consider some of the notes and questions below.

4. *Promise versus benefit?* "On one hand Britton has not kept his promise; on the other Turner has had a substantial benefit at his expense. The promise and restitution principles appear to point in opposite directions in this situation."* Where the promise-based principle conflicts with the benefit-based principle, which theory do you think should generally prevail, and why? How about as applied to the facts of *Britton v. Turner*? Why?

5. *Thinking tools applied.* What policy arguments were advanced by the court in *Britton v. Turner* for changing the default rule from (a) one that did not allow laborers to recover unless they fully performed their contracts to (b) one that allowed them to recover a pro rata share of their completed performance? If you were representing the defendant, what policy arguments would you have made to support your client's position? In answering these questions, try to draw on some of the thinking tools we examined earlier.

6. *Policy considerations.* Was it the court's job to change the default rule, or should this have been left to the legislative branch? Why?

7. *The purpose of contract law.* Do you think contract law should encourage parties to perform their promises by deterring and/or punishing breaching parties, or should it merely ensure that injured parties are compensated for damages resulting from the promisor's breach?

8. *Recovery for unjust enrichment?* As the excerpt above points out, although it was once a minority rule, the rule announced by the court in *Britton v. Turner* is now widely accepted. A more difficult question, however, is determining how the recovery should be measured. Professor Farnsworth provides the following guidelines:

> If the party in breach seeks the return of money paid, the value of the benefit is clear. But if the party in breach seeks to recover the value of the benefit conferred by a performance of some other kind, measurement of that value may pose a difficult problem. Since it is the party seeking restitution that is responsible for the problem, courts resolve doubts against that party and generally limit recovery to net enrichment and do not allow cost avoided. In contrast to claims based on substantial performance or divisibility, where recovery is on the contract, here the contract price is not conclusive. Still, it is often taken as evidence of the value of the benefit had the contract been performed. Recovery will then equal the contract price, minus diminution in value resulting from the breach. The result is as generous as if recovery were allowed on the contract on the ground that performance was substantial. When courts can determine a ratable portion of the contract price, they have sometimes allowed recovery of

* CHARLES FRIED, CONTRACT AS PROMISE 27 (1981).

that amount. Then the result is as generous as if recovery were allowed on the contract on the ground that the contract was divisible. But unlike the situation in which the injured party seeks restitution, a court will not allow recovery to exceed the ratable portion of the price.*

9. ***Previewing remedies.*** We will explore the issue of measuring the restitution interest in greater detail in the next chapter. For now, drawing on the previous case and accompanying materials, see if you can answer the following questions:

a. How much would Turner owe Britton if Turner had to pay another hand $25 to complete Britton's unfinished work?

b. How much would Turner owe Britton if Turner provided evidence to the court that Britton's labor was only worth $5 per month, and that he only agreed to pay Britton the equivalent of $10 per month "to be nice," in the hope that Britton would stay on for the entire year?

c. How much would Turner owe Britton if Britton provided evidence to the court that his labor was worth $20 per month, and that he only agreed to work for Turner for less because he was having a hard time finding another job?

THINKING TOOL: THE COASE THEOREM, TRANSACTION COSTS, AND DISTRIBUTIVE JUSTICE

Recall that the court in *Britton v. Turner* stated that "[i]t is easy, if parties so choose, to provide by an express agreement that nothing shall be earned, if the laborer leaves his employer without having performed the whole service contemplated. . . ." The court, in other words, recognized that the rule it adopted was simply a default rule, one that could be contracted around by the parties if they so desired. This brings up an important question: If the parties can simply contract around the default rule chosen by the court, how should a court select the default rule in the first place? How, for instance, should a court choose between the competing default rules embodied in *Stark v. Parker* and *Britton v. Turner*?

* E. ALLAN FARNSWORTH, CONTRACTS § 8.14 (4th ed. 2004). *See also* RESTATEMENT (THIRD) OF RESTITUTION AND UNJUST ENRICHMENT § 49 cmt. f (2011) ("Liability in restitution for the market value of goods or services is the remedy traditionally known as quantum meruit. . . . The measurement of unjust enrichment is significantly affected by the fact that the defendant requested the benefits in question and—implicitly, at least—expressed a willingness to pay for them.")

We touched on the issue of setting default rules in an earlier chapter,[120] but another way of approaching this question was provided by Nobel Prize winner Ronald Coase, whose "Coase theorem"[122] provides us with our next thinking tool. According to the Coase theorem, we should begin (for the sake of simplicity) by assuming a world in which there are no transaction costs, in which bargaining is costless to the parties. In such a world, if a court is only concerned with promoting efficiency, then the Coase theorem tells us that our choice of the default rule is irrelevant—we could even pick it by flipping a coin![124] Why? Because, in such a world, whenever two parties contracted with one another, whichever party valued a particular rule the most would bargain with the other party to have that rule included in their contract. This, in turn, would have the result of increasing efficiency[126] and minimizing waste. (Can you see why?)

To see how this works, let's return to the facts of *Britton v. Turner* and see some Coasean bargaining in action. Assume that two parties live in a jurisdiction that adopted the *Stark v. Parker* default rule, which requires its laborers to work a full year before collecting their salary. A worker like Britton, of course, would prefer to live in a jurisdiction with the opposite rule, allowing him to earn his salary (i.e., $120) on a pro-rata basis (i.e., $10 per month) as he labored for Turner, and might be willing to pay as much as $12 for this right. In such a case, Britton would approach Turner and propose something like the following: "Turner, if you agree to pay me monthly, rather than yearly, I will accept a salary of $108, rather than $120 (or $9 per month, rather than $10)." Turner now has the opportunity to save $12 in labor costs. What will he do? Well, that depends. If Turner values paying Britton at the end of the year *more* than $12, he will reject Britton's offer. From the standpoint of efficiency, this makes sense because any other result would result in taking a legal entitlement from a party who valued it more (Turner) and giving it to a party who valued it less (Britton). On the other hand, if Turner valued paying Britton once a year at, say, $10, then Turner would accept Britton's $12 offer (because it would make him better off by $2), which again makes sense from the standpoint of efficiency as the bargain would result in a benefit to both parties.

So, is there anything wrong with this picture? Well, recall that the example just discussed assumed a world with zero transaction costs (i.e., a world in which bargaining was costless). But in the real world, of course, bargaining often entails at least *some* transaction costs. Does this mean that the Coase theorem is irrelevant? Not at all. As a model, it remains useful because it focuses our attention on what's important from the standpoint of efficiency: transaction costs. In the real world, some transactions will entail low transaction costs (e.g., purchasing a computer at Best Buy), whereas others will entail high transaction costs (e.g.,

120. *See* "Thinking Tool: Gap Filling and Default Rules" in Part II.2.E, *supra* (p. 126) .

122. Although the Coase theorem was given its name by other scholars, the ideas behind it were first outlined by Ronald Coase in an important work, Coase, R.H., *The Problem of Social Cost*, J. LAW ECON. 3, 1-44 (1960).

124. Specifically, according to Coase: "With costless market transactions, the decision of the courts concerning liability for damage would be without effect on the allocation of resources." Ronald Coase, *The Problem of Social Cost*, 3 JOURNAL OF LAW AND ECONOMICS 1, 10 (1960).

126. For more on "efficiency," *see* "Thinking Tool: Marginal Analysis and Efficiency," in Part II.2.B.2, *supra* (p. 64).

negotiating a billion-dollar merger). Where transaction costs are low (e.g., $1 in the last Britton-Turner hypo given above), the Coase theorem suggests that the parties are still likely to strike an efficient bargain. Why? Because such parties will often be able to gain from trade even after paying these small transaction costs. For instance, if Britton placed a value on the right of getting paid monthly at $12, then he could forgo $10 in yearly salary *and* incur $1 in transaction costs and still strike an efficient bargain, as the resulting contract would still result in a $1 net benefit to him (can you see why?) Where transactions costs are high, however, it is less likely that parties will be able to reach an efficient bargain. Specifically, the parties will *not* strike an efficient bargain whenever the transaction costs exceed the difference between the values each party assigns to the contract right at issue (can you see why?) So, for instance, if Britton values the right of getting paid monthly at $12 but Turner values the right of paying Britton yearly at $10, then whenever transaction costs exceed the difference between these two amounts (i.e., $12–$10=$2), the parties will not be able to reach an efficient bargain.

What can we take away from all this? At the very least, we should recognize that because high transaction costs often prevent parties from reaching efficient bargains, courts concerned with efficiency should not select default rules arbitrarily (e.g., by flipping a coin) whenever transaction costs are high. Instead, courts concerned with efficiency should attempt to arrive at a default rule that assigns initial entitlements to the party likely to value them most. Why? Because if they don't, and high transaction costs prevent the parties from bargaining with one another, then these entitlements may inefficiently remain in the hands of parties who value them less.

Applying these insights to *Britton v. Turner*, this means that unless the parties can bargain with one another cheaply, courts should (1) adopt the *Britton v. Turner* rule where the Brittons of the world tend to value getting paid monthly *more* than the Turners of the world value paying their employees yearly, and (2) adopt the *Stark v. Parker* rule where the opposite is true. Stated differently, courts concerned with efficiency should adopt the default rule the parties themselves would have adopted if they could bargain with one another costlessly.

Up until now, however, we have only concerned ourselves with efficiency, concluding that the court's selection of default rules is irrelevant where transaction costs are zero, but become increasingly important as transaction costs increase. While efficiency is important, however, the law is also concerned with advancing other important public policy goals, such as distributive justice, which is concerned with ensuring that legal entitlements are distributed justly among society's members. Given these other concerns, the court's selection of default rules again becomes relevant, even in a world with zero transaction costs. Why? Recall that, even in a world with no transaction costs, an entitlement will only end up in the hands of the party who values it most (1) if that party *pays* the other party for that entitlement or (2) if the entitlement just so happens to already be assigned to that party by the court. Thus, efficiency concerns aside, this means that the manner in which a court selects a default rule constitutes a real form of wealth for the party to whom the default rule assigns the entitlement. To see how, let's return to an earlier example.

Suppose, once again, that Britton values being paid monthly at $12, whereas Turner values paying Britton yearly at $10. Suppose further that transaction costs are zero, so that a Coasean bargain will take place regardless of which default rule is adopted by the court. From the standpoint of efficiency, all is well and good; as we have previously seen, an efficient contract will be reached. From the standpoint of distributive justice, however, if the court adopts the *Stark v. Parker* default rule, then Britton will find himself $12 *poorer* after bargaining with Turner, whereas if the court adopts the *Britton v. Turner* default rule, then Britton will get the default rule he desires *without* paying $12 to do so. From Britton's perspective, the court's choice of selecting the "wrong" default rule will result in his becoming poorer (and Turner becoming richer) by $12.

What can we take away from the analysis above? At the very least, it suggests that courts should not only take transaction costs into account when selecting default rules, but should also weigh the competing concerns of efficiency with other important public policy goals, such as distributive justice. As you read through cases in this and other classes, you should be on the lookout for these issues, and ask yourself whether you agree with the default rule that has been selected by the court both in terms of (1) efficiency and (2) other public policy goals.

NOTES AND QUESTIONS

1. ***Choosing the best default rule.*** In light of the considerations raised in the excerpt above, do you think the *Stark v. Parker* or the *Britton v. Turner* default rule is better from the standpoint of (a) efficiency, (b) distributive justice, and (c) the combination of efficiency and distributive justice? Why?

2. ***Coasean bargaining in action.*** Assume that the parties lived in a jurisdiction that adopted the *Britton v. Turner* default rule, but that Britton only valued this right (to get paid on a pro rata basis) at $5, whereas Turner valued the right (to pay Britton yearly) at $10. Assume transaction costs were $3. Provide your own numbers, and write two dialogues, one in which Coasean bargaining takes place, and another where it does not.

2. Quasi-Contracts

In the previous case, Britton and Turner actually *had* a contract with each other at one point in time. Although their contract was ultimately breached, the fact that one once existed signaled to the court that the parties (at one time, anyway) intended to have a legal relationship with each other. But what should a court do where one party confers a benefit on another party where a contract has never been made? Should the court treat the benefit as a gift, for which the recipient need not pay, or should it treat it as an instance of unjust enrichment, requiring the recipient to pay for the value of the benefit received? Should the answer depend on why the benefit was conferred, or on why the parties never contracted with each other in the first place? The next well-known case explores some of these issues.

Cotnam v. Wisdom

Supreme Court of Arkansas
104 S.W. 164 (1907)

> ***Intestate and Administrator***
>
> An intestate is a party who has died without a will, requiring another party (the administrator) to wind up the affairs of decedent's estate. Can you now see why the case is "Cotnam v. Wisdom" rather than "Harrison v. Wisdom"?

Action by F. L. Wisdom and another against T. T. Cotnam, **administrator** of A. M. Harrison, deceased, for services rendered by plaintiffs as surgeons to defendant's **intestate**. Judgment for plaintiffs. Defendant appeals. Reversed and remanded.

Instructions 1 and 2, given at the instance of plaintiffs, are as follows: "(1) If you find from the evidence that plaintiffs rendered professional services as physicians and surgeons to the deceased, A. M. Harrison, in a sudden emergency following the deceased's injury in a street car wreck, in an endeavor to save his life, then you are instructed that plaintiffs are entitled to recover from the estate of the said A. M. Harrison such sum as you may find from the evidence is a reasonable compensation for the services rendered. (2) The character and importance of the operation, the responsibility resting upon the surgeon performing the operation, his experience and professional training, and the ability to pay of the person operated upon, are elements to be considered by you in determining what is a reasonable charge for the services performed by plaintiffs in the particular case."

HILL, C.J. (after stating the facts). . . . [I]nstruction 1 amounted to a peremptory instruction to find for the plaintiff in some amount.

1. The first question is as to the correctness of this instruction. As indicated therein the facts are that Mr. Harrison, appellant's intestate, was thrown from a street car, receiving serious injuries which rendered him unconscious, and while in that condition the appellees were notified of the accident and summoned to his assistance by some spectator, and performed a difficult operation in an effort to save his life, but they were unsuccessful, and he died without regaining consciousness. The appellant says:

> Harrison was never conscious after his head struck the pavement. He did not and could not, expressly or impliedly, assent to the action of the appellees. He was without knowledge or will power. However merciful or benevolent may have been the intention of the appellees, a new rule of law, of contract by implication of law, will have to be established by this court in order to sustain the recovery.

Appellant is right in saying that the recovery must be sustained by a contract by implication of law, but is not right in saying that it is a new rule of law, for such contracts are almost as old as the English system of jurisprudence. They are usually called "implied contracts." More properly they should be called "quasi contracts" or "constructive contracts."

The following excerpts from *Sceva v. True*, 53 N. H. 627, are peculiarly applicable here:

> We regard it as well settled by the cases . . . that an insane person, an idiot, or a person utterly bereft of all sense and reason by the sudden stroke of an accident or disease may be held liable, in assumpsit, for necessaries furnished to him in good faith while in that unfortunate and helpless condition. And the reasons upon which this rest are too broad, as well as too sensible and humane, to be overborne by any deductions which a refined logic may make from the circumstances that in such cases there can be no contract or promise, in fact, no meeting of the minds of the parties. The cases put it on the ground of an implied contract; and by this is not meant . . . an actual contract—that is, an actual meeting of the minds of the parties, an actual, mutual understanding, to be inferred from language, acts, and circumstances by the jury—but a contract and promise, said to be implied by the law, where, in point of fact, there was no contract, no mutual understanding, and so no promise. The defendant's counsel says it is usurpation for the court to hold, as a matter of law, that there is a contract and a promise, when all the evidence in the case shows that there was not a contract, nor the semblance of one. It is doubtless a legal fiction, invented and used for the sake of the remedy. If it was originally usurpation, certainly it has now become very inveterate, and firmly fixed in the body of the law. Illustrations might be multiplied, but enough has been said to show that when a contract or promise implied by law is spoken of, a very different thing is meant from a contract in fact, whether express or tacit. The evidence of an actual contract is generally to be found either in some writing made by the parties, or in verbal communications which passed between them, or in their acts and conduct considered in the light of the circumstances of each particular case. **A contract implied by law, on the contrary, rests upon no evidence. It has no actual existence. It is simply a mythical creation of the law. The law says it shall be taken that there was a promise, when in point of fact, there was none. Of course this is not good logic, for the obvious and sufficient reason that it is not true. It is a legal fiction, resting wholly for its support on a plain legal obligation, and a plain legal right. If it were true, it would not be a fiction. . . .**

Quasi Contract

Also called a **constructive** or **implied-in-law contracts**, a quasi-contract is not a contract at all, but rather "an obligation imposed by law because of some special relationship between the parties or because one of them would otherwise be unjustly enriched." BLACK'S LAW DICTIONARY (10th ed. 2014).

Assumpsit

From the Latin *assumere*, to "take on" or "assume." A common-law form of action (see "Forms of action" at 89, *supra*) to recover damages for the breach of contract (here, a constructive contract) not under seal.

A mythical creation

Where policy dictates recovery, but the prevailing legal doctrine (i.e., consideration) suggests otherwise, what should a court do? Is employing a legal fiction for the sake of recovery justified here? Why or why not?

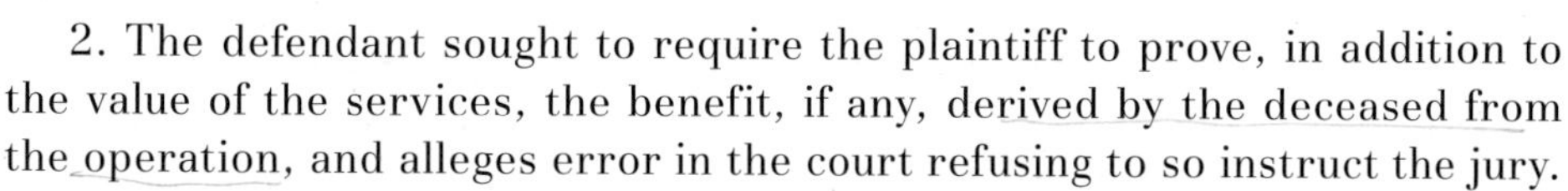

2. The defendant sought to require the plaintiff to prove, in addition to the value of the services, the benefit, if any, derived by the deceased from the operation, and alleges error in the court refusing to so instruct the jury.

The court was right in refusing to place this burden upon the physicians. The same question was considered in *Ladd v. Witte*, 92 N.W. 365, where the court said:

> That is not at all the test. So that a surgical operation be conceived and performed with due skill and care, the price to be paid therefor does not depend upon the result. The event so generally lies with the forces of nature that all intelligent men know and understand that the surgeon is not responsible therefor. In absence of express agreement, the surgeon, who brings to such a service due skill and care, earns the reasonable and customary price therefor, whether the outcome be beneficial to the patient or the reverse.

3. The court permitted to go to the jury the fact that Mr. Harrison was a bachelor, and that his estate would go to his collateral relatives, and also permitted proof to be made of the value of the estate, which amounted to about $18,500, including $10,000 from accident and life insurance policies. [Although there was a conflict of authorities on this question, this court found] that the financial condition of a patient cannot be considered where there is no contract and recovery is sustained on a legal fiction which raises a contract in order to afford a remedy which the justice of the case requires. . . .

[The court noted that although physicians sometimes "graduate[d] their charges by the ability of the patient to pay," this could only be the case in an actual contract, where "the financial condition of the patient [could be] a factor to be contemplated by both parties when the services were rendered and accepted."] This could not apply to a physician called in an emergency by some bystander to attend a stricken man whom he never saw or heard of before; and certainly the unconscious patient could not, in fact or in law, be held to have contemplated what charges the physician might properly bring against him. In order to admit such testimony, it must be assumed that the surgeon and patient each had in contemplation that the means of the patient would be one factor in determining the amount of the charge for the services rendered. While the law may admit such evidence as throwing light upon the contract and indicating what was really in contemplation when it was made, yet a different question is presented when there is no contract to be ascertained or construed, but a mere fiction of law creating a contract where none existed in order that there might be a remedy for a right. This fiction merely requires a reasonable compensation for the services rendered. The services are the same be the patient prince or pauper, and for them the surgeon is entitled to fair compensation for his time, service, and skill. It was therefore error to admit this evidence, and to instruct the jury in the second instruction that in determining what was a reasonable charge they could consider the "ability to pay of the person operated upon."

It was improper to let it go to the jury that Mr. Harrison was a bachelor and that his estate was left to nieces and nephews. This was relevant to no issue in the case, and its effect might well have been prejudicial. While this verdict is no higher than some of the evidence would justify, yet it is much higher than some of the other evidence would justify, and hence it is impossible to say that this was a harmless error.

Judgment is reversed, and cause remanded.

BATTLE AND WOOD, JJ., concur in sustaining the recovery, and in holding that it was error to permit the jury to consider the fact that his estate would go to collateral heirs; but they do not concur in holding that it was error to admit evidence of the value of the estate, and instructing that it might be considered in fixing the charge.

RELEVANT PROVISIONS

For the *Restatement (Second) of Contracts,* consult § 370. For the *Restatement (Third) of Restitution and Unjust Enrichment,* consult §§ 1 and 20.

NOTES AND QUESTIONS

1. *What happened?* Who sued whom for what? Procedurally, how did the case get before this court? Factually, what happened between the parties? What arguments did the plaintiff and defendant make? What rule or rules did the court apply? How did the court analyze the dispute between the parties? How did the court decide the case?

2. *Was this case correctly decided?* Do you agree with the result reached in this case? Why or why not? Do you agree with the court's reasoning? Why or why not? How, if at all, would you have written the opinion differently?

3. *Unjust enrichment?* Was Harrison unjustly enriched? Imagine if Harrison could come back to life for a moment: What would he say? Maybe something like the following: "Thanks for trying to save me, doc, but you didn't. I'm dead, about as far away from being 'unjustly enriched' as one could imagine. I don't owe you diddly squat." How would the plaintiffs respond?

4. *Three different types of contracts.* Make sure you know the difference between an express contract, an implied-in-fact contract, and an implied-in-law contract (sometimes also called a "quasi-contract" or "constructive contract.")

5. *Who summoned the doctors?* The facts tell us that the doctors who rendered emergency services to Harrison "were notified of the accident and summoned to his assistance by some spectator." What result if the doctors sued this spectator instead? Would it matter who the spectator was? Suppose it was a close friend or family member of Harrison. Same result?

6. *Should defendant's financial condition have been relevant?* Do you think the court should have considered Harrison's financial condition in determining what Harrison's estate owes to the plaintiffs? Why or why not?

7. *Thinking tools.* Drawing on any of the thinking tools we previously examined, do you think this case was correctly decided? Ex post, did it do justice between these parties? Ex ante, will it provide the right incentives for future parties?

8. *Illustrations.* This case now appears as Illustrations 1, 2, and 8 to *Restatement (Third) of Restitution and Unjust Enrichment* § 20 as follows:

> 1. Doctor is summoned by Bystander to attend accident Victim, who is lying unconscious. Doctor performs emergency surgery. Doctor's reasonable and customary charge for the services rendered is $1000, which Victim refuses to pay. Doctor has a claim in restitution for $1000 against Victim.
>
> 2. Same facts as Illustration 1, except that the circumstances of the accident are such that both Bystander and Doctor act courageously and at great personal risk in coming to the aid of Victim. Their heroic intervention is not, in itself, a source of unjust enrichment. Bystander has no claim in restitution under this section, while Doctor's entitlement to restitution is limited (as in Illustration 1) to his reasonable and customary charge of $1000 for professional services rendered.
>
> 8. Physician provides emergency medical assistance to unconscious accident Victim. The services are medically appropriate and properly performed, but Victim dies without regaining consciousness. Physician seeks restitution from Victim's Estate by the rule of this section. Resisting the claim, Estate argues that Physician's unsuccessful intervention conferred no benefit; accordingly . . . restitution would leave Estate worse off (by the amount of Physician's eventual recovery) than if Physician had not intervened. The objection is misplaced. Medical services provided in an emergency are presumed to be desirable; though unrequested (the recipient having no opportunity to request them), they are valued for restitution purposes as if they had been requested. Physician is entitled to restitution from Estate in the amount of his reasonable and customary charge.

9. *When is enrichment unjust?* One interesting issue raised by this case is how a court should determine when enrichment is unjust. Can an encyclopedia salesperson, for instance, simply run up to an unconscious customer and place a set of the Encyclopedia Britannica on his chest along with a bill, claiming that the benefit should be paid for because it will "enrich the customer's mind"? Well, of course not! But why? What principle allows plaintiffs to recover in a case like *Cotnam v. Wisdom*, but would deny recovery to the encyclopedia salesperson? The "relevant provisions" cited above, along with the next case, *Bailey v. West*, and the excerpt following *Bailey* should shed some light—and a little bit of history—on this important question.

Bailey v. West

Supreme Court of Rhode Island
249 A.2d 414 (1969)

PAOLINO, JUSTICE. This is a civil action wherein the plaintiff alleges that the defendant is indebted to him for the reasonable value of his services rendered in connection with the feeding, care and maintenance of a certain race horse named "Bascom's Folly" from May 3, 1962 through July 3, 1966. The case was tried before a justice of the superior court sitting without a jury, and resulted in a decision for the plaintiff for his cost of boarding the horse for the five months immediately subsequent to May 3, 1962, and for certain expenses incurred by him in trimming its hoofs. The cause is now before us on the plaintiff's appeal and defendant's cross appeal from the judgment entered pursuant to such decision.

The facts material to a resolution of the precise issues raised herein are as follows. In late April 1962, defendant, accompanied by his horse trainer, went to Belmont Park in New York to buy race horses. On April 27, 1962, defendant purchased "Bascom's Folly" from a Dr. Strauss and arranged to have the horse shipped to Suffolk Downs in East Boston, Massachusetts. Upon its arrival defendant's trainer discovered that the horse was lame, and so notified defendant, who ordered him to reship the horse by van to the seller at Belmont Park. The seller refused to accept delivery at Belmont on May 3, 1962, and thereupon, the van driver, one Kelly, called defendant's trainer and asked for further instructions. Although the trial testimony is in conflict as to what the trainer told him, it is not disputed that on the same day Kelly brought "Bascom's Folly" to plaintiff's farm where the horse remained until July 3, 1966, when it was sold by plaintiff to a third party.

While "Bascom's Folly" was residing at his horse farm, plaintiff sent bills for its feed and board to defendant at regular intervals. According to testimony elicited from defendant at the trial, the first such bill was received by him some two or three months after "Bascom's Folly" was placed on plaintiff's farm. He also stated that he immediately returned the bill to plaintiff with the notation that he was not the owner of the horse nor was it sent to plaintiff's farm at his request. The plaintiff testified that he sent bills monthly to defendant and that the first notice he received from him disclaiming ownership was ". . . maybe after a month or two or so" subsequent to the time when the horse was left in plaintiff's care.

In his decision the trial judge found that defendant's trainer had informed Kelly during their telephone conversation of May 3, 1962, that ". . . he would have to do whatever he wanted to do with the horse, that he wouldn't be on any farm at the defendant's expense. . . ." He also found, however, that when "Bascom's Folly" was brought to his farm, plaintiff was not aware of the telephone conversation between Kelly and defendant's trainer, and hence, even though he knew there was a controversy surrounding the ownership of the horse, he was entitled to assume that ". . . there is an implication here that, 'I am to take care of this horse.'" Continuing his decision, the trial justice stated that in view of the result reached by this court in a recent opinion[1] wherein we

1. *See Strauss v. West*, 216 A.2d 366 (1966). [Specifically, "[t]he trial justice found as a fact that the horse was sound at the time it was purchased and rendered decision for plaintiff in the sum of $1,800 with interest."—ED.]

held that the instant defendant was liable to the original seller, Dr. Strauss, for the purchase price of this horse, there was a contract "implied in fact" between the plaintiff and defendant to board "Bascom's Folly" and that this contract continued until plaintiff received notification from defendant that he would not be responsible for the horse's board. The trial justice further stated that ". . . I think there was notice given at least at the end of the four months, and I think we must add another month on there for a reasonable disposition of his property." In view of the conclusion we reach with respect to defendant's first two contentions, we shall confine ourselves solely to a discussion and resolution of the issues necessarily implicit therein, and shall not examine other subsidiary arguments advanced by plaintiff and defendant.

I

The defendant alleges in his brief and oral argument that the trial judge erred in finding a contract "implied in fact" between the parties. We agree.

The following quotation from 17 C.J.S. *Contracts* § 4, illustrates the elements necessary to the establishment of a contract "implied in fact":

> . . . A "contract implied in fact," . . . or an implied contract in the proper sense, arises where the intention of the parties is not expressed, but an agreement in fact, creating an obligation, is implied or presumed from their acts, or, as it has been otherwise stated, where there are circumstances which, according to the ordinary course of dealing and the common understanding of men, show a mutual intent to contract.
>
> It has been said that a contract implied in fact must contain all the elements of an express contract. So, such a contract is dependent on mutual agreement or consent, and on the intention of the parties: and a meeting of the minds is required. A contract implied in fact is to every intent and purpose an agreement between the parties, and it cannot be found to exist unless a contract status is shown. Such a contract does not arise out of an implied legal duty or obligation, but out of facts from which consent may be inferred; there must be a manifestation of assent arising wholly or in part from acts other than words, and a contract cannot be implied in fact where the facts are inconsistent with its existence.

Therefore, essential elements of contracts "implied in fact" are mutual agreement, and intent to promise, but the agreement and the promise have not been made in words and are implied from the facts.

In the instant case, plaintiff sued on the theory of a contract "implied in law." There was no evidence introduced by him to support the establishment of a contract "implied in fact," and he cannot now argue solely on the basis of the trial justice's decision for such a result.

The source of the obligation in a contract "implied in fact," as in express contracts, is in the intention of the parties. We hold that there was no mutual agreement and "intent to promise" between the plaintiff and defendant so as to establish a contract "implied in fact" for defendant to pay plaintiff for the maintenance of this horse. From the time Kelly delivered the horse to him plaintiff knew there was a dispute as to its ownership, and his subsequent actions indicated he did not know with whom, if anyone, he had a contract. After he had accepted the horse, he made inquiries as to its ownership and, initially, and for some time thereafter, sent his bills to both defendant and Dr. Strauss, the original seller.

There is also uncontroverted testimony in the record that prior to the assertion of the claim which is the subject of this suit neither defendant nor his trainer had ever had any business transactions with plaintiff, and had never used his farm to board horses. Additionally, there is uncontradicted evidence that this horse, when found to be lame, was shipped by defendant's trainer not to plaintiff's farm, but back to the seller at Belmont Park. What is most important, the trial justice expressly stated that he believed the testimony of defendant's trainer that he had instructed Kelly that defendant would not be responsible for boarding the horse on any farm.

From our examination of the record we are constrained to conclude that the trial justice overlooked and misconceived material evidence which establishes beyond question that there never existed between the parties an element essential to the formulation of any true contract, namely, an "intent to contract."

II

The defendant's second contention is that, even assuming the trial justice was in essence predicating defendant's liability upon a quasi-contractual theory, his decision is still unsupported by competent evidence and is clearly erroneous.

The following discussion of quasi-contracts appears in 12 Am. Jur., *Contracts* § 6 (1938):

> . . . A quasi contract has no reference to the intentions or expressions of the parties. The obligation is imposed despite, and frequently in frustration of, their intention. For a quasi contract neither promise nor privity, real or imagined, is necessary. In quasi contracts the obligation arises, not from consent of the parties, as in the case of contracts, express or implied in fact, but from the law of natural immutable justice and equity. The act, or acts, from which the law implies the contract must, however, be voluntary. Where a case shows that it is the duty of the defendant to pay, the law imputes to him a promise to fulfil that obligation. The duty, which thus forms the foundation of a quasicontractual obligation, is frequently based on the doctrine of unjust enrichment. . . .
>
> . . . The law will not imply a promise against the express declaration of the party to be charged, made at the time of the supposed undertaking, unless such party is under legal obligation paramount to his will to perform some duty, and he is not under such legal obligation unless there is a demand in equity and good conscience that he should perform the duty.

Therefore, the essential elements of a quasi-contract are a benefit conferred upon defendant by plaintiff, appreciation by defendant of such benefit, and acceptance and retention by defendant of such benefit under such circumstances that it would be inequitable to retain the benefit without payment of the value thereof.

The key question raised by this appeal with respect to the establishment of a quasi-contract is whether or not plaintiff was acting as a "volunteer" at the time he accepted the horse for boarding at his farm. There is a long line of authority which has clearly enunciated the general rule that ". . . if a performance is rendered by one person without any request by another, it is very unlikely that this person will be under a legal duty to pay compensation." 1 A Corbin, *Contracts* § 234.

The *Restatement of Restitution* § 2 (1937) provides: "A person who officiously confers a benefit upon another is not entitled to restitution therefor." Comment a in the above-mentioned section states in part as follows:

> . . . Policy ordinarily requires that a person who has conferred a benefit . . . by way of giving another services . . . should not be permitted to require the other to pay therefor, unless the one conferring the benefit had a valid reason for so doing. A person is not required to deal with another unless he so desires and, ordinarily, a person should not be required to become an obligor unless he so desires.

Applying those principles to the facts in the case at bar it is clear that plaintiff cannot recover. The plaintiff's testimony on cross-examination is the only evidence in the record relating to what transpired between Kelly and him at the time the horse was accepted for boarding. The defendant's attorney asked plaintiff if he had any conversation with Kelly at that time, and plaintiff answered in substance that he had noticed that the horse was very lame and that Kelly had told him: "That's why they wouldn't accept him at Belmont Track." The plaintiff also testified that he had inquired of Kelly as to the ownership of "Bascom's Folly," and had been told that "Dr. Strauss made a deal and that's all I know." It further appears from the record that plaintiff acknowledged receipt of the horse by signing a uniform livestock **bill of lading**, which clearly indicated on its face that the horse in question had been **consigned** by defendant's trainer not to plaintiff, but to Dr. Strauss's trainer at Belmont Park. Knowing at the time he accepted the horse for boarding that a controversy surrounded its ownership, plaintiff could not reasonably expect remuneration from defendant, nor can it be said that defendant acquiesced in the conferment of a benefit upon him. **The undisputed testimony was that defendant, upon receipt of plaintiff's first bill, immediately notified him that he was not the owner of "Bascom's Folly" and would not be responsible for its keep.**

Bill of lading

"A document acknowledging the receipt of goods by a carrier or by the shipper's agent and the contract for the transportation of those goods; a document that indicates the receipt of goods for shipment and that is issued by a person engaged in the business of transporting or forwarding goods." BLACK'S LAW DICTIONARY (10th ed. 2014).

Consigned

"1. To transfer to another's custody or charge. 2. To give (goods) to a carrier for delivery to a designated recipient. 3. To give (merchandise or the like) to another to sell, usu. with the understanding that the seller will pay the owner for the goods from the proceeds." BLACK'S LAW DICTIONARY (10th ed. 2014).

Would silence have constituted acceptance?

How important was this fact to the court? Do you think the case would have turned out differently if the defendant, upon receipt of the plaintiff's first bill, simply remained silent? Is *Hobbs v. Massasoit Whip Co.* of any help here?

It is our judgment that the plaintiff was a mere volunteer who boarded and maintained "Bascom's Folly" at his own risk and with full knowledge that he might not be reimbursed for expenses he incurred incident thereto.

The plaintiff's appeal is denied and dismissed, the defendant's cross appeal is sustained, and the cause is remanded to the superior court for entry of judgment for the defendant.

NOTES AND QUESTIONS

1. ***What happened?*** Who sued whom for what? Procedurally, how did the case get before this court? Factually, what happened between the parties? What arguments did the plaintiff and defendant make? What rule or rules did the court apply? How did the court analyze the dispute between the parties? How did the court decide the case?

2. ***Was this case correctly decided?*** Do you agree with the result reached by Judge Paolino? What about his reasoning? What are the strengths and weaknesses of his approach? How, if at all, would you have decided the case, and written the opinion, differently?

3. ***Plaintiff's arguments.*** Plaintiff brought two separate claims against defendant. What were they? Which argument was stronger? Was the court right to reject both theories of liability? Had plaintiff won, what would he have recovered? Would his recovery have been the same under either theory?

4. ***Comparing the cases.*** Why did plaintiffs in *Cotnam* recover whereas the plaintiff in *Bailey* did not? Are these rulings consistent? If so, what explains the different result?

5. ***In praise of folly?*** The court said plaintiff was "a mere volunteer." Do you agree? Doesn't the fact that plaintiff sent bills to defendant for the care of "Bascom's Folly" show he wasn't acting as a mere volunteer? On the other hand, doesn't the fact that defendant refused to pay these bills show that plaintiff's belief was unreasonable? And if this is true, then wouldn't a judgment for plaintiff have been a ruling in praise of folly?

6. ***Comparative perspective.*** Many Europeans do not seem to think so. Indeed, Professor Dawson notes that, "[u]nlike his American counterpart . . . the European volunteer who without request intervenes in another's affairs has been, under the doctrine of *negotiorum gestio,* rewarded for his efforts and encouraged in his behavior." He goes on to explain:

> It is well known that in the treatment they accord to altruists there is a major difference between the Anglo-American common law and most legal systems of western Europe. An altruist can be defined in this context as a good neighbor who renders a service to another, acting without request and through purely unselfish motives, but not intending a gift. The disapproval with which

> most Englishmen and North Americans regard such persons is reflected in the words we use to describe them. The mildest comment will probably be that the unsolicited intervenor is "a mere volunteer." It is even more likely that he will be described as an "officious intermeddler," and he will be lucky if he is not described as an outright tortfeasor. In French or German, Italian or Dutch he is apt to be described as a "manager of another's affair," and the impulse will be both to praise and reward him.*

Which approach seems better to you, the American approach reflected in *Bailey v. West* or the European approach reflected in the doctrine of *negotiorum gestio*? To answer this, you may want to draw on some . . .

7. *Thinking tools.* Drawing on any of the thinking tools we previously examined, do you think the rule adopted by the *Bailey* court is a good one? Should the defendant get to reap all the benefits of selling "Bascom's Folly" years down the road without having to pay any of the expenses for its upkeep? As with *Cotnam*, you can think about this question in two different ways. From an ex post or after-the-fact perspective, which focuses on doing justice between the parties involved in this dispute, one could ask whether the court's resolution was a just one. Or, from an ex ante or before-the-fact perspective, which is more concerned with establishing a default rule to govern future disputes, one could ask whether the rule announced in *Bailey* is a good one. Going down this road, one could ask, for instance, how such a rule would likely affect similarly situated parties in future cases. Would the *Bailey* rule provide such parties with the right incentives, or would the European approach be better? One could ask the same questions about the parties in *Cotnam*. Was the rule announced there a good one? Why or why not?

8. *Counseling.* If plaintiff came to you for advice while he was boarding and caring for "Bascom's Folly," what would you have told him? Would your advice have been different if Bailey and West had a previous relationship, à la Hobbs and the Massasoit Whip Company (see p. 282, *supra*)? Why or why not?

WHEN IS ENRICHMENT UNJUST?†

The principle is now fully recognized in this country that a "person who has been unjustly enriched at the expense of another is required to make restitution to the other." This is the language of the first section of the Restatement of Restitution. When one person confers a benefit upon another without the latter's solicitation, the benefit received constitutes an enrichment—a windfall, so to speak. This

* John P. Dawson, *Negotiorum Gestio: The Altruistic Intermeddler,* 74 HARV. L. REV. 817, 817 (1961).

† Excerpted John W. Wade, *Restitution for Benefits Conferred Without Request,* 19 VAND. L. REV. 1183, 1183-84, 1211-12 (1966).

benefit may take one of several forms. It may involve (1) transferring property to the defendant, (2) saving, preserving or improving his property, (3) rendering personal services for him, or (4) performing for him a duty imposed directly by law or by his own contractual arrangements. In any of these situations there is an enrichment, and the principle quoted above comes into play if the enrichment is "unjust." When is it unjust? Obviously, it would not be so characterized if it were intended as a gift; just as obviously, the opposite is true if the plaintiff acted under legal compulsion and against his will. In making the determination, considerable weight is given to the circumstance that the benefit was not requested by the defendant.

The common law has long had a pronounced policy that benefits may not be forced upon a party against his will, so as to require him to pay for them. This idea has been forcefully expressed on a number of occasions. Said the court in the leading English case, "Liabilities are not to be forced upon people behind their backs any more than you can confer a benefit upon a man against his will."[3] Most of the time this idea has been indicated by applying an epithet to the plaintiff. The term most frequently used is that of "volunteer." Applied to the plaintiff, particularly if it carries the adjective "mere," it has proved the "kiss of death" and the sure indication that he will not be allowed to recover. Other derogatory terms used include meddler, intermeddler, interloper, mere stranger, mere impertinence. The Restatement uses the adjective, "officious," which carries a somewhat more restricted connotation.[6] All of these terms embody the policy that one should not be required to pay for benefits which he did not solicit and does not desire. . . . The restrictions on recovery . . . have all been presented from a negative standpoint. It may now be possible to summarize them and present a general principle stated in a positive fashion.

Perhaps the following two sentences will prove helpful in this regard:

> One who, without intent to act gratuitously, confers a measurable benefit upon another, is entitled to restitution, if he affords the other an opportunity to decline the benefit or else has a reasonable excuse for failing to do so. If the other refuses to receive the benefit, he is not required to make restitution unless the actor justifiably performs for the other a duty imposed upon him by law.

PROBLEM: YOU DON'T CHOOSE YOUR FAMILY

Doris Briggs lived alone in a small house in Nashville, Tennessee. Doris supported herself on social security benefits and had a small amount of investment income. Occasionally, if Doris grew sick her nieces and nephews would stay with her. In April 2008, Doris prepared a will leaving her valuable antiques collection to her

3. Falcke v. Scottish Imperial Ins. Co., 34 Ch. D. 234, 248 (C.A. 1886) (Bowen, L.J.). . . .

6. "A person who officiously confers a benefit upon another is not entitled to restitution therefor." RESTATEMENT, RESTITUTION § 2 (1937). "Officiousness means interference in the affairs of others not justified by the circumstances under which the interference takes place." *Id.*, comment a.

nieces, Elizabeth Carlton and Sarah Watson. The remainder of her estate Doris planned to leave to Cross Point Church. In January 2009, Doris became seriously ill and her niece Elizabeth traveled to Nashville as there was no one else to take care of Doris. Elizabeth tried to look after Doris for three weeks but found she was unable to provide the continuous specialized care that Doris required. Elizabeth placed Doris in a nursing home where she could be near her friends and more distant relatives. In February 2009, when Doris's social security and investment income was not enough to pay the nursing home bills, Elizabeth began using her own funds to pay. Elizabeth set up a separate account for Doris's expenses and maintained detailed expense records. Doris was aware that Elizabeth was using her own funds to pay Doris's nursing home costs and told Elizabeth she "would get everything she had, if there was anything left." In March 2012, Doris died in the nursing home. Her will was admitted to probate and Elizabeth filed a timely claim seeking reimbursement of $47,024 she spent on Doris's behalf from February 2009 to March 2012. The administrator of the estate opposed the claim on the grounds that the expenditures were gift since Doris never agreed to reimburse Elizabeth.

How would Elizabeth respond to the administrator's claim? What is Elizabeth's best argument in favor of being reimbursed? What additional facts, if proved, would help Elizabeth's case? The estate administrator's?

PROBLEM: PAID AID

Brandon Knight was admitted to Saint Luke's Hospital of Kansas City with an abdominal aneurysm. When Brandon was brought to the hospital by EMTs, his condition was grave so for his health and safety he was placed in the intensive care unit. His condition was serious enough that the hospital ordered around-the-clock nursing care for two weeks. During this two-week period, Brandon was monitored with various medical equipment attached to his body. Following the two-week inpatient stay, Brandon had two weeks of at-home care. Brandon never complained about the nurses' presence during the at-home care period or tried to fire them. Once the hospital was sufficiently satisfied that Brandon was out of danger, the hospital withdrew the at-home nursing care. Shortly afterwards, the hospital sent Brandon a bill for $8,545. Brandon refused to pay, arguing that he never signed a written contract nor orally agreed to be liable for the hospital's inpatient or at-home services.

What argument would the hospital raise in response to Brandon's assertion that he never signed a written contract? How might Brandon respond to the hospital's argument? As the judge in this case, how would you rule?

PROBLEM: INVOLUNTARY HOSPITALIZATION

On Thursday, January 8, 2015, at 3:00 a.m., the county magistrate ("Magistrate") was contacted by a doctor from General Hospital ("Hospital") in regard to one of their patients, Kylo Stimpy. The record indicates that Kylo left his marital residence, after having an argument with his wife, and checked into a motel. Kylo later telephoned his wife "making threats of self harm" and purchased a shotgun. Kylo was subsequently taken to Hospital by the police, who had been advised of his threats.

Pursuant to an emergency hospitalization procedure code, Magistrate found probable cause that Kylo was seriously mentally impaired and likely to physically injure himself. Magistrate therefore entered an emergency hospitalization order on January 8, requiring that Kylo be detained in custody at Hospital's psychiatric unit for examination and care for a period not to exceed forty-eight hours.

During admission to Hospital, Kylo was given a hospital release form to sign which would have made either Kylo or his insurance company responsible for the bill. Kylo refused to sign the form. According to Kylo, at approximately five o'clock that morning, a nurse awakened him and demanded that he sign the hospital release form or Hospital could not insure the safety or return of his personal items. Kylo eventually read and signed the form. The form stated that Kylo understood he remained liable for any charges not covered by insurance.

Thereafter, Kylo's wife filed an application for involuntary hospitalization of Kylo, and an order for immediate hospitalization was entered by a hospitalization referee.

An evidentiary hearing was held before the judicial hospitalization referee on January 13, concerning Kylo's commitment status. Medical reports and testimony were received by the referee. Pursuant to a written order, the hospitalization referee found that Kylo suffers from mental illness described as bipolar disorder, an illness from which Kylo has suffered for many years. In addition, the referee concluded "that although Kylo Stimpy clearly is in need of and would benefit from treatment for a serious mental illness, the required elements for involuntary hospitalization are lacking," and that further involuntary hospitalization was not authorized. Kylo was released from Hospital and court jurisdiction as of January 13, 1995.

Hospital later sought compensation from Kylo in the amount of $2,775.79 for medical services provided to him from January 8 to January 13, 1995. Kylo got very angry and refused to pay the bill or authorize his health insurance carrier to do so. Hospital filed a petition against Kylo seeking judgment on the hospital bill.

At a hearing concerning Hospital's petition, Kylo admitted that he was hospitalized from January 8 through January 13, 1995, but argued that he made no agreement to pay for services provided to him. Kylo explained that upon being admitted to the hospital, he refused to complete the hospital release form so that his health insurance carrier could be contacted for payment because he believed that he did not need evaluation or treatment. Kylo argued he later signed the release form under duress and that he did not agree to pay for medical services provided. Kylo stated he had health insurance and was not indigent at the time he was hospitalized.

Ignore the duress defense for the moment (we will discuss duress in greater detail in Chapter 8. Do you think Kylo Stimpy should be liable to General Hospital under a theory of quasi contract?

3. Past and Moral Consideration

In Section A of this chapter, which covered bargain-based contracts, we learned that promises involving past or moral consideration were generally not enforceable because they were unsupported by consideration. We reexamine the issue here to consider whether an enterprising plaintiff might have a more promising avenue of recovery under a theory of unjust enrichment. In an ideal case, a plaintiff pursuing this theory would ignore the doctrine of consideration altogether and argue that it is entitled to recover because (a) it conferred a benefit for which (b) the other party promised to pay, such that (c) it would be unjust to allow the other party to break its promise and retain the benefit. The next case, *Webb v. McGowin*, provides an ideal fact pattern for a court receptive to such an argument. But before we read *Webb*, let's consider a brief excerpt, which helps illustrate why the doctrine of consideration is probably not the ideal way to treat cases involving "past" or "moral" consideration. This, in turn, may shed light on why the *Webb* court decided the case as it did.

PAST PROMISES AND UNJUST ENRICHMENT*

In spite of impressive efforts to organize and classify the grounds for enforcement of promises, the law of contracts has failed to deal effectively with the wide range of problems which arise typically under the labels of "past consideration" and "moral obligation." Most of the difficulties are traceable to the historical assumption that promises made in response to earlier events require, indeed demand, the application of conventional contract rules and modes of analysis. The assumption of course sets the stage for a hostile reception in court for the promise grounded in the past, for it is familiar that the element of present exchange which is central to consideration doctrine precludes enforcement of a promise made in recognition of something previously received.

Thus the promise supported solely by an earlier receipt of benefit has come to occupy a curious and uncertain position in the scheme of contractual liabilities. We insist that such promises be consumed by, and reconciled with, orthodox doctrine. Yet the structure of the rules of contract denies any real exploration of

* Excerpted from Stanley Henderson, *Promises Grounded in the Past: The Idea of Unjust Enrichment and the Law of Contracts*, 57 Va. L. Rev. 1115, 1115-16 (1971).

the value choices that point toward enforcement. At the same time, though the doctrinal presumption against promises to return a benefit is made to appear conclusive, the decisions, as well as the literature they produce, perpetuate ideas which tend to cut inroads into the presumption. Consequently, as students of contract have long been aware, unless the past transaction is viewed independently of standard theories of bargain contract, the purposes to be served in imposing liability for benefit conferred will continue to be obscured by doctrinal attitudes which glance away from basic issues of policy.

Mills v. Wyman

Supreme Judicial Court of Massachusetts
20 Mass. 207 (1825)

For a report of the case, see p. 367, *supra*.

Webb v. McGowin

Court of Appeals of Alabama
168 So. 196 (1935)

BRICKEN, PRESIDING JUDGE. This action is in **assumpsit**. The complaint as originally filed was amended. The demurrers to the complaint as amended were sustained, and because of this adverse ruling by the court the plaintiff took a **nonsuit**, and the assignment of errors on this appeal are predicated upon said action or ruling of the court.

> **Assumpsit**
>
> From the Latin *assumere*, to "take on" or "assume." A common-law form of action (see "Forms of action" at 89, *supra*) to recover damages for the breach of contract not under seal.

> **Nonsuit**
>
> A nonsuit can be either voluntary or involuntary. As the court uses the term here, it refers to "[a] plaintiff's voluntary dismissal of a case . . . or of a defendant, without a decision on the merits." BLACK'S LAW DICTIONARY (10th ed. 2014).

A fair statement of the case presenting the questions for decision is set out in appellant's brief, which we adopt.

> On the 3d day of August, 1925, appellant while in the employ of the W. T. Smith Lumber Company, a corporation, and acting within the scope of his employment, was engaged in clearing the upper floor of mill No. 2 of the company. While so engaged he was in the act of dropping a pine block from the upper floor of the mill to the ground below; this being the usual and ordinary way of clearing the floor, and it being the duty of the plaintiff in the course of his employment to so drop it. The block weighed about 75 pounds.
>
> As appellant was in the act of dropping the block to the ground below, he was on the edge of the upper floor of the mill. As he started to turn the block loose so that it would drop to the ground, he saw J. Greeley McGowin, testator of the defendants, on the ground below and directly under where the block would have fallen had appellant turned it loose. Had he turned it loose it would

> have struck McGowin with such force as to have caused him serious bodily harm or death. Appellant could have remained safely on the upper floor of the mill by turning the block loose and allowing it to drop, but had he done this the block would have fallen on McGowin and caused him serious injuries or death. The only safe and reasonable way to prevent this was for appellant to hold to the block and divert its direction in falling from the place where McGowin was standing and the only safe way to divert it so as to prevent its coming into contact with McGowin was for appellant to fall with it to the ground below. Appellant did this, and by holding to the block and falling with it to the ground below, he diverted the course of its fall in such way that McGowin was not injured. In thus preventing the injuries to McGowin appellant himself received serious bodily injuries, resulting in his right leg being broken, the heel of his right foot torn off and his right arm broken. He was badly crippled for life and rendered unable to do physical or mental labor.
>
> On September 1, 1925, in consideration of appellant having prevented him from sustaining death or serious bodily harm and in consideration of the injuries appellant had received, McGowin agreed with him to care for and maintain him for the remainder of appellant's life at the rate of $15 every two weeks from the time he sustained his injuries to and during the remainder of appellant's life; it being agreed that McGowin would pay this sum to appellant for his maintenance. Under the agreement McGowin paid or caused to be paid to appellant the sum so agreed on up until McGowin's death on January 1, 1934. After his death the payments were continued to and including January 27, 1934, at which time they were discontinued. Thereupon plaintiff brought suit to recover the unpaid installments accruing up to the time of the bringing of the suit. . . .

In other words, the complaint as amended averred in substance: (1) That on August 3, 1925, appellant saved J. Greeley McGowin, appellee's testator, from death or grievous bodily harm; (2) that in doing so appellant sustained bodily injury crippling him for life; (3) that in consideration of the services rendered and the injuries received by appellant, McGowin agreed to care for him the remainder of appellant's life, the amount to be paid being $15 every two weeks; (4) that McGowin complied with this agreement until he died on January 1, 1934, and the payments were kept up to January 27, 1934, after which they were discontinued.

The action was for the unpaid installments accruing after January 27, 1934, to the time of the suit.

The principal grounds of demurrer to the original and amended complaint are: (1) It states no cause of action; (2) its averments show the contract was without consideration; (3) it fails to allege that McGowin had, at or before the services were rendered, agreed to pay appellant for them; (4) the contract declared on is void under the statute of frauds.

1. The averments of the complaint show that appellant saved McGowin from death or grievous bodily harm. This was a material benefit to him of infinitely more value than any financial aid he could have received. Receiving this benefit, McGowin became morally bound to compensate appellant for the services rendered. Recognizing his moral obligation, he expressly agreed to pay

appellant as alleged in the complaint and complied with this agreement up to the time of his death; a period of more than 8 years.

Had McGowin been accidentally poisoned and a physician, without his knowledge or request, had administered an antidote, thus saving his life, a subsequent promise by McGowin to pay the physician would have been valid. Likewise, McGowin's agreement as disclosed by the complaint to compensate appellant for saving him from death or grievous bodily injury is valid and enforceable.

Where the promisee cares for, improves, and preserves the property of the promisor, though done without his request, it is sufficient consideration for the promisor's subsequent agreement to pay for the service, because of the material benefit received. . . .

It follows that if, as alleged in the complaint, appellant saved J. Greeley McGowin from death or grievous bodily harm, and McGowin subsequently agreed to pay him for the service rendered, it became a valid and enforceable contract.

2. It is well settled that a moral obligation is a sufficient consideration to support a subsequent promise to pay where the promisor has received a material benefit, although there was no original duty or liability resting on the promisor. . . .

The case at bar is clearly distinguishable from that class of cases where the consideration is a mere moral obligation or conscientious duty unconnected with receipt by promisor of benefits of a material or pecuniary nature. Here the promisor received a material benefit constituting a valid consideration for his promise.

3. Some authorities hold that, for a moral obligation to support a subsequent promise to pay, there must have existed a prior legal or equitable obligation, which for some reason had become unenforceable, but for which the promisor was still morally bound. This rule, however, is subject to qualification in those cases where the promisor, having received a material benefit from the promisee, is morally bound to compensate him for the services rendered and in consideration of this obligation promises to pay. In such cases the subsequent promise to pay is an affirmance or ratification of the services rendered carrying with it the presumption that a previous request for the service was made.

McGowin's express promise to pay appellant for the services rendered was an affirmance or ratification of what appellant had done raising the presumption that the services had been rendered at McGowin's request.

4. The averments of the complaint show that in saving McGowin from death or grievous bodily harm, appellant was crippled for life. This was part of the consideration of the contract declared on. McGowin was benefited. Appellant was injured. Benefit to the promisor or injury to the promisee is a sufficient legal consideration for the promisor's agreement to pay.

5. Under the averments of the complaint the services rendered by appellant were not gratuitous. The agreement of McGowin to pay and the acceptance of payment by appellant conclusively shows the contrary. . . .

From what has been said, we are of the opinion that the court below erred in the ruling complained of; that is to say, in sustaining the demurrer, and for this error the case is reversed and remanded.

Reversed and remanded.

SAMFORD, **Judge (concurring)**. The questions involved in this case are not free from doubt, and perhaps the strict letter of the rule, as stated by judges, though not always in accord, would bar a recovery by plaintiff, but following the principle announced by Chief Justice Marshall in *Hoffman v. Porter*, Fed. Cas. No. 6,577, 2 Brock. 156, 159, where he says, "I do not think that law ought to be separated from justice, where it is at most doubtful," I concur in the conclusions reached by the court.

Webb v. McGowin

Supreme Court of Alabama
168 So. 199 (1936)

FOSTER, JUSTICE. . . . The opinion of the Court of Appeals here under consideration recognizes and applies the distinction between a supposed moral obligation of the promisor, based upon some refined sense of ethical duty, without material benefit to him, and one in which such a benefit did in fact occur. We agree with that court that if the benefit be material and substantial, and was to the person of the promisor rather than to his estate, it is within the class of material benefits which he has the privilege of recognizing and compensating either by an executed payment or an executory promise to pay. The cases are cited in that opinion. The reason is emphasized when the compensation is not only for the benefits which the promisor received, but also for the injuries either to the property or person of the promisee by reason of the service rendered.

Writ denied.

RELEVANT PROVISIONS

For the *Restatement (Second) of Contracts,* consult § 86.

NOTES AND QUESTIONS

1. ***What happened?*** Who sued whom for what? Procedurally, how did the case get before this court? Factually, what happened between the parties? What arguments did the plaintiff and defendant make? What rule or rules did the court apply? How did the court analyze the dispute between the parties? How did the court decide the case?

2. *Was this case correctly decided?* Do you agree with the result reached in this case? How about the reasoning used? What are the strengths and weaknesses of Judge Bricken's approach? Can it be reconciled with *Mills v. Wyman*? How, if at all, would you have decided the case, and written the opinion, differently?

3. *Consideration?* According to the bargain-based theory of consideration, plaintiff should only recover if he could prove that there was a bargained-for exchange. Should it matter that no such exchange took place in *Webb*? Should it matter *why* no such exchange took place?

4. *Other theories of liability.* If plaintiff could not recover under a traditional, bargain-based contract, do any of the theories for enforcing promises offered in Cohen's article, excerpted as "Justifying Contract Law" in Part II.2.C, *supra* (p. 81), or Fuller's article, excerpted as "The Role of Legal Formalities" in Section A.1, *supra* (p. 341), explain the result here?

5. *The material benefit rule.* A cleaner (though far from perfect) doctrinal solution to the type of problem posed in *Webb* was set forth in *Restatement (Second) of Contracts* § 86. Sometimes called the "material benefit rule," § 86 tests the enforceability of a promise not by asking whether there was a bargain, but by asking whether the promisor made a subsequent promise to pay for a benefit already received. Read this provision carefully. Would it have changed the result, or the amount recovered, in *Webb*? How about in *Mills v. Wyman*? What about *Bailey v. West*? Grant Gilmore doesn't seem to think so (see next note). If he is correct, is § 86 much ado about nothing, merely changing the form without altering the function of the doctrines we already studied above? Or does it have anything new to offer?

6. *Evaluating the material benefit rule.* What are some of the strengths and weaknesses of the material benefit rule? Professor Gilmore, after quoting § 86 in full, offered the following harsh (but colorful) criticism. Do you agree?

> This is far from going the whole hog on the unjust enrichment idea. For one thing, the ungrateful recipient may keep whatever he has received without paying for it so long as he is clever enough to avoid making a "promise" to repay. (Of course courts which have learned how easy it is to imply promises to make contracts could easily use the same technique in this context.) For another thing what Subsection (1) giveth, Subsection (2) largely taketh away: the promise, even if made, will be "binding" only within narrow limits. Furthermore, the use which is made in the Commentary of two of our best known Good Samaritan cases contributes a perhaps desirable confusion:
>
> > A gives emergency care to B's adult son while the son is sick and without funds far from home. B subsequently promises to reimburse A for his expenses. The promise is not binding under this section.
> >
> > A saves B's life in an emergency and is totally and permanently disabled in so doing: One month later B promises to pay A $15 every two weeks for the rest of A's life, and B makes the payment for eight years until he dies. The promise is binding.

The idea that [§ 86] has succeeded in "codifying" both the nineteenth century Massachusetts case and the twentieth century Alabama case is already sufficiently surprising but we are not yet finished:

> A finds B's escaped bull and feeds and cares for it. B's subsequent promise to pay reasonable compensation to A is binding.

Are we to believe that my promise to pay the stranger who takes care of my bull is binding but that my promise to pay the stranger who takes care of my dying son is not? Or that "adult sons" are supposed to be able to take care of themselves while "escaped bulls" are not? Or that, as in maritime salvage law, saving property is to be rewarded but saving life is not?

Enough has been said to make the point that *Restatement (Second)*, at least in [§ 86], is characterized by the same "schizophrenic quality" for which *Restatement (First)* was so notable. This may well be all to the good. A wise draftsman, when he is dealing with novel issues in course of uncertain development, will deliberately retreat into ambiguity. The principal thing is that *Restatement (Second)* gives overt recognition to an important principle whose existence *Restatement (First)* ignored and, by implication denied. By the time we get to *Restatement (Third)* it may well be that [§ 86] will have flowered like Jack's bean-stalk in the same way that § 90 did between *Restatement (First)* and *Restatement (Second)*.*

7. ***Illustrations.*** *Webb v. McGowin* is now enshrined as Illustration 7 to both the *Restatement (Second) of Contracts* § 86 and the *Restatement (Third) of Restitution and Unjust Enrichment* § 20, respectively, as follows:

> 7. A saves B's life in an emergency and is totally and permanently disabled in so doing. One month later B promises to pay A $15 every two weeks for the rest of A's life, and B makes the payments for 8 years until he dies. The promise is binding.
>
> 7. A acts in an emergency to save the lives of B and C, sustaining crippling injuries as a result. In gratitude for A's assistance, B promises to pay him a weekly pension of $100. B's promise is unsupported by consideration, but it may nevertheless be enforceable as a matter of contract law. (If such a promise is enforceable, B's recognition of the fact and value of the benefit conferred by A is a significant part of the rationale. See *Restatement Second, Contracts* § 86, Comment d, Illustration 7.) Unlike B, C makes no promise of compensation and later rejects A's suggestion that he is entitled to a reward. A is possibly entitled to enforce B's promise, but A has no claim in restitution against either B or C.

PROBLEM: CONCERT CONCERN

Carlton Properties, Inc. filed suit against singer Arnold Hennessey and his management company Phillip Higham Management, LLC to recover a $2.3 million

* GRANT GILMORE, THE DEATH OF CONTRACT 82-84 (1974).

advance fee that Carlton Properties paid to Arnold for a concert that Arnold was later unable to perform due to his diagnosis and treatment for prostate cancer. The agreement between Carlton Properties and Arnold contained a broad force majeure provision that stated in part:

> Any cause beyond such parties' reasonable control (excepting causes of which Carlton Properties had knowledge, or in the exercise of due diligence should have had knowledge), then there shall be no claim for damages by either party to this Agreement, and the performance shall be rescheduled to a mutually agreeable time.

Arnold agreed to reschedule the performance and argued that the force majeure clause should allow him to keep the advance as long as he eventually does the performance. Carlton Properties sought recovery of the advanced fee under an unjust enrichment theory.

Has Arnold been unjustly enriched if he agreed to reschedule the concert? Drawing on any assigned cases or materials, how do you think this dispute should be resolved, and why? What should the court award as a remedy?

PROBLEM: SHOW SOME CONSIDERATION

Drew assaulted his wife, Whitney, who took refuge in Perry's house. The next day, Drew gained access to Perry's house and began another assault upon Whitney. In the scuffle, Whitney knocked Drew to floor with an axe, where he lay unconscious. She then raised the axe high above her head and brought it down swiftly in an attempt to decapitate Drew. At the last moment, Perry intervened and caught the axe with her hand, mutilating it badly, but saving Drew's life.

Subsequently, Drew orally promised to pay Perry for her significant hospital bills. However, when those bills arrived, Drew only paid a small fraction of the total amount due, and refused to pay the rest. Perry sued Drew, and Drew filed a motion to dismiss Perry's complaint, alleging that Perry failed to state a cause of action because his promise was unsupported by consideration.

Drawing on the cases and *Restatement* provisions above, how should the court rule, and why?

D. CHAPTER CAPSTONE: PUTTING IT ALL TOGETHER

As with the previous chapter, we once again end with an interesting and recent case that brings together many of the issues and themes we've explored in this chapter. Bargain-based contracts and the doctrine of consideration? Check. Reliance-based contracts and the doctrine of promissory estoppel? Check. Benefit-based contracts and the doctrine of unjust enrichment? Check. It's all there, with a little past consideration and intellectual property law (which is related to plaintiff's unjust enrichment claim) sprinkled in for flavoring. As before, there are no notes at the end; just read and enjoy. Also, as you read, put your book down every now and again and try to figure out how you would resolve the issue before the court. Then, pick your book back up and check your answer against the court's.

Blackmon v. Iverson

United States District Court, Eastern District of Pennsylvania
324 F. Supp. 2d 602 (2003)

MCLAUGHLIN, DISTRICT JUDGE. The plaintiff, Jamil Blackmon, has sued the defendant, basketball player Allen Iverson, for idea misappropriation, breach of contract, and quantum meruit (unjust enrichment), all arising out of the defendant's use of "The Answer," both as a nickname and as a logo or slogan. The plaintiff, who describes himself as Mr. Iverson's "surrogate father," alleges that Mr. Blackmon came up with the idea that Mr. Iverson use "The Answer" as a nickname, and that Mr. Iverson promised that he would pay Mr. Blackmon twenty-five percent of the proceeds from the sale of merchandise using "The Answer."

Presently before the Court is the defendant's motion to dismiss. The Court will grant the motion.

I. BACKGROUND

The facts, according to the amended complaint are as follows.[1] Mr. Blackmon met Mr. Iverson and his family in 1987. At that time, Mr. Iverson was a young high school student who showed tremendous promise as an athlete. Mr. Blackmon maintained a close personal friendship and relationship with Mr. Iverson and his family from 1987 forward. At various times in their friendship, Mr. Blackmon provided Mr. Iverson and his family with financial support, allowed Mr. Iverson and his family members to live in Mr. Blackmon's home, and provided other support to Mr. Iverson, such as picking him up from school and providing him with a tutor. In July of 1994, Mr. Blackmon suggested that Mr. Iverson use "The Answer" as a nickname in the summer league basketball tournaments in which Mr. Iverson would be playing. Mr. Blackmon told Mr. Iverson that Mr. Iverson would be "The Answer" to all of the National Basketball Association's ("NBA's") woes. Mr. Blackmon and Mr. Iverson also discussed the fact that the nickname "The Answer" had immediate applications as a label, brand name, or other type of marketing slogan for use in connection with clothing, sports apparel, and sneakers. The parties also discussed using "The Answer" as a logo.

---

1. The defendant brought his motion to dismiss pursuant to Federal Rule of Civil Procedure 12(b)(6). In considering a motion to dismiss under Rule 12(b)(6), the Court "take[s] all well pleaded allegations as true, construe[s] the complaint in the light most favorable to the plaintiff, and determine[s] whether under any reasonable reading of the pleadings, the plaintiff may be entitled to relief." *Colburn v. Upper Darby Township*, 838 F.2d 663, 665 (3d Cir. 1988).

Later that evening, Mr. Iverson promised to give Mr. Blackmon twenty-five percent of all proceeds the merchandising of products sold in connection with the term "The Answer." The parties understood that in order to "effectuate Mr. Iverson's agreement to compensate" Mr. Blackmon, Mr. Iverson would have to be drafted by the NBA.

Mr. Blackmon thereafter began to invest significant time, money, and effort in the refinement of the concept of "The Answer." Mr. Blackmon continued to develop and refine the marketing strategy for the sale of merchandise, such as athletic wear and sneakers, in connection with the term "The Answer."

Mr. Blackmon retained a graphic designer to develop logos bearing "The Answer" as well as conceptual drawings for sleeveless t-shirts, adjustable hats, and letterman jackets for sale in connection with "The Answer."

In 1994 and 1995, during Mr. Iverson's freshman year at Georgetown University and the summer thereafter, there were numerous conversations between Mr. Blackmon and Mr. Iverson regarding Mr. Blackmon's progress in refining the marketing concept for "The Answer."

In 1996, just prior to the NBA draft, during which Mr. Iverson was drafted by the Philadelphia 76ers, Mr. Iverson advised Mr. Blackmon that Mr. Iverson intended to use the phrase "The Answer" in connection with a contract with Reebok for merchandising of athletic shoes and sports apparel. Mr. Iverson repeated his promise to pay Mr. Blackmon twenty-five percent of all proceeds from merchandising goods that incorporated "The Answer" slogan or logo.

On July 10, 1996, Mr. Iverson's lawyers wrote to Mr. Blackmon and stated that, despite the fact that Mr. Iverson and Mr. Blackmon reached an agreement regarding "The Answer," Mr. Iverson would not use "The Answer" because it was already a federally protected trademark.

Many months later, Reebok began manufacturing, marketing, and selling a line of athletic sportswear and sneakers using and incorporating "The Answer" slogan and logo. On numerous occasions thereafter, Mr. Iverson repeated his promise to pay Mr. Blackmon.

In the fall of 1997, Mr. Iverson told a third party that Mr. Blackmon had told him, "you need to call yourself 'The Answer,'" and had then explained to him the many marketing applications of "The Answer." During the week of Thanksgiving 1997, Mr. Iverson again promised to give Mr. Blackmon twenty-five percent of the "Reebok deal."

During the 1997-1998 NBA season, there were numerous conversations regarding Mr. Blackmon's marketing plan for merchandise, such as athletic wear and sneakers, sold in connection with "The Answer." Mr. Iverson also continued to repeat his promise to pay Mr. Blackmon.

Also during the 1997-1998 season, Mr. Iverson persuaded Mr. Blackmon to relocate to Philadelphia so that Mr. Blackmon could "begin seeking the profits from his ideas." Mr. Iverson also wanted to pay Mr. Blackmon back for the benefits the Iverson family had received when they had lived with Mr. Blackmon.

In the fall of 1998, Mr. Iverson advised Mr. Blackmon that Mr. Iverson had instructed his attorney to account for the number of "The Answer" units sold by Reebok and to distribute proceeds from those units to the plaintiff. At Thanksgiving of that year, Mr. Iverson told a third party that Mr. Blackmon was about to be a rich man, and that Mr. Blackmon could have twenty-five percent of Mr. Iverson's proceeds from the Reebok deal.

During the 1998-1999 NBA season, Mr. Blackmon again presented Mr. Iverson with logos incorporating "The Answer." Mr. Iverson advised Mr. Blackmon that Mr. Iverson intended to have Reebok incorporate the logo, that Mr. Iverson would give the logos to his lawyer, Lawrence Woodward, "Woody," and that Woody would present them to Reebok.

Thereafter, a meeting took place between Mr. Blackmon, Mr. Iverson, Mr. Woodward, and another individual. Mr. Blackmon told Mr. Woodward that Mr. Blackmon wanted to present him with some things Mr. Blackmon had produced for "The Answer" project. Mr. Blackmon then gave him with a package containing logos and graphics for jackets, t-shirts, and other items relating to "The Answer" project. Mr. Woodward agreed to discuss the matter with David Falk, Mr. Iverson's agent.

During the 1998-1999 and 1999-2000 NBA seasons, Mr. Iverson told Mr. Blackmon and a third party that Mr. Iverson was going to make sure that Mr. Blackmon got his due compensation from the Reebok proceeds. Mr. Iverson also told someone that he was happy that Mr. Blackmon would receive compensation from the exploitation of "The Answer" because he would not have to pay Mr. Blackmon directly from his basketball contract. Mr. Iverson stressed that the proceeds from "The Answer" were the vehicle for Mr. Blackmon's financial independence and restoration.

On or about November of 2000, Mr. Iverson was questioned as to why he had not talked to Mr. Blackmon about "The Answer" deal. Mr. Iverson stated that his attorney, Woody, had instructed him to cease all communications with Mr. Blackmon.

Reebok has continued to sell products bearing "The Answer" slogan and Mr. Iverson has continued to receive profits from the sale of products bearing "The Answer" slogan. Despite repeated requests and demands from Mr. Blackmon, Mr. Iverson has never compensated Mr. Blackmon and continues to deny Mr. Blackmon twenty-five percent of the proceeds from the merchandising of products incorporating "The Answer."

The plaintiff has not alleged that either Mr. Iverson or Reebok used any of the graphics or logos that he designed using "The Answer." At oral argument, the plaintiff conceded that his graphics were not incorporated into any of Reebok's products sold in connection with "The Answer." Transcript of September 5, 2003 Oral Argument (hereinafter "T.") at 62-64.

As damages for his misappropriation claim, the plaintiff requests all gains, profits, and advantages the defendant derived from the misappropriation. For the breach of contract claim, the plaintiff seeks compensation in an amount equal to twenty-five percent of the profits received by Mr. Iverson from the sale of goods using "The Answer." For the unjust enrichment claim, the plaintiff seeks compensation in an amount equal to the defendant's unjust enrichment.

II. ANALYSIS

The essence of all three of the plaintiff's claims is that the defendant took and used the plaintiff's ideas without compensating the plaintiff. This case raises the question of what legal protection is given to ideas—products of the mind.

Judicial decisions in this area of intellectual property attempt to "balanc[e] the rights of the creator of ideas or information to exploit them for commercial gain against the public's right to free access in these ideas." *United States Golf Ass'n v. St. Andrews Sys.*, 749 F.2d 1028, 1035 (3d Cir. 1984).

The three established statutory systems for protecting intellectual property are copyright, patent, and trademark/deception as to origin. Courts have also been willing to give protection to ideas under various other legal theories: idea misappropriation; contract; quasi-contract or unjust enrichment; implied contracts; property theories; and confidential relationship theories. The plaintiff's claims fall into this latter category of protection.

A. Idea Misappropriation

The elements of an idea misappropriation claim are that (1) the plaintiff had an idea that was novel and concrete, and (2) his idea was misappropriated by the defendant. *Sorbee Int'l Ltd. v. Chubb Custom Ins. Co.*, 735 A.2d 712 (1999).

1. Was the Plaintiff's Idea Novel?

A threshold requirement for an idea misappropriation claim is that the plaintiff's idea be novel and concrete. The *Sorbee* court, taking guidance from *Thomas v. R.J. Reynolds Tobacco Co.*, 38 A.2d 61 (1944), held that novelty and concreteness are required so that the court could identify the idea as having been created by one party and stolen by another.

Denying recovery for the use of ideas that are not novel properly confines protection to those ideas that are truly valuable to society. An idea is novel and merits protection when it is truly innovative, inventive, and new. An idea is not novel if it is merely a clever version or variation of already existing ideas.

The idea for which the plaintiff seeks compensation is that the defendant use the nickname "The Answer" as a professional basketball player in a marketing strategy scheme to sell various products, such as sneakers and sportswear. The use of a nickname by a professional sports figure is not novel; nor is the idea of selling products labeled with a nickname. The plaintiff concedes that these ideas are not novel but argues that the particular nickname he suggested was not in use so it is novel.

The defendant argues that there is nothing innovative or novel in the words "The Answer," or using them as a nickname. The defendant contends that it is common for basketball players to use nicknames that consist of ordinary words with ordinary meanings.

It is doubtful that the suggestion of a nickname to a professional athlete could ever be novel; but, the Court need not decide this issue here because the complaint fails to allege other elements of idea misappropriation.

2. *Was the Plaintiff's Idea Misappropriated?*

The doctrine of idea misappropriation is derived from the seminal Supreme Court case of *Int'l News Svc. v. The Associated Press,* 248 U.S. 215 (1918). The complainant in *Int'l News,* the AP newswire service, put time and effort into collecting information and transmitting this information to its subscribers, which were news publications. The defendant, a competing newswire service, took the information from the early editions of the news publications put out by the plaintiff's subscribers and transmitted the information to its own paying customers.

The Supreme Court held that, under federal common law, although any member of the general public had a right to use and retransmit the ideas contained in the publications, a competitor did not. The Court found that equitable relief was warranted under an unfair competition theory; the defendant had acquired the information at little or no cost, used it to make a profit, and gained an unfair advantage over the complainant who was burdened with the expense of gathering the news. This amounted to an unauthorized interference with the complainant's business—a diversion of a portion of profits from the complainant. The Supreme Court held that the misappropriation of ideas was actionable as a subset of unfair competition.

Under the Supreme Court's reasoning in *Int'l News Svc.,* direct competition is an essential element of idea misappropriation. The Court of Appeals for the Third Circuit also held that under New Jersey law direct competition is required for idea misappropriation, absent a substantial justification for making an exception, because "it properly balances the competing concerns of providing incentives to producers of information while protecting free access." *United States Golf Ass'n,* 749 F.2d at 1039. The Third Circuit reasoned that requiring direct competition "protects the public interest in free access to information except where protection of the creator's interest is required in order to assure that the information is produced." *Id.* at 1039, n. 17.

With this background, the Court examines Pennsylvania law to determine if Pennsylvania requires that the plaintiff and the defendant be direct competitors before a plaintiff may bring a claim for idea misappropriation.

In *Sorbee Int'l Ltd. v. Chubb Custom Ins. Co.,* 735 A.2d 712 (1999), the Pennsylvania Superior Court, in the context of an insurance policy, explored the meaning of the term "misappropriation of advertising ideas." The Superior Court quoted with approval the three elements of a common law tort of misappropriation:

> (1) the plaintiff "has made a substantial investment of time, effort, and money into creating the thing misappropriated such that the court can characterize the 'thing' as a kind of property right," (2) the defendant "has appropriated the 'thing' at little or no cost, such that the court can characterize defendant's actions as 'reaping where it has not sown,'" and (3) the defendant "has injured the plaintiff by the misappropriation."

Id. (quoting *Lebas Fashion Imports of USA Inc. v. ITT Hartford Ins. Group,* 59 Cal. Rptr. 2d 36 (1996)).

The Superior Court then cited a Wisconsin case, again apparently with approval:

> *See also Atlantic Mutual Ins. Co. v. Badger Medical Supply Co.*, 528 N.W.2d 486 (1995) (essence of cause of action of misappropriation is the defendant's use of the plaintiff's product, into which plaintiff has put time, skill and money; and the defendant's use of the plaintiff's product or a copy of it in competition with the plaintiff and gaining an advantage in that competition because the plaintiff, and not the defendant, has expended the energy to produce it.)

Sorbee, 735 A.2d 712.

These two definitions arguably are different. Under the first, the plaintiff may not have to be a competitor of the defendant; but, he must have been "injured" by the misappropriation. Under the second, the plaintiff and the defendant must be competitors, as was required by the Supreme Court in *Int'l News* and by the Third Circuit in *United States Golf Ass'n.*

The Court does not have to decide between the two definitions in *Sorbee* because under either definition, the plaintiff has failed to make out the element of misappropriation that requires that the plaintiff suffer a loss of competitive advantage or otherwise be injured in his business.

It is not alleged that either the defendant or Reebok is in direct competition with the plaintiff. The plaintiff has admitted that he wanted and intended for the defendant to use his idea. The plaintiff does not allege that he had any use for the idea himself or that he would have been able to sell it to anyone else. The plaintiff, therefore, has not alleged that he suffered any competitive or other financial loss when the defendant took his idea.

The plaintiff instead alleges that he suffered a loss when the defendant did not pay him for the use of the idea. This is insufficient. In order to state a claim for idea misappropriation, it must be the taking of the idea itself that causes the plaintiff a competitive or other financial harm. This occurs only when the defendant's use of the idea deprives the plaintiff of some competitive or financial benefit or causes some other detriment separate from the misappropriation. The loss must be independent of a defendant's failure to pay; to hold otherwise would render the third element of misappropriation superfluous. Because there is no allegation that the plaintiff was harmed competitively or financially by the misappropriation, the plaintiff has not properly pled misappropriation.

The complaint also fails to allege the first two elements of a misappropriation claim: a substantial investment of time, effort, and money into creating an idea that the defendant has appropriated at little or no cost. The complaint does allege a substantial investment of time, effort, and money but not in the creation of anything the defendant appropriated. The plaintiff alleges that he spent time and money coming up with graphics and marketing ideas. There is no allegation, however, that the defendant or Reebok appropriated any of these graphics or marketing ideas.

B. Breach of Contract

The plaintiff claims that he entered into an express contract with the defendant pursuant to which he was to receive twenty-five percent of the proceeds that the defendant received from marketing products with "The Answer" on them. The defendant argues that there was not a valid contract because the claim was not timely filed under the Pennsylvania statute of limitations, the terms of the contract were not sufficiently definite, and there was no consideration alleged.

Under Pennsylvania law, a plaintiff must present clear and precise evidence of an agreement in which both parties manifested an intent to be bound, for which both parties gave consideration, and which contains sufficiently definite terms.

Consideration confers a benefit upon the promisor or causes a detriment to the promisee and must be an act, forbearance, or return promise bargained for and given in exchange for the original promise. *See also Restatement of Contracts 2d,* § 71. Under Pennsylvania and Virginia law, past consideration is insufficient to support a subsequent promise.

It is difficult to analyze the alleged contract because the complaint describes various promises that were made by the defendant at various times. This problem with the plaintiff's alleged contract became even clearer at the hearing on the motion. Counsel for the plaintiff gave various dates for the formation of the alleged contract. T., at 80-95 (the "agreement and the discussions took place in early 1994"; "the last part of the contract didn't really take place until 1997"; "there was a meeting of the minds that took place in 1994, albeit the last . . . part of that contract didn't really take place until after Mr. Iverson had gotten into the pros"; "there was an initial understanding in 1994 that is then modified for a more specific situation in 1996"; "in Philadelphia in 1997 there is a modification of the original understanding"; "the original contract could have been rescinded, it could have been modified by the parties"; and the contract "most importantly came into being in 1996"). On this basis alone, the complaint fails adequately to set forth the elements required for a contract claim.

The Court, nevertheless, will consider whether there was consideration at the various times the plaintiff alleges the formation of a contract.

The plaintiff has argued that, in exchange for the defendant's promise to pay the twenty-five percent, the plaintiff gave three things as consideration: (1) the plaintiff's idea to use "The Answer" as a nickname to sell athletic apparel; (2) the plaintiff's assistance to and relationship with the defendant and his family; and (3) the plaintiff's move to Philadelphia. T., at 94, 97.

According to the facts alleged by the plaintiff, he made the suggestion that the defendant use "The Answer" as a nickname and for product merchandising one evening in 1994. This was before the defendant first promised to pay; according to the plaintiff, the promise to pay was made later that evening. The disclosure of the idea also occurred before the defendant told the plaintiff that he was going to use the idea in connection with the Reebok contract in 1996, and before the sales of goods bearing "The Answer" actually began in 1997.

Regardless of whether the contract was formed in 1994, 1996, or 1997, the disclosure of "The Answer" idea had already occurred and was, therefore, past consideration insufficient to create a binding contract.

The plaintiff also argued that the plaintiff's relationship with and assistance to the defendant and his family and the defendant's move to Philadelphia during the 1997-1998 season constituted consideration for the defendant's promise to pay. There is no allegation in the complaint that these actions by the plaintiff were in exchange for the defendant's promise to pay.

According to the complaint, the plaintiff's relationship and support for the defendant, his "surrogate father" role, began in 1987, seven years before the first alleged promise to pay was made. There is no allegation that the plaintiff began engaging in this conduct because of any promise by the defendant, or that the plaintiff continued his gratuitous conduct in 1994, 1996, or 1997 in exchange for the promise to pay. These actions are not valid consideration. *Greene v. Oliver Realty*, 526 A.2d 1192 (1987) (promise is only binding if made in exchange for consideration); *Brewer v. First Nat. Bank of Danville*, 120 S.E.2d 273 (1961) (consideration is something given in exchange for the promise to pay).

The plaintiff also alleged at oral argument that his move to Philadelphia during the 1997-1998 season was consideration for the promise to pay. If the parties reached a mutual agreement in 1994, the plaintiff has not properly alleged that the move was consideration because there is no allegation that the parties anticipated that the plaintiff would move to Philadelphia three or four years later, or that the plaintiff promised to do so in exchange for the defendant's promise to pay.

Nor is there any allegation that the move was part of the terms of any contract created in 1996 or 1997. The complaint states only that the defendant "persuaded" him to move to Philadelphia to "begin seeking the profits from his ideas." Even when the complaint is construed broadly, there is no allegation that the move was required in exchange for any promise by the defendant to pay. In the absence of valid consideration, the plaintiff has no claim for breach of an express contract.

The plaintiff has not made a claim of promissory estoppel. At the hearing, the plaintiff confirmed that he was not making an argument based on detrimental reliance or promissory estoppel because he would only be entitled to reliance damages, an amount far less than what the plaintiff is seeking here. T., at 107.

If the plaintiff wishes to amend the complaint to state a claim of promissory estoppel, the Court will permit him to do so. The Court does note, however, that in order for the Court to have jurisdiction under 28 U.S.C. § 1332, the plaintiff's damages must exceed $75,000.00.

C. Unjust Enrichment

The plaintiff has also brought a claim for unjust enrichment. Under Pennsylvania law, the elements of a claim for unjust enrichment are "benefits conferred on defendant by plaintiff, appreciation of such benefits by the defendant, and the acceptance and retention of such benefits as it would be inequitable for the defendant to retain the benefit without payment of value." *Wiernik v. PHH U.S. Mortgage Corp.*, 736 A.2d 616, 622 (1999).

The alleged benefit in this case was the use of the plaintiff's idea. Several courts require that a plaintiff show that his idea was novel and concrete before the court will find unjust enrichment based on the use of that idea.

These courts reason that, absent novelty and concreteness, the plaintiff has not provided the defendant with anything that can be properly be deemed the property of the plaintiff; upon their release from the brain, non-novel and non-concrete ideas are common property. In the absence of novelty and concreteness, the plaintiff cannot show that he enriched the defendant; the defendant has only received an idea that he was already free to use.

Although the Pennsylvania Supreme Court has not opined on whether a claim of unjust enrichment based on the use of an idea requires novelty, it has required novelty in an implied contract case involving the use of an idea. *Thomas,* 38 A.2d 61. The *Thomas* court reasoned that novelty was required for the creator to have a property right in the idea used by the other party. *Id.* I hold that the Pennsylvania Supreme Court would reach the same conclusion in an unjust enrichment case.

As discussed above, it is very doubtful that the plaintiff's idea was novel. Even if the idea to use "The Answer" as a nickname were novel, the plaintiff would still not have made out a claim for unjust enrichment. The facts alleged in the complaint do not include an allegation that the plaintiff expected payment if the defendant used the nickname "The Answer." The plaintiff's facts show that he wanted and intended the defendant to use the nickname in summer league basketball tournaments, starting in 1994, without expecting any payment for that use. The plaintiff cannot make out a claim that the defendant was unjustly enriched by the use of a nickname that the plaintiff freely offered.

It is the use of the nickname on products for which the plaintiff claims damages. But the use of the nickname on products came years after the defendant began using the nickname. If the plaintiff concedes, as he does, that the idea of putting a nickname on products is not novel; and if the plaintiff is not claiming any damages for merely suggesting the use of the nickname to the defendant, and he is not, there is no unjust enrichment alleged in the complaint. Any benefit to the defendant from the marketing of products with "The Answer" on them comes from his fame as a basketball player and the investment in marketing the products by Reebok.

An appropriate order follows.

ORDER

AND NOW, this 4th day of April, 2003, upon consideration of the defendant's Motion to Dismiss, the plaintiff's opposition thereto, and all supplemental filings by the parties, and following oral argument, IT IS HEREBY ORDERED that the motion is GRANTED and the plaintiff's first amended complaint is DISMISSED for the reasons set forth in a memorandum of today's date.

AND IT IS FURTHER ORDERED THAT, if the plaintiff wishes to amend his complaint to state a claim for promissory estoppel, he may do so on or before May 2, 2003.

CHAPTER 5

REMEDIES

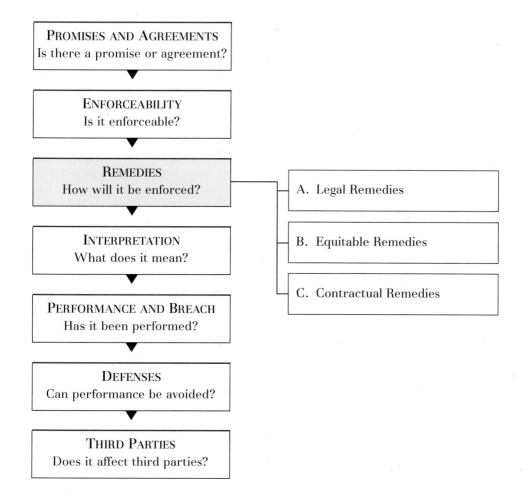

PROMISES AND AGREEMENTS
Is there a promise or agreement?

ENFORCEABILITY
Is it enforceable?

REMEDIES
How will it be enforced?

- A. Legal Remedies
- B. Equitable Remedies
- C. Contractual Remedies

INTERPRETATION
What does it mean?

PERFORMANCE AND BREACH
Has it been performed?

DEFENSES
Can performance be avoided?

THIRD PARTIES
Does it affect third parties?

Breach of contract is naturally the slightest of all injuries, because we naturally depend more on what we possess than what is in the hands of others. A man robbed of five pounds thinks himself much more injured than if he had lost five pounds by a contract.

Adam Smith, LECTURES ON JUSTICE, POLICY, REVENUE AND ARMS 131 (Cannan ed. 1896)

One of the many evil effects of the confusion between legal and moral ideas . . . is that theory is apt to get the cart before the horse, and to consider the right or the duty as something existing apart from and independent of the consequences of its breach, to which certain sanctions are added afterward. But . . . a legal duty so called is nothing but a prediction that if a man does or omits certain things he will be made to suffer in this or that way by judgment of the court; and so of a legal right. . . . The duty to keep a contract at common law means a prediction that you must pay damages if you do not keep it—and nothing else. If you commit a tort, you are liable to pay a compensatory sum. If you commit a contract, you are liable to pay a compensatory sum unless the promised event comes to pass, and that is all the difference. But such a mode of looking at the matter stinks in the nostrils of those who think it advantageous to get as much ethics into the law as they can. . . .

Oliver Wendell Holmes, *Path of the Law*, 10 Harv. L. Rev. 457 (1897)

In the memorable case of *Hawkins v. McGee*, discussed in Part II.2.D "Introduction to Remedies" and in the related materials,* you learned how courts sometimes use *property rules* (i.e., specific relief) to protect contractual rights—usually by issuing an injunction requiring the promisor to perform or refrain from performing a specified act—but more often than not they protect contractual rights with *liability rules* (i.e., substitutionary relief), usually through an award of expectation damages, but sometimes through an award of reliance or restitution damages instead. In the materials that follow, we will study each of these remedial concepts in greater depth, and in the process learn about (1) some of the ways courts decide to protect a party's contractual right with a property rule or liability rule, (2) how to understand and calculate each of the three damage interests, (3) the three limitations an injured promisee must overcome when trying to recover damages (foreseeability, certainty, and avoidability), (4) how to distinguish between several different methods of measuring expectation damages, and (5) the controversial role played by the doctrine of efficient breach. As you read the cases throughout this chapter, try to see the relation between the contractual right the court is trying to protect and the remedy the judge is using to protect that right, and ask yourself whether you believe the remedy awarded by the court seems to over- or underprotect the promisee's contractual rights. Would a different remedy have done a better job of protecting the promisee's rights? If so, which remedy, and why

* *See* "Thinking Tool: Property Rules and Liability Rules," p. 109, *infra*.

do you think the court did not award this alternative remedy? But before we delve into the cases, let us pause for a moment to consider the purpose of contract remedies as outlined in the following excerpt.

DOCTRINAL OVERVIEW: THE PURPOSE OF CONTRACT REMEDIES*

Why do people keep their promises? Sometimes the reason has little to do with the legal remedies available to the promisee of a broken promise. One may simply regard keeping promises as the "right" thing to do. Or one may fear that if one breaks one's promise the promisee will not keep the return promise, that the promisee and others will not deal with one in the future, or that one's general reputation will suffer.

It might be supposed that the law would add to these extra-legal compulsions a system of sanctions of its own, designed to compel promisors to keep their promises. Somewhat surprisingly, our system of contract remedies rejects, for the most part, compulsion of the promisor as a goal. It does not impose criminal penalties on one who refuses to perform one's promise, nor does it generally require one to pay punitive damages. Our system of contract remedies is not directed at *compulsion* of *promisors* to *prevent* breach; it is aimed, instead, at *relief* to *promisees* to *redress* breach. Its preoccupation is not with the question: how can promisors be made to keep their promises? Its concern is with a different question: how can people be encouraged to deal with those who make promises? The result may sometimes be to compel a promisor to keep a promise, but this is only the incidental effect of a system designed to serve other ends. Perhaps it is more consistent with free enterprise to promote the use of contract by encouraging promisees to rely on the promises of others instead of by compelling promisors to perform their promises. In any event, along with the celebrated freedom to make contracts goes a considerable freedom to break them as well.

How do courts encourage promisees to rely on promises? Ordinarily they do so by protecting the expectation that the injured party had when making the contract by attempting to put that party in as good a position as it would have been in had the contract been performed, that is, had there been no breach. The interest measured in this way is called the *expectation interest* and is said to give the injured party the "benefit of the bargain."[5] The expectation interest is based not on the injured party's hopes at the time of making the contract, but on the actual value that the contract would have had to the injured party had it been performed. The expectation of the foolishly optimistic landowner who contracted to have an oil well

---

* Excerpted from E. ALLAN FARNSWORTH, CONTRACTS § 12.1 (4th ed. 2004).

5. For a statement of the expectation interest, *see* UCC 1-305(a) ("remedies provided . . . must be liberally administered to the end that the aggrieved party may be put in as good a position as if the other party had fully performed"). For another statement, *see* Restatement Second § 344. *Cf. Contempo Design v. Chicago & Northeast Ill. Dist. Council*, 226 F.3d 535 (7th Cir. 2000) (rule that "injured party is to be placed in as good a position as he would have been had the contract been performed . . . applies in the labor context"). The seminal article on the expectation, reliance, and restitution interests is Fuller & Perdue, *The Reliance Interest in Contract Damages* (pts. 1, 2), 46 YALE L.J 52, 373 (1936, 1937).

dug is not the gusher that the landowner hoped for but the *dry* well that actually would have resulted. Since the circumstances at the time for performance, rather than those at the time of the making of the contract, are determinative, changes in the market adverse to the promisee that occur between the time of making and the time for performance diminish the promisee's expectation interest. . . .

At times, a court will enforce a promise by protecting the promisee's reliance instead of the promisee's expectation. The injured party may, for example, have changed position in reliance on the contract by incurring expenses in preparation or in performance. In that case, the court may attempt to put the injured party back in the position in which that party would have been had the contract not been made. The interest measured in this way is called the *reliance interest*. . . .

[T]he reliance interest is ordinarily smaller than the expectation interest because, while the expectation interest takes account of the injured party's lost profit as well as reliance, the reliance interest includes nothing for lost profit. In this connection it is important to understand that the law has not generally recognized yet another kind of reliance—reliance that consists in forgoing opportunities to make other contracts [due, in part, to the difficulty of proving these types of damages]. Situations in which damages have been measured by the reliance interest have characteristically been those in which damages measured by the full expectation are for some reason regarded as inappropriate and the court turns to the reliance interest as a lesser included component that will give a measure of relief. . . .

Sometimes a court will recognize a third interest in cases of breach of contract by granting restitution to the injured party. However, the object of restitution is not the enforcement of a promise, but an entirely distinct goal—the prevention of unjust enrichment. The focus is on the party in breach rather than on the injured party, and the attempt is to put the party in breach back in the position in which that party would have been had the contract not been made. The party in breach is required to disgorge what that party has received in money or services by, for example, returning the benefit to the injured party that conferred it. The interest of the injured party that is measured in this way is called the *restitution interest*. It is ordinarily smaller than either the expectation interest or the reliance interest. . . .

For a simple illustration of the three interests—expectation, reliance, and restitution—consider a contract by a builder to build a building on an owner's land for $100,000. If it would have cost the builder $90,000 to build the building, and the owner repudiates the contract before the builder has done anything in reliance on it, the builder's only loss is the $10,000 profit that the builder would have made. This is the builder's expectation interest, since this is the amount it will take to put the builder in as good a position as if the contract had been performed. Since the builder has done nothing in reliance and no benefit has been conferred on the owner, the builder's reliance and restitution interests are both zero.[23] If, however, the owner does not repudiate until the builder has spent $60,000 of the $90,000 it would have cost to build it, the builder's expectation interest is now $70,000, since this is the amount it will take to put the builder

23. The builder may have relied on the contract by forgoing opportunities to make other contracts but, as noted earlier, courts generally have not recognized this kind of reliance.

in as good a position as if the contract had been performed. The builder's reliance interest is now $60,000, the amount spent on past performance. And if the benefit to the owner of the partly finished building is, say, $40,000, the builder's restitution interest is now $40,000. . . .

A. LEGAL REMEDIES

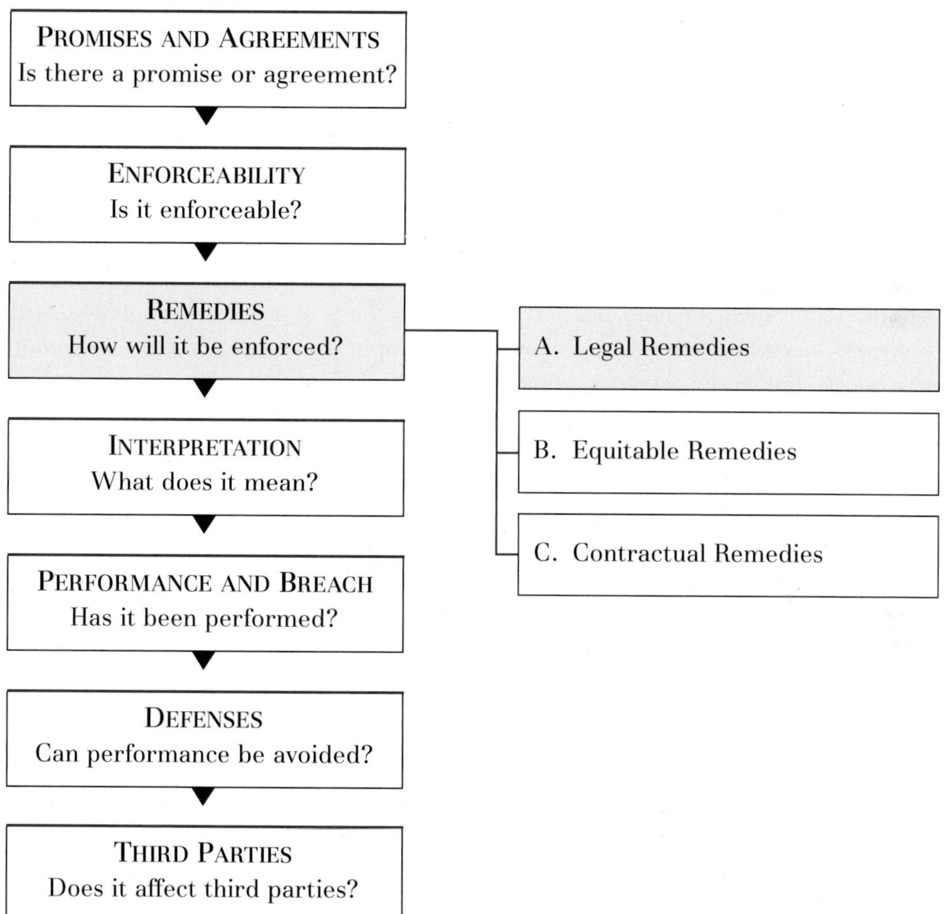
PROMISES AND AGREEMENTS
Is there a promise or agreement?
ENFORCEABILITY
Is it enforceable?
REMEDIES
How will it be enforced?
INTERPRETATION
What does it mean?
PERFORMANCE AND BREACH
Has it been performed?
DEFENSES
Can performance be avoided?
THIRD PARTIES
Does it affect third parties?
A. Legal Remedies
B. Equitable Remedies
C. Contractual Remedies

The traditional goal of the law of contract remedies has not been compulsion of the promisor to perform his promise but compensation of the promisee for the loss resulting from breach. "Willful" breaches have not been distinguished from other breaches, punitive damages have not been awarded for breach of contract, and specific performance has not been granted where compensation in damages is an adequate substitute for the injured party. In general, therefore, a party may find it advantageous to refuse to perform a contract if he will still have a net gain after he has fully compensated the injured party for the resulting loss.

RESTATEMENT (SECOND) OF CONTRACTS, ch. 16, Introductory Note

Where one party, through its breach, injures another party, courts have two main methods of making the injured party whole. First, courts can protect the injured party's right to the breaching party's performance with a property rule, requiring the promisor to give the injured party "specific relief," or the very thing that party contracted for. Second, a court can protect the injured party's right with a liability rule, requiring the breaching party to give the injured party "substitutionary relief," or an amount of money reflecting the value of the contracted-for performance. Historically, specific relief was generally (but not always) awarded in a court of equity, whereas substitutionary relief was generally (but not always) awarded in a common-law court. You will see why this matters in just a moment.

Now, as a general matter, most of us would find specific relief to be the obvious remedy: If you promised to sell me your car, I paid for your car, and you failed to deliver your car, most of us would think that a court should require you to hand over your car. But here, our intuition would be wrong. Historically, our courts, influenced less by prevailing common sense than by several centuries of tradition, tended to favor awarding substitutionary over specific relief. In an overly simplistic summary bordering on libel, but perhaps of some value in helping you make sense of the cases below, the story is as follows: Two completely separate courts—common-law courts (generally favoring substitutionary relief) and the Court of Chancery (generally favoring specific relief)—grew up alongside each other in England.* Each court had its own set of rules, procedures, and remedies. Litigants, who were aware of these differences, would take advantage of this system by filing their suit in whichever court was likely to be most favorable to their case. The courts, in turn, competed for the business of the litigants, and a rivalry ensued.

As a result of this rivalry, and after much fighting between the courts, something like the following rule emerged several hundred years ago in England: Parties were entitled to equitable relief only where they could demonstrate that legal relief would be inadequate.† So, what does any of this have to do with contract law in America in the twenty-first century? Suffice it to say that our courts have never gotten around to changing the rule, so that, even today, when litigants seek an equitable remedy, they must still first show that legal relief would be inadequate. Why? One can chalk it up to inertia, I suppose. As Holmes famously quipped over a century ago:

> The life of the law has not been logic; it has been experience. . . . The law embodies the story of a nation's development through many centuries, and it

* There were other courts as well, but we can ignore these for the time being.

† One might think that this would have been the beginning of the end for equity, but then one would be wrong. In practice, it was not the common-law judges but the Chancellor who determined whether legal relief was adequate. Clever! And the Chancellor, of course, wanting litigants to file in the Court of Chancery rather than in common-law courts, was obviously inclined to find the legal remedy to be adequate less often than would have been the case if the common-law courts were called upon to decide the issue.

> cannot be dealt with as if it contained only the axioms and corollaries of a book of mathematics.*

So, for purely historical reasons, legal remedies (e.g., substitutionary relief) are still preferred over equitable remedies (e.g., specific relief) to this day. For this reason, we begin our study of remedies by looking at legal remedies. Also, because equitable remedies are only awarded where legal remedies are inadequate, we are in no position to know whether an equitable remedy should be awarded unless we first understand whether the legal remedy that could have been awarded in its place was (or was not) inadequate. Thus, on to legal remedies!

In this section, we will explore in greater depth the most common legal remedies available, including the three damage interests (expectation, reliance, and restitution). In addition, we will practice calculating damages, consider several alternative ways of thinking about "expectation damages," and learn about the theory of efficient breach.

Three Damage Interests†

For a report of the excerpt, see p. 117, *supra*.

RELEVANT PROVISIONS

For the *Restatement (Second) of Contracts*, consult § 344.

1. Expectation Damages

a. Expectation Damages: The General Rule

DOCTRINAL OVERVIEW: GENERAL MEASURE OF DAMAGES‡

How is the injured party's expectation to be measured in terms of money? What sum will put the injured party in as good a position as if the contract had been performed? . . .

If the injured party has not terminated the contract, damages need only compensate that party for the loss caused by the shortfall in the other party's performance. Thus if a builder has finished work on a building and been paid but has not done the work on time or in conformity with the contract, the owner is entitled to damages for partial breach. . . . But if the breach is material, the owner can choose instead to terminate, refuse to render any further performance, and claim

* Oliver Wendell Holmes, Common Law 1 (1881).

† Excerpted from Lon L. Fuller and William R. Perdue, Jr., *The Reliance Interest in Contract Damages: I,* 46 Yale L.J. 52, 53-54, 56-57 (1936).

‡ Excerpted from E. Allan Farnsworth, Contracts § 12.9 (4th ed. 2004).

damages for total breach, based on a more complex calculation that takes account of savings as well as loss[, subject to the limitations of certainty, foreseeability, and avoidability, which we explore in greater detail in subsection D.1 below]. . . . We examine in this section the general elements of a claim for damages, with emphasis on damages for total breach.

A claim of damages for total breach may have four elements because the breach may affect an injured party in four ways. First, the breach may cause that party loss in value. Second, it may cause that party other loss. Third, it may enable that party to avoid some cost. Fourth, it may enable that party to avoid some loss. The first two of these effects may also apply to an injured party's claim for partial breach. We take them up in order.

First, the breach may cause the injured party a loss by depriving that party, at least to some extent, of the performance expected under the contract. The difference between the value to the injured party of the performance that should have been received and the value to that party of what, if anything, actually was received will be referred to as the *loss in value*. If, for example, a buyer of goods has a claim for damages for partial breach because the goods were nonconforming, the *loss in value* equals the difference between the value to the buyer of the goods that were to have been delivered and the value of the goods that were actually delivered.[3] . . .

Second, the breach may cause the injured party loss other than loss in value, and the party is also entitled to recovery for this, subject again to limitations such as that of unforeseeability. Such loss will be referred to as other loss and is sometimes said to give rise to "incidental" and "consequential" damages. Incidental damages include additional costs incurred after the breach in a reasonable attempt to avoid loss, even if the attempt is unsuccessful. If, for example, the injured party who has not received the promised performance pays a fee to a broker in a reasonable but unsuccessful attempt to obtain a substitute, that expense is recoverable.[10] Consequential damages include such items as injury to person or property caused by the breach. If, for example, services furnished to the injured party are defective and cause damage to that party's property, that loss is recoverable.[11] The terms used to characterize the loss should not, however, be critical, for the general principle is that all loss, however characterized, is recoverable.

What has been said in the two preceding paragraphs applies regardless of whether or not the injured party chooses to treat the breach as total. It applies to both claims for partial breach and claims for total breach. If the injured party does terminate the

3. Under UCC 2-714(2) the general measure of damages for breach of warranty in the case of accepted goods is "the difference at the time and place of acceptance between the value of the goods accepted and the value they would have had if they had been as warranted."

10. . . . UCC 2-715(1) provides: "Incidental damages resulting from the seller's breach include expenses reasonably incurred in inspection, receipt, transportation and care and custody of goods rightfully rejected, any commercially reasonable charges, expenses or commissions in connection with effecting cover and any other reasonable expense incident to the delay or other breach."

11. *See* UCC 2-715(2), under which the buyer can recover "consequential damages resulting from the seller's breach" including "injury to person or property proximately resulting from any breach of warranty."

contract, however, the breach may have a third or a fourth effect because that party is relieved of the duty of rendering whatever remains of its own performance. What is said in the two following paragraphs applies only to claims for total breach.

Third, then, if the injured party terminates and claims damages for total breach, the breach may have a beneficial effect on that party by saving it the further expenditure that would otherwise have been incurred. This saving will be referred to as *cost avoided.* If, for example, the injured party is a builder that stops work after terminating a construction contract because of the owner's breach, the additional expenditure the builder saves is *cost avoided.*

Fourth, if the injured party terminates and claims damages for total breach, the breach may have a further beneficial effect on that party by allowing it to avoid some loss by salvaging and reallocating some or all of the resources that otherwise it would have had to devote to performance of the contract. The saving that results will be referred to as *loss avoided.* If, for example, the injured party is a builder that, after stopping work after terminating a construction contract, uses some of the leftover materials on another contract, the resulting saving to the builder is *loss avoided.* Or if the injured party is an employee who, after being wrongfully discharged by an employer, takes other employment, the net amount that has been earned or will be earned from that employment is *loss avoided.* If the injured party has actually saved money, the saving is treated as *loss avoided* even though another person might not have been able to effect that saving. If, for example, the injured party happens to make especially favorable arrangements to dispose of leftover materials, and thereby avoids more loss than another person might have succeeded in doing, the *loss avoided* will be based on the actual favorable arrangements. . . .

The general measure of damages for total breach can therefore be expressed in terms of these four effects, two of which (loss in value and other loss) are adverse to the injured party and therefore increase damages, and two of which (cost avoided and loss avoided) are beneficial to the injured party and therefore decrease that party's damages. Formula (A) therefore reads:

(A) *general measure = loss in value + other loss – cost avoided – loss avoided*

Hawkins v. McGee

Supreme Court of New Hampshire
146 A. 641 (1929)

For a report of the case and accompanying materials, see p. 105, *supra*.

RELEVANT PROVISIONS

For the *Restatement (Second) of Contracts,* consult §§ 344 and 347. For the UCC, consult § 1-305. For the CISG, consult Article 74. For the UNIDROIT Principles, consult Article 7.4.2.

PROBLEM: CALCULATING EXPECTATION DAMAGES

Leonardo agrees to sell Michelangelo his *Mona Lisa*, in return for Michelangelo's agreement to pay Leonardo 35 florins and give Leonardo an exact replica of his statue *David*. Assume that the *Mona Lisa* has a market value of 50 florins, that a replica of Michelangelo's *David* would have a market value of 1 florin, and that it would cost Michelangelo 3 florins to hire a skillful artisan to produce a replica of the *David*. Assume that Michelangelo paid Leonardo 35 florins and, after paying an artisan 3 florins to create a replica of the *David*, also gave Leonardo the replica. Bitter rivals to the end, Leonardo refused to deliver the *Mona Lisa* to Michelangelo, and also refused to return Michelangelo's money or the replica of the *David*. Further, to prevent Michelangelo from obtaining the *Mona Lisa*, Leonardo sold it to the French King François I. Michelangelo, figuring that an action for specific performance against the king of France would prove futile, sued Leonardo for damages instead.

Q1: What are Michelangelo's expectation damages?

Q2: Same facts as before, but assume that Michelangelo paid an artisan 3 florins to replicate the *David*, but did not give that replica to Leonardo and had not yet paid Leonardo the 35 florins. On this set of facts, what are Michelangelo's expectation damages?

Q3: Assume that the market value of the *Mona Lisa* fell to 30 florins, but that Michelangelo already paid Leonardo 35 florins and also already gave him a replica of the *David*. What are Michelangelo's expectation damages?

b. Expectation Damages: The Sale of Goods

For the most part, expectation damages under Article 2 of the UCC mirrors expectation damages under the common law, but there are a few important scenarios that tend to arise more frequently where goods are involved, two of which will be explored below. First, we will explore how courts calculate expectation damages where a buyer breaches a contract with a "lost volume" seller (i.e., a seller with a virtually unlimited inventory) who goes on to sell the good to a third party, and second, we will explore the related problem of how courts calculate expectation damages where a seller breaches a contract with a buyer who is prevented from reselling the goods to a third party.

i. Sellers' Remedies

The following case considers two different ways of calculating "expectation damages," and explores how such damages should be assessed where the injured party is a "lost volume" seller. As you read it, ask yourself whether you agree with the way the court assessed damages, and how (if at all) you would have assessed them differently.

Neri v. Retail Marine Corp.

Court of Appeals of New York
285 N.E.2d 311 (1972)

GIBSON, JUDGE. . . . The plaintiffs contracted to purchase from defendant a new boat of a specified model for the price of $12,587.40, against which they made a deposit of $40. They shortly increased the deposit to $4,250 in consideration of the defendant dealer's agreement to arrange with the manufacturer for immediate delivery on the basis of "a firm sale," instead of the delivery within approximately four to six weeks originally specified. Some six days after the date of the contract plaintiffs' lawyer sent to defendant a letter rescinding the sales contract for the reason that plaintiff Neri was about to undergo hospitalization and surgery, in consequence of which, according to the letter, it would be "impossible for Mr. Neri to make any payments." The boat had already been ordered from the manufacturer and was delivered to defendant at or before the time the attorney's letter was received. Defendant declined to refund plaintiffs' deposit and this action to recover it was commenced. Defendant counterclaimed, alleging plaintiffs' breach of the contract and defendant's resultant damage in the amount of $4,250. . . .

[T]he boat ordered and received by defendant in accordance with plaintiffs' contract of purchase was sold some four months later to another buyer for the same price as that negotiated with plaintiffs. From this proof the plaintiffs argue that defendant's loss on its contract was recouped, while defendant argues that but for plaintiffs' default, it would have sold two boats and [would] have earned two profits instead of one. Defendant proved, without contradiction, that its profit on the sale under the contract in suit would have been $2,579 and that during the period the boat remained unsold incidental expenses aggregating $674 for storage, upkeep, finance charges and insurance were incurred. . . .

The issue is governed in the first instance by § 2-718 of the Uniform Commercial Code which provides, among other things, that the buyer, despite his breach, may have restitution of the amount by which his payment exceeds: (a) reasonable liquidated damages stipulated by the contract or (b) absent such stipulation, 20% of the value of the buyer's total performance or $500, whichever is smaller. . . . [T]he trial court awarded defendant an offset in the amount of $500 under paragraph (b) and directed restitution to plaintiffs of the balance. [However, § 2-718(a)(3)] establishes an alternative right of offset in favor of the seller, as follows: "(3) The buyer's right to restitution under subsection (2) is subject to offset to the extent that the seller establishes (a) a right to recover damages under the provisions of this Article other than subsection (1)."

Among "the provisions of this Article other than subsection (1)" are those to be found in § 2-708, which the courts below did not apply. Subsection (1) of that section provides that

> the measure of damages for non-acceptance or repudiation by the buyer is the difference between the market price at the time and place for tender and the unpaid contract price together with any incidental damages provided in this

> Article (Section 2-710), but less expenses saved in consequence of the buyer's breach.

However, this provision is made expressly subject to subsection (2), providing:

> (2) If the measure of damages provided in subsection (1) is inadequate to put the seller in as good a position as performance would have done then the measure of damages is the profit (including reasonable overhead) which the seller would have made from full performance by the buyer, together with any incidental damages provided in this Article (Section 2-710), due allowance for costs reasonably incurred and due credit for payments or proceeds of resale.

. . . The buyer's right to restitution was established at Special Term . . . , as was the seller's right to proper offsets, in each case pursuant to § 2-718; and, as the parties concede, the only question before us . . . is that as to the proper measure of damage to be applied. The conclusion is clear from the record—indeed with mathematical certainty—that "the measure of damages provided in subsection (1) is inadequate to put the seller in as good position as performance would have done," § 2-708(2), and hence . . . that the seller is entitled to its "profit (including reasonable overhead) . . . together with any incidental damages . . . , due allowance for costs reasonably incurred and due credit for payments or proceeds of resale."

It is evident, first, that this retail seller is entitled to its profit and, second, that the last sentence of [§ 2-718(2)] referring to "due credit for payments or proceeds of resale" is inapplicable to this retail sales contract.[2] Closely parallel to the factual situation now before us is that hypothesized by Dean Hawkland as illustrative of the operation of the rules:

> Thus, if a private party agrees to sell his automobile to a buyer for $2,000, a breach by the buyer would cause the seller no loss (except incidental damages, i.e., expense of a new sale) if the seller was able to sell the automobile to another buyer for $2,000. But the situation is different with dealers having an unlimited supply of standard-priced goods. Thus, if an automobile dealer agrees to sell a car to a buyer at the standard price of $2,000, a breach by the buyer injures the dealer, even though he is able to sell the automobile to another for $2,000. If the dealer has an inexhaustible supply of cars, the resale to replace the breaching buyer costs the dealer a sale, because, had the breaching buyer performed, the dealer would have made two sales instead of one. The buyer's breach, in such a case, depletes the dealer's sales to the extent of one, and the measure of damages should be the dealer's profit on one sale. Section 2-708 recognizes this, and it rejects the rule developed under the Uniform Sales Act by many courts that the profit cannot be recovered in this case.

Hawkland, *Sales and Bulk Sales* 153-154 (1958).

---

2. The concluding clause, "due credit for payments or proceeds of resale," is intended to refer to "the privilege of the seller to realize junk value when it is manifestly useless to complete the operation of manufacture." [See UCC § 2-704(2).]

The record which in this case establishes defendant's entitlement to damages in the amount of its prospective profit, at the same time confirms defendant's cognate right to "any incidental damages provided in this Article (Section 2-710)."[3] [UCC § 2-708(2).] From the language employed it is too clear to require discussion that the seller's right to recover loss of profits is not exclusive and that he may recoup his "incidental" expenses as well. . . .

It follows that plaintiffs are entitled to restitution of the sum of $4,250 paid by them on account of the contract price less an offset to defendant in the amount of $3,253 on account of its lost profit of $2,579 and its incidental damages of $674. . . .

> ***Three damage interests***
>
> Make sure you can identify how all three of the damage interests — expectation, reliance, and restitution — are represented here.

RELEVANT PROVISIONS

For the UCC, consult §§ 2-706, 2-708, 2-710, 2-718. For the *Restatement (Second) of Contracts,* consult § 347. For the CISG, consult Article 74.

NOTES AND QUESTIONS

1. ***What happened?*** Who sued whom for what? Procedurally, how did the case get before this court? Factually, what happened between the parties? What arguments did the plaintiff and defendant make? What rule or rules did the court apply? How did the court analyze the dispute between the parties? How did the court decide the case?

2. ***Was this case correctly decided?*** Do you agree with the result reached in this case? Why or why not? Do you agree with the court's reasoning? Why or why not? How, if at all, would you have written the opinion differently? Do you think the court could have reached the same result much more easily by simply apply the general rule of expectation damages and putting the injured party (Retail Marine Corp.) in the position it would have occupied had the promisor (Neri) performed?

3. ***Thinking tools.*** Can expectation damages be justified in a case like this? If so, on what grounds?

---

3. "Incidental damages to an aggrieved seller include any commercially reasonable charges, expenses or commissions incurred in stopping delivery, in the transportation, care and custody of goods after the buyer's breach, in connection with return or resale of the goods or otherwise resulting from the breach." UCC § 2-710.

4. *Lost-volume sellers under the* Restatement (Second) of Contracts. As with the UCC, a lost-volume seller may also recover lost profits under the *Restatement. See, e.g., Restatement (Second) of Contracts* § 347, Comment f and Illustration 16:

Comment:

f. Lost volume. Whether a subsequent transaction is a substitute for the broken contract sometimes raises difficult questions of fact. If the injured party could and would have entered into the subsequent contract, even if the contract had not been broken, and could have had the benefit of both, he can be said to have "lost volume" and the subsequent transaction is not a substitute for the broken contract. The injured party's damages are then based on the net profit that he has lost as a result of the broken contract. Since entrepreneurs try to operate at optimum capacity, however, it is possible that an additional transaction would not have been profitable and that the injured party would not have chosen to expand his business by undertaking it had there been no breach. It is sometimes assumed that he would have done so, but the question is one of fact to be resolved according to the circumstances of each case. See Illustration 16. See also Uniform Commercial Code § 2-708(2).

Illustration:

16. A contracts to pave B's parking lot for $10,000. B repudiates the contract and A subsequently makes a contract to pave a similar parking lot for $10,000. A's business could have been expanded to do both jobs. Unless it is proved that he would not have undertaken both, A's damages are based on the net profit he would have made on the contract with B, without regard to the subsequent transaction.

ii. Buyers' Remedies

In many ways, the next case presents the opposite problem posed in the previous case. Whereas the *Neri* court had to choose between two different measures of expectation damages, one of which would arguably put Retail Marine in a *worse* position than if the Neris had performed, here the court must choose (once again) between two different measures of expectation damages, but one of which would arguably put the plaintiff in a *better* position than if the defendant performed. This case also introduces us to the concept of efficient breach, which we will explore in greater detail in the notes and materials following the case. As you read it, ask yourself whether you agree with the way the court assessed damages, and how (if at all) you would have assessed them differently.

Tongish v. Thomas

Supreme Court of Kansas

840 P.2d 471 (1992)

[Dennis Tongish agreed to grow, and the Decatur Coop Association ("Coop") agreed to purchase, sunflower seeds at $8 per hundredweight for small seeds and $13 per hundredweight for large seeds. In a separate transaction, Coop agreed to deliver the seeds it purchased from Tongish to Bambino Bean & Seed, Inc. for the same price it paid Tongish plus a 55 cent per hundredweight handling fee. Coop's only anticipated profit in this second contract was the handling fee.

Due to a short crop, bad weather, and other factors, the market price of sunflower seeds in January 1989 was double that set forth in the Tongish/Coop contract. On January 13, Tongish notified Coop he would not deliver any more sunflower seeds. Then, to take advantage of the higher prices prevailing in the market, Tongish sold and delivered 82,820 pounds of sunflower seeds to Danny Thomas for approximately $20 per hundredweight. Tongish was to receive $14,714.89, or $5,153.13 more than the Coop contract price. Thomas, however, only paid for approximately one-half of the seeds, and Tongish brought suit to collect the balance due. Thomas paid the balance of $7,359.61 into court and was ultimately dismissed from the action.

Meanwhile, Coop intervened in the action, seeking damages for Tongish's breach of their original contract. The district court held that Tongish breached the contract, and awarded Coop damages of $455.51, reflecting its loss of handling charges. Coop appealed. The Court of Appeals reversed, finding that Coop was entitled to damages reflecting the difference between the market price and the contract price. Tongish appealed, and the case comes before the Supreme Court of Kansas.]

McFarland, Justice. This case presents the narrow issue of whether . . . the buyer is entitled to its actual loss of profit or the difference between the market price and the contract price. . . .

The analyses and rationale of the Court of Appeals utilized in resolving the issue are sound and we adopt the following portion thereof:

> The trial court decided the damages to Coop should be the loss of expected profits. Coop argues that [UCC § 2-713] entitles it to collect as damages the difference between the market price and the contract price. Tongish argues that the trial court was correct and cites [UCC § 1-106] as support for the contention that a party should be placed in as good a position as it would be in had the other party performed. Therefore, the only disagreement is how the damages should be calculated.
>
> The measure of damages in this action involves two sections of the Uniform Commercial Code: [UCC § 1-106 and UCC § 2-713]. The issue to be determined is which statute governs the measure of damages. Stated in another way, if the statutes are in conflict, which statute should prevail? The answer involves an ongoing academic discussion of two contending positions. The issues in this case disclose the problem.
>
> If Tongish had not breached the contract, he may have received under the contract terms with Coop about $5,153.13 less than he received from Danny Thomas. Coop in turn had an oral contract with Bambino to sell whatever seeds it received from Tongish to Bambino for the same price Coop paid for them.

Therefore, if the contract had been performed, Coop would not have actually received the extra $5,153.13.

We first turn our attention to the conflicting statutes and the applicable rules of statutory construction. [UCC § 1-106] states:

> The remedies provided by this act shall be liberally administered to the end that the aggrieved party may be put in as good a position as if the other party had fully performed but neither consequential or special nor penal damages may be had except as specifically provided in this act or by other rule of law.

If a seller breaches a contract and the buyer does not "**cover**," the buyer is free to pursue other available remedies. [UCC § 2-711] and [UCC § 2-712]. One remedy, which is a complete alternative to "cover," is [UCC § 2-713(1)], which provides:

> [T]he measure of damages for nondelivery or repudiation by the seller is the difference between the market price at the time when the buyer learned of the breach and the contract price together with any incidental and consequential damages provided in this article [UCC § 2-715], but less expenses saved in consequence of the seller's breach.

Neither party argues that the Uniform Commercial Code is inapplicable. Both agree that the issue to be determined is which provision of the UCC should be applied. . . .

The statutes do contain conflicting provisions. On the one hand, [UCC § 1-106] offers a general guide of how remedies of the UCC should be applied, whereas [UCC § 2-713] specifically describes a damage remedy that gives the buyer certain damages when the seller breaches a contract for the sale of goods.

The cardinal rule of statutory construction, to which all others are subordinate, is that the purpose and intent of the legislature govern. When there is a conflict between a statute dealing generally with a subject and another statute dealing specifically with a certain phase of it, the specific statute controls unless it appears that the legislature intended to make the general act controlling. . . .

[UCC § 2-713] allows the buyer to collect the difference in market price and contract price for damages in a breached contract. For that reason, it seems impossible to reconcile the decision of the district court that limits damages to lost profits with this statute.

Therefore, because it appears impractical to make [UCC § 1-106] and [UCC § 2-713] harmonize in this factual situation, [UCC § 2-713] should prevail as the more specific statute according to statutory rules of construction.

As stated, however, Coop protected itself against market price fluctuations through its contract with Bambino. Other than the minimal handling charge, Coop suffered no lost profits from the breach. Should the protection require an exception to the general rule under [UCC § 2-713]? . . .

Cover

Rather than suing under UCC § 2-712, the buyer, at its election, could try to "cover" by "making in good faith and without unreasonable delay any reasonable purchase of or contract to purchase goods in substitution for those due from the seller." UCC § 2-712(1). Had the buyer done so, it could "recover from the seller as damages the difference between the cost of cover and the contract price together with any incidental or consequential damages as hereinafter defined (§ 2-715), but less expenses saved in consequence of the seller's breach." UCC § 2-712(2). This remedy is completely optional, and the "[f]ailure of the buyer to effect cover within this section does not bar him from any other remedy," (UCC § 2-712(3)), which is why the buyer was entitled to seek expectation damages under UCC § 2-713 instead.

There is authority for [Tongish's] position that [UCC § 2-713] should not be applied in certain circumstances. In *Allied Canners & Packers, Inc. v. Victor Packing Co.*, 162 Cal. App. 3d 905 (1984), Allied contracted to purchase 375,000 pounds of raisins from Victor for 29.75 cents per pound with a 4% discount. Allied then contracted to sell the raisins for 29.75 cents per pound expecting a profit of $4,462.50 from the 4% discount it received from Victor.

Heavy rains damaged the raisin crop and Victor breached its contract, being unable to fulfill the requirement. The market price of raisins had risen to about 80 cents per pound. Allied's buyers agreed to rescind their contracts so Allied was not bound to supply them with raisins at a severe loss. Therefore, the actual loss to Allied was the $4,462.50 profit it expected, while the difference between the market price and the contract price was about $150,000.

The California appellate court, in writing an exception, stated: "It has been recognized that the use of the market-price contract-price formula under section 2-713 does not, absent pure accident, result in a damage award reflecting the buyer's actual loss." 162 Cal. App. 3d at 912. The court indicated that section 2-713 may be more of a statutory liquidated damages clause and, therefore, conflicts with the goal of section 1-106. The court discussed that in situations where the buyer has made a resale contract for the goods, which the seller knows about, it may be appropriate to limit 2-713 damages to actual loss. **However, the court cited a concern that a seller not be rewarded for a bad faith breach of contract.**

In *Allied*, the court determined that if the seller knew the buyer had a resale contract for the goods, and the seller did not breach the contract in bad faith, the buyer was limited to actual loss of damages under section 1-106. . . .

[However,] [t]he *Allied* decision . . . has been sharply criticized. In Schneider, *UCC Section 2-713: A Defense of Buyers' Expectancy Damages*, 22 Cal. W. L. Rev. 233, 266 (1986), the author stated that *Allied* "adopted the most restrictive [position] on buyer's damages." . . . Schneider argued that by following section 1-106, "the court ignored the clear language of section 2-713's compensation scheme to award expectation damages in accordance with the parties' allocation of risk as measured by the difference between contract price and market price on the date set for performance." 22 Cal. W. L. Rev. at 264.

> **Bad faith breach?**
>
> We began Section A of this chapter with a quote from the *Restatement (Second) of Contracts*, where we were told that "[t]he traditional goal of the law of contract remedies has not been compulsion of the promisor to perform his promise but compensation of the promisee for the loss resulting from breach," with the result that "'[w]illful' breaches have not been distinguished from other breaches." But is this true? As you read the cases in this chapter, ask yourself whether the courts are holding true to the principle of not distinguishing between willful and non-willful breaches, or if they are instead awarding plaintiffs more generous damage judgments where defendants breaches are willful. Stay tuned.

Recently in Scott, *The Case for Market Damages: Revisiting the Lost Profits Puzzle*, 57 U. Chi. L. Rev. 1155, 1200 (1990), the *Allied* result was called "unfortunate." Scott argues that section 1-106 is "entirely consistent" with the market damages remedy of 2-713. 57 U. Chi. L. Rev. at 1201. According to Scott, it is possible to harmonize sections 1-106 and 2-713. Scott states, "Market damages measure the expectancy ex ante, and thus reflect the value of the option; lost profits, on the other hand, measure losses ex post, and thus only reflect the value of the completed exchange." 57 U. Chi. L. Rev. at 1174. The author argues that if the nonbreaching party has laid off part of the market risk (like Coop did) the lost profits rule creates instability because the other party is now encouraged to breach the contract if the market fluctuates to its advantage.

> We are not persuaded that the lost profits view under *Allied* should be embraced. It is a minority rule that has received only nominal support. We believe the majority rule or the market damages remedy as contained in [UCC § 2-713] is more reasoned and should be followed as the preferred measure of damages. While application of the rule may not reflect the actual loss to a buyer, it encourages a more efficient market and discourages the breach of contracts.

Tongish v. Thomas, 16 Kan. App. 2d at 811-17.

At first blush, the result reached herein appears unfair. However, closer scrutiny dissipates this impression. By the terms of the contract Coop was obligated to buy Tongish's large sunflower seeds at $13 per hundredweight whether or not it had a market for them. Had the price of sunflower seeds plummeted by delivery time, Coop's obligation to purchase at the agreed price was fixed. If loss of actual profit pursuant to [UCC § 1-106(1)] would be the measure of damages to be applied herein, it would enable Tongish to consider the Coop contract price of $13 per hundredweight plus 55 cents per hundredweight handling fee as the "floor" price for his seeds, take advantage of rapidly escalating prices, ignore his contractual obligation, and profitably sell to the highest bidder. Damages computed under [UCC § 2-713] encourage the honoring of contracts and market stability.

As an additional argument, Tongish contends that the application of [UCC § 2-713] would result in the unjust enrichment of Coop. This argument was not presented to the trial court.

Even if properly before us, the argument lacks merit. We discussed the doctrine of unjust enrichment in *J. W. Thompson Co. v. Welles Products Corp.*, 243 Kan. 503 (1988), stating:

> The basic elements on a claim based on a theory of unjust enrichment are threefold: (1) a benefit conferred upon the defendant by the plaintiff; (2) an appreciation or knowledge of the benefit by the defendant; and (3) the acceptance or retention by the defendant of the benefit under such circumstances as to make it inequitable for the defendant to retain the benefit without payment of its value.

243 Kan. at 512.

Before us is which statutory measure of damages applies. This is not a matter of one party conferring a benefit upon another.

The judgment of the Court of Appeals [requiring that damages be determined per UCC § 2-713] is affirmed. The judgment of the district court is reversed.

RELEVANT PROVISIONS

For the UCC, consult §§ 1-106, 2-711, 2-712, 2-713, 2-715, and 2-717. For the CISG, consult Articles 50, 74, 75, and 76. For the UNIDROIT Principles, consult Articles 7.4.2, 7.4.4, 7.4.5, and 7.4.6.

NOTES AND QUESTIONS

1. ***What happened?*** Who sued whom for what? Procedurally, how did the case get before this court? Factually, what happened between the parties? What arguments did the plaintiff and defendant make? What rule or rules did the court apply? How did the court analyze the dispute between the parties? How did the court decide the case?

2. ***Was this case correctly decided?*** Do you agree with the result reached in this case? Why or why not? Do you agree with the court's reasoning? Why or why not? How, if at all, would you have written the opinion differently?

3. ***What to do when the UCC conflicts.*** Should the court have awarded lost profits per UCC § 1-106, or the difference between the market and contract prices per UCC § 2-713? Why? Which measure better reflects Coop's expectation damages? Why? Which measure seems most just? Why?

4. *UCC § 2-713.* The Court of Appeals' decision, which was heavily quoted by the Supreme Court of Kansas, noted that although UCC § 2-713 "may not reflect the actual loss to a buyer, it encourages a more efficient market and discourages the breach of contracts." Do you agree? Why or why not? Should courts try to discourage promisors from breaching their contracts, or simply ensure that, if they do, the promisee is made whole?

5. *UCC § 1-106.* The Supreme Court of Kansas rejected Tongish's argument that awarding damages per UCC § 2-713 would result in the unjust enrichment of Coop. Do you agree? Would an award issued per § 2-713 unjustly enrich Coop? If not, would it overcompensate Coop? Why or why not? A slightly different question: would awarding damages per § 1-106 result in undercompensation to Coop? Why or why not? Try to look at this question from the perspective of each party, and from the perspective of the judicial system as a whole. Which measure of damages makes the most sense, and why?

6. *UCC § 2-712.* How would damages have been calculated under § 2-712 if the injured party would have "covered"?

7. *Seller's and buyer's remedies compared.* Compare § 2-706 with § 2-712, and §§ 2-708 with § 2-713. What differences, if any, can you detect? Does the CISG (see "Relevant Provisions," above) provide a better solution to the problem that this court faced? Why or why not?

8. *Efficient breach?* Once the price of sunflower seeds rose, Tongish realized that it would be better off breaching its contract with Coop, paying Coop damages (its 55 cent per hundredweight handling fee), and selling the sunflower seeds to another party at a higher price. If the goal of expectation damages is not to punish the promisor, but to put the injured party in the position it would have occupied had the contract been performed, then, according to advocates of the theory of efficient breach, the court should not only

have allowed, but *encouraged* (by awarding damages under § 1-106) Tongish to breach its contract. Why? Because such a breach would result in Pareto efficiency in that all parties involved would either benefit, or be made no worse off, as a result of the breach. Let's see how. Tongish, so goes the theory, would be better off (even after paying damages to Coop) because he would be able to sell sunflower seeds to Thomas for nearly twice as much as he would have sold them to Coop under the original contract. Thomas would benefit because he would obtain something he valued (i.e., the sunflower seeds) more than he valued the money he needed to pay to obtain them. Society would also benefit because scarce resources (i.e., the sunflower seeds) would move from a party who valued them less (Coop) to a party who valued them more (Thomas), as reflected by the higher price Thomas agreed to pay. And finally, if expectation damages are accurately assessed by the court, then Coop would be no worse off than if the contract had been performed, in that it would have received its 55 cent per hundredweight handling fee as a damages award from Tongish. Or, so goes the theory, anyway. In the following two excerpts, we will take a critical look at the theory of efficient breach, the first from an economic perspective, and the second from a moral one. As you read these excerpts, ask yourself whether you think courts should allow parties to efficiently breach their contracts (i.e., allow them to breach so long as they can pay expectation damages to the injured party), or whether they should try to calibrate the remedy to achieve other important policy objectives, such as encouraging promisors to keep their promises. Your answer will probably depend, at least in part, on whether you think the purpose of contract law is to protect the disappointed expectations of promisees, or to encourage promisors to keep their promises.

THE ECONOMIC BASIS OF CONTRACT REMEDIES*

Economic theory is a useful adjunct to legal analysis in the field of contract remedies. The important role that contracts play in the economy has inspired much economic analysis, which tends, to a surprising extent, to confirm the choices that common law judges made without the benefit of such insights.[1]

According to traditional economic theory, the mechanism of bargained-for exchange plays a vital role in the voluntary reallocation of goods, labor, and other resources in a socially desirable manner. The basic notion is that an economy will operate "efficiently" only to the extent that available goods and resources are utilized in their most productive manner. Ideally, each good must be consumed by the person who values it most highly, and each factor of production must be employed in the way that produces the most valued output. However, actual allocations of wealth rarely meet this test of efficiency, since assets are often owned by persons who place lower values on them than do others. Through voluntary agreements, in

* Excerpted from E. Allan Farnsworth, Contracts § 12.3 (4th ed. 2004).

1. The most frequently cited work is Richard Posner, Economic Analysis of Law ch. 4 (6th ed. 2003).

which individuals exchange assets that they own for others that they value more, society progresses toward the goal of economic efficiency. A bargained-for exchange from which both parties benefit is socially desirable in the sense that it results in a gain in efficiency by moving the assets that are exchanged to higher valued uses.

Economic theory presupposes rational parties that strive to maximize their own welfare. Such parties will not freely enter into agreements that are detrimental to their own interests. Absent some impediment, such as mistake, misrepresentation, or duress, each party will place a value on the other's performance that is greater than the anticipated cost of its own performance. At the time the agreement is made, each party has reason to suppose that it will be profitable for that party. A party may, however, err in calculating the net benefit to be anticipated from performance of the agreement, or circumstances may change so as to disappoint that party's initial hopes. A contract that the party once thought would be profitable may turn out to be unprofitable. If it is still profitable for the other party, should the reluctant party be compelled to perform?

If nonperformance of the agreement would result in a gain by the reluctant party at the expense of a loss by the other party, the result of nonperformance is economically efficient only if the value of the gain to the reluctant party is greater than the value of the loss to the other party. However, since individuals differ in their value judgments, the gain and the loss cannot be simply compared in absolute terms. One of the principles that has been developed to overcome this difficulty states that a redistribution of wealth is desirable if the party that benefits values its gains more than the loser values its losses.[2] This principle can be applied to the redistribution of wealth that follows from a breach of contract and to the payment of damages for that breach. The party in breach may gain enough from the breach to have a net benefit, even though that party compensates the injured party for resulting loss, calculated according to the subjective preferences of the injured party. If this is so, nonperformance and the consequent reallocation of resources is socially desirable, and economic theory not only sanctions but encourages breach. The breach is often called an "efficient breach."[3] To prevent such a breach by compelling performance would result in an undesirable wealth distribution, since the party in breach would lose more than the injured party would gain.

This notion accords remarkably with the traditional assumptions of the law of contract remedies. The principal interest protected by that law is the expectation interest, measured by the amount of money required to put the injured party in as good a position as that party would have been in had the contract been performed. This amount is the counterpart of the compensation that economic

---

2. This is known as the Kaldor or Kaldor-Hicks criterion, initially stated in Kaldor, *Welfare Propositions of Economics and Interpersonal Comparisons of Utility*, 49 ECON. J. 549 (1939), and in Hicks, *The Foundations of Welfare Economics*, 49 ECON. J. 696 (1939). [This concept was also discussed in "Thinking Tool: Marginal Analysis and Efficiency" in Part II, p. 64, *supra*.—ED.]

3. For judicial endorsement of the notion of efficient breach by one of its leading advocates, *see Patton v. Mid-Continent Sys.*, 841 F.2d 742 (7th Cir. 1988) (Posner, J.: "Even if the breach is deliberate, it is not necessarily blameworthy. The promisor may simply have discovered that his performance is worth more to someone else. If so, efficiency is promoted by allowing him to break his promise, provided he makes good the promisee's actual losses."). . . .

analysis suggests. The effect is to give the reluctant party an incentive to break the contract if, but only if, that party gains enough from the breach that it can compensate the injured party for its losses yet still retain some of the benefits from the breach. Since the goal is compensation and not compulsion, the promisor who could have performed, but chose not to for financial reasons, should not be dealt with harshly. Punitive damages should not be awarded for breach of contract because they will encourage performance when breach would be socially more desirable. "Willful" breaches should not be distinguished from other breaches. And specific performance should generally not be required, at least where compensation in damages is an adequate substitute for the injured party. All of these conclusions mirror traditional contract doctrine.

This economic analysis is not without shortcomings. First, its focus on the relative pecuniary benefits from breach leaves no place for notions of the sanctity of contract and the moral obligation to honor one's promises.[8] Second, analysis in economic terms assumes an ability to measure value with a certainty that is often not possible in the judicial process. Third, the economic analysis suggested here may be affected by "transaction costs," such as the cost of negotiation and the costs of search.[9]

The impact of transaction costs has attracted considerable attention. Suppose, for example, that a seller, under contract to deliver specific goods to a buyer, is offered a better price for the goods from another buyer, which values the goods more highly than the first buyer and therefore should end up with the goods if efficiency is to be served. Under the notion of "efficient breach," it is desirable that the seller break the contract and sell the goods to the second buyer, using part of the difference in price to pay damages to the first buyer and keeping whatever is left of the difference. Only in this way, the argument runs, will the goods end up in the hands of the second buyer, which values them more highly than does the first buyer. But if transaction costs are ignored, the argument is doubly flawed for, under either of two scenarios, the second buyer will end up with the goods even if the seller is not permitted to break the contract. First, if the costs of search are ignored, even if the seller performs the contract, the first buyer will costlessly find the second buyer and sell it the goods for the higher price. Second, if the costs of negotiation are ignored, the seller will costlessly negotiate a release from the contract with the first buyer, enabling the seller to sell the goods to the second buyer for the higher price. These scenarios would result in different allocations, as between the seller and the first buyer, of the gain from the sale to the second buyer, but since in all scenarios the goods end up in the hands of the buyer that values them more highly, there is no difference in economic efficiency. In

8. *See* CHARLES FRIED, CONTRACT AS PROMISE 36 (1981) (conception of contract rooted in bargain "challenges my thesis that the basis of contract is promise by locating that basis now in a distinct collective policy, the furtherance of economic exchange"). [Sanctity of contract and the notion of honoring one's moral obligations was also discussed in "Justifying Contract Law" in Part II, p. 81, *supra*.—ED.]

9. The seminal work is Ronald Coase, *The Problem of Social Cost*, 3 J.L. & ECON. 1 (1960). [Transaction costs were also discussed in "Thinking Tool: The Coase Theorem, Transaction Costs, and Distributive Justice" in Part III, p. 460, *supra*.—ED.]

life, however, transaction costs are not negligible. Furthermore, thorough analysis must also take account of the costs inherent in negotiating the contract in the first instance, if parties feel compelled to insist on protective clauses to assure performance. This is a particularly significant defect if the amount involved is small. However, the main thrust of the analysis and its support of traditional contract doctrine in this area are clear. And the lawyer who, acting in a client's interest, advises the client to break a contract or assists the client in breaking it is not liable to the aggrieved party. . . .

EFFICIENT BREACH AND THE "BAD MAN'S" THEORY OF CONTRACTS*

What constitutes the law? You will find some text writers telling you that it is something different from what is decided by the courts[,] . . . that it is a system of reason, that it is a deduction from principles of ethics or admitted axioms or what not, which may or may not coincide with the decisions. But if we take the view of our friend the bad man we shall find that he does not care two straws for the axioms or deductions, but that he does want to know what the . . . courts are likely to do in fact. I am much of his mind. The prophecies of what the courts will do in fact, and nothing more pretentious, are what I mean by the law.

— Oliver Wendell Holmes, *Path of the Law*, 10 Harv. L. Rev. 457, 460-61 (1897)

Although Holmes's bad man theory of law has come to permeate Anglo-American legal thought, perhaps nowhere has the bad man had more influence than in the realm of contracts, where scholars and judges alike have spilled so much ink fleshing out and giving shape to Holmes's vision that it is difficult to think or write about contract law without the bad man standing over one's shoulders, monitoring one's action, and attempting to influence one's thought. But how, exactly, does Holmes's bad man approach contract law, and what, if anything, can his views tell us about the way Holmes thinks we are to understand contract law?

Perhaps the best way of understanding the bad man's view of contract law is to contrast it with the way his counterpart, the good man, understands the subject. Unlike the bad man, the good man performs his promise not because of the benefits he might receive, nor because of the costs he might incur, but because, quite simply, performing one's promise is the right thing to do. And because the good man is guided by the moral law emanating from within, rather than the positive law imposed from without, he believes that moral principles governing the institution of promise-keeping (e.g., the idea that "there is something inherently despicable" about not

* Excerpted from Marco Jimenez, *Finding the Good in Holmes' Bad Man*, 79 FORDHAM L. REV. 2069, 2080-87 (2011) (internal citations omitted).

keeping one's promises) should guide, or at the very least inform, the legal principles governing contract law (e.g., "a properly organized society should not tolerate this").

The bad man, in contrast, sees matters quite differently. Holmes, in his monumental speech, famously dismissed this type of moralistic thinking as unhelpful and confusing, and invited his audience to understand contract law as the bad man himself would understand it. In language now immortalized in the contract law canon, Holmes wrote:

> Nowhere is the confusion between legal and moral ideas more manifest than in the law of contract. Among other things, here again the so called primary rights and duties are invested with a mystic significance beyond what can be assigned and explained. The duty to keep a contract at common law means a prediction that you must pay damages if you do not keep it,—and nothing else. . . . But such a mode of looking at the matter stinks in the nostrils of those who think it advantageous to get as much ethics into the law as they can.

. . . What Holmes meant by these words, and whether he was speaking normatively or descriptively, is a matter of much debate. . . . What is not in debate, however, is the enormous influence these words, as interpreted by generations of contracts scholars and judges, have had on the subsequent history of contract law. . . . According to the standard interpretation, Holmes meant to suggest that a promisor, upon entering into a contract, is not obligated to uphold his promissory commitment, but rather has a choice between performing, on the one hand, and breaching while paying money damages, on the other. The truth is that the bad man, of course, does see matters this way, and will probably, as a descriptive matter, choose his course of conduct based not on moral considerations, but by performing a cost-benefit analysis.

Although some scholars lament the fact that morality does not play a larger role in Holmes's theory, most scholars (even if only reluctantly) concede that modern contract law is essentially Holmesian and ultimately does "exclude[] considerations of morality" in order to "advance the objective of economic efficiency." Today, the most ardent supporters of Holmes's theory are those working within the law and economics paradigm, who have applied Holmes's bad man view of contracts with particular force to the modern theory of efficient breach, which acts as the bad man's shibboleth in distinguishing those who would invoke morality when determining one's contractual obligations from those who would not.

For instance, the strongest proponents of efficient breach theory not only acknowledge, as a descriptive point, the promisor's right to breach a contract where doing so is efficient, but even go so far as to claim that the law should encourage, as a normative matter, such breaches. Putting aside for the moment Holmes's own views on the matter, it is in large part due to such statements that many scholars have opposed this theory as morally wanting and, worse yet, damaging to the institution of promise-keeping.

PROBLEM: I CHANGED MY MIND

Buyer entered into a contract to purchase a sophisticated piece of medical diagnostic equipment from Seller for for $1,000,000. As part of the agreement, Buyer paid a $250,000 deposit to Seller. Several days later, Builder, who agreed to build a medical facility for Buyer, breached its contract with Buyer, so Buyer subsequently breached its contract with Seller, refusing (a) to take delivery of the medical diagnostic equipment and (b) to pay the balance due under the Buyer-Seller contract. Seller subsequently resold the equipment to a third party for $1,000,000. As a result, Buyer brought suit against Seller to recover its $250,000 down payment under UCC 2-718(2), but Seller alleges it is entitled to an offset under UCC 2-718(3). Specifically, Seller alleges it is a "lost volume seller" and Buyer's breach caused it to lose the profit from one additional sale.

How should a judge rule, and why? Which additional facts, if any, do you think a court would like to know before reaching its decision?

c. Expectation Damages Revisited: Cost of Completion v. Diminution in Value

As we have seen throughout this chapter, the goal of expectation damages is to give the injured party the "benefit of his bargain" by putting him "in as good a position as he would have been in had the contract been performed." *Restatement (Second) of Contracts* § 344. But, as we have also seen in cases like *Neri v. Retail Marine Corp.* and *Tongish v. Thomas,* expectation damages can sometimes be measured in several different ways, with quite different results. In this unit, we will look at several cases in which the promisor's performance is defective (i.e., there is a breach), and courts are called upon to protect an injured party's expectation interest by choosing between (1) awarding them the "cost to complete" their bargained-for performance, or (2) by awarding them the "difference" or "diminution in value" between the performance that was promised and the performance that was received.

It is important to keep in mind that, as a theoretical matter, both ways of measuring expectation damages are designed to put the injured party in the position it would have occupied but for the breach, but, as a practical matter, the actual difference between the two values is often quite drastic. For instance, if I contract for you to install birch cabinets in my kitchen, but you accidentally install maple cabinets instead, which (let's assume) look identical and are of similar quality, it might cost you several thousand dollars to rip out the maple cabinets and install birch cabinets, even though the value of my kitchen will (let's assume) remain unchanged. Here, because you are in breach, I am clearly entitled to a remedy, but the court's choice of protecting my contractual right with a cost-of-completion or a diminution-in-value measure of damages will differ dramatically, although both are, technically speaking, "expectation" damages. Keep your eyes out for these issues as you read the cases below, and ask yourself which of the two measures you believe to be most appropriate based on the facts of each case, and why.

DOCTRINAL OVERVIEW: AVOIDABILITY AND COST TO REMEDY DEFECT*

An especially troublesome aspect of the limitation of avoidability may arise if the recipient is the injured party and seeks damages for partial breach based on the cost to remedy the defect in the other party's performance. If the breach consists merely of incomplete, rather than defective, performance, the cost at which the recipient can arrange a substitute transaction to have the performance completed will ordinarily be less than the *loss in value* to the recipient. So the limitation of avoidability will have the effect of restricting the recipient to damages based on that lesser cost to complete performance, rather than on *loss in value*. Suppose, for example, that a builder breaks a contract to construct a factory by failing to finish the roof, making the factory unusable. The owner cannot recover the relatively enormous loss resulting from the inability to use the factory, but is instead relegated to the relatively small amount that it will cost to get another builder to finish the roof. Trouble may arise, however, if the performance under such a contract is defective, rather than merely incomplete. In that case, part of the cost to remedy the defect and complete the performance as agreed will probably be the cost of undoing some of the work already done. The total cost to remedy the defect may then exceed the *loss in value* to the injured party, so an award based on that cost would to that extent be a windfall.

Jacob & Youngs v. Kent is a striking example of this. . . .

Jacob & Youngs, Inc. v. Kent

Court of Appeals of New York
129 N.E. 889 (1921)

For a report of the case and accompanying materials, see p. 133, *supra*.

NOTES AND QUESTIONS

1. *The relationship between performance and remedy?* Did you notice how, in *Jacob & Youngs v. Kent*, the type of performance that the contractor rendered (i.e., substantial performance versus material breach), along with whether its breach was willful, affected the type of remedy it could get from the

* Excerpted from E. ALLAN FARNSWORTH, CONTRACTS § 12.13 (4th ed. 2004).

homeowner (i.e., cost of completion versus diminution in value)? Indeed, the relationship between the nature of the performance rendered by the breaching party, and the remedy available to the injured party, will be a theme that runs through the rest of the cases in this section (*Groves v. John Wunder Co.*, *Peevyhouse v. Garland Coal Mining Co.*, and *American Standard, Inc. v. Schectman*). The following two excerpts explore some of these issues in greater depth, and are designed to help you get the most out of your reading of the remaining cases in this unit.

Before reading the excerpt below, you may wish to review "Thinking Tool: Thinking Clearly About Legal Relationships" at p. 96, *supra*.

THINKING TOOL APPLIED: SORTING OUT COMPLEX LEGAL RELATIONS*

Complex legal relations come in two types—multiple issues between two parties and issues involving three or more parties. A Hohfeldian analysis, which demands separation of issues and is built on the premise that a legal relation is always between two persons, provides a mechanism for sorting out these relations.

As an example of multiple issues between two parties, consider Illustration 11 to Section 237 of the *Restatement (Second) of Contracts*:

> A contracts to build a house for B, for which B promises to pay $50,000 in monthly progress payments equal to 85% of the value of the work with the balance to be paid on completion. When A completes the construction, B refuses to pay the $7,500 balance claiming that there are defects that amount to an uncured material breach. If the breach is material, A's performance is not substantial and he has no claim under the contract against B, although he may have a claim in restitution (§ 374). If the breach is not material, A's performance is said to be substantial, he has a claim under the contract against B for $7,500, and B has a claim against A for damages because of the defects.[39]

This illustration implicates issues of full performance, substantial performance, breach, recovery *on* the contract, recovery *off* the contract (restitution), and damages. The key to teaching these issues is separating them. If A builds the house without defects, she will have a right to recover the $7,500 balance without deduction, and B will have a duty to pay. If the construction is defective, the next issue is whether A's performance is substantial. If it is, then A has a right to recover the $7,500 balance but also has a duty to pay damages for the defects. If A's performance is not substantial, then A does not have a right to recover on the contract, and B is privileged not to pay. In that case, however, to avoid unjust enrichment A has a right to recover off the contract in restitution for the value

* Excerpted from Curtis Nyquist, *Teaching Wesley Hohfeld's Theory of Legal Relations*, 52 J. Legal Educ. 238, 249-50 (2002).

39. Restatement (Second) of Contracts § 237 cmt., illus. 11 (1981).

of the benefit received by B. It is worth repeating here that Hohfeld provides no resolution of these issues, but offers a method of separating, clarifying, and stating them. Once issues have been stated, then the difficult work of confronting the law's gaps, conflicts, and ambiguities begins.

When expectation damages can be measured in two different ways, as either the cost of completion or diminution in value, then what remedy should a court award to return an injured party to its rightful position? After reviewing the facts in Jacob & Youngs v. Kent, *the excerpt below tries to answer this question. As you read it, ask yourself whether you agree or disagree with the author's characterization of the case as presenting an invitation for courts to not only compensate injured parties, but also to punish breaching parties. It is universally believed, you will remember, that contract damages are intended to compensate, not punish. Does the author's example rebut this presumption? How do you think damages in cases like* Jacob & Youngs v. Kent *should be measured, and why? In the absence of a principled justification for choosing between competing measures of the expectancy, might the "split the baby" approach criticized by the author actually be the best solution? Does the author's suggestion that courts may be doing more than just compensating victims (i.e., they may be sneakily punishing wrongdoers) help explain the cases following the excerpt?*

COMPENSATION OR PUNISHMENT? COST OF COMPLETION VERSUS DIMINUTION IN VALUE DAMAGES IN *JACOB & YOUNGS V. KENT**

Consider . . . *Jacob & Youngs, Inc. v. Kent,* in which the parties entered into a contract pursuant to which the plaintiff-builder, Jacob & Youngs, agreed to build a country residence for the defendant-homeowner, Kent. In their contract, Jacob & Youngs further promised to install only pipe manufactured by the Reading Pipe Company. The defendant completed the construction, but throughout much of the house unintentionally installed Cohoes pipe, which was of the same quality, appearance, market value, and cost as Reading pipe. After Kent took possession of the residence, he discovered that some of the pipe did not conform to the contract, claimed that Jacob & Youngs failed to satisfy a condition in the contract, and refused to pay the balance due.

Judge Cardozo, writing for the court, found that although Jacob & Youngs breached the contract by failing to install the specific brand of pipe requested by the defendant, its mistake was both unintentional and harmless. Therefore, according to Cardozo, the real issue was whether, in such a situation, the court should imply a condition, the nonsatisfaction of which would result in a forfeiture, or whether the court should merely find that Jacob & Youngs breached the

* Excerpted from Marco Jimenez, *Remedial Consilience*, 62 EMORY L.J. 1309, 1328-34 (2013) (internal citations omitted).

contract (but did not violate an implied condition), and hold it liable for compensatory damages. In a memorable passage, Cardozo wrote:

> The courts never say that one who makes a contract fills the measure of his duty by less than full performance. They do say, however, that an omission, both trivial and innocent, will sometimes be atoned for by allowance of the resulting damage, and will not always be the breach of a condition to be followed by a forfeiture. The distinction is akin to that between dependent and independent promises, or between promises and conditions.

Framed in such a manner, the issue that now confronted Judge Cardozo was whether the language in the contract constituted (a) a condition that had not been satisfied, in which case Jacob & Youngs would not be entitled to recover the balance due under the contract unless it replaced the nonconforming pipe with Reading pipe, or (b) a promise that had been breached, in which case Jacob & Youngs could recover the balance due under the contract, but would be liable to Kent for any damages he might have suffered due to the installation of nonconforming pipe. In making this determination, Cardozo set forth the following rubric for distinguishing conditions from promises:

> Some promises are so plainly independent that they can never by fair construction be conditions of one another. Others are so plainly dependent that they must always be conditions. Others, though dependent and thus conditions when there is departure in point of substance, will be viewed as independent and collateral when the departure is insignificant. Considerations partly of justice and partly of presumable intention are to tell us whether this or that promise shall be placed in one class or in another.

Here, because Cardozo found that considerations of justice (the departure was insignificant in point of substance, the defect was insignificant in its relation to the project, and the cost of replacing the nonconforming pipe was great) and presumable intention (the breach was unintentional rather than willful) favored Jacob & Youngs, Cardozo held that the language used in the contract requesting Reading pipe was a promise, rather than a condition, and that Jacob & Youngs was entitled to payment of the balance due under the contract. Because Jacob & Youngs breached, however, they were still liable to Kent for money damages. In determining the measure of those damages, Cardozo wrote:

> [T]he measure of the allowance is not the cost of replacement, which would be great, but the difference in value, which would be either nominal or nothing. . . . The owner is entitled to the money which will permit him to complete, unless the cost of completion is grossly and unfairly out of proportion to the good to be attained.

Here, because the breach was insignificant, and because the difference between these two measures of damages was disproportional, Kent could only recover diminution in value damages (i.e., the difference in value between the house with Reading pipe and the house with Cohoes pipe) rather than the more generous cost of completion damages (i.e., the amount it would cost Kent to tear out the nonconforming Cohoes pipe and replace it with Reading pipe). Because

Cohoes and Reading pipe were of the same quality, appearance, value, and cost, the expectation damages awarded by the court "would be either nominal or nothing."

This case, and others like it, is commonly understood by many commentators as presenting a choice between two different measures of expectation damages—cost of completion versus diminution in value—both of which are restorative . . . in that they attempt to measure the injured party's loss by restoring that party to the position he or she would have occupied but for the breach. Viewed in this manner, the case seems to read like other contracts cases in which the court is confronted with a policy choice between two different measures of a restorative remedy. . . . Faced with this decision—again, still viewing the problem through the lens of restoration—it does not seem unreasonable to make this policy choice on economic (or other) grounds. Thus, according to some commentators, where the "[l]oss in value to the owner is likely to be only a small fraction of the cost to complete," then "diminution in market price [is] probably the better approximation of this loss." Not only is it frequently thought that a cost of completion remedy might lead, in some cases, to "economic waste," but even where it does not, such a remedy may be criticized as "result[ing] in a 'windfall' to the injured party."

On the other hand, many of these same commentators also recognize that where diminution in value damages do not fully reflect the loss suffered by the promisee, it will result in undercompensation. Like the notion of "windfall" discussed above, this too is unacceptable if the goal is restoration. [Looking at this problem through the] lens of restoration, then, seems to provide no clear answers to distinguish between cost of completion and diminution in value cases, and has even led some commentators to suggest that we might resolve the issue by splitting the remedial baby:

> Rather than accept the draconian choice between overcompensation through cost [of completion] and undercompensation through diminution in market price, the trier of the facts ought to be allowed at least to fix an intermediate amount as its best estimate, in the light of all the circumstances, of the loss in value to the injured party.

This approach, however, seems to be without a principled justification, as it seems to advocate awarding a remedy in between two principled amounts for the sake of awarding a remedy, rather than forcing courts to grapple with the underlying justification for the remedy itself. Unlike King Solomon, whose order to split the baby achieved justice precisely because it was not carried out, a "splitting the baby" remedy, if carried out (either by King Solomon, then, or by a judge, today), would seem to result in injustice because it would give to one party only half as much as that party deserved while leaving the wrongdoing party with a half share too much. Might there be a better solution to this problem?

This Article suggests that the answer is yes: the seemingly intractable problem presented by *Jacob & Youngs, Inc. v. Kent* and other similar cases seems to be an illusion created by viewing the problem exclusively through the restorative lens itself, which becomes obfuscated when presented with legal problems that cannot clearly be discerned through the lens by which it is viewed. By changing our remedial lens, however, and viewing these problems through other remedial lenses (e.g., the . . . lens of retribution), these seemingly thorny remedial questions become both clearer and more interesting as well.

So how might our analysis of the remedial problem set forth in *Jacob & Youngs, Inc. v. Kent* be affected by viewing the matter through a different remedial lens—say, the retributive lens? First of all, such an approach would invite the judge to consider, for instance, the fact that a cost of completion remedy, rather than overcompensating the victim, may be just what was necessary to take ill-gotten gains from a wrongdoing party; or that a diminution in value remedy, rather than undercompensating a victim, may be one way for a court to ensure that no more is taken from a relatively innocent wrongdoing party than what is absolutely necessary. So, for example, by taking the retributive interest seriously, we could look at a case like *Jacob & Youngs* with fresh eyes, and would reexamine Cardozo's rhetoric concerning the cause of the default, the willfulness of the breach, and the builder's insistence to exercise its own discretion by installing pipe it perceived to be "'just as good'" not as the obscure and peripheral musings of an all-too- clever judge (as it often seems to my students when viewed through the restorative lens of compensation).

Instead, when viewed through the retributive lens, such rhetoric becomes central to unlocking the case's meaning. Words that otherwise seemed strange and aberrational in the context of contract law, such as Cardozo's refusal to visit this particular builder's "venial faults with oppressive retribution" while admonishing others that "[t]he willful transgressor must accept the penalty of his transgression," are given new meaning and hold a potentially powerful sway over private law. By recasting *Jacob & Youngs* as a case not only (or even primarily) about restoration, but also about retribution, it reveals that punishing the breaching party by taking from the wrongdoer what the wrongdoer himself took from the injured party (i.e., Reading pipe, measured by the cost of completion remedy) is not warranted where the breach was both unintentional and trivial.

If this is correct, and courts take seriously the notion of retributive relief in private law, then there should be instances in which courts, when faced with a choice between two different restorative remedies, decide the issue on retributive grounds by punishing more severely defendants who intentionally breached their contracts, or otherwise behaved badly, by taking from the wrongdoing parties what they themselves have taken from their victim, either in-kind or substitutionarily, by way of a dollar equivalent. A perfect test case, it would seem, would be one in which a judge would seem to be guided by retributive concerns and where an intentional breach is both trivial and incidental to the main purpose of the contract, and even more conclusive still would be a case in which the cost of completion damages are grossly disproportional to the diminution in value damages. The law, it turns out, is replete with such cases.

Consider, for instance, *Groves v. John Wunder Co.* . . .

Groves v. John Wunder Co.

Supreme Court of Minnesota
286 N.W. 235 (1939)

STONE, JUSTICE. Action for breach of contract. Plaintiff got judgment for a little over $15,000. Sorely disappointed by that sum, he appeals.

In August, 1927, S. J. Groves & Sons Company, a corporation (hereinafter mentioned simply as Groves), owned a tract of 24 acres of Minneapolis suburban real estate. It was served or easily could be reached by railroad trackage. It is zoned as heavy industrial property. But for lack of development of the neighborhood its principal value thus far may have been in the deposit of sand and gravel which it carried. The Groves company had a plant on the premises for excavating and screening the gravel. Nearby defendant owned and was operating a similar plant.

In August, 1927, Groves and defendant made the involved contract. For the most part it was a lease from Groves, as lessor, to defendant, as lessee; its term seven years. Defendant agreed to remove the sand and gravel and to leave the property "at a uniform grade, substantially the same as the grade now existing at the roadway . . . on said premises, and that in stripping the overburden . . . it will use said overburden for the purpose of maintaining and establishing said grade." . . .

Defendant breached the contract deliberately. It removed from the premises only "the richest and best of the gravel" and wholly failed, according to the findings, "to perform and comply with the terms, conditions, and provisions of said lease . . . with respect to the condition in which the surface of the demised premises was required to be left." Defendant surrendered the premises, not substantially at the grade required by the contract "nor at any uniform grade." Instead, the ground was "broken, rugged, and uneven." Plaintiff sues as assignee and successor in right of Groves.

As the contract was construed below, the finding is that to complete its performance 288,495 cubic yards of overburden would need to be excavated, taken from the premises, and deposited elsewhere. The reasonable cost of doing that was found to be upwards of $60,000. But, if defendant had left the premises at the uniform grade required by the lease, the reasonable value of the property on the determinative date would have been only $12,160. The judgment was for that sum, including interest, thereby nullifying plaintiff's claim that cost of completing the contract rather than difference in value of the land was the measure of

Deliberate, willful, and bad-faith breaches

When you read *Tongish v. Thomas*, one of the sidebar notes asked you to look at whether courts take into account the moral nature of defendant's breach, or whether they follow the principles of damages announced by the *Restatement (Second) of Contracts* and ignore the manner in which the contract has been breached. The truth is, some judges (being human, after all) seem to care about why parties breach contracts, whereas others, not so much. The majority opinion in *Groves* fell into the former category, the dissent into the latter. Here, for the remainder of the cases in this section, I have underlined every time a judge has used the word "deliberately" or "willfully" or "bad-faith," or has announced some other similar concept indicating that the court cares, or does not care, about the nature of the breach. Doing so, I hope, will allow you to notice the sharp divide between the way the majority and dissenting opinions in these cases are really divided — in no

damages. The gauge of damage adopted by the decision was the difference between the market value of plaintiff's land in the condition it was when the contract was made and what it would have been if defendant had performed. The one question for us arises upon plaintiff's assertion that he was entitled, not to that difference in value, but to the reasonable cost to him of doing the work called for by the contract which defendant left undone.

> small part, over the *purpose* contract remedies are designed to serve.

1. Defendant's breach of contract was wilful. There was nothing of good faith about it. Hence, that the decision below handsomely rewards bad faith and deliberate breach of contract is obvious. That is not allowable. Here the rule is well settled, . . . where the contractor wilfully and fraudulently varies from the terms of a construction contract, he cannot sue thereon and have the benefit of the equitable doctrine of substantial performance. That is the rule generally. *See* Annotation, "Wilful or intentional variation by contractor from terms of contract in regard to material or work as affecting measure of damages," 6 A.L.R. 137.

Jacob & Youngs, Inc. v. Kent, 230 N.Y. 239, 243, 244, is typical. It was a case of substantial performance of a building contract. (This case is distinctly the opposite.) Mr. Justice Cardozo, in the course of his opinion, stressed the distinguishing features. "Nowhere," he said, "will change be tolerated, however, if it is so dominant or pervasive as in any real or substantial measure to frustrate the purpose of the contract." Again, "the willful transgressor must accept the penalty of his transgression."

2. In reckoning damages for breach of a building or construction contract, the law aims to give the disappointed promisee, so far as money will do it, what he was promised. . . .

Even in case of substantial performance in good faith, the resulting defects being remediable, it is error to instruct that the measure of damage is "the difference in value between the house as it was and as it would have been if constructed according to contract." The "correct doctrine" is that the cost of remedying the defect is the "proper" measure of damages. . . .

The summit from which to reckon damages from trespass to real estate is its actual value at the moment. The owner's only right is to be compensated for the deterioration in value caused by the tort. That is all he has lost. But not so if a contract to improve the same land has been breached by the contractor who refuses to do the work, especially where, as here, he has been paid in advance. The summit from which to reckon damages for that wrong is the hypothetical peak of accomplishment (not value) which would have been reached had the work been done as demanded by the contract.

The owner's right to improve his property is not trammeled by its small value. It is his right to erect thereon structures which will reduce its value. If that be the result, it can be of no aid to any contractor who declines performance. As said long ago in *Chamberlain v. Parker*, 45 N.Y. 569, 572:

> A man may do what he will with his own, . . . and if he chooses to erect a monument to his caprice or folly on his premises, and employs and pays another to do

it, it does not lie with a defendant who has been so employed and paid for building it, to say that his own performance would not be beneficial to the plaintiff.

[I]n such a case as this, the owner is entitled to compensation for what he has lost, that is, the work or structure which he has been promised, for which he has paid, and of which he has been deprived by the contractor's breach.

To diminish damages recoverable against him in proportion as there is presently small value in the land would favor the faithless contractor. It would also ignore and so defeat plaintiff's right to contract and build for the future. . . .

It is suggested that because of little or no value in his land the owner may be unconscionably enriched by such a reckoning. The answer is that there can be no unconscionable enrichment, no advantage upon which the law will frown, when the result is but to give one party to a contract only what the other has promised; particularly where, as here, the delinquent has had full payment for the promised performance.

3. It is said by the *Restatement, Contracts,* § 346, comment b:

> Sometimes defects in a completed structure cannot be physically remedied without tearing down and rebuilding, at a cost that would be imprudent and unreasonable. The law does not require damages to be measured by a method requiring such economic waste. If no such waste is involved, the cost of remedying the defect is the amount awarded as compensation for failure to render the promised performance.

The "economic waste" declaimed against by the decisions applying that rule has nothing to do with the value in money of the real estate, or even with the product of the contract. The waste avoided is only that which would come from wrecking a physical structure, completed, or nearly so, under the contract. The cases applying that rule go no further. Absent such waste, as it is in this case, the rule of the *Restatement, Contracts,* § 346, is that "the cost of remedying the defect is the amount awarded as compensation for failure to render the promised performance." That means that defendants here are liable to plaintiff for the reasonable cost of doing what defendants promised to do and have wilfully declined to do.

It follows that there must be a new trial. . . .

A court divided

Take note of the fundamental disagreement between the majority's and the dissent's approach regarding the purpose of contract damages. Note also how the dissent's fundamentally different philosophical approach to damages influences the rest of its opinion. You will see the same fundamental differences appear in the next case as well, but there, the positions of the majority and dissent are reversed.

JULIUS J. OLSON, Justice (dissenting). . . . As the **rule of damages to be applied in any given case has for its purpose compensation, not punishment,** we must be ever mindful that, "If the application of a particular rule for measuring damages to given facts results in more than compensation, it is at once apparent that the wrong rule has been adopted." [Citation omitted.]

We have here then a situation where, concededly, if the contract had been performed, plaintiff would have had property worth, in round numbers, no more than $12,000. If he is to be awarded damages in an amount exceeding $60,000 he will be receiving at least 500 per cent more than his property, properly leveled to grade by actual performance, was intrinsically worth when the breach occurred. To so conclude is to give him something far beyond what the parties had in mind or contracted for. . . .

The theory upon which plaintiff relies for application of the cost of performance rule must have for its basis cases where the property or the improvement to be made is unique or personal instead of being of the kind ordinarily governed by market values. His action is one at law for damages, not for specific performance. As there was no affirmative showing of any peculiar fitness of this property to a unique or personal use, the rule to be applied is . . . this: Damages recoverable for breach of a contract to construct is the difference between the market value of the property in the condition it was when delivered to and received by plaintiff and what its market value would have been if defendant had fully complied with its terms. . . .

And the same thought was expressed by Mr. Justice Cardozo in *Jacob & Youngs, Inc. v. Kent,* 230 N.Y. 239, 244, thus: "The owner is entitled to the money which will permit him to complete, unless the cost of completion is grossly and unfairly out of proportion to the good to be attained. When that is true, the measure is the difference in value." . . .

No one doubts that a party may contract for the doing of anything he may choose to have done (assuming what is to be done is not unlawful) "although the thing to be produced had no marketable value." [Citing *Chamberlain v. Parker,* 45 N.Y. 569, 572]. . . . But that is not what plaintiff's predecessor in interest contracted for. Such a provision might well have been made, but the parties did not. . . .

In what manner has plaintiff been hurt beyond the damages awarded? As to him "economic waste" is not apparent. Assume that defendant abandoned the entire project without taking a single yard of gravel therefrom but left the premises as they were when the lease was made, could plaintiff recover damages upon the basis here established? The trouble with the prevailing opinion is that here plaintiff's loss is not made the basis for the amount of his recovery but rather what it would cost the defendant. No case has been decided upon that basis until now. . . .

I think the judgment should be affirmed.

Peevyhouse v. Garland Coal Mining Co.

Supreme Court of Oklahoma
382 P.2d 109 (1962)

JACKSON, JUSTICE. In the trial court, plaintiffs Willie and Lucille Peevyhouse sued the defendant, Garland Coal and Mining Company, for damages for breach of contract. Judgment was for plaintiffs in an amount considerably less than was sued for. Plaintiffs appeal and defendant cross-appeals.

In the briefs on appeal, the parties present their argument and contentions under several propositions; however, they all stem from the basic question of whether the trial court properly instructed the jury on the measure of damages.

Briefly stated, the facts are as follows: plaintiffs owned a farm containing coal deposits, and in November, 1954, leased the premises to defendant for a period of five years for coal mining purposes. A "stripmining" operation was contemplated in which the coal would be taken from pits on the surface of the ground, instead of from underground mine shafts. In addition to the usual covenants found in a coal mining lease, defendant specifically agreed to perform certain restorative and remedial work at the end of the lease period. It is unnecessary to set out the details of the work to be done, other than to say that it would involve the moving of many thousands of cubic yards of dirt, at a cost estimated by expert witnesses at about $29,000. However, plaintiffs sued for only $25,000.

During the trial, it was stipulated that all covenants and agreements in the lease contract had been fully carried out by both parties, except the remedial work mentioned above; defendant conceded that this work had not been done.

Plaintiffs introduced expert testimony as to the amount and nature of the work to be done, and its estimated cost. Over plaintiffs' objections, defendant thereafter introduced expert testimony as to the "diminution in value" of plaintiffs' farm resulting from the failure of defendant to render performance as agreed in the contract—that is, the difference between the present value of the farm, and what its value would have been if defendant had done what it agreed to do.

At the conclusion of the trial, the court instructed the jury that it must return a verdict for plaintiffs, and left the amount of damages for jury determination. On the measure of damages, the court instructed the jury that it might consider the cost of performance of the work defendant agreed to do, "together with all of the evidence offered on behalf of either party."

It thus appears that the jury was at liberty to consider the "diminution in value" of plaintiffs' farm as well as the cost of "repair work" in determining the amount of damages.

It returned a verdict for plaintiffs for $5,000—only a fraction of the "cost of performance," *but more than the total value of the farm even after the remedial work is done.*

On appeal, the issue is sharply drawn. Plaintiffs contend that the true measure of damages in this case is what it will cost plaintiffs to obtain performance of the work that was not done because of defendant's default. Defendant argues that the measure of damages is the cost of performance "limited, however, to the total difference in the market value before and after the work was performed."

It appears that this precise question has not heretofore been presented to this court. In *Ardizonne v. Archer*, 178 P. 263, this court held that the measure of damages for breach of a contract to drill an oil well was the reasonable cost of drilling the well, but here a slightly different factual situation exists. The drilling of an oil well will yield valuable geological information, even if no oil or gas is found, and of course if the well is a producer, the value of the premises increases. In the case before us, it is argued by defendant with some force that the performance of the remedial work defendant agreed to do will add at the most only a few hundred dollars to the value of plaintiffs' farm, and that the damages should be limited to that amount because that is all plaintiffs have lost.

Plaintiffs rely on *Groves v. John Wunder Co.*, 205 Minn. 163. In that case, the Minnesota court, in a substantially similar situation, adopted the "cost of performance" rule as opposed to the "value" rule. The result was to authorize a jury to give plaintiff damages in the amount of $60,000, where the real estate concerned would have been worth only $12,160, even if the work contracted for had been done.

It may be observed that *Groves v. John Wunder Co., supra*, is the only case which has come to our attention in which the cost of performance rule has been followed under circumstances where the cost of performance greatly exceeded the diminution in value resulting from the breach of contract. Incidentally, it appears that this case was decided by a plurality rather than a majority of the members of the court.

Defendant relies principally upon *Sandy Valley & E. R. Co., v. Hughes*, 175 Ky. 320; *Bigham v. Wabash-Pittsburg Terminal Ry. Co.*, 223 Pa. 106, and *Sweeney v. Lewis Const. Co.*, 66 Wash. 490. These were all cases in which, under similar circumstances, the appellate courts followed the "value" rule instead of the "cost of performance" rule. Plaintiff points out that in the earliest of these cases (*Bigham*) the court cites as authority on the measure of damages an earlier Pennsylvania *tort* case, and that the other two cases follow the first, with no explanation as to why a measure of damages ordinarily followed in cases sounding in tort should be used in contract cases. **Nevertheless, it is of some significance that three out of four appellate courts have followed the diminution in value rule under circumstances where, as here, the cost of performance greatly exceeds the diminution in value.**

The explanation may be found in the fact that the situations presented are artificial ones. **It is highly unlikely that the ordinary property owner would agree to pay $29,000 (or its equivalent) for the construction of "improvements" upon his property that would increase its value only about ($300) three hundred dollars.** The result is that we are called upon to apply principles of law theoretically based upon reason and reality to a situation which is basically unreasonable and unrealistic.

In *Groves v. John Wunder Co., supra*, in arriving at its conclusions, the Minnesota court apparently

Some significance?

Is it really? First, there were two cases favoring the plaintiff's position—*Ardizonne v. Archer* and *Groves v. John Wunder Co.*—not just one. Second, *Groves* was factually more analogous to the facts of *Peevyhouse* than any of the other opinions cited by the court. Third, the court never directly responded to the plaintiff's point that of the three cases favoring the defendant's position, the first relies on a tort case, and the rest follow suit. Which brings us to the last point: how statistically significant is it, really, that three out of four appellate courts (or three out of five, if you count *Ardizonne*) support the defendant's position? Is this how courts should decide cases, by comparing the quantity, rather than the quality, of the opinions favoring one party over the other?

Do you agree?

How do we know what the Peevyhouses would have done with the money? If they did not value their land in its restored condition more than they valued having $29,000 in their bank, then the court is right, but wrong otherwise. First, is it even relevant how much the Peevyhouses valued their restored property? Why not say "a deal is a deal," and because Garland Coal Mining Co. promised to restore it, that's what they should do? And second, if knowing how much the Peevyhouses valued their restored land *is* relevant to the court, how could it figure out the value the Peevyhouses placed on their restored property? (Hint: what would happen if the court awarded specific performance to the Peevyhouses and then let the Peevyhouses and Garland Coal Mining Co. bargain with one another as to whether the repairs should be made?) Finally, is any of this economic mumbo-jumbo even relevant? As Professor Linzer explained: "When people enter into contracts, they also may be motivated by non-monetary considerations. The end to be achieved by performance may be desired in and of itself, not as a means to an increase in wealth measured by conventional methods of valuation. . . . [After discussing *Peevyhouse*, Professor Linzer goes on to explain that] "[a]ny economic analysis that assigns no value to their love of home or treats the promise to restore the land as merely instrumental to protecting its market value is incapable of measuring the true costs and benefits of breach."[26]

considered the contract involved to be analogous to a building and construction contract, and cited authority for the proposition that the cost of performance or completion of the building as contracted is ordinarily the measure of damages in actions for damages for the breach of such a contract.

In an annotation following the Minnesota case beginning at 123 A.L.R. 515, the annotator places the three cases relied on by defendant (*Sandy Valley*, *Bigham* and *Sweeney*) under the classification of cases involving "grading and excavation contracts."

We do not think either analogy is strictly applicable to the case now before us. The primary purpose of the lease contract between plaintiffs and defendant was neither "building and construction" nor "grading and excavation." It was merely to accomplish the economical recovery and marketing of coal from the premises, to the profit of all parties. The special provisions of the lease contract pertaining to remedial work were incidental to the main object involved.

Even in the case of contracts that are unquestionably building and construction contracts, the authorities are not in agreement as to the factors to be considered in determining whether the cost of performance rule or the value rule should be applied. The American Law Institute's *Restatement of the Law, Contracts*, Volume 1, §§ 346(1)(a)(i) and (ii) submits the proposition that the cost of performance is the proper measure of damages "if this is possible and does not involve *unreasonable economic waste*;" and that the diminution in value caused by the breach is the proper measure "if construction and completion in accordance with the contract would involve *unreasonable economic waste*." (Emphasis supplied.) In an explanatory comment immediately following the text, the *Restatement* makes it clear that the "economic waste" referred to consists of the destruction of a substantially completed building or other structure. Of course no such destruction is involved in the case now before us.

On the other hand, in McCormick, *Damages* § 168, it is said with regard to building and construction contracts that ". . . in cases where the defect is one that can be repaired or cured without *undue expense*" the cost of performance is the proper measure of damages, but where ". . . the defect in material or construction is one that cannot be remedied without *an expenditure for*

26. Peter Linzer, *On the Amorality of Contract Remedies—Efficiency, Equity, and the Second Restatement*, 81 COLUM. L. REV. 111, 117 (1981).

reconstruction disproportionate to the end to be attained" (emphasis supplied) the value rule should be followed. The same idea was expressed in *Jacob & Youngs, Inc. v. Kent*, 230 N.Y. 239, as follows:

> The owner is entitled to the money which will permit him to complete, unless the cost of completion is grossly and unfairly out of proportion to the good to be attained. When that is true, the measure is the difference in value.

It thus appears that the prime consideration in the *Restatement* was "economic waste;" and that the prime consideration in McCormick, *Damages*, and in *Jacob & Youngs, Inc. v. Kent, supra*, was the relationship between the expense involved and the "end to be attained"—in other words, the "relative economic benefit."

In view of the unrealistic fact situation in the instant case, and certain Oklahoma statutes to be hereinafter noted, we are of the opinion that the "relative economic benefit" is a proper consideration here. This is in accord with the recent case of *Mann v. Clowser*, 190 Va. 887, 59 S.E.2d 78, where, in applying the cost rule, the Virginia court specifically noted that ". . . the defects are remediable from a practical standpoint and the costs *are not grossly disproportionate to the results to be obtained.*" (Emphasis supplied.) . . .

We therefore hold that where, in a coal mining lease, lessee agrees to perform certain remedial work on the premises concerned at the end of the lease period, and thereafter the contract is fully performed by both parties except that the remedial work is not done, the measure of damages in an action by lessor against lessee for damages for breach of contract is ordinarily the reasonable cost of performance of the work; however, where the contract provision breached was merely incidental to the main purpose in view, and where the economic benefit which would result to lessor by full performance of the work is grossly disproportionate to the cost of performance, the damages which lessor may recover are limited to the diminution in value resulting to the premises because of the non-performance.

We believe the above holding is in conformity with the intention of the Legislature as expressed in the statutes mentioned, and in harmony with the better-reasoned cases from the other jurisdictions where analogous fact situations have been considered. It should be noted that the rule as stated does not interfere with the property owner's right to "do what he will with his own" *Chamberlain v. Parker*, 45 N.Y. 569 (1871), or his right, if he chooses, to contract for "improvements" which will actually have the effect of reducing his property's value. Where such result is in fact contemplated by the parties, and is a main or principal purpose of those contracting, it would seem that the measure of damages for breach would ordinarily be the cost of performance.

The above holding disposes of all of the arguments raised by the parties on appeal.

Under the most liberal view of the evidence herein, the diminution in value resulting to the premises because of non-performance of the remedial work was $300. After a careful search of the record, we have found no evidence of a higher figure, and plaintiffs do not argue in their briefs that a greater diminution in value was sustained. It thus appears that the judgment was clearly excessive, and that the amount for which judgment should have been rendered is definitely and satisfactorily shown by the record. . . .

We are of the opinion that the judgment of the trial court for plaintiffs should be, and it is hereby, modified and reduced to the sum of $300, and as so modified it is affirmed.

IRWIN, JUSTICE **(dissenting)**. By the specific provisions in the coal mining lease under consideration, the defendant agreed as follows:

> 7b Lessee agrees to make fills in the pits dug on said premises on the property line in such manner that fences can be placed thereon and access had to opposite sides of the pits.
>
> 7c Lessee agrees to smooth off the top of the spoil banks on the above premises.
>
> 7d Lessee agrees to leave the creek crossing the above premises in such a condition that it will not interfere with the crossings to be made in pits as set out in 7b. . . .
>
> 7f Lessee further agrees to leave no shale or dirt on the high wall of said pits. . . .

Following the expiration of the lease, plaintiffs made demand upon defendant that it carry out the provisions of the contract and to perform those covenants contained therein.

Defendant admits that it failed to perform its obligations that it agreed and contracted to perform under the lease contract and there is nothing in the record which indicates that defendant could not perform its obligations. Therefore, in my opinion defendant's breach of the contract was willful and not in good faith.

Although the contract speaks for itself, there were several negotiations between the plaintiffs and defendant before the contract was executed. Defendant admitted in the trial of the action, that plaintiffs insisted that the above provisions be included in the contract and that they would not agree to the coal mining lease unless the above provisions were included.

In consideration for the lease contract, plaintiffs were to receive a certain amount as royalty for the coal produced and marketed and in addition thereto their land was to be restored as provided in the contract.

Defendant received as consideration for the contract, its proportionate share of the coal produced and marketed and in addition thereto, the *right to use* plaintiffs' land in the furtherance of its mining operations.

The cost for performing the contract in question could have been reasonably approximated when the contract was negotiated and executed and there are no conditions now existing which could not have been reasonably anticipated by the parties. Therefore, defendant had knowledge, when it prevailed upon the plaintiffs to execute the lease, that the cost of performance might be disproportionate to the value or benefits received by plaintiff for the performance.

Defendant has received its benefits under the contract and now urges, in substance, that plaintiffs' measure of damages for its failure to perform should be the economic value of performance to the plaintiffs and not the cost of performance.

If a peculiar set of facts should exist where the above rule should be applied as the proper measure of damages, (and in my judgment those facts do not exist in the instant case) before such rule should be applied, consideration should be given to the benefits received or contracted for by the party who asserts the application of the rule.

Defendant did not have the right to mine plaintiffs' coal or to use plaintiffs' property for its mining operations without the consent of plaintiffs. Defendant had knowledge of the benefits that it would receive under the contract and the approximate cost of performing the contract. With this knowledge, it must be presumed that defendant thought that it would be to its economic advantage to enter into the contract with plaintiffs and that it would reap benefits from the contract, or it would have not entered into the contract.

Therefore, if the value of the performance of a contract should be considered in determining the measure of damages for breach of a contract, the value of the benefits received under the contract by a party who breaches a contract should also be considered. However, in my judgment, to give consideration to either in the instant action, completely rescinds and holds for naught the solemnity of the contract before us and makes an entirely new contract for the parties. . . .

In my judgment, we should follow the case of *Groves v. John Wunder Company*, 205 Minn. 163, which defendant agrees "that the fact situation is apparently similar to the one in the case at bar," and where the Supreme Court of Minnesota held:

> The owner's or employer's damages for such a breach (i.e. breach hypothesized in 2d syllabus) are to be measured, not in respect to the value of the land to be improved, but by the reasonable cost of doing that which the contractor promised to do and which he left undone.

The hypothesized breach referred to states that where the contractor's breach of a contract is willful, that is, in bad-faith, he is not entitled to any benefit of the equitable doctrine of substantial performance.

In the instant action defendant has made no attempt to even substantially perform. The contract in question is not immoral, is not tainted with fraud, and was not entered into through mistake or accident and is not contrary to public policy. It is clear and unambiguous and the parties understood the terms thereof, and the approximate cost of fulfilling the obligations could have been approximately ascertained. There are no conditions existing now which could not have been reasonably anticipated when the contract was negotiated and executed. The defendant could have performed the contract if it desired. It has accepted and reaped the benefits of its contract and now urges that plaintiffs' benefits under the contract be denied. If plaintiffs' benefits are denied, such benefits would inure to the direct benefit of the defendant.

Therefore, in my opinion, the plaintiffs were entitled to specific performance of the contract and since defendant has failed to perform, the proper measure of damages should be the cost of performance. Any other measure of damage would be holding for naught the express provisions of the contract; would be taking from the plaintiffs the benefits of the contract and placing those benefits in defendant which has failed to perform its obligations; would be granting benefits to defendant without a resulting obligation; and would be completely rescinding the solemn obligation of the contract for the benefit of the defendant to the detriment of the plaintiffs by making an entirely new contract for the parties.

I therefore respectfully dissent to the opinion promulgated by a majority of my associates.

RELEVANT PROVISIONS

For the *Restatement (Second) of Contracts,* consult § 348.

NOTES AND QUESTIONS

1. *What happened?* For each of the above three cases, make sure you can answer the following questions: Who sued whom for what? Procedurally, how did the case get before this court? Factually, what happened between the parties? What arguments did the plaintiff and defendant make? What rule or rules did the court apply? How did the court analyze the dispute between the parties? How did the court decide the case?

2. *Which (if any) of the three previous cases was correctly decided?* Do you agree with the results reached in these cases? Why or why not? Do you agree with the courts' reasoning? Why or why not? How, if at all, would you have written the opinions differently?

3. *Can the previous three cases be reconciled?* If so, how?

4. *Cost of completion or diminution in value?* Which damages rule best promotes justice among the parties? Which rule best protects their ex ante expectations? Which best promotes efficiency?

5. *Behind the scenes.* Here are a few more interesting facts left out of the *Peevyhouse* opinion in a thoughtful article by Professor Maute (the entire article is worth reading) undertaking a detailed exploration of the background of *Peevyhouse*. Does it change your views on whether the case was decided correctly?

> The record omitted evidence regarding consideration for remediation, course of performance, and breach. To obtain Garland's promises of remediation, the Peevyhouses waived the right to receive $3,000 cash upon executing the lease. This amount equals $50 per acre and represents the amount coal operators customarily paid landowners for any surface damages caused by the mining. Upon executing the contract, the Peevyhouses received $2,000 for advance royalties, and

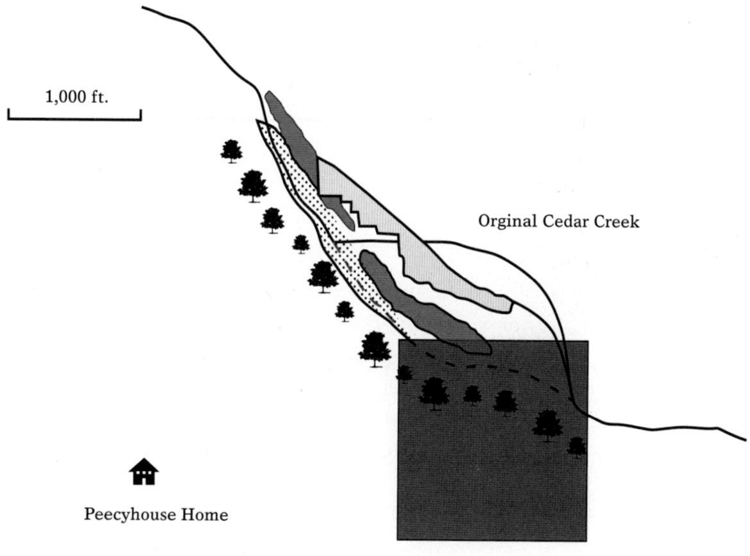

they later received an additional $500 royalty calculated on the total quantity of coal removed. Within days, Garland diverted a bothersome creek onto the Peevyhouse land so that it could continue elsewhere, unimpeded by water flow. Eventually Garland mined a small portion of the leased Peevyhouse land, but left the property earlier than expected, claiming the coal ran too deep. Heavy spring rains saturated the low-lying worksite, making it dangerously unstable. Garland made little effort to complete the promised remedial work. A bulldozer spent one day knocking off sharp peaks from the highwall and constructing a makeshift dirt fill to prevent the diverted creek from running into the pit, causing further damage. Settlement efforts failed. Upon conclusion of the lease term, the Peevyhouses sued for damages. After their attorney paid the litigation costs from the $300 judgment, nothing remained for distribution to the Peevyhouses. They still live on the land, which has not been restored.*

6. ***Illustrations.*** *Peevyhouse v. Garland Coal Mining Co.* now appears as Illustration 5 to the *Restatement (Third) of Restitution and Unjust Enrichment* § 39 as follows:

> 5. Landowner and Mining Company enter a contract for strip-mining. The agreement authorizes Mining Company to remove coal from Blackacre in exchange for payment of a specified royalty per ton. A further provision of the agreement, included at Landowner's insistence, obliges Mining Company to restore the surface of Blackacre to its preexisting contours on the completion of mining operations. Mining Company removes the coal from Blackacre, pays the stipulated royalty, and repudiates its obligation to restore the land. In Landowner's action against Mining Company it is established that the cost of restoration would be $25,000, and that the diminution in the value of Blackacre if the restoration is not performed would be negligible. The contract is not affected by

* Judith Maute, Peevyhouse v. Garland Coal & Mining Co. *Revisited: The Ballad of Willie and Lucille*, 89 NW. L. REV. 1341, 1347-48 (1995)

mistake or impracticability. The cost of restoration is in line with what Mining Company presumably anticipated, and the available comparisons suggest that Mining Company took this cost into account in calculating the contractual royalty. Landowner is entitled to recover $25,000 from Mining Company by the rule of this section. It is not a condition to Landowner's recovery in restitution that the money be used to restore Blackacre.

In the following excerpt, ask yourself how the parties would bargain with each other if a property rule (i.e., specific performance) rather than a liability rule (i.e., expectation damages) were the default remedy in cost of completion versus diminution in value cases. Should the common law's traditional default rule in favor of damages be replaced with a more equitable rule in favor of injunctions? What do you think are the pros and cons of such an approach?

THINKING TOOL APPLIED: COASEAN BARGAINING AND SPECIFIC PERFORMANCE*

Two law school favorites, *Groves v. John Wunder Co.* and *Peevyhouse v. Garland Coal & Mining Co.*, show that liberal application of specific performance can, in many cases, work both fairer and more efficient results than the traditional remedy of money damages. In *Groves*, the Wunder Company had leased land from the Groves Company for $105,000, for which it had received the right to remove sand and gravel for seven years, and had covenanted to restore the land to uniform grade at road level by the end of the lease term. Wunder "breached the contract deliberately. It removed . . . only 'the richest and best of the gravel' and wholly failed to perform its duty to regrade. . . . Instead, the ground was 'broken, rugged, and uneven.'" The trial court found that the cost of restoring the land was more than $60,000, but that the reasonable value of the property had Wunder properly regraded it would have been only $12,160. The Minnesota Supreme Court, with two justices vigorously dissenting, reversed a judgment of $15,053.58 for Groves and held that if a wilful breach was proven, the proper measure of damages was the cost of remedying the "defect," not the smaller loss in value of the property.

In *Peevyhouse*, a farmer and his wife gave a coal company a stripmining lease that required the company to make fills in the pits and do other restorative work on the land. The company failed to perform, causing a substantial part of the property to be washed out, and leaving a 45-foot water-filled trench, which made it difficult to use much of the remaining land. The cost of restoring the land would have been about $29,000, while the increase in value from the restoration would have been only about $300. The Oklahoma Supreme Court, in a five-to-four decision, expressly rejected *Groves* and limited the Peevyhouses' recovery to $300.

Groves and *Peevyhouse* have been damned, praised, and rationalized for years; this is not the place to repeat the discussions. It is sufficient to note that the key argument against giving the victim the cost of completion of the broken promise rather than the property's diminution in value is that this permits the victim to sell the property, buy a fairly comparable substitute, and pocket the profit.

* Excerpted from Peter Linzer, *On the Amorality of Contract Remedies—Efficiency, Equity, and the Second Restatement*, 81 Colum. L. Rev. 111, 134-39 (1981)

This might be labeled punitive damages against a wilful but efficient breacher, especially given what actually happened after the *Groves* decision. The parties settled for $55,000 and Groves left the land barren for twelve years, until 1951, when a successor corporation partially restored it at a cost of $6,000 and then sold about three-fifths of the land for $45,000.

But, as both Farnsworth and Birmingham have recognized, had the agreement been that Wunder pay $165,000 for the lease with an option to reduce the price to $105,000 by restoring the land, no one would have had difficulty holding Wunder to the higher price upon its failure to restore the property. The same argument could be made on behalf of the Peevyhouses. Since the condition triggering the "net" amount had not occurred, the promisees would get the greater amount (contract price plus cost of restoration), regardless of what they did with the additional money. Having bargained for performance and not money, the promisees should be able to risk the real estate market with the unrestored land, if they so please.

There is still an argument, however, that the court awarded too much money to Groves and that the amount sought by the Peevyhouses was too high. This is the familiar efficiency argument, which suggests that the moral approach—enforcing performance by awarding the higher cost of performance—is inefficient. The way to respond to this argument and the proper way of dealing with *Groves, Peevyhouse*, and all but the most egregious substantial performance cases is to order specific performance of the promise. This is especially appropriate when the breach was premeditated or deliberate; despite all the talk that wilfulness is irrelevant, many courts and even the *Restatement (Second)*[175] treat wilful breachers more severely than "innocent" breachers. But even innocents should normally be held to their bargains; if there are excuses, such as impracticability, mistake, duress, and unconscionability, the courts should state that they are the reasons for denying relief. When people make bargains that *they* thought valuable when executed, courts, after the fact, should not apply incomplete notions of value by limiting the remedy to money damages. Such a limit is unfair and will often lead to an inefficient result; there are many values that courts, like economists, cannot quantify, particularly non-productive ones like esthetic, humanistic, and emotional values, such as the value to the Peevyhouses of their family farm, or the value of a living room of particular size and shape to the owners of a house. This is true even of some commercial judgments, such as the effect of physical improvements on the future value of land held for investment, as in *Groves*. . . . The amoral approach is unfair when it allows the Peevyhouses to bargain with a coal company for restoration of their family farm, and then be told that the coal company may deliberately refuse to do what it promised and pay only nominal damages.

Specific performance was not sought in either *Groves* or *Peevyhouse*. Nonetheless, a court may decree specific performance against both parties' desires, and in similar cases in the future, aggrieved parties presumably would ask for specific performance more often if they thought it were more readily available.

175. *See Restatement (Second)* § 237 comment b, illustrations 6 & 7. The second *Restatement* uses as a criterion of materiality of breach whether or not conduct "comports with standards of good faith and fair dealing," *id.* § 241(e), and says that "[i]n giving weight to this factor courts have often used such less precise terms as 'willful.'" *Id.* § 241 comment f. . . .

Had specific performance been decreed in *Groves* and *Peevyhouse*, the plaintiffs would not have received a windfall. If the land restorations were of little value to the plaintiffs, they would presumably have been willing to negotiate to relieve the defendants of their obligations. Perhaps Groves would have demanded $40,000 with the rubble to relieve Wunder of the $60,000 restoration job. Perhaps the Peevyhouses would have taken $20,000 and their ruined farm. If the promisee had a clear right to specific performance, we would learn the true value of the promised actions to him, namely, the greatest dollar amount that he would refuse rather than release the promisor from his obligation. We need not consider whether the promisee's values are good or bad, productive or consumptive, materialistic or metaphysical, hardheaded or sentimental. The promisee *proves* the value to him of that performance by refusing money to give up his right. . . .

The general use of specific performance will produce truer economic efficiency than a system that counts the money cost of performance to the promisor but not the unquantifiable emotional and other costs of nonperformance to the promisee. Money damages lend themselves to the selective valuation so often used by economists, discounting things that are important to some people but that do not easily translate into money. By holding the parties to their bargain, but permitting them to negotiate out, specific performance lets no outsiders substitute their values for those of the parties. Except in the most fungible of commercial transactions, courts should encourage this self-regulating and thus more efficient method of valuation and dispute resolution.

More important, it is simply right that one get what he was promised. This is not the place to figure out why we enforce promises, but surely there is a reason beyond efficient allocation of resources. The origins of enforcement may be religious, or religion may have been used to achieve utility, but I think that today most people believe that one should stand by one's word. This is as it should be, for when a person bargains for a promise he puts trust in the promisor. This is especially true in noncommercial transactions and in transactions involving idiosyncratic values, yet often these are the situations where courts are most likely to remit the victim to inadequate money damages, rather than to compel the promisor to carry out his bargain.

Predictability is an important value in law, as should be the promotion of economic efficiency. But most important are fairness and justice. If courts take the amoral approach of Holmes or the second *Restatement*, defaulting promisors will often be able to shift costs ignored by the law to promisees, parties who trusted their promisors and who must now take second best through money damages. If, instead, the courts regularly order specific performance and hold promisors to their promises rather than to a diluted substitute in money damages, predictability, economic efficiency, and fairness all will be achieved.

As you read the next case, ask yourself how the court should resolve the dispute applying the principles you have learned from *Jacob & Youngs*, *Groves*, and *Peevyhouse*.

American Standard, Inc. v. Schectman

Supreme Court of New York, Appellate Division
439 N.Y.S.2d 529 (1981)

HANCOCK, Jr. Plaintiffs have recovered a judgment on a jury verdict of $90,000 against defendant for his failure to complete grading and to take out certain foundations and other subsurface structures to one foot below the grade line as promised. Whether the court should have charged the jury, as defendant Schectman requested, that the difference in value of plaintiffs' property with and without the promised performance was the measure of the damage is the main point in his appeal. We hold that the request was properly denied and that the cost of completion—not the difference in value—was the proper measure. Finding no basis for reversal, we affirm.

Until 1972, plaintiffs operated a pig iron manufacturing plant on land abutting the Niagara River in Tonawanda. On the 26-acre parcel were, in addition to various industrial and office buildings, a 60-ton blast furnace, large lifts, hoists and other equipment for transporting and storing ore, railroad tracks, cranes, diesel locomotives and sundry implements and devices used in the business. Since the 1870's plaintiffs' property, under several different owners, had been the site of various industrial operations. Having decided to close the plant, plaintiffs on August 3, 1973 made a contract in which they agreed to convey the buildings and other structures and most of the equipment to defendant, a demolition and excavating contractor, in return for defendant's payment of $275,000 and his promise to remove the equipment, demolish the structures and grade the property as specified.

We agree with Trial Term's interpretation of the contract as requiring defendant to remove all foundations, piers, headwalls, and other structures, including those under the surface and not visible and whether or not shown on the map attached to the contract, to a depth of approximately one foot below the specified grade lines. The proof from plaintiffs' witnesses and the exhibits, showing a substantial deviation from the required grade lines and the existence above grade of walls, foundations and other structures, support the finding, implicit in the jury's verdict, that defendant failed to perform as agreed. Indeed, the testimony of defendant's witnesses and the position he has taken during his performance of the contract and throughout this litigation (which the trial court properly rejected), *viz.*, that the contract did not require him to remove all subsurface foundations, allow no other conclusion.

We turn to defendant's argument that the court erred in rejecting his proof that plaintiffs suffered no loss by reason of the breach because it makes no difference in the value of the property whether the old foundations are at grade or one foot below grade and in denying his offer to show that plaintiffs succeeded in selling the property for $183,000—only $3,000 less than its full fair market value. **By refusing this testimony and charging the jury that the cost of completion (estimated at $110,500 by plaintiffs' expert), not diminution in value of the property, was the measure of damage the court, defendant contends, has unjustly**

> ***Is the windfall argument convincing?***
>
> While enforcing the contract and awarding cost of completion damages would certainly benefit plaintiffs and arguably

result in a windfall, wouldn't it also be the case that not enforcing the contract, or awarding diminution in value damages, would give defendant a similar windfall? At least one commentator thinks so. *See* RICHARD POSNER, ECONOMIC ANALYSIS OF LAW 121 (7th ed. 2007). If this is correct, and the court is merely deciding which party should receive the windfall, the question becomes: How should it do that? What do you think?

permitted plaintiffs to reap a windfall at his expense. Citing the definitive opinion of Judge Cardozo in *Jacob & Youngs v. Kent* (230 N.Y. 239), he maintains that the facts present a case "of substantial performance" of the contract with omissions of "trivial or inappreciable importance" and that because the cost of completion was "grossly and unfairly out of proportion to the good to be attained," the proper measure of damage is diminution in value.

The general rule of damages for breach of a construction contract is that the injured party may recover those damages which are the direct, natural and immediate consequence of the breach and which can reasonably be said to have been in the contemplation of the parties when the contract was made (see *Chamberlain v. Parker*, 45 N.Y. 569; *Hadley v. Baxendale*, 9 Exch. 341; *Restatement, Contracts*, § 346). In the usual case where the contractor's performance has been defective or incomplete, the reasonable cost of replacement or completion is the measure. . . . When, however, there has been a substantial performance of the contract made in good faith but defects exist, the correction of which would result in economic waste, courts have measured the damages as the difference between the value of the property as constructed and the value if performance had been properly completed. *Jacob & Youngs* is illustrative. There, plaintiff, a contractor, had constructed a house for the defendant which was satisfactory in all respects save one: the wrought iron pipe installed for the plumbing was not of Reading manufacture, as specified in the contract, but of other brands of the same quality. Noting that the breach was unintentional and the consequences of the omission trivial, and that the cost of replacing the pipe would be "grievously out of proportion" to the significance of the default, the court held the breach to be immaterial and the proper measure of damage to the owner to be not the cost of replacing the pipe but the nominal difference in value of the house with and without the Reading pipe.

Not in all cases of claimed "economic waste" where the cost of completing performance of the contract would be large and out of proportion to the resultant benefit to the property have the courts adopted diminution in value as the measure of damage. Under the *Restatement* rule, the completion of the contract must involve "unreasonable economic waste" and the illustrative example given is that of a house built with pipe different in name but equal in quality to the brand stipulated in the contract as in *Jacob & Youngs v. Kent* (230 N.Y. 239, *supra*). In *Groves v. Wunder Co.* (205 Minn. 163), plaintiff had leased property and conveyed a gravel plant to defendant in exchange for a sum of money and for defendant's commitment to return the property to plaintiff at the end of the term at a specified grade—a promise defendant failed to perform. Although the cost of the fill to complete the grading was $60,000 and the total value of the property, graded as specified in the contract, only $12,160 the court rejected the "diminution in value" rule, stating:

> The owner's right to improve his property is not trammeled by its small value. It is his right to erect thereon structures which will reduce its value. If that be the result, it can be of no aid to any contractor who declines performance. As said long ago in *Chamberlain v. Parker*, 45 N.Y. 569, 572: "A man may do what he will with his own, . . . and if he chooses to erect a monument to his caprice or folly on his premises, and employs and pays another to do it, it does not lie with a defendant who has been so employed and paid for building it, to say that his own performance would not be beneficial to the plaintiff."

The "economic waste" of the type which calls for application of the "diminution in value" rule generally entails defects in construction which are irremediable or which may not be repaired without a substantial tearing down of the structure as in *Jacob & Youngs*.

Where, however, the breach is of a covenant which is only incidental to the main purpose of the contract and completion would be disproportionately costly, courts have applied the diminution in value measure even where no destruction of the work is entailed.

It is also a general rule in building and construction cases, at least under *Jacob & Youngs* in New York, that a contractor who would ask the court to apply the diminution of value measure "as an instrument of justice" must not have breached the contract intentionally and must show substantial performance made in good faith.

In the case before us, plaintiffs chose to accept as part of the consideration for the promised conveyance of their valuable plant and machines to defendant his agreement to grade the property as specified and to remove the foundations, piers and other structures to a depth of one foot below grade to prepare the property for sale. It cannot be said that the grading and the removal of the structures were incidental to plaintiffs' purpose of "achieving a reasonably attractive vacant plot for resale" (cf. *Peevyhouse v. Garland Coal & Min. Co., supra*). Nor can defendant maintain that the damages which would naturally flow from his failure to do the grading and removal work and which could reasonably be said to have been in the contemplation of the parties when the contract was made would not be the reasonable cost of completion (see *Hadley v. Baxendale*, 9 Exch. 341, *supra*). That the fulfillment of defendant's promise would (contrary to plaintiffs' apparent expectations) add little or nothing to the sale value of the property does not excuse the default.

As in the hypothetical case, posed in *Chamberlain v. Parker* (45 N.Y. 569, *supra*) of the man who "chooses to erect a monument to his caprice or folly on his premises, and employs and pays another to do it," it does not lie with defendant here who has received consideration for his promise to do the work "to say that his own performance would not be beneficial to the [plaintiffs]."

Defendant's completed performance would not have involved undoing what in **good faith** was done improperly but only doing what was promised and left undone. That the burdens of performance were heavier than anticipated and the cost of completion disproportionate to the end to be obtained does not, without more, alter the rule that the measure of plaintiffs' damage is the cost of completion. Disparity in relative economic benefits is not the equivalent of "economic waste" which will invoke the rule in *Jacob & Youngs v. Kent*. Moreover, faced with the jury's finding that the reasonable cost of removing the large concrete and stone walls and other structures extending above grade was $90,000, defendant can hardly assert that he has rendered substantial performance of the contract or that what he left unfinished was "of trivial or inappreciable importance" (*Jacob & Youngs v. Kent, supra*, p 245). Finally, defendant, instead of attempting in good faith to complete the removal of the underground structures, contended that he was not obliged by the contract to do so and, thus, cannot claim to be a "transgressor whose default is unintentional and trivial [and who] may hope for mercy if he will offer atonement for his wrong" (*Jacob & Youngs v. Kent, supra*, p 244). We conclude, therefore, that the proof pertaining to the value of plaintiffs' property was properly rejected and the jury correctly charged on damages.

The judgment and order should be affirmed.

NOTES AND QUESTIONS

1. ***What happened?*** Who sued whom for what? Procedurally, how did the case get before this court? Factually, what happened between the parties? What arguments did the plaintiff and defendant make? What rule or rules did the court apply? How did the court analyze the dispute between the parties? How did the court decide the case?

2. ***Was this case correctly decided?*** Do you agree with the result reached in this case? Why or why not? Do you agree with the court's reasoning? Why or why not? How, if at all, would you have written the opinion differently?

PROBLEM: A DISAPPOINTED HOMEOWNER

Homeowners entered into a written contract with Builder to furnish the materials and construct a house upon their lot in St. Petersburg, Florida, for the sum of $250,000. During the course of construction, Builder was paid $200,000. As the project was nearing completion, however, Homeowner soon became aware of defective workmanship. Specifically, Homeowner realized that the patio wall, though it was non-weight-bearing and nonstructural, would need to be rebuilt (at an estimated cost of $15,000), the patio floor would need to be repaired (at an estimated cost of $1,000), and several prominent cracks in the ceiling of the living room and kitchen would need to be repaired (at an estimated cost of $4,000). Based on these defects, Homeowner refused to continue payment, and Builder refused to complete the house, and instead brought suit to recover the unpaid balance of the contract price.

As the judge assigned to this case, how would you rule? Are there any additional facts you would like to know in reaching your decision?

2. Reliance Damages

DOCTRINAL OVERVIEW: RELIANCE AS AN ALTERNATIVE MEASURE OF DAMAGES*

[Allowing an injured party to recover damages incurred based on reliance] is of particular importance if the *cost of reliance* is an appreciable part of the expectation interest. In this situation, as generally in contract law, the reliance interest is regarded as affording a means for giving some relief when the full expectation interest is for some reason inappropriate.

Sometimes the injured party is a supplier, such as a builder under a construction contract, that cannot prove lost profits with sufficient certainty. If the builder has already begun work when the owner repudiates, the builder can recover as damages any expenditures for labor and materials and other costs of preparation and part performance, even though the builder cannot prove lost profits. . . . However, claims for recovery based on such essential reliance are not common, since . . . a supplier does not often encounter difficulty in proving lost profits.

Recovery based on incidental reliance is more significant in practice. An injured party that is a recipient, such as an entrepreneur attempting to establish a new business, will often encounter difficulty in proving lost profits on collateral transactions. If the recipient has relied on the contract by spending money or making commitments for advertising, acquiring premises and equipment, hiring employees, and the like, it is important to be able to recover these costs as damages if the breach frustrates the venture. Reliance has often been used as the basis for measuring recovery. An early example is *Nurse v. Barns,* a seventeenth-century English case in which an entrepreneur promised to pay £10 for the use of an owner's iron mills. When the owner denied him their use, the entrepreneur recovered £500 for the stock he had laid in.[8] Of course any benefit to the injured party from preparation should be deducted. . . . Damages measured by reliance may, however, still be denied if the party in breach did not have reason at the time the contract was made to foresee them as a probable result of the breach.

Since it is a fundamental tenet of the law of contract damages that an injured party should not be put in a better position than if the contract had been performed, this alternative measure of damages rests on the premise that the injured party's reliance interest is no greater than that party's expectation interest. The classic analysis of reliance losses puts it in this fashion: "We will not, in a suit for reimbursement for losses incurred in reliance on a contract knowingly put the plaintiff in a better position than he would have occupied had the contract been fully performed."[14] Therefore, to the extent that the party in breach can prove with reasonable certainty that the injured party's expectation interest was less than its reliance interest so that performance of the contract would have resulted in a net loss to that party rather than a net profit, the amount of that loss will be subtracted from the cost of reliance. . . .

---

* Excerpted from E. ALLAN FARNSWORTH, CONTRACTS §§ 12.16 (4th ed. 2004).

8. 83 Eng. Rep. 43 (K.B. 1664).

14. Fuller & Perdue, *The Reliance Interest in Contract Damages (pt. 1)*, 46 YALE L.J. 52, 79 (1936).

Sullivan v. O'Connor

Supreme Judicial Court of Massachusetts
296 N.E.2d 183 (1973)

KAPLAN, JUSTICE. The plaintiff patient secured a jury verdict of $13,500 against the defendant surgeon for breach of contract in respect to an operation upon the plaintiff's nose. The substituted consolidated bill of exceptions presents questions about the correctness of the judge's instructions on the issue of damages.

The declaration was in two counts. In the first count, the plaintiff alleged that she, as patient, entered into a contract with the defendant, a surgeon, wherein the defendant promised to perform plastic surgery on her nose and thereby to enhance her beauty and improve her appearance; that he performed the surgery but failed to achieve the promised result; rather the result of the surgery was to disfigure and deform her nose, to cause her pain in body and mind, and to subject her to other damage and expense. The second count, based on the same transaction, was in the conventional form for malpractice, charging that the defendant had been guilty of negligence in performing the surgery. Answering, the defendant entered a general denial.

On the plaintiff's demand, the case was tried by jury. At the close of the evidence, the judge put to the jury, as special questions, the issues of liability under the two counts, and instructed them accordingly. The jury returned a verdict for the plaintiff on the contract count, and for the defendant on the negligence count. The judge then instructed the jury on the issue of damages.

As background to the instructions and the parties' exceptions, we mention certain facts as the jury could find them. The plaintiff was a professional entertainer, and this was known to the defendant. The agreement was as alleged in the declaration. More particularly, judging from exhibits, the plaintiff's nose had been straight, but long and prominent; the defendant undertook by two operations to reduce its prominence and somewhat to shorten it, thus making it more pleasing in relation to the plaintiff's other features. Actually the plaintiff was obliged to undergo three operations, and her appearance was worsened. Her nose now had a concave line to about the midpoint, at which it became bulbous; viewed frontally, the nose from bridge to midpoint was flattened and broadened, and the two sides of the tip had lost symmetry. This configuration evidently could not be improved by further surgery. The plaintiff did not demonstrate, however, that her change of appearance had resulted in loss of employment. Payments by the plaintiff covering the defendant's fee and hospital expenses were stipulated at $622.65.

The judge instructed the jury, first, that the plaintiff was entitled to recover her out-of-pocket expenses incident to the operations. Second, she could recover the damages flowing directly, naturally, proximately, and foreseeably from the defendant's breach of promise. These would comprehend damages for any disfigurement of the plaintiff's nose—that is, any change of appearance for the worse—including the effects of the consciousness of such disfigurement on the plaintiff's mind, and in this connection the jury should consider the nature of the plaintiff's profession. Also consequent upon the defendant's breach, and compensable, were the pain and suffering involved in the third operation, but not in the first two. As there was no proof that any loss of earnings by the plaintiff resulted from the breach, that element should not enter into the calculation of damages.

By his exceptions the defendant contends that the judge erred in allowing the jury to take into account anything but the plaintiff's out-of-pocket expenses (presumably at the stipulated amount). The defendant excepted to the judge's refusal of his request for a general charge to that effect, and, more specifically, to the judge's refusal of a charge that the plaintiff could not recover for pain and suffering connected with the third operation or for impairment of the plaintiff's appearance and associated mental distress.

The plaintiff on her part excepted to the judge's refusal of a request to charge that the plaintiff could recover the difference in value between the nose as promised and the nose as it appeared after the operations. However, the plaintiff in her brief expressly waives this exception and others made by her in case this court overrules the defendant's exceptions; thus she would be content to hold the jury's verdict in her favor.

We conclude that the defendant's exceptions should be overruled.

It has been suggested on occasion that agreements between patients and physicians by which the physician undertakes to effect a cure or to bring about a given result should be declared unenforceable on grounds of public policy. But there are many decisions recognizing and enforcing such contracts, and the law of Massachusetts has treated them as valid, although we have had no decision meeting head on the contention that they should be denied legal sanction. These causes of action are, however, considered a little suspect, and thus we find courts straining sometimes to read the pleadings as sounding only in tort for negligence, and not in contract for breach of promise, despite sedulous efforts by the pleaders to pursue the latter theory.

It is not hard to see why the courts should be unenthusiastic or skeptical about the contract theory. Considering the uncertainties of medical science and the variations in the physical and psychological conditions of individual patients, doctors can seldom in good faith promise specific results. Therefore it is unlikely that physicians of even average integrity will in fact make such promises. Statements of opinion by the physician with some optimistic coloring are a different thing, and may indeed have therapeutic value. But patients may transform such statements into firm promises in their own minds, especially when they have been disappointed in the event, and testify in that sense to sympathetic juries. If actions for breach of promise can be readily maintained, doctors, so it is said, will be frightened into practising

A middle ground?

Note that, on the one hand, the court does not want to cut off the possibility of patients suing doctors who make and breach contracts but, on the other hand, they are generally skeptical about doctors making such contracts in the first place. So, rather than raising the bar on liability on the front end by making it more difficult for patients to prove that there was really a contract, the court allows such claims to go forward but raises the bar on recovery on the back end by "insisting on clear proof" of damages. If you remember our exploration of promissory estoppel under the *Restatement (Second) of Contracts*, you will recall that the drafters of § 90 did something remarkably similar: They made it easier for plaintiffs to bring a cause of action under promissory estoppel under the new *Restatement*, thus allowing more plaintiffs in through the front door of contractual enforcement while allowing judges to limit the remedy of such plaintiffs "as justice requires," with the result that, in some cases (e.g., recall *Hoffman v. Red Owl*), plaintiffs would walk out the back door with much less than they would have under the *Restatement (First) of Contracts*. Is this generally a good way of handling cases where courts are skeptical about liability — allowing claims on the front end but reducing the remedy available on the back end?

"defensive medicine." On the other hand, if these actions were outlawed, leaving only the possibility of suits for malpractice, there is fear that the public might be exposed to the enticements of charlatans, and confidence in the profession might ultimately be shaken. The law has taken the middle of the road position of allowing actions based on alleged contract, but insisting on clear proof. Instructions to the jury may well stress this requirement and point to tests of truth, such as the complexity or difficulty of an operation as bearing on the probability that a given result was promised.

If an action on the basis of contract is allowed, we have next the question of the measure of damages to be applied where liability is found. Some cases have taken the simple view that the promise by the physician is to be treated like an ordinary commercial promise, and accordingly that the successful plaintiff is entitled to a standard measure of recovery for breach of contract—"compensatory" ("expectancy") damages, an amount intended to put the plaintiff in the position he would be in if the contract had been performed, or, presumably, at the plaintiff's election, "restitution" damages, an amount corresponding to any benefit conferred by the plaintiff upon the defendant in the performance of the contract disrupted by the defendant's breach. *See Restatement: Contracts* § 329 and comment a, §§ 347, 384(1). Thus in *Hawkins v. McGee*, 84 N.H. 114, the defendant doctor was taken to have promised the plaintiff to convert his damaged hand by means of an operation into a good or perfect hand, but the doctor so operated as to damage the hand still further. The court, following the usual expectancy formula, would have asked the jury to estimate and award to the plaintiff the difference between the value of a good or perfect hand, as promised, and the value of the hand after the operation. (The same formula would apply, although the dollar result would be less, if the operation had neither worsened nor improved the condition of the hand.) If the plaintiff had not yet paid the doctor his fee, that amount would be deducted from the recovery. There could be no recovery for the pain and suffering of the operation, since that detriment would have been incurred even if the operation had been successful; one can say that this detriment was not "caused" by the breach. But where the plaintiff by reason of the operation was put to more pain that he would have had to endure, had the doctor performed as promised, he should be compensated for that difference as a proper part of his expectancy recovery. It may be noted that on an alternative count for malpractice the plaintiff in the *Hawkins* case had been nonsuited; but on ordinary principles this could not affect the contract claim, for it is hardly a defence to a breach of contract that the promisor acted innocently and without negligence. . . .

Other cases, including a number in New York, without distinctly repudiating the *Hawkins* type of analysis, have indicated that a different and generally more lenient measure of damages is to be applied in patient-physician actions based on breach of alleged special agreements to effect a cure, attain a stated result, or employ a given medical method. This measure is expressed in somewhat variant ways, but the substance is that the plaintiff is to recover any expenditures made by him and for other detriment (usually not specifically described in the opinions) following proximately and foreseeably upon the defendant's failure to carry out his promise. This, be it noted, is not a "restitution" measure, for it is not limited to restoration of the benefit conferred on the defendant (the fee paid) but includes other expenditures, for example, amounts paid for medicine and nurses; so also it would seem according to its logic to take in damages for any worsening of the plaintiff's condition due to the breach. Nor is it an "expectancy" measure, for it does not appear to contemplate recovery of the whole difference in value between the condition as promised and the condition actually resulting from the treatment. Rather the tendency of the formulation is to put the plaintiff back in the position he occupied just before the parties entered upon the agreement, to compensate him for the detriments he suffered in reliance upon the agreement. This kind of intermediate pattern of recovery for breach of contract is discussed in the suggestive article by Fuller and Perdue, *The Reliance Interest in Contract Damages*, 46 Yale L.J. 52, 373, where the authors show that, although not attaining the currency of the standard measures, a "reliance" measure has for special reasons been applied by the courts in a variety of settings, including noncommercial settings. *See* 46 Yale L.J. at 396-401.[4]

For breach of the patient-physician agreements under consideration, a recovery limited to restitution seems plainly too meager, if the agreements are to be enforced at all. On the other hand, an expectancy recovery may well be excessive. The factors, already mentioned, which have made the cause of action somewhat suspect, also suggest moderation as to the breadth of the recovery that should be permitted. Where, as in the case at bar and in a number of the reported cases, the doctor has been absolved of negligence by the trier, an expectancy measure may be thought harsh. We should recall here that the fee paid by the patient to the doctor for the alleged promise would usually be quite disproportionate to the putative expectancy recovery. To attempt, moreover, to put a value on the condition that would or might have resulted, had the treatment succeeded as promised, may sometimes put an exceptional strain on the imagination of the

> ***Reliance and the Goldilocks principle?***
>
> The court seems to be saying that, at least in the context of a patient-physician contract, restitution and expectation damages may be like the porridges that Goldilocks rejected as being too cold and too hot, whereas the nice and warm reliance damages are "just right." What is it about the patient-physician relationship, or about the facts of this case, that caused the court to favor a reliance measure of recovery? Do you agree that this was the appropriate measure here? Why or why not?

4. Some of the exceptional situations mentioned where reliance may be preferred to expectancy are those in which the latter measure would be hard to apply or would impose too great a burden; performance was interfered with by external circumstances; the contract was indefinite. *See* 46 YALE L.J. at 373-386; 394-396.

fact finder. As a general consideration, Fuller and Perdue argue that the reasons for granting damages for broken promises to the extent of the expectancy are at their strongest when the promises are made in a business context, when they have to do with the production or distribution of goods or the allocation of functions in the market place; they become weaker as the context shifts from a commercial to a noncommercial field.

There is much to be said, then, for applying a reliance measure to the present facts, and we have only to add that our cases are not unreceptive to the use of that formula in special situations. We have, however, had no previous occasion to apply it to patient-physician cases.

The question of recovery on a reliance basis for pain and suffering or mental distress requires further attention. We find expressions in the decisions that pain and suffering (or the like) are simply not compensable in actions for breach of contract. The defendant seemingly espouses this proposition in the present case. True, if the buyer under a contract for the purchase of a lot of merchandise, in suing for the seller's breach, should claim damages for mental anguish caused by his disappointment in the transaction, he would not succeed; he would be told, perhaps, that the asserted psychological injury was not fairly foreseeable by the defendant as a probable consequence of the breach of such a business contract. *See Restatement: Contracts* § 341, and comment a. But there is no general rule barring such items of damage in actions for breach of contract. It is all a question of the subject matter and background of the contract, and when the contract calls for an operation on the person of the plaintiff, psychological as well as physical injury may be expected to figure somewhere in the recovery, depending on the particular circumstances. . . . Suffering or distress resulting from the breach going beyond that which was envisaged by the treatment as agreed, should be compensable on the same ground as the worsening of the patient's condition because of the breach. Indeed it can be argued that the very suffering or distress "contracted for"—that which would have been incurred if the treatment achieved the promised result—should also be compensable. . . . For that suffering is "wasted" if the treatment fails. Otherwise stated, compensation for this waste is arguably required in order to complete the restoration of the status quo ante.

In the light of the foregoing discussion, all the defendant's exceptions fail: the plaintiff was not confined to the recovery of her out-of-pocket expenditures; she was entitled to recover also for the worsening of her condition,[7] and for the pain and suffering and mental distress involved in the third operation. These items were compensable on either an expectancy or a reliance view. We might have been required to elect between the two views if the pain and suffering connected with the first two operations contemplated by the agreement, or the whole difference in value between the present and the promised conditions, were being claimed as elements of damage. But the plaintiff waives her possible claim to the former element, and to so much of the latter as represents the

7. That condition involves a mental element and appraisal of it properly called for consideration of the fact that the plaintiff was an entertainer.

difference in value between the promised condition and the condition before the operations.

Plaintiff's exceptions waived.

Defendant's exceptions overruled.

RELEVANT PROVISIONS

For the *Restatement (Second) of Contracts,* consult § 349.

NOTES AND QUESTIONS

1. ***What happened?*** Who sued whom for what? Procedurally, how did the case get before this court? Factually, what happened between the parties? What arguments did the plaintiff and defendant make? What rule or rules did the court apply? How did the court analyze the dispute between the parties? How did the court decide the case?

2. ***Was this case correctly decided?*** Do you agree with the result reached in this case? Why or why not? Do you agree with the court's reasoning? Why or why not? How, if at all, would you have written the opinion differently?

3. ***Back to*** **Hawkins.** The case cites *Hawkins v. McGee,* in which expectation damages were awarded. Why were expectation damages not awarded here? How, if at all, can the two cases be reconciled?

4. ***Pain and suffering.*** Why was pain and suffering awarded at all here? And, since the court did award it, why weren't pain and suffering damages awarded for the first two surgeries? K b/c waived?

5. ***Reliance or expectation.*** Why, broadly speaking, did the court (mostly) award reliance rather than expectation damages? Do any of the thinking tools we previously examined shed light on this issue? Do you find any of the following explanations convincing?

> *Explanation #1*: Enforcement of a promise does not necessarily mean Specific Performance. It does not necessarily mean Damages for breach. Moreover the amount allowed as Damages may be determined by the plaintiff's expenditures or change of position in reliance as well as by the value to him of the promised performance. Restitution is also an "enforcing" remedy, although it is often said to be based upon some kind of a rescission. In determining what justice requires, the court must remember all of its powers, derived from equity, law merchant, and other sources, as well as the common law. Its decree should be molded accordingly.*

* 1A Corbin, Contracts § 200 (1963).

Explanation #2: The wrong is not primarily in depriving the plaintiff of the promised reward but in causing the plaintiff to change position to his detriment. It would follow that the damages should not exceed the loss caused by the change of position, which would never be more in amount, but might be less, than the promised reward.*

3. Restitution Damages

DOCTRINAL OVERVIEW: RESTITUTION AS A REMEDY FOR BREACH†

Restitution is a substantial subject with a literature of its own, and this treatise addresses only those aspects that are of special importance to the law of contracts. . . .

When a court grants this remedy for breach, the party in breach is required to account for a benefit that has been conferred by the injured party. Sometimes this is accomplished by requiring the party in breach to return the very benefit received and sometimes by requiring that party instead to pay a sum of money that represents the value of that benefit. In contrast to cases in which the court grants specific performance or awards damages as a remedy for breach, the effort is not to enforce the promise by protecting the injured party's expectation or reliance interest, but to prevent unjust enrichment of the party in breach by protecting the injured party's restitution interest. The objective is not to put the *injured* party in as good a position as that party would have been in if the contract had been performed, nor even to put the *injured* party back in the position that party would have been in if the contract had not been made. It is, rather, to put the party *in breach* back in the position that party would have been in if the contract had not been made.

Since the restitution interest is ordinarily the smallest of the three interests, the injured party will usually find restitution less attractive than enforcement of the other party's broken promise, either by specific relief or by an award of damages based on the injured party's expectation or reliance interest.[15] However, if the bargain has turned out to favor the party in breach rather than the injured party, the injured party may prefer restitution. Cases of this kind are rare since the party who is favored by the bargain has every reason to keep it, not to break it. . . .

---

* Seavey, *Reliance on Gratuitous Promises or Other Conduct*, 64 HARV. L. REV., 913, 926 (1951).

† Excerpted from E. ALLAN FARNSWORTH, CONTRACTS § 12.19 (4th ed. 2004).

15. In one exceptional situation, that of the losing contract, the injured party prefers restitution because that party's restitution interest exceeds its expectation interest. . . . In another exceptional situation, the injured party prefers restitution because it wants specific restitution of what the other party has received, rather than money damages, because the other party is financially insecure. Furthermore, in rare cases an injured party that has no claim for damages based on a repudiation until the time for performance has come may prefer an immediate claim in restitution. . . .

When such cases have arisen, however, courts have often granted restitution to the injured party. The injured party uses the breach as a basis for claiming that its remaining duties under the contract are discharged, and that party pursues an alternative remedy that is generally regarded as inconsistent with relief based on the contract itself. Restitution as a remedy for breach is therefore limited to cases in which the injured party has a claim for damages for total breach, so that that party's remaining duties are discharged. If the claim is only one for damages for partial breach, the injured party's remaining duties are not discharged, and restitution is not available as an alternative. . . .

Bush v. Canfield

Supreme Court of Errors
2 Conn. 485 (1818)

This was an action on the case, brought by the plaintiffs as the only surviving partners of the late firm of Norton & Bush. The declaration stated, that Norton & Bush, on the 20th of February 1812, entered into a contract in writing with the defendant, in these words:

> It is agreed by and between the parties here subscribing, that Judson Canfield agrees to deliver to the order of Norton & Bush, at New-Orleans, 2000 barrels superfine wheat flour, to be delivered in good shipping order, on or before the first day of May next: the flour to be regularly inspected at New-Orleans, at the time of delivery; the price of the superfine to be 7 dollars per barrel; and in case the whole quantity to be delivered should not pass as superfine, but should pass as good merchantable fine flour, the said Canfield will have a right to deliver of the above named 2000, say 1000, barrels, that should be inspected and branded fine, at 50 cents less than the price of superfine, as above. And Norton & Bush do agree to receive the flour as here described, at the port of New-Orleans, and to pay therefor 5000 dollars in advance, as is agreed by us, calculating to be in 15 or 20 days from this date; 3000 dollars more to be advanced at four months from the date of the first advance for the said flour; and the balance then remaining due to be paid in six months from the date of the delivery of the said flour. It is agreed, that Norton & Bush shall be allowed four months interest on 1000 dollars.
>
> Judson Canfield.
>
> Norton & Bush.

That in pursuance of this contract, Norton & Bush paid over to the defendant, on the 12th of March 1812, the sum of 5000 dollars; and were ready, at New-Orleans, on the 1st of May 1812, to receive the flour; and have kept and performed all the covenants on their part; concluding with a general assignment of breach, on the part of the defendant, and a demand of damages.

The defendant pleaded Not guilty, and several special pleas, on which issues were taken. . . .

On the trial, it was proved, that the price of superfine flour at New-Orleans, on the 1st of May, 1812, was 5 dollars, 50 cents, per barrel, and no more. The court, in their charge to the jury, directed them, that if they should find the issues in favour of the plaintiffs, the rule of damages would be, the amount of the sum advanced by the plaintiffs to the defendant, and the interest thereof, from the time it was so advanced. The jury found a verdict for the plaintiffs, with 6,771 dollars damages; and the defendant moved for a new trial, on the ground of a misdirection.

SWIFT, CH. J. Where a man contracts to deliver any article besides money, and fails to do it, the rule of damages is the value of the article at the time and place of delivery, and the interest for the delay. Though the promissee may have suffered a great disappointment and loss, by the failure to fulfil the contract; yet these remote consequences cannot, in such cases, be taken into consideration by courts, in estimating the damages. It is always supposed, that the party could have supplied himself with the article at that price; and if he intends to provide against the inconvenience arising from such a disappointment, he must make a contract adapted to such objects. In the present case, if the plaintiffs had paid to the defendants the full sum for the two thousand barrels of flour contracted for, then they would have been entitled to recover the value of it at New-Orleans, where it was to have been delivered. If the price had risen between the time of purchase and delivery, they would have made a profitable speculation; otherwise, if it had fallen. If they had paid nothing, if the flour had advanced in price, they would have been entitled to recover the amount of such advance. If the price had fallen, they would have been entitled to recover nominal damages for the breach of the contract; though they might have been subjected to a great loss, if the contract had been fulfilled. This proves, that the actual damages suffered by a party cannot always be the rule of estimating damages for a breach of contract.

In this case, the plaintiffs advanced a part of the purchase money; that is, the sum of five thousand dollars; and no parallel case has been adduced to shew what ought to be the rule of damages for not delivering the flour. I think the one adopted by the court at the circuit, to be just and reasonable. The defendant has violated his contract; and it is not for him to say, that if he had fulfilled it, the plaintiffs would have sustained a great loss, and that this ought to be deducted from the money advanced. It is not for him to say, that the plaintiffs shall only recover the reduced value of a part of the flour which was to have been delivered, in proportion to the advanced payment. The contract was for the delivery of an entire quantity of flour; and no rule can be found for an apportionment in such manner. The plaintiffs have been disappointed in their arrangements; the defendant has neglected his duty; and retains in his hands five thousand dollars of the money of the plaintiffs, without consideration. Nothing can be more just than that he should refund it; and I am satisfied, that a better rule cannot be adopted in similar cases. . . .

HOSMER, J. [dissenting]. This is an action on an express contract, to recover damages for its non-performance. On the 20th day of February 1812, the defendant agreed to deliver to *Norton & Bush*, at *New-Orleans*, two thousand barrels of superfine flour, on or before the 1st day of May then next. On their part, they contracted to pay 7 dollars per barrel. Of this sum 5,000 dollars were advanced, and the residue was payable at different periods, posterior to the time prefixed for the delivery of the flour. It was not delivered, and the jury have given their verdict for damages in the sum of 6,771 dollars. At the time when the flour should have been delivered, the price of that article, at *New-Orleans*, was 5 dollars, 50 cents, per barrel, and no more. The court directed the jury, that "if they found the issues joined in favour of the plaintiffs, they should find for them to recover of the defendant 5,000 dollars, being the amount of the sum advanced by the plaintiffs to the defendant, and the interest thereof from the time the same was so advanced." For a supposed misdirection, the defendant now applies for a new trial.

Had the contract been rescinded, in an action for money had and received to recover the sum advanced, the charge to the jury would have been precisely correct. The agreement, however, was open; the action is founded upon it, and damages are demanded for the breach of it. So long as the agreement is open, it must be stated specially; and the consideration paid cannot be recovered. . . .

The jury should have been directed to give the plaintiffs the damages sustained by the breach of the agreement, on the day when it should have been performed. In other words, the plaintiffs were entitled to the price of the flour estimated at 5 dollars, 50 cents, per barrel; and on this basis, connected with the other circumstances relative to the point of damages, the verdict should have been founded. . . .

That the plaintiffs have sustained a considerable loss on the supposed legal result, is unquestionably manifest. A fallacy has existed in not ascribing it to the right cause. It did not arise from the non-performance of the defendant's agreement. Before the period had arisen when the flour was to have been delivered, the loss had accrued by the fall of it in the market. It is equally obvious, that the defendant had derived a correspondent benefit. The verdict of the jury, in opposition to the contract of the parties, reverses their condition. It rescues the plaintiffs from their loss, and deprives the defendant of his gain. In effect, it arbitrarily subjects the defendant to a warranty, that flour shall not sink in price, and renders him the victim of the plaintiffs' unfortunate speculation.

It has been contended, that in as much as the defendant did not fulfil his contract, he ought not to derive a profit from it. To this I reply, that the obligations of the parties depend exclusively upon their own voluntary agreement.

Rescission and restitution.

The dissent is making a bit of a technical argument here. Had the plaintiff properly *rescinded* the contract and sought *restitution*, rather than suing *on* the contract for *damages*, the dissent seemingly would have had no problem with allowing the plaintiff to recover its $5,000 deposit plus interest. However, the dissent's point is that because the plaintiff sued for breach of *contract*, he should get a breach of contract remedy, i.e., expectation damages. Here, expectation damages would mean deducting from plaintiff's deposit a $3,000 market loss due to the drop in the price of flour from $7.00 to $5.50 per barrel, even though the defendant never performed its end of the contract. Is there any sense in that? Should the plaintiff be punished because its lawyer didn't ask for the right remedy?

There was a hazard accompanying the contract. If flour rose in the market, the defendant would become, proportionably, a loser; and if it fell, he would be a gainer. The event on which the result was suspended, was favourable to him; and of this he cannot be deprived, unless it is the duty of courts to *make* contracts, *not to enforce* them.

I am clear in my opinion, that a new trial ought to be granted.

RELEVANT PROVISIONS

For the *Restatement (Third) of Restitution and Unjust Enrichment*, consult §§ 37 and 38. For the *Restatement (Second) of Contracts*, consult §§ 371 and 373. For the UCC, consult § 2-711. For the CISG, consult Article 81(2). For the UNIDROIT Principles, consult Article 7.3.6.

NOTES AND QUESTIONS

1. *What happened?* Who sued whom for what? Procedurally, how did the case get before this court? Factually, what happened between the parties? What arguments did the plaintiff and defendant make? What rule or rules did the court apply? How did the court analyze the dispute between the parties? How did the court decide the case?

2. *Was this case correctly decided?* Do you agree with the result reached in this case? Why or why not? Do you agree with the court's reasoning? Why or why not? How, if at all, would you have written the opinion differently?

3. *Hosmer's dissent.* Pay careful attention to Hosmer's dissent. What, exactly, is he arguing? Is he against giving the injured party relief in every similar case, or only in this case?

Vickery v. Ritchie

Supreme Court of Massachusetts
88 N.E. 835 (1909)

KNOWLTON, C.J. This is an action to recover a balance of $10,467.16, alleged to be due the plaintiff as a contractor, for the construction of a Turkish bath house on land of the defendant. The parties signed duplicate contracts in writing, covering the work. At the time when the plaintiff signed both copies of the contract, the defendant's signature was attached, and the contract price therein named was $33,721. When the defendant signed them the contract price stated in each was $23,200. Until the building was completed, the plaintiff held a contract under which he was to receive the larger sum, while the defendant held a contract for the same work, under which he was to pay only the smaller sum. This resulted from the fraud of the architect who drew the contracts, and did all the business and made all the payments for the defendant. The contracts were on typewritten sheets, and it is supposed that the architect accomplished the fraud by changing the sheets on which the price was written, before the signing by the plaintiff, and before the delivery to the defendant. The parties did not discover the discrepancy between the two writings until after the building was substantially completed. Each of them acted honestly and in good faith, trusting the statements of the architect. The architect was indicted, but he left the commonwealth and escaped punishment.

The auditor found that the market value of the labor and materials furnished by the plaintiff, not including the customary charge for the supervision of the work, was $33,499.30, and that their total cost to the plaintiff was $32,950.96. He found that the land and building have cost the defendant much more than their market value. The findings indicate that it was bad judgment on the part of the defendant to build such a structure upon the lot, and that the increase in the market value of the real estate, by reason of that which the plaintiff put upon it, is only $22,000. The failure of the parties to discover the difference between their copies of the contract was caused by the frequently repeated fraudulent representations of the architect to each of them.

The plaintiff and defendant were mistaken in supposing that they had made a binding contract for the construction of this building. Their minds never met in any agreement about the price. The labor and materials were furnished at the defendant's request and for the defendant's benefit. From this alone the law would imply a contract on the part of the defendant to pay for them. The fact that the parties supposed the price was fixed by a contract, when in fact there was no contract, does not prevent this implication, but leaves it as a natural result of their relations. Both parties understood and agreed that the work should be paid for, and both parties thought that they had agreed upon the price. Their mutual mistake in this particular left them with no express contract by which their rights and liabilities could be determined. The law implies an obligation to pay for what has been done and furnished under such circumstances, and the defendant, upon whose property the work was done, has no right to say that it is not to be paid for. . . .

We think it plain that, under such circumstances as were shown in the present case, the law implies a contract on the part of the defendant to pay for that which the plaintiff furnished.

If the law implies an agreement to pay, how much is to be paid? There is but one answer. The fair value of that which was furnished. No other rule can be applied. Under certain conditions the price fixed by the contract might control in such cases. In this case there was no price fixed. . . .

The right of recovery depends upon the plaintiff's having furnished property or labor, under circumstances which entitle him to be paid for it, not upon the ultimate benefit to the property of the owner at whose request it was furnished.

It follows that the plaintiff is entitled to recover the fair value of his labor and materials.

NOTES AND QUESTIONS

1. ***What happened?*** Who sued whom for what? Procedurally, how did the case get before this court? Factually, what happened between the parties? What arguments did the plaintiff and defendant make? What rule or rules did the court apply? How did the court analyze the dispute between the parties? How did the court decide the case?

2. ***Was this case correctly decided?*** Do you agree with the result reached in this case? Why or why not? Do you agree with the court's reasoning? Why or why not? How, if at all, would you have written the opinion differently?

PROBLEM: A PROMISE FOR A DAUGHTER

Martha ("Mattie") Waters was the niece of the wife of John Cline. The Clines had no children. In March, 1872, Mr. Cline and wife went to visit Mrs. Cline's sister, Mrs. Rogers. Mrs. Rogers and her husband and their daughter Mattie (now Mrs. Waters) constituted the family. Mrs. Cline was in poor health—had heart trouble and asthma—and she and her husband were both very fond of Mattie, who was then a girl about 13 years old. They proposed to her parents that if they would let her come and live with them, just the same as their own child, and stay with them until she was 21 years old, they would clothe her, and give her a musical education; and he also agreed that by his will at his death he would give her a farm known as the "Alfred Gregg Farm," and put buildings on it and stock it at an expense of $4,000, and give her $5,000 to run it with. The Gregg Farm was worth about $8,000. Finally, after much persuading, the parents agreed to the proposition; and they took the child home with them, to be just the same as if she was their own child. She lived with them until she was 24 years old; being treated as a daughter by Mr. Cline and his wife, transforming their home with her presence, her music, her joyousness, and her dutiful attention in nursing and taking care of her aunt. In 1883, when she was 24 years old, she married Richard Waters, and has since lived with her husband. Mr. Cline faithfully carried out his contract as to the girl, except that he died in August, 1902, without making the provision for her by his will as he had agreed to do. He left a large estate, which went to his collateral kindred, as he died intestate. In the suit to settle up his estate, Martha Waters filed her petition, setting up the above facts, and alleging that his estate was worth from $500,000 to $700,000, and praying judgment against the estate for the sum of $8,000, the value of the farm, also the further sum of $4,000, which Cline had agreed he would spend in putting buildings on it, and the further sum of $5,000 for her to run it with. The allegations of her petition were denied. The case was set for trial by a jury, and, at the conclusion of the evidence on both sides, the court instructed the jury to find for the defendants, and Mrs. Waters appeals.

The case comes before your court on appeal. How would you rule, and why?

United States v. Algernon Blair, Inc.

United States Court of Appeals, Fourth Circuit
479 F.2d 638 (1973)

Craven, Circuit Judge. May a subcontractor, who justifiably ceases work under a contract because of the prime contractor's breach, recover in quantum meruit the value of labor and equipment already furnished pursuant to the contract irrespective of whether he would have been entitled to recover in a suit on the contract? We think so, and, for reasons to be stated, the decision of the district court will be reversed.

The subcontractor, Coastal Steel Erectors, Inc., brought this action . . . in the name of the United States against Algernon Blair, Inc., and its **surety**, United States Fidelity and Guaranty Company. Blair had entered a contract with the United States for the construction of a naval hospital in Charleston County, South Carolina. Blair had then contracted with Coastal to perform certain steel erection and supply certain equipment in conjunction with Blair's contract with the United States. Coastal commenced performance of its obligations, supplying its own cranes for handling and placing steel. Blair refused to pay for crane rental, maintaining that it was not obligated to do so under the subcontract. Because of Blair's failure to make payments for crane rental, and after completion of approximately 28 percent of the subcontract, Coastal terminated its performance. Blair then proceeded to complete the job with a new subcontractor. Coastal brought this action to recover for labor and equipment furnished.

> ***Surety***
>
> "Someone who is primarily liable for paying another's debt or performing another's obligation; specif., a person who becomes a joint obligor, the terms of the undertaking being identical with the other obligor's, and the circumstances under which the joint obligation is assumed being such that, if the joint obligor becomes required to pay anything, he or she will be entitled to complete reimbursement. Although a surety is similar to an insurer, one important difference is that a surety often receives no compensation for assuming liability. A surety differs from a guarantor, who is liable to the creditor only if the debtor does not meet the duties owed to the creditor; the surety is directly liable." Black's Law Dictionary (10th ed. 2014).

The district court found that the subcontract required Blair to pay for crane use and that Blair's refusal to do so was such a material breach as to justify Coastal's terminating performance. This finding is not questioned on appeal. The court then found that under the contract the amount due Coastal, less what had already been paid, totaled approximately $37,000. Additionally, the court found Coastal would have lost more than $37,000 if it had completed performance. Holding that any amount due Coastal must be reduced by any loss it would have incurred by complete performance of the contract, the court denied recovery to Coastal. While the district court correctly stated the "'normal' rule of contract damages,"[1] we think Coastal is entitled to recover in quantum meruit. In *United States for Use of Susi Contracting Co. v. Zara Contracting Co.*, 146 F.2d 606

1. Fuller & Perdue, *The Reliance Interest in Contract Damages*, 46 Yale L.J. 52 (1936); *Restatement of Contracts* § 333 (1932).

(2d Cir. 1944), . . . the court was faced with a situation similar to that involved here—the prime contractor had unjustifiably breached a subcontract after partial performance by the subcontractor. The court stated:

> For it is an accepted principle of contract law, often applied in the case of construction contracts, that the promisee upon breach has the option to forego any suit on the contract and claim only the reasonable value of his performance.

146 F.2d at 610. The Tenth Circuit has also stated that the right to seek recovery under quantum meruit . . . is clear. Quantum meruit recovery is not limited to an action against the prime contractor but may also be brought against the . . . surety, as in this case. Further, that the complaint is not clear in regard to the theory of a plaintiff's recovery does not preclude recovery under quantum meruit. A plaintiff may join a claim for quantum meruit with a claim for damages from breach of contract.

In the present case, Coastal has, at its own expense, provided Blair with labor and the use of equipment. Blair, who breached the subcontract, has retained these benefits without having fully paid for them. On these facts, Coastal is entitled to restitution in quantum meruit.

> The "restitution interest," involving a combination of unjust impoverishment with unjust gain, presents the strongest case for relief. If, following Aristotle, we regard the purpose of justice as the maintenance of an equilibrium of goods among members of society, the restitution interest presents twice as strong a claim to judicial intervention as the reliance interest, since if A not only causes B to lose one unit but appropriates that unit to himself, the resulting discrepancy between A and B is not one unit but two.

Fuller & Perdue, *The Reliance Interest in Contract Damages,* 46 Yale L.J. 52, 56 (1936).[6] The impact of quantum meruit is to allow a promisee to recover the value of services he gave to the defendant irrespective of whether he would have lost money on the contract and been unable to recover in a suit on the contract. The measure of recovery for quantum meruit is the reasonable value of the performance, *Restatement of Contracts* § 347 (1932); and recovery is undiminished by any loss which would have been incurred by complete performance. 12 *Williston on Contracts* § 1485, at 312 (3d ed. 1970). While the contract price may be evidence of reasonable value of the services, it does not measure the value of the performance or limit recovery.[7] Rather, the standard for measuring the reasonable value of the services rendered is the amount for which such services could have been purchased from one in the plaintiff's

6. This case also comes within the requirements of the Restatements for recovery in quantum meruit. *Restatement of Restitution* § 107 (1937); *Restatement of Contracts* §§ 347-357 (1932).

7. It should be noted, however, that in suits for restitution there are many cases permitting the plaintiff to recover the value of benefits conferred on the defendant, even though this value exceeds that of the return performance promised by the defendant. In these cases it is no doubt felt that the defendant's breach should work a forfeiture of his right to retain the benefits of an advantageous bargain. Fuller & Perdue, *supra* at 77.

position at the time and place the services were rendered. Since the district court has not yet accurately determined the reasonable value of the labor and equipment use furnished by Coastal to Blair, the case must be remanded for those findings. When the amount has been determined, judgment will be entered in favor of Coastal, less payments already made under the contract. Accordingly, for the reasons stated above, the decision of the district court is

Reversed and remanded with instructions.

RELEVANT PROVISIONS

For the *Restatement (Third) of Restitution and Unjust Enrichment,* consult § 36. For the *Restatement (Second) of Contracts,* consult §§ 371 and 373. For the UCC, consult § 2-718(2) and (3). For the CISG, consult Article 81(2). For the UNIDROIT Principles, consult Article 7.3.6.

NOTES AND QUESTIONS

1. *What happened?* Who sued whom for what? Procedurally, how did the case get before this court? Factually, what happened between the parties? What arguments did the plaintiff and defendant make? What rule or rules did the court apply? How did the court analyze the dispute between the parties? How did the court decide the case?

2. *Was this case correctly decided?* Do you agree with the result reached in this case? Why or why not? Do you agree with the court's reasoning? Why or why not? How, if at all, would you have written the opinion differently?

3. *How would this case have been decided . . .* under the *Restatement (Third) of Restitution and Unjust Enrichment*? What about under the CISG? The UNIDROIT Principles?

4. *Thinking tools.* Applying the thinking tools we have discussed, which of the above approaches do you most favor, and why?

Ventura v. Titan Sports, Inc.

United States Court of Appeals, Eighth Circuit
65 F.3d 725 (1995)

MAGILL, CIRCUIT JUDGE. This appeal arises out of a match between wrestler/commentator Jesse "The Body" Ventura and Titan Sports, Inc., which operates "The World Wrestling Federation" (WWF). Titan appeals the district court's judgment in favor of Ventura, arguing that (1) Ventura was not entitled to recovery under quantum meruit because an express contract covers the subject matter for which Ventura sought recovery; and (2) the district court erroneously admitted and relied upon the testimony of Ventura's damages expert. . . . We affirm in all respects.[1]

I. BACKGROUND

During July 1984, Titan entered into a licensing agreement with LJN Toys authorizing LJN Toys to manufacture dolls using the images of WWF wrestlers. Titan also entered a "master licensing" agreement with DIC Enterprises that resulted in WWF T-shirts, trading cards, calendars, a computer game and numerous other items. In December 1984, Titan entered into a licensing agreement with A & H Video Sales (d/b/a Coliseum Video) for the production of videotapes of WWF matches. Agreements with A & H and Columbia House resulted in the production of approximately ninety videotapes of WWF performances involving Ventura.

Ventura began wrestling for Titan in Spring 1984 under an oral contract with Vincent K. McMahon, Titan's President and sole shareholder. In late 1984, Ventura suffered medical problems and ceased to work as a wrestler, although Titan continued to pay him during his convalescence. After Ventura recovered, he returned to work for Titan as a "color" or "heel"[2] commentator under an oral agreement with Titan. He was paid a flat rate of $1000 per week and there was no discussion of videotape royalties or licenses. Shortly after returning to work for Titan, Ventura executed a "Wrestling Booking Agreement" (WBA) with an effective date of January 1, 1985. Ventura subsequently resumed wrestling for Titan, for which he was paid according to the terms of the WBA. In March 1986, Ventura terminated his relationship with Titan in order to pursue an acting career.Ventura's foray into movies was moderately successful, but in fall 1986 he returned to Titan as a commentator, again under an oral agreement that made no mention of videotape royalties or licenses. In fall 1987, Ventura hired Barry Bloom as his talent agent. Bloom negotiated on Ventura's behalf with Dick Ebersol, Titan's partner in producing the "Saturday Night's Main Event" show. However, the negotiations quickly broke down, and as a result, the first show of the 1987-88 season aired without Ventura. A few weeks later, Titan's Vice-President of Business Affairs, Dick Glover, contacted Bloom concerning Ventura and represented to Bloom that Titan's policy was to pay royalties only to "feature" performers. Because Ventura was interested in working for Titan, Bloom thought it wise not to attempt to "break the policy." Ventura returned to work for Titan under a new contract that waived royalties and continued to work as a commentator for Titan until August 1990. Since that time he has worked as a commentator for WCW, Titan's main competitor.

In December 1991, Ventura filed an action in Minnesota state court seeking royalties for the use of his likeness on videotapes produced by Titan. The

1. We refer to the contracts negotiated by Ventura's agent, Barry Bloom, during the 1987-90 period as "post-Bloom" contracts. The earlier oral agreements between Ventura and McMahon we refer to as the "pre-Bloom" contracts.

2. A color commentator provides the story of the wrestling match, which is in essence a stage show. A heel commentator is a color commentator who plays the role of "the bad guy."

original complaint contained causes of action for fraud,[3] misappropriation of publicity rights and quantum meruit. Titan removed the case to federal court, and the case was tried before a jury. Although only the quantum meruit claim was submitted to the jury, the jury was given a special verdict form concerning misrepresentation. Using this form, the jury found that Titan had defrauded Ventura and that $801,333.06 would compensate Ventura for Titan's videotape exploitation of his commentary. The jury also determined that Titan exploited Ventura's name, voice or likeness as a commentator in other merchandise and concluded that $8,625.60 would compensate Ventura for this exploitation. After the jury rendered its verdict, the district court concluded that Ventura was not entitled to a jury trial on his quantum meruit claim. Accordingly, the court vacated the jury verdict and entered findings of fact and conclusions of law that were consistent with the verdict. . . . Titan appealed. . . .

II. DISCUSSION

Titan raises three claimed errors on appeal. First, Titan argues that Ventura was not entitled to quantum meruit recovery of royalties for the videotape[4] exploitation of his performance as color commentator during the 1985-87 (pre-Bloom) period because Ventura provided his commentating services under an express contract. Second, Titan claims that the district court erroneously applied the law of quantum meruit when it rescinded an express contract and awarded Ventura royalties for the videotape exploitation of his performance as color commentator during the 1987-90 (post-Bloom) period. Third, Titan alleges that the district court abused its discretion in qualifying and relying upon Ventura's expert witness in awarding damages. . . . We address each of these issues in turn.

A. Is Quantum Meruit Available During the Pre-Bloom Period?

. . . The basic contours of the law of quantum meruit, or unjust enrichment, are well settled under Minnesota law:

> An action for unjust enrichment may be based on failure of consideration, fraud, mistake, and situations where it would be morally wrong for one party to enrich himself at the expense of another. However, a claim of unjust enrichment does not lie simply because one party benefits from the efforts or obligations of others, but instead lies where one party was unjustly enriched in the sense that the term "unjustly" could mean illegally or unlawfully.

Hesselgrave v. Harrison, 435 N.W.2d 861, 863-64 (Minn. App. 1989). Although the applicable law is well settled, the facts of this case are rather unique and therefore require us to address some preliminary issues.

---

3. The fraud pleaded in Ventura's Complaint and Second Amended Complaint is that Titan fraudulently misrepresented to Ventura that Ventura was employed for no purpose other than a live performance.

4. For the sake of simplicity, we discuss the issues only in terms of the videotapes. However, the principles applied to videotape licenses and royalties apply equally to other merchandise.

The first unique aspect of this appeal involves defining the benefit received (allegedly unjustly) by Titan. Titan makes much of the fact that Ventura provided no services for Titan other than pursuant to the Ventura-Titan contracts. While it is true that the Ventura-Titan contracts governed all the services provided by Ventura (*i.e.,* his acts of appearing at the wrestling match and commentating), the agreements do not necessarily address all the benefits created by Ventura's services. Ventura's services created several varieties of intellectual property rights. In defining the "benefit" conferred upon Titan, the proper focus is not merely Ventura's labor as he performed, but must also include the intellectual property rights created by Ventura's performance. Thus, we find that the intellectual property rights to Ventura's commentary are benefits upon which an action for unjust enrichment may be based.

We next must determine whether Titan, in taking this benefit, was *unjustly* enriched. Ventura's quantum meruit claim may succeed only if Titan's rights to use Ventura's performance are limited so that Titan is not entitled to use the performance without Ventura's consent. . . .

[W]e believe . . . Titan's use of Ventura's commentary without his consent unjust.

However, quantum meruit is not available simply because Titan may have been unjustly enriched. Minnesota law is clear that "[w]here an express contract exists, there can be no implied [in law] contract with respect to the same subject matter." *Reese Design v. I-94 Highway 61 Eastview Center Partnership*, 428 N.W.2d 441, 446 (Minn. App. 1988). On the other hand, if an existing contract does not address the benefit for which recovery is sought, quantum meruit is available regarding those items about which the contract is silent.[7] Between 1985 and 1987, Ventura performed services for Titan under two different agreements. Ventura's services as a wrestler are governed by the WBA; his services as a commentator are governed by his oral agreements with McMahon. Thus, two contracts existed between Ventura and Titan between 1985 and March 1986, when the WBA was terminated. Whether quantum meruit recovery was proper depends upon whether or not the two agreements between Ventura and Titan were of limited scope, addressing only televised live performances, or also included subsequent videotape releases of the performances. The district court found that the WBA precluded royalties for the videotape exploitation of Ventura's performance *as a wrestler.* The district court also found that Ventura and Titan had no agreement concerning the payment of royalties for videotape exploitation of Ventura's performance *as a commentator.* This finding concerns the intent of the parties, and as such, is a factual finding which we review only for clear error.

We have reviewed the record, and are left with no definite and firm conviction that a mistake has been made. From 1985 to 1987, there was no discussion

7. A corollary of this rule is that quantum meruit is available if the benefit is conferred unknowingly, but not if the benefit is conferred merely as part of a bad bargain. For the reasons discussed below, we conclude that Ventura conferred the videotape rights upon Titan unknowingly.

of Titan's right to use Ventura's color commentary. At least initially,[8] Ventura was not aware of the impending videotape sales, as merchandising was not part of the industry practice. These facts support the conclusion that Ventura's contract for commentating services did not contemplate a license for videotape distribution. Accordingly, we hold that the district court's finding that the pre-Bloom Ventura-Titan contracts did not address videotape licenses or royalties is not clearly erroneous. We believe that the judgment of the district court was correct insofar as it awarded damages for the exploitation of Ventura's pre-Bloom commentating performances.

B. Is Quantum Meruit Available for the Post-Bloom Period?

[This portion of the court's opinion, which involves a lengthy discussion of fraud, is omitted. Fraud and misrepresentation will be taken up in Chapter 8, *infra*.]

C. Did the District Court Abuse Its Discretion When It Relied upon the Testimony of Ventura's Damages Expert?

Titan makes two challenges to the testimony of Ventura's damages expert, Weston Anson. First, Titan argues that the district court abused its discretion when it admitted Anson's testimony that was "without foundation, speculative and irrelevant." Titan also argues that the district court "ignored all of the reliable, relevant evidence." Although not specifically so labeled by Titan, we interpret this second argument as a challenge to the sufficiency of the evidence relating to damages. . . .

Titan's challenge to the admissibility of Anson's testimony is two-pronged. First, Titan argues that the testimony, which had to do with the market rate for royalties for licensing intellectual property, was irrelevant to the damages issue at trial. Second, in what appears to be a reliability-based challenge, Titan argues that the testimony was impermissibly speculative. We review the district court's decision to admit expert testimony for abuse of discretion.

We believe that the district court did not abuse its discretion when it found Anson's testimony to be relevant. . . . Anson's testimony is relevant if it makes any material fact more likely than the fact would be in the absence of his testimony.

Anson's testimony concerned a material fact. Minnesota cases generally state the amount of recovery in quantum meruit as the reasonable value of the benefit (or services) to the defendant. Section 152 of the *Restatement of Restitution,* which applies in cases of conscious torts, defines the measure of recovery as the market value of the plaintiff's services irrespective of their benefit to the recipient. *Restatement of Restitution* § 152 (1937). Thus, regardless of whether Titan's actions rise to the level of a conscious tort, Anson's

8. Ventura stated that he was aware that tapes were being distributed in 1985. App. at 99-100.

testimony concerning the market value of Ventura's videotape license relates to material facts: the value of the license to Titan . . . and the value of royalties to Ventura. . . .

Anson's testimony is relevant because it tended to fix the value of the license/royalty. By providing evidence of the market rate for videotape royalties, Anson's testimony (1) provided direct evidence of the market value of Ventura's license, which is the measure of Ventura's recovery if Titan's conduct was consciously tortious; and (2) assisted the jury in determining the reasonable amount that Ventura's license is worth to Titan by providing the competitive background against which Titan is operating. Titan argues that Anson's testimony is irrelevant because Glover and Bloom negotiated an arm's length deal that should be used as the measure of royalties and, alternatively, because Titan's policy which provides for a royalty rate of less than five percent should be used to determine the amount of the royalty. We reject these arguments. The proof identified by Titan simply provides evidence of a reasonable royalty rate; it does not render competing evidence irrelevant. Accordingly, we conclude that the district court did not abuse its discretion when it concluded that Anson's testimony was relevant.

We now turn to the related question whether Anson's testimony was reliable. Titan argues that Anson's testimony is unreliable because it is impermissibly speculative. In order to assess whether Anson's testimony is reliable, we must focus on the methodology and principles underlying the testimony, not the conclusions they generate. Anson arrived at his estimate of damages by applying a royalty percentage to Titan's revenues from wholesale distribution of the tapes. The sales figures for the ninety videotapes upon which Ventura appeared were not available, but net profits (a more conservative measure) were established to the penny ($25,733,527.94). The main dispute concerns the royalty rate applied to this figure to generate the royalty that is the measure of damages. Titan's expert figured damages in a similar fashion, applying varying royalty percentages and formulas to base amounts keyed to sales. Anson testified that a five percent royalty was the minimum that he would be satisfied with as an agent and was the single most likely rate, but that rates could range from 3.5% to 7.5%. When applied to the profits figure, these rates yield: $865,723.00 (3.5%), $1,236,747.00 (5%), and $1,855,121.00 (7.5%).

We believe that Anson's methodology in arriving at the royalty percentages was reliable. Anson based his opinion as to the reasonable royalty upon a survey of thousands of licensing agreements. It is common practice to prove the value of an article (*e.g.*, a videotape license) by introducing evidence of transactions involving other "substantially similar" articles (*i.e.*, other licenses). Anson surveyed licensing agreements involving numerous sports and entertainment figures, as well as various other types of characters. Although no individual arrangement examined by Anson was "on all fours" with the predicted Ventura-Titan license, in the aggregate, the licenses provided sufficient information to allow Anson to predict a royalty range for a wrestling license. We believe that this methodology is sufficiently reliable to support the admission of Anson's testimony.

Titan's other arguments go mostly to Anson's qualifications as an expert. Anson's qualifications are quite impressive, and certainly more so than those of some experts whose testimony this court has permitted. Titan's arguments boil down to an argument that Anson cannot be qualified and his methodology cannot be trusted because he did not personally handle Ventura's licenses. This argument is meritless. Accordingly, we find no abuse of discretion in the district court's admission of Anson's testimony. We also find no merit to Titan's challenge to the sufficiency of the evidence to support the damages award. . . .

III. CONCLUSION

The district court did not clearly err when it determined that Ventura's pre-Bloom contracts did not address videotape licensing and royalties. Accordingly, it did not err in permitting quantum meruit recovery of videotape royalties for the pre-Bloom period. Nor did the district court err when it awarded quantum meruit recovery for the post-Bloom period. We also find that the district court did not abuse its discretion in qualifying Anson, nor did it abuse its discretion in determining that Anson's testimony was relevant and that the methods used by Anson were reliable. . . .

MORRIS SHEPPARD ARNOLD, **Circuit Judge, dissenting.** I dissent from so much of the court's opinion as allows Mr. Ventura a recovery for royalties before Mr. Bloom negotiated a contract for him. To state a cause of action for unjust enrichment in Minnesota, a plaintiff must show either on legal or equitable grounds, or based on principles of natural justice, that a defendant's retention of a benefit would be unjust. . . .

Mr. Ventura [has not] shown that it would be inequitable or violate natural justice for Titan to reproduce and sell the videotapes that it produced and on which Mr. Ventura was already paid to appear as an announcer without paying him additional consideration. The doctrine of unjust enrichment, it is true, may provide recovery for performing extra services not specified in an original contract, but Mr. Ventura does not argue that he performed any duties in addition to his commentary. One may also recover to prevent unjust enrichment if a benefit is conferred "unknowingly" or "unwillingly," but Mr. Ventura's own testimony shows that he did not confer the alleged benefit unknowingly or unwillingly. More important, it is hardly unjust, from an economic viewpoint, that Titan should receive the full benefit from selling copies of the videotapes that it created. Titan, as entrepreneur, staged the wrestling matches, hired the various wrestlers, hired the announcers, and, above all, took the risks that the venture would fail to turn a profit. Now that Titan has been successful, Mr. Ventura wants additional compensation for having performed no additional work. If there is any unjust enrichment in this case, it is in allowing Mr. Ventura a recovery under these circumstances. . . .

Nelson v. Radio Corp. of Am., 148 F. Supp. 1 (S.D. Fla. 1957) is an instructive case. Nelson, a vocalist, was hired to perform with the Glenn Miller Orchestra. Miller paid him weekly according to union scale. Nelson sang six selections for a recording session and two more for a broadcast that also was recorded. Miller assigned all his rights in the records to the defendant, and in due course, defendant made copies of the recordings for sale. Nelson sued for an accounting for the sale of the recordings on which he sang, a 5 percent royalty on the records, as well as injunctive relief and damages. The evidence established that Nelson had no agreement with Miller entitling him to receive any royalties on the sale of photograph records. The court ruled that "any right in and to phonograph records or other recordings in connection with the production of which plaintiff worked were the property of the plaintiff's employer Miller. . . ." 148 F. Supp. at 3. The court therefore rejected Nelson's claim for royalties.

The reasoning of *Nelson* is highly persuasive and our case is strikingly similar to it. Mr. Ventura agreed to receive weekly pay to perform wrestling commentary. He does not dispute, as far as I can discern, that the videotapes belong to Titan. Mr. Ventura, like Nelson, is suing for a royalty on the sales of the recordings on which he performed. And like Nelson, Mr. Ventura deserves no recovery because he and Titan both performed under their contract and the recordings of Mr. Ventura's performances now belong to Titan and it may profit from them as it sees fit.

Finally, . . . I still doubt that Mr. Ventura should recover. Mr. Ventura himself testified that he was employed to "broadcast wrestling." The agreement was therefore clearly susceptible to the construction that it authorized the sale of videotapes to end users. . . . Mr. Ventura testified that he was hired to perform commentary for television broadcasts. "Television broadcasts" under these circumstances must reasonably include dissemination of the videotapes containing the commentary that Mr. Ventura performed as part of his employment. Indeed, this seems to me utterly implicit in the original contractual arrangement.

For the foregoing reasons, I believe that Mr. Ventura's claim for additional compensation for his announcing duties in the period before Mr. Bloom negotiated a contract for him fails as a matter of law. I would therefore reverse that part of the judgment allowing Mr. Ventura's recovery for his role as a commentator before he entered into the written contract.

NOTES AND QUESTIONS

1. *What happened?* Who sued whom for what? Procedurally, how did the case get before this court? Factually, what happened between the parties? What arguments did the plaintiff and defendant make? What rule or rules did the court apply? How did the court analyze the dispute between the parties? How did the court decide the case?

2. *Was this case correctly decided?* Do you agree with the result reached in this case? Why or why not? Do you agree with the court's reasoning? Why or why not? How, if at all, would you have written the opinion differently?

3. *Majority or dissent?* Which judge makes the better argument, and why? Try to draw on any of the thinking tools we have previously examined in answering this question.

4. *Reconcilable?* Can this case be reconciled with the previous cases in this unit?

4. Limiting Damages

DOCTRINAL OVERVIEW: LIMITING DAMAGES*

To the general principle of recovery based on the promisee's expectation there emerged three important limitations that now serve as a basis not merely for instructing jurors, but for passing on the admissibility of evidence and for withdrawing some elements of damage from the jury's consideration altogether.

One of these limitations is that the injured party cannot recover damages for loss that could have been avoided if that party had taken appropriate steps to do so. To take an obvious case, the builder who stubbornly continues work after the owner has repudiated the contract cannot recover for expenditures in doing work after the repudiation. A second limitation denies the injured party recovery for loss that the party in breach did not have reason to foresee as a probable result of the breach at the time the contract was made. The classic, if apocryphal, case is that in which "a man going to be married to an heiress, his horse having cast a shoe on the journey, employed a blacksmith to replace it, who did the work so unskillfully that the horse was lamed, and, the rider not arriving in time, the lady married another"—the blacksmith would not be liable for the loss of the marriage.[14] The third limitation is that the injured party cannot recover damages for loss beyond the amount proved with reasonable certainty. . . . The effect of these three limitations is to reduce the amount of damages recoverable under the general principle that the law protects the injured party's expectation. . . .

Before reading the excerpt below, you may wish to review "Thinking Tool: Thinking Clearly About Legal Relationships" at p. 96, supra. Earlier, we learned that expectation damages are traditionally awarded for breach of contract to put the promisee in the position it would have occupied had the promise been performed. But, as we shall soon see, these damages are subject to some important limitations, with the result that injured promisees often aren't put in their rightful position. These limitations have had important implications for contract law, as discussed below.

---

* Excerpted from E. ALLAN FARNSWORTH, CONTRACTS § 12.8 (4th ed. 2004).

14. 'Saw Mill Co. v. Nettleship, 3 L.R. C.P. 499, 508 (1868).

THINKING TOOL APPLIED: INJURY WITHOUT COMPENSATION AND HOHFELD'S ATTACK ON FORMALISM*

Damnum Absque Injuria

The nineteenth-century classical analytical jurisprudence of Jeremy Bentham, John Stuart Mill, and John Austin assumed that a privilege (they used the term *liberty*) also imposed a duty of noninterference. In other words, they assumed that once society had determined an act was privileged, it meant *both* that others had no effective claim against the person exercising the privilege *and* that others had a duty of noninterference. . . .

This system created the illusion that injury without compensation (damnum absque injuria) was of marginal importance in law. Hohfeld's insight that privileges can, and often do, conflict moved damnum absque injuria to center stage. We now understand that damnum absque injuria is fundamental to our legal system, both in terms of the sheer scale of uncompensated injury we tolerate and as a policy.

In contracts, for example, many losses inflicted by breach are damnum absque injuria because of three limiting principles in awarding damages. The requirement that contract damages be foreseeable means that injuries caused by breach, but unforeseeable at the time of contracting, are uncompensated.[56] The obligation to mitigate damages denies recovery for injuries that, in the court's view, could reasonably have been avoided.[57] And the rule that contract damages must be proven within a reasonable degree of certainty allows parties, in many instances, to breach and pay minimal damages although it is clear the breach inflicted substantial injury.[58] These three concepts (foreseeability, mitigation, certainty) do not lurk at the borders of contract doctrine, but are core principles reflecting significant policies.

Hohfeld as Antiformalist

Nineteenth-century American legal formalism argued that rules in a particular area of law (e.g., contracts) could be formulated through a two-step process. First, a small number of high-level principles were established inductively from the cases. Langdell, for example, remarks that "the number of fundamental legal doctrines is much less than is commonly supposed. . . . It seemed to me, therefore, to be possible . . . to select, classify, and arrange all the cases which had contributed in any important degree to the growth, development, or establishment of any of its essential doctrines."[59] Once the principles had been

---

* Excerpted from Curtis Nyquist, *Teaching Wesley Hohfeld's Theory of Legal Relations*, 52 J. Legal Educ. 238, 253-55 (2002).

56. *Restatement (Second) of Contracts* § 351 (1981). In *Hadley v. Baxendale*, 156 Eng. Rep. 145 (1854), the plaintiff failed to recover profits lost when the defendant delayed delivery of a mill crank shaft, because the loss was not foreseeable.

57. *Restatement (Second) of Contracts* § 350 (1981).

58. *Restatement (Second) of Contracts* § 352 (1981). In *Chicago Coliseum Club v. Dempsey*, 265 Ill. App. 542 (1932), the plaintiff recovered only a few hundred dollars for its expenses, not the $1.6 million lost profits it claimed, because the profits were held to be speculative.

59. C. C. Langdell, A Selection of Cases on the Law of Contracts vi-vii (Birmingham, Ala., 1983) (1871).

established, particular rules could be logically deduced from the principles. The goal was a system of rules that was complete and applicable in a determinate way. In deciding a case, the judge sorted through rules and found the one that applied; the rule dictated the result.In contracts, for example, two high-level principles held that liability was based on promise (reflecting the will of the promisor) and that only promises supported by a bargained consideration should be enforced. Many particular rules were logically derived from these principles: offers could be revoked at any time before acceptance (unless consideration made the offer irrevocable); modifications were unenforceable unless the agreed performances of both parties changed; a promise to discharge an obligation by agreeing to pay an amount less than originally promised was unenforceable; an agreement to agree was unenforceable; and if the promise of one of the parties was illusory (e.g., output and requirements contracts), the contract was unenforceable.

Hohfeld's system provided weaponry for the progressive/realist assault on formalism. Duties could not be deduced from privileges "without fresh exercise of ethical judgment."[65] Duties also could not be deduced from injury since many injuries are uncompensated. "The very process of recognizing more and more instances of *damnum absque injuria* in the legal system demonstrated that a series of classical conceptualist deductions were logical errors."[66]

a. Foreseeability

DOCTRINAL OVERVIEW: UNFORESEEABILITY AS A LIMITATION*

[U]ntil the nineteenth century judges left the assessment of damages for breach of contract largely to the discretion of the jury. With the advent of the industrial revolution, a solicitude for burgeoning enterprise led to the development of rules to curb this discretion and the "outrageous and excessive" verdicts to which it led. The limitation of unforeseeability is an apt example. Under this limitation, a party in breach is not liable for damages, whether for partial or for total breach, that the party did not at the time of contracting have reason to foresee as a probable result of the breach. The development of such a limitation was encouraged by a realization that liability for unforeseeable loss might impose upon an entrepreneur a burden greatly out of proportion to the risk that the entrepreneur originally supposed was involved and to the corresponding benefit that the entrepreneur stood to gain.

65. Frank I. Michelman, *Commentary*, in Fred R. Shapiro, *The Most Cited Articles from the Yale Law Journal*, 100 YALE L.J. 1449, 1512 (1991).

66. Joseph William Singer, *The Legal Rights Debate in Analytical Jurisprudence from Bentham to Hohfeld*, 1982 WIS. L. REV. 975, 1051.

* Excerpted from E. ALLAN FARNSWORTH, CONTRACTS § 12.14 (4th ed. 2004).

> The fountainhead of the limitation of foreseeability is the famous English case of *Hadley v. Baxendale,* which in 1854 laid down general principles that are still honored today. . . .
>
> *For want of a nail, the shoe was lost;*
> *For want of a shoe, the horse was lost;*
> *For want of a horse, the rider was lost;*
> *For want of a rider the battle is lost;*
> *For want of a battle the kingdom is lost.*
> *All for the loss of a horseshoe nail.*
>
> George Herbert, THE TEMPLE (1633)

Hadley v. Baxendale

In the Court of Exchequer
156 Eng. Rep. 145 (1854)

Joseph and Jonah Hadley's flour mill, as operated by Priday Metford & Co. in the 1920s.

At the trial before CROMPTON, J., . . . it appeared that the plaintiffs carried on an extensive business as millers at Gloucester; and that, on the 11th of May, their mill was stopped by a breakage of the crank shaft by which the mill was worked. The steam-engine was manufactured by Messrs. Joyce & Co., the engineers, at Greenwich, and it became necessary to send the shaft as a pattern for a new one to Greenwich. The fracture was discovered on the 12th, and on the 13th the plaintiffs sent one of their servants to the office of the defendants, who are the well-known carriers trading under the name of **Pickford & Co.**, for the purpose of having the shaft carried to Greenwich. The plaintiffs' servant told the clerk that the mill was stopped, and that the shaft must be sent immediately; and in answer to the inquiry when the shaft would be taken, the answer was, that if it was sent up by twelve o'clock any day, it would be delivered at Greenwich on the following day. On the following day the shaft was taken by the defendants, before noon, for the purpose of being conveyed to Greenwich, and the sum of £2. 4s. was paid for its carriage for the whole distance; at the same time the defendants' clerk was told that a special entry, if required, should be made to hasten its delivery. The delivery of the shaft at

Why didn't Hadley sue Pickford & Co.?

The short answer, as explained in a wonderful article by Professor Danzig, an excerpt of which appears after this case, is that the limited liability company, though recognized, was still in its infancy, and nothing like the limited liability company of today. Pickford itself did not even formally incorporate until 1901. As an injured plaintiff, therefore, your best chance of recovery was to bring suit against the individual owners of such firms. Baxendale, as senior partner of Pickford & Co., would have been a natural target for such litigation,

Greenwich was delayed by some neglect; and the consequence was, that the plaintiffs did not receive the new shaft for several days after they would otherwise have done, and the working of their mill was thereby delayed, and they thereby lost the profits they would otherwise have received.* On the part of the defendants, it was objected that these damages were too remote, and that the defendants were not liable with respect to them. The learned Judge left the case generally to the jury, who found a verdict with £25 damages beyond the amount paid into Court.† [Defendant appealed, seeking a new trial on the ground of misdirection. Specifically, defendant argued that "the jury ought to have been told that these damages were too remote; and that, in the absence of the proof of any other damage, the plaintiffs were entitled to nominal damages only."]

and there are, in fact, a number of other "Plaintiff v. Baxendale" cases from this period. This meant that the owners of such firms, who "were personally liable for the misfeasance of their companies," were exposed to an extremely high amount of risk. Indeed, in 1854, when this case was decided, a jury award "might lead to damages that could significantly diminish annual profits or even destroy the personal fortunes of those sharing in thinly financed ventures." Richard Danzig, *Hadley v. Baxendale: A Study in the Industrialization of the Law*, 4 J. LEGAL STUD. 249 (1975).

ALDERSON, B. We think that there ought to be a new trial in this case; but, in so doing, we deem it to be expedient and necessary to state explicitly the rule which the Judge, at the next trial, ought, in our opinion, to direct the jury to be governed by when they estimate the damages.

It is, indeed, of the last importance that we should do this; for, if the jury are left without any definite rule to guide them, it will, in such cases as these, manifestly lead to the greatest injustice. . . .

"There are certain establishing rules," this Court says, in *Alder v. Keighley* (15 M. & W. 117), "according to which the jury ought to find." And the Court, in that case, adds: "and here there is a clear rule, that the amount which would have been received if the contract had been kept, is the measure of damages if the contract is broken."

Now we think the proper rule is such as the present is this: Where two parties have made a contract which one of them has broken, the damages which the other party ought to receive in respect of such breach of contract should be such as may fairly and reasonably be considered either arising naturally, i.e., according to the usual course of things, from such breach of contract itself, or such as may reasonably be supposed to have been in the contemplation of both parties, at the time they made the contract, as the probable result of the breach of it.

The "rule" of Hadley v. Baxendale

In one of the most important sentences ever written about contract damages, the *Hadley* court changed an old, time-worn default rule, which allowed juries some discretion in determining damages, and replaced it with a new, more mechanical rule limiting recoverable damages to the harm the promisor, at the time of entering into the contract, could reasonably foresee would

---

* [Specifically, plaintiff sued for £300 for lost profits and wages.—ED.]

† [Defendant previously paid £25 into court to satisfy plaintiff's claim, so the total amount of damages assessed by the jury was £50.—ED.]

result as a probable consequence of its breach. If you read this sentence carefully, you'll notice that the court actually announces two separate rules, one rule governing "direct" or "general" damages, and another governing "special," "consequential," or "indirect" damages (the terms are used interchangeably). What's the difference between these two categories of damages? Suppose I agree to rent my car to you for $25, which you plan to use to pick up a $10,000 check from your uncle, who promised it to you on condition that you drive to his house this evening.[47] If I don't know about the "deal" you have with your uncle and breach my contract with you, a reasonable person in my position ought to have foreseen that you would have to rent a car from someone else (this is generally foreseeable), but would not have foreseen that you would lose $10,000 as a result of my breach (only someone with special knowledge would have foreseen this). Therefore, in terms of recovery, *Hadley* says you should get the difference between the price you paid Hertz or Avis to rent another car (e.g., $100) and the amount you would have paid me (i.e., $25), because these general damages arise "directly" from my breach "according to the usual course of things," but you should not recover the $10,000 in consequential damages because they were neither foreseeable to me, or to a reasonable person in my position, when we first entered into our contract. What do you suppose is the justification behind the court's test? In what ways might such a rule incentivize the Hadleys and Baxendales of the world to behave differently in the future? Once you've thought through these questions, you'll be in a good position to appreciate the materials and Notes and Questions following the case.

Now, if the special circumstances under which the contract was actually made were communicated by the plaintiffs to the defendants, and thus known to both parties, the damages resulting from the breach of such a contract, which they would reasonably contemplate, would be the amount of injury which would ordinarily follow from a breach of contract under these special circumstances so known and communicated. But, on the other hand, if these special circumstances were wholly unknown to the party breaking the contract, he, at the most, could only be supposed to have had in his contemplation the amount of injury which would arise generally, and in the great multitude of cases not affected by any special circumstances, from such a breach of contract. For, had the special circumstances been known, the parties might have specially provided for the breach of contract by special terms as to the damages in that case; and of this advantage it would be very unjust to deprive them. . . .

Now, in the present case, if we are to apply the principles above laid down, we find that the only circumstances here communicated by the plaintiffs to the defendants at the time the contract was made, were, that the article to be carried was the broken shaft of a mill, and that the plaintiffs were the millers of that mill. But how do these circumstances shew reasonably that the profits of the mill must be stopped by an unreasonable delay in the delivery of the broken shaft by the carrier to the third person? Suppose the plaintiffs had another shaft in their possession put up or putting up at the time, and that they only wished to send back the broken shaft to the engineer who made it; it is clear that this would be quite consistent with the above circumstances, and yet the unreasonable delay in the delivery would have no effect upon the intermediate profits of the mill. Or, again, suppose that, at the time of the delivery to the carrier, the machinery of the mill had been in other respects defective, then, also, the same results would follow. Here it is true that the shaft was actually sent back to serve as a model for a new one, and that the want of a new one was the only cause of the stoppage of the mill, and that

47. Is your uncle's promise enforceable? Consult *Hamer v. Sidway*, along with the materials discussed in Section II.2.C, and Sections III.4.A-B.

the loss of profits really arose from not sending down the new shaft in proper time, and that this arose from the delay in delivering the broken one to serve as a model. But it is obvious that, in the great multitude of cases of millers sending off broken shafts to third persons by a carrier under ordinary circumstances, such consequences would not, in all probability, have occurred; and these special circumstances were here never communicated by the plaintiffs to the defendants.

It follows, therefore, that the loss of profits here cannot reasonably be considered such a consequence of the breach of contract as could have been fairly and reasonably contemplated by both the parties when they made this contract. For such loss would neither have flowed naturally from the breach of this contract in the great multitude of such cases occurring under ordinary circumstances, nor were the special circumstances, which, perhaps, would have made it a reasonable and natural consequence of such breach of contract, communicated to or known by the defendants. The Judge ought, therefore, to have told the jury, that, upon the facts then before them, they ought not to take the loss of profits into consideration at all in estimating the damages. There must therefore be a new trial in this case. . . .

CONTEXTUAL PERSPECTIVE: MORE ON *HADLEY V. BAXENDALE**

Hadley v. Baxendale *is still, and presumably always will be, a fixed star in the jurisprudential firmament.*

Grant Gilmore, THE DEATH OF CONTRACT 83 (1974)

Of the many thousands of students who graduate from American law schools every year, probably all save a few hundred are required to read the 1854 English Exchequer case of *Hadley v. Baxendale.* It is, indeed, one of a startlingly small number of opinions to which graduates from law school will almost assuredly have been exposed even if they attended different institutions, used a variety of textbooks, and opted for disparate electives. The exceptional pedagogical centrality of the case is further underscored by the similarly widespread attention the case receives in the curricula of all Commonwealth law schools.

But if the case is unusually widely read, it is typically narrowly studied. In the first-year law curriculum, where the opinion usually appears, cases are normally treated like doctrinal fruits on a conceptual tree: some bulk large, some are almost insignificant; some display a wondrous perfection of development, others are shown to be rotten at the core; some are further out along conceptual branches than others; but all are quite erroneously treated as though they blossomed at the same time, and for the same harvest.

* Excerpted from Richard Danzig, Hadley v. Baxendale*: A Study in the Industrialization of the Law,* 4 J. LEG. STUD. 249, 249-51, 254-55, 259-60, 267-68, 271-76, 284 (1975) (some internal citations omitted).

This ahistorical view may have some didactic advantages, but it overlooks much that is important. Cases are of different vintages; they arise in different settings. It matters that *Hadley v. Baxendale* was decided in 1854 in England, and not in 1974 in California. Without reflecting on the ramifications of these facts of timing and setting, perhaps teachers and students can understand black letter law as it now is, but neither can comprehend the processes of doctrinal innovation, growth, and decay.

By focusing on one central case in its historical setting I hope . . . to provide an experiential supplement to the legal reader's steady diet of logic. My theme is that *Hadley v. Baxendale* can usefully be analyzed as a judicial invention in an age of industrial invention. . . . [M]y concern . . . is to discuss why the "rule of the case" was invented in its particular form and in this particular case, to assess the relationship between this judicial invention and the existing legal and economic technology, to underscore the impact of the rule in effecting a specialization of judicial labor and a standardization, centralization, and mass production of judicial products, and to demonstrate that the rule of the case became widely known and generally accepted because, as with other successful inventions, it was well advertised and marketed. . . .

II.

The novelty of the changes effected in procedural and substantive law by *Hadley v. Baxendale* suggests that the opinion may be examined as an invention. The innovation effected in the law is here unusually stark. Baron Alderson, in support of the central proposition he advanced, cited no precedent and invoked no British legislative or academic authority in favor of the rule he articulated. Nor was this due to oversight. The opinion broke new ground by establishing a rule for decision by judges in an area of law—the calculation of damages in contracts suits—which had previously been left to almost entirely unstructured decision by English juries. . . .

III.

To understand the origins and the limitations of the rule in *Hadley v. Baxendale* we must appreciate the industrial and legal world out of which it came and for which it was designed. In 1854 Great Britain was in a state of extraordinary flux. Between 1801 and 1851 its population rose from 10.6 to 20.9 million people and its gross national product increased from £10.7 to £523.3 million. By 1861 its population was 23.2 million and its GNP £668.0 million. Contemporaries saw the magnitude of this change and were aware of its impact on the law. As one writer, surveying the scene in 1863, put it:

> What our Law was then [in 1828], it is not now; and what it is now, can best be understood by seeing what it was, then. It is like the comparison between England under former, and present, systems of transit, for persons, property, and intelligence: between the days of lumbering wagons, stage coaches, and a creeping post—and of swift, luxurious railroads and lightening telegraphs. All is altered: material, inducing corresponding moral and social changes.

Arising squarely in the middle of the "industrial revolution" and directly in the midst of the "Great Boom" of 1842-1874, *Hadley v. Baxendale* was a product of these times. The case was shaped by the increasing sophistication of the economy and the law—and equally significantly by the gaps, the naiveté, and the crudeness of the contemporary system.

The raw facts of the case should alert the reader to the half-matured and unevenly developing nature of the economy in which the decision was rendered. For example, the Hadley mill was steam-powered. While it was not hand-run, animal-driven, wind-powered, or water-powered, as in an earlier age, it was also not powered by electricity as it would be in the next century. So with the now famous broken shaft. It was a complicated piece of machinery, manufactured by a specialized company on the other side of England. But it was neither a standardized nor a mass-produced machine. It was handcrafted. Thus, the transaction in *Hadley v. Baxendale:* the old shaft had to be brought to eastern England as the "model" for the new one.

The circumstances of the breach similarly reflect a half-way modernized society. The breach occurred because the shaft was sent by canal, the early industrial transport form, rather than by rail, the mature industrial transport form. That both co-existed as significant means of shipment suggests the transitional nature of the period. The ready acceptance of the notion that delay gave rise to damages, that time meant money, suggests the affinity of the modes of thought of this age to our own. But the units of account for measuring time in *Hadley v. Baxendale* suggest the distance between our period and this one: speed for a trip across England was measured in days, not hours.

If the facts of the case offer us a glimpse of an economic world in transition, what of the legal system which had to deal with that transition? This system was also modernizing, but, at the time of *Hadley v. Baxendale,* it was still strikingly underdeveloped. . . .

IV.

I think the rule in *Hadley v. Baxendale* may have had its most significant contemporary effects not for the entrepreneurs powering a modernizing economy, but rather for the judges caught up in their own problems of modernization.

By the middle of the nineteenth century Parliament had acted to modernize the judicial system in a number of important ways. . . . But the size and case disposition capacity of the common law courts remained remarkably stagnant.

In 1854 the national judiciary of Britain and Wales sitting in courts of general jurisdiction numbered fifteen. These judges, distributed equally between three benches—the Court of Common Pleas, the Queen's Bench and the Exchequer—sat individually to hear all cases in London and at Assize (court held in major provincial towns) for two terms of about four weeks each year. They convened as panels of three or four to hear appeals in London at other times. They sat in panels usually numbering seven . . . to hear appeals from the panels of three or four. Only appeals from the panels of seven would be heard by another body of men: The House of Lords. . . .

In 1854 it must have been apparent to the fifteen judges who composed the national judicial system that they had no hope of reviewing half a million cases or even that fraction of them which dealt with genuinely contested issues. Moreover the relatively small stakes involved in County Court cases left all but a miniscule proportion of litigants disinclined to incur the costs of appeal. Under these conditions it is not surprising that *ad hoc* review gave way to attempts at a crystallized delineation of instructions for dispute resolution which more closely resembled legislation than they did prior common law adjudication.

In its centralization of control, the judicial invention here examined paralleled the industrial developments of the age. The importance of the centralization of control is particularly evident when the rule is put back into the context in which it was promulgated: in terms of judges' control over juries. . . . [Indeed, the] resolution of this case . . . [led] to a rule of procedure and review which shifted power from more parochial to more cosmopolitan decision-makers. As Baron Alderson put the matter, "we deem it to be expedient and necessary to state explicitly the rule which . . . the jury [ought] to be governed by . . . for if the jury are left without any definite rule to guide them, it will, in such cases as these, manifestly lead to the greatest injustice."[100] From a less personal perspective the invention also effected a modernization by enhancing efficiency as a result of taking matters out of the hands of the jurors. Whatever its other characteristics, jury justice is hand-crafted justice. Each case is mulled on an *ad hoc* basis with reference to little more than, as Chitty put it, "the circumstances of the case." In an age of rapidly increasing numbers of transactions and amounts of litigation, a handcrafted system of justice had as little durability as the hand-crafted system of tool production on which the Hadleys relied for their mill parts. By moving matters from a special jury—which cost £24, untold time to assemble, and a half hour to decide—to a judge, the rule in *Hadley v. Baxendale* facilitated the production of the judicial product. And by standardizing the rule which a judge employed, the decision compounded the gain—a point of particular importance in relation to the County Courts where juries were rarely called.

Thus, the judicial advantages of *Hadley v. Baxendale* can be summarized: after the opinion the outcome of a claim for damages for breach of contract could be more readily predicted (and would therefore be less often litigated) than before; when litigated the more appropriate court could more often be chosen; the costs and biases of a jury could more often be avoided; and County Court judges and juries alike could be more readily confined in the exercise of their discretion. Clearly the rule invented in the case offered substantial rewards to the judges who promulgated it and in later years reaffirmed it. . . .

VII.

My aim in this article has been to supplement the 120 years of doctrinal explication lavished on the text of *Hadley v. Baxendale* with a sufficient understanding of context to afford some insights—albeit speculative ones—into the process of law-change. I would hope that this discussion would serve as a counterpoise to the tendency to regard some rules of law as "fixed stars" in our legal system. Judicial rules are more like inventions, designed to serve particular functions in particular

100. 156 Eng. Rep. 145, 150 (1854).

settings. I have tried to demonstrate that an analysis of the original setting and functions of one particular rule will enhance an understanding of that rule even when it has long outlived that setting and those functions. Further, I have sought to suggest that if a rule is to be regarded as an invention, then it ought to be subject to review, lest we make too big an investment in it even as it is becoming outmoded.

RELEVANT PROVISIONS

For the *Restatement (Second) of Contracts,* consult § 351. For the UCC, consult § 2-715. For the CISG, consult Article 74. For the UNIDROIT Principles, consult Article 7.4.4.

NOTES AND QUESTIONS

1. *What happened?* Who sued whom for what? Procedurally, how did the case get before this court? Factually, what happened between the parties? What arguments did the plaintiff and defendant make? What rule or rules did the court apply? How did the court analyze the dispute between the parties? How did the court decide the case?

2. *Was this case correctly decided?* Do you agree with the result reached in this case? Why or why not? Do you agree with the court's reasoning? Why or why not? How, if at all, would you have written the opinion differently?

3. *The two rules of* Hadley. *Hadley* stands for the general idea that a promisee may only recover damages that would foreseeably result from the promisor's breach. More specifically, the *Hadley* court distinguished between two types of damages, "general" or "direct" damages, and "special" or "consequential" or "non-direct" damages. The court defined "general" damages as those that "naturally" flow from a breach "according to the usual course of things." These damages, in turn, can always be recovered. "Special" or "consequential" damages, on the other hand, could only be recovered if the promisor knew when it made the contract that these damages would flow "as the probable result of the breach." What type of damages are at issue in *Hadley,* general or consequential? Can you think of any good reasons for distinguishing between them? Try to think of a few examples to discuss in class in which both general and consequential damages flow as a result of the promisor's breach.

4. *In praise of* Hadley. Professor Danzig has argued that the *Hadley* rule may make possible social gains by allowing sellers to make more informed decisions about whether to perform or breach their contracts. To illustrate, he provides the following example:

> [C]onsider the position of a truck owner, A, who has a contract to sell his truck to B, and assume that B would suffer a "normal" net loss of $200 if the truck were

> not made available as scheduled. If C arrives on the scene and bids to preempt the truck for an urgent need, A can estimate the damages he will "normally" owe B. He will presumably sell to C only if the new sale price will exceed the old sale price plus $200 in damages. If C is willing to buy for such a high price, it is to everybody's advantage to let him do so. C benefits because he values the truck more highly than he values the money he is paying for it; B benefits because he receives his expected profits by way of damages; A benefits because he makes more money, even after paying damages than he would have made had the truck not been sold to C. Society benefits because one party, C, has gained while no other party has lost. If B were in an abnormal situation and so expected to suffer greater damages than $200, the rule of *Hadley v. Baxendale* would coerce him into signalling these higher damages, so that the proper damage calculation and subsequent truck allocation would be made. Thus, in theory, by facilitating an accurate calculus of breach, the rule optimizes resource allocation.*

5. *A critical look at* Hadley. Fuller and Purdue had a more critical view of *Hadley,* suggesting that the foreseeability "rule" announced by the court was, in point of fact, quite manipulable by the courts:

> [I]t is clear that the test of foreseeability is less a definite test itself than a cover for a developing set of tests. As in the case of all "reasonable man" standards there is an element of circularity about the test of foreseeability. "For what items of damage should the court hold the defaulting promisor? Those which he should as a reasonable man have foreseen. But what should he have foreseen as a reasonable man? Those items of damage for which the court feels he ought to pay." The test of foreseeability is therefore subject to manipulation by the simple device of defining the characteristics of the hypothetical man who is doing the foreseeing. By a gradual process of judicial inclusion and exclusion this "man" acquires a complex personality; we begin to know just what "he" can "foresee" in this and that situation, and we end, not with one test but with a whole set of tests. This has obviously happened in the law of negligence, and it is happening, although less obviously, to the reasonable man postulated by *Hadley v. Baxendale.*†

6. Hadley *and its aftermath.* Those who know about the *Hadley* rule typically limit their liability by contracting around it. For instance, UCC § 2-719(3) provides that: "Consequential damages may be limited or excluded unless the limitation or exclusion is unconscionable. Limitation of consequential damages for injury to the person in the case of consumer goods is *prima facie* unconscionable but limitation of damages where the loss is commercial is not." While this may, at first glance, appear to take some of the bite out of the *Hadley* rule by allowing more-informed parties to contract out of consequential damages, it is still significant in that it has an important information-revealing effect, which

---

* Richard Danzig, Hadley v. Baxendale*: A Study in the Industrialization of the Law,* 4 J. LEG. STUD. 249, 282 (1975).

† Lon L. Fuller and William R. Perdue, Jr., *The Reliance Interest in Contract Damages: I,* 46 YALE L.J. 52, 85 (1936).

may lead to the formation of more efficient contracts. For instance, when a well-informed party contracts around the *Hadley* default rule (e.g., by disclaiming consequential damages or providing a limitation of liability clause), the less well-informed party will now learn about an important but invisible default term that it might not otherwise have been made aware of. This knowledge, in turn, will give the less well-informed party the opportunity to decide whether it wants to protect itself against any contract risks for which it will be responsible by, for example, taking extra precautions or purchasing insurance.

7. *Tacit agreement?* Holmes thought that mere notice of the risk of special damages was not enough to make the promisor liable for those damages. Rather, he thought that there should be some indication that the promisor has agreed to assume these risks. *See Morrow v. First National Bank of Hot Springs*, 550 S.W.2d 429 (1977) (applying tacit-agreement test to preclude plaintiff's recovery of consequential damages because defendant never tacitly agreed to assume responsibility for them). *See also Globe Ref. Co. v. Landa Cotton Oil Co.*, 190 U.S. 540, 544 (1903) (recovery "depends on what liability the defendant fairly may be supposed to have assumed consciously, or to have warranted the plaintiff reasonably to suppose that it assumed, when the contract was made"). Although it is the minority approach, is Holmes's test a better test? Why or why not? Here is how Holmes justified the tacit-agreement test in *The Common Law*. Are you persuaded?

> A more practical advantage in looking at a contract as the taking of a risk is to be found in the light which it throws upon the measure of damages. If a breach of contract were regarded in the same light as a tort, it would seem that if, in the course of performance of the contract the promisor should be notified of any particular consequence which would result from its not being performed, he should be held liable for that consequence in the event of non-performance. Such a suggestion has been made. But it has not been accepted as the law. On the contrary, according to the opinion of a very able judge, which seems to be generally followed, notice, even at the time of making the contract, of special circumstances out of which special damages would arise in case of breach, is not sufficient unless the assumption of that risk is to be taken as having fairly entered into the contract.*

Most common law jurisdictions, along with the UCC (specifically, § 2-715, comment 2) reject the tacit agreement test.

8. *Penalty default rules.* Under the *Hadley* default rule, the authors of the excerpt below argue that it is the high-damage millers who have the incentive to reveal to carriers information about the potential loss they might suffer in the event of breach. Why? Because only in this way can they make the shippers liable for their consequential losses. But what if the high-damage millers probably would not have contracted for such a default rule had they bargained with

* Oliver W. Holmes, The Common Law 236 (Howe ed. 1963).

the shipper in advance? According to the excerpt below, this may be even *more* reason to adopt the default rule. Can you see why?

Where parties do not allocate the risk of delay between them, as in Hadley v. Baxendale, *and it is not clear that a court can ascertain how they would have allocated such a risk had they foreseen it in advance, how should a court select the default rule? The excerpt below explores a powerful but somewhat counterintuitive idea: In such cases, courts should deliberately apply a* penalty *default rule, or a default rule that is in all likelihood* inconsistent *with what the parties themselves would have selected had they foreseen the contingency that ultimately arose. As you read the following excerpt, try to understand the justification for what appears to be, on its face, a rather bizarre approach to selecting default rules. Can you see how, under the right circumstances, such a strategy might actually be a good idea? Once you understand (even if you don't agree with) the argument below, ask yourself (1) whether you think the rule adopted by the court in* Hadley v. Baxendale *is a penalty default rule, and (2) whether you think courts should use penalty default rules where the parties do not provide their own rules, or whether courts should use a different technique, such as trying to figure out what the parties would have intended had they foreseen the contingency that ultimately arose.*

PENALTY DEFAULT RULES*

The holding in *Hadley* operates as a penalty default. The miller could have informed the carrier of the potential consequential damages and contracted for full damage insurance. The *Hadley* default of denying unforeseeable damages may not be consistent with what fully informed parties would have wanted. The miller's consequential damages were real and the carrier may have been the more efficient bearer of this risk. As a general matter, millers may want carriers to compensate them for consequential damages that carriers can prevent at lower cost. The default can instead be understood as a purposeful inducement to the miller as the more informed party to reveal that information to the carrier. Informing the carrier creates value because if the carrier foresees the loss, he will be able to prevent it more efficiently. At the same time, however, revealing the information to the carrier will undoubtedly increase the price of shipping. Nonetheless, so long as transaction costs are not prohibitive, a miller with high consequential damages will gain from revealing this information and contracting for greater insurance from the carrier because the carrier is the least-cost avoider. . . .

9. Hadley *and economic efficiency.* According to Professor Posner, *Hadley* stands for the principle that "where a risk of loss is known to only one party to the contract, the other party is not liable for the loss if it occurs." He goes on to note that this principle is economically efficient in that it "induces the party

* Robert Gertner & Ian Ayres, *Filling Gaps in Incomplete Contracts: An Economic Theory of Default Rules*, 99 YALE L.J. 87, 101-03 (1989).

with knowledge of the risk either to take any appropriate precautions himself or, if he believes that the other party might be the more efficient loss avoider, to disclose the risk to that party." To illustrate this point, see Posner provides the following example:

> A commercial photographer purchases a roll of film to take pictures of the Himalayas for a magazine. The cost of development of the film by the manufacturer is included in the purchase price. The photographer incurs heavy expenses (including the hire of an airplane) to complete the assignment. He mails the film to the manufacturer but it is mislaid in the developing room and never found.
>
> Compare the incentive effects of allowing the photographer to recover his full losses and of limiting him to recovery of the price of the film. The first alternative creates little incentive to avoid similar losses in the future. The photographer will take no precautions. He is indifferent as between successful completion of his assignment and the receipt of adequate compensation for its failure. The manufacturer of the film will probably not take additional precautions either; the aggregate costs of such freak losses are probably too small to justify substantial efforts to prevent them. The second alternative, in contrast, should induce the photographer to take precautions that turn out to be at once inexpensive and effective: using two rolls of film or requesting special handling when he sends the roll in for development.*

Try to apply what you have learned above to the following problem.

PROBLEM: A WIDGET FROM TIBET

While on vacation in Tibet, you develop an exciting new widget, which a large Fortune 500 company has learned about. The company offers you $10 million if you can deliver your widget to their headquarters in the United States within two days so they can beat a competitor to market. You call a private courier and relate the details above, tell them you have a package (with your new widget design) that must be delivered right away, and explain as follows: "Please handle this package with care, and please make sure to ship it right away. If this package doesn't get there in two days, I'm gonna lose ten million dollars—it's *that* important." The clerk on the other end of the phone assures you that everything will be fine, tells you not to worry, and sends someone by to pick up the widget later that day. On the courier's way to the airport, to his great surprise, he is intercepted by a marauding band of barbarians descended from Genghis Khan and the package containing the widget design is stolen. Of course, because the widget never makes it to the U.S. in time, you never get paid the $10 million. So, naturally, you bring suit against the courier for breach of contract, asking for consequential damages of $10 million.

The courier claims that it does not owe you consequential damages because (1) mere *notice* of the possible damages is not equivalent to an *agreement* to

* RICHARD A. POSNER, ECONOMIC ANALYSIS OF THE LAW 60-61 (1972).

accept liability, and (2) it was completely unforeseeable that a band of marauding barbarians, who were thought to be extinct, should intercept the courier and prevent the delivery of the widget, and so these damages should be unrecoverable. How should the court address the defendant's claims?

PROBLEM: THE CASE OF THE STOLEN COINS

Plaintiff collected coins for many years, and had metal cabinets built in a closet in his house to store the coins. These cabinets were arranged so that a burglar would have to go through eleven sets of locks to reach the coins. As insurance rates were becoming prohibitive, however, Plaintiff began to look for large safety-deposit boxes in which to keep his coins, and discussed the problem with Defendant Bank, where he was a regular customer.

During their conversation, Bank explained to Plaintiff that it was planning to move into a new building that included safety-deposit boxes. On June 25 Plaintiff reserved three large boxes in the new building, paying $25 for each box. It was expected that the boxes would be available within 30 to 60 days. Plaintiff explained his need for the boxes, adding that he particularly wanted them by September 1, when his husky teenage son would leave for college. The bank was perhaps on notice, through a loan application to a different department, that the coins were worth at least $12,000.

One or two employees of the bank promised to notify Plaintiff as soon as the boxes were available. Unfortunately, although the boxes became available on August 30, Plaintiff was never notified. This was doubly unfortunate because on September 4 someone broke into Plaintiff's house and stole coins valued at $32,000 when he and his wife were out to dinner. Plaintiff brought this action against Defendant Bank to recover the value of the stolen coins. Specifically, Plaintiff alleges a breach of contract on the ground that Bank failed to notify Plaintiff of the availability, on August 30, of safety-deposit boxes in a new bank building as they promised to do.

How should a court rule Plaintiff's claim? What, if anything, should Plaintiff recover, and why?

INTERNATIONAL PERSPECTIVE: FORESEEABILITY AND THE CISG*

Ever since *Hadley v. Baxendale*, the common law has limited expectation damages with a principle of foreseeability. *Hadley* expressed these damages as those that

* Excerpted from William S. Dodge, *Teaching the CISG in Contracts*, 50 J. LEGAL EDUC. 72, 90-91 (2000).

"may reasonably be supposed to have been in the contemplation of both parties, at the time they made the contract, as the probable result of the breach of it."[97] The *Restatement (Second)* changes the phrasing somewhat but continues to focus on those damages one could foresee as "probable,"[98] and the UCC appears to be in accord.[99]

The CISG's foreseeability limitation is even less strict: "Such damages may not exceed the loss which the party in breach foresaw or ought to have foreseen at the time of the conclusion of the contract . . . as a *possible* consequence of the breach of contract."[100] This means that the breaching party ought to be liable for a greater range of consequential damages under the CISG (those that were foreseeable as a "possible" consequence of the breach) than under the common law or UCC (only those that were foreseeable as a "probable" consequence of the breach).[101] Indeed, one commentator has cautioned, "U.S. judges should try to divorce themselves from the influence of *Hadley* as much as possible; its rules are not the same as those under the consequential damages article of the C.I.S.G."[102]

Would a court really find a party liable for those damages that could have *possibly* been foreseen by a party at the time of the conclusion of the contract? After all, the world of possibility, even as apprehended by a reasonable person, is nearly infinite. In the next case, the court is confronted with this issue. As you read it, pay careful attention to the court's language whenever foreseeability is discussed, and ask yourself what standard of foreseeability the court is using: the standard found in *Hadley*, or the standard set out in CISG Article 74. As an aside, you should also note that, in the course of reaching its decision, the court also discusses several other concepts from the CISG with which you should be familiar, such as fundamental breach and the absence of a perfect tender rule. Finally, if you look carefully, you will see traces of *Neri v. Retail Marine Corp.* in its decision.

97. 156 Eng. Rep. 145, 151 (Ex. 1854).

98. "Damages are not recoverable for loss that the party in breach did not have reason to foresee as a probable result of the breach when the contract was made:." *Restatement (Second) of Contracts* § 351(1) (1981).

99. UCC § 2-715(2)(a) states that "consequential damages resulting from the seller's breach include . . . any loss resulting from general or particular requirements and needs of which the seller at the time of contracting had reason to know and which could not reasonably be prevented by cover or otherwise. . . ." Although this language omits the word "probable," White and Summers explain that this provision does not supply a complete definition of consequential damages and must be read against the background of *Hadley*. James J. White & Robert S. Summers, Uniform Commercial Code, 4th ed., v. 1, § 104, at 573-74 (St. Paul, 1995). Even more specifically, they state that "'the test is one of reasonable foreseeability of probable consequences.'" *Id.* § 104, at 569.

100. CISG Art. 74 (emphasis added).

101. This difference is noted by Arthur G. Murphey, Jr., *Consequential Damages in Contracts for the International Sale of Goods and the Legacy of* Hadley, 23 GEO. WASH J. INT'L L. & ECON. 415, 439-40 (1989).

102. *Id.* at 417.

Delchi Carrier S.p.A. v. Rotorex Corp.

United States Court of Appeals, Second Circuit
71 F.3d 1024 (1995)

Winter, Circuit Judge. Rotorex Corporation, a New York corporation, appeals from a judgment of $1,785,772.44 in damages for lost profits and other consequential damages awarded to Delchi Carrier SpA following a bench trial before Judge Munson. The basis for the award was Rotorex's delivery of nonconforming compressors to Delchi, an Italian manufacturer of air conditioners. Delchi cross-appeals from the denial of certain incidental and consequential damages. We affirm the award of damages; we reverse in part on Delchi's cross-appeal and remand for further proceedings.

BACKGROUND

In January 1988, Rotorex agreed to sell 10,800 compressors to Delchi for use in Delchi's "Ariele" line of portable room air conditioners. The air conditioners were scheduled to go on sale in the spring and summer of 1988. Prior to executing the contract, Rotorex sent Delchi a sample compressor and accompanying written performance specifications. The compressors were scheduled to be delivered in three shipments before May 15, 1988.

Rotorex sent the first shipment by sea on March 26. Delchi paid for this shipment, which arrived at its Italian factory on April 20, by **letter of credit.** Rotorex sent a second shipment of compressors on or about May 9. Delchi also remitted payment for this shipment by letter of credit. While the second shipment was en route, Delchi discovered that the first lot of compressors did not conform to the sample model and accompanying specifications. On May 13, after a Rotorex representative visited the Delchi factory in Italy, Delchi informed Rotorex that 93 percent of the compressors were rejected in quality control checks because they had lower cooling capacity and consumed more power than the sample model and specifications. After several unsuccessful attempts to cure the defects in the compressors, Delchi asked Rotorex to supply new compressors conforming to the original sample and specifications. Rotorex refused, claiming that the performance specifications were "inadvertently communicated" to Delchi.

> ***Letter of credit***
>
> "An instrument under which the issuer (usu. a bank), at a customer's request, agrees to honor a draft or other demand for payment made by a third party (the *beneficiary*), as long as the draft or demand complies with specified conditions, and regardless of whether any underlying agreement between the customer and the beneficiary is satisfied." BLACK'S LAW DICTIONARY (10th ed. 2014).

In a faxed letter dated May 23, 1988, Delchi cancelled the contract. Although it was able to expedite a previously planned order of suitable compressors from Sanyo, another supplier, Delchi was unable to obtain in a timely fashion substitute compressors from other sources and thus suffered a loss in its sales volume of Arieles during the 1988 selling season. Delchi filed the instant action under the United Nations Convention on Contracts for the International Sale of Goods ("CISG" or "the Convention") for breach of contract and failure to deliver conforming goods. On January 10, 1991, Judge Cholakis granted Delchi's motion for partial summary judgment, holding Rotorex liable for breach of contract.

After three years of discovery and a bench trial on the issue of damages, Judge Munson, to whom the case had been transferred, held Rotorex liable to Delchi for $1,248,331.87. This amount included consequential damages for: (i) lost profits resulting from a diminished sales level of Ariele units, (ii) expenses that Delchi incurred in attempting to remedy the nonconformity of the compressors, (iii) the cost of expediting shipment of previously ordered Sanyo compressors after Delchi rejected the Rotorex compressors, and (iv) costs of handling and storing the rejected compressors. The district court also awarded **prejudgment interest** under CISG art. 78.

> ***Prejudgment interest***
>
> "Statutorily prescribed interest accrued either from the date of the loss or from the date when the complaint was filed up to the date the final judgment is entered." BLACK'S LAW DICTIONARY (10th ed. 2014).

The court denied Delchi's claim for damages based on other expenses, including: (i) shipping, customs, and incidentals relating to the two shipments of Rotorex compressors; (ii) the cost of obsolete insulation and tubing that Delchi purchased only for use with Rotorex compressors; (iii) the cost of obsolete tooling purchased only for production of units with Rotorex compressors; and (iv) labor costs for four days when Delchi's production line was idle because it had no compressors to install in the air conditioning units. The court denied an award for these items on the ground that it would lead to a double recovery because "those costs are accounted for in Delchi's recovery on its lost profits claim." It also denied an award for the cost of modification of electrical panels for use with substitute Sanyo compressors on the ground that the cost was not attributable to the breach. Finally, the court denied recovery on Delchi's claim of 4000 additional lost sales in Italy.

On appeal, Rotorex argues that it did not breach the agreement, that Delchi is not entitled to lost profits because it maintained inventory levels in excess of the maximum number of possible lost sales, that the calculation of the number of lost sales was improper, and that the district court improperly excluded fixed costs and depreciation from the manufacturing cost in calculating lost profits. Delchi cross-appeals, claiming that it is entitled to the additional out-of-pocket expenses and the lost profits on additional sales denied by Judge Munson.

DISCUSSION

The district court held, and the parties agree, that the instant matter is governed by the CISG, a self-executing agreement between the United States and other signatories, including Italy.[1] Because there is virtually no caselaw under

1. Generally, the CISG governs sales contracts between parties from different signatory countries. However, the Convention makes clear that the parties may by contract choose to be bound by a source of law other than the CISG, such as the Uniform Commercial Code. *See* CISG art. 6 ("The parties may exclude the application of this Convention or . . . derogate from or vary the effect of any of its provisions.") If, as here, the agreement is silent as to choice of law, the Convention applies if both parties are located in signatory nations. *See* CISG art. 1.

the Convention, we look to its language and to "the general principles" upon which it is based. *See* CISG art. 7(2). The Convention directs that its interpretation be informed by its "international character and . . . the need to promote uniformity in its application and the observance of good faith in international trade." *See* CISG art. 7(1). Caselaw interpreting analogous provisions of Article 2 of the Uniform Commercial Code ("UCC"), may also inform a court where the language of the relevant CISG provisions tracks that of the UCC. However, UCC caselaw "is not *per se* applicable."

We first address the liability issue. We review a grant of summary judgment *de novo*. Summary judgment is appropriate if "there is no genuine issue as to any material fact" regarding Rotorex's liability for breach of contract.

Under the CISG, "[t]he seller must deliver goods which are of the quantity, quality and description required by the contract," and "the goods do not conform with the contract unless they . . . [p]ossess the qualities of goods which the seller has held out to the buyer as a sample or model." CISG art. 35. The CISG further states that "[t]he seller is liable in accordance with the contract and this Convention for any lack of conformity." CISG art. 36.

Judge Cholakis held that "there is no question that [Rotorex's] compressors did not conform to the terms of the contract between the parties" and noted that "[t]here are ample admissions [by Rotorex] to that effect." We agree. The agreement between Delchi and Rotorex was based upon a sample compressor supplied by Rotorex and upon written specifications regarding cooling capacity and power consumption. After the problems were discovered, Rotorex's engineering representative, Ernest Gamache, admitted in a May 13, 1988 letter that the specification sheet was "in error" and that the compressors would actually generate less cooling power and consume more energy than the specifications indicated. Gamache also testified in a deposition that at least some of the compressors were nonconforming. The president of Rotorex, John McFee, conceded in a May 17, 1988 letter to Delchi that the compressors supplied were less efficient than the sample and did not meet the specifications provided by Rotorex. Finally, in its answer to Delchi's complaint, Rotorex admitted "that some of the compressors . . . did not conform to the nominal performance information." There was thus no genuine issue of material fact regarding liability, and summary judgment was proper.

Under the CISG, if the breach is "fundamental" the buyer may either require delivery of substitute goods, CISG art. 46, or declare the contract void, CISG art. 49, and seek damages. With regard to what kind of breach is fundamental, Article 25 provides:

> A breach of contract committed by one of the parties is fundamental if it results in such detriment to the other party as substantially to deprive him of what he is entitled to expect under the contract, unless the party in breach did not foresee and a reasonable person of the same kind in the same circumstances would not have foreseen such a result.

In granting summary judgment, the district court held that "[t]here appears to be no question that [Delchi] did not substantially receive that which [it] was entitled to expect" and that "any reasonable person could foresee that shipping non-conforming goods to a buyer would result in the buyer not receiving that which he expected and was entitled to receive." Because the cooling power and energy consumption of an air conditioner compressor are important determinants of the product's value, the district court's conclusion that Rotorex was liable for a fundamental breach of contract under the Convention was proper.

We turn now to the district court's award of damages following the bench trial. A reviewing court must defer to the trial judge's findings of fact unless they are clearly erroneous. However, we review questions of law, including "the measure of damages upon which the factual computation is based," *de novo*.

The CISG provides:

> Damages for breach of contract by one party consist of a sum equal to the loss, including loss of profit, suffered by the other party as a consequence of the breach. Such damages may not exceed the loss which the party in breach foresaw or ought to have foreseen at the time of the conclusion of the contract, in the light of the facts and matters of which he then knew or ought to have known, as a possible consequence of the breach of contract.

CISG art. 74. This provision is "designed to place the aggrieved party in as good a position as if the other party had properly performed the contract." John Honnold, *Uniform Law for International Sales Under the 1980 United Nations Convention* 503 (2d ed. 1991).

Rotorex argues that Delchi is not entitled to lost profits because it was able to maintain inventory levels of Ariele air conditioning units in excess of the maximum number of possible lost sales. In Rotorex's view, therefore, there was no actual shortfall of Ariele units available for sale because of Rotorex's delivery of nonconforming compressors. Rotorex's argument goes as follows. The end of the air conditioner selling season is August 1. If one totals the number of units available to Delchi from March to August 1, the sum is enough to fill all sales. We may assume that the evidence in the record supports the factual premise. Nevertheless, the argument is fallacious. Because of Rotorex's breach, Delchi had to shut down its manufacturing operation for a few days in May, and the date on which particular units were available for sale was substantially delayed. For example, units available in late July could not be used to meet orders in the spring. As a result, Delchi lost sales in the spring and early summer. We therefore conclude that the district court's findings regarding lost sales are not clearly erroneous. A detailed discussion of the precise number of lost sales is unnecessary because the district court's findings were, if anything, conservative.

Rotorex contends, in the alternative, that the district court improperly awarded lost profits for unfilled orders from Delchi affiliates in Europe and from sales agents within Italy. We disagree. The CISG requires that damages be limited by the familiar principle of foreseeability established in *Hadley v. Baxendale*, 156 Eng. Rep. 145 (1854). CISG art. 74. However, it was objectively foreseeable that Delchi would take orders for Ariele sales based on the number of compressors it had ordered and expected to have ready for the season. The district court was entitled to rely upon the documents and testimony regarding these lost sales and was well within its authority in deciding which orders were proven with sufficient certainty.

Rotorex also challenges the district court's exclusion of fixed costs and depreciation from the manufacturing cost used to calculate lost profits. The trial judge calculated lost profits by subtracting the 478,783 lire "manufacturing cost"—the total variable cost—of an Ariele unit from the 654,644 lire average sale price. The CISG does not explicitly state whether only variable expenses, or both fixed and variable expenses, should be subtracted from sales revenue in calculating lost profits. However, courts generally do not include fixed costs in the calculation of lost profits. This is, of course, because the fixed costs would have been encountered whether or not the breach occurred. In the absence of a specific provision in the CISG for calculating lost profits, the district court was correct to use the standard formula employed by most American courts and to deduct only variable costs from sales revenue to arrive at a figure for lost profits.

In its cross-appeal, Delchi challenges the district court's denial of various consequential and incidental damages, including reimbursement for: (i) shipping, customs, and incidentals relating to the first and second shipments—rejected and returned—of Rotorex compressors; (ii) obsolete insulation materials and tubing purchased for use only with Rotorex compressors; (iii) obsolete tooling purchased exclusively for production of units with Rotorex compressors; and (iv) labor costs for the period of May 16-19, 1988, when the Delchi production line was idle due to a lack of compressors to install in Ariele air conditioning units. The district court denied damages for these items on the ground that they "are accounted for in Delchi's recovery on its lost profits claim," and, therefore, an award would constitute a double recovery for Delchi. We disagree.

The Convention provides that a contract plaintiff may collect damages to compensate for the full loss. This includes, but is not limited to, lost profits, subject only to the familiar limitation that the breaching party must have foreseen, or should have foreseen, the loss as a probable consequence. CISG art. 74; *see Hadley v. Baxendale, supra*.

An award for lost profits will not compensate Delchi for the expenses in question. Delchi's lost profits are determined by calculating the hypothetical revenues to be derived from unmade sales less the hypothetical variable costs that would have been, but were not, incurred. This figure, however, does not compensate for costs actually incurred that led to no sales. Thus, to award damages for costs actually incurred in no way creates a double recovery and instead furthers the purpose of giving the injured party damages "equal to the loss." CISG art. 74.

The only remaining inquiries, therefore, are whether the expenses were reasonably foreseeable and legitimate incidental or consequential damages. The expenses incurred by Delchi for shipping, customs, and related matters for the two returned shipments of Rotorex compressors, including storage expenses for the second shipment at Genoa, were clearly foreseeable and recoverable incidental expenses. These are up-front expenses that had to be paid to get the goods to the manufacturing plant for inspection and were thus incurred largely before the nonconformities were detected. To deny reimbursement to Delchi for these incidental damages would effectively cut into the lost profits award. The same is true of unreimbursed tooling expenses and the cost of the useless insulation and tubing materials. These are legitimate consequential damages that in no way duplicate lost profits damages.

The labor expense incurred as a result of the production line shutdown of May 16-19, 1988 is also a reasonably foreseeable result of delivering nonconforming compressors for installation in air conditioners. However, Rotorex argues that the labor costs in question were fixed costs that would have been incurred whether or not there was a breach. The district court labeled the labor costs "fixed costs," but did not explore whether Delchi would have paid these wages regardless of how much it produced. Variable costs are generally those costs that "fluctuate with a firm's output," and typically include labor (but not management) costs. Whether Delchi's labor costs during this four-day period are variable or fixed costs is in large measure a fact question that we cannot answer because we lack factual findings by the district court. We therefore remand to the district court on this issue.

The district court also denied an award for the modification of electrical panels for use with substitute Sanyo compressors. It denied damages on the ground that Delchi failed to show that the modifications were not part of the regular cost of production of units with Sanyo compressors and were therefore attributable to Rotorex's breach. This appears to have been a credibility determination that was within the court's authority to make. We therefore affirm on the ground that this finding is not clearly erroneous.

Finally, Delchi cross-appeals from the denial of its claimed 4000 additional lost sales in Italy. The district court held that Delchi did not prove these orders with sufficient certainty. The trial court was in the best position to evaluate the testimony of the Italian sales agents who stated that they would have ordered more Arieles if they had been available. It found the agents' claims to be too speculative, and this conclusion is not clearly erroneous.

CONCLUSION

We affirm the award of damages. We reverse in part the denial of incidental and consequential damages. We remand for further proceedings in accord with this opinion.

NOTES AND QUESTIONS

1. *What happened?* Who sued whom for what? Procedurally, how did the case get before this court? Factually, what happened between the parties? What arguments did the plaintiff and defendant make? What rule or rules did the court apply? How did the court analyze the dispute between the parties? How did the court decide the case?

2. ***Was this case correctly decided?*** Do you agree with the result reached in this case? Why or why not? Do you agree with the court's reasoning? Why or why not? How, if at all, would you have written the opinion differently?

b. Certainty

The most fundamental rule with regard to damages is that of Certainty. Damages must be certain, both in their nature and in respect to the cause from which they spring. It is more fundamental than any rule of compensation, because compensation is allowed or disallowed subject to it.

Sedgwick, ELEMENTS OF THE LAW OF DAMAGES, 2d ed. 13 (1909)

DOCTRINAL OVERVIEW: UNCERTAINTY AS A LIMITATION*

In the middle of the nineteenth century, while English judges were introducing the requirement of foreseeability in order to control the discretion of juries in awarding contract damages, American judges were engaged in fashioning an additional doctrine to the same end—the requirement of certainty. This limitation has been characterized by an authority on remedies as "probably the most distinctive contribution of the American courts to the common law of damages."[1] As formulated in 1858 in a leading New York case, the doctrine required damages for breach of contract to "be shown, by clear and satisfactory evidence, to have been actually sustained" and to "be shown with certainty, and not left to speculation or conjecture."[2] It thus imposed on the injured party a distinctly more onerous burden than that imposed in tort cases[3] and manifested a judicial reluctance to recognize interests that are difficult or impossible to measure in money.

Recent decades, however, have seen a relaxation of the requirement. Contemporary statements insist only on "reasonable certainty" rather than on certainty itself. The Restatement Second, for example, precludes recovery "for loss beyond an amount that the evidence permits to be established with reasonable certainty."[4] The comments to the Uniform Commercial Code explain that damages need not "be calculable with mathematical accuracy," are "at best approximate," and "have to be proved with whatever definiteness and accuracy the facts permit, but no more."[5] Doubts are generally resolved against the party in breach on the rationale, as Judge Amalya Kearse put it, that it is "not improper, given the inherent uncertainty, to exercise generosity in favor of the injured party

* Excerpted from E. ALLAN FARNSWORTH, CONTRACTS § 12.15 (4th ed. 2004).

1. C. McCormick, Law of Damages 124 (1935).

2. Griffin v. Colver. 16 N.Y. 489, 491 (1858).

3. *See* Restatement (Second) of Torts § 912 ("with as much certainty as the nature of the tort and the circumstances permit"). . . .

4. Restatement Second § 352.

5. 1-106 cmt. 1. *See also* UCC 2-715 cmt. 4 ("Loss may be determined in any manner which is reasonable under the circumstances.").

rather than in favor of the breaching party."[6] Courts are therefore less demanding in applying the requirement if the breach was "willful," in spite of the general tenet that the amount of contract damages does not turn on the character of the breach. . . .

Freund v. Washington Square Press, Inc.

Court of Appeals of New York
314 N.E.2d 419 (1974)

RABIN, J. In this action for breach of a publishing contract, we must decide what damages are recoverable for defendant's failure to publish plaintiff's manuscript. In 1965, plaintiff, an author and a college teacher, and defendant, Washington Square Press, Inc., entered into a written agreement which, in relevant part, provided as follows. Plaintiff ("author") granted defendant ("publisher") exclusive rights to publish and sell in book form plaintiff's work on modern drama. Upon plaintiff's delivery of the manuscript, defendant agreed to complete payment of a nonreturnable $2,000 "advance." Thereafter, if defendant deemed the manuscript not "suitable for publication," it had the right to terminate the agreement by written notice within 60 days of delivery. Unless so terminated, defendant agreed to publish the work in hardbound edition within 18 months and afterwards in paperbound edition. The contract further provided that defendant would pay royalties to plaintiff, based upon specified percentages of sales. (For example, plaintiff was to receive 10% of the retail price of the first 10,000 copies sold in the continental United States.) If defendant failed to publish within 18 months, the contract provided that "this agreement shall terminate and the rights herein granted to the Publisher shall revert to the Author. In such event all payments theretofore made to the Author shall belong to the Author without prejudice to any other remedies which the Author may have." . . .

Plaintiff performed by delivering his manuscript to defendant and was paid his $2,000 advance. Defendant thereafter merged with another publisher and ceased publishing in hardbound. Although defendant did not exercise its 60-day right to terminate, it has refused to publish the manuscript in any form.

Plaintiff . . . initially sought specific performance of the contract. The Trial Term Justice denied specific performance but, finding a valid contract and a breach by defendant, set the matter down for trial on the issue of monetary damages, if any, sustained by the plaintiff. At trial, plaintiff sought to prove: (1) delay of his academic promotion; (2) loss of royalties which would have been earned; and (3) the cost of publication if plaintiff had made his own arrangements to

6. United States Naval Inst. v. Charter Communications. 936 F.2d 692. 697 (2d Cir. 1991). For a similar view, *see* Locke v. United States, 283 F.2d 521, 524 (Ct. Cl. 1960) (one "who has wrongfully broken a contract should not be permitted to reap advantage from his own wrong by insisting on proof which by reason of his breach is unobtainable").

publish. The trial court found that plaintiff had been promoted despite defendant's failure to publish, and that there was no evidence that the breach had caused any delay. Recovery of lost royalties was denied without discussion. The court found, however, that the cost of hardcover publication to plaintiff was the natural and probable consequence of the breach and, based upon expert testimony, awarded $10,000 to cover this cost. It denied recovery of the expenses of paperbound publication on the ground that plaintiff's proof was conjectural.

The Appellate Division, (3 to 2) affirmed, finding that the cost of publication was the proper measure of damages. In support of its conclusion, the majority analogized to the construction contract situation where the cost of completion may be the proper measure of damages for a builder's failure to complete a house or for use of wrong materials. The dissent concluded that the cost of publication is not an appropriate measure of damages and consequently, that plaintiff may recover nominal damages only. We agree with the dissent. In so concluding, we look to the basic purpose of damage recovery and the nature and effect of the parties' contract.

It is axiomatic that, except where punitive damages are allowable, the law awards damages for breach of contract to compensate for injury caused by the breach—injury which was foreseeable, i.e., reasonably within the contemplation of the parties, at the time the contract was entered into. Money damages are substitutional relief designed in theory

> to put the injured party in as good a position as he would have been put by full performance of the contract, at the least cost to the defendant and without charging him with harms that he had no sufficient reason to foresee when he made the contract. 5 Corbin, *Contracts*, § 1002, pp. 31-32.

In other words, so far as possible, the law attempts to secure to the injured party the benefit of his bargain, subject to the limitations that the injury—whether it be losses suffered or gains prevented—was foreseeable, and that the amount of damages claimed be measurable with a reasonable degree of certainty and, of course, adequately proven. But it is equally fundamental that the injured party should not recover more from the breach than he would have gained had the contract been fully performed.

Measurement of damages in this case according to the cost of publication to the plaintiff would confer greater advantage than performance of the contract would have entailed to plaintiff and would place him in a far better position than he would have occupied had the defendant fully performed. Such measurement bears no relation to compensation for plaintiff's actual loss or anticipated profit. Far beyond compensating plaintiff for the interests he had in the defendant's performance of the contract—whether restitution, reliance or expectation (see Fuller &

> ***Courts care about defendants too!***
>
> Note how the court states its concern (1) with restoring the injured party to its rightful (i.e., contracted-for) position, which is concerned with ensuring that the plaintiff is not *undercompensated*, but (2) also with ensuring that the plaintiff is not *overcompensated*, which is an indirect way of caring about the defendant's rightful position, as it is the defendant who must pay these damages. Did the court strike the proper balance between the plaintiff's and defendant's rightful positions in this case? Why or why not?

Perdue, *Reliance Interest in Contract Damages*, 46 Yale L.J. 52, 53-56)—an award of the cost of publication would enrich plaintiff at defendant's expense.

Pursuant to the contract, plaintiff delivered his manuscript to the defendant. In doing so, he conferred a value on the defendant which, upon defendant's breach, was required to be restored to him. Special Term, in addition to ordering a trial on the issue of damages, ordered defendant to return the manuscript to plaintiff and plaintiff's restitution interest in the contract was thereby protected.

At the trial on the issue of damages, plaintiff alleged no reliance losses suffered in performing the contract or in making necessary preparations to perform. Had such losses, if foreseeable and ascertainable, been incurred, plaintiff would have been entitled to compensation for them.

As for plaintiff's expectation interest in the contract, it was basically twofold—the "advance" and the royalties. (To be sure, plaintiff may have expected to enjoy whatever notoriety, prestige or other benefits that might have attended publication, but even if these expectations were compensable, plaintiff did not attempt at trial to place a monetary value on them.) There is no dispute that plaintiff's expectancy in the "advance" was fulfilled—he has received his $2,000. His expectancy interest in the royalties—the profit he stood to gain from sale of the published book—while theoretically compensable, was speculative. Although this work is not plaintiff's first, at trial he provided no stable foundation for a reasonable estimate of royalties he would have earned had defendant not breached its promise to publish. In these circumstances, his claim for royalties falls for uncertainty.

Since the damages which would have compensated plaintiff for anticipated royalties were not proved with the required certainty, we agree with the dissent in the Appellate Division that nominal damages alone are recoverable. Though these are damages in name only and not at all compensatory, they are nevertheless awarded as a formal vindication of plaintiff's legal right to compensation which has not been given a sufficiently certain monetary valuation.

In our view, the analogy by the majority in the Appellate Division to the construction contract situation was inapposite. In the typical construction contract, the owner agrees to pay money or other consideration to a builder and expects, under the contract, to receive a completed building in return. The value of the promised performance to the owner is the properly constructed building. In this case, unlike the typical construction contract, the value to plaintiff of the promised performance—publication—was a percentage of sales of the books published and not the books themselves. Had the plaintiff contracted for the printing, binding and delivery of a number of hardbound copies of his manuscript, to be sold or disposed of as he wished, then perhaps the construction analogy, and measurement of damages by the cost of replacement or completion, would have some application.

Here, however, the specific value to plaintiff of the promised publication was the royalties he stood to receive from defendant's sales of the published book. Essentially, publication represented what it would have cost the defendant to

confer that value upon the plaintiff, and, by its breach, defendant saved that cost. The error by the courts below was in measuring damages not by the value to plaintiff of the promised performance but by the cost of that performance to defendant. Damages are not measured, however, by what the defaulting party saved by the breach, but by the natural and probable consequences of the breach *to the plaintiff*. In this case, the consequence to plaintiff of defendant's failure to publish is that he is prevented from realizing the gains promised by the contract—the royalties. But, as we have stated, the amount of royalties plaintiff would have realized was not ascertained with adequate certainty and, as a consequence, plaintiff may recover nominal damages only.

Accordingly, the order of the Appellate Division should be [affirmed but] modified to the extent of reducing the damage award of $10,000 for the cost of publication to six cents, but with costs and disbursements to the plaintiff. . . .

RELEVANT PROVISIONS

For the *Restatement (Second) of Contracts,* consult § 352. For the UNIDROIT Principles, see Article 7.4.3.

NOTES AND QUESTIONS

1. *What happened?* Who sued whom for what? Procedurally, how did the case get before this court? Factually, what happened between the parties? What arguments did the plaintiff and defendant make? What rule or rules did the court apply? How did the court analyze the dispute between the parties? How did the court decide the case?

2. *Was this case correctly decided?* Do you agree with the result reached in this case? Why or why not? Do you agree with the court's reasoning? Why or why not? How, if at all, would you have written the opinion differently?

3. *Denying recovery.* The plaintiff tried to recover damages for (1) delay of his academic promotion, (2) the loss of royalties he would have earned if the publisher published his work, and (3) the cost of publication if plaintiff made his own arrangements to publish his work. What justifications did the court provide for denying each item of recovery, and do you agree with the court's analysis? Are the justifications offered by the court the same or different with respect to each item? Can you think of any additional justifications?

4. *Thinking about the certainty requirement.* Although the plaintiff could not prove his damages with a reasonable degree of certainty in the above case, the non-publication of his book must certainly have caused him *some* harm. Yet, the plaintiff cannot recover damages for this harm. The logical question, of course, is why? Can you think of any policy justifications for the current rule? Or, perhaps, can you think of a better rule? Here are a few questions to

get you started in thinking about these considerations: First, why should the *defendant* get the benefit of the plaintiff's inability to prove his damages with certainty? As the defendant is the party that breached, why not place the burden on it, rather than on the plaintiff? We could do this, for instance, by having a rule whereby the plaintiff is allowed to suggest a figure that roughly approximates the harm caused by the defendant, and then put the burden on the defendant to prove, with reasonable certainty, that certain of these damages are excessive. And second, where it seems clear that the plaintiff suffered some harm from the defendant's breach, then why not allow the plaintiff to recover what the defendant saved? Doesn't the court's rule allow breaching parties to benefit at the expense of non-breaching parties?

5. *Justifying certainty?* Drawing on any thinking tools we've discussed, why should the onus be put on the injured party to prove their damages with reasonable certainty? It is, after all, the promisor that caused the breach.

Kenford Co., Inc. v. County of Erie

Court of Appeals of New York
493 N.E.2d 234 (1986)

PER CURIAM. The issue in this appeal is whether a plaintiff, in an action for breach of contract, may recover loss of prospective profits for its contemplated 20-year operation of a domed stadium which was to be constructed by defendant County of Erie (County).

On August 8, 1969, pursuant to a duly adopted resolution of its legislature, the County of Erie entered into a contract with Kenford Company, Inc. (Kenford) and Dome Stadium, Inc. (DSI) for the construction and operation of a domed stadium facility near the City of Buffalo. The contract provided that construction of the facility by the County would commence within 12 months of the contract date and that a mutually acceptable 40-year lease between the County and DSI for the operation of said facility would be negotiated by the parties and agreed upon within three months of the receipt by the County of preliminary plans, drawings and cost estimates. It was further provided that in the event a mutually acceptable lease could not be agreed upon within the three-month period, a separate management contract between the County and DSI, as appended to the basic agreement, would be executed by the parties, providing for the operation of the stadium facility by DSI for a period of 20 years from the completion of the stadium and its availability for use.

Although strenuous and extensive negotiations followed, the parties never agreed upon the terms of a lease, nor did construction of a domed facility begin within the one-year period or at any time thereafter. A breach of the contract thus occurred and this action was commenced in June 1971 by Kenford and DSI.

Prolonged and extensive pretrial and preliminary proceedings transpired throughout the next 10 years, culminating with the entry of an order which affirmed the grant of summary judgment against the County on the issue of liability and directed a trial limited to the issue of damages. The ensuing trial ended some nine months later with a multimillion dollar jury verdict in plaintiffs' favor. An appeal to the Appellate Division resulted in a modification of the judgment. That court reversed portions of the judgment awarding damages for loss of profits and for certain out-of-pocket expenses incurred, and directed a new trial upon other issues. On appeal to this court, we are concerned only with that portion of the verdict which awarded DSI money damages for loss of prospective profits during the 20-year period of the proposed management contract, as appended to the basic contract. That portion of the verdict was set aside by the Appellate Division and the cause of action dismissed. The court concluded that the use of expert opinion to present statistical projections of future business operations involved the use of too many variables to provide a rational basis upon which lost profits could be calculated and, therefore, such projections were insufficient as a matter of law to support an award of lost profits. We agree with this ultimate conclusion, but upon different grounds.

Loss of future profits as damages for breach of contract have been permitted in New York under long-established and precise rules of law. First, it must be demonstrated with certainty that such damages have been caused by the breach and, second, the alleged loss must be capable of proof with reasonable certainty. In other words, the damages may not be merely speculative, possible or imaginary, but must be reasonably certain and directly traceable to the breach, not remote or the result of other intervening causes. In addition, there must be a showing that the particular damages were fairly within the contemplation of the parties to the contract at the time it was made. If it is a new business seeking to recover for loss of future profits, a stricter standard is imposed for the obvious reason that there does not exist a reasonable basis of experience upon which to estimate lost profits with the requisite degree of reasonable certainty.

These rules must be applied to the proof presented by DSI in this case. We note the procedure for computing damages selected by DSI was in accord with contemporary economic theory and was presented through the testimony of recognized experts. Such a procedure has been accepted in this State and many other jurisdictions. DSI's economic analysis employed historical data, obtained from the operation of other domed stadiums and related facilities throughout the country, which was then applied to the results of a comprehensive study of the marketing prospects for the proposed facility in the Buffalo area. The quantity of proof is massive and, unquestionably, represents business and industry's most advanced and sophisticated method for predicting the probable results of contemplated projects. Indeed, it is difficult to conclude what additional relevant proof could have been submitted by DSI in support of its attempt to establish, with reasonable certainty, loss of prospective profits. Nevertheless, DSI's proof is insufficient to meet the required standard.

The reason for this conclusion is twofold. Initially, the proof does not satisfy the requirement that liability for loss of profits over a 20-year period was in the contemplation of the parties at the time of the execution of the basic contract or at the time of its breach. Indeed, the provisions in the contract providing remedy for a default do not suggest or provide for such a heavy responsibility on the part of the County. In the absence of any provision for such an eventuality, the commonsense rule to apply is to consider what the parties would have concluded had they considered the subject. The evidence here fails to demonstrate that liability for loss of profits over the length of the contract would have been in the contemplation of the parties at the relevant times.

Next, we note that despite the massive quantity of expert proof submitted by DSI, the ultimate conclusions are still projections, and as employed in the present day commercial world, subject to adjustment and modification. We of course recognize that any projection cannot be absolute, nor is there any such requirement, but it is axiomatic that the degree of certainty is dependent upon known or unknown factors which form the basis of the ultimate conclusion. Here, the foundations upon which the economic model was created undermine the certainty of the projections. DSI assumed that the facility was completed, available for use and successfully operated by it for 20 years, providing professional sporting events and other forms of entertainment, as well as hosting meetings, conventions and related commercial gatherings. At the time of the breach, there was only one other facility in this country to use as a basis of comparison, the Astrodome in Houston. Quite simply, the multitude of assumptions required to establish projections of profitability over the life of this contract require speculation and conjecture, making it beyond the capability of even the most sophisticated procedures to satisfy the legal requirements of proof with reasonable certainty.

The economic facts of life, the whim of the general public and the fickle nature of popular support for professional athletic endeavors must be given great weight in attempting to ascertain damages 20 years in the future. New York has long recognized the inherent uncertainties of predicting profits in the entertainment field in general and, in this case, we are dealing, in large part, with a new facility furnishing entertainment for the public. It is our view that the record in this case demonstrates the efficacy of the principles set forth [above], principles to which we continue to adhere. In so doing, we specifically reject the "rational basis" test . . . adopted by the Appellate Division.

Accordingly, that portion of the order of the Appellate Division being appealed from should be affirmed.

NOTES AND QUESTIONS

1. ***What happened?*** Who sued whom for what? Procedurally, how did the case get before this court? Factually, what happened between the parties? What arguments did the plaintiff and defendant make? What rule or rules did the court apply? How did the court analyze the dispute between the parties? How did the court decide the case?

2. *Was this case correctly decided?* Do you agree with the result reached in this case? Why or why not? Do you agree with the court's reasoning? Why or why not? How, if at all, would you have written the opinion differently?

3. *Rational basis test?* What, exactly, is the rational basis test, and what is the relationship between that doctrine and the doctrine that damages must be proved with reasonable certainty? Do you agree with the court in rejecting the rational basis test? Why or why not?

Drews Company, Inc. v. Ledwith-Wolfe Associates, Inc.

Supreme Court of South Carolina
371 S.E.2d 532 (1988)

HARWELL, JUSTICE. This case involves the breach of a construction contract. . . . The Drews Company, Inc. ("Contractor") contracted to renovate a building owned by Ledwith-Wolfe Associates, Inc. ("Owner"). Owner intended to convert the building into a restaurant. From its inception, the project was plagued by construction delays, work change orders, and general disagreement over the quality of work performed. Contractor eventually pulled its workers off the project [and] . . . sued to foreclose[] a **mechanic's lien** for labor and materials used in renovating the building. Owner counterclaimed, alleging Contractor breached the contract and forced Owner to rework part of the job. Owner also claimed that Contractor's delays in performance caused Owner to lose profits from the restaurant.

> ***Mechanic's lien***
>
> "A statutory lien that secures payment for labor or materials supplied in improving, repairing, or maintaining real or personal property, such as a building, an automobile, or the like." BLACK'S LAW DICTIONARY (10th ed. 2014).

The jury returned an $18,000 verdict for Contractor on its complaint. The jury awarded Owner $22,895 on its counterclaim for re-doing and completing the work and $14,000 in lost profits caused by Contractor's delays. The trial judge denied Contractor's new trial motion. . . . [We affirm the trial court's refusal to grant a new trial, but reverse the jury's award of lost profits.]

[This case] presents this Court with an opportunity to address a legal issue unsettled in South Carolina: Does the "new business rule" operate to automatically preclude the recovery of lost profits by a new business or enterprise? We hold that it does not.

We begin our analysis of the lost profits issue by recognizing an elementary principle of contract law. The purpose of an award of damages for breach is "to give compensation, that is, to put the plaintiff in as good a position as he would have been in had the contract been performed." 11 S. Williston, *A Treatise on the Law of Contracts,* § 1338 (3d ed. 1968). The proper measure of that compensation, then, "is the loss actually suffered by the contractee as the result of the breach." *South Carolina Finance Corp. v. West Side Finance Co.,* 236 S.C. 109, 122 (1960).

"Profits" have been defined as "the net pecuniary gain from a transaction, the gross pecuniary gains diminished by the cost of obtaining them." *Restatement of Contracts* § 331, Comment B (1932). Profits lost by a business as the result of a contractual breach have long been recognized as a species of recoverable consequential damages in this state. The issue is more difficult, however, when a new or unestablished business is the aggrieved party seeking projected lost profits as damages.

The new business rule as a per se rule of nonrecoverability of lost profits was firmly established in this state in *Standard Supply Co. v. Carter & Harris,* 81 S.C. 181, 187 (1907): "When a business is in contemplation, but not established or not in actual operation, profit merely hoped for is too uncertain and conjectural to be considered." . . .

Modern cases, however, reflect [a] willingness . . . to view the new business rule as a rule of evidentiary sufficiency rather than an automatic bar to recovery of lost profits by a new business. . . . [Indeed, a number of modern] cases have so eroded the new business rule as an absolute bar to recovery of lost profits that the rigid *Standard Supply Co.* rule is no longer good law.

South Carolina has not been alone in developing its evidentiary view of the new business rule. Numerous authorities and commentators have tracked a similar trend nationwide: "Courts are now taking the position that the distinction between established businesses and new ones is a distinction that goes to the weight of the evidence and not a rule that automatically precludes recovery of profits by a new business." D. Dobbs, *Handbook on the Law of Remedies,* § 3.3, at 155 (1973). . . .

We believe South Carolina should now unequivocally join those jurisdictions applying the new business rule as a rule of evidentiary sufficiency and not as an automatic preclusion to recovery of lost profits by a new business or enterprise.

The same standards that have for years governed lost profits awards in South Carolina will apply with equal force to cases where damages are sought for a new business or enterprise. First, profits must have been prevented or lost "as a natural consequence of" the breach of contract. *South Carolina Finance Corp., supra,* at 122.

The second requirement is foreseeability; a breaching party is liable for those damages, including lost profits, "which may reasonably be supposed to have been within the contemplation of the parties at the time the contract was made as a probable result of the breach of it." *National Tire & Rubber Co. v. Hoover,* 128 S.C. 344, 348 (1924); *see also Sitton v. MacDonald,* 25 S.C. 68 (1885) (lost profits cases citing the "knowledge of special circumstances" rule of *Hadley v. Baxendale,* 156 Eng. Rep. 154 (1854)).

The crucial requirement in lost profits determinations is that they be "established with reasonable certainty, for recovery cannot be had for profits that are conjectural or speculative." *South Carolina Finance Corp.*, supra, at 122. "The proof must pass the realm of conjecture, speculation, or opinion not founded on facts, and must consist of actual facts from which a reasonably accurate conclusion regarding the cause and the amount of the loss can be logically and rationally drawn." 22 Am. Jur. 2d *Damages* § 641 (1988).

Numerous proof techniques have been discussed and accepted in different factual scenarios. *See, e.g., Upjohn v. Rachelle Laboratories, Inc.*, 661 F.2d 1105, 1114 (6th Cir.1981) (proof of future lost profits based on marketing forecasts by employees specializing in economic forecasting); *Petty v. Weyerhaeuser Co.*, [288 S.C. 349 (Ct. App. 1986)] (skating rink's projected revenues compared to those of another arena in a nearby town); *see also Restatement (Second) of Contracts* § 352, at 146 (1981) (proof of lost profits "may be established with reasonable certainty with the aid of expert testimony, economic and financial data, market surveys and analyses, business records of similar enterprises, and the like."); Note, [*The New Business Rule And The Denial Of Lost Profits*, 48 Ohio St. L.J. 855, 872-73 (1987)] (means of proving prospective profits include (1) "yardstick" method of comparison with profit performance of business similar in size, nature, and location; (2) comparison with profit history of plaintiff's successor, where applicable; (3) comparison of similar businesses owned by plaintiff himself, and (4) use of economic and financial data and expert testimony). While the factual contexts in which new business/lost profits cases arise will undoubtedly vary, these methods of proof and the "reasonable certainty" requirement bear an inherent flexibility facilitating the just assessment of profits lost to a new business due to contractual breach.

Applying this standard to the facts before us, we find that Owner's proof failed to clear the "reasonable certainty" hurdle. Owner's projections of the profits lost by the restaurant because of the breach were based on nothing more than a sheet of paper reflecting the gross profits the restaurant made in the first 11 months of operation after construction was completed. These figures were not supplemented with corresponding figures for overhead or operating expenditures, but only with Owner's testimony that he "would expect at least a third of that [gross figure] to be" net profit. Owner's expectations, unsupported by any particular standard or fixed method for establishing net profits, were wholly insufficient to provide the jury with a basis for calculating profits lost with reasonable certainty.

The trial judge erred in failing to rule that, as a matter of law, Owner's proof was insufficient to merit submission to the jury. The $14,000 award of lost profits must therefore be reversed. . . .

NOTES AND QUESTIONS

1. *What happened?* Who sued whom for what? Procedurally, how did the case get before this court? Factually, what happened between the parties? What arguments did the plaintiff and defendant make? What rule or rules did the court apply? How did the court analyze the dispute between the parties? How did the court decide the case?

2. *Was this case correctly decided?* Do you agree with the result reached in this case? Why or why not? Do you agree with the court's reasoning? Why or why not? How, if at all, would you have written the opinion differently?

3. ***Reasonable certainty standard not satisfied.*** Here, the court found that the reasonable certainty standard was not satisfied. First, do you agree? Second, what will the plaintiff recover on remand?

PROBLEM: THE CASE OF PRE-RELIANCE EXPENDITURES

In 1968, plaintiff Anglia Television Ltd. decided to make a film of a play for television entitled "The Man in the Wood." It portrayed an American man married to an English woman. The American has an adventure in an English wood. The film was to last for 90 minutes. Anglia Television made many arrangements in advance. They arranged for a place where the play was to be filmed. They employed a director, a designer and a stage manager, and so forth. They involved themselves in much expense. All this was done before they got the leading man. They required a strong actor capable of holding the play together. He was to be on the scene the whole time. Anglia Television eventually found the man. He was Mr. Robert Reed, the defendant, an American who has a very high reputation as an actor. He was very suitable for this part. By telephone conversation on August 30, 1968, it was agreed by Mr. Reed through his agent that he would come to England and be available between September 9 and October 11, 1968, to rehearse and play in this film. He was to get a performance fee of £1,050, living expenses of £100 a week, his first class fares to and from the United States, and so forth. Unfortunately, after the contract was concluded, it was realized that there was some confusion with the bookings. It appears that Mr. Reed's agents had already booked him in America for another play. So on September 3, 1968, the agent said that Mr. Reed would not come to England to perform in this play, and repudiated his contract. Anglia Television tried hard to find a substitute but could not do so. So on September 11 they accepted his repudiation, abandoned the proposed film, and sued Mr. Reed for damages. Mr. Reed did not dispute his liability, but a question arose as to the damages. Anglia Television do not claim their profit. They cannot say what their profit would have been on this contract if Mr. Reed had come here and performed it. So instead of claim for loss of profits, they claim for the wasted expenditure. They had incurred the director's fees. the designer's fees, the stage manager's and assistant manager's fees, and so on. It comes in all to £2,750. Anglia Television say that all that money was wasted because Mr. Reed did not perform his contract.

Mr. Reed's lawyer's argue that Anglia Television cannot recover for expenditure incurred *before* the contract was concluded with Mr. Reed. They can only recover the expenditure *after* the contract was concluded. They say that the expenditure *after* the contract was only £854.65, and that is all that Anglia Television can recover.

How should the court rule, and why?

c. Avoidability

DOCTRINAL OVERVIEW: AVOIDABILITY AS A LIMITATION*

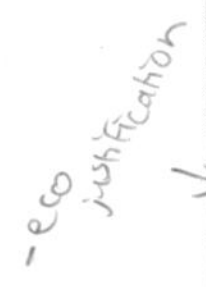

A court ordinarily will not compensate an injured party for loss that that party could have avoided by making efforts appropriate, in the eyes of the court, to the circumstances. A quaint English case from over three centuries ago makes this point. The plaintiff had contracted to carry goods to Ipswich and to deliver them to a place to be appointed by the defendant. When the plaintiff arrived in Ipswich, however, "the defendant delayed by the space of six hours the appointment of the place; insomuch that his horses being so hot . . . and standing in *aperto aere,* they died soon after." The plaintiff sued for damages, but the court denied recovery on the ground that "it was the plaintiff's folly to let the horses stand," for he "might have taken his horses out of the cart or laid down the [goods] anywhere in Ipswich."[1] The economic justification of such a rule is plain, for it encourages the injured party to act so as to minimize the wasteful results of breach. Looked at in another way, the rule allows the obligor to call upon the obligee's efforts to reduce the cost of satisfying the obligors duty to perform. The Third Circuit has suggested that if "both the plaintiff and the defendant have had equal opportunity to reduce the damages by the same act and it is equally reasonable to expect the defendant to minimize damages, the defendant is in no position to contend that the plaintiff failed to mitigate,"[3] but this view has not escaped criticism. The limitation of avoidability applies to damages measured by reliance as well as to damages based on expectation.

It is sometimes said that in such cases the injured party is under a "duty" to take appropriate steps to mitigate damages. This is misleading, however, for the injured party incurs no liability to the party in breach by failing to take such steps. That party is simply precluded from recovering damages for loss that it could have avoided, had it taken such steps. Since the injured party is in some sense responsible for such loss, this conclusion might seem to be no more than a corollary of the requirement that an injured party's damages must have been caused by the other party's breach, but it is not commonly thought of in this way. The burden of showing that the injured party could have, but has not, taken appropriate steps generally rests upon the party in breach. . . .

What steps the injured party is expected to take depends on the circumstances.[10] Just as the plaintiff who carried the goods to Ipswich could not recover for loss he could have avoided by taking his horses out of the cool Ipswich air, a buyer of oil that discovers that the barrels are leaking cannot recover for loss it could have avoided by transferring the oil to other available barrels,[11] and a

* Excerpted from E. ALLAN FARNSWORTH, CONTRACTS § 12.12 (4th ed. 2004).

1. Vertue v. Bird, 84 Eng. Rep. 1000 (same case), 86 Eng. Rep. 200 (K.B. 1677).

3. S.J. Groves & Sons Co. v. Warner Co., 576 F.2d 524, 530 (3d Cir. 1978).

10. Restatement Second § 3.50(1) bars recovery of "loss that the injured party could have avoided without undue risk, burden or humiliation." The Vienna Convention bars recoverv of loss that could have been avoided by such measures as were "reasonable in the circumstances." CISC 77. *See* UNIDROIT Principles 7.4.8(1) ("reasonable steps").

11. *See* Restatement Second § 350 ill. 3.

baker that knowingly uses seriously defective flour cannot recover from the seller for loss due to claims by dissatisfied customers.[12] The injured party is not, however, expected to guard against unforeseeable risks nor to take steps that involve undue burden, risk, or humiliation. Furthermore, a party that takes steps that seemed reasonable at the time will not be judged by hindsight. As the Third Circuit has said:

> When a choice has been required between two reasonable courses, the person whose wrong forced the choice cannot complain that one rather than the other was chosen. The rule of mitigation of damages may not be invoked by a contract breaker as a basis for hypercritical examination of the conduct of the injured party, or merely for the purpose of showing that the injured person might have taken steps which seemed wiser or would have been more advantageous to the defaulter. One is not obligated to exalt the interest of the defaulter to his probable detriment.[15]

Rockingham County v. Luten Bridge Co.

Circuit Court of Appeals, Fourth Circuit
35 F.2d 301 (1929)

[Plaintiff Luten Bridge Company contracted with defendant Rockingham County, North Carolina to build a bridge. After the contract was awarded, the composition of the Board of County Commissioners, which originally voted 3-2 in favor of giving the contract to plaintiff, was altered. The new board members voted to cancel the original contract, and instructed plaintiff to immediately stop work on the bridge. At this time, plaintiff had already spent $1,900 performing the contract. Despite being instructed to stop by the new board members, plaintiff, perhaps confused about which of the two boards it should have listened to, continued to build the bridge. Once it was complete, defendant refused to pay, and plaintiff brought suit to recover the $18,301.07 it alleged was due under the contract. Defendant took the position that it was only liable for the damages plaintiff sustained prior to being instructed to abandon construction of the bridge.]

PARKER, CIRCUIT JUDGE. [Regarding] the measure of plaintiff's recovery—we do not think that, after the county had given notice, while the contract was still executory, that it did not desire the bridge built and would not pay for it, plaintiff could proceed to build it and recover the contract price. **It is true that the county had no right to rescind the contract, and the notice given plaintiff amounted to a breach on its part; but, after plaintiff had received notice of the breach, it was its duty to do nothing to increase the damages flowing therefrom.** If A enters into a binding contract to build a house for B, B, of

> ***Hohfeld to the rescue!***
>
> This sentence, and indeed this entire paragraph, makes use of the terms "no right" and "duty" in several places, but it is not clear that the court is using these terms in an analytically precise manner, with the unfortunate result

12. *See* Restatement Second § 350 ill. 4.
15. In re Kellett Aircraft Corp., 186 F.2d 197. 198-99 (3d Cir. 1950).

that this lack of clarity can spread to the unwary reader as well. Using Hohfeld's juridical concepts, which we examined in "Thinking Tool: Thinking Clearly About Legal Relationships" (p. 96, *supra*), replace the underlined terms with the correct Hohfeldian terms the court should have used instead.

Economic waste

Note here the court's concern with economic waste, a concept we explored when we examined the cost of completion versus diminution in value cases of *Groves v. John Wunder Co.*, *Peevyhouse v. Garland Coal Mining Co.*, and *American Standard, Inc. v. Schectman* earlier in this chapter. Note also how the court's concern with enforcing inefficient contracts links up with some earlier thinking tools, such as "Thinking Tool: Marginal Analysis and Efficiency" (p. 64, *supra*), and even provides a relatively uncontroversial example of efficient breach. If one of the reasons that courts enforce promises is to allow parties to enter into wealth-maximizing, Pareto-efficient contracts, it stands to reason that once there is evidence that the contract will no longer accomplish these objectives (i.e., the road will no longer be built, with the result that there would be no access to the newly built bridge), efficiency considerations should allow a party to breach and pay damages, rather than being forced to perform its contractual obligations. Do you agree?

course, has no right to rescind the contract without A's consent. But if, before the house is built, he decides that he does not want it, and notifies A to that effect, A has no right to proceed with the building and thus pile up damages. His remedy is to treat the contract as broken when he receives the notice, and sue for the recovery of such damages, as he may have sustained from the breach, including any profit which he would have realized upon performance, as well as any other losses which may have resulted to him. **In the case at bar, the county decided not to build the road of which the bridge was to be a part, and did not build it. The bridge, built in the midst of the forest, is of no value to the county because of this change of circumstances.** When, therefore, the county gave notice to the plaintiff that it would not proceed with the project, plaintiff should have desisted from further work. It had no right thus to pile up damages by proceeding with the erection of a useless bridge.

The contrary view was expressed by Lord Cockburn in *Frost v. Knight*, L.R. 7 Ex. 111, but, as pointed out by Prof. Williston (*Williston on Contracts*, vol. 3, p. 2347), it is not in harmony with the decisions in this country. The American rule and the reasons supporting it are well stated by Prof. Williston as follows:

> There is a line of cases running back to 1845 which holds that, after an absolute repudiation or refusal to perform by one party to a contract, the other party cannot continue to perform and recover damages based on full performance. This rule is only a particular application of the general rule of damages that a plaintiff cannot hold a defendant liable for damages which need not have been incurred; or, as it is often stated, the plaintiff must, so far as he can without loss to himself, mitigate the damages caused by the defendant's wrongful act. The application of this rule to the matter in question is obvious. If a man engages to have work done, and afterwards repudiates his contract before the work has been begun or when it has been only partially done, it is inflicting damage on the defendant without benefit to the plaintiff to allow the latter to insist on proceeding with the contract. The work may be useless to the defendant, and yet he would be forced to pay the full contract price. On the other hand, the plaintiff is interested only in the profit he will make out of the contract. If he receives this it is equally advantageous for him to use his time otherwise.

The leading case on the subject in this country is the New York case of *Clark v. Marsiglia*, 1 Denio 317 (N.Y. 1845). In that case defendant had employed

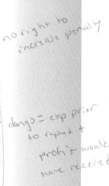

plaintiff to paint certain pictures for him, but countermanded the order before the work was finished. Plaintiff, however, went on and completed the work and sued for the contract price. In reversing a judgment for plaintiff, the court said:

> The plaintiff was allowed to recover as though there had been no countermand of the order; and in this the court erred. The defendant, by requiring the plaintiff to stop work upon the paintings, violated his contract, and thereby incurred a liability to pay such damages as the plaintiff should sustain. Such damages would include a recompense for the labor done and materials used, and such further sum in damages as might, upon legal principles, be assessed for the breach of the contract; but the plaintiff had no right, by obstinately persisting in the work, to make the penalty upon the defendant greater than it would otherwise have been.

. . . It follows that there was error in directing a verdict for plaintiff for the full amount of its claim. The measure of plaintiff's damage, upon its appearing that notice was duly given not to build the bridge, is an amount sufficient to compensate plaintiff for labor and materials expended and expense incurred in the part performance of the contract, prior to its repudiation, plus the profit which would have been realized if it had been carried out in accordance with its terms. . . .

The judgment below will accordingly be reversed, and the case remanded for a new trial. Reversed.

RELEVANT PROVISIONS

For the *Restatement (Second) of Contracts*, consult § 350. For the UCC, consult § 2-704(2). For the CISG, consult Article 77. For the UNIDROIT Principles, consult 7.4.8.

NOTES AND QUESTIONS

1. ***What happened?*** Who sued whom for what? Procedurally, how did the case get before this court? Factually, what happened between the parties? What arguments did the plaintiff and defendant make? What rule or rules did the court apply? How did the court analyze the dispute between the parties? How did the court decide the case?

2. ***Was this case correctly decided?*** Do you agree with the result reached in this case? Why or why not? Do you agree with the court's reasoning? Why or why not? How, if at all, would you have written the opinion differently?

3. ***Damages?*** Assume that the Luten Bridge Co. stopped working the moment it was requested to do so. How would their damages be computed?

4. ***Double recovery?*** If the Luten Bridge Co. stopped work when it was told, could it not then immediately go out and build a bridge for someone else, resulting in a double recovery? If so, should this be taken into account by the court in determining damages? Why or why not?

5. ***UCC § 2-704(2).*** Does the UCC change the rule in *Luten Bridge*?

Before reading the excerpt below, you may wish to review "Thinking Tool: Thinking Clearly About Legal Relationships" at p. 96, supra. Recalling the Hohfeldian definition of a legal duty developed in that excerpt, can you see why the so-called "duty" to mitigate damages referred to in Rockingham County v. Luten Bridge Co. *is not, strictly speaking, a duty?*

THINKING TOOL APPLIED: READING CRITICALLY*

Once students have grasped Hohfeld's vocabulary, they tend to assume, as they encounter the terms in their reading, that the author has used them in a way consistent with Hohfeld's definitions. This is incorrect. Hohfeld's work is built on the premise that the words *right, privilege, power,* and *immunity* have no generally agreed meaning, that they are "chameleon-hued."[28] A reader must investigate further to determine the underlying meaning. Hohfeld provides an opportunity to teach students to read with a skeptical eye.[29] . . .

In a first-year course, Hohfeld can provide a platform for the class's first foray into critical reading and, in any course, this reading beneath the language can model other types of critical reading. . . . In Contracts, for example, the obligation imposed on a nonbreaching party to act reasonably to reduce damages is commonly known as the "duty" to mitigate, as illustrated in *Rockingham County v. Luten Bridge Co.* The plaintiff had agreed to build a bridge for a price of $18,300 and had expended $1,900 in beginning the project when the defendant breached. Despite the breach the plaintiff continued construction, finished the project, and sued for the contract price. The court held that since the plaintiff had not complied with its "duty" to mitigate, damages would be limited to its prebreach reliance expenses ($1,900) plus *profits* it would have made from full performance.

In the classroom students invariably use the word *duty* to describe the plaintiff's obligation to mitigate. I allow the discussion to proceed for a few minutes and then ask whether the duty of mitigation is a Hohfeldian duty. The ensuing analysis clarifies the difference. Breach of a Hohfeldian duty results in a claim by the rightholder. A failure to mitigate, on the other hand, does not result in a claim, but means that a claim, or a portion of a claim, is ineffective. In Hohfeldian terms, a failure to mitigate means the party in breach is privileged not to pay damages that could have been avoided. As applied in *Rockingham County,* the defendant has a duty to pay prebreach reliance expenses ($1,900) plus profits it would have made from full performance, but it is privileged not to pay postbreach expenses.

* Excerpted from Curtis Nyquist, *Teaching Wesley Hohfeld's Theory of Legal Relations,* 52 J. LEGAL EDUC. 238, 246-47 (2002).

28. Wesley Newcomb Hohfeld, *Some Fundamental Legal Conceptions as Applied in Judicial Reasoning,* 23 YALE L.J. 16, 29 (1913). Hohfeld comments: "Just how accurate the distinctions in the mind of the draftsman may have been it is, of course, impossible to say." *Id.* at 31.

29. Skepticism is an essential first step to critical reading. *See, e.g.,* Elizabeth Fajans & Mary R. Falk, *Against the Tyranny of Paraphrase: Talking Back to Texts,* 78 CORNELL L. REV. 163, 163-65 (1995).

Drennan v. Star Paving Co.

Supreme Court of California
333 P.2d 757 (1958)

For a report of the case and accompanying materials, see p. 300, *supra*.

TRAYNOR, JUSTICE. . . . There is no merit in defendant's contention that plaintiff failed to state a cause of action, on the ground that the complaint failed to allege that plaintiff attempted to mitigate the damages or that they could not have been mitigated. Plaintiff alleged that after defendant's default, "plaintiff had to procure the services of the L & H Co. to perform said asphaltic paving for the sum of $10,948.60." Plaintiff's uncontradicted evidence showed that he spent several months trying to get bids from other subcontractors and that he took the lowest bid. Clearly he acted reasonably to mitigate damages. . . .

Parker v. Twentieth Century-Fox Film Corp.

Supreme Court of California
474 P.2d 689 (1970)

BURKE, J. Defendant Twentieth Century-Fox Film Corporation appeals from a summary judgment granting to plaintiff the recovery of agreed compensation under a written contract for her services as an actress in a motion picture. As will appear, we have concluded that the trial court correctly ruled in plaintiff's favor and that the judgment should be affirmed.

Plaintiff [Shirley MacLaine] is well known as an actress, and in the contract between plaintiff and defendant is sometimes referred to as the "Artist." Under the contract, dated August 6, 1965, plaintiff was to play the female lead in defendant's contemplated production of a motion picture entitled "Bloomer Girl." The contract provided that defendant would pay plaintiff a minimum "guaranteed compensation" of $53,571.42 per week for 14 weeks commencing May 23, 1966, for a total of $750,000. Prior to May 1966 defendant decided not to produce the picture and by a letter dated April 4, 1966, it notified plaintiff of that decision and that it would not "comply with our obligations to you under" the written contract.

By the same letter and with the professed purpose "to avoid any damage to you," defendant instead offered to employ plaintiff as the leading actress in another film tentatively entitled "Big Country, Big Man" (hereinafter, "Big Country"). The compensation offered was identical, as were 31 of the 34 numbered provisions or articles of the original contract.[1] Unlike "Bloomer Girl," however, which was to have been a musical production, "Big Country" was a dramatic

1. Among the identical provisions was the following found in the last paragraph of Article 2 of the original contract: "We [defendant] shall not be obligated to utilize your [plaintiff's] services in or in connection with the Photoplay hereunder, our sole obligation, subject to the terms and conditions of this Agreement, being to pay you the guaranteed compensation herein provided for."

"western type" movie. "Bloomer Girl" was to have been filmed in California; "Big Country" was to be produced in Australia. Also, certain terms in the proffered contract varied from those of the original.[2] Plaintiff was given one week within which to accept; she did not and the offer lapsed. Plaintiff then commenced this action seeking recovery of the agreed guaranteed compensation.

The complaint sets forth two causes of action. The first is for money due under the contract; the second, based upon the same allegations as the first, is for damages resulting from defendant's breach of contract. Defendant in its answer admits the existence and validity of the contract, that plaintiff complied with all the conditions, covenants and promises and stood ready to complete the performance, and that defendant breached and "anticipatorily repudiated" the contract. It denies, however, that any money is due to plaintiff either under the contract or as a result of its breach, and pleads as an affirmative defense to both causes of action plaintiff's allegedly deliberate failure to mitigate damages, asserting that she unreasonably refused to accept its offer of the leading role in "Big Country."

Plaintiff moved for summary judgment . . . , the motion was granted, and summary judgment for $750,000 plus interest was entered in plaintiff's favor. This appeal by defendant followed. . . .

As stated, defendant's sole defense to this action which resulted from its deliberate breach of contract is that in rejecting defendant's substitute offer of employment plaintiff unreasonably refused to mitigate damages.

The general rule is that the measure of recovery by a wrongfully discharged employee is the amount of salary agreed upon for the period of service, less the amount which the employer affirmatively proves the employee has earned or with reasonable effort might have earned from other employment. However, before projected earnings from other employment opportunities not sought or accepted by the discharged employee can be applied in mitigation, the employer

---

2. Article 29 of the original contract specified that plaintiff approved the director already chosen for "Bloomer Girl" and that in case he failed to act as director plaintiff was to have approval rights of any substitute director. Article 31 provided that plaintiff was to have the right of approval of the "Bloomer Girl" dance director, and Article 32 gave her the right of approval of the screenplay.Defendant's letter of April 4 to plaintiff, which contained both defendant's notice of breach of the "Bloomer Girl" contract and offer of the lead in "Big Country," eliminated or impaired each of those rights. It read in part as follows: "The terms and conditions of our offer of employment are identical to those set forth in the 'Bloomer Girl' Agreement, Articles 1 through 34 and Exhibit A to the Agreement, except as follows:

"1. Article 31 of said Agreement will not be included in any contract of employment regarding 'Big Country, Big Man' as it is not a musical and it thus will not need a dance director.

"2. In the 'Bloomer Girl' agreement, in Articles 29 and 32, you were given certain director and screenplay approvals and you had preapproved certain matters. Since there simply is insufficient time to negotiate with you regarding your choice of director and regarding the screenplay and since you already expressed an interest in performing the role in 'Big Country, Big Man,' we must exclude from our offer of employment in 'Big Country, Big Man' any approval rights as are contained in said Articles 29 and 32; however, we shall consult with you respecting the director to be selected to direct the photoplay and will further consult with you with respect to the screenplay and any revisions or changes therein, provided, however, that if we fail to agree . . . the decision of . . . [defendant] with respect to the selection of a director and to revisions and changes in the said screenplay shall be binding upon the parties to said agreement."

must show that the other employment was comparable, or substantially similar, to that of which the employee has been deprived; the employee's rejection of or failure to seek other available employment of a different or inferior kind may not be resorted to in order to mitigate damages.

In the present case defendant has raised no issue of *reasonableness of efforts* by plaintiffs to obtain other employment; the sole issue is whether plaintiff's refusal of defendant's substitute offer of "Big Country" may be used in mitigation. Nor, if the "Big Country" offer was of employment different or inferior when compared with the original "Bloomer Girl" employment, is there an issue as to whether or not plaintiff acted reasonably in refusing the substitute offer. Despite defendant's arguments to the contrary, no case cited or which our research has discovered holds or suggests that reasonableness is an element of a wrongfully discharged employee's option to reject, or fail to seek, different or inferior employment lest the possible earnings therefrom be charged against him in mitigation of damages.[5]

Applying the foregoing rules to the record in the present case, with all intendments in favor of the party opposing the summary judgment motion—here, defendant—it is clear that the trial court correctly ruled that plaintiff's failure to accept defendant's tendered substitute employment could not be applied in mitigation of damages because the offer of the "Big Country" lead was of employment both different and inferior, and that no factual dispute was presented on that issue. The mere circumstance that "Bloomer Girl" was to be a musical review calling upon plaintiff's talents as a dancer as well as an actress, and was to be produced in the City of Los Angeles, whereas "Big Country" was a straight dramatic role in a "Western Type" story taking place in an opal mine in Australia, demonstrates the difference in kind between the two employments; the female lead as a dramatic actress in a western style motion picture can by no stretch of imagination be considered the equivalent of or substantially similar to the lead in a song-and-dance production.

Additionally, the substitute "Big Country" offer proposed to eliminate or impair the director and screenplay approvals accorded to plaintiff under the original "Bloomer Girl" contract (see fn. 2, *ante*), and thus constituted an offer of inferior employment. No expertise or judicial notice is required in order to hold that the deprivation or infringement of an employee's rights held under an original employment contract converts the available "other employment" relied upon by the employer to mitigate damages, into inferior employment which the employee need not seek or accept. . . .

In view of the determination that defendant failed to present any facts showing the existence of a factual issue with respect to its sole defense—plaintiff's rejection of its substitute employment offer in mitigation of damages—we need not consider plaintiff's further contention that for various reasons, including the provisions of the original contract set forth in footnote 1, *ante*, plaintiff was excused from attempting to mitigate damages.

5. Instead, in each case the reasonableness referred to was that of the *efforts* of the employee to obtain other employment that was not different or inferior; his right to reject the latter was declared as an unqualified rule of law. . . .

The judgment is affirmed.

SULLIVAN, ACTING C.J., **dissenting.** The basic question in this case is whether or not plaintiff acted reasonably in rejecting defendant's offer of alternate employment. The answer depends upon whether that offer (starring in "Big Country, Big Man") was an offer of work that was substantially similar to her former employment (starring in "Bloomer Girl") or of work that was of a different or inferior kind. To my mind this is a factual issue which the trial court should not have determined on a motion for summary judgment. The majority have not only repeated this error but have compounded it by applying the rules governing mitigation of damages in the employer-employee context in a misleading fashion. Accordingly, I respectfully dissent.

The familiar rule requiring a plaintiff in a tort or contract action to mitigate damages embodies notions of fairness and socially responsible behavior which are fundamental to our jurisprudence. Most broadly stated, it precludes the recovery of damages which, through the exercise of due diligence, could have been avoided. Thus, in essence, it is a rule requiring reasonable conduct in commercial affairs. This general principle governs the obligations of an employee after his employer has wrongfully repudiated or terminated the employment contract. Rather than permitting the employee simply to remain idle during the balance of the contract period, the law requires him to make a reasonable effort to secure other employment.[1] He is not obliged, however, to seek or accept any and all types of work which may be available. Only work which is in the same field and which is of the same quality need be accepted.[2]

Over the years the courts have employed various phrases to define the type of employment which the

Mitigation and Public Policy

Here, Chief Justice Sullivan, in his dissent, provides a nice summary of the public policy considerations animating the mitigation "rule." Based on these considerations, do you think the majority or the dissent does a better job of ensuring that these public policy considerations are taken into account in this case? Why? And, speaking of public policy, be sure to take a look at Footnote 2. In it, the dissent suggests that allowing the mitigating employee to reject so-called "inferior" employment while only accepting work "in the same field and . . . of the same quality" as his or her previous employment "may have had its origin in the bourgeois fear of resubmergence in lower economic classes." Is this a consideration that courts should take into account in today's society, which strives to be much more egalitarian than our society was in the days of yore? Why or why not?

1. The issue is generally discussed in terms of a duty on the part of the employee to minimize loss. The practice is long-established and there is little reason to change despite Judge Cardozo's observation of its subtle inaccuracy. "The servant is free to accept employment or reject it according to his uncensored pleasure. What is meant by the supposed duty is merely this, that if he unreasonably reject, he will not be heard to say that the loss of wages from then on shall be deemed the jural consequence of the earlier discharge. He has broken the chain of causation, and loss resulting to him thereafter is suffered through his own act." *McClelland* v. *Climax Hosiery Mills*, 252 N.Y. 347, 359 (1930) (concurring opinion).

2. This qualification of the rule seems to reflect the simple and humane attitude that it is too severe to demand of a person that he attempt to find and perform work for which he has no training or experience. Many of the older cases hold that one need not accept work in an inferior rank or position nor work which is more menial or arduous. This suggests that the rule may have had its origin in the bourgeois fear of resubmergence in lower economic classes.

employee, upon his wrongful discharge, is under an obligation to accept. Thus in California alone it has been held that he must accept employment which is "substantially similar." . . .

The relevant language excuses acceptance only of employment which is of a *different kind*. It has never been the law that the mere existence of *differences between two jobs in the same field* is sufficient, as a matter of law, to excuse an employee wrongfully discharged from one from accepting the other in order to mitigate damages. Such an approach would effectively eliminate any obligation of an employee to attempt to minimize damage arising from a wrongful discharge. The only alternative job offer an employee would be required to accept would be an offer of his former job by his former employer.

Although the majority appear to hold that there was a difference "in kind" between the employment offered plaintiff in "Bloomer Girl" and that offered in "Big Country," an examination of the opinion makes crystal clear that the majority merely point out differences between the two *films* (an obvious circumstance) and then apodically assert that these constitute a difference in the *kind* of *employment*. The entire rationale of the majority boils down to this: that the "*mere circumstances*" that "Bloomer Girl" was to be a musical review while "Big Country" was a straight drama "demonstrates the difference in kind" since a female lead in a western is not "the equivalent of or substantially similar to" a lead in a musical. This is merely attempting to prove the proposition by repeating it. It shows that the vehicles for the display of the star's talents are different but it does not prove that her employment as a star in such vehicles is of necessity different *in kind* and either inferior or superior.

I believe that the approach taken by the majority (a superficial listing of differences with no attempt to assess their significance) may subvert a valuable legal doctrine.[5] The inquiry in cases such as this should not be whether differences between the two jobs exist (there will always be differences) but whether the differences which are present are substantial enough to constitute differences in the *kind* of employment or, alternatively, whether they render the substitute work employment of an *inferior kind*.

It seems to me that *this* inquiry involves, in the instant case at least, factual determinations which are improper on a motion for summary judgment. Resolving whether or not one job is substantially similar to another or whether, on the other hand, it is of a different or inferior kind, will often (as here) require a critical appraisal of the similarities and differences between them in light of the importance of these differences to the employee. This necessitates a weighing of the evidence, and it is precisely this undertaking which is forbidden on summary judgment.

5. The values of the doctrine of mitigation of damages in this context are that it minimizes the unnecessary personal and social (e.g., nonproductive use of labor, litigation) costs of contractual failure. If a wrongfully discharged employee can, through his own action and without suffering financial or psychological loss in the process, reduce the damages accruing from the breach of contract, the most sensible policy is to require him to do so. I fear the majority opinion will encourage precisely opposite conduct.

This is not to say that summary judgment would never be available in an action by an employee in which the employer raises the defense of failure to mitigate damages. No case has come to my attention, however, in which summary judgment has been granted on the issue of whether an employee was obliged to accept available alternate employment. Nevertheless, there may well be cases in which the substitute employment is so manifestly of a dissimilar or inferior sort, the declarations of the plaintiff so complete and those of the defendant so conclusionary and inadequate that no factual issues exist for which a trial is required. This, however, is not such a case.

It is not intuitively obvious, to me at least, that the leading female role in a dramatic motion picture is a radically different endeavor from the leading female role in a musical comedy film. Nor is it plain to me that the rather qualified rights of director and screenplay approval contained in the first contract are highly significant matters either in the entertainment industry in general or to this plaintiff in particular. . . .

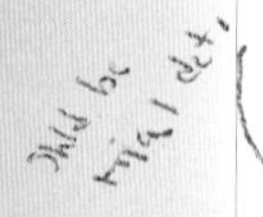

I believe that the judgment should be reversed so that the issue of whether or not the offer of the lead role in "Big Country, Big Man" was of employment comparable to that of the lead role in "Bloomer Girl" may be determined at trial.

NOTES AND QUESTIONS

1. *What happened?* Who sued whom for what? Procedurally, how did the case get before this court? Factually, what happened between the parties? What arguments did the plaintiff and defendant make? What rule or rules did the court apply? How did the court analyze the dispute between the parties? How did the court decide the case?

2. *Was this case correctly decided?* Do you agree with the result reached in this case? Why or why not? Do you agree with the majority or the dissent's reasoning? Why? How, if at all, would you have written the opinion differently?

3. *From bridges to people.* Should the rule of *Luten Bridge* be equally applicable to cover the so-called "duty" to mitigate for the non-performance of personal services? Why or why not?

4. *Critical reading.* Note that the dissent does not necessarily disagree with the conclusion reached by the majority. Instead the Chief Justice is arguing that the reasonableness of mitigation is a question for a jury or for a judge as a fact-finder, and therefore is inappropriate on summary judgment. Do you agree?

5. *The reasonable person.* In tort law, what the "reasonable person" would do is generally a question of law (this is generally true in contract law as well, *see, e.g., Embry v. Hargadine*), and not one of fact for a jury. How, if at all, should this affect your analysis of *Parker*?

THE "DUTY" TO MITIGATE*

It has frequently been said that the employee is under a "duty" to mitigate damages by looking for other work and accepting it if it can be obtained. Accurately speaking, however, this is not the case. It makes no difference whatever whether the employee actually uses the time that is set free for his use by the employer's discharge or does not use it. His recoverable damages are exactly the same in either case. He is legally privileged to throw away his time if he so desires.

B. EQUITABLE REMEDIES

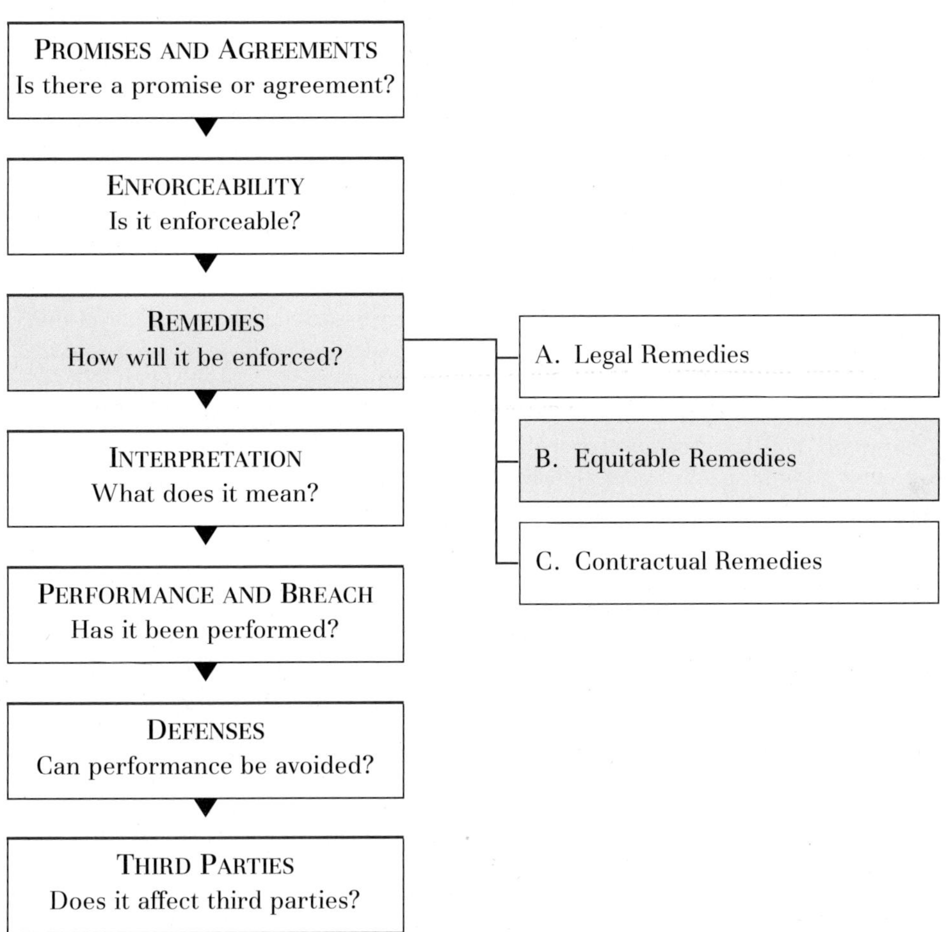
PROMISES AND AGREEMENTS
Is there a promise or agreement?
ENFORCEABILITY
Is it enforceable?
REMEDIES
How will it be enforced?
INTERPRETATION
What does it mean?
PERFORMANCE AND BREACH
Has it been performed?
DEFENSES
Can performance be avoided?
THIRD PARTIES
Does it affect third parties?
A. Legal Remedies
B. Equitable Remedies
C. Contractual Remedies

* Excerpted from ARTHUR L. CORBIN, CORBIN ON CONTRACTS § 1095 (1964).

DOCTRINAL OVERVIEW: HISTORICAL DEVELOPMENT OF EQUITABLE RELIEF*

Although in some cases damages will permit the injured party to arrange an adequate substitute for the expected performance, specific relief is plainly better suited to the objective of putting the promisee in the position in which it would have been had the promise been performed. There are, however, some situations in which specific relief is simply not possible. The promise may, for example, have been one to deliver particular goods that are defective, destroyed, or owned by a third person. Even if specific relief is possible, performance will usually be delayed, and the passage of time may reduce its effectiveness. But there remain many instances in which specific relief will be both feasible and timely.

The common law courts did not generally grant specific relief for breach of contract. The usual form of relief at common law was substitutional, and the typical judgment declared that the plaintiff recover from the defendant a sum of money. This, in effect, imposed a new obligation on the defendant for the breach of the old. This new obligation could be enforced even without cooperation on the defendant's part. If the sum was not paid, a writ of execution was issued, empowering the sheriff to seize and sell so much of the defendant's property as was required to pay the plaintiff. Of course if the promise was simply to pay a sum of money, the effect of such a judgment was to give the plaintiff specific relief. For example, if a seller had judgment for the price of goods delivered but not paid for, the seller had, in effect, specific relief. And occasionally specific relief was granted by means of proprietary actions, in which a party asserted rights as owner of the property concerned. For example, if a buyer was granted replevin of goods sold to him but not delivered, the sheriff would seize them from the seller and turn them over to the buyer, and the judgment would declare that the buyer was entitled to them. But these instances were exceptional, and even when the common law courts granted specific relief, they were unwilling to exert pressure directly on the defendant to compel performance. The judgment was seen as a mere declaration of rights as between the parties, and the process for its execution was directed, not at the defendant, but at the sheriff, ordering the sheriff to put the plaintiff in possession of real or personal property or to seize the defendant's property and sell so much of it as was necessary to satisfy a money judgment.

Promises were enforced in equity in a very different way. Prior to the development of assumpsit by the common law courts in the sixteenth century, most of the cases brought before the chancellor were based on promises that would not have been enforceable at common law, and the question was whether they would nevertheless be enforced in equity. After the development of assumpsit, equity accepted the doctrine of consideration, the test for enforcement that had been developed by the rival common law courts. To this extent, the jurisdiction of equity in contract cases became concurrent with that of the common law courts, and its concern shifted from the enforceability of promises to the nature of their enforcement. Claimants then sought relief from the chancellor as an alternative to the judgment for damages to which they were entitled at common law. Under the influence of canon law—for the early chancellors were usually clerics—decrees in equity came

* Excerpted from E. ALLAN FARNSWORTH, CONTRACTS § 12.4 (4th ed. 2004).

to take the form of the chancellor's personal command to the defendant to do or not to do something. The defendant that disobeyed could be punished not only for criminal contempt, at the instance of the court, but also for civil contempt, at the instance of the plaintiff. This put into the plaintiff's hands the extreme sanction of imprisonment, which might be supplemented by fines payable to the plaintiff and by sequestration of the defendant's goods. So it was said that equity acted *in personam,* against the person of the defendant, while the law acted *in rem,* against the defendant's property. But it did not follow that the chancellor stood ready to order every defaulting promisor to perform its promise. Equitable relief was confined to special cases by both historical and practical limitations.

The most important historical limitation grew out of the circumstance that the chancellor had originally granted equitable relief in order to supply the deficiencies of the common law. Equitable remedies were therefore readily characterized as "extraordinary." When, during the long jurisdictional struggle between the two systems of courts, some means of accommodation was needed, an adequacy test was developed to prevent the chancellor from encroaching on the powers of the common law judges. Equity would stay its hand if the remedy of an award of damages at law was "adequate." To this test was added the gloss that damages were ordinarily adequate—a gloss encouraged by the philosophy of free enterprise with its confidence that a market economy ought to enable the injured party to arrange a substitute transaction. As one writer put it:

> The law, concerning itself more and more with merchandise bought or sold for money, with things having a definite and calculable exchange value, came to conceive that the money compensation, which was an entirely adequate remedy in the common case, and in many cases the only possible one when once the wrong complained of had been committed, was [generally] the only remedy available for their use. . . .[12]

So English courts came to regard money damages as the norm and specific relief as the deviation. Only for land, which English courts regarded with particular esteem, was a general exception made, on the ground that each parcel of land was "unique" so money damages were inadequate. This strong preference of English courts for substitutional relief stands in sharp contrast to the preference of civil law systems, those derived from the Roman law, for specific relief.

A second historical limitation, or group of limitations, is based on the concept that equitable relief is discretionary. Since the chancellor was to act according to "conscience" (which prompted the notorious charge that his conscience might vary with the length of his foot), he might withhold relief if considerations of fairness or morality dictated. Gradually these equitable restrictions became more precise and hardened into rules. Some of the most renowned are embodied in equity's colorful maxims: "one who seeks equity must do equity"; "one who comes into equity must come with clean hands"; and "equity aids the vigilant." One of the most troublesome of these rules was the now discredited "mutuality of remedy" rule, under which the injured party's right to specific relief depended on whether it would have been available to the other party, had the breach been on the other side.

12. C. Huston, The Enforcement of Decrees in Equity 74 (1915).

The practical limitations on specific relief in equity grew out of the problems inherent in coercing the defendant to perform its promise. In some cases, of course, specific relief does not require the defaulting promisor's cooperation. If, for example, the promise is to convey land, the court can transfer the title by virtue of its own decree, or it can be transferred by a deed executed by an officer of the court. But there is no such simple solution if the performance is personal in nature, and courts have bridled at coercing such performances. They will not, for example, compel a singer to perform a promise to sing, although they have been willing to order the singer not to act inconsistently with the promise, by enjoining the singer from singing elsewhere. Courts have also been reluctant to order performance if difficulties of supervision or enforcement are foreseen, as may be the case under a building contract, especially if the absence of clear standards may lead to conflict and unfairness. Moreover, the practical exigencies of drafting decrees to guide future conduct under the threat of the severe sanctions available for contempt have moved courts to require that contract terms be expressed with greater certainty if specific relief is to be ordered than if damages are to be awarded.

Thus it came to be that, although the injured party can always claim damages for breach of contract, that party's right to specific relief as an alternative is much more limited. The historical development of parallel systems of law and equity may afford an adequate explanation for the reluctance of our courts to grant specific relief more widely, but it is scant justification for it. A more rational basis can today be found in the severity of the sanctions available for enforcement of equitable orders. Nevertheless, the modern trend is clearly in favor of the extension of specific relief at the expense of the traditional primacy of damages.

The limits on specific relief that grew out of the parallel systems of law and equity in England are peculiar to the common law and are unknown in other legal systems. Therefore the Vienna Convention ignores those limits in its broad provisions under which a "buyer may require performance by the seller of his obligations"[24] and a "seller may require the buyer to pay the price, take delivery or perform his other obligations."[25] In order to placate common law countries, however, "a court is not bound to enter a judgment for specific performance unless the court would do so under its own law in respect of similar contracts of sale."[26] This means that if suit is brought in a common law country in a case governed by the Convention, specific performance may be denied even though it would be granted were jurisdiction obtained elsewhere and suit brought there. Although the UNIDROIT Principles proclaim the general availability of specific performance, this is undercut by an exception, accommodating the common law position, if the injured party "may reasonably obtain performance from another source."[27]

In this section, we will look at the concept of equitable remedies as an alternative to legal remedies, and will explore the historical reasons for the differences that continue to influence our common law today. This section should also go some way towards exploring many of the similarities between contract law, property

24. CISG 46(1).
25. CISG 62.
26. CISG 28.
27. UNIDROIT Principles 7.2.2(c).

law, and tort law. My hope is that by looking at some cases in which these areas of law overlap, we can help bridge some of the divide that artificially separates many of your first year classes, and reveal that many areas of the law, although taught in isolation for pedagogical purposes, are really part of a larger whole.

THINKING TOOL: PROPERTY RULES AND LIABILITY RULES*

How should the legal system decide which way to protect a right? How should a *judge* decide in cases where there is a choice? . . . First is the idea of efficiency: the notion that it's a good thing for rights to be in the hands of whoever values them the most. Of course the people in charge of the legal system often may not know who values rights the most, and that leads to a second idea familiar from earlier . . . : the Coase theorem, which holds that rights will automatically end up in the hands of whoever values them most if people can bargain over them easily. The high bidder will win the rights in court or buy them from whoever does.

What do these ideas have to do with the choice between property rules and liability rules? Well, if goods can change hands easily through bargaining, there is a natural argument for protecting them with property rules. That means they can be taken from their owner only with consent; so they will pass from me to you only if you offer to pay me enough. The great thing about this, at least so far as efficiency is concerned, is that when we consent to a trade of this kind we *know* the goods are moving from someone who values them less to someone who values them more. Otherwise we wouldn't have agreed to whatever exchange we made. The world could be run differently; we could say that if you want my things, you can just take them, and then I sue you for the value: they all are protected just by liability rules. One problem with this idea is that if you drive off with my car, we don't know that you valued it more than I did. We only know that you valued it more than the price the law will make you pay for it—its market value.

1. Land

DOCTRINAL OVERVIEW: SPECIFIC PERFORMANCE FOR LAND†

Land was viewed by English courts with particular esteem and was therefore singled out for special treatment. Each parcel, however ordinary, was considered "unique," and its value was regarded as to some extent speculative. From this it

* Excerpted from WARD FARNSWORTH, THE LEGAL ANALYST: A TOOLKIT FOR THINKING ABOUT THE LAW 190-191 (2007).

† Excerpted from E. ALLAN FARNSWORTH, CONTRACTS § 12.6 (4th ed. 2004).

followed that, if a vendor broke a promise to convey an interest in land, money would not enable the injured purchaser to buy a substitute, and specific performance would generally be granted. Under this traditional view, the purchaser has the right to specific performance, even if the purchaser has made a contract to resell the land to a third person. A purchaser who cannot convey the land to another purchaser will be held for damages for breach of the resale contract, and, at least so it is argued, these damages cannot be accurately determined without litigation. Although the arguments for allowing the vendor specific performance when the purchaser defaults are less compelling, equity also granted the vendor relief. The arguments run: because the value of land is to some extent speculative, it may be difficult for the vendor to prove damages with sufficient certainty; even if the vendor can make this proof, the land may not be immediately convertible into money, depriving the vendor of funds with which to make other investments; and, until the vendor gets a judgment, the existence of the contract, even if broken by the purchaser, may impair the saleability of the land, making it difficult to sell. But after the vendor has transferred the interest in the land to the purchaser and all that remains is for the purchaser to pay the price, a money judgment is an adequate remedy for the vendor. The traditional view that land contracts are generally specifically enforceable has been challenged and is particularly difficult to defend if the vendor is the injured party.

Van Wagner Advertising Corp. v. S&M Enterprises

Court of Appeals of New York
492 N.E.2d 756 (1986)

KAYE, JUDGE. Specific performance of a contract to lease "unique" billboard space is properly denied when damages are an adequate remedy to compensate the tenant and equitable relief would impose a disproportionate burden on the defaulting landlord. However, owing to an error in the assessment of damages, the order of the Appellate Division should be modified so as to remit the matter to Supreme Court, New York County, for further proceedings with respect to damages.

By agreement dated December 16, 1981, Barbara Michaels leased to plaintiff, Van Wagner Advertising, for an initial period of three years (plus option periods totaling seven additional years) space on the eastern exterior wall of a building on East 36th Street in Manhattan. Van Wagner was in the business of erecting and leasing billboards, and the parties anticipated that Van Wagner would erect a sign on the leased space, which faced an exit ramp of the Midtown Tunnel and was therefore visible to vehicles entering Manhattan from that tunnel.

In early 1982 Van Wagner erected an illuminated sign and leased it to Asch Advertising for a three-year period commencing March 1, 1982. However, by agreement dated January 22, 1982, Michaels sold the building to defendant S&M Enterprises. Michaels informed Van Wagner of the sale in early August

1982, and on August 19, 1982 S&M sent Van Wagner a letter purporting to cancel the lease as of October 18. . . .

[H]aving already acquired other real estate on the block, S&M purchased the subject building in 1982 for the ultimate purpose of demolishing existing buildings and constructing a mixed residential-commercial development. The project is to begin upon expiration of a lease of the subject building in 1987, if not sooner. . . .

S&M's cancellation of Van Wagner's lease constituted a breach of contract.

Given defendant's unexcused failure to perform its contract, we next turn to a consideration of remedy for the breach: Van Wagner seeks specific performance of the contract, S&M urges that money damages are adequate but that the amount of the award was improper.[2]

Whether or not to award specific performance is a decision that rests in the sound discretion of the trial court, and here that discretion was not abused. Considering first the nature of the transaction, specific performance has been imposed as the remedy for breach of contracts for the sale of real property, but the contract here is to lease rather than sell an interest in real property. While specific performance is available, in appropriate circumstances, for breach of a commercial or residential lease, specific performance of real property leases is not in this State awarded as a matter of course. ***See Gardens Nursery School v. Columbia University***, 404 N.Y.S.2d 833 (N.Y. City Civ. Ct. 1978).[3]

Van Wagner argues that specific performance must be granted in light of the trial court's finding that the "demised space is unique as to location for the particular advertising purpose intended." The word "uniqueness" is not, however, a magic door to specific performance. A distinction must be drawn between physical difference and economic interchangeability. The trial court found that the leased property is physically unique, but so is every parcel of real property and so are many consumer goods. Putting aside contracts for the sale of real property, where specific performance has traditionally been the remedy

> ***Hmmmm...***
>
> Why do you think the highest court of the state is citing the lowest court of the state for a proposition of law? If you read *Gardens Nursery School*, you will find the citation even stranger, as it is, at best, only tangentially related to the case at hand. Finally, take a look at the eminent sources cited for the contrary proposition of law in footnote 3 after the "But see" signal. What do you think is going on here?

2. We note that the parties' contentions regarding the remedy of specific performance in general, mirror a scholarly debate that has persisted throughout our judicial history, reflecting fundamentally divergent views about the quality of a bargained-for promise. While the usual remedy in Anglo-American law has been damages, rather than compensation "in kind", the current trend among commentators appears to favor the remedy of specific performance, but the view is not unanimous.

3. *But see* 5A Arthur L. Corbin, *Contracts* § 1143 at 131 (West 1964); 11 Samuel Williston, *Contracts* § 1418A (3d ed., Baker Voorhis 1968); John N. Pomeroy & John C. Mann, *Specific Performance* § 9 at 18-19 (3d ed., Banks & Co. 1926); *Restatement (Second) of Contracts* § 360 cmt. *a*, illus. 2 (1981); *id.* § 360 cmt. *e*; *cf. City Stores Co. v. Ammerman*, 266 F. Supp. 766 (D.D.C. 1967), *aff'd per curiam*, 394 F.2d 950 (D.C. Cir. 1968).

for breach, uniqueness in the sense of physical difference does not itself dictate the propriety of equitable relief.

By the same token, at some level all property may be interchangeable with money. Economic theory is concerned with the degree to which consumers are willing to substitute the use of one good for another, the underlying assumption being that "every good has substitutes, even if only very poor ones," and that "all goods are ultimately commensurable." *See* Anthony T. Kronman, *Specific Performance*, 45 U. CHI. L. REV. 351, 359 (1978). Such a view, however, could strip all meaning from uniqueness, for if all goods are ultimately exchangeable for a price, then all goods may be valued. Even a rare manuscript has an economic substitute in that there is a price for which any purchaser would likely agree to give up a right to buy it, but a court would in all probability order specific performance of such a contract on the ground that the subject matter of the contract is unique.

The point at which breach of a contract will be redressable by specific performance thus must lie not in any inherent physical uniqueness of the property but instead in the uncertainty of valuing it:

> What matters, in measuring money damages, is the volume, refinement, and reliability of the available information about substitutes for the subject matter of the breached contract. When the relevant information is thin and unreliable, there is a substantial risk that an award of money damages will either exceed or fall short of the promisee's actual loss. Of course this risk can always be reduced—but only at great cost when reliable information is difficult to obtain. Conversely, when there is a great deal of consumer behavior generating abundant and highly dependable information about substitutes, the risk of error in measuring the promisee's loss may be reduced at much smaller cost. In asserting that the subject matter of a particular contract is unique and has no established market value, a court is really saying that it cannot obtain, at reasonable cost, enough information about substitutes to permit it to calculate an award of money damages without imposing an unacceptably high risk of undercompensation on the injured promisee. Conceived in this way, the uniqueness test seems economically sound.

45 U. CHI. L. REV., at 362. This principle is reflected in the case law, and is essentially the position of the *Restatement (Second) of Contracts* [§ 360(a)], which lists "the difficulty of proving damages with reasonable certainty" as the first factor affecting adequacy of damages.

Thus, the fact that the subject of the contract may be "unique as to location for the particular advertising purpose intended" by the parties does not entitle a plaintiff to the remedy of specific performance.

Here, the trial court correctly concluded that the value of the "unique qualities" of the demised space could be fixed with reasonable certainty and without imposing an unacceptably high risk of undercompensating the injured tenant. Both parties complain: Van Wagner asserts that while lost revenues on the Asch contract may be adequate compensation, that contract expired February 28, 1985, its lease with S&M continues until 1992, and the value of the demised space cannot reasonably be fixed for the balance of the term. S&M urges that future rents and continuing damages are necessarily conjectural. . . . Both parties' contentions were properly rejected.

First, it is hardly novel in the law for damages to be projected into the future. Particularly where the value of commercial billboard space can be readily determined by comparisons with similar uses—Van Wagner itself has more than 400 leases—the value of this property between 1985 and 1992 cannot be regarded as speculative. Second, S&M having successfully resisted specific performance on the ground that there is an adequate remedy at law, cannot at the same time be heard to contend that damages beyond 60 days must be denied because they are conjectural. If damages for breach of this lease are indeed conjectural, and cannot be calculated with reasonable certainty, then S&M should be compelled to perform its contractual obligation by restoring Van Wagner to the premises. . . .

The trial court, additionally, correctly concluded that specific performance should be denied on the ground that such relief "would be inequitable in that its effect would be disproportionate in its harm to defendant and its assistance to plaintiff." It is well settled that the imposition of an equitable remedy must not itself work an inequity, and that specific performance should not be an undue hardship. . . . Here, . . . there was no abuse of discretion; the finding that specific performance would disproportionately harm S&M and benefit Van Wagner has been affirmed by the Appellate Division and has support in the proof regarding S&M's projected development of the property.

While specific performance was properly denied, the court erred in its assessment of damages. . . .

Damages should have been awarded through the expiration of Van Wagner's lease. . . .

RELEVANT PROVISIONS

For the *Restatement (Second) of Contracts, consult* §§ 359 and 360 (especially comment e). For the UNIDROIT Principles, consult Article 7.2.2.

NOTES AND QUESTIONS

1. ***What happened?*** Who sued whom for what? Procedurally, how did the case get before this court? Factually, what happened between the parties? What arguments did the plaintiff and defendant make? What rule or rules did the court apply? How did the court analyze the dispute between the parties? How did the court decide the case?

2. ***Was this case correctly decided?*** Do you agree with the result reached in this case? Why or why not? Do you agree with the court's reasoning? Why or why not? How, if at all, would you have written the opinion differently?

3. ***Irreplaceability.*** Specific performance is usually the remedy for land because damages are traditionally thought to never be adequate to put the injured party in the position they would have occupied had the contract been performed. Why was this case different?

4. *Uniqueness.* Consider the following explanation from Professor Laycock. Are you convinced?

> Any case where the loss is irreplaceable on the market can also be described as a case where damages are hard to measure. The actual cost of cover is the most easily applied measure of damages. Value in an active market is nearly as easy. But value in an inactive or nonexistent market is difficult, and if plaintiff is unable to replace the item lost, there may be no actual transaction to support an assessment of value. Consequential damages can also be difficult to measure, and they arise only when plaintiff cannot immediately replace what was lost.*

Walgreen Co. v. Sara Creek Property Co.

United States Court of Appeals, Seventh Circuit
966 F.2d 273 (1992)

POSNER, CIRCUIT JUDGE. This appeal from the grant of a permanent injunction raises fundamental issues concerning the propriety of injunctive relief. The essential facts are simple. Walgreen has operated a pharmacy in the Southgate Mall in Milwaukee since its opening in 1951. Its current lease, signed in 1971 and carrying a 30-year, 6-month term, contains, as had the only previous lease, a clause in which the landlord, Sara Creek, promises not to lease space in the mall to anyone else who wants to operate a pharmacy or a store containing a pharmacy. . . .

In 1990, fearful that its largest tenant—what in real estate parlance is called the "anchor tenant"—having gone broke was about to close its store, Sara Creek informed Walgreen that it intended to buy out the anchor tenant and install in its place a discount store operated by Phar-Mor Corporation, a "deep discount" chain, rather than, like Walgreen, just a "discount" chain. Phar-Mor's store would occupy 100,000 square feet, of which 12,000 would be occupied by a pharmacy the same size as Walgreen's. The entrances to the two stores would be within a couple of hundred feet of each other.

Walgreen filed this **diversity suit** for breach of contract against Sara Creek and Phar-Mor and asked for an injunction against Sara Creek's letting the anchor premises to Phar-Mor. After an evidentiary hearing, the judge found a breach of Walgreen's lease and entered a permanent injunction against Sara Creek's letting the anchor tenant premises to Phar-Mor until the expiration of Walgreen's lease. He did this over the defendants' objection that Walgreen had failed to

> ***Diversity suit***
>
> A federal court may only adjudicate a dispute if (1) the dispute contains a federal question, or (2) if the parties are citizens of different states and the amount in controversy is greater than $75,000. *See* 28 U.S.C.A. § 1332.

*DOUGLAS LAYCOCK, THE DEATH OF THE IRREPARABLE INJURY RULE 44-45 (Oxford Univ. Press 1991).

show that its remedy at law—damages—for the breach of the exclusivity clause was inadequate. Sara Creek had put on an expert witness who testified that Walgreen's damages could be readily estimated, and Walgreen had countered with evidence from its employees that its damages would be very difficult to compute, among other reasons because they included intangibles such as loss of goodwill.

Sara Creek reminds us that damages are the norm in breach of contract as in other cases. Many breaches, it points out, are "efficient" in the sense that they allow resources to be moved into a more valuable use. Perhaps this is one—the value of Phar-Mor's occupancy of the anchor premises may exceed the cost to Walgreen of facing increased competition. If so, society will be better off if Walgreen is paid its damages, equal to that cost, and Phar-Mor is allowed to move in rather than being kept out by an injunction. That is why injunctions are not granted as a matter of course, but only when the plaintiff's damages remedy is inadequate. Walgreen's is not, Sara Creek argues; the projection of business losses due to increased competition is a routine exercise in calculation. Damages representing either the present value of lost future profits or (what should be the equivalent) the diminution in the value of the leasehold have either been awarded or deemed the proper remedy in a number of reported cases for breach of an exclusivity clause in a shopping-center lease. Why, Sara Creek asks, should they not be adequate here?

Sara Creek makes a beguiling argument that contains much truth, but we do not think it should carry the day. For if, as just noted, damages have been awarded in some cases of breach of an exclusivity clause in a shopping-center lease, injunctions have been issued in others. The choice between remedies requires a balancing of the costs and benefits of the alternatives. The task of striking the balance is for the trial judge, subject to deferential appellate review in recognition of its particularistic, judgmental, fact-bound character. As we said in an appeal from a grant of a preliminary injunction—but the point is applicable to review of a permanent injunction as well—"The question for us [appellate judges] is whether the [district] judge exceeded the bounds of permissible choice in the circumstances, not what we would have done if we had been in his shoes." *Roland Machinery Co. v. Dresser Industries, Inc.*, 749 F.2d 380, 390 (7th Cir. 1984).

The plaintiff who seeks an injunction has the burden of persuasion—damages are the norm, so the plaintiff must show why his case is abnormal. [W]hen, as in this case, the issue is whether to grant a permanent injunction, . . . the burden is to show that damages are inadequate. . . .

The benefits of substituting an injunction for damages are twofold. First, it shifts the burden of determining the cost of the defendant's conduct from the court to the parties. If it is true that Walgreen's damages are smaller than the gain to Sara Creek from allowing a second pharmacy into the shopping mall, then there must be a price for dissolving the injunction that will make both parties better off. Thus, the effect of upholding the injunction would be to substitute for the costly processes of forensic fact determination the less costly processes of private negotiation. Second, a premise of our free-market system, and the lesson of experience here and abroad as well, is that prices and costs are more accurately determined by the market than by government. A battle of experts is a less reliable method of determining the actual cost to Walgreen of facing new competition than negotiations between Walgreen and Sara Creek over the price at which Walgreen would feel adequately compensated for having to face that competition.

That is the benefit side of injunctive relief but there is a cost side as well. Many injunctions require continuing supervision by the court, and that is costly. . . . Some injunctions are problematic because they impose costs on third parties. A more subtle cost of injunctive relief arises from the situation that economists call "bilateral monopoly," in which two parties can deal only with each other: the situation that an injunction creates. The sole seller of widgets selling to the sole buyer of that product would be an example. But so will be the situation confronting Walgreen and Sara Creek if the injunction is upheld. Walgreen can "sell" its injunctive right only to Sara Creek, and Sara Creek can "buy" Walgreen's surrender of its right to enjoin the leasing of the anchor tenant's space to Phar-Mor only from Walgreen. The lack of alternatives in bilateral monopoly creates a bargaining range, and the costs of negotiating to a point within that range may be high. Suppose the cost to Walgreen of facing the competition of Phar-Mor at the Southgate Mall would be $1 million, and the benefit to Sara Creek of leasing to Phar-Mor would be $2 million. Then at any price between those figures for a waiver of Walgreen's injunctive right both parties would be better off, and we expect parties to bargain around a judicial assignment of legal rights if the assignment is inefficient. R.H. Coase, "The Problem of Social Cost," 3 *J. Law & Econ.* 1 (1960). But each of the parties would like to engross as much of the bargaining range as possible—Walgreen to press the price toward $2 million, Sara Creek to depress it toward $1 million. With so much at stake, both parties will have an incentive to devote substantial resources of time and money to the negotiation process. The process may even break down, if one or both parties want to create for future use a reputation as a hard bargainer; and if it does break down, the injunction will have brought about an inefficient result. All these are in one form or another costs of the injunctive process that can be avoided by substituting damages.

The costs and benefits of the damages remedy are the mirror of those of the injunctive remedy. The damages remedy avoids the cost of continuing supervision and third-party effects, and the cost of bilateral monopoly as well. It imposes costs of its own, however, in the form of diminished accuracy in the determination of value, on the one hand, and of the parties' expenditures on preparing and presenting evidence of damages, and the time of the court in evaluating the evidence, on the other.

The weighing up of all these costs and benefits is the analytical procedure that is or at least should be employed by a judge asked to enter a permanent injunction, with the understanding that if the balance is even the injunction should be withheld. The judge is not required to explicate every detail of the analysis and he did not do so here, but as long we are satisfied that his approach is broadly consistent with a proper analysis we shall affirm; and we are satisfied here. The determination of Walgreen's damages would have been costly in forensic resources and inescapably inaccurate. The lease had ten years to run. So Walgreen would have had to project its sales revenues and costs over the next ten years, and then project the impact on those figures of Phar-Mor's competition, and then discount that impact to present value. All but the last step would have been fraught with uncertainty. . . .

It is difficult to forecast the profitability of a retail store over a decade, let alone to assess the impact of a particular competitor on that profitability over that period. Of course one can hire an expert to make such predictions, and if injunctive relief is infeasible the expert's testimony may provide a tolerable basis for an award of damages. We cited cases in which damages have been awarded for the breach of an exclusivity clause in a shopping-center lease. But they are awarded in such circumstances not because anyone thinks them a clairvoyant forecast but because it is better to give a wronged person a crude remedy than none at all. It is the same theory on which damages are awarded for a disfiguring injury. No one thinks such injuries readily monetizable, but a crude estimate is better than letting the wrongdoer get off scot-free (which, not incidentally, would encourage more such injuries). . . .

Damages are not always costly to compute, or difficult to compute accurately. In the standard case of a seller's breach of a contract for the sale of goods where the buyer covers by purchasing the same product in the market, damages are readily calculable by subtracting the contract price from the market price and multiplying by the quantity specified in the contract. But this is not such a case and here damages would be a costly and inaccurate remedy; and on the other side of the balance some of the costs of an injunction are absent and the cost that is present seems low. The injunction here, like one enforcing a covenant not to compete (standardly enforced by injunction), is a simple negative injunction—Sara Creek is not to lease space in the Southgate Mall to Phar-Mor during the term of Walgreen's lease—and the costs of judicial supervision and enforcement should be negligible. There is no contention that the injunction will harm an *unrepresented* third party. It may harm Phar-Mor but that harm will be reflected in Sara Creek's offer to Walgreen to dissolve the injunction. (Anyway Phar-Mor *is* a party.) The injunction may also, it is true, harm potential customers of Phar-Mor—people who would prefer to shop at a deep-discount store than an ordinary discount store—but their preferences, too, are registered indirectly. The more business Phar-Mor would have, the more rent it will be willing to pay Sara Creek, and therefore the more Sara Creek will be willing to pay Walgreen to dissolve the injunction.

The only substantial cost of the injunction in this case is that it may set off a round of negotiations between the parties. In some cases, illustrated by *Boomer v. Atlantic Cement Co.*, 26 N.Y.2d 219 (1970), this consideration alone would be enough to warrant the denial of injunctive relief. The defendant's factory was emitting cement dust that caused the plaintiffs harm monetized at less than \$200,000, and the only way to abate the harm would have been to close down the factory, which had cost \$45 million to build. An injunction against the nuisance could therefore have created a huge bargaining range (could, not would, because it is unclear what the current value of the factory was), and the costs of negotiating to a point within it might have been immense. If the market value of the factory was actually $45 million, the plaintiffs would be tempted to hold out for a price to dissolve the injunction in the tens of millions and the factory would be tempted to refuse to pay anything more than a few hundred thousand dollars. Negotiations would be unlikely to break down completely, given such a bargaining range, but they might well be protracted and costly. There is nothing so dramatic here. Sara Creek does not argue that it will have to close the mall if enjoined from leasing to Phar-Mor. Phar-Mor is not the only potential anchor tenant. . . .

To summarize, the judge did not exceed the bounds of reasonable judgment in concluding that the costs (including forgone benefits) of the damages remedy would exceed the costs (including forgone benefits) of an injunction. We need not consider whether, as intimated by Walgreen, exclusivity clauses in shopping-center leases should be considered presumptively enforceable by injunctions. Although we have described the choice between legal and equitable remedies as one for case-by-case determination, the courts have sometimes picked out categories of case in which injunctive relief is made the norm. The best-known example is specific performance of contracts for the sale of real property. The rule that specific performance will be ordered in such cases as a matter of course is a generalization of the considerations discussed above. Because of the absence of a fully liquid market in real property and the frequent presence of subjective values (many a homeowner, for example, would not sell his house for its market value), the calculation of damages is difficult; and since an order of specific performance to convey a piece of property does not create a continuing relation between the parties, the costs of supervision and enforcement if specific performance is ordered are slight. The exclusivity clause in Walgreen's lease relates to real estate, but we hesitate to suggest that every contract involving real estate should be enforceable as a matter of course by injunctions. Suppose Sara Creek had covenanted to keep the entrance to Walgreen's store free of ice and snow, and breached the covenant. An injunction would require continuing supervision, and it would be easy enough if the injunction were denied for Walgreen to hire its own ice and snow remover and charge the cost to Sara Creek. On the other hand, injunctions to enforce exclusivity clauses are quite likely to be justifiable by just the considerations present here—damages are difficult to estimate with any accuracy and the injunction is a one-shot remedy requiring no continuing judicial involvement. So there is an argument for making injunctive relief presumptively appropriate in such cases, but we need not decide in this case how strong an argument.

Affirmed.

NOTES AND QUESTIONS

1. ***What happened?*** Who sued whom for what? Procedurally, how did the case get before this court? Factually, what happened between the parties?

What arguments did the plaintiff and defendant make? What rule or rules did the court apply? How did the court analyze the dispute between the parties? How did the court decide the case?

2. ***Was this case correctly decided?*** Do you agree with the result reached in this case? Why or why not? Do you agree with the court's reasoning? Why or why not? How, if at all, would you have written the opinion differently?

3. ***Property rules and liability rules.*** Note how Judge Posner's opinion canvasses the economic arguments for and against granting an injunction, mirroring and adding to the arguments made in the excerpt at the beginning of this section entitled "Thinking Tool: Property Rules and Liability Rules." How would you summarize these arguments? Can you think of any rules of thumb to guide our courts in determining the circumstances in which they should protect a party's expectancy with a property rule, and when they should protect it with a liability rule? Do our current rules do a good job of taking into account these considerations? How do these considerations influence, if at all, the way you think about the cost of completion versus diminution in value cases (e.g., *Jacob & Youngs v. Kent, Groves v. John Wunder Co., Peevyhouse v. Garland Coal Mining Co.*, and *American Standard, Inc. v. Schectman*) we explored earlier in this chapter (Subsection A.1.c)?

2. Goods

DOCTRINAL OVERVIEW: SPECIFIC PERFORMANCE FOR GOODS*

The traditional attitude toward contracts for the sale of goods is quite the opposite of the attitude toward contracts for the sale of land. In a market economy it was supposed that, with rare exceptions for such "unique" items as heirlooms and objects of art, substantially similar goods were available elsewhere. The trend, however, has been to relax this restriction on the availability of specific performance. The commentary to the Uniform Commercial Code explains that it "seeks to further a more liberal attitude than some courts have shown in connection with the specific performance of contracts of sale."[27] It goes on to assert that it introduces "a new concept of what are 'unique' goods" with a test of uniqueness that "must be made in terms of the total situation which characterizes the contract," adding that the buyer's "inability to cover is strong evidence" of the propriety of granting specific performance.[28] It notes that "where the unavailability of a market price is caused by a scarcity of goods of the type involved, a good case is normally made for specific performance under this Article."[29] But the text of the Code is

* Excerpted from E. ALLAN FARNSWORTH, CONTRACTS § 12.6 (4th ed. 2004).

27. UCC 2-716 cmt. 1.

28. UCC 2-716 cmt. 2.

29. UCC 2-713 cmt. 3.

more circumspect, stating only, "Specific performance may be decreed where the goods are unique or in other proper circumstances."[30] The Code does not reject the adequacy test, and specific performance remains the exception rather than the rule under contracts for the sale of goods. If the seller fails to deliver the goods, the typical buyer must still content itself with money as a substitute.

Campbell Soup Co. v. Wentz

United States Court of Appeals, Third Circuit
172 F.2d 80 (1948)

GOODRICH, CIRCUIT JUDGE. These are appeals from judgments of the District Court denying equitable relief to the buyer under a contract for the sale of carrots. . . .

On June 21, 1947, Campbell Soup Company . . . entered into a written contract with George B. Wentz and Harry T. Wentz, who are Pennsylvania farmers, for delivery by the Wentzes to Campbell of all the Chantenay red cored carrots to be grown on fifteen acres of the Wentz farm during the 1947 season. . . . The prices specified in the contract ranged from $23 to $30 per ton according to the time of delivery. The contract price for January, 1948, was $30 a ton.

The Wentzes harvested approximately 100 tons of carrots from the fifteen acres covered by the contract. Early in January, 1948, they told a Campbell representative that they would not deliver their carrots at the contract price. The market price at that time was at least $90 per ton, and Chantenay red cored carrots were virtually unobtainable. The Wentzes then sold approximately 62 tons of their carrots to the defendant Lojeski, a neighboring farmer. Lojeski resold about 58 tons on the open market, approximately half to Campbell and the balance to other purchasers.

On January 9, 1948, Campbell, suspecting that Lojeski was selling it "contract carrots," refused to purchase any more, and instituted these suits against the Wentz brothers and Lojeski to enjoin further sale of the contract carrots to others, and to compel specific performance of the contract. The trial court denied equitable relief.[1] We agree with the result reached, but on a different ground from that relied upon by the District Court. . . .

30. UCC 2-716(1). *See* UCC 1-305(a) (remedies provided "must be liberally administered to the end that the aggrieved party may be put in as good a position as if the other party had fully performed").

1. The issue is preserved on appeal by an arrangement under which Campbell received all the carrots held by the Wentzes and Lojeski, paying a stipulated market price of $90 per ton, $30 to the defendants, and the balance into the registry of the District Court pending the outcome of these appeals.

> **Chattels**
>
> "Movable or transferable property; personal property; esp., a physical object capable of manual delivery and not the subject matter of real property." BLACK'S LAW DICTIONARY (10th ed. 2014).

A party may have specific performance of a contract for the sale of **chattels** if the legal remedy is inadequate. Inadequacy of the legal remedy is necessarily a matter to be determined by an examination of the facts in each particular instance.

We think that on the question of adequacy of the legal remedy the case is one appropriate for specific performance. It was expressly found that at the time of the trial it was "virtually impossible to obtain Chantenay carrots in the open market." This Chantenay carrot is one which the plaintiff uses in large quantities, furnishing the seed to the growers with whom it makes contracts. It was not claimed that in nutritive value it is any better than other types of carrots. Its blunt shape makes it easier to handle in processing. And its color and texture differ from other varieties. The color is brighter than other carrots. The trial court found that the plaintiff failed to establish what proportion of its carrots is used for the production of soup stock and what proportion is used as identifiable physical ingredients in its soups. We do not think lack of proof on that point is material. It did appear that the plaintiff uses carrots in fifteen of its twenty-one soups. It also appeared that it uses these Chantenay carrots diced in some of them and that the appearance is uniform. The preservation of uniformity in appearance in a food article marketed throughout the country and sold under the manufacturer's name is a matter of considerable commercial significance and one which is properly considered in determining whether a substitute ingredient is just as good as the original.

The trial court concluded that the plaintiff had failed to establish that the carrots, "judged by objective standards," are unique goods. This we think is not a pure fact conclusion like a finding that Chantenay carrots are of uniform color. It is either a conclusion of law or of mixed fact and law and we are bound to exercise our independent judgment upon it. That the test for specific performance is not necessarily "objective" is shown by the many cases in which equity has given it to enforce contracts for articles—family heirlooms and the like—the value of which was personal to the plaintiff.

Judged by the general standards applicable to determining the adequacy of the legal remedy we think that on this point the case is a proper one for equitable relief. There is considerable authority, old and new, showing liberality in the granting of an equitable remedy. We see no reason why a court should be reluctant to grant specific relief when it can be given without supervision of the court or other time-consuming processes against one who has deliberately broken his agreement. Here the goods of the special type contracted for were unavailable on the open market, the plaintiff had contracted for them long ahead in anticipation of its needs, and had built up a general reputation for its products as part of which reputation uniform appearance was important. We think if this were all that was involved in the case specific performance should have been granted.

[The court ultimately refused to specifically enforce Campbell's contract because it found several of its clauses to be unconscionable. We will take up this part of the court's opinion when we discuss unconscionability in Chapter 8.D.4, *infra*.]

RELEVANT PROVISIONS

For the *Restatement (Second) of Contracts, consult* § 360, especially comment c. For the UCC, consult § 2-716. For the CISG, consult Articles 28, 46, and 62. For the *Restatement (Third) of Restitution and Unjust Enrichment,* consult § 39.

NOTES AND QUESTIONS

1. *What happened?* Who sued whom for what? Procedurally, how did the case get before this court? Factually, what happened between the parties? What arguments did the plaintiff and defendant make? What rule or rules did the court apply? How did the court analyze the dispute between the parties? How did the court decide the case?

2. *Was this case correctly decided?* Do you agree with the result reached in this case? Why or why not? Do you agree with the court's reasoning? Why or why not? How, if at all, would you have written the opinion differently?

3. *Specific performance.* It is important to note that the court would have enforced the promise by awarding Campbell's specific performance but for the fact that it behaved unconscionably.

4. *Replaceability.* But should the court have done this? The carrots were actually being purchased on the open market by Campbell Soup, so money damages *were* an adequate substitute here. But isn't it silly to award money damages so Campbell Soup could buy carrots, especially when it could just require the Wentzes to deliver the carrots? Professor Laycock seems to think so. According to him:

> Courts have escaped the rule by defining adequacy in such a way that damages are never an adequate substitute for plaintiff's loss. Thus, our law embodies a preference for specific relief if plaintiff wants it.*

5. *Efficient breach.* What do you think the court would have (or should have) made of the Wentzes' argument that their breach was efficient? Part of the answer, probably, depends on what you think the Wentzes' duty was to Campbell Soup. Holmes, for instance, understood the duty to perform a contracts in the following way. Would you agree?

> The duty to keep a contract at common law means a prediction that you must pay damages if you do not keep it,—and nothing else. If you commit a tort, you are liable to pay a compensatory sum. If you commit a contract, you are liable to pay a compensatory sum unless the promised event comes to pass, and that is all the difference.†

---

* Douglas Laycock, *The Death of the Irreparable Injury Rule,* 103 HARV. L. REV. 687 (1990).

† Oliver Wendell Holmes, *The Path of the Law,* 10 HARV. L. REV. 457, 462 (1897).

Do you agree with Holmes? If not, then you probably approve of the court's inclination to award specific performance, even for goods that are replaceable on the open market. But if you see the world as Holmes did, then you might be in favor of the Wentzes' attempt at efficient breach. And, while we are on that topic, *was* the Wentzes' breach efficient (if you think so, how can you tell?), or was it opportunistic? Professor Dodge defines the difference this way:

> An opportunistic breach does not increase the size of the economic pie; the breaching party gains simply by capturing a larger share of the pie at the expense of the nonbreaching party. An efficient breach, on the other hand, increases the size of the pie, allowing the breaching party more without decreasing the amount that the nonbreaching party receives.*

6. *Opportunistic versus efficient breach.* Why does the distinction between efficient and opportunistic breach matter? The short answer is that under *Restatement (Third) of Restitution and Unjust Enrichment* § 39:

> (1) If a deliberate breach of contract results in profit to the defaulting promisor and the available damage remedy affords inadequate protection to the promisee's contractual entitlement, the promisee has a claim to restitution of the profit realized by the promisor as a result of the breach. Restitution by the rule of this section is an alternative to a remedy in damages.
>
> (2) A case in which damages afford inadequate protection to the promisee's contractual entitlement is ordinarily one in which damages will not permit the promisee to acquire a full equivalent to the promised performance in a substitute transaction.
>
> (3) Breach of contract is profitable when it results in gains to the defendant (net of potential liability in damages) greater than the defendant would have realized from performance of the contract. Profits from breach include saved expenditure and consequential gains that the defendant would not have realized but for the breach, as measured by the rules that apply in other cases of disgorgement (§ 51(5)).

This distinction is even supported by no less of a proponent of efficient breach than Judge Posner, who recognized that "opportunistic" breach, unlike efficient breach, should be deterred by means of a more generous remedy to the promisee:

> If a promisor breaks his promise merely to take advantage of the promisee's vulnerability in a setting (the normal contract setting) in which performance is sequential rather than simultaneous, we might as well throw the book at him. An example would be where A pays B in advance for goods and instead of delivering them B uses the money to build a swimming pool for himself. An attractive remedy in such a case is restitution. We can deter A's opportunistic behavior by making it worthless to him, which we can do by making him hand over all his

* William S. Dodge, *The Case for Punitive Damages in Contracts*, 48 DUKE L. J. 629 (1999).

profits from the breach to the promisee. No lighter sanction would deter. (Why not make his conduct criminal as well or instead?)*

7. *UCC.* UCC § 2-716(1) allows specific performance "if the goods are unique or in other proper circumstances." The Official Comment notes that this section "seeks to further a more liberal attitude" and that "inability to cover is strong evidence of 'other proper circumstances.'"

King Aircraft Sales, Inc. v. Lane

Court of Appeals of Washington
68 Wash. App. 706 (1993)

PEKELIS, ACTING CHIEF JUDGE. Joe Lane, Jr., d/b/a The Lane Company, and Lane Aviation, Inc. (Lane) appeal the judgment of the trial court awarding King Aircraft Sales, Inc., d/b/a King Aviation Services (King) $338,280.60 in damages. . . . The principal issue presented in this appeal, one of first impression in Washington, is whether the trial court may award money damages as a remedy in a claim for specific performance under [UCC § 2-716]. The trial court found King was entitled to specific performance and, because the planes were no longer available, awarded relief in the form of "value." The trial court determined value by using a lost expectation of profit approach resulting in an award of $157,010 plus return of the $10,000 deposit. . . .

Lane appeals the award of these amounts. King cross-appeals from the trial court's determination of value using the expectation of lost profit approach instead of the wholesale "blue book" value. We affirm all of the trial court's rulings. . . .

FACTS

The trial court found that in October 1988, King made a written offer to purchase two "quality, no damage" aircraft from Lane for $870,000. The offer was accompanied by a $10,000 deposit. Lane accepted the King offer both in writing and by depositing the $10,000 deposit. The acceptance created a contract of sale between the parties. King was to perform certain requirements but prior to the expiration of the time to perform, Lane advised King it was backing out of the agreement and that it had reached agreement with another party, Western Aircraft (Western), for the sale of the planes. Because at the time Lane backed out of the contract the time for King's performance had not yet expired, the trial court concluded that Lane's action was a breach of the contract. . . .

In January of 1989, long before trial, Lane sold both planes "as is" to Priester Aviation (Priester) for $870,000. Priester put the planes on the market and resold them separately in a series of transactions. . . .

* POSNER, ECONOMIC ANALYSIS OF LAW § 4.10.

King's claim for specific performance and "other appropriate relief" was tried before the court without a jury. After trial, the court in its oral opinion ruled that Lane had breached the contract between the parties and that King should recover the "value" of the planes, as measured by the profit made by Priester, on its resale of the planes. . . .

The trial court entered findings of fact that a contract was formed and that Lane breached the contract before the time for King's performance expired. In addition, the trial court found the planes were fairly characterized as "one of a kind" or "possibly the best" in the U.S.; however, it was not proven that the planes were "unique" because there were others of the same make and model available. However, the planes were so rare in terms of their exceptional condition that King had no prospect to cover its anticipated re-sales by purchasing alternative planes, because there was no possibility of finding similar or better planes.

Therefore, the trial court concluded that under the total surrounding circumstances this case appropriately fell within the "other proper circumstances" clause of the specific performance statute of [UCC § 2-716(1)] and therefore King was entitled to specific performance. Relying on the Official Comments to [UCC § 2-716], the trial court noted that the inability to cover was strong evidence of "other proper circumstances" for an action/award of specific performance. Because the planes were no longer available the trial court concluded that specific performance should take the form of the value of the aircraft at the time of the breach. The trial court concluded this value could be measured either by the blue book value, including increased price adjustments for the prime condition of the planes, or by King's expectation of profit. The trial court chose the latter and awarded judgment to King as set forth above.

I.

Lane's principal claim on appeal is that because this was solely an action for specific performance under the UCC, and because the goods had been sold and thus inaccessible, no remedy was available to King. Lane contends the trial court had no authority to make a dollar value award. Its argument is as follows: Because King failed to plead a claim for monetary damages in its original complaint and had twice been denied permission by the court to add such a claim, no right to a damages remedy existed. However, because an adequate remedy at law existed, albeit not one available to King, specific performance was not proper here either.

We disagree and find that the remedy fashioned by the trial court was proper under the UCC and Washington common law.

The UCC § 2-716 provides:

Buyer's right to specific performance or replevin.

(1) *Specific performance may be decreed where the goods are unique or in other proper circumstances.*

(2) The decree for specific performance may include such terms and conditions as to payment of the price, *damages,* or other relief as the court may deem just.

(3) The buyer has a right of replevin for goods identified to the contract if after reasonable effort he is unable to effect cover for such goods or the circumstances reasonably indicate that such effort will be unavailing or if the goods have been shipped under reservation and satisfaction of the security interest in them has been made or tendered.

(Emphasis added.)

The UCC, like its predecessor, the Uniform Sales Act, does not expressly require that the remedy at law be inadequate in order to invoke specific performance. However, the stated intent of the drafters of the UCC was to continue "in general prior policy as to specific performance and injunction against breach", and also "to further *a more liberal attitude* than some courts have shown" toward specific performance. (Emphasis added.) Official Comment 1, [UCC § 2-716].

Nevertheless, there is a split of authority among those jurisdictions which have considered whether a buyer's remedy at law must be inadequate before specific performance can be granted.

We find [*Sedmak v. Charlie's Chevrolet, Inc.*, 622 S.W.2d 694 (Mo. App. 1981)] particularly instructive both on its facts and on the law. There, Mr. and Mrs. Sedmak were told they could buy a limited edition "pace car" when it arrived at the dealership for the suggested retail price of approximately $15,000. Factory changes were made to the car at the Sedmaks' request before delivery to the dealer. When the car arrived at the dealership the Sedmaks were told they could *bid* on the car, but its popularity had increased the price. The Sedmaks did not bid, but sued for specific performance. The court held that the pace car was not unique in the traditional legal sense, however, its "mileage, condition, ownership and appearance" did make it difficult, if not impossible, to obtain the replication without considerable expense, delay, and inconvenience. The court ordered specific performance even though the legal remedy of damages may have been available to make the Sedmaks "whole."

The *Sedmak* court also addressed the UCC's adoption of the term "in other proper circumstances" and Official Comment 2, [UCC § 2-716]:[2]

The general term "in other proper circumstances" expresses the drafters' intent to "further a more liberal attitude than some courts have shown in connection with the specific performance of contracts of sale." [§ 2-716], U.C.C., Comment 1. This Comment was not directed to the courts of this state, for long before the Code, we, in Missouri, took a practical approach in determining whether specific performance would lie for the breach of contract for the sale of goods and did not limit this relief only to the sale of "unique" goods.

2. Official Comment 2 states: "In view of this Article's emphasis on the commercial feasibility of replacement, a new concept of what are 'unique' goods is introduced under this section. Specific performance is no longer limited to goods which are already specific or ascertained at the time of contracting. The test of uniqueness under this section must be made in terms of the total situation which characterizes the contract. . . . [U]niqueness is not the sole basis of the remedy under this section for the relief may also be granted 'in other proper circumstances' and inability to cover is strong evidence of 'other proper circumstances.'"

We agree with the *Sedmak* court's interpretation of § 2-716 and, like that court, find the liberal interpretation urged by the UCC drafters to be entirely consistent with the common law of our state. Prior to adoption of the UCC, our cases did not always require the absence of a legal remedy before awarding specific performance nor did these cases require the goods to be absolutely "unique." Hence, the liberal approach to "other proper circumstances" suggested in Official Comment 2, [UCC § 2-716] is not a departure from our law.[3] . . .

Nevertheless, Lane claims that King has not met the requirements of § 2-716 because it has not shown an inability to cover. Lane contends that King could have covered by accepting Lane's "as is" proposal of November 4. King's failure to do so, argues Lane, was "commercially unreasonable." Lane cites [UCC §§ 1-203, 2-103(1)(b)] and the case of *Saboundjian v. Bank Audi (USA)*, 157 A.D.2d 278 (1990) for the proposition that the buyer has the duty to act reasonably and to mitigate damages. Lane contends that King should have "covered" with the "as is" offer of November 4 and if there were additional repair costs or other expenses, it could have sued for the difference. Furthermore, Lane argues that even if the trial court was correct in finding that King did not have to cover by accepting its November 4 proposal, [UCC § 2-713] sets forth the measure of damages for a buyer who does not cover—the difference between the market price when the buyer learned of the breach and the contract price. In addition, however, a buyer for resale cannot recover more than his expected profit. Washington Comments, [UCC § 2-713]; *Allied Canners & Packers, Inc. v. Victor Packing Co.*, 162 Cal. App. 3d 905 (1984) (§ 1-106 limits damages under § 2-713 to buyer's expected profit where purchase is for resale).

Here, the trial court held in conclusion that King was under no obligation to purchase the planes on terms other than as contained in the contract. Specifically, the trial court found that King was under no obligation to accept the new November 4 proposal, which the trial court deemed to be considerably different from the original contract agreement. . . . Therefore, the findings and conclusions listed above will not be disturbed on appeal.

We conclude the trial court properly determined that specific performance was an appropriate remedy here. At the time King commenced its action for specific performance Lane was still in possession of the planes; thus, the court properly acquired equity jurisdiction. The airplanes, although not necessarily "unique", were rare enough so as to make the ability to cover virtually impossible. Furthermore, Lane, by its own act of selling the planes, incapacitated

3. This distinguishes our situation from the case relied on by Lane, *Klein v. PepsiCo, Inc.*, 845 F.2d 76 (4th Cir. 1988). There, the Fourth Circuit reversed a trial court decision awarding specific performance in the form of damages in the sale of a corporate jet which, as in the instant case, was no longer available. Despite the trial court's finding that the plane was unique, or in the alternative, that the plaintiff's inability to cover with another plane was strong evidence of "other circumstances" for purposes of awarding specific performance under § 2-716, the Fourth Circuit held that Virginia's adoption of the UCC did not abrogate the common law rule that specific performance is inappropriate where damages are recoverable and adequate. *Klein*, 845 F.2d at 80.

itself from performance. Under these circumstances, the court of equity did not err in finding that "other proper circumstances" were present for issuance of relief under a claim of specific performance under the UCC. The trial court had the discretion to award the legal remedy of damages or other relief deemed just by the trial court. For the reasons above, we conclude that under [UCC § 2-716] and Washington common law the trial court's determination that "other proper circumstances" existed is correct and permitted it to fashion the relief it did.

II.

Next, we address King's cross appeal. King contends that the trial court erred in using lost expectation of profits as the basis for its monetary award, rather than the market value of the planes at the time of trial, or alternatively, the retail value set forth in the blue book, adjusted upward for the planes' special "rareness."

King alleges it met its burden of proof as to the market value of the planes at trial. However, it does not cite any authority, or support its contention that because the planes were unavailable, the closest replacement value of them is the value of them *at the time of trial.* As such King is not entitled to consideration of its contention. . . .

The decision of the trial court is affirmed. . . .

RELEVANT PROVISIONS

For the UCC, consult §§ 2-709 and 2-716.

NOTES AND QUESTIONS

1. *What happened?* Who sued whom for what? Procedurally, how did the case get before this court? Factually, what happened between the parties? What arguments did the plaintiff and defendant make? What rule or rules did the court apply? How did the court analyze the dispute between the parties? How did the court decide the case?

2. *Was this case correctly decided?* Do you agree with the result reached in this case? Why or why not? Do you agree with the court's reasoning? Why or why not? How, if at all, would you have written the opinion differently?

3. *CISG?* Would this case have been decided differently under the CISG? If so, how?

4. *Equivalent remedies?* Note that whereas the buyer has a right to specific performance under UCC § 2-716, the most analogous remedy for a seller is "action on the price" under UCC § 2-709. Do these remedies seem equivalent?

PROBLEM: LITTLE RED CORVETTE

Plaintiff entered into a contract with Dealership to purchase a Corvette for $75,000. The Corvette was one of a limited number manufactured to commemorate the selection of the Corvette as the Pace Car for the Indianapolis 500. The car turned out to be much more popular than Dealership expected, and some customers expressed a willingness to pay as much as $100,000 for this car when it was delivered to Dealership. When the automobile was delivered, Dealership breached its contract with Plaintiff, telling them that they could not purchase it for $75,000, but would have to bid on it.

If Plaintiff prevails on its breach of contract suit against Dealership, what remedy should Plaintiff receive, and why?

INTERNATIONAL PERSPECTIVE: SPECIFIC PERFORMANCE AND THE CISG*

At common law, specific performance is available only if damages would be an inadequate remedy, and the UCC also reflects this limitation. The CISG by contrast allows both the buyer and the seller to elect specific performance rather than damages.[85] But this specific performance remedy is subject to a substantial limitation contained in Article 28, which provides that "a court is not bound to enter a judgement for specific performance unless the court would do so under its own law in respect of similar contracts of sale not governed by this Convention." Although this provision would not require a U.S. court to deny specific performance unless the goods at issue were unique, it would allow the court to do so without violating the CISG. . . .

[T]he CISG's provisions on specific performance [invites one] to question the common law and UCC limitations on this remedy. A number of scholars have argued that American law should make specific performance more readily available.[86] The CISG is an example of a system of contract law that actually does so.[87]

---

* Excerpted from William S. Dodge, *Teaching the CISG in Contracts*, 50 J. LEGAL EDUC. 72, 90 (2000).

85. See CISG Art. 46(1) ("The buyer may require performance by the seller of his obligations unless the buyer has resorted to a remedy which is inconsistent with this requirement."); *id.* Art. 62 ("The seller may require the buyer to pay the price, take delivery or perform his other obligations, unless the seller has resorted to a remedy which is Inconsistent with this requirement."). Article 46(2), however, allows a buyer to "require delivery of substitute goods only if the lack of conformity constitutes a fundamental breach of contract."

86. *See, e.g.*, Alan Schwartz, *The Case for Specific Performance*, 89 YALE L.J. 271 (1979); Thomas S. Ulen, *The Efficiency of Specific Performance: Toward a Unified Theory of Contract Remedies*, 83 MICH. L. REV. 341 (1984).

87. Of course, civil law countries also more routinely make specific performance available for breach of contract, *see* RUDOLPH B. SCHLESINGER ET AL., COMPARATIVE LAW: CASES—TEXT—MATERIALS, 5th ed., 663-84 (Mineola, 1988), and this aspect of the CISG is really just a reflection of the civil law tradition.

3. Services

DOCTRINAL OVERVIEW: SPECIFIC PERFORMANCE FOR SERVICES*

The most direct form of equitable relief for breach of contract is specific performance. By ordering the promisor to render the promised performance, the court attempts to produce, as nearly as is practicable, the same effect as if the contract had been performed. A court will not order a performance that has become impossible, unreasonably burdensome, or unlawful, nor will it issue an order that can be frustrated by the defendant through exercise of a power of termination or otherwise. Specific performance may be granted after there has been a breach of contract by either nonperfonnance or repudiation.

Instead of ordering specific performance, a court may, by injunction, direct a party to refrain from doing a specified act. If the performance due under the contract consists simply of forbearance, the effect of an injunction is to order specific performance. Often, however, an injunction is used as an indirect means of enforcing a duty to act. Instead of ordering that the act be done, as a court would in granting specific performance, the court orders forbearance from inconsistent action. This is done most often in cases in which specific performance is objectionable on some ground that can be avoided by the use of an injunction. Difficulties in supervising compliance with the order may, for example, be fewer if an injunction is issued than if specific performance is ordered.

The classic case is *Lumley v. Wagner,* arising out of a contract in which Johanna Wagner, an opera singer from the court of Prussia, agreed to sing exclusively for Benjamin Lumley, proprietor of Her Majesty's Theatre in London, for a period of three months. . . .

Lumley v. Wagner

Chancery Division
42 Eng. Rep. 687 (1852)

The bill in this suit was filed on the 22nd April 1852, by Benjamin Lumley, the lessee of Her Majesty's Theatre, against Johanna Wagner, Albert Wagner, her father, and Frederick Gye, the lessee of Covent Garden Theatre: it stated that in November 1851 Joseph Bacher, as the agent of the Defendants Albert Wagner and Johanna Wagner, came to and concluded at Berlin an agreement in writing in the French language, bearing date the 9th November 1851, and which agreement, being translated into English, was as follows:

> The undersigned Mr. Benjamin Lumley, possessor of Her Majesty's Theatre at London, and of the Italian Opera at Paris, of the one part and Mademoiselle

* Excerpted from E. ALLAN FARNSWORTH, CONTRACTS § 12.5 (4th ed. 2004).

Johanna Wagner, cantatrice of the Court of His Majesty the King of Prussia, with the consent of her father, Mr. A. Wagner, residing at Berlin, of the other part, have concerted and concluded the following contract:

The Opera House at Her Majesty's Theatre on Haymarket, where Benjamin Lumley engaged Mademoiselle Wagner to sing.

First, Mademoiselle Johanna Wagner binds herself to sing [six parts over] three months at the theatre of Mr. Lumley, Her Majesty's, at London, to date from the 1st of April 1852. . . .
Third, these six parts belong exclusively to Mademoiselle Wagner, and any other cantatrice shall not presume to sing them during the three months of her engagement. If Mr. Lumley happens to be prevented by any cause soever from giving these operas, he is, nevertheless, held to pay Mademoiselle Johanna Wagner the salary stipulated lower down for the number of her parts as if she had sung them. . . .
Fifth, Mademoiselle Johanna Wagner binds herself to sing twice a week during the run of the three months; however, if she herself was hindered from singing twice in any week whatever, she will have the right to give at a later period the omitted representation.
Sixth, if Mademoiselle Wagner, fulfilling the wishes of the direction, consent to sing more than twice a week in the course of three months, this last will give to Mademoiselle Wagner £50 sterling for each representation extra.
Seventh, Mr. Lumley engages to pay Mademoiselle Wagner a salary of £400 sterling per month, and payment will take place in such manner that she will receive £100 sterling each week. . . .

JOHANNA WAGNER
ALBERT WAGNER

Berlin, the 9th November 1851

The bill then stated that in November 1851 Joseph Bacher met the Plaintiff in Paris, when the Plaintiff objected to the agreement as not containing an usual and necessary clause, preventing the Defendant Johanna Wagner from exercising her professional abilities in England without the consent of the Plaintiff, whereupon Joseph Bacher, as the agent of the Defendants Johanna Wagner and Albert Wagner, and being fully authorized by them for the purpose, added an article in writing in the French language to the agreement, and which, being translated into English, was as follows:

Mademoiselle Wagner engages herself not to use her talents at any other theatre, nor in any concert or reunion, public or private, without the written authorization of Mr. Lumley.

Dr. JOSEPH BACHER, for Mademoiselle Johanna Wagner, and authorized by her.

The bill then stated that J. and A. Wagner subsequently made another engagement with the Defendant F. Gye, by which it was agreed that the Defendant J. Wagner should, for a larger sum than that stipulated by the agreement with the Plaintiff, sing at the Royal Italian Opera, Covent Garden, and abandon the agreement with the Plaintiff. The bill then stated that the Defendant F. Gye had full knowledge of the previous agreement with the Plaintiff, and that the Plaintiff had received a protest from the Defendants J. and A. Wagner, repudiating the agreement on the allegation that the Plaintiff had failed to fulfil the pecuniary portion of the agreement.*

The bill prayed that the Defendants Johanna Wagner and Albert Wagner might be restrained from violating or committing any breach of the last article of the agreement; that the Defendant Johanna Wagner might be restrained from singing and performing or singing at the Royal Italian Opera, Covent Garden, or at any other theatre or place without the sanction or permission in writing of the Plaintiff during the existence of the agreement with the Plaintiff; and that the Defendant Albert Wagner might be restrained from permitting or sanctioning the Defendant Johanna Wagner singing and performing or singing as aforesaid; that the Defendant Frederick Gye might be restrained from accepting the professional services of the Defendant Johanna Wagner as a singer and performer or singer at the said Royal Italia Opera, Covent Garden, or at any other theatre or place, and from permitting her to sing and perform or to sing at the Royal Italian Opera, Covent Garden, during the existence of the agreement with the Plaintiff, without the permission or sanction of the Plaintiff. . . .

THE LORD CHANCELLOR.† The question which I have to decide in the present case arises out of a very simple contract, the effect of which is, that the Defendant Johanna Wagner should sing at Her Majesty's Theatre for a certain number of nights, and that she should not sing elsewhere (for that is the true construction) during that period. . . .

The present is a mixed case, consisting not of two correlative acts to be done—one by the Plaintiff, and the other by the Defendants . . . —but of an act to be done by J. Wagner alone, to which is superadded a negative stipulation on her part to abstain from the commission of any act which will break in upon her affirmative covenant; the one being ancillary to, concurrent and operating together with, the other. The agreement to sing for the Plaintiff during three months at his theatre, and during that time not to sing for anybody else, is not a correlative contract, it is in effect one contract; and though beyond all doubt this Court could not interfere to enforce the specific performance of the whole of this contract, yet in all sound construction, and according to the true spirit of the agreement, the engagement to perform for three months at one theatre

* [In a separate case, Lumley sued Gye for tortious interference with contract. The case is reproduced at 653, *infra*.—ED.]

† [Lord St. Leonards.—ED.]

must necessarily exclude the right to perform at the same time at another theatre. It was clearly intended that J. Wagner was to exert her vocal abilities to the utmost to aid the theatre to which she agreed to attach herself. I am of opinion that if she had attempted, even in the absence of any negative stipulation, to perform at another theatre, she would have broken the spirit and true meaning of the contract as much as she would now do with reference to the contract into which she was actually entered.

Wherever this Court has not proper jurisdiction to enforce specific performance, it operates to bind men's consciences, as far as they can be bound, to a true and literal performance of their agreements; and it will not suffer them to depart from their contracts at their pleasure, leaving the party with whom they have contracted to the mere chance of any damages which a jury may give. The exercise of this jurisdiction has, I believe, had a wholesome tendency towards the maintenance of that good faith which exists in this country to a much greater degree perhaps than in any other. . . .

> **"Bind Men's Consciences"**
>
> This language might remind you of *Mills v. Wyman*. In that case, Parker, writing for the court, noted that "What a man ought to do, generally he ought to be made to do, whether he promise or refuse." However, he somewhat reluctantly commented that, be that as it may, "the law of society has left most of such obligations to the *interior* forum, as the tribunal of conscience has been aptly called." Here, the Lord Chancellor seems much more ambitious, stating that courts should "bind men's consciences, as far as they can be bound, to a true and literal performance of their agreements," which will have a "a wholesome tendency towards the maintenance of . . . good faith." Which approach seems better to you, and why?

It was objected that the operation of the injunction in the present case was mischievous, excluding the Defendant J. Wagner from performing at any other theatre while this Court had no power to compel her to perform at Her Majesty's Theatre. It is true that I have not the means of compelling her to sing, but she has no cause of complaint if I compel her to abstain from the commission of an act which she has bound herself not to do, and thus possibly cause her to fulfil her engagement. . . . The effect, too, of the injunction in restraining J. Wagner from singing elsewhere may, in the event of an action being brought against her by the Plaintiff, prevent any such amount of vindictive damages being given against her as a jury might probably be inclined to give if she had carried her talents and exercised them at the rival theatre: the injunction may also, as I have said, tend to the fulfilment of her engagement; though, in continuing the injunction, I disclaim doing indirectly what I cannot do directly. . . .

I may at once declare that if I had only to deal with the affirmative covenant of the Defendant J. Wagner that she would perform at Her Majesty's Theatre, I should not have granted any injunction. . . .

NOTES AND QUESTIONS

1. ***What happened?*** Who sued whom for what? Procedurally, how did the case get before this court? Factually, what happened between the parties?

What arguments did the plaintiff and defendant make? What rule or rules did the court apply? How did the court analyze the dispute between the parties? How did the court decide the case?

2. *Was this case correctly decided?* Do you agree with the result reached in this case? Why or why not? Do you agree with the court's reasoning? Why or why not? How, if at all, would you have written the opinion differently?

3. *Almost specific performance?* Although the court did not specifically enforce the contract, it did the next best thing (from the promisee's perspective). Does the court's remedy put too much, or not enough, pressure on breaching promisors?

4. *Meanwhile* . . . On the other side of the Atlantic, about two decades before this case was decided, a Chancellor in New York took the opposite approach in a case involving a male opera singer, but recognized the inherent problems in doing so, writing that:

> [T]he law appears to have been long since settled that a bird that can sing and will not sing must be made to sing. (*Old adage*). In this case it is charged in the bill, not only that the defendant can sing, but also that he has expressly agreed to sing, and to accompany that singing with such appropriate gestures as may be necessary and proper to give an interest to his performance. And from the facts disclosed, I think it is very evident also that he does not intend to gratify the citizens of New York, who may resort to the Italian opera, either by his singing, or by his gesticulations. Although the authority before cited shows the law to be in favor of the complainant, so far at least as to entitle him to a decree for the singing, I am not aware that any officer of his court has that perfect knowledge of the Italian language, or possesses that exquisite sensibility in the auricular nerve which is necessary to understand, and to enjoy with a proper zest, the peculiar beauties of the Italian opera, so fascinating to the fashionable world. There might be some difficulty, therefore, even if the defendant was compelled to sing under the direction and in the presence of a master in chancery, in ascertaining whether he performed his engagement according to its spirit and intent. It would also be very difficult for the master to determine what effect coercion might produce upon the defendant's singing, especially in live livelier airs: although the fear of imprisonment would unquestionably deepen his seriousness in the graver parts of the drama. But one thing at least is certain; his songs will be neither comic, or even semi-serious, while he remains confined in that dismal cage, the debtor's prison of New York.*

5. *Public policy.* Note the court's remark about enforcing promises having a wholesome effect on the polity at large. Do you agree that the judiciary's role is as important as this court believes it to be? If so, why? If not, what does it say about the remedy that ought to have been awarded here?

---

* De Rivafinoli v. Corsetti, 4 Paige Ch. (N.Y.) 264, 270 (1833).

Be sure to look at the footnotes in the excerpt below: many of them review concepts and thinking tools to which you were previously exposed.

THINKING TOOLS: PROPERTY RULES, LIABILITY RULES, AND EFFICIENT BREACH*

The only universal consequence of a legally binding promise is, that the law makes the promisor pay damages if the promised event does not come to pass. In every case it leaves him free from interference until the time for fulfillment has gone by, and therefore free to break his contract if he chooses.

— Oliver Wendell Holmes, THE COMMON LAW 301 (1881)

What does it really mean to make a contract? Is the promisor legally and/or morally obligated to perform her promise, or is she merely obligated to choose between keeping her promise, on the one hand, or breaching and paying damages, on the other? Throughout history, this question has been answered in several ways, two of which I shall focus on in this Article.

The first way of answering this question is to hold that a promisor, upon entering into a contract, is and ought to be both legally and morally bound to keep his or her promise, as the very institution of contract law is, and ought to be, one of promise-keeping. This position, which has been maintained by nonconsequentialist thinkers stretching back hundreds of years, has been justified on the grounds that the rightness or wrongness of an act ought not depend (at least exclusively) upon the good or bad consequences that follow from the act, but rather upon some quality intrinsic to the act itself. It is a rough, but not entirely inaccurate, characterization to say that whereas a consequentialist would focus on the end of a given act to determine whether or not that act is just or unjust, a nonconsequentialist making a similar determination would focus instead on the means used to achieve that end. And because nonconsequentialist theories do "not appeal to the consequences of our actions," but rather "to conformity with certain rules of duty," this philosophy provides an important process by which we can obtain answers to our initial inquiry concerning the meaning of enforceable promises (that is, contracts). Specifically, under the nonconsequentialist view, a promisor ought to keep his or her promise because, simply stated, it is the right thing to do. Stated differently, under this view, one ought to keep one's promise if only for promise's sake. This view was powerfully expressed by Immanuel Kant over two centuries ago, who argued that . . . "promises made and accepted must be kept," even though "the other party might not be able to compel [him or her] to do so." Kant's ideas have continued to hold sway, not only over modern contract-law

* Excerpted from Marco Jimenez, *The Value of a Promise: A Utilitarian Approach to Contract Law Remedies*, 56 UCLA L. REV. 59, 63-72 (2008) (internal citations omitted).

theorists,[20] but, even more importantly for our purposes, over the law itself[21] and the way that judges decide contract-law disputes.

Consider, for instance, the famous case of *Lumley v. Wagner*, in which Benjamin Lumley, the lessee and manager of Her Majesty's Theatre, entered into a series of contracts with opera singer Johanna Wagner, pursuant to which Wagner promised to sing in Lumley's theatre for a period of three months (the affirmative covenant), and promised not to sing at another competitor's theatre (the negative covenant) during this time, in exchange for a consideration of several hundred pounds. Wagner was subsequently approached by one of Lumley's competitors, Frederick Gye, who offered Wagner more money to sing at his rival theatre, the Royal Italian Opera, if she would agree to abandon her agreement with Lumley. She did, and Lumley brought a breach of contract action against her, seeking to indirectly enforce the affirmative covenant by obtaining direct enforcement of the negative covenant. In its decision, the court began by stating that, although it did not have the power to specifically enforce the Lumley-Wagner contract, it did have the power to "bind men's consciences, as far as they can be bound, to a true and literal performance of their agreements; and [that] it w[ould] not suffer them to depart from their contracts at their pleasure, leaving the party with whom they have contracted to the mere chance of any damages which a jury may give." In refusing to allow Wagner to breach her contract with Lumley, it is not without significance that the Lord Chancellor not only proclaimed Wagner to be legally bound to perform her agreement (or, at least, legally unable to perform for Lumley's competitor, Gye)—but morally bound to uphold her end of the bargain with Lumley. Even more notable is the fact that the Lord Chancellor explicitly rejected the view—popular among law and economics scholars today—that Wagner was free to choose between performance, on the one hand, and nonperformance plus a payment of money damages, on the other.

Although the nonconsequentialist position reflected in the Lord Chancellor's decision still exercises powerful influence over many jurists today, it has come under increasing attack from consequentialists, who, in sharp contrast to nonconsequentialists, hold that the goodness or justness of an act is determined solely by reference to its consequences. Simply put, an act that maximizes good consequences is just, and one that does not is unjust. As applied to contract law, the implications of consequentialist thought are readily apparent. A promisor, under this view, should not be obligated, either morally or legally, to absolutely perform

20. The most popular and generally accessible modern expression of this view can be found in CHARLES FRIED, CONTRACT AS PROMISE: A THEORY OF CONTRACTUAL OBLIGATION 17 (1981) ("If I make a promise to you, I should do as I promise; and if I fail to keep my promise, it is fair that I should be made to hand over the equivalent of the promised performance.").

21. The Uniform Commercial Code, for example, appears to take a similar stance. *See, e.g.*, Melvin Eisenberg, *The Theory of Efficient Breach and the Theory of Efficient Termination* 43 (Law & Econ. Workshop, Univ. of Cal. Berkeley, Paper No. 14, 2004), available at http://repositories.cdlib.org/berkeley_law_econ/spring2004/14 ("As stated in the Comments to the U.C.C., 'the essential purpose of a contract between commercial [actors] is actual performance and they do not bargain merely for a promise, or for a promise plus the right to win a lawsuit.' Accordingly, 'a continuing sense of reliance and security that the promised performance will be forthcoming when due . . . is an important feature of the bargain.'" (citing U.C.C. § 2-609, cmt. 1 (2004)).

his or her promise, but should instead be obligated to choose between performance, on the one hand, and breach plus a payment of money damages, on the other, depending on which of the two choices leads to better consequences. It was this approach that was championed by Holmes over a century ago, who forcefully sought to ameliorate the "evil effects of the confusion between legal and moral ideas . . . in the law of contract" by holding that "[t]he duty to keep a contract at common law means a prediction that you must pay damages if you do not keep it,—and nothing else." By disambiguating the word "obligation" into its normative and descriptive components, Holmes sought to deemphasize the promisor's moral obligation to keep her promises by emphasizing instead her legal right to choose between performance, on the one hand, and breach plus a payment of money damages to the aggrieved party, on the other. Without exaggeration, it can be said that this approach revolutionized Anglo-American contract law by creating a rift between legal and moral ideas whose aftershocks can still be felt on the legal landscape to this day.

Although Holmes' jurisprudential contribution was profound—especially for the history of Anglo-American contract law—his insight was not unique, but can, I think, best be characterized as a weighing in on a deep and longstanding philosophical struggle between the two diametrically opposed schools of thought just discussed: consequentialism and nonconsequentialism. With Holmes' encouragement, this war, which was once fought in the realm of philosophy, has since been waged on the jurisprudential battlefield as well. There, over the past hundred years, each side has sent its champion to do battle, and, although bloodied, scarred, and exhausted from the fight, each is still standing, with no clear winner or end in sight.

This battle, and the resulting doctrinal differences that have manifested themselves in our law, can perhaps best be illustrated by examining the contrasting views of each camp through the lens of efficient breach theory. Let us suppose, for example, that A has agreed to sell to B his last one hundred widgets for $10 per widget, but C then approaches A and offers to buy these widgets for $12 per widget. A, of course, is confronted with the following question: Should he perform his contract with B, or should he breach his contract and pay damages instead, the amount of which should be more than compensated by the additional profit he makes from C? The answer, of course, will largely be determined by whether the legal system will allow A to breach his contract with B at all. And this, as I suggest, depends on whether the legal system has adopted a nonconsequentialist theory of contract law (whereby A would be morally and legally obligated to perform his contract with B,[38] thereby protecting B's right to A's performance with a property rule[39]), or whether it has instead adopted a consequentialist theory

38. This approach was taken by the Lord Chancellor in *Lumley v. Wagner*, . . . who noted: "The moralist of duty thus posits a general obligation to keep promises, of which the obligation of contract will only be a special case—that special case in which certain promises have attained legal as well as moral force." Fried, *supra* note 20, at 17.

39. As Professors Calabresi and Melamed explained in their seminal article:

> An entitlement is protected by a property rule to the extent that someone who wishes to remove the entitlement from its holder must buy it from him in a voluntary transaction

of contract law (whereby A would be free to choose between performance and breach, protecting B's right to A's performance with a liability rule instead[41]).

If the legal system has adopted a nonconsequentialist property rule, it has, in effect, decided to protect B's interest in A's performance in such a way that "someone [C] who wishes to remove the entitlement [to A's performance] from its holder [B] must buy it from [B] in a voluntary transaction in which the value of the entitlement is agreed upon by the seller [B]."[42] In doing so, it should be noted that C will not be entitled to buy the widgets from A for $12, but will instead be forced to negotiate with B to reach a mutually agreeable price. And, in the course of these negotiations, it should be noted that C will only be entitled to purchase these widgets if he values them more than B does. Thus, for example, if B values A's widgets at $11 per widget, whereas C values them at $13 per widget, B and C should be able to negotiate a mutually agreeable price between these two amounts.[43] If, on the other hand, B values A's widgets at $14 per widget, whereas C only values them at $13 per widget, the parties would not reach an agreement through their negotiations, because C did not value the widgets more than B did.

> in which the value of the entitlement is agreed upon by the seller. It is the form of entitlement which gives rise to the least amount of state intervention: once the original entitlement is decided upon, the state does not try to decide its value. It lets each of the parties say how much the entitlement is worth to him, and gives the seller a veto if the buyer does not offer enough. Property rules involve a collective decision as to who is to be given an initial entitlement but not as to the value of the entitlement.

Guido Calabresi & A. Douglas Melamed, Property Rules, Liability Rules, and Inalienability: One View of the Cathedral, 85 HARV. L. REV. 1089, 1092 (1972).

41. As explained by Professors Calabresi and Melamed:

> Whenever someone may destroy the initial entitlement if he is willing to pay an objectively determined value for it, an entitlement is protected by a liability rule. This value may be what it is thought the original holder of the entitlement would have sold it for. But the holder's complaint that he would have demanded more will not avail him once the objectively determined value is set. Obviously, liability rules involve an additional stage of state intervention: not only are entitlements protected, but their transfer or destruction is allowed on the basis of a value determined by some organ of the state rather than by the parties themselves.

Calabresi & Melamed, *supra* note 39, at 1092.

42. *Id.*

43. This argument excludes, but does not ignore, transaction costs, the inclusion of which would likely strengthen the claims made in this Article. Many scholars—including law and economics scholars—who have considered transaction costs, have persuasively challenged the remedial implications of wealth maximization theory on the grounds that WMT sometimes does not, in practice, lead to the most efficient outcome once transactions costs are taken into account. This approach is not, properly speaking, either consequentialist or nonconsequentialist, but it does have important implications for the way damages are awarded under either regime. Of particular importance is the fact that, once the practical implications of transaction costs are added to the theoretical conclusions reached here, the argument against the applicability of WMT to contract law becomes all the more powerful. And where transaction costs cannot be determined at all, or where the empirical evidence is mixed, this would seem to suggest determining rights based on noneconomic factors, which would also seem to favor a property rule. For the seminal article discussing the importance of taking into account transaction costs in a remedial regime, see R.H. Coase, *The Problem of Social Cost*, 3 J.L. & ECON. 1 (1960).

If, on the other hand, the legal system has adopted a consequentialist liability rule, it has, in effect, stated that B's interest in A's performance is protected in such a way that "[A] may destroy [B's] initial entitlement if he is willing to pay an objectively determined value for it."[44] In our Anglo-American legal system, the "objectively determined value" that A would be required to pay to B would be measured by the expectation interest, which is the amount of money needed "to put [B] in as good a position as [B] would have been in had the contract been performed"—but with an important caveat. This "objectively determined value" would be "determine[d] by some organ of the state rather than by the parties themselves" based upon what courts determine "the original holder of the entitlement [B] would have sold it for."[46] This, of course, "necessitates a prediction [by the court] of what the injured party's [B's] situation would have been had the contract been performed," so that if the court predicts that B values A's widgets at $11, for example, A will be able breach his contract with B and sell the widgets to C, so long as A agrees to pay B the difference between what B objectively valued the widgets at ($11), and the contract price ($10), multiplied by the number of widgets, one hundred, or $100.

[It should be noted that] the subjective value that B attaches to A's widgets will often deviate (with important implications) from the court's objectively determined value, but for present purposes, it is sufficient to note that it is at least possible, by adopting [a] liability rule, that C will sometimes be able to obtain A's widgets over B's objection, even though B values the widgets more than C does. It is this rather counterintuitive[48] scenario that has been popularly described as efficient breach theory, which, in its weak form, allows promisors to breach their

44. Calabresi & Melamed, *supra* note 39.

46. Calabresi & Melamed, *supra* note 39.

48. The theory is intriguing in more ways than one: Despite the pecuniary advantages guaranteed to its practitioners, many people who make contracts in the real world consider the practice to be unethical and refuse to follow the theory's dictates, preferring instead, it would seem, wealth-minimizing intuition over wealth-maximizing logic. For example,

> [t]he conclusion that a contracting promisee normally expects that the promisor is committed to performance, rather than performance or damages at the promisor's election, is backed not only by experience and theory, but by empirical evidence. In 1990, David Baumer and Patricia Marschall surveyed 119 North Carolina corporations about their attitudes towards willful breach. One question was, "If a trading partner deliberately breaches a contract because a better deal can be had elsewhere, is such behavior unethical?" One hundred and five respondents said Yes.

Eisenberg, *supra* note 21, at 41 (*citing* David Baumer & Patricia Marschall, *Willful Breach of Contract for the Sale of Goods: Can the Bane of Business Be an Economic Bonanza?*, 65 TEMP. L. REV. 159, 165-66 (1992)). In addition, eighty-six respondents said that they would always or almost always withhold future business from a party who had willfully breached. Eisenberg, *supra* note 21, at 42 n.48 (citing Baumer & Marschall, *supra*, at 166).

contracts[49] whenever it is efficient[50] to do so,[51] and, in its strong form, actually encourages promisors to breach their contracts whenever it is efficient to do so, without regard to whether or not it is the right thing to do.

But ought we take the "ought" of promise-keeping into account, as the nonconsequentialist would suggest, or is it enough to seek efficiency, as the consequentialist would hold? This question, of course, brings us back full circle to where we began, and it is easy to see why Holmes so eagerly desired to take morality out of contract law in the first place. Indeed, whether we parse the issue in terms of consequentialism versus nonconsequentialism, in terms of liability rules versus property rules, or in terms of those who favor efficient breach versus those who oppose it, when we return to the inquiry posed at the beginning of this [excerpt] and consider the modern debate over what it really means to make a contract, we can appreciate why a resolution over the meaning of contract law has appeared to be intractable.

PROBLEM: THE OBLITERATOR*

You are a publisher. Your largest source of revenue is a series of action-adventure novels written by Author X, featuring a protagonist known as "The Obliterator." One day, Author X announces that he is tired of the series and plans to kill off The Obliterator in the next installment. Not wanting to lose your top moneymaker, you make a deal with Author X: He will allow in-house authors to write

49. *See, e.g., Patton v. Mid-Continent Systems,* 841 F.2d 742, 750 (7th Cir. 1988) (Posner, J.) ("Even if the breach is deliberate, it is not necessarily blameworthy. The promisor may simply have discovered that his performance is worth more to someone else. If so, efficiency is promoted by allowing him to break is promise, provided he makes good the promisee's actual losses.").

50. The concept of efficiency is usually defined in one of two ways, and there is no agreement even among efficient breach theorists as to which of the two definitions should control. First, under the Paretian model of efficiency, a breach of contract is efficient if it is Pareto superior, that is, if the breaching party's gains exceed, and are actually used to compensate, the nonbreaching party's losses. *See, e.g.,* Posner, Richard A. Posner, Utilitarianism, Economics, and Legal Theory, 8 J. Legal Stud. 103, 114 (1979) ("[A] transaction is Pareto optimal if it makes at least one person better off and no one worse off."). Second, under the less-restrictive Kaldor-Hicks test, a breach of contract is efficient (and social welfare is maximized) if the breaching party's gains exceed the nonbreaching party's losses, regardless of whether the breaching party compensates the nonbreaching party for her losses. *See, e.g.,* Nicholas Kaldor, *Welfare Propositions of Economics and Interpersonal Comparisons of Utility,* 49 ECON. J. 549 (1939) (stating that allocation A is preferable to allocation B if the gainers from A could theoretically compensate the losers from B while still remaining better off); J.R. Hicks, *The Foundations of Welfare Economics,* 49 ECON. J. 696 (1939) (stating that allocation A is preferable to allocation B if those who would lose from allocation A could not profitably bribe the gainers into not switching from B to A).

51. Whether or not the breach is efficient, of course, will be determined by using the court's—and not the parties'—"objectively determined value."

* The following problem was taken from Kevin M. Kelly, *Drafting Enforceable Covenants Not to Compete in Author-Publisher Agreements Under New York Law,* 36 UCLA L. REV. 119, 119-20 (1988).

new "Obliterator" novels. They will be uncredited "ghostwriters" whose names will not appear anywhere on the books. Instead, the books will refer to "Author X's 'Obliterator,'" creating the impression that Author X is still writing the series. In return for letting you continue the series, Author X will receive a lump sum of $200,000 each time a new installment is published. This way, Author X is relieved of his writing duties, yet both he and you continue to profit from the series. As part of the deal, Author X agrees not to write any competing novels—that is, novels that might draw a substantial number of readers away from the series.

Six months later, you publish the next installment in the series—the first not actually written by Author X—and sales are good . . . for the first two weeks, that is. Then one of your competitors publishes a new novel by Author X, advertising it as "The Latest Blockbuster by Author X, Creator of 'The Obliterator,' Featuring His New Hero!" Sales of your latest installment drop dramatically. You immediately call your attorney, tell him that Author X has breached the covenant not to compete, and demand that sales and distribution of the competing novel be stopped.* The new novel is drawing away so many readers that soon there will be no market left for future adventures of The Obliterator. He responds by informing you that the enforceability of a noncompetition covenant in a publishing contract has not been litigated before, and that he has serious doubts about its validity. He does tell you, however, that he has always wanted to litigate a question of first impression. Somehow, you do not find this reassuring.

How do you think a court would rule if you brought suit against Author X for breaching his noncompete agreement?

4. Contorts: Tortious Interference with Contract

After Gye enticed Wagner to break her contract with Lumley and sing at Gye's theatre, Lumley brought an action against Gye for tortious interference with contract, as related in the case below.

Lumley v. Gye

Queen's Bench

118 Eng. Rep. 749 (1853)

Erle J. The question raised . . . is [w]hether an action will lie by the proprietor of a theatre against a person who maliciously procures an entire abandonment of a contract to perform exclusively at that theatre for a certain time; whereby damage was sustained? And it seems to me that it will. . . . He who maliciously procures a damage to another by violation of his right ought to be

* It is important to note in this hypothetical that aside from the express covenant not to compete, there is no basis for stopping publication of the competing novel. Author X has not violated copyright laws because he is using a new protagonist, not "The Obliterator," and his story line is presumably not substantially similar to any he has used in the past. Also, he has not committed trademark infringement: the publisher may own the exclusive rights to "The Obliterator," but she does not own the exclusive rights to Author X's name.

made to indemnify. . . . He who procures the non-delivery of goods according to contract may inflict an injury, the same as he who procures the abstraction of goods after delivery; and both ought on the same ground to be made responsible. The remedy on the contract may be inadequate, as where the measures of damages is restricted; . . . or, in the case of the non-delivery of the goods, the disappointment may lead to a heavy forfeiture under a contract to complete a work within a time, but the measure of damages against the vendor of the goods for non-delivery may be only the difference between the contract price and the market value of the goods in question at the time of the breach. In such cases, he who procures the damage maliciously might justly be made responsible beyond the liability of the contractor. . . .

The result is that there ought to be, in my opinion, judgment for the plaintiff.

COLERIDGE J. **[dissenting]**. . . . [I]n respect of breach of contract the general rule of our law is to confine its remedies by action to the contracting parties, and to damages directly and proximately consequential on the act of him who is sued. . . .

[I]f there be any remedy by action against a stranger, . . . there must be both injury in the strict sense of the word (that is a wrong done), and loss resulting from that injury: the injury or wrong done must be the act of the defendant; and the loss must be a direct and natural, not a remote and indirect, consequence of the defendant's act. Unless there be a loss thus directly and proximately connected with the act, the mere intention, or even the endeavour, to produce it will not found the action. . . . If a contract has been made between A. and B. that the latter should go **supercargo** for the former on a voyage to China, and C., however maliciously, persuades B. to break his contract, but in vain, no one, I suppose, would contend that any action would lie against C. On the other hand, suppose a contract of the same kind made between the same parties to go to Sierra Leone, and C. urgently and bona fide advises B. to abandon his contract, which on consideration B. does, whereby loss results to A.; I think no one will be found bold enough to maintain that an action would lie against C. In the first case no loss has resulted; the malice has been ineffectual; in the second, though a loss has resulted from the act, that act was not C.'s, but entirely and exclusively B.'s own. If so, let malice be added, and let C. have persuaded, not bona fide but mala fide and maliciously, still, all other circumstances remaining the same, the same reason applies; for it is **malitia sine damno**, if the hurtful act is entirely and exclusively B.'s, which last circumstance cannot be affected by the presence or absence of malice in C. . . .

> ***Supercargo***
>
> "A person specially employed and authorized by a cargo owner to sell cargo that has been shipped and to purchase returning cargo, at the best possible prices; the commercial or foreign agent of a merchant." BLACK'S LAW DICTIONARY (10th ed. 2014).]

> ***Malitia sine damno***
>
> Malice without harm.

To draw a line between advice, persuasion, enticement and procurement is practically impossible in a court of justice; who shall say how much of a free agent's resolution flows from the interference of other minds, or the independent resolution of his own? This is a matter for the casuist rather than the jurist; still less is it for the juryman. . . . Again, if, instead of limiting our recourse to the agent, actual or constructive, we will go back to the person who immediately persuades or procures him one step, why are we to stop there? The first mover, and the malicious mover too, may be removed several steps backward from the party actually induced to break the contract: why are we not to trace him out? Morally he may be the most guilty. . . . I[f] we go the first step, we can shew no good reason for not going fifty. . . .

I conclude then that this action cannot be maintained, because . . . [m]erely to induce or procure a free contracting party to break his covenant, whether done maliciously or not, to the damage of another, . . . is not actionable. . . .

[O]ur judgment ought to be for the defendant: though it must be pronounced for the plaintiff.

Judgment for plaintiff.

RELEVANT PROVISIONS

For the *Restatement (Second) of Torts*, consult § 766.

NOTES AND QUESTIONS

1. *YouTube.* A very entertaining clip summarizing both *Lumley v. Wagner* and *Lumley v. Gye* was put together by Professor Craswell and can be found at https://www.youtube.com/watch?v=sTmCaqIgM8s.

2. *What happened?* Who sued whom for what? Procedurally, how did the case get before this court? Factually, what happened between the parties? What arguments did the plaintiff and defendant make? What rule or rules did the court apply? How did the court analyze the dispute between the parties? How did the court decide the case?

3. *Was this case correctly decided?* Do you agree with the result reached in this case? Why or why not? Do you agree with the court's reasoning? Why or why not? How, if at all, would you have written the opinion differently?

4. *Majority or dissent?* What is the dissent's main argument against the position taken by the majority? Do you agree?

5. *Slippery slope?* Is there any way of *really* getting to the bottom of why, exactly, a party chooses not to perform? If not, do you think that tortious interference with contracts as a cause of action make sense? Why or why not?

6. *Punitive damages?* It should be noted that courts ordinarily do not award punitive damages for an ordinary breach of contract. In Holmes' words,

"If a contract is broken the measure of damages generally is the same, whatever the cause of the breach."* However, punitive damages are sometimes available in tort actions, usually where defendant's actions are particularly egregious (i.e., beyond mere negligence). This means that where a breach of contract is also tortious, as in *Lumley v. Gye*, or is accompanied by an independent tort, punitive damages may sometimes be available to punish the breaching party and, by making an example of that party, deter other similarly situated parties from behaving in a like manner in the future. Do you think punitive damages should be available in *Lumley v. Gye*? Why or why not?

C. CONTRACTUAL REMEDIES

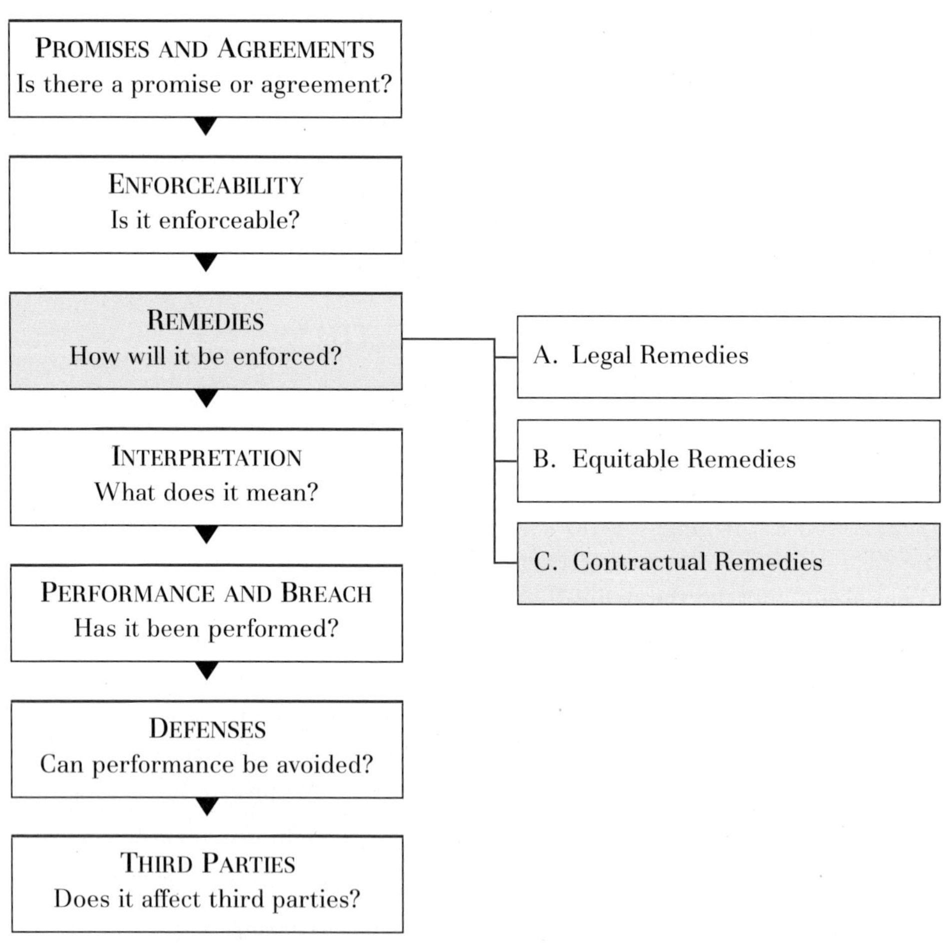
PROMISES AND AGREEMENTS
Is there a promise or agreement?
ENFORCEABILITY
Is it enforceable?
REMEDIES
How will it be enforced?
INTERPRETATION
What does it mean?
PERFORMANCE AND BREACH
Has it been performed?
DEFENSES
Can performance be avoided?
THIRD PARTIES
Does it affect third parties?
A. Legal Remedies
B. Equitable Remedies
C. Contractual Remedies

* Globe Ref. Co. v. Landa Cotton Oil Co., 190 U.S. 540, 544 (1903).

In this section we will explore one of the main alternatives to the legal remedies previously discussed: contractual or party-based remedies, or remedies agreed upon by the parties in their contract. Specifically, we will explore the conditions in which such remedies will be enforced by the court. In so doing, some of the topics that will be covered in this section include contracting around the default rule of damages, limiting consequential and incidental damages, liquidated damages versus penalty clauses, punitive damages, and arbitration clauses.

DOCTRINAL OVERVIEW: LIQUIDATED DAMAGES, PENALTIES, AND OTHER AGREED REMEDIES*

To what degree is the law of remedies for breach of contract amenable to contrary agreements by the parties? Compared with the extensive power that contracting parties have to bargain over their substantive contract rights and duties, their power to bargain over their remedial rights is surprisingly limited. The most important restriction is the one denying them the power to stipulate in their contract a sum of money payable as damages that is so large as to be characterized as a "penalty."

The advantages of stipulating in advance a sum payable as damages are manifold. For both parties, stipulating a sum may facilitate the calculation of risks and reduce the cost of proof. For the injured party, it may afford the only possibility of compensation for loss that is not susceptible of proof with sufficient certainty. For the party in breach, it may have the effect of limiting damages to the sum stipulated. For society as a whole, it may save the time of judges, juries, and witnesses, as well as the parties, and may cut the expense of litigation. These advantages are of special significance when the amount in controversy is small.

If, however, the stipulated sum is significantly larger than the amount required to compensate the injured party for its loss, the stipulation may have quite a different advantage to that party—an *in terrorem* effect on the other party that will deter breach by compelling performance. Enforcement of such a provision would allow the parties to depart from the fundamental principle that the law's goal on breach of contract is not to deter breach by compelling the promisor to perform, but rather to redress breach by compensating the promissee. It is this departure that is proscribed when a court characterizes such a provision as a penalty. Since it is the *in terrorem* effect that is objectionable, the proscription applies only if the stipulated sum is on the high, rather than the low, side of conventional damages, although a provision stipulating an "unreasonably small amount . . . might be stricken under the section on unconscionable contracts or clauses."[4] This hostile attitude toward penalties is peculiar to common law countries and is not generally shared by other legal systems. . . .

If a provision is condemned as a penalty, it is unenforceable. But the rest of the agreement stands, and the injured party is remitted to the conventional damage

---

* Excerpted from E. ALLAN FARNSWORTH, CONTRACTS § 12.18 (4th ed. 2004).

4. UCC 2-718 cmt. 1.

remedy for breach of that agreement, just as if the provision had not been included. If the provision is sustained as one for liquidated damages, both parties are bound by it, and it displaces the conventional damage remedy for breach. This is so whether it provides for damages that are larger or smaller than would otherwise have been awarded. The same distinction is now often applied to clauses providing that a sum of money deposited as security shall be forfeit in the case of breach.

1. Liquidating Damages

As discussed in the previous excerpt, courts are frequently called upon to distinguish between liquidated damages clauses and penalty clauses whenever parties to a contract stipulate their own remedies. But how, exactly, do courts do this? The cases in this subsection explore this issue in further depth, and set forth several principles courts rely on to distinguish between valid liquidated damages clauses and invalid penalty clauses.

Kemble v. Farren

Court of Common Pleas
130 Eng. Rep. 1234 (1829)

Assumpsit by the manager of Covent Garden Theatre against an actor, to recover liquidated damages for the violation of an engagement to perform at Covent Garden for four seasons.

By an agreement between the Plaintiff and Defendant, the Defendant had engaged himself to act as a principal comedian at Covent Garden Theatre for four seasons, commencing with October 1828, and in all things to conform to the regulations of the theatre. The Plaintiff agreed to pay the Defendant £3. 6s. 8d. every night on which the theatre should be open for theatrical performances during the ensuing four seasons; and that the Defendant should be allowed one benefit night during each season, on certain terms therein specified. And the agreement contained a clause, that if either of the parties should neglect or refuse to fulfil the said agreement, or any part thereof, or any stipulation therein contained, such party should pay to the other the sum of £1000, to which sum it was thereby agreed that the damages sustained by any such omission, neglect, or refusal should amount; and which sum was thereby declared by the said parties to be liquidated and ascertained damages, and not a penalty or penal sum, or in the nature thereof.

The breach alleged was, that the Defendant refused to act during the second season; and at the trial the jury gave a verdict for the Plaintiff for £750 damages, subject to a motion for increasing them to £1000, if the Court should be of opinion that, upon this agreement, the Plaintiff was entitled to the whole sum claimed as liquidated damages.

TINDAL C.J. This is a rule which calls upon the Defendant to shew cause why the verdict, which has been entered for the Plaintiff for £750, should not be increased to £1000. . . .

It is, undoubtedly, difficult to suppose any words more precise or explicit than those used in the agreement; the same declaring not only affirmatively that the sum of £1000 should be taken as liquidated damages, but negatively also that it should not be considered as a penalty, or in the nature thereof. And if the clause had been limited to breaches which were of an uncertain nature and amount, we should have thought it would have had the effect of ascertaining the damages upon any such breach at £1000. For we see nothing illegal or unreasonable in the parties, by their mutual agreement, settling the amount of damages, uncertain in their nature, at any sum upon which they may agree. In many cases, such an agreement fixes that which is almost impossible to be accurately ascertained; and in all cases, it saves the expense and difficulty of bringing witnesses to that point. But in the present case, the clause is not so confined; it extends to the breach of any stipulation by either party. If, therefore, on the one hand, the Plaintiff had neglected to make a single payment of £3. 6s. 8d. per day, or on the other hand, the Defendant had refused to conform to any usual regulation of the theatre, however minute or unimportant, it must have been contended that the clause in question, in either case, would have given the stipulated damages of £1000. But that a very large sum should become immediately payable, in consequence of the nonpayment of a very small sum, and that the former should not be considered as a penalty, appears to be a contradiction in terms; the case being precisely that in which courts of equity have always relieved, and against which courts of law have, in modern times, endeavoured to relieve, by directing juries to assess the real damages sustained by the breach of the agreement. It has been argued at the bar, that the liquidated damages apply to those breaches of the agreement only which are in their nature uncertain, leaving those which are certain to a distinct remedy, by the verdict of a jury. But we can only say, if such is the intention of the parties, they have not expressed it; but have made the clause relate, by express and positive terms, to all breaches of every kind. . . . The consequence is, we think the present verdict should stand, and the rule for increasing the damages be discharged.

Rule discharged.

RELEVANT PROVISIONS

For the *Restatement (Second) of Contracts,* consult §§ 356 and 361. For the UCC, consult §§ 2-718 and 2-719. For the UNIDROIT Principles, consult Article 7.4.13.

NOTES AND QUESTIONS

1. ***What happened?*** Who sued whom for what? Procedurally, how did the case get before this court? Factually, what happened between the parties?

What arguments did the plaintiff and defendant make? What rule or rules did the court apply? How did the court analyze the dispute between the parties? How did the court decide the case?

2. ***Was this case correctly decided?*** Do you agree with the result reached in this case? Why or why not? Do you agree with the court's reasoning? Why or why not? How, if at all, would you have written the opinion differently?

3. ***What was the breach?*** How, exactly, was the contract breached here? Was it the type of breach contemplated by the rather hefty liquidated damages provision? If so, why wasn't the provision enforced?

4. ***Comparative analysis.*** How, if at all, would this case have been decided differently under the UNIDROIT Principles? Which outcome do you prefer, and why?

Truck Rent-A-Center, Inc. v. Puritan Farms 2nd, Inc.

Court of Appeals of New York
361 N.E.2d 1015 (1977)

JASEN, JUDGE. The principal issue on this appeal is whether a provision in a truck lease agreement which requires the payment of a specified amount of money to the lessor in the event of the lessee's breach is an enforceable liquidated damages clause, or, instead, provides for an unenforceable penalty.

Defendant Puritan Farms 2nd, Inc. (Puritan), was in the business of furnishing milk and milk products to customers through home delivery. In January, 1969, Puritan leased a fleet of 25 new milk delivery trucks from plaintiff Truck Rent-A-Center for a term of seven years commencing January 15, 1970. Under the provisions of a truck lease and service agreement entered into by the parties, the plaintiff was to supply the trucks and make all necessary repairs. Puritan was to pay an agreed upon weekly rental fee. It was understood that the lessor would finance the purchase of the trucks through a bank, paying the prime rate of interest on the date of the loan plus 2%. The rental charges on the trucks were to be adjusted in the event of a fluctuation in the interest rate above or below specified levels. The lessee was granted the right to purchase the trucks, at any time after 12 months following commencement of the lease, by paying to the lessor the amount then due and owing on the bank loan, plus an additional $100 per truck purchased.

Article 16 of the lease agreement provided that if the agreement should terminate prior to expiration of the term of the lease as a result of the lessee's breach, the lessor would be entitled to damages, "liquidated for all purposes," in the amount of all rentals that would have come due from the date of termination to the date of normal expiration of the term less the "re-rental value" of the vehicles, which was set at 50% of the rentals that would have become due. In effect, the lessee would be obligated to pay the lessor, as a consequence of breach, one half of all rentals that would have become due had the agreement run its full course. The agreement recited that, in arriving at the settled amount of damage, "the parties hereto have considered, among other factors, Lessor's substantial initial investment in purchasing or reconditioning for Lessee's service the demised motor vehicles, the uncertainty of Lessor's ability to re-enter the said vehicles, the costs to Lessor during any period the vehicles may remain idle until re-rented, or if sold, the uncertainty of the sales price and its possible attendant loss. The parties have also considered, among other factors, in so liquidating the said damages, Lessor's saving in expenditures for gasoline, oil and other service items."

The bulk of the written agreement was derived from a printed form lease which the parties modified by both filling in blank spaces and typing in alterations. The agreement also contained several typewritten indorsements which also made changes in the provisions of the printed lease. The provision for lessee's purchase of the vehicles for the bank loan balance and $100 per vehicle was contained in one such indorsement. The liquidated damages clause was contained in the body of the printed form.

Puritan tendered plaintiff a security deposit, consisting of four weeks' rent and the lease went into effect. After nearly three years, the lessee sought to terminate the lease agreement. On December 7, 1973, Puritan wrote to the lessor complaining that the lessor had not repaired and maintained the trucks as provided in the lease agreement. Puritan stated that it had "repeatedly notified" plaintiff of these defaults, but plaintiff had not cured them. Puritan, therefore, exercised its right to terminate the agreement "without any penalty and Without purchasing the trucks." (Emphasis added.) On the date set for termination, December 14, 1973, plaintiff's attorneys replied to Puritan by letter to advise it that plaintiff believed it had fully performed its obligations under the lease and, in the event Puritan adhered to the announced breach, would commence proceedings to obtain the liquidated damages provided for in article 16 of the agreement. Nevertheless, Puritan had its drivers return the trucks to plaintiff's premises, where the bulk of them have remained ever since. At the time of termination, plaintiff owed $45,134.17 on the outstanding bank loan.

Plaintiff followed through on its promise to commence an action for the payment of the liquidated damages. Defendant counterclaimed for the return of its security deposit. At the nonjury trial, plaintiff contended that it had fully performed its obligations to maintain and repair the trucks. Moreover, it was submitted, Puritan sought to cancel the lease because corporations allied with Puritan had acquired the assets, including delivery trucks, of other dairies and Puritan believed it cheaper to utilize this "shadow fleet." The home milk delivery business was on the decline and plaintiff's president testified that efforts to either re-rent or sell the truck fleet to other dairies had not been successful. Even with modifications in the trucks, such as the removal of the milk racks and a change in the floor of the trucks, it was not possible to lease the trucks to other industries, although a few trucks were subsequently sold. The proceeds of the sales were applied to the reduction of the bank balance. The other trucks remained at plaintiff's premises, partially protected by a fence plaintiff erected to discourage vandals. The defendant countered with proof that plaintiff had not repaired the trucks promptly and satisfactorily.

At the close of the trial, the court found, based on the evidence it found to be credible, that plaintiff had substantially performed its obligations under the lease and that defendant was not justified in terminating the agreement. Further, the court held that the provision for liquidated damages was reasonable and represented a fair estimate of actual damages which would be difficult to ascertain precisely. "The parties, at the time the agreement was entered into, considered many factors affecting damages, namely: the uncertainty of the plaintiff's ability to re-rent the said vehicles; the plaintiff's investment in purchasing and reconditioning the vehicles to suit the defendant's particular purpose; the number of man hours not utilized in the non-service of the vehicles in the event of a breach; the uncertainty of reselling the vehicles in question; the uncertainty of the plaintiff's savings or expenditures for gasoline, oil or other service items, and the amount of fluctuating interest on the bank loan." The court calculated that plaintiff would have been entitled to $177,355.20 in rent for the period remaining in the lease and, in accordance with the liquidated damages provision, awarded plaintiff half that amount, $88,677.60. The resulting judgment was affirmed by the Appellate Division, with two Justices dissenting.

The primary issue before us is whether the "liquidated damages" provision is enforceable. Liquidated damages constitute the compensation which, the parties have agreed, should be paid in order to satisfy any loss or injury flowing from a breach of their contract. In effect, a liquidated damage provision is an estimate, made by the parties at the time they enter into their agreement, of the extent of the injury that would be sustained as a result of breach of the agreement. Parties to a contract have the right to agree to such clauses, provided that the clause is neither unconscionable nor contrary to public policy. Provisions for liquidated damage have value in those situations where it would be difficult, if not actually impossible, to calculate the amount of actual damage. In such cases, the contracting parties may agree between themselves as to the amount of damages to be paid upon breach rather than leaving that amount to the calculation of a court or jury.

On the other hand, liquidated damage provisions will not be enforced if it is against public policy to do so and public policy is firmly set against the imposition of penalties or forfeitures for which there is no statutory authority. It is plain that a provision which requires, in the event of contractual breach, the payment of a sum of money grossly disproportionate to the amount of actual damages provides for penalty and is unenforceable. A liquidated damage provision has its basis in the principle of just compensation for loss. A clause which provides for an amount plainly disproportionate to real damage is not intended to provide fair compensation but to secure performance by the compulsion of the very disproportion. A promisor would be compelled, out of fear of economic devastation, to continue performance and his promisee, in the event of default, would reap a windfall well above actual harm sustained. As was stated eloquently long ago, to permit parties, in their unbridled discretion, to utilize penalties as damages, "would lead to the most terrible oppression in pecuniary dealings."

The rule is now well established. A contractual provision fixing damages in the event of breach will be sustained if the amount liquidated bears a reasonable proportion to the probable loss and the amount of actual loss is incapable or difficult of precise estimation. If, however, the amount fixed is plainly or grossly disproportionate to the probable loss, the provision calls for a penalty and will not be enforced. In interpreting a provision fixing damages, it is not material whether the parties themselves have chosen to call the provision one for "liquidated damages," as in this case, or have styled it as a penalty. Such an approach would put too much faith in form and too little in substance. Similarly, the agreement should be interpreted as of the date of its making and not as of the date of its breach.

In applying these principles to the case before us, we conclude that the amount stipulated by the parties as damages bears a reasonable relation to the amount of probable actual harm and is not a penalty. Hence, the provision is enforceable and the order of the Appellate Division should be affirmed.

Looking forward from the date of the lease, the parties could reasonably conclude, as they did, that there might not be an actual market for the sale or re-rental of these specialized vehicles in the event of the lessee's breach. To be sure, plaintiff's lost profit could readily be measured by the amount of the weekly rental fee. However, it was permissible for the parties, in advance, to agree that the re-rental or sale value of the vehicles would be 50% of the weekly rental. Since there was uncertainty as to whether the trucks could be re-rented or sold, the parties could reasonably set, as they did, the value of such mitigation at 50% of the amount the lessee was obligated to pay for rental of the trucks. This would take into consideration the fact that, after being used by the lessee, the vehicles would no longer be "shiny, new trucks," but would be used, possibly battered, trucks, whose value would have declined appreciably. The parties also considered the fact that, although plaintiff, in the event of Puritan's breach, might be spared repair and maintenance costs necessitated by Puritan's use of the trucks, plaintiff would have to assume the cost of storing and maintaining trucks idled by Puritan's refusal to use them. Further, it was by no means certain, at the time of the contract, that lessee would peacefully return the trucks to the lessor after lessee had breached the contract.

With particular reference to the dissent at the Appellate Division, it is true that the lessee might have exercised an option to purchase the trucks. However, lessee would not be purchasing 25 "shiny, new trucks" for a mere $2,500. Rather, lessee, after the passage of one year from the commencement of the term, could have purchased trucks that had been used for at least one year for the amount outstanding on the bank loan, in addition to the $2,500. Of course, the purchase price would be greater if the option were exercised early in the term rather than towards the end of the term since plaintiff would be making payments to the bank all the while. More fundamental, the existence of the option clause has absolutely no bearing on the validity of the discrete, liquidated damages provision. The lessee could have elected to purchase the trucks but elected not to do so. In fact, the lessee's letter of termination made a point of the fact that the lessee did not want to purchase the trucks. The reality is that the lessee sought, by its wrongful termination of the lease, to evade all obligations to the plaintiff, whether for rent or for the agreed upon purchase price. Its effort to do so failed. That lessee could have made a better bargain for itself by purchasing the trucks for $48,134.17 pursuant to the option, instead of paying $92,341.79 in damages for wrongful breach of the lease is not availing to it now. Although the lessee might now wish, with the benefit of hindsight, that it had purchased the trucks rather than default on its lease obligations, the simple fact is that it did not do so.

We attach no significance to the fact that the liquidated damages clause appears on the preprinted form portion of the agreement. The agreement was fully negotiated and the provisions of the form, in many other respects, were amended. There is no indication of any disparity of bargaining power or of unconscionability. The provision for liquidated damages related reasonably to potential harm that was difficult to estimate and did not constitute a disguised penalty. We also find no merit in the claim of trial error advanced by Puritan.

Accordingly, the order of the Appellate Division should be affirmed, with costs.

BREITEL, C.J., and GABRIELLI, JONES, WACHTLER, FUCHSBERG and COOKE, J.J. concur.

Order affirmed.

NOTES AND QUESTIONS

1. ***What happened?*** Who sued whom for what? Procedurally, how did the case get before this court? Factually, what happened between the parties? What arguments did the plaintiff and defendant make? What rule or rules did the court apply? How did the court analyze the dispute between the parties? How did the court decide the case?

2. ***Was this case correctly decided?*** Do you agree with the result reached in this case? Why or why not? Do you agree with the court's reasoning? Why or why not? How, if at all, would you have written the opinion differently?

3. ***Discussion.*** For an interesting discussion of the previous cases, see generally Comment, *Liquidated Damages: A Comparison of the Common Law and the Uniform Commercial Code*, 45 FORDHAM L. REV. 1349, 1350 (1977).

Lake River Corp. v. Carborundum Co.

United States Court of Appeals, Seventh Circuit
769 F.2d 1284 (1985)

POSNER, CIRCUIT JUDGE. This diversity suit between Lake River Corporation and Carborundum Company requires us to consider questions of Illinois commercial law, and in particular to explore the fuzzy line between penalty clauses and liquidated-damages clauses.

Carborundum manufactures "Ferro Carbo," an abrasive powder used in making steel. To serve its midwestern customers better, Carborundum made a contract with Lake River by which the latter agreed to provide distribution services in its warehouse in Illinois. Lake River would receive Ferro Carbo in bulk from Carborundum, "bag" it, and ship the bagged product to Carborundum's customers. The Ferro Carbo would remain Carborundum's property until delivered to the customers.

Carborundum insisted that Lake River install a new bagging system to handle the contract. In order to be sure of being able to recover the cost of the new system ($89,000) and make a profit of 20 percent of the contract price, Lake River insisted on the following minimum-quantity guarantee:

> In consideration of the special equipment [i.e., the new bagging system] to be acquired and furnished by LAKE-RIVER for handling the product, CARBORUNDUM shall, during the initial three-year term of this Agreement, ship to LAKE-RIVER for bagging a minimum quantity of [22,500 tons]. If, at the end of the three-year term, this minimum quantity shall not have been shipped, LAKE-RIVER shall invoice CARBORUNDUM at the then prevailing rates for the difference between the quantity bagged and the minimum guaranteed.

If Carborundum had shipped the full minimum quantity that it guaranteed, it would have owed Lake River roughly $533,000 under the contract.

After the contract was signed in 1979, the demand for domestic steel, and with it the demand for Ferro Carbo, plummeted, and Carborundum failed to ship the guaranteed amount. When the contract expired late in 1982, Carborundum had shipped only 12,000 of the 22,500 tons it had guaranteed. Lake River had bagged the 12,000 tons and had billed Carborundum for this bagging, and Carborundum had paid, but by virtue of the formula in the minimum-guarantee clause Carborundum still owed Lake River $241,000—the contract price of $533,000 if the full amount of Ferro Carbo had been shipped, minus what Carborundum had paid for the bagging of the quantity it had shipped.

When Lake River demanded payment of this amount, Carborundum refused, on the ground that the formula imposed a penalty. At the time, Lake River had in its warehouse 500 tons of bagged Ferro Carbo, having a market value of $269,000, which it refused to release unless Carborundum paid the $241,000 due under the formula. . . .

Lake River brought this suit for $241,000, which it claims as liquidated damages. Carborundum counterclaimed for the value of the bagged Ferro Carbo when Lake River impounded it and the additional cost of serving the customers affected by the impounding. . . . The district judge, after a bench trial, gave judgment for both parties. Carborundum ended up roughly $42,000 to the good: $269,000 + $31,000 − $241,100 − $17,000, the last figure representing prejudgment interest on Lake River's damages. (We have rounded off all dollar figures to the nearest thousand.) Both parties have appealed. . . .

The hardest issue in the case is whether the formula in the minimum-guarantee clause imposes a penalty for breach of contract or is merely an effort to liquidate damages. Deep as the hostility to penalty clauses runs in the common law, *see* Loyd, *Penalties and Forfeitures*, 29 HARV. L. REV. 117 (1915), we still might be inclined to question, if we thought ourselves free to do so, whether a modern court should refuse to enforce a penalty clause where the signator is a substantial corporation, well able to avoid improvident commitments. Penalty clauses provide an earnest of performance. The clause here enhanced Carborundum's credibility in promising to ship the minimum amount guaranteed by showing that it was willing to pay the full contract price even if it failed to ship anything. On the other side it can be pointed out that by raising the cost of a breach of contract to the contract breaker, a penalty clause increases the risk to his other creditors; increases (what is the same thing and more, because bankruptcy imposes "deadweight" social costs) the risk of bankruptcy; and could amplify the business cycle by increasing the number of bankruptcies in bad times, which is when contracts are most likely to be broken. But since little effort is made to prevent businessmen from assuming risks, these reasons are no better than makeweights.

A better argument is that a penalty clause may discourage efficient as well as inefficient breaches of contract. Suppose a breach would cost the promisee $12,000 in actual damages but would yield the promisor $20,000 in additional profits. Then there would be a net social gain from breach. After being fully compensated for his loss the promisor would be no worse off than if the contract had been performed, while the promisor would be better off by $8,000. But now suppose the contract contains a penalty clause under which the promisor if he breaks his promise must pay the promisee $25,000. The promisor will be discouraged from breaking the contract, since $25,000, the penalty, is greater than $20,000, the profits of the breach; and a transaction that would have increased value will be forgone.

On this view, since compensatory damages should be sufficient to deter inefficient breaches (that is, breaches that cost the victim more than the gain to the contract breaker), penal damages could have no effect other than to deter some efficient breaches. But this overlooks the earlier point that the willingness to agree to a penalty clause is a way of making the promisor and his promise credible and may therefore be essential to inducing some value-maximizing contracts to be made. It also overlooks the more important point that the parties (always assuming they are fully competent) will, in deciding whether to include a penalty clause in their contract, weigh the gains against the costs—costs that include the possibility of discouraging an efficient breach somewhere down the road—and will include the clause only if the benefits exceed those costs as well as all other costs.

On this view the refusal to enforce penalty clauses is (at best) paternalistic—and it seems odd that courts should display parental solicitude for large corporations. But however this may be, we must be on guard to avoid importing our own ideas of sound public policy into an area where our proper judicial role is more than usually deferential. The responsibility for making innovations in the common law of Illinois rests with the courts of Illinois, and not with the federal courts in Illinois. And like every other state, Illinois, untroubled by academic skepticism of the wisdom of refusing to enforce penalty clauses against sophisticated promisors, *see, e.g.*, Goetz & Scott, *Liquidated Damages, Penalties and the Just Compensation Principle*, 77 COLUM. L. REV. 554 (1977), continues steadfastly to insist on the distinction between penalties and liquidated damages. To be valid under Illinois law a liquidation of damages must be a reasonable estimate at the time of contracting of the likely damages from breach, and the need for estimation at that time must be shown by reference to the likely difficulty of measuring the actual damages from a breach of contract after the breach occurs. If damages would be easy to determine then, or if the estimate greatly exceeds a reasonable upper estimate of what the damages are likely to be, it is a penalty.

The distinction between a penalty and liquidated damages is not an easy one to draw in practice but we are required to draw it and can give only limited weight to the district court's determination. Whether a provision for damages is a penalty clause or a liquidated-damages clause is a question of law rather than fact, and unlike some courts of appeals we do not treat a determination by a federal district judge of an issue of state law as if it were a finding of fact, and reverse only if persuaded that clear error has occurred, though we give his determination respectful consideration.

Mindful that Illinois courts resolve doubtful cases in favor of classification as a penalty, we conclude that the damage formula in this case is a penalty and not a liquidation of damages, because it is designed always to assure Lake River more than its actual damages. The formula—full contract price minus the amount already invoiced to Carborundum—is invariant to the gravity of the breach. When a contract specifies a single sum in damages for any and all breaches even though it is apparent that all are not of the same gravity, the specification is not a reasonable effort to estimate damages; and when in addition the fixed sum greatly exceeds the actual damages likely to be inflicted by a minor breach, its character as a penalty becomes unmistakable. This case is within the gravitational field of these principles even though the minimum-guarantee clause does not fix a single sum as damages. . . .

The fact that the damage formula is invalid does not deprive Lake River of a remedy. The parties did not contract explicitly with reference to the measure of damages if the agreed-on damage formula was invalidated, but all this means is that the victim of the breach is entitled to his common law damages. In this case that would be the unpaid contract price of $241,000 minus the costs that Lake River saved by not having to complete the contract (the variable costs on the other 45 percent of the Ferro Carbo that it never had to bag). The case must be remanded to the district judge to fix these damages. . . .

The judgment of the district court is affirmed in part and reversed in part, and the case is returned to that court to redetermine both parties' damages in accordance with the principles in this opinion. . . .

NOTES AND QUESTIONS

1. ***What happened?*** Who sued whom for what? Procedurally, how did the case get before this court? Factually, what happened between the parties? What arguments did the plaintiff and defendant make? What rule or rules did the court apply? How did the court analyze the dispute between the parties? How did the court decide the case?

2. ***Was this case correctly decided?*** Do you agree with the result reached in this case? Why or why not? Do you agree with the court's reasoning? Why or why not? How, if at all, would you have written the opinion differently?

3. ***Policy justifications.*** Try to summarize Judge Posner's policy justifications for and against enforcing penalty clauses. Based on the cases you've read so far in this chapter, do you think that, in general, courts should or should not enforce these clauses?

In the previous cases in this section, we learned that overliquidating damages is generally not allowable as it constitutes a "penalty." Does the same hold true when a party tries to underliquidate damages, i.e., to provide a remedy well below the damage that would be caused in the event of breach? The following case explores this question. As you read it, ask yourself if you think the same public policy concerns are raised in both types of cases. If so, would you say they should be policed the same way? If not, would you say they should be policed differently? Do you agree with the court's resolution of this case?

Samson Sales, Inc. v. Honeywell, Inc.

Supreme Court of Ohio
465 N.E.2d 392 (1984)

[Plaintiff Samson Sales, Inc., ("Samson") entered into a contract with Morse Signal Devices whereby Morse installed a burglar alarm system at the plaintiff's pawn shop in exchange for $1,500 and $150 each month for a period of five years. Paragraph 18 of the contract contained the following clause:

> It is agreed by and between the Parties that Company is not an insurer; and that this Agreement in no way binds Company as an insurer of the premises or of the property of the Subscriber, and that all charges are based solely on the value of the service, maintenance and installation of the system. In the event of loss or damage to Subscriber resulting by reason of failure of the performance of such service or the failure of the system to properly operate, Company's liability, if any, shall be limited to the sum of Fifty Dollars ($50.00) as liquidated damages and not as a penalty and this liability shall be exclusive.

Subsequently, Morse Signal Devices was purchased by the defendant Honeywell, Inc. ("Honeywell"), which assumed responsibility under the agreement. While the contract was in force, a burglary occurred at Samson's business establishment, but Honeywell failed to transmit a burglar alarm signal to the police as required by the contract. Nevertheless, Honeywell refused to pay any more than $50 toward the loss.

Samson brought suit, alleging breach of contract against Honeywell for failing to transmit a burglar alarm signal, and sought damages in the amount of $68,303 for loss of merchandise occasioned by the burglary. In defense, defendant Honeywell claimed that its liability was limited to liquidated damages in the amount of $50 as set forth in Paragraph 18 of the contract.

The trial court entered summary judgment for Samson, but limited damages to the sum of $50. Samson appealed, and the trial court's judgment was reversed by the court of appeals, which found that the provision for liquidated damages, under the facts of this case, was in the nature of a penalty.]

KERNS, JUSTICE. The only issue of any consequence in this appeal is whether the exculpatory clause limiting Honeywell's liability to $50 is valid and enforceable.

While some jurisdictions have rejected such contract provisions on policy grounds, clauses in contracts providing for reasonable liquidated damages are recognized in Ohio as valid and enforceable. However, reasonable compensation for actual damages is the legitimate objective of such liquidated damage provisions and where the amount specified is manifestly inequitable and unrealistic, courts will ordinarily regard it as a penalty. Hence, Honeywell's standard reference "to the sum of Fifty Dollars ($50.00) as liquidated damages and not as a penalty" is by no means conclusive or controlling in this case.

Whether a particular sum specified in a contract is intended as a penalty or as liquidated damages depends upon the operative facts and circumstances surrounding each particular case, but time has apparently had no undermining influence upon the guiding principles initially set forth in *Jones v. Stevens,* [112 Ohio St. 43 (1925),] where the court held at paragraph two of the syllabus:

> Where the parties have agreed on the amount of damages, ascertained by estimation and adjustment, and have expressed this agreement in clear and unambiguous terms, the amount so fixed should be treated as liquidated damages and not as a penalty, if the damages would be (1) uncertain as to amount and difficult of proof, and if (2) the contract as a whole is not so manifestly unconscionable,

unreasonable, and disproportionate in amount as to justify the conclusion that it does not express the true intention of the parties, and if (3) the contract is consistent with the conclusion that it was the intention of the parties that damages in the amount stated should follow the breach thereof.

With reference to the initial test suggested in *Jones,* the court of appeals expressly noted that "the damages here are patently estimable," and this finding is attuned to the indisputable fact that the damages in this case would be as readily ascertainable as the damages in a multitude of other conceivable situations involving negligence and/or breach of contract. As to the second guideline recommended by this court, the stated sum of $50 in the contract involved in this case is manifestly disproportionate to either the consideration paid by Samson or the possible damage that reasonably could be foreseen from the failure of Honeywell to notify the police of the burglary. And with particular emphasis upon the third condition proposed in *Jones,* it is beyond comprehension that the parties intended that damages in the amount of $50 should follow the negligent breach of the contract.

In other words, an examination of the minute type used in the standard contract issued by Morse, as well as a fair construction of the contract provision as a whole, fails to evince a conscious intention of the parties to consider, estimate, or adjust the damages that might reasonably flow from the negligent breach of the agreement. Surely, Samson, which apparently had some business experience, did not pay $10,500 for the mere possibility of recouping $50 if Honeywell provided no service at all under the terms of the contract. Characteristically, therefore, and by way of analysis, the nominal amount set forth in the contract between Samson and Honeywell has the nature and appearance of a penalty.

Accordingly, the judgment of the court of appeals is affirmed.

NOTES AND QUESTIONS

1. *What happened?* Who sued whom for what? Procedurally, how did the case get before this court? Factually, what happened between the parties? What arguments did the plaintiff and defendant make? What rule or rules did the court apply? How did the court analyze the dispute between the parties? How did the court decide the case?

2. *Was this case correctly decided?* Do you agree with the result reached in this case? Why or why not? Do you agree with the court's reasoning? Why or why not? How, if at all, would you have written the opinion differently?

3. *Policy justification.* Can you think of any policy justifications as to why over- and underliquidated remedies should be treated differently? If not, should the rule change? If so, what rule should apply? Why?

PROBLEM: SILENCE AT THE BAR MITZVAH

Plaintiff and defendant James Haber entered into a contract pursuant to which plaintiff agreed to provide a designated 16-piece band on a specified date to perform at Mr. Haber's son's bar mitzvah. Mr. Haber was to pay approximately $30,000 for the band's services. The contract contained a liquidated damages clause stating, in pertinent part,

> If [the contract] is terminated in writing by [Mr. Haber] for any reason within ninety (90) days prior to the engagement, the remaining balance of the contract will be immediately due and payable. If [the contract] is terminated in writing by [Mr. Haber] for any reason before the ninety (90) days period, 50% of the balance will be immediately due and payable.

Less than 90 days prior to the date of the bar mitzvah, Mr. Haber sent a letter to plaintiff notifying it that he was cancelling the contract. After Mr. Haber refused plaintiff's demand that he pay the remaining amount due under the contract—approximately $25,000—plaintiff commenced this action against Mr. Haber and his wife, defendant Jill Haber.

Should the liquidated damages clause be enforced, or is it unenforceable as a penalty clause?

PROBLEM: SUMMER CAMP

Pacheco had sent his son to Camp Wekeela, a summer camp owned and operated by the Scoblionkos in Canton for several years. In 1985, Pacheco paid a full camp fee of $3,100 prior to February 1, 1985. This early payment allowed Pacheco to receive a discount on the regular camp fee, the amount of which is not specified in the record. The contract Pacheco signed in registering his son with the camp was on a pre-printed form. In one clause of the contract it was specified that if notice of a camper's withdrawal was received after May 1, 1985, the amount paid to the camp up to the time of the receipt of the notice would be retained by the camp.

On June 14, Pacheco was informed that because his son, a high school student, had failed his final exam in Spanish, he would be required to attend summer school. That same day, Pacheco telephoned Eric Scoblionko, informing him that his son would be unable to attend camp and asking for the return of the fees paid to the camp. Scoblionko refused to refund any portion of the $3,100, and Pacheco brought suit seeking the return of the deposit.

As the judge assigned to this case, how would you rule, and why? Is this clause a valid liquidated damages clause or an unenforceable penalty? Are there any additional facts you would like to know before reaching your decision?

2. Limiting Damages

Note that the issues raised in the next case, like *Samson*, are sometimes treated as *liquidated damages* provisions, in which case the rules discussed in *Samson* apply. But sometimes they are also treated as *limitation of liability* clauses, in which case the analysis is altered, as demonstrated in the case below. As you read it, ask yourself whether such a distinction can be maintained. If not, how should such cases be policed?

Wedner v. Fidelity Security Systems, Inc.

Superior Court of Pennsylvania
307 A.2d 429 (1973)

WATKINS, JUDGE, in support of affirmance. This is an appeal from the judgment of the [trial court] entered after a non-jury trial on a burglar alarm system contract, in the amount of $312.00 in favor of Charles Wedner, doing business as Wedner Furs, the appellant, and against Fidelity Security Systems, Inc., the appellee.

This action involved a contract for a burglar alarm system. There was a burglary involving the loss of $46,180.00 in furs. It was . . . tried by Judge McLean without a jury and although he found the contract had been negligently breached, the appellant was only entitled to liquidated damages in the amount of $312.00 by the terms of the contract. Exceptions were filed and the Court En Banc by a majority vote dismissed the exceptions. This appeal followed.

The appellant suffered a loss of $46,180.00 due to the appellee's wrongful failure to perform under a burglary protection service contract, but because of a contract provision he was allowed recovery of only $312.00. The contract provided that the appellee, FEPS, was not to be liable for any loss or damages to the goods of the appellant and then continued:

> If there shall, notwithstanding the above provisions, at any time arise any liability on the part of FEPS by virtue of this agreement, whether due to the negligence of FEPS or otherwise, such liability is and shall be limited to a sum equal in amount to the yearly service charge hereunder, which sum shall be paid and received by the Subscriber as liquidated damages.

The appellant contends that this is an unreasonable forecast of the probable damages resulting from a breach of the contract.

The court below treated the matter as one of liquidated damages and said:

> In his decision the trial judge pointed out, and the parties agree, that there is a well settled general principle that courts will not give effect to a provision in a contract which is a penalty, but will give effect to a provision in a contract which is deemed a liquidated damages provision. The trial judge further noted that deciding which is which can be difficult. In the absence of any Pennsylvania cases making the determination in the context of a contract for burglary alarm protection, the trial judge determined that the instant provision was one for liquidated damages, rather than a penalty.

However, although he ably supported his judgment on the theory of liquidated damages, he did not have to decide the matter on the premise alone.

Much reliance is placed upon the *Restatement of Contracts* § 339, but the appellant disregards Comment [g], which provides:

> An agreement limiting the amount of damages recoverable for breach is not an agreement to pay either liquidated damages or a penalty. Except in the case of certain public service contracts, the contracting parties can by agreement limit their liability in damages to a specified amount, either at the time of making their principal contract, or subsequently thereto. Such a contract, or subsequent thereto, does not purport to make an estimate of the harm caused by a breach; nor is its purpose to operate in terrorem to induce performance.

It can hardly be contended that the words "liability is and shall be limited" to the yearly service charge of $312 are anything but a limitation of liability and not really a liquidated damage clause. Surely, if the loss to the customer was $150, the expressed mutual assent was that recovery should be $150 and not $312.

The fact that the words "liquidated damages" were used in the contract has little bearing on the nature of the provision. It is well settled that in determining whether a particular clause calls for liquidated damages or for a penalty, the name given to the clause by the parties "is but of slight weight, and the controlling elements are the intention of the parties and the special circumstances of the case." *Laughlin v. Baltalden, Inc.*, 191 Pa. Super. 611, 617 (1960). The same principle applies here. Nor can it be argued that the use of these words automatically creates an ambiguity to be resolved against the appellee as the drafter of the instrument. The meaning of the words is clear—the fixed limit of liability was $312. We are, therefore, not dealing with a liquidated damage problem.

The real question is whether any reason exists why the limitation on liability should not be given effect. There is no doubt as to its legality as between ordinary business men. "The *validity* of a contractual provision which exculpates a person from liability for his own acts of negligence is well settled if the contract is between persons relating entirely to their own private affairs." *Dilks v. Flohr Chevrolet*, 411 Pa. 425, 433 (1963). That was the common law rule and is illustrated by *Bechtold v. Murray Ohio Mfg. Co.*, 321 Pa. 423, 428-29 (1936), where the court stated:

> It is not suggested that the transaction is affected by fraud or mistake. The parties agree that they said what they meant. Both parties and their counsel participated in stating the terms of the contract. The seller says that it was performed, but, if it has not done so in the respect complained of, the buyer has agreed that he shall have no right to recover damages.

In accord is the *Restatement of Contracts* §§ 574, 575. It is also the rule with respect to the sale of goods under [UCC § 2-719(3)], which provides:

> Consequential damages may be limited or excluded unless the limitation or exclusion is unconscionable. Limitation of consequential damages for injury to

> the person in the case of consumer goods is prima facie unconscionable but limitation of damages where the loss is commercial is not.

The common law exception as to public utilities has been expanded to some extent by *Thomas v. First Nat. Bank of Scranton*, 376 Pa. 181, 185-86 (1954), where the court concluded:

> Banks, like common carriers, utility companies, etc., perform an important public service. The United States Government and the Commonwealth respectively stipulate how banks under their respective jurisdictions shall be incorporated and organized. All banks are examined and supervised by government or state officers with extreme particularity. The United States insures deposits in banks up to a stipulated amount. If a person desires to deposit money in a bank, necessarily, he is relegated to a governmental or state regulated banking institution. The situation of a depositor is quite analogous to that of a passenger on a public carrier who is required to accept such means of transportation and to purchase a ticket in the nature of a contract. This Court has consistently decided that it is against public policy to permit a common carrier to limit its liability for its own negligence.

In this case, however, we have a private arrangement between two firms without the attendant state regulation that exists with banks and public utilities. The appellant had a choice as to how to protect his property, and whether or not he should obtain insurance. Although protection against burglary is becoming increasingly important, we believe that it has not yet reached the level of necessity comparable to that of banking and other public services.

Nor do we consider this a case of an unconscionable provision, assuming that unconscionability is applicable by adoption of the prevailing rule with respect to the sale of goods. Even under the foregoing reference to the Uniform Commercial Code the limitation of liability under the facts of the case is prima facie conscionable. Furthermore, there is this significant fact pointed out in the opinion of the trial judge:

> In our case both plaintiff and defendant are experienced, established business persons. Additionally, plaintiff had for some 20 years prior to the instant contract had a similar type protection service with similar type clause, with a competitor of defendant.

Thus in this respect the case is comparable to *K & C, Inc. v. Westinghouse Elec. Corp.*, 437 Pa. 303, 308 (1970), where the court concluded that "it is clear that the exclusion was not unconscionable here, where the buyer was hardly the sheep keeping company with wolves that it would have us believe."

I would affirm the judgment of the court below.

CERCONE, JUDGE, in support of reversal. . . . Neither the court below nor any of the parties to this action at any time prior to oral argument before this court regarded the provision in question as other than what the parties expressed it to be, to-wit: a "liquidated damages" clause. The affirming opinion, however, views the language differently than did the lower court and the parties and refers to it as a "limitation of liability" clause. It apparently views a "limitation of liability" clause as more binding than a "liquidated damages" clause under the circumstances. I cannot agree. If the parties can escape their contractual provisions for liquidated damages because the amount stated is unreasonably disproportionate (either higher or lower) to the actual damages involved, there is no logical reason why the same test of reasonableness should not apply to a contractual limitation of liability. I would hold therefore, that a contractual Limitation, as well as a contractual Liquidation of damages, is not binding where unreasonable and bearing no relation to the loss that would result from defendant's failure to fulfill the terms of its contract. The limitation in this case "to a sum equal in amount to the yearly service charge hereunder" was clearly unreasonable and arbitrary, bearing no relationship whatever to the damages flowing from defendant's breach. In my opinion this provision, whether viewed as one of liquidated damages or as a limitation of damages, should not be enforced.

[UCC § 2-718], which by its expressed title "Liquidation or Limitation of Damages" necessarily refers to limitation as well as liquidation of damages, provides:

> (1) Damages for breach by either party may be liquidated in the agreement but only at an amount which is reasonable in the light of the anticipated or actual harm caused by the breach, the difficulties of proof of loss, and the inconvenience or nonfeasibility of otherwise obtaining an adequate remedy. A term fixing unreasonably large liquidated damages is void as a penalty.

The Uniform Commercial Code comment to that subsection 1 is:

> A term fixing unreasonably large liquidated damages is expressly made void as a penalty. An unreasonably small amount would be subject to similar criticism and might be stricken under the section on unconscionable contracts or clauses.

[UCC § 2-719], is entitled "Contractual Modification or Limitation of Remedy" and subsection 1 of that section states that

> Subject to the provisions . . . of the preceding section on liquidation and limitation of damages, (a) the agreement . . . may limit or alter the measure of damages recoverable under this Article . . .

The official comment to that section is:

> 1. Under this section parties are left free to shape their remedies to their particular requirements and Reasonable agreements Limiting or modifying remedies are to be given effect.
>
> However, it is of the very essence of a sales contract that at least minimum adequate remedies be available. If the parties intend to conclude a contract for sale within this Article they must accept the legal consequence that there be at least a fair quantum of remedy for breach of the obligations or duties outlined in the contract. Thus any clause purporting to modify or limit the remedial provisions of this Article in an unconscionable manner is subject to deletion and in that event the remedies made available by this Article are applicable as if the

stricken clause had never existed. Similarly, under subsection (2), where an apparently fair and reasonable clause because of circumstances fails in its purpose or operates to deprive either party of the substantial value of the bargain, it must give way to the general remedy provisions of this Article.

The clause here in question (whether viewed as a liquidated damages clause or a limitation of damages clause) unreasonably limits plaintiff's recovery to a return of the service charge and deprives plaintiff of the bargain of his contract. As construed in the affirming opinion, the clause in effect works a rescission of the contract, completely freeing defendant from proper performance of its terms and requiring only a return of the service charge when defendant has failed to properly perform thereunder. The contract thus becomes, in effect, an illusory one with defendant not being bound to perform and plaintiff not being entitled to performance by defendant. By limiting plaintiff's remedy upon defendant's breach to a return of the service charge, the defendant is permitted to effectuate a cancellation of its duties to perform under the contract, leaving plaintiff without the bargained-for performance and without any reasonable compensation for defendant's failure to perform as contracted.

It is my opinion, therefore, that the clause in question is unreasonable and unconscionable and should not be enforced.

I therefore respectfully, but vigorously, dissent from the affirming opinion in this case.

RELEVANT PROVISIONS

For the UCC, consult §§ 2-718 and 2-719.

NOTES AND QUESTIONS

1. ***What happened?*** Who sued whom for what? Procedurally, how did the case get before this court? Factually, what happened between the parties? What arguments did the plaintiff and defendant make? What rule or rules did the court apply? How did the court analyze the dispute between the parties? How did the court decide the case?

2. ***Was this case correctly decided?*** Do you agree with the result reached in this case? Why or why not? Do you agree with the court's reasoning? Why or why not? How, if at all, would you have written the opinion differently?

3. ***Who has the better argument?*** Who has the better argument, the majority or the dissent? Do you think limitation of liability clauses should be treated the same was as liquidated damages clauses? Why or why not?

4. ***Reconciling the cases.*** Which approach do you agree with, this court or the court's opinion in *Samson Sales, Inc. v. Honeywell, Inc.*?

3. Punitive Damages

Allapattah Services, Inc. v. Exxon Corporation

United States District Court, Southern District of Florida
61 F. Supp. 2d 1326 (1999)

GOLD, DISTRICT JUDGE. This cause is before the Court upon Plaintiffs' Motion for Leave to Assert Claim for Punitive Damages Against Defendant Exxon Corporation. Plaintiffs seek to recover punitive damages, alleging that Exxon tortiously and oppressively breached its contracts with Plaintiffs, substantiating punitive relief which is purportedly available under the laws of twenty-three of the thirty-six jurisdictions implicated in this diversity action. Having carefully considered the arguments of the parties, the relevant portions of the record and prior positions asserted by Plaintiffs, and having reviewed and applied the relevant law, the Court concludes that punitive damages are not appropriate or timely under the circumstances giving rise to Plaintiffs' claims, and therefore, should be denied.

Although Plaintiffs acknowledge that damages for breaches of a contract are generally limited to those that equate to the benefit of the bargain intended to be realized under the terms of the contract, or, in other words, that which the non-breaching party would have received had the contract been performed, Plaintiffs argue that the majority of the states' laws applicable to many of the Plaintiffs' contract claims recognize a more liberal standard, leaning toward awards of punitive damages on breaches of contractual obligations. In support of their argument, Plaintiffs cited to several cases which are distinguishable from the facts underlying the case before the Court. Significantly, rather than relying on cases involving contractual claims predicated on Article 2 of the Uniform Commercial Code, which Plaintiffs have repeatedly contended is the applicable law, Plaintiffs rely on the Restatement (Second) on Contracts to support their demand for punitive damages.

Exxon opposes Plaintiffs' attempt to interject punitive elements in the absence of any tort claims. Additionally, Exxon argues that Plaintiffs should be precluded from adding a claim for punitive damages so close to trial, because not giving Exxon a corresponding benefit of conducting necessary discovery thereon would severely prejudice Exxon in its defense of such a claim. Exxon points out that the various jurisdictions apply differing standards of proof, which will likely require numerous separate trials and individualized jury instructions, undermining the propriety of class certification.

A. GENERAL CONTRACT PRINCIPLES REGARDING PUNITIVE DAMAGES

The underlying purpose of damages in actions premised on a breach of contract is to place the non-breaching party in the same position it would have occupied if the contract had not been breached. *See Mortgage Finance, Inc. v. Podleski*, 742 P.2d 900, 902 (Colo. 1987) (breach of contract remedies serve only to provide compensation for loss, not to punish the wrongdoer). Recognizing this central purpose, courts have uniformly rejected requests for punitive damages for mere breach of contract, regardless of the breaching party's conduct or motives. *See id.* Thus, well established principles of contract law dictate that punitive damages are generally not available for a breach of contract claim unless the defendant's conduct in breaching the contract also violated a non-contractual legal duty, thereby constituting a tort. *See Restatement (Second) of Contracts* § 355 (1981).[1] Even under the common law, tort remedies are not awarded in a contract dispute absent conduct which separately and independently substantiates the commission of a tort. *See id.; see also Vanwyk Textile Sys., B.V. v. Zimmer Machinery America, Inc.*, 994 F. Supp. 350, 362 (W.D.N.C. 1997) ("To state a claim in tort, a plaintiff must allege a duty owed him by the defendant separate and distinct from any duty owed under a contract."). "Whether an action is characterized as one in tort or on contract is determined by the nature of the complaint, not by the form of the pleadings, and consideration must be given to the facts which constitute the cause of action." *Thomas v. Countryside of Hastings, Inc.*, 524 N.W.2d 311, 313 (1994).

Notably, the breach of a duty is an element in both contractual and tort causes of action. *See Splitt v. Deltona Corp.*, 662 F.2d 1142, 1145 (5th Cir. 1981). The distinction is that "duties involved in [tort actions] are raised by law and social policy and owed to an entire class of persons . . . [while] [c]ontractual duties are created by the contract terms and [are] owed to the parties thereto." *Id.*

Not only are intentional breaches exempt from punitive claims, they are sometimes encouraged. "The law has long recognized the view that a contracting party has the option to breach a contract and pay damages if it is more efficient to do so." *L.L. Cole & Son, Inc. v. Hickman*, 665 S.W.2d 278, 280 (1984) (citing Holmes, "The Path of the Law" in *Collected Legal Papers* 167, 175 (1920)).[2] **The logical result of this theory is a "limitation of breach of contract damage exposure to losses contemplated by the contracting parties, and for which a defendant 'at least tacitly agreed to assume responsibility.'"** *Delta Rice Mill, Inc. v. General Foods Corp.*, 763 F.2d 1001, 1006 (8th Cir. 1985) (quoting *Morrow v. First Nat'l Bank of Hot Springs*, 550 S.W.2d 429, 430 (1977)).

Tacit agreement test

Recall that we discussed the "tacit agreement" test in the notes after *Hadley v. Baxendale* earlier in this chapter. *See* Subsection A.4.a.

---

1. The Restatement specifically provides that: "Punitive damages are not recoverable for a breach of contract unless the conduct constituting the breach is also a tort for which punitive damages are recoverable." *Restatement (Second) of Contracts* § 355. As commentary, the restatement expresses that "the purposes of awarding contract damages is to compensate the injured party." *Id.* § 355, cmt. a. It goes on to reiterate that "the purpose of awarding damages is still compensation and not punishment, and punitive damages are not appropriate. In exceptional instances, departures have been made from this general policy . . . notably in situations involving consumer transactions or arising under insurance policies." *Id.*

2. Justice Homes articulated that "[t]he duty to keep a contract at common law means a prediction that you must pay damages if you do not keep it—and nothing else."

This acceptance of intentional, efficient breaches has been uniformly adopted among the jurisdictions. *See, e.g., Thyssen, Inc. v. SS Fortune Star*, 777 F.2d 57, 63 (2d Cir. 1985) ("Breaches of contract that are in fact efficient and wealth-enhancing should be encouraged, and . . . such 'efficient breaches' occur when the breaching party will still profit after compensating the other party for its 'expectation interest.' The addition of punitive damages to traditional contract remedies would prevent many such beneficial actions from being taken."); *Reiver v. Murdoch & Walsh, P.A.*, 625 F. Supp. 998, 1015 (D. Del. 1985) ("some breaches may be intentional and . . . efficient [ ] when the payment of damages would be less costly than performance . . . that fact alone does not entitle a plaintiff to seek punitive damages unless the intentional breach is similar in character to an intentional tort."); *Harris v. Atlantic Richfield Co.*, 17 Cal. Rptr. 2d 649, 653 (1993) ("The traditional goal of contract remedies is compen sation of the promisee for the loss resulting from the breach, not compulsion of the promisor to perform his promises." Therefore, "willful" breaches have not been distinguished from other breaches. The restrictions on contract remedies serve purposes not found in tort law. They protect the parties' freedom to bargain over special risks and they promote contract formation by limiting liability to the value of the promise. This encourages efficient breaches, resulting in "increased production of goods and services at lower cost to society.") (internal citations omitted); *Kutzin v. Pirnie*, 591 A.2d 932, 941 (1991) ("The approach that we adopt is suggested to have the added benefit of promoting economic efficiency: penalties deter 'efficient' breaches of contract 'by making the cost of the breach to the contract breaker greater than the cost of the breach to the victim.'") (quoting Posner, *Economic Analysis of Law* § 4.10 (3d ed. 1986)).

In sum, in the normal commercial situation, damages for breach of contract are limited to the pecuniary loss sustained, since the damage is usually financial, susceptible of accurate estimation, and the wrong suffered by the plaintiff is the same, regardless of the defendant's motive. Although this is the general rule, courts have, nevertheless carved out exceptions, which are not applicable to the instant contractual dispute.[3]

B. PUNITIVE DAMAGES UNDER THE UCC

For the sale of goods, remedies for breach of contract are addressed in UCC § 1-106, which provides:

> The remedies provided by the Act shall be liberally administered to the end that the aggrieved party may be put in as good a position as if the other party had

3. For instance, courts have most commonly awarded tort damages for a breach of the duty of good faith in cases involving first-party and third-party insurance claims. Many courts have fashioned a tort of bad faith in certain narrowly defined situations, such as when a liability insurer violates its duty to defend its insured or to settle a claim within the policy limits. Plaintiffs' survey of state law cites to several cases involving bad faith breach of contract claims derived from a obligations under insurance policies. Several states have enacted statutes providing punitive relief for an insurer's bad faith.

> fully performed but *neither consequential or special nor penal damages may be had except as specifically provided in this Act or by other rule of law.*

UCC § 106(1) (emphasis added). While consistently relying on UCC principles of law throughout this litigation, Plaintiffs now seek to utilize the common contract laws of the various states to obtain punitive relief. Since various states permit recovery of punitive damages for independently tortious conduct, Plaintiffs argue that Exxon's intentional and willful breach of its good faith obligation supports a claim for punitive damages. In essence, Plaintiffs aver that Exxon's willful breach of the covenant of good faith, implied in contracts governed by the UCC, constitutes an independent tort for which punitive damages are recoverable. The Court does not agree with Plaintiffs' assessment of the law.

As articulated in prior orders of this Court, the Uniform Commercial Code (the "UCC") imposes a duty of good faith and fair dealing on all contracts governed thereunder. *See* UCC § 1-203 ("Every contract or duty within this Act imposes an obligation of good faith in its performance and enforcement."). Every state in the union, except Louisiana, which has codified a good faith obligation similar to that imposed by the UCC, has enacted statutes adopting the UCC. However, Plaintiffs have not called attention to, nor can the Court find, a provision of the UCC that specifically permits punitive damages in circumstances similar to the instant case.

Case law interpreting the UCC in the context of the **implied duty of good faith performance** expressly discounts Plaintiffs' argument that a breach of a contractual covenant of good faith can be treated as an independent tort. The Official Comment to § 1-203 disclaims any provision of an additional cause of action for failure to act in good faith. *See* UCC § 1-203, cmt. ("This section does not support an independent cause of action for failure to perform in good faith."); *see also Duquesne Light Co. v. Westinghouse Elec. Corp.*, 66 F.3d 604, 617 (3d Cir. 1995) (good faith is an interpretive tool to determine the parties' justified expectations, and is not to be used for enforcement of "an independent duty divorced from the specific clauses of the contract.").

Implied duty of good faith

We will discuss the implied duty of good faith in greater detail in Chapter 6.

Thus, the UCC itself does not allow punishment for bad faith conduct that breaches the covenant of good faith, thereby breaching the underlying contract. Absent an independent tort, which Plaintiffs have not identified, punitive damages under the UCC are not available, unless Plaintiffs otherwise demonstrate that they would be allowed "by other rule of law." UCC § 1-106.

C. PUNITIVE DAMAGES FOR BREACH OF CONTRACT UNDER STATE COMMON LAW

Plaintiffs have also consistently relied on the UCC to support their position that class certification "is superior to other available methods for the fair and efficient adjudication of this controversy because it will avoid multiplicity of litigation and will enhance judicial economy." First Amended Complaint, at ¶ 118. Nevertheless, they now seek to invoke the common law principles of various states to bolster an argument that Exxon's conduct rose to the level warranting punitive damages.

While Plaintiffs correctly point out that various states permit punitive damages when a breach of contract is also found to constitute independently tortious conduct, the variety of approaches to punitive damages among the states indicates less consensus than Plaintiffs admit. *See, e.g., Feinstein v. Firestone Tire & Rubber Co.*, 535 F.Supp. 595, 605 n.14 (S.D.N.Y. 1982) (noting that "the doctrine of punitive damages takes different forms, and requires different showings, in different states."). Notwithstanding some jurisdictional variation, the state laws still preclude punitive damages absent an affirmative showing of the commission of a tort independent of any obligation under the contract. *See, e.g., Atchison Casting Corp. v. Dofasco, Inc.*, 889 F. Supp. 1445, 1461 (D. Kan. 1995) ("The general rule in Kansas and elsewhere is that the existence of a contract relationship bars the assertion of tort claims covering the same subject matter governed by the contract."); *Foreign Mission Bd. v. Wade*, 409 S.E.2d 144, 148 (1991) (a tort claim arising out of a contractual agreement may only stand as an independent claim where "the duty tortiously or negligently breached [is] a common law duty, not one existing between the parties solely by virtue of the contract."); *Kamlar Corp. v. Haley*, 299 S.E.2d 514, 518 (1983) (punitive damages in an action for breach of contract are only appropriate where there is "proof of an independent, wilful tort, beyond the mere breach of a duty imposed by contract."). The purpose of the independent tort exception to the rule barring punitive damages in contract cases is to separate mere wilful breaches of contract, which require no more than an unwilling breach to make the plaintiff whole, and other wanton or malicious acts that cause a distinct injury and merit the deterrent of punitive damages. *See Hardin, Rodriguez & Boivin Anesthesiologists, Ltd. v. Paradigm*, 962 F.2d 628, 639 (7th Cir. 1992). Thus, a general rule allowing tort damages whenever a court perceives some amorphous quality such as "bad faith" invites uncertainty and inhibits commerce without a counterbalancing economic benefit. *See id.*

An overview of state law, on which Plaintiffs rely to addend their claim for punitive damages convinces the Court that Plaintiffs cannot be awarded punitive damages for Exxon's alleged breach of its Sales Agreement with its dealers. . . .

It is clear that, based on the UCC, as well as the common law of the various states, a breach of the implied covenant of good faith, no matter the degree of intent involved, is not a tort independent of the obligations required by the contract.[6] . . .

---

6. *See Chambers v. NASCO, Inc.*, 501 U.S. 32, 54 (1991) (Louisiana law does not permit punitive damages for breach of contract, "even when a party has acted in bad faith in breaching the agreement"); *Kahal v. J.W. Wilson & Assoc., Inc.*, 673 F.2d 547, 548 (D.C. Cir. 1982) (punitive damages were not recoverable simply because the defendant breached a contract in bad faith); *Davis Cattle Co. v. Great Western Sugar Co.*, 393 F. Supp. 1165, 1181 (D. Colo. 1975) (punitive damages were unavailable to a plaintiff's claims that the defendant breached an implied contractual duty to deal in good faith in determining the highest practicable price to be paid for sugar beets); *Barry v. Posi-Seal Intern., Inc.*, 672 A.2d 514, 519 (1996) (punitive damages were not available for a breach premised on the implied covenant of good faith).

In the typical contract case, such as the one before the Court, "punitive damages are inappropriate and counter-productive" in light of contract law favoring the reliance on promises freely negotiated. *See Ennen v. Public Service Mut. Ins. Co.*, 774 F.2d 321, 326 (8th Cir. 1985) (citation omitted). The use of punitive damages as legal compulsion to perform contractual obligations "would tend to substitute the coercive power of the courts for the freedom of the marketplace." *Id.* Such an undesirable result was not contemplated by the UCC and shall not be adopted by this Court. Moreover, because the Court finds that, should they prevail, Plaintiffs will be adequately compensated by a damage award representing their expectation interest provided under traditional contract law, Plaintiffs cannot recover punitive damages.

Accordingly, it is

Ordered and adjudged that Plaintiffs' Motion for Leave to Assert Claim for Punitive Damages Against Defendant Exxon Corporation is denied.

RELEVANT PROVISIONS

For the *Restatement (Second) of Contracts*, consult §§ 355 and 356. For the UCC, consult § 2-718(1). For the UNIDROIT Principles, consult Article 7.4.13.

NOTES AND QUESTIONS

1. *What happened?* Who sued whom for what? Procedurally, how did the case get before this court? Factually, what happened between the parties? What arguments did the plaintiff and defendant make? What rule or rules did the court apply? How did the court analyze the dispute between the parties? How did the court decide the case?

2. *Was this case correctly decided?* Do you agree with the result reached in this case? Why or why not? Do you agree with the court's reasoning? Why or why not? How, if at all, would you have written the opinion differently?

3. *Policy justification.* Do you agree that punitive damages should generally not be recoverable for breach of contract? Why or why not? Ought there to be any exceptions to this general rule? If so, which ones, and why?

4. *Comparative analysis.* How does the traditional rule compare to the rule under the UNIDROIT Principles? Drawing on any thinking tools we have previously examined, which rule seems best? Why?

CHAPTER 6

INTERPRETATION

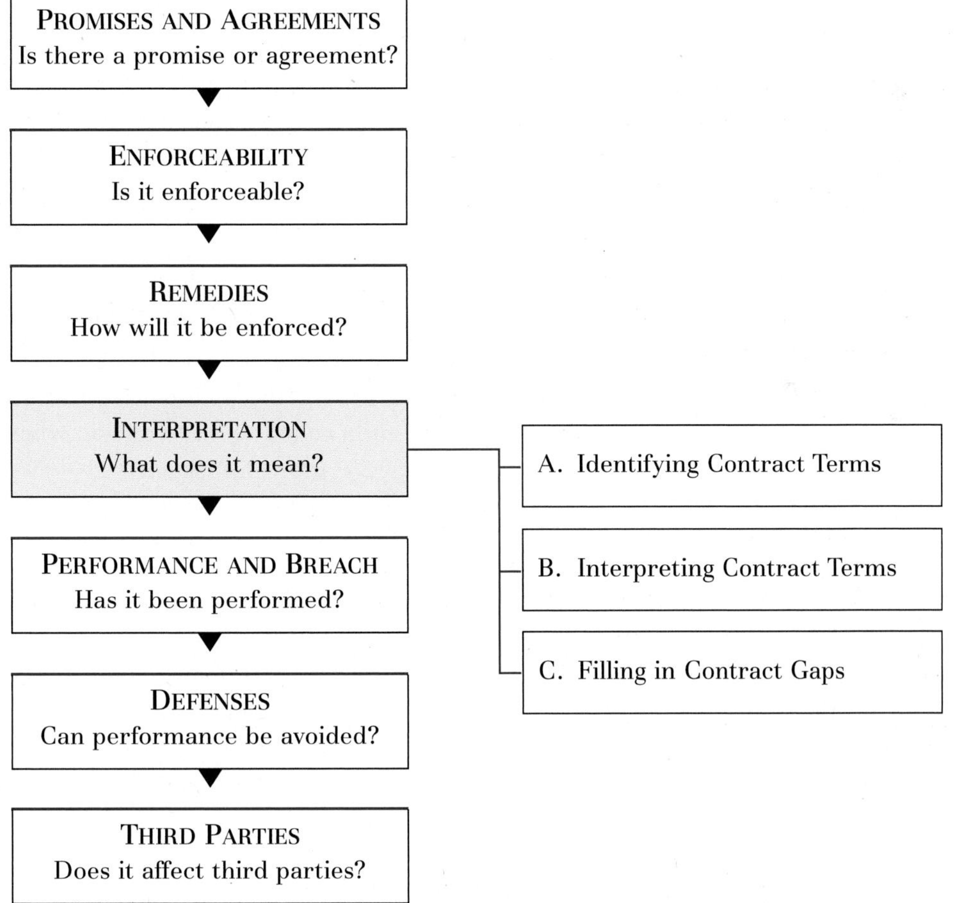

PROMISES AND AGREEMENTS
Is there a promise or agreement?
ENFORCEABILITY
Is it enforceable?
REMEDIES
How will it be enforced?
INTERPRETATION
What does it mean?
PERFORMANCE AND BREACH
Has it been performed?
DEFENSES
Can performance be avoided?
THIRD PARTIES
Does it affect third parties?
A. Identifying Contract Terms
B. Interpreting Contract Terms
C. Filling in Contract Gaps

> *Whoever hath an absolute authority to interpret any written or spoken laws, it is he who is truly the Law-giver to all intents and purposes, and not the person who first wrote or spoke them.*
>
> Bishop Benjamin Hoadly to King George I, 1717

In this chapter we will explore the principles of interpretation, seeking to understand how courts and legal practitioners interpret contracts.

Although the term "interpretation," in the context of contract law, is often generally understood as a somewhat vague process whereby courts ascertain the meaning of the words, texts, or actions employed by parties to manifest their assent, there are at least three broad techniques by which such manifestations can be "interpreted" by judges to give meaning to a contract. First, a judge can give meaning to a contract by identifying *which* words, clauses, paragraphs, or actions should be given interpretive weight in the first place, and also by determining *how much* interpretive weight these terms should be given. Second, once the court identifies the language or conduct it deems relevant, the judge must then decide what the language or conduct *means*, and this "meaning" may vary from judge to judge. So, for example, one judge might interpret a word according to its plain and ordinary meaning, whereas another judge might interpret it according to a more specialized, technical meaning; or one judge might give each word and clause in a contract roughly equal weight, whereas another might treat some words and clauses as more important than others; or one judge might believe that only the terms she identified in a written contract should give meaning to the parties' agreement, whereas another judge might believe that these words must be interpreted in light of other facts that did not find their way into the written agreement. Finally, the third broad technique by which a judge may interpret or give meaning to a contract is by filling in the gaps where the parties themselves did not speak. For example, courts are frequently called upon to decide what policies, standards, or rules should be imposed to govern an important issue that the parties themselves failed to foresee, or—if they foresaw it—failed to address in their contract.

The materials in this chapter are organized along these three broad interpretive categories. As you read the cases below, ask yourself which (if any) of the three types of interpretive problems judges are best suited to deal with, and which techniques seem most appropriate for ascertaining the "meaning" of a contract.

A. IDENTIFYING CONTRACT TERMS

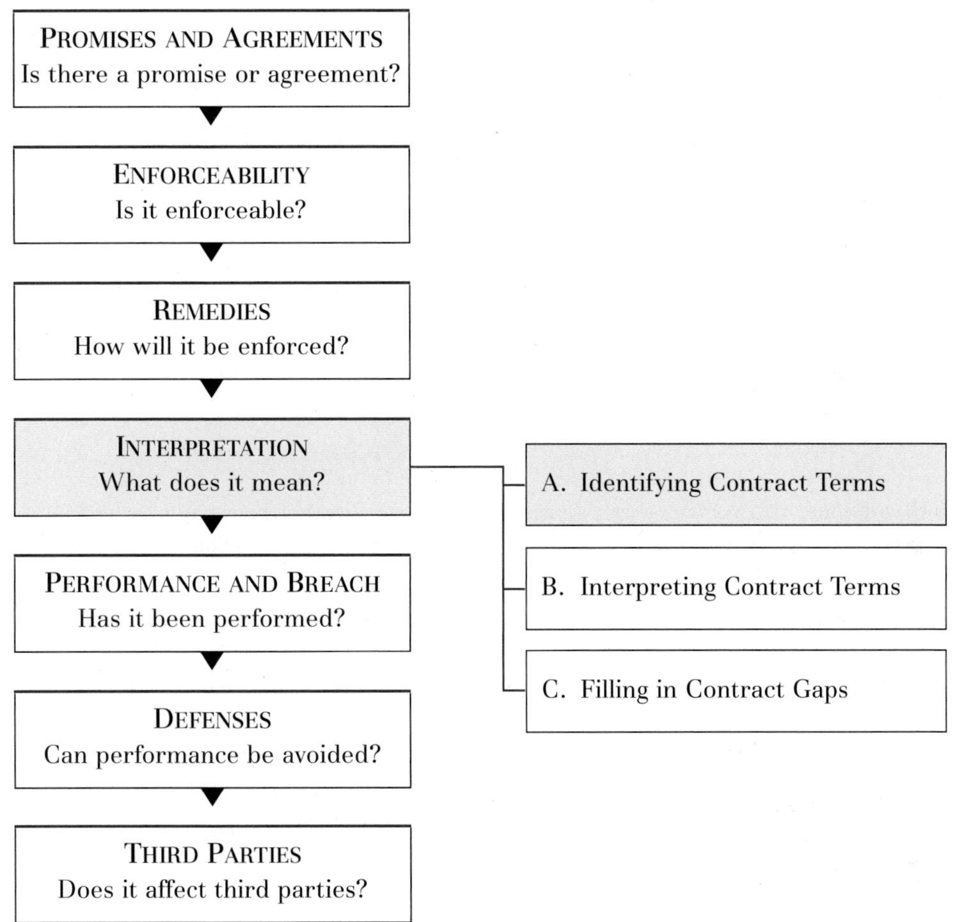
PROMISES AND AGREEMENTS
Is there a promise or agreement?
ENFORCEABILITY
Is it enforceable?
REMEDIES
How will it be enforced?
INTERPRETATION
What does it mean?
PERFORMANCE AND BREACH
Has it been performed?
DEFENSES
Can performance be avoided?
THIRD PARTIES
Does it affect third parties?
A. Identifying Contract Terms
B. Interpreting Contract Terms
C. Filling in Contract Gaps

1. Standardized Contracts

> *Instead of thinking about "assent" to boiler-plate clauses, we can recognize that so far as concerns the specific, there is no assent at all. What has in fact been assented to specifically are the few dickered terms, the broad type of the transaction, and but one thing more. That one thing more is a blanket assent (not a specific assent) to any not unreasonable or indecent terms the seller may have on his form, which do not alter or eviscerate the reasonable meaning of the dickered terms.*
>
> Karl Llewellyn, THE COMMON LAW TRADITION 370 (1960)

Standardized contracts, also called form contracts, boilerplate contracts, or contracts of adhesion, are fill-in-the-blank, pre-negotiated forms offered by one party (often with superior bargaining power) to another party (often with inferior bargaining power) on a take-it-or-leave-it basis. As such, these contracts pose particular problems to the classical conception of contracts, which operates under the presumption that agreements are the result of freely negotiated bargains between consenting parties with roughly equal bargaining power. Courts are frequently called upon to determine not only whether such form contracts are enforceable but, where they are, which of their numerous standardized terms should govern the parties' agreement. These issues become particularly interesting when parties form a contract via an exchange of standardized forms, each with their own pre-printed (and often conflicting) terms. These and other issues will be taken up in the cases and materials below. As you read these materials, ask yourself whether (and under what circumstances) you believe such agreements should be enforceable, and how you would determine which (if any) of the numerous terms appearing in these forms should be found to constitute part of the agreement between the parties.

DOCTRINAL OVERVIEW: STANDARDIZED AGREEMENTS*

Traditional contract law was designed for a paradigmatic agreement that had been reached by two parties of equal bargaining power by a process of free negotiation. Today, however, in routine transactions the typical agreement consists of a standard form containing terms prepared by one party and assented to by the other with little or no opportunity for negotiation. Commonplace examples range from automobile purchase orders and credit card agreements to confirmations for goods ordered over the telephone and license agreements for software acquired online. Sometimes basic terms relating to quality, quantity, and price are negotiable. But the standard terms the standard terms—the *boilerplate*—are not subject to bargain. They must simply be adhered to if the transaction is to go forward.

As with goods, standardization and mass production of contracts may serve the interest of both parties. Since standard forms can be tailored to fit office routines and mechanical equipment, they simplify operations and reduce costs. The product of the skilled drafter becomes available throughout the enterprise and frees sales and office personnel from responsibility for contract terms.

Because a judicial interpretation of one standard form serves as an interpretation of similar forms, standardization facilitates the accumulation of experience. It helps to make risks calculable and, as one scholar put it, "increases that real security which is the necessary basis of initiative and the assumption of tolerable risks."[2]. . .

Dangers are inherent in standardization, however, for it affords a means by which one party may impose terms on another unwitting or even unwilling party. Several circumstances facilitate this imposition. First, the party that proffers the form has had the advantage of time and expert advice in preparing it, almost inevitably producing a form slanted in its favor. Second, the other

---

* Excerpted from E. ALLAN FARNSWORTH, CONTRACTS § 4.26 (4th ed. 2004).

2. Morris Cohen. *The Basis of Contract*, 46 HARV. L. REV. 553, 588 (1933).

party is usually completely or at least relatively unfamiliar with the form and has scant opportunity to read it—an opportunity often diminished by the use of fine print and convoluted clauses. Third, bargaining over terms of the form may not be between equals or, as is more often the case, there may be no possibility of bargaining at all. The form may be used by an enterprise with such disproportionately strong economic power that it simply dictates the terms. Or the form may be a take-it-or-leave-it proposition, often called a *contract of adhesion*, under which the only alternative to complete adherence is oubight rejection.[5] It would, indeed, defeat the purpose of standardization if the other party were free to negotiate over its terms. This impact of the phenomenon of standardization in reducing the possibility of negotiation over terms has prompted one observer to suggest that, in contrast to the "movement *from Status to Contract*" that Sir Heniy Maine detected in 1861,[6] there is now a "distinct veering back to status."[7]

Courts steeped in traditional contract doctrine have not been receptive to the argument that a party should be relieved of an agreement on the grounds of such imposition. A party that signs an agreement is regarded as manifesting assent to it and may not later complain about not having read or understood it, even if the agreement is on the other party's standard form. Since the requirement of bargain under the bargain theory of consideration is plainly met by simple adherence, the doctrine of consideration offers no ground for such relief. And since the objective theory of contracts imposes no requirement that one intend or even understand the legal consequences of one's actions, one is not entitled to relief merely because one neither read the standard form nor considered the legal consequence of adhering to it. As Maryland's highest court put it, "the law presumes that a person knows the contents of a document that he executes and understands at least the literal meaning of its terms."[8] This principle has been applied to standard forms,[9] and it has been adhered to even when the party seeking to be relieved of the agreement is poorly educated or illiterate.[10] Nevertheless, in hard cases, courts have strained to avoid applying this principle and, in doing so, they have developed several techniques. . . .

5. Disproportionately strong economic power is not necessary to the dictation of terms on a take-it-or-leave-it basis, as is illustrated when a large corporation, in order to park its truck, adheres to the terms of a small operator of a parking lot.

6. Henry Maine, Ancient Law 170 (1861).

7. Nathan Isaacs, *The Standardizing of Contracts*, 27 Yale L.J. 34, 40 (1917).

8. Merit Music Serv. v. Sonneborn, 225 A.2d 470, 474 (Md. 1967) (handwritten clauses added to standard form lease signed by tavern owners).

9. Heller Fin. v. Midwhey Powder Co., 883 F.2d 1286 (7th Cir. 1989) (no reason to treat "adhesion contracts or form contracts differently").

10. Mitchell Nissan, Inc. v. Foster, 775 So. 2d 138 (Ala. 2000) (car buyer with "only a sixth-grade reading level" was bound by arbitration clause where he "did not tell a representative of [seller] that he was unable to read or to understand any portion of the contract").

Carnival Cruise Lines v. Shute

United States Supreme Court
499 U.S. 585 (1991)

JUSTICE BLACKMUN delivered the opinion of the court.

In this admiralty case we primarily consider whether the United States Court of Appeals for the Ninth Circuit correctly refused to enforce a forum-selection clause contained in tickets issued by petitioner Carnival Cruise Lines, Inc., to respondents Eulala and Russel Shute.

I

The Shutes, through an Arlington, Wash., travel agent, purchased passage for a 7-day cruise on petitioner's ship, the *Tropicale*. Respondents paid the fare to the agent who forwarded the payment to petitioner's headquarters in Miami, Fla. Petitioner then prepared the tickets and sent them to respondents in the State of Washington. The face of each ticket, at its left-hand lower corner, contained this admonition:

> SUBJECT TO CONDITIONS OF CONTRACT ON LAST PAGES IMPORTANT! PLEASE READ CONTRACT—ON LAST PAGES 1, 2, 3.

The following appeared on "contract page 1" of each ticket:

> TERMS AND CONDITIONS OF PASSAGE CONTRACT TICKET
>
> 3. (a) The acceptance of this ticket by the person or persons named hereon as passengers shall be deemed to be an acceptance and agreement by each of them of all of the terms and conditions of this Passage Contract Ticket. . . .
>
> 8. It is agreed by and between the passenger and the Carrier that all disputes and matters whatsoever arising under, in connection with or incident to this Contract shall be litigated, if at all, in and before a Court located in the State of Florida, U. S. A., to the exclusion of the Courts of any other state or country.

The last quoted paragraph is the forum-selection clause at issue.

II

Respondents boarded the *Tropicale* in Los Angeles, Cal. The ship sailed to Puerto Vallarta, Mexico, and then returned to Los Angeles. While the ship was in international waters off the Mexican coast, respondent Eulala Shute was injured when she slipped on a deck mat during a guided tour of the ship's galley. Respondents filed suit against petitioner in the United States District Court for the Western District of Washington, claiming that Mrs. Shute's injuries had been caused by the negligence of Carnival Cruise Lines and its employees.

Petitioner moved for summary judgment, contending that the forum clause in respondents' tickets required the Shutes to bring their suit against petitioner in a court in the State of Florida. Petitioner contended, alternatively, that the District Court lacked personal jurisdiction over petitioner because petitioner's contacts with the State of Washington were insubstantial. The District Court granted the motion, holding that petitioner's contacts with Washington were constitutionally insufficient to support the exercise of personal jurisdiction.

The Court of Appeals reversed. Reasoning that "but for" petitioner's solicitation of business in Washington, respondents would not have taken the cruise and Mrs. Shute would not have been injured, the court concluded that petitioner had sufficient contacts with Washington to justify the District Court's exercise of personal jurisdiction.

Turning to the forum-selection clause, the Court of Appeals acknowledged that a court concerned with the enforceability of such a clause must begin its analysis with *The Bremen v. Zapata Off-Shore Co.*, 407 U.S. 1 (1972), where this Court held that forum-selection clauses, although not "historically . . . favored," are "prima facie valid." *Id.*, at 9-10. The appellate court concluded that the forum clause should not be enforced because it "was not freely bargained for." As an "independent justification" for refusing to enforce the clause, the Court of Appeals noted that there was evidence in the record to indicate that "the Shutes are physically and financially incapable of pursuing this litigation in Florida" and that the enforcement of the clause would operate to deprive them of their day in court and thereby contravene this Court's holding in *The Bremen*.

We granted certiorari to address the question whether the Court of Appeals was correct in holding that the District Court should hear respondents' tort claim against petitioner. Because we find the forum-selection clause to be dispositive of this question, we need not consider petitioner's constitutional argument as to personal jurisdiction.

III

We begin by noting the boundaries of our inquiry. First, this is a case in admiralty, and federal law governs the enforceability of the forum-selection clause we scrutinize. **Second, we do not address the question whether respondents had sufficient notice of the forum clause before entering the contract for passage. Respondents essentially have conceded that they had notice of the forum-selection provision. . . .**

Within this context, respondents urge that the forum clause should not be enforced because, contrary to this Court's teachings in *The Bremen*, the clause was not the product of negotiation, and enforcement effectively would deprive respondents of their day in court. . . .

Litigation strategy

Ought respondents to have conceded this? Do you think the Shutes had notice of the forum selection clause when they when they first purchased their cruise tickets? Or only after they received their tickets in the mail? If you represented the Shutes, what arguments would you make to the court as to why the forum selection clause should not be enforced? How do you think Carnival Cruise Lines would respond?

IV

In evaluating the reasonableness of the forum clause at issue in this case, we must refine the analysis of *The Bremen* to account for the realities of form

> **Whither bargain?**
>
> Pay careful attention to the reasons the court offers for permitting a party to include a non-bargained-for forum selection clause in a contract. What kind of reasons are these? Are any of them *contractual* reasons? Do you think they justify abandoning the bargain requirement? Why or why not?

passage contracts. **As an initial matter, we do not adopt the Court of Appeals' determination that a nonnegotiated forum-selection clause in a form ticket contract is never enforceable simply because it is not the subject of bargaining. Including a reasonable forum clause in a form contract of this kind well may be permissible for several reasons:** First, a cruise line has a special interest in limiting the fora in which it potentially could be subject to suit. Because a cruise ship typically carries passengers from many locales, it is not unlikely that a mishap on a cruise could subject the cruise line to litigation in several different fora. Additionally, a clause establishing *ex ante* the forum for dispute resolution has the salutary effect of dispelling any confusion about where suits arising from the contract must be brought and defended, sparing litigants the time and expense of pretrial motions to determine the correct forum and conserving judicial resources that otherwise would be devoted to deciding those motions. Finally, it stands to reason that passengers who purchase tickets containing a forum clause like that at issue in this case benefit in the form of reduced fares reflecting the savings that the cruise line enjoys by limiting the fora in which it may be sued. . . .

It bears emphasis that forum-selection clauses contained in form passage contracts are subject to judicial scrutiny for fundamental fairness. In this case, there is no indication that petitioner set Florida as the forum in which disputes were to be resolved as a means of discouraging cruise passengers from pursuing legitimate claims. Any suggestion of such a bad-faith motive is belied by two facts: Petitioner has its principal place of business in Florida, and many of its cruises depart from and return to Florida ports. Similarly, there is no evidence that petitioner obtained respondents' accession to the forum clause by fraud or overreaching. Finally, respondents have conceded that they were given notice of the forum provision and, therefore, presumably retained the option of rejecting the contract with impunity. In the case before us, therefore, we conclude that the Court of Appeals erred in refusing to enforce the forum-selection clause. . . .

The judgment of the Court of Appeals is reversed.

It is so ordered.

JUSTICE STEVENS, with whom JUSTICE MARSHALL joins, dissenting.

The Court prefaces its legal analysis with a factual statement that implies that a purchaser of a Carnival Cruise Lines passenger ticket is fully and fairly notified about the existence of the choice of forum clause in the fine print on the back of the ticket. Even if this implication were accurate, I would disagree with the Court's analysis. But, given the Court's preface, I begin my dissent by noting that only the most meticulous passenger is likely to become aware of the forum-selection provision. I have therefore appended to this opinion a facsimile of the relevant text, using the type size that actually appears in the ticket itself.

A careful reader will find the forum-selection clause in the 8th of the 25 numbered paragraphs.

Of course, many passengers, like the respondents in this case, will not have an opportunity to read paragraph 8 until they have actually purchased their tickets. By this point, the passengers will already have accepted the condition set forth in paragraph 16(a), which provides that "the Carrier shall not be liable to make any refund to passengers in respect of . . . tickets wholly or partly not used by a passenger." Not knowing whether or not that provision is legally enforceable, I assume that the average passenger would accept the risk of having to file suit in Florida in the event of an injury, rather than canceling—without a refund—a planned vacation at the last minute. The fact that the cruise line can reduce its litigation costs, and therefore its liability insurance premiums, by forcing this choice on its passengers does not, in my opinion, suffice to render the provision reasonable. . . .

Exculpatory clauses in passenger tickets have been around for a long time. These clauses are typically the product of disparate bargaining power between the carrier and the passenger, and they undermine the strong public interest in deterring negligent conduct. For these reasons, courts long before the turn of the century consistently held such clauses unenforceable under federal admiralty law. Thus, in a case involving a ticket provision purporting to limit the shipowner's liability for the negligent handling of baggage, this Court wrote:

> It is settled in the courts of the United States that exemptions limiting carriers from responsibility for the negligence of themselves or their servants are both unjust and unreasonable, and will be deemed as wanting in the element of voluntary assent; and, besides, that such conditions are in conflict with public policy. This doctrine was announced so long ago, and has been so frequently reiterated, that it is elementary. . . .

Clauses limiting a carrier's liability or weakening the passenger's right to recover for the negligence of the carrier's employees come in a variety of forms. Complete exemptions from liability for negligence or limitations on the amount of the potential damage recovery, requirements that notice of claims be filed within an unreasonably short period of time, provisions mandating a choice of law that is favorable to the defendant in negligence cases, and forum-selection clauses are all similarly designed to put a thumb on the carrier's side of the scale of justice.[4] Forum-selection clauses in passenger tickets involve the intersection of two strands of traditional contract law that qualify the general rule that courts will enforce the terms of a contract as written. Pursuant to the first strand, courts traditionally have reviewed with heightened scrutiny the terms of contracts of adhesion, form contracts offered on a take-or-leave basis by

4. All these clauses will provide passengers who purchase tickets containing them with a "benefit in the form of reduced fares reflecting the savings that the cruise line enjoys by limiting [its exposure to liability]." Under the Court's reasoning, all these clauses, including a complete waiver of liability, would be enforceable, a result at odds with longstanding jurisprudence.

a party with stronger bargaining power to a party with weaker power. Some commentators have questioned whether contracts of adhesion can justifiably be enforced at all under traditional contract theory because the adhering party generally enters into them without manifesting knowing and voluntary consent to all their terms.

The common law, recognizing that standardized form contracts account for a significant portion of all commercial agreements, has taken a less extreme position and instead subjects terms in contracts of adhesion to scrutiny for reasonableness. Judge J. Skelly Wright set out the state of the law succinctly in *Williams v. Walker-Thomas Furniture Co.*, 350 F.2d 445, 449-450 (1965) (footnotes omitted):

> Ordinarily, one who signs an agreement without full knowledge of its terms might be held to assume the risk that he has entered a one-sided bargain. But when a party of little bargaining power, and hence little real choice, signs a commercially unreasonable contract with little or no knowledge of its terms, it is hardly likely that his consent, or even an objective manifestation of his consent, was ever given to all of the terms. In such a case the usual rule that the terms of the agreement are not to be questioned should be abandoned and the court should consider whether the terms of the contract are so unfair that enforcement should be withheld.

The second doctrinal principle implicated by forum-selection clauses is the traditional rule that "contractual provisions, which seek to limit the place or court in which an action may . . . be brought, are invalid as contrary to public policy." *See* Dougherty, *Validity of Contractual Provision Limiting Place or Court in Which Action May Be Brought*, 31 A.L.R. 4th 404, 409, § 3 (1984). Although adherence to this general rule has declined in recent years, particularly following our decision in *The Bremen v. Zapata Off-Shore Co.*, 407 U.S. 1 (1972), the prevailing rule is still that forum-selection clauses are not enforceable if they were not freely bargained for, create additional expense for one party, or deny one party a remedy. A forum-selection clause in a standardized passenger ticket would clearly have been unenforceable under the common law before our decision in *The Bremen*, and, in my opinion, remains unenforceable under the prevailing rule today. . . .

I respectfully dissent.

RELEVANT PROVISIONS

For the *Restatement (Second) of Contracts*, consult § 211. For the UNIDROIT Principles, consult Articles 2.1.19, 2.1.20, and 2.1.21.

NOTES AND QUESTIONS

1. ***What happened?*** Who sued whom for what? Procedurally, how did the case get before this court? Factually, what happened between the parties? What arguments did the plaintiff and defendant make? What rule or rules did the court apply? How did the court analyze the dispute between the parties? How did the court decide the case?

2. ***Was this case correctly decided?*** Do you agree with the result reached in this case? Why or why not? More specifically, in the "Doctrinal Overview" that appeared before this case, it was noted that sometimes, "in hard cases, courts have strained to avoid" enforcing such standard-form contracts. Do you think the Court should have refused to enforce this particular contract? Why or why not? Do you agree with the court's reasoning? Why or why not? How, if at all, would you have written the opinion differently?

3. ***Policy implications?*** Consider the policy implications of this decision. Do you agree with the majority or dissent, or neither? Next, review the materials below. What policies surround the issue of form contracts? How does it seem they are addressed in various statutes, treaties, and the common law?

STANDARD FORM CONTRACTS*

Standard form contracts probably account for more than ninety-nine percent of all the contracts now made. Most persons have difficulty remembering the last time they contracted other than by standard form; except for casual oral agreements, they probably never have. But if they are active, they contract by standard form several times a day. Parking lot and theater tickets, package receipts, department store charge slips, and gas station credit card purchase slips are all standard form contracts.

Moreover, standard forms have come to dominate more than just routine transactions. For individuals, if not quite yet for corporations, form contracts are in common use for even such important matters as insurance, leases, deeds, mortgages, automobile purchases, and all of the various forms of consumer credit. The contracting still imagined by courts and law teachers as typical, in which both parties participate in choosing the language of their entire agreement, is no longer of much more than historical importance.

The privately made law imposed by standard form has not only engulfed the law of contract; it has become a considerable portion of all the law to which we are subject. If by making law we mean imposing officially enforceable duties or creating or restricting officially enforceable rights, then automobile manufacturers make more warranty law in a day than most legislatures or courts make in a year.

---

* Excerpted from W. David Slawson, *Standard Form Contracts and Democratic Control of Law Making Power*, 84 HARV. L. REV. 529, 529-32 (1971).

The predominance of standard forms is the best evidence of their necessity. They are characteristic of a mass production society and an integral part of it. They provide information and enforce order. A typical automobile insurance policy, for example, informs the policyholder how to conduct himself should he become involved in an accident or other kind of occurrence from which liability of the kind covered may arise. It enforces all or a part of such conduct by the sanction of denying insurance protection unless it is performed. These services are essential, and if they are to be provided at reasonable cost, they must be standardized and mass-produced like other goods and services in an industrial economy. The need for order could, in theory, be fully satisfied by officially drafted rules—by laws in the traditional sense. One of the beliefs by which our society is organized, however, is that at least some lawmaking is better accomplished in a decentralized manner. We therefore prefer that the economy be controlled privately to a large extent, and private control today means control largely by standard form.

Since so much law is made by standard form it is important that it be made democratically—*i.e.*, in accordance with the desires of the immediate parties to the contract. Private law which is made by contract in the traditional sense is democratic because a traditional contract must be the agreement of both parties. Unless a contract is coerced, therefore, the "government" it creates is by its nature "government by and with the consent of the governed." But the overwhelming proportion of standard forms are not democratic because they are not, under any reasonable test, the agreement of the consumer or business recipient to whom they are delivered. Indeed, in the usual case, the consumer never even reads the form, or reads it only after he has become bound by its terms. Even the fastidious few who take the time to read the standard form may be helpless to vary it. The form may be part of an offer which the consumer has no reasonable alternative but to accept.

The prevalence of uncontrollable standard forms also has unfortunate economic results. The effect of mass production and mass merchandising is to make all consumer forms standard, and the combined effect of economics and the present law is to make all standard forms unfair. Mass production and mass merchandising work to make all forms standard because a nonstandard form is characteristically just as expensive for a seller to make and sell as is a nonstandard tangible product. . . .

It would be unrealistic to try to make the law of contract fair and legitimate by insisting that a standard form, to be enforceable, must be an uncoerced, informed agreement. The extreme specialization of function of modern life requires that we contract with each other too frequently to take the time to reach even a mildly complicated agreement every time we do, and the complexity of modern life and modern law combine to demand that even minor agreements usually be complicated. There are other situations, moreover, in which even if we were willing to devote the time, any agreement reached would be without the consent of one of the parties because the other would have possessed the power to dictate the terms without question. . . . The power to contract in this situation is the power of one party to impose whatever terms he likes on the other.

It would be equally unrealistic to confer on courts broad powers to rewrite standard forms. This alternative would destroy the essential order that forms create if courts were permitted to rewrite with a large scope of discretion, or it would replace it by a centrally controlled and inflexible order if their discretion were bounded by narrow rules of law.

PROBLEM: PROBLEM AT THE BANK

When a customer opens a bank account, he or she is frequently required to sign a form contract with a number of pre-printed terms, discussing the bank's fees, etc., along with language allowing the bank to periodically change these terms by giving a 30-day notice to its customers. Suppose that a year after you open an account, your bank decides to (a) resolve all of its disputes via arbitration in which (b) class-action claims are disallowed, and sends its customers notice to this effect. At the same time, buried in fine print, the bank also begins charging its customers a small, monthly "administrative" fee. A few months later, you and several other customers carefully read through your statements and, noticing this new fee, bring a class-action suit against the bank to disallow these charges. The bank, of course, files a motion to dismiss and argues that you and the other members of the class are compelled to arbitrate your dispute.

What result? Does it matter that you and the other customers were given a 30-day notice within which you could reject the bank's new terms?

2. The Battle of the Forms

Where one party makes an offer, and the other party sends a purported acceptance that varies the terms in the offer, is there a contract, and, if so, on what terms? When we discussed the mirror image rule in Chapter 3, we learned that, to be valid, the terms of the acceptance must exactly mirror the terms of the offer; where they do not, the purported "acceptance" is treated as a rejection of the original offer, and a counteroffer on the new terms provided therein, which must themselves be accepted to form a contract. But it is frequently the case that the parties who exchange such forms believe they have a contract, which means that they often follow such defective "acceptances" with performance. Where this happens, it is more difficult for a court to simply find that there is no contract; even if the parties' *words* did not form an express contract, many courts will use the parties' subsequent *conduct* to imply one in fact. But even if a court is inclined to find that the parties formed a contract through their conduct, the question still remains: What terms should govern the parties' agreement? The logical corollary of the mirror image rule is what is sometimes referred to as the "last shot" doctrine: The party who fired the last shot (i.e., the party who made the last offer prior to performance) will have its terms govern the agreement. But this rule has come under harsh criticism over the years; although it is easy to apply, it may sometimes lead to injustices between the parties, and may also provide perverse incentives to parties in the know to fire the last shot prior to the other party's performance. But coming up with a better rule has proven to be quite a challenge.

Indeed, the problems discussed above have only been exacerbated in the Internet age, where individuals are frequently said to "agree" to a contract they may or may not have read by clicking on an "I agree" button before purchasing an item, downloading software, or simply navigating a website's digital content. And, as we saw in *Nguyen v. Barnes & Noble Inc.*, it is even sometimes argued that parties manifest their assent to a website's terms and conditions by simply *using* a website. Are the traditional rules of contract law—and in particular the mirror image rule and last shot doctrine—useful in such situations? Or should a new set of rules be developed to handle such transactions? We will explore these and other issues in the cases and materials below, and will conclude this section by looking at how these cases are handled in the international arena.

DOCTRINAL OVERVIEW: BATTLE OF THE FORMS*

We have seen that traditional contract doctrine requires that the offeree's commitment be one on the terms proposed by the offer with no variation. An attempt to add to or change the terms of the offer turns the offeree's response from an acceptance into a counteroffer and a rejection of the offer. This rule is sometimes called the "mirror image" rule because it requires that an acceptance be the mirror image of the offer. It has been applied even though the variation is unintentional, as when the offeree makes a mistake in repeating the terms of the offer.

Courts have, however, developed techniques to mitigate the harshness of the mirror image rule. One technique is to interpret the offeree's language relating to the variation as a "mere suggestion," which the offeror might accept or reject, and to find an acceptance on the offerer's terms coupled with a further offer by the original offeree to modify that contract. . . . Another technique is to read the offer as already containing by interpretation or implication the apparent variation made by the offeree and to find an acceptance of a contract on the offeree's terms, which are also regarded as those of the offerer. Finally, the rule does not seem appropriate in the case of a variation, such as a price concession, that is solely to the offerer's advantage.

Even as mitigated by these techniques, however, the impact of the mirror goods image rule on negotiations for the sale of goods has caused concern. A study of Wisconsin businesses, for instance, revealed that most firms have their own forms with standard terms for such transactions:

> Typically, these terms and conditions are lengthy and printed in small type on the back of the forms. . . . If the seller does not object to this planning and accepts the order, the buyer's "fine print" will control. If the seller does object, differences can be settled by negotiation. . . . However, the seller may fail to read the buyer's . . . fine print and may accept the buyer's order on the seller's own acknowledgement-of-order form.

* Excerpted from E. ALLAN FARNSWORTH, CONTRACTS § 3.21 (4th ed. 2004).

The seller's form will then have different terms that favor the seller. The buyer's clerk who handles the seller's form has neither the time nor training to analyze the small print on back of the many forms received each day.

> The face of the acknowledgment—where the goods and the price are specified—is likely to correspond with the face of the purchase order. If it does, the two forms are filed away. At this point, both buyer and seller are likely to assume thev have planned an exchange and made a contract. Yet they have done neither, as they are in disagreement about all that appears on the back of their forms. This practice is common enough to have a name. Law teachers call it "the battle of the forms."[8]

Though it would be impractical for either party on receipt of such a preprinted form to read and consider its terms, it is inevitable that the forms will contain terms on which there has been no agreement. In practice, most of these transactions are carried out without incident, even though there may be no contract. But how is contract law to resolve those disputes that do arise?

THE PROBLEM OF CONFLICTING FORMS*

Article 2—Sales, of the Uniform Commercial Code may very well be called "the businessman's Article." It attacks, for the first time, many of the technical rules of contract law whose application has disappointed the reasonable expectations and frustrated the intentions of the businessman in commercial transactions. It attacks, for example, the concept of consideration in the areas of the firm offer[1] and of modification of a contract of sale already made,[2] upon both of which reliance is placed in the business world. It attacks the concept of indefiniteness in the areas of the open price term,[3] of output, requirements and exclusive dealing contracts[4] and of options and cooperation respecting performance.[5] Probably the most technical concept Article 2 assails, however, is the common law concept that the terms of an acceptance must match those of the offer exactly. It is this point of attack with which we are solely concerned herein. We shall consider, in order, the common law concept, the practical problem created by it, the attack made upon the concept by the Uniform Commercial Code in § 2-207, the scope of § 2-207

8. Stewart Macaulay, *Non-Contractual Relations in Business: A Preliminary Study*, 28 AM. SOC. REV. 55, 58-59 (1963).

* Excerpted from William B. Davenport, *How to Handle Sales of Goods: The Problem of Conflicting Purchase Orders and Acceptances and New Concepts in Contract Law*, 19 BUS. LAW. 75, 75-76, 77-78 (1963).

1. UCC § 2-205.
2. UCC § 2-209.
3. UCC § 2-305.
4. UCC § 2-306.
5. UCC § 2-311. Other attacks upon the concept of indefiniteness are found in UCC § 2-308, which deals with the absence of a specified place for delivery, and UCC § 2-309, which deals with the absence of a specified time for delivery.

(including both offer-acceptance and written confirmation problems), the success of the attack as measured by the decisions applying this Code provision and suggestions on handling in practice problems involving conflicting forms.

The Common Law Concept—The "Mirror Image" Rule

The common law concept is sometimes referred to as the "mirror image" rule—i.e., an acceptance of an offer repeating the terms of the offer must reflect those terms precisely. It cannot add to, subtract from or change those terms. If it does any one of these things, it is no longer an acceptance but a counter-offer rejecting the original offer and requiring in turn acceptance itself for the formation of a contract. . . .

The Problem

The "mirror image" rule understandably produced many commercial disappointments at common law. While both parties to an exchange of communications in a commercial transaction undoubtedly intended a contract at the time of the exchange, intentions change with a change in fortune or with a rapid rise or fall in the market. The safest way for an offeree to make a contract "stick" was to indorse the single word "accepted" and his signature on a copy of the offer or to write simply, "I accept your offer."

The practical problem presented, however, was that businessmen do not have forms so tersely worded. The forms used by businessmen are much more elaborate. Also they are understandably slanted in favor of the drafting party. In both the buyer's and the seller's forms the quantity, description, price, payment and delivery terms are usually contained on the front side. The front side of the form is generally free of other printed matter except the billhead (containing the name, address and similar information identifying the drafting party) and a line, generally in conspicuous type, incorporating the printed terms on the reverse side as part of the agreement. The most likely point of difference on the front side of the buyer's and seller's forms is the payment or credit term. The seller's form probably provides for payment at a short date; the buyer's form, at a more remote date. The quantity, description, price and shipment terms are the most likely to coincide. The principal difference between the buyer's and seller's forms is found in the terms on the reverse side which are incorporated by the conspicuous legend on the front side. Frequently the seller's form contains a clause making some kind of express warranty and disclaiming all other warranties, express or implied. It may also contain a provision that overshipment or undershipment by a small percentage will fill the order. It may also have a paragraph that the buyer will inspect the goods and give notice of all claimed defects within a short period of time. The buyer's form probably has clauses on the same subjects but slanted in the opposite direction. These forms, whether they be labeled "Sales Order," "Purchase Order," "Acknowledgment," "Acceptance," or "Confirmation," are frequently exchanged almost without reference to each other. An unceasing conflict in offer and acceptance forms has been the necessary result of this practice of businessmen. The conflict has become known as the "battle of the forms."[14] In

---

14. Fuller, *Basic Contract Law*, 178-80 (1947); Apsey, *The Battle of the Forms*, 34 Notre Dame L. Rev. 556 (1959).

addition to problems of contract formation, the "battle" has raised problems of contract content where the parties (or either of them) have begun performance before completion of the exchange of all forms. This, then, was the commercial reality with which the common law of offer and acceptance had not kept pace. An updating of the law to bring it into alignment with commercial practice was in order.

Step-Saver Data Systems, Inc. v. Wyse Technology

United States Court of Appeals, Third Circuit
939 F.2d 91 (1991)

WISDOM, CIRCUIT JUDGE. The "Limited Use License Agreement" printed on a package containing a copy of a computer program raises the central issue in this appeal. The trial judge held that the terms of the Limited Use License Agreement governed the purchase of the package, and, therefore, granted the software producer, The Software Link, Inc. ("TSL"), a directed verdict on claims of breach of warranty brought by a disgruntled purchaser, Step-Saver Data Systems, Inc. We disagree with the district court's determination of the legal effect of the license, and reverse and remand the warranty claims for further consideration. . . .

I. FACTUAL AND PROCEDURAL BACKGROUND

The growth in the variety of computer hardware and software has created a strong market for these products. It has also created a difficult choice for consumers, as they must somehow decide which of the many available products will best suit their needs. To assist consumers in this decision process, some companies will evaluate the needs of particular groups of potential computer users, compare those needs with the available technology, and develop a package of hardware and software to satisfy those needs. Beginning in 1981, Step-Saver performed this function as a value added retailer for International Business Machine (IBM) products. It would combine hardware and software to satisfy the word processing, data management, and communications needs for offices of physicians and lawyers. It originally marketed single computer systems, based primarily on the IBM personal computer.

As a result of advances in micro-computer technology, Step-Saver developed and marketed a multi-user system. With a multi-user system, only one computer is required. Terminals are attached, by cable, to the main computer. From these terminals, a user can access the programs available on the main computer.

After evaluating the available technology, Step-Saver selected a program by TSL, entitled Multilink Advanced, as the operating system for the multi-user system. Step-Saver selected WY-60 terminals manufactured by Wyse, and used an IBM AT as the main computer. For applications software, Step-Saver included in the package several off-the-shelf programs, designed to run under

Microsoft's Disk Operating System ("MS-DOS"), as well as several programs written by Step-Saver. Step-Saver began marketing the system in November of 1986, and sold one hundred forty-two systems mostly to law and medical offices before terminating sales of the system in March of 1987. Almost immediately upon installation of the system, Step-Saver began to receive complaints from some of its customers.

Step-Saver, in addition to conducting its own investigation of the problems, referred these complaints to Wyse and TSL, and requested technical assistance in resolving the problems. After several preliminary attempts to address the problems, the three companies were unable to reach a satisfactory solution, and disputes developed among the three concerning responsibility for the problems. As a result, the problems were never solved. At least twelve of Step-Saver's customers filed suit against Step-Saver because of the problems with the multi-user system.

Once it became apparent that the three companies would not be able to resolve their dispute amicably, Step-Saver filed suit for declaratory judgment, seeking indemnity from either Wyse or TSL, or both, for any costs incurred by Step-Saver in defending and resolving the customers' law suits. [Among other allegations, Step-Saver claims that Wyse and TSL have breached their warranties to Step-Saver, and that] Step-Saver and TSL did not intend the box-top license to be a complete and final expression of the terms of their agreement. . . .

II. THE EFFECT OF THE BOX-TOP LICENSE

The relationship between Step-Saver and TSL began in the fall of 1984 when Step-Saver asked TSL for information on an early version of the Multilink program. TSL provided Step-Saver with a copy of the early program, known simply as Multilink, without charge to permit Step-Saver to test the program to see what it could accomplish. Step-Saver performed some tests with the early program, but did not market a system based on it.

In the summer of 1985, Step-Saver noticed some advertisements in Byte magazine for a more powerful version of the Multilink program, known as Multilink Advanced. Step-Saver requested information from TSL concerning this new version of the program, and allegedly was assured by sales representatives that the new version was compatible with ninety percent of the programs available "off-the-shelf" for computers using MS-DOS. The sales representatives allegedly made a number of additional specific representations of fact concerning the capabilities of the Multilink Advanced program.

Based on these representations, Step-Saver obtained several copies of the Multilink Advanced program in the spring of 1986, and conducted tests with the program. After these tests, Step-Saver decided to market a multi-user system which used the Multilink Advanced program. From August of 1986 through March of 1987, Step-Saver purchased and resold 142 copies of the Multilink Advanced program. Step-Saver would typically purchase copies of the program in the following manner. First, Step-Saver would telephone TSL and place an order. (Step-Saver would typically order twenty copies of the program at a time.) TSL would accept the order and promise, while on the telephone, to ship the goods promptly. After the telephone order, Step-Saver would send a purchase order, detailing the items to be purchased, their price, and shipping and payment terms. TSL would ship the order promptly, along with an invoice. The invoice would contain terms essentially identical with those on Step-Saver's purchase order: price, quantity, and shipping and payment terms. No reference was made during the telephone calls, or on either the purchase orders or the invoices with regard to a disclaimer of any warranties.

Printed on the package of each copy of the program, however, would be a copy of the box-top license. The box-top license contains five terms relevant to this action:

> (1) The box-top license provides that the customer has not purchased the software itself, but has merely obtained a personal, non-transferable license to use the program.
>
> (2) The box-top license, in detail and at some length, disclaims all express and implied warranties except for a warranty that the disks contained in the box are free from defects.
>
> (3) The box-top license provides that the sole remedy available to a purchaser of the program is to return a defective disk for replacement; the license excludes any liability for damages, direct or consequential, caused by the use of the program.
>
> (4) The box-top license contains an integration clause, which provides that the box-top license is the final and complete expression of the terms of the parties's agreement.
>
> (5) The box-top license states: "Opening this package indicates your acceptance of these terms and conditions. If you do not agree with them, you should promptly return the package unopened to the person from whom you purchased it within fifteen days from date of purchase and your money will be refunded to you by that person."

The district court, without much discussion, held, as a matter of law, that the box-top license was the final and complete expression of the terms of the parties's agreement. Because the district court decided the questions of contract formation and interpretation as issues of law, we review the district court's resolution of these questions *de novo*.

> ***The "last shot" doctrine***
>
> This result is a logical consequence of the last shot doctrine, discussed in the introductory materials to this subsection.

Step-Saver contends that the contract for each copy of the program was formed when TSL agreed, on the telephone, to ship the copy at the agreed price.[9] The box-top license, argues Step-Saver, was a material alteration to

9. *See* UCC § 2-206(1)(b) and comment 2. Note that under UCC § 2-201, the oral contract would not be enforceable in the absence of a writing or part performance because each order typically involved more than $500 in goods. However, courts have typically treated the questions of formation and interpretation as separate from the question of when the contract becomes enforceable.

the parties's contract which did not become a part of the contract under UCC § 2-207. . . . TSL argues that the contract between TSL and Step-Saver did not come into existence until Step-Saver received the program, saw the terms of the license, and opened the program packaging. TSL contends that too many material terms were omitted from the telephone discussion for that discussion to establish a contract for the software. Second, TSL contends that its acceptance of Step-Saver's telephone offer was conditioned on Step-Saver's acceptance of the terms of the box-top license. Therefore, TSL argues, it did not accept Step-Saver's telephone offer, but made a counteroffer represented by the terms of the box-top license, which was accepted when Step-Saver opened each package. Third, TSL argues that, however the contract was formed, Step-Saver was aware of the warranty disclaimer, and that Step-Saver, by continuing to order and accept the product with knowledge of the disclaimer, assented to the disclaimer. . . .

A. *Does UCC § 2-207 Govern the Analysis?*

As a basic principle, we agree with Step-Saver that UCC § 2-207 governs our analysis. **We see no need to parse the parties's various actions to decide exactly when the parties formed a contract. TSL has shipped the product, and Step-Saver has accepted and paid for each copy of the program. The parties's performance demonstrates the existence of a contract. The dispute is, therefore, not over the existence of a contract, but the nature of its terms.** When the parties's conduct establishes a contract, but the parties have failed to adopt expressly a particular writing as the terms of their agreement, and the writings exchanged by the parties do not agree, UCC § 2-207 determines the terms of the contract.

As stated by the official comment to § 2-207:

> 1. This section is intended to deal with two typical situations. The one is the written confirmation, where an agreement has been reached either orally or by informal correspondence between the parties and is followed by one or more of the parties sending formal memoranda embodying the terms so far as agreed upon and adding terms not discussed. . . .
>
> 2. Under this Article a proposed deal which in commercial understanding has in fact been closed is recognized as a contract. Therefore, any additional matter contained in the confirmation or in the acceptance falls within subsection (2) and must be regarded as a proposal for an added term unless the acceptance is made conditional on the acceptance of the additional or different terms.

Critical reading

Read UCC § 2-207 carefully. According to the language of the statute, is the court correct that it is not important to "decide exactly when the parties formed a contract" because "the parties' performance demonstrates the existence of a contract"? To ask a slightly more leading question, is the issue in this case (1) *whether* there is a contract, or (2) *what terms* were agreed to? If the latter, how might the terms of the contract vary depending on whether the contract was formed through an acceptance, on the one hand, or through conduct, on the other?

[A] writing will be a final expression of, or a binding modification to, an earlier agreement only if the parties so intend. It is undisputed that Step-Saver never expressly agreed to the terms of the box-top license, either as a final expression of, or a modification to, the parties's agreement. In fact, Barry Greebel, the President of Step-Saver, testified without dispute that he objected to the terms of the box-top license as applied to Step-Saver. In the absence of evidence demonstrating an express intent to adopt a writing as a final expression of, or a modification to, an earlier agreement, we find UCC § 2-207 to provide the appropriate legal rules for determining whether such an intent can be inferred from continuing with the contract after receiving a writing containing additional or different terms.

To understand why the terms of the license should be considered under § 2-207 in this case, we review briefly the reasons behind § 2-207. Under the common law of sales, and to some extent still for contracts outside the UCC, an acceptance that varied any term of the offer operated as a rejection of the offer, and simultaneously made a counteroffer. This common law formality was known as the mirror image rule, because the terms of the acceptance had to mirror the terms of the offer to be effective. If the offeror proceeded with the contract despite the differing terms of the supposed acceptance, he would, by his performance, constructively accept the terms of the "counteroffer," and be bound by its terms. As a result of these rules, the terms of the party who sent the last form, typically the seller, would become the terms of the parties's contract. This result was known as the "last shot rule."

The UCC, in § 2-207, rejected this approach. Instead, it recognized that, while a party may desire the terms detailed in its form if a dispute, in fact, arises, most parties do not expect a dispute to arise when they first enter into a contract. As a result, most parties will proceed with the transaction even if they know that the terms of their form would not be enforced. The insight behind the rejection of the last shot rule is that it would be unfair to bind the buyer of goods to the standard terms of the seller, when neither party cared sufficiently to establish expressly the terms of their agreement, simply because the seller sent the last form. Thus, UCC § 2-207 establishes a legal rule that proceeding with a contract after receiving a writing that purports to define the terms of the parties's contract is not sufficient to establish the party's consent to the terms of the writing to the extent that the terms of the writing either add to, or differ from, the terms detailed in the parties's earlier writings or discussions. In the absence of a party's express assent to the additional or different terms of the writing, § 2-207 provides a default rule that the parties intended, as the terms of their agreement, those terms to which both parties have agreed, along with any terms implied by the provisions of the UCC.

The reasons that led to the rejection of the last shot rule, and the adoption of § 2-207, apply fully in this case. TSL never mentioned during the parties's negotiations leading to the purchase of the programs, nor did it, at any time, obtain Step-Saver's express assent to, the terms of the box-top license. Instead, TSL contented itself with attaching the terms to the packaging of the software, even though those terms differed substantially from those previously discussed by the parties. Thus, the box-top license, in this case, is best seen as one more form in a battle of forms, and the question of whether Step-Saver has agreed to be bound by the terms of the box-top license is best resolved by applying the legal principles detailed in § 2-207.

B. *Application of § 2-207*

TSL advances several reasons why the terms of the box-top license should be incorporated into the parties's agreement under a § 2-207 analysis. First, TSL argues that the parties's contract was not formed until Step-Saver received the package, saw the terms of the box-top license, and opened the package, thereby consenting to the terms of the license. TSL argues that a contract defined without reference to the specific terms provided by the box-top license would necessarily fail for indefiniteness. Second, TSL argues that the box-top license was a conditional acceptance and counter-offer under § 2-207(1). Third, TSL argues that Step-Saver, by continuing to order and use the product with notice of the terms of the box-top license, consented to the terms of the box-top license.

1. Was the contract sufficiently definite?

TSL argues that the parties intended to license the copies of the program, and that several critical terms could only be determined by referring to the box-top license. Pressing the point, TSL argues that it is impossible to tell, without referring to the box-top license, whether the parties intended a sale of a copy of the program or a license to use a copy. TSL cites *Bethlehem Steel Corp. v. Litton Industries* in support of its position that any contract defined without reference to the terms of the box-top license would fail for indefiniteness.

From the evidence, it appears that the following terms, at the least, were discussed and agreed to, apart from the box-top license: (1) the specific goods involved; (2) the quantity; and (3) the price. TSL argues that the following terms were only defined in the box-top license: (1) the nature of the transaction, sale or license; and (2) the warranties, if any, available. TSL argues that these two terms are essential to creating a sufficiently definite contract. We disagree.

Section 2-204(3) of the UCC provides:

> Even though one or more terms are left open a contract for sale does not fail for indefiniteness if the parties have intended to make a contract and there is a reasonably certain basis for giving an appropriate remedy.

Unlike the terms omitted by the parties in *Bethlehem Steel Corp.*, the two terms cited by TSL are not "gaping holes in a multi-million dollar contract that no one but the parties themselves could fill." First, the rights of the respective parties under the federal copyright law if the transaction is characterized as a sale of a copy of the program are nearly identical to the parties's respective rights under the terms of the box-top license. Second, the UCC provides for express and implied warranties if the seller fails to disclaim expressly those warranties.[24] Thus, even though warranties are an important term left blank by the parties, the default rules of the UCC fill in that blank. We hold that contract was sufficiently definite without the terms provided by the box-top license.

2. The box-top license as a counter-offer?

TSL advances two reasons why its box-top license should be considered a conditional acceptance under UCC § 2-207(1). First, TSL argues that the express language of the box-top license, including the integration clause and the phrase "opening this product indicates your acceptance of these terms", made TSL's acceptance "expressly conditional on assent to the additional or different terms". Second, TSL argues that the box-top license, by permitting return of the product within fifteen days if the purchaser does not agree to the terms stated in the license (the "refund offer"), establishes that TSL's acceptance was conditioned on Step-Saver's assent to the terms of the box-top license, citing *Monsanto Agricultural Products Co. v. Edenfield*.[28] While we are not certain that a conditional acceptance analysis applies when a contract is established by performance,[29] we assume that it does and consider TSL's arguments.

To determine whether a writing constitutes a conditional acceptance, courts have established three tests. . . .

Under the first test, an offeree's response is a conditional acceptance to the extent it states a term "materially altering the contractual obligations solely to the disadvantage of the offeror." . . .

[W]e note that adopting this test would conflict with the express provision of UCC § 2-207(2)(b). Under § 2-207(2)(b), additional terms in a written confirmation that "materially alter [the contract]" are construed "as proposals for addition to the contract," not as conditional acceptances.

A second approach considers an acceptance conditional when certain key words or phrases are used, such as a written confirmation stating that the terms of the confirmation are "the only ones upon which we will accept orders."[34] The

24. *See* UCC §§ 2-312, 2-313, 2-314 & 2-315.

28. 426 So. 2d 574 (Fla. Dist. Ct. App. 1982).

29. Even though a writing is sent after performance establishes the existence of a contract, courts have analyzed the effect of such a writing under UCC § 2-207. The official comment to UCC 2-207 suggests that, even though a proposed deal has been closed, the conditional acceptance analysis still applies in determining which writing's terms will define the contract.

> 2. Under this Article a proposed deal which in commercial understanding has in fact been closed is recognized as a contract. Therefore, any additional matter contained in the confirmation or in the acceptance falls within subsection (2) and must be regarded as a proposal for an added term *unless the acceptance is made conditional on the acceptance of the additional or different terms.*

34. *Ralph Shrader, Inc. v. Diamond Int'l Corp.*, 833 F.2d 1210, 1214 (6th Cir. 1987). Note that even though an acceptance contains the key phrase, and is conditional, these courts typically avoid finding a contract on the terms of the counteroffer by requiring the offeree/counterofferor to establish that the offeror assented to the terms of the counteroffer. Generally, acceptance of the goods, alone, is not sufficient to establish assent by the offeror to the terms of the counteroffer. If the sole evidence of assent to the terms of the counteroffer is from the conduct of the parties in proceeding with the transaction, then the courts generally define the terms of the parties's agreement under § 2-207(3).

third approach requires the offeree to demonstrate an unwillingness to proceed with the transaction unless the additional or different terms are included in the contract. Although we are not certain that these last two approaches would generate differing answers,[36] we adopt the third approach for our analysis because it best reflects the understanding of commercial transactions developed in the UCC. Section 2-207 attempts to distinguish between: (1) those standard terms in a form confirmation, which the party would like a court to incorporate into the contract in the event of a dispute; and (2) the actual terms the parties understand to govern their agreement. The third test properly places the burden on the party asking a court to enforce its form to demonstrate that a particular term is a part of the parties's commercial bargain. Using this test, it is apparent that the integration clause and the "consent by opening" language is not sufficient to render TSL's acceptance conditional. As other courts have recognized, this type of language provides no real indication that the party is willing to forego the transaction if the additional language is not included in the contract. . . .

[Indeed,] the undisputed evidence in this case demonstrates that the terms of the license were not sufficiently important that TSL would forego its sales to Step-Saver if TSL could not obtain Step-Saver's consent to those terms.

As discussed, Mr. Greebel testified that TSL assured him that the box-top license did not apply to Step-Saver, as Step-Saver was not the end user of the Multilink Advanced program. Supporting this testimony, TSL on two occasions asked Step-Saver to sign agreements that would put in formal terms the relationship between Step-Saver and TSL. Both proposed agreements contained warranty disclaimer and limitation of remedy terms similar to those contained in the box-top license. Step-Saver refused to sign the agreements; nevertheless, TSL continued to sell copies of Multilink Advanced to Step-Saver. . . .

Thus, TSL was willing to proceed with the transaction despite the fact that one of the terms of the box-top license was not included in the contract between TSL and Step-Saver. . . .

Based on these facts, we conclude that TSL did not clearly express its unwillingness to proceed with the transactions unless its additional terms were incorporated into the parties's agreement. The box-top license did not, therefore, constitute a conditional acceptance under UCC § 2-207(1). . . .

4. Public policy concerns

TSL has raised a number of public policy arguments focusing on the effect on the software industry of an adverse holding concerning the enforceability

36. Under the second approach, the box-top license might be considered a conditional acceptance, but Step-Saver, by accepting the product, would not be automatically bound to the terms of the box-top license. Instead, courts have applied UCC § 2-207(3) to determine the terms of the parties's agreement. The terms of the agreement would be those "on which the writings of the parties agree, together with any supplementary terms incorporated under any other provisions of this Act." UCC § 2-207(3). Because the writings of the parties did not agree on the warranty disclaimer and limitation of remedies terms, the box-top license version of those terms would not be included in the parties's contract; rather, the default provisions of the UCC would govern.

of the box-top license. We are not persuaded that requiring software companies to stand behind representations concerning their products will inevitably destroy the software industry. We emphasize, however, that we are following the well-established distinction between conspicuous disclaimers made available before the contract is formed and disclaimers made available only after the contract is formed. When a disclaimer is not expressed until after the contract is formed, UCC § 2-207 governs the interpretation of the contract, and, between merchants, such disclaimers, to the extent they materially alter the parties's agreement, are not incorporated into the parties's agreement.

If TSL wants relief for its business operations from this well-established rule, their arguments are better addressed to a legislature than a court. . . .

C. The Terms of the Contract

Under section 2-207, an additional term detailed in the box-top license will not be incorporated into the parties's contract if the term's addition to the contract would materially alter the parties's agreement.[47] Step-Saver alleges that several representations made by TSL constitute express warranties, and that valid implied warranties were also a part of the parties's agreement. Because the district court considered the box-top license to exclude all of these warranties, the district court did not consider whether other factors may act to exclude these warranties. The existence and nature of the warranties is primarily a factual question that we leave for the district court, but assuming that these warranties were included within the parties's original agreement, we must conclude that adding the disclaimer of warranty and limitation of remedies provisions from the box-top license would, as a matter of law, substantially alter the distribution of risk between Step-Saver and TSL. Therefore, under UCC § 2-207(2)(b), the disclaimer of warranty and limitation of remedies terms of the box-top license did not become a part of the parties's agreement.Based on these considerations, we reverse the trial court's holding that the parties intended the box-top license to be a final and complete expression of the terms of their agreement. Despite the presence of an integration clause in the box-top license, the box-top license should have been treated as a written confirmation containing additional terms. Because the warranty disclaimer and limitation of remedies terms would materially alter the parties's agreement, these terms did not become a part of the parties's agreement. We remand for further consideration the express and implied warranty claims against TSL.

47. UCC § 2-207(2)(b).

RELEVANT PROVISIONS

For the *Restatement (Second) of Contracts,* consult §§ 39 and 59. For the UCC, consult §§ 2-204, 2-206, and 2-207.

NOTES AND QUESTIONS

1. *What happened?* Who sued whom for what? Procedurally, how did the case get before this court? Factually, what happened between the parties? What arguments did the plaintiff and defendant make? What rule or rules did the court apply? How did the court analyze the dispute between the parties? How did the court decide the case?

2. *Was this case correctly decided?* Do you agree with the result reached in this case? Why or why not? Do you agree with the court's reasoning? Why or why not? How, if at all, would you have written the opinion differently?

3. *History of the UCC.* In its decision, the court explains the history of the UCC. Do you understand its development and how it differs from the common law mirror image and last shot rules? Do you understand why? The policy governing the UCC will help you build arguments with it, and will help guide your understanding of this complicated issue of contract law.

4. *Public policy.* Near the end of the case the court discusses TSL's public policy arguments. When courts are willing to entertain such arguments, they can go far towards bolstering your legal argument, especially where a court is being asked by the parties to choose between competing rules to govern the dispute. Other times, however, a court will brush aside such policy arguments, stating (as this court did) that they are better addressed by the legislative branch. In general, under what circumstances (if any) do you think courts, rather than legislatures, are better equipped to consider public policy arguments, and which arguments (if any) are better suited to be addressed by the legislative branch? Was the court above right to punt TSL's public policy argument to the legislative branch? Why or why not?

In the following excerpt, Professors Baird and Weisberg helpfully explain many contexts in which "battle of the forms" questions typically arise, and suggest that UCC § 2-207 can best be viewed as moving away from the rule-based paradigm of the mirror image rule and towards a more flexible standards-based approach to offer and acceptance. If they are correct, it would explain a good deal of the confusion reigning among courts attempting to apply the rule—er, standard.*

* We first examined the difference between standards and rules in "Thinking Tool: Administrative Costs and Standards v. Rules," p. 75, *supra,* which you may want to review at this time.

Although we don't have the space to consider whether the authors are correct in their underlying assumption about § 2-207 operating as a standard, the very possibility of it operating in this fashion raises a number of important questions with which you should be concerned. For instance, as you read, you should ask yourself (1) whether you think viewing § 2-207 as a standard would make it more or less workable/user-friendly to the judges and lawyers attempting to apply it, and (2) whether you think a standard- or rule-based approach would be the best way of solving the offer-acceptance problem. Keep your answer in mind, for we will revisit the mirror image rule one more time at the end of this unit in a well-known case, Filanto v. Chilewich International, *which was decided under the CISG's version of that rule.*

THINKING TOOL APPLIED: RULES, STANDARDS, AND THE BATTLE OF THE FORMS*

Buyers and sellers of commercial goods sometimes bargain only on basic matters such as price and delivery date, and leave the details of the transaction, including warranties and arbitration provisions, to standardized term in preprinted forms. The buyer's and seller's forms do not coincide, and may even contradict one another, creating two types of disputes for courts to resolve. First, one party may seek to renege on the deal before performance and may point to inconsistencies between the purchase order and the acknowledgment to show that the minds of the parties never met clearly enough to form a contract.[1] In such a case, a court facing disagreement between two printed forms must decide whether a contract even exists. Second, after the seller has sent the goods or the buyer has used them, the parties may fall into dispute over a term on which the forms failed to agree.[2]

* Excerpted from Douglas G. Baird, *Rules, Standards, and the Battle of the Forms: A Reassessment of § 2-207,* 68 VA. L. REV. 1217, 1217-23 (1982) (internal citations omitted).

1. For example, a maker of gaskets orders 100 pounds of rubber and uses a purchase order drafted by its lawyer. The order form might be silent on the warranty question, or it might say that "Seller warrants goods suitable for use in the manufacture of gaskets." The rubber manufacturer, in return, sends an acknowledgment form that disclaims all warranties, including the implied warranty of merchantability (UCC § 2-314) and the implied warranty of fitness for a particular purpose (UCC § 2-315). The parties explicitly agree on a delivery date six months in the future. After the exchange of forms but before delivery, a sudden worldwide shortage of rubber causes the price of the commodity to triple. Seller then tries to avoid selling to the gasket manufacturer at the now bargain price. He asserts that no contract exists between the parties because his form and that of the buyer disagree on the issue of warranty. The practicing commercial lawyer frequently confronts a client that has exchanged forms and wants to know whether it is bound. . . . Though in principle battles of the forms might arise in consumer transactions, such cases are rare. We assume throughout this article that the parties involved are merchants, and thus that the special concerns that arise when a consumer is a party are not present.

2. This type of case is litigated much more frequently than the first. Most of the disputes involve a warranty disclaimer in one of the forms, or a term in one of the forms mandating arbitration in the event of a dispute. Cases have arisen in which one of the forms included an indemnity clause; in which a form required the other party to pay attorneys' fees in the event of litigation; and in which one of the forms sought to set New York as the jurisdiction in which any disputes would be litigated. All these clauses have been found to be 'material' (thus materially altering the contract), as have those in most recent cases involving disclaimers and arbitration under UCC § 2-207(2). . . .

In these cases where the parties have already performed, the court must supply a term that the parties never agreed on; the court may have to decide, for example, which party will bear the loss resulting from a defect in the goods or whether the dispute will go to arbitration. Each of these two types of disputes is commonly called a "battle of the forms." These disputes arise only when the parties do not explicitly dicker over the terms at issue. Thus, the law cannot resolve the battle of the forms with a simple inquiry into the parties' intent. It is useless to ask what terms the parties intended to govern this transaction.[5] The buyer and seller were content to leave their mutual rights uncertain, because greater certainty would have come only with negotiations, the cost of which probably would have exceeded the expected cost of leaving things open to dispute.The law cannot avoid choosing among terms that the parties never explicitly agreed on; any approach to the battle of the forms that allows each party to insist on its own contract terms is doomed to failure. If, for example, the buyer wants a warranty on the goods and the seller does not, the lawmaker has several choices. A rule could say that the buyer wins, that the seller wins, that the first party to send its form wins, or that the last party to send its form wins. No rule of law, however, can allow both parties to prevail. Likewise, a rule that purports to enforce one party's clause saying "My terms govern or there is no deal" cannot resolve the many cases where both parties have such a clause and the deal has already gone through.

This article joins an extensive literature examining the Uniform Commercial Code's response to the battle of the forms—U.C.C. § 2-207. The conventional wisdom of the commentators on 2-207 runs roughly as follows: The drafters of 2-207 had the salutary, indeed the unexceptionable purpose of overcoming the rigidity of one of the oldest and most mechanical common-law rules of offer and acceptance—the mirror-image rule. The commentators argue, however, that serious drafting errors,[7] compounded by occasional judicial errors, have hampered 2-207's effectiveness and contravened the drafters' purpose in a significant number of cases. This article shows that the conventional wisdom is wrong or, at least, seriously incomplete. We argue that 2-207 and the battle of the forms must be understood in light of a fundamental question in jurisprudence—whether to use

5. It is also of limited value even to have a legal rule that determines whether a contract exists by focusing exclusively on the parties' intent. The intent of the parties may not be independent of the legal rule. As is true in many areas of the law, when parties do reflect on the legal consequences of their acts, their expectations depend in some measure on what they assume the legal rule to be. If, for example, as a matter of common knowledge, courts enforced only those contracts executed under a seal, parties would never think they had formed binding contracts unless they had used a seal. Where the rules of contract formation are less certain, the intent of the parties may be no more than their rough prediction of how the court will treat their exchange.

7. Grant Gilmore, one of the drafters of the Uniform Commercial Code (though not of 2-207), said that, if anything, commentators have been too forgiving of 2-207: "[They] treat the section much too respectfully—as if it had sprung, all of a piece, like Minerva from the brow of Jove. The truth is that it was a miserable, bungled, patched-up job—both text and comment—to which various hands—Llewellyn, Honnold, Braucher and my anonymous hack—contributed at various points, each acting independently of the others (like the blind men and the elephant). It strikes me as ludicrous to pretend that the section can, or should, be construed as an integrated whole in the light of what 'the draftsman' 'intended.'" Letter from Grant Gilmore to Robert Summers (Sept. 10, 1980), *in* R. Speidel, R. Summers & J. White, Teaching Materials on Commercial and Consumer Law 54-55 (3d ed. 1981).

formal "rules" or open-ended "standards" to resolve the mutual rights of private parties. The drafters of the Code intended to do more than overcome the formalist excesses of the mirror-image rule; indeed, that purpose only poorly explains the history and final language of 2-207. Instead, the drafters sought to break dramatically with traditional formal rules of offer and acceptance and, with those rules, dependence on the parties' documented expressions. The drafters sought to treat the battle of the forms with an open-textured "standard" similar to the one they applied to another recurrent problem in contract formation—the case where the parties have unquestionably contracted but have left some of the terms of their agreement incomplete.

The drafters decided, however, to put 2-207 to double-duty. They wrote the section to resolve not only battles of the forms, but also disputes in which the parties make a binding oral agreement and later disagree when they attempt to record or fine-tune the agreement through post-bargain "confirming letters." The drafters chose to resolve this type of dispute with a relatively formal rule, yet the final language of 2-207 applies the formal rule to both confirmation cases and battles of the forms. Most of the flaws that the commentators have seen in the Code's treatment of the battle of the forms stem from this intrusion of a formal rule in situations that the drafters initially intended to resolve with a flexible standard.

Nevertheless, the judicial history of 2-207 in battle of the forms cases reveals that the courts have generally overcome these flaws and have construed 2-207 consistently with the drafters' intent—though at the sacrifice of literal construction of the section's language. To determine whether a contract exists, courts in practice look at the terms that the parties expressly agreed on and then decide whether agreement on these terms shows that a contract was in the mutual interest of the parties, viewed ex ante. When the agreement leaves certain terms of the contract in dispute, courts supply the terms that the Code posits parties would have agreed to had they dickered over them. We conclude then that, if one accepts the drafters' goals for 2-207, redrafting its language may be unnecessary.

We challenge, however, the assumption of many commentators that the goal of 2-207 is correct and argue that the formalist principles of offer and acceptance underlying the mirror-image rule are fundamentally sound. Commentators assume that the mirror-image rule cannot resolve the problem of the welsher satisfactorily, but the problem of the party that wants to back out of a bargain on a technicality can be handled within the framework of the mirror-image rule and does not require abandoning the very idea of a rule, as the Code's drafters intended. Perhaps more important, the mirror-image rule may yield a better result than 2-207 in the second battle of the forms problem, in which both parties have performed and a dispute exists over terms. In theory, at least, formal rules such as the mirror-image rule allow parties to a contract to avoid the off-the-rack terms the Code supplies in the absence of express agreement; such ready-made terms may be poorly suited to the transaction and consequently advance the interest of neither party. Compared with 2-207, the mirror-image rule encourages parties to adapt the terms in their forms to the needs and abilities of buyers and sellers in their particular market. Thus, we believe that a formal rule of contract formation, applied consistently in battles of the forms, may produce terms that are better suited to particular transactions than does 2-207.

Application of Doughboy Industries, Inc. to Stay Arbitration

New York Supreme Court, Appellate Division
233 N.Y.S.2d 488 (1962)

BREITEL, J. This case involves a conflict between a buyer's order form and a seller's acknowledgment form, each memorializing a purchase and sale of goods. The issue arises on whether the parties agreed to arbitrate future disputes. The seller's form had a general arbitration provision. The buyer's form did not. The buyer's form contained a provision that only a signed consent would bind the buyer to any terms thereafter transmitted in any commercial form of the seller. The seller's form, however, provided that silence or a failure to object in writing would be an acceptance of the terms and conditions of its acknowledgment form. The buyer never objected to the seller's acknowledgment, orally or in writing. In short, the buyer and seller accomplished a legal equivalent to the irresistible force colliding with the immovable object.

Special Term denied the buyer's motion to stay arbitration on the ground that there was no substantial issue whether the parties had agreed to arbitrate. For the reasons to be stated, the order should be reversed and the buyer's motion to stay arbitration should be granted. As a matter of law, the parties did not agree in writing to submit future disputes to arbitration.

Of interest in the case is that both the seller and buyer are substantial businesses—a "strong" buyer and a "strong" seller. This is not a case of one of the parties being at the bargaining mercy of the other.

The facts are:

During the three months before the sale in question the parties had done business on two occasions. On these prior occasions the buyer used its purchase-order form with its insulating conditions, and the seller used its acknowledgment form with its self-actuating conditions. Each ignored the other's printed forms, but proceeded with the commercial business at hand.

The instant transaction began with the buyer, on May 6, 1960, mailing from its office in Wisconsin to the seller in New York City two purchase orders for plastic film. Each purchase order provided that some 20,000 pounds of film were to be delivered in the future on specified dates. In addition, further quantities were ordered on a "hold basis," that is, subject to "increase, decrease, or cancellation" by the buyer. On May 13, 1960 the seller orally accepted both purchase orders without change except to suggest immediate shipment of the first part of the order. The buyer agreed to the request, and that day the seller shipped some 10,000 pounds of film in partial fulfillment of one purchase order. On May 16, 1960, the buyer received the seller's first acknowledgment dated May 13, 1960, and on May 19, 1960 the seller's second acknowledgment dated May 16, 1960. Although the purchase orders called for written acceptances and return of attached acknowledgments by the seller no one paid any attention to these requirements. Neither party, orally or in writing, objected to the conditions printed on the other's commercial form. Later, the buyer sent change orders with respect to so much of the orders as had been, according to the buyer, on a "hold basis."

The dispute, which has arisen and which the parties wish determined, the seller by arbitration, and the buyer by court litigation, is whether the buyer is bound to accept all the goods ordered on a "hold basis." The arbitration would take place in New York City. The litigation might have to be brought in Wisconsin, the buyer's home State.

The buyer's purchase-order form had on its face the usual legends and blanks for the ordering of goods. On the reverse was printed a pageful of terms and conditions. The grand defensive clause reads as follows:

> ALTERATION OF TERMS—None of the terms and conditions contained in this Purchase Order may be added to, modified, superseded or otherwise altered except by a written instrument signed by an authorized representative of Buyer and delivered by Buyer to Seller, and each shipment received by Buyer from Seller shall be deemed to be only upon the terms and conditions contained in this Purchase Order except as they may be added to, modified, superseded or otherwise altered, notwithstanding any terms and conditions that may be contained in any acknowledgment, invoice or other form of Seller and notwithstanding Buyer's act of accepting or paying for any shipment or similar act of Buyer.

The buyer's language is direct; it makes clear that no variant seller's acknowledgment is to be binding. But the seller's acknowledgment form is drafted equally carefully. On its front in red typography one's attention is directed to the terms and conditions on the reverse side; and it advises the buyer that he, the buyer, has full knowledge of the conditions and agrees to them unless within 10 days he objects in writing.

The seller's clause reads:

> IMPORTANT
>
> Buyer agrees he has full knowledge of conditions printed on the reverse side hereof; and that the same are part of the agreement between buyer and seller and shall be binding if either the goods referred to herein are delivered to and accepted by buyer, or if buyer does not within ten days from date hereof deliver to seller written objection to said conditions or any part thereof.

On the reverse side the obligations of the buyer set forth above are carefully repeated. Among the conditions on the reverse side is the general arbitration clause.

This case involves only the application of the arbitration clause. Arguably, a different principle from that applied here might, under present law,* govern other of the terms and conditions in either of the commercial forms. The reason is the special rule that the courts have laid down with respect to arbitration clauses, namely, that the agreement to arbitrate must be direct and

* *See*, as to future law, discussion, *infra*, of applicable provisions of the Uniform Commercial Code, effective in this State on September 27, 1964.

the intention made clear, without implication, inveiglement or subtlety. The severability of arbitration clauses from other provisions in commercial documentation would, of course, follow, if it be true that the threshold for clarity of agreement to arbitrate is greater than with respect to other contractual terms.It should be evident, as the buyer argues, that a contract for the sale of goods came into existence on May 13, 1960 when the seller made a partial shipment, especially when following upon its oral acceptance of the buyer's purchase order. The contract, at such time, was documented only by the buyer's purchase-order form. However, that is not dispositive. It is equally evident from the prior transactions between these parties, and general practices in trade, that more documents were to follow. Such documents may help make the contract, or modify it. Whether the subsequent documents were necessary to complete the making of the contract (as would be true if there had been no effective or valid acceptance by partial shipment), or whether they served only to modify or validate the terms of an existing contract (as would be true if there had been a less formal written acceptance, merely an oral acceptance, or an acceptance by partial shipment of goods) is not really too important once the commercial dealings have advanced as far as they had here. By that time, there is no question whether there was a contract, but only what was the contract.

Recognizing, as one should, that the business men in this case acted with complete disdain for the "lawyer's content" of the very commercial forms they were sending and receiving, the question is what obligation ought the law to attach to the arbitration clause. And in determining that question the traditional theory is applicable, namely, that of constructive knowledge and acceptance of contractual terms, based on prior transactions and the duty to read contractual instruments to which one is a party.

But, and this is critical, it is not only the seller's form which should be given effect, but also the buyer's form, for it too was used in the prior transactions, and as to it too, there was a duty to read. Of course, if the two commercial forms are given effect, they cancel one another. (Certainly, the test is not which is the later form, because here the prior form said the buyer would not be bound by the later form unless it consented in writing. It needs little discussion that silence, a weak enough form of acceptance, effective only when misleading and there is a duty to speak, can be negatived as a misleading factor by announcing in advance that it shall have no effect as acceptance.

As pointed out earlier, an agreement to arbitrate must be clear and direct, and must not depend upon implication, inveiglement or subtlety. It follows then that the existence of an agreement to arbitrate should not depend solely upon the conflicting fine print of commercial forms which cross one another but never meet.

Matter of Wachusett Spinning Mills (*Blue Bird Silk Mfg. Co.*), 7 A.D. 2d 382, provides no applicable rule. There the seller's acknowledgment of the buyer's purchase order (which included an arbitration clause) expressly accepted the purchase order by reference and designation. Although the acknowledgment contained additional terms, the specific reference to the purchase order was held determinative that the acknowledgment was an acceptance of the purchase order with all its terms. Thus, it was said:

> The position of the petitioners might be sound if the confirmation orders made no reference to the original orders containing the arbitration clause. On the contrary however, the confirmation orders were in such form as to show an intent to incorporate all the terms of the original orders—except, of course, as to specific changes stated.

In this case, the supposed condition happened, the acknowledgment made no reference to the purchase order, and, moreover, the prior purchase order disavowed the future application of any subsequent differing acknowledgment. And, the arbitration clause was one of the "specific changes" from the purchase order, which even under the rule in the *Wachusett* case would not be binding on the other party.

Consequently, as a matter of law there was no agreement to arbitrate in this case, if one applies existing principles.

But the problem of conflicting commercial forms is one with which there has been much concern before this, and a new effort at rational solution has been made. The new solution would yield a similar result. The Uniform Commercial Code takes effect in this State September 27, 1964. It reflects the latest legislative conclusions as to what the law ought to be. It provides:

> **§ 2-207. Additional Terms in Acceptance or Confirmation.**
>
> (1) A definite and seasonable expression of acceptance or a written confirmation which is sent within a reasonable time operates as an acceptance even though it states terms additional to or different from those offered or agreed upon, unless acceptance is expressly made conditional on assent to the additional or different terms.
>
> (2) The additional terms are to be construed as proposals for addition to the contract. Between merchants such terms become part of the contract unless:
>
> (a) the offer expressly limits acceptance to the terms of the offer;
>
> (b) they materially alter it; or
>
> (c) notification of objection to them has already been given or is given within a reasonable time after notice of them is received.
>
> (3) Conduct by both parties which recognizes the existence of a contract is sufficient to establish a contract for sale although the writings of the parties do not otherwise establish a contract. In such case the terms of the particular contract consist of those terms on which the writings of the parties agree, together with any supplementary terms incorporated under any other provisions of this Act.

While this new section is not in its entirety in accordance with New York law in effect when the events in suit occurred, in its particular application to the problem at hand it is quite useful. The draftsmen's comments to section

2-207 are in precise point (Uniform Commercial Code § 2-207, comments 3 and 6). Thus, it is said:

> 3. Whether or not additional or different terms will become part of the agreement depends upon the provisions of subsection (2). If they are such as materially to alter the original bargain, they will not be included unless expressly agreed to by the other party. If, however, they are terms which would not so change the bargain they will be incorporated unless notice of objection to them has already been given or is given within a reasonable time. . . .
>
> 6. If no answer is received within a reasonable time after additional terms are proposed, it is both fair and commercially sound to assume that their inclusion has been assented to. Where clauses on confirming forms sent by both parties conflict each party must be assumed to object to a clause of the other conflicting with one on the confirmation sent by himself. As a result the requirement that there be notice of objection which is found in subsection (2) is satisfied and the conflicting terms do not become a part of the contract. The contract then consists of the terms originally expressly agreed to, terms on which the confirmations agree, and terms supplied by this Act, including subsection (2).

On this exposition, the arbitration clause, whether viewed as a material alteration under subsection (2), or as a term nullified by a conflicting provision in the buyer's form, would fail to survive as a contract term. In the light of the New York cases, at least, there can be little question that an agreement to arbitrate is a material term, one not to be injected by implication, subtlety or inveiglement. And the conclusion is also the same if the limitation contained in the offer (the buyer's purchase order) is given effect, as required by paragraph (a) of subsection 2 of the new section.

Accordingly, the order denying petitioner-appellant buyer's motion to stay arbitration should be reversed, on the law, with costs to petitioner-appellant and the motion should be granted.

RELEVANT PROVISIONS

For the *Restatement (Second) of Contracts,* consult §§ 39 and 59. For the UCC, consult §§ 2-204, 2-206, and 2-207.

NOTES AND QUESTIONS

1. ***What happened?*** Who sued whom for what? Procedurally, how did the case get before this court? Factually, what happened between the parties? What arguments did the plaintiff and defendant make? What rule or rules did

the court apply? How did the court analyze the dispute between the parties? How did the court decide the case?

2. *Was this case correctly decided?* Do you agree with the result reached in this case? Why or why not? Do you agree with the court's reasoning? Why or why not? How, if at all, would you have written the opinion differently?

3. *2-207 in the real world.* The excerpt below offers some practical advice on handling "battle of the forms" problems under UCC § 2-207.

HANDLING "BATTLE OF THE FORMS" PROBLEMS UNDER THE UCC*

(1) If your client is the sender of a sales or purchase order form (or an offeror) and wants no contract except upon his terms, he should include a clause in conspicuous type limiting acceptance to the exact terms of the offer. The clause set forth in the opinion in *Doughboy Industries* is a good model for drafting purposes. Any acceptance other than an expressly conditional one forms a contract on your client's terms.

(2) If your client is the recipient of a sales or purchase order form (or an offeree) and wants no contract except upon his terms, he need reply only as follows: "I accept your offer (identifying it) provided you agree to the following additional [or substitute] terms:"[39] Or he may reply, "I accept upon the express condition that you agree," or, "I accept if and only if you agree, etc." The exact words must depend upon the preference of the draftsman. Any of these replies should make the conditional character of the acceptance clear. This then becomes the Code counter-offer, and acceptance of it on the standards of § 2-207 is required for contract formation.

(3) If your client may be willing to accept some terms that may be proposed by the other party after he sees what they are, he may use a clause of the type in *Doughboy Industries* or he may omit it and merely object promptly to the terms that he doesn't want. If he doesn't want a particular term he should always object promptly. He should never assume that the term will not become part of the contract because it will "materially alter" the contract. His so assuming will only invite an opportunity for re-examination of the correctness of his assumption.

(4) In order that your client may be doubly sure that the contract contains all of the terms which he wants included, he should not begin performance or do any act recognizing a contract before all forms have crossed and the terms are settled.

(5) In the case of written confirmations, they should be mailed promptly and preferably by registered mail. The foregoing suggestions, to the extent that they apply to written confirmations, should also be followed.

---

* Excerpted from William B. Davenport, *How to Handle Sales of Goods: The Problem of Conflicting Purchase Orders and Acceptances and New Concepts in Contract Law*, 19 BUS. LAW. 75, 88-89 (1963).

39. Section 2-207 does not change the rule of pre-Code case law in this respect. . . .

(6) Finally, any legend on the front side of the form incorporating by reference any terms on the reverse side should be in conspicuous type. Moreover, the terms on the reverse side should be in as large and clear type as possible. In drafting these terms on the reverse side, attention must be paid to other provisions of the Code—for example, § 2-316, with respect to the size or color of type and the language used to disclaim or limit warranties.

Before wrapping up this subsection, let's explore how the types of cases considered above are dealt with in the international context.

INTERNATIONAL PERSPECTIVE: THE BATTLE OF THE FORMS AND THE CISG*

Under the common law's mirror-image rule, an acceptance that added to or changed the terms of the offer was deemed to be a rejection and a counteroffer. In practice this resulted in a last-shot rule, with each new form constituting a counteroffer until the last one was accepted by conduct. The UCC, of course, changed this rule, providing that "[a] definite and seasonable expression of acceptance . . . operates as an acceptance even though it states terms additional to or different from those offered. . . ."[47] The additional terms in the acceptance may become part of the contract if expressly accepted by the offeror or (so long as both parties are merchants) automatically so long as the offer does not expressly limit acceptance to the terms of the offer, the additional terms do not materially alter the contract, and the offeror does not object to the additional terms.[48] Finally, if the parties act as though there is a contract although their writings fail to establish one (for example, because the acceptance was expressly conditional on the offeror's assent to the additional or different terms), the UCC employs a strikeout rule so that the terms of the contract are those on which the parties' writings agree, supplemented by the UCC's gap fillers.[49] The CISG, by contrast, adopts what is essentially a mirror-image rule.[50] Article 19(1) provides: "A reply

* Excerpted from William S. Dodge, *Teaching the CISG in Contracts*, 50 J. LEGAL EDUC. 72, 82-83 (2000).

47. UCC § 2-207(1). Such an expression of acceptance does not operate as an acceptance if it is "expressly made conditional on [the offeror's] assent to the additional or different terms." *Id.*

48. UCC § 2-207(2). What to do with "different" terms, which are not mentioned In the text of § 2-207(2), has divided the courts. The majority rule is that conflicting terms cancel each other out and are replaced by the UCC's gap fillers. The leading minority view does not allow different terms to become part of the contract automatically, since they are not mentioned in § 2-207(2). And California treats different terms like additional terms, allowing them to become part of the contract automatically unless the offer expressly limits acceptance to the terms of the offer, the different terms materially alter the contract, or the offeror objects. . . .

49. UCC § 2-207(3).

50. The mirror-image rule is found in both the common and civil law traditions. Britain and France still adhere to it, even with respect to contracts for the sale of goods. Germany, by contrast, has adopted a solution very similar to that of UCC 2-207(3). *See* Arthur Taylor von Mehren, *The "Battle of the Forms": A Comparative View*, 38 AM. J. COMP. L. 265, 269, 294-98 (1990).

to an offer which purports to be an acceptance but contains additions, limitations or other modifications is a rejection of the offer and constitutes a counter-offer." Article 19(2) attempts to soften this rule a little by providing that if the additional or different terms are not material *and* the offeror does not object to them, then the purported acceptance is an acceptance and the additional or different terms become part of the contract. But Article 19(3) defines materiality so broadly that it is hard to imagine a change that the CISG would not consider material.[51] This means that, in almost every case, an acceptance that varies the terms of the offer will be a counteroffer which will be accepted by the other party's conduct.[52]

In the following case, a number of forms passed back and forth between the parties, ultimately establishing a contract between them. A dispute arose, however, and the court was called on to determine (1) when the contract was formed, and (2) whether it included or excluded an arbitration clause requiring the parties to arbitrate their disputes in Moscow. In reaching its conclusion, the court relies on many of the CISG provisions discussed in the excerpt above.

Filanto, S.p.A. v. Chilewich International Corp.

United States District Court, Southern District of New York
789 F. Supp. 1229 (1992)

BRIEANT, CHIEF JUDGE. By motion fully submitted on December 11, 1991, defendant Chilewich International Corp. moves to stay this action pending arbitration in Moscow. Plaintiff Filanto has moved to enjoin arbitration or to order arbitration in this federal district.

This case is a striking example of how a lawsuit involving a relatively straightforward international commercial transaction can raise an array of complex questions. Accordingly, the Court will recount the factual background of the case, derived from both parties' memoranda of law and supporting affidavits, in some detail.

Plaintiff Filanto is an Italian corporation engaged in the manufacture and sale of footwear. Defendant Chilewich is an export-import firm incorporated in the state of New York with its principal place of business in White Plains. On February 28, 1989, Chilewich's agent in the United Kingdom, Byerly Johnson, Ltd., signed a contract with Raznoexport, the Soviet Foreign Economic Association, which obligated Byerly Johnson to supply footwear to Raznoexport.

51. It reads: "Additional or different terms relating, among other things, to the price, payment, quality and quantity of the goods, place and time of delivery, extent of one party's liability to the other or the settlement of disputes are considered to alter the terms of the offer materially."

52. CISG Article 18(1) provides for acceptance by conduct: "A statement made by or other conduct of the offeree indicating assent to an offer is an acceptance. Silence or inactivity does not in itself amount to acceptance."

Section 10 of this contract—the "Russian Contract"—is an arbitration clause, which reads in pertinent part as follows:

> All disputes or differences which may arise out of or in connection with the present Contract are to be settled, jurisdiction of ordinary courts being excluded, by the Arbitration at the USSR Chamber of Commerce and Industry, Moscow, in accordance with the Regulations of the said Arbitration.

The first exchange of correspondence between the parties to this lawsuit is a letter dated July 27, 1989 from Mr. Melvin Chilewich of Chilewich International to Mr. Antonio Filograna, chief executive officer of Filanto. This letter refers to a recent visit by Chilewich and Byerly Johnson personnel to Filanto's factories in Italy, presumably to negotiate a purchase to fulfill the Russian Contract, and then states as follows:

> Attached please find our contract to cover our purchase from you. Same is governed by the conditions which are enumerated in the standard contract in effect with the Soviet buyers [the Russian contract], copy of which is also enclosed.

The next item in the record is a letter from Filanto to Chilewich dated September 2, 1989. . . . This letter refers to a letter from Chilewich to Filanto of August 11, 1989, which "you [Chilewich] sent me with the contracts n 10001-10002-10003." These numbers do not correspond to the contract sued on here, but refer instead to other, similar contracts between the parties.[2] None of these contracts, or their terms, are in the record, both parties having been afforded ample opportunity to submit whatever they wished. The last paragraph of the September 2, 1989 letter from Filanto to Chilewich states as follows:

> Returning back the enclosed contracts n 10001-10002-10003 signed for acceptance, we communicate, if we do not misunderstood [sic], the Soviet's contract that you sent us together with your above mentioned contract, that of this contract we have to respect only the following points of it:
> -n 5 Packing and marking
> -n 6 Way of Shipment
> -n 7 Delivery—Acceptance of Goods
> We ask for your acceptance by return of post.

The intent of this paragraph, clearly, was to exclude from incorporation by reference inter alia section 10 of the Russian contract, which provides for arbitration. Chilewich, for its part, claims never to have received this September 2 letter. In any event, it relates only to prior course of conduct.

It is apparent from the record that further negotiations occurred in early 1990, but the content of these negotiations is unclear; it is, however, clear that deliveries of boots from Filanto to Chilewich were occurring at this time,

2. In his affidavit dated October 29, 1991, Mr. Filograna states that there were actually six contracts between the parties.

pursuant to other contracts, since there is a reference to a shipment occurring between April 23, 1990 and June 11, 1990.

The next document in this case, and the focal point of the parties' dispute regarding whether an arbitration agreement exists, is a Memorandum Agreement dated March 13, 1990. This Memorandum Agreement, number 9003002, is a standard merchant's memo prepared by Chilewich for signature by both parties confirming that Filanto will deliver 100,000 pairs of boots to Chilewich at the Italian/Yugoslav border on September 15, 1990, with the balance of 150,000 pairs to be delivered on November 1, 1990. Chilewich's obligations were to open a Letter of Credit in Filanto's favor prior to the September 15 delivery, and another letter prior to the November delivery. This Memorandum includes the following provision:

> It is understood between Buyer and Seller that USSR Contract No. 32-03/93085 [the Russian Contract] is hereby incorporated in this contract as far as practicable, and specifically that any arbitration shall be in accordance with that Contract.

Chilewich signed this Memorandum Agreement, and sent it to Filanto. Filanto at that time did not sign or return the document. Nevertheless, on May 7, 1990, Chilewich opened a Letter of Credit in Filanto's favor in the sum of $2,595,600.00. The Letter of Credit itself mentions the Russian Contract, but only insofar as concerns packing and labeling.

Again, on July 23, 1990, Filanto sent another letter to Chilewich, which reads in relevant part as follows:

> We refer to Point 3, Special Conditions, to point out that: returning back the above-mentioned contract, signed for acceptance, from Soviet Contract 32-03/93085 we have to respect only the following points of it:
> -No. 5-Packing and Marking
> -No. 6-Way of Shipment
> -No. 7-Delivery-Acceptance of Goods.

It should be noted that the contract referred to in this letter is apparently another contract between the parties, as the letter refers to "Sub. Contract No. 32-03/03122," while the contract sued on in the present action is No. 32-03/03123.

This letter caused some concern on the part of Chilewich and its agents: a July 30, 1990 fax from Byerly Johnson, Chilewich's agent, to Chilewich, mentions Filanto's July 23 letter, asserts that it "very neatly dodges" certain issues, other than arbitration, covered by the Russian Contract, and states that Johnson would "take it up" with Filanto during a visit to Filanto's offices the next week.

Then, on August 7, 1990, Filanto returned the Memorandum Agreement, sued on here, that Chilewich had signed and sent to it in March; though Filanto had signed the Memorandum Agreement, it once again appended a covering letter, purporting to exclude all but three sections of the Russian Contract.

There is also in the record an August 7, 1990 telex from Chilewich to Byerly Johnson, stating that Chilewich would not open the second Letter of Credit unless it received from Filanto a signed copy of the contract without any exclusions. In order to resolve this issue, Byerly Johnson on August 29, 1990 sent a fax to Italian Trading SRL, an intermediary, reading in relevant part:

> We have checked back through our records for last year, and can find no exclusions by Filanto from the Soviet Master Contract and, in the event, we do not believe that this has caused any difficulties between us. We would, therefore, ask you to . . . accept all points of the Soviet Master Contract . . . as far as practicable. . . .

Filanto later confirmed to Italian Trading that it received this fax.

As the date specified in the Memorandum Agreement for delivery of the first shipment of boots—September 15, 1990—was approaching, the parties evidently decided to make further efforts to resolve this issue: what actually happened, though, is a matter of some dispute. Mr. Filograna, the CEO of Filanto, asserts that [Simon Chilewich agreed that the Filanto-Chilewich Contract would incorporate only the packing, shipment and delivery terms of the Russian Contract.] Mr. Simon Chilewich [stated Mr. Filograna agreed to Chilewich's position].

On September 27, 1990, Mr. Filograna faxed a letter to Chilewich. This letter . . . complains that Chilewich had not yet opened the second Letter of Credit for the second delivery, which it had supposedly promised to do by September 25. Mr. Chilewich responded by fax on the same day; his fax states that he is "totally cognizant of the contractual obligations which exist," but goes on to say that Chilewich had encountered difficulties with the Russian buyers, that Chilewich needed to "reduce the rate of shipments," and denies that Chilewich promised to open the Letter of Credit by September 25.

According to the Complaint, what ultimately happened was that Chilewich bought and paid for 60,000 pairs of boots in January 1991, but never purchased the 90,000 pairs of boots that comprise the balance of Chilewich's original order. It is Chilewich's failure to do so that forms the basis of this lawsuit, commenced by Filanto on May 14, 1991.

There is in the record, however, one document that post-dates the filing of the Complaint: a letter from Filanto to Chilewich dated June 21, 1991. This letter is in response to claims by Byerly Johnson that some of the boots that had been supplied by Filanto were defective. The letter expressly relies on a section of the Russian contract which Filanto had earlier purported to exclude—Section 9 regarding claims procedures.

This letter must be regarded as an admission in law by Filanto, the party to be charged. A litigant may not blow hot and cold in a lawsuit. The letter of June 21, 1991 clearly shows that when Filanto thought it desirable to do so, it recognized that it was bound by the incorporation by reference of portions of the Russian Contract, which, prior to the Paris meeting, it had purported to exclude. This letter shows that Filanto regarded itself as the beneficiary of the claims adjustment provisions of the Russian Contract. This legal position is entirely inconsistent with the position which Filanto had professed prior to the

Paris meeting, and is inconsistent with its present position. Consistent with the position of the defendant in this action, Filanto admits that the other relevant clauses of the Russian Contract were incorporated by agreement of the parties, and made a part of the bargain. Of necessity, this must include the agreement to arbitrate in Moscow. In the June 21, 1991 letter, Mr. Filograna writes:

> The April Shipment and the September Shipment are governed by the Master Purchase Contract of February 28, 1989 N. 32-03-93085 (the "Master Purchase Contract") The Master Purchase Contract provides that claims for inferior quality must be made within six months of the arrival of the goods at the USSR port.

Against this background based almost entirely on documents, defendant Chilewich on July 24, 1991 moved to stay this action pending arbitration, while plaintiff Filanto on August 22, 1992 moved to enjoin arbitration, or, alternatively, for an order directing that arbitration be held in the Southern District of New York rather than Moscow, because of unsettled political conditions in Russia.

JURISDICTION/APPLICABLE LAW

. . . The United States, Italy and the USSR are all signatories to [the New York Convention on the Recognition and Enforcement of Foreign Arbitral Awards] and its implementing legislation makes clear that the Arbitration Convention governs disputes regarding arbitration agreements between parties to international commercial transactions. . . .

The Arbitration Convention specifically requires courts to recognize any "agreement in writing under which the parties undertake to submit to arbitration. . . ." The term "agreement in writing" is defined as "an arbitral clause in a contract or an arbitration agreement, signed by the parties or contained in an exchange of letters or telegram." . . .

Courts interpreting this "agreement in writing" requirement have generally started their analysis with the plain language of the Convention, which requires "an arbitral clause in a contract or an arbitration agreement, signed by the parties or contained in an exchange of letters or telegrams" and have then applied that language in light of federal law, which consists of generally accepted principles of contract law, including the Uniform Commercial Code. . . .

However, as plaintiff correctly notes, the "general principles of contract law" relevant to this action, do *not* include the Uniform Commercial Code; rather, the "federal law of contracts" to be applied in this case is found in the United Nations Convention on Contracts for the International Sale of Goods (the "Sale of Goods Convention"), codified at 15 U.S.C. Appendix (West Supp. 1991).[5] This Convention, ratified by the Senate in 1986, is a self-executing agreement

5. Of course, as with the Arbitration Convention, the Sale of Goods Convention is also "state law." U.S. Const. art. VI cl. 2; *Hauenstein v. Lynham*, 100 U.S. 483, 490 (1880) ("[T]he Constitution, laws, and treaties of the United States are as much a part of the law of every state as its own local laws and Constitution").

which entered into force between the United States and other signatories, including Italy, on January 1, 1988. Although there is as yet virtually no U.S. case law interpreting the Sale of Goods Convention, it may safely be predicted that this will change: absent a choice-of-law provision, and with certain exclusions not here relevant, the Convention governs *all* contracts between parties with places of business in different nations, so long as both nations are signatories to the Convention. Sale of Goods Convention Article 1(1)(a). Since the contract alleged in this case most certainly was formed, if at all, after January 1, 1988, and since both the United States and Italy are signatories to the Convention, the Court will interpret the "agreement in writing" requirement of the Arbitration Convention in light of, and with reference to, the substantive international law of contracts embodied in the Sale of Goods Convention. Not surprisingly, the parties offer varying interpretations of the numerous letters and documents exchanged between them. The Court will briefly summarize their respective contentions.

Defendant Chilewich contends that the Memorandum Agreement dated March 13 which it signed and sent to Filanto was an offer. It then argues that Filanto's retention of the letter, along with its subsequent acceptance of Chilewich's performance under the Agreement—the furnishing of the May 11 letter of credit—estops it from denying its acceptance of the contract. Although phrased as an estoppel argument, this contention is better viewed as an acceptance by conduct argument, e.g., that in light of the parties' course of dealing, Filanto had a duty timely to inform Chilewich that it objected to the incorporation by reference of all the terms of the Russian contract. Under this view, the return of the Memorandum Agreement, signed by Filanto, on August 7, 1990, along with the covering letter purporting to exclude parts of the Russian Contract, was ineffective as a matter of law as a rejection of the March 13 offer, because this occurred some five months after Filanto received the Memorandum Agreement and two months after Chilewich furnished the Letter of Credit. Instead, in Chilewich's view, this action was a proposal for modification of the March 13 Agreement. Chilewich rejected this proposal, by its letter of August 7 to Byerly Johnson, and the August 29 fax by Johnson to Italian Trading SRL, which communication Filanto acknowledges receiving. Accordingly, Filanto under this interpretation is bound by the written terms of the March 13 Memorandum Agreement; since that agreement incorporates by reference the Russian Contract containing the arbitration provision, Filanto is bound to arbitrate.

Plaintiff Filanto's interpretation of the evidence is rather different. While Filanto apparently agrees that the March 13 Memorandum Agreement was indeed an offer, it characterizes its August 7 return of the signed Memorandum Agreement with the covering letter as a counteroffer. While defendant contends that under Uniform Commercial Code § 2-207 this action would be viewed as an acceptance with a proposal for a material modification, the Uniform Commercial Code, as previously noted does not apply to this case, because the State Department undertook to fix something that was not broken by helping to create the Sale of Goods Convention which varies from the Uniform Commercial Code in many significant ways. Instead, under this analysis, Article 19(1) of the Sale of Goods Convention would apply. That section, as the Commentary to the Sale of Goods Convention notes, reverses the rule of Uniform Commercial Code § 2-207, and reverts to the common law rule that "A reply to an offer which purports to be an acceptance but contains additions, limitations or other modifications is a rejection of the offer and constitutes a counter-offer." Sale of Goods Convention Article 19(1). Although the Convention, like the Uniform Commercial Code, does state that non-material terms do become part of the contract unless objected to, Sale of Goods Convention Article 19(2), the Convention treats inclusion (or deletion) of an arbitration provision as "material," Sale of Goods Convention Article 19(3). The August 7 letter, therefore, was a counteroffer which, according to Filanto, Chilewich accepted by its letter dated September 27, 1990. Though that letter refers to and acknowledges the "contractual obligations" between the parties, it is doubtful whether it can be characterized as an acceptance.

More generally, both parties seem to have lost sight of the narrow scope of the inquiry required by the Arbitration Convention. All that this Court need do is to determine if a sufficient "agreement in writing" to arbitrate disputes exists between these parties. . . .

The Court is satisfied on this record that there *was* indeed an agreement to arbitrate between these parties.

There is simply no satisfactory explanation as to why Filanto failed to object to the incorporation by reference of the Russian Contract in a timely fashion. As noted above, Chilewich had in the meantime commenced its performance under the Agreement, and the Letter of Credit it furnished Filanto on May 11 itself mentioned the Russian Contract. An offeree who, knowing that the offeror has commenced performance, fails to notify the offeror of its objection to the terms of the contract within a reasonable time will, under certain circumstances, be deemed to have assented to those terms. *Restatement (Second) of Contracts* § 69 (1981). The Sale of Goods Convention itself recognizes this rule: Article 18(1), provides that "A statement made by or other conduct of the offeree indicating assent to an offer is an acceptance." Although mere "silence or inactivity" does not constitute acceptance, Sale of Goods Convention Article 18(1), the Court may consider previous relations between the parties in assessing whether a party's conduct constituted acceptance, Sale of Goods Convention Article 8(3). In this case, in light of the extensive course of prior dealing between these parties, Filanto was certainly under a duty to alert Chilewich in timely fashion to its objections to the terms of the March 13 Memorandum Agreement—particularly since Chilewich had repeatedly referred it to the Russian Contract and Filanto had had a copy of that document for some time.

There [is another] convincing manifestation[] of Filanto's true understanding of the terms of this agreement. . . .

Filanto, in a letter to Byerly Johnson dated June 21, 1991, explicitly stated that "[t]he April Shipment and the September shipment are governed by the Master Purchase Contract of February 28, 1989 [the Russian Contract]." Furthermore, the letter, which responds to claims by Johnson that some of the boots that were supplied were defective, expressly relies on section 9 of the Russian Contract—another section which Filanto had in its earlier correspondence purported to exclude. The Sale of Goods Convention specifically directs that "[i]n determining the intent of a party . . . due consideration is to be given to . . . any subsequent conduct of the parties," Sale of Goods Convention Article 8(3). In this case, as the letter post-dates the partial performance of the contract, it is particularly strong evidence that Filanto recognized itself to be bound by all the terms of the Russian Contract.

In light of these factors, and heeding the presumption in favor of arbitration, which is even stronger in the context of international commercial transactions, the Court holds that Filanto is bound by the terms of the March 13 Memorandum Agreement, and so must arbitrate its dispute in Moscow.

RELEVANT PROVISIONS

For the CISG, consult Articles 8, 18, and 19. For the UNIDROIT Principles, consult Articles 2.1.12, 2.1.19, 2.1.20, 2.1.21, and 2.1.22.

NOTES AND QUESTIONS

1. *What happened?* Who sued whom for what? Procedurally, how did the case get before this court? Factually, what happened between the parties? What arguments did the plaintiff and defendant make? What rule or rules did the court apply? How did the court analyze the dispute between the parties? How did the court decide the case?

2. *Was this case correctly decided?* Do you agree with the result reached in this case? Why or why not? Do you agree with the court's reasoning? Why or why not? How, if at all, would you have written the opinion differently?

3. *Comparative analysis.* Do you think the solution adopted by the common law, the UCC, or the CISG is better for resolving battle of the forms problems? Why?

4. *Thinking tools.* Drawing on any of the thinking tools we have previously examined, which method of resolving battle of the forms problems seems best? Why?

PROBLEM: MAY THE FORCE BE WITH YOU

Luke Skywalker sends the Jawas (a band of merchants trading in scavenged, technological goods) an offer to buy a lightsaber. On the back of his "Purchase Order" Skywalker includes the following term: "All disputes arising out of or relating to this contract shall be arbitrated before the Jedi Council on the planet of Coruscant under the Rules of the Galactic Arbitration Association." The Jawas, no strangers to such tactics themselves, shipped the lightsaber to Luke Skywalker along with an "Acknowledgement of Order Form," on the back of which states it wrote that "All disputes relating to the conformity of the lightsaber shall be arbitrated in Mos Eisley, on the planet of Tatooine, under the rules of the Tatooine Chamber of Commerce." The lightsaber was destroyed in transit and each party claimed the other should bear the risk of loss. The Jawas brought suit against Skywalker on Tatooine to recover the price. Skywalker filed a motion to stay litigation pending arbitration and a motion to compel arbitration on Coruscant.

1. Assume Luke Skywalker is located on Coruscant and the Jawas are located on the planet of Tatooine. How should this dispute be resolved under UCC § 2-207?

2. Assume that Luke Skywalker's place of business is in Coruscant and the Jawas' place of business is in Tatooine, and that both are CISG signatory states. How should this dispute be resolved under the CISG?

PROBLEM: WHAT TERMS APPLY?

Pablo, a law student, went online to buy a new computer from Dynamic Computing ("DC"). DC allows its customers to build their own computers by choose their hard drive, RAM, monitor, etc. When Pablo finished building his computer online, he was quoted a price of $2,000 and was asked to call a customer service representative to place his order. Pablo did so, was again quoted a price of $2,000 by the customer service representative, and paid for his order by providing his credit card information over the phone. At no point during this transaction were any terms and conditions discussed besides price and the computer components selected by Pablo. When the computer arrived at Pablo's house three days later, he immediately opened it up and noticed that a contract with several pages of fine print (in 10-point font) was attached to his monitor. Although Pablo never read this contract, buried in the fine print were clauses (a) requiring that any disputes between DC and its customers be settled by binding arbitration under the rules of the American Arbitration Association, and (b) exclaiming liability for consequential damages. Another term that Pablo did not read states as follows: "If you do not accept any of these terms, please return the computer to us, at our own expense, within 14 days. Failure to do so indicates your acceptance of the terms in this agreement."

Pablo used the computer for several months without having ever read any of the terms DC attached to his monitor. As Pablo was getting ready to print out his outlines for his final exams, his computer crashed, and he lost all of his data. Consequently, he did poorly on his final exams and got kicked out of law school. If Pablo brings suit against DC for breach of contract, would his contract be governed by the arbitration clause and the clause excluding consequential damages?

3. Identifying Contract Terms in the Internet Age

This subsection is a continuation of the previous subsection on "The Battle of the Forms," but with a special emphasis on contracts created in the Internet age. In particular, we will be examining the extent to which the traditional principles of contract law are applicable to relatively recent developments in our economy, such as e-commerce.

ProCD v. Zeidenberg

United States Court of Appeals, Seventh Circuit
86 F.3d 1447 (1996)

EASTERBROOK, **Circuit Judge.** Must buyers of computer software obey the terms of shrinkwrap licenses? The district court held not, for two reasons: first, they are not contracts because the licenses are inside the box rather than printed on the outside; second, federal law forbids enforcement even if the licenses are contracts. The parties and numerous ***amici curiae*** have briefed many other issues, but these are the only two that matter—and we disagree with the district judge's conclusion on each. Shrinkwrap licenses are enforceable unless their terms are objectionable on grounds applicable to contracts in general (for example, if they violate a rule of positive law, or if they are unconscionable). Because no one argues that the terms of the license at issue here are troublesome, we remand with instructions to enter judgment for the plaintiff.

> ***Amicus curiae***
>
> "[Latin 'friend of the court'] (17c) Someone who is not a party to a lawsuit but who petitions the court or is requested by the court to file a brief in the action because that person has a strong interest in the subject matter. Often shortened to *amicus*." BLACK'S LAW DICTIONARY (10th ed. 2014).

I

[Plaintiff ProCD compiled information from over 3,000 telephone directories into a database, which it then sold on CD-ROM discs. These discs were "shrinkwrapped," or covered with plastic or cellophane packaging, and each package contained an end-user licensing agreement. This licensing agreement, which also appeared on the user's computer screen every time the software runs, limited the use of the application program and listings to non-commercial purposes. Matthew Zeidenberg bought this software from ProCD and, ignoring the license, formed his own company to resell the information for less than ProCD charged its commercial customers. ProCD sought an injunction against Zeidenberg against further dissemination of the software that exceeded the rights specified in the licenses. The district court denied the injunction, holding that the licenses were without effect because their terms did not appear on the outside of the packages.]

II

Following the district court, we treat the licenses as ordinary contracts accompanying the sale of products, and therefore as governed by the common law of contracts and the Uniform Commercial Code. . . . Zeidenberg . . . argue[s], and the district court held, that placing the package of software on the shelf is an "offer," which the customer "accepts" by paying the asking price and leaving the store with the goods. In Wisconsin, as elsewhere, a contract includes only the terms on which the parties have agreed. One cannot agree to hidden terms, the judge concluded. So far, so good—but one of the terms to which Zeidenberg agreed by purchasing the software is that the transaction was subject to a license. Zeidenberg's position therefore must be that the printed terms on the outside of a box are the parties' contract—except for printed terms that refer to or incorporate other terms. But why would Wisconsin fetter the parties' choice in this way? Vendors can put the entire terms of a contract on the outside of a box only by using microscopic type, removing other information that buyers might find more useful (such as what the software does, and on which computers it works), or both. The "Read Me" file included with most software, describing system requirements and potential incompatibilities, may be equivalent to ten pages of type; warranties and license restrictions take still more space. Notice on the outside, terms on the inside, and a right to return the software for a refund if the terms are unacceptable (a right that the license expressly extends), may be a means of doing business valuable to buyers and sellers alike. *See* E. Allan Farnsworth, 1 *Farnsworth on Contracts* § 4.26 (1990); *Restatement (2d) of Contracts* § 211 comment a (1981) ("Standardization of agreements serves many of the same functions as standardization of goods and services; both are essential to a system of mass production and distribution. Scarce and costly time and skill can be devoted to a class of transactions rather than the details of individual transactions."). Doubtless a state could forbid the use of standard contracts in the software business, but we do not think that Wisconsin has done so.

Transactions in which the exchange of money precedes the communication of detailed terms are common. Consider the purchase of insurance. The buyer goes to an agent, who explains the essentials (amount of coverage, number of years) and remits the premium to the home office, which sends back a policy. On the district judge's understanding, the terms of the policy are irrelevant because the insured paid before receiving them. Yet the device of payment, often with a "binder" (so that the insurance takes effect immediately even though the home office reserves the right to withdraw coverage later), in advance of the policy, serves buyers' interests by accelerating effectiveness and reducing transactions costs. Or consider the purchase of an airline ticket. The traveler calls the carrier or an agent, is quoted a price, reserves a seat, pays, and gets a ticket, in that order. The ticket contains elaborate terms, which the traveler can reject by canceling the reservation. To use the ticket is to accept the terms, even terms that in retrospect are disadvantageous. See *Carnival Cruise Lines, Inc. v. Shute,* 499 U.S. 585 (1991). Just so with a ticket to a concert. The back of the ticket states that the patron promises not to record the concert; to attend is to agree. A theater that detects a violation will confiscate the tape and escort the violator to the exit. One *could* arrange things so that every concertgoer signs this promise before forking over the money, but that cumbersome way of doing things not only would lengthen queues and raise prices but also would scotch the sale of tickets by phone or electronic data service.

Consumer goods work the same way. Someone who wants to buy a radio set visits a store, pays, and walks out with a box. Inside the box is a leaflet containing some terms, the most important of which usually is the warranty, read for the first time in the comfort of home. By Zeidenberg's lights, the warranty in the box is irrelevant; every consumer gets the standard warranty implied by the UCC in the event the contract is silent; yet so far as we are aware no state disregards warranties furnished with consumer products. Drugs come with a list of ingredients on the outside and an elaborate package insert on the inside. The package insert describes drug interactions, contraindications, and other vital information—but, if Zeidenberg is right, the purchaser need not read the package insert, because it is not part of the contract.

Next consider the software industry itself. Only a minority of sales take place over the counter, where there are boxes to peruse. A customer may place an order by phone in response to a line item in a catalog or a review in a magazine. Much software is ordered over the Internet by purchasers who have never seen a box. Increasingly software arrives by wire. There is no box; there is only a stream of electrons, a collection of information that includes data, an application program, instructions, many limitations, and the terms of sale. The user purchases a serial number, which activates the software's features. On Zeidenberg's arguments, these unboxed sales are unfettered by terms—so the seller has made a broad warranty and must pay consequential damages for any shortfalls in performance, two "promises" that if taken seriously would drive prices through the ceiling or return transactions to the horse-and-buggy age.

According to the district court, the UCC does not countenance the sequence of money now, terms later. . . . To judge by the flux of law review articles discussing shrinkwrap licenses, uncertainty is much in need of reduction—although businesses seem to feel less uncertainty than do scholars, for only three cases (other than ours) touch on the subject, and none directly addresses it. *See Step-Saver Data Systems, Inc. v. Wyse Technology,* 939 F.2d 91 (3d Cir. 1991). As their titles suggest, these are not consumer transactions. *Step-Saver* is a battle-of-the-forms case, in which the parties exchange incompatible forms and a court must decide which prevails. **Our case has only one form; UCC § 2-207 is irrelevant.** . . .

> **Critical reading**
>
> Read UCC § 2-207 carefully. Does the text support Judge Easterbrook's interpretation that the UCC is irrelevant where there is only one form? Judge Vratil, who we will meet in *Klocek v. Gateway, infra,* doesn't seem to think so, and addresses this point at length in her opinion.

What then does the current version of the UCC have to say? We think that the place to start is § 2-204(1): "A contract for sale of goods may be made in any manner sufficient to show agreement, including conduct by both parties which recognizes the existence of such a contract." A vendor, as master of the offer, may invite acceptance by conduct, and may propose limitations on the kind of conduct that constitutes acceptance. A buyer may accept by performing the acts the vendor proposes to treat as acceptance. And that is what happened. ProCD proposed a contract that a buyer would accept by *using* the software after having an opportunity to read the license at leisure. This Zeidenberg did. He had no choice, because the software splashed the license on the screen and would not let him proceed without indicating acceptance. So although the district judge was right to say that a contract can be, and often is, formed simply by paying the price and walking out of the store, the UCC permits contracts to be formed in other ways. ProCD proposed such a different way, and without protest Zeidenberg agreed. Ours is not a case in which a consumer opens a package to find an insert saying "you owe us an extra $10,000" and the seller files suit to collect. Any buyer finding such a demand can prevent formation of the contract by returning the package, as can any consumer who concludes that the terms of the license make the software worth less than the purchase price. Nothing in the UCC requires a seller to maximize the buyer's net gains.

Section 2-606, which defines "acceptance of goods," reinforces this understanding. A buyer accepts goods under § 2-606(1)(b) when, after an opportunity to inspect, he fails to make an effective rejection under § 2-602(1). ProCD extended an opportunity to reject if a buyer should find the license terms unsatisfactory; Zeidenberg inspected the package, tried out the software, learned of the license, and did not reject the goods. We refer to § 2-606 only to show that the opportunity to return goods can be important; acceptance of an offer differs from acceptance of goods after delivery, but the UCC consistently permits the parties to structure their relations so that the buyer has a chance to make a final decision after a detailed review. . . .

Zeidenberg has not located any Wisconsin case—for that matter, any case in any state—holding that under the UCC the ordinary terms found in shrinkwrap licenses require any special prominence, or otherwise are to be undercut rather than enforced. In the end, the terms of the license are conceptually identical to the contents of the package. Just as no court would dream of saying that SelectPhone (trademark) must contain 3,100 phone books rather than 3,000, or must have data no more than 30 days old, or must sell for $100 rather than $150—although any of these changes would be welcomed by the customer, if all other things were held constant—so, we believe, Wisconsin would not let the buyer pick and choose among terms. Terms of use are no less a part of "the product" than are the size of the database and the speed with which the software compiles listings. Competition among vendors, not judicial revision of a package's contents, is how consumers are protected in a market economy. ProCD has rivals, which may elect to compete by offering superior software, monthly updates, improved terms of use, lower price, or a better compromise among these elements. As we stressed above, adjusting terms in buyers' favor might help Matthew Zeidenberg today (he already has the software) but would lead to a response, such as a higher price, that might make consumers as a whole worse off. . . .

REVERSED AND REMANDED.

RELEVANT PROVISIONS

For the UCC, consult §§ 2-204, 2-207 and 2-606.

NOTES AND QUESTIONS

1. *What happened?* Who sued whom for what? Procedurally, how did the case get before this court? Factually, what happened between the parties? What arguments did the plaintiff and defendant make? What rule or rules did the court apply? How did the court analyze the dispute between the parties? How did the court decide the case?

2. *Was this case correctly decided?* Do you agree with the result reached in this case? Why or why not? Do you agree with the court's reasoning? Why or why not? How, if at all, would you have written the opinion differently?

3. *Reason by analogy?* To what extent should the rules developed in *Step-Saver* be applicable to problems of assent in the context of electronic commerce?

4. *Comparative analysis.* How would this case be resolved under the CISG? Would the CISG provide a better approach? Why or why not?

PROCD AND COGNITIVE OVERLOAD IN CONTRACTUAL BARGAINING*

Sellers often find it useful to sell products without revealing the terms of the contract to buyers until after buyers have taken the products home or begun to use them. These transactions take a number of forms. A buyer might purchase a box

* Excerpted from Eric A. Posner, *ProCD v. Zeidenberg and Cognitive Overload in Contractual Bargaining*, 77 U. Chi. L. Rev. 1181, 1181-83 (2010).

containing software or a database from a store. The box's skin bears the name of the software and a description of its function, and perhaps a statement that other terms are inside, or perhaps not. The buyer learns the terms only after he takes the box home and opens it; if he does not like the terms, he can return the product as long as he has not yet begun to use it, and sometimes not even then. A buyer might order a computer or appliance or airplane ticket over the phone. The operator tells him none of the terms other than price and a few others; again, he learns those terms when the product or ticket arrives and may (or may not) have an opportunity at that point to repudiate the transaction.

The evident business reason for these "terms later" or "rolling" contracts, as they are sometimes called, is that sellers cannot communicate all the relevant information to the buyer on the outsides of boxes or in telephone conversations. Buyers do not have the time or patience to listen to or read and understand the terms. The optimal terms cannot be disclosed without causing cognitive overload. To avoid driving off buyers, sellers provide minimal information in advance of purchase. Yet when buyers learn of unfavorable arbitration clauses or other adverse terms, they complain that they never consented to those terms, and therefore should not be bound to them.

This problem is not entirely new. The earlier manifestation involved lengthy standard form contracts that consumers signed when they purchased automobiles, appliances, and other complex products. Consumers were given the opportunity to read the terms before they signed the contracts, but clearly many did not. They could not make their way through the legalese, the complex sentences, the fine print, the sheer length of the document. Under the common law duty to read they were nonetheless bound, but courts gradually relaxed the rule, holding that buyers could be bound to especially unfavorable terms only if they were conspicuous (and not unconscionable).[2] What is different about the new group of cases is that the terms are not even inconspicuous—they are invisible.It would seem to follow that these contracts are invalid. And that is what the district court held in the case of *ProCD v. Zeidenberg*. ProCD created a database consisting of names, telephone numbers, and other information, from more than three thousand telephone directories. It sold two versions of this database: a cheaper version to the public, and a more expensive version to businesses. The first contract limited use of the database to noncommercial purposes; the contract with businesses had no such limitation. ProCD stated on the outside of the box that the database was subject to restrictions in a license in the box but did not state what those restrictions were. Zeidenberg bought the consumer version of the product and sought to resell ProCD's database to customers over the Internet. ProCD brought a lawsuit based on breach of contract.

The district court refused to enforce the license restriction, holding that the "offer," which included only the visible terms on the outside of the box, did not include the restriction to noncommercial uses. Zeidenberg "accepted" this offer

2. *See*, for example, *Williams v Walker-Thomas Furniture Co*, 350 F.2d 445, 449 (D.C. Cir. 1965) ("[W]hen a party of little bargaining power, and hence little real choice, signs a commercially unreasonable contract with little or no knowledge of its terms, it is hardly likely that his consent, or even an objective manifestation of his consent, was ever given to all the terms.").

by handing money over to the store. Because he could not see and learn of the restriction at the time that he accepted, he could not be bound by it.

The court's decision was vulnerable to two objections, one logical and one practical. In his opinion reversing the decision, Judge Frank Easterbrook pressed both of these points. The logical objection is that the offer did include the terms in the box by reference. If Zeidenberg did not like the idea that he could be bound to terms that he has not seen, he was free to refuse to buy the product.

In Wisconsin, as elsewhere, a contract includes only the terms on which the parties have agreed. One cannot agree to hidden terms, the [district] judge concluded. So far, so good—but one of the terms to which Zeidenberg agreed by purchasing the software is that the transaction was subject to a license. Zeidenberg's position therefore must be that the printed terms on the outside of a box are the parties' contract—except for printed terms that refer to or incorporate other terms. But why would Wisconsin fetter the parties' choice in this way?

If contracts rest on consent, then parties should be able to consent to be bound by hidden terms.

The practical objection is that all the terms of a contract can rarely be put on the outside of a box. Contracts are long and detailed by necessity. To sell goods, manufacturers need to be able to put just the crucial terms on the box (such as the price) along with useful information, and to omit information of little use to consumers, including obvious information.

Do you think the logical and practical objections identified above are enough to overcome traditional rules of offer and acceptance? Can you think of a better rule? Some of the practical objections will be further discussed in the case below.

Hill v. Gateway 2000

United States Court of Appeals, Seventh Circuit
105 F.3d 1147 (1997)

EASTERBROOK, **Circuit Judge.** A customer picks up the phone, orders a computer, and gives a credit card number. Presently a box arrives, containing the computer and a list of terms, said to govern unless the customer returns the computer within 30 days. Are these terms effective as the parties' contract, or is the contract term-free because the order-taker did not read any terms over the phone and elicit the customer's assent?

One of the terms in the box containing a Gateway 2000 system was an arbitration clause. Rich and Enza Hill, the customers, kept the computer more than 30 days before complaining about its components and performance. They filed suit in federal court arguing, among other things, that the product's shortcomings make Gateway a racketeer (mail and wire fraud are said to be the predicate offenses), leading to treble damages under RICO for the Hills and a class of all other purchasers. Gateway asked the district court to enforce the arbitration clause; the judge refused, writing that "the present record is insufficient to support a finding of a valid arbitration agreement between the parties or that the plaintiffs were given adequate notice of the arbitration clause." Gateway took an immediate appeal, as is its right.

The Hills say that the arbitration clause did not stand out: they concede noticing the statement of terms but deny reading it closely enough to discover the agreement to arbitrate, and they ask us to conclude that they therefore may go to court. . . . A contract need not be read to be effective; people who accept take the risk that the unread terms may in retrospect prove unwelcome. Terms inside Gateway's box stand or fall together. If they constitute the parties' contract because the Hills had an opportunity to return the computer after reading them, then all must be enforced.

ProCD, Inc. v. Zeidenberg, 86 F.3d 1447 (7th Cir. 1996), holds that terms inside a box of software bind consumers who use the software after an opportunity to read the terms and to reject them by returning the product. Likewise, *Carnival Cruise Lines, Inc. v. Shute*, 499 U.S. 585 (1991) enforces a forum-selection clause that was included among three pages of terms attached to a cruise ship ticket. *ProCD* and *Carnival Cruise Lines* exemplify the many commercial transactions in which people pay for products with terms to follow; *ProCD* discusses others. The district court concluded in *ProCD* that the contract is formed when the consumer pays for the software; as a result, the court held, only terms known to the consumer at that moment are part of the contract, and provisos inside the box do not count. Although this is one way a contract could be formed, it is not the only way: "A vendor, as master of the offer, may invite acceptance by conduct, and may propose limitations on the kind of conduct that constitutes acceptance. A buyer may accept by performing the acts the vendor proposes to treat as acceptance." *Id.* at 1452. Gateway shipped computers with the same sort of accept-or-return offer ProCD made to users of its software. *ProCD* relied on the Uniform Commercial Code rather than any peculiarities of Wisconsin law; both Illinois and South Dakota, the two states whose law might govern relations between Gateway and the Hills, have adopted the UCC; neither side has pointed us to any atypical doctrines in those states that might be pertinent; *ProCD* therefore applies to this dispute.

Plaintiffs ask us to limit *ProCD* to software, but where's the sense in that? *ProCD* is about the law of contract, not the law of software. Payment preceding the revelation of full terms is common for air transportation, insurance, and many other endeavors. Practical considerations support allowing vendors to enclose the full legal terms with their products. Cashiers cannot be expected to read legal documents to customers before ringing up sales. If the staff at the other end of the phone for direct-sales operations such as Gateway's had to read the four-page statement of terms before taking the buyer's credit card number, the droning voice would anesthetize rather than enlighten many potential buyers. Others would hang up in a rage over the waste of their time. And oral recitation would not avoid customers' assertions (whether true or feigned) that the clerk did not read term X to them, or that they did not remember or understand it. Writing provides benefits for both sides of commercial transactions. Customers as a group are better off when vendors skip costly and ineffectual steps such as telephonic recitation, and use instead a simple approve-or-return device. Competent adults are bound by such documents, read or unread. For what little it is worth, we add that the box from Gateway was crammed with software. The computer came with an operating system, without which it was useful only as a boat anchor. Gateway also included many application programs. So the Hills' effort to limit *ProCD* to software would not avail them factually, even if it were sound legally—which it is not.

For their second sally, the Hills contend that *ProCD* should be limited to executory contracts (to licenses in particular), and therefore does not apply because both parties' performance of this contract was complete when the box arrived at their home. This is legally and factually wrong: legally because the question at hand concerns the *formation* of the contract rather than its *performance*, and factually because both contracts were incompletely performed. *ProCD* did not depend on the fact that the seller characterized the transaction as a license rather than as a contract; we treated it as a contract for the sale of goods and reserved the question whether for other purposes a "license" characterization might be preferable. 86 F.3d at 1450. All debates about characterization to one side, the transaction in *ProCD* was no more executory than the one here: Zeidenberg paid for the software and walked out of the store with a box under his arm, so if arrival of the box with the product ends the time for revelation of contractual terms, then the time ended in *ProCD* before Zeidenberg opened the box. But of course ProCD had not completed performance with delivery of the box, and neither had Gateway. One element of the transaction was the warranty, which obliges sellers to fix defects in their products. The Hills have invoked Gateway's warranty and are not satisfied with its response, so they are not well positioned to say that Gateway's obligations were fulfilled when the motor carrier unloaded the box. What is more, both ProCD and Gateway promised to help customers to use their products. Long-term service and information obligations are common in the computer business, on both hardware and software sides. Gateway offers "lifetime service" and has a round-the-clock telephone hotline to fulfil this promise. Some vendors spend more money helping customers use their products than on developing and manufacturing them. The document in Gateway's box includes promises of future performance that some consumers value highly; these promises bind Gateway just as the arbitration clause binds the Hills.

Next the Hills insist that *ProCD* is irrelevant because Zeidenberg was a "merchant" and they are not. Section 2-207(2) of the UCC, the infamous battle-of-the-forms section, states that "additional terms [following acceptance of an offer] are to be construed as proposals for addition to a contract. Between merchants such terms become part of the contract unless. . . ." Plaintiffs tell us that *ProCD* came out as it did only because Zeidenberg was a "merchant" and the terms inside ProCD's box were not excluded by the "unless" clause. This argument pays scant attention to the opinion in *ProCD*, which concluded that, when there is only one form, "§ 2-207 is irrelevant." 86 F.3d at 1452. The question in *ProCD* was not whether terms were added to a contract after its formation, but how and when the contract was formed—in particular, whether a vendor may propose that a contract of sale be formed, not in the store (or over the phone) with the payment of money or a general "send me the product," but after the customer has had a chance to inspect both the item and the terms. *ProCD* answers "yes," for merchants and consumers alike. Yet again, for what little it is worth we observe that the Hills misunderstand the setting of *ProCD*. A "merchant" under the UCC "means a person who deals in goods of the kind or otherwise by his occupation holds himself out as having knowledge or skill peculiar to the practices or goods involved in the transaction," § 2-104(1). Zeidenberg bought the product at a retail store, an uncommon place for merchants to acquire inventory. His corporation put ProCD's database on the Internet for anyone to browse, which led to the litigation but did not make Zeidenberg a software merchant.

At oral argument the Hills propounded still another distinction: the box containing ProCD's software displayed a notice that additional terms were within, while the box containing Gateway's computer did not. The difference is functional, not legal. Consumers browsing the aisles of a store can look at the box, and if they are unwilling to deal with the prospect of additional terms can leave the box alone, avoiding the transactions costs of returning the package after reviewing its contents. Gateway's box, by contrast, is just a shipping carton; it is not on display anywhere. Its function is to protect the product during transit, and the information on its sides is for the use of handlers ("Fragile!" "This Side Up!") rather than would-be purchasers.

> ***Do you agree?***
>
> Should it be of no legal significance that the customer wasn't notified, before opening the box, that there would be terms within the box to which it might be legally bound? How do you think Judge Easterbrook would respond to a customer's argument that it never became aware of the terms inside the box, perhaps because they mistook them for assembly instructions and threw them away, or perhaps because they never saw them (e.g., the instructions got lost or somehow became attached to the bottom of the hard drive)?

Perhaps the Hills would have had a better argument if they were first alerted to the bundling of hardware and legal-ware after opening the box and wanted to return the computer in order to avoid disagreeable terms, but were dissuaded by the expense of shipping. What the remedy would be in such a case—could it exceed the shipping charges?—is an interesting question, but one that need not detain us because the Hills knew before they ordered the computer that the carton would include *some* important terms, and they did not seek to discover these in advance. Gateway's ads state that their products come with limited warranties and lifetime support. How limited was the warranty—30 days, with service contingent on shipping the computer back, or five years, with free onsite service? What sort of support was offered? Shoppers have three principal ways to discover these things. First, they can ask the vendor to send a copy before deciding whether to buy. The Magnuson-Moss Warranty Act requires firms to distribute their warranty terms on request, 15 U.S.C. § 2302(b)(1)(A); the Hills do not contend that Gateway would have refused to enclose the remaining terms too. Concealment would be bad for business, scaring some customers away and leading to excess returns from others. Second, shoppers can consult public sources (computer magazines, the Web sites of vendors) that may contain this information. Third, they may inspect the documents after the product's delivery. Like Zeidenberg, the Hills took the third option. By keeping the computer beyond 30 days, the Hills accepted Gateway's offer, including the arbitration clause. . . .

The decision of the district court is vacated, and this case is remanded with instructions to compel the Hills to submit their dispute to arbitration.

RELEVANT PROVISIONS

For the UCC, consult §§ 2-104 and 2-207.

NOTES AND QUESTIONS

1. *What happened?* Who sued whom for what? Procedurally, how did the case get before this court? Factually, what happened between the parties? What arguments did the plaintiff and defendant make? What rule or rules did the court apply? How did the court analyze the dispute between the parties? How did the court decide the case?

2. *Was this case correctly decided?* Do you agree with the result reached in this case? Why or why not? Do you agree with the court's reasoning? Why or why not? How, if at all, would you have written the opinion differently?

3. ProCD *as precedent.* Can you see how the reasoning in *ProCD* affected the outcome in this case? Should it have? Why or why not?

4. *Economic theory.* As with *ProCD,* Judge Easterbrook's economic leanings shine through. Do his economic arguments make sound legal sense? To what extent do you think economic considerations should factor into the law? To what extent do you think economic arguments can sway judges to adopt a particular legal rule?

5. Carnival *revisited.* Notice that Judge Easterbrook cites *Carnival Cruise Lines v. Shute* as precedent. Does it matter that *Shute* is a maritime case? How (if at all) can you reconcile the result in this case with the fact that the ticket in *Carnival* was *not* refundable?

Klocek v. Gateway

United States District Court, District of Kansas
104 F. Supp. 2d 1332 (2000)

VRATIL, **District Judge.** William S. Klocek brings suit against Gateway, Inc. and Hewlett-Packard, Inc. on claims arising from purchases of a Gateway computer and a Hewlett-Packard scanner. . . .

Gateway asserts that plaintiff must arbitrate his claims under Gateway's Standard Terms and Conditions Agreement ("Standard Terms"). Whenever it sells a computer, Gateway includes a copy of the Standard Terms in the box which contains the computer battery power cables and instruction manuals. At the top of the first page, the Standard Terms include the following notice:

> NOTE TO THE CUSTOMER:
> This document contains Gateway 2000's Standard Terms and Conditions. By keeping your Gateway 2000 computer system beyond five (5) days after the date of delivery, you accept these Terms and Conditions.

The notice is in emphasized type and is located inside a printed box which sets it apart from other provisions of the document. The Standard Terms are four pages long and contain 16 numbered paragraphs. Paragraph 10 provides the following arbitration clause:

> DISPUTE RESOLUTION. Any dispute or controversy arising out of or relating to this Agreement or its interpretation shall be settled exclusively and finally by arbitration. The arbitration shall be conducted in accordance with the Rules of Conciliation and Arbitration of the International Chamber of Commerce. The arbitration shall be conducted in Chicago, Illinois, U.S.A. before a sole arbitrator. Any award rendered in any such arbitration proceeding shall be final and binding on each of the parties, and judgment may be entered thereon in a court of competent jurisdiction.

Gateway urges the Court to dismiss plaintiff's claims under the Federal Arbitration Act ("FAA"). The FAA ensures that written arbitration agreements in maritime transactions and transactions involving interstate commerce are "valid, irrevocable, and enforceable." 9 U.S.C. § 2. Federal policy favors arbitration agreements and requires that we "rigorously enforce" them. . . .

Before granting a stay or dismissing a case pending arbitration, the Court must determine that the parties have a written agreement to arbitrate. . . . The existence of an arbitration agreement "is simply a matter of contract between the parties; [arbitration] is a way to resolve those disputes—but only those disputes—that the parties have agreed to submit to arbitration." *Avedon*, 126 F.3d at 1283 (quoting *Kaplan*, 514 U.S. at 943-945). . . .

The Uniform Commercial Code ("UCC") governs the parties' transaction under both Kansas and Missouri law. Regardless whether plaintiff purchased the computer in person or placed an order and received shipment of the computer, the parties agree that plaintiff paid for and received a computer from

Gateway. This conduct clearly demonstrates a contract for the sale of a computer. See, e.g., *Step-Saver Data Sys., Inc. v. Wyse Techn.*, 939 F.2d 91, 98 (3d Cir. 1991). Thus the issue is whether the contract of sale includes the Standard Terms as part of the agreement.

State courts in Kansas and Missouri apparently have not decided whether terms received with a product become part of the parties' agreement. Authority from other courts is split. It appears that at least in part, the cases turn on whether the court finds that the parties formed their contract *before* or *after* the vendor communicated its terms to the purchaser.

Gateway urges the Court to follow the Seventh Circuit decision in *Hill*. That case involved the shipment of a Gateway computer with terms similar to the Standard Terms in this case, except that Gateway gave the customer 30 days—instead of 5 days—to return the computer. In enforcing the arbitration clause, the Seventh Circuit relied on its decision in *ProCD*, where it enforced a software license which was contained inside a product box. See *Hill*, 105 F.3d at 1148-50. In *ProCD*, the Seventh Circuit noted that the exchange of money frequently precedes the communication of detailed terms in a commercial transaction. Citing UCC § 2-204, the court reasoned that by including the license with the software, the vendor proposed a contract that the buyer could accept by using the software after having an opportunity to read the license. Specifically, the court stated:

> A vendor, as master of the offer, may invite acceptance by conduct, and may propose limitations on the kind of conduct that constitutes acceptance. A buyer may accept by performing the acts the vendor proposes to treat as acceptance.

The *Hill* court followed the *ProCD* analysis, noting that "practical considerations support allowing vendors to enclose the full legal terms with their products." *Hill*, 105 F.3d at 1149.

The Court is not persuaded that Kansas or Missouri courts would follow the Seventh Circuit reasoning in *Hill* and *ProCD*. In each case the Seventh Circuit concluded without support that UCC § 2-207 was irrelevant because the cases involved only one written form. This conclusion is not supported by the statute or by Kansas or Missouri law. Disputes under § 2-207 often arise in the context of a "battle of forms," but nothing in its language precludes application in a case which involves only one form. [UCC § 2-207] provides:

> *Additional terms in acceptance or confirmation*.
>
> (1) A definite and seasonable expression of acceptance or a written confirmation which is sent within a reasonable time operates as an acceptance even though it states terms additional to or different from those offered or agreed upon, unless acceptance is expressly made conditional on assent to the additional or different terms.
>
> (2) The additional terms are to be construed as proposals for addition to the contract [if the contract is not between merchants]. . . .

By its terms, § 2-207 applies to an acceptance or written confirmation. It states nothing which requires another form before the provision becomes effective. In fact, the official comment to the section specifically provides that §§ 2-207(1) and (2) apply "where an agreement has been reached orally . . . and is followed by one or both of the parties sending formal memoranda embodying the terms so far agreed and adding terms not discussed." Official Comment 1 of UCC § 2-207. Kansas and Missouri courts have followed this analysis. Thus, the Court concludes that Kansas and Missouri courts would apply § 2-207 to the facts in this case.

In addition, the Seventh Circuit provided no explanation for its conclusion that "the vendor is the master of the offer." See *ProCD,* 86 F.3d at 1452 (citing nothing in support of proposition). In typical consumer transactions, the purchaser is the offeror, and the vendor is the offeree. While it is possible for the vendor to be the offeror, Gateway provides no factual evidence which would support such a finding in this case. The Court therefore assumes for purposes of the motion to dismiss that plaintiff offered to purchase the computer (either in person or through catalog order) and that Gateway accepted plaintiff's offer (either by completing the sales transaction in person or by agreeing to ship and/or shipping the computer to plaintiff).[11] Under § 2-207, the Standard Terms constitute either an expression of acceptance or written confirmation. As an expression of acceptance, the Standard Terms would constitute a counter-offer only if Gateway expressly made its acceptance conditional on plaintiff's assent to the additional or different terms. "The conditional nature of the acceptance must be clearly expressed in a manner sufficient to notify the offeror that the offeree is unwilling to proceed with the transaction unless the additional or different terms are included in the contract." *Brown Machine,* 770 S.W.2d at 420. Gateway provides no evidence that at the time of the sales transaction, it informed plaintiff that the transaction was conditioned on plaintiff's acceptance of the Standard Terms. Moreover, the mere fact that Gateway shipped the goods with the terms attached did not communicate to plaintiff any unwillingness to proceed without plaintiff's agreement to the Standard Terms.

Because plaintiff is not a merchant, additional or different terms contained in the Standard Terms did not become part of the parties' agreement unless plaintiff expressly agreed to them. *See* K.S.A. § 84-2-207, Kansas Comment 2 (if either party is not a merchant, additional terms are proposals for addition to the contract that do not become part of the contract unless the original offeror expressly agrees).[13] Gateway argues that plaintiff demonstrated acceptance of the arbitration provision by keeping the computer more than five days after the date of delivery. Although the Standard Terms purport to work that result,

11. UCC § 2-206(b) provides that "an order or other offer to buy goods for prompt or current shipment shall be construed as inviting acceptance either by a prompt promise to ship or by the prompt or current shipment. . . ." The official comment states that "either shipment or a prompt promise to ship is made a proper means of acceptance of an offer looking to current shipment." UCC § 2-206, Official Comment 2.

13. The Court's decision would be the same if it considered the Standard Terms as a proposed modification under UCC § 2-209.

Gateway has not presented evidence that plaintiff expressly agreed to those Standard Terms. Gateway states only that it enclosed the Standard Terms inside the computer box for plaintiff to read afterwards. It provides no evidence that it informed plaintiff of the five-day review-and-return period as a condition of the sales transaction, or that the parties contemplated additional terms to the agreement.[14] See *Step-Saver*, 939 F.2d at 99 (during negotiations leading to purchase, vendor never mentioned box-top license or obtained buyer's express assent thereto). The Court finds that the act of keeping the computer past five days was not sufficient to demonstrate that plaintiff expressly agreed to the Standard Terms. Thus, because Gateway has not provided evidence sufficient to support a finding under Kansas or Missouri law that plaintiff agreed to the arbitration provision contained in Gateway's Standard Terms, the Court overrules Gateway's motion to dismiss.

RELEVANT PROVISIONS

For the UCC, consult §§ 2-204, 2-207 and 2-606.

NOTES AND QUESTIONS

1. *What happened?* Who sued whom for what? Procedurally, how did the case get before this court? Factually, what happened between the parties? What arguments did the plaintiff and defendant make? What rule or rules did the court apply? How did the court analyze the dispute between the parties? How did the court decide the case?

2. *Was this case correctly decided?* Do you agree with the result reached in this case? Why or why not? Do you agree with the court's reasoning? Why or why not? How, if at all, would you have written the opinion differently?

3. *Can these cases be reconciled?* Compare Judge Vratil's decision here with Judge Easterbrook's in *ProCD* and *Hill*. With whom do you agree? Do you find one judge's interpretation of § 2-207's "battle of the forms" more correct than the other?

4. *Practical considerations.* Notice that, in Footnote 14 of her opinion, Judge Vratil indicates that she *does* weigh practical considerations in reaching her decision. Contrast this with Judge Easterbrook's approach. Who has the better argument here, and why?

---

14. The Court is mindful of the practical considerations which are involved in commercial transactions, but it is not unreasonable for a vendor to clearly communicate to a buyer—at the time of sale—either the complete terms of the sale or the fact that the vendor will propose additional terms as a condition of sale, if that be the case.

5. *Thinking tools.* Can you draw on any of the thinking tools we previously examined to come up with a better solution? Do you agree with the approach suggested in the excerpt below?

IMPROVING THE ROLLING CONTRACT*

Courts and commentators have typically either embraced or rejected rolling contracts.† This Article offers a third alternative: improving the rolling contract.

Courts have failed to develop a satisfactory approach for determining which contract terms sellers may provide after purchase—a failure of significance given the proliferation of rolling contracts. Courts enforcing rolling contracts have given sellers nearly unfettered ability to delay disclosure of contract terms. Buyers now routinely find important contract terms, such as arbitration provisions and limitations on damages, inside the box of a newly purchased item instead of learning about the terms before or during purchase or order (as would be the case in a traditional contract).

In this Article, I propose a mechanism that will ensure that sellers continue to have needed flexibility to defer some contract terms, but that will also protect purchasers against the unfair imposition of unexpected and important contract terms arriving at a time when purchasers are very unlikely to read or act on them.

The proposal, which I refer to as "Template Notice," is an intermediate form of disclosure that meets the pressing concerns of both buyers and sellers. It would not require sellers to provide the full text of all contract terms before or during purchase or order. It would, however, require sellers to do more than merely give notice that unspecified additional terms will be forthcoming. Sellers would be required to provide the following vital information before or during purchase or order: a brief and clear list or summary of important terms being deferred (but not the full text), a statement that the buyer will have the right to reject the terms and avoid the transaction, and a description of how to exercise that right. For example, a potential purchaser of a computer placing an order over the telephone might be told by the sales representative that:

> Inside the box with your computer there will be some additional contract terms. Among other things, those terms limit the time you would have to sue us if there is a problem, limit the damages you could be awarded, and require binding arbitration of any disputes between us. Those terms will be in the box and you can return the computer if they are not acceptable. You can also obtain them now if you would like through our website, or I will send them to you.

I choose the term "Template Notice" because the information provided at purchase or order should establish the overall form or template of the transaction. It

---

* Excerpted from Stephen E. Friedman, *Improving the Rolling Contract*, 56 AM. U. L. REV. 1, 2-3 (2006).

† [Elsewhere in his article, the author defines "rolling contracts" as "contracts [that are] formed over time, with the seller presenting the terms in batches. Some terms are provided before or during the purchase or order, while others are provided later." Stephen E. Friedman, *Improving the Rolling Contract*, 56 AM. U. L. REV. 1, 4 (2006).—ED.]

recognizes the primacy of the purchase to the transaction, while also recognizing that the contract is not completely closed to new terms at that point. Sellers can and should be able to defer some terms until after purchase or order, but only to a more limited extent than is currently permitted. Template Notice provides an appropriate limitation on the ability of sellers to defer terms: sellers would have the flexibility to delay terms, but could do so only for terms that flesh out details of the information provided at purchase. Terms beyond the structure established at purchase or order could not be added "out of the blue."

B. INTERPRETING CONTRACT TERMS

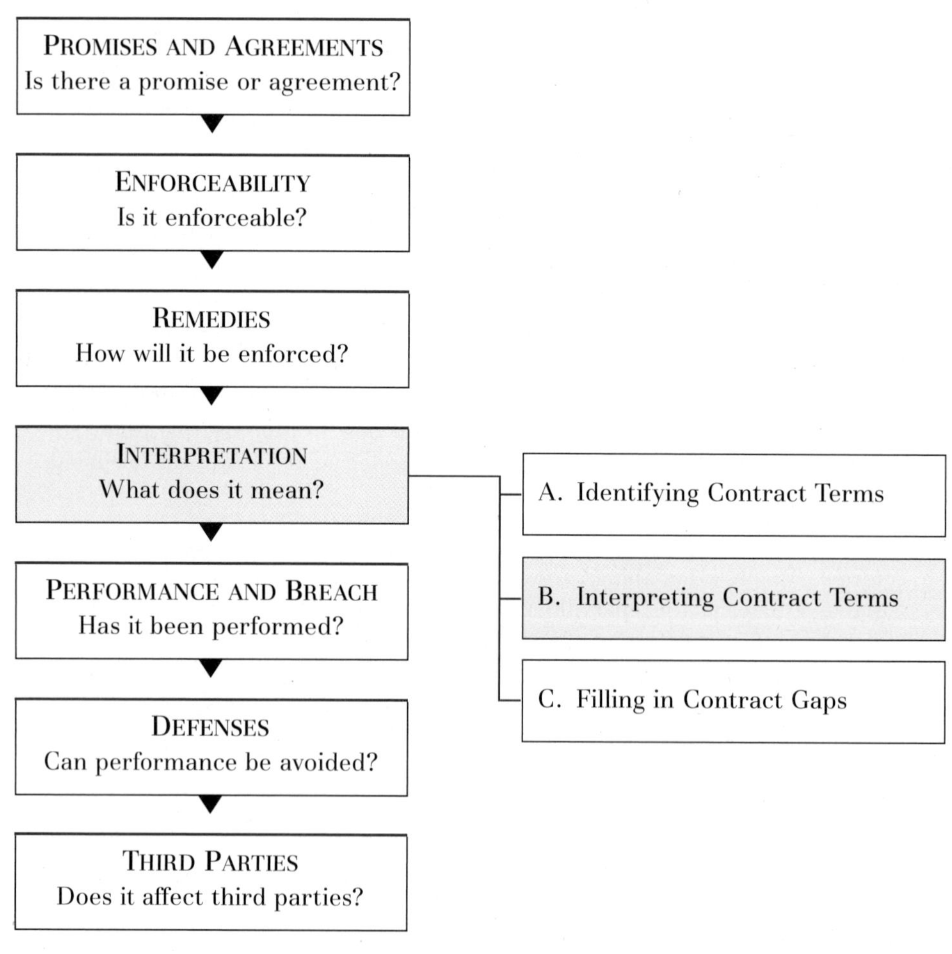

In this section we will learn to distinguish between ambiguous and vague terms, examine how these terms are treated by judges (and how they ought to be treated by lawyers in drafting contracts for their clients), and explore the parol evidence rule, which governs the admissibility of prior or contemporaneous non-written evidence offered to contradict, add to, detract from, or otherwise vary the terms of a written agreement.

DOCTRINAL OVERVIEW: THE PROCESS OF INTERPRETATION*

Interpretation is the process by which a court ascertains the meaning that it will give to the language used by the parties in determining the legal effect of the contract. It is not the only technique used by a court to determine the legal effect of a contract, for even in the absence of relevant contract language a court may, by the process of implication, supply a term to govern an omitted case. Furthermore, the interpretation may not even be decisive as to the legal effect of the contract language itself, for a court may refuse to enforce part or all of the contract because of some overriding legal rule.

The word *interpretation* is sometimes used more narrowly to refer to the process by which a court determines the meaning that the parties themselves attached to their language. This enables the court to determine what the Uniform Commercial Code calls the *agreement,* meaning "the bargain of the parties in fact, as found in their language or inferred from other circumstances."[4] The meaning attached by the parties is not necessarily controlling, however, because a court may take account of factors that are unrelated to the parties' intentions. The word *construction* is then used to refer to the process by which a court determines the meaning that will be given to the language of the contract in giving it legal effect. This enables the court to determine what the Code calls the *contract,* meaning "the total legal obligation that results from the parties' agreement as affected by [the Uniform Commercial Code] as supplemented by any other applicable laws."[6] Under this terminology, while the process of interpretation might lead to one meaning (the one that the parties themselves attached to their language), the process of construction might lead to a different one (the one that would be decisive in determining the legal effect of the contract). Although courts have sometimes endorsed this distinction, they have often ignored it by characterizing the process of construction as that of "interpretation" in order to obscure the extent of their control over private agreement. . . .

* Excerpted from E. ALLAN FARNSWORTH, CONTRACTS § 7.7 (4th ed. 2004).
4. UCC § 1-201(3).
6. UCC § 1-201(12).

1. Vagueness and Ambiguity

DOCTRINAL OVERVIEW: VAGUENESS AND AMBIGUITY*

It is a rare contract that needs no interpretation. It has been wisely observed that there is no "lawyer's Paradise [where] all words have a fixed, precisely ascertained meaning, . . . and where, if the writer has been careful, a lawyer, having a document referred to him may sit in his chair, inspect the text, and answer all questions without raising his eyes."[1] As Holmes cautioned, "A word is not a crystal, transparent and unchanged, it is the skin of a living thought and may vary greatly in color and content according to the circumstances and the time in which it is used."[2]

A particularly perceptive student of language has emphasized a distinction between *vagueness* and *ambiguity* that is also useful in contract interpretation. According to this distinction, a word is vague to the extent that it defines "not a neatly bounded class but a distribution about a central norm." Thus the word *green* is vague as it shades into yellow at the one extreme and into blue at the other, so that its applicability in marginal situations is uncertain. Ambiguity is an entirely distinct concept. A word may have two entirely different connotations, so that it may be at the same time both appropriate and inappropriate. Thus the word *light* is ambiguous when considered in the context of dark feathers.[3]

Try to define, in your own words, the difference between vagueness and ambiguity. Then, as you read the next two cases, try to determine whether the word "chicken" in Frigaliment *and the word "Peerless" in* Raffles *is being used vaguely or ambiguously, and how, if at all, this distinction should affect the way a judge understands and interprets those terms. We will explore both vagueness and ambiguity in greater detail in the materials following these cases.*

Frigaliment Importing Co. v. B.N.S. International Sales Corp.

United States District Court, Southern District of New York

190 F. Supp. 116 (1960)

For a report of the case and accompanying materials, see p. 120, *supra*.

RELEVANT PROVISIONS

For the *Restatement (Second) of Contracts*, consult §§ 200, 201, and 202. For the UCC, consult §§ 1-205 and 2-208. For the CISG, consult Articles 8 and 9. For the UNIDROIT Principles, consult Articles 1.9, 4.1, 4.2, and 4.3.

---

* Excerpted from E. ALLAN FARNSWORTH, CONTRACTS § 7.8 (4th ed. 2004).

1. JAMES BRADLEY THAYER, A PRELIMINARY TREATISE ON THE LAW OF EVIDENCE 428-29 (1898).
2. Towne v. Eisner, 245 U.S. 418, 425 (1918).
3. WILLARD VAN ORMAN QUINE, WORD AND OBJECT 85, 129 (1960).

Raffles v. Wichelhaus

Court of Exchequer
159 Eng. Rep. 375 (1864)

Declaration. For that it was agreed between the plaintiff and the defendants, to wit, at Liverpool, that the plaintiff should sell to the defendants, and the defendants buy of the plaintiff, certain goods, to wit, 125 bales of Surat cotton, guaranteed middling fair merchant's Dhollorah, to arrive ex "Peerless" from Bombay; and that the cotton should be taken from the quay, and that the defendants would pay the plaintiff for the same at a certain rate, to wit, at the rate of 17½d. per pound, within a certain time then agreed upon after the arrival of the said goods in England. Averments: that the said goods did arrive by the said ship from Bombay in England, to wit, at Liverpool, and the plaintiff was then and there ready, and willing and offered to deliver the said goods to the defendants, &c. Breach: that the defendants refused to accept the said goods or pay the plaintiff for them.

Plea. That the said ship mentioned in the said agreement was meant and intended by the defendants to be the ship called the "Peerless," which sailed from Bombay, to wit, in October; and that the plaintiff was not ready and willing and did not offer to deliver to the defendants any bales of cotton which arrived by the last mentioned ship, but instead thereof was only ready and willing and offered to deliver to the defendants 125 bales of Surat cotton which arrived by another and different ship, which was also called the "Peerless," and which sailed from Bombay, to wit, in December.

Demurrer, and joinder therein.

> ***Who's Milward?***
>
> Milward is the attorney for the plaintiff, Raffles. Notice how, throughout Milward's argument, he is continually interrupted by two of the judges (Pollock and Martin) listening to his argument.

MILWARD, **in support of the demurrer.** The contract was for the sale of a number of bales of cotton of a particular description, which the plaintiff was ready to deliver. It is immaterial by what ship the cotton was to arrive, so that it was a ship called the "Peerless." The words "to arrive ex 'Peerless,'" only mean that if the vessel is lost on the voyage, the contract is to be at an end. [POLLOCK, C. B. It would be a question for the jury whether both parties meant the same ship called the "Peerless."] That would be so if the contract was for the sale of a ship called the "Peerless"; but it is for the sale of cotton on board a ship of that name. [POLLOCK, C. B. The defendant only bought that cotton which was to arrive by a particular ship. It may as well be said, that if there is a contract for the purchase of certain goods in warehouse A., that is satisfied by the delivery of goods of the same description in warehouse B.] In that case there would be goods in both warehouses; here it does not appear that the plaintiff had any goods on board the other "Peerless." [MARTIN, B. It is imposing on the defendant a contract different from that which he entered into. POLLOCK, C. B. It is like a contract for the purchase of wine coming from a particular estate in France or Spain, where there are two estates of that name.] The defendant has no right to contradict by parol evidence a written contract good upon the face of it. He does not impute misrepresentation or fraud, but only says that he fancied the ship was a different one. Intention is of no avail, unless stated at the time of the contract. [POLLOCK, C. B. One vessel sailed in October and the other in December.] The time of sailing is no part of the contract.

Who's Mellish?

Mellish is the attorney for the defendant, Wichelhaus. You may also recall him as one of the judges who decided *Dickinson v. Dodds* (p. 287) twelve years after *Raffles* was decided. Unlike Milward, the judges allow Mellish's argument to continue unimpeded, until he hits on the powerful idea that there was no "consensus ad idem," or meeting of the minds, and therefore no binding contract. This argument so impresses the court that they stop him and immediately pronounce judgment for defendants. For a colorful account of this case, see Professor Gilmore's take on it in Note 3 below.

MELLISH (COHEN **with him), in support of the plea.** There is nothing on the face of the contract to shew that any particular ship called the "Peerless" was meant; but the moment it appears that two ships called the "Peerless" were about to sail from Bombay there is a latent ambiguity, and parol evidence may be given for the purpose of shewing that the defendant meant one "Peerless," and the plaintiff another. That being so, there was no *consenus ad idem*, and therefore no binding contract. He was then stopped by the Court.

PER CURIAM. There must be judgment for the defendants.

RELEVANT PROVISIONS

For the *Restatement (Second) of Contracts*, consult § 20.

NOTES AND QUESTIONS

1. *What happened?* Who sued whom for what? Procedurally, how did the case get before this court? Factually, what happened between the parties? What arguments did the plaintiff and defendant make? What rule or rules did the court apply? How did the court analyze the dispute between the parties? How did the court decide the case?

2. *Was this case correctly decided?* Do you agree with the result reached in this case? Why or why not? Do you agree with the court's reasoning? Why or why not? How, if at all, would you have written the opinion differently?

3. *Professor Gilmore's take on* Raffles:

> The "fairly simple" point which Milward tried to make was that, under the contract term "to arrive ex Peerless," "it was immaterial by what ship the cotton was to arrive, so that it was a ship called the Peerless" and that the term meant only that "if the vessel is lost on the voyage, the contract is to be at an end" [that

is, the seller would bear the loss but the buyer would have no claim for damages for non-delivery]. In commercial understanding, that is exactly what the terms mean today and there is no reason to believe that they meant anything else a hundred years ago. In technical language, Milward's argument was that the identity of the carrying ship was not a true condition of the contract. Thus, even on the assumption that the buyer had meant the October Peerless (and that his meaning was entitled to prevail), he would not have been justified in rejecting the tender of the cotton which arrived on the December Peerless. For mistake to justify rescission of a contract the mistake must relate to some fundamental aspect of the contractual performance; it was, as Milward said, given the commercial meaning of the contract term and the fact that no issue relating to the time of tender was raised, "immaterial" on which Peerless the cotton arrived.

Milward got absolutely nowhere in explaining this point to the court. Two of the judges, Pollock and Martin, kept interrupting him with questions which suggest that they had no idea what he was talking about. Their evident assumption was that if the contract said Peerless, then Peerless was a fundamental term (or condition) of the contract and Milward could go on talking until he was blue in the face without shaking them. There seems to be an air increasing desperation in Milward's attempts to deal with the wooly-headed [sic] questions from the bench. Toward the end of his argument, perhaps distracted, he suddenly switched to an obviously unsound line: that parol evidence was not admissible to show which Peerless was meant—a diversionary tactic which the Court treated with the silent contempt it deserved.

Mellish, as counsel for the buyer, answered Milward. His first sentence effectively demolished Milward's unfortunate attempt to drag in the parol evidence rule. His second sentence was:

> That being so [i.e. the parol evidence being admissible], there was no consensus ad idem, and therefore no binding contract.

At that point he was stopped by the Court which forthwith announced judgment for Mellish's client.

There are really only two things we can make out of this curious case. One is that the judges, no doubt mistakenly, believed that the identity of the carrying ship was important—a true condition of the contract. The other is that they seem to have been immediately convinced by Mellish's consensus ad idem argument—that if buyer "meant" the October Peerless while seller "meant" the December Peerless (which was admitted by the demurrer), then there could be no contract since their minds had never met. None of these judges thought of asking Mellish what would seem to be obvious questions. Would a reasonably well-informed cotton merchant in Liverpool have known that there were two ships called Peerless? Ought this buyer to have known? If in fact the October Peerless had arrived in Liverpool first, had the buyer protested the seller's failure to tender the cotton? The failure of the judges, who had given Milward such a hard time, to put any questions to Mellish suggests that they were entirely content to let the case go off on the purely subjective failure of the minds to meet at the time the contract was entered into.*

* Grant Gilmore, The Death of Contract 41-44 (1995).

4. *Holmes's take on* Raffles. Holmes has a much simpler explanation of *Raffles*. Do you agree?

> It is commonly said that such a contract is void, because of mutual mistake as to the subject-matter, and because therefore the parties did not consent to the same thing. But this way of putting it seems to me misleading. The law has nothing to do with the actual state of the parties' mind. In contract, as elsewhere, it must go by externals, and judge parties by their conduct. If there had been but one "Peerless," and the defendant had said "Peerless" by mistake, meaning "Peri," he would have been bound. The true ground of the decision was not that each party meant a different thing from the other, as is implied by the explanation which has been mentioned, but that each said a different thing. The plaintiff offered one thing, the defendant expressed his assent to another.*

5. *Illustration.* The *Restatement (Second) of Contracts* § 20 offers the following helpful illustrations:

> 1. A offers to sell B goods shipped from Bombay ex steamer "Peerless." B accepts. There are two steamers of the name "Peerless," sailing from Bombay at materially different times. If both parties intend the same Peerless, there is a contract, and it is immaterial whether they know or have reason to know that two ships are named Peerless.
>
> 2. The facts being otherwise as stated in Illustration 1, A means Peerless No. 1 and B means Peerless No. 2. If neither A nor B knows or has reason to know that they mean different ships, or if they both know or if they both have reason to know, there is no contract.
>
> 3. The facts being otherwise as stated in Illustration 1, A knows that B means Peerless No. 2 and B does not know that there are two ships named Peerless. There is a contract for the sale of the goods from Peerless No. 2, and it is immaterial whether B has reason to know that A means Peerless No. 1. . . . Conversely, if B knows that A means Peerless No. 1 and A does not know that there are two ships named Peerless, there is a contract for the sale of the goods from Peerless No. 1, and it is immaterial whether A has reason to know that B means Peerless No. 2, but the contract may be voidable by A for misrepresentation.
>
> 4. The facts being otherwise as stated in Illustration 1, neither party knows that there are two ships Peerless. A has reason to know that B means Peerless No. 2 and B has no reason to know that A means Peerless No. 1. There is a contract for the sale of goods from Peerless No. 2. In the converse case, where B has reason to know and A does not, there is a contract for sale from Peerless No. 1. . . .
>
> 5. A says to B, "I offer to sell you my horse for $100." B, knowing that A intends to offer to sell his cow for that price, not his horse, and that the word "horse" is a slip of the tongue, replies, "I accept." The price is a fair one for either the horse or the cow. There is a contract for the sale of the cow and not of the horse. . . .

---

* OLIVER WENDELL HOLMES, JR., THE COMMON LAW 242 (1963).

PROMISES, PREDICTIONS, AND MEANING*

We must now notice two of the most persistent sources of difficulty in the law of contracts: first, the fact that words frequently mean different things to the speaker and to the hearer; second, the fact that promise and prediction are often inextricably mixed up in the same phrase.

When merchant *A* promises merchant *B* that he will deliver 125 bales of cotton "ex *Peerless*," both parties understand this as an assertion that *B*, by virtue of the promise, possesses a power to command cotton which he did not previously possess. But to *A* this may mean a power to obtain cotton from a ship which sailed from Bombay in October, while to *B* it may mean a power to obtain cotton from an entirely different vessel which left Bombay two months later.[6] There are, in fact, two distinct assertions—the one uttered and the one heard—and legal consequences may conceivably be predicated on either, on neither, or on both. This becomes vividly apparent whenever parties are negotiating at a distance so that the utterance and the hearing are separated by an appreciable interval of time. Most of the controversies which have arisen from this kind of situation revolve about the question whether the utterance or the hearing of some promise is to be given controlling force. Even if both *A* and *B* refer to the same *Peerless*, *A*'s assertion is a compound of promise and prediction; *B*'s power to command cotton is asserted to exist partly because *A*'s word binds him to a certain course of conduct and partly because *A* expects the *Peerless* to arrive. No one understands *A* to assert, however, that the *Peerless* will come in because he promises that it will. That part of his assertion is a prediction of the same order as that of astronomer X. The promissory part of an assertion about the future is confined to that portion of the events predicted which are asserted to be under the promisor's control.[9] It will be convenient to pause at this point to define four phrases which will be used henceforth throughout this essay as terms of art. By "apparent promise" is meant the promise as heard and understood by the promisee—in the illustrative case just stated the promise to deliver cotton from that *Peerless* which sailed in October from Bombay. By "actual promise" is meant the promise as uttered and understood by the promisor—the promise to deliver cotton from the December *Peerless*. By "power predicted" is meant the entire power which any expression either wholly or partly promissory attributes to the promisee—in our illustration the power to obtain cotton at the time when the designated vessel would normally arrive. By "power asserted" is meant that portion of the power predicted which the promisor purports to be creating by force of the promissory utterance. In the illustrative case the power asserted is limited by the continued existence of the cotton and possibly by other facts as well.

---

* Excerpted from George K. Gardner, *An Inquiry into the Principles of the Law of Contracts*, 46 HARV. L. REV. 1, 6-7 (1932).

6. *Raffles v. Wichelhaus*, 2 H. & C. 906 (1864).

9. This, of course, is not the same as saying that the promissory part of an assertion about the future is confined to that portion of the events predicted which are under the promisor's control in fact. If the *Peerless* arrives safely and *A* does not deliver the cotton, he will be liable whether he owned any cotton on board or not.

The following excerpt reveals that both Frigaliment *and* Raffles *can be understood not only in terms of a court's quest to ascertain meaning in contract law, but can also provide us with a valuable way of thinking about and distinguishing between vagueness and ambiguity, concepts that plague not only contract law, but law in general. The sooner you grasp the distinction between these related but distinct ideas, the better you will be able to navigate, draft, and understand legal texts of every variety.*

An important part of coming to grips with the meaning of any legal text is to begin by understanding the manner in which the words and phrases that constitute that text may be subject to multiple and varied interpretations, due in no small part to the vagueness and ambiguity of those words and phrases. As you read the following excerpt, note the variety of circumstances in which vague and ambiguous terms, phrases, and even concepts may arise in contract law, ideas we will return to time and again throughout this casebook.

MEANING, VAGUENESS, AND AMBIGUITY IN CONTRACT LAW*

The very concept of plain meaning finds scant support in semantics, where one of the cardinal teachings is the fallibility of language as a means of communication. Waismann lamented that,

> Ordinary language simply has not got the "hardness," the logical hardness, to cut axioms in it. It needs something like a metallic substance to carve a deductive system out of it such as Euclid's. But common speech? If you begin to draw inferences it soon begins to go "soft" and fluffs up somewhere. You may just as well carve cameos on a cheese *souffle*.[52]

Much of this softness of language comes from the differing ways in which we learn to use words, for the use of a symbol for communication is ordinarily preceded by an elaborate process of conditioning which may vary greatly with the individual. . . .

[There are at least] two reasons why vagueness pervades language. First, each person learns words on the basis of different sets of stimuli. To borrow Quine's example of the word "red," some will have learned this word in situations where red was sharply contrasted with other colors that differ greatly; others will have learned it by being rewarded for distinguishing red from other reddish colors. It seems clear that the former group will use "red" more freely than the latter group. Second, the abilities of people to group stimulations into sets differ somewhat. Thus, some children will simply respond "red" when either a red object or a crimson object comes into view and will remain incapable of distinguishing them.

---

* Excerpted from E. Allan Farnsworth, *"Meaning" in the Law of Contracts*, 76 YALE L.J. 939, 952-57 (1967)

52. Waismann, *How I See Philosophy*, in LOGICAL POSITIVISM 345 (A. Ayer ed. 1959).

[This analysis helps] explain the concept of vagueness. According to Quine, "stimulations eliciting a verbal response, say 'red,' are best depicted as forming not a neatly bounded class but a distribution about a central *norm*." The idea of a central norm is useful in explaining the concept of vagueness, for a word is vague to the extent that it can apply to stimuli that depart from its central norm.

Contract language abounds in perturbing examples of vagueness. The parties provide for the removal of "all the dirt" on a tract; may sand from a stratum of subsoil be taken?[55] An American seller and a Swiss buyer agree upon the sale of "chicken"; is stewing chicken "chicken"?[56] Vagueness may even infect a term that has an apparently precise connotation. The parties contract for the sale of horse-meat scraps "Minimum 50% protein"; may evidence be admitted to show that by trade usage scraps containing 49.5% or more conform?[57]

Ambiguity, properly defined, is an entirely distinct concept from that of vagueness. A word that may or may not be applicable to marginal objects is vague. But a word may also have two entirely different connotations so that it may be applied to an object and be at the same time both clearly appropriate and inappropriate, as the word "light" may be when applied to dark feathers. Such a word is ambiguous.

Whether an ambiguity arises may depend upon the medium of communication. Some ambiguities (ordinarily homonyms), such as "beer" and "bier" arise only in speech and disappear in writing; others such as "tear" (a rip or a drop), arise only in writing and disappear in speech. Speech will do much to remove the ambiguity from sentences. . . . Gestures also play a part in normal face-to-face conversation, and habits of speech have been shown to change when conversation is over a telephone and normal gesture reinforcement is lost. Ambiguity may arise in a telegram because of the lack of punctuation which would ordinarily be supplied in a letter. And even given an ambiguity, it may be resolved by its context: one drinks a beer, not a bier, and sheds a tear (drop) not a tear (rip).

Ambiguities may be classified into those of term and those of syntax. As Young has pointed out, true examples of ambiguity of term are rare in contract cases. A contract specifies "tons"; are they to be long or short tons?[64] A charter party provides that a vessel must be "double-rigged," which by usage can refer to either two winches and two booms per hatch, or four of each per hatch; how many must the vessel have?[65] An important variety of ambiguity of term, for our purposes, is proper name ambiguity, the kind of ambiguity that plagued Shakespeare's Cinna,[66]

---

55. *See* Highley v. Phillips, 176 Md. 463, 5 A.2d 824 (1939) (held: yes).

56. *See* Frigaliment Importing Co. v. B.N.S. Int'l Sales Corp., 190 F. Supp. 116 (S.D.N.Y. 1960) (held: for seller).

57. *See* Hurst v. Lake & Co., 141 Ore. 306, 16 P.2d 627 (1932) (held: yes).

64. *Compare* Chemung Iron & Steel Co. v. Mersereau Metal Bed Co., 179 N.Y.S. 577 (App. Div. 1920) (short tons) *with* The Miantinomi, 17 Fed. Cas. 254 (No. 9,521) (C.C.W.D. Pa. 1855) (long tons).

65. *See* Amicizia Societa Navegazione v. Chilean Nitrate & Iodine Sales Corp., 184 F. Supp. 116 (S.D.N.Y. 1959) (held: arbitrators' decision that two of each per hatch suffices sustained).

66. "*Cinna*: I am Cinna the poet. . . . I am not Cinna the conspirator! *Second Plebian*: It is no matter, his name's Cinna; pluck but his name out of his heart and turn him going." JULIUS CAESAR, III, iii.

the kind of ambiguity that we deliberately create when we name a child after someone. It was this kind of ambiguity that was involved in the celebrated case of the ships "Peerless."

An ambiguity of syntax is, in the strictest sense, an ambiguity of grammatical structure, of what is syntactically connected with what. A classic example is, "And Satan trembles when he sees The weakest saint upon his knees," in which the ambiguity is that of pronominal reference. Ambiguity of syntax is probably a more common cause of contract disputes than is ambiguity of term. An insurance policy covers any "disease of organs of the body not common to both sexes"; does it include a fibroid tumor (which can occur on any organ) of the womb?[68] A contract provides that, "Before the livestock is removed from the possession of the carrier or mingled with other livestock, the shipper . . . shall inform in writing the delivery carrier of any visible injuries to the livestock"; is it enough that he notify before mingling although after removal?[69]

Syntactical ambiguity is often the result of inadequate punctuation. Note, for example, the confusion that sometimes results from contracts concluded by an unpunctuated telegram. Sometimes the ambiguity is caused by the dropping of words to make shorthand expressions. A contract for the sale of "approx. 10,000" heaters adds "All in perfect condition"; is this, as buyer contends, an express warranty ("All *to be* in perfect condition") or, as seller contends, a limitation on the quantity ("All *that are* in perfect condition")?[70]

Particularly hazardous as a source of ambiguity for the contract draftsman are the words "and" and "or." Layman Allen's extensive analysis of the ambiguities associated with these terms suggests three that are particularly likely.[71] The first is the ambiguity between "or" as a disjunctive (P *or else* Q) and as a coimplicative (P, *that is to say* Q). The second ambiguity is that between "or" as an exclusive disjunctive (P *or else* Q, *but not both)* and as an inclusive disjunctive (P *or else* Q, *or else both)*. The third is that between "and" as a conjunctive (only both P *and* Q) and as an inclusive disjunctive (P *or else* Q, *or else* both). The classic case of *Cuthbert v. Cumming*[72] shows the complexity that can occur in a single case of this type. A charter party obliged the charterer "to load a full and complete cargo of sugar [A], molasses [B], *and/or* other lawful produce [C]"; what may he load? A and B and C, or else A and B, or else C? A and B and C, or else A and B? A and

68. Business Men's Assur. Ass'n v. Read, 48 S.W.2d 678 (Tex. Civ. App. 1932) (held: yes).

69. *See* Atlantic Coast Line R. Co. v. Holman, 33 Ala. App. 319, 33 So. 2d 365 (1946), *rev'd,* 250 Ala. 1, 33 So. 2d 367 (1947), analyzed in Allen, *Symbolic Logic and Law: A Reply,* 15 J. LEGAL ED. 47, 50-51 (1962). The lower court read it: "*either* before the livestock is removed from the possession of the carrier, *or* before it is mingled with livestock" and answered in the negative. 33 Ala. App. at 322, 33 So. 2d at 367 (emphasis added).

70. *See* Udell v. Cohen, 282 App. Div. 685, 122 N.Y.S.2d 552 (1953) (mem. dec.) (held: parol evidence admissible to resolve ambiguity).

71. Allen, *Symbolic Logic: A Razor-Edged Tool for Drafting and Interpreting Legal Documents,* 66 YALE L.J. 833 (1957).

72. 11 Ex. 405, 156 Eng. Rep. 889 (Ex. Ch. 1855) (held: he performed by loading sugar and molasses). The case is discussed along with related ones in D. MELLINKOFF, THE LANGUAGE OF THE LAW 150-52 (1963).

B? A or else B or else C? A or else A and B or else A and C? A or else B or else C or any combination of two or three?

Ambiguity in contracts may also result from inconsistent or conflicting language. A buyer agrees to pay "at the rate of $1.25 per M" for all the timber on a designated tract, and that "the entire sale and purchase price of said lumber is $1400.00"; how much must he pay for 4,000 M feet?[79] In many of these cases the conflict is between language in a form contract and that added by the parties for the particular transaction. A printed warranty in the sale of a house requires the owner to give notice of breach "within one year from . . . the date of initial occupancy" and also provides that "notice of nonconformity must be delivered no later than January 6, 1957," the date having been inserted by hand; when must the buyer give notice if he moves in on May 16, 1955?[80]

It would be wrong to assume that the failure of contract language to dispose of a dispute that later arises is invariably due to some inherent fallibility of language as a means of communication. The parties may simply not have foreseen the problem at the time of contracting. An insurance contract on a motor vessel covers "collision with any other ship or vessel"; is a collision with an anchored flying boat included?[81] Or one or both may have foreseen the problem but deliberately refrained from raising it during the negotiations for fear that they might fail—the lawyer who "wakes these sleeping dogs" by insisting that they be resolved may cost his client the bargain. An elderly lady enters a home for the aged, paying a lump sum, to be returned to her "if it should be found advisable to discontinue her stay" during a two-month probationary period; must the home refund her money if she dies within that time?[82] Or both may have foreseen the problem but chosen to deal with it only in general terms, delegating the ultimate resolution of particular controversies to the appropriate forum. A contract for the sale of wool requires "prompt" shipment from New Zealand to Philadelphia; does shipment in 52 days conform?[83] It is interesting to note that while either ambiguity or vagueness may result from the other causes just suggested, only vagueness is suitable for use in such a conscious attempt at delegation. . . .

In the previous excerpt, we learned that ambiguity arises where a contract provision is subject to two or more different interpretations. This ambiguity, in turn, may be created by (a) ***semantic*** *or* ***lexical ambiguity****, or the use of a term with more than one meaning (such as the word "light" in the excerpt above), (b)* ***syntactical ambiguity****, or ambiguity resulting from inadequate or confusing punctuation or word order (the excerpt above gives the example of an unpunctuated telegram), or* ***contextual ambiguity****, which arises from a word or provision being used in an inconsistent or conflicting manner in different parts of the contract (the excerpt above gives the example of a contract stating both that (i) buyer will*

---

79. *See* Hardin v. Dimension Lumber Co., 140 Ore. 385, 13 P.2d 602 (1932).

80. *See* McNeely v. Claremont Management Co., 210 Cal. App. 2d 749, 27 Cal. Rptr. 87 (1962).

81. *See* Polpen Shipping Co. v. Commercial Union Assurance Co., [1943] 1 K.B. 161 (1942) (held: no).

82. *See* First Nat'l Bank v. Methodist Home, 181 Kan. 100, 309 P.2d 389 (1957) (held: yes).

83. *See* Kreglinger & Fernau v. Charles J. Webb Sons Co., 162 F. Supp. 695 (E.D. Pa. 1957) (held: yes).

buy timber "at the rate of $1.25 per M" and (ii) that "the entire sale and purchase price of said lumber is $1400.00"). It's now time to turn to some problems to put this knowledge into practice!

DRAFTING PROBLEMS: IDENTIFYING AND AVOIDING AMBIGUITY

The first five problems should be treated as part of a single transaction between an American Seller and a Canadian Buyer. For each problem, please (a) identify the type of ambiguity/ambiguities at issue (e.g., semantic ambiguity), and (b) suggest how the provision might be redrafted to remove the ambiguity/ambiguities.

1. **Goods:** Seller agrees to ship 5,000 black or white widgets, fit for use in Buyer's Widgetorama 5,000 Machine, in exchange for $50,000.
2. **Description of Goods:** The widgets delivered shall consist of 1-pound black widgets or 2-pound white widgets manufacturered after 2015.
3. **Price and Delivery:** Buyer agrees to pay Seller, on the first day of each month:
   (a) $10,000 after receipt of the first 1,000 pounds of widgets,
   (b) $10,000 after receipt of the second 1,000 pounds of widgets, and
   (c) a proportion of the remaining $30,000 based on the proportional weight of widgets delivered each month.
4. **Warranty:** These widgets are being sold "as is," and Seller disclaims any and all express and/or implied warranties.
5. **Dispute Resolution:** All disputes arising under this contract shall be resolved by arbitration, and the arbitrators shall apply the substantive law of the State of Florida. The arbitration panel shall consist of three aribtrators, two laywers and one expert in commercial law.

Please consider each of the remaining problems independently. As before, please remember to (a) identify the potential ambiguity/ambiguities at issue and (b) suggest how the provision might be redrafted to remove the ambiguity/ambiguities.

6. On December 31, a $5,000 bonus shall be paid to each Employee that has been with the Company during the entire calendar year (i.e., since January 1 of the same year), except temporary and part-time employees.
7. Seller shall deliver to Buyer 10,000 pounds of widgets, consisting of 1-pound white widgets and 2-pound red widgets or 5-pound black widgets.
8. Seller shall deliver to Buyer 100 widgets of each of the following colors: white, red, black and blue.
9. Buyer agrees to buy 1,000 additional widgets from Seller if the price of widgets remains under $10 per widget between June 1 and June 30.
10. Employee agrees to communicate and assign his or her rights to the Company of any and all inventions conceived by Employee at any time during his or her employment by the Company.
11. This offer can only be accepted by individuals who are not over 21 years of age.
12. The contract shall continue in force for a period of five (5) years from the date it is made, and thereafter for successive five (5) year terms, unless and until terminated by one year prior notice in writing by either party.

2. Parol Evidence Rule

DOCTRINAL OVERVIEW: THE PAROL EVIDENCE RULE*

The parties to a contract often reduce to writing part or all of their agreement, following negotiations during which they have given assurances, made promises, and reached understandings. They do this in order to provide trustworthy evidence of the fact and terms of their agreement and to avoid reliance on uncertain memory. However, should litigation ensue, one party may seek to introduce evidence of the earlier negotiations in an effort to show that the terms of the agreement are other than as shown on the face of the writing. The party will be met with a rule known as the "parol evidence rule," which may bar the use of such extrinsic evidence to contradict and perhaps even to supplement the writing.

Gianni v. R. Russel & Co. is a classic example of the rule in operation. Frank Gianni sold tobacco, fruit, candy, and soft drinks in a Pittsburgh office building. When the building was sold, Gianni had discussions with the new owner's rental agent and signed a three-year lease that provided that Gianni could "use the premises only for the sale of fruit, candy [and] soda water" but that he was "not allowed to sell tobacco." Later, when a drugstore leased space in the building and began to sell soft drinks, Gianni sued the owner for breach of an alleged promise that Gianni was to have the exclusive right to sell soft drinks in the building. Gianni sought to show that before he had signed the lease the rental agent had made this promise in return for Gianni's promises not to sell tobacco and to pay an increased rent. This would have, in effect, added a term to the lease. The Supreme Court of Pennsylvania held that it was error to admit testimony to this effect. "As the written lease is the complete contract of the parties and since it embraces the field of the alleged oral contract, evidence of the latter is inadmissible under the parol evidence rule."[2] Even if the agent had in fact made the promise, the rule barred Gianni from using evidence of the negotiations to prove it.

The parol evidence rule is universally recognized and is embodied in the Uniform Commercial Code in a statutory formula applicable to contracts for the sale of goods.[3] If kept within sensible limits, the rule has much to commend it. It has, however, generated its share of criticism. . . .

Thompson v. Libbey

Supreme Court of Minnesota

26 N.W. 1 (1885)

MITCHELL, J. The plaintiff being the owner of a quantity of logs marked "H. C. A.," cut in the winters of 1882 and 1883, and lying in the Mississippi river,

* Excerpted from E. ALLAN FARNSWORTH, CONTRACTS § 7.2 (4th ed. 2004).

2. 126 A. 791, 792 (Pa. 1924).

3. UCC § 2-202.

or on its banks, above Minneapolis, defendant and the plaintiff, through his agent, D. S. Mooers, having fully agreed on the terms of a sale and purchase of the logs referred to, executed the following written agreement:

> AGREEMENT.
>
> Hastings, Minn., June 1, 1883.
>
> I have this day sold to R. C. Libbey, of Hastings, Minn., all my logs marked "H. C. A.," cut in the winters of 1882 and 1883, for ten dollars a thousand feet, boom scale at Minneapolis, Minnesota. Payments cash as fast as scale bills are produced.
>
> J. H. Thompson,
> Per D. S. Mooers.
> R. C. Libbey.

This action having been brought for the purchase-money, the defendant—having pleaded a warranty of the quality of the logs, alleged to have been made at the time of the sale, and a breach of it—offered on the trial oral testimony to prove the warranty, which was admitted, over the objection of plaintiff that it was incompetent to prove a verbal warranty, the contract of sale being in writing. This raises the only point in the case.

No ground was laid for the reformation of the written contract, and any charge of fraud on part of plaintiff or his agent in making the sale was on the trial expressly disclaimed. No rule is more familiar than that "parol contemporaneous evidence is inadmissible to contradict or vary the terms of a valid written instrument," and yet none has given rise to more misapprehension as to its application. It is a rule founded on the obvious inconvenience and injustice that would result if matters in writing, made with consideration and deliberation, and intended to embody the entire agreement of the parties, were liable to be controlled by what Lord Coke expressively calls "the uncertain testimony of slippery memory." Hence, where the parties have deliberately put their engagements into writing in such terms as to import a legal obligation, without any uncertainty as to the object or extent of such engagement, it is conclusively presumed that the whole engagement of the parties, and the manner and extent of their undertaking, was reduced to writing. Of course, the rule presupposes that the parties intended to have the terms of their complete agreement embraced in the writing, and hence it does not apply where the writing is incomplete on its face and does not purport to contain the whole agreement, as in the case of mere bills of parcels, and the like.

But in what manner shall it be ascertained whether the parties intended to express the whole of their agreement in writing? It is sometimes loosely stated that where the whole contract be not reduced to writing, parol evidence may be admitted to prove the part omitted. But to allow a party to lay the foundation for such parol evidence by oral testimony that only part of the agreement was reduced to writing, and then prove by parol the part omitted, would be to work in a circle, and to permit the very evil which the rule was designed to prevent. **The only criterion of the completeness of the written contract as a full expression of the agreement of the parties is the writing itself.** If it imports on its face to be a complete expression of the whole agreement,—that is, contains such language as imports a complete legal obligation,—it is to be presumed that the parties have introduced into it every material item and term; and parol evidence cannot be admitted to add another term to the agreement, although the writing contains nothing on the particular one to which the parol evidence is directed. The rule forbids to add by parol where the writing is silent, as well as to vary where it speaks.

The written agreement in the case at bar, as it appears on its face, in connection with the law controlling its construction and operation, purports to be a complete expression of the whole agreement of the parties as to the sale and purchase of these logs, solemnly executed by both parties. There is nothing on its face (and this is a question of law for the court) to indicate that it is a mere informal and incomplete memorandum. Parol evidence of extrinsic facts and circumstances would, if necessary, be admissible, as it always is, to apply the contract to its subject-matter, or in order to a more perfect understanding of its language. But in that case such evidence is used, not to contradict or vary the written instrument, but to aid, uphold, and enforce it as it stands. The language of this contract "imports a legal obligation, without any uncertainty as to its object or the extent of the engagement," and therefore "it must be conclusively presumed that the whole engagement of the parties, and the manner and extent of the undertaking, was reduced to writing." No new term, forming a mere incident to or part of the contract of sale, can be added by parol. . . .

Our conclusion therefore is that the court erred in admitting parol evidence of a warranty, and therefore the order refusing a new trial must be reversed.

Circular reasoning?

In general, do you think it makes sense to look to a written contract to see whether the parties' entire agreement is contained within it? Suppose you and I make a written contract by which I agree to sell you my car for $10,000, delivery to take place tomorrow. Before tomorrow arrives, I remove an expensive radio system that, in part, motivated you to buy the car, but the contract says nothing about an expensive radio system (or, for that matter, about any radio system at all, or a steering wheel, or tires, or. . .). Is the expensive radio system part of our contract? Is it your fault for not making sure that the expensive radio system was specifically included in the contract? Finally, if you sue me, should a court decide the case only by looking to the writing between us, or should it consider parol or extrinsic evidence (such as oral testimony) not included within the four corners of the written agreement?

RELEVANT PROVISIONS

For the *Restatement (Second) of Contracts,* consult §§ 209, 210, 213, 214, and 216. For the UCC, consult § 2-202. For the CISG, consult Articles 8(3) and 11. For the UNIDROIT Principles, consult Articles 1.2 and 2.1.17.

NOTES AND QUESTIONS

1. *What happened?* Who sued whom for what? Procedurally, how did the case get before this court? Factually, what happened between the parties?

What arguments did the plaintiff and defendant make? What rule or rules did the court apply? How did the court analyze the dispute between the parties? How did the court decide the case?

2. *Was this case correctly decided?* Do you agree with the result reached in this case? Why or why not? Do you agree with the court's reasoning? Why or why not? How, if at all, would you have written the opinion differently?

3. *Come again?* What, exactly, did the court mean when it said that "[n]o rule is more familiar than that 'parol contemporaneous evidence is inadmissible to contradict or vary the terms of a valid written instrument'"? Does the excerpt below shed any light on this?

THE ADMISSIBILITY OF PAROL EVIDENCE FOR PURPOSES OF INTERPRETATION*

No parol evidence that is offered can be said to vary or contradict a writing until by process of interpretation the meaning of the writing is determined. The "parol evidence rule" is not, and does not purport to be, a rule of interpretation or a rule as to the admission of evidence for the purpose of interpretation. Even if a written document has been assented to as the complete and accurate integration of the terms of a contract, it must still be interpreted and all those factors that are of assistance in this process may be proved by oral testimony.

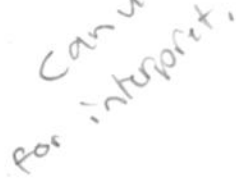

It is true that the language of some agreements has been believed to be so plain and clear that the court needs no assistance in interpretation. Even in these case, however, the courts seem to have had the aid of parol evidence of surrounding circumstances. The meaning to be discovered and applied is that which each party had reason to know would be given to the words by the other party. Antecedent and surrounding factors that throw light upon this question may be proved by any kind of relevant evidence.

The more bizarre and unusual an asserted interpretation is, the more convincing must be the testimony that supports it. At what point the court should cease listening to testimony that white is black and that a dollar is fifty cents is a matter for sound judicial discretion and common sense. Even these things may be true for some purposes. As long as the court is aware that there may be doubt and ambiguity and uncertainty in the meaning and application of agreed language, it will welcome testimony as to antecedent agreements, communications, and other factors that may help to decide the issue. Such testimony does not vary or contradict the written words; it determines that which cannot afterwards be varied or contradicted.

Mr. Justice Holmes once gave us the dictum that

* Excerpted from Arthur Linton Corbin, *The Parol Evidence Rule*, 53 YALE L.J. 603, 622-624 (1944).

> you cannot prove a mere private convention between the two parties to give language a different meaning from its common one. It would open too great risks if evidence were admissible to show that when they said five hundred feet they agreed it should mean one hundred inches, or that Bunker Hill Monument should signify the Old South Church.

It is believed, however, that the great judge was in error. The risks which he says would be "too great" are in fact being borne; they are not so great as he feared. We must remember that a person asserting that "five hundred feet" was used to mean "one hundred inches" bears the heavy risk of not being able to persuade the court and jury that it is true. . . .

Masterson v. Sine

Supreme Court of California
436 P.2d 561 (1968)

TRAYNOR, CHIEF JUSTICE. Dallas Masterson and his wife Rebecca owned a ranch as tenants in common. On February 25, 1958, they conveyed it to Medora and Lu Sine by a grant deed "Reserving unto the Grantors herein an option to purchase the above described property on or before February 25, 1968" for the "same consideration as being paid heretofore plus their depreciation value of any improvements Grantees may add to the property from and after two and a half years from this date." Medora is Dallas' sister and Lu's wife. Since the conveyance Dallas has been adjudged bankrupt. His trustee in bankruptcy and Rebecca brought this declaratory relief action to establish their right to enforce the option.

The case was tried without a jury. Over defendants' objection the trial court admitted extrinsic evidence that by "the same consideration as being paid heretofore" both the grantors and the grantees meant the sum of $50,000 and by "depreciation value of any improvements" they meant the depreciation value of improvements to be computed by deducting from the total amount of any capital expenditures made by defendants grantees the amount of depreciation allowable to them under United States income tax regulations as of the time of the exercise of the option.

The court also determined that the parol evidence rule precluded admission of extrinsic evidence offered by defendants to show that the parties wanted the property kept in the Masterson family and that the option was therefore personal to the grantors and could not be exercised by the trustee in bankruptcy.

The court entered judgment for plaintiffs, declaring their right to exercise the option, specifying in some detail how it could be exercised, and reserving jurisdiction to supervise the manner of its exercise and to determine the amount that plaintiffs will be required to pay defendants for their capital expenditures if plaintiffs decide to exercise the option.

Defendants appeal. They contend that the option provision is too uncertain to be enforced and that extrinsic evidence as to its meaning should not have been admitted. The trial court properly refused to frustrate the obviously declared intention of the grantors to reserve an option to repurchase by an overly meticulous insistence on completeness and clarity of written expression. It properly admitted extrinsic evidence to explain the language of the deed to the end that the consideration for the option would appear with sufficient certainty to permit specific enforcement. The trial court erred, however, in excluding the extrinsic evidence that the option was personal to the grantors and therefore nonassignable.

When the parties to a written contract have agreed to it as an "integration"—a complete and final embodiment of the terms of an agreement—parol evidence cannot be used to add to or vary its terms. When only part of the agreement is integrated, the same rule applies to that part, but parol evidence may be used to prove elements of the agreement not reduced to writing.

The crucial issue in determining whether there has been an integration is whether the parties intended their writing to serve as the exclusive embodiment of their agreement. The instrument itself may help to resolve that issue. It may state, for example, that "there are no previous understandings or agreements not contained in the writing," and thus express the parties' "intention to nullify antecedent understandings or agreements." (See 3 Corbin, *Contracts* (1960) § 578, p. 411.) Any such collateral agreement itself must be examined, however, to determine whether the parties intended the subjects of negotiation it deals with to be included in, excluded from, or otherwise affected by the writing. Circumstances at the time of the writing may also aid in the determination of such integration.

California cases have stated that whether there was an integration is to be determined solely from the face of the instrument, and that the question for the court is whether it "appears to be a complete . . . agreement." (See *Ferguson v. Koch* (1928) 204 Cal. 342.) Neither of these strict formulations of the rule, however, has been consistently applied. The requirement that the writing must appear incomplete on its face has been repudiated in many cases where parol evidence was admitted "to prove the existence of a separate oral agreement as to any matter on which the document is silent and which is not inconsistent with its terms"—even though the instrument appeared to state a complete agreement. Even under the rule that the writing alone is to be consulted, it was found necessary to examine the alleged collateral agreement before concluding that proof of it was precluded by the writing alone. It is therefore evident that "The conception of a writing as wholly and intrinsically self-determinative of the parties' intent to make it a sole memorial of one or seven or twenty-seven subjects of negotiation is an impossible one." (9 Wigmore, *Evidence* (3d ed. 1940) § 2431, p. 103.) For example, a promissory note given by a debtor to his creditor may integrate all their present contractual rights and obligations, or it may be only a minor part of an underlying executory contract that would never be discovered by examining the face of the note.

In formulating the rule governing parol evidence, several policies must be accommodated. One policy is based on the assumption that written evidence is more accurate than human memory. This policy, however, can be adequately served by excluding parol evidence of agreements that directly contradict the writing. Another policy is based on the fear that fraud or unintentional invention by witnesses interested in the outcome of the litigation will mislead the finder of facts. *Mitchill v. Lath,* 247 N.Y. 377 (1928) (dissenting opinion by Lehman, J.). McCormick has suggested that the party urging the spoken as against the written word is most often the economic underdog, threatened by severe hardship if the writing is enforced. In his view the parol evidence rule arose to allow the court to control the tendency of the jury to find through sympathy and without a dispassionate assessment of the probability of fraud or faulty memory that the parties made an oral agreement collateral to the written contract, or that preliminary tentative agreements were not abandoned when omitted from the writing. He recognizes, however, that if this theory were adopted in disregard of all other considerations, it would lead to the exclusion of testimony concerning oral agreements whenever there is a writing and thereby often defeat the true intent of the parties.

Evidence of oral collateral agreements should be excluded only when the fact finder is likely to be misled. The rule must therefore be based on the credibility of the evidence. One such standard, adopted by section 240(1)(b) of the *Restatement of Contracts,* permits proof of a collateral agreement if it "is such an agreement as might Naturally be made as a separate agreement by parties situated as were the parties to the written contract." The draftsmen of the Uniform Commercial Code would exclude the evidence in still fewer instances: "If the additional terms are such that, if agreed upon, they would Certainly have been included in the document in the view of the court, then evidence of their alleged making must be kept from the trier of fact." (Com. 3, § 2-202.)

The option clause in the deed in the present case does not explicitly provide that it contains the complete agreement, and the deed is silent on the question of assignability. Moreover, the difficulty of accommodating the formalized structure of a deed to the insertion of collateral agreements makes it less likely that all the terms of such an agreement were included. The statement of the reservation of the option might well have been placed in the recorded deed solely to preserve the grantors' rights against any possible future purchasers and this function could well be served without any mention of the parties' agreement that the option was personal. There is nothing in the record to indicate that the parties to this family transaction, through experience in land transactions or otherwise, had any warning of the disadvantages of failing to put the whole agreement in the deed. This case is one, therefore, in which it can be said that a collateral agreement such as that alleged "might naturally be made as a separate agreement." A fortiori, the case is not one in which the parties "would certainly" have included the collateral agreement in the deed. . . .

In the present case defendants offered evidence that the parties agreed that the option was not assignable in order to keep the property in the Masterson family. The trial court erred in excluding that evidence.

The judgment is reversed.

PETERS, TOBRINER, MOSK, and SULLIVAN, JJ., concur.

BURKE, JUSTICE (dissenting). I dissent. The majority opinion:

(1) Undermines the parol evidence rule as we have known it in this state since at least 1872 by declaring that parol evidence should have been admitted by the trial court to show that a written option, absolute and unrestricted in form, was intended to be limited and nonassignable;

(2) Renders suspect instruments of conveyance absolute on their face;

(3) Materially lessens the reliance which may be placed upon written instruments affecting the title to real estate; and

(4) Opens the door, albeit unintentionally to a new technique for the defrauding of creditors.

The opinion permits defendants to establish by parol testimony that their grant to their brother (and brother-in-law) of a written option, absolute in terms, was nevertheless agreed to be nonassignable by the grantee (now a bankrupt), and that therefore the right to exercise it did not pass, by operation of the bankruptcy laws, to the trustee for the benefit of the grantee's creditors.

And how was this to be shown? By the proffered testimony of the bankrupt optionee himself! Thereby one of his assets (the option to purchase defendants' California ranch) would be withheld from the trustee in bankruptcy and from the bankrupt's creditors. Understandably the trial court, as required by the parol evidence rule, did not allow the bankrupt by parol to so contradict the unqualified language of the written option.

The court properly admitted parol evidence to explain the intended meaning of the "same consideration" and "depreciation value" phrases of the written option to purchase defendants' land, as the intended meaning of those phrases was not clear. However, there was nothing ambiguous about the Granting language of the option and not the slightest suggestion in the document that the option was to be nonassignable. Thus, to permit such words of limitation to be added by parol is to contradict the absolute nature of the grant, and to directly violate the parol evidence rule.

Just as it is unnecessary to state in a deed to "lot X" that the house located thereon goes with the land, it is likewise unnecessary to add to "I grant an option to Jones" the words "and his assigns" for the option to be assignable. As hereinafter emphasized in more detail, California statutes expressly declare that it is assignable, and only if I add language in writing showing my intent to withhold or restrict the right of assignment may the grant be so limited. Thus, to seek to restrict the grant by parol is to contradict the written document in violation of the parol evidence rule.

The majority opinion arrives at its holding via a series of false premises which are not supported either in the record of this case or in such California authorities as are offered.

The parol evidence rule is set forth in clear and definite language in the statutes of this state. It "is not a rule of evidence but is one of substantive law. . . . The rule as applied to contracts is simply that as a matter of substantive law, a certain act, the act of embodying the complete terms of an agreement in a writing (the 'integration'), becomes the contract of the parties." (*Hale v. Bohannon,* 38 Cal. 2d 458, 465 (1952), quoting from *In re Estate of Gaines,* 15 Cal. 2d 255, 264-65 (1940).) The rule is based upon the sound principle that the parties to a written instrument, after committing their agreement to or evidencing it by the writing, are not permitted to add to, vary or *contradict* the terms of the writing by parol evidence. As aptly expressed by the author of the present majority opinion, speaking for the court in *Parsons v. Bristol Development Co.,* 62 Cal. 2d 861, 865 (1965), such evidence is "admissible to interpret the instrument, but *not* to give it a meaning to which it is not reasonably susceptible." (Italics added.) Or, as stated by the same author, concurring in *Laux v. Freed,* 53 Cal. 2d 512, 527 (1960), "extrinsic evidence is not admissible to 'add to, *detract* from, or vary its terms.'" (Italics added.)

At the outset the majority in the present case reiterate that the rule against contradicting or varying the terms of a writing remains applicable when only part of the agreement is contained in the writing, and parol evidence is used to prove elements of the agreement not reduced to writing. But having restated this established rule, the majority opinion inexplicably proceeds to subvert it. . . .

The contract of sale and purchase of the ranch property here involved was carried out through a title company upon written escrow instructions executed by the respective parties after various preliminary negotiations. The deed to defendant grantees, in which the grantors expressly reserved an option to repurchase the property within a ten-year period and upon a specified consideration, was issued and delivered in consummation of the contract. In neither the written escrow instructions nor the deed containing the option is there any language even suggesting that the option was agreed or intended by the parties to be personal to the grantors, and so nonassignable. The trial judge, on at least three separate occasions, correctly sustained objections to efforts of defendant optionors to get into evidence the testimony of Dallas Masterson (the bankrupt holder of the option) that a part of the agreement of sale of the parties was that the option to repurchase the property was personal to him, and therefore unassignable for benefit of creditors. But the majority hold that that testimony should have been admitted, thereby permitting defendant optionors to limit, detract from and contradict the plain and unrestricted terms of the written option in clear violation of the parol evidence rule and to open the door to the perpetration of fraud. . . .

The majority opinion attempts to buttress its approach by asserting that "California cases have stated that whether there was an integration is to be determined solely from the face of the instrument, and that the question for the court is whether it 'appears to be a complete . . . agreement,'" but that "Neither of these strict formulations of the rule has been consistently applied."

The majority's claim of inconsistent application of the parol evidence rule by the California courts fails to find support in the examples offered. . . .

Upon this structure of incorrect premises and unfounded assertions the majority opinion arrives at its climax: The pronouncement of "several policies [to] be accommodated . . . *[i]n formulating the rule governing parol evidence.*" (Italics added.) Two of the "policies" as declared by the majority are: Written evidence is more accurate than human memory; fraud or unintentional invention by interested witnesses may well occur.

I submit that these purported "policies" are in reality two of the basic and obvious reasons for adoption by the legislature of the parol evidence rule as the policy in this state. Thus the speculation of the majority concerning the views of various writers on the subject and the advisability of following them in this state is not only superfluous but flies flatly in the face of established California law and policy. It serves only to introduce uncertainty and confusion in a field of substantive law which was codified and made certain in this state a century ago.

However, despite the law which until the advent of the present majority opinion has been firmly and clearly established in California and relied upon by attorneys and courts alike, that parol evidence may *not* be employed to vary or contradict the terms of a written instrument, the majority now announce that such evidence "should be excluded only when the fact finder is *likely* to be misled," and that "the rule must therefore be based on the *credibility* of the evidence." (Italics added.) But was it not, *inter alia*, to avoid misleading the fact finder, and to further the introduction of only the evidence which is most likely to *be* credible (the written document), that the Legislature adopted the parol evidence rule as a part of the substantive law of this state? . . .

I would hold that the trial court ruled correctly on the proffered parol evidence, and would affirm the judgment.

McComb, J., concurs.

Rehearing denied; McComb and Burke, JJ., dissenting.

NOTES AND QUESTIONS

1. *What happened?* Who sued whom for what? Procedurally, how did the case get before this court? Factually, what happened between the parties? What arguments did the plaintiff and defendant make? What rule or rules did the court apply? How did the court analyze the dispute between the parties? How did the court decide the case?

2. *Was this case correctly decided?* Do you agree with the result reached in this case? Why or why not? Do you agree with the court's reasoning? Why

or why not? Do you think the majority or dissenting opinion has the better argument? Why? How, if at all, would you have written the opinion differently?

3. *Reconciled?* Can this case be reconciled with *Thompson v. Libby*? If so, how? If not, which rule seems best, and why?

Pacific Gas and Electric Co. v. G.W. Thomas Drayage & Rigging Co.

Supreme Court of California
442 P.2d 641 (1968)

TRAYNOR, C.J. Defendant appeals from a judgment for plaintiff in an action for damages for injury to property under an indemnity clause of a contract.

In 1960 defendant entered into a contract with plaintiff to furnish the labor and equipment necessary to remove and replace the upper metal cover of plaintiff's steam turbine. Defendant agreed to perform the work "at [its] own risk and expense" and to "indemnify" plaintiff "against all loss, damage, expense and liability resulting from . . . injury to property, arising out of or in any way connected with the performance of this contract." Defendant also agreed to procure not less than $50,000 insurance to cover liability for injury to property. Plaintiff was to be an additional named insured, but the policy was to contain a cross-liability clause extending the coverage to plaintiff's property.

During the work the cover fell and injured the exposed rotor of the turbine. Plaintiff brought this action to recover $25,144.51, the amount it subsequently spent on repairs. During the trial it dismissed a count based on negligence and thereafter secured judgment on the theory that the indemnity provision covered injury to all property regardless of ownership.

Defendant offered to prove by admissions of plaintiff's agents, by defendant's conduct under similar contracts entered into with plaintiff, and by other proof that in the indemnity clause the parties meant to cover injury to property of third parties only and not to plaintiff's property. Although the trial court observed that the language used was "the classic language for a third party indemnity provision" and that "one could very easily conclude that . . . its whole intendment is to indemnify third parties," it nevertheless held that the "plain language" of the agreement also required defendant to indemnify plaintiff for injuries to plaintiff's property. Having determined that the contract had a plain meaning, the court refused to admit any extrinsic evidence that would contradict its interpretation.

When the court interprets a contract on this basis, it determines the meaning of the instrument in accordance with the ". . . extrinsic evidence of the judge's own linguistic education and experience." (3 *Corbin on Contracts* (1960 ed.) [1964 Supp. § 579, p. 225, fn. 56].) The exclusion of testimony that might contradict the linguistic background of the judge reflects a judicial belief in the possibility of perfect verbal expression. This belief is a remnant of a primitive faith in the inherent potency and inherent meaning of words.

The test of admissibility of extrinsic evidence to explain the meaning of a written instrument is not whether it appears to the court to be plain and unambiguous on its face, but whether the offered evidence is relevant to prove a meaning to which the language of the instrument is reasonably susceptible.

Charge!

This language constitutes a direct frontal assault on the "four corners" approach we first explored in *Thompson v. Libbey* (p. 757). Do you agree or disagree with Chief Justice Traynor?

A rule that would limit the determination of the meaning of a written instrument to its four corners merely because it seems to the court to be clear and unambiguous, would either deny the relevance of the intention of the parties or presuppose a degree of verbal precision and stability our language has not attained.

Some courts have expressed the opinion that contractual obligations are created by the mere use of certain words, whether or not there was any intention to incur such obligations.[4] Under this view, contractual obligations flow, not from the intention of the parties but from the fact that they used certain magic words. Evidence of the parties' intention therefore becomes irrelevant. In this state, however, the intention of the parties as expressed in the contract is the source of contractual rights and duties.[5] A court must ascertain and give effect to this intention by determining what the parties meant by the words they used. Accordingly, the exclusion of relevant, extrinsic, evidence to explain the meaning of a written instrument could be justified only if it were feasible to determine the meaning the parties gave to the words from the instrument alone. If words had absolute and constant referents, it might be possible to discover contractual intention in the words themselves and in the manner in which they were arranged. Words, however, do not have absolute and constant referents. "A word is a symbol of thought but has no arbitrary and fixed meaning like a symbol of algebra or chemistry. . . ." (*Pearson v. State Social Welfare Board* (1960) 54 Cal. 2d 184, 195.) The meaning of particular words or groups of words varies with the ". . . verbal context and surrounding circumstances and purposes in view of the linguistic education and experience of their users and their hearers or readers (not excluding judges). . . . A word has no meaning apart from these factors; much less does it have an objective meaning, one true meaning." (Corbin, *The Interpretation of Words and the Parol Evidence Rule* (1965) 50 Cornell L.Q. 161, 187.) Accordingly, the meaning of a writing ". . . can only be found by interpretation in the light of all the circumstances that reveal the sense in which

4. "A contract has, strictly speaking, nothing to do with the personal, or individual, intent of the parties. A contract is an obligation attached by the mere force of law to certain acts of the parties, usually words, which ordinarily accompany and represent a known intent." (Hotchkiss v. National City Bank of New York (S.D.N.Y. 1911) 200 F. 287, 293.

5. "A contract must be so interpreted as to give effect to the mutual intention of the parties as it existed at the time of contracting, so far as the same is ascertainable and lawful." (Civ. Code, § 1636.)

the writer used the words. The exclusion of parol evidence regarding such circumstances merely because the words do not appear ambiguous to the reader can easily lead to the attribution to a written instrument of a meaning that was never intended." (*Universal Sales Corp. v. California Press Mfg. Co., supra,* 20 Cal. 2d 751, 776 (concurring opinion).)

Although extrinsic evidence is not admissible to add to, detract from, or vary the terms of a written contract, these terms must first be determined before it can be decided whether or not extrinsic evidence is being offered for a prohibited purpose. The fact that the terms of an instrument appear clear to a judge does not preclude the possibility that the parties chose the language of the instrument to express different terms. That possibility is not limited to contracts whose terms have acquired a particular meaning by trade usage,[6] but exists whenever the parties' understanding of the words used may have differed from the judge's understanding. Accordingly, rational interpretation requires at least a preliminary consideration of all credible evidence offered to prove the intention of the parties.[7] Such evidence includes testimony as to the "circumstances surrounding the making of the agreement . . . including the object, nature and subject matter of the writing . . ." so that the court can "place itself in the same situation in which the parties found themselves at the time of contracting." (*Universal Sales Corp. v. California Press Mfg. Co., supra,* 20 Cal. 2d 751, 761.) If the court decides, after considering this evidence, that the language of a contract, in the light of all the circumstances, "is fairly susceptible of either one of the two interpretations contended for . . ." (*Balfour v. Fresno C. & I. Co.* (1895) 109 Cal. 221, 225), extrinsic evidence relevant to prove either of such meanings is admissible.[8] In the present case the court erroneously refused to consider extrinsic evidence offered to show that the indemnity clause in the contract was not intended to cover injuries to plaintiff's property. Although that evidence was not necessary to show that the indemnity clause was reasonably susceptible of the meaning contended for by defendant, it was nevertheless

6. Extrinsic evidence of trade usage or custom has been admitted to show that the term "United Kingdom" in a motion picture distribution contract included Ireland; that the word "ton" in a lease meant a long ton or 2,240 pounds and not the statutory ton of 2,000 pounds; that the word "stubble" in a lease included not only stumps left in the ground but everything "left on the ground after the harvest time"; that the term "north" in a contract dividing mining claims indicated a boundary line running along the "magnetic and not the true meridian" and that a form contract for purchase and sale was actually an agency contract.

7. When objection is made to any particular item of evidence offered to prove the intention of the parties, the trial court may not yet be in a position to determine whether in the light of all of the offered evidence, the item objected to will turn out to be admissible as tending to prove a meaning of which the language of the instrument is reasonably susceptible or inadmissible as tending to prove a meaning of which the language is not reasonably susceptible. In such case the court may admit the evidence conditionally by either reserving its ruling on the objection or by admitting the evidence subject to a motion to strike.

8. Extrinsic evidence has often been admitted in such cases on the stated ground that the contract was ambiguous. This statement of the rule is harmless if it is kept in mind that the ambiguity may be exposed by extrinsic evidence that reveals more than one possible meaning.

relevant and admissible on that issue. Moreover, since that clause was reasonably susceptible of that meaning, the offered evidence was also admissible to prove that the clause had that meaning and did not cover injuries to plaintiff's property. Accordingly, the judgment must be reversed. . . .

The judgment is reversed.

NOTES AND QUESTIONS

1. *What happened?* Who sued whom for what? Procedurally, how did the case get before this court? Factually, what happened between the parties? What arguments did the plaintiff and defendant make? What rule or rules did the court apply? How did the court analyze the dispute between the parties? How did the court decide the case?

2. *Was this case correctly decided?* Do you agree with the result reached in this case? Why or why not? Do you agree with the court's reasoning? Why or why not? How, if at all, would you have written the opinion differently?

3. *Thinking tools applied.* At one point in his opinion, Chief Justice Traynor states that "rational interpretation requires at least a preliminary consideration of all credible evidence offered to prove the intention of the parties." Do you think such an approach is workable? Why or why not? *See* "Thinking Tool: Administrative Costs and Standards v. Rules" and "Thinking Tool: Marginal Analysis and Efficiency" (pp. 75 and 64, *supra*). *See also* Chief Judge Kozinski's opinion in *Trident*, following the excerpt below.

4. *Policy.* Do you prefer the formalist approach of *Thompson v. Libbey*, or the more flexible approach adopted here? Why? If the latter, do you think the flexible approach can go too far? For one court adopting this view, see *Trident*, after the excerpt.

> *As you may recall, we met Justice Traynor earlier in this course when we discussed the firm offer rule in* Drennan v. Star Paving Co. *(See p. 300,* infra.*) Now that we have had the opportunity to examine a couple more of his opinions, it is worth pausing to examine his approach to contract law, an approach that is not unique to him, but shared by other members of the bench and bar. It is not, however, an uncontroversial approach, as indicated by Judge Kozinski's opinion in the case* (Trident Center) *following the excerpt below. As you read the following excerpt and case, ask yourself whether you agree with Justice Traynor's approach to adjudication, or whether you agree with some of the criticisms raised by Judge Kozinski. Try to be as clear as possible about what you like or dislike about Justice Traynor's approach, and feel free to draw on any of the thinking tools we previously examined to shed light on this issue.*

JUSTICE TRAYNOR AND THE LAW OF CONTRACTS*

In his twenty years on the Supreme Court of California Justice Roger J. Traynor has become one of the country's best known state judges. A number of his contracts opinions have been exhibited as prize specimens in casebooks and have been the subject of discussion in the law reviews. His work in contracts excites all this academic interest because he is willing, perhaps even eager, to strike out in new directions, overturning and modifying old rules and establishing new ones. A critical review of Justice Traynor's work in this area is appropriate at this time, since the innovations of a famous judge tend to influence the development of the law far beyond the boundaries of his own state.

The work of such an innovator can best be appraised by asking what he is trying to accomplish by his lawmaking and then considering the appropriateness of his goals. Unfortunately for easy analysis, Justice Traynor has not explained his design for California contract law fully. As a result, one must pull his goals out of his opinions and writings, seeking clues in the pattern of positions he accepts or rejects either explicitly or implicitly. Of course, the danger of reading too much into this material is great, and it would be most surprising if Justice Traynor would agree with all my conclusions as to his purposes. It is necessary first to consider the ends a lawmaker might try to achieve through contract law and then to look for the pattern of choices, if any, that emerges from Justice Traynor's opinions in this area. After this is done, the question of appropriateness remains.

I. The Functions of Contract Law

It is helpful at the outset to set up some tentative categories of goals and means of implementing them that a judge or legislator might seek to attain through contract law. An important goal in this society is the achievement of the best balance of economic freedom and order. We seek the best proportion of (a) individual and corporate freedom to make choices in the market to (b) governmental action to promote general economic welfare.[3] Contract law reflects this problem of proportioning. Clearly, contract is a legal device primarily designed to support the market institution; yet it shows as well the impact of ideas of economic planning and control apart from the market process. Further, within both the market and nonmarket sectors divergent policies, or strategies of reaching these goals, are sometimes pursued. More particularly, it is a commonplace that contract law serves to support the market system, but one can isolate usefully at least three not always consistent policies concerning how that support ought to be given. *The self-reliance policy* dictates that courts should support the market by leaving it alone as much as possible. Wherever a rational economic man could have protected himself or made a choice the court should not protect the individual or

* Excerpted from Stewart Macaulay, *Justice Traynor and the Law of Contracts*, 13 STAN. L. REV. 812, 812-18 (1961).

3. "The most general objective of policy in our democratic society is twofold—freedom with order. . . . But the nature of the problem comes out as soon as we ask, how much freedom and in what connections and how much order and how it is to be achieved and maintained 'in a changing world.'" Knight, Economic Objectives in a Changing World, in Economics and Public Policy 49, 50 (1955).

make a choice for him. Responsibility is developed by giving it to individuals and making them take the consequences. If people behave rationally and responsibly, the market will work without disruption as people will either cover possible losses or take them. Common examples of this policy are the doctrine of caveat emptor, the rule imposing a heavy responsibility to check all representations for accuracy, and the dogma that courts do not make contracts for the parties.

The transactional policy calls for courts to support the market by taking action to carry out the particular transaction brought before them. The court should discover the bargain that was made and enforce it. If this discovery is not possible, the court should work out a result involving the least disruption of plans and causing the least amount of reliance loss in light of the situation at the time of the dispute. The market is supported by transactional policy because the legal system is directed to seek the result which best solves the problem in the particular case in market terms. A court following this policy will be eager to look at all the "legislative history" of a written contract and will confine or overturn rules which let people back out of bargains or disrupt plans.

Finally, *the functional policy* calls for the lawmaker to create generally applicable rules which facilitate bargaining by producing a system or structure in which exchanges can take place. Rules should be adopted which aid quick and rational bargaining and allow the parties to consider the impact of contract law in their planning. The courts should not seek the best result case-by-case since predictable law is a more important means of supporting the market. Most functional rules fill in gaps left in making contracts, or draw lines indicating when reliance will be protected or when a contract has been performed, and the like.

In sum, transactional policy calls for a case-by-case approach, and functional policy the creation of generally applicable rules. Of course, these are only extreme points on a scale useful for analysis. Few, if any, decisions turn on either an application of a general rule to facts with no judicial choice involved or on an application of pure discretion unfettered by any standard. It is the tendency in either the direction of rules to promote individual planning or discretion to reach good results which is significant in the analysis presented here.

As in the case of the market-oriented policies, the strategies designed to promote general economic welfare through social control can be divided into the particular and the general. *The relief-of-hardship policy* calls for courts to let one party out of his bargain in exceptional cases where enforcement would be unduly harsh, or, where the content of the bargain is in doubt, to place the burden on the party best able to spread the loss or absorb it. This case-by-case approach is based not on considerations of market functioning but on ethical ideals and emotional reactions to the plight of the underdog, to pressing an advantage too far, to making undue profit, or to inequality of resources. It is reflected in some aspects of the impossibility-of-performance doctrine, of the certainty and foreseeability limitations on contract damages, of the requirement of mutuality of performance, and of the application of many other devices which let bargainers out of contracts.

The economic planning policy is the other nonmarket strategy and the one calling for generalized rules to promote economic welfare. This policy is something of a catchall as these goals can range from wealth redistribution to regulation of particular industries or types of transactions. The most obvious examples involve a change in the market context by removing certain types of bargains from the kinds which will be legally enforced or by requiring particular terms in some bargains. More subtly the policy may shape the construction of contracts in desirable directions or affect other general rules.

A great deal of overlap among these policies is possible. A particular result may be justified by reference to several different policies, both market and non-market in orientation. For example, in the typical employment contract the employee must work before the employer must pay for the service—the employer's duty to pay is constructively conditional on the employee's performance.[8] One could justify this rule by reference to the market-oriented functional policy. It is likely that the result accords with the tacit assumptions of the parties because of well-established custom, and courts have adopted such a rule to fill the gap in the agreement. While the parties are free to contract differently, bargaining is facilitated if they need not bother to spell out such things. On the other hand, one can see here some economic planning. Employers as a class are probably better credit risks than employees paid in advance. Moreover, employers are more likely to be performing an entrepreneurial function, and in one view this risk taking and coordination is important enough to the general economic welfare to justify favoring the employer. Even though this overlap of policies exists, the classification suggested here may have utility. It serves to clarify the issues and separates distinct arguments so that they reinforce each other rather than confuse the issue. It also may serve as a checklist to avoid neglecting relevant arguments.

FIG. 1—AN ANALYSIS OF CONTRACT POLICY

Goals	Means
Support of the market institution	1. *The self-reliance policy.* The legal system should take minimum action, as bargainers must protect themselves.
	2. *The transactional policy.* The legal system should seek the best resolution of particular disputes in terms of minimizing disruption of plans and reliance loss, on a case-by-case basis.
	3. *The functional policy.* The legal system should create general rules designed to promote market functioning.
Social control to achieve economic welfare	1. *The relief-of-hardship policy.* The legal system should grant relief from unduly harsh obligations and allocate losses to the party who can best spread or absorb them, on a case-by-case basis.
	2. *The economic planning policy.* The legal system should adopt general rules which promote economic welfare apart from supporting the market system.

However, the policies listed can point to conflicting results. Obviously, the transactional and relief-of-hardship policies will always be difficult to reconcile.

8. *Restatement (First) of Contracts* § 270 (1932).

Where such a policy conflict is present, a choice must be made which should turn on the law- maker's views as to the weight to give market and nonmarket goals and the various means of attaining these goals. In this situation the classification should sharpen the issues. Yet the classification does not tell anyone when one policy ought to prevail over another. This remains in the realm of value judgments.[11]

II. Justice Traynor's Contracts Decisions

Most of Justice Traynor's approximately fifty-six contracts opinions are market-oriented, as one would expect in view of the major purposes of contract law. He gives a remarkably high priority to supporting the market through the transactional policy, seeking the best result in market terms in each case. Of course, transactional policy is built into much of contract law as it is administered by all judges, but a significant chunk of orthodox contract doctrine is inconsistent with upholding particular transactions and minimizing disruption of plans and reliance loss—prime examples are much of the consideration doctrine and the Statute of Frauds. What makes Justice Traynor's emphasis on the transactional policy worth comment is his reengineering of contract doctrine which overturns bargains. When he is finished reshaping this kind of rule, it will overturn very few transactions.

The other strategies for supporting the market are not employed too often. Only a few of Justice Traynor's contracts decisions seem based on functional policy. He seems unwilling to create many general rules which would interfere with a case-by-case approach. Relatively few of his opinions merely follow established rules. Also, there is no clear example of the self-reliance policy to be found in his contracts decisions, and many of them reach results directly contrary to those called for by this policy.

Even though Justice Traynor's positions in bargaining situations often can be explained in nonmarket social control terms, such explanations are almost always secondary and only reinforce market-oriented ones. Yet a few of his positions may be grounded on the relief-of-hardship or economic planning policies. . . .

Trident Center v. Connecticut General Life Insurance Co.

United States Court of Appeals, Ninth Circuit

847 F.2d 564 (1988)

KOZINSKI, CIRCUIT JUDGE. The parties to this transaction are, by any standard, highly sophisticated business people: Plaintiff is a partnership consisting of an insurance company and two of Los Angeles' largest and most prestigious law firms; defendant is another insurance company. Dealing at arm's length and from positions of roughly equal bargaining strength, they negotiated a commercial loan amounting to more than $56 million. The contract documents are

11. "Ideals are not unitary, they conflict; and the problem is to secure the best balance and compromise, for which there is no simple formula; it is a matter of *judgment*." Knight, *Book Review*, 39 VA. L. REV. 871, 875-76 (1953).

lengthy and detailed; they squarely address the precise issue that is the subject of this dispute; to all who read English, they appear to resolve the issue fully and conclusively.

Plaintiff nevertheless argues here, as it did below, that it is entitled to introduce extrinsic evidence that the contract means something other than what it says. This case therefore presents the question whether parties in California can ever draft a contract that is proof to parol evidence. Somewhat surprisingly, the answer is no.

FACTS

The facts are rather simple. Sometime in 1983 Security First Life Insurance Company and the law firms of Mitchell, Silberberg & Knupp and Manatt, Phelps, Rothenberg & Tunney formed a limited partnership for the purpose of constructing an office building complex on Olympic Boulevard in West Los Angeles. The partnership, Trident Center, the plaintiff herein, sought and obtained financing for the project from defendant, Connecticut General Life Insurance Company. The loan documents provide for a loan of $56,500,000 at 12¼ percent interest for a term of 15 years, secured by a deed of trust on the project. The promissory note provides that "[m]aker shall not have the right to prepay the principal amount hereof in whole or in part" for the first 12 years. In years 13-15, the loan may be prepaid, subject to a sliding prepayment fee. The note also provides that in case of a default during years 1-12, Connecticut General has the option of accelerating the note and adding a 10 percent prepayment fee.

Everything was copacetic for a few years until interest rates began to drop. The 12¼ percent rate that had seemed reasonable in 1983 compared unfavorably with 1987 market rates and Trident started looking for ways of refinancing the loan to take advantage of the lower rates. Connecticut General was unwilling to oblige, insisting that the loan could not be prepaid for the first 12 years of its life, that is, until January 1996.

Trident then brought suit in state court seeking a declaration that it was entitled to prepay the loan now, subject only to a 10 percent prepayment fee. Connecticut General promptly removed to federal court and brought a motion to dismiss, claiming that the loan documents clearly and unambiguously precluded prepayment during the first 12 years. The district court agreed and dismissed Trident's complaint. The court also "*sua sponte,* sanction[ed] the plaintiff for the filing of a frivolous lawsuit." Trident appeals both aspects of the district court's ruling.

DISCUSSION

I

Trident makes two arguments as to why the district court's ruling is wrong. First, it contends that the language of the contract is ambiguous and proffers a construction that it believes supports its position. Second, Trident argues that, under California law, even seemingly unambiguous contracts are subject to modification by parol or extrinsic evidence. Trident faults the district court for denying it the opportunity to present evidence that the contract language did not accurately reflect the parties' intentions.

A. The Contract

As noted earlier, the promissory note provides that Trident "shall not have the right to prepay the principal amount hereof in whole or in part before January 1996." It is difficult to imagine language that more clearly or unambiguously expresses the idea that Trident may not unilaterally prepay the loan during its first 12 years. Trident, however, argues that there is an ambiguity because another clause of the note provides that "[i]n the event of a prepayment resulting from a default hereunder or the Deed of Trust prior to January 10, 1996 the prepayment fee will be ten percent (10%)." Trident interprets this clause as giving it the option of prepaying the loan if only it is willing to incur the prepayment fee.

We reject Trident's argument out of hand [because, first, Trident's interpretation would result in a contradiction between two clauses of the contract (in that the default clause would swallow up the clause prohibiting Trident from prepaying during the first 12 years of the contract), and the normal rule of construction is to interpret contracts to avoid internal conflict where such an interpretation is possible. And second, because the clause on which Trident relied was not on its face reasonably susceptible to Trident's proffered interpretation.]

B. Extrinsic Evidence

Trident argues in the alternative that, even if the language of the contract appears to be unambiguous, the deal the parties actually struck is in fact quite different. It wishes to offer extrinsic evidence that the parties had agreed Trident could prepay at any time within the first 12 years by tendering the full amount plus a 10 percent prepayment fee. As discussed above, this is an interpretation to which the contract, as written, is not reasonably susceptible. Under traditional contract principles, extrinsic evidence is inadmissible to interpret, vary or add to the terms of an unambiguous integrated written instrument.

Trident points out, however, that California does not follow the traditional rule. Two decades ago the California Supreme Court in *Pacific Gas & Electric Co. v. G.W. Thomas Drayage & Rigging Co.*, 69 Cal. 2d 33, 442 P.2d 641, 69 Cal. Rptr. 561 (1968), turned its back on the notion that a contract can ever have a plain meaning discernible by a court without resort to extrinsic evidence. The court reasoned that contractual obligations flow not from the words of the contract, but from the intention of the parties. "Accordingly," the court stated, "the exclusion of relevant, extrinsic, evidence to explain the meaning of a written instrument could be justified only if it were feasible to determine the meaning the parties gave to the words from the instrument alone." This, the California Supreme Court concluded, is impossible: "If words had absolute and constant referents, it might be possible to discover contractual intention in the words themselves and in the manner in which they were arranged. Words, however, do not have absolute and constant referents." In the same vein, the court noted that "[t]he exclusion of testimony that might contradict the linguistic background of the judge reflects a judicial belief in the possibility of perfect verbal expression. This belief is a remnant of a primitive faith in the inherent potency and inherent meaning of words."

Under *Pacific Gas,* it matters not how clearly a contract is written, nor how completely it is integrated, nor how carefully it is negotiated, nor how squarely it addresses the issue before the court: the contract cannot be rendered impervious to attack by parol evidence. If one side is willing to claim that the parties intended one thing but the agreement provides for another, the court must consider extrinsic evidence of possible ambiguity. If that evidence raises the specter of ambiguity where there was none before, the contract language is displaced and the intention of the parties must be divined from self-serving testimony offered by partisan witnesses whose recollection is hazy from passage of time and colored by their conflicting interests. We question whether this approach is more likely to divulge the original intention of the parties than reliance on the seemingly clear words they agreed upon at the time.

Pacific Gas casts a long shadow of uncertainty over all transactions negotiated and executed under the law of California. As this case illustrates, even when the transaction is very sizeable, even if it involves only sophisticated parties, even if it was negotiated with the aid of counsel, even if it results in contract language that is devoid of ambiguity, costly and protracted litigation cannot be avoided if one party has a strong enough motive for challenging the contract. While this rule creates much business for lawyers and an occasional windfall to some clients, it leads only to frustration and delay for most litigants and clogs already overburdened courts.

It also chips away at the foundation of our legal system. By giving credence to the idea that words are inadequate to express concepts, *Pacific Gas* undermines the basic principle that language provides a meaningful constraint on public and private conduct. If we are unwilling to say that parties, dealing face to face, can come up with language that binds them, how can we send anyone to jail for violating statutes consisting of mere words lacking "absolute and constant referents"? How can courts ever enforce decrees, not written in language understandable to all, but encoded in a dialect reflecting only the "linguistic background of the judge"? Can lower courts ever be faulted for failing to carry out the mandate of higher courts when "perfect verbal expression" is impossible? Are all attempts to develop the law in a reasoned and principled fashion doomed to failure as "remnant[s] of a primitive faith in the inherent potency and inherent meaning of words"?

Be that as it may. While we have our doubts about the wisdom of *Pacific Gas,* we have no difficulty understanding its meaning, even without extrinsic evidence to guide us. As we read the rule in California, we must reverse and remand to the district court in order to give plaintiff an opportunity to present extrinsic evidence as to the intention of the parties in drafting the contract.[6]

II

In imposing sanctions on plaintiff, the district court stated:

> Pursuant to Fed. R. Civ. P. 11, the Court, *sua sponte,* sanctions the plaintiff for the filing of a frivolous lawsuit. The Court concludes that the language in the note and deed of trust is plain and clear. No reasonable person, much less firms of able attorneys, could possibly misunderstand this crystal-clear language. Therefore, this action was brought in bad faith.

Having reversed the district court on its substantive ruling, we must, of course, also reverse it as to the award of sanctions. While we share the district judge's impatience with this litigation, we would suggest that his irritation may have been misdirected. It is difficult to blame plaintiff and its lawyers for bringing this lawsuit. With this much money at stake, they would have been foolish not to pursue all remedies available to them under the applicable law. At fault, it seems to us, are not the parties and their lawyers but the legal system that encourages this kind of lawsuit. By holding that language has no objective meaning, and that contracts mean only what courts ultimately say they do, *Pacific Gas* invites precisely this type of lawsuit. With the benefit of 20 years of hindsight, the California Supreme Court may wish to revisit the issue. If it does so, we commend to it the facts of this case as a paradigmatic example of why the traditional rule, based on centuries of experience, reflects the far wiser approach.

CONCLUSION

The judgment of the district court is REVERSED. The case is REMANDED for reinstatement of the complaint and further proceedings in accordance with this opinion. The parties shall bear their own costs on appeal.

NOTES AND QUESTIONS

1. *What happened?* Who sued whom for what? Procedurally, how did the case get before this court? Factually, what happened between the parties? What arguments did the plaintiff and defendant make? What rule or rules did

6. Nothing we say should be construed as foreclosing Connecticut General from moving for summary judgment after completion of discovery; given the unambiguous language of the contract itself, such a motion would succeed unless Trident were to come forward with extrinsic evidence sufficient to render the contract reasonably susceptible to Trident's alternate interpretation, thereby creating a genuine issue of fact resolvable only at trial.

the court apply? How did the court analyze the dispute between the parties? How did the court decide the case?

2. *Was this case correctly decided?* Do you agree with the result reached in this case? Why or why not? Do you agree with the court's reasoning? Why or why not? How, if at all, would you have written the opinion differently?

3. *Did Kozinski misread* Pacific Gas*?* Pay careful attention to how Kozinski characterizes *Pacific Gas*. Did he get it right? Why or why not?

4. *Reconciled?* Can the frameworks adopted by *Pacific Gas* and *Trident* be reconciled? If so, how? If not, drawing on any thinking tools we covered, which approach do you prefer, and why? Does the following excerpt shed any light on which approach you think best?

PLAIN MEANING AND THE PAROL EVIDENCE RULE*

In Contract Interpretation

The concept of a plain meaning of language has found a more hospitable climate in the field of contract law than it has in semantics. . . .

While courts engaged in contract interpretation . . . have not adopted the idea that there is *always* a fixed and inevitable connection between word and object, they have found it difficult to rid themselves of the influence of this view. They have tended to attribute a definitive quality to written words. This tendency is exemplified by the parol evidence rule, which deserves close examination in light of the points we have just discussed.

Of the parol evidence rule, Thayer wrote: "Few things are darker than this, or fuller of subtle difficulties."[85] Typically, the rule is called into play where the parties have reduced their contract to writing after oral or written negotiations in which they have given assurances, made promises, or reached understandings. When, in the event of litigation, one of them seeks to introduce evidence of these negotiations to support his version of the contract, he will be met with this rule which, if it applies, will preclude his reliance on such "parol evidence," that is to say, on prior oral or written or contemporaneous oral negotiations. . . . For the rule to apply at all, a court must first conclude that the parties regarded the documents as a sort of exclusive memorial of their transaction, an "integration." This happens if the parties adopt a writing as the final, complete, and exclusive expression of their agreement. Once it is judicially determined that the agreement is "integrated," then the parol evidence rule applies, and prior oral or written and contemporaneous oral agreements are "inoperative to add to or to vary the agreement."[88] It is generally recognized, however, that this prohibition against addition and variation

* Excerpted from E. Allan Farnsworth, *"Meaning" in the Law of Contracts,* 76 YALE L.J. 939, 957-63, 65 (1967)

85. J. THAYER, A PRELIMINARY TREATISE ON EVIDENCE 390 (1898).

88. *Restatement* § 237. On partial integration, *see Restatement* §§ 228 and 229.

does not necessarily preclude resort to parol evidence when it is offered for the purpose of interpretation of language. Here there are two conflicting views.Under the older and more restrictive, parol evidence may only be used for the purpose of interpretation where the language in the writing is "ambiguous." The decision to admit parol evidence, that is, consists of two steps: first, one decides whether the language is ambiguous; second, if it is ambiguous, then one admits parol evidence only for the purpose of clearing up that ambiguity. This is the view adopted both by Williston and by the *Restatement of Contracts*[, which] provides that in the absence of ambiguity, the standard of interpretation to be applied to an integration is "the meaning that would be attached . . . by a reasonably intelligent person" familiar with all operative usages and knowing all the circumstances other than oral statements by the parties about what they intended the words to mean.[89] Under the newer and more liberal view championed by Corbin, the parol evidence rule is not applicable at all to matters of interpretation. On this view there is only one standard, applicable alike to integrated and unintegrated agreements, and parol evidence is always admissible in either of these two cases so long as it is used for the purpose of interpretation. The court need not first determine that the language is "ambiguous." This latter version of the rule seems more meaningful.[90] The principal instance in which the two views give conflicting results occurs when the parties reach an oral understanding whose meaning differs from what would be inferred by the *Restatement's* "reasonably intelligent person." This can be illustrated by another example based on the Peerless case.

> *Illustration 6.* A, by an agreement evidenced by an integration, contracted to sell B goods shipped from Bombay "ex Peerless." There were two steamers of the name "Peerless" sailing from Bombay at materially different times. A and B orally agreed that they were referring to Peerless No. 1, but a reasonably intelligent person acquainted with all operative usages and knowing all the circumstances, other than the oral agreement, would have referred to Peerless No. 2.[91]

Under the more restrictive view, it will be remembered, the court must determine whether "Peerless" as used in the writing is ambiguous. Assuming that it would conclude that it is not, parol evidence would be excluded. And since the reasonably intelligent person would have referred to Peerless No. 2, the court will find that to be the meaning of "Peerless." Under the more liberal view, however,

---

89. Restatement § 230.

90. Corbin, *The Interpretation of Words and the Parol Evidence Rule*, 50 CORNELL L.Q. 161 (1965). This view seems to be supported by Uniform Commercial Code § 2-202, which states the parol evidence rule so as to forbid contradiction but not interpretation, without regard to "ambiguity."

91. The comparable *Restatement* example is Illustration 1 to § 230, which involves an integrated agreement for the sale of certain patents, which A, the seller, understands to be only the English, but B, the buyer, understands to be the English, French and American. If a reasonable person under the standard of limited usage would understand this as a sale of the English and American, but not French, patents, then A and B are bound by the meaning. As Corbin points out, this example seems to be a distortion of *Preston v. Luck*, 27 Ch. D. 497 (1884). *See* 3 Corbin § 539 n.60.

since the purpose for which the evidence is offered is clearly that of "interpretation" of "Peerless," the court will admit evidence of the oral agreement and find the "meaning" of "Peerless" to be Peerless No. 1.

Under the more restrictive view, therefore, the parties do not have absolute freedom to attach special meanings to ordinary words. This view is kin to the much discredited "plain meaning" rule in the field of statutory interpretation, which excludes from consideration the statute's legislative history where the meaning of the statutory language is "plain." For if parol evidence may only be used to interpret the language of an integrated agreement where that language is ambiguous, the effect is to exclude the "transactional history" of the contract where the meaning of the integration is "plain."

The problem then becomes one of determining what constitutes ambiguity for this purpose. . . .

Generally, the term "ambiguity" is used loosely under the more restrictive view of the parol evidence rule, so that it includes not only patent and latent ambiguities, but vagueness as well. In one recent case, for example, the issue was whether the word "liabilities" included liabilities that were unknown and unforeseen and not stated on the balance sheet. Strictly, the problem was one of the vagueness of "liabilities" and not of its ambiguity. The court, nevertheless, held that parol evidence was admissible because the word "liability" was ambiguous, explaining: "An ambiguous contract is one capable of being understood in more senses than one; an agreement obscure in meaning through in-definiteness of expression, or having a double meaning."[95] In other words, the court defined "ambiguity" to include vagueness as well as ambiguity, and then admitted parol evidence where only vagueness existed. Indeed, some formulations of the traditional view specifically use the term "uncertainty" in addition to "ambiguity." Furthermore, courts have become increasingly willing to recognize the presence of both ambiguity and vagueness.

In spite of this liberalization of the more restrictive view, is there any excuse for the continued insistence upon ambiguity or vagueness in the integration in an era when the concept of a "plain" meaning of words has become justifiably suspect? Williston defended the more restrictive view on the ground that in unintegrated contracts the parties are not primarily paying attention to the symbols which they are using but have in mind the things for which the symbols stand. He claimed that just the opposite is true in the case of an integration. The basis for this assumption does not appear, and the image of the parties considering the things for which the symbols stand rather than the symbols themselves seems as appropriate to a contract made on a standard printed form containing an integration clause among its boilerplate as to a more informal sort of transaction. On a more practical level, Williston suggested that exclusion of parol evidence, even for the purpose of interpretation, may be dictated by two factors: first by fairness to the other party, who may have been justified in assuming an intention different from that which actually existed; and second, by the desirability of a reasonable certainty of proof of the terms of the contract. The first argument is scarcely

95. *Gerhart v. Henry Disston & Sons*, 290 F.2d 778, 784 (3d Cir. 1961).

compelling if it has been determined that *both* parties used words in a way different from that dictated by general or limited usage. As to the second, the curious fact that the *Restatement* formulation of the more restrictive view speaks only to "oral statements," while the parol evidence rule generally applies to prior written statements as well, suggests that this branch of the rule places more reliance on the desirability of certainty of proof for its justification. Since, however, interpretation is ordinarily regarded as a matter of law rather than one of fact, so that it falls within the province of judge rather than of jury, there is an adequate safeguard, if one is needed, against the risk of insubstantial evidence.

The more liberal view is more persuasive. This view makes it unnecessary to determine whether the language of an integrated writing is "plain" as opposed to "ambiguous" or "vague." Instead the task is to characterize the process involved as that of "interpreting" the writing on the one hand, or as that of "adding to" or "varying" it on the other. The distinction can be justified on the ground that although the writing is an integration and the parties have assented to it as a complete and exclusive statement of terms, the imprecise nature of language still leaves room for interpretation.

The question is then, when does "interpretation" end and "addition" or "variation" begin? The answer under the definition of "interpretation" arrived at earlier must be, interpretation ends with the resolution of problems which derive from the failure of language, that is to say with the resolution of ambiguity and vagueness. Accordingly, even under the liberal view, parol evidence is admissible only where vagueness or ambiguity is claimed. In many cases this will produce the same result as the restrictive view—that parol evidence is admissible only where the meaning of the writing is not "plain." The principal departure is that while the restrictive view confines the court to the language of the integration itself and requires it to decide whether there is ambiguity or vagueness, the liberal view simply requires the court to look to the purpose for which the parol evidence is sought to be introduced, without the necessity of deciding beforehand whether the language is, in fact, ambiguous or vague. . . .

It is increasingly difficult to justify the restrictive view of the parol evidence rule. Once it is recognized that all language is infected with ambiguity and vagueness, it is senseless to ask a court to determine whether particular language is "ambiguous" or "vague" as opposed to "plain." But it is possible to give content to the terms "ambiguity" and "vagueness," and it does make sense to ask a court to determine whether evidence is offered for the purpose of resolving ambiguity or vagueness. By limiting "interpretation" to the resolution of ambiguity or vagueness, we can give meaningful content to the more liberal rule.

Now that you have considered a number of different approaches to parol evidence, how do you think the problem of whether (and when) to introduce parol evidence should be approached? Should it be governed by a standard or a rule? And what should the standard or rule seek to accomplish? You may find the excerpt below to be of some assistance in helping you think about these issues.

Professor Farnsworth suggests that lawmakers should take into account a number of factors (detailed below) when deciding whether to regulate the conduct of parties with a rule (such as a rule prohibiting the consideration of parol evidence outside the four corners of a written document where the document appears to be clear and unambiguous) or a standard (such as a standard inquiring into the intention of a party to see whether parol evidence should be admitted). As you read the following excerpt, ask yourself whether you think the benefits of a clear but less flexible rule outweigh the benefits of a somewhat muddy but flexible standard, and how your answer influences the way you believe courts should think about parol evidence. Specifically, what light does the excerpt below shed on the debate we saw played out between Justice Traynor in Pacific Gas *and Judge Kozinski in* Trident Center?

THINKING TOOL APPLIED: RULES V. STANDARDS*

The choice between rules and standards comes up all the time in law. Most laws—whether made by legislatures, courts, agencies, or anyone else—can be understood as if-then statements. Usually they are commands enforced by penalties if they aren't obeyed. Whoever drafts the directives has to decide whether to put them in the form of rules or standards or some combination, whether it's a speed limit, a judicial decision about free speech, or a determination that the defendant in a case involving a car accident was negligent and should pay damages. . . . [Some of the trade-offs between regulating conduct with a rule or a standard include]:

1. *Potential for abuse*. . . . [W]hich danger is greater—the abuse of a standard's vagueness or of a rule's precision. . . .
2. *Precision and notice*. . . . Rules tend to be clear in advance but crude in application. At their edges they often cover some cases one wishes they would miss, and miss some cases one wishes they would cover. In the classic shorthand, rules are overinclusive and underinclusive. . . . But use of a standard makes the result less clear in advance, and the uncertainty can create costs of its own. Giving everyone clear notice makes it easier to comply with the law and easier to resolve disputes without help from a judge. . . .
3. *Blame and accountability*. Rules gain ground in another respect when it comes time for their enforcement by a court. A judge confronted with an odious defendant might be inclined, consciously or not, to bend the application of a standard [whereas a] rule helps avoid these risks. It leaves less room for discretion and its abuses not only by those it governs but by the judge called on to enforce it, and it gives the judge a way to enforce the law without worrying about blame: he isn't doing much; he merely is applying the rule, and the rule, or perhaps its authors (anyone but the judge), should bear any blame from the public. By the same token the existence of a rule makes accountability easier. When a standard is applied, a judge can blame

* Excerpted from WARD FARNSWORTH, THE LEGAL ANALYST: A TOOLKIT FOR THINKING ABOUT THE LAW 164-69, 171 (2007). We first examined the difference between standards and rules in "Thinking Tool: Administrative Costs and Standards v. Rules," p. 75, *supra*, which you may want to review at this time.

its author for blundering in the writing of it, and the author can blame the judge for blundering in its application. Rules tend to make it harder to point fingers back and forth in this way. . . . And yet it also is possible for rules to have the perverse effect of pushing discretion out of view and thus making its exercise less accountable. A standard often requires the users of it to explain their thinking; a rule doesn't. And if a rule seems a bad fit to a case, the enforcer may be tempted to bend its interpretation, or bend the facts, or bend the exercise of discretion, to avoid applying it. . . .

4. *Uncertainty and conflict.* Sometimes it makes sense to proceed case-by-case because we aren't ready to settle on a rule. Maybe we can't yet figure out what the right rule would be and would rather try to close in on it one situation at a time; good judgments require the sort of information about the facts that a trial judge will have but that is beyond the reach of rule makers further away from the action. Or maybe we disagree about what the right rule would be but can agree on what outcome is best in particular cases; we would rather go case-by-case and make do with "incompletely theorized agreements"—in other words, agreements on results that might not extend to agreements about first principles. Taking one case at a time, rather than insisting on a clear rule, can be a helpful way of getting through the business of life, and of government, despite deep political conflict.
5. *Costs of creation and application.* The choice between rules and standards also has a more explicitly economic side. For example, it often involves tradeoffs between accuracy and finality, or—roughly the same thing—how seriously one worries about administrative costs. Standards are more precise than rules, but they also are more expensive to use. . . . [whereas rules may be] simpler, easier to understand, clearer in advance to everyone, and cheaper to apply. The standard may be more likely to produce results that seem fair on all the facts, which is a point in its favor—maybe a decisive one. But then someone—chiefly the parties, but also the public—has to pay for all the extra efforts to be fair. The standard also makes cases less predictable and harder to settle. Here and elsewhere, standards thus are more expensive than rules; that is why an increase in the use of standards is sometimes associated with an increase in the wealth of a society. When resources are in short supply, there is less interest in spending them on arguments about choice of law or any other feature of litigation. It is easier to live with rules that sometimes produce wrong answers than with standards that cause some of the pie to be destroyed by the efforts to carve it up too precisely. . . . There can be hidden costs to rules, too. They have to be made in the first place—a process that takes time and investigation, especially if the rules are going to apply to lots of situations with different details. If one proceeds with rules rather than standards, there often have to be many more rules, and they will be less intuitive; compare the standard of "reasonable care" in tort law—a single idea used to judge just about every mistake a driver can make—to all the formal rules of the road, the violation of which will result in criminal penalties. Rules also have to be rewritten more often than standards to keep up with changes in the world. A standard delegates that task of adjustment to judges or whoever else applies them on the front lines, which might be the

cheapest way to go if the adjustments have to be made often, or if the rule is hard to work out in advance, or if the rule makers face a large risk of botching it when they try to get too precise.

Many of the points just considered suggest a general and useful way to think about rules. They involve three parties: one who makes the rule, another who applies it, and another to whom it is applied. . . . [For instance, a rule may be made by the legislature, applied by a judge, and used against a defendant.] Sometimes the maker and enforcer of the rule can be the same, as when a court makes a rule one day and then applies it the next; but even then the rule usually gets carried out by at least some actors besides the ones who wrote it—other judges, perhaps. As a result of these divided functions, sometimes the costs of using or avoiding a rule aren't fully felt by the party who makes it. Using standards rather than rules might sometimes sound good to a court, which then leaves itself wiggle room in future cases; but the standards might create costs for others—for example, litigants trying to settle their cases—that the court doesn't feel or (to say it in economics) internalize. . . .

Another consequence of the divided manner in which rules are made and applied is that the wishes of the maker may not get expressed accurately once the rule falls into the hands of the enforcer. . . .

Another reason why courts sometimes prefer rules to standards has to do with notice. Rules tell people in advance what consequences will follow from their acts, and clarity of this kind is more important in some areas than others. . . .

INTERNATIONAL PERSPECTIVE: THE PAROL EVIDENCE RULE AND THE CISG*

Although the CISG does not require the parties to put their contract in writing,† they will frequently choose to do so anyway, and so a court may have to decide whether to allow one of the parties to argue that their actual agreement differed from the written terms. Under the parol evidence rule found in both the common law and the UCC, the parties may not contradict the terms of a final written agreement with evidence of prior or contemporaneous negotiations or agreements. CISG Article 8(3), by contrast, directs a court interpreting a contract to give "due consideration . . . to all relevant circumstances of the case including the negotiations, any practices which the parties have established between themselves, usages and any subsequent conduct of the parties." In other words, the CISG lacks a parol evidence rule and allows a court interpreting a written contract to consider not just trade usage, course of dealing, and course of performance, but even the parties' prior negotiations.

* Excerpted from William S. Dodge, *Teaching the CISG in Contracts*, 50 J. LEGAL EDUC. 72, 86-87 (2000).

† [*See* "International Perspective: The Statute of Frauds and the CISG" at p. 1147, *infra*.—ED.]

In the next case, we examine a famous U.S. case in which a court dealt with a party's argument that extrinsic evidence should be considered under the CISG, even where such evidence may contradict or vary the terms of a written contract.

MCC-Marble Ceramic Center v. Ceramica Nuova D'Agostino

United States Circuit Court of Appeals, Eleventh Circuit
144 F.3d 1384 (1998)

[We previously considered whether the court could look into the subjective intention of the parties under the CISG to see whether there was mutual assent. To review that portion of the opinion, see p. 181, *supra*. In this portion of the opinion, we examine the applicability of the parol evidence rule under the CISG.]

DISCUSSION

II. Parol Evidence and the CISG

Given our determination that the magistrate judge and the district court should have considered MCC's affidavits regarding the parties' subjective intentions, we must address a question of first impression in this circuit: whether the parol evidence rule, which bars evidence of an earlier oral contract that contradicts or varies the terms of a subsequent or contemporaneous written contract,[12] plays any role in cases involving the CISG. We begin by observing that the parol evidence rule, contrary to its title, is a substantive rule of law, not a rule of evidence. *See* II E. Allen Farnsworth, *Farnsworth on Contracts*, § 7.2 at 194 (1990). The rule does not purport to exclude a particular type of evidence as an "untrustworthy or undesirable" way of proving a fact, but prevents a litigant from attempting to show "the fact itself—the fact that the terms of the agreement are other than those in the writing." *Id.* As such, a federal district court cannot simply apply the parol evidence rule as a procedural matter—as it might if excluding a particular type of evidence under the Federal Rules of Evidence, which apply in federal court regardless of the source of the

12. The Uniform Commercial Code includes a version of the parol evidence rule applicable to contracts for the sale of goods in most states:Terms with respect to which the confirmatory memoranda of the parties agree or which are otherwise set forth in a writing intended by the parties as a final expression of their agreement with respect to such terms as are included therein may not be contradicted by evidence of any prior agreement or of a contemporaneous oral agreement but may be explained or supplemented(a) by course of dealing or usage of trade . . . or by course of performance . . . ; and

> (b) by evidence of consistent additional terms unless the court finds the writing to have been intended also as a complete and exclusive statement of the terms of the agreement.

U.C.C. § 2-202.

substantive rule of decision. *Cf. id.* § 7.2 at 196.[13] The CISG itself contains no express statement on the role of parol evidence. It is clear, however, that the drafters of the CISG were comfortable with the concept of permitting parties to rely on oral contracts because they eschewed any statutes of fraud provision and expressly provided for the enforcement of oral contracts. *Compare* CISG, art. 11 (a contract of sale need not be concluded or evidenced in writing) with U.C.C. § 2-201 (precluding the enforcement of oral contracts for the sale of goods involving more than $500). Moreover, article 8(3) of the CISG expressly directs courts to give "due consideration . . . to all relevant circumstances of the case including the negotiations . . ." to determine the intent of the parties. Given article 8(1)'s directive to use the intent of the parties to interpret their statements and conduct, article 8(3) is a clear instruction to admit and consider parol evidence regarding the negotiations to the extent they reveal the parties' subjective intent. . . .

Our reading of article 8(3) as a rejection of the parol evidence rule, however, is in accordance with the great weight of academic commentary on the issue. As one scholar has explained:

> The language of Article 8(3) that "due consideration is to be given to *all relevant* circumstances of the case" seems adequate to override any domestic rule that would bar a tribunal from considering the relevance of other agreements. . . . Article 8(3) relieves tribunals from domestic rules that might bar them from "considering" any evidence between the parties that is relevant. This added flexibility for interpretation is consistent with a growing body of opinion that the "parol evidence rule" has been an embarrassment for the administration of modern transactions.

Honnold, *Uniform Law* § 110 at 170-71. . . . One of the primary factors motivating the negotiation and adoption of the CISG was to provide parties to international contracts for the sale of goods with some degree of certainty as to the principles of law that would govern potential disputes and remove the previous doubt regarding which party's legal system might otherwise apply. Courts applying the CISG cannot, therefore, upset the parties' reliance on the Convention by substituting familiar principles of domestic law when the Convention requires a different result. We may only achieve the directives of good faith and uniformity in contracts under the CISG by interpreting and applying the plain language of article 8(3) as written and obeying its directive to consider this type of parol evidence.

---

13. An example demonstrates this point. The CISG provides that a contract for the sale of goods need not be in writing and that the parties may prove the contract "by any means, including witnesses." CISG, art. 11. Nevertheless, a party seeking to prove a contract in such a manner in federal court could not do so in a way that violated in the rule against hearsay. *See* Fed. R. Evid. 802 (barring hearsay evidence). A federal district court applies the Federal Rules of Evidence because these rules are considered procedural, regardless of the source of the law that governs the substantive decision. *Cf. Farnsworth on Contracts* § 7.2 at 196 & n.16 (citing cases).

This is not to say that parties to an international contract for the sale of goods cannot depend on written contracts or that parol evidence regarding subjective contractual intent need always prevent a party relying on a written agreement from securing summary judgment. To the contrary, most cases will not present a situation (as exists in this case) in which both parties to the contract acknowledge a subjective intent not to be bound by the terms of a pre-printed writing. In most cases, therefore, article 8(2) of the CISG will apply, and objective evidence will provide the basis for the court's decision. *See* Honnold, *Uniform Law* § 107 at 164-65. Consequently, a party to a contract governed by the CISG will not be able to avoid the terms of a contract and force a jury trial simply by submitting an affidavit which states that he or she did not have the subjective intent to be bound by the contract's terms. Moreover, to the extent parties wish to avoid parol evidence problems they can do so by including a merger clause in their agreement that extinguishes any and all prior agreements and understandings not expressed in the writing.

Considering MCC's affidavits in this case, however, we conclude that the magistrate judge and the district court improperly granted summary judgment in favor of D'Agostino. Although the affidavits are, as D'Agostino observes, relatively conclusory and unsupported by facts that would *objectively* establish MCC's intent not to be bound by the conditions on the reverse of the form, article 8(1) requires a court to consider evidence of a party's subjective intent when the other party was aware of it, and the Silingardi and Copelli affidavits provide that evidence. This is not to say that the affidavits are conclusive proof of what the parties intended. A reasonable finder of fact, for example, could disregard testimony that purportedly sophisticated international merchants signed a contract without intending to be bound as simply too incredible to believe and hold MCC to the conditions printed on the reverse of the contract. Nevertheless, the affidavits raise an issue of material fact regarding the parties' intent to incorporate the provisions on the reverse of the form contract. If the finder of fact determines that the parties did not intend to rely on those provisions, then the more general provisions of the CISG will govern the outcome of the dispute.

MCC's affidavits, however, do not discuss all of the transactions and orders that MCC placed with D'Agostino. Each of the affidavits discusses the parties' subjective intent surrounding the initial order MCC placed with D'Agostino in October 1990. The Copelli affidavit also discusses a February 1991 requirements contract between the parties and reports that the parties subjectively did not intend the terms on the reverse of the D'Agostino order form to apply to that contract either. D'Agostino, however, submitted the affidavit of its chairman, Vincenzo Maselli, which describes at least three other orders from MCC on form contracts dated January 15, 1991, April 27, 1991, and May 4, 1991, in addition to the October 1990 contract. MCC's affidavits do not discuss the subjective intent of the parties to be bound by language in those contracts, and D'Agostino, therefore, argues that we should affirm summary judgment to the extent damages can be traced to those order forms. It is unclear from the record, however, whether all of these contracts contained the terms that appeared in the October 1990 contract. Moreover, because article 8 requires a court to consider any "practices which the parties have established between themselves, usages and any subsequent conduct of the parties" in interpreting contracts, CISG, art. 8(3), whether the parties intended to adhere to the ten day limit for complaints, as stated on the reverse of the initial contract, will have an impact on whether MCC was bound to adhere to the limit on subsequent deliveries. Since material issues of fact remain regarding the interpretation of the remaining contracts between MCC and D'Agostino, we cannot affirm any portion of the district court's summary judgment in D'Agostino's favor.

CONCLUSION

MCC asks us to reverse the district court's grant of summary judgment in favor of D'Agostino. The district court's decision rests on pre-printed contractual terms and conditions incorporated on the reverse of a standard order form that MCC's president signed on the company's behalf. Nevertheless, we conclude that the CISG, which governs international contracts for the sale of goods, precludes summary judgment in this case because MCC raised a material issue of material fact concerning the parties' subjective intent to be bound by the terms on the reverse of the pre-printed contract.* The CISG also precludes the application of the parol evidence rule, which would otherwise bar the consideration of evidence concerning a prior or contemporaneously negotiated oral agreement. Accordingly, we REVERSE the district court's grant of summary judgment and REMAND this case for further proceedings consistent with this opinion.

NOTES AND QUESTIONS

1. ***What happened?*** Who sued whom for what? Procedurally, how did the case get before this court? Factually, what happened between the parties? What arguments did the plaintiff and defendant make? What rule or rules did the court apply? How did the court analyze the dispute between the parties? How did the court decide the case?

2. ***Was this case correctly decided?*** Do you agree with the result reached in this case? Why or why not? Do you agree with the court's reasoning? Why or why not? How, if at all, would you have written the opinion differently?

3. *Trick question.* How would you articulate the parol evidence rule under the CISG?

4. *Comparative Perspective.* What are the pros and cons of the CISG's approach to parol evidence? In your opinion, is this approach better or worse

* [This portion of the court's decision was discussed in Chapter 3, on p.181, *supra*.]

than the common law's approach? What criticisms do you think Judge Kozinski (who wrote the opinion in *Trident Center*) might offer, and how do you think Justice Traynor (who wrote the opinion in *Pacific Gas*) would respond?

5. *Best approach.* Of all the approaches to parol evidence that we have examined in this chapter, what approach to parol evidence do you think works best, and why?

PROBLEM: THE ICEHOUSE

The Petersons wanted to purchase a farm owned by the Davidsons, but wanted the Davidsons to remove an icehouse that was located across the street, on a neighboring farm, which the Petersons found objectionable. The Davidsons orally promised, in consideration of the purchase of their farm by the Petersons, to remove the icehouse after the closing. Relying upon the promise, the Petersons entered into a written contract to buy the property for $100,000, and the closing followed 30 days later. The written contract, however, was silent as to the icehouse. Since the closing, the Petersons have spent considerable sums in improving the property for use as a summer residence. The Davidsons, however, have not fulfilled their promise as to the icehouse, and do not intend to do so.

If the Petersons sue the Davidsons, should the oral agreement between the parties with respect to the icehouse be enforced?

PROBLEM: NO HORSING AROUND

Seller and Buyer made a contract for the sale of horse meat scraps. According to the terms of the contract, if any of the scraps tested at less than "50% protein," Buyer was to receive a discount of $5.00 per ton. Roughly 170 tons of the scraps delivered by Seller contained less than 50 percent protein; of these 170 tons, 140 contained between 49.53 and 49.96 percent protein. Buyer took a $5.00 discount on the entire 170 tons, contrary to Seller's claim that he was entitled to do so on 30 tons only. When Buyer refused to pay the balance allegedly due, Seller brought an action against him. In his complaint Seller alleged:

That at the time the written contract was entered into, both Seller and Buyer were engaged in the business of buying and selling horse meat scraps; that at the time the contract was entered into there was a custom and usage of trade in said business well known to both Seller and Buyer as to the meaning of the terms "minimum 50 per cent protein" and "less than 50 per cent protein" used in the agreement between Seller and Buyer; that, by virtue of this custom, it was well known and understood among all members of the trade, including Seller and Buyer, that the terms "minimum 50 per cent protein" and "less than 50 percent protein" when used in a contract for the sale of horse meat scraps with reference to a test of its protein content, meant that a protein content of not less than 49.5 per cent was equal to and the same as a content of 50 per cent protein.

Analyze whether the contract between Seller and Buyer is ambiguous? If it is, should the court allow Seller to introduce parol evidence as to the meaning of "minimum 50 per cent protein"? How would you redraft the contract to remove any potential ambiguity in the future?

PROBLEM: BUYING A CAR

Buyer and Seller entered into a signed written contract whereby Buyer agreed to purchase Seller's car for $10,000, delivery to take place at the end of the month, once Seller retired as an Uber driver. The written contract was silent as to whether the Bose stereo system that was installed by Seller would be included in the sale price, and further provided that "any previous representations made between Buyer and Seller are superseded by this agreement." When Seller delivered the car to Buyer, the Bose stereo had been removed, and the standard stock stereo, which was in perfect condition, was installed in its place.

Buyer brings suit against Seller, and seeks to introduce evidence that, before signing the written agreement, the parties agreed that the Bose stereo would be included in the purchase price. How should a court should rule, and why? Would your answer change if Seller, after signing the contract, assured Buyer that the Bose stereo system would be included? Why or why not?

PROBLEM: MOVING THE EARTH

Plaintiff Peyton Earthworks ("Peyton") contracted with Defendant Dallas Construction ("Dallas") to do certain earth-moving work involved in the construction of housing units. Peyton contends that while it was examining the building site in preparation for submitting a bid on this project, a representative of Dallas told it that there were 25,000 cubic yards of excavation to be performed on the job. Peyton claims that its bid of $100,000 on the contract was made in reliance on that representation. Dallas denies that its representative made any such statement to Peyton.

Peyton's bid was submitted and accepted. Peyton began work before a written contract was signed. While performing the earthwork, Peyton discovered that the quantity of work far exceeded 25,000 cubic yards. When the written contract was finally presented to Peyton, it provided that Peyton would perform all earthwork for the consideration of $100,000. Peyton contends that it signed the contract, even though by then it knew that the job involved more than 25,000 cubic yards of earthwork, because a Dallas officer verbally represented that a deal would be worked out wherein Peyton would be paid more than the sum provided for in the contract.

In its "Standard Provisions," the contract provided that:

No verbal agreement with any agent either before or after the execution of this Contract shall affect or modify any of the terms or obligations herein contained and this contract shall be conclusively considered as containing and expressing all of the terms and conditions agreed upon by the parties hereto. No changes shall be valid unless reduced to writing and signed by the parties hereto.

Upon completion of the work, Peyton was paid the $100,000 provided for in the contract, but brought suit to recover for the additional work performed. Dallas moves for summary judgment. What are Peyton's and Dallas's best arguments as to why parol evidence should be included or excluded, respectively? How do you think the court should rule, and why?

C. FILLING IN CONTRACT GAPS

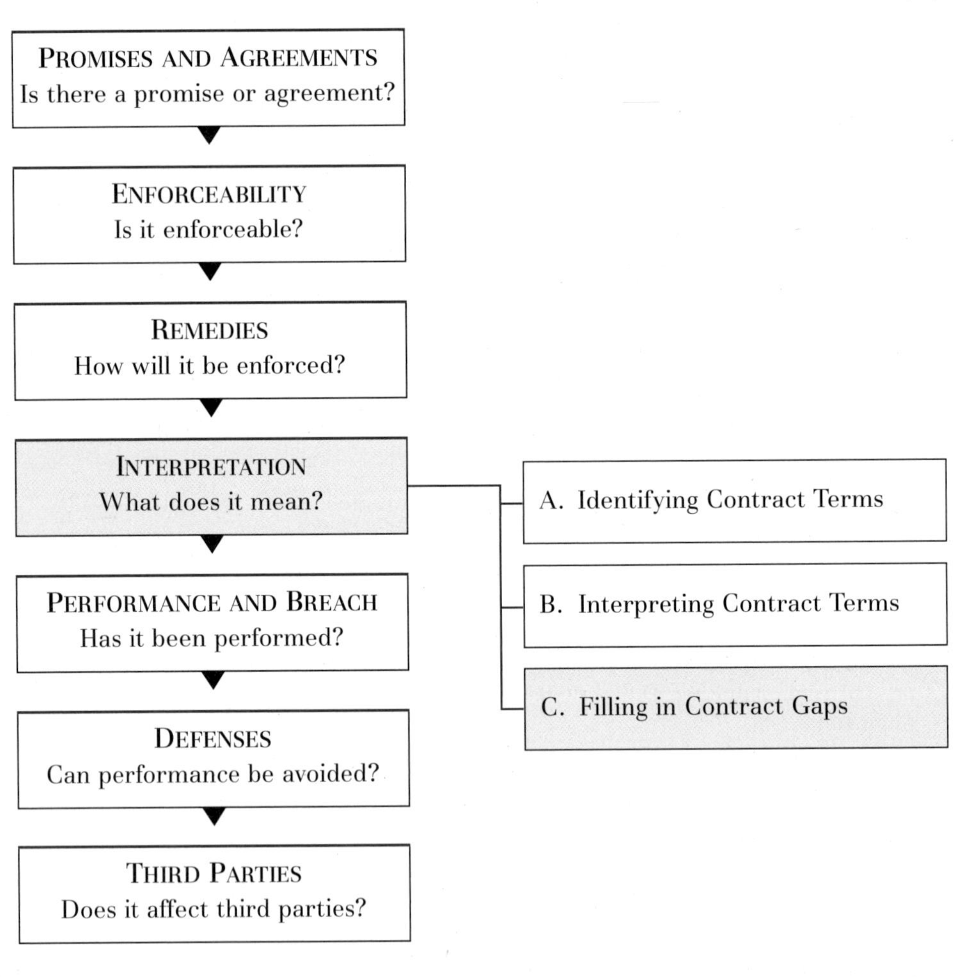

In this section, we will look at the process by which judges imply (or refuse to imply) terms into contracts where the parties themselves have failed to do so—either for strategic reasons or through inadvertence—and will cover topics such as agreements to agree, "illusory promises," the implied duty of good faith performance, and implied and express warranties. But first, let's begin with a broad overview as to why gaps appear in contracts, and the various techniques courts use to plug them.

DOCTRINAL OVERVIEW: FILLING IN CONTRACT GAPS*

Omissions in contracts occur in two types of situations. Sometimes a potential dispute is foreseen but there is a conscious decision not to deal with it. Sometimes the potential dispute is simply not foreseen. In both types of situations, courts supply rules that are commonly described as *default* rules, though in situations of the latter type they might more accurately be styled *gap-filling* rules.

In informal agreements much goes without saying. When a consumer buys a can of tuna in a grocery store, the terms of the transaction are left to be supplied by law—the buyer does not demand express warranties nor does the seller disclaim implied warranties. If all terms were expressly agreed to, even the simplest contracts would become intolerably long.

Even in a complex transaction, a party that foresees a potential dispute may decide not to deal with it if the dispute seems unlikely to arise. Parties tend to expect that the prescribed performances will be rendered. . . .

Sometimes conscious omissions can also be explained by a party's reluctance to raise the matter in negotiations. Thus, it has been suggested, "contractual incompleteness" may occur "when one party to a contract knows more than the other" and "strategically decide[s] not to contract around even an inefficient default" because to do so "can reveal information."[9] A party may fear that to raise the point will result in delay or the addition of an unfavorable provision or even the loss of the entire bargain. . . .

When contract language fails to cover a situation because the parties did not foresee it, they may simply have overlooked the obvious through haste or inadvertence. . . .

At other times when the situation is not foreseen, even the most sibylline drafter would not have anticipated the turn of events. . . . Not surprisingly, the risk of unforeseen and unforeseeable developments grows as the lifetime of the contract increases. . . .

Our present concern is with the process that is involved in dealing with an omitted case.

Interpretation is necessarily the first step in that process, since a court will supply a term only after it has determined that the language of the agreement

---

* Excerpted from E. ALLAN FARNSWORTH, CONTRACTS §§ 7.15-7.16 (4th ed. 2004).

9. Ayres & Gertner, *Filling Gaps in Incomplete Contracts: An Economic Theory of Default Rules*, 99 YALE L.J. 87, 127 (1989).

does not cover the case at hand. It follows that any term that a court would supply can be derogated from by agreement of the parties, either explicitly or by necessary inference. The resulting rule is therefore a default rule rather than a mandatory rule. . . .

Once the court has determined through interpretation that it is faced with an omitted case, it must supply a term to deal with that case. The process by which a court supplies a term is commonly called "implication" and the resulting term is called an "implied term." (Such terms are also called "implied-in-law" terms to distinguish them from "implied-in-fact" terms, which are derived from the behavior of the parties and are treated in the same way as "express" terms.) The process of implication may have two bases.

The first basis for implication is the actual expectations of the parties. If the court is persuaded that the parties shared a common expectation with respect to the omitted case, the court will give effect to that expectation, even though the parties did not reduce it to words. However, if the parties' expectations were significantly different or if one party had no expectation, the court will substitute for the subjective test of shared expectation an objective test of whether one party should reasonably have known of the other's expectation. Expectation can sometimes be gleaned from the agreement itself. Thus a recital or a provision dealing with a related case may suggest the parties' intention with respect to the omitted case. Their intention may also be deduced from a course of performance, course of dealing, or usage, or from the negotiations that led up to the agreement if the parol evidence rule permits. In many cases, however, no reliable indication of expectation can be found. The court must then seek some other basis for implication.

It is sometimes suggested that if a court cannot determine the actual expectations of the parties, it should implement the expectations that it thinks they would have had if they had considered the matter, thereby remedying "the shortsightedness of individuals, by doing for them what they would have done for themselves if their imagination had anticipated the march of nature."[17] However, even if the parties did not foresee the situation, it is often naïve to assume that a court can determine how the parties would have dealt with it had they foreseen it. And even if a court could determine this, it might find that the term the parties would have chosen would be unjust for a court to supply because of the greater bargaining power of one *of* the parties.

In such situations, it should not be hypothetical expectations or fictitious intentions, but basic principles of justice that guide a court in extrapolating from the situations for which the parties provided to the one for which they did not. . . . Where do courts find these basic principles of justice? Often they look to the idea of fairness in the exchange. In searching for what Lord Mansfield called "the essence of the agreement,"[21] a court seeks a fair bargain—a bargain that an economist would describe as maximizing the expected value of the transaction. A court may, for example, justify the term it supplies on the ground that

---

17. J. BENTHAM, A GENERAL VIEW OF A COMPLETE CODE OF LAWS, in 3 WORKS OF JEREMY BENTHAM 191 (J. Bowring ed. 1843).

21. Kingston v. Preston, 98 Eng. Rep. 606, 608, 99 Eng. Rep. 437, 438 (K.B. 1773).

the term prevents one party from being in a position of "economic servility" and "completely at the mercy" of the other.[22] It may supply a term that is suitable for a particular market or other segment of society or even for society in general.

1. Implied Terms

Wood v. Lucy, Lady Duff-Gordon

Court of Appeals of New York
118 N.E. 214 (1917)

Appeal from a judgment entered April 24, 1917 upon an order of the Appellate Division of the Supreme Court in the first judicial department, which reversed an order of Special Term denying a motion by defendant for judgment in her favor upon the pleadings and granted said motion.

John Jerome Rooney for appellant. Assuming that the contract does not contain an express covenant and agreement on the part of the plaintiff to use his best endeavors and efforts to place indorsements, make sales or grant licenses to manufacture, nevertheless such a covenant must necessarily be implied from the terms of the contract itself and all the circumstances.

Edward E. Hoenig and William M. Sullivan for respondent. The motion for judgment on the pleadings was properly granted and the demurrer properly sustained by the appellate court, as the agreement upon which the action is based is *nudum pactum* and not binding upon this defendant for lack of mutuality and consideration. The order of the Appellate Division should be affirmed, for under the contract the appellant assumes no obligation and there is no provision therein enforceable as against him.

CARDOZO, J. The defendant styles herself "a creator of fashions." Her favor helps a sale. Manufacturers of dresses, millinery and like articles are glad to pay for a certificate of her approval. The things which she designs, fabrics, parasols and what not, have a new value in the public mind when issued in her name. She employed the plaintiff to help her to turn this vogue into money. He was to have the exclusive right, subject always to her approval, to place her indorsements on the designs of others. He was also to have the exclusive right to place her own designs on sale, or to license others to market them. In return, she was to have one-half of 'all profits and revenues' derived from any contracts he might make. The exclusive right was to last at

Lady Duff-Gordon in 1917.

22. Perkins v. Standard Oil Co., 383 P.2d 107, 112 (Or. 1963).

least one year from April 1, 1915, and thereafter from year to year unless terminated by notice of ninety days. The plaintiff says that he kept the contract on his part, and that the defendant broke it. She placed her indorsement on fabrics, dresses and millinery without his knowledge, and withheld the profits. He sues her for the damages, and the case comes here on demurrer.

The agreement of employment is signed by both parties. It has a wealth of recitals. The defendant insists, however, that it lacks the elements of a contract. She says that the plaintiff does not bind himself to anything. It is true that he does not promise in so many words that he will use reasonable efforts to place the defendant's indorsements and market her designs. We think, however, that such a promise is fairly to be implied. The law has outgrown its primitive stage of formalism when the precise word was the sovereign talisman, and every slip was fatal. It takes a broader view to-day. A promise may be lacking, and yet the whole writing may be "instinct with an obligation," imperfectly expressed (Scott, J., *in McCall Co. v. Wright*, 133 App. Div. 62). If that is so, there is a contract.

The implication of a promise here finds support in many circumstances. The defendant gave an *exclusive* privilege. She was to have no right for at least a year to place her own indorsements or market her own designs except through the agency of the plaintiff. The acceptance of the exclusive agency was an assumption of its duties. We are not to suppose that one party was to be placed at the mercy of the other. Many other terms of the agreement point the same way. We are told at the outset by way of recital that "the said Otis F. Wood possesses a business organization adapted to the placing of such indorsements as the said Lucy, Lady Duff-Gordon has approved." The implication is that the plaintiff's business organization will be used for the purpose for which it is adapted. But the terms of the defendant's compensation are even more significant. Her sole compensation for the grant of an exclusive agency is to be one-half of all the profits resulting from the plaintiff's efforts. Unless he gave his efforts, she could never get anything. **Without an implied promise, the transaction cannot have such business "efficacy as both parties must have intended that at all events it should have"** (Bowen, L.J., in *The Moorcock*, 14 P. D. 64, 68). But the contract does not stop there. The plaintiff goes on to promise that he will account monthly for all moneys received by him, and that he will take out all such patents and copyrights and trademarks as may in his judgment be necessary to protect the rights and articles affected by the agreement. It is true, of course, as the Appellate Division has said, that if he was under no duty to try to market designs or to place certificates of indorsement, his promise to account for profits or take out

Interpreting silence

Here, Cardozo suggests that the court must imply a promise (that Wood will use reasonable efforts to bring about profits, as Cardozo reveals later in this paragraph) to make sense of this contract. On the one hand, this idea has an attractive quality, in that, if the court did not read such a duty into the parties' contract, the apparently sensible business arrangement between the parties would be illusory, i.e., would not result in any contractual obligations. On the other hand, if the parties intended for Wood to use reasonable efforts, why didn't they just indicate that this was their understanding in their contract? Was it simply so obvious to both of the parties

copyrights would be valueless. But in determining the intention of the parties, the promise *has* a value. It helps to enforce the conclusion that the plaintiff *had* some duties. His promise to pay the defendant one-half of the profits and revenues resulting from the exclusive agency and to render accounts monthly, was a promise to use reasonable efforts to bring profits and revenues into existence. For this conclusion, the authorities are ample.

that Wood would use reasonable efforts that neither party even considered memorializing this understanding in writing? In short, how do you think Cardozo should have interpreted the silence between the parties, and why? Whatever you think about what Cardozo should or should not have done here, keep this case in mind when you read *Sun Printing,* our next principal case, and ask yourself whether Cardozo is being consistent.

The judgment of the Appellate Division should be reversed, and the order of the Special Term affirmed, with costs in the Appellate Division and in this court.

CUDDEBACK, MCLAUGHLIN and ANDREWS, JJ., concur; HISCOCK, C.J., CHASE and CRANE, JJ., dissent.

RELEVANT PROVISIONS

For the *Restatement (Second) of Contracts,* consult § 77. For the UCC, consult § 2-306(2).

NOTES AND QUESTIONS

1. *YouTube.* A fun musical summary of the case, written as a rag, was put together by Professor Craswell and posted at https://www.youtube.com/watch?v=yLe3wWrBUMk.

2. *What happened?* Who sued whom for what? Procedurally, how did the case get before this court? Factually, what happened between the parties? What arguments did the plaintiff and defendant make? What rule or rules did the court apply? How did the court analyze the dispute between the parties? How did the court decide the case?

3. *Was this case correctly decided?* Do you agree with the result reached in this case? Why or why not? Do you agree with the court's reasoning? Why or why not? How, if at all, would you have written the opinion differently?

4. *Critical reading.* Go back and reread the first few lines of the opinion. Does it seem obvious whom Cardozo will rule for? Why do you think Cardozo set up the case the way he did?

We've previously examined (in earlier thinking tools, in various contextual perspectives, and in the Notes and Questions throughout the book) how courts can influence the result in a case by carefully selecting which facts to focus on, and then by choosing how they will interpret those facts. In a brilliant lecture on appellate advocacy (the entire article is worth reading), Professor Llewellyn described how Cardozo did exactly this in Wood v. Lucy, Lady Duff-Gordon.

THINKING TOOL APPLIED: READING *WOOD* CRITICALLY*

[T]he statement of facts, be it in the brief or be it oral, is the complete guts of your case. And I'm going to give you two statements of fact, one by an utter master, and another in the exactly same case, as an effort to show you how it can be done just the other way on the same facts and the same case.

The statement by the master is Cardozo in *Wood v. Lady Duff-Gordon*. And you will get that, as I read it to you. You must remember that Cardozo was a truly great advocate, and the fact that he became a great judge didn't at all change the fact that he was a great advocate. And if you will watch, in the very process of your listening to the facts, you will find two things happening. The one is that according to principle number one, you arrive at the conclusion that the case has to come out one way. And the other is, that it fits into a legal frame that says, "How comfortable it will be, to bring it out that way. No trouble at all. No trouble at all."

"The defendant styles herself"—now watch the way in which she is subtly made into a pasty person—"The defendant styles herself 'a creator of fashions.' Her favor helps a sale. Manufacturers of dresses, millinery, and like articles are glad to pay for a certificate of her approval. The things which she designs, fabrics, parasols, and what not, have a new value in the public mind when issued in her name. She employed the plaintiff to help her turn this vogue into money."

Does this sound—this is an interposition—does this sound like a business deal? Does a business deal sound like a legally enforceable view? Nothing is being said about that. But watch it grow on you. And if I hadn't stopped to tell you about it, it would have grown until you just took it, without a word.

"He was to have the exclusive right"—watch this language—"exclusive right"—what wonderful legal language, to make it legally enforceable—"He was to have the exclusive right . . . to place her own designs on sale, or to license others to market them. In return, she was to have one-half of 'all profits and revenues' derived from any contracts he might make. The exclusive right was to last at least one year from April 1, 1915, and thereafter from year to year unless terminated by notice of ninety days."

My heavens, isn't this legal?

"The plaintiff says that he kept the contract on his part, and that the defendant broke it. She placed her indorsement on fabrics, dresses and millinery without his knowledge, and withheld the profits. He sues her for the damages, and the case comes here on demurrer.

* Excerpted from Karl N. Llewellyn, *A Lecture on Appellate Advocacy*, 29 U. CHI. L. REV. 627, 637-38 (1962). We first examined critical reading in "Thinking Tool: Reading Critically," p. 31, *supra*, which you may want to review at this time.

"The agreement of employment is signed by both parties. It has a wealth of recitals. The defendant insists, however, that it lacks the elements of a contract. She says that the plaintiff does not bind himself to anything. It is true that he does not promise in so many words that he will use reasonable efforts to place the defendant's indorsements and market her designs."

Now, is there any way to bring that case out, except one? Isn't it obvious that we are going to imply a promise on the part of the plaintiff which will satisfy the requirment [sic] of consideration and the decency of the situation?

All right, now try this: "The plaintiff in this action rests his case upon his own carefully prepared form agreement, which has as its first essence his own omission of any expression whatsoever of any obligation of any kind on the part of this same plaintiff. We thus have the familiar situation of a venture in which one party, here the defendant, has an asset, with what is, in advance, of purely speculative value. The other party, the present plaintiff, who drew the agreement, is a marketer eager for profit, but chary of risk. The legal question presented is whether the plaintiff, while carefully avoiding all risk in the event of failure, can nevertheless claim full profit in the event that the market may prove favorable in its response. The law of consideration joins with the principles of business decency in giving the answer. And the answer is no."

Same case. Entirely the same case. But it brings me to the next fundamental point, which is that if you have an intelligent appellant, to rest upon his statement of the facts, if you are the respondent, is suicide. Did you hear me? If he is any good, you're cooked. (Laughter.) You have a positive case to make, and you can only make it by restating the facts so that they fit into your picture of what the whole thing is. And I think with that I can practically stop, can't I, because I've made the fundamental point.

Sun Printing & Publishing Ass'n. v. Remington Paper & Power Co.

Court of Appeals of New York

139 N.E. 470 (1923)

Appeal, by permission, from an order of the Appellate Division of the Supreme Court in the first judicial department, entered April 24, 1922, which reversed an order of Special Term denying a motion by plaintiff for judgment on the pleadings and granted said motion.

The following question was **certified**: "Does the complaint state facts sufficient to constitute a cause of action?"

Certification

"A procedure by which a federal appellate court asks the U.S. Supreme Court or the highest state court to review a question of law arising in a case pending before the appellate court and on which it needs guidance." BLACK'S LAW DICTIONARY (10th ed. 2014).

Nathan L. Miller for appellant. No exclusive option was given to respondent under the agreement. The language used in the agreement set forth in the complaint does not sufficiently define the price to create an enforceable obligation. In the absence of prices and terms agreed upon by the parties as provided for in the agreement, the court will not determine prices and terms for them. The case at bar shows a contract with express contemplation of a further agreement to fix the price and the term and until such further agreement was made there could be no breach of obligation and no damages assessable.

Archibald R. Watson, John M. Harrington and Ralph O. Willguss for respondent. By virtue of the agreement in suit, the plaintiff acquired, for a valuable consideration, an option to purchase from the defendant 1,000 tons of newsprint paper per month during the year 1920 at a readily ascertainable price, namely, the contract price for newsprint paper charged by the Canadian Export Paper Company to the large consumers. The agreement in suit prescribes the criterion whereby the maximum price for paper deliverable during each month of the year 1920 was definitely ascertainable; and thereby the defendant irrevocably agreed upon a price to the extent of fixing the maximum price at which it would make deliveries during 1920. Courts favor a construction that renders contracts operative rather than that which nullifies them; and in order to justify disregarding a promise on the ground of uncertainty, indefiniteness must reach the point where construction becomes futile. The agreement in suit, when construed in accordance with its legal meaning, conferred upon the plaintiff the right, at its election, to demand of the defendant the delivery of 1,000 tons of newsprint paper per month during the year 1920 at a definitely ascertainable price, namely, the maximum price provided for in the agreement. The plaintiff having, in the exercise of its option, duly demanded the delivery of the paper, the parties thereupon became mutually bound, the defendant to deliver, and the plaintiff to pay for, the paper at the maximum price provided for in the agreement.

CARDOZO, J. Plaintiff agreed to buy and defendant to sell 1,000 tons of paper per month during the months of September, 1919, to December, 1920, inclusive, 16,000 tons in all. Sizes and quality were adequately described. Payment was to be made on the 20th of each month for all paper shipped the previous month. The price for shipments in September, 1919, was to be \$3.73 3/4 per 100 pounds, and for shipments in October, November and December, 1919, \$4 per 100 pounds. "For the balance of the period of this agreement the price of the paper and length of terms for which such price shall apply shall be agreed upon by and between the parties hereto fifteen days prior to the expiration of each period for which the price and length of term thereof have been previously agreed upon, said price in no event to be higher than the contract price for newsprint charged by the Canadian Export Paper Company to the large consumers, the seller to receive the benefit of any differentials in freight rates."

Between September, 1919, and December of that year, inclusive, shipments were made and paid for as required by the contract. The time then arrived when there was to be an agreement upon a new price and upon the term of its duration. The defendant in advance of that time gave notice that the contract was imperfect, and disclaimed for the future an obligation to deliver. Upon this, the plaintiff took the ground that the price was to be ascertained by resort to an established standard. It made demand that during each month of 1920 the defendant deliver 1,000 tons of paper at the contract price for newsprint charged by the Canadian Export Paper Company to the large consumers, the defendant to receive the benefit of any differentials in freight rates. The demand was renewed month by month till the expiration of the year. This action has been brought to recover the ensuing damage.

Seller and buyer left two subjects to be settled in the middle of December and at unstated intervals thereafter. One was the price to be paid. The other was the length of time during which such price was to govern. Agreement as to the one was insufficient without agreement as to the other. If price and nothing more had been left open for adjustment, there might be force in the contention that the buyer would be viewed, in the light of later provisions, as the holder of an option. This would mean that in default of an agreement for a lower price, the plaintiff would have the privilege of calling for delivery in accordance with a price established as a maximum. The price to be agreed upon might be less, but could not be more than "the contract price for newsprint charged by the Canadian Export Paper Company to the large consumers." The difficulty is, however, that ascertainment of this price does not dispense with the necessity for agreement in respect of the term during which the price is to apply. Agreement upon a maximum payable this month or to-day is not the same as an agreement that it shall continue to be payable next month or to-morrow. Seller and buyer understood that the price to be fixed in December for a term to be agreed upon, would not be more than the price then charged by the Canadian Export Paper Company to the large consumers. They did not understand that if during the term so established the price charged by the Canadian Export Paper Company was changed, the price payable to the seller would fluctuate accordingly. This was conceded by plaintiff's counsel on the argument before us. The seller was to receive no more during the running of the prescribed term, though the Canadian maximum was raised. The buyer was to pay no less during that term, though the maximum was lowered. In brief, the standard was to be applied at the beginning of the successive terms, but once applied was to be maintained until the term should have expired. While the term was unknown, the contract was inchoate.

The argument is made that there was no need of an agreement as to time unless the price to be paid was lower than the maximum. We find no evidence of this intention in the language of the contract. The result would then be that the defendant would never know where it stood. The plaintiff was under no duty to accept the Canadian standard. It does not assert that it was. What it asserts is that the contract amounted to the concession of an option. Without an agreement as to time, however, there would be not one option, but a dozen. The Canadian price to-day might be less than the Canadian price to-morrow. Election by the buyer to proceed with performance at the price prevailing in one month would not bind it to proceed at the price prevailing in another. Successive options to be exercised every month would thus be read into the contract. Nothing in the wording discloses the intention of the seller to place itself to that extent at the mercy of the buyer. Even if, however, we were to interpolate the restriction that the option, if exercised at all, must be exercised only once, and for the entire quantity permitted, the difficulty would not be ended. Market prices in 1920 happened to rise. The importance of the time element becomes apparent when we ask ourselves what the seller's position would be if they had happened to fall. Without an agreement as to time, the maximum would be lowered from one shipment to another with every reduction of the standard. With such an agreement, on the other hand, there would be stability and certainty. The parties attempted to guard against the contingency of failing to come together as to price. They did not guard against the contingency of failing to come together as to time. Very likely they thought the latter contingency so remote that it could safely be disregarded. In any event, whether through design or through inadvertence, they left the gap unfilled. The result was nothing more than "an agreement to agree." Defendant "exercised its legal right" when it insisted that there was need of something more. The right is not affected by our appraisal of the motive.

We are told that the defendant was under a duty, in default of an agreement, to accept a term that would be reasonable in view of the nature of the transaction and the practice of the business. To hold it to such a standard is to make the contract over. The defendant reserved the privilege of doing its business in its own way, and did not undertake to conform to the practice and beliefs of others. We are told again that there was a duty, in default of other agreement, to act as if the successive terms were to expire every month. The contract says they are to expire at such intervals as the agreement may prescribe. There is need, it is true, of no high degree of ingenuity to show how the parties, with little change of language, could have framed a form of contract to which obligation would attach. The difficulty is that they framed another. We are not at liberty to revise while professing to construe.

We do not ignore the allegation of the complaint that the contract price charged by the Canadian Export Paper Company to the large consumers "constituted a definite and well defined standard of price that was readily ascertainable." The suggestion is made by members of the court that the price so charged may have been known to be one established for the year, so that fluctuation would be impossible. If that was its character, the complaint should so allege. The writing signed by the parties calls for an agreement as to time. The complaint concedes that no such agreement has been made. The result, *prima facie*, is the failure of the contract. In that situation, the pleader has the burden of setting forth the extrinsic circumstances, if there are any, that make agreement unimportant. There is significance, moreover, in the attitude of counsel. No point is made in brief or in argument that the Canadian price, when once established, is constant through the year. On the contrary, there is at least a tacit assumption that it varies with the market. The buyer acted on the same assumption when it renewed the demand from month to month, making tender of performance at the prices then prevailing. If we misconceive the course of dealing, the plaintiff by amendment of its pleading can correct our misconception. **The complaint as it comes before us leaves no escape from the conclusion that agreement in respect of time is as essential to a completed contract as agreement in respect of price. The agreement was not reached, and the defendant is not bound.**

The question is not here whether the defendant would have failed in the fulfilment of its duty by an arbitrary refusal to reach any agreement as to time after notice from the plaintiff that it might make division of the terms in any way it pleased. No such notice was given so far as the complaint discloses. The action is not based upon a refusal to treat with the defendant and attempt to arrive at an agreement. Whether any such theory of liability would be tenable we need not now inquire. Even if the plaintiff might have stood upon the defendant's denial of obligation as amounting to such a refusal, it did not elect to do so. Instead, it gave its own construction to the contract, fixed for itself the length of the successive terms, and thereby coupled its demand with a condition which there was no duty to accept. We find no allegation of readiness and offer to proceed on any other basis. The condition being untenable, the failure to comply with it cannot give a cause of action.

The order of the Appellate Division should be reversed and that of the Special Term affirmed, with costs in the Appellate Division and in this court, and the question certified answered in the negative.

CRANE, J. **(dissenting).** I cannot take the view of this contract that has been adopted by the majority. The parties to this transaction beyond question thought they were making a contract for the purchase and sale of 16,000 tons rolls news print. The contract was upon a form used by the defendant in its business, and we must suppose that it was intended to be what it states to be, and not a trick or device to defraud merchants. It begins by saying that in consideration of the mutual covenants and agreements herein set forth the Remington Paper and Power Company, Incorporated, of Watertown, state of New

Can this case be reconciled with Wood?

In *Wood*, Cardozo implied a promise to find a contract, but here, he refused to do so. Why? In a series of lectures given the next year, this is how Cardozo explained it:

> Here was a case where advantage had been taken of the strict letter of a contract to avoid an onerous engagement. Not inconceivably a sensitive conscience would have rejected such an outlet of escape. We thought this immaterial. The court subordinated the equity of a particular situation to the overmastering need of certainty in the transactions of commercial life. The end to be attained in the development of the law of contract is the supremacy, not of some hypothetical, imaginary will, apart from external manifestations, but of will outwardly revealed in the spoken or the written word. The loss to business would in the long run be greater than the gain if judges were clothed with power to revise as well as to interpret. Perhaps, with a higher conception of business and its needs, the time will come when even revision will be permitted if it is revision in consonance with established standards of fair dealing, but the time is not yet. In this department of activity, the current axiology still places stability and certainty in the forefront of the virtues. "The field is one where the law should hold fast to fundamental conceptions of contract and of duty, and follow them with loyalty to logical conclusions." *Imperator Realty Co. v. Tull*, 228 N.Y. 447, 455.*

* Benjamin Cardozo, GROWTH OF THE LAW 110-11 (1924)

York, hereinafter called the seller, agrees to sell and hereby does sell and the Sun Printing and Publishing Association of New York city, state of New York, hereinafter called the purchaser, agrees to buy and pay for and hereby does buy the following paper, 16,000 tons rolls news print. The sizes are then given. Shipment is to be at the rate of 1,000 tons per month to December, 1920, inclusive. There are details under the headings consignee, specifications, price and delivery, terms, miscellaneous, cores, claims, contingencies, cancellations.

Under the head of miscellaneous comes the following:

> The price agreed upon between the parties hereto, for all papers shipped during the month of September, 1919, shall be $3.73 3/4 per hundred pounds gross weight of rolls on board cars at mills.
>
> The price agreed upon between the parties hereto for all shipments made during the months of October, November and December, 1919, shall be $4.00 per hundred pounds gross weight of rolls on board cars at mills.
>
> For the balance of the period of this agreement the price of the paper and length of terms for which such price shall apply shall be agreed upon by and between the parties hereto fifteen days prior to the expiration of each period for which the price and length of term thereof has been previously agreed upon, said price in no event to be higher than the contract price for newsprint charged by the Canadian Export Paper Company to the large consumers, the seller to receive the benefit of any differentials in freight rates.
>
> It is understood and agreed by the parties hereto that the tonnage specified herein is for use in the printing and publication of the various editions of the Daily and Sunday New York Sun, and any variation from this will be considered a breach of contract."

After the deliveries for September, October, November and December, 1919, the defendant refused to fix any price for the deliveries during the subsequent months, and refused to deliver any more paper. It has taken the position that this document was no contract, that it meant nothing, that it was formally executed for the purpose of permitting the defendant to furnish paper or not, as it pleased.

Surely these parties must have had in mind that some binding agreement was made for the sale and delivery of 16,000 tons rolls of paper, and that the instrument contained all the elements necessary to make a binding contract. It is a strain upon reason to imagine the paper house, the Remington Paper and Power Company, Incorporated, and the Sun Printing and Publishing Association, formally executing a contract drawn up upon the defendant's prepared form which was useless and amounted to nothing. We must, at least, start the examination of this agreement by believing that these intelligent parties intended to make a binding contract. If this be so, the court should spell out a binding contract, if it be possible.

I not only think it possible, but think the paper itself clearly states a contract recognized under all the rules at law. It is said that the one essential element of price is lacking; that the provision above quoted is an agreement to agree to a price, and that the defendant had the privilege of agreeing or not, as it pleased;

that if it failed to agree to a price there was no standard by which to measure the amount the plaintiff would have to pay. The contract does state, however, just this very thing. Fifteen days before the first of January, 1920, the parties were to agree upon the price of the paper to be delivered thereafter, and the length of the period for which such price should apply. However, the price to be fixed was not "to be higher than the contract price for newsprint charged by the Canadian Export Paper Company to large consumers." Here surely was something definite. The 15th day of December arrived. The defendant refused to deliver. At that time there was a price for newsprint charged by the Canadian Export Paper Company. If the plaintiff offered to pay this price, which was the highest price the defendant could demand, the defendant was bound to deliver. This seems to be very clear.

But while all agree that the price on the 15th day of December could be fixed, the further objection is made that the period during which that price should continue was not agreed upon. There are many answers to this.

We have reason to believe that the parties supposed they were making a binding contract; that they had fixed the terms by which one was required to take and the other to deliver; that the Canadian Export Paper Company price was to be the highest that could be charged in any event. These things being so, the court should be very reluctant to permit a defendant to avoid its contract.

On the 15th of the fourth month, the time when the price was to be fixed for subsequent deliveries, there was a price charged by the Canadian Export Paper Company to large consumers. As the defendant failed to agree upon a price, made no attempt to agree upon a price and deliberately broke its contract, it could readily be held to deliver the rest of the paper, a thousand rolls a month, at this Canadian price. There is nothing in the complaint which indicates that this is a fluctuating price, or that the price of paper as it was on December 15th was not the same for the remaining twelve months.

Or we can deal with this contract, month by month. The deliveries were to be made 1,000 tons per month. On December 15th 1,000 tons could have been demanded. The price charged by the Canadian Export Paper Company on the 15th of each month on and after December 15th, 1919, would be the price for the thousand ton delivery for that month.

Or again, the word as used in the miscellaneous provision quoted is not "price," but "contract price"—"in no event to be higher than the contract price." Contract implies a term or period and if the evidence should show that the Canadian contract price was for a certain period of weeks or months, then this period could be applied to the contract in question.

Failing any other alternative, the law should do here what it has done in so many other cases, apply the rule of reason and compel parties to contract in the light of fair dealing. It could hold this defendant to deliver its paper as it agreed to do, and take for a price the Canadian Export Paper Company contract price for a period which is reasonable under all the circumstances and conditions as applied in the paper trade.

To let this defendant escape from its formal obligations when any one of these rulings as applied to this contract would give a practical and just result is to give the sanction of law to a deliberate breach. (*Wood v. Duff-Gordon*, 222 N.Y. 88.)

For these reasons I am for the affirmance of the courts below.

RELEVANT PROVISIONS

For the *Restatement (Second) of Contracts,* consult §§ 33, 34, and 204. For the UCC, consult §§ 2-204, 2-305, 2-306, and 2-309. For the UNIDROIT Principles, consult Article 2.1.1.

NOTES AND QUESTIONS

1. *What happened?* Who sued whom for what? Procedurally, how did the case get before this court? Factually, what happened between the parties? What arguments did the plaintiff and defendant make? What rule or rules did the court apply? How did the court analyze the dispute between the parties? How did the court decide the case?

2. *Was this case correctly decided?* In light of the sidebar above, asking whether this case can be reconciled with *Wood,* are you persuaded that Judge Cardozo decided this case correctly? Why or why not? How, if at all, would you have written the opinion differently?

3. *Comparative perspective?* How, if at all, would this case be resolved differently under either (a) the UCC or (b) the UNIDROIT Principles?

4. *Thinking tools.* Do you think this case can be reconciled with Cardozo's decision in *Wood*? If so, how? If not, why not? How would you explain, in short, why Cardozo enforced the contract in *Wood,* but not the contract in *Sun Printing*? Can this be justified on the basis of any of the thinking tools we have previously examined? In what ways does the following excerpt shed light on Cardozo's opinion?

Before reading the excerpt below, you may wish to review "Thinking Tool: The Coase Theorem, Transaction Costs, and Distributive Justice" at p. 460, supra, *and "Thinking Tool: Gap Filling and Default Rules" at p. 126,* supra.

THINKING TOOLS APPLIED: THE COASE THEOREM AND DEFAULT RULES*

Suppose we make a contract but leave some parts of it unspecified. Should the law fill in the blanks with default terms that amount to guesses at what we would

* Excerpted from WARD FARNSWORTH, THE LEGAL ANALYST: A TOOLKIT FOR THINKING ABOUT THE LAW 80-81 (2007).

have wanted? That would be consistent with the Coase theorem: it would save the parties the bother and expense of negotiating over all the terms. But here is another idea: maybe the law sometimes should supply default terms for contracts that probably aren't what the parties would want. Why? Because then the parties will be more likely to negotiate over the point (since they don't want what the law will give them if they don't). And perhaps we want them to negotiate because we think that talks between them will lead to better results than any background rule the law might come up with.

[Consider, for instance, a contract in which] I agree to sell you a million widgets but we don't mention the price. The courts will fill in a price that seems "reasonable" at the time of delivery. Now suppose the opposite: we do mention the price but we don't specify the number of widgets involved. This time the court's reply will be different. It won't try to speculate about what a reasonable number would have been; it won't enforce the contract at all. In effect the court fills in the blank with a zero. Obviously this isn't an effort to simulate what the parties would have wanted; zero isn't the quantity that either party to a contract has in mind. But whereas a court can figure out a reasonable price fairly easily (by just finding out what the market price was for widgets), it will be much more trouble to figure out what a reasonable *number* of widgets would have been. The court probably would have to learn all about the situation each party is in. It's cheaper (if not for the parties, then cheaper *overall*) for the parties to take the time to work out the quantity in advance. So the default rule is deliberately made inaccurate—perhaps it's a "penalty" default—to force the parties to do their own negotiating. (There is some controversy about whether the "zero quantity" rule is a default rule or is simply a formal requirement of making an enforceable contract—and indeed about whether there are many, or any, true penalty default rules in contract law. But however that debate ever gets resolved, the example at least illustrates why and how the law might force people to negotiate over a point.)

Or suppose the issue is employment. In the United States the usual rule is employment at will: unless there is a contract saying otherwise, an employer can fire an employee for any reason or no reason. Yet there is evidence that most employees don't realize this. It has therefore been suggested that the default rule be changed so that employees can be fired only for cause—unless (again) they sign a contract saying otherwise. Either way the employer and employee can make any contract they like. But a presumption that an employee can be fired only for cause might have the good property of forcing a negotiation. The employer, who more likely knows the default rule, would be obliged to bring it up if he wanted it changed; and employees would then get clearer information than most of them now seem to have. The default rule might not mimic what the parties want (we may not really *know* what they want—that's the point). Instead it is "information forcing"; it prods the parties to reveal things to each other.

In the next case, a new and unforeseen development arises in a long-established contractual relationship, and a court struggles, in a thoughtful opinion, with whether (and how) it should imply a term in the parties' contract to take this development into account. In addition to discussing intention, the case also dovetails nicely with the implied obligation of good faith, which we take up next.

Parev Products Co. v. I. Rokeach & Sons

United States Court of Appeals, Second Circuit
124 F.2d 147 (1941)

CLARK, CIRCUIT JUDGE. This appeal involves the question whether or not an injunction should issue to enforce an asserted implied negative covenant in a contract granting an exclusive license to use a secret formula for a food product. In the District Court the complaint was dismissed on the merits on the ground that the parties to the contract did not intend a negative covenant. Although the District Court may perhaps have emphasized "intent" more than is realistic as to matters concerning which the parties have not revealed their thinking processes, it is, of course, obvious that the terms of the contract and the status arising out of those terms are of paramount importance. We turn, therefore, at once to the facts of the case.

In 1924, plaintiff, Parev Products Co., Inc., entered into a contract with defendant, I. Rokeach & Sons, Inc. At that time, as can be reasonably inferred from some of the terms of the contract, plaintiff was not in the best of financial condition. So far as appears, its principal product of manufacture was Parev Schmaltz, a cooking oil made from coconut oil in such a way as to be Kosher, that is, usable with meat and dairy products without violation of the Jewish dietary laws. Parev Schmaltz was then supposed to be manufactured by a secret formula made by plaintiff's president, Aaron Proser, and, as the contract warranted, known only to him, Solomon Proser, and Julius Proser, though at the time a patent had been applied for on the formula and process. Defendant, on the other hand, was a successful business house of long standing. It engaged in extensive merchandising of food and cleansing products, mostly to orthodox Jews. The purpose of the contract, so far as appears, was to enable plaintiff to get out of its difficulties and to provide defendant with a Kosher semisolid vegetable oil.

By the terms of the contract, defendant obtained the exclusive use of all the necessary secret formulae, etc., for a period of twenty-five years, with an option to renew for another twenty-five years. In return, plaintiff was to receive royalties on all sales of Parev Schmaltz. Defendant had several powers to terminate, however. It could terminate the contract at any time it found the formula not to have been secret. Up to two years after the date of the contract, it could terminate the contract without cause upon payment of $100; and after two years, upon payment of $500. If any patents were judicially declared invalid, the contract was to terminate automatically. In defending any patent actions, plaintiff was to bear the full cost if suits arose during the first two years; after that, costs were to be split.

Under the agreement, defendant was privileged to use Parev Schmaltz as it should "think fit for its use and benefit absolutely." This same privilege was restated in another part of the contract with a complete specification of what was included, such as labels, trademarks, good will, and so on. For its part, plaintiff agreed not to engage or aid in the manufacture or sale of any product "similar" to Parev Schmaltz or in any business incidental thereto during the life of the contract; moreover, it agreed to deliver the agreement of the three Prosers not to "engage or aid, either severally or collectively, directly or indirectly, in the manufacture, sale or distribution of any article that might be in competition with (defendant) in the sale, manufacture and distribution of Parev Schmaltz or of any similar product." Defendant promised after termination or expiration of the contract "not to engage in, directly or indirectly, in (sic) the manufacture, sale or distribution of the product Parev Schmaltz, or any product of a similar nature." Defendant was privileged to discard the name Parev Schmaltz, however, and any name which was substituted would always remain defendant's property.

It should be noted that the contract therefore contained at least three express negative covenants, none directly applicable to the case before the court, and that the one to be made by the Prosers as individuals is the more extensive in mode of expression at least.

Thereafter defendant immediately dropped the name Parev Schmaltz, adopted Nyafat in its stead, and commenced production. From the beginning, Nyafat was a success and during the fifteen-year period from 1924 to 1939, royalties of approximately $135,000 were paid over. In 1940, however, a disturbing factor entered the picture. Defendant began the distribution of Kea, a semisolid cooking oil made almost wholly from cottonseed oil. Although defendant does not manufacture Kea, it distributes it under its own label as a Kosher product to the same orthodox Jewish trade. Defendant, of course, has not paid any royalties to plaintiff on its sales of Kea. Plaintiff claims that, since the royalties on Nyafat are based on an absolute sum per ounce and since the price obtained by defendant has been falling, defendant has undertaken the sale of Kea to avoid its royalty obligation. Defendant, on the other hand, asserts that Crisco and Spry, widely selling cooking oils, were cutting into the Nyafat market. This was aggravated, defendant says, by a nationwide price war which occurred as soon as Spry went on the market. Consequently, it is urged, defendant had to obtain a new product "similar" to Spry and Crisco, and in the same price range.

In this action, plaintiff seeks an injunction against any further sales of Kea by defendant. The theory is that we should imply a negative covenant on the part of defendant not to compete with its own Nyafat, or in any other way to interfere with the sales of Nyafat. Defendant's argument is that no covenant should be implied beyond what it calls conduct on its part of a "tortious" nature, or, in the alternative, that any covenant would forbid only the sale of products of a "similar nature." Kea, it says, is not similar. One is made from coconut oil, one from cottonseed oil. One is yellow, one is white; one is neutral in flavor, the other has an onion flavor. Other, somewhat esoteric, differences can be spelled out.

Although the District Court placed considerable reliance on this argument, we do not think that this should be finally conclusive. If any covenant is to be implied, it must be one which reaches the core of this dispute, which is the claim that a directly competitive product is produced by defendant. Whatever reasons there are for imposing on defendant such a strict obligation are hardly vitiated by the difference in composition of the two products. They are used for exactly the same purpose— shortening; if any covenant is to be implied, it would be hollow unless it took note of this fact. Thus, it seems rather unlikely that had plaintiff undertaken the manufacture of Kea today a court would have been content to say, as against a suit by the defendant, that the products were not similar under plaintiff's express covenant not to distribute a similar shortening.

Should, therefore, a covenant be implied under all the present circumstances? When we turn to the precedents we are met at once with the confusion of statement whether a covenant can be implied only if it was clearly "intended" by the parties, or whether such a covenant can rest on principles of equity. Expressions can be found which insist on "intention," which seem to combine both a requirement of "intention" and of "equity and justice," and which by-pass "intention" and rely solely on equity. One may perhaps conclude that in large measure this confusion arises out of the reluctance of courts to admit that they were to a considerable extent "remaking" a contract in situations where it seemed necessary and appropriate so to do. "Intention of the parties" is a good formula by which to square doctrine with result. That this is true has long been an open secret. See 3 *Williston on Contracts,* Rev. Ed. 1936, § 825; Holmes, *The Path of the Law,* 10 HARV. L. REV. 457, 466; Fuller, *Legal Fictions,* 25 ILL. L. REV. 363, 369; Chafee, *The Disorderly Conduct of Words,* 41 COL. L. REV. 381, 398.[2] Of course, where intent, though obscure, is nevertheless discernible, it must be followed; but a certain sophistication must be recognized—if we are to approach the matter frankly—where we are dealing with changed circumstances, fifteen years later, with respect to a contract which does not touch this exact point and which has at most only points of departure for more or less pressing analogies. Here defendant has a strong point in stressing the various extensive grants to it of the contract, as well as the express negative covenants which do not touch the present case. Undoubtedly extensive freedom of action was intended it. And yet that could not have been wholly unlimited, as indeed, defendant properly concedes when it admits that at least tortious competition or destruction of the Nyafat market was not open to it. And we must consider that in the period of time since the making of the contract there have been various developments which present a situation not clearly, if at all, within the contemplation of the parties at the time. Here a status exists upon which each party should be entitled to rely. What we should

2. Cf. Chafee, loc. cit.: "My first suggestion is, that we should firmly resolve never to speak of the intention of a testator or other writer on a given point except after we have carefully convinced ourselves that that point was actually in his mind when he wrote the words in question. For example, we will never say, 'He intended this result' when we merely think that if he had foreseen the present contingency (which he didn't) then he would have intended this result. That consideration may be helpful, but it is not his intention."

seek is therefore that which will most nearly preserve the status created and developed by the parties.

If we thus emphasize the situation existing today, two facts stand out. Plaintiff must clearly rely on defendant for any future benefit to be derived from its original formula; and defendant, if it is to continue to remain in the vegetable oil market, must be able to prevent the inroads of outside products, such as Crisco and Spry. So far as the plaintiff is concerned, it has long since lost its hold on its own formula. Nyafat is known to the public as a Rokeach product. Even were the defendant to release the formula, plaintiff would have some difficulty. This is not the controlling factor, for if it were, defendant might very well terminate the contract. Instead, the sales of Nyafat continue. And yet if no covenant is found, defendant to some extent can let Nyafat slip in sales, while Kea is boosted. In other words, if the defendant does not terminate the contract, it can keep Nyafat under its control until Kea is successfully built up, and then it can safely forget Nyafat. The advantage is all to defendant. But a court of equity should grant some protection to a person who parts with his formula for exploitation. Thus, a court would hardly have permitted the defendant from the inception of this contract to lock up the plaintiff's formula in a vault and freely market Kea. There is no reason to do so now.

But defendant has an equally justifiable complaint to make. Kea, it asserts, is marketed only to compete with other products; and no attempt is made to injure Nyafat's market. Certainly we cannot say that defendant must market Nyafat, come what may, down to the sale of a mere can a year, while the vegetable oil business goes to outsiders. That would as violently alter the status of the parties as would a decree of complete freedom to defendant. It is thus clear that a strict injunction against any marketing of Kea is unjustified. Yet a complete denial of relief to the plaintiff under any circumstances would not be fair either.

As we have previously suggested, defendant indirectly acknowledges the need for a middle ground when it argues that cases implying a negative covenant have as their rationale the requirement that the conduct enjoined be tortious. This presumably, amounts to saying that so long as defendant acts in good faith in judging the extent to which Kea must be sold to meet the competition of Crisco and Spry, no cause of action lies. But this, it seems to us, is to state the rule too narrowly; a limited rule of good faith, valid so far as it goes, does not exhaust the possibilities. The really equitable solution is to permit defendant to sell Kea so long as it does not invade Nyafat's market if that point is susceptible of proof, as we think it is. Thus, assuming that defendant is correct in its assertions, Kea sells only to people who no longer buy Nyafat.[3] Hence, all the plaintiff is entitled to is the market Nyafat has created and will

3. It is only fair to state that plaintiff produced two housewives who said they had discontinued the use of Nyafat because Kea was cheaper. These witnesses did not say, however, that they would not have switched to Spry or Crisco.

retain, regardless of outside competition. An injunction to reach such a conclusion would be so vague as to be meaningless under present circumstances. Its practical effect would be to restrain defendant from any sales of Kea—which we have held to be unfair. Only by inserting "good faith" in the restraining order could defendant be protected; and this would be equivalent to the rule we have found too narrow. It follows, then, that on the present record plaintiff cannot obtain an injunction. A broad one would be unfair to defendant; a narrow one would be an empty gesture.

But plaintiff should not be denied the opportunity to show a loss of the Nyafat market as we have thus defined it. Plaintiff may be protected if it can be determined what sales of Kea represent loss to outside products, what sales represent loss to Nyafat. Expert appraisal of market conditions would, it seems to us, answer this.[4] If loss were established, the measure of damages would be the amount of royalties on the displaced jars of Nyafat. On this record, the evidence is too fragmentary to be conclusive. Since an injunction was sought, the action was brought too soon to reflect the nature of the competition among the various cooking oils. If the plaintiff has further evidence of the inroads of Kea, it should be entitled to present it, either hereinafter in this case or in a later actionJudgment affirmed, with costs to defendant and with leave to plaintiff either to move to reopen the action, or to bring a subsequent action, for relief not inconsistent with this opinion.

NOTES AND QUESTIONS

1. ***What happened?*** Who sued whom for what? Procedurally, how did the case get before this court? Factually, what happened between the parties? What arguments did the plaintiff and defendant make? What rule or rules did the court apply? How did the court analyze the dispute between the parties? How did the court decide the case?

2. ***Was this case correctly decided?*** Do you agree with the result reached in this case? Why or why not? Do you agree with the court's reasoning? Why or why not? How, if at all, would you have written the opinion differently?

3. ***Why not imply a term?*** Why didn't the court simply imply a term (à la *Wood v. Lucy, Lady Duff-Gordon*) to enforce this contract? For instance, it could have implied a negative covenant on the part of defendant not to compete, à la *Lumley v. Wagner*. Professor Corbin, citing *Parev Products*, provides

4. Assume, for example, that sales of Nyafat dropped steadily from 1933 to 1936, then from 1936 to 1939 Nyafat held its own. And assume Kea was introduced in 1939. If from 1939 on, Nyafat still held its own, Kea was not injuring Nyafat. On the other hand, if Nyafat again declined while Kea went up, kea would be invading Nyafat's own irreducible minimum market. To be sure, this is an oversimplified example, and many extraneous factors affecting marketing would have to be eliminated. This would be the task of expert witnesses.

one explanation: "The exact terms of the promise that is 'implied' must frequently be determined by what equity and morality appear to require after the parties have come into contact."* How helpful is this? Is it clear what equity and morality require here? Professor Gergen offers another explanation, excerpted below. Are you convinced?

> The near universal refusal to imply a term of exclusive dealing in a best efforts contract can be explained on these grounds. *Parev Products Co. v. I. Rokeach & Sons* is a well-reasoned decision illustrating both the attraction of and the problem with implying exclusivity. Rokeach gave Parev an exclusive license to sell its recipe for kosher schmaltz (rendered chicken fat). Parev sold the product under its own brand name, Nyafat. About twenty years into the relationship, Parev began to sell Kea, a kosher cottonseed cooking oil. The contract had an exclusivity clause but it did not unambiguously apply to other cooking oils. Canceling the contract was not a viable solution: Nyafat's value was by then dependent upon the Parev tradename and distribution network. Barring Parev from selling other cooking oils also was unattractive: the decline in sales of schmaltz was an industry-wide trend, and prohibiting Parev from selling other cooking oils would have prevented it from carrying an important product line. Rokeach was left with a damage remedy, which also was unsatisfactory given the problems of proving breach and damages. However, there was no clearly better solution to the conflict.†

4. *Best efforts?* According to Professor Goetz, "The competition cases reveal a sensitivity by the courts to limitations inherent in a best efforts obligation. Most courts have held that the introduction of a competing product by the best efforts promisor is not a per se breach of the contractual arrangement."‡ Why not? Citing *Parev Products*, Professor Goetz explains: "Best efforts . . . does not require the agent to consider the principal's interests either ahead of or instead of his own interests."§

2. The Implied Duty of Good Faith

DOCTRINAL OVERVIEW: THE IMPLIED DUTY OF GOOD FAITH¶

Courts have often supplied a term requiring both parties to a contract to exercise what is called "good faith" or sometimes "good faith and fair dealing," and the Uniform Commercial Code provides that every contract governed by it "imposes

* CORBIN, CONTRACTS § 19 (1963).

† Mark P. Gergen, *The Use of Open Terms in Contract*, 92 COLUM. L. REV. 997, 1073-74 (1992)

‡ Charles J. Goetz, *Principles of Relational Contracts*, 67 VA. L. REV. 1089, 1124 (1981).

§ *Id.* at 1125-26.

¶ Excerpted from E. ALLAN FARNSWORTH, CONTRACTS § 7.17 (4th ed. 2004).

an obligation of good faith in its performance."[4] This implied duty is based on fundamental notions of fairness. Under the Code it "may not be disclaimed by agreement," though the "parties, by agreement, may determine the standards by which the performance of [that obligation] is to be measured if those standards are not manifestly unreasonable."[5] A similar restriction has been imposed outside the scope of the Code.[6]

The following excerpt provides a nice historical introduction to the implied covenant of good faith.

HISTORICAL PERSPECTIVE: THE IMPLIED COVENANT OF GOOD FAITH AND FORMALIST CONTRACT INTERPRETATION*

Although the notion of a good faith purchaser is traceable to ancient times, the implication of a covenant of good faith in contract performance is a relatively recent development in the law of contracts, arising in the second half of the Nineteenth Century. In its earliest uses, the covenant was applied to a variety of situations in which the express contract language, interpreted strictly, appeared to grant unbridled discretion to one of the parties and could reduce or eliminate the other party's contract benefits. These situations arose when the promisor's duty was conditioned on its satisfaction with the promisee's performance; when the duty to buy or sell goods was measured by the needs of the purchaser or the output of the seller; when the promisor's duty to pay was dependent on when he chose to sell property; when an insurer was granted discretion to dispute or settle claims against the insured; when the promisor reserved the right to interpret the contract; and when the promisor attempted to manipulate its profits so as to defeat the promisee's rights based on the existence of such profits. In all of these cases the good faith obligation overrode the unqualified discretion that a strict reading of the contract terms seemed to vest in one of the parties. In such cases, the good faith requirement could be used to change the outcome, so that "if the person [who reserved discretion] decide[d], not on the question submitted, but on some question of interest or advantage not made the basis of rights or obligations by the contract, the decision [was] outside of the contract and [was] given no effect by it."

4. UCC § 1-304. According to Comment 1, "This section sets forth a basic principle running throughout the Uniform Commercial Code."

5. UCC § 1-302(b).

6. Carmichael v. Adirondack Bottled Gas Corp., 635 A.2d 1211 (Vt. 1993) (though contract with distributor terminated with his death, supplier still owed "duties with respect to winding down," and "duty of good faith is imposed by law and is not a contractual term that the parties are free to bargain in or out as they see fit").

* Excerpted from Harold Dubroff, *The Implied Covenant of Good Faith in Contract Interpretation and Gap-Filling: Reviling A Revered Relic*, 80 St. John's L. Rev. 559, 564-71 (2006).

By the early Twentieth Century, the New York Court of Appeals had announced "a contractual obligation of universal force . . . the obligation of good faith in carrying out what is written," as well as its view that, for purposes of implying contract terms, one would be incorrect to "suppose that one party was to be placed at the mercy of the other."[23] Then, in 1933, the New York Court of Appeals decided *Kirk La Shelle Co. v. Paul Armstrong Co.*,[24] often cited as the leading early case on the implied covenant of good faith, in which the court declared that:

> [I]n every contract there is an implied covenant that neither party shall do anything which will have the effect of destroying or injuring the right of the other party to receive the fruits of the contract, which means that in every contract there exists an implied covenant of good faith and fair dealing.

In *Kirk La Shelle*, the defendant settled a lawsuit by agreeing to pay, to the plaintiff, half of all receipts from the revival of a play. The settlement also gave, to the plaintiff, approval power over all arrangements affecting the rights to the play, except for "motion picture rights." At the time of the settlement, all motion pictures were silent. After the development of talking motion pictures, the defendant sold, to MGM, the talking motion picture rights to the play without providing plaintiff with a right of approval, and without sharing any of the revenues from the sale. The court held that talking motion pictures could not have been within the contemplation of the parties at the time of the settlement, and that production of the talking motion picture reduced the value of the revival right payments to the plaintiff. By selling these rights without the approval of the plaintiff, the defendant breached its obligation "not to render valueless" the benefit given the plaintiff by the contract. Accordingly, the defendant was required to hold, for the plaintiff, the revenue received from violation of the right of approval.

In 1932, one year before the decision in *Kirk La Shelle*, the American Law Institute adopted *Restatement of Contracts* ("*Restatement First*"). There are provisions in *Restatement First* with regard to bona fide purchasers and assignees, and conditions based on the personal satisfaction of the promisor—all of which involve the question of good faith—and there are other specific references to "good faith" in *Restatement First*, but no provision of *Restatement First* imposes a universal obligation of good faith in contract performance or enforcement. In a sense, the absence of an implied covenant of good faith from *Restatement First*, which embodies a formalistic approach to contract interpretation and gap-filling, undermines a central theme of this Article—that the covenant was inspired by the desire of courts to soften the sometimes harsh results of formalistic jurisprudence. Nevertheless, since only New York and a few other states had recognized the covenant by the time *Restatement First* was adopted, the omission of the covenant is readily explained as consistent with the primary objective of *Restatement*

23. *Wood v. Lucy, Lady Duff-Gordon*, 118 N.E. 214, 214 (1917) (referencing nowhere an application of the implied covenant of good faith, but demonstrating the willingness of a court to recognize the imposition, upon contracting parties, of principles of fairness in dealing).

24. 188 N.E. 163 (1933).

First, to set forth the then extant common law of contracts.[33] The formalistic approach to interpretation placed great weight on the supposed capability of language to perfectly express the intentions of the parties as determined from the perspective of an objective third person. As such, its application could result in disregarding the actual intention of the parties if that intention was inconsistent with what a reasonable third person would assume the parties intended in light of their overt actions and words. The rationale behind this approach was a belief that strict formalism led to consistency and predictability—a desirable attribute in the administration of contract law that permitted parties to arrange their affairs with clear and certain expectations of legal consequences.

At the heart of the formalistic approach to contract interpretation was "the plain meaning" rule, which was based on two presumptions. The first was a presumption that words have a finite number of ordinary or commonly understood meanings, and the second was that parties intend that the words included in their contracts be given those meanings. Operating under these presumptions allowed questions of interpretation to be treated as questions of law not requiring factual determination regarding the context in which the contract was formed or the actual intentions of the parties. Judge Hand's often-quoted observation regarding the plain meaning rule was particularly candid:

> It makes not the least difference whether a promisor actually intends that meaning which the law will impose upon his words. The whole House of Bishops might satisfy us that he had intended something else, and it would make not a particle of difference in his obligation. . . . Hence it follows that no declaration of the promisor as to his meaning when he used the words is of the slightest relevancy, however formally competent it may be as an admission. Indeed, if both parties severally declared that their meaning had been other than the natural meaning, and each declaration was similar, it would be irrelevant . . . [and w]hen the court came to assign the meaning to their words, it would disregard such declarations, because they related only to their state of mind when the contract was made, and that has nothing to do with their obligations.[39]

The parol evidence rule, which applies when the parties reach a final written agreement on some or all of the terms of the contract, intensified the importance of the plain meaning rule by barring proof of prior, or contemporaneous oral, agreements, whether or not such agreements could be proved to have been actually made. As applied by the formalists, the parol evidence rule also barred extrinsic evidence intended to interpret the integration itself, unless a court found the

33. *See* E. Allan Farnsworth, *Good Faith Performance and Commercial Reasonableness Under the Uniform Commercial Code*, 30 U. CHI. L. REV. 666, 671 (1963) (noting that the duty of good faith performance was applied in only a few jurisdictions, and then generally in cases "in which one party's compensation was fixed in terms of a percentage of the other's profits, receipts, sales or production and the obligation of good faith was the basis of implying a condition of cooperation by the party who was to pay"); *see also Restatement of Contracts* vi ("The function of the courts is to decide the controversies brought before them. The function of the Institute is to state clearly and precisely in the light of the decisions the principles and rules of the common law.").

39. *Eustis Mining Co. v. Beer, Sondheimer & Co.*, 239 F. 976, 984-85 (S.D.N.Y. 1917).

writing to be ambiguous on its face.[41] Thus, extrinsic evidence was often barred, even when introduced to demonstrate an ambiguity in the language of the contract. Courts would apply the plain meaning rule, and if a court concluded that the language employed had a plain meaning then there was no ambiguity. Although courts acknowledged the potential injustice and harshness of the rule, classic contract law and Restatement First applied it rigorously as a necessary prophylactic against fraud and faulty memories. As one court noted:

> [A]pplication of the [parol evidence] rule can work to create harsh results. However, the policies behind the rule compel its consistent, uniform application. Commercial stability requires that parties to a contract may rely upon its express terms without worrying that the law will allow the other party to change the terms of the agreement at a later date.[42]

A party relying upon the plain meaning and parol evidence rules could seek to enforce rights that contract language, literally interpreted, conferred upon it despite the fact that the literal interpretation was not an accurate reflection of the actual intent of the parties at the time of contracting. Implication of a covenant of good faith, however, provided a justification for courts to look beyond the plain language of an agreement to inquire into the context of a particular bargain and determine the actual intentions and expectations of the parties, although they may have been expressed imperfectly. Two early New York Court of Appeals cases provide interesting illustrations of how changes in the common law evolve—in this case to limit the plain meaning rule so as to achieve reasonable results without abandoning the principles of formalistic jurisprudence. In one of the earliest of the good faith cases, New York Central Iron Works Co. v. United States Radiator Co.,[43] the defendant was required to fill the "entire radiator needs" of the plaintiff. When iron prices rose beyond the defendant's expectations, it refused to fill the plaintiff's "needs" above those in prior years. Interpreting the contract language under the plain meaning rule, the court concluded that the plaintiff's "needs" consisted of all radiators that it could sell at a profit. Nevertheless, it stated in dictum that, had the defendant properly raised the issue, it could have defended on the grounds that the plaintiff was not acting in good faith in attempting to exploit market conditions that were beyond the contemplation of the parties when the contract was formed:

> [W]e do not mean to assert that the plaintiff had the right, under the contract, to order goods to any amount. Both parties in such a contract are bound to carry it out in a reasonable way. The obligation of good faith and fair dealing towards each other is implied in every contract of this character. The plaintiff could not use the contract for the purpose of speculation in a rising market, since that would be a plain abuse of the rights conferred, and something like a fraud upon the seller.

41. E. Allan Farnsworth, *"Meaning" in the Law of Contracts*, 76 YALE L.J. 939, 959 (1967); Eric A. Posner, *The Parol Evidence Rule, the Plain Meaning Rule, and the Principles of Contractual Interpretation*, 146 U. PA. L. REV. 533, 535 (1998).

42. *Baker v. Bailey*, 782 P.2d 1286, 1288 (Mont. 1989).

43. 66 N.E. 967 (1903).

The court cited no authority for its view that bad faith contract enforcement was "something like a fraud."

In the later case of *Kirk La Shelle Co. v. Paul Armstrong Co.*, the court took a different approach. It did not address the question whether "motion picture rights" had a plain meaning that favored the defendant, but it did not deny such plain meaning. The court was, however, persuaded that when the parties entered into their contract they did not contemplate the development of talking motion pictures. The court was further convinced that to adopt the defendant's position would enable the defendant to deprive the plaintiff of the benefits of its bargain. How then to reach a just result without questioning the underlying validity of the plain meaning rule? The court found its answer in the same source as it did in its earlier famous decision in Lawrence v. Fox[45]—the law of trusts: "By entering into the contract and accepting and retaining the consideration therefor, the respondents assumed a fiduciary relationship which had its origin in the contract, and which imposed upon them the duty of utmost good faith."[46] Prior to the adoption of the U.C.C., some two decades after the promulgation of *Restatement First*, the common law of most states had not yet recognized a general implied covenant of good faith. In fact, at that time, the covenant was still largely the creation of the common law of New York, a jurisdiction not noted for its liberal approach to contract interpretation and the parol evidence rule. For this reason, the U.C.C. represented a watershed in the history of the implied covenant because of its inclusion of a general implied covenant of good faith—"Every contract or duty within this Act imposes an obligation of good faith in its performance or enforcement."[48] The implied obligation of good faith ultimately then became part of the statutory commercial law of every state. Equally significant, in the half century following promulgation of the U.C.C., the implied covenant has been accepted as part of the common law of most states.

Eastern Air Lines, Inc. v. Gulf Oil Corporation

United States District Court, Southern District of Florida
415 F. Supp. 429 (1975)

JAMES LAWRENCE KING, **District Judge**. Eastern Air Lines, Inc., hereafter Eastern, and Gulf Oil Corporation, hereafter Gulf, have enjoyed a mutually advantageous business relationship involving the sale and purchase of aviation fuel for several decades.

This controversy involves the threatened disruption of that historic relationship and the attempt, by Eastern, to enforce the most recent contract between the parties. On March 8, 1974 the correspondence and telex communications

45. 20 N.Y. 268, 274 (1859).
46. *Kirk La Shelle Co. v. Paul Armstrong Co.*, 188 N.E. 163, 166 (1933).
48. U.C.C. § 1-203 (2005).

between the corporate entities culminated in a demand by Gulf that Eastern must meet its demand for a price increase or Gulf would shut off Eastern's supply of jet fuel within fifteen days.

Eastern responded by filing its complaint with this court, alleging that Gulf had breached its contract and requesting preliminary and permanent mandatory injunctions requiring Gulf to perform the contract in accordance with its terms. By agreement of the parties, a preliminary injunction preserving the status quo was entered on March 20, 1974, requiring Gulf to perform its contract and directing Eastern to pay in accordance with the contract terms, pending final disposition of the case.

Gulf answered Eastern's complaint, alleging that the contract was not a binding requirements contract, was void for want of mutuality. . . .

The extraordinarily able advocacy by the experienced lawyers for both parties produced testimony at the trial from internationally respected experts who described in depth economic events that have, in recent months, profoundly affected the lives of every American.*

THE CONTRACT

On June 27, 1972, an agreement was signed by the parties which, as amended, was to provide the basis upon which Gulf was to furnish jet fuel to Eastern at certain specific cities in the Eastern system. Said agreement supplemented an existing contract between Gulf and Eastern which, on June 27, 1972, had approximately one year remaining prior to its expiration.

The contract is Gulf's standard form aviation fuel contract and is identical in all material particulars with the first contract for jet fuel, dated 1959, between Eastern and Gulf and, indeed, with aviation fuel contracts antedating the jet age. It is similar to contracts in general use in the aviation fuel trade. The contract was drafted by Gulf after substantial arm's length negotiation between the parties. Gulf approached Eastern more than a year before the expiration of the then-existing contracts between Gulf and Eastern, seeking to preserve its historic relationship with Eastern. Following several months of negotiation, the contract, consolidating and extending the terms of several existing contracts, was executed by the parties in June, 1972, to expire January 31, 1977. . . .

Against this factual background we turn to a consideration of the legal issues.

I. THE "REQUIREMENTS" CONTRACT

Gulf has taken the position in this case that the contract between it and Eastern is not a valid document in that it lacks mutuality of obligation; it is vague and indefinite; and that it renders Gulf subject to Eastern's whims

* [The court is referring to the 1973 oil crisis triggered by an embargo among several large oil-producing nations in the Middle East. The embargo created worldwide oil shortages and caused prices to soar.—ED.]

respecting the volume of jet fuel Gulf would be required to deliver to the purchaser Eastern.

The contract talks in terms of fuel "requirements."[4] The parties have interpreted this provision to mean that any aviation fuel purchased by Eastern at one of the cities covered by the contract, must be bought from Gulf. Conversely, Gulf must make the necessary arrangements to supply Eastern's reasonable good faith demands at those same locations. This is the construction the parties themselves have placed on the contract and it has governed their conduct over many years and several contracts.In early cases, requirements contracts were found invalid for want of the requisite definiteness, or on the grounds of lack of mutuality. Many such cases are collected and annotated at 14 A.L.R. 1300.

As reflected in the foregoing annotation, there developed rather quickly in the law the view that a requirements contract could be binding where the purchaser had an operating business. The "lack of mutuality" and "indefiniteness" were resolved since the court could determine the volume of goods provided for under the contract by reference to objective evidence of the volume of goods required to operate the specified business. Therefore, well prior to the adoption of the Uniform Commercial Code, case law generally held requirements contracts binding.

The Uniform Commercial Code, adopted in Florida in 1965, specifically approves requirements contracts in F.S. 672.306 (U.C.C. § 2-306(1)).

> (1) A term which measures the quantity by the output of the seller or the requirements of the buyer means such actual output or requirements as may occur in good faith, except that no quantity unreasonably disproportionate to any stated estimate or in the absence of a stated estimate to any normal or otherwise comparable prior output or requirements may be tendered or demanded.

The Uniform Commercial Code Official Comment interprets § 2-306(1) as follows:

> 2. Under this Article, a contract for output or requirements is not too indefinite since it is held to mean the actual good faith output or requirements of the particular party. Nor does such a contract lack mutuality of obligation since, under this section, the party who will determine quantity is required to operate his plant or conduct his business in good faith and according to commercial standards of fair dealing in the trade so that his output or requirements will approximate a reasonably foreseeable figure. Reasonable elasticity in the requirements is expressly envisaged by this section and good faith variations from prior requirements are permitted even when the variation may be such as to result in discontinuance. A shut-down by a requirements buyer for lack of orders might be permissible when a shut-down merely to curtail losses would not. The essential test is whether the party is acting in good faith. Similarly, a

4. "Gulf agrees to sell and deliver to Eastern, and Eastern agrees to purchase, receive and pay for their requirements of Gulf Jet A and Gulf Jet A-1 at the locations listed. . . ."

sudden expansion of the plant by which requirements are to be measured would not be included within the scope of the contract as made but normal expansion undertaken in good faith would be within the scope of this section. One of the factors in an expansion situation would be whether the market price has risen greatly in a case in which the requirements contract contained a fixed price. Reasonable variation of an extreme sort is exemplified in *Southwest Natural Gas Co. v. Oklahoma Portland Cement Co.*, 102 F.2d 630 (C.C.A. 10, 1939)."

Some of the prior Gulf-Eastern contracts have included the estimated fuel requirements for some cities covered by the contract while others have none. The particular contract contains an estimate for Gainesville, Florida requirement.

The parties have consistently over the years relied upon each other to act in good faith in the purchase and sale of the required quantities of aviation fuel specified in the contract. During the course of the contract, various estimates have been exchanged from time to time, and, since the advent of the petroleum allocations programs, discussions of estimated requirements have been on a monthly (or more frequent) basis.[5]

The court concludes that the document is a binding and enforceable requirements contract.

II. BREACH OF CONTRACT

Gulf suggests that Eastern violated the contract between the parties by manipulating its requirements through a practice known as "fuel freighting" in the airline industry. Requirements can vary from city to city depending on whether or not it is economically profitable to freight fuel. This fuel freighting practice in accordance with price could affect lifting from Gulf stations by either raising such liftings or lowering them. If the price was higher at a Gulf station, the practice could have reduced liftings there by lifting fuel in excess of its actual operating requirements at a prior station, and thereby not loading fuel at the succeeding high price Gulf station. Similarly where the Gulf station was comparatively cheaper, an aircraft might load more heavily at the Gulf station and not load at other succeeding non-Gulf stations.

The court however, finds that Eastern's performance under the contract does not constitute a breach of its agreement with Gulf and is consistent with good faith and established commercial practices as required by U.C.C. § 2-306.

5. A requirements contract under the U.C.C. may speak of "requirements" alone, or it may include estimates, or it may contain maximums and minimums. In any case, the consequences are the same, as Official Comments 2 and 3 indicate. Comment 2 is set out in the text above. Comment 3 provides: "3. If an estimate of output or requirements is included in the agreement, no quantity unreasonably disproportionate to it may be tendered or demanded. Any minimum or maximum set by the agreement shows a clear limit on the intended elasticity. In similar fashion, the agreed estimate is to be regarded as a center around which the parties intend the variation to occur."

"Good Faith" means "honesty in fact in the conduct or transaction concerned" U.C.C. § 1-201(19). Between merchants, "good faith" means "honesty in fact and the observance of reasonable commercial standards of fair dealing in the trade"; U.C.C. § 2-103(1)(b) and Official Comment 2 of U.C.C. § 2-306. The relevant commercial practices are "courses of performance," "courses of dealing" and "usages of trade."[6]

Throughout the history of commercial aviation, including 30 years of dealing between Gulf and Eastern, airlines' liftings of fuel by nature have been subject to substantial daily, weekly, monthly and seasonal variations, as they are affected by weather, schedule changes, size of aircraft, aircraft load, local airport conditions, ground time, availability of fueling facilities, whether the flight is on time or late, passenger convenience, economy and efficiency of operation, fuel taxes, into-plane fuel service charges, fuel price, and, ultimately, the judgment of the flight captain as to how much fuel he wants to take.

All these factors are, and for years have been, known to oil companies, including Gulf, and taken into account by them in their fuel contracts. . . .

The court concludes that fuel freighting is an established industry practice, inherent in the nature of the business. The evidence clearly demonstrated that the practice has long been part of the established courses of performance and dealing between Eastern and Gulf. As the practice of "freighting" or "tankering" has gone on unchanged and unchallenged for many years accepted as a fact of life by Gulf without complaint, the court is reminded of Official Comment 1 to U.C.C. § 2-208:

> The parties themselves know best what they have meant by their words of agreement and their action under that agreement is the best indication of what that meaning was.

. . . If a customer's demands under a requirements contract become excessive, U.C.C. § 2-306 protects the seller and, in the appropriate case, would allow him to refuse to deliver unreasonable amounts demanded (but without eliminating his basic contract obligation); similarly, in an appropriate case, if a customer repeatedly had no requirements at all, the seller might be excused from performance if the buyer suddenly and without warning should descend upon him and demand his entire inventory, but the court is not called upon to decide those cases here.

---

6. U.C.C. § 2-208(1) defines "course of performance" as those "repeated occasions for performance by either party with knowledge of the nature of the performance and opportunity for objection to it by the other." U.C.C. § 1-205(1) defines "course of dealing" as "a sequence of previous conduct be-tween the parties to a particular transaction which is fairly to be regarded as establishing a common basis of understanding for interpreting their expressions and other conduct." U.C.C. § 1-205(2) defines "usage of trade" as "any practice or method of dealing having such regularity of observance in a place, vocation or trade as to justify an expectation that it will be observed with respect to the transaction in question."

U.C.C. § 2-208(2) provides that "express terms shall control course of performance and course of performance shall control both course of dealings and usage of trade."

Rather, the case here is one where the established courses of performance and dealing between the parties, the established usages of the trade, and the basic contract itself all show that the matters complained of for the first time by Gulf after commencement of this litigation are the fundamental given ingredients of the aviation fuel trade to which the parties have accommodated themselves successfully and without dispute over the years.

> The practical interpretation given to their contracts by the parties to them while they are engaged in their performance, and before any controversy has arisen concerning them, is one of the best indications of their true intent, and courts that adopt and enforce such a construction are not likely to commit serious error.

Manhattan Life Ins. Co. of New York v. Wright, 126 F. 82, 87 (8th Cir. 1903).

The court concludes that Eastern has not violated the contract. . . .

RELEVANT PROVISIONS

For the *Restatement (Second) of Contracts,* consult § 205. For the UCC, consult §§ 1-201(b)(20), 1-304, and 2-306. For the CISG, consult Article 7. For the UNIDROIT Principles, consult Article 1.7.

NOTES AND QUESTIONS

1. *What happened?* Who sued whom for what? Procedurally, how did the case get before this court? Factually, what happened between the parties? What arguments did the plaintiff and defendant make? What rule or rules did the court apply? How did the court analyze the dispute between the parties? How did the court decide the case?

2. *Was this case correctly decided?* Do you agree with the result reached in this case? Why or why not? Do you agree with the court's reasoning? Why or why not? How, if at all, would you have written the opinion differently?

3. *Importance of good faith?* Do you understand why courts believe the role of good faith is so important in a requirement contract? Would these contracts be possible without implying such a requirement as good faith? Why or why not?

4. *Requirements and output contracts.* Requirements contracts are related to output contracts. The former require a supplier to fulfill a buyer's reasonable requirements, whereas the latter require a buyer to purchase a supplier's reasonable output. But why, exactly, are such contracts used? The following excerpts discuss some of these issues in a bit more depth.

REQUIREMENTS AND OUTPUT CONTRACTS*

The ordinary type of agreement for the sale of goods specifies a fixed quantity for a fixed price. Buyers and sellers of goods in a community where production and distribution are on a small scale and for a limited market find such arrangements sufficient for their dealings. Large-scale production and expanding markets create greater uncertainties and more business hazards. There has arisen a demand for a more complex allocation of these new risks determined by the ability of the parties to bear certain risks conveniently and by their respective bargaining positions. To meet this demand many types of contracts have come into use containing various provisions for the fixing of terms with reference to future events. Among these we find contracts to supply raw materials for manufacture or finished products for resale in which the quantity term is subject to variation according to the needs of the buyer's business. A similar variable quantity term is to be found in contracts for all the products which a manufacturer or producer may turn out in his business during a specified period.

The advantages of contracts without a fixed quantity term are most apparent in the case of a manufacturer who makes a contract for his requirements of raw material. If he is manufacturing for a market whose demand is incapable of certain prediction, the task of correlating his supply of materials with his sales may prove something of a burden if he is compelled to contract for fixed quantities. If his supply is assured and at the same time variable, he is relieved of the necessity of providing against insufficiency or of disposing of a surplus in a market with which he is unfamiliar and in which he has no regular customers. These reasons hold also to some extent when the buyer is a jobber. He is relieved of the necessity of predicting his sales over a period. The advantage to the seller is not so clear. The press of competition and the large quantities usually involved lead him to accede to provisions of this type in order to make his proposition more attractive. Furthermore the fact that he is usually dealing with the commodity in question in larger quantities and is acquainted with the market makes it easier for him to effect the adjustments necessary because of the variations in the needs of the buyer's business.

Output contracts have much in common with those for requirements, but there are differences. The seller's position is comparable to that of the buyer in the requirement contract, but his motives are not precisely the same. The purpose here seems to be to turn over the marketing of the product to the buyer, thus effecting a greater division of labor. Buyers do not enter into such contracts so much because of the competition of other prospective buyers, but because of the lower price the seller is able to make due to the elimination of marketing expense. The buyer's increased profit is for assuming the market risk and performing the marketing service with the attendant expense.

The risks of price fluctuation are of course also present in these contracts as in the ordinary contract of sale over a period. But whereas in the contract for a fixed amount the parties stand to lose or gain in equal amounts according to

---

* Excerpted from Harold C. Havighurst and Sidney Berman, *Requirement and Output Contracts*, 27 ILL. L. REV. 1, 1-3 (1932).

whether the market rises or falls, the requirement buyer and the output seller have a distinct advantage in that they have a measure of control over the quantity. The market price of finished products usually bears a direct relation to the market price of raw materials. But in a rising market the requirement buyer, whose costs are in a measure stabilized by the contract, enjoys an advantage that will probably be reflected in business expansion. The output seller, operating at a higher cost but selling at the contract price, will tend to produce less. On the other hand, in a falling market the requirement buyer, who is obliged to pay the contract price for his materials, will purchase less goods and the output seller will increase his production. This aspect is even more marked when the buyer of requirements is a jobber. Business men without doubt are fully conscious of this inequality. But the party thus at a disadvantage is usually led to take his chances by the pressure of competition and the commercially desirable features already discussed. It is this effect of price fluctuation, however, that has led to much friction and litigation under these contracts. Doubtless from a commercial standpoint the loss from this source has not been sufficient to outweigh the advantages that are realized by the use of such agreements.

Does the following excerpt shed any light on why courts imply the duty of good faith in requirements and outputs contracts? Pay particular attention to the last paragraph—the author may very well have had Eastern Air Lines, Inc. v. Gulf Oil Corporation *in mind when he wrote it.*

THINKING TOOL: THE SINGLE OWNER*

[P]eople often create waste for others in the course of creating gains for themselves. Suppose that an accident occurs because the defendant skips some precaution: he doesn't put a fence around his ballpark, so balls sometimes break the windows of the neighboring houses. The owner gains by omitting the fence; he saves some money. The neighbors have a different experience of the situation: broken windows. Looking at the situation from the outside in, we can call it a waste if the gains from skipping the fence are smaller than the losses from the smashed windows. We view these things in the aggregate; we decide whether there is waste by comparing the gains to everyone with the losses to everyone. The challenge is to get the ballpark's owner to think that way, too. That is what the law accomplishes if it holds the owner liable for the broken windows. We make the costs experienced by the neighbors costs to him; to say it more technically, we force him to internalize the cost of omitting the fence. If he weren't held liable for the broken windows, he wouldn't worry about breaking them, which we then could call an external cost, or externality—a cost of his behavior that isn't brought home to him. Try thinking of that as the point of many legal rules, and

* Excerpted from WARD FARNSWORTH, THE LEGAL ANALYST: A TOOLKIT FOR THINKING ABOUT THE LAW 37-38, 44-45 (2007).

of holding people liable for expenses they create: the purpose is to bring home to them the full costs of their choices rather than letting them foist the costs onto other people they don't care about.

There is a nice tool for thinking about this type of situation. It is known generally as the single owner. . . . The idea is to picture all the interests at stake in a case having just one owner, and to ask what that single owner of them would do.

The useful thought experiment is to imagine that the ballpark and the neighboring houses had a single owner. Would he have built a fence? Notice how this solves the problem. A single owner of all the properties would take the cost of the broken windows just as seriously as the cost of the fence. He would build the fence if it were cheaper than replacing windows, and otherwise not. Put differently, a single owner of all the interests at stake would be careful to minimize waste, or (the same) to do the efficient thing. On this view the law's goal should be to make a rule that gets the owner of the ballpark to think the way a single owner would when he decides what precautions to take. Making him pay for every window broken by his baseballs (whether or not he builds a fence) might do the trick; that would be known as strict liability. Making him pay only if he fails to think like a single owner—that is, making him pay only if he doesn't build the fence, and it's found that the fence would have paid for itself in the broken windows it would have prevented—probably would do it, too. That would be called liability for negligence. . . .

Here is another limit on the single-owner principle. Suppose we make a contract in which you agree to supply me with as much rubber as I need at a fixed price for the next five years. A year later the price of rubber unexpectedly skyrockets; the price of most things made out of rubber naturally goes way up, too. But not for me: I can keep getting rubber from you at the same price, so I do; I can't get enough of the stuff. You complain that I'm not behaving the way I would if I were a single owner of all the resources involved—my manufacturing plant *and* your rubber supply concern. If I owned both, I would be conserving rubber because it has become scarce; instead I'm using it like mad. I shrug and say that I made a long-term contract with you so that I wouldn't have to worry about acting like a single owner. The law tends to agree. When we make a contract we are gambling, and sometimes we are gambling against each other. If I started demanding lots more rubber, a court eventually might hold that I'm breaching the contract because the point of it wasn't to let me go wild in this way; but even then the benchmark wouldn't be the behavior of a single owner.

Dalton v. Educational Testing Service

Court of Appeals of New York
663 N.E.2d 289 (1995)

CHIEF JUDGE KAYE. The primary question before us is whether defendant, Educational Testing Service (ETS), a standardized testing firm, complied with procedures specified in its contract with high school senior Brian Dalton in refusing to release Dalton's Scholastic Aptitude Test (SAT) score. Because the factual findings underlying the trial court's determination that ETS failed to act in good faith in following those procedures were affirmed by the Appellate Division, have support in the record and are consequently beyond the scope of our review, we conclude—as did the trial court and Appellate Division—that ETS breached its contract with Dalton. Though we agree, moreover, with the courts below that specific performance is the appropriate remedy, we nevertheless conclude that the promised performance was good-faith compliance with the stated procedures, not release of the questioned scores as ordered by those courts.

I

In May 1991, Brian Dalton took the SAT, which was administered by ETS. . . . Six months later, in November, he took the examination a second time . . . , and his combined score increased 410 points.

Because Dalton's score increased by more than 350 points, his test results fell within the ETS category of "Large Score Differences" or "discrepant scores." In accordance with ETS policy, [ETS] reviewed his May and November answer sheets. Upon a finding of disparate handwriting, the answer sheets were submitted to a document examiner, who opined that they were completed by separate individuals. Dalton's case was then forwarded to the Board of Review, which preliminarily decided that substantial evidence supported cancelling Dalton's November score.

Upon registering for the November SAT, Dalton had signed a statement agreeing to the conditions in . . . the Registration Bulletin, which reserved to ETS "the right to cancel any test score . . . if ETS believes that there is reason to question the score's validity." The Registration Bulletin further provided that, if "the validity of a test score is questioned because it may have been obtained unfairly, ETS [will] notif[y] the test taker of the reasons for questioning the score" and offer the test-taker the following five options: (1) the opportunity to provide additional information, (2) confirmation of the score by taking a free retest, (3) authorization for ETS to cancel the score and refund all fees, (4) third-party review by any institution receiving the test score or (5) arbitration.

As specified in the Registration Bulletin, ETS apprised Dalton of its preliminary decision to cancel his November SAT score in a letter from Test Security Specialist Celeste M. Eppinger. Noting the handwriting disparity and the substantial difference between his May and November test results, Eppinger informed Dalton that "[t]he evidence suggests that someone else may have completed your answer sheet and that the questioned scores may be invalid." She advised him that he could supply "any additional information that will help explain" this or, alternatively, elect one of the other options.

Eppinger enclosed the Procedures for Questioned Scores pamphlet with her letter, which reiterated the test-taker's right to "submit additional relevant information" to the Board of Review supporting the validity of questioned scores. In cautioning test-takers to provide only information "relevant to the questions being raised," the Procedures for Questioned Scores explained, "[f]or example, character references or testimonial letters do not explain handwriting differences." As to the four additional options, the guide further explained, "ETS also offers other options . . . if additional information doesn't resolve the questions about the validity of the scores. The option to provide additional information to resolve these questions may be used in combination with one or more of the[se] options."

Dalton opted to present additional information to the Board of Review, including the following: verification that he was suffering from mononucleosis during the May examination; diagnostic test results from a preparatory course he took prior to the November examination (he had taken no similar course prior to the May SAT) that were consistent with his performance on that test, a statement from an ETS proctor who remembered Dalton's presence during the November examination; and statements from two students . . . that he had been in the classroom during that test. Dalton further provided ETS with a report from a document examiner obtained by his family who concluded that Dalton was the author of both sets of answer sheets.

ETS, after several Board of Review meetings, submitted the various handwriting exemplars to a second document examiner who, like its first, opined that the May and November tests were not completed by the same individual. As a result, ETS continued to question the validity of Dalton's November score.

At this point plaintiff Peter Dalton, father and natural guardian of Brian Dalton, filed a [lawsuit] to prohibit ETS from cancelling Dalton's November SAT score and to compel immediate release of the score. Following a 12-day nonjury trial, the trial court found that ETS failed "to make even rudimentary efforts to evaluate or investigate the information" furnished by Dalton and thus concluded that ETS failed to act in good faith in determining the legitimacy of Dalton's score, thereby breaching its contract. The trial court premised this conclusion on its determination that the ETS Board of Review members failed to evaluate the information submitted because they believed Dalton's presence at the November SAT to be wholly irrelevant to the handwriting issue. . . . As a remedy for the contractual breach, the trial court ordered ETS to release the November SAT score.

The Appellate Division affirmed. It too found that ETS ignored the documentation provided by Dalton and considered only the reports of its own document examiners. Like the trial court, the Appellate Division concluded that this failure to evaluate as well as to investigate Dalton's information constituted a breach of contract. In light of these factual determinations, we agree that ETS breached its contract with Dalton but differ as to the scope of the relief.

II

By accepting ETS' standardized form agreement when he registered for the November SAT, Dalton entered into a contract with ETS. Implicit in all contracts is a covenant of good faith and fair dealing in the course of contract performance.

Encompassed within the implied obligation of each promisor to exercise good faith [is] a pledge that "neither party shall do anything which will have the effect of destroying or injuring the right of the other party to receive the fruits of the contract" (*Kirke La Shelle Co. v Armstrong Co.*, 263 N.Y. 79, 87). Where the contract contemplates the exercise of discretion, this pledge includes a promise not to act arbitrarily or irrationally in exercising that discretion. The duty of good faith and fair dealing, however, is not without limits, and no obligation can be implied that "would be inconsistent with other terms of the contractual relationship" (*Murphy v American Home Prods. Corp.*, 58 N.Y.2d 293, 304).

The parties here agreed to the provisions in the Registration Bulletin, which expressly permit cancellation of a test score so long as ETS found "reason to question" its validity after offering the test-taker the five specified options. . . .

The contract, however, did require that ETS consider any relevant material that Dalton supplied to the Board of Review. The Registration Bulletin explicitly afforded Dalton the option to provide ETS with relevant information upon notification that ETS questioned the legitimacy of his test score. Having elected to offer this option, it was certainly reasonable to expect that ETS would, at the very least, consider any relevant material submitted in reaching its final decision.

Dalton triggered this implied-in-law obligation on the part of ETS by exercising his contractual option to provide ETS with information. Significantly, Dalton heeded the advice in the Procedures for Questioned Scores and tendered numerous documents that did more than simply deny allegations of wrongdoing or attest to his good character, such as medical evidence regarding his physical condition, statements by fellow test-takers, the statement of a classroom proctor and consistent diagnostic test results.

Nevertheless, with the exception of the document examiner's report, ETS disputes the relevancy of this information. Specifically, ETS maintains that the sole issue before the Board of Review was the disparate handwriting and that evidence regarding Dalton's health (apart from a damaged arm) or presence during both examinations is irrelevant to resolving that issue. . . .

Thus, ETS expressly framed the dispositive question as one of suspected impersonation. Because the statements from the classroom proctor and November test-takers corroborated Dalton's contention that he was present at and in fact took the November examination, they were relevant to this issue.

Likewise, inasmuch as the medical documentation concerning Dalton's health at the time of the May SAT provided an explanation for his poor performance on that examination, and the consistent diagnostic test results demonstrated his ability to achieve such a dramatic score increase, these items were also germane to the question whether it was Dalton or an imposter who completed the November examination. Indeed, in its manual . . . ETS offers several examples of "relevant information" that a test-taker might provide, including "a doctor's report that the candidate was under the influence of medication at the time the low score was earned." Regarding "a case of possible impersonation" in particular, the manual suggests that "other test results might demonstrate that the questioned score is not inconsistent with other measures of the candidate's abilities." Thus, Dalton's material fell within ETS' own definition of relevancy, as expressed in its manual and letter to Dalton.

The critical question then is whether the Board of Review made any effort to consider this relevant information submitted by Dalton. That is a factual inquiry. Both the trial court and the Appellate Division concluded that the Board utterly failed to evaluate the material. . . .

When ETS fulfills its contractual obligation to consider relevant material provided by the test-taker and otherwise acts in good faith, the testing service—not the courts—must be the final arbiter of both the appropriate weight to accord that material and the validity of the test score. This Court will not interfere with that discretionary determination unless it is performed arbitrarily or irrationally.

Where, however, ETS refuses to exercise its discretion in the first instance by declining even to consider relevant material submitted by the test-taker, the legal question is whether this refusal breached an express or implied term of the contract, not whether it was arbitrary or irrational. Here, the courts below agreed that ETS did not consider the relevant information furnished by Dalton. By doing so, ETS failed to comply in good faith with its own test security procedures, thereby breaching its contract with Dalton. . . .

III

We agree with the trial court and Appellate Division that Dalton is entitled to specific performance of the contract. Dalton is not, however, entitled to release of his score as though fully validated. The goal of specific performance is to produce "as nearly as is practicable, the same effect as if the contract had been performed" (Farnsworth, *Contracts* § 12.5, at 823 [1982]). Had the contract here been performed, ETS would have considered the information provided by Dalton in reaching a final decision. ETS never promised to release a score believed to be invalid, and the validity of Dalton's November SAT score has yet to be determined. Indeed, the trial court specifically noted that it was not resolving the question whether Dalton in fact took the November test. . . .

When a standardized testing service reports a score, it certifies to the world that the test-taker possesses the requisite knowledge and skills to achieve the particular score. Like academic credentials, if courts were to require testing services to release questioned scores, "the value of these credentials from the point of view of society would be seriously undermined" ([*Matter of Olsson v. Board of Higher Educ.*, 49 N.Y.2d 408, 413]). Given the reliance that students, educational institutions, prospective employers and others place on the legitimacy of scores released by ETS, requiring challenged scores to be reported would be contrary to the public interest and exceed the scope of ETS' promised performance.

While courts as a matter of policy are reluctant to intrude upon academic discretion in educational matters, they stand ready as a matter of law and equity to enforce contract rights. Where a contract is breached, moreover, and the injured party is entitled to specific performance, the remedy must be a real one, not an exercise in futility.

Dalton is entitled to relief that comports with ETS' contractual promise—good-faith consideration of the material he submitted to ETS. We cannot agree with Dalton's assumption that ETS will merely rubber-stamp its prior determination without good-faith attention to his documentation and that reconsideration by ETS will be an empty exercise. Our conclusion that the contract affords Dalton a meaningful remedy rests also on the provision in the Procedures for Questioned Scores allowing Dalton to utilize one or more of the remaining four options in combination with renewed consideration by the Board of Review. Those options—including third-party review by any institution receiving the test score as well as arbitration—remain available should ETS determine that the information submitted fails to resolve its concerns about the validity of the November score.

Accordingly, the Appellate Division order should be modified in accordance with this opinion and, as so modified, affirmed, without costs.

RELEVANT PROVISIONS

For the *Restatement (Second) of Contracts,* consult § 205. For the UCC, consult §§ 1-201(b)(20), 1-304, and 2-306. For the CISG, consult Article 7. For the UNIDROIT Principles, consult Article 1.7.

NOTES AND QUESTIONS

1. *What happened?* Who sued whom for what? Procedurally, how did the case get before this court? Factually, what happened between the parties? What arguments did the plaintiff and defendant make? What rule or rules did the court apply? How did the court analyze the dispute between the parties? How did the court decide the case?

2. *Was this case correctly decided?* Do you agree with the result reached in this case? Why or why not? Do you agree with the court's reasoning? Why or why not? How, if at all, would you have written the opinion differently?

3. *Comparative perspective.* How, if at all, does the implied duty of good faith and fair dealing vary under the Restatement, UCC, CISG, or UNIDROIT Principles?

4. *Thinking tools.* Drawing on any of the thinking tools we previously examined, which approach to good faith seems best, and why?

THE IMPLIED COVENANT OF GOOD FAITH IN CONTRACT INTERPRETATION*

The implied covenant of good faith contract performance has become a fundamental concept of modern contract jurisprudence. Originally applied in late Nineteenth Century common law contracts cases, the covenant gained increased acceptance when it was incorporated into the *Uniform Commercial Code* ("U.C.C.") and later adopted by the American Law Institute as part of the *Restatement (Second) of Contracts* ("Restatement Second"). Since the middle of the Twentieth Century it has attracted the attention of scholars and has become an increasingly familiar issue in commercial litigation. The attention lavished on the implied covenant has not, however, resulted in the emergence of a clear consensus on what it is. As Judge Posner put it, "[t]he . . . cases are cryptic as to [the meaning of good faith] though emphatic about its existence."

One of the important roles perceived for the implied covenant has been the resolution of disputes that arise after contract formation. Such disputes generally arise when the express contract either does not address the nature of the dispute, or the application of the express contract language would seem to give rise to an unfair result, which, the disadvantaged party argues, was not contemplated when the express contract language was adopted. The assertion is then made that the party seeking to take advantage of the omission or the unanticipated application of express contract terms is not acting in good faith, thereby breaching the implied covenant. In arguing and deciding these disputes based on the implied covenant, the parties and courts frequently ignore the fundamental question of how the meaning of the agreement ought to be determined based on principles of interpretation and gap-filling.

In the early stages of the development of the covenant, it served a salutary role in affording a rationale for courts (primarily in New York) to avoid the sometimes harsh results that would otherwise have occurred under the conservative interpretation and gap-filling rules prevalent in the Nineteenth and early Twentieth Centuries, which were grounded in a formalistic approach to contract interpretation and enforcement. But at the same time that the implied covenant of good faith was gaining prominence in the Twentieth Century, the process of contract interpretation was also evolving by moving away from formalism toward an approach based on dual realities: one, language, because of its inherent ambiguity, cannot always express perfectly the actual agreement of the parties, and two, foreseeing all eventualities that may arise in contract performance is beyond the capacity of humans and gaps in contract provisions inevitably will arise. This newer approach to contract interpretation, exemplified by the U.C.C. and Restatement Second, which not only tolerates but encourages the exercise of judicial power in facilitating contract interpretation and enforcement, also emphasizes the context of an agreement—usage, course of dealing, course of performance, and other factors present in the relationship that gave rise to the agreement.

---

* Excerpted from Harold Dubroff, *The Implied Covenant of Good Faith in Contract Interpretation and Gap-Filling: Reviling A Revered Relic*, 80 St. John's L. Rev. 559, 559-62 (2006).

INTERNATIONAL PERSPECTIVE: GOOD FAITH IN INTERNATIONAL COMMERCIAL LAW*

The Vienna Convention does not contain a provision imposing a duty of good faith in the performance of an agreement. It does however, state that in the interpretation of the Convention, "regard is to be had to . . . the observance of good faith in international trade."[7] This provision, which falls short of imposing any duty of good faith performance on the *parties,* resolved a stalemate between those representatives, primarily from civil law countries, who favored the imposition of such a duty and those, primarily from common law countries, who opposed the imposition of such a duty. There are three views as to what this compromise means. One view, supported by the drafting history, is that since there was no agreement on imposing such a duty none was imposed. At the other extreme is the view that the duty of good faith performance is so fundamental that the language of compromise should be tortured to impose it. In between these extremes is the view that though the language of compromise does not impose a duty of good faith performance, such a duty underlies a number of the Convention's specific provisions so that it can be said to be one of "the general principles on which [the Convention] is based" and which are to govern matters not "expressly settled" by the Convention.[9] The UNIDROIT Principles avoid such uncertainty by stating that each party "must act in accordance with good faith and fair dealing in international trade."[10]

3. Warranties and Consumer Legislation

a. Express and Implied Warranties

As we have seen in a number of cases, parties are always free to make promises to one another, and this includes making warranties to one another, i.e., that the thing contracted for shall possess certain characteristics, or be of a certain quality. It should therefore come as no surprise that, under the UCC, parties remain free to create express warranties, and the UCC lists three particular ways in which they may do so: by (1) affirming a fact or making a promise relating to goods, (2) describing goods, or (3) providing a sample of goods, where the affirmance, promise, description, or sample become a basis of the bargain. (*See* UCC § 2-313.)

In addition to allowing parties to create express warranties, there are two important types of warranties that the UCC will imply in sales contracts unless these warranties are contracted around by the parties. First, in all contracts

* Excerpted from William S. Dodge, *Teaching the CISG in Contracts,* 50 J. LEGAL EDUC. 72, 82-83 (2000).

7. CISG Art. 7(1).

9. CISG Art. 7(2).

10. UNIDROIT Principles 1.7(1).

where the seller is a merchant, the UCC will imply (unless excluded or modified) a warranty of merchantability, which represents to the buyer that the goods sold will be "merchantable." What does this mean? According to the UCC, it means that they must "pass without objection in the trade," be of "fair average quality," be "fit for the ordinary purposes for which such goods are used," must "run, within the variations permitted by the agreement, of even kind, quality, and quantity within each unit and among all units involved," be "adequately contained, packaged, and labeled as the agreement may require," and "conform to the promises or affirmations of fact made on the container or label if any." (*See* UCC § 2-314.)

In addition, where (1) the seller knows of a "particular purpose" for which a buyer needs goods, and (2) the buyer is "relying on the seller's skill or judgment to select or furnish suitable goods," the UCC will also imply, "unless excluded or modified," a warranty of fitness for a particular purpose "that the goods shall be fit for such purpose." (*See* UCC § 2-315.) But what if a party does not want such implied warranties to become part of their contract? May a party exclude them and—if so—how, and under what circumstances? The question is explored in greater detail in the following case and accompanying materials.

RELEVANT PROVISIONS

For the UCC, consult §§ 2-313, 2-314, 2-315.

b. Limiting or Disclaiming Warranties and Remedies

Henningsen v. Bloomfield Motors

Supreme Court of New Jersey
161 A.2d 69 (1960)

FRANCIS, J. [Plaintiff Clause H. Henningsen purchased a Plymouth, manufactured by defendant Chrysler Corporation, from defendant Bloomfield Motors, Inc., as a Mother's Day gift to his wife, Helen. When the purchase order or contract was prepared and presented, the husband executed it alone. The purchase order consisted of a one-page form. The front of the form contained blanks to be filled in, and the printed portion of the form became smaller in size, different in style, and less readable toward the bottom where the line for the purchaser's signature was placed. The smallest type on the page consisted of two paragraphs, which the court described as "the least legible and the most difficult to read in the instrument, but the . . . most important in the evaluation of the rights of the contesting parties. They do not attract attention and there is nothing about the format which would draw the reader's eye to them. In fact, a studied and concentrated effort would have to be made to read them. De-emphasis seems the motive rather than emphasis." In fact, although "most of the printing in the body of the order appears to be 12 point block type, and easy to read," the following two paragraphs appeared in six-point script:

> The front and back of this Order comprise the entire agreement affecting this purchase and no other agreement or understanding of any nature concerning same has been made or entered into, or will be recognized. I hereby certify that no credit has been extended to me for the purchase of this motor vehicle except as appears in writing on the face of this agreement.
>
> I have read the matter printed on the back hereof and agree to it as a part of this order the same as if it were printed above my signature. I certify that I am 21 years of age, or older, and hereby acknowledge receipt of a copy of this order.

The back of the contract referring to in the second-paragraph quoted above was also written in fine print (although not as small as the six-point script in the paragraphs above), and stated as follows:

> 7. It is expressly agreed that there are no warranties, express or implied, Made by either the dealer or the manufacturer on the motor vehicle, chassis, of parts furnished hereunder except as follows.
>
> "The manufacturer warrants each new motor vehicle (including original equipment placed thereon by the manufacturer except tires), chassis or parts manufactured by it to be free from defects in material or workmanship under normal use and service. Its obligation under this warranty being limited to making good at its factory any part or parts thereof which shall, within ninety (90) days after delivery of such vehicle to the original purchaser or before such vehicle has been driven 4,000 miles, whichever event shall first occur, be returned to it with transportation charges prepaid and which its examination shall disclose to its satisfaction to have been thus defective; This warranty being expressly in lieu of all other warranties expressed or implied, and all other obligations or liabilities on its part, and it neither assumes nor authorizes any other person to assume for it any other liability in connection with the sale of its vehicles. . . ." (Emphasis ours.)

Mr. Henningsen did not read any of the paragraphs above, and the defendants did not otherwise reference or called his attention to these clauses.

After purchasing the automobile, Mr. Henningsen's wife was injured while driving when the steering mechanism failed, causing the steering wheel to spin and the car to veer sharply to the right and crash into a brick wall. Mr. and Mrs. Henningsen brought suit against both defendants to recover damages on account of her injuries, basing their complaint, among other things, on the defendants' breach of the implied warranty of merchantability. The defendants, referencing the fine-print on the back of the contract, argued that they disclaimed this warranty. At trial, the jury returned verdicts against both defendants, and defendants appealed.]

II. THE EFFECT OF THE DISCLAIMER AND LIMITATION OF LIABILITY CLAUSES ON THE IMPLIED WARRANTY OF MERCHANTABILITY.

[W]hat effect should be given to the express warranty in question which seeks to limit the manufacturer's liability to replacement of defective parts, and which disclaims all other warranties, express or implied? In assessing its significance we must keep in mind the general principle that, in the absence of fraud, one who does not choose to read a contract before signing it, cannot later relieve himself of its burdens. And in applying that principle, the basic tenet of freedom of competent parties to contract is a factor of importance. But in the framework of modern commercial life and business practices, such rules cannot be applied on a strict, doctrinal basis. The conflicting interests of the buyer and seller must be evaluated realistically and justly, giving due weight to the social policy evinced by the Uniform Sales Act [a precursor to Article 2 of the Uniform Commercial Code], the progressive decisions of the courts engaged in administering it, the mass production methods of manufacture and distribution to the public, and the bargaining position occupied by the ordinary consumer in such an economy. This history of the law shows that legal doctrines, as first expounded, often prove to be inadequate under the impact of later experience. In such case, the need for justice has stimulated the necessary qualifications or adjustments.

In these times, an automobile is almost as much a servant of convenience for the ordinary person as a household utensil. For a multitude of other persons it is a necessity. Crowded highways and filled parking lots are a commonplace of our existence. There is no need to look any farther than the daily newspaper to be convinced that when an automobile is defective, it has great potentiality for harm.

No one spoke more graphically on this subject than Justice Cardozo in the landmark case of *MacPherson v. Buick Motor Co.*, 217 N.Y. 382 (Ct. App. 1916):

> Beyond all question, the nature of an automobile gives warning of probable danger if its construction is defective. This automobile was designed to go 50 miles per hour. Unless its wheels were sound and strong, injury was almost certain. It was as much a thing of danger as a defective engine for a railroad. . . . The dealer was indeed the one person of whom it might be said with some approach to certainty that by him the car would not be used. . . . Precedents drawn from the days of travel by stagecoach do not fit the conditions of travel to-day. The principle that the danger must be imminent does not change, but the things subject to the principle do change. They are whatever the needs of life in a developing civilization require them to be.

In the 44 years that have intervened since that utterance, the average car has been constructed for almost double the speed mentioned; 60 miles per hour is permitted on our parkways. The number of automobiles in use has multiplied many times and the hazard to the user and the public has increased proportionately. The Legislature has intervened in the public interest, not only to regulate the manner of operation on the highway but also to require periodic inspection of motor vehicles and to impose a duty on manufacturers to adopt certain safety devices and methods in their construction. It is apparent that the public has an interest not only in the safe manufacture of automobiles, but also, as shown by the Sales Act, in protecting the rights and remedies of purchasers, so far as it can be accomplished consistently with our system of free enterprise. In a society such as ours, where the automobile is a common and necessary adjunct of daily life, and where its use is so fraught with danger to the driver, passengers and the public, the manufacturer is under a special obligation in connection with the construction, promotion and sale of his cars. Consequently, the courts must examine purchase agreements closely to see if consumer and public interests are treated fairly.

What influence should these circumstances have on the restrictive effect of Chrysler's express warranty in the framework of the purchase contract? As we have said, warranties originated in the law to safeguard the buyer and not to limit the liability of the seller or manufacturer. It seems obvious in this instance that the motive was to avoid the warranty obligations which are normally incidental to such sales. The language gave little and withdrew much. In return for the delusive remedy of replacement of defective parts at the factory, the buyer is said to have accepted the exclusion of the maker's liability for personal injuries arising from the breach of the warranty, and to have agreed to the elimination of any other express or implied warranty. An instinctively felt sense of justice cries out against such a sharp bargain. But does the doctrine that a person is bound by his signed agreement, in the absence of fraud, stand in the way of any relief?

In the modern consideration of problems such as this, Corbin suggests that practically all judges are "chancellors" and cannot fail to be influenced by any equitable doctrines that are available. And he opines that "there is sufficient flexibility in the concepts of fraud, duress, misrepresentation and undue influence, not to mention differences in economic bargaining power" to enable the courts to avoid enforcement of unconscionable provisions in long printed standardized contracts. 1 *Corbin on Contracts* (1950) § 128, p. 188. Freedom of contract is not such an immutable doctrine as to admit of no qualification in the area in which we are concerned. As Chief Justice Hughes said in his dissent in *Morehead v. People of State of New York ex rel. Tipaldo*, 298 U.S. 587, 627 (1936):

> We have had frequent occasion to consider the limitations on liberty of contract. While it is highly important to preserve that liberty from arbitrary and capricious interference, it is also necessary to prevent its abuse, as otherwise it could be used to override all public interests and thus in the end destroy the very freedom of opportunity which it is designed to safeguard.

That sentiment was echoed by Justice Frankfurter in his dissent in *United States v. Bethlehem Steel Corp.*, 315 U.S. 289, 326 (1942):

> It is said that familiar principles would be outraged if Bethlehem were denied recovery on these contracts. But is there any principle which is more familiar or more firmly embedded in the history of Anglo-American law than the basic doctrine that the courts will not permit themselves to be used as instruments of inequity and injustice? Does any principle in our law have more universal application than the doctrine that courts will not enforce transactions in which

> the relative positions of the parties are such that one has unconscionably taken advantage of the necessities of the other?
>
> These principles are not foreign to the law of contracts. Fraud and physical duress are not the only grounds upon which courts refuse to enforce contracts. The law is not so primitive that it sanctions every injustice except brute force and downright fraud. More specifically, the courts generally refuse to lend themselves to the enforcement of a "bargain" in which one party has unjustly taken advantage of the economic necessities of the other. . . .

The traditional contract is the result of free bargaining of parties who are brought together by the play of the market, and who meet each other on a footing of approximate economic equality. In such a society there is no danger that freedom of contract will be a threat to the social order as a whole. But in present-day commercial life the standardized mass contract has appeared. It is used primarily by enterprises with strong bargaining power and position. "The weaker party, in need of the goods or services, is frequently not in a position to shop around for better terms, either because the author of the standard contract has a monopoly (natural or artificial) or because all competitors use the same clauses. His contractual intention is but a subjection more or less voluntary to terms dictated by the stronger party, terms whose consequences are often understood in a vague way, if at all." Kessler, *Contracts of Adhesion—Some Thoughts About Freedom of Contract,* 43 Colum. L. Rev. 629, 632 (1943). Such standardized contracts have been described as those in which one predominant party will dictate its law to an undetermined multiple rather than to an individual. They are said to resemble a law rather than a meeting of the minds.

Vold, in the recent revision of his *Law of Sales* (2d ed. 1959) at page 447, wrote of this type of contract and its effect upon the ordinary buyer:

> In recent times the marketing process has been getting more highly organized than ever before. Business units have been expanding on a scale never before known. The standardized contract with its broad disclaimer clauses is drawn by legal advisers of sellers widely organized in trade associations. It is encountered on every hand. Extreme inequality of bargaining between buyer and seller in this respect is now often conspicuous. Many buyers no longer have any real choice in the matter. They must often accept what they can get though accompanied by broad disclaimers. The terms of these disclaimers deprive them of all substantial protection with regard to the quality of the goods. In effect, this is by force of contract between very unequal parties. It throws the risk of defective articles on the most dependent party. He has the least individual power to avoid the presence of defects. He also has the least individual ability to bear their disastrous consequences.

The warranty before us is a standardized form designed for mass use. It is imposed upon the automobile consumer. He takes it or leaves it, and he must take it to buy an automobile. No bargaining is engaged in with respect to it. In fact, the dealer through whom it comes to the buyer is without authority to alter it; his function is ministerial—simply to deliver it. The form warranty is not only standard with Chrysler but, as mentioned above, it is the uniform warranty of the Automobile Manufacturers Association. Members of the Association are: General Motors, Inc., Ford, Chrysler, Studebaker-Packard, American Motors, (Rambler), Willys Motors, Checker Motors Corp., and International Harvester Company. Of these companies, the 'Big Three' (General Motors, Ford, and Chrysler) represented 93.5% of the passenger-car production for 1958. . . .

The gross inequality of bargaining position occupied by the consumer in the automobile industry is thus apparent. There is no competition among the car makers in the area of the express warranty. Where can the buyer go to negotiate for better protection? Such control and limitation of his remedies are inimical to the public welfare and, at the very least, call for great care by the courts to avoid injustice through application of strict common-law principles of freedom of contract. Because there is no competition among the motor vehicle manufacturers with respect to the scope of protection guaranteed to the buyer, there is no incentive on their part to stimulate good will in that field of public relations. Thus, there is lacking a factor existing in more competitive fields, one which tends to guarantee the safe construction of the article sold. Since all competitors operate in the same way, the urge to be careful is not so pressing.

Although the courts, with few exceptions, have been most sensitive to problems presented by contracts resulting from gross disparity in buyer-seller bargaining positions, they have not articulated a general principle condemning, as opposed to public policy, the imposition on the buyer of a skeleton warranty as a means of limiting the responsibility of the manufacturer. They have endeavored thus far to avoid a drastic departure from age-old tenets of freedom of contract by adopting doctrines of strict construction, and notice and knowledgeable assent by the buyer to the attempted exculpation of the seller. Accordingly to be found in the cases are statements that disclaimers and the consequent limitation of liability will not be given effect if "unfairly procured," if not brought to the buyer's attention and he was not made understandingly aware of it, or if not clear and explicit. . . .

[The court then discussed a number of cases in which disclaimers of implied warranties that were not brought to the attention of purchasers were found to be not binding.]

It is undisputed that the president of the dealer with whom Henningsen dealt did not specifically call attention to the warranty on the back of the purchase order. The form and the arrangement of its face, as described above, certainly would cause the minds of reasonable men to differ as to whether notice of a yielding of basic rights stemming from the relationship with the manufacturer was adequately given. The words 'warranty' or 'limited warranty' did not even appear in the fine print above the place for signature, and a jury might well find that the type of print itself was such as to promote lack of attention rather than sharp scrutiny. . . .

But there is more than this. Assuming that a jury might find that the fine print referred to reasonably served the objective of directing a buyer's attention to the warranty on the reverse side, and, therefore, that he should be charged with awareness of its language, can it be said that an ordinary layman would realize what he was relinquishing in return for what he was being granted? . . . Any ordinary layman of reasonable intelligence, looking at the phraseology, might well conclude that Chrysler was agreeing to replace defective parts and perhaps replace anything that went wrong because of defective workmanship during the first 90 days or 4,000 miles of operation, but that he would not be entitled to a new car. It is not unreasonable to believe that the entire scheme being conveyed was a proposed remedy for physical deficiencies in the car. In the context of this warranty, only the abandonment of all sense of justice would permit us to hold that, as a matter of law, the phrase "its obligation under this warranty being limited to making good at its factory any part or parts thereof" signifies to an ordinary reasonable person that he is relinquishing any personal injury claim that might flow from the use of a defective automobile. Such claims are nowhere mentioned. The draftsmanship is reflective of the care and skill of the Automobile Manufacturers Association in undertaking to avoid warranty obligations without drawing too much attention to its effort in that regard. No one can doubt that if the will to do so were present, the ability to inform the buying public of the intention to disclaim liability for injury claims arising from breach of warranty would present no problem. . . .

The role of the courts

Would you agree with this court that the judiciary ought to "protect the ordinary man against the loss of important rights" against those with unequal bargaining power? Why or why not? How does Judge Francis' approach here compare to the approach advocated by Judge Easterbrook in cases like *Pro CD v. Zeidenberg* and *Hill v. Gateway?* Which approach is better, and why?

The task of the judiciary is to administer the spirit as well as the letter of the law. On issues such as the present one, part of that burden is to protect the ordinary man against the loss of important rights through what, in effect, is the unilateral act of the manufacturer. The status of the automobile industry is unique. Manufacturers are few in number and strong in bargaining position. In the matter of warranties on the sale of their products, the Automotive Manufacturers Association has enabled them to present a united front. From the standpoint of the purchaser, there can be no arms length negotiating on the subject. Because his capacity for bargaining is so grossly unequal, the inexorable conclusion which follows is that he is not permitted to bargain at all. He must take or leave the automobile on the warranty terms dictated by the maker. He cannot turn to a competitor for better security.

Public policy is a term not easily defined. Its significance varies as the habits and needs of a people may vary. It is not static and the field of application is an ever increasing one. A contract, or a particular provision therein, valid in one era may be wholly opposed to the public policy of another. Courts keep in mind the principle that the best interests of society demand that persons should not be unnecessarily restricted in their freedom to contract. But they do not hesitate to declare void as against public policy contractual provisions which clearly tend to the injury of the public in some way.

Public policy at a given time finds expression in the Constitution, the statutory law and in judicial decisions. In the area of sale of goods, the legislative will has imposed an implied warranty of merchantability as a general incident of sale of an automobile by description. The warranty does not depend upon the affirmative intention of the parties. It is a child of the law; it annexes itself to the contract because of the very nature of the transaction. The judicial process has recognized a right to recover damages for personal injuries arising from a breach of that warranty. The disclaimer of the implied warranty and exclusion of all obligations except those specifically assumed by the express warranty signify a studied effort to frustrate that protection. True, the Sales Act authorizes agreements between buyer and seller qualifying the warranty obligations. But quite obviously the Legislature contemplated lawful stipulations (which are determined by the circumstances of a particular case) arrived at freely by parties of relatively equal bargaining strength. The lawmakers did not authorize the automobile manufacturer to use its grossly disproportionate bargaining power to relieve itself from liability and to impose on the ordinary buyer, who in effect has no real freedom of choice, the grave danger of injury to himself and others that attends the sale of such a dangerous instrumentality as a defectively made automobile. In the framework of this case, illuminated as it is by the facts and the many decisions noted, we are of the opinion that Chrysler's attempted disclaimer of an implied warranty of merchantability and of the obligations arising therefrom is so inimical to the public good as to compel an adjudication of its invalidity. . . .

Under all of the circumstances outlined above, the judgments in favor of the plaintiffs and against the defendants are affirmed.

RELEVANT PROVISIONS

For the UCC, consult § 2-316.

NOTES AND QUESTIONS

1. What happened? Who sued whom for what? Procedurally, how did the case get before this court? Factually, what happened between the parties? What arguments did the plaintiff and defendant make? What rule or rules did the court apply? How did the court analyze the dispute between the parties? How did the court decide the case?

2. Was this case correctly decided? Do you agree with the result reached in this case? Why or why not? Do you agree with the court's reasoning? Why or why not? How, if at all, would you have written the opinion differently?

CONTRACTS OF FRUSTRATION*

Two factors combine to bring about the modern consumer's lack of effective legal power when be buys a product which is faulty but does not cause physical injury. Both of them stem from the fact that he is a little man in the scheme of things. First, there is an all-pervasive difficulty: our machinery of justice is simply not designed for easy use by the average citizen with a minor claim of any kind. If anything, it is designed to discourage him. He is not apt to know a lawyer and he does not particularly want to know one. And if he does muster up his courage and finds a lawyer, he will almost surely discover that his small claim is of no interest to that lawyer unless he is prepared to guarantee what to him will seem a preposterous sum. Even in those localities where small claims courts are supposed to be readily available, the use of the law remains a mysterious and a frightening prospect for the average citizen. It is especially frightening for the below-average citizen, for "the poor man looks upon the law as an enemy, not as a friend. For him the law is always taking something away."

The unavailability of simple process handicaps the little man regardless of the nature of his small claim, and it is handicap enough. But when he claims as a consumer against a seller, he encounters a second difficulty. Unless his claim is based on accidental injury to person or property caused by a defective product and is thus eligible for relief in tort, he claims in contract and must use a deck of doctrine that is stacked against him.

Most of his losing cards are colored "freedom of contract." Contract (says the jurisprudence) is a voluntary association, and the parties are therefore free within broad limits to adopt such terms as they see fit.[16] The reasonably equal bargaining power that is manifestly required to support this basic principle is presumed,[17] as is the fact that parties to a written agreement know, or ought to know, the terms of their agreement. The ultimate consumer faced with a defective appliance or product, is almost sure to find that his seller has taken full advantage of these presumptions. He will discover that the printed contract that he "made" with his dealer contained one or more variously labeled terms and conditions designed by lawyers to give the dealer and everyone above him in the distribution pipeline maximum protection against consumer claims. He has, in short, entered into what we have come to call a contract of adhesion. Professor Patterson, who coined the phrase in 1919 in an article discussing life insurance policies, described such a contract as one "drawn up by the insurer, and the insured, who merely 'adheres' to it, has little choice as to its terms." In less elegant but no less accurate language, a contract of adhesion is a contract that sticks the helpless consumer

* Excerpted from Addison Mueller, *Contracts of Frustration*, 78 YALE L.J. 576, 578-81 (1969).

16. "The law will not make a better contract for the parties than they themselves have seen fit to enter into, or alter it for the benefit of one party and to the detriment of the other. The judicial function of a court of law is to enforce a contract as it is written." Gummere, C.J., in *Kupfersmith v. Delaware Ins. Co.*, 86 A. 399, 401 (1913).

17. Perhaps the neatest, though oblique, expression of this presumption is the "rule" that the law will not question the adequacy of consideration. The presumption is, of course, rebuttable. *See* 1 A. CORBIN, CONTRACTS § 127, at 541 (1964).

with standard form clauses that he might not have agreed to if he had actually had free choice. Some of this printed boilerplate is apt to come in an envelope containing assorted other literature that is sealed in the carton or is taped to the chassis of the purchased equipment. In consequence it is seldom seen by the buyer until after delivery. Clearly, then, the buyer might persuasively claim that he cannot be bound by it because he never accepted it as part of his bargain. But it would make little practical difference if he not only saw it but read it and even understood it before his purchase. The result of an attempt on his part to reject it would be no purchase; it would be a rare and imaginative dealer indeed (to say nothing of a rare and imaginative customer) who would act in so non-institutional a fashion as to agree to a special warranty arrangement. Even if a dealer were willing to do so, his action would almost surely be held not to have involved the deeper pockets of his supplier or the manufacturer of the product.[21] And though theoretically the buyer could go elsewhere and buy from a merchant who did not so limit his obligations, he would almost certainly find that all competing goods were similarly limited.[22] So to turn the matter on the buyer's lack of knowledge would simply put dealers to the useless task of saying, "Look at this," before they say, "Sign here." A requirement that full disclosure be made concerning terms that can in fact be accepted or rejected is a meaningful and important element of contract law. But standard disclaimers and limitation of remedy clauses[23] such as make up the bulk of the printed boilerplate in contracts for the sale of consumer goods are not such choice-offering terms. The problem with such clauses is not lack of notice but lack of consumer power to bargain about them. The problem is that they are parts of contracts of adhesion.

21. Manufacturers' warranties usually state explicitly that a dealer is not authorized to alter or make additional warranties on behalf of the manufacturer. Such limitations should at least be given effect against a claim over by a dealer who is held to such altered or additional obligation by his customer. Whether a consumer should be entitled to claim directly against the manufacturer in such a case depends on whether an agency relationship (express or apparent) can reasonably be spelled out. The problem ties into that arising when a dealer warrants that a product is fit for a use not reasonably encompassed by the nature of the product. In such a case, a remote seller's defense of no privity to a consumer claim based on product failure under the stress of such special use makes some sense.

22. The clause limiting remedy to repair or replacement is now as much a fixture in business literature as those old friends the *force majeure* clause, the offer subject to prior sale and acceptance clause, standard invocations of the parol evidence rule, and "very truly yours." The feeling about them is that they—like so much contractual language—can do no harm and might do some good.

23. Broad disclaimers of warranty are frowned upon by the UCC; limitations of remedy, on the other hand, are encouraged. *Compare* UCC § 2-316 (exclusion or modification of warranties) *with* §§ 2-718 (liquidation or limitation of damages) *and* 2-719 (contractual modification or limitation of remedy).

c. Consumer Legislation

DOCTRINAL OVERVIEW: CONSUMER LEGISLATION*

The Uniform Commercial Code was not initially intended to deal with problems of consumer protection. . . . [However, i]ncreasing awareness of the need to protect contracting parties against unfair terms has . . . resulted in a plethora of other legislation, both state and federal, to supplement the protections afforded by the common law and the Uniform Commercial Code. Most of this legislation, such as the Uniform Consumer Credit Code, is designed to protect consumers, though other parties, such as franchisees, are protected under some federal and state statutes. The discussion here will be confined to consumer legislation.

In contrast with UCC 2-302, which condemns unconscionable terms in general, consumer legislation is usually directed at specific terms, such as finance charges or warranty disclaimers, singled out as likely to be unfair. Statutes deal with such terms in two principal ways. Some attempt to control the terms directly, by limiting the parties' freedom to determine them in a way unfavorable to the consumer. Others leave the parties free to determine the terms but attempt to give the consumer an informed choice as to whether to make the contract, by requiring that the terms be clearly disclosed in advance. Legislatures have sometimes delegated to government agencies some discretion in administering both types of statutes.

Most legislation designed to control terms has done so by specifying terms that are considered unfair and then prohibiting them. Classic examples are statutes that prohibit employers from fixing wages below a minimum level or prohibit public utilities from fixing rates above a maximum. Occasionally, however, legislation has taken a different course and has specified terms that are considered fair and then required them. A classic example is legislation prescribing standard terms for insurance policies.

Common examples of consumer legislation of this type include state statutes that prohibit provisions setting finance charges in excess of a specified rate, fixing balloon payments, or cutting off defenses on assignment. A few states have enacted statutes prohibiting disclaimers of implied warranties, such as the one attacked in *Henningsen*. Legislation requiring specified terms is less common, though a number of states have statutes providing for application of payments in such a way as to prevent sellers from such repossessions as took place in *Williams*.[12]

On the whole, however, legislatures have favored the second type of solution—disclosure of terms, rather than control of terms—as more consistent with a market economy. Given adequate information, the premise runs, a consumer will make an informed choice. It can he argued that elaborate and burdensome disclosure requirements tell the sophisticated consumer little that such a consumer

---

* Excerpted from E. ALLAN FARNSWORTH, CONTRACTS § 4.29 (4th ed. 2004).

12. *See* Uniform Consumer Credit Code § 3.303 (payments under debts secured by cross-collateral "deemed . . . to have been applied first to the payment of the debts arising from the sales first made").

does not already know and tell the unsophisticated consumer little that such a consumer can or will use. Nevertheless, disclosure requirements have proved an attractive compromise between the extremes of protection through control of terms and no protection at all. Two examples are especially significant.

The first is the Truth in Lending Act, enacted in 1968. It is designed to allow a consumer contemplating the purchase of goods or services on credit to make an informed choice as to whether to buy on credit and, if so, among sources of credit. It therefore requires a creditor, before extending credit to the consumer, to disclose any finance charge as an annual percentage rate, together with other essential terms.[16] It is essentially a disclosure statute, however, and leaves the creditor free to impose any charges for credit that state law permits.

Another federal disclosure statute is the Magnuson-Moss Act, enacted in 1975. It is designed to prevent a consumer who is contemplating the purchase of durable goods from being confused or misled as to the warranties of the manufacturer or seller. Where it applies, it controls if there is a conflict with the Uniform Commercial Code. It requires a supplier of a consumer product who gives a written warranty to designate it as either a "full" or a "limited" warranty.[18] In either case, the supplier cannot disclaim implied warranties; and, if the supplier designates a written warranty as "full," it must meet stated requirements, including an undertaking to provide a remedy without charge by repair, replacement, or refund. This act too is essentially a disclosure statute. Thus a supplier's written warranty need not conform to the requirements for a full warranty if it is designated as limited. Moreover, a supplier need not make any written warranty, and, if the supplier does not, the act does not limit the power to disclaim warranties.

Advocates of consumer legislation such as the Truth in Lending Act and the Magnuson-Moss Act have recognized the shortcomings of the conventional private lawsuit as a means of enforcement. The amount in dispute is often small, and many consumers are deterred from pursuing their rights by ignorance, apathy, and inability to pay for legal services. One kind of solution is to "sweeten the pot" by allowing the consumer a civil penalty or multiple (e.g., treble) damages and attorneys fees and other costs of litigation. Another is to give each consumer the support of others by allowing them to join with claimants similarly situated in a class action. Yet another is to reduce the cost of litigation by instituting a system of informal dispute-settlement procedures.

Beyond encouraging consumers to press their own claims, consumer legislation often provides for investigation and enforcement by the government. Thus a public official or agency may be empowered to enjoin violations and other objectionable practices or to seek criminal sanctions.

---

16. Truth in Lending Act §§ 127, 128.
18. Magnuson-Moss Act § 10.3. (This provision is limited to products costing more than $10.)

CHAPTER 7

PERFORMANCE AND BREACH

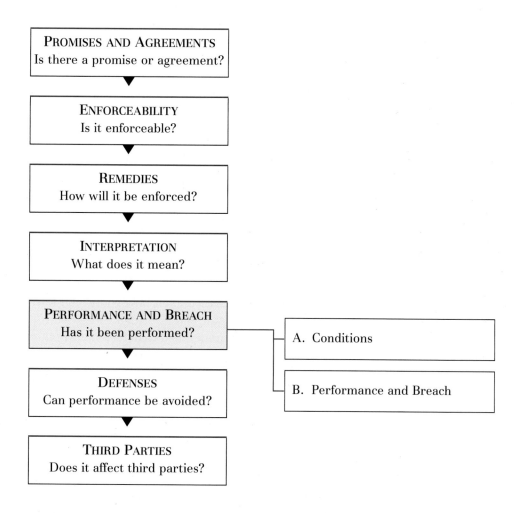

PROMISES AND AGREEMENTS
Is there a promise or agreement?

ENFORCEABILITY
Is it enforceable?

REMEDIES
How will it be enforced?

INTERPRETATION
What does it mean?

PERFORMANCE AND BREACH
Has it been performed?

- A. Conditions
- B. Performance and Breach

DEFENSES
Can performance be avoided?

THIRD PARTIES
Does it affect third parties?

The materials on interpretation in the previous chapter provide a nice segue into the materials in this chapter on performance and breach, because before a court can determine whether a breach has occurred, it must first identify, interpret, and fill in missing terms in the parties' agreement to see what a contract *means*. Only then can a court identify what rights and duties existed between the parties, which, in turn, enables it to determine whether the parties have or have not performed their obligations.

Indeed, we saw this principle in action in Chapter 2 when we examined the venerable case of *Jacob & Youngs v. Kent*. There, as you will recall, the question that confronted the court was whether the contractor's installation of nonconforming pipe (though of the same price and quality) constituted substantial performance, as the general contractor Jacob & Youngs argued, or whether it constituted material breach, as the homeowner Kent argued. But to determine whether Jacob & Youngs substantially performed or materially breached its obligations under the contract, we were interested in knowing whether Kent was bargaining for high-quality pipe, using the brand name "Reading Pipe" as a proxy for that quality, or whether he was bargaining for the brand name "Reading Pipe," perhaps (though unlikely) even without regard to its quality. In the absence of Kent's clear expression of intent that he was contracting for the brand "Reading Pipe," which he could have made clear by using "apt and certain words," the most likely scenario is that he was probably contracting for quality and price. And if he was contracting for quality and price, then Jacob & Youngs substantially performed (i.e., did not materially breach) its obligations under the contract. The problem of performance, in other words, is, in large part, a problem of contract *interpretation* (Chapter 6). And the problem of interpretation, in no small part, is a problem of figuring out what the parties *intended* when they entered into their agreement with one another in the first place (Chapter 3).

In the cases and materials that follow, we will explore more deeply the issue of material breach, and take a closer look at the circumstances that compel a court to determine when a party has (or has not) fulfilled its contractual obligations. As you read the cases below, try to ask yourself how you would have argued these issues to a court, or how you would have decided these issues if you were the judge. What test(s) would you have applied to determine whether or not the promisor's actions constituted performance or breach?

DOCTRINAL OVERVIEW: PERFORMANCE IN GENERAL*

When parties negotiate agreements, they usually assume that they will perform their obligations. Therefore they devote more attention to spelling out the required performances than to detailing what is to happen if those performances are not forthcoming. . . .

Frequently, then, it is left to the courts to determine the consequences of any nonperformance. Our focus here is on the rules courts fashion to deal with the nonperformance of bilateral contracts.

When parties make a bilateral contract, they exchange promises in the expectation of a subsequent exchange of performances. Although the consideration for each party's promise is the other party's return promise, each party enters into the transaction only because of the expectation that the return promise will be performed. The principal goal of the rules applicable to the performance stage of such contracts is to protect that expectation against a possible failure of the other party to perform. It would be possible, of course, to leave a party who has not received the expected performance to pursue a claim for damages. But the injured party bargained for performance rather than for a lawsuit. Therefore courts have developed rules to afford the injured party, in addition to any claim for damages, a variety of types of self-help, the most important of which is the right to suspend its own performance and ultimately to refuse to perform if the other party fails to perform.

In developing these rules, courts have relied on the concept of a *condition,* an event that must occur before performance of a contractual duty becomes due. In general, a party whose duty is conditioned on such an event is not required to perform unless the event has occurred. Suppose that the owner of a house pays $1,000 to an insurance company in return for the company's promise to pay the owner $100,000 if the house is destroyed by fire. The burning of the house is a condition of the company's duty to pay. If the house burns, payment becomes due; if it does not burn, payment does not become due.

By analogy to conditions, courts developed a concept of constructive (i.e., implied) conditions of exchange. To the extent practicable, a court will supply terms under which a party's duties are conditioned on the performance to be given in return. A party whose duty is in this way impliedly conditional on the other party's performance is afforded the security of not having to perform unless the other party has performed. Suppose that a house painter promises to paint a house in return for the owners promise to pay $1,000. Even though the language of the contract does not make the owner's promise to pay conditional on the painter's performance, it is impliedly conditional on that performance. If the painter paints the house, payment becomes due; if the painter does not paint it, payment does not become due. . . .

* Excerpted from E. ALLAN FARNSWORTH, CONTRACTS § 8.1 (4th ed. 2004).

A. CONDITIONS

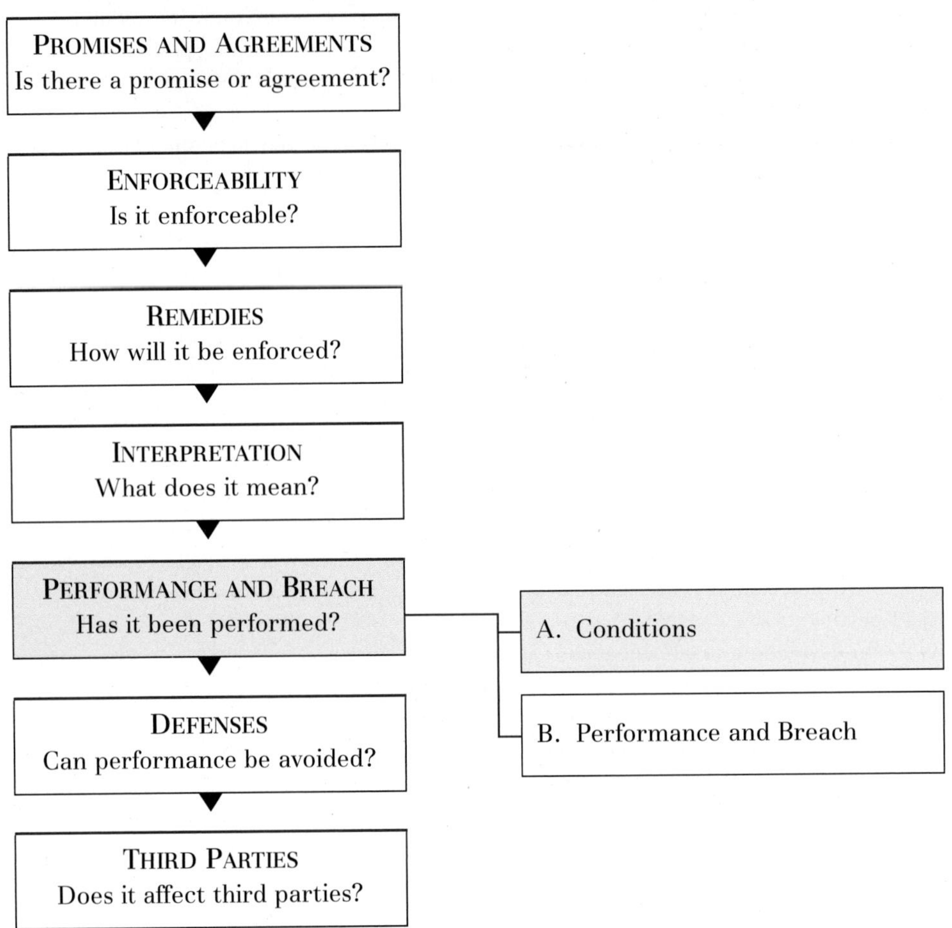

In this section, we will look at an extremely important area of contract law: the law of conditions. Specifically, after reading this section, you should have a good understanding of what conditions are, how they work, how to draft them, and, if need be, how to avoid them. Some of the topics we will cover include: the effects of condition, determining what events constitute conditions, and avoiding conditions through the doctrines of waiver, estoppel, and excuse.*

* You should note that the doctrines of waiver, estoppel, and excuse also could have been covered in Chapter 8 ("Defenses"), and should appear in both places (i.e., under "Conditions" and under "Defenses") in your outline for this course.

DOCTRINAL OVERVIEW: PERFORMANCE IN GENERAL*

Promises and the duties they generate can be either unconditional ("I promise to pay you $100,000") or conditional ("I promise to pay you $100,000 if your house burns down"). Lawyers use *condition* in several senses. Sometimes they use it to refer to the term in the agreement that makes the promise conditional. . . . However, lawyers also use *condition* to refer to an operative fact rather than to a term. According to the *Restatement Second* a condition is "an event, not certain to occur, which must occur, unless occurrence is excused, before performance under a contract becomes due."[2] This use of the word has the support of leading writers. . . .

Almost any event may be made a condition. The event may be largely within the control of the obligor, as when the owner of a house conditions the duty to pay for painting the house on the owner's "honest satisfaction" with the job. It may be largely within the control of the obligee, as when an insurer conditions its duty to pay for loss due to fire on the insureds furnishing proof of loss within 60 days of the loss. It may be largely within the control of a third person, as when a purchaser of a house conditions the promise to go through with the deal on a bank's approval of a mortgage application. Or it may be largely beyond the control of anyone, as when an insurer conditions its duty to pay under a fire insurance policy on damage as a result of fire. Each obligor comes under a duty as soon as the contract is made, but that duty is conditional. The obligor need not render performance until the occurrence of the event on which the obligor's duty is conditioned–the homeowner's honest satisfaction with the paint job, the insured's furnishing of proof of loss, the bank's approval of the mortgage application, or damage as a result of fire.

Although a condition is usually an event of significance to the obligor, this need not be the case. In exercising their freedom of contract the parties are not fettered by any test of materiality or reasonableness. If they agree, they can make even an apparently insignificant event a condition. . . .

UNDERSTANDING AND CLASSIFYING CONDITIONS†

The word "condition" is used in the law of property as well as in the law of contract and it is used with some variation in meaning. In the law of contract it is sometimes used in a very loose sense as synonymous with "term," "provision,"

---

* Excerpted from E. ALLAN FARNSWORTH, CONTRACTS § 8.2 (4th ed. 2004).

2. *Restatement Second* § 224. . . . For a less precise definition based on The Cat in the Hat by Dr. Seuss, *see* Northern Heel Corp. v. Compo Indus., 851 F.2d 456 (1st Cir. 1988) (defining condition as "something (Thing One) which, by its terms, is made a condition to the performance of some corresponding obligation (Thing Two) by the other party, as where the latter agrees to do Thing Two if the former shall carry out Thing One").

† Excerpted from Arthur Corbin, *Conditions in the Law of Contracts*, 28 YALE L.J. 739, 743-44 (1969).

or "clause." In such a sense it performs no useful service; instead, it affords one more opportunity for slovenly thinking. In its proper sense the word *"condition" means some operative fact subsequent to acceptance and prior to discharge*, a fact upon which the rights and duties of the parties depend. Such a fact may be an act of one of the two contracting parties, an act of a third party, or any other fact of our physical world. It may be a performance that has been promised or a fact as to which there is no promise.

It will be observed that any operative fact may with some propriety be said to be a cause or condition of the legal relations that are consequent thereon. This does not mean that these legal relations will infallibly follow the existence of this fact irrespective of its combination with other antecedent facts; but it does mean that with the same combination of antecedent facts legal relations will infallibly result. An offer is a cause (or condition) of the power in the offeree. An acceptance is a cause (or condition) of contractual rights and duties. Nevertheless in contract law it is not common to speak of these facts as conditions, although such usage is not unknown. The term condition is more properly restricted to facts subsequent to acceptance and prior to discharge.

Express, implied and constructive conditions. A certain fact may operate as a condition, because the parties intended that it should and said so in words.[9] It is then an express condition. It may operate as a condition because the parties intended that it should, such intention being reasonably inferable from conduct other than words. It is then a condition implied in fact. Lastly, it may operate as a condition because the court believes that the parties would have intended it to operate as such if they had thought about it at all, or because the court believes that by reason of the *mores* of the time justice requires that it should so operate. It may then be described as a condition implied by law, or better as a *constructive condition*.

In addition to classifying conditions by how they are *created* (expressly, impliedly, and constructively), we can also classify them according to how they *operate* to alter legal relationships. Here, once again, we can classify conditions into three different categories: conditions *precedent*, conditions *concurrent*, and conditions *subsequent*. What's the difference? Let's start with some definitions.

We can define a condition precedent as "an operative fact that must exist prior to the existence of some legal relation in which we are interested,"* a condition subsequent as "an operative fact that causes the termination of some previous legal relation in which we are interested,"† and where "the performances of the two parties are required to be concurrent in time and neither party can

9. If they used words that are now interpreted by the court as creating a condition, but in fact the parties did not intend the words to be thus interpreted, the condition is *express* even though it was *unintended*.

* Arthur L. Corbin, *Conditions in the Law of Contract*, 28 YALE L.J. 739, 747 (1919).

† *Id.*

be charged with a breach until after a tender of performance by the other, both promises are dependent and the conditions are said to be concurrent."*

There's quite a bit of information packed into that last paragraph, but if you recall that all presently-existing legal relationships must be either (1) right/duty or (2) privilege/no right relationships,† then the definitions above fall into place quite nicely. To see how, let's recast the definition of a condition precedent into Hohfeldian terms. Doing so, we might rewrite our definition to say something like the following: A condition precedent is an operative fact that, once triggered, converts a presently-existing privilege/no right relationship into a right/duty relationship (or vice versa). How, exactly, does it do this? An example should help clarify things.

Right now, I have the privilege of not buying your car, and you have no right to force me to do so. The legal relationship existing between us is therefore a privilege/no right relationship. Suppose, however, that you offer to sell your car to me for $10,000. Your offer has created in me the power‡ to convert our privilege/no right relationship into a right/duty relationship through the operative fact of acceptance (i.e., by accepting your offer, I would now have the right to buy—and you would have the corresponding duty to sell—your car for $10,000). But what if I'm not ready to take this step just yet? Suppose I want to accept your offer, but I'm worried about financing, and don't want to be bound if I can't pay. What can I do? One idea is to make my promise *conditional* on financing, by saying something like "I accept your offer subject to the bank approving a $10,000 loan." If you agree, we've now added a condition precedent to our contract. Only if this condition is triggered (i.e., only if the bank approves the loan—the operative fact) will our previous privilege/no right relationship be converted into a right/duty relationship. If the bank does not approve the loan, I am privileged to simply walk away from the transaction, and you have no right to take any legal action against me for doing so.

Drafting Exercise: The example above should help illustrate the tremendous power of conditions as a risk-allocation device. Can you see how I used the condition precedent to allocate the risk that *I* wouldn't get financing to *you*? Without that clause, the risk of not obtaining financing would have fallen on *me* (i.e., if I couldn't obtain a loan and therefore didn't buy your car after agreeing to do so, a court would have found *me* in breach). So, now that you know a bit about how conditions work, you shouldn't let me have all the fun. Try to come up with a few examples of your own (like the car example above) and then recast the definitions of both (1) conditions concurrent and (2) conditions

* *Id.* at 751. *See also* 6 SAMUEL WILLISTON, CONTRACTS § 832 (3d ed. 1961). "It is one of the consequences of concurrent conditions that a situation may arise where no right of action ever arises against either party. Since a conditional tender is necessary to put either party in default, so long as both parties remain inactive, neither is liable and neither has acquired a right of action."

† *See* "Thinking Tool: Thinking Clearly About Legal Relationships", p. 96, *supra*.

‡ Which means that you have the corresponding liability. *Id.*

subsequent into Hohfeldian terms, using the paragraphs above as a guide. This exercise should not only help you grasp the material in this chapter, but will get you thinking about the power of conditions as a risk-allocation device, an important fact that should come in handy whenever you negotiate or draft contracts.

1. Conditions in General

> *Since an express condition, like a condition implied in fact, depends for its validity on the manifested intention of the parties, it has the same sanctity as the promise itself. Though the court may regret the harshness of such a condition, as it may regret the harshness of a promise, it must, nevertheless, generally enforce the will of the parties unless to do so would violate public policy.*
>
> Samuel Williston, CONTRACTS, Vol. 5, § 6-619 (3d ed. 1961)

In the cases and materials in this unit, we will explore the law of conditions in some detail by examining how conditions differ from promises, and how the legal effect of the non-fulfilment of a condition differs from the legal effect of the non-fulfillment of a promise.

Luttinger v. Rosen

Supreme Court of Connecticut
316 A.2d 757 (1972)

LOISELLE, ASSOCIATE JUSTICE. The plaintiffs contracted to purchase for $85,000 premises in the city of Stamford owned by the defendants and paid a deposit of $8500. The contract was "subject to and conditional upon the buyers obtaining first mortgage financing on said premises from a bank or other lending institution in an amount of $45,000 for a term of not less than twenty (20) years and at an interest rate which does not exceed 8½ percent per annum." The plaintiffs agreed to use due diligence in attempting to obtain such financing. The parties further agreed that if the plaintiffs were unsuccessful in obtaining financing as provided in the contract, and notified the seller within a specific time, all sums paid on the contract would be refunded and the contract terminated without further obligation of either party.

In applying for a mortgage which would satisfy the contingency clause in the contract, the plaintiffs relied on their attorney who applied at a New Haven lending institution for a $45,000 loan at 8¼ percent per annum interest over a period of twenty-five years. The plaintiffs' attorney knew that this lending institution was the only one which at that time would lend as much $45,000 on a mortgage for a single-family dwelling. A mortgage commitment was obtained for $45,000 with "interest at the prevailing rate at the time of closing but not less than 8¾%." Since this commitment failed to meet the contract requirement, timely notice was given to the defendants and demand was made for the return of the down payment. The defendants' counsel thereafter offered to make up the difference between the interest rate offered by the bank and the 8 1/2 percent rate provided in the contract for the entire twenty-five years by a funding arrangement, the exact terms of which were not defined. The plaintiffs did not accept this offer and on the defendants' refusal to return the deposit an action was brought. From a judgment rendered in favor of the plaintiffs the defendants have appealed.

The defendants claim that the plaintiffs did not use due diligence in seeking a mortgage within the terms specified in the contract. The unattacked findings by the court establish that the plaintiffs' attorney was fully informed as to the conditions and terms of mortgages being granted by various banks and lending institutions in and out of the area and that the application was made to the only bank which might satisfy the mortgage conditions of the contingency clause at that time. These findings adequately support the court's conclusion that due diligence was used in seeking mortgage financing in accordance with the contract provisions. . . . The defendants assert that notwithstanding the plaintiffs' reliance on their counsel's knowledge of lending practices, applications should have been made to other lending institutions. This claim is not well taken. The law does not require the performance of a futile act. . . .

The remaining assignment of error briefed by the defendants is that the court erred in concluding that the mortgage contingency clause of the contract, a condition precedent, was not met and, therefore, the plaintiffs were entitled to recover their deposit. "A condition precedent is a fact or event which the parties intend must exist or take place before there is a right to performance." *Lach v. Cahill*, 138 Conn. 418, 421. . . . In this case the language of the contract is unambiguous and clearly indicates that the parties intended that the purchase of the defendants' premises be conditioned on the obtaining by the plaintiffs of a mortgage as specified in the contract. From the subordinate facts found the court could reasonably conclude that since the plaintiffs were unable to obtain a $45,000 mortgage at no more than 8 1/2 percent per annum interest "from a bank or other lending institution" the condition precedent to performance of the contract was not met and the plaintiffs were entitled to the refund of their deposit. Any additional offer by the defendants to fund the difference in interest payments could be rejected by the plaintiffs. . . . There was no error in the court's exclusion of testimony relating to the additional offer since the offer was obviously irrelevant.

There is no error.

NOTES AND QUESTIONS

1. *What happened?* Who sued whom for what? Procedurally, how did the case get before this court? Factually, what happened between the parties? What arguments did the plaintiff and defendant make? What rule or rules did

the court apply? How did the court analyze the dispute between the parties? How did the court decide the case?

2. ***Was this case correctly decided?*** Do you agree with the result reached in this case? Why or why not? Do you agree with the court's reasoning? Why or why not? How, if at all, would you have written the opinion differently?

3. ***Promise versus condition.*** In your own words, how would you distinguish between a promise and a condition? Legally speaking, how is the non-performance of a promise different from a non-satisfaction of a condition?

PROBLEM: MUST THE BUYER BUY?

On January 1, Deborah entered into a written contract to sell Patricia real estate for $105,000. The agreement contained a clause conditioning Patricia's obligation to purchase on her obtaining a thirty-year, $84,000 first mortgage at prevailing interest rates. This clause also required Patricia to make immediate application for the loan and to pursue the application with diligence. Further, pursuant to the contract, Patricia had until January 31 to obtain such a commitment or to inform Deborah that the commitment was not received.*

Patricia applied for the mortgage at a bank, but was turned down because the amount requested was excessive in view of the bank's appraisal of the property of $100,000. The bank, however, approved an $80,000 mortgage.

Patricia requested either an extension of time within which to obtain a mortgage commitment which met the terms of the agreement or a reduction in the purchase price to reflect the bank's appraisal. Deborah refused the plaintiff's requests. When the three weeks expired, the plaintiff timely requested that her deposit be returned. The defendant refused.

How should the court rule, and why?

---

* The clause in full provided as follows: "This agreement is contingent upon the Buyer obtaining a commitment for a loan, to be secured by a first mortgage on the premises in the amount of $84,000, at prevailing % interest per annum, to be amortized over a 30 year term and to be on such other terms and conditions, including prepayment limitations, institutional financing charges and interest rate charges, as are imposed by any lending institution where the Buyer makes application for such a loan at the time the Buyer makes such application. The Buyer agrees to make immediate application for such a loan and to pursue said application with diligence. In the event such commitment is not obtained by the Buyer on or before April 30, 1979, the Buyer, to take advantage of this contingency, must cause notice of the Buyer's inability to obtain such a commitment to be given to the Seller, by the Buyer's Attorney. Receipt of such notice by the Seller shall constitute receipt by the Seller of such notice. If the Seller does not receive such notice prior to 5:00 p.m. on said date, this agreement shall remain in full force and effect as if this paragraph had not been included herein. If the Seller does receive such notice prior to 5:00 p.m., on said date, The Seller shall return to the Buyer all sums paid hereunder without interest thereon, and upon receipt of said sums by the Buyer this agreement shall terminate and be of no further force or effect and the Buyer and Seller shall be discharged of all liability, each to the other, hereunder."

Howard v. Federal Crop Insurance Corp.

United States Court of Appeals, Fourth Circuit
540 F.2d 695 (1976)

WIDENER, **Circuit Judge**. Plaintiff-appellants sued to recover for losses to their 1973 tobacco crop due to alleged rain damage. The crops were insured by defendant-appellee, Federal Crop Insurance Corporation (FCIC). . . . The district court granted summary judgment for the defendant and dismissed all three actions. We remand for further proceedings. . . .

Federal Crop Insurance Corporation, an agency of the United States, in 1973, issued three policies to the Howards, insuring their tobacco crops, to be grown on six farms, against weather damage and other hazards.

The Howards (plaintiffs) established production of tobacco on their acreage, and have alleged that their 1973 crop was extensively damaged by heavy rains, resulting in a gross loss to the three plaintiffs in excess of $35,000. The plaintiffs harvested and sold the depleted crop and timely filed notice and proof of loss with FCIC, but, prior to inspection by the adjuster for FCIC, the Howards had either plowed or disked under the tobacco fields in question to prepare the same for sowing a cover crop of rye to preserve the soil. When the FCIC adjuster later inspected the fields, he found the stalks had been largely obscured or obliterated by plowing or disking and denied the claims, apparently on the ground that the plaintiffs had violated a portion of the policy which provides that the stalks on any acreage with respect to which a loss is claimed shall not be destroyed until the corporation makes an inspection.

The holding of the district court is best capsuled in its own words:

> The inquiry here is whether compliance by the insureds with this provision of the policy was a condition precedent to the recovery. The court concludes that it was and that the failure of the insureds to comply worked a forfeiture of benefits for the alleged loss.

There is no question but that apparently after notice of loss was given to defendant, but before inspection by the adjuster, plaintiffs plowed under the tobacco stalks and sowed some of the land with a cover crop, rye. The question is whether, under paragraph 5(f) of the tobacco endorsement to the policy of insurance, the act of plowing under the tobacco stalks forfeits the coverage of the policy. Paragraph 5 of the tobacco endorsement is entitled *Claims*. Pertinent to this case are subparagraphs 5(b) and 5(f), which are as follows:

> 5(b) *It shall be a condition precedent* to the payment of any loss that the insured establish the production of the insured crop on a unit and that such loss has been directly caused by one or more of the hazards insured against during the insurance period for the crop year for which the loss is claimed, and furnish any other information regarding the manner and extent of loss as may be required by the Corporation. (Emphasis added)
>
> 5(f) The tobacco stalks on any acreage of tobacco of types 11a, 11b, 12, 13, or 14 with respect to which a loss is claimed *shall not be destroyed until the Corporation makes an inspection.* (Emphasis added)

The arguments of both parties are predicated upon the same two assumptions. First, if subparagraph 5(f) creates a condition precedent, its violation caused a forfeiture of plaintiffs' coverage. Second, if subparagraph 5(f) creates an obligation (variously called a promise or covenant) upon plaintiffs not to plow under the tobacco stalks, defendant may recover from plaintiffs (either in an original action, or, in this case, by a counterclaim, or as a matter of defense) for whatever damage it sustained because of the elimination of the stalks. However, a violation of subparagraph 5(f) would not, under the second premise, standing alone, cause a forfeiture of the policy.

Generally accepted law provides us with guidelines here. There is a general legal policy opposed to forfeitures. Insurance policies are generally construed most strongly against the insurer. When it is doubtful whether words create a promise or a condition precedent, they will be construed as creating a promise. The provisions of a contract will not be construed as conditions precedent in the absence of language plainly requiring such construction.

> ***Promise or condition?***
>
> Here, the court states a strong policy preference for interpreting ambiguous language as a promise rather than as a condition. Similarly, when we examined *Jacob & Youngs v. Kent* in Chapter 2 (which we will turn to again in the following subsection), we saw a similar preference stated by Judge Cardozo, who stated that if parties intended their language to operate as a condition rather than a promise, they ought to have used "apt and certain words to effectuate a purpose that performance of every term shall be a condition of recovery." Absent such an expression, courts were more likely to interpret such terms as promises. Do you agree that there should be a presumption in favor of construing ambiguous language as promissory rather than conditional, and what do you suppose accounts for this strong policy preference against interpreting contract language as conditional?

Plaintiffs rely most strongly upon the fact that the term "condition precedent" is included in subparagraph 5(b) but not in subparagraph 5(f). It is true that whether a contract provision is construed as a condition or an obligation does not depend entirely upon whether the word "condition" is expressly used. However, the persuasive force of plaintiffs' argument in this case is found in the use of the term "condition precedent" in subparagraph 5(b) but not in subparagraph 5(f). Thus, it is argued that the ancient maxim to be applied is that the expression of one thing is the exclusion of another.

The defendant places principal reliance upon the decision of this court in *Fidelity-Phenix Fire Insurance Company v. Pilot Freight Carriers*, 193 F.2d 812 (4th Cir. 1952). Suit there was predicated upon a loss resulting from theft out of a truck covered by defendant's policy protecting plaintiff from such a loss. The insurance company defended upon the grounds that the plaintiff had left the truck unattended without the alarm system being on. The policy contained six paragraphs limiting coverage. Two of those imposed what was called a "condition precedent." They largely related to the installation of specified safety equipment. Several others, including paragraph 5, pertinent in that case, started with the phrase, "It is further warranted." In paragraph 5, the insured warranted that the alarm system would be on whenever the vehicle was left unattended. Paragraph 6 starts with the language: "The assured agrees, by acceptance of this policy, that the foregoing conditions precedent relate to matters material to the acceptance of the risk by the insurer." Plaintiff recovered in the district court, but judgment on its behalf was reversed because of a breach of warranty of paragraph 5, the truck had been left unattended with the alarm off. In that case, plaintiff relied upon the fact that the words "condition precedent" were used in some of the paragraphs but the word "warranted" was used in the paragraph in issue. In rejecting that contention, this court said that "warranty" and "condition precedent" are often used interchangeably to create a condition of the insured's promise, and "manifestly the terms 'condition precedent' and 'warranty' were intended to have the same meaning and effect." 193 F.2d at 816.

Fidelity-Phenix thus does not support defendant's contention here. Although there is some resemblance between the two cases, analysis shows that the issues are actually entirely different. Unlike the case at bar, each paragraph in *Fidelity-Phenix* contained either the term "condition precedent" or the term "warranted." We held that, in that situation, the two terms had the same effect in that they both involved forfeiture. That is well established law. In the case at bar, the term "warranty" or "warranted" is in no way involved, either in terms or by way of like language, as it was in *Fidelity-Phenix*. The issue upon which this case turns, then, was not involved in *Fidelity-Phenix*.

The *Restatement of the Law of Contracts* states:

> § 261. INTERPRETATION OF DOUBTFUL WORDS AS PROMISE OR CONDITION.
> Where it is doubtful whether words create a promise or an express condition, they are interpreted as creating a promise; but the same words may sometimes mean that one party promises a performance and that the other party's promise is conditional on that performance.

Two illustrations (one involving a promise, the other a condition) are used in the *Restatement*:

> 2. A, an insurance company, issues to B a policy of insurance containing promises by A that are in terms conditional on the happening of certain events. The policy contains this clause: "provided, in case differences shall arise touching any loss, *the matter shall be submitted to impartial arbitrators*, whose award shall be binding on the parties." This is a promise to arbitrate and does not make an award a condition precedent of the insurer's duty to pay.
>
> 3. A, an insurance company, issues to B an insurance policy in usual form containing this clause: "In the event of disagreement as to the amount of loss it shall be ascertained by two appraisers and an umpire. The loss shall *not be payable until 60 days after the award of the appraisers when such an appraisal is required*." This provision is not merely a promise to arbitrate differences but makes an award a condition of the insurer's duty to pay in case of disagreement. (Emphasis added)

We believe that subparagraph 5(f) in the policy here under consideration fits illustration 2 rather than illustration 3. Illustration 2 specifies something to be done, whereas subparagraph 5(f) specifies something not to be done. Unlike illustration 3, subparagraph 5(f) does not state any conditions under which the insurance shall "not be payable," or use any words of like import. We hold that the district court erroneously held, on the motion for summary judgment, that subparagraph 5(f) established a condition precedent to plaintiffs' recovery which forfeited the coverage.[2] . . . Nothing we say here should preclude FCIC from asserting as a defense that the plowing or disking under of the stalks caused damage to FCIC if, for example, the amount of the loss was thereby made more difficult or impossible to ascertain whether the plowing or disking under was done with bad purpose or innocently. To repeat, our narrow holding is that merely plowing or disking under the stalks does not of itself operate to forfeit coverage under the policy.

The case is remanded for further proceedings not inconsistent with this opinion.

Vacated and Remanded.

RELEVANT PROVISIONS

For the *Restatement (Second) of Contracts*, consult § 2-227. For the UCC, consult § 2-615.

NOTES AND QUESTIONS

1. ***What happened?*** Who sued whom for what? Procedurally, how did the case get before this court? Factually, what happened between the parties? What arguments did the plaintiff and defendant make? What rule or rules did the court apply? How did the court analyze the dispute between the parties? How did the court decide the case?

2. ***Was this case correctly decided?*** Do you agree with the result reached in this case? Why or why not? Do you agree with the court's reasoning? Why or why not? How, if at all, would you have written the opinion differently?

3. ***Consequences?*** What consequence would have followed if the court interpreted clause 5(f) as a condition rather than a promise? Because the court interpreted clause 5(f) as a promise, how much will the promisor (FCIC) have to pay?

4. ***Drafting.*** In the previous case, you saw how the interpretation of language as a condition, rather than a promise, would have had particularly severe consequences for the promisee. If you were representing the promisor, how would you redraft this language to ensure that it would be construed by a court as a condition rather than a promise?

---

2. The district court also referred to subparagraph 5(f) as a condition subsequent. The difference in terminology is of no consequence here. [These terms of often used interchangeably, but incorrectly. Other cases will further elucidate this point, and it is likely to be the subject of substantial class discussion.—Ed.]

5. *Counseling.* In light of this case, what advice would you give to future clients in the promisee's and promisor's condition?

PROBLEM: LET'S HAVE A BALL

Plaintiff Solid Concepts, LLC invested in "The African & International Friends Inaugural Ball" ("Ball") that was to be held on January 20, 2009, to commemorate the inauguration of President Barack Obama. Defendant Gaylord National, LLC ("Gaylord") owns and operates the Gaylord National Resort and Convention Center where the Ball was to be held. On December 26, 2008, at the direction and insistence of a group who organized the Ball ("Organizers"), Plaintiff entered into the Inaugural Ball Gaylord National Hotel Block Contract (the "contract") with Gaylord to reserve a block of 500 rooms at the Convention Center for January 20 and 21, 2009. Plaintiff paid a non-refundable deposit of $1,000,000, one hundred percent of the full amount, to reserve the rooms, with the understanding that Organizers would resell the rooms as part of sponsorship packages for the Ball and repay Plaintiff double its investment. Ultimately the entirety of Plaintiff's block of rooms was not reserved by guests of the Ball, and Plaintiff alleges that its 500 reserved rooms were sold to other guests by Gaylord National. Plaintiff is suing Organizers in a separate action, but here files a complaint against Defendant Gaylord National for breach of contract and unjust enrichment.

Defendant Gaylord moves to dismiss the complaint, arguing that Plaintiff did not contract to reserve specific, identifiable pre-assigned rooms, but rather that the contract specified that Gaylord would make 500 rooms available to any of Plaintiff's guests upon their arrival at the hotel. Consequently, because none of Plaintiff's guests showed up to the hotel and were denied rooms, Gaylord never breached the contract. More specifically, Gaylord maintains that the contract contained an implied (but necessary) condition precedent to the hotel's obligation to furnish an actual room for occupancy—namely, that a guest had to present himself or herself at the hotel with a reservation and demand to occupy a room. Gaylord argues that because Plaintiff never alleged that any guests completed this condition precedent, Gaylord's duty to perform was not triggered and a breach of the contract never occurred.

Should the court imply a condition precedent? Why or why not?

DISTINGUISHING BETWEEN PROMISES AND CONDITIONS*

The purpose of a promise is the creation of a duty or a disability in the promisor;[13] the purpose of constituting some fact as a condition is always the postponement of an instant duty (or other specified legal relation). The fulfilment of a promise

* Excerpted from Arthur Corbin, *Conditions in the Law of Contracts*, 28 YALE L.J. 739, 745-46 (1969).

discharges a duty; the occurrence of a condition creates a duty. The non-fulfilment of a promise is called a breach of contract, and creates in the other party a secondary right to damages; it is the failure to perform that which was required by a previous duty. The non-occurrence of a condition will prevent the existence of a duty in the other party. . . .

Of course a contract can be so constructed as to create a duty that the fact operative as a condition shall come into existence. . . . Such a condition might be described as a promissory condition.

It may be observed that both a promise and a condition are means that are used to bring about certain desired action by another person. For example, an insurance company desires the payment of premiums. One means of securing this desired object would be to obtain a promise by the insured to pay premiums; on failure to pay them an action would lie. In fact, however, insurance policies seldom contain such a promise; the payment of the premiums is secured in a more effective way than that. The insurance company makes its own duty to pay the amount of the policy expressly conditional upon the payment of premiums. Here is no express promise of the insured creating a duty to pay premiums, but there is an express condition precedent to his right to recover on the policy. Payment by the insured is obtained not by holding a lawsuit over him *in terrorem* but by hanging before him a purse of money to be reached only by climbing the ladder of premiums. Before bilateral contracts became enforceable this was the only contractual way for a promisor to secure his desired object. He might offer his promise and specify the desired performance as the one mode of acceptance; or he might deliver his own sealed promise, making it expressly conditional upon the desired performance. In either case the promisee would have no legal right against the promisor, and could not get the purse of money, unless he first performed as desired. But as soon as bilateral contracts (mutual promises creating mutual duties) became enforceable, the courts observed that a promisor now had a new remedy and a new means of securing his desired object. Previously, in getting a return promise he got nothing; now he got a legally enforceable right. Hence, it did not appear unjust to declare mutual promises to be independent, and to compel a defendant to perform as he had agreed even though the plaintiff had failed to perform his part; the defendant had a like remedy in his turn against the plaintiff. It gradually became evident, however, that the contracting parties usually made no conscious choice of remedies, choosing the remedy on a promise rather than the advantage given by a condition. Often the remedy on a promise is very inadequate, and it is not surprising that the courts reverted to the earlier form. At first they seized upon such words as "for" and "in consideration of," construing these to create express conditions. Later, by reading wholly between the lines, they found a supposed intention of the parties that the defendant's promise should be conditional, or in the absence of any intention whatever they frankly constructed a condition in order to do justice according to the *mores* of the time. Thus grew up the rules of law concerning implied and constructive conditions.

2. Constructive Conditions

You can always imply a condition in a contract. But why do you imply it? It is because of some belief as to the practice of the community or of a class, or because of some opinion as to policy, or, in short, because of some attitude of yours upon a matter not capable of exact quantitative measurement, and therefore not capable of founding exact logical conclusions. Such matters really are battle grounds where the means do not exist for determinations that shall be good for all time, and where the decision can do no more than embody the preference of a given body at a given time and place. We do not realize how large a part of our law is open to reconsideration upon a slight change in the habit of the public mind.

Justice Holmes, *The Path of the Law,* 10 HARV. L. REV. 466 (1897)

Where . . . the law itself has imposed the condition, in absence of or irrespective of the manifested intention of the parties, it can deal with its creation as it pleases, shaping the boundaries of the constructive condition in such a way as to do justice and avoid hardship.

SAMUEL WILLISTON, CONTRACTS § 6-619, Vol. 5 (3d ed. 1961)

DOCTRINAL OVERVIEW: CONSTRUCTIVE CONDITIONS*

If the only consequence of a party's nonperformance were liability for breach of contract, a party to a bilateral contract would have little assurance of receiving the promised return performance. If the other party failed to perform, the injured party would still be bound to perform. If the builder failed to build the house, the owner would still be bound to pay the price. The injured party would have a remedy for breach, but this remedy might be no more than a claim for damages, collectible only after much delay. Were the injured party to refuse to perform in response to the other party's breach, the injured party would be exposed to a claim for damages that might exceed the injured party's own claim.

[Indeed, in early English law, courts routinely held that a party's promised performance was independent of (or not conditioned on) the other party's performance. Thus, for example, an employee could sue his employer for wages owed without first performing the work that was promised,[†] or a seller could sue a buyer for the purchase price of a cow without first delivering the cow.[‡]] The cases that applied this literalistic solution were later said by an English judge to "outrage common sense,"[7] but English courts applied it for over a century and a half, sometimes softening it by finding that the parties had expressed a condition in their agreement.

It was left to Lord Mansfield to set the law right in the great case *of Kingston v. Preston,* decided by the Court of King's Bench in 1773. . . .

---

* Excerpted from E. ALLAN FARNSWORTH, CONTRACTS § 8.9 (4th ed. 2004).

† Anon, Y.B. 15 Hen. VII, fo. 10b, pl. 17 (1500) (Fineux, C.J.).

‡ *Nichols v. Raynbred,* 80 Eng. Rep. 238 (K.B. 1615).

7. Lord Kenyon in Goodisson v. Nunn. 100 Eng. Rep. 1288, 1289 (K.B. 1792).

Kingston v. Preston

Court of King's Bench
99 Eng. Rep. 437 (1773)

It was an action of debt, for non-performance of covenants contained in certain articles of agreement between the plaintiff and the defendant.

The declaration stated: [1] [t]hat, by articles made the 24th of March, 1770, the plaintiff, for the considerations therein-after mentioned, covenanted, with the defendant, to serve him for one year and a quarter next ensuing, as a covenant-servant, in his trade of a silk-mercer, at £200 a year, and in consideration of the premises, the defendant covenanted, that at the end of the year and a quarter, he would give up his business of a mercer to the plaintiff, and a nephew of the defendant, or some other person to be nominated by the defendant, and give up to them his stock in trade, at a fair valuation; and [2] that, between the young traders, deeds of partnership should be executed for 14 years, and from and immediately after the execution of, the said deeds, the defendant would permit the said young traders to carry on the said business in the defendant's house.

Then the declaration stated a covenant by the plaintiff, that he would accept the business and stock in trade, at a fair valuation, with the defendant's nephew, or such other person, &c. and execute such deeds of partnership, and, further, that the plaintiff should, and would, at, and before, the sealing and delivery of the deeds, cause and procure good and sufficient security to be given to the defendant, to be approved of by the defendant, for the payment of £250 monthly, to the defendant, in lieu of a moiety of the monthly produce of the stock in trade, until the value of the stock should be reduced to £4000.

Then the plaintiff averred, that he had performed, and been ready to perform, his covenants, and assigned for breach on the part of the defendant, that he had refused to surrender and give up his business, at the end of the said year and a quarter.

The defendant pleaded, 1. That the plaintiff did not offer sufficient security; and, 2. That he did not give sufficient security for the payment of the £250, &c.

[T]he plaintiff demurred generally to both pleas.

On the part of the plaintiff, the case was argued by Mr. Buller, who contended, that the covenants were mutual and independent, and, therefore, a plea of the breach of one of the covenants to be performed by the plaintiff was no bar to an action for a breach by the defendant of one of which he had bound himself to perform, but that the defendant might have his remedy for the breach by the plaintiff, in a separate action.

On the other side, Mr. Grose insisted, that the covenants were dependent in their nature, and, therefore, performance must be alleged: the security to be given for the money, was manifestly the chief object of the transaction, and it would be highly unreasonable to construe the agreement, so as to oblige the defendant to give up a beneficial business, and valuable stock in trade, and trust to the plaintiff's personal security, (who might, and, indeed, was admitted to be worth nothing,) for the performance of his part.

In delivering the judgment of the Court, Lord Mansfield expressed himself to the following effect: There are three kinds of covenants: 1. Such as are called mutual and independent, where either party may recover damages from the other, for the injury he may have received by a breach of the covenants in his favor, and where it is no excuse for the defendant, to allege a breach of the covenants on the part of the plaintiff. 2. There are covenants which are conditions and dependent, in which the performance of one depends on the prior performance of another, and, therefore, till this prior condition is performed, the other party is not liable to an action on his covenant. 3. There is also a third sort of covenants, which are mutual conditions to be performed at the same time; and, in these, if one party was ready, and offered, to perform his part, and the other neglected, or refused, to perform his, he who was ready, and offered, has fulfilled his engagement, and may maintain an action for the default of the other; though it is not certain that either is obliged to do the first act.

His Lordship then proceeded to say, that the dependence, or independence, of covenants, was to be collected from the evident sense and meaning of the parties, and, that, however transposed they might be in the deed, their precedency must depend on the order of time in which the intent of the transaction requires their performance. That, in the case before the Court, it would be the greatest injustice if the plaintiff should prevail: the essence of the agreement was, that the defendant should not trust to the personal security of the plaintiff, but, before he delivered up his stock and business, should have good security for the payment of the money. The giving such security, therefore, must necessarily be a condition precedent.

Judgment was accordingly given for the defendant, because the part to be performed by the plaintiff was clearly a condition precedent.

NOTES AND QUESTIONS

1. ***What happened?*** Who sued whom for what? Procedurally, how did the case get before this court? Factually, what happened between the parties? What arguments did the plaintiff and defendant make? What rule or rules did the court apply? How did the court analyze the dispute between the parties? How did the court decide the case?

2. ***Was this case correctly decided?*** Do you agree with the result reached in this case? Why or why not? Do you agree with the court's reasoning? Why or why not? How, if at all, would you have written the opinion differently?

3. ***Concurrent conditions.*** The "third sort of covenants" referred to by Lord Mansfield are commonly referred to as concurrent conditions. In your own words, how would you define a condition concurrent? How do they differ

from conditions precedent and concurrent? Where a contract does not specify the order in which the parties are to perform, can you see why an implied condition concurrent is important in giving meaning to that contract?

Jacob & Youngs v. Kent

Court of Appeals of New York
129 N.E. 889 (1921)

For a report of the case and accompanying materials, see p. 133, *supra*.

K&G Construction Co. v. Harris

Court of Appeals of Maryland
164 A.2d 451 (1960)

PRESCOTT, **Judge**. . . . [Plaintiff/appellant K&G Construction Company, Inc. ("Contractor") was owner and general contractor of a housing subdivision project being constructed ("Project"). Defendants/appellees Harris and Brooks ("Subcontractor") entered into a contract with Contractor to do excavating and earth-moving work on the Project. The contract provided, in relevant part, as follows:]

> **Section 3.** The Subcontractor agrees to complete the several portions and the whole of the work herein sublet by the time or times following: (a) Without delay, as called for by the Contractor. (b) It is expressly agreed that time is of the essence of this contract, and that the Contractor will have the right to terminate this contract and employ a substitute to perform the work in the event of delay on the part of Subcontractor, and Subcontractor agrees to indemnify the Contractor for any loss sustained thereby, provided, however, that nothing in this paragraph shall be construed to deprive Contractor of any rights or remedies it would otherwise have as to damage for delay.
>
> **Section 4.** (b) Progress payments will be made each month during the performance of the work. Subcontractor will submit to Contractor, by the 25th of each month, a requisition for work performed during the preceding month. Contractor will pay these requisitions, less a retainer equal to ten per cent (10%), by the 10th of the months in which such requisitions are received. (c) No payments will be made under this contract until the insurance requirements of Sec. 9 hereof have been complied with. . . .
>
> **Section 5.** The Contractor agrees—(1) That no claim for services rendered or materials furnished by the Contractor to the Subcontractor shall be valid unless written notice thereof is given by the Contractor to the Subcontractor during the first ten days of the calendar month following that in which the claim originated.
>
> **Section 8.** . . . All work shall be performed in a workmanlike manner, and in accordance with the best practices.
>
> **Section 9.** Subcontractor agrees to carry, during the progress of the work, . . . liability insurance against . . . property damage, in such amounts and with such companies as may be satisfactory to Contractor and shall provide Contractor with certificates showing the same to be in force.

While in the course of his employment by the Subcontractor on the Project, a bulldozer operator drove his machine too close to Contractor's house while grading the yard, causing the immediate collapse of a wall and other damage to the house. The resulting damage to contractor's house was $3,400.00. Subcontractor had complied with the insurance provision (Sec. 9) of the aforesaid contract [and] reported said damages to their liability insurance carrier. [However, both] Subcontractor and its insurance carrier refused to repair damage or compensate Contractor for damage to the house, claiming that there was no liability on the part of the Subcontractor. . . .

Contractor was generally satisfied with Subcontractor's work and progress as required under Sections 3 and 8 of the contract until September 12, 1958, with the exception of the bulldozer accident of August 9, 1958. . . . [Prior to the bulldozer accident, Contractor made all scheduled payments to Subcontractor. However,] Contractor refused to pay Subcontractor's requisition due on August 10, 1958, because the bulldozer damage to Contractor's house had not been repaired or paid for. Subcontractor continued to work on the project until the 12th of September, 1958, at which time they discontinued working on the project because of Contractor's refusal to pay[.] [Subcontractor] notified Contractor . . . of their position and willingness to return to the job, but only upon payment. At that time, September 12, 1958, the value of the work completed by Subcontractor on the project for which they had not been paid was $1,484.50. . . .

It was stipulated that Subcontractor had completed work on the Project under the contract for which they had not been paid in the amount of $1,484.50 and that if they had completed the remaining work to be done under the contract, they would have made a profit of $1,340.00 on the remaining uncompleted portion of the contract. It was further stipulated that it cost the Contractor $450.00 above the contract price to have another excavating contractor complete the remaining work required under the contract. . . .

Contractor filed suit against the Subcontractor in two counts: (1) for the aforesaid bulldozer damage to Contractor's house, alleging negligence of the Subcontractor's bulldozer operator, and (2) for the $450.00 costs above the contract price in having another excavating subcontractor complete the uncompleted work in the contract. Subcontractor filed a counter-claim for recovery of work of the value of $1,484.50 for which they had not received payment and for loss of anticipated profits on uncompleted portion of work in the amount of $1,340.00.

By agreement of the parties, the first count of Contractor's claim, i.e., for aforesaid bulldozer damage to Contractor's house, was submitted to jury who found in favor of Contractor in the amount of $3,400.00. Following the finding by the jury, the second count of the Contractor's claim and the counter-claims of the Subcontractor, by agreement of the parties, were submitted to the Court for determination, without jury. All of the facts recited herein above were stipulated to by the parties to the Court. Circuit Court Judge Fletcher found for . . .

Subcontractor in the amount of $2,824.50 from which Contractor has entered this appeal. . . .

The subcontractor contends, of course, that when the contractor failed to make the payment due on August 10, 1958, he breached his contract and thereby released him (the subcontractor) from any further obligation to perform. The contractor, on the other hand, argues that the failure of the subcontractor to perform his work in a workmanlike manner constituted a material breach of the contract, which justified his refusal to make the August 10 payment; and, as there was no breach on his part, the subcontractor had no right to cease performance on September 12, and his refusal to continue work on the project constituted another breach, which rendered him liable to the contractor for damages. The vital question, more tersely stated, remains: Did the contractor have a right, under the circumstances, to refuse to make the progress payment due on August 10, 1958?

Independent and dependent promises

For a review of these concepts, consult the introductory materials for this section. The careful reader may also have noticed the extent to which the language here mirrors the language in the third paragraph of Cardozo's opinion in *Jacob & Youngs v. Kent.*

The answer involves interesting and important principles of contract law. **Promises and counter-promises made by the respective parties to a contract have certain relations to one another, which determine many of the rights and liabilities of the parties. Broadly speaking, they are (1) independent of each other, or (2) mutually dependent, one upon the other. They are independent of each other if the parties intend that *performance* by each of them is in no way conditioned upon *performance* by the other. In other words, the parties exchange promises for promises, not the *performance* of promises for the *performance* of promises. A failure to perform an independent promise does not excuse non-performance on the part of the adversary party, but each is required to perform his promise, and, if one does not perform, he is liable to the adversary party for such non-performance. . . . Promises are mutually dependent if the parties intend *performance* by one to be conditioned upon *performance* by the other, and, if they be mutually dependent, they may be (a) precedent, i.e., a promise that is to be performed before a corresponding promise on the part of the adversary party is to be performed, (b) subsequent, i.e., a corresponding promise that is not to be performed until the other party to the contract has performed a precedent covenant, or (c) concurrent, i.e., promises that are to be performed at the same time by each of the parties, who are respectively bound to perform each. . . .**

In the early days, it was settled law that covenants and mutual promises in a contract were *prima facie* independent, and that they were to be so construed in the absence of language in the contract clearly showing that they were intended to be dependent. In the case of *Kingston v. Preston*, 2 Doug. 689 (1774), Lord Mansfield, contrary to three centuries of opposing precedents, changed the rule, and decided that performance of one covenant might be dependent on prior performance of another, although the contract contained no express condition to that effect. The modern rule, which seems to be of almost universal application, is that there is a presumption that mutual promises in a contract are dependent and are to be so regarded, whenever possible.

While the courts assume, in deciding the relation of one or more promises in a contract to one or more counter-promises, that the promises are dependent rather than independent, **the intention of the parties, as shown by the entire contract as construed in the light of the circumstances of the case, the nature of the contract, the relation of the parties thereto, and the other evidence which is admissible to assist the court in determining the intention of the parties, is the controlling factor in deciding whether the promises and counter-promises are dependent or independent.**

Considering the presumption that promises and counter-promises are dependent and the statement of the case, we have no hesitation in holding that the promise and counter-promise under consideration here were mutually dependent, that is to say, the parties intended performance by one to be conditioned on performance by the other; and the subcontractor's promise was, by the explicit wording of the contract, precedent to the promise of payment, monthly, by the contractor. In *Shapiro Engineering Corp. v. Francis O. Day Co.*, 137 A.2d 695, we stated that it is the general rule that where a total price for work is fixed by a contract, the work is not rendered **divisible** by progress payments. It would, indeed present an unusual situation if we were to hold that a building contractor, who has obtained someone to do work for him and has agreed to pay each month for the work performed in the previous month, has to continue the monthly payments, irrespective of the degree of skill and care displayed in the performance of work, and his only recourse is by way of suit for ill-performance. If this were the law, it is conceivable, in fact, probable, that many contractors would become insolvent before they were able to complete their contracts. As was stated by the Court in *Measures Brothers Ltd. v. Measures*, 2 Ch. 248 (1910): "Covenants are to be construed as dependent or independent according to the intention of the parties and the good sense of the case."

Ascertaining intention

Note all of the circumstances courts are asked to take into account when determining whether the parties intended for their promises to be independent or dependent. In addition, because we are ultimately concerned with the parties' intentions, you should consider these factors in light of the *Embry* test and the accompanying materials on intention examined in Part II.2.B and in Part III.3.A.1. In a close case, to what extent do you think it is likely that two judges, considering these factors, will reach the same result? Note once again the extent to which the language here tracks the language on intention discussed in the third paragraph of Cardozo's opinion in *Jacob & Youngs v. Kent.*

Divisibility

"A contract is said to be divisible if the performances to be exchanged can be divided into corresponding pairs of part performances in such a way that a court will treat the parts of each pair as if the parties had agreed that they were equivalents." E. ALLAN FARNSWORTH, CONTRACTS § 8.13 (3d ed. 2004). Finding a contract to be divisible allows a party that renders some, but not all, of the performance due to avoid forfeiture by allowing it to receive a "pro rata recovery based on the contract price for the proportion of the performance rendered." *Id.* Professor Farnsworth provides the following illustration: "Suppose . . . that a builder has made a contract to build three houses at $100,000 each for a total price of $300,000. The builder breaks the contract by building only one of the houses and claims its price of $100,000. Will a court allow the builder to recover on the contract to build three houses, even though the builder has not substantially performed it? It will, if it regards the contract as divisible into three pairs of part performances, each pair consisting of the building of a house and the payment of $100,000. The builder is then entitled to recover $100,000 on the contract for the house that was built, less such damages as they owner can prove were suffered by the builder's breach in not building the other two." *Id.* Do you think the contract in *K&G Construction Co. v. Harris* has been treated as divisible? Why or why not?

We hold that when the subcontractor's employee negligently damaged the contractor's wall, this constituted a breach of the subcontractor's promise to perform his work in a "workmanlike manner, and in accordance with the best practices." And there can be little doubt that the breach was material: the damage to the wall amounted to more than double the payment due on August 10. 3A Corbin, *Contracts*, § 708, says:

> The failure of a contractor's [in our case, the subcontractor's] performance to constitute "substantial" performance may justify the owner [in our case, the contractor] in refusing to make a progress payment. . . . If the refusal to pay an installment is justified on the owner's [contractor's] part, the contractor [subcontractor] is not justified in abandoning work by reason of that refusal. His abandonment of the work will itself be a wrongful repudiation that goes to the essence, even if the defects in performance did not.

Professor Corbin, in § 954, states further:

> The unexcused failure of a contractor to render a promised performance when it is due is always a breach of contract. . . . Such failure may be of such great importance as to constitute what has been called herein a "total" breach. . . . For a failure of performance constituting such a "total" breach, an action for remedies that are appropriate thereto is at once maintainable. Yet the injured party is not required to bring such action. He has the option of treating the nonperformance as a "partial" breach only. . . .

In permitting the subcontractor to proceed with work on the project after August 9, the contractor, obviously, treated the breach by the subcontractor as a partial one. As the promises were mutually dependent and the subcontractor had made a material breach in his performance, this justified the contractor in refusing to make the August 10 payment; hence, as the contractor was not in default, the subcontractor again breached the contract when he, on September 12, discontinued work on the project, which rendered him liable (by the express terms of the contract) to the contractor for his increased cost in having the excavating done—a stipulated amount of $450. . . .

Judgment against the appellant reversed; and judgment entered in favor of the appellant against the appellees for $450, the appellees to pay the costs.

RELEVANT PROVISIONS

For the *Restatement (Second) of Contracts*, consult §§ 237 and 240. For the UCC, consult § 2-717.

NOTES AND QUESTIONS

1. *What happened?* Who sued whom for what? Procedurally, how did the case get before this court? Factually, what happened between the parties? What arguments did the plaintiff and defendant make? What rule or rules did the court apply? How did the court analyze the dispute between the parties? How did the court decide the case?

2. *Was this case correctly decided?* Do you agree with the result reached in this case? Why or why not? Do you agree with the court's reasoning? Why or why not? How, if at all, would you have written the opinion differently?

3. *Who goes first?* In the introductory materials that began this chapter, we discussed how a savvy party can use the law of conditions to shift risks to the *other* party by making them perform first. Here, can you tell which party—K&G or Harris—had to perform first?

4. *Material breach?* Did Harris materially breach the contract? The court certainly thought so ("there can be little doubt that the breach was material"), but do you agree? How can you tell?

5. *Suspending performance?* Do you think the suspension of performance was justified here? Why or why not? We will look at some of the circumstances in which a party is justified in suspending its performance in much greater detail in Section B of this chapter, "Performance and Breach."

6. *Counseling.* In light of this case, how would you advise a client in an uncertain position about whether to suspend performance to proceed?

PROBLEM: THE DEFECTIVE MACHINE

Plaintiff and Defendant entered into a lease agreement whereby Defendant agreed to lease a large widget engraving machine from Plaintiff for a three-year term and to pay the rental fees in twelve installments due in advance at the beginning of each quarter. The contract provided that the equipment was leased subject to certain terms and conditions, among which were the following:

TERMS AND CONDITIONS

8. MAINTENANCE SERVICE: The Lessor shall render regular maintenance service to the equipment during Lessor's normal working hours and keep such equipment in good working order providing a specific charge is made therefor.

9. DEFAULT: Upon default by Lessee in any term or covenant herein, on the part of the Lessee to be performed, lessor may, at its option, cancel and terminate this lease and repossess the equipment. Upon such default and termination the total payments contracted for hereunder shall immediately become due and payable.

Pursuant to the provisions of Paragraph 8, a separate maintenance charge was added to the quarterly rental payments. The lease further provided that

Defendant had the option of obtaining one-year renewal leases, at significantly lower rates, upon the expiration of the principal lease, and it stated that "each new lease shall be subject to terms and conditions identical with those of this lease except that maintenance will not be a part of this agreement but may be covered in a separate agreement." Defendant paid seven of the twelve installments and then refused to pay any more. Plaintiff brought suit to recover the balance of the contract price and Defendant answered by contending that he stopped paying rent for the machine because it never worked properly and was constantly in a state of disrepair. He claimed that he made numerous calls to Plaintiff about the condition of the machine, but that even after repairs were made it failed to operate properly.

Assuming that the machine was constantly in a state of disrepair from the beginning of the contract and that the Plaintiff's repair personnel were unable to keep the machine in a state of repair, was Defendant allowed to stop paying rent for the machine without itself materially breaching the contract? Stated differently, should Defendant's duty to pay rent on the machine be treated as an independent duty, or should it depend on Plaintiff's obligation to keep the machine in good repair? (Hint: In answering this question, ask whether you think Plaintiff's obligation should be treated as a promise or as a constructive condition precedent to Defendant's duty to pay.)

3. Excusing Conditions

Because the strict application of a condition often results in forfeiture, courts have developed a number of doctrines to mitigate their harshness, such as waiver and estoppel. In the next colorful case, a law professor made a contract to write a book whereby he would receive $6 per page if he abstained from alcohol while writing, but only $2 per page otherwise. Of course, he drank. As you read the case, ask yourself if whether you think the professor's obligation to write while sober was a promise or a condition, and, if the latter, whether you think publishing company, who was alleged to have known about the professor's drinking while writing, waived this condition. But first, a quick doctrinal overview of waiver to get us started.

DOCTRINAL OVERVIEW: EXCUSING CONDITIONS BY WAIVER*

[E]ven if a duty is conditional at the time a contract is made, subsequent events may excuse the condition, causing performance to become due even though the condition has not occurred at all or even though it has not occurred within the required time. A common ground for excuse of a condition is that, after the contract was made, the obligor promised to perform despite the nonoccurrence of

* Excerpted from E. ALLAN FARNSWORTH, CONTRACTS § 8.5 (4th ed. 2004).

the condition or despite a delay in its occurrence. Such a promise is known as a *waiver.* If an owner whose duty to make progress payments is conditional on the contractors furnishing architect's certificates excuses that condition by promising to make payments without certificates, the owner is said to waive the condition. The promise may be made either before or after expiration of the time during which the condition must occur. The obligor's promise to perform is not effective unless the obligor knows or at least has reason to know of the essential facts, but the obligor's knowledge of its legal situation and of the legal effect of the promise is immaterial.[2] A party can waive a condition only if the condition is for that party's own benefit, i.e., only if that party is the obligor that owes the duty that is subject to the condition. If the duty of the purchaser of a house is conditional on the purchaser's obtaining a mortgage, that condition can be waived by the purchaser, but not by the vendor. And in the unusual situation in which the condition is a condition of the duties of both parties, it cannot be waived by one party alone.

The meaning of *waiver* has provoked much discussion. Although it has often been said that a waiver is "the intentional relinquishment of a known right,"[5] this is a misleading definition. What is involved is not the relinquishment of a right and the termination of the reciprocal duty but the excuse of the nonoccurrence of or a delay in the occurrence of a condition of a duty.[6] The owner that leads the builder to believe that progress payments will be made without architect's certificates "waives" the condition, since the owner's duty to pay is no longer conditional on certificates. But the creditor that discharges a debt by release or renunciation does not "waive" the debt in the sense in which that term is used here. It is desirable to confine the use of *waiver* in this way to avoid confusion. "Waiver is then properly described as consent to [give] up a condition of one's duty, and when one gives such consent one can be said to waive the condtion."[8] . . .

Clark v. West

Court of Appeals of New York

86 N.E. 1 (1908)

WERNER, J. The contract before us, stripped of all superfluous verbiage, binds the plaintiff [prolific author, itinerant professor, and avid drinker William L. Clark] to total abstention from the use of intoxicating liquors during the continuance of the work which he was employed to do [for defendant John B. West, founder of West Publishing]. The stipulations relating to the plaintiff's

2. According to *Restatement Second* § 93, though the promisor must know or have reason to know the essential facts, "his knowledge of the legal effect of the facts is immaterial."

5. Clark v. West, 86 N.E. 1 (N.Y. 1908) ("A waiver has been defined to be the intentional relinquishment of a known right.").

6. The quoted definition is also misleading in that the word *known* must be read as going only to the facts and not to their legal effect.

8. *See* E. FARNSWORTH, CHANGING YOUR MIND, ch. 16 at 155 (1998).

compensation provide that if he does not observe this condition he is to be paid at the rate of $2 per page, and if he does comply therewith he is to receive $6 per page. The plaintiff has written one book under the contract known as "Clark & Marshall on Corporations," which has been accepted, published and copies sold in large numbers by the defendant. The plaintiff admits that while he was at work on this book he did not entirely abstain from the use of intoxicating liquors. He has been paid only $2 per page for the work he has done. He claims that, despite his breach of this condition, he is entitled to the full compensation of $6 per page because the defendant, with full knowledge of plaintiff's non-observance of this stipulation as to total abstinence, has waived the breach thereof and cannot now insist upon strict performance in this regard. This plea of waiver presents the underlying question which determines the answers to the questions certified.

Briefly stated, the defendant's position is that the stipulation as to plaintiff's total abstinence is the consideration for the payment of the difference between $2 and $6 per page and therefore could not be waived except by a new agreement to that effect based upon a good consideration; that the so-called waiver alleged by the plaintiff is not a waiver but a modification of the contract in respect of its consideration. The plaintiff on the other hand argues that the stipulation for his total abstinence was merely a condition precedent intended to work a forfeiture of the additional compensation in case of a breach and that it could be waived without any formal agreement to that effect based upon a new consideration.

The subject-matter of the contract was the writing of books by the plaintiff for the defendant. The duration of the contract was the time necessary to complete them all. The work was to be done to the satisfaction of the defendant, and the plaintiff was not to write any other books except those covered by the contract unless requested so to do by the defendant, in which latter event he was to be paid for that particular work by the year. The compensation for the work specified in the contract was to be $6 per page, unless the plaintiff failed to totally abstain from the use of intoxicating liquors during the continuance of the contract, in which event he was to receive only $2 per page. That is the obvious import of the contract construed in the light of the purpose for which it was made, and in accordance with the ordinary meaning of plain language. **It is not a contract to write books in order that the plaintiff shall keep sober, but a contract containing a stipulation that he shall keep sober so that he may write satisfactory books. When we view the contract from this standpoint it will readily be perceived that the particular stipulation is not the consideration for the contract, but simply one of its conditions** which fits in with those relating to time and method of delivery of manuscript, revision of proof, citation of cases, assignment of copyrights, keeping track of new cases

Promise versus condition

How did (or should) the court determine whether the professor's abstention from alcohol was merely a promise (i.e., part of the bargained-for consideration), or a condition, the non-satisfaction of which would result in the professor earning $2 per page, rather than $6? Courts generally answer this question by looking into the *purpose* behind why the parties included a particular provision in the contract, which, of course, requires them

and citations for new editions, and other details which might be waived by the defendant, if he saw fit to do so. This is made clear, it seems to us, by the provision that, "In consideration of the above promises," the defendant agrees to pay the plaintiff $2 per page on each book prepared by him, and if he "abstains from the use of intoxicating liquor and otherwise fulfills his agreements as hereinbefore set forth, he shall be paid an additional $4 per page in manner hereinbefore stated." The compensation of $2 per page, not to exceed $250 per month, was an advance or partial payment of the whole price of $6 per page, and the payment of the two-thirds which was to be withheld pending the performance of the contract, was simply made contingent upon the plaintiff's total abstention from the use of intoxicants during the life of the contract. It is possible, of course, by segregating that clause of the contract from the context, to give it a wider meaning and a different aspect than it has when read in conjunction with other stipulations. But this is also true of other paragraphs of the contract. . . . The contract read as a whole, however, shows that it is modified by the preceding provisions making the compensation in excess of the $2 per page dependent upon the plaintiff's total abstinence, and upon the performance by him of the other conditions of the contract. It is obvious that the parties thought that the plaintiff's normal work was worth $6 per page. That was the sum to be paid for the work done by the plaintiff and not for total abstinence. If the plaintiff did not keep to the condition as to total abstinence, he was to lose part of that sum. Precisely the same situation would have risen if the plaintiff had disregarded any of the other essential conditions of the contract. The fact that the particular stipulation was emphasized did not change its character. It was still a condition which the defendant could have insisted upon, as he has apparently done in regard to some others, and one which he could waive just as he might have waived those relating to the amount of the advance payments, or the number of pages to be written each month. A breach of any of the substantial conditions of the contract would have entailed a loss or forfeiture similar to that consequent upon a breach of the one relating to total abstinence, in case of the defendant's insistence upon his right to take advantage of them. This, we think, is the fair interpretation of the contract, and it follows that the stipulation as to the plaintiff's total abstinence was nothing more nor less than a condition precedent. If that conclusion is well founded there can be no escape from the corollary that this condition could be waived; and if it was waived the defendant is clearly not in a position to insist upon the forfeiture which his waiver was intended to annihilate. The forfeiture must stand or fall with the condition. If the latter was waived, the former is no longer a part of the contract. . . .

> to inquire into the parties' *intent*. And, as we have learned, courts inquire into the parties' intent by using the sorts of tools we discussed when we examined *Embry* and the accompanying materials on intention in Part II.2.B and in Part III.3.A.1.

This whole discussion is predicated of course upon the theory of an express waiver. We assume that no waiver could be implied from the defendant's mere acceptance of the books and his payment of the sum of $2 per page without objection. It was the defendant's duty to pay that amount in any event after acceptance of the work. The plaintiff must stand upon his allegation of an express waiver and if he fails to establish that he cannot maintain his action.

The theory upon which the defendant's attitude seems to be based is that even if he has represented to the plaintiff that he would not insist upon the condition that the latter should observe total abstinence from intoxicants, he can still refuse to pay the full contract price for his work. The inequity of this position becomes apparent when we consider that this contract was to run for a period of years, during a large portion of which the plaintiff was to be entitled only to the advance payment of $2 per page, the balance being contingent, among other things, upon publication of the books and returns from sales. Upon this theory the defendant might have waived the condition while the first book was in process of production, and yet when the whole work was completed, he would still be in a position to insist upon the forfeiture because there had not been strict performance. Such a situation is possible in a case where the subject of the waiver is the very consideration of a contract, but not where the waiver relates to something that can be waived. In the case at bar, as we have seen, the waiver is not of the consideration or subject-matter, but of an incident to the method of performance. The consideration remains the same. The defendant has had the work he bargained for, and it is alleged that he has waived one of the conditions as to the manner in which it was to have been done. He might have insisted upon literal performance and then he could have stood upon the letter of his contract. If, however, he has waived that incidental condition, he has created a situation to which the doctrine of waiver very precisely applies. . . .

> ***Not so fast!***
>
> Although the court defines waiver as "the intentional relinquishment of a known right," Professor Farnsworth, in the Doctrinal Overview before this case, takes issue with this definition. Make sure you know why.

A waiver has been defined to be the intentional relinquishment of a known right. It is voluntary and implies an election to dispense with something of value, or forego some advantage which the party waiving it might at its option have demanded or insisted upon, and this definition is supported by many cases in this and other states. In the recent case of *Draper v. Oswego Co. Fire R. Assn.*, 190 N.Y. 12, 16, Chief Judge Cullen, in speaking for the court upon this subject, said:

> While [the doctrine of waiver] and the doctrine of equitable estoppel are often confused . . . , there is a clear distinction between the two. A waiver is the voluntary abandonment or relinquishment by a party of some right or advantage. As said by my brother Vann in the *Kiernan Case*, 150 N.Y. 190: "The law of waiver seems to be a technical doctrine, introduced and applied by the court for the purpose of defeating forfeitures. . . . While the principle may not be easily classified, it is well established that if the words and acts of the insurer reasonably justify the conclusion that with full knowledge of all the facts it intended to abandon or not to insist upon the particular defense afterwards relied upon, a verdict or finding

to that effect establishes a **waiver, which, if it once exists, can never be revoked.**" The doctrine of equitable estoppel, or estoppel *in pais*, is that a party may be precluded by his acts and conduct from asserting a right to the detriment of another party who, entitled to rely on such conduct, has acted upon it. . . . As already said, the doctrine of waiver is to relieve against forfeiture; it requires no consideration for a waiver, nor any prejudice or injury to the other party.

> ***Are waivers irrevocable?***
>
> Despite the strong language used here, the common law has tried to move away from the position that waivers cannot be revoked, so long as the party to whom the waiver has been given has not relied on the waiver. *See Restatement (Second) of Contracts* § 84, Illustration 6. The UCC is even clearer, and states that "A party who has made a waiver affecting an executory portion of the contract may retract the waiver by reasonable notification received by the other party that strict performance will be required of any term waived, unless the retraction would be unjust in view of a material change of position in reliance on the waiver." UCC § 2-209(5).

It remains to be determined whether the plaintiff has alleged facts which, if proven, will be sufficient to establish his claim of an express waiver by the defendant of the plaintiff's breach of the condition to observe total abstinence. In the 12th paragraph of the complaint, the plaintiff alleges facts and circumstances which we think, if established, would prove defendant's waiver of plaintiff's performance of that contract stipulation. These facts and circumstances are that long before the plaintiff had completed the manuscript of the first book undertaken under the contract, the defendant had full knowledge of the plaintiff's non-observance of that stipulation, and that with such knowledge he not only accepted the completed manuscript without objection, but

> repeatedly avowed and represented to the plaintiff that he was entitled to and would receive said royalty payments (*i. e.*, the additional $4 per page), and plaintiff believed and relied upon such representations . . . and at all times during the writing of said treatise on corporations, and after as well as before publication thereof as aforesaid, it was mutually understood, agreed and intended by the parties hereto that notwithstanding plaintiff's said use of intoxicating liquors, he was nevertheless entitled to receive and would receive said royalty as the same accrued under said contract.

. . . [W]e think it cannot be doubted that the allegations contained in the 12th paragraph of the complaint, if proved upon the trial, would be sufficient to establish an express waiver by the defendant of the stipulation in regard to plaintiff's total abstinence. . . .

RELEVANT PROVISIONS

For the *Restatement (Second) of Contracts*, consult §§ 84, cmt. *b*, and 229. For the UCC, consult §§ 1-306, 2-208(3) and 2-209(4) and (5).

NOTES AND QUESTIONS

1. *What happened?* Who sued whom for what? Procedurally, how did the case get before this court? Factually, what happened between the parties? What arguments did the plaintiff and defendant make? What rule or rules did

the court apply? How did the court analyze the dispute between the parties? How did the court decide the case?

2. *Was this case correctly decided?* Do you agree with the result reached in this case? Why or why not? Do you agree with the court's reasoning? Why or why not? How, if at all, would you have written the opinion differently?

3. *What's the difference?* What is the difference between waiver, estoppel, and excuse? Which seems most applicable in the above case?

4. *Classifying the condition.* Was the condition in *Clark v. West* a condition precedent or condition subsequent? How can you tell?

5. *Drafting exercise.* Try to redraft the condition precedent/subsequent (whichever you think it is) into its opposite (a condition subsequent/precedent). What effect, if any, would this have on the case's outcome?

B. PERFORMANCE AND BREACH

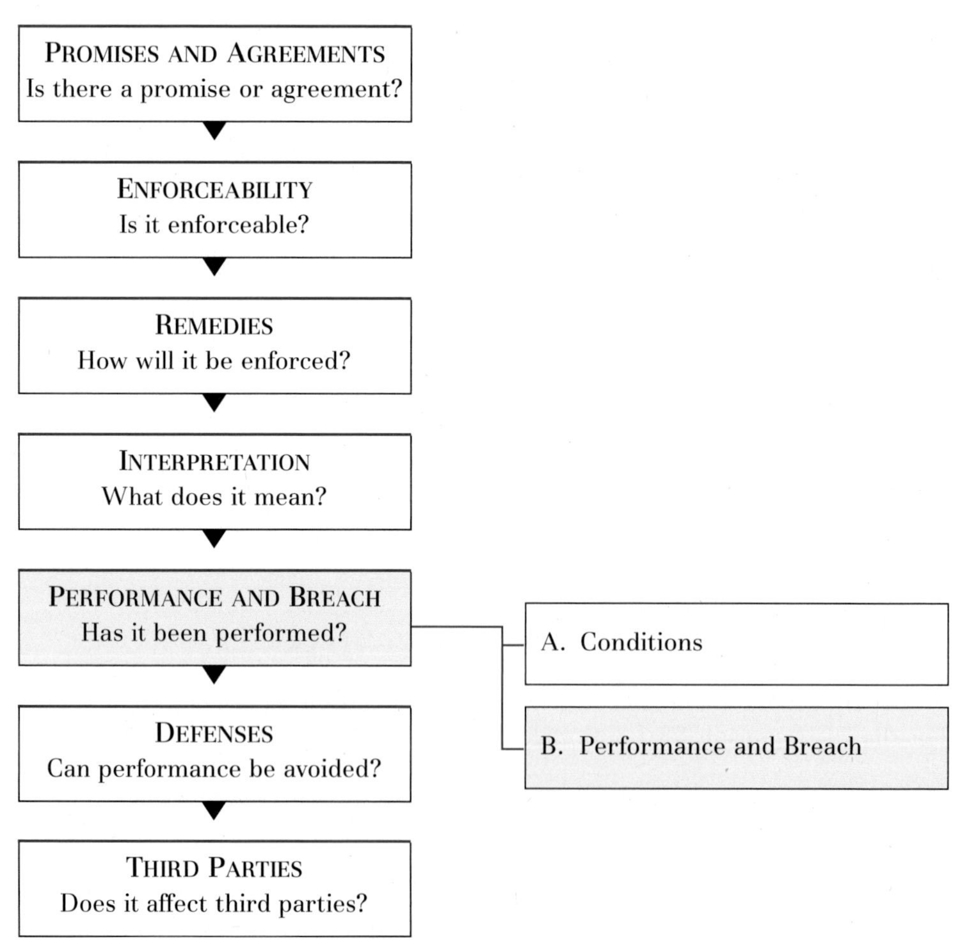

In this section we will examine what, exactly, constitutes material breach, and some of the options parties have when they believe the other party has materially breached the contract. Specific topics that will be covered in this section include suspending performance, material breach, terminating the contract, anticipatory repudiation, adequate assurances of performance, and the perfect tender rule.

1. Material Breach, Suspending Performance, and Terminating the Contract

In this subsection we are concerned with what types of breaches authorize a party to suspend their performance, or to otherwise avoid, rescind, cancel, or terminate the contract. In general, a court will allow a party to do any of these things where their contractual partner has materially breached its contract. But, how, exactly, should courts (and the party wondering whether they should withhold their own performance) go about determining whether the other party has *materially* breached its obligation, as opposed to merely committing a trivial or non-material breach? After all, if Party A withholds its performance due to its belief that Party B has materially breached its contract, and this belief turns out to be false, then it will be Party A who will have breached. There is therefore much at stake, for both parties and courts, in being able to ascertain with some clarity whether a material breach has taken place, which might suggest that this area of law be governed by a clear, black letter rule. On the other hand, breach can take place in myriad unforeseeable ways, and if we want to allow courts to take into account both the individual contract between the parties and the unique facts that arose in each particular case, then perhaps courts should ascertain whether there is a material breach not with a rule, but with a standard. As you read the cases and materials below, try to ask yourself how courts should ascertain whether a material breach has taken place, and whether a rule or a standard would provide the best tool for doing so.

The next two cases explore the issues raised in this paragraph in much greater depth, and also build on our discussion of conditions in the previous section. But, before diving into the cases, we will begin with a doctrinal overview to get the lay of the land.

DOCTRINAL OVERVIEW: MATERIAL BREACH, SUSPENDING PERFORMANCE, AND TERMINATING THE CONTRACT*

Courts developed the doctrine of substantial performance to deal with the relatively simple case in which the party in breach had finished performing and the injured party refused to pay the price because the performance was

* Excerpted from E. ALLAN FARNSWORTH, CONTRACTS §§ 8.15-16 (4th ed. 2004).

defective or incomplete. Often the dispute arises at a much earlier stage of performance, however, and the question is whether a breach justifies the injured party in exercising a right to self-help by terminating the contract and refusing either to render any remaining performance or to accept any further performance by the party in breach. The injured party may be the defendant, seeking merely to justify its nonperformance in an action that has been brought by the other party. Or the injured party may be the plaintiff, seeking to justify its nonperformance in an action that it has brought against the other party for damages for total breach.

Suppose that in breach of a construction contract the owner has delayed making a required progress payment, and the builder, after first refusing to go forward with the work, has finally terminated the contract, leaving the building unfinished. Has the builder a defense if sued by the owner? Has the builder a claim against the owner for damages for total breach? Under the concept of constructive conditions of exchange, the owner's payment of progress payments is an implied condition of the builder's duty to continue to work. Therefore, the owner's breach in failing to make a progress payment may have two effects on the builder's duty. First, further performance will not become due, so the builder will be justified in exercising a right to self-help by suspending performance. Second, after an appropriate period of time, the builder can choose to treat its remaining duties of performance under the contract as discharged and can exercise a right to self-help by terminating the contract. Two distinct issues are therefore raised. First, was the owner's breach in failing to make the progress payments significant enough to justify the builder's suspending performance? Second, did the owner's breach continue long enough to justify the builder's terminating the contract? If the answer to both questions is yes, the builder was entitled to terminate the contract and claim damages for total breach against the owner. But if the answer to either is no, the builder's action was precipitous and unjustified, itself amounting to a breach that gave the owner a right to terminate and claim damages for total breach against the builder.

This sensible two-step analysis is carefully articulated in the *Restatement Second*.[6] It is in society's interest to accord each party to a contract reasonable security for the protection of that party's justified expectations. But it is not in society's interest to permit a party to abuse this protection by using an insignificant breach as a pretext for evading its contractual obligations. If the other party relied on the agreement, by performance or otherwise, "keeping the deal together" avoids the risk of forfeiture. Courts encourage this course as long as it will not seriously disappoint justified expectations. They do this by allowing the injured party to suspend performance only if the breach is *material,* that is, sufficiently serious to warrant this response. . . . An injured party that chooses to exercise a right of self-help either by suspending or by electing to terminate takes the risk that a court may later regard the exercise as precipitous. According to the Supreme Court of Michigan, that party's decision "is fraught with peril, for should

6. *See Restatement Second* § 237 & cmt. *a.* In older terminology it was said that the injured party could terminate if the breach was material. No special term existed to describe a breach that justified suspension.

such determination, as viewed by a later court in the calm of its contemplation, be unwarranted, the repudiator himself will have been guilty of material breach and himself have become the aggressor, not an innocent victim."[10] . . .

How significant must a breach be in order to justify suspension?

In order for a breach to justify the injured party's suspension of performance, the breach must be significant enough to amount to the nonoccurrence of a constructive condition of exchange. Such a breach is termed "material." . . .

The doctrine of material breach is simply the converse of the doctrine of substantial performance. Substantial performance is performance without a material breach, and a material breach results in performance that is not substantial. . . .

Whether a breach is material is a question of fact, with the answer depending on circumstances similar to those used to determine whether a performance has been substantial. The *Restatement Second* looks to the injured party and asks to what extent that party will be deprived of the benefit it reasonably expected, account being taken of the possibility of adequate compensation for that part. It also looks to the other party—to the possibility that it will suffer forfeiture, to the likelihood that it will cure its failure, and to the degree that its behavior comported with standards of good faith and fair dealing.[6] Most significant is the extent to which the breach will deprive the injured party of the benefit that it justifiably expected, a factor that is often decisive in determining whether a breach is material or not. This may depend in turn on the adequacy of damages. A court is less likely to characterize a breach as material where, in Mansfield's words, the "breach may be paid for in damages."[10]

Walker & Co. v. Harrison

Supreme Court of Michigan
81 N.W.2d 352 (1957)

SMITH, JUSTICE. This is a suit on a written contract. The defendants are in the dry-cleaning business. Walker & Company, plaintiff, sells, rents, and services advertising signs and billboards. These parties entered into an agreement pertaining to a sign. The agreement is in writing and is termed a "rental agreement." It specifies in part that:

> The lessor agrees to construct and install, at its own cost, one 18′9″ high x 8′8″ wide pylon type d.f. neon sign with electric clock and flashing lamps. . . . The lessor agrees to and does hereby lease or rent unto the said lessee the said SIGN for the term, use and rental and under the conditions, hereinafter set out, and the lessee agrees to pay said rental . . .
>
> (a) The term of this lease shall be 36 months. . . .
>
> (b) The rental to be paid by lessee shall be $148.50 per month for each and every calendar month during the term of this lease. . . .

10. Walker & Co. v. Harrison. 81 N.W.2d 352, 355 (Mich. 1957).
6. *Restatement Second* § 241.
10. Boone v. Eyre, 126 Eng. Rep. 160(a) (K.B. 1777).

> (d) Maintenance. Lessor at its expense agrees to maintain and service the sign together with such equipment as supplied and installed by the lessor to operate in conjunction with said sign under the terms of this lease; this service is to include cleaning and repainting of sign in original color scheme as often as deemed necessary by lessor to keep sign in first class advertising condition and make all necessary repairs to sign and equipment installed by lessor. . . .

At the "expiration of this agreement," it was also provided, "title to this sign reverts to lessee." This clause is in addition to the printed form of agreement and was apparently added as a result of defendants' concern over title, they having expressed a desire "to buy for cash" and the salesman, at one time, having "quoted a cash price."

The sign was completed and installed in the latter part of July, 1953. The first billing of the monthly payment of $148.50 was made August 1, 1953, with payment thereof by defendants on September 3, 1953. This first payment was also the last. Shortly after the sign was installed, someone hit it with a tomato. Rust, also, was visible on the chrome, complained defendants, and in its corners were "little spider cobwebs." In addition, there were "some children's sayings written down in here." Defendant Herbert Harrison called Walker for the maintenance he believed himself entitled to under subparagraph (d) above. It was not forthcoming. He called again and again. "I was getting, you might say, sorer and sorer. . . . Occasionally, when I started calling up, I would walk around where the tomato was and get mad again. Then I would call up on the phone again." Finally, on October 8, 1953, plaintiff not having responded to his repeated calls, he telegraphed Walker that:

> You Have Continually Voided Our Rental Contract By Not Maintaining Signs As Agreed As We No Longer Have A Contract With You Do Not Expect Any Further Remuneration.

Walker's reply was in the form of a letter. After first pointing out that "your telegram does not make any specific allegations as to what the failure of maintenance comprises," and stating that "We certainly would appreciate your furnishing us with such information," the letter makes reference to a prior collateral controversy between the parties, "wondering if this refusal on our part prompted your attempt to void our rental contract," and concludes as follows:

> We would like to call your attention to paragraph G in our rental contract, which covers procedures in the event of a Breach of Agreement. In the event that you carry out your threat to make no future monthly payments in accordance with the agreement, it is our intention to enforce the conditions outlined under

1. **(g) Breach of Agreement.** Lessee shall be deemed to have breached this agreement by default in payment of any installment of the rental herein provided for; abandonment of the sign or vacating premises where the sign is located; termination or transfer of lessee's interest in the premises by insolvency, appointment of a receiver for lessee's business; filing of a voluntary or involuntary petition in bankruptcy with respect to lessee or the violation of any of the other terms or conditions hereof. In the event of such default, the lessor may, upon notice to the lessee, which

> paragraph G[1] through the proper legal channels. We call to your attention that your monthly rental payments are due in advance at our office not later than the 10th day of each current month. You are now approximately 30 days in arrears on your September payment. Unless we receive both the September and October payments by October 25th, this entire matter will be placed in the hands of our attorney for collection in accordance with paragraph G which stipulates that the entire amount is forthwith due and payable.

No additional payments were made and Walker sued in assumpsit for the entire balance due under the contract, $5,197.50, invoking paragraph (g) of the agreement. Defendants filed answer and claim of recoupment, asserting that plaintiff's failure to perform certain maintenance services constituted a prior material breach of the agreement, thus justifying their repudiation of the contract and grounding their claim for damages. The case was tried to the court without a jury and resulted in a judgment for the plaintiff. The case is before us on a general appeal.

Defendants urge upon us again and again, in various forms, the proposition that Walker's failure to service the sign, in response to repeated requests, constituted a material breach of the contract and justified repudiation by them. Their legal proposition is undoubtedly correct. Repudiation is one of the weapons available to an injured party in event the other contractor has committed a material breach. **But the injured party's determination that there has been a material breach, justifying his own repudiation, is fraught with peril, for should such determination, as viewed by a later court in the calm of its contemplation, be unwarranted, the repudiator himself will have been guilty of material breach and himself have become the aggressor, not an innocent victim.**

What is our criterion for determining whether or not a breach of contract is so fatal to the undertaking

A Catch-22?

As we have previously seen in cases like *K&G Construction Co. v. Harris* (p. 866), a party who withholds its own performance due to its belief that the other party has materially breached may subsequently learn to its horror that it, and not the other party, is in material breach of the contract. So what ought a party who

notice shall conclusively be deemed sufficient if mailed or delivered to the premises where the sign was or is located, take possession of the sign and declare the balance of the rental herein provided for to be forthwith due and payable, and lessee hereby agrees to pay such balance upon any such contingencies. Lessor may terminate this lease and without notice, remove and repossess said sign and recover from the lessee such amounts as may be unpaid for the remaining unexpired term of this agreement. Time is of the essence of this lease with respect to the payment of rentals herein provided for. Should lessee after lessor has declared the balance of rentals due and payable, pay the full amount of rental herein provided, he shall then be entitled to the use of the sign, under all the terms and provisions hereof, for the balance of the term of this lease. No waiver by either party hereto of the nonperformance of any term, condition or obligation hereof shall be a waiver of any subsequent breach of, or failure to perform the same, or any other term, condition or obligation hereof. It is understood and agreed that the sign is especially constructed for the lessee and for use at the premises now occupied by the lessee for the term herein provided; that it is of no value unless so used and that it is a material consideration to the lessor in entering into this agreement that the lessee shall continue to use the sign for the period of time provided herein and for the payment of the full rental for such term.

finds itself in such an unfortunate position do? How would *you* advise a client (like Harrison) in such a position? One possibility, which we will discuss in Subsection B.3, *infra*, is to request that the other party provide adequate assurance of its own performance. Can you think of any others?

Material breach and the Restatement (Second) of Contracts

This provision of the *Restatement* now appears in *Restatement (Second) of Contracts* § 241, and has undergone a few minor changes (e.g., courts are now asked to consider five factors rather than six). We will see the *Restatement (Second) of Contracts* in action in our next principal case, *Shah v. Cover-It, Inc.*

of the parties that it is to be classed as "material"? There is no single touchstone. Many factors are involved. They are well stated in ***Restatement (First) of Contracts*** § 275 in the following terms:

> In determining the materiality of a failure fully to perform a promise the following circumstances are influential:
>
> (a) The extent to which the injured party will obtain the substantial benefit which he could have reasonably anticipated;
>
> (b) The extent to which the injured party may be adequately compensated in damages for lack of complete performance;
>
> (c) The extent to which the party failing to perform has already partly performed or made preparations for performance;
>
> (d) The greater or less hardship on the party failing to perform in terminating the contract;
>
> (e) The wilful, negligent or innocent behavior of the party failing to perform;
>
> (f) The greater or less uncertainty that the party failing to perform will perform the remainder of the contract.

We will not set forth in detail the testimony offered concerning the need for servicing. Granting that Walker's delay (about a week after defendant Herbert Harrison sent his telegram of repudiation Walker sent out a crew and took care of things) in rendering the service requested was irritating, we are constrained to agree with the trial court that it was not of such materiality as to justify repudiation of the contract, and we are particularly mindful of the lack of preponderant evidence contrary to his determination. The trial court, on this phase of the case, held as follows:

> Now Mr. Harrison phoned in, so he testified, a number of times. He isn't sure of the dates but he sets the first call at about the 7th of August and he complained then of the tomato and of some rust and some cobwebs. The tomato, according to the testimony, was up on the clock; that would be outside of his reach, without a stepladder or something. The cobwebs are within easy reach of Mr. Harrison and so would the rust be. I think that Mr. Bueche's argument that these were not materially a breach would clearly be true as to the cobwebs and I really can't believe in the face of all the testimony that there was a great deal of rust seven days after the installation of this sign. And that really brings it down to the tomato. And, of course, when a tomato has been splashed all over your clock, you don't like it. But he says he kept calling their attention to it, although the rain probably washed some of the tomato off. But the stain remained, and they didn't come. I really can't find that that was such a material breach of the contract as to justify rescission. I really don't think so.

Nor, we conclude, do we. There was no valid ground for defendants' repudiation and their failure thereafter to comply with the terms of the contract was itself a material breach, entitling Walker, upon this record, to judgment.

The question of damages remains. . . . [T]he parties before us have agreed, with particularity, as to remedies in event of breach, the remedy here sought, as provided, being acceleration of "rentals" due. The trial court cut down such sum by the amount that service would have cost Walker during the unexpired portion of the agreement and as to such diminution Walker does not complain or cross-appeal. Judgment was, therefore, rendered for the cash price of the sign, for such services and maintenance as were extended and accepted, and interest upon the amount in default. There was no error.

RELEVANT PROVISIONS

For the *Restatement (Second) of Contracts*, consult §§ 235 and 241. For the UCC, consult §§ 2-601, 2-608, and 2-612. For the CISG, consult Articles 25 and 49. For the UNIDROIT Principles, consult Articles 7.3.1 and 7.3.5.

NOTES AND QUESTIONS

1. *What happened?* Who sued whom for what? Procedurally, how did the case get before this court? Factually, what happened between the parties? What arguments did the plaintiff and defendant make? What rule or rules did the court apply? How did the court analyze the dispute between the parties? How did the court decide the case?

2. *Was this case correctly decided?* Do you agree with the result reached in this case? Why or why not? Do you agree with the court's reasoning? Why or why not? How, if at all, would you have written the opinion differently?

3. *Classifying conditions.* What type of condition was at stake in the previous case? How, if at all, did it affect the outcome of the dispute?

4. *Drafting question.* How could you have redrafted the contract to avoid the problem that arose in this case?

Shah v. Cover-It, Inc.

Appellate Court of Connecticut
859 A.2d 959 (2004)

SCHALLER, JUDGE. The plaintiff, Khalid Shah, appeals from the judgment of the trial court, rendered after a trial to the court, in favor of the defendants Cover-It, Inc., and Brian Goldwitz. On appeal, the plaintiff claims that the court improperly found that he materially breached the employment contract between the parties. We disagree and, accordingly, affirm the judgment of the trial court.

The following facts and procedural history are relevant to our discussion. On November 12, 1997, the parties entered into an employment contract by which the plaintiff became the structural engineering manager of Cover-It, Inc. Pursuant to the terms of the employment contract, the plaintiff was to receive an annual salary of $70,000, payable weekly, for a period of five years and subject to cost of living adjustments. In addition to his salary, the plaintiff was entitled to a commission of 2 percent of the sales generated from those products that he designed while employed, up to $1.5 million.

In addition to standard company benefits, the plaintiff also received three paid weeks of vacation on the completion of his first year of employment and the use of a company car. Furthermore, the plaintiff was permitted to work a flexible full-time schedule of thirty-five hours per week. He also was allowed to take time off from work to attend professional workshops and activities, and to resolve any prior professional obligations. The employment contract was subject to termination by either party with ninety days written notice. If the defendants terminated the contract, the plaintiff, on the completion of his first year of employment, was to receive monthly salary payments for the remainder of the five-year period pursuant to a schedule.[2] In June, 1998, the plaintiff requested and received permission for a period of vacation time. Goldwitz approved the time off with the understanding that the plaintiff would be gone for several weeks. At the end of August, 1998, the plaintiff had not returned. Goldwitz believed that the plaintiff had abandoned the employment contract and sent him notice that his health benefits were cancelled. The plaintiff returned to work in early September, 1998, and continued working until the middle of October. During that time period, the plaintiff worked two or three days per week and spent long periods of time visiting Internet web sites that were unrelated to his employment duties. The plaintiff also refused to use a time clock to document his attendance; instead, he simply indicated on his time card that he was present. On October 14, 1998, Goldwitz asked the plaintiff if certain designs would be completed. The plaintiff stated that he was not sure when the designs would be completed and that he would take his time in completing them. Goldwitz then terminated the plaintiff's employment.

The plaintiff commenced the present action on October 6, 1999. By way of a fourteen count amended complaint filed on November 20, 2001, the plaintiff alleged various causes of action against the defendants, including breach of contract, breach of the implied covenant of good faith and fair dealing, failure to pay wages in violation of General Statutes § 31–72 and negligent misrepresentation. The defendants filed an answer and a two count counterclaim. With respect to the plaintiff's claims, the court found in favor of the defendants on all counts and rendered judgment accordingly. As to the counterclaim, the court

2. The contract provided that for up to two years of service, the plaintiff would be paid $20,000 per year, for three years of service, $30,000 per year and for four years of service, $40,000 per year.

concluded that the defendants had failed to prove damages and rendered judgment in favor of the plaintiff. This appeal followed.

On appeal, the plaintiff claims that the court improperly found that he had breached the contract or, in the alternative, that any breach was not material. Specifically, the plaintiff argues that the court failed to identify an express term or condition that was breached and instead merely found that certain acts, considered together, demonstrated a material breach prior to the termination of his employment. Therefore, according to the plaintiff, the defendants were not relieved of their obligations, under the terms of the contract, to pay his full salary for ninety days and to pay his posttermination salary pursuant to the schedule set forth in the contract. We disagree.

As a preliminary matter, we identify the applicable standard of review.

> The determination of whether a contract has been materially breached is a question of fact that is subject to the clearly erroneous standard of review. . . . A finding of fact is clearly erroneous when there is no evidence in the record to support it . . . or when although there is evidence to support it, the reviewing court on the entire evidence is left with the definite and firm conviction that a mistake has been committed.

Efthimiou v. Smith, 846 A.2d 216 (2004). "Our authority, when reviewing the findings of a judge, is circumscribed by the deference we must give to decisions of the trier of fact, who is usually in a superior position to appraise and weigh the evidence." *LaVelle v. Ecoair Corp.*, 814 A.2d 421 (2003).

"It is a general rule of contract law that a total breach of the contract by one party relieves the injured party of any further duty to perform further obligations under the contract." (Emphasis added.) *Rokalor, Inc. v. Connecticut Eating Enterprises, Inc.*, 558 A.2d 265 (1989); *see also* 2 *Restatement (Second) Contracts* § 237 (1981).

In *Bernstein v. Nemeyer*, 570 A.2d 164 (1990), our Supreme Court endorsed the use of the multifactor test set forth in the *Restatement (Second) of Contracts, supra*, § 241, when determining whether a breach is material.

> Section 241 of the *Restatement (Second) of Contracts* provides: "In determining whether a failure to render or to offer performance is material, the following circumstances are significant: (a) the extent to which the injured party will be deprived of the benefit which he reasonably expected; (b) the extent to which the injured party can be adequately compensated for the part of that benefit of which he will be deprived; (c) the extent to which the party failing to perform or to offer to perform will suffer forfeiture; (d) the likelihood that the party failing to perform or to offer to perform will cure his failure, taking account of all the circumstances including any reasonable assurances;

Standards versus rules

In a previous thinking tool (see "Thinking Tool: Administrative Costs and Standards Versus Rules," p. 75, *supra*), we explored the difference between standards and rules, and noted that standards provide courts with more discretion than rules, allowing them to shape the standard before it to fit the contours of the case, but that this discretion comes at a cost, as standards are more difficult and costly to administer than rules. Rules, of course, are much easier (and inexpensive) to administer, but do not allow courts to take into consideration relevant factors outside of the rule's scope, leading both to injustices and to results inconsistent with the purpose behind the rule in a number of particular cases. Here, the drafters of the *Restatement (Second) of Contracts* thought it would be better for courts to determine whether there is a material breach by using a standard rather than a rule, but when we attempt to apply this standard, we can see first-hand some of the problems mentioned in the thinking tool. For instance, how, exactly, are courts supposed to apply these five factors? What weight should judges give to each of these factors, and how should a court treat a case where only one or two of these factors are present, but to a significant extent, or where all five factors are present, but only to a minor extent? The *Restatement* provides no guidance, leaving each judge to apply the standard in a slightly different way, with both benefits and costs. So, what do you think? Should courts use a standard or a rule to determine material breach? If the former, can you improve on the standard offered by the *Restatement*? If the latter, what would the rule look like?

[and] (e) the extent to which the behavior of the party failing to perform or to offer to perform comports with standards of good faith and fair dealing."

Bernstein v. Nemeyer, supra, 570 A.2d 164.

The standards of materiality [are] to be applied in the light of the facts of each case in such a way as to further the purpose of securing for each party his expectation of an exchange of performances. [§ 241] therefore states circumstances, not rules, which are to be considered in determining whether a particular failure is material. 2 *Restatement (Second), supra,* § 241, comment (a).

Strouth v. Pools by Murphy & Sons, Inc., 829 A.2d 102, 105 (2003).

In the present case, the court found that the plaintiff took a ten-week vacation, which exceeded the time authorized. After the plaintiff returned, he reported for work only two or three days per week and spent long periods of time visiting Internet web sites that were unrelated to his professional duties. Additionally, after being instructed by the human resources manager to document his attendance by use of a time clock, the plaintiff refused and simply marked his time sheets with a "P" for present. Last, the court found that when Goldwitz asked when certain designs would be completed, the plaintiff responded that he was not sure and that he would take his time in completing them. When reviewing those findings in light of the factors set forth in § 241 of the *Restatement (Second) of Contracts,* we conclude that the court's finding of a material breach was not clearly erroneous.

It is clear from the court's findings that the plaintiff failed to perform under the obligations of the employment contract. As the court properly stated: "[O]ne cannot recover upon a contract unless he has fully performed his own obligation under it, has tendered performance or has some legal excuse for not performing." *See Automobile Ins. Co. v. Model Family Laundries, Inc.,* 52 A.2d 137 (1947). As a result of the material breach by the plaintiff, the defendants were excused from further performance under the contract, and were relieved of the obligation to pay the plaintiff his full salary for ninety days and to pay his posttermination salary pursuant to the schedule set forth in the contract.

The judgment is affirmed.

RELEVANT PROVISIONS

For the *Restatement (Second) of Contracts,* consult §§ 237 and 241. For the CISG, consult Article 25. For the UNIDROIT Principles, consult Articles 7.3.1 and 7.3.5.

NOTES AND QUESTIONS

1. ***What happened?*** Who sued whom for what? Procedurally, how did the case get before this court? Factually, what happened between the parties? What arguments did the plaintiff and defendant make? What rule or rules did the court apply? How did the court analyze the dispute between the parties? How did the court decide the case?

2. ***Was this case correctly decided?*** Do you agree with the result reached in this case? Why or why not? Do you agree with the court's reasoning? Why or why not? How, if at all, would you have written the opinion differently?

3. ***Applying the*** **Restatement.** If you were the judge in the case, how, exactly, would you apply *Restatement (Second) of Contracts* § 241 to determine whether there was a breach?

PROBLEM: TO BUILD OR NOT TO BUILD . . .

Pursuant to a written contract, Plaintiff agreed to do build a cellar and three-story house for Defendant for $150,000. Defendant agreed to make a payment of $50,000 when the cellar was finished, a payment of $50,000 when the house was plastered, and the balance of $50,000 when the work was completed.

Plaintiff began work on the cellar in April, and by May 17, after the cellar was completed, started work on the house. The work continued until June 10, when Plaintiff stopped because Defendant did not make the first $50,000 payment due. On June 27, Defendant paid Plaintiff $50,000, and Plaintiff resumed work. The house was plastered by the middle of August, and on September 3, Plaintiff asked Defendant for the second $50,000 installment. Defendant, on account of several minor defects it had spotted with Plaintiff's work, refused, but reassured Plaintiff that it would pay the entire $100,000 owed when the house was completed and these defects were fixed. Plaintiff acknowledged these defects, but refused to continue working until it was paid the second installment. Defendant treated Plaintiff's refusal to continue work as a breach of contract, and hired another firm to finish building the house.

Plaintiff now brings suit to recover the value of materials furnished and labor performed in the partial construction of the cellar and house for which it has not yet received compensation, in addition to any lost profits. Defendant maintains that Plaintiff breached the contract by not fully performing the work required by the contract, and was therefore not entitled to the second or third payments. Defendant adds that, upon Plaintiff's willful and voluntary refusal to finish building the house, Plaintiff forfeited its right to recover, either on the contract or on a quantum meruit.

Consulting the cases and materials in this subsection, how do you think the court should rule?

2. Anticipatory Repudiation

DOCTRINAL OVERVIEW: ANTICIPATORY REPUDIATION AS A BREACH*

We now turn to the effects of a party's repudiation of its duty before the time for performance has arrived. Such a repudiation, occurring before there has been any breach by nonperformance, is called an "anticipatory breach" or, more precisely, an "anticipatory repudiation."

It has long been accepted that an anticipatory repudiation discharges any remaining duties of performance of the injured party. In other words, the repudiation has the same effect as the nonoccurrence of a condition of those remaining duties. Once there has been a repudiation, the injured party is no longer expected to hold itself ready to perform; that party is free to make such substitute arrangements as may be appropriate. It was less clear, however, that the repudiation gave the injured party an immediate action for damages for total breach, so that that party would not have to await the time for performance to sue for damages.

In 1853 the Court of Queen's Bench allowed such an action in the celebrated case of *Hochster v. De la Tour*. . . .

Hochster v. De La Tour

Queen's Bench

118 Eng. Rep. 922 (1853)

[On April 12, 1852, plaintiff agreed, for £10 per month, to travel throughout Europe with defendant for three months as his courier. Performance was scheduled to begin on June 1, 1852. Plaintiff alleges that although he remained ready and willing to perform, the defendant wrote to him on May 11, 1852 and told him that he changed his mind, breaching his contract, but refusing to compensate plaintiff. Plaintiff argues that defendant's breach "absolved, exonerated and discharged the plaintiff from the performance of his agreement." On May 22, 1852, before the performance of the contract would have commenced, Plaintiff brought a breach of contract action against defendant. Meanwhile, between May 22 and June 1, plaintiff obtained employment with Lord Ashburton on equally good terms, although this performance was not

* Excerpted from E. ALLAN FARNSWORTH, CONTRACTS § 8.20 (4th ed. 2004).

scheduled to commence until July 4, 1852. Defendant argues that there could be no breach of the contract before June 1, 1852, but the court below rejected this argument, finding for plaintiff. Defendant appeals.]

John Campbell, 1st Baron Campbell.

LORD CAMPBELL, C.J. On this motion in arrest of judgment, the question arises, whether, if there be an agreement between A and B, whereby B engages to employ A on and from a future day for a given period of time, to travel with him into a foreign country as a courier and to start with him in that capacity on that day, A being to receive a monthly salary during the continuance of such service, B may, before the day, refuse to perform the agreement and break and renounce it so as to entitle A, before the day, to commence an action against B to recover damages for breach of the agreement, A having been ready and willing to perform it till it was broken and renounced by B.

The defendant's counsel very powerfully contended that, if the plaintiff was not contented to dissolve the contract and to abandon all remedy upon it, he was bound to remain ready and willing to perform it till the day when the actual employment as courier in the service of the defendant was to begin, and that there could be no breach of the agreement, before that day, to give a right of action. **But it cannot be laid down as a universal rule that, where by agreement an act is to be done on a future day, no action can be brought for a breach of the agreement till the day for doing the act has arrived.** If a man promises to marry a woman on a future day and before that day marries another woman, he is instantly liable to an action for breach of promise of marriage. If a man contracts to execute a lease on and from a future day for a certain term, and, before that day, executes a lease to another for the same term, he may be immediately sued for breaking the contract. So, if a man contracts to sell and deliver specific goods on a future day, and before the day he sells and delivers them to another, he is immediately liable to an action at the suit of the person with whom he first contracted to sell and deliver them.

> ***A new rule***
>
> Prior to this case, a promisee generally could *not* sue a promisor for anticipatorily repudiating its contract, in part because the promisor has, technically speaking, not *yet* breached any of its obligations, and in part because allowing the promisee to immediately bring suit would cut off the promisor's ability to change its mind and retract its repudiation. Note that, unlike in this case, in all three of the examples used by the court in the remainder of this paragraph, it was virtually (though not technically) impossible for the promisor to perform when its performance came due because the promisor had already (a) married another, (b) rented land to another, or (c) sold goods to another.

One reason alleged in support of such an action is that the defendant has, before the day, rendered it impossible for the plaintiff to perform the contract at the day, but this does not necessarily follow, for, prior to the day fixed for doing the act, the first wife may have died, a surrender of the lease executed might be obtained, and the defendant might have re-purchased the goods so as to be in a situation to sell and deliver them to the plaintiff.

Another reason may be that where there is a contract to do an act on a future day there is a relation constituted between the parties in the meantime by the contract, and that they impliedly promise that in the meantime neither will do any thing to the prejudice of the other inconsistent with that relation. As an example, a man and woman engaged to marry are affianced to one another during the period between the time of the engagement and the celebration of the marriage.

In this very case, of traveller and courier, from the day of the hiring till the day when the employment was to begin, the parties were engaged to each other, and it seems to be a breach of an implied contract if either of them renounces the engagement. . . . **If the plaintiff has no remedy for breach of the contract unless he treats the contract as in force, and acts upon it down to 1 June 1852, it follows that, till then, he must enter into no employment which will interfere with his promise "to start with the defendant on such travels on the day and year," and that he must then be properly equipped in all respects as a courier for a three months' tour on the continent of Europe.**

But it is surely much more rational, and more for the benefit of both parties, that, after the renunciation of the agreement by the defendant, the plaintiff should be at liberty to consider himself absolved from any future performance of it, retaining his right to sue for any damage he has suffered from the breach of it. Thus, instead of remaining idle and laying out money in preparations which must be useless, he is at liberty to seek service under another employer, which would go in mitigation of the damages to which he would otherwise be entitled for a breach of the contract. It seems strange that the defendant, after renouncing the contract, and absolutely declaring that he will never act under it, should be permitted to object that faith is given to his assertion, and that an opportunity is not left to him of changing his mind. . . .

> ***Mitigation and avoidability, redux***
>
> Note the policy considerations supporting the court's new rule (allowing the promisee to bring suit before the promisor's performance has come due where the latter has anticipatorily repudiated the contract), and how closely these justifications link up with the policy considerations explored in Part III.5.A.4.c, where we examined limiting a promisee's recoverable damages to those that it could not avoid by taking reasonable measures to mitigate. In both cases, the court seems concerned with preventing (or allowing recovery for) wasteful behavior, a concept we have encountered many times throughout these materials, especially in cost of completion versus diminution in value cases we explored in Part III.5.A.1.c. For more on the concept of waste and its opposite, efficiency, see "Thinking Tool: Marginal Analysis and Efficiency," p. 64, *supra*.

The man who wrongfully renounces a contract into which he has deliberately entered cannot justly complain if he is immediately sued for a compensation in damages by the man whom he has injured: and it seems reasonable to allow an option to the injured party, either to sue immediately or to wait till the time when the act was to be done, still holding it as prospectively binding for the exercise of this option, which may be advantageous to the innocent party, and cannot be prejudicial to the wrongdoer.

An argument against the action before June 1 is urged from the difficulty of calculating the damages, but this argument is equally strong against an action before Sept 1, when the three months would expire. In either case, the jury in assessing the damages would be justified in looking to all that had happened, or was likely to happen, to increase or mitigate the loss of the plaintiff down to the day of trial. . . .

If it should be held that, upon a contract to do an act on a future day, a renunciation of the contract by one party dispenses with a condition to be performed in the meantime by the other, there seems no reason for requiring that other to wait till the day arrives before seeking his remedy by action, and the only ground on which the condition can be dispensed with seems to be that the renunciation may be treated as a breach of the contract.

Upon the whole, we think that the declaration in this case is sufficient. It gives us great satisfaction to reflect that, the question being on the record, our opinion may be reviewed in a court of error. In the meantime we must give judgment for the plaintiff.

Judgment for plaintiff.

RELEVANT PROVISIONS

For the *Restatement (Second) of Contracts,* consult § 250. For the UCC, consult §§ 2-610 and 2-611. For the CISG, consult Articles 71-73. For the UNIDROIT Principles, consult Article 7.3.3.

NOTES AND QUESTIONS

1. *What happened?* Who sued whom for what? Procedurally, how did the case get before this court? Factually, what happened between the parties? What arguments did the plaintiff and defendant make? What rule or rules did the court apply? How did the court analyze the dispute between the parties? How did the court decide the case?

2. *Was this case correctly decided?* Do you agree with the result reached in this case? Why or why not? Do you agree with the court's reasoning? Why or why not? How, if at all, would you have written the opinion differently?

3. *Remedies.* Thinking back to remedies, why might it make a difference that the plaintiff made a new contract with Lord Ashburton for similar services?

4. *Changing the default rule.* Prior to *Hochster,* a plaintiff would have had to wait for an actual breach before bringing suit; i.e., the plaintiff would have had to wait to see if the defendant would perform when performance was due, and only if the defendant did not perform at that time could the plaintiff bring suit. Did the old rule make any sense? What were some of its advantages and disadvantages? For a critical response to the new rule, see the excerpt "Repudiation of Contracts" following these Notes and Questions.

5. *When to sue?* Should the plaintiff have been allowed to (1) immediately sue defendant for damages, or should he have had to wait until either (2) performance was scheduled to begin or (3) performance was scheduled

to end? If you answered (1) or (2), does this mean that plaintiff could have obtained a double recovery by (a) suing first and then (b) seeking work elsewhere? Can you see how different answers to the questions above could change the remedy available to the injured party? You should also note that if the plaintiff obtained employment elsewhere and then sued, the money he made in his substitute employment would reduce the damages owed by defendant, as we explored when we examined mitigation of damages in Part III.5.A.4.c.

6. *Retraction?* Does the fact that the promisee is allowed to sue immediately mean that the promisor's privilege to retract his repudiation is now cut off? If so, does it seem fair that the promisor can be sued *now*, even though his promise was to be performed at some *future* date and therefore has not yet been technically broken?

7. *What's the rule?* So what, exactly, is the rule of the case? Here's how one treatise defined anticipatory repudiation:

> An anticipatory breach occurs if a party to a contract, expressly or by implication, repudiates the contract before the time for performance arrives. To justify treating a renunciation as a total breach, a refusal to perform must be of the whole contract or a promise or obligation going to the whole consideration, and it must be distinct, unequivocal, and absolute. There must be an unqualified refusal, or declaration of inability, to perform substantially according to the terms of the contract. A party who sues for the total breach of a contract that is executory in part must show an absolute repudiation by language or act making it futile to proceed. As more than statements expressing a doubt about the obligor's willingness or ability to perform are required, a threat to abandon contract obligations or a mere assertion that one will be unable or will refuse to perform is not sufficient. A simple suggestion that performance of a contract should be delayed to a future time is not a repudiation of its obligations. Similarly, statements that other executives of a company that is a party to the contract wanted to terminate the relationship are not sufficiently definite to constitute an anticipatory repudiation, as they do not state that the party would not perform its duties under the contract. Ordinarily, the renunciation need not be made at the place of performance specified in the contract.*

8. *Justifying the rule.* What are the advantages and disadvantages of the doctrine of anticipatory repudiation as set forth by the court? Citing *Hochster v. De La Tour,* here is how one court justified the rule:

> The real sanctity of any contract rests only in the mutual willingness of the parties to perform. Where this willingness ceases to exist, any attempt to prolong or preserve the status between them will usually be unsatisfactory and mechanical. Generally speaking, it is far better in such a situation, for the individuals and for society, that the rights and obligations between them should be promptly and definitely settled, if the injured party so desires, unless there is some provision in the contract that, as a matter of mutual intention, can be said to prevent this

* 17A Am. Jur. 2d Contracts § 723.

> from being done. The commercial world has long since learned the desirability of fixing its liabilities and losses as quickly as possible, and the law similarly needs to remind itself that, to be useful, it too must seek to be practical.*

Do you agree? What kind of argument is this? How can it be defended?

9. *Criticism.* Do you agree with Professor Williston's criticism of *Hochster v. De La Tour*, reproduced below? Or are you more inclined to agree with the second excerpt by Professor Vold?

WILLISTON, REPUDIATION OF CONTRACTS†

The reasoning in *Hochster v. De la Tour* . . . illustrates a distinction, which it is important to observe—the distinction between a defence and a right of action. This seems obvious, but it is frequently lost sight of, as it was in that case. Every consideration of justice requires that repudiation or inability to perform should immediately excuse the innocent party from performing, nor is any technical rule violated if the excuse is allowed. But it does not follow from this that he has an immediate right of action. It is a consequence of allowing such an excuse that when he brings an action he shall not be defeated by reason of the fact that he himself has not performed, since that failure to perform was excused by the defendant's fault. But though the defendant cannot defeat the action on this ground, any other defence is as effectual as ever, and that the action is prematurely brought is an entirely different defence. . . .

The reason most strongly urged in support of the doctrine of anticipatory breach is, however, its practical convenience. It is said that it is certain that the plaintiff is going to have an action, it is better for both parties to have it disposed of at once. It may be conceded that practical convenience is of more importance than logical exactness, but yet the considerations of practical convenience must be very weighty to justify infringing the underlying principles of the law of contracts. The law is not important solely or even chiefly for the just disposal of litigated cases. The settlement of the rights of a community without recourse to the courts can only be satisfactorily arranged when logic is respected. But it is not logic only which is injured. The defendant is injured. He is held liable on a promise he never made. He has only promised to do something at a future day. He is held to have broken his contract by doing something before that day. Enlarging the obligation of contracts is perhaps as bad as impairing it. This may be of great importance. Suppose the defendant, after saying that he will not perform, changes his mind and concludes to keep his promise. Unless the plaintiff relying on the repudiation, as he justly may, has so changed his position that he cannot go on with the contract without injury, the defendant ought surely to be allowed to do this. But if the plaintiff is allowed to bring an action at once this possibility is cut off. . . . A promise to perform in June does not preclude changing position in May.

---

* *Hawkinson v. Johnston*, 122 F.2d 724, 729-30 (8th Cir. 1941).

† Excerpted from Samuel Williston, *Repudiation of Contracts, Pt. 2*, 14 HARV. L. REV. 421, 434, 438-39 (1936).

VOLD, *REPUDIATION OF CONTRACTS**

The substantial practical reason for permitting the aggrieved promise to sue at once for anticipatory repudiation is that allowing an action at once tends to conserve available resources and prevent waste. If not legal recognition is extended to the promisee's valuable contractual relation pending performance, if no cause of action is recognized until there is a failure to perform at the time for performance, large losses may be incurred which suing promptly might avoid. Merely recognizing repudiation as an excuse to aggrieved party for future non-performance is not enough since frequently there is a dispute over who is in the wrong which only litigation can settle. Unless the aggrieved promisee can at once come to court in an action for anticipatory repudiation he must either struggle on with hostile or possibly insolvent parties, incurring expense and loss of time in preparation which may be of no use to anybody, or he must cease such further preparations for performance at the peril of being found in default after all in later litigation at the time for performance. In long-time contracts which now in the business world are becoming more and more important, the importance of getting a reasonably prompt settlement of controversies over repudiation is hard to exaggerate. Very often by such settlement through litigation, the controversy can be adjusted and the productive work of the business in hand continued without serious interruption.

Even should the law's delays through appeals to the higher courts absorb more than the time outstanding between repudiation and the date for performance the general consideration of conserving available resources and avoiding waste continues applicable in favor of an immediate action for the repudiation. The sooner the controversy can be disposed of the sooner the parties can know their obligations and the sooner they can in accordance therewith adjust their affairs to practical productive efforts, instead of remaining idle or engaging in misdirected futile activity while awaiting the results of distant future litigation.

First National Bank of Omaha v. Three Dimension Systems Products, Inc.

United States Court of Appeals, Eighth Circuit
289 F.3d 542 (2002)

KYLE, CIRCUIT JUDGE. In 1996 and 1997, the First National Bank of Omaha (the Bank) and Three Dimension Systems Products, Inc. (3D) entered into a series of written agreements by which 3D was to develop, customize, and deliver to the Bank three software computer programs intended for the use of the Bank's affiliates, subsidiaries and clients. Two of the programs, known as PPS and Teller, were successfully installed by 3D at the Bank and are not the subject of the litigation below.

* Excerpted from Lawrence Vold, *Repudiation of Contracts*, 5 NEB. L. BULL. 269, 279-85 (1927).

It is the third program, known as Platform, which is at the heart of the lawsuit. Following 3D's delivery of the first stage (Stage I) of the Platform program to the Bank, a dispute concerning contract performance arose between the parties. In this litigation, the Bank claimed that 3D had breached the contract by (a) refusing to "performance test" that part of the program, Stage I, which had been delivered and (b) demanding the payment of $250,000 as a condition of its continued performance. 3D denied any breach and counterclaimed for breach of contract by the Bank, copyright infringement, and conversion. Among the defenses asserted by 3D was the Bank's failure to give 3D the contractual opportunity to cure the alleged breach.

Although there were several issues between the parties, each of which was the subject of extensive testimony during the two-week jury trial, the heart of this appeal is whether there was sufficient evidence to support the Bank's assertion, and the jury's determination, that 3D's conduct constituted an anticipatory breach of the contract justifying the Bank's decision to terminate the contract and excusing the Bank from giving 3D the opportunity to cure the conduct which constituted the breach.

Following the jury's verdict, in which it found that 3D had anticipatorily breached the contract, the District Court determined that "given the evidence presented at trial, no reasonable jury could have arrived at the conclusion that 3D had anticipatorily breached the contract with [the Bank]." Accordingly, it granted 3D's motion for judgment as a matter of law, which had been taken under advisement at the close of all the evidence. The Bank now appeals from that determination. Because our review of the entire record satisfies us that there was sufficient evidence to support the jury's finding that 3D had anticipatorily breached the contract, we reverse and reinstate the jury's verdict.

Before reviewing the evidentiary bases for the jury's determination, it is well to understand what is *not* at issue in this appeal. The parties, and the District Court, agreed that Arizona law governs the contract and all issues relating to anticipatory breach. Under Arizona law, anticipatory breach may be proven by evidence that a party has "expressed a positive and unequivocal manifestation that [it would] not render the required performance when it [was] due." *Oldenburger v. Del E. Webb Dev. Co.,* 159 Ariz. 129, 765 P.2d 531, 533 (Ct. App. 1988). Not only do the parties agree on the foregoing principle of law, but they also agree that the Court's instructions to the jury accurately reflected that legal principle. The sole disagreement is whether there was sufficient evidence to support the jury's factual determination.

We review *de novo* the District Court's grant of judgment as a matter of law and view the evidence and draw all reasonable inferences in the light most favorable to the nonmoving party—the Bank.

As this Court has recently stated

> [T]he law places a high standard on overturning a jury verdict because of the danger that the jury's rightful province will be invaded when judgment as a matter of law is misused. Where conflicting inferences reasonably can be drawn from the evidence, it is the role of the jury, not the court, to determine which

> inference shall be drawn. Only where "all of the evidence points in one direction and is susceptible to no reasonable interpretation supporting the jury verdict" should the grant of a motion for judgment as a matter of law be affirmed. Thus, it is improper to overturn a jury verdict unless, after giving the nonmoving party the benefit of all reasonable inferences and resolving all conflicts in the evidence in the nonmoving party's favor, there still exists "*a complete absence of probative facts* to support the conclusion reached so that no reasonable juror could have found for the nonmoving party."

Hunt v. Nebraska Pub. Power Dist., 282 F.3d 1021, 1029 (8th Cir. 2002) (citations omitted and emphasis in original).

To establish anticipatory breach of a contract under Arizona law, it was necessary for the Bank to prove (1) an unequivocal intent on the part of 3D not to perform as promised and (2) its own willingness and ability to perform the contract in the absence of the anticipatory breach. The Bank asserted that 3D had refused to give the required support for Stage I and had refused to continue performing under the contract unless and until the Bank paid an additional $250,000 invoice, which the Bank contended was not called for by the contract. To support these claims, the Bank presented testimony that 3D's President had stated to the Bank that he "wasn't going to fix any errors" in Stage I, and that "he might consider fixing these errors after stage three or four was delivered." There was also evidence in the form of a written communication from 3D to the Bank that there would be "no support of stage one deliverables after Friday 10/30/98, (10 days from delivery of stage 1)." To "support" a "deliverable" means to correct errors in the product which has been delivered. The Bank also presented testimony that correction of errors in Stage I was essential to the moving on to subsequent stages called for by the contract between the parties. There was also testimony that 3D's President stated to the Bank, with respect to a $250,000 invoice—"if you are not going to pay [the invoice], I'm not moving on to stage two development of this project." The Bank introduced into evidence a written communication dated November 3, 1998, stating that failure to pay this outstanding invoice would "probably cause a delay to the delivery of stage 2." Another verbal communication from 3D's President stated that in order to bring the project to a conclusion, the Bank would have to pay the $250,000 invoice. There was also evidence from which the jury could conclude that the $250,000 payment was not authorized by the contract between the parties.

In response to the foregoing, 3D argued and presented testimony to the effect that the written and verbal communication relating to Stage I errors did not state, nor could they be reasonably construed as stating, that Stage I errors would never be corrected. Rather, they would be corrected in the later stages and that process would neither delay nor impede the completion of the project. 3D also denied that the payment of the $250,000 was ever made a condition of continued performance. At most, 3D claimed, it was a subject discussed by the parties.

The record shows sharp disagreement between the parties as to what was said, intended, and understood with respect to these two issues. Each was given wide latitude by the District Court to put before the jury evidence in support of its respective position. The jury was instructed in accordance with Arizona law and neither party had substantive objections to those instructions. The jury was asked, in effect, to resolve the conflicting testimony, and it did so.

We have made a thorough review of the entire record and are satisfied that the jury's determination that there was an anticipatory breach of the contract by 3D was supported by the evidence before it. It is not within the province of a trial court to replace a jury's reasonable findings with its own, but that appears to be what occurred here when the jury verdict was set aside. We recognize that this jury could have reached a different result—this was a close case—but the need to resolve factual issues in close cases is the very reason we have juries. Both parties had ample opportunity to present evidence on the issue of anticipatory breach. The jury resolved that issue in favor of the Bank and we are satisfied that the decision has support in the record and should be allowed to stand.

We therefore reverse the District Court's granting of judgment as a matter of law and reinstate the jury verdict in favor of the Bank on the claim of anticipatory breach of contract by 3D.

NOTES AND QUESTIONS

1. *What happened?* Who sued whom for what? Procedurally, how did the case get before this court? Factually, what happened between the parties? What arguments did the plaintiff and defendant make? What rule or rules did the court apply? How did the court analyze the dispute between the parties? How did the court decide the case?

2. *Was this case correctly decided?* Do you agree with the result reached in this case? Why or why not? Do you agree with the court's reasoning? Why or why not? How, if at all, would you have written the opinion differently?

The next problem requires you to wrestle with one of the issues that sometimes comes up when a party anticipatorily repudiates its contractual obligations: At what point in time should a court measure damages? Some possibilities include: (a) when the anticipatory breach is announced, (b) when performance was scheduled to begin, and (c) when performance would have been completed. As you read the question below, ask yourself whether you think there is a principled approach to this problem, or whether injured parties are simply allowed to hop around the calendar looking for the best market price.

PROBLEM: WHEN SHOULD DAMAGES BE MEASURED?

Defendant Brewer agreed to buy from Plaintiff Farmer certain quantities of hops at specified prices, for delivery in October 2015, 2016, and 2017, of the crops of those respective years. On January 1, 2016, Defendant notified Plaintiff that because of the inferior hops delivered by Plaintiff in 2015, Defendant was repudiating each of their agreement would accept no more hops under any of the contracts. After unsuccessfully negotiating with Defendant to keep the contracts in force, Plaintiff brought suit against Defendant for breach of contract, and the court must determine how Plaintiff's damages should be measured.

Defendant contends that the correct measure of damages is the difference between the contract price and the market price as of the time when the deliveries were to have been made under the contracts. Plaintiff urges that where, as here, the hops were bought and sold for future delivery, the correct measure of damages is the difference between the contract price and the market price of the hops as of January 1, 2016, the time of repudiation.

At what point in time should the court measure damages, and why?

3. Adequate Assurance of Performance

DOCTRINAL OVERVIEW: ADEQUATE ASSURANCE OF PERFORMANCE*

. . . Under UCC 2-609, when "reasonable grounds for insecurity arise with respect to the performance of either party," the other party may "demand adequate assurance of due performance" and until receiving such assurance the other party "may if commercially reasonable suspend any performance" for which it has not received the agreed return. "After receipt of a justified demand failure to provide within a reasonable time not exceeding thirty days such assurance of due performance as is adequate under the circumstances of the particular case is a repudiation of the contract."[10] . . .

Even without the benefit of the rule of UCC § 2-609, a party that believes that the other party will not perform is free to act on that belief. If the belief turns out to be correct, the party is shielded from liability, even if it failed to render a performance of its own that was due at an earlier time. If the belief turns out to be wrong, however, the party's own failure to perform may subject it to liability for

* Excerpted from E. ALLAN FARNSWORTH, CONTRACTS § 8.23 (4th ed. 2004).

10. . . . Under the Vienna Convention, a party may suspend performance where, "after the conclusion of the contract, it becomes apparent that the other party will not perform a substantial part of his obligations," but must continue performance "if the other party provides adequate assurance of his performance." CISG 71. For a comparable provision, *see* UNIDROIT Principles 7.3.4 (giving party that "reasonably believes that there will be a fundamental non-performance by the other party" a right to "demand adequate assurance of due performance").

damages for total breach. The Code spares a party this dilemma by empowering it to demand assurance that performance will be forthcoming, allowing it thereby to avoid the risk that it would otherwise run in acting on its belief. As Ellen Peters has counselled, "If there is reasonable doubt about whether the buyer's default is substantial, the seller may be well advised to temporize by suspending future performance until it can ascertain whether the buyer is able to offer adequate assurance of further payments."[15] If it is reasonable for a party to suspend its own performance while it awaits assurance, it may do so. And a failure by the other party to give adequate assurance will be a repudiation. . . .

Whether there is a right to assurance under contracts other than those for the sale of goods is still unclear, some courts extending UCC § 2-609 by analogy and others declining to do so. . . . The *Restatement Second* states a broader rule inspired by and similar to the Code rule, applicable to contracts of all kinds.[28] . . .

AMF, Inc. v. McDonald's Corp.

United States Court of Appeals, Seventh Circuit
536 F.2d 1167 (1976)

CUMMINGS, CIRCUIT JUDGE. AMF, Incorporated, filed this case in the Southern District of New York in April 1972. It was transferred to the Northern District of Illinois in May 1973. AMF seeks damages for the alleged wrongful cancellation and repudiation of McDonald's Corporation's ("McDonald's") orders for sixteen computerized cash registers for installation in restaurants owned by wholly-owned subsidiaries of McDonald's and for seven such registers ordered by licensees of McDonald's for their restaurants. In July 1972, McDonald's of Elk Grove, Inc. sued AMF to recover the $20,385.28 purchase price paid for a prototype computerized cash register and losses sustained as a result of failure of the equipment to function satisfactorily. Both cases were tried together during a fortnight in December 1974. A few months after the completion of the bench trial, the district court rendered a memorandum opinion and order in both cases in favor of each defendant. The only appeal is from the eight judgment orders dismissing AMF's complaints against McDonald's and the seven licensees. We affirm.

The district court's memorandum opinion and order are unreported. Our statement of the pertinent facts is culled from the 124 findings of fact contained therein or from the record itself.

In 1966, AMF began to market individual components of a completely automated restaurant system, including its model 72C computerized cash register

15. Cherwell-Ralli v. Rytman Grain Co., 433 A.2d 984, 987 (Conn. 1980).

28. *Restatement Second* § 251 ("where reasonable grounds arise to believe that the obligor will commit a breach by non-performance that would of itself give the obligee a claim for damages for total breach . . . , the obligee may demand adequate assurance of due performance. . . .").

involved here. The 72C cash register then consisted of a central computer, one to four input stations, each with a keyboard and cathode ray tube display, plus the necessary cables and controls.

In 1967 McDonald's representatives visited AMF's plant in Springdale, Connecticut, to view a working "breadboard" model 72C to decide whether to use it in McDonald's restaurant system. Later that year, it was agreed that a 72C should be placed in a McDonald's restaurant for evaluation purposes.

In April 1968, a 72C unit accommodating six input stations was installed in McDonald's restaurant in Elk Grove, Illinois. This restaurant was a wholly-owned subsidiary of McDonald's and was its busiest restaurant. Besides functioning as a cash register, the 72C was intended to enable counter personnel to work faster and to assist in providing data for accounting reports and bookkeeping. McDonald's of Elk Grove, Inc. paid some $20,000 for this prototype register on January 3, 1969. AMF never gave McDonald's warranties governing reliability or performance standards for the prototype.

At a meeting in Chicago on August 29, 1968, McDonald's concluded to order sixteen 72C's for its company-owned restaurants and to cooperate with AMF to obtain additional orders from its licensees. In December 1968, AMF accepted McDonald's purchase orders for those sixteen 72C's. In late January 1969, AMF accepted seven additional orders for 72C's from McDonald's licensees for their restaurants. Under the contract for the sale of all the units, there was a warranty for parts and service. AMF proposed to deliver the first unit in February 1969, with installation of the remaining twenty-two units in the first half of 1969. However, AMF established a new delivery schedule in February 1969, providing for deliveries to commence at the end of July 1969 and to be completed in January 1970, assuming that the first test unit being built at AMF's Vandalia, Ohio, plant was built and satisfactorily tested by the end of July 1969. This was never accomplished.

During the operation of the prototype 72C at McDonald's Elk Grove restaurant, many problems resulted, requiring frequent service calls by AMF and others. Because of its poor performance, McDonald's had AMF remove the prototype unit from its Elk Grove restaurant in late April 1969.

At a March 18, 1969, meeting, McDonald's and AMF personnel met to discuss the performance of the Elk Grove prototype. AMF agreed to formulate a set of performance and reliability standards for the future 72C's, including "the number of failures permitted at various degrees of seriousness, total permitted downtime, maximum service hours and cost." Pending mutual agreement on such standards, McDonald's personnel asked that production of the twenty-three units be held up and AMF agreed.

On May 1, 1969, AMF met with McDonald's personnel to provide them with performance and reliability standards. However, the parties never agreed upon such standards. At that time, AMF did not have a working machine and could not produce one within a reasonable time because its Vandalia, Ohio, personnel were too inexperienced. After the May 1st meeting, AMF concluded that McDonald's had cancelled all 72C orders. The reasons for the cancellation were the poor performance of the prototype, the lack of assurances that a workable machine was available and the unsatisfactory conditions at AMF's Vandalia, Ohio, plant where the twenty-three 72C's were to be built.

On July 29, 1969, McDonald's and AMF representatives met in New York. At this meeting it was mutually understood that the 72C orders were cancelled and that none would be delivered.

In its conclusions of law, the district court held that McDonald's and its licensees had entered into contracts for twenty-three 72C cash registers but that AMF was not able to perform its obligations under the contracts (see note, 1, supra). Citing § 2-610 of the [UCC][3] and Comment 1 thereunder, the court concluded that on July 29, McDonald's justifiably repudiated the contracts to purchase all twenty-three 72C's.

Relying on §§ 2-609 and 2-610 of the [UCC],[5] the court decided that McDonald's was warranted in repudiating the contracts and therefore had a right to cancel the orders by virtue of § 2-711 of the [UCC].[6] Accordingly, judgment was entered for McDonald's.

---

3. Section 2-610 provides: Anticipatory Repudiation. When either party repudiates the contract with respect to a performance not yet due the loss of which will substantially impair the value of the contract to the other, the aggrieved party may

(a) for a commercially reasonable time await performance by the repudiating party; or

(b) resort to any remedy for breach (§ 2-703 or § 2-711), even though he has notified the repudiating party that he would await the latter's performance and has urged retraction; and

(c) in either case suspend his own performance or proceed in accordance with the provisions of this Article on the seller's right to identify goods to the contract notwithstanding breach or to salvage unfinished goods (§ 2-704).

5. Section 2-609 provides: Right to Adequate Assurance of Performance. (1) A contract for sale imposes an obligation on each party that the other's expectation of receiving due performance will not be impaired. When reasonable grounds for insecurity arise with respect to the performance of either party the other may in writing demand adequate assurance of due performance and until he receives such assurance may if commercially reasonable suspend any performance for which he has not already received the agreed return.

(2) Between merchants the reasonableness of grounds for insecurity and the adequacy of any assurance offered shall be determined according to commercial standards.

(3) Acceptance of any improper delivery or payment does not prejudice the aggrieved party's right to demand adequate assurance of future performance.

(4) After receipt of a justified demand failure to provide within a reasonable time not exceeding 30 days such assurance of due performance as is adequate under the circumstances of the particular case is a repudiation of the contract.

6. Section 2-711 provides: Buyer's Remedies in General; Buyer's Security Interest in Rejected Goods. (1) Where the seller fails to make delivery or repudiates or the buyer rightfully rejects or justifiably revokes acceptance then with respect to any goods involved, and with respect to the whole if the breach goes to the whole contract (§ 2-612), the buyer may cancel and whether or not he has done so may in addition to recovering so much of the price as has been paid

(a) "cover" and have damages under the next section as to all the goods affected whether or not they have been identified to the contract; or

(b) recover damages for non-delivery as provided in this Article (§ 2-713).

(2) Where the seller fails to deliver or repudiates the buyer may also

(a) if the goods have been identified recover them as provided in this Article (§ 2-502); or

(b) in a proper case obtain specific performance or replevy the goods as provided in this Article (§ 2-716).

The findings of fact adopted by the district court were a mixture of the court's own findings and findings proposed by the parties, some of them modified by the court. AMF has assailed ten of the 124 findings of fact, but our examination of the record satisfies us that all have adequate support in the record and support the conclusions of law.

> ***Another question of fact***
>
> What constitutes an "adequate" assurance of performance is also a question of fact.

Whether in a specific case a buyer has reasonable grounds for insecurity is a question of fact. Comment 3 to UCC § 2-609; Anderson, *Uniform Commercial Code*, § 2-609 (2d Ed. 1971). On this record, McDonald's clearly had "reasonable grounds for insecurity" with respect to AMF's performance. At the time of the March 18, 1969, meeting, the prototype unit had performed unsatisfactorily ever since its April 1968 installation. Although AMF had projected delivery of all twenty-three units by the first half of 1969, AMF later scheduled delivery from the end of July 1969 until January 1970. When McDonald's personnel visited AMF's Vandalia, Ohio, plant on March 4, 1969, they saw that none of the 72C systems was being assembled and learned that a pilot unit would not be ready until the end of July of that year. They were informed that the engineer assigned to the project was not to commence work until March 17th. AMF's own personnel were also troubled about the design of the 72C, causing them to attempt to reduce McDonald's order to five units. Therefore, under § 2-609 McDonald's was entitled to demand adequate assurance of performance by AMF.[7] However, AMF urges that § 2-609 of the UCC (note 5 *supra*) is inapplicable because McDonald's did not make a written demand of adequate assurance of due performance. In *Pittsburgh-Des Moines Steel Co. v. Brookhaven Manor Water Co.*, 532 F.2d 572, 581 (7th Cir. 1976), we noted that the Code should be liberally construed[8] and therefore rejected such "a formalistic approach" to § 2-609. McDonald's failure to make a written demand was excusable because AMF's Mr. Dubosque's testimony and his April 2 and 18, 1969, memoranda about the March 18th meeting showed AMF's clear understanding that McDonald's had suspended performance until it should receive adequate assurance of due performance from AMF.After the March 18th demand, AMF never repaired the Elk Grove unit satisfactorily nor replaced it. Similarly, it was unable to satisfy McDonald's that the twenty-three

7. McDonald's was justified in seeking assurances about performance standards at the March 18th meeting. The parts and service warranty in the contracts for the twenty-three 72C's was essentially a limitation of remedy provision. Under UCC § 2-719(2) if the 72C cash registers failed to work or could not be repaired within a reasonable time, the limitation of remedy provision would be invalid, and McDonald's would be entitled to pursue all other remedies provided in Article 2. Because McDonald's would have a right to reject the machines if they proved faulty after delivery and then to cancel the contract, it was consistent with the purposes of § 2-609 for McDonald's to require assurances that such eventuality would not occur. See Comment 1 to UCC § 2-719.

8. UCC § 1-102(1) provides that the Code "shall be liberally construed and applied to promote its underlying purposes and policies."

machines on order would work. At the May 1st meeting, AMF offered unsatisfactory assurances for only five units instead of twenty-three. The performance standards AMF tendered to McDonald's were unacceptable because they would have permitted the 72C's not to function properly for 90 hours per year, permitting as much as one failure in every fifteen days in a busy McDonald's restaurant. Also, as the district court found, AMF's Vandalia, Ohio, personnel were too inexperienced to produce a proper machine. Since AMF did not provide adequate assurance of performance after McDonald's March 18th demand, UCC § 2-609(1) permitted McDonald's to suspend performance. When AMF did not furnish adequate assurance of due performance at the May 1st meeting, it thereby repudiated the contract under § 2-609(4). At that point, § 2-610(b) (note 3 *supra*) permitted McDonald's to cancel the orders pursuant to § 2-711 (note 6, *supra*), as it finally did on July 29, 1969.

In seeking reversal, AMF relies on *Pittsburgh-Des Moines Steel Co. v. Brookhaven Manor Water Co., supra,* 532 F.2d at 581. There we held a party to a contract could not resort to UCC § 2-609 since there was no demonstration that reasonable grounds for insecurity were present. That case is inapt where, as here, McDonald's submitted sufficient proof in that respect. But that case does teach that McDonald's could cancel the orders under §§ 2-610 and 2-711 because of AMF's failure to give adequate assurance of due performance under § 2-609.

AMF also relies heavily on *Stewart-Decatur Security Systems v. Von Weise Gear Co.,* 517 F.2d 1136 (8th Cir. 1975), but it did not involve the provisions of the Commercial Code that are before us. There the buyer had agreed to purchase production line models of a previously approved prototype. Here McDonald's contracted to purchase workable 72C's, not copies of the worthless Elk Grove prototype.

Judgment Affirmed.

RELEVANT PROVISIONS

For the *Restatement (Second) of Contracts,* consult § 251. For the UCC, consult §§ 2-609 and 2-610. For the CISG, consult Article 71. For the UNIDROIT Principles, consult Article 7.3.4.

NOTES AND QUESTIONS

1. ***What happened?*** Who sued whom for what? Procedurally, how did the case get before this court? Factually, what happened between the parties? What arguments did the plaintiff and defendant make? What rule or rules did the court apply? How did the court analyze the dispute between the parties? How did the court decide the case?

2. *Was this case correctly decided?* Do you agree with the result reached in this case? Why or why not? Do you agree with the court's reasoning? Why or why not? How, if at all, would you have written the opinion differently?

3. *An improvement over pre-Code law.* In previous cases like *Walker & Co. v. Harrison*, we have seen how a party's decision to repudiate its obligations due to its belief that the other party has breached "is fraught with peril," for, as the *Walker* court explained, "should such determination, as viewed by a later court in the calm of its contemplation, be unwarranted, the repudiator himself will have been guilty of material breach and himself have become the aggressor, not an innocent victim." What was a skeptical party to do when they believed the other party to be in breach? Under pre-Code law, the answer was, unfortunately, not much. It could withhold its own performance based on its fears that the other party would not perform but, as we have just seen, doing so would put it at risk of being the party in breach. Or, it could take its chances and perform its obligations in the hopes that its contractual partner did the same. But if the doubtful party's skepticism turned out to be justified, and the other party did not perform, then it was left to seek its remedy in court—hardly an efficient solution. § 2-609 of the UCC attempts to solve this problem by allowing a party with "reasonable grounds for insecurity" to demand adequate assurance of the other party's "due performance." Although the section is far from perfect—there are problems with defining the scope of "due performance," for example, and sometimes there will be a good-faith dispute between the parties as to the meaning of an ambiguous or vague term, with each party alleging, in good faith, that it will only perform based on its understanding of such a term—but, all in all, it marks a big improvement over pre-Code law. As explained in a Comment written not too long after the promulgation of UCC § 2-609:

> That § 2-609 offers a regime of certainty where commercial anarchy previously reigned, is one of the section's greatest merits. Professor Llewellyn has said:
>
> > If there is one thing that makes trouble in . . . contracts of any kind for future delivery, it is in situations where you are beginning to wonder whether he [the other party to the contract] is going to perform and you have not yet got up to the place . . . where you can say either he is insolvent or he has repudiated. . . .
> >
> > § 2-609 gives you the werewithal [sic] for finding out where you are within a reasonable time. This is certainty. This is the kind of certainty that eliminates litigation that has to go to the Appellate Court.
>
> § 2-609 has also been complimented because it conforms to the desires and practices of businessmen.*

---

* Ralph D. Smith, *Comment: Commercial Law—Uniform Commercial Code—Section 2-609: Right to Adequate Assurance of Performance*, 7 NAT'L RES. J. 397, 398-99 (1967).

PROBLEM: WHO BREACHED?

During February, Scott (Seller) and Barbara (Buyer) entered into contract No. 1 ("K1") for the sale of 16,000 bushels of wheat. Pursuant to the contract, Buyer paid Seller $2,000 as an advanced payment. With respect to payment of the contract balance, the agreement reads in part:

> Payment by Buyer is conditioned upon Seller's completion of Delivery of total quantity as set forth in this contract. Any payment made prior to completion of delivery is merely an accommodation. In making such accommodation, Buyer does not waive any condition of this contract to be performed by Seller.

Elsewhere, the contract provided that the full balance would be paid 30 days after shipment of the total contract quantity of grain.

By March 13, Seller had delivered all the wheat called for in K1. Payment of the full contract balance of approximately $49,000 was due on April 13.

On March 1, Seller and Buyer executed contract No. 2 ("K2") for the sale of 13,500 bushels of wheat and contract No. 3 ("K3") for the sale of approximately 30 truckloads of wheat. With the exception of quantity, the contracts had identical terms and conditions as those in K1, including the above-quoted provision and the provision for full payment by Buyer 30 days after complete performance by Seller.

In early March 2013, Seller commenced performance of K2. By March 15, 2013, he had delivered to Buyer approximately 10,000 bushels of wheat. However, he ceased performance because of his belief that Buyer could not pay for the wheat. More specifically, Seller was contracting with other grain dealers while working with Buyer, and suffered a loss on an unrelated contract. When reviewing this loss with his banker, Seller was told that Buyer was not the "best grain trader" and was advised to contact an agent from the Department of Agriculture for additional information about Buyer. The agent told Seller there was an active complaint against Buyer concerning payments to other farmers.

The next day, one of Buyer's trucks appeared at Seller's farm to take another load of grain, but Seller refused to load the grain. Instead, he told the driver that, per his attorney's advice, he was trying to get in touch with Barbara, and would not load any grain until he made contact with Barbara to settle some questions he had about her ability to pay.

From March 21 through April 6, Seller and Seller's attorney unsuccessfully attempted to contact Buyer several times by telephone.

Meanwhile, by a letter dated March 23, 1983, Buyer responded to Seller's refusal to load the wheat. Buyer stated that she had not breached the contracts; however, Seller had breached the agreements. Buyer pointed out the payment terms requiring shipment of the full quantity before payment was due and requested that Seller resume performance. Otherwise, Buyer would be forced to "resort to cover."

Buyer followed up this letter with another dated April 4, in which she notified Seller that she was cancelling the contracts. However, she assured Seller that, if the contracts were performed, she would pay according to the contract terms.

On April 6, Seller, through counsel, replied to Buyer, informing Buyer that his client had not been paid on the contracts, and demanding assurances of performance that Buyer would pay for the grain shipped on the fully performed K1 and the partially performed K2. However, under the contract terms, payment was not due on K1 until April 13, and was not due on K2 until 30 days after full performance.

Upon receiving this letter, Buyer cancelled contracts K2 and K3 on April 7. She had previously contacted grain sellers in Denver and Salt Lake City to effect cover, but by this date the grain was no longer available.

Seller instituted suit against Buyer on April 25, alleging breach of contract by Buyer in not paying in full for the grain prior to delivery pursuant to his demand for adequate assurance of performance.

Applying the material discussed in this subsection (especially UCC § 2-609), how do you think the court should resolve this dispute?

4. The Perfect Tender Rule

DOCTRINAL OVERVIEW: THE PERFECT TENDER RULE*

During the nineteenth century a rule developed that a buyer was entitled to reject goods unless the seller made a "perfect tender." The requirement of perfection covered not only the quantity and quality of the goods but also the details of shipment. In the words of Learned Hand, "There is no room in commercial contracts for the doctrine of substantial performance."[28] This rule of strict performance remained unchallenged during the first half of the twentieth century. In its terms, it applied even though it was not practical for the seller to resell the rejected goods as, for example, if the goods were perishable or specially manufactured. Because the buyer's right to reject did not depend on the buyer's having been harmed by the breach, the rule offered an inviting pretext for buyers that sought to escape their contract obligations on discovering that they no longer needed the goods or that the market price had fallen. The shortcomings of the rule did not escape criticism.

Nevertheless, the Code adopts the perfect tender rule. The buyer can reject "if the goods or the tender of delivery fail in any respect to conform to the contract."[33] However, the rule has been eroded by a number of related sections that soften its impact. Among the most significant are those that subject a buyer that has accepted goods to a standard of substantial performance if the buyer chooses to

---

* Excerpted from E. ALLAN FARNSWORTH, CONTRACTS § 8.12 (4th ed. 2004).

28. Mitsubishi Goshi Kaisha v. J. Aron & Co., 16 F.2d 185. 186 2d Cir. 1926) (seller of soy bean oil, to be shipped "f.o.b. . . . Pacific Coast" and paid for against documents, presented documents showing shipment from Dallas).

33. UCC § 2-601. (The Code slightly limits the perfect tender rule as to details of shipment in UCC § 2-504.)

revoke the acceptance,[35] that subject a buyer under an installment contract to a similar standard if the buyer chooses to reject an installment,[36] and that grant a seller the right to "cure" after the buyer has rejected the goods.[37]

Ramirez v. Autosport

Supreme Court of New Jersey
440 A.2d 1345 (1982)

POLLOCK, J. This case raises several issues under the Uniform Commercial Code ("the Code" and "UCC") concerning whether a buyer may reject a tender of goods with minor defects and whether a seller may cure the defects. We consider also the remedies available to the buyer, including cancellation of the contract. The main issue is whether plaintiffs, Mr. and Mrs. Ramirez, could reject the tender by defendant, Autosport, of a camper van with minor defects and cancel the contract for the purchase of the van.

The trial court ruled that Mr. and Mrs. Ramirez rightfully rejected the van and awarded them the fair market value of their trade-in van. The Appellate Division affirmed in a brief per curiam decision which, like the trial court opinion, was unreported. We affirm the judgment of the Appellate Division.

I

Following a mobile home show at the Meadowlands Sports Complex, Mr. and Mrs. Ramirez visited Autosport's showroom in Somerville. On July 20, 1978 the Ramirezes and Donald Graff, a salesman for Autosport, agreed on the sale of a new camper and the trade-in of the van owned by Mr. and Mrs. Ramirez. Autosport and the Ramirezes signed a simple contract reflecting a \$14,100 purchase price for the new van with a \$4,700 trade-in allowance for the Ramirez van, which Mr. and Mrs. Ramirez left with Autosport. After further allowance for taxes, title and documentary fees, the net price was \$9,902. Because Autosport needed two weeks to prepare the new van, the contract provided for delivery on or about August 3, 1978.

On that date, Mr. and Mrs. Ramirez returned with their checks to Autosport to pick up the new van. Graff was not there so Mr. White, another salesman, met them. Inspection disclosed several defects in the van. The paint was scratched, both the electric and sewer hookups were missing, and the hubcaps were not installed. White advised the Ramirezes not to accept the camper because it was not ready.

35. UCC § 2-608(1) (buyer can revoke acceptance only if non-conformity "substantially impairs" the value of the goods to buyer).

36. UCC § 2-612(2) (buyer can reject installment only "if the non-conformity substantially impairs the value of that installment," unless the defect is in the required documents).

37. UCC § 2-508.

Mr. and Mrs. Ramirez wanted the van for a summer vacation and called Graff several times. Each time Graff told them it was not ready for delivery. Finally, Graff called to notify them that the camper was ready. On August 14 Mr. and Mrs. Ramirez went to Autosport to accept delivery, but workers were still touching up the outside paint. Also, the camper windows were open, and the dining area cushions were soaking wet. Mr. and Mrs. Ramirez could not use the camper in that condition, but Mr. Leis, Autosport's manager, suggested that they take the van and that Autosport would replace the cushions later. Mrs. Ramirez counteroffered to accept the van if they could withhold $2,000, but Leis agreed to no more than $250, which she refused. Leis then agreed to replace the cushions and to call them when the van was ready.

On August 15, 1978 Autosport transferred title to the van to Mr. and Mrs. Ramirez, a fact unknown to them until the summer of 1979. Between August 15 and September 1, 1978 Mrs. Ramirez called Graff several times urging him to complete the preparation of the van, but Graff constantly advised her that the van was not ready. He finally informed her that they could pick it up on September 1.

When Mr. and Mrs. Ramirez went to the showroom on September 1, Graff asked them to wait. And wait they did—for one and a half hours. No one from Autosport came forward to talk with them, and the Ramirezes left in disgust.

On October 5, 1978 Mr. and Mrs. Ramirez went to Autosport with an attorney friend. Although the parties disagreed on what occurred, the general topic was whether they should proceed with the deal or Autosport should return to the Ramirezes their trade-in van. Mrs. Ramirez claimed they rejected the new van and requested the return of their trade-in. Mr. Lustig, the owner of Autosport, thought, however, that the deal could be salvaged if the parties could agree on the dollar amount of a credit for the Ramirezes. Mr. and Mrs. Ramirez never took possession of the new van and repeated their request for the return of their trade-in. Later in October, however, Autosport sold the trade-in to an innocent third party for $4,995. Autosport claimed that the Ramirez' van had a book value of $3,200 and claimed further that it spent $1,159.62 to repair their van. By subtracting the total of those two figures, $4,159.62, from the $4,995.00 sale price, Autosport claimed a $600-700 profit on the sale.

On November 20, 1978 the Ramirezes sued Autosport seeking, among other things, rescission of the contract. Autosport counterclaimed for breach of contract.

II

Our initial inquiry is whether a consumer may reject defective goods that do not conform to the contract of sale. The basic issue is whether under the UCC, . . . a seller has the duty to deliver goods that conform precisely to the contract. **We conclude that the seller is under such a duty to make a "perfect tender" and that a buyer has the right to reject goods that do not conform to the contract.** That conclusion, however, does not resolve the entire dispute between buyer and seller. A more complete answer requires a brief

The Perfect Tender Rule

Note that, in contrast to contracts for land and/or services (*see, e.g., Jacob & Youngs v. Kent*) there is no room for the doctrine of substantial performance in the UCC. Per UCC § 2-601, the buyer

statement of the history of the mutual obligations of buyers and sellers of commercial goods.

> has the right to perfect tender, and can reject goods for any non-conformity whatsoever. This seemingly harsh doctrine (from the seller's perspective, anyway) is mitigated somewhat by other provisions in the UCC, such as §§ 2-508 and 2-608, as discussed elsewhere in the court's opinion.

In the nineteenth century, sellers were required to deliver goods that complied exactly with the sales agreement. See *Filley v. Pope,* 115 U.S. 213, 220 (1885) (buyer not obliged to accept otherwise conforming scrap iron shipped to New Orleans from Leith, rather than Glasgow, Scotland, as required by contract); *Columbian Iron Works & Dry-Dock Co. v. Douglas,* 84 Md. 44, 47 (1896) (buyer who agreed to purchase steel scrap from United States cruisers not obliged to take any other kind of scrap). That rule, known as the "perfect tender" rule, remained part of the law of sales well into the twentieth century. By the 1920's the doctrine was so entrenched in the law that Judge Learned Hand declared "(t)here is no room in commercial contracts for the doctrine of substantial performance." *Mitsubishi Goshi Kaisha v. J. Aron & Co., Inc.,* 16 F.2d 185, 186 (2d Cir. 1926).

The harshness of the rule led courts to seek to ameliorate its effect and to bring the law of sales in closer harmony with the law of contracts, which allows rescission only for material breaches. . . . The chief objection to the continuation of the perfect tender rule was that buyers in a declining market would reject goods for minor nonconformities and force the loss on surprised sellers.

To the extent that a buyer can reject goods for any nonconformity, the UCC retains the perfect tender rule. Section 2-106 states that goods conform to a contract "when they are in accordance with the obligations under the contract." [UCC § 2-106]. Section 2-601 authorizes a buyer to reject goods if they "or the tender of delivery fail in any respect to conform to the contract." **The Code, however, mitigates the harshness of the perfect tender rule and balances the interests of buyer and seller.** See *Restatement (Second), Contracts,* § 241 comment (b) (1981). The Code achieves that result through its provisions for revocation of acceptance and cure. [UCC §§ 2-608 and 2-508].

> ***Striking a Balance, Part 1***
>
> Although the UCC retains the perfect tender rule, it is critical to note how its drafters attempted to strike a balance between the buyer's and seller's interests depending on whether the buyer attempted to reject any non-conforming goods *before* formally accepting them (e.g., during inspection, as discussed in the next two paragraphs) or *after* accepting them (discussed in the following paragraph).

Initially, the rights of the parties vary depending on whether the rejection occurs before or after acceptance of the goods. Before acceptance, the buyer may reject goods for any nonconformity. [UCC § 2-601]. Because of the seller's right to cure, however, the buyer's rejection does not necessarily discharge the contract. [UCC § 2-508]. Within the time set for performance in the contract, the seller's right to cure is unconditional. *Id.,* subsec. (1); see *id.,* Official Comment 1. Some authorities recommend granting a breaching party a right to cure in all contracts, not merely those for the sale of goods. *Restatement (Second), Contracts,* ch. 10, especially §§ 237 and 241. Underlying the right to cure in both kinds of contracts is the recognition that parties should be encouraged to communicate with each other and to resolve their own problems. *Id.*, Introduction p. 193.

The rights of the parties also vary if rejection occurs after the time set for performance. After expiration of that time, the seller has a further reasonable time to cure if he believed reasonably that the goods would be acceptable with or without a money allowance. [UCC § 2-508(2)]. The determination of what constitutes a further reasonable time depends on the surrounding circumstances, which include the change of position by and the amount of inconvenience to the buyer. [UCC § 2-508], Official Comment 3. Those circumstances also include the length of time needed by the seller to correct the nonconformity and his ability to salvage the goods by resale to others. See *Restatement (Second), Contracts*, § 241 comment (d). Thus, the Code balances the buyer's right to reject nonconforming goods with a "second chance" for the seller to conform the goods to the contract under certain limited circumstances. [UCC § 2-508], New Jersey Study Comment 1.

After acceptance, the Code strikes a different balance: the buyer may revoke acceptance only if the nonconformity substantially impairs the value of the goods to him. [UCC § 2-608]. This provision protects the seller from revocation for trivial defects. It also prevents the buyer from taking undue advantage of the seller by allowing goods to depreciate and then returning them because of asserted minor defects. Because this case involves rejection of goods, we need not decide whether a seller has a right to cure substantial defects that justify revocation of acceptance.

Other courts agree that the buyer has a right of rejection for any nonconformity, but that the seller has a countervailing right to cure within a reasonable time.

One New Jersey case, *Gindy Mfg. Corp. v. Cardinale Trucking Corp.*, suggests that, because some defects can be cured, they do not justify rejection. 111 N.J. Super. 383, 387 n.1 (Law Div. 1970). Nonetheless, we conclude that the perfect tender rule is preserved to the extent of permitting a buyer to reject goods for any defects. Because of the seller's right to cure, rejection does not terminate the contract. Accordingly, we disapprove the suggestion in *Gindy* that curable defects do not justify rejection.

A further problem, however, is identifying the remedy available to a buyer who rejects goods with insubstantial defects that the seller fails to cure within a reasonable time. The Code provides expressly that when "the buyer rightfully rejects, then with respect to the goods involved, the buyer may cancel." [UCC § 2-711]. "Cancellation" occurs when either party puts an end to the contract for breach by the other. [UCC § 2-106(4)]. Nonetheless, some confusion exists whether the equitable remedy of rescission survives under the Code.

Striking a Balance, Part 2

Note that regardless of whether the buyer has attempted to reject non-conforming goods before or after accepting them, the seller may still, under certain circumstances (outlined in UCC § 2-508), cure any defects.

The Code eschews the word "rescission" and substitutes the terms "cancellation," "revocation of acceptance", and "rightful rejection". [UCC §§ 2-106(4); 2-608; and 2-711] & Official Comment 1. Although neither "rejection" nor "revocation of acceptance" is defined in the Code, rejection includes both the buyer's refusal to accept or keep delivered goods and his notification to the seller that he will not keep them. Revocation of acceptance is like rejection, but occurs after the buyer has accepted the goods. Nonetheless, revocation of acceptance is intended to provide the same relief as rescission of a contract of sale of goods. [UCC § 2-608,] Official Comment 1; N.J. Study Comment 2. In brief, revocation is tantamount to rescission. Similarly, subject to the seller's right to cure, a buyer who rightfully rejects goods, like one who revokes his acceptance, may cancel the contract. [UCC § 2-711] & Official Comment 1. We need not resolve the extent to which rescission for reasons other than rejection or revocation of acceptance, e.g. fraud and mistake, survives as a remedy outside the Code. . . .

Although the complaint requested rescission of the contract, plaintiffs actually sought not only the end of their contractual obligations, but also restoration to their pre-contractual position. That request incorporated the equitable doctrine of restitution, the purpose of which is to restore plaintiff to as good a position as he occupied before the contract. In UCC parlance, plaintiffs' request was for the cancellation of the contract and recovery of the price paid. [UCC §§ 2-106(4), 2-711].

General contract law permits rescission only for material breaches, and the Code restates "materiality" in terms of "substantial impairment." The Code permits a buyer who rightfully rejects goods to cancel a contract of sale. [UCC § 2-711]. Because a buyer may reject goods with insubstantial defects, he also may cancel the contract if those defects remain uncured. Otherwise, a seller's failure to cure minor defects would compel a buyer to accept imperfect goods and collect for any loss caused by the nonconformity. [UCC § 2-714].

Although the Code permits cancellation by rejection for minor defects, it permits revocation of acceptance only for substantial impairments. That distinction is consistent with other Code provisions that depend on whether the buyer has accepted the goods. Acceptance creates liability in the buyer for the price, [UCC § 2-709(1)], and precludes rejection. [UCC §§ 2-607(2); 2-606], New Jersey Study Comment 1. Also, once a buyer accepts goods, he has the burden to prove any defect. [UCC § 2-607(4)]. By contrast, where goods are rejected for not conforming to the contract, the burden is on the seller to prove that the nonconformity was corrected.

Underlying the Code provisions is the recognition of the revolutionary change in business practices in this century. The purchase of goods is no longer a simple transaction in which a buyer purchases individually-made goods from a seller in a face-to-face transaction. Our economy depends on a complex system for the manufacture, distribution, and sale of goods, a system in which manufacturers and consumers rarely meet. Faceless manufacturers mass-produce goods for unknown consumers who purchase those goods from merchants exercising little or no control over the quality of their production. In an age of assembly lines, we are accustomed to cars with scratches, television sets without knobs and other products with all kinds of defects. Buyers no longer expect a "perfect tender." If a merchant sells defective goods, the reasonable expectation of the parties is that the buyer will return those goods and that the seller will repair or replace them.

Recognizing this commercial reality, the Code permits a seller to cure imperfect tenders. Should the seller fail to cure the defects, whether substantial or not, the balance shifts again in favor of the buyer, who has the right to cancel or seek damages. [UCC § 2-711]. In general, economic considerations would induce sellers to cure minor defects. Assuming the seller does not cure, however, the buyer should be permitted to exercise his remedies under [UCC § 2-711]. The Code remedies for consumers are to be liberally construed, and the buyer should have the option of cancelling if the seller does not provide conforming goods. [UCC § 1-106].

To summarize, the UCC preserves the perfect tender rule to the extent of permitting a buyer to reject goods for any nonconformity. Nonetheless, that rejection does not automatically terminate the contract. A seller may still effect a cure and preclude unfair rejection and cancellation by the buyer. [UCC § 2-508], Official Comment 2; [UCC § 2-711], Official Comment 1.

III

The trial court found that Mr. and Mrs. Ramirez had rejected the van within a reasonable time under [UCC § 2-602]. The court found that on August 3, 1978 Autosport's salesman advised the Ramirezes not to accept the van and that on August 14, they rejected delivery and Autosport agreed to replace the cushions. Those findings are supported by substantial credible evidence, and we sustain them. Although the trial court did not find whether Autosport cured the defects within a reasonable time, we find that Autosport did not effect a cure. Clearly the van was not ready for delivery during August, 1978 when Mr. and Mrs. Ramirez rejected it, and Autosport had the burden of proving that it had corrected the defects. Although the Ramirezes gave Autosport ample time to correct the defects, Autosport did not demonstrate that the van conformed to the contract on September 1. In fact, on that date, when Mr. and Mrs. Ramirez returned at Autosport's invitation, all they received was discourtesy.

On the assumption that substantial impairment is necessary only when a purchaser seeks to revoke acceptance under [UCC § 2-608], the trial court correctly refrained from deciding whether the defects substantially impaired the van. The court properly concluded that plaintiffs were entitled to "rescind"—i.e., to "cancel"—the contract.

Because Autosport had sold the trade-in to an innocent third party, the trial court determined that the Ramirezes were entitled not to the return of the trade-in, but to its fair market value, which the court set at the contract price of \$4,700. . . .

Although the value of the trade-in van as set forth in the sales contract was not the only possible standard, it is an appropriate measure of fair market value.

For the preceding reasons, we affirm the judgment of the Appellate Division.

RELEVANT PROVISIONS

For the *Restatement (Second) of Contracts,* consult §§ 237 and 241. For the UCC, consult §§ 2-106(2)-(4), 2-508, 2-601, 2-602, 2-606, 2-607, 2-608, 2-709, and 2-711. For the CISG, consult Articles 25, 49(1)(a), and 64(1)(a). For the UNIDROIT Principles, consult Article 7.3.1.

NOTES AND QUESTIONS

1. *What happened?* Who sued whom for what? Procedurally, how did the case get before this court? Factually, what happened between the parties? What arguments did the plaintiff and defendant make? What rule or rules did the court apply? How did the court analyze the dispute between the parties? How did the court decide the case?

2. *Was this case correctly decided?* Do you agree with the result reached in this case? Why or why not? Do you agree with the court's reasoning? Why or why not? How, if at all, would you have written the opinion differently?

3. *Counseling.* How would you have advised the Ramirezes during the resolution of this dispute? How would you advise Autosport?

4. *Perfect tender.* Do you agree that the Ramirezes should be entitled to a perfect tender, or were they being too nitpicky?

5. *From the casebook to the silver screen.* There is a wonderful scene from the movie *National Lampoon's Vacation* that is remarkably similar to the fact pattern in *Ramirez.* In it, the protagonist Clark has traded in his old family wagon and is haggling with a shady car dealer for delivery of the Antarctic Blue Super Sports Wagon he has ordered. The rest of the tragi-comic scene can be seen here: http://www.youtube.com/watch?v=pTaTitRENDM.

PROBLEM: THE BRIDESMAID'S GOWN

Plaintiff Patty seeks to recover from Defendant Dressmaker the purchase price of a bridesmaid's gown that Plaintiff alleges was not been properly altered. Specifically, Patty states that she had had two fittings at Dressmaker's salon and that she picked up the gown three days before the wedding. When she picked it up, the gown was ironed and on a hanger, and she did not try it on in the store.

Patty claims that a salesperson assured her that it was perfect. On the day of the wedding, however, Patty tried the gown on for the first time and discovered that it did not fit properly. Dressmaker claims that the problem with the fit of the gown (which could be seen in the photograph of Patty taken on the day of the wedding) would only be apparent when Patty tried it on.

Drawing on the material discussed in this subsection (especially on the UCC provisions cited under "Relevant Provisions," *supra*), how do you think the court should resolve this dispute?

INTERNATIONAL PERSPECTIVE: THE PERFECT TENDER RULE AND THE CISG*

Under the common law doctrine of substantial performance, one party's obligations under a contract are not affected by the other party's breach of its obligations unless the second party's breach is material.[88] Under the UCC's perfect tender rule, by contrast, a buyer may reject a delivery of goods if they "fail in any respect to conform to the contract."[89] The UCC's adoption of a perfect tender rule was simply a continuation of the different treatment the common law had given to contracts for the sale of goods, which Karl Llewellyn[†] unsuccessfully proposed replacing with a substantial performance rule. . . . In contrast to the UCC, the CISG [rejects the perfect tender rule and] does not allow one party to declare a contract avoided unless the other party's failure to perform its obligations amounts to a "fundamental breach."[93] A breach is considered fundamental "if it results in such detriment to the other party as substantially to deprive him of what he is entitled to expect under the contract,"[94] a standard that appears almost indistinguishable from the common law notion of material breach.

---

* Excerpted from William S. Dodge, *Teaching the CISG in Contracts,* 50 J. Legal Educ. 72, 90-91 (2000).

88. *See Restatement (Second) of Contracts* § 237 (1981). A nonmaterial breach may, however, give rise to a claim for damages.

89. UCC § 2-601. But the seller typically has the right to cure any nonconformity. *See id.* § 2-508. Moreover, once a buyer has accepted the goods, he may revoke his acceptance only if the "non-conformity substantially impairs its value to him." *Id.* § 2-608.

† [Karl Llewellyn served as the principal drafter of the U.C.C.–Ed.]

93. CISG Art. 49(1)(a) (seller's breach); *id.* Art. 64(1)(a) (buyer's breach). The CISG allows one method for the nonbreaching party to avoid the contract in the absence of a fundamental breach. Under the so-called *Nachfrist* procedure (borrowed from German law), the nonbreaching party may fix an additional, reasonable period of time for the breaching party to perform its obligations. *Id.* Arts. 47 & 63. If the breaching party falls to perform or declares he will not perform within that period of time, the nonbreaching party may declare the contract avoided. *Id.* Arts. 49(1)(b) & 64(1)(b).

94. CISG Art. 25. [Importantly, even where a party has been "substantially deprive[d]" of what it expected under the contract, Article 25 goes on state that a breach will not be treated as fundamental "unless the party in breach did not foresee and a reasonable person of the same kind in the same circumstances would not have foreseen such a result." *See also* UNIDROIT Principles 7.3.1(2)(a).–Ed.]

CHAPTER 8

DEFENSES

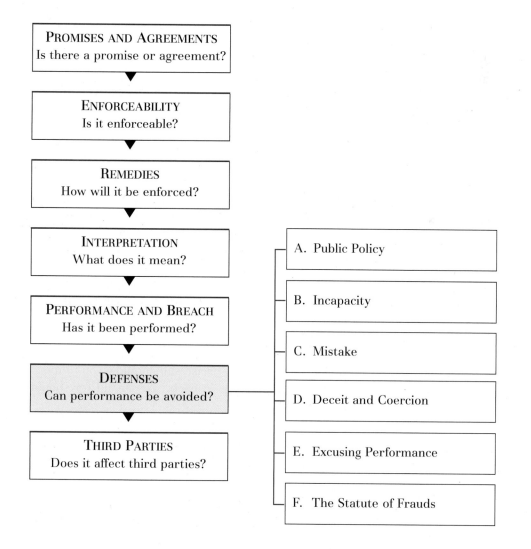

PROMISES AND AGREEMENTS
Is there a promise or agreement?

ENFORCEABILITY
Is it enforceable?

REMEDIES
How will it be enforced?

INTERPRETATION
What does it mean?

PERFORMANCE AND BREACH
Has it been performed?

DEFENSES
Can performance be avoided?

- A. Public Policy
- B. Incapacity
- C. Mistake
- D. Deceit and Coercion
- E. Excusing Performance
- F. The Statute of Frauds

THIRD PARTIES
Does it affect third parties?

Generally speaking, the ideal contract would be formed between two well-informed parties of roughly equal bargaining power, in which (following Adam Smith) each party proposes to the other something like the following: "Give me that which I want, and you shall have this which you want." This is so because it is believed that, on the whole, transactions made in such a manner would result in mutually beneficial trades. In the real world, of course, bargains do not always conform to such lofty ideals. Perhaps, for instance, one of the parties is not particularly well-informed about the transaction (as might be the case whenever a party is mistaken about or, worse, misled about the substance of a transaction), or perhaps one of the parties has much more bargaining power than the other and uses this power to coerce the weaker party into agreeing to an unfair exchange. Where these considerations arise, the question becomes what, if anything, should contract law *do* about it. Think about that question for a moment. At one extreme, contract law could attempt to prevent *every* unfair exchange or refuse to enforce *every* deal struck between parties of unequal bargaining power. Doing so, of course, would reduce party autonomy by allowing little legal space in which parties could bargain with one another. But if we move to the opposite extreme, and only prevent *egregiously* unfair exchanges, or contracts where a party has *forced* another party to agree to an exchange against its will, we will surely be sacrificing justice in the process. The answer, of course, probably lies somewhere in the middle, and the tough question for lawmakers is where, exactly, to draw the line.

So, for just a moment, let's put ourselves in the shoes of these lawmakers. Suppose that you are a judge responsible, in part, for the development of common law. Under what conditions do you think it would be wise to force parties to follow through with their promises, and under what conditions do you think their promises should be excused? Are there certain promises that we, as a society, should—or should not—enforce? Should we refuse to enforce bargains between parties where there is a great disparity in bargaining power? Should it matter if such a bargain results in fair or unfair terms? What sorts of public policy considerations do you think should guide these decisions? Brainstorm for a moment and try to come up with a set of rules or principles capable of guiding how you think courts should handle such cases. Then, as you read the cases and materials in this chapter, test your intuitions against how the courts have, in fact, treated such cases. Besides providing insight into the conceptual space in which contract law and justice meet, this exercise should allow you to more critically examine whether you think the judge in each case should (or should not) have enforced the promise at issue.

DOCTRINAL OVERVIEW: POLICING AGREEMENT FOR UNFAIRNESS*

[Here we are] concerned with the extent to which courts "police" agreements against unfairness by placing limits on their enforceability. Such an interference in the bargaining process requires courts to consider competing policies. On the side of enforcing the bargain as made stand the policies favoring the autonomy of the parties, the protection of justified expectations, and the stability of transactions. On the other side stand the policies favoring the prevention of unfairness and the protection of the parties from overreaching. No single formula has evolved to reconcile these competing policies, and often the factors that contribute to a particular decision can be separated, if at all, only with difficulty. Nevertheless, it is possible to distinguish three different perspectives from which courts view the task of policing agreements: substance, status, and behavior.

Of these three, courts have been most reluctant to view the problem in the first perspective, that of substantive unfairness. The rise of the bargain theory contributed to this reluctance by helping to strip from the doctrine of consideration any vestige of concern with the substance of the exchange on which the parties had agreed, thereby eliminating a possible basis for policing the agreement for substantive unfairness. The doctrine of consideration shields the improvident promisor from liability if the promise is gratuitous, but not if the promisor has received something, however small, by way of bargained-for exchange. One legal scholar identified three reasons for the willingness of courts to enforce the bargain of the parties without inquiring into substance:

> (1) the efficient administration of the law of contracts requires that courts shall not be required to prescribe prices. (2) The test of enforceability should be certain and should not be beclouded by such vague terms as "fair" or "reasonable" as tests of validity. (3) There is still the somewhat old-fashioned theory that persons of maturity and sound mind should be free to contract imprudently as well as prudently.[3]

Furthermore, judges are aware that they are not well equipped to redress fundamental imbalances in the distribution of wealth. Another scholar, Melvin Eisenberg, conceded the bargain principle's "conceptual simplicity and the ease with which it can be administered," since for its application "it need only be determined whether a bargain was made and, if so, what remedy is required to put the innocent party in the position he would have been in had the bargain been performed." But he concluded that while placing limits on the principle "involves costs of administration," failing to do so "involves still greater costs to the system of justice."[4]

[However,] the traditional reluctance of common law courts to police agreements for substantive unfairness was never shared by courts of equity and over the years this traditional reluctance has declined. Nevertheless, the established

---

* Excerpted from E. ALLAN FARNSWORTH, CONTRACTS § 4.1 (4th ed. 2004).

3. Edwin W. Patterson, *An Apology for Consideration*, 58 COLUM. L. REV. 929, 953 (1958).

4. Melvin Eisenberg, *The Bargain Principle and Its Limits*, 95 HARV. L. REV. 741, 800-01 (1982).

perspectives for policing agreements have been those of status and behavior rather than of substance. That of *status* focuses on the characteristics of the party involved. Classic examples are the restrictions on the capacity of specified classes of persons, such as minors and the mentally incompetent, whose power to contract has been limited in order to shield them from the consequences of unwise bargains. The perspective of *behavior* focuses on how the parties acted during the bargaining process. Classic examples are the rules that allow a party to avoid the contract on the ground that the party has been induced to make the contract by misrepresentation or duress, the most flagrant examples of misbehavior during the bargaining process. . . .

A. PUBLIC POLICY, FREEDOM OF CONTRACT, AND THE LIMITS OF PUBLIC POLICY

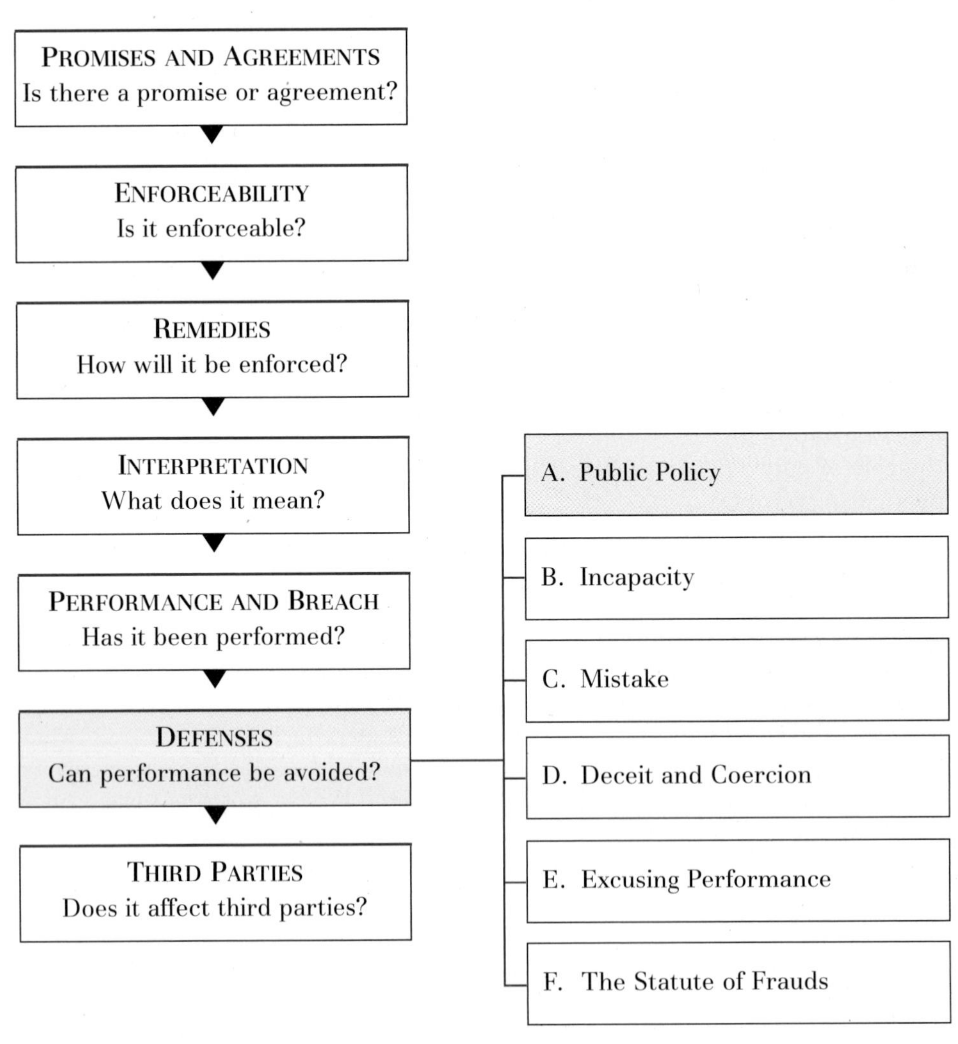

In general, when a party gets slapped with a lawsuit ("You breached your contract to pay me $5,000") and does not want to admit legal liability, it can do one of three things. First, it can deny the truth of the plaintiff's allegations ("No, I never promised you $5,000"). Second, it can admit the truth of the plaintiff's allegations but challenge their legal sufficiency ("Yes, I promised you $5,000, but the promise was gratuitous and therefore unenforceable"). Third, it can admit both the truth and legal sufficiency of plaintiff's allegations, but raise an additional matter undermining the legal significance ordinarily attached to these allegations ("Yes, I promised you $5,000, but I was drunk, had a gun to my head, and thought I was signing something else").* It is this third option—traditionally called entering a "plea in avoidance" but more commonly known today as asserting a "defense"—that we will be concerned with in this chapter. Specifically, in addition to exploring what kind of defenses exist, we will be interested in exploring *why* they exist, which is the only way to truly get a handle on what these defenses are designed to accomplish, and whether they are meeting their goals.

Indeed, when conceived of broadly, all of the traditional defenses (e.g., duress, unconscionability, undue influence, fraud) rest on the basic notion that a court should not enforce some particular promise due to the presence of one or more broader public policy considerations (e.g., a promisor's coercive or deceptive behavior) that undermine the traditional significance a court would otherwise give to that promise. Understood this way, all defenses are, at their core, specific iterations of much broader public policy concerns against enforcing certain types of promises, often because such promises, made in particular circumstances, undermine some of the objectives or assumptions upon which contract law rests. It is for this reason that we shall begin our chapter on defenses by taking a look at some of these broader public policy issues in our next two cases, *In the Matter of Baby "M"* and *Flood v. Fidelity & Guaranty Life Ins. Co.* But, before we dive into the cases, let's begin with a brief overview of the role of public policy in contract law. As you read the following excerpt, pay particular attention to the last sentence. Do you agree that this should be the test for determining whether or not to enforce a contract on grounds of public policy? Why or why not? Can you think of a better test?

DOCTRINAL OVERVIEW: PUBLIC POLICY AS A GROUND FOR UNENFORCEABILITY†

A court may be moved by two considerations in refusing to enforce an agreement on grounds of public policy. First, it may see its refusal as an appropriate sanction

---

* For an excellent discussion of a defendant's options to deny a plaintiff's allegations, admit them while challenging their legal sufficiency, or enter a defense or "plea in avoidance" alleging some additional fact undermining the legal significance ordinarily attached to the plaintiff's allegations, *see* Richard Epstein, *Pleadings and Presumptions*, 40 U. CHI. L. REV. 556 (1973).

† Excerpted from E. ALLAN FARNSWORTH, CONTRACTS § 5.1 (4th ed. 2004).

to discourage undesirable conduct, either by the parties or by others. Second, it may regard enforcement of the promise as an inappropriate use of the judicial process to uphold an unsavory agreement. . . .

When a court refuses to enforce an agreement on grounds of public policy, it sometimes characterizes the agreement as "void." . . . [However,] a court will not necessarily condemn the entire agreement as unenforceable by both parties merely because it offends public policy. A court may hold instead that the agreement can be enforced by one of the parties though it cannot be enforced by the other. Or it may hold that part of the agreement is enforceable, though another part of it is not. It is therefore more accurate to say that the agreement or some part of it is unenforceable by one or both parties than to say that it is "void."

Courts are also fond of condemning the unenforceable agreement as "illegal." This is misleading insofar as it suggests that some penalty is necessarily imposed on one of the parties, apart from the court's refusal to enforce the agreement. . . . It is therefore preferable to attribute unenforceability to grounds of public policy rather than to "illegality."

How does a court determine that all or part of an agreement is unenforceable on grounds of public policy? Occasionally the legislature simplifies the court's task by saying explicitly in a statute that agreements or portions of agreements that violate the statute are unenforceable. Statutes dealing with gambling and usury, for example, often state that agreements that violate their provisions are "void." The courts function is then merely statutory interpretation. In most cases, however, the court alone must decide whether a contravention of public policy is grave enough to warrant unenforceability.

If the agreement involves the commission of a serious crime or tort, it may be clear that unenforceability is warranted; and if the agreement involves only a trivial contravention of policy, it may be clear that unenforceability is unwarranted. In doubtful cases, however, the court's decision must rest on a delicate balancing of factors for and against enforcement of the particular agreement. Enforcement should not be refused unless the potential benefit in deterring misconduct or avoiding an inappropriate use of the judicial process outweighs the factors favoring enforceability.

In the Matter of Baby "M" (A Pseudonym for an Actual Person)

Supreme Court of New Jersey
537 A.2d 1227 (1988)

For a report of the case and accompanying materials, see p. 36, *supra*.

Flood v. Fidelity & Guaranty Life Ins. Co.,

Court of Appeal of Louisiana
394 So. 2d 1311 (1981)

LEAR, JUDGE. Fidelity & Guaranty Life Insurance Company (hereinafter called Fidelity), the defendant-appellant, seeks reversal of the decision of the lower court which upheld the validity of a life insurance policy issued on the life of the late Richard Alvin Flood which, appellant contends, was fraudulently procured. The estate of decedent, Flood, instituted these proceedings to recover the proceeds of the policy of life insurance. The estate is now postured as plaintiff-appellees.

In 1971, Richard Alvin Flood resided with his wife and family in Houma, Louisiana. Mr. Flood was employed by the Transcontinental Gas Pipeline Corporation. Ellen Flood, his wife, was employed by Houtz Insurance Agency as an underwriter of personal casualty insurance.

In February, 1971, defendant, Fidelity, received an application for life insurance purportedly bearing the signature of Richard Flood. A policy of life insurance was issued, and Ellen Flood was designated as the beneficiary. In August, 1971, a change of ownership form was submitted to defendant-appellant purportedly bearing the signature of Richard Flood and changing the ownership of the policy to Ellen Flood.

Subsequent to these events, Richard Alvin Flood was murdered (in 1972) at the hands of his wife, Ellen Flood. The details of the homicide and the findings and adjudications of the guilt of Ellen Flood are found in *State v. Flood,* 301 So. 2d 637 (La. 1974). Suffice it to say that Richard Flood was poisoned by the use of arsenic. His wife was tried for his murder and convicted in 1973.

Fidelity denied Mrs. Flood's request for payment of the insurance policy based upon her being charged with her husband's death. It returned all premiums to Mrs. Flood.

In 1977, a demand for payment of the policy was brought on behalf of the estate of Richard Flood or in the alternative for the benefit of the minor child of Richard and Ellen Flood. It was denied by Fidelity which reasoned that the policy had been obtained through the forgery and fraud of Mrs. Flood. This suit followed.

Plaintiff's evidence consisted of the certificate of death, the application and insurance policy and its demand letter. The theory of plaintiff's case was that the policy of insurance is valid because the insurer is estopped from denying coverage when, as here, its agent has signed the application purporting to witness the signature of the insured (Richard Flood).

The defendant, in an effort to prove forgery and fraud, called several witnesses. The agent, David Coignet, testified that Mrs. Flood presented him with an application which she represented was signed by her husband. Acting upon that representation, he testified that he signed his name as a witness to the signature. He further admitted that the change of ownership form, which changed ownership of the policy from Mr. Flood to Mrs. Flood, bore a signature purporting to be that of Mr. Flood which wasn't in fact witnessed by him; that all transactions concerning the policy of life insurance herein complained of were handled by Mrs. Flood.

Defendant-appellant also adduced evidence to establish the handwriting style of Mr. Flood and called as a witness Mr. Gilbert J. Portier, Jr. of New Orleans, Louisiana. Mr. Portier was qualified as an expert in handwriting identification. He testified that the known signature of Mr. Flood was not the same as the signature on the insurance policy nor that found on the change of ownership form. Finally, appellant offered without objection the opinion of the Louisiana Supreme Court, rendered in *State of Louisiana v. Ellen Flood*, and reported at 301 So. 2d 637.

The lower court rendered judgment in favor of plaintiff in the amount of $9,000.00. In his written reasons for judgment, the trial judge concluded that it would be sheer speculation on the part of the court to conclude that Mr. Flood had no knowledge of the application and policy of insurance and did not approve and authorize the action taken by his wife in obtaining the said insurance. It further found that there was no direct provable evidence to establish the wife's motive at the time the policy was applied for and, finally, construed defendant's failure to call Mrs. Flood as a factor militating against defendant's claim.

We must decide whether or not the policy of insurance was fraudulently obtained and, if so, whether such fraud voids the contract under Louisiana law.

The case at bar involves a calculated attempt by Ellen Flood to subvert the laws of Louisiana in order to realize a pecuniary gain. Life insurance policies are procured because life is, indeed precarious and uncertain. But our law does not and cannot sanction any scheme which has as its purpose the certain infliction of death for, inter alia, financial gain through receipt of the proceeds of life insurance.

The genesis of this litigation is the escalating criminal action of Ellen Flood, bent on taking the life of her lawful husband. Our courts have previously adjudicated (1) the issue of the cause of death of Richard Flood, (2) the culprit in that death, and (3) the motives for the death.[1] Under the peculiar circumstances of the case, it was unreasonable of the trial court not to consider and to assign great weight to the mountain of circumstantial evidence tending to prove Mrs. Flood's scheme to defraud both the insurer, Fidelity, and the insured, Mr. Flood.

---

1. We have excerpted the pertinent part of the findings of the Supreme Court per Justice Marcus:

> "Richard and Ellen Flood were married in 1965. At the time of Richard's death on June 2, 1972, he was about 27 years old. Richard was described as a healthy robust man about 5'10", weighing about 190 pounds with a 'fantastic build.' Defendant was described as good looking. Mr. Flood was employed at Transcontinental Gas Pipeline Company as a maintenance man earning an annual salary of $8,745.00. Defendant was employed at Houtz Insurance Agency as an underwriter of personal casualty insurance, with a salary of $475.00 per month. The couple lived in a house trailer. The evidence is that defendant was unhappy in marriage and was having sexual relations with other men. There is further evidence that, during April of 1972 (about two months prior to Richard's death), defendant made inquiry in regard to obtaining a $100,000.00 life insurance policy on the life of her husband. The inquiry included questions by her as to whether her husband would have to be apprised of the policy. She was given an affirmative answer to this line of questioning. The evidence reveals that thereafter no further action was taken by her in regard to the policy."
>
> "Richard Flood had two life insurance policies. One was a group policy through his employment calculated at three times his annual base pay ($8,745.00), or about $25,000.00.

Louisiana follows the majority rule which holds, as a matter of public policy, that a beneficiary named in a life insurance policy is not entitled to the proceeds of the insurance if the beneficiary feloniously kills the insured.

Article 1881 of our Civil Code[2] provides that contracts made through fraud are voidable by the parties.[3] Article 1847(7) defines, in pertinent part, fraud and an instance in which its invocation will nullify a contract.[4]

Additionally, Title 22 of the Revised Statutes, Section 619(B) governs the standard for life insurance applications:

> B. In any application for life or health and accident insurance made in writing by the insured, all statements therein made by the insured shall, in the absence of fraud, be deemed representations and not warranties. The falsity of any such statement shall not bar the right to recovery under the contract unless such false statement was made with actual intent to deceive or unless it materially affected either the acceptance of the risk or the hazard assumed by the insurer.

The other policy was a $5,000.00 whole life type policy with a $5,000.00 declining term rider, under which policy, the beneficiary would receive approximately $9,300.00 at the time of Flood's death. The ownership of this latter policy was changed from Richard Flood to Ellen Flood on August 2, 1971. Defendant was the beneficiary under both of these policies."

"Without attempting to point out the significance of the aforesaid evidence, we simply say that there is some evidence upon which the jury could reasonably conclude that defendant murdered her husband by arsenic poisoning. The motive was there. She was unhappy and going out with other men. There was some evidence that she was fearful of her husband. Further, her attempt to take out a large life insurance policy on his life without his knowledge is certainly evidence which indicates a motive, as well as the fact that she would receive about $35,000.00 as the beneficiary under the other two policies then in effect. There is also some evidence upon which the jury could conclude that she did, in fact, administer the arsenic. The evidence that six medicine bottles found in her trailer contained arsenic is revealing. This is particularly significant in view of the fact that the medicines called for by the labels on these bottles would not have contained any arsenic. Two of the medicines in these bottles, tylenol and paregoric, are the types which the jury could infer that Flood was taking for relief of headaches and diarrhea, some of the symptoms of his illness. Also noteworthy is the evidence of defendant feeding Richard ice at the hospital when no feeding had been ordered. At that time, his condition had been improving; however, from then on, he deteriorated and died several hours later. Finally, there is no dispute that he died of arsenic poisoning. The remaining evidence is also directed at proving the crime charged."

2. C.C. Art. 12: "Whatever is done in contravention of a prohibitory law, is void, although the nullity be not formally directed."

3. C.C. Art. 1881: "Engagements made through error, violence, fraud or menace, are not absolutely null, but are voidable by the parties, who have contracted under the influence of such error, fraud, violence or menace, or by the representatives of such parties."

4. C.C. Art. 1847(7): "Art. 1847. Fraud, as applied to contracts, is the cause of an error bearing on a material part of the contract, created or continued by artifice, with design to obtain some unjust advantages to the one party, or to cause an inconvenience or loss to the other. From which definition are drawn the following rules:

> 7. The artifice must be designed to obtain either an unjust advantage to the party for whose benefit the artifice is carried on, or a loss or inconvenience to him against whom it is practiced, although attended with advantage to no one."

It is clear to us that the entirety of the transaction here reviewed is tainted with the intendment of Ellen Flood to contravene the prohibitory law. The fact that plaintiff seeks to install in her stead a contingent beneficiary is of no consequence. To sanction this policy in any way would surely shackle the spirit, letter and life of our laws.

For the foregoing reasons, the decision of the lower court is reversed, and judgment is entered in favor of defendant-appellant, Fidelity & Guaranty Life Insurance Company, dismissing the suit of plaintiff-appellee, Succession of Richard Alvin Flood, all costs to be paid by the plaintiff-appellee.

REVERSED.

NOTES AND QUESTIONS

1. ***What happened?*** Who sued whom for what? Procedurally, how did the case get before this court? Factually, what happened between the parties? What arguments did the plaintiff and defendant make? What rule or rules did the court apply? How did the court analyze the dispute between the parties? How did the court decide the case?

2. ***Was this case correctly decided?*** Do you agree with the result reached in this case? Why or why not? Do you agree with the court's reasoning? Why or why not? How, if at all, would you have written the opinion differently?

GAMBLING: OCTOGENARIAN POWERBALL SISTERS*

Judges have long been averse to enforcing bargains founded in illegal activity, ranging from prostitution to murder. But some behavior once widely condemned as criminal, such as adultery, gambling, or possessing marijuana, becomes decriminalized or legalized. While society's attitudes slowly change, judges sometimes struggle with whether to enforce bargains based on those activities.[26]

Gambling has been an especially interesting setting in recent years. After all, millions of Americans play the lottery, often teaming up with siblings or colleagues to buy tickets with agreement to share the winnings. Most lottery tickets are worthless, but when they pay off, fights often break out and at least one of the

---

* Excerpted from LAWRENCE A. CUNNINGHAM, CONTRACTS IN THE REAL WORLD: STORIES OF POPULAR CONTRACTS AND WHY THEY MATTER 49-52 (2012).

26. What once was considered immoral and prohibited by statute is often viewed differently generations later. Through the twentieth century, statutes made adultery criminal. Promises surrounding those affairs were not legally binding either. But those statutes have either been repealed or fallen into disuse, presenting challenges to judges when asked to enforce related bargains. Courts could overtly declare that the bargains are valid, but many judges remain squeamish about the subject. That sometimes leads them to avoid declaring an arrangement illegal and instead to find it unenforceable on more traditional contract law grounds. . . .

parties asserts the deal was illegal and unenforceable. That is the sad story of the octogenarian sisters, Terry Sokaitis and Rose Bakaysa.

Terry and Rose grew up in the 1920s in a family of ten children in New Britain, Connecticut, a small middle-class town near Hartford famous for its Polish community and locally referred to as "Hard Hittin' New Britain." The sisters were close. Both married; Terry raised six kids; Rose's husband died in 1981. After Foxwoods Casino opened in 1986, the sisters gambled there several times weekly, Terry playing Black Jack, Rose the slots. They informally shared all of their winnings.

In January 1995, Terry hit a poker jackpot paying $165,000. She shared that nearly equally with Rose, giving her $75,000. In April of that year, Terry proposed signing a winnings-sharing contract, perhaps to ensure that Rose would be likewise obligated to split her winnings in the future. An accountant typed and printed the terms, proclaiming the sisters were "partners in any winning" in slots, cards, or lotteries, with gains "to be shared equally." The sisters signed and notarized the writing. Terry and Rose continued their trips to Foxwoods, bought lottery tickets, and shared winnings.

In 2004, however, Rose faced health challenges requiring surgery and weeks in rehab. Terry visited daily. During her visits, Terry borrowed some money from Rose. After leaving the facility, Rose still needed assistance and so stayed for three weeks with Terry. In exchange, Rose forgave Terry an earlier $650 loan she had made. After Rose went home, she phoned Terry to say she and their brother Joe were coming over to recover the $250 Rose had lent her in the rehab facility. Terry said she had borrowed only $100 and told Rose not to come because she had no money anyway.

A disputed dialogue ensued. Rose reported a heated yelling match whereas Terry recalled a calm chat. Rose said Terry hollered "I don't want to be your partner anymore," and Rose said "okay." Their brother Joe reported conflicting versions of events, possibly because of how his own fortunes may have turned on later interpretations of what really happened. Rose, upset by the call, contacted Joe and said, "Terry doesn't want to be my partner anymore," and Joe responded, "I'll be partners with you."

The sisters never spoke again. Terry bought some scratch lottery tickets afterward but less often, preferring to put any extra money she had in the church collection basket. She also sent Rose a check for $250. Rose began buying tickets with Joe, biweekly, always selecting the same number to bet.

On June 15, 2005, Joe bought Powerball tickets that won $500,000, promptly calling Rose to share the news. They split the winnings as agreed, each receiving five days later checks for $175,000 (the other $150,000 going to the government, as income tax). They did not tell Terry, however, who learned about it from her daughter, Eileen, Rose's godchild, to whom Rose had given $10,000 as a gift from the winnings. Within weeks of hearing the news, on August 19, 2005, Terry sued Rose for breach of contract. They fought a pitched and ultimately tearful battle in a tortured case lasting five years until its final resolution on May 11, 2010.

The first skirmish in the sisters' legal battle was over the validity of their 1995 winnings-sharing contract. Rose argued it was invalid because it violated a state statute rendering void any contract whose consideration was money won in a bet. Terry denied that the consideration was money won in a bet. The deal involved an exchange of promises—to buy together and share winnings. Given that no winnings existed when the contract was formed, that fruit was not the consideration—the exchange of promises was. So, Terry argued, the contract was valid.

Terry coupled that hair-splitting defense with a more practical one: Even if the consideration was money won in a bet in apparent violation of the statute, the statute cannot make contracts like these illegal, because many other state statutes legalize gambling in various forms. Read literally, the statute would void all kinds of bargains made every day and lawfully statewide, like betting on horse races, at jai alai frontons, and in tribal casinos.

Every legal wager is a gambling contract, including the very lottery ticket being fought over—a contract in which buyers pay the purchase price in exchange for the lottery commission's promise to pay the holder of the winning ticket. The parties to it engage in a gamble, and the consideration is a "money bet." Taken at face value, the statute would bar anyone from buying state lottery tickets. Looking at all the other statutes legalizing various forms of gambling, the Supreme Court of Connecticut determined that the statute voids only contracts for gambling unauthorized by those statutes. As a result, the court held that even if Terry and Rose's bargain were a gambling contract, it was outside the statute's proscription.

But after losing the gambling defense, Rose vouched a firmer defense in the trial of her case with Terry. She said the two, although originally bound to the lawful contract written up in 1995, had mutually rescinded it during the disputed 2004 telephone conversation. The trial judge, Cynthia Sweinton [sic], accepted that argument, characterizing Terry's declaration, "I don't want to be your partner anymore," as an offer to rescind the deal, which Rose accepted by saying, "okay." The two were legally free of each other.

Judge Sweinton thus found for Rose, concluding her opinion with: "There is something in this tragedy that touches most people. While the court may be able to resolve the legal dispute, it is powerless to repair the discord and strife that now overshadows the once harmonious sisterly relationship." Judge Sweinton also reprinted a tear-jerking letter Terry wrote to Rose during the case:

> Rose,
>
> I hope you get this letter because I have plenty to say—the most important thing is I am so sick over what is happening with you and I going to court. None of this would have happened if you were not so greedy. All I know is we should both be ashamed of ourselves. We are sisters. Going to court is not right. All I know is I am entitled to my share of the money and you know it.
>
> I remember when I was pregnant. We went to Raphel's and you bought me my dress. It was navy blue and it had pink flowers on it. You and I used to go to the casino all the time and to Old Saybrook and look at all the houses and get hot dogs out there at the restaurants.
>
> Well Ro Ro, I don't know what is going to happen. I want you to know I will always love you. But if you wanted to hurt me you did. My kids are so good to me and they do send me any money I need. They can't do enough for me so I guess I am rich with a lot of love and that is something you can't buy.

I hope you feel good and have good health. I have a disease that is incurable. It is called neuropathy. I can't walk at all. It is really painful. But Ma always said other people have worse problems so I just ask God to let me be able to handle it all.

Take care of yourself. Mom would be sick over all of this. It would never happen if you at least shared some of the money with me. Do you think I would have done that to you? Never.

See you in court.

Terry

B. INCAPACITY

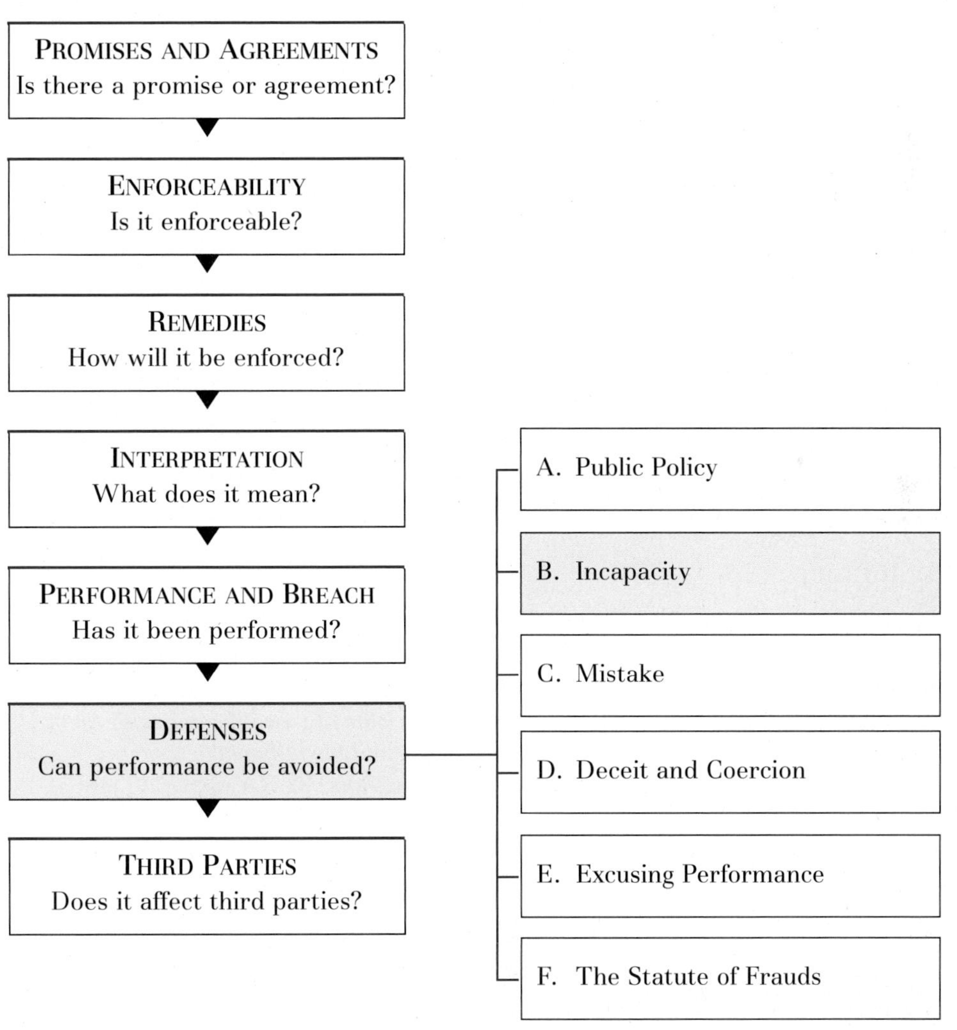

When we discussed mutual assent in Chapter 3, it was taken for granted that the courts were dealing with competent adults capable of exercising their faculties in forming mutually beneficial agreements. Where one of the parties to a contract lacks this basic level of competency, however, there is reason to believe that the agreement reached may not be in that party's best interest, thereby undermining both the moral and legal significance of that party's "consent." In this section, we will examine how courts treat cases in which one of the parties may lack the legal capacity to give their consent to an agreement. Specifically, in the materials that follow, we will examine two main forms of contractual incapacity, both of which can operate as defenses to contract formation: infancy and incompetence.

DOCTRINAL OVERVIEW: INCAPACITY IN GENERAL*

Even though individuals differ markedly in their ability to represent their own interests in the bargaining process, one is generally assumed to have full power to bind oneself contractually. Only in extreme instances is one's power regarded as impaired because of an inability to participate meaningfully in the bargaining process. One whose power is so impaired is said to lack capacity to contract and is subject to special rules that allow one to avoid the contracts that one makes in order to give protection from one's own improvident acts and from imposition by others. What kinds of defects are recognized as impairing the power to contract?

Two principal kinds of defects are today recognized as impairing the power to contract: immaturity and mental infirmity. . . .

As with other instances of policing, the law relating to capacity to contract involves difficult choices between competing policies—on the one side favoring protection of the party that lacks capacity, and on the other favoring protection of the other party's expectation, reliance, and restitution interests.

1. Infancy

> *[A] protracted struggle has been maintained in the courts, on the one hand to protect infants or minors from their own improvidence and folly, and to save them from the depredations and frauds practiced upon them by the designing and unprincipled, and on the other to protect the rights of those dealing with them in good faith and on the assumption that they could lawfully make contracts.*
>
> *Henry v. Root*, 33 N.Y. 526, 536 (1865)

DOCTRINAL OVERVIEW: INFANCY AS A DEFENSE TO ENFORCEMENT†

With respect to immaturity the law has tenaciously adhered to an arbitrary standard—the attainment of a prescribed age at the time of the making of the

* Excerpted from E. ALLAN FARNSWORTH, CONTRACTS § 4.2 (4th ed. 2004).

† Excerpted from E. ALLAN FARNSWORTH, CONTRACTS §§ 4.3-4.5 (4th ed. 2004).

contract—ignoring the obvious differences in maturity among individuals of the same age. At common law that age was 21 [but has since been reduced to 18 in a number of states]. Before the age of majority, one is a "minor" or an "infant" who lacks the capacity to contract and who therefore can avoid [by "disaffirming"] one's contracts, regardless of their fairness. A minor's apparent age or maturity is irrelevant, as is the other party's knowledge of the minor's age. One's incapacity is not terminated by emancipation by one's parents or by marriage. . . .

The resulting rules evidence an indulgence toward minors that is not always easy to justify. . . . [Indeed], these rules may disadvantage minors by discouraging others from contracting with them. . . . The rules may also work hardship on those who have dealt fairly with minors. . . .

[What, exactly, are these rules?]

[T]he prevailing view that a minor's contract is "voidable" at the instance of the minor. By this is meant that there is a contract if no further action is taken at the minor's instance, but that the effects of the contract can be avoided if [it the contract is disaffirmed by the minor]. . . . The minor may avoid the contract even if it has been fully performed on both sides, as where the minor has received and paid for goods. However, the other party is bound unless the minor avoids the contract. . . . The result is to allow the minor to enforce transactions that have proved advantageous while avoiding those that have proved disadvantageous. . . .

Since a minor may avoid even after having received some or all of the other party's performance under a contract, a court must often determine the extent to which the minor is accountable for the benefit conferred by that performance. At the very least, the minor is expected to return what remains of anything that was received from the other party. . . . But what if the minor received services, such as transportation or lessons, that cannot be returned? Or what if the minor received goods, such as an automobile or a house trailer, that have been resold or damaged or that have depreciated with use? Is the minor accountable for the difference between the value of whatever remains and its original value? The traditional answer has been that the minor is not accountable for such loss or depreciation. A minor who has used services is not accountable for anything. A minor who has smashed an automobile or house trailer need only return the wreck. . . .

The law in this area would surely be simpler and arguably fairer if the minor were accountable in full for the benefit received. . . . [Such is the position adopted by New Hampshire and a few other states, but] in most states the other party's right to full restitution depends on whether that party can bring the case within one of several exceptions.

The most universal of these exceptions to the traditional rule holds the minor accountable for the reasonable value of what are called *necessaries*. . . .

Kiefer v. Fred Howe Motors, Inc.

Supreme Court of Wisconsin
158 N.W.2d 288 (1968)

On August 9, 1965, the plaintiff, Steven Kiefer, entered into a contract with the defendant, Fred Howe Motors, Inc., ("dealer" hereinafter) for the purchase of a 1960 Willys station wagon. Kiefer paid the contract price of $412 and took possession of the car. At the time of the sale Kiefer was twenty years old, married, and the father of one child.

Kiefer had difficulty with the car which he claimed was caused by a cracked block. Kiefer contacted the dealer and asked it to take the car back. Several other attempts to secure some adjustment with the dealer failed and Kiefer contacted Attorney Paul C. Konnor. The attorney wrote a letter to the dealer advising it that Kiefer was under twenty-one at the time of the sale. The letter declared the contract void, tendered return of the automobile and demanded repayment of the purchase price. There was no response so this action was commenced to recover the $412 purchase price. After a trial to the court, a judgment for the plaintiff was entered and the defendant appeals.

WILKIE, JUSTICE. Three issues are presented on this appeal. They are:

1. Should an emancipated minor over the age of eighteen be legally responsible for his contracts?
2. Was the contract effectively disaffirmed?
3. Is the plaintiff liable in tort for misrepresentation?

LEGAL RESPONSIBILITY OF EMANCIPATED MINOR.

The law governing agreements made during infancy reaches back over many centuries. The general rule is that ". . . the contract of a minor, other than for necessaries, is either void or voidable at his option."[2] The only other exceptions to the rule permitting disaffirmance are statutory or involve contracts which deal with duties imposed by law such as a contract of marriage or an agreement to support an illegitimate child. The general rule is not affected by the minor's status as emancipated or unemancipated.

Appellant does not advance any argument that would put this case within one of the exceptions to the general rule, but rather urges that this court, as a matter of public policy, adopt a rule that an emancipated minor over eighteen years of age be made legally responsible for his contracts.

The underpinnings of the general rule allowing the minor to disaffirm his contracts were undoubtedly the protection of the minor. It was thought that the minor was immature in both mind and experience and that, therefore, he should be protected from his own bad judgments as well as from adults who would take advantage of him. The doctrine of the voidability of minors' contracts often seems commendable and just. If the beans that the young naive Jack purchased from the crafty old man in the fairy tale "Jack and the Bean Stalk" had been worthless rather than magical, it would have been only fair to allow Jack to disaffirm the bargain and reclaim his cow. However, in today's

2. *Grauman, Marx & Cline Co. v. Krienitz*, 142 Wis. 556, 560 (1910).

modern and sophisticated society the "infancy doctrine" seems to lose some of its gloss.

Paradoxically, we declare the infant mature enough to shoulder arms in the military, but not mature enough to vote; mature enough to marry and be responsible for his torts and crimes, but not mature enough to assume the burden of his own contractual indiscretions. In Wisconsin, the infant is deemed mature enough to use a dangerous instrumentality—a motor vehicle—at sixteen, but not mature enough to purchase it without protection until he is twenty-one.

No one really questions that a line as to age must be drawn somewhere below which a legally defined minor must be able to disaffirm his contracts for nonnecessities. The law over the centuries has considered this age to be twenty-one. Legislatures in other states have lowered the age. We suggest that the appellant might better seek the change it proposes in the legislative halls rather than this court. . . .

Undoubtedly, the infancy doctrine is an obstacle when a major purchase is involved. However, we believe that the reasons for allowing that obstacle to remain viable at this point outweigh those for casting it aside. Minors require some protection from the pitfalls of the market place. Reasonable minds will always differ on the extent of the protection that should be afforded. For this court to adopt a rule that the appellant suggests and remove the contractual disabilities from a minor simply because he becomes emancipated, which in most cases would be the result of marriage, would be to suggest that the married minor is somehow vested with more wisdom and maturity than his single counterpart. However, logic would not seem to dictate this result especially when today a youthful marriage is oftentimes indicative of a lack of wisdom and maturity.

> ***Paradoxical indeed!***
>
> A similar concern was expressed by the court in *Porter v. Wilson*, 209 A.2d 730, 731 (1965), which stated that "A stranger must think it strange that a minor in certain cases may be liable for his torts and responsible for his crimes and yet is not bound by his contracts. . . . However, the common law conception that a minor does not possess the discretion and experience of adults and therefore must be protected from his own contractual follies generally holds sway today." Throughout this casebook we have explored some of the pros and cons in choosing between regulating party conduct with a standard or a rule (see, e.g., "Thinking Tool: Administrative Costs and Standards versus Rules," p. 75, *supra*), and contract law has chosen, for better or worse, to use a rule rather than a standard in regulating contracts made with infants. Does this seem like a wise policy choice? Why or why not? If you think such contracts should be regulated with a standard instead, what would that standard look like?

DISAFFIRMANCE.

The appellant questions whether there has been an effective disaffirmance of the contract in this case.

Williston, while discussing how a minor may disaffirm a contract, states:

> Any act which clearly shows an intent to disaffirm a contract or sale is sufficient for the purpose. Thus a notice by the infant of his purpose to disaffirm . . . a tender or even a offer to return the consideration or its proceeds to the vendor, . . . is sufficient."[10]

---

10. 2 Williston, *Contracts* (3d ed.), p. 26, § 234.

The testimony of Steven Kiefer and the letter from his attorney to the dealer clearly establish that there was an effective disaffirmance of the contract.

MISREPRESENTATION.

Appellant's last argument is that the respondent should be held liable in tort for damages because he misrepresented his age. Appellant would use these damages as a setoff against the contract price sought to be reclaimed by respondent.

The 19th-century view was that a minor's lying about his age was inconsequential because a fraudulent representation of capacity was not the equivalent of actual capacity. This rule has been altered by time. There appear to be two possible methods that now can be employed to bind the defrauding minor: He may be **estopped** from denying his alleged majority, in which case the contract will be enforced or contract damages will be allowed; or he may be allowed to disaffirm his contract but be liable in tort for damages. Wisconsin follows the latter approach. . . .

> ***Estoppel***
>
> Recall from our discussion of cases like *Ricketts v. Scothorn* (p. 392) that equitable estoppel, where it applies, prevents a party (here, the minor) from making an assertion inconsistent with an earlier representation (e.g., "I was actually a minor when I signed that contract even though I represented that I was 21 years of age") where the other party (the adult) is induced to detrimentally rely on that representation, where doing so is necessary to prevent an injustice. Do you think equitable estoppel ought to have been allowed here? Why or why not?

Having established that there is a remedy against the defrauding minor, the question becomes whether the requisites for a tort action in misrepresentation are present in this case.

The trial produced conflicting testimony regarding whether Steven Kiefer had been asked his age or had replied that he was "twenty-one." Steven and his wife, Jacqueline, said "No," and Frank McHalsky, appellant's salesman, said "Yes." Confronted with this conflict, the question of credibility was for the trial court to decide, which it did by holding that Steven did not orally represent that he was "twenty-one." This finding is not contrary to the great weight and clear preponderance of the evidence and must be affirmed.

Even accepting the trial court's conclusion that Steven Kiefer had not orally represented his age to be over twenty-one, the appellant argues that there was still a misrepresentation. The "motor vehicle purchase contract" signed by Steven Kiefer contained the following language just above the purchaser's signature:

> I represent that I am 21 years of age or over and recognize that the dealer sells the above vehicle upon this representation.

Whether the inclusion of this sentence constitutes a misrepresentation depends on whether elements of the tort have been satisfied. They were not. In *First Nat. Bank in Oshkosh v. Scieszinski*[15] it is said:

15. 25 Wis. 2d 569 (1964).

A party alleging fraud has the burden of proving it by clear and convincing evidence. The elements of fraud are well established:

> To be actionable the false representation must consist, first of a statement of fact which is untrue; second, that it was made with intent to defraud and for the purpose of inducing the other party to act upon it; third, that he did in fact rely on it and was induced thereby to act, to his injury or damage.

No evidence was adduced to show that the plaintiff had an intent to defraud the dealer. To the contrary, it is at least arguable that the majority of minors are, as the plaintiff here might well have been, unaware of the legal consequences of their acts.

Without the element of **scienter** being satisfied, the plaintiff is not susceptible to an action in misrepresentation. Furthermore, the reliance mentioned in Scieszinski must be, as Prosser points out, "justifiable reliance."[17] We fail to see how the dealer could be justified in the mere reliance on the fact that the plaintiff signed a contract containing a sentence that said he was twenty-one or over. The trial court observed that the plaintiff was sufficiently immature looking to arouse suspicion. The appellant never took any affirmative steps to determine whether the plaintiff was in fact over twenty-one. It never asked to see a draft card, identification card, or the most logical indicium of age under the circumstances, a driver's license. Therefore, because there was no intent to deceive, and no justifiable reliance, the appellant's action for misrepresentation must fail.

> ***Scienter***
>
> "[Latin 'knowingly'] 1. A degree of knowledge that makes a person legally responsible for the consequences of his or her act or omission; the fact of an act's having been done knowingly, esp. as a ground for civil damages or criminal punishment. . . . 2. A mental state consisting in an intent to deceive, manipulate, or defraud. In this sense, the term is used most often in the context of securities fraud. . . ." BLACK'S LAW DICTIONARY (10th ed. 2014).

Judgment affirmed.

HALLOWS, CHIEF JUSTICE **(dissenting)**. The majority opinion on the issue of whether an emancipated minor legally should be responsible for his contracts "doth protest too much." After giving very cogent reasons why the common-law rule should be abandoned, the opinion refrains from reshaping the rule to meet reality. Minors are emancipated by a valid marriage and also by entering military service. If they are mature enough to become parents and assume the responsibility of raising other minors and if they are mature enough to be drafted or volunteer to bear arms and sacrifice their life for their country, then they are mature enough to make binding contracts in the market place. The magical age limit of 21 years as an indication of contractual maturity no longer has a basis in fact or in public policy.

My second ground of the dissent is that an automobile to this respondent was a necessity and therefore the contract could not be disaffirmed. Here, we have a minor, aged 20 years and 7 months, the father of a child, and working.

17. Prosser, *Law of Torts* (3d ed.), p. 731, § 103.

While the record shows there is some public transportation to his present place of work, it also shows he borrowed his mother's car to go to and from work. Automobiles for parents under 21 years of age to go to and from work in our current society may well be a necessity and I think in this case the record shows it is. An automobile as a means of transportation to earn a living should not be considered a nonnecessity because the owner is 5 months too young. I would reverse.

RELEVANT PROVISIONS

For the *Restatement (Second) of Contracts*, consult §§ 7, 12, and 14.

NOTES AND QUESTIONS

1. *What happened?* Who sued whom for what? Procedurally, how did the case get before this court? Factually, what happened between the parties? What arguments did the plaintiff and defendant make? What rule or rules did the court apply? How did the court analyze the dispute between the parties? How did the court decide the case?

2. *Was this case correctly decided?* Do you agree with the result reached in this case? Why or why not? Do you agree with the court's reasoning? Why or why not? How, if at all, would you have written the opinion differently?

3. *Justifying the infancy defense.* Does this defense of allowing minors to avoid their contractual obligations, at their election, make sense to you? As best as you can tell, what is the purpose of the defense, and what are its pros and cons? Try to frame your answer from the perspective of (a) the minor, (b) the person with whom the minor is contracting, and (c) the best rule for society in general. In thinking about this question, you may find it helpful to think about how this defense interacts with some of the bedrock principles of contract law, such as the freedom of contract, the capacity to consent, and the ability to exercise one's judgment and experience to form welfare-maximizing agreements. In addition, you may want to draw upon some of the thinking tools discussed earlier to consider what justifications exist for shifting the risk of nonperformance from the minor to the party contracting with the minor. Do these reasons still hold up in a case like *Kiefer* where the minor falsely represented himself as being 21? Why or why not?

4. *Necessaries?* Towards the beginning of its opinion, the court wrote that "the contract of a minor, other than for necessaries, is either void or voidable at his option." Why the exception for "necessaries", and what, exactly, is a "necessary" anyway? As it turns out, there is no easy answer to such a seemingly simple question. Consider the following excerpt from the court's opinion in *Webster Street Partnership, Ltd. v. Sheridan*, 368 N.W.2d 439, 442-43 (1985):

Just what are necessaries, however, has no exact definition. The term is flexible and varies according to the facts of each individual case. In *Cobbey v. Buchanan*, 48 Neb. 391, 397, 67 N.W. 176, 178 (1896), we said:

> The meaning of the term "necessaries" cannot be defined by a general rule applicable to all cases; the question is a mixed one of law and fact, to be determined in each case from the particular facts and circumstances in such case.

A number of factors must be considered before a court can conclude whether a particular product or service is a necessary. As stated in *Schoenung v. Gallet*, 206 Wis. 52, 54 (1931):

> The term "necessaries," as used in the law relating to the liability of infants therefor, is a relative term, somewhat flexible, except when applied to such things as are obviously requisite for the maintenance of existence, and depends on the social position and situation in life of the infant, as well as upon his own fortune and that of his parents. The particular infant must have an actual need for the articles furnished; not for mere ornament or pleasure. The articles must be useful and suitable, but they are not necessaries merely because useful or beneficial. Concerning the general character of the things furnished, to be necessaries the articles must supply the infant's personal needs, either those of his body or those of his mind. However, the term "necessaries" is not confined to merely such things as are required for a bare subsistence. There is no positive rule by means of which it may be determined what are or what are not necessaries, for what may be considered necessary for one infant may not be necessaries for another infant whose state is different as to rank, social position, fortune, health, or other circumstances, the question being one to be determined from the particular facts and circumstances of each case.

This appears to be the law as it is generally followed throughout the country. In *Ballinger v. Craig*, 95 Ohio App. 545 (1953), the defendants were husband and wife and were 19 years of age at the time they purchased a house trailer. Both were employed. However, prior to the purchase of the trailer, the defendants were living with the parents of the husband. The Court of Appeals for the State of Ohio held that under the facts presented the trailer was not a necessary. The court stated:

> To enable an infant to contract for articles as necessaries, he must have been in actual need of them, and obliged to procure them for himself. They are not necessaries as to him, however necessary they may be in their nature, if he was already supplied with sufficient articles of the kind, or if he had a parent or guardian who was able and willing to supply them. The burden of proof is on the plaintiff to show that the infant was destitute of the articles, and had no way of procuring them except by his own contract. . . .

In 42 Am. Jur. 2d *Infants* § 67 at 68-69 (1969), the author notes:

> Thus, articles are not necessaries for an infant if he has a parent or guardian who is able and willing to supply them, and an infant residing

> with and being supported by his parent according to his station in life is not absolutely liable for things which under other circumstances would be considered necessaries.

5. *More examples of necessaries.* In *Williams v. Buckler*, 264 S.W.2d 279, 280 (Ky. 1954), the court wrote:

> However, in the instant case we regard this farm machinery as a necessity for the infant, therefore he could be held liable on this contract. At the time he made his contract with Williams, defendant was married and had a wife and child dependent upon him for support. He was supporting himself and family by tilling the soil and in order to do that in this machine age it was necessary for him to have a tractor, disc and cultipacker. Years ago we held a work horse was necessary for an infant who was earning a living for himself and family by farming and he was liable for the reasonable value of the horse on his contract to purchase it. *Young v. Gudgell*, 2 Ky. Opin. 264. True, in even an earlier case, *Beeler v. Young*, 1 Bibb 519, 4 Ky. 519, decided in 1809, this court held a horse, saddle and bridle sold an infant were not necessaries, "and the moment after they were received they might have been converted to the purposes of an extravagant, dissipated and idle inclination." We see a distinction between a pleasure horse and a work horse just as we see a distinction between an automobile and a farm tractor, and while a pleasure horse and an automobile cannot ordinarily be termed necessaries, we think a work horse and a tractor may be so considered.

6. *Reexamining necessaries.* Does the "necessary" doctrine make sense in light of the thinking tools we have previously examined? If so, which ones, and why?

7. *A Victorian holdover?* Even if the doctrine of necessaries makes sense, do you think recovery for them should depend on the socio-economic status of individuals, so that what a "necessary" is to me may not be a "necessary" to you? Why or why not?

PROBLEM: WHAT RECOVERY IS OWED, AND BY WHOM?

Must a minor who disaffirms a contract for the purchase of a vehicle (which is not a necessity) make restitution to the vendor for damage sustained by the vehicle prior to the time the contract was disaffirmed?

On or about July 13, 2013, Plaintiff Minnie, a minor, entered into an agreement with Defendant Goofy whereby Goofy agreed to sell Minnie a used car for the sum of $12,500. Goofy was the manager of a used-car dealership, and Minnie was an employee at the dealership. At the time the agreement was made Minnie paid Goofy $10,000 cash and took possession of the car. Arrangements were made for Minnie to pay $250 per week until the balance was paid. About five weeks after the purchase agreement, and after Minnie had paid a total of $11,000 of the purchase price, a connecting rod on the vehicle's engine broke. Goofy, while denying any obligation, offered to assist Minnie in installing a used engine in the vehicle if Minnie, at her expense, could secure one. Minnie declined the offer and in September took the vehicle to a garage where it was repaired at a cost of $750. Minnie did not pay the repair bill.

On October 15, 2013, Minnie returned the title to Goofy and disaffirmed the purchase contract, demanding the return of all money paid by Minnie. Goofy did not return the money paid by Minnie.

The repair bill remained unpaid, and the vehicle remained in the garage where the repairs had been made. In the spring of 2014, in satisfaction of a garageman's lien for the outstanding amount, the garage elected to remove the vehicle's engine and transmission and then towed the vehicle to the residence of Disney, the father of the plaintiff minor. Goofy was asked several times to remove the vehicle from the Disney's home, but he declined to do so, claiming he was under no legal obligation to remove it. During the period when the vehicle was at the garage and then subsequently at the home of the plaintiff's father, it was subjected to vandalism, making it unsalvageable.

Minnie initiated this action seeking the return of the $11,000 she had paid toward the purchase of the vehicle, and Goofy counterclaimed for $1,500, the amount still owing on the contract.

How should the court rule? Consult *Kiefer* and the provisions from the *Restatement (Second) of Contracts* following that case.

Berg v. Traylor

California Court of Appeal
56 Cal. Rptr. 3d 140 (2007)

DOI TODD, J. Appellants Meshiel Cooper Traylor (Meshiel) and her minor son Craig Lamar Traylor (Craig) appeal the judgment confirming an arbitration award in favor of Craig's former personal manager, respondent Sharyn Berg (Berg), for unpaid commissions under a contract between Berg, Meshiel and Craig and unrepaid loans from Berg. Because we find that Craig had the statutory right as a minor to disaffirm both the original contract and the arbitration award, we reverse the judgment against Craig. We affirm the judgment against Meshiel.

FACTUAL AND PROCEDURAL BACKGROUND

The Agreement

On January 18, 1999, Berg entered into a two-page "Artist's Manager's Agreement" (agreement) with Meshiel and Craig, who was then 10 years old. Meshiel signed the agreement and wrote Craig's name on the signature page where he was designated "Artist." Craig did not sign the agreement. Pursuant to the agreement, Berg was to act as Craig's exclusive personal manager in exchange for a commission of 15 percent of all gross monies or other consideration paid to him as an artist during the three-year term of the agreement, as well as income from merchandising or promotional efforts or offers of employment made during the term of the agreement, regardless of when

Craig received such monies. The agreement expressly provided that any action Craig "may take in the future pertaining to disaffirmance of this agreement, whether successful or not," would not affect Meshiel's liability for any commissions due Berg. The agreement also provided that any disputes concerning payment or interpretation of the agreement would be determined by arbitration in accordance with the rules of Judicial Arbitration and Mediation Services, Inc. (JAMS).

Termination of the Agreement

On or about June 13, 2001, Craig obtained a recurring acting role on the Fox Television Network show "Malcolm in the Middle" (show). On September 11, 2001, four months prior to the expiration of the agreement, Meshiel sent a certified letter to Berg stating that while she and Craig appreciated her advice and guidance, they no longer needed her management services and could no longer afford to pay Berg her 15 percent commission because they owed a "huge amount" of taxes. On September 28, 2001, Berg responded, informing appellants that they were in breach of the agreement.

The Lawsuit

In 2004, Berg filed suit against Meshiel and Craig for breach of the agreement, breach of the implied covenant of good faith and fair dealing, breach of an oral loan agreement, conversion and declaratory relief. In July 2004, the law firm of White O'Connor Curry & Avanzado represented Meshiel and Craig when the parties stipulated to submit the matter to binding arbitration before JAMS. But in November 2004, the trial court granted that firm's motion to withdraw due to appellants' refusal to pay legal fees or communicate with the firm.

The Arbitration

The arbitration hearing was originally scheduled for December 7, 2004. In order to accommodate Meshiel's hospitalization for the premature delivery of her third child and to give appellants time to find new counsel, JAMS continued the hearing to February 7, 2005. In the meantime, appellants' second counsel, the law firm of Cohen & Gardner, represented appellants in unsuccessful settlement negotiations.

The arbitration hearing commenced on February 7, 2005. Because appellants had failed to pay their share of the arbitration fees, Berg did not anticipate their appearance and did not retain a court reporter. Though Meshiel and Craig's counsel failed to appear at the hearing, Meshiel personally appeared with Craig's talent agent, Steven Rice. Craig did not appear. According to Meshiel, the arbitrator denied her request for a two-week continuance. The arbitrator permitted Meshiel to use Rice's assistance and advice in presenting her case. Rice asserted that the agreement was invalid because Craig was a minor at the time it was executed and there had been no court approval of the agreement.

The Arbitration Award

On February 11, 2005, the arbitrator issued his award, which was served on the parties on February 14, 2005. Noting that Craig had not appeared at the hearing "despite personal service of summons and notice from JAMS," the arbitrator stated that the award was "issued against him through prove-up and default as provided for in the JAMS Rules" incorporated by reference. After briefly summarizing the testimonial and documentary evidence presented, the arbitrator found that Berg had proven her case by a preponderance of the evidence and reiterated that "Craig did not appear at the arbitration and the award of the undersigned is made on the basis of the evidence produced during the prove-up and is deemed a default judgment." The arbitrator awarded Berg commissions and interest of $154,714.15, repayment of personal loans and interest of $5,094, and attorney fees and costs of $13,762. He also awarded Berg $405,000 "for future earnings projected on a minimum of 6 years for national syndication earnings," and stated that this part of the award would "vest and become final, as monies earned after February 7, 2005, become due and payable." On February 20, 2005, the arbitrator served a clarification of the award, stating that "all monies earned by Craig Traylor, pursuant to the contract with Ms. Berg, are paid directly to Ms. Berg. . . . After deduction of fees and commissions, etc., the balance of the funds shall be forwarded to the client."

Stipulated Order

Following issuance of the arbitration award, appellants hired their third counsel, the law firm of White Bordy & Levey. The parties then entered into a stipulated order signed by the court in March 2005, which contained the following provisions:

> (1) Appellants would pay Berg $50,000 plus 50 percent of compensation earned by Craig on the show until the award was satisfied and thereafter 15 percent of all future compensation related to the show; (2) the award of unpaid commissions could not be reduced below $50,000 and the award of attorney fees and costs could not be modified; (3) appellants could only seek an adjustment of the amount of the award if they disclosed all of Craig's earnings from the show with verified declarations; and (4) the arbitration award would be treated as final for all purposes until the parties agreed on any correction to the award or the arbitrator recalculated the commissions and interest due.

Pursuant to the stipulated order, appellants' counsel directed Fox Television Network to pay Berg $50,000, and Meshiel signed an "Authorization Re: One-Time Payment" to this effect on behalf of Craig as his "legal guardian."

Petitions to Confirm and Vacate the Arbitration Award

After appellants' third counsel filed a motion to withdraw in June 2005 on the grounds that appellants refused to follow legal advice, pay legal fees or communicate with them, Meshiel and her counsel filed a substitution of attorney on

July 7, 2005 indicating that Meshiel was representing herself. The substitution of attorney did not address Craig's representation.

On July 8, 2005, Berg served a petition to confirm the arbitration award, which was filed on July 12, 2005. The petition sought confirmation of the award and a judgment entered thereon, together with a "permanent injunction (i) prohibiting Defendants from accepting compensation for Malcolm in the Middle and (ii) requiring Defendants to direct all Malcolm in the Middle payors to pay all compensation directly into Berg's Counsel's Client Trust Account for distribution to Defendants after deduction of monies owed to Berg."

On August 8, 2005, the Law Offices of Robert N. Pafundi substituted in as appellants' fourth counsel. The same day, appellants filed a "Notice of Disaffirmance of Arbitration Award by Minor," which stated that in addition to his disaffirmance of the agreement on September 11, 2001, Craig was also disaffirming the arbitration award and all other proceedings and orders arising out of the parties' dispute, including the stipulation to submit the action to binding arbitration and the March 2005 stipulated order following the arbitration. Also on that day, appellants filed a "Notice of Intention to File Documents in Opposition to Petition to Confirm Arbitration Award and to File Petition to Vacate Arbitration Award."

On August 18, 2005, appellants filed a petition/response seeking to vacate the arbitration award. The petition to vacate was based primarily on the grounds that Craig had exercised his statutory right to disaffirm both the original agreement with Berg and the arbitration award and that Berg was illegally practicing as an unlicensed talent agent. Following a hearing, the trial court took the matter under submission and the next day issued an order denying the petition to vacate the arbitration award as untimely and granting Berg's petition to confirm the award. Thereafter, the trial court entered a judgment in favor of Berg consistent with the arbitrator's award.

Appellants then filed a motion to vacate the judgment pursuant to Code of Civil Procedure section 473. While the motion was pending, appellants filed a notice of appeal from the judgment. In a January 2006 order, the trial court determined that it had no jurisdiction to rule on the matter in light of the appeal and ordered the motion off calendar.

DISCUSSION

Simply stated, one who provides a minor with goods and services does so at her own risk. The agreement here expressly contemplated this risk, requiring that Meshiel remain obligated for commissions due under the agreement regardless of whether Craig disaffirmed the agreement. Thus, we have no difficulty in reaching the conclusion that Craig is permitted to and did disaffirm the agreement and any obligations stemming therefrom, while Meshiel remains liable under the agreement and resulting judgment. Where our difficulty lies is in understanding how counsel, the arbitrator and the trial court repeatedly and systematically ignored Craig's interests in this matter. From the time Meshiel signed the agreement, her interests were not aligned with Craig's. That no one—counsel, the arbitrator or the trial court—recognized this conflict and sought appointment of a guardian ad litem for Craig is nothing short of stunning. It is the court's responsibility to protect the rights of a minor who is a litigant in court.

I. Standard of Review.

Our review of an arbitrator's award is generally limited. In *Aguilar v. Lerner*, 88 P.3d 24 (2004), the Supreme Court stated:

> When parties choose to forgo the traditional court system and arbitrate their claims, it is assumed they wish to have a final and conclusive resolution of their dispute. The Legislature has recognized this underlying assumption of finality and has, by statute, limited the grounds for judicial review of an arbitrator's award. Consistent with this legislative intent, we recognized the general rule that "an arbitrator's decision cannot be reviewed for errors of fact or law." *Moncharsh v. Heily & Blase*, 832 P.2d 899 (1992). We explained that because the Legislature has provided certain statutory grounds to overturn or modify an arbitrator's decision, courts should not subject such decisions to standard judicial review. In addition, however, to the statutory grounds for vacating an arbitrator's award, we explained in *Moncharsh* "that there may be some limited and exceptional circumstances justifying judicial review of an arbitrator's decision. . . . Such cases would include those in which granting finality to an arbitrator's decision would be inconsistent with the protection of a party's statutory rights." *Id.*

Although appellants cite neither *Aguilar* nor *Moncharsh v. Heily & Blase*, this exception appears to be the primary basis on which appellants rely in seeking judicial relief from the arbitrator's award.

II. The Judgment is Reversed as to the Minor.

The trial court denied appellants' petition to vacate the arbitration award on the ground that it was untimely. Code of Civil Procedure section 1288 provides that a petition to vacate or correct an arbitration award must be served and filed no later than 100 days after the date of service of a signed copy of the award on the petitioner. Code of Civil Procedure section 1290.6 provides that a response to a petition to confirm an award must be served and filed within 10 days after service of the petition. Here, the arbitration award was served on February 14, 2005 and the clarification of the award was served on February 20, 2005. Berg's petition to confirm the award was served on July 8, 2005 and filed on July 12, 2005. It is undisputed that by the time appellants' fourth and current counsel substituted into the action and thereafter filed a petition to vacate the arbitration award and response to the petition to confirm it on August 18, 2005, both of these statutory deadlines had passed.

Appellants contend that despite the lapse of these deadlines, Craig had the statutory right as a minor to disaffirm both the original agreement with Berg containing the arbitration provision and the arbitration award itself. We agree. Craig's minority status entitled him to disaffirm the agreement and his minority status coupled with the absence of the appointment of guardian ad litem entitled him to disaffirm the arbitration award and judgment even after the statutory deadline for moving to vacate the arbitration award had passed.

A. Disaffirmance of the Agreement.

"As a general proposition, parental consent is required for the provision of services to minors for the simple reason that minors may disaffirm their own contracts to acquire such services." *Ballard v. Anderson*, 484 P.2d 1345 (1971). According to Family Code section 6700, "a minor may make a contract in the same manner as an adult, subject to the power of disaffirmance" provided by Family Code section 6710. In turn, Family Code section 6710 states: "Except as otherwise provided by statute, a contract of a minor may be disaffirmed by the minor before majority or within a reasonable time afterwards or, in case of the minor's death within that period, by the minor's heirs or personal representative." Sound policy considerations support this provision:

> The law shields minors from their lack of judgment and experience and under certain conditions vests in them the right to disaffirm their contracts. Although in many instances such disaffirmance may be a hardship upon those who deal with an infant, the right to avoid his contracts is conferred by law upon a minor "for his protection against his own improvidence and the designs of others." It is the policy of the law to protect a minor against himself and his indiscretions and immaturity as well as against the machinations of other people and to discourage adults from contracting with an infant. Any loss occasioned by the disaffirmance of a minor's contract might have been avoided by declining to enter into the contract.

Niemann v. Deverich, 221 P.2d 178 (1950). . . .

Berg argues that Craig cannot disaffirm the agreement because it was for his and his family's necessities. Family Code section 6712 provides that a valid contract cannot be disaffirmed by a minor if all of the following requirements are met: the contract is to pay the reasonable value of things necessary for the support of the minor or the minor's family, the things have actually been furnished to the minor or the minor's family, and the contract is entered into by the minor when not under the care of a parent or guardian able to provide for the minor or the minor's family. These requirements are not met here. The agreement was not a contract to pay for the necessities of life for Craig or his family. While such necessities have been held to include payment for lodging and even payment of attorneys' fees, we cannot conclude that a contract to secure personal management services for the purpose of advancing Craig's acting career constitutes payment for the type of necessity contemplated by Family Code section 6712. Nor is there any evidence that Meshiel was unable to provide for the family in 1999 at the time of the agreement. As such, Family Code section 6712 does not bar the minor's disaffirmance of the contract.

No specific language is required to communicate an intent to disaffirm. "A contract (or conveyance) of a minor may be avoided by any act or declaration disclosing an unequivocal intent to repudiate its binding force and effect." *Spencer v. Collins,* 104 P. 320 (1909). Express notice to the other party is unnecessary. We find that the "Notice of Disaffirmance of Arbitration Award by Minor" filed on August 8, 2005 was sufficient to constitute a disaffirmance of the agreement by Craig. Although the notice assumed that Meshiel's September 11, 2001 letter to Berg stating that Meshiel and Craig were no longer going to honor their obligations under the agreement acted as a prior disaffirmance of the agreement, the notice further stated that Craig "disaffirms all other documents filed under his name or affecting him as a minor in this litigation. . . ." This language adequately conveyed Craig's intent to repudiate the binding force and effect of the agreement.

We find that Craig was entitled to and did disaffirm the agreement which, among other things, required him to arbitrate his disputes with Berg. On this basis alone, therefore, the judgment confirming the arbitration award must be reversed.

B. Disaffirmance of the Arbitration Award.

[In this omitted portion of its opinion, the court went on to find (although doing so was unnecessary to the court's disposition of the case) that Craig was entitled to and did disaffirm the arbitration award because he was never represented by an appointed guardian ad litem.]

III. The Judgment is Affirmed as to the Mother.

Appellants do not generally distinguish their arguments between mother and son, apparently assuming that if Craig disaffirms the agreement and judgment, Meshiel would be permitted to escape liability as well. But a disaffirmance of an agreement by a minor does not operate to terminate the contractual obligations of the parent who signed the agreement. *Raden v. Laurie,* 262 P.2d 61 (1953). The agreement Meshiel signed provided that Craig's disaffirmance would not serve to void or avoid Meshiel's obligations under the agreement and that Meshiel remained liable for commissions due Berg regardless of Craig's disaffirmance. Accordingly, we find no basis for Meshiel to avoid her independent obligations under the agreement. . . .

While we conclude that Craig nevertheless had the right to disaffirm the arbitration award and the subsequent judgment as an unrepresented minor, Meshiel has not provided us with any authority that would permit her now to challenge the award against her. Accordingly, the judgment confirming the arbitration award is affirmed as to Meshiel.

DISPOSITION

The judgment is reversed as to Craig and affirmed as to Meshiel. The parties to bear their own costs on appeal.

NOTES AND QUESTIONS

1. *What happened?* Who sued whom for what? Procedurally, how did the case get before this court? Factually, what happened between the parties? What arguments did the plaintiff and defendant make? What rule or rules did the court apply? How did the court analyze the dispute between the parties? How did the court decide the case?

2. *Was this case correctly decided?* Do you agree with the result reached in this case? Why or why not? Do you agree with the court's reasoning? Why or why not? How, if at all, would you have written the opinion differently?

3. *YouTube.* This case made quite a splash in the entertainment industry when it was first decided, and is still consulted by minors and parents of minors who are considering entering into entertainment contracts. Robert N. Pafundi, the lawyer who served as appellants' fourth counsel, put up a short (8 minutes) video on YouTube (https://www.youtube.com/watch?v=oWt145Uddxk) explaining how he was finally able to bring the issue of Craig's minority to the appellate court—an issue that incredibly had been missed by the trial judge, the arbitrator, and all of the lawyers prior to his taking on the case.

2. Incompetence

DOCTRINAL OVERVIEW: INCOMPETENCY AS A DEFENSE TO ENFORCEMENT*

According to the Supreme Court of Arkansas, "Perhaps no branch of jurisprudence is more elusive than that dealing with one's mental capacity to contract."[1] The intrinsic elusiveness of this subject is compounded by a patchwork of statutes that, as is the case for minors, vary considerably from one jurisdiction to another.

Although the older cases were concerned mainly with "lunacy" and "insanity," it is now recognized that incapacity due to mental infirmity may result from a variety of causes, including mental retardation, mental illness, brain damage, brain deterioration due to old age, and the use of alcohol or drugs. The mere presence of such a disability, however, does not itself impair the capacity to contract. In the colorful words of the Supreme Court of Arkansas, the fact that a man may have been "filthy, forgetful and eccentric, . . . believed in witchcraft, and had dogs eat at the same table with him . . . does not establish lack of capacity."[3] Something more must be shown, and it has been difficult to formulate a single test of that additional element to encompass diverse types of mental disorders.

The traditional test is a "cognitive" one. Did the party lack the capacity to understand the nature and consequences of the transaction in question? Was

---

* Excerpted from E. ALLAN FARNSWORTH, CONTRACTS § 4.6 (4th ed. 2004).

1. Waggoner v. Atkins, 162 S.W.2d 55, 58 (Ark. 1942).

3. Simmons First Natl. Bank v. Luzader, 438 S.W.2d 25, 30 (Ark. 1969). . . .

the party unable to know what he or she was doing and to appreciate its effects? Since it is competency at the time the agreement was made that is critical, it is enough if the party had a "lucid interval" at that moment. The cognitive test has been attacked as unscientific, and one legal scholar has condemned it as setting up a standard that is "ambiguous, self-contradictory and practically meaningless" and that "defies accurate verbal formulation."[6] Nevertheless, the cognitive test is almost universally accepted by courts. In view of the difficulty in applying the test, it is especially significant that it is irrelevant whether the other party knew or had reason to know of the mental disability.

The principal challenges to the cognitive test have come from instances in which mentally infirm persons understand the nature and consequences of their actions, but nevertheless lack effective control of them, a situation characteristic of manic-depressives. Should a "volitional" test be applied in such cases, as an alternative to the cognitive one? In a seminal lower court New York case, a previously frugal and cautious businessman passed from the depressed to the manic phase of a manic-depressive psychosis and suddenly refused to see his psychiatrist, went on a buying spree, and embarked on ambitious construction projects. As part of one of these projects he contracted, against his lawyer's advice, to buy land for $51,500. Two weeks later he was sent to a mental hospital, and he later sued to rescind the contract. The court concluded that he understood the transaction since the "manic-depressive psychosis affects motivation rather than ability to understand." It nevertheless held that "capacity to understand is not . . . the sole criterion. Incompetence to contract also exists when a contract is entered into under the compulsion of a mental disease or disorder but for which the contract would not have been made."[8]

The *Restatement Second* takes a compromise position by adding to the traditional cognitive test a qualified volitional test: "if by reason of mental illness or defect . . . he is unable to act in a reasonable manner in relation to the transaction and the other party has reason to know of his condition."[9] The qualification that the other party have reason to know of the condition—one that does not figure in the *Restatement Second's* formulation of the cognitive test—was reaffirmed by the New York Court of Appeals in *Ortelere v. Teachers' Retirement Board,* the leading case applying the volitional branch of the *Restatement Second* formulation. . . .

Ortelere v. Teachers' Retirement Board of New York

Court of Appeals of New York
250 N.E.2d 460 (1969)

BREITEL, JUDGE. This appeal involves the revocability of an election of benefits under a public employees' retirement system and suggests the need for a

6. Milton D. Green, *Judicial Tests of Mental Incompetency,* 6 MO. L. REV. 141, 147, 165 (1941).
8. Faber v. Sweet Style Mfg. Corp., 242 N.Y.S.2d 763, 768 (Sup. Ct. 1963).
9. *Restatement Second* § 15(1). . . .

renewed examination of the kinds of mental incompetency which may render voidable the exercise of contractual rights. **The particular issue arises on the evidently unwise and foolhardy selection of benefits by a 60-year-old teacher, on leave for mental illness and suffering from cerebral arteriosclerosis, after service as a public schoolteacher and participation in a public retirement system for over 40 years.** The teacher died a little less than two months after making her election of maximum benefits, payable to her during her life, thus causing the entire reserve to fall in. She left surviving her husband of 38 years of marriage and two grown children.

> ***Unwise and foolhardy?***
>
> As you read the rest of the court's opinion, ask yourself whether you agree that Grace Ortelere's decision was "unwise and foolhardy." Is the court making this claim in light of subsequent events, events which, by definition, Grace could not have been aware of when she made her election? Or is the court saying that, regardless of subsequent events, making this particular election was a poor decision on Grace's part? Which of these two questions (if any) do you think it is appropriate for the court to ask, and why?

There is no doubt that any retirement system depends for its soundness on an actuarial experience based on the purely prospective selections of benefits and mortality rates among the covered group, and that retrospective or adverse selection after the fact would be destructive of a sound system. It is also true that members of retirement systems are free to make choices which to others may seem unwise or foolhardy. The issue here is narrower than any suggested by these basic principles. It is whether an otherwise irrevocable election may be avoided for incapacity because of known mental illness which resulted in the election when, except in the barest actuarial sense, the system would sustain no unfavorable consequences.

The husband and executor of Grace W. Ortelere, the deceased New York City schoolteacher, sues to set aside her application for retirement without option, in the event of her death. It is alleged that Mrs. Ortelere, on February 11, 1965, two months before her death from natural causes, was not mentally competent to execute a retirement application. By this application, effective the next day, she elected the maximum retirement allowance. She thus revoked her earlier election of benefits under which she named her husband a beneficiary of the unexhausted reserve upon her death. Selection of the maximum allowance extinguished all interests upon her death.

Following a nonjury trial in Supreme Court, it was held that Grace Ortelere had been mentally incompetent at the time of her February 11 application, thus rendering it "null and void and of no legal effect". The Appellate Division, by a divided court, reversed the judgment of the Supreme Court and held that, as a matter of law, there was insufficient proof of mental incompetency as to this transaction.

Mrs. Ortelere's mental illness, indeed, psychosis, is undisputed. It is not seriously disputable, however, that she had complete cognitive judgment or awareness when she made her selection. **A modern understanding of mental illness, however, suggests that incapacity to contract or exercise contractual rights may exist, because of volitional and affective**

> ***Expanding the defense***
>
> Note carefully how, according to this court, the defense of mental incapacity,

impediments or disruptions in the personality, despite the intellectual or cognitive ability to understand. It will be recognized as the civil law parallel to the question of criminal responsibility which has been the recent concern of so many and has resulted in statutory and decisional changes in the criminal law.

> which was once only concerned with a party's ability to *understand*, has evolved to encompass situations where a party may possess understanding yet lack the ability or willpower to *control* their behavior, sort of like a hypothetical contracts casebook author who knows too much apple pie is not good for him but indulges nevertheless (but only during the holidays, he assures me, or rather, he would assure me if he were not hypothetical).

Mrs. Ortelere, an elementary schoolteacher since 1924, suffered a "nervous breakdown" in March, 1964 and went on a leave of absence expiring February 5, 1965. She was then 60 years old and had been happily married for 38 years. On July 1, 1964 she came under the care of Dr. D'Angelo, a psychiatrist, who diagnosed her breakdown as involutional psychosis, melancholia type. Dr. D'Angelo prescribed, and for about six weeks decedent underwent, tranquilizer and shock therapy. Although moderately successful, the therapy was not continued since it was suspected that she also suffered from cerebral arteriosclerosis, an ailment later confirmed. However, the psychiatrist continued to see her at monthly intervals until March, 1965. On March 28, 1965 she was hospitalized after collapsing at home from an aneurysm. She died 10 days later; the cause of death was "Cerebral thrombosis due to H(ypertensive) H(eart) D(isease)."

As a teacher she had been a member of the Teachers' Retirement System of the City of New York. This entitled her to certain annuity and pension rights, preretirement death benefits, and empowered her to exercise various options concerning the payment of her retirement allowance.

Some years before, on June 28, 1958, she had executed a "Selection of Benefits under Option One" naming her husband as beneficiary of the unexhausted reserve. Under this option upon retirement her allowance would be less by way of periodic retirement allowances, but if she died before receipt of her full reserve the balance of the reserve would be payable to her husband. On June 16, 1960, two years later, she had designated her husband as beneficiary of her service death benefits in the event of her death prior to retirement.

Then on February 11, 1965, when her leave of absence had just expired and she was still under treatment, she executed a retirement application, the one here involved, selecting the maximum retirement allowance payable during her lifetime with nothing payable on or after death. She also, at this time, borrowed from the system the maximum cash withdrawal permitted, namely, $8,760. Three days earlier she had written the board, stating that she intended to retire on February 12 or 15 or as soon as she received "the information I need in order to decide whether to take an option or maximum allowance." She then listed eight specific questions, reflecting great understanding of the retirement system, concerning the various alternatives available. An extremely detailed reply was sent, by letter of February 15, 1965, although by that date it was technically impossible for her to change her selection. However, the board's chief clerk, before whom Mrs. Ortelere executed the application, testified that the questions were "answered verbally by me on February 11th." Her retirement reserve totaled $62,165 (after deducting the $8,760 withdrawal), and the difference between electing the maximum retirement allowance (no option) and the allowance under "option one" was $901 per year or $75 per month. That is, had the teacher selected "option one" she would have received an annual allowance of $4,494 or $375 per month, while if no option had been selected she would have received an annual allowance of $5,395 or $450 per month. Had she not withdrawn the cash the annual figures would be $5,247 and $6,148 respectively.

Following her taking a leave of absence for her condition, Mrs. Ortelere had become very depressed and was unable to care for herself. As a result her husband gave up his electrician's job, in which he earned $222 per week, to stay home and take care of her on a full-time basis. She left their home only when he accompanied her. Although he took her to the Retirement Board on February 11, 1965, he did not know why she went, and did not question her for fear "she'd start crying hysterically that I was scolding her. That's the way she was. And I wouldn't upset her."

The Orteleres were in quite modest circumstances. They owned their own home, valued at $20,000, and had $8,000 in a savings account. They also owned some farm land worth about $5,000. Under these circumstances, as revealed in this record, retirement for both of the Orteleres or the survivor of them had to be provided, as a practical matter, largely out of Mrs. Ortelere's retirement benefits.

According to Dr. D'Angelo, the psychiatrist who treated her, Mrs. Ortelere never improved enough to "warrant my sending her back (to teaching)." A physician for the Board of Education examined her on February 2, 1965 to determine her fitness to return to teaching. Although not a psychiatrist but rather a specialist in internal medicine, this physician "judged that she had apparently recovered from the depression" and that she appeared rational. However, before allowing her to return to teaching, a report was requested from Dr. D'Angelo concerning her condition. It is notable that the Medical Division of the Board of Education on February 24, 1965 requested that Mrs. Ortelere report to the board's "panel psychiatrist" on March 11, 1965.

Dr. D'Angelo stated "(a)t no time since she was under my care was she ever mentally competent"; that "(m)entally she couldn't make a decision of any kind, actually, of any kind, small or large." He also described how involutional melancholia affects the judgment process:

> They can't think rationally, no matter what the situation is. They will even tell you, "I used to be able to think of anything and make any decision. Now," they say, "even getting up, I don't know whether I should get up or whether I should stay in bed." Or, "I don't even know how to make a slice of toast anymore." Everything is impossible to decide, and everything is too great an effort to even think of doing. They just don't have the effort, actually, because their nervous breakdown drains them of all their physical energies.

While the psychiatrist used terms referring to "rationality," it is quite evident that Mrs. Ortelere's psychopathology did not lend itself to a classification under the legal test of irrationality. It is undoubtedly, for this reason, that the Appellate Division was unable to accept his testimony and the trial court's finding of irrationality in the light of the prevailing rules as they have been formulated.

The well-established rule is that contracts of a mentally incompetent person who has not been adjudicated insane are voidable. Even where the contract has been partly or fully performed it will still be avoided upon restoration of the *status quo*.

> ***Voidable, not void***
>
> As the defense of infancy, once again it is important to note that contractual obligations undertaken by parties who lack the mental capacity to form contracts are not void *ab initio*, but rather voidable at the option of the party asserting the defense. *See, e.g., Restatement (Second) of Contracts* § 15. Why do you suppose this is?

Traditionally, in this State and elsewhere, contractual mental capacity has been measured by what is largely a cognitive test. Under this standard the "inquiry" is whether the mind was "so affected as to render him wholly and absolutely incompetent to comprehend and understand the nature of the transaction" [*Aldrich v. Bailey*, 132 N.Y. 85, 89 (1892)]. A requirement that the party also be able to make a rational judgment concerning the particular transaction qualified the cognitive test. Conversely, it is also well recognized that contractual ability would be affected by insane delusions intimately related to the particular transaction.

These traditional standards governing competency to contract were formulated when psychiatric knowledge was quite primitive. They fail to account for one who by reason of mental illness is unable to control his conduct even though his cognitive ability seems unimpaired. When these standards were evolving it was thought that all the mental faculties were simultaneously affected by mental illness. This is no longer the prevailing view.

Of course, the greatest movement in revamping legal notions of mental responsibility has occurred in the criminal law. The nineteenth century cognitive test embraced in the *M'Naghten* rules has long been criticized and changed by statute and decision in many jurisdictions (see *M'Naghten's Case*, 8 Eng. Rep. 718 (House of Lords, 1843)).

While the policy considerations for the criminal law and the civil law are different, both share in common the premise that policy considerations must be based on a sound understanding of the human mind and, therefore, its illnesses. Hence, because the cognitive rules are, for the most part, too restrictive and rest on a false factual basis they must be re-examined. Once it is understood that, accepting plaintiff's proof, Mrs. Ortelere was psychotic and because of that psychosis could have been incapable of making a voluntary selection of her retirement system

> ***The M'Naghten Rules***
>
> For those of you who have not yet taken criminal law (or have not yet covered this material), the *M'Naghten* rules were developed by the British House of Lords in response to the acquittal of Daniel M'Naghten's murder of Edward Drummond, whom he mistook for the British Prime Minister. Specifically, the Rules were originally designed to test the whether criminal defendants possessed the *mens rea* (or mindset) to be found guilty of certain crimes, and was originally formulated as follows: "to establish a defense on the ground of insanity, it must be clearly proved that, at the time of the committing of the act, the party accused was laboring under such a defect of reason, from disease of the mind, as not to know the nature and quality of the act

he was doing; or, if he did know it, that he did not know he was doing what was wrong." *M'Naghten's Case, 8 Eng. Rep. 718 (House of Lords, 1843).* Since it was first announced in 1843, of course, the logic animating this defense has expanded well beyond its original concern with the criminal insane and now encompasses civil law defendants as well, who can now, as in *Ortelere*, assert the defense of incompetence where they can show that they lacked the ability (or, in some cases, even possessed a diminished capacity) to give their consent to a contract.

Note the "and"

Note that, under the *Restatement (Second) of Contracts*, one cannot void their contractual obligations *simply* by possessing a mental illness or defect. Rather, note the "and" that the drafters of the *Restatement* have added, which requires that the party with whom the defendant is contracting *also* "has reason to know of his condition." Why do you suppose the *Restatement* has been drafted in such a manner, and do you think this is a good rule? Why or why not?

benefits, there is an issue that a modern jurisprudence should not exclude, merely because her mind could pass a "cognition" test based on nineteenth century psychology. . . .

It is quite significant that *Restatement, 2d, Contracts,* states the modern rule on competency to contract. This is in evident recognition, and the Reporter's Notes support this inference, that, regardless of how the cases formulated their reasoning, the old cognitive test no longer explains the results. Thus, the new *Restatement* section reads:

> **(1) A person incurs only voidable contractual duties by entering into a transaction if by reason of mental illness or defect . . . (b) he is unable to act in a reasonable manner in relation to the transaction and the other party has reason to know of his condition.**

Restatement, 2d, Contracts § [15].

The avoidance of duties under an agreement entered into by those who have done so by reason of mental illness, but who have understanding, depends on balancing competing policy considerations. There must be stability in contractual relations and protection of the expectations of parties who bargain in good faith. On the other hand, it is also desirable to protect persons who may understand the nature of the transaction but who, due to mental illness, cannot control their conduct. Hence, there should be relief only if the other party knew or was put on notice as to the contractor's mental illness. Thus, the Restatement provision for avoidance contemplates that "the other party has reason to know" of the mental illness. *Id.*

When, however, the other party is without knowledge of the contractor's mental illness and the agreement is made on fair terms, the proposed Restatement rule is:

> The power of avoidance under subsection (1) terminates to the extent that the contract has been so performed in whole or in part or the circumstances have so changed that avoidance would be inequitable. In such a case a court may grant relief on such equitable terms as the situation requires.

Restatement, 2d, Contracts § [15(2)].

The system was, or should have been, fully aware of Mrs. Ortelere's condition. They, or the Board of Education, knew of her leave of absence for medical reasons and the resort to staff psychiatrists by the Board of Education. Hence, the other of the conditions for avoidance is satisfied.

Lastly, there are no significant changes of position by the system other than those that flow from the barest actuarial consequences of benefit selection.

Nor should one ignore that in the relationship between retirement system and member, and especially in a public system, there is not involved a commercial, let alone an ordinary commercial, transaction. Instead the nature of the system and its announced goal is the protection of its members and those in whom its members have an interest. It is not a sound scheme which would permit 40 years of contribution and participation in the system to be nullified by a one-instant act committed by one known to be mentally ill. This is especially true if there would be no substantial harm to the system if the act were avoided. On the record none may gainsay that her selection of a "no option" retirement while under psychiatric care, ill with cerebral arteriosclerosis, aged 60, and with a family in which she had always manifested concern, was so unwise and foolhardy that a factfinder might conclude that it was explainable only as a product of psychosis.

On this analysis it is not difficult to see that plaintiff's evidence was sufficient to sustain a finding that, when she acted as she did on February 11, 1965, she did so solely as a result of serious mental illness, namely, psychosis. Of course, nothing less serious than medically classified psychosis should suffice or else few contracts would be invulnerable to some kind of psychological attack. Mrs. Ortelere's psychiatrist testified quite flatly that as an involutional melancholiac in depression she was incapable of making a voluntary "rational" decision. Of course, as noted earlier, the trial court's finding and perhaps some of the testimony attempted to fit into the rubrics of the traditional rules. For that reason rather than reinstatement of the judgment at Trial Term there should be a new trial under the proper standards frankly considered and applied.

Accordingly, the order of the Appellate Division should be reversed, without costs, and the action remanded to Special Term for a new trial.

JASEN, JUDGE **(dissenting)**. Where there has been no previous adjudication of incompetency, the burden of proving mental incompetence is upon the party alleging it. I agree with the majority at the Appellate Division that the plaintiff, the husband of the decedent, failed to sustain the burden incumbent upon him of proving deceased's incompetence.

The evidence conclusively establishes that the decedent, at the time she made her application to retire, understood not only that she was retiring, but also that she had selected the maximum payment during her lifetime.

Indeed, the letter written by the deceased to the Teachers' Retirement System prior to her retirement demonstrates her full mental capacity to understand and to decide whether to take on option or the maximum allowance. The full text of the letter reads as follows:

> February 8, 1965
>
> Gentlemen:
>
> I would like to retire on Feb. 12 or Feb. 15. In other words, just as soon as possible after I receive the information I need in order to decide whether to take an option or maximum allowance. Following are the questions I would like to have answered:
>
> 1. What is my "average" five-year salary?
>
> 2. What is my maximum allowance?
>
> 3. I am 60 years old. If I select option four-a with a beneficiary (female) 27 years younger, what is my allowance?
>
> 4. If I select four-a on the pension part only, and take the maximum annuity, what is my allowance?
>
> 5. If I take a loan of 89% Of my year's salary before retirement, what would my maximum allowance be?
>
> 6. If I take a loan of $5,000 before retiring, and select option four-a on both the pension and annuity, what would my allowance be?
>
> 7. What is my total service credit? I have been on a leave without pay since Oct. 26, 1964.
>
> 8. What is the "factor" used for calculating option four-a with the above beneficiary?
>
> Thank you for your promptness in making the necessary calculations. I will come to your office on Thursday afternoon of this week.

It seems clear that this detailed, explicit and extremely pertinent list of queries reveals a mind fully in command of the salient features of the Teachers' Retirement System. Certainly, it cannot be said that the decedent could possess sufficient capacity to compose a letter indicating such a comprehensive understanding of the retirement system, and yet lack the capacity to understand the answers.

As I read the record, the evidence establishes that the decedent's election to receive maximum payments was predicated on the need for a higher income to support two retired persons—her husband and herself. Since the only source of income available to decedent and her husband was decedent's retirement pay, the additional payment of $75 per month which she would receive by electing the maximal payment was a necessity. Indeed, the additional payments represented an increase of 20% over the benefits payable under option 1. Under these circumstances, an election of maximal income during decedent's lifetime was not only a rational, but a necessary decision.

Further indication of decedent's knowledge of the financial needs of her family is evidenced by the fact that she took a loan for the maximum amount ($8,760) permitted by the retirement system at the time she made application for retirement.

Moreover, there is nothing in the record to indicate that the decedent had any warning, premonition, knowledge or indication at the time of retirement that her life expectancy was, in any way, reduced by her condition.

Decedent's election of the maximum retirement benefits, therefore, was not so contrary to her best interests so as to create an inference of her mental incompetence.

Indeed, concerning election of options under a retirement system, it has been held:

> Even where no previous election has been made, the court must make the election for an incompetent which would be in accordance with what would have been his manifest and reasonable choice if he were sane, and, in the absence of convincing evidence that the incompetent would have made a different selection, it is *presumed that he would have chosen the option yielding the largest returns in his lifetime.*

Schwartzberg v. Teachers' Retirement Bd., 76 N.Y.S.2d 488, *aff'd*, 298 N.Y. 741, 83 N.E.2d 146; emphasis supplied.

Nor can I agree with the majority's view that the traditional rules governing competency to contract "are, for the most part, too restrictive and rest on a false factual basis."

The issue confronting the courts concerning mental capacity to contract is under what circumstances and conditions should a party be relieved of contractual obligations freely entered. This is peculiarly a legal decision, although, of course, available medical knowledge forms a datum which influences the legal choice. It is common knowledge that the present state of psychiatric knowledge is inadequate to provide a fixed rule for each and every type of mental disorder. Thus, the generally accepted rules which have evolved to determine mental responsibility are general enough in application to encompass all types of mental disorders, and phrased in a manner which can be understood and practically applied by juries composed of laymen.

The generally accepted test of mental competency to contract which has thus evolved is whether the party attempting to avoid the contract was capable of understanding and appreciating the nature and consequences of the particular act or transaction which he challenges. This rule represents a balance struck between policies to protect the security of transactions between individuals and freedom of contract on the one hand, and protection of those mentally handicapped on the other hand. In my opinion, this rule has proven workable in practice and fair in result. A broad range of evidence including psychiatric testimony is admissible under the existing rules to establish a party's condition. In the final analysis, the lay jury will infer the state of the party's mind from his observed behavior as indicated by the evidence presented at trial. Each juror instinctively judges what is normal and what is abnormal conduct from his own experience, and the generally accepted test harmonizes the competing policy considerations with human experience to achieve the fairest result in the greatest number of cases.

As in every situation where the law must draw a line between liability and nonliability, between responsibility and nonresponsibility, there will be borderline cases, and injustices may occur by deciding erroneously that an individual belongs on one side of the line or the other. To minimize the chances of such injustices occurring, the line should be drawn as clearly as possible.

The Appellate Division correctly found that the deceased was capable of understanding the nature and effect of her retirement benefits, and exercised rational judgment in electing to receive the maximum allowance during her lifetime. I fear that the majority's refinement of the generally accepted rules will prove unworkable in practice, and make many contracts vulnerable to psychological attack. Any benefit to those who understand what they are doing, but are unable to exercise self-discipline, will be outweighed by frivolous claims which will burden our courts and undermine the security of contracts. The reasonable expectations of those who innocently deal with persons who appear rational and who understand what they are doing should be protected.

Accordingly, I would affirm the order appealed from. . . .

Order reversed, without costs, and a new trial granted.

RELEVANT PROVISIONS

For the *Restatement (Second) of Contracts,* consult § 15.

NOTES AND QUESTIONS

1. ***What happened?*** Who sued whom for what? Procedurally, how did the case get before this court? Factually, what happened between the parties? What arguments did the plaintiff and defendant make? What rule or rules did the court apply? How did the court analyze the dispute between the parties? How did the court decide the case?

2. ***Was this case correctly decided?*** Do you agree with the result reached in this case? Why or why not? Do you agree with the court's reasoning? Why or why not? How, if at all, would you have written the opinion differently?

3. ***Majority or dissent.*** What, exactly, is the dispute between the majority and the dissent? Who has the better argument? Why?

4. ***Sound mind?*** Was Mrs. Ortelere of sound mind when she signed the retirement papers? Should it have mattered according to the majority? To the dissent?

5. ***Dissent.*** In his dissent, Judge Jasen writes that: "As in every situation where the law must draw a line between liability and nonliability, between responsibility and nonresponsibility, there will be borderline cases, and injustices may occur by deciding erroneously that an individual belongs on one side of the line or the other. To minimize the chances of such injustices occurring, the line should be drawn as clearly as possible." Do you agree?

Farnum v. Silvano

Appeals Court of Massachusetts
540 N.E.2d 202 (1989)

KASS, JUSTICE. On the basis of a finding that Viola Farnum enjoyed a lucid interval when she conveyed her house to Joseph Silvano, III, for approximately half its market value, a Probate Court judge decided that Farnum had capacity to execute the deed. A different test measures competence to enter into a contract and we, therefore, reverse the judgment. . . .

When she sold her real estate in South Yarmouth on July 14, 1986, Farnum was ninety years of age. The sale price was $64,900. At that time, the fair market value of the property was $115,000. Indeed, at the closing, the buyer, Silvano, obtained a mortgage loan from a bank of $65,000. Silvano, age twenty-four, knew Farnum from mowing her lawn and doing other landscape work. Farnum trusted him and had confidence in him. Before entering into the transaction, Silvano had been put on notice of the inadequacy of the price he was going to pay. He had been warned not to proceed by Farnum's nephew, Harry Gove, who is now Farnum's guardian and is pressing this action for rescission on her behalf.

Farnum's mental competence had begun to fail seriously in 1983, three years before she delivered a deed to the South Yarmouth real estate. That failure manifested itself in aberrant conduct. She would lament not hearing from sisters who were dead. She would wonder where the people upstairs in her house had gone, but there was no upstairs to her house. She offered to sell the house to a neighbor for $35,000. (He declined, recognizing the property was worth much more.) She became abnormally forgetful. Frequently she locked herself out of her house and broke into it, rather than calling on a neighbor with whom she had left a key (on one occasion, she broke and entered through a basement window). She hid her cat to protect it from "the cops . . . looking for my cat." She would express a desire to return to Cape Cod although she was on Cape Cod. She easily became lost. Payment of her bills required the assistance of her sister and her nephew, who also balanced her check book.

There were several hospitalizations during the three-year period preceding the conveyance in 1986. On May 2, 1985, a brain scan examination disclosed organic brain disease. By January, 1987, some six months after the conveyance, Farnum was admitted to Cape Cod Hospital for treatment of dementia and seizure disorder. She was discharged to a nursing home.

In connection with drawing the deed and effecting the transfer of real estate, Farnum was represented by a lawyer selected and paid by Silvano. That lawyer, and a lawyer for the bank which was making a loan to Silvano, attended the closing at Farnum's house. At the closing Farnum was, as the trial judge expressed it, "aware of what was going on." She was cheerful, engaged in pleasantries, and made instant coffee for those present. After the transaction, however, Farnum insisted to others—her sister and nephew, for example—that she still owned the property. That may have been consistent with Farnum's ambivalence about giving up her home and going to a nursing home.

It was not unusual, the judge concluded, for Farnum to be perfectly coherent and "two minutes later" be confused. When she signed the deed, "she was coherent or in a lucid interval."

Acting during a lucid interval can be a basis for executing a will. "[A] person of pathologically unsound mind may possess testamentary capacity at any given time and lack it at all other times." *Daly v. Hussey*, 275 Mass. 28, 29 (1931).

Competence to enter into a contract presupposes something more than a transient surge of lucidity. It involves not merely comprehension of what is "going on," but an ability to comprehend the nature and quality of the transaction, together with an understanding of its significance and consequences. From a testator we ask awareness of the natural objects of bounty. The choice among those objects may be seen by others as arbitrary, but arbitrariness or capriciousness may be allowed a donor. In the act of entering into a contract there are reciprocal obligations, and it is appropriate, when mental incapacity, as here, is manifest, to require a baseline of reasonableness.

In *Krasner v. Berk*, [366 Mass. 464, 468 (1974)], the court cited with approval the synthesis of those principles now appearing in the *Restatement (Second) of Contracts* § 15(1), which regards as voidable a transaction entered into with a person who, "by reason of mental illness or defect (a) . . . is unable to understand in a reasonable manner the nature and consequences of the transaction, or (b) . . . is unable to act in a reasonable manner in relation to the transaction and the other party has reason to know of [the] condition."

Applied to the case at hand, Farnum could be aware that she was selling her house to Silvano for much less than it was worth, while failing to understand the unreasonableness of doing so at a time when she faced serious cash demands for rent, home care, or nursing home charges. That difference between awareness of the surface of a transaction, i.e., that it was happening, and failure to comprehend the unreasonableness and consequences of the transaction by a mentally impaired person was recognized and discussed in an opinion for the court by Judge Breitel, in *Ortelere v. Teachers' Retirement Bd.*, 25 N.Y.2d 196, 202-206 (1969). In the *Ortelere* case, a teacher who was enrolled in a retirement plan suffered a psychotic break. Her age was sixty and she also suffered from cerebral arteriosclerosis. While thus afflicted, Grace Ortelere changed her selection of benefit to choose the maximum retirement allowance payable during her lifetime with nothing payable after her death—this in the face of severely diminished life expectancy and her husband having given up his employment to care for her full time. The court observed that "her selection of a 'no option' retirement while under psychiatric care, ill with cerebral arteriosclerosis, aged 60, and with a family in which she had always manifested concern, was so unwise and foolhardy that a factfinder might conclude that it was explainable only as a product of psychosis." *Id.* at 206. A major factor in the court's decision was that the retirement board "was, or should have been, fully aware of Mrs. Ortelere's condition." *Id.* at 205.

On the basis of the trial judge's findings, we think Farnum did not possess the requisite contextual understanding. She suffered mental disease which had manifested itself in erratic and irrational conduct and was confirmed by diagnostic test. Her physician did not think she was competent to live alone. Relatively soon after the transaction, Farnum's mental deficits grew so grave that it became necessary to hospitalize her. The man to whom she sold her property for less than its value was not a member of her family or someone who had cared for her for long duration. Silvano's explanation that he gave Farnum the additional consideration of agreeing to let her stay in the house for some time after the closing is unpersuasive, as the purchase and sale agreement and the deed are silent about any such agreement. Farnum was not represented by a lawyer who knew her and considered her over-all interests as a primary concern. The mission of the lawyer secured by Silvano, and paid by him, was to effect the transaction. As we have observed, Farnum faced growing cash demands for her maintenance, and, in her circumstances, it was not rational to part with a major asset for a cut-rate price.

The decisive factor which we think makes Farnum's delivery of her deed to Silvano voidable was his awareness of Farnum's inability to act in a reasonable manner. See *Restatement (Second) of Contracts* § 15(1)(b). Silvano knew or had reason to know of Farnum's impaired condition from her conduct, which at the times material caused concern to her relatives, her neighbors, and her physician. Silvano was aware that he was buying the house for about half its value.[1] He had been specifically warned by Farnum's nephew about the unfairness of the transaction and Farnum's mental disability.

> ***The decisive factor***
>
> This point was already brought up in a sidebar in *Ortelere*, but it bears repeating here. Given the evidence of Viola Farnum's diminished mental capacity, should her ability to void the contract be made to depend on Silvano's knowledge of her mental condition? Stated differently, what if Silvano left for college and his cousin, who knew nothing about Farnum's condition, began helping her out with her lawn and landscape work. Then, one day, overhearing Farnum indicate that she would like to sell her land, made the same offer that Silvano made in this case. First, regardless of the language of *Restatement (Second) of Contracts* § 15, do you think such a transaction *should* be allowed to stand? Second, even if we take the language of the *Restatement* as a given, what do you think a court confronted with such a case would *actually* do, and why?

In view of our conclusion that Farnum lacked the capacity to enter into contractual arrangements for the sale of her house, we need not and do not consider the arguments of fraud, undue influence, and constructive trust which Farnum has advanced.

Farnum is entitled to rescission of the conveyance. Silvano shall deliver a deed to the real estate in question to Farnum's guardian in his capacity as such, in return for the consideration paid by Silvano. The

1. The judge's finding of a fair market value of $115,000 was based on an appraisal of the real estate received in evidence. Under the purchase and sale agreement, Silvano was to receive the furniture and furnishings as well for his purchase price.

object of rescission is to arrive so far as possible at full restoration of the status quo before the transaction which is being cancelled. In achieving rescission, it is appropriate to give account to the value of possessing or the rental value of the real estate from July 14, 1986, to the date a revised judgment is entered. Consideration must be given to accounting for benefits which the claimant for rescission (i.e., Farnum) may have received, e.g., taxes paid on the real estate. Generally, consideration ought not to be given to any improvements in the property which Silvano may have made, because they were not requested by the plaintiff, or to Silvano's mortgage payments. But compare *Thibbitts v. Crowley*, 405 Mass. 222, 230 (1989), which authorizes making allowance for improvements when the equities of a particular case so indicate. When a defendant-buyer wrongly acquires real estate and rescission is ordered, it does not appear, on a review of the cases, that interest is generally required to be paid on the returned purchase price, although we do not hold that so to order would go beyond the discretion of a trial judge who is framing an order designed to effect a fair restoration of the status quo. The judgment is vacated, and the case is remanded to the Probate Court for the entry of a judgment of rescission consistent with this opinion.

NOTES AND QUESTIONS

1. ***What happened?*** Who sued whom for what? Procedurally, how did the case get before this court? Factually, what happened between the parties? What arguments did the plaintiff and defendant make? What rule or rules did the court apply? How did the court analyze the dispute between the parties? How did the court decide the case?

2. ***Was this case correctly decided?*** Do you agree with the result reached in this case? Why or why not? Do you agree with the court's reasoning? Why or why not? How, if at all, would you have written the opinion differently?

3. ***Lucid interval?*** Recall that the probate court judge ruled against Viola Farnum because he found that she "enjoyed a lucid interval when she conveyed her house to Joseph Silvano, III, for approximately half its market value." Although the court of appeals rejected this line of reasoning, the basic legal doctrine espoused by the probate judge is good law: If an otherwise incompetent party makes a contract during a lucid interval, that contract is not voidable. But this, of course, begs the following question: How can courts determine whether a particular promisor had a "lucid interval" when making its contract? Is this the sort of fact finding courts are equipped to deal with? Or, to ask a slightly different question, is this the sort of question that our judicial system can answer while keeping the administrative costs manageable?

C. MISTAKE

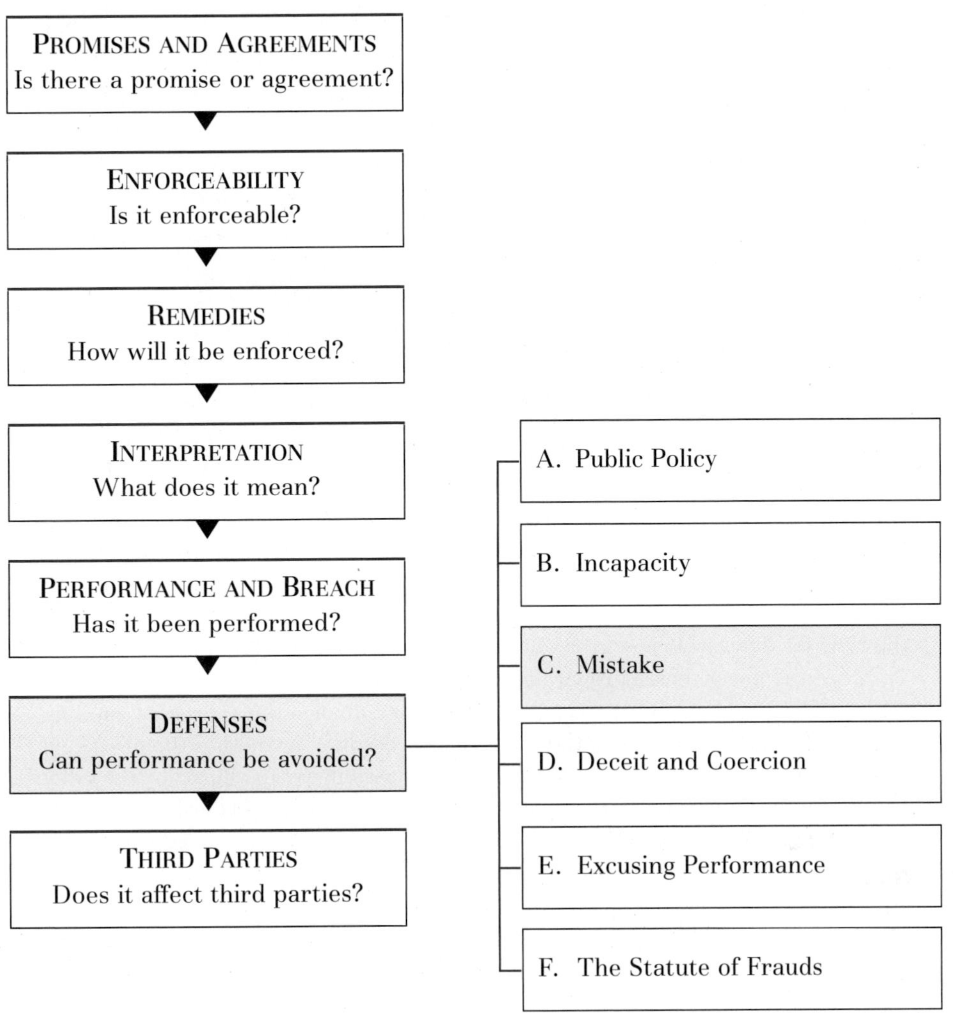

Having now examined the defenses of infancy and incompetence, which concern a party's inability to manifest their assent due to lack of legal capacity, the defenses in this section are concerned with instances in which the parties possess the legal capacity to manifest their assent but in doing so one or both parties make certain assumptions about presently existing facts that subsequently turn out to be erroneous. Such an erroneous assumption is called a "mistake," and in our coverage of this doctrine, we will learn about mutual mistake, unilateral mistake, and the duty to disclose. As we shall see, the failure to disclose information where there is a duty to do so constitutes a form of misrepresentation, and dovetails nicely with Section D on "Deceit and Coercion," which immediately follows these materials.

DOCTRINAL OVERVIEW: MISTAKE AS A DEFENSE TO ENFORCEMENT*

The word *mistake* is generally used in the law of contracts to refer to an erroneous perception—what the *Restatement Second* calls "a belief that is not in accord with the facts."[1] To avoid confusion, it should not be used, as it sometimes is in common speech, to refer to an improvident act, such as the making of a contract, which results from such a perception. Nor should it be used, as it sometimes is by courts and writers, to refer to what is more properly called a misunderstanding, a situation in which two parties attach different meanings to their language. . . .

An erroneous perception is not a mistake unless it relates to the facts as they exist at the time the contract is made. A misprediction—a poor prediction of events that are expected to occur or circumstances that are expected to exist after the contract is made—is not a mistake. The law of mistake deals only with the risk of error relating to the factual basis of agreement—the state of affairs at the time of agreement. It does not deal with the risk of error as to future matters. Such mispredictions are dealt with by the doctrines of impracticability and frustration, which are thought to be more suited to adjusting the relationship between the parties under their agreement. Thus an erroneous perception as to the existence of specific goods that are the subject of a contract for sale is plainly a mistake as to an existing fact; an erroneous belief that the goods will remain in existence until the time for delivery is just as plainly a misprediction as to the future. . . .

Once the party seeking relief has convinced the court that a mistake and not a misprediction is involved, the party must also convince the court that the mistake justifies relief. As to this, the law differs according to whether the mistake is "mutual" or "unilateral." If one party's mistaken assumption is shared by the other party, the mistake is mutual. If one party's mistaken assumption is not shared by the other party, the mistake is unilateral. Within these two broad categories, however, are situations of almost infinite variety. Because the law of mistake was shaped largely in equity, courts have considerable discretion in applying it to these situations, as we shall see. . . .

MISTAKE, DISCLOSURE, INFORMATION, AND THE LAW OF CONTRACTS†

Every contractual agreement is predicated upon a number of factual assumptions about the world. Some of these assumptions are shared by the parties to the contract and some are not. It is always possible that a particular factual assumption is mistaken. From an economic point of view, the risk of such a mistake (whether it be the mistake of only one party or both) represents a cost. It is a cost to the

---

* Excerpted from E. ALLAN FARNSWORTH, CONTRACTS § 9.2 (4th ed. 2004).

1. *Restatement Second* § 151.

† Excerpted from Anthony T. Kronman, *Mistake, Disclosure, Information, and the Law of Contracts*, 7 J. LEGAL STUDIES 1, 2-3, 4-5 (1978).

contracting parties themselves and to society as a whole since the actual occurrence of a mistake always (potentially) increases the resources which must be devoted to the process of allocating goods to their highest-valuing users. . . .

Information is the antidote to mistake. Although information is costly to produce, one individual may be able to obtain relevant information more cheaply than another. If the parties to a contract are acting rationally, they will minimize the joint costs of a potential mistake by assigning the risk of its occurrence to the party who is the better (cheaper) information-gatherer. Where the parties have actually assigned the risk—whether explicitly, or implicitly through their adherence to trade custom and past patterns of dealing—their own allocation must be respected. Where they have not—and there is a resulting gap in the contract—a court concerned with economic efficiency should impose the risk on the better information-gatherer. This is so for familiar reasons: by allocating the risk in this way, an efficiency-minded court reduces the transaction costs of the contracting process itself.

The most important doctrinal distinction in the law of mistake is the one drawn between "mutual" and "unilateral" mistakes. Traditionally, courts have been more reluctant to excuse a mistaken promisor where he alone is mistaken than where the other party is mistaken as to the same fact. Although relief for unilateral mistake has been liberalized during the last half-century (to the point where some commentators have questioned the utility of the distinction between unilateral and mutual mistake and a few have even urged its abolition), it is still "black-letter" law that a promisor whose mistake is not shared by the other party is less likely to be relieved of his duty to perform than a promisor whose mistake happens to be mutual.[12]

Viewed broadly, the distinction between mutual and unilateral mistake makes sense from an economic point of view. Where both parties to a contract are mistaken about the same fact or state of affairs, deciding which of them would have been better able to prevent the mistake may well require a detailed inquiry regarding the nature of the mistake and the (economic) role or position of each of the parties involved. But where only one party is mistaken, it is reasonable to assume that he is in a better position than the other party to prevent his own error. As we shall see, this is not true in every case, but it provides a useful beginning point for analysis and helps to explain the generic difference between mutual and unilateral mistakes.

1. Mutual Mistake

These cases in this subsection concern assumptions made by both parties about facts in existence at the time of entering into the contract which subsequently turn out to be erroneous. Later in this chapter* we will consider some defenses that may excuse a party's performance where unanticipated circumstances materialize in the future that neither party took into account when they entered into their contract.

12. Although it liberalizes relief for unilateral mistake, the *Second Restatement of Contracts* preserves the basic doctrinal distinction between unilateral and mutual mistake, and makes relief less freely available in the former case than in the latter.

* See "Excusing Performance," beginning on p. 1073, *infra*.

DOCTRINAL OVERVIEW: MUTUAL MISTAKE AS A DEFENSE TO ENFORCEMENT*

A mutual mistake occurs when both parties are under substantially the same erroneous perception as to the facts. (If both parties are mistaken, but their mistakes are materially different, the case is one of unilateral mistake.) The cases in which an adversely affected party has been allowed to avoid the contract on this ground are not marked by their consistency in either reasoning or result. . . .

Because courts have had great difficulty in formulating rules for mutual mistake cases, it will be helpful to look at the three requirements established by the *Restatement Second* for avoidance on this ground. The party adversely affected must show that: (1) the mistake goes to a basic assumption on which the contract was made; (2) the mistake has a material effect on the agreed exchange of performances; and (3) the mistake is not one of which that party bears the risk.[3]. . .

A landmark case on mutual mistake is *Sherwood v. Walker*, which arose out of a contract for the sale of a cow known as "Rose 2d of Aberlone." According to the seller, both he and the buyer believed that Rose could not breed and therefore the price was fixed at $80, about one-tenth of what the cow would otherwise have been worth. When the seller discovered that Rose was in fact with calf, he attempted to avoid the contract and refused to deliver the cow to the buyer. . . .

So, what did the court ultimately do? Keep reading to find out! As you do, try to apply the *Restatement (Second) of Contracts* § 152 to the facts to see how (if at all) the court's result (or reasoning) would have come out differently.

Sherwood v. Walker

Supreme Court of Michigan
33 N.W. 919 (1887)

MORSE, J. **Replevin** for a cow. Suit commenced in justice's court; judgment for plaintiff; appealed to circuit court of Wayne county, and verdict and judgment for plaintiff in that court. The defendants bring error, and set out 25 assignments of the same. . . .

> ***Replevin***
>
> "1. An action for the repossession of personal property wrongfully taken or detained by the defendant, whereby the plaintiff gives security for and holds the property until the court decides who owns it. . . . 2. A writ obtained from a court authorizing the retaking of personal property wrongfully taken or detained. Also termed (in sense 2) writ of replevin." BLACK'S LAW DICTIONARY (10th ed. 2014).

The Walkers [defendants] are importers and breeders of polled Angus cattle.

The plaintiff is a banker living at Plymouth, in Wayne county. He called upon the defendants at Walkerville for the purchase of some of their stock, but found none there that suited him. Meeting one of the defendants afterwards, he was informed that they had a few head upon their Greenfield farm. He

* Excerpted from E. ALLAN FARNSWORTH, CONTRACTS § 9.3 (4th ed. 2004).
3. *Restatement Second* § 152.

was asked to go out and look at them, with the statement at the time that they were probably barren, and would not breed. May 5, 1886, plaintiff went out to Greenfield, and saw the cattle. A few days thereafter, he called upon one of the defendants with the view of purchasing a cow, known as "Rose 2d of Aberlone." After considerable talk, it was agreed that defendants would telephone Sherwood at his home in Plymouth in reference to the price. The second morning after this talk he was called up by telephone, and the terms of the sale were finally agreed upon. He was to pay five and one-half cents per pound, live weight, fifty pounds shrinkage. . . . He requested defendants to confirm the sale in writing, which they did by sending him the following letter:

WALKERVILLE, May 15, 1886.

T.C. Sherwood, President, etc.

DEAR SIR:

We confirm sale to you of the cow Rose 2d of Aberlone, lot 56 of our catalogue, at five and half cents per pound, less fifty pounds shrink. We enclose herewith order on Mr. Graham for the cow. You might leave check with him, or mail to us here, as you prefer.

Yours, truly,

HIRAM WALKER & SONS.

The order upon Graham enclosed in the letter read as follows:

WALKERVILLE, May 15, 1886.

George Graham: You will please deliver at King's cattle-yard to Mr. T.C. Sherwood, Plymouth, the cow Rose 2d of Aberlone, lot 56 of our catalogue. Send halter with the cow, and have her weighed.

Yours truly,

HIRAM WALKER & SONS.

On the twenty-first of the same month the plaintiff went to defendants' farm at Greenfield, and presented the order and letter to Graham, who informed him that the defendants had instructed him not to deliver the cow. Soon after, the plaintiff tendered to Hiram Walker, one of the defendants, $80, and demanded the cow. Walker refused to take the money or deliver the cow. The plaintiff then instituted this suit [and] secured possession of the cow under the writ of replevin. . . .

The defendants . . . introduced evidence tending to show that at the time of the alleged sale it was believed by both the plaintiff and themselves that the cow was barren and would not breed; that she cost $850, and if not barren would be worth from $750 to $1,000. . . . The cow had a calf in the month of October following. . . .

It appears from the record that both parties supposed this cow was barren and would not breed, and she was sold by the pound for an insignificant sum as compared with her real value if a breeder. She was evidently sold and purchased on the relation of her value for beef, unless the plaintiff had learned of her true condition, and concealed such knowledge from the defendants. Before the plaintiff secured the possession of the animal, the defendants learned that she was with calf, and therefore of great value, and undertook to rescind the sale by refusing to deliver her. The question arises whether they had a right to do so.

The circuit judge ruled that this fact did not avoid the sale and it made no difference whether she was barren or not. I am of the opinion that the court erred in this holding. I know that this is a close question, and the dividing line between the adjudicated cases is not easily discerned. But it must be considered as well settled that a party who has given an apparent consent to a contract of sale may refuse to execute it, or he may avoid it after it has been completed, if the assent was founded, or the contract made, upon the mistake of a material fact,—such as the subject-matter of the sale, the price, or some collateral fact materially inducing the agreement; and this can be done when the mistake is mutual.

If there is a difference or misapprehension as to the substance of the thing bargained for; if the thing actually delivered or received is different in substance from the thing bargained for, and intended to be sold,—then there is no contract; but if it be only a difference in some quality or accident, even though the mistake may have been the actuating motive to the purchaser or seller, or both of them, yet the contract remains binding. . . .

It has been held, in accordance with the principles above stated, that where a horse is bought under the belief that he is sound, and both vendor and vendee honestly believe him to be sound, the purchaser must stand by his bargain, and pay the full price, unless there was a warranty.

It seems to me, however, in the case made by this record, that the mistake or misapprehension of the parties went to the whole substance of the agreement. If the cow was a breeder, she was worth at least $750; if barren, she was worth not over $80. The parties would not have made the contract of sale except upon the understanding and belief that she was incapable of breeding, and of no use as a cow. It is true she is now the identical animal that they thought her to be when the contract was made; there is no mistake as to the identity of the creature. Yet the mistake was not of the mere quality of the animal, but went to the very nature of the thing. A

Substance versus quality

Does this distinction make sense? In your own words, how would you draw the distinction between substance and quality, and what do you suppose the court is really trying to get at with this test? Do you think this is the best way (or, at least, a good way) of ascertaining whether the defense of mutual mistake should apply? How would such a case be resolved today? See "Relevant Provisions" following *Wood v. Boynton*, p. 971, *infra*.

Critical reading

Pay close and careful attention to this entire paragraph, as there are, on the surface at least, some seemingly strange things being said. For instance, on the one hand the court notes that "[i]t is true she is now the identical animal that they thought her to be when the contract was made," but on the other hand, it notes both that "[a] barren cow is substantially a different creature than a breeding one" and that "[t]he thing sold and bought had in fact no existence." What does the court mean? The court also notes that "the mistake was not of the mere quality of the animal, but went to the very nature of the thing." Again, what, exactly, does the court mean by this, and why do you suppose this is relevant?

barren cow is substantially a different creature than a breeding one. There is as much difference between them for all purposes of use as there is between an ox and a cow that is capable of breeding and giving milk. If the mutual mistake had simply related to the fact whether she was with calf or not for one season, then it might have been a good sale, but the mistake affected the character of the animal for all time, and for its present and ultimate use. She was not in fact the animal, or the kind of animal, the defendants intended to sell or the plaintiff to buy. She was not a barren cow, and, if this fact had been known, there would have been no contract. The mistake affected the substance of the whole consideration, and it must be considered that there was no contract to sell or sale of the cow as she actually was. The thing sold and bought had in fact no existence. She was sold as a beef creature would be sold; she is in fact a breeding cow, and a valuable one.

The court should have instructed the jury that if they found that the cow was sold, or contracted to be sold, upon the understanding of both parties that she was barren, and useless for the purpose of breeding, and that in fact she was not barren, but capable of breeding, then the defendants had a right to rescind, and to refuse to deliver, and the verdict should be in their favor.

The judgment of the court below must be reversed, and a new trial granted, with costs of this court to defendants.

SHERWOOD, J., **(dissenting).** I do not concur in the opinion given by my brethren in this case. . . . [I agree that] the plaintiff was entitled to a delivery of the property to him when the suit was brought, unless there was a mistake made which would invalidate the contract, [but] I can find no such mistake. . . .

In the spring of 1886 the plaintiff, learning that the defendants had some "polled Angus cattle" for sale, was desirous of purchasing some of that breed, and meeting the defendants, or some of them, at Walkerville, inquired about them, and was informed that they had none at Walkerville, "but had a few head left on their farm in Greenfield, and asked the plaintiff to go and see them, stating that in all probability they were sterile and would not breed." In accordance with said request, the plaintiff, on the fifth day of May, went out and looked at the defendants' cattle at Greenfield, and found one called "Rose, Second," which he wished to purchase, and the terms were finally agreed upon at five and a half cents per pound, live weight, 50 pounds to be deducted for shrinkage. The sale was in writing, and the defendants gave an order to the plaintiff directing the man in charge of the Greenfield farm to deliver the cow to plaintiff. This was done on the fifteenth of May. On the twenty-first of May plaintiff went to get his cow, and the defendants refused to let him have her; claiming at the time that the man in charge at the farm thought the cow was with calf, and, if such was the case, they would not sell her for the price agreed upon. The record further shows that the defendants, when they sold the cow, believed the cow was not with calf, and barren; that from what the plaintiff had been told by defendants (for it does not appear he had any other knowledge or facts from which he could form an opinion) he believed the cow was farrow, but still thought she could be made to breed. The foregoing shows the entire interview and treaty between the parties as to the sterility and qualities of the cow sold to the plaintiff. The cow had a calf in the month of October.

There is no question but that the defendants sold the cow representing her of the breed and quality they believed the cow to be, and that the purchaser so understood it. And the buyer purchased her believing her to be of the breed represented by the sellers, and possessing all the qualities stated, and even more. He believed she would breed. There is no pretense that the plaintiff bought the cow for beef, and there is nothing in the record indicating that he would have bought her at all only that he thought she might be made to breed. Under the foregoing facts,—and these are all that are contained in the record material to the contract,—it is held that because it turned out that the plaintiff was more correct in his judgment as to one quality of the cow than the defendants, and a quality, too, which could not by any possibility be positively known at the time by either party to exist, the contract may be annulled by the defendants at their pleasure. . . .

In this case neither party knew the actual quality and condition of this cow at the time of the sale. . . . [N]either knew she was with calf or whether she would breed. The defendants thought she would not, but the plaintiff says that he thought she could be made to breed, but believed she was not with calf. The defendants sold the cow for what they believed her to be, and the plaintiff bought her as he believed she was, after the statements made by the defendants. No conditions whatever were attached to the terms of sale by either party. It was in fact as absolute as it could well be made. . . .

It is not the duty of courts to destroy contracts when called upon to enforce them, after they have been legally made. There was no mistake of any material fact by either of the parties in the case as would license the vendors to rescind. There was no difference between the parties, nor misapprehension, as to the substance of the thing bargained for, which was a cow supposed to be barren by one party, and believed not to be by the other. As to the quality of the animal, subsequently developed, both parties were equally ignorant, and as to this each party took his chances. If this were not the law, there would be no safety in purchasing this kind of stock.

I entirely agree with my brethren that the right to rescind occurs whenever "the thing actually delivered or received is different in substance from the thing bargained for, and intended to be sold; but if it be only a difference in some quality or accident, even though the misapprehension may have been the actuating motive" of the parties in making the contract, yet it will remain binding. In this case the cow sold was the one delivered. What might or might not happen to her after the sale formed no element in the contract. . . .

According to this record, whatever the mistake was, if any, in this case, it was upon the part of the defendants, and while acting upon their own judgment.

It is, however, elementary law, and very elementary, too, "that the mistaken party, without any common understanding with the other party in the premises as to the quality of an animal, is remediless if he is injured through his own mistake." *Leake*, Cont. 338. . . .

The case of *Huthmacher v. Harris*, 38 Pa.St. 491, is this: A party purchased at an administrator's sale a drill-machine, which had hidden away in it by the deceased a quantity of notes, to the amount of $3,000, money to the amount of over $500, and two silver watches and a pocket compass of the value of $60.25. In an action of **trover** for the goods, it was held that nothing but the machine was sold or passed to the purchasers, neither party knowing that the machine contained any such articles. . . .

> ***Trover***
>
> "A common-law action for the recovery of damages for the conversion of personal property, the damages generally being measured by the property's value." BLACK'S LAW DICTIONARY (10th ed. 2014).

I fail to discover any similarity between [this case] and the present case; and . . . I have found no adjudicated case going to the extent, either in law or equity, that has been held in this case. In this case, if either party had superior knowledge as to the qualities of this animal to the other, certainly the defendants had such advantage.

I understand the law to be well settled that "there is no breach of any implied confidence that one party will not profit by his superior knowledge as to facts and circumstances" actually within the knowledge of both, because neither party reposes in any such confidence unless it be specially tendered or required, and that a general sale does not imply warranty of any quality, or the absence of any; and if the seller represents to the purchaser what he himself believes as to the qualities of an animal, and the purchaser buys relying upon his own judgment as to such qualities, there is no warranty in the case, and neither has a cause of action against the other if he finds himself to have been mistaken in judgment.

The only pretense for avoiding this contract by the defendants is that they erred in judgment as to the qualities and value of the animal. . . .

The judgment should be affirmed.

RELEVANT PROVISIONS

For the *Restatement (Second) of Contracts*, consult §§ 151-152, 154-158. For the *Restatement (Third) Restitution and Unjust Enrichment*, consult § 34. For the UNIDROIT Principles, consult Articles 3.2.1 and 3.2.2.

NOTES AND QUESTIONS

1. ***What happened?*** Who sued whom for what? Procedurally, how did the case get before this court? Factually, what happened between the parties?

What arguments did the plaintiff and defendant make? What rule or rules did the court apply? How did the court analyze the dispute between the parties? How did the court decide the case?

2. *Was this case correctly decided?* Do you agree with the result reached in this case? Why or why not? Do you agree with the court's reasoning? Why or why not? How, if at all, would you have written the opinion differently? Would the result have changed if the plaintiff, despite learning that the cow was pregnant, nevertheless still intended to slaughter it for meat?

3. *What was the holding?* Read the end of the decision carefully. What, exactly, did the court hold? Do you agree? Why or why not?

4. *Distinguishing precedent.* To what extent do you think the facts in *Huthmacher* ought to have been relevant in resolving the dispute between Sherwood and Walker?

5. *Majority versus dissent?* Who has the better argument here? Why? Read both opinions closely. What, exactly, are the two judges arguing about? Or, to ask a leading question, are they really arguing about anything at all? And why is the dissenting judge's last name Sherwood?

6. *An interesting aside.* Speaking of Judge Sherwood, in a dispute that came up before the same court just one year later, a party relied on *Sherwood v. Walker* in support of its position and Judge Sherwood, now writing for the majority, had this to say:

> We know of no case which will sustain the complainant's case upon the facts before us. That of *Sherwood v. Walker*, 33 N.W. Rep. 919, (in this court,) will come the nearest to it of any referred to. That is, however, somewhat different upon its facts, and the rule applied in that case can never be resorted to except in a case where all the facts and circumstances are precisely the same as in that.*

7. *Risk analysis.* Had the parties foreseen the possibility of the cow being pregnant when they entered into their contract, the seller would have probably asked for a risk premium, or a bit more money to compensate him for the possibility of the pregnancy. Where the parties fail to consider and allocate such risks between them, should the courts step in and do it for them? Professor Posner, in the short excerpt below, believes that they should, with the result being that the risk should fall on the seller. Do you agree?

> This approach decomposes the contract into two distinct agreements: an agreement respecting the basic performance (the transfer of the cow) and an agreement respecting a risk associated with the transfer (that the cow will turn out to be different from what the parties believed). In fact there was some evidence

* *Nester v. Michigan Land & Iron Co.*, 37 N.W. 278, 280 (1888).

that Rose's sale price included her value if pregnant, discounted (very drastically of course) by the probability of that happy eventuality. This evidence, if believed, would have justified the court in concluding that the parties had intended to transfer the risk of the cow's turning out to be pregnant to the buyer, in which event delivery should have been enforced. Even in the absence of any such evidence, there would be an argument for placing on the seller the risk that the cow is not what it seems. In general, if not in every particular case, the owner will have superior access to information concerning the actual or probable characteristics of his property. This is the theory on which the seller of a house is liable to the buyer for any latent (as distinct from obvious) defects; a similar principle could be used to decide cases of mutual mistake.*

Wood v. Boynton

Supreme Court of Wisconsin
25 N.W. 42 (1885)

TAYLOR, J. This action was brought in the circuit court for Milwaukee county to recover the possession of an uncut diamond of the alleged value of $1,000. The case was tried in the circuit court, and after hearing all the evidence in the case, the learned circuit judge directed the jury to find a verdict for the defendants. The plaintiff excepted to such instruction, and, after a verdict was rendered for the defendants, moved for a new trial upon the minutes of the judge. The motion was denied, and the plaintiff duly excepted, and after judgment was entered in favor of the defendants, appealed to this court. The defendants are partners in the jewelry business. On the trial it appeared that on and before the twenty-eighth of December, 1883, the plaintiff was the owner of and in the possession of a small stone of the nature and value of which she was ignorant; that on that day she sold it to one of the defendants for the sum of one dollar. Afterwards it was ascertained that the stone was a rough diamond, and of the value of about $700. After hearing this fact the plaintiff tendered the defendants the one dollar, and ten cents as interest, and demanded a return of the stone to her. The defendants refused to deliver it, and therefore she commenced this action.

The plaintiff testified to the circumstances attending the sale of the stone to Mr. Samuel B. Boynton, as follows:

> The first time Boynton saw that stone he was talking about buying the topaz, or whatever it is, in September or October. I went into the store to get a little pin mended, and I had it in a small box,—the pin,—a small ear-ring; . . . this stone, and a broken sleeve-button were in the box. Mr. Boynton turned to give me a check for my pin. I thought I would ask him what the stone was, and I took it out of the box and asked him to please tell me what that was. He took it in his hand and seemed some time looking at it. I told him I had been told it was a

* RICHARD POSNER, ECONOMIC ANALYSIS OF LAW 73 (2d ed. 1977).

> topaz, and he said it might be. He says, "I would buy this; would you sell it?" I told him I did not know but what I would. What would it be worth? And he said he did not know; he would give me a dollar and keep it as a specimen, and I told him I would not sell it; and it was certainly pretty to look at. He asked me where I found it, and I told him in Eagle. He asked about how far out, and I said right in the village, and I went out. Afterwards, and about the twenty-eighth of December, I needed money pretty badly, and thought every dollar would help, and I took it back to Mr. Boynton and told him I had brought back the topaz, and he says, "Well, yes; what did I offer you for it?" and I says, "One dollar;" and he stepped to the change drawer and gave me the dollar, and I went out.

In another part of her testimony she says:

> Before I sold the stone I had no knowledge whatever that it was a diamond. I told him that I had been advised that it was probably a topaz, and he said probably it was. The stone was about the size of a canary bird's egg, nearly the shape of an egg,—worn pointed at one end; it was nearly straw color,—a little darker.

She also testified that before this action was commenced she tendered the defendants $1.10, and demanded the return of the stone, which they refused. This is substantially all the evidence of what took place at and before the sale to the defendants, as testified to by the plaintiff herself. She produced no other witness on that point.

The evidence on the part of the defendant is not very different from the version given by the plaintiff, and certainly is not more favorable to the plaintiff. Mr. Samuel B. Boynton, the defendant to whom the stone was sold, testified that at the time he bought this stone, he had never seen an uncut diamond; had seen cut diamonds, but they are quite different from the uncut ones; "he had no idea this was a diamond, and it never entered his brain at the time." Considerable evidence was given as to what took place after the sale and purchase, but that evidence has very little if any bearing, upon the main point in the case.

This evidence clearly shows that the plaintiff sold the stone in question to the defendants, and delivered it to them in December, 1883, for a consideration of one dollar. By such sale the title to the stone passed by the sale and delivery to the defendants. How has that title been divested and again vested in the plaintiff? The contention of the learned counsel for the appellant is that the title became vested in the plaintiff by the tender to the Boyntons of the purchase money with interest, and a demand of a return of the stone to her. Unless such tender and demand revested the title in the appellant, she cannot maintain her action. The only question in the case is whether there was anything in the sale which entitled the vendor (the appellant) to rescind the sale and so revest the title in her. The only reasons we know of for rescinding a sale and revesting the title in the vendor so that he may maintain an action at law for the recovery of the possession against his vendee are (1) that the vendee was guilty of some fraud in procuring a sale to be made to him; (2) that there was a mistake made by the vendor in delivering an article which was not the article sold,—a mistake in fact as to the identity of the thing sold with the thing delivered upon the sale. This last is not in reality a rescission of the sale made, as the thing delivered was not the thing sold, and no title ever passed to the vendee by such delivery.

In this case, upon the plaintiff's own evidence, there can be no just ground for alleging that she was induced to make the sale she did by any fraud or unfair dealings on the part of Mr. Boynton. Both were entirely ignorant at the time of the character of the stone and of its intrinsic value. Mr. Boynton was not an expert in uncut diamonds, and had made no examination of the stone, except to take it in his hand and look at it before he made the offer of one dollar, which was refused at the time, and afterwards accepted without any comment or further examination made by Mr. Boynton. The appellant had the stone in her possession for a long time, and it appears from her own statement that she had made some inquiry as to its nature and qualities. If she chose to sell it without further investigation as to its intrinsic value to a person who was guilty of no fraud or unfairness which induced her to sell it for a small sum, she cannot repudiate the sale because it is afterwards ascertained that she made a bad bargain. There is no pretense of any mistake as to the identity of the thing sold. It was produced by the plaintiff and exhibited to the vendee before the sale was made, and the thing sold was delivered to the vendee when the purchase price was paid. Suppose the appellant had produced the stone, and said she had been told it was a diamond, and she believed it was, but had no knowledge herself as to its character or value, and Mr. Boynton had given her $500 for it, could he have rescinded the sale if it had turned out to be a topaz or any other stone of very small value? Could Mr. Boynton have rescinded the sale on the ground of mistake? Clearly not, nor could he rescind it on the ground that there had been a breach of warranty, because there was no warranty, nor could he rescind it on the ground of fraud, unless he could show that she falsely declared that she had been told it was a diamond, or, if she had been so told, still she knew it was not a diamond.

It is urged, with a good deal of earnestness, on the part of the counsel for the appellant that, because it has turned out that the stone was immensely more valuable than the parties at the time of the sale supposed it was, such fact alone is a ground for the rescission of the sale, and that fact was evidence of fraud on the part of the vendee. Whether inadequacy of price is to be received as evidence of fraud, even in a suit in equity to avoid a sale, depends upon the facts known to the parties at the time the sale is made. When this sale was made the value of the thing sold was open to the investigation of both parties, neither knowing its intrinsic value, and, so far as the evidence in this case shows, both supposed that the price paid was adequate. How can fraud be predicated upon such a sale, even though after investigation showed that the intrinsic value of the thing sold was hundreds of times greater than the price paid? It certainly shows no such fraud as would authorize the vendor to rescind the contract and bring an action at law to recover the possession of the thing sold. Whether that fact would have any influence in an action in equity to avoid the sale we need not consider.

We can find nothing in the evidence from which it could be justly inferred that Mr. Boynton, at the time he offered the plaintiff one dollar for the stone, had any knowledge of the real value of the stone, or that he entertained even a belief that the stone was a diamond. It cannot, therefore, be said that there was a suppression of knowledge on the part of the defendant as to the value of the stone which a court of equity might seize upon to avoid the sale. The following cases show that, in the absence of fraud or warranty, the value of the property sold, as compared with the price paid, is no ground for a rescission of a sale. However unfortunate the plaintiff may have been in selling this valuable stone for a mere nominal sum, she has failed entirely to make out a case either of fraud or mistake in the sale such as will entitle her to a rescission of such sale so as to recover the property sold in an action at law.

The judgment of the circuit court is affirmed.

NOTES AND QUESTIONS

1. *What happened?* Who sued whom for what? Procedurally, how did the case get before this court? Factually, what happened between the parties? What arguments did the plaintiff and defendant make? What rule or rules did the court apply? How did the court analyze the dispute between the parties? How did the court decide the case?

2. *Was this case correctly decided?* Do you agree with the result reached in this case? Why or why not? Do you agree with the court's reasoning? Why or why not? How, if at all, would you have written the opinion differently?

3. *Risk analysis.* Do you think the risk of mistake was placed on the correct party? Why or why not? According to Professor Posner (see Note 7 following *Sherwood*), on which party should the risk of mistake have fallen? According to the *Restatement (Second) of Contracts*, on which party should the risk of mistake have been placed?

4. *Illustrations.* *Sherwood v. Walker* now appears as Illustration 1 to *Restatement (Third) of Restitution and Unjust Enrichment* § 20, whereas Illustration 2 comes from the holding of *Wood v. Boynton*:

> 1. Rose 2d of Aberlone, a purebred cow belonging to Farmer, fails to breed in season; on examination by a veterinarian she is determined to be barren. Farmer sells Rose to Breeder for $300, a price based on her value as beef. Before the day fixed for delivery and payment, Rose is discovered to be with calf; her value as a breeding animal is not less than $3000. Farmer repudiates the sale, and Breeder sues for specific performance or damages. Breeder's claim is in contract, not restitution; Farmer's defense asserts a theory of mistake as the ground for avoidance. Breeder's claim will predictably be denied.
>
> 2. Same facts as Illustration 1, except that Rose's fertility is discovered after Rose has been delivered and paid for. Farmer brings suit to rescind the

completed exchange. The plaintiff's claim is now in restitution, not contract, though it alleges the identical mistake as the ground for avoidance. Farmer's claim will predictably be denied.

5. ***Reconciling the cases.*** Can *Sherwood* and *Wood* be reconciled? In the excerpt below, Professor Kull thinks they can, but on non-legalistic grounds. Do you agree? It should be pointed out that Professor Kull thinks the same analysis can also be applied to the defenses excusing performance: impossibility, impracticability, and frustration of purpose.

MISTAKE, FRUSTRATION, AND THE WINDFALL PRINCIPLE OF CONTRACT REMEDIES*

[T]he characteristic and traditional response of our legal system to cases of mistaken . . . contracts is neither to relieve the disadvantaged party nor to assign the loss to the superior risk bearer, but to leave things alone. The party who has balked at performing will not be forced to proceed, but the completed exchange will not be recalled. Walker will not be forced to deliver to Sherwood a breeding cow sold for the price of beef; but neither will Wood be allowed to recover the yellow diamond, already delivered, unwittingly sold to Boynton for the price of a topaz. . . .

The principle of inertia that frequently seems to guide the remedies for mutual mistake . . . may seem harsh in some particular applications, but it is neither arbitrary nor illogical. Disparities between anticipation and realization in contractual exchange, the risk of which has not been allocated by the parties, are in the nature of "windfalls" (including those, carrying adverse consequences, that might more properly be described as "casualties"). The law will not act to enforce such windfalls—to compel an exchange on terms that were not bargained for—because its objective is limited to giving effect to the parties' agreement. But if the parties have not allocated the risk of a particular windfall or casualty to one of them, neither have they allocated it to the other. There is thus no basis in their bargain on which to justify a court's intervention to shift windfall benefits and burdens in either direction. As a matter of social utility, excluding for the moment considerations of fairness, it will ordinarily be a matter of indifference whether the windfall cost or benefit, once realized, falls to A or to B. Reallocation after the event thus involves significant administrative costs while achieving no compelling social advantage. The judicial disposition to let windfalls lie—to answer the claim of mistake or frustration by confirming the status quo—is here referred to as the "windfall principle."

The more things change, the more they stay the same. The following excerpt discusses the defense of mistake as it existed in ancient Roman law. If the laws used by the Romans to resolve their legal disputes appear to be strikingly modern, it is because our law still indebted to Rome, as many of their rules and legal

* Excerpted from Andrew Kull, *Mistake, Frustration, and the Windfall Principle of Contract Remedies*, 43 HASTINGS L.J. 1, 5-6 (1991).

principles were imported wholesale during the Victorian era by common-law judges familiar with Roman law. [*] *It is only when we come to the subject matter of some of their contracts (i.e., the purchase of virgins and slaves) that we realize we are dealing with a completely foreign legal system.*

HISTORICAL PERSPECTIVE: MISTAKE IN ANCIENT ROMAN LAW[†]

Digest, Book 18, 1, 9-14

9. ULPIAN, *Sabinus, book 28*: It is obvious that agreement is of the essence in sale and purchase; the purchase is not valid if there be disagreement over the contract itself, the price, or any other element of the sale. Hence, if I thought that I was buying the Cornelian farm and you that you were selling the Sempronian, the sale is void because we were not agreed upon the thing sold. The same is true if I intended to sell Stichus and you thought I was selling you Pamphilus, the slave himself not being there: Because there is no agreement on the object of sale, there is manifestly no sale. 1. Of course, if we are merely in disagreement over the name but at one on the actual thing, there is no doubt that the sale is good; for if the thing be identified, a mistake over its name is irrelevant. 2. The next question is whether there is a good sale when there is no mistake over the identity of the thing but there is over its substance: Suppose that vinegar is sold as wine, copper as gold or lead, or something else similar to silver as silver. Marcellus, in the sixth book of his *Digest*, writes that there is a sale because there is agreement on the thing despite the mistake over its substance. I would agree in the case of the wine, because the essence is much the same, that is, if the wine has gone sour; if it be not sour wine, however, but was vinegar from the beginning such as brewed vinegar; then it emerges that one thing has been sold as another. But in the other cases, I think that there is no sale by reason of the error over the material.

10. PAUL, *Sabinus, book 5*: It would be different if the thing was gold, although of a quality inferior to that supposed by the purchaser. In such a case, the sale is good.

11. ULPIAN, *Sabinus, book 28*: Now what if the purchaser were blind or a mistake over the material were made by a purchaser unskilled in distinguishing materials? Do we say that the parties are agreed on the thing? How can a man agree who cannot see it? 1. If, however, I think that I am buying a virgin when she is, in fact, a woman, the sale is valid, there being no mistake over her sex. But if I sell you a woman and you think that you are buying a male slave, the error over sex makes the sale void.

12. POMPONIUS, *Quintus Mucius, book 31*: In questions of this kind, we must look to the persons of the actual contracting parties, not to those to whom an action will accrue from the contract; if, say, my slave or son-in-power buy

* *See, e.g.*, CATHARINE MACMILLAN, MISTAKES IN CONTRACT LAW 1-26 (2010).

† Excerpted from THE INSTITUTES OF JUSTINIAN (533 A.D.), translated by T.C. Sandars (7th ed. 1883).

something in my presence but in his own name, it is his intention not mine which must be investigated.

13. POMPONIUS, *Sabinus, book 9*: However, it is true that if you knowingly sell a fugitive to my slave or mandatory who is ignorant of the fact but I do know, you will not be liable to the action on purchase.

14. ULPIAN, *Sabinus, book 28*: Now what are we to say when both parties are in error over both the material and its quality? Suppose that I think that I am selling and you that you are buying gold, when it is, in fact, copper, or, again, that co-heirs sell to one of their number, for a substantial price, a bracelet said to be gold which proves to be largely copper? It is settled law that the sale holds good because there is some gold in it. Even if a thing be of gold alloy, though I think it solid gold, the sale is good. But if copper be sold as gold, there is no contract.

Lenawee County Board of Health v. Messerly

Supreme Court of Michigan
331 N.W.2d 203 (1982)

RYAN, JUSTICE. In March of 1977, Carl and Nancy Pickles, appellees, purchased from appellants, William and Martha Messerly, a 600-square-foot tract of land upon which is located a three-unit apartment building. Shortly after the transaction was closed, the Lenawee County Board of Health condemned the property and obtained a permanent injunction which prohibits human habitation on the premises until the defective sewage system is brought into conformance with the Lenawee County sanitation code.

We are required to determine whether appellees should prevail in their attempt to avoid this land contract on the basis of mutual mistake and failure of consideration. We conclude that the parties did entertain a mutual misapprehension of fact, but that the circumstances of this case do not warrant rescission.

The facts of the case are not seriously in dispute. In 1971, the Messerlys acquired approximately one acre plus 600 square feet of land. A three-unit apartment building was situated upon the 600-square-foot portion. The trial court found that, prior to this transfer, the Messerlys' predecessor in title, Mr. Bloom, had installed a septic tank on the property without a permit and in violation of the applicable health code. The Messerlys used the building as an income investment property until 1973 when they sold it, upon land contract, to James Barnes who likewise used it primarily as an income-producing investment.

Mr. and Mrs. Barnes, with the permission of the Messerlys, sold approximately one acre of the property in 1976, and the remaining 600 square feet and building were offered for sale soon thereafter when Mr. and Mrs. Barnes defaulted on their land contract. Mr. and Mrs. Pickles evidenced an interest in the property, but were dissatisfied with the terms of the Barnes-Messerly land contract. Consequently, to accommodate the Pickleses' preference to enter into a land contract directly with the Messerlys, Mr. and Mrs. Barnes executed a quit-claim deed which conveyed their interest in the property back to the Messerlys. After inspecting the property, Mr. and Mrs. Pickles executed a new land contract with the Messerlys on March 21, 1977. It provided for a purchase price of $25,500. A clause was added to the end of the land contract form which provides:

> 17. Purchaser has examined this property and agrees to accept same in its present condition. There are no other or additional written or oral understandings.

Five or six days later, when the Pickleses went to introduce themselves to the tenants, they discovered raw sewage seeping out of the ground. Tests conducted by a sanitation expert indicated the inadequacy of the sewage system. The Lenawee County Board of Health subsequently condemned the property and initiated this lawsuit in the Lenawee Circuit Court against the Messerlys as land contract vendors, and the Pickleses, as vendees, to obtain a permanent injunction proscribing human habitation of the premises until the property was brought into conformance with the Lenawee County sanitation code. The injunction was granted, and the Lenawee County Board of Health was permitted to withdraw from the lawsuit by stipulation of the parties.

When no payments were made on the land contract, the Messerlys filed a cross-complaint against the Pickleses seeking foreclosure, sale of the property, and a deficiency judgment. Mr. and Mrs. Pickles then counterclaimed for rescission against the Messerlys, and filed a third-party complaint against the Barneses, which incorporated, by reference, the allegations of the counterclaim against the Messerlys. In count one, Mr. and Mrs. Pickles alleged failure of consideration. Count two charged Mr. and Mrs. Barnes with willful concealment and misrepresentation as a result of their failure to disclose the condition of the sanitation system. Additionally, Mr. and Mrs. Pickles sought to hold the Messerlys liable in equity for the Barneses' alleged misrepresentation. The Pickleses prayed that the land contract be rescinded.

After a bench trial, the court concluded that the Pickleses had no cause of action against either the Messerlys or the Barneses as there was no fraud or misrepresentation. This ruling was predicated on the trial judge's conclusion that none of the parties knew of Mr. Bloom's earlier transgression or of the resultant problem with the septic system until it was discovered by the Pickleses, and that the sanitation problem was not caused by any of the parties. The trial court held that the property was purchased "as is," after inspection and, accordingly, its "negative . . . value cannot be blamed upon an innocent seller." Foreclosure was ordered against the Pickleses, together with a judgment against them in the amount of $25,943.09.

Mr. and Mrs. Pickles appealed from the adverse judgment. The Court of Appeals unanimously affirmed the trial court's ruling with respect to Mr. and Mrs. Barnes but, in a two-to-one decision, reversed the finding of no cause of action on the Pickleses' claims against the Messerlys. It concluded that the mutual mistake between the Messerlys and the Pickleses went to a basic, as opposed to a collateral, element of the contract, and that the parties intended to transfer income-producing rental property but, in actuality, the vendees paid $25,500 for an asset without value.

We granted the Messerlys' application for leave to appeal.

We must decide initially whether there was a mistaken belief entertained by one or both parties to the contract in dispute and, if so, the resultant legal significance.

A contractual mistake "is a belief that is not in accord with the facts." 1 *Restatement Contracts 2d* § 151. The erroneous belief of one or both of the parties must relate to a fact in existence at the time the contract is executed. *Sherwood v. Walker,* 66 Mich. 568, 580 (1887) (Sherwood, J., dissenting). That is to say, the belief which is found to be in error may not be, in substance, a prediction as to a future occurrence or non-occurrence.

The Court of Appeals concluded, after a *de novo* review of the record, that the parties were mistaken as to the income-producing capacity of the property in question. We agree. The vendors and the vendees each believed that the property transferred could be utilized as income-generating rental property. All of the parties subsequently learned that, in fact, the property was unsuitable for any residential use. . . .

Having determined that when these parties entered into the land contract they were laboring under a mutual mistake of fact, we now direct our attention to a determination of the legal significance of that finding.

A contract may be rescinded because of a mutual misapprehension of the parties, but this remedy is granted only in the sound discretion of the court. Appellants argue that the parties' mistake relates only to the quality or value of the real estate transferred, and that such mistakes are collateral to the agreement and do not justify rescission, citing *A & M Land Development Co. v. Miller,* 354 Mich. 681 (1959).

In that case, the plaintiff was the purchaser of 91 lots of real property. It sought partial rescission of the land contract when it was frustrated in its attempts to develop 42 of the lots because it could not obtain permits from the county health department to install septic tanks on these lots. This Court refused to allow rescission because the mistake, whether mutual or unilateral, related only to the value of the property. . . .

Appellees contend, on the other hand, that in this case the parties were mistaken as to the very nature of the character of the consideration and claim that the pervasive and essential quality of this mistake renders rescission appropriate. They cite in support of that view *Sherwood v. Walker,* 66 Mich. 568 (1887), the famous "barren cow" case. . . .

As the parties suggest, the foregoing precedent arguably distinguishes mistakes affecting the essence of the consideration from those which go to its quality or value, affording relief on a per se basis for the former but not the latter.

However, the distinctions which may be drawn from *Sherwood* and *A & M Land Development Co.* do not provide a satisfactory analysis of the nature of a mistake sufficient to invalidate a contract. Often, a mistake relates to an underlying factual assumption which, when discovered, directly affects value, but simultaneously and materially affects the essence of the contractual consideration. It is disingenuous to label such a mistake collateral.

Appellant and appellee both mistakenly believed that the property which was the subject of their land contract would generate income as rental property. The fact that it could not be used for human habitation deprived the property of its income-earning potential and rendered it less valuable. However, this mistake, while directly and dramatically affecting the property's value, cannot accurately be characterized as collateral because it also affects the very essence of the consideration. "The thing sold and bought [income generating rental property] had in fact no existence." *Sherwood v. Walker,* 66 Mich. 578.

We find that the inexact and confusing distinction between contractual mistakes running to value and those touching the substance of the consideration serves only as an impediment to a clear and helpful analysis for the equitable resolution of cases in which mistake is alleged and proven. Accordingly, the holdings of *A & M Land Development Co.* and *Sherwood* with respect to the material or collateral nature of a mistake are limited to the facts of those cases.

Instead, we think the better-reasoned approach is a case-by-case analysis whereby rescission is indicated when the mistaken belief relates to a basic assumption of the parties upon which the contract is made, and which materially affects the agreed performances of the parties. 1 *Restatement Contracts 2d* § 152. Rescission is not available, however, to relieve a party who has assumed the risk of loss in connection with the mistake. 1 *Restatement Contracts 2d* §§ 152, 154.

All of the parties to this contract erroneously assumed that the property transferred by the vendors to the vendees was suitable for human habitation and could be utilized to generate rental income. The fundamental nature of these assumptions is indicated by the fact that their invalidity changed the character of the property transferred, thereby frustrating, indeed precluding, Mr. and Mrs. Pickles' intended use of the real estate. Although the Pickleses are disadvantaged by enforcement of the contract, performance is advantageous to the Messerlys, as the property at issue is less valuable absent its income-earning potential. Nothing short of rescission can remedy the mistake. Thus, the parties' mistake as to a basic assumption materially affects the agreed performances of the parties.

Despite the significance of the mistake made by the parties, we reverse the Court of Appeals because we conclude that equity does not justify the remedy sought by Mr. and Mrs. Pickles.

Rescission is an equitable remedy which is granted only in the sound discretion of the court. A court need not grant rescission in every case in which the mutual mistake relates to a basic assumption and materially affects the agreed performance of the parties.

In cases of mistake by two equally innocent parties, we are required, in the exercise of our equitable powers, to determine which blameless party should assume the loss resulting from the misapprehension they shared.[13] Normally that can only be done by drawing upon our "own notions of what is reasonable and just under all the surrounding circumstances".[14]

Equity suggests that, in this case, the risk should be allocated to the purchasers. We are guided to that conclusion, in part, by the standards announced in § 154 of the *Restatement of Contracts 2d,* for determining when a party bears the risk of mistake. § 154(a) suggests that the court should look first to whether the parties have agreed to the allocation of the risk between themselves. While there is no express assumption in the contract by either party of the risk of the property becoming uninhabitable, there was indeed some agreed allocation of the risk to the vendees by the incorporation of an "as is" clause into the contract which, we repeat, provided:

> Purchaser has examined this property and agrees to accept same in its present condition. There are no other or additional written or oral understandings.

That is a persuasive indication that the parties considered that, as between them, such risk as related to the "present condition" of the property should lie with the purchaser. If the "as is" clause is to have any meaning at all, it must be interpreted to refer to those defects which were unknown at the time that the contract was executed.[15] Thus, the parties themselves assigned the risk of loss to Mr. and Mrs. Pickles.[16]

We conclude that Mr. and Mrs. Pickles are not entitled to the equitable remedy of rescission and, accordingly, reverse the decision the Court of Appeals.

NOTES AND QUESTIONS

1. ***What happened?*** Who sued whom for what? Procedurally, how did the case get before this court? Factually, what happened between the parties? What arguments did the plaintiff and defendant make? What rule or rules did

13. This risk-of-loss analysis is absent in both *A & M Land Development Co.* and *Sherwood,* and this omission helps to explain, in part, the disparate treatment in the two cases. Had such an inquiry been undertaken in *Sherwood,* we believe that the result might have been different. Moreover, a determination as to which party assumed the risk in *A & M Land Development Co.* would have alleviated the need to characterize the mistake as collateral so as to justify the result denying rescission. Despite the absence of any inquiry as to the assumption of risk in those two leading cases, we find that there exists sufficient precedent to warrant such an analysis in future cases of mistake.

14. *Hathaway v. Hudson,* 256 Mich. 702.

15. An "as is" clause waives those implied warranties which accompany the sale of a new home, or the sale of goods. Since implied warranties protect against latent defects, an "as is" clause will impose upon the purchaser the assumption of the risk of latent defects, such as an inadequate sanitation system, even when there are no implied warranties.

16. An "as is" clause does not preclude a purchaser from alleging fraud or misrepresentation as a basis for rescission. However, Mr. and Mrs. Pickles did not appeal the trial court's finding that there was no fraud or misrepresentation, so we are bound thereby.

the court apply? How did the court analyze the dispute between the parties? How did the court decide the case?

2. *Was this case correctly decided?* Do you agree with the result reached in this case? Why or why not? Do you agree with the court's reasoning? Why or why not? How, if at all, would you have written the opinion differently?

3. *Quite the pickle.* What should the Pickleses have done once they discovered the problem with the apartment building? Or was it simply too late to do anything?

4. *Counseling.* How would you advise future clients in the Pickles' position in light of the outcome in this case?

5. *Thinking tools.* Is the rule adopted above a good one? Why or why not? Where the parties are silent, do you think the risk of mistake should lie with the buyer or the seller? Why?

PROBLEM: SELLING A "STRADIVARIUS" VIOLIN

Plaintiff Peter, who was 86 years of age, although not a dealer in violins, had been a collector of rare violins for many years. Defendant Daniel was a violinist of great prominence, internationally known, and himself the owner and collector of rare and old violins made by the old masters. At the suggestion of a third person, and without Plaintiff's knowledge of Defendant's intention, Defendant visited Plaintiff's home and asked Plaintiff if he might see Plaintiff's collection of old violins. As Plaintiff showed Defendant his collection, Defendant picked up a violin and asked Plaintiff what he would take for it, calling it a "Stradivarius." Plaintiff, upon being asked this question, said he would not charge as much as a regular dealer, but that he would sell it for $50,000. Defendant then picked up another violin, calling it a "Guarnerius," and asked Plaintiff what he would take for it. Plaintiff responded by saying that if Defendant took both violins, he could have them for $80,000. To this the Defendant said "all right." Defendant then explained his financial condition to Plaintiff and asked if he could pay $20,000 cash in a week and the balance in monthly payments of $10,000." The parties agreed, and a memorandum was signed by defendant as follows:

> I hereby acknowledge receipt of one violin by Joseph Guarnerius and one violin by Stradivarius dated 1717 purchased by me, Daniel, from Peter for the total sum of Eighty Thousand Dollars toward which purchase price I have paid Twenty Thousand Dollars the balance I agree to pay at the rate of ten thousand dollars on the fifteenth day of each month until paid in full.

In addition thereto, the following "bill of sale" was also signed by Plaintiff:

> This certifies that I have on this date sold to Daniel one Joseph Guarnerius violin and one Stradivarius violin dated 1717, for the full price of $80,000 on which has been paid $20,000.00.

> The balance of $60,000 to be paid $10,000 fifteenth of each month until paid in full, I agree that Daniel shall have the right to exchange these for any others in my collection should he so desire.

At the time the transaction was consummated, each party fully believed that the violins were made one by Antonius Stradivarius and one by Josef Guarnerius. Further, at the closing of the transaction, Plaintiff made no representations and/or warranties as to either of the violins, or as to who their makers were, but believed them to have been made one by Antonius Stradivarius and one by Josef Guarnerius in the early part of the eighteenth century. The violins, however, were not Stradivarius or Guarnerius violins, but were in fact made as imitations thereof, and were not worth more than $3,000.

Plaintiff brings suit against Defendant to recover the unpaid balance of the purchase price of the two violins. Defendant responds by claiming that Plaintiff is not entitled to recover judgment on account of their being a mutual mistake of fact. Consulting the cases and materials in this subsection, how would you analyze this problem?

PROBLEM: WHEN A PICTURE IS WORTH MORE THAN A THOUSAND WORDS

Plaintiff Patricia's estate (hereinafter "Estate") seeks to rescind the sale of two paintings to Defendant Demeter, alleging that the sale was based upon a mutual mistake.

The facts are these. After Plaintiff died, Ronald Representative, the representatives of her estate, employed Alphonse the Appraiser to appraise the Estate's personal property in preparation for an estate sale. Alphonse told Ronald that he did not appraise fine art and that, if he saw any, Ronald would need to hire an additional appraiser. Alphonse did not report finding any fine art, and relying on his silence and his appraisal, Ronald priced and sold the Estate's personal property.

Responding to a newspaper advertisement, Demeter attended the public estate sale and paid the asking price of $60 for two oil paintings. Although Demeter had bought and sold some art, she was not an educated purchaser, had never made more than $55 on any single piece, and had bought many pieces that had "turned out to be frauds, forgeries or . . . to have been created by less popular artists." She assumed the paintings were not originals given their price and the fact that the Estate was managed by professionals, but was attracted to the subject matter of one of the paintings and the frame of the other. At home, she compared the signatures on the paintings to those in a book of artists' signatures, noticing they "appeared to be similar" to that of Martin Johnson Heade. As she had done in the past, Demeter sent pictures of the paintings to Christie's in New York, hoping they might be Heade's work. Christie's authenticated the paintings, Magnolia Blossoms on Blue Velvet and Cherokee Roses, as paintings by Heade and offered to sell them on consignment. Christie's subsequently sold the paintings at auction for $1,000,000. After subtracting the buyer's premium and the commission, Demeter realized $900,000 from the sale.

Ronald learned about the sale in February 2007 and thereafter sued Alphonse on behalf of the Estate, believing he was entirely responsible for the Estate's loss. The following November, they settled the lawsuit because Alphonse had no assets with which to pay damages. During 2007, Demeter paid income taxes on the profit from the sale of the paintings, purchased a home, created a family trust, and spent some of the funds on living expenses.

The Estate sued Demeter in late January 2008, alleging the sale contract should be rescinded or reformed on grounds of mutual mistake. Specifically, the Estate argued the parties were not aware the transaction had involved fine art, believing instead that the items exchanged were "relatively valueless, wall decorations." Demeter argued the Estate bore the risk of mistake.

Assuming that both of the parties had been mistaken about the value of the paintings, which party should bear the risk of that mistake, and why?

PROBLEM: A SAFE BET?

The Mitchells, who operate a second-hand store, attended an auction and purchased a safe for $100. They subsequently delivered it to a locksmith who, upon opening a locked inner door, found $50,000. Both the Mitchells and the estate that owned the safe made a claim to the funds.

The Mitchells were regular customers at the auction and were familiar with a sign that appeared behind the auction block which read: "All Sales Are Final." In their affidavit, they stated that:

> At the auction we saw, among other things, two safes. Regarding the one we ultimately purchased, we saw that the top outer-most door with a combination lock was open, and that the inner door was locked shut. That inner door required a key to open, and we learned that the safe would have to be taken to a locksmith to get the inner door opened because no key was available. We also learned that the combination for the outer lock was unknown. The auctioneer told the bidders that both this and the other safe had come from an estate, that both were still locked, that neither had been opened, and that the required combinations and key were unavailable for either. They were both like a "pig-in-a-poke" because of the equal possibilities that: (1) The inner contents or condition would be detrimental to its value to us; (2) would increase its value to us; (3) it would be empty or its contents without significance. In any event, we did know that its ultimate value to us depended in part upon whether a locksmith could make it operable or could only damage it in opening the inner drawer. The cost of the locksmith's effort was also a factor. The purchase of this safe was a gamble on our part in these respects.

At the auction the auctioneer he told the crowd that the safes were from an estate, that an inner door was locked and had never been opened, and that he did not have the combination.

The personal representative of the estate stated in an affidavit that he had hired the auctioneer as an agent to sell certain personal property belonging to the estate, but that he "only intended to sell the safe, not the contents."

Which party should bear the risk of the safe containing valuable contents? If you were a judge deciding this case, would you allow the estate to rescind the sale on the grounds of mutual mistake? Why or why not?

2. Unilateral Mistake

Whereas the cases in the previous subsection examined the defense of mutual mistake, which concerned mistakes made by *both* parties relating to some presently-existing fact, the materials in this subsection will look at circumstances in which the mistake was unilateral, or made by a *single* party. Specifically, we will explore whether, and under what circumstances, a unilateral mistake can offer a defense to the mistaken party's performance.

DOCTRINAL OVERVIEW: UNILATERAL MISTAKE AS A DEFENSE TO ENFORCEMENT?*

A unilateral mistake occurs when only one party has an erroneous perception as to the facts. . . . In general, courts have been reluctant to allow a party to avoid a contract for a mistake that was not shared by the other party. . . .

Many courts, however, have abandoned this strict view and recognized a limited right of avoidance for unilateral mistake.[2]

Most of the cases in which avoidance has been granted for unilateral mistake have involved errors in the calculation of bids by general contractors on construction contracts. . . . [Here, courts sometimes allow those preparing construction bids to avoid their contract for unilateral mistake where (1) no significant reliance has yet taken place on the mistaken bid and (2) hardship would otherwise result to the mistaken party. But even here] relief for unilateral mistake, like that for mutual mistake, is not available if the party seeking relief bears the risk of the mistake. For example, if a bidder's mistake is one of "judgment," the bidder bears the risk and cannot avoid. . . .

Not all of the cases allowing relief for unilateral mistake have involved mistaken bids. The Supreme Court of California, while recognizing that "the most common types of mistakes falling within this category" of unilateral mistake "occur in bids on construction contracts," noted that *Restatement Second* § 153 "is not limited to such cases" and granted relief to an automobile dealer that had mistakenly offered a more expensive Jaguar for $25,995. Other courts have

* Excerpted from E. ALLAN FARNSWORTH, CONTRACTS § 9.4 (4th ed. 2004).

2. *See Restatement Second* § 153.

reached a similar conclusion, granting relief to a purchaser that contracts to buy a tract of land under a unilateral mistake as to the identity of the tract or as to its boundaries and to a holder of a patent that settles a patent infringement claim under a unilateral mistake as to whether the patent would withstand challenge. There is even authority that a party to a contract that has arisen in spite of a misunderstanding may, in some circumstances, be able to avoid it on the ground of a unilateral mistake. The general principles applicable to the mistaken bid cases apply to such cases as well. . . .

The mistaken party's remedy for unilateral mistake is avoidance, although if the other party actually knew of the mistake it would seem that no contract was formed at all. This power of avoidance is subject to the restrictions applicable to avoidance for mutual mistake, including the requirement of restitution of anything received from the other party. In return, the party seeking avoidance is entitled to restitution for any benefit conferred on the other party. Occasionally, as in the case of mutual mistake, courts have been impelled to shape more inventive solutions.

Laidlaw v. Organ

United States Supreme Court
15 U.S. 178 (1817)

ERROR to the district court for the Louisiana district.

The defendant in error filed his petition, or libel, in the court below, stating, that on the 18th day of February, 1815, he purchased of the plaintiffs in error one hundred and eleven hogsheads of tobacco, as appeared by the copy of a bill of parcels annexed, and that the same were delivered to him by the said Laidlaw & Co., and that he was in the lawful and quiet possession of the said tobacco, when, on the 20th day of the said month, the said Laidlaw & Co., by force, and of their own wrong, took possession of the same, and unlawfully withheld the same from the petitioner, notwithstanding he was at all times, and still was, ready to do and perform all things on his part stipulated to be done and performed in relation to said purchase, and had actually tendered to the said Laidlaw & Co. bills of exchange for the amount of the purchase money, agreeably to the said contract; to his damage, &c. Wherefore the petition prayed that the said Laidlaw & Co. might be cited to appear and answer to his plaint, and that judgment might be rendered against them for his damages, &c. And inasmuch as the petitioner did verily believe that the said one hundred and eleven hogsheads of tobacco would be removed, concealed, or disposed of by the said Laidlaw & Co., he prayed that a writ of sequestration might issue, and that the same might be sequestered in the hands of the marshal, to abide the judgment of the court, and that the said one hundred and eleven hogsheads of tobacco might be finally adjudged to the petitioner, together with his damages, &c., and costs of suit, and that the petitioner might have such other and farther relief as to the court should seem meet, &c. . . .

On the 20th of April, 1815, the cause was tried by a jury, who returned the following verdict, to wit: "The jury find for the plaintiff, for the tobacco named in the petition, without damages, payable as per contract." Whereupon the court rendered judgment

> that the plaintiff recover of the said defendants the said 111 hogsheads of tobacco, mentioned in the plaintiff's petition, and sequestered in this suit, with his costs of suit to be taxed; and ordered, that the marshal deliver the said tobacco to the said plaintiff, and that he have execution for his costs aforesaid, upon the said plaintiff's depositing in this court his bills of exchange for the amount of the purchase money endorsed, &c., for the use of the defendants, agreeably to the verdict of the jury.

On the 29th of April, 1815, the plaintiffs in error filed the following bill of exceptions, to wit:

> . . . [O]n the night of the 18th of February, 1815, Messrs. Livingston, White, and Shepherd brought from the British fleet the news that a treaty of peace had been signed at Ghent by the American and British commissioners, contained in a letter from Lord Bathurst to the Lord Mayor of London, published in the British newspapers, and that Mr. White caused the same to be made public in a handbill on Sunday morning, 8 o'clock, the 19th of February, 1815, and that the brother of Mr. Shepherd, one of these gentlemen, and who was interested in one-third of the profits of the purchase set forth in said plaintiff's petition, had, on Sunday morning, the 19th of February, 1815, communicated said news to the plaintiff; that the said plaintiff, on receiving said news, called on Francis Girault, (with whom he had been bargaining for the tobacco mentioned in the petition, the evening previous,) said Francis Girault being one of the said house of trade of Peter Laidlaw & Co., soon after sunrise on the morning of Sunday, the 19th of February, 1815, before he had heard said news. Said Girault asked if there was any news which was calculated to enhance the price or value of the article about to be purchased; and that the said purchase was then and there made, and the bill of parcels annexed to the plaintiff's petition delivered to the plaintiff between 8 and 9 o'clock in the morning of that day; and that in consequence of said news the value of said article had risen from 30 to 50 per cent. There being no evidence that the plaintiff had asserted or suggested anything to the said Girault, calculated to impose upon him with respect to said news, and to induce him to think or believe that it did not exist; and it appearing that the said Girault, when applied to, on the next day, Monday, the 20th of February, 1815, on behalf of the plaintiff, for an invoice of said tobacco, did not then object to the said sale, but promised to deliver the invoice to the said plaintiff in the course of the forenoon of that day; the court charged the jury to find for the plaintiff. Wherefore, that justice, by due course of law, may be done in this case, the counsel of said defendants, for them, and on their behalf, prays the court that this bill of exceptions be filed, allowed, and certified as the law directs. . . .

On the 29th of April, 1815, a writ of error was allowed to this court, and on the 3d of May, 1815, the defendant in error deposited in the court below, for the use of the plaintiffs in error, the bills of exchange mentioned in the pleadings, according to the verdict of the jury and the judgment of the court thereon, which bills were thereupon taken out of court by the plaintiffs in error. . . .

Mr. *C. J. Ingersoll*, for the plaintiffs in error. 1. The first question is, whether the sale, under the circumstances of the case, was a valid sale; whether fraud, which vitiates every contract, must be proved by the communication of positive misinformation, or by withholding information when asked. Suppression of material circumstances within the knowledge of the vendee, and not accessible to the vendor, is equivalent to fraud, and vitiates the contract. **Pothier**, in discussing this subject, adopts the distinction of the forum of conscience, and the forum of law; but he admits that *fides est servanda*. The parties treated on an unequal footing, as the one party had received intelligence of the peace of Ghent, at the time of the contract, and the other had not. This news was unexpected, even at Washington, much more at New-Orleans, the recent scene of the most sanguinary operations of the war. In answer to the question, whether there was any news calculated to enhance the price of the article, the vendee was silent. This reserve, when such a question was asked, was equivalent to a false answer, and as much calculated to deceive as the communication of the most fabulous intelligence. Though the plaintiffs in error, after they heard the news of peace, still went on, in ignorance of their legal rights, to complete the contract, equity will protect them. 2. Mr. Girault was improperly rejected as a witness, because he and his partner had *disclaimed*, and Messrs. Boorman & Johnston, the real owners of the tobacco, had *intervened* and taken the place of the original defendants. Girault was not obliged to disclose his character of agent, and, as such, he was an admissible witness. The tendency of the modern decisions to let objections go to the *credibility*, and not to the *competency* of witnesses, ought to be encouraged as an improvement in the jurisprudence on this subject. Besides, the proceedings are essentially *in rem*, according to the course of the civil law, and that consideration is conclusive as to the admissibility of the witness. 3. The court below had no right to charge the jury absolutely to find for the plaintiff. It was a mixed question of fact and law, which ought to have been left to the jury to decide. 4. There is error in the judgment of the court, in decreeing a deposit of the bills of exchange by the vendee for the tobacco, no such agreement being proved.

Mr. *Key* contra, 1. Though there be no testimony in the record to show a contract for payment in bills of exchange, still the court may infer that such was the contract from the petition of the plaintiff below, supported as it is by his oath, and uncontradicted, as to this fact, by the defendant's answer. The decree was for a specific performance, and the vendors took the bills out of court. 2. The judge's charge was right, there being no evidence of fraud. The vendee's silence was not legal evidence of fraud, and, therefore, there was no conflict of testimony on this point: it was exclusively a question of law; the law was with the plaintiff; and, consequently, the court did right to instruct the jury to find for the plaintiff. 3. Mr. Girault was an inadmissible witness. He and his partners were general merchants as well as factors. They sold in their own names, and might call the article their own or the property of their principals, as

Robert Joseph Pothier

Robert Joseph Pothier (1699-1772) was a French judge and jurist who was probably the leading contract theorist of his time. His views on contract law, which were greatly influenced by his study of Roman law, had a direct and traceable impact not only on French law, but on the development of English and American contract law as well.

Francis Scott Key

The "Mr. Key" being referred to by the Court is none other than Francis Scott Key, the author of the United States' national anthem, "The Star-Spangled Banner." Interestingly, Key wrote the poem during the War of 1812, the war that was ended by the Treaty of Ghent about which the defendant remained silent, thus leading to the dispute in this case.

it suited them. But they were parties to the suit, and the intervention of their principals did not abate the suit as to them. On every ground, therefore, Mr. Girault was an inadmissible witness. 4. The only real question in the cause is, whether the sale was invalid because the vendee did not communicate information which he received precisely as the vendor *might* have got it had he been equally diligent or equally fortunate? And, surely, on this question there can be no doubt. Even if the vendor had been entitled to the disclosure, he waived it by not insisting on an answer to his question; and the silence of the vendee might as well have been interpreted into an *affirmative* as a *negative* answer. But, on principle, he was not bound to disclose. Even admitting that his conduct was unlawful, in *foro conscientiae*, does that prove that it was so in the civil forum? Human laws are imperfect in this respect, and the sphere of morality is more extensive than the limits of civil jurisdiction. The maxim of *caveat emptor* could never have crept into the law, if the province of ethics had been co-extensive with it. There was, in the present case, no circumvention or maneuver practiced by the vendee, unless rising earlier in the morning, and obtaining by superior diligence and alertness that intelligence by which the price of commodities was regulated, be such. It is a romantic equality that is contended for on the other side. Parties never can be precisely equal in knowledge, either of facts or of the inferences from such facts, and both must concur in order to satisfy the rule contended for. The absence of all authority in England and the United States, both great commercial countries, speaks volumes against the reasonableness and practicability of such a rule.

MR. *C. J. Ingersoll,* in reply. Though the record may not show that anything tending to mislead by positive assertion was said by the vendee, in answer to the question proposed by Mr. Girault, yet it is a case of maneuver; of mental reservation; of circumvention. The information was monopolized by the messengers from the British fleet, and not imparted to the public at large until it was too late for the vendor to save himself. The rule of law and of ethics is the same. It is not a romantic, but a practical and legal rule of equality and good faith that is proposed to be applied. The answer of Boorman & Johnston denies the whole of the petition, and consequently denies that payment was to be in bills of exchange; and their taking the bills out of court, ought not to prejudice them. There is nothing in the record to show that the vendors were general merchants, and they disclosed their principals when they came to plead. The judge undertook to decide from the testimony, that there was no fraud; in so doing he invaded the province of the jury; he should have left it to the jury, expressing his opinion merely.

John Marshall

John Marshall was the Chief Justice of the U.S. Supreme Court from 1801-1835 and not only had a profound impact on

MR. CHIEF JUSTICE MARSHALL **delivered the opinion of the court**. The question in this case is, whether the intelligence of extrinsic circumstances, which might influence the price of the commodity, and which was exclusively within the knowledge of the vendee, ought to have been communicated by

the development of American law and legal thought but, by strengthening the judiciary vis-à-vis the legislative and executive branches, had a lasting impact on the balance of power among the three branches as well. Alas, his impact on contract law—which is a creature of state rather than federal law—was slightly less profound, but in at least this one case, his legacy continues to endure.

Critical reading

Make sure you can distinguish between Chief Justice Marshall's holding of the case, on the one hand, and his personal view about how he thinks the case should be resolved, on the other. What do you suppose he means when he says that "each party must take care not to say or do anything tending to impose upon the other"?

him to the vendor? **The court is of opinion that he was not bound to communicate it. It would be difficult to circumscribe the contrary doctrine within proper limits, where the means of intelligence are equally accessible to both parties. But at the same time, each party must take care not to say or do anything tending to impose upon the other.** The court thinks that the absolute instruction of the judge was erroneous, and that the question, whether any imposition was practiced by the vendee upon the vendor ought to have been submitted to the jury. For these reasons the judgment must be reversed, and the cause remanded to the district court of Louisiana, with directions to award a *venire facias de novo*.

Venire de novo awarded.

RELEVANT PROVISIONS

For the *Restatement (Second) of Contracts*, consult §§ 153, 160, and 161. For the *Restatement (Third) Restitution and Unjust Enrichment*, consult § 34.

NOTES AND QUESTIONS

1. *What happened?* Who sued whom for what? Procedurally, how did the case get before this court? Factually, what happened between the parties? What arguments did the plaintiff and defendant make? What rule or rules did the court apply? How did the court analyze the dispute between the parties? How did the court decide the case?

2. *Was this case correctly decided?* Do you agree with the result reached in this case? Why or why not? Do you agree with the court's reasoning? Why or why not? How, if at all, would you have written the opinion differently?

3. *Was the buyer's behavior acceptable?* According to Professor Keeton, the buyer simply acted the way you or I would have acted in the same situation, stating that

> the case of *Laidlaw v. Organ* has received a storm of criticism, but it seems that the buyer in that case acted in the way in which buyers generally would

> be expected to act. If those facts were given to a normal person, as an abstract question, he would probably say that the buyer's conduct was unethical; on the other hand, if the same individual were given the opportunity that the buyer had in *Laidlaw v. Organ,* he would do precisely the same thing.*

First, do you agree with Professor Keeton's observation? Second, do you think that his observation, even if true, is relevant? Should courts, in other words, seek to establish rules that reflect how parties *already* behave, or should they formulate rules to influence how parties *ought* to behave? If the latter, is this the way buyers *ought* to behave? Why or why not?

4. *To disclose or not to disclose.* So, do you think that disclosure ought or ought not to have been required? More specifically, how should a court determine when a party should, or should not, be required to disclose privately held information? Are you satisfied with Chief Justice Marshall's solution? If not, can you think of a better approach? Is the approach put forward by the *Restatement (Second) of Contracts* (see "Relevant Provisions" following the case) a workable approach? What do you make of the approach adopted by Professor Kronman in the excerpt below? Is it workable?

As you read the following excerpt, ask yourself whether you agree with Professor Kronman's solution of governing the disclosure requirement by placing the burden on the knowledgeable party to show how they acquired their information. Would his proposal tend to result in more efficient contracts, or would the large administrative costs associated with enforcing this proposal wipe out (at least some of) the efficiency gains?

MISTAKE, DISCLOSURE, INFORMATION, AND THE LAW OF CONTRACTS†

It is appropriate to begin a discussion of fraud and nondisclosure in contract law with the celebrated case of *Laidlaw v. Organ.*

Allocative efficiency is promoted by getting information of changed circumstances to the market as quickly as possible. Of course, the information doesn't just "get" there. Like everything else, it is supplied by individuals. . . .

* W. Page Keeton, *Fraud—Concealment and Non-Disclosure,* 15 TEX. L. REV. 1, 32, 34 (1936).

† Excerpted from Anthony T. Kronman, *Mistake, Disclosure, Information, and the Law of Contracts,* 7 J. LEGAL STUD. 1, 9, 13-18 (1978).

In some cases, the individuals who supply information have obtained it by a deliberate search; in other cases, their information has been acquired casually. . . .

[T]he term "deliberately acquired information" means information whose acquisition entails costs which would not have been incurred but for the likelihood, however great, that the information in question would actually be produced. . . . If the costs incurred in acquiring the information . . . would have been incurred in any case . . . the information may be said to have been casually acquired. . . .

If information has been deliberately acquired . . . and its possessor is denied the benefits of having and using it, he will have an incentive to reduce . . . his production of such information in the future. . . .

One effective way of insuring that an individual will benefit from the possession of information . . . is to assign him a property right in the information itself—a right or entitlement to invoke the coercive machinery of the state in order to exclude others from its use and enjoyment. The benefits of possession become secure only when the state transforms the possessor of information into an owner by investing him with a legally enforceable property right of some sort or other. . . .

One . . . way in which the legal system can establish property rights in information is by permitting an informed party to enter—and enforce—contracts which his information suggests are profitable, without disclosing the information to the other party. Imposing a duty to disclose upon the knowledgeable party deprives him of a private advantage which the information would otherwise afford. A duty to disclose is tantamount to a requirement that the benefit of the information be publicly shared and is thus antithetical to the notion of a property right which—whatever else it may entail—always requires the legal protection of private appropriation. . . .

The only feasible way of assigning property rights in [a] short-lived market [such as that which occurred in *Laidlaw v. Organ*] is to permit those with such information to contract freely without disclosing what they know.

It is unclear, from the report of the case, whether the buyer in *Laidlaw* casually acquired his information or made a deliberate investment in seeking it out (for example, by cultivating a network of valuable commercial "friendships"). If we assume the buyer casually acquired his knowledge of the treaty, requiring him to disclose the information to his seller (that is, denying him a property right in the information) will have no significant effect on his future behavior. Since one who casually acquires information makes no investment in its acquisition, subjecting him to a duty to disclose is not likely to reduce the amount of socially useful information which he actually generates. Of course, if the buyer in *Laidlaw* acquired his knowledge of the treaty as the result of a deliberate and costly search, a disclosure requirement will deprive him of any private benefit which he might otherwise realize from possession of the information and should discourage him from making similar investments in the future. . . .

If we assume that courts can easily discriminate between those who have acquired information casually and those who have acquired it deliberately, plausible economic considerations might well justify imposing a duty to disclose on a case-by-case basis (imposing it where the information has been casually acquired, refusing to impose it where the information is the fruit of a deliberate search). . . .

Indeed, . . . a rule permitting nondisclosure (which has the effect of imposing the risk of a mistake on the mistaken party) corresponds to the arrangement the parties themselves would have been likely to adopt if they had negotiated an explicit allocation of the risk at the time they entered the contract. The parties to a contract are always free to allocate this particular risk by including an appropriate disclaimer in the terms of their agreement. Where they have failed to do so, however, the object of the law of contracts should be (as it is elsewhere) to reduce transaction costs by providing a legal rule which approximates the arrangement the parties would have chosen for themselves if they had deliberately addressed the problem. This consideration, coupled with the reduction in the production of socially useful information which is likely to follow from subjecting him to a disclosure requirement, suggests that allocative efficiency is best served by permitting one who possesses deliberately acquired information to enter and enforce favorable bargains without disclosing what he knows.

A rule which calls for case-by-case application of a disclosure requirement is likely, however, to involve factual issues that will be difficult (and expensive) to resolve. *Laidlaw* itself illustrates this point nicely. On the facts of the case, as we have them, it is impossible to determine whether the buyer actually made a deliberate investment in acquiring information regarding the treaty. The cost of administering a disclosure requirement on a case-by-case basis is likely to be substantial.

As an alternative, one might uniformly apply a blanket rule (of disclosure or nondisclosure) across each class of cases involving the same sort of information (for example, information about market conditions or about defects in property held for sale). In determining the appropriate blanket rule for a particular class of cases, it would first be necessary to decide whether the kind of information involved is (on the whole) more likely to be generated by chance or by deliberate searching. The greater the likelihood that such information will be deliberately produced rather than casually discovered, the more plausible the assumption becomes that a blanket rule permitting nondisclosure will have benefits that outweigh its costs.

In *Laidlaw*, for example, the information involved concerned changing market conditions. The results in that case may be justified (from the more general perspective just described) on the grounds that information regarding the state of the market is typically (although not in every case) the product of a deliberate search. The large number of individuals who are actually engaged in the production of such information lends some empirical support to this proposition.

First Baptist Church of Moultrie v. Barber Contracting Co.

Court of Appeals of Georgia
377 S.E.2d 717 (1989)

McMurray, Presiding Judge. The First Baptist Church of Moultrie, Georgia, invited bids for the construction of a music, education and recreation building. The bids were to be opened on May 15, 1986. They were to be accompanied by a bid bond in the amount of 5 percent of the base bid. The bidding instructions provided, in pertinent part:

> Negligence on the part of the bidder in preparing the bid confers no right for the withdrawal of the bid after it has been opened.

Barber Contracting Company ("Barber") submitted a bid for the project in the amount of $1,860,000. The bid provided, in pertinent part: "For and in consideration of the sum of $1.00, the receipt of which is hereby acknowledged, the undersigned agrees that this proposal may not be revoked or withdrawn after the time set for the opening of bids but shall remain open for acceptance for a period of thirty-five (35) days following such time." The bid also provided that if it was accepted within 35 days of the opening of bids, Barber would execute a contract for the construction of the project within 10 days of the acceptance of the bid.

A bid bond in the amount of 5 percent of Barber's bid ($93,000) was issued by The American Insurance Company to cover Barber's bid. With regard to the bid bond, the bid submitted by Barber provided:

> If this proposal is accepted within thirty-five (35) days after the date set for the opening of bids and the undersigned [Barber] fails to execute the contract within ten (10) days after written notice of such acceptance . . . the obligation of the bid bond will remain in full force and effect and the money payable thereon shall be paid into the funds of the Owner as liquidated damages for such failure. . . .

The bids were opened by the church on May 15, 1986, as planned. Barber submitted the lowest bid. The second lowest bid, in the amount of $1,975,000, was submitted by H & H Construction and Supply Company, Inc. ("H & H").

Barber's president, Albert W. Barber, was present when the bids were opened, and of course, he was informed that Barber was the low bidder. Members of the church building committee informally asked President Barber if changes could be made in the contract to reduce the amount of the bid. He replied that he was sure such changes could be made.

On May 16, 1986, Albert W. Barber informed the architect for the project, William Frank McCall, Jr., that the amount of the bid was in error—the bid should have been $143,120 higher. In Mr. Barber's words:

> [T]he mistake in Barber's bid was caused by an error in totaling the material costs on page 3 of Barber's estimate work sheets. The subtotal of the material cost listed on that page is actually $137,990. The total listed on Barber's summary sheet for the material cost subtotal was $19,214. The net error in addition was $118,776. After adding in mark-ups for sales tax (4 percent), overhead and profit (15 percent), and bond procurement costs (.75 percent), the error was compounded to a total of $143,120. . . .

The architect immediately telephoned Billy G. Fallin, co-chairman of the church building committee, and relayed the information which he received from President Barber.

On May 20, 1986, Barber delivered letters to the architect and the church. In the letter to the architect, Barber enclosed copies of its estimate sheets and requested that it be permitted to withdraw its bid. In the letter to the church, Barber stated that it was withdrawing its bid on account of "an error in adding certain estimated material costs." In addition, Barber sought the return of the bid bond from the church.

On May 29, 1986, the church forwarded a construction contract, based upon Barber's bid, to Barber. The contract had been prepared by the architect and executed by the church. The next day, Barber returned the contract to the church without executing it. In so doing, Barber pointed out that its bid had been withdrawn previously.

On July 25, 1986, the church entered into a construction contract for the project with H & H, the second lowest bidder. Through deletions and design changes, the church was able to secure a contract with H & H for $1,919,272.

In the meantime, the church demanded that Barber and The American Insurance Company pay it $93,000 pursuant to the bid bond. The demand was refused.

On May 26, 1987, the church brought suit against Barber and The American Insurance Company seeking to recover the amount of the bid bond. Answering the complaint, defendants denied they were liable to plaintiff.

Thereafter, defendants moved for summary judgment and so did the plaintiff. In support of their summary judgment motions, defendants submitted the affidavit of Albert W. Barber. He averred that in preparing its bid, Barber exercised the level of care ordinarily exercised by contractors submitting sealed bids. In support of its summary judgment motion, the church submitted the affidavit of a building contractor who averred that he would never submit a bid of any magnitude without obtaining assistance in verification and computation.

The trial court denied the summary judgment motions, certified its rulings for immediate review and we granted these interlocutory appeals. *Held:* The question for decision is whether Barber was entitled to rescind its bid upon discovering that it was based upon a miscalculation or whether Barber should forfeit its bond because it refused to execute the contract following the acceptance of its bid by the church. We hold that Barber was entitled to rescind its bid.

That equity will rescind a contract upon a unilateral mistake is a generally accepted principle. As it is said:

> Where a mistake of one party at the time a contract was made as to a basic assumption on which he made the contract has a material effect on the agreed exchange of performances that is adverse to him, the contract is voidable by him if he does not bear the risk of the mistake . . . and (a) the effect of the mistake is such that enforcement of the contract would be unconscionable, or (b) the other party had reason to know of the mistake or his fault caused the mistake.

Restatement (2d) of Contracts § 153.

The following illustration demonstrates the rule:

> In response to B's invitation for bids on the construction of a building according to stated specifications, A submits an offer to do the work for $150,000. A believes that this is the total of a column of figures, but he has made an error by inadvertently omitting a $50,000 item, and in fact the total is $200,000. B, having no reason to know of A's mistake, accepts A's bid. If A performs for $150,000, he will sustain a loss of $20,000 instead of making an expected profit of $30,000. If the court determines that enforcement of the contract would be unconscionable, it is voidable by A.

Restatement (2d) of Contracts § 153 (Illustration 1).

Corbin explains:

> Suppose . . . a bidding contractor makes an offer to supply specified goods or to do specified work for a definitely named price, and that he was caused to name this price by an antecedent error of computation. If, before acceptance, the offeree knows, or has reason to know, that a material error has been made, he is seldom mean enough to accept; and if he does accept, the courts have no difficulty in throwing him out. He is not permitted 'to snap up' such an offer and profit thereby. If, without knowledge of the mistake and before any revocation, he has accepted the offer, it is natural for him to feel a sense of disappointment at not getting a good bargain, when the offeror insists on withdrawal; but a just and reasonable man will not insist upon profiting by the other's mistake. There are now many decisions to the effect that if the error was a substantial one and notice is given before the other party has made such a change of position that he cannot be put substantially in status quo, the bargain is voidable and rescission will be decreed.

Corbin on Contracts § 609 (1960).

Georgia law is no different. It provides for rescission and cancellation "upon the ground of mistake of fact material to the contract of one party only." OCGA § 23-2-31. The mistake must be an "unintentional act, omission, or error arising from ignorance, surprise, imposition, or misplaced confidence." OCGA § 23-2-21(a). But relief will be granted even in cases of negligence if the opposing party will not be prejudiced. OCGA § 23-2-32.

We can see these principles at work in *M.J. McGough Co. v. Jane Lamb Memorial Hosp.*, 302 F. Supp. 482 (S.D. Iowa 1969). In that case, a bid of $1,957,000 was submitted for a hospital improvement by a contractor. A bond in the amount of $100,000 was given to secure the contractor's bid. The contractor submitted the lowest bid. After the bids were opened, but before its bid was accepted, the contractor informed the hospital that it erroneously transcribed numbers in computing the bid and that, therefore, it underbid the project by $199,800. Nevertheless, the hospital tried to hold the contractor to its bid. When the contractor refused to execute a contract, the hospital awarded the contract to the next lowest bidder. The contractor and surety sought rescission of the bid and the return of the bond. The hospital sued the contractor and surety for damages. The district court allowed the contractor to rescind. Its decision is noteworthy and illuminating. We quote it at length:

> By the overwhelming weight of authority a contractor may be relieved from a unilateral mistake in his bid by rescission under the proper circumstances. The prerequisites for obtaining such relief are: (1) the mistake is of such consequence that enforcement would be unconscionable; (2) the mistake must relate to the substance of the consideration; (3) the mistake must have occurred regardless of the exercise of ordinary care; (4) it must be possible to place the other party in status quo. It is also generally required that the bidder give prompt notification of the mistake and his intention to withdraw. . . .
>
> Applying the criteria for rescission for a unilateral mistake to the circumstances in this case, it is clear that [the contractor] and his surety . . . are

> entitled to equitable relief. The notification of mistake was promptly made, and [the contractor] made every possible effort to explain the circumstances of the mistake to the authorities of [the hospital]. Although [the hospital] argues to the contrary, the Court finds that notification of the mistake was received before acceptance of the bid. The mere opening of the bids did not constitute the acceptance of the lowest bid. . . . Furthermore, it is generally held that acceptance prior to notification does not bar the right to equitable relief from a mistake in the bid.
>
> The mistake in this case was an honest error made in good faith. While a mistake in and of itself indicates some degree of lack of care or negligence, under the circumstances here there was not such a lack of care as to bar relief. . . .
>
> The mistake here was a simple clerical error. To allow [the hospital] to take advantage of this mistake would be unconscionable. This is especially true in light of the fact that they had actual knowledge of the mistake before the acceptance of the bid. Nor can it be seriously contended that a $199,800 error, amounting to approximately 10% of the bid, does not relate directly to the substance of the consideration. Furthermore, [the hospital] has suffered no actual damage by the withdrawal of the bid of [the contractor]. The Hospital has lost only what it sought to gain by taking advantage of [the contractor's] mistake. Equitable considerations will not allow the recovery of the loss of bargain in this situation.

M.J. McGough Co. v. Jane Lamb Memorial Hosp., 302 F. Supp. 482, 485, 486.

In the case ***sub judice***, Barber, the contractor, promptly notified the plaintiff that a mistake was made in calculating the amount of the bid. The plaintiff had actual knowledge of the mistake before it forwarded a contract to Barber. The mistake was a "simple clerical error." *M.J. McGough Co. v. Jane Lamb Memorial Hosp.*, 302 F. Supp. 482, 485. It did not amount to negligence preventing equitable relief. Furthermore, it was a mistake which was material to the contract—it went to the substance of the consideration. (The mistake amounted to approximately 7 percent of the bid.) To allow the plaintiff to take advantage of the mistake would not be just.

> ***Sub judice***
>
> "[Latin 'under a judge'] Before the court or judge for determination; at bar [in the case sub judice, there have been no out-of-court settlements]. Legal writers sometimes use case sub judice where the present case would be more comprehensible." BLACK'S LAW DICTIONARY (10th ed. 2014).

The contention is made that Barber's miscalculation constituted negligence sufficient to prevent relief in equity. Assuming, arguendo, that the error stemmed from such a want of prudence as to violate a legal duty, we must nevertheless conclude that Barber is entitled to rescission.

Relief in equity "may be granted even in cases of negligence by the complainant if it appears that the other party has not been prejudiced thereby." OCGA § 23-2-32(b). It cannot be said that plaintiff was prejudiced by Barber's rescission. After all, plaintiff "lost only what it sought to gain by taking advantage of [the contractor's] mistake." *M.J. McGough Co. v. Jane Lamb Memorial Hosp.*, at 486.

The plaintiff takes the position that rescission is improper since, pursuant to the language set forth in the bid, Barber agreed not to withdraw the bid for a period of 35 days after the bids were opened. It also asserts that the language set forth in the bidding instructions prohibited Barber from withdrawing the bid on the ground of "negligence." We disagree. "[P]rovisions such as these have been considered many times in similar cases, and have never been held effective when equitable considerations dictate otherwise." *M.J. McGough Co. v. Jane Lamb Memorial Hosp.*, 302 F. Supp. 482, 487.

The trial court properly denied the plaintiff's (the church's) motion for summary judgment. It erred in denying defendants' (Barber's and The American Insurance Company's) motions for summary judgment.

NOTES AND QUESTIONS

1. *What happened?* Who sued whom for what? Procedurally, how did the case get before this court? Factually, what happened between the parties? What arguments did the plaintiff and defendant make? What rule or rules did the court apply? How did the court analyze the dispute between the parties? How did the court decide the case?

2. *Was this case correctly decided?* Do you agree with the result reached in this case? Why or why not? Do you agree with the court's reasoning? Why or why not? How, if at all, would you have written the opinion differently?

3. Baird *and* Drennan, *redux?* This case should remind you a lot of the *Baird* and *Drennan* decisions we read when we explored mutual assent in Part III.3.D.2, both of which also discussed mistake. This indicates the close relationship between mutual assent and the defense of mistake: where one (or both) parties have made a mistake regarding an important fact in the underlying transaction, it is easy to understand why the party negatively impacted by the mistake would assert that they should be allowed to rescind the contract because they did not manifest their assent regarding the true nature of the transaction before them. The question, of course, is whether courts should allow such a defense to stand, and, if so, under what conditions. Can these sorts of issues be resolved by applying the *Embry* test, to see whether the parties manifested their assent to one another, or do you think we need a separate doctrine to specifically deal with mistake?

4. *Thinking tools.* Is this case consistent with the analysis proposed by Professor Kronman in the excerpt above? If not, how would this case be resolved under Kronman's approach? Can you think of any other thinking tools that would help shed light on the resolution of this case, or of other similar cases?

PROBLEM: THE BASEBALL CARD CASE*

Twelve-year-old card collector Bryan Wrzesinski, owner of some 40,000 baseball cards, spotted a 1968 Nolan Ryan/Jerry Koosman rookie card at the Ball-Mart, a newly opened baseball card store in Itasca, Illinois. The price of the card was marked as "1200/." An inexperienced sales clerk interpreted this figure to mean $12.00 and accepted that amount in exchange for the card. The proprietor of the Ball-Mart, Joe Irmen, claimed that the card had been offered for sale at $1,200 (a price in line with its market value) and asked for it back. Wrzesinski refused to reverse the transaction.

Irmen sues Wrzesinski for return of the card or money damages. Who should win, and why?

D. DECEIT AND COERCION

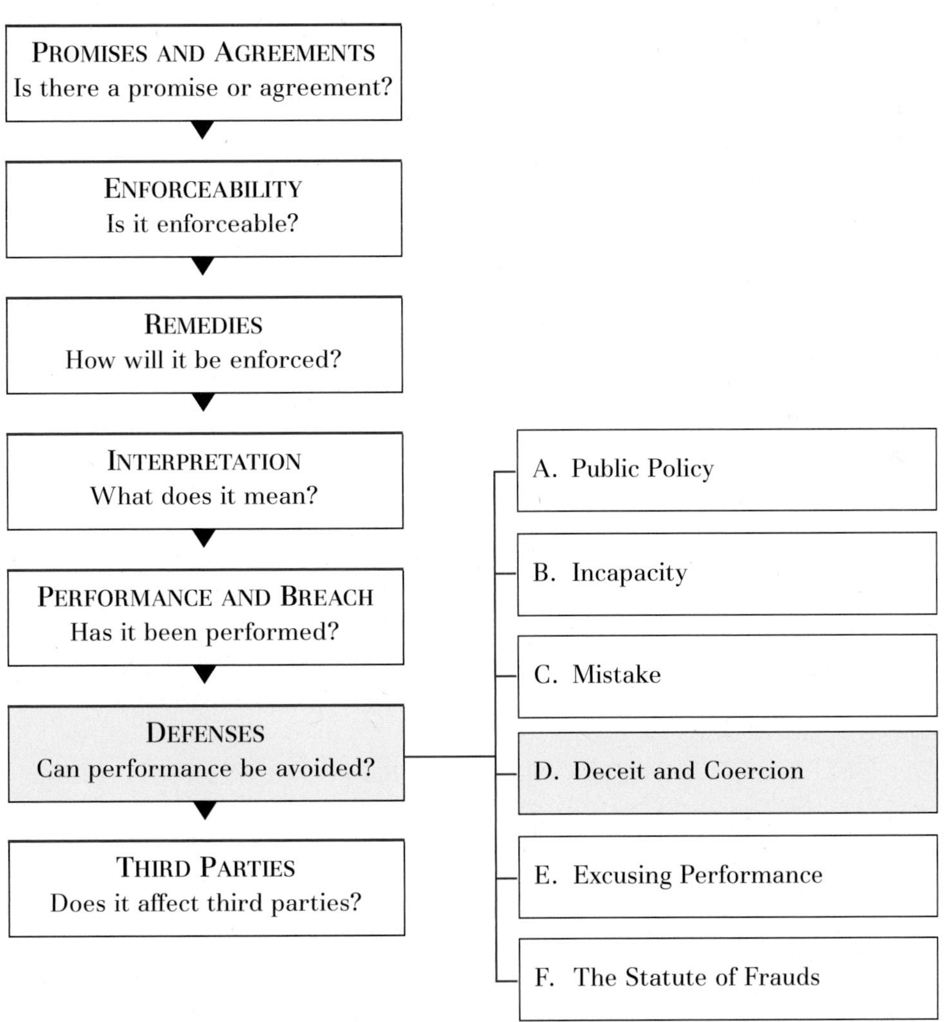

* This problem is taken from Andrew Kull, *Unilateral Mistake: The Baseball Card Case*, 70 Wash. U. L.Q. 57 (1992).

When we discussed enforceability in Chapter 4, it was taken for granted that the contracting parties possessed the judgment, experience, and capacity to enter into a contract,* were of roughly equal bargaining power,† and that, as a result, the contract entered into was a mutually beneficial transaction.‡ Where one party has superior mental, physical, or economic resources, however, and uses these to its advantage to maximize its wellbeing at the expense of the other party, many of these basic assumptions no longer hold, and the question becomes what the court should do about it, if anything. The cases discussed in this section are concerned with instances in which one party may have overstepped its contractual prerogative vis-à-vis the other party by violating one or more of the above-stated assumptions, typically through deceit, coercion, or some combination of the two. Where this is the case, the affected party may be able to avoid having to perform its contractual obligations by asserting one of the defenses we will explore in this section, such as misrepresentation, duress, undue influence, or unconscionability—all of which are, at their core, related to one party having obtained the assent of another party by improper means.

RELEVANT PROVISIONS

For the *Restatement (Second) of Contracts*, consult § 19(3).

1. Misrepresentation

No rogue should enjoy his ill-gotten plunder for the simple reason that his victim is by chance a fool.

Chamberlin v. Fuller, 9 A. 832 (1887)

The state of adjudicated cases in this state and elsewhere is such that the question whether fraudulent representations . . . can ever be actionable is not without some difficulty. To that question we pass. Fraud is kaleidoscopic, infinite. Fraud being infinite and taking on protean form at will, were courts to cramp themselves by defining it with a hard and fast definition, their jurisdiction would be cunningly circumvented at once by new schemes beyond the definition. . . . Accordingly definitions of fraud are of set purpose left general and flexible, and thereto courts match their astuteness against the versatile inventions of fraud-doers.

Stonemets v. Head, 154 S.W. 108, 114 (1913)

* *See* Section B ("Incapacity") earlier in this chapter.

† *See, e.g.*, Selznick, *The Ethos of American Law*, included in THE AMERICANS: 1976, at 221 (I. Kristol & P. Weaver eds. 1976) ("The contract model presumes a world of independent, roughly equal actors who enter relationships of limited duration and limited commitment.")

‡ *See, e.g.*, ADAM SMITH, WEALTH OF NATIONS 423 (Cannan ed. 1937) ("By pursuing his own interest the individual member of society promotes that of the society more effectively than when he really intends to promote it.")

DOCTRINAL OVERVIEW: MISREPRESENTATION AS A DEFENSE TO ENFORCEMENT*

A distinction is drawn between misrepresentation that goes only to the "inducement" and misrepresentation that goes to the "execution" (or the "factum"). In the typical case, as when a seller misrepresents the quality of goods, the misrepresentation is said to go to the "inducement." The effect of such a misrepresentation is to make the contract voidable at the instance of the recipient. In rare cases, however, the misrepresentation is regarded as going to the very character of the proposed contract itself, as when one party induces the other to sign a document by falsely stating that it has no legal effect. Such a misrepresentation is said to go to the "execution" (or the "factum"[1]). If the other party neither knows nor has reason to know of the character of the proposed agreement, the effect of such a misrepresentation is that there is no contract at all—what is sometimes anomalously described as a "void," as opposed to a voidable, contract. The same result would follow from the general principles relating to assent. The distinction is mainly of significance to such third parties as good faith purchasers, who generally take property free of claims and defenses based on misrepresentation if the misrepresentation goes only to the inducement, but not if it goes to the factum or the execution. Only rarely, however, is a misrepresentation seen as going to the very nature of the contract itself. Even the identity of the other party is not usually regarded as sufficiently central, so that a mere misrepresentation as to identity, as when a buyer of goods obtains credit by impersonating a person of means, may make the contract voidable but is not ordinarily seen as preventing a manifestation of assent.

In the great bulk of cases, the misrepresentation is seen as going only to the inducement, with the result that the contract is voidable. The requirements for avoidance can be grouped under four headings. First, there must be an assertion that is not in accord with the facts. Second, the assertion must be either fraudulent or material. Third, the assertion must be relied on by the recipient in manifesting assent. Fourth, the reliance of the recipient must be justified. . . .

Leonard v. Pepsico

United States District Court, Southern District of New York
88 F. Supp. 2d 116 (1999)

For a report of the case and accompanying materials, see p. 217, *infra*.

E. PLAINTIFF'S FRAUD CLAIM

In addition to moving for summary judgment on plaintiff's claim for breach of contract, defendant has also moved for summary judgment on plaintiff's fraud claim. The elements of a cause of action for fraud are "'representation of

* Excerpted from E. ALLAN FARNSWORTH, CONTRACTS § 4.10 (4th ed. 2004).

1. *See Restatement Second* § 163 ("misrepresentation as to the character or essential terms of a proposed contract").

a material existing fact, falsity, scienter, deception and injury.'" *New York Univ. v. Continental Ins. Co.,* 662 N.E.2d 763 (1995).

To properly state a claim for fraud, "plaintiff must allege a misrepresentation or material omission by defendant, on which it relied, that induced plaintiff" to perform an act. *See NYU,* 662 N.E.2d at 769. "General allegations that defendant entered into a contract while lacking the intent to perform it are insufficient to support the claim." *See id.*; *see also Grappo v. Alitalia Linee Aeree Italiane, S.p.A.,* 56 F.3d 427, 434 (2d Cir. 1995) ("A cause of action does not generally lie where the plaintiff alleges only that the defendant entered into a contract with no intention of performing it"). Instead, the plaintiff must show the misrepresentation was collateral, or served as an inducement, to a separate agreement between the parties. *See Bridgestone/Firestone v. Recovery Credit,* 98 F.3d 13, 20 (2d Cir. 1996) (allowing a fraud claim where plaintiff "'demonstrate[s] a fraudulent misrepresentation collateral or extraneous to the contract'").

For example, in *Stewart v. Jackson & Nash,* 976 F.2d 86 (2d Cir. 1992), the Second Circuit ruled that plaintiff had properly stated a claim for fraud. In the course of plaintiff's negotiations for employment with defendant, a law firm, defendant represented to plaintiff not only that plaintiff would be hired (which she was), but also that the firm had secured a large environmental law client, that it was in the process of establishing an environmental law department, and that plaintiff would head the environmental law department. *See id.* at 89-90. The Second Circuit concluded that these misrepresentations gave rise to a fraud claim, because they consisted of misrepresentations of present fact, rather than future promises.

Plaintiff in this case does not allege that he was induced to enter into a contract by some collateral misrepresentation, but rather that defendant never had any intention of making good on its "offer" of a Harrier Jet. Because this claim "alleges only that the defendant entered into a contract with no intention of performing it," *Grappo,* 56 F.3d at 434, judgment on this claim should enter for defendant.

RELEVANT PROVISIONS

For the *Restatement (Second) of Contracts,* consult §§ 159-164 and 167. For the UNIDROIT Principles, consult Article 3.2.5.

NOTES AND QUESTIONS

1. *What happened?* Who sued whom for what? Procedurally, how did the case get before this court? Factually, what happened between the parties? What arguments did the plaintiff and defendant make? What rule or rules did

the court apply? How did the court analyze the dispute between the parties? How did the court decide the case?

2. *Was this case correctly decided?* Do you agree with the result reached in this case? Why or why not? Do you agree with the court's reasoning? Why or why not? How, if at all, would you have written the opinion differently?

Vokes v. Arthur Murray, Inc.

District Court of Appeal of Florida
212 So. 2d 906 (1968)

PIERCE, JUDGE. This is an appeal by Audrey E. Vokes, plaintiff below, from a final order dismissing with prejudice, for failure to state a cause of action, her fourth amended complaint, hereinafter referred to as plaintiff's complaint.

Defendant Arthur Murray, Inc., a corporation, authorizes the operation throughout the nation of dancing schools under the name of "Arthur Murray School of Dancing" through local franchised operators, one of whom was defendant J. P. Davenport whose dancing establishment was in Clearwater.

Plaintiff Mrs. Audrey E. Vokes, a widow of 51 years and without family, had a yen to be "an accomplished dancer" with the hopes of finding "new interest in life." So, on February 10, 1961, a dubious fate, with the assist of a motivated acquaintance, procured her to attend a "dance party" at Davenport's "School of Dancing" where she whiled away the pleasant hours, sometimes in a private room, absorbing his accomplished sales technique, during which her grace and poise were elaborated upon and her rosy future as "an excellent dancer" was painted for her in vivid and glowing colors. As an incident to this interlude, he sold her eight 1/2-hour dance lessons to be utilized within one calendar month therefrom, for the sum of $14.50 cash in hand paid, obviously a baited "come on."

Thus she embarked upon an almost endless pursuit of the **terpsichorean** art during which, over a period of less than sixteen months, she was sold fourteen "dance courses" totaling in the aggregate 2302 hours of dancing lessons for a total cash outlay of $31,090.45, all at Davenport's dance emporium. All of these fourteen courses were evidenced by execution of a written "Enrollment Agreement—Arthur Murray's School of Dancing" with the addendum in heavy black print, "No one will be informed that you are taking dancing lessons. Your relations with us are held in strict confidence," setting forth the number of "dancing lessons" and the "lessons in rhythm sessions" currently sold to her from time to time, and always of course accompanied by payment of cash of the realm.

> ***Terpsichorean***
>
> According to Greek mythology, there were nine Muses responsible for inspiring humans in such widely divergent pursuits as poetry, history, and astronomy. Terpsichore, as the goddess of song and dance, was the Muse responsible for inspiring those who, like Vokes, wished to excel in their "terpsichorean" pursuits. Judge Pierce might just as well have conjured Melpomene, the Muse of tragedy, given what happened to Vokes at the hands of Arthur Murray, or perhaps Erato, the Muse of lyric poetry, given Judge Pierce's florid writing throughout his opinion.

These dance lesson contracts and the monetary consideration therefor of over $31,000 were procured from her by means and methods of Davenport and his associates which went beyond the unsavory, yet legally permissible, perimeter of "sales puffing" and intruded well into the forbidden area of undue influence, the suggestion of falsehood, the suppression of truth, and the free exercise of rational judgment, if what plaintiff alleged in her complaint was true. From the time of her first contact with the dancing school in February, 1961, she was influenced unwittingly by a constant and continuous barrage of flattery, false praise, excessive compliments, and panegyric encomiums, to such extent that it would be not only inequitable, but unconscionable, for a Court exercising inherent chancery power to allow such contracts to stand.

She was incessantly subjected to overreaching blandishment and cajolery. She was assured she had "grace and poise"; that she was "rapidly improving and developing in her dancing skill"; that the additional lessons would "make her a beautiful dancer, capable of dancing with the most accomplished dancers"; that she was "rapidly progressing in the development of her dancing skill and gracefulness," etc., etc. She was given "dance aptitude tests" for the ostensible purpose of "determining" the number of remaining hours instructions needed by her from time to time.

At one point she was sold 545 additional hours of dancing lessons to be entitled to award of the "Bronze Medal" signifying that she had reached "the Bronze Standard," a supposed designation of dance achievement by students of Arthur Murray, Inc.

Later she was sold an additional 926 hours in order to gain the "Silver Medal," indicating she had reached "the Silver Standard," at a cost of $12,501.35.

At one point, while she still had to her credit about 900 unused hours of instructions, she was induced to purchase an additional 24 hours of lessons to participate in a trip to Miami at her own expense, where she would be "given the opportunity to dance with members of the Miami Studio."

She was induced at another point to purchase an additional 123 hours of lessons in order to be not only eligible for the Miami trip but also to become "a life member of the Arthur Murray Studio," carrying with it certain dubious emoluments, at a further cost of $1,752.30.

At another point, while she still had over 1,000 unused hours of instruction she was induced to buy 151 additional hours at a cost of $2,049.00 to be eligible for a "Student Trip to Trinidad," at her own expense as she later learned.

Also, when she still had 1100 unused hours to her credit, she was prevailed upon to purchase an additional 347 hours at a cost of $4,235.74, to qualify her to receive a "Gold Medal" for achievement, indicating she had advanced to "the Gold Standard."

On another occasion, while she still had over 1200 unused hours, she was induced to buy an additional 175 hours of instruction at a cost of $2,472.75 to be eligible "to take a trip to Mexico."

Finally, sandwiched in between other lesser sales promotions, she was influenced to buy an additional 481 hours of instruction at a cost of $6,523.81 in order to "be classified as a Gold Bar Member, the ultimate achievement of the dancing studio."

All the foregoing sales promotions, illustrative of the entire fourteen separate contracts, were procured by defendant Davenport and Arthur Murray, Inc., by false representations to her that she was improving in her dancing ability, that she had excellent potential, that she was responding to instructions in dancing grace, and that they were developing her into a beautiful dancer, whereas in truth and in fact she did not develop in her dancing ability, she had no "dance aptitude," and in fact had difficulty in "hearing that musical beat." The complaint alleged that such representations to her "were in fact false and known by the defendant to be false and contrary to the plaintiff's true ability, the truth of plaintiff's ability being fully known to the defendants, but withheld from the plaintiff for the sole and specific intent to deceive and defraud the plaintiff and to induce her in the purchasing of additional hours of dance lessons." It was averred that the lessons were sold to her "in total disregard to the true physical, rhythm, and mental ability of the plaintiff." In other words, while she first exulted that she was entering the "spring of her life," she finally was awakened to the fact there was "spring" neither in her life nor in her feet.

The complaint prayed that the Court decree the dance contracts to be null and void and to be cancelled, that an accounting be had, and judgment entered against, the defendants "for that portion of the $31,090.45 not charged against specific hours of instruction given to the plaintiff." The Court held the complaint not to state a cause of action and dismissed it with prejudice. We disagree and reverse.

The material allegations of the complaint must, of course, be accepted as true for the purpose of testing its legal sufficiency. Defendants contend that contracts can only be rescinded for fraud or misrepresentation when the alleged misrepresentation is as to a material fact, rather than an opinion, prediction or expectation, and that the statements and representations set forth at length in the complaint were in the category of "trade puffing," within its legal orbit.

It is true that "generally a misrepresentation, to be actionable, must be one of fact rather than of opinion." ***Tonkovich v. South Florida Citrus Industries, Inc.***, **185 So. 2d 710 (Fla. App. 1966). But this rule has significant qualifications, applicable here. It does not apply where there is a fiduciary relationship between the parties, or where there has been some artifice or trick employed by the representor, or where the parties do not in general deal at "arm's length" as we understand the phrase, or where the representee does not have equal opportunity to become apprised of the truth or falsity of the fact**

Rule and exceptions

Make sure you are aware of both the general rule and the exceptions to the general rule that a statement of opinion ordinarily cannot constitute a misrepresentation. First, why do you suppose we have this general rule, and second, why do you suppose we have these exceptions? Given these exceptions, how easy is it to distinguish between a misrepresentation, on the one hand, and mere puffery, on the other? Do you agree with the court that the defendant's representations to Vokes *may** have gone too far? Why or why not? To what extent (if any) should the reasonableness of Vokes's reliance on the defendant's representations be relevant?

represented. As stated by Judge Allen of this Court in *Ramel v. Chasebrook Construction Company*, 135 So.2d 876 (Fla. App. 1961):

> . . . A statement of a party having . . . superior knowledge may be regarded as a statement of fact although it would be considered as opinion if the parties were dealing on equal terms.

It could be reasonably supposed here that defendants had "superior knowledge" as to whether plaintiff had "dance potential" and as to whether she was noticeably improving in the art of terpsichore. And it would be a reasonable inference from the undenied averments of the complaint that the flowery eulogiums heaped upon her by defendants as a prelude to her contracting for 1944 additional hours of instruction in order to attain the rank of the Bronze Standard, thence to the bracket of the Silver Standard, thence to the class of the Gold Bar Standard, and finally to the crowning plateau of a Life Member of the Studio, proceeded as much or more from the urge to "ring the cash register" as from any honest or realistic appraisal of her dancing prowess or a factual representation of her progress.

Even in contractual situations where a party to a transaction owes no duty to disclose facts within his knowledge or to answer inquiries respecting such facts, the law is if he undertakes to do so he must disclose the *whole truth*. From the face of the complaint, it should have been reasonably apparent to defendants that her vast outlay of cash for the many hundreds of additional hours of instruction was not justified by her slow and awkward progress, which she would have been made well aware of if they had spoken the "whole truth." . . .

We repeat that where parties are dealing on a contractual basis at arm's length with no inequities or inherently unfair practices employed, the Courts will in general "leave the parties where they find themselves." But in the case sub judice, from the allegations of the unanswered complaint, . . . plaintiff is entitled to her day in Court.

---

* It is by no means a forgone conclusion that the defendant's actions in *Vokes* constituted misrepresentation. In *Parker v. Arthur Murray, Inc.*, 295 N.E.2d 487, 490 (Ill. App. Ct. 1973), a remarkably similar case involving similar representations made to a youngish (37-year-old) man rather than an elderly woman, the Appellate Court of Illinois affirmed the trial court's dismissal of plaintiff's fraud count, noting that:

> Generally, a mere expression of opinion will not support an action for fraud. (I.L.P. Fraud § 8.) In addition, misrepresentations, in order to constitute actionable fraud, must pertain to present or pre-existing facts, rather than to future or contingent events, expectations or probabilities. (Hayes v. Disque, 401 Ill. 479, 82 N.E.2d 350.) Whether particular language constitutes speculation, opinion or averment of fact depends upon all the attending facts and circumstances of the case. (Buttitta v. Lawrence, 346 Ill. 164, 178 N.E.2d 390.) Mindful of these rules, and after carefully considering the representations made to plaintiff, and taking into account the business relationship of the parties as well as the educational background of plaintiff, we conclude that the instructors' representations did not constitute fraud. The trial court correctly dismissed Count II. We affirm.

It accordingly follows that the order dismissing plaintiff's last amended complaint with prejudice should be and is reversed.

Reversed.

RELEVANT PROVISIONS

For the *Restatement (Second) of Contracts,* consult § 168.

NOTES AND QUESTIONS

1. *What happened?* Who sued whom for what? Procedurally, how did the case get before this court? Factually, what happened between the parties? What arguments did the plaintiff and defendant make? What rule or rules did the court apply? How did the court analyze the dispute between the parties? How did the court decide the case? Be careful here. What, exactly, is the court's holding? Did the court hold that the defendant made misrepresentations to the plaintiff?

2. *Was this case correctly decided?* Do you agree with the result reached in this case? Why or why not? Do you agree with the court's reasoning? Why or why not? How, if at all, would you have written the opinion differently?

3. *Opinion as "fact."* According to the court, when can statements of opinion be treated as assertions of fact? Do you agree with this approach? Why or why not?

4. *Counseling.* What *should* the Arthur Murray Studios have done when approached by the dancer about her progress? What would you have advised them to do?

5. *Not one of a kind.* Unfortunately, this case was not unique. For a strikingly similar case involving strikingly similar parties, see *Syester v. Banta,* 133 N.W.2d 666 (1965). Like *Vokes,* the plaintiff in that case was "a lonely and elderly widow who fell for the blandishments and flattery of those who saw some 'easy money' available." And, like *Vokes,* the defendant was the Arthur Murray Dance Studio, but this time the case involved a branch in Des Moines, Iowa.

Swinton v. Whitinsville Savings Bank

Supreme Judicial Court of Massachusetts
42 N.E.2d 808 (1942)

Action by Neil W. Swinton against Whitinsville Savings Bank to recover damages for alleged fraudulent concealment by defendant in sale of a house to plaintiff. From an order sustaining a demurrer to plaintiff's declaration, the plaintiff appeals.

Order sustaining demurrer affirmed, and judgment entered for defendant.

QUA, JUSTICE. The declaration alleges that on or about September 12, 1938, the defendant sold the plaintiff a house in Newton to be occupied by the plaintiff and his family as a dwelling; that at the time of the sale the house "was infested with termites, an insect that is most dangerous and destructive to buildings"; that the defendant knew the house was so infested; that the plaintiff could not readily observe this condition upon inspection; that "knowing the internal destruction that these insects were creating in said house," the defendant falsely and fraudulently concealed from the plaintiff its true condition; that the plaintiff at the time of his purchase had no knowledge of the termites, exercised due care thereafter, and learned of them about August 30, 1940; and that, because of the destruction that was being done and the dangerous condition that was being created by the termites, the plaintiff was put to great expense for repairs and for the installation of termite control in order to prevent the loss and destruction of said house.

There is no allegation of any false statement or representation, or of the uttering of a half truth which may be tantamount to a falsehood. There is no intimation that the defendant by any means prevented the plaintiff from acquiring information as to the condition of the house. There is nothing to show any fiduciary relation between the parties, or that the plaintiff stood in a position of confidence toward or dependence upon the defendant. So far as appears the parties made a business deal at arm's length. The charge is concealment and nothing more; and it is concealment in the simple sense of mere failure to reveal, with nothing to show any peculiar duty to speak. The characterization of the concealment as false and fraudulent of course adds nothing in the absence of further allegations of fact.

If this defendant is liable on this declaration every seller is liable who fails to disclose any nonapparent defect known to him in the subject of the sale which materially reduces its value and which the buyer fails to discover. Similarly it would seem that every buyer would be liable who fails to disclose any nonapparent virtue known to him in the subject of the purchase which materially enhances its value and of which the seller is ignorant. The law has not yet, we believe, reached the point of imposing upon the frailties of human nature a standard so idealistic as this. That the particular case here stated by the plaintiff possesses a certain appeal to the moral sense is scarcely to be denied. Probably the reason is to be found in the facts that the infestation of buildings by termites has not been common in Massachusetts and constitutes a concealed risk against which buyers are off their guard. But the law cannot provide special rules for termites and can hardly attempt to determine liability according to the varying probabilities of the existence and discovery of different possible defects in the subjects of trade. . . .

The order sustaining the demurrer is affirmed, and judgment is to be entered for the defendant.

So ordered.

RELEVANT PROVISIONS

For the *Restatement (Second) of Contracts*, consult §§ 159 and 161. For the *Restatement (Second) of Torts*, consult § 551.

NOTES AND QUESTIONS

1. ***What happened?*** Who sued whom for what? Procedurally, how did the case get before this court? Factually, what happened between the parties? What arguments did the plaintiff and defendant make? What rule or rules did the court apply? How did the court analyze the dispute between the parties? How did the court decide the case?

2. ***Was this case correctly decided?*** Do you agree with the result reached in this case? Why or why not? Do you agree with the court's reasoning? Why or why not? How, if at all, would you have written the opinion differently?

3. Caveat emptor? As we shall see in the next case, the principle of caveat emptor (or "let the buyer beware") animating *Swinton* has increasingly come under attack by the courts during the twentieth century, and its scope has been substantially reduced. Before reading the next case, brainstorm for a moment and try to come up with the best arguments for and against a default rule of caveat emptor. What are the merits of such a rule, and what are its drawbacks? When you buy a product from a merchant, do you think it should be the merchant's responsibility to sell you a non-defective product, or your responsibility to discover any possible defects? Which approach would make the most sense in light of some of the thinking tools we have previously examined? Then, as you read the next case, compare your logic to the court's logic. Does the rule it articulates make sense? Why or why not? Can you think of any way to improve the rule?

Obde v. Schlemeyer

Supreme Judicial Court of Washington
353 P.2d 672 (1960)

FINLEY, JUDGE. Plaintiffs, Mr. and Mrs. Fred Obde, brought this action to recover damages for the alleged fraudulent concealment of termite infestation in an apartment house purchased by them from the defendants, Mr. and Mrs. Robert Schlemeyer. Plaintiffs assert that the building was infested at the time of the purchase; that defendants were well apprised of the termite condition, but fraudulently concealed it from the plaintiffs.

After a trial on the merits, the trial court entered findings of fact and conclusions of law sustaining the plaintiffs' claim, and awarded them a judgment for damages in the amount of $3,950. The defendants appealed. Their assignments of error may be compartmentalized, roughly, into two categories: (1)

those going to the question of liability, and (2) those relating to the amount of damages to be awarded if liability is established.

First, as to the question of liability: The Schlemeyers concede that, shortly after they purchased the property from a Mr. Ayars on an installment contract in April 1954, they discovered substantial termite infestation in the premises. The Schlemeyers contend, however, that they immediately took steps to eradicate the termites, and that, at the time of the sale to the Obdes in November 1954, they had no reason to believe that these steps had not completely remedied the situation. We are not convinced of the merit of this contention.

The record reveals that when the Schlemeyers discovered the termite condition they engaged the services of a Mr. Senske, a specialist in pest control. He effected some measures to eradicate the termites, and made some repairs in the apartment house. Thereafter, there was no easily apparent or surface evidence of termite damage. However, portions of the findings of fact entered by the trial court read as follows:

> Senske had advised Schlemeyer that in order to obtain a complete job it would be necessary to drill the holes and pump the fluid into all parts of the basement floors as well as the basement walls. Part of the basement was used as a basement apartment. Senske informed Schlemeyer that the floors should be taken up in the apartment and the cement flooring under the wood floors should be treated in the same manner as the remainder of the basement. Schlemeyer did not care to go to the expense of tearing up the floors to do this and therefore this portion of the basement was not treated.
>
> Senske also told Schlemeyer even though the job were done completely, including treating the portion of the basement which was occupied by the apartment, to be sure of success, it would be necessary to make inspections regularly for a period of a year. Until these inspections were made for this period of time the success of the process could not be determined. Considering the job was not completed as mentioned, Senske would give Schlemeyer no assurance of success and advised him that he would made no guarantee under the circumstances.

No error has been assigned to the above findings of fact. Consequently, they will be considered as the established facts of the case. The pattern thus established is hardly compatible with the Schlemeyers' claim that they had no reason to believe that their efforts to remedy the termite condition were not completely successful.

The Schlemeyers urge that, in any event, as sellers, they had no duty to inform the Obdes of the termite condition. They emphasize that it is undisputed that the purchasers asked no questions respecting the possibility of termites. They rely on a Massachusetts case involving a substantially similar factual situation, *Swinton v. Whitinsville Savings Bank*, 42 N.E.2d 808 (1942). Applying the traditional doctrine of *caveat emptor*—namely, that, as between parties dealing at arms length (as vendor and purchaser), there is no duty to speak, in the absence of a request for information—the Massachusetts court held that a vendor of real property has no duty to disclose to a prospective purchaser the fact of a latent termite condition in the premises.

Without doubt, the parties in the instant case were dealing at arms length. Nevertheless, and notwithstanding the reasoning of the Massachusetts court above noted, we are convinced that the defendants had a duty to inform the plaintiffs of the termite condition. In *Perkins v. Marsh*, 37 P.2d 689, 690 (1934), a case involving parties dealing at arms length as landlord and tenant, we held that,

> Where there are concealed defects in demised premises, dangerous to the property, health, or life of the tenant, which defects are known to the landlord when the lease is made, but unknown to the tenant, and which a careful examination on his part would not disclose, it is the landlord's duty to disclose them to the tenant before leasing, and his failure to do so amounts to a fraud.

We deem this rule to be equally applicable to the vendor-purchaser relationship. *See*, Keeton: *Fraud—Concealment and Non-Disclosure*, 15 TEX. LAW REVIEW 1, 14-16 (1936). In this article Professor Keeton also aptly summarized the modern judicial trend away from a strict application of *caveat emptor* by saying:

> It is of course apparent that the content of the maxim "caveat emptor," used in its broader meaning of imposing risks on both parties to a transaction, has been greatly limited since its origin. When Lord Cairns stated in Peek v. Gurney that there was no duty to disclose facts, however morally censurable their non-disclosure may be, he was stating the law as shaped by an individualistic philosophy based upon freedom of contract. It was not concerned with morals. In the present stage of the law, the decisions show a drawing away from this idea, and there can be seen an attempt by many courts to reach a just result in so far as possible, but yet maintaining the degree of certainty which the law must have. The statement may often be found that if either party to a contract of sale conceals or suppresses a material fact which he is in good faith bound to disclose then his silence is fraudulent.
>
> The attitude of the courts toward non-disclosure is undergoing a change and contrary to Lord Cairns' famous remark it would seem that the object of the law in these cases should be to impose on parties to the transaction a duty to speak whenever justice, equity, and fair dealing demand it. (page 31.)

A termite infestation of a frame building, such at that involved in the instant case, is manifestly a serious and dangerous condition. One of the Schlemeyers' own witnesses, Mr. Hoefer, who at the time was a building inspector for the city of Spokane, testified that ". . . if termites are not checked in their damage, they can cause a complete collapse of a building, . . . they would simply eat up the wood." Further, at the time of the sale of the premises, the condition was clearly latent—not readily observable upon reasonable inspection. As we have noted, all superficial or surface evidence of the condition had been removed by reason of the efforts of Senske, the pest control specialist. Under the circumstances, we are satisfied that "justice, equity, and fair dealing," to use Professor Keeton's language, demanded that the Schlemeyers speak—that they inform prospective purchasers, such as the Obdes, of the condition, regardless of the latter's failure to ask any questions relative to the possibility of termites. . . .

Schlemeyers' final contentions, relating to the issue of liability, emphasize the Obdes' conduct after they discovered the termite condition. Under the purchase agreement with the Schlemeyers, the Obdes paid $5,000 in cash, and gave their promissory note for $2,250 to the Schlemeyers. In addition, they assumed the balance due on the installment contract, under which the Schlemeyers had previously acquired the property from Ayars. This amounted to $34,750. After they discovered the termites (some six weeks subsequent to taking possession of the premises in November 1954), the Obdes continued for a time to make payments on the Ayars contract. They then called in Senske to examine the condition—not knowing that he had previously worked on the premises at the instance of the Schlemeyers. From Senske the Obdes learned for the first time that the Schlemeyers had known of the termite infestation prior to the sale. Obdes then ceased performance of the Ayars contract, and allowed the property to revert to Ayars under a forfeiture provision in the installment contract.

The Schlemeyers contend that by continuing to make payments on the Ayars contract after they discovered the termites the Obdes waived any right to recovery for fraud. This argument might have some merit if the Obdes were seeking to rescind the purchase contract. However, this is not an action for rescission; it is a suit for damages, and thus is not barred by conduct constituting an affirmance of the contract.

Contrary to the Schlemeyers['] final argument relative to the question of liability, the Obdes' ultimate default and forfeiture on the Ayars contract does not constitute a bar to the present action. The rule governing this issue is well stated in 24 Am. Jur. 39, *Fraud and Deceit,* § 212, as follows:

> Since the action of fraud or deceit in inducing the entering into a contract or procuring its execution is not based upon the contract, but is independent thereof, although it is regarded as an affirmance of the contract, it is a general rule that a vendee is entitled to maintain an action against the vendor for fraud or deceit in the transaction even though he has not complied with all the duties imposed upon him by the contract. His default is not a bar to an action by him for fraud or deceit practiced by the vendor in regard to some matter relative to the contract.

For the reasons hereinbefore set forth, we hold that the trial court committed no error in determining that the respondents (Obdes) were entitled to recover damages against the appellants (Schlemeyers) upon the theory of fraudulent concealment. However, there remains the question of the proper amount of damages to be awarded. The trial court found that,

> . . . because of the termite condition the value [of the premises] has been reduced to the extent of $3950.00 and the plaintiffs have been damaged to that extent, and in that amount.

As hereinbefore noted, judgment was thereupon entered for the respondents in that amount.

The appellants concede that the measure of damages in a case of this type is the difference between the actual value of the property and what the property would have been worth had the misrepresentations been true. However, they urge that the only evidence introduced to show the diminution in value of the premises on account of the termite condition—namely, the testimony of one Joseph P. Wieber—was incompetent. Wieber qualified as an expert witness on the basis of substantial experience as a realtor and appraiser. He examined the premises in question, and estimated that the termite condition had reduced the value of the property by some thirty per cent. Applying this estimate to an assumption (as posed in a hypothetical question propounded by respondents' counsel) that the property had been purchased twice during the year 1954 by persons who were unaware of the termite condition for approximately $40,000, Wieber rendered an opinion that the actual value of the premises (taking into account the termite condition) was about $25,000.

Appellants' sole objection to Wieber's testimony is based upon a claim that the facts (two purchases in 1954 for approximately $40,000, by persons who were unaware of the termite condition) supporting the hypothetical question were never supplied. We find no merit in this claim. The record fully discloses the two purchases in question: namely, the Obdes' purchase from the Schlemeyers in November 1954; and the Schlemeyers' purchase from Ayars in April 1954.

The judgment awarding damages of $3,950 is well within the limits of the testimony in the record relating to damages. The Obdes have not cross-appealed. The judgment of the trial court should be affirmed in all respects. It is so ordered.

NOTES AND QUESTIONS

1. ***What happened?*** Who sued whom for what? Procedurally, how did the case get before this court? Factually, what happened between the parties? What arguments did the plaintiff and defendant make? What rule or rules did the court apply? How did the court analyze the dispute between the parties? How did the court decide the case?

2. ***Was this case correctly decided?*** Do you agree with the result reached in this case? Why or why not? Do you agree with the court's reasoning? Why or why not? How, if at all, would you have written the opinion differently?

3. Caveat emptor. Latin for "let the buyer beware." Despite its epigrammatic quality and ostensible ancient pedigree, however, it is neither a rule of law (except when explicitly adopted as such by courts), nor, according to one author, of a very distinguished lineage, only really coming into its own as a principle affecting (or infecting) contract law in the nineteenth century. *See* Walton H. Hamilton, *The Ancient Maxim Caveat Emptor,* 40 YALE L.J. 1133 (1931).

4. ***Reconciled?*** Do you think this case and the previous case can be reconciled? If not, which approach towards nondisclosure do you most agree with,

and why? Do either of the following excerpts offer any assistance in thinking about such issues?

As we have seen in a few other places in this casebook, many of the legal problems we struggle with today were grappled with long ago by the ancient Romans, who possessed a sophisticated understanding of the arguments that could be made on both sides of an issue. In the fascinating excerpt below, Cicero, the famous orator, philosopher, and statesman, struggles with two separate but related problems of non-disclosure, the first bearing a striking resemblance to the facts in Laidlaw v. Organ, *and the second bearing an uncanny similarity to both* Swinton *and* Obde. *As you read the excerpt, ask yourself (a) how Cicero would resolve these problems, (b) how our current law would resolve them, and (c) how you think they should be resolved, and why.*

HISTORICAL PERSPECTIVE: THE ROMANS WERE HERE FIRST*

12 . . . [S]uppose . . . a time of dearth and famine at Rhodes, with provisions at fabulous prices; and suppose that an honest man has imported a large cargo of grain from Alexandria and that to his certain knowledge also several other importers have set sail from Alexandria, and that on the voyage he has sighted their vessels laden with grain and bound for Rhodes; is he to report the fact to the Rhodians or is he to keep his own counsel and sell his own stock at the highest market price? I am assuming the case of a virtuous, upright man, and I am raising the question how a man would think and reason who would not conceal the facts from the Rhodians if he thought that it was immoral to do so, but who might be in doubt whether such silence would really be immoral.

In deciding cases of this kind Diogenes of Babylonia, a great and highly esteemed Stoic, consistently holds one view; his pupil Antipater, a most profound scholar, holds another. According to Antipater all the facts should be disclosed, that the buyer may not be uninformed of any detail that the seller knows; according to Diogenes the seller should declare any defects in his wares, in so far as such a course is prescribed by the common law of the land; but for the rest, since he has goods to sell, he may try to sell them to the best possible advantage, provided he is guilty of no misrepresentation.

"I have imported my stock," Diogenes's merchant will say; "I have offered it for sale; I sell at a price no higher than my competitors—perhaps even lower, when the market is overstocked. Who is wronged?"

"What say you?" comes Antipater's argument on the other side; "it is your duty to consider the interests of your fellow-men and to serve society; you were brought into the world under these conditions and have these inborn principles which you are in duty bound to obey and follow, that your interest shall be the

* Excerpted from Marcus Tullius Cicero, De Officiis, Book III, §§ 12-13, *translated by* Walter Miller (1913).

interest of the community and conversely that the interest of the community shall be your interest as well; will you, in view of all these facts, conceal from your fellow-men what relief in plenteous supplies is close at hand for them?"

"It is one thing to conceal," Diogenes will perhaps reply; "not to reveal is quite a different thing. At this present moment I am not concealing from you, even if I am not revealing to you, the nature of the gods or the highest good; and to know these secrets would be of more advantage to you than to know that the price of wheat was down. But I am under no obligation to tell you everything that it may be to your interest to be told."

"Yea," Antipater will say, "but you are, as you must admit, if you will only bethink you of the bonds of fellowship forged by Nature and existing between man and man."

"I do not forget them," the other will reply; "but do you mean to say that those bonds of fellowship are such that there is no such thing as private property? If that is the case, we should not sell anything at all, but freely give everything away."

13. In this whole discussion, you see, no one says, "However wrong morally this or that may be, still, since it is expedient, I will do it"; but the one side asserts that a given act is expedient, without being morally wrong, while the other insists that the act should not be done, because it is morally wrong.

Suppose again that an honest man is offering a house for sale on account of certain undesirable features of which he himself is aware but which nobody else knows; suppose it is unsanitary, but has the reputation of being healthful; suppose it is not generally known that vermin are to be found in all the bedrooms; suppose, finally, that it is built of unsound timber and likely to collapse, but that no one knows about it except the owner; if the vendor does not tell the purchaser these facts but sells him the house for far more than he could reasonably have expected to get for it, I ask whether his transaction is unjust or dishonorable.

"Yes," says Antipater, "it is; for to allow a purchaser to be hasty in closing a deal and through mistaken judgment to incur a very serious loss, if this is not refusing 'to set a man right when he has lost his way' (a crime which at Athens is prohibited on pain of public execration), what is? It is even worse than refusing to set a man on his way: it is deliberately leading a man astray."

"Can you say," answers Diogenes, "that he compelled you to purchase, when he did not even advise it? He advertised for sale what he did not like; you bought what you did like. If people are not considered guilty of swindling when they place upon their placards FOR SALE: A FINE VILLA, WELL BUILT, even when it is neither good nor properly built, still less guilty are they who say nothing in praise of their house. For where the purchaser may exercise his own judgment, what fraud can there be on the part of the vendor? But if, again, not all that is expressly stated has to be made good, do you think a man is bound to make good what has not been said? What, pray, would be more stupid than for a vendor to recount all the faults in the article he is offering for sale? And what would be so absurd as for an auctioneer to cry, at the owner's bidding, 'Here is an unsanitary house for sale'?"

In this way, then, in certain doubtful cases moral rectitude is defended on the one side, while on the other side the case of expediency is so presented as to make it appear not only morally right to do what seems expedient, but even morally wrong not to do it. This is the contradiction that seems often to arise between the expedient and the morally right. But I must give my decision in these two cases; for I did not propound them merely to raise the questions, but to offer a solution.

I think, then, that it was the duty of that grain-dealer not to keep back the facts from the Rhodians, and of this vendor of the house to deal in the same way with his purchaser. The fact is that merely holding one's peace about a thing does not constitute concealment, but concealment consists in trying for your own profit to keep others from finding out something that you know, when it is for their interest to know it. And who fails to discern what manner of concealment that is and what sort of person would be guilty of it? At all events he would be no candid or sincere or straightforward or upright or honest man, but rather one who is shifty, sly, artful, shrewd, underhand, cunning, one grown old in fraud and subtlety. Is it not inexpedient to subject oneself to all these terms of reproach and many more besides?

HONESTY IN FACT*

The Uniform Commercial Code defines good faith as honesty in fact. On the face of it honesty has nothing to do with sharing, with altruism, or with an active concern for one's fellow man. An honest man may drive a hard bargain, but does so openly, candidly. It might be said that honesty is the virtue most closely associated with classical individualism, and with the principle of autonomy: If a person is well informed and in secure enjoyment of his rights, then whatever arrangements he chooses to make deserve to be honored. They represent a free man's rational decision about how to dispose of what is his, how to bind himself. The quintessence of honesty is the Victorian gentleman, who though rigid, perhaps ungenerous, a hard bargainer, keeps his word and does not lie. Honesty assures, first, that one will not mislead another as to the facts in order to profit by the other's misinformed decision. It assures also that engagements once made will be honored. Good faith as honesty may be viewed as a manifestation of the liberal belief in the objectivity of facts, in individual autonomy, and in the importance of keeping one's word.

Consider the leading case of *Obde v. Schlemeyer*. The seller knew that his house was infested by termites, and knew also that he had done no more by way of treatment than to cover up and repair all visible signs of that infestation. The buyer had not, however, asked about termites, nor had the seller given any assurances about the condition of his house. Nevertheless a court held that the buyer had been defrauded and awarded him damages for the losses he had suffered.

What are we to say of this case? The seller certainly acted dishonestly, and if Schlemeyer had told an outright lie neither lawyer nor moralist would have the least difficulty with the case. Lying is wrong, and thus it is an inadmissible way of

* Excerpted from CHARLES FRIED, CONTRACT AS PROMISE 64-66 (1981).

procuring an advantage. . . . A liar seeks to accomplish his purpose by creating a false belief in his interlocutor, and so he may be said to do harm by touching the mind, as an assailant does harm by laying hands on his victim's body. Further, a liar procures this advantage by preying on the other person's trust, for it is only by invoking the expectation of truthfulness that the lie does its work. This vice is compounded when the lie does its work in the context of a promise. A simple lie does harm because it is believed; a lie that is believed and so elicits the victim's promise does harm only if that promise is enforced. But to enforce the promise is to invoke *against the victim* the very morality of respect and trust that the liar betrayed in eliciting the promise. . . .

So lying is an easy case, but did Schlemeyer lie? He appears to have done "no more" than fail to disclose information he knew would be very helpful to the buyer. One can lie otherwise than in words. Schlemeyer covered up (literally) the traces of termite infestation, knowing that this would create a wrong impression on the buyer and surely intending that it should. Is this a lie? The critics of the conception of contract as promise argue that the concept of fraud is unstable, that it cannot be limited to some analytically defined or intuitively clear domain of clearly wrongful conduct, that it inevitably implies a duty to share information, which in turn inevitably admits a duty to share advantages in general. The *Obde* case might be thought to be the first step down this slippery slope to a general duty of sharing.

Consider this case:

> I. An oil company has made extensive geological surveys seeking to identify possible oil and gas reserves. These surveys are extremely expensive. Having identified one promising site, the oil company (acting through a broker) buys a large tract of land from its prosperous farmer owner, revealing nothing about its survey, its purposes, or even its identity. The price paid is the going price for farmland of that quality in that region.

Is the purchaser's conduct here different from the seller's in *Obde*? Should we hold the seller here to his promise to sell the land, as we would *not* hold the buyer in *Obde*? Would it be correct to say that the purchaser deceived the seller? Unlike Schlemeyer, the oil company studiously avoided deceiving the farmer. It did not send its agent around dressed in overalls and chewing on a straw. Its inquiries were placed through a broker known to be acting for an unidentified purchaser. Now as a general matter the prohibition on lying can hardly entail a general duty to remove all instances of ignorance and error that might swim within your reach; you do no greater wrong if you fail to remove a stranger's error than if you fail to go out of your way to relieve some other unfulfilled want of a random stranger. If in Columbus, Ohio, there is a child who would be made happier if presented with an ice cream cone, this makes no moral claim upon you. . . . You did not cause the distress; you are not using it for your purposes—and so also you did not cause the ignorance. The distress and the ignorance of themselves make no generalized claim on all those who might possibly relieve them. In hypothetical case I, however, the oil company is not simply failing to relieve distress, not simply failing officiously to remove ignorance, it is making that ignorance the means by which it achieves its ends, increases its profits.

NOTES AND QUESTIONS

1. *Lying.* In the excerpt above, Fried argues that lying is wrong, and that courts should not allow a party to procure an advantage by doing so. Do you agree? If so, do you think that a failure to disclose is equivalent to lying, or does the answer depend on the circumstances? If the latter, which ones? Even if you agree with Fried that lying is wrong and should be forbidden, how can you tell what constitutes a lie? Or is this even the right test? Can it help us resolve *Swinton* or *Obde*? Can it help us resolve Fried's oil company hypothetical?

2. Swinton *versus* Obde. The *Swinton* court placed the risk of nondisclosure on the buyer, and the *Obde* court placed it on the seller. Can these cases be reconciled, or do they represent two fundamentally different approaches to the problem of nondisclosure? If you think they can be reconciled, how? If not, then which case was correctly decided, and why?

3. *Risk allocation.* At their core, *Swinton* and *Obde* are about how courts should allocate the risk of nondisclosure. A court's choices are: (1) always require a party with superior information to disclose that information, (2) never require a party with superior information to disclose that information, or (3) find a method of determining the circumstances in which disclosure is required. The third approach, it turns out, is very tricky, and courts and scholars have devoted much attention to identifying the circumstances in which disclosure is required. Can you think of a workable approach? Professor Keeton, who was cited extensively in *Obde*, suggests one approach to this problem in the excerpt below. As you read it, ask yourself if his approach is workable? Which factors, if any, do you think courts should consider, and why? Are there any other factors you think important that Professor Keeton did not mention?

FRAUD—CONCEALMENT AND NON-DISCLOSURE*

[We should test the propriety of a party's conduct not by asking whether remaining silent was ethical], but [by asking] what the man of ordinary moral sensibilities would have done; would he have disclosed the information or would he have remained silent? . . .

[To know whether "the man of ordinary moral sensibilities would . . . have disclosed the information or . . . remained silent," a number of factors should be taken into consideration by the court, including]:

(1) The difference in the degree of intelligence of the parties to the transaction. If one possesses more than the normal amount of intelligence, whereas the other is unusually ignorant, that circumstance tends to impose a greater duty of disclosure on the intelligent party. This is simply because our sense of justice demands it.

---

* Excerpted from W. Page Keeton, *Fraud—Concealment and Non-Disclosure,* 15 TEX. L. REV. 1, 32, 34-37 (1936).

(2) The relation that the parties bear to each other. . . . [I]f A and B are friends, should not B be entitled to require a fuller disclosure than would be the case where A and B are rivals and bitter enemies?

(3) The manner in which the information is acquired. . . . [I]nformation which affects the value of the subject-matter of the contract may have been acquired by chance, by effort, or by an illegal act. If, in any of these cases, a duty of disclosure exists, it should be in the last instance. . . . Where, however, the buyer has gained the knowledge or information as a result of his bringing to bear the skill and experience acquired by diligent effort, no one would contend that a duty of disclosure should always exist.

(4) The nature of the fact not disclosed. For example, in contracts of sale, if the vendor conceals an intrinsic defect in the property sold, there is a much greater likelihood of the existence of a duty to speak than where the circumstance not disclosed, is extrinsic. . . .

(5) The general class to which the person who is concealing the information belongs. Was he a buyer, or was he a seller? The buyer is not ordinarily expected to disclose information greatly affecting the value of the property which is the subject-matter of the sale, whereas the seller is expected to disclose defects in the property sold which greatly decrease the value of the property.

(6) The nature of the contract itself. . . .

(7) The materiality of the fact not disclosed. In contracts of sale, a proper inquiry would be whether the defect concealed by the vendor was a minor one or one of a serious nature. . . .

(8) The type of damage which the ignorant person will, or is likely to, suffer from a non-disclosure. If the only injury that will probably result from a non-disclosure is an economic loss resulting from the fact that the ignorant person will receive less of value than what he gave in return, there is not as great a likelihood of a duty to speak as where personal injury is likely to result from the non-disclosure.

(9) Finally, the conduct of the person with knowledge of the fact not disclosed. Has he by his affirmative conduct prevented the other person from discovering what otherwise would have been obvious? This brings up the cases of active concealment. There should be a greater duty of disclosing what a person has hidden by his own conduct, than there is where the fact was hidden without his connivance, and certainly this is the law. The active concealment of anything that might prevent the purchaser from buying at the price agreed on, is, and should be, as a matter of law fraudulent.

PROBLEM: A ROACH-INFESTED HOME

For the past five years, Seller Sally owned and occupied a house that she placed in the hands of a real estate broker for sale. Peter was interested in purchasing the home, examined it while it was illuminated and found it suitable. On June 30, 2011, Sally, as seller, and Peter, as the purchaser, entered into a contract for the sale of the property for $425,000. The contract provided that the purchaser had inspected the property and was fully satisfied with its physical condition, that no representations had been made and that no responsibility was assumed by the seller as to the present or future condition of the premises. A deposit of $42,500 was sent by the Peter to the broker to be held in escrow pending the closing of the transaction. Peter requested that the seller have the house fumigated and that was done.

During the evening of August 25, 2011, prior to closing, Peter entered the house, then unoccupied, and as he turned the lights on he was astonished to see roaches literally running in all directions, up the walls, drapes, etc. On the following day his attorney wrote a letter to Sally advising her that on the previous day "it was discovered that the house is infested with vermin despite the fact that an exterminator has only recently serviced the house" and asserting that "the presence of vermin in such great quantities, particularly after the exterminator was done, rendered the house as unfit for human habitation at this time and therefore, the contract is rescinded." On September 2, 2011 an exterminator wrote to Sally advising her that he had examined the premises and that "cockroaches were found to have infested the entire house." The exterminator said he could eliminate them for a relatively modest charge by two treatments with a twenty-one day interval but that it would be necessary to remove the carpeting "to properly treat all the infested areas."

Peter seeks rescission, claiming fraudulent concealment or nondisclosure by the seller as the basis for their rescission. Specifically, Peter points out that every time he inspected the house prior to discovering the infestation, every light in the place was turned on, with the consequence that, because roaches are nocturnal by nature, keeping the lights on kept them out of sight. Peter further points out that Sally had to know she had this problem, as she could not possibly have lived in a house this infested without knowing about it. Sally rejected the rescission by the purchasers and sought damages in the sum of $42,500, representing the deposit held in escrow by the broker.

Drawing on the cases and materials presented above, how do you think this case should be resolved?

Before reading the excerpt below, you may wish to review "Thinking Tool: Thinking Clearly About Legal Relationships" at p. 96, supra.

THINKING TOOL APPLIED: ON REGULATION*

At first glance, in might appear that, in moving from Swinton *to* Obde, *our society has moved from a non-regulatory to a regulatory regime. Indeed, this is a*

* Excerpted from Curtis Nyquist, *Teaching Wesley Hohfeld's Theory of Legal Relations*, 52 J. LEGAL EDUC. 238, 254-55 (2002).

common way of thinking, both in popular culture and (less excusably) in the legal world itself, but, strictly speaking, this is wrong. If you recall our earlier discussion of Hohfeld's fundamental legal relationships, then you will recall that a court must always choose between two different methods of regulating the presently-existing relationship between two parties: It can regulate it with a right/duty relationship or with a privilege/no-right relationship. There are no other choices. Seen in this light, it becomes clear that the choice between Swinton *and* Obde *is not a choice between non-regulation and regulation, but a choice about how the parties' relationship should be governed, as explained more fully in the short excerpt below.*

Hohfeld created a semiotic system with the four legal relations enjoying coequal status and terms deriving meaning from their correlatives and opposites. Privilege, for example, is the correlative of no-right and the opposite of duty. Power is the correlative of liability and the opposite of disability. And so on. The consequences of this system for classical analytical jurisprudence were profound. The classics focused on privilege and duty. Hohfeld demonstrated that they were discussing opposite ends of two different legal relations. The classics defined law as the command of the sovereign. Hohfeld's system pointed out (in Corbin's words) "that society not only commands, but also *permits* and *enables* and *disables*."[70] The classics viewed rights as fundamental. Hohfeld demoted rights to the status of a correlative and an opposite. The classics deduced duties from privileges and from injury. Hohfeld exposed the logical errors underlying this system.

Furthermore, Hohfeld's work was fundamental to the progressive/realist critique of the formalist notion that laissez faire was not a regulatory system. "A rule of law that *permits* is just as real as a rule of law that *forbids*."[71] In other words, privilege/no-right and right/duty are both legal relations. In a sale of goods by a merchant, for example, the late-nineteenth-century rule of caveat emptor (no implied warranty of quality) has now been replaced by an implied warranty of merchantability.[73] But in these transactions we have not moved from an unregulated to a regulated market; we have merely changed how we regulate. The choice between imposing liability on a merchant seller for defective goods or allowing the loss to fall on the buyer is not a choice between having a policy and not having a policy. It is a choice of which policy to have.

Before reading the excerpt below, you may wish to review "Thinking Tool: Thinking Clearly About Legal Relationships" at p. 96, supra. *What light, if any, does the following thinking tool shed on the problem of the duty to disclose?*

70. Arthur L. Corbin, Jural Relations and Their Classification, 30 Yale L.J. 226, 237 (1921). . . .
71. Wesley Newcomb Hohfeld, *Some Fundamental Legal Conceptions as Applied in Judicial Reasoning*, 23 YALE L.J. 16, 42 n.59 (1913).
73. U.C.C. § 2-314 (1999).

THINKING TOOL: BASELINES*

"Doing nothing" is one of those expressions like "leaving people alone" that requires a baseline: we need to know what counts as action and inaction. Many people imagine that the government is doing nothing—is leaving them alone—when they go about their ordinary business: buying and selling things, watching television, and so forth. In a sense they are being left alone, but in a sense they aren't: all their conduct is played out against a background of laws and regulations. The regulations aren't visible most of the time because they create fairly simple boundaries within which those activities take place. But you probably would notice right away if the boundaries weren't there. Someone would steal your television or break a contract with you—or not enter into the contract in the first place because they have no reason to think you will go through with it. The rules of property, contract, and criminal law are a deep part of the state of things that we take for granted, and they are responsible for everyone's ability to walk around feeling unmolested most of the time. They are also a necessary condition for some people amassing large amounts of wealth while others don't end up with as much; for large amounts of wealth usually involve lots of contracts to create, and require protections of the criminal law to be kept secure. Of course we might find similar inequalities—or greater—if those rules didn't exist, but the winners and losers probably would be different. Anyway, the point is that the government is engaged in a certain sort of acting all the time, even if you don't notice.

[W]here does the principle stop? . . . The government is constrained when it acts—but when it "acts" is a hard question. An action is a departure from some state of inaction, but it's hard to find any situation where the government is entirely inactive.

[H]ow *do* we figure out whether the government is "acting" if it isn't as simple as asking whether it is visibly in motion?

In the next case—a playfully written decision with a wonderful set of facts—if the court believed that the seller had no duty to disclose, why did the seller lose the case?

Stambovsky v. Ackley

New York Supreme Court, Appellate Division
572 N.Y.S.2d 672 (1991)

RUBIN, J. Plaintiff, to his horror, discovered that the house he had recently contracted to purchase was widely reputed to be possessed by poltergeists, reportedly seen by defendant seller and members of her family on numerous occasions over the last nine years. Plaintiff promptly commenced this action

* Excerpted from WARD FARNSWORTH, THE LEGAL ANALYST: A TOOLKIT FOR THINKING ABOUT THE LAW 198-204 (2007).

seeking rescission of the contract of sale. Supreme Court reluctantly dismissed the complaint, holding that plaintiff has no remedy at law in this jurisdiction.

The unusual facts of this case, as disclosed by the record, clearly warrant a grant of equitable relief to the buyer who, as a resident of New York City, cannot be expected to have any familiarity with the folklore of the Village of Nyack. Not being a "local," plaintiff could not readily learn that the home he had contracted to purchase is haunted. **Whether the source of the spectral apparitions seen by defendant seller are parapsychic or psychogenic, having reported their presence in both a national publication (Readers' Digest) and the local press (in 1977 and 1982, respectively), defendant is estopped to deny their existence and, as a matter of law, the house is haunted.** More to the point, however, no divination is required to conclude that it is defendant's promotional efforts in publicizing her close encounters with these spirits which fostered the home's reputation in the community. In 1989, the house was included in five-home walking tour of Nyack and described in a November 27th newspaper article as "a riverfront Victorian (with ghost)." The impact of the reputation thus created goes to the very essence of the bargain between the parties, greatly impairing both the value of the property and its potential for resale. The extent of this impairment may be presumed for the purpose of reviewing the disposition of this motion to dismiss the cause of action for rescission and represents merely an issue of fact for resolution at trial.

> ***A legally haunted house?***
>
> How can a house be haunted as a matter of law? The answer lies in the doctrine of equitable estoppel. Just as that doctrine prevented the grandfather's estate in *Ricketts v. Scothorn* from denying that the grandfather's promise to his granddaughter was supported consideration (even though it wasn't), so, too, does that doctrine prevent the defendant in *Stambovsky* from denying that the house is haunted due to earlier representations that it was (even if it isn't).

While I agree with Supreme Court that the real estate broker, as agent for the seller, is under no duty to disclose to a potential buyer the phantasmal reputation of the premises and that, in his pursuit of a legal remedy for fraudulent misrepresentation against the seller, plaintiff hasn't a ghost of a chance, I am nevertheless moved by the spirit of equity to allow the buyer to seek rescission of the contract of sale and recovery of his down payment. New York law fails to recognize any remedy for damages incurred as a result of the seller's mere silence, applying instead the strict rule of caveat emptor. Therefore, the theoretical basis for granting relief, even under the extraordinary facts of this case, is elusive if not ephemeral. "Pity me not but lend thy serious hearing to what I shall unfold." William Shakespeare, *Hamlet,* Act I, Scene V [Ghost].

From the perspective of a person in the position of plaintiff herein, a very practical problem arises with respect to the discovery of a paranormal phenomenon: "Who you gonna' call?" as a title song to the movie "Ghostbusters" asks. Applying the strict rule of caveat emptor to a contract involving a house possessed by poltergeists conjures up visions of a psychic or medium routinely accompanying the structural engineer and Terminix man on an inspection of

> ***An economic argument for disclosure?***
>
> The court is having quite a bit of fun in this paragraph, but, at its heart, is really making an important economic argument against the rule of caveat emptor. Translating the courts language from Ghostese to ordinary English, it is saying something like the following: If

the doctrine of caveat emptor held sway, and buyers weren't let out of contracts where defects later turned up that weren't easily discoverable upon an ordinary inspection, a buyer would be forced to waste precious resources both (a) in its initial inspection of the contracted-for item to discover any potentially hidden defects, and (b) in insurance premiums to protect it against any defects that later turned up. Understood this way, a rule requiring sellers to discover such defects during the initial bargaining stages (by allowing buyers to get out of contracts where they did not) could lead to much greater efficiencies, and, arguably, a rule that is much easier to apply. Notwithstanding these points, is the court being too cute here? Was the fact that the house was haunted ("as a matter of law," in the court's words) *really* as difficult for the buyer to discover as the court suggests?

every home subject to a contract of sale. It portends that the prudent attorney will establish an escrow account lest the subject of the transaction come back to haunt him and his client—or pray that his malpractice insurance coverage extends to supernatural disasters. In the interest of avoiding such untenable consequences, the notion that a haunting is a condition which can and should be ascertained upon reasonable inspection of the premises is a hobgoblin which should be exorcised from the body of legal precedent and laid quietly to rest.

It has been suggested by a leading authority that the ancient rule which holds that mere nondisclosure does not constitute actionable misrepresentation "finds proper application in cases where the fact undisclosed is patent, or the plaintiff has equal opportunities for obtaining information which he may be expected to utilize, or the defendant has no reason to think that he is acting under any misapprehension" (Prosser, *Torts* § 106, at 696 [4th ed. 1971]). However, with respect to transactions in real estate, New York adheres to the doctrine of caveat emptor and imposes no duty upon the vendor to disclose any information concerning the premises unless there is a confidential or fiduciary relationship between the parties or some conduct on the part of the seller which constitutes "active concealment." Normally, some affirmative misrepresentation or partial disclosure is required to impose upon the seller a duty to communicate undisclosed conditions affecting the premises.

Caveat emptor is not so all-encompassing a doctrine of common law as to render every act of nondisclosure immune from redress, whether legal or equitable. . . . Even as a principle of law, long before exceptions were embodied in statute law (*see, e.g.*, UCC §§ 2-312, 2-313, 2-314, 2-315; 3-417(2)(e)), the doctrine was held inapplicable to [a number of cases]. Common law is not moribund. *Ex facto jus oritur* (law arises out of facts). Where fairness and common sense dictate that an exception should be created, the evolution of the law should not be stifled by rigid application of a legal maxim.

The doctrine of caveat emptor requires that a buyer act prudently to assess the fitness and value of his purchase and operates to bar the purchaser who fails to exercise due care from seeking the equitable remedy of rescission. For the purposes of the instant motion to dismiss . . . , plaintiff is entitled to every favorable inference which may reasonably be drawn from the pleadings, specifically, in this instance, that he met his obligation to conduct an inspection of the premises and a search of available public records with respect to title. It should be apparent, however, that the most meticulous inspection and the search would not reveal the presence of poltergeists at the premises or unearth the property's ghoulish reputation in the community. Therefore, there is no sound policy reason to deny plaintiff relief for failing to discover a state of affairs which the most prudent purchaser would not be expected to even contemplate.

The case law in this jurisdiction dealing with the duty of a vendor of real property to disclose information to the buyer is distinguishable from the matter under review. The most salient distinction is that existing cases invariably deal with the physical condition of the premises, defects in title, liens against the property, expenses or income and other factors affecting its operation. No case has been brought to this court's attention in which the property value was impaired as the result of the reputation created by information disseminated to the public by the seller (or, for that matter, as a result of possession by poltergeists).

Where a condition which has been created by the seller materially impairs the value of the contract and is peculiarly within the knowledge of the seller or unlikely to be discovered by a prudent purchaser exercising due care with respect to the subject transaction, nondisclosure constitutes a basis for rescission as a matter of equity. Any other outcome places upon the buyer not merely the obligation to exercise care in his purchase but rather to be omniscient with respect to any fact which may affect the bargain. No practical purpose is served by imposing such a burden upon a purchaser. To the contrary, it encourages predatory business practice and offends the principle that equity will suffer no wrong to be without a remedy.

Defendant's contention that the contract of sale, particularly the merger or "as is" clause, bars recovery of the buyer's deposit is unavailing. Even an express disclaimer will not be given effect where the facts are peculiarly within the knowledge of the party invoking it. Moreover, a fair reading of the merger clause reveals that it expressly disclaims only representations made with respect to the physical condition of the premises and merely makes general reference to representations concerning "any other matter or things affecting or relating to the aforesaid premises". As broad as this language may be, a reasonable interpretation is that its effect is limited to tangible or physical matters and does not extend to paranormal phenomena. Finally, if the language of the contract is to be construed as broadly as defendant urges to encompass the presence of poltergeists in the house, it cannot be said that she has delivered the premises "vacant" in accordance with her obligation under the provisions of the contract rider.

To the extent New York law may be said to require something more than "mere concealment" to apply even the equitable remedy of rescission, the case of *Junius Constr. Corp. v Cohen*, 257 NY 393 (1931) . . . provides some guidance. In that case, the seller disclosed that an official map indicated two as yet unopened streets which were planned for construction at the edges of the parcel. What was not disclosed was that the same map indicated a third street which, if opened, would divide the plot in half. The court held that, while the seller was under no duty to mention the planned streets at all, having undertaken to disclose two of them, he was obliged to reveal the third.

In the case at bar, defendant seller deliberately fostered the public belief that her home was possessed. Having undertaken to inform the public-at-large, to whom she has no legal relationship, about the supernatural occurrences on her property, she may be said to owe no less a duty to her contract vendee. It has been remarked that the occasional modern cases which permit a seller to take unfair advantage of a buyer's ignorance so long as he is not actively misled are "singularly unappetizing" (Prosser, *Torts* § 106, at 696 [4th ed. 1971]). **Where, as here, the seller not only takes unfair advantage of the buyer's ignorance but has created and perpetuated a condition about which he is unlikely to even inquire, enforcement of the contract (in whole or in part) is offensive to the court's sense of equity. Application of the remedy of rescission, within the bounds of the narrow exception to the doctrine of caveat emptor set forth herein, is entirely appropriate to relieve the unwitting purchaser from the consequences of a most unnatural bargain.**

> ***Caveat emptor lives!***
>
> Although the court is willing to invoke the spirit of equity to get around the consequences of the caveat emptor rule, it is unwilling to send this rule to its grave, leaving its specter free to haunt future parties in similar cases who find themselves occupying the unfortunate position of buyer's doppelganger.

Accordingly, the judgment of the [trial court], which dismissed the complaint . . . , should be modified, . . . and the first cause of action seeking rescission of the contract reinstated, without costs.

SMITH, J. (dissenting). I would affirm the dismissal of the complaint by the motion court.

Plaintiff seeks to rescind his contract to purchase defendant Ackley's residential property and recover his down payment. Plaintiff alleges that Ackley and her real estate broker, defendant Ellis Realty, made material misrepresentations of the property in that they failed to disclose that Ackley believed that the house was haunted by poltergeists. Moreover, Ackley shared this belief with her community and the general public through articles published in *Reader's Digest* (1977) and the local newspaper (1982). In November 1989, approximately two months after the parties entered into the contract of sale but subsequent to the scheduled October 2, 1989 closing, the house was included in a five-house walking tour and again described in the local newspaper as being haunted.

Prior to closing, plaintiff learned of this reputation and unsuccessfully sought to rescind the $650,000 contract of sale and obtain return of his $32,500 down payment without resort to litigation. The plaintiff then commenced this action for that relief and alleged that he would not have entered into the contract had he been so advised and that as a result of the alleged poltergeist activity, the market value and resaleability of the property was greatly diminished. Defendant Ackley has counterclaimed for specific performance.

"It is settled law in New York State that the seller of real property is under no duty to speak when the parties deal at arm's length. The mere silence of the seller, without some act or conduct which deceived the purchaser, does not amount to a concealment that is actionable as a fraud. The buyer has the duty to satisfy himself as to the quality of his bargain pursuant to the doctrine of caveat emptor, which in New York State still applies to real estate transactions." (*London v. Courduff*, 141 A.D.2d 803, 804 (1988)).

The parties herein were represented by counsel and dealt at arm's length. This is evidenced by the contract of sale which, *inter alia,* contained various riders and a specific provision that all prior understandings and agreements between the parties were merged into the contract, that the contract completely expressed their full agreement and that neither had relied upon any statement by anyone else not set forth in the contract. There is no allegation that defendants, by some specific act, other than the failure to speak, deceived the plaintiff. Nevertheless, a cause of action may be sufficiently stated where there is a confidential or fiduciary relationship creating a duty to disclose and there was a failure to disclose a material fact, calculated to induce a false belief. However, plaintiff herein has not alleged and there is no basis for concluding that a confidential or fiduciary relationship existed between these parties to an arm's length transaction such as to give rise to a duty to disclose. In addition, there is no allegation that defendants thwarted plaintiff's efforts to fulfill his responsibilities fixed by the doctrine of caveat emptor.

Finally, if the doctrine of caveat emptor is to be discarded, it should be for a reason more substantive than a poltergeist. The existence of a poltergeist is no more binding upon the defendants than it is upon this court.

Based upon the foregoing, the motion court properly dismissed the complaint.

NOTES AND QUESTIONS

1. *What happened?* Who sued whom for what? Procedurally, how did the case get before this court? Factually, what happened between the parties? What arguments did the plaintiff and defendant make? What rule or rules did the court apply? How did the court analyze the dispute between the parties? How did the court decide the case?

2. *Was this case correctly decided?* Do you agree with the result reached in this case? Why or why not? Do you agree with the court's reasoning? Why or why not? How, if at all, would you have written the opinion differently?

3. *As is?* Recall that defendant argued that the fact that the property was sold "as is" should have prevented the buyer from getting out of the contract. Why did the court reject this argument, and do you think the court was correct in doing so? Why or why not?

4. *Best solution?* Now that you've read a number of cases about the problem of disclosure, which of the above courts do you think approached this question most effectively?

5. Thinking tools. Do you think the problem of non-disclosure should be governed by a standard or a rule? Why? Follow up: Which standard or rule should govern it?

PROBLEM: MUST A KING CONFESS A MURDER?

Buyer (Reed) purchased a house from Seller (King), but King never disclosed that a woman and her four children were murdered there ten years earlier. However, Reed soon learned of the gruesome murders from a neighbor after the sale, and sought rescission and damages.

Drawing on the cases and materials presented above, should King be required to disclose that the home was the site of a multiple murder? Why or why not?

In previous case, *Stambovsky v. Ackley*, the court found that there was no duty to disclose. But under what circumstances will a court impose such a duty? The decision below, which draws on the *Restatement (Second) of Contracts* for guidance, seeks to answer this question.

2. Duress

DOCTRINAL OVERVIEW: DURESS AS A DEFENSE TO ENFORCEMENT*

Coercive behavior may take the form of physical compulsion or of threat. Under the general principles of contract law relating to assent, if a victim acts under physical compulsion, for instance, by signing a writing under such force that the victim is "a mere mechanical instrument," the victim's actions are not effective to manifest assent.[1] Such duress by physical compulsion results in no contract at all or in what is sometimes anomalously described as a "void contract."[2] [More specifically, the contract becomes voidable at the election of the victim.] More difficult and important questions arise when the coercion is by threat rather than by physical compulsion.

The requirements for a showing of duress by threat can be grouped under four headings. First, there must be a threat. Second, the threat must be improper.

---

* Excerpted from E. ALLAN FARNSWORTH, CONTRACTS § 4.16 (4th ed. 2004).

1. . . . The quoted phrase appears in *Restatement* § 494(b) and in *Restatement Second* § 174 cmt. *a*.

2. If *contract* is defined in terms of an enforceable promise, a "void contract" is not a "contract" at all. Duress that "nullifies the obligation of the obligor" is a *real* defense to an asserted obligation on a negotiable instrument, i.e., a good defense even when the instrument is in the hands of a good faith purchaser (known as a *holder in due course*). UCC § 3-305(a)(1),(b).

Third, the threat must induce the victim's manifestation of assent. Fourth, it must be sufficiently grave to justify the victim s assent.[3]

First, what is a threat? A threat is a manifestation of an intent to inflict some loss or harm on another. It need not be expressed in words but may be inferred from words or other conduct. Thus if one person strikes or imprisons another, the conduct may amount to duress because of the threat of further blows or continued imprisonment that is implied. But a mere prediction of the probable consequences of a course of action may not amount to a threat. . . .

Second, when is a threat improper? The kind of threat with which we are concerned is one that is made to induce the victim to manifest assent to a contract. But not all such threats are improper . . . . The problem then becomes one of distinguishing impermissible threats from legitimate offers. [For example], the seller that offers to deliver cotton to the buyer if the buyer promises to pay $10,000, but not otherwise, is not ordinarily thought of as making an improper threat. But what if cotton is scarce? If the buyer's need is desperate? If $10,000 is exorbitant? If the seller is already bound by a contract to deliver the same cotton to the buyer for $5,000? . . .

Third, when does a threat induce the manifestation of assent? The requirement is simply one of causation. Did the threat actually induce assent on the part of the victim? Threats that would induce assent on the part of one person may not induce it in the case of another. . . .

Fourth, when is a threat sufficiently grave to justify the victim in succumbing to it? The early common law imposed a very strict test. According to Lord Coke, the victim might avoid a contract only:

> 1. for fear of losse of life, 2. of losse of member, 3. of mayhem, and 4. of imprisonment; otherwise it is for fear of battery, which might be very light, or for burning of his houses, or taking away, or destroying of his goods or the like, for there he may have satisfaction in damages.[9]

Assent in the face of that kind of fear was sometimes said to be "voluntary." The notion that the victim of a threat to property might always be expected to refuse to assent and resort to an action for damages gave way in the eighteenth century with the recognition of "duress of goods," the wrongful detention of the victim's property. This presaged a "radical change" in the doctrine of duress and paved the way to a more liberal doctrine of "economic duress," or "business compulsion," under which the threat went, not to the victim's person, but to the victim's economic interests. . . .

[We will discuss all three forms of duress—duress of person, duress of goods, and economic duress—in the cases and materials that follow.]

3. *See Restatement Second* § 175(1) (the manifestation of assent must be "induced by an improper threat by the other party that leaves the victim no reasonable alternative").

9. EDWARD COKE, SECOND INSTITUTE 482-83 (1642). *Accord:* Rubenstein v. Rubenstein, 120 A.2d 11 (N.J. 1956) (threats included gangster violence and arsenic poisoning).

ON DURESS*

A person who does something under the most severe constraints (such as throwing his cargo overboard to save his ship during a storm), is, said Aristotle, still acting voluntarily, of his own free will. He is choosing between two very unpalatable courses, but he is still making a free choice. Similarly, a person who signs a contract at the point of a gun may be said to be simply choosing between being shot and signing the document. He signs, not because he has no will—indeed, the more strongly he believes in the gunman's threats, the more willing he is likely to be to sign—but because it is the lesser of two evils open to him.

But this analysis leads to a new difficulty. If even the gunman's victim is acting of his free will, then we must say that all (or anyhow nearly all) contracts are made voluntarily, but we must also admit that all contracts are made under pressure of some sort. Not only is there no such thing as a totally involuntary contract, there is equally no such thing as a totally unconstrained choice. Every contract we make is made under some form of pressure, every contractual offer is made backed by some sort of threat. The pressure and the threats are implicit in the whole concept of exchange, because the offeror is always demanding something in return for his offer, which is only another way of saying that he is threatening not to supply what you want, unless you can give him what he wants in return. This means that some way must be found of distinguishing between the kinds of pressure and the kinds of threats which will be permissible, which will not invalidate a contract, and those pressures and threats which will be ruled out, and which will invalidate a contract. The distinction which the law seeks to draw, therefore, must be that between legitimate and illegitimate pressure, or threats, and has nothing to do with "overborne wills."

This excursion into theory is not without practical import, because the question raised by these two possible approaches are quite different. If the law were truly concerned with the degree to which a choice was an exercise of free will, the question before the court would presumably be a psychological (or even philosophical) question of no little difficulty, and it would also be a question of fact in each case: has the will been overborne? On the other hand, if the true question concerns the legitimacy of the pressure of threats used, the question must be one of law which has nothing to do with the psychological state of mind of the party in question.

a. Duress of Person

Duress, in its broad sense, now includes all instances where a condition of mind of a person, caused by fear of personal injury or loss of limb, or injury to such person's property, wife, child or husband, is produced by the wrongful conduct of another, rendering such person incompetent to contract with the exercise of his free will power, whether formerly relievable at law on the ground of duress or in equity on the ground of wrongful compulsion.

---

* Excerpted from P.S. ATIYAH, AN INTRODUCTION TO THE LAW OF CONTRACT 265-67 (1995).

The making of a contract requires the free exercise of the will power of the contracting parties, and the free meeting and blending of their minds. In the absence of that, the essential of a contract is wanting; and if such absence be produced by the wrongful conduct of one party to the transaction, or conduct for which he is responsible, whereby the other party, for the time being, through fear, is bereft of his free will power, for the purpose of obtaining the contract, and it is thereby obtained, such contract may be avoided on the ground of duress. . . . The question in each case is, was the alleged injured person, by being put in fear by the other party to the transaction for the purpose of obtaining an advantage over him, deprived of the free exercise of his will power, and was such advantage thereby obtained? If the proposition be determined in the affirmative, no matter what the nature of the threatened injury to such person, or his property, or the person or liberty of his wife or child, the advantage thereby obtained cannot be retained. . . .

Galusha v. Sherman, 81 N.W. 495, 500 (1900)

Rubenstein v. Rubenstein

Supreme Court of New Jersey
120 A.2d 11 (1956)

[At the close of evidence, on defendant's motion, the trial court found that plaintiff failed to make out a cause of action for duress and dismissed plaintiff's complaint. The Appellate Division affirmed the trial court, and plaintiff appealed the case to the Supreme Court of New Jersey.]

HEHER, J. . . . The gravamen of the complaint is that plaintiff, while "in fear of his safety and under duress" practiced by his defendant wife, . . . conveyed to her . . . all his right, title and interest in a farm of 126½ acres containing a 14-room dwelling house and several farm buildings, . . . known as the "Marlboro Manor Farm," of the value of $90,000, and a plot of ground and a factory building . . . , of the value of $12,000, both tracts then being held by plaintiff and his wife in a tenancy by the entirety. . . .

If these conveyances were procured by means of duress, they are inoperative and voidable. Actual violence is not an essential element of duress of the person, even at common law, because consent is the very essence of a contract and, if there be compulsion, there is no actual consent. And moral compulsion, such as that produced by threats to take life or to inflict great bodily harm, as well as that produced by imprisonment, came to be regarded everywhere as sufficient in law to destroy free agency, indispensable to the consent without which there can be no contract. Duress in its more extended sense means that degree of constraint or danger, either actually inflicted or threatened and impending, sufficient in severity or in apprehension to overcome the mind or will of a person of ordinary firmness, according to the earlier rule, but now, by the weight of modern authority, such as in fact works control of the will.

There are two categories under the common law: duress *per minas* and duress of imprisonment. Duress *per minas* at common law "is where the party enters into a contract (1) For fear of loss of life; (2) For fear of loss of limb; (3) For fear of mayhem; (4) For fear of imprisonment"; and some of the later English cases confine the rule within these limits, while the American rule is more liberal and contracts procured by threats of battery to the person, or the destruction of property, were early held to be voidable on the ground of duress, "because in such a case there is nothing but the form of a contract, without the substance." *Brown v. Pierce*, 74 U.S. 205 (1869). In many cases it was found to be enough that there was moral compulsion "sufficient to overcome the mind and will of a person entirely competent, in all other respects, to contract," for "it is clear that a contract made under such circumstances is as utterly without the voluntary consent of the party menaced as if he were induced to sign it by actual violence. . . ." *United States v. Huckabee*, 83 U.S. 414 (1873).

It would seem to be basic to the legal concept of duress, proceeding as it does from the unreality of the apparent consent, that the controlling factor be the condition at the time of the mind of the person subjected to the coercive measures, rather than the means by which the given state of mind was induced, and thus the test is essentially subjective.

> The test of duress is not so much the means by which the party was compelled to execute the contract as it is the state of mind induced by the means employed—the fear which made it impossible for him to exercise his own free will. . . . The threat must be of such a nature and made under such circumstances as to constitute a reasonable and adequate cause to control the will of the threatened person, and must have that effect; and the act sought to be avoided must be performed by such person while in such condition. *Fountain v. Bigham*, 235 Pa. 35 (Sup. Ct. 1912).

In the modern view, moral compulsion or psychological pressure may constitute duress if, thereby, the subject of the pressure is overborne and he is deprived of the exercise of his free will. The question is whether consent was coerced; that is, was the person complaining "induced by the duress or undue influence to give his consent, and would not have done so otherwise." *Williston on Contracts* (rev. ed.) § 1604. It was said in the early books that there could not be duress by threats unless the threats were such as "to put a brave man in fear"; then came the qualified standard of something sufficient to overcome the will of a person of "ordinary firmness"; but the tendency of the more recent cases, and the rule comporting with reason and principle, is that any "unlawful threats" which do "in fact overcome the will of the person threatened, and induce him to do an act which he would not otherwise have done, and which he was not bound to do, constitute duress. The age, sex, capacity, relation of the parties and all the attendant circumstances must be considered. This follows the analogy of the modern doctrine of fraud which tends to disregard the question whether misrepresentations were such as would have deceived a reasonable person, and confines the question to whether the misrepresentations were intended to deceive and did so." *Williston on Contracts* § 1605. . . .

But the pressure must be wrongful, and not all pressure is wrongful. And means in themselves lawful must not be so oppressively used as to constitute, e.g., an abuse of legal remedies. The act or conduct complained of need not be "unlawful" in the technical sense of the term; it suffices if it is "wrongful in the sense that it is so oppressive under given circumstances as to constrain one to do what his free will would refuse." *First State Bank v. Federal Reserve Bank*, 174 Minn. 535 (Sup. Ct. 1928). It was said in a recent case that duress is tested, not by the nature of the threats, but rather by the state of mind induced thereby in the victim. *Ensign v. Home for Jewish Aged*, 274 S.W.2d 502 (Mo. App. 1955). . . .

[After remarking on the trial court's refusal to allow evidence regarding the plaintiff's state of mind, on account that doing so "would be opening a door wide and entering into a very dangerous area," this court proceeds to examine such evidence.]

There is no occasion now to set down the plaintiff's evidence in detail. It suffices to say that he gave a circumstantial account of threats of gangster violence, arsenic poisoning, and a course of action designed to overcome his will. . . . The arsenic threat, he said, had a background that filled him with an overpowering sense of foreboding and dread. His wife's father was then serving a life sentence in a Pennsylvania prison for murder committed while he was identified with an "arsenic ring" engaged in killings to defraud life insurers. The threats were first made in December 1952. The demand for the conveyances came in April 1953, and was refused. It was repeated at intervals until the following July, when the arsenic threat was made. He was seized with a great fear for his life and, so conditioned, he agreed the following day to make the conveyance. . . .

These findings suggest psychological factors bearing on the subjective standard of free will. . . .

There was a Prima facie showing here of a compulsive yielding to the demand for the conveyances, rather than the volitional act of a free mind, which called for a full disclosure by the defendant wife; and so it was error to entertain the motion to dismiss at the close of the plaintiff's case. . . .

The judgment is reversed; and the cause is remanded for further proceedings in conformity with this opinion.

RELEVANT PROVISIONS

For the *Restatement (Second) of Contracts*, consult §§ 174-176. For the UNIDROIT Principles, consult Article 3.2.6.

NOTES AND QUESTIONS

1. ***What happened?*** Who sued whom for what? Procedurally, how did the case get before this court? Factually, what happened between the parties? What arguments did the plaintiff and defendant make? What rule or rules did

the court apply? How did the court analyze the dispute between the parties? How did the court decide the case?

2. *Was this case correctly decided?* Do you agree with the result reached in this case? Why or why not? Do you agree with the court's reasoning? Why or why not? How, if at all, would you have written the opinion differently?

b. Duress of Goods

> *Duress exists where one by the unlawful act of another is induced to make a contract or perform or forego some act under circumstances which deprive him of the exercise of free will. Duress is commonly said to be of the person where it is manifested by imprisonment, or by threats, or by an exhibition of force which apparently cannot be resisted. Or it may be of the goods, when one is obliged to submit to an illegal exaction in order to obtain possession of his goods and chattels from one who has wrongfully taken them into possession.*
>
> *Smithwick v. Whitley*, 67 S.E. 913, 914 (1910)

Hackley v. Headley

Supreme Court of Michigan
8 N.W. 511 (1881)

COOLEY, J. Headley sued Hackley & McGordon to recover compensation for cutting, hauling and delivering in the Muskegon river a quantity of logs. The performance of the labor was not disputed, but the parties were not agreed as to the construction of the contract in some important particulars, and the amount to which Headley was entitled depended largely upon the determination of these differences. The defendants also claimed to have had a full and complete settlement with Headley, and produced his receipt in evidence thereof. Headley admitted the receipt, but insisted that it was given by him under duress, and the verdict which he obtained in the circuit court was in accordance with this claim. . . .

The [receipt] reads as follows:

> MUSKEGON, MICH., August 3, 1875.
>
> Received from Hackley & McGordon their note for four thousand dollars, payable in thirty days, at First National Bank, Grand Rapids, which is in full for all claims of every kind and nature which I have against Hackley & McGordon.
>
> Witness: THOMAS HUME. JOHN HEADLEY.

Headley's account of the circumstances under which this receipt was given is in substance as follows: On August 3, 1875, he went to Muskegon, . . . for the purpose of collecting the balance which he claimed was due him under the contract. The amount he claimed was upwards of $6,200, estimating the logs by the Scribner scale. [Hackley, however,] insisted that the estimate should be according to the Doyle scale, and . . . also claimed that he had made payments to others amounting to some $1,400 which Headley should allow. Headley did not admit these payments, and denied his liability for them if they had been made. Hackley told Headley to come in again in the afternoon, and when he did so Hackley said to him: "My figures show there is 4,260 and odd dollars in round numbers your due, and I will just give you $4,000. I will give you our note for $4,000." To this Headley replied: "I cannot take that; it is not right, and you know it. There is over $2,000 besides that belongs to me, and you know it." Hackley replied: "That is the best I will do with you." Headley said: "I cannot take that, Mr. Hackley," and Hackley replied, "You do the next best thing you are a mind to. You can sue me if you please." Headley then said, "I cannot afford to sue you, because I have got to have the money, and I cannot wait for it. If I fail to get the money to-day, I shall probably be ruined financially, because I have made no other arrangement to get the money only on this particular matter." Finally he took the note and gave the receipt, because at the time he could do nothing better, and in the belief that he would be financially ruined unless he had immediately the money that was offered him, or paper by means of which the money might be obtained.

If this statement is correct, the defendants not only took a most unjust advantage of Headley, but they obtained a receipt which, to the extent that it assumed to discharge anything not honestly in dispute between the parties and known by them to be owing to Headley beyond the sum received, was without consideration and ineffectual. But was it a receipt obtained by duress? That is the question which the record presents. The circuit judge was of opinion that if the jury believed the statement of Headley they would be justified in finding that duress existed. . . .

Duress exists when one by the unlawful act of another is induced to make a contract or perform some act under circumstances which deprive him of the exercise of free will. It is commonly said to be of either the person or the goods of the party. Duress of the person is either by imprisonment, or by threats, or by an exhibition of force which apparently cannot be resisted. It is not pretended that duress of the person existed in this case; it is if anything duress of goods, or at least of that nature, and properly enough classed with duress of goods. Duress of goods may exist when one is compelled to submit to an illegal exaction in order to obtain them from one who has them in possession but refuses to surrender them unless the exaction is submitted to.

The leading case involving duress of goods is *Astley v. Reynolds*, 2 Strange 915. The plaintiff had pledged goods for £20, and when he offered to redeem them, the pawnbroker refused to surrender them unless he was paid £10 for interest. The plaintiff submitted to the exaction, but was held entitled to recover back all that had been unlawfully demanded and taken. "This," say the court,

The expansion of duress

We covered physical duress, or duress of the person, in the previous subsection in our examination of *Rubenstein* (p. 1031), and in this case we are shown how some of the same concerns (though present to a lesser degree) that justified the original defense can operate to expand the doctrine to include a new form of duress, duress of goods, which must have been of primary importance in the industrializing, goods-based economy of 1881 when this case was decided. In fact, the expansion is still ongoing, and in the next subsection, we will see how the defense of duress of goods has expanded to include economic duress, or duress against a party's economic interests, which, once again, became of primary importance in the post-industrial, capitalist society of the twentieth and twenty-first centuries. As we have seen throughout this casebook (with the Danzig excerpt following *Hadley v. Baxendale* providing perhaps the most striking example), legal doctrines must constantly evolve to keep pace with (and be relevant to) the modern society in which we operate. To balance this need, which suggests legal progressivism, against the need for maintaining predictability and stability for those planning their affairs according to the laws currently in existence, which suggests legal conservatism, is a challenge faced by our judges and legislators, who must constantly walk a tightrope between these two very different though equally important ideas.

Volenti non fit injuria

"[Law Latin 'to a willing person it is not a wrong,' i.e., a person is not wronged by that to which he or she consents] The principle that a person who knowingly and voluntarily risks danger cannot recover for any resulting injury." BLACK'S LAW DICTIONARY (10th ed. 2014).

is a payment by compulsion: the plaintiff might have such an immediate want of his goods that an action of trover would not do his business: where the rule ***volenti non fit injuria*** is applied, it must be when the party had his freedom of exercising his will, which this man had not: we must take it he paid the money relying on his legal remedy to get it back again.

The principle of this case was approved in . . . *Ashmore v. Wainwright*, 2 Q.B. 837[,] . . . a suit to recover back excessive charges paid to common carriers who refused until payment was made to deliver the goods for the carriage of which the charges were made. There has never been any doubt but recovery could be had under such circumstances. The case is like it of one having securities in his hands which he refuses to surrender until illegal commissions are paid. So if illegal tolls are demanded, for passing a raft of lumber, and the owner pays them to liberate his raft, he may recover back what he pays.

So one may recover back money which he pays to release his goods from an attachment which is sued out with knowledge on the part of the plaintiff that he has no cause of action. Nor is the principle confined to payments made to recover goods: it applies equally well when money is extorted as a condition to the exercise by the party of any other legal right. . . . And the mere threat to employ colorable legal authority to compel payment of an unfounded claim is such duress as will support an action to recover back what is paid under it.

But where the party threatens nothing which he has not a legal right to perform, there is no duress. When therefore a judgment creditor threatens to levy his execution on the debtor's goods, and under fear of the levy the debtor executes and delivers a note for the amount, with sureties, the note cannot be avoided for duress. Many other cases might be cited, but it is wholly unnecessary. . . .

In what did the alleged duress consist in the present case? Merely in this: that the debtors refused to pay on demand a debt already due, though the plaintiff was in great need of the money and might be financially ruined in case he failed to obtain it. It is not pretended that Hackley & McGordon had done anything to bring Headley to the condition which made this money so important to him at this very time, or that they were in any manner responsible for his pecuniary embarrassment except as they failed to pay this demand. The duress, then, is to be found exclusively in their failure to meet promptly their pecuniary obligation. But this, according to the plaintiff's claim, would have constituted no duress whatever if he had not happened to be in pecuniary straits; and the validity of negotiations, according to this claim, must be determined, not by the defendants' conduct, but by the plaintiff's necessities. The same contract which would be valid if made with a man easy in his circumstances, becomes invalid when the contracting party is pressed with the necessity of immediately meeting his bank paper. But this would be a most dangerous, as well as a most unequal doctrine; and if accepted, no one could well know when he would be safe in dealing on the ordinary terms of negotiation with a party who professed to be in great need. . . .

These views render a reversal of the judgment necessary, and the case will be remanded for a new trial with costs to the plaintiffs in error.

NOTES AND QUESTIONS

1. ***What happened?*** Who sued whom for what? Procedurally, how did the case get before this court? Factually, what happened between the parties? What arguments did the plaintiff and defendant make? What rule or rules did the court apply? How did the court analyze the dispute between the parties? How did the court decide the case?

2. ***Was this case correctly decided?*** Do you agree with the result reached in this case? Why or why not? Do you agree with the court's reasoning? Why or why not? How, if at all, would you have written the opinion differently?

3. ***Why is there no duress?*** Why did the court find that there was no duress of goods in this case, even though the defendants (a) owed the money, and (b) knew the plaintiff would be in severe financial straits if the plaintiff was not paid?

4. ***Fear of expansion.*** Does the court have good reason for fearing the expansion of the defense of duress to cover cases involving the duress of goods and/or duress of property? Why or why not? What thinking tools that we have previously examined shed light on whether this doctrine should, or should not, be expanded?

5. ***Duress of goods.*** What facts could be changed above so that there would be duress of goods?

PROBLEM: WASHERS AND DRYERS

Plaintiff manufactured washing machines and dryers, and Defendant was the sole supplier of knobs for Plaintiff's appliances. Defendant, however, was not contractually obligated to supply Plaintiff with knobs, but would simply fill Plaintiff's purchase orders as they came in.

In March 2013, Defendant prepared a bid to supply Plaintiff with knobs for its new product line, but that bid was rejected in favor of a lower bidder. In

November 2014, Defendant notified Plaintiff that it was increasing the price of its knobs because the volume of parts Plaintiff purchased fell below the level Defendant originally quoted. Plaintiff claims the price increase was in retaliation for its rejection of Defendant's bid.

In December, 2014, Defendant began threatening to interrupt Plaintiff's manufacturing operations by refusing to sell Plaintiff its knobs unless Plaintiff agreed to its price increase. On January 1, 2015, Defendant informed Plaintiff that it would cancel their supply chain relationship by January 31, 2015. On January 31, 2015, Defendant refused to accept any new purchase orders from Plaintiff but continued to honor Plaintiff's previously scheduled orders.

Faced with a potential parts shortage and production stoppage, Plaintiff negotiated a parts agreement ("the Agreement") with Defendant in February, 2015. The Agreement called for an average price-per-part-increase of 300%. Plaintiff also agreed to make a $50,000 advance payment to Defendant. Eventually, Plaintiff found an alternative knob supplier and ceased sending Defendant purchase orders.

In November, 2015, Defendant shipped Plaintiff its existing knob inventory that it had specifically produced for Plaintiff under the Agreement. Defendant also informed Plaintiff of its intentions to invoice Plaintiff for raw materials and knobs partially produced pursuant to the Agreement.

Plaintiff sues Defendant, alleging that the Agreement with Defendant is void and it is not obligated to accept Defendant's shipped inventory or make any payments under the Agreement because Defendant procured the Agreement via duress. Defendant, in turn, files a motion to dismiss Plaintiff's suit. Drawing on *Hackley v. Headley* and the materials in this subsection, how should the court rule?

c. Economic Duress

Austin Instrument, Inc. v. Loral Corp.

Court of Appeals of New York
272 N.E.2d 533 (1971)

FULD, CHIEF JUDGE. The defendant, Loral Corporation, seeks to recover payment for goods delivered under a contract which it had with the plaintiff Austin Instrument, Inc., on the ground that the evidence establishes, as a matter of law, that it was forced to agree to an increase in price on the items in question under circumstances amounting to economic duress.

In July of 1965, Loral was awarded a $6,000,000 contract by the Navy for the production of radar sets. The contract contained a schedule of deliveries, a liquidated damages clause applying to late deliveries and a cancellation clause in case of default by Loral. The latter thereupon solicited bids for some 40 precision gear components needed to produce the radar sets, and awarded Austin a subcontract to supply 23 such parts. That party commenced delivery in early 1966.

In May, 1966, Loral was awarded a second Navy contract for the production of more radar sets and again went about soliciting bids. Austin bid on all 40 gear components but, on July 15, a representative from Loral informed Austin's president, Mr. Krauss, that his company would be awarded the subcontract only for those items on which it was low bidder. The Austin officer refused to accept an order for less than all 40 of the gear parts and on the next day he told Loral that Austin would cease deliveries of the parts due under the existing subcontract unless Loral consented to substantial increases in the prices provided for by that agreement—both retroactively for parts already delivered and prospectively on those not yet shipped—and placed with Austin the order for all 40 parts needed under Loral's second Navy contract. Shortly thereafter, Austin did, indeed, stop delivery. After contacting 10 manufacturers of precision gears and finding none who could produce the parts in time to meet its commitments to the Navy,[1] Loral acceded to Austin's demands; in a letter dated July 22, Loral wrote to Austin that "We have feverishly surveyed other sources of supply and find that because of the prevailing military exigencies, were they to start from scratch as would have to be the case, they could not even remotely begin to deliver on time to meet the delivery requirements established by the Government. . . . Accordingly, we are left with no choice or alternative but to meet your conditions."

Loral thereupon consented to the price increases insisted upon by Austin under the first subcontract and the latter was awarded a second subcontract making it the supplier of all 40 gear parts for Loral's second contract with the Navy.[2] Although Austin was granted until September to resume deliveries, Loral did, in fact, receive parts in August and was able to produce the radar sets in time to meet its commitments to the Navy on both contracts. After Austin's last delivery under the second subcontract in July, 1967, Loral notified it of its intention to seek recovery of the price increases.

On September 15, 1967, Austin instituted this action against Loral to recover an amount in excess of $17,750 which was still due on the second subcontract. On the same day, Loral commenced an action against Austin claiming damages of some $22,250—the aggregate of the price increases under the first subcontract—on the ground of economic duress. The two actions were consolidated and, following a trial, Austin was awarded the sum it requested and Loral's complaint against Austin was dismissed on the ground that it was not shown that "it could not have obtained the items in question from other sources in time to meet its commitment to the Navy under the first contract." A closely divided Appellate Division affirmed. There was no material disagreement concerning the facts; as Justice Steuer stated in the course of his dissent below, "(t)he facts are virtually undisputed, nor is there any serious question of law. The difficulty lies in the application of the law to these facts."

---

1. The best reply Loral received was from a vendor who stated he could commence deliveries sometime in October.

2. Loral makes no claim in this action on the second subcontract.

> ***Economic duress***
>
> Note carefully the elements of economic duress. A party asserting this defense must show more than a mere wrongful withholding of goods. It must also show that (1) cover is not possible, *and* (2) "the ordinary remedy" (which will usually be expectation damages as limited by certainty, foreseeability, and avoidability [see Part III.5.A.4]) would not be adequate to put it back in its rightful position. Are each of these elements satisfied in this case? *See also Restatement (Second) of Contracts* §§ 174-176.

The applicable law is clear and, indeed, is not disputed by the parties. A contract is voidable on the ground of duress when it is established that the party making the claim was forced to agree to it by means of a wrongful threat precluding the exercise of his free will. The existence of economic duress or business compulsion is demonstrated by proof that "immediate possession of needful goods is threatened" (*Mercury Mach. Importing Corp. v. City of New York*, 3 N.Y.2d 418, 425 (1957)) or, more particularly, in cases such as the one before us, by proof that one party to a contract has threatened to breach the agreement by withholding goods unless the other party agrees to some further demand. However, a mere threat by one party to breach the contract by not delivering the required items, though wrongful, does not in itself constitute economic duress. It must also appear that the threatened party could not obtain the goods from another source of supply and that the ordinary remedy of an action for breach of contract would not be adequate.

We find without any support in the record the conclusion reached by the courts below that Loral failed to establish that it was the victim of economic duress. On the contrary, the evidence makes out a classic case, as a matter of law, of such duress.

It is manifest that Austin's threat—to stop deliveries unless the prices were increased—deprived Loral of its free will. As bearing on this, Loral's relationship with the Government is most significant. As mentioned above, its contract called for staggered monthly deliveries of the radar sets, with clauses calling for liquidated damages and possible cancellation on default. Because of its production schedule, Loral was, in July, 1966, concerned with meeting its delivery requirements in September, October and November, and it was for the sets to be delivered in those months that the withheld gears were needed. Loral had to plan ahead, and the substantial liquidated damages for which it would be liable, plus the threat of default, were genuine possibilities. Moreover, Loral did a substantial portion of its business with the Government, and it feared that a failure to deliver as agreed upon would jeopardize its chances for future contracts. These genuine concerns do not merit the label "self-imposed, undisclosed and subjective" which the Appellate Division majority placed upon them. It was perfectly reasonable for Loral, or any other party similarly placed, to consider itself in an emergency, duress situation.

Austin, however, claims that the fact that Loral extended its time to resume deliveries until September negates its alleged dire need for the parts. A Loral official testified on this point that Austin's president told him he could deliver some parts in August and that the extension of deliveries was a formality. In any event, the parts necessary for production of the radar sets to be delivered in September were delivered to Loral on September 1, and the parts needed for the October schedule were delivered in late August and early September. Even so, Loral had to "work . . . around the clock" to meet its commitments. Considering that the best offer Loral received from the other vendors it contacted was commencement of delivery sometime in October, which, as the record shows, would have made it late in its deliveries to the Navy in both September and October, Loral's claim that it had no choice but to accede to Austin's demands is conclusively demonstrated.

We find unconvincing Austin's contention that Loral, in order to meet its burden, should have contacted the Government and asked for an extension of its delivery dates so as to enable it to purchase the parts from another vendor. Aside from the consideration that Loral was anxious to perform well in the Government's eyes, it could not be sure when it would obtain enough parts from a substitute vendor to meet its commitments. The only promise which it received from the companies it contacted was for Commencement of deliveries, not full supply, and, with vendor delay common in this field, it would have been nearly impossible to know the length of the extension it should request. It must be remembered that Loral was producing a needed item of military hardware. Moreover, there is authority for Loral's position that nonperformance by a subcontractor is not an excuse for default in the main contract. In light of all this, Loral's claim should not be held insufficiently supported because it did not request an extension from the Government.

Loral, as indicated above, also had the burden of demonstrating that it could not obtain the parts elsewhere within a reasonable time, and there can be no doubt that it met this burden. The 10 manufacturers whom Loral contacted comprised its entire list of "approved vendors" for precision gears, and none was able to commence delivery soon enough.[6] As Loral was producing a highly sophisticated item of military machinery requiring parts made to the strictest engineering standards, it would be unreasonable to hold that Loral should have gone to other vendors, with whom it was either unfamiliar or dissatisfied, to procure the needed parts. As Justice Steuer noted in his dissent, Loral "contacted all the manufacturers whom it believed capable of making these parts," and this was all the law requires.

It is hardly necessary to add that Loral's normal legal remedy of accepting Austin's breach of the contract and then suing for damages would have been inadequate under the circumstances, as Loral would still have had to obtain the gears elsewhere with all the concomitant consequences mentioned above. In other words, Loral actually had no choice, when the prices were raised by Austin, except to take the gears at the "coerced" prices and then sue to get the excess back.

---

6. Loral, as do many manufacturers, maintains a list of "approved vendors," that is, vendors whose products, facilities, techniques and performance have been inspected and found satisfactory.

Austin's final argument is that Loral, even if it did enter into the contract under duress, lost any rights it had to a refund of money by waiting until July, 1967, long after the termination date of the contract, to disaffirm it. It is true that one who would recover moneys allegedly paid under duress must act promptly to make his claim known. In this case, Loral delayed making its demand for a refund until three days after Austin's last delivery on the second subcontract. Loral's reason—for waiting until that time—is that it feared another stoppage of deliveries which would again put it in an untenable situation. Considering Austin's conduct in the past, this was perfectly reasonable, as the possibility of an application by Austin of further business compulsion still existed until all of the parts were delivered.

In sum, the record before us demonstrates that Loral agreed to the price increases in consequence of the economic duress employed by Austin. Accordingly, the matter should be remanded to the trial court for a computation of its damages.

The order appealed from should be modified, with costs, by reversing so much thereof as affirms the dismissal of defendant Loral Corporation's claim and, except as so modified, affirmed.

BERGAN, JUDGE **(dissenting)**. Whether acts charged as constituting economic duress produce or do not produce the damaging effect attributed to them is normally a routine type of factual issue.

Here the fact question was resolved against Loral both by the Special Term and by the affirmance at the Appellate Division. It should not be open for different resolution here.

In summarizing the Special Term's decision and its own, the Appellate Division decided that "the conclusion that Loral acted deliberately and voluntarily, without being under immediate pressure of incurring severe business reverses, precludes a recovery on the theory of economic duress."

When the testimony of the witnesses who actually took part in the negotiations for the two disputing parties is examined, sharp conflicts of fact emerge. Under Austin's version the request for a renegotiation of the existing contract was based on Austin's contention that Loral had failed to carry out an understanding as to the items to be furnished under that contract and this was the source of dissatisfaction which led both to a revision of the existing agreement and to entering into a new one.

This is not necessarily and as a matter of law to be held economic duress. On this appeal it is needful to look at the facts resolved in favor of Austin most favorably to that party. Austin's version of events was that a threat was not made but rather a request to accommodate the closing of its plant for a customary vacation period in accordance with the general understanding of the parties.

Moreover, critical to the issue of economic duress was the availability of alternative suppliers to the purchaser Loral. The demonstration is replete in the direct testimony of Austin's witnesses and on cross-examination of Loral's principal and purchasing agent that the availability of practical alternatives was a highly controverted issue of fact. On that issue of fact the explicit findings made by the Special Referee were affirmed by the Appellate Division. Nor is the issue of fact made the less so by assertion that the facts are undisputed and that only the application of equally undisputed rules of law is involved.

Austin asserted and Loral admitted on cross-examination that there were many suppliers listed in a trade registry but that Loral chose to rely only on those who had in the past come to them for orders and with whom they were familiar. It was, therefore, at least a fair issue of fact whether under the circumstances such conduct was reasonable and made what might otherwise have been a commercially understandable renegotiation an exercise of duress.

The order should be affirmed.

NOTES AND QUESTIONS

1. ***What happened?*** Who sued whom for what? Procedurally, how did the case get before this court? Factually, what happened between the parties? What arguments did the plaintiff and defendant make? What rule or rules did the court apply? How did the court analyze the dispute between the parties? How did the court decide the case?

2. ***Was this case correctly decided?*** Do you agree with the result reached in this case? Why or why not? Do you agree with the court's reasoning? Why or why not? How, if at all, would you have written the opinion differently?

3. ***Wrongful threat.*** Was the threat here wrongful? Why or why not?

4. Stilk ***and*** Alaska Packers***, Revisited.*** Recall how, in cases like *Stilk* (p. 376) and *Alaska Packers* (p. 378), the court policed contract modifications by testing whether they were supported by consideration, even though the courts *really* seemed to be worried about the type of coercive, hold-up behavior we have been exploring in this subunit on duress. We are now in a better position to appreciate why consideration is probably not the best doctrine with which to police duress: Any sophisticated party could easily support a contract modification with new consideration (the modification in *Austin,* for instance, was supported by consideration), which means that these modifications would be enforceable if consideration were the only thing that courts looked for.

5. ***Distinguishing precedents.*** Can this case be distinguished from *Hackley*? Can it be distinguished from the next case, *Rich & Whillock*?

Rich & Whillock, Inc. v. Ashton Development, Inc.

California Court of Appeal
204 Cal. Rptr. 86 (1984)

WIENER, ASSOCIATE JUSTICE. Ashton Development, Inc. and Bob Britton, Inc. appeal from the judgment awarding Rich & Whillock, Inc. $22,286.45 for the balance due under a grading and excavating contract. Following a nonjury trial the court entered judgment after it found a settlement agreement and release signed by Rich & Whillock, Inc. were the products of economic duress and thus provided no defense to its contract claim. We conclude substantial evidence supports the court's finding and affirm the judgment.

FACTUAL AND PROCEDURAL BACKGROUND

On February 17, 1981, Bob Britton, president of Bob Britton, Inc., signed a contract for grading and excavating services to be provided by Rich & Whillock, Inc. at a price of $112,990. The work was to be done on a project by Ashton Development, Inc. Bob Britton, Inc. was general contractor on the project and the agent for Ashton Development, Inc. in all dealings with Rich & Whillock, Inc. Work began the day the contract was signed.

In late March 1981 Rich & Whillock, Inc. encountered rock on the project site. A meeting was held at the site to discuss the problem. In attendance were Greg Whillock and Jim Rich, president and vice-president of Rich & Whillock, Inc., Bob Britton, Berj Aghadjian, president of Ashton Development, Inc., and a man from a blasting company. Everyone agreed the rock would have to be blasted. The $112,990 contract price expressly excluded blasting. The contract also stated "[a]ny rock encountered will be considered an extra at current rental rates." In response to Britton's inquiry, Whillock and Rich estimated the extra cost to remove the rock would be about $60,000, for a total contract price of approximately $172,000. They also emphasized, however, the estimate was not firm and the actual cost could go much higher due to the unpredictable nature of rock work.

Britton directed Whillock and Rich to go ahead with the rock work and bill him for the extra costs and said they would be paid. Rich & Whillock, Inc. proceeded accordingly, submitting invoices and receiving payments every other week. The invoices separately stated the charges for the regular contract work and the extra rock work and were supported by attached employee time sheets. Toward the end of April Whillock asked Britton if he had any questions about any of the billings. Britton had no questions and told Whillock to continue with the rock work because it had to be done.

By June 17, 1981, after receiving payments totaling $190,363.50, Rich & Whillock, Inc. submitted a final billing for an additional $72,286.45. After consulting with Aghadjian, Britton refused to pay. When Whillock asked why, Britton explained he and Aghadjian were short on funds for the project and had no money left to pay the final billing. Up until he received that billing, Britton had no complaints about the work done or the invoices submitted by Rich &

Whillock, Inc. and had never asked for any accounting of charges in addition to that already provided. Whillock told Britton he and Rich would "go broke" if not paid because they were a new company, the project was a big job for them, they had rented most of their equipment and they had numerous subcontractors waiting to be paid. Britton replied he and Aghadjian would pay them $50,000 or nothing, and they could sue for the full amount if unsatisfied with the compromise.

On July 10, 1981, Britton presented Rich with an agreement for a final compromise payment of $50,000. The agreement provided $25,000 would be paid "upon receipt of this signed agreement," to be followed by a second $25,000 payment on August 10, 1981 "upon receipt of full and unconditional releases for all labor, material, equipment, supplies, etc., purchased, acquired or furnished for this contract up to and including August 10, 1981." Rich repeated Whillock's earlier statements about the probable effects of nonpayment on their business. Britton replied: "I have a check for you, and just take it or leave it, this is all you get. If you don't want this, you have got to sue me." Rich then signed the agreement and received a $25,000 check after telling Britton the agreement was "blackmail" and he was signing it only because he had to in order to survive. Rich & Whillock, Inc. received the second $25,000 payment on August 20, 1981, at which time Whillock signed a standard release form.

In December 1981 Rich & Whillock, Inc. filed this action for damages for breach of contract. The court found Ashton Development, Inc. and Bob Britton, Inc. were liable for the $22,286.45 balance due under the contract, and that the July 10 agreement and August 20 release were unenforceable due to economic duress. On the latter point the court found Britton and Aghadjian "never really disputed the amount of plaintiff's charge in that they never asked for an accounting nor documentation concerning the extra work." The court also stated it disbelieved Britton when he testified Rich & Whillock, Inc. had agreed to do the extra work for a sum not to exceed $90,000. By disbelieving Britton and finding no dispute about the actual amount owed, the court impliedly found Britton and Aghadjian acted in bad faith when they refused to pay Rich & Whillock, Inc.'s final billing and offered instead to pay a compromise amount of $50,000. Based upon its finding of bad faith, the court concluded the July 10 agreement and August 20 release were signed "under duress in that plaintiff felt they would face financial ruin if they did not accept the lesser sum and that defendants, knowing this, threatened no further payment unless plaintiff accepted the lesser sum."

DISCUSSION

"At the outset it is helpful to acknowledge the various policy considerations which are involved in cases involving economic duress. Typically, those claiming such coercion are attempting to avoid the consequences of a modification of an original contract or of a settlement and release agreement. On the one hand, courts are reluctant to set aside agreements because of the notion of freedom of contract and because of the desirability of having private dispute resolutions be final. On the other hand, there is an increasing recognition of the law's role in correcting inequitable or unequal exchanges between parties of disproportionate bargaining power and a greater willingness to not enforce agreements which were entered into under coercive circumstances." *Totem Marine T. & B. v. Alyeska Pipeline, Etc.*, 584 P.2d 15, 21 (Alaska 1978).

California courts have recognized the economic duress doctrine in private sector cases for at least 50 years. The doctrine is equitably based and represents "but an expansion by courts of equity of the old common-law doctrine of duress." *Sistrom v. Anderson*, 51 Cal. App. 2d 213, 220 (1942). As it has evolved to the present day, the economic duress doctrine is not limited by early statutory and judicial expressions requiring an unlawful act in the nature of a tort or a crime. Civ. Code § 1569 (2).[2] Instead, the doctrine now may come into play upon the doing of a wrongful act which is sufficiently coercive to cause a reasonably prudent person faced with no reasonable alternative to succumb to the perpetrator's pressure. The assertion of a claim known to be false or a bad faith threat to breach a contract or to withhold a payment may constitute a wrongful act for purposes of the economic duress doctrine. Further, a reasonably prudent person subject to such an act may have no reasonable alternative but to succumb when the only other alternative is bankruptcy or financial ruin.

The underlying concern of the economic duress doctrine is the enforcement in the marketplace of certain minimal standards of business ethics. Hard bargaining, "efficient" breaches and reasonable settlements of good faith disputes are all acceptable, even desirable, in our economic system. That system can be viewed as a game in which everybody wins, to one degree or another, so long as everyone plays by the common rules. Those rules are not limited to precepts of rationality and self-interest. They include equitable notions of fairness and propriety which preclude the wrongful exploitation of business exigencies to obtain disproportionate exchanges of value. Such exchanges make a mockery of freedom of contract and undermine the proper functioning of our economic system. The economic duress doctrine serves as a last resort to correct these aberrations when conventional alternatives and remedies are unavailing. The necessity for the doctrine in cases such as this has been graphically described:

> Nowadays, a wait of even a few weeks in collecting on a contract claim is sometimes serious or fatal for an enterprise at a crisis in its history. The business of a creditor in financial straits is at the mercy of an unscrupulous debtor, who need only suggest that if the creditor does not care to settle on the debtor's own hard terms, he can sue. This situation, in which promptness in payment is vastly

---

2. Originally enacted in 1872 and never since amended, Civil Code § 1569 provides:

> Duress consists in:
>
> 1. Unlawful confinement of the person of the party, or of the husband or wife of such party, or of an ancestor, descendant, or adopted child of such party, husband, or wife;
>
> 2. Unlawful detention of the property of any such person; or,
>
> 3. Confinement of such person, lawful in form, but fraudulently obtained, or fraudulently made unjustly harassing or oppressive.

> more important than even approximate justice in the settlement terms, is too common in modern business relations to be ignored by society and the courts. Dalzell, *Duress by Economic Pressure II,* 20 N. Carolina L. Rev. 340, 370 (1942).

Totem Marine T. & B. v. Alyeska Pipeline, Etc., 584 P.2d 15 (1978), presents an example of economic duress remarkably parallel to the circumstances of this case. Totem, a new corporation, contracted with Alyeska to transport pipeline construction materials from Houston, Texas to a port in southern Alaska, with the possibility of one or two cargo stops along the way. Totem chartered the equipment necessary to perform the contract. Unfortunately, numerous unanticipated problems arose from the outset which impeded Totem's performance. When Totem's chartered tugs and barge arrived in the port of Long Beach, California, Alyeska caused the barge to be unloaded and unilaterally terminated the contract. Totem then submitted termination invoices totaling somewhere between $260,000 and $300,000. At the same time, Totem notified Alyeska it was in urgent need of cash to pay creditors and that without immediate payment it would go bankrupt. After some negotiations, Alyeska offered to settle Totem's account for $97,500. In order to avoid bankruptcy, Totem accepted Alyeska's compromise offer and signed an agreement releasing Alyeska from all claims under the contract.

About four months after signing the release agreement Totem sued Alyeska for the balance due under the contract. The trial court entered summary judgment for Alyeska based on the release agreement. The Supreme Court of Alaska reversed, explaining:

> [W]e believe that Totem's allegations, if proved, would support a finding that it executed a release of its contract claims against Alyeska under economic duress. Totem has alleged that Alyeska deliberately withheld payment of an acknowledged debt, knowing that Totem had no choice but to accept an inadequate sum in settlement of that debt; that Totem was faced with impending bankruptcy; that Totem was unable to meet its pressing debts other than by accepting the immediate cash payment offered by Alyeska; and that through necessity, Totem thus involuntarily accepted an inadequate settlement offer from Alyeska and executed a release of all claims under the contract. If the release was in fact executed under these circumstances, we think that under the legal principles discussed above that this would constitute the type of wrongful conduct and lack of alternatives that would render the release voidable by Totem on the ground of economic duress.

Id. at 23-24.

Here, Britton and Aghadjian acted in bad faith when they refused to pay Rich & Whillock, Inc.'s final billing and offered instead to pay a compromise amount of $50,000. At the time of their bad faith breach and settlement offer, Britton, and through him, Aghadjian, knew Rich & Whillock, Inc. was a new company overextended to creditors and subcontractors and faced with imminent bankruptcy if not paid its final billing. Whillock and Rich strenuously protested Britton's and Aghadjian's coercive tactics, and succumbed to them only to avoid economic disaster to themselves and the adverse ripple effects of their bankruptcy on those to whom they were indebted. Under these circumstances, the trial court found the July 10 agreement and August 20 release were the products of economic duress. That finding is consistent with the legal principles discussed above and is supported by substantial evidence. Accordingly, the court correctly concluded Ashton Development, Inc. and Bob Britton, Inc. were liable for the $22,286.45 balance due under the contract.

NOTES AND QUESTIONS

1. ***What happened?*** Who sued whom for what? Procedurally, how did the case get before this court? Factually, what happened between the parties? What arguments did the plaintiff and defendant make? What rule or rules did the court apply? How did the court analyze the dispute between the parties? How did the court decide the case?

2. ***Was this case correctly decided?*** Do you agree with the result reached in this case? Why or why not? Do you agree with the court's reasoning? Why or why not? How, if at all, would you have written the opinion differently?

3. ***Distinguishing* Rich & Whillock *from* Hackley.** In your judgment, what distinguishes this case from *Hackley*? In both cases, payments were withheld, but whereas the *Hackley* court found no duress of goods, here, the *Rich & Whillock* court found economic duress. First, why did the first case involve duress of goods, whereas this case involves economic duress? And second, why did the *Hackley* court find no duress of goods, but this court find economic duress?

Do you find the doctrine of economic duress a bit vague? If so, what do you suppose accounts for this vagueness? Is it the lack of clear thinking by judges? The difficulty of defining such an amorphous concept? The author below suggests that perhaps the answer lies in the fact that, if economic duress were defined clearly, it might prove to be too unruly a horse, swallowing up our modern conception of contract law. Do you agree?

THE VAGUENESS OF ECONOMIC DURESS*

The most characteristic result of [the expansion of the doctrine of duress] has been the doctrine of economic duress with its key concept of equal bargaining power. According to this doctrine, a contract may be voidable for economic duress whenever a significant inequality of bargaining power exists between the

* Excerpted from Roberto Mangabeira Unger, *The Critical Legal Studies Movement*, 96 HARV. L. REV. 561, 629 (1983).

parties. Gross inequalities of bargaining power, however, are all too common in the current forms of market economy, a fact shown not only by the dealings between individual consumers and large corporate enterprises, but also by the huge disparities of scale and market influence among enterprises themselves. Thus, the doctrine of economic duress must serve as a roving commission to correct the most egregious and overt forms of an omnipresent type of disparity. But the unproven assumption of the doctrine is that the amount of corrective intervention needed to keep a contractual regime from becoming a power order will not be so great that it destroys the vitality of decentralized decision making through contract. If this assumption proved false, no compromise between correction and abstention could achieve its intended effect. The only solution would be the one that every such compromise is meant to avoid: the remaking of the institutional arrangements that define the market economy. The doctrinal manifestation of this problem is the vagueness of the concept of economic duress. The cost of preventing the revised duress doctrine from running wild and from correcting almost everything is to draw unstable, unjustified, and unjustifiable lines between the contracts that are voidable and those that are not. In the event, the law draws these lines by a strategy of studied indefinition, though it might just as well have done so—as it so often does elsewhere—through precise but makeshift distinctions.

PROBLEM: ECONOMIC DURESS

Pursuant to a requirements contract, Defendant Demosthenes agreed to be the sole supplier of olives to Plaintiff Pericles, who is a producer of olive oil in Athens, Georgia. Three years into their 5-year contract, several articles in the mainstream media came out highlighting the health benefits of olive oil, causing the demand for olive oil to spike. Trying to capitalize on this demand, a number of olive oil manufacturers approached Demosthenes and offered to buy his olives at a price 50% higher than that currently being paid by Pericles. Demosthenes approached Pericles, told him about these offers, but explained that, due to their long relationship, he would "split the difference" by continuing to sell Pericles all the olives he should require if Pericles agreed to a 25% price increase. Otherwise, explained Demosthenes, he would be forced to sell his olives to someone else. Pericles looked around for another supplier, but couldn't find anyone that could beat Demosthenes's new price. Pericles, therefore, agreed to buy olives from Demosthenes for 25% more than provided in the contract, and continued to do so until the contract expired 2 years later, at which time Pericles brought suit against Demosthenes, seeking restitution of the additional amounts paid on account of economic duress.

Drawing on the cases and materials presented above, how do you think this case should be resolved, and why?

3. Undue Influence

DOCTRINAL OVERVIEW: UNDUE INFLUENCE AS A DEFENSE TO ENFORCEMENT*

The concept of undue influence developed in courts of equity to give relief to victims of unfair transactions that were induced by improper persuasion. In contrast to the common law notion of duress, the essence of which was simple fear induced by threat, the equitable concept of undue influence was aimed at the protection of those affected with a weakness, short of incapacity, against improper persuasion, short of misrepresentation or duress, by those in a special position to exercise such persuasion. By the end of the nineteenth century it had been carried over to actions at law as well as equity. Like duress, undue influence makes a contract voidable and may serve as a defense or as the basis of a claim in restitution. Two elements are commonly required: first, a special relation between the parties; second, improper persuasion of the weaker by the stronger.

A finding of undue influence is generally said to require a special relation between the parties that makes one of them peculiarly susceptible to persuasion by the other. . . . The classical case involves a relation of trust or confidence in which the weaker party is justified in assuming that the stronger will not act in a manner inconsistent with the weaker's welfare.[5] Examples include the relations between parent and child, member of the clergy and communicant, physician and patient, husband and wife, and—according to some courts—one engaged person and the other. In an illustrative case, the mother of a child born out of wedlock testified that during a period of emotional distress following the birth of the child, representatives of the maternity home, including her individual counsellor, had sought her agreement to give up the child. The Texas court observed that her counsellor was "a person to whom plaintiff was encouraged to look for guidance" and upheld a jury verdict based on this testimony, which was "rendered credible by the fact that an unwed mother who has just given birth is usually emotionally distraught and peculiarly vulnerable to efforts, well meaning or unscrupulous, to persuade her to give up her child."[9]

The protection afforded by the doctrine has been extended beyond relations characterized by trust and confidence to those in which the weaker party is for some reason under the domination of the stronger.[10] [For instance, in the next case we shall read,] a schoolteacher alleged that after he had been arrested on criminal charges of homosexual activity, questioned by the police, booked, released on bail, and gone for 40 hours without sleep, the superintendent of the school district and the principal of his school came to his apartment to ask for his resignation. The California court noted the possibility "that exhaustion and

* Excerpted from E. ALLAN FARNSWORTH, CONTRACTS § 4.20 (4th ed. 2004).

5. *See Restatement Second* § 177 (party "who by virtue of the relation between them is justified in assuming that (the other) person will not act in a manner inconsistent with his welfare").

9. Methodist Mission Home v. B., 451 S.W.2d 539, 543-44 (Tex. Civ. App. 1970).

10. *See Restatement Second* § 177 ("a party who is under the domination of the person exercising the persuasion").

emotional turmoil may wholly incapacitate a person from exercising his judgment" and held that the pleadings sufficed to show the required relation of "a dominant subject to a servient object."

Once the requisite relation is shown, it must then be shown that the assent of the weaker party was induced by unfair persuasion on the part of the stronger. What are the limits of persuasion in this context? The degree of persuasion that will be characterized as "unfair" depends on a variety of circumstances, but the ultimate question is whether the result was produced by means that seriously impaired the free and competent exercise of judgment. A particularly important factor in showing unfairness in persuasion is imbalance in the resulting bargain. As one authority has expressed it, "Transactions must be judged not only in terms of motive but in terms of their effects."[13] Other factors include the unavailability of independent advice, the lack of time for reflection, and the susceptibility of the weaker party. . . .

In the case of the unwed mother, the court noted that:

> Because the unfair persuasion required falls short of what is required for misrepresentation or duress, undue influence affords protection in some situations where those other doctrines would not. However, the extraordinary expansion of the scope of duress has to a considerable extent undercut the importance of the concept of undue influence.[16]

Because the unfair persuasion required falls short of what is required for misrepresentation or duress, undue influence affords protection in some situations where those other doctrines would not. However, the extraordinary expansion of the scope of duress has to a considerable extent undercut the importance of the concept of undue influence. . . .

Odorizzi v. Bloomfield School District

California District Court of Appeal
54 Cal. Rptr. 533 (1996)

FLEMING, J. Appeal from a judgment dismissing plaintiff's amended complaint on demurrer.

Plaintiff Donald Odorizzi was employed during 1964 as an elementary school teacher by defendant Bloomfield School District and was under contract with the district to continue to teach school the following year as a permanent employee. On June 10 he was arrested on criminal charges of homosexual activity, and on June 11 he signed and delivered to his superiors his written resignation as a teacher, a resignation which the district accepted on June 13. In July the criminal charges against Odorizzi were dismissed . . . , and in September

13. John Dawson, *Economic Duress—An Essay in Perspective*. 45 MICH. L. REV. 253, 264 (1947).
16. 451 S.W.2d at 544.

he sought to resume his employment with the district. On the district's refusal to reinstate him he filed suit for declaratory and other relief.

Odorizzi's amended complaint asserts his resignation was invalid because obtained through duress, fraud, mistake, and undue influence and given at a time when he lacked capacity to make a valid contract. Specifically, Odorizzi declares he was under such severe mental and emotional strain at the time he signed his resignation, having just completed the process of arrest, questioning by the police, booking, and release on bail, and having gone for 40 hours without sleep, that he was incapable of rational thought or action. While he was in this condition and unable to think clearly, the superintendent of the district and the principal of his school came to his apartment. They said they were trying to help him and had his best interests at heart, that he should take their advice and immediately resign his position with the district, that there was no time to consult an attorney, that if he did not resign immediately the district would suspend and dismiss him from his position and publicize the proceedings, his "aforedescribed arrest" and cause him "to suffer extreme embarrassment and humiliation"; but that if he resigned at once the incident would not be publicized and would not jeopardize his chances of securing employment as a teacher elsewhere. Odorizzi pleads that because of his faith and confidence in their representations they were able to substitute their will and judgment in place of his own and thus obtain his signature to his purported resignation. A demurrer to his amended complaint was sustained without leave to amend.

By his complaint plaintiff in effect seeks to rescind his resignation . . . , on the ground that his consent had not been real or free . . . , but had been obtained through duress, menace, fraud, undue influence, or mistake. . . . In our view the facts in the amended complaint are insufficient to state a cause of action for duress, menace, fraud, or mistake, but they do set out sufficient elements to justify rescission of a consent because of undue influence. We summarize our conclusions on each of these points.

1. No duress or menace has been pleaded. Duress consists in unlawful confinement of another's person, or relatives, or property, which causes him to consent to a transaction through fear. Duress is often used interchangeably with menace, but in California menace is technically a threat of duress or a threat of injury to the person, property, or character of another. We agree with respondent's contention that neither duress nor menace was involved in this case, because the action or threat in duress or menace must be unlawful, and a threat to take legal action is not unlawful unless the party making the threat knows the falsity of his claim. The amended complaint shows in substance that the school representatives announced their intention to initiate suspension and dismissal proceedings . . . at a time when the filing of such proceedings was not only their legal right but their positive duty as school officials. Although the filing of such proceedings might be extremely damaging to plaintiff's reputation, the injury would remain incidental so long as the school officials acted in good faith in the performance of their duties. Neither duress nor menace was present as a ground for rescission.

2. **Nor do we find a cause of action for fraud, either actual or constructive.** Actual fraud involves conscious misrepresentation, or concealment, or non-disclosure of a material fact which induces the innocent party to enter the contract. A complaint for fraud must plead misrepresentation, knowledge of falsity, intent to induce reliance, justifiable reliance, and resulting damage. While the amended complaint charged misrepresentation, it failed to assert the elements of knowledge of falsity, intent to induce reliance, and justifiable reliance. A cause of action for actual fraud was therefore not stated.

Constructive fraud arises on a breach of duty by one in a confidential or fiduciary relationship to another which induces justifiable reliance by the latter to his prejudice. Plaintiff has attempted to bring himself within this category, for the amended complaint asserts the existence of a confidential relationship between the school superintendent and principal as agents of the defendant, and the plaintiff. Such a confidential relationship may exist whenever a person with justification places trust and confidence in the integrity and fidelity of another. Plaintiff, however, sets forth no facts to support his conclusion of a confidential relationship between the representatives of the school district and himself, other than that the parties bore the relationship of employer and employee to each other. Under prevailing judicial opinion no presumption of a confidential relationship arises from the bare fact that parties to a contract are employer and employee; rather, additional ties must be brought out in order to create the presumption of a confidential relationship between the two. The absence of a confidential relationship between employer and employee is especially apparent where, as here, the parties were negotiating to bring about a termination of their relationship. In such a situation each party is expected to look after his own interests, and a lack of confidentiality is implicit in the subject matter of their dealings. We think the allegations of constructive fraud were inadequate.

3. **As to mistake, the amended complaint fails to disclose any facts which would suggest that consent had been obtained through a mistake of fact or of law.** The material facts of the transaction were known to both parties. Neither party was laboring under any misapprehension of law of which the other took advantage. The discussion between plaintiff and the school district representatives principally attempted to evaluate the probable consequences of plaintiff's predicament and to predict the future course of events. The fact that their speculations did not forecast the exact pattern which events subsequently took does not provide the basis for a claim that they were acting under some sort of mistake. The doctrine of mistake customarily involves such errors as the nature of the transaction, the identity of the parties, the identity of the things to which the contract relates, or the occurrence of collateral happenings. Errors of this nature were not present in the case at bench.

4. **However, the pleading does set out a claim that plaintiff's consent to the transaction had been obtained through the use of undue influence.** Undue influence, in the sense we are concerned with here, is a shorthand legal phrase used to describe persuasion which tends to be coercive in nature,

persuasion which overcomes the will without convincing the judgment. The hallmark of such persuasion is high pressure, a pressure which works on mental, moral, or emotional weakness to such an extent that it approaches the boundaries of coercion. In this sense, undue influence has been called overpersuasion. Misrepresentations of law or fact are not essential to the charge, for a person's will may be overborne without misrepresentation. By statutory definition undue influence includes "taking an unfair advantage of another's weakness of mind, or . . . taking a grossly oppressive and unfair advantage of another's necessities or distress." [Citations omitted.] While most reported cases of undue influence involve persons who bear a confidential relationship to one another, a confidential or authoritative relationship between the parties need not be present when the undue influence involves unfair advantage taken of another's weakness or distress.

We paraphrase the summary of undue influence given the jury by Sir James P. Wilde in *Hall v. Hall,* L.R. 1, P. & D. 481, 482 (1868):

> To make a good contract a man must be a free agent. Pressure of whatever sort which overpowers the will without convincing the judgment is a species of restraint under which no valid contract can be made. Importunity or threats, if carried to the degree in which the free play of a man's will is overborne, constitute undue influence, although no force is used or threatened. A party may be led but not driven, and his acts must be the offspring of his own volition and not the record of someone else's.

In essence undue influence involves the use of excessive pressure to persuade one vulnerable to such pressure, pressure applied by a dominant subject to a servient object. In combination, the elements of undue susceptibility in the servient person and excessive pressure by the dominating person make the latter's influence undue, for it results in the apparent will of the servient person being in fact the will of the dominant person.

Undue susceptibility may consist of total weakness of mind which leaves a person entirely without understanding; or, a lesser weakness which destroys the capacity of a person to make a contract even though he is not totally incapacitated; or, the first element in our equation, a still lesser weakness which provides sufficient grounds to rescind a contract for undue influence. Such lesser weakness need not be long-lasting nor wholly incapacitating, but may be merely a lack of full vigor due to age, physical condition, emotional anguish, or a combination of such factors. The reported cases have usually involved elderly, sick, senile persons alleged to have executed wills or deeds

The Jedi Defense

Personally, I like to think of undue influence as the Jedi defense. Why? There's a wonderful scene in *Star Wars: Episode IV—A New Hope,* in which Ben Obi-Wan Kenobi, a Jedi of extraordinary mental abilities, comes face to face with several stormtroopers, soldiers in the Imperial Army, who are of at least average mental ability. Here's what happens:

> Stormtrooper: Let me see your identification.
> Ben Obi-Wan Kenobi: [with a small wave of his hand] You don't need to see his identification.
> Stormtrooper: We don't need to see his identification.
> Ben Obi-Wan Kenobi: These aren't the droids you're looking for.
> Stormtrooper: These aren't the droids we're looking for.
> Ben Obi-Wan Kenobi: He can go about his business.
> Stormtrooper: You can go about your business.

under pressure. In some of its aspects this lesser weakness could perhaps be called weakness of spirit. But whatever name we give it, this first element of undue influence resolves itself into a lessened capacity of the object to make a free contract.

In the present case plaintiff has pleaded that such weakness at the time he signed his resignation prevented him from freely and competently applying his judgment to the problem before him. Plaintiff declares he was under severe mental and emotional strain at the time because he had just completed the process of arrest, questioning, booking, and release on bail and had been without sleep for forty hours. It is possible that exhaustion and emotional turmoil may wholly incapacitate a person from exercising his judgment. As an abstract question of pleading, plaintiff has pleaded that possibility and sufficient allegations to state a case for rescission.

Undue influence in its second aspect involves an application of excessive strength by a dominant subject against a servient object. Judicial consideration of this second element in undue influence has been relatively rare, for there are few cases denying persons who persuade but do not misrepresent the benefit of their bargain. Yet logically, the same legal consequences should apply to the results of excessive strength as to the results of undue weakness. Whether from weakness on one side, or strength on the other, or a combination of the two, undue influence occurs whenever there results

> that kind of influence or supremacy of one mind over another by which that other is prevented from acting according to his own wish or judgment, and whereby the will of the person is overborne and he is induced to do or forbear to do an act which he would not do, or would do, if left to act freely.

Webb v. Saunders, 79 Cal. App. 2d 863, 871 (1947). Undue influence involves a type of mismatch which our statute calls unfair advantage. Whether a person of subnormal capacities has been subjected to ordinary force or a person of normal capacities subjected to extraordinary force, the match is equally out of balance. If will has been overcome against judgment, consent may be rescinded.

The difficulty, of course, lies in determining when the forces of persuasion have overflowed their normal banks and become oppressive flood waters. There are second thoughts to every bargain, and hindsight is still better than foresight. Undue influence cannot be used as a pretext to avoid bad bargains or escape from bargains which refuse to come up to expectations. A woman who

> Ben Obi-Wan Kenobi: Move along.
> Stormtrooper: Move along . . .
> move along.
>
> Note that the stormtroopers do not suffer from the sort of deficiencies in mental capacity that would allow them to assert the defense of incompetence that we explored in subsection 8.B.2 — they are, after all, soldiers in the imperial army — yet they were clearly no match for the mind of a Jedi. Had the stormtroopers been contracting with Obi-Wan, they could easily have been made to give him anything he wanted for, say, a meager galactic credit. Because courts don't generally inquire into the adequacy of consideration, the stormtroopers would be at the Jedi's mercy without a defense like undue influence available to them, which measures not the absolute strength of the stronger party's will, nor the absolute weakness of the weaker party's will, but *the relative difference between them*. More evidence for this view is provided in a bolded sentence three paragraphs down.

buys a dress on impulse, which on critical inspection by her best friend turns out to be less fashionable than she had thought, is not legally entitled to set aside the sale on the ground that the saleswoman used all her wiles to close the sale. A man who buys a tract of desert land in the expectation that it is in the immediate path of the city's growth and will become another Palm Springs, an expectation cultivated in glowing terms by the seller, cannot rescind his bargain when things turn out differently. If we are temporarily persuaded against our better judgment to do something about which we later have second thoughts, we must abide the consequences of the risks inherent in managing our own affairs.

Characteristics accompanying undue influence

Where Jedi aren't involved, overpersuasion is traditionally accompanied (as in *Odorizzi*) by one or more of the seven characteristics noted by the court. Whenever you see any of these factors present, you should be on the lookout for the possibility of undue influence. Which of these factors were present in *Odorizzi*?

However, **overpersuasion is generally accompanied by certain characteristics which tend to create a pattern. The pattern usually involves several of the following elements: (1) discussion of the transaction at an unusual or inappropriate time, (2) consummation of the transaction in an unusual place, (3) insistent demand that the business be finished at once, (4) extreme emphasis on untoward consequences of delay, (5) the use of multiple persuaders by the dominant side against a single servient party, (6) absence of third-party advisers to the servient party, (7) statements that there is no time to consult financial advisers or attorneys. If a number of these elements are simultaneously present, the persuasion may be characterized as excessive.** . . .

The difference between legitimate persuasion and excessive pressure, like the difference between seduction and rape, rests to a considerable extent in the manner in which the parties go about their business. For example, if a day or two after Odorizzi's release on bail the superintendent of the school district had called him into his office during business hours and directed his attention to those provisions of the Education Code compelling his leave of absence and authorizing his suspension on the filing of written charges, had told him that the district contemplated filing written charges against him, had pointed out the alternative of resignation available to him, had informed him he was free to consult counsel or any adviser he wished and to consider the matter overnight and return with his decision the next day, it is extremely unlikely that any complaint about the use of excessive pressure could ever have been made against the school district.

But, according to the allegations of the complaint, this is not the way it happened, and if it had happened that way, plaintiff would never have resigned. Rather, the representatives of the school board undertook to achieve their objective by overpersuasion and imposition to secure plaintiff's signature but not his consent to his resignation through a high-pressure carrot-and-stick technique—under which they assured plaintiff they were trying to assist him, he should rely on their advice, there wasn't time to consult an attorney, if he didn't resign at once the school district would suspend and dismiss him from his position and publicize the proceedings, but if he did resign the incident wouldn't jeopardize his chances of securing a teaching post elsewhere.

Plaintiff has thus pleaded both subjective and objective elements entering the undue influence equation and stated sufficient facts to put in issue the question whether his free will had been overborne by defendant's agents at a time when he was unable to function in a normal manner. It was sufficient to pose ". . . the ultimate question . . . whether a free and competent judgment was merely influenced, or whether a mind was so dominated as to prevent the exercise of an independent judgment." *Williston on Contracts* § 1625 [rev. ed.]. The question cannot be resolved by an analysis of pleading but requires a finding of fact.

We express no opinion on the merits of plaintiff's case, or the propriety of his continuing to teach school, or the timeliness of his rescission. We do hold that his pleading, liberally construed, states a cause of action for rescission of a transaction to which his apparent consent had been obtained through the use of undue influence.

The judgment is reversed.

RELEVANT PROVISIONS

For the *Restatement (Second) of Contracts,* consult § 177.

NOTES AND QUESTIONS

1. ***What happened?*** Who sued whom for what? Procedurally, how did the case get before this court? Factually, what happened between the parties? What arguments did the plaintiff and defendant make? What rule or rules did the court apply? How did the court analyze the dispute between the parties? How did the court decide the case?

2. ***Was this case correctly decided?*** Do you agree with the result reached in this case? Why or why not? Do you agree with the court's reasoning? Why or why not? How, if at all, would you have written the opinion differently?

3. ***Importance of the*** Odorizzi ***factors?*** How important are the seven factors listed in *Odorizzi* for establishing the defense of undue influence? Here's one court's take:

> The district court erred in two ways in dismissing Kelly's rescission claim as inadequate under California law. The first was in concluding that Kelly failed to state a claim for undue influence because his complaint did not include some or all of the seven factors from *Odorizzi v. Bloomfield School Dist.*, 54 Cal. Rptr. 533 (Cal. App. 1966). *Odorizzi* did not hold that undue influence can be found only if some of the seven factors are present. Rather, the California court suggested that most, but not necessarily all, situations constituting undue

influence involve those factors. *Id.* at 133, 54 Cal. Rptr. 533 ("[O]verpersuasion is *generally* accompanied by certain characteristics which tend to create a pattern. The pattern *usually* involves several of the following elements.") (emphasis added). The *Odorizzi* list was not described as exhaustive. Some contracts might be formed through undue influence even if most or all of the *Odorizzi* factors are absent. For example, if a contract is the sort for which undue influence must be presumed, the contract would be presumed illegal even if no *Odorizzi* factors were present. *See O'Neil v. Spillane*, 119 Cal. Rptr. 245 (Cal. App. 1975) (the presumption of undue influence "is, by itself, sufficient to support the finding of undue influence"). We do not hold that Kelly did state a valid cause of action for undue influence under California law, let alone that he can prove it, but we are satisfied that Kelly's failure to allege *Odorizzi* factors does not support the conclusion that he did not.*

4. *Distinguishing defenses.* How, if at all, would you distinguish between the defenses of duress and undue influence?

5. *Public policy.* How can this defense be justified, if at all, on grounds different than those used to justify the defense of physical duress? We encountered a similar issue when we examined *Vokes v. Arthur Murray* in subsection 8.D.1, *supra*, but, once again, how (if at all) can courts draw the line between permissible and impermissible methods of persuasion?

PROBLEM: UNDUE INFLUENCE?

Plaintiff Paula was 80 years old and very feeble, under the influence of medicines, and being confined to her bed most of the time, when she deeded her house to her daughter-in-law, Defendant Diana, of whom she was very fond. Diana had, at the request of Paula, left her home, and devoted her time and attention to Paula as her companion and nurse for some weeks prior to the time the deed was made. Diana was kind, patient, and attentive during the days and nights she nursed and cared for Paula. During this time, Paula talked a great deal, and at times incoherently, and seemed to fear that she would lose all her property. She told Diana that there were evil spirits in the house and that the spirits kept her from sleeping. She said that a web was being woven against her, and that the pills the doctor gave her had legs; she could feel them crawling in her stomach. While Paula was not mentally incompetent, she was delirious at times, weak, and very nervous. It is not clear whether Diana made any hints or suggestions to gain Paula's confidence and take advantage of her during the many days and nights during which she appeared faithful and lovingly attended and nursed Paula. However, Diana had the deed prepared by her own attorney, and that this fact was never mentioned to Paula's husband or daughter, who also lived in the house. Further, Paula never obtained any advice from a third party before signing the deed, nor did Paula ever suggest that she do so. By the same token, Paula never prevented her from

* *Kelly v. Provident Life & Acc. Ins.*, 245 F. App'x 637, 639 (9th Cir. 2007).

consulting anyone, and never suggested that she not do so. The notary who took the acknowledgment was brought to the house while Diana's husband and daughter were absent. The deed was executed, acknowledged, delivered, and recorded before any one was informed of it other than the notary.

Drawing on *Odorizzi* and the materials in this subunit, do you think the deed made by plaintiff was procured by undue influence? Why or why not?

4. Unconscionability

Society, when granting freedom of contract, does not guarantee that all members of the community will be able to make use of it to the same extent. On the contrary, the law, by protecting the unequal distribution of property, does nothing to prevent freedom of contract from becoming a one-sided privilege. Society, by proclaiming freedom of contract, guarantees that it will not interfere with the exercise of power by contract. Freedom of contract enables enterprisers to legislate by contract and, what is even more important, to legislate in a substantially authoritarian manner without using the appearance of authoritarian forms. Standard contracts in particular could thus become effective instruments in the hands of powerful industrial and commercial overlords enabling them to impose a new feudal order of their own making upon a vast host of vassals.

Friedrich Kessler, *Contracts of Adhesion—Some Thoughts about Freedom of Contract*, 43 COLUM. L. REV. 629, 640 (1943)

DOCTRINAL OVERVIEW: UNCONSCIONABILITY AS A DEFENSE TO ENFORCEMENT*

Courts of equity did not share the reluctance of common law courts to police bargains for substantive unfairness. Though mere "inadequacy of consideration" alone was not a ground for withholding equitable relief, a contract that was "inequitable" or "unconscionable"—one that was so unfair as to "shock the conscience of the court"—would not be enforced in equity. . . .

The equitable concept of unconscionability inspired one of the most innovative sections of the Uniform Commercial Code—UCC § 2-302, which deals with unconscionable contracts and terms, provides in Subsection (1):

> If the court as a matter of law finds the contract or any clause of the contract to have been unconscionable at the time it was made the court may refuse to enforce the contract, or it may enforce the remainder of the contract without the unconscionable clause, or it may so limit the application of any unconscionable clause as to avoid any unconscionable result.[1]

* Excerpted from E. ALLAN FARNSWORTH, CONTRACTS §§ 4.27 and 4.28 (4th ed. 2004).

1. UCC § 2-302.

Thus the Code recognizes a doctrine of unconscionability that is not limited to equity and that invites courts to police bargains overtly for unfairness. . . . In the words of the comments to the Code:

> This section is intended to enable courts to police explicitly against the contracts or clauses which they find to be unconscionable. In the past such policing has been accomplished by adverse construction of language, by manipulation of the rules of offer and acceptance or by determinations that the clause is contrary to public policy or to the dominant purpose of the contract.[3]

Llewellyn, who is credited with authorship of UCC § 2-302, described it as "perhaps the most valuable section in the entire Code."[4] As scholars lavished more ink on this section than on any comparable passage in the Code, the doctrine of unconscionability rapidly gained wide acceptance.

Although § UCC 2-302 is not one of the general articles of the Code and so strictly speaking governs only "transactions in goods," it has wisely been applied, either by analogy or as an expression of a general doctrine, to many other kinds of contracts, including contracts that fall under other articles of the Code. The *Restatement Second* contains a section on unconscionability patterned after the Code's and applicable to contracts generally,[8] and several uniform laws contain similar provisions applicable to contracts within their purview. . . .

Nowhere among the Code's many definitions is there one of *unconscionability.* That the term is incapable of precise definition is a source of both strength and weakness. The comments to UCC § 2-302 give only the most general guidance on the meaning of the term. They tell the reader that the "basic test is whether, in the light of the general commercial background and the commercial needs of the particular trade or case, the clauses involved are so one-sided as to be unconscionable under the circumstances existing at the time of the making of the contract."[15] The commentary then gives a series of examples based on pre-Code cases, confirming the reader's suspicion that the term is undefinable. UCC § 2-302 does at least make it clear that any unfairness in the terms is to be judged at the time the contract is made and not at some later time. The analogous provision of the UNIDROIT Principles on "gross disparity," in contrast, lists at least a few factors relevant to the determination of whether a contract or term "unjustifiably gave the other party an excessive advantage."[17]

The most noted of these pre-Code cases is *Campbell Soup Co. v. Wentz.* . . .

---

3. UCC § 2-302 cmt. 1.
4. 1 N.Y.L. Revision Comm'n, Hearings on the Uniform Commercial Code 121 (1954).
8. *Restatement Second* § 208.
15. UCC § 2-302 cmt. 1.
17. UNIDROIT Principles [3.2.7(1)]. However, these factors include, in addition to the nature and purpose of the contract, only taking unfair advantage of the other party.

Campbell Soup Co. v. Wentz

United States Court of Appeals, Third Circuit
172 F.2d 80 (1948)

[We previously considered whether Campbell was entitled to specific performance of their contract. To review that portion of the opinion, see p. 632, *supra*. In this portion of the opinion, we examine whether Campbell's contract was unconscionable.]

GOODRICH, CIRCUIT JUDGE. . . . The reason that we shall affirm instead of reversing with an order for specific performance is found in the contract itself. We think it is too hard a bargain and too one-sided an agreement to entitle the plaintiff to relief in a court of conscience. For each individual grower the agreement is made by filling in names and quantity and price on a printed form furnished by the buyer. This form has quite obviously been drawn by skillful draftsmen with the buyer's interests in mind.

Paragraph 2 provides for the manner of delivery. Carrots are to have their stalks cut off and be in clean sanitary bags or other containers approved by Campbell. This paragraph concludes with a statement that Campbell's determination of conformance with specifications shall be conclusive. . . .

The next paragraph allows Campbell to refuse carrots in excess of twelve tons to the acre. The next contains a covenant by the grower that he will not sell carrots to anyone else except the carrots rejected by Campbell nor will he permit anyone else to grow carrots on his land. Paragraph 10 provides liquidated damages to the extent of $50 per acre for any breach by the grower. There is no provision for liquidated or any other damages for breach of contract by Campbell.

The provision of the contract which we think is the hardest is paragraph 9, set out in the margin.[11] It will be noted that Campbell is excused from accepting carrots under certain circumstances. But even under such circumstances the grower, while he cannot say Campbell is liable for failure to take the carrots, is not permitted to sell them elsewhere unless Campbell agrees. This is the kind of provision which the late Francis H. Bohlen would call "carrying a good joke too far." What the grower may do with his product under the circumstances set out is not clear. He has covenanted not to store it anywhere except on his own farm and also not to sell to anybody else.

11. "Grower shall not be obligated to deliver any Carrots which he is unable to harvest or deliver, nor shall Campbell be obligated to receive or pay for any Carrots which it is unable to inspect, grade, receive, handle, use or pack at or ship in processed form from its plants in Camden (1) because of any circumstance beyond the control of Grower or Campbell, as the case may be, or (2) because of any labor disturbance, work stoppage, slow-down, or strike involving any of Campbell's employees. Campbell shall not be liable for any delay in receiving Carrots due to any of the above contingencies. During periods when Campbell is unable to receive Grower's Carrots, Grower may with Campbell's written consent, dispose of his Carrots elsewhere. Grower may not, however, sell or otherwise dispose of any Carrots which he is unable to deliver to Campbell."

We are not suggesting that the contract is illegal. Nor are we suggesting any excuse for the grower in this case who has deliberately broken an agreement entered into with Campbell. We do think, however, that a party who has offered and succeeded in getting an agreement as tough as this one is, should not come to a chancellor and ask court help in the enforcement of its terms. That equity does not enforce unconscionable bargains is too well established to require elaborate citation. . . .

[T]he sum total of [this contract's] provisions drives too hard a bargain for a court of conscience to assist.

This disposition of the problem makes unnecessary further discussion of the separate liability of Lojeski, who was not a party to the contract, but who purchased some of the carrots from the Wentzes.

The judgments will be affirmed.

RELEVANT PROVISIONS

For the *Restatement (Second) of Contracts*, consult §§ 208 and 364. For the UCC, consult §§ 1-103, 2-302. For the UNIDROIT Principles, consult Article 3.2.7.

NOTES AND QUESTIONS

1. *What happened?* Who sued whom for what? Procedurally, how did the case get before this court? Factually, what happened between the parties? What arguments did the plaintiff and defendant make? What rule or rules did the court apply? How did the court analyze the dispute between the parties? How did the court decide the case?

2. *Was this case correctly decided?* Do you agree with the result reached in this case? Why or why not? Do you agree with the court's reasoning? Why or why not? How, if at all, would you have written the opinion differently?

Williams v. Walker-Thomas Furniture Co.

United States Court of Appeals, D.C. Circuit
350 F.2d 445 (1965)

For a report of the case and accompanying materials, see p. 144, *supra*.

Higgins v. Superior Court of Los Angeles County

California Court of Appeal
45 Cal. Rptr. 3d 293 (2006)

RUBIN, J. In this writ proceeding, five siblings who appeared in an episode of the television program "Extreme Makeover: Home Edition" (Extreme

Makeover) challenge an order compelling them to arbitrate most of their claims against various entities involved with the production and broadcast of the program. Petitioners claim the arbitration clause contained in a written agreement they executed before the program was broadcast is unconscionable. We agree. Accordingly, we grant the petition for **writ of mandate**.

> ***Mandamus***
>
> "[Latin 'we command'] A writ issued by a court to compel performance of a particular act by a lower court or a governmental officer or body, usu. to correct a prior action or failure to act. Also termed writ of mandamus; mandate." BLACK'S LAW DICTIONARY (10th ed. 2014).

FACTUAL AND PROCEDURAL BACKGROUND

Petitioners Charles, Michael, Charis, Joshua, and Jeremiah Higgins are siblings. In February 2005, when they executed the agreement whose arbitration provision is at issue, they were 21, 19, 17, 16, and 14 years old, respectively.

Real parties in interest, to whom we refer collectively as the television defendants, are (1) American Broadcasting Companies, Inc., the network that broadcasts Extreme Makeover; (2) Disney/ABC International Television, Inc., which asserts it had no involvement with the Extreme Makeover program in which petitioners appeared; (3) Lock and Key Productions, the show's producer; (4) Endemol USA, Inc., which is also involved in producing the program; and (5) Pardee Homes, which constructed the home featured in the Extreme Makeover episode in which petitioners appeared.

Petitioners' parents died in 2004. The eldest sibling, Charles, became the guardian for the then three minor children. . . . Shortly thereafter, petitioners moved in with church acquaintances, Firipeli and Lokilani Leomiti, a couple with three children of their own. The Leomitis are defendants in the litigation but are not involved in the present writ proceeding.

According to Charles Higgins, after moving in with the Leomitis, he was advised by members of his church that producers of Extreme Makeover had contacted the church and had asked to speak to him about the production of a show based on the loss of petitioners' parents and that petitioners were now living with the Leomitis.[1] In July or August 2004, Charles called and spoke with an associate producer of Lock and Key about the program and petitioners' living situation.

Over the next several months, there were additional contacts between petitioners and persons affiliated with the production of the program, including in-person interviews and the filming of a casting tape. By early 2005, petitioners and the Leomitis were chosen to participate in the program in which the Leomitis' home would be completely renovated.

---

1. Lock and Key's executive producer describes Extreme Makeover as a "'reality' based television series" whose "premise . . . is to find needy and deserving families who live in a home which does not serve their needs. The Program takes the selected families' existing homes and land and radically improves them by demolishing and rebuilding the home."

On February 1, 2005, a Lock and Key producer sent by Federal Express to each of the petitioners and to the Leomitis an "Agreement and Release" for their signatures.[2] The Agreement and Release contains 24 single-spaced pages and 72 numbered paragraphs. Attached to it were several pages of exhibits, including an authorization for release of medical information, an emergency medical release, and, as Exhibit C, a one-page document entitled "Release." To avoid confusion with the one-page Exhibit C Release, we refer to the 24-page Agreement and Release simply as the "Agreement," and to Exhibit C as the "Release."

At the top of the first page of the Agreement, the following appears in large and underlined print:

> NOTE: DO NOT SIGN THIS UNTIL YOU HAVE READ IT COMPLETELY.

The second-to-last numbered paragraph also states in pertinent part:

> I have been given ample opportunity to read, and I have carefully read, this entire agreement. . . . I certify that I have made such an investigation of the facts pertinent to this Agreement and of all the matters pertaining thereto as I have deemed necessary. . . . I represent and warrant that I have reviewed this document with my own legal counsel prior to signing (or, IN THE ALTERNATIVE, although I have been given a reasonable opportunity to discuss this Agreement with counsel of my choice, I have voluntarily declined such opportunity).

The last section of the Agreement, which includes 12 numbered paragraphs, is entitled "MISCELLANEOUS." None of the paragraphs in that section contains a heading or title. Paragraph 69 contains the following arbitration provision:

> 69. I agree that any and all disputes or controversies arising under this Agreement or any of its terms, any effort by any party to enforce, interpret, construe, rescind, terminate or annul this Agreement, or any provision thereof, and any and all disputes or controversies relating to my appearance or participation in the Program, shall be resolved by binding arbitration in accordance with the following procedure. . . . All arbitration proceedings shall be conducted under the auspices of the American Arbitration Association. . . . I agree that the arbitrator's ruling, or arbitrators' ruling, as applicable, shall be final and binding and not subject to appeal or challenge. . . . The parties hereto agree that, notwithstanding the provisions of this paragraph, Producer shall have a right to injunctive or other equitable relief as provided for in California Code of Civil Procedure § 1281.8 or other relevant laws.

There is nothing in the Agreement that brings the reader's attention to the arbitration provision. Although a different font is used occasionally to highlight certain terms in the Agreement, that is not the case with the paragraph

---

2. The version of the agreement intended for the three minor petitioners was slightly different than the one intended for the two adult petitioners and the Leomitis. The slight variations between the two versions are not relevant to the issue before us. In this opinion, we quote from, and cite to, the adult version.

containing the arbitration provision. Six paragraphs in the Agreement contain a box for the petitioners to initial; initialing is not required for the arbitration provision.

The Agreement also contains a provision limiting petitioners' remedies for breach of the Agreement to money damages.

The one-page Release is typed in a smaller font than the Agreement. It consists of four single-spaced paragraphs, the middle of which contains the following arbitration clause:

> I agree that any and all disputes or controversies arising under this Release or any of its terms, any effort by any party to enforce, interpret, construe, rescind, terminate or annul this Release, or any provision thereof, shall be resolved exclusively by binding arbitration before a single, neutral arbitrator, who shall be a retired judge of a state or federal court. All arbitration proceedings shall be conducted under the auspices of the American Arbitration Association, under its Commercial Arbitration Rules, through its Los Angeles, California office. I agree that the arbitration proceedings, testimony, discovery and documents filed in the course of such proceedings, including the fact that the arbitration is being conducted, will be treated as confidential. . . .

There is no evidence that any discussions took place between petitioners and any representative of the television defendants regarding either the Agreement or the Release, or that any of the television defendants directly imposed any deadline by which petitioners were required to execute the documents.

On February 5, 2005, a field producer from Lock and Key and a location manager for the program went to the Leomitis' home and met with the Leomitis. Although physically present at the house, petitioners did not participate in the meeting. During the meeting, one of the Leomitis asked about the documents they had received, and the producer and location manager advised the Leomitis that they should read the documents carefully, call if they had questions, and then execute and return the documents.

According to Charles, after this meeting, the Leomitis emerged with a packet of documents, which they handed to petitioners. Mrs. Leomiti instructed petitioners to "flip through the pages and sign and initial the document where it contained a signature line or box." Charles stated that from the time Mrs. Leomiti "handed the document to us and the time we signed it, approximately five to ten minutes passed." The document contained complex legal terms that he did not understand. He did not know what an arbitration agreement was and did not understand its significance or the legal consequences that could flow from signing it. He did not specifically state whether or not he saw the arbitration provisions contained either in paragraph 69 or the Release before he signed the documents.

Each of the petitioners executed the Agreement and signed all exhibits, including the Release.

On February 16, 2005, representatives from the show appeared and started to reconstruct the Leomitis' home. When the new home was completed, it had nine bedrooms, including one for each of the five petitioners. The existing mortgage was also paid off.

The program featuring petitioners and the Leomitis was broadcast on Easter Sunday, 2005.

Petitioners allege that, after the show was first broadcast, the Leomitis informed petitioners that the home was theirs (the Leomitis'), and the Leomitis ultimately forced petitioners to leave. Charles contacted Lock and Key's field producer and asked for help. The producer responded that he could not assist petitioners. Sometime thereafter, the Extreme Makeover episode was rebroadcast.

In August 2005, petitioners filed this action against the television defendants and the Leomitis. According to the record before us, the complaint includes claims for, among other things, intentional and negligent misrepresentation, breach of contract, unfair competition, and false advertising. With respect to the television defendants, the complaint appears to allege that those defendants breached promises to provide petitioners with a home, exploited petitioners, and portrayed petitioners in a false light (by rebroadcasting the episode when they knew the episode no longer reflected petitioners' living situation).

The television defendants petitioned to compel arbitration pursuant to the Federal Arbitration Act (FAA). The television defendants maintained that all claims against both them and the Leomitis should be arbitrated. The Leomitis joined in the petition.

Petitioners opposed the petition, claiming, among other things, that the arbitration provision was unconscionable. They claimed it was procedurally unconscionable because the parties had unequal bargaining power, the arbitration provision was "buried" in the Agreement, petitioners were given only five to ten minutes before they were asked to sign the Agreement, none of the television defendants explained the Agreement to them, and copies of the executed documents were "withheld" from them.

Petitioners also argued the Agreement was substantively unconscionable because its terms were so one-sided as to shock the conscience. They claimed the Agreement requires only them and not the television defendants to arbitrate, limits petitioners' remedies to damages (while the television defendants' remedies are not so limited), precludes only petitioners from appealing, provides that the arbitration will be in accordance with the rules of the American Arbitration Association (which unfairly requires arbitration costs to be borne equally by the parties), and allows the television defendants to change the terms of the Agreement at any time.

After argument, the trial court issued an order granting [defendants'] petition in most respects, conditioned on the television defendants' paying all arbitration costs. . . . The trial court also stated that "since defendants have shown that plaintiffs signed the releases having had an opportunity to read them, the arbitration provisions are found by this court to be enforceable." . . .

Petitioners then filed this writ petition challenging the trial court's ruling. We issued an alternative writ, received additional briefing from the parties, and heard oral argument.

DISCUSSION

A. *Unconscionability as a Defense to Enforcement of Arbitration Provisions*

The trial court ruled, and petitioners do not dispute, that the enforceability of the arbitration clause is governed by the FAA. . . .

[U]nder both the FAA and California law, "arbitration agreements are valid, irrevocable, and enforceable, save upon such grounds as exist at law or in equity for the revocation of any contract." *Armendariz v. Foundation Health Psychcare Services, Inc.*, 24 Cal. 4th 83, 98 (2000).

One ground is unconscionability. . . . As is frequently the case with inquiries into unconscionability, our analysis begins—although it does end—with whether the Agreement and Release are contracts of adhesion. Petitioners contend that they are and that the arbitration provisions are unconscionable. A contract of adhesion is a standardized contract that is imposed and drafted by the party of superior bargaining strength and relegates to the other party "'only the opportunity to adhere to the contract or reject it.'" *Ibid.* . . . If a court finds a contract to be adhesive, it must then determine whether "'other factors are present which, under established legal rules—legislative or judicial—operate to render it'" unenforceable. *Armendariz,* at p. 113.

One "established rule" is that a court need not enforce an adhesion contract that is unconscionable. As our Supreme Court explained in *Armendariz,* the Legislature has now codified the principle, historically developed in case law, that a court may refuse to enforce an unconscionable provision in a contract. Code Civ. Proc., § 1670.5.[8] . . .

Unconscionability has both a procedural and a substantive element, the former focusing on "oppression" or "surprise" due to unequal bargaining power, the latter on "overly harsh" or "one-sided" results. *Armendariz,* supra, 24 Cal. 4th at p. 114. "'The prevailing view is that [procedural and substantive unconscionability] must *both* be present in order for a court to exercise its discretion to refuse to enforce a contract or clause under the doctrine of unconscionability.' But they need not be present in the same degree. 'Essentially a sliding scale is invoked which disregards the regularity of the procedural process of the contract formation, that creates the terms, in proportion to the greater harshness or unreasonableness of the substantive terms themselves.' In other words, the more substantively oppressive the contract term, the less evidence of procedural unconscionability is required to come to the conclusion that the term is unenforceable, and vice versa." *Ibid.* . . .

8. Civil Code § 1670.5(a) provides: "If the court as a matter of law finds the contract or any clause of the contract to have been unconscionable at the time it was made the court may refuse to enforce the contract, or it may enforce the remainder of the contract without the unconscionable clause, or it may so limit the application of any unconscionable clause as to avoid any unconscionable result."

D. *The Arbitration Provision Is Unconscionable*

1. *The Adhesive Nature of the Parties' Agreement*

We begin with whether the parties' agreement was adhesive. See *Armendariz,* supra, 24 Cal. 4th at p. 113. As discussed above, "'[t]he term [contract of adhesion] signifies a standardized contract, which, imposed and drafted by the party of superior bargaining strength, relegates to the subscribing party only the opportunity to adhere to the contract or reject it.'" *Ibid.*

In this case, it is undisputed that the lengthy Agreement was drafted by the television defendants. It is a standardized contract; none of the petitioners' names or other identifying information is included in the body of the document. There is no serious doubt that the television defendants had far more bargaining power than petitioners.

The remaining question is whether petitioners were relegated only to signing or rejecting the Agreement. The television defendants note that there is no evidence petitioners were told they could not negotiate any terms of the Agreement or that petitioners made any attempt to do so. Although literally correct, the uncontested evidence was that on the day petitioners signed the Agreement the television defendants initially met with the Leometis alone. Inferentially, at the television defendants' urging, immediately after the meeting concluded, the Leomitis gave the Agreement and exhibits to petitioners with directions to "flip through the pages and sign." The documents were returned in five to ten minutes. One of the producers testified that he told the Leomitis "that these agreements must be executed as a condition to their further participation in the program."

From these facts, we conclude the Agreement was presented to petitioners on a take-it-or-leave-it basis by the party with the superior bargaining position who was not willing to engage in negotiations. Accordingly, we conclude the Agreement and exhibits constitute a contract of adhesion.

2. *Procedural Unconscionability*

"Procedural unconscionability focuses on the factors of surprise and oppression, with surprise being a function of the disappointed reasonable expectations of the weaker party." *Harper v. Ultimo,* 113 Cal. App. 4th 1402, 1406 (2003).

In this case, the arbitration provision appears in one paragraph near the end of a lengthy, single-spaced document. The entire agreement was drafted by the television defendants, who transmitted copies of it to the petitioners. The television defendants knew petitioners were young and unsophisticated, and had recently lost both parents. Indeed, it was petitioners' vulnerability that made them so attractive to the television defendants. The latter made no effort to highlight the presence of the arbitration provision in the Agreement. It was one of 12 numbered paragraphs in a section entitled "miscellaneous." In contrast to several other paragraphs, no text in the arbitration provision is highlighted. No words are printed in bold letters or larger font; nor are they capitalized. Although petitioners were required to place their initials in boxes adjacent to six other paragraphs, no box appeared next to the arbitration provision.

It is true that the top of the first page advises petitioners to read the entire agreement before signing it and the second-to-last paragraph states that the person signing acknowledges doing so. This language, although relevant to our inquiry, does not defeat the otherwise strong showing of procedural unconscionability.

We now turn to substantive unconscionability, utilizing our Supreme Court's sliding scale approach. See *Armendariz*, supra, 24 Cal. 4th at p. 114. Procedural and substantive unconscionability "need not be present in the same degree. 'Essentially a sliding scale is invoked which disregards the regularity of the procedural process of the contract formation, that creates the terms, in proportion to the greater harshness or unreasonableness of the substantive terms themselves.'" *Ibid.*

3. *Substantive Unconscionability*

"Substantively unconscionable terms may 'generally be described as unfairly one-sided.' For example, an agreement may lack 'a modicum of bilaterality' and therefore be unconscionable if the agreement requires 'arbitration only for the claims of the weaker party but a choice of forums for the claims of the stronger party.'" *Fitz v. NCR Corp.*, 118 Cal. App. 4th 702, 713 (2004), quoting *Armendariz*, supra, 24 Cal. 4th at p. 119.

In this case, the arbitration provision requires only petitioners to submit their claims to arbitration. The clause repeatedly includes "I agree" language, with the "I" being a reference to the "applicant" (i.e., each of the petitioners). The only time the phrase "the parties" is used is in the last sentence, where "the parties" agree that, notwithstanding the arbitration provision, the producer has the right to seek injunctive or other equitable relief in a court of law as provided for in Code of Civil Procedure § 1281.1 or other relevant laws.

The television defendants claim that the arbitration provision is bilateral, because "all disputes or controversies arising under this Agreement or any of its terms, any effort by any party to enforce . . . this Agreement . . . and any and all disputes or controversies relating to my appearance or participation in the Program, shall be resolved by binding arbitration." (¶69.) Thus, "all disputes" are subject to arbitration, and either side may move to compel. But they miss the point: only one side (petitioners) agreed to that clause. . . .

Additional elements of substantive unconscionability are found in the provision barring only petitioners from seeking appellate review of the arbitrator's decision and, at least insofar as it could impact petitioners' statutory claims, the provision requiring arbitration in accordance with the rules of the American Arbitration Association, which provide that arbitration costs are to be borne equally by the parties.[13] The harsh, one-sided nature of the arbitration

13. As noted above, the trial court shifted all arbitration costs to the television defendants. See *Gutierrez v. Autowest, Inc.*, 114 Cal. App. 4th 77, 92-93 (2003) (unconscionable requirement for payment of arbitration costs may be severed).

provision, combined with the elements of procedural unconscionability earlier discussed, leads us to conclude that the arbitration provision is unconscionable and, therefore, unenforceable. Accordingly, it was error for the trial court to have granted the petition to compel arbitration.

DISPOSITION

The petition for writ of mandate is granted. The respondent court is directed to vacate that part of its December 1, 2005 order granting the petition of the television defendants to compel arbitration and staying certain claims, and to thereafter enter a new and different order denying the petition to compel arbitration. Petitioners are entitled to recover their costs in this writ proceeding.

NOTES AND QUESTIONS

1. *What happened?* Who sued whom for what? Procedurally, how did the case get before this court? Factually, what happened between the parties? What arguments did the plaintiff and defendant make? What rule or rules did the court apply? How did the court analyze the dispute between the parties? How did the court decide the case?

2. *Was this case correctly decided?* Do you agree with the result reached in this case? Why or why not? Do you agree with the court's reasoning? Why or why not? How, if at all, would you have written the opinion differently?

3. *Procedural and substantive unconscionability.* Does the "procedural" prong of the unconscionability test (i.e., finding a contract of adhesion) seem to be doing any analytical work in these cases? Why or why not? If not, does the defense of unconscionability really boil down to examining its substantive prong? If so, to what extent does this challenge the traditional rule that the substance of a bargain will not be inquired into by courts? Remember, courts generally do not inquire into the adequacy of consideration. *See Schnell, Batsakis,* and related materials in Part III.4.A.2.a.

4. *Media attention.* This heart-wrenching case garnered a lot of media attention, and there is a wonderful Dan Abrams video that should be consulted as a supplement to the written case above. The video can be found here: http://www.nbcnews.com/id/8973501/ns/msnbc-the_abrams_report/t/extreme-makeover-lawsuit/#.VZ3T-0bw92A.

5. *A case in a poem.* Having still more fun with the case, a law student at the University of Minnesota Law School was inspired to turn the facts above into a darn good poem! Here is the poem as it appears on the website "Above the Law":

'TWAS THE CASE BRIEF BEFORE CHRISTMAS

'Twas 2006, in the court of appeal

When California decided to rule on this deal.
The story at hand has some tragic beginnings,
Where both parents had died and left behind these 5 siblings
A family at church made their troubles their own,
And invited the family to stay at their home.
A network caught wind of the troubles they faced,
And offered to build for these kids a new place.
The family from church was briefly consulted
Much less so the kids, which is how this resulted.
For after the studio built them a house
The church family decided to kick these kids out.
The children were shocked and cried "that's not fair!"
"In the contract we signed, we weren't told of what's there."
In the papers they signed, there contained an agreement
That arbitration would rule when one side sought appeasement.
The trial court said that the signed clause would rule,
And the provision within was judged to be cool.
At this point in the case, this court intervened,
And decided the claims of these children redeemed.
Unconscionability, this court has decided,
Henceforth shall be present with two things provided:
First, the two parties must not be the same
When deciding which terms on the contract remain.
And next all those terms that are contained herein,
Must be oppressive for the plaintiff to win.
The trial court was correct, if as they assumed,
The plaintiff had thought the whole contract was doomed.
But their beef was not with the thing as a whole,
But arbitration, they claimed, was all that was null.
So the court of appeal turned back the dial,
And ruled that this case be remanded for trial.*

PROBLEM: CONTRACTING IN ANOTHER LANGUAGE

Plaintiff Gas Company is suing Diego Defendant for breach of contract to collect money owed. Specifically, Gas Company entered into a contract on June 15, 2011 to deliver and install a Gas Conversion Burner in an apartment complex owned by Diego. According to the contract, Diego's payments were deferred for twelve months, and the Gas Conversion Burner had a one-year unconditional satisfaction guarantee.

The written contract was presented to Diego in English only. Diego, who did not speak or write English but spoke and wrote Spanish fluently, admits to signing

* *See* "'Twas The Night Before Finals, And Law Students Were Freaking Out" at http://abovethelaw.com/2012/12/twas-the-night-before-finals-and-law-students-were-freaking-out/ (last accessed December 4, 2015).

the contract but claims that no one ever explained it to him. Diego further asserts that when he asked for an interpretation and explanation of the contract, an agent of the Gas Company named Carmen told him to sign it. It should be noted that Gas Company never sold or negotiated directly with Diego, but induced Diego's tenants to pressure Diego into signing the contract. It should also be pointed out that Carmen had Diego sign the contract at her office, which was a few blocks away from the Gas Company's main office, where a Spanish interpreter would have been available.

One month after purchasing the Gas Conversion Burner, Diego attempted to make a payment but was told by an employee of the Gas Company that he need not pay for another year. After one year passed, on June 15, 2012, Diego started to make payment. On or about May 22, 2013, Diego complained to Gas Company that the Gas Conversion Buner was not functioning. Gas Company's field repairmen found that a transformer burned out, and an order for the part was placed with Gas Company office. However, after discovering that Diego had made no payments past December 2012, no further action was taken by Gas Company to supply the necessary part. Diego, not receiving satisfaction, made no attempt to make further payments and Gas Company made no attempt to repair. Diego further claims that one of Gas Company's employees told him that if anything ever happened to the unit it would be repaired.

How would you analyze Diego's defense of unconscionability in response to Gas Company's suit against him for breach of contract?

PROBLEM: THE DESPERATE TRAVELER?*

T, a symphony musician, is driving through the desert on a recreational trip when he suddenly hits a rock jutting out from the sand. *T*'s vehicle is disabled and his ankle is fractured. He has no radio and little water, and will die if he is not soon rescued. The next day, *G,* a university geologist who is returning to Tucson from an inspection of desert rock formations, adventitiously passes within sight of the accident and drives over to investigate. *T* explains the situation and asks *G* to take him back to Tucson, which is sixty miles away. *G* replies that he will help only if *T* promises to pay him two-thirds of his wealth or $100,000, whichever is more. *T* agrees, but after they return to Tucson he refuses to keep his promise, and *G* brings an action to enforce it.

Applying the principles developed above, how should a court decide the previous dispute, and why?

* The following problem is from Melvin Aaron Eisenberg, *The Bargain Principle and Its Limits,* 95 HARV. L. REV. 741, 755 (1982).

E. EXCUSING PERFORMANCE

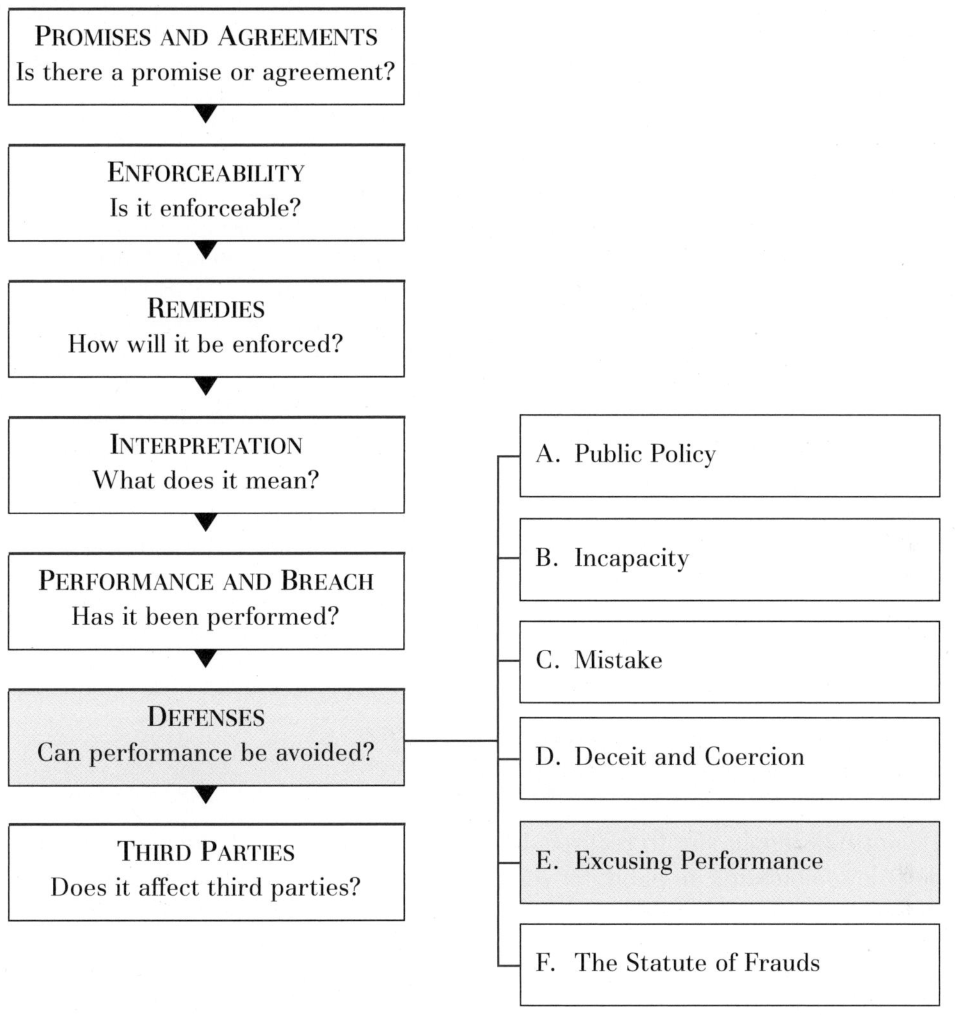

Contrary to our examination of mistake, where we were concerned with whether one or both of the parties were mistaken about a basic assumption regarding presently existing facts, the defenses we will cover in this section concern assumptions the parties have made about facts as they will exist in the future. Although nobody can predict the future with certainty, contract law presumes that parties enter into contracts with certain background assumptions in mind about what the future world will look like, and that their bargain is based, at least in part, on these assumptions. Therefore, when the future that arrives deviates sufficiently from the parties' assumptions about the future they thought would arrive, and this deviation relates to some material aspect of the parties' contract, courts will sometimes excuse a party's performance due to these unexpected circumstances, on the grounds that they either render performance (1) impossible, (2) impracticable, or (3) frustrate a party's purpose in making a contract. We will explore each of these three defenses in turn in the materials below.

1. Discharging Contractual Obligations: The Traditional Rule

One who makes a contract never can be absolutely certain that he will be able to perform it when the time comes, and the very essence of it is that he takes the risk within the limits of his undertaking. The modern cases may have abated somewhat the absoluteness of the older ones in determining the scope of the undertaking by the literal meaning of the words alone. . . . But when the scope of the undertaking is fixed, that is merely another way of saying that the contractor takes the risk of the obstacles to that extent.

Day v. United States, 245 U.S. 159, 161 (1917) (Holmes, J.)

A man may contract to do what is impossible, as well as what is difficult, and be liable for failure to perform. The important question is whether an unanticipated circumstance has made performance of the promise vitally different from what should reasonably have been within the contemplation of both parties when they entered into the contract.

Samuel Williston, ON CONTRACTS, vol. 6, § 1931 (rev. ed. 1938)

Stees v. Leonard

Supreme Court of Minnesota
20 Minn. 494 (1874)

[Plaintiffs brought suit to recover damages for defendants' failure to erect and complete a building on plaintiffs' lot according to plans and specifications. The defendants commenced the construction of the building, and had carried it to the height of three stories, when it fell to the ground. The next year, they began again and carried it to the same height, when it again fell to the ground, whereupon defendants refused to perform the contract. Defendants claimed that in attempting to erect the building their work was performed according to the plans and specifications, and that the failure to complete the building and its fall on the two occasions was due to the fact that the soil upon which it was to be constructed was composed of quicksand, and when water flowed into it, was incapable of sustaining the building. The jury found for plaintiffs and awarded $5,214.80 in damages, consisting of (1) $3,745.80 already paid to defendants, (2) $1,000 for loss of use of the lot, and (3) $469 reflecting damage to an adjacent house owned by plaintiffs. Defendants moved for a new trial, and now appeal an order denying that motion.]

Risk analysis

It's difficult to imagine a more unforgiving rule, but to say a rule is unforgiving is not to say that it is good or bad—that's

YOUNG, J. **The general principle of law which underlies this case is well established. If a man bind himself, by a positive, express contract, to do an**

act in itself possible, he must perform his engagement, unless prevented by the act of God, the law, or the other party to the contract. No hardship, no unforeseen hindrance, no difficulty short of absolute impossibility, will excuse him from doing what he has expressly agreed to do. This doctrine may sometimes seem to bear heavily upon contractors; but, in such cases, the hardship is attributable, not to the law, but to the contractor himself, who has improvidently assumed an absolute, when he might have undertaken only a qualified, liability. The law does no more than enforce the contract as the parties themselves have made it. . . .

for *you* to decide. What do you think are the advantages and disadvantages to such a rule? Throughout the cases in this section, we will be examining the extent to which courts have chipped away at this rule, and explore the extent to which you think these changes are good or bad for contract law.

The rule has been applied in several recent cases, closely analogous to the present in their leading facts. In *Adams v. Nichols,* 19 Pick. 275, the defendant, Nichols, contracted to erect a dwelling-house for plaintiff on plaintiff's land. The house was nearly completed, when it was destroyed by accidental fire. It was held that the casualty did not relieve the contractor from his obligation to perform the contract he had deliberately entered into. The court clearly stated and illustrated the rule, as laid down in the note to *Walton v. Waterhouse,* 2 Wms. Saunders, 422, and added:

> In these and similar cases, which seem hard and oppressive, the law does no more than enforce the exact contract entered into. If there be any hardship, it arises from the indiscretion or want of foresight of the suffering party. It is not the province of the law to relieve persons from the improvidence of their own acts.

In *School District* v. *Dauchy,* 25 Conn. 530, the defendant contracted to build and complete a school-house. When nearly finished, the building was struck by lightning, and consumed by the consequent fire, and the defendant refused to rebuild, although plaintiffs offered to allow him such further time as should be necessary. It was held that this non-performance was not excused by the destruction of the building. The court thus stated the rule:

> If a person promise absolutely, without exception or qualification, that a certain thing shall be done by a given time, or that a certain event shall take place, and the thing to be done, or the event, is neither impossible nor unlawful at the time of the promise, he is bound by his promise, unless the performance, before that time, becomes unlawful.

School Trustees v. Bennett, 3 Dutcher, 513, is almost identical, in its material facts, with the present case. The contractors agreed to build and complete a school-house, and find all materials therefor, according to specifications annexed to the contract; the building to be located on a lot owned by plaintiff, and designated in the contract. When the building was nearly completed it was blown down by a sudden and violent gale of wind. The contractors again began to erect the building, when it fell, solely on account of the soil on which it stood having become soft and miry, and unable to sustain the weight of the building;

although, when the foundations were laid, the soil was so hard as to be penetrated with difficulty by a pickax, and its defects were latent. The plaintiff had a verdict for the amount of the installments paid under the contract as the work progressed. The verdict was sustained by the supreme court, which held that the loss, although arising solely from a latent defect in the soil, and not from a faulty construction of the building, must fall on the contractor.

In the opinion of the court, the question is fully examined, many cases are cited, and the rule is stated

> that where a party by his own contract creates a duty or charge upon himself he is bound to make it good if he may, notwithstanding any accident by inevitable necessity, because he might have provided against it by his contract. . . . If, before the building is completed or accepted, it is destroyed by fire or other casualty, the loss falls upon the builder; he must rebuild. The thing may be done, and he has contracted to do it. . . . No matter how harsh and apparently unjust in its operation the rule may occasionally be, it cannot be denied that it has its foundations in good sense and inflexible honesty. He that agrees to do an act should do it, unless absolutely impossible. He should provide against contingencies in his contract. Where one of two innocent persons must sustain a loss, the law casts it upon him who has agreed to sustain it; or, rather, the law leaves it where the agreement of the parties has put it. . . . Neither the destruction of the incomplete building by a tornado, nor its falling by a latent softness of the soil, which rendered the foundation insecure, *necessarily* prevented the performance of the contract to build, erect, and complete this building for the specified price. It can still be done, for aught that was opened to the jury as a defense, and overruled by the court.

In *Dermott v. Jones*, 2 Wall. 1, the foundation of the building sank, owing to a latent defect in the soil, and the owner was compelled to take down and rebuild a portion of the work. The contractor having sued for his pay, it was held that the owner might recoup the damages sustained by his deviation from the contract. The court refers with approval to the cases cited, and says:

> The principle which controlled them rests upon a solid foundation of reason and justice. It regards the sanctity of contracts. It requires a party to do what he has agreed to do. If unexpected impediments lie in the way, and a loss ensue, it leaves the loss where the contract places it. If the parties have made no provision for a dispensation, the rule of law gives none. It does not allow a contract fairly made to be annulled, and it does not permit to be interpolated what the parties themselves have not stipulated.

Nothing can be added to the clear and cogent arguments we have quoted in vindication of the wisdom and justice of the rule which must govern this case, unless it is in some way distinguishable from the cases cited. . . .

[Here] defendants contracted to "erect and complete the building." Whatever was necessary to be done in order to complete the building, they were bound by the contract to do. . . .

[T]he order appealed from is affirmed.

NOTES AND QUESTIONS

1. ***What happened?*** Who sued whom for what? Procedurally, how did the case get before this court? Factually, what happened between the parties? What arguments did the plaintiff and defendant make? What rule or rules did the court apply? How did the court analyze the dispute between the parties? How did the court decide the case?

2. ***Was this case correctly decided?*** Do you agree with the result reached in this case? Why or why not? Do you agree with the court's reasoning? Why or why not? How, if at all, would you have written the opinion differently?

3. ***Too harsh?*** Does this result seem overly harsh? Does it seem fair? Do you agree with the approach taken by the court? What are the pros and cons of this approach? Can you think of a better rule?

4. ***Risk.*** Where should the risk lie? In fact, many of the cases you will read in this section deal with this seemingly basic question: When a future risk materializes that neither party has foreseen, which party should bear it? At the end of this unit, some materials will be presented that offer potential answers to this question. For the time being, try to formulate a rule or principle that could assist courts with the difficult task of determining on which party an unforeseen risk that materializes should lie.

5. ***The sound of silence?*** Where a risk befalls the parties, and neither party has provided against this risk in their contract, how should the contract be interpreted? Should the court simply assign the risk ex post to the party on whom it happened to fall, or is there a principled way to think about this risk ex ante, so that a court could determine which party should bear a risk before the risk materialized?

6. ***Antecedents.*** This ostensibly harsh principle has antecedents going back to a famous English case, *Paradine v. Jane*, 82 Eng. Rep. 897 (K.B., 1647), in which defendant (Jane) was forced off land he was leasing from plaintiff (Paradine) by a Royalist army during the English Civil War. The Royalist army held the land for three years, and because Jane could not occupy the land during this time, he stopped paying rent. Paradine brought suit against Jane for breaching the lease agreement, and, in memorable language, the court sided with Paradine, finding that Jane was liable for the unpaid rent:

> [T]hough the whole army had been alien enemies, yet he ought to pay his rent. . . . [W]hen the party by his own contract creates a duty or charge upon himself, he is bound to make it good, if he may, notwithstanding any accident by inevitable necessity, because he might have provided against it by his contract. And therefore if the lessee covenant to repair a house, though it be burnt by lightning, or thrown down by enemies, yet he ought to repair it. Now the rent is a duty created by the parties . . . , there [is] no question but the lessee must have made it good, notwithstanding the interruption by enemies, for the law

would not protect him beyond his own agreement. . . . [T]hough the land be surrounded, or gained by the sea, or made barren by wildfire, yet the lessor shall have his whole rent: and judgment was given for the plaintiff.

2. Impossibility and Impracticability

DOCTRINAL OVERVIEW: EXCUSING PERFORMANCE DUE TO IMPOSSIBILITY OR IMPRACTICABILITY*

The common law was slow to give effect to the maxim *impossibilium nulla obligatio est* ("there is no obligation to do the impossible"). Courts were less receptive to claims of excuse based on events occurring after the making of the contract than they were to claims of excuse based on facts that existed at the time of the agreement. In a seventeenth-century dictum that was to gain wide acceptance, the Court of King's Bench declared that:

> when the party by his own contract creates a duty or charge upon himself, he is bound to make it good, if he may, notwithstanding any accident by inevitable necessity, because he might have provided against it by his contract. And therefore if the lessee covenant to repair a house, though it be burnt by lightning, or thrown down by enemies, yet he ought to repair it.[1]

The same court, however, had already admitted three important exceptions to this strict view that impossibility is no excuse.

The first of these exceptions can be traced back to an even earlier case, in which the Court of King's Bench said that if a seller undertakes to deliver wheat by a stated day in a foreign country and before that day performance is made illegal by statute, the seller's duty is discharged.[2] It subsequently became established that if supervening governmental action prevents a party's performance by prohibiting it or imposing requirements that make it impossible, that party is excused. . . .

The second exception to the strict view that impossibility is no excuse was announced by Queen's Bench in the sixteenth century. In dictum, that court stated that if a contract requires performance by the promisor, no action will lie for its breach if the promisor dies before performing.[7] It later became accepted that if a particular person's existence is necessary for performance of a duty, and performance is prevented by that person's death or disability, the duty is discharged. . . . Whether the existence of a particular person is necessary for performance may be determined by the agreement itself. . . . The services of a

* Excerpted from E. ALLAN FARNSWORTH, CONTRACTS § 9.5 (4th ed. 2004).

1. *Paradine v. Jane*, 82 Eng. Rep. 897, 897 (K.B. 1647). That case arose, the court said, when a lessee sought to be excused from paying rent because a "German prince, by name Prince Rupert, an alien born, enemy to the King and kingdom," ousted him from the land, so that he could not take income from it, but it did not involve impossibility because lie could still have paid the rent. . . .

2. *Abbot of Westminster v. Clerke*, 73 Eng. Rep. 59, 63 (K.B. 1536).

7. *Hyde v. Dean of Windsor*, 78 Eng. Rep. 798 (Q.B. 1597).

portrait painter are clearly personal, and the portrait painter is therefore excused if prevented by illness or death from painting the portrait. The services of a house painter, on the other hand, are usually not personal, and the house painter is therefore not excused by illness or death. If a party can delegate a duty to perform to another, the party's own death or incapacity will not be an excuse.

The third exception to the strict rule that impossibility is no excuse was laid down by King's Bench in the seventeenth century. The court held that a bailee's duty to return a horse was discharged when, without the bailee's fault, the horse died, because "that is become impossible by the act of God."[12] The rule came to be that if the existence of a particular thing is necessary for a party's performance, the party is excused if the destruction or deterioration of that thing prevents performance.[13] This rule was confirmed and elaborated in the celebrated case of *Taylor v. Caldwell*, the fountainhead of the modern law of impossibility. . . .

Taylor v. Caldwell

Queen's Bench

112 Eng. Rep. 309 (1863)

BLACKBURN J. In this case the plaintiffs and defendants had, on the 27th May, 1861, entered into a contract by which the defendants agreed to let the plaintiffs have the use of The Surrey Gardens and Music Hall on four days then to come, *viz.*, the 17th June, 15th July, 5th August and 19th August, for the purpose of giving a series of four grand concerts, and day and night fetes at the Gardens and Hall on those days respectively; and the plaintiffs agreed to take the Gardens and Hall on those days, and pay £100 for each day.

Surrey Music Hall ca. 1858

The parties inaccurately call this a "letting," and the money to be paid a "rent"; but the whole agreement is such as to shew that the defendants were to retain the possession of the Hall and Gardens so that there was to be no demise of them, and that the contract was merely to give the plaintiffs the use of them on those days. Nothing however, in our opinion, depends on this. The agreement then proceeds to set out various stipulations between the parties as to what each was to supply for these concerts and entertainments, and as to the manner in which they should be carried on. The effect of the whole is to shew

12. *Williams v. Lloyd*, 82 Eng. Rep. 95 (K.B. 1629). . . .

13. *See Restatement Second* § 263. The result is the same if the thing does not come into existence, as in [a crop failure case].

that the existence of the Music Hall in the Surrey Gardens in a state fit for a concert was essential for the fulfilment of the contract—such entertainments as the parties contemplated in their agreement could not be given without it.

After the making of the agreement, and before the first day on which a concert was to be given, the Hall was destroyed by fire. This destruction, we must take it on the evidence, was without the fault of either party, and was so complete that in consequence the concerts could not be given as intended. **And the question we have to decide is whether, under these circumstances, the loss which the plaintiffs have sustained is to fall upon the defendants.** The parties when framing their agreement evidently had not present to their minds the possibility of such a disaster, and have made no express stipulation with reference to it, so that the answer to the question must depend upon the general rules of law applicable to such a contract.

Risk analysis

As we have seen throughout the cases in this chapter, the court here understands that the critical issue it is being tasked with is deciding which party should bear a risk that neither party has foreseen when they entered into the contract. On which party do you think the risk of loss should fall, and why? Can you think of any thinking tools that we have examined in this casebook, or any concepts we have explored in this chapter, that can shed light on how the court should answer this question?

There seems no doubt that where there is a positive contract to do a thing, not in itself unlawful, the contractor must perform it or pay damages for not doing it, although in consequence of unforeseen accidents, the performance of his contract has become unexpectedly burthensome or even impossible. But this rule is only applicable when the contract is positive and absolute, and not subject to any condition either express or implied: and there are authorities which, as we think, establish the principle that where, from the nature of the contract, it appears that the parties must from the beginning have known that it could not be fulfilled unless when the time for the fulfilment of the contract arrived some particular specified thing continued to exist, so that, when entering into the contract, they must have contemplated such continuing existence as the foundation of what was to be done; there, in the absence of any express or implied warranty that the thing shall exist, the contract is not to be construed as a positive contract, but as subject to an implied condition that the parties shall be excused in case, before breach, performance becomes impossible from the perishing of the thing without default of the contractor.

There seems little doubt that this implication tends to further the great object of making the legal construction such as to fulfil the intention of those who entered into the contract. For in the course of affairs men in making such contracts in general would, if it were brought to their minds, say that there should be such a condition.

Accordingly, in the Civil law, such an exception is implied in every obligation . . . of which the subject is a certain thing. The general subject is treated of by Pothier, who . . . states the result to be that the debtor . . . is freed from his obligation when the thing has perished, . . . unless by some stipulation he has taken on himself the risk of the particular misfortune which has occurred.

Although the Civil law is not of itself authority in an English Court, it affords great assistance in investigating the principles on which the law is grounded. And it seems to us that the common law authorities establish that in such a contract the same condition of the continued existence of the thing is implied by English law.

There is a class of contracts in which a person binds himself to do something which requires to be performed by him in person; and such promises, e.g. promises to marry, or promises to serve for a certain time, are never in practice qualified by an express exception of the death of the party; and therefore in such cases the contract is in terms broken if the promisor dies before fulfilment. Yet it was very early determined that, if the performance is personal, the executors are not liable; See 2 Wms. Exors. 1560, 5th ed., where a very apt illustration is given. "Thus," says the learned author,

> if an author undertakes to compose a work, and dies before completing it, his executors are discharged from this contract: for the undertaking is merely personal in its nature, and, by the intervention of the contractor's death, has become impossible to be performed.

. . . In *Hall v. Wright* (E. B. & E. 746, 749), Crompton J., in his judgment, puts another case.

> Where a contract depends upon personal skill, and the act of God renders it impossible, as, for instance, in the case of a painter employed to paint a picture who is struck blind, it may be that the performance might be excused.

. . . These are instances where the implied condition is of the life of a human being, but there are others in which the same implication is made as to the continued existence of a thing. For example, where a contract of sale is made amounting to a bargain and sale, transferring presently the property in specific chattels, which are to be delivered by the vendor at a future day; there, if the chattels, without the fault of the vendor, perish in the interval, the purchaser must pay the price and the vendor is excused from performing his contract to deliver, which has thus become impossible.

That this is the rule of the English law is established by the case of *Rugg v. Minett* (11 East, 210). . . .

This also is the rule in the Civil law, and it is worth noticing that Pothier . . . treats this as merely an example of the more general rule that every obligation [of which the subject is a certain thing] is extinguished when the thing ceases to exist. . . .

It may, we think, be safely asserted to be now English law, that in all contracts of loan of chattels or bailments if the performance of the promise of the borrower or bailee to return the things lent or bailed, becomes impossible because it has perished, this impossibility (if not arising from the fault of the borrower or bailee from some risk which he has taken upon himself) excuses the borrower or bailee from the performance of his promise to redeliver the chattel. . . .

The principle seems to us to be that, in contracts in which the performance depends on the continued existence of a given person or thing, a condition is implied that the impossibility of performance arising from the perishing of the person or thing shall excuse the performance.

In none of these cases is the promise in words other than positive, nor is there any express stipulation that the destruction of the person or thing shall excuse the performance; but that excuse is by law implied, because from the nature of the contract it is apparent that the parties contracted on the basis of the continued existence of the particular person or chattel. In the present case, looking at the whole contract, we find that the parties contracted on the basis of the continued existence of the Music Hall at the time when the concerts were to be given; that being essential to their performance.

We think, therefore, that the Music Hall having ceased to exist, without fault of either party, both parties are excused, the plaintiffs from taking the gardens and paying the money, the defendants from performing their promise to give the use of the Hall and Gardens and other things. Consequently the rule must be absolute to enter the verdict for the defendants.

The power of constructive conditions

Note that, in both *Stees* (p. 1074) and here, the parties did not themselves allocate the risk that ultimately materialized, leaving the courts to figure out how the parties' silence should be interpreted. In *Stees*, although the court did not write its opinion in these terms, what it actually did was interpret the parties' silence to mean that the *builder* implied a warranty to complete the building, come what may. In *Taylor*, by way of contrast, the court, instead of implying a warranty that the music hall would continue in existence (which it certainly *could* have done), implied a condition that, if the music hall did *not* continue to exist, the defendants' obligation to let the hall would be excused. Note that, in both cases, the court was *not* being (could not be!) neutral between the parties, as neither contract stated what was to be done where a particular risk materialized that Note that, in both *Stees* (p. 1074) and here, the parties did not themselves allocate the risk that ultimately materialized, leaving the courts to figure out how the parties' silence should be interpreted. In *Stees*, although the court did not write its opinion in these terms, what it actually did was interpret the parties' silence to mean that the *builder* implied a warranty to complete the building, come what may. In *Taylor*, by way of contrast, the court, instead of implying a warranty that the music hall would continue in existence (which it certainly *could* have done), implied a condition that, if the music hall did *not* continue to exist, the defendants' obligation to let the hall would be excused. Note that, in both cases, the court was *not* being (could not be!) neutral between the parties, as neither contract stated what was to be done where a particular risk materialized that the parties did not foresee. Therefore, in both cases, it was not the contract between the parties that dictated the court's outcome, and the court could not resolve the dispute by simply "applying" the terms of the contract. Instead, in both cases, the court's decision came

RELEVANT PROVISIONS

For the *Restatement (Second) of Contracts*, consult §§ 261 and 263. For the UCC, consult §§ 1-103(b), 2-509, 2-510, 2-613, 2-614(1), and 2-615. For the CISG, consult Articles 66-69 and 79. For the UNIDROIT Principles, consult Articles 6.2.1, 6.2.2, 6.2.3, and 7.1.7.

NOTES AND QUESTIONS

1. *What happened?* Who sued whom for what? Procedurally, how did the case get before this court? Factually, what happened between the parties? What arguments did the plaintiff and defendant make? What rule or rules did the court apply? How did the

court analyze the dispute between the parties? How did the court decide the case?

2. *Was this case correctly decided?* Do you agree with the result reached in this case? Why or why not? Do you agree with the court's reasoning? Why or why not? How, if at all, would you have written the opinion differently?

3. *Risk analysis.* Did the court place the risk on the right party? Why or why not? Which party was in the best position to prevent the risk that materialized here—the fire? In general, how do you think the court should determine on which party the risk should lie? Do any of the thinking tools we previously examined shed light on this question?

down to a choice between what type of constructive term it would write into the parties' contract as a matter of law. And how should the court make *this* decision? Should it look at what the parties would have intended had they foreseen the risk that materialized? Should they ask which of the two parties could have avoided the risk at the least cost? There is no single "right" answer to this question, so we end this sidebar with Holmes's musing on the subject (which may by now start to look familiar to you), who perhaps put it best when he said: "You can always imply a condition in a contract. But why do you imply it? It is because of some belief as to the practice of the community or of a class, or because of some opinion as to policy, or, in short, because of some attitude of yours upon a matter not capable of exact quantitative measurement, and therefore not capable of founding exact logical conclusions." Oliver Wendell Holmes, *The Path of the Law*, 10 HARV. L. REV. 466 (1897).

Facto v. Pantagis

Superior Court of New Jersey, Appellate Division
390 N.J. Super. 227 (2007)

SKILLMAN, J. This is a breach of contract action arising out of the cancellation of a wedding reception due to a power failure.

Plaintiffs contracted with defendant Snuffy Pantagis Ent., Inc., t/a Pantagis Renaissance, a banquet hall in Scotch Plains, for a wedding reception for 150 people, to be held between 6 p.m. and 11 p.m. on Saturday, August 3, 2002. The total contract price was $10,578, all of which was to be paid in advance. The contract contained a *force majeure* clause, which stated: "Snuffy's will be excused from performance under this contract if it is prevented from doing so by an act of God (e.g., flood, power failure, etc.), or other unforeseen events or circumstances."

Less than forty-five minutes after the reception began, there was a power failure in the area where the Pantagis Renaissance is located. At the time, plaintiffs were in an upstairs room with the bridal party, and their guests were downstairs being served alcoholic beverages and hors d'oeuvres. The power failure caused all the lights, except emergency lights, to go out and the air conditioning system to shut off. In addition, the band plaintiffs had hired for the reception refused to play without lights or the electricity required to operate their instruments, and the lack of lighting impeded the wedding photographer and videographer from taking pictures.

On the day of the reception, the temperature was in the upper 80s or low 90s and the humidity was high. As a result, plaintiffs and their guests became extremely uncomfortable within a short time after the power failure. According to plaintiffs, some of the guests resorted to pouring water over their heads to keep cool.

When it became evident that electricity would not be restored quickly, the manager of the Pantagis Renaissance offered to reschedule the reception. However, many of plaintiffs' guests had traveled a substantial distance to attend the wedding and would not have been able to return on another date. Therefore, plaintiffs declined the offer.

There was some dispute regarding the services provided after the power failure. Plaintiffs testified that the Pantagis Renaissance stopped serving alcoholic beverages around 7:30 p.m. and that the only food it served in addition to hors d'oeuvres was salad. However, the banquet hall's general manager testified that the facility continued to serve alcoholic beverages until after 9 p.m. and that it served plaintiffs and their guests salad and pasta and started to serve them dinner.

Shortly after 9 p.m., there was some kind of altercation between one of plaintiffs' guests and an employee of the Pantagis Renaissance. As a result, the banquet hall called the police, who arrived around 9:30 p.m. By this time, the batteries operating the emergency lights had begun to run out of power, and the only illumination was provided by candelabras on the tables. Therefore, the manager of the Pantagis Renaissance asked the police to evacuate the facility, which was then occupied not only by plaintiffs and their guests but also the attendees at four other wedding receptions.

Plaintiffs subsequently brought this breach of contract action seeking recovery of the $10,578 they prepaid for the wedding reception plus the $6,000 paid to the band, $3,810 paid to the wedding photographer and $3,242.09 paid to the videographer. Plaintiffs' complaint also asserted a negligence claim.

The case was tried in a half-day bench trial. The trial court concluded in a brief oral opinion that plaintiffs' breach of contract claim was barred by the *force majeure* clause of the contract because the power failure was an "unusual extraordinary unexpected circumstance" that could not be avoided by "reasonable human foresight." The court dismissed plaintiffs' negligence claim on the ground there was no evidence the Pantagis Renaissance was responsible for the power failure or failed to take reasonable measures to respond to this unforeseen circumstance. Accordingly, the court entered judgment dismissing plaintiffs' complaint.

On appeal, plaintiffs challenge the dismissal of both their negligence and contract claims. Plaintiffs' arguments in support of their negligence claim are clearly without merit and do not warrant extended discussion. Plaintiffs failed to present any evidence that could support a finding that defendants were negligent. Moreover, even if defendants had been negligent, their liability for failure to perform the contract would still be governed solely by the law of contracts.

Plaintiffs' contract claim presents more difficult issues. We agree with the trial court's conclusion that the power failure relieved the banquet hall of the obligation to provide plaintiffs with a wedding reception. Therefore, the banquet hall's failure to perform the contract due to the absence of electricity did not constitute a breach. But even though there was no breach, the banquet hall's inability to perform the contract also relieved plaintiffs of their obligation to pay the contract price. Consequently, plaintiffs are entitled to recovery of the $10,578 they prepaid the banquet hall, less the value of the services they did receive.

Even if a contract does not expressly provide that a party will be relieved of the duty to perform if an unforeseen condition arises that makes performance impracticable, "a court may relieve him of that duty if performance has unexpectedly become impracticable as a result of a supervening event." *Restatement (Second) of Contracts* § 261 cmt. a (1981). In deciding whether a party should be relieved of the duty to perform a contract, a court must determine whether "the existence of a specific thing is necessary for the performance of a duty" and "its . . . destruction, or . . . deterioration . . . makes performance impracticable[.]" *Restatement (Second) of Contracts* § 263 (1981). As explained in *Corbin*: "If the contract contains no words of express condition to either party's duty of performance, the court may have to fill the gap and determine whether the continued availability of certain means of performance should be deemed a constructive or implied condition." 14 *Corbin on Contracts* § 75.7 (Perillo rev. 2001). One court has recognized that even in the absence of a *force majeure* clause, a power failure is the kind of unexpected occurrence that may relieve a party of the duty to perform if the availability of electricity is essential for satisfactory performance. *See Opera Co. of Boston, Inc. v. Wolf Trap Found. for Performing Arts*, 817 F.2d 1094 (4th Cir. 1987) (power failure that prevented safe performance of concert).

A *force majeure* clause, such as contained in the Pantagis Renaissance contract, provides a means by which the parties may anticipate in advance a condition that will make performance impracticable. *See* 8 *Corbin on Contracts* § 31.4 (Perillo rev. 1999). Such a clause conditions a party's duty to perform upon the non-occurrence of some event beyond its control and serious enough to interfere materially with performance. *Ibid.*

A *force majeure* clause must be construed, like any other contractual provision, in light of "the contractual terms, the surrounding circumstances, and the purpose of the contract." *Marchak v. Claridge Commons, Inc.*, 134 N.J. 275, 282, 633 A.2d 531 (1993). When an unforeseen event affecting performance of a contract occurs, such a clause will be given a reasonable construction in light of the circumstances. *See* 8 *Corbin, supra*, § 31.4.

The *force majeure* clause in the Pantagis Renaissance contract provided: "Snuffy's will be excused from performance under this contract if it is prevented from doing so by an act of God (e.g., flood, power failure, etc.), or other unforeseen events or circumstances." Thus, the contract specifically identified a "power failure" as one of the circumstances that would excuse the Pantagis Renaissance's performance. We do not attribute any significance to the fact the *force majeure* clause refers to a power failure as an example of an "act of God." This term has been construed to refer not just to natural events such as storms but to "comprehend[ ] all misfortunes and accidents arising from inevitable necessity which human prudence could not foresee or prevent[.]" *Meyer Bros. Hay & Grain Co. v. Nat'l Malting Co.*, 11 A.2d 840 (Sup. Ct. 1940); *see also* 14 *Corbin, supra*, § 74.4 (noting that "[t]he kinds of impossibility that [excuse performance under a contract] in many instances are caused by human beings, although the court might still refer to the event as an 'act of

God.'"). Furthermore, the *force majeure* clause in the Pantagis Renaissance contract excuses performance not only for "acts of God" but also "other unforeseen events or circumstances." Consequently, even if a power failure caused by circumstances other than a natural event were not considered to be an "act of God," it still would constitute an unforeseen event or circumstance that would excuse performance.

The fact that a power failure is not absolutely unforeseeable during the hot summer months does not preclude relief from the obligation to perform. Indeed, even in the absence of a *force majeure* clause, absolute unforeseeability of a condition is not a prerequisite to the defense of impracticability. The party seeking to be relieved of the duty to perform only needs to show that "the 'destruction, or . . . deterioration' of a 'specific thing necessary for the performance' of the contract 'makes performance impracticable.'" *Id.* at 1100 (quoting *Restatement (Second) of Contracts* § 263 (1981)). In this case, the Pantagis Renaissance sought to eliminate any possible doubt that the availability of electricity was a "specific thing necessary" for the wedding reception by specifically referring to a "power failure" as an example of an "act of God" that would excuse performance.

It is also clear that the Pantagis Renaissance was "prevented from" substantial performance of the contract. The power failure began less than forty-five minutes after the start of the reception and continued until after it was scheduled to end. The lack of electricity prevented the band from playing, impeded the taking of pictures by the photographer and videographer and made it difficult for guests to see inside the banquet hall. Most significantly, the shutdown of the air conditioning system made it unbearably hot shortly after the power failure began. It is also undisputed that the power failure was an area-wide event that was beyond the Pantagis Renaissance's control. These are precisely the kind of circumstances under which the parties agreed, by inclusion of the *force majeure* clause, that the Pantagis Renaissance would be excused from performance. Therefore, the trial court correctly concluded that defendants did not breach the contract.

However, the court erred in concluding that because defendants did not breach the contract, plaintiffs are not entitled to recover the money they prepaid for the wedding reception. Where one party to a contract is excused from performance as a result of an unforeseen event that makes performance impracticable, the other party is also generally excused from performance. *Restatement (Second) of Contracts* §§ 237, 239, 267 (1981). As explained in *Corbin*:

> A promisor should not be compelled to give something for nothing. The parties agreed upon an exchange of performances, and an exchange cannot now take place. Even if not stated in express terms, the promisor's duty is constructively conditional on the return performance by the promisee. Even though the non-performing promisee is not in default because the impossibility doctrine discharges the duty, it cannot demand something for nothing from the other party.

14 *Corbin*, supra, § 78.2.

The same rule applies if a party to a contract is excused from performance by a *force majeure* clause that expressly sets forth certain categories of unforeseen events that will render performance impracticable. *See* 8 *Corbin, supra,* § 31.4 at 62. Therefore, the power failure that relieved the Pantagis Renaissance of the obligation to furnish plaintiffs with a wedding reception also relieved plaintiffs of the obligation to pay the contract price for the reception.

Nevertheless, since the Pantagis Renaissance partially performed the contract by starting the reception before the power failure, it is entitled, under principles of quantum meruit, to recover the value of the services it provided to plaintiffs. *See Shapiro v. Solomon,* 42 N.J. Super. 377, 383, 126 A.2d 654 (App.Div.1956) (noting that "where an express contract for work or services is abortive for . . . impossibility, or invalidity for other reasons, the plaintiff not being at fault . . . may have recovery for the value of his services[.]"); *see also Restatement (Second) of Contracts* § 272 (1981). The measure of damages is the benefit conferred upon the party against whom the quantum meruit claim is asserted.

Accordingly, the final judgment dismissing plaintiffs' complaint is reversed and the case is remanded to the trial court for further proceedings in conformity with this opinion.

NOTES AND QUESTIONS

1. *What happened?* Who sued whom for what? Procedurally, how did the case get before this court? Factually, what happened between the parties? What arguments did the plaintiff and defendant make? What rule or rules did the court apply? How did the court analyze the dispute between the parties? How did the court decide the case?

2. *Was this case correctly decided?* Do you agree with the result reached in this case? Why or why not? Do you agree with the court's reasoning? Why or why not? How, if at all, would you have written the opinion differently?

3. *Force majeure clause.* Make sure you know what a force majeure clause is, and how it can be used to allocate the risk between the parties. Alas, the risks covered by a force majeure clause will still only include those that the parties could foresee at the time they entered into the contract, and will therefore still require courts to fill gaps where risks materialize that were not foreseen by the parties.

4. *Risk analysis.* Did the court place the risk of loss on the right party? Why or why not?

5. *Illustration.* This case now appears as Illustration 10 to *Restatement (Third) of Restitution and Unjust Enrichment* § 20 as follows:

Plaintiffs hire Banquet Hall for a wedding reception, paying the full contract price of $10,000 in advance. The reception is disrupted by a power failure 45 minutes after it begins, when the failure of air conditioning makes conditions intolerable. Plaintiffs sue Banquet Hall for breach of contract, seeking to recover both the prepaid price and (as consequential damages) further amounts they had paid in advance to the band, the wedding photographer, and the videographer. The contract between Plaintiffs and Banquet Hall contains a force majeure clause specifically excusing performance in the event of a power failure; the existence of this provision disposes of Plaintiffs' claim for breach of contract and for contract damages. The court finds, however, that the parties' agreement does not authorize Banquet Hall to retain the prepaid price if its own performance is excused. Plaintiffs are entitled to restitution by the rule of this section. Recovery is in the amount of $10,000 less the value of the goods and services provided to Plaintiffs and their guests before performance was interrupted.

6. ***Thinking tools.*** Where it is not clear on which party to place the risk of loss, do any of the thinking tools we've previously examined shed light on either (a) that question, or (b) the broader question of how courts should decide such disputes?

THINKING TOOL APPLIED: EFFICIENCY, FORESEEABILITY, AND IMPOSSIBILITY*

The foreseeability doctrine appears to raise a number of difficulties. To some extent every occurrence is foreseeable. There is always some probability that a fire will destroy the anticipated source of supply, that a key person will die, that various acts of God—like floods—will occur, that there will be an embargo or war, etc. In an objective sense, virtually nothing is truly unforeseeable to the extent that theoretically every possible state of the world could be enumerated and some probability assigned to its occurrence.

The foreseeability requirement may only make sense if we introduce the concept of "bounded rationality." Following Simon and Williamson, the concept of bounded rationality recognizes that human beings cannot evaluate all possible states of the world or all available information that might affect a particular situation. One way of thinking about the foreseeability doctrine is as delineating the boundary between those contingencies that are reasonably part of the decision-making process and those that are not. This recognizes that most contracts are not complete contingent claims contracts, commonly including only some subset of all possible occurrences as a reasonable basis for decisionmaking and appropriately included either explicitly or implicitly in the terms of the contract.

The foreseeability doctrine is therefore more of a "contemplation" doctrine. What occurrences were or should have been included in the negotiations

* Excerpted from Paul L. Joskow, *Commercial Impossibility, the Uranium Market and the Westinghouse Case*, 6 J. LEGAL STUD. 119, 157-58 (1977).

underlying the contract and what contingencies were not?[84] In recognizing such cognitive realities, the courts effectively enforce the contract only over that set of contingencies that was or should have been part of the decisionmaking process. Such a requirement makes good sense because it recognizes the realities of voluntary exchange. To require performance under contingencies that could not efficiently be part of the decisionmaking process would encourage the costly and difficult enumeration of a large number of contingencies, raising the costs of private exchange.

Under a "contemplation" test we would ask: "Did one of the parties to the contract contemplate or should one of the parties to the contract have contemplated a certain occurrence based on his superior economic ability to do so and make the probability of this occurrence one of the bases on which the terms of the contract (including the price) were negotiated?" If the answer is no, then an additional requirement for excuse has been satisfied, the occurrence not being covered by the contract. If the answer is yes, then the reverse is the case, and we would assume that the risk of the occurrence which has now occurred was covered in the contract.

Under the circumstances it would appear that the "foreseen" interpretation of this requirement would be sufficient. We would ask the evidentiary question of whether one or both parties contemplated the occurrence and whether it formed the basis of their negotiating position. However, a "foreseen, should have foreseen, or reason to know" test appears in principle to have certain advantages. It allows us to ask a normative question: whether one or more of the parties *should* have contemplated such occurrences and made them a basis of the terms of the contract. This stronger interpretation provides an incentive to both parties to carefully evaluate available information about uncertain occurrences involving supply and demand and make this information part of the dickered terms of the contract. The test then is not only whether the parties contemplate an occurrence and made it a basis of the contract, but stronger, should they have done so? This stronger test should encourage more efficient use of available information and help to insure that contingencies are properly reflected in contract terms. This has the effect of not penalizing a shrewd buyer (or, alternatively, rewarding an incompetent seller) who recognizes that the possibility of certain occurrences which should increase the price of the contract even if the seller fails to. In the long run this will serve to eliminate those sellers from the market who do not utilize information about alternative states of the world efficiently, as would occur in a competitive market without transactions costs.

In the problem below, do you agree that the risk of loss was placed on the correct party? Why or why not?

84. The U.C.C. has this "contemplation" or "reason to know" standard running through it. See for example U.C.C. § 2-715.

PROBLEM: HORSING AROUND*

A supplier leased a team of horses which were to be returned by the lessee "in as good condition as they are at present." One of the horses was later found to have spinal meningitis and was shot to death—against the express wishes of the lessee—by an agent of the Society for the Prevention of Cruelty to Animals. The agreement to return the horse was held to have been discharged. The result was to place the risk of death by disease on the horse's owner.

Did the court place the rule of loss an the appropriate party? Why or why not?

PROBLEM: A CANCELLED CRUISE

Plaintiff, a corporation that chartered a cruise ship for $1 million, seeks to recover money it paid to Defendant Cruise Line for a cruise that Plaintiff subsequently cancelled because of the September 11, 2001 terrorist attacks. Specifically, the cruise was scheduled to depart on October 2, 2001 from Piraeus, Greece, and to disembark in Istanbul, Turkey on October 9, 2001, with intermediate ports of call in several Greek and Turkish islands.

Plaintiff claims that its performance should be excused under the contract, and that it should get its prepaid deposit of $1 million back, which represents the total price of the cruise. Defendant, however, argues that it should be entitled to keep the deposit, and that Plaintiff cannot recover under the doctrines of impossibility of performance or commercial frustration of purpose.

The contract between the parties includes a provision, clause #1, stating that the entire cruise hire price becomes payable to Defendant if Plaintiff cancels the agreement. Another provision, clause #2, the force majeure clause, relieves Defendant of any liability for failure to perform in the event of acts of God, war, fire, acts or threats of terrorism, or order or restraint by government authorities, among other things. Finally, clause #3, the integration clause, incorporates into the agreement "all prior understandings and agreements heretofore entered into between [defendant] and [plaintiff] whether written or oral." It further provides that "no course of dealing between the parties shall operate as a waiver by either party of any right of such party."

Before entering into the agreement, Plaintiff asked Defendant how Defendant would treat Plaintiff in regard to refunds or rescheduling if there was an outbreak of terrorism or war at the time of the cruise. In response, Defendant's director of sales (David) told Plaintiff that Defendant would never put its vessels or guests in danger and would work with Plaintiff to reschedule the location or dates of the cruise as necessary to assure safety and to satisfy the safety concerns of Plaintiff's guests. Alternatively, David explained that Defendant would give Plaintiff a refund.

On April 29, 1999, David sent a letter to Plaintiff memorializing his response to Plaintiff's inquiries, stating, in relevant part:

* The following problem is taken from Richard A. Posner & Andrew M. Rosenfield, *Impossibility And Related Doctrines In Contract Law: An Economic Analysis*, 6 J. LEGAL STUD. 83, 106 (1977).

> It goes without saying that Defendant would never go to an area where we have been officially advised not to go, as we would never place our guests, crew and vessel in harm's way.
>
> If we are advised not to go to a scheduled port, we would always work with our charterers to move (if operationally possible) to another port for the better of all involved. As you can see, there are quite a few behind the scenes professionals who monitor all security aspects of our operation.
>
> It should be noted that a charterer may decide on their own to cancel or reschedule their cruise, but our agreement does not allow for any release of financial responsibility unless we have been officially directed by the government and can't perform.

On May 3, 1999, Plaintiff signed the agreement with Defendant for the cruise. Plaintiff completed the prepayment of $1 million and the cruise was scheduled to occur until the intervention of the terrorist attacks destroying the World Trade Center in New York City and damaging the Pentagon in Washington, D.C. Several days after the attacks, the United States declared a "war on terrorism." The United States government mobilized substantial resources in and around the eastern Mediterranean and Middle East and elsewhere, and placed its military units on a high state of alert and battle readiness. During the scheduled time of the cruise the United States launched a major military action against Afghanistan.

In response to the September 11 attacks, the United States Department of State issued formal warnings to Americans abroad and to those who were considering traveling abroad, instructing them to exercise heightened caution and vigilance while traveling abroad and urging that Americans avoid such travel. However, the United States government did not issue any orders requiring Defendant to cancel its October 2, 2001 cruise.

In the three-week period between the September 11 attacks and the scheduled cruise date, many of Plaintiff's employees, guests and their spouses informed Plaintiff that they would not go on the cruise because they believed it would be unsafe. Plaintiff made repeated efforts to persuade Defendant to work with Plaintiff to reschedule the cruise dates or to refund some or all of the prepayment. Defendant refused to make any adjustment to the date or location of the cruise. In addition, Defendant informed Plaintiff that it would retain the entire amount of Plaintiff's prepayment whether or not the cruise took place.

Plaintiff notified Defendant formally before the scheduled departure date that it was cancelling the cruise and demanded that Defendant mitigate its losses and provide Plaintiff a return of money equal to the amount of cost savings effected by cancellation. Defendant refused to remit any refund or cost savings.

Should Defendant have to refund the $1 million deposit? Stated differently, should Plaintiff's performance be excused? How, if at all, would your answer change if clause #3 were removed from the contract? How would it change if clauses #3 and #2 were removed? Finally, what if all three clauses were removed?

IMPOSSIBILITY AND RELATED DOCTRINES IN CONTRACT LAW*

Section 2-615 of the Uniform Commercial Code (U.C.C.) states a general impossibility doctrine for sales cases, limited, however, to cases where the seller of the goods is seeking discharge. The Code provides:

> Except so far as a seller may have assumed a greater obligation . . .
> (a) Delay in delivery or non-delivery in whole or part by a seller . . . is not a breach of his duty under a contract for sale if performance as agreed has been made impracticable by the occurrence of a contingency the non-occurrence of which was a basic assumption on which the contract was made. . . .[83]

This language, which is similar to that employed by the *Restatement of Contracts*,[84] uses impracticability rather than impossibility or commercial frustration as the controlling concept. The Code makes clear that the parties to the contract can control the assignment of risk by inserting appropriate terms in their agreement.[85]

Section 2-615 appears to add little to the common law doctrines and indeed is completely silent on many important issues. As noted above, the entire section is developed exclusively from the seller's point of view. No buyer's relief is specifically contemplated in the Code.[86] This omission has been explained as a cautious reaction on the part of the Code's draftsmen to the then undecided state of the common law with regard to buyers' claims of impossibility. One consequence of the omission, however, is that cases similar to our specialized-machinery hypothetical are not controlled by any provision in the Code.

The general view is that, where it does apply, section 2-615 is consistent with the non-Code case law. Professor Murray has written:

> Though the Code language is not expressed in terms of risk allocation there is little question but that the courts will interpret it in keeping with the now generally recognized basic inquiry of whether the risk created by the occurrence of the contingency should be allocated to the promisor.[89]

The U.C.C. also contains several more specific sections that are relevant to the discharge of a contract on impossibility or related grounds when the event allegedly justifying discharge is the destruction of specific goods identified in the contract.[90]

---

* Excerpted from Richard A. Posner & Andrew M. Rosenfield, *Impossibility and Related Doctrines In Contract Law: An Economic Analysis*, 6 J. LEGAL STUD. 83, 108-09 (1977).

83. U.C.C. § 2-615. *See* Paul L. Joskow, *Commercial Impossibility, the Uranium Market and the Westinghouse Case*, 6 J. LEG. STUDIES 119, at pt. II (1977), for a fuller economic analysis of § 2-615.

84. See *Restatement of Contracts* § 454 (1932).

85. U.C.C. § 1-102.

86. U.C.C. § 2-615, Comment 9, contains a fleeting reference to the possibility of a buyer's claim of discharge, but the issue is never pursued.

89. John Murray, Jr., *supra* note 21, at 412.

90. See U.C.C. §§ 2-319, 2-509, 2-510, and § 2-615, Comment 9, supra note 80.

The Code abandons the traditional approach of making the risk of loss from destruction follow the title to the goods—an approach related, although loosely, to the ability to prevent destruction—in favor of a similarly mechanical approach but one avowedly based on risk-allocation concepts.

The Westinghouse *case referred to in Note 83 of the previous excerpt has a fascinating history, as discussed below.*

JUDICIAL REVISION OF FRUSTRATED CONTRACTS*

Miscalculation by a supplier reached a new scale of magnitude in the contracts of Westinghouse Electric to supply 49 nuclear power plants with their requirements of uranium. The 27 utilities that owned the sites where these plants were projected wanted assurances before making the necessary huge investment in nuclear plant and equipment, of which Westinghouse was a major supplier. The assurances they received took the form of contracts, mostly made in the early 1970's, for Westinghouse to supply the requirements of uranium for these plants when in operation, at fixed prices—$8.00 or $10.00 (up to $12.00) a pound. They were mostly made in the early 1970's and the market price of uranium began to rise sharply in 1974. In September, 1975, when Westinghouse announced that it could not and would not perform further, the market price approached $40.00 a pound and later went higher. The guesses as to how much Westinghouse would lose if it performed all its contracts for their full terms (on the doubtful assumption they could procure the supplies) started from a base of two billion dollars and went considerably higher. In actions for damages by thirteen power companies, consolidated in a trial that lasted six months, the conclusion reached by the trial judge was that Westinghouse had no sufficient excuse and was liable full scale for expectancy damages.[60] Unfortunately for posterity a reasoned opinion was not filed but this may have been just as well for Westinghouse, since its damage-claim creditors, motivated presumably by their own self-interest in preserving it as a fully functioning enterprise, agreed to settlements that were vastly more lenient than any that a court would have been bold enough to propose.[61]

---

* Excerpted from John P. Dawson, *Judicial Revision of Frustrated Contracts: The United States*, 64 B.U. L. REV. 1, 25-26 (1984).

60. Since this decision has not been reported, the main events have been described only in newspaper reports. The 13 actions for damages brought in different parts of the country were consolidated for trial in Virginia in *In re Westinghouse Elec. Corp. Uraniam Contracts Litig.*, 405 F. Supp. 316 (J.P.M.D.L. 1975). A useful comment on this aspect appears in Note, *In Re* Westinghouse: *Commercial Impractibility as a Contractual Defense*, 47 UMKC L. REV. 650 (1979). An excellent account of the economic and legal background and of the astonishing lack of foresight shown by the Westinghouse management is given by Joskow, *Commercial Impossibility, The Uranium Market and the Westinghouse Case*, 6 J. LEGAL STUD. 119, 143-50 (1977).

61. Extremely lenient terms in the settlements that Westinghouse was able to secure assisted it greatly in wiping out the effects of this potentially fatal episode. N.Y. TIMES, March 15, 1981, § 3, at 1.

So the question becomes whether, as the interests at stake rise higher on a scale of magnitude and the complexities of the performances multiply, these are reasons for judges to intervene and impose new terms that to them will seem more workable and fair.

3. Frustration of Purpose

DOCTRINAL OVERVIEW: EXCUSING PERFORMANCE DUE TO FRUSTRATION OF PURPOSE*

The fountainhead of the doctrine of frustration of purpose is the English case *of Krell v. Henry.* In 1902, when King Edward VII succeeded Queen Victoria, Britons awaited their first coronation in more than 60 years. Henry saw in the window of Krell's flat an announcement of windows to be let to view the coronation processions. He arranged with Krell's housekeeper to take the suite for the daytime of June 26 and 27 for £75, of which £25 was paid in advance. On June 22, the House of Commons was informed that the King had been required to undergo an operation for appendicitis, and the coronation was indefinitely postponed. Henry refused to pay the balance of £50, and Krell sued in what became the most noted of the coronation cases. The Court of Appeal held for Henry on the ground that his duty to pay had been discharged because "the coronation procession was the foundation of this contract, and . . . the object of the contract was frustrated by the non-happening of the coronation and its procession on the days proclaimed."

The doctrine announced in *Krell v. Henry* has come to be known as that of frustration of purpose. Cancellation of the procession did not make performance by either party impracticable; it did not prevent Krell from letting Henry use his rooms or Henry from paying Krell the £50. Rather, its effect was to deprive one party entirely of the benefit he expected from the other's performance, since it made the use of Krell's rooms during the period for which they were let virtually worthless to Henry. . . .

The doctrine of frustration has been generally accepted by American courts. Although the doctrine is not explicitly recognized by the Uniform Commercial Code, there is little doubt that it is applicable to contracts for the sale of goods.[6] It has been incorporated in both the first and second Restatements.[7] It appears to be recognized by the exemption provision of the Vienna Convention, which applies to either party.[8]

---

* Excerpted from E. ALLAN FARNSWORTH, CONTRACTS § 9.7 (4th ed. 2004).

6. UCC 1-103(b) (unless displaced by the Code's particular provisions, "the principles of law and equity . . . supplement its provisions").

7. *Restatement* § 288; *Restatement Second* § 265.

8. [*See* CISG Article 79 ("A party is not liable for a failure to perform any of his obligations if he proves that the failure was due to an impediment beyond his control and that he could not

The *Restatement Second* synthesis of the doctrine of frustration of purpose is strikingly similar to that of the doctrine of impracticability of performance.[9] . . .

Krell v. Henry

Court of Appeals
2 K.B. 740 (1903)

[After occupying the English throne since 1837, Queen Victoria died in 1901, and coronation processions for her eldest son, Edward VII, were scheduled for June 26 and 27, 1902. Plaintiff (Krell) advertised his third-floor premises at 56A, Pall Mall, in an announcement to the effect that windows to view the Royal coronation procession were to be let. Defendant (Henry) was induced by this announcement to apply to the housekeeper on the premises, who said that the owner was willing to let the suite of rooms for the purpose of seeing the Royal procession for both days, but not nights, of June 26 and 27.

Edward VII and Alexandra of Denmark in their coronation robes

The contract is contained in two letters of June 20 that passed between the defendant and the plaintiff's agent, Mr. Cecil Bisgood. These letters do not mention the coronation, but speak merely of the taking of Mr. Krell's chambers, or, rather, of the use of them, in the daytime of June 26 and 27, for the sum of £75. £25 was paid immediately, and the balance £50 was to be paid on June 24th. Prior to that date, however, Edward VII was diagnosed with appendicitis, and had to undergo surgery. The coronation was consequently postponed, and plaintiff sued for the £50 due, which defendant refused to pay. Defendant, in fact, counterclaimed for the return of his £25 deposit, but subsequently withdrew this request.]

VAUGHAN WILLIAMS, L.J. **read the following written judgment:**—The real question in this case is the extent of the application in English law of the principle of the Roman law which has been adopted and acted on in many English

reasonably be expected to have taken the impediment into account at the time of the conclusion of the contract or to have avoided or overcome it or its consequences." It should be noted that this language applies not only to excuse performance due to frustration of purpose, but due to impossibility or impracticability as well.—ED.]

9. Compare *Restatement Second* § 265 *with* § 261.

decisions, and notably in the case of *Taylor v. Caldwell*. That case at least makes it clear that

> where, from the nature of the contract, it appears that the parties must from the beginning have known that it could not be fulfilled unless, when the time for the fulfilment of the contract arrived, some particular specified thing continued to exist, so that when entering into the contract they must have contemplated such continued existence as the foundation of what was to be done; there, in the absence of any express or implied warranty that the thing shall exist, the contract is not to be considered a positive contract, but as subject to an implied condition that the parties shall be excused in case, before breach, performance becomes impossible from the perishing of the thing without default of the contractor.

Thus far it is clear that the principle of the Roman law has been introduced into the English law. The doubt in the present case arises as to how far this principle extends. . . .

It is said, on the one side, that the specified thing, state of things, or condition the continued existence of which is necessary for the fulfilment of the contract, so that the parties entering into the contract must have contemplated the continued existence of that thing, condition, or state of things as the foundation of what was to be done under the contract, is limited to things which are either the subject-matter of the contract or a condition or state of things, present or anticipated, which is expressly mentioned in the contract.

But, on the other side, it is said that the condition or state of things need not be expressly specified, but that it is sufficient if that condition or state of things clearly appears by extrinsic evidence to have been assumed by the parties to be the foundation or basis of the contract, and the event which causes the impossibility is of such a character that it cannot reasonably be supposed to have been in the contemplation of the contracting parties when the contract was made. In such a case the contracting parties will not be held bound by the general words which, though large enough to include, were not used with reference to a possibility of a particular event rendering performance of the contract impossible.

I do not think that the principle of the civil law as introduced into the English law is limited to cases in which the event causing the impossibility of performance is the destruction or non-existence of something which is the subject-matter of the contract or of some condition or state of things expressly specified as a condition of it. I think that you first have to ascertain, not necessarily from the terms of the contract, but, if required, from necessary inferences, drawn from surrounding circumstances recognized by both contracting parties, what is the substance of the contract, and then to ask the question whether that substantial contract needs for its foundation the assumption of the existence of a particular state of things. If it does, this will limit the operation of the general words, and in such case, if the contract becomes impossible of performance by reason of the non-existence of the state of things assumed by both contracting parties as the foundation of the contract, there will be no breach of the contract thus limited. . . .

In my judgment the use of the rooms was let and taken for the purpose of seeing the Royal procession. It was not a demise of the rooms, or even an agreement to let and take the rooms. It is a license to use rooms for a particular purpose and none other. And in my judgment the taking place of those processions on the days proclaimed along the proclaimed route, which passed 56A, Pall Mall, was regarded by both contracting parties as the foundation of the contract; and I think that it cannot reasonably be supposed to have been in the contemplation of the contracting parties, when the contract was made, that the coronation would not be held on the proclaimed days, or the processions not take place on those days along the proclaimed route; and I think that the words imposing on the defendant the obligation to accept and pay for the use of the rooms for the named days, although general and unconditional, were not used with reference to the possibility of the particular contingency which afterwards occurred.

It was suggested in the course of the argument that if the occurrence, on the proclaimed days, of the coronation and the procession in this case were the foundation of the contract, and if the general words are thereby limited or qualified, so that in the event of the non-occurrence of the coronation and procession along the proclaimed route they would discharge both parties from further performance of the contract, it would follow that if a cabman was engaged to take someone to Epsom on Derby Day at a suitable enhanced price for such a journey, say £10, both parties to the contract would be discharged in the contingency of the race at Epsom for some reason becoming impossible; but I do not think this follows, for I do not think that in the cab case the happening of the race would be the foundation of the contract. No doubt the purpose of the engager would be to go to see the Derby, and the price would be proportionately high; but the cab had no special qualifications for the purpose which led to the selection of the cab for this particular occasion. Any other cab would have done as well. Moreover, I think that, under the cab contract, the hirer, even if the race went off, could have said, "Drive me to Epsom; I will pay you the agreed sum; you have nothing to do with the purpose for which I hired the cab," and that if the cabman refused he would have been guilty of a breach of contract, there being nothing to qualify his promise to drive the hirer to Epsom on a particular day.

Whereas in the case of the coronation, there is not merely the purpose of the hirer to see the coronation procession, but it is the coronation procession and the relative position of the rooms which is the basis of the contract as much for the lessor as the hirer; and I think that if the King, before the coronation day and after the contract, had died, the hirer could not have insisted on having the rooms on the days named. It could not in the cab case be reasonably said that seeing the Derby race was the foundation of the contract, as it was of the license in this case. Whereas in the present case, where the rooms were offered and taken, by reason of their peculiar suitability from the position of the rooms for a view of the coronation procession, surely the view of the coronation procession was the foundation of the contract, which is a very different thing from the purpose of the man who engaged the cab—namely, to see the race—being held to be the foundation of the contract.

> ***The frustration of purpose test***
>
> According to this court, three requirements must be met before a court will excuse a party's performance on account of the defense of frustration of purpose. How does the court's test differ from the test adopted by the *Restatement (Second) of Contracts* § 265? Is it a good test? Is the court's test consistent with putting the risk on the party in the best position to avoid it? Is it consistent with what the parties would themselves have done had they foreseen the risk when they made their contract?

Each case must be judged by its own circumstances. In each case one must ask oneself, first, what, having regard to all the circumstances, was the foundation of the contract? Secondly, was the performance of the contract prevented? Thirdly, was the event which prevented the performance of the contract of such a character that it cannot reasonably be said to have been in the contemplation of the parties at the date of the contract? If all these questions are answered in the affirmative (as I think they should be in this case), I think both parties are discharged from further performance of the contract.

I think that the coronation procession was the foundation of this contract, and that the non-happening of it prevented the performance of the contract; and, secondly, I think that the non-happening of the procession . . . was an event "of such a character that it cannot reasonably be supposed to have been in the contemplation of the contracting parties when the contract was made." . . .

The test seems to be whether the event which causes the impossibility was or might have been anticipated and guarded against. . . . I myself am clearly of opinion that in this case, where we have to ask ourselves whether the object of the contract was frustrated by the non-happening of the coronation and its procession on the days proclaimed, parol evidence is admissible to shew that the subject of the contract was rooms to view the coronation procession, and was so to the knowledge of both parties. . . .

This disposes of the plaintiff's claim for £50 unpaid balance of the price agreed to be paid for the use of the rooms. The defendant at one time set up a cross-claim for the return of the £25 he paid at the date of the contract. As that claim is now withdrawn it is unnecessary to say anything about it. . . . I think this appeal ought to be dismissed.

[Various concurring opinions are omitted.]

Appeal dismissed.

RELEVANT PROVISIONS

For the *Restatement (Second) of Contracts*, consult § 265.

NOTES AND QUESTIONS

1. *What happened?* Who sued whom for what? Procedurally, how did the case get before this court? Factually, what happened between the parties? What arguments did the plaintiff and defendant make? What rule or rules did

the court apply? How did the court analyze the dispute between the parties? How did the court decide the case?

2. *Was this case correctly decided?* Do you agree with the result reached in this case? Why or why not? Do you agree with the court's reasoning? Why or why not? How, if at all, would you have written the opinion differently?

3. *Epsom on Derby Day.* The court spends some time distinguishing this case from the Epsom on Derby Day example brought up by counsel in oral argument. According to the judge, how does the hypothetical differ from the actual dispute, and are you convinced by the judge's explanation as to the differences between these two cases?

4. *Frustration of purpose and impossibility/impracticability, compared.* In what way is this case different from *Taylor v. Caldwell,* which was cited in *Krell*? In general, what are the similarities and differences between the defenses of impossibility and impracticability, on the one hand, and the defense of frustration of purpose, on the other?

5. *Risk of loss.* Who should bear the risk of loss for the cancellation of the coronation? Why? Do any of the thinking tools we've previously discussed shed light on this question?

6. *Deposit.* What result if the deposit had not been paid at all? What if it had been paid in full? Should these "practical" facts affect the legal doctrine? Why or why not?

One way of understanding Krell v. Henry *is through an economic lens. Would you agree with the following analysis of the coronation cases?*

IMPOSSIBILITY AND RELATED DOCTRINES IN CONTRACT LAW*

In many individual, and perhaps some classes of, cases economic analysis—at least of the casual sort employed by the judges and lawyers in contract cases—will fail to yield a definite answer, or even a guess, as to which party is the superior risk bearer. A good example is provided by the coronation cases. Neither party was in a superior position to foresee the event (the illness of Edward VII) that prevented completion of the contract. To be sure, the building owner had a superior ability to compute the loss, which depended on his ability to re-rent the rooms on short notice, and could in principle have bought a single insurance policy on Edward's health at lower cost than the renters could have insured. However, the renters may well have been superior self-insurers: enforcing the contracts would have spread the loss among a relatively large number of renters rather

* Excerpted from Richard A. Posner & Andrew M. Rosenfield, *Impossibility and Related Doctrines In Contract Law: An Economic Analysis,* 6 J. LEGAL STUD. 83, 110-11 (1977).

than concentrate it on a relatively few building owners. It is not surprising that the courts divided on whether discharge should be allowed.[94]

The choice in doubtful cases between treating nonperformance as breach or as discharge is similar to the choice in tort law between strict liability and no liability for unavoidable accidents. Pending definitive empirical study, we are inclined to consider the strict-liability solution better in the contract context, though in the tort context the choice must be considered indeterminate on the basis of present knowledge.

The performing party to a contract is generally the superior risk bearer. Typically, though not invariably, he is better able both to prevent the occurrence of the event rendering performance uneconomical and, if it cannot be prevented at reasonable cost, to estimate the probability of its occurrence. Often, too, he is at least as able as the payor to estimate the magnitude of the loss if the event occurs. True, the payor (that is, the buyer) will have better knowledge of the consequences of nonperformance for his business, but the rule of *Hadley v. Baxendale* properly assigns the risk of consequential injury to the payor in any event. Finally, the performer can often self-insure at low cost simply by diversifying the risk across the full range of his contractual obligations.

The performer is not always the superior risk bearer; otherwise there would be no place in contract law for impossibility and related doctrines. But as long as the performer is generally the superior risk bearer, assigning the risk to him in cases of doubt—that is, refusing discharge in those cases—can be expected to yield correct results more often than the contrary rule. Accordingly, one is not surprised to find that the courts indeed treat discharge as an excuse, so that nonperformance is a breach of contract unless the case fits one of the exceptions to liability carved out by the impossibility or some other excuse doctrine.

This discussion raises the broader question why in general notions of strict liability seem much more important in contract than in tort law. The concept of breach of contract is one of strict liability rather than of negligence. The difference in this regard between tort and contract law appears to be related to the fact that tort cases typically involve interactive activities and contract cases typically do not. An automobile accident, for example, is produced by a collision between two automobiles or between an automobile and a pedestrian, and there is no presumption that the injurer could have avoided the accident more cheaply than the victim. But in the typical contract case the only relevant actors are performer and payor and the productive activity under the contract is controlled and conducted entirely by the former. There is a strong presumption therefore that he is better able than the payor to prevent a mishap that will render performance uneconomical. The presumption is not absolute but it is sufficient to make strict liability the appropriate general rule defining breach of contract.

---

94. Compare *Krell v. Henry*, [1903] 2 K.B. 740 (C.A.), with *Chandler v. Webster*, (1904] 1 K.B. 493 (L.R.), and *Herne Bay S.S. Co. v. Hutton*, [1903] 2 K.B. 683 (C.A.). While the coronation cases on their peculiar facts could have gone either way on an economic analysis—which may explain the division in the courts—the case against discharge is much stronger in the related but more common case where, for example, a skier books a room at a ski lodge and, having paid his deposit, seeks a refund because of poor ski conditions. Skiers as a class are superior self-insurers against poor ski conditions compared to ski lodges; the skier can find adequate conditions somewhere but the lodge cannot diversify away the risk of poor conditions (save by merger with lodges in other ski areas); market insurance may also be unavailable. . . .

Northern Indiana Public Service Co. v. Carbon County Coal Co.

United States Court of Appeals, Seventh Circuit
799 F.2d 265 (1986)

POSNER, CIRCUIT JUDGE. These appeals bring before us various facets of a dispute between Northern Indiana Public Service Company (NIPSCO), an electric utility in Indiana, and Carbon County Coal Company, a partnership that until recently owned and operated a coal mine in Wyoming. In 1978 NIPSCO and Carbon County signed a contract whereby Carbon County agreed to sell and NIPSCO to buy approximately 1.5 million tons of coal every year for 20 years, at a price of $24 a ton subject to various provisions for escalation which by 1985 had driven the price up to $44 a ton.

NIPSCO's rates are regulated by the Indiana Public Service Commission. In 1983 NIPSCO requested permission to raise its rates to reflect increased fuel charges. Some customers of NIPSCO opposed the increase on the ground that NIPSCO could reduce its overall costs by buying more electrical power from neighboring utilities for resale to its customers and producing less of its own power. Although the Commission granted the requested increase, it directed NIPSCO, in orders issued in December 1983 and February 1984 (the "economy purchase orders"), to make a good faith effort to find, and wherever possible buy from, utilities that would sell electricity to it at prices lower than its costs of internal generation. The Commission added ominously that "the adverse effects of entering into long-term coal supply contracts which do not allow for renegotiation and are not requirement contracts, is a burden which must rest squarely on the shoulders of NIPSCO management." Actually the contract with Carbon County did provide for renegotiation of the contract price—but one-way renegotiation in favor of Carbon County; the price fixed in the contract (as adjusted from time to time in accordance with the escalator provisions) was a floor. And the contract was indeed not a requirements contract: it specified the exact amount of coal that NIPSCO must take over the 20 years during which the contract was to remain in effect. NIPSCO was eager to have an assured supply of low-sulphur coal and was therefore willing to guarantee both price and quantity.

Unfortunately for NIPSCO, as things turned out it was indeed able to buy electricity at prices below the costs of generating electricity from coal bought under the contract with Carbon County; and because of the "economy purchase orders," of which it had not sought judicial review, NIPSCO could not expect to be allowed by the Public Service Commission to recover in its electrical rates the costs of buying coal from Carbon County. NIPSCO therefore decided to stop accepting coal deliveries from Carbon County, at least for the time being; and on April 24, 1985, it brought this diversity suit against Carbon County in a federal district court in Indiana, seeking a declaration that it was excused from its obligations under the contract either permanently or at least until the economy purchase orders ceased preventing it from passing on the costs of the contract to its ratepayers. In support of this position it argued that . . .

NIPSCO's performance was excused or suspended—either under the contract's *force majeure* clause or under the doctrines of frustration or impossibility—by reason of the economy purchase orders. . . .

The contract permits NIPSCO to stop taking delivery of coal "for any cause beyond [its] reasonable control . . . including but not limited to . . . orders or acts of civil . . . authority . . . which wholly or partly prevent . . . the utilizing . . . of the coal." This is what is known as a *force majeure* clause. NIPSCO argues that the Indiana Public Service Commission's "economy purchase orders" prevented it, in whole or part, from using the coal that it had agreed to buy, and it complains that the district judge instructed the jury incorrectly on the meaning and application of the clause. . . .

All that those orders do is tell NIPSCO it will not be allowed to pass on fuel costs to its ratepayers in the form of higher rates if it can buy electricity cheaper than it can generate electricity internally using Carbon County's coal. Such an order does not "prevent," whether wholly or in part, NIPSCO from using the coal; it just prevents NIPSCO from shifting the burden of its improvidence or bad luck in having incorrectly forecasted its fuel needs to the backs of the hapless ratepayers. The purpose of public utility regulation is to provide a substitute for competition in markets (such as the market for electricity) that are naturally monopolistic. Suppose the market for electricity were fully competitive, and unregulated. Then if NIPSCO signed a long-term fixed-price fixed-quantity contract to buy coal, and during the life of the contract competing electrical companies were able to produce and sell electricity at prices below the cost to NIPSCO of producing electricity from that coal, NIPSCO would have to swallow the excess cost of the coal. It could not raise its electricity prices in order to pass on the excess cost to its consumers, because if it did they would buy electricity at lower prices from NIPSCO's competitors. By signing the kind of contract it did, NIPSCO gambled that fuel costs would rise rather than fall over the life of the contract; for if they rose, the contract price would give it an advantage over its (hypothetical) competitors who would have to buy fuel at the current market price. If such a gamble fails, the result is not *force majeure*.

This is all the clearer when we consider that the contract price was actually fixed just on the downside; it put a floor under the price NIPSCO had to pay, but the escalator provisions allowed the actual contract prices to rise above the floor, and they did. This underscores the gamble NIPSCO took in signing the contract. It committed itself to paying a price at or above a fixed minimum and to taking a fixed quantity at that price. It was willing to make this commitment to secure an assured supply of low-sulphur coal, but the risk it took was that the market price of coal or substitute fuels would fall. A *force majeure* clause is not intended to buffer a party against the normal risks of a contract. The normal risk of a fixed-price contract is that the market price will change. If it rises, the buyer gains at the expense of the seller (except insofar as escalator provisions give the seller some protection); if it falls, as here, the seller gains at the expense of the buyer. The whole purpose of a fixed-price contract is to allocate risk in this way. A *force majeure* clause interpreted to excuse the buyer from the consequences of the risk he expressly assumed would nullify a central term of the contract. . . .

If the Commission had ordered NIPSCO to close a plant because of a safety or pollution hazard, we would have a true case of *force majeure*. As a regulated firm NIPSCO is subject to more extensive controls than unregulated firms and it therefore wanted and got a broadly worded *force majeure* clause that would protect it fully (hence the reference to partial effects) against government actions that impeded its using the coal. But as the only thing the Commission did was prevent NIPSCO from using its monopoly position to make consumers bear the risk that NIPSCO assumed when it signed a long-term fixed-price fuel contract, NIPSCO cannot complain of *force majeure;* the risk that has come to pass was one that NIPSCO voluntarily assumed when it signed the contract.

[The court then turned to NIPSCO's defenses of impracticability and frustration of purpose.] In the early common law a contractual undertaking unconditional in terms was not excused merely because something had happened (such as an invasion, the passage of a law, or a natural disaster) that prevented the undertaking. See *Paradine v. Jane,* 82 Eng. Rep. 897 (K.B. 1647). Excuses had to be written into the contract; this is the origin of *force majeure* clauses. Later it came to be recognized that negotiating parties cannot anticipate all the contingencies that may arise in the performance of the contract; a legitimate judicial function in contract cases is to interpolate terms to govern remote contingencies—terms the parties would have agreed on explicitly if they had had the time and foresight to make advance provision for every possible contingency in performance. Later still, it was recognized that physical impossibility was irrelevant, or at least inconclusive; a promisor might want his promise to be unconditional, not because he thought he had superhuman powers but because he could insure against the risk of nonperformance better than the promisee, or obtain a substitute performance more easily than the promisee. Thus the proper question in an "impossibility" case is not whether the promisor could not have performed his undertaking but whether his nonperformance should be excused because the parties, if they had thought about the matter, would have wanted to assign the risk of the contingency that made performance impossible or uneconomical to the promisor or to the promisee; if to the latter, the promisor is excused.

UCC § 2-615 takes this approach. It provides that "delay in delivery . . . by a seller . . . is not a breach of his duty under a contract for sale if performance as agreed has been made impracticable by the occurrence of a contingency the non-occurrence of which was a basic assumption on which the contract was made. . . ." Performance on schedule need not be impossible, only infeasible—provided that the event which made it infeasible was not a risk that the promisor had assumed. Notice, however, that the only type of promisor referred to is a seller; there is no suggestion that a buyer's performance might be excused by reason of impracticability. The reason is largely semantic. Ordinarily all the buyer has to do in order to perform his side of the bargain is pay, and while one can think of all sorts of reasons why, when the time came to pay, the buyer might not have the money, rarely would the seller have intended to assume the risk that the buyer might, whether through improvidence or bad luck, be unable to pay for the seller's goods or services. To deal with the rare case where the buyer or (more broadly) the paying party might have a good excuse based on some unforeseen change in circumstances, a new rubric was thought necessary, different from "impossibility" (the common law term) or "impracticability" (the Code term, picked up in *Restatement (Second) of Contracts* § 261), and it received the name "frustration." Rarely is it impracticable or impossible for the payor to pay; but if something has happened to make the performance for which he would be paying worthless to him, an excuse for not paying, analogous to impracticability or impossibility, may be proper. *See Restatement, supra,* § 265, comment a.

The leading case on frustration remains *Krell v. Henry,* 2 K.B. 740 (C.A. 1903). Krell rented Henry a suite of rooms for watching the coronation of Edward VII, but Edward came down with appendicitis and the coronation had to be postponed. Henry refused to pay the balance of the rent and the court held that he was excused from doing so because his purpose in renting had been frustrated by the postponement, a contingency outside the knowledge, or power to influence, of either party. The question was, to which party did the contract (implicitly) allocate the risk? Surely Henry had not intended to insure Krell against the possibility of the coronation's being postponed, since Krell could always relet the room, at the premium rental, for the coronation's new date. So Henry was excused. . . .

Since impossibility and related doctrines are devices for shifting risk in accordance with the parties' presumed intentions, which are to minimize the costs of contract performance, one of which is the disutility created by risk, they have no place when the contract explicitly assigns a particular risk to one party or the other. As we have already noted, a fixed-price contract is an explicit assignment of the risk of market price increases to the seller and the risk of market price decreases to the buyer, and the assignment of the latter risk to the buyer is even clearer where, as in this case, the contract places a floor under price but allows for escalation. If, as is also the case here, the buyer forecasts the market incorrectly and therefore finds himself locked into a disadvantageous contract, he has only himself to blame and so cannot shift the risk back to the seller by invoking impossibility or related doctrines. It does not matter that it is an act of government that may have made the contract less advantageous to one party. Government these days is a pervasive factor in the economy and among the risks that a fixed-price contract allocates between the parties is that of a price change induced by one of government's manifold interventions in the economy. Since "the very purpose of a fixed price agreement is to place the risk of increased costs on the promisor (and the risk of decreased costs on the promisee)," the fact that costs decrease steeply (which is in effect what happened here—the cost of generating electricity turned out to be lower than NIPSCO thought when it signed the fixed-price contract with Carbon County) cannot allow the buyer to walk away from the contract. . . .

NOTES AND QUESTIONS

1. ***What happened?*** Who sued whom for what? Procedurally, how did the case get before this court? Factually, what happened between the parties? What arguments did the plaintiff and defendant make? What rule or rules did the court apply? How did the court analyze the dispute between the parties? How did the court decide the case?

2. ***Was this case correctly decided?*** Do you agree with the result reached in this case? Why or why not? Do you agree with the court's reasoning? Why or why not? How, if at all, would you have written the opinion differently?

3. ***Reconciling cases.*** Can this case be reconciled with *Krell v. Henry*?

4. ***Distinguishing the doctrines.*** How can frustration of purpose cases be distinguished, if at all, from the impossibility/impracticability cases? How, if at all, are the doctrines governing each type of case similar, and how, if at all, are they different? The following two excerpts should prove to be of some value in helping you think through these questions.

LETTING THE LOSS LIE WHERE IT FALLS*

One response of classical theory has been to deny any title to relief in such cases, insisting instead on a "strict," "literal" construction of the contract, come what may. Gilmore gives *Stees v. Leonard* as an example of this Draconian attitude. A contractor, encountering unexpectedly swampy terrain, almost completes a promised structure, but it collapses. He rebuilds. It collapses again. Finally, he throws up his hands. Williston and other hard-liners have it that the builder is not excused from his promised performance. (In the actual case, the owner sued primarily for a return of progress payments.) Since the contractor's bond obligates him to build, he must build, build and build again. This harsh, silly result is a stock example for critics of just where the liberal, or will, or promissory theory leads. Such harsh results are unacceptable, but the theory of contract as promise does not require them. Indeed *no* coherent theory can require such a conclusion. By demonstrating the incoherence of this so-called strict view, I show that no merely harsh theory could entail it.

The strict or literal view always enforces or ratifies *some* distribution of risk. In *Stees v. Leonard* the court allocated the risk of collapse to the builder. If no relief is granted to licensees of rooms along the route of the canceled coronation procession, the risk of cancellation is by implication imposed on them and not on those who hire out these rooms. Now why is that allocation of risks more "strict" than its opposite? Is it really because the contract says "to build a house" or "to rent rooms on . . ."? Is it because the builder or hirer implies a term such as "unless the ground is altogether softer than either of us considers reasonably likely" or "unless there is no procession to view"? But if this is the point why not

* Excerpted from CHARLES FRIED, CONTRACT AS PROMISE 64-67 (1981).

argue the contrary; that there *should* be relief since the contract does not say "to build a house, whatever the condition of the ground," or "to hire the rooms on the date presently scheduled for the coronation, whether or not the coronation is subsequently canceled"? It is true that the actual words used admit of either interpretation, but why does that make the "harsher" interpretation the more eligible of the two possibilities? I suspect because of a lingering prejudice that the harsher interpretation is the simpler, the more unqualified, the more natural interpretation, while that which allows an excuse requires the court to add language, to superimpose something on the will of the parties. But it is just the point that on the issues in question the parties *had not will at all*, so that any resolution of the problem is necessarily imposed by the court. In short there has just been an accident, and any resolution of the accident is a kind of judgment, a kind of intervention.

I suspect that the strict or literal view is related to the belief that accident losses in general should lie where they fall. The usual domain for letting the loss lie where it falls is the law of torts, and commentators have noted that the attitude that gave rise to the strict view in contracts displayed itself as well in an aversion to shifting losses in the law of torts. As Gilmore puts it, on this view ideally nobody was ever liable for anything. But what does it mean to say even in tort law that the loss lies where it falls? It is worth clarifying this, since it is my contention that mistake and impossibility are a species of accident too—contractual accident.

The intuitive idea is that the burden of an accident should remain with whoever happens to have been hurt. Now, the injured party may decide to take the matter into his own hands and shift the loss to someone else (the injurer or a third party) so that thereafter the loss lies *there*. If a thief steals, unless the law helps the victim or the victim helps herself, the loss will lie with the victim. If an assailant punches you in the nose, the loss absent redress lies with you. Thus letting the loss lie where it falls does not describe an order at all, since nothing intrinsically tells us where this nonlegal imposition of burdens should stop. After all, why should it stop after the first link in the chain of events, why should not the victim at the end of the first link pass it on to someone else and then to someone else? This point is vital in the domain of contracts. For if losses were truly to be allowed to lie where they fall, then no contract would ever be enforced. If somebody ended up losing because he trusted in the promise of another, why the more fool he! Contract law enforces promises and does not allow a disappointed party to bear his disappointments simply because it has fallen upon him, any more than the law of torts allows the victim of an assault or a reckless act to bear the costs that another would force on him. Some losses, on the other hand, are allowed to lie where they fall: If I trip and fall while walking along the beach, or if my business is ruined by a more efficient competitor, or if I make an unlucky speculation in the currency markets. The reasons why some losses are shifted and others not are as various as the law itself, but there must *be* reasons. Letting the loss lie where if falls is not an argument, a reason; at best it restates one possible conclusion of an argument.

There are several general attitudes behind the inclination to let losses lie where they fall. One such attitude shrinks from the intervention that shifting losses entails, but this is only an attitude, not a theory, since as we have seen it cannot be systematically adhered to. At most it expresses a preference for nonintervention other things being equal, but then we need a theory of when things are indeed equal. A related attitude sees in loss shifting a threat to individual autonomy, since forcing others to share losses correspondingly threatens the chances of enjoying the gains from individual talents, efforts, and accomplishments. Yet this too is only a vague attitude until it is fleshed out by a theory of responsibility and of rights, a theory that identifies when a particular individual is responsible for his own or another's good or ill fortune and when an act is an exercise of one's own or a violation of another's right. Finally, the confused attitude of social Darwinism, which once enjoyed a certain currency, may have suggested that refusing to shift losses would allow the stronger to triumph over the less fit and the race—or whatever—to improve. Since this last posture would make all law and all morality irrelevant, we need consider it no further.

This same set of confused attitudes lurks behind the notion that if an agreement is expressed in general words, and if those general words appear to cover a surprising specific case, then the burden of this surprise should lie where it will fall as a result of taking those general words as covering that specific case, even when neither party meant them to. To the extent that his notion has any appeal at all, it is as a rather confused and approximate statement of another, more coherent conception—a conception that, however, will often lead to quite different results. Now why should we take those words to include the unintended, surprising, specific results? The general words might usually imply this specific result. But in the instance of this contract and these parties, by hypothesis neither party meant or foresaw that these general words should cover this specific case. Perhaps a promisor should not be allowed to claim that she did not mean by a term what is generally implied by that term. But if she is not allowed to excuse herself by showing this private, special intention, it is not because we doubt that sometimes people truly have such special intentions. Rather we may bar such a claim as a matter of fairness to the other party or as a matter of practical convenience. We rather suspect either (1) that the claimant did mean what is usually meant, took her chances, and is now trying to get out of what has turned into a bad deal; or (2) that though she didn't mean it, her opposite number did, and reasonably assumed that she did mean it, so that it would be unfair to disappoint the opposite party's expectations now by urging some surprising, unexpected, secret intention. But this is not turning your back and allowing the loss to lie where it falls. These are perfectly reasonable, practical grounds for administering a system that in general seeks to effectuate the true intentions of the parties. Where we really can be confident that neither party intended to cover this particular case, and where we can reach that conclusion without fearing a spreading disintegration of confidence in contractual obligations generally, no reason remains for enforcing this contract.

THINKING TOOL: THE LEAST COST AVOIDER*

Ordinarily the failure of one party to a contract to fulfill the performance required of him constitutes a breach of contract for which he is liable in damages to the other party. But sometimes the failure to perform is excused and the contract is said to be discharged rather than breached. This study uses economic theory to investigate three closely related doctrines in the law of contracts that operate to discharge a contract: "impossibility," "impracticability," and "frustration." . . .

"Impossibility" is the rubric used when the carrying out of a promise is no longer "physically possible,"[7] and "frustration of purpose" when performance of the promise is physically possible but the underlying purpose of the bargain is no longer attainable.[8] Impracticability—a catch-all for any discharge case that does not fit snugly into either the impossibility or the frustration pigeonhole—is the term used when performance of the promise is physically possible and the underlying purpose of the bargain achievable but as a result of an unexpected event enforcement of the promise would entail a much higher cost than originally contemplated.[9]

---

* Excerpted from Richard A. Posner & Andrew M. Rosenfield, *Impossibility And Related Doctrines In Contract Law: An Economic Analysis*, 6 J. LEGAL STUD. 83, 83, 85-86, 88-82 (1977).

7. *See* 6 Samuel Williston, *supra* note 6, at §§ 1931-1979; 6 Arthur Linton Corbin, *supra* note 6, at §§ 1320-1372; and *Restatement of Contracts* § 454 (1932). The leading case is *Taylor v. Caldwell*, 122 Eng. Rep. 309 (1863), in which a contract for a musical performance in a specified auditorium was discharged on grounds of impossibility when the music hall was destroyed by fire. Similar American cases include *Siegel v. Eaton & Prince Co.*, 46 N.E. 449 (1896) (discussed infra pp. 105-06), in which a contract calling for the manufacture of an elevator and its installation in a department store was discharged on grounds of impossibility when the store was destroyed by fire. *See also*, for example, *Texas Co. v. Hogarth Shipping Co.*, 256 U.S. 619 (1921); and Emerich Co. v. Siegal, Cooper & Co., 237 Il. 610, 86 N.E. 1104 (1908). These cases illustrate one prominent group of impossibility decisions, in which the continued existence of some material thing is considered essential; if the thing ceases to exist, performance is then said to be impossible. The other principal group of impossibility cases involves contracts discharged because of supervening illegality. The courts thus treat what is illegal as impossible, illustrating great judicial respect for the law but a disregard for normal uses of language. *See*, for example, *Columbus Ry. Power & Light Co. v. City of Columbus*, 249 U.S. 399 (1919); *Stamey v. State Highway Comm'n of Kansas*, 76 F. Supp. 946 (D. Kan. 1948); and *Phelps v. School District*, 134 N.E. 312 (1922) (discussed infra p. 101).

8. *See* 6 Arthur Linton Corbin, *supra* note 6, at §§ 1353-1361; *Restatement of Contracts* § 288 (1932). The case law develops from the "coronation cases," for example, *Krell v. Henry*, [1903] 2 K.B. 740 (C.A.). *See* R. G. McElroy & Glanville Williams. *The Coronation Cases*, I, 4 MOD. L. REV. 241 (1941). In each of these cases, an apartment was rented to view the coronation procession of Edward VU. The procession was cancelled due to Edward's illness and discharge was sought on the ground that the underlying purpose (the viewing of the procession) had been frustrated. For further discussion of these cases see text at notes 93-94, 108 infra. And for similar American cases *see*, for example, *La Cumbre Golf & Country Club v. Santa Barbara Hotel Co.*, 271 P. 476 (1928); and *Alfred Marks Realty Co. v. Hotel Hermitage Co.*, 156 N.Y.S. 179 (1915).

9. *See* 6 Arthur Linton Corbin, *supra* note 6, at § 1325; and 6 Samuel Williston, *supra* note 6, at § 1935. The early impracticability cases stressed that when performance became sufficiently difficult or costly, it could be treated as impossible. See *Restatement of Contracts* § 454 (1932). Thus in *Mineral Park Land Co. v. Howard*, 156 P. 458 (1916), a contractor agreed to haul from the plaintiff's land all of the gravel necessary for the construction of a concrete bridge. The contractor took all of the immediately available gravel from plaintiff's land but purchased on the open

This categorization is unhelpful. . . . In every discharge case the basic problem is the same: to decide who should bear the loss resulting from an event that has rendered performance by one party uneconomical. . . .

The process by which goods and services are shifted into their most valuable uses is one of voluntary exchange. The distinctive problems of contract law arise when the agreed-upon exchange does not take place instantaneously (for example, A agrees to build a house for B and construction will take several months). The fact that performance is to extend into the future introduces uncertainty, which in turn creates risks. A fundamental purpose of contracts is to allocate these risks between the parties to the exchange. . . .

1. Of contract law in general. One purpose of contract *law*, but not a particularly interesting one here, is to assure compliance with the allocation of risks that the parties have agreed upon. . . . A second purpose, central to our subject, is to reduce the costs of contract negotiation by supplying contract terms that the parties would probably have adopted explicitly had they negotiated over them. . . .

This function of contract *law* is analogous to that performed by standard or form *contracts*. The form contract economizes on the costs of contract negotiation by providing a set of terms to govern in the absence of explicit negotiations. The parties can of course vary the terms of the form contract, but to the extent that they do not, finding the terms suitable for their needs, contracting costs are reduced. It is much the same with the law of contracts. Judicial decisions, the Uniform Commercial Code, and other sources of contract law operate to define the parties' contractual obligations in the absence of express provisions in the contract. Every contract automatically incorporates a host of (generally) appropriate terms, over which the parties do not have to negotiate explicitly unless they want to vary the standard terms supplied by the law. Incidentally, the role of contract law in supplying contract terms, like the role of the standard or form contract, is less important the larger the stakes in the contract and hence the smaller the ratio of the costs of transacting to the value of the exchange. The larger the stakes, the more it will pay the parties to negotiate contract terms finely adapted to the particular circumstances of their contract.

If the purpose of the law of contracts is to effectuate the desires of the contracting parties, then the proper criterion for evaluating the rules of contract law is surely that of economic efficiency. Since the object of most voluntary exchanges

---

market about half of the amount necessary to complete the project. He claimed that all of the additional gravel in plaintiff's land was below water and its extraction would have required the use of extremely expensive techniques. The Supreme Court of California held the contract discharged on the ground that, "[a]lthough there was gravel on the land, it was so situated that the defendants could not take it by ordinary means, nor except at a prohibitive cost. To all fair intents then, it was impossible for defendants to take it." 172 Cal. 293, 156 P. 459-60. However, the courts have been unable to articulate a standard as to what magnitude of cost change is necessary to justify discharge on grounds of impracticability, except to say that "mere hardship is not enough." *See*, for example, *Wischhusen v. American Medicinal Spirits Co.*, 163 A. 685 (1933); *Piaggio v. Somerville*, 80 So. 342 (1919); and *Browne & Bryan Lumber Co. v. Toney*, 194 So. 296 (1940). *See also* Kronprinzessin Cecilie, 244 U.S. 12 (1917); *Comment*, 4 CALIF. L. REV. 407 (1916). 10 6 Arthur Linton Corbin, *supra* note 6, at § 1325. It makes little sense to speak of an event being impossible until it is first accomplished, and possible thereafter.

is to increase value or efficiency, contracting parties may be assumed to desire a set of contract terms that will maximize the value of the exchange. It is true that each party is interested only in the value of the contract to it. However, the more efficiently the exchange is structured, the larger is the potential profit of the contract for the parties to divide between them.

The use of economic efficiency as a criterion for legal decision-making is of course controversial. In the area of contract, however, the criterion is well nigh inevitable once it is conceded that the parties to a contract have the right to vary the terms at will. If the rules of contract law are inefficient, the parties will (save as transaction costs may sometimes outweigh the gains from a more efficient rule) contract around them. A law of contract not based on efficiency considerations will therefore be largely futile. This is a powerful reason for expecting that the law of contract has, in fact, been informed by efficiency considerations, even if judges and lawyers may have found it difficult to articulate the underlying economic premises of the law.

Moreover, the spirit of our analysis is severely positive. We are interested not in whether a contract law based on efficiency is ultimately a good law, but in whether the assumption that contract law has been shaped by a concern with economic efficiency is a fruitful one in explaining the doctrinal positions and typical case outcomes of that law.

2. *The economics of impossibility.* The typical case in which impossibility or some related doctrine is invoked is one where, by reason of an unforeseen or at least unprovided-for event, performance by one of the parties of his obligations under the contract has become so much more costly than he foresaw at the time the contract was made as to be uneconomical (that is, the costs of performance would be greater than the benefits). The performance promised may have been delivery of a particular cargo by a specified delivery date—but the ship is trapped in the Suez Canal because of a war between Israel and Egypt. Or it may have been a piano recital by Gina Bachauer—and she dies between the signing of the contract and the date of the recital. The law could in each case treat the failure to perform as a breach of contract, thereby in effect assigning to the promisor the risk that war, or death, would prevent performance (or render it uneconomical). Alternatively, invoking impossibility or some related notion, the law could treat the failure to perform as excusable and discharge the contract, thereby in effect assigning the risk to the promisee.

From the standpoint of economics—and disregarding, but only momentarily, administrative costs—discharge should be allowed where the promisee is the superior risk bearer; if the promisor is the superior risk bearer, nonperformance should be treated as a breach of contract. "Superior risk bearer" is to be understood here as the party that is the more efficient bearer of the particular risk in question, in the particular circumstances of the transaction. Of course, if the parties have expressly assigned the risk to one of them, there is no occasion to inquire which is the superior risk bearer. The inquiry is merely an aid to interpretation.

A party can be a superior risk bearer for one of two reasons. First, he may be in a better position to prevent the risk from materializing. . . . Discharge would be inefficient in any case where the promisor could prevent the risk from materializing at a lower cost than the expected cost of the risky event. In such a case efficiency would require that the promisor bear the loss resulting from the occurrence of the event, and hence that occurrence should be treated as precipitating a breach of contract.

But the converse is not necessarily true. It does not necessarily follow from the fact that the promisor could not at any reasonable cost have prevented the risk from materializing that he should be discharged from his contractual obligations. Prevention is only one way of dealing with risk; the other is insurance. The promisor may be the superior insurer. If so, his inability to prevent the risk from materializing should not operate to discharge him from the contract, any more than an insurance company's inability to prevent a fire on the premises of the insured should excuse it from its liability to make good the damage caused by the fire.

To understand how it is that one party to a contract may be the superior (more efficient) risk bearer even though he cannot prevent the risk from materializing, it is necessary to understand the fundamental concept of risk aversion. Compare a 100 percent chance of having to pay $10 with a one percent chance of having to pay $1000. The expected cost is the same in both cases, yet not everyone would be indifferent as between the two alternatives. Many people would be willing to pay a substantial sum to avoid the uncertain alternative—for example, $15 to avoid having to take a one percent chance of having to pay $1000. Such people are risk averse. The prevalence of insurance is powerful evidence that risk aversion is extremely common, for insurance is simply trading an uncertain for a certain cost. Because of the administrative expenses of insurance, the certain cost (that is, the insurance premium) is always higher, often much higher, than the uncertain cost that it avoids—the expected cost of the fire, of the automobile accident, or whatever. Only a risk-averse individual would pay more to avoid bearing risk than the expected cost of the risk.

The fact that people are willing to pay to avoid risk shows that risk is a cost. Accordingly, insurance is a method (alternative to prevention) of reducing the costs associated with the risk that performance of a contract may be more costly than anticipated. It is a particularly important method of cost avoidance in the impossibility context because the risks with which that doctrine is concerned are generally not preventable by the party charged with nonperformance. As mentioned, if they were, that would normally afford a compelling reason for treating nonperformance as a breach of contract. . . .

The factors relevant to determining which party to the contract is the cheaper insurer are (1) risk-appraisal costs and (2) transaction costs.[25] The former comprise the costs of determining (a) the probability that the risk will materialize and (b) the magnitude of the loss if it does materialize. The amount of risk is the product of the probability of loss and of the magnitude of the loss if it occurs. Both elements—probability and magnitude—must be known in order for the insurer to know how much to ask from the other party to the contract as compensation for bearing the risk in question.

The relevant transaction costs are the costs involved in eliminating or minimizing the risk through pooling it with other uncertain events, that is, diversifying away the risk. This can be done [by purchasing insurance]. . . .

25. The appraisal costs are really part of the transaction costs, but to facilitate exposition we exclude them from the latter concept.

The foregoing discussion indicates the factors that courts and legislatures might consider in devising efficient rules for the discharge of contracts. An easy case for discharge would be one where (1) the promisor asking to be discharged could not reasonably have prevented the event rendering his performance uneconomical, and (2) the promisee could have insured against the occurrence of the event at lower cost than the promisor because the promisee (a) was in a better position to estimate both (i) the probability of the event's occurrence and (ii) the magnitude of the loss if it did occur, and (b) could have self-insured, whereas the promisor would have had to buy more costly market insurance. As we shall see, not all cases are this easy.

NOTES AND QUESTIONS

1. ***Summarizing the least-cost avoider approach.*** In your own words, how would you summarize Posner's least-cost avoider approach developed in the previous excerpt as it applies to the doctrines of impossibility, impracticability, and frustration of purpose? Is his approach workable? What are its pros and cons? Does it provide any insight into how the cases we have discussed in this section have been, or ought to have been, decided? How would you apply Judge Posner's approach to resolve the problems below?

PROBLEM: THE PRINTING MACHINE*

A, a manufacturer of printing machinery, contracts with *B*, a commercial printer, to sell and install a printing machine on *B*'s premises. As *B* is aware, the machine will be custom-designed for *B*'s needs and once the machine has been completed its value to any other printer will be very small. After the machine is completed, but before installation, a fire destroys *B*'s premises and puts *B* out of business, precluding *B* from accepting delivery of the machine. The machine has no salvage value and *A* accordingly sues for the full price. *B* defends on the ground that the fire, which the fire marshal has found occurred without negligence on B's part—indeed (the same point, in an economic sense), which could not have been prevented by *B* at any reasonable cost—should operate to discharge *B* from its obligations under the contract.

How should this dispute be resolved? Specifically, how should a court determine the party on which to place the risk?

* Excerpted from Richard A. Posner & Andrew M. Rosenfield, *Impossibility and Related Doctrines in Contract Law: An Economic Analysis*, 6 J. LEGAL STUD. 83, 92-94 (1977).

PROBLEM: COAL MINING*

For our second hypothetical case, let *C* be a large and diversified business concern engaged in both coal mining and the manufacture and sale of large coal-burning furnaces. *C* executes contracts for the sale of furnaces to *D*, *E*, *F*, etc. in which it also agrees to supply coal to them for a given period of time at a specified price. The price, however, is to vary with and in proportion to changes in the consumer price index.

A few years later the price of coal unexpectedly quadruples and *C* repudiates the coal-supply agreements arguing that if forced to meet its commitments to supply coal at the price specified in its contracts it will be bankrupted. Each purchaser sues *C* seeking as damages the difference between the price of obtaining coal over the life of *C*'s commitment and the contract price. *C* argues that the rise in the price of coal was unforeseeable and ought to operate to discharge it from its obligations.

As before, how should this dispute be resolved? Specifically, how should a court determine the party on which to place the risk?

PROBLEM: A FRUSTRATED CAR DEALER

On August 4, 1941 Plaintiff leased to Defendant for a five-year term beginning September 15, 1941, certain premises located at a prominent corner in Beverly Hills, Los Angeles County,

> for the sole purpose of conducting thereon the business of displaying and selling new automobiles (including the servicing and repairing thereof and of selling the petroleum products of a major oil company) and for no other purpose whatsoever without the written consent of the lessor except to make an occasional sale of a used automobile.

Defendant agreed not to sublease or assign without Plaintiff's written consent. On January 8, 1942 the federal government ordered that the sale of new automobiles be permitted only to those engaged in military activities, and on January 20, 1942, it established a system of priorities restricting sales to persons having preferential ratings of A-1-j or higher. On March 10, 1942, Defendant explained the effect of these restrictions on his business to Plaintiff, who orally waived the restrictions in the lease as to use and subleasing and offered to reduce the rent if Defendant should be unable to operate profitably. Nevertheless Defendant vacated the premises on March 15, 1942, giving oral notice of repudiation of the lease to Plaintiff. Plaintiff affirmed in writing on March 26th their oral waiver and, failing to persuade Defendant to perform his obligations, they rented the property to other tenants to mitigate damages. On May 11, 1942, Plaintiff brought

* Excerpted from Richard A. Posner & Andrew M. Rosenfield, *Impossibility and Related Doctrines in Contract Law: An Economic Analysis*, 6 J. LEGAL STUD. 83, 94-95 (1977).

suit against Defendant for unpaid rent. Defendant claims that its performance should be excused because the purpose for which the premises were leased was frustrated by the restrictions placed on the sale of new automobiles by the federal government, thereby terminating his duties under the lease.

Did war conditions terminate Defendant's obligations under the contract? In short, should Defendant's performance be excused on account of frustration of purpose?

F. THE STATUTE OF FRAUDS

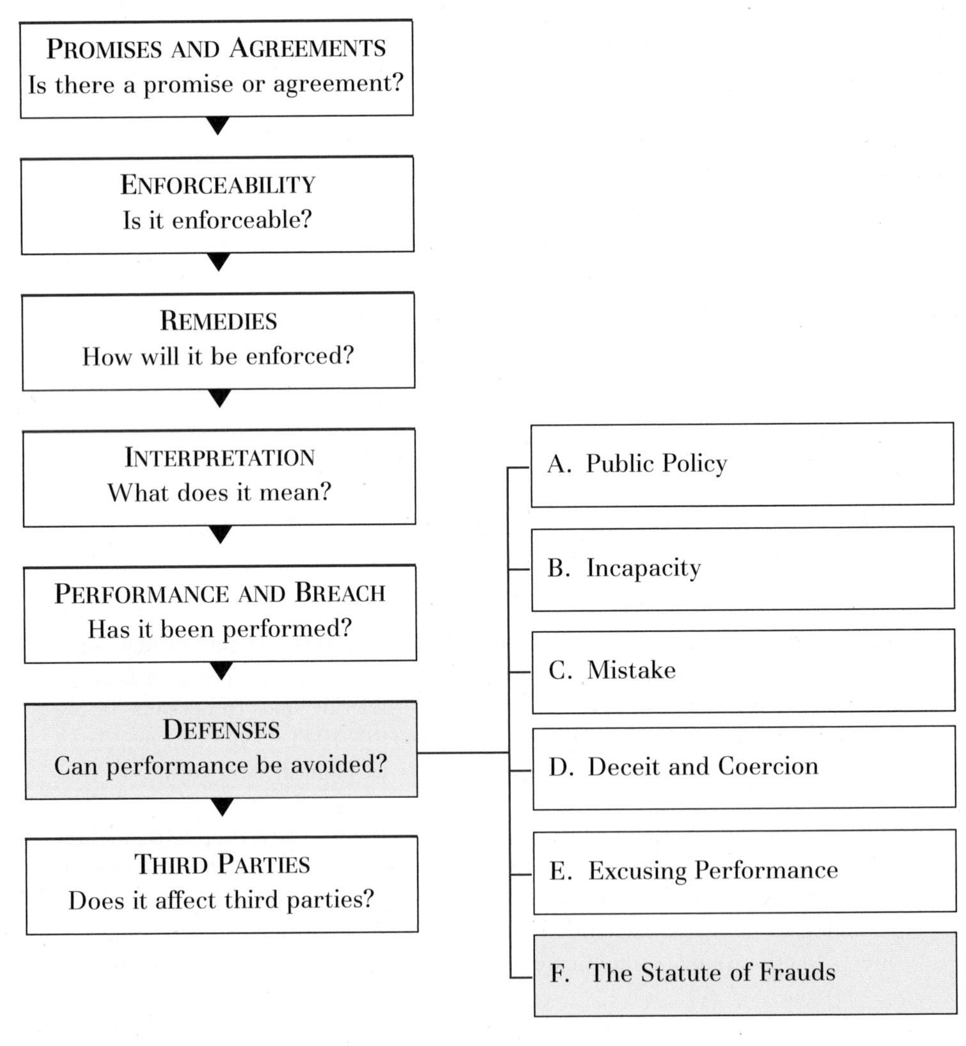

In the final substantive section of this chapter, we will study the statute of frauds, which requires that certain types of agreements, to be enforceable, must be in writing. Indeed, the idea behind the statute of frauds is as old as written law itself, and appears in some of the earliest known legal codes. For instance, in the Laws of Hammurabi, perhaps the most well-known legal code from the ancient world written about 1750 B.C., two memorable provisions provided that:

> ¶ 122 If a man intends to give silver, gold, or anything else to another man for safekeeping, he shall exhibit before witnesses anything which he intends to give, he shall draw up a written contract, and (in this manner) he shall give goods for safekeeping.
>
> ¶ 123 If he gives goods for safekeeping without witnesses or a written contract, and they deny that he gave anything, that case has no basis for a claim.*

But why should certain promises only be enforceable if memorialized in a written document? At least part of the reason is that a written document satisfies the evidentiary, channeling, and cautionary functions of legal formalities we explored in a previous chapter.† This explanation is good as far as it goes, but it cannot tell us why courts sometimes enforce promises that are *not* reduced to writing, or why courts sometimes fail to enforce promises that *are* reduced to writing. Therefore, as you read the cases and materials below, try to think critically about the policy considerations involved in requiring that some promises, but not others, be put in writing to be enforceable, and the kind of black-letter doctrine that would best reflect these policy considerations. This—even more than knowing the black-letter doctrines enshrined in the cases below—will help you understand why courts sometimes apply the statute of frauds and require a writing before enforcing a promise, and why they sometimes apply an exception to the statute of frauds and enforce a promise even without a writing.

DOCTRINAL OVERVIEW: THE STATUTE OF FRAUDS AND THE WRITING REQUIREMENT‡

It would be difficult to imagine a question more important to a person expecting to make agreements in an unfamiliar legal system than this: When is a writing needed for an enforceable agreement? The answer will determine both one's willingness to give unwritten assurances and one's insistence that the other party put its undertaking in writing. This question whether a writing is needed for an enforceable agreement should not be confused with the question whether a writing excludes evidence of prior negotiations. The latter is governed by the parol evidence rule [discussed in chapter 6.B.2.]. The former, which is discussed here,

* From the Laws of Hammurabi (LH), ca. 1750 B.C.E., Babylon, *in* MARTHA ROSS, LAW COLLECTIONS FROM MESOPOTAMIA AND ASIA MINOR (2d ed. 1997).

† See "The Role of Legal Formalities" on p. 341, *supra*, excerpted from Lon L. Fuller, *Consideration and Form*, 41 COL. L. REV. 799, 800-06 (1941).

‡ Excerpted from E. ALLAN FARNSWORTH, CONTRACTS § 6.1 (4th ed. 2004).

is governed by "statutes of frauds," patterned after the English Statute of Frauds of more than three centuries ago.

[Specifically, the Statute of Frauds, enacted by Parliament in 1677, was designed to prevent fraud by refusing to enforce certain categories of contracts (e.g., contracts for the sale of land, contracts that could not be performed within a year of being made) unless the contract was written and signed by the party against whom enforcement was sought. Interestingly, although the Statute of Frauds found its way into all 50 states, i]n 1954, after 277 years, Parliament repealed most of the Statute of Frauds. . . .

The rules for international contracts contained in the Vienna Convention and the UNIDROIT Principles reflect the absence of writing requirements for commercial contracts in most civil law countries as well as the repeal of the sale of goods provision in England. The Convention, which displaces the Uniform Commercial Code with respect to contracts for the sale of goods within the Convention's scope, provides that such a contract "need not be concluded in or evidenced by writing and is not subject to any other requirement as to form."[9] The UNIDROIT Principles follow suit by stating that "Nothing in these Principles requires a contract to be concluded in or evidenced by a writing."[10]

Statutes of frauds remain in this country despite their many critics. During the period England was moving to abolish most of the Statute, including the sale of goods provision, the drafters of the Uniform Commercial Code were deciding to retain that part of the Statute, albeit in a less rigorous form. . . .

Attempts at justifying the statute of frauds in this country stress the functions of a formality such as a writing. Its original purpose was evidentiary, providing some proof that the alleged agreement was actually made, and all its provisions perform this function to some degree. A few provisions perform other functions as well. . . . [For instance, t]he land contract provision performs a significant channeling function, by furnishing a simple test of enforceability to mark off unenforceable agreements from enforceable ones. It is noteworthy that the most durable and well-regarded of the statute's provisions are those that fulfill more than just the original evidentiary purpose.

During its long life, the statute has occasioned an enormous amount of litigation, and critics have disagreed over how well it has served its purposes. One English jurist opined that the statute "promotes fraud rather than prevents it,"[16] and another thought that had it "been always carried into execution according to the letter, it would have done ten times more mischief than it has done good, by protecting, rather than by preventing, frauds."[17] An American critic agreed that the statute's provisions "are no longer preventing fraud, if they ever did, but rather are a cause of fraud."[18] On the other side, Karl Llewellyn argued that "after two centuries and a half the statute stands, in essence better adapted to our needs than when it first was passed."[19] Another observer suggested that the

9. CISG Article 11

10. UNIDROIT Principles Article 1.2.

16. Marvin v. Wallis, 119 Eng. Rep. 1035, 1038 (Ch. 1856).

17. Simon v. Metivier, 96 Eng. Rep. 347, 348 (K.B. 1766) (Wilmot, J.).

18. Huge Evander Willis, *The Statute of Frauds—A Legal Anachronism (pt. 2)*, 3 IND. L.J. 528, 541 (1928).

19. Karl Llewellyn, *What Price Contract?—An Essay in Perspective*, 40 YALE L.J. 704, 747 (19:51).

statute was justified by "the thousands of uncontested current transactions where misunderstanding and controversy are avoided by the presence of a writing which the statute at least indirectly aided to procure."[20] After more than three centuries, the statute still plays to mixed reviews.

Although the statute is not likely to be subjected to wholesale repeal in this country, it has been the subject of constant erosion. Courts have long been receptive to pleas that the statute should be narrowly interpreted so as not to cover the contract in question. They have more recently become receptive to arguments that, even if the statute covers the contract in question, the statute's requirement of a writing has been met or the claimant's reliance on the contract dispenses with the requirement. This process of erosion promises to continue in the future. . . .

1. The General Rule and Some Important Exceptions

Rosenthal v. Fonda

United States Court of Appeals, Ninth Circuit
862 F.2d 1398 (1988)

CANBY, CIRCUIT JUDGE. Richard Rosenthal appeals the district court's grant of summary judgment in favor of Jane Fonda and four of her related corporations. The district court determined that New York law controlled this dispute and that New York's statute of frauds barred Rosenthal's claim against Fonda for breach of an oral contract. . . . We affirm. . . .

FACTUAL BACKGROUND

This action arises out of the twelve year relationship between Jane Fonda and her former attorney and general business manager, Richard Rosenthal. In 1968, Fonda, a California resident, retained the services of a New York law firm. She entered into an oral agreement with the firm that she would pay five percent of her earnings as compensation for the firm's services. Rosenthal, an attorney with the firm, assumed responsibility for a large share of the firm's activities on Fonda's behalf. In 1971, the law firm dissolved and in 1972, Rosenthal began to represent Fonda as an independent private practitioner. Rosenthal alleges that in April of 1972, he and Fonda entered into an oral contract whereby he agreed to continue performing a variety of services for Fonda and she, in turn, agreed to pay him ten percent of all gross professional income derived from the projects that were initiated during his tenure.

Rosenthal continued to represent Fonda from his New York office. In 1978, Rosenthal and his family moved to California, at Fonda's request, so that he could be closer to her and represent her more efficiently. Despite relocating,

20. L. Vold, *The Application of the Statute of Frauds Under the Uniform Sales Act*, 15 MINN. L. REV. 391, 394 (1931).

Rosenthal maintained a home and an office in New York. Fonda discharged Rosenthal approximately two years later, on May 30, 1980.

Rosenthal brought suit against Fonda in California district court to recover commissions on projects that were initiated during his tenure and produced or continued to produce income after his termination. The district court granted Fonda's motion for partial summary judgment, holding that New York's statute of frauds applied and served to bar Rosenthal's oral contract claim unless Fonda was equitably estopped from asserting the statute as a defense. After a bench trial on the equitable estoppel issue, the district court granted Fonda's motion for a directed verdict, ruling that she was not equitably estopped from asserting the defense. Accordingly, the court entered judgment for Fonda.

DISCUSSION

. . . Rosenthal contends that the district court should have applied California, not New York, law to resolve this dispute. . . .

I. *Do The Laws of the Two States Differ?*

The principal issue in this dispute is whether Rosenthal's breach of oral contract claim is barred under the statute of frauds provision that requires that all contracts not to be performed within one year be in writing. Textually, the relevant New York and California provisions of the statute of frauds are essentially identical. New York's statute of frauds provides that "[e]very agreement, promise or undertaking is void or unenforceable unless it or some note or memorandum thereof be in writing and subscribed by the party to be charged therewith, or his agent, if such agreement, promise or undertaking, by its terms is not to be performed within one year from making thereof . . ." N.Y. Gen. Oblig. Law § 5-701. Similarly, California's statute provides that "[t]he following contracts are invalid, unless the same, or some note or memorandum thereof, is in writing and subscribed by the party to be charged or by his agent: 1. An agreement that by its terms is not to be performed within a year from the making thereof. . . ." Cal. Civ. Code § 1624.1.

The district court found that while these two provisions are facially identical, they are interpreted differently. The court correctly determined that in California, Rosenthal's employment contract with Fonda, terminable at the will of either party, would fall outside the bar of the state's statute of frauds because it is *capable* of being performed within a year. California's one year provision is interpreted literally and narrowly. Only those oral contracts which "expressly preclude performance within one year" or that "cannot possibly be performed within one year" are unenforceable. In this case, Fonda could have discharged Rosenthal after he had worked for her for six months; therefore, this contract was capable of being performed within one year. Moreover, California's statute of frauds does not invalidate oral employment contracts that call for the payment of commissions after one year or upon termination of the employment relationship. Thus, Rosenthal's oral contract with Fonda would not be barred under California's statute of frauds.

In New York, however, while a typical employment contract with no fixed term is not barred by the statute of frauds, a commission sales arrangement that extends beyond the employee's termination or that has no specific time frame has repeatedly been held to be one that cannot be performed within one year. The New York rule was enunciated in *McCollester v. Chisholm*, 478 N.Y.S.2d 691 (1984):

> A service contract of indefinite duration, in which one party agrees to procure customers, or accounts, or orders on behalf of the second party, is not by its terms performable within one year—and hence must be in writing and signed by the party to be charged—since performance is dependent, not upon the will of the parties to the contract, but on that of a third party.

Id. at 692.

The key element in deciding whether New York's statute of frauds applies to bar a commission sales agreement is whether the defendant can unilaterally terminate the contract, discharging all promises made to the plaintiff including the promise to make commission payments. If commission payments are due under the contract after one party has fully performed, the contract, by its own terms, cannot be performed within a year because there is no way the defendant can unilaterally terminate the contract. *See Shirley Polykoff Advertising, Inc. v. Houbigant, Inc.*, 374 N.E.2d 625, 626 (1978) (contract providing that advertising agency receive $5,000 a year for every year the advertisement is used cannot be performed within one year). *See also Urvant*, 325 F. Supp. 677, 685-86 (1970) (Under New York law, the statute of frauds is applicable "where nothing in the commission contract contemplates its fulfillment within a year and no term or event controlled by the parties will bring the contract to an end with its promises discharged.").

In the present case, Rosenthal contends that Fonda promised him a percentage fee every time a project initiated during his tenure generated income. Fonda could not unilaterally terminate this contract once Rosenthal performed because she would continue to owe Rosenthal money under the contract for as long as his projects generated income. Moreover, Fonda's liability to perform under the contract and make commission payments to Rosenthal is dependent not upon her will, but upon the will of others who may elect, for example, to exhibit her works. This contract, therefore, would be barred under New York's statute of frauds as one that by its own terms could not be performed within a year. . . .

CONCLUSION

[T]he relevant statute of frauds provisions in California and New York produce different results when applied to this transaction, each state has an interest in having its own law applied, and New York's interest would be most impaired if its policies were subordinated to California's policies. Thus, the district court correctly determined that New York's law should govern this dispute. Rosenthal's oral fee agreement with Fonda would be barred under New

York's statute of frauds as an agreement that cannot, by its own terms, be performed within one year. Accordingly, the district court's grant of summary judgment in favor of Fonda is affirmed.

RELEVANT PROVISIONS

For the *Restatement (Second) of Contracts,* consult §§ 110, 125, 129, 130, 131, 139, and 143. For the UCC, consult § 2-201.

NOTES AND QUESTIONS

1. ***What happened?*** Who sued whom for what? Procedurally, how did the case get before this court? Factually, what happened between the parties? What arguments did the plaintiff and defendant make? What rule or rules did the court apply? How did the court analyze the dispute between the parties? How did the court decide the case?

2. ***Was this case correctly decided?*** Do you agree with the result reached in this case? Why or why not? Do you agree with the court's reasoning? Why or why not? How, if at all, would you have written the opinion differently?

3. ***The policy behind the statute of frauds.*** Do you think the statute of frauds ought to have applied here? Why or why not? In general, what should courts do where it is clear that the purpose for which the statute of frauds exists (i.e., to prevent frauds) is a non sequitur in the case before them? Should they ignore the doctrine to apply the policy?

McInerney v. Charter Golf, Inc.

Supreme Court of Illinois
680 N.E.2d 1347 (1997)

[We previously considered whether an employee's promise to forgo another job opportunity in exchange for a guarantee of lifetime employment constituted sufficient consideration to modify an existing employment-at-will relationship. To review that portion of the opinion, see p. 335, *supra*. In this portion of the opinion, we examine whether the agreement must be in writing to satisfy the requirements of the statute of frauds.]

JUSTICE HEIPLE **delivered the opinion of the court. . . .**

B. STATUTE OF FRAUDS

So there is a contract, but should we enforce it? Charter Golf argues that the oral contract at issue in this case violates the statute of frauds and is unenforceable because it is not capable of being performed within one year of its making. By statute in Illinois, "[n]o action shall be brought . . . upon any agreement that is not to be performed within the space of one year from the making thereof, unless . . . in writing and signed by the party to be charged." 740 ILCS 80/1 (West 1994). Our statute tracks the language of the original English Statute of Frauds and Perjuries. 29 Charles II ch. 3 (1676). The English statute enacted by Parliament had as its stated purpose the prohibition of those "many fraudulent practices, which are commonly endeavored to be upheld by perjury and subordination of perjury." 29 Charles II ch. 3, introductory clause (1676). Illinois' statute of frauds seeks to do the same by barring actions based upon nothing more than loose verbal statements.

The period of one year, although arbitrary, recognizes that with the passage of time evidence becomes stale and memories fade. The statute proceeds from the legislature's sound conclusion that while the technical elements of a contract may exist, certain contracts should not be enforced absent a writing. It functions more as an evidentiary safeguard than as a substantive rule of contract. As such, the statute exists to protect not just the parties to a contract, but also—perhaps more importantly—to protect the fact finder from charlatans, perjurers and the problems of proof accompanying oral contracts.

There are, of course, exceptions to the statute of frauds' writing requirement which permit the enforcement of certain oral contracts required by the statute to be in writing. One such exception is the judicially created exclusion for contracts of uncertain duration. In an effort to significantly narrow the application of the statute, many courts have construed the words "not to be performed" to mean "not capable of being performed" within one year. See *Restatement (Second) of Contracts* § 130. These cases hold that if performance is possible by its terms within one year, the contract is not within the statute regardless of how unlikely it is that it will actually be performed within one year. Under this interpretation, the actual course of subsequent events and the expectations of the parties are entirely irrelevant. *Restatement (Second) of Contracts* § 130, Comment a. A contract for lifetime employment would then be excluded from the operation of the statute because the employee could, in theory, die within one year, and thus the contract would be "capable of being performed."[1]

We find such an interpretation hollow and unpersuasive. A "lifetime" employment contract is, in essence, a permanent employment contract. Inherently, it anticipates a relationship of long duration—certainly longer than one year. In the context of an employment-for-life contract, we believe that the better view is to treat the contract as one "not to be performed within the space of one year

1. In attempting to rein in this exception to the statute of frauds, some courts have made a distinction—at times quite attenuated—between death as full performance and death operating to terminate or excuse the contract. Under this view, an oral contract for employment for a stated period longer than one year will not be enforced because, although the employee could die within one year of the making of the contact, these courts elect to treat that contingency as an excuse or termination of the contract and not as performance. This distinction, while perhaps logical in other contexts, is meaningless in our case where the complete performance contemplated by the parties, i.e., employment for life, is identical to the event giving rise to termination or excuse. Under the terms of the oral contract alleged in this case, the employee's death would have resulted in full performance.

from the making thereof." To hold otherwise would eviscerate the policy underlying the statute of frauds and would invite confusion, uncertainty and outright fraud. Accordingly, we hold that a writing is required for the fair enforcement of lifetime employment contracts.

The plaintiff argues that the statute of frauds' writing requirement is nonetheless excused because he performed, either fully or partially, according to the terms of the oral contract. Illinois courts have held that a party who has fully performed an oral contract within the one-year provision may nonetheless have the contract enforced. Full or complete performance of the instant contract, by its terms, would have required the plaintiff to work until his death, but our plaintiff lives.

A party's partial performance generally does not bar application of the statute of frauds, unless it would otherwise be "impossible or impractical to place the parties in status quo or restore or compensate" the performing party for the value of his performance. *Mapes v. Kalva Corp.*, 68 Ill. App. 3d 362, 368 (1979). This so-called exception resembles the doctrines of restitution, estoppel and fraud, and exists to avoid a "virtual fraud" from being perpetrated on the performing party. *Barrett v. Geisinger*, 35 N.E. 354 (1893); see also *Restatement (Second) of Contracts* § 130, Comment e. In any event, our plaintiff has been fully compensated for the work that he performed. Accordingly, part performance—on these facts—will not take the case out of the statute of frauds.

Finally, the plaintiff argues that the defendant should be estopped from asserting the defense of statute of frauds. Traditionally, a party's reliance estopped the other party from asserting the statute only under the doctrine of equitable estoppel. Equitable estoppel is available if one party has relied upon another party's misrepresentation or concealment of a material fact. Absent such misrepresentation or fraud, the defense is not available. No misrepresentation has been alleged here.

Rather, the plaintiff complains that he relied upon the oral promises of his employer and makes much of the injustice done him—indeed, too much. While agreeing to work for an employer and giving up other employment opportunities can clearly be described as reliance on the employer's oral promises concerning the terms of employment, promissory estoppel does not bar the application of the statute of frauds in Illinois. *See Ozier v. Haines*, 103 N.E.2d 485 (1952); *Sinclair v. Sullivan Chevrolet Co.*, 202 N.E.2d 516 (1964) (rejecting, at least implicitly, the suggestion that promissory estoppel bars the application of the statute of frauds). In the context of an employment relationship, reasonable reliance is insufficient to bar the application of the statute of frauds. Some authorities—reflected in the view of the Second Restatement—have used promissory estoppel to bar the application of the statute of frauds in a narrow class of cases in which a performing party would otherwise be without an adequate remedy and there is some element of unjust enrichment. *Restatement (Second) of Contracts* § 139, Comment *c*. We do not believe that this case is one which requires us to adopt such a rule. As we have observed, McInerney has been compensated for his services, and the sole injustice of which he complains is his employer's failure to honor its promise of lifetime employment. Our plaintiff, however, is a salesman—a sophisticated man of commerce—and arguably should have realized that his employer's oral promise was unenforceable under the statute of frauds and that his reliance on that promise was misplaced. Our parties entered into this disputed oral contract freely and without any hint of coercion, fraud or misrepresentation, and thus we adhere to the rule of *Ozier* and *Sinclair* and hold that the statute of frauds operates even where there has been reliance on a promise.

In sum, though an employee's promise to forgo another job opportunity in exchange for a guarantee of lifetime employment is consideration to support the formation of a contract, the statute of frauds requires that contracts for lifetime employment be in writing. Accordingly, we affirm the judgment of the appellate court.

Appellate court judgment affirmed.

Justice Nickels, **dissenting.** I agree with the majority's conclusion that plaintiff's promise to forgo another job opportunity is sufficient consideration in return for defendant's promise of lifetime employment to plaintiff. However, I disagree with the majority's holding that the employment contract in the case at bar must be in writing because it falls within the requirements of the statute of frauds.

The writing requirement applies to "any agreement that is not to be performed within the space of one year from the making thereof." 740 ILCS 80/1 (West 1994). Commenting on this language, the *Restatement (Second) of Contracts* observes:

> [T]he enforceability of a contract under the one-year provision does not turn on the actual course of subsequent events, nor on the expectations of the parties as to the probabilities. Contracts of uncertain duration are simply excluded; the provision covers only those contracts whose performance cannot possibly be completed within a year.

Restatement (Second) of Contracts § 130, Comment *a*.

A contract of employment for life is necessarily one of uncertain duration. Since the employee's life may end within one year, and, as the majority acknowledges, the contract would be fully performed upon the employee's death, the contract is not subject to the statute of frauds' one-year provision. See *Restatement (Second) of Contracts* § 130, Illustration 2; see also 72 Am. Jur. 2d *Statute of Frauds* § 14, at 578 (1974) ("The rule generally accepted by the authorities is that an agreement or promise the performance or duration of which is contingent on the duration of human life is not within the statute"); J. Calamari & J. Perillo, *The Law of Contracts* § 19-20 (3d ed. 1987) ("if A promises . . . to employ X for life, the promise is not within the Statute because it is not for a fixed term and the contract by its terms is conditioned upon the continued life of X and the condition may cease to exist within a year because X may die within a year"). It is irrelevant whether the parties anticipate that the employee will live for more than a year or whether the employee actually does so.

The majority acknowledges that "many courts" subscribe to this view. More accurately, the Restatement rule represents "the prevailing interpretation" of the statute of frauds' one-year provision. *Restatement (Second) of Contracts* § 130, Comment *a*. Only a "distinct minority" of cases have ascribed significance to whether the parties expected that a contract would take more than a year to perform. J. Calamari & J. Perillo, *The Law of Contracts* § 19-18, at 808 (3d ed. 1987). According to *Williston on Contracts*:

> It is well settled that the oral contracts invalidated by the Statute because not to be performed within a year include only those which cannot be performed within that period. A promise which is not likely to be performed within a year, and which in fact is not performed within a year, is not within the Statute if at the time the contract is made there is a possibility in law and in fact that full performance such as the parties intended may be completed before the expiration of a year.
>
> In the leading case on this section of the Statute the Supreme Court of the United States said: 'The parties may well have expected that the contract would continue in force for more than one year; it may have been very improbable that it would not do so; and it did in fact continue in force for a much longer time. But they made no stipulation which in terms, or by reasonable inference, required that result. The question is not what the probable, or expected, or actual performance of the contract was; but whether the contract, according to the reasonable interpretation of its terms, required that it should not be performed within the year.'"

3 W. Jaeger, *Williston on Contracts* § 495, at 575-79 (3d ed. 1960), quoting *Warner v. Texas & Pacific Ry. Co.*, 164 U.S. 418, 434 (1896).

Although the majority brands this interpretation "hollow and unpersuasive," it has a sound basis in the plain language of the statute. Corbin notes:

> [Courts] have observed the exact words of [the one-year] provision and have interpreted them literally and very narrowly. The words are "agreement that is not to be performed." They are not "agreement that is not in fact performed" or "agreement that may not be performed" or "agreement that is not at all likely to be performed." To fall within the words of the provision, therefore, the agreement must be one of which it can truly be said at the very moment that it is made, "This agreement is not to be performed within one year"; in general, the cases indicate that there must not be the slightest possibility that it can be fully performed within one year.

2 A. Corbin, *Corbin on Contracts* § 444, at 535 (1950).

It is well established that where the words of a statutory provision are unambiguous, there is no need to resort to external aids of interpretation in order to glean the legislature's purpose. Although the statutory language at issue in this case is clear and unambiguous, the majority improperly relies upon policies identified in the introductory clause to the original English statute of frauds in order to significantly expand the scope of the one-year provision. Even assuming, *arguendo,* that it is proper to look beyond the language of the statute in order to determine its meaning, I do not find the majority's policy analysis to be persuasive justification for the broad construction it gives the statute.

The majority notes the dangers of stale evidence and faded memories. But the one-year provision does not effectively guard against these dangers because "'[t]here is no necessary relationship between the time of the making of the contract, the time within which its performance is required and the time when it might come to court to be proven.'" J. Calamari & J. Perillo, *The Law of Contracts* § 19-17, at 807 (3d ed. 1987), quoting *D & N Boening, Inc. v. Kirsch Beverages, Inc.*, 472 N.E.2d 992, 993 (1984).

Courts have tended to give the one-year provision a narrow construction precisely because of the lack of a discernable rationale for it. J. Calamari & J. Perillo, *The Law of Contracts* § 19-17, at 807 (3d ed. 1987); see also *Restatement (Second) of Contracts* § 130, Comment *a* ("The design was said to be not to trust to the memory of witnesses for a longer time than one year, but the statutory language was not appropriate to carry out that purpose. The result has been a tendency to construction narrowing the application of the statute"). I am inclined to do likewise. Since the one-year provision is so poorly suited to the aims it was ostensibly designed to accomplish, I see no compelling reason to expand the provision's scope beyond the class of contracts to which it applies by its terms. The narrow and literal interpretation that most courts have given to the language of the one-year provision is entirely appropriate under these circumstances.

Lacking any reasoned basis for its holding, the majority resorts to nearly tautological wordplay, declaring that because a "lifetime" employment contract is essentially a "permanent" employment contract, it inherently anticipates a relationship of long duration. Merely labelling a lifetime employment contract "permanent" should not change the result that the statute of frauds is inapplicable. See 2 A. Corbin, *Corbin on Contracts* § 446, at 549-50 (1950) ("A contract for 'permanent' employment is not within the one-year clause for the reason that such a contract will be fully performed, according to its terms, upon the death of the employee. The word 'permanent' has, in this connection, no more extended meaning than 'for life'"); 3 W. Jaeger, *Williston on Contracts* § 495, at 582 (3d ed. 1960) ("A promise of permanent personal performance is on a fair interpretation a promise of performance for life, and therefore not within the Statute"). The parties in this case allegedly agreed to plaintiff's employment for life. But with suitable modesty befitting mere mortals, the parties did not stipulate how long plaintiff's life should be. They left that matter—and hence the duration of the contract—to a higher power (I do not refer to this court).

The majority also suggests that its holding is necessary to avoid confusion and uncertainty. I fail to see how the generally accepted rule that lifetime employment contracts need not be in writing is any more confusing or uncertain than the contrary rule adopted by the majority. Indeed, the majority's reasoning is likely to cause greater confusion and uncertainty. A lifetime employment contract is only one example of a broader general category of contracts of uncertain duration. While the majority has declared that lifetime employment contracts anticipate a relationship of longer than one year, the decision in this case supplies no guidance as to other types of contracts that do not, by their terms, set forth a specific time frame for performance. Contracting parties can no longer simply look to the actual terms of their agreement to ascertain whether it must be in writing. Instead, they are left to guess whether the type of contract they have entered into will be viewed by a court as inherently anticipating a relationship of more than one year.

In summary, the majority's holding: (1) is contrary to the relevant statutory language and the great weight of authority; (2) finds no justification in the policy considerations ostensibly underlying the statute of frauds; and (3) is likely to increase, rather than reduce, uncertainty regarding the application of the one-year provision. I would hold that the statute of frauds does not require the contract in this case to be in writing, and I would reverse the judgments of the courts below. Accordingly, I respectfully dissent.

NOTES AND QUESTIONS

1. *What happened?* Who sued whom for what? Procedurally, how did the case get before this court? Factually, what happened between the parties? What arguments did the plaintiff and defendant make? What rule or rules did the court apply? How did the court analyze the dispute between the parties? How did the court decide the case?

2. *Was this case correctly decided?* Do you agree with the result reached in this case? Why or why not? Do you agree with the court's reasoning? Why or why not? How, if at all, would you have written the opinion differently?

3. *Majority or dissent?* Who has the better argument, between the majority and the dissent? If you were deciding the case, how would you decide it, and why?

4. *What's the disagreement?* The majority believes that (1) the statute of frauds applies to this case, requiring the contract between the parties to be in writing, and (2) that none of the exceptions to the statute of frauds apply here. The dissent disagrees on both counts. Why, exactly? What are the best arguments for and against applying the statute of frauds here? What, exactly, are the exceptions to the statute of frauds? What explains their existence? Why does the majority believe that they do not apply here? Does the dissent take issue with the majority's treatment of (1), (2), or both?

Dewberry v. George

Washington Court of Appeals
62 P.3d 525 (2003)

COLEMAN, J. At issue in this dissolution case is whether an oral prenuptial agreement to treat income earned during marriage as separate property is enforceable. Because the trial court found by clear, cogent, and convincing evidence supported by the record that the parties fully performed their separate property agreement during their marriage, we conclude that their oral prenuptial agreement is enforceable. The trial court did not err when it characterized the parties' property acquired during marriage as separate property in accordance with the agreement. In addition, we conclude that the trial court did not abuse its discretion by allocating the parties' separate property to the spouse who acquired it. Accordingly, we affirm the trial court's property division. . . .

FACTS

Emanuel George, Jr. and Carla DewBerry started dating in 1980 while they were both living in California. DewBerry had just graduated from Boalt Hall School of Law and was working toward becoming a CPA at Arthur Andersen. George was a college-educated music industry executive.

In 1981, the parties were discussing marriage and George told DewBerry that, because a friend had been wronged in a divorce settlement and lost his house, he insisted on the following conditions of marriage: (1) DewBerry would always be fully employed; (2) each party's income and property would be treated as separate property; (3) each party would own a home to return to if the marriage failed; and (4) DewBerry would not get fat. DewBerry agreed to these conditions. This discussion took place in California, a community property state. Neither party was particularly wealthy at the beginning of their relationship. George and DewBerry married in 1986.

Between 1981 and 2000, George and DewBerry continually affirmed this agreement through words and actions. The record reflects painstaking and meticulous effort to maintain separate finances and property. During their marriage, DewBerry and George deposited their incomes into separate accounts which they used for their personal expenses and investments. In 1990, after the birth of their first child, they opened a joint checking account in order to handle certain agreed household expenses. George and DewBerry deposited a specified amount to the joint account, and they reimbursed their personal accounts from the joint account if they happened to use personal funds for household expenses. They took turns managing that account. By 2000, when George and DewBerry separated, they had accumulated minimal community property in the form of joint accounts and jointly purchased possessions. They held numerous investment, bank, and retirement accounts as individuals, and the spouse who had created and contributed to those accounts was considered the sole owner and manager of the assets in those accounts. The primary beneficiaries of their individual accounts were the parties' children, or alternatively, the estate of the spouse who funded them.

During their relationship, DewBerry purchased three houses as her separate property, securing financing separately in all instances by signing promissory notes or asking her sister to co-sign. The first house that she bought was a duplex in Oakland, which she purchased in 1982 in order to fulfill the third condition of the prenuptial agreement. The latter two houses, both located in

Seattle, served as the family's primary residences. In accordance with the parties' agreement, DewBerry treated these houses as her separate property by paying for maintenance, improvements, and the down payment and mortgage with funds from her separate accounts. George paid DewBerry a set amount each month toward living expenses, such as utilities, and DewBerry repaid George for any maintenance costs he incurred. The only involvement George had with these properties was to sign documents at various times indicating either that he had no interest in the properties . . . , or, in the case of the parties' most recent residence . . . , that he consented to being listed on the purchase documents as husband and wife per the bank's requirements. There was no intent that George be personally liable, however, for any of the indebtedness on the properties. George already owned real property in Texas and California that he had acquired before their marriage.

In 1985, DewBerry left Arthur Andersen to become an associate in a Seattle law firm. Meanwhile, George worked in sales and marketing in the entertainment and hospitality industries, and his salary was comparable to DewBerry's initial law firm salary, around $40,000 to $50,000 per year. By the 1990s, however, after DewBerry became a partner at her law firm, her annual salary increased rapidly, totaling over $1 million in 2000. Meanwhile, George's salary remained constant in the $40,000 to $50,000 range. Both parties worked full-time while sharing parenting responsibilities for their two children.

The trial court entered detailed findings of fact and conclusions of law regarding the parties' property and oral prenuptial agreement. Specifically, the trial court found by clear, cogent, and convincing evidence that the parties had entered into an oral prenuptial agreement, despite George's denial of the agreement's existence. The trial court also found that there had been "complete performance" of that agreement during the parties' marriage and, thus, the parties' property consisted primarily of separate property. The trial court ordered that the parties' property be divided roughly in accordance with its status as separate or community property. It awarded DewBerry $2.3 million, or approximately 82 percent of the parties' property, which consisted almost entirely of real and personal property that DewBerry had acquired during the marriage, as well as her pre-marriage separate property. George received property worth $600,000 [and appeals the trial court's property division].

DECISION

George argues that the trial court erred when it found by clear, cogent, and convincing evidence that an oral separate property agreement had been made by the parties prior to marriage and that it had been fully performed during their marriage, making it an enforceable agreement. He claims that such an agreement is void under . . . the statute of frauds. . . . We find no error and affirm.

There is nothing in Washington law that prohibits parties from entering into prenuptial agreements that alter the status of community property. Furthermore, there is substantial evidence to support the trial court's findings and conclusions regarding the existence and complete performance of the parties' oral prenuptial agreement. Thus, the part performance exception to the statute of frauds applies and the parties' oral agreement is enforceable.

Oral separate property agreements made *after* marriage have consistently been enforced by Washington courts when clear and convincing evidence shows both the existence of the agreement and mutual observance of the agreement.

But Washington courts have not yet addressed a situation where parties have orally agreed *prior* to marriage to have a separate property agreement during their marriage. Accordingly, this is a matter of first impression, and we address both the statute of frauds and Washington law concerning prenuptial agreements.

The statute of frauds requires certain agreements, including agreements made in consideration of marriage, to be in writing. Failure to put such agreements into writing renders them void. *Koontz v. Koontz,* 83 Wash. 180, 184-85 (1915). In *Koontz,* the husband's heirs alleged that his surviving spouse had orally agreed prior to marriage that she would not claim any interest in her husband's estate. *Koontz,* 83 Wash. at 184-85. The Washington Supreme Court held that any such agreement, if made orally, would violate the statute of frauds and declined to enforce the agreement. *Koontz,* 83 Wash. at 184-85. The alleged agreement took effect only upon the husband's death; thus, there was no performance during the parties' marriage.

The statute of frauds also barred enforcement of an alleged separate property agreement in *Graves v. Graves,* 48 Wash. 664 (1908). In *Graves,* several years after a husband and wife had divorced, the wife claimed that she was a co-owner of a parcel of real property that was acquired during marriage, but which was not disposed of in the parties' dissolution decree. The ex-husband contended that he and his ex-wife had entered into an oral agreement to treat each spouse's property as separate property; thus, he was the sole owner of the parcel in question because he purchased it in his name. The husband conceded, however, that community funds were used to purchase the property, and the court found that the wife had continuously asserted that the property was jointly owned. Thus, the alleged oral prenuptial agreement was void under the statute requiring agreements in consideration of marriage, as well as agreements transferring an interest in real property, to be in writing. . . .

Although we hold that the statute of frauds applies to the agreement in question, we conclude that it is enforceable under the part performance exception to the statute of frauds. The doctrine of part performance is an equitable doctrine which provides the remedies of damages or specific performance for agreements that would otherwise be barred by the statute of frauds.

The first requirement of the doctrine of part performance of oral contracts is that the contract must be proven by clear, cogent, and convincing evidence. The second requirement is that:

> the acts relied upon as constituting part performance must unmistakably point to the existence of the claimed agreement. If they point to some other relationship,

> such as that of landlord and tenant, or may be accounted for on some other hypothesis, they are not sufficient.

Granquist, 29 Wash. 2d 440, 445 (1947). Where the evidentiary standard is clear, cogent, and convincing, the appellate court must determine whether the substantial evidence in support of the findings of fact is "highly probable." *In re Marriage of Schweitzer*, 132 Wash. 2d 318, 329 (1997). . . .

Here, the terms of the agreement were clear and simple. Several witnesses testified that the parties created an oral prenuptial agreement and that George and DewBerry acted in accordance with that agreement. Furthermore, despite George's denial of the agreement, the steps taken by the parties to avoid commingling of their assets were unusually strong evidence of a separate property agreement. It was undisputed that the parties meticulously accounted for and handled their individual incomes as separate property and created minimal joint accounts to handle certain family-related expenses and requirements. The husband and wife relationship cannot account for such painstaking efforts to establish and maintain separate property. We conclude that the trial court's determination that an oral agreement was made is supported by substantial evidence that is "highly probable."

George also contends that there was no finding of complete performance to take the agreement out of the statute of frauds. This contention lacks merit, as the trial court expressly stated in its oral opinion that it found complete performance:

> So, then, looking at whether or not under Washington law the oral contract can be enforced, we have to look then at the exceptions that will allow for an enforcement for such a contract. Performance is certainly one of them. I find that there was really complete performance at least up to the present. I won't go back though all of the factors that I listed, but the parties did clearly keep their property separate.

The oral opinion is expressly integrated into the written findings of fact and conclusions of law. Thus, the trial court's decision to enforce the oral prenuptial agreement was based upon a recognized exception to the statute of frauds and is supported by the proper evidentiary standard. . . .

We affirm.

NOTES AND QUESTIONS

1. *What happened?* Who sued whom for what? Procedurally, how did the case get before this court? Factually, what happened between the parties? What arguments did the plaintiff and defendant make? What rule or rules did the court apply? How did the court analyze the dispute between the parties? How did the court decide the case?

2. *Was this case correctly decided?* Do you agree with the result reached in this case? Why or why not? Do you agree with the court's reasoning? Why or why not? How, if at all, would you have written the opinion differently?

3. *Reconciling the cases.* Can this case be reconciled with the decision in *Rosenthal* or *McInerney*? Why or why not?

4. *Thinking tools.* Thinking about administrative costs and efficiency, on the one hand, and the justice between the two parties, on the other, what doctrine do you think should courts adopt to govern cases where important transactions are at stake? Should all such transactions be required to be in writing to be enforceable? Or is it enough if the parties can prove that the transaction being alleged did, in fact, take place?

Browning v. Poirier

Supreme Court of Florida
165 So. 3d 663 (May 28, 2015)

POLSTON, J. We review the decision of the Fifth District Court of Appeal in *Browning v. Poirier*, 128 So. 3d 144 (Fla. 5th DCA 2013), a case in which the Fifth District certified a question of great public importance. We rephrase the certified question to the following as suggested by Chief Judge Torpy:

> Is a terminable-at-will agreement to pool lottery winnings unenforceable in the absence of an express agreement to continue the agreement for a period of time exceeding one year, when full performance of the agreement is possible within one year from the inception of the agreement[?]

Id. at 155. We answer the rephrased question in the negative and quash the Fifth District's decision.

I. BACKGROUND

Petitioner Howard Browning and Respondent Lynn Anne Poirier lived together in a romantic relationship beginning in 1991. In approximately 1993, the parties entered into an oral agreement in which they each agreed to purchase lottery tickets and to equally share in the proceeds of any winning lottery tickets. On June 2, 2007, Poirier purchased a winning ticket and "collected one million dollars minus deductions for taxes." *Id.* When Browning requested half of the proceeds, Poirier refused, and Browning filed the underlying suit for breach of an oral contract and unjust enrichment. However, Poirier denied the existence of any oral agreement to split lottery proceeds and raised the defense of the statute of frauds.

At the close of Browning's case, Poirier moved for a directed verdict on two counts in Browning's complaint, and the trial court granted the directed verdict on both counts. Specifically, the trial court granted a directed verdict on Browning's claim for breach of an oral contract, finding that the action was barred by the statute of frauds. Additionally, the trial court "granted a directed verdict on Browning's claim for unjust enrichment, holding that a party seeking to enforce an express contract cannot simultaneously disavow the contract and seek equitable relief in quasi-contract." *Id.* The trial court entered final judgment in favor of Poirier.

On appeal, a panel of the Fifth District entered an opinion on March 8, 2013, reversing the trial court. *Browning v. Poirier*, 113 So. 3d 976 (Fla. 5th DCA 2013), *withdrawn and superseded on reh'g en banc* by 128 So. 3d 144 (Fla. 5th DCA 2013). However, the Fifth District granted a motion for rehearing en banc, withdrew the panel opinion, and substituted an opinion in its place on November 8, 2013. *Browning*, 128 So. 3d at 145.

Regarding Browning's claim for breach of an oral contract, the Fifth District looked to the statute of frauds as stated in section 725.01, Florida Statutes, and the "leading case interpreting this statute," *Yates v. Ball*, 132 Fla. 132, 181 So. 341 (1937), to find that "the trial court was correct in granting a directed verdict" and correct to "conclude[ ] that 'the intent was that the contract was to last and it did last, as it turns out, much longer than a year.'" *Browning*, 128 So. 3d at 145-46. Specifically, the Fifth District discussed that Browning and Poirier intended the oral contract to last as long as they were in a romantic relationship, and "'the parties contemplated that the relationship would last more than one year. . . .'" *Id.* at 146 (quoting *Browning*, 113 So. 3d at 979).

Therefore, the Fifth District "affirm[ed] the judgment under review regarding the count for breach of the alleged oral contract, but reverse[d] that part of the judgment regarding the count for unjust enrichment and remand[ed] this case to the trial court for further proceedings." *Id.*

II. ANALYSIS

In this Court, Browning argues that his oral agreement with Poirier to equally share in the proceeds of any winning lottery tickets they purchased falls outside the statute of frauds. We agree.

Section 725.01, Florida Statutes, commonly referred to as the statute of frauds, provides the following:

> No action shall be brought . . . upon any agreement that is *not to be performed within the space of 1 year from the making thereof* . . . unless the agreement or promise upon which such action shall be brought, or some note or memorandum thereof shall be in writing and signed by the party to be charged therewith or by some other person by her or him thereunto lawfully authorized.

(Emphasis added.) The issue here focuses on interpreting the one year performance provision of the statute of frauds for oral agreements of indefinite duration, where no time is fixed by the parties for the performance of their agreement.

In 1937, with its decision in *Yates*, 181 So. 341, this Court interpreted the one year performance provision of the statute of frauds. Yates, the plaintiff, was the holder by assignment of second mortgage bonds secured by a trust deed, falling due approximately four years from the date of entering the agreement. The defendant contended that the agreement was within the statute of frauds. In its analysis, this Court in *Yates* set out the following general and qualifying rules for interpreting the statute of frauds:

> When, as in this case, no definite time was fixed by the parties for the performance of their agreement, and there is nothing in its terms to show that it could not be performed within a year according to its intent and the understanding of the parties, it should not be construed as being within the statute of frauds.
>
> The general rule so stated is subject to the qualifying rule that when no time is agreed on for the complete performance of the contract, if from the object to be accomplished by it and the surrounding circumstances, it clearly appears that the parties intended that it should extend for a longer period than a year, it is within the statute of frauds, though it cannot be said that there is any impossibility preventing its performance within a year.

Id. After setting out these rules, this Court in Yates reversed a directed verdict and held that the oral agreement at issue was not subject to the statute of frauds. This Court stated that "[w]hile the second mortgage bonds were not due for four years and the interest was payable semi-annually, they were by their terms susceptible of payment in full at any time upon notice given. . . ." *Id.* at 344. This Court reasoned as follows:

> In our view, the agreement sued on was clearly within the general rule as here stated. It contains no express provision that it should not be performed within a year, nor is there anything embraced within its terms that shows conclusively that it was intended to run for more than a year. Under its terms, it is susceptible of performance within a year, and the evidence shows that it was expected to have been performed within that time. When such is the case, even if actual performance runs beyond the year, it is not within the statute of frauds.

Id. at 344-45. Although the *Yates* decision was inartful in its discussion of a general and qualifying rule, the manner in which this Court applied the statute of frauds in *Yates* is in accord with the majority approach to interpreting a statute of frauds:

> It is well settled that the oral contracts made unenforceable by the statute because they are not to be performed within a year include only those which cannot be performed within that period. A promise which is not likely to be performed within a year, and which in fact is not performed within a year, is not within the statute if at the time the contract is made there is a possibility in law and in fact that full performance such as the parties intended may be completed before the expiration of a year.

9 *Williston on Contracts* § 24:3 (4th ed. 2011) (emphasis in original) (footnotes omitted). Stated otherwise, judging from the time the oral contract of indefinite duration is made, if the contract's full performance is possible within one year from the inception of the contract, then it falls outside the statute of frauds.

In this case, the oral agreement between Browning and Poirier is one of indefinite duration because, as the general rule in *Yates* states, "no definite time was fixed by the parties for the performance of their agreement." *Yates*, 181 So. at 344. Additionally, "at the time the contract [was] made there is a possibility in law and in fact that full performance" of the agreement between Browning and Poirier could have been "completed before the expiration of a year." 9 *Williston on Contracts* § 24:3. For example, if Browning or Poirier purchased a winning lottery ticket and they split the proceeds before the expiration of one year, the agreement would have been fully performed before the expiration of one year. Alternatively, either Browning or Poirier could have ended the agreement at any time. Accordingly, judging from the time the oral contract was made, nothing in the terms of their contract demonstrates that it could not be performed within one year.

III. CONCLUSION

Because the oral agreement between Browning and Poirier could have possibly been performed within one year, it falls outside the statute of frauds. Accordingly, we answer the rephrased question in the negative. We quash the Fifth District's decision and remand for further proceedings.

It is so ordered.

NOTES AND QUESTIONS

1. *What happened?* Who sued whom for what? Procedurally, how did the case get before this court? Factually, what happened between the parties? What arguments did the plaintiff and defendant make? What rule or rules did the court apply? How did the court analyze the dispute between the parties? How did the court decide the case?

2. *Was this case correctly decided?* Do you agree with the result reached in this case? Why or why not? Do you agree with the court's reasoning? Why or why not? How, if at all, would you have written the opinion differently?

3. *The one-year rule.* The court held that because the agreement could have *possibly* been performed within one year, it fell outside the statute of frauds. What do you think was really going on in this case? Would the court have ruled the same way if it were clear that a contract was not well evidenced?

2. Satisfying the Writing and Signature Requirements

Crabtree v. Elizabeth Arden Sales Corp.

New York Court of Appeals
110 N.E.2d 551 (1953)

FULD, JUDGE. In September of 1947, Nate Crabtree entered into preliminary negotiations with Elizabeth Arden Sales Corporation, manufacturers and sellers of cosmetics, looking toward his employment as sales manager. Interviewed on September 26th, by Robert P. Johns, executive vice-president and general manager of the corporation, who had apprised him of the possible opening, Crabtree requested a three-year contract at $25,000 a year. Explaining that he would be giving up a secure well-paying job to take a position in an entirely new field of endeavor—which he believed would take him some years to master—he insisted upon an agreement for a definite term. And he repeated his desire for a contract for three years to Miss Elizabeth Arden, the corporation's president. When Miss Arden finally indicated that she was prepared to offer a two-year contract, based on an annual salary of $20,000 for the first six months, $25,000 for the second six months and $30,000 for the second year, plus expenses of $5,000 a year for each of those years, Crabtree replied that that offer was "interesting." Miss Arden thereupon had her personal secretary make this memorandum on a telephone order blank that happened to be at hand:

EMPLOYMENT AGREEMENT WITH NATE CRABTREE
Date Sept. 26, 1947 6: PM
At 681 5th Ave

Begin 20000.
6 months 25000.
6 months 30000.

5000. per year Expense money (2 years to make good)

Arrangement with Mr. Crabtree
By Miss Arden

Present: Miss Arden, Mr. John, Mr. Crabtree, Miss O'Leary

A few days later, Crabtree phoned Mr. Johns and telegraphed Miss Arden; he accepted the "invitation to join the Arden organization," and Miss Arden wired back her "welcome." When he reported for work, a "pay-roll change" card was made up and initialed by Mr. Johns, and then forwarded to the payroll department. Reciting that it was prepared on September 30, 1947, and was to be effective as of October 22d, it specified the names of the parties, Crabtree's "Job Classification" and, in addition, contained the notation that

This employee is to be paid as follows:

First six months of employment: $20,000 per annum
Next six months of employment: $25,000 per annum
After one year of employment: $30,000 per annum

Approved by RPJ (initialed)

After six months of employment, Crabtree received the scheduled increase from $20,000 to $25,000, but the further specified increase at the end of the year was not paid. Both Mr. Johns and the comptroller of the corporation, Mr. Carstens, told Crabtree that they would attempt to straighten out the matter with Miss Arden, and, with that in mind, the comptroller prepared another "pay-roll change" card, to which his signature is appended, noting that there was to be a "Salary increase" from $25,000 to $30,000 a year, "per contractual arrangements with Miss Arden." The latter, however, refused to approve the increase and, after further fruitless discussion, plaintiff left defendant's employ and commenced this action for breach of contract.

At the ensuing trial, defendant denied the existence of any agreement to employ plaintiff for two years, and further contended that, even if one had been made, the statute of frauds barred its enforcement. The trial court found against defendant on both issues and awarded plaintiff damages of about $14,000, and the Appellate Division, two justices dissenting, affirmed. Since the contract relied upon was not to be performed within a year, the primary question for decision is whether there was a memorandum of its terms, subscribed by defendant, to satisfy the statute of frauds, *Personal Property Law* § 31.

Each of the two payroll cards—the one initialed by defendant's general manager, the other signed by its comptroller—unquestionably constitutes a memorandum under the statute. That they were not prepared or signed with the intention of evidencing the contract, or that they came into existence subsequent to its execution, is of no consequence; it is enough, to meet the statute's demands, that they were signed with intent to authenticate the information contained therein and that such information does evidence the terms of the contract. Those two writings contain all of the essential terms of the contract—the parties to it, the position that plaintiff was to assume, the salary that he was to receive—except that relating to the duration of plaintiff's employment. Accordingly, we must consider whether that item, the length of the contract, may be supplied by reference to the earlier unsigned office memorandum, and, if so, whether its notation, "2 years to make good," sufficiently designates a period of employment.

The statute of frauds does not require the "memorandum . . . to be in one document. It may be pieced together out of separate writings, connected with one another either expressly or by the internal evidence of subject-matter and occasion." *Marks v. Cowdin*, 123 N.E. 139, 141 (1919). Where each of the separate writings has been subscribed by the party to be charged, little if any difficulty is encountered. Where, however, some writings have been signed, and others have not—as in the case before us—there is basic disagreement as to what constitutes a sufficient connection permitting the unsigned papers to be considered as part of the statutory memorandum. The courts of some jurisdictions insist that there be a reference, of varying degrees of specificity, in the signed writing to that unsigned, and, if there is no such reference, they refuse to permit consideration of the latter in determining whether the memorandum satisfies the statute. That conclusion is based upon a construction of the statute which requires that the connection between the writings and defendant's acknowledgment of the one not subscribed, appear from examination of the papers alone, without the aid of parol evidence. The other position—which has gained increasing support over the years—is that a sufficient connection between the papers is established simply by a reference in them to the same subject matter or transaction. The statute is not pressed "to the extreme of a literal and rigid logic," *Marks v. Cowdin, supra*, 123 N.E. 139, 141, and oral testimony is admitted to show the connection between the documents and to establish the acquiescence, of the party to be charged, to the contents of the one unsigned.

The view last expressed impresses us as the more sound, and, indeed—although several of our cases appear to have gone the other way—this court has on a number of occasions approved the rule, and we now definitively adopt it, permitting the signed and unsigned writings to be read together, provided that they clearly refer to the same subject matter or transaction.

The language of the statute—"Every agreement . . . is void, unless . . . some note or memorandum thereof be in writing, and subscribed by the party to be charged," *Personal Property Law* § 31—does not impose the requirement that the signed acknowledgment of the contract must appear from the writings alone, unaided by oral testimony. The danger of fraud and perjury, generally attendant upon the admission of parol evidence, is at a minimum in a case such as this. None of the terms of the contract are supplied by parol. All of them must be set out in the various writings presented to the court, and at least one writing, the one establishing a contractual relationship between the parties, must bear the signature of the party to be charged, while the unsigned document must on its face refer to the same transaction as that set forth in the one that was signed. Parol evidence—to portray the circumstances surrounding the making of the memorandum—serves only to connect the separate documents and to show that there was assent, by the party to be charged, to the contents of the one unsigned. If that testimony does not convincingly connect the papers, or does not show assent to the unsigned paper, it is within the province of the judge to conclude, as a matter of law, that the statute has not been satisfied. True, the possibility still remains that, by fraud or perjury, an agreement never in fact made may occasionally be enforced under the subject matter or transaction test. It is better to run that risk, though, than to deny enforcement to all agreements, merely because the signed document made no specific mention of the unsigned writing. As the United States Supreme Court declared, in sanctioning the admission of parol evidence to establish the connection between the signed and unsigned writings.

> There may be cases in which it would be a violation of reason and common sense to ignore a reference which derives its significance from such (parol) proof. If there is ground for any doubt in the matter, the general rule should be enforced. But where there is no ground for doubt, its enforcement would aid, instead of discouraging, fraud.

Beckwith v. Talbot, 95 U.S. 289, 292 (1877).

Turning to the writings in the case before us—the unsigned office memo, the payroll change form initialed by the general manager Johns, and the paper signed by the comptroller Carstens—it is apparent, and most patently, that all three refer on their face to the same transaction. The parties, the position to be filled by plaintiff, the salary to be paid him, are all identically set forth; it is hardly possible that such detailed information could refer to another or a different agreement. Even more, the card signed by Carstens notes that it was prepared for the purpose of a "Salary increase per contractual arrangements with Miss Arden." That certainly constitutes a reference of sorts to a more comprehensive "arrangement," and parol is permissible to furnish the explanation.

The corroborative evidence of defendant's assent to the contents of the unsigned office memorandum is also convincing. Prepared by defendant's agent, Miss Arden's personal secretary, there is little likelihood that that paper was fraudulently manufactured or that defendant had not assented to its contents. Furthermore, the evidence as to the conduct of the parties at the time it was prepared persuasively demonstrates defendant's assent to its terms. Under such circumstances, the courts below were fully justified in finding that the three papers constituted the "memorandum" of their agreement within the meaning of the statute.

Nor can there be any doubt that the memorandum contains all of the essential terms of the contract. Only one term, the length of the employment, is in dispute. The September 26th office memorandum contains the notation, "2 years to make good." What purpose, other than to denote the length of the contract term, such a notation could have, is hard to imagine. Without it, the employment would be at will, and its inclusion may not be treated as meaningless or purposeless. Quite obviously, as the courts below decided, the phrase signifies that the parties agreed to a term, a certain and definite term, of two years, after which, if plaintiff did not "make good," he would be subject to discharge. And examination of other parts of the memorandum supports that construction. Throughout the writings, a scale of wages, increasing plaintiff's salary periodically, is set out; that type of arrangement is hardly consistent with the hypothesis that the employment was meant to be at will. The most that may be argued from defendant's standpoint is that "2 years to make good," is a cryptic and ambiguous statement. But, in such a case, parol evidence is admissible to explain its meaning. Having in mind the relations of the parties, the course of the negotiations and plaintiff's insistence upon security of employment, the purpose of the phrase—or so the trier of the facts was warranted in finding—was to grant plaintiff the tenure he desired.

The judgment should be affirmed, with costs.

RELEVANT PROVISIONS

For the *Restatement (Second) of Contracts,* consult §§ 131, 133, 134, and 136. For the UCC, consult § 2-201.

NOTES AND QUESTIONS

1. *What happened?* Who sued whom for what? Procedurally, how did the case get before this court? Factually, what happened between the parties? What arguments did the plaintiff and defendant make? What rule or rules did the court apply? How did the court analyze the dispute between the parties? How did the court decide the case?

2. *Was this case correctly decided?* Do you agree with the result reached in this case? Why or why not? Do you agree with the court's reasoning? Why or why not? How, if at all, would you have written the opinion differently?

3. *Legal formalities and the statute of frauds.* Can you see how the statute of frauds, in general, and the writing requirement, in particular, help satisfy all three functions of legal formalities discussed in the excerpt "The Role of Legal Formalities" in Part III.4.A.1?

4. *The writing requirement.* After consulting the *Restatement (Second)* provisions above, do you think the writing requirement was satisfied here? Why or why not?

5. *Illustrations.* The *Restatement (Second) of Contracts* § 133 provides the following illustrations:

> 1. A and B enter into an oral contract for the sale of Blackacre. A writes and signs a letter to his friend C containing an accurate statement of the contract. The letter is a sufficient memorandum to charge A even though it is never mailed.
>
> 2. A writes to B the following letter: "Dear B: I will employ you as superintendent of my mill for a term of three years from date, at a salary of $28,000 a year. Let me know if you wish to accept this offer. [Signed] A." B accepts the offer orally. The letter is a sufficient memorandum to charge A.
>
> 3. A writes and signs a letter to his agent C authorizing C to make the offer stated in Illustration 2. C orally makes the offer, and B orally accepts it. A's letter is not a sufficient memorandum to charge him.
>
> 4. A and B enter into an oral contract by which A promises to sell and B promises to buy Blackacre for $5,000. A writes and signs a letter to B in which he states accurately the terms of the bargain, but adds "our agreement was oral. It, therefore, is not binding upon me, and I shall not carry it out." The letter is a sufficient memorandum to charge A.

Leonard v. Pepsico

United States District Court, Southern District of New York
88 F. Supp. 2d 116 (1999)

For a report of the case and accompanying materials, see p. 217, *supra*.

D. THE ALLEGED CONTRACT DOES NOT SATISFY THE STATUTE OF FRAUDS

The absence of any writing setting forth the alleged contract in this case provides an entirely separate reason for granting summary judgment. Under the New York Statute of Frauds,

> a contract for the sale of goods for the price of $500 or more is not enforceable by way of action or defense unless there is some writing sufficient to indicate that a contract for sale has been made between the parties and signed by the party against whom enforcement is sought or by his authorized agent or broker.

N.Y.U.C.C. § 2-201(1). Without such a writing, plaintiff's claim must fail as a matter of law.

There is simply no writing between the parties that evidences any transaction. Plaintiff argues that the commercial, plaintiff's completed Order Form, and perhaps other agreements signed by defendant which plaintiff has not yet seen, should suffice for Statute of Frauds purposes, either singly or taken together. For the latter claim, plaintiff relies on *Crabtree v. Elizabeth Arden Sales Corp.*, 110 N.E.2d 551 (N.Y. 1953). *Crabtree* held that a combination of signed and unsigned writings would satisfy the Statute of Frauds, "provided that they clearly refer to the same subject matter or transaction." *Id.* at 55. Yet the Second Circuit emphasized in *Horn & Hardart Co. v. Pillsbury Co.*, 888 F.2d 8 (2d Cir. 1989), that this rule "contains two strict threshold requirements." *Id.* at 11. First, the signed writing relied upon must by itself establish "'a contractual relationship between the parties.'" *Id.* (quoting *Crabtree*). The second threshold requirement is that the unsigned writing must "'on its face refer to the same transaction as that set forth in the one that was signed.'" *Horn & Hardart*, 888 F.2d at 11 (quoting *Crabtree*).

None of the material relied upon by plaintiff meets either threshold requirement. The commercial is not a writing; plaintiff's completed order form does not bear the signature of defendant, or an agent thereof; and to the extent that plaintiff seeks discovery of any contracts between defendant and its advertisers, such discovery would be unavailing: plaintiff is not a party to, or a beneficiary of, any such contracts. Because the alleged contract does not meet the requirements of the Statute of Frauds, plaintiff has no claim for breach of contract or specific performance. . . .

RELEVANT PROVISIONS

For the UCC, consult §§ 1-201(37) and (43) and 2-201.

NOTES AND QUESTIONS

1. *What happened?* Who sued whom for what? Procedurally, how did the case get before this court? Factually, what happened between the parties? What arguments did the plaintiff and defendant make? What rule or rules did the court apply? How did the court analyze the dispute between the parties? How did the court decide the case?

2. *Was this case correctly decided?* Do you agree with the result reached in this case? Why or why not? Do you agree with the court's reasoning? Why or why not? How, if at all, would you have written the opinion differently?

3. *Writing requirement.* Do you agree with the court that the writing requirement was not satisfied here? Or do you think the preposterousness of the plaintiff's allegation might have motivated the court's analysis here?

4. *UCC.* How, if at all, does the writing requirement under the UCC differ from the writing requirement under the *Restatement (Second)*?

Rosenfeld v. Basquiat

United States Court of Appeals, Second Circuit
78 F.3d 84 (1996)

CARDAMONE, CIRCUIT JUDGE. Artist Jean-Michel Basquiat's short-lived career left a lasting impression on the art world. A so-called neo-expressionist, he was remarkable in his precocious talent, his prolificacy, and his eccentricity. His rapid rise to fame and premature death at age 27 left a number of mysteries. One of them, which is the subject of this appeal, is whether Basquiat contracted to sell three of his paintings to Michelle Rosenfeld, an art dealer and plaintiff in the instant action. These artworks that Rosenfeld alleges she contracted to buy were entitled "Separation of the 'K'" (a diptych), "Atlas," and "Untitled Head." Their whereabouts—if indeed they still actually exist—are unknown. On November 20, 1989 Rosenfeld sued Gerard Basquiat, as administrator of the estate of his son Jean-Michel, for damages or specific performance of the contract.

BACKGROUND

[During the trial, Rosenfeld] stated she went to Basquiat's apartment on October 25, 1982, and while she was there he agreed to sell her three paintings for $4,000 each, and that she picked out the three works identified in her complaint. She testified further that Basquiat asked for a cash deposit of ten percent; she left his loft and later returned with $1,000 in cash, which she paid him. When she asked for a receipt, he insisted on drawing up a "contract," and got down on the floor and wrote it out in crayon on a large piece of paper, remarking that "some day this contract will be worth money." She identified a handwritten document listing the three paintings, bearing her signature and that of Basquiat, which stated: "$12,000—$1000 DEPOSIT—OCT 25 82." Rosenfeld also testified that she later returned to Basquiat's loft to discuss delivery, but Basquiat convinced her to wait for at least two years so that he could show the paintings at exhibitions.

Plaintiff's evidence presented at this first trial included the testimony of Rosenfeld's driver, Ron Belfrom, who corroborated plaintiff's story by stating he had been present and participated in the October 25, 1982 meeting between Rosenfeld and Basquiat. A forensic document examiner, Paul Osborn, opined that the handwritten "contract" was in Basquiat's hand. Although plaintiff maintained that at one time she had photographs of the paintings, she was unable to produce them at trial, and introduced reconstructions of the works instead. To rebut plaintiff's evidence, defendant relied primarily on cross-examination and attempted to show that the alleged contract was a fraud.

When the jury reported it was deadlocked, a mistrial was declared. The case was then reassigned to Judge Baer for a new trial. . . .

The evidence offered at the second trial was substantially the same as that offered at the first trial, except that the estate called its own handwriting expert and an art gallery manager who had been responsible for keeping an inventory of Basquiat's works for the estate. When Rosenfeld was called, however, her counsel carefully avoided asking about anything that occurred between her and the artist. She testified she went to Basquiat's loft in October 1982 and "picked out" the three paintings. She also indicated she returned to the loft ten days later, but did not pick up the paintings. After Rosenfeld was excused, the trial court allowed portions of her former testimony to be read to the jury. The portions read into evidence dealt primarily with the personal transactions allegedly occurring between Rosenfeld and Basquiat on October 25, 1982 and those occurring ten days later when she returned to his loft. Counsel for the estate did not object when plaintiff's counsel asked to have the testimony read into evidence.

The jury in the second trial reached a verdict in favor of Rosenfeld, returning answers to special interrogatories as follows: Basquiat entered into a written agreement in October 1982 to sell the three paintings to Rosenfeld for $12,000; although there was no initial agreement establishing a delivery date, they made a separate oral agreement approximately ten days later setting the delivery date; a reasonable delivery date was October 1987; Rosenfeld first learned of the breach in August 1988, when Jean-Michel Basquiat died; and the market price of the three works at that time was $395,000.

Following defendant's post-trial motion for judgment as a matter of law, the district court ruled that the contract did not violate the Statute of Frauds and that there was sufficient proof of damages to support the verdict. It subsequently entered a judgment in favor of Rosenfeld in the amount of $384,000, representing the current market value of the artworks, discounted by the outstanding portion of the purchase price. In addition, interest in the amount of $217,301.92 was awarded to plaintiff in the judgment.

On appeal, the estate argues it was error for the trial court to admit Rosenfeld's testimony into evidence and that the alleged contract between plaintiff and Basquiat violated the Statute of Frauds. We conclude that what has already been once repeated must now be repeated again. Accordingly, we reverse and remand for a new trial.

DISCUSSION

II The Statute of Frauds

We pass now to the estate's point respecting the Statute of Frauds. The estate avers it is entitled to judgment as a matter of law because the Statute of Frauds makes the alleged agreement between plaintiff and the artist unenforceable. It states that a written contract for the sale of goods must include the date of delivery if the parties have indeed agreed on a specific date, although a reasonable delivery time will be inferred in the absence of an express provision. Because the jury found that there was an oral agreement regarding a particular delivery date, the argument continues, the document bearing the signatures of Rosenfeld and Basquiat is legally insufficient. In addition, defendant maintains the oral agreement regarding the delivery date was invalid because it could not be performed within a year. None of these contentions has merit.

Because this case involves an alleged contract for the sale of three paintings, any question regarding the Statute of Frauds is governed by the U.C.C. *See* N.Y. U.C.C. § 2-102 (applicability to "transactions in goods") (McKinney 1988); § 2-201 (contract for $500 or more is unenforceable "unless there is some writing sufficient to indicate that a contract for sale has been made between the parties and signed by the party [charged]"). Under the U.C.C., the only term that *must* appear in the writing is the quantity. *See* N.Y. U.C.C. § 2-201 cmt. 1. Beyond that, "[a]ll that is required is that the writing afford a basis for believing that the offered oral evidence rests on a real transaction." *Id.* The writing supplied by the plaintiff indicated the price, the date, the specific paintings involved, and that Rosenfeld paid a deposit. It also bore the signatures of the buyer and seller. Therefore, the writing satisfied the requirements of § 2-201.

Citing *Berman Stores Co. v. Hirsh*, 240 N.Y. 209 (1925), the estate claims that a specific delivery date, if agreed upon, must be in the writing. *Berman Stores* was decided before the enactment of the U.C.C. and was based on the principle that "the note or memorandum . . . should completely evidence the contract which the parties made." 240 N.Y. at 214. The rule that a specific delivery date is "an essential part of the contract and must be embodied in the memorandum," *Berman Stores*, 240 N.Y. at 215, was rejected by the legislature—at least for sale-of-goods cases—when it enacted the U.C.C. That rule and the statute upon which it was based were repealed to make way for the U.C.C. The U.C.C. "[c]ompletely re-phrased" the provisions of prior legislation and "intended to make it clear that . . . [t]he required writing need not contain all the material terms." N.Y. U.C.C. § 2-201 cmt. 1.

The estate also urges that the alleged agreement is unenforceable because it could not be performed within a year. It relies on § 5-701(a)(1) of the New York

General Obligations Law, which requires a signed writing for an agreement "not to be performed within one year from the making thereof." But a contract for the sale of goods is not subject to the one-year rule because a "writing covering the sale of goods which is sufficient . . . under U.C.C. 2-201 is valid despite its insufficiency under General Obligation Law § 5-701." *AP Propane, Inc. v. Sperbeck,* 157 A.D.2d 27, 29-30 (1990). Hence, the provisions of § 5-701 do not control here.

To support the relevance of statutes other than the U.C.C., the estate relies extensively on cases applying pre-U.C.C. law. All are inapposite.

Because the writing, allegedly scrawled in crayon by Jean-Michel Basquiat on a large piece of paper, easily satisfied the requirements of § 2-201 of the U.C.C., the estate is not entitled to judgment as a matter of law. It is of no real significance that the jury found Rosenfeld and Basquiat settled on a particular time for delivery and did not commit it to writing; nor is it of any moment that performance may not have been possible within one year of when the agreement was made. As a consequence, though this case must be retried, the alleged contract is not invalid on Statute of Frauds grounds.

CONCLUSION

The arguments advanced by the estate relating to discretionary evidentiary rulings by the trial judge need not be addressed. Nor do we find any merit in its contention that the evidence of the paintings' market value was insufficient. For the reasons stated, the judgment is reversed and the case remanded for a new trial not inconsistent with this opinion.

NOTES AND QUESTIONS

1. *What happened?* Who sued whom for what? Procedurally, how did the case get before this court? Factually, what happened between the parties? What arguments did the plaintiff and defendant make? What rule or rules did the court apply? How did the court analyze the dispute between the parties? How did the court decide the case?

2. *Was this case correctly decided?* Do you agree with the result reached in this case? Why or why not? Do you agree with the court's reasoning? Why or why not? How, if at all, would you have written the opinion differently?

3. *The writing requirement.* Should an artistic scribbling in crayon satisfy the writing requirement? Why or why not? Does the context in which the crayon was used cast doubt on whether the promisor truly intended to make a promise? For an even stranger case (though one, alas, not supported by consideration), keep reading.

A CONTRACT WRITTEN IN BLOOD*

A bloody dispute is underway in Orange County Superior Court.

It centers on a promise—written in blood—by a Korean businessman to pay back $170,000 to an investor.

"Please forgive me. Because of my deeds, you have suffered financially," Stephen Son wrote in Korean. "I will pay you back to the best of my ability."

Jinsoo Kim filed suit in January alleging that he never received the money promised him for investing in a children's clothing company.

This month, Judge Corey S. Cramin ruled that the case could go forward.

Although a blood contract carries no additional legal weight, Kim's attorney, Richard J. Radcliffe, is trying to use the once-crimson ink to boost his client's case.

The defendant took the effort "to solemnify his promise in blood, which seems to be communicating an intent more serious than one expressed in pen," Radcliffe said in an interview. "So it's ironic that he is not abiding by his commitment."

Son's attorney, Vladimir Khiterer, said the promise didn't mention a repayment deadline. He added that the contract was drawn in a bar when the two men were drunk, and Kim demanded the promise in blood.

Radcliffe said the scene in the bar never occurred.

Both lawyers in the case say the blood promise stems from Korean culture.

"I don't think so," said Kyeyoung Park, a UCLA anthropology professor, with a laugh. "Even in the past, a blood contract was pretty rare" in Korea.

Though blood oaths have been taken by mobsters, teen lovers and others, examples are elusive.

That's "a new one for me," said Michael Asimow, UCLA law professor who specializes in contracts. "I've never heard of a promise made in blood."

PERCEPTION AS REALITY: PROMISSORY ESTOPPEL AND THE STATUTE OF FRAUDS†

In some instances, even where all of the elements of promissory estoppel have been satisfied, judges have nevertheless refused to enforce promissory estoppel claims on the grounds that doing so would circumvent some other contract-related defense. For example, the Statute of Frauds requires that certain agreements, such as contracts for the sale of land,[128] service contracts that take longer than one year

* Excerpted from Jennifer Delson, *Landing in an O.C. Court, This IOU Was Red All Over*, Los Angeles Times, May 31, 2006.

† Excerpted from Marco Jimenez, *The Many Faces of Promissory Estoppel: An Empirical Analysis Under the Restatement (Second) of Contracts*, 57 UCLA L. Rev. 669, 704-06 (2010) (internal citations omitted).

128. *Restatement (Second) of Contracts* § 110(1)(d) (1981).

to perform,[129] and contracts for the sale of goods over $500,[130] be put in writing. Notably, even though the drafters of the Restatement (Second) adopted § 139 to specifically deal with this issue by allowing the enforcement of non-written promises under a theory of promissory estoppel, where the non-enforcement would otherwise lead to an "injustice,"[131] the courts themselves are split on this important issue.

Why is this significant? Back in 1974, Professor Gilmore noted that some of the then-recent cases were "beginning to suggest that liability under § 90 . . . is somehow different from liability in contract," and pointed out that certain contract-based defenses, such as the Statute of Frauds and the parol evidence rule, would not be available in promissory estoppel actions if the promissory estoppel action itself was not thought to be "contractual." In other words, Gilmore was suggesting that, so long as judges were conceptualizing promissory estoppel claims as essentially contractual causes of action, it was natural to suppose that traditional, contract-based defenses (such as the Statute of Frauds and the parol evidence rule) would continue to apply (as would traditional contract-based remedies, such as expectation damages). However, once judges began conceptualizing promissory estoppel actions as non-contractual causes of action, then the entire normative basis upon which promissory estoppel rested would shift, so that traditional contract-based defenses, along with traditional contract-based remedies, would no longer be available. Here, as in other areas, Professor Gilmore's prophesying proved to be extraordinarily prescient.

[In an empirical analysis of 383 promissory estoppel cases decided between 1981 and 2007], [t]he data reveal that in twenty-six (or 17 percent) of the cases, relief was denied to a promissory estoppel claimant where he or she was unable to show that the promise being relied upon complied with the strictures of the Statute of Frauds (the relied-upon promise was not in writing). This result only makes sense if promissory estoppel is conceptualized as a "contractual" cause of action, but would defy logic if it is viewed as a distinct, non-contractual theory of recovery.

Notably, in about 8 percent of the cases, the Statute of Frauds was raised as a defense to the enforcement of a promissory estoppel claim, but the defense was found inapplicable, and the action was nevertheless allowed to proceed, in large part because the judge deciding the dispute did not conceptualize the promissory estoppel cause of action as a contractual action. This, of course, indicates that there is something much deeper going on in these cases and that the promissory estoppel action is, in many instances, succeeding (or failing) not because the litigants are able (or unable) to satisfy the black-letter prongs of the promissory estoppel test, but because the judge is conceptualizing promissory estoppel in a way that favors (or disfavors) the parties to the litigation before the judge has ever had a chance to hear the litigant's promissory estoppel claim! In short, the

129. *Id.* § 110(1)(e).

130. *Id.* § 110(2)(a); *see also* U.C.C. § 2-201 (2007).

131. *Restatement (Second) of Contracts* § 139(1) (1981) ("A promise which the promisor should reasonably expect to induce action or forbearance on the part of the promisee or a third person and which does induce the action or forbearance is enforceable notwithstanding the Statute of Frauds if injustice can be avoided only be enforcement of the promise. The remedy granted for breach is to be limited as justice requires.").

seemingly academic questions "what, really, is a contract" and "why should we enforce them" turn out to be of much more practical importance than may have been previously supposed.[136]

This finding not only illustrates the extraordinary role that is (or should be) played by contract theory in what might otherwise be thought of as a traditional, run-of-the-mill case, but highlights the importance of judges coming to grips with this reality in their decisions and acknowledging that their answers to seemingly theoretical questions like "what is a contract" play a significant role in their decisions.

This finding is also relevant because, if this trend continues, courts may be slowly creating a new strain of "super contracts" capable of obtaining for the promisee a more extensive, contract-like remedy for an essentially easier-to-prove promissory estoppel action. In addition to the damage that such an action may inflict on a promisor, in those instances in which a court conceptualizes the promissory estoppel action as non-contractual, the promisor will be without the protection of traditional, contract-based defenses, thus making his or her immunity to this super contract all the more alarming.

INTERNATIONAL PERSPECTIVE: THE STATUTE OF FRAUDS AND THE CISG*

Ignorance of the CISG can be costly. Take as an example the case of *GPL Treatment, Ltd. v. Louisiana-Pacific Corp?* GPL and its two co-plaintiffs were Canadian companies engaged in the manufacture and sale of wood shakes and shingles. Plaintiffs alleged that the defendant Louisiana-Pacific, a U.S. company, had agreed orally to

---

136. This point was beautifully captured by Professors Blum and Bushaw, who noted that some legal scholars:

> argue that [promissory estoppel] is (or should be) a substitute for consideration—that is, an alternative means of determining if a promise is worthy of enforcement as a contract. Others argue that it is (or should be) an independent theory of recovery more akin to tort law or general equitable principles than to contract law. This debate is long-standing, and continues to the current day. This is not simply an academic exercise, fascinating to scholars alone; it potentially has profound real-world implications. If the elements of promissory estoppel merely substitute for consideration, once they are present a contract should be present. This means that all of the trappings that go along with a contract should be present as well. So if particular procedures apply to contract actions but not to others, they should apply to promissory estoppel actions. If certain defenses are available in contract actions but not in others, they should be available in promissory estoppel actions. Or if certain remedies lie in contract actions but not in others, they should lie in promissory estoppel actions. If, on the other hand, promissory estoppel is a separate theory of recovery related to but independent from contract, the trappings of contract law do not necessarily carry over and rules from other areas of law might apply.

BRIAN A. BLUM & AMY C. BUSHAW, CONTRACTS: CASES, DISCUSSION, AND PROBLEMS 323-24 (2d ed. 2008).

* Excerpted from William S. Dodge, *Teaching the CISG in Contracts*, 50 J. LEGAL EDUC. 72, 74-75 (2000).

buy eighty-eight truckloads of cedar shakes. But Louisiana-Pacific accepted only thirteen truckloads and denied making an agreement for any more. When the plaintiffs sued for their lost profits on the remaining seventy-five truckloads, Louisiana-Pacific raised the UCC statute of frauds as a defense.[8] The plaintiffs in tum argued that the merchant's exception to the UCC statute of frauds applied because they had sent a written confirmation of the agreement for eighty-eight truckloads of cedar shakes to which Louisiana-Pacific had not objected.[9] Louisiana-Pacific responded that, although the plaintiffs' form was captioned "Order Confirmation," it was not actually a confirmation because it required the buyer to sign and return it.

Determining when a writing is "in confirmation" of a contract has troubled the courts, and the Oregon courts in *GPL Treatment* were no exception. The Oregon Court of Appeals affirmed the trial court's ruling that, as a matter of law, plaintiffs' Order Confirmation was a writing in confirmation despite the sign-and-return clause. This ruling was affirmed by the Oregon Supreme Court, but both the Supreme Court and the Court of Appeals were closely divided. Although ultimately the plaintiffs won their case, doing so required them to prevail on a dose question and to win two appeals.

There was an easier way. Because the plaintiffs had their places of business in Canada and the defendant had its in the United States, and because both Canada and the United States have ratified the CISG, the CISG rather than the UCC was applicable to this sale-of-goods transaction. CISG Article 11 states: "A contract of sale need not be concluded in or evidenced by writing and is not subject to any other requirement as to form. It may be proved by any means, including witnesses." In other words, the CISG does not have a statute of frauds and would have allowed the plaintiffs to submit their evidence of an oral contract for the sale of cedar shakes to the jury without the need to produce a writing of any sort. Apparently the plaintiffs raised the argument that the CISG rather than the UCC applied, but they raised it so late that the trial judge ruled the argument had been waived. It is likely that the delay in raising the applicability of the CISG was attributable to the unfamiliarity of plaintiffs' counsel with the CISG. The result was that the plaintiffs gave up an argument that was a sure winner and were forced to rely instead on the merchant's exception to the UCC statute of frauds, which presented a much closer question leading to two appeals and presumably costing the plaintiffs a good deal more in attorney's fees.

NOTES AND QUESTIONS

1. *Opting out.* A country may, by filing an Article 96 declaration, opt out of Article 11. If a country files such a declaration, then its domestic law, rather

8. Uniform Commercial Code § 2-201 [hereinafter UCC].

9. The "merchant's exception" provides: "Between merchants, if within a reasonable time a writing in confirmation of the contract and sufficient against the sender is received and the party receiving it has reason to know its contents, it satisfies the requirements of subsection (1) of this section against such party unless written notice of objection to its contents Is given within 10 days after it is received." *Id.* § 2-201(2).

than the CISG, would govern whether contracts must be committed to writing (and in what form) to be enforceable. Currently, only Argentina, Armenia, Belarus, Chile, Estonia, Hungary, Lithuania, the Russian Federation, and Ukraine have filed such a declaration.* This means that when a party in the United States contracts with a party in another CISG country, their contract will be governed by CISG Article 11 *unless* the foreign party is from of one of the countries that has filed an Article 96 declaration.

2. ***Should we keep the statute of frauds?*** The *Restatement (Second) of Contracts* and the UCC retain a statute of frauds, but the CISG and many other countries around the world have rejected such a rule. Even England, which gave us the original Statute of Frauds in 1677, has largely repealed most of its provisions. So, should we retain it? Why or why not? What are the pros and cons of having, and not having, such a rule? Again, you may find it helpful to consult some of the thinking tools developed earlier.

G. CHAPTER CAPSTONE: PUTTING IT ALL TOGETHER

We end this chapter with an interesting case that brings together many of the issues and themes we've explored in this chapter. Although the case does not explore *every* defense covered in this chapter, some of the defenses from this chapter that make an appearance include unconscionability, fraud, undue influence, and mistake, and from previous chapters we get a discussion of gift promises, the adequacy or fairness of consideration, and principles of equity. All in all, it's a really neat case with which to conclude this chapter. So, to repeat what has been written regarding previous capstone cases, no notes or questions will be included at the end: just read and enjoy. Also, as you read, put your book down every now and again and try to figure out how you would resolve the issue before the court. Then, pick your book back up and check your answer against the court's opinion.

Ryan v. Weiner

Court of Chancery of Delaware
610 A.2d 1377 (1992)

ALLEN, CHANCELLOR. In this action Robert Ryan seeks, *inter alia,* an order canceling a deed to his house that he gave to Norman Weiner in May 1984. Ryan asserts that in making that transfer he was deceived by Weiner and only recently came to understand that the deed in question was not simply a

3. Well, sort of. China (PRC) also filed an Article 96 declaration, but did not couch it in the language required by Article 96.

security interest. Mr. Weiner denies all aspects of the complaint. The case has been through a brief trial.

While I do not reach the question whether Weiner in fact deceived Ryan by making false statements to him upon which Ryan relied, I do conclude that the transfer in question represents a shocking and oppressive transaction; that Mr. Weiner took the grossest advantage of Mr. Ryan, who found himself in weakened and distressed circumstances, and that Weiner manipulated their dealings to accomplish that result. In short, for the reasons set forth below, I conclude, that this represents that unusual case in which a court of equity cannot let stand an executed contract but is obligated to grant the remedy of rescission.

I.

Mr. Ryan is a 69-year-old man with a ninth grade education. He retired about ten years ago from his work as a laborer and subsists on a small pension and social security benefits. In 1971, Ryan and his now deceased wife purchased a modest house located at 928 Pine Street in Wilmington, Delaware to live in. The price was $8,600. Most of that was borrowed and repayment was secured by a first mortgage.

After about 12 years of mortgage payments, Mr. Ryan (who had become a widower in the interim) fell badly behind in his mortgage payments. The monthly payment was $98 per month at that time. By April 1984, he owed in excess of $1,000 in arrearages.

It is agreed that Ryan's house had a fair market value at that time of $19,800. The balance of the loan secured by the mortgage was less than $8,000. In March 1984, the mortgage lender instituted foreclosure proceedings. Mr. Ryan did not answer the complaint and, on April 16, 1984, a default judgment in the amount of $7,843.26 was entered. A sheriff's sale was scheduled for June 12, 1984.

Ryan testified that throughout this period he was an active alcoholic.

Defendant, Norman Weiner, was (and is) a licensed real estate broker who engages in the business, *inter alia,* of buying and leasing inner-city houses. On Sunday, May 13, 1984, Weiner arrived at Ryan's home unannounced and informed Ryan that he could help him keep his house. The parties had not met prior to that. They disagree about what was said at that meeting. Ryan reports that he understood that Weiner offered to lend him the money to make up the back payments and to take a deed to secure repayment. Weiner reports that he offered to buy the house and to let Ryan continue to live in it as a tenant. They agree, however, that Weiner did not offer to make a cash payment to Ryan.

Weiner showed Ryan no papers but told him he would pick him up the following morning to complete the transaction. When Weiner left that afternoon, he took Ryan's original deed to the property which he said he would hold in his safe deposit box.

At 8:00 a.m. the following day, Weiner picked Ryan up at his house and drove him to the office of Harold Green, a Delaware lawyer, who represented

Weiner in real estate transactions and is also a close personal friend and relative. At Green's office, Ryan was asked to sign several documents which Weiner explained were necessary. Green did not explain any of the documents to Ryan, nor did he speak to him during their ten-minute meeting. Neither Weiner nor Green advised Ryan of his right to seek independent legal advice concerning the transaction. At trial, Green testified that he had no specific recollection of his meeting with Ryan and was unable to confirm any of the alleged conversations or events that took place between the parties. Ryan says that he signed the documents without reading them because he trusted the defendant's statements that the papers were loan documents.

In fact, Ryan did not sign loan documents on May 14, 1984, but signed a deed transferring the Pine Street property to Weiner. According to Ryan, he did not see the front page of the deed containing the property description when he signed the back of the deed and neither Weiner nor Green told him that he was signing a deed. He also claims that he did not understand a one-sentence document that he signed in Green's office, assigning all money held in escrow to Weiner. Ryan also signed a document which he later learned was a settlement sheet. He testified that when he signed the document on May 14, 1984, it contained no figures and only had about two inches of writing on it. The document now bears the date May 15, 1984 and contains many figures. Ryan was not given any copies of documents that he had signed.

Before Weiner had gone to Ryan's house, Mr. Green had requested and received from the mortgagee two documents: a "Sale Subject to Mortgage" document (now dated May 14, 1984) and an "Insurance Information and Assignment of Escrow." The assignment form required Ryan's signature and required that Seller's address be set forth. But, Weiner, not Ryan, signed the Assignment of Escrow form, completing the section which requested the seller's forwarding address with Weiner's own P.O. box number. The forms were then sent back to the mortgage company as an enclosure with a letter from Green of May 15, 1984. Ryan never saw the Sale Subject to Mortgage Statement or Insurance Information and Assignment of Escrow form.

The May 14, 1984 deed signed by Ryan recites that $7,000 in consideration was paid to him. He did not, however, receive any cash, nor did Mr. Weiner ever pay off the balance of the outstanding mortgage on the property or satisfy the default judgment entered against Ryan. Weiner did thereafter pay the mortgage company $1,898.30 in order to bring the loan current. But Weiner did not sign any documents assuming the legal obligations of the mortgage.

The result of the transaction was that Ryan transferred ownership of his property to Weiner without receiving any part of the financial value of the then equity in the property of approximately $12,000. Ryan has remained personally liable for paying off the mortgage balance under the mortgage bond and note.

Following the May 13 and 14 meetings with Weiner, Ryan continued to live in the house. A lease was executed with an effective date of May 14, 1984. Weiner steadily increased Ryan's monthly payments over intervening seven years from $100 a month to $310 per month. During the same period the mortgage payment also increased, but only from $93 in 1984 to $120 in 1991. . . .

Over the years, while Ryan paid him a total of $21,480, Mr. Weiner expended $12,149.27 on the mortgage, insurance, taxes, sewer and water charges, including the amount paid to bring the mortgage up to date in 1984.

The two parties had a significant amount of contact—Weiner transported Ryan to and from his bank on the third day of each month so that Ryan could cash his Social Security check in order to make monthly payments, and Weiner hired Ryan to do odd jobs at Weiner's residence. The issue of ownership of the property arose only on two occasions. On both occasions, Ryan asked for his deed to the property in order to apply for a loan, and on each occasion, he was put-off by Weiner but, he says, nevertheless left with the impression that he was still the rightful owner of the property.

Before his May, 1991 payment was due, Ryan concluded that he had paid Weiner a total amount in excess of the amount of the mortgage on the property and the amount of Weiner's "loan." He refused to make any more monthly payments to Weiner in May, 1991. Weiner promptly commenced a summary action in the justice of peace court to evict Ryan. On Ryan's motion, this court stayed that proceeding, concluding that issues of the quality of Weiner's title itself and Ryan's alleged right to have Weiner's deed canceled were remedies not available in the justice of peace court.

II.

The right of competent persons to make contracts and thus privately to acquire rights and obligations is a basic part of our general liberty. This ability to enter and enforce contracts is universally thought not only to reflect and promote liberty, but as well to promote the production of wealth. Thus, the right to make and enforce contracts is elemental in our legal order. But not every writing purporting to contain a promise or every document purporting to make a transfer will be given legal effect. A large body of law defines when valid contracts are formed and when and how they can be enforced.

Contracts or transfers induced by fraudulent misrepresentations, for example, can be avoided. Similarly, a lack of legal capacity or the existence of duress can lead a court to declare a promise unenforceable or a transfer voidable. *See, e.g.*, A. Farnsworth, *Contracts* §§ 4.1-4.20 (1982). Ordinarily, an evaluation of relative values of the bargain to the parties will not provide a basis for such judicial action.

It is general rule, recited by courts for well over a century, that the adequacy or fairness of the consideration that adduces a promise or a transfer is not alone grounds for a court to refuse to enforce a promise or to give effect to a transfer. This rule, present in 17th and 18th century cases, achieved its greatest dignity in the jurisprudence of 19th century classical liberalism. Thus, the classical liberal's premise concerning the subjectivity (and thus non-reviewability) of value has plainly been a dominant view in our contract law for a very long time. Countless cases from the 19th and 20th centuries could be cited for the proposition that "mere inadequacy of price" will not invalidate a contract or a transfer. But as standard as that generalization is, it has not precluded courts, on occasion, from striking down contracts or transfers in which inadequacy of price is coupled with some circumstance that amounts to inequitable or oppressive conduct. That is, the "rule" that courts will not weigh consideration or assess the wisdom of bargains, has not fully excluded the opposite proposition, that at some point courts will do so even in the absence of actual fraud, duress or incapacity.

The notion that a court can and will review contracts for fairness is apt for good reason to strike us as dangerous, subjecting negotiated bargains to the loosely constrained review of the judicial process. Perhaps for this reason, courts have evoked this doctrine with extreme reluctance and then only when all of the facts suggest a level of unfairness that is unconscionable.

The applicable principle is ancient. It was old when Justice Story summarized it in 1835:

> Of a kindred nature, to the cases already considered, are cases of bargains of such an unconscionable nature, and of such gross inequality, as naturally lead to the presumption of fraud, imposition, or undue influence. This is the sort of fraud, to which Lord Hardwicke alluded in the passage already cited, when he said, that they were such bargains, as no man in his senses and not under delusion would make on the one hand, and as no honest and fair man would accept on the other, being inequitable and unconscientious bargains. Mere inadequacy of price, or any other inequality in the bargain, is not, however, to be understood as constituting *per se* a ground to avoid a bargain in Equity. . . .
>
> Inadequacy of consideration is not then, of itself, a distinct principle of relief in Equity. The Common Law knows no such principle. The consideration more or less supports the contract. Common sense knows no such principle. The value of a thing is, what it will produce; and it admits of no precise standard. It must be in its nature fluctuating, and will depend upon ten thousand different circumstances.
>
> Still, however, there may be such unconscionableness or inadequacy in a bargain, as to demonstrate some gross imposition or undue influence; and in such cases Courts of Equity ought to interfere, upon the satisfactory ground of fraud. But then such unconscionableness or such inadequacy should be made out, as would, to use an expressive phrase, shock the conscience, and amount in itself to conclusive and decisive evidence of fraud. And where there are other ingredients in the case of a suspicious nature, or peculiar relations between the parties, gross inadequacy of price must necessarily furnish the most vehement presumption of fraud.

Story, *Commentaries on Equity Jurisprudence, supra,* §§ 244-246 (footnotes omitted).

A more recent statement of the principle is set forth in *Johnson v. Woodworth,* 119 N.Y.S. 146 (1909), a case in which the consideration for a deed by an elderly woman equaled 25% of the fair value of the property:

> An arrangement so unusual and unnatural cannot be lightly regarded, without some explanation on the part of the person claiming the benefit thereof, and not much evidence is necessary to impose on such person the duty of an explanation. In 6 *American and English Encyclopedia of Law*, 701, it is said:
>
>> When the inadequacy of consideration is very gross, fraud will be presumed; for though in such a case there may be no positive evidence of it, yet when the inequality is so great as to shock the conscience, the mind cannot resist the inference that the bargain must in some way have been improperly obtained. As to what degree of inequality constitutes gross inadequacy, no rule can be laid down. Between the parties, it has been said, "to set aside a conveyance, there must be an inequality so strong, gross, and manifest that it must be impossible to state it to a man of common sense without producing an exclamation at the inequality of it."

Substantially the same rule was declared in [other cases]. It is true that mere inadequacy of consideration is insufficient to avoid a sale; but that rule is not an unqualified one, and may not in all cases prevail where the inadequacy is very great. In *Byers v. Surget*, 15 L. Ed. 670 (1856), the court said:

> It is insisted that inadequacy of consideration, singly, cannot amount to proof of fraud. This position, however, is scarcely reconcilable with the qualification annexed to it by the courts, namely, unless such inadequacy be so gross as to shock the conscience; for this qualification implies necessarily the affirmation that, if the inadequacy be of a nature so gross as to shock the conscience, it will amount to proof of fraud.

The degree or extent of the inadequacy is to be considered with reference to the relations existing between the parties and the apparent reasons which may exist for such inadequacy. A consideration which may not be inadequate as between parties bound by the ties of affection and kinship may be grossly inadequate as between strangers, unless some explanation is vouchsafed. . . .

Thus, while affirming as a general rule the position that, absent fraud or duress, the court will enforce the agreement reached, American courts have continued the centuries old practice of inferring constructive fraud from shockingly oppressive contracts, at least when they could find sharp practice or overreaching present. Indeed the very language of Lord Hardwicke (in *Chesterfield v. Janssen*, 28 Eng. Rep. 82, 100 (1750)) quoted by Justice Story above was employed by the Delaware Supreme Court in 1978 to define an unconscionable contract:

> The traditional test is this: a contract is unconscionable if it is "such as no man in his senses and not under a delusion would make on the one hand, and as no honest or fair man would accept on the other." *Williams v. Walker-Thomas Furniture Co.*, 350 F.2d 445, 450 (1965). "It is generally held that the unconscionability test involves the question of whether the provision amounts to a taking of an unfair advantage by one party over the other." *J.A. Jones Construction Co. v. City of Dover*, Del. Super., 372 A.2d 540, 552 (1977).

Tulowitzki v. Atlantic Richfield Co., Del. Supr., 396 A.2d 956, 960 (1978).

Limiting our search to real estate contracts and to cases arising over the last fifty-years, without being exhaustive, we [have found numerous] cases in which courts have set aside or refused to enforce conveyances because of the unfairness of price and other circumstances of inequitable or oppressive conduct.

These cases give a flavor for the application of this judicial nullification of contract. *Lampley v. Pertuit*, Miss. Supr., 199 So. 2d 452 (1967), for example, involved an alleged sale of a house, valued in excess of $1600, for $400. While plaintiffs had given a deed absolute, they testified that they had intended a loan not a sale and had intended the deed as security. In canceling the deed, the court concluded that the parties must have entered a loan transaction, reasoning that, a $400 purchase price would represent "grossly inadequate" consideration for the plaintiffs' house. The court gave weight to the trial court's finding that the defendant had a far superior education and understanding of the intricacies of real estate transactions than the plaintiffs. *Id.* at 454.

Another apt case is, *Daniels v. Forston*, 95 S.W.2d 1075 (1936). Plaintiff, a sixty-four year old woman, had fallen behind in her mortgage payments on her house. Her young cousin allegedly offered to lend her the necessary funds to pay off the mortgage. When she met with the young man and his attorney, however, she signed a deed of sale reserving to herself only a life estate in the property. Although the court found no direct evidence of duress or fraud, it did find the sale transaction to be unconscionable, since the market value for the house was far in excess of the small consideration paid. The court reasoned, in part, that no mutual agreement could have been reached since "this trusting old woman thought she was executing a mortgage; this scheming young man knew he was getting a deed." *Id.*, 95 S.W.2d at 1076.

Statutory developments over the last thirty years reflect an explicit legislative endorsement of this ancient equitable doctrine. The most important example of this mid-twentieth century codification is the unconscionability provision contained in UCC § 2-302. That provision has, of course, been adopted in almost all of the states and applies to sale of all goods. § 2-302 provides, in part:

> (1) If the court as a matter of law finds the contract or any clause . . . to have been unconscionable [when] . . . made the court may refuse to enforce the contract. . . .

§ 2-302. The drafters' comments note that

> the basic test is whether, in light of the general commercial background and the commercial needs of the particular trade or case, the clauses involved are so one-sided as to be unconscionable under the circumstances existing at the time of the making of the contract.

Id.

While the UCC does not, of course, apply to sales of land, there is good reason to assume that the legislature's solicitude for parties who are disadvantaged by bargains that are unconscionably oppressive should not be entirely ignored where sales of land are concerned. Such transactions are obviously enormously more significant than a purchase of goods to the average person. They will occur rarely in the typical life and will often involve a person's largest single asset. *See* Leff, *Unconscionability and the Code—The Emperor's New Clause*, 115 U. PA. L. REV. 485, 537 (1967).[3]

Indeed traditionally the common law has been more protective of grantors of real property than of commercial bargainers. Thus, in discussing the general rule that the court will not generally evaluate the adequacy of consideration, Justice Story long-ago quoted a civil law scholar who touched on the special case of land sales:

> [F]or the most part, [civil law jurists] seem silently to abandon cases of inadequacy in bargains, where there is no fraud, to the forum of conscience, and morals, and religion. Thus, Domat, after remarking, that the law of nature obliges us not to take advantage of necessities of the seller, to buy at too low a price, adds, "But because of the difficulties in fixing the just price of things, and of the inconveniences, which would be too many and too great, if all sales were annulled, in which the things were not sold at their just value, *the laws connive at the injustice of buyers, except in the sale of lands, where the price given for them is less than half of their just value.*" So that sales of personal property are usually without redress; and even sales of immovable property are in the same predicament, unless the inadequacy of price amounts to one half the value; a rule purely artificial, and which must leave behind it many cases of gross hardship, and unconscionable advantage.

Story, *Commentary on Equity Jurisprudence, supra,* § 247 (emphasis added). The common law system has always regarded land as an asset of special significance. It is not surprising therefore to find echoes of the old civil law rule referred to above reverberating in contemporary American law. For example, it is a common practice for courts today to refuse to confirm judicial sales of realty in which the price is less than 50% of the fair market value of the land. *See, e.g., Girard Trust Bank v. Castle Apartments, Inc.*, Del. Super., 379 A.2d 1144 (1977).

Thus, while the statutory provision of UCC § 2-302 does not itself reach sales of land, it is appropriate to read that statute as consistent with and reflective of the traditional equitable doctrines quoted above.

One structure within which the common law has sanctioned courts in evaluating the fairness of an exchange is presented by the law of unilateral mistake. As our Supreme Court has recently restated that doctrine, it provides that:

---

3. ". . . real property is likely to be the only thing that relatively unsophisticated people have which is worth tricking them out of . . . the equity cases are replete with factual patterns involving the old being bilked and farmers sweet-talked into ruinous trades." 115 U. PA. L. REV. at 536.

> Generally, a party may rescind an agreement based on its unilateral mistake if the following conditions are met: (1) the enforcement of the agreement would be unconscionable; (2) the mistake relates to the substance of the consideration; (3) the mistake occurred regardless of the exercise of ordinary care; and (4) it is possible to place the other party in the status quo. 13 *Williston on Contracts* § 1573 (3d ed. 1970).

In the Matter of the Appraisal of Enstar Corporation, Del. Supr., 604 A.2d 404, 411 (1992). This structure has been employed in land sale cases.

Arguably Professor Williston's formulation of this unilateral mistake doctrine forms one available structure for addressing the issues of this case.

1. *The transaction was unconscionable.* (a) *The substance:* the financial aspects of the sale are shocking. Mr. Ryan had lived for more than 13 years in this modest house and had until relatively shortly before the sale regularly made his mortgage payment. The house had a fair market value of $19,800 and a mortgage of about $7,800.00. Thus, at the time it represented some $12,000 of equity which, one can safely assume, represented all of the assets that Ryan had acquired over a long life as an employed laborer.

In exchange for the conveyance of this asset, Ryan received no cash, and no release of liability. He received only a promise to be able to occupy the same house at a market-rate rent. That rent was, at first, modestly in excess of the mortgage payment ($100) but within 15 months it had been raised twice, first to $160 (60% increase) then to $260 per month (additional 62% increase).

What, on the other hand, did Mr. Weiner get from the transaction and what did he give? He received, of course, the value of the property net of the mortgage. He paid out some cash (about $1,900) but that amount, in large measure, reduced the amount of the mortgage lien on the property and thus immediately accrued to the financial interest, not of Ryan, but of the new equity owner—Weiner himself. Therefore if the transaction is valid all that Weiner extended as consideration to Ryan was the right to be a tenant in his house at a fair market rate in excess of the mortgage amortization cost.

From a financial perspective this transaction is as close to a gift as one is likely to encounter.

(b) *The process:* the process that lead to this one-sided bargain, in part, appears to explain and account for it. Ryan was, of course, vulnerable, and unsophisticated, but those facts do not prevent him from making valid contracts. But Ryan's circumstances—his age, his obvious lack of sophistication, his poverty, his distress and his fear of being dispossessed—are factors that one who initiates a transaction concerning transfer of the other's home should take into account, in order to offer some assurance that whatever deal may be made is made knowingly and with due consideration. But instead of offering Ryan sufficient time to consider his proposal (and to perhaps consult with others), Mr. Weiner moved with urgent speed. He did not give Ryan time to consider the matter, perhaps to seek advice from a Legal Aid lawyer or to consider alternatives. Weiner rushed Ryan. He picked him up at his home early the next day and took Ryan to Weiner's lawyer to sign papers. I am convinced that Ryan did not understand the nature and effect of the papers he signed.

2. *Ryan's mistake relates to the substance of the consideration.* He misunderstood the very nature of the transaction. Ryan believed he was giving security for a loan; that Weiner would manage the property and that Ryan would only have to pay a monthly amount that would cover the mortgage and, in time, repay Weiner. In this, the documents show he was mistaken.

3. *Ryan was not culpable.* The third item in Professor Williston's statement of a unilateral mistake test as recited by our Supreme Court is whether the party who was mistaken exercised ordinary care. I take this element of the structure of inquiry to direct our attention to the question who, if either party, is most responsible for the material mistake. The justification for this element, in the context of an unconscionable contract, is not readily apparent at least where the party benefitting from the contract is actively involved in securing the unconscionable term. Presumably it is grounded in a perception of fairness to the beneficiary of unconscionable contracts. That is, if the result of the analysis may be to deprive the defendant of the benefit of the bargain he thought was reached, then it may be thought that in fairness to him, even if in all events he will at least be restored to his prior position, this result ought not obtain if plaintiff is more responsible for the mistake than was he. On this formulation, I understand this element, in the context of an unconscionable contract, to permit a comparative assessment of fault.

It is hard to say that Ryan exercised ordinary care of a prudent man in entering this transaction. He did not understand the transaction and appears to have naively placed himself entirely into Mr. Weiner's hands. But while Ryan appears as a financial innocent upon whom Mr. Weiner could practice his skills, Weiner appears a manipulative and skillful predator. When one with substantially greater knowledge, experience, and resources himself seeks out the powerless to deal with them directly on matters of vital importance, he assumes some responsibility to assure, to the extent circumstances permit, that they do understand the nature of the transaction proposed. If he does not do this and if the transaction he initiates is oppressive and shockingly one-sided, he cannot retain the bargain. Even if Weiner did not affirmatively deceive Mr. Ryan (as to which I make no finding), he did not assure that the party from whom he attempted to extract so much understood the nature of this transaction. It was this fact more than Ryan's lack of care that accounts for Mr. Ryan's unilateral mistake of thinking he was signing a secured loan.

4. *It is possible to restore the status quo.* On one level, the transaction was entirely financial. Ryan never moved out of his house. The mortgage was not paid off by Mr. Weiner; rather he made monthly payments from the payments that Ryan made to him. Thus it is not difficult to return the parties to the status quo as of May, 1984. All that is required is for Mr. Weiner to establish what he paid on account of the house: mortgage, taxes, insurance, heat, utilities and maintenance. These amounts, including the expenditures necessary to bring the mortgage up to date in May 1984 appear to total $12,149.27. They

will be credited to him. On the other hand the $21,480.00 paid by Mr. Ryan to Mr. Weiner should be credited to him. After this operation is gone through (and tax adjusted) a net amount will be owing to Mr. Ryan. Interest is a matter upon which the parties should be heard, if they cannot resolve it. Surely Mr. Weiner is entitled to a fair rate of interest on any amounts of credit that he had extended, for so long as he was a net lender into the transaction. It is, however, not clear in the record how long a time passed before all net expenditures were fully recovered from "rental" payments in excess of mortgage payments. Counsel can work out those details. The significant point is that there is no factor that would preclude the entry of an order that will return defendant, financially speaking, to the position he occupied when he went to Mr. Ryan's home to induce a transaction.

Thus I conclude that this transaction is one that, under principles applied for more than two hundred years, cannot in equity be allowed to stand. I conclude that it involves shockingly unconscionable financial terms, coupled with innocent failure to understand the transaction on one side and sharp and predatory practices on the other. I am satisfied that these facts clearly are the equivalent of cases in which courts have set aside land transfers as fraudulent or constructively fraudulent.

The plaintiff may submit a form of order consistent with the foregoing, on notice.

CHAPTER 9

THIRD PARTIES

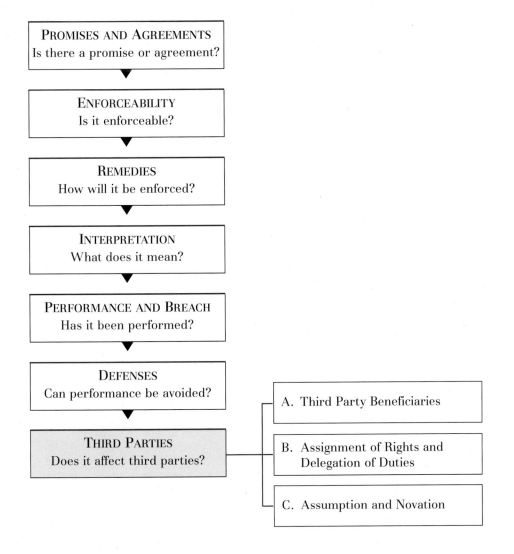

PROMISES AND AGREEMENTS
Is there a promise or agreement?

▼

ENFORCEABILITY
Is it enforceable?

▼

REMEDIES
How will it be enforced?

▼

INTERPRETATION
What does it mean?

▼

PERFORMANCE AND BREACH
Has it been performed?

▼

DEFENSES
Can performance be avoided?

▼

THIRD PARTIES
Does it affect third parties?

- A. Third Party Beneficiaries
- B. Assignment of Rights and Delegation of Duties
- C. Assumption and Novation

A. THIRD PARTY BENEFICIARIES

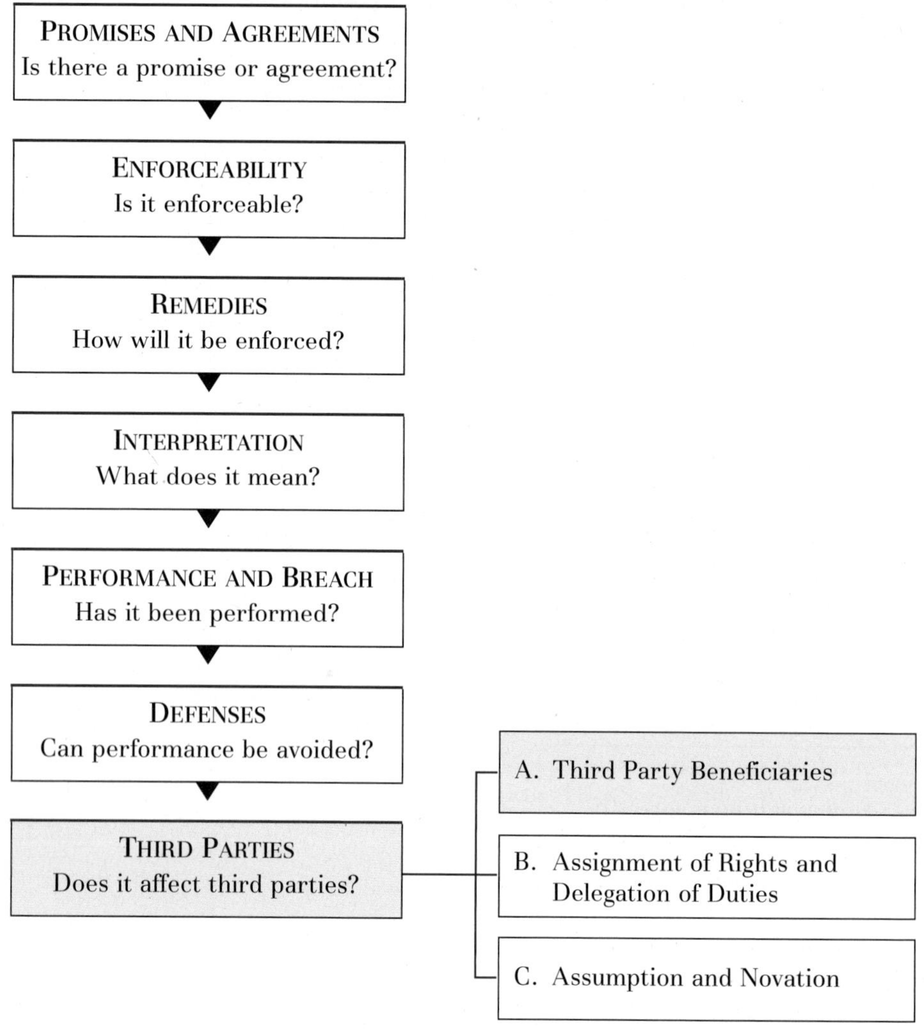

DOCTRINAL OVERVIEW: THIRD PARTY BENEFICIARIES*

The performance of a contract usually benefits persons other than the parties who made it, but they cannot ordinarily enforce it. The prompt construction of an office building will benefit prospective tenants by allowing them to move in on schedule, but they cannot recover damages from the builder that wrongfully fails to complete performance on time. A labor union's performance of a collective bargaining agreement with a transit system will benefit riders of the system by making transportation available, but the riders cannot recover damages from the

* Excerpted from E. ALLAN FARNSWORTH, CONTRACTS §§ 10.1-10.2 (4th ed. 2004).

union if it wrongfully calls a strike that paralyzes the system. It is sometimes said that such persons cannot enforce the contract because they are not in "privity" with the promisor, but this begs the question: When does the duty of a promisor extend to one other than the promisee? This troublesome question is raised in what has become a small flood of cases. . . .

The right of a third person (C) to sue as a beneficiary of a contract to which that person was not a party—a contract between a promisor (A) and a promisee (B—was upheld as early as 1677 by the King's Bench in *Dutton v. Poole.* A father (B) planned to sell wood to raise a dowry for his daughter (C). The eldest son (A), who wanted to inherit the wood, promised the father to pay the daughter £1,000 if the father would not sell it. When the son failed to pay the £1,000, the daughter sued him. It was argued for the son that "the action ought not to be brought by the daughter but by the father . . . for the promise was made to the father, and the daughter is neither privy nor interested in the consideration. The court rejected the argument, noting that "there was such apparent consideration of affection from the father to his children, for whom nature obliges him to provide, that the consideration and promise to the father may well extend to the children."[2] Later English cases approved of *Dutton v. Poole*. . . .

[With respect to the law of third-party beneficiaries in America, t]he New York Court of Appeals led the way in *Lawrence v. Fox,* decided in 1859. . . . Holly (B) owed Lawrence (C) $300. Holly then lent Fox (A) $300, in return for which Fox promised Holly to pay Holly's debt to Lawrence. When Fox did not do so, Lawrence sued him. The Court of Appeals noted that if Fox had made his promise to Lawrence instead of to, or in addition to, Holly, there would have been a clear precedent for recovery by Lawrence against Fox. Since the consideration for a promise need not move from the promisee to the promisor, the loan by Holly to Fox would have been consideration for Fox's promise to Lawrence. But Fox's promise had not been made to Lawrence. Nevertheless, the court allowed him to recover directly against Fox.[13] It applied a principle from the law of trusts to the effect that, in the case of "a promise made to one for the benefit of another, he for whose benefit it is made may bring an action for its breach."[14] Because the beneficiary, Lawrence, was a creditor to whom the promisee, Holly, sought to have his debt paid, claimants in the position of Lawrence came to be called "creditor beneficiaries." . . .

Nearly 60 years after *Lawrence v. Fox,* the New York Court of Appeals handed down another influential case involving a contract beneficiary . . . [i]n *Seaver v. Ransom*. . . .

Lawrence v. Fox

Court of Appeals of New York
20 N.Y. 268 (1859)

For a report of the case and accompanying materials, see p. 157, *supra*.

2. 83 Eng. Rep. 523, 523, 524 (K.B. 1677).
13. Since Holly's debt to Lawrence had not been paid, Lawrence clearly had an action against Holly.
14. 20 N.Y. 268, 274 (1859) (6-2 decision).

Seaver v. Ransom

Court of Appeals of New York
120 N.E. 639 (1918)

POUND, J. Judge Beman and his wife were advanced in years. Mrs. Beman was about to die. She had a small estate, consisting of a house and lot in Malone and little else. Judge Beman drew his wife's will according to her instructions. It gave $1,000 to plaintiff, $500 to one sister, plaintiff's mother, and $100 each to another sister and her son, the use of the house to her husband for life, and remainder to the American Society for the Prevention of Cruelty to Animals. She named her husband as residuary legatee and executor. Plaintiff was her niece, 34 years old in ill health sometimes a member of the Beman household. When the will was read to Mrs. Beman, she said that it was not as she wanted it. She wanted to leave the house to plaintiff. She had no other objection to the will, but her strength was waning, and, although the judge offered to write another will for her, she said she was afraid she would not hold out long enough to enable her to sign it. So the judge said, if she would sign the will, he would leave plaintiff enough in his will to make up the difference. He avouched the promise by his uplifted hand with all solemnity and his wife then executed the will. When he came to die, it was found that his will made no provision for the plaintiff.

This action was brought, and plaintiff recovered judgment in the trial court, on the theory that Beman had obtained property from his wife and induced her to execute the will in the form prepared by him by his promise to give plaintiff $6,000, the value of the house, and that thereby equity impressed his property with a trust in favor of plaintiff. Where a legatee promises the testator that he will use property given him by the will for a particular purpose, a trust arises. Beman received nothing under his wife's will but the use of the house in Malone for life. Equity compels the application of property thus obtained to the purpose of the testator, but equity cannot so impress a trust, except on property obtained by the promise. Beman was bound by his promise, but no property was bound by it; no trust in plaintiff's favor can be spelled out.

An action on the contract for damages, or to make the executors trustees for performance, stands on different ground. The Appellate Division properly passed to the consideration of the question whether the judgment could stand upon the promise made to the wife, upon a valid consideration, for the sole benefit of plaintiff. The judgment of the trial court was affirmed by a return to the general doctrine laid down in the great case of *Lawrence v. Fox*, 20 N.Y. 268, which has since been limited as herein indicated.

Contracts for the benefit of third persons have been the prolific source of judicial and academic discussion. The general rule, both in law and equity, was that privity between a plaintiff and a defendant is necessary to the maintenance of an action on the contract. The consideration must be furnished by the party to whom the promise was made. The contract cannot be enforced against the third party, and therefore it cannot be enforced by him. On the other hand, the right of the beneficiary to sue on a contract made expressly for his benefit has been fully recognized in many American jurisdictions, either by judicial decision or by legislation, and is said to be "the prevailing rule in this country." *Hendrick v. Lindsay*, 93 U.S. 143. It has been said that "the establishment of this doctrine has been gradual, and is a victory of practical utility over theory, of equity over technical subtlety." *Brantly on Contracts* (2d Ed.) p. 253. The reasons for this view are that it is just and practical to permit the person for whose benefit the contract is made to enforce it against one whose duty it is to pay. Other jurisdictions still adhere to the present English rule that a contract cannot be enforced by or against a person who is not a party.

In New York the right of the beneficiary to sue on contracts made for his benefit is not clearly or simply defined. It is at present confined: First, to cases where there is a pecuniary obligation running from the promisee to the beneficiary, "a legal right founded upon some obligation of the promisee in the third party to adopt and claim the promise as made for his benefit." *Farley v. Cleveland*, 4 Cow. 432; *Lawrence v. Fox, supra*. Secondly, to cases where the contract is made for the benefit of the wife, affianced wife, or child of a party to the contract. The close relationship cases go back to the early King's Bench case (1677), long since repudiated in England, of *Dutton v. Poole*, 2 Lev. 211. The natural and moral duty of the husband or parent to provide for the future of wife or child sustains the action on the contract made for their benefit. "This is the furthest the cases in this state have gone," says Cullen, J., in the marriage settlement case of *Borland v. Welch*, 56 N.E. 556, 557 (1900).

The right of the third party is also upheld in, thirdly, the public contract cases, where the municipality seeks to protect its inhabitants by covenants for their benefit; and, fourthly, the cases where, at the request of a party to the contract, the promise runs directly to the beneficiary although he does not furnish the consideration. It may be safely said that a general rule sustaining recovery at the suit of the third party would include but few classes of cases not included in these groups, either categorically or in principle.

The desire of the childless aunt to make provision for a beloved and favorite niece differs imperceptibly in law or in equity from the moral duty of the parent to make testamentary provision for a child. The contract was made for the plaintiff's benefit. She alone is substantially damaged by its breach. The representatives of the wife's estate have no interest in enforcing it specifically. It is said in *Buchanan v. Tilden* that the common law imposes moral and legal obligations upon the husband and the parent not measured by the necessaries of life. It was, however, the love and affection or the moral sense of the husband and the parent that imposed such obligations in the cases cited, rather than any common-law duty of husband and parent to wife and child. If plaintiff had been a child of Mrs. Beman, legal obligation would have required no testamentary provision for her, yet the child could have enforced a covenant in her favor identical with the covenant of Judge Beman in this case. The constraining power of conscience is not regulated by the degree of relationship alone. The dependent or faithful niece may have a stronger claim than the affluent or unworthy son. No sensible theory of moral obligation denies arbitrarily to the former what would be conceded to the latter. We might consistently either refuse or allow the claim of both, but I cannot reconcile a decision in favor of the wife in *Buchanan v. Tilden*, based on the moral obligations arising out of near relationship, with a decision against the niece here on the ground that the relationship is too remote for equity's ken. No controlling authority depends upon so absolute a rule. In *Sullivan v. Sullivan,* the grandniece lost in a litigation with the aunt's estate, founded on a certificate of deposit payable to the aunt "or in case of her death to her niece"; but what was said in that case of the relations of plaintiff's intestate and defendant does not control here, any more than what was said in *Durnherr v. Rau,* supra, on the relation of husband and wife, and the inadequacy of mere moral duty, as distinguished from legal or equitable obligation, controlled the decision in *Buchanan v. Tilden. Borland v. Welch,* deals only with the rights of volunteers under a marriage settlement not made for the benefit of collaterals. Kellogg, P. J., writing for the court below well said:

> The doctrine of *Lawrence v. Fox* is progressive, not retrograde. The course of the late decisions is to enlarge, not to limit, the effect of that case.

The court in that leading case attempted to adopt the general doctrine that any third person, for whose direct benefit a contract was intended, could sue on it. The headnote thus states the rule. Finch, J., in *Gifford v. Corrigan,* 22 N.E. 756, says that the case rests upon that broad proposition; Edward T. Bartlett, J., in *Pond v. New Rochelle Water Co.*, 76 N.E. 211, 213, calls it "the general principle"; but *Vrooman v. Turner* confined its application to the facts on which it was decided. "In every case in which an action has been sustained," says Allen, J., "there has been a debt or duty owing by the promisee to the party claiming to sue upon the promise." As late as *Townsend v. Rackham,* 38 N.E. 731, 733, we find Peckham, J., saying that, "to maintain the action by the third person, there must be this liability to him on the part of the promisee." *Buchanan v. Tilden* went further than any case since *Lawrence v. Fox* in a desire to do justice rather than to apply with technical accuracy strict rules calling for a legal or equitable obligation. In *Embler v. Hartford Steam Boiler Inspection & Ins. Co.,* 53 N.E. 212, it may at least be said that a majority of the court did not avail themselves of the opportunity to concur with the views expressed by Gray, J., who wrote the dissenting opinion in *Buchanan v. Tilden,* to the effect that an employee could not maintain an action on an insurance policy issued to the employer, which covered injuries to employs.

In *Wright v. Glen Telephone Co.,* 95 N.Y. Supp. 101, the learned presiding justice who wrote the opinion in this case said at Trial Term:

> The right of a third person to recover upon a contract made by other parties for his benefit must rest upon the peculiar circumstances of each case rather than upon the law of some other case.

"The case at bar is decided upon its peculiar facts." Edward T. Bartlett, J., in *Buchanan v. Tilden.*

But, on principle, a sound conclusion may be reached. If Mrs. Beman had left her husband the house on condition that he pay the plaintiff $6,000, and he had accepted the devise, he would have become personally liable to pay the legacy, and plaintiff could have recovered in an action at law against him, whatever the value of the house. That would be because the testatrix had in substance bequeathed the promise to plaintiff, and not because close relationship or moral obligation sustained the contract. The distinction between an implied promise to a testator for the benefit of a third party to pay a legacy and an unqualified promise on a valuable consideration to make provision for the third party by will is discernible, but not obvious. The tendency of American authority is to sustain the gift in all such cases and to permit the donee beneficiary to recover on the contract. The equities are with the plaintiff, and they may be enforced in this action, whether it be regarded as an action for damages or an action for specific performance to convert the defendants into trustees for plaintiff's benefit under the agreement.

The judgment should be affirmed, with costs.

HOGAN, CARDOZO, and CRANE, JJ., concur. HISCOCK, C.J., and COLLIN and ANDREWS, JJ., dissent.

Judgment affirmed.

RELEVANT PROVISIONS

For the *Restatement (Second) of Contracts,* consult §§ 302, 309, 311, and 315. For the UNIDROIT Principles, consult Article 3.2.6.

NOTES AND QUESTIONS

1. *What happened?* Who sued whom for what? Procedurally, how did the case get before this court? Factually, what happened between the parties? What arguments did the plaintiff and defendant make? What rule or rules did the court apply? How did the court analyze the dispute between the parties? How did the court decide the case?

2. *Was this case correctly decided?* Do you agree with the result reached in this case? Why or why not? Do you agree with the court's reasoning? Why or why not? How, if at all, would you have written the opinion differently?

3. *Reconciling precedents.* Can this case be reconciled with *Lawrence v. Fox*? In what ways do the two cases differ from one another? Based on these two cases, can you tell what test courts use to determine which beneficiaries may bring suit? How, if at all, does the *Restatement (Second) of Contracts* provisions cited above change the test for third-party beneficiaries?

Rouse v. United States

United States Court of Appeals, D.C. Circuit
215 F.2d 872 (1954)

EDGERTON, CIRCUIT JUDGE. Bessie Winston gave Associated Contractors, Inc., her promissory note for $1,008.37, payable in monthly installments of $28.01, for a heating plant in her house. The Federal Housing Administration guaranteed the note and the payee endorsed it for value to the lending bank, the Union Trust Company.

Winston sold the house to Rouse. In the contract of sale Rouse agreed to assume debts secured by deeds of trust and also "to assume payment of $850 for heating plant payable $28 per Mo." Nothing was said about the note.

Winston defaulted on her note. The United States paid the bank, took an assignment of the note, demanded payment from Rouse, and sued him for $850 and interest.

Rouse alleged as defenses (1) that Winston fraudulently misrepresented the condition of the heating plant and (2) that Associated Contractors did not install it satisfactorily. The District Court struck these defenses and granted summary judgment for the plaintiff. The defendant Rouse appeals.

Since Rouse did not sign the note he is not liable on it. He is not liable to the United States at all unless his contract with Winston makes him so. The contract says the parties to it are not "bound by any terms, conditions, statements, warranties or representation, oral or written" not contained in it. But this means only that the written contract contains the entire agreement. It does not mean that fraud cannot be set up as a defense to a suit on the contract. Rouse's promise to "assume payment of $850 for heating plant" made him liable to Associated Contractors, Inc., only if and so far as it made him liable to Winston; one who promises to make a payment to the promisee's creditor can assert against the creditor any defense that the promisor could assert against the promisee. Accordingly Rouse, if he had been sued by the corporation, would have been entitled to show fraud on the part of Winston. He is equally entitled to do so in this suit by an assignee of the corporation's claim. It follows that the court erred in striking the first defense. We do not consider whether Winston's alleged fraud, if shown, would be a complete or only a partial defense to this suit, since that question has not arisen and may not arise.

We think the court has right in striking the second defense.

> If the promisor's agreement is to be interpreted as a promise to discharge whatever liability the promisee is under, the promisor must certainly be allowed to show that the promisee was under no enforceable liability. . . . On the other hand, if the promise means that the promisor agrees to pay a sum of money to A, to whom the promisee says he is indebted, it is immaterial whether the promisee is actually indebted to that amount or at all. . . . Where the promise is to pay a specific debt . . . this interpretation will generally be the true one.[3]

The judgment is reversed and the cause remanded with instructions to reinstate the first defense.

Reversed and remanded.

3. 2 Williston, Contracts § 399 (Rev. Ed. 1936).

NOTES AND QUESTIONS

1. *What happened?* Who sued whom for what? Procedurally, how did the case get before this court? Factually, what happened between the parties? What arguments did the plaintiff and defendant make? What rule or rules did the court apply? How did the court analyze the dispute between the parties? How did the court decide the case?

2. *Was this case correctly decided?* Do you agree with the result reached in this case? Why or why not? Do you agree with the court's reasoning? Why or why not? How, if at all, would you have written the opinion differently?

3. *A counterfactual.* Assume that Winston, and not Rouse, still owned the house. If the seller would have sued Winston in this case, rather than Rouse, there is little doubt that Winston could raise faulty installation as a defense. Should that matter here, now that Rouse owns it?

4. *Liability.* Why was Rouse not liable on Winston's note?

5. *Revisiting* Lawrence v. Fox. In light of this precedent, should Fox have been able to plead any defense that Holly had against Lawrence? Why or why not?

6. *Application.* How would you apply the principles you learned thus far to resolve the following dispute?

PROBLEM: THE WRECKING BALL

Plaintiff Percy owned the Park Place Hotel. In 2010, the hotel was severely damaged by fire, and the Town Commission ("Commission"), acting under a Commission ordinance so authorizing, obtained a court order compelling Percy to remove the structure as a public nuisance and as a dangerous, unsafe fire hazard. When Percy failed to demolish the structure within the time required, Commission entered into a demolition contract with Wrecking Crew, Inc. ("Wrecking") as authorized by the ordinance.

The contract between Commission and Wrecking called for Wrecking to demolish and remove buildings and boardwalk and stated that as demolition progressed all materials and debris were to be removed from the premises and that the lot, after demolition, was to be compacted and graded to "grade level" with dirt. The parties also agreed that, "All walls and foundations shall be removed one (1) foot below the elevation of the existing grade of the sidewalk adjacent to it. The slab will be crushed for drainage and all large pieces removed." Before demolition commenced, Percy brought an action for injunction to prevent it, but after a preliminary injunction was denied, the action was abandoned. Demolition was concluded in July 2010, at a cost of $100,000 to the Commission, which subsequently recovered that sum from Percy.

In March 2012, Percy began constructing Boardwalk Hotel on the site formerly occupied by the Park Place Hotel. During initial excavation work it discovered that the walls and foundations had not been removed one foot below existing grade nor had the slab been crushed and all large pieces removed as required by the contract. In September 2012, Percy brought suit against both Commission and Wrecking for breach of contract. Specifically, Percy alleged that he was a third-party beneficiary of the Commission-Wrecking demolition contract, that Wrecking failed to remove the concrete foundation and boardwalk, to crush the slab and to remove the large pieces, and that the Commission breached its obligation to the plaintiff in failing to supervise and to insure that the contract and the judgment were fully complied with.

Was Plaintiff Percy a third-party beneficiary? Why or why not?

B. ASSIGNMENT OF RIGHTS AND DELEGATION OF DUTIES

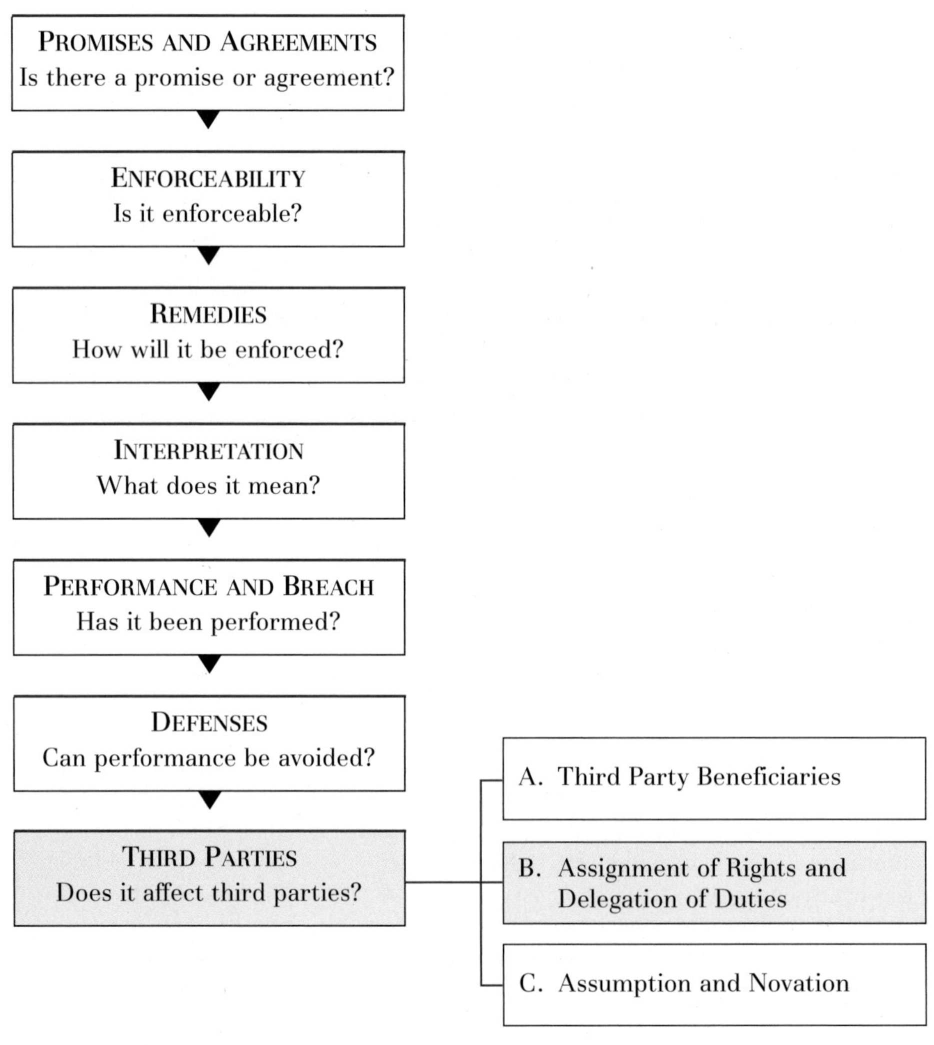

In the previous Section, we discussed *Lawrence v. Fox, Seaver v. Ransom,* and *Rouse v. United States,* and looked at some of the ways in which third parties may obtain rights pursuant to a contract made between two other parties. Here, we will take a closer look at some of the third-party issues that come up when parties attempt to assign their rights, delegate their duties, or otherwise involve third parties in their affairs. The typical fact pattern we will be examining in these cases looks something like the following: *A* and *B* have a contract in which *A* has a right to *B*'s performance, and *B* has the corresponding duty to perform for *A*. Then, once the contract is formed, either (1) *A* decides that she wants to assign her right (to *B*'s performance) to another party, *C*; or (2) *B* decides that he wants to delegate his duty to perform (to *A*) to another party, *D*. In such cases, the question for the courts becomes whether, and under what circumstances, *A* or *B* can assign or delegate their respective rights and duties to *C* and/or *D*. We will orient ourselves with the lay of the land in the following excerpt, and then take a look at some cases.

DOCTRINAL OVERVIEW: ASSIGNMENT OF RIGHTS AND DELEGATION OF DUTIES*

At the outset, it is vital to distinguish the *assignment of rights* from the *delegation of performance of duties.* An obligee's transfer of a contract right is known as an *assignment* of the right. By an assignment, the obligee as *assignor* (B) transfers to an *assignee* (C) a right that the assignor has against an *obligor* (A). An obligor's empowering of another to perform the obligor's duty is known as a *delegation* of the performance of that duty. By a delegation, the obligor as *delegating party* (B) empowers a *delegate* (C) to perform a duty that the delegating party owes to an *obligee* (A).[5] A party to a contract that both assigns rights and delegates performance to another person will be referred to as a *transferor* (B); the other person will be referred to as a *transferee* (C); and the transaction will be called a *transfer* of the contract. . . .

We examine first the law of assignment and then that of delegation. . . .

The word *assignment* here refers to the act by which an assignor transfers a contract right to an assignee.[1] Such an act will sometimes also be referred to as an *effective assignment,* as distinguished from an *attempted* or *purported assignment.* What is necessary for an effective assignment?

To make an effective assignment of a contract right, the owner of that right must manifest an intention to make a present transfer of the right without further action

---

* Excerpted from E. ALLAN FARNSWORTH, CONTRACTS §§ 11.1, 11.3, and 11.10 (4th ed. 2004).

5. The terms *delegating party* and *delegate* are not as well established as *assignor* and *assignee. See* UCC § 2-210 (using *party delegating* and *delegate*) . . . ; *Restatement Second* § 318(3) (using *delegating obligor* and *person delegated*). . . .

1. The *Restatement Second* uses it in this sense. *See Restatement Second* § 317(1) ("assignment of a right is a manifestation of the assignor's intention to transfer it by virtue of which the assignor's right" is transferred). The word is sometimes also used to refer to the transfer itself or to a writing evidencing the transfer.

by the owner or by the obligor. The owner may manifest this intention directly to the assignee or to a third person. No words of art are required; the assignor need not even use the word *assign*. Whether the owner of a right has manifested an intention to transfer it is a question of interpretation to be answered from all the circumstances, including words and other conduct. To transfer a contract right is, in essence, to take from the assignor (B) and to give to the assignee (C) the right to performance by the obligor (A). Put in another way, the transfer of a contract right extinguishes the assignor's right to performance by the obligor and gives the assignee a right to that performance. It is important not to confuse an assignment, which is a present transfer, with a contract, which is a promise of future performance. . . .

The term *delegation* . . . refers to the act by which one owing a duty (B) manifests an intention to confer upon another person (C) the power to perform that duty. If the delegating party accomplishes that intention, the delegation is said to be "effective." It is important not to confuse delegation with assignment. The term *delegate* should be used in connection with performance, while the term *assign* should be reserved for rights, though courts often fail to use these terms with precision.

No particular language is necessary for an effective delegation of performance. Thus, the parties may not observe the distinction between the terms *assign* and *delegate*, and language by which one purports to "assign" one's duties may suffice to effect a delegation. Furthermore, it is not uncommon for a party to purport to assign in general terms "the contract," and, under both Article 2 of the Code and the Restatement Second, such language ordinarily will delegate performance as well as assign rights.[4] If, however, the language or the situation indicates the contrary, as in the case of an assignment for security, an assignment of rights but no delegation of performance results.

Even an effective delegation does not relieve the delegating party (B) of its duty; that requires either consent by the obligee (A) or performance by the delegate (C). As the Uniform Commercial Code makes clear, a delegation of performance does not relieve the delegating party of "any duty to perform" or of any "liability for breach."[6] While an obligee can rid itself of a right merely by making an effective assignment, an obligor cannot rid itself of a duty merely by making an effective delegation. If obligors could do so, they could discharge their duties simply by finding obliging insolvents to whom performance could be delegated. . . .

From the perspective of the delegating party, the significance of an effective delegation is not that the delegation itself discharges the duty of the delegating party, but that the subsequent performance of that duty by the delegate will discharge the duty.[12] Thus, from the obligee's perspective, an effective delegation means that the obligee must accept performance by the delegate as performance of the duty owed by the delegating party. If the obligee were to refuse to accept performance by the delegate and insist on performance by the delegating party, the refusal would be a repudiation.

4. UCC § 2-210(4) . . . ; *Restatement Second* § 328(1).

6. UCC § 2-210(1).

12. If a third person (C) offers performance to an obligee (A), but does not do so on behalf of the obligor (B), the obligor's duty is discharged only if the obligee accepts the performance in satisfaction. *See Restatement Second* § 278(2).

Macke Co. v. Pizza of Gaithersburg, Inc.

Court of Appeals of Maryland
270 A.2d 645 (1970)

SINGLEY, JUDGE. The appellees and defendants below, Pizza of Gaithersburg, Inc.; Pizzeria, Inc.; The Pizza Pie Corp., Inc. and Pizza Oven, Inc., four corporations under the common ownership of Sidney Ansell, Thomas S. Sherwood and Eugene Early and the same individuals as partners or proprietors (the Pizza Shops) operated at six locations in Montgomery and Prince George's Counties. The appellees and arranged to have installed in each of their locations cold drink vending machines owned by Virginia Coffee Service, Inc., and on 30 December 1966, this arrangement was formalized at five of the locations, by contracts for terms of one year, automatically renewable for a like term in the absence of 30 days' written notice. A similar contract for the sixth location, operated by Pizza of Gaithersburg, Inc., was entered into on 25 July 1967.

On 30 December 1967, Virginia's assets were purchased by The Macke Company (Macke) and the six contracts were assigned to Macke by Virginia. In January, 1968, the Pizza Shops attempted to terminate the five contracts having the December anniversary date, and in February, the contract which had the July anniversary date.

Macke brought suit in the Circuit Court for Montgomery County against each of the Pizza Shops for damages for breach of contract. From judgments for the defendants, Macke has appealed.

The lower court based the result which it reached on two grounds: first, that the Pizza Shops, when they contracted with Virginia, relied on its skill, judgment and reputation, which made impossible a delegation of Virginia's duties to Macke; and second, that the damages claimed could not be shown with reasonable certainty. These conclusions are challenged by Macke.

In the absence of a contrary provision—and there was none here—rights and duties under an executory bilateral contract may be assigned and delegated, subject to the exception that duties under a contract to provide personal services may never be delegated, nor rights be assigned under a contract where *delectus personae* was an ingredient of the bargain. *Crane Ice Cream Co. v. Terminal Freezing & Heating Co.*, 128 A. 280 (1925) held that the right of an individual to purchase ice under a contract which by its terms reflected a knowledge of the individual's needs and reliance on his credit and responsibility could not be assigned to the corporation which purchased his business. In *Eastern Advertising Co. v. McGaw& Co.*, 42 A. 923 (1899), our predecessors held that an advertising agency could not delegate its duties under a contract which had been entered into by an advertiser who had relied on the agency's skill, judgment and taste.

The six machines were placed on the appellees' premises under a printed "Agreement-Contract" which identified the "customer," gave its place of business, described the vending machine, and then provided:

TERMS

1. The Company will install on the Customer's premises the above listed equipment and will maintain the equipment in good operating order and stocked with merchandise.

2. The location of this equipment will be such as to permit accessibility to persons desiring use of same. This equipment shall remain the property of the Company and shall not be moved from the location at which installed, except by the Company.

3. For equipment requiring electricity and water, the Customer is responsible for electrical receptacle and water outlet within ten (10) feet of the equipment location. The Customer is also responsible to supply the Electrical Power and Water needed.

4. The Customer will exercise every effort to protect this equipment from abuse or damage.

5. The Company will be responsible for all licenses and taxes on the equipment and sale of products.

6. This Agreement-Contract is for a term of one (1) year from the date indicated herein and will be automatically renewed for a like period, unless thirty (30) day written notice is given by either party to terminate service.

7. Commission on monthly sales will be paid by the Company to the Customer at the following rate: . . .

The rate provided in each of the agreements was "30% of Gross Receipts to $300.00 monthly(,) 35% over ($)300.00," except for the agreement with Pizza of Gaithersburg, Inc., which called for "40% of Gross Receipts."

We cannot regard the agreements as contracts for personal services. They were either a license or concession granted Virginia by the appellees, or a lease of a portion of the appellees' premises, with Virginia agreeing to pay a percentage of gross sales as a license or concession fee or as rent, and were assignable by Virginia unless they imposed on Virginia duties of a personal or unique character which could not be delegated.

The appellees earnestly argue that they had dealt with Macke before and had chosen Virginia because they preferred the way it conducted its business. Specifically, they say that service was more personalized, since the president of Virginia kept the machines in working order, that commissions were paid in cash, and that Virginia permitted them to keep keys to the machines so that minor adjustments could be made when needed. Even if we assume all this to be true, the agreements with Virginia were silent as to the details of the working arrangements and contained only a provision requiring Virginia to "install . . . the above listed equipment and . . . maintain the equipment in good operating order and stocked with merchandise." We think the Supreme Court of California put the problem of personal service in proper focus a century ago when it upheld the assignment of a contract to grade a San Francisco street:

> All painters do not paint portraits like Sir Joshua Reynolds, nor landscapes like Claude Lorraine, nor do all writers write dramas like Shakespeare or fiction like Dickens. Rare genius and extraordinary skill are not transferable, and contracts

> for their employment are therefore personal, and cannot be assigned. But rare genius and extraordinary skill are not indispensable to the workmanlike digging down of a sand hill or the filling up of a depression to a given level, or the construction of brick sewers with manholes and covers, and contracts for such work are not personal, and may be assigned.

Taylor v. Palmer, 31 Cal. 240 at 247-248 (1866). Moreover, the difference between the service the Pizza Shops happened to be getting from Virginia and what they expected to get from Macke did not mount up to such a material change in the performance of obligations under the agreements as would justify the appellees' refusal to recognize the assignment.

In support of the proposition that the agreements were for personal services, and not assignable, the Pizza Shops rely on three Supreme Court cases, *Burck v. Taylor*, 152 U.S. 634 (1894); *Delaware County Comm'r v. Diebold Safe & Lock Co.*, 133 U.S. 473 (1890); and *Arkansas Valley Smelting Co. v. Belden Mining Co.*, 127 U.S. 379 (1888), all of which were cited with approval by our predecessors in *Tarr v. Veasey*, 93 A. 428 (1915). We find none of these cases persuasive. *Burck* held that the contractor for the state capitol in Texas, who was prohibited by the terms of his contract from assigning it without the state's consent, could not make a valid assignment of his right to receive three-fourths of the proceeds. In *Delaware County*, Diebold Safe and Lock, which was a subcontractor in the construction of a county jail, was barred from recovering from the county commissioners for its work on the theory that there had been a partial assignment of the construction contract by the prime contractor, which had never been assented to by the commissioners. This result must be limited to the facts: i.e., to the subcontractor's right to recover under the assignment, and not to the contractor's right to delegate. *Arkansas Valley*, which held invalid an attempt to assign a contract for the purchase of ore, is clearly distinguishable, because of a contract provision which stipulated that payment for the ore was to be made after delivery, based on an assay to be made by the individual purchaser named in the contract. The court concluded that this was a confidence imposed in the individual purchaser's credit and responsibility and that his rights under the contract could not be transferred to another. *Tarr v. Veasey* involved a situation where duties were delegated to one person and rights assigned to another and our predecessors held the rights not to be assignable, because of the parties' intention that duties and rights were interdependent.

We find more apposite two cases which were not cited by the parties. In *The British Waggon Co. & The Parkgate Waggon Co. v. Lea & Co.*, 5 Q.B.D. 149 (1880), Parkgate Waggon Company, a lessor of railway cars, who had agreed to keep the cars "in good and substantial repair and working order," made an assignment of the contract to British Waggon Company. When British Waggon Company sued for rent, the lessee contended that the assignment had terminated the lease. The court held that the lessee remained bound under the lease, because there was no provision making performance of the lessor's duty to keep in repair a duty personal to it or its employees.

Except for the fact that the result has been roundly criticized, the Pizza Shops might have found some solace in the facts found in *Boston Ice Co. v.*

Potter, 123 Mass. 28 (1877). There, Potter, who had dealt with the Boston Ice Company, and found its service unsatisfactory, transferred his business to Citizens' Ice Company. Later, Citizens' sold out to Boston, unbeknown to Potter, and Potter was served by Boston for a full year. When Boston attempted to collect its ice bill, the Massachusetts court sustained Potter's demurrer on the ground that there was no privity of contract, since Potter had a right to choose with whom he would deal and could not have another supplier thrust upon him. Modern authorities do not support this result, and hold that, absent provision to the contrary, a duty may be delegated, as distinguished from a right which can be assigned, and that the promisee cannot rescind, if the quality of the performance remains materially the same.

Restatement, Contracts § 160(3) (1932) reads, in part:

> Performance or offer of performance by a person delegated has the same legal effect as performance or offer of performance by the person named in the contract, unless,
>
> (a) performance by the person delegated varies or would vary materially from performance by the person named in the contract as the one to perform, and there has been no . . . assent to the delegation. . . .

In cases involving the sale of goods, the Restatement rule respecting delegation of duties has been amplified by Uniform Commercial Code § 2-210(5), which permits a promisee to demand assurances from the party to whom duties have been delegated.

As we see it, the delegation of duty by Virginia to Macke was entirely permissible under the terms of the agreements. In so holding, we do not put ourselves at odds with *Eastern Advertising Co. v. McGaw, supra,* 42 A. 923, for in that case, the agreement with the agency contained a provision that "the advertising cards were to be subject to the approval of Eastern Advertising Company as to style and contents," which the court found to import that reliance was being placed on the agency's skill, judgment and taste.

Having concluded that the Pizza Shops had no right to rescind the agreements, we turn to the question of damages.

The assessment of damages for loss of profits following the breach of an executory contract has been a relatively recent development.

Under the concept of "foreseeability" enunciated by *Hadley v. Baxendale,* 156 Eng. Rep. 145 (1854), which was followed in *United States Telegraph Co. v. Gildersleve,* 29 Md. 232 (1868), in order to recover unrealized profits a plaintiff had to show that the breach of contract caused the loss and that the loss of profits was in the contemplation of the parties and the probable result of a breach. Some of the early American cases superimposed a test of certainty on the concept of foreseeability. . . .

In the last hundred years, however, courts have modified the rule that anticipated profits were not an element of damages because of their inherent uncertainty, and have turned from the requirement of "certainty" to a more flexible test of "reasonable certainty." See Restatement, Contracts § 311 (1932).

This Court, speaking through Judge Horney in *M & R Contractors & Builders, Inc. v. Michael*, 138 A.2d 350, said:

> Courts have modified the "certainty" rule into a more flexible one of "reasonable certainty." In such instances, recovery may often be based on opinion evidence, in the legal sense of that term, from which liberal inferences may be drawn. Generally, proof of actual or even estimated costs is all that is required with certainty.
>
> Some of the modifications which have been aimed at avoiding the harsh requirements of the "certainty" rule include: (a) if the fact of damage is proven with certainty, the extent or the amount thereof may be left to reasonable inference; (b) where a defendant's wrong has caused the difficulty of proving damage, he cannot complain of the resulting uncertainty; (c) mere difficulty in ascertaining the amount of damage is not fatal; (d) mathematical precision in fixing the exact amount is not required; (e) it is sufficient if the best evidence of the damage which is available is produced; and (f) the plaintiff is entitled to recover the value of his contract as measured by the value of his profits. McCormick, Damages, Sec. 27 (1935), at 348-349, 138 A.2d at 354.

To recover direct profits in a case such as this, the measure of damages is the difference between what it would have cost Macke to perform and what it would have received had the Pizza Shops not repudiated.

We can understand why the court below was "not satisfied that the claim for damages (was) shown with reasonable certainty, since it (was) based upon conjecture." Macke attempted to prove damages by the testimony of two witnesses. The first was Arnold Harlem, the general manager of Macke's Chesapeake area, in which the Pizza Shops were located. His testimony related to gross sales figures for the cold drink vending machines at the six locations for the month of January, 1968, when the machines were still under Macke's control. He produced a computer print-out (which was not introduced in evidence) in support of his statement that Macke's cost of goods for January 1968 was 23.62% of gross sales. From this testimony, it might have been possible to extrapolate what Macke's profit would have been on five of the machines for the 11 months commencing 1 February 1968 and ending 31 December 1968 and on one of the machines for the period February 1968 to 24 July 1968 when the Virginia agreements respectively ended, assuming that cold drink sales in the Pizza Shops remained uniform during the year, as Mr. Harlem said they did, and that cost of goods did not vary.

No such extrapolation was introduced in evidence, but one had been supplied in answer to an interrogatory. For some unaccountable reason, it projected sales and profits for 10 months only, included the Gaithersburg location for five months, which, for reasons to be developed, should not have been included at all, and failed to reflect that five of the agreements provided for an increase in commission rates from 30% to 35% on gross receipts in excess of $300 in any month.

Macke then called Thomas S. Sherwood, one of the individual defendants, as an adverse witness. He testified, without objection, to the commissions received by five of the Pizza Shops during the calendar year 1967, and by the sixth shop, at Gaithersburg, for the last five months of that year. Based on this testimony, Macke's counsel prepared, and submitted to the court, a "Memorandum of Damages Claimed," an extrapolation of 1967 figures intended to show profits lost in 1968.

The fact that the projection from Harlem's testimony showed lost profits of $5,286.80, and the extrapolation from Sherwood's testimony showed lost profits of $9,047.00 was surely enough to give the lower court pause. Factually, the situation was not dissimilar from that in *Prescon Corp. v. Savoy Constr. Co.*, supra, 259 Md. 52, at 55, 267 A.2d 222, where the plaintiff attempted to establish a prima facie case of lost profits by having its vice president testify from a computer print-out which was never introduced in evidence. The opinion in *Prescon*, delivered more than six months after the trial of the case before us, was, of course, not available to the trial court. In *Prescon*, we affirmed the judgment as to liability, but remanded the case so that additional evidence could be taken on the question of damages.

There is ample authority for the proposition that loss of profits may be projected from past performance, assuming, of course, that past performance has continued long enough to the best evidence of damage which is available..

We cannot agree with the lower court's conclusion that the claim for damages could not be shown with reasonable certainty because it was based on conjecture. For this reason, we propose to remand the case in order that damages may properly be assessed. On remand, the court may wish to take several factors into consideration. First, it seems clear to us that no damages should be allowed with respect to the repudiation of the agreement covering the vending machine at 16523 North Frederick Road, Gaithersburg. The uncontroverted testimony of the Pizza Shop's manager established that the agreement covering this machine was breached in January, 1968 by Macke's failure to stock and service the machine.

Then, too, the record is deficient as regards Macke's duty to mitigate damages. Harlem's testimony as to what disposition was made of the vending machines removed from the Pizza Shops was vague and inconclusive. It may well be that the machines were placed at other locations prior to the time when the agreements would have expired by their terms, and this, of course, may have to be taken into account in assessing damages, subject, however, to the limitation that gains made by Macke could not have been made, save for the breach.

Finally, it is not an implausible inference that Macke's machines were replaced in the Pizza Shops by comparable machines provided by another concern. If this is the case, a more appropriate measure of damages might be that grounded on the five Pizza Shops' actual experience for the period February through December 1968, rather than one based on extrapolating profits from the results experienced in the year 1967 or in January 1968, particularly in the light of testimony that the seating capacity of one or more of the shops may have been altered in 1967 and the conflicting testimony as to whether cold drink sales remain constant in pizza shops. Authority for the use of a defendant's future earnings as an appropriate method of determining lost profits may be found in *Pace Corp. v. Jackson*, 284 S.W.2d 340 (1955); *Sinclair Refining Co. v. Jenkins Petroleum Process Co.*, 289 U.S. 689 (1933).

The appellees make two other points which can be summarily disposed of. The first is that the agreements were terminable at any time on 30 days' notice. A careful examination of the agreements shows that this was simply not the case, despite the fact that the president of Virginia and the Pizza Shops may have thought so. The second point is that the assignments were invalidated by Virginia's failure to comply with the provisions of the U.C.C. relating to bulk transfers. The short answer to this is that the Pizza Shops were not creditors in the context of their relationships with Virginia, since they had control of the machines and were accountable to Virginia for their contents. Additionally, see U.C.C. § 6-102(3) and Official Comment to this subsection, indicating that the primary thrust of the bulk transfer provisions of the U.C.C. is directed at enterprises whose principal business is the sale of merchandise from stock.

Judgment reversed as to liability; judgment entered for appellant for costs, on appeal and below; case remanded for a new trial on the question of damages.

RELEVANT PROVISIONS

For the *Restatement (Second) of Contracts,* consult §§ 317 and 318. For the UCC, consult § 2-210.

NOTES AND QUESTIONS

1. *What happened?* Who sued whom for what? Procedurally, how did the case get before this court? Factually, what happened between the parties? What arguments did the plaintiff and defendant make? What rule or rules did the court apply? How did the court analyze the dispute between the parties? How did the court decide the case?

2. *Was this case correctly decided?* Do you agree with the result reached in this case? Why or why not? Do you agree with the court's reasoning? Why or why not? How, if at all, would you have written the opinion differently?

3. Delectus personae. What, exactly, is the "*delectus personae* rule," and how is it relevant to resolving this dispute?

4. *Assignment of right or delegation of duty?* Was this case about the validity of the assignment or the validity of the delegation? How can you tell?

5. *Drafting.* What language should have been provided in the contract (by either party) to avoid an assignment of right or delegation of duty?

6. *Policy.* What policy arguments can you think of as to why contracts are generally assignable unless the assignment somehow materially alters a party's rights or duties? What policy arguments can you think of that stand against this principle?

Sally Beauty Co. v. Nexxus Products Co.

United States Court of Appeals, Seventh Circuit
801 F.2d 1001 (1986)

CUDAHY, CIRCUIT JUDGE. Nexxus Products Company ("Nexxus") entered into a contract with Best Barber & Beauty Supply Company, Inc. ("Best"), under which Best would be the exclusive distributor of Nexxus hair care products to barbers and hair stylists throughout most of Texas. When Best was acquired by and merged into Sally Beauty Company, Inc. ("Sally Beauty"), Nexxus cancelled the agreement. Sally Beauty is a wholly-owned subsidiary of Alberto-Culver Company ("Alberto-Culver"), a major manufacturer of hair care products and a competitor of Nexxus'. Sally Beauty claims that Nexxus breached the contract by cancelling; Nexxus asserts by way of defense that the contract was not assignable or, in the alternative, not assignable to Sally Beauty. The district court granted Nexxus' motion for summary judgment, ruling that the contract was one for personal services and therefore not assignable. We affirm on a different theory—that this contract could not be assigned to the wholly-owned subsidiary of a direct competitor under § 2-210 of the Uniform Commercial Code.

I.

Only the basic facts are undisputed and they are as follows. Prior to its merger with Sally Beauty, Best was a Texas corporation in the business of distributing beauty and hair care products to retail stores, barber shops and beauty salons throughout Texas. Between March and July 1979, Mark Reichek, Best's president, negotiated with Stephen Redding, Nexxus' vice-president, over a possible distribution agreement between Best and Nexxus. Nexxus, founded in 1979, is a California corporation that formulates and markets hair care products. Nexxus does not market its products to retail stores, preferring to sell them to independent distributors for resale to barbers and beauticians. On August 2, 1979, Nexxus executed a distributorship agreement with Best, in the form of a July 24, 1979 letter from Reichek, for Best, to Redding, for Nexxus:

> Dear Steve:
>
> It was a pleasure meeting with you and discussing the distribution of Nexus Products. The line is very exciting and we feel we can do a substantial job with it—especially as the exclusive distributor in Texas (except El Paso).
>
> If I understand the pricing structure correctly, we would pay $1.50 for an item that retails for $5.00 (less 50%, less 40% off retail), and Nexus will pay the freight charges regardless of order size. This approach to pricing will enable us to price the items in the line in such a way that they will be attractive and profitable to the salons.
>
> Your offer of assistance in promoting the line seems to be designed to simplify the introduction of Nexus Products into the Texas market. It indicates a sincere desire on your part to assist your distributors. By your agreeing to underwrite the cost of training and maintaining a qualified technician in our territory, we should be able to introduce the line from a position of strength. I am sure you will let us know at least 90 days in advance should you want to change

> this arrangement.
>
> By offering to provide us with the support necessary to conduct an annual seminar (i.e., mailers, guest artists) at your expense, we should be able to reinforce our position with Nexus users and introduce the product line to new customers in a professional manner.
>
> To satisfy your requirement of assured payment for merchandise received, each of our purchase orders will be accompanied by a Letter of Credit that will become negotiable when we receive the merchandise. I am sure you will agree that this arrangement is fairest for everybody concerned.
>
> While we feel confident that we can do an outstanding job with the Nexus line and that the volume we generate will adequately compensate you for your continued support, it is usually best to have an understanding should we no longer be distributing Nexus Products—either by our desire or your request. Based on our discussions, cancellation or termination of Best Barber & Beauty Supply Co., Inc. as a distributor can only take place on the anniversary date of our original appointment as a distributor—and then only with 120 days prior notice. If Nexus terminates us, Nexus will buy back all of our inventory at cost and will pay the freight charges on the returned merchandise.
>
> Steve, we feel that the Nexus line is exciting and very promotable. With the program outlined in this letter, we feel it can be mutually profitable and look forward to a long and successful business relationship. If you agree that this letter contains the details of our understanding regarding the distribution of Nexus Products, please sign the acknowledgment below and return one copy of this letter to me.
>
> Very truly yours,
> /s/ Mark E. Reichek
> President
> Acknowledged /s/ Stephen Redding Date 8/2/79.

Appellant's Appendix at 2-3.

In July 1981 Sally Beauty acquired Best in a stock purchase transaction and Best was merged into Sally Beauty, which succeeded to Best's rights and interests in all of Best's contracts. Sally Beauty, a Delaware corporation with its principal place of business in Texas, is a wholly-owned subsidiary of Alberto-Culver. Sally Beauty, like Best, is a distributor of hair care and beauty products to retail stores and hair styling salons. Alberto-Culver is a major manufacturer of hair care products and, thus, is a direct competitor of Nexxus in the hair care market.

Shortly after the merger, Redding met with Michael Renzulli, president of Sally Beauty, to discuss the Nexxus distribution agreement. After the meeting, Redding wrote Renzulli a letter stating that Nexxus would not allow Sally Beauty, a wholly-owned subsidiary of a direct competitor, to distribute Nexxus products:

> As we discussed in New Orleans, we have great reservations about allowing our NEXXUS Products to be distributed by a company which is, in essence, a direct competitor. We appreciate your argument of autonomy for your business, but the fact remains that you are totally owned by Alberto-Culver.

> Since we see no way of justifying this conflict, we cannot allow our products to be distributed by Sally Beauty Company.

Appellant's Appendix at 475.

In August 1983 Sally Beauty commenced this action by filing a complaint in the Northern District of Illinois, claiming that Nexxus had violated the federal antitrust laws and breached the distribution agreement. In August 1984 Nexxus filed a counterclaim alleging violations of the Lanham Act, the Racketeer Influenced and Corrupt Organizations Act ("RICO") and the unfair competition laws of North Carolina, Tennessee and unidentified "other states." On October 22, 1984 Sally Beauty filed a motion to dismiss the counterclaims arising under RICO and "other states' law." Nexxus filed a motion for summary judgment on the breach of contract claim the next day.

The district court ruled on these motions in a Memorandum Opinion and Order dated January 31, 1985. It granted Sally's motion to dismiss the two counterclaims and also granted Nexxus' motion for summary judgment. In May 1985 it dismissed the remaining claims and counterclaims (pursuant to stipulation by the parties) and directed the entry of an appealable final judgment on the breach of contract claim.

II.

Sally Beauty's breach of contract claim alleges that by acquiring Best, Sally Beauty succeeded to all of Best's rights and obligations under the distribution agreement. It further alleges that Nexxus breached the agreement by failing to give Sally Beauty 120 days' notice prior to terminating the agreement and by terminating it on other than an anniversary date of its formation. Nexxus, in its motion for summary judgment, argued that the distribution agreement it entered into with Best was a contract for personal services, based upon a relationship of personal trust and confidence between Reichek and the Redding family. As such, the contract could not be assigned to Sally without Nexxus' consent.

In opposing this motion Sally Beauty argued that the contract was freely assignable because (1) it was between two corporations, not two individuals and (2) the character of the performance would not be altered by the substitution of Sally Beauty for Best. It also argued that "the Distribution Agreement is nothing more than a simple, non-exclusive contract for the distribution of goods, the successful performance of which is in no way dependent upon any particular personality, individual skill or confidential relationship."

In ruling on this motion, the district court framed the issue before it as "whether the contract at issue here between Best and Nexxus was of a personal nature such that it was not assignable without Nexxus' consent." It ruled:

> The court is convinced, based upon the nature of the contract and the circumstances surrounding its formation, that the contract at issue here was of such a nature that it was not assignable without Nexxus's consent. First, the very nature of the contract itself suggests its personal character. A distribution agreement is a contract whereby a manufacturer gives another party the right to distribute its products. It is clearly a contract for the performance of a service. In the court's

> view, the mere selection by a manufacturer of a party to distribute its goods presupposes a reliance and confidence by the manufacturer on the integrity and abilities of the other party. . . . In addition, in this case the circumstances surrounding the contract's formation support the conclusion that the agreement was not simply an ordinary commercial contract but was one which was based upon a relationship of personal trust and confidence between the parties. Specifically, Stephen Redding, Nexxus's vice-president, travelled to Texas and met with Best's president personally for several days before making the decision to award the Texas distributorship to Best. Best itself had been in the hair care business for 40 years and its president Mark Reichek had extensive experience in the industry. It is reasonable to conclude that Stephen Redding and Nexxus would want its distributor to be experienced and knowledgeable in the hair care field and that the selection of Best was based upon personal factors such as these.

The district court also rejected the contention that the character of performance would not be altered by a substitution of Sally Beauty for Best: "Unlike Best, Sally Beauty is a subsidiary of one of Nexxus' direct competitors. This is a significant distinction and in the court's view, it raises serious questions regarding Sally Beauty's ability to perform the distribution agreement in the same manner as Best."

We cannot affirm this summary judgment on the grounds relied on by the district court. Under Fed. R. Civ. P. 56(c) summary judgment may be granted only where there is no genuine issue as to any material fact and the moving party is entitled to judgment as a matter of law. The burden on the movant is stringent: "all doubts as to the existence of material fact must be resolved against the movant." *Moore v. Marketplace Restaurant, Inc.,* 754 F.2d 1336, 1339 (7th Cir. 1985). Nexxus did not meet its burden on the question of the parties' reasons for entering into this agreement. Although it might be "reasonable to conclude" that Best and Nexxus had based their agreement on "a relationship of personal trust and confidence," and that Reichek's participation was considered essential to Best's performance, this is a finding of fact. Since the parties submitted conflicting affidavits on this question,[3] the district court

3. Reichek stated the following in an affidavit submitted in support of Sally Beauty's Memorandum in Opposition to Nexxus' Motion for Summary Judgment:

> At no time prior to the execution of the Distribution Agreement did Steve Redding tell me that he was relying upon my personal peculiar tastes and ability in making his decision to award a Nexxus distributorship to Best. Moreover, I never understood that Steve Redding was relying upon my skill and ability in particular in choosing Best as a distributor.
>
> I never considered the Distribution Agreement to be a personal service contract between me and Nexxus or Stephen Redding. I always considered the Distribution Agreement to be between Best and Nexxus as expressly provided in the Distribution Agreement which was written by my brother and me. At all times I conducted business with Nexxus on behalf of Best and not on my own behalf. In that connection, when I sent correspondence to Nexxus, I invariably signed it as president of Best.
>
> Neither Stephen Redding nor any other Nexxus employee ever told me that Nexxus was relying on my personal financial integrity in executing the Distribution Agreement or in shipping Nexxus products to Best. . . .

Affidavit of Mark Reichek, ¶¶ 19-21, Appellant's Appendix at 189-190.

erred in relying on Nexxus' view as representing undisputed fact in ruling on this summary judgment motion.

We may affirm this summary judgment, however, on a different ground if it finds support in the record. Sally Beauty contends that the distribution agreement is freely assignable because it is governed by the provisions of the Uniform Commercial Code (the "UCC" or the "Code"), as adopted in Texas. We agree with Sally that the provisions of the UCC govern this contract and for that reason hold that the assignment of the contract by Best to Sally Beauty was barred by the UCC rules on delegation of performance, UCC § 2-210(1).

III.

The UCC codifies the law of contracts applicable to "transactions in goods." UCC § 2-102. Texas applies the "dominant factor" test to determine whether the UCC applies to a given contract or transaction: was the essence of or dominant factor in the formation of the contract the provision of goods or services? No Texas case addresses whether a distribution agreement is a contract for the sale of goods, but the rule in the majority of jurisdictions is that distributorships (both exclusive and non-exclusive) are to be treated as sale of goods contracts under the UCC.

Several of these courts note that "a distributorship agreement is more involved than a typical sales contract," *Quality Performance Lines,* 609 P.2d at 1342, but apply the UCC nonetheless because the sales aspect in such a contract is predominant. This is true of the contract at issue here (as embodied in the July 24, 1979 letter from Reichek to Redding). Most of the agreed-to terms deal with Nexxus' sale of its hair care products to Best. We are confident that a Texas court would find the sales aspect of this contract dominant and apply the majority rule that such a distributorship is a contract for "goods" under the UCC.

IV.

The fact that this contract is considered a contract for the sale of goods and not for the provision of a service does not, as Sally Beauty suggests, mean that it is freely assignable in all circumstances. The delegation of performance under a sales contract (whether in conjunction with an assignment of rights, as here, or not) is governed by UCC § 2-210(1). The UCC recognizes that in many cases an obligor will find it convenient or even necessary to relieve himself of the duty of performance under a contract, *see* Official Comment 1, UCC § 2-210 ("[T]his section recognizes both delegation of performance and assignability as normal and permissible incidents of a contract for the sale of goods."). The Code therefore sanctions delegation except where the delegated performance would be unsatisfactory to the obligee: "A party may perform his duty through a delegate unless otherwise agreed to or unless the other party has a substantial interest in having his original promisor perform or control the acts required by the contract." UCC § 2-210(1). Consideration is given to balancing the policies of free alienability of commercial contracts and protecting the obligee from having to accept a bargain he did not contract for.

We are concerned here with the delegation of Best's duty of performance under the distribution agreement, as Nexxus terminated the agreement because it did not wish to accept Sally Beauty's substituted performance.[6] Only one Texas case has construed § 2-210 in the context of a party's delegation of performance under an executory contract. In *McKinnie v. Milford,* 597 S.W.2d 953 (Tex. Civ. App. 1980), the court held that nothing in the Texas Business and Commercial Code prevented the seller of a horse from delegating to the buyer a pre-existing contractual duty to make the horse available to a third party for breeding. "[I]t is clear that Milford [the third party] had no particular interest in not allowing Stewart [the seller] to delegate the duties required by the contract. Milford was only interested in getting his two breedings per year, and such performance could only be obtained from McKinnie [the buyer] after he bought the horse from Stewart." *Id.* at 957. In *McKinnie,* the Texas court recognized and applied the UCC rule that bars delegation of duties if there is some reason why the non-assigning party would find performance by a delegate a substantially different thing than what he had bargained for.

In the exclusive distribution agreement before us, Nexxus had contracted for Best's "best efforts" in promoting the sale of Nexxus products in Texas. UCC § 2-306(2) states that

> [a] lawful agreement by either buyer or seller for exclusive dealing in the kind of goods concerned imposes unless otherwise agreed an obligation by the seller to use best efforts to supply the goods and by the buyer to use best efforts to promote their sale.

This implied promise on Best's part was the consideration for Nexxus' promise to refrain from supplying any other distributors within Best's exclusive area. *See* Official Comment 5, UCC § 2-306. It was this contractual undertaking which Nexxus refused to see performed by Sally.

In ruling on Nexxus' motion for summary judgment, the district court noted: "Unlike Best, Sally Beauty is a subsidiary of one of Nexxus' direct competitors. This is a significant distinction and in the court's view, it raises serious questions regarding Sally Beauty's ability to perform the distribution agreement in the same manner as Best." In *Berliner Foods Corp. v. Pillsbury Co.,* 633 F. Supp. 557 (D. Md. 1986), the court stated the same reservation more strongly on similar facts. Berliner was an exclusive distributor of Haagen-Dazs ice cream when it was sold to Breyer's, manufacturer of a competing ice cream line. Pillsbury Co., manufacturer of Haagen-Dazs, terminated the distributorship and Berliner sued. The court noted, while weighing the factors for and against a preliminary

6. If this contract is assignable, Sally Beauty would also, of course, succeed to Best's rights under the distribution agreement. But the fact situation before us must be distinguished from the assignment of contract rights that are no longer executory (e.g., the right to damages for breach or the right to payment of an account), which is considered in UCC section 2-210(2), and in several of the authorities relied on by appellants. The policies underlying these two situations are different and, generally, the UCC favors assignment more strongly in the latter. See UCC § 2-210(2) (non-executory rights assignable even if agreement states otherwise).

injunction, that "it defies common sense to require a manufacturer to leave the distribution of its products to a distributor under the control of a competitor or potential competitor." *Id.* at 559-60. We agree with these assessments and hold that Sally Beauty's position as a wholly-owned subsidiary of Alberto-Culver is sufficient to bar the delegation of Best's duties under the agreement.

We do not believe that our holding will work the mischief with our national economy that the appellants predict. We hold merely that the duty of performance under an exclusive distributorship may not be delegated to a competitor in the market place—or the wholly-owned subsidiary of a competitor—without the obligee's consent. We believe that such a rule is consonant with the policies behind § 2-210, which is concerned with preserving the bargain the obligee has struck. Nexxus should not be required to accept the "best efforts" of Sally Beauty when those efforts are subject to the control of Alberto-Culver. It is entirely reasonable that Nexxus should conclude that this performance would be a different thing than what it had bargained for. At oral argument, Sally Beauty argued that the case should go to trial to allow it to demonstrate that it could and would perform the contract as impartially as Best. It stressed that Sally Beauty is a "multi-line" distributor, which means that it distributes many brands and is not just a conduit for Alberto-Culver products. But we do not think that this creates a material question of fact in this case. When performance of personal services is delegated, the trier merely determines that it is a personal services contract. If so, the duty is *per se* nondelegable. There is no inquiry into whether the delegate is as skilled or worthy of trust and confidence as the original obligor: the delegate was not bargained for and the obligee need not consent to the substitution. And so here: it is undisputed that Sally Beauty is wholly owned by Alberto-Culver, which means that Sally Beauty's "impartial" sales policy is at least acquiesced in by Alberto-Culver—but could change whenever Alberto-Culver's needs changed. Sally Beauty may be totally sincere in its belief that it can operate "impartially" as a distributor, but who can guarantee the outcome when there is a clear choice between the demands of the parent-manufacturer, Alberto-Culver, and the competing needs of Nexxus? The risk of an unfavorable outcome is not one which the law can force Nexxus to take. Nexxus has a substantial interest in not seeing this contract performed by Sally Beauty, which is sufficient to bar the delegation under § 2-210. Because Nexxus should not be forced to accept performance of the distributorship agreement by Sally, we hold that the contract was not assignable without Nexxus' consent.[10]

The judgment of the district court is Affirmed.

POSNER, CIRCUIT JUDGE, **dissenting.** My brethren have decided, with no better foundation than judicial intuition about what businessmen consider reasonable, that the Uniform Commercial Code gives a supplier an absolute right

10. This disposition makes it unnecessary to address Nexxus' argument that Sally Beauty breached the distribution agreement by not giving Nexxus 120 days' notice of the Best-Sally Beauty merger.

to cancel an exclusive-dealing contract if the dealer is acquired, directly or indirectly, by a competitor of the supplier. I interpret the Code differently.

Nexxus makes products for the hair and sells them through distributors to hair salons and barbershops. It gave a contract to Best, cancellable on any anniversary of the contract with 120 days' notice, to be its exclusive distributor in Texas. Two years later Best was acquired by and merged into Sally Beauty, a distributor of beauty supplies and wholly owned subsidiary of Alberto-Culver. Alberto-Culver makes "hair care" products, too, though they mostly are cheaper than Nexxus's, and are sold to the public primarily through grocery stores and drugstores. My brethren conclude that because there is at least a loose competitive relationship between Nexxus and Alberto-Culver, Sally Beauty cannot—as a matter of law, cannot, for there has been no trial on the issue—provide its "best efforts" in the distribution of Nexxus products. Since a commitment to provide best efforts is read into every exclusive-dealing contract by § 2-306(2) of the Uniform Commercial Code, the contract has been broken and Nexxus can repudiate it. Alternatively, Nexxus had "a substantial interest in having his original promisor perform or control the acts required by the contract," and therefore the delegation of the promisor's (Best's) duties to Sally Beauty was improper under § 2-210(1).

My brethren's conclusion that these provisions of the Uniform Commercial Code entitled Nexxus to cancel the contract does not leap out from the language of the provisions or of the contract; so one would expect, but does not find, a canvass of the relevant case law. My brethren cite only one case in support of their conclusion: a district court case from Maryland, *Berliner Foods Corp. v. Pillsbury Co.*, 633 F. Supp. 557 (D. Md. 1986), which, since it treated the contract at issue there as one for personal services, *id.* at 559 (a characterization my brethren properly reject for the contract between Nexxus and Best), is not helpful. *Berliner* is the latest in a long line of cases that make the propriety of delegating the performance of a distribution contract depend on whether or not the contract calls for the distributor's personal (unique, irreplaceable, distinctive, and therefore nondelegable) services. By rejecting that characterization here, my brethren have sawn off the only limb on which they might have sat comfortably.

A slightly better case for them (though not cited by them) is *Wetherell Bros. Co. v. United States Steel Co.*, 200 F.2d 761, 763 (1st Cir. 1952), which held that an exclusive sales agent's duties were nondelegable. The agent, a Massachusetts corporation, had agreed to use its "best endeavors" to promote the sale of the defendant's steel in the New England area. The corporation was liquidated and its assets sold to a Pennsylvania corporation that was not shown to be qualified to conduct business in Massachusetts, the largest state in New England. On these facts the defendant was entitled to treat the liquidation and sale as a termination of the contract. The *Wetherell* decision has been understood to depend on its facts. The facts of the present case are critically different. So far as appears, the same people who distributed Nexxus's products for Best (except for Best's president) continued to do so for Sally Beauty. Best was acquired, and continues, as a going concern; the corporation was dissolved, but the business wasn't. Whether there was a delegation of performance in any sense may be doubted. The general rule is that a change of corporate form—including a merger—does not in and of itself affect contractual rights and obligations.

The fact that Best's president has quit cannot be decisive on the issue whether the merger resulted in a delegation of performance. The contract between Nexxus and Best was not a personal-services contract conditioned on a particular individual's remaining with Best. If Best had not been acquired, but its president had left anyway, as of course he might have done, Nexxus could not have repudiated the contract.

No case adopts the per se rule that my brethren announce. The cases ask whether, as a matter of fact, a change in business form is likely to impair performance of the contract. *Green v. Camlin,* 92 S.E.2d 125, 127 (1956), has some broad language which my brethren might have cited; but since the contract in that case forbade assignment it is not an apt precedent.

My brethren find this a simple case—as simple (it seems) as if a lawyer had undertaken to represent the party opposing his client. But notions of conflict of interest are not the same in law and in business, and judges can go astray by assuming that the legal-services industry is the pattern for the entire economy. The lawyerization of America has not reached that point. Sally Beauty, though a wholly owned subsidiary of Alberto-Culver, distributes "hair care" supplies made by many different companies, which so far as appears compete with Alberto-Culver as vigorously as Nexxus does. Steel companies both make fabricated steel and sell raw steel to competing fabricators. General Motors sells cars manufactured by a competitor, Isuzu. What in law would be considered a fatal conflict of interest is in business a commonplace and legitimate practice. The lawyer is a fiduciary of his client; Best was not a fiduciary of Nexxus.

Selling your competitor's products, or supplying inputs to your competitor, sometimes creates problems under antitrust or regulatory law—but only when the supplier or distributor has monopoly or market power and uses it to restrict a competitor's access to an essential input or to the market for the competitor's output. . . . There is no suggestion that Alberto-Culver has a monopoly of "hair care" products or Sally Beauty a monopoly of distributing such products, or that Alberto-Culver would ever have ordered Sally Beauty to stop carrying Nexxus products. Far from complaining about being squeezed out of the market by the acquisition, Nexxus is complaining in effect about Sally Beauty's refusal to boycott it!

How likely is it that the acquisition of Best could hurt Nexxus? Not very. Suppose Alberto-Culver had ordered Sally Beauty to go slow in pushing Nexxus products, in the hope that sales of Alberto-Culver "hair care" products would rise. Even if they did, since the market is competitive Alberto-Culver would not reap monopoly profits. Moreover, what guarantee has Alberto-Culver that consumers would be diverted from Nexxus to it, rather than to products closer in price and quality to Nexxus products? In any event, any trivial gain in profits to Alberto-Culver would be offset by the loss of goodwill to Sally Beauty; and a cost to Sally Beauty is a cost to Alberto-Culver, its parent. Remember that Sally Beauty carries beauty supplies made by other competitors of Alberto-Culver; Best alone carries "hair care" products manufactured by Revlon,

Clairol, Bristol-Myers, and L'Oreal, as well as Alberto-Culver. Will these powerful competitors continue to distribute their products through Sally Beauty if Sally Beauty displays favoritism for Alberto-Culver products? Would not such a display be a commercial disaster for Sally Beauty, and hence for its parent, Alberto-Culver? Is it really credible that Alberto-Culver would sacrifice Sally Beauty in a vain effort to monopolize the "hair care" market, in violation of section 2 of the Sherman Act? Is not the ratio of the profits that Alberto-Culver obtains from Sally Beauty to the profits it obtains from the manufacture of "hair care" products at least a relevant consideration?

Another relevant consideration is that the contract between Nexxus and Best was for a short term. Could Alberto-Culver destroy Nexxus by failing to push its products with maximum vigor in Texas for a year? In the unlikely event that it could and did, it would be liable in damages to Nexxus for breach of the implied best-efforts term of the distribution contract. Finally, it is obvious that Sally Beauty does not have a bottleneck position in the distribution of "hair care" products, such that by refusing to promote Nexxus products vigorously it could stifle the distribution of those products in Texas; for Nexxus has found alternative distribution that it prefers—otherwise it wouldn't have repudiated the contract with Best when Best was acquired by Sally Beauty.

Not all businessmen are consistent and successful profit maximizers, so the probability that Alberto-Culver would instruct Sally Beauty to cease to push Nexxus products vigorously in Texas cannot be reckoned at zero. On this record, however, it is slight. And there is no principle of law that if something happens that trivially reduces the probability that a dealer will use his best efforts, the supplier can cancel the contract. Suppose there had been no merger, but the only child of Best's president had gone to work for Alberto-Culver as a chemist. Could Nexxus have canceled the contract, fearing that Best (perhaps unconsciously) would favor Alberto-Culver products over Nexxus products? That would be an absurd ground for cancellation, and so is Nexxus's actual ground. At most, so far as the record shows, Nexxus may have had grounds for "insecurity" regarding the performance by Sally Beauty of its obligation to use its best efforts to promote Nexxus products, but if so its remedy was not to cancel the contract but to demand assurances of due performance. See UCC § 2-609; Official Comment 5 to § 2-306. No such demand was made. An anticipatory repudiation by conduct requires conduct that makes the repudiating party unable to perform. Farnsworth, *Contracts* 636 (1982). The merger did not do this. At least there is no evidence it did. The judgment should be reversed and the case remanded for a trial on whether the merger so altered the conditions of performance that Nexxus is entitled to declare the contract broken.

RELEVANT PROVISIONS

For the *Restatement (Second) of Contracts,* consult § 328. For the UCC, consult §§ 2-210 and 2-306(b).

NOTES AND QUESTIONS

1. *What happened?* Who sued whom for what? Procedurally, how did the case get before this court? Factually, what happened between the parties? What arguments did the plaintiff and defendant make? What rule or rules did the court apply? How did the court analyze the dispute between the parties? How did the court decide the case?

2. *Was this case correctly decided?* Do you agree with the result reached in this case? Why or why not? Are you more inclined to agree with the majority or the dissent in this case? Why? How, if at all, would you have written the opinion differently?

3. *UCC.* Why did the court apply Article 2 of the UCC? Was this really a contract for the sale of goods?

4. *Drafting.* What language would you have added to the original contract to prevent it from being assigned in this case?

5. *Application.* How would you apply the principles you learned in this chapter to resolve the following dispute?

PROBLEM: STANDARDS AT WAL-MART

Plaintiffs, who are employees of Wal-Mart's foreign suppliers in countries including China, Bangladesh, Indonesia, Swaziland, and Nicaragua, allege the following facts:

In 1992, Wal-Mart developed a code of conduct for its suppliers, entitled "Standards for Suppliers" ("Standards"). These Standards were incorporated into its supply contracts with foreign suppliers. The Standards require foreign suppliers to adhere to local laws and local industry standards regarding working conditions like pay, hours, forced labor, child labor, and discrimination. The Standards also include a paragraph entitled "RIGHT OF INSPECTION":

> To further assure proper implementation of and compliance with the standards set forth herein, Wal-Mart or a third party designated by Wal-Mart will undertake affirmative measures, such as on-site inspection of production facilities, to implement and monitor said standards. Any supplier which fails or refuses to comply with these standards or does not allow inspection of production facilities is subject to (1) immediate cancellation of any and all outstanding orders, (2) have any of its shipments refused or returned, , and (3) may have its business relationship with Wal-Mart terminated.

Thus, each supplier must acknowledge that its failure to comply with the Standards could result in cancellation of orders and termination of its business relationship with Wal-Mart.

Wal-Mart represents to the public that it improves the lives of its suppliers' employees and that it does not condone any violation of the Standards. However, Plaintiffs allege that Wal-Mart does not adequately monitor its suppliers and that

Wal-Mart knows its suppliers often violate the Standards. Specifically, Plaintiffs claim that only eight percent of audits were unannounced, and that workers are often coached on how to respond to auditors. Additionally, Plaintiffs allege that Wal-Mart's inspectors were pressured to produce positive reports of factories that were not in compliance with the Standards. Finally, Plaintiffs allege that the short deadlines and low prices in Wal-Mart's supply contracts force suppliers to violate the Standards to satisfy the terms of the contracts.

Plaintiffs filed a class action against Wal-Mart arguing that they are third-party beneficiaries of the Standards contained in Wal-Mart's supply contracts, and that Wal-Mart both (a) negligently breached a duty to monitor the suppliers and protect Plaintiffs from the suppliers' working conditions, and (b) was unjustly enriched by Plaintiffs' mistreatment.

How do you think the court should rule?

C. ASSUMPTION AND NOVATION

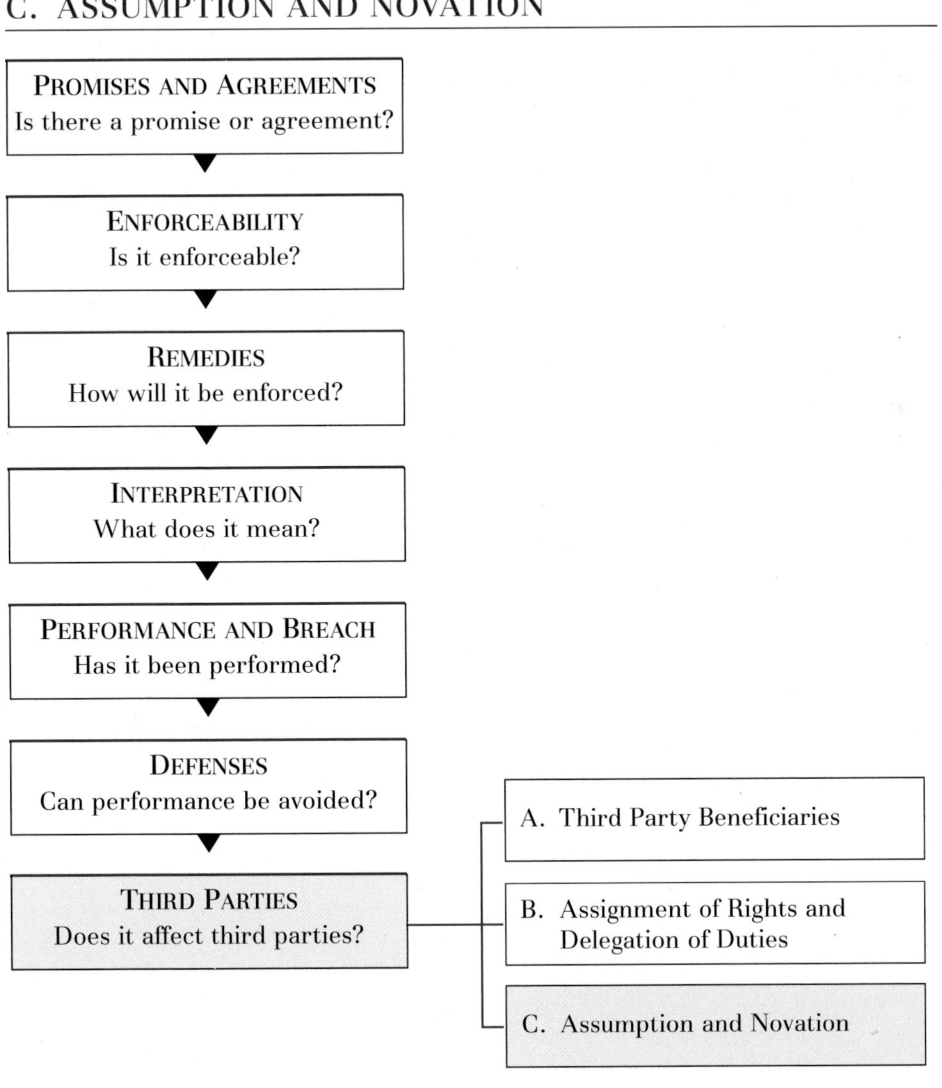

DOCTRINAL OVERVIEW: ASSUMPTION AND NOVATION*

We have seen that an effective delegation empowers the delegate (C) to tender on behalf of the delegating party (B) the performance due the obligee (A) but leaves the delegating party liable to the obligee in the event of the delegates nonperformance. We now consider whether the delegate is also liable in the event of its nonperformance.

The mere delegation of a performance imposes no duty on the delegate to perform. If the delegate performs the duty, the duty is discharged. If the delegate does not perform the duty, the duty is not discharged, but any claim of the obligee for breach is against the delegating party and not against the delegate. The delegate is under no duty to perform unless it has undertaken to do so.

Often, as part of the transaction delegating performance, the delegate expressly promises the delegating party to perform that party's duties. The delegate is then said to have *assumed* the duties of the delegating party. It follows from the delegate's assumption that the delegate is under a duty to the delegating party, and it usually follows that the delegate is also under a duty to the obligee, as an intended beneficiary of the assumption agreement. But though the delegate's assumption makes the delegate liable to the obligee, it does not discharge the duty to the obligee of the delegating party; and if the delegating party repudiates its duty, it is liable to the obligee. Thus, as a result of the assumption, the delegate and the delegating party are now both under a duty to the obligee to render the same performance. But the obligee is entitled to only one performance, and, as between the delegate and the delegating party, it is the delegate that should render the performance because the delegate promised to do so by its assumption. The relationship is thus one of suretyship, in which the delegate is the principal and the delegating party is the surety, and all of the consequences of a suretyship relationship follow. . . .

Although neither an effective delegation by a delegating party nor an assumption by a delegate results in the discharge of the duty of the delegating party, a discharge may result if the obligee consents to it. The transaction usually takes the form of a novation, in which the promise of the delegate (C) to perform the duty of the delegating party (B) is the consideration for the discharge of that duty by the obligee (A). . . . However, more is required for a novation than the mere consent of the obligee to performance by the delegate. . . . [T]o discharge the *duty* of the delegating party[,] . . . assent by the obligee to release the delegating party, in exchange for the new liability of the delegate, is required. Thus, in the example of the sale of a business, the mere consent of the customer (A) to performance by the buyer of the business (C), instead of by the seller (B), will not amount to a novation that will discharge the duty of the seller to the customer; for that the customer must assent to the substitution of the buyer's duty in place of the seller's, thereby discharging the seller's duty. . . .

---

* Excerpted from E. Allan Farnsworth, Contracts § 11.10 (4th ed. 2004).

Rosenberg v. Son, Inc.

Supreme Court of North Dakota
491 N.W.2d 71 (1992)

ERICKSTAD, CHIEF JUSTICE. Harold Rosenberg and Gladys E. Rosenberg (Rosenbergs) appeal two district court decisions granting summary judgment in favor of Son, Inc., and Mary Pratt. We reverse and remand for further proceedings.

On February 8, 1980, Pratt entered into a contract for the sale of a business with the Rosenbergs, agreeing to purchase the Rosenbergs' Dairy Queen located in the City Center Mall in Grand Forks. The terms of the sales contract for the franchise, inventory, and equipment were a purchase price totaling $62,000, a $10,000 down payment, and $52,000 due in quarterly payments at 10 percent interest over a 15-year-period. The sales contract also contained a provision denying the buyer a right to prepayment for the first five years of the contract.

Mary Pratt assigned her rights and delegated her duties under the sales contract to Son, Inc., on October 1, 1982.[1] The assignment agreement contained a "Consent To Assignment" clause which was signed by the Rosenbergs on October 14, 1982.[2] The assignment agreement also included a "save harmless" clause in which Son, Inc., promised to indemnify Pratt.[3] Subsequent to this

---

1. The term "assign" is normally associated with a party's rights under a contract (*i.e.*, getting paid, receiving goods); whereas the term "delegate" is associated with a party's duties under a contract (*i.e.*, making a payment, performing a service). However, it is a common practice to call the assigning of rights and delegating of duties merely an "assignment of contract." This is especially true when language such as "all right, title and interest" is used. This was the exact language contained in the assignment agreement between Pratt and Son, Inc., and also in the assignment agreement between Son, Inc., and Merit, Corporation (to be discussed later):

> An assignment of "the contract" or of "all my rights under the contract" or an assignment in similar general terms is an assignment of rights and unless the language or the circumstances (as in an assignment for security) indicate the contrary, it is a delegation of performance of the duties of the assignor and its acceptance by the assignee constitutes a promise by him to perform those duties. This promise is enforceable by either the assignor or the other party to the original contract.

Section 41-02-17(4), N.D.C.C. *See also* 67 Am.Jur.2d *Sales* § 383 at 650. Thus, the assignment agreements in this case not only assigned rights, they also delegated duties to the assignees.

2. The language of the consent clause was very brief and direct. In full, it read: "The undersigned, Harold Rosenberg and Gladys E. Rosenberg, sellers in the above described Contract of Sale, do hereby consent to the above assignment."

3. The indemnification clause reads as follows:

> And the said party of the second part [Son, Inc.] covenants and agrees to and with the said party of the first part [Pratt] that the said party of the second part will pay the said purchase price and will observe and perform all the terms, conditions and stipulations in the said agreement mentioned which are thereunder by the said party of the first part to be observed and performed, and will save harmless and keep indemnified the said party of the first part against all claims, demands and actions by reason of the failure of the said party of the second part to observe and perform the said agreement.

transaction, Mary Pratt moved to Arizona and had no further knowledge of, or involvement with, the Dairy Queen business. Also following the assignment, the Dairy Queen was moved from the City Center Mall to the corner of DeMers and North Fifth Street in Grand Forks.

The sales contract was then assigned by Son, Inc., to Merit, Corporation (Merit) on June 1, 1984. This assignment agreement did not contain a consent clause for the Rosenbergs to sign. However, the Rosenbergs had knowledge of the assignment and apparently acquiesced. They accepted a large prepayment from Merit, reducing the principal balance due to $25,000. Following this assignment, Merit pledged the inventory and equipment of the Dairy Queen as collateral for a loan from Valley Bank and Trust of Grand Forks.

Payments from Merit to the Rosenbergs continued until June of 1988, at which time the payments ceased, leaving an unpaid principal balance of $17,326.24 plus interest. The Rosenbergs attempted collection of the balance from Merit, but the collection efforts were precluded when Merit filed bankruptcy. The business assets pledged as collateral for the loan from Valley Bank and Trust of Grand Forks were repossessed. The Rosenbergs brought this action for collection of the outstanding debt against Son, Inc., and Mary Pratt.

The trial court denied a summary judgment motion by the Rosenbergs, stating that there were questions of fact remaining which could not be resolved by a summary judgment motion. Several months later, Pratt and Son, Inc., renewed their summary judgment motions. The trial court granted Pratt's motion on December 2, 1991, and granted Son, Inc.'s motion on January 10, 1992, dismissing the Rosenbergs' claims against both parties. The trial court based its decision on the case of *Tri-Continental Leasing Corp. v. Gunter*, 472 N.W.2d 437 (N.D. 1991). It concluded that once Pratt assigned her contract she became a guarantor. Under *Tri-Continental* and North Dakota guaranty law, any alteration in the original obligation exonerates a guarantor. The trial court found that moving the business, the second assignment to Merit, and pledging business assets as collateral, all without Pratt's knowledge, constituted alterations in the underlying obligation. Therefore, because it determined that Pratt was a guarantor on the contract, she was exonerated by the trial court. We disagree with the trial court's analysis and decision to grant summary judgment.

It is a well-established principle in the law of contracts that a contracting party cannot escape its liability on the contract by merely assigning its duties and rights under the contract to a third party. This principle is codified in Section 41-02-17(1), N.D.C.C.:

> *Delegation of performance-Assignment of rights.*
>
> 1. A party may perform his duty through a delegate unless otherwise agreed or unless the other party has a substantial interest in having his original promisor perform or control the acts required by the contract. *No delegation of performance relieves the party delegating of any duty to perform or any liability for breach* [Emphasis added.].

Professor Corbin explained this point succinctly in his treatise on contract law.

> An assignment is an expression of intention by the assignor that his duty shall immediately pass to the assignee. Many a debtor wishes that by such an expression he could get rid of his debts. Any debtor can express such an intention, but it is not operative to produce such a hoped-for result. It does not cause society to relax its compulsion against him and direct it toward the assignee as his substitute. In spite of such an "assignment," the debtor's duty remains absolutely unchanged. The performance required by a duty can often be delegated; but by such a delegation the duty itself is not escaped.

4 Corbin on Contracts § 866 at 452.

This rule of law applies to all categories of contracts, including contracts for the sale or lease of real property, service contracts, and contracts for the sale of goods, which is present in the facts of this case.

> In the case of a contract for the sale of goods, the assignment and delegation may be by the buyer as well as by the seller. The buyer's assignment of his right to the goods and his delegation of the duty to pay the price are both effective; but he himself remains bound to pay the price just as before. If the assignee contracts with the assignor to pay the price, the seller can maintain suit for the price against the assignee also, as a creditor beneficiary of the assumption contract; *the seller has merely obtained a new and additional security.*

Id. at 454-455 (emphasis added) (footnotes omitted).

Thus, when Pratt entered into the "assignment agreement" with Son, Inc., a simple assignment alone was insufficient to release her from any further liability on the contract.

It is not, however, a legal impossibility for a contracting party to rid itself of an obligation under a contract. It may seek the approval of the other original party for release, and substitute a new party in its place. In such an instance, the transaction is no longer called an assignment; instead, it is called a novation.[7] If a novation occurs in this manner, it must be clear from the terms of

---

7. There are three statutes applicable to novation in the present case. The first statute defines the concept of novation.

> "*Novation defined.* Novation is the substitution of a new obligation for an existing one."

Section 9-13-08, N.D.C.C. The second statute explains how a novation is created.

> "*Novation-Created by contract.* Novation is made by contract and is subject to all the rules concerning contracts in general."

Section 9-13-09, N.D.C.C. The third and final statute points out the various methods for making a novation.

> "*How novation made.* Novation is made by the substitution of:
> 1. A new obligation between the same parties with intent to extinguish the old obligation;
> 2. A new debtor in the place of the old one with intent to release the latter; or
> 3. A new creditor in place of the old one with intent to transfer the rights of the latter to the former."

Section 9-13-10, N.D.C.C.

the agreement that a novation is intended by all parties involved. "An obligor is discharged by the substitution of a new obligor only if the contract so provides or if the obligee makes a binding manifestation of assent, forming a novation." *Restatement (Second) of Contracts* § 318 cmt. d. Therefore, both original parties to the contract must intend and mutually assent to the discharge of the obligor from any further liability on the original contract.

It is evident from the express language of the assignment agreement between Pratt and Son, Inc., that only an assignment was intended, not a novation.[8] The agreement made no mention of discharging Pratt from any further liability on the contract. To the contrary, the latter part of the agreement contained an indemnity clause holding Pratt harmless in the event of a breach by Son, Inc. Thus, it is apparent that Pratt contemplated being held ultimately responsible for performance of the obligation.

Furthermore, the agreement was between Pratt and Son, Inc.; they were the parties signing the agreement, not the Rosenbergs. An agreement between Pratt and Son, Inc., cannot unilaterally affect the Rosenbergs' rights under the contract.

As mentioned earlier, the Rosenbergs did sign a consent to the assignment at the bottom of the agreement. However, by merely consenting to the assignment, the Rosenbergs did not consent to a discharge of the principal obligor—Pratt. Nothing in the language of the consent clause supports such an allegation. A creditor is free to consent to an assignment without releasing the original obligor.

> Where the obligee consents to the delegation, the consent itself does not release the obligor from liability for breach of contract. More than the obligee's consent to a delegation of performance is needed to release the obligor from liability for breach of contract. For the obligor to be released from liability, the obligee must agree to the release. If there is an agreement between the obligor, obligee and a third party by which the third party agrees to be substituted for the obligor and the obligee assents thereto, the obligor is released from liability and the third person takes the place of the obligor. Such an agreement is known as a novation.

Brooks v. Hayes, 395 N.W.2d at 167 (1986). Thus, the express language of the agreement and intent of the parties at the time the assignment was made did not contemplate a novation by releasing Pratt and substituting Son, Inc., in her stead.

---

8. The agreement itself was titled "ASSIGNMENT OF CONTRACT FOR SALE." Following the standard introduction of the parties involved (Pratt and Son, Inc.), it read:

> That the said party of the first part [Pratt], in consideration of the sum of One Dollar ($1.00) and other valuable consideration to her paid by the said party of the second part [Son, Inc.], the receipt whereof is hereby acknowledged, does hereby assign, transfer and set over unto the said party of the second part the above recited agreement or Contract of Sale and all the right, title and interest of the said party of the first part to the business above described, to have and to hold the same unto the said party of the second part, its successors and assigns, forever, subject, nevertheless, to the terms, conditions and stipulations in the said agreement contained. [Indemnification clause set forth in footnote 3.]

Without thoroughly acknowledging the above principles and their importance, the trial court concluded that once Pratt assigned her contract she became a guarantor on the contract. The trial court proceeded to apply North Dakota guaranty statutes and guaranty case law to Pratt, and exonerated her under that authority. We do not believe that the trial court appropriately applied the law.

As stressed above, a party assigning its rights and delegating its duties is still a party to the original contract. An assignment will not extinguish the relationship and obligations between the two original contracting parties. However, an assignment does result in the assignor having a surety relationship, albeit involuntary, *with the assignee,* but not with the other original contracting party.

> A common instance of involuntary suretyship, *at least as between the principal and surety themselves,* occurs where one party to a contract [Son, Inc.], as a part of the agreement, assumes an indebtedness owing by the other [Pratt] to a third person [the Rosenbergs], the one assuming the indebtedness becoming the principal [Son, Inc.], and the former debtor a surety [Pratt].

72 C.J.S. *Principal and Surety* § 35 (emphasis added). Therefore, in the present facts, Pratt enjoyed a surety position as to Son, Inc., but remained a principal on the contract with the Rosenbergs.

The inquiry as to Pratt's liability does not end at this juncture. Pursuant to guaranty law, the trial court released Pratt from any liability on the contract due to the changes or alterations which took place following her assignment to Son, Inc. While it is true that Pratt cannot be forced to answer on the contract irrespective of events occurring subsequent to her assignment, it is also true that she cannot be exonerated for *every* type of alteration or change that may develop.

> The buyer can assign his right to the goods or land and can delegate performance of his duty to pay the price. He himself remains bound as before by his duty to pay that price. But observe that he remains bound "as before"; the assignee and the seller cannot, by agreement or by waiver, make it the assignor's duty to pay a different price or on different conditions. If the seller is willing to make such a change, he must trust to the assignee alone. It has been held that, if a tender of delivery by a certain time is a condition precedent to the buyer's duty to pay, the assignee of the buyer has no power to waive this condition, and substantial delay by the seller will prevent his getting judgment against the assignor for the price. If the assignee has contracted to pay the price, his waiver of the condition will be effective in a suit against him, *but it will not be allowed to prejudice the position of the assignor,* who now occupies substantially the position of surety.

4 Corbin on Contracts § 866 at 458-459 (emphasis added) (footnotes omitted).

The trial court decided pursuant to guaranty statutes, Section 22-01-15, N.D.C.C., and case law, *Tri-Continental Leasing Corp. v. Gunter,* 472 N.W.2d 437, that any alteration in the underlying obligation resulted in a release of Pratt on the contract. It appears that an assignor occupies a much different position from that of a guarantor; not every type of alteration is sufficient to warrant discharge of the assignor. As suggested by Professor Corbin in the language highlighted above, the alteration must "prejudice the position of the assignor." 4 Corbin on Contracts § 866 at 459.

> Accordingly, unless the other contracting party has consented to release him, the assignor remains bound by his obligations under the contract and is liable to the other party if the assignee defaults,. . . . However, the assignor is responsible only for the obligation which he originally contracted to assume, and the assignee cannot, without the assignor's knowledge, *increase the burden.*

6A C.J.S. *Assignments* § 97 at 753-754 (emphasis added) (footnotes omitted).

Further authority for this principle is found in *Jedco,* 441 N.W.2d 664 (1989). The facts in *Jedco* involved an assignment of the lease of a building, to which the lessor consented. Various changes occurred following the assignment of the lease. When the assignee defaulted, the lessor sued the assignor for uncollected rental payments. This Court reversed the summary judgment of the trial court, which judgment was in favor of the assignor, and remanded for further proceedings. Justice VandeWalle, speaking for the Court, said:

> Thus, if the lessor and assignee materially change the terms of the lease as it existed between the lessor and assignor, a new tenancy relationship is established and the assignor is released from his obligations under the original lease. This rule of law is qualified, however, in that:
>
> > The [assignor] is not discharged, however, by *variations which inure to his benefit.* Nor is the [assignor] discharged by agreements between lessor and assignee which may increase the liability of the [assignor], but which are permitted by the terms of the original lease, to the benefits of which the assignee is entitled. *Walker v. Rednalloh Co.,* 13 N.E.2d 394, 397 (1938).

Jedco, 441 N.W.2d at 667 (emphasis added) (footnote omitted). *See also Boswell v. Lyon,* 401 N.E.2d 735 (Ind. 1980) (subsequent assignments do not relieve the assignor of any liability on the contract because it is not a change in the time or manner of payment).

If the changes in the obligation prejudicially affect the assignor, a new agreement has been formed between the assignee and the other original contracting party. More concisely, a novation has occurred and the assignor's original obligation has been discharged. This is consistent with our previous decisions and statutory authority. *See* Section 9-13-09, N.D.C.C. Although we have previously determined that the terms of the assignment agreement between Pratt and Son, Inc., did not contemplate a novation, there are additional methods of making a novation besides doing so in the express terms of an agreement. In *Jedco,* we held that:

> The intent to create a novation may be shown not only by the terms of the agreement itself, but also by the character of the transaction and by the facts and circumstances surrounding the transaction.

441 N.W.2d at 666.

The question of whether or not there has been a novation is a question of fact, as decided by this Court in *Herb Hill Ins., Inc. v. Radtke*, 380 N.W.2d 651.

> [T]he question of whether or not there has been a novation is a question of fact if the evidence is such that reasonable persons can draw more than one conclusion.

Id. at 654.

The trial court should not have granted summary judgment on the basis of guaranty law. First of all, guaranty law does not apply to contract assignments without more. Further, there are questions of fact remaining as to the result of the changes in the contract. These issues were not addressed by the trial court. In reversing and remanding in *Jedco*, we said:

> We cannot determine as a matter of law that the assignment was intended to be a novation which resulted in a release of [the assignor's] liability under the lease. Because there are different inferences to be drawn from the undisputed facts, reasonable persons could draw more than one conclusion in this case. Therefore, the summary judgment is reversed and the case is remanded for further proceedings.

441 N.W.2d at 668. We must do the same in this case. Thus, we reverse the summary judgment and remand for further proceedings.

RELEVANT PROVISIONS

For the *Restatement (Second) of Contracts*, consult § 329.

NOTES AND QUESTIONS

1. *What happened?* Who sued whom for what? Procedurally, how did the case get before this court? Factually, what happened between the parties? What arguments did the plaintiff and defendant make? What rule or rules did the court apply? How did the court analyze the dispute between the parties? How did the court decide the case?

2. *Was this case correctly decided?* Do you agree with the result reached in this case? Why or why not? Do you agree with the court's reasoning? Why or why not? How, if at all, would you have written the opinion differently?

3. *A note on novation.* So what, exactly, is novation? According to the court in *Wells Fargo Bank v. Bank of Am.*, 38 Cal. Rptr. 2d 521, 525 (1995) (internal citations omitted):

> "Novation is the substitution of a new obligation for an existing one." The substitution is by agreement and with the intent to extinguish the prior obligation. The substitution of a new obligation for an existing one may be either (1) a new

obligation between the same parties, or (2) a new obligation arising because of new parties, either a new debtor or new creditor. "Novation is made by contract, and is subject to all the rules concerning contracts in general." A novation thus amounts to a new contract which supplants the original agreement and "completely *extinguishes* the original obligation. . . ."

It must "'clearly appear' that the parties intended to extinguish rather than merely modify the original agreement." Where novation is in the form of a substitution of a new debtor for an old one, the release of the old debtor is sufficient to constitute the requisite consideration for the new debtor's promise. Moreover, to constitute a novation, rather than a mere assignment, in the context of a new debtor, the former debtor must be released of his obligation by consent of the former debtor as well as the creditor. However, a creditor may, in advance in the underlying contract, assent to the substitution of a new debtor and discharge from liability the old debtor, thus causing a novation.

APPENDIX A

RESTATEMENT (SECOND) OF CONTRACTS (1981)

FOREWORD

The Restatement of the Law of Contracts was approved and promulgated by the American Law Institute in May 1932, the first of the original Restatements to be finished. With Professor Samuel Williston as Chief Reporter and Professor Arthur L. Corbin as a Special Adviser and the Reporter on Remedies, the work was a legendary success, exercising enormous influence as an authoritative exposition of the subject. . . .

Restatement, Second, of the Law of Contracts was begun in 1962 and completed by the Institute in 1979. . . . Professor Robert Braucher of the Harvard Law School served as Reporter for approximately the first half of this period, resigning on his appointment to the Supreme Judicial Court of Massachusetts in January 1971. He was succeeded as Reporter by Professor E. Allan Farnsworth of Columbia University School of Law, who carried the project to completion . . . .

The Reporters had the benefit of the criticisms and suggestions of Professor Corbin, who served as Consultant until his death in 1967 and left a rich legacy in his elaborate written notes. They also had the aid of a strong Committee of Advisers whose annual review of the preliminary drafts substantially enhanced their quality. Professor Peter Linzer of the University of Detroit School of Law, serving as Editorial Reviser, assumed responsibility for checking, updating and to some extent expanding the Reporter's Notes, and participated in reading the proofs as they appeared, tasks that were performed with diligence and skill. The index was prepared by Philip C. Oxley of the Columbia University Law Library staff. . . .

The Reporters, their Advisers and the Institute approached the text of the first Restatement with the respect and tenderness that are appropriate in dealing with a classic. As the work proceeded, it uncovered relatively little need for major substantive revision, in the sense of changing the positions taken on important issues, although the Uniform Commercial Code inspired a number of significant additions. . . .

CHAPTER 1. MEANING OF TERMS (§§ 1-8)

Introductory Note: A persistent source of difficulty in the law of contracts is the fact that words often have different meanings to the speaker and to the hearer. Most words are commonly used in more than one sense, and the words used in this Restatement are no exception. It is arguable that the difficulty is increased rather than diminished by an attempt to give a word a single definition and to use it only as defined. But where usage varies widely, definition makes it possible to avoid circumlocution in the statement of rules and to hold ambiguity to a minimum.

In the Restatement, an effort has been made to use only words with connotations familiar to the legal profession, and not to use two or more words to express the same legal concept. Where a word frequently used has a variety of distinct meanings, one meaning has been selected and indicated by definition. But it is obviously impossible to capture in a definition an entire complex institution such as "contract" or "promise." The operative facts necessary or sufficient to create legal relations and the legal relations created by those facts will appear with greater fullness in the succeeding chapters.

§ 1 Contract Defined

A contract is a promise or a set of promises for the breach of which the law gives a remedy, or the performance of which the law in some way recognizes as a duty.

§ 2 Promise; Promisor; Promisee; Beneficiary

(1) A promise is a manifestation of intention to act or refrain from acting in a specified way, so made as to justify a promisee in understanding that a commitment has been made.

(2) The person manifesting the intention is the promisor.

(3) The person to whom the manifestation is addressed is the promisee.

(4) Where performance will benefit a person other than the promisee, that person is a beneficiary.

Comment:

a. *Acts and resulting relations.* If . . . there is a legal duty to perform [the promise], the promise is a contract; but the word "promise" is not limited to acts having legal effect. . . .

b. *Manifestation of intention.* Many contract disputes arise because different people attach different meanings to the same words and conduct. The phrase "manifestation of intention" adopts an external or objective standard for interpreting conduct; it means the external expression of intention as distinguished from undisclosed intention. A promisor manifests an intention if he believes or has reason to believe that the promisee will infer that intention from his words or conduct. . . .

d. *Promise of event beyond human control; warranty.* Words which in terms promise that an event not within human control will occur may be interpreted to include a promise to answer for harm caused by the failure of the event to occur. . . .

Illustrations:

1. A, the builder of a house, or the inventor of the material used in part of its construction, says to B, the owner of the house, "I warrant that this house will never burn down." This includes a promise to pay for harm if the house should burn down.

2. A, by a charter-party, undertakes that the "good ship Dove," having sailed from Marseilles a week ago for New York, shall take on a cargo for B on her arrival in New York. The statement of the quality of the ship and the statement of her time of sailing from Marseilles include promises to pay for harm if the statement is untrue.

e. Illusory promises; mere statements of intention. Words of promise which by their terms make performance entirely optional with the "promisor" whatever may happen, or whatever course of conduct in other respects he may pursue, do not constitute a promise. . . .

f. Opinions and predictions. A promise must be distinguished from a statement of opinion or a mere prediction of future events. . . .

Illustration:

4. A, on seeing a house of thoroughly fireproof construction, says to B, the owner, "This house will never burn down." This is not a promise but merely an opinion or prediction. If A had been paid for his opinion as an expert, there might be an implied promise that he would employ reasonable care and skill in forming and giving his opinion.

g. Promisee and beneficiary. The word promisee is used repeatedly in discussion of the law of contracts, and it cannot be avoided here. In common usage the promisee is the person to whom the promise is made. . . .

The promisor and promisee are the "parties" to a promise; a third person who will benefit from performance is a "beneficiary." A beneficiary may or may not have a legal right to performance; like "promisee", the term is neutral with respect to rights and duties. . . .

§ 3 Agreement Defined; Bargain Defined

An agreement is a manifestation of mutual assent on the part of two or more persons. A bargain is an agreement to exchange promises or to exchange a promise for a performance or to exchange performances.

Comment:

b. Manifestation of assent. Manifestation of assent may be made by words or by any other conduct. Even silence in some circumstances is such a manifestation.

§ 4 How a Promise May Be Made

A promise may be stated in words either oral or written, or may be inferred wholly or partly from conduct.

§ 7 Voidable Contracts

A voidable contract is one where one or more parties have the power, by a manifestation of election to do so, to avoid the legal relations created by the contract, or by ratification of the contract to extinguish the power of avoidance.

Chapter 2. Formation of Contracts—Parties and Capacity (§§ 9-16)

§ 12 Capacity to Contract

(1) No one can be bound by contract who has not legal capacity to incur at least voidable contractual duties. Capacity to contract may be partial and its existence in respect of a particular transaction may depend upon the nature of the transaction or upon other circumstances.

(2) A natural person who manifests assent to a transaction has full legal capacity to incur contractual duties thereby unless he is

(a) under guardianship, or

(b) an infant, or

(c) mentally ill or defective, or

(d) intoxicated.

Comment:

a. *Total and partial incapacity.* Capacity, as here used, means the legal power which a normal person would have under the same circumstances. Incapacity may be total, as in cases where extreme physical or mental disability prevents manifestation of assent to the transaction, or in cases of mental illness after a guardian has been appointed. Often, however, lack of capacity merely renders contracts voidable. Incapacity sometimes relates only to particular types of transactions; on the other hand, persons whose capacity is limited in most circumstances may be bound by particular types of transactions. In cases of partial disability, the law of mistake or of misrepresentation, duress and undue influence may be relevant.

§ 14 Infants

Unless a statute provides otherwise, a natural person has the capacity to incur only voidable contractual duties until the beginning of the day before the person's eighteenth birthday.

§ 15 Mental Illness or Defect

(1) A person incurs only voidable contractual duties by entering into a transaction if by reason of mental illness or defect

(a) he is unable to understand in a reasonable manner the nature and consequences of the transaction, or

(b) he is unable to act in a reasonable manner in relation to the transaction and the other party has reason to know of his condition.

(2) Where the contract is made on fair terms and the other party is without knowledge of the mental illness or defect, the power of avoidance under Subsection (1) terminates to the extent that the contract has been so performed in whole or in part or the circumstances have so changed that avoidance would be unjust. In such a case a court may grant relief as justice requires.

Comment:

a. Rationale. A contract made by a person who is mentally incompetent requires the reconciliation of two conflicting policies: the protection of justifiable expectations and of the security of transactions, and the protection of persons unable to protect themselves against imposition. Each policy has sometimes prevailed to a greater extent than is stated in this Section. At one extreme, it has been said that a lunatic has no capacity to contract because he has no mind; this view has given way to a better understanding of mental phenomena and to the doctrine that contractual obligation depends on manifestation of assent rather than on mental assent. At the other extreme, it has been asserted that mental incompetency has no effect on a contract unless other grounds of avoidance are present, such as fraud, undue influence, or gross inadequacy of consideration; it is now widely believed that such a rule gives inadequate protection to the incompetent and his family, particularly where the contract is entirely executory.

b. The standard of competency. It is now recognized that there is a wide variety of types and degrees of mental incompetency. Among them are congenital deficiencies in intelligence, the mental deterioration of old age, the effects of brain damage caused by accident or organic disease, and mental illnesses evidenced by such symptoms as delusions, hallucinations, delirium, confusion and depression. Where no guardian has been appointed, there is full contractual capacity in any case unless the mental illness or defect has affected the particular transaction: a person may be able to understand almost nothing, or only simple or routine transactions, or he may be incompetent only with respect to a particular type of transaction. Even though understanding is complete, he may lack the ability to control his acts in the way that the normal individual can and does control them; in such cases the inability makes the contract voidable only if the other party has reason to know of his condition. Where a person has some understanding of a particular transaction which is affected by mental illness or defect, the controlling consideration is whether the transaction in its result is one which a reasonably competent person might have made.

Illustration:

1. A, a school teacher, is a member of a retirement plan and has elected a lower monthly benefit in order to provide a benefit to her husband if she dies first. At age 60 she suffers a "nervous breakdown," takes a leave of absence, and is treated for cerebral arteriosclerosis. When the leave

expires she applies for retirement, revokes her previous election, and elects a larger annuity with no death benefit. In view of her reduced life expectancy, the change is foolhardy, and there are no other circumstances to explain the change. She fully understands the plan, but by reason of mental illness is unable to make a decision based on the prospect of her dying before her husband. The officers of the plan have reason to know of her condition. Two months after the changed election she dies. The change of election is voidable.

§ 16 Intoxicated Persons

A person incurs only voidable contractual duties by entering into a transaction if the other party has reason to know that by reason of intoxication

(a) he is unable to understand in a reasonable manner the nature and consequences of the transaction, or

(b) he is unable to act in a reasonable manner in relation to the transaction.

Comment:

a. *Rationale.* Compulsive alcoholism may be a form of mental illness; and when a guardian is appointed for the property of a habitual drunkard, his transactions are treated like those of a person under guardianship by reason of mental illness. If drunkenness is so extreme as to prevent any manifestation of assent, there is no capacity to contract. It would be possible to treat voluntary intoxication as a temporary mental disorder in all cases, but voluntary intoxication not accompanied by any other disability has been thought less excusable than mental illness. Hence a contract made by an intoxicated person is enforceable by the other party even though entirely executory, unless the other person has reason to know that the intoxicated person lacks capacity. Elements of overreaching or other unfair advantage may be relevant on the issues of competency, of the other party's reason to know, and of the appropriate remedy. Use of drugs may raise similar problems.

b. *What contracts are voidable.* The standard of competency in intoxication cases is the same as that in cases of mental illness. If the intoxication is so extreme as to prevent any manifestation of assent, there is no contract. Otherwise the other party is affected only by intoxication of which he has reason to know. A contract made by a person who is so drunk he does not know what he is doing is voidable if the other party has reason to know of the intoxication. Where there is some understanding of the transaction despite intoxication, avoidance depends on a showing that the other party induced the drunkenness or that the consideration was inadequate or that the transaction departed from the normal pattern of similar transactions; if the particular transaction in its result is one which a reasonably competent person might have made, it cannot be avoided even though entirely executory.

Illustrations:

1. A, while in a state of extreme intoxication, signs and mails a written offer on fair terms to B, who has no reason to know of the intoxication. B accepts the offer. A has no right to avoid the contract.

2. A is ill and confined to his bed. B, knowing that the illness is incurable, plies A with intoxicating liquor for a week and then purports to treat him by rubbing him with oil. While intoxicated, A executes by mark a contract to sell land to B for a grossly inadequate consideration. Six days later A dies. A's heirs may avoid the contract.

3. A has been drinking heavily. B, who has also been drinking, meets A, offers to buy A's farm for $50,000, a fair price, and offers A a drink which A accepts. In drunken exhilaration A, as a joke, writes out and signs a memorandum of agreement to sell, gets his wife to sign it, and delivers it to B, who understands the transaction as a serious one. A's intoxication is no defense to B's suit for specific performance.

CHAPTER 3. FORMATION OF CONTRACTS—MUTUAL ASSENT (§§ 17-70)

§ 17 Requirement of a Bargain

(1) Except as stated in Subsection (2), the formation of a contract requires a bargain in which there is a manifestation of mutual assent to the exchange and a consideration.

(2) Whether or not there is a bargain a contract may be formed under special rules applicable to formal contracts or under the rules stated in §§ 82-94.

Comment:

c. *"Meeting of the minds."* The element of agreement is sometimes referred to as a "meeting of the minds." The parties to most contracts give actual as well as apparent assent, but it is clear that a mental reservation of a party to a bargain does not impair the obligation he purports to undertake. The phrase used here, therefore, is "manifestation of mutual assent," as in the definition of "agreement" in § 3.

§ 18 Manifestation of Mutual Assent

Manifestation of mutual assent to an exchange requires that each party either make a promise or begin or render a performance.

§ 19 Conduct as Manifestation of Assent

(1) The manifestation of assent may be made wholly or partly by written or spoken words or by other acts or by failure to act.

(2) The conduct of a party is not effective as a manifestation of his assent unless he intends to engage in the conduct and knows or has reason to know that the other party may infer from his conduct that he assents.

(3) The conduct of a party may manifest assent even though he does not in fact assent. In such cases a resulting contract may be voidable because of fraud, duress, mistake, or other invalidating cause.

§ 20 Effect of Misunderstanding

(1) There is no manifestation of mutual assent to an exchange if the parties attach materially different meanings to their manifestations and

(a) neither party knows or has reason to know the meaning attached by the other; or

(b) each party knows or each party has reason to know the meaning attached by the other.

(2) The manifestations of the parties are operative in accordance with the meaning attached to them by one of the parties if

(a) that party does not know of any different meaning attached by the other, and the other knows the meaning attached by the first party; or

(b) that party has no reason to know of any different meaning attached by the other, and the other has reason to know the meaning attached by the first party.

Comment:

d. Error in expression. The basic principle governing material misunderstanding is stated in Subsection (1): no contract is formed if neither party is at fault or if both parties are equally at fault. Subsection (2) deals with cases where both parties are not equally at fault. . . .

Illustrations:

1. A offers to sell B goods shipped from Bombay ex steamer "Peerless". B accepts. There are two steamers of the name "Peerless", sailing from Bombay at materially different times. If both parties intend the same Peerless, there is a contract, and it is immaterial whether they know or have reason to know that two ships are named Peerless.

2. The facts being otherwise as stated in Illustration 1, A means Peerless No. 1 and B means Peerless No. 2. If neither A nor B knows or has reason to know that they mean different ships, or if they both know or if they both have reason to know, there is no contract.

3. The facts being otherwise as stated in Illustration 1, A knows that B means Peerless No. 2 and B does not know that there are two ships named Peerless. There is a contract for the sale of the goods from Peerless No. 2, and it is immaterial whether B has reason to know that A means Peerless No. 1. . . . Conversely, if B knows that A means Peerless No. 1 and A does not know that there are two ships named Peerless, there is a contract for the sale of the goods from Peerless No. 1, and it is immaterial whether A has reason to know that B means Peerless No. 2, but the contract may be voidable by A for misrepresentation.

4. The facts being otherwise as stated in Illustration 1, neither party knows that there are two ships Peerless. A has reason to know that B means Peerless No. 2 and B has no reason to know that A means Peerless No. 1. There is a contract for the sale of goods from Peerless No. 2. In the converse case, where B has reason to know and A does not, there is a contract for sale from Peerless No. 1. . . .

5. A says to B, "I offer to sell you my horse for $100." B, knowing that A intends to offer to sell his cow for that price, not his horse, and that the word "horse" is a slip of the tongue, replies, "I accept." The price is a fair one for either the horse or the cow. There is a contract for the sale of the cow and not of the horse. . . .

§ 22 Mode of Assent: Offer and Acceptance

(1) The manifestation of mutual assent to an exchange ordinarily takes the form of an offer or proposal by one party followed by an acceptance by the other party or parties.

(2) A manifestation of mutual assent may be made even though neither offer nor acceptance can be identified and even though the moment of formation cannot be determined.

§ 24 Offer Defined

An offer is the manifestation of willingness to enter into a bargain, so made as to justify another person in understanding that his assent to that bargain is invited and will conclude it.

Illustration:

1. A says to B, "That book you are holding is yours if you promise to pay me $5 for it." This is an offer empowering B, by making the requested promise, to make himself owner of the book and thus complete A's performance. . . .

§ 25 Option Contracts

An option contract is a promise which meets the requirements for the formation of a contract and limits the promisor's power to revoke an offer.

Comment:

a. *"Option."* A promise which constitutes an option contract may be contained in the offer itself, or it may be made separately in a collateral offer to keep the main offer open. . . .

Illustrations:

1. A promises B under seal or in return for $100 paid or promised by B that A will sell B 100 shares of stock in a specified corporation for $5,000 at any time within thirty days that B selects. There is an option contract under which B has an option.

2. A offers to sell B Blackacre for $5,000 at any time within thirty days. Subsequently A promises under seal or in return for $100 paid or promised by B that the offer will not be revoked. There is an option contract under which B has an option.

b. The need for irrevocable offers. To provide the offeree with a dependable basis for decision whether or not to accept, the rule in many legal systems is that an offer is irrevocable unless it provides otherwise. The common-law rule, on the other hand, resting on the requirement of consideration, permits the revocation of offers even though stated to be firm. . . .

§ 26 Preliminary Negotiations

A manifestation of willingness to enter into a bargain is not an offer if the person to whom it is addressed knows or has reason to know that the person making it does not intend to conclude a bargain until he has made a further manifestation of assent.

Comment:

a. Interpretation of proposals for exchange. The rule stated in this Section is a special application of the definition in § 24 and of the principles governing the interpretation of manifestations of assent. . . .

b. Advertising. Business enterprises commonly secure general publicity for the goods or services they supply or purchase. Advertisements of goods by display, sign, handbill, newspaper, radio or television are not ordinarily intended or understood as offers to sell. The same is true of catalogues, price lists and circulars, even though the terms of suggested bargains may be stated in some detail. It is of course possible to make an offer by an advertisement directed to the general public (see § 29), but there must ordinarily be some language of commitment or some invitation to take action without further communication.

Illustrations:

1. A, a clothing merchant, advertises overcoats of a certain kind for sale at $50. This is not an offer, but an invitation to the public to come and purchase. The addition of the words "Out they go Saturday; First Come First Served" might make the advertisement an offer.

2. A advertises that he will pay $5 for every copy of a certain book that may be sent to him. This is an offer, and A is bound to pay $5 for every copy sent while the offer is unrevoked.

§ 29 To Whom an Offer is Addressed

(1) The manifested intention of the offeror determines the person or persons in whom is created a power of acceptance.

(2) An offer may create a power of acceptance in a specified person or in one or more of a specified group or class of persons, acting separately or together, or in anyone or everyone who makes a specified promise or renders a specified performance.

§ 30 Form of Acceptance Invited

(1) An offer may invite or require acceptance to be made by an affirmative answer in words, or by performing or refraining from performing a specified act, or may empower the offeree to make a selection of terms in his acceptance.

(2) Unless otherwise indicated by the language or the circumstances, an offer invites acceptance in any manner and by any medium reasonable in the circumstances.

Comment:

b. General offers. An offer may create separate powers of acceptance in an unlimited number of persons, and the exercise of the power by one person may or may not extinguish the power of another. Where one acceptor only is to be selected, various methods of selection are possible: for example, "first come, first served" (see Illustration 1 to § 26), the highest bidder, or the winner of a contest. Who can accept, and how, is determined by interpretation of the offer.

Illustrations:

1. A publishes an offer of reward to whoever will give him certain information. There is no indication that A intends to pay more than once. Any person learning of the offer has power to accept, but the giving of the information by one terminates the power of every other person. . . .

3. A, the proprietor of a medical preparation, offers $100 to anyone who contracts a certain disease after using the preparation as directed. B, C and D use it as directed. Each has made a contract independent of the others, and is entitled to the $100 if he later contracts the disease.

§ 32 Invitation of Promise or Performance

In case of doubt an offer is interpreted as inviting the offeree to accept either by promising to perform what the offer requests or by rendering the performance, as the offeree chooses.

Comment:

a. Promise or performance. In the ordinary commercial bargain a party expects to be bound only if the other party either renders the return performance or binds himself to do so either by express words or by part performance or other conduct. Unless the language or the circumstances indicate that one party is to have an option, therefore, the usual offer invites an acceptance which either amounts to performance or constitutes a promise. The act of acceptance may be merely symbolic of assent and promise, or it may also be part or all of the performance bargained for. See §§ 2, 4, 18, 19. In either case notification of the offeror may be necessary. See §§ 54, 56.

The rule of this Section is a particular application of the rule stated in § 30(2). The offeror is often indifferent as to whether acceptance takes the form of words of promise or acts of performance, and his words literally referring to one are often intended and understood to refer to either. Where performance takes time, however, the beginning of performance may constitute a promise to complete it. See § 62.

Illustrations:

1. A writes B, "If you will mow my lawn next week, I will pay you $10." B can accept A's offer either by promptly promising to mow the lawn or by mowing it as requested.

2. A says to B: "If you finish that table you are making and deliver it to my house today, I will give you $100 for it." B replies, "I'll do it." There is a contract. B could also accept by delivering the table as requested.

b. Offer limited to acceptance by performance only. Language or circumstances sometimes make it clear that the offeree is not to bind himself in advance of performance. His promise may be worthless to the offeror, or the circumstances may make it unreasonable for the offeror to expect a firm commitment from the offeree. In such cases, the offer does not invite a promissory acceptance, and a promise is ineffective as an acceptance. Examples are found in offers of reward or of prizes in a contest, made to a large number of people but to be accepted by only one. Non-commercial arrangements among relatives and friends and offers which leave important terms to be fixed by the offeree in the course of performance provide other examples.

It is a separate question whether the offeree undertakes any responsibility to complete performance once begun, or whether he takes any responsibility for the quality of the performance when completed.

Illustrations:

3. A publishes the following offer: "I will pay $50 for the return of my diamond bracelet lost yesterday on State Street." B sees this advertisement and at once sends a letter to A, saying "I accept your offer and will search for this bracelet." There is no acceptance.

4. A writes to B, his nephew aged 16, that if B will refrain from drinking, using tobacco, swearing, and playing cards or billiards for money until he becomes 21 years of age, A will pay B $5,000. B makes a written reply promising so to refrain. There is probably no contract. But if B begins to refrain, A may be bound by an option contract under § 45; and if B refrains until he becomes 21, A is bound to pay him $5,000.

c. Shipment of goods. An order or other offer to buy goods for prompt or current shipment normally invites acceptance either by a prompt promise to ship or by prompt or current shipment. Uniform Commercial Code § 2-206(1)(b). If non-conforming goods are shipped, the shipment may be an acceptance and at the same time a breach. But there is no acceptance if the offeror has reason to know that none is intended, as where the offeree promptly notifies him that non-conforming goods are being shipped and are offered only as an accommodation to him.

Illustrations:

5. A mails a written order to B, offering to buy specified machinery on specified terms. The order provides, "Ship at once." B immediately mails a letter to A, saying "I accept your offer and will ship at once." This is a sufficient acceptance to form a contract. See Uniform Commercial Code § 2-206(1).

6. In Illustration 5, instead of mailing a letter of acceptance, B immediately ships the machinery as requested. This is a sufficient acceptance to form a contract. If the machinery is defective, the shipment is both an acceptance forming a contract and a breach of that contract, unless B promptly notifies A that the shipment is offered only as an accommodation to A. See Uniform Commercial Code § 2-206(1).

§ 33 Certainty

(1) Even though a manifestation of intention is intended to be understood as an offer, it cannot be accepted so as to form a contract unless the terms of the contract are reasonably certain.

(2) The terms of a contract are reasonably certain if they provide a basis for determining the existence of a breach and for giving an appropriate remedy.

(3) The fact that one or more terms of a proposed bargain are left open or uncertain may show that a manifestation of intention is not intended to be understood as an offer or as an acceptance.

Comment:

a. *Certainty of terms.* It is sometimes said that the agreement must be capable of being given an exact meaning and that all the performances to be rendered must be certain. Such statements may be appropriate in determining whether a manifestation of intention is intended to be understood as an offer. But the actions of the parties may show conclusively that they have intended to conclude a binding agreement, even though one or more terms are missing or are left to be agreed upon. In such cases courts endeavor, if possible, to attach a sufficiently definite meaning to the bargain.

An offer which appears to be indefinite may be given precision by usage of trade or by course of dealing between the parties. Terms may be supplied by factual implication, and in recurring situations the law often supplies a term in the absence of agreement to the contrary. . . . Where the parties have intended to conclude a bargain, uncertainty as to incidental or collateral matters is seldom fatal to the existence of the contract. If the essential terms are so uncertain that there is no basis for deciding whether the agreement has been kept or broken, there is no contract. But even in such cases partial performance or other action in reliance on the agreement may reinforce it under § 34.

b. *Certainty in basis for remedy.* The rule stated in Subsection (2) reflects the fundamental policy that contracts should be made by the parties, not by the courts, and hence that remedies for breach of contract must have a basis in the agreement of the parties. Where the parties have intended to make a contract and there is a reasonably certain basis for granting a remedy, the same policy supports the granting of the remedy. The test is not certainty as to what the parties were to do nor as to the exact amount of damages due to the plaintiff; uncertainty may preclude one remedy without affecting another. See Uniform Commercial Code § 2-204(3) and Comment.

Thus the degree of certainty required may be affected by the dispute which arises and by the remedy sought. Courts decide the disputes before them, not other hypothetical disputes which might have arisen. . . .

Illustrations:

1. A agrees to sell and B to buy goods for $2,000, $1,000 in cash and the "balance on installment terms over a period of two years," with a provision for liquidated damages. If it is found that both parties manifested an intent to conclude a binding agreement, the indefiniteness of the quoted language does not prevent the award of the liquidated damages.

2. A agrees to sell and B to buy a specific tract of land for $10,000, $4,000 in cash and $6,000 on mortgage. A agrees to obtain the mortgage loan for B or, if unable to do so, to lend B the amount, but the terms of loan are not stated, although both parties manifest an intent to conclude a binding agreement. The contract is too indefinite to support a decree of specific performance against B, but B may obtain such a decree if he offers to pay the full price in cash.

c. Preliminary negotiations. The rule stated in Subsection (3) is a particular application of the rule stated in § 26 on preliminary negotiations. Incompleteness of terms is one of the principal reasons why advertisements and price quotations are ordinarily not interpreted as offers. Similarly, if the parties to negotiations for sale manifest an intention not to be bound until the price is fixed or agreed, the law gives effect to that intention. Uniform Commercial Code § 2-305(4). The more terms the parties leave open, the less likely it is that they have intended to conclude a binding agreement. See Uniform Commercial Code § 2-204 and Comment.

d. Uncertain time of performance. Valid contracts are often made which do not specify the time for performance. Where the contract calls for a single performance such as the rendering of a service or the delivery of goods, the time for performance is a "reasonable time." . . .

Illustrations:

3. A and B promise that certain performances shall be mutually rendered by them "immediately" or "at once," or "promptly," or "as soon as possible," or "in about one month." All these promises are sufficiently definite to form contracts.

4. A promises B to sell certain goods to him, and B promises to pay a specified price therefor. No time of performance is fixed. The time for delivery and payment is a reasonable time. Uniform Commercial Code

§§ 2-309(1), 2-310(a). What is a reasonable time depends on the nature, purpose and circumstances of the action to be taken. Uniform Commercial Code § 1-204(2).

5. A offers to employ B for a stated compensation as long as B is able to do specified work, or as long as a specified business is carried on, and B accepts the terms offered. The length of the engagement is sufficiently definite for the formation of a contract.

6. A promises B to serve B as chauffeur, and B promises to pay him $100 a month. Nothing further is stated as to the duration of the employment. There is at once a contract for one month's service. At the end of the first month, in the absence of revocation, there is a contract for a second month. But circumstances may show that such an agreement merely specifies the rate of compensation for an employment at will.

e. Indefinite price. Where the parties manifest an intention not to be bound unless the amount of money to be paid by one of them is fixed or agreed and it is not fixed or agreed there is no contract. Uniform Commercial Code § 2-305(4). Where they intend to conclude a contract for the sale of goods, however, and the price is not settled, the price is a reasonable price at the time of delivery if (a) nothing is said as to price, or (b) the price is left to be agreed by the parties and they fail to agree, or (c) the price is to be fixed in terms of some agreed market or other standard as set or recorded by a third person or agency and it is not so set or recorded. Uniform Commercial Code § 2-305(1). Or one party may be given power to fix the price within limits set by agreement or custom or good faith. Similar principles apply to contracts for the rendition of service. But substantial damages cannot be recovered unless they can be estimated with reasonable certainty (§ 352), and if the contract is entirely executory and specific performance is not an appropriate remedy, relief may be limited to the recovery of benefits conferred and specific expense incurred in reliance on the contract.

Illustrations:

7. A promises to sell and B to buy goods "at cost plus a nice profit." The quoted words strongly indicate that the parties have not yet concluded a bargain.

8. A promises to do a specified piece of work and B promises to pay a price to be thereafter mutually agreed. The provision for future agreement as to price strongly indicates that the parties do not intend to be bound. If they manifest an intent to be bound, the price is a reasonable price at the time for doing the work.

f. Other indefinite terms. Promises may be indefinite in other aspects than time and price. The more important the uncertainty, the stronger the indication is that the parties do not intend to be bound; minor items are more likely to be left to the option of one of the parties or to what is customary or reasonable. Even when the parties intend to enter into a contract, uncertainty may be so great as to frustrate their intention. . . .

Illustrations:

10. A promises to sell and B to buy all goods of a certain character which B shall need in his business during the ensuing year. The quantity to be sold is sufficiently definite to provide a basis for remedy, since the promises are interpreted to refer to B's actual good-faith requirements. Uniform Commercial Code § 2-306.

11. A promises B to construct a building according to stated plans and specifications, and B promises A to pay $30,000 therefor. It is also provided that the character of the window fastenings shall be subject to further agreement of the parties. Unless a contrary intention is manifested, the indefiniteness of the agreement with reference to this matter will not prevent the formation of a contract.

§ 34 Certainty and Choice of Terms; Effect of Performance or Reliance

(1) The terms of a contract may be reasonably certain even though it empowers one or both parties to make a selection of terms in the course of performance.

(2) Part performance under an agreement may remove uncertainty and establish that a contract enforceable as a bargain has been formed.

(3) Action in reliance on an agreement may make a contractual remedy appropriate even though uncertainty is not removed.

§ 35 The Offeree's Power of Acceptance

(1) An offer gives to the offeree a continuing power to complete the manifestation of mutual assent by acceptance of the offer.

(2) A contract cannot be created by acceptance of an offer after the power of acceptance has been terminated in one of the ways listed in § 36.

§ 36 Methods of Termination of the Power of Acceptance

(1) An offeree's power of acceptance may be terminated by
  (a) rejection or counter-offer by the offeree, or
  (b) lapse of time, or
  (c) revocation by the offeror, or
  (d) death or incapacity of the offeror or offeree.

(2) In addition, an offeree's power of acceptance is terminated by the non-occurrence of any condition of acceptance under the terms of the offer.

§ 37 Termination of Power of Acceptance Under Option Contract

Notwithstanding §§ 38-49, the power of acceptance under an option contract is not terminated by rejection or counter-offer, by revocation, or by death or incapacity of the offeror, unless the requirements are met for the discharge of a contractual duty.

§ 38 Rejection

(1) An offeree's power of acceptance is terminated by his rejection of the offer, unless the offeror has manifested a contrary intention.

(2) A manifestation of intention not to accept an offer is a rejection unless the offeree manifests an intention to take it under further advisement.

Comment:

a. *The probability of reliance.* The legal consequences of a rejection rest on its probable effect on the offeror. An offeror commonly takes steps to prepare for performance in the event that the offer is accepted. If the offeree states in effect that he declines to accept the offer, it is highly probable that the offeror will change his plans in reliance on the statement. The reliance is likely to take such negative forms as failure to prepare or failure to send a notice of revocation, and hence is likely to be difficult or impossible to prove. To protect the offeror in such reliance, the power of acceptance is terminated without proof of reliance. This rule also protects the offeree in accordance with his manifested intention that his subsequent conduct is not to be understood as an acceptance.

Illustrations:

1. A makes an offer to B and adds: "This offer will remain open for a week." B rejects the offer the following day, but later in the week purports to accept it. There is no contract unless the offer was itself a contract. B's purported acceptance is itself a new offer.

2. A makes an offer to sell water rights to B, and states, "You may accept this offer by applying to the appropriate authority for a permit to use the water." B rejects the offer, obtains water rights elsewhere, and later applies for the permit contemplated by the offer. There is no contract. Even if A's offer was a binding option, B has not exercised it.

b. *Contrary statement of offeror or offeree.* The rule of this Section is designed to give effect to the intentions of the parties, and a manifestation of intention on the part of either that the offeree's power of acceptance is to continue is effective. Thus if the offeree states that he rejects the offer for the present but will reconsider it at a future time, there is no basis for a change of position by the offeror in reliance on a rejection, and under Subsection (2) there is no rejection. Similarly a statement in the offer that it will continue in effect despite a rejection is effective, and a similar statement after a rejection makes a new offer.

Where the manifestation of intention of either party is misunderstood by the other, the principles underlying § 20 apply. If the offeror is justified in inferring from the words or conduct of the offeree, interpreted in the light of the offeror's prior words or conduct, that the offeree intends not to accept the offer and not to take it under further advisement, the power of acceptance is terminated. Compare § 39.

§ 39 Counter-Offers

(1) A counter-offer is an offer made by an offeree to his offeror relating to the same matter as the original offer and proposing a substituted bargain differing from that proposed by the original offer.

(2) An offeree's power of acceptance is terminated by his making of a counter-offer, unless the offeror has manifested a contrary intention or unless the counter-offer manifests a contrary intention of the offeree.

Comment:

a. *Counter-offer as rejection.* It is often said that a counter-offer is a rejection, and it does have the same effect in terminating the offeree's power of acceptance. But in other respects a counter-offer differs from a rejection. A counter-offer must be capable of being accepted; it carries negotiations on rather than breaking them off. The termination of the power of acceptance by a counter-offer merely carries out the usual understanding of bargainers that one proposal is dropped when another is taken under consideration; if alternative proposals are to be under consideration at the same time, warning is expected.

Illustration:

1. A offers B to sell him a parcel of land for $5,000, stating that the offer will remain open for thirty days. B replies, "I will pay $4,800 for the parcel," and on A's declining that, B writes, within the thirty day period, "I accept your offer to sell for $5,000." There is no contract unless A's offer was itself a contract (see § 37), or unless A's reply to the counter-offer manifested an intention to renew his original offer.

b. *Qualified acceptance, inquiry or separate offer.* A common type of counter-offer is the qualified or conditional acceptance, which purports to accept the original offer but makes acceptance expressly conditional on assent to additional or different terms. See § 59. Such a counter-offer must be distinguished from an unqualified acceptance which is accompanied by a proposal for modification of the agreement or for a separate agreement. A mere inquiry regarding the possibility of different terms, a request for a better offer, or a comment upon the terms of the offer, is ordinarily not a counter-offer. Such responses to an offer may be too tentative or indefinite to be offers of any kind; or they may deal with new matters rather than a substitution for the original offer; or their language may manifest an intention to keep the original offer under consideration.

Illustration:

2. A makes the same offer to B as that stated in Illustration 1, and B replies, "Won't you take less?" A answers, "No." An acceptance thereafter by B within the thirty-day period is effective. B's inquiry was not a counter-offer, and A's original offer stands.

c. *Contrary statement of offeror or offeree.* An offeror may state in his offer that it shall continue for a stated time in any event and that in the meanwhile he will be glad to receive counter-offers. Likewise an offeree may state that he is holding the offer under advisement, but that if the offeror desires to close a bargain at once the offeree makes a specific counter-offer. Such an answer will not extend the time that the original offer remains open, but will not cut that time short. Compare § 38.

Illustration:

3. A makes the same offer to B as that stated in Illustration 1. B replies, "I am keeping your offer under advisement, but if you wish to close the matter at once I will give you $4,800." A does not reply, and within the thirty-day period B accepts the original offer. B's acceptance is effective.

§ 40 Time When Rejection or Counter-Offer Terminates the Power of Acceptance

Rejection or counter-offer by mail or telegram does not terminate the power of acceptance until received by the offeror, but limits the power so that a letter or telegram of acceptance started after the sending of an otherwise effective rejection or counter-offer is only a counter-offer unless the acceptance is received by the offeror before he receives the rejection or counter-offer.

Comment:

a. Receipt essential. A rejection terminates the offeree's power of acceptance because of the probability of reliance by the offeror, and there is no possibility of reliance until the rejection is received. See § 38. Hence the power continues until receipt. The same rule is applied by analogy to a counter-offer, although the reason is somewhat different: a counter-offer cannot be taken under consideration as a substitute proposal until it is received. See § 39. As to when a rejection is received, see § 68; compare Restatement, Second, Agency §§ 268-83, Uniform Commercial Code §§ 1-201(25) to (27).

b. Subsequent acceptance. Since a rejection or counter-offer is not effective until received, it may until that time be superseded by an acceptance. But the probability remains that the offeror will rely on the rejection or counter-offer if it is received before the acceptance. To protect the offeror in such reliance, the offeree who has dispatched a rejection is deprived of the benefit of the rule that an acceptance may take effect on dispatch (§ 63). The rule of this Section only applies, however, to a rejection or counter-offer which is otherwise effective. A rejection or counter-offer may be denied effect to terminate the power of acceptance if the original offer is itself a contract or if the offeror or offeree manifests an intention that the power continue. See §§ 37-39. Similarly, a purported rejection or counter-offer dispatched after an effective acceptance is in effect a revocation of acceptance, governed by § 63 rather than by this Section.

Illustration:

1. A makes B an offer by mail. B immediately after receiving the offer mails a letter of rejection. Within the time permitted by the offer B accepts. This acceptance creates a contract only if received before the rejection, or if the power of acceptance continues under §§ 37-39.

§ 41 Lapse of Time

(1) An offeree's power of acceptance is terminated at the time specified in the offer, or, if no time is specified, at the end of a reasonable time.

(2) What is a reasonable time is a question of fact, depending on all the circumstances existing when the offer and attempted acceptance are made. . . .

§ 42 Revocation by Communication From Offeror Received by Offeree

An offeree's power of acceptance is terminated when the offeree receives from the offeror a manifestation of an intention not to enter into the proposed contract.

Comment:

a. *Revocability of offers.* Most offers are revocable. Revocability may rest on the express or implied terms of the offer, as in the case of bids at an auction. But the ordinary offer is revocable even though it expressly states the contrary, because of the doctrine that an informal agreement is binding as a bargain only if supported by consideration. . . .

Illustration:

1. A makes a written offer to B to sell him a piece of land. The offer states that it will remain open for thirty days and is not subject to countermand. The next day A orally informs B that the offer is terminated. B's power of acceptance is terminated unless the offer is a contract under § 25.

c. *Purported revocation after acceptance.* Once the offeree has exercised his power to create a contract by accepting the offer, a purported revocation is ineffective as such. Where an acceptance by mail is effective on dispatch, for example, it is not deprived of effect by a revocation subsequently received by the offeree. See § 63. . . .

Illustration:

2. A sends B an offer by mail to buy a piece of land for $5,000. The next day A sends B a letter stating that unless B has already accepted A revokes the offer and makes a new offer to buy the same land for $4,800. B receives A's second letter after he has duly mailed a letter of acceptance, but promptly sells the land to C without further communication with A. The sale is a breach of contract by B.

d. *What constitutes revocation.* The word "revoke" is not essential to a revocation. Any clear manifestation of unwillingness to enter into the proposed bargain is sufficient. Thus a statement that property offered for sale has been otherwise disposed of is a revocation. But equivocal language may not be sufficient.

Illustration:

5. A makes an offer to B, and later says to B, "Well, I don't know if we are ready. We have not decided, we might not want to go through with it." The offer is revoked.

§ 43 Indirect Communication of Revocation

An offeree's power of acceptance is terminated when the offeror takes definite action inconsistent with an intention to enter into the proposed contract and the offeree acquires reliable information to that effect.

Comment:

b. Sale of land. The rule of this Section has been applied most frequently to offers for the sale of an interest in land. If the offeror, after making such an offer, sells or contracts to sell the interest to another person than the offeree, his act manifests an intention not to perform in accordance with the offer and creates a probable inability to perform. . . .

Illustration:

1. A offers a parcel of land to B at a stated price, and gives B a week in which to consider the proposal. Within the week A contracts to sell the parcel to C, and B is informed of that fact by a tenant of the premises. B nevertheless sends a formal acceptance which is received by A within the week. There is no contract between A and B.

c. Other transactions. The considerations applicable to offers to sell land are equally applicable to offers to sell other specific property, if the offeror enters into a transaction which confers on a third person rights prior to those of the offeree. But the rule stated is not limited to such cases. . . .

Illustration:

2. A offers to employ B to replace C, an employee of A who has given A a month's notice of intention to quit. A gives B a week to consider the proposal. C changes his mind and makes a contract with A for continued employment for a year. B asks C about his duties, and C informs B of the new contract. B immediately mails a letter of acceptance to A, which arrives within the week allowed for acceptance. There is no contract between A and B.

d. Definite action; reliable information. This Section does not apply to cases where the offeror takes no action or takes equivocal action. Thus mere negotiations with a third person, or even a definite offer to a second offeree, may be consistent with an intention on the part of the offeror to honor an acceptance by the original offeree. . . . Moreover, a mere rumor does not terminate the power of acceptance, if the offeree disbelieves it and is reasonable in doing so, even though the rumor is later verified. The basic standard to which the offeree is held is that of a reasonable person acting in good faith.

Illustration:

3. A offers to sell B a hundred shares of stock at a fixed price, and states that the offer will not be revoked for a week. Within the week C offers A a

higher price for the same stock, and B learns of the higher offer. B's power of acceptance is not terminated, since he is entitled to assume that A will honor his commitment regardless of its legal effect.

§ 45 Option Contract Created by Part Performance or Tender

(1) Where an offer invites an offeree to accept by rendering a performance and does not invite a promissory acceptance, an option contract is created when the offeree tenders or begins the invited performance or tenders a beginning of it.

(2) The offeror's duty of performance under any option contract so created is conditional on completion or tender of the invited performance in accordance with the terms of the offer.

Comment:

a. *Offer limited to acceptance by performance only.* This Section is limited to cases where the offer does not invite a promissory acceptance. Such an offer has often been referred to as an "offer for a unilateral contract." Typical illustrations are found in offers of rewards or prizes and in non-commercial arrangements among relatives and friends. See Comment *b* to § 32. As to analogous cases arising under offers which give the offeree power to accept either by performing or by promising to perform, as he chooses, see §§ 32, 62. . . .

c. *Tender of performance.* A proposal to receive a payment of money or a delivery of goods is an offer only if acceptance can be completed without further cooperation by the offeror. If there is an offer, it follows that acceptance must be complete at the latest when performance is tendered. A tender of performance, so bargained for and given in exchange for the offer, ordinarily furnishes consideration and creates a contract. See §§ 17, 71, 72.

This is so whether or not the tender carries with it any incidental promises. See §§ 54, 62. If no commitment is made by the offeree, the contract is an option contract. See § 25.

Illustration:

3. A promises B to sell him a specified chattel for $5, stating that B is not to be bound until he pays the money. B tenders $5 within a reasonable time, but A refuses to accept the tender. There is a breach of contract.

d. *Beginning to perform.* If the invited performance takes time, the invitation to perform necessarily includes an invitation to begin performance. In most such cases the beginning of performance carries with it an express or implied promise to complete performance. See § 62. In the less common case where the offer does not contemplate or invite a promise by the offeree, the beginning of performance nevertheless completes the manifestation of mutual assent and furnishes consideration for an option contract. See § 25. If the beginning of performance requires the cooperation of the offeror, tender of part performance has the same effect. Part performance or tender may also create an option contract in a situation where the offeree is invited to take up the option by making a promise, if the offer invites a preliminary performance before the time for the offeree's final commitment.

Illustrations:

4. A offers a reward for the return of lost property. In response to the offer, B searches for the property and finds it. A then notifies B that the offer is revoked. B makes a tender of the property to A conditional on payment of the reward, and A refuses. There is a breach of contract by A.

5. A, a magazine, offers prizes in a subscription contest. At a time when B has submitted the largest number of subscriptions, A cancels the contest. A has broken its contract with B.

6. A writes to her daughter B, living in another state, an offer to leave A's farm to B if B gives up her home and cares for A during A's life, B remaining free to terminate the arrangement at any time. B gives up her home, moves to A's farm, and begins caring for A. A is bound by an option contract.

7. A offers to sell a piece of land to B, and promises that if B incurs expense in employing experts to appraise the property the offer will be irrevocable for 30 days. B hires experts and pays for their transportation to the land. A is bound by an option contract.

8. In January A, an employer, publishes a notice to his employees, promising a stated Christmas bonus to any employee who is continuously in A's employ from January to Christmas. B, an employee hired by the week, reads the notice and continues at work beyond the expiration of the current week. A is bound by an option contract, and if B is continuously in A's employ until Christmas a notice of revocation of the bonus is ineffective.

e. Completion of performance. Where part performance or tender by the offeree creates an option contract, the offeree is not bound to complete performance. The offeror alone is bound, but his duty of performance is conditional on completion of the offeree's performance. If the offeree abandons performance, the offeror's duty to perform never arises. See § 224, defining "condition," and Illustration 4 to that Section. But the condition may be excused, for example, if the offeror prevents performance, waives it, or repudiates. See Comment *b* to § 225 and §§ 239, 278.

f. Preparations for performance. What is begun or tendered must be part of the actual performance invited in order to preclude revocation under this Section. Beginning preparations, though they may be essential to carrying out the contract or to accepting the offer, is not enough. Preparations to perform may, however, constitute justifiable reliance sufficient to make the offeror's promise binding under § 87(2).

In many cases what is invited depends on what is a reasonable mode of acceptance. See § 30. The distinction between preparing for performance and beginning performance in such cases may turn on many factors: the extent to which the offeree's conduct is clearly referable to the offer, the definite and substantial character of that conduct, and the extent to which it is of actual or prospective benefit to the offeror rather than the offeree, as well as the terms of the communications between the parties, their prior course of dealing, and any relevant usages of trade.

Illustration:

9. A makes a written promise to pay $5,000 to B, a hospital, "to aid B in its humanitarian work." Relying upon this and other like promises, B proceeds in its humanitarian work, expending large sums of money and incurring large liabilities. Performance by B has begun, and A's offer is irrevocable.

§ 50 Acceptance of Offer Defined; Acceptance by Performance; Acceptance by Promise

(1) Acceptance of an offer is a manifestation of assent to the terms thereof made by the offeree in a manner invited or required by the offer.

(2) Acceptance by performance requires that at least part of what the offer requests be performed or tendered and includes acceptance by a performance which operates as a return promise.

(3) Acceptance by a promise requires that the offeree complete every act essential to the making of the promise.

Comment:

a. *Mode of acceptance.* The acceptance must manifest assent to the same bargain proposed by the offer, and must also comply with the terms of the offer as to the identity of the offeree and the mode of manifesting acceptance. Offers commonly invite acceptance in any reasonable manner, but a particular mode of acceptance may be required. See § 30. In case of doubt, the offeree may choose to accept either by promising or by rendering the requested performance. See § 32.

b. *Acceptance by performance.* Where the offer requires acceptance by performance and does not invite a return promise, as in the ordinary case of an offer of a reward, a contract can be created only by the offeree's performance. In such cases the act requested and performed as consideration for the offeror's promise ordinarily also constitutes acceptance; under § 45 the beginning of performance or the tender of part performance of what is requested may both indicate assent and furnish consideration for an option contract. In some other cases the offeree may choose to create a contract either by making a promise or by rendering or tendering performance; in most such cases the beginning of performance or a tender of part performance operates as a promise to render complete performance. See §§ 32, 62. Mere preparation to perform, however, is not acceptance, although in some cases preparation may make the offeror's promise binding under § 87(2).

Illustrations:

1. A, who is about to leave on a month's vacation, tells B that A will pay B $50 if B will paint A's porch while A is away. B says he may not have time,

and A says B may decide after A leaves. If B begins the painting, there is an acceptance by performance which operates as a promise to complete the job. See §§ 32, 62.

2. In Illustration 1, B also expresses doubt whether he will be able to finish the job, and it is agreed that B may quit at any time but will be paid only if he finishes the job during A's vacation. If B begins the painting, there is an acceptance by performance creating an option contract. See § 45.

c. Acceptance by promise. The typical contract consists of mutual promises and is formed by an acceptance constituting a return promise by the offeree. A promissory acceptance may be explicitly required by the offer, or may be the only type of acceptance which is reasonable under the circumstances, or the offeree may choose to accept by promise an offer which invites acceptance either by promise or by performance. See §§ 30, 32. The promise may be made in words or other symbols of assent, or it may be implied from conduct, other than acts of performance, provided only that it is in a form invited or required by the offer. An act of performance may also operate as a return promise, but the acceptance in such a case is treated as an acceptance by performance rather than an acceptance by promise; thus the requirement of notification is governed by § 54 rather than by § 56. As appears from § 63, acceptance by promise may be effective when a written promise is started on its way, but the offeree must complete the acts necessary on his part to constitute a promise by him. Similarly, in cases where communication to the offeror is unnecessary under § 69, the acts constituting the promise must be complete.

Illustrations:

3. A sends to B plans for a summer cottage to be built on A's land in a remote wilderness area, and writes, "If you will undertake to build a cottage in accordance with the enclosed plans, I will pay you $5,000." B cannot accept by beginning or completing performance, since A's letter calls for acceptance by promise. See § 58.

4. A mails a written order to B, offering to buy on specified terms a machine of a type which B regularly sells from stock. The order provides, "Ship at once." B immediately mails a letter of acceptance. This is an acceptance by promise, even though under § 32 B might have accepted by performance.

5. A gives an order to B Company's traveling salesman which provides, "This proposal becomes a contract without further notification when approval by an executive officer of B Company is noted hereon at its home office." The notation of approval is an acceptance by promise. See §§ 56, 69 as to the requirement of notification.

§ 52 Who May Accept an Offer

An offer can be accepted only by a person whom it invites to furnish the consideration.

Comment:

a. Rationale. This Section states a negative fairly implied in § 29. The offeror is the master of his offer, and the power of acceptance rests on his manifested intention. The rule that the power of acceptance is personal to the offeree is applied strictly. . . .

Illustrations:

1. A makes an offer to B, who dies after receiving it. His executor, though acting within the permitted time, cannot accept.
2. A offers to guarantee payment for goods delivered to B by C. D cannot accept by delivering goods to B.

b. Identity of the offeree. Just as the person to whom a promise is addressed is the promisee (§ 2), so the person to whom an offer is addressed is the offeree. An offer which is itself a promise may contemplate the furnishing of consideration by a person other than the promisee. See § 71(4). That other person is then the offeree.

In case of misunderstanding as to identity of the offeree, the principles stated in § 20 are applicable. An offeror who knows or has reason to know that he is apparently making an offer to a particular person may be bound by that appearance. But one who knows that he is not the intended offeree cannot take advantage of such an appearance, and one who has reason to know the offeror's meaning can accept only if the offeror in fact knows of the offeree's contrary understanding.

Illustrations:

3. A promises B that A will sell and deliver a set of books to B if B's father C will promise to pay $150 for the set. B is the promisee of A's promise; C is the offeree of A's offer. Only C can accept the offer by making the return promise invited by A.
4. A sends B an order for goods. C, from whom A has previously refused to buy such goods, has purchased B's business. Without notifying A of the change of proprietorship, C ships the goods as ordered. Neither B nor C has accepted A's offer.
5. A, in Illustration 4, before using the goods, discovers that they have come from C. A's retention or use of them is an acceptance of an offer from C, and a contract arises.

§ 53 Acceptance by Performance; Manifestation of Intention Not to Accept

(1) An offer can be accepted by the rendering of a performance only if the offer invites such an acceptance. . . .

Comment:

a. Invitation of acceptance by performance. Subsection (1) makes explicit with respect to acceptance by performance the offeror's power to control the mode of acceptance. See §§ 30(1), 50(1). In the absence of contrary indication, the question is whether acceptance by performance is reasonable under the circumstances. See § 30(2). Where either acceptance by performance or acceptance by promise is reasonable, the offeree may choose between them. Where no return commitment is invited and the invited performance takes time, the beginning of performance creates an option contract. See § 45. In other cases the beginning of performance may carry with it a promise to complete performance. See § 62. . . .

§ 54 Acceptance by Performance; Necessity of Notification to Offeror

(1) Where an offer invites an offeree to accept by rendering a performance, no notification is necessary to make such an acceptance effective unless the offer requests such a notification.

(2) If an offeree who accepts by rendering a performance has reason to know that the offeror has no adequate means of learning of the performance with reasonable promptness and certainty, the contractual duty of the offeror is discharged unless

(a) the offeree exercises reasonable diligence to notify the offeror of acceptance, or

(b) the offeror learns of the performance within a reasonable time, or

(c) the offer indicates that notification of acceptance is not required.

Comment:

a. Rationale. In the usual commercial bargain the offeror expects and receives prompt notification of acceptance, and such notification is ordinarily essential to an acceptance by promise. See § 56. But where an offer invites the offeree to accept by rendering a performance, the offeree needs a dependable basis for his decision whether to accept. When the offeree performs or begins to perform in response to such an offer, there is need for protection of his justifiable reliance. Compare § 45. Those needs are met by giving the performance the effect of temporarily barring revocation of the offer; but ordinarily notification of the offeror must follow in due course. See Uniform Commercial Code § 2-206 Comment 3.

b. Performance operating as return promise. This Section applies only to offers which invite acceptance by performance. Where the offeree is empowered to choose between acceptance by performance and acceptance by promise (see § 32), this Section applies only if he chooses to accept by performance. See § 50(2). In such a case the acceptance often carries with it a return commitment (see § 62), and it is rare that the offer dispenses with notification of such a commitment. Compare §§ 56, 69. Unless the performance will come to the offeror's attention in normal course, it is not likely to be a reasonable mode of acceptance. See § 30. In the exceptional case where acceptance is invited by a performance which will not come promptly to the offeror's attention, Subsection (2) usually requires notification of acceptance. Uniform Commercial Code § 2-206(2) provides that if no notification is sent within a reasonable time in such a case, the offeror may treat the offer as having lapsed before acceptance. Compare § 41.

Illustration:

1. A mails a written order to B for goods to be manufactured specially for A, and requests B to begin at once since manufacture will take several weeks. Under § 62 acceptance is complete when B begins, but A's contractual duty is discharged and he may treat the offer as having lapsed before acceptance unless within a reasonable time B sends notification of acceptance or unless the offer or a prior course of dealing indicates that notification is not required.

c. *Where no return promise is contemplated.* Performance may be invited as an alternative mode of acceptance or as the exclusive mode of acceptance. See §§ 30, 32. Where no return commitment is involved, the only notification of acceptance called for is often that necessarily involved in performance by the offeree, or that which accompanies the offeree's request for performance by the offeror. Performance itself both manifests assent and furnishes consideration. Notification is requisite only where the offeror has no convenient means of ascertaining whether the requisite performance has taken place. Even then, it is not the notification which creates the contract, but lack of notification which ends the duty. Compare § 224. Moreover, the offeror may effectively waive notification either before or after the time when it would otherwise be due. See § 84.

Illustrations:

2. A, the proprietor of a medical preparation, offers $100 to anyone who contracts a certain disease after using the preparation as directed. B uses it as directed. B has accepted the offer, and is entitled to the $100 if she later contracts the disease. No notification to A is required until after B has contracted the disease.

3. A, a newspaper, requests B to discontinue distribution of a rival newspaper, and offers to pay B $10 per week as long as B abstains from such distribution. B discontinues the distribution. B has accepted the offer, and no notification to A is required. . . .

§ 58 Necessity of Acceptance Complying with Terms of Offer

An acceptance must comply with the requirements of the offer as to the promise to be made or the performance to be rendered.

Comment:

a. *Scope.* This rule applies to the substance of the bargain the basic principle that the offeror is the master of his offer. That principle rests on the concept of private autonomy underlying contract law. It is mitigated by the interpretation of offers, in accordance with common understanding, as inviting acceptance in any reasonable manner unless there is contrary indication.

See §§ 20, 30(2), 32. Usage of trade or course of dealing may permit inconsequential variations; or a variation clearly to the offeror's advantage, such as a reduction in the price of ordered goods, may be within the scope of the offer. But even in such cases the offeror is entitled, if he makes his meaning clear, to insist on a prescribed type of acceptance.

Illustrations:

1. A offers to sell a book to B for $5 and states that no other acceptance will be honored but the mailing of B's personal check for exactly $5. B personally tenders $5 in legal tender, or mails a personal check for $10. There is no contract.

2. A offers to pay B $100 for plowing Flodden field, and states that acceptance is to be made only by posting a letter before beginning work and before the next Monday noon. Before Monday noon B completes the requested plowing and mails to A a letter stating that the work is complete. There is no contract.

§ 59 Purported Acceptance Which Adds Qualifications

A reply to an offer which purports to accept it but is conditional on the offeror's assent to terms additional to or different from those offered is not an acceptance but is a counter-offer.

Comment:

a. *Qualified acceptance.* A qualified or conditional acceptance proposes an exchange different from that proposed by the original offeror. Such a proposal is a counter-offer and ordinarily terminates the power of acceptance of the original offeree. See § 39. The effect of the qualification or condition is to deprive the purported acceptance of effect. But a definite and seasonable expression of acceptance is operative despite the statement of additional or different terms if the acceptance is not made to depend on assent to the additional or different terms. See § 61; Uniform Commercial Code § 2-207(1). The additional or different terms are then to be construed as proposals for modification of the contract. See Uniform Commercial Code § 2-207(2). Such proposals may sometimes be accepted by the silence of the original offeror. See § 69.

Illustration:

1. A makes an offer to B, and B in terms accepts but adds, "This acceptance is not effective unless prompt acknowledgement is made of receipt of this letter." There is no contract, but a counter-offer.

§ 61 Acceptance Which Requests Change of Terms

An acceptance which requests a change or addition to the terms of the offer is not thereby invalidated unless the acceptance is made to depend on an assent to the changed or added terms.

Comment:

a. *Interpretation of acceptance.* An acceptance must be unequivocal. But the mere inclusion of words requesting a modification of the proposed terms does not prevent a purported acceptance from closing the contract unless, if fairly interpreted, the offeree's assent depends on the offeror's further acquiescence in the modification. See Uniform Commercial Code § 2-207(1).

Illustrations:

1. A offers to sell B 100 tons of steel at a certain price. B replies, "I accept your offer. I hope that if you can arrange to deliver the steel in weekly installments of 25 tons you will do so." There is a contract, but A is not bound to deliver in installments.

2. A offers to sell specified hardware to B on stated terms. B replies: "I accept your offer; ship in accordance with your statement. Please send me also one No. 5 hand saw at your list price." The request for the saw is a separate offer, not a counter-offer.

§ 62 Effect of Performance by Offeree Where Offer Invites Either Performance or Promise

(1) Where an offer invites an offeree to choose between acceptance by promise and acceptance by performance, the tender or beginning of the invited performance or a tender of a beginning of it is an acceptance by performance.

(2) Such an acceptance operates as a promise to render complete performance.

Comment:

a. *The offeree's power to choose.* The offeror normally invites a promise by the offeree for the purpose of obtaining performance of the promise. Full performance fulfills that purpose more directly than the promise invited, and hence constitutes a reasonable mode of acceptance. The offeror can insist on any mode of acceptance, but ordinarily he invites acceptance in any reasonable manner; in case of doubt, an offer is interpreted as inviting the offeree to choose between acceptance by promise and acceptance by performance. See §§ 30, 32, 58.

b. *Part performance or tender.* Where acceptance by performance is invited and no promise is invited, the beginning of performance or the tender of part performance creates an option contract and renders the offer irrevocable. See §§ 37, 45. Under Subsection (1) of this Section the offer is similarly rendered irrevocable where it invites the offeree to choose between acceptance by promise and acceptance by performance. But unless an option contract is contemplated, the offeree is expected to be bound as well as the offeror, and Subsection (2) of this Section states the implication of promise which results from that expectation. See Illustration 5 to § 32. . . .

c. *Manifestation of contrary intention.* The rule of Subsection (1), like the rule of § 45, is designed to protect the offeree in justifiable reliance on the offeror's promise; both rules yield to a manifestation of intention which makes such reliance unjustified. . . . Similarly, the rule of Subsection (2) is designed to preclude the offeree from speculating at the offeror's expense where no option contract is contemplated by the offer (compare § 63), and to protect the offeror in justifiable reliance on the offeree's implied promise. . . .

d. Preparations for performance. As under § 45, what is begun or tendered must be part of the actual performance invited, rather than preparation for performance, in order to make the rule of this Section applicable. See Comment *f* to § 45. But preparations to perform may bring the case within § 87(2) on justifiable reliance.

Illustrations:

1. A, a merchant, mails B, a carpenter in the same city, an offer to employ B to fit up A's office in accordance with A's specifications and B's estimate previously submitted, the work to be completed in two weeks. The offer says, "You may begin at once," and B immediately buys lumber and begins to work on it in his own shop. The next day, before B has sent a notice of acceptance or begun work at A's office or rendered the lumber unfit for other jobs, A revokes the offer. The revocation is timely, since B has not begun to perform.

2. A, a regular customer of B, orders fragile goods from B which B carries in stock and ships in his own trucks. Following his usual practice, B selects the goods ordered, tags them as A's, crates them and loads them on a truck at substantial expense. Performance has begun, and A's offer is irrevocable. See Uniform Commercial Code § 2-206 and Comment 2.

§ 63 Time When Acceptance Takes Effect

Unless the offer provides otherwise,

(a) an acceptance made in a manner and by a medium invited by an offer is operative and completes the manifestation of mutual assent as soon as put out of the offeree's possession, without regard to whether it ever reaches the offeror; but

(b) an acceptance under an option contract is not operative until received by the offeror.

Comment:

a. Rationale. It is often said that an offeror who makes an offer by mail makes the post office his agent to receive the acceptance, or that the mailing of a letter of acceptance puts it irrevocably out of the offeree's control. Under United States postal regulations, however, the sender of a letter has long had the power to stop delivery and reclaim the letter. A better explanation of the rule that the acceptance takes effect on dispatch is that the offeree needs a dependable basis for his decision whether to accept. In many legal systems such a basis is provided by a general rule that an offer is irrevocable unless it provides otherwise. The common law provides such a basis through the rule that a revocation of an offer is ineffective if received after an acceptance has been properly dispatched. Acceptance by telegram is governed in this respect by the same considerations as acceptance by mail.

Illustration:

1. A makes B an offer, inviting acceptance by telegram, and B duly telegraphs an acceptance. A purports to revoke the offer in person or by telephone or telegraph, but the attempted revocation is received by B after the telegram of acceptance is dispatched. There is no effective revocation.

b. Loss or delay in transit. In the interest of simplicity and clarity, the rule has been extended to cases where an acceptance is lost or delayed in the course of transmission. The convenience of the rule is less clear in such cases than in cases of attempted revocation of the offer, however, and the language of the offer is often properly interpreted as making the offeror's duty of performance conditional upon receipt of the acceptance. Indeed, where the receipt of notice is essential to enable the offeror to perform, such a condition is normally implied.

Illustrations:

2. A offers to buy cotton from B, the operator of a cotton gin, B to accept by specifying the number of bales in a telegram sent before 8 p.m. the same day. B duly sends a telegram of acceptance and ships the cotton, but the telegram is not delivered. There is a contract, and A is bound to take and pay for the cotton.

3. A mails to B an offer to lease land, stating, "Telegraph me Yes or No. If I do not hear from you by noon on Friday, I shall conclude No." B duly telegraphs "Yes," but the telegram is not delivered until after noon on Friday. Any contract formed by the telegraphic acceptance is discharged.

4. A offers to buy cattle for B, on an understanding that if B telegraphs "Yes" A will notify B of the amount of money needed and B will supply it. B's "Yes" telegram is duly dispatched but does not arrive within a reasonable time. Any contract formed by the dispatch of the telegram is discharged.

c. Revocation of acceptance. The fact that the offeree has power to reclaim his acceptance from the post office or telegraph company does not prevent the acceptance from taking effect on dispatch. Nor, in the absence of additional circumstances, does the actual recapture of the acceptance deprive it of legal effect, though as a practical matter the offeror cannot assert his rights unless he learns of them. An attempt to revoke the acceptance by an overtaking communication is similarly ineffective, even though the revocation is received before the acceptance is received. After mailing an acceptance of a revocable offer, the offeree is not permitted to speculate at the offeror's expense during the time required for the letter to arrive.

A purported revocation of acceptance may, however, affect the rights of the parties. It may amount to an offer to rescind the contract or to a repudiation of it, or it may bar the offeree by estoppel from enforcing it. In some cases it may be justified as an exercise of a right of stoppage in transit or a demand for assurance of performance. Compare Uniform Commercial Code §§ 2-609, 2-702, 2-705. Or the contract may be voidable for mistake or misrepresentation, §§ 151-54, 164. See particularly the provisions of § 153 on unilateral mistake.

Illustrations:

5. A mails to B a note payable by C with instructions to collect the amount of the note and remit by mailing B's own check. At C's request B mails his own check as instructed. Subsequently, at C's request, B recovers his letter and check from the post office. The recovery does not discharge the contract formed by the mailing of B's check. But if B is a bank, its remittance may be provisional under Uniform Commercial Code § 4-211.

6. The facts being otherwise as stated in Illustration 5, B recovers his letter and check from the post office because he has learned that C is insolvent and cannot reimburse B. B is entitled to rescind the contract for mistake. See §§ 153-54; compare Uniform Commercial Code § 4-212.

7. A mails an offer to B to appoint B A's exclusive distributor in a specified area. B duly mails an acceptance. Thereafter B mails a letter which is received by A before the acceptance is received and which rejects the offer and makes a counter-offer. On receiving the rejection and before receiving the acceptance, A executes a contract appointing C as exclusive distributor instead of B. B is estopped to enforce the contract. Compare § 40.

8. The Government mails to A an offer to pay the amount quoted by him for the manufacture of two sets of ship propellers, and A mails an acceptance. A then discovers that by mistake he has quoted the price for a single set, and so informs the Government by a telegram which arrives before the acceptance. A's mailing the acceptance created a contract. The question whether the contract is voidable for mistake is governed by the rules stated in §§ 153-54. . . .

e. The offeree's possession. The rule of Subsection (1) gives effect to an acceptance when "put out of the offeree's possession." Its principal application is to the use of mail and telegraph, but it would apply equally to any other similar public service instrumentality, even though the instrumentality may for some purposes be the offeree's agent. It may also apply to a private messenger service which is independent of the offeree and can be relied on to keep accurate records. But, except where the Government or a telegraph company can make use of its own postal or telegraph facilities, communication by means of the offeree's employee is excluded; the employee's possession is treated as that of the employer.

Illustration:

11. A makes B an offer by mail, or messenger, and B promptly sends an acceptance by his own employee. There is no contract until the acceptance is received by the offeror. As to receipt, see § 68.

f. Option contracts. An option contract provides a dependable basis for decision whether to exercise the option, and removes the primary reason for the rule of Subsection (1). Moreover, there is no objection to speculation at the expense of a party who has irrevocably assumed that risk. Option contracts are commonly subject to a definite time limit, and the usual understanding is that the notification that the option has been exercised must be received by the offeror before that time. Whether or not there is such a time limit, in the absence of a contrary provision in the option contract, the offeree takes the risk of loss or delay in the transmission of the acceptance and remains free to revoke the acceptance until it arrives. Similarly, if there is such a mistake on the part of the offeror as justifies the rescission of his unilateral obligation, the right to rescind is not lost merely because a letter of acceptance is posted. See §§ 151- 54.

Illustrations:

12. A, for consideration, gives B an option to buy property, written notice to be given on or before a specified date. Notice dispatched before but not received until after that date is not effective to exercise the option.

13. A submits a bid to supply goods to the Government, which becomes irrevocable when bids are opened. Within a reasonable time the Government mails a notice of award of the contract to A. Until A receives the notice, there is no contract binding on the Government.

§ 68 What Constitutes Receipt of Revocation, Rejection, or Acceptance

A written revocation, rejection, or acceptance is received when the writing comes into the possession of the person addressed, or of some person authorized by him to receive it for him, or when it is deposited in some place which he has authorized as the place for this or similar communications to be deposited for him.

Comment:

a. *Point of receipt*. Under § 42, a revocation if sent from a distance must be received in order to be effectual. Under § 63 acceptance from a distance need not be received if started on its way in a method authorized, unless receipt is made a condition of the offer. . . . What amounts to receipt in all these cases is defined by the present Section, under which a written communication may be received though it is not read or though it does not even reach the hands of the person to whom it is addressed. . . .

Illustrations:

1. A sends B by mail an offer dated from A's house and states as a condition of the offer that an acceptance must be received within three days. B mails an acceptance which reaches A's house and is delivered to a servant or is deposited in a mail box at the door within three days; but A has been called away from home and does not personally receive the letter for a week. There is a contract.

2. A sends B by mail an offer, but later, desiring to revoke the offer, telegraphs B to that effect. The messenger boy carrying the telegram from the receiving office meets C, B's neighbor, who volunteers to carry the telegram to B, and accordingly is given it by the messenger boy. C forgets to deliver it to B until the following morning. An acceptance by B mailed prior to this time creates a contract.

§ 69 Acceptance by Silence or Exercise of Dominion

(1) Where an offeree fails to reply to an offer, his silence and inaction operate as an acceptance in the following cases only:

(a) Where an offeree takes the benefit of offered services with reasonable opportunity to reject them and reason to know that they were offered with the expectation of compensation.

(b) Where the offeror has stated or given the offeree reason to understand that assent may be manifested by silence or inaction, and the offeree in remaining silent and inactive intends to accept the offer.

(c) Where because of previous dealings or otherwise, it is reasonable that the offeree should notify the offeror if he does not intend to accept.

(2) An offeree who does any act inconsistent with the offeror's ownership of offered property is bound in accordance with the offered terms unless they are manifestly unreasonable. But if the act is wrongful as against the offeror it is an acceptance only if ratified by him.

Comment:

a. Acceptance by silence is exceptional. Ordinarily an offeror does not have power to cause the silence of the offeree to operate as acceptance. . . . The exceptional cases where silence is acceptance fall into two main classes: those where the offeree silently takes offered benefits, and those where one party relies on the other party's manifestation of intention that silence may operate as acceptance. . . .

b. Acceptance of offered services. Services rendered cannot be recovered in specie, and there is in general no right to restitution of the value of services rendered officiously or gratuitously. . . . But when the recipient knows or has reason to know that the services are being rendered with an expectation of compensation, and by a word could prevent the mistake, his privilege of inaction gives way; under Subsection (1)(a) he is held to an acceptance if he fails to speak. The resulting duty is not merely a duty to pay fair value, but a duty to pay or perform according to the terms of the offer.

Illustration:

1. A gives several lessons on the violin to B's child, intending to give the child a course of twenty lessons, and to charge B the price. B never requested A to give this instruction but silently allows the lessons to be continued to their end, having reason to know A's intention. B is bound to pay the price of the course.

c. Intent to accept. The mere fact that an offeror states that silence will constitute acceptance does not deprive the offeree of his privilege to remain silent without accepting. But the offeree is entitled to rely on such a statement if he chooses. The case for acceptance is strongest when the reliance is definite and substantial or when the intent to accept is objectively manifested though not communicated to the offeror. Even though the intent to accept is manifested only by silent inaction, however, the offeror who has invited such an acceptance cannot complain of the resulting uncertainty in his position.

Illustrations:

2. A offers by mail to sell to B a horse already in B's possession for $250, saying: "I am so sure that you will accept that you need not trouble to write me. Your silence alone will operate as acceptance." B makes no reply, but he does not intend to accept. There is no contract.

d. Prior conduct of the offeree. Explicit statement by the offeree, usage of trade, or a course of dealing between the parties may give the offeror reason to understand that silence will constitute acceptance. In such a situation the offer may tacitly incorporate that understanding, and if the offeree intends to accept the case then falls within Subsection (1)(b). Under Subsection (1)(c) the offeree's silence is acceptance, regardless of his actual intent, unless both parties understand that no acceptance is intended. . . .

Illustrations:

5. A, through salesmen, has frequently solicited orders for goods from B, the orders to be subject to A's personal approval. In every case A has shipped the goods ordered within a week and without other notification to B than billing the goods to him on shipment. A's salesman solicits and receives another order from B. A receives the order and remains silent. B relies on the order and forbears to buy elsewhere for a week. A is bound to fill the order.

6. A has for years insured B's property against fire under annual policies. At the expiration of one policy, in accordance with the usual practice, A sends B a renewal policy and a bill for the premium. B retains the policy for two months and then refuses to pay the premium on demand. B is liable for the premium accrued prior to his rejection.

e. Exercise of dominion. An offeree in possession of offered property commonly has a duty or privilege to hold it for the offeror, or, if storage is inconvenient or hazardous, to return it, sell it for the offeror's account, or otherwise dispose of it. . . .

Illustrations:

7. A sends B a one-volume edition of Shakespeare with a letter, saying, "If you wish to buy this book send me $6.50 within one week after receipt hereof, otherwise notify me and I will forward postage for return." B examines the book and without replying makes a gift of it to his wife. B owes A $6.50.

8. The facts being otherwise as stated in Illustration 7, B examines the book and without replying carefully lays it on a shelf to await A's messenger. There is no contract.

CHAPTER 4. FORMATION OF CONTRACTS—CONSIDERATION (§§ 71-109)

§ 71 Requirement of Exchange; Types of Exchange

(1) To constitute consideration, a performance or a return promise must be bargained for.

(2) A performance or return promise is bargained for if it is sought by the promisor in exchange for his promise and is given by the promisee in exchange for that promise.

(3) The performance may consist of

(a) an act other than a promise, or

(b) a forbearance, or

(c) the creation, modification, or destruction of a legal relation.

(4) The performance or return promise may be given to the promisor or to some other person. It may be given by the promisee or by some other person.

Comment:

b. "Bargained for." In the typical bargain, the consideration and the promise bear a reciprocal relation of motive or inducement: the consideration induces the making of the promise and the promise induces the furnishing of the consideration. Here, as in the matter of mutual assent, the law is concerned with the external manifestation rather than the undisclosed mental state: it is enough that one party manifests an intention to induce the other's response and to be induced by it and that the other responds in accordance with the inducement. See § 81. But it is not enough that the promise induces the conduct of the promisee or that the conduct of the promisee induces the making of the promise; both elements must be present, or there is no bargain. Moreover, a mere pretense of bargain does not suffice, as where there is a false recital of consideration or where the purported consideration is merely nominal. In such cases there is no consideration and the promise is enforced, if at all, as a promise binding without consideration under §§ 82-94.

Illustrations:

1. A offers to buy a book owned by B and to pay B $10 in exchange therefor. B accepts the offer and delivers the book to A. The transfer and delivery of the book constitute a performance and are consideration for A's promise. This is so even though A at the time he makes the offer secretly intends to pay B $10 whether or not he gets the book, or even though B at the time he accepts secretly intends not to collect the $10. . . .

4. A desires to make a binding promise to give $1,000 to his son B. Being advised that a gratuitous promise is not binding, A writes out and signs a false recital that B has sold him a car for $1,000 and a promise to pay that amount. There is no consideration for A's promise.

5. A desires to make a binding promise to give $1000 to his son B. Being advised that a gratuitous promise is not binding, A offers to buy from B for $1,000 a book worth less than $1. B accepts the offer knowing that the purchase of the book is a mere pretense. There is no consideration for A's promise to pay $1,000.

c. Mixture of bargain and gift. In most commercial bargains there is a rough equivalence between the value promised and the value received as consideration. But the social functions of bargains include the provision of opportunity for free individual action and exercise of judgment and the fixing of values by private action, either generally or for purposes of the particular transaction. Those functions would be impaired by judicial review of the values so fixed. Ordinarily, therefore, courts do not inquire into the adequacy of consideration, particularly where one or both of the values exchanged are difficult to measure. Even where both parties know that a transaction is in part a bargain and in part a gift, the element of bargain may nevertheless furnish consideration for the entire transaction. . . .

Illustration:

6. A offers to buy a book owned by B and to pay B $10 in exchange therefor. B's transfer and delivery of the book are consideration for A's promise even though both parties know that such books regularly sell for $5 and that part of A's motive in making the offer is to make a gift to B.

d. Types of consideration. Consideration may consist of a performance or of a return promise. Consideration by way of performance may be a specified act of forbearance, or any one of several specified acts or forbearances of which the offeree is given the choice, or such conduct as will produce a specified result. Or either the offeror or the offeree may request as consideration the creation, modification or destruction of a purely intangible legal relation. Not infrequently the consideration bargained for is an act with the added requirement that a certain legal result shall be produced. Consideration by way of return promise requires a promise as defined in § 2. Consideration may consist partly of promise and partly of other acts or forbearances, and the consideration invited may be a performance or a return promise in the alternative. Though a promise is itself an act, it is treated separately from other acts. See § 75.

Illustrations:

9. A promises B, his nephew aged 16, that A will pay B $1,000 when B becomes 21 if B does not smoke before then. B's forbearance to smoke is a performance and if bargained for is consideration for A's promise.

10. A says to B, the owner of a garage, "I will pay you $100 if you will make my car run properly." The production of this result is consideration for A's promise.

11. A has B's horse in his possession. B writes to A, "If you will promise me $100 for the horse, he is yours." A promptly replies making the

requested promise. The property in the horse at once passes to A. The change in ownership is consideration for A's promise.

12. A promises to pay B $1,000 if B will make an offer to C to sell C certain land for $25,000 and will leave the offer open for 24 hours. B makes the requested offer and forbears to revoke it for 24 hours, but C does not accept. The creation of a power of acceptance in C is consideration for A's promise.

13. A mails a written order to B, offering to buy specified machinery on specified terms. The order provides "Ship at once." B's prompt shipment or promise to ship is consideration for A's promise to pay the price.

§ 73 Performance of Legal Duty

Performance of a legal duty owed to a promisor which is neither doubtful nor the subject of honest dispute is not consideration; but a similar performance is consideration if it differs from what was required by the duty in a way which reflects more than a pretense of bargain.

§ 74 Settlement of Claims

(1) Forbearance to assert or the surrender of a claim or defense which proves to be invalid is not consideration unless

(a) the claim or defense is in fact doubtful because of uncertainty as to the facts or the law, or

(b) the forbearing or surrendering party believes that the claim or defense may be fairly determined to be valid. . . .

(2) The execution of a written instrument surrendering a claim or defense by one who is under no duty to execute it is consideration if the execution of the written instrument is bargained for even though he is not asserting the claim or defense and believes that no valid claim or defense exists.

Comment:

b. Requirement of good faith. The policy favoring compromise of disputed claims is clearest, perhaps, where a claim is surrendered at a time when it is uncertain whether it is valid or not. Even though the invalidity later becomes clear, the bargain is to be judged as it appeared to the parties at the time; if the claim was then doubtful, no inquiry is necessary as to their good faith. Even though the invalidity should have been clear at the time, the settlement of an honest dispute is upheld. But a mere assertion or denial of liability does not make a claim doubtful, and the fact that invalidity is obvious may indicate that it was known. In such cases Subsection (1)(b) requires a showing of good faith.

§ 77 Illusory and Alternative Promises

A promise or apparent promise is not consideration if by its terms the promisor or purported promisor reserves a choice of alternative performances unless

(a) each of the alternative performances would have been consideration if it alone had been bargained for; or

(b) one of the alternative performances would have been consideration and there is or appears to the parties to be a substantial possibility that before the promisor exercises his choice events may eliminate the alternatives which would not have been consideration.

§ 79 Adequacy of Consideration; Mutuality of Obligation

If the requirement of consideration is met, there is no additional requirement of

(a) a gain, advantage, or benefit to the promisor or a loss, disadvantage, or detriment to the promisee; or

(b) equivalence in the values exchanged; or

(c) "mutuality of obligation."

Comment:

a. Rationale. In such typical bargains as the ordinary sale of goods each party gives up something of economic value, and the values exchanged are often roughly or exactly equivalent by standards independent of the particular bargain. Quite often promise is exchanged for promise, and the promised performances are sometimes divisible into matching parts. Hence it has sometimes been said that consideration must consist of a "benefit to the promisor" or a "detriment to the promisee"; it has frequently been claimed that there was no consideration because the economic value given in exchange was much less than that of the promise or the promised performance; "mutuality of obligation" has been said to be essential to a contract. But experience has shown that these are not essential elements of a bargain or of an enforceable contract, and they are negated as requirements by the rules stated in §§ 71-78. This Section makes that negation explicit.

b. Benefit and detriment. Historically, the common law action of debt was said to require a quid pro quo, and that requirement may have led to statements that consideration must be a benefit to the promisor. But contracts were enforced in the common-law action of assumpsit without any such requirement; in actions of assumpsit the emphasis was rather on the harm to the promisee, and detrimental reliance on a promise may still be the basis of contractual relief. See § 90. But reliance is not essential to the formation of a bargain, and remedies for breach have long been given in cases of exchange of promise for promise where neither party has begun to perform. Today when it is said that consideration must involve a detriment to the promisee, the supposed requirement is often qualified by a statement that a "legal detriment" is sufficient even though there is no economic detriment or other actual loss. It is more realistic to say simply that there is no requirement of detriment.

c. Exchange of unequal values. To the extent that the apportionment of productive energy and product in the economy are left to private action, the parties to transactions are free to fix their own valuations. The resolution of disputes often requires a determination of value in the more general sense of market value, and such values are commonly fixed as an approximation based on a multitude of private valuations. But in many situations there is no reliable external standard of value, or the general standard is inappropriate to the precise circumstances of the parties. Valuation is left to private action in part because the parties are thought to be better able than others to evaluate the circumstances of particular transactions. In any event, they are not ordinarily bound to follow the valuations of others.

Ordinarily, therefore, courts do not inquire into the adequacy of consideration. This is particularly so when one or both of the values exchanged are uncertain or difficult to measure. But it is also applied even when it is clear that the transaction is a mixture of bargain and gift. Gross inadequacy of consideration may be relevant to issues of capacity, fraud and the like, but the requirement of consideration is not a safeguard against imprudent and improvident contracts except in cases where it appears that there is no bargain in fact.

Illustrations:

3. A borrows $300 from B to enable A to begin litigation to recover a gold mine through litigation, and promises to repay $10,000 when he recovers the mine. The loan is consideration for the promise.

4. A is pregnant with the illegitimate child of B, a wealthy man. A promises to give the child A's surname and B's given name, and B promises to provide for the support and education of the child and to set up a trust of securities to provide the child with a minimum net income of $100 per week until he reaches the age of 21. The naming of the child is consideration for B's promise.

d. Pretended exchange. Disparity in value, with or without other circumstances, sometimes indicates that the purported consideration was not in fact bargained for but was a mere formality or pretense. Such a sham or "nominal" consideration does not satisfy the requirement of § 71. Promises are enforced in such cases, if at all, either as promises binding without consideration under §§ 82-94 or as promises binding by virtue of their formal characteristics under § 6. See, for example, §§ 95-109 on contracts under seal.

Illustrations:

5. In consideration of one cent received, A promises to pay $600 in three yearly installments of $200 each. The one cent is merely nominal and is not consideration for A's promise.

6. A dies leaving no assets and owing $4,000 to the B bank. C, A's widow, promises to pay the debt, and B promises to make no claim against A's estate. Without some further showing, B's promise is a mere formality and is not consideration for C's promise.

e. Effects of gross inadequacy. Although the requirement of consideration may be met despite a great difference in the values exchanged, gross inadequacy of consideration may be relevant in the application of other rules. Inadequacy "such as shocks the conscience" is often said to be a "badge of fraud," justifying a denial of specific performance. Inadequacy may also help to justify rescission or cancellation on the ground of lack of capacity, mistake, misrepresentation, duress or undue influence. Unequal bargains are also limited by the statutory law of usury, by regulation of the rates of public utilities and some other enterprises, and by special rules developed for the sale of an expectation of inheritance, for contractual penalties and forfeitures, and for agreements between secured lender and borrower.

§ 81 Consideration as Motive or Inducing Cause

(1) The fact that what is bargained for does not of itself induce the making of a promise does not prevent it from being consideration for the promise.

(2) The fact that a promise does not of itself induce a performance or return promise does not prevent the performance or return promise from being consideration for the promise.

Comment:

a. "Bargained for." Consideration requires that a performance or return promise be "bargained for" in exchange for a promise; this means that the promisor must manifest an intention to induce the performance or return promise and to be induced by it, and that the promisee must manifest an intention to induce the making of the promise and to be induced by it. See § 71 and Comment *b*. In most commercial bargains the consideration is the object of the promisor's desire and that desire is a material motive or cause inducing the making of the promise, and the reciprocal desire of the promisee for the making of the promise similarly induces the furnishing of the consideration.

b. Immateriality of motive or cause. This Section makes explicit a limitation on the requirement that consideration be bargained for. Even in the typical commercial bargain, the promisor may have more than one motive, and the person furnishing the consideration need not inquire into the promisor's motives. Unless both parties know that the purported consideration is mere pretense, it is immaterial that the promisor's desire for the consideration is incidental to other objectives and even that the other party knows this to be so. Subsection (2) states a similar rule with respect to the motives of the promisee.

§ 82 Promise to Pay Indebtedness; Effect on the Statute of Limitations

(1) A promise to pay all or part of an antecedent contractual or quasi-contractual indebtedness owed by the promisor is binding if the indebtedness is still enforceable or would be except for the effect of a statute of limitations. . . .

Illustrations:

2. A owes B three debts of $500 each. All of the debts are barred by the statute of limitations. A writes to B, "I promise to pay you one of those $500 debts which I owe; the other two I shall not pay." A's promise of $500 is binding.

3. A owes B a debt for some work which B has done but the amount due is in dispute. A writes to B, "I will pay you whatever I owe." The promise is

binding during the statutory period of limitation from the time when it was made, and subjects A to a duty to pay whatever amount B can prove was due him.

§ 83 Promise to Pay Indebtedness Discharged in Bankruptcy

An express promise to pay all or part of an indebtedness of the promisor, discharged or dischargeable in bankruptcy proceedings begun before the promise is made, is binding.

Illustrations:

1. A owes B $100 and is about to go into bankruptcy. Immediately before filing his petition he promises B to pay the debt in spite of any discharge that he may get in bankruptcy. The promise is not binding but would have been binding if it had been made after the petition in bankruptcy was filed.

2. A owes B $100, and the debt is discharged in A's bankruptcy. Thereafter A promises in writing to pay the debt "as soon as I sell the mill." Two years later A sells the mill. B can recover the debt from A by an action brought within the period fixed by the statute of limitations after the sale. If the subsequent promise were oral, B would be limited in most States to an action within the statutory period after the original debt became due.

§ 84 Promise to Perform a Duty in Spite of Non-Occurrence of a Condition

(1) Except as stated in Subsection (2), a promise to perform all or part of a conditional duty under an antecedent contract in spite of the non-occurrence of the condition is binding, whether the promise is made before or after the time for the condition to occur, unless

(a) occurrence of the condition was a material part of the agreed exchange for the performance of the duty and the promisee was under no duty that it occur; or

(b) uncertainty of the occurrence of the condition was an element of the risk assumed by the promisor.

(2) If such a promise is made before the time for the occurrence of the condition has expired and the condition is within the control of the promisee or a beneficiary, the promisor can make his duty again subject to the condition by notifying the promisee or beneficiary of his intention to do so if

(a) the notification is received while there is still a reasonable time to cause the condition to occur under the antecedent terms or an extension given by the promisor; and

(b) reinstatement of the requirement of the condition is not unjust because of a material change of position by the promisee or beneficiary; and

(c) the promise is not binding apart from the rule stated in Subsection (1).

Comment:

b. "Waiver" and "estoppel"; mistake. "Waiver" is often inexactly defined as "the voluntary relinquishment of a known right." When the waiver is reinforced by reliance, enforcement is often said to rest on "estoppel." Compare §§ 89, 90. Since the more common definition of estoppel is limited to reliance on a misrepresentation of an existing fact, reliance on a waiver or promise as to the future is sometimes said to create a "promissory estoppel." The common definition of waiver may lead to the incorrect inference that the promisor must know his legal rights and must intend the legal effect of the promise. But under § 93 it is sufficient if he has reason to know the essential facts. And if the waiver is supported by reliance or by consideration, the effect of mistake on the part of the promisor depends on the rules stated in Chapter 6.

Illustrations:

4. A, an insurance company, insures B's house for $5,000 against loss by fire. The insurance policy provides that it shall be payable only if B gives written notification of any loss within thirty days after its occurrence. An insured loss occurs and B gives only oral notification thereof within thirty days. A tells him, either before or after the lapse of thirty days from the loss, that this notification is sufficient. A cannot thereafter rely upon B's failure to give written notification as an excuse for failure to pay for the loss. . . .

6. In Illustration 4, A can restore the requirement of the condition by notifying B of his intention to do so if there still remains a reasonable time for the occurrence of the condition before the expiration of the thirty-day period, unless such action would be unjust in view of a material change of position by B in reliance on A's waiver. If a reasonable time does not remain, A cannot restore the requirement of the condition by extending the time.

§ 86 Promise for Benefit Received

(1) A promise made in recognition of a benefit previously received by the promisor from the promisee is binding to the extent necessary to prevent injustice.

(2) A promise is not binding under Subsection (1)

(a) if the promisee conferred the benefit as a gift or for other reasons the promisor has not been unjustly enriched; or

(b) to the extent that its value is disproportionate to the benefit.

Comment:

a. *"Past consideration"; "moral obligation."* Enforcement of promises to pay for benefit received has sometimes been said to rest on "past consideration" or on the "moral obligation" of the promisor, and there are statutes in such terms in a few states. Those terms are not used here: "past consideration" is inconsistent with the meaning of consideration stated in § 71, and there seems to be no consensus as to what constitutes a "moral obligation." The mere fact of promise has been thought to create a moral obligation, but it is clear that not all promises are enforced. Nor are moral obligations based solely on gratitude or sentiment sufficient of themselves to support a subsequent promise.

Illustrations:

1. A gives emergency care to B's adult son while the son is sick and without funds far from home. B subsequently promises to reimburse A for his expenses. The promise is not binding under this Section.

2. A lends money to B, who later dies. B's widow promises to pay the debt. The promise is not binding under this Section.

3. A has immoral relations with B, a woman not his wife, to her injury. A's subsequent promise to reimburse B for her loss is not binding under this Section.

b. Rationale. Although in general a person who has been unjustly enriched at the expense of another is required to make restitution, restitution is denied in many cases in order to protect persons who have had benefits thrust upon them. In other cases restitution is denied by virtue of rules designed to guard against false claims, stale claims, claims already litigated, and the like. In many such cases a subsequent promise to make restitution removes the reason for the denial of relief, and the policy against unjust enrichment then prevails. . . .

d. Emergency services and necessaries. The law of restitution in the absence of promise severely limits recovery for necessaries furnished to a person under disability and for emergency services. A subsequent promise in such a case may remove doubt as to the reality of the benefit and as to its value, and may negate any danger of imposition or false claim. A positive showing that payment was expected is not then required; an intention to make a gift must be shown to defeat restitution.

Illustrations:

6. A finds B's escaped bull and feeds and cares for it. B's subsequent promise to pay reasonable compensation to A is binding.

7. A saves B's life in an emergency and is totally and permanently disabled in so doing. One month later B promises to pay A $15 every two weeks for the rest of A's life, and B makes the payments for 8 years until he dies. The promise is binding.

i. Partial enforcement. . . . [W]here a benefit received is a liquidated sum of money, a promise is not enforceable under this Section beyond the amount of the benefit. Where the value of the benefit is uncertain, a promise to pay the value is binding and a promise to pay a liquidated sum may serve to fix the amount due if in all the circumstances it is not disproportionate to the benefit. See Illustration 7. A promise which is excessive may sometimes be enforced to the extent of the value of the benefit, and the remedy may be thought of as quasi-contractual rather than contractual. In other cases a promise of disproportionate value may tend to show unfair pressure or other conduct by the promisee such that justice does not require any enforcement of the promise.

Illustrations:

12. A, a married woman of sixty, has rendered household services without compensation over a period of years for B, a man of eighty living alone

and having no close relatives. B has a net worth of three million dollars and has often assured A that she will be well paid for her services, whose reasonable value is not in excess of $6,000. B executes and delivers to A a written promise to pay A $25,000 "to be taken from my estate." The promise is binding.

13. The facts being otherwise as stated in Illustration 12, B's promise is made orally and is to leave A his entire estate. A cannot recover more than the reasonable value of her services.

§ 87 Option Contracts

(1) An offer is binding as an option contract if it

(a) is in writing and signed by the offeror, recites a purported consideration for the making of the offer, and proposes an exchange on fair terms within a reasonable time; or

(b) is made irrevocable by statute.

(2) An offer which the offeror should reasonably expect to induce action or forbearance of a substantial character on the part of the offeree before acceptance and which does induce such action or forbearance is binding as an option contract to the extent necessary to avoid injustice.

Comment:

a. *Consideration and form.* The traditional common-law devices for making a firm offer or option contract are the giving of consideration and the affixing of a seal. . . . The erosion of the formality of the seal has made it less and less satisfactory as a universal formality. As literacy has spread, the personal signature has become the natural formality and the seal has become more and more anachronistic. The rules stated in this section reflect the judicial and legislative response to this situation.

e. *Reliance.* Subsection (2) states the application of § 90 to reliance on an unaccepted offer, with qualifications which would not be appropriate in some other types of cases covered by § 90. It is important chiefly in cases of reliance that is not part performance. If the beginning of performance is a reasonable mode of acceptance, it makes the offer fully enforceable under § 45 or § 62; if not, the offeror commonly has no reason to expect part performance before acceptance. But circumstances may be such that the offeree must undergo substantial expense, or undertake substantial commitments, or forego alternatives, in order to put himself in a position to accept by either promise or performance. The offer may be made expressly irrevocable in contemplation of reliance by the offeree. If reliance follows in such cases, justice may require a remedy. But the reliance must be substantial as well as foreseeable.

Full-scale enforcement of the offered contract is not necessarily appropriate in such cases. Restitution of benefits conferred may be enough, or partial or full reimbursement of losses may be proper. Various factors may influence the remedy: the formality of the offer, its commercial or social context, the extent to which the offeree's reliance was understood to be at his own risk, the relative competence and the bargaining position of the parties, the degree of fault on the part of the offeror, the ease and certainty of proof of particular items of damage and the likelihood that unprovable damages have been suffered.

Illustration:

6. A submits a written offer for paving work to be used by B as a partial basis for B's bid as general contractor on a large building. As A knows, B is required to name his subcontractors in his general bid. B uses A's offer and B's bid is accepted. A's offer is irrevocable until B has had a reasonable opportunity to notify A of the award and B's acceptance of A's offer.

§ 89 Modification of Executory Contract

A promise modifying a duty under a contract not fully performed on either side is binding

(a) if the modification is fair and equitable in view of circumstances not anticipated by the parties when the contract was made; or

(b) to the extent provided by statute; or

(c) to the extent that justice requires enforcement in view of material change of position in reliance on the promise.

Comment:

b. Performance of legal duty. . . . The limitation to a modification which is "fair and equitable" goes beyond absence of coercion and requires an objectively demonstrable reason for seeking a modification. Compare Uniform Commercial Code § 2-209 Comment. The reason for modification must rest in circumstances not "anticipated" as part of the context in which the contract was made. . . .

The same result called for by paragraph (a) is sometimes reached on the ground that the original contract was "rescinded" by mutual agreement and that new promises were then made which furnished consideration for each other. That theory is rejected here because it is fictitious when the "rescission" and new agreement are simultaneous, and because if logically carried out it might uphold unfair and inequitable modifications.

Illustrations:

1. By a written contract A agrees to excavate a cellar for B for a stated price. Solid rock is unexpectedly encountered and A so notifies B. A and B then orally agree that A will remove the rock at a unit price which is reasonable but nine times that used in computing the original price, and A completes the job. B is bound to pay the increased amount.

2. A contracts with B to supply for $300 a laundry chute for a building B has contracted to build for the Government for $150,000. Later A discovers that he made an error as to the type of material to be used and should have bid $1,200. A offers to supply the chute for $1,000, eliminating overhead and profit. After ascertaining that other suppliers would charge more, B agrees. The new agreement is binding.

3. A is employed by B as a designer of coats at $90 a week for a year beginning November 1 under a written contract executed September 1. A is offered $115 a week by another employer and so informs B. A and B then agree that A will be paid $100 a week and in October execute a new written contract to that effect, simultaneously tearing up the prior contract. The new contract is binding.

4. A contracts to manufacture and sell to B 2,000 steel roofs for corn cribs at $60. Before A begins manufacture a threat of a nationwide steel strike raises the cost of steel about $10 per roof, and A and B agree orally to increase the price to $70 per roof. A thereafter manufactures and delivers 1700 of the roofs, and B pays for 1,500 of them at the increased price without protest, increasing the selling price of the corn cribs by $10. The new agreement is binding.

5. A contracts to manufacture and sell to B 100,000 castings for lawn mowers at 50 cents each. After partial delivery and after B has contracted to sell a substantial number of lawn mowers at a fixed price, A notifies B that increased metal costs require that the price be increased to 75 cents. Substitute castings are available at 55 cents, but only after several months delay. B protests but is forced to agree to the new price to keep its plant in operation. The modification is not binding.

§ 90 Promise Reasonably Inducing Action or Forbearance

(1) A promise which the promisor should reasonably expect to induce action or forbearance on the part of the promisee or a third person and which does induce such action or forbearance is binding if injustice can be avoided only by enforcement of the promise. The remedy granted for breach may be limited as justice requires.

(2) A charitable subscription or a marriage settlement is binding under Subsection (1) without proof that the promise induced action or forbearance.

Comment:

a. *Relation to other rules.* Obligations and remedies based on reliance are not peculiar to the law of contracts. This Section is often referred to in terms of "promissory estoppel," a phrase suggesting an extension of the doctrine of estoppel. Estoppel prevents a person from showing the truth contrary to a representation of fact made by him after another has relied on the representation. Reliance is also a significant feature of numerous rules in the law of negligence, deceit and restitution. In some cases those rules and this Section overlap; in others they provide analogies useful in determining the extent to which enforcement is necessary to avoid injustice. . . .

Illustration:

1. A, knowing that B is going to college, promises B that A will give him $5,000 on completion of his course. B goes to college, and borrows and spends more than $5,000 for college expenses. When he has nearly completed his

course, A notifies him of an intention to revoke the promise. A's promise is binding and B is entitled to payment on completion of the course without regard to whether his performance was "bargained for" under § 71.

b. Character of reliance protected. The principle of this Section is flexible. The promisor is affected only by reliance which he does or should foresee, and enforcement must be necessary to avoid injustice. Satisfaction of the latter requirement may depend on the reasonableness of the promisee's reliance, on its definite and substantial character in relation to the remedy sought, on the formality with which the promise is made, on the extent to which the evidentiary, cautionary, deterrent and channeling functions of form are met by the commercial setting or otherwise, and on the extent to which such other policies as the enforcement of bargains and the prevention of unjust enrichment are relevant. The force of particular factors varies in different types of cases: thus reliance need not be of substantial character in charitable subscription cases, but must in cases of firm offers and guaranties.

Illustrations:

2. A promises B not to foreclose, for a specified time, a mortgage which A holds on B's land. B thereafter makes improvements on the land. A's promise is binding and may be enforced by denial of foreclosure before the time has elapsed. . . .

4. A has been employed by B for 40 years. B promises to pay A a pension of $200 per month when A retires. A retires and forbears to work elsewhere for several years while B pays the pension. B's promise is binding.

c. Reliance by third persons. If a promise is made to one party for the benefit of another, it is often foreseeable that the beneficiary will rely on the promise. Enforcement of the promise in such cases rests on the same basis and depends on the same factors as in cases of reliance by the promisee. Justifiable reliance by third persons who are not beneficiaries is less likely, but may sometimes reinforce the claim of the promisee or beneficiary. . . .

d. Partial enforcement. A promise binding under this section is a contract, and full-scale enforcement by normal remedies is often appropriate. But the same factors which bear on whether any relief should be granted also bear on the character and extent of the remedy. In particular, relief may sometimes be limited to restitution or to damages or specific relief measured by the extent of the promisee's reliance rather than by the terms of the promise. Unless there is unjust enrichment of the promisor, damages should not put the promisee in a better position than performance of the promise would have put him. . . .

Illustrations:

8. A applies to B, a distributor of radios manufactured by C, for a "dealer franchise" to sell C's products. Such franchises are revocable at will. B erroneously informs A that C has accepted the application and will soon award the franchise, that A can proceed to employ salesmen and solicit orders,

and that A will receive an initial delivery of at least 30 radios. A expends $1,150 in preparing to do business, but does not receive the franchise or any radios. B is liable to A for the $1,150 but not for the lost profit on 30 radios.

9. The facts being otherwise as stated in Illustration 8, B gives A the erroneous information deliberately and with C's approval and requires A to buy the assets of a deceased former dealer and thus discharge C's "moral obligation" to the widow. C is liable to A not only for A's expenses but also for the lost profit on 30 radios.

10. A, who owns and operates a bakery, desires to go into the grocery business. He approaches B, a franchisor of supermarkets. B states to A that for $18,000 B will establish A in a store. B also advises A to move to another town and buy a small grocery to gain experience. A does so. Later B advises A to sell the grocery, which A does, taking a capital loss and foregoing expected profits from the summer tourist trade. B also advises A to sell his bakery to raise capital for the supermarket franchise, saying "Everything is ready to go. Get your money together and we are set." A sells the bakery taking a capital loss on this sale as well. Still later, B tells A that considerably more than an $18,000 investment will be needed, and the negotiations between the parties collapse. At the point of collapse many details of the proposed agreement between the parties are unresolved. The assurances from B to A are promises on which B reasonably should have expected A to rely, and A is entitled to his actual losses on the sales of the bakery and grocery and for his moving and temporary living expenses. Since the proposed agreement was never made, however, A is not entitled to lost profits from the sale of the grocery or to his expectation interest in the proposed franchise from B.

f. Charitable subscriptions, marriage settlements, and other gifts. One of the functions of the doctrine of consideration is to deny enforcement to a promise to make a gift. Such a promise is ordinarily enforced by virtue of the promisee's reliance only if his conduct is foreseeable and reasonable and involves a definite and substantial change of position which would not have occurred if the promise had not been made. In some cases, however, other policies reinforce the promisee's claim. Thus the promisor might be unjustly enriched if he could reclaim the subject of the promised gift after the promisee has improved it.

Subsection (2) identifies two other classes of cases in which the promisee's claim is similarly reinforced. American courts have traditionally favored charitable subscriptions and marriage settlements, and have found consideration in many cases where the element of exchange was doubtful or nonexistent. Where recovery is rested on reliance in such cases, a probability of reliance is enough, and no effort is made to sort out mixed motives or to consider whether partial enforcement would be appropriate.

Illustrations:

16. A orally promises to give her son B a tract of land to live on. As A intended, B gives up a homestead elsewhere, takes possession of the land,

lives there for a year and makes substantial improvements. A's promise is binding.

17. A orally promises to pay B, a university, $100,000 in five annual installments for the purposes of its fund-raising campaign then in progress. The promise is confirmed in writing by A's agent, and two annual installments are paid before A dies. The continuance of the fund-raising campaign by B is sufficient reliance to make the promise binding on A and his estate.

§ 95 Requirements for Sealed Contract or Written Contract or Instrument

(1) In the absence of statute a promise is binding without consideration if

(a) it is in writing and sealed; and

(b) the document containing the promise is delivered; and

(c) the promisor and promisee are named in the document or so described as to be capable of identification when it is delivered.

CHAPTER 5. THE STATUTE OF FRAUDS (§§ 110-150)

§ 110 Classes of Contracts Covered

(1) The following classes of contracts are subject to a statute, commonly called the Statute of Frauds, forbidding enforcement unless there is a written memorandum or an applicable exception:

(a) a contract of an executor or administrator to answer for a duty of his decedent (the executor-administrator provision);

(b) a contract to answer for the duty of another (the suretyship provision);

(c) a contract made upon consideration of marriage (the marriage provision);

(d) a contract for the sale of an interest in land (the land contract provision);

(e) a contract that is not to be performed within one year from the making thereof (the one-year provision).

(2) The following classes of contracts, which were traditionally subject to the Statute of Frauds, are now governed by Statute of Frauds provisions of the Uniform Commercial Code:

(a) a contract for the sale of goods for the price of $500 or more (Uniform Commercial Code § 2-201);

(b) a contract for the sale of securities (Uniform Commercial Code § 8-319);

(c) a contract for the sale of personal property not otherwise covered, to the extent of enforcement by way of action or defense beyond $5,000 in amount or value of remedy (Uniform Commercial Code § 1-206).

(3) In addition the Uniform Commercial Code requires a writing signed by the debtor for an agreement which creates or provides for a security interest in personal property or fixtures not in the possession of the secured party.

(4) Statutes in most states provide that no acknowledgment or promise is sufficient evidence of a new or continuing contract to take a case out of the

operation of a statute of limitations unless made in some writing signed by the party to be charged, but that the statute does not alter the effect of any payment of principal or interest.

(5) In many states other classes of contracts are subject to a requirement of a writing.

§ 125 Contract to Transfer, Buy, or Pay for an Interest in Land

(1) A promise to transfer to any person any interest in land is within the Statute of Frauds.

(2) A promise to buy any interest in land is within the Statute of Frauds, irrespective of the person to whom the transfer is to be made.

(3) When a transfer of an interest in land has been made, a promise to pay the price, if originally within the Statute of Frauds, ceases to be within it unless the promised price is itself in whole or in part an interest in land.

(4) Statutes in most states except from the land contract and one-year provisions of the Statute of Frauds short-term leases and contracts to lease, usually for a term not longer than one year.

§ 129 Action in Reliance; Specific Performance

A contract for the transfer of an interest in land may be specifically enforced notwithstanding failure to comply with the Statute of Frauds if it is established that the party seeking enforcement, in reasonable reliance on the contract and on the continuing assent of the party against whom enforcement is sought, has so changed his position that injustice can be avoided only by specific enforcement.

§ 130 Contract Not to Be Performed Within a Year

(1) Where any promise in a contract cannot be fully performed within a year from the time the contract is made, all promises in the contract are within the Statute of Frauds until one party to the contract completes his performance.

(2) When one party to a contract has completed his performance, the one-year provision of the Statute does not prevent enforcement of the promises of other parties.

§ 131 General Requisites of a Memorandum

Unless additional requirements are prescribed by the particular statute, a contract within the Statute of Frauds is enforceable if it is evidenced by any writing, signed by or on behalf of the party to be charged, which

(a) reasonably identifies the subject matter of the contract,

(b) is sufficient to indicate that a contract with respect thereto has been made between the parties or offered by the signer to the other party, and

(c) states with reasonable certainty the essential terms of the unperformed promises in the contract.

§ 133 Memorandum Not Made as Such

Except in the case of a writing evidencing a contract upon consideration of marriage, the Statute may be satisfied by a signed writing not made as a memorandum of a contract.

§ 134 Signature

The signature to a memorandum may be any symbol made or adopted with an intention, actual or apparent, to authenticate the writing as that of the signer.

§ 136 Time of Memorandum

A memorandum sufficient to satisfy the Statute may be made or signed at any time before or after the formation of the contract.

§ 139 Enforcement by Virtue of Action in Reliance

(1) A promise which the promisor should reasonably expect to induce action or forbearance on the part of the promisee or a third person and which does induce the action or forbearance is enforceable notwithstanding the Statute of Frauds if injustice can be avoided only by enforcement of the promise. The remedy granted for breach is to be limited as justice requires.

(2) In determining whether injustice can be avoided only by enforcement of the promise, the following circumstances are significant:

(a) the availability and adequacy of other remedies, particularly cancellation and restitution;

(b) the definite and substantial character of the action or forbearance in relation to the remedy sought;

(c) the extent to which the action or forbearance corroborates evidence of the making and terms of the promise, or the making and terms are otherwise established by clear and convincing evidence;

(d) the reasonableness of the action or forbearance;

(e) the extent to which the action or forbearance was foreseeable by the promisor.

§ 143 Unenforceable Contract as Evidence

The Statute of Frauds does not make an unenforceable contract inadmissible in evidence for any purpose other than its enforcement in violation of the Statute.

CHAPTER 6. MISTAKE (§§ 151-154)

§ 151 Mistake Defined

A mistake is a belief that is not in accord with the facts.

Comment:

a. *Belief as to facts.* In this Restatement the word "mistake" is used to refer to an erroneous belief. A party's erroneous belief is therefore said to be a "mistake" of that party. The belief need not be an articulated one, and a party may have a belief as to a fact when he merely makes an assumption with respect to it, without being aware of alternatives. The word "mistake" is not used here, as it is sometimes used in common speech, to refer to an improvident act, including the making of a contract, that is the result of such an erroneous belief. This usage is avoided here for the sake of clarity and consistency. Furthermore, the erroneous belief must relate to the facts as they exist at the time of the making of the contract. A party's prediction or judgment as to events to occur in the future, even if erroneous, is not a "mistake" as that word is defined here. An erroneous belief as to the contents or effect of a writing that expresses the agreement is, however, a mistake. Mistake alone, in the sense in which the word is used here, has no legal consequences. The legal consequences of mistake in connection with the creation of contractual liability are determined by the rules stated in the rest of this Chapter.

Illustrations:

1. A contracts with B to raise and float B's boat which has run aground on a reef. At the time of making the contract, A believes that the sea will remain calm until the work is completed. Several days later, during a sudden storm, the boat slips into deep water and fills with mud, making it more difficult for A to raise it. Although A may have shown poor judgment in making the contract, there was no mistake of either A or B, and the rules stated in this Chapter do not apply. Whether A is discharged by supervening impracticability is governed by the rules stated in Chapter 11. See Illustration 5 to § 261. If, however, the boat had already slipped into deep water at the time the contract was made, although they both believed that it was still on the reef, there would have been a mistake of both A and B. Its legal consequences, if any, would be governed by the rule stated in § 152.

2. A contracts to sell and B to buy stock amounting to a controlling interest in C Corporation. At the time of making the contract, both A and B believe that C Corporation will have earnings of $1,000,000 during the following fiscal year. Because of a subsequent economic recession, C Corporation earns less than $500,000 during that year. Although B may have shown poor judgment in making the contract, there was no mistake of either A or B, and the rules stated in this Chapter do not apply. See Uniform Commercial Code § 8-306(2).

§ 152 When Mistake of Both Parties Makes a Contract Voidable

(1) Where a mistake of both parties at the time a contract was made as to a basic assumption on which the contract was made has a material effect on the agreed exchange of performances, the contract is voidable by the adversely affected party unless he bears the risk of the mistake under the rule stated in § 154.

(2) In determining whether the mistake has a material effect on the agreed exchange of performances, account is taken of any relief by way of reformation, restitution, or otherwise.

§ 153 When Mistake of One Party Makes a Contract Voidable

Where a mistake of one party at the time a contract was made as to a basic assumption on which he made the contract has a material effect on the agreed exchange of performances that is adverse to him, the contract is voidable by him if he does not bear the risk of the mistake under the rule stated in § 154, and

(a) the effect of the mistake is such that enforcement of the contract would be unconscionable, or

(b) the other party had reason to know of the mistake or his fault caused the mistake.

§ 154 When a Party Bears the Risk of a Mistake

A party bears the risk of a mistake when

(a) the risk is allocated to him by agreement of the parties, or

(b) he is aware, at the time the contract is made, that he has only limited knowledge with respect to the facts to which the mistake relates but treats his limited knowledge as sufficient, or

(c) the risk is allocated to him by the court on the ground that it is reasonable in the circumstances to do so.

§ 155 When Mistake of Both Parties as to Written Expression Justifies Reformation

Where a writing that evidences or embodies an agreement in whole or in part fails to express the agreement because of a mistake of both parties as to the contents or effect of the writing, the court may at the request of a party reform the writing to express the agreement, except to the extent that rights of third parties such as good faith purchasers for value will be unfairly affected.

§ 156 Mistake as to Contract Within the Statute of Frauds

If reformation of a writing is otherwise appropriate, it is not precluded by the fact that the contract is within the Statute of Frauds.

§ 157 Effect of Fault of Party Seeking Relief

A mistaken party's fault in failing to know or discover the facts before making the contract does not bar him from avoidance or reformation under the rules stated in this Chapter, unless his fault amounts to a failure to act in good faith and in accordance with reasonable standards of fair dealing.

§ 158 Effect of Fault of Party Seeking Relief

Note: The current position of the American Law Institute concerning every form of restitution in a contractual context is set forth in Restatement Third, Restitution and Unjust Enrichment *(R3RUE), formally adopted in 2010 and published in 2011. On the topic of this section, see especially R3RUE § 34.*

(1) In any case governed by the rules stated in this Chapter, either party may have a claim for relief including restitution under the rules stated in §§ 240 and 376.

(2) In any case governed by the rules stated in this Chapter, if those rules together with the rules stated in Chapter 16 will not avoid injustice, the court may grant relief on such terms as justice requires including protection of the parties' reliance interests.

Chapter 7. Misrepresentation, Duress and Undue Influence (§§ 159-177)

§ 159 Misrepresentation Defined

A misrepresentation is an assertion that is not in accord with the facts.

§ 160 When Action is Equivalent to an Assertion (Concealment)

Action intended or known to be likely to prevent another from learning a fact is equivalent to an assertion that the fact does not exist.

Comment:

a. Scope. Concealment is an affirmative act intended or known to be likely to keep another from learning of a fact of which he would otherwise have learned. Such affirmative action is always equivalent to a misrepresentation and has any effect that a misrepresentation would have under the rules stated in §§ 163, 164 and 166. The rule stated in the following section applies to non-disclosure, where one person simply fails to inform another of a fact relating to the transaction. Non-disclosure is equivalent to a misrepresentation only in the circumstances enumerated in that section.

b. Common situations. The rule stated in this Section is commonly applied in two situations, although it is not limited to them. In the first, a party actively hides something from the other, as when the seller of a building paints over a defect. See Illustration 1. In such a case his conduct has the same effect as an assertion that the defect does not exist, and it is therefore a misrepresentation. Similarly, if the offeror reads a written offer to the offeree and omits a portion of it, his conduct has the same effect as an assertion that the omitted portion is not contained in the writing and is therefore a misrepresentation. In the second situation, a party prevents the other from making an investigation that would have disclosed a defect. An analogous situation arises where a party frustrates an investigation made by the other, for example by sending him in search of information where it cannot be found. Even a false denial of knowledge by a party who has possession of the facts may amount to a misrepresentation as to the facts that he knows, just as if he had actually misstated them, if its effect on the other is to lead him to believe that the facts do not exist or cannot be discovered. Action may be considered as likely to prevent another from learning of a fact even though it does not make it impossible to learn of it.

Illustrations:

1. A, seeking to induce B to make a contract to buy his house, paints the basement floor in order to prevent B from discovering that the foundation is cracked. B is prevented from discovering the defect and makes the contract.

The concealment is equivalent to an assertion that the foundation is not cracked, and this assertion is a misrepresentation. Whether the contract is voidable by B is determined by the rule stated in § 164.

2. A, seeking to induce B to make a contract to buy his house, convinces C, who, as A knows, is about to tell B that the foundation is cracked, to say nothing to B about the foundation. B is prevented from discovering the defect and makes the contract. A's conduct is equivalent to an assertion that the foundation is not cracked, and this assertion is a misrepresentation. Whether the contract is voidable by B is determined by the rule stated in § 164.

§ 161 When Non-Disclosure Is Equivalent to an Assertion

A person's non-disclosure of a fact known to him is equivalent to an assertion that the fact does not exist in the following cases only:

(a) where he knows that disclosure of the fact is necessary to prevent some previous assertion from being a misrepresentation or from being fraudulent or material.

(b) where he knows that disclosure of the fact would correct a mistake of the other party as to a basic assumption on which that party is making the contract and if non-disclosure of the fact amounts to a failure to act in good faith and in accordance with reasonable standards of fair dealing.

(c) where he knows that disclosure of the fact would correct a mistake of the other party as to the contents or effect of a writing, evidencing or embodying an agreement in whole or in part.

(d) where the other person is entitled to know the fact because of a relation of trust and confidence between them.

Comment:

a. Concealment distinguished. Like concealment, non-disclosure of a fact may be equivalent to a misrepresentation. Concealment necessarily involves an element of non-disclosure, but it is the act of preventing another from learning of a fact that is significant and this act is always equivalent to a misrepresentation (§ 160). Non-disclosure without concealment is equivalent to a misrepresentation only in special situations. A party making a contract is not expected to tell all that he knows to the other party, even if he knows that the other party lacks knowledge on some aspects of the transaction. His nondisclosure, as such, has no legal effect except in the situations enumerated in this Section. He may not, of course, tell half-truths and his assertion of only some of the facts without the inclusion of such additional matters as he knows or believes to be necessary to prevent it from being misleading is itself a misrepresentation. See Comment *a* to § 159. In contrast to the rule applicable to liability in tort for misrepresentation, it is not enough, where disclosure is expected, merely to make reasonable efforts to disclose the relevant facts. Actual disclosure is required. Compare Restatement, Second, Torts § 551, Comment *d*.

b. Fraudulent or material. In order to make the contract voidable under the rule stated in § 164(1), the non-disclosure must be either fraudulent or material. The notion of disclosure necessarily implies that the fact in question is known to the person expected to disclose it. But the failure to disclose the fact may be unintentional, as when one forgets to disclose a known fact, and it is then equivalent to an innocent misrepresentation. Furthermore, one is expected to disclose only such facts as he knows or has reason to know will influence the other in determining his course of action. See § 162(2). Therefore, he need not disclose facts that the ordinary person would regard as unimportant unless he knows of some peculiarity of the other person that is likely to lead him to attach importance to them. There is, however, no such requirement of materiality if it can be shown that the non-disclosure was actually fraudulent. If a fact is intentionally withheld for the purpose of inducing action, this is equivalent to a fraudulent misrepresentation.

c. Failure to correct. One who has made an assertion that is neither a fraudulent nor a material misrepresentation may subsequently acquire knowledge that bears significantly on his earlier assertion. He is expected to speak up and correct the earlier assertion in three cases. First, if his assertion was not a misrepresentation because it was true, he may later learn that it is no longer true. See Illustration 1. Second, his assertion may have been a misrepresentation but may not have been fraudulent. If this was because he believed that it was true, he may later learn that it was not true. See Illustration 2. If this was because he did not intend that it be relied upon, he may later learn that the other is about to rely on it. See Illustration 3. Third, if his assertion was a misrepresentation but was not material because he had no reason to know of the other's special characteristics that made reliance likely, he may later learn of such characteristics. If a person fails to correct his earlier assertion in these situations, the result is the same as it would have been had he had his newly acquired knowledge at the time he made the assertion. The rule stated in Clause (a), like that stated in Clause (d), extends to non-disclosure by persons who are not parties to the transaction.

Illustrations:

1. A makes to B, a credit rating company, a true statement of his financial condition, intending that its substance be published to B's subscribers. B summarizes the information and transmits the summary to C, a subscriber. Shortly thereafter, A's financial condition becomes seriously impaired, but he does not disclose this to B. C makes a contract to lend money to A. A's non-disclosure is equivalent to an assertion that his financial condition is not seriously impaired, and this assertion is a misrepresentation. Whether the contract is voidable by B is determined by the rule stated in § 164.

2. A, seeking to induce B to make a contract to buy a thoroughbred mare, tells B that the mare is in foal to a well-known stallion. Unknown to A, the mare has miscarried. A learns of the miscarriage but does not disclose it to B. B makes the contract. A's non-disclosure is equivalent to an assertion that the

mare has not miscarried, and this assertion is a misrepresentation. Whether the contract is voidable by B is determined by the rule stated in § 164.

3. A, in casual conversation with B, tells B that a tract of land owned by A contains thirty acres. A knows that it contains only twenty-nine acres but misstates its area because he does not regard the figure as important. A's statement is not fraudulent because it is not made with the intention of inducing B to buy the land (§ 162(1)). B later offers to buy the tract from A. A does not disclose its true area to B, for fear that B will not buy it, and accepts B's offer. A's non-disclosure is equivalent to a new assertion that the tract contains thirty acres, and this assertion is a fraudulent misrepresentation (§ 162(1)). Whether the contract is voidable by B is determined by the rule stated in § 164.

d. Known mistake as to a basic assumption. In many situations, if one party knows that the other is mistaken as to a basic assumption, he is expected to disclose the fact that would correct the mistake. A seller of real or personal property is, for example, ordinarily expected to disclose a known latent defect of quality or title that is of such a character as would probably prevent the buyer from buying at the contract price. An owner is ordinarily expected to disclose a known error in a bid that he has received from a contractor. See Comment *e* to § 153. The mistake must be as to a basic assumption, as is also required by the rules on mistake stated in § 152 (see Illustrations 4, 5 and 6) and § 153 (see Illustrations 8 and 9). The rule stated in Clause (b), is, however, broader than these rules for mistake because it does not require a showing of a material effect on the agreed exchange and is not affected by the fact that the party seeking relief bears the risk of the mistake (§ 154). Nevertheless, a party need not correct all mistakes of the other and is expected only to act in good faith and in accordance with reasonable standards of fair dealing, as reflected in prevailing business ethics. A party may, therefore, reasonably expect the other to take normal steps to inform himself and to draw his own conclusions. If the other is indolent, inexperienced or ignorant, or if his judgment is bad or he lacks access to adequate information, his adversary is not generally expected to compensate for these deficiencies. A buyer of property, for example, is not ordinarily expected to disclose circumstances that make the property more valuable than the seller supposes. Compare Illustrations 10 and 11. In contrast to the rules stated in Clauses (a) and (d), that stated in Clause (b) is limited to non-disclosure by a party to the transaction. Actual knowledge is required for the application of the rule stated in Clause (b). The case of a party who does not know but has reason to know of a mistake is governed by the rule stated in § 153(b). As to knowledge in the case of an organization, see the analogous rule in Uniform Commercial Code § 1-201(27).

Illustrations:

4. A, seeking to induce B to make a contract to buy land, knows that B does not know that the land has been filled with debris and covered

but does not disclose this to B. B makes the contract. A's non-disclosure is equivalent to an assertion that the land has not been filled with debris and covered, and this assertion is a misrepresentation. Whether the contract is voidable by B is determined by the rule stated in § 164.

5. A, seeking to induce B to make a contract to buy A's house, knows that B does not know that the house is riddled with termites but does not disclose this to B. B makes the contract. A's non-disclosure is equivalent to an assertion that the house is not riddled with termites, and this assertion is a misrepresentation. Whether the contract is voidable by B is determined by the rule stated in § 164.

6. A, seeking to induce B to make a contract to buy a food-processing business, knows that B does not know that the health department has given repeated warnings that a necessary license will not be renewed unless expensive improvements are made but does not disclose this to B. B makes the contract. A's non-disclosure is equivalent to an assertion that no warnings have been given by the health department, and this assertion is a misrepresentation. Whether the contract is voidable by B is determined by the rule stated in § 164.

7. A, seeking to induce B to make a contract to sell land, knows that B does not know that the land has appreciably increased in value because of a proposed shopping center but does not disclose this to B. B makes the contract. Since B's mistake is not one as to a basic assumption (see Comment *b* to § 152 and Comment *b* to § 261), A's non-disclosure is not equivalent to an assertion that the value of the land has not appreciably increased, and this assertion is not a misrepresentation. The contract is not voidable by B. See Illustration 13.

8. In response to B's invitation for bids on the construction of a building according to stated specifications, A submits an offer to do the work for $150,000. A believes that this is the total of a column of figures, but he has made an error by inadvertently omitting a $5,000 item, and in fact the total is $155,000. B knows this but accepts A's bid without disclosing it. B's non-disclosure is equivalent to an assertion that no error has been made in the total, and this assertion is a misrepresentation. Whether the contract is voidable by A is determined by the rule stated in § 164. See Illustrations 1 and 2 to § 153. See also Comment *a* to § 167.

9. In answer to an inquiry from "J.B. Smith Company," A offers to sell goods for cash on delivery. A mistakenly believes that the offeree is John B. Smith, who has an established business of good repute, but in fact it is a business run by his son, with whom A has refused to deal because of previous disputes. The son learns of A's mistake but accepts A's offer without disclosing his identity. The son's non-disclosure is equivalent to an assertion that the business is run by the father, and this assertion is a misrepresentation. Whether the contract is voidable by A is determined by the rule stated in § 164. See Illustration 11 to § 153. See also Comment *a* to § 167.

10. A, seeking to induce B to make a contract to sell A land, learns from government surveys that the land contains valuable mineral deposits and knows that B does not know this, but does not disclose this to B. B makes the contract. A's non-disclosure does not amount to a failure to act in good faith and in accordance with reasonable standards of fair dealing and is therefore not equivalent to an assertion that the land does not contain valuable mineral deposits. The contract is not voidable by B.

11. The facts being otherwise as stated in Illustration 10, A learns of the valuable mineral deposits from trespassing on B's land and not from government surveys. A's non-disclosure is equivalent to an assertion that the land does not contain valuable mineral deposits, and this assertion is a misrepresentation. Whether the contract is voidable by B is determined by the rule stated in § 164.

§ 162 When a Misrepresentation Is Fraudulent or Material

(1) A misrepresentation is fraudulent if the maker intends his assertion to induce a party to manifest his assent and the maker

(a) knows or believes that the assertion is not in accord with the facts, or

(b) does not have the confidence that he states or implies in the truth of the assertion, or

(c) knows that he does not have the basis that he states or implies for the assertion.

(2) A misrepresentation is material if it would be likely to induce a reasonable person to manifest his assent, or if the maker knows that it would be likely to induce the recipient to do so.

§ 163 When a Misrepresentation Prevents Formation of a Contract

If a misrepresentation as to the character or essential terms of a proposed contract induces conduct that appears to be a manifestation of assent by one who neither knows nor has reasonable opportunity to know of the character or essential terms of the proposed contract, his conduct is not effective as a manifestation of assent.

§ 164 When a Misrepresentation Makes a Contract Voidable

(1) If a party's manifestation of assent is induced by either a fraudulent or a material misrepresentation by the other party upon which the recipient is justified in relying, the contract is voidable by the recipient.

(2) If a party's manifestation of assent is induced by either a fraudulent or a material misrepresentation by one who is not a party to the transaction upon which the recipient is justified in relying, the contract is voidable by the recipient, unless the other party to the transaction in good faith and without reason to know of the misrepresentation either gives value or relies materially on the transaction.

§ 167 When a Misrepresentation Is an Inducing Cause

A misrepresentation induces a party's manifestation of assent if it substantially contributes to his decision to manifest his assent.

§ 168 Reliance on Assertions of Opinion

(1) An assertion is one of opinion if it expresses only a belief, without certainty, as to the existence of a fact or expresses only a judgment as to quality, value, authenticity, or similar matters.

(2) If it is reasonable to do so, the recipient of an assertion of a person's opinion as to facts not disclosed and not otherwise known to the recipient may properly interpret it as an assertion

(a) that the facts known to that person are not incompatible with his opinion, or

(b) that he knows facts sufficient to justify him in forming it.

§ 169 When Reliance on an Assertion of Opinion Is Not Justified

To the extent that an assertion is one of opinion only, the recipient is not justified in relying on it unless the recipient

(a) stands in such a relation of trust and confidence to the person whose opinion is asserted that the recipient is reasonable in relying on it, or

(b) reasonably believes that, as compared with himself, the person whose opinion is asserted has special skill, judgment or objectivity with respect to the subject matter, or

(c) is for some other special reason particularly susceptible to a misrepresentation of the type involved.

§ 174 When Duress by Physical Compulsion Prevents Formation of a Contract

If conduct that appears to be a manifestation of assent by a party who does not intend to engage in that conduct is physically compelled by duress, the conduct is not effective as a manifestation of assent.

§ 175 When Duress by Threat Makes a Contract Voidable

(1) If a party's manifestation of assent is induced by an improper threat by the other party that leaves the victim no reasonable alternative, the contract is voidable by the victim.

(2) If a party's manifestation of assent is induced by one who is not a party to the transaction, the contract is voidable by the victim unless the other party to the transaction in good faith and without reason to know of the duress either gives value or relies materially on the transaction.

§ 176 When a Threat Is Improper

(1) A threat is improper if

(a) what is threatened is a crime or a tort, or the threat itself would be a crime or a tort if it resulted in obtaining property,

(b) what is threatened is a criminal prosecution,

(c) what is threatened is the use of civil process and the threat is made in bad faith, or

(d) the threat is a breach of the duty of good faith and fair dealing under a contract with the recipient.

(2) A threat is improper if the resulting exchange is not on fair terms, and

(a) the threatened act would harm the recipient and would not significantly benefit the party making the threat,

(b) the effectiveness of the threat in inducing the manifestation of assent is significantly increased by prior unfair dealing by the party making the threat, or

(c) what is threatened is otherwise a use of power for illegitimate ends.

§ 177 When Undue Influence Makes a Contract Voidable

(1) Undue influence is unfair persuasion of a party who is under the domination of the person exercising the persuasion or who by virtue of the relation between them is justified in assuming that that person will not act in a manner inconsistent with his welfare.

(2) If a party's manifestation of assent is induced by undue influence by the other party, the contract is voidable by the victim.

(3) If a party's manifestation of assent is induced by one who is not a party to the transaction, the contract is voidable by the victim unless the other party to the transaction in good faith and without reason to know of the undue influence either gives value or relies materially on the transaction.

Chapter 8. Unenforceability on Grounds of Public Policy (§§ 178-199)

§ 178 When a Term is Unenforceable on Grounds of Public Policy

(1) A promise or other term of an agreement is unenforceable on grounds of public policy if legislation provides that it is unenforceable or the interest in its enforcement is clearly outweighed in the circumstances by a public policy against the enforcement of such terms.

(2) In weighing the interest in the enforcement of a term, account is taken of

(a) the parties' justified expectations,

(b) any forfeiture that would result if enforcement were denied, and

(c) any special public interest in the enforcement of the particular term.

(3) In weighing a public policy against enforcement of a term, account is taken of

(a) the strength of that policy as manifested by legislation or judicial decisions,

(b) the likelihood that a refusal to enforce the term will further that policy,

(c) the seriousness of any misconduct involved and the extent to which it was deliberate, and

(d) the directness of the connection between that misconduct and the term.

§ 179 Bases of Public Policies Against Enforcement

A public policy against the enforcement of promises or other terms may be derived by the court from

(a) legislation relevant to such a policy, or

(b) the need to protect some aspect of the public welfare, as is the case for the judicial policies against, for example,

(i) restraint of trade (§§ 186-188),

(ii) impairment of family relations (§§ 189-191), and

(iii) interference with other protected interests (§§ 192-196, 356).

§ 191 Promise Affecting Custody

A promise affecting the right of custody of a minor child is unenforceable on grounds of public policy unless the disposition as to custody is consistent with the best interest of the child.

CHAPTER 9. THE SCOPE OF CONTRACTUAL OBLIGATIONS (§§ 200-230)

§ 200 Interpretation of Promise or Agreement

Interpretation of a promise or agreement or a term thereof is the ascertainment of its meaning.

§ 201 Whose Meaning Prevails

(1) Where the parties have attached the same meaning to a promise or agreement or a term thereof, it is interpreted in accordance with that meaning.

(2) Where the parties have attached different meanings to a promise or agreement or a term thereof, it is interpreted in accordance with the meaning attached by one of them if at the time the agreement was made

(a) that party did not know of any different meaning attached by the other, and the other knew the meaning attached by the first party; or

(b) that party had no reason to know of any different meaning attached by the other, and the other had reason to know the meaning attached by the first party.

(3) Except as stated in this Section, neither party is bound by the meaning attached by the other, even though the result may be a failure of mutual assent.

Comment:

a. The meaning of words. Words are used as conventional symbols of mental states, with standardized meanings based on habitual or customary practice. Unless a different intention is shown, language is interpreted in accordance with its generally prevailing meaning. See § 202(3). Usages of varying degrees of generality are recorded in dictionaries, but there are substantial differences between English and American usages and between usages in different parts of the United States. Differences of usage also exist in various localities and in different social, economic, religious and ethnic groups. All these usages change over time, and persons engaged in transactions with each other often develop temporary usages peculiar to themselves. Moreover, most words are commonly used in more than one sense.

b. The problem of context. Uncertainties in the meaning of words are ordinarily greatly reduced by the context in which they are used. The same is true of other conventional symbols, and the meaning of conduct not used as a conventional symbol is even more dependent on its setting. But the context of words and other conduct is seldom exactly the same for two different people, since connotations depend on the entire past experience and the attitudes and expectations of the person whose understanding is in question. In general, the context relevant to interpretation of a bargain is the context common to both parties. More precisely, the question of meaning in cases of misunderstanding depends on an inquiry into what each party knew or had reason to know, as stated in Subsections (2) and (3). See § 20 and Illustrations. Ordinarily a party has reason to know of meanings in general usage.

c. Mutual understanding. Subsection (1) makes it clear that the primary search is for a common meaning of the parties, not a meaning imposed on them by the law. To the extent that a mutual understanding is displaced by government regulation, the resulting obligation does not rest on "interpretation" in the sense used here. The objective of interpretation in the general law of contracts is to carry out the understanding of the parties rather than to impose obligations on them contrary to their understanding: "the courts do not make a contract for the parties." Ordinarily, therefore, the mutual understanding of the parties prevails even where the contractual term has been defined differently by statute or administrative regulation. But parties who used a standardized term in an unusual sense obviously run the risk that their agreement will be misinterpreted in litigation.

d. Misunderstanding. Subsection (2) follows the terminology of § 20, referring to the understanding of each party as the meaning "attached" by him to a term of a promise or agreement. Where the rules stated in Subsections (1) and (2) do not apply, neither party is bound by the understanding of the other. The result may be an entire failure of agreement or a failure to agree as to a term. There may be a binding contract despite failure to agree as to a term, if the term is not essential or if it can be supplied. See § 204. In some cases a party can waive the misunderstanding and enforce the contract in accordance with the understanding of the other party.

Illustrations:

4. A agrees to sell and B to buy a quantity of eviscerated "chicken." A tenders "stewing chicken" or "fowl"; B rejects on the ground that the contract calls for "broilers" or "fryers." Each party makes a claim for damages against the other. It is found that each acted in good faith and that neither had reason to know of the difference in meaning. Both claims fail.

5. A orders goods from B, using A's standard form. B acknowledges the order, using his own standard form. Each form provides that no terms are agreed to except those on the form and that the other party agrees to

the form. One form contains an arbitration clause; the other does not. The goods are delivered and paid for. Later a dispute arises as to their quality. There is no agreement to arbitrate the dispute.

§ 202 Rules in Aid of Interpretation

(1) Words and other conduct are interpreted in the light of all the circumstances, and if the principal purpose of the parties is ascertainable it is given great weight.

(2) A writing is interpreted as a whole, and all writings that are part of the same transaction are interpreted together.

(3) Unless a different intention is manifested,

(a) where language has a generally prevailing meaning, it is interpreted in accordance with that meaning;

(b) technical terms and words of art are given their technical meaning when used in a transaction within their technical field.

(4) Where an agreement involves repeated occasions for performance by either party with knowledge of the nature of the performance and opportunity for objection to it by the other, any course of performance accepted or acquiesced in without objection is given great weight in the interpretation of the agreement.

(5) Wherever reasonable, the manifestations of intention of the parties to a promise or agreement are interpreted as consistent with each other and with any relevant course of performance, course of dealing, or usage of trade.

§ 204 Supplying an Omitted Essential Term

When the parties to a bargain sufficiently defined to be a contract have not agreed with respect to a term which is essential to a determination of their rights and duties, a term which is reasonable in the circumstances is supplied by the court.

§ 205 Duty of Good Faith and Fair Dealing

Every contract imposes upon each party a duty of good faith and fair dealing in its performance and its enforcement.

Comment:

a. *Meanings of "good faith."* Good faith is defined in Uniform Commercial Code § 1-201(19) as "honesty in fact in the conduct or transaction concerned." "In the case of a merchant" Uniform Commercial Code § 2-103(1)(b) provides that good faith means "honesty in fact and the observance of reasonable commercial standards of fair dealing in the trade." The phrase "good faith" is used in a variety of contexts, and its meaning varies somewhat with the context. Good faith performance or enforcement of a contract emphasizes faithfulness to an agreed common purpose and consistency with the justified expectations of the other party; it excludes a variety of types of conduct characterized as involving "bad faith" because they violate community standards of decency, fairness or reasonableness. The appropriate remedy for a breach of the duty of good faith also varies with the circumstances. . . .

d. Good faith performance. Subterfuges and evasions violate the obligation of good faith in performance even though the actor believes his conduct to be justified. But the obligation goes further: bad faith may be overt or may consist of inaction, and fair dealing may require more than honesty. A complete catalogue of types of bad faith is impossible, but the following types are among those which have been recognized in judicial decisions: evasion of the spirit of the bargain, lack of diligence and slacking off, willful rendering of imperfect performance, abuse of a power to specify terms, and interference with or failure to cooperate in the other party's performance.

Illustrations:

1. A, an oil dealer, borrows $100,000 from B, a supplier, and agrees to buy all his requirements of certain oil products from B on stated terms until the debt is repaid. Before the debt is repaid, A makes a new arrangement with C, a competitor of B. Under the new arrangement A's business is conducted by a corporation formed and owned by A and C and managed by A, and the corporation buys all its oil products from C. The new arrangement may be found to be a subterfuge or evasion and a breach of contract by A.

2. A, owner of a shopping center, leases part of it to B, giving B the exclusive right to conduct a supermarket, the rent to be a percentage of B's gross receipts. During the term of the lease A acquires adjoining land, expands the shopping center, and leases part of the adjoining land to C for a competing supermarket. Unless such action was contemplated or is otherwise justified, there is a breach of contract by A.

3. A Insurance Company insures B against legal liability for certain bodily injuries to third persons, with a limit of liability of $10,000 for an accident to any one person. The policy provides that A will defend any suit covered by it but may settle. C sues B on a claim covered by the policy and offers to settle for $9,500. A refuses to settle on the ground that the amount is excessive, and judgment is rendered against B for $20,000 after a trial defended by A. A then refuses to appeal, and offers to pay $10,000 only if B satisfies the judgment, impairing B's opportunity to negotiate for settlement. B prosecutes an appeal, reasonably expending $7,500, and obtains dismissal of the claim. A has failed to deal fairly and in good faith with B and is liable for B's appeal expense.

4. A and B contract that A will perform certain demolition work for B and pay B a specified sum for materials salvaged, the contract not to "become effective until" certain insurance policies "are in full force and effect." A makes a good faith effort to obtain the insurance, but financial difficulty arising from injury to an employee of A on another job prevents A from obtaining them. A's duty to perform is discharged.

5. B submits and A accepts a bid to supply approximately 4000 tons of trap rock for an airport at a unit price. The parties execute a standard form

of "Invitation, Bid, and Acceptance (Short Form Contract)" supplied by A, including typed terms "to be delivered to project as required," "delivery to start immediately," "cancellation by A may be effected at any time." Good faith requires that A order and accept the rock within a reasonable time unless A has given B notice of intent to cancel.

6. A contracts to perform services for B for such compensation "as you, in your sole judgment, may decide is reasonable." After A has performed the services, B refuses to make any determination of the value of the services. A is entitled to their value as determined by a court.

7. A suffers a loss of property covered by an insurance policy issued by B, and submits to B notice and proof of loss. The notice and proof fail to comply with requirements of the policy as to form and detail. B does not point out the defects, but remains silent and evasive, telling A broadly to perfect his claim. The defects do not bar recovery on the policy.

e. *Good faith in enforcement.* The obligation of good faith and fair dealing extends to the assertion, settlement and litigation of contract claims and defenses. See, e.g., §§ 73, 89. The obligation is violated by dishonest conduct such as conjuring up a pretended dispute, asserting an interpretation contrary to one's own understanding, or falsification of facts. It also extends to dealing which is candid but unfair, such as taking advantage of the necessitous circumstances of the other party to extort a modification of a contract for the sale of goods without legitimate commercial reason. See Uniform Commercial Code § 2-209, Comment 2. Other types of violation have been recognized in judicial decisions: harassing demands for assurances of performance, rejection of performance for unstated reasons, willful failure to mitigate damages, and abuse of a power to determine compliance or to terminate the contract. For a statutory duty of good faith in termination, see the federal Automobile Dealer's Day in Court Act, 15 U.S.C. §§ 1221-25 (1976).

Illustrations:

8. A contracts to sell and ship goods to B on credit. The contract provides that, if B's credit or financial responsibility becomes impaired or unsatisfactory to A, A may demand cash or security before making shipment and may cancel if the demand is not met. A may properly demand cash or security only if he honestly believes, with reason, that the prospect of payment is impaired.

9. A contracts to sell and ship goods to B. On arrival B rejects the goods on the erroneous ground that delivery was late. B is thereafter precluded from asserting other unstated grounds then known to him which A could have cured if stated seasonably.

§ 208 Unconscionable Contract or Term

If a contract or term thereof is unconscionable at the time the contract is made a court may refuse to enforce the contract, or may enforce the remainder of the contract without the unconscionable term, or may so limit the application of any unconscionable term as to avoid any unconscionable result.

Comment:

a. Scope. Like the obligation of good faith and fair dealing (§ 205), the policy against unconscionable contracts or terms applies to a wide variety of types of conduct. The determination that a contract or term is or is not unconscionable is made in the light of its setting, purpose and effect. Relevant factors include weaknesses in the contracting process like those involved in more specific rules as to contractual capacity, fraud, and other invalidating causes; the policy also overlaps with rules which render particular bargains or terms unenforceable on grounds of public policy. Policing against unconscionable contracts or terms has sometimes been accomplished "by adverse construction of language, by manipulation of the rules of offer and acceptance or by determinations that the clause is contrary to public policy or to the dominant purpose of the contract." Uniform Commercial Code § 2-302 Comment 1. Particularly in the case of standardized agreements, the rule of this Section permits the court to pass directly on the unconscionability of the contract or clause rather than to avoid unconscionable results by interpretation.

b. Historic standards. Traditionally, a bargain was said to be unconscionable in an action at law if it was "such as no man in his senses and not under delusion would make on the one hand, and as no honest and fair man would accept on the other;" damages were then limited to those to which the aggrieved party was "equitably" entitled. Even though a contract was fully enforceable in an action for damages, equitable remedies such as specific performance were refused where "the sum total of its provisions drives too hard a bargain for a court of conscience to assist." *Campbell Soup Co. v. Wentz,* 172 F.2d 80, 84 (3d Cir.1948). Modern procedural reforms have blurred the distinction between remedies at law and in equity. For contracts for the sale of goods, Uniform Commercial Code § 2-302 states the rule of this Section without distinction between law and equity. Comment 1 to that section adds, "The principle is one of the prevention of oppression and unfair surprise (Cf. *Campbell Soup Co. v. Wentz,* . . .) and not of disturbance of allocation of risks because of superior bargaining power."

c. Overall imbalance. Inadequacy of consideration does not of itself invalidate a bargain, but gross disparity in the values exchanged may be an important factor in a determination that a contract is unconscionable and may be sufficient ground, without more, for denying specific performance. Such a disparity may also corroborate indications of defects in the bargaining process, or may affect the remedy to be granted when there is a violation of a more specific rule. Theoretically it is possible for a contract to be oppressive taken as a whole, even though there is no weakness in the bargaining process and no single term which is in itself unconscionable. Ordinarily, however, an unconscionable contract involves other factors as well as overall imbalance.

Illustration:

1. A, an individual, contracts in June to sell at a fixed price per ton to B, a large soup manufacturer, the carrots to be grown on A's farm. The contract, written on B's standard printed form, is obviously drawn to protect B's interests and not A's; it contains numerous provisions to protect B against various contingencies and none giving analogous protection to A. Each of the clauses can be read restrictively so that it is not unconscionable, but several can be read literally to give unrestricted discretion to B. In January, when the market price has risen above the contract price, A repudiates the contract, and B seeks specific performance. In the absence of justification by evidence of commercial setting, purpose, or effect, the court may determine that the contract as a whole was unconscionable when made, and may then deny specific performance.

d. Weakness in the bargaining process. A bargain is not unconscionable merely because the parties to it are unequal in bargaining position, nor even because the inequality results in an allocation of risks to the weaker party. But gross inequality of bargaining power, together with terms unreasonably favorable to the stronger party, may confirm indications that the transaction involved elements of deception or compulsion, or may show that the weaker party had no meaningful choice, no real alternative, or did not in fact assent or appear to assent to the unfair terms. Factors which may contribute to a finding of unconscionability in the bargaining process include the following: belief by the stronger party that there is no reasonable probability that the weaker party will fully perform the contract; knowledge of the stronger party that the weaker party will be unable to receive substantial benefits from the contract; knowledge of the stronger party that the weaker party is unable reasonably to protect his interests by reason of physical or mental infirmities, ignorance, illiteracy or inability to understand the language of the agreement, or similar factors.

e. Unconscionable terms. Particular terms may be unconscionable whether or not the contract as a whole is unconscionable. Some types of terms are not enforced, regardless of context; examples are provisions for unreasonably large liquidated damages, or limitations on a debtor's right to redeem collateral. See Uniform Commercial Code §§ 2-718, 9-501(3). Other terms may be unconscionable in some contexts but not in others. Overall imbalance and weaknesses in the bargaining process are then important.

Illustrations:

5. A, a retail furniture store, sells furniture on installment credit to B, retaining a security interest. As A knows, B is a woman of limited education, separated from her husband, maintaining herself and seven children by means of $218 per month public assistance. After 13 purchases over a period of five years for a total of $1,200, B owes A $164. B then buys a stereo set for $514. Each contract contains a paragraph of some 800 words in extremely fine print, in the middle of which are the words "all payments . . . shall be

credited pro rata on all outstanding . . . accounts." The effect of this language is to keep a balance due on each item until all are paid for. On B's default, A sues for possession of all the items sold. It may be determined that either the quoted clause or the contract as a whole was unconscionable when made.

6. A, a corporation with its principal office in State X, contracts with B, a resident of State X, to make improvements on B's home in State X. The contract is made on A's standard printed form, which contains a clause by which the parties submit to the jurisdiction of a court in State Y, 200 miles away. No reason for the clause appears except to make litigation inconvenient and expensive for B. The clause is unconscionable.

f. Law and fact. A determination that a contract or term is unconscionable is made by the court in the light of all the material facts. Under Uniform Commercial Code § 2-302, the determination is made "as a matter of law," but the parties are to be afforded an opportunity to present evidence as to commercial setting, purpose and effect to aid the court in its determination. Incidental findings of fact are made by the court rather than by a jury, but are accorded the usual weight given to such findings of fact in appellate review. An appellate court will also consider whether proper standards were applied.

g. Remedies. Perhaps the simplest application of the policy against unconscionable agreements is the denial of specific performance where the contract as a whole was unconscionable when made. If such a contract is entirely executory, denial of money damages may also be appropriate. But the policy is not penal: unless the parties can be restored to their pre-contract positions, the offending party will ordinarily be awarded at least the reasonable value of performance rendered by him. Where a term rather than the entire contract is unconscionable, the appropriate remedy is ordinarily to deny effect to the unconscionable term. In such cases as that of an exculpatory term, the effect may be to enlarge the liability of the offending party.

§ 211 Standardized Agreements

(1) Except as stated in Subsection (3), where a party to an agreement signs or otherwise manifests assent to a writing and has reason to believe that like writings are regularly used to embody terms of agreements of the same type, he adopts the writing as an integrated agreement with respect to the terms included in the writing.

(2) Such a writing is interpreted wherever reasonable as treating alike all those similarly situated, without regard to their knowledge or understanding of the standard terms of the writing.

(3) Where the other party has reason to believe that the party manifesting such assent would not do so if he knew that the writing contained a particular term, the term is not part of the agreement.

Comment:

a. *Utility of standardization.* Standardization of agreements serves many of the same functions as standardization of goods and services; both are essential to a system of mass production and distribution. Scarce and costly time and skill can be devoted to a class of transactions rather than to details of individual transactions. Legal rules which would apply in the absence of agreement can be shaped to fit the particular type of transaction, and extra copies of the form can be used for purposes such as record-keeping, coordination and supervision. Forms can be tailored to office routines, the training of personnel, and the requirements of mechanical equipment. Sales personnel and customers are freed from attention to numberless variations and can focus on meaningful choice among a limited number of significant features: transaction-type, style, quantity, price, or the like. Operations are simplified and costs reduced, to the advantage of all concerned.

b. Assent to unknown terms. A party who makes regular use of a standardized form of agreement does not ordinarily expect his customers to understand or even to read the standard terms. One of the purposes of standardization is to eliminate bargaining over details of individual transactions, and that purpose would not be served if a substantial number of customers retained counsel and reviewed the standard terms. Employees regularly using a form often have only a limited understanding of its terms and limited authority to vary them. Customers do not in fact ordinarily understand or even read the standard terms. They trust to the good faith of the party using the form and to the tacit representation that like terms are being accepted regularly by others similarly situated. But they understand that they are assenting to the terms not read or not understood, subject to such limitations as the law may impose.

c. Review of unfair terms. Standardized agreements are commonly prepared by one party. The customer assents to a few terms, typically inserted in blanks on the printed form, and gives blanket assent to the type of transaction embodied in the standard form. He is commonly not represented in the drafting, and the draftsman may be tempted to overdraw in the interest of his employer. The obvious danger of overreaching has resulted in government regulation of insurance policies, bills of lading, retail installment sales, small loans, and other particular types of contracts. Regulation sometimes includes administrative review of standard terms, or even prescription of terms. Apart from such regulation, standard terms imposed by one party are enforced. But standard terms may be superseded by separately negotiated or added terms (§ 203), they are construed against the draftsman (§ 206), and they are subject to the overriding obligation of good faith (§ 205) and to the power of the court to refuse to enforce an unconscionable contract or term (§ 208). Moreover, various contracts and terms are against public policy and unenforceable.

d. Non-contractual documents. The same document may serve both contractual and other purposes, and a party may assent to it for other purposes without understanding that it embodies contract terms. He may nevertheless be bound if he has reason to know that it is used to embody contract terms. Insurance policies, steamship tickets, bills of lading, and warehouse receipts are commonly so obviously contractual in form as to give the customer reason to know their character. But baggage checks or automobile parking lot tickets may appear to be mere identification tokens, and a party without knowledge or reason to know that the token purports to be a contract is then not bound by terms printed on the token. Documents such as invoices, instructions for use, and the like, delivered after a contract is made, may raise similar problems.

§ 209 Integrated Agreements

(1) An integrated agreement is a writing or writings constituting a final expression of one or more terms of an agreement.

(2) Whether there is an integrated agreement is to be determined by the court as a question preliminary to determination of a question of interpretation or to application of the parol evidence rule.

(3) Where the parties reduce an agreement to a writing which in view of its completeness and specificity reasonably appears to be a complete agreement, it is taken to be an integrated agreement unless it is established by other evidence that the writing did not constitute a final expression.

§ 210 Completely and Partially Integrated Agreements

(1) A completely integrated agreement is an integrated agreement adopted by the parties as a complete and exclusive statement of the terms of the agreement.

(2) A partially integrated agreement is an integrated agreement other than a completely integrated agreement.

(3) Whether an agreement is completely or partially integrated is to be determined by the court as a question preliminary to determination of a question of interpretation or to application of the parol evidence rule.

§ 213 Effect of Integrated Agreement on Prior Agreements (Parol Evidence Rule)

(1) A binding integrated agreement discharges prior agreements to the extent that it is inconsistent with them.

(2) A binding completely integrated agreement discharges prior agreements to the extent that they are within its scope.

(3) An integrated agreement that is not binding or that is voidable and avoided does not discharge a prior agreement. But an integrated agreement, even though not binding, may be effective to render inoperative a term which would have been part of the agreement if it had not been integrated.

§ 214 Evidence of Prior or Contemporaneous Agreements and Negotiations

Agreements and negotiations prior to or contemporaneous with the adoption of a writing are admissible in evidence to establish

(a) that the writing is or is not an integrated agreement;

(b) that the integrated agreement, if any, is completely or partially integrated;

(c) the meaning of the writing, whether or not integrated;

(d) illegality, fraud, duress, mistake, lack of consideration, or other invalidating cause;

(e) ground for granting or denying rescission, reformation, specific performance, or other remedy.

§ 216 Consistent Additional Terms

(1) Evidence of a consistent additional term is admissible to supplement an integrated agreement unless the court finds that the agreement was completely integrated.

(2) An agreement is not completely integrated if the writing omits a consistent additional agreed term which is

(a) agreed to for separate consideration, or

(b) such a term as in the circumstances might naturally be omitted from the writing.

§ 227 Standards of Preference with Regard to Conditions

(1) In resolving doubts as to whether an event is made a condition of an obligor's duty, and as to the nature of such an event, an interpretation is preferred that will reduce the obligee's risk of forfeiture, unless the event is within the obligee's control or the circumstances indicate that he has assumed the risk.

(2) Unless the contract is of a type under which only one party generally undertakes duties, when it is doubtful whether

(a) a duty is imposed on an obligee that an event occur, or

(b) the event is made a condition of the obligor's duty, or

(c) the event is made a condition of the obligor's duty and a duty is imposed on the obligee that the event occur, the first interpretation is preferred if the event is within the obligee's control.

(3) In case of doubt, an interpretation under which an event is a condition of an obligor's duty is preferred over an interpretation under which the non-occurrence of the event is a ground for discharge of that duty after it has become a duty to perform.

§ 229 Excuse of a Condition to Avoid Forfeiture

To the extent that the non-occurrence of a condition would cause disproportionate forfeiture, a court may excuse the non-occurrence of that condition unless its occurrence was a material part of the agreed exchange.

Illustrations:

1. A contracts to build a house for B, using pipe of Reading manufacture. In return, B agrees to pay $75,000 in progress payments, each payment to be made "on condition that no pipe other than that of Reading manufacture has been used." Without A's knowledge, a subcontractor mistakenly uses pipe of Cohoes manufacture which is identical in quality and is distinguishable only by the name of the manufacturer which is stamped on it. The

mistake is not discovered until the house is completed, when replacement of the pipe will require destruction of substantial parts of the house. B refuses to pay the unpaid balance of $10,000. A court may conclude that the use of Reading rather than Cohoes pipe is so relatively unimportant to B that the forfeiture that would result from denying A the entire balance would be disproportionate, and may allow recovery by A subject to any claim for damages for A's breach of his duty to use Reading pipe.

2. A, an ocean carrier, carries B's goods under a contract providing that it is a condition of A's liability for damage to cargo that "written notice of claim for loss or damage must be given within 10 days after removal of goods." B's cargo is damaged during carriage and A knows of this. On removal of the goods, B notes in writing on the delivery record that the cargo is damaged, and five days later informs A over the telephone of a claim for that damage and invites A to participate in an inspection within the ten day period. A inspects the goods within the period, but B does not give written notice of its claim until 25 days after removal of the goods. Since the purpose of requiring the condition of written notice is to alert the carrier and enable it to make a prompt investigation, and since this purpose had been served by the written notice of damage and the oral notice of claim, the court may excuse the non-occurrence of the condition to the extent required to allow recovery by B.

Chapter 10. Performance and Non-Performance (§§ 231-260)

§ 235 Effect of Performance as Discharge and of Non-Performance as Breach

(1) Full performance of a duty under a contract discharges the duty.

(2) When performance of a duty under a contract is due any non-performance is a breach.

Comment:

a. Discharge by performance. Under the rule stated in Subsection (1), a duty is discharged when it is fully performed. Nothing less than full performance, however, has this effect and any defect in performance, even an insubstantial one, prevents discharge on this ground. The defect need not be wilful or even negligent. . . .

Illustration:

1. A contracts to build a house for B for $50,000 according to specifications furnished by B. A builds the house according to the specifications. A's duty to build the house is discharged.

2. The facts being otherwise as stated in Illustration 1, A builds the house according to the specifications except for an inadvertent variation in kitchen fixtures which can easily be remedied for $100. A's non-performance is a breach.

§ 237 Effect on Other Party's Duties of a Failure to Render Performance

Except as stated in § 240, it is a condition of each party's remaining duties to render performances to be exchanged under an exchange of promises that there be no uncured material failure by the other party to render any such performance due at an earlier time.

Comment:

a. *Effect of non-occurrence of condition.* Under the rule stated in this Section, a material failure of performance, including defective performance as well as an absence of performance, operates as the non-occurrence of a condition. . . . [T]he non-occurrence of a condition has two possible effects on the duty subject to that condition. The first is that of preventing performance of the duty from becoming due, at least temporarily. The second is that of discharging the duty when the condition can no longer occur. A material failure of performance has, under this Section, these effects on the other party's remaining duties of performance with respect to the exchange. It prevents performance of those duties from becoming due, at least temporarily, and it discharges those duties if it has not been cured during the time in which performance can occur. The occurrence of conditions of the type dealt with in this Section is required out of a sense of fairness rather than as a result of the agreement of the parties. Such conditions are therefore sometimes referred to as "constructive conditions of exchange." . . . Circumstances significant in determining whether a failure is material are set out in § 241. . . .

Illustrations:

1. A contracts to build a house for B for $50,000, progress payments to be made monthly in an amount equal to 85% of the price of the work performed during the preceding month, the balance to be paid on the architect's certificate of satisfactory completion of the house. Without justification B fails to make a $5,000 progress payment. A thereupon stops work on the house and a week goes by. A's failure to continue the work is not a breach and B has no claim against A. B's failure to make the progress payment is an uncured material failure of performance which operates as the non-occurrence of a condition of A's remaining duties of performance under the exchange. If B offers to make the delayed payment and in all the circumstances it is not too late to cure the material breach, A's duties to continue the work are not discharged. A has a claim against B for damages for partial breach because of the delay.

2. The facts being otherwise as stated in Illustration 1, B fails to make the progress payment or to give any explanation or assurances for one month. If, in all the circumstances, it is now too late for B to cure his material failure of performance by making the delayed payment, A's duties to continue the work are discharged. Because B's failure to make the progress payment was a breach, A also has a claim against B for total breach of contract.

§ 240 Part Performances as Agreed Equivalents

If the performances to be exchanged under an exchange of promises can be apportioned into corresponding pairs of part performances so that the parts of each pair are properly regarded as agreed equivalents, a party's performance of his part of such a pair has the same effect on the other's duties to render performance of the agreed equivalent as it would have if only that pair of performances had been promised.

§ 241 Circumstances Significant in Determining Whether a Failure Is Material

In determining whether a failure to render or to offer performance is material, the following circumstances are significant:

(a) the extent to which the injured party will be deprived of the benefit which he reasonably expected;

(b) the extent to which the injured party can be adequately compensated for the part of that benefit of which he will be deprived;

(c) the extent to which the party failing to perform or to offer to perform will suffer forfeiture;

(d) the likelihood that the party failing to perform or to offer to perform will cure his failure, taking account of all the circumstances including any reasonable assurances;

(e) the extent to which the behavior of the party failing to perform or to offer to perform comports with standards of good faith and fair dealing.

§ 250 When a Statement or an Act Is a Repudiation

A repudiation is

(a) a statement by the obligor to the obligee indicating that the obligor will commit a breach that would of itself give the obligee a claim for damages for total breach under § 243, or

(b) a voluntary affirmative act which renders the obligor unable or apparently unable to perform without such a breach.

§ 251 When a Failure to Give Assurance May Be Treated as a Repudiation

(1) Where reasonable grounds arise to believe that the obligor will commit a breach by non-performance that would of itself give the obligee a claim for damages for total breach under § 243, the obligee may demand adequate assurance of due performance and may, if reasonable, suspend any performance for which he has not already received the agreed exchange until he receives such assurance.

(2) The obligee may treat as a repudiation the obligor's failure to provide within a reasonable time such assurance of due performance as is adequate in the circumstances of the particular case.

(a) a statement by the obligor to the obligee indicating that the obligor will commit a breach that would of itself give the obligee a claim for damages for total breach under § 243, or

(b) a voluntary affirmative act which renders the obligor unable or apparently unable to perform without such a breach.

Chapter 11. Impracticability of Performance and Frustration of Purpose (§§ 261-272)

§ 261 Discharge by Supervening Impracticability

Where, after a contract is made, a party's performance is made impracticable without his fault by the occurrence of an event the non-occurrence of which was a basic assumption on which the contract was made, his duty to render that performance is discharged, unless the language or the circumstances indicate the contrary.

Comment:

. . .

b. Basic assumption. In order for a supervening event to discharge a duty under this Section, the non-occurrence of that event must have been a "basic assumption" on which both parties made the contract. This is the criterion used by Uniform Commercial Code § 2-615(a). Its application is simple enough in the cases of the death of a person or destruction of a specific thing necessary for performance. The continued existence of the person or thing (the non-occurrence of the death of destruction) is ordinarily a basic assumption on which the contract was made, so that death or destruction effects a discharge. . . . In borderline cases this criterion is sufficiently flexible to take account of factors that bear on a just allocation of risk. The fact that the event was foreseeable, or even foreseen, does not necessarily compel a conclusion that its non-occurrence was not a basic assumption. . . .

d. Impracticability. Events that come within the rule stated in this Section are generally due either to "acts of God" or to acts of third parties. . . . Although the rule stated in this Section is sometimes phrased in terms of "impossibility," it has long been recognized that it may operate to discharge a party's duty even though the event has not made performance absolutely impossible. This Section, therefore, uses "impracticable," the term employed by Uniform Commercial Code § 2-615(a), to describe the required extent of the impediment to performance. Performance may be impracticable because extreme and unreasonable difficulty, expense, injury, or loss to one of the parties will be involved. A severe shortage of raw materials or of supplies due to war, embargo, local crop failure, unforeseen shutdown of major sources of supply, or the like, which either causes a marked increase in cost or prevents performance altogether may bring the case within the rule stated in this Section. Performance may also be impracticable because it will involve a risk of injury to person or to property, of one of the parties or of others, that is disproportionate to the ends to be attained by performance. However, "impracticability" means more than "impracticality." A mere change in the degree of difficulty or expense due to such causes as increased wages, prices of raw materials, or costs of construction, unless well beyond the normal range, does not amount to impracticability since it is this sort of risk that a fixed-price contract is intended to cover. Furthermore, a party is expected to use reasonable efforts to surmount obstacles to performance (see § 205), and a performance is impracticable only if it is so in spite of such efforts.

Illustrations:

6. A contracts to repair B's grain elevator. While A is engaged in making repairs, a fire destroys the elevator without A's fault, and A does not finish the repairs. A's duty to repair the elevator is discharged, and A is not liable to B for breach of contract. See Illustration 3 to § 263.

7. A contracts with B to carry B's goods on his ship to a designated foreign port. A civil war then unexpectedly breaks out in that country and the rebels announce that they will try to sink all vessels bound for that port. A refuses to perform. Although A did not contract to sail on the vessel, the risk of injury to others is sufficient to make A's performance impracticable. A's duty to carry the goods to the designated port is discharged, and A is not liable to B for breach of contract.

8. The facts being otherwise as stated in Illustration 7, the rebels announce merely that they will confiscate all vessels found in the designated port. The goods can be bought and sold on markets throughout the world. A refuses to perform. Although there is no risk of injury to persons, the court may conclude that the risk of injury to property is disproportionate to the ends to be attained. A's duty to carry the goods to the designated port is then discharged, and A is not liable to B for breach of contract. If, however, B is a health organization and the goods are scarce medical supplies vital to the health of the population of the designated port, the court may conclude that the risk is not disproportionate to the ends to be attained and may reach a contrary decision.

9. Several months after the nationalization of the Suez Canal, during the international crisis resulting from its seizure, A contracts to carry a cargo of B's wheat on A's ship from Galveston, Texas to Bandar Shapur, Iran for a flat rate. The contract does not specify the route, but the voyage would normally be through the Straits of Gibraltar and the Suez Canal, a distance of 10,000 miles. A month later, and several days after the ship has left Galveston, the Suez Canal is closed by an outbreak of hostilities, so that the only route to Bandar Shapur is the longer 13,000 mile voyage around the Cape of Good Hope. A refuses to complete the voyage unless B pays additional compensation. A's duty to carry B's cargo is not discharged, and A is liable to B for breach of contract.

10. The facts being otherwise as in Illustration 9, the Suez Canal is closed while A's ship is in the Canal, preventing the completion of the voyage. A's duty to carry B's cargo is discharged, and A is not liable to B for breach of contract.

§ 263 Discharge by Supervening Impracticability

If the existence of a specific thing is necessary for the performance of a duty, its failure to come into existence, destruction, or such deterioration as makes performance impracticable is an event the non-occurrence of which was a basic assumption on which the contract was made.

Comment:

a. Rationale. This Section, like the preceding one, states a common specific instance for the application of the rule stated in § 261. If, as both parties understand, the existence of a specific thing is necessary for the performance of a duty it is "a basic assumption on which the contract was made" that that thing will come into existence if it does not already exist and will remain in existence until the time for performance. Therefore, if its failure to come into existence or its destruction or deterioration makes performance impracticable, the obligor's duty to render that performance is discharged, subject to the qualifications stated in § 261. Each party bears some of the risk that the transaction will not be carried out for such a reason. . . .

Illustrations:

1. A contracts to sell and B to buy cloth. A expects to manufacture the cloth in his factory, but before he begins manufacture the factory is destroyed by fire without his fault. Although cloth meeting the contract description is available on the market, A refuses to buy and deliver it to B. A's duty to deliver the cloth is not discharged, and A is liable to B for breach of contract.

2. The facts being otherwise as stated in Illustration 1, A contracts to sell cloth to be manufactured in the factory that is later destroyed. A's duty to deliver the cloth is discharged, and A is not liable to B for breach of contract.

3. A contracts with B to shingle the roof of B's house. When A has done part of the work, much of the house including the roof is destroyed by fire without his fault, so that he is unable to complete the work. A's duty to shingle the roof is discharged, and A is not liable to B for breach of contract.

4. A contracts with B to build a house for B. When A has done part of the work, much of the structure is destroyed by fire without his fault. A refuses to finish building the house. A's duty to build the house is not discharged, and A is liable to B for breach of contract.

5. A contracts to sell a specified machine to B for $10,000. Before A tenders the machine to B, a fire destroys it without A's fault. A's duty to deliver the machine is discharged (Uniform Commercial Code § 2-613), and A is not liable for breach of contract.

§ 265 Discharge by Supervening Frustration

Where, after a contract is made, a party's principal purpose is substantially frustrated without his fault by the occurrence of an event the non-occurrence of which was a basic assumption on which the contract was made, his remaining duties to render performance are discharged, unless the language or the circumstances indicate the contrary.

Comment:

a. Rationale. This Section deals with the problem that arises when a change in circumstances makes one party's performance virtually worthless to the other, frustrating his purpose in making the contract. It is distinct from the problem of impracticability . . . because there is no impediment to performance by either party. . . . The rule stated in this Section sets out the requirements for the discharge of that party's duty. First, the purpose that is frustrated must have been a principal purpose of that party in making the contract. It is not enough that he had in mind some specific object without which he would not have made the contract. The object must be so completely the basis of the contract that, as both parties understand, without it the transaction would make little sense. Second, the frustration must be substantial. It is not enough that the transaction has become less profitable for the affected party or even that he will sustain a loss. The frustration must be so severe that it is not fairly to be regarded as within the risks that he assumed under the contract. Third, the non-occurrence of the frustrating event must have been a basic assumption on which the contract was made. This involves essentially the same sorts of determinations that are involved under the general rule on impracticability. The foreseeability of the event is here, as it is there, a factor in that determination, but the mere fact that the event was foreseeable does not compel the conclusion that its non-occurrence was not such a basic assumption.

Illustration:

1. A and B make a contract under which B is to pay A $1,000 and is to have the use of A's window on January 10 to view a parade that has been scheduled for that day. Because of the illness of an important official, the parade is cancelled. B refuses to use the window or pay the $1,000. B's duty to pay $1,000 is discharged, and B is not liable to A for breach of contract.

CHAPTER 14. CONTRACT BENEFICIARIES (§§ 302-315)

Introductory Note: Historically, the rights of contract beneficiaries have been the subject of doctrinal difficulties in both England and the United States. In both countries, decisions in the latter part of the nineteenth century overruled or limited earlier precedents recognizing such rights. In England, but not in the United States (see § 71), the rule was established that consideration must move from the plaintiff. That rule has sometimes been avoided by an artificial holding that the promisee held a contract right in trust for the beneficiary, but it seems to retain some force.

In the United States the principal difficulty was that the beneficiary was not a party to the contract, since the promise was not addressed to him. Some decisions recognized a right only in a "sole" beneficiary or "donee" beneficiary, such as the person to whom the proceeds of a life insurance policy are made payable. Others recognized the beneficiary's right only if the promisor was to satisfy a duty of the promisee to the beneficiary, who was then called a "creditor" beneficiary, or if there was some other relationship between promise and beneficiary.

These difficulties have now been largely resolved in the United States by recognition of the power of promisor and promisee to create rights in a beneficiary by manifesting an intention to do so. Since the terms "donee" beneficiary and "creditor" beneficiary carry overtones of obsolete doctrinal difficulties, they are avoided in the statement of rules in this Chapter. Instead, the terms "intended" beneficiary and "incidental" beneficiary are used to distinguish beneficiaries who have rights from those who do not. . . .

§ 302 Intended and Incidental Beneficiaries

(1) Unless otherwise agreed between promisor and promisee, a beneficiary of a promise is an intended beneficiary if recognition of a right to performance in the beneficiary is appropriate to effectuate the intention of the parties and either

(a) the performance of the promise will satisfy an obligation of the promisee to pay money to the beneficiary; or

(b) the circumstances indicate that the promisee intends to give the beneficiary the benefit of the promised performance.

(2) An incidental beneficiary is a beneficiary who is not an intended beneficiary.

§ 304 Creation of Duty to Beneficiary

A promise in a contract creates a duty in the promisor to any intended beneficiary to perform the promise, and the intended beneficiary may enforce the duty.

§ 309 Defenses Against the Beneficiary

(1) A promise creates no duty to a beneficiary unless a contract is formed between the promisor and the promisee; and if a contract is voidable or unenforceable at the time of its formation the right of any beneficiary is subject to the infirmity.

(2) If a contract ceases to be binding in whole or in part because of impracticability, public policy, non-occurrence of a condition, or present or prospective failure of performance, the right of any beneficiary is to that extent discharged or modified.

(3) Except as stated in Subsections (1) and (2) and in § 311 or as provided by the contract, the right of any beneficiary against the promisor is not subject to the promisor's claims or defenses against the promisee or to the promisee's claims or defenses against the beneficiary.

(4) A beneficiary's right against the promisor is subject to any claim or defense arising from his own conduct or agreement.

§ 311 Variation of a Duty to a Beneficiary

(1) Discharge or modification of a duty to an intended beneficiary by conduct of the promisee or by a subsequent agreement between promisor and promisee is ineffective if a term of the promise creating the duty so provides.

(2) In the absence of such a term, the promisor and promisee retain power to discharge or modify the duty by subsequent agreement.

(3) Such a power terminates when the beneficiary, before he receives notification of the discharge or modification, materially changes his position in justifiable reliance on the promise or brings suit on it or manifests assent to it at the request of the promisor or promisee.

(4) If the promisee receives consideration for an attempted discharge or modification of the promisor's duty which is ineffective against the beneficiary, the beneficiary can assert a right to the consideration so received. The promisor's duty is discharged to the extent of the amount received by the beneficiary.

§ 315 Effect of a Promise of Incidental Benefit

An incidental beneficiary acquires by virtue of the promise no right against the promisor or the promisee.

CHAPTER 15. ASSIGNMENT AND DELEGATION (§§ 316-343)

§ 317 Assignment of a Right

(1) An assignment of a right is a manifestation of the assignor's intention to transfer it by virtue of which the assignor's right to performance by the obligor is extinguished in whole or in part and the assignee acquires a right to such performance.

(2) A contractual right can be assigned unless

(a) the substitution of a right of the assignee for the right of the assignor would materially change the duty of the obligor, or materially increase the burden or risk imposed on him by his contract, or materially impair his chance of obtaining return performance, or materially reduce its value to him, or

(b) the assignment is forbidden by statute or is otherwise inoperative on grounds of public policy, or

(c) assignment is validly precluded by contract.

§ 318 Delegation of Performance of Duty

(1) An obligor can properly delegate the performance of his duty to another unless the delegation is contrary to public policy or the terms of his promise.

(2) Unless otherwise agreed, a promise requires performance by a particular person only to the extent that the obligee has a substantial interest in having that person perform or control the acts promised.

(3) Unless the obligee agrees otherwise, neither delegation of performance nor a contract to assume the duty made with the obligor by the person delegated discharges any duty or liability of the delegating obligor.

§ 328 Interpretation of Words of Assignment; Effect of Acceptance of Assignment

(1) Unless the language or the circumstances indicate the contrary, as in an assignment for security, an assignment of "the contract" or of "all my rights under the contract" or an assignment in similar general terms is an assignment of the assignor's rights and a delegation of his unperformed duties under the contract.

(2) Unless the language or the circumstances indicate the contrary, the acceptance by an assignee of such an assignment operates as a promise to the assignor to perform the assignor's unperformed duties, and the obligor of the assigned rights is an intended beneficiary of the promise.

Caveat:

The Institute expresses no opinion as to whether the rule stated in Subsection (2) applies to an assignment by a purchaser of his rights under a contract for the sale of land.

§ 329 Repudiation by Assignor and Novation with Assignee

(1) The legal effect of a repudiation by an assignor of his duty to the obligor of the assigned right is not limited by the fact that the assignee is a competent person and has promised to perform the duty.

(2) If the obligor, with knowledge of such a repudiation, accepts any performance from the assignee without reserving his rights against the assignor, a novation arises by which the duty of the assignor is discharged and a similar duty of the assignee is substituted.

Chapter 16. Remedies (§§ 344-385)

§ 344 Purpose of Remedies

Note: The current position of the American Law Institute concerning "restitution" as a remedy for breach of contract is set forth in Restatement Third, Restitution and Unjust Enrichment (R3RUE), formally adopted in 2010 and published in 2011. Contract remedies treated in the new Restatement include rescission for material breach (R3RUE §§ 37, 54) and damages to protect both the "reliance interest" and the "restitution interest" (R3RUE § 38), as well as a potential liability in unjust enrichment to disgorge the profits of an "opportunistic" breach of contract (R3RUE § 39).

Judicial remedies under the rules stated in this Restatement serve to protect one or more of the following interests of a promisee:

(a) his "expectation interest," which is his interest in having the benefit of his bargain by being put in as good a position as he would have been in had the contract been performed,

(b) his "reliance interest," which is his interest in being reimbursed for loss caused by reliance on the contract by being put in as good a position as he would have been in had the contract not been made, or

(c) his "restitution interest," which is his interest in having restored to him any benefit that he has conferred on the other party.

Comment:

a. *Three interests.* The law of contract remedies implements the policy in favor of allowing individuals to order their own affairs by making legally enforceable promises. Ordinarily, when a court concludes that there has been a breach of contract, it enforces the broken promise by protecting the expectation that the injured party had when he made the contract. It does this by attempting to put him in as good a position as he would have been in had the contract been performed, that is, had there been no breach. The interest protected in this way is called the "expectation interest." It is sometimes said to give the injured party the "benefit of the bargain." This is not, however, the only interest that may be protected.

The promisee may have changed his position in reliance on the contract by, for example, incurring expenses in preparing to perform, in performing, or in foregoing opportunities to make other contracts. In that case, the court may recognize a claim based on his reliance rather than on his expectation. It does this by attempting to put him back in the position in which he would have been had the contract not been made. The interest protected in this way is called "reliance interest." Although it may be equal to the expectation interest, it is ordinarily smaller because it does not include the injured party's lost profit.

In some situations a court will recognize yet a third interest and grant relief to prevent unjust enrichment. This may be done if a party has not only changed his own position in reliance on the contract but has also conferred a benefit on the other party by, for example, making a part payment or furnishing services under the contract. The court may then require the other party to disgorge the benefit that he has received by returning it to the party who conferred it. The interest of the claimant protected in this way is called the "restitution interest." Although it may be equal to the expectation or reliance interest, it is ordinarily smaller because it includes neither the injured party's lost profit nor that part of his expenditures in reliance that resulted in no benefit to the other party.

The interests described in this Section are not inflexible limits on relief and in situations in which a court grants such relief as justice requires, the relief may not correspond precisely to any of these interests. See §§ 15, 87, 89, 90, 139, 158 and 272.

Illustrations:

1. A contracts to build a building for B on B's land for $100,000. B repudiates the contract before either party has done anything in reliance on it. It would have cost A $90,000 to build the building. A has an expectation interest of $10,000, the difference between the $100,000 price and his savings of $90,000 in not having to do the work. Since A has done nothing in reliance, A's reliance interest is zero. Since A has conferred no benefit on B, A's restitution interest is zero.

2. The facts being otherwise as stated in Illustration 1, B does not repudiate until A has spent $60,000 of the $90,000. A has been paid nothing and can salvage nothing from the $60,000 that he has spent. A now has an expectation interest of $70,000, the difference between the $100,000 price and his saving of $30,000 in not having to do the work. A also has a reliance interest of $60,000, the amount that he has spent. If the benefit to B of the partly finished building is $40,000, A has a restitution interest of $40,000.

b. Expectation interest. In principle, at least, a party's expectation interest represents the actual worth of the contract to him rather than to some reasonable third person. Damages based on the expectation interest therefore take account of any special circumstances that are peculiar to the situation of the injured party, including his personal values and even his idiosyncracies, as well as his own needs and opportunities. See Illustration 3. In practice, however, the injured party is often held to a more objective valuation of his expectation interest because he may be barred from recovering for loss resulting from such special circumstances on the ground that it was not foreseeable or cannot be shown with sufficient certainty. See §§ 351 and 352. Furthermore, since he cannot recover for loss that he could have avoided by arranging a substitute transaction on the market (§ 350), his recovery is often limited by the objective standard of market price. See Illustration 4. The expectation interest is not based on the injured party's hopes when he made the contract but on the actual value that the contract would have had to him had it been performed. See Illustration 5. It is therefore based on the circumstances at the time for performance and not those at the time of the making of the contract.

Illustrations:

3. A, who is about to produce a play, makes a contract with B, an actor, under which B is to play the lead in the play at a stated salary for the season. A breaks the contract and has the part played by another actor. B's expectation interest includes the extent to which B's reputation would have been enhanced if he had been allowed to play the lead in A's play, as well as B's loss in salary, both subject to the limitations stated in Topic 2.

4. A contracts to construct a monument in B's yard for $10,000 but abandons the work after the foundation has been laid. It will cost B $6,000 to have another contractor complete the work. The monument planned is so ugly that it would decrease the market price of the house. Nevertheless, B's expectation interest is the value of the monument to him, which, under the rule stated in § 348(2)(b), would be measured by the cost of completion, $6,000.

5. A makes a contract with B under which A is to pay B for drilling an oil well on B's land, adjacent to that of A, for development and exploration purposes. Both A and B believe that the well will be productive and will substantially enhance the value of A's land in an amount that they estimate to be $1,000,000. Before A has paid anything, B breaks the contract by

refusing to drill the well. Other exploration then proves that there is no oil in the region. A's expectation interest is zero.

c. *Reliance interest.* If it is reliance that is the basis for the enforcement of a promise, a court may enforce the promise but limit the promisee to recovery of his reliance interest. See §§ 87, 89, 90, 139. There are also situations in which a court may grant recovery based on the reliance interest even though it is consideration that is the basis for the enforcement of the promise. These situations are dealt with in §§ 349 and 353.

d. *Restitution interest.* Since restitution is the subject of a separate Restatement, this Chapter is concerned with problems of restitution only to the extent that they arise in connection with contracts. Such problems arise when a party, instead of seeking to enforce an agreement, claims relief on the ground that the other party has been unjustly enriched as a result of some benefit conferred under the agreement. In some cases a party's choice of the restitution interest is dictated by the fact that the agreement is not enforceable, perhaps because of his own breach (§ 374), as a result of impracticability of performance or frustration of purpose (§ 377(1)), under the Statute of Frauds (§ 375), or in consequence of the other party's avoidance for some reason as misrepresentation, duress, mistake or incapacity (§ 376). Occasionally a party chooses the restitution interest even though the contract is enforceable because it will give a larger recovery than will enforcement based on either the expectation or reliance interest. These rare instances are dealt with in § 373. Sometimes the restitution interest can be protected by requiring restoration of the specific thing, such as goods or land, that has resulted in the benefit. See § 372. Where restitution in kind is not appropriate, however, a sum of money will generally be allowed based on the restitution interest. See § 371.

§ 346 Availability of Damage

(1) The injured party has a right to damages for any breach by a party against whom the contract is enforceable unless the claim for damages has been suspended or discharged.

(2) If the breach caused no loss or if the amount of the loss is not proved under the rules stated in this Chapter, a small sum fixed without regard to the amount of loss will be awarded as nominal damages.

§ 347 Measure of Damages in General

Subject to the limitations stated in §§ 350-53, the injured party has a right to damages based on his expectation interest as measured by

(a) the loss in the value to him of the other party's performance caused by its failure or deficiency, plus

(b) any other loss, including incidental or consequential loss, caused by the breach, less

(c) any cost or other loss that he has avoided by not having to perform.

Comment:

a. Expectation interest. Contract damages are ordinarily based on the injured party's expectation interest and are intended to give him the benefit of his bargain by awarding him a sum of money that will, to the extent possible, put him in as good a position as he would have been in had the contract been performed. See § 344(1)(a). In some situations the sum awarded will do this adequately as, for example, where the injured party has simply had to pay an additional amount to arrange a substitute transaction and can be adequately compensated by damages based on that amount. In other situations the sum awarded cannot adequately compensate the injured party for his disappointed expectation as, for example, where a delay in performance has caused him to miss an invaluable opportunity. The measure of damages stated in this Section is subject to the agreement of the parties, as where they provide for liquidated damages (§ 356) or exclude liability for consequential damages.

b. Loss in value. The first element that must be estimated in attempting to fix a sum that will fairly represent the expectation interest is the loss in the value to the injured party of the other party's performance that is caused by the failure of, or deficiency in, that performance. If no performance is rendered, the loss in value caused by the breach is equal to the value that the performance would have had to the injured party. See Illustrations 1 and 2. If defective or partial performance is rendered, the loss in value caused by the breach is equal to the difference between the value that the performance would have had if there had been no breach and the value of such performance as was actually rendered. In principle, this requires a determination of the values of those performances to the injured party himself and not their values to some hypothetical reasonable person or on some market. See Restatement, Second, Torts § 911. They therefore depend on his own particular circumstances or those of his enterprise, unless consideration of these circumstances is precluded by the limitation of foreseeability (§ 351). Where the injured party's expected advantage consists largely or exclusively of the realization of profit, it may be possible to express this loss in value in terms of money with some assurance. In other situations, however, this is not possible and compensation for lost value may be precluded by the limitation of certainty. See § 352. In order to facilitate the estimation of loss with sufficient certainty to award damages, the injured party is sometimes given a choice between alternative bases of calculating his loss in value. The most important of these are stated in § 348. See also §§ 349 and 373.

Illustrations:

1. A contracts to publish a novel that B has written. A repudiates the contract and B is unable to get his novel published elsewhere. Subject to the limitations stated in §§ 350-53, B's damages include the loss of royalties that he would have received had the novel been published together with the value to him of the resulting enhancement of his reputation. But see Illustration 1 to § 352.

2. A, a manufacturer, contracts to sell B, a dealer in used machinery, a used machine that B plans to resell. A repudiates and B is unable to obtain a similar machine elsewhere. Subject to the limitations stated in §§ 350-53, B's damages include the net profit that he would have made on resale of the machine.

c. Other loss. Subject to the limitations stated in §§ 350-53, the injured party is entitled to recover for all loss actually suffered. Items of loss other than loss in value of the other party's performance are often characterized as incidental or consequential. Incidental losses include costs incurred in a reasonable effort, whether successful or not, to avoid loss, as where a party pays brokerage fees in arranging or attempting to arrange a substitute transaction. See Illustration 3. Consequential losses include such items as injury to person or property resulting from defective performance. See Illustration 4. The terms used to describe the type of loss are not, however, controlling, and the general principle is that all losses, however described, are recoverable.

Illustrations:

3. A contracts to employ B for $10,000 to supervise the production of A's crop, but breaks his contract by firing B at the beginning of the season. B reasonably spends $200 in fees attempting to find other suitable employment through appropriate agencies. B can recover the $200 incidental loss in addition to any other loss suffered, whether or not he succeeds in finding other employment.

4. A leases a machine to B for a year, warranting its suitability for B's purpose. The machine is not suitable for B's purpose and causes $10,000 in damage to B's property and $15,000 in personal injuries. B can recover the $25,000 consequential loss in addition to any other loss suffered. See Uniform Commercial Code § 2-715(2)(b).

d. Cost or other loss avoided. Sometimes the breach itself results in a saving of some cost that the injured party would have incurred if he had had to perform. See Illustration 5. Furthermore, the injured party is expected to take reasonable steps to avoid further loss. See § 350. Where he does this by discontinuing his own performance, he avoids incurring additional costs of performance. See Illustrations 6 and 8. This cost avoided is subtracted from the loss in value caused by the breach in calculating his damages. If the injured party avoids further loss by making substitute arrangements for the use of his resources that are no longer needed to perform the contract, the net profit from such arrangements is also subtracted. See Illustration 9. The value to him of any salvageable materials that he has acquired for performance is also subtracted. See Illustration 7. Loss avoided is subtracted only if the saving results from the injured party not having to perform rather than from some unrelated event. See Illustration 10. If no cost or other loss has been avoided, however, the injured party's damages include the full amount of the loss in value with no subtraction, subject to the limitations stated in §§ 350-53. See Illustration 11. The intended "donee" beneficiary of a gift promise usually suffers loss to the full extent of the value of the promised performance, since he is ordinarily not required to do anything, and so avoids no cost on breach. See § 302(1)(b).

Illustrations:

5. A contracts to build a hotel for B for $500,000 and to have it ready for occupancy by May 1. B's occupancy of the hotel is delayed for a month because of a breach by A. The cost avoided by B as a result of not having to operate the hotel during May is subtracted from the May rent lost in determining B's damages.

6. A contracts to build a house for B for $100,000. When it is partly built, B repudiates the contract and A stops work. A would have to spend $60,000 more to finish the house. The $60,000 cost avoided by A as a result of not having to finish the house is subtracted from the $100,000 price lost in determining A's damages. A has a right to $40,000 in damages from B, less any progress payments that he has already received. See Illustration 2 to § 344.

7. The facts being otherwise as stated in Illustration 6, A has bought materials that are left over and that he can use for other purposes, saving him $5,000. The $5,000 cost avoided is subtracted in determining A's damages, resulting in damages of only $35,000 rather than $40,000.

8. A contracts to convey land to B in return for B's working for a year. B repudiates the contract before A has conveyed the land. The value to A of the land is subtracted from the value to A of B's services in determining A's damages.

9. A contracts to employ B for $10,000 to supervise the production of A's crop, but breaks his contract by firing B at the beginning of the season. B instead takes another job as a supervisor at $9,500. The $9,500 is subtracted from the $10,000 loss of earnings in determining B's damages. See Illustration 8 to § 350.

10. A contracts to build a machine for B and deliver it to be installed in his factory by June 30. A breaks the contract and does not deliver the machine. B's factory is destroyed by fire on December 31 and the machine, if it had been installed there, would also have been destroyed. The fact that the factory was burned is not considered in determining B's damages.

11. A contracts to send his daughter to B's school for $5,000 tuition. After the academic year has begun, A withdraws her and refuses to pay anything. A's breach does not reduce B's instructional or other costs and B is unable to find another student to take the place of A's daughter. B has a right to damages equal to the full $5,000.

e. Actual loss caused by breach. The injured party is limited to damages based on his actual loss caused by the breach. If he makes an especially favorable substitute transaction, so that he sustains a smaller loss than might have been expected, his damages are reduced by the loss avoided as a result of that transaction. See Illustration 12. If he arranges a substitute transaction that he would not have been expected to do under the rules on avoidability (§ 350), his damages are similarly limited by the loss so avoided. See Illustration 13. Recovery can be had only for loss that would not have occurred but for the breach. See § 346. If, after the breach, an event occurs that would have discharged the party in breach on grounds of impracticability of performance or frustration of purpose, damages are limited to the loss sustained prior to that event. See Illustration 15. Compare § 254(2). The principle that a party's liability is not reduced by payments or other benefits received by the injured party from collateral sources is less compelling in the case of a breach of contract than in the case of a tort. See Restatement, Second, Torts § 920A. The effect of the receipt of unemployment benefits by a discharged employee will turn on the court's perception of legislative policy rather than on the rule stated in this Section. See Illustration 14.

Illustrations:

12. A contracts to build a house for B for $100,000, but repudiates the contract after doing part of the work and having been paid $40,000. Other builders would charge B $80,000 to finish the house, but B finds a builder in need of work who does it for $70,000. B's damages are limited to the $70,000 that he actually had to pay to finish the work less the $60,000 cost avoided or $10,000, together with damages for any loss caused by the delay. See Illustration 2 to § 348.

13. A contracts to employ B for $10,000 to supervise the production of A's crop. A breaks the contract by firing B at the beginning of the season, and B, unable to find another job, instead takes a job as a farm laborer for the entire season at $6,000. The $6,000 that he made as a farm laborer is subtracted from the $10,000 loss of earnings in determining B's damages. See Illustration 8 to § 350.

14. A contracts to employ B for $10,000 to supervise the production of A's crop, but breaks his contract by firing B at the beginning of the season. B is unable to find another similar job but receives $3,000 in state unemployment benefits. Whether the $3,000 will be subtracted from the $10,000 loss of earnings depends on the state legislation under which it was paid and the policy behind it.

15. On April 1, A and B make a personal service contract under which A is to employ B for six months beginning July 1 and B is to work for A during that period. On May 1, B repudiates the contract. On August 1, B falls ill and is unable to perform the contract for the remainder of the period. A can only recover damages based on his loss during the month of July since his loss during subsequent months was not caused by B's breach. Compare Illustration 2 to § 254.

f. Lost volume. Whether a subsequent transaction is a substitute for the broken contract sometimes raises difficult questions of fact. If the injured party could and would have entered into the subsequent contract, even if the contract had not been broken, and could have had the benefit of both, he can be said to have "lost volume" and the subsequent transaction is not a substitute for the broken contract. The injured party's damages are then based on the net profit that he has lost as a result of the broken contract. Since entrepreneurs try to operate at optimum capacity, however, it is possible that an additional transaction would not have been profitable and that the injured party would not have chosen to expand his business by undertaking it had there been no breach. It is sometimes assumed that he would have done so, but the question is one of fact to be resolved according to the circumstances of each case. See Illustration 16. See also Uniform Commercial Code § 2-708(2).

Illustration:

16. A contracts to pave B's parking lot for $10,000. B repudiates the contract and A subsequently makes a contract to pave a similar parking lot for $10,000. A's business could have been expanded to do both jobs. Unless it is proved that he would not have undertaken both, A's damages are based on the net profit he would have made on the contract with B, without regard to the subsequent transaction.

§ 348 Alternatives to Loss in Value of Performance

(2) If a breach results in defective or unfinished construction and the loss in value to the injured party is not proved with sufficient certainty, he may recover damages based on.

(a) the diminution in the market price of the property caused by the breach, or

(b) the reasonable cost of completing performance or of remedying the defects if that cost is not clearly disproportionate to the probable loss in value to him.

§ 349 Damages Based on Reliance Interest

As an alternative to the measure of damages stated in § 347, the injured party has a right to damages based on his reliance interest, including expenditures made in preparation for performance or in performance, less any loss that the party in breach can prove with reasonable certainty the injured party would have suffered had the contract been performed.

§ 350 Avoidability as a Limitation on Damages

(1) Except as stated in Subsection (2), damages are not recoverable for loss that the injured party could have avoided without undue risk, burden or humiliation.

(2) The injured party is not precluded from recovery by the rule stated in Subsection (1) to the extent that he has made reasonable but unsuccessful efforts to avoid loss.

§ 351 Unforeseeability and Related Limitations on Damages

(1) Damages are not recoverable for loss that the party in breach did not have reason to foresee as a probable result of the breach when the contract was made.

(2) Loss may be foreseeable as a probable result of a breach because it follows from the breach

(a) in the ordinary course of events, or

(b) as a result of special circumstances, beyond the ordinary course of events, that the party in breach had reason to know.

(3) A court may limit damages for foreseeable loss by excluding recovery for loss of profits, by allowing recovery only for loss incurred in reliance, or otherwise if it concludes that in the circumstances justice so requires in order to avoid disproportionate compensation.

§ 352 Uncertainty as a Limitation on Damages

Damages are not recoverable for loss beyond an amount that the evidence permits to be established with reasonable certainty.

§ 355 Punitive Damages

Punitive damages are not recoverable for a breach of contract unless the conduct constituting the breach is also a tort for which punitive damages are recoverable.

§ 356 Liquidated Damages and Penalties

(1) Damages for breach by either party may be liquidated in the agreement but only at an amount that is reasonable in the light of the anticipated or actual loss caused by the breach and the difficulties of proof of loss. A term fixing unreasonably large liquidated damages is unenforceable on grounds of public policy as a penalty.

§ 358 Form of Order and Other Relief

(3) In addition to specific performance or an injunction, damages and other relief may be awarded in the same proceeding and an indemnity against future harm may be required.

§ 359 Effect of Adequacy of Damages

(1) Specific performance or an injunction will not be ordered if damages would be adequate to protect the expectation interest of the injured party.

(2) The adequacy of the damage remedy for failure to render one part of the performance due does not preclude specific performance or injunction as to the contract as a whole.

§ 360 Factors Affecting Adequacy of Damages

In determining whether the remedy in damages would be adequate, the following circumstances are significant:

(a) the difficulty of proving damages with reasonable certainty,

(b) the difficulty of procuring a suitable substitute performance by means of money awarded as damages, and

(c) the likelihood that an award of damages could not be collected.

Comment:

a. Principal factors. Under the rule stated in § 359, specific performance or an injunction will not be ordered if damages would be adequate to protect the injured party's expectation interest. This Section lists the principal factors that enter into a decision as to the adequacy of damages. The enumeration does not purport to be exclusive of other factors. A court may also consider, for example, the probability that full compensation cannot be had without multiple litigation, although this is an unusual circumstance in contract cases.

b. Difficulty in proving damages. The damage remedy may be inadequate to protect the injured party's expectation interest because the loss caused by the breach is too difficult to estimate with reasonable certainty (§ 352). If the injured party has suffered loss but cannot sustain the burden of proving it, only nominal damages will be awarded. If he can prove some but not all of his loss, he will not be compensated in full. In either case damages are an inadequate remedy. Some types of interests are by their very nature incapable of being valued in money. Typical examples include heirlooms, family treasures and works of art that induce a strong sentimental attachment. Examples may also be found in contracts of a more commercial character. The breach of a contract to transfer shares of stock may cause a loss in control over the corporation. The breach of a contract to furnish an indemnity may cause the sacrifice of property and financial ruin. The breach of a covenant not to compete may cause the loss of customers of an unascertainable number or importance. The breach of a requirements contract may cut off a vital supply of raw materials. In such situations, equitable relief is often appropriate.

Illustrations:

1. A contracts to sell to B a painting by Rembrandt for $1,000,000. A repudiates the contract and B sues for specific performance. Specific performance will be granted.

2. A contracts to sell to B the racing sloop "Columbia," this sloop being one of a class of similar boats manufactured by a particular builder. Although other boats of this class are easily obtainable, their racing characteristics differ considerably and B has selected the "Columbia" because she is regarded as a witch in light airs and, therefore, superior to most of the others. A repudiates the contract and B sues for specific performance. Specific performance may properly be granted.

3. A contracts to sell to B his interest as holder of a franchise to operate a hamburger stand. Because A has not yet opened his stand for business, it would be difficult to prove his expected profits with reasonable certainty. A repudiates the contract and B sues for specific performance. Specific performance may properly be granted.

4. A, a manufacturer of steel, contracts to sell B all of its output of steel scrap for a period of five years. After one year, A repudiates the contract and B sues A for specific performance. The uncertainty in A's output over

the remaining four years would make it very difficult for B to prove damages. Specific performance may properly be granted.

5. A contracts to supply B with water for irrigation. In reliance on his contract, B sows his land with rice. A repudiates the contract although he has water that he can supply and B sues for specific performance. The loss that B will suffer as a result of A's failure to supply water is difficult of estimation. Specific performance may properly be granted.

c. *Difficulty of obtaining substitute.* If the injured party can readily procure by the use of money a suitable substitute for the promised performance, the damage remedy is ordinarily adequate. Entering into a substitute transaction is generally a more efficient way to prevent injury than is a suit for specific performance or an injunction and there is a sound economic basis for limiting the injured party to damages in such a case. Furthermore, the substitute transaction affords a basis for proving damages with reasonable certainty, eliminating the factor stated in Paragraph (a). The fact that the burden of financing the transaction is cast on the injured party can usually be sufficiently compensated for by allowing interest. There are many situations, however, in which no suitable substitute is obtainable, and others in which its procurement would be unreasonably difficult or inconvenient or would impose serious financial burdens or risks on the injured party. A suitable substitute is never available for a performance that consists of forbearance, such as that under a contract not to compete. If goods are unique in kind, quality or personal association, the purchase of an equivalent elsewhere may be impracticable, and the buyer's "inability to cover is strong evidence of" the propriety of granting specific performance. Comment 2 to Uniform Commercial Code § 2-716. Shares of stock in a corporation may not be obtainable elsewhere. Patents and copyrights are unique. In all these situations, damages may be regarded as inadequate.

Illustrations:

6. A contracts to sell B 10,000 bales of cotton. A repudiates the contract on the day for delivery. B can buy cotton on the market at a somewhat higher price. B will not be granted specific performance.

7. A contracts to sell to B 1,000 shares of stock in the X Corporation for $10,000. A repudiates the contract and B sues for specific performance. Other shares of X Corporation are not readily obtainable and B will suffer an uncertain loss as a result of diminished voting power. Specific performance may properly be granted. If other shares were readily obtainable, even though at a considerably higher price, specific performance would be refused.

8. A contracts to obtain a patent for his invention and to assign a half interest in it to B, who promises to pay A's expenses and $100,000. A repudiates the contract and threatens to assign the patent when it is issued to others. B sues A for specific performance. Specific performance may properly be granted. The decree may enjoin A from assigning the patent to others and order him to proceed with the application and, on its issuance to execute an assignment to B, all conditional on appropriate payment by B.

d. Difficulty of collecting damages. Even if damages are adequate in other respects, they will be inadequate if they cannot be collected by judgment and execution. The party in breach may be judgment proof or may conceal his assets. Statutes may exempt some or all of his property from execution. If he is insolvent, specific performance may result in a preferential transfer to the party seeking relief and will then be denied on grounds of public policy. See Comment *b* to § 365 and Illustration 4 to that Section. If, however, the contract is unperformed on both sides and provides for a fair exchange, performance will not result in a preferential transfer and may benefit other creditors and help prevent insolvency.

Illustrations:

9. A contracts to sell his stock of goods together with good will to B for $100,000, a fair price, payable on delivery. Before the time for performance, A becomes insolvent and repudiates the contract. B sues A for specific performance. A's insolvency is a factor tending to show that damages are inadequate. But see Illustration 4 to § 365.

10. A owns an interest in a shop, the title to which is held by B in trust for A and others. B is insolvent. A assigns his interest to C and B contracts with C to effectuate the transfer of that interest to C and to terminate his own power. B then refuses to do so and C sues B for specific performance. B's insolvency is a factor tending to show that damages are inadequate.

e. Contracts for the sale of land. Contracts for the sale of land have traditionally been accorded a special place in the law of specific performance. A specific tract of land has long been regarded as unique and impossible of duplication by the use of any amount of money. Furthermore, the value of land is to some extent speculative. Damages have therefore been regarded as inadequate to enforce a duty to transfer an interest in land, even if it is less than a fee simple. Under this traditional view, the fact that the buyer has made a contract for the resale of the land to a third person does not deprive him of the right to specific performance. If he cannot convey the land to his purchaser, he will be held for damages for breach of the resale contract, and it is argued that these damages cannot be accurately determined without litigation. Granting him specific performance enables him to perform his own duty and to avoid litigation and damages.

Similarly, the seller who has not yet conveyed is generally granted specific performance on breach by the buyer. Here it is argued that, because the value of land is to some extent speculative, it may be difficult for him to prove with reasonable certainty the difference between the contract price and the market price of the land. Even if he can make this proof, the land may not be immediately convertible into money and he may be deprived of funds with which he could have made other investments. Furthermore, before the seller gets a judgment, the existence of the contract, even if broken by the buyer, operates as a clog on saleability, so that it may be difficult to find a purchaser at a fair price. The fact that specific performance is available to the buyer has sometimes been regarded as of some weight under the now discarded doctrine of "mutuality of remedy" (see Comment *c* to § 363), but this is today of importance only because it enables a court to assure the vendee that he will receive the agreed performance if he is required to pay the price. The fact that legislation may have prohibited imprisonment as a means of enforcing a decree for the payment of money does not affect the seller's right to such a decree. After the seller has transferred the interest in the land to the buyer, however, and all that remains is for the buyer to pay the price, a money judgment for the amount of the price is an adequate remedy for the seller.

Illustrations:

11. On February 1, A contracts to sell his farm to B for $500,000, of which $100,000 is paid when the contract is signed and $400,000 is to be paid on A's delivery of a deed on August 1. On March 1, A repudiates the contract. B sues A for specific performance. Specific performance will be granted immediately, A's performance not to take place until August 1 and to be conditional on the simultaneous payment by B of the $400,000 balance when the deed is tendered at that time. A may also be enjoined from making a conveyance to anyone else.

12. The facts being otherwise as stated in Illustration 11, B rather than A repudiates the contract on March 1 and A sues B for specific performance. Specific performance will be granted immediately, B's performance not to take place until August 1 and to be conditional on the simultaneous tender by A of the deed when the $400,000 balance is tendered at that time.

13. A contracts to sell land to B, a dealer in land, who contracts to sell it to C. C plans to build a home on the land and would be granted specific performance against B if B refused to convey the land to him. A repudiates the contract and refuses to convey the land to B and B sues A for specific performance. Specific performance will be granted.

§ 361 Effect of Provision for Liquidated Damages

Specific performance or an injunction may be granted to enforce a duty even though there is a provision for liquidated damages for breach of that duty.

§ 364 Effect of Unfairness

(1) Specific performance or an injunction will be refused if such relief would be unfair because

(a) the contract was induced by mistake or by unfair practices,

(b) the relief would cause unreasonable hardship or loss to the party in breach or to third persons, or

(c) the exchange is grossly inadequate or the terms of the contract are otherwise unfair.

(2) Specific performance or an injunction will be granted in spite of a term of the agreement if denial of such relief would be unfair because it would cause unreasonable hardship or loss to the party seeking relief or to third persons.

Comment:

a. Types of unfairness. Courts have traditionally refused equitable relief on grounds of unfairness or mistake in situations where they would not necessarily refuse to award damages. Some of these situations involve elements of mistake (§§ 1, 153), misrepresentation (§ 164), duress (§ 175) or undue influence (§ 177) that fall short of what is required for avoidance under those doctrines. See Paragraph (a) and Illustrations 1, 2 and 3. Others involve elements of impracticability of performance or frustration of purpose that fall short of what is required for relief under those doctrines. See Paragraph (b) and Illustration 4. Still others involve elements of substantive unfairness in the exchange itself or in its terms that fall short of what is required for unenforceability on grounds of unconscionability (§ 208). See Paragraph (c) and Comment *b*. The gradual expansion of these doctrines to afford relief in an increasing number of cases has resulted in a contraction of the area in which this traditional distinction is made between the availability of equitable and legal relief. Nevertheless, the discretionary nature of equitable relief permits its denial when a variety of factors combine to make enforcement of a promise unfair, even though no single legal doctrine alone would make the promise unenforceable. Such general equitable doctrines as those of laches and "unclean hands" supplement the rule stated in this Section. See Comment *c* to § 357.

Illustrations:

1. A is an aged, illiterate farmer, inexperienced in business. B is an experienced speculator in real estate who knows that a developer wants to acquire a tract of land owned by A and will probably pay a price considerably above the previous market price. B takes advantage of A's ignorance of this fact and of his general inexperience and persuades A not to seek advice. He induces A to contract to sell the land at the previous market price, which is considerably less than the developer later agrees to pay B. A refuses to perform, and B sues A for specific performance. Specific performance may properly be refused on the ground of unfairness.

2. A and B make a contract under which A is to sell B a tract of land for $100,000. B does not tell A that he intends to combine the tract with others as part of a large development in order to prevent A from asking a higher price. $100,000 is a fair price for the tract at existing market prices. A refuses to perform and B sues A for specific performance. Specific performance will not be refused on the ground of unfairness. Cf. Illustration 2 to § 171.

3. A writes B offering to sell for $100,000 a tract of land that A owns known as "201 Lincoln Street." B, who mistakenly believes that this description contains an additional tract of land worth $30,000, accepts A's offer. On discovery of his mistake, B refuses to perform and A sues for specific performance. Even if the court determines that enforcement of the contract would not be unconscionable under the rule stated in § 153, specific

performance may properly be refused on the ground of unfairness. Cf. Illustration 5 to § 153.

4. A, a milkman, and B, a dairy farmer make a contract under which B is to sell and A to buy all of A's requirements of milk, but not less than 200 quarts a day, for one year. B may deliver milk from any source but expects to deliver milk from his own herd. B's herd is destroyed because of hoof and mouth disease and he fails to deliver any milk. A sues B for specific performance. Even though B's duty to deliver milk is not discharged and B is liable to A for breach of contract, specific performance may properly be refused on the ground of unfairness. Cf. Illustration 12 to § 261.

b. Unfairness in the exchange. Unfairness in the exchange does not of itself make an agreement unenforceable. See Comment *c* to § 208. If it is extreme, however, it may be a sufficient ground, without more, for denying specific performance or an injunction. See Illustration 5. A contract, other than an option contract on fair terms (§§ 2, 87), that is binding solely because of a nominal payment or by reason of some formality such as a seal or a signed writing will not ordinarily be enforced by specific performance or an injunction. It is, however, unusual to find such unfairness in the exchange itself without some mistake or unfairness in its inducement. In determining the fairness of an exchange, account will be taken of the risks taken by both parties at the time the agreement was made. An exchange that might otherwise seem unfairly favorable to one party may in fact be fair if there is a substantial risk that the other party's performance may never become due. This is so for insurance and other aleatory contracts. See also Illustration 6. Where the agreement is one of modification between parties who are already bound by a contract (§ 89), the overriding duty of good faith and fair dealing (§ 205) imposes a requirement of fairness.

Illustrations:

5. A, an individual, contracts in June to sell at a fixed price per ton to B, a large soup manufacturer, carrots to be grown on A's farm. The contract, written on B's standard printed form, is obviously drawn to protect B's interests and not A's; it contains numerous provisions to protect B against various contingencies and none giving analogous protection to A. Each of the clauses can be read restrictively so that it is not unconscionable, but several can be read literally to give unrestricted discretion to B. In January, when the market price has risen above the contract price, A repudiates the contract, and B seeks specific performance. In the absence of justification by evidence of commercial setting, purpose or effect, the court may determine that the contract as a whole was unconscionable when made and may properly deny specific performance on the ground of unfairness regardless of whether it would award B damages for breach.

6. A, a childless widow in her seventies suffering from Parkinson's disease, contracts with B, her niece, to leave B her farm in her will in return for B's promise to care for A for the rest of her life. B immediately resigns

her job and begins to care for A, but deterioration of A's condition requires her to go to the hospital within a week and she dies without changing her will. B sues A's estate for specific performance. If the court concludes that the contract was fair when made, in view of the burden of caring for A in her condition and the risk that she might live for a considerable time, it will order specific performance.

c. *Unfair term.* Sometimes a party relies upon an unfair term as a defense in a suit for specific performance or injunction. Even if the term is not unconscionable (§ 208), the court may disregard it and grant the relief sought. See Illustration 7.

Illustration:

7. A contracts to sell land to B for $100,000, payable in five annual $20,000 installments with conveyance to be at the time of the last payment. The contract contains a term providing that "time is of the essence with respect to each installment, and B shall lose all his rights under the contract if he fails to pay any installment when due." See Comment *d* to § 242. B pays the first installment and takes possession, making improvements and paying the next two installments on time. When he tenders the fourth payment one month late, A refuses it and brings an action of ejectment. B sues for specific performance. The court may refuse to enforce the quoted term on the ground of unfairness. Specific performance may then properly be granted conditional on payment into court of the fourth installment with interest from maturity and on payment of the last installment on conveyance.

§ 370 Requirement That Benefit Be Conferred

Note: The current position of the American Law Institute concerning every form of restitution in a contractual context is set forth in Restatement Third, Restitution and Unjust Enrichment *(R3RUE), formally adopted in 2010 and published in 2011. On the topic of this section, see especially R3RUE §§ 31-36 and 49-50.*

A party is entitled to restitution under the rules stated in this Restatement only to the extent that he has conferred a benefit on the other party by way of part performance or reliance.

Comment:

a. *Meaning of requirement.* A party's restitution interest is his interest in having restored to him any benefit that he has conferred on the other party. Restitution is, therefore, available to a party only to the extent that he has conferred a benefit on the other party. The benefit may result from the transfer of property or from services, including forbearance. The benefit is ordinarily conferred by performance by the party seeking restitution, and receipt by the other party of performance that he bargained for is regarded as a benefit. However, a benefit may also be conferred if the party seeking restitution relies on the contract in some other way, as where he makes improvements on property that does not ultimately become his. However, a party's expenditures in preparation for performance that do not confer a benefit on the other party do not give rise to a restitution interest. See Illustration 1. If, for example, the performance consists of the manufacture and delivery of goods and the buyer wrongfully prevents its completion, the seller is not entitled to restitution because no benefit has been conferred on the buyer. See Illustration 2. The injured party may, however, have an action for damages, including one for recovery based on his reliance interest. The requirement of this Section is generally satisfied if a benefit has been conferred, and it is immaterial that it was later lost, destroyed or squandered. See Illustration 3. The benefit must have been conferred by the party claiming restitution. It is not enough that it was simply derived from the breach. See Illustration 4. The other party is considered to have had a benefit conferred on him if a performance was rendered at his request to a third person. See Illustration 5. If the contract is for the benefit of a third person, the promisee is entitled to restitution unless the duty to the beneficiary cannot be varied. . . .

Illustrations:

1. A, who holds a mortgage on B's house, makes a contract with B under which A promises not to foreclose the mortgage for a year. In reliance on this promise, B invests money that he would have used to pay the mortgage in improving other land that he owns. A repudiates the contract and forecloses. B cannot get restitution based on the improvements since making them conferred no benefit on A.

2. A contracts to sell B a machine for $100,000. After A has spent $40,000 on the manufacture of the machine but before its completion, B repudiates the contract. A cannot get restitution of the $40,000 because no benefit was conferred on B.

3. A promises to deposit $100,000 to B's credit in the X Bank in return for B's promise to render services. A deposits the $100,000, the X Bank fails, and B refuses to perform. A can get restitution of the $100,000 because a benefit was to that extent conferred on B even though it was lost by B when the X Bank failed.

4. A contracts to work full time for B as a bookkeeper. In breach of this contract, A uses portions of the time that he should spend working for B in keeping books for C, who pays him an additional salary. B sues A for breach of contract. B cannot recover from A the amount of the salary paid by C because it was not a benefit conferred by B.

5. A, a social worker, promises B to render personal services to C in return for B's promise to educate A's children. B repudiates the contract after A has rendered part of the services. A can get restitution from B for the services, even though they were not rendered to B, because they conferred a benefit on B.

§ 371 Measure of Restitution Interest

If a sum of money is awarded to protect a party's restitution interest, it may as justice requires be measured by either

(a) the reasonable value to the other party of what he received in terms of what it would have cost him to obtain it from a person in the claimant's position, or

(b) the extent to which the other party's property has been increased in value or his other interests advanced.

§ 373 Restitution When Other Party Is in Breach

(1) Subject to the rule stated in Subsection (2), on a breach by non-performance that gives rise to a claim for damages for total breach or on a repudiation, the injured party is entitled to restitution for any benefit that he has conferred on the other party by way of part performance or reliance.

(2) The injured party has no right to restitution if he has performed all of his duties under the contract and no performance by the other party remains due other than payment of a definite sum of money for that performance.

§ 374 Restitution in Favor of Party in Breach

Note: The current position of the American Law Institute concerning every form of restitution in a contractual context is set forth in Restatement Third, Restitution and Unjust Enrichment *(R3RUE), formally adopted in 2010 and published in 2011. On the topic of this section, see especially R3RUE § 36.*

(1) Subject to the rule stated in Subsection (2), if a party justifiably refuses to perform on the ground that his remaining duties of performance have been discharged by the other party's breach, the party in breach is entitled to restitution for any benefit that he has conferred by way of part performance or reliance in excess of the loss that he has caused by his own breach.

(2) To the extent that, under the manifested assent of the parties, a party's performance is to be retained in the case of breach, that party is not entitled to restitution if the value of the performance as liquidated damages is reasonable in the light of the anticipated or actual loss caused by the breach and the difficulties of proof of loss.

Comment:

a. Restitution in spite of breach. The rule stated in this Section applies where a party, after having rendered part performance, commits a breach by either non-performance or repudiation that justifies the other party in refusing further performance. It is often unjust to allow the injured party to retain the entire benefit of the part performance rendered by the party in breach without paying anything in return. The party in breach is, in any case, liable for the loss caused by his breach. If the benefit received by the injured party does not exceed that loss, he owes nothing to the party in breach. If the benefit received exceeds that loss, the rule stated in this Section generally gives the party in breach the right to recover the excess in restitution. If the injured party has a right to specific performance and remains willing and able to perform, he may keep what he has received and sue for specific performance of the balance. . . .

b. Measurement of benefit. If the party in breach seeks restitution of money that he has paid, no problem arises in measuring the benefit to the other party. See Illustration 1. If, however, he seeks to recover a sum of money that represents the benefit of services rendered to the other party, measurement of the benefit is more difficult. Since the party seeking restitution is responsible for posing the problem of measurement of benefit, doubts will be resolved against him and his recovery will not exceed the less generous of the two measures stated in § 370, that of the other party's increase in wealth. See Illustration 3. If no value can be put on this, he cannot recover. See Illustration 5. Although the contract price is evidence of the benefit, it is not conclusive. However, in no case will the party in breach be allowed to recover more than a ratable portion of the total contract price where such a portion can be determined.

A party who intentionally furnishes services or builds a building that is materially different from what he promised is properly regarded as having acted officiously and not in part performance of his promise and will be denied recovery on that ground even if his performance was of some benefit to the other party. This is not the case, however, if the other party has accepted or agreed to accept the substitute performance. See §§ 278, 279.

Illustrations:

1. A contracts to sell land to B for $100,000, which B promises to pay in $10,000 installments before transfer of title. After B has paid $30,000 he fails to pay the remaining installments and A sells the land to another buyer for $95,000. B can recover $30,000 from A in restitution less $5,000 damages for B's breach of contract, or $25,000. . . .

3. A contracts to make repairs to B's building in return for B's promise to pay $10,000 on completion of the work. A makes repairs costing him $8,000 but inadvertently fails to follow the specifications in such material respects that there is no substantial performance. The defects cannot be corrected without the destruction of large parts of the building, but the work confers a benefit on B by increasing the value of the building to him by $4,000. A can recover $4,000 from B in restitution. . . .

5. A contracts to tutor B's son for six months in preparation for an examination, in return for which B promises to pay A $2,000 at the end of that time. After A has worked for three months, he leaves to take another job and B is unable to find a suitable replacement. In the absence of any reliable basis for measuring the benefit to B from A's part performance, restitution will be denied.

APPENDIX B

UNIFORM COMMERCIAL CODE

§ 1-103 Construction of Uniform Commercial Code to Promote its Purposes and Policies: Applicability of Supplemental Principles of Law

(a) The Uniform Commercial Code must be liberally construed and applied to promote its underlying purposes and policies, which are: (1) to simplify, clarify, and modernize the law governing commercial transactions; (2) to permit the continued expansion of commercial practices through custom, usage, and agreement of the parties; and (3) to make uniform the law among the various jurisdictions.

(b) Unless displaced by the particular provisions of the Uniform Commercial Code, the principles of law and equity, including the law merchant and the law relative to capacity to contract, principal and agent, estoppel, fraud, misrepresentation, duress, coercion, mistake, bankruptcy, and other validating or invalidating cause supplement its provisions.

§ 1-201 General Definitions

(a) Unless the context otherwise requires, words or phrases defined in this section, or in the additional definitions contained in other articles of the Uniform Commercial Code that apply to particular articles or parts thereof, have the meanings stated.

(b) Subject to definitions contained in other articles of the Uniform Commercial Code that apply to particular articles or parts thereof: . . .

> (3) **"Agreement"**, as distinguished from "contract", means the bargain of the parties in fact, as found in their language or inferred from other circumstances, including course of performance, course of dealing, or usage of trade as provided in Section 1-303. . . .

(12) **"Contract"**, as distinguished from "agreement", means the total legal obligation that results from the parties' agreement as determined by the Uniform Commercial Code as supplemented by any other applicable laws. . . .

(20) **"Good faith"**, except as otherwise provided in Article 5, means honesty in fact and the observance of reasonable commercial standards of fair dealing. . . .

(37) "**Signed**" includes using any symbol executed or adopted with present intention to adopt or accept a writing. . . .

(43) "**Writing**" includes printing, typewriting, or any other intentional reduction to tangible form. "Written" has a corresponding meaning.

§ 1-205 Course of Dealing and Usage of Trade

(1) A course of dealing is a sequence of previous conduct between the parties to a particular transaction which is fairly to be regarded as establishing a common basis of understanding for interpreting their expressions and other conduct.

(2) A usage of trade is any practice or method of dealing having such regularity of observance in a place, vocation, or trade as to justify an expectation that it will be observed with respect to the transaction in question. The existence and scope of such a usage are to be proved as facts. If it is established that such a usage is embodied in a written trade code or similar writing, the interpretation of the writing is for the court.

(3) A course of dealing between parties and any usage of trade in the vocation or trade in which they are engaged or of which they are or should be aware give particular meaning to and supplement or qualify terms of an agreement.

(4) The express terms of an agreement and an applicable course of dealing or usage of trade shall be construed wherever reasonable as consistent with each other; but when such construction is unreasonable express terms control both course of dealing and usage of trade and course of dealing controls usage of trade.

(5) An applicable usage of trade in the place where any part of performance is to occur shall be used in interpreting the agreement as to that part of the performance.

(6) Evidence of a relevant usage of trade offered by one party is not admissible unless and until he has given the other party such notice as the court finds sufficient to prevent unfair surprise to the latter.

§ 1-303 Course of Performance, Course of Dealing, and Usage of Trade

(a) A "course of performance" is a sequence of conduct between the parties to a particular transaction that exists if: (1) the agreement of the parties with respect to the transaction involves repeated occasions for performance by a party; and (2) the other party, with knowledge of the nature of the performance and opportunity for objection to it, accepts the performance or acquiesces in it without objection.

(b) A "course of dealing" is a sequence of conduct concerning previous transactions between the parties to a particular transaction that is fairly to be regarded as establishing a common basis of understanding for interpreting their expressions and other conduct.

(c) A "usage of trade" is any practice or method of dealing having such regularity of observance in a place, vocation, or trade as to justify an expectation that it will be observed with respect to the transaction in question. The existence and scope of such a usage must be proved as facts. If it is established that such a usage is embodied in a trade code or similar record, the interpretation of the record is a question of law.

(d) A course of performance or course of dealing between the parties or usage of trade in the vocation or trade in which they are engaged or of which they are or should be aware is relevant in ascertaining the meaning of the parties' agreement, may give particular meaning to specific terms of the agreement, and may supplement or qualify the terms of the agreement. A usage of trade applicable in the place in which part of the performance under the agreement is to occur may be so utilized as to that part of the performance.

(e) Except as otherwise provided in subsection (f), the express terms of an agreement and any applicable course of performance, course of dealing, or usage of trade must be construed whenever reasonable as consistent with each other. If such a construction is unreasonable: (1) express terms prevail over course of performance, course of dealing, and usage of trade; (2) course of performance prevails over course of dealing and usage of trade; and (3) course of dealing prevails over usage of trade.

(f) Subject to Section 2-209, a course of performance is relevant to show a waiver or modification of any term inconsistent with the course of performance.

(g) Evidence of a relevant usage of trade offered by one party is not admissible unless that party has given the other party notice that the court finds sufficient to prevent unfair surprise to the other party.

§ 1-304 Obligation of Good Faith

Every contract or duty within the Uniform Commercial Code imposes an obligation of good faith in its performance and enforcement.

§ 1-305 Remedies to Be Liberally Administered

(a) The remedies provided by [the Uniform Commercial Code] shall be liberally administered to the end that the aggrieved party may be put in as good a position as if the other party had fully performed but neither consequential or special nor penal damages may be had except as specifically provided in [the Uniform Commercial Code] or by other rule of law. . . .

§ 1-306 Waiver or Renunciation of Claim or Right After Breach

A claim or right arising out of an alleged breach may be discharged in whole or in part without consideration by agreement of the aggrieved party in an authenticated record.

§ 2-104 Definitions: "Merchant"; "Between Merchants"; "Financing Agency"

(1) "Merchant" means a person who deals in goods of the kind or otherwise by his occupation holds himself out as having knowledge or skill peculiar to the practices or goods involved in the transaction or to whom such knowledge or skill may be attributed by his employment of an agent or broker or other intermediary who by his occupation holds himself out as having such knowledge or skill. . . .

§ 2-106 Definitions: "Contract"; "Agreement"; "Contract for sale"; "Sale"; "Present sale"; "Conforming" to Contract; "Termination"; "Cancellation"

. . .

(2) Goods or conduct including any part of a performance are "**conforming**" or conform to the contract when they are in accordance with the obligations under the contract.

(3) "**Termination**" occurs when either party pursuant to a power created by agreement or law puts an end to the contract otherwise than for its breach. On "termination" all obligations which are still executory on both sides are discharged but any right based on prior breach or performance survives.

(4) "**Cancellation**" occurs when either party puts an end to the contract for breach by the other and its effect is the same as that of "termination" except that the cancelling party also retains any remedy for breach of the whole contract or any unperformed balance.

§ 2-201 Formal Requirements; Statute of Frauds

(1) Except as otherwise provided in this section a contract for the sale of goods for the price of $500 or more is not enforceable by way of action or defense unless there is some writing sufficient to indicate that a contract for sale has been made between the parties and signed by the party against whom enforcement is sought or by his authorized agent or broker. A writing is not insufficient because it omits or incorrectly states a term agreed upon but the contract is not enforceable under this paragraph beyond the quantity of goodss-hown in such writing.

(2) Between merchants if within a reasonable time a writing in confirmation of the contractand sufficient against the sender is received and the party receiving it has reason to know its contents, it satisfies the requirements of subsection (1) against such party unless written notice of objection to its contents is given within 10 days after it is received.

(3) A contract which does not satisfy the requirements of subsection (1) but which is valid in other respects is enforceable

(a) if the goods are to be specially manufactured for the buyer and are not suitable for sale to others in the ordinary course of the seller'sbusiness and the seller, before notice of repudiation is received and under circumstances which reasonably indicate that the goods are for the buyer, has made either a substantial beginning of their manufacture or commitments for their procurement; or

(b) if the party against whom enforcement is sought admits in his pleading, testimony or otherwise in court that a contract for sale was made, but the contract is not enforceable under this provision beyond the quantity of goodsadmitted; or

(c) with respect to goods for which payment has been made and accepted or which have been received and accepted (Sec. 2-606).

§ 2-202 Final Written Expression: Parol or Extrinsic Evidence

Terms with respect to which the confirmatory memoranda of the parties agree or which are otherwise set forth in a writing intended by the parties as a final expression of their agreement with respect to such terms as are included therein may not be contradicted by evidence of any prior agreement or of a contemporaneous oral agreement but may be explained or supplemented

(a) by course of dealing or usage of trade (Section 1-205) or by course of performance (Section 2-208); and

(b) by evidence of consistent additional terms unless the court finds the writing to have been intended also as a complete and exclusive statement of the terms of the agreement.

§ 2-204 Formation in General

(1) A contract for sale of goods may be made in any manner sufficient to show agreement, including offer and acceptance, conduct by both parties which recognizes the existence of a contract, the interaction of electronic agents, and the interaction of an electronic agent and an individual.

(2) An agreement sufficient to constitute a contract for sale may be found even if the moment of its making is undetermined.

(3) Even if one or more terms are left open, a contract for sale does not fail for indefiniteness if the parties have intended to make a contract and there is a reasonably certain basis for giving an appropriate remedy.

§ 2-205 Firm Offers

An offer by a merchant to buy or sell goods in a signed writing which by its terms gives assurance that it will be held open is not revocable, for lack of consideration, during the time stated or if no time is stated for a reasonable time, but in no event may such period of irrevocability exceed three months; but any such term of assurance on a form supplied by the offeree must be separately signed by the offeror.

§ 2-206 Offer and Acceptance in Formation of Contract

(1) Unless otherwise unambiguously indicated by the language or circumstances

(a) an offer to make a contract shall be construed as inviting acceptance in any manner and by any medium reasonable in the circumstances;

(b) an order or other offer to buy goods for prompt or current shipment shall be construed as inviting acceptance either by a prompt promise to ship or by the prompt or current shipment of conforming or non-conforming goods, but such a shipment of non-conforming goods does not constitute an acceptance if the seller seasonably notifies the buyer that the shipment is offered only as an accommodation to the buyer.

(2) Where the beginning of a requested performance is a reasonable mode of acceptance an offeror who is not notified of acceptance within a reasonable time may treat the offer as having lapsed before acceptance.

§ 2-207 Additional Terms in Acceptance or Confirmation

(1) A definite and seasonable expression of acceptance or a written confirmation which is sent within a reasonable time operates as an acceptance even though it states terms additional to or different from those offered or agreed upon, unless acceptance is expressly made conditional on assent to the additional or different terms.

(2) The additional terms are to be construed as proposals for addition to the contract. Between merchants such terms become part of the contract unless:

(a) the offer expressly limits acceptance to the terms of the offer;

(b) they materially alter it; or

(c) notification of objection to them has already been given or is given within a reasonable time after notice of them is received.

(3) Conduct by both parties which recognizes the existence of a contract is sufficient to establish a contract for sale although the writings of the parties do not otherwise establish a contract. In such case the terms of the particular contract consist of those terms on which the writings of the parties agree, together with any supplementary terms incorporated under any other provisions of this Act.

Official Comment

1. This section is intended to deal with two typical situations. The one is the written confirmation, where an agreement has been reached either orally or by informal correspondence between the parties and is followed by one or both of the parties sending formal memoranda embodying the terms so far as agreed upon and adding terms not discussed. The other situation is offer and acceptance, in which a wire or letter expressed and intended as an acceptance or the closing of an agreement adds further minor suggestions or proposals such as "ship by Tuesday," "rush," "ship draft against bill of lading inspection allowed," or the like. A frequent example of the second situation is the exchange of printed purchase order and acceptance (sometimes called "acknowledgment") forms. Because the forms are oriented to the thinking of the respective drafting parties, the terms contained in them often do not correspond. Often the seller's form contains terms different from or additional to those set forth in the buyer's form. Nevertheless, the parties proceed with the transaction. [Comment 1 was amended in 1966.]

2. Under this Article a proposed deal which in commercial understanding has in fact been closed is recognized as a contract. Therefore, any additional matter contained in the confirmation or in the acceptance falls within subsection (2) and must be regarded as a proposal for an added term unless the acceptance is made conditional on the acceptance of the additional or different terms. [Comment 2 was amended in 1966.]

3. Whether or not additional or different terms will become part of the agreement depends upon the provisions of subsection (2). If they are such as materially to alter the original bargain, they will not be included unless

expressly agreed to by the other party. If, however, they are terms which would not so change the bargain they will be incorporated unless notice of objection to them has already been given or is given within a reasonable time.

4. Examples of typical clauses which would normally "materially alter" the contract and so result in surprise or hardship if incorporated without express awareness by the other party are: a clause negating such standard warranties as that of merchantability or fitness for a particular purpose in circumstances in which either warranty normally attaches; a clause requiring a guaranty of 90% or 100% deliveries in a case such as a contract by cannery, where the usage of the trade allows greater quantity leeways; a clause reserving to the seller the power to cancel upon the buyer's failure to meet any invoice when due; a clause requiring that complaints be made in a time materially shorter than customary or reasonable.

5. Examples of clauses which involve no element of unreasonable surprise and which therefore are to be incorporated in the contract unless notice of objection is seasonably given are: a clause setting forth and perhaps enlarging slightly upon the seller's exemption due to supervening causes beyond his control, similar to those covered by the provision of this Article on merchant's excuse by failure of presupposed conditions or a clause fixing in advance any reasonable formula of proration under such circumstances; a clause fixing a reasonable time for complaints within customary limits, or in the case of a purchase for sub-sale, providing for inspection by the sub-purchaser; a clause providing for interest on overdue invoices or fixing the seller's standard credit terms where they are within the range of trade practice and do not limit any credit bargained for; a clause limiting the right of rejection for defects which fall within the customary trade tolerances for acceptance "with adjustment" or otherwise limiting remedy in a reasonable manner (see Sections 2-718 and 2-719).

6. If no answer is received within a reasonable time after additional terms are proposed, it is both fair and commercially sound to assume that their inclusion has been assented to. Where clauses on confirming forms sent by both parties conflict each party must be assumed to object to a clause of the other conflicting with one on the confirmation sent by himself. As a result the requirement that there be notice of objection which is found in subsection (2) is satisfied and the conflicting terms do not become a part of the contract. The contract then consists of the terms originally expressly agreed to, terms on which the confirmations agree, and terms supplied by this Act, including subsection (2). The written confirmation is also subject to Section 2-201. Under that section a failure to respond permits enforcement of a prior oral agreement; under this section a failure to respond permits additional terms to become part of the agreement. [Comment 6 was amended in 1966.]

7. In many cases, as where goods are shipped, accepted and paid for before any dispute arises, there is no question whether a contract has been made. In such cases, where the writings of the parties do not establish a contract, it is not necessary to determine which act or document constituted the offer and which the acceptance. See Section 2-204. The only question is what terms

are included in the contract, and subsection (3) furnishes the governing rule. [Comment 7 was added in 1966.]

§ 2-208 Course of Performance or Practical Construction

(1) Where the contract for sale involves repeated occasions for performance by either party with knowledge of the nature of the performance and opportunity for objection to it by the other, any course of performance accepted or acquiesced in without objection shall be relevant to determine the meaning of the agreement.

(2) The express terms of the agreement and any such course of performance, as well as any course of dealing and usage of trade, shall be construed whenever reasonable as consistent with each other; but when such construction is unreasonable, express terms shall control course of performance and course of performance shall control both course of dealing and usage of trade (Section 1-205).

(3) Subject to the provisions of the next section on modification and waiver, such course of performance shall be relevant to show a waiver or modification of any term inconsistent with such course of performance.

§ 2-209 Modification, Rescission and Waiver

(1) An agreement modifying a contract within this Article needs no consideration to be binding.

(2) A signed agreement which excludes modification or rescission except by a signed writing cannot be otherwise modified or rescinded, but except as between merchants such a requirement on a form supplied by the merchant must be separately signed by the other party.

(3) The requirements of the statute of frauds section of this Article (Section 2-201) must be satisfied if the contract as modified is within its provisions.

(4) Although an attempt at modification or rescission does not satisfy the requirements of subsection (2) or (3) it can operate as a waiver.

(5) A party who has made a waiver affecting an executory portion of the contract may retract the waiver by reasonable notification received by the other party that strict performance will be required of any term waived, unless the retraction would be unjust in view of a material change of position in reliance on the waiver.

Official Comment:

1. This section seeks to protect and make effective all necessary and desirable modifications of sales contracts without regard to the technicalities which at present hamper such adjustments.

2. Subsection (1) provides that an agreement modifying a sales contract needs no consideration to be binding.

However, modifications made thereunder must meet the test of good faith imposed by this Act. The effective use of bad faith to escape performance on the original contract terms is barred, and the extortion of a "modification" without legitimate commercial reason is ineffective as a violation of the duty of good faith. Nor can a mere technical consideration support a modification made in bad faith.

The test of "good faith" between merchants or as against merchants includes "observance of reasonable commercial standards of fair dealing in the trade" (Section 2-103), and may in some situations require an objectively demonstrable reason for seeking a modification. But such matters as a market shift which makes performance come to involve a loss may provide such a reason even though there is no such unforeseen difficulty as would make out a legal excuse from performance under Sections 2-615 and 2-616. . . .

§ 2-210 Delegation of Performance; Assignment of Rights

(1) A party may perform his duty through a delegate unless otherwise agreed or unless the other party has a substantial interest in having his original promisor perform or control the acts required by the contract. No delegation of performance relieves the party delegating of any duty to perform or any liability for breach.

(2) Unless otherwise agreed all rights of either seller or buyer can be assigned except where the assignment would materially change the duty of the other party, or increase materially the burden or risk imposed on him by his contract, or impair materially his chance of obtaining return performance. A right to damages for breach of the whole contract or a right arising out of the assignor's due performance of his entire obligation can be assigned despite agreement otherwise.

(3) Unless the circumstances indicate the contrary a prohibition of assignment of "the contract" is to be construed as barring only the delegation to the assignee of the assignor's performance.

(4) An assignment of "the contract" or of "all my rights under the contract" or an assignment in similar general terms is an assignment of rights and unless the language or the circumstances (as in an assignment for security) indicate the contrary, it is a delegation of performance of the duties of the assignor and its acceptance by the assignee constitutes a promise by him to perform those duties. This promise is enforceable by either the assignor or the other party to the original contract.

(5) The other party may treat any assignment which delegates performance as creating reasonable grounds for insecurity and may without prejudice to his rights against the assignor demand assurances from the assignee (Section 2-609).

§ 2-302 Unconscionable Contract or Clause

(1) If the court as a matter of law finds the contractor any clause of the contract to have been unconscionable at the time it was made the court may refuse to enforce the contract, or it may enforce the remainder of the contract without the unconscionable clause, or it may so limit the application of any unconscionable clause as to avoid any unconscionable result.

(2) When it is claimed or appears to the court that the contractor any clause thereof may be unconscionable the parties shall be afforded a reasonable opportunity to present evidence as to its commercial setting, purpose and effect to aid the court in making the determination.

Official Comment

1. This section is intended to make it possible for the courts to police explicitly against the contracts or clauses which they find to be unconscionable. In the past such policing has been accomplished by adverse construction of language, by manipulation of the rules of offer and acceptance or by determinations that the clause is contrary to public policy or to the dominant purpose of the contract. This section is intended to allow the court to pass directly on the unconscionability of the contract or particular clause therein and to make a conclusion of law as to its unconscionability. The basic test is whether, in the light of the general commercial background and the commercial needs of the particular trade or case, the clauses involved are so one-sided as to be unconscionable under the circumstances existing at the time of the making of the contract. Subsection (2) makes it clear that it is proper for the court to hear evidence upon these questions. The principle is one of the prevention of oppression and unfair surprise (*Cf. Campbell Soup Co. v. Wentz*, 172 F.2d 80, 3d Cir.1948) and not of disturbance of allocation of risks because of superior bargaining power. . . .

2. Under this section the court, in its discretion, may refuse to enforce the contract as a whole if it is permeated by the unconscionability, or it may strike any single clause or group of clauses which are so tainted or which are contrary to the essential purpose of the agreement, or it may simply limit unconscionable clauses so as to avoid unconscionable results.

3. The present section is addressed to the court, and the decision is to be made by it. The commercial evidence referred to in subsection (2) is for the court's consideration, not the jury's. Only the agreement which results from the court's action on these matters is to be submitted to the general triers of the facts.

§ 2-305 Open Price Term

(1) The parties if they so intend can conclude a contract for sale even though the price is not settled. In such a case the price is a reasonable price at the time for delivery if

(a) nothing is said as to price; or

(b) the price is left to be agreed by the parties and they fail to agree; or

(c) the price is to be fixed in terms of some agreed market or other standard as set or recorded by a third person or agency and it is not so set or recorded.

(2) A price to be fixed by the seller or by the buyer means a price for him to fix in good faith.

(3) When a price left to be fixed otherwise than by agreement of the parties fails to be fixed through fault of one party the other may at his option treat the contract as cancelled or himself fix a reasonable price.

(4) Where, however, the parties intend not to be bound unless the price be fixed or agreed and it is not fixed or agreed there is no contract. In such a case the buyer must return any goods already received or if unable so to do must pay their reasonable value at the time of delivery and the seller must return any portion of the price paid on account.

§ 2-306 Output, Requirements and Exclusive Dealings

(1) A term which measures the quantity by the output of the seller or the requirements of the buyer means such actual output or requirements as may occur in good faith, except that no quantity unreasonably disproportionate to any stated estimate or in the absence of a stated estimate to any normal or otherwise comparable prior output or requirements may be tendered or demanded.

(2) A lawful agreement by either the seller or the buyer for exclusive dealing in the kind of goods concerned imposes unless otherwise agreed an obligation by the seller to use best efforts to supply the goods and by the buyer to use best efforts to promote their sale.

§ 2-309 Absence of Specific Time Provisions; Notice of Termination

(1) The time for shipment or delivery or any other action under a contract if not provided in this Article or agreed upon shall be a reasonable time.

(2) Where the contract provides for successive performances but is indefinite in duration it is valid for a reasonable time but unless otherwise agreed may be terminated at any time by either party.

(3) Termination of a contract by one party except on the happening of an agreed event requires that reasonable notification be received by the other party and an agreement dispensing with notification is invalid if its operation would be unconscionable.

§ 2-316 Exclusion or Modification of Warranties

(1) Words or conduct relevant to the creation of an express warranty and words or conduct tending to negate or limit warranty shall be construed wherever reasonable as consistent with each other; but subject to the provisions of this Article on parol or extrinsic evidence (Section 2-202) negation or limitation is inoperative to the extent that such construction is unreasonable.

(2) Subject to subsection (3), to exclude or modify the implied warranty of merchantability or any part of it the language must mention merchantability and in case of a writing must be conspicuous, and to exclude or modify any implied warranty of fitness the exclusion must be by a writing and conspicuous. Language to exclude all implied warranties of fitness is sufficient if it states, for example, that "There are no warranties which extend beyond the description on the face hereof."

(3) Notwithstanding subsection (2)

(a) unless the circumstances indicate otherwise, all implied warranties are excluded by expressions like "as is", "with all faults" or other language which in common understanding calls the buyer's attention to the exclusion of warranties and makes plain that there is no implied warranty; and

(b) when the buyer before entering into the contract has examined the goods or the sample or model as fully as he desired or has refused to examine the goods there is no implied warranty with regard to defects which an examination ought in the circumstances to have revealed to him; and

(c) an implied warranty can also be excluded or modified by course of dealing or course of performance or usage of trade.

(4) Remedies for breach of warranty can be limited in accordance with the provisions of this Article on liquidation or limitation of damages and on contractual modification of remedy (Sections 2-718 and 2-719).

§ 2-328 Sale by Auction

(1) In a sale by auction if goods are put up in lots each lot is the subject of a separate sale.

(2) A sale by auction is complete when the auctioneer so announces by the fall of the hammer or in other customary manner. Where a bid is made while the hammer is falling in acceptance of a prior bid the auctioneer may in his discretion reopen the bidding or declare the goods sold under the bid on which the hammer was falling.

(3) Such a sale is with reserve unless the goods are in explicit terms put up without reserve. In an auction with reserve the auctioneer may withdraw the goods at any time until he announces completion of the sale. In an auction without reserve, after the auctioneer calls for bids on an article or lot, that article or lot cannot be withdrawn unless no bid is made within a reasonable time. In either case a bidder may retract his bid until the auctioneer's announcement of completion of the sale, but a bidder's retraction does not revive any previous bid.

(4) If the auctioneer knowingly receives a bid on the seller's behalf or the seller makes or procures such a bid, and notice has not been given that liberty for such bidding is reserved, the buyer may at his option avoid the sale or take the goods at the price of the last good faith bid prior to the completion of the sale. This subsection shall not apply to any bid at a forced sale.

§ 2-508 Cure by Seller of Improper Tender or Delivery; Replacement

(1) Where any tender or delivery by the seller is rejected because non-conforming and the time for performance has not yet expired, the seller may seasonably notify the buyer of his intention to cure and may then within the contract time make a conforming delivery.

(2) Where the buyer rejects a non-conforming tender which the seller had reasonable grounds to believe would be acceptable with or without money allowance the seller may if he seasonably notifies the buyer have a further reasonable time to substitute a conforming tender.

§ 2-509 Risk of Loss in the Absence of Breach

(1) Where the contract requires or authorizes the seller to ship the goods by carrier

(a) if it does not require him to deliver them at a particular destination, the risk of loss passes to the buyer when the goods are duly delivered to the carrier even though the shipment is under reservation (Section 2-505); but

(b) if it does require him to deliver them at a particular destination and the goods are there duly tendered while in the possession of the carrier, the risk of loss passes to the buyer when the goods are there duly so tendered as to enable the buyer to take delivery.

(2) Where the goods are held by a bailee to be delivered without being moved, the risk of loss passes to the buyer

(a) on his receipt of a negotiable document of title covering the goods; or

(b) on acknowledgment by the bailee of the buyer's right to possession of the goods; or

(c) after his receipt of a non-negotiable document of title or other written direction to deliver, as provided in subsection (4)(b) of Section 2-503.

(3) In any case not within subsection (1) or (2), the risk of loss passes to the buyer on his receipt of the goods if the seller is a merchant; otherwise the risk passes to the buyer on tender of delivery.

(4) The provisions of this section are subject to contrary agreement of the parties and to the provisions of this Article on sale on approval (Section 2-327) and on effect of breach on risk of loss (Section 2-510).

§ 2-510 Effect of Breach on Risk of Loss

(1) Where a tender or delivery of goods so fails to conform to the contract as to give a right of rejection the risk of their loss remains on the seller until cure or acceptance.

(2) Where the buyer rightfully revokes acceptance he may to the extent of any deficiency in his effective insurance coverage treat the risk of loss as having rested on the seller from the beginning.

(3) Where the buyer as to conforming goods already identified to the contract for sale repudiates or is otherwise in breach before risk of their loss has passed to him, the seller may to the extent of any deficiency in his effective insurance coverage treat the risk of loss as resting on the buyer for a commercially reasonable time.

§ 2-601 Buyer's Rights on Improper Delivery

Subject to the provisions of this Article on breach in installment contracts (Section 2-612) and unless otherwise agreed under the sections on contractual limitations of remedy (Sections 2-718 and 2-719), if the goods or the tender of delivery fail in any respect to conform to the contract, the buyer may

(a) reject the whole; or

(b) accept the whole; or

(c) accept any commercial unit or units and reject the rest.

§ 2-602 Manner and Effect of Rightful Rejection

(1) Rejection of goods must be within a reasonable time after their delivery or tender. It is ineffective unless the buyer seasonably notifies the seller.

(2) Subject to the provisions of the two following sections on rejected goods (Sections 2-603 and 2-604),

(a) after rejection any exercise of ownership by the buyer with respect to any commercial unit is wrongful as against the seller; and

(b) if the buyer has before rejection taken physical possession of goods in which he does not have a security interest under the provisions of this Article (subsection (3) of Section 2-711), he is under a duty after rejection to hold them with reasonable care at the seller's disposition for a time sufficient to permit the seller to remove them; but

(c) the buyer has no further obligations with regard to goods rightfully rejected.

(3) The seller's rights with respect to goods wrongfully rejected are governed by the provisions of this Article on seller's remedies in general (Section 2-703).

§ 2-606 What Constitutes Acceptance of Goods

(1) Acceptance of goods occurs when the buyer

(a) after a reasonable opportunity to inspect the goods signifies to the seller that the goods are conforming or that he will take or retain them in spite of their non-conformity; or

(b) fails to make an effective rejection (subsection (1) of Section 2-602), but such acceptance does not occur until the buyer has had a reasonable opportunity to inspect them; or

(c) does any act inconsistent with the seller's ownership; but if such act is wrongful as against the seller it is an acceptance only if ratified by him. . . .

§ 2-607 Effect of Acceptance; Notice of Breach; Burden of Establishing Breach After Acceptance; Notice of Claim or Litigation to Person Answerable Over

(1) The buyer must pay at the contract rate for any goods accepted.

(2) Acceptance of goods by the buyer precludes rejection of the goods accepted and if made with knowledge of a non-conformity cannot be revoked because of it unless the acceptance was on the reasonable assumption that the non-conformity would be seasonably cured but acceptance does not of itself impair any other remedy provided by this Article for non-conformity.

(3)Where a tender has been accepted

(a) the buyer must within a reasonable time after he discovers or should have discovered any breach notify the seller of breach or be barred from any remedy; and

(b) if the claim is one for infringement or the like (subsection (3) of Section 2-312) and the buyer is sued as a result of such a breach he must so notify the seller within a reasonable time after he receives notice of the litigation or be barred from any remedy over for liability established by the litigation.

(4) The burden is on the buyer to establish any breach with respect to the goods accepted.

(5) Where the buyer is sued for breach of a warranty or other obligation for which his seller is answerable over

(a) he may give his seller written notice of the litigation. If the notice states that the seller may come in and defend and that if the seller does not do so he will be bound in any action against him by his buyer by any determination of fact common to the two litigations, then unless the seller after seasonable receipt of the notice does come in and defend he is so bound.

(b) if the claim is one for infringement or the like (subsection (3) of Section 2-312) the original seller may demand in writing that his buyer turn over to him control of the litigation including settlement or else be barred from any remedy over and if he also agrees to bear all expense and to satisfy any adverse judgment, then unless the buyer after seasonable receipt of the demand does turn over control the buyer is so barred.

(6) The provisions of subsections (3), (4) and (5) apply to any obligation of a buyer to hold the seller harmless against infringement or the like (subsection (3) of Section 2-312).

§ 2-608 Revocation of Acceptance in Whole or in Part

(1) The buyer may revoke his acceptance of a lot or commercial unit whose non-conformity substantially impairs its value to him if he has accepted it

(a) on the reasonable assumption that its non-conformity would be cured and it has not been seasonably cured; or

(b) without discovery of such non-conformity if his acceptance was reasonably induced either by the difficulty of discovery before acceptance or by the seller's assurances.

(2) Revocation of acceptance must occur within a reasonable time after the buyer discovers or should have discovered the ground for it and before any substantial change in condition of the goods which is not caused by their own defects. It is not effective until the buyer notifies the seller of it.

(3) A buyer who so revokes has the same rights and duties with regard to the goods involved as if he had rejected them.

§ 2-609 Right to Adequate Assurance of Performance

(1) A contract for sale imposes an obligation on each party that the other's expectation of receiving due performance will not be impaired. When reasonable grounds for insecurity arise with respect to the performance of either party the other may in writing demand adequate assurance of due performance and until he receives such assurance may if commercially reasonable suspend any performance for which he has not already received the agreed return.

(2) Between merchants the reasonableness of grounds for insecurity and the adequacy of any assurance offered shall be determined according to commercial standards.

(3) Acceptance of any improper delivery or payment does not prejudice the aggrieved party's right to demand adequate assurance of future performance.

(4) After receipt of a justified demand failure to provide within a reasonable time not exceeding thirty days such assurance of due performance as is adequate under the circumstances of the particular case is a repudiation of the contract.

§ 2-610 Anticipatory Repudiation

When either party repudiates the contract with respect to a performance not yet due the loss of which will substantially impair the value of the contract to the other, the aggrieved party may

(a) for a commercially reasonable time await performance by the repudiating party; or

(b) resort to any remedy for breach (Section 2-703 or Section 2-711), even though he has notified the repudiating party that he would await the latter's performance and has urged retraction; and

(c) in either case suspend his own performance or proceed in accordance with the provisions of this Article on the seller's right to identify goods to the contract notwithstanding breach or to salvage unfinished goods (Section 2-704).

§ 2-611 Retraction of Anticipatory Repudiation

(1) Until the repudiating party's next performance is due he can retract his repudiation unless the aggrieved party has since the repudiation cancelled or materially changed his position or otherwise indicated that he considers the repudiation final.

(2) Retraction may be by any method which clearly indicates to the aggrieved party that the repudiating party intends to perform, but must include any assurance justifiably demanded under the provisions of this Article (Section 2-609).

(3) Retraction reinstates the repudiating party's rights under the contract with due excuse and allowance to the aggrieved party for any delay occasioned by the repudiation.

§ 2-612 "Installment contract"; Breach

(1) An "installment contract" is one which requires or authorizes the delivery of goods in separate lots to be separately accepted, even though the contractcontains a clause "each delivery is a separate contract" or its equivalent.

(2) The buyer may reject any installment which is non-conforming if the non-conformity substantially impairs the value of that installment and cannot be cured or if the non-conformity is a defect in the required documents; but if the non-conformity does not fall within subsection (3) and the seller gives adequate assurance of its cure the buyer must accept that installment.

(3) Whenever non-conformity or default with respect to one or more installments substantially impairs the value of the whole contract there is a breach of the whole. But the aggrieved party reinstates the contract if he accepts a non-conforming installment without seasonably notifying of cancellation or if he brings an action with respect only to past installments or demands performance as to future installments.

§ 2-613 Casualty to Identified Goods

Where the contract requires for its performance goods identified when the contract is made, and the goods suffer casualty without fault of either party before the risk of loss passes to the buyer, or in a proper case under a "no arrival, no sale" term (Section 2-324) then

(a) if the loss is total the contract is avoided; and

(b) if the loss is partial or the goods have so deteriorated as no longer to conform to the contract the buyer may nevertheless demand inspection and at his option either treat the contract as avoided or accept the goods with due allowance from the contract price for the deterioration or the deficiency in quantity but without further right against the seller.

§ 2-614 Substituted Performance

(1) Where without fault of either party the agreed berthing, loading, or unloading facilities fail or an agreed type of carrier becomes unavailable or the agreed manner of delivery otherwise becomes commercially impracticable but a commercially reasonable substitute is available, such substitute performance must be tendered and accepted.

(2) If the agreed means or manner of payment fails because of domestic or foreign governmental regulation, the seller may withhold or stop delivery unless the buyer provides a means or manner of payment which is commercially a substantial equivalent. If delivery has already been taken, payment by the means or in the manner provided by the regulation discharges the buyer's obligation unless the regulation is discriminatory, oppressive or predatory.

§ 2-615 Excuse by Failure of Presupposed Conditions

Except so far as a seller may have assumed a greater obligation and subject to the preceding section on substituted performance:

(a) Delay in delivery or non-delivery in whole or in part by a seller that complies with paragraphs (b) and (c) is not a breach of his duty under a contract for sale if performance as agreed has been made impracticable by the occurrence of a contingency the non-occurrence of which was a basic assumption on which the contract was made or by compliance in good faith with any applicable foreign or domestic governmental regulation or order whether or not it later proves to be invalid.

(b) Where the causes mentioned in paragraph (a) affect only a part of the seller's capacity to perform, he must allocate production and deliveries among his customers but may at his option include regular customers not then under contract as well as his own requirements for further manufacture. He may so allocate in any manner which is fair and reasonable.

(c) The seller must notify the buyer seasonably that there will be delay or non-delivery and, when allocation is required under paragraph (b), of the estimated quota thus made available for the buyer.

§ 2-702 Seller's Remedies on Discovery of Buyer's Insolvency

(1) Where the seller discovers the buyer to be insolvent he may refuse delivery except for cash including payment for all goods theretofore delivered under the contract, and stop delivery under this Article (Section 2-705).

(2) Where the seller discovers that the buyer has received goods on credit while insolvent he may reclaim the goods upon demand made within ten days after the receipt, but if misrepresentation of solvency has been made to the particular seller in writing within three months before delivery the ten day limitation does not apply. Except as provided in this subsection the seller may not base a right to reclaim goods on the buyer's fraudulent or innocent misrepresentation of solvency or of intent to pay.

(3) The seller's right to reclaim under subsection (2) is subject to the rights of a buyer in ordinary course or other good faith purchaser under this Article (Section 2-403). Successful reclamation of goods excludes all other remedies with respect to them.

§ 2-704 Seller's Right to Identify Goods to the Contract Notwithstanding Breach or to Salvage Unfinished Goods

(1) An aggrieved seller under the preceding section may

(a) identify to the contract conforming goods not already identified if at the time he learned of the breach they are in his possession or control;

(b) treat as the subject of resale goods which have demonstrably been intended for the particular contract even though those goods are unfinished.

(2) Where the goods are unfinished an aggrieved seller may in the exercise of reasonable commercial judgment for the purposes of avoiding loss and of effective realization either complete the manufacture and wholly identify the goods to the contract or cease manufacture and resell for scrap or salvage value or proceed in any other reasonable manner.

§ 2-706 Seller's Resale Including Contract for Resale

(1) Under the conditions stated in Section 2-703 on seller's remedies, the seller may resell the goods concerned or the undelivered balance thereof. Where the resale is made in good faith and in a commercially reasonable manner the seller may recover the difference between the resale price and the contract price together with any incidental damages allowed under the provisions of this Article (Section 2-710), but less expenses saved in consequence of the buyer's breach.

(2) Except as otherwise provided in subsection (3) or unless otherwise agreed resale may be at public or private sale including sale by way of one or more contracts to sell or of identification to an existing contract of the seller.

Sale may be as a unit or in parcels and at any time and place and on any terms but every aspect of the sale including the method, manner, time, place and terms must be commercially reasonable. The resale must be reasonably identified as referring to the broken contract, but it is not necessary that the goods be in existence or that any or all of them have been identified to the contract before the breach.

(3) Where the resale is at private sale the seller must give the buyer reasonable notification of his intention to resell.

(4) Where the resale is at public sale

(a) only identified goods can be sold except where there is a recognized market for a public sale of futures in goods of the kind; and

(b) it must be made at a usual place or market for public sale if one is reasonably available and except in the case of goods which are perishable or threaten to decline in value speedily the seller must give the buyer reasonable notice of the time and place of the resale; and

(c) if the goods are not to be within the view of those attending the sale the notification of sale must state the place where the goods are located and provide for their reasonable inspection by prospective bidders; and

(d) the seller may buy.

(5) A purchaser who buys in good faith at a resale takes the goods free of any rights of the original buyer even though the seller fails to comply with one or more of the requirements of this section.

(6) The seller is not accountable to the buyer for any profit made on any resale. A person in the position of a seller (Section 2-707) or a buyer who has rightfully rejected or justifiably revoked acceptance must account for any excess over the amount of his security interest, as hereinafter defined (subsection (3) of Section 2-711).

§ 2-708 Seller's Damages for Non-acceptance or Repudiation

(1) Subject to subsection (2) and to the provisions of this Article with respect to proof of market price (Section 2-723), the measure of damages for nonacceptance or repudiation by the buyer is the difference between the market price at the time and place for tender and the unpaid contract price together with any incidental damages provided in this Article (Section 2-710) but less expenses saved in consequence of the buyer's breach.

(2) If the measure of damages provided in subsection (1) is inadequate to put the seller in as good a position as performance would have done then the measure of damages is the profit (including reasonable overhead) which the seller would have made from full performance by the buyer, together with any incidental damages provided in this Article (Section 2-710), less due allowance for costs reasonably incurred and due credit for payments or proceeds of resale.

§ 2-709 Action for the Price

(1) When the buyer fails to pay the price as it becomes due the seller may recover, together with any incidental damages under the next section, the price

(a) of goods accepted or of conforming goods lost or damaged within a commercially reasonable time after risk of their loss has passed to the buyer; and

(b) of goods identified to the contract if the seller is unable after reasonable effort to resell them at a reasonable price or the circumstances reasonably indicate that such effort will be unavailing.

(2) Where the seller sues for the price he must hold for the buyer any goods which have been identified to the contract and are still in his control except that if resale becomes possible he may resell them at any time prior to the collection of the judgment. The net proceeds of any such resale must be credited to the buyer and payment of the judgment entitles him to any goods not resold.

(3) After the buyer has wrongfully rejected or revoked acceptance of the goods or has failed to make a payment due or has repudiated (Section 2-610), a seller who is held not entitled to the price under this section shall nevertheless be awarded damages for non-acceptance under the preceding section.

§ 2-710. Seller's Incidental Damages

Incidental damages to an aggrieved seller include any commercially reasonable charges, expenses or commissions incurred in stopping delivery, in the transportation, care and custody of goods after the buyer's breach, in connection with return or resale of the goods or otherwise resulting from the breach.

§ 2-711 Buyer's Remedies in General; Buyer's Security Interest in Rejected Goods

(1) Where the seller fails to make delivery or repudiates or the buyer rightfully rejects or justifiably revokes acceptance then with respect to any goods involved, and with respect to the whole if the breach goes to the whole contract (Section 2-612), the buyer may cancel and whether or not he has done so may in addition to recovering so much of the price as has been paid

(a) "cover" and have damages under the next section as to all the goods affected whether or not they have been identified to the contract; or

(b) recover damages for non-delivery as provided in this Article (Section 2-713).

(2) Where the seller fails to deliver or repudiates the buyer may also

(a) if the goods have been identified recover them as provided in this Article (Section 2-502); or

(b) in a proper case obtain specific performance or replevy the goods as provided in this Article (Section 2-716).

(3) On rightful rejection or justifiable revocation of acceptance a buyer has a security interest in goods in his possession or control for any payments made on their price and any expenses reasonably incurred in their inspection, receipt, transportation, care and custody and may hold such goods and resell them in like manner as an aggrieved seller (Section 2-706).

2706 - sell resale v. contract price

§ 2-712 "Cover"; Buyer's Procurement of Substitute Goods

(1) After a breach within the preceding section the buyer may "cover" by making in good faith and without unreasonable delay any reasonable purchase of or contract to purchase goods in substitution for those due from the seller.

(2) The buyer may recover from the seller as damages the difference between the cost of cover and the contract price together with any incidental or consequential damages as hereinafter defined (Section 2-715), but less expenses saved in consequence of the seller's breach.

(3) Failure of the buyer to effect cover within this section does not bar him from any other remedy.

2-708/

§ 2-713 Buyer's Damages for Non-delivery or Repudiation

(1) Subject to the provisions of this Article with respect to proof of market price (Section 2-723), the measure of damages for non-delivery or repudiation by the seller is the difference between the market price at the time when the buyer learned of the breach and the contract price together with any incidental and consequential damages provided in this Article (Section 2-715), but less expenses saved in consequence of the seller's breach.

(2) Market price is to be determined as of the place for tender or, in cases of rejection after arrival or revocation of acceptance, as of the place of arrival.

§ 2-715 Buyer's Incidental and Consequential Damages

(1) Incidental damages resulting from the seller's breach include expenses reasonably incurred in inspection, receipt, transportation and care and custody of goods rightfully rejected, any commercially reasonable charges, expenses or commissions in connection with effecting cover and any other reasonable expense incident to the delay or other breach.

(2) Consequential damages resulting from the seller's breach include

(a) any loss resulting from general or particular requirements and needs of which the seller at the time of contracting had reason to know and which could not reasonably be prevented by cover or otherwise; and

(b) injury to person or property proximately resulting from any breach of warranty.

§ 2-716 Buyer's Right to Specific Performance or Replevin

(1) Specific performance may be decreed where the goods are unique or in other proper circumstances.

(2) The decree for specific performance may include such terms and conditions as to payment of the price, damages, or other relief as the court may deem just.

(3) The buyer has a right of replevin for goods identified to the contract if after reasonable effort he is unable to effect cover for such goods or the circumstances reasonably indicate that such effort will be unavailing or if the goods

have been shipped under reservation and satisfaction of the security interest in them has been made or tendered.

§ 2-717 Deduction of Damages From the Price

The buyer on notifying the seller of his intention to do so may deduct all or any part of the damages resulting from any breach of the contract from any part of the price still due under the same contract.

§ 2-718 Liquidation or Limitation of Damages; Deposits

(1) Damages for breach by either party may be liquidated in the agreement but only at an amount which is reasonable in the light of the anticipated or actual harm caused by the breach, the difficulties of proof of loss and the inconvenience or nonfeasibility of otherwise obtaining an adequate remedy. A term fixing unreasonably large liquidated damages is void as a penalty.

(2) Where the seller justifiably withholds delivery of goods because of the buyer's breach, the buyer is entitled to restitution of any amount by which the sum of his payments exceeds:

(a) the amount to which the seller is entitled by virtue of terms liquidating the seller's damages in accordance with subsection (1); or

(b) in the absence of such terms, twenty percent of the value of the total performance for which the buyer is obligated under the contract or $500, whichever is smaller.

(3) The buyer's right to restitution under subsection (2) is subject to offset to the extent that the seller establishes:

(a) a right to recover damages under the provisions of this Article other than subsection (1); and

(b) the amount or value of any benefits received by the buyer directly or indirectly by reason of the contract.

(4) Where a seller has received payment in goods, their reasonable value or the proceeds of their resale shall be treated as payments for the purposes of subsection (2); but if the seller has notice of the buyer's breach before reselling goods received in part performance, his resale is subject to the conditions laid down in this Article on resale by an aggrieved seller (Section 2-706).

§ 2-719 Contractual Modification or Limitation of Remedy

(1) Subject to the provisions of subsections (2) and (3) of this section and of the preceding section on liquidation and limitation of damages,

(a) the agreement may provide for remedies in addition to or in substitution for those provided in this Article and may limit or alter the measure of damages recoverable under this Article, as by limiting the buyer's remedies to return of the goods and repayment of the price or to repair and replacement of non-conforming goods or parts; and

(b) resort to a remedy as provided is optional unless the remedy is expressly agreed to be exclusive, in which case it is the sole remedy.

(2) Where circumstances cause an exclusive or limited remedy to fail of its essential purpose, remedy may be had as provided in this Act.

(3) Consequential damages may be limited or excluded unless the limitation or exclusion is unconscionable. Limitation of consequential damages for injury to the person in the case of consumer goods is prima facie unconscionable but limitation of damages where the loss is commercial is not.

APPENDIX C

UNITED NATIONS CONVENTION ON CONTRACTS FOR THE INTERNATIONAL SALE OF GOODS ("CISG")

Article 1

(1) This Convention applies to contracts of sale of goods between parties whose places of business are in different States:

(a) when the States are Contracting States; or

(b) when the rules of private international law lead to the application of the law of a Contracting State.

(2) The fact that the parties have their places of business in different States is to be disregarded whenever this fact does not appear either from the contract or from any dealings between, or from information disclosed by, the parties at any time before or at the conclusion of the contract.

(3) Neither the nationality of the parties nor the civil or commercial character of the parties or of the contract is to be taken into consideration in determining the application of this Convention.

Article 7

(1) In the interpretation of this Convention, regard is to be had to its international character and to the need to promote uniformity in its application and the observance of good faith in international trade.

(2) Questions concerning matters governed by this Convention which are not expressly settled in it are to be settled in conformity with the general principles on which it is based or, in the absence of such principles, in conformity with the law applicable by virtue of the rules of private international law.

Article 8

(1) For the purposes of this Convention statements made by and other conduct of a party are to be interpreted according to his intent where the other party knew or could not have been unaware what that intent was.

(2) If the preceding paragraph is not applicable, statements made by and other conduct of a party are to be interpreted according to the understanding that a reasonable person of the same kind as the other party would have had in the same circumstances.

(3) In determining the intent of a party or the understanding a reasonable person would have had, due consideration is to be given to all relevant circumstances of the case including the negotiations, any practices which the parties have established between themselves, usages and any subsequent conduct of the parties.

Secretariat Commentary

1. Article [8] on interpretation furnishes the rules to be followed in interpreting the meaning of any statement or other conduct of a party which falls within the scope of application of this Convention. Interpretation of the statements or conduct of a party may be necessary to determine whether a contract has been concluded, the meaning of the contract, or the significance of a notice given or other act of a party in the performance of the contract or in respect of its termination.

2. Article [8] states the rules to be applied in terms of interpreting the unilateral acts of each party, i.e., communications in respect of the proposed contract, the offer, the acceptance, notices, etc. Nevertheless article [8] is equally applicable to the interpretation of "the contract" when the contract is embodied in a single document. Analytically, this Convention treats such an integrated contract as the manifestation of an offer and an acceptance. Therefore, for the purpose of determining whether a contract has been concluded as well as for the purpose of interpreting the contract, the contract is considered to be the product of two unilateral acts.

3. Since article [8] states rules for interpreting the unilateral acts of each party, it does not rely upon the common intent of the parties as a means of interpreting those unilateral acts. However, article [8(1)] recognizes that the other party often knows or could not be unaware of the intent of the party who made the statement or engaged in the conduct in question. Where this is the case, that intent is to be ascribed to the statement or conduct.

4. Article [8] cannot be applied if the party who made the statement or engaged in the conduct had no intention on the point in question or if the other party did not know and had no reason to know what that intent was. In such a case, article [8(2)] provides that the statements made by and conduct of a party are to be interpreted according to the understanding that a reasonable person *[of the same kind as the other party]* would have had in the same circumstances.

[The italicized phrase *"a reasonable person of the same kind as the other party"* . . . is said to refer to "a person from the same background as the person concerned and engaged in the same occupation, the same trade activities for example". *Kopac states:* "[T]he words 'a reasonable person of the same kind' were intended to refer to the party to whom the statement was addressed and not to the party making the statement or performing the conduct. . . ." *Honnold states:* "A person with technical skill and knowledge [is] required to make his statement in such a way as to make his meaning clear to a person not possessed of such skill and knowledge". . . .]

5. In determining the intent of a party or the intent a reasonable person *[of the same kind as the other party]* would have had in the same circumstances, it is necessary to look first to the words actually used or the conduct engaged in. However, the investigation is not to be limited to those words or conduct even if they appear to give a clear answer to the question. It is common experience that a person may dissimulate or make an error and the process of interpretation set forth in this article is to be used to determine the true content of the communication. If, for example, a party offers to sell a quantity of goods for Swiss francs 50,000 and it is obvious that the offeror intended Swiss francs 500,000 and the offeree knew or could not have been unaware of it, the price term in the offer is to be interpreted as Swiss francs 500,000.

[Suppose the intent is not readily recognizable? *Farnsworth states:* "If a seller mistakenly offers to sell goods for `68,000 francs' when he intended to offer to sell them for 86,000 francs, a reasonable person of the same kind and in the same circumstances of the buyer might not realize that the seller has made a mistake in expression. If the buyer accepts, the rule of Article 19(2) would result in a contract at 68,000 francs as a matter of interpretation." . . .]

6. In order to go beyond the apparent meaning of the words or the conduct by the parties, article [8(3)] states that "due consideration is to be given to all relevant circumstances of the case." It then goes on to enumerate some, but not necessarily all circumstances of the case which are to be taken into account. These include the negotiations, any practices which the parties have established between themselves, usages and any subsequent conduct of the parties.

Article 9

(1) The parties are bound by any usage to which they have agreed and by any practices which they have established between themselves.

(2) The parties are considered, unless otherwise agreed, to have impliedly made applicable to their contract or its formation a usage of which the parties knew or ought to have known and which in international trade is widely known to, and regularly observed by, parties to contracts of the type involved in the particular trade concerned.

Article 11

A contract of sale need not be concluded in or evidenced by writing and is not subject to any other requirement as to form. It may be proved by any means, including witnesses.

Article 14

(1) A proposal for concluding a contract addressed to one or more specific persons constitutes an offer if it is sufficiently definite and indicates the intention of the offeror to be bound in case of acceptance. A proposal is sufficiently definite if it indicates the goods and expressly or implicitly fixes or makes provision for determining the quantity and the price.

(2) A proposal other than one addressed to one or more specific persons is to be considered merely as an invitation to make offers, unless the contrary is clearly indicated by the person making the proposal.

Article 15

(1) An offer becomes effective when it reaches the offeree.

(2) An offer, even if it is irrevocable, may be withdrawn if the withdrawal reaches the offeree before or at the same time as the offer.

Article 16

(1) Until a contract is concluded an offer may be revoked if the revocation reaches the offeree before he has dispatched an acceptance.

(2) However, an offer cannot be revoked:

(a) if it indicates, whether by stating a fixed time for acceptance or otherwise, that it is irrevocable; or

(b) if it was reasonable for the offeree to rely on the offer as being irrevocable and the offeree has acted in reliance on the offer.

Article 17

An offer, even if it is irrevocable, is terminated when a rejection reaches the offeror.

Article 18

(1) A statement made by or other conduct of the offeree indicating assent to an offer is an acceptance. Silence or inactivity does not in itself amount to acceptance.

(2) An acceptance of an offer becomes effective at the moment the indication of assent reaches the offeror. An acceptance is not effective if the indication of assent does not reach the offeror within the time he has fixed or, if no time is fixed, within a reasonable time, due account being taken of the circumstances of the transaction, including the rapidity of the means of communication employed by the offeror. An oral offer must be accepted immediately unless the circumstances indicate otherwise.

(3) However, if, by virtue of the offer or as a result of practices which the parties have established between themselves or of usage, the offeree may indicate assent by performing an act, such as one relating to the dispatch of the goods or payment of the price, without notice to the offeror, the acceptance is effective at the moment the act is performed, provided that the act is performed within the period of time laid down in the preceding paragraph.

Article 19

(1) A reply to an offer which purports to be an acceptance but contains additions, limitations or other modifications is a rejection of the offer and constitutes a counter-offer.

(2) However, a reply to an offer which purports to be an acceptance but contains additional or different terms which do not materially alter the terms of the offer constitutes an acceptance, unless the offeror, without undue delay, objects orally to the discrepancy or dispatches a notice to that effect. If he does not so object, the terms of the contract are the terms of the offer with the modifications contained in the acceptance.

(3) Additional or different terms relating, among other things, to the price, payment, quality and quantity of the goods, place and time of delivery, extent of one party's liability to the other or the settlement of disputes are considered to alter the terms of the offer materially.

Article 22

An acceptance may be withdrawn if the withdrawal reaches the offeror before or at the same time as the acceptance would have become effective.

Article 23

A contract is concluded at the moment when an acceptance of an offer becomes effective in accordance with the provisions of this Convention.

Article 24

For the purposes of this Part of the Convention, an offer, declaration of acceptance or any other indication of intention "reaches" the addressee when it is made orally to him or delivered by any other means to him personally, to his place of business or mailing address or, if he does not have a place of business or mailing address, to his habitual residence.

Article 25

A breach of contract committed by one of the parties is fundamental if it results in such detriment to the other party as substantially to deprive him of what he is entitled to expect under the contract, unless the party in breach did not foresee and a reasonable person of the same kind in the same circumstances would not have foreseen such a result.

Article 29

(1) A contract may be modified or terminated by the mere agreement of the parties. . . .

Secretariat Commentary

1. This article governs the modification and abrogation *[termination by agreement]* of a contract.

General rule, paragraph (1)

2. Paragraph (1), which states the general rule that a contract may be modified or abrogated *[terminated]* merely by agreement of the parties, is intended to eliminate an important difference between the civil law and the common law in respect of the modification of existing contracts. In the civil law an agreement between the parties to modify the contract is effective if there is sufficient cause even if the modification relates to the obligations of only one of the parties. In the common law a modification of the obligations of only one of the parties is in principle not effective because "consideration" is lacking.

3. Many of the modifications envisaged by this provision are technical modifications in specifications, delivery dates, or the like which frequently arise in the course of performance of commercial contracts. Even if such modifications of the contract may increase the costs of one party, or decrease the value of the contract to the other, the parties may agree that there will be no change in the price. Such agreements according to [CISG article 29(1)] are effective, thereby overcoming the common law rule that "consideration" is required. . . .

5. A proposal to modify the terms of an existing contract by including additional or different terms in a confirmation or invoice should be distinguished from a reply to an offer which purports to be an acceptance but which contains additional or different terms. This latter situation is governed by [CISG article 19].

Article 49

(1) The buyer may declare the contract avoided:

(a) if the failure by the seller to perform any of his obligations under the contract or this Convention amounts to a fundamental breach of contract; or

(b) in case of non-delivery, if the seller does not deliver the goods within the additional period of time fixed by the buyer in accordance with paragraph (1) of article 47 or declares that he will not deliver within the period so fixed.

(2) However, in cases where the seller has delivered the goods, the buyer loses the right to declare the contract avoided unless he does so:

(a) in respect of late delivery, within a reasonable time after he has become aware that delivery has been made;

(b) in respect of any breach other than late delivery, within a reasonable time:

(i) after he knew or ought to have known of the breach;

(ii) after the expiration of any additional period of time fixed by the buyer in accordance with paragraph (1) of article 47, or after the seller has declared that he will not perform his obligations within such an additional period; or

(iii) after the expiration of any additional period of time indicated by the seller in accordance with paragraph (2) of article 48, or after the buyer has declared that he will not accept performance.

Article 50

If the goods do not conform with the contract and whether or not the price has already been paid, the buyer may reduce the price in the same proportion as the value that the goods actually delivered had at the time of the delivery bears to the value that conforming goods would have had at that time. However, if the seller remedies any failure to perform his obligations in accordance with article 37 or article 48 or if the buyer refuses to accept performance by the seller in accordance with those articles, the buyer may not reduce the price.

Article 66

Loss of or damage to the goods after the risk has passed to the buyer does not discharge him from his obligation to pay the price, unless the loss or damage is due to an act or omission of the seller.

Article 67

(1) If the contract of sale involves carriage of the goods and the seller is not bound to hand them over at a particular place, the risk passes to the buyer when the goods are handed over to the first carrier for transmission to the buyer in accordance with the contract of sale. If the seller is bound to hand the goods over to a carrier at a particular place, the risk does not pass to the buyer until the goods are handed over to the carrier at that place. The fact that the seller is authorized to retain documents controlling the disposition of the goods does not affect the passage of the risk.

(2) Nevertheless, the risk does not pass to the buyer until the goods are clearly identified to the contract, whether by markings on the goods, by shipping documents, by notice given to the buyer or otherwise.

Article 68

The risk in respect of goods sold in transit passes to the buyer from the time of the conclusion of the contract. However, if the circumstances so indicate, the risk is assumed by the buyer from the time the goods were handed over to the carrier who issued the documents embodying the contract of carriage. Nevertheless, if at the time of the conclusion of the contract of sale the seller knew or ought to have known that the goods had been lost or damaged and did not disclose this to the buyer, the loss or damage is at the risk of the seller.

Article 69

(1) In cases not within articles 67 and 68, the risk passes to the buyer when he takes over the goods or, if he does not do so in due time, from the time when the goods are placed at his disposal and he commits a breach of contract by failing to take delivery.

(2) However, if the buyer is bound to take over the goods at a place other than a place of business of the seller, the risk passes when delivery is due and the buyer is aware of the fact that the goods are placed at his disposal at that place.

(3) If the contract relates to goods not then identified, the goods are considered not to be placed at the disposal of the buyer until they are clearly identified to the contract.

Article 71

(1) A party may suspend the performance of his obligations if, after the conclusion of the contract, it becomes apparent that the other party will not perform a substantial part of his obligations as a result of:

(a) a serious deficiency in his ability to perform or in his creditworthiness; or

(b) his conduct in preparing to perform or in performing the contract.

(2) If the seller has already dispatched the goods before the grounds described in the preceding paragraph become evident, he may prevent the handing over of the goods to the buyer even though the buyer holds a document which entitles him to obtain them. The present paragraph relates only to the rights in the goods as between the buyer and the seller.

(3) A party suspending performance, whether before or after dispatch of the goods, must immediately give notice of the suspension to the other party and must continue with performance if the other party provides adequate assurance of his performance.

Article 72

(1) If prior to the date for performance of the contract it is clear that one of the parties will commit a fundamental breach of contract, the other party may declare the contract avoided.

(2) If time allows, the party intending to declare the contract avoided must give reasonable notice to the other party in order to permit him to provide adequate assurance of his performance.

(3) The requirements of the preceding paragraph do not apply if the other party has declared that he will not perform his obligations.

Article 73

(1) In the case of a contract for delivery of goods by instalments, if the failure of one party to perform any of his obligations in respect of any instalment constitutes a fundamental breach of contract with respect to that instalment, the other party may declare the contract avoided with respect to that instalment.

(2) If one party's failure to perform any of his obligations in respect of any instalment gives the other party good grounds to conclude that a fundamental breach of contract will occur with respect to future instalments, he may declare the contract avoided for the future, provided that he does so within a reasonable time.

(3) A buyer who declares the contract avoided in respect of any delivery may, at the same time, declare it avoided in respect of deliveries already made or of future deliveries if, by reason of their interdependence, those deliveries could not be used for the purpose contemplated by the parties at the time of the conclusion of the contract.

Article 74

Damages for breach of contract by one party consist of a sum equal to the loss, including loss of profit, suffered by the other party as a consequence of the breach. Such damages may not exceed the loss which the party in breach foresaw or ought to have foreseen at the time of the conclusion of the contract, in the light of the facts and matters of which he then knew or ought to have known, as a possible consequence of the breach of contract.

Article 75

If the contract is avoided and if, in a reasonable manner and within a reasonable time after avoidance, the buyer has bought goods in replacement or the seller has resold the goods, the party claiming damages may recover the difference between the contract price and the price in the substitute transaction as well as any further damages recoverable under article 74.

Article 76

(1) If the contract is avoided and there is a current price for the goods, the party claiming damages may, if he has not made a purchase or resale under article 75, recover the difference between the price fixed by the contract and the current price at the time of avoidance as well as any further damages recoverable under article 74. If, however, the party claiming damages has avoided the contract after taking over the goods, the current price at the time of such taking over shall be applied instead of the current price at the time of avoidance.

(2) For the purposes of the preceding paragraph, the current price is the price prevailing at the place where delivery of the goods should have been made or, if there is no current price at that place, the price at such other place as serves as a reasonable substitute, making due allowance for differences in the cost of transporting the goods.

Article 77

A party who relies on a breach of contract must take such measures as are reasonable in the circumstances to mitigate the loss, including loss of profit, resulting from the breach. If he fails to take such measures, the party in breach may claim a reduction in the damages in the amount by which the loss should have been mitigated.

Article 79

(1) A party is not liable for a failure to perform any of his obligations if he proves that the failure was due to an impediment beyond his control and that

he could not reasonably be expected to have taken the impediment into account at the time of the conclusion of the contract or to have avoided or overcome it or its consequences.

(2) If the party's failure is due to the failure by a third person whom he has engaged to perform the whole or a part of the contract, that party is exempt from liability only if:

(a) he is exempt under the preceding paragraph; and

(b) the person whom he has so engaged would be so exempt if the provisions of that paragraph were applied to him.

(3) The exemption provided by this article has effect for the period during which the impediment exists.

(4) The party who fails to perform must give notice to the other party of the impediment and its effect on his ability to perform. If the notice is not received by the other party within a reasonable time after the party who fails to perform knew or ought to have known of the impediment, he is liable for damages resulting from such non-receipt.

(5) Nothing in this article prevents either party from exercising any right other than to claim damages under this Convention.

Article 81

(1) Avoidance of the contract releases both parties from their obligations under it, subject to any damages which may be due. Avoidance does not affect any provision of the contract for the settlement of disputes or any other provision of the contract governing the rights and obligations of the parties consequent upon the avoidance of the contract.

(2) A party who has performed the contract either wholly or in part may claim restitution from the other party of whatever the first party has supplied or paid under the contract. If both parties are bound to make restitution, they must do so concurrently.

APPENDIX D

UNIDROIT PRINCIPLES OF INTERNATIONAL COMMERCIAL CONTRACTS ("UNIDROIT PRINCIPLES 2010")

Article 1.2 No form required

Nothing in these Principles requires a contract, statement or any other act to be made in or evidenced by a particular form. It may be proved by any means, including witnesses.

Article 1.7 Good faith and fair dealing

(1) Each party must act in accordance with good faith and fair dealing in international trade.

(2) The parties may not exclude or limit this duty.

Article 1.9 Usages and practices

(1) The parties are bound by any usage to which they have agreed and by any practices which they have established between themselves.

(2) The parties are bound by a usage that is widely known to and regularly observed in international trade by parties in the particular trade concerned except where the application of such a usage would be unreasonable.

Article 2.1.1 Manner of formation

A contract may be concluded either by the acceptance of an offer or by conduct of the parties that is sufficient to show agreement.

Article 2.1.2 Definition of offer

A proposal for concluding a contract constitutes an offer if it is sufficiently definite and indicates the intention of the offeror to be bound in case of acceptance.

Article 2.1.3 Withdrawal of offer

(1) An offer becomes effective when it reaches the offeree.

(2) An offer, even if it is irrevocable, may be withdrawn if the withdrawal reaches the offeree before or at the same time as the offer.

Article 2.1.4 Revocation of offer

(1) Until a contract is concluded an offer may be revoked if the revocation reaches the offeree before it has dispatched an acceptance.

(2) However, an offer cannot be revoked

(a) if it indicates, whether by stating a fixed time for acceptance or otherwise, that it is irrevocable; or

(b) if it was reasonable for the offeree to rely on the offer as being irrevocable and the offeree has acted in reliance on the offer.

Article 2.1.5 Revocation of offer

An offer is terminated when a rejection reaches the offeror.

Article 2.1.6 Mode of acceptance

(1) A statement made by or other conduct of the offeree indicating assent to an offer is an acceptance. Silence or inactivity does not in itself amount to acceptance.

(2) An acceptance of an offer becomes effective when the indication of assent reaches the offeror.

(3) However, if, by virtue of the offer or as a result of practices which the parties have established between themselves or of usage, the offeree may indicate assent by performing an act without notice to the offeror, the acceptance is effective when the act is performed.

Article 2.1.7 Time of acceptance

An offer must be accepted within the time the offeror has fixed or, if no time is fixed, within a reasonable time having regard to the circumstances, including the rapidity of the means of communication employed by the offeror. An oral offer must be accepted immediately unless the circumstances indicate otherwise.

Article 2.1.10 Withdrawal of acceptance

An acceptance may be withdrawn if the withdrawal reaches the offeror before or at the same time as the acceptance would have become effective.

Article 2.1.11 Modified acceptance

(1) A reply to an offer which purports to be an acceptance but contains additions, limitations or other modifications is a rejection of the offer and constitutes a counter-offer.

(2) However, a reply to an offer which purports to be an acceptance but contains additional or different terms which do not materially alter the terms of the offer constitutes an acceptance, unless the offeror, without undue delay, objects to the discrepancy. If the offeror does not object, the terms of the contract are the terms of the offer with the modifications contained in the acceptance.

Article 2.1.12 Writings in confirmation

If a writing which is sent within a reasonable time after the conclusion of the contract and which purports to be a confirmation of the contract contains additional or different terms, such terms become part of the contract, unless they materially alter the contract or the recipient, without undue delay, objects to the discrepancy.

Article 2.1.17 Merger clauses

A contract in writing which contains a clause indicating that the writing completely embodies the terms on which the parties have agreed cannot be contradicted or supplemented by evidence of prior statements or agreements. However, such statements or agreements may be used to interpret the writing.

Article 2.1.19 Contracting under standard terms

(1) Where one party or both parties use standard terms in concluding a contract, the general rules on formation apply, subject to Articles 2.1.20-2.1.22.

(2) Standard terms are provisions which are prepared in advance for general and repeated use by one party and which are actually used without negotiation with the other party.

Article 2.1.20 Surprising terms

(1) No term contained in standard terms which is of such a character that the other party could not reasonably have expected it, is effective unless it has been expressly accepted by that party.

(2) In determining whether a term is of such a character regard shall be had to its content, language and presentation.

Article 2.1.21 Conflict between standard terms and non-standard terms

In case of conflict between a standard term and a term which is not a standard term the latter prevails.

Article 2.1.22 Battle of forms

Where both parties use standard terms and reach agreement except on those terms, a contract is concluded on the basis of the agreed terms and of any standard terms which are common in substance unless one party clearly indicates in advance, or later and without undue delay informs the other party, that it does not intend to be bound by such a contract.

Article 3.1.2 Validity of mere agreement

A contract is concluded, modified or terminated by the mere agreement of the parties, without any further requirement.

Article 3.2.1 Definition of mistake

Mistake is an erroneous assumption relating to facts or to law existing when the contract was concluded.

Article 3.2.2 Relevant mistake

(1) A party may only avoid the contract for mistake if, when the contract was concluded, the mistake was of such importance that a reasonable person in the same situation as the party would not have concluded it at all if the true state of affairs had been known, and

(a) the other party made the same mistake, or caused the mistake, or knew or ought to have known of the mistake and it was contrary to reasonable commercial standards of fair dealing to leave the mistaken party in error; or

(b) the other party had not at the time of avoidance acted in reliance on the contract

(2) However, a party may not avoid the contract if

(a) it was grossly negligent in committing the mistake; or

(b) the mistake relates to a matter in regard to which the risk of mistake was assumed or, having regard to the circumstances, should be borne by the mistaken party.

Article 3.2.5 Fraud

A party may avoid the contract when it has been led to conclude the contract by the other party's fraudulent representation, including language or practices, or fraudulent non-disclosure of circumstances which, according to reasonable commercial standards of fair dealing, the latter party should have disclosed.

Article 3.2.6 Threat

A party may avoid the contract when it has been led to conclude the contract by the other party's unjustified threat which, having regard to the circumstances, is so imminent and serious as to leave the first party no reasonable alternative. In particular, a threat is unjustified if the act or omission with which a party has been threatened is wrongful in itself, or it is wrongful to use it as a means to obtain the conclusion of the contract.

Article 3.2.7 Gross disparity

(1) A party may avoid the contract or an individual term of it if, at the time of the conclusion of the contract, the contract term unjustifiably gave the other party an excessive advantage. Regard is to be had, among other factors, to

(a) the fact that the other party has taken unfair advantage of the first party's dependence, economic distress or urgent needs, or of its improvidence, ignorance, inexperience or lack of bargaining skill; and

(b) the nature and purpose of the contract.

(2) Upon the request of the party entitled to avoidance, a court may adapt the contract or term in order to make it accord with reasonable commercial standards of fair dealing.

(3) A court may also adapt the contract or term upon the request of the party receiving notice of avoidance, provided that that party informs the other party of its request promptly after receiving such notice and before the other party has acted in reliance on it. The provisions of Article 3.2.10 (2) apply accordingly.

Article 4.1 Intention of the parties

(1) A contract shall be interpreted according to the common intention of the parties.

(2) If such an intention cannot be established, the contract shall be interpreted according to the meaning that reasonable persons of the same kind as the parties would give to it in the same circumstances.

Article 4.2 Interpretation of statements and other conduct

(1) The statements and other conduct of a party shall be interpreted according to that party's intention if the other party knew or could not have been unaware of that intention.

(2) If the preceding paragraph is not applicable, such statements and other conduct shall be interpreted according to the meaning that a reasonable person of the same kind as the other party would give to it in the same circumstances.

Article 4.3 Relevant circumstances

In applying Articles 4.1 and 4.2, regard shall be had to all the circumstances, including

(a) preliminary negotiations between the parties;

(b) practices which the parties have established between themselves;

(c) the conduct of the parties subsequent to the conclusion of the contract;

(d) the nature and purpose of the contract;

(e) the meaning commonly given to terms and expressions in the trade concerned;

(f) usages.

Article 5.2.1 Contracts in favour of third parties

(1) The parties (the "promisor" and the "promisee") may confer by express or implied agreement a right on a third party (the "beneficiary").

(2) The existence and content of the beneficiary's right against the promisor are determined by the agreement of the parties and are subject to any conditions or other limitations under the agreement.

Article 5.2.2 Third party identifiable

The beneficiary must be identifiable with adequate certainty by the contract but need not be in existence at the time the contract is made.

Article 6.2.1 Contract to be observed

Where the performance of a contract becomes more onerous for one of the parties, that party is nevertheless bound to perform its obligations subject to the following provisions on hardship.

Article 6.2.2 Definition of hardship

There is hardship where the occurrence of events fundamentally alters the equilibrium of the contract either because the cost of a party's performance has increased or because the value of the performance a party receives has diminished, and

(a) the events occur or become known to the disadvantaged party after the conclusion of the contract;

(b) the events could not reasonably have been taken into account by the disadvantaged party at the time of the conclusion of the contract;

(c) the events are beyond the control of the disadvantaged party; and

(d) the risk of the events was not assumed by the disadvantaged party.

Article 6.2.3 Effects of hardship

(1) In case of hardship the disadvantaged party is entitled to request renegotiations. The request shall be made without undue delay and shall indicate the grounds on which it is based.

(2) The request for renegotiation does not itself entitle the disadvantaged party to withhold performance.

(3) Upon failure to reach agreement within a reasonable time either party may resort to the court.

(4) If the court finds hardship it may, if reasonable,

(a) terminate the contract at a date and on terms to be fixed; or

(b) adapt the contract with a view to restoring its equilibrium.

Article 7.1.7 Force majeure

(1) Non-performance by a party is excused if that party proves that the non-performance was due to an impediment beyond its control and that it could not reasonably be expected to have taken the impediment into account at the time of the conclusion of the contract or to have avoided or overcome it or its consequences.

(2) When the impediment is only temporary, the excuse shall have effect for such period as is reasonable having regard to the effect of the impediment on performance of the contract.

(3) The party who fails to perform must give notice to the other party of the impediment and its effect on its ability to perform. If the notice is not received by the other party within a reasonable time after the party who fails to perform knew or ought to have known of the impediment, it is liable for damages resulting from such non-receipt.

(4) Nothing in this article prevents a party from exercising a right to terminate the contract or to withhold performance or request interest on money due.

Article 7.2.2 Performance of non-monetary obligation

Where a party who owes an obligation other than one to pay money does not perform, the other party may require performance, unless

(a) performance is impossible in law or in fact;

(b) performance or, where relevant, enforcement is unreasonably burdensome or expensive;

(c) the party entitled to performance may reasonably obtain performance from another source;

(d) performance is of an exclusively personal character; or

(e) the party entitled to performance does not require performance within a reasonable time after it has, or ought to have, become aware of the non-performance.

Article 7.3.1 Right to terminate the contract

(1) A party may terminate the contract where the failure of the other party to perform an obligation under the contract amounts to a fundamental non-performance.

(2) In determining whether a failure to perform an obligation amounts to a fundamental non-performance regard shall be had, in particular, to whether

(a) the non-performance substantially deprives the aggrieved party of what it was entitled to expect under the contract unless the other party did not foresee and could not reasonably have foreseen such result;

(b) strict compliance with the obligation which has not been performed is of essence under the contract;

(c) the non-performance is intentional or reckless;

(d) the non-performance gives the aggrieved party reason to believe that it cannot rely on the other party's future performance;

(e) the non-performing party will suffer disproportionate loss as a result of the preparation or performance if the contract is terminated.

(3) In the case of delay the aggrieved party may also terminate the contract if the other party fails to perform before the time allowed it under Article 7.1.5 has expired.

Article 7.3.3 Anticipatory non-performance

Where prior to the date for performance by one of the parties it is clear that there will be a fundamental non-performance by that party, the other party may terminate the contract.

Article 7.3.4 Adequate assurance of due performance

A party who reasonably believes that there will be a fundamental non-performance by the other party may demand adequate assurance of due performance and may meanwhile withhold its own performance. Where this assurance is not provided within a reasonable time the party demanding it may terminate the contract.

Article 7.3.5 Effects of termination in general

(1) Termination of the contract releases both parties from their obligation to effect and to receive future performance.

(2) Termination does not preclude a claim for damages for non-performance.

(3) Termination does not affect any provision in the contract for the settlement of disputes or any other term of the contract which is to operate even after termination.

Article 7.3.6 Restitution

(1) On termination of the contract either party may claim restitution of whatever it has supplied, provided that such party concurrently makes restitution of whatever it has received. If restitution in kind is not possible or appropriate allowance should be made in money whenever reasonable.

(2) However, if performance of the contract has extended over a period of time and the contract is divisible, such restitution can only be claimed for the period after termination has taken effect.

Article 7.4.2 Full compensation

(1) The aggrieved party is entitled to full compensation for harm sustained as a result of the non-performance. Such harm includes both any loss which it suffered and any gain of which it was deprived, taking into account any gain to the aggrieved party resulting from its avoidance of cost or harm.

(2) Such harm may be non-pecuniary and includes, for instance, physical suffering or emotional distress.

Article 7.4.3 Certainty of harm

(1) Compensation is due only for harm, including future harm, that is established with a reasonable degree of certainty.

(2) Compensation may be due for the loss of a chance in proportion to the probability of its occurrence.

(3) Where the amount of damages cannot be established with a sufficient degree of certainty, the assessment is at the discretion of the court.

Article 7.4.4 Foreseeability of harm

The non-performing party is liable only for harm which it foresaw or could reasonably have foreseen at the time of the conclusion of the contract as being likely to result from its non-performance.

Article 7.4.5 Proof of harm in case of replacement transaction

Where the aggrieved party has terminated the contract and has made a replacement transaction within a reasonable time and in a reasonable manner it may recover the difference between the contract price and the price of the replacement transaction as well as damages for any further harm.

Article 7.4.6 Proof of harm by current price

(1) Where the aggrieved party has terminated the contract and has not made a replacement transaction but there is a current price for the performance contracted for, it may recover the difference between the contract price and the price current at the time the contract is terminated as well as damages for any further harm.

(2) Current price is the price generally charged for goods delivered or services rendered in comparable circumstances at the place where the contract should have been performed or, if there is no current price at that place, the current price at such other place that appears reasonable to take as a reference.

Article 7.4.8 Mitigation of harm

(1) The non-performing party is not liable for harm suffered by the aggrieved party to the extent that the harm could have been reduced by the latter party's taking reasonable steps.

(2) The aggrieved party is entitled to recover any expenses reasonably incurred in attempting to reduce the harm.

Article 7.4.13 Agreed payment for non-performance

(1) Where the contract provides that a party who does not perform is to pay a specified sum to the aggrieved party for such non-performance, the aggrieved party is entitled to that sum irrespective of its actual harm.

(2) However, notwithstanding any agreement to the contrary the specified sum may be reduced to a reasonable amount where it is grossly excessive in relation to the harm resulting from the non-performance and to the other circumstances.

APPENDIX E

RESTATEMENT (THIRD) OF RESTITUTION AND UNJUST ENRICHMENT (2011)

§ 1 Restitution and Unjust Enrichment

A person who is unjustly enriched at the expense of another is subject to liability in restitution.

Comment:

a. Liability in restitution. Liability in restitution derives from the receipt of a benefit whose retention without payment would result in the unjust enrichment of the defendant at the expense of the claimant. While the paradigm case of unjust enrichment is one in which the benefit on one side of the transaction corresponds to an observable loss on the other, the consecrated formula "at the expense of another" can also mean "in violation of the other's legally protected rights," without the need to show that the claimant has suffered a loss.

The usual consequence of a liability in restitution is that the defendant must restore the benefit in question or its traceable product, or else pay money in the amount necessary to eliminate unjust enrichment.

The identification of unjust enrichment as an independent basis of liability in common-law legal systems—comparable in this respect to a liability in contract or tort—was the central achievement of the 1937 Restatement of Restitution. That conception of the subject is carried forward here. The use of the word "restitution" to describe the cause of action as well as the remedy is likewise inherited from the original Restatement, despite the problems this usage creates. There are cases in which the essence of a plaintiff's right and remedy is the reversal of a transfer, and thus a literal "restitution," without regard to whether the defendant has been enriched by the transfer in question. Conversely, there are cases in which the remedy for unjust enrichment gives the plaintiff something—typically, the defendant's wrongful gain—that the plaintiff did not previously possess.

Such is the inherent flexibility of the concept of unjust enrichment that almost every instance of a recognized liability in restitution might be referred to the broad rule of the present section. The same flexibility means that the concept of unjust enrichment will not, by itself, yield a reliable indication of the nature and scope of the liability imposed by this part of our legal system. It is by no means obvious, as a theoretical matter, how "unjust enrichment" should best be defined; whether it constitutes a rule of decision, a unifying theme, or something in between; or what role the principle would ideally play in our legal system. Such questions preoccupy much academic writing on the subject. This Restatement has been written on the assumption that the law of restitution and unjust enrichment can be usefully described without insisting on answers to any of them. . . .

b. Unjust enrichment. The law of restitution is predominantly the law of unjust enrichment, but "unjust enrichment" is a term of art. The substantive part of the law of restitution is concerned with identifying those forms of enrichment that the law treats as "unjust" for purposes of imposing liability.

A significant tradition within English and American law refers to unjust enrichment as if it were something identifiable *a priori*, by the exercise of a moral judgment anterior to legal rules. This equitable conception of the law of restitution is crystallized by Lord Mansfield's famous statement in Moses v. Macferlan, 97 Eng. Rep. 676, 681 (K.B. 1760): "In one word, the gist of this kind of action is, that the defendant, upon the circumstances of the case, is obliged by the ties of natural justice and equity to refund the money." Explaining restitution as the embodiment of natural justice and equity gives the subject an undoubted versatility, an adaptability to new situations, and (in the eyes of many observers) a special moral attractiveness. Restitution in this view is the aspect of our legal system that makes the most direct appeal to standards of equitable and conscientious behavior as a source of enforceable obligations.

At the same time, the purely equitable account of the subject is open to substantial objections. Saying that liability in restitution is imposed to avoid unjust enrichment effectively postpones the real work of definition, leaving to a separate inquiry the question whether a particular transaction is productive of unjust enrichment or not. In numerous cases natural justice and equity do not in fact provide an adequate guide to decision, and would not do so even if their essential requirements could be treated as self-evident. Unless a definition of restitution can provide a more informative generalization about the nature of the transactions leading to liability, it is difficult to avoid the objection that sees in "unjust enrichment," at best, a name for a legal conclusion that remains to be explained; at worst, an open-ended and potentially unprincipled charter of liability.

In reality, the law of restitution is very far from imposing liability for every instance of what might plausibly be called unjust enrichment. The law's potential for intervention in transactions that might be challenged as inequitable is narrower, more predictable, and more objectively determined than the unconstrained implications of the words "unjust enrichment." Equity and good conscience might see an unjust enrichment in the performance of a valid but unequal bargain, or in the legally protected refusal to perform an equal one (as where the statute of limitations bars enforcement of a valid debt). Beyond these merely legal instances, moreover, "unjust enrichment" (in the natural and nontechnical sense of the words) might seem to be a pervasive fact of human experience—given any prior standard (such as equality or merit) by which people's relative entitlements might be measured.

The concern of restitution is not, in fact, with unjust enrichment in any such broad sense, but with a narrower set of circumstances giving rise to what might more appropriately be called *unjustified enrichment*. Compared to the open-ended implications of the term "unjust enrichment," instances of unjustified enrichment are both predictable and objectively determined, because the justification in question is not moral but legal. Unjustified enrichment is enrichment that lacks an adequate legal basis; it results from a transaction that the law treats as ineffective to work a conclusive alteration in ownership rights. Broadly speaking, an ineffective transaction for these purposes is one that is *nonconsensual*. Such a transaction may occur when the claimant's consent to the transaction is impaired for some reason; or when the claimant confers unrequested benefits without obtaining the recipient's agreement to pay for them; or when an attempted contractual exchange miscarries after partial performance; or when the defendant acquires benefits by wrongful interference with the claimant's rights. . . .

Because of its greater explanatory power, the term *unjustified enrichment* might thus be preferred to *unjust enrichment*, were it not for the established usage imposed by the first Restatement of Restitution. But while the choice between the two expressions may indicate a preferred vantage point, it implies no difference in legal outcomes. As descriptions of the circumstances that give rise to legal liability, the terms *unjust enrichment* and *unjustified enrichment* are precisely coextensive, identifying the same transactions and the same legal relationships. This is because—notwithstanding the potential reach of the words, and Lord Mansfield's confident reference to "natural justice"—the circumstances in which American law has in fact identified an *unjust enrichment* resulting in legal liability have been those and only those in which there might also be said to be *unjustified enrichment*, meaning the transfer of a benefit without adequate legal ground.

The two expressions, moreover, point to mutually reinforcing explanations of liability. Enrichment is unjust, in legal contemplation, to the extent it is without adequate legal basis; and the law supplies a remedy for unjustified enrichment because such enrichment cannot conscientiously be retained. In no instance does the fact or extent of liability in restitution depend on whether the source of that liability is conceived or described as unjust enrichment, as unjustified enrichment, or as a combination of the two.

c. Restitution and restoration. Employed to denote liability based on unjust enrichment, the word "restitution" is a term of art that has frequently proved confusing. . . .

In short, most of the law of restitution might more helpfully be called the law of unjust or unjustified enrichment. See Comment *b*. . . .

§ 20 Protection of Another's Life or Health

(1) A person who performs, supplies, or obtains professional services required for the protection of another's life or health is entitled to restitution from the other as necessary to prevent unjust enrichment, if the circumstances justify the decision to intervene without request.

(2) Unjust enrichment under this section is measured by a reasonable charge for the services in question.

Comment:

a. General principles and scope; relation to other sections. The claim for emergency medical services rendered in the absence of contract is one of restitution's paradigms. Its significance lies not in its practical utility—a litigated claim under this section being a rarity—but in the clarity with which it reflects the general principles that justify a claim to compensation for nonbargained benefits voluntarily conferred. An emergency that threatens life or health offers the ultimate justification for conferring a benefit in the absence of contract, if need be, asserting a claim for payment only after services have been rendered. Under ordinary circumstances, this reversal of the normal sequence of an exchange transaction is not tolerated: a transferor or provider who neglects a suitable opportunity to bargain with the recipient ahead of time will be deemed to have acted gratuitously. The significance of the medical emergency is not only that the provider is amply justified in proceeding without first making a contract, but that the benefit to the recipient is unmistakable, even if its measurement is sometimes debated. . . .

b. Professional services. Emergency assistance rendered by a nonprofessional, however valuable, does not give rise to a claim in restitution under existing law. . . .

Illustrations:

1. Doctor is summoned by Bystander to attend accident Victim, who is lying unconscious. Doctor performs emergency surgery. Doctor's reasonable and customary charge for the services rendered is $1,000, which Victim refuses to pay. Doctor has a claim in restitution for $1,000 against Victim.

2. Same facts as Illustration 1, except that the circumstances of the accident are such that both Bystander and Doctor act courageously and at great personal risk in coming to the aid of Victim. Their heroic intervention is not, in itself, a source of unjust enrichment. Bystander has no claim in restitution under this section, while Doctor's entitlement to restitution is limited (as in Illustration 1) to his reasonable and customary charge of $1,000 for professional services rendered. . . .

5. Daughter, a minor living with and supported by her Parents, is injured in an automobile accident. She is transported by helicopter to Hospital

where she receives emergency medical attention. Daughter lacks capacity to contract, and Hospital renders services before Parents can be informed. Daughter and Parents are jointly liable in restitution to Hospital for the reasonable cost of Daughter's care. . . .

7. A acts in an emergency to save the lives of B and C, sustaining crippling injuries as a result. In gratitude for A's assistance, B promises to pay him a weekly pension of $100. B's promise is unsupported by consideration, but it may nevertheless be enforceable as a matter of contract law. (If such a promise is enforceable, B's recognition of the fact and value of the benefit conferred by A is a significant part of the rationale. See Restatement Second, Contracts § 86, Comment *d*, Illustration 7.) Unlike B, C makes no promise of compensation and later rejects A's suggestion that he is entitled to a reward. A is possibly entitled to enforce B's promise, but A has no claim in restitution against either B or C.

c. Measure of benefit. Because the ultimate benefits of medical treatment are both contingent and difficult to value, marginal cases within the rule of § 20 may pose problems in measuring enrichment. The practical answer to what is largely a classroom paradox is that services that are medically necessary are presumed to be beneficial, without regard to their ultimate outcome; moreover, that it is appropriate to value such services as if the recipient had requested them. The result, as in most cases of quantum meruit, is a liability measured by market value.

Illustration:

8. Physician provides emergency medical assistance to unconscious accident Victim. The services are medically appropriate and properly performed, but Victim dies without regaining consciousness. Physician seeks restitution from Victim's Estate by the rule of this section. Resisting the claim, Estate argues that Physician's unsuccessful intervention conferred no benefit; accordingly . . . restitution would leave Estate worse off (by the amount of Physician's eventual recovery) than if Physician had not intervened. The objection is misplaced. Medical services provided in an emergency are presumed to be desirable; though unrequested (the recipient having no opportunity to request them), they are valued for restitution purposes as if they had been requested. Physician is entitled to restitution from Estate in the amount of his reasonable and customary charge.

d. Refusal. There can be no claim under this section for services that a recipient having full legal capacity has attempted to refuse; or for which such a recipient has communicated to the provider, before the services were rendered, an unwillingness to pay. Capacity to consent is capacity to refuse. . . .

§ 34 Mistake or Supervening Change of Circumstances

(1) A person who renders performance under a contract that is subject to avoidance by reason of mistake or supervening change of circumstances has

a claim in restitution to recover the performance or its value, as necessary to prevent unjust enrichment. If the case is one in which the requirements of § 54 can be met, the remedy of rescission and restitution permits the reversal of the transaction without the need to demonstrate unjust enrichment.

(2) For purposes of subsection (1):

(a) the value of a nonreturnable contractual performance is measured by reference to the recipient's contractual expectations; and

(b) the recipient's liability in restitution may be reduced to allow for loss incurred in reliance on the contract.

Illustrations:

1. Rose 2d of Aberlone, a purebred cow belonging to Farmer, fails to breed in season; on examination by a veterinarian she is determined to be barren. Farmer sells Rose to Breeder for $300, a price based on her value as beef. Before the day fixed for delivery and payment, Rose is discovered to be with calf; her value as a breeding animal is not less than $3,000. Farmer repudiates the sale, and Breeder sues for specific performance or damages. Breeder's claim is in contract, not restitution; Farmer's defense asserts a theory of mistake as the ground for avoidance. Breeder's claim will predictably be denied.

2. Same facts as Illustration 1, except that Rose's fertility is discovered after Rose has been delivered and paid for. Farmer brings suit to rescind the completed exchange. The plaintiff's claim is now in restitution, not contract, though it alleges the identical mistake as the ground for avoidance. Farmer's claim will predictably be denied. . . .

10. Plaintiffs hire Banquet Hall for a wedding reception, paying the full contract price of $10,000 in advance. The reception is disrupted by a power failure 45 minutes after it begins, when the failure of air conditioning makes conditions intolerable. Plaintiffs sue Banquet Hall for breach of contract, seeking to recover both the prepaid price and (as consequential damages) further amounts they had paid in advance to the band, the wedding photographer, and the videographer. The contract between Plaintiffs and Banquet Hall contains a force majeure clause specifically excusing performance in the event of a power failure; the existence of this provision disposes of Plaintiffs' claim for breach of contract and for contract damages. The court finds, however, that the parties' agreement does not authorize Banquet Hall to retain the prepaid price if its own performance is excused. Plaintiffs are entitled to restitution by the rule of this section. Recovery is in the amount of $10,000 less the value of the goods and services provided to Plaintiffs and their guests before performance was interrupted.

§ 36 Restitution to a Party in Default

(1) A performing party whose material breach prevents a recovery on the contract has a claim in restitution against the recipient of performance, as necessary to prevent unjust enrichment.

(2) Enrichment from receipt of an incomplete or defective contractual performance is measured by comparison to the recipient's position had the contract been fully performed. The claimant has the burden of establishing the fact and amount of any net benefit conferred.

(3) A claim under this section may be displaced by a valid agreement of the parties establishing their rights and remedies in the event of default.

(4) If the claimant's default involves fraud or other inequitable conduct, restitution may on that account be denied (§ 63).

Comment:

a. *General principles and scope; relation to contract law.* Standard contract remedies do not impose forfeiture as a punishment for default. Expectation damages reflect the injured party's net entitlement, subtracting what was received from what had been promised; the consequence is that the defaulting party normally receives credit (against a liability for breach) for the value of an incomplete or defective performance, measured at the contract rate. Yet if circumstances are such that it is the defaulting party (rather than the recipient of the defective performance) who appears as plaintiff, contract law affords no claim by which the same value may be reached. The absence of any claim on the contract for the value of a defaulted performance results from the contractual theory of conditions, according to which—either expressly or by implication—substantial performance by each party is a precondition of the other's obligation to perform. Where a defective performance confers a net benefit, and the parties have not validly contracted for forfeiture in the event of breach, one consequence of the theory of conditions may be the unjust and extracontractual enrichment of the recipient at the expense of the party in default.

Contract law affords the party in default no direct recourse, but it mitigates this untoward result by a number of ancillary doctrines whose common effect is to reduce the frequency with which a party in default must resort to an action "off the contract" on a restitution theory. Among them are the doctrine of substantial performance, allowing an action for damages by a party who would otherwise be barred by default or failure of condition; rules of severability, permitting a court to find that the performing party has an enforceable claim for a part performance; and judicial hostility toward contractual forfeitures, stemming not only from notions of equity but from a realistic skepticism about the likelihood that Draconian penalties have been intentionally negotiated. The theory and application of all such rules are technically matters of contract law, outside the scope of this Restatement; although the context is one in which rules of contract and restitution may be effectively congruent.

For purposes of organization, however, the rule of the present section applies exclusively to cases not governed by contract. In other words, this section applies to cases in which (i) the performing party has no enforceable rights under the contract, whether by a rule of substantial performance, of severability, or otherwise; and (ii) the claim based on unjust enrichment is not displaced by a valid contractual provision imposing forfeiture or liquidated damages. Where a remedy to the party in default is neither conferred nor foreclosed by valid terms of the agreement, restitution authorizes a claim as necessary to avoid unjust enrichment. The principal task confronting the restitution claimant is to establish that an incomplete or defective performance has in fact conferred a net benefit on the recipient, taking into account the various costs to which the defendant has been subjected in the wake of the claimant's default.

Except where the party in default has engaged in fraud or inequitable conduct (see Comment *b*), a claimant under this section is not generally viewed as a wrongdoer. The most important constraints on the availability of relief under this section relate, therefore, not to the quality of the claimant's conduct, but to the nature of the benefit conferred and the position of the recipient in light of the claimant's breach. The ultimate question is whether the court may order a remedy in restitution that does not prejudice the defendant, in light of the defendant's protected expectations under the defaulted contract. Factors relevant to this determination are common to other areas of restitution. Thus a party whose (partial) contractual performance involved the payment of money will more readily recover by the rule of this section than one whose defaulted performance consisted of nonreturnable services or improvements to real property. See Comments *d*, *e*, and *f*.

A restitution claim based on a contractual performance starts with certain inherent advantages, because the benefit in question may be shown—in some cases at least—to be something that the recipient both requested and offered to pay for. Conversely, a claim based on a *defective* performance may encounter the objection that restitution would subject the defendant to a forced exchange (§ 2(4)). A defendant who is obliged to pay the court-determined value of the claimant's nonconforming performance—if a significant purpose of the agreement was to obtain something else—is denied the fundamental right to choose the performance he will pay for. Restitution in such a case might leave the defendant worse off than if the transaction had not taken place at all—an outcome that is not authorized against an innocent recipient. See § 50(3).

b. Willful or deliberate default. Courts in many jurisdictions continue to state that restitution is unavailable to a party whose contractual default is willful or deliberate. The quality of the breach in a particular case manifestly determines the claimant's equitable posture in seeking restitution. The claimant's conduct may be culpable or excusable; it may reflect opportunism or merely inadequate resources; it may manifest a conscious disregard of the defendant's legal entitlement, on the one hand, or simple inadvertence, on the other. The court's sense of the claimant's relative equitable position will in many instances determine the success or failure of the claim.

It is potentially misleading, however, to describe willful or deliberate default as an absolute bar to the claim under this section. In the large and significant class of cases where the claimant's defaulted obligation is to pay money, the breach of contract—the failure to pay a debt when due—is most often the result of a conscious election. Even a debtor who faces financial hardship normally has a choice to pay one creditor rather than another. It can be difficult to explain why breach in such instances should not be qualified as "willful" or "deliberate"; yet the same instances include some of the foremost illustrations of cases in which modern American law authorizes restitution to the party in default. See Comment *d*.

Although restitution is undeniably available in some cases of deliberate default, there remain many circumstances in which the quality of the claimant's breach will effectively bar the claim. The significance of "deliberateness" in this context lies in the extraordinary costs that will frequently be imposed by an election to discontinue a contractual performance already under way. Assuming a simple choice between performance and breach, the election to perform yields a straightforward claim to the price specified by contract, securing contractual expectations on both sides; while the election to default, and then to pursue a claim in restitution, draws the litigants and the court into a complex, extracontractual evaluation of both benefit conferred and injury inflicted. The remedial inefficiency of the latter course is obvious, as is the risk that the innocent party will incur substantial uncompensated costs in consequence of the claimant's election to breach. Judicial awareness of these factors accounts for the traditional rule that denies restitution whenever default is "willful or deliberate." The omission of this condition from § 36 must not be taken to imply that such factors have somehow become irrelevant.

As already noted, the present section forgoes an inquiry into "willfulness" in order to accommodate numerous decisions allowing restitution to claimants whose contractual default was evidently the result of conscious choice. At the same time, the recipient of the defaulted performance is protected against prejudice by overlapping safeguards:

(1) There is liability in restitution only to the extent of a net benefit conferred, and the claimant bears the burden of demonstrating that a net benefit exists. Where the net enrichment of the defendant remains doubtful, the claim in restitution must fail. The broad rule of § 50(3) affords the same guarantee. See Comment *c*.

(2) A liability in restitution will not impose a forced exchange-requiring the defendant to pay for something which, under the circumstances, the defendant should have been free to refuse (§ 2(4)). See Comment *f* and Illustrations 19-20.

(3) If the party in default has engaged in fraud or inequitable conduct, a claim under § 36 may be barred, notwithstanding the existence of net enrichment by some measures. See Comment *e*, Illustration 17; Comment *f*, Illustration 19. Denial of restitution in such cases is an instance of the rule of equitable disqualification described in § 63.

c. Amount of recovery; burden of proof. There is a claim in restitution in respect of defaulted contractual performance only if and to the extent the claimant can prove that the benefit thereby conferred, net of losses attributable to claimant's default, results in the enrichment of the defendant. Requiring the claimant to carry the burden of proof on the key issue of net enrichment does not mean that the claimant must produce evidence within the knowledge of the defendant. It does mean that if the net enrichment of the defendant cannot be clearly established, restitution will be denied.

Net enrichment is measured by reference to the defendant's contractual expectation. Because the award is net of damages caused by claimant's default, the particular items entering into the account reflect the standard calculation of damages in the relevant transactional setting: lost profits in one case, cost of cure or completion in another. The uniform test is to compare the defendant's actual position with the position the defendant would have occupied in the absence of breach. See Illustration 1. Given the difficulty in many circumstances of quantifying the injury to the defendant from the claimant's breach, the appropriate reduction may be liberally estimated. The object is to insure that the nonbreaching defendant will under no circumstance be left with a net loss from the transaction; and a party who has elected not to perform the contract cannot insist on a nice calculation of extracontractual benefits conferred. See Illustration 2.

When properly applied, a contractual provision for liquidated damages serves the same function, protecting the innocent party against loss when injury is difficult to quantify. Rules governing the enforceability of liquidated damages are a matter of contract law, but the enforcement of such a provision may properly decide the scope of restitution in the present context. See Illustration 3.

When the claimant seeks restitution of the value of a nonreturnable performance, it may be necessary to choose between alternative measures of the benefit conferred. To the extent the claimant's breach of contract includes an element of fault, the equities of the claim under § 36 will tend to favor the application of the most restrictive test among those proposed by § 49(3). This will ordinarily mean either (i) a ratable portion of the contract price, (ii) the market value of the benefit conferred, or (iii) the resulting addition to the defendant's wealth, whichever is least. See Illustrations 4-5.

Illustrations:

1. Owner and Builder contract for specified work at a price of $235,000. Builder abandons the job after part performance, and Owner has the work completed by a third party. Builder sues Owner seeking damages for breach of contract or, in the alternative, restitution by the rule of this section. The jury finds that Builder committed a material breach; that the value of labor and materials furnished by Builder is $200,000, for which Owner has paid $150,000; that Owner has been obliged to spend a further $100,000 to have the work completed according to contract specifications; and that the value of the completed work is $260,000. Because Owner was entitled to have the work done for $235,000 (and has spent $250,000), Owner has not been unjustly enriched by Builder's part performance (§ 36(2)). Builder has no claim in restitution.

2. Painter agrees to paint Owner's house for $20,000. During the course of the work, Owner makes progress payments of $15,000. When the job is 90 percent complete Painter demands another $10,000, announcing that

he will suspend work until this additional sum is paid. Owner refuses, and Painter moves his equipment to another job across town. Owner has the work completed by someone else at a cost of $2,000. Painter sues Owner in restitution. The value of Painter's work on a quantum meruit basis is $18,000. If Painter's claim is not barred outright by his inequitable conduct, Painter might be able to demonstrate enrichment in the amount of $3,000—in that Owner has obtained performance worth $20,000 for an aggregate expenditure of $17,000 (§ 36(2)). On the facts supposed, however, the court might reasonably allow $3,000 in incidental damages to compensate Owner for the delay and aggravation caused by Painter's willful breach. On this view there is no net benefit to Owner, and Painter is not entitled to restitution.

3. Mechanic contracts with Owner on January 1 for the restoration of Owner's 1931 Duesenberg roadster. The price of the work is $50,000, payable on completion; the job is to be completed by June 30; Owner may terminate the contract for lack of timely performance; Mechanic will pay liquidated damages of $100 for each day that the work remains unfinished after June 30. Mechanic performs only part of the work specified. On October 1, Owner regains possession of the vehicle by legal process, then has the work completed elsewhere at a cost of $25,000 and a further delay of three months. Mechanic sues Owner in restitution, offering to prove that his uncompensated work on the car had a reasonable value of $25,000. The provision of the parties' agreement fixing damages of $100 for each day of delay is valid and enforceable by the contract law of the jurisdiction. Calculating on the basis of 180 days' delay, there is no net enrichment of Owner (and Mechanic has no claim in restitution) except to the extent that the value of Mechanic's uncompensated labor and materials exceeds $18,000.

4. A agrees to use his earthmoving equipment to clear and grade Blackacre, the property of B, making the land suitable for subdivision; in return, A will share in the proceeds from the sale of the improved lots. A improves a number of lots before the parties' agreement dissolves in acrimony, each claiming breach by the other. Regulatory obstacles prevent sale of the lots as originally contemplated, with the result that neither party would be able to prove expectation damages from the other's breach. A sues B seeking damages for breach of contract or, in the alternative, restitution by the rule of this section. If B is liable for breach of contract, A is entitled to performance-based damages measured by the cost or value of his uncompensated services (§ 38), without regard to any resulting increase in the value of Blackacre. If on the other hand A is the party in default, A's recovery under § 36 is limited to B's net enrichment, which cannot exceed the increased value of Blackacre attributable to A's services.

5. Architect undertakes to prepare plans for Owner's building for a fee of eight percent of the cost of construction. The parties' agreement stipulates that the total cost of the building shall not exceed $1 million. Architect

spends 250 hours preparing plans for a building that would cost at least $2 million to construct. The reasonable value of Architect's services is $200 per hour. Owner makes no use of the plans and refuses to pay for them. Architect's services have not resulted in Owner's enrichment, and Architect has no claim in restitution.

d. Benefit conferred in money. Restitution to a party in default is most readily available where there has been incomplete performance of an obligation to pay money, because the net enrichment of the defendant is easiest to demonstrate in such cases. The principal question in this setting is normally not the fact of enrichment but the validity of a contractual provision providing (at least in the view of the nonbreaching party) for forfeiture or liquidated damages in the event of default. The extent to which such a provision is enforceable is a question of contract law, though one to which considerations of unjust enrichment have an obvious relevance.

The classic illustration of restitution in this setting is the claim by a defaulting purchaser of real property. See Illustrations 6-7. Analogous claims may be asserted by a defaulting buyer of goods, or by a claimant who has paid money due under the contract but defaulted in some subsequent aspect of that party's obligation. See Illustrations 8-10.

Illustrations:

6. Purchaser agrees to buy a condominium apartment from Vendor, making an initial payment of $15,000 against the contract price of $150,000. Two months later, having discovered another apartment he likes better, Purchaser repudiates his agreement with Vendor and requests the return of his initial payment. Vendor promptly sells the apartment to another buyer for $160,000 and refuses to refund any money to Purchaser. The parties' contract provides that "In the event of default by Purchaser, Vendor shall retain all sums of money paid hereunder as liquidated damages." By the law of the jurisdiction, a clause in a real estate sales contract establishing liquidated damages for the purchaser's default at 10 percent of the sales price is presumptively valid; the presumption may be rebutted by evidence that the vendor's actual damages are substantially less than the amount stipulated by contract. Purchaser introduces evidence of the $10,000 realized by Vendor on resale of the apartment as proof that Vendor sustained no damages from the breach. Vendor offers evidence of incidental damages associated with the necessity of resale, but the damages established do not exceed $5,000. Purchaser has a claim in restitution to recover $10,000 of the $15,000 initial payment. If local law were more favorable to liquidated damages in this context, or if the court were free to presume (with reasonable limits) the existence of unquantifiable injury to the disappointed seller, restitution to Purchaser might be further reduced or denied altogether.

7. On signing an agreement to buy Blackacre at a price of $100,000, Purchaser pays Vendor $5,000. The parties' agreement contains no provision

specifying remedies in the event of default. Purchaser later changes her mind, repudiates the contract, and brings suit for restitution of $5,000. In support of her claim, Purchaser proves only that Vendor resold the property, six months following Purchaser's default, at a price of $110,000. Purchaser's liability for breach of contract is measured at the time of the breach; it is not reduced by a subsequent increase in the market value of Vendor's property. For this reason, proof of a profitable resale is insufficient (by itself) to prove net enrichment of Vendor as a result of Purchaser's down payment. Purchaser is not entitled to restitution.

8. Buyer purchases standing timber on land owned by Seller. The price to Buyer is to be determined by the price Buyer eventually receives from the mill for the harvested timber. Buyer makes a substantial payment in advance, to be credited against the purchase price as subsequently determined. After half the timber has been harvested, the relationship breaks down. Buyer and Seller sue each other for breach of contract. The court determines that Buyer is liable to Seller for breach of contract; that Buyer's default has caused damages to Seller of $30,000; and that Buyer's payment to Seller exceeds Buyer's payment obligation under the contract by $100,000. Buyer's claim in restitution is governed by the Uniform Commercial Code, which (as applied to these facts) authorizes Buyer to recover $70,000 from Seller. U.C.C. § 2-718(3).

9. Buyer agrees to purchase Seller's used car for $10,000. Buyer pays $1,000 down and promises to pay $9,000 on taking delivery in 10 days. The parties' agreement contains no provision specifying remedies in the event of default. Buyer is unable to finance the purchase and seeks return of his down payment. Seller refuses to return the money and resells the car to another purchaser for $12,000 cash. Buyer's claim in restitution is governed by the Uniform Commercial Code, which (as applied to these facts) displaces any inquiry into Seller's net enrichment. Buyer is entitled to restitution of $500, being the amount of his payment less $500 in statutory liquidated damages. U.C.C. §§ 2-706(6), 2-718(2).

10. As part of its employment benefits for professional staff, Company offers (i) to make an interest-free loan to Employee to cover the cost of approved graduate education, (ii) to rehire Employee after the degree has been obtained, and (iii) to forgive the principal of the loan if Employee remains with Company for 24 months thereafter. Employee borrows $20,000 under this program and obtains the intended degree; but on returning to work, Employee is assigned to a menial position at a reduced salary. Employee refuses this employment and refuses to repay the loan. The court determines that it was an implied but essential term of the parties' agreement that Employee's post-degree employment would be at least equal in salary and responsibility to the position previously occupied; that Employee's loan obligation is not severable from the rest of the agreement; and that Company's breach of contract has caused Employee $12,000 in damages. Company has a claim in restitution to recover $8,000 from Employee.

Repudiation after partial performance of a contract involving other financial obligations may present a case that is ultimately analogous to the standard case of payment default. See Illustration 11.

Illustration:

11. Borrower lends to its Franchisees and takes their promissory Notes. Borrower finances its loans by selling the Notes to Bank, while assuming an obligation to repurchase any Notes on which Franchisees might default. As part of the transaction, the parties create a "reserve account" to secure the performance of Borrower's repurchase obligation. The agreement between Borrower and Bank provides that—in the absence of a default by Borrower—Borrower shall be entitled to any balance of the reserve account, once Bank has recovered its advances, interest, and fees. Borrower files for bankruptcy and rejects the executory contract with Bank (Bankruptcy Code § 365). Because rejection constitutes a breach of contract by the debtor, Borrower cannot enforce the contract to recover the net surplus in the reserve account. By contrast, Borrower has a claim by the rule of this section to any surplus in the account once Bank has been indemnified. The inchoate restitution claim is part of Borrower's bankruptcy estate.

Occasionally a buyer of goods or services who has paid the full price in advance will repudiate the exchange and seek to recover that portion of the payment that exceeds the seller's contractual expectation. Such a claim cannot be brought within the literal terms of § 36 because the claimant is not in default. But the present section governs the case *a fortiori,* since a party who has fully performed must have at least the rights of a party in default. See Illustration 12.

Illustration:

12. Member reserves a place on a "wilderness tour" of Alaska, organized by Society and operated by Carrier. Terms and conditions set forth in Society's brochure specify that each reservation must be accompanied by a nonrefundable $500 deposit, and that the balance of $4,500 per person must be paid not later than 30 days before the scheduled departure, on penalty of cancellation. Member instead pays the full price of $5,000 six months in advance, then changes his mind and attempts to cancel the reservation 60 days before the tour is to begin. Society refuses to refund any part of the payment. On suit for restitution, Member establishes that Society made no payment to Carrier in respect of his reservation, and that the tour operated at full capacity, as the place he paid for was resold to someone on a waiting list. Interpreting the parties' agreement, the court concludes that Society made no promise, express or implied, to make any refunds in respect of a canceled reservation; but also that the parties agreed to no forfeiture or liquidated damages beyond the $500 deposit that was stated to be nonrefundable. The rule of this section applies *a fortiori* to authorize Member's claim, since Member would be entitled to restitution had he paid something

less than the full contract price. Member can recover $4,500 from Society by the rule of this section.

e. *Benefit conferred in goods or services.* Under the Uniform Commercial Code, a seller of goods who defaults after partial performance—typically, by choosing to sell to another buyer at a higher price—is entitled to recovery "on the contract," notwithstanding what may be a willful and deliberate breach. This outcome is achieved by enforcing the buyer's liability to "pay at the contract rate for any goods accepted" (U.C.C. § 2-607(1)), reduced by the resulting damages, such as buyer's cost to obtain higher-priced cover (U.C.C. § 2-712).

A party in default under a contract to render personal services is ordinarily entitled to restitution by the rule of this section unless the nature of the default indicates fraud or inequitable conduct. Even if the claimant has been guilty of conscious wrongdoing, the tendency of more recent decisions—where the facts permit—is to distinguish periods of faithful and disloyal service, awarding the value of services performed during the former but not the latter. See Illustrations 13-14.

Claims in respect of legal services make up an important subcategory of cases within this section. One reason is practical: lawyers' contingent-fee arrangements account for a large proportion of transactions in which the performance of personal services substantially outruns the payment of compensation. Another reason for the salience of cases involving lawyers is the particular gravity attached to the lawyer's breach of an obligation to a client. From the perspective of professional responsibility, the question is whether the character of the lawyer's default is such as to make it appropriate that the lawyer forfeit some or all of the lawyer's claim to compensation. See Restatement Third, The Law Governing Lawyers § 37. Within the terms of the present section, the question is whether the lawyer's breach of duty involves fraud or inequitable conduct: professional and fiduciary obligations to the client increase the likelihood that a lawyer's default may be of this character. Absent such a bar, even a lawyer discharged for cause may recover for the value of services rendered, provided that those services have conferred a net benefit on the client. By contrast, restitution will uniformly be denied to a lawyer who abandons a representation without justification. See Illustrations 15-17.

Illustrations:

13. A and his wife B move onto C's farm. By written agreement, they undertake to care for C and C's property for the rest of her life, in exchange for C's promise to leave them her real and personal property by will. Relations between the parties are harmonious for several years: A and B are conscientious caretakers, and C makes a will in accordance with her promise. Later, following a domestic dispute, A and B terminate the arrangement and vacate the premises. In subsequent litigation between the parties, the court determines that A and B breached their contract with C; but that (given the difficulty of apportioning blame for the breakdown in the

relationship) their wrongful termination did not cause compensable injury. A and B have a claim in restitution to the reasonable value of their services and expenditures in the care of C and her property, net of the compensation they have already received—in the form of room and board—over the course of the relationship.

14. A is employed by B Co. as regional manager, receiving a monthly salary plus a commission on B's sales in A's region. The commission is calculated and paid quarterly in arrears. On April 15, B discovers that A has been engaged since February 15 in organizing a new company to compete with B. B immediately discharges A and refuses to pay him further compensation. A sues B to recover commissions on sales from January 1 to April 15. The court determines that (i) A was in breach of his duty of loyalty to B on February 15 and thereafter, but (ii) A continued to perform valuable services for B until the date of his discharge. A has a claim in restitution for the commissions otherwise payable in respect of sales prior to February 15. A's restitution claim in respect of services performed after that date is precluded by A's inequitable conduct toward B.

15. Attorney represents Client in litigation on a contingent-fee basis. Becoming dissatisfied with Attorney's handling of the matter, Client discharges Attorney and retains another lawyer to take over the representation. When substitute counsel obtains a favorable settlement, Attorney sues Client to recover a fee. Attorney's remedy depends on whether his discharge was with or without cause. Because public policy demands that a client be free to discharge an attorney, there is no breach of contract by Client in either event. If Attorney was discharged without cause, Attorney is entitled to restitution as if he had been performing under an unenforceable contract (§ 31): he recovers the reasonable value of his interrupted services in quantum meruit (§ 50(2)(b)). If Attorney was discharged with cause, his claim to a fee is within the rule of this section. As such it is limited to the net benefit, if any, conferred on Client by Attorney's interrupted services. (If Client has been obliged to pay the same contingent fee to substitute counsel, the services of an attorney previously discharged for cause are not a source of benefit to Client.) If Attorney's performance prior to discharge for cause involved professional misconduct, the claim in restitution may be denied on that account (§ 36(4)).

16. Same facts as Illustration 15, except that Client obtains no recovery on its underlying claim, and no contingent fee is payable to successor counsel. If Attorney was discharged without cause, he may or may not be entitled to restitution for the value of his interrupted services, depending on the court's assessment of the reasons for the failure of Client's underlying claim. If Attorney was discharged for cause he has no claim to have conferred a net benefit.

17. Attorney represents Client in litigation on a contingent-fee basis. Attorney recommends that Client accept a settlement offer that Client rejects. Attorney withdraws from the representation. Client engages other counsel and eventually obtains a settlement; Attorney sues Client to recover a fee.

The court finds that Attorney's withdrawal was without justification and a violation of Attorney's fiduciary duty to Client. Although Attorney's services conferred a net benefit on Client, Attorney is not entitled to restitution.

f. Improvements to property. The peculiar difficulties associated with restitution in respect of improvements to property are largely the same, whether they arise in the present context or in that of mistaken improvements (§ 10). Where restitution is sought by a party in default under a contract, there is a greater likelihood that the improvement (or something like it) is one the defendant both wanted and expressed a willingness to pay for. So long as the defendant's contractual expectations may be respected, restitution encounters no particular obstacle. See Illustration 18. On the other hand, improvements by a party in default may be the result of bad faith; while the improver who was merely mistaken is at most guilty of carelessness. Fundamental principles of restitution preclude any recovery by a party who has deliberately and fraudulently promised one thing and delivered another. See Illustration 19.

If the law imposes a liability to pay for nonconforming improvements, it requires the defendant to pay for something different from what was promised under the contract. The propriety of doing so depends not only on the claimant's equitable position but on the position of the defendant if restitution is allowed. Resolution of such a controversy inevitably turns on the court's sense of what justice requires, and the potentially relevant factors are too numerous to be specified by rule. Along the range of possible outcomes, the extreme positions are occupied by contract remedies: on the one hand, finding substantial performance by the builder and measuring damages by diminution of value, possibly nil; on the other, finding breach by the builder and measuring damages by the cost of demolition and replacement. Restitution affords a set of intermediate possibilities, for cases in which the equities of the parties are more closely balanced.

A recovery in restitution is subject to restitution's inherent limits. As is true of every claim within § 36, therefore, restitution in respect of nonconforming improvements may not exceed the defendant's net enrichment as a result of the claimant's defaulted performance; as stated in § 50(3), the defendant may not be left worse off than if the transaction had not taken place. Where the nonconformity relates to an aspect of performance about which the parties have specifically bargained, so that the defendant has chosen one thing and been given another, restitution is limited not only by the difficulty of measuring net enrichment but by the need to protect the defendant against a forced exchange. See Illustration 20.

Illustrations:

18. Builder and Owner contract for the remodeling of Owner's house at a price of $25,000. Work is interrupted when the project is 80 percent completed and $15,000 of the price has been paid. In subsequent litigation the parties accuse each other of breach. The court finds that there has been

no substantial performance; Builder breached the contract by performing portions of the work in a manner that was not workmanlike. On the other hand, Builder furnished labor and materials having a value of $20,000 before performance was interrupted; and Owner's cost to complete the work and correct the defects of Builder's performance will not exceed $8,000. Builder has a claim in restitution to recover $2,000.

19. Builder and Owner contract for the construction of an apartment house at a price of $2 million. Upon completion of the work, when $1.5 million of the price has been paid, a final inspection reveals that the building fails to conform to specifications: Builder has placed floor joists 18 inches apart when the plans required joists every 12 inches. When Owner refuses to pay the balance of the price, Builder sues for breach of contract and (alternatively) for restitution by the rule of this section. The court finds that the Builder's deviations from specifications constitute a material breach; in consequence, Builder has no claim on the contract. On the restitution claim, it is conceded that joists on 18-inch centers are standard for construction of this type, and that the difference in the appraised value of the property as a result of the nonconformity is nil. The court finds, however, that the deviation from specifications was intentional and fraudulent: Builder's object was to economize on labor and materials by making unauthorized changes that would not be readily apparent. The fact that Builder's inequitable conduct resulted in no diminution in the value of the structure is irrelevant. Builder is not entitled to restitution.

20. Builder agrees to install a swimming pool in Owner's backyard. Pools of this type are normally eight feet deep, a depth that is adequate for diving and meets all building code requirements. Such a pool costs $25,000. Owner informs Builder that, for reasons of personal preference, he wants a pool nine feet deep. Builder agrees to construct a nine-foot pool at a cost of $30,000, payable $10,000 in advance and the balance on completion. Builder's foreman misreads the order, and the completed pool is only eight feet deep. Owner refuses to pay the balance of the price. Builder sues Owner in restitution, seeking the $25,000 price of an eight-foot pool less $10,000 already paid. Builder establishes by expert testimony that the eight-foot pool is fully as suitable as a nine-foot pool for all uses to which Owner or anyone else will put it. The difference in depth makes no difference to the appraised value of Owner's property, to which the completed pool has added $15,000. Owner can prove no quantifiable damages as a result of Builder's breach. Because the depth of the pool is an element of Builder's performance for which Owner specifically bargained, however, restitution by the rule of this section (measured by the usual price or market value of Builder's labor and materials) would subject Owner to an unacceptable forced exchange, imposing the very bargain that Owner had rejected. A court sympathetic to Builder might permit him to recover instead by the rule of § 10. Treating the eight-foot pool as a mistaken improvement yields a recovery of $5,000 in restitution ($15,000 added value less $10,000 already paid).

§ 37 Rescission for Material Breach

(1) Except as provided in subsection (2), a plaintiff who is entitled to a remedy for the defendant's material breach or repudiation may choose rescission as an alternative to enforcement if the further requirements of § 54 can be met.

(2) Rescission as a remedy for breach of contract is not available against a defendant whose defaulted obligation is exclusively an obligation to pay money.

§ 38 Performance-Based Damages

(1) As an alternative to damages based on the expectation interest (*Restatement Second, Contracts* § 347), a plaintiff who is entitled to a remedy for material breach or repudiation may recover damages measured by the cost or value of the plaintiff's performance.

(2) Performance-based damages are measured by

(a) uncompensated expenditures made in reasonable reliance on the contract, including expenditures made in preparation for performance or in performance, less any loss the defendant can prove with reasonable certainty the plaintiff would have suffered had the contract been performed (*Restatement Second, Contracts* § 349); or

(b) the market value of the plaintiff's uncompensated contractual performance, not exceeding the price of such performance as determined by reference to the parties' agreement.

(3) A plaintiff whose damages are measured by the rules of subsection (2) may also recover for any other loss, including incidental or consequential loss, caused by the breach.

§ 39 Profit From Opportunistic Breach

(1) If a deliberate breach of contract results in profit to the defaulting promisor and the available damage remedy affords inadequate protection to the promisee's contractual entitlement, the promisee has a claim to restitution of the profit realized by the promisor as a result of the breach. Restitution by the rule of this section is an alternative to a remedy in damages.

(2) A case in which damages afford inadequate protection to the promisee's contractual entitlement is ordinarily one in which damages will not permit the promisee to acquire a full equivalent to the promised performance in a substitute transaction.

(3) Breach of contract is profitable when it results in gains to the defendant (net of potential liability in damages) greater than the defendant would have realized from performance of the contract. Profits from breach include saved expenditure and consequential gains that the defendant would not have realized but for the breach, as measured by the rules that apply in other cases of disgorgement (§ 51(5)).

Comment:

. . .

Illustrations:

5. Landowner and Mining Company enter a contract for strip-mining. The agreement authorizes Mining Company to remove coal from Blackacre in exchange for payment of a specified royalty per ton. A further provision of the agreement, included at Landowner's insistence, obliges Mining Company to restore the surface of Blackacre to its preexisting contours on the completion of mining operations. Mining Company removes the coal from Blackacre, pays the stipulated royalty, and repudiates its obligation to restore the land. In Landowner's action against Mining Company it is established that the cost of restoration would be $25,000, and that the diminution in the value of Blackacre if the restoration is not performed would be negligible. The contract is not affected by mistake or impracticability. The cost of restoration is in line with what Mining Company presumably anticipated, and the available comparisons suggest that Mining Company took this cost into account in calculating the contractual royalty. Landowner is entitled to recover $25,000 from Mining Company by the rule of this section. It is not a condition to Landowner's recovery in restitution that the money be used to restore Blackacre. . . .

13. Builder and Owner agree on the construction of a house at a price of $2 million. The specifications call for foundations to be made of Vermont granite, and the work has been bid and priced on that basis. By mistake and inadvertence, Builder constructs the foundations of granite quarried in New Hampshire. This fact comes to light when construction has been completed. The difference in the appraised value of Owner's property as a result of the nonconformity is nil. The cost to cure the default would far exceed the total price of the house. Because New Hampshire granite is less expensive than comparable stone from Vermont, Builder has saved $15,000 as a result of his negligent breach of contract. Owner may recover damages of $15,000 for Builder's breach. The case is not within the rule of § 39 (because Builder's default is unintentional), but principles of unjust enrichment reinforce the conclusion that saved expenditure makes an appropriate measure of contract damages in such a case.

h. Efficient breach. Modern American contract scholarship devotes considerable attention to a hypothetical case in which breach of contract is "efficient." The scenario most often debated involves a seller who is offered a higher price for goods or services that he has sold but not yet delivered to the buyer. The seller—it is suggested—ought to breach the contract whenever the anticipated profits from resale at the higher price would be more than sufficient to pay the buyer's damages, thereby leaving some parties better off and nobody worse off. An efficient breach of contract by this definition is easy to hypothesize but difficult to find in real life. In a market context, gain to one party is normally offset or exceeded by loss to the other; while the test of efficiency will not be met unless the injured party is fully indemnified against the cost of resolving the resulting dispute. American practice regarding the allocation of litigation expense makes satisfaction of the latter condition especially unlikely.

(There are other circumstances, typically involving an unexpected increase in the seller's individualized costs, in which a deliberate and profitable breach of contract may be not only efficient but uncontroversial. See Illustration 16. Cases of this kind satisfy the usual definition of "efficient breach," but they are not the ones in question when a general conception of "efficient breach" tends to be invoked.)

The rationale of the disgorgement liability in restitution, in a contractual context or any other, is inherently at odds with the idea of efficient breach in its usual connotation. Given the pervasive risk of undercompensation by standard damage measures, not to mention the deadweight loss from the cost of litigation, the law of restitution strongly favors voluntary over involuntary transactions in the adjustment of conflicts over any form of legal entitlement. A voluntary transaction in the present context requires a negotiated release or modification of the existing obligation. The obligor who elects instead to take without asking—calculating that his anticipated liability for breach is less than the price he would have to pay to purchase the rights in question, and leaving the obligee to the chance of a recovery in damages—engages in precisely the conduct that the law of restitution normally condemns.

Whether the promisor's decision to modify or withhold a given performance infringes the contract rights of the promisee is a preliminary question of contract law and interpretation. If it does, the promisor's liability in restitution follows from the same principles as restitution for other instances of conscious and profitable interference with legally protected rights. See Illustration 14. The rule of § 39 does not automatically punish every "efficient breach" with a disgorgement remedy, because it applies only when a remedy in damages is inadequate to protect the promisee's entitlement. See Illustration 15; compare Illustrations 16-17.

Illustrations:

14. Farmer sells Buyer his entire crop of carrots for the coming season at a price of $500 per ton. It is in Buyer's interest to be the exclusive distributor of Farmer's carrots, and Farmer's obligation to tender his entire output is a material term of the parties' agreement. Bad weather results in a reduced harvest and higher prices. Farmer delivers 20 tons of carrots to Buyer, then sells a further 10 tons to a competing buyer at $800 per ton. (Had Buyer discovered the facts in time, Buyer would have been entitled to a decree of specific performance. See U.C.C. § 2-716, Official Comment 2.) Buyer is entitled to recover $3,000 from Farmer by the rule of this section. It is irrelevant to the recovery in restitution that Buyer's provable contract damages (measured by the contract-market differential or by Buyer's cost to cover) might be less than $3,000.

15. On April 1, Farmer sells his entire crop of wheat to A at a price of $5 per bushel, for delivery after the June harvest. On May 1, an unexpected rise in the price of June wheat allows Farmer to sell the same crop to B at $10 per bushel. On June 15, Farmer harvests his wheat and delivers it to B. On June 16, when A learns of the breach, the spot price of wheat of the kind grown by Farmer has fallen back to $6 per bushel. A is entitled to market or cover damages of $1 per bushel (plus incidental damages as appropriate). On the assumption that Farmer's wheat is fungible with goods readily available on the market—and that Farmer has assets from which a damage judgment can be satisfied—A is not entitled to restitution of Farmer's profit from the sale to B, because A's contractual entitlement (wheat at $5 per bushel) is fully protected by a damage award. Assuming on the contrary that Farmer's wheat is unique, or that Farmer's wheat crop was his only asset at the time of the sale to B, A is entitled to restitution of the profit realized by Farmer's breach ($5 per bushel).

APPENDIX F

RESTATEMENT (SECOND) OF TORTS (1965)

§ 551 Liability for Nondisclosure

(1) One who fails to disclose to another a fact that he knows may justifiably induce the other to act or refrain from acting in a business transaction is subject to the same liability to the other as though he had represented the nonexistence of the matter that he has failed to disclose, if, but only if, he is under a duty to the other to exercise reasonable care to disclose the matter in question.

(2) One party to a business transaction is under a duty to exercise reasonable care to disclose to the other before the transaction is consummated,

(a) matters known to him that the other is entitled to know because of a fiduciary or other similar relation of trust and confidence between them; and

(b) matters known to him that he knows to be necessary to prevent his partial or ambiguous statement of the facts from being misleading; and

(c) subsequently acquired information that he knows will make untrue or misleading a previous representation that when made was true or believed to be so; and

(d) the falsity of a representation not made with the expectation that it would be acted upon, if he subsequently learns that the other is about to act in reliance upon it in a transaction with him; and

(e) facts basic to the transaction, if he knows that the other is about to enter into it under a mistake as to them, and that the other, because of the relationship between them, the customs of the trade or other objective circumstances, would reasonably expect a disclosure of those facts.

Comment:

. . .

k. Nondisclosure of basic facts. The rule stated in Subsection (1) reflects the traditional ethics of bargaining between adversaries, in the absence of any special reason for the application of a different rule. When the facts are patent, or when the plaintiff has equal opportunity for obtaining information that he may be expected to utilize if he cares to do so, or when the defendant has no reason to think that the plaintiff is acting under a misapprehension, there is no obligation to give aid to a bargaining antagonist by disclosing what the defendant has himself discovered. To a considerable extent, sanctioned by the customs and mores of the community, superior information and better business acumen are legitimate advantages, which lead to no liability. The defendant may reasonably expect the plaintiff to make his own investigation, draw his own conclusions and protect himself; and if the plaintiff is indolent, inexperienced or ignorant, or his judgment is bad, or he does not have access to adequate information, the defendant is under no obligation to make good his deficiencies. This is true, in general, when it is the buyer of land or chattels who has the better information and fails to disclose it. Somewhat less frequently, it may be true of the seller.

Illustrations:

6. A is a violin expert. He pays a casual visit to B's shop, where second-hand musical instruments are sold. He finds a violin which, by reason of his expert knowledge and experience, he immediately recognizes as a genuine Stradivarius, in good condition and worth at least $50,000. The violin is priced for sale at $100. Without disclosing his information or his identity, A buys the violin from B for $100. A is not liable to B.

7. The same facts as in Illustration 6, except that the violin is sold at auction and A bids it in for $100. The same conclusion.

8. B has a shop in which he sells second-hand musical instruments. In it he offers for sale for $100 a violin, which he knows to be an imitation Stradivarius and worth at most $50. A enters the shop, looks at the violin and is overheard by B to say to his companion that he is sure that the instrument is a genuine Stradivarius. B says nothing, and A buys the violin for $100. B is not liable to A.

§ 766 Intentional Interference with Performance of Contract by Third Person

One who intentionally and improperly interferes with the performance of a contract (except a contract to marry) between another and a third person by inducing or otherwise causing the third person not to perform the contract, is subject to liability to the other for the pecuniary loss resulting to the other from the failure of the third person to perform the contract.

TABLE OF CASES

Principal cases are italicized.

INDEX